VARIETY
Film Reviews
1907-1980

A SIXTEEN-VOLUME SET,
Including an Index to Titles

Garland Publishing, Inc.
New York and London
1983

Contents

OF THE SIXTEEN-VOLUME SET

Film Reviews
1978-1980

VOLUME FIFTEEN

Garland Publishing, Inc.
New York and London
1983

Library of Congress Cataloging in Publication Data
Main entry under title:

Variety film reviews.
  Includes index.

  1. Moving-pictures—Reviews.   I. Daily variety.
PN1995.V34   1982   791.43'75   82-15691
ISBN 0-8240-5200-5 (v. 1)
ISBN 0-8240-5214-5 (v. 15)

Manufactured in the United States of America

Printed on acid-free,
250-year-life paper

User's Guide

The reviews in this collection are published in chronological order, by the date on which the review appeared. The date of each issue appears at the top of the column where the reviews for that issue begin. The reviews continue through that column and all following columns until a new date appears at the top of the page. Where blank spaces occur at the end of a column, this indicates the end of that particular week's reviews. An index to film titles, giving date of review, is published as the last volume in this set.

1978

The Incredible Melting Man
(COLOR)

One more in the gruesome genre. R Rating may diminish its normal trade.

Chicago, Jan. 3.

An American International Pictures Release of a Rosenberg-Gelfman Production. Produced by Samuel W. Gelfman. Features entire cast. Written and directed by William Sachs. Camera (color) Willy Curtis; special effects, Rick Baker, Harry Woolman; make-up, Rick Baker; music, Arlon Ober; art direction, Michael Levesque. Reviewed at the Roosevelt Theatre, Chicago, Dec. 29, '77. (MPAA Rating: R.). Running time: 86 MINS.

The Incredible

Melting Man	Alex Rebar
Dr. Ted Nelson	Burr DeBenning
General Perry	Myron Healey
Sheriff Blake	Michael Alldredge
Judy Nelson	Ann Sweeny
Dr. Loring	Lisle Wilson
The Model	Rainbeaux Smith
Carol	Julie Drazen
Little Boy	Stuart Edmond Rodgers
Little Boy	Chris Whitney
Harold	Edwin Max
Helen	Dorothy Love
Nell	Janus Blythe
Matt	Jonathon Demme

Taken as one of hundreds of horror films, "The Incredible Melting Man" more often than not succeeds in telling a story and sustaining audience interest. But cult fans might be disappointed with plot and special effects that aren't always gruesome enough to measure up to monstrosity peaks.

Like many works of the genre, "Melting Man" is presented on two levels. On the surface it is a scary adventure of astronaut Steve West, who returns to Earth from Saturn as a melting man who must feed on the flesh of humans in order to survive. But aside from the initial shock of the man's face, the haunting music and a number of other horror trappings, the film is also a human story attempting to leave a moral message as to whether society or the horrible creature it is chasing is really the most destructive.

As pure horror, the film disappoints by lingering too long on ordinary characters and not spending enough time on the melting man and the reasons he is melting. In scenes where he is shown, he is in human form with the exception of a melting face, hands and feet. Instead of making him a horror creature, make-up artist Rick Baker, has created a strange-looking human who is just not scary enough for this film.

Surprisingly, "Melting Man" is at its strongest when making moral comments. Although William Sach's dialog is trite and some scenes are technically incorrect (one instance has light shining through a kitchen window in the middle of the night), the twist ending is just corny enough to work.

Part of the credit for this is Alex Rebar, who provides the only outstanding acting job as the melting man. —Berg.

Doppio Delitto
(Double Murder)
(ITALIAN-FRENCH-COLOR)

Rome, Jan. 2.

A PIC (WB) release produced by Roberto Infascelli for Primex (Rome) and PECF (Paris). Stars Marcello Mastroianni, Agostina Belli, Ursula Andress, Peter Ustinov, Jean-Claude Brialy. Directed by Steno. Screenplay, Age-Scarpelli-Steno; camera (Eastmancolor). Luigi Kuveiller; art director, Mario Ambrosino; editor, Antonio Siciliano; music, Riz Ortolani. Reviewed at Cinema Fiamma, Rome, Jan. 2, '78. Running time, 113 MINS.

Bruno Baldassare	Marcello Mastroianni
Teresa	Agostina Belli
Princess Dell'Orso	Ursula Andress
Harry Hellman	Peter Ustinov
Van Nijlen	Jean-Claude Brialy
Cantalamessa	Gianfranco Barra
"Sorcio"	Mario Scaccia

The late Roberto Infascelli produced "Double Murder" as a comedy-satire-murder mystery like his earlier "Sunday Woman." In current entry, scene shifts from Turin to Rome with basic ingredients repeated. Formula, linking crime with real estate speculation (a sort of ecological warfare to preserve national monuments), bans violence, blood and suspense in favor of character study, background fresco, light comedy situations and wit, where possible.

Marcello Mastroianni holds up the story thread as a disgraced detective who wins back his spurs. His name along with Ursula Andress, Peter Ustinov, Agostina Belli, and Jean-Claude Brialy should give the WB release an audience prop in many markets. Stateside, pic has dualler chances and a sure slot on tv.

Without throwing a punch or pulling a gun, detective Baldassare (Marcello Mastroianni) and bumbling aide, Cantalamessa (Gianfranco Barra) in strong comedy support, are entertaining sleuths who successfully unravel a double electrocution — almost filed and forgotten as a lightning act of God. Along the way, Steno intertwines an array of odd characters — especially Peter Ustinov as a cynical, down-at-the-heels screenwriter and Ursula Andress as the Dietrich type spouse of the assassinated prince .

Suspense is minimal but film races to an unpredictable unravelling on the flavor of characters, lively satire and Roman situation. Two hours of entertainment, however light, is nothing to sneeze at in an Italian film these days. Cast is strong right down the line with special mention for Mario Scaccia as a neighborhood bookshop owner who knows what's inside everyone's closet.

Technical assist in lensing, sets, music and editing are all vital to the pace, breeze and local hues of the Roberto Infascelli production.
—Werb.

La Part Du Feu
(The Fire's Share)
(FRENCH-COLOR)

Paris, Jan. 10.

Planfilm release of Les Films De La Tour — FR3 — Films 66 production. Stars Michel Piccoli, Claudia Cardinale, Jacques Perrin. Directed by Etienne Perrier. Screenplay, Perrier, Dominique Fabre; camera (Eastmancolor), Jean Charvein; editor, Renee Lichtig; music, Paul Misraki. Reviewed at Publicis, Paris, Dec. 23, '77. Running time, 105 MINS.

Hansen	Michel Piccoli
Catherine	Claudia Cardinale
Jacques	Jacques Perrin
Delbaut	Rufus
Edouard	Roland Bertin
William	Gabriel Cattand
Giselle	Veronique Silver

Several films have worked about unsavory and corrupt parliamentarians lately. This item is mainly a rather glossy melodrama about abominable, ruthless business ethnics plus an equivocal friendship and a wife seen as a pawn for both husband and her lover, the latter working for the husband.

Michel Piccoli is the middleaged business man who enjoys manipulation and power as much as making money. He had used his wife's money to get started in the building business. His assistant, apparently as he was in his younger days, is seemingly still a little unsure of himself. The wife is in love with the younger man, but the husband finds out about their affair and decides to use it rather than get excited about it.

Questions of possible homosexuality between Piccoli and Perrin are quashed in talk and other characters are surface. There have been big building scandals here, so pic could enjoy local exploitation aspects, helped by its name cast. Outsize look at immorality is more well meaning rather than getting the spark of life into it. Pic has Asian and Latino American possibilities.
—Mosk.

The Private Files Of J. Edgar Hoover
(COLOR)

Cheap, lurid, sensationalized look at J. Edgar Hoover. For fast selloff.

Hollywood, Dec. 23.

An American International release of a Larco Production. Produced, directed and written by Larry Cohen. Camera (Movielab color), Paul Glickman; editor, Christopher Lebenzon; associate producer, Arthur Mandelberg, Peter Sabiston; sound, Robert Geraldini, Jane Landis; assistant director, Reid Freeman; set design, Cathy Davis; set decorator, Carolyn Loewenstein; costumes, Lewis Friedman; technical advisor, John M. Crewdson; music, Miklos Rozsa. Reviewed at AIP Screening Room, Dec. 22, '77. (MPAA rating: PG.) Running time; 112 MINS.

J. Edgar Hoover	Broderick Crawford
Lionel McCoy	Jose Ferrer
Robert F. Kennedy	Michael Parks
Carrie DeWitt	Ronee Blakley
Dwight Webb	Rip Torn
Florence Hollister	Celeste Holm
Melvin Purvis	Michael Sacks
Clyde Tolson	Dan Dailey
Martin Luther King, Jr.	Raymond St. Jacques
Lyndon B. Johnson	Andrew Duggan
Dave Hindley	John Marley
Franklin D. Roosevelt	Howard Da Silva
Hoover's Mother	June Havoc
Young Hoover	James Wainwright
Attorney General Stone	Lloyd Nolan
FBI Secretary	Ellen Barber
Walter Winchell	Lloyd Gough
Alvin Karpas	Brad Dexter
Ethel Brunette	Jennifer Lee
Quentin Reynolds	George Plimpton
Damon Runyon	Jack Cassidy

For months now Larry Cohen has been touting himself as cinema's answer to Woodward and Bernstein. Well, on the basis of "The Private Files of J. Edgar Hoover" alone, if the National Enquirer ever decides to hire an investigative reporter Cohen's got the job locked up. He needs no more credentials than this tawdry "expose."

According to Cohen, who wrote, produced and directed this 114-minute, $3,000,000 look at America's top cop, Hoover was a public relations gimmick. As a vindictive, puritanical paranoid he shipped agents off to Knoxville for reading Playboy magazine. Privately, he was a mama's boy and a homosexual who got his jollies by sitting in the dark with a bottle of bourbon and a tape recorder playing the sounds of a powerful government official's hotel liaisons.

Matching the picture's sleazy sensationalism in story is its sleazy sensationalistic look and sound. This may be the motion picture industry's first historical horror story. Cohen and cameraman Paul Glickman have adopted two visual styles. There's the "backlot look" used to reenact great moments in J. Edgar Hoover's life, like the shooting of John Dillinger in front of the Biograph Theatre in Chicago and Hoover's first arrest.

Then there's the documentary look: Hoover in the FBI building; that's the real FBI building. Hoover in the apartment of his lifelong friend Lionel McCoy; that's the real McCoy's apartment. Hoover in the office of Attorney General Stone; that's the real Attorney General's office. At least Cohen knows how to scout locations.

He also knew enough to cast Broderick Crawford in the lead. As Hoover, the jowly Crawford turns in a fine performance. (The temptation is to call it a credible performance, but nothing about this picture is credible.)

However, the remainder of the

performances, starting with Michael Parks' Robert Kennedy, are grotesque attempts to mimic well known public officials. For example, Howard Da Silva turns FDR into a flitty fop. Were it not in such bad taste, William Jordon and Parks could take their silly Massachusetts Kennedy accents with some comic lines and start a nightclub act in Las Vegas.

American International Pictures picked up Cohen's film a few months back and reportedly is pushing it as a class picture, complete with bid letters and six-week playtimes. Like the sensational tabloids, movies like "The Private Files of J. Edgar Hoover," need quick sales. Eye catching headlines sell that kind of literature, not word of mouth. The same goes for this film. —Hege.

Holocaust 2000
(ITALIAN-BRITISH-COLOR)

Rome, Dec. 26.

A Fida release (AIP in the U.S.A.), produced by Edmondo Amati for Embassy Productions (Rome) and Aston Film (London). Stars Kirk Douglas, Agostina Belli, Simon Ward. Directed by Alberto De Martino. Screenplay by Sergio Donati, Aldo De Martino, Michael Robson; camera (Technicolor), Enrico Menczer; art director, Umberto Betacca; editor, Vincenzo Tomassi; music, Ennio Morricone. Reviewed at Fida screening room, Rome, Dec. 26, '77. Running time **102 MINS.**

Robert Caine	Kirk Douglas
Sara Golan	Agostina Belli
Angel Ciane	Simon Ward
Prof. Griffith	Anthony Quayle
Eva Caine	Virginia McKenna
Meyer	Alexander Knox
Msgr. Charrier	Romolo Valli
Arab Assassin	Massimo Foschi

Take the threat of nuclear disaster, the ecological deterioration of the earth, the terror of an all-powerful Antichrist; mix it with an international cast topped by Kirk Douglas, Agostina Belli (Italy) and a number of convincing British actors like Simon Ward, Anthony Quayle, Alexander Knox and Virginia McKenna and shake well. What emerges is an entertainment product viable in all film markets and for all tv audiences.

Producer Edmondo Amati and Alberto De Martino are old hands at terrifying general audiences with the Antichrist. They did one under that title several years ago and established market merit for this type of fare. With heightened cast and production values, eerie special effects — the Antichrist in "Holocaust" takes on a more spectacular dimension as a supernatural force insidious enough to settle for no less than the "purification of mankind" by setting off a chain of nuclear explosions to destroy the world.

The conflict is between Robert Caine (Kirk Douglas), an idealist in the realm of nuclear power plants and his demon son Angelo, (Simon Ward) with tenebrous plans to push dad's project for fission power to wipe out human life. The supernatural pushes superficial arguments about nuclear power to the side and gives the spectator a feature long feeling of harrowing anguish, a sense of human helplessness to contend with such an evil and destructive force as the Antichrist.

This makes the film and complements for a loose, obscure story peppered with banal characters, situations and especially dialog. As striking a beauty as Agostina Belli is catapulted into the conflict with only symbolic story roots in a Biblical-like finale and with a slow, pronounced accent for her lines. The dramatic picture-long father-son duel between Kirk Douglas with a mid-American accent and Simon Ward with a British lilt keeps the plot in place right up to the inconclusive finale.

Ward takes over the Robert Caine Enterprises, ritually increases the board of directors from 12 to 21 and orders completion of the nuclear power complex for his 33d birthday in the year 2000. Douglas escapes with Belli and newly-born daughter to Mediterranean shores.

A variety of accents (pic plays off in England, Europe and vaguely, in the Middle East) does not necessarily give a film international identity. At times it is an aural handicap. On the other hand, special effects, sound and music track provide more credibility than a big and zealous cast. —Werb.

Preparez Vos Mouchoirs
(Get Your Handkerchiefs Ready)
(FRENCH-COLOR)

Paris, Jan. 2.

GEF-CCFC release of Les Films Ariane-CAPAC production. Stars Gerard Depardieu, Patrick Dewaere, Carole Laure. Written and directed by Bertrand Blier. Camera (Eastmancolor), Jean Peuzer; editor, Claudine Merlin; music, Georges Delerue. Reviewed at Club 13, Paris, Dec. 29, '77. Running time, **108 MINS.**

Raoul	Gerard Depardieu
Stephane	Patrick Dewaere
Solange	Carole Laure
Christian	Riton
Neighbor	Michel Serrault
Mother	Eleonore Hirt
Passerby	Sylvie Joly
Father	Jean Rougerie

A rather bizarre mixture of gritty comedy, satire and delving into female status makes this a literary film. There is a lot of talk, sometimes good, but often edgy and too often pointless in lieu of a more robust visual dynamism and life.

Film manages to be provocative and could stir interest locally with some offshore chances indicated. Director-writer Bertrand Blier's first film was a sort of docu in which he interviewed people, with a few actor ringers, and then intercut giving an impression the people were answering questions together or to each other. It was called "Hitler, Don't Know Him."

This film has a bit of that feeling. People act and talk at cross currents. Gerard Depardieu is first seen in closeup talking to his pretty but vacant-looking wife in a restaurant. She is nibbling on food and he insists she is off her feed, indifferent and he loves her enough to give her to another man.

He picks on a bespectacled young man, Patrick Dewaere, and talks him into going with his wife. The wife, the lovely Canadian thesp Carole Laure, accepts. But it does not quite work out for all she seems to want is a baby and a completely feminine life of washing, cooking, knitting, etc.

The three go off to a summer camp run by Dewaere where there is a 13-year-old quiz kid picked on by the others for he is the only one from a rich family. Laure warms to him and to protect him let's him sleep with her as her husband and suitor read books together. The boy, a long-haired, shrewd innocent, manages to tap her need for a child and uses it to become her lover. Scene avoids vulgarity or bad taste.

But it is apparently a symbol. The boy does not want to go home and is finally packed off to a boarding school from which he is kidnapped when Laure becomes inconsolable. She and the boy run off while Depardieu and Dewaere are briefly jailed as kidnappers. The boy's mother, who rushes out to look for him, ends up eloping with a friend of the group.

It does not have the accessible glib bonhommie of the family mate changing of "Cousin, Cousine" or Lina Wertmuller's more flamboyant, vulgar social and politico comedic styling. Still, film is ambiguous enough to possibly catch interest on its hitting on the themes of permissiveness, teenage precocity and male macho tactics.

Blier did the more anarchic tale of two semi-delinquents living on women and society, "Going Places," which launched Dewaere and Depardieu. Now they do a sort of comedy team number rather than imbuing their roles with human insight. Film stays in the realm of ideas.

It is well produced technically. The title seems to say that Blier also wanted to both use and send up old film melodramas and tearjerkers. It does not quite make it on either plane. —Mosk.

Sasquatch
(COLOR)

Excellent scenery camerawork almost compensates for naive screenplay and generally bad acting.

North American Film Enterprises release of a John Fabian Production. Executive producer, Ronald B. Olson. Directed by Ed Ragozzini. Features entire cast. Screenplay, Edward H. Hawkins, based on story by Ronald B. Olson; camera (De Luxe), John Fabian, Bill Farmer; editors, Fabian, Farmer; sound, Steve Winitzky. Reviewed at New Embassy Theatre, New York, Jan. 11, '78. (MPAA Rating - G). Running time: **102 MINS.**

Chuck Evans	George Lauris
Hank Parshall	Steve Boergadine
Barney Snipe	Jim Bradford
Josh Bigsby	Ken Kenzle
Dr. Paul Markham	William Emmons
Techka Blackhawk	Joe Morello

Taking advantage of the proven interest in "wilderness" films, North American Film Enterprises of Eugene, Oregon is throwing this variation on the "Bigfoot" legend onto the nation's screens in what appears to be a rather hurried manner. In the New York area, it bowed two days early at the New Embassy, then went onto a widespread showcase. In its genre, it rates about average — high on scenery, low on every other category.

Filmed for the most part in the U.S. and Canadian Northwest, the film almost annihilates the fantastic scenery with its banal story of a group of computer-happy scientists in search of "Sasquatch," the Indian name for "Bigfoot," the giant-sized missing link who may provide anthropological links to man's ancient past. It figures that the expedition is a failure with the primeval brute a faster thinker and quicker mover than the gear-laden and over-cautious adventurers.

Indeed, there's a considerable disparity between the long shots of the mountains and plains and the action footage involving Sasquatch — the latter conceivably having been shot in a close-to-civilization California woods where the plastic boulders and rampages as well as the fleeting glimpses of the ape-like giant could be controlled. It doesn't figure they'd take all this on location.

Other than the photography, all other areas are bad to amateurish. —Robe.

Il ... Bel Paese
(ITALIAN-COLOR)

Rome, Dec. 22.

77 Cinematografica Rome release, produced by Fulvio Lucisano for Italian International Film. Stars Paolo Villaggio. Directed by Luciano Salce. Screenplay, Castlelano and Pipolo; camera (Eastmancolor), Ennio Guarnieri; art director, Ezio Altieri; music, Gianni Boncompagni, Giorgio Farina, Paolo Ormi; editor, Antonio Siciliano. Reviewed at Ariston Cin-

ema, Rome, Dec. 21, '77. Running time: 11? MINS.
Guido . . . . .Paolo Villaggio
Mia . . . . .Silvia Dionisio

This is a fast-paced, very funny film about national disaster, with off-shore chances in Latino and other markets.

"Il Bel Paese," the affectionate term Italians use for the mother country, is falling apart at the seams, with murder, robbery, kidnapping and violence now everyday occurrences.

After eight years away from all this on a Persian Gulf oil rig, Guido (Paolo Villaggio) returns to his native Milan to invest his savings in a jewelry shop. The tone is set, right from his arrival at the airport. Terrorists open up machine gun fire on the plane's other passengers, but Villaggio, having knelt to kiss his native soil, escapes the slaughter. Unfazed, unconscious of what has happened, he proceeds into a fearcrazed and violence-ridden city where police battle rioters, tear-gas and bombs fly through the air, and Villaggio can't get past the barricades of his own sister's apartment until he manages to come up with the password.

It doesn't sound very funny, but somehow it all works. In the best tradition of Italian slapstick, director Luciano Salce keeps the madcap pace under tight control and manages not to cross that perilous line between comic vulgarity and plain bad taste. Salce is ably assisted by his lead actor. Villaggio combines a superb sense of timing with all the characteristics of the little man surviving in a world he neither controls nor comprehends.

Other actors, from featured players to bit parts, measure up to Villaggio's standards, particularly the ravishing Silvia Dionisio as Mia the politically polymorphic girlfriend, blithely moving from feminism to radical politics to ecology. Anna Mazzamauro is extremely funny as a well-heeled, materialistic Italian businesswoman. Here again, Salce lifts the role above screechy caricature. And Massimo Boldi is delightfully stupid as Villaggio's dopey addict nephew.

Ennio Guarnieri's highly competent camera work reinforces the zany pace of the comedy. Musical scoring is particularly effective as punk rock passages intercut with the kind of rapid-fire deejay commentary that characterizes Italy's left-wing pirate radio stations.

Despite local setting and local actors, the film has a broad comic appeal. And media coverage that Italy's unfortunate political problems have had recently might well attract foreign distribs. —*Ancy.*

La Vie Parisienne
(The Parisian Life)
(FRENCH-COLOR)

Paris, Jan. 10.

UGC/CFD release of Belles Rives-SFP-Bavaria Atelier production. Features entire cast. Directed by Christian-Jaque. Screenplay, Jaque, Jacques Emmanuel from the operetta by Meilhac and Halevy; camera (Eastmancolor), Michel Carre; editor, Michel Nezick, Christine Monge; music, Jacques Offenbach; choreography, Michel Ardan. Reviewed at UGC-Biarritz, Paris, Dec. 26, '77. Running time: **100 MINS.**
Gardefeu . . . . Bernard Alane
Brazilian . . . . .·. . . . . Georges Aminel
Urbain .·. . . . . Jacques Balutin
Gabrielle . . . . Evelyne Buyle
Baron . . . . Jean-Pierre Darras
Baroness . . . . Martine Sarcey
Pauline . . . . Dany Saval

This last century Offenbach operetta that introduced the music now associated with that high kicking dance, the can-can, lacks the dynamism, timing and joyfulness of that terping. It is a lame tale of upper class doings in cahoots with their servants. Any social bite is absent in this bland pic made by vet Christian-Jaque.

Two disingenuous rich young men decide they have had enough of Paris nightlife when they find a mistress they share with another. They decide to get back to their own class. Book tells of one picking up members of foreign aristocracy at a station and passing off his house as a hotel to seduce the wife of a visiting Swedish nobleman.

The farcical aspects get repetitive, the songs just stop the action and pic goes its way for one of mainly local chances on the Offenbach music and the 19th century insouciant carryings-on that remain innocent in the end. It opens with a bright can-can number and then slows down to tell its vapid tale which, however, made for a hit legit revival some years ago. Mainly for the record. —*Mosk.*

Yeti
(ITALIAN-COLOR)

Rome, Dec. 27.

A Stefano release, produced by Nicolo Pomilia and Wolfranco Coccia for Stefano Film. Features entire cast. Directed by Frank Kramer. Screenplay, Mario Di Nardo, Frank Kramer; camera (Technicolor), Sandro Mancori; art director, Claudio De Santis; special effects Ermanno Biamonte; music, Santa Maria Romitelli. Reviewed at Cinema Fiammetta, Rome, Dec. 26, '77. Running time **105 MINS.**
Yeti . . . . Mimmo Crau
Jane . . . . Phoenix Grant
Herbie . . . . Jim Sillivan
Prof Wassermann . . . . .John Stacey
Hunnicut . . . . Eddie Faye
Cliff . . . . Tony Kendall

Frank Kramer (ne Gianfranco Parolini) has attempted the impossible — to bring in a monster film without a monster. His protagonist, hosed back into existence from an ice pack after a millenium of inter-red hibernation, is played by Mimmo Crau inside a wig and costume mainly against models or at lowangle or high-angle photography through the big lens. "Yeti" leans too heavily on blue-black projection with the monster often blown up in special photography to fill the screen. Kramer intends to perfect flaw-filled blue blacks in original English version before taking print to U.S.A.

Producer Nicolo Pomilia started the film last summer with apparently one idea in mind — to get a family film into 100 Italian cinemas for the holidays. "Yeti" is strictly a moppet entry despite feeble plot effort to woo adolescents with cornball romance and adults with some ineffectual criminology.

The kids, however, can disregard the blue backing to lap up real life screen-filling monster — befriending a little mute boy, a sweet 16 lass (son and niece of multinational, multimillionaire Hunnicut) a collie dog and a goodhearted wildlife conservationist, Professor Wassermann.

Kramer has an out. The stark inadequacies of the screenplay he wrote with Mario Di Nardo, the rush, rush helming (with crowds sometimes panicking and police cars speeding in the wrong direction) and the limp pace (placating tension before each successive, accessible gimmick) — can all be attributed to the filmmaker's basic plan of giving spectators under 10 a chance to shed a tear or cheer. But even infants today are wiser than their years and more than once laughed when they should have cried.

Withal, Yeti is a b.o. answer to the eternal parental quiz "Where do I take my children during the holidays?" It's exploitable, and in nationwide saturation (100 cinemas) — could even be quite profitable — not only in this market but at odd hiliday moments in most other territories as well.

Santa Maria Romitelli's score undercuts the monster and goes heavy on the schmalz. Art direction is built around a snowman without snow trapped in the summer sun of a major city.

Of the cast, only Eddie Faye is smart enough to laugh through the role of money-crazed Hunnicut.

Finale has Phoenix Grant (pretty daughter of Franco Interlenghi and Antonella Lualdi) on a hilltop outside Toronto convincing Yeti to big foot it back to the Himalayas ... on foot!

Similarities .to "King Kong" in plot motivation, and monster movement-expression show through. By comparison, "Kong" was unfairly under-rated. —*Werb.*

The Hazing
(COLOR)

Indie entry creditably produced with lightweight story of illegal fraternity hazing. Punch ending.

Kansas City, Jan. 4.

The Miraleste Company release of a Robert Fridley/Dick Davis Production. Produced by Douglas Curtis, Bruce Shelly. Screenplay, Shelly, David Ketchum, based on an idea by Shelly. Features entire cast. Directed by Curtis. Music, Ian Freebairn-Smith. Released to selected theatres in the Kansas City, Des Moines and Omaha exchange areas, no national trade screening. Reviewed at Valley View Theatre, Kansas City, Dec. 29, '77. (MPAA rating PG). Running time: **90 MINS.**
Craig Lewis . . . . .Jeff East
Rod . . . . Brad David
Carl . . . . David Hayward
Barney . . . . Charlie Martin Smith
Dworsky . . . . .Sandra Vacey
Wendy . . . . Kelly Moran
Phil . . . . .Jim Boelsen

First film production venture of two Des Moines-based theatremen has packaged a slice of campus life around a hazing episode of The Delts. The stunt backfires when one of the pledges is accidentally killed, seemingly, and crux of the plot is for those involved to keep it quiet until it can be believably explained and the reputation of the fraternity be saved from complicity in an illegal hazing.

High-school track star Jeff East on an athletic scholarship to State U and his brother, David Hayward, have planned, instead, to raze the fraternity house to settle a score for a wrong unjustly settled on the brother earlier by the fraternity. They bring about their intent and the manner of levelling the frat house in the final five minutes gives the picture a punch that somewhat saves the stretchy interior of the film. It would be a drag, however, for television to make an hour show of this idea.

This is the first feature film for young director Doug Curtis, who has a career of commercial films and documentaries behind him. He has put it together creditably, if at length, and given it minor names in Jeff East, a Kansas City native, and Charlie Martin Smith, of "American "Grafitti," Brad David is good as the frat prez, and others are satisfactory.

For a film in a campus setting "The Hazing" is very short of girl stuff, only two femmes being Kelly Moran as East's traditional girl friend back home and Sandra Vacey as the pushy Dworsky. There also is some question about the title as a word not readily known by the average filmgoer.

Film has had some try-out dates in the midwest home territory of the producers and will be released through subdistributors in other sections later this spring. It should have some appeal in college towns and other youth-predominant spots.

—*Quin.*

The Foreigner

Plodding, depressing film with limited appeal.

An Amos Poe Visions release. Produced, written and directed by Amos Poe. Features entire cast. Screenplay, Amos Poe, Eric Mitchell; camera (16m-black & white), Chirine El Khadem; editor, Michael Penland, Amos Poe, Johanna Heer; stills photographs, Fernando Natalici; music, composed and performed by Ivan Kral. Reviewed at Tisch Hall, New York U., Jan. 11, '78. (No MPAA rating). Running time: **101 MINS.**

Max Menace	Eric Mitchell
Fili Harlow	Patti Astor
Dee Trick	Deborah Harry
Zazu Weather	Terens Severine
Doll	Anya Phillips
Shake	Duncan Hannah
Forbag	David Forshtay
The German	Klaus Mettig
Rumanian	Ana Marton
Rumanian	Pusante Byzantium
The Arab	Chirine ed Khadem

"The Foreigner" is a lugubrious film whose depressing story bores more than it scores. Photography, of New York City scenes, and sound are not of the best quality.

Story, which is not always clear, is about a Frenchman, played serviceably by Eric Mitchell, on the run for some reason or other. New York hardly proves pleasant as he's pursued and terrorized by Gotham lowlifes as well as apparently by crime bigshots.

Featured billing is given three femmes, although one, Deborah Harry, probably the best known as member of the New Wave rock combo Blondie, appears only briefly, singing Brecht's "Bilbao Song" well. Patti Astor, as a detective in constant pursuit, and Terens Severine, as an ill-fated sadist, are capable.

The lead character is in constant state of harried depression as the film goes on and on. Score by Ivan Kral of the Patti Smith Group is forgettable, although the Erasers, one of Gotham's better New Wave rock combos, do a couple of their numbers well at C.B.G.B. & OM-FUG, the city's top underground cafe. Max, the name of Mitchell's character, is beaten up in the john there during part of the music, one of the film's better action sequences, but, for the most part, "The Foreigner" can hit limited cult favor at most. —*Kirb.*

Il Gatto
(The Cat)
(ITALIAN-COLOR)

Rome, Jan. 6.

A UA release produced by Sergio Leone for Rafran Cinematografica. Stars Ugo Tognazzi, Mariangela Melato. Directed by Luigi Comencini. Screenplay, Rodolfo Sonego, Augusto Caminito, Fulvio Marcolin; camera (Eastmancolor), Ennio Guarnieri; art director, Dante Ferretti; editor, Nino Baragli; music, Ennio Morricone. Reviewed at Cinema Barberini, Rome, Jan. 5, '78. Running time: **106 MINS.**

Amedeo	Ugo Tognazzi
Ofelia	Mariangela Melato
Police Chief	Michel Galabrue
Wanda	Dalila Di Lazzaro

The collaboration of Sergio Leone as producer and Luigi Comencini as director has brought forth an entertaining suspense comedy slanted primarily to the Italian market although the ensemble of Roman vignettes, sitcoms, performance and technical quality should give the UA Europa entry a toehold in many territories. The flavor could even prove contagious in special Yank situations.

Drawing on his hit two years ago — "Sunday Woman" — Comencini again gets embroiled with real estate speculation, this time in old Rome and then proceeds to build it into a satiric crosscut of contemporary life and manners. A wacky couple, sister and brother (Mariangela Melato and Ugo Tognazzi) must get rid of a half-dozen remaining tenants in their old building in old Rome in order to sell the property for high stakes.

"The Cat" becomes a series of interspersed sketches tracking the odd couple on the move to eliminate the last handful of oddball tenants. Before they're through, holdout dwellers (at old, very low blocked rents) are fingered for prostitution, drug traffic, sodomy, Mafia connections, blackmailed priesthood and an odor of CIA covert action. As the property transfer checks are being written, however, a lovely Yugoslav tenant (Dalila Di Lazzaro) who fled to her homeland to beat the mob, reappears in her little penthouse apartment to gum up the deal.

Tognazzi is a vet social comic who knows where the laughs are buried. Mariangelo Melato wraps a smile around her thesp talent and teams more convincingly in the sister act. Di Lazzaro is an eyefull, clothed or in deshabille, with self-styled inner thesp springs that are worth noting and watching.

Script by Rodolfo Sonego and Augusto Caminito with an assist by Fulvio Marcolin is a few pegs higher in novelty and imagination than the average Italian comedy. Other plus factors are Ennio Guarnieri's tints, the lightly mocking music score of Ennio Morricone and the sharp pace of editor Nino Baragli.

—*Werb.*

On Peut Le Dire Sans Se Facher
(One Can Say It Without Getting Angry)
(FRENCH-COLOR)

Paris, Jan. 10.

Filmologies release of Oliane Productions-Gerland Productions-Filmologies production. Stars Roger Coggio, Elisabeth Huppert. Directed by Roger Coggio. Screenplay, Coggio, Elisabeth Huppert, Bernard Landry; camera (Eastmancolor), Etienne Becker; editor, Denise De Casablanca; music, Michel Legrand. Reviewed at Club 13, Paris, Dec. 25, '77. Running time, **91 MINS.**

Peppo	Roger Coggio
Pauline	Elisabeth Huppert
Mother	Madeleine Robinson
Desmarais	Louisa Colpeyn
La Mamma	Jole Silvani
Bianca	Andriana Innocenti

Roger Coggio and Elisabeth Huppert try hard to add some spark to a tale of an ill-assorted couple, who bring it off despite her suicidal tendencies and his being married with a teenage son. But pic is more shrill than charming with not enough pacing and social insight to lift this sitcom out of the ordinary.

The rather self-absorbed characters and their problems could catch local fancies though foreign possibilities are chancier. Director Coggio just piles on the imbroglios and upsets that stave off the suicide and lead to a happy ending.

Huppert comes from a fairly well-off family, has a lovely apartment, a job in a Ministry and a straitlaced boy friend. But she is unhappy and decides to commit suicide one weekend. She buys a coffin, sends letters and prepares for her Sunday ritual of slashed wrists before people receive her cards about her death and her mother a letter.

But she goes out on a Saturday night bender and finds Coggio in her car. He has just laid down in it. It seems he is an alcoholic on a cure and had heisted a few. He drives her home and plot has an awakening of desire but with her still determined to do the suicide bit. Neighbors break in and plumbing problems keep putting it off.

He confesses to having a wife and a family of Italo emigrants as they become lovers. But she is late in stopping the letters as the coffin and mourners arrive for a last-minute free-for-all. On their way to the cemetery, to confess all, there is an accident and they end up bandaged in a hospital where they decide to share their lives.

The timing lacks the balance of comedy and character perception to bring this off though technical aspects are good and acting, besides the leads, is an asset. —*Mosk.*

Nippon No Don-Yabohen
(The Don of Japan — Big Schemes)
(JAPANESE-COLOR)

Tokyo, Dec. 22.

A Toei release. Produced by Koji Shundo, Goro Kusakabe, Norimichi Matsudaira, Mitsuru Taoka. Directed by Sadao Nakajima. Features entire cast. Camera (color), Toshio Matsuda; screenplay, Koji Takada; costumes, Jun Ashida; music, Toshiro Mayuzumi. Reviewed at Toei Palace, Nov. 30, '77. Running time: **141 MINS.**

Cast: Saburi Shin, Toshiro Mifune, Kyoko Kishida, Hiroki Matsukata, Bunta Sugawara.

In parts 1 and 2 of "The Godfather," director Francis Coppola drew parallels between what he felt are two "totally capitalistic phenomena" — corporate America and the Mafia.

Similarly, it is suggested in this Toei release that the daily operations of both Japan's underworld and aboveboard capitalist organizations are strikingly alike. As is the case with an exec at Japan, Inc., an average day in the life of a criminal biggie is filled not so much with stabbing, stompings and knifings as with interminable business meetings.

Aside from this insight into corporate behavior, gangland-style (if, indeed, an insight it is), the film has very little to recommend it. Its windy plot of labyrinthine, interlocking relationships and its innumerable scenes of shirt-and-tie yakuza (gangsters) seated at conference tables make you long for 1930s Warner Bros. gangster films, which were not only more valuable as social documents, but were livelier.

Scenarist Koji Tokada, when not being tedious or risible, is busy repeating himself. On two different occasions, criminal types are executed by excitable hitmen who perform their deeds in the middle of crowded thoroughfares in broad daylight. Apparently the reason there are so few unsolved gangland slayings in Japan and so many in Chicago has less to do with the relative merits of the respective police forces than the relative demerits of the respective criminal elements.

What is ultimately so disappointing about this film, the second in a series, is its refusal to get down to the yakuza nitty-gritty. The pervasive influence of this country's criminal syndicates is a story that, for sheer excitement, cannot be beat. It may be too much to hope for, but perhaps the next installment of "Nippon No Don" will demonstrate that truth is not only stranger than fiction, it makes better drama.

—*Bail.*

Coma
(COLOR)

Excellent suspenser from Michael Crichton. Genevieve Bujold super. Strong outlook.

Hollywood, Jan. 18.

United Artists release of a Metro-Goldwyn-Mayer picture, produced by Martin Erlichman. Stars Genevieve Bujold, Michael Douglas. Screenplay and direction, Michael Crichton, based on the novel by Robin Cook. Camera (Metrocolor), Victor J. Kemper; Gerald Hirschfeld; editor, David Bretherton; Music, Jerry Goldsmith; production design, Albert Brenner; set decoration, Rick Simpson; sound, Bill Griffith, William McCaughey, Michael J. Kohut, Aaron Rochin; costumes-wardrobe, Eddie Marks, Yvonne Kubis; asst. directors, William McGarry, Ron Grow. Reviewed at MGM Studios, Culver City, Calif. Jan. 17, '78. (MPAA Rating: PG.) Running time. 113 MINS.

Dr. Susan Wheeler	Genevieve Bujold
Dr. Mark Bellows	Michael Douglas
Mrs. Emerson	Elizabeth Ashley
Dr. George	Rip Torn
Dr. Harris	Richard Widmark
Nancy Greenly	Lois Chiles
Dr. Morelind	Harry Rhodes
Computer Technician	Gary Barton
Kelly	Frank Downing
Jim	Richard Doyle
Dr. Marcus	Alan Haufrect
Vince	Lance Le Gault
Chief Resident	Michael MacRae
Nurse	Betty McGuire
Murphy	Tom Selleck
Dr. Goodman	Charles Siebert
Lab Technician	William Wintersole

"Coma" is an extremely entertaining suspense drama in the Hitchcock tradition. Director-adapter Michael Crichton neatly builds mystery and empathy around star Genevieve Bujold, a doctor who grows to suspect her superiors of deliberate surgical error. Michael Douglas also stars as her disbelieving lover. Martin Erlichman's handsome production, right down to that consistently great Metro-Goldwyn-Mayer post-production and color finish, looks like a very good commercial bet for United Artists release in general situations.

Robin Cook's novel was adapted by Crichton into a smartly paced tale which combines traditional Hitchcock elements with contemporary personal relationships. Thus, Bujold and Douglas wrestle in sub-plot with separate identity and mutual romantic problems while she becomes the innocent enmeshed in suspicious medical wrongdoing. When lifelong friend Lois Chiles goes into permanent coma during an otherwise routine operation, Bujold begins probing a series of similar incidents.

Arrayed against her are hospital superiors Richard Widmark and Rip Torn, and even Douglas himself. Lance Le Gault is a hired killer whom Bujold outwits to the relief of the entire audience. Elizabeth Ashley is notable as the head of a dubious medical experimental centre where the comatose victims vegetate pending ghoulish, but all-too-plausible disposition.

The precise nature of the threat unfolds slowly, and both script and players tantalizingly confuse Bujold and an audience; all we know is that she's in trouble and we want her to escape.

Victor J. Kemper finished photographing the 113-minute film in Metrocolor, replacing Gerald Hirschfeld who was initial cinematographer. Albert Brenner's production design is up to his usual outstanding level of achievement; far more of the film is actually studio set than one might imagine.

Entire cast, down through minor supporting roles, contributes to the impact; Sam Christensen and Joyce Robinson rate their solo credit card for the casting work. Bujold, whose self-assurance can often work against much audience sympathy, herein balances quiet determination and emotional vulnerability.

There are a couple of awkward lurches in the plot, but that never stopped a good film from being forgiven a few lapses. Similarly, Crichton's direction is not the type that calls attention to its trickiness; it tells the story well and that's really all that matters.

Jerry Goldsmith's score does not come in until the pic is well underway, but when it does it's effective. All production credits are solid.
—*Murf.*

El Paso Wrecking Corp.
(COLOR)

Hollywood, Jan. 10.

A Joe Gage Films release. Produced by Sam Gage. Written and directed by Joe Gage. Features entire cast. Camera (Eastmancolor), Nick Elliott; music, Al Steinman; sound, Harlan Archer, Glen Nathan. Reviewed at Century Theatre, L.A. Jan. 9, '78. (Self-imposed X rating.) Running time: 94 MINS.

Gene	Fred Halsted
Hank	Richard Locke
Roadhouse Owner	Georgina Spelvin
Voyeuristic Couple	Steve King, Jeanne Marie Marchaud
Boys In Car	Robert Snowden, Aaron Taylor
Bike Rider	Keith Anthoni
Stranded Motorist	Ken Brown
Mechanic	Rob Carter
Park Ranger	Clay Russell
Ranger's Sister	Veronica Compton
Gardener	Guillermo Ricardo
Repairman	Lou Davis
Foreman	Stan Braddock
Mr. Harris	Mike Morris
Seth Harris	Jared Benson
Receptionist	Beth McDyer

Conceived as a followup to last year's highly successful "Kansas City Trucking Co." "El Paso Wrecking Corp." is the rare example of a sequel being a better film. Writer-director Joe Gage and producer Sam Gage have again made a male porno feature that is erotic, artful and commercial. Richard Locke, a familiar face in the genre and holding over from the first film, is now teamed with underground filmmaker Fred Halsted, appearing most effectively in top-featured spot. The project should enjoy strong b.o. in gay sexfilm houses, and both pix have a good outlook later in nontheatrical markets.

What distinguishes the Gage films is the refreshing simplicity with which the various sequences of male sexual activity are motivated. No ponderous and pretentious environment is suggested; no Wagner, no Dante, no De Sade here. instead the rather honest attitude that casual sexual encounters are sufficiently motivating in themselves, considering the transiency involved. The longer psychological effect and the morality involved are right where they belong — in the conscience of the viewer.

Thus, Halsted and Locke are truckers enroute to Texas, and their 94-minute odyssey is spotted with hardcore vignettes in which they separately become involved with a series of passing strangers. Selection of sexual environments covers a good array of contemporary turn-on situations. Al Steinman's original score is a strong asset, providing a wide range of c&w, rock and other beats appropriate to the sexual tempo. Chuck Thatcher played the harmonica solos to good effect.

Quite apart from the specifics of the film itself, Halsted's screen presence is excellent. It's in a comfortable middle ground, far from the extremes either of pretty-boy or the grotesque. The acting demands on him are light and he does okay in this area (as does Locke). It would be interesting to see Halsted in a conventional film role.

It's fairly well known that the Gages (noms-de-film) are making these films as practical exercises on the way to broader goals. That they do so well in a field that limits their audience to a quasi-captive market is some measure of proven as well as latent talent. **This seems to be the second in a trilogy, for end-title card promises. "L.A. Tool & Die" as the next project. —*Murf.***

The Boys In Company C
(U.S.-HONG KONG-COLOR)

Good if long action programmer about U.S. Marines in Vietnam.

Hollywood, Jan. 12.

A Columbia Pictures release of a Golden Harvest production, produced by Andre Morgan; executive producer, Raymond Chow. Directed by Sidney J. Furie. Features entire cast. Screenplay. Rick Natkin. Furie; camera (Technicolor), Godfrey A. Godar; editors, Michael Berman. Frank J. Urioste, Alan Pattillo. James Benson; music, Jaime Mendoza-Nava; song, Craig Wasson; production design, Robert Lang; art direction, Laida Perez; sound, Bob Litt, Danny Daniel; costumes-wardrobe, Erwin Arenas; asst. directors, Fred Slark, Hernan Robles. Reviewed at The Burbank Studios, Burbank, Calif., Jan. 11, '78. (MPAA Rating: R.) Running time: 125 MINS.

Tyrone Washington	Stan Shaw
Billy Ray Pike	Andrew Stevens
Alvin Foster	James Canning
Vinnie Fazio	Mihcael Lembeck
Dave Bisbee	Craig Wasson
Capt. Collins	Scott Hylands
Lt. Archer	James Whitmore Jr.
Sgt. Curry	Noble Willingham
Sgt. Loyce	Lee Ermey
Sgt. Aquilla	Santos Morales
Col. Metcalfe	Drew Michaels
Betsy	Karen Hilger
Nancy Bisbee	Peggy O'Neal
Col. Dong	Jose Avellana
Col. Trang	Vic Diaz

"The Boys In Company C" is a spotty but okay popcorn trade drama about five young Marines and how their lives were changed by duty in the Vietnam war. Laden with barracks dialog and played at the enlisted man's level, the Raymond Chow production, directed well by Sidney J. Furie, features strong performances by some very fine actors. The futility of the conflict emerges steadily during the longish 125-minute length. The Columbia release, first of this year's parade of Vietnam era films, looks like a good bet in the general action market via expeditious playoff.

Chow's Hong Kong-based Golden Harvest Films is trying to make a dent in the international film market, and one important achievement in this film is that Chow and producer Andre Morgan have avoided a major pitfall of others seeking such global appeal. To be specific, the film (though shot in the Philippines) has a totally made-in-Hollywood production look; no washed out titles, mushy sound, nervous color tones, slightly "off" looping/dubbing, etc. In fact, a lot of Hollywood technical work was done. All that adds up to a big commercial plus since the film, being about Americans, seems totally indigenous. This is no small point in its favor in North America and Europe, as the slew of ambitious failures dating from J. Arthur Rank down to present times can attest.

Not that "The Boys In Company C" is anywhere near a definitive film about the Vietnam debacle. No geopolitics or other cosmic matters intrude; instead, it's a deliberate action programmer, made effective within its intentions by the Rick Natkin and Furie screenplay collaboration and the topnotch performances.

Stan Shaw heads the cast as a dope pusher who sees Vietnam as a major new connection, until he matures into a natural leader. Andrew Stevens, son of Stella Stevens, is a Southern athlete who turns junkie in action. James Canning is an aspiring writer who records the bewildering and unnatural warfare. Michael Lembeck, son of Harvey Lembeck, plays a street-smart promoter. Craig Wasson is a hippie who accommodates to military service while retaining his peaceful nature. All of them are excellent.

At higher levels of authority are Scott Hylands, gung-hot to the point of mental imbalance as company commander; James Whitmore Jr., superb as a counter-balancing force in the company; Lee Ermey, originally hired as a technical advisor but outstanding as the boot camp drill instructor who shapes up the recruits for combat.

Too many films thus far have, besides avoiding any direct and developed story line about the war itself, spotlighted psychotic veterans in anti-social postwar behavior. But, after all, there were hundreds of thousands of persons who experienced the mismanaged war, hated it, yet returned hom with strengthened, if bruised, ideals and values. It's about time some of them were presented on the screen in the milieu which sorted out the men from the stooges.

Credits are all good. —*Murf.*

Running Fence
(DOCU-COLOR)

Fascinating cinematic description of Christo's immense nylon curtain project. Necessarily limited appeal.

Maysles Film Production and release of a film by David Maysles, Charlotte Zwerin, Albert Maysles. Associated editor, Kate Hirson; asst. editor, Donald Klocek; filming teams, Albert and David Maysles; camera (color), Robert Elfstrom, Donald Lenzer, Stephen Lighthill, Richard Pearce; sound, Petur Hliddal, Larry Johnson, David MacMillan, Nelson Stoll; location producer, Stanley Hirson; location production manager, Mike Giovingo; music, arranged and conducted by Jim Dickinson; singer, Jill Lancaster; sound mixer, Lee Dichter. Reviewed at Maysles screening room, New York, Jan. 20, '77. (No MPAA Rating). Running time: 57 MINS.

Having won an Academy Award nomination with their documentary on Bulgarian-born artist Christo's Colorado River project, it's little wonder that the Maysles brothers wouldn't team up again on an even bigger scheme — the artist's building a 24-mile long nylon fence across the landscape of northern California, eventually trailing off into the Pacific ocean.

Christo is an artist who has been successful in many areas of art, particularly graphics, but whose visual concept refuses to be limited to the confines of canvases or even the walls of a building. The only way to properly appreciate these huge projects, thrown across an entire countryside, is to take a helicopter ride along the route of the work. This is highly impractical for the general public, especially considering the short lifespan of the project (it was intended to be, and

was, taken down after two weeks of existence). This film, therefore, is not only its history but, ultimately, the best way to view Christo's handiwork.

There's more to it, however, than the construction as the artist expectedly ran into plenty of red tape, especially at the very beginning when he had to overcome the apathy and some resentment of ranch owners whose property he would need and at the ending when his teams of volunteers and young workers had to race against a time limit when some environmentalists try to get a court injunction to prevent the completion (the coast sequence) of the curtain.

This is a far more engrossing film than the Maysles' "Gray Gardens," in which many felt they exploited the subject. Even those indifferent to Christo's artistic concept will get caught up in an individual's heroic efforts to fulfill his own beliefs and, finally, the scenic sweep of the 18-foot high curtain, stretching beyond one's vision over miles and miles of countryside, is with considerable visual impact of its own.

All technical aspects of the film are superior, even the live sound which must have been extremely difficult to control under such circumstances. A fascinating film. It's being shown in its 16m size, initially, starting March 1 at a San Francisco theatre and will be blown up to 35m when it gets a national release. —*Robe.*

Les Liens De Sang
(Blood Relatives)
(FRENCH-CANADIAN-COLOR)

Paris, Jan. 24.

SNC release of Filmel-Cinevideo-Classic Films production. Stars Donald Sutherland. Directed by Claude Chabrol. Screenplay, Chabrol, R. Sydeny, from the novel by Ed McBain; camera (Eastmancolor), Jean Rabier; editor, Yves Langlois; music, Paul Jensen. Reviewed at CELTEC, Paris, Jan. 12, '78. Running time, 100 MINS.
Carella . . . . Donald Sutherland
Patricia . . . . Aude Landry
Muriel . . . . Lisa Langlois
Andrew . . . . Laurent Malet
Mrs. Carella . . . . Micheline Lanctot
Mother . . . . Stephane Audran
Doniac . . . . Donald Pleasence
Armstrong . . . . David Hemmings
(In English)

Claude Chabrol has made two pix locally in French and English but considers this one, made in Canada and based on a Yank police precinct novel of Ed McBain, his first film made directly in English albeit some of the actors appear dubbed. He is aiming at finally making a film in the U.S. but has said he thought it best to make his first North American venture in Canada with its mixed English, American and French backgrounds.

Film is not a hybrid but the Eng-

lish seems a bit strained at the beginning. It settles down as an inspector, played with a low profile and humanity by Donald' Sutherland, probes a knife killing of a teen-age girl and the wounding of another girl who was with her. At first it is felt to be the work of a psychotic but then segues into a middle-class family that might have been the crucible for the gory carryings-on.

Chabrol has often used murder as a catalyst in his grim pix about upper class French life. But here it is more psychosis, repression and jealousy than the more absorbing social patterns of his French work. It makes the pic somewhat ambivalent for it is a sudden revelation of madness rather than having more depth in characterization and a harder edge focused on its police work.

The girl killed was a first cousin to a 19-year-old boy and his younger sister, about 15. The dead girl was 17 and had lived as sister to the others. A slovenly drinking mother and a stern father make up this family that is shown to breed sudden dramatic unhinging and killing.

The cousin, wounded with the girl, says they were in a doorway escaping rain after going home from a party, when a man suddenly appeared with a knife and forced her cousin to commit fellatio before being knifed as she managed to escape after being cut up.

Later she blames her brother, but seemingly after an outburst at the cousin's funeral when he throws himself on the grave sobbing for her. But dogged Sutherland manages to unearth the dead firl's diary, helped by a garbage strike, which allows for a playback of their home life. The boy and cousin become lovers, have a pregnancy scare and he wants to marry her despite their blood ties.

But she is mixed up with an older man at her office. Chabrol unveils the real killer, the girl, logically along with Sutherland to finally show the killing itself for the girl was apparently jealous of her brother's attachment. Things have to be read into it as the lack of love given by the parents and the young girl's twisting of family and sexual love to a final murderous action.

Film could have playoff legs in most climes and is generally well played but does not quite get the hard edged balance of police work and the life centered around a case that caused it. Chabrol shows a narrative and atmospheric flair, rings in some solid sidebar feel in Donald Pleasence's rendering of a middleaged man who likes 13-year-old girls picked up as sex deviates are questioned and David Hemmings as the older man falling for the victim.

Film has mainly supporting pos-

sibilities in Anglo marts but posits some name values and a pic that keeps up interest throughout. Playing is generally good. Some more feeling for the tempo of the English lingo should have Chabrol ready for that Hollywood pic he hankers to do.
—*Mosk.*

The One And Only
(COLOR)

Very commercial Carl Reiner comedy.

Hollywood, Jan. 20.

Paramount Pictures release of a First Artists Production, produced by Steve Gordon, David V. Picker; executive producer, Robert Halmi. Stars Henry Winkler, Kim Darby. Directed by Carl Reiner. Screenplay, Gordon; camera (Movielab Color), Victor J. Kemper; editor, Bud Molin; music, Patrick Williams; new song, Alan and Marilyn Bergman; production design, Edward Carfagno; set decoration, Ruby Levitt; sound, John K. Wilkinson, Bud Alper; asst. director, Bob Birnbaum. Reviewed at Paramount Studios, L.A., Jan. 19, '78. (MPAA Rating: PG.) Running time, 98 MINS.
Andy Schmidt . . . . Henry Winkler
Mary Crawford . . . . Kim Darby
Sidney Seltzer . . . . Gene Saks
Mary's Parents . . . . William Daniels,
Polly Holliday
Moses . . . . Harold Gould
Milton Miller . . . . Herve Villechaize
Wrestling Announcers . . . . . Dick Lane, Bill Baldwin, Dennis James
Andy as Kid . . . . Anthony Battaglia
Arnold . . . . Ed Begley Jr.
Mary's Brother . . . . Brandon Cruz
Paul Harris . . . . Charles Frank

With Warners' "Oh, God!" having come off so well, "The One And Only" makes it two in a row for director Carl Reiner. And with the b.o. on Universal's "Heroes" so rewarding, Henry Winkler's star position, shared with Kim Darby, in "The One And Only" augurs well commercially for the First Artists project. Film is an amusing '50s comedy about a stage-struck egomaniac and his steadfast, though puzzled wife. Writer Steve Gordon produced with David V. Picker. Good outlook everywhere.

Apart from the film itself, Paramount now appears to be back in the business of making and releasing a regular series of films to various segments of the general audience. This is important to exhibitors particularly, and contrasts with an m.o. for several years of appearing to vault between heavily promoted event pix arriving every 12-18 months.

Story has Winkler an irrepressible showoff who sets his mind on winning Darby, and together they hit N.Y. where he hopes to make it big. But his success comes from carnival-type garishness in the wrestling ring, under the guidance of promoter Gene Saks who is excellent as a jaded entrepreneur. Also excellent is Herve Villechaize as a small, but urbane and horny wrestler.

Based on Winkler's two most recent films, there seems to be a pattern emerging; in early scenes he is introduced as an apparent kook, while later story development presents a more sensitive side which thereupon alternates with the nuttiness to lead to a serio-comic, low-key and upbeat fadeout. His less flamboyant acting abilities are obvious, so one hopes there will not come to pass the generic description of a "Henry Winkler role."

Darby, offscreen for about seven years, returns as a more mature performer and a good match for Winkler, neither competitive nor submissive in the interaction of characters. Her reaction dialog and expressions are extremely important to the credibility and viability of the story; she becomes every young girl in the audience. One of her best delivered lines comes when, after Winkler has done a number on her parents (William Daniels and Polly Holliday, both very effective), he asks if she still wants to get married. She says they have to — "I'm too embarrassed to have you as a date."

Production credits are all very good, including a well-chosen supporting cast. Unbilled but a never-to-be-forgotten point of reference in the 50's wrestling milieu is Dick Lane, vet L.A. sportscaster (and before that, longtime feature film character actor more formally known as Richard Lane). Wayne Fitzgerald designed the good titles, featuring b&w stills. —Murf.

Reina Zanahoria
(The Carrot Queen)
(SPANISH-COLOR)

Madrid, Jan. 13.

Labarone Films production. Written and directed by Gonzalo Suarez. Features entire cast. Exec producers, Oscar Kidelan and Leonardo Echegaray; camera (Eastmancolor), Carlos Suarez; music, Luis de Pablo; editor, Antonio Gimeno; sets, Alberto Corazon. Reviewed at Sala Carreno, Madrid, Jan. 12, '78. Running time: 90 MINS.

Cast: Jose Sacristan, Marilina Ross, Fernando Fernan Gomez, Diana Polakov, Fernando Hilbeck.

After successfully handling drama and a wry sort of humor in "Parranda," helmer-scribe Gonzalo Suarez has now reverted to a brand of slapstick humor and not-very-droll gags which some may find to be in the realm of "surrealism" and others deem more fitting for sophomoric charades. Either way, the effect is of a self-conscious and stilted film with a rambling story and some parodies which fail to evoke a laugh.

The hare-brained plot involves an American millionairess who owns a carrot empire, (played by Marilina Ross using a thick Yank accent), a bungling agency that wants to get the Spanish rights for the carrots, and a dazed and dim-witted salesman (Jose Sacristan) who, the ad hawks imagine, has the composite face of the "Carrot Queen's" four ex-husbands. The salesman is dubbed Jacinto 03 and is taught how to play tennis, make love, etc. There are a lot of people running into doors and getting hit in the crotch and other slapstick antics and ham acting, none of it adding up to even a social message, as in a far better film on a similar subject by Jose Luis Dibildos, "The New Spaniards." —Besa.

Po Mai Tidet
(The Widower)
(THAI-COLOR)

Bangkok, Jan. 11.

A New Five Star Productions release. Produced by Kiat Iampungporn. Directed by Sakka Charuchinda. Features entire cast. Story, Kanok Rekka; screenplay, Settawit; camera (color) Sompote Akarapan; editor, Narong Charuchinda; music, Prasert Chulaketr; sound recording, Pong Asavinikul, Kasem Militachinda; art director, Supote Charuchinda. Reviewed at Athens Theatre, Bangkok, Jan. 10, '77. Running time: 115 MINS.

Payap	Pairoj Sangvoributr
Taksina	Lalana Sulawan
Vien	Setta Sirachaiya
Kajit	Kamol Ngarmphinit
Khunphai Tileukdetr	Chuangyod Kolakit
Jok	Poompat Tamsekat
Jak	Poonthep Tamsekat

Following the tremendous success of "Wai Olawon" (Only 16) and "Rak Otaroot" (Only Sixteen 2), Pairoj Sangvoributr and Lalana Sulawan became the country's number one love team. Their predecessors, Sombat Metanee and Aranya Namwong, have never quite generated the same b.o. fever.

Director Sakka Charuchinda did not have to invent a new plot for his young lovers. All that was necessary was to keep things in a light-hearted vein, as close as possible to the comic nonsense of the "Wai Olawon" series.

There is one major difference, "Wai Olawon" had the quality to surprise. It built on stock situations, but most details used were fresh and spontaneous, as though director Piac Poster just thought of something good to add on the set, and simply tacked it on, with often very funny results.

Piac doesn't forget in most of his films to add local color. Even when Pairoj and Lalana were caught up in the modern world of haute couture and advertising in "Rak Otaroot," they still did not shed their typically Thai way of life, and without experiencing any cultural shock.

On the other hand, the popular twosome are again two modern youngsters moving in the world of local television in "Po Mai Tidet." Their milieu is entirely Hollywood-ish, making many scenes appear quaint. Whatever is Thai is lost. Pic deemphasizes it to make Pairoj and Lalana look like two completely westernized kids. —Cano.

Pae Kao
(The Scar)
(THAI-COLOR)

Bangkok, Jan. 10.

A Cherdchai Productions release. Produced by Thomchant Thanyachart. Directed by Cherd Songsri. Features entire cast. Story, Mai Muang Derm; screenplay, Rapeeporn and Thom Thatree; music, Samarn Karnchanapalin, Sanga Arampee, Chalie Intravichit, Cholmoo Chalanukroh; camera (color), Kavee Kiattinan, Suthat Buréepakdee and Somchai Leelanuruk; art directors, Urai Sirisombat and Sathorn Srichan; editor, Rom Ramnee. Reviewed at Paramount Theatre, Bangkok, Jan. 9, '77. Running time: 105 MINS.

Kwan	Sorapong Chatri
Riam	Nantana Ngaokrachang
Pooyay Tien	So Asanachinda
Gharman	Suwin Swangrat
Rom	Sirinthip Siriwan
Khun Nai Tongkam	Suphan Buranaphim
Ron	Kitti Daskorn
Chao	Setta Sirachaiya
Somchai	Chalit Fuangarom

Cherd Songsri's beautifully photographed film of "Pae Kao" (The Scar) immediately invites comparison with "Romeo and Juliet." Which is why the story and script of "Pae Kao" work against the picture.

A romantic tragedy about two young lovers who cannot marry because their fathers have sworn eternal enmity, "Pae Kao" lacks the poetic and profound dialog to raise shopworn material to the level of art.

Cherd's version tries to compensate by making the hero, Sorapong Chatri, sing humorous and bawdy country songs, mixed with some tender, very poignant ballads.

Nevertheless, they are not enough to keep the viewer interested, making the pic seem too long at 105 minutes. Every time the film quickens its pace, it is slowed down by musical numbers. —Cano.

Renaldo & Clara
(COLOR)

Four hour Dylan film that begs indulgence.

A Circuit Films release of a Lombard Street Films production, supervised by Jack Baran and Mel Howard. Written and directed by Bob Dylan. Camera, David Myers, Paul Goldsmith, Howard Alk, Michael Levine; editing, Dylan, Alk; sound, Gary Bourgeois, L.A. Johnson; sound editors, Bruce Nyznik, Peter Thillaye; mixers, Arthur Piantadosi, Les Fresholtz, Michael Minkler; blow up, Osvaldo Zornizer. Reviewed at Magno Screening Room, N.Y., Jan. 19, '78. (MPAA rating: R). Running time: 232 MINS.

Renaldo	Bob Dylan
Clara	Sara Dylan
Woman in White	Joan Baez
Bob Dylan	Ronnie Hawkins
Mrs. Dylan	Ronee Blakely

Also Jack Elliott, Harry Dean Stanton, Bob Neuwirth, Helena Kalloaniotes, Allen Ginsberg, David Blue, Roger McGuinn, Sam Shepard, Arlo Guthrie, Roberta Flack, others.

Here we have a film in which Bob Dylan is played by 300 pound Ronnie Hawkins and Bob Dylan plays somebody named Renaldo, a man with vague hair and sharp fingernails who doesn't give anyone straight answers. Somewhere on the back of this four-hour elephantine release rides a notion that Dylan wanted to say something about Existence, Truth and maybe even Beauty.

What really comes through is an attitude that the world is populated by slaves and icon worshippers, and realization that he is one more icon doesn't really serve as Dylan's saving grace. In fact, Dylan's making a film in which he is Renaldo, a man — when you can pin him down — who is a man you can't pin down, only serves to confuse the audience over whether he is being falsely humble or humbly false. Confusing? You bet.

In "Renaldo & Clara" Dylan is only capitalizing on audience regard for his private life, though he insists that it is not his intent.

In four hours of anything, including a deserted stadium, there are bound to be interesting moments, but that doesn't mean one can charge admission on the strength of these few. Most of the concert footage of his Rolling Thunder Revue, which would create a furious subtension if the sequences weren't so far apart, are good, though his wearing a mask to indicate he's wearing a mask gets a bit tiring.

Enough said, save that Allen Ginsberg playing the center of the universe really is the center of the universe. He is a haven of sanity in the midst of self-indulgence by an artist who fought many battles for the young against the Big Lie. As Ginsberg — bare-chested in a room with a lady wearing a feather boa she considers to be an extension of the ego — says, "This is a very strange situation to be in." Right on.

One other saving grace is David Blue, stuck at a pinball machine, recalling the lost days of Greenwich Village and the illusions that needed to be shed to grow up. Much of the improvisation in the film has a bigger payoff to the actors than to the audience, which can detect the lie in the slight smile at the corners of many mouths. —*Jac.*

La Criatura
(The Creature)
(SPANISH-COLOR)

Jan. 31.

Alborada P.C. and Guion P.C. production (Madrid). Directed by Eloy de la Iglesia. Features entire cast. Screenplay, Enrique Barreiro; editor, Julip Pena; camera (Eastmancolor), Raul Artigaut; music, Victor Aute. Reviewed at Minicine 3 (Madrid), Jan. '78. Running time: **100 MINS.**

Cast: Ana Belen, Juan Diego, Claudia Gravi, Ramon Reparaz, Manuel Pereiro, Barbara Lys, Francisco Melgares.

"The Creature" has a few embryonic ideas in it which, if properly developed, might have resulted in a significant statement on present-day Spain, but they are lost in an inchoate jumble of pointless symbolism, sex, political caricature and at times even suggested supernaturalism, all of it ultimately unconvincing and at times painfully contrived.

Story revolves around a famous tv emcee (a dead ringer for Jose Maria Inigo) played by Juan Diego, his sexually and intellectually unfulfilled wife (Ana Belen) and an eponymous black cur. During a car trip, the wife goes over to pet a dog at a gas station, but the hound snarls and frightens her, and she loses the unborn baby she is carrying. Bereft, the couple take a vacation, where they see a similar dog on the beach. Wife befriends dog and takes him back to her Madrid duplex, where the pet soon takes on the importance of her lost child, and ultimately of her lover. The latter is unimaginatively suggested by the very obviously-trained dog (he keeps on looking back at the camera and tilting his head) pulls her bathtowel away, and jumps up on her bed at night.

It all ends with the emcee, who by the way is strictly Catholic and a member of a party which is a take-off on Manuel Fraga's Alianza Popular, raping his wife and making her pregnant again. They temporarily get rid of the dog, but at the end she goes to the dog (or dogs) to live alone in her El Escorial villa with her unborn child. So? None of it adds up to anything, and the political and video ends are left dangling embarrassingly, while the trained mutt presumably is sent back to the kennels in filmic disgrace. Thesping

and technical credits are merely okay and offshore sales prospects seem dim. —*Besa.*

Yompaban Cha
(Heaven and Hell)
(THAI-COLOR)

Bangkok, Jan. 18.

An Asvin Pictures release. Produced, idea and story by Prince Bhanubhandu Yugala. Written and directed by Niramitr. Features entire cast. Executive producer, Mom Prim Yugala; camera (color), Anant Inroah; editor, Prom Rungrangsri; music, Chalie Intravijit and Sanga Arampi; sound recordist, Kasem Militachinda. Reviewed at Siri Hall theatre, Bangkok, Jan. 17, '78. Running time: **135 MINS.**

Pisawon	Krung Srivilai
Remrudee	Aranya Namwong
Phaya Yom	Manop Assawathep
Ramjai	Choosri Misomon
Om	Chinadit Bunnag
Thep	Pairoj Jaising
Kada	Anant Samasap
Stranger	Sayant Chantrawiboon
Dao	Orsa Issarangkul Na Ayudhya

Krung Srivilai plays the reincarnation of a heartbroken farmer, Chinadit Bunnag, who pleads with the god of the dead, Manop Assawathep, to let him return to life to be reunited with his loved one, Aranya Namwong.

Manop decides to make Chinadit handsomer by turning him into Krung. Later, this results in embarrassing complications, because Krung's other identity is that of a married man. The latter's deserted wife breaks up the wedding

On his return visit to Earth, Krung suddenly finds himself dangling from the top of the Suthat Temple giant swing (a famous landmark in Bangkok). Deluded into thinking that Aranya loves him, she has to betray Krung twice before he realizes the truth.

"Yompaban Cha" has sex, comedy, action, fantasy — a little of everything. Which has been the standard approach to local film-making, until producers began to concentrate on either action-drama or action-comedy during the past two years.

Krung Srivilai gives his best performance since his award-winning role in "Choo" (The Adulterer). Manop is outstanding in a character role. —*Cano.*

Jubilee
(BRITISH-COLOR)

London, Jan. 26.

A Cinegate release of a Megalovision Film. Produced by Howard Malin and James Whaley. Directed by Derek Jarman. Features entire cast. Camera (color), Peter Middleton; sound, John Hayes; supervising editor, Tom Priestley; editor, Nick Barnard; design, Christopher Hobbs; continuity, Judy Futrille; asst. director, Guy Ford; prod. manager, Mordechai Schreiber; music, Suzi Pinns, Brian Eno, Adam and the Ants, Siouxsie and the Banshees, Chelsea, Wayne County, Electric Chairs, Maneaters, and Amilcar. Re-

viewed at the Gate Cinema, London, Jan. 24, '78. Running time: **103 MINS.**

Queen Elizabeth I	Jenny Runacre
Amyl Nitrite	Jordan
Crabs	Little Nell
Viv	Linda Spurrier
Chaos	Hermine Demoriane
Mad	Toyah Willcox
John Dee	Richard O'Brien
Kid	Adam Ant
Angel	Ian Charleson
Sphinx	Karl Johnson
Max	Neil Kennedy
Borgia Ginz	Orlando
Cabaret	Lindsay Kemp and troupe

Derek Jarman's "Jubilee" is one of the most original, bold, and exciting features to have come out of Britain this decade.

The industry proper may be napping, but Jarman, along with a highly-gifted cast and crew, has forged a film which through its brutal and lyrical vision of contemporary England, should help to restore native and international faith in British cinema.

Produced by Howard Malin and James Whaley of Megalovision Films whose first effort was the financially successful "Sebastiane," also directed by Jarman, the film's unique aspects of design, music, and action assure a broad popular and critical response.

With its punkish soundtrack, attitudes, and vision of urban disintegration, "Jubilee" could duplicate the cultural impact that "Easy Rider" had upon the young generation of approximately 10 years ago. While the film's electric performances, operatic elegance, and narrative sophistication should appeal to both older audiences and film buffs alike.

The year is 1578. Queen Elizabeth I is transported by an angel into the future (roughly our present), where she has "the shadow of the time" revealed to her.

Observing a renegade women's collective (a pyromaniac, a punk star, a nympho, a bent historian, etc.), Her Majesty watches as the "ladies" and their friends go about their picaresque misadventures — disrupting a cafe, a punk audition, a murder spree.

Through this process of disemboweling the present through the memory of the past and the anticipation of the future, Jarman unravels the nation's social history in a way that other features haven't even attempted.

At times, amidst the story's violence (there are two vicious killings), black humor, and loose fire hose energy, the film — like the characters—seems to career out of control.

In fact, not only is this equilibrium evident in the delicate dreamlike juggling of time, location and musical modes (for which large credit rests with the film's editors), but also within the feature's conclusion, which despite the overall

bleakness of the vision, turns out to be enchanting.

As noted, much of the spell into which "Jubilee" casts the viewer must go to the film's superb production values, work, and performances.

Peter Middleton's photography is versatile and evocative as it shifts between the lush garden world of Elizabeth I and the gristle of the modern streets. The editing by Tom Priestley and Nick Barnard is extraordinary. And the music by Suzi Pinns, Brian Eno, and Adam and the Ants is vital and refreshingly used.

Toyah Willcox, as an over the edge firebug, gives the film's finest performance. Jenny Runacre, in a demanding dual role as Elizabeth I and the leader of the collective, is marvelous. And Orlando, as the world-owning impresario Borgia Ginz, steals every scene he's in.
—*Coli.*

La Coquito
(SPANISH-COLOR)

Madrid, Jan. 31.

Impala and Pedro Maso P.C. (Madrid) production. Directed by Pedro Maso. Features entire cast. Screenplay, Pedro Maso, Antonio Vich, based on novel by Joaquin Belda; camera (Eastmancolor), Alejandro Ulloa; music, Gregorio Garcia Segura; sets, Ramiro Gomez; editor, Alfonso Santacana. Reviewed at Cine Fantasio (Madrid), Jan. 21, '78. Running time: **105 MINS.**

La Coquito	Ilyana Ross
Micaela	Amparo Rivelles
Julio	Fernando Allende
Gonzalo	Carlos Bracho
Raimundo	Juanito Navarro
Don Alejo	Pancho Cordova
Vidriales	Rafael Navarro

Handsome production values, magnificent photography by Alejandro Ulloa, top supporting cast and a mesmerizing Ilyana Ross (a former Miss Puerto Rico) in the title role make "La Coquito" one of the year's most attractive Spanish films for offshore sales, especially in Latin and Hispano circuits, but also apt for the less-sophisticated non-Latin spin-offs.

Admittedly the story is a bit soap-operaish and the ending unsatisfactory, and more could have been done with as fascinating a subject as the "cupletistas" of the 1920s, but Pedro Maso has been largely successful in evoking what in retrospect was an exciting period; with taste, talent and expertise, he chronicles the life of one of these "cupletistas," based loosely on the life of "La Chelito."

The cuple (couplet) was a genre which in some ways might be compared to the cabaret phenomenon in Germany in the 20s, though the former was generally erotic rather than political in its intent. Different from Yank variety acts, or French chansonniers or German cabaret performers, the famous cupletistas shared with their foreign siblings an aura of illrepute and scandal as they titillated audiences with risque songs and flimsy costumes.

The times in Spain were as stormy and tumultuous as in pre-Hitler Germany, and Maso touches in passing on anarchist and socialist unrest in Madrid, the life of the fancy clubs and casinos and the glamor of the era.

Using footage shot in Puerto Rico, Maso traces the rise of what was a voluptuous but ignorant farmgirl from Cuba to her local success in Havana and then her rise to fame in pre-war Madrid. Ilyana Ross is a knock-out in the part; her moody, provocative songs combined with her saftige physical allures make her the sultry sex bomb of the year. Her singing style is at times reminiscent of Sara Montiel. Others in the cast are perfect foils for the cupletista. These include a doddering septuagenarian who buys a theatre for her, a dashing count playing the local politics of the time, a Socialist student, and a protective mother-agent.

Maso, art director Ramiro Gomez and lenser Alejandro Ulloa have lavishly recreated the Madrid of the 20s, and scenes range from a demonstration in front of the North Railroad Station to a chotis dance at Mingo's. The script isn't much, but that doesn't matter since the musical numbers are eye-catchers. Pic has a few scenes that might run into censorship problems in some countries, but even these are handled with decorous taste. —Besa.

Deal
(DOCU-COLOR)

A Schott-Vaughn production presented by Document/CB. Produced by E.J. Vaughn. No distributor. Directed by John Schott and Vaughn in collaboration with Robert M. Young. Conceived by Robert Horvitz, Schott and Vaughn. Camera (color), Young and Tom McDonough; editor, Schott; sound, Larry Loewinger and Vic Losick. Reviewed at Ford Foundation screening room, New York, Jan. 26, '78. (No MPAA Rating). Running time: 95 MINS.

As a means of showing commercial television's impact upon American society, "Deal" focuses on one of the industry's top gameshows. The behind the scenes techniques, preparation and physical organization of Hatos-Hall Productions' "Let's Make a Deal" television show is painstakingly chronicled in a 95-minute color documentary.

To some of the less informed public, this $250,000 independently financed film may provide an education. But whether the average filmgoer wants such an education is questionable. For this probing venture into advertisers' needs, what the public wants, what the network

nabobs want, and the profits that ride on the right decisions appears a bit too trady for most audiences.

Film was produced by E.J. Vaughn who also directed with John Schott in collaboration with Robert M. Young. Both Vaughn and Schott, with broad academic backgrounds, have lectured on films at such cultural showcases as the Museum of Modern Art, N.Y., and the Dayton Art Institute.

For the time being, "Deal" reportedly will be distributed theatrically by Vaughn, Schott and their associates on their own, with a March opening envisioned in New York. An adroit promotional campaign, promising to unveil the commercial mysteries behind the box, could be effective in generating patron interest. However, the subject appears to lend itself primarily to intimate houses that cater to a more literate clientele.

In what might be considered a foreword, the film reproduces a quote from Les Brown's book, "Television, the Business Behind the Box": "In day-to-day commerce, television is not so much interested in the business of communications as in the business of delivering people to advertisers. People are the merchandise, not the shows. The shows are merely the bait...".

That quote from a former tv editor of Variety, now with N.Y. Times, aptly sets the stage and Vaughn & Schott take it from there. They toss in a variety of interviews with key personnel of "Let's Make a Deal" including Monty Hall, who emcees and co-owns the show with producer Stefan Hatos; the program's writers, announcer, Hatos himself and sundry ABC-TV execs, among others.

And it can't be said that anyone was self-effacing. For exampel, Hall says laconically: "Grant us the fact that what we do, we do very, very well." Lloyd Gaines, ABC Director of Daytime Programming, West Coast, also comes to the point. "'Deal's" success is very simple," he said, "it's based on greed. Good old American greed. That's the success of the show."

Vaughn and Schott use a "candid camera" technique in developing their subject. It ably captures the mood and excitement that surrounds this show which has been on the tube for 14 years. Schott's editing could have been tighter since the 95-minute running time seems to belabor the point, even though he and Vaughn believe this gameshow has been "pivotal in the history of television." —Gilb.

The End of the World in Our Usual Bed in a Night Full of Rain
(COLOR)

Wertmuller's English-language debut. Should click in art situations but wider appeal unlikely.

———

Hollywood, Jan. 21.

A Warner Bros. release of a Liberty Film, produced by Gil Shiva. Written and directed by Lina Wertmuller. Stars Giancarlo Giannini, Candice Bergen. Executive producer, Harry Colombo; camera (technicolor), Giuseppe Rotunno; editor, Franco Fraticelli; art director, Enrico Job; music, G.B. Pergolesi, Roberto De Simone; assistant director, Gianni Arduini; costume designer, Benito Persico; set designer; Gianni Giovagnoni; production manager, Jone Tuzi; Reviewed at The Burbank Studios, Jan. 20, '78. (MPAA Rating: R.) Running time: 104MINS.
Paolo .... Giancarlo Giannini
Lizzy .... Candice Bergen
The Friends: Michael Tucker, Mario Scarpetta, Lucio Amelio, Massimo Wertmuller, Anna Papa, Anne Byrne, Flora Carabella, Anita Paltrinieri, Giuliana Carnescecchi, Alice Colombo Oxman.

By couching mankind's oldest conflict — the battle of the sexes — in Marxist and feminist rhetoric, Italian director Lina Wertmuller has carved herself a reputation as a political filmmaker. It's now called "the crisis of the couple," but in the end it amounts to no more than a husband and wife arguing about who should do the dishes.

In "A Night Full of Rain" Wertmuller has them arguing in ideological terms and Warner Bros. has them fight in English. Removing the subtitles and casting Candice Bergen in one of the two leads should broaden Wertmuller's art circuit appeal somewhat. Still, this work is more of a tract than an entertainment — a salon movie — and that's a turnoff to the general audience.

None of this is to downplay Wertmuller's obvious technical talents. She is a proficient filmmaker and this work, as with "Swept Away," "Love and Anarchy" and "The Seduction of Mimi," for example, is stylish and settings and Giuseppe Rotunno's photography radiant.

It is the talky, dense, precious dialog which is so much a part of her script that makes this film ponderous and should prevent crossover beyond her sizable cult.

The film opens at a festival in Italy. Candice Bergen, an American photographer, and Giancarlo Giannini, an Italian journalist, meet after Bergen intercedes in a fight between a local girl and her fiance. Giannini, Wertmuller's regular collaborator, helps Bergen escape the brawl, attempts to seduce her, meets her again in San Francisco where the two fall in love and marry.

This does not turn out to be a mar-

riage made in heaven. The two are constantly in conflict — Bergen wants to commit herself to the feminist movement, Giannini is a Communist chauvinist who likes his shirts hand-laundered. They feud. Somehow serving as a chorus to their conflict is a collection of friends — straight out of Wertmuller's previous association with Fellini — seen in fantasy scenes and in flashbacks.

"A Night Full of Rain" is the first of three pictures Wertmuller is scheduled to make for Warner Bros. Her initial English-language effort does not translate well. It's a foreign film with the actors reciting subtitles rather than dialogue.

With two films remaining on her pact with Warners, it would be interesting to see Wertmuller tackle someone else's script, to see how she would shape an American subject with her point of view. By continuing to direct her own scripts, especially English ones, she seems headed towards repetition and superficial repetition at that. — Hege.

———

In Kluis
(The Enclosure)
(BELGIAN-COLOR)

———

Brussels, Jan. 21.

Progres Films release of Visie-Filmproduction. Produced by Roland Verhavert. Written and directed by Jan Gruyaert. Features entire cast. Camera (Eastmancolor), Ben Tenniglo; art directors, Bob Van Reeth, Herman Jacobs; assistant director, Mary Hehuat; editor, Gust Malfliet; sound, Joos Suetens. Reviewed at 5th International Film Festival, Brussels, Jan. 20, '78. Running time: 100 MINS.
Keeper .... Bert Andre
Painter .... Herman Jacobs
Young Woman .... Mirjam Nuyten
Photographer ....Mary Hehuat

This film has the trappings of a little jewel: an original story, tasteful locations and it dares turn its back to the generalities and conventions of Belgian filmmaking. In his first long feature Jan Gruyaert proves not only a filmic flair but perfect taste: no vulgarity here, no concessions to permissive tastes.

Nudity there is but justified but no violent love making because there is simply no need for it. Unfortunately, this young director has all the flaws of his undeniable qualities, first being that he has not yet mastered the art of ellipsis and is apparently unable to resist the lure of framing beautiful pictures in attractive canvases. Result is that built on an extremely frail story line, his film quickly becomes repetitive, hence irritating.

A pity this for there is great visual beauty in "In Kluis," made with a substantial subsidy from the Flemish Ministry of Culture — slightly over $150,000, the rest provided by private investment — which eloquently shows on the screen with excellent use of an attractive location. A far better director than script writer, Gruyaert should in his next film concentrate more on courting his camera than dabbling with pen or typewriter.

Hero here concerned is a deaf-and-dumb nature keeper living in what remains of a medieval castle. Through telescope and binoculars he keeps a vigilant eye on his territory and hardly ever something happens in his solitary life. Till the day when a painter starts building a strange house across the river in full view of the recluse's refuge. From that very moment, the man becomes a peeping tom, all the more fascinated since the painter's model frolicks about in the altogether. Thus he also watches the progressive deterioration in the couple's behaviour, finally sees the woman pack and leave and the unsociable painter, having taken great pains in building an enclosure around his domain, destroying it in a frenzy, wounding himself in the process.

Technically, pic is handsomely mounted and there is first-rate camerawork, shots through the watching lenses being especially fine. To make more perceptible the strange world of the deaf-and-mute, dialogue has been entirely done away with in favor of sound only. Thus a subtle atmosphere, well suited to the cause of events, is created and maintained till the end. Sounds are vaguely perceived, mostly provided by nature, and the late Keon De Bruyne score — he died while film was being edited — proves extremely effective. It really is a great pity that this film proves so desperately slow. Trimmed of its superfluous and reduced to its essentials, this could indeed prove a gem.

Outside Bert Andre, importantly featured and quite good as the deaf-and-mute, playing is nondescript, which is unimportant, nature assuming star importance here.

—Flor.

Fingers
(COLOR)

Unimpressive character study. Thin outlook.

Hollywood, Jan. 10.
Brut Productions release, produced by George Barrie. Stars Harvey Keitel. Written and directed by James Toback. Camera (Eastmancolor), Mike Chapman; editor, Robert Lawrence; production design, Gene Rudolf; set decoration, Fred Weiler; sound, Bill Varney, Lee Lasarowitz; costumes-wardrobe, Albert Wolsky; asst. director, Dan McCauley. Reviewed at Frankovich Screening Room, L.A., Jan. 10, '78. (MPAA Rating: R). Running time, 90 MINS.
Jimmy Angelilli .... Harvey Keitel
Carol .... Tisa Farrow
Deems .... Jim Brown
Ben Angelelli .... Michael V. Gazzo
Mother .... Marian Seldes
Christa .... Carole Francis

Anita .... Georgette Muir
Butch .... Danny Aiello
Arthur Fox .... Dominick Chianese
Riccamonza .... Anthony Siroco
Julie .... Tanya Roberts
Gino .... Ed Marinaro
Cop .... Zack Norman
Dr. Fry .... Murray Mosten
Esther .... Jane Elder
Luchino .... Lenny Montana
Raymond .... Frank Pesche

"Fingers" is an uneven and confused R-rated melodrama starring Harvey Keitel as a 32-year-old teenager whose classical pianist ambitions, sexual immaturity and gangland family origins collide in an artistic mess. Writer James Toback ("The Gambler") makes his directorial bow for producer George Barrie's Brut Prods. Toback's talent periodically flashes through the undisciplined confusion. Performances overall are very good, but the film is an offbeat item with limited outlook in some urban situations.

The character Keitel plays is torn between several strong influences: Michael V. Gazzo, his aging hood father; Tisa Farrow, a passing stranger on whom he focusses extreme fractured macho sexual pathology; his own ambitions to be a serious musician as was mother Marian Seldes, long ago committed to an asylum. In the course of 90 minutes, Keitel must make this character plausible. He can't; nobody could.

Basic problem is script's lack of simplicity. To be sure, everyone is a mixture of periodically conflicting emotions and hangups; that's life. But art must select, spotlight, focus and place these pieces in some sort of organized perspective. As written, Keitel's character is a ticking time bomb. Who cares about time bombs, other than being as far away as possible?

Jim Brown, as ever a strong screen presence, has a few good scenes as the man whom Farrow cannot leave despite occasional revulsion. That's just another of the many cluttered plot lines.

Production credits are okay.

—Murf.

Avoriaz Fest

L'Ange et La Femme
(Angel and Woman)
(CANADIAN-B&W-16m)

Avoriaz, Jan. 31.
Carle release and production. Stars Carole Laure, Lewis Furey. Written and directed by Gilles Carle. Camera (black and white), Francois Portat; music, Lewis Furey. Reviewed at Avoriaz Fantastic Film Fest, Jan. 20, '78. Running time, 90 MINS.
Girl .... Carole Laure
Man .... Lewis Furey
Boss .... Steve Lack

Made in black-and-white and in seven days, a protest reportedly, of

director Gilles Carle towards the difficulties of making personal films in French-speaking Quebec in Canada, this is still a rather outmoded, vague and finally self indulgent pic that will not help the situation in Quebec.

A girl is shot down on a snowy hill by a machine gun and picked up by a long-haired youth. He takes her to his isolated cabin where he reanimates her by breathing on her wounds. They become lovers and Carole Laure, now making films here, looks good although the love scenes are finally exploited rather than laced into the fabric of this meandering precious affair.

It seems she had worked as a dancer in a club and been murdered because she expressed dangerous social ideas about Chile and corruption to her audiences instead of attending to her suggestive dancing. *— Mosk.*

Photo Souvenir
(FRENCH-COLOR-16m)

Avoriaz, Jan. 31.
FR3 Lyon release and production. Features entire cast. Directed by Edmond Sechan. Screenplay, Jean-Claude Carriere, Sechan; camera (Color), Guy Delattre; music, Georges Delerue. Reviewed at Avoriaz Fantastic Film Fest, Jan. 22, '78. Running time, 90 MINS.
Doctor .... Jean-Claude Carriere
Patient .... Vania Vilers
Niece .... Daniele Ayme
Wife .... Ginette Mathieu
Groom .... Bernard Lecoq

Made as a tv film, pic does not have the vitality, inventiveness or flair in direction and story to make this fantasy tale of viable theatrical voltage. On video, its discursiveness, repetitiveness and stolid playing may be acceptable.

A noted heart doctor is handed a Polaroid camera by a patient whose heart he had transplanted after the latter had had an accident. The man is apparently alright but dies when his photograph shows up after the doctor has taken the picture of a friend for whom he is planning a transplant.

He keeps the camera when he cannot return it and finds pictures can seem to predict death and a just-married couple do not appear on one. Finally it is the doctor's demise that is trying to be warned of by the camera. The idea is good but somewhat too dragged out.

— Mosk.

The Other Side of the Mountain - Part 2
(COLOR)

Sequel to "Other Side of The Mountain" is a weeper. Strong performance by Marilyn Hassett.

Hollywood, Jan. 24.
Universal release of a Filmways Production. Produced by Edward S. Feldman. Directed by Larry Peerce. Stars Marilyn Hassett, Timothy Bottoms. Screenplay, Douglas Day Stewart; camera (Technicolor), Ric Waite; editor, Eve Newman, Walter Hannemann; art director, William Campbell; music, Lee Holdridge; set decoration, John Dwyer; sound, Don Sharpless, Robert L. Hoyt; sound effects editor, Gordon Ecker Jr.; special effects, Art Brewer. Reviewed in Hollywood, Jan. 24, '78. (MPAA Rating - PG). Running time: 105 MINS.
Jill Kinmont .... Marilyn Hassett
John Boothe .... Timothy Bottoms
June Kinmont .... Nan Martin
Audra-Jo .... Belinda J. Montgomery
Linda .... Gretchen Corbett
Bill Kinmont .... William Bryant
Mr. Boothe .... James A. Bottoms
Mrs. Boothe .... June Dayton
Roy Boothe .... Curtis Credel
Beverly Boothe .... Carol Tru Foster
Mel .... Charles Frank
Doctor .... George Petrie
Presenter at luncheon .... Ross Durfee
Woman at bar .... Jackie Russell
Waitress .... Gerri Nelson
Bob Kinmont .... Tom Jordan
Jerry Kinmont .... Harry Moses
Doctor .... Myron Healey
Minister .... Rev. Bee Landis
Wrangler .... Steve Conte
Gary .... Craig Chudy
Indian boy .... David Yanez
Indian girl .... Marlina Vega

"The Other Side Of The Mountain — Part 2" is a four-hankie weepie in the tradition of formula "Women's Films." Commercially, it's got everything this kind of film should have — attractive sick people who eventually get happy if not better, picture postcard settings, a 99-minute running time and a built-in audience from the original 1975 Universal release. Outlook for the Filmways Production starring Marilyn Hassett and Timothy Bottoms is strong for all markets.

Producer Edward S. Feldman has reunited a number of the talents who helped make the original — the story of skier Jill Kinmont's refusal to give up after a near fatal skiing accident put her in a wheelchair for life — a simple, compassionate and inspiring tale. Larry Peerce returns to direct; Hassett again commands in the lead role; Belinda J. Montgomery plays a courageous friend, who was struck down by polio; Nan Martin repeats as Kinmont's mother; and Eve Newmann edits. Technical credits are fine. Much of the lensing once again took place on location in Bishop, California, where Kinmont now lives.

Basic weakness of the followup lies in Douglas Day Stewart's screenplay. To be fair, Stewart didn't have as much to work with as did David Seltzer, who scripted the original. The crucial dramatic events in Kinmont's life have occurred already in Part One — her competitive skiing triumphs, her accident, her recovery, her struggle through college, her achievements as a teacher, and the death of her fiancee, daredevil Dick Buek.

So what Stewart has created, albeit from Kinmont's real life, is basically a love story, complete with hokum and a degree of implausibility. A certain percentage of the audience that enjoyed the original will return for the follow up; those in the market for a good cry will not be disappointed.

The film picks up a few years after the original left off. Kinmont, now teaching in L.A., has been named "Woman of the Year." She takes a vacation in Bishop, sees some old friends and makes a new one, Timothy Bottoms, a long haul trucker and her summer landlord.

Kinmont reluctantly falls in love ("every man I've ever loved has died"). They court, vacation together in Reno and Canada where Kinmont, a quadraplegic, gets to "feel like a woman for the first time," split up and have a reconciliation on the road between Bishop and L.A. in a scene sure to swell eyes from coast to coast.

Bottoms is the film's second weakness. Again, his part is not as vital as the Dick Buek role played so well by Jeff Bridges in the original. But Bottoms is not Bridges and he's also slightly miscast as the taciturn trucker.

One of the strengths of this sequel is that it can stand by itself. Kinmont's story is now wellknown and the film gives enough information through flashbacks and subtle exposition to be accessible to those who missed the original. And the original was strong enough to draw audiences back to the theatre for this one. —*Hege.*

The Medusa Touch
(BRITISH-COLOR)

Brussels, Jan. 28.

Elan Film release of ITC Entertainment Production. Produced by Lew Grade, Arnon Milchan, Elliot Kastner. Directed by Jack Gold. Features entire cast. Screenplay, John Briley, Jack Gold, from novel by Peter Van Greenaway: camera (Technicolor, Panavision), Arthur Ibbetson: editor, Anne V Coate: art director, Peter Mullins. Reviewed at Burssels Film Festival, Passage 44, Brussels, Jan. 27, '78. Running time: 110 MINS.

John Morlar	Richard Burton
Brunel	Lino Ventura
Dr. Zonfeld	Lee Remick
Assistant commissioner	Harry Andrews
Patricia	Marie-Christine Barrault
Atropos	Michael Hordern
Dr. Johnson	Gordon Jackson
Townley	Derek Jacobi
Duff	Michael Byrne
Parrish	Jeremy Brett
Pennington	Robert Lang

Another disaster film? Not exactly, even if at the end a London cathedral caves in, with many victims trapped underneath the rubble but with the Queen of England saved in the nick of time. These scenes, realistically treated and technically good, are among the highlights of this lavishly-produced film. There are other impressive scenes, including the crashing of a jet into a skyscraper on the London skyline. There are also sufficient dramatic moments to keep interest alive in the story itself.

It all starts with a murder. John Morlar (Richard Burton) is attacked by an unknown intruder who bashes in his skull. Why? The man didn't seem to have a single enemy and there seems to be no motive. Therefore Inspector Brunel is puzzled. Why a French detective instead of British? Apparently due to French financial participation in this film. In any case, it allows Lino Ventura to make his British film debut and very good he is.

Brunel finally discovers a clue leading to a psychiatrist Dr. Zonfeld played by Lee Remick. She had treated Morlar for reasons not stated at once.

It turns out that Morlar is not dead at all. His mind is fighting a desperate battle to survive. Even as a child, Morlar proved a very odd number indeed. His files relate to a vast series of disasters and apparently unsolved mysteries. Brunel is slowly but surely put on the right track. Will more innocent people have to be sacrificed by a monster whose body is almost dead but whose mind is plotting ever more awful deeds?

Tension mounts in this well-paced story. Director Jack Gold controls all the angles of this improbable story. Slick production assets abound and there is very good acting by the four principals, main part here being played by Ventura, at ease in a typical British atmosphere. Burton has some very effective moments too as does Remick.

Technically, "The Medusa Touch" is highly professional with excellent camera work. —*Flor.*

Blue Collar
(COLOR)

Impressive directorial debut by Paul Schrader. Urban market appeal.

Hollywood, Jan. 17.

Universal release of a T.A.T. Communications Co. production. Executive producer, Robin French. Produced by Don Guest. Directed by Paul Schrader. Stars Richard Pryor, Harvey Keitel, Yaphet Kotto. Screenplay, Paul Schrader, Leonard Schrader, based on source material by Sydney A. Glass; camera (Technicolor), Bobby Byrne; music, Jack Nitzsche; film editor, Tom Rolf; production designer, Lawrence G. Paull; set decorator, Peggy Cummings; sound, Willie Burton, Marvin Lewis, Winfred Tennison; special musical arrangements, Ry Cooder. Reviewed in Hollywood, Jan. 17, '78. (MPAA Rating: R) Running time: 110 MINS.

Zeke	Richard Pryor
Jerry	Harvey Keitel
Smokey	Yaphet Kotto
Bobby Joe	Ed Begley Jr.
Eddie Johnson	Harry Bellaver
Jenkins	George Memmoli
Arlene Bartowski	Lucy Saroyan
Clarence Hill	Lane Smith
John Burrows	Cliff De Young
Dogshit Miller	Borah Silver
Caroline Brown	Chip Fields
Hank	Harry Northup
IRS Man	Leonard Gaines
Sumabitch	Milton Selzer
Barney	Sammy Warren
Charlie T. Hernandez	Jimmy Martinez
Superintendent	Jerry Dahlmann

Also: Denny Arnold, Rock Riddle, Stacey Baldwin, Steve Butts, Stephen P. Dunn, Speedy Brown, Davone Florence, Eddie Singleton, Rya Singleton, Vermettya Royster, Jaime Carreire.

Paul Schrader's directorial debut is an artistic triumph. Best known as the scripter of "Taxi Driver" and "Obsession," in "Blue Collar" Schrader has transformed a carefully researched original screenplay penned by him and his brother, Leonard Schrader, into a powerful, gritty, seamless profile of three automobile assembly line workers banging their heads against the monotony and corruption that is the factory system.

In one sense, the T.A.T. Communications production succeeds where documentaries have usually failed. It is a picture about the monotony and routine of factory life that isn't monotonous, but is realistic. Regardless of where individual scenes are set — at the after-work tavern, at a bowling alley, at a worker's home, in the union headquarters, or in a Detroit street — the factory dominates every frame of this film. Schrader, along with cinematographer Bobby Byrne and production designer Lawrence G. Paull, establish this from shot number one.

Notwithstanding reports of conflict among cast and crew during location shooting at the Checker Motor Company plant in Kalamazoo, Michigan, the film's three stars — Richard Pryor, Harvey Keitel and Yaphet Kotto — all turn in outstanding and disciplined performances.

Rough language, an underlayer of violence and the picture's setting will limit the appeal of the Universal release mostly to big cities. But slow and careful buildup, coupled with almost certain critical praise and subsequent word-of-mouth, should help.

Also, Keitel, who's getting lotsa notice for his work in two other films, "Fingers," and "The Duellists," is beginning to have some marquee value. Pryor, in his strongest dramatic performance to date, continues to draw in many areas. Still, "Blue Collar" will be a tough sell outside large urban markets.

In many ways it is a hopeless film. For the worker who remains on the line his whole life, the future holds second jobs, loan sharks and an unhappy family life. The union, which is supposed to protect the workers, is out to exploit them just as much as management. Government, as represented by IRS and FBI men, offers no relief.

Plot of "Blue Collar" centers around the three workers' attempts to confront and battle the reality of this system as Schrader views it. The three devise a plan to rob the union, which in the end turns into another helpless action.

"Blue Collar" is a powerful film that marks the entry of a major American film talent. Schrader, who rolls "Hardcore" later this month and who has another script, "Old Boyfriends," set to enter production under Joan Tewkesbury's direction in March, is someone to watch. —*Hege.*

Beyond And Back
(COLOR)

Another incredibly amateurish four-wall item from Sunn Classic. Watch the marketing, not the film.

Hollywood, Feb. 2.

A Sunn Classic Pictures release, produced by Charles E. Sellier Jr. Directed by James L. Conway. Written by Stephen Lord, based in part on the book by Ralph Wilkerson. Camera (Technicolor), Henning Schellerup; editor, James D. Wells; music, Bob Summers; art director, Charles Bennett; assistant director, Jerry Fleck; sound, Robert Eber; special effects, Doug Hubbard; stunt coordinator, Alan Biss. Reviewed at Fairfax Theatre, Los Angeles, Feb. 2, '78 (MPAA Rating: G.) Running time: 93 MINS.

Narrator	Brad Crandall
Plato	Vern Adix
Army Nurse	Linda Bishop
Nurse	Janet Bylund
Physician	Richard Cannaday
Dr. Stevens	Maxilyn Capell
Doctor	Bill Carroll
Nobleman	David Chandler
Sam	Hyde Clayton
Janice	Elaine Daniels
Little Girl	Lori Davis
Dr. Meyers	Stewart Falconer

It happens two or three times a year. The market research department at Sunn Classic Pictures determines that the public is aching for an examination of some pseudo-scientific phenomenon. It puts aside a few hundred thousand dollars to produce a 90-minute documentary featuring "real experts," usually carts out director James Conway and narrator Brad Crandall, and assembles — inevitably — "the most incredible story you have ever heard."

"Beyond and Back" is the latest "astounding" chapter in the incredible Sunn Classic economics. The topic: Is there life after death?

The answer: Yes. And the revelations: The soul weighs between one-half and three-quarters of an ounce; people who miraculously recover from death have about a 10 minute period when they resemble Caspar the Friendly Ghost and look straight at a white arc lamp which they somehow find peaceful; and the soul looks like a puff of smoke, probably the same well known puff of smoke often photographed by unidentified flying object watchers.

The only element of this dramatized documentary that rightly could be described as incredible is that Sunn Classic is able to sell it and films like "In Search of Noah's Ark" and "The Mysterious Monsters" so successfully.

Once again Sunn is proving that the real art behind four-walling is hardly the film itself — they're unimportant and amateurish in every way from scripting, acting, direction to the socalled special effects — but the television trailer and the big budget marketing.

That theatre owners will for a week or two lend out their houses and alienate the same patrons they hope to recapture later on, and that the public lays down first run admission prices for this nonsense can only be described with that word. Incredible. —*Hege.*

Les Petits Calins
(The Little Wheedlers)
(FRENCH-COLOR)

———

Paris, Feb. 7.
Gaumont release of Gaumont International-Les Productions De La Gueville productions. Features entire cast. Written and directed by Jean-Marie Poire. Camera (Eastmancolor), Edmon Sechan; editor, Marie-Josephe Yoyotte. Reviewed at Marignan-Pathe, Paris, Jan. 25, '78. Running time, 95 MINS.
Sophie .... Dominique Laffin
Sylvie ....Caroline Cartier
Corinne .... Josiane Balasko
Antoine .... Roger Mirmont
Marck .... Jacques Frantz
Jean-Pierre .... Patrick Cartie
Mother .... Claire Maurier
Father ....Jean Bouise

———

Writer-director Jean-Marie Poire does not seem to know where he is going with this sitcom which tries to be a comedy or satire about so-called liberated women. It just reverses things with the women pursuing men but does not add much insight, comic spirit or story to give this the insouciant tang it strives for.

Locally, it might fare acceptably but with offshore chances looming mainly for playoff. Dominique Laffin rides a motorcycle. She lives with two friends. Her main object seems to be trying to pick up men she desires. Family money keeps her solvent though her friends work at odd jobs.

Laffin mainly smiles wryly as she tries to find her own way in a macho world. Her advances turn some men off but she finally does win one after a series of on and off again adventures and even other men on the side.

Too much stuffing in the pic that avoids getting down to a truly comic and lively treatment of the hang-ups that can come with permissiveness in re men and women relations. Dialog is no help though this is ably produced. —*Mosk.*

La Ragazza In Pigiama Giallo
(The Girl in the Yellow Pajamas)
(ITALIAN-COLOR)

———

Rome, Feb. 4.
Distributed by Capitol in Italy, Medusa worldwide. A Zodiac (Rome)-Picasa (Madrid) production, produced by Giorgio Salvioni. Directed by Flavio Mogherini. Screenplay, Mogherini & Rafael Sanchez Campoy; camera (Microstampa-Color), Raul Arteguy; editor, Adriano Tagliavia; music, Riz Ortolani. Reviewed at Empire Theatre, Rome, Feb. 2, 1978. Running time: 101 MINS.
Cast: Ray Milland, Dalila di Lazzaro, Michele Placido, Howard Ross, Ramiro Oliveros, Rod Mullinar, Mel Ferrer.

———

"The Girl in the Yellow Pajamas" is both a chilling police thriller and, more successfully, an unusual love story about two young immigrants to Australia.

The body of a young woman, nude but for a scrap of silk from her yellow pajamas, her face horribly charred beyond recognition, is discovered in an abandoned car on a Sydney beach. Who is she, who killed her, and why? Ray Milland gives a strong performance as retired police inspector Simpson, called in from his orchid garden to help find out the answers. Milland suffers competition from younger detectives who prefer beating up suspects to solving crimes.

Meanwhile, as Milland tracks the identity of the girl and her killer, in a series of flashbacks the young immigrant couple, played by Dalila di Lazzaro and Michele Placido, meet, fall in love, marry, and split up. Di Lazzaro's enigmatic features are well cast as the Dutch girl who goes from loving wife to nympho to roadside prostitute, and Michele Placido is particularly effective as the quiet, timid Italian waiter who explodes violently when he wakes up to his wife's infidelities.

Director Flavio Mogherini exploits the Australian locale, both as picturesque background, particularly Sydney harbor and opera house, and as a comment on the action. Milland's pursuit of the murderer gives Mogherini a chance to play with a gamut of weird minor characters and bizarre incidents. Mogherini, whose work heretofore has been mostly comedy, has a sure handling of these grotesques, though his overall control is less forceful. Raul Artegry's camera work is stunning, and the color has a rare freshness and clarity to it.

Despite these strong points, the film suffers a real drawback: editing has weakened an already feeble script to the point that the story is confused, verging on the unintelligible. The relationship between the love affair and the murder is obscure until the very end. Thus, tension and suspense build up continuously, only to be interrupted and dissipated by the flashbacks.

The Australian background should give the film good play in Australian and U.K. markets, perhaps in other English-speaking countries as well. Judicious cutting might clear up the confusion and make this stylish but flawed effort more attractive to an international audience. —*Ancy.*

Deux Super Flics
(Two Super Cops)
(ITALIAN-COLOR)

———

Paris, Feb. 7.
WB-Col release of Triton Cinematografica production. Produced by Salvatore Alabiso. Stars Terence Hill, Bud Spencer. Written and directed by E.B. Clucher (Enzo Barboni). Camera (Color), laudio Cirillo; music, Guido and Maurizio DeAngelis. Reviewed at Mercury, Paris, Jan. 30, '78. Running time: 115 MINS.
Matt .... Terence Hill
Wilber .... Bud Spencer
Susy Lee .... Laura Gemser
Fred ....Luciano Catenacci

———

Terence Hill and Bud Spencer, Americanized Italo names, made it in oaters that even spoofed the already parodic pasta oaters in the "Trinity" series. Hill even managed to make two Yank pics. Now both are reunited for a sort of pasta police opus shot in the U.S.

It has all the naive, outlandish aspects of the oaters with Hill a brash would-be criminal and Spencer a long-suffering big sidekick to Hill's attempts at criminality. They end up in the police force when they mistakenly raid their offices thinking it is a supermarket.

Pair finally break up a dope racket and have the usual fight scenes which are more slapabout than trying to simulate fisticuffs. This naive, childish romp is doing right well locally which may explain the difficulties for more demanding pix. WB-Col has an English version too and it could be a quick playoff item on its obvious but good natured proceedings in less demanding orbits. Technically passable. —*Mosk.*

L'Hotel De La Plage
(The Beach Hotel)
(FRENCH-COLOR)

———

Paris, Feb. 7.
Gaumont release of Production 2000-Gaumont production. Features entire cast. Written and directed by Michel Lang. Camera (Eastmancolor), Daniel Gaudry; editor, Helene Plemiannikov. Reviewed at Paris, Jan. 25, '78. Running time, 115 MINS.
Cast: Myriam Boyer, Daniel Ceccaldi, Martine Sarcey, Michele Grellier, Rosine Cadoret, Guy Marchand, Sophie Barjac, Blanche Ravalec.

———

Michel Lang, who hit a sleeper bonanza with his first pic on teenage sex shenanigans through French students studying English in Britain, "Let's Get the Little English Girls," which drew top youthful attendance, came-a-cropper with a weak melodrama on the effect of the death of a young woman on her family, "A Strait-Laced Girl," and now comes up with a cross-section look at French stereotypes of all ages on vacation with sex the main thing on their minds from seven and up to 50 with oldsters mere figures of fun.

It looks mainly a local item, for, though Lang manages to juggle all his characters to have their actions coherent, they are more exploited than developing or shedding any true humor or more probing revelations on people at play. The married men try for adventure, the young men are after older women while younger ones cat around finding love until the season is over.

Lang is a populariser and may become an okay staple at home if there is no personalized or more insouciant deftness for more than quick playoff in some offshore spots. However he does keep his disparate cast in harness even if it is all predictable, gently boring and easily forgettable. —*Mosk.*

Bare Knuckles
(COLOR)

———

Classless, violent programmer.

———

Hollywood, Jan. 31.
An Intercontinental Releasing Corp. release. Produced, directed and written by Don Edmonds. Camera (Metrocolor), Dean Cundey; editor, Robert Freeman; assistant director, Buck Flower; music, Vic Caesar; production design; Michael Riva; sound, Al Ramierz' stunt coordinator, Jim Winburn. Reviewed at Pacific Theatre, Hollywood, Jan. 31, '78. (MPAA Rating: R.) Running time: 90 MINS.
Zachary Kane ....Robert Viharo
Jennifer Randall .... Sherry Jackson
Richard Devlin .... Michael Heit
Barbara Darrow ....Gloria Hendry
Black ....John Daniels

———

"Bare Knuckles" is an ugly, incompetent, styleless, nonsensical exploitation item about a modern day urban bounty hunter. It panders to the lowest elements without providing anything even remotely related to cheap thrills. Technical and artistic merits of this low-budget programmer writteff, directed and produced by Don Edmonds should assure it third spot on drive-in double bills across the country.

Periodically interrupting the Intercontinental release is a plot. There's a grubby Robert Viharo (trying his best to be a low-budget Charles Bronson) tracking down a maniac best known for slashing up women with a butcher knife. The ladies come from various walks of life, but share one trait: they all have an uncanny ability to bleed a thick red dye which photographs something like blood.

The real heart (or stomach, as it were) of this production are the fight scenes. And the fight scenes. There's the above-mentioned butcher knife work, kung fu scraps, the fist to fist variety, fag beatups, and car crashes, if you want to include those.

Technical credits match the acting credits. —*Hege.*

The Betsy
(COLOR)

Screen adaptation of Harold Robbins novel that's nice, rather than naughty.

Hollywood, Feb. 7.

An Allied Artists release of an Allied Artists/Harold Robbins International production, produced by Robert R. Weston. Stars Laurence Olivier, Robert Duvall, Katharine Ross, Tommy Lee Jones, Jane Alexander. Directed by Daniel Petrie. Screenplay, William Bast, Walter Bernstein; based on the novel by Harold Robbins; Camera (Technicolor), Mario Tosi; editor, Rita Roland; production designer, Herman A. Bluemnthal; music, John Barry; costume designer, Dorothy Jeakins; set decorators, James Payne, Sal Blydenburgh; associate producer, Jack Grossberg; assistant director, Wolfgang Glattes; sound, Lee Alexander, Rimas Tumasonis; stunt coordinator, William Couch. Reviewed at Aidikoff Screening Room, Beverly Hills, Feb. 7, 1978. (MPAA Rating: R.) Running time: 125 MIN.
Loren Hardeman, Sr. ... Laurence Olivier
Loren Hardeman 3d .... Robert Duvall
Sally Hardeman .... Katharine Ross
Angelo Perino .... Tommy Lee Jones
Alicia Hardeman .... Jane Alexander
Lady Bobby Ayres ..... Lesley-Ann Down
Jake Weinstein .... Joseph Wiseman
Betsy Hardeman .... Kathleen Beller
Dan Weyman .... Edward Herrmann
Loren Hardeman, Jr. .... Paul Rudd
Also: Roy Poole, Richard Venturo, Titos Vandis, Clifford David, Inga Swenson, Whitney Blanke, Carol Williard, Read Morgan, Charlie Fields.

It's a backhanded criticism, but there's something too classy about the Robert Weston-produced version of "The Betsy." It's too tame. And too solemn. Allied Artists, which is releasing the film domestically, and United Artists, which has it overseas, are using the Harold Robbins association as their main selling point; after all, Robbins has a possessory credit. But, to be blunt, where's the raunch? This should be Peyton Place with plenty of flesh. Don't entice audiences with the name of an author associated with a long list of best-selling seamy novels and then deliver a 125-minute film you wouldn't be embarrassed to bring your mother to. "The Betsy" is a guilty movie — it's got an acute case of the soft Rs. That will hurt at the b.o.

The William Bast-Walter Bernstein script has four main interests: cars, sex, money and power. It's an American movie. Laurence Olivier is retired auto tycoon Loren Hardeman, Sr., founder of Bethlehem Motor Co., now interested in manufacturing a revolutionary car — one too efficient, too practical and too benevolent for American industry. It is to be called the Betsy, after his great-granddaughter.

Through a series of flashbacks, Olivier ages from 40 to 90. Complete with midwest accent, he's on target, maybe too much so. Ditto for Robert Duvall as his grandson and current president of the auto company, Jane Alexander as Duvall's

wife and Katharine Ross as Olivier's daughter-in-law and lover.

Tommy Lee Jones as a daredevil race driver hired by Olivier to build the dream car plays his role with a mixture of edginess and offhandedness — a combination of Burt Reynolds and Harvey Keitel. His style — it's got a sense of humor and a campy quality to it — seems more to the point. It's almost trashy. (Now that's Harold Robbins.) Lesley-Anne Down, as a jetsetting designer who becomes involved with both Jones and Duvall, adapts the same tone, as does Edward Herrmann, Duvall's righthand man.

These characters are entangled through business and family relations. All are jockeying for power of one sort or another.

Technical credits, from Herman Blumenthal's lush production design to John Barry's soft opening piano music which accompanies a lovely montage of classic cars by Daniel Petrie's direction are all plush, dignified. —*Hege.*

Coming Home
(COLOR)

Excellent home-front drama of Vietnam war.

Hollywood, Feb. 7.

United Artists release, produced by Jerome Hellman. Directed by Hal Ashby. Features entire cast. Screenplay, Waldo Salt, Robert C. Jones, based on a story by Nancy Dowd; camera (DeLuxe Color), Haskell Wexler; editor, Don Zimmerman; production design, Mike Haller; set decoration, George Gaines; sound, Buzz Knudson; costumes-wardrobe, Ann Roth, Mike Hoffman, Silvio Scarano, Jennifer Parson; asst. director, Chuck Myers. Reviewed at MGM Studios, Culver City, Feb. 7, '78. (MPAA Rating: R.) Running time, 126 MINS.
Sally Hyde .... Jane Fonda
Luke Martin .... Jon Voight
Capt. Bob Hyde .... Bruce Dern
Sgt. Dink Mobley .... Robert Ginty
Viola Munson .... Penelope Milford
Bill Munson .... Robert Carradine

"Coming Home" is in general an excellent Hal Ashby film which illuminates the conflicting attitudes on the Vietnam debacle from the standpoint of three participants. Jerome Hellman's fine production has Jane Fonda in another memorable and moving performance; Jon Voight, back on the screen much more matured, assured and effective; Bruce Dern, continuing to forge new career dimension. The United Artists release is a compelling and absorbing film which should enjoy good response. Even though there are no battle scenes, the pic must overcome a psychic revulsion to reliving a major national embarrassment.

Nancy Dowd's story was adapted by Waldo Salt and former film editor Robert C. Jones into a home-front drama. Gung-ho Marine officer Dern goes to Vietnam while

loyal wife Fonda decides to work in a veteran's hospital where she meets high-school classmate Voight, now an embittered cripple from the war. Their lives become transformed completely.

Fonda's real-life identification with Vietnam protest could obscure full appréciation of her performance here, since audiences may tend to add in that extraneous element. That would be unfortunate, because, if anything, she and Ashby have reined in any tendencies to be smug or pedantic. Instead, she provides a superb characterization by a magnificent actress.

Voight no longer seems either an adolescent in grownup clothing or else a slightly neurotic adult. This is his finest acting to date. His character evolves as he and Fonda become lovers. A sex scene between the two is a masterpiece of discreet romantic eroticism.

Dern's character is the trigger for certain major events, but there remains enough exposure for him to be convincing as a career soldier disillusioned by Vietnam. Among the large supporting cast are Penelope Milford, excellent as another hospital worker keeping an eye on brother Robert Carradine, very effective as a pitiful, freaked-out and ultimately suicidal case. Robert Ginty is good as Milford's boyfriend.

Haskell Wexler's superb cinematography (front end work by MGM, prints by DeLuxe) highlights uniformly excellent production achievement. The music is a series of contemporary songs of a decade back, properly and dramatically interpolated to support the sotry without becoming a pretentious distraction.

Ending of the story is flat compared to what has preceded; but then, that era in this country didn't so much end as it faded away. Better to end flat than pat, but one misses a stronger wrap. —*Murf.*

L'Amant De Poche
(The Pocket Lover)
(FRENCH-COLOR)

Paris, Feb. 14.

Gaumont release of Progefi-SFP-Gaumont production. Features entire cast. Directed by Bernard Queysanne. Screenplay, Pierre Pelegri, Queysanne from the book by Voldemar Lestienne; camera (Eastmancolor), Alain Levent; editor, Agnes Molinard; music, Laurent Petitgirard. Reviewed at Publicis, Paris, Feb. 1, '78. Running time: 90 MINS.
Helena .... Mimsy Farmer
Julien .... Pascal Sellier
Mother .... Andrea Ferreol
Father .... Serge Sauvion
Gisbert .... Bernard Fresson
Josee .... Madeleine Robinson
Capo .... Stephane Jobert
Martine .... Eva Ionesco

The news that youthful audiences are a good percentage of

filmgoers has led to a spate of so-called youth oriented films. This one may try to fit that category, but it just takes up that old theme of an older woman and a young boy as lovers. Here, it is a world-weary American call girl of 25 living in incredible luxury and a 15-year-old high school boy.

Hard to tell what the director's outlook is and whether this is a comedy of sex mores, a romantic film or a drama. Mimsy Farmer does have her vulnerable air to stave off ridicule in her love for a bespectacled young boy. She is picked up by the boy's brash, macho, vulgar friend one night but chooses the former and then decides to keep him on tap.

The boy thinks she is married at first but finally finds out her line of work. However, even after she shows him up by playing a cheap prostie before his friends, he runs off with her for a last idyll as she leaves him because she loves him and he is recuperated by his easygoing, understanding, taxi-driving father.

Pascal Sellier lacks the mixture of youthful brashness, drive and passion to give this more bite in any of its various outlooks that deal in satire of jaded worldly types, the tasteless sexual attitudes of the adolescents and the lack of understanding of the few parents seen.

Its theme might just give this okay local legs and foreign playoff despite its flaws. Production side is good. —*Mosk.*

15 Yok Yok
(Only 15)
(THAI-COLOR)

Bangkok, Feb. 4.

A Nakorn Ping Films release. Produced, directed and edited by Chana Krapayun. Story, Prai Maliwan; screenplay, Seeda Wichanupop; camera (color), Sophon Jaenpanit; music, Seksan Sonimsart; theme song, "15 Yok Yok," music and lyrics by Seksan, sung by Suda Chuenban. Reviewed at Siam theatre, Bangkok, Feb. 3, '78. Running time: 115 MINS.
Sakda .... Sorapong Chatri
Saowitree .... Tasawan Seniwong
Nati .... Suriya Chinaphan
Kanya .... Nawarat Yukthanan
Rerngchai .... Niroot Sirichanya

A b.o. winner, "15 Yok Yok" has several new pretty faces. It was banned earlier, which helped in the publicity.

What the censors found morally objectionable was the fact that it depicts five young Thai schoolgirls committing all sorts of wayward acts. Pic was passed only after underscoring the fact that the lives these misguided girls led were wrong, and should not be copied.

In the end, the repentant girls see five other young schoolgirls about to play truant, but a female superior shouts at the latter and sends them all back to school.

Pic is okay for thrill seekers. —*Cano.*

An Unmarried Woman
(COLOR)

Excellent Paul Mazursky film. Strong outlook.

Hollywood, Feb. 2.

Twentieth Century-Fox release. Written, produced (with Tony Ray) and directed by Paul Mazursky. Features entire cast. Camera (Movielab Color), Arthur Ornitz; editor, Stuart H. Pappe; music, Bill Conti; production design, Pato Guzman; set decoration, Edward Stewart; sound, Arthur Piantadosi, Dennis Maitland; costumes-wardrobe, Albert Wolsky, Max Solomon, Beverly Cycon; asst. director, Terry Donnelly. Reviewed at 20th-Fox Studios, L.A., Feb. 2, '78. (MPAA Rating: R.) Running time: 124 MINS.
Erica .... Jill Clayburgh
Saul .... Alan Bates
Martin .... Michael Murphy
Charlie .... Cliff Gorman
Sue .... Pat Quinn
Elaine .... Kelly Bishop
Patti .... Lisa Lucas
Jeanette .... Linda Miller
Bob .... Andrew Duncan
Dr. Jacobs .... Daniel Seltzer
Phil .... Matthew Arkin
Tanya .... Penelope Russianoff
Jean .... Novelle Nelson
Edward .... Raymond J. Barry
Hal .... Paul Mazursky
Lady MacBeth .... Ultra Violet

"An Unmarried Woman" adds further strong momentum to the current trend of superb films centered around admirable heroines. Paul Mazursky's film gives Jill Clayburgh an excellent opportunity to arrive as a major screen star. Alan Bates is equally outstanding as her ultimate lover after abandonment by weak-willed husband Michael Murphy. The literate and mature story-telling gives 20th-Fox three in a row—following "Julia" and "The Turning Point"—in a very strong commercial market for this revived film genre.

Mazursky's excellent screenplay presents Clayburgh in a most demanding role where she is torn between conflicting forces following the surprise confession of Murphy that he has fallen in love with another woman.

Daughter Lisa Lucas needs her mother's support just as she herself is coming on to adolescent love; Clayburgh's girlfriends, Pat Quinn, Kelly Bishop and Linda Miller, offer well-meaning advice not necessarily of the best calibre; blind date Andrew Duncan's premature pass falls flat; therapist Penelope Russianoff's probing strikes raw nerves; neighborhood stud Cliff Gorman, in an excellent though brief role, comes to realize that the only thing worse than not getting what you want can be getting it.

Finally, artist Bates arrives in Clayburgh's life. A thoughtful and deep attachment evolves which survives the early resentment of the daughter and the lover's increasing demands on her time. Resolution avoids the pat but portents for happiness are strong.

Bill Conti's score is spare but most effective. The Arthur Ornitz cinematography and Pato Guzman's production design are outstanding. All production credits are tops.

Mazursky is a native New Yorker who, both here and in "Next Stop Greenwich Village," adds a rather lovely touch in showing some of the quiet delights of the city, instead of the almost obligatory noise, dirt and garbage environment. It's just one of the many evidences of super filmmaking. —*Murf.*

Et Vive La Liberte
(And Long Live Liberty)
(FRENCH-COLOR)

Paris, Feb. 14.

Gaumont release of Belstar Productions production. Stars Les Charlots (3). Directed by Serge Korber. Screenplay, Albert Kantoff, Jacques Lanzmann, Korber; camera (Eastmancolor), Jean-Jacques Tarbes; eidtor, Marie-Claire Korber. Reviewed at Ambassade-Gaumont, Paris, Feb. 6, '78. Running time: 90 MINS.
Les Charlots (3) .... Themselves
Captain .... Claude Pieplu
Sergeant .... Georges Geret

Les Charlots started out as a comedy team of five young innocents spreading havoc due to a certain shrewdness in getting out of scrapes and commitments. They clicked and did well for a few pix but then two dropped out. After this rather lame jabe, there may be more dropouts.

The three here start in the Foreign Legion as they manage to emerge heroes in a daring escape from Arab captors who turn out to be allies. In civilian life, they are misfits but get a call from an old buddy to come live on some land as gamekeepers in a rustic commune. But they are hired to stave off the Foreign Legion, now back in France.

They succeed in holding off their own commander. There are some fair gags albeit all familiar, even, including a pie fight. Flat direction loses this a needed comic grounding for its themes of military intransigence and false heroics. Chalk it up as mainly local, with some chances in Latino and Asian outlets where Charlots have scored in the past as The Crazy Boys. —*Mosk.*

The Last Challenge Of The Dragon
(HONG KONG-COLOR)

Chopsocky actioner with standard fight scenes and atrocious dubbing.

Hollywood, Jan. 31.

A CineWorld Pictures International release. Produced by Alex Gouw and Chow Hiap Hou. Directed by Steve Chan. Features entire cast. Screenplay, Chan, Kung Ming; camera (uncredited color), Lee Man Kit; editor, Hu Kie Chan; music, Frankie Chan; action director, Haung Peichi. Reviewed at Hollywood Screening Room, Hollywood, Jan. 31, '78. (MPAA Rating: R.) Running time: 90 MINS.
The Godfather .... Shi Chien
Kung-fu champion son .... Ou Yang So Fei
Mr. Wong .... Kuan Shan
Addict son .... Steve Chan
Wong's accomplice .... Chang Li
Daughter .... Chen Li Li
Addict's girlfriend .... Anna Jones

Exhibs should be warned to never lose the final reel of a chopsocky film. That can will inevitably contain the climactic fight scene, which also involves at least one character nicknamed "The Dragon." Cine-World pick-up of a 1976 Hong Kong pic lives up to formula expectations, delivering a grisly final battle that measures comparably with similar scenes in Bruce Lee pix.

"Dragon" of this title is gray-haired Shih Chien, who distinguished himself as one-armed villain in "Enter the Dragon," Bruce Lee-starrer that inaugurated chopsocky genre. Here, Chien plays a Chinese godfather with a headstrong family that repeatedly gets him into hot water with rival gangster Kuan Shan. Number One son, Ou Yang So Fei, demolishes champion of his father's rival in opening scenes, setting the stage for usual excesses of revenge.

Sinologists might find heavy symbolism in the Oriental creed of an eye for an eye, but for chopsocky fans, drumming their fingers on the seat until the next battle, "Last Challenge Of the Dragon" might seem like a long 90 minutes. The stylized fights themselves are well-choreographed by Haung Peichi, but contain little actual excitement.

Not helping matters is the worst dubbed soundtrack in memory. It's one thing to have the dialog way out of synch, but the popping noises designed to accompany the flurries of strikes, blows and punches often precede or antedate the actual action.

Writer-director-actor Steve Chan has concocted an involved plot that eventually brings in almost every member of Chien's large family, in a style reminiscent of Chinese soap-operas. Chan himself plays a son who studied in Europe and comes back a drug addict (so much for the Western style of life), but that's about the only new wrinkle in a plot as predictable as the old Republic sagebrushers used to grind out.

Only with that final battle does "Challenge" take on any spark, as Chien's entire family battles a Japanese martial arts expert who specializes in ripping flesh with his claw-like fingers. The unnamed expert (who exhibits considerable stage presence) decimates the Chien clan, until modern weapons put an end to an age-old fighting style.

Outlook outside of chopsocky revivals or actioner double bills seems extremely poor. Only bright spot is Lee Man Kit's attractive lensing of Hong Kong locales. Thanks to gory finale, R rating is fully deserved.

—Poll.

Mean Dog Blues
(COLOR)

Effective but predictable prison work farm meller. Gregg Henry shines in pic debut.

Hollywood, Feb. 15.

American International Pictures release of a Bing Crosby Productions film, produced by Charles A. Pratt and George Lefferts. Directed by Mel Stuart. Features entire cast. Screenplay, Lefferts; camera (DeLuxe Color), Robert B. Hauser; editor, Houseley Stevenson; art director, J.S. Poplin; sound, Dwight Mobley; music, Fred Karlin; set decorator, Don Sullivan; costumes, Bill Milton, Chris Zamiara; stunt coordinator, Bill Couch; assistant director, Kenneth Swor. Reviewed at AIP Screening Room, Beverly Hills, Feb. 14, '78. (MPAA Rating: R.) Running time: 108 MINS.
Paul Ramsey . . . . Gregg Henry
Linda Ramsey . . . . Kay Lenz
Captain Omar Kinsman . George Kennedy
Mudcat . . . . Scatman Crothers
Donna Lacey . . . . Tina Louise
Jake Turner . . . . Felton Perry
Jesus Gonzales . . . . Gregory Sierra
Sgt. Hubbell Wacker . . James Wainwright
Victor Lacey . . . . William Windom
Yakima Jones . . . . John Daniels

Prisoner on the run pix have long been a Hollywood staple, and "Mean Dog Blues" draws upon one of the originals, "I Am A Fugitive From A Chain Gang," for its inspiration and plot line. Familiar tale of a wronged man fighting the injustice and brutality of the work farm system has been turned into an effective, if predictable, meller with a good outlook in urban situations.

Gregg Henry plays a young c&w musician headed for Nashville via thumb. He's picked up by odd couple William Windom and Tina Louise; after a roadside stop, boozer Windom plows into a little girl, and poor Henry ends up taking the rap, leaving wife Kay Lenz in the lurch.

He's sentenced to one to five years on a prison work farm in some nameless state, where he's greeted by fellow inmate Gregory Sierra, camp commandant George Kennedy, and ex-Marine James Wainwright. It's "Cool Hand Luke" all over again, with Kennedy on the other side of the bullwhip, and Henry taking the lumps. Only unique angle is Kennedy's unhealthy fascination with a killer Doberman

Scripter George Lefferts and director Mel Stuart have fashioned the stock elements of the plot into an involving, and sometimes amusing, story that has few surprises. Only the open acceptance of prison homosexuality (Sierra warns Henry that "It helps to be a little queer") distinguishes "Mean Dog Blues" from a bunch of similarly-themed pix, and provides the plot angle that leads to Henry's inevitable escape attempt.

Thrown into the pot are the usual BCP ingredients of violence, sadism, sexual innuendo and final revenge, although Henry is con-

siderably more sympathetic than the usual heroes of these actioners. In his film debut after stints on tv's "Rich Man, Poor Man, Book II," Henry proves himself a natural, handling a hackneyed part with ease and freshness. As his nemesis, Wainwright is excellent, providing numerous shadings to a one-dimensional role. Both Kennedy and Kay Lenz are given little to do, and the parts of Windom and Louise are too cliched to be very believable.

What counts is that the mixture works on screen, right down to the final chase between Henry and the snarling dog, well coached by trainers Cindy James and Carl Spitz. This may not have the power of the 1932 Mervyn LeRoy pic, but the plot holds the same appeal for audiences.

Technical credits are good, with Robert Hauser's lensing of Southern California locations doubling nicely for presumed Southwest setting. Other production credits are fine. *—Poll.*

Rabbit Test
(COLOR)

Joan Rivers comedy about a pregnant man. Slim idea, slim result, slim outlook.

Hollywood, Jan. 24.

An Avco Embassy Pictures release of a Laugh or Die production in association with Mel Simon Productions. Produced by Edgar Rosenberg. Features entire cast. Directed by Joan Rivers. Screenplay, Rivers, Jay Redack; camera (CFI Color), Lucien Ballard; editor, Stanford C. Allen; music, Mike Post, Pete Carpenter; art director, Robert Kinoshita; asst. director, Joseph M. Ellis. Reviewed at CFI, Los Angeles, Jan. 23, '78. (MPAA Rating - PG). Running time: 84 MINS.
Lionel . . . . Billy Crystal
Segoynia . . . . Joan Prather
Danny . . . . Alex Rocco
Mrs. Carpenter . . . . Doris Roberts

For her directorial debut, Joan Rivers has taken a slim concept — a full-length comedy, scripted by her and Jay Redack about the first pregnant man — and come up with a generally slim feature. To be sure, it contains a few yocks, but the humor — from one liner to one liner — never emerges; it's 84 minutes of forced setups. Outlook for the Avco Embassy release depends on how anxious audiences are for an extended Joan Rivers monolog with throwaway pictures.

Billy Crystal plays a schlemiel turned celebrity and ambassador thanks to macho motherhood. Doris Roberts is the mother of the mother. Joan Prather portrays of the fiancee and Alex Rocco an ex-Green Beret turned agent. The four featured performances have a likable, if shrill quality to them. Dozens of guest appearances, including George Gobel as President of the U.S., Tom Poston as a priest,

Imogene Coca, Larry Gelman, Jimmie Walker and Roosevelt Grier, are occasionally amusing, but make the pic seem slapdash, as if Rivers had to finish their scenes because these performers had something better to do in an hour.

Like a rambling Rivers monolog the film's humor has a number of targets — doctors, religion, mothers, movies. And, of course, there are Polish jokes, fat jokes and homosexual jokes. Most of it is pretty tame stuff and the PG rating is appropriate. Some of it is funny.

For example, there's this question from Doris Roberts to her son, Billy Crystal: "Have you eaten? Because it's no trouble to fix you a coke and a banana?"

Technical credits are dull. Rivers' direction is limited mostly to long takes of head shots.

For the record, this is not the first movie about a pregnant man. Jacques Demy did it first in "The Single Most Important Event Since Man Walked on the Moon." *—Hege.*

Avantazh
(The Advantage)
(BULGARIAN-COLOR)

Sofia, Feb. 3.

A Film Bulgaria Production, Sofia. Features entire cast. Directed by Georgi Dyulgerov. Screenplay, Roussi Chanev, Dyulgerov; camera (color), Radoslav Spassov; sets, Roussi Doundakov, Georgi Todorov; music, Bozhidar Petrov. Reviewed at Bulgaro Films, Sofia Feb. 2, '78. Running time: 142 MINS.
Cast: Roussi Chanev (Lazar Kassabov), Maria Statulov (his wife), Plamena Getova (Zhela), Radosvetz Vassileva (Tanya), Plamen Donchev (Gerchev), Dimiter Ganev (Lyubo), Velyo Goranov, Stepan Popov.

Considered by some to be Bulgaria's most promising young helmer, Georgi Dyulgerov's "Advantage" places him within the circle of East Europe's talent to watch by virtue of the theme alone: a remarkable historical review of the 1950s when the country was going through its birth-pains as a Socialist state.

"Advantage" is underworld jargon for "work that pays off" — namely, the ability to pick a pocket cleanly without risk of getting caught. A legendary "king of the pickpockets," nicknamed Cock or Rooster, plied his trade on trains, at fairgrounds, and places where people gathered in crowds. Little is known about the real man, Lazar Kassabov, except for the hazy memories of friends and acquaintances, along with police records of the time.

Dyulgerov went to police officials and petty thieves for enough material to put together three lengthy episodes in the Cock's life through the eyes of women who knew him. This allowed for some freedom to fantasize about the man himself, to touch upon the petty criminal's dream-world and capture the feelings of an outsider trying, against fate, to fit into society and live with the woman he loves.

The story is both comic and tragic, but the fascinating element is the accurate portrait of the times. The pickpocket moves easily from place to place, changing disguises and girlfriends as necessity demands or whim takes him. One of his romances is with an adept lady thief, another with an idealistic girl at a summer camp, and a third (a more lasting relationship) with a young mother of an illegitimate child who, unfortunately for his profession, wins his heart. He betrays his friends and tries to go straight, but fails.

Pic opens with a prison scene, in which a real criminal tells a story about the past and the exploits of the Cock. Dyulgerov, mixing truth with illusion, introduces Kassabov in the prison group, and we are back in the 1950s with a police official reviewing the Cock's life and adventures in flashbacks. The young director chose unknown actors for the lead roles: his scriptwriter, Roussi Chanev, plays the pickpocket, and debut-thesps the women in his life, and there are real criminals in actual prison locations.

The end result is a compelling psychological portrait of a petty criminal, bearing comparison with Robert Bresson's classic "Pickpocket." The shift between good and evil in the man's character, the honesty and cruelty of the profession, and the human aspects of an outsider in a society demanding social integration — these conflicts alone make for comedy and drama. Dyulgerov's ability to improvise on the spot adds an extra richness and excuses the over-length of the film.

A "Citizen Kane" reporter-interview framework interprets past history and the mystery of a man who became a legend in his own time. The same unique mixture of memory and fact occupied the attention of Andrei Tarkovsky in "The Mirror" (Soviet Union) and Andrzej Wajda in "Man of Marble" (Poland). This is the third in that series, a film not to be missed by observers attentive to historic events in East Europe in the immediate postwar period.

Lensing and acting are big pluses — pic could do well on fest circuit or find a place in art houses and campuses programming.

Film is Bulgaria's entry at the Berlin Film Festival. —*Holl.*

Zmierc Prezydenta
(Death of the President)
(POLISH-COLOR)

Warsaw, Feb. 1.

A Film Polski Production, Warsaw, Film Group Kadr. Features entire cast. Directed by Jerzy Kawalerowicz. Screenplay, Boleslaw Michalek, Kawalerowicz; camera (color), Witold Sobocinski, Jerzy, Lukaszewicz; editing, Wieslawa Otocka; ets, Wojceich Krysztofiak, Adam Nowakowski; music, Adam Walacinski. Reviewed at Film Polski, Warsaw, Jan. 30, '78. Running time: 144 MINS.

Cast: Zdzislaw Mrozewski (President Narutowicz), Marek Walczewski (Eligiusz Niewieadomski), Czeslaw Byszewski (Prime Minister Nowak), Jerzy Duszynski (Jozef Pilsudzski), Zbigniew Krynski (Stanislaw Thugutt), Tomasz Zaliwski (Rataj), Erwin Kohkund (Isselin), Hans-Gerd Kuebel (Wyuling), Henryk Bista (Father Lutoslawski), Edmund Fetting (Jozef Haller), Kazimierz Iwor (Libermann), Julian Jabszynski (Przezdziecki), Wlodzimierz Saar (Stanislaw Stronski), Jerzy Sagan (Wicinty Witos), Roman Sikora (Tarpczynski), Janusz Sykutera (Stanislaw Car), Marek Dowmunt (Polkowski), Lucjan Dytrych (Daszynski), Marian Godlewski (Prof. Limanowski), Andrzej Krasicki (Kamienski), Leszek Kubanek (Barlicki), Marian Nosek (Piotrowski), Tadeusz Sabara (Kozlowski), Jozef Zbirog (Lancucki), Antoni Lewek (Sadzewicz), Marek Prazanowski (Narutowicza), Jacek Reknitz (Delagneau), Mieczyslaw Szargan (Dr. Thon).

The period in European history between 1918 and 1939 marked the rebirth of historic Poland, achieved to a great extent by the efforts of General Jozef Pilsudski who held political power up to 1922 and again in 1926 as a dictator after a coup d'etat. In the short period in between, Polish democracy was given a severe test when the newly organized National Assembly elected Gabriel Narutowicz, a professor returning home from Switzerland to enter public life, as the first President in the history of the Polish Republic.

Kawalerowicz's "Death of the President" focuses on the turmoil leading up to Narutowicz's election by a National Assembly divided between Polish Nationalists and the minorities of Germans, Ukrainians, White Russians, and Jews comprising one-third of the population. The engineering professor's election to the presidency came as a surprise: his candidacy, supported by the Left Wing of the Peasant Movement, the Central Party, and the National Minorities, infuriated the Right-wing supporters of Pilsudski. A few days after the election, the President was assassinated by a fanatic Nationalist while opening an art exhibit.

Pic recounts the drama in November and December of 1922 leading up to the assassination in the style of an on-the-spot tv-docu, covering the important events day-by-day. It's an historical document coming to life. The assassin, Eligiusz Niewiadomski, appears throughout the story as a connecting link, his defence-speech in the courtroom proposed as a "portrait" of fascist thinking sweeping Europe at that time.

Film reps Poland at this year's Berlin Film Festival. —*Holl.*

Toi Ippon no Michi
(The Far Road)
(JAPANESE-COLOR)

Planned, produced and directed by Sachiko Hidari. Features entire cast. Screenplay, Ken Miyamoto; camera (color), Junichi Segawa; art director, Shigeichi Ikuno; music, Minoru Miki. Screened at Japan House, New York, Feb. 15, '78. No MPAA rating. Running time: 115 MINS.
Ichizo Takinogami .... Hisashi Igawa
His wife, Satoko .... Sachiko Hidari
Their daughter, Yuki .... Yoshie Shimo
Their son, Tetsu .... Kenji Isomura
Sata-sen .... Kyozo Nagatsuka
Tokujiro Iwata .... Masaaki Maeda
His wife, Tome .... Kazuko Imai

(English subtitles)

Although Japanese actress Sachiko Hidari's first attempt at directing was sponsored by the Japanese National Railway Workers Union, when they got a look at the result, they withdrew their patronage until critics' reviews convinced them that they'd better offer token support at least. Indeed, it's not exactly a complimentary look at one of Japan's most overworked and underpaid labor areas. The end result, which proves that Hidari-san is as talented behind the cameras as in front of it, has been chosen as the Japanese entry at the Berlin Film Festival where Hidari is well known for her acting roles (she won best actress award there for Susumu Hani's "She And He").

For American audiences the film will have greater impact as an example of Hidari's ongoing work as one of the most militant feminists in Japanese films—her study of a Japanese railway worker's wife tells us more about domestic conditions there than they do about the labor situations. She's superb in her portrayal, so much so that one tends to forget she also helmed the film. As one person said it is a "sharply etched portrait of a family, and a country, in transition."

"The Far Road," shot almost entirely on location in northern Japan, offers viewers some previously little-seen scenery and the last look at a now bygone era — that of steam trains. The last one has been retired from service. In addition to Hidari, the performances are uniformly good especially that of Hisashi Igawa as her husband (although he doesn't age at all in some 20 to 30 years), whose tie to his menial labor is as much his lack of education as the class restrictions that mean to keep him in his place.

The technical aspects of the film are all superior, the color photography of Junichi Segawa being particularly outstanding. It is one of the best films to be shown at New York's Japan House's ongoing presentation of contemporary Japanese cinema. —*Robe.*

Pas Koji Je Voleo Vozove
(The Dog That Liked Trains)
(YUGOSLAV-COLOR)

Belgrade, Feb. 5.

A Centar Film Production, Belgrade, world rights, Yugoslavia Film, Belgrade. Features entire cast. Directed by Goran Paskaljevic. Screenplay, Gordan Mihic; camera (Eastmancolor), Aleksandar Petkovic; editing, Olga Skrigin; sets, Dragoljub Ivkov; music, Zoran Hristic. Reviewed at Yugoslavia Films, Belgrade, Feb. 4, '78. Running time: 89 MINS.

Cast: Svetlana Bojokvic (Mika), Irfan Mensur (The Boy), Bata Zivojinovic (The Cowboy), Dusan Janicijevic (Zuki), Bata Stojkovic (The Father), Pavle Vujisic (The Uncle), Gordana Pavlov (The Sister), Ljiljana Jovanovic (The Mother).

In the front line of new directors emerging from Yugoslavia at present, Goran Paskaljevic made a name for himself two years ago at the Berlin Fest with the tragicomedy "Beach Guard in Winter." Now he's back (pic is Yugoslav entry in Berlin) with another bitter-sweet, satirical, warmly human story about three outsiders who can't seem to find their way to luck or fortune: "The Dog That Liked Trains," which should score on the coming fest circuit and may get legs for solid off-shore chances to boot.

As the titles of Paskaljevic's two pix indicate, this is a helmer who likes the metaphor and the symbol with a passion: scenes are packed with layers of meaning to comment on life and the twists of fate that lead people astray. Pic is vaguely Fellini-esque ("La Strada" comes to mind), save that the film is in the best tradition of recent Yugoslav cinema. Further, the film's distinctly personal style signals a new generation in Yugoslav cinema, which bears watching in the future.

Mika (Svetlana Bojokvic) escapes from a prison train carrying women inmates to a work camp. Determined to seek a better life and at any costs, she has learned little from the lesson of bad company and peddled drugs that got her into trouble in the first place. She meets a wandering rodeo cowboy (a refugee from Yugoslav-produced Italo-and-Winnetou Westerns), who needs an assistant to hawk his Buffalo Bill tricks on fair grounds in provincial towns — that is, until the police appear on the scene hot on the girl's tracks.

She is then befriended by a naive young lad fresh from an orphans home: he's searching for a dog which his deceased father, a railway crossing guard, trained to jump on passing trains. The boy takes her to Belgrade on his motorbike, simply because he is alone and longing for a friend of any kind. The girl treats his kindness matter of factly, as she tries to hustle cash and a false passport from her old cronies.

"The Dog That Liked Trains" weaves its magic around drifters and drifting, the kind of theme Raoul Walsh and the early Fellini exploited to perfection. Paskaljevic relies heavily on his shooting team: vet scriptwriter Gordan Mihic, lenser Aleksander Petrovic, and thesps who have made names in Yugoslav cinema (Zivojinovic, Stojkovic, Vujisic, the talented Svetlana Bojkavic and Irfan Mensur) give his slight tale flesh-and-blood, an irresistible zest for life even when the outlook is dim. It's a story aiming for tears and laughs. —Holl.

Rheingold
(WEST GERMAN-COLOR)

Munich, Feb. 10.

A Visual Filmproduktion, Munich. Elke Haltaufderheide, producer. Distributor, Cine International, Munich. Features entire cast. Written and directed by Niklaus Schilling. Camera (Eastmancolor). Ernst Wild; editing, Thomas Nikel; sets, Gretel Zeppel; music, Eberhard Schoener; sound, Rolf Maas. Reviewed at Bavaria Ateliers, Munich, Feb. 9, '78. Running time: **91 MINS.**

Wolfgang
Friedrichs . . . . Ruediger Kirschstein
Karl-Heinz
Drossbach . . . . Gunther Malzacher
Elisabeth
Drossbach . . . . . . Elke Haltaufderheide
Mother . . . . Alice Treff
Inventor . . . . Reinfried Keilich
Astrologer . . . . Alfred Baarovy
Young Woman . . . . Petra Maria Gruehn
Grandfather . . . . Franz Zimmermann
Granddaughter . . . . Ulrike Quien

For Niklaus Schilling — the Swiss helmer living in West Germany who scored critically at the Berlin fest last summer with "The Expulsion from Paradise," an original, metaphysical fable on the German film industry — "Rheingold" was conceived as a similar metaphorical portrait of Germany via the fate of typical passengers on a luxury train.

Besides the motifs of Rhine legends in the story itself (a grandfather tells the story of Lorelei to his granddaughter as the train sweeps by the legendary bend in the river), the Wagner opera on the soundtrack, and the appearance of a Death Angel and a Gretchen out of Goethe at appropriate moments to thicken this crime-and-passion plot, there's the detective thriller surface-narrative about people-and-places that really could have happened. Three people — a career diplomat, his sensuous wife, and her lover — get on the same train, the TEE Rheingold, at different times and quite by accident. When the train arrives at Basel, a murder has taken place — and the public is no wiser.

The fascination lies more in the deed than the human cargo woven into the story: the train's usual clientele of businessmen, tourists, and odd-fellows like fortune-telling astrologers and crazy inventors.

One stylistic element, however, puts schilling in a class by himself.

The time-table of the TEE train brings a compelling rhythm and drive to the narrative. Since the film was shot in a fortnight or more by travelling with the shooting crew up and down the Rhine on the Rheingold, dialog matches scenery and locations in a spellbinding, eery, "thriller" context. An extra dose of tension is added when the husband, in a panic, leaves the train and must then suddenly rent a taxi to race across West Germany to get back on the Rheingold before Basel and recover his precious attache case, a condemning bit of evidence left behind.

The wife (played by producer Elke Haltaufderheide), meanwhile, tries to stop the external bleeding and remain composed at the same time before lover and unsuspecting passengers. As the train whistles past rendezvous spots, flashbacks reveal that this proper lady is a nymphomaniac in chic boutique garb: self-respect prevents her getting off the train and running to a doctor — until she reaches Geneva. Too late.

The end comes at Basel, after legends and illusions have been woven intricately into the story to present a sardonic portrait of the middle-class, career-obsessed, moral-minded citizen in refined filmic terms. Schilling, already an established cameraman, has now secured a position in New German Cinema as a writer-director with a personal vision. Acting by three principle thesps is tops, and lensing and soundtrack are both added pluses.

A commercial, as well as critical, winner. —Holl.

The Manitou
(COLOR)

Another "Exorcist" copycat. Oke credits. Limited appeal.

Hollywood, Feb. 23.

An Avco Embassy Pictures release of a Herman Weist/Melvin Simon presentation. Produced and directed by William Girdler. Executive producer, Melvin G. Gordy. Screenplay, Girdler, Jon Cedar, Tom Pope, based on novel by Graham Masterton; camera (CFI color), Michel Hugo; editor, Bub Asman; music, Lalo Schifrin; conceptual designer and second unit director, Nikita Knatz; production designer, Walter Scott Herndon; associate producers, Cedar, Gilles A. DeTurenne; assistant director, Bob Bender; set decorator, Cheryal Kearney; costumes, Michael Faeth, Agnes Lyon; sound, Glenn Anderson. Reviewed at MGM Studios, Culver City, Feb. 23, '78. (MPAA Rating: PG.) Running time, **104 MINS.**

Harry Erskine . . . . Tony Curtis
Singing Rock . . . . Michael Ansara
Karen Tandy . . . . Susan Strasberg
Amelia Crusoe . . . . Stella Stevens
Dr. Jack Hughes . . . . Jon Cedar
Mrs. Karmann . . . . Ann Southers
Dr. Ernest Snow . . . . Burgess Meredith
Dr. Robert McEvoy . . . . Paul Mantee

Nearly five years after "The Exorcist" was first released, new versions of the Warner Brothers religious supernatural thriller continue to surface. Now there's Avco Embassy's "The Manitou," produced, directed and coauthored with Jon Cedar and Tom Pope from Graham Masterton's novel by the late William Girdler, who was also responsible for "Abby," a black version of "The Exorcist." This bout between good and Satan includes some scares, camp and better than average credits, including a Lalo Schifrin score. That should be enough for inner city houses and the drive-in circuit, both of which can still exploit this kind of fare.

This time the demon is a 400-year-old American Indian medicine man. He's a little devil in the literal sense, thanks to over-exposure to x-rays which has shriveled him into a three-foot tall redskin monster. Until he makes a rather dramatic entrance onto the floor of a hospital bedroom, he can be found — growing as a fetus — on Susan Strasberg's upper back. .

Michael Ansara, a modern day medicine man is imported from South Dakota to deliver the evil spirit and return him to the place where 400-year-old medicine men hibernate. He'll have difficulty getting reacquainted with his old friends when he does return: he doesn't look so good, again thanks to those x-rays.

Tony Curtis plays a charlatan of the supernatural, reading tarot cards for rich old ladies. He's romantically involved with Strasberg and does most of the coordinating for the exorcism — booking the medicine man, arranging for cooperation from the hospital, etc. His character is a nice twist —

bogus genie in a situation where the unseen powers really are controlling things. But in general Curtis is too serious about it all. Only Burgess Meredith as a befuddled professor of anthropology has any fun; with his part.

Special effects are included mostly for shock falue and they do occasionally shock. Good use of Dolby sound will also aid in bringing audiences to screeching. —Hege.

Follow The Star
(HONG KONG-COLOR)

Hong Kong, Feb. 15.

A Golden Harvest production and release. Produced by Raymond Chow. Directed by John Y.S. Woo. Screenplay, John Y.S. Woo, T.C. Lau; camera, (color), Franki Cheung; editor, Chang Yiu Chung; music, Frank Chan. Reviewed at Golden Harvest Theatre, Hong Kong, Feb. 10, '78. Running time: **96 MINS.**

Cast: Rowena Cortes, Roy Chiao, Fung Huk On, Lee Hoi Shen, Wong Ching, Chan Yu Shen, Chan Pa Sun.

(English subtitles)

John Woo, the young director who surprised everyone with the 1977 b.o. success of "Money Crazy," follows with a mildly amusing effort that features debut of teeny bopper singer Rowena Cortes. Cute-looking, Cortes portrays a rich and popular recording artist who gets entangled in a wild romp to recover a fortune of hidden stolen money.

The story is paper thin and fun sequences are prolonged to boredom through repeated fights and gags. Cortes' friend and protector is versatile performer Roy Chiao as an uncouth, unkempt garage repairman, more geared to drinking.

"Follow The Star" has the necessary ingredients to draw local and Asian moviegoers. The charms and mannerism of Cortes will surely appeal to the juvenile crowd.

Woo shows some rich and original visuals that seem to pay tribute to Mel Brooks and Blake Edwards. Included are rousing moments such as the motorcycle stunts and chases. There is no doubt that Woo is one of the major comedy talents of Hong Kong.

"Follow The Star" unfortunately offers too much of the same thing. Following the star becomes a tedious process as chase after chase, fight after fight with bizarre characters become a weary 96 minutes of Cantonese "blah." The lightweight film has limited potential in other foreign countries besides South East Asia, maybe Korea and Japan. The technical aspects are average and are often overshadowed by gimmicky situations.

—Mel.

Dora Et La Lanterne Magique
(Dora and the Magic Lantern)
(FRENCH-COLOR)

Paris, Feb. 21.

Cinema 9 release and production. Features entire cast. Directed by Pascal Kane. Screenplay, Kane, Raoul Ruiz; camera (Eastmancolor), Gilberto Azvedo; editor, Martine Giordano; music, Daniel Vangarde. Reviewed at Celtec, Paris, Feb. 9, '78. Running time, 100 MINS.
Valentine .... Valerie Mairesse
Dora .... Nathalie Manet
Magdelieine .... Rita Maiden
Slurp .... Gerard Boucaron
Tutor ..../......... Alain David
Zorrito .... Fabrice Herrero
Sultan .... Michel Peyrelon

There are some good ideas in this attempt to blend comic strip characters, old films, the fairy tale and the inevitable atmosphere of "Alice in Wonderland" into film form. However, director Pascal Kane has not been able to match his disarming narrative with the inventiveness, ease and charm to keep it from falling into repetitiveness and finally archness.

Quite intellectual in its collage of docu footage and allusions to old films, pic might be above moppets, yet not brisk enough for demanding adult appeal. It could have some tv possibilities.

A teenage girl's inventor father dies and may have left a great secret confided to her. She has some clues and is chased by hoods repping big industrial interests for the invention might have been a motor to replace those using oil or gas. She escapes after a kidnapping and is helped by a fairy whereupon film jumps about to Arab and Latino climes and rings in Rudolph Valentino and Douglas Fairbanks, who are intercut with the girl's friend, a film-struck starlet.

Painted backdrops, narrators, editing all keep this slippant or engaging but it is more a clever exercise than a successful delving into childhood innocence. The teen thesp is properly self assured sans preciosity and others accept the stereotyped images they are called on to limn. —*Mosk.*

Tomorrow Never Comes
(BRITISH-CANADIAN-COLOR)

Police meller. Okay for dualers.

London, Feb. 20.

Rank Film Distributors release of an Anglo-Canadian production, produced by Julian Melzack and Michael Klinger. Stars Oliver Reed, Susan George, Raymond Burr, John Ireland, Donald Pleasence, Stephen McHattie, Paul Koslo, John Osborne. Directed by Peter Collinson. Screenplay, David Pursall, Jack Seddon, Sydney Banks; camera (Eastmancolor), Francois Protat; editor, John Shirley; art director, Michael Proulx; set dresser, Norman Sarrazin; associate producers, Denis Heroux, Bob Sterne; stunt director, Jerome Tiber-ghien; ass't directors, Peter Price, Avde Chiriaeff, Michele St.-Arnaud. Reviewed at Audley Sq. screening room, London, Feb. 20, '78. Running time: 107 MINS.
Wilson .... Oliver Reed
Janie .... Susan George
Burke .... Raymond Burr
Captain .... John Ireland
Frank .... Stephen McHattie
Dr. Todd .... Donald Pleasence
Willy ....,.......... Paul Koslo
Milton .... Cec Linder
Ray .... Richard Donat
Hilde .... Dolores Etienne
Joey .... Sammy Snyder
Lois .... Jane Eastwood
Doug .... Mario Di Iorio
Vic ....·...... Stephen Mendel
Sergeant .... Walter Massey
First waiter .... Earl Pennington
Hotel manager .... Jack Fisher
Robert Lynn .... John Osborne

"Tomorrow Never Comes" is undistinguished melodrama about a struggle for the soul of a smalltown police department caught in a crunch between a corrupt bigshot civilian and a crazed gunman holding his girlfriend hostage after he has critically wounded a cop. Oliver Reed plays a patient and humane lieutenant who succeeds in flushing his quarry out peaceably, only for both to be crossed up by Raymond Burr as the hack chief of the force who orders the gunman cut down in a hail of lead.

Reed's dedication to the contrary, the film is only apt to reinforce an image of cops as trigger-happy pigs with more brawn than brain. Despite some self-justifying sociology, the Anglo-Canadian entry adds up to routine suspense for the dualer trade.

Pic was coproduced on Canadian locations by Julian Melzack and Michael Klinger. Peter Collinson's direction is assured, wringing the utmost from a contrived and cliched screenplay by David Pursall, Jack Seddon and Sydney Banks. One overdone angle are the reactions of bloodthirsty tourists who collect at the siege scene.

Burr is okay as the eccentric and corrupt police commander. Reed's character is unremittingly grim, the result of losing his wife and too many years on a brutish force. Actor plays it to the hilt.

John Ireland as Burr's nervous number two, Susan George as the terrified hostage, Donald Pleasence as a philosophical quack, and Paul Koslo as a vicious plainclothes cop all acquit in seasoned fashion. But nobody's gonna win any honors.

Stephen McHattie, young Canadian thesp, is impressive as the nice guy who goes off his rocker as result of a brutal barroom brawl when he learns that George has jilted him for rich and politically influential John Osborne. The battered McHattie catches up with the girl in a resort hotel beach cabana, where he inadvertently shoots a uniformed cop summoned by George's frightened maid. Thereafter it's the cat and mouse number between Mc-Hattie and Reed. Osborne, on one of his thespic outings between playwriting chores, throws in a neat study of uppercrust slime.

What we have here, along with a lot of nasty people and rough albeit credible language, is one of those hunks of overripe pulp with stock characterization to match.

Technical credits, including Francois Protat's photography, are all pro. There's an effective but uncredited score, also a song, "Alone Am I," sung by Matt Munro over front and end credits. —*Pit.*

Firmaskovturen
(The Factory Outing)
(DANISH-COLOR)

Copenhagen, Feb. 10.

A Klaus Pagh and Just Betzer production, A/S as a Filmudlejning release. Features entire cast. Co-written (with Ole Boje), directed and edited by John Hilbard. Camera (Eastmancolor) Claus Loof and Alex Henningsen; music, Ole Hoeyer; production manager, Leif Jul. Reviewed at Saga Bio, Copenhagen, Feb. 9, '78. Running time: 84 MINS.
Cast: Joergen Ryg, Preben Kaas, Torben Jensen, Jesper Langberg, Lisbeth Dahl, Judy Gringer, Bjoern Puggaard-Mueller, Birgitte Federspiel, Kirsten Norholt.

After "The Office Christmas Party," producers Klaus Pagh and Just Betzer send the same actors off on "The Factory Outing," an annual summer party in the Copenhagen Deer-park, where the staff gets gloriously (or obnoxiously, according to taste) drunk, clumsily amorous and often belligerent. Everybody winds up in the drunk tank of a nearby amusement park and slouch off to work the next morning, surprisingly unharmed.

This is after all a straight and crude farce about a crude Danish tradition and only few attempts at social comment or deeper humanistic insights are attempted by writer-director John Hilbard and his often witty cowriter Ole Boje.

The actors all perform with obvious private gusto and Torben Jensen is outstanding in a short sequence where he fights both the social system and himself — in a hall of mirrors. Sales prospects abroad would seem rather limited although some territories, especially within Scandinavia, might find common grounds for giggling empathy. —*Kell.*

Skytten
(The Marksman)
(DANISH-COLOR)

Copenhagen, Feb. 15.

A Steen Herdel production, Warner & Constantin distribution. Directed by Tom Hedegaard. Features entire cast. Original story and script, Anders Bodelsen; camera (Eastmancolor) Mikael Salomon; production manager, Helge Sten Knudsen; no music score credit. Reviewed at Noerre-port Bio, Copenhagen, Feb. 14, '78. Running time, 87 MINS.
Niels .... Peter Sten
Monica·,.............Pia Maria Wohlert
The Marksman ....Jens Okking
Police inspector .... Ebbe Langberg
Police lieutenant .... Per Pallesen

"The Marksman" could have been the political thriller to more than match Bo Widerberg's "Man On The Roof" were it not for Tom Hedegaard's rather pedestrian helming (he took over after the shooting started from coscripter-director Franz Ernst who soured on the project) and for an embarrassingly bad performance in the female lead.

As it stands, however, "The Marksman" should be a good sales item in practically all situations. It might also inspire Hollywood to buy its almost perfect script to have it reshot by a director of international renown. Writer Anders Bodelsen, already a novelist of some international renown and much movie experience, has fashioned a thriller of poignant political relevance to our times and also a good old fashioned police yarn.

Story has a good guy (solid Jens Okking as a swimming instructor for handicapped children) who also happens to be an excellent rifle shot plus an anti-nuclear-power fanatic, happen to tune in on a tv panel dis-cussion that has Peter Steen as science editor of a leading daily be goaded into declaring that if need be he would find it worthwhile to sacrifice human life to save all of mankind (a referendum has just by a wide popular margin cleared the way for the building of Denmark's first nuclear power plant).

The marksman now communicates through mailed tapes with the journalist, hoping to have the later give his ventures wide publicity as political, not criminal acts. What the marksman has started is a series of killings that will escalate until the government halts the power plant plans.

The first victims of the marksman, who works like Widerberg's fanatic, from rooftops, are the dolls in an outdoor Punch & Judy Show, the next is a Golden Retriever being aired by a little girl, the third a very old lady, the fourth a businessman in his prime, the fourth an idolized football hero.

Early on, the journalist's unexpected dilemma becomes clear and tough. Although his wife is a true-hearted Ban-The-Atom activist (and almost nine months pregnant), the newsman goes to the police with the tapes he receives. He simultaneously fights his superiors at the daily who refuse to stress the political aspect of the case.

His wife is in hysterics while the police close in on the killer through studying of background noises of a church bell and a carnival shouter's voice on the tapes. All screws are tightened for a climactic chase sequence at the hospital where the marksman at first holds the journalist's wife, now in the actual stage of giving birth, as hostage, and later the journalist himself.

Film ends in only partial tragedy, while scripter Bodelsen cops out a bit on the dilemma he so efficiently leaves the audience with by having the surviving mother and child take part in a later lie down on the road in front of the wheels demonstration on the day work on the nuclear power plant is to begin. All the kids wave little paper windmills.

By trying to please everybody, Bodelsen may please no one. But the thrill and the real dilemma of the film's central idea remain clean and intriguing. —*Kell.*

Jo-Bachi
(Queen Bee)
(JAPANESE-COLOR)

Tokyo, Feb. 15.

A Toho release. Produced by Kazuo Baba and Osamu Tanaka. Directed by Kon Ichikawa. Features entire cast. Screenplay, Masaya Hidaka, Chiho Katsura, Kon Ichikawa, based on novel by Yokomizo Seishi, camera (color), Kiyoshi Hasegawa; music, Shinichi Tanabe; asst. director, Mune Matsubayashi; art director, Iwao Akune. Reviewed at Toho screening room, Tokyo, Feb. 7, '77. Running time: **140 MINS.**

Kosuke Kindaichi	Koji Ishikawa
Hideko Kamio	Keiko Kishi
Ginzo Daidoji	Tatsuya Nakadai
Tomoko Daidoji	Kie Nakae

The opening credits for "Jo-bachi" announced that it was "planned by the relentlessly self-promoting Kadokawa Publishing Co. and directed by respected veteran Kon Ichikawa, a juxtaposition suggesting a meeting of showmanship and art. Unfortunately, what follows is often in desperate need of both.

This is the fourth in a series of Toho mysteries based on novels by the prolific Yokomizo Seishi (the other three: "Inugami-Ke No Ichizoku," "Gokumonto" and "Akuma No Temari Uta," all helmed by Ichikawa). As before, the drama unfolds in a remote, but scenic, area of post-war Japan, on the estate of a well-to-do, but troubled, family. As before, a series of murders is solved by untangling a complicated web of relationships, getting back to the roots of the problem and establishing, once and for all, who fathered (or mothered) whom. As before, essential elements in the mystery are: a pure and simple young woman; a suspect — but, as it turns out, completely innocent — young man; a "wrong" ultimately "righted" a generation or two after the fact.

And this is the major failing of the film: too much of it is "as before." No suspense or sense of dread or danger is conveyed, as murder suspects simply go through a prescribed and familiar roundelay until

all assemble in a large room to weep, wail and confess.

Save for a few bravura moments, "Jo-bachi" could have been directed by any reasonably competent technician. If the circumstantial evidence presented here is any indication, Ichikawa has already grown tired of this series and is just going through the paces. The formerly eloquent creator of "Fires on the Plain" and "The Burmese Harp" apparently no longer has anything to say.

In marked contrast to the abysmal performance by Koji Ishikawa, repeating his role as detective Kosuke Kindaichi, are those by Keiko Kishi and Tatsuya Nakadai. Kishi, portraying a governess, is an Oriental `Mme. Defarge, calmly knitting while heads are split open. Nakadai brings to his role as head of the star-crossed Daidoji family the same low-keyed assurance that was a trademark of those many features in which he co-starred with Toshiro Mifune.

Reasonably talented, but physically miscast, is "new face" Kie Nakae as Tomoko Daidoji, the "Queen Bee" of the title. While not unattractive, she hardly looks the sort capable of, as the plot requires, exerting a fatal attraction over men. —*Bail.*

Questo Si Che E' Amore
(The Night Before Christmas)
(ITALIAN-COLOR)

Rome, Feb. 7.

Columbia Pictures release. Produced by Ovidio Assonitis for Creative Films Century-Roma. Stars Christopher George, Gay Hamilton, Sven Valsecchi. Directed by Filippo Ottoni. Screenplay, Francesco Vanorio; camera (Technicolor), Mario Vulpiani; editor, Angelo Curi; music, Steve Powder; title song by Sefano Torossi. Reviewed at Cinema Rouge et Noir, Rome, Feb. 6, '78. Running time: **99 MINS.**

Mike Thompson	Christopher George
Gwen Thompson	Gay Hamilton
Tommy	Sven Valsecchi
Larry	Mauro Curi

A well-filmed tear-jerker, "Night Before Christmas" is family entertainment with the makings of long-play success: an enchanting pair of little boys, one with a genetic disease requiring life-long isolation in a germ-free hospital environment; a large and lovable mutt named Pelouche; a catchy title song; and a climactic Christmas Eve reunion of the sick child's separated parents.

Blond, eight-year-old Sven Valsecchi, already a film veteran, has seductive charm and instant appeal as Tommy, the victim of a rare blood condition. Even the most innocuous germ could kill him. His life is confined to a lavish hospital room where he rollerskates, watches his father's daily moppet show on television, plays his guitar — but always alone. Even his visiting parents (Christopher George and

Gay Hamilton), must embrace him through a cumbersome pair of sterile gloves. His chum Larry, played by endearing Mauro Curi, smuggles the fluffy shepherd dog into the hospital.

Tommy and Larry Scheme to reunite parents to bring them back together. Tommy enters a song contest on Dad's show with title song, an appealing plaint that his father never visits him anymore. Touched, Mike tries and fails to effect a reconciliation with Tommy's mother.

Desperate to spend Christmas Eve with his parents, Tommy manages to escape from the hospital. Mario Vulpiani's proficient camera work conveys Tommy's hallucinatory joy at the freedom to see, touch, smell, roll in the grass, visit the zoo. Finally, visibly weakening, with the help of Larry and Pelouche, he reaches the parental cottage on Thames for final fireplace suds, as he strokes his mother's cheek for the first and last time. It's guaranteed not to leave a dry eye in the house.

Exteriors, perhaps reflecting Tommy's mood, are shot in a evergreen London with appropriate Yule snowdrifts. Filippo Ottoni's direction is smooth and professional without cynicism, and he paces child actors for maximum appeal. Tot thesps overshadow adult leads, who insert maudlin soap extremities. Against skill of young Valsecchi and Curi, George and Hamilton are just plain outclassed. Attempted reconciliation is facile and unconvincing. But motivation is not a strongpoint in family entertainment and film should do well on the solid kiddie tandem alone. —*Ancy.*

Lille Spejl
(Mirror, Mirror)
(DANISH-COLOR)

Copenhagen, Feb. 17.

A Crone Film production, A/S Palladium release. Coproduced, written and directed by Edward Felming. Star Frits Helmuth, Preben Kaas, Bodil Kjer. Camera (Eastmancolor), executive producer, Nina Crone; edited by Fleming, Gert Fredholm, Grete Moeldrup; music, Ole Hoeyer; production designer, Peper Hoeimark; costumes, Ulla-Britt Soederlund. Reviewed at Ankerstjerne Film Laboratories, Copenhagen, Feb. 17, '78. Running time: **106 MINS.**

Bent	Frits Helmuth
The Mother	Bodil Kjer
Sandra	Preben Kaas
Maona	Bent Reiner
Bettina	Poul-Kristian
Greengrocer	Ole Ernst
The Graduate	Jesper Klein

Writer-director Edward Fleming once again shows his technical mastery of the folksy entertainment feature along with his true-blue compassion for life's oddballs, in this case the lowerclass fags in a rundown part of Copenhagen who seek solace in preparing for their annual transvestite ball.

There is also a lot of bickering and quite some ill-will among them. Actually, the heterosexuals around them (a greengrocer, a cafe waitress) treat them much nicer than they treat each other. In the center are Bent (played by Frits Helmuth in a way sure to catch him some of the year's more important Danish film awards), who is mostly out of work, which gives him time to shoplift little gifts for his many friends. He is balding and running to fat and generally finds it hard to cope.

He also has a mother, a terminal cancer case who is constantly daydreaming of imagined past glories as an international ballet star (Bodil Kjer, real life prima donna of The Royal Danish Theatre). Bent does much to humor and encourage her, but she is impatient with him, especially for not having been born a girl so that they could have conquered the world as a dancing team.

Plot is mostly a series of episodes, most true to life, some overcrowded with characters and some definitely expendable. But all told, "Mirror, Mirror" allows general audiences to feel empathy for its offbeat protagonists and film could be a good, if minor, sales item is most popular situations anywhere. It never runs counter to accepted good taste and it studiously avoids any kind of hard-core visuals. —*Kell.*

Vota A Gundisalvo
(Vote For Gundisalvo)
(SPANISH-COLOR)

Madrid, Jan. 31.

An Agata Films - Jose Luis Dibildos production. Directed by Pedro Lazaga. Features entire cast. Screenplay, Jose Luis Dibildos, Antonio Mingote; camera (Eastmancolor), Manuel Rojas; editor, Petra de Nieva; music, Antonio Garcia Abril. Reviewed at Cine Amaya, Madrid, Jan. 30, '78. Running time: **90 MINS.**

Cast: Antonio Ferrandis, Emilio Gutierrez Caba, Laly Soldevila, Tina Sainz, Yolanda Rios, Ivonne Sentis, Silvia Tortosa, Rafael Hernandez, Manuel Alexandre, Jose Ruiz Lifante.

Mildly droll spoof on the selection of candidates for last year's Spanish elections. Some laffs are generated as a stodgy building and construction company owner named Gundisalvo is enlisted as a candidate for one of the political parties. We then witness party leaders trying to whip him into shape, both physically and ideologically, for the elections.

But all Gundisalvo really wants is to eat and be with his pretty mistress, instead of being dragged to political rallies. His politics are an alternation of left and rightwing doctrine, as best suits the moment, and he practices his hollow oratory, first on his large local household in Malaga, with its maids, cook and butler, and then on groups in the street, who are paid to listen to him.

Through all the kidding, the Dibildos-Mingote team throw in some election footage showing Carrillo, Suarez, Fraga and Gonzalez; Gundisalvo's bumbling speeches often sound no worse than the gobbledegook given by the political pros. A few sex scenes, also played for humor, are thrown in, and it is all done with the lighthearted, mildly mocking tone that marks all of Dibildos's productions.

Thesping and direction and technical credits are fine throughout, and the pacing and dialogs are kept brisk. — *Besa.*

Haro
(Hue and Cry)
(FRENCH-COLOR)

Paris, Feb. 21.

Filmologies release of Cine Groupe 76-Audio-Spectacle Co-op production. Features entire cast. Directed by Gilles Behat. Screenplay, Behat, Dominique Delpierre; camera (Fujicolor), Bernard Malaisy; editor, Genevieve Vaury; music, Jean-Michel Cayre. Reviewed at Publicis, Paris, Feb. 7. '78. Running time, 100 MINS.
Guillaume . . . . Jean-Claude Bouillon
Jeanne . . . . Nathalie Courval
Jill . . . . Laurent Malet
Marie . . . . : . . . Valerie Mairesse

A first film by an actor, Gilles Behat, this is a lineal period drama, solidly carpentered and played, with no concessions to today's changing tastes in its look at small town repression and feudal hangovers in the France of 1920, and at militaristic and patriotic excesses.

A 23-year-old youth, a savage who poaches on the land of a nobleman and a nouveau riche, seems slightly mad to the small-minded peasants. His older brother, wounded in the war, tries to get him to settle down as resentment builds against him. When the youth, getting out of the rain in the nobleman's barn, flees it after lightning starts a fire, he is accused of arson.

But it seems he was never registered at birth and is arrested for army desertion. His brother, in an attempt to get him out of prison, brings on his own slaying and that of two women in their lives, while the solitary youth escapes.

Solid, sometimes stolid, pic looks mainly a local theatrical item though its dense tale could slant it for tv abroad. Pic also underscores new young actor Laurent Malet, who could develop into an unusual film talent with more maturity and the right roles. —*Mosk.*

Berlin Festival

Birjuk
(Lone Wolf)
(USSR-COLOR)

Moscow, Jan. 21.

A Dovzhenko Film Studio Production, Kiev. Leonid Korezski and Valentina Grishokin, producers. Features entire cast. Directed by Roman Balaian. Screenplay, Balaian, Ivan Mikolaitchuk, based on a story by Ivan Sergeyevich Turgenev; camera (color), Vilen Kaliuta; editing, E. Lukasheiko; sets, Vitali Kaliuta; music, V. Guba; sound, S. Sergijenko. Reviewed at Goskino, Moscow, Jan. 20, '78. Running time: 77 MINS.
Foma . . . . Michael Golubovich
Bersenev . . . . Oleg Tabakov
Ulita . . . . . : . . . . Lana Chrol
First Peasant . . . . Juri Dubrovin
Second Peasant . . . . Alexei Saizev

"Lone Wolf" — a free translation from an ancient word for "Wolf," which also can be interpreted as "morose" or "gloomy" in reference to a man who never smiles — is taken from the same collection of Ivan Turgenev short stories, "A Sportsman's Sketches," that provided the inspirational source for Eisenstein's aborted, destroyed masterpiece "Bezhin Meadow." It's a debut pic by a talented young helmer, Roman Balaian, and is, far and away, the best filmic adaptation of the great Russian author's writings to date. Pic (making its preem at the Berlin fest) has solid chances to score commercially at home and abroad.

The Soviet cinema is justly proud of its remarkable literary adaptations — Iosif Heifitz's "Lady with a Dog" (Chekhov), Sergei Bondarchuk's "War and Peace" (Tolstoy), and Andrei Mikhalkov-Konchalovski's "A Nest of Gentlefolk" (Turgenev) and "Uncle Vanya" (Chekhov) are just a few that come to mind. The secret of these films' success abroad is the accurate reflection of Russian life in the period before the turn of the century that fostered such diverse genius as Turgenev and Dostoievsky, Tolstoy and Chekhov, among several minor but talented writers. In short, they are saved from the curse of costume dramas.

In the case of "Lone Wolf," the accent is on poetic realism in the spirit of the original short story, published between 1847-'51 in the literary magazine, The Contemporary, and lated edited into "A Sportsman's Sketches" (1952). The collection dealt with the question of serfdom and with the country's serious problem of the absentee landlords, the "superfluous men" talking and dreaming their lives and fortunes away, while the poor peasant remains in bondage. Turgenev's sensitive portraits of peasant life (written in his early 30s) won him instant fame and wielded considerable influence to abolish serfdom.

"Lone Wolf" captures the atmosphere of Central Russia as it was then: the wooded estates placed under the care of a forester, an "outsider" in the service of a rich landlord whose duty is principally to prevent the poor from "stealing" wood or poaching for food. Because of the loneliness of his trade, he lives apart from the villagers and communicates with his young daughter and infant son through feelings rather than words. Their rustic cottage has only the bare necessities of life — and when the giant of a man needs milk or eggs for his children, he barters fish he catches in ponds with his bare hands.

The story is more a series of impressions than a narrative. In the opening scene, the giant Foma releases a poacher rather than punishing him: it is the only time dialog is used (save at the end when the estate's gentry speak French on a picnic-outing). He cares for his infant son (the loss of the mother is experienced rather than explained), plays on a carved flute to accompany his daughter's silent dance, and looks after the life processes in nature with the same minute, sensitive attention.

Life in the nearby village is beyond the grasp of this lonely giant.

At the close, Foma accompanies the gentry on a warm summer day to a picnic-area. When his chores are done, he rests under a tree — then a departing young hunter fires carelessly at a pheasant on the ground, misses his quarry, and kills the "lone wolf" inadvertently. This closing sequence — plus scenes at the pond while fishing, in the village at daybreak, and in the dwelling with shafts of light pouring through the window — sticks to the memory like an impressionist painting by Monet or Renoir.

"Lone Wolf" deserves praise as poetic, lyrical, pastoral, enchanting, and compassionate. Its main virtue, however, lies in another direction: here is an unassuming work of art in which the viewer excuses a story froth with sentiment. Lensing is superb and the acting is unpretentiously professional. A Soviet film that will travel with ease on the coming fest circuit. —*Holl.*

Gray Lady Down
(COLOR)

Nuclear sub rescue. So-so outlook.

Hollywood, Feb. 22.

A Universal Pictures release of a Mirisch Corp. production, produced by Walter Mirisch. Stars Charlton Heston, David Carradine, Stacy Keach. Directed by David Greene. Screenplay, James Whittaker, Howard Sackler, based upon the novel, "Event 1000" by David Lavallee, with adaptation by Frank P. Rosenberg; camera (Technicolor), Steven Larner; editor, Robert Swink; music, Jerry Fielding; production designer, William Tuntke; set decoration, John Dwyer; sound, John Kean, Kevin F. Cleary; sound effects editor, Peter Berkos; assistant director, Mack Bing; special effects, Curtis Dickson. Reviewed at Universal Studios, L.A., Feb. 22, '78. (MPAA Rating: PG.) Running time: 111 MINS.
Captain Paul Blanchard . . Charlton Heston
Captain Gates . . . . David Carradine
Captain Bennett . . . . Stacy Keach
Mickey . . . . Ned Beatty
Murphy . . . . Stephen McHattie
Commander Samuelson . . . . Ronny Cox
Fowler . . . . Dorian Harewood
Vickie . . . . Rosemary Forsyth
Page . . . . Hilly Hicks
Admiral Barnes . . . . Charles Cioffi

Charlton Heston is back in jeopardy. He's 60 miles off the coast of Connecticut stuck with 41 other sailors on the edge of an ocean canyon in a nuclear submarine, waiting for Stacy Keach to organize a rescue mission. If Keach doesn't hurry one of three disasters will soon happen: water pressure will crush the sub's hull, oxygen will run out, or the boat will slip off the ledge. Ultimately, it's David Carradine and Ned Beatty, not Keach, who save the day and rescue the Walter Mirisch production of "Gray Lady Down" from the plodding and predictable tedium of the disaster genre.

Carradine and Beatty enter the scene after Heston and crew suffer a pair of double setbacks. First their surfacing vessel is rammed by a Norwegian freighter and plunges straight down. Then an earth tremor covers the sub's escape hatch, making it impossible for the Navy's Deep Submergence Rescue Vehicle to rescue the trapped men.

Up to this point things are fairly routine. Heston looks courageous; Ronny Cox, the second in command, freaks out; some crew members get sick, and a handful die; Heston's on-shore wife is informed of her husband's condition and adopts a visage of sadness; Stacy Keach, a very formal officer, promises Heston and crew that everything will be all right. Everyone plays his assigned stereotype as prescribed by a pedestrian screenplay by James Whittaker and Howard Sackler.

Technically, director David Greene has the film chug along and shakes the camera when the tremor hits and manipulates the models in their tubs for special effects.

But the second disaster — the escape hatch burial — calls for special action. Enter Carradine, a subdued Navy captain and inventor of an experimental diving vessel known as the Snark, and his assistant, Ned Beatty.

Carradine and Beatty resemble a disaster movie's Laurel and Hardy. They're non-conformists who get the job done. They're something special, although their non-formal style rubs Keach the wrong way. Carradine is quiet and internal — it's "Kung-Fu" with a Navy uniform. Beatty is his blabbering, loyal assistant. They're a nice twist.

This duo adds the only sparkle to the production, and it is considerable sparkle. Commercial outlook appears to be so-so, although the public continues to maintain some fascination with the big production disaster movies. Television sale — a certainty at a premium — will add some additional bucks.

—*Hege.*

Laserblast
(COLOR)

Sci-fi exercise for quick play-off.

Hollywood, March 1.
Irwin Yablans release of a Charles Band production. Directed by Michael Rae. Features entire cast. Screenplay, Franne Schact, Frank Ray Perilli; camera (Technicolor), Terry Bowen; editor, Jodie Copelan; sound, Jerry Wolfe; wardrobe, Jill Sheridan, Barbara Scott; special effects make-up and props, Steve Neill; asst. director, Andy Gallerani. Reviewed at World Theatre, Hollywood, March 1, '78. (MPAA Rating: PG.) Running time: **85 MINS.**
Billy Duncan .... Kim Milford
Kathy Farley .... Cheryl Smith
Tony Craig .... Gianni Russo
Sheriff .... Ron Masak
Peter Ungar .... Dennis Burkley
Jesse Jeep .... Barry Cutler
Chuck Boran .... Mike Bobenko
Froggy .... Eddie Deezen
Col. Farley .... Keenan Wynn
Dr. Mellon .... Roddy McDowall

If Steven Spielberg advanced the likelihood of intelligent extra-terrestrial life in "Close Encounters Of The Third Kind," then Charles Band sets it back 20 years with his production of "Laserblast." This poorly-made sci-fier, which reverts to the image of aliens as sub-human monsters, should have audiences screaming for their money back.

But "Laserblast" does live up to its name. There is a whole fleet of cars destroyed by laser rays in this tale of a California teenager who stumbles on a zapped-out alien's gun in the desert, and uses it for revenge purposes. But while most of the special effects can pass muster, the script by Franne Schacht and

Frank Ray Perilli has more holes than the laser-ravaged landscape.

Kim Milford limns the troubled teener, beset by an uncaring mother, taunting friends, a brutish cop and assorted everyday problems. But when he stumbles on a laser bazooka and accompanying pendant (debris from an otherworldly battle gilmpsed in the opening scene), Milford's got "the power," as the ad campaign trumpets, and it's "Carrie" time all over again.

Girlfriend Cheryl Smith perceives something "dark" inside Milford, which may be why he only emerges, green-faced and grinning, as a nighttime alien, out to literally blow away his tormentors. Local doc Roddy McDowall is intrigued by the pendant's effects on Milford's body, but he's eliminated after a brief scene. Even the appearance of mysterious Federal agent Gianni Russo doesn't clear up the mystery of who Milford is becoming and why he's doing all these terrible things.

Instead of answers, however, director Michael Rae keeps dishing up "action," herein defined as exploding vehicle after vehicle. He also favors Hitchcockian camera angles, but there's nothing of the master's touch in this hackneyed tale. Neither Milford nor Smith do anything to distinguish themselves, while Russo primarily poses in three-piece suits (he's garbed in a different one for every scene).

Animation of original aliens, who view all the proceedings on giant-screen tv in the safety of their spaceship, is along "Godzilla" lines, but Dave Allen's work is cleaner than the rest of the pic. Steve Neill's makeup for Milford is effective while used sparingly, but becomes tiresome by the final titles.

Other tech credits range from okay to poor, with Jodie Copelan's editing coming off as particularly haphazard. As a quick playoff item, "Laserblast" might take off in initial situations, but word of mouth is bound to cut its journey short. Resentful of the success of its betters, pic has Milford completely obliterate a "Star Wars" poster.
—*Poll.*

Sextette
(COLOR)

Another screen return for Mae West. Embarrassing "camp" by the lady who invented the word. Loaded with names and awkwardnesses.

Hollywood, Feb. 28.
A Briggs and Sullivan presentation, produced by Daniel Briggs and Robert Sullivan; executive producer, Warner G. Toub. Stars Mae West. Directed by Ken Hughes. Screenplay, Herbert Baker, based on the play by Mae West; camera (Metro color),

James Crabe; music, Artie Butler; editor, Argyle Nelson; art director, James F. Claytor; set decorator, Reg Allen; associate producer, Harry Weiss; choreographer, Marc Breaux; production manager-assistant director, Gene Marum; music coordinator, Michael Arciaga; music, Gene Cantamessa. Reviewed at Aidkoff Screening Room, Beverly Hills, Feb. 28, '78. (M-PAA Rating: PG.) Running time: **91 mins.**
Marlo Manners .... Mae West
Sir Michael Barrington ... Timothy Dalton
Dan Turner .... Dom DeLuise
Alexei Karansky .... Tony Curtis
Laslo Karolny .... Ringo Starr
Vance .... George Hamilton
Waiter .... Alice Cooper
Waiter (in Alexei's suite) .... Keith Allison
Rona Barrett .... Herself
Delegate .... Van McCoy
Dress Designer .... Keith Moon
Regis Philbin .... Himself
The Chairman .... Walter Pidgeon
George Raft .... Himself

"Sextette" is a cruel, unnecessary and mostly unfunny musical comedy. Mae West made the mistake in 1970 of returning to the screen after a 26-year absence in 20th Century-Fox's "Myra Breckenridge" and she's blundered again, this time for a pair of first-time out film producers, Daniel Briggs and Robert Sullivan.

The Herbert Baker screenplay based on a play by West, concerns a sexy Hollywood movie star who has married a young British nobleman. It's her sixth marriage and in the course of attempting to consummate the liaison she's interrupted by numbers four and five, fans, newspapermen, Rona Barrett, an American gymnastic team and a group of international diplomats meeting at her London hotel. She's also in the middle of dictating her memoirs when the tape of her recorded autobiography gets out of her hands, a fate which could shorten her latest marriage, cause international turmoil, and even worse, make Xaviera Hollander blush.

West is on screen for most of the film's 91 minutes, mostly attempting Mae West imitations and lip-syncing a series of undistinguished musical numbers. It's an embarrassing attempt at camp from the lady who helped invent the word.

Only Dom DeLuise is occasionally amusing as West's agent. The remainder of the cast — Tony Curtis as a Soviet delegate to the peace conference, Timothy Dalton as West's new husband, Ringo Starr and George Hamilton as former husbands, among others — will hardly enhance their reputations with this project. Nor will director Ken Hughes, director of photography James Crabe or any of the other technical crew. —*Hege.*

Word Is Out
(COLOR-DOCU)

Intelligent and well-handled series of interviews with 26 homosexuals. No attempt to preach or teach.

A Mariposa Film Group production. Produced by Peter Adair. Directed by Mariposa Film Group (Peter Adair, Nancy Adair, Veronica Selver, Andrew Brown, Robert Epstein, Lucy Massie Phenix). Camera (color), sound, interviews, editing by Lucy Massie Phenix, Robert Epstein, Andrew Brown, Veronica Selver, Nancy Adair, Peter Adair; technical services, Fantasy Films, Ferco Inc., Monaco Labs; women's music composed by Trish Nugent; men's music performed by Buena Vista. Reviewed in screening room, New York, Feb. 16, '78. (No MPAA rating). Running time: **135 MINS.**

Careful to avoid as much as possible most of the cliches and stereotypes of the homosexual world, a team of San Francisco-based young filmmakers have made a fascinating and intelligent documentary in which they interview 26 individuals who have "come out of the closet." Of the group only a few are of the outre or obvious types who would have disclosed their proclivities in sexual preference and lifestyle to even the uninformed. Most are only "gay" in their declarations, certainly not in their appearance or behavior and could have, seemingly, pretended to lead "normal" lives.

The film, budgeted at $250,000, looks considerably more expensive and in every technical area is outstanding. The color photography is crisp and clean and, with the exception of some murky shots in a gay discotheque and a recording studio, is one of the major assets of the film.

The Mariposa Film Group, made up of six documentary filmmakers, are never shown during their interviews, but their voices indicate they're all quite young. Their subjects are from every spectrum — an actor, a college professor, a filmmaker, a veterinarian, two factory operators, a secretary, a Chinese-American student, a black Princeton student, a singer, a waitress, a militant feminist, a corporation official, a worker in a factory, a former member of the Frisco Board of Permit Appeals and lawyer, a writer, a female impersonator, a comedienne and former WAC, a truckdriver, and a musician. Some have been married, several have children. In some instances, coming out of the closet has meant being parted from their kids; in some rare instances, with an understanding former mate, they still have visiting privileges.

An equal share of the film is given to such side issues as the ethnic gay (both sexes) and feminism from both the viewpoint of the lesbian and the heterosexual feminist. With such a mixed bag, some of the subjects come across more interestingly than do others. Carrying the most emotional impact are two New Mexican lesbians (one evidently of Mexican origin) who live in a house without plumbing or electricity, but don't mind it and just want to be left alone. As the "oddities" in a small community, they rarely are, however, left to themselves.

Some of the descriptions of the subjects of methods some of them used in the past to avoid a final commitment to homosexuality skirts on the macabre — one young man allowing himself to be committed to a mental institute and shock treatments.

A powerful answer to why more of the militant homosexuals are declaring themselves, it's a generally fascinating film. Overlong, it could be edited, with care, to a more manageable length. Because of its subject matter, bookings may be difficult to find. —*Robe.*

Take All Of Me
(ITALIAN-COLOR)

Hollywood, Feb. 25.

A Group 1 International release, produced by Mario Cotone. Features entire cast. Directed by Luigi Cozzi. Screenplay, Cozzi, Michele Delle Aie, Daniele Del Giudice, Sonia Molteni; camera (Technicolor), Roberto Piazzoli; music, Stelvio Cipriani. Reviewed at Joe Shores Screening Room, L.A., Feb. 24, '78. (No MPAA rating). Running Time: **90 MINS.**
Richard Lasky . . . . Richard Johnson
Stella Glisset . . . . Pamela Vincent
Simone . . . . .Maria Antonietta Beluzzi

It's tempting to make fun of any film that would dare put forward such a cornball cliche of a tragic live story as "Take All Of Me." But the effort seems so sincere, and Richard Johnson and Pamela Vincent try so hard in fairly solid performances, you have to give this group credit for going for 10 handerchiefs of sobs, whether successful or not.

The plot speaks for itself: Johnson, a middle-aged, bitter, failed concert pianist, meets vibrant young Vincent, dying of leukemia. She restores his faith in his music, staying beside him through thick and thin until the eve of his big chance to intro his concerto in Paris.

Alas, her time is running out and she's on her deathbed in the hospital, where Johnson refuses to leave her side to get to the stage. "Do the concert," she pleads weakly. "Do it for me — for my life." As the flashbacks of their brief romance roll by, we hear his answer, "You'll stay in my heart and my blood forever."

In one final effort, she musters her strength to sit weakly backstage at his moment of triumph. As the violins sing and Johnson plays beautifully, she dies.

Vincent is very good and hopefully will be around more with a better scripts. And Johnson, too, makes his character believable and touching through the threadbare dialog. If this picture were the first of its kind done several generations ago, it would have been a smash.
—*Har.*

Legacy Of Blood
(COLOR)

Tedious, amateurish gothic melodrama.

Ken Lane Films release of a Take One Film Group presentation. Produced, written, directed, photographed and edited by Andy Milligan. Features entire cast. Reviewed at Anco Theatre, N.Y., Feb. 28, '78. (No MPAA Rating.) Running Time: **82 MINS.**
Cast: Elaine Boies, Chris Broderick, Marilee Troncone, Jeannie Cusick, Pete Barcia, Louise Gallandra, Stanley Schwartz, Dale Hansen, Joe Downing, Julia Curry, Martin Reymert.

Though its bloody, entrail-strewn finale is theoretically the stuff that litters the dreams of hardcore violence buffs, even the least discriminating subrun audience is unlikely to stay with "Legacy of Blood" long enough to see the butchers go to town. Commercial prospects for this plodding, amateurish stab at gothic horror are poor.

Allowing the pic all the excuses of a miniscule budget, what soon emerges through the washed-out color and muddled soundtrack is nothing more than a long-winded tale of sibling rivalry plotted and acted like a junior high school assembly play. Whodunit storyline finds three sisters and their mates progressively murdered and disembowled as they gather in a deserted inn for the reading of their murderously misogynistic father's will. Time is supposed to be turn-of-the-century, conveyed through ill-fitting costumes and little else.

Film was written, produced, directed, shot and edited by Andy Milligan. The buck stops there.
—*Step.*

Casey's Shadow
(COLOR)

Offbeat Americana lacks spark.

Hollywood, Jan. 18.

Columbia Pictures release, produced by Ray Stark; executive producer, Michael Levee. Stars Walter Matthau. Directed by Martin Ritt. Screenplay, Carol Sobieski, based on short story, "Ruidoso," by John McPhee; camera (Metrocolor), John A. Alonzo; editor — second unit director, Sidney Levin; music, Patrick Williams; production design, Robert Luthardt; set decoration, Charles Pierce; sound, Al Overton Jr.; costumes-wardrobe, Moss Mabry, Michael Harte, Gail Viola; asst. director, Ronald L. Schwary Reviewed at The Bur-

bank Studios, Jan. 18, '78. (MPAA Rating: PG.) Running time: **116 MINS.**
Lloyd Bourdelle . . . . Walter Matthau
Sarah Blue . . . . Alexis Smith
Mike Marsh . . . . .Robert Webber
Tom Patterson . . . . Murray Hamilton
Buddy Bourdelle . . . . .Andrew A. Rubin
Randy Bourdelle . . . . Stephen Burns
Kelly Marsh . . . . Susan Myers
Casey Bourdelle . . . . . .Michael Hershewe
Calvin Lebec . . . . Harry Caesar
Jimmy Judson . . . . .Joel Fluellen
Dr. Williamson . . . . .Whit Bissell

The subject matter of "Casey's Shadow" is more compelling than its realization on the screen. The annual quarter-horse race at Ruidoso, New Mexico, is an event that draws rich and poor alike, united in their common interest. Walter Matthau stars effectively as a poor Cajun in this pastoral Ray Stark production which, under Martin Ritt's direction, comes over nicely in its down-home sequences but lacks spirit and zest in its dramatic highlights. Alexis Smith is very good as a wealthy horse-owner who wants to buy Matthau's promising animal. The Columbia release, competing with Matthau in Universal's "House Calls," may limp in its b.o. payoff.

Carol Sobieski's script, based on John McPhee's story, "Ruidoso," updates a film genre in which a humble family, against all odds, breeds a champion. Matthau has three sons—Andrew A. Rubin in an excellent film showcase debut as the eldest; Stephan Burns as the middle boy and an aspiring jockey; Michael Hershewe as the baby named Casey whose devotion to the horse inspired the film's title. They finally get the big race, despite attempts by Smith and Murray Hamilton to buy the horse, and by cruel trainer Robert Webber to kill the animal.

The story is as much that of a close-knit family as it is of this Americana event. An unusual and underplayed plot twist has Matthau working for black chicken farmer Harry Caesar instead of the other way around. Production credits and music are all supportive of the story. Too bad the film seems to just creak through its 116 minutes until low-key fadeout.
— *Murf*

Solo
(NEW ZEALAND-AUSTRALIAN-COLOR)

Auckland, Feb. 19.

A Hannay-Williams Production. Features entire cast. Directed by Tony Williams. Screenplay, Williams, Martyn Sanderson; camera (color), John Blick. Produced by Williams and David Hannay. Reviewed at Amalgamated Theaterett, Auckland, Feb. 15, '78. Running time: **97 MINS.**
Jules . . . . .Martyn Sanderson
Judy . . . . Lisa Peers
Radio operator . . . . .Jock Spence
Paul . . . . .Vincent Gil
Billy . . . . Perry Armstrong
Schoolteacher . . . . .Frances Edmund
Rohana Beaulieu . . . . . Davina Whitehouse

Crispin Beaulieu . . . . .Maxwell Fernie
Woman on train . . . . Gillian Hope
Sue . . . . .Veronica Lawrence
Anita .Val Murphy

The romance of a girl hitch-hiker and a widower who flies a forest plantation fire-spotting plane opens up all kinds of possibilities for scenic photography, given the spectacular nature of the New Zealand locations used in "Solo." Tony Williams, noted for his visual flair among New Zealand filmmakers, makes the most of every chance. This element displays more professionalism than does the acting or the writing.

Hitch-hiker Lisa Peers and airman Vincent Gil, a flying buff of Richard Bach dimensions, are doomed by the rules of this kind of plot to part after the briefest interlude. Part they do, but not before Gil's adolescent son has proved himself by flying, single-handed, a Tiger Moth. The boy survives a crash landing and also an avowal of love that the accident wrenches from his father, an undemonstrative man until that point.

The script works other changes on the title "Solo." Martyn Sanderson as a man who has worked out his own philosophy in the isolation of a fire-watching tower, does well by what he has to work with, delivering a credible picture of a loner. His advice to the disconsolate girl, when she visits his aerie after her brief, unsatisfactory affair, is that she let her tension and grief go by indulging in some scream therapy. It's a good moment, and makes the film come alive.

Peer's acting does not suffer from the flaw of professional gloss, and she carries off the obligatory nude swim sequence with aplomb. This is wheeled on so abruptly, within three minutes of the opening credits, that it is as though the writers are saying let's get this out of the way and get on with the film. They may be underestimating their audience.

Gil saves two scenes that would otherwise have been mawkish by the power and conviction of his acting. The first is the episode with his son, the second his confession to the girl that he may not be up to the physical demands of an affair.

Davina Whitehouse and Maxwell Fernie are polished as a well-to-do elderly couple. They introduce a welcome new dimension to the plot. —*Dub.*

Raoni
(FRENCH-BELGIAN-COLOR-DOCU)

Paris, Feb. 28.

SBD release and production. Conceived and directed by Jean-Pierre Dutilleux. Camera (Eastmancolor-Scope), Carlos Saldanha; music, Egberto Gismonti. Reviewed at UGC-Marbeuf, Paris, Feb. 17, '78. Running time, **82 MINS.**

A documentary on the vanishing Indians of the Amazon section of Brazil, as roads are built through their land and socalled civilized people move in, is mainly surface in its look at the everyday life of the original inhabitants of Brazil.

It rings in a hippy type captured by Indians in a mock scene. Nothing much is done with this except to note the Indians have accepted to be filmed to help them with their demands against the loss of their lands.

The titled Raoni is a tribe chieftain with a disked lower lip, a la the Ubangis, who gives the Indian side. He meets with a seemingly understanding government Indian Bureau chief who wants to help them. Raoni says if not helped the tribes will unite and fight.

Film does have some good footage on the Indians in their native habitat, but does not add much to the theme of the drama of their conflicts.

It's mainly for possible tv public service outings and some specialized usage on its Indian life footage. Might fare okay theatrically in Europe, where docus get more attention than in more demanding house setups in other climes. —*Mosk.*

Du er ikke alene
(You Are Not Alone)
(DANISH-COLOR)

Copenhagen, Feb. 21.
A Steen Herdel Production/Warner-Constantin release. Directed by Lasse Nielsen, Ernst Johansen. Story, script, Lasse Nielsen, Bent Petersen; camera (Eastmancolor) Henrik Herbert; music (composed, sung and played) by Sebastian (Knud Christensen); editor, Hanne. Reviewed at Warner-Constantin screening room, Copenhagen, Feb. 21, '78. Running time: **89 MINS.**
Bo .... Anders Agensoe
Kim .... Peter Bjerg
The Headmaster .... Ove Sprogoe

"You Are Not Alone" is Lasse Nielsen's third feature for the youth market, which it should appeal to worldwide. Without being preachy about the film's main issue (that boys at a boys' boarding school may let off the pressures of their submerged tenderness in sexual approaches to each other without necessarily being programmed for lifelong homosexuality), Nielsen gives a vivid picture of the boys' everyday life in joy and trouble.

Plot is skimpy but lets one see a relationship develop while other episodes like a pupils' strike in protest of a boy's being sent down are equally well covered.

The children generally give unforced performances while the teachers, played by professionals, are left with cliches to speak and act. —*Kell.*

Mais Qu'Est-Ce Qu'Elles Veulent?
(But What Do They Want?)
(FRENCH-DOCU-COLOR)

Paris, March 7.
SND release of INA-Copra Films-SND production. Conceived and directed by Coline Serreau. Camera (Eastmancolor), Jean-Francoise Robin; editor, Sophie Tatischeff, Joelle Hache, Francoise Collin. Reviewed at Publicis, Paris, Feb. 22, '78. Running time, **90 MINS.**

Coline Serreau, on the strength of her first fiction pic, "Why Not?," a whimsical, satirical, sometimes cumbersome, but generally engaging look at commune living, has had her first film blown up from 16m and released. It is a documentary made up of interviews or conversations with women from various social strata and walks of life.

There is no sexist overkill here. Film cannily orchestrates a lively woman worker in a pants factory who points up inequities in pay and exploitation counterpointed by the boss who feels women should be happy enough to work. A peasant woman, whose husband has left her, must run the farm but cannot touch any social payments or buy or sell anything without her husband's consent.

A middleaged upper middle-class woman talks of being a good condescending wife though a certain feeling of uselessness creeps in and regrets of having nothing to turn to with her children grown up. A widow speaks frankly of her unsatisfactory sex life and a porno **actress expresses disappointment at being just exploited rather than help free people of repression.**

This docu, cinema verite, or whatever labels one wants to put on it, has a spontaneous flair and makes a statement on woman's problems, places and outlooks without stridency. The interviewer has about been cut out which perhaps can leave it in for a change of manipulation in the editing and juxtaposition of discussions.

But the articulateness, even if perhaps the camera may bring out a play to it, makes salient points on women in particular and in general. Pic could find good tv outlets as well as fest and specialized chances. A leitmotiv of rising waves is an acceptable symbol of these women as a token of their rising anger that could lead to revolt, here strikes and demonstrations in the streets, as well as political movements and women lib groups. —*Mosk.*

La Barricade Du Point Du Jour
(The Barricade At Point Du Jour)
(FRENCH-COLOR)

Paris, Feb. 28.
Lugofilms release of Les Films Du Point Du Jour production. Features entire cast. Directed by Rene Richon. Screenplay, Richon, Yves Oppenheim; camera (Eastmancolor-Panavision), Ramon Suarez; editor, Annie Baronnet; music, Antoine Duhamel, Pascal Auberson. Reviewed at Publicis, Paris, Feb. 15, '78. Running time 110 **MINS.**
Elise .... Anicee Alvina
Bouillon .... Jean-Luc Bideau
Pottier .... Philippe Noiret
Madrou .... Claude Brosset
Frankel .... Laszlo Szabo
Dumbrowksi .... Julian Negulesco
Leila ....Cecile Vassort
Flora .... Eliane Boeri
Henriette .... Monique Chaumette

The Paris Commune, the short-lived, 73-day uprising of workers, helped by military men and guardsmen after the French defeat in the Franco-Prussian War in 1871, has not often been treated in films despite its historical importance. It was a scene in the many film versions of Victor Hugo's "Les Miserables," but now is showing up more as a subject for young filmmakers.

It was bloodily put down by the French military under the new conservative Republic of Adolphe Thiers. Film treats the building of a barricade in a suburban Montmartre section of Paris of the time. It tries for Brechtian didactic treatment, even working in a song on the barricades and the stating of the simple needs of exploited workers as well as by socialist foreign workers who have come to fight for the Commune.

Director Rene Richon, for his first film, goes in more for tableaus and historically-typed characters. There is a certain compassion for them, but the pic does not give them a more human form and stays theatrical rather than giving a needed visual flurry of life within its historical form.

An artist paints the barricade and imagines the song, a poet recites his work, a baby is born and trysting lovers escape but they are all wiped out by a sudden barrage of firing from unseen soldiers who have bypassed the skimpy barricade. In these pre-election days, with the left making what could be a successful bid for power, it may have local legs. Foreign chances appear specialized at best.

However, it might do the festival route this year and does show a new director with ambition and a pictorial flair. Players, mostly little known, are adequate with the more noted Philippe Noiret etching a fine bit as a poet who reads his work to the Commune people. —*Mosk.*

Coach
(COLOR)

Youth market programmer about a female coach of a high school basketball team.

Hollywood, Feb. 2.
A Crown International Picture Release produced by Mark Tenser; executive producer, Newton P. Jacobs. Features entire cast. Directed by Bud Townsend. Screenplay, Stephen Bruce Rose and Nancy Larson, based on an idea by Mark Tenser; camera (Metrocolor), Mike Murphy; editor, Bob Gordon; art director, Ken Hergenroeder; music, Anthony Harris; production manager assistant director, Mike Castle. Reviewed at UA Cinema, L.A., Feb. 2, '78 MPAA Rating: PG. Running time: 100 MINS.
Randy .... Cathy Lee Crosby
Jack .... Michael Biehn
Fenton .... Keenan Wynn
Ralph .... Steve Nevil
Bradley .... Channing Clarkson
Ned .... Jack David Walker
Janet .... Meredith Baer
Danny .... Myron McGill
Candy .... Robyn Pohle
Darlene .... Kristine Greco

With dominant women characters in the sports films no longer out, Crown International Pictures has taken a calculated risk with its latest entry for the youth market, "Coach." Cathy Lee Crosby toplines in the Mark Tenser produced low budgeter about the distaff coach of a boy's high school basketball team. Technical quality has always been optional on the drive-in and wide break circuit and once again Crown has decided not to pick up the option. Nonetheless, "Coach" has a likable, good-natured tone, some cute moments and an exploitable concept, making it a contender in the youth market.

The Stephen Bruce Rose-Nancy Larson script, based on an idea by Tenser includes enough elements from the standard youth exploitation formula to insure a certain degree of success. Namely, there are enough young people in the cast, a touch of nudity and slapdash subplots about the basketball team's center being hypnotized into a star athlete and a bumbling team member's encounter with the opposite sex.

Keenan Wynn plays the leading citizen of Granger, who fires the coach of his grandson's high school basketball team. Through a computer analysis he hires a former Olympic track star, Randy Rawlings, to put the team back into contention. Randy turns out to be a woman, but she knows her rights and Wynn can't fire her, at least not without a chance.

Randy also turns out to be a good coach and a physical turn-on to the team, especially one member, affably portrayed by Michael Biehn, making her a combination Jerry West-Mrs. Robinson.

Crosby is given little more to do than display some tight-fitting warm-up clothes, look healthy and occasionally recite some basketball terms like "high post" and "jumper," all of which she does with sufficient enthusiasm. Rest of the acting credits are standard. Item's outlook is oke, if Crown does not attempt to expand outside the youth market. —*Hege.*

The Big Sleep
(BRITISH-COLOR)

So-so but handsome re-make of Raymond Chandler wise-guy sleuth, moved from California to London locale. Name cast. May do best overseas after okay U.S. saturation opening.

Hollywood, March 8.

United Artists release, produced by Elliott Kastner, Michael Winner. Stars Robert Mitchum, Sarah Miles, Richard Boone, Candy Clark, Joan Collins, Edward Fox, John Mills, James Stewart. Adapted and directed by Winner. Based on the novel by Raymond Chandler; camera (DeLuxe Color), Robert Paynter; editor, Freddie Wilson; music, Jerry Fielding; production design, Harry Pottle; art direction, John Graysmark; sound, Hugh Strain, Brian Marshall; costumes-wardrobe, Ron Beck; asst. director, Michael Dryhurst. Reviewed at MGM Studios, Culver City, March 8, '78. (MPAA Rating: R.) Running time, 99 MINS.

Philip Marlowe	Robert Mitchum
Charlotte Sternwood	Sarah Miles
Lash Canino	Richard Boone
Camilla Sternwood	Candy Clark
Agnes Lozelle	Joan Collins
Joe Brody	Edward Fox
Inspector Carson	John Mills
Gen. Sternwood	James Stewart
Eddie Mars	Oliver Reed
Butler Norris	Harry Andrews
Harry Jones	Colin Blakely
Barker	Richard Todd
Mona Grant	Diana Quick
Inspector Gregory	James Donald
Arthur Geiger	John Justin
Karl Lundgren	Simon Turner
Owen Taylor	Martin Potter
Rusty Regan	David Savile
Lanny	Dudley Sutton
Lou	Don Henderson
Croupier	Nik Forster
Taxi Driver	Joe Ritchie
Reg	Patrick Durkin
Man In Bookstore	Derek Deadman

Howard Hawks' lusty, if confusing, 1946 filming of Raymond Chandler's "The Big Sleep" takes on even more filmic history in light of the Lord Lew Grade-Elliott Kastner-Jerry Bick-Michael Winner remake which transplants from 1940-California to 1970-London. The move denatures the Chandler environment. Robert Mitchum encores as he did in the 1975 "Farewell My Lovely" remake. The United Artists release may perform better abroad, though fast saturation playoff in the domestic U.S. market may yield okay results.

Chandler buffs can debate whether Winner's adaptation closes better story loops which failed William Faulkner, Leigh Brackett and Jules Furthman in the earlier Warner Bros. screenplay. One thing that hasn't changed: Every so often there's a high-speed dialog transmission sequence that is supposed to illuminate what's happening.

Mitchum (Humphrey Bogart earlier) is hired by wealthy cripple James Stewart to probe possible blackmail. This leads him into the tangled lives of the client's daughters — semi-nympho Candy Clark

(Martha Vickers) and the more mature Sarah Miles (Lauren Bacall). Latter has a relationship with gambler Oliver Reed whose wife Diana Quick has disappeared. Edward Fox was once in love with Clark; he is killed by Simon Turner. Bookstore staff includes Joan Collins.

Weak-willed Colin Blakely is no match for hitman Richard Boone. Pornographer John Justin now runs the bookstore where Collins works; the Dorothy Malone character seems not to have been replicated here.

As for the police, the shift to London introduces John Mills, Richard Todd and James Donald. Back at the mansion, butler Harry Andrews acts officiously, while chauffeur Martin Potter dies in attempt to help Clark avoid implication in Justin's murder; she has been posing for nude pix.

The production is handsome, but in the updating and relocation a lot has been lost. In particular, gone is the '40s L.A. feel — where, befitting the middle west smalltown seaport metropolis that once was the essence of the city, nude photos and gambling were quite racy. Today, in any large city, such things are not quite as scandalous, and in London, such matters would seem to have been handled routinely and discreetly for centuries. So, no big deal anymore. Wise-guy detectives have been rendered moot by time.

Remaking a film classic is dangerous business under even optimum conditions. The effort here seems a mixture of dedication and canned elements. While the cast is filled with known players, only Clark seems to project the requisite spoiled-rotten youthful spark. Nearly every other principal seems beyond the point of really caring. The film doesn't even qualify as camp, though someone, somewhere, is likely to engage in such a delusion. —*Murf.*

Va Voir Maman ... Papa Travaille
(Go See Mother ... Father is Working)
(FRENCH-COLOR)

Paris, March 14.

Gaumont release of Action Films-Gaumont production. Stars Marlene Jobert, Philippe Leotard. Directed by Francois Leterrier. Screenplay, Daniele Thompson, Francoise Dorin, Leterrier from book by Dorin; camera (Eastmancolor), Jean Penzer; editor, Marie-Josephe Yoyotte; music, Georges Delerue. Reviewed at Salle Ponthieu, Paris, March 3, '78. Running time: 95 MINS.

Agnes	Marlene Jobert
Vincent	Philippe Leotard
Vava	Micheline Presle
Marianne	Macha Meril
Laurence	Catherine Rich
Stephane	Sylvie Joly
Jerome	Vladimir Andres

Christine	Albina Du Boisrouvray
Serge	Daniel Duval

Francoise Dorin is known as the local Neil Simon. She has had a string of legit hits using one-liners and shrewd theatrical knowhow around what could be construed as serious themes. Here, in a script she worked on adapted from her first book, such themes as awakening femme consciousness, macho husbands and romantic love are again created lightly, on the surface. Pic emerges more a sitcom or romantic comedy than one going more robustly into the issues tackled.

Director Francois Leterrier has kept his distance though adding some visual insights to this tale of a thirtyish mother of a seven-year-old with a cheating, forgetful husband who meets the man of her life. They meet as their cars lock while driving through a game reserve outside of Paris.

He is divorced and has a daughter. The meeting strikes chords and the plot advances as the woman's husband gets suspicious. Latter, in turn, decides to turn the boy away from her and she finally gives in so as not to lose the boy as her lover goes off on a job to Canada. But, at the end, as she goes to pick up her now teenage boy at the airport, she sees her lover once again, and they eye each other with love.

Marlene Jobert has the right mixture of wistfulness, vulnerability and underlying strength to make the protagonist effective, while Phillippe Leotard, a resourceful actor, here gets one of his best, sympathetic roles in some time as the lover. Others are adquate and children escape preciosity.

Quintessentially French in its general insouciance, pic should catch fancies at home. It is not to be overlooked for offshore chances where its very refusal to probe issues might get to those who found the family love antics of "Cousin-Cousine" so effective. —*Mosk.*

Return From Witch Mountain
(COLOR)

Entertaining Disney hijinks that should find solid juve and adult appeal.

Hollywood, March 3.

Buena Vista Distributing release of a Walt Disney production. Produced by Ron Miller, Jerome Courtland. Features entire cast. Directed by John Hough. Screenplay, Malcolm Marmorstein, based on characters created by Alexander Key; camera (Technicolor), Frank Phillips; editor, Bob Bring; music, Lalo Schifrin; art direction, John B. Mansbridge, Jack Senter; set decoration, Frank R. McKelvy; sound, Herb Taylor, Ron Ronconi; costumes, Chuck Keehne, Emily Sundby; asst. director, Michael Dmytryk; special effects, Eustace Lycett, Art Cruickshank, Danny Lee. Reviewed at Walt Disney Studios, March 3, '78. (MPAA Rating: G.) Running time: **93** MINS.

Letha .... Bette Davis
Victor .... Christopher Lee
Tia .... Kim Richards
Tony .... Ike Eisenmann
Mr. Yokomoto .... Jack Soo
Sickle .... Anthony James
Eddie .... Dick Bakalyan
Mr. Clearcole .... Ward Costello
Dazzler .... Christian Juttner
Crusher .... Poindexter
Muscles .... Brad Savage
Rocky .... Jeffrey Jacquet

"Return From Witch Mountain," sequel to the popular "Escape To Witch Mountain," 1975 Disney release that has returned more than $9,000,000 in rentals, should do as well as its precessor, if not better. Pic is loaded with the kind of visual hijinks juve audiences love, and appeal should hold for adults, as well. Playoff looks bright in most situations.

Kim Richards and Ike Eisenmann reprise their roles as sister and brother from another world, this time back on Earth for a vacation, courtesy of space traveler Uncle Bene (Denver Pyle). Siblings get a quick test of their psychic powers as mad scientist Christopher Lee and accomplice Bette Davis are testing their mind-control device on henchman Anthony James — when Eisenmann saves James from falling off a building by anti-gravity display, Lee sees the youngster as his meal ticket to world power.

Film is basically a chase caper, as sister Richards tries to find her brother, aided by a junior bunch of Dead End kids, Christian Juttner, Brad Savage, Poindexter and Jeffrey Jacquet. Despite an extrasensory link between the siblings (they communicate via telepathy, and can also make objects move at will), Lee has Eisenmann straitjacketed with his device, so he can use youngster's "molecular reorganization" powers to his own purposes.

Davis, however, is in it for the money, and with aid of James, snatches Eisenmann off to a museum displaying a horde of gold bullion. Ensuing scene is one of the film's highpoints, as Eisenmann creates total chaos with museum displays coming to life, and gold bars floating through the air.

Richards arrives in time to foil that escapade, leading up to a superbattle between the siblings at a nuclear reactor Lee wants Eisenmann to blow up. Stop motion animation by Joe Hale is flawless, and special effects by Disney Stalwarts Eustace Lycett, Art Cruickshank and Danny Lee are superb. One has the feeling the objects and people really are doing the oddball movements, and that suspension of disbelief is crucial to pic's success. Kudos to director John Hough in that respect.

Eisenmann and Richards have matured considerably since original, but they still should attract moppet empathy. Lee makes one of the best Disney villains in years, but Davis doesn't quite click as his partner in crime. It's interesting to note that Disney villainesses are triumphantly cruel in animation, a quality difficult to duplicate in live action. For the men, it's the opposite way around, which should give sociologists something to ponder.

Anthony James is well cast as a heavy, and Jack Soo adds a nice, light touch as a truant officer in pursuit of the youthful gang members, of whom Poindexter, Savage and Jacquet are standouts. Malcom Marmorstein's script keeps the emphasis light, although it's ironic that a Disney pic is one of the first to dwell on nuclear terrorism as a plot angle.

Ron Miller-Jerome Courtland production is rich in visuals, and L.A. locations were chosen to good effect, especially dilapidated Victorian manse located near Union Station.

Ending is ripe for a third pic in the series, and if high standards of first two are any indication, Disney org should push ahead. —*Poll.*

Io Sono Mia
(I Belong To Me)
(ITALIAN-GERMAN-SPANISH-COLOR)

Rome, Feb. 13.

Titanus release of Clesi Cinematografica-Albatros Produktion-Munder Film production. Produced by Lu Leone for Spirale 76. Stars Stefania Sandrelli, Maria Schneider, Michele Placido. Directed by Sofia Scandurra. Screenplay, Elena Ricci Poccetto, Giorgia Onofri, based on novel by Dacia Maraini; camera (Technospes color), Nurith Aviv; editor, Gabriella Cristiani; music, Giovanna Marini. Reviewed at Cinema Ariston, Rome, 12 Feb. '78. Running time: **99 MINS.**

Vanina .... Stefania Sandrelli
Suna .... Maria Schneider
Giacinto .... Michele Placido

Hailed in Italy as the first film made entirely by women, "Io Sono Mia" is unfortunately both bad cinema and bad feminism. Based on Dacia Maraini's novel, "Donna in Guerra," film stars Maria Schneider as a poor little crippled rich girl and Stefania Sandrelli as a young housewife whose consciousness is raised.

The decks are stacked against men right from the start with Michele Placido as the heavy, playing Sandrelli's incredibly loutish husband who takes her off to an island cottage on vacation and leaves her to scrub floors while he goes skin diving. Why she wants to scrub floors on her holiday is unclear but, left to her own devices, she meets up with Schneider who flounders about on her crutches like an incongruous

March of Dimes poster girl dressed in flowing white robes and high-heeled pink boots.

Schneider is a feminist, though she lives on Daddy's money, and she encourages Sandrelli in the right directions. Discovering, with the help of an adolescent native, that she can too have an orgasm, Sandrelli wakes up to her oppression, joins a group to investigate women's working conditions, leaves her husband, has an abortion, and goes back to teaching nursery school.

This is thin material on which to hang a 99-minute film, but attempts to expand it, such as the death of the adolescent lover, seem absurd. The actors, with the best of intentions, can only struggle with the ludicrous story. Placido, who's been an effective Mr. Nice Guy in several films recently, is particularly ill at ease as the caricature of a male chauvinist, and Sandrelli, whose features have a plain and honest appeal, is earnest and committed but unsure of the character she plays.

Nurith Aviv's camera work is competent but static and makes no attempt to exploit the interesting Costa Brava locations. Music by Giovanna Marini is at best inappropriate, a cheerful, bouncy tune providing the background for chneider's suicide decision. —*Ancy.*

The Fury
(COLOR)

Psychic powers mixed up with superspies. Good Brian DePalma film. Outlook bright and fast.

Hollywood, March 7.

Twentieth Century-Fox release, produced by Frank Yablans, executive producer, Ron Preissman. Directed by Brian DePalma. Features entire cast. Screenplay, John Farris, based on his novel; camera (DeLuxe Color), Richard H. Kline; editor, Paul Hirsch; music, John Williams; production design, Bill Malley; art direction, Richard Lawrence; set decoration, Audrey Blasdel-Goddard; sound, Richard Vorisek, Hal Etherington; costumes-wardrobe, Theoni V. Aldridge, Seth Banks, Margo Baxley; asst. director, Donald E. Heitzer; stunt coordinator, Mickey Gilbert; special effects, A. D. Flowers. Reviewed at 20th-Fox Studios, L.A., March 7, '78. (MPAA Rating: R.) Running time, 117 MINS.

Peter .... Kirk Douglas
Childress .... John Cassavetes
Hester .... Carrie Snodgress
Dr. McKeever ....,.... Charles Durning
Gillian ....: ...... Amy Irving
Susan .... Fiona Lewis
Robin .... Andrew Stevens
Dr. Lindstrom .... Carol Rossen
Kristen .... Rutanya Alda
Mrs. Bellaver .... Joyce Easton
Raymond .... William Finley
Mrs. Nuckells .... Jane Lambert
Kidnapped Cops .... Dennis Franz, Michael O'Dwyer
CIA Agent .... Mickey Gilbert
Goon on Radio .... Frank Yablans

"The Fury" is a good spring vacation season b.o. meller combining the psychic elements of "Carrie" with the superspy chase elements of a hundred other films. Frank Yablans' latest production features Kirk Douglas and John Cassavetes as adversaries in an elaborate game of mind control. Director Brian DePalma is on home ground in moving the plot pieces around effectively. John Williams' score is outstanding, as is the special effects team work. The 20th-Fox release will make its smart money fast.

John Farris adapted his novel for the screen. Most viewers will enjoy the razzle-dazzle of the lengthy pursuit by Douglas of son Andrew Stevens, kidnapped by Cassavetes because of his mystical powers. But those who have to write about the film are confronted with a gaping hole in the script: Apart from a few throwaway references to government agencies and psychic phenomena, there is never, anywhere, a coherent exposition of what all the running and jumping is about. The more one analyzes the picture, the less substantive its story becomes. Better not to think too much about this one.

Strong cast also includes Carrie Snodgress, returning to films as a staffer in Charles Durning's research institute where Amy Irving (also blessed/cursed with psychic powers) is being readied as a substitute for Stevens. Seems that Stevens is freaking out, despite the attentions and care of Fiona Lewis, and he is targeted for elimination.

Excellent effects have been provided by A. D. Flowers, Rick Baker's special makeup, Bill Hansard's process coordination and Mickey Gilbert's action staging. Lots of wrecked cars, furniture and bodies mark the film's 117-minute trail of ambiguous strange-goings-on. But, to repeat, the film plays very well to an undemanding escapist audience.

Chicago locations give a refreshing new look to the various sequences; one tires of Manhattan and L.A. after a few thousand films, and Chi certainly seems to have a total urban ambience for a wide spectrum of film plots.

Productions credits are all very good. Fox gave "The Fury" the nationwide public preview treatment last Fri. (10), which should set it up for holiday runs. —*Murf.*

American Hot Wax
(COLOR)

Easygoing early rock era songalog film. Good Easter outlook.

Hollywood, March 6.

Paramount Pictures release, produced by Art Linson. Directed by Floyd Mutrux.

Features entire cast. Screenplay, John Kaye; camera (Metrocolor), William A. Fraker; editors, Melvin Shapiro, Ronald J. Fagan; music supervision, Kenny Vance; art direction, Elayne Barbara Ceder; set decoration, George Gaines; sound, Robert Knudsen, Thomas Overton; costumes-wardrobe, Robert DeMora, Don Vargas, Mina Mittelman; asst. director, Joe Wallenstein. Reviewed at Paramount Studio, L.A., March 6, '78. (MPAA Rating: PG.) Running time, 91 MINS.

Alan Freed ... . Tim McIntire
Sheryl .... Fran Drescher
Mookie...................... Jay Leno
Teenage Louise ....Laraine Newman
The Chesterfields ......Carl Earl Weaver,
              Al Chalk, Sam Harkness,
                      Arnold McCuller
Lennie Richfield ....Jeff Altman
Artie Moress ....Moosie Drier
District Attorney.............John Lehne
Themselves ......Chuck Berry, Jerry Lee
             Lewis, Screamin'
                    Jay Hawkins
Prof. La Plano ....Kenny Vance

"American Hot Wax" is an unpretentious and enjoyable salute to the Big Beat era of 20-25 years ago when rock and roll was in its infancy. Art Linson's production is pegged around pioneer rock deejay Alan Freed, impersonated well by Tim McIntire. Floyd Mutrux directed John Kaye's deliberately skimpy script which allows for a slew of vintage R&R song interpolations. The 91-minute Paramount release is a good commercial bet for the Easter holiday-spring vacation period. Exhibitors should play the film at very high sound volume for maximum audience impact.

The simple conflict in the story centers around efforts by the police to censor rock music. To the authorities, Freed was a Mongol at the city gates; to kids, he was Columbus opening up a new world. Guest appearances by Chuck Berry, Jerry Lee Lewis and Screamin' Jay Hawkins add verisimilitude to the era portrayed.

Of particular interest is McIntire. The son of John McIntire and Jeanette Nolan, he's a genuine Renaissance man — actor, musician and also busy in trailer voiceovers. The one element recalled from "The Choirboys" is McIntire's memorable performance as a truly despicable cop. In "American Hot Wax," his gruff charisma manifests a warmer and more sympathetic side. He's the latest second-generation performer to arrive — as usual, after a decade or more of hard work — at the brink of broad public and trade recognition.

Production credits are all good. Kenny Vance supervised the strong music production. Rest of featured cast is up to the easy demands of the script: Fran Drescher and Jay Leno as McIntire's sides; Laraine Newman as an aspiring songwriter; Jeff Altman as a hustling record promoter; Moosie Drier as a Buddy Holly groupie; John Lehne as a smut-crusading district attorney.

Freed has often been credited with "inventing" the phrase rock-and-roll. He didn't. It can be heard in Depression era song lyrics of a lot earlier. However, as a popularizer of the phrase in relation to a new music era, he indeed has a secure place in history. —*Murf.*

House Calls
(COLOR)

———

Sluggish comedy.

———

Hollywood, Feb. 16.

Universal Pictures release, produced by Alex Winitsky, Arlene Sellers. Executive producer, Jennings Lang. Stars Walter Matthau, Glenda Jackson, Art Carney, Richard Benjamin. Directed by Howard Zieff. Screenplay, Max Shulman, Julius J. Epstein, Alan Mandel, Charles Shyer, based on a story by Shulman, Epstein; camera (Technicolor), David M. Walsh; editor, Edward Warschilka; music, Henry Mancini; production design, Henry Bumstead; set decoration, Mickey S. Michaels; sound, Don Sharpless, Robert L. Hoyt; costumes-wardrobe, Burton Miller; asst. director, Gary Daigler. Reviewed at Universal Studios, L.A., Feb. 15, '78. (MPAA Rating: PG.) Running time, 98 MINS.

Dr. Nichols .... Walter Matthau
Ann Atkinson .... Glenda Jackson
Dr. Willoughby ....Art Carney
Dr. Solomon ....Richard Benjamin
Ellen Grady .... Candice Azzara
Irwin Owett ....Dick O'Neill
Pogostin .... Thayer David

Despite some horsepower casting which at least will help opening weeks, "House Calls" is overall a silly and uneven comedy about doctors which wants to be as macabre as, say, "Hospital," and at the same time as innocuous as a tv sitcom. It manages to be neither. Alex Winitsky and Arlene Sellers produced the Universal release, directed by Howard Zieff, with Jennings Lang exec producer. Commercial outlook is okay for spring holiday playoff. Walter Matthau by the way is competing with himself in Columbia's "Casey's Shadow," concurrently in release.

Max Shulman and Julius J. Epstein, credited with story, share script credit with Alan Mandel and Charles Shyer. Matthau, engaging as a middle-aged lech, is one of four stars in the film, herein a newly-widowed medic out to make up for lost infidelity time; Glenda Jackson, divorced from a philanderer, seeks a faithful new mate; Art Carney is a near-senile hospital chief of staff whose mistakes are supposed to be funny but come off as really nasty; Richard Benjamin is a young doctor whose part is essentially to provide plot exposition.

The 98-minute film is thus a middle-years comedy-romance vehicle for Matthau and Jackson, latter in her first made-in-Hollywood project and appearing none too comfortably either; the lightness of her "A Touch Of Class" Oscar-winning performance is gone. In fact, had not "A Touch Of Class" been yet made, her performance in "House Calls" would certainly suggest that straight comedy is not her bag.

Carney also huffs and puffs his way uncomfortably through an unsympathetic part. Benjamin relaxes and Matthau seems mellow enough. Candice Azzara is very good as the showgirl wife of sportsman Lloyd Gough, whose operating table death cues a malpractice scandal around Carney and hospital administrator Dick O'Neill.

A few good sketches — Matthau and Jackson, both clothed, maneuvering atop a bed is one — can't overcome a general impression of inconsistent plotting and direction. Production credits are okay.

—*Murf.*

Berlin Festival

Las Palabras De Max
(What Max Said)
(SPANISH-COLOR)

———

Berlin, March 3.

An Elias Querejeta P.C. production, produced by Elias Querejeta. Directed by Emilio Martinez Lazaro. Screenplay, Elias Querejeta, Emilio Martinez Lazaro; camera, (color), Teo Escamilla; music, Luis de Pablo; editor, Pablo del Amor; art director, Antonio Belizon. Reviewed at Berlin Film Festival (in competition) March 2, '78. Running time: 97 MINS.

Max ...... Ignacio Fernandez de Castro
Sara .... Gracia Querejeta
Luisa .... Miriam Maeztu
Laura .... Cecilia Villarean
Julian .... Hector Alterio
Conductor ....Raul Sender
Jacoba .... Maria de la Riva

Maximo Gascon is 50 and alone in the world. Whatever relationships he had in his life, have crumbled and he spends his time brooding about his past in quiet anguish. Occasionally he attempts to reestablish links with people he knew in the past, only to discover that he has long since been forgotten.

The closest he comes to a relationship is with Sara, his 13 year old daughter, but even she — although fond of him — tires of his unrelenting egotism and the self-centeredness that aborts any relationship he tries to establish.

"What Max Said" is a loosely structured film that does not sentimentalize or pity Maximo. But, behind its apparent gentleness and objectivity there is a harsh and uncompromising view of the main character. No solution to his quandary is offered because, at this stage there can be no way out for the loneliness and isolation which is, after all, his own handiwork.

There is no narrative plot: just a series of gropings, frustrated — even half-hearted — attempts to reach out towards people, Although this is an original screenplay, it has the feeling of a short story or novel brought to life with considerable shadings and nuances. It is definitely an art house film and, if well handled, could find its possibilities on this level. Pic has already been sold to several European countries. Pic is enhanced by Fernandez de Castro's intelligent performance; in actual life he is not an actor but a sociologist.—*Amig.*

Las Truchas
(Trout)
(SPANISH-COLOR)

———

Berlin, March 1

A Cinema 2000 S.A. release produced by Luis Megino for Arandano S.A. Directed by Luis Garcia Sanchez. Features entire cast. Screenplay, Manuel Gutierrez Aragon, Garcia Sanchez, Luis Megino Grande; camera (color), Magi Torruella; music, Victor Manuel; editor, Eduardo Biurrun; art director, Jose Antonio de la Guerra. Reviewed at Berlin Film Festival (in competition), March 1, '78. Running Time: 99 MINS.

Cast: Hector Alterio, Juan Amigo, Ofelia Angelica, Maria Carmen Arevalo, Maria Teresa Arteche, Norma Bacaicoa, Pedro Basanta, Mari Carrillo, Francisco Casares, Fernando Chinarro, Carla Cristi, Luis Ciges, Maria Luisa de la Cruz, Julian del Monte, Emilio de Diego, Juan Estelrich, Maria Elena Flores, Roberto Font, Veronica Forque, Irene Foster, Javier Gallifa, Antonio Gamero, Enrique Gregor, Yolanda Guardione, Manuel Garcia, Manuel Huete, Paloma Hurtado, Montserrat Julio, Irina Kouberskaya, Elisa Laguna, Conchita Leza, Veronica Llimera, Alejo Loren, Eduardo MacGregor, Federico Mendez, Amparo Merino, Lautaro Murua, Jesus Munarriz, Aramis Ney, Carlos Oller, Antonio Passy, Raul Pazos, Luis Politti, Quino Pueyo, Antonio Requena, Jose Maria Riera, Marichu Rosado, Juan Sala, Yelena Samarina, Kike San Francisco, Amparo Valle, Alfonso Vallejo, Juan J. Valverde, Walter Vidarte and the children Maria and Susana Prados, Javier Romero, Federico Ruiz, J. Carlos Sanchez, Cristina Torres.

A fishing club's annual banquet is turned into a parable for Franco Spain or any other country that refuses to see the writing on the wall and stubbornly hangs on to its status quo. The high point of the proceedings, beside long-winded speeches and a prizegiving, is to be the ingestion of the delicious trout fished by the Club's very own.

Trouble brews from the beginning: upstairs, a crowd of outsiders tries to crash the party, while downstairs the cooks go on strike. The trout is finally cooked and served, but no amount of sauce can disguise the fact that the fish is rotten and stinks. Yet the club members refuse to admit there can be something wrong with their own handiwork; these are their fish, caught by the club, and nothing is happening, nothing could go wrong, although some break out in a rash, while others fall sick and even die. Up to the very end they refuse to discard their blinkers and realize that their society is crumbling.

With these ingredients, there was every chance of heavy symbolism. Instead, thanks to Luis Garcia Sanchez's sense of comedy, "Trout" becomes an entertaining film that constantly draws laughter from the audience. In fact, it can even be enjoyed by those who do not care about ulterior meanings.

In casting, the pic eats its cake and keeps it at the same time. Garcia Sanchez did not want familiar faces breaking up the ensemble work. The film is full of rich character details and little episodes and a well-known actor would have stressed some of these at the expense of others. The solution lay in using a lot of exiled Latin-Americans, who are celebrities in their own countries, but still unfamiliar in Spain. Among these, Argentine Hector Alterio (although his acting award at San Sebastian in 1977 somewhat changed the situation), Walter Vidarte from Uruguay, Carla Cristi from Chile and Lautaro Murua, a Chilean whose career unfolded in Buenos Aires.

Technical credits are good, although the editing could have been a little tighter. Given the present interest in post Franco Spanish cinema, "Trout" stands a fair chance abroad, equally due to its entertainment values and to its parable. An interesting point may well be that this is a typical film in the transition from Franco to a democratic Spain: not direct or explicit, it uses the symbolisms that were frequent in some Spanish cinema while the "Caudillo" was still in power.

—Amig.

Flores de Papel
(Paper Flowers)
(MEXICAN-COLOR)

Berlin, March 5.

A Comacine Uno production. Directed by Gabriel Retes. Screenplay, Ignacio Retes, Rosa del Caudillo, in adaptation of plays "The Invaders" and "Paper Flowers" by Egon Wolff; camera (color), Daniel Lopez, music, Mario Lavista, Raul Lavista, Javier Mateos; editor, Eugenio Rivera; art director, Felida Medina. Reviewed at Berlin Festival (in competition), March 4, '78. Running time: 98 MINS.
Cast: Ana Luisa Peluffo, Gabriel Retes, Tina Romero, Claudio Brook, Adriana Role, Ignacio Retes and Silva Mariscal.

When making a political film, it helps to have a little understanding of politics. This certainly did not occur in the case of "Paper Flowers."

It deals with an explosion of the Lumpen who, expelled from their miserable slums, invade a prosperous section of the city, taking over the property of the resident bourgeoie; specifically, the large house of Hector Trejo, an industrialist and the small apartment of Eva, an attractive, lonely woman.

At first, Trejo tries to resist, as does Eva when the man who carries her shopping bags from the supermarket decides not to leave her apartment. Shortly, however, both give in and are assimilated by the Lumpen. The invaders sack and destroy Trejo's home and garden in what is meant to be a Walpurgis night of terror; in the morning they leave, loading their booty on a cart, drawn by its former owner, who has somehow been reduced to their level. Eva has come to a similar end because to her, having a man is primary consideration that matters more than worldly goods.

The film is based on two dramas by Chilean playwright Egon Wolff and, in telescoping both into one pic, it does justice to neither of the plays. Director Retes is strong on violence, but omits the motivations, character development and ideas that made the plays interesting, without substituting anything of similar interest. It does not matter from which angle of the political spectrum one beholds the film; whether viewed from the left, the right or the North Pole, it simply is not consistent.

Acting ranges from unimpressive to the weak; the nightmare atmosphere is only partially sustained and boxoffice prospects are limited on the pic's homeground. Even more so, abroad. —Amig.

El Brigadista
(The Teacher)
(CUBAN-COLOR)

Berlin, March 5.

An ICAIC production, produced by Sergio San Pedro. Directed by Octavio Cortazar. Screenplay, Louis Rogelio Nogueras, Cortazar; camera, (color), Pablo Martinez; music, Sergio Vitier; editor, Roberto Bravo; art director, Carlos Arditi. Reviewed at Berlin Film Festival (competition). Running time: 119 MINS.
Cast: Salvador Wood, Patricio Wood, Rene de la Cruz, Louis Alberto Ramirez, Luis Rielo, Mario Balmaseda and others.

On its homeground, "The Teacher" drew over 500,000 spectators in less than a month, making it the most successful film ever shot by ICAIC, the Cuban Film Institute. As a festival choice and for exploitation abroad, its chances are limited, for a very simple reason. What to Cubans is nostalgia, history or reality will, in part, hit Western audiences as heavy-handed propaganda.

Cuban films have often explored and analyzed the country's past in terms of the present. Now, after almost 20 years of revolution, they no longer need to go back to pre-Castro days. The massive 1961 campaign to eradicate illiteracy forms part of a collective memory: 100,000 students were sent into the countryside to teach the peasants to read and write and, at the same time, work with them in their daily chores. They and their students now make up a large part of Cuba's adult population.

In "The Teacher" Mario, a city-bred and 15-year-old high-school student is sent to Maniadero Chiquito, a small village in the Zapata swamps, to teach the peasants to read and write. At first they reject him, feeling that a youngster like that should bat at school himself instead of trying to teach others. But eventually they accept him and Mario himself also learns a great deal while sharing in the villagers' work. If Cortazar had stuck to this aspect of the story he might have had a better film; but he adds other angles: a little, in itself interesting, documentary on crocodile hunting, and then the background of the Bay of Pigs and the fighting with the counter-revolutionaries. Historically this, of course, coincided with the anti-illiteracy campaign, but this part of the story is unfortunately handled in a style reminiscent of some low-budget war pix from Hollywood in the Forties and Fifties. During the last few minutes the film returns to documentary, emphasizing that the fictionalized events form part of reality. However, with its speech extracts, etc., this also creates an excessive propaganda effect.

"The Teacher" has some good parts and Octavio Cortazar is a director to watch. Beyond the film's flaws, there is a freshness of approach, a belief in what he is doing, that is pretty powerful in spite of the underlying oldfashioned socialist realism which, unfortunately, is still one of the tendencies of Cuban cinema. —Amig.

La Tierra y el Cielo
(The Earth and the Sky)
(CUBAN-COLOR)

Berlin, March 1.

An ICAIC production. Directed by Manuel Octavio Gomez. Features entire cast. Camera (color), Livio Delgado; Music, Sergio Vitier (songs), Martha Jean Claude; editor, Nelson Rodriguez. At Berlin Film Festival (out of competition) March 1, '78. Running Time: 87 MINS.
Cast Samuel Claxton, Tito Junco, Martha Jean Claude.

There are still some 50,000 Haitians and their direct descendants living in Cuba and the film deals with them on a double level: their background as a minority and the struggle against superstition (also the subject of "The Days of Water," a previous film by Gomez) in post-Batista Cuba.

During the '40s, thousands of Haitians were brought in as cheap labor for the "zafra" (sugar harvest); many of them stayed on in Cuba, hoping to eventually save money, before returning home. Instead, they faced poverty, found great difficulty in adapting to an alien civilization and often were forcibly repatriated.

The story is developed on several time levels: during the present, Pedro Limon returns to his native village as a teacher and faces the changes that have taken place after several years of absence. The past is brought in through childhood memories, the Sierra Maestra where Pedro and his friend Ariston fought on the side of Castro's guerrillas and, later, the Bay of Pigs where Pedro is seriously wounded. The flashbacks may at times be complicated for those not well acquainted with Cuban history.

Basic idea is a contrast between Pedro, who is educated by the Revolution, and Ariston, who hangs on to his background of superstitious which, at a given moment, turn him into an antisocial element and bring on his end. This is the choice between heaven and the earth in the title. Within the Cuban film industry this is a minor film, a sort of social footnote to history; this does not prevent it from making its point clearly, but — except for perhaps some black or politically attracted audiences — it is of limited interest in other countries. —Amig.

Straight Time
(COLOR)

Distasteful and misfired Dustin Hoffman drama about crime and parole. Thin outlook.

Hollywood, March 16.

Warner Bros. release of a First Artists-Sweetwall film, produced by Stanley Beck, Tim Zinnemann; executive producer, Howard B. Pine. Stars Dustin Hoffman. Directed by Ulu Grosbard. Screenplay, Alvin Sargent, Edward Bunker, Jeffrey Boam, based on Bunker's novel, "No Beast So Fierce;" camera (Technicolor, Owen Roizman; editors, Sam O'Steen, Randy Roberts; music, David Shire; song lyrics, Norma Helms; production design, Stephen Grimes; art direction, Dick Lawrence; set decoration, Marvin March; sound, Richard Portman, Jim Webb; costumes-wardrobe, Bernie Pollack; asst. director, Jack Roe; stunt coordinators, Everett Creach, Dick Ziker. Reviewed at The Burbank Studios, March 16, '78. (MPAA Rating: R.) Running time: **114 MINS.**

Max Dembo	Dustin Hoffman
Jenny Mercer	Theresa Russell
Willy Darin	Gary Busey
Jerry Schue	Harry Dean Stanton
Earl Frank	M. Emmet Walsh
Carol Schue	Rita Taggart
Selma Darin	Kathy Bates
Manny	Sandy Baron
Henry Darin	Jacob Busey
Mickey	Edward Bunker
Jewelry Store Personnel	James Ray, Stuart I. Berton, Barry Cahill
Carlos	Corey Rand
Cafe Owner	Fran Ryan

"Straight Time" is a most unlikable film because Dustin Hoffman, starring as a paroled and longtime criminal, cannot overcome the essentially distasteful and increasingly unsympathetic elements in the character. Ulu Grosbard's sluggish direction doesn't help. Hoffman has already sued First Artists and Warner Bros. for allegedly taking the film away from him, the presumption being that the released version, running 114 minutes, is not his cut. Whoever did what, the result is bland and unappealing. Commercial outlook is thin.

The screenplay is credited to Alvin Sargent, Edward Bunker (who wrote the source novel, "No Beast So Fierce," long planned by Hoffman on his First Artists schedule) and Jeffrey Boam. One can easily argue that there were story problems right at the start. Apparent plot peg is that a parolee suffers os many indignities that a return to crime is easier. That would be okay if the principal character did not ultimately emerge as a lifelong lawbreakers — armed robbery — given to paranoid and psychotic behavior. This film is enough to set back the philosophy of parole for two centuries.

Viewers are asked initially to believe that M. Emmet Walsh, the assigned parole officer, is a sadistic person who delights in hassling his charges. But given the circumstances, he does not emerge as a heavy. Indeed, Hoffman's too-easy lapse into his old ways absolves any blame on The System. Thus, "Straight Time" is by no means an updated "Invisible Stripes," to mention just one old WB film where an ex-con is forced by events into new criminality. Hoffman's character would have defied the parole supervision of a saint.

Among the featured cast, Theresa Russell is very good as Hoffman's girl; Harry Dean Stanton is excellent as a reformed hood who (nobody explains why) is being suffocated in the life of a successful suburban businessman; Gary Busey is good as a weak ex-con who bungles a climactic robbery plan (and "friend" Hoffman kills him for that goof in the midst of a supposedly fraternal embrace).

David Shire's music is very good and physical production details are strong. Film ends with Hoffman sending the girl away from him — his only gesture in the story. He then drives off as a curtain montage shows his jail mug shots dating back to juvenile crime. One leaves the theatre hoping the character will die painfully and slowly in a hail of bullets — that's the effect of this nothing film. —*Murf.*

Skateboard
(COLOR)

Uninspired, poorly-made juve sport pic.

Hollywood, Feb. 24.

A Universal release of a Blum Group production. Produced by Harry N. Blum, Richard A. Wolf. Directed by George Gage. Screenplay by Richard A. Wolf and George Gage, based on a story by Wolf; camera, Ross Kelsay; editor, Robert Angus; sound, Galen Handy, Roger Heman; costume design, Elizabeth Gage. Reviewed at Writer's Guild Theatre, Beverly Hills, Calif., Feb. 24, '78. (MPAA Rating: PG.) Running time: **97 MINS.**

Manny Bloom	Allen Garfield
Millicent Broderick	Kathleen Lloyd
Brad Harris	Leif Garrett
Jason Maddox	Richard Van Der Wyk
Tony Bluetile	Tony Alva
Peter Steffens	Steve Monahan
Dennis	David Hyde
Jenny Bradshaw	Ellen Oneal
Randi	Pam Kenneally
Sol	Anthony Carbone

If "Skateboard" is any indication, most producers still don't give socalled "youth"market much credit for discriminating taste. Riding on the wheels of the skateboard craze, this Blum Group production, picked up by Universal, is short on action, long on talk and unsatisfying in both respects.

Idea by Richard Wolf is a good one — down-and-out Allen Garfield is backed into a corner by bookie Anthony Carbone, who holds big markers on the would-be agent. Garfield hits on the scheme of fielding a professional skateboard team, since players are there for the asking, schussing down city streets on custom-made skateboards, or hanging around those hair-raising curves at parks especially suite for the sport.

Plot, however, goes steadily downhill. Once Garfield has roped in skaters Tony Alva, Ellen Oneal Steve Monahan, David Hyde, Pam Kenneally and hotshot Richard Van Der Wyk, and scrounged up a bus, uniforms, matches and crowds, situation would seem ripe for a "Bad News Bears" take-off.

But director George Gage (who coscripted with Wolf) elicits no tension from the situation, in either internecine warfare among the kids, nor resolution of conflicts between stern taskmaster Garfield and his laid back charges. Garfield creates a totally unsympathetic character, and Kathleen Lloyd (wasted in another role) is tossed in as a superfluous character, a nurse for the team.

Kids who attend this pic aren't that interested in the dramatics, of course, but even the skateboard action, while technically impressive, holds no excitement. "Skateboard" builds to final race, which mobster Carbone, in the best fight film tradition, wants Garfield to throw. Since ace skateboarder Van Der Wyk has taken off because of Garfield's harassment (another conflict never resolved), young Leif Garrett is drafted and comes back a winner. Gage doesn't provide any suspense, however, and Robert Angus' editing makes Garrett's actual victory come off as confusing rather than impressive.

Lensing by Ross Kelsay is okay, but other tech credits are poor, with microphones clearly visible in several shots, and a choppy feeling permeating entire pic. Another important factor with youth audience, music soundtrack, is anemic, further depriving skateboard scenes of any punch.

"Skateboard" should do well in matinee and early evening slots, but most tykes will walk away with same feeling as when they wipe out on their skateboards: they've been burned. —*Poll.*

Bomsalva
(Misfire)
(SWEDISH-COLOR)

Malmoe, March 9.

A Svenska Filminstitutet/Europa Film production, Europa Film release. Features entire cast. Written and directed by Lars Molin. Camera (Eastmancolor), Hans Welin, Roland Sterner; executive producers, Bo Jonsson, Per Berglund; music, Kaj Chydenius; editor, Wic Kjellin. Reviewed at Rio Bio, Malmore, March 9, '78. Running time: **106 MINS.**

Rune	Lars Hjelt
Alma	Gunnel Lindblom
Pilander	Folke Asplund
Jaegner	Carl-Axel Heiknert

Lars Molin, novelist and tv scripter, comes out as a feature film helmer in an impressive way with "Misfire," which deals with the rising anger, frustrations and compromises among mine workers and management members when a minor explosion, probably caused by meteorological circumstances but also not averted due to a mining engineer's negligence, costs the lives of three men.

Moods and matters are worsened when it turns out that several tons of dynamite have been "trapped" inside the mountain and perilous work has to be done to neutralize the explosives.

"Misfire" works both as an indictment of management mismanagement and good dramatic story-telling and is sure to have appeal to all situations catering to films with a political charge.

The miners as well as the in-between foremen and engineers and even the management members are sharply drawn, true-to-life characters, well played by Lars Hjelt, Folke Asplund and Carl-Axel Heiknert with Gunnel Lindblom doing a weepy cameo as the canteen caretaker who cares for the workers' cause and longs to belong to the young engineer. —*Kell.*

En och en
(One Plus One)
(SWEDISH-COLOR)

Copenhagen, March 15.

A Josephson . . Nykvist/Swedish Film Institute/AB Sandrews production, AB Sandrews release. Stars Erland Josephson, Ingrid Thulin, Erland Josephson Directed by Josephson, Sven Nykvist, Ingrid Thulin. Camera (Eastmancolor), Nykvist. Executive producer, Katinka Farago. Reviewed during Nordic Film Days at private screening, Copenhagen, March 14, '78. Running time, **90 MINS.**

A couple of major Ingmar Bergman actors, Erland Josephson and Ingrid Thulin, and Bergman cinematographer Sven Nykvist insist on "One Plus One" being a feature film "by" this threesome. But most obviously Nykvist has directed his own magnificent cinematography, while Josephson has done most of the direction from his own script. He has already written and directed a few works for Swedish television.

The story is vague. It tells of a close to middle-age woman artist (Ingrid Thulin) who more or less forces her slightly older cousin (Erland Josephson) to abandon his self-chosen life of an eccentric hermit (of private means) to follow her on a voyage to first Copenhagen and then to the idyllic Danish island of Bornholm.

The woman has guilt feelings about how she and other children once treated the cousin who was always the shy, bespectacled one and the victim in all games. She is also now running away from a long-time lover and a newly-acquired one. Plus she is escaping from working at her art.

The odd couple taunt each other and make shy approaches to each other and go through endless dialogues of intellectual pallor when they don't stage confrontations of sexual or otherwise challenging kinds. The affair is not meant to be an affair and is doomed from the start.

Both main actors and a couple of lesser performers shine in great style. Nykvist's cinematography makes sequences come almost alive that are otherwise devoid of natural dramatics. Bergman's ghosts moans from cupboards in hotel rooms or from behind sand dunes on beaches or out of pictures at museums. Film is a footnote to the Bergman production of the early seventies, nothing more and of interest to hardly anybody but Bergman scholars. The title, "One Plus One," is heavily explained to have Two as an impossible equation. No new views here, no news anywhere in this series of dialog-shaped essays from the graveyard of modern love. —*Kell.*

Doctor Vlimmen
(DUTCH-BELGIAN-COLOR)

Brussels, March 8.
A Cinecentrum (Amsterdam) — Kunst en Kino (Brussels) production. Produced by Gerrit Visscher, Jef Vliegen, Jan Van Raemdonck. Directed by Guido Pieters. Features entire cast. Screenplay, Guido Pieters, Ben Verbong, from novel by A. Roothaert; camera (Kodacolor), Theo van de Sande; editor, Ton Ruys; music, Pim Koopman; art director, Dick Schillemans; asst. director, Eefje Cornelis. Reviewed at Cinema Marivaux, Brussels, March 7, '78. Running time: **70 MINS.**
Doctor Vlimmen . . . . .Peter Faber
Dacka . . . . Roger Van Hool
Truus . . . . Chris Lomme
Mientje . . . . Brigitte de Man
Dop (5 years) . . . . .Mattijn Hallers
Dop . . . . Erik van 't Wout
Van Bemmel . . . . . . .Helmert Woudenberg
Van der Kalck . . . . Leo Beyers
Dr. Treeborg . . . . Manfred de Graaf
Pietje Mulder . . . . .Serge Henri Valcke
Keeke Mulder . . . . .Reinhilde Decleir
Stein . . . . Frans Vorstman
Van Heusden . . . . .Tim Beekman
Tilly . . . . Yolande Bertsch
Paula .Cox Habbema
Leonieke . . . . Monique van de Ven
Baron . . . . .Hein Fentener van
Vlissingen
Tiest . . . . .Guy Lavreysen
Bonneke . . . . Michel van Rooy
Singer . . . . .Dorien van der Klei

As a convincing adaptation of a popular novel, "Dr. Vlimmen" can't fail. It's a well made, adroitly scripted film. It has a realistic approach to the problems of the hero, a veterinarian facing the stupidity, bigotry, distrust of backward peasants of a Dutch-Belgian border village. What happens is not very original but it has enough human aspects to please and interest those

who, fed-up with sex, seek renewed contact with old values.

To these, "Dr. Vlimmen" will appeal very much, all the more since Guido Pieters has avoided many pitfalls. Not a film for sophisticates, but a great many people will enjoy it and word of the mouth will be its best publicity.

Not a great deal outside everyday events happen in this tale of a dedicated vet who, in 20 years, tries to survive in a world of pettiness and small intrigues. He is not popular because his wife left him, because he speaks his mind and fights unorthodox methods of local slaughterers, and cruelty to animals.. And then, one day, he is falsely accused by a young maid of having fathered her child. It takes a long time for him to establish his innocence, in which he finally succeeds.

It's all but it's enough. The rustic charm of some scenes is ingratiating, charmingly photographed by Theo van de Sande. The happy-end, in true classical style, seems a little forced and quite unnecessary. As a nice change, there is no cruelty to animals here and even their trainers are credited.

Acting is quite good, with Peter Faber convincingly depicting the hero and Roger Van Hool exactly right as his friend. The others don't have much to do, being more cliches than anything else. The Dutch and Antwerp locations are attractive and all technical aspects are good.
—*Flor.*

In Nome Del Papa Re
(In the Name of the Pope King)
(ITALIAN-COLOR)

Rome, March 21.
A Rizzoli Film release (Italy) produced by Franco Committeri for Juppiter Generale Cinematografica (Italy). Stars Nino Manfredi. Written and directed by Luigi Magni. Camera (Eastmancolor), Danilo Desideri; editor, Ruggero Mastroianni; music, Armando Trovaioli. Reviewed at Cinema Cola di Reinzo, Rome, March 8, '78. Running time: **107 MINS.**
Don Colombo . . . . Nino Manfredi
Cesare Costa . . . . Danilo Mattei
Contessa Flaminia . . . . . Carmen Scarpitta
Teresa . . . . Giovanella Grifeo
Perpetuo . . . . Carlo Bagno
Papa Nero . . . . Salvo Randone

All of Luigi Magni's films are centered in Rome and the specialization has paid off. In turning back the pages 100 years or so to the closing days of a long period when the Vatican exercised temporal as well as spiritual authority, Magni wrote and directed "Pope-King" with one eye on history and the other on the box-office.

For youth, he offers a parallel between extremism then and now by dosing dialog and youth behaviour to contemporary student rebels and revolutionaries, using a group of young actors who ob-

viously endorse this affiliation. For other age brackets, the Cineriz entry is an all purpose dramatic comedy with melodramatic moments giving popular thesp Nino Manfredi a free hand to run the gamut of his personal comic style and still capture the serious tones of an Inquisition judge no longer tolerant of authoritarianism and routine bureaucracy. The combination certainly works for Italy — more so in southern cinemas — and should find a toehold in Mediterranean and Latin American markets with Manfredi's name.

"Pope King" takes place just before Garibaldi's troops entered Rome with ensuing separation of Church and State. According to Magni, youth were on the rampage for liberty. Historically true is the bombing of a Zouave garrison in Rome and beheading of two young Romans after a Vatican court found them guilty of spreading death among the troops. From there in, it's fiction and fantasy.

Manfredi, already troubled in conscience learns after 20 years that he is the father of one of the arrested youths—born of an illicit affair. The mother — later wed into a top noble family (and convincingly played by legit actress Carmen Scarpitta) makes an unwilling ally of Manfredi to save the boy. The son-father dialogue and the boy's girlfriend give the filmmaker a chance to align past kids with radical youth today.

Scenes between the countess and the bishop cover melodramatic ground from their original transgression to the critical danger for their grown son, whose sweet and liberated young girlfriend (Giovanella Grifeo) gets her big permissive moment in a final love scene with the boy.

Effort to content all audience age groups limits plausibility — particulary so in all characterizations. Magni goes overboard in dressing young radicals of a century back with the hard nose generational-gap reactions and verbiage of 1978. Manfredi is fine as Manfredi but whittles away the portrayal of a bishop searching for more tolerance and freedom, resorting frequently to his standard comedy routines. Two excellent support roles are played by Carlo Bagno and Salvo Randone.

Magni provides authentic background of old Rome for his costumer. Armando Trovaioli stirring score — among other solid technical credits — is an infusion of opera bits, folk songs and patriotic tunes. —*Werb.*

Starhops
(COLOR)

Fast moving exploitationer.

Hollywood, March 14.
First American Films release of a Grodnik/Sharpe production of a Roseworld film. Produced by John B. Kelley, Robert D. Krintzman; exec producers, Daniel Grodnik, Robert Sharpe. Features entire cast. Directed by Barbara Peeters. Screenplay, Dallas Meredith; camera (CFI Color), Eric Saarinen; editor, Steve Zaillian; sound, Mike C. Moore; costumes-wardrobe, Elan. Reviewed at Culver Triplex, Culver City, March 14, '78. (MPAA Rating: R.) Running time: **82 MINS.**
Danielle . . . . .Dorothy Buhrman
Cupcake . . . . Sterling Frazier
Angel .Jillian Kesner
Ron .Peter Paul Iapis
Kong . . . . Anthony Mannino
Norman . . . . Paul Ryan
Carter Axe . . . . .Al Hobson
Jerry . . . . Dick Miller

"Starhops" is a breezy, deftly-directed exploitation comedy with fetching girls, skimpy outfits, risque dialog and a general permeation of sexual innuendo, but there's very little that couldn't easily transferred to "Charlie's Angels" on tv.

Pic was originally rated PG last September, leading First American Films to loop in that four letter word which auomatically guarantees an R tag. Audience will have to be all ears to catch the vulgarism, however, since it slides by virtually unnoticed. There is no nudity and little simulated sex — considering the pic is being double-billed with more rauchy items.

Threadbare plot has Sterling Frazier and Jillian Kesner as two carhops who take over a failing drive-in from beleaguered owner Dick Miller. Endowed with monickers like Cupcake and Angel La-Plante, the feminine duo has no trouble seducing a bank loan out of a willing financier, obtaining the start-up money take over the operation by themselves.

They're joined by French gourmet chef Dorothy Buhrman, and with the addition of some flesh-exposing uniforms and roller skates, business is booming. As usual, there's a heavy lurking about, in this case, oil mogul Carter Axe (Al Hobson), whose Axeon Oil wants the drive-in site for a prototype gas station of the future designed by architect Peter Paul Liapis.

Axe sends dumbbell son Paul Ryan in to collect dirt on the femmes, but their operation is so squeaky clean that violence is eventually resorted to, with biker Anthony Mannino (as a character apropriately named Kong) coming to the rescue, aided by the reformed son, won over to the cause thanbks to Frazier's charms.

All this is directed in upbeat fashion by Peeters, who employs rapid cutting and lotsa visual humor to keep the mixture bubbling away.

Several of the jokes (such as a mock "Star Wars" crawl) are never milked for all they're worth, but Peeters is smart enough to toss in elements from several successful pix, such as a flashy disco dancing scene.

Presence of one of few active femme directors also might explain lack of overt sexual intimations. If First American is eyeing a future tv sale, they should have no problems. Even the vid censors won't find too much to excise from "Starhops."

Cast acquits itself in competent fashion, with Frazier evincing some actual acting ability and a fresh personality that could rise above this kind of typecasting. Mannino, Ryan and Hobson add flair, while Dick Miller ("Little Shop Of Horrors") contributes a finely-crafted bit as the hassled entrepreneur driven out of biz by the fast-food conglomerates.

Tech credits are fine, with Eric Saarinen's sharp lensing around Marina Del Rey locations. —*Poll.*

Queridos Companeros
(Dear Comrades)
(CHILE-VENEZUELA-COLOR)

Berlin, March 6.

A Cinematografica Proa C.A. and Grupo Rent-a-cine C.A. production. Directed by Pablo de la Barra. Screenplay, De la Barra, Ione Borg; camera (color), Wellinta Dinis; music, Jesus Sanoja Jr.; editor, Giuliano Ferrioli; art director, Sergio Zapata. Viewed at Berlin Festival (International Forum of Young Film) March 5, '78. Running Time: **90 MINS.**
Cast: Marcelo Romo, Hugo Medina, Andrea Bacay, Eduardo Duran, Paz Irarazabal.

At the time of the military takover in Chile, (Sept., 1973), Pablo de la Barra had not finished shooting his feature. His production company was searched and 90% of his soundtracks destroyed. It took him almost three years to get his material to Caracas, where he himself has lived since 1974. Under these conditions it would appear almost impossible to finish a film. But, with the aid of a deaf-and-dumb lip-reader the dialog was reconstructed and then dubbed by Chilean residents in Venezuela.

The action takes place in 1967, several years before Allende's "Unidad Popular" government; it is focussed on a direct action revolutionary group and also goes into the dilemma of the left between direct action and electoral means. The protagonists fail in one venture, have to go into hiding, then prepare and carry out a bank robbery to collect funds for their political work.

Action scenes are well handled, but what gives the film its special dimension are the director's reflections on them. He looks back with serene hindsight, relates the events

of the film with those taking place at hte actual sight, relates the events of the film with those taking place at the actual time of shooting, and observes both periods from his present Venezuelan vantage point. These interpolations are unobtrusively used to cover up the gaps in the narrative.

Almost 50 films have been made on the subject of Chile over the last four years: short and long, documentaries and features, in both Germanies, in the Soviet Union, in Mexico, in Sweden, in France, Canada, Cuba and Rumania. As far as documentaries are concerned, a saturation point may well have been reached, but a lot of ground can still be covered in fiction and semi-fiction features. In this field, de la Barra's film covers new ground and is likely to gain considerable international exposures at festivals, film archives and some art houses. He is also a director worth watching, as "Queridos Companeros" is a promising first feature. —*Amig.*

Doubles
(COLOR)

Confusing suspenser. Good points, however, for Seattle production.

Seattle, March 16.

Cinema World Releasing release of Doppleganger Production Associates production in association with Skylight Productions. Produced, written and directed by Bruce Wilson. Features entire cast Story consultant, Ed Leimbacher; caemra, (Eastman Color) P. Kip Anderson; music, Jim Bredouw and Martin Lund; editors, Art Coburn and Skeets McGrew; asst. director-production manager, Pat Fay; script supervisor, Karen Thorndike. Reviewed at Broadway Theatre, Seattle, March 15, '78. (No MPAA rating). Running time: **90 MINS.**
Dennis Cooley .... Ted D'Arms
Raymond
    Randolph .... Martin La Platney
Linda .... Ann Bowden
Dick .... Dean Melang
Sandra .... Peggy Nielsen
Nick .... Glen Mazen
Carol .... Sally Prtichard
Bob .... Niles Brewster

This, the first feature film entirely financed and produced in Seattle (Washington State) is a good try, auguring well for future ventures, but it never gets off the ground, caught between an exposition of chase-type hustle and art house moodiness.

The story has a group of people, led by protagonist Ted D'Arms, a dentist, setting up a parlor game to alleviate boredom. The scenario for the game gets out of hand, resulting in a deadly confrontation between the dentist and a hired hit man who is stalking him.

The script is based on a real incident in 1921, brought up to date. That real life incident involved a Dennis Cooley, who was tried and con-

victed of murder. Documentary device, a scratchy recording of Cooley's plea of innocence and justification for his act, supposedly made in 1921, doesn't add much to the proceedings, only confusion.

Action, such as it is, switches from the party planning the scenario to chases and confrontations, ending in the death of the hit man at Cooley's hand, then back to the party. If it sounds confusing, it is. It's not clear how much is fantasy and how much is "real," and finally, there is no answer to the question.

However, there are certianly promising aspects to the production. Camera work by P. Kip Anderson is good, especially in depiction of locations in the Skagit Valley, where most of the film was shot. Music by Bredouw and Lund is a definite asset. Overall look of the film belies its less-than-$100,000 cost, and if Wilson can produce this quality for that price his future is promising.

D'Arms underplays his leading role to the level of dullness, but La Platney does a fine job of his dual hit man role, bringing touch of smooth menace that has strong impact. None of the femme parts are big. Ann Bowden is effective and appealing in her larger role as Cooley's lover.

As noted, it's a good try, and with low budget will not require much playing time to get into the black. Prospects difficult to assess, but should be good second in dual situations, and could do particularly well in the Pacific Northwest, which is a pretty big area. —*Reed.*

The Stud
(BRITISH-COLOR)

London, March 16.

Brent Walker Film Productions release, produced by Ronald S. Kass; executive in charge of production, Oscar S. Lerman; executive producers, George A. Walker, Edward D. Simons. Features entire cast. Directed by Quentin Masters. Screenplay, Jackie Collins; camera, (color), Peter Hannan; art director, Michael Bastow; editor, David Camplin; music Sammy Cahn and Biddu; wardrobe, Penny Rose; Sound, Stan Phillips; assistant director, Vincent Winter; Reviewed at Century Theatre, Soho Square, London, March 15, '78. Running time: **90 MINS.**
Fontaine Khaled .... Joan Collins
Tony Blake .... Oliver Tobias
Alex Khaled .... Emma Jacobs
Vanessa .... Sue Lloyd
Ben Khaled .... Walter Gotell
Leonard .... Mark Burns
Maddy .... Nathalie Ogle
Deborah .... Felicity Buirski
Sammy .... Doug Fisher
Hal .... Tony Allyn
Ian Thane .... Peter Lukas
Lord Newton ...... Constantin De Goguel
Peter .... Guy Ward
Molly .... Minah Bird
Mum .... Hilda Fenemore
Dad .... Bernard Stone
Staton .... Hugh Morton
Sandro .... Howard Nelson
Anne Khaled .... Sarah Lawson
Doctor .... Leonard Trolley
Lawyer Scott .... Jeremy Child
Franco .... Franco De Rosa
Flowers .... Shango Baku
Janine .... Tania Rogers
Vicar .... Michael Barrington
Meter Maid .... Rynagh O'Grady
Tailor .... Edmond Warwick
Mario .... Robert Tayman
Chef .... Giorgio Bosso

"The Stud," maiden production of Britain's Brent Walker filmery, goes a long way toward transcending the softcore sexpo genre, but ultimately doesn't quite make it. It's a shame because the producers have obviously tried hard to avoid low-budget seediness of routine skinflicks. That element is thankfully missing from this one, with production given a thoroughly professional gloss with an expensive-looking, albeit slightly dated, veneer of swinging London chic.

The Ron Kass production, directed by Australian Quentin Masters, should be okay in fast playoff. Based on the novel by Jackie Collins (sister of Joan, who toplines) film has Oliver Tobias in title role as a virile manager of a London nitery.

Joan Collins is the lady who pulls the strings to manipulate him as her own sexual marionette. Her husband, played by Walter Gotell, owns the nightclub and if the stud wants to keep his perquisites he must toe the line and keep the lady happy. And quite a few others, too.

Film is short on titillation and is neither erotic nor arty enough to join the "Emmanuelle" class. Nevertheless, it's quality stuff as such pix go and a fair proportion of the $1,000,000 budget can be seen on screen. There are some sumptuous interiors, imaginatively lensed by Peter Hannan, who maintains a high standard of photography throughout.

On the debit side "The Stud" lacks a credible script. Penned by the author herself, the plotline often borders on the banal.

Masters' direction could have leaned more toward humor in perhaps the same way achieved by Lewis Gilbert directing Michael Caine in "Alfie" a dozen or so years back.

Tobias himself is short on sensitivity and would be Lotharios, seeking useful tips might be excused for wondering what, apart from rakish good looks, is the secret of lad's success in persuading so many eligibles into the sack. He, in fact, seems faintly embarrassed about the whole thing. Joan Collins sails through her part giving just what was demanded but adding no dimension.

Most notable performance (and natural) came from Doug Fisher as Tobias' buddy.

Songwriting team of Sammy Cahn and Biddu are responsible for pic's original music which works well enough, but producers have been overzealous in pushing a bunch of established disco clicks too. Presumably to cash in on exploitation values, the numbers are often too loud and alien to pic's dialog. —*Swan.*

Moritz, Lieber Moritz
(Moritz, Dear Moritz)
(WEST GERMAN-COLOR)

Berlin, March 7.
A Production of the Hamburger Kino Kompanie/Hark Bohm Film Productions; world rights, Filmverlag der Auoren, Munich. Features entire cast. Written and directed by Hark Bohm. Camera (Eastmancolor), Wolfgang Treu; editing, Jane Sperri; sets, Hans Zillmann; music, Klaus Doldinger; sound, Peter Kellerhals; animal trainer, Natalia Bowakow. Reviewed at Cinema Paris, Berlin, March 6, '78. Running time: 96 MINS.
Moritz ....:.......Michael Kebschull
Mother Stuckmann .... Myra Mladeck
Father Stuckmann .... Walter Klosterfelde
Aunt .... Elvira Thom
Barbara ....:...... Kerstin Wehlmann
Uwe .... Uwe Enkelmann
Dschingis .... Dschingis Bowakow
Bass .... Armand Hacaturyan
Drummer .... Nico Lafrentz
Guitar .... Richard Schuhmacher
Teacher .... Wolf-Dietrich Berg
Widow .... Eva Fiebig
Kantor .... Uwe Dallmeier
Nurse .... Christa Siems
Grandmother .... Grete Mosheim

The only consistent commercial director in New German Cinema, Hark Bohm has another winner in "Moritz, Dear Moritz," an entry at the Berlin Film Festival, drawing immediate approval from the young auds at the preem.

Bohm makes films that are close to home: they usually star one or both of his step-sons and deal directly with their world in a straightforward, no-punches-pulled, semi-

docu style. His b.o. winners thus far — "Chetan, the Indian Boy" (1973) and "North Sea Is Death Sea" (1975) — are about boys growing up, the first set in the Wild West and the second in the harbor-city of Hamburg. He is a master at blending milieu with story to render that necessary touch of credibility.

"Moritz, Dear Moritz" is again set in Hamburg. It's the story of a rich kid at the crisis age of 15 who can't get along with anyone, save for a pet rat in the basement (where he goes to practice his saxophone). His father, who married into wealth, has gone bankrupt; the mother cares little about the youngster's weird habits; the grandmother has grown weary of life in an Old Peoples Home and asks Moritz for an extra supply of sleeping pills on his next visit; the aunt has sex on her mind and tries to seduce the boy; and his schoolmates and teacher only tend to make things more miserable than they really are.

Moritz uses his fantasies to get even. He daydreams violence upon his teacher (a ghoulish scene in which he dissects his tormentor on a geometric cross), imagines how to get the best of the neighbor's cat (kill it, of course), and even fantasizes — or is it reality? — an automobile crack-up with a lovely girl's decapitation to boot.

The boy's salvation is a girl his own age and a pop band on the waterfront who could use a hot sax. He is able to break out of his closed inner world, Bohm supplying a nice finishing touch with a fight scene as his school chums appear at the teenage club to jeer the band's first outing with Moritz.

Credits are top-flight across the board. Pic is in mainstream of new trend in German cinema towards an original narrative style. Directors like Bohm, Niklaus Schilling, Reinhard Hauff, and Sohrab Shahid Saless, among others, are joining ground to prove NGC is viable commercially as well as critically. "Moritz" could score offshore with proper handling. —*Holl.*

Mig og Charly
(Me and Charly)
(DANISH-COLOR)

Copenhagen, March 16.
A Steen Herdel Production/Warner-Constantin release. Features entire cast. Written, directed and lensed (Eastmancolor) by Henning Kristiansen and Morten Arnfred, based on Ben Rasmussen's novel "The White Hands." Production manager Lars Kolvig; editor, Anders Refn; music, Kasper Winding, with song and lyrics by C.V. Jorgensen. Reviewed at private screening during Nordic Film Days at Copenhagen, March 16, '78. Running time: 98 MINS.
Steffen .... Kim Eduard Jensen
Charly .... Allan Olsen
Steffen's mother .... Ghita Noerby
Majbritt .... Helle Nielsen
Car Dealer .... Jens Okking

Henning Kristiansen and Morten Arnfred, professional cinematographers of high standing, have written and directed this handsome, humorous and mildly tragic feature about people, young and old, in a Danish provincial town and the surrounding landscape with the latter playing an actual dramatic part in all proceedings.

Steffen (Kim Eduard Jensen) is a teenager living with his widowed mother, a newspaperwoman (Ghita Noerby). Steffen is out of school, but only halfheartedly looking for work. He is no drifter, however. He handles himself well when his girlfriend gets jealous about his befriending Charly, a boy from a reform school, and equally well when his mother, who sees her late husband in the son, one night gets slightly drunk and more than slightly amourous. A sequence involving, possibly, a bit of incest, is handled with tact and good taste.

Charly (Allan Olsen, like Kim Jensen an amateur player who does well among professionals such as, the excellent Ghita Noerby) gets into trouble when Steffen gains him access to the outskirts of bourgeois life in the provincial town.

But Steffen stands by Charly and though no happy ending is promised or even in sight, audiences everywhere will leave theatres with moist eyes and unashamed pleasure at having been in the company of very real people.

"Me and Charly" is an obvious fest contender, but a broader appeal in commercial situations everywhere should also be assured. —*Kell.*

La Chambre Verte
(The Green Room)
(FRENCH-COLOR)

Paris, March 28.
United Artists release of Les Films Du Carrosse-UA production. Stars Francois Truffaut, Nathalie Baye. Directed by Francois Truffaut. Screenplay, Truffaut, Jean Gruault from two themes in stories by Henry James; camera (Eastmancolor), Nestor Almendros; editor, Martine Barraque-Curie; music, Maurice Jaubert. Reviewed at Publicis, Paris, March 20, '78. Running time: 94 MINS.
Julien .... Francois Truffaut
Cecilia .... Nathalie Baye
Humbert .... Jean Daste
Gerard .... Jean-Pierre Moulin
Rambaud .... Jane Lobre
Georges .... Patrick Maleon

Francois Truffaut, probably one of the most popular French directors in the U.S., who also recently scored as a thesp in the hit sci-fier, "Close Encounters of the Third Kind" (WB-Col), must have had some intimations of mortality.

In this film, based on themes of expatriate U.S. writer Henry James, he again directs and for the third time plays a lead in his own pic, a pared-down, sometimes-labored tale of a man whose love for

his dead wife takes precedence over the living.

It is a decade after the end of World War I, and Truffaut is a quiet, almost asocial man working on a fading provincial magazine for which he excels at obits. It becomes clear he has been affected by having come back intact from the murderous war where most of his friends died. His young wife had died soon after their marriage and he has constructed a room in her memory full of her photos and memorabilia.

Looking for one of her rings, when her family's possessions are sold off, he meets a young woman whom he met as an adolescent and a relationship of sorts springs up.

Truffaut's outlook is not sentimental or based on charity or religious dogma. He makes this clear when a friend breaks down at his wife's wake and Truffaut upbraids a priest for promises of an after life. The dead have to be respected and loved, is his credo.

He gets permission from the church to restore an old chapel and to dedicate it to his dead wife and friends, but when he finds out that his new aquaintance has previously loved a man Truffaut did not respect, it leads to his withdrawal and sickness. Eventually, he meets her again in the chapel, where he dies while asking her to carry on his work and light a candle for him.

The James themes of repressiveness and cultural conflicts are just underpinnings to the film. There is the insidey scene when his chapel shows pictures of some deceased people who helped, influenced or were friends of Truffaut, including James himself. It is well lensed in stark hues. Nathalie Bayle is effective as a woman who loves life but she also respects death. Pic has fine period recreation.

But its sombre, ritualistic, sometimes over-explicative aspects make this an item that needs delicate handling for best results. There is the Truffaut name but it is more for selective than general audiences. Truffaut displays his eclectic and prolific tendencies but the film remains an uneven though exacting exercise —*Mosk.*

Kloden rokker
(This Rockin' Globe)
(DANISH-COLOR)

Copenhagen, March 21.
An Ebbe Preisler/Film & Lyd production, Constantin-Warner distribution. Written and directed by a collective headed by John Menzer. Camera (Eastmancolor), Morten Bruus Pedersen, Henrik Herbert, Dirk Bruel, Simon Plum, Freddy Tornberg, Andreas Fischer-Hansen, Bo Riemer, Dan Lausten, Jimmy Andreasen; editor, Lars Brydesen; music by performing groups and soloists: Gnags, Culpepper, Lone Kellerman, Stig Moeller, Tania Maria

Trio, The Jack Bruce Band, The Chieftains, Karsten Vogel & Birds of Beauty, Troels Trier, C. V. Joergensen, Skousen & Ingemann, Starfuckers. Reviewed at Cinema 1, Copenhagen, March 21, '78. Running time, **88 MINS.**

"This Rockin' Globe" is an on the spot report on the 1977 Danish Roskilde Rock Festival, done by a collective and suffering from that fact.

Film emerges as an unmusical mess of badly-edited and sloppily-filmed concert excerpts interspersed with glimpses of the audience dancing, sleeping, eating, showering and, mostly, swilling beer. Serving as a framework and interviews with three roadies and sequences showing these truly working class rockers at work and at (very little) play. Apart from Brasil's Tania Maria, Ireland's Chieftains, Denmark's Birds of Beauty and the English Jack Bruce Band very little music is heard to its advantage. Dim offshore sales prospects for this one, but it may serve in youth slots at minor festivals. —*Kell.*

Taugenichts
(Good-for-Nothings)
(WEST GERMAN-COLOR)

Berlin, March 7.

An ABS/Solaris-Film Production, Munich; world rights, Filmverlag der Autoren, Munich. Features entire cast. Directed by Bernhard Sinkel. Screenplay, Alf Brustellin, Sinkel, based on Joseph Freiherr von Eichendorff's novel, "Memoirs of a Good-for-Nothing;" camera (color), Dietrich Lohmann; editing, Dagmar Hirtz; sets, Nicos Perakis; costumes, Barbara Matthee; music, Hans Werner Henze; sound, Ed Parente. Reviewed at Cinema Paris, Berlin, March 6, '78. Running time: **91 MINS.**
Good-for-Nothing .... Jacques Breuer
Countess .... Eva-Maria Meineke
Aurelie ..'................. Sybil Schreiber
Flora .... Mareike Carriere
Leonard .... Matthias Habich
Porter .... Wolfgang Reichman
Painter .... Peter Berling
Chambermaid .... Pizi Adam
Dwarf Gouffino .... Jiri Kritnar
Castle Administratrix ...... Maria Grazia
de Giorgi

Among NGC helmers, Bernhard Sinkel has a reputation after four films for lovely pictures and a story set more to images than words. His "Lina Braake" ended with a sunset scene in a pastoral Italian village; "Berlinger" needed open spaces to give this "German Adventure" room to breathe; "The Maidens' War" depended on the baroque beauty of Prague as a stunning backdrop. And now "Good-for-Nothing" leans heavily on the major achievement of German Romantic narrative fiction to pump some life into a fragile, rather stiff story.

"Good-for-Nothing" (written in 1826) wins readers even today as a naive, optimistic, fun-loving, sometimes simple-minded fairy tale embracing the late Romantic period. Its author, a nobleman by birth, was both a Prussian official and the

greatest lyricist of his day (his poems have inspired Richard Strauss, Schumann, and Mendelssohn).

The German Democratic Republic filmed a version of the novel in 1973, at a time when Sinkel and his scriptwriter Alf Brustellin (they codirected "Berlinger" and "Maidens' War") had already finished their screenplay but couldn't find a backer. Now that Sinkel-Brustellin have made a rep as two of the most "cinema-minded" (in contrast to tv film-making) of German helmers, the way was open to rework an old project.

It's the story of a lad leaving his father's mill, a "good-for-nothing" finding his way into the wide world. Eventually he winds up at the castle of a bankrupt countess, learns about the ways of life and love, and scampers off to Italy with a broken heart. There he encounters the seamy underworld of poets and painters, gets caught under the spell of the reckless life, and finally finds comfort and reward in the arms of the lovely Aurelia.

Pic moves at a shaky pace, lacking a Tom Jones flamboyance to get it off and running. What pulls it down is the weight of a costume melodrama; Sinkel hasn't caught the light spirit of the novel. Humor, in particular, is lacking in the make-believe romps of principle characters. Like Helma Sanders's "Heinrich" (on Prussian poet Heinrich von Kleist) and Heidi Genee's "Grete Minde," costume pictures and literary adaptations don't seem to be a strong suit in New German Cinema.

"Good-for-Nothing" special-screened at Berlin Fest. —*Holl.*

Bluff Stop
(SWEDISH-COLOR)

Copenhagen, March 20.

A Swedish Film Institute production and release. Written and directed by Jonas Cornell. Features entire cast. Camera (Eastmancolor) Lars Svanberg; production manager, Jutta Ekman; executive producer, Jorn Donner. Reviewed during Nordic Film Days at Copenhagen at Cinema 1, March 20, '78. Running time, **104 MINS.**
Stefan .... Bjoern Andresen
Rachel .... Barbro Skarp
Stefan's father .... Keve Hjelm
Stefan's mother .... Maj-Britt Nilsson
The father's
second wife .... Agneta Ekmanner
Uncle .... Jan Malmsjoe

The cinematography of Lars Svanberg recalls some of the more lyrical passages in the works of Visconti and Bertolucci: beauty filtered through a temperament. The story and the direction of Jonas Cornell has wit, flashes of vibrant originality and a rather run of the mill human compassion plus not much of anywhere to go. Still, with some necessary editing, "Bluff Stop"

ought easily to rate art house showings even in the U.S.

Editing would be necessary since one flashback to childhood sequence, brief as it is, is absolutely inexplicable. Another puzzling sequence in a classroom with the Latin teacher, is placed after the class has graduated. Sloppy editing here? Or did the director have to leave on some other film job before this one was finished?

"Bluff Stop," an expression from a card game, is also an ill-chosen though nice sounding title. It indicates that everybody in the story is bluffing, but the plot itself defeats that indication.

Cornell recalls his own last year in school before graduating to enter either a university or life itself. It happened in the '50s, and film's production dress as well as acting in all roles bear the mark of the exquisite.

Still, "Bluff Stop" is not just another nostalgia exploiter but a thing of beauty and wit unto itself, faults notwithstanding. Bjoern Andresen (the boy of Visconti's "Death In Venice") ducks his school chores, beds down with his father's new wife (Agneta Ekmanner), clowns with his pals and is, with them, much puzzled at adult behavior and its general shallowness.

The youngster decides to run away from all the bluffing. He and his girlfriend actually buy tickets to go to Rome in search of a new life when she gets trapped by her family while he waits on the platform as the train pulls out. Those two were not bluffing and they are drawn as characters who will not bluff in the future, either. —*Kell.*

Tod Oder Freiheit
(Death Or Freedom)
(WEST GERMAN-COLOR)

Berlin, March 2.

A Regina Ziegler Film Production, Berlin, in collaboration with Paramount Films, Germany, distributed by Cinema International Corporation. Features entire cast. Written and directed by Wolf Gremm. Camera (color), Jost Vacano; editing, Siegrun Jaeger; sets, Goetz Heymann, Juergen Henze; costumes, Ingrid Zore; sound, Gunther Kortwich. Reviewed at Pallette cinema, Berlin, March 1, '78. Running time: **90 MINS.**
Fritz von Buttlar .... Peter Sattmann
Nicole von Beck .... Erika Pluhar
Ludwig von Buttlar Wolfgang Schumacher
Supreme Commander .... Harold Leipnitz
Maria .... Christine Boehm
Max .... Mario Adorf
Count von Buttlar .... Gert Frobe
Bartel .... Dieter Schidor
Angelo .... Guido de Angelis
Mopp .... George Meyer-Goll
Nickel .... Seidenschwan
Anton .... Stefan Ostertag
Pfeiffer .... Volker Bogdan

Wolf Gremm scored on the commercial circuit the last try out with the thriller-melodrama "The

Brothers." It helped him raise a cool $1 million for his backer, Berlin producer Regina Ziegler, for "Death or Freedom," an action film set in Schiller's "The Robbers" times and our own Revolutionary War period. The film is an attempt to find and win support from a new cinema audience for German-made commercial fare — but unfortunately it loses sight of the rules of the action-film genre and never quite stands on its own feet.

The only trouble is that Gremm doesn't have a large Hollywood studio of action professionals to keep things moving. The one good swordfight at the beginning of the film awakens hopes of more to come, but the rest is but a shade of the good old days when Errol Flynn and Cornel Wilde (to say nothing of Douglas Fairbanks) ran all over the place every ten minutes or so. Gremm relies on letting his story do the drifting, so much so that it's hard to keep the main plot with multiple characters straight. And dialog weakens many promising scenes with flat, banal lines or unpredictable twists or irony.

The story is about two brothers, a good one and a bad one, who both love the same girl. The supreme commander in the area is herding young men off to serve the British in the Revolutionary War, and Fritz (Peter Sattmann) runs him through with his sword in a fit of anger. A group of outlaws join Fritz in this fight for freedom, while Ludwig, his evil brother, tells lies to his father back home and causes a fortunate heart attack. Fritz squares matters in the end, but loses his best friend in a rescue attempt; then he sets prisoners free in a raid against the authorities, and takes to the hills to continue the fight for justice under the motto "Death or Freedom."

Pluses are ace lensing and some credible acting by top German film thesps. A recutting and rewriting of the dialogue might save enough to win the auds intended at home and offshore. —*Holl.*

Mackan
(Mackan)
(SWEDISH-COLOR)

Malmoe, March 17.

A Drakfilm (Hans Iveberg) — Swedish Film Institute — AB Svensk Film production, AB Svensk Film release. Features entire cast. Written and directed by Birgitta Svensson. Camera (Eastmancolor), Peter Davidson, Lasse Karlsson; music, Jan Lindell with special arrangements by Christer Boustedt; editor, Thomas Holewa; executive producer, Pelle Berglund. Reviewed at Fontanen, Malmo, Sweden, March 17, '78. Running time: **106 MINS.**
Mackan .... Maria Andersson
Kenneth .... Kare Molder
Gudrun .... Franciskan von Koch

Writer-director Birgitta Svensson seems to have no other point of view except general pessimism in her flimsy sketches of 14-year-old "Mackan" (nickname for Margretha) in various encounters with sex (never an inkling of love), parents (invariably stupid and sometimes vicious), teachers (the same) and girl schoolmates (dull and vapid except for sickly Gudrun whom Mackan befriends).

Mackan's 18-year-old boyfriend is a nice enough guy although sexually stupid. He gets her maneuvred into sex on his creaky bed every so often, managing only to make her look bored. Mackan is probably a nice enough girl, too, but she does seem dull beyond anybody's responsibility.

Film has good, natural performances from its young actors and is sharp and precise in its evoking of 1960 moods, manners, etc. such as they were on the surface. Sales prospects offshore would seem very slim even in youth situations. —*Kell.*

Deutschland Im Herbst
(Germany In Autumn)
(WEST GERMAN-COLOR)

Berlin, March 14.

A Projekt Film Production in Filmverlag der Autoren, Munich, together with Hallelujah-Film, Munich, and Kairos-Film, Munich; world rights, Filmverlag der Autoren, Munich. Produced by Theo Hinz and Eberhard Junkersdorf. Features entire cast. Directed (as Omnibus film) by Alf Brustellin, Bernhard Sinkel, Rainer Werner Fassbinder, Alexander Kluge, Beate Mainka-Jellinghaus, Maximiliane Mainka, Peter Schubert, Edgar Reitz, Katja Rupe, Hans Peter Cloos, and Volker Schloendorff. Screenplay, Heinrich Boell, Peter Steinbach; camera (color), Michael Ballhaus, Juergen Juerges, Bodo Kessler, Dietrich Lohmann, Colin Mounier, Joerg Schmidt-Reitwein; editing Heidi Genee, Mulle Goetz-Dickopp, Tanja Schmidbauer, Christina Warnick; sets, Winfried Henning, Henning von Gierke, Toni Luedi; sound, Roland Hentschke, Martin Mueller, Guenther Stadelmann; production manager, Heinz Badewitz, Karl Helmer, Herbert Kerz. Reviewed at Die Kurbel, Berlin, March 13, '78. Running time: 134 MINS.

Cast: Caroline Chaniolleau, Hildegard Friese, Petra Kiener, Lisi Mangold, Eva Meier, Katja Rupe, Franziska Walser, Angela Winkler, Wolfgang Baechler, Heinz Bennent, Wolf Biermann, Joachim Bissmeyer, Hans Peter Cloos, Otto Friebel, Michael Gahr, Vadim Glowna, Helmut Griem, Horatius Heberle, Hannelore Hoger, Dieter Laser, Horst Mahler, Enno Patalas, Franz Priegel, Werner Possardt, Leon Rainer, Walter Schmiedinger, Gerhard Schneider, Eric Vilgertshofer, Manfred Zapatka, Joey Buschmann, and the Collective "Rote Ruebe."

One of the two important political-minded films at the Berlin Film Festival (the other was Georgi Dyulgerov's "Advantage" from Bulgaria), the West German omnibus film, "Germany in Autumn," seeks to do the same thing the Chris Marker SLON film group did in 1967: "Loin de Vietnam," produced as a protest against continuation of the war in Vietnam, involved such names as Marker, Resnais, Lelouch, Ivens, Klein, Varda, and Godard. The drum-beater for "Germany in Autumn" is Alexander Kluge, the "chronicler" in New German Cinema, who knitted together a strong, representative film group of top NGC names — including Nobel Prize winner Heinrich Boell — to observe and comment on the tragic events last autumn, when public official Hanns Martin Schleyer was kidnapped and murdered by terrorists and the remaining core of the Baader-Meinhof terrorists group died rather mysteriously in a Stuttgart-Stammheim prison.

Unlike the French counterpart, "Germany in Autumn" is not a protest; it is more an outcry against hysteria, hypocrisy, and inhumanity. Further, it touches on that sensitive nerve in postwar Germany history: that terrorism here owes much to the sins of the parents. In this sense, the film is a complicated thesis that requires repeated viewings by the uninitiated and a close examination of the printed dialogue text (readily available in German and English from Filmverlag der Autoren).

Not all the episodes are to the point or worth inclusion; some are embarrassing rehashes of known, televised events or vague reports of how fear gripped the land. Worse still, the bleeding-heart, let's-get-socially-engaged, melodramatic outpourings by safely ensconced Left-thinking intellectuals nearly tip the boat in the opposite direction with some make-believe compassion for ideas rather than persons. It appears as though each director has his own private axe to grind, and the initial reason for making the film (it was the idea of Theo Hinz) is lost sight of by some along the way. (The mass storming of the stage for the spotlight at the Berlin preem by the collaborating directors seems odd in view of the tragic events depicted in the film.)

The Kluge-Schloendorff frame-like episodes at the beginning and end of the film, dealing with the burials of Schleyer and the Baader-Meinhof group, are very strong documentary passages revealing more about the occasions than anything else reported by the media at the time. Kluge's sense for irony — his brilliant idea to resurrect archive footage of the funeral ceremonies for Field Marshal Rommel, showing the general's son, Manfred, whose father was poisoned by the state, in order to contrast this with the grown Manfred Rommel, Mayor of Stuttgart, granting burial privileges in a city cemetery to the dead terrorists in the name of human decency — gives the film breath and proportion: the viewer is witnessing an historical document that will make "Germany in Autumn" a prized bit of archive footage in the future.

In addition to the valuable Kluge-Schloendorff passages covering both funerals from contrasting perspectives (a minute-pause in a Mercedes plant where nearly everyone on the assembly line is a foreign-worker, an interview with an officious head-waiter at the Schleyer funeral banquet, students and young people attending the burial of the Baader-Meinhof group, a couple humanely offering their restaurant to the bereaved Ensslin family), there's a commendable live interview with Horst Mahler in the Berlin-Tegel prison (he is considered to be the co-founder of the RAF antifascist, revolutionary movement) and a stinging satire on television hysteria written by Heinrich Boell, in which a tv production of Sophocles's "Antigone" is cancelled because it's considered too "pro-terrorists."

Pic also includes a Fassbinder episode in which he draws a personal confession from his mother that life under a "benevolent dictator" was not so bad after all — but then the director mixes his own sexual neuroses into the sequence.

"Germany in Autumn" is already a controversial film. No doubt it will be seen and discussed by thousands in Germany. It might even lead to a more politically committed New German cinema. For these reasons alone, it stands as one of the unique undertakings of the year on the European scene. But it's also a film of distorted feelings and raw pain, of semiengaged, commercial-minded mumbling on politics and ideals, of despair and confusion. —*Holl.*

Lyftet
(The Score)
(SWEDISH-COLOR)

Malmoe, March 10.

An Europa Film/Ri-Film production, Europa Film release. Directed by Christer Dahl. Screenplay, Kennet Ahl; based on novel by Kennet Ahl (pseudonym for Christer Dahl and Lasse Storemstedt); camera, (Eastmancolor); Lass Bjoerne; music, Robert Cornford; editors, Kennet Ahl, Roger Sellberg. Stars Bodil Martensson and Anders Loennbro. Reviewed at Rio Bio, Malmoe, March 9, '78. Running time: 118 MINS.

Kennet	Anders Loennbro
Karin	Bodil Martensson
Eleganten	Roland Jansson
Karlin's father	Karl-Erik Heiknert
Karin's mother	Siv Eriks

An English-language version of "Lyftet" (The Score) has already been made in New York, but even in its original version this unusual feature about a young man trapped by prison even when he is at large will surely find its way into commercial as well as artistically more demanding situations throughout the world.

Film has elementary drama, humor, compassion plus a gut appeal to anybody's sense of the obviously right and wrong. It is a proud addition to the output of a country that even without a Bergman or a Widerberg or Troell would be in the forefront of European cinema art.

"The Score" is not truly the correct translation of the newly-minted Swedish word, "Lyftet," which has to do with the dream that feeds energy to planned deeds toward a better life. In this case, Kennet, a young prisoner, keeps himself going by constantly working one day at a time making it in an honest way on the outside, hand in hand with his faithful, beloved one, Karin, who is pregnant.

She got pregnant during prison visiting hours. The prison is a thoroughly modern one, but is it really any better at restoring to a prisoner his soul than any medieval institution when that same prisoner is being watched day and night by electronic eyes and ears?

"The Score" is never a drab social-indictment tract. Kennet (Anders Loennbro) is drawn as being of such violent temper that even when injustice thwarts his plans and dreams, audiences will be apt to put a good deal of the blame on him.

This, of course, does not really lessen the injustices (such as red tape keeping Kennet longer in prison than he was given to expect, resulting in a temper outburst on his part that puts him back in solitary), but neither director Christer Dahl or the collective behind the entire production wanted to sweeten the pill of their story with easy jerkings of the tear ducts.

The production dress is excellent throughout and actual prison locations are used to an effect of maximum chill. Lars Bjoerne's cinematography is especially good when the director allows him to move his camera. Too many dialog sequences are filmed so squarely head-on that it clutters up the fluency of an otherwise rhythmically composed film.

The music score is used sparingly and well and the players, including ex con author Lass Stroemstedt in a cameo, all perform with the right touch of personal involvement.

—*Kell.*

The Evil
(COLOR)

Highly effective suspenser. Outlook solid for exploitation booking.

Hollywood, March 17.

New World Pictures release of a Rangoon production, produced by Ed Carlin; executive producers, Paul A. Joseph, Malcolm Levinthal. Directed by Gus Trikonis. Features entire cast. Screenplay, Donald G. Thompson; camera (Movie Lab Color), Mario Di Leo; editor, Jack Kirshner; music, Johnny Harris; art director, Peter Jamison; sound, Kill Kaplan Jr.; wardrobe, Barbara Andrews, James Alvarez; assistant director, Scott Adam; stunts, Buddy Joe Hooker. Reviewed at Culver Triplex, Culver City, March 17, '78. (MPAA Rating: R.) Running time: **89 MINS.**

C.J. .... Richard Crenna
Caroline .... Joanna Pettet
Raymond .... Andrew Prine
Mary .... Cassie Yates
Felecia .... Lynne Moddy
Devil .... Victor Buono
Pete .... George O'Hanlon Jr.
Laurie .... Mary Louise Weller
Dwight .... Robert Viharo
Realtor .... Milton Selzer
Vargas .... Galen Thompson

Any satanic-oriented film that actually has the nerve to display the Wicked One in the flesh can't be all bad, and in fact, "The Evil" is quite good. New World Pictures release effectively blends moments of suspense and horror with sold psychological plotting, in the tradition of "Legend Of Hell House," which has become a cult classic in this genre. Outlook is auspicious for exploitation booking. It was shot last year as "Cry Demon."

Donald G. Thompson's screenplay has psychologist Richard Crenna, accompanied by wife (also a medico) Joanna Pettet, picking up a lease on the proverbial haunted house, despite real estate agent Milton Selzer's recounting of the grisly horrors that took place there.

Crenna and Pettet are soon joined by college prof Andrew Prine with student/companion Mary Louise Weller, and several of Crenna's patients, including Cassie Yates, Lynne Moddy, George O'Hanlon Jr. and Robert Viharo. Just what they're all up to is never clearly delineated, but once the house (or something in it) begins to act up, it really doesn't matter.

Stumbling on a trap door in the cellar, Crenna unwittingly releases a force akin to a mild earthquake, which immediately traps the group in the manse, a foreboding thought on a sunny day. As it is, a storm rages throughout the pic, further adding to the ominous atmosphere carefully constructed by director Gus Trikonis.

One by one, Crenna's cohorts are eliminated, some by electrocution, some by incineration, and some just by fear. Throughout, there is a spirit on the loose (resembling the White Tornado) in communication with Pettet, trying to warn her of the dangers ahead. But Crenna is a stubborn skeptic, only admitting his own helplessness in dealing with the situation when there is no other recourse.

This type of psychological insight is rare in suspensers, and is a credit to both Crenna, who delivers a strong performance, and Trikonis. Fulcrum of pic's success or failure comes in final scenes, when Crenna and Pettet confront the devil himself, played with sinister angelicism by Victor Buono.

A silly idea? Maybe, but Trikonis and Buono make it click, except for seeming demise of the evil spirit, which comes off as forced and hokey.

Other scenes in "The Evil" are top notch horror stuff, such as a harrowing attempted rape perpetrated on Moddy by the unseen spirit, and a blood-curdling shot of Cassie Yates arising, momentarily, from the dead. Trikonis makes these scenes even more effective by throwing in a few fake scares to keep the audience on the edge of its seat. The ploy works.

Pettet and Prine offer complete characterizations, and Moddy is very effective as the put-upon femme. Robert Viharo adds a nice bit, but is wiped out early. Buono, of course, sets a new standard for a rarely-depicted character.

Production values are high, with Mario Di Leo's atmospheric camerawork adding to the suspense, as does Jack Kirshner's editing. Johnny Harris' score is strictly pro forma, however. —*Poll.*

Lemon Popsicle
(ISRAELI-COLOR)

Berlin, March 7.
A Noah Film Production, Tel-Aviv; producers, Menahem Golan, Yoram Globus. Features entire cast. Directed by Boaz Davidson. Screenplay, Davidson, Eli Tabor; camera (Eastmancolor), Adam Greenberg; editing, Alain Jakubowicz; sets, Ariel Roshko, Alfred Gershoni; sound, Eli Yarkoni. Reviewed at Tonfilm Studio, Berlin, March 6, '78. Running time: **100 MINS.**

Benz .... Yiftach Katzur
Nili .... Anat Atzmon
Momo .... Jonathan Segal
Yudaleh .... Zachi Noy

A light comedy about boyhood initiation to sex set in the 1950s, Boaz Davidson's "Lemon Popsicle" is the best film to emerge from Israel in recent times. Davidson graduated from the London Film School in 1970, and since then has been working in television, doing musical shows, making documentaries, and turning out advertising films on the side. He is the youngest and most productive director working today in Israel.

"Lemon Popsicle" takes place in Tel Aviv in the late 1950s. Three youths — Benz, Momo, and Yudaleh — have only girls on their mind, while the hit-parade on the radio (Elvis Presley) reflects their own emotional engagement in the world. Benz, a shy, sensitive lad, falls in love with Nili, who prefers his best chum, Momo. Momo gets Nili pregnant, then drops her as the summer vacation starts; Benz stays behind to arrange the necessary abortion. He confesses his love

and things appear running his way, when the school term starts and Nili is back again in the arms of Momo.

The schoolboy romance also has a funnier side to it. It's in the search for an initial sexual experience — first with a middle-age nympho where Benz delivers ice, then with a prostitute who gives them the crabs — both handled with appropriate gags to put the scenes over. This is another twist on "American Graffiti" that will find response abroad as well as at home. —*Holl.*

Man kan inte valtas
(Manrape)
(SWEDISH-COLOR)

Malmoe, March 17.
A Stockholm Film production, Fox-Stockholm Film release. Features entire cast. Written and directed by Jorn Donner, based on Marta Tikkanen novel. Executive producers, Jorn and Jeanette Donner. Camera (Eastmancolor) Bille August; music, Heiki Valpola; editor, Irma Taina; production management, Anssi Mantari, Jaako Talaskivi. Reviewed at Rio Bio, Malmoe, March 10 '78. Running time: **95 MINS.**

Eva Randers .... Anna Godenius
Martin Wester .... Gosta Bredefeldt

Assured by its subject matter (direct title translation would be "Can Men Be Raped?") and by its raw thriller values of world-wide sales, Jorn Donner's "Manrape" is also an obvious debate-raiser on the festival circuit and may be a major competition contender to boot.

Slightly squarish and dry of dialog where its theme is theoretically approached among the protagonists, story gathers momentum and meaning where straight action and good acting are allowed to take over.

Anna Godenius performs with strength and sensitivity as the divorced librarian who, on the eve of her 40th birthday, in an expansive mood, lets herself be picked up by a stranger and goes with him rather beyond the flirtatious stage. The man, a middleaged bachelor of the roaming kind, rapes her in frustration at meeting resistance where he truly expected none. Afterwards, he loses all interest in the woman.

Anna, the woman, digests her humiliation only slowly, but in such a way that she coolly plans to take revenge in direct kind. She dons a black wig and heavy make-up and starts stalking Martin, the rapist, making him increasingly nervous and causing him, in a witty scene, to lose in an international bowling competition.

When Anna has Martin sufficiently cornered, she points a gun at him and ties him to his bed in a humiliating posture for his expected guests to later come and stare at.

But has Martin really been raped? Has his humiliation in any deeper sense corresponded to what a woman suffers through this crime? Donner, otherwise no prude, has shown the original rape only sketchily and now shows the man's humiliation only in partly indirect telling.

Actually, audiences may here, and quite legitimately so, let out a sigh of frustration. Stronger visuals would not have hurt the story's serious aim. After all, we all need to be taught something about the horrors experienced by a rape victim if we are to understand the total scope of this particular aggression.

"Manrape," filmed on Helsinki, Finland, locations, has a nice production dress, and as the rapist, Gosta Bredefeldt radiates innocent stupidity as well as stupid innocence. — *Kell.*

Apam Nehany Boldog Eve
(My Father's Happy Years)
(HUNGARIAN-COLOR)

Budapest, March 9.
An Hungarofilm, Budapest, Production, Hunnia Studio. Features entire cast. Written and directed by Sandor Simo. Camera (Eastmancolor), Tamas Andor; editing, Eva Karmento; sets, Jozsef Romvary; music, Zdenko Tamassy. Reviewed at Hungarofilm, Budapest, March 8, '78. Running time: **98 MINS.**

Father (Janos Torok) .. Lorand Lohinszky
Mother .... Eszter Szakacs
Son .... Peter Hollo
Ilus .... Judit Meszleri
Ede .... Jozsef Madaras
Zsiga .... Istvan Bujtor
Old Woman .... Irma Patkos
Jutka .... Gyorgyi Tarjan

The Hungarian entry at the Berlin Film Festival, Sandor Simo's "My Father's Happy Years" won the FIPRESCI Critics Prize and deservedly so: it looks back frankly at the postwar years, 1945 to 1949, when Hungary experienced a democratic government before switching to the Communist Party. This period has interested a number of Hungarian directors — Miklos Jancso's "The Confrontation" and Istvan Szabo's "Budapest Tales," to mention two — and each time a degree of autobiographical remembrance enters into the story.

"My Father's Happy Years" is based on a son's (Simo himself) recollection of his father's attempts to go it alone as an educated and independent-minded chemist, who acquires a small chemical plant and is obsessed with experiments to develop new products, among them a new female hormone. His small successes are painfully earned and lack of ready cash slows down prograss, but somehow his friends are able to lend a hand in need.

What the chemist doesn't notice is that the political climate is changing. The Communist Party's victory closes down credit at the bank for private enterprise, and he goes bankrupt. Attempts to raise support from other sources leads, one day, to arrest and internment in a labor camp. Letters home remain cheerful and in hopes of continuing his chemical experiments, a passion that has consumed his entire "happy years."

Simo's reserved handling of actors and observant camera techniques are major pluses in this story of a key moment in modern Hungarian history. Pic is slow-moving but warming and compassionately rendered. A cinch for the fest circuit, Hungarian film weeks, and art houses — where it could score with proper handling. —*Holl.*

Joerg Ratgeb, Maler
(Joerg Ratgeb, Painter)
(EAST GERMAN-COLOR)

Berlin, March 8.

A DEFA-FILM, Group "Berlin," Production. Features entire cast. Directed by Bernhard Stephan. Screenplay, Manfred Freitag, Jochen Nestler; camera (color), Otto Hanisch; editing, Brigitte Krex; sets, Peter Wilde; music, Andrzej Korzynski; sound, Bernd-Dieter Henning, Christfried Sobczyk, Guenter Witt; production manager, Helmut Klein, Rolf Martius. Reviewed at DEFA-Export DDR, East Berlin, March 7, '78. Running time: 101 MINS.
Joerg Ratgeb . . . . Alois Svehlik
Barbara . . . . Margrit Tenner
Joss Fritz . . . . Guenter Naumann
Bishop . . . . Olgierd Lukaszewicz
Young Peasant Girl . . Malgorzata Braunek
Thomas Niedler . . . . Henry Huebchen
Clown . . . . Rolf Hoppe
His Wife . . . . Marylu Poolman
Albrecht Durer . . . . Martin Trettau
Agnes Durer . . . . Helga Goering
Vogt . . . . : . . . . Hilmar Baumann
Christopher Ederlin . . . . Thomas Neumann
Mrs. Ratgeb . . . . Monika Hildebrand
Commander . . . . Giso Weissbach
Bagpiper . . . . Werner Pauli
Fiddler . . . . Guenter Rueger

"Joerg Ratgeb, Painter" deals with a contemporary of Albrecht Durer who leaned as much to the cause of the peasants as the former did to the rights of the establishment. Little was known about the painter, and only recently is it possible to credit some paintings directly to his name. What's known is that Joerg Ratgeb existed and was drawn into the current of the times on the side of the common man. The rest of the film is fiction.

But it's fiction of a particular sort. Bernhard Stephen is aiming at the contemporary audience — what this painter means to audiences today — rather than making an historical biography or costume epic. He depicts a man in the middle-age crisis, one easy to identify with, and lets the rest of the story compose itself around this man's search for his revolutionary self.

The year is 1517, a few years before the bloody put-down of the Peasants' Revolt. Ratgeb lives in the small town of Herrenberg in Wurtenberg, where he is working on an altar painting. He is contacted by a secret organization of peasant revolutionaries, who want him to paint a flag for them. Ratgeb refuses, as his own passion is painting. Later, when he journeys to visit his idol, Albrecht Durer, he experiences the suppression of the peasants under feudal landlords and is appalled at Durer's indifference to the injustice around him. Back in Herrenberg, he works with new eyes and passion on the altar painting, now a painter who believes in revolt.

The weakness of the film is its predictable line of development from pure artist to committed artist. But Stephan imbues the film with moments of psychological realism as the character and vision of a man change in response to the human needs about him. Ratgeb, however, was not a Goya, and the story can only go so far. It's remarkable enough that the man and his paintings have been rescued from the confusing maze of history in the turbulent 16th century. Pic preemed at Berlin fest. —*Holl.*

Berlin Festival

Feuer Um Mitternacht
(Red Midnight)
(WEST GERMAN-COLOR)

Berlin, March 2.

An Ehmck-Film Production, Munich, world rights, Transocean International, Munich. Features entire cast. Directed by Gustav Ehmck. Screenplay, Ehmck, Boy Lornsen, Hansch Schmid, Andrea Wagner; camera (color), Hubs Hagen; editing, K.H. Fugunt, Monika Gussner; music, Gunter Hampel and the Galaxie Dream Band; sound, Rainer Wiehr; sets, Margarete Fackelmann; art direction, Michael Fackelmann; production manager, Martin Haeussler. Reviewed at Berlin Film Fest, German Section, March 1, '78. Running time: 100 MINS.
Cast: Andreas Nutzhorn (Markus Unschlitt), Ina Trautmann (Sylvia Tackert), Joachim Dietman Mues (Theo Bank), Carsta Loeck (Aunt Lena), Horst Gnekow (Peter Soenderop), Nann Soederberg (Titus Unschlitt), Anke Joldrichsen (Nelli Unschlitt), Joachim Richart (Willi Tackert), Heinz Joachim Klein (Niklas Hageldom), Gerhard Olschewski (David Kueppers), Uwe Michael Wiebking (Tim Weppler), Annemie Winger (Hannah Postel), Joerg Zimmer (Fred Rueckert).

Gustav Ehmck has made a solid rep as a children's filmmaker whose stories appeal equally to grown-ups. Perhaps his best known film to date is "The Robber Hotzenplotz" (1973), unspooled at the Moscow Film Fest in 1975 in the Children's Program.

"Red Midnight" excels anything he has done to date for psychological realism and narrative tension emanating from the story itself. It's about a youth on a Frisian island in the North Sea, whose hero-worship of his father goes back to learning the secrets of the island, sailing and fishing, and close companionship. When his father hangs himself, Markus is sure that a neighbor is to blame, an old eccentric living in a thatched house.

To get even, the boy sends anonymous letters threatening fire, a danger that troubles the entire village. Markus's aunt, in particular, is troubled as she knows the real reasons for the father's death. When fire does break out at the neighbor's home and he dies in the blaze, Markus is suspected of wrongdoing and goes to the aunt for help, thereby learning his father was not as blameless as he thought he was. He knows how the fire was started, but also realizes that revealing the culprit's name wouldn't help anyone.

Thesp performances are all topnotch, particularly the boy Andreas Nutzhorn who carries the film effortlessly. Lensing of natural beauty helps, but Ehmck has also caught the daily pace of ife on a North Sea island. A commercial film with good off-shore chances. —*Holl.*

Strauberg Ist Da
(Strauberg Is Here)
(WEST GERMAN-B&W)

Berlin, March 2.

A Galle Film Production, Munich, in collaboration with Suedwestfunk, Baden-Baden. Features entire cast. Written and directed by Mischa Galle. Camera, Dieter Matzka; editing, Dieter Matzka, Beate Schlegel; music, Stefan Melbinger; sound, Rolf Schwarze, Vladimir Vizner; production manager, Demetrio Mathiopoulos, Dieter Matzka. Reviewed at Berlin Film Fest, German Section, March 1, '78. Running time: 120 MINS.
Cast: Michel Piccoli (Strauberg, Publisher), Theodor Kotulla (Panek, Writer), Bernadette Lafont (Anne, Children's Book Author), Udo Heiland (Volkart, Director), Karl-Heinz Heitmann (Gromberg, Actor), Joerg Richter (Felix).

Occasionally a film comes along dealing with the creative process — or lack of it. Mischa Galle's "Strauberg Is Here" fascinates on both scores: it's an attempt to group a bunch of would-be talent together from theatre, publishing, acting, and writing — then confront them with a successful publisher they are all secretly jealous of.

The scene — to make it even better — is the Mediterranean isle of Mykonos, where a stifling boredom sets in to eat at each individual's nerves. Added to this, nearly everyone in the enclosed, isolated group is an intolerable egoist. The filmmaker herself has published short stories; one of the actors, Theodor Kotulla, is a prominent German director ("Aus einem deutschen Leben"); and no less than Michel Piccoli and Bernadette Lafont have lent their thespian skills to the project.

The film itself, by the way, has become a legend in its own time. An open quarrel between the femme helmer and Suedwestfunk (SWF), the tv backer, delayed release of the film after shooting was finished in 1975. Now that the smoke has cleared, a closer view of this "cause celebre" is possible.

"Strauberg Is Here" never gets off the ground as a narrative film with something dramatic to say. It depends entirely on mood and atmosphere. Because this is Strauberg's summer house, the would-be artists feel they have to prove themselves and so they decide to give up their usual habits (smoking and drinking) and depend on the island's natural resources instead. The result is that their latent aggressions break out, and when Strauberg appears they murder him.

Some tense moments mount towards the end of the film, but the waiting may not seem worth it — even for Michel Piccoli fans. Little chances commercially, but a sure bet for art-minded fests on the summer circuit. — *Holl.*

Winterspelt
(WEST GERMAN-COLOR)

Berlin, March 4.

An Ullstein AV, Berlin, Production in collaboration with Sender Freies Berlin and Hessischer Rundfunk, Frankfurt. Features entire cast. Written and directed by Eberhard Fechner, based on novel of same name by Alfred Andersch. Camera (color), Rudolf Korosi, Kurt Weber; editing, Barbara Grimm; music, Gyorgy Ligeti; sound, Jochen Schwarzat, Peter Kellerhals; sets, Hans-Huergen Kiebach; costumes, Elisabeth Schewer; production manager, Dieter Graber. Reviewed at Berlin Film Fest, German Section, March 3, '78. Running time: 108 MINS.
Major Joseph
Dincklage . . . . Ulrich von Dobschuetz
Kaethe Lenk . . . . Katherina Thalbach
Wenzel Hainstock . . . Hans-Christian Blech
Dr. Bruno Schefold . . . . . Henning Schlueter
Captain John Kimbrough George Roubicek
Major Robert Wheeler . . Frederick Jaeger
Corp. Hubert Reidel . . Claus Theo Gaertner
Rifleman Fritz Borek Andreas von Studnitz
Sgt. Kammerer . . . . Ulrich Radke

Based on a recent novel by Alfred Andersch which many critics consider to be a key book on the Second World War from a European point of view, Eberhard Fechner's "Winterspelt" scores as a remarkable page on the 1944 Ardenne Offensive as German and American troops prepared for the Battle of the Bulge. Winterspelt is the name of a village near the German-Belgian border in the Eifel, a place where American and German battalions are quartered a short walking distance away from each other.

It's the story of a German major's attempt to surrender his battalion to the American unit without firing a shot, as he knows that the war is lost and further resistance would led to senseless bloodshed (in fact, 75,000 lost their lives in the Battle of the Bulge). The question is how to do it?

Five people get involved in the complicated move to contact the Americans and convince them that the surrender is in good faith. Major Dincklage reveals his plan to a schoolteacher with whom he is having an affair, a woman with Left sympathies who readily supports the idea. She has a close friend with similar sympathies, who receives visits on occasion from an art historian who freely crosses the lines (as he already fled to the American side). The plan for the surrender flows through these people to an American captain, who is acquainted with the art historian.

So far, so good. The complications arise when the officer's code of honor is mocked by such a humanitarian gesture: surrender is thus militarily impossible. The human possibility is also ruined by a homosexual corporal who shoots the art historian while conducting him back to the lines in order to win favor with his commander and avoid imprisonment. A few weeks later, the Battle of the Bulge begins.

Pic is a good literary adaptation of a novel that is difficult to film, due to lengthy passages of dialogue and commentary. Andersch's autobiographical trace is also present: as a Communist he was imprisoned in Dachau for six months, forced to join the German army upon release, but deserted in 1944 to become an American prisoner-of-war in the U.S. His knowledge of the military thinking on both side makes both the novel and the film worth a close inspection.

Eberhard Fechner has made a career in television reviewing past German history back to 1900 through a story-telling interview style. His "Testimonials to Klara Heydebreck" (1969), "Class Picture" (1970), "Under Landmark Protection" (1975), and "The Comedian Harmonists" (1976) form a intricate Panorama of German Society from 1900 to 1975. His "Tadelloeser & Wolff" (1975), a tv prize-winner, viewed the Nazi years from inside via Walter Kempowski's autobiographical novel. Now Fechner has done the same with Alfred Andersch in focusing on the closing years of the war and a German major's dilemma. A pic for both history-minded viewers and war buffs. —*Holl.*

Flammende Herzen
(Flaming Hearts)
(WEST GERMAN-COLOR)

Berlin, March 7.
An Enten-Production, Cologne, in collaboration with Das kleine Fernsehspiel (ZDF), Wiesbaden-Mainz; world rights, Filmverlag der Autoren, Munich. Features Barbara Valentin, Peter Kern. Written and directed by Walter Bockmayer, Rolf Buehr-mann. Production manager, Rolf Buehr-mann; camera (color), Horst Knechtel, Peter Mertin; editing & assistant director, Ila von Hasperg; sound, Gary Steel. Reviewed at Cinema Paris, Berlin, March 6, '78. Running time: 95 MINS.
Cast: Peter Kern (Peter Huber), Barbara Valentin (Karola Faber), Enzi Fuchs (Anna Schlaetel), Katja Rupe (Magda Weberscheid), Anneliese and Peter Geisler (Mr. & Mrs. Geisler), Rolf Buehrmann (Master of Ceremonies), Armin Meyer (Driver), Ila von Hasperg (Salesgirl), Evelyn Kuenneke (singer), and Bessie the Cow.

Walter Bockmayer's film career is one of those success stories that makes filmmaking and moviegoing all the more enjoyable. The owner of a Cologne bar who turned to making Super-8 films as a hobby, the home-made stories packed with humor and nostalgic musical soundtracks about and starring his circle of gay friends became an instant hit at an art-house cinema in nearby Duesseldorf. Bockmayer and his co-director, Rolf Buehrmann, then got the recognition they needed to shoot "Jane Is Jane Forever," the story of a woman in an Old Peoples Home who believes she's married to Tarzan; this camp-pic ended up at the Locarno Film Festival.

The pair have scored at the Berlin fest with a hilarious, quaint bit of Bavarian kitsch. "Flaming Hearts" is melodrama of the squarest sort, but everything Bockmayer-Buehmann touches these days turns to gold. Picture the timid owner of a newspaper kiosk in Upper Bavaria who wins a trip to New York in a magazine competition. Off he goes, but Gotham isn't quite what he thought it would be. Further disillusionment sets in when he meets a German girl who contemplates suicide; she came to the States as the wife of a G.I. and now works as a prostitute in Manhattan dives. The two try to go it alone as a pair of romantic outsiders.

The German immigrant community throws an October-Fest. It provides an occasion for Peter Kern and Barbara Valentin (both top acting and singing talent) to show their stuff: they are crowned Cornfield King and Queen of the festival and given a cow as their prize. After wandering through the night-streets of New York with Bessie — a Bavarian version of Orpheus in Hades — the pair reaches the end of their monetary rope, and our hero longs to be back at his newspaper stand.

Somehow, all this fruitcake meandering works — probably because Bockmayer takes his characters seriously and plays everything with an impishly straight face. Pic has good possibilities as an oddity on the fest circuit, while offshore chances require some care-and-attention. —*Holl.*

Halbe-Halbe
(Fifty-Fifty)
(WEST GERMAN-B & W)

Berlin, March 5.
A Production of DNS-Film Munich, in collaboration with Norddeutscher Rundfunk, Hamburg; distributed by Filmverlag der Autoren, Munich, world rights, Cine International, Munich. Features entire cast. Written and directed by Uwe Brandner. Camera (black and white), Juergen Juerges; editing, Helga Beyer; music, J.J. Cale, Munich Factory, Peer Raben; production manager, Denyse Noever. Reviewed at Berlin Film Fest, German Section, March 4, '78. Running time: 105 MINS.
Cast: Hans Peter Hallwachs (Bert Maschkara), Bernd Tauber (Thomas Berger), Agnes Duenneisen (Katrin Adams), Masch Gonska (Eva Hauff), Kai Fischer (Hedi Brunner), Gerhard Olschewski (Walter Brunner), Nikolaus Dutsch (Axel Hauff) Alexandra Bogojevich (Sylvia), Beva McNeely (Naguna), Joachim Regelien (Fred Leitner), Adrian Hoven (Begger), Ivan Desny (Baron Wurlitzer), Alexander Allerson (Buettner), Glenn Moray (Ravi), Eva Schuckhardt (Sociology Teacher).

"Fifty-Fifty" marks Uwe Brand-Brandner's return to filmmaking. The writer-director scored a hit back in 1970 with "I Love You, I'll Kill You," winning critical approval at Cannes's Week of the Critics. His next, "Kopf oder Zahl," was disappointing, and he disappeared temporarily from sight.

"Fifty-Fifty" is quite literary in style and leans perhaps too heavily on word-games to make it with foreign auds. But there's a lot of raw energy in the film, and it's strongly acted by two coming film thesps, Hans Peter Hallwachs and Bernd Tauber, to guarantee some success at home, if not abroad.

It's the story of a middle-aged loser facing a crisis he has not expected, nor is he prepared for. Bert is 36 and has just lost a well-paying job in a profession he enjoys (apparently an architect). His severance pay of $15,000 leaves him discontented, and his penthouse studios seem s superfluous. He meets Thomas, a new neighbor, 26, in a similar predicament: after seven years in the military as a traffic controller, he has to go through several exams to qualify for the same civilian position; his military service also brought him $15,000, but nowhere to go. Both have to start from scratch.

The film is shot in Munich, primarily in modern apartment buildings (the penthouse is at the Olympic Village), on streets before imposing concrete facades, and in-and-out of elevators. Thus, the pic also presents a portrait of modern man in cold, inhuman surroundings, not just the middle-age crises of two outsiders in search of themselves.

Women enter casually into the story: both have girlfriends who come and go (as in a Bogart film or a Chandler detective story), one of whom innocently gets Tom into a fight with another boyfriend and lands him in a hospital. Bert, meanwhile, figures he can double his money by swindling a swindler, but ends up in jail — and Tom posts bond with the remainder of his cash reserved. When Bert breaks his parole accidentally, he drifts into a tramp existence on the outskirts of town. And while begging for a handout, he meets Tom again and the two seem to be ready to wrestle in earnest with life.

"Fifty-Fifty" in its greyish, black-and-white tones comes across as a tough street film, one that holds to a tight, unfolding, pessimistic revelation of character. It's quite in line with Brandner's published cycle of novels: pic can be taken as an outcry against an indifferent society, as well as a search for an inner truth through a purgation of self.

Acting and lensing are tops. With proper handling there's a possibility for art houses, and pic could score this summer on the fest circuit. —*Holl.*

Johnny West
(WEST GERMAN-COLOR)

Berlin, March 3.
A Peter Welz Production of Multimedia, Hamburg in coproduction with Sunny Point Film, Berlin, Faust Film, Munich, and Terra Filmkunst, Berlin. Features entire cast. Written and directed by Roald Koller. Camera (color), Bahram Manocherie; sets and costumes, Harold Waistnage; title song "Moving" composed by Winfried Lovett, sung by "The Manhattans." Reviewed at Berlin Film Fest, German Section, March 2, '78. Running time: 129 MINS.
Cast: Rio Reiser (Johnny West), Kristina van Eyck (Monika), Jess Hahn (Manager), Karl Maslo (Max), Rainer Westerfield (Rainer), Birgit Bergen (Linda), the Groups The Manhattans, Missus Beastly, and, as guests, The Platters.

Roald Koller — whose "Johnny West" is a debut film — is well known on the New German Cinema scene: he's made documentaries on filmmakers (John Ford and Eric Rohmer), wrote a script for Hans W. Geissendoerfer ("A Rose for Jane"), contributed to Filmkritik, and worked on tv film-reportage programs. His first love is music and pop bands (he's a saxophonist), which led to the "Johnny West" project.

Pic is about a travelling group of "roadies" who set up and dismantle the complicated electronic devices accompanying a soul group known as "The Manhattans." Johnny West (real name is Hans-Michael Westerfield) hopes to become a musician himself one day. On one of his trips he meets Monika, an upper-class looker who falls for him; they go on the road together to Cologne and on to Bochum in the Ruhr Valley. Johnny neglects his job in catering to Monika and his guitar lessons; he is nearly fired and the couple separates for the time being.

Travelling across Germany, Johnny makes both friends and enemies. One day he fights with the road manager and is fired for good, along with his buddy Max. Johnny tries to go it alone in a Frankfurt rock club, and does all right on his first time out as a rock musician. For a while, it goes to his head — but the presence of Monika brings him back to earth again.

Not a narrative story with pace and action, "Johnny West" does, however, catch the atmosphere of two-night stands in jazz-and-rock clubs across Germany. Rio Reiser obviously knows this music scene inside out too, but he doesn't have enough charisma to carry the film on personality alone. Lensing is also a notch under professional standards. But the semi-docu realism boosts the film into a "cinema" category and tends to draw its supporters from the "in" music crowd.

A worthy attempt to go commercial: something New German Cinema should be doing more of.
— *Holl.*

Ein Verdammt Gutes Leben
(A Hell of a Life)
(WEST GERMAN-COLOR-16m)

Berlin, March 3.

A Sunset Mark Production, Munich, in collaboration with Bayerischer Rundfunk, Munich. Written and directed by Hans C. Blumenberg. Camera (color), Bodo Kessler; editing, Inge Gielow; sound, Pat Shea; production coordinator, Juergen Hellwig; tv editor, Silvia Koller. Reviewed at Berlin Film Fest, German Section, March 2, '78. Running time: **58 MINS.**

"A Hell of a Good Life" (if the clue in the title hasn't already given it away) is about Howard Hawks, interviewed and filmed in November of 1977 just six weeks before he died. It's a fitting testimonial to a pantheon director, as film jargon goes, made by a vet tv-journalist, Hans C. Blumenberg, who has now completed 20 docus on filmmaking the majority about Hollywood.

Blumenberg has perfected the art of the movie documentary. For one thing, he as interviewer seldom appears in his own films (as many in West German television do). For another, he lets the material determine the style: once he only showed excerpts in documenting Hollywood's "cine noir" series, and for the Hawks film he restrained from using any excerpt at all.

"A Hell of a Good Life" focuses solely on the great personality that Hawks was by dividing the story of his creative life into 19 chapters, pretty much as the director himself outlined it. He was in to shape for his 81 years (he died Dec. 26 after an accident), spent five days with Blumenberg, and told a number of unknown personal stories about his colorful career.

Among them ws his beginning as a prop-boy for Mary Pickford, his passion for hunting and plane-and-motor racing, his friendship with writers (Ernest Hemingway, William Faulkner, Arymond Chandler), actors (John Wayne, Cary Grant, Gary Cooper), actresses (Carole Lombard, Lauren Bacall), and top bosses at Paramount (for whom he did most of his filming) and other Hollywood studios. Stories about F.W. Murnau, the making of "Sergeant York," and a long-standing friendship with Victor Fleming are just some of the odds-and-ends this docu contributes to vital footnotes on Hollywood history.

It should not be missed when docu makes the rounds of fests and German films weeks. —*Holl.*

The Sea Gypsies
(COLOR)

First class G-rated film. Outstanding animal footage.

Hollywood, March 29.

A Warner Bros. release of a Raffill Production, produced by Joseph C. Raffill; executive producer, Peter R. Simpson. Features entire cast. Written and directed by Stewart Raffill. Camera (CFI Color), Thomas McHugh; editor, Dan Greer, R. Hansel Brown, Art Stafford; music, Fred Steiner; associate producer-second unit director, Gerard Alcan; production supervisor-assistant director, Hal Schwartz; animal supervision, Hubert Wells; animal trainers, Wells, Lloyd Beebe, Cheryl Shawver, George Toth, Gwen Johnson, Marinho Correia, Mickey Bailey, Helena Walsh, Sonny Allen; sound, Craig Felburg. Reviewed at The Burbank Studios, Burbank, March 28, '78. (MPAA Rating: G.) Running time: **101 MINS.**

Travis	Robert Logan
Kelly	Mikki Jamison-Olsen
Courtney	Heather Rattray
Jesse	Cjon Damitri Patterson
Samantha	Shannon Saylor

Every so often a small independent production company comes along and proves that quality family films aren't the exclusive domain of the Walt Disney Studios. Joe Camp demonstrated that in 1974 with "Benji" and the latest example comes from the father-son team of Stewart and Joseph Raffill.

"The Sea Gypsies," which was picked up by Warner Bros. about a month ago, is a sometimes touching, sometimes frightening adventure tale about a father, his two daughters, a female photojournalist, and a stowaway who set off on a round-the-world sail and wind up stranded on a desert island off the coast of Alaska.

The film comes as a surprise, only because it arrives with so little fanfare. It's a superior effort in every way — credible story, effective acting, first rate technical credits. Thomas McHugh's photography is worthy of picture postcards and Stewart Raffill's direction is expertly paced. (NBC not only helped finance in return for tube rights but, upon viewing full print, ordered 13 hours for an episode series, a firm order for fall. - Ed.)

Loosely adapted by the director from a true story about a group of animal trainers and actors sailing from Jamaica to California, the plot opens with Robert Logan about to embark on his voyage with his two daughters, Heather Rattry and Shannon Saylor.

The trip is being financed partly by a magazine and Logan is waiting for the correspondent to arrive — the male correspondent who is also a crack sailor — when his replacement shows up. She's an attractive, ambitious female journalist. Not good news for Logan, a male chauvinist, but he needs the money for the trip so he can't turn away Mikki Jamison-Olsen. Needless to say she and Logan get better acquainted and fall in love in appropriate G-rated fashion.

Shortly into the voyage a stowaway is found on board, but you've got to love him — he's an orphan — and everyone on board does. A storm hits, the ship goes down and suddenly it's survival time off the coast of Alaska.

Not to downplay the talents of the five featured actors, but once the survivors reach the island the stars become some backstage humans. The island is raw, inhabited with wild bear, moose, caribou, sea lions and an assortment of other animals. Thanks to the considerable talents of Hubert Wells, credited as animal supervisor, and a group of animal trainers, their threats are trained for the cameras.

Logan hunts a pack o.̇ caribou, he's attacked by a Kodiak bear, threatened by a killer whale while diving for tools in the sunken wrecked ship and has his food eaten by a pack of wolves. It all amounts to wonderfully exciting footage, especially when juxtaposed with some of the film's good-natured lighter moments.

This is a fine G-rated film and also an important one because it introduces some fresh acting talent. The Raffills have worked before as producers of outdoor adventure films and as suppliers of animals for Disney productions. But their technical achievement here simply as filmmakers who know their craft and can develop an engaging story and work with actors is also formidable. —*Hege.*

A Queda
(The Fall)
(BRAZILIAN-COLOR)

Berlin, March 23.

A Zoom Cinematografica production, produced by Nei Sroulevich. Directed by Ruy Guerra, Nelson Xavier. Screenplay, Guerra, Xavier; camera (color), Edgar Moura; editor, Ruy Guerra; art director, Carlos Prieto; music, Milton Nascimento and Ruy Guerra. Reviewed at Berlin Film Festival (in competition) March 22, '78. Running time: **120 MINS.**

Mario	Nelson Xavier
Salatiel	Lima Duarte
Laura	Isabel Ribeiro
The widow	Maria Silvia
Jose	Hugo Carvana

Latin American cinema is by no means in healthy shape, mainly due to the restrictions on freedom of expression that come as a direct result of military dictatorships. But Brazil, after a lean period during which it was feared that the "cinema novo" had died, is again doing well with some of the same names (Pereira dos Santos, Diegues, Andrade) that once helped it earn a considerable international reputation among film buffs.

In fact, it is the most socio-politically (barring Cuba) and sexually (barring none) explicit cinema in Latin America, in spite of its military rulers. Which once again shows the contradictory, almost surrealist, qualities of this huge country.

"The Fall" deals with an accident on a construction where the pace is being forced to finish the job on schedule. Speed is given precedence over compliance with safety regulations and, as a result, a worker falls to his death. Mario, the foreman's son-in-law, gets involved. He knew the man, although they were by no means friends and, while the construction company tries to pass off the death as a fortuitous accident, Mario attempts to help the widow to obtain compensation, an experience that increasingly resembles the banging of one's head against a cement wall.

The impotence of an individual, when faced with the closed ranks of the establishment; the effect this has on his personal life and development, the theory and practice of social justice, are among the very valid themes of this Guerra-Xavier film, shot in 16m and blown up to 35m.

Mario and the accident victim were characters in an early Ruy Guerra film ("Os Fuzis" (The Guns) 1964) and interspersed black and white footage from same tries to build up the continuity. This attempt to link the pic with its characters' past was unsuccessful. After all, how many people can be expected to remember a 1964 Brazilian film, even in that country? On the other hand, if the aim was to show the characters' past as soldiers and to insinuate how the oppressors had become the oppressed, there were better ways of accomplishing this within the context of "The Fall."

Besides, editing should have been far tighter. At its present 120 minutes the film often lingers excessively; shots are held too long and, in this shape, international exposure would appear limited.
—*Amig.*

Pretty Baby
(COLOR)

———

Boring Louis Malle film about a pre-teener's brothel upbringing. Thin outlook.

———

Hollywood, March 27.

Paramount Pictures release, produced and directed by Louis Malle. Features entire cast. Screenplay, Polly Platt, based on a story by Platt, Malle from material in "Storyville," by Al Rose; camera (Metrocolor), special photography, Maureen Lambray; editors, Suzanne Baron, Suzanne Fenn; music supervision, Jerry Wexler; piano solos, Bob Greene; production design, Trevor Williams; set decoration,

Jim Berkey; sound, Richard Vorisek, Don Johnson; costumes-wardrobe, Mina Mittelman; asst. directors, John M. Poer, Don Heitzer. Reviewed at Paramount Studio, L.A., March 27, '78. (MPAA Rating: R.) Running time: **109 MINS.**
Bellocq .... Keith Carradine
Hattie .... Susan Sarandon
Violet .... Brooke Shields
Nell .... Frances Faye
Piano Player .... Antonio Fargas
Highpockets .... Gerrit Graham
Mama Mosebery .... Mae Mercer
Frieda .... Diana Scarwid
Josephine .... Barbara Steele
Red Top .... Matthew Anton
Flora .... Seret Scott
Gussie .... Cheryl Markowitz
Fanny .... Susan Manskey
Agnes .... Laura Zimmerman
Odette .... Miz Mary
Alfred Fuller .... Don Hood

The Louis Malle-Polly Platt collaboration on "Pretty Baby" has yielded an offbeat depiction of life in New Orleans' Storyville red-light district circa 1917, as experienced by a lifelong resident — a 12-year-old girl. The film is handsome, the players nearly all effective, but the story highlights are confined within a narrow range of ho-hum dramatization. This seems a deliberate style, but what it produces is a tedious, overlong and eventually boring film which Paramount may experience difficulty in marketing.

Al Rose's "Storyville" is credited for source material for the Platt screenplay from a story written by her and Malle. The time of the plot is just before Josephis Davids, Secretary of the U.S. Navy closed Storyville as a bad influence; the black musicians who found employment in the brothels there drifted north to Kansas City, Memphis and Chicago, later east to N.Y., and thereby changed forever the direction and the fabric of American popular music that continues today in its evolution. Such are the odd results of moral crusades, but that potentially strong film plot is not what's here.

Instead, Malle and Platt have created a placid milieu in the barrelhouse owned by Frances Faye (it would be nice to say that her presence makes the film worth seeing, but unfortunately this great entertainer seems used mostly for gothic effect). There, Susan Sarandon is one of the girls who, in residence, has given birth to a child, in this case Brooke Shields, who gives either an extraordinarily subtle or else a totally perplexed performance as a pre-teenager whose entire world is that of the brothel.

Keith Carradine is cast as a catatonic photographer who only likes to shoot portraits of the girls. Life for Shields is a series of minor joys and sorrows — a drunken customer here, a friendly piano player there (Antonio Fargas as a Jelly Roll Morton-inspired character, with Bob Greene playing the piano solos which comprise a major part of Jerry Wexler's superb musical environment). Eventually she and

Carradine live together, but the relationship ends when Sarandon, who left to marry a customer, returns in respectability to claim the underage child. That's it.

Sven Nykvist and other craft personnel supported the project well. Too bad there never was a solid script —*Murf.*

La Zizanie
(The Spat)
(FRENCH-COLOR)

———

Paris, March 25.

AMLF release of Films Christian Fechner production. Stars Louis De Funes, Annie Girardot. Directed by Claude Zidi. Screenplay, Zidi, Michel Fabre, Pascal Jardin; camera (Eastmancolor), Claude Renoir; editor, Monique and Robert Isnardon; music, Vladimir Cosma. Reviewed at Ambassade-Gaumont, Paris, March 24, '78. Running time, **95 MINS.**
Guillaume .... Louis De Funes
Wife .... Annie Girardot
Assistant .... Maurice Ritsch
Doctor .... Julien Guiomar

Film puts top comic draw Louis De Funes in with Annie Girardot, a lead femme performer these days. It is a broad slapstick comedy with pollution as a unifying theme.

As usual, this will have to depend on its main take from home marts, some European countries where De Funes has a name, and Latin and Asian outlets. U.S. chances again are summed up as possible playoff on its theme, though the needed comic elan, invention and drive are only intermittent.

This is De Funes' second pic since his heart attack. He now can do more physical things and his double takes, bird-like movements and rages are accentuated by his thin silhouette. He is still patronizing to employees, selfish and devious with a thin streak of tenderness that may explain his popularity to all classes.

Annie Girardot is somewhat out of her element though she tries valiantly to play the foil to De Funes's hardnosed demands and authoritativeness. He has invented something to harness air pollution but sets off dust discharges to be able to display the efficacy of his invention.

He browbeats Japanese reps to order over 3,000 of them and then tries to find land to build up his factory. Not getting the space, the factory moves into his house as he ruins his wife's garden and tries to keep her as the factory even invades their bedroom.

It lacks that artful pacing and coordinated playing to bring it off. The couple just do not strike sparks, even when they run against each other politically. He is the mayor and a good bit has people he is marrying forced to also promise to vote for him before they can make their marital vows. —*Mosk.*

Ne Pleure Pas
(Don't Cry)
(FRENCH-COLOR)

———

Paris, March 26.

Gaumont release of Gaumont-TF1-SFP production. Features entire cast. Directed by Jacques Ertaud. Screenplay, Ertaud, Guy Lagorce from the book by Lagorce. No other credits available. Reviewed at Colisee, Paris, March 25, '78. Running time, **105 MINS.**
Thomas .... Sylvain Joubert
Grandpa .... Charles Vanel
Brother .... Xavier Labouze
Girlfriend .... Christine Laruent
Hippie .... Marc Chapiteau
Father .... Andre Falcon

———

Supposedly a test case coproduction between tv and a regular industry producer, with the main production control in the hands of one vid web and its production arm, film flounders between the two and, summing up, tips it more for tv than for theatrical outlets. Film was shown on tv two days before being released, which seems not to have boosted its chances.

Gaumont (a minority coproducer) apparently felt this was a way of using tv while sharing a theatrical film at lower cost.

Pic tells a cautionary tale of a jock who boxes in his spare time but wants to be a veterinarian. He uses his fisticuffs against some punk thieves he runs into and some leftists-cum-hippies who trespass on his grandpa's land. He is fascist around the edges.

But pic segues into his getting badly hurt in an anti-nuclear demonstration and choosing to die rather than be a cripple. So is this tough guy brave or a coward? The generally meandering, predictable tale and the lacklustre direction do not set up much emotion or clarity in the film's attitudes. Venerable actor Charles Vanel is rung in as a grandfather who does not understand his hysterically violent grandson.

Sylvain Joubert is effective as the tough guy, with others adequate. Technically it is passable. For tv its inconclusive script may be acceptable but it emerges tedious on a big screen. Mainly local chances for this early tv-film coprod. —*Mosk.*

Sale Reveur
(Dirty Dreamer)
(FRENCH-COLOR)

———

Paris, March 25.

Gaumont release of Les Productions De La Gueville-FR3 production. Stars Jacques Dutronc, Lea Massari. Directed by Jean-Marie Perier. Screenplay, Pascal Jardin, Lucien Elia, Perier; camera (Eastmancolor), Yves Lafaye; editor, Nicole Saulnier; music, Jacques Dutronc. Reviewed at Club 13, Paris, March 24, '78. Running time, **90 MINS.**
Jerome .... Jacques Dutronc
Josephe .... Lea Massari
Taupin .... Maurice Benichou
Cesar .... Greg Germain

Anne .... Nathalie Perier
Gardener .... Jacques Dichamp

Jean-Marie Perier is a maverick in the film picture. He was a still photog and then turned to tv, making docus and fiction entries. In the last eight years he has made three features but kept a low profile in the film milieu. Here he comes up with an ambivalent tale of a born loser.

Somewhat mannered and romanticizing lowlife, film concerns a 30-year-old orphan and reform school product who cannot seem to grow up. He lives with an earthy, attractive 40-year-old woman, Lea Massari, who indulges his daydreams based on American movies, especially "Hud," which he knows by heart, where Paul Newman played a mean man embittered by life who finally got his comeuppance.

Jacques Dutronc has a fine presence and a sort of offbeat, introverted stare that adds some dimension to his anti-hero role. He can drive off some operators who want to buy the woman's land by using a razor but cannot face up to life and any emotional maturity.

He develops a crush on a lovely, seemingly upper-class girl he sees eating pastries every day in a posh shop and then is driven off by a chauffeur. He fantasizes and lies to his mistress that he is having an affair with a rich woman.

Dutronc emerges racist, full of quirks, such as drowning puppies when he is jealous of the black, and finally breaking in on the rich girl's house only to find she is a governess. This enrages him, for he apparently wants her unattainable and above him. Film schematizes its characters rather than bringing them to life which gives the pic a cold and prettied-up look rather than the tang of life and the sentimentality sans bathos it strives for.
—*Mosk.*

La Jument Vapeur
(The Steam Mare)
(FRENCH-COLOR)

Paris, April 4.
Planfilm release of Stephane Films production. Stars Carole Laure. Written and directed by Joyce Bunuel. Camera (Eastmancolor), Francois Protat; editor, Jean-Bernard Bonis; music, Jean-Marie Senia. Reviewed at I.P. projection room, Paris, March 28, '78. Running time, **92 MINS.**
Wife .... Carole Laure
Husband .... Pierre Santini
Friend .... Liliane Roveyre

Another Bunuel to be reckoned with. Joyce Bunuel is the daughter-in-law of the noted Luis and her husband Juan also directs pix. She is American and has now made her first film in France. It consists of a zesty, tangy few pages from the life of a pretty housewife with two kids who rebels out of instinct or inchoat

need rather than from consciousness raising or women's lib didactics.

No use trying to compare Bunuels, for they share mainly a name. However, she does start the film with a sudden gust of violence as she and her family are enjoying themselves at a picnic. A man drives up, insults them and then almost runs them down, chasing them in his car. This everyday violence and general public indifference catalyses her growing need for self awareness and standing as a person rather than an object.

Her good-natured macho husband insists on sex even when she does not feel like it and he does not understand her needs. It finally leads to an explosive negation of her status as she starts all the kitchen gadgets going and a suitor in the house happens to walk in and seduce her at her point of disarray.

It ends in her running to the basement of their impersonal big tenement house where she sobs on the shoulder of a man she runs into. Her husband arrives for a battle as they seem to come to some accord as the pic ends.

There is a tendency to gloss over events and to add scenes to pointedly goad the distraught housewife to her final recognition of the everyday flirting of a man who lives in the house. However, its notations of everyday household frictions, an escape by her and friends to a porno film and her realization that she has really no talents for a job when she hunts for one are well noted.

Pic could strike chords locally for good returns but it needs more care in handling abroad on this by-now familiar theme. It eschews sentimentality and the personal hermetic tics sometimes prevalent in first pix. Carole Laure is pretty as the muddled ex-nightclub dancer who wanted a family, but now cannot cope with her life and feelings.

The new Bunuel appears promising. --*Mosk.*

The Last Waltz
(COLOR)

Outstanding rock duo. Big outlook.

Hollywood, April 5.
United Artists release, produced by Robbie Robertson; executive producer, Jonathan Taplin. Stars The Band. Directed by Martin Scorsese. Camera (Deluxe), Michael Chapman, Laszlo Kovacs, Vilmos Zsigmond, David Myers, Bobby Byrne, Michale Watkins, Hiro Narita; editor, Yeu-Bun Yee, Jan Roblee; production design, Boris Leven; concert producer, Bill Graham; associate producer, Steven Prince; audio production, Rob Fraboni; concert music production, John Simon; assistant director, Jerry Grandey, James Quinn; set decorator, Anthony Mondell. Reviewed at MGM Studios, Culver City, April 5, '78. (No MPAA Rating.) Running time: 115 MINS.
With Bob Dylan, Joni Mitchell, Neil Diamond, Emmylou Harris, Neil Young, Van Morrison, Ron Wood, Muddy Waters, Eric Clapton, the Staples, Ringo Starr, Dr. John, Ronnie Hawkins, Paul Butterfield, The Band.

"The Last Waltz" is an outstanding rock documentary of the last concert by The Band on Thanksgiving, 1976 at Winterland in San Francisco.

Eight years after Warner Bros. released "Woodstock," United Artists, director Martin Scorsese and some of the film industry's top technical talent have combined forces to produce a concert documentary that earns comparisons to the watershed rock n' roll picture. Commercial outlook is strong in the youth market.

By itself The Band performs 12 numbers. The group backs up guest artists on another dozen. They include Ronnie Hawkins, Dr. John, Neil Young, the Staples, Neil Diamond, Joni Mitchell, Paul Butterfield, Muddy Waters, Eric Clapton, Emmylou Harris, Van Morrison, Bob Dylan, Ringo Starr and Ron Wood.

UA claims this is the first film to use a 24-track recording system, mixed down to four-track Dolby and the result will help bring theatres out of the audio dark ages.

Warner Bros. is releasing the soundtrack album. The LP should move quickly up the charts, further aiding the film's b.o.

Second, Scorsese and producer Tour" and was one of the three editors of "Woodstock," has succeeded on a number of fronts. First, he recognized that this concert deserved cinematic preservation. The Band was an important and intelligent force in rock music on its own and as a backup group for Bob Dylan and Ronnie Hawkins.

Intelligent is a key word here. This film is something more than a rock documentary. It's a chronicle of one important group very much a part of the music of the late '60s and '70s and it's also a commentary on those times. It's 90% concert film and 10% history. Unlike so many of their colleagues, the mem-

bers of The Band are competent musicians and spokesmen.

Second, Scorses and producer Robbie Robertson, lead guitarist for The Band, assembled a first class crew to shoot the concert. Credited as director of photography is Michael Chapman with Laszlo Kovacs, Vilmos Zsigmond, David Myers, Bobby Byrne, Michael Watkins and Hiro Narita adding their talents as additional directors of photography.

Third, Scorsese actually directed his large crew. It's obvious from what's up on the screen that he didn't just let his cameramen run wild and worry later about coverage in the cutting room, as so often is the case with these films. This is a recording of a live event, so some of the footage is the result of serendipity and good fortune; most of it, however, was obviously planned, maybe choreographed is a better word.

Most of the film was shot the night of the concert, but there are also interviews with the members of the group as well as a few scenes shot at the MGM Studios. As a package it fits together beautifully.

The film is a series of highlights. Except for Dylan, none of the guests perform more than one number with The Band. There are no dull moments and at 115 minutes the picture is tight and exciting.

After 16 years together, most of that time on the road, The Band has dissolved and the group has promised never to perform together publicly. The individual members are pursuing careers independently. This is one time, however, when breaking a promise would be okay.
— *Hege.*

Breakfast In Bed
(16M-COLOR)

Well done examination of a disintegrating marriage. Too short for most theatre bookings.

Hollywood, April 7.
A William Haugse production, produced by Catherine Coulson. Written, directed and edited by William Haugse. Camera (Metrocolor), Frederick Elmes; music, Tom Grant. No other credits available. Reviewed at the Royal Theatre, West L.A., April 7, '78. (NO MPAA rating.) Running time: 56 MINS.
Sara .... Jenny Sullivan
Paul .... John Ritter
Mimi .... V. Phipps-Wilson
Hairdresser .... Mitchell Breit
Marcja .... Timothy Near
Man in car .... Buckline Beery

Thanks to the recent emergence in ABC's "Three's Company," of John Ritter "Breakfast in Bed" should find an audience beyond the film festival circuit, and deservedly so. Theatrical booking is precluded by the film's 56-minute running time, 30 minutes too short, but a spot could be found on public television for this honest and mostly realistic examination of a disintegrating marriage.

Ritter and Sullivan play a young L.A. couple whose marriage has gone sour. They're trying to decide whether to split up or continue with the new arrangement, that is, live together, date others and get on each other's nerves every few minutes. The characters are introduced on a Sunday when the problems of their marriage come to a head.

Each half of the couple does some soul searching this Sunday: they bicker, daydream, discuss their thoughts with friends and remember better days.

William Haugse wrote, directed and edited the film. Technically he displays competence and agility and some innovation with the integration of still photographs into the narrative.

Ritter and Sullivan each deliver acceptable performances, more as "types," however, than as people. That's the fault of Haugse's underdeveloped script which pegs Sullivan as the young, frustrated artist who could be but lacks courage, and Ritter as a young wiseguy, a frustrated craftsman who'd rather be a lawyer but lacks courage. This couple's situation is real and deserves examination, so it's a shame Haugse didn't take more care with the writing.

"Breakfast in Bed" will be screened April 16 as part of the 1978 Los Angeles International Film Exposition. —Hege.

The Popovich Brothers of South Chicago
(DOCUMENTARY)

Chicago, April 4.

Ethel Raim, Martin Koenig and Jill Godmillow production for the Balkan Arts Center. Directed by Jill Godmillow. Camera, Tom Hurwitz, sound, Chat Gunter. No other credits available. Reviewed at the Film Center of the Art Institute of Chicago, March 28, '77. Running time: 60 MINS.

Jill Godmillow, who with folk singer Judy Collins helmed the 1975 Oscar-nominated documentary "Antonia," is sole director of a new hour-long documentary, "The Popovich Brothers of South Chicago." The film provides an interesting but not always clear look at the American Serbian community through the ethnic music of the Popovich Brothers — three laborer-musicians whose music has been a mainstay of the Serbs for almost 50 years.

Godmillow showcases the brothers and friends playing at various Serb functions over a year illustrating the importance of music to the culture. The film interlaces interviews with three generations of

the Popovich family and other Serbs with going on at social and religious get-togethers and the technique works well in capturing the spirit of the people. But the film needs to be pulled together by some objective narration about the history of the family and how music became important to them. Infrequent comments by a third generation Popovich who has left most of the traditions behind is not enough to clarify some confusing moments.

Part of the problem might be the Popovichs themselves who didn't seem comfortable speaking about their personal lives, especially after one of the brothers died during the year the film was being made. Their reluctance makes it difficult to figure out the personal relationships between members of the family, an interesting sidelight unexplored.

Camera work is good throughout, especially in photographing large social events where a less-skilled filmmaker might have gotten caught up with crowd shots. Godmillow also scores points with several interviews with younger members of the Serb community and in a scene where the brothers are rehearsing in the kitchen of one of their homes.

Distribution has thus far been limited to museums and art centers in a few major cities, perfect for this entry. Commercial prospects seem doubtful. Further possibility exists at schools and libraries where film could add to study of an ethnic group. —Berg.

F.I.S.T.
(COLOR)

Excellent Norman Jewison drama. Sylvester Stallone great as corrupt union leader. Long, but strong outlook.

Hollywood, April 12.

United Artists release, produced and directed by Norman Jewison; executive producer, Gene Corman. Stars Sylvester Stallone, Rod Steiger, Peter Boyle. Screenplay, Joe Eszterhas, Stallone, from a story by Eszterhas; camera (Technicolor), Laszlo Kovacs; editors, Tony Gibbs, Graeme Clifford; music, Bill Conti; production design, Richard MacDonald; art direction, Angelo Graham; set decoration, George Bob Nelson; sound, Chuck Wilborn; costumes-wardrobe, Anthea Sylbert, Tony Scarano, Thalia Phillips; asst. director, Andrew Stone. Reviewed at MGM Studios, Culver City, April 12, '78. (MPAA Rating: PG.) Running time: 145 MINS.
Johnny Kovak . . . . Sylvester Stallone
Sen. Madison . . . . Rod Steiger
Max Graham . . . . Peter Boyle
Anna Zerinkas . . . . Melinda Dillon
Abe Belkin . . . . David Huffman
Babe Milano . . . . Tony Lo Bianco
Vince Doyle . . . . Kevin Conway
Molly . . . . Cassie Yates
Arthur St. Claire . . . . Peter Donat
Win Talbot . . . . Henry Wilcoxon
Gant . . . . John Lehne
Mike Monahan . . . . Richard Herd
Mrs. Zerinkas . . . . Elena Karam
Bernie Marr . . . . Ken Kercheval
Tom Higgins . . . . Tony Mockus
Frank Vasko . . . . Brian Dennehy
Andrews . . . . James Karen

In its superb telling of how a humble but idealistic young man escalates to the corrupt heights of unbridled power. "F.I.S.T." is to the labor movement in the United States what "All The King's Men" was to an era in American politics. Norman Jewison's excellent film stars Sylvester Stallone in a characterization every bit as powerful as that of Broderick Crawford in the earlier Robert Rossen picture. Rod Steiger and Peter Boyle, also above title, head a very effective cast. Strong and handsome production values recreate brilliantly a quarter century of Americana. The United Artists release has a big commercial outlook, though its overlong running time (145 minutes) may restrict b.o. turnover. Pic opened Filmex here last Thursday (13).

Executive producer Gene Corman's initial concept of an epochal American labor melodrama was based on magazine articles by author Joe Eszterhas. Corman's presentation credit rewards this highlight example of a career-long astuteness, and the input of Jewison, again joined by associate producer Patrick Palmer and several key technicians, has carried the ball to full realization through the Eszterhas-Stallone final screenplay.

The first hour of the film presents the milieu of unorganized labor circa 1937, a time when the phrase "property rights" was as persistent (and often as shrill) a

harangue as "human rights" later became. Stallone and lifelong friend David Huffman (excellent in film debut) are among the workers in Henry Wilcoxon's trucking company, where foreman John Lehne personifies an attitude that still has not died away. Stallone and Huffman drift into organizing drivers for local union rep Richard Herd, whose assassination during a brawl triggered by management goons drives Stallone into league with Kevin Conway, a local hood. Thus, in desperation, came the inroads of organized crime into legitimate labor union activities.

This portion of the film strongly evokes Warner Bros. social melodramas of the time; one almost expects Barton MacLane, Pat O'Brien, Ann Sheridan, James Cagney and the rest to appear at any moment, under the direction of Raoul Walsh.

The next act depicts the militant labor response of Stallone and Conway, highlighted by a well-staged riot, after which the tentacles of mobsterism — Tony Lo Bianco personifying them well — parallel the growth and power of the truckers' union.

Concurrent sub-plot features Stallone and Melinda Dillon in evolving romance; good as it is, it's too much — and a drag on the pace — and too bad some further pruning didn't occur. (Put it this way: Warners told these stories in less than two hours.) Cassie Yates and Huffman also develop a lesser romantic sub-plot.

Action then cuts to the late '50s, when Stallone pushes international union leader Boyle out of office by some private blackmail, only to run head-on into Steiger, crusading U.S. Senator with a nicely ambivalent eye both for headlines and genuine union reform. (Insert Jimmy Hoffa, Robert Kennedy, Dave Beck, et al., as you like throughout, of course.)

This final hour of the film illuminates Stallone's ultimate tragedy and downfall, and poses a legitimate and timeless question: When a person sells out enroute to the top, even for an initially good principle, how much (or how little) a sellout is too much? Fadeout finds Stallone gunned down and kidnapped, his fate uncertain.

Richard MacDonald's production design and Laszlo Kovacs' cinematography are both outstanding, the highlights of superior technical work. Bill Conti's music is effective, along with a few period poptunes to help anchor the time frames. Technicolor toning is tops — a quasi-roto look in the early reels and more contemporary hues later.
—Murf.

Five Days From Home
(COLOR)

Meller with George Peppard as man on the run. Thin outlook.

Hollywood, April 7.

Universal Pictures release, produced and directed by George Peppard; executive producer, Robert S. Bremson. Stars Peppard, Neville Brand. Screenplay, William Moore; camera (CFI Color), Harvey Genkins; editor, Samuel E. Beetley; music, Bill Conti; song lyric, Norman Gimbel; sound, Jay Harding. Reviewed at Universal Studios, L.A., April 7, '78. (MPAA Rating: PG). Running time, 108 MINS.

T.M. Pryor	George Peppard
Insp. Markley	Neville Brand
Wanda Dulac	Sherry Boucher
Jose Stover	Victor Campos
Baldwin	Robert Donner
Marian	Ronnie Claire Edwards
Mrs. Peabody	Jessie Lee Fulton
J.J. Bester	William Larsen
The Colonel	Robert Magruder
Georgie Haskin	Savannah Smith
Howie	Don Wyse
TV newsman	Ralph Story

For all the hardships endured by George Peppard in producing, directing and starring in his indie-made "Five Days From Home," the film emerges as a modest and ultimately overripe meller about an escaped convict crossing the country to get to the bedside of his seriously-ill son. The Universal release has limited commercial outlook.

A script, credited to William Moore, loads up sympathy for Peppard, an ex-cop who killed his wife's lover and, six days left on his prison time, runs through swamp and mire to see his sick kid. The odyssey involves him with an assortment of characters, the most interesting his friendly kidnap of Savannah Smith, a plain-Jane girl who has never had anybody pay any attention to her. Smith delivers a very creditable performance and her sequence is the highlight of the picture.

Otherwise, things proceed from bland to bathos. Neville Brand, also billed above title, plays an unconvincing meanie sent to capture Peppard. In the final reels, Peppard, just happening by, rescues a mother and child from a burning house. — *Murf.*

I Wanna Hold Your Hand
(COLOR)

Lively comedy about Beatlemania. Youth appeal. Fresh acting and technical talent debut.

Hollywood, April 13.

Universal release, produced by Tamara Asseyev and Alex Rose; executive producer, Steven Spielberg. Directed by Robert Zemeckis. Features entire cast. Screenplay, Zemeckis, Bob Gale; camera (Technicolor), Donald M. Morgan; art director, Peter Jamison; editor, Frank Morriss; special visual effects, Albert Whitlock; associate producer, Bob Gale; set decoration, John Dwyer; assistant director, Newton Arnold; costume design, Roseanna Norton' special effects, Curtis Dickson; sound, Don Sharpless. Reviewed at Universal Studios, L.A., April 13, '77. (MPAA Rating: PG). Running time: 104 MINS.

Pam Mitchell	Nancy Allen
Tony Smerko	Bobby DiCicco
Larry Dubois	Marc McClure
Janis Goldman	Susan Kendall Newman
Grace Corrigan	Theresa Saldana
Rosie Petrofsky	Wendie Jo Sperber
Richard "Ringo" Klaus	Eddie Deezen
Peter Plimpton	Christian Juttner
Ed Sullivan	Will Jordan
Peter's father	Read Morgan
Al	Claude Earl Jones
Eddie	James Houghton
Neil	Michael Hewitson

"I Wanna Hold Your Hand" is a good-natured, lighthearted backward glance at a 1960s phenomenon — Beatlemania. That's a subject best tackled by youth, so it's appropriate — and encouraging — that Universal and producers Tamara Asseyev and Alex Rose had the foresight and the guts, to assign this picture to filmmakers who know something about that decade. Featuring mostly untried talent on both sides of the camera, "I Wanna Hold Your Hand" is a fresh, clever comedy which should score modestly with the youth market.

Budgeted at under $2,500,000 — rock bottom for a major studio production — modest will be enough. Universal should easily recoup its investment plus a profit at the boxoffice. But it'll reap an even larger profit with the discovery of fresh acting talent, especially Bobby DiCicco, Wendie Jo Sperber and Eddie Deezen, and director Robert Zemeckis, who coscripted with Bob Gale, the associate producer.

Zemeckis and Gale, both in their mid-20s, are proteges of Steven Spielberg, who helped bring this film to the attention of Universal and also served as an active executive producer and mentor on the production. Zemeckis and Gale are currently writing "Growing Up" with Spielberg and have penned, with John Milius, "1941," Spielberg's feature following "Growing Up."

"I Wanna Hold Your Hand" is a day-in-the-life film, in this case a day in the life of some New Jersey teenagers. It's February, 1964 and The Beatles will be appearing for the first time on the "Ed Sullivan Show" that night.

Everyone's got a mission in this film and all of them have to do with The Beatles debut. Theresa Saldana is a budding photographer who's got to meet the boys to launch her career by snapping some exclusive photos; Wendie Jo Sperber is a Beatles groupie without equal, unless it's Richard "Ringo" Klaus, played by Eddie Deezen as the classic nerd; Nancy Allen is about to get married, but is looking for a final fling; and Susan Kendall Newman and Bobby DiCicco are Beatles haters bent on sabotaging the show.

It takes a while to accept the situation and the film's early development is too slow and the humor initially too broad. But it develops into a lively entertainment with many memorable lines and scenes.

The film's biggest problem, the fact that The Beatles can't be shown, is turned into its greatest asset through Zemekis' creativity. He shoots scenes in their hotel room from under the bed, where Allen is hiding, and he handles the actual performance on the Sullivan show by mixing long shots and various angles with a monitor of the 1964 performance.

Technical credits are fine. Peter Jamison and John Dwyer did a formidable job recreating the Plaza Hotel (where the Beatles stayed during their visit) and other locales on the backlot at Universal and the Burbank Studios, although it's too bad at least the Plaza scenes couldn't have been done on location. — *Hege.*

Maternale
(Mother And Daughter)
(ITALIAN-COLOR)

Inaction dims any U.S. prospect. 'Smother hood,' Italian style.

A Rai-Radiotelevisione Italiana, Cooperative AATA and Pantheon I production. Written and directed by Giovanna Gagliardo; camera (color) Giuseppe Lanci; artdirection, Maria-Palo Maino; music, Stelvio Cipriani; editing, Roberto Perpignani; sound, Gianni Sardo; artistic collaboration, Giorgio Barattolo. Reviewed at Museum of Modern Art, N.Y., April 11, '78. Running time: 95 MINS.

With Carla Gravina, Anna Maria Gherardi, Marino Mase, Francesca Muzio, Benedetta Fantoli, Francesco, Lajos Balaszovits and Umberto Silva.

(English Subtitles)

"Maternale" is one more in the long line of good ideas affecting filmmakers in the area of family relationships that simply is executed poorly. Director and scripter Giovanna Gagliardo has brought this psychological item about a day in the lives of a young girl and her destructive mother in just over 90 minutes, though it conveys through a "longer" feeling.

Carla Gravina, the mother, has a problem. Her daughter, Benedetta Fantoli, who has reached young womanhood wants to quit limping and get out from underneath the blanket her mother is sure she needs. Fantoli wants to dance and have a good time. This is not good, because Gravina can't accept the idea that the baby she has made sick doesn't want to fulfill those expectations anymore.

Gravina has further problems cutting up vegetables. Hard to tell why this is such a big deal, but maybe to Italian women cutting up vegetables is meaningful. In any event, Gagliardo spends a lot of time taking the viewer into the sumptuous boring life of an upper class home to prove how boring it is.

This one adheres to the school of the meaningful gesture, which is a branch of heavy symbolism department. That usually means many closeups, which are here in abundance. Problem here really is that Gagliardo's sensibilities are better suited to the novel than to film. American audiences insist that a picture move. No one ever enters a room or a scene honestly; it's always a close encounter of the thud kind.

Maria-Paolo Maino's art direction and Lanci's camerawork are quite nice, limning in bright, soft colors the rotten, good time the rich are having. (Pic was one offering in the New Directors series of the Film Society of Lincoln Center and the Museum of Modern Art. It is also slated to unspool at Cannes Fest.)
—*Jac.*

A Different Story
(COLOR)

Boy meets girl, but they're both gay. Good premise that falters in resolution. Some b.o. potential.

Hollywood, April 11.

Avco Embassy Pictures release, produced by Alan Belkin; executive producer, Michael F. Leone. Stars Perry King, Meg Foster. Directed by Paul Aaron. Features entire cast. Screenplay, Henry Olek; camera (CFI Color), Philip Lathrop; second unit camera, Michael Werk; editor, Lynn McCallon; music, David Frank; songs, Bob Wahler; set decoration, Lee Poll; sound, William Teague, Thomas Dodington; costumes-wardrobe, Robert Demora, Agnes Lyon; Reviewed at CFI, L.A., April 11, '78. (MPAA Rating: R.) Running time, 106 MINS.

Albert	Perry King
Stella	Meg Foster
Phyllis	Valerie Curtin
Sills	Peter Donat
Stella's Parents	Richard Bull, Barbara Collentine
Ned	Guerin Barry
Roger	Doug Higgins
Chris	Lisa James
Sam	Eugene Butler

"A Different Story" certainly is. Stars Perry King and Meg Foster are excellent as a couple whose budding romance has just one problem: they are both gay. Feature film newcomers Alan Belkin, who produced for the Peterson Co. teleblurbery and exec producer Michael F. Leone, and director Paul Aaron have made a first-class production whose only — but serious — flaw is a Henry Olek script that begins with brilliant cleverness but dissolves by fadeout into formula banality. However, the Avco Embassy release has sufficient offbeat charm and appeal to start off well in certain situations, though overall results may be spotty.

The early genius in the script is the casual springing of the basic situation and the clever reversal of timeless film romantic-comedy plot turns. Real estate agent Foster, showing a mansion, discovers squatter tenant King after he has been dropped by wealthy Peter Donat, who evidently changes "chauffeurs" with regularity. An illegal alien, King is vulnerable to deportation.

She takes King home to help him out; he thinks she is straight, only to be as surprised as the audience when date Lisa James — and later, irate lover Valerie Curtin — arrive. The couple evolve a sincere friendship, he keeping house (his talents include cooking and clothes design) while she's in the real estate office. Her parents don't know that he has cooked the dinner when they come to call; the door-to-door salesman is puzzled. Foster marries King to prevent deportation when jealous Donat calls the police.

But half way through the film, after a birthday party, the two married friends accidently wind up having sex (shades of "I must have been drunk"); they like it, get serious, have a child and the rest of the film is not much better than an updated tv sitcom with superficial marital problems and resolutions. The abrupt plot change — which abandons everything that has come earlier, except for Curtin's freakout stereotype of the neurotic and suicidal homosexual ex-lover — dissipates most of the earlier appeal of the story. One would think that both Foster and King are "cured," or "born again"

The film would have sustained itself throughout had the plot probed deeper into the far more intriguing and complex situation of a dissolving gay and straight domestic and romantic environment.

Nevertheless, save for this severe script problem, director and performers have done admirable work. Phil Lathrop's cinematography highlights the superior production polish. — *Murf.*

Nunzio
(COLOR)

Warm-hearted but intermittently contrived urban meller. Thin outlook.

Universal Pictures release. Produced by Jennings Lang. Features entire cast. Directed by Paul Williams. Camera (Color), Ed Brown; screenplay, James Andronica; editor, Johanna Demetrakas; sound, Les Lazarowitz; production designer, Mel Bourne; music, Lalo Schifrin; costumes, Ann Roth; set decorator, George DeTitta; first asst. director, J. Allan Hopkins. Reviewed at Universal screening room, N.Y., April 24, '78. (MPAA Rating: R.) Running time: 86 MINS.
Nunzio .... David Proval
Jamesie ....James Andronica
Mrs. Sabatino .... Morgana King
Michele .... Tovah Feldshuh
Jo Jo ....Vincent Russo
Carol .... Maria Smith
Bobby .... Jamie Alba
Angelo .... Joe Spinell
Maryann .... Theresa Saldana
Georgie ....Glenn Scarpelli
Priest .... Joseph Sullivan

Nunzio is an Italo-American with the mentality of a pre-teenager and the body of a man in his early twenties. In James Adronica's film about him, directed by Paul Williams, the character's obvious asymmetry is the source of genuine sentiment and, unfortunately, a good deal of pre-engineered sentimentality. Thin outlook looms.

"Nunzio" is the somewhat constricted tradition of the "small" urban meller set against an ethnic, New York City backround — substantial parts of this film were lensed in Brooklyn's Borough Park section. In the most successful such outings — "Marty" immediately comes to mind — the dreariness of the physical surroundings was more than offset by sharply-etched, rich and warm characterizations.

This Jennings Lang production shines in its depictions of Nunzio and his family. But the subsidiary characters are merely stereotypes designed to propel Nunzio (David Proval) to a pre-ordained finale (he saves the infant of a paraplegic mother from a burning apartment house). From a promising premise, we are left with mawkishness.

Nunzio helps support his widowed mother (played with delicate feeling by Morgana King) by delivering groceries for a local store. He functions rather ably, sustaining himself often by fantasizing he's superman.

The luxury of this fantasy is afforded by Nunzio's supportive family, especially his older brother (author Andronica) and protector. Had the film focussed more intently on these familial relationships, the rewards would have increased geometrically.

The film's best performance is that of Andronica, who best combines the sense of desperation in those assigned to minutely oversee a retarded person profoundly loved. Andronica's muscular cockiness in the part is well contrasted with overriding compassion, and his portrayal is totally convincing.

Much less so are the auxiliary roles — a group of local toughs who harass Nunzio, a neighborhood doxy (Theresa Saldana) who seduces him on a dining-room table (scene is the reason for the R rating), a Jansenist priest who equates sex with unmitigated evil (Joseph Sullivan), the owner of the grocery store (Joe Spinell) — not because of acting deficiencies but because the script dooms them to the strictly utilitarian. Characters are there to give "Nunzio" an upbeat ending. In the title role, Proval is generally strong as the hulking retard. But it's tough to fully assess this kind of portrayal — it's Actors Studio taken to a minimalist extreme.

Director Paul Williams helms in straightforward style that occasionally allows the pic to drag unnecessarily. Ed Brown's photography is workmanlike, Lalo Schifrin's score, however, is intrusive in the sense its contrasting grittiness and lyricism dictate rather than enhance audience response.

— *Sege.*

Le Beaujolais Nouveau Est Arrive ...
(The New Beaujolais Wine Has Arrived ...)
(FRENCH-COLOR)

Paris, April 25.

CIC release of Camera One-Les Films De L'Alma production. Stars Jean Carmet, Michel Galabru. Directed by Jean-Luc Voulfow. Screenplay, Marco Pico, voulfow from book by Rene Fallet' camera (Eastmancolor), Jean-Paul Schwartz; editor, Armand Psenny; music, Carlo Rustichelli. Reviewed at CIC screening room, Paris, April 13, '78. Running time, 92 MINS.
Camadule .... Jean Carmet
Captatin .... Michel Galabru
Georges .... Pierre Mondy
Kamel .... Rabah Loucif
Wife ....Pascale Roberts
Prunelle .... Kathy Mongadin

The film might be a stab at French nostalgia in a tale of two middleaged, anarchic dreamers on the road to find some new wine for their local Paris cafe which will soon be condemned as new buildings encroach on the old parts of the city. But it rarely captures the insuciance, poetic individuality and comedic finesse of such pre-war items as "Boudou Saved from Drowning" by Jean Renoir or Rene Clair's "A Nous La Liberte."

Too much padding in the pic and also a somewhat too deliberate approach to comedy by transplanted tv director Jean-Luc Voulfow. Like many French wines, this might not travel well abroad but could click with general audiences at home. Then again, that complacent comedy of family mores and love among cousins "Cousin, Cousine" was a solid hit Stateside. So this might be tried to see if its winey French bouquet might catch on.

Jean Carmet is a little man dreamer who has concocted a beautiful countess who writes to him from the Beaujolais wine country. People in his cafe believe him and he comes to believe she exists also. So when the cafe's new wine is destroyed in a big ricochet traffic accident, caused by Carmet and pals crossing the road, they promise to go and get the wine from the Countess's chateau vineyard themselves.

Carmet has a gruff ex-military friend called the Captain, played with bombastic overbearing bonhommie by Michel Galabru. Neither seems to work and they pick up a young innocent Arab who is fired by Carmet's bumbling interference with his work on a building site. They run into all sorts of adventures including meeting a distraught tie salesman with a girl in all of his town sites; vendor has to report to his wife every two hours in Paris.

Old style French macho has Galabru slapping the wife when she finds them and also uses a sex fling to put her in her place of accepting her husband's work and ways. There is also the sentimental streak as Carmet's illusion is discovered about the countess and Galabru admits he was never a Captain and never served abroad.

It has moments of fun and the Arab character brings out the paternalistic French racism as he is accepted despite insults. A brief romantic interlude the Arab has with a pretty little farm girl can, of course, have no future. A determinedly French populist pic that just misses the fillip of human insight, pacing and more easygoing adventurousness. However, director Voulfow is a rare tv director with some filmic knowhow but needing more roadwork before he can be judged. — *Mosk.*

Local Color
(B&W 16M)

Self-indulgent independent film.

Hollywood, April 16.

Produced, directed, written and edited by Mark Rappaport. Camera (black and white), Fred Murphy. Features entire cast. No other credits available. Reviewed at the Academy of Motion Picture Arts and Sciences Little Theater, Beverly Hills, April 16, '78. (No MPAA rating). Running time: 116 MINS.
Andrea .... Jane Campbell
Fred .... Bob Herron
Lil .... Dolores Kenan
Alvin .... Michael Burg

This year Filmex is featuring a series on American independent filmmakers. That assures at least one picture the charitable label of "interesting" and the more forthright boring and confusing. And so we come to Mark Rappaport's "Local Color."

It's a surreal soap opera in black and white. There are eight characters, including two married couples, two woman and a gay pair. One half of the gay couple is the brother of the female member of a married couple. She has an affair with her brother's lover, etc.

Floating around is a gun, which changes hands frequently. And there are dreams, which meld into reality. It all very confusing.

— *Hege.*

Los Dias Del Pasado
(Days of the Past)
(SPANISH-COLOR)

Madrid, April 16.

Impala production. directed by Mario Camus. Screenplay, Antonio Betancort, Mario Camus; camera (Eastmancolor), Hans Burmann; music, Anton Garcia Abril; sets, Rafael Palmero; editor, Javier Moran. Reviewed at Cine Paz (Madrid) April 15, '78. Running time: 105MINS.
Juana .... Marisol
Antonio .... Antonio Gades
Also: Gustavo Berges, Antonio Iranzo, Fernando Sanchez-Polack, Saturnino Cerra, Manuel Alexandre and Mario Pardo.

Dull, monotonous film set in a rainy northern Spanish province shortly after the Civil War when pockets of Republican partisans were still holding out against the Civil Guards. Though the subject could have lent itself to some interesting comments and asides, Camus's film instead plods along flatly making no points, never really delving into the wheretofore of the guerrillas, and unsuccessfully treating a love story which never arouses the filmgoer's interest or compassion.

To make the film even more unbearable, it seems to have been shot in a constant, dready downpour of rain, with next to no light. When there is any light, Hans Burmann shoots against it.

An aging Marisol, at 28 shorn of her youthful puppetlike attractions, gives a deadpan performance, though compared to that put in by Antonio Gades, she's a live wire.

Story, briefly, is of an Andalusian schoolteacher who takes on a job in a miserable village in Santander province, in hope of meeting a former lover who's now a guerrilla. She does finally track him down through a boy in her class and,

far-fetched though it may seem, spends a night with him in the village room where she lives. He's off in the morning to fight the Civil Guards.

Camus does throw in one emotionless shoot-out, and then ends the film inconclusively with the teacher going back to a sunny Andalusian village, leaving Antonio to fight it out pointlessly to the end.
— *Besa.*

Deathsport
(COLOR)

Carradine in trouble in 30th Century.

Hollywood, April 17.

A New World picture, produced by Roger Corman. Stars David Carradine. Directed by Henry Suso, Allen Arkush. Screenplay, Suso, Donald Stewart, from a story by Francis Doel; camera (Metrocolor), Gary Graver; editor, Larry Bock; music, Andrew Stein; art director, Sharon Compton; special effects, Jack Rabin, asst. director, Tom Jacobson, Jim Burnett; sound, Paul Hunt. Reviewed at the Music Hall Theatre, Beverly Hills, April 17. (MPAA Rating R.) Running time: 83 MINS.
Kaz Oshay .... David Carradine
Deneer .... Claudia Jennings
Ankar Moor .... Richard Lynch
Doctor Karl .... William Smithers
Marcus Karl .... Will Walker
Lord Zirpola .... David McLean
Polna .... Jesse Vint
Jailer .... H.B. Haggerty
Tritan President .... John Himes

"Deathsport" is Roger Corman's futuristic science fiction gladiator picture. And what is a futuristic science fiction gladiator picture? It's a film set 1,000 years into the future, post neutron wars, where the good warriors ride horses and wield see-through sabres fighting bad guys known as Statesmen who drive lethal motorcycles known as "Death Machines."

The good guys are quiet, live by a code, make temporary unions and roam desert wastelands trying to avoid the cannibal mutants and those motorcycles, which are very noisy.

The good guys are known as Ranger Guides and they just want to be left alone. Anything to avoid those motorcycles. Statesmen have other plans. They have two ways of amusing themselves; beating up Ranger Guides — no easy task since Ranger Guides are superior warriors — and capturing female rangers, who they strip, lock up in dark room with metal chandeliers and then apply electricity and special effects. Nice guys.

New World topper Corman produced this low-budget "Rollerball," "Star Wars," "Deathrace" combination imitation. Francis Doel wrote the story with Henry Suso and Donald Stewart scripting. Direction is by Suso and Allan Arkush. In true New World fashion there are a number of motorcycle

crashes, which are almost as spectacular as car crashes. Lots of flames engulf the screen every few minutes.

David Carradine is the quiet good guy and the best thing that can be said about his acting and his part is that he doesn't say much. Claudia Jennings is his partner good guy, the one who gets to amuse the bad guy in the dark room. The best thing that can be said about her performance is that she gets to take off her clothes, twice.

Outlook is strictly quick playoff, which shouldn't be that difficult since the film runs only 83 minutes.
—*Hege.*

Jane Bleibt Jane
(Jane Is Jane Forever)
(W. GERMAN-COLOR)

An Enten Production produced by Rolf Buhrmann. Written and directed by Walter Bockmayer and Buhrmann. Features cast. Camera (color). Peter Martin; editor, Inge Gielow; music, David Bowie, Asha Putli, Mandingo, Stomu Yamahia; art direction, Norbert Schaub. Reviewed at Museum of Modern Art, N.Y. April 9, '78. Running time: 85 MINS.
With: Johanna Konig, Peter Chatel, Karl Blomer, Evelyn Hall, Hannelore Lubeck, Anita Riotte and Brigitte Gonsior.

"Jane Is Jane Forever" is a lovely, funny film about an elderly woman who checks into what appears to be the most unstructured old folks home in West Germany, where this pic was made, and fantasizes about her past and future life with Tarzan, he of the Apes. Young filmmaker Walter Bockmayer has nicely crafted for 90,000 marks (about $45,000) a filmic portrait not unlike the job the better-known Rainer Werner Fassbinder did in "Mother Kusters Goes To Heaven," but arguably did better.

For one thing, Bockmayer is less concerned with examining the political spectrum than he is in promoting the right to thrive in one's own world. There are many comic, bittersweet moments of Johanna Konig as a brilliant Jane acting out her fantasy life — learning to talk Ape, confronting some befuddled monkeys in the zoo, flashing her leopard-skin toga from beneath her raincoat, showing a family photo album of old Hollywood stills of "my husband" Tarzan to an incredulous journalist — but one in particular is a slapstock standout: Konig and Tarzan rushing toward each other across a snowfallen field, until Tarzan gets a closer look at her and backs off.

But much of what passes for simple Tarzaniness — and there is plenty — actually touches a deeper nerve. That is the expression of the ubermensch — the philosophical underpinning of Nazi Germany — which has been recast into a loon's delusion. It is rendered harmless

and comical, and so forgotten for the power it once possesed. Anyone wanting a clue to W. Germans' enjoyment of their prosperity and their essential change into the Swiss mentality, need only check this film out.

But for one grisly eight-minute scene of a snake allegorically chomping into a mouse — a scene that prompted one aud member to ask Bockmayer after the screening at the Museum of Modern Art how he got it to be so real? — this film is a real art crowd pleaser.

Konig is superb as Jane, as is Peter Chatel as the reporter and Karl Blomer as Tarzan. —*Jac.*

The Great Rocky Mountain Jazz Party
(COLOR-16M)

Hollywood, April 14.

A Great Rocky Mountain Jazz Party production, produced by Dick and Maddie Gibson. Directed and photographed by Vilis Lapenieks. Editor, Rich and Bobby Meyer. No other credits available. Reviewed at the Suncrest Cinema screening room, L.A., April 14, '78. (No MPAA rating.) Running time: 103 MINS.
Features: Clark Terry, Zoot Sims, Phil Woods, Eubie Blake, Jon Faddis, Joe Venuti, Dick Hyman, Roger Kellaway, Ray Brown, Roland Hanna, Milt Hinton, Bob Wilder, Buddy DeFranco, Ruby Braff, Joe Newman, Ralph Sutton, Carl Fontana, Buddy Tate, Bill Watrous, Billy Butterfield, Budd Johnson, Pee Wee Erwin, Trummy Young.

Every Labor Day weekend Dick and Maddie Gibson invite some of the country's best jazz musicians and most enthusiastic jazz buffs to the Broadmoor Hotel in Colorado Springs for a four-day jazz orgy. In "The Great Rocky Mountain Jazz Party" Vilis Lapenieks focuses his cinema-verite camera on the event and the result is a cinematic equivalent to the sponteneous affair.

It's anything but a slick documentary, but it's anything but a slick party. The Gibsons, who produced the film, also act as narrators and they come off as homey, friendly people. It really seems like a party, not a concert, and the couple are unobtrusive and cooperative hosts.

Nearly all of the documentary's 103 minutes are devoted to music, which is strictly traditional jazz. More than 50 musicians attended the party, including Clark Terry, Zoot Sims, Ray Brown and Eubie Blake, and there are various combinations and jam sessions. Again, this is not a slick rock docu, so no one should expect sophisticated or elaborate sound mixing or direction. Main appeal of this item will be film festivals and clubs. — *Hege.*

Almost Summer
(COLOR)

Dull "high-school" programmer.

Hollywood, April 6.

Universal Pictures release of a Motown Production, produced by Rob Cohen; executive producer, Steve Tisch. Stars Bruno Kirby, Lee Purcell, John Friedrich, Didi Conn, Thomas Carter, Tim Matheson. Directed by Martin Davidson. Screenplay, Judith Berg, Sandra Berg, Davidson, Marc Reid Rubel; camera (Technicolor), Stevan Larner; editor, Lynzee Klingman; music, Charles Lloyd, Ron Altbach; art direction, William M. Hiney; set decoration, Mary Ann Biddle; sound, Jim Alexander, Bill Varney; costumes-wardrobe, Sandra Davidson; asst. director, Gary Daigler; stunt coordinator, Conrad Palmisano. Reviewed at Universal Studios, L.A., April 6, '78. (MPAA Rating: PG.) Running time: **88 MINS.**

Bobby DeVito .... Bruno Kirby
Christine Alexander .... Lee Purcell
Darryl Fitzgerald .... John Friedrich
Donna DeVito .... Didi Conn
Dean Hampton .... Thomas Carter
Kevin Hawkins .... Tim Matheson
Nicole Henderson .... Petronia Paley
Duane Jackson .... David Wilson
Lori Ottinger .... Sherry Hursey
Stanley Lustgarten .... Harvey Lewis

"Almost Summer" is an innocuous and harmless children's film about the perils of first love, acne and high-school politics, featuring many players a trifle long of tooth to be thus employed. The film is the merger — or shotgun marriage, if you will — of a Martin Davidson-Steve Tisch project, "Senior Prom," and a Rob Cohen-Motown property, "High School." The Universal release, at 88 minutes, is a good triple-bill item for undiscriminating teenagers.

Judith and Sandra Berg ("High School") and director Davidson with Marc Reid Rubel ("Senior Prom") get writing credit. The cosmic plot issue is a class election, with Bruno Kirby a conniving campaign manager opposing the candidacy of Lee Purcell, his former inamorata and just as cold a cookie as he. Tim Matheson is Purcell's jock b.m.o.c. flame. Thomas Carter is Kirby's sidekick, and Didi Conn, every bit as appealing as in "You Light Up My Life," plays Kirby's awkward sister.

John Friedrich, who gives the best acting impression, is a shy student recruited by Kirby to oppose Purcell. The script recreates in playpen terms the same machinations by which grownups maneuver; that may be the redeeming feature of the plot — the recognition that the child is indeed the parent of the adult. Put another way, the film is cloying in a seamy grownup sort of way.

Lots of 45 rpm record tunes recur. Production credits are adequate.

The picture first hits the screen in the Dallas and Oklahoma City territory. —*Murf.*

Rituals
(CANADIAN-COLOR)

Hollywood, April 12.

Day and Date International release, produced by Lawrence Dane. Directed by Peter Carter. Features entire cast. Screenplay, Ian Sutherland; camera (Bellevue Pathe color), Rene Verzier; art direction, Karen Bromley; assistant director, John Eckert. No other credits provided. Reviewed at Studio I Screening Room, Beverly Hills, April 11, '78. (No MPAA rating.) Running time: **94 MINS.**

Harry .... Hal Holbrook
Mitzi .... Lawrence Dane
Martin .... Robin Gammell
Able .... Ken James
D.J. .... Gary Reineke

"Rituals" has the same ingredients of "Deliverance," except the excitement and suspense. As the picture trails its agony and bloodshed endlessly through the wilds, there's little worth following the path for, except for those fascinated by how many ways doctors can be bumped off by a madman prosecuting his malpractice complaints outdoors.

Title comes from the habits of Hal Holbrook and four other unpleasant physicians who vacation together annually. Since none of them seems to like the other very much, it is not clear why they choose to do this. But something has to get the story started.

An airplane deposits the quintet in a foresaken area where a lurking person steals their shoes, then sics the bees on the four left behind after the fifth goes for help wearing a spare pair of tennies.

The bees don't seem to sting anybody, but one doctor breaks his neck running away. This leaves three doctors, the minimum necessary so one can step in a beaver trap and two can quarrel unceasingly about whether to leave him behind. They don't.

But the other doctor comes back in time to join Holbrook and the stretcher case in discovering the impaled form of the doctor who went for help. Apparently overloaded with patients for the moment, Holbrook strangles him. And the other doctor runs off again.

Holbrook comes upon a cabin where a blind man says the unseen person is his brother. Amazingly, Holbrook never asks the blind man exactly what his brother is so upset about.

Never mind, for here comes a knife in the unseen hand, slashing Holbrook's leg through the artery. As it gushes, the other doctor turns up again, dangling and screaming from a tree outside.

The unseen person sets that doctor on fire as Holbrook explodes a shotgun shell in his wound to stop the bleeding, obviously a wilderness trick he didn't pick up at med school.

Finally, the unseen person gets to be seen, an apparent error on some-body's operating table. He's also missing a hand Holbrook just blew away with the shotgun.

Skipping over the conclusion, Holbrook finally makes it back to the highway, where he sits on the median stripe, seemingly grateful for no more holidays in store with that bunch. The gratitude is widely shared. —*Har.*

The March On Paris 1914
(COLOR-16M)

Hollywood, April 18.

Hawk Serpant Prods., Ltd., produced, directed and written by Walter Gutman. Features entire cast; camera (color), Gutman, Mike Cuchar; editor, Gutman, Shirley Clarke; music, Jessie Holladay Duane. No other credits available. Reviewed at the Royal Theatre, West L.A., April 18, '78. (No MPAA rating.) Running time: **75 MINS.**

Young von Kluck .... Wulf Brandes
Jessie Holladay ....Jessie Holladay Duane
Old von Kluck .... Barrows Mussey
Baroness von Dohop Frau Barrows Mussey

This is a witty and intriguing combination of history, romance, reverie and fantasy from Walter Gutman, 74-year-old stock market analyst, art critic and philosopher turned independent filmmaker. Using German General Alexander von Kluck's memoirs as source material and his own imagination to mold and reshape that history, Gutman has constructed a demanding film, one that will turn off most, but will appeal and fascinate the limited market for independent and experimental cinema.

The history behind this work is that von Kluck led the advance on Paris in 1914 and was turned back before he reached the city. Gutman probes that defeat using only his imagination, a very fertile source material. According to the filmmaker, von Kluck's downfall was a young American woman he met a few years before 1914.

The picture mixes contemporary settings in the French countryside and depictions of the love affair with military maps, remembrances by the filmmaker and narration taken from von Kluck's book. —*Hege.*

Attention, Les Enfants Regardent
(Attention, the Kids Are Watching)
(FRENCH-COLOR)

Paris, April 25.

United Artists release of Adel Productions-UA production. Stars Alain Delon. Directed by Serge Leroy. Screenplay, Christopher Frank, Leroy, from a book by Laird Koenig, Peter Dixon; camera (Eastmancolor), Claude Renoir; editor, Fernand Cespi. Reviewed at Publicis-Elysees, Paris, April 13, '78. Running time: **100 MINS.**

Man .... Alain Delon
Secretary .... Francoise Brion
Dimitri .... Richard Constantini
Marlene .... Sophie Renoir
Boule .... Thierry Torchet
Laetitia ....Tiphaine Leroux
Gardener ....Henri Vilbert
Policeman .... Marco Perrin

Alain Delon, star and producer of this tale of child psychology and suspense, does not really come into the pic until midway and is then dispatched by a batch of four supposedly rich, well-brought-up kids from 5 to 13 before the end. Pic lacks a true edge of menace and insight and is a predictable, familiar affair.

The film industry, fighting against too many pix shown on tv, too low prices for films and too many prime filmgoing time showings, may be trying to get back at video in this pic.

The kids live in a big house near the ocean with only a Spanish maid and the occasional visit of a secretary. They spend their time looking at tv, especially violent pix, from morn to night when they are not on the beach. Alongside the water one day they push the sleeping maid, on a rubber raft, into the water as a lark. But she floats out and awakes and gets hysterical for she cannot swim. The kids do make an attempt to save her, but she drowns.

Apparently an unkempt stranger, Delon, may have seen it. They decide to hush it up and go on an orgy of eating sweets in the well-stocked kitchen and making a mess of things. They manage to stave off people looking for the maid and even the secretary until one day Delon comes into the house. He had seen the drowning.

He terrorizes the kids and is apparently preparing to go off with the family car when he finds the key. The older girl decides to vamp him while the older boy, 12, gets one of daddy's guns, he is a collector, and starts shooting at Delon. Ironically, it is the exploding tv set that really gets him. Kids dispose of his body, insist the maid ran off, get the house cleaned up before acting angelic at the return of the parents.

Done better in "A High Wind in Jamaica," "Lord of the Flies," "Our Mother's House" and other films on moppet susceptibilities and cruelty, film still might have okay returns locally and in spots where Delon has a following. Delon cannot create the menace and disturbing qualities a film of this kind needs. Playoff in other climes is also indicated. — *Mosk.*

Solos En La Madrugada
(Alone At Daybreak)
(SPANISH-COLOR)

Madrid, April 16.

Jose Luis Tafur production. Directed by Jose Luis Garci. Screenplay, J.M. Gonzalez Sinde, J.L. Garci; camera (Eastmancolor), Manuel Rojas; music, Jesus Gluck; sets, Ramiro Gomez; editor, Miguel Gonzalez Sinde. Reviewed at Cine Carlos III (Madrid), April 15, '78. Running time: 103MINS.

Jose	Jose Sacristan
Elena	Fiorella Faltoyano
Maite	Emma Cohen
Lola	Maria Casanova
Antonio	Claudio Rodriguez

This film was largely made by the same group that scored with "Asignatura Pendiente" and is in a similar vein in that it nicely captures the feel and pulse of modern Madrid and bounces along with sprightly, intelligent dialogs and a winsome spontaneity.

However, script is less varied than its predecessor and the story more rambling and ultimately downbeat as its authors explore Spain's "postpartum blues" and delve into the world of disillusion and shattered college-day hopes.

Story gyrates about a loquacious disk jockey who broadcasts a radio show "Alone at Daybreak" every night during the wee hours. He is separated from his wife, has a fling at an affair with a "progressive" anthropologist and learns that his coworker at the radio station has been sweet on him since college days.

Garci purposely tries to keep the film as matter-of-fact as possible, but livens it up throughout with humor and wise cracking from Jose, who becomes a kind of symbol of the aimless "new Spain," and also of a generation of Spaniards now in their 30s who, once revolutionaries, have now slipped into a dull middle-class routine (home bickerings, intolerable Sunday outings with the kids and the patterns of tedium familiar to the Western world).

Pic nonetheless ends on a hopeful note, as the disk jockey ends his last program on the air and refuses a job in London, as he vows to live' life to the hilt and make improvements, starting with himself.

Sacristan plays the part of the alternately weary and ebullient deejay to perfection, and despite his overexposure on Spanish screens, comes across beautifully. Support by Fiorella Faltoyano and Emma Cohen are good and technical credits fine.

Though the pic is full of allusions to the local Spanish scene, and couched in a slang and jargon proper of Madrid, it might generate some interest on the fest circuits and other select playoff as a good example of contemporary Spanish cinema. — Besa.

Ann Arbor Film Fest

Showboat 1988
(COLOR)
Ann Arbor, March 20.
A Living Legend production. Filmed, directed, edited, and produced by Richard Schmidt. A film created by Henry Bean, Bill Farley, Nick Kazan, Joe DiVincenzo, Richard Schmidt, William Walker II, and Richard Richardson. Scripted by Bean, Farley, Kazan, and Schmidt. Cast: Ed Nylund, Skip Covington, Carolyn Zaremba, Richard A. Richardson, Willy Walker, others. No other credits provided. Reviewed at the Ann Arbor Film Festival, March 19, '78. Running time: 94 MINS.

For the second year running, feature film played a predominant role in Ann Arbor's experimental film festival. Rick Schmidt's "Showboat 1988" falls under the avant-garde category, but bears enough popular touches to make it with a crossover audience, even if the mixed format is somewhat unusual.

Financed with AFI funds, "Showboat 1988" recounts the fictitious tale of a middle-aged librarian's attempts to finance and remake the film musical, "Showboat," in contemporary terms. The auditions are arranged on a San Francisco stage, and range from incredible to merely bizarre. Director Rick Schmidt, under the remake pretext, actually enticed Bay Area would-be performers to these auditions which for the most part are "Gong Show" material, tap-dancing turtles and nuns and nudists. These frequently hilarious acts form the central core of the film, and are highly entertaining.

Since San Francisco tv stations picked up on the auditions, Schmidt managed to obtain their tapes and mix his footage with their interviews. The actual and the staged are often confused, and the layers of references pile up. Schmidt, in effect, has made a film about the remake of a film and added outsiders' footage of auditions. Nevertheless, the put-on is pulled off.
— Pege.

One Way Boogie Woogie
(COLOR)
Ann Arbor, April 1.
All technical credits by James Benning. Reviewed at Ann Arbor Film Festival, March 15, '78. Running time: 60 MINS.

James Benning took home last year's top prize at Ann Arbor for his mutated narrative, "11 x 14." "One Way Boogie Woogie" bears an unmistakably similar style with a bright, lab-treated colorization, an obsession with urban objects such as smokestacks and street signs, and the unexplained actions of characters. Whereas the barely perceptible story of "11 x 14" made these elements intriguing, Benning has removed any trace of overall connection in this new film. Instead, 60 one-minute shots contain as many visual anecdotes and puns, with little or no thematic segue.

A train is partially seen through a window, construction workers carry Mondrian works of art down the street, an industrial stack spews fire as Johnny Mathis croons "Chances Are," several Volkswagens drive into scenes. Every shot is a carefully-planned technical or illusionistic wonder, precisely staged and altered with negative, double exposure, or other lab technique, and most aim for a laugh.

The humor is highly accessible to those already conversant with the avant-garde scene, and while any one of the segments might tempt the interest of the mainstream, 60 at a shot makes the exercise more formally aesthetic than popularly aimed. —Pege.

The End
(COLOR)
Burt Reynolds stars-directs. Thin outlook.

Hollywood, April 24.
United Artists release, produced by Lawrence Gordon; executive producer, Hank Moonjean. Stars Burt Reynolds. Directed by Reynolds. Screenplay, Jerry Belson; camera (DeLuxe Color), Bobby Byrne; editor, Donn Cambern; music, Paul Williams; production design, Jan Scott; set decoration, John Franco Jr.; sound, Richard Portman, Jack Solomon; costumes-wardrobe, Norman Salling, Gene Deardorff, Violet Cane; asst. director, Kurt Baker; stunt coordinator, Hal Needham. Reviewed at MGM Studios. Culver City, April 24, '78. (MPAA Rating: R.) Running time: 100 MINS.

Sonny Lawson	Burt Reynolds
Marlon Borunki	Dom DeLuise
Mary Ellen	Sally Field
Dr. Kling	Strother Martin
Marty Lieberman	David Steinberg
Jessica	Joanne Woodward
Dr. Krugman	Norman Fell
Maureen Lawson	Myrna Loy
Julie Lawson	Kristy McNichol
Ben Lawson	Pat O'Brien
Priest	Robby Benson
Dr. Maneet	Carl Reiner
Pacemaker Patient	James Best
Old Man	Jock Mahoney

The rather complete failure of Jerry Belson's script — which seems a trunk item from those cute-weird cinema days a decade back — makes "The End" of "The End" come none too soon. Star-director Burt Reynolds, as a medically-doomed sharpie, exercises and exorcises his fears while milking sympathy from everyone available. Lawrence Gordon's production is a tasteless and overripe comedy that disintegrates very early into hysterical, undisciplined hamming. The United Artists release has limited commercial appeal.

For a few frames of the 100-minute film, Reynolds' bearded face suggests that there was some effort to project a different image; to transform his familiar and likable charisma into something different, befitting the last days of a carefree, selfish person who has been informed of fatal illness. Rather than improve the person's character, the script, direction and acting only make him even more shallow and selfish (save for a few flop attempts to make him warm and human).

There's little more to do now than list the featured players: Dom DeLuise, absolutely dreadful; Sally Field, phoning in a kooky-pretty role; David Steinberg, an outtake that crept back into the print; Joanne Woodward, poorly utilized though adroitly cast; Robby Benson, Carl Reiner, Strother Martin Myrna Loy and Pat O'Brien, all good ideas that got plowed under; Norman Fell, palatable.

Reynolds might be well advised to either act or direct, but not simultaneously. There's got to be something really wrong when a viewer, beyond simply turning off on a film, becomes embarrassed for the people on the screen. — *Murf.*

Petey Wheatstraw
(COLOR)

Comic black exploitation film. Crossover potential slight.

Hollywood, April 27.

A Tronsue Pictures Corp. release. Produced by Theadore Toney; exec producer, Burt Steiger. Stars Rudy Ray Moore. Written and directed by Cliff Roquemore; camera (Pacific Film Lab Color) Nickolas Von Sternberg; editors, Cecella Hall, Jack Tucker; assistant director, Ayanna Du-Laney. Reviewed at The Burbank Studios, Burbank, April 26, '78. (MPAA Rating: R.) Running time: **93 MINS.**

Cast: Rudy Ray Moore, Jimmy Lynch, Leroy & Skillet, Eboni Wryte, Wildman Steve, G. Tito Shaw, Lady Reed, Doc Watson.

Inspiration and intended audience for this film is black, hence this "comedy" should do well in those venues. White cross-over potential would seem to be nil.

Rudy Ray Moore, who has established a name for himself as Mr. "Dolemite" returns as the title character, affectionately dubbed "the devil's son-in-law," a status Moore spends most of the film trying to avoid. Like Redd Foxx, Moore began on the chitterlin' circuit and built up his following via X-rated party records.

From its voodoo hoodoo beginning, "Wheatstraw" apparently gives Moore's fans what they're looking for: broad, slapstick humor based around every sexual, racial and toilet joke imaginable. Pic opens with the birth of Petey (Moore), a scene right out of "Uncle Tom's Cabin," as the boy is preceded by a watermelon, while family and friends roll their eyes and mug for the camera.

The youngster gets some karate training from an elderly black guru, but then, everybody in the film seems a karate expert, too, if the many fight scenes are any indication. These come to the fore when Petey arrives in an unnamed burg just when the black comedy team of Leroy and Skillet are planning a big show of their own.

Since the comedy team's show is financed by the only white character in the pic (appropriately named Mr. White), they have to get Petey out of the way, a feat accomplished by murdering an eight-year-old boy and then wiping out the mourners at the child's funeral.

Some 20 bleeding bodies might not qualify as comedy in some people's minds, but the fun is just beginning. Lucifer appears to restore everyone to life, on the condition that Petey marry his ugly-as-sin daughter and give him a grandchild. In exchange, he gives Petey a magic

cane, with which Moore destroys Leroy and Skillet's show (one of the few genuinely humorous scenes in the pic).

Attempting to welsh on Satan, Petey and friends try to hightail it out of town, but the devil sends his minions after him to collect on the wedding promise. These junior devils resemble a bad "Gong Show" act, with taped-on little horns and pink tights, and they prove just as ineffectual. Only frightening moment results in pic's final scene, in which Petey finally gets his just desserts.

Moore is by no means a polished actor, but he delivers his particular brand of humor forcefully. Supporting cast can't break out of the racial stereotypes forced on them by writer-director Cliff Roquemore, other than G. Tito Shaw, who registers strongly as the devil. Eboni Wryte adds some flash as Moore's good-looking girlfriend.

Tech credits are generally poor, exception being sturdy lensing by Nickolas Von Sternberg. Dialog looping was way, off, however, and uncredited r&b score especially strident.

One doesn't hear too much about black exploitation pictures any more, although "Petey Wheatstraw" threatens to bring the genre back single-handedly. —*Poll.*

Sweeney 2
(BRITISH-COLOR)

Entertaining cops-and-crooks action for the program trade.

London, April 19.

EMI Film Distributors release of a Euston Films production, produced by Ted Childs. Features entire cast. Exec producers, Lloyd Shirley, George Taylor. Directed by Tom Clegg. Screenplay, Troy Kennedy Martin; camera (Technicolor), Dusty Miller; music, Tony Hatch; art director, Bill Alexander; editor, Chris Burt; sound, Derek Rye; assistant director, Bill Westley. Reviewed at ABC Shaftesbury Ave. Theatre, London, April 18, '78. Running time: **108 MINS.**

Regan	John Thaw
Carter	Dennis Waterman
Jupp	Denholm Elliott
Switchboard girl	Georgina Hale
Dilke	Nigel Hawthorne
Gorran	Lewis Fiander
Jellyneck	James Warrior
Willard	John Flanagan
Goodyear	David Casey
Llewlyn	Derrick O'Connor
Daniels	John Alkin
Soames	Michal Jackson
Hill	Ken Hutchison
White	Brian Gwaspari
Duncan Mead	John Lyons
Morris Haughton	Brian Hall
Jefferson	Matthew Scurfield
Mrs. Hill	Anna Gael
Mrs. White	Lynn Dearth
Mrs. Haughton	Fiona Mollison
Mrs. Mead	Sarah Atkinson

With: George Mikell, Marc Zuber, Leon Lissek, Stefan Gryff, Diana Weston, Anna Nygh, George Innes, Roddy McMillan.

"Sweeney 2" is excellent British cops and robbers stuff in which a

special squad of Scotland Yard detectives ultimately crack and demolish a gang of bank robbers whose hallmarks include gold-plated shotguns. Good action well-spaced and paced; good characterization played with finesse; a witty script and stylish direction all lend the Ted Childs production a degree of distinction.

Prospects are bright in Blighty and certain other territories where the title and key characters have strong longrun tv series identification. But the heavily idiomatic and occasionally slurred lingo figures to dim potential U.S. appreciation, as and when a distrib is lined up. Not for the first time with an Anglo entry, Yankee subtitles would be very much in order. No kidding.

The villains of the piece are a quirky bunch of lammisters who've set their families up as a colony on a Mediterranean island from which they commute to London for periodic bank jobs to pay the rent. A farfetched angle, but it doesn't damage the basic plot.

Thesping is good to excellent. John Thaw, top-featured, is credible and appealing as the hardbitten cop who leads the police team on the case. Also notably fine are Denholm Elliott as a corrupt police officer who lands in the jug, Dennis Waterman as Thaw's number two, and Georgina Hale as a pickup promoted by the unattached Thaw.

Tom Clegg's direction is not only professionally accomplished but often acutely observant. There's some naturalistic rough language but never in gratuitous amounts. Also mayhem and gore, particularly at the end when the remaining bandits are vanquished, but again within acceptable limits overall. There's no apparent attempt, in short, to suck up to baser emotions — just one point in the film's favor.

The script by Troy Kennedy Martin abounds with humorous touches, and the plotting contains some amusing tangents — a go-between dame with a Hitler fetish, for one; a bomb-defusing sequence in a hotel for another.

Dusty Miller's photography, though at times overlighted, is generally firstrate, ditto the unobtrusive music by Tony Hatch. All other craft elements are fine.

The digit in the title, of course, marks a sequel to the initial theatrical spinoff of a couple years back, but never picked up in the U.S. Modest as to budget, the new one nonetheless crams a lot of value up on the screen. —*Pit.*

Giselle
(W. GERMAN-COLOR)

Uneven adaptation of ballet. Appeal limited to dance clubs and retrospectives.

Hollywood, April 26.

International TV Trading Corp. release of a Unitel production. Exec producer, Fritz Buttenstedt. Director, Hugo Niebeling. Based on the ballet "Giselle" by Adolphe Adam, libretto by Vernoy de Saint-Georges, Theophile L. Gautier, Jean Coralli; camera (uncredited color), Wolfgang Treu; editor Niebeling; set design, Georges Wakhevitch, Oliver Smith; costumes, Peter Hall, Jeanne Renucci-Wakhevitch. Reviewed at Westland I Theatre, West L.A., April 25, '78. (No MPAA rating) Running time: **95 MINS.**

Giselle	Carla Fracci
Count Albrecht	Eric Bruhn
Hklarion	Bruce Marks
Myrtha	Toni Lander
Peasant	Eleanor D'Antuono
Peasant	Ted Kivitt

Ballet is not the easiest art form to transfer to film. That adage is reaffirmed with "Giselle," an ambitious production that attempts to meet the requirements of both dance and cinema, and ends up satisfying neither. Outlook would seem confined to ballet groups and repetory houses doing dance retrospectives. (Pic was shown in N.Y. recently on a "dance film" series — Ed.)

This American Ballet Theatre production was filmed in Spain in 1968 for German tv by Munich's Unitel, while the American dance company was on a European tour. "Giselle," of course, is a classic in ballet repertory, and original choreography by Jules Perrot and Jean Coralli is very stylish.

Unfortunately, at least for filmmakers, ballet is best appreciated when viewer can take in the entire scope fo the production, and not isolated shots of feet, arms or single dancers. Director Hugo Niebeling alternates between expansive camera angles (with even some Busby Berkeley overhead shots) and tight closeups, but the power and thrust of Adolphe Adam's work is greatly diminished.

Not helping matters is Niebeling's Bergman-esque sense of editing. This version of "Giselle" is full of crooked angles, half-lit visages and a running string of shots that resemble a face behind barbed wire. Against the extreme naturalism of Georges Wakhevitch and Oliver Smith's sets, German expressionist stylings give the pic an unreal, choppy look.

Costumes by Peter Hall and Jeanne Renucci-Wakhevitch are stunners, and give viewers something to look at for 95 minutes, because as presented, the story line of the ballet is difficult to follow. After all, when shots of various legs predominate, it's difficult to tell which gams belong to whom.

There is no dialog whatsoever in "Giselle," and even balletomanes may find themselves listening for the applause after various solos that never comes. But Carla Fracci is superb as Giselle, Eric Bruhn commendable as her aristocrat-in-disguise lover, and Ted Kivitt and Eleanor D'Antuono shine in their peasant pas de deux.

As ballet, "Giselle" is stunning. As a film, however, it borders on the tedious. — *Poll.*

La Ultima Cena
(The Last Supper)
(CUBAN-COLOR)

Tricontinental Film Center release of a production by the Instituto Cubano Del Arte y Industria Cinematograficos. Produced by Santiago Llapur and Camilo Vives. Directed by Tomas Gutierrez Alea. Features entire cast. Screenplay, Tomas Gonzalez, Maria Eugenia Haya and Alea; camera (color) Mario Garcia Joya; editor, Nelson Rodriguez; music, Leo Brouwer. Reviewed at Magno Theatre, N.Y., April 19, '78. Running time: **110 MINS.**
With Nelson Villagra, Silvano Rey, Luis Alberto Garcia, Jose Antonio Rodriguez, Samuel Claxton and Mario Balmaseda.
(Spanish language — English subtitles)

The parable behind "The Last Supper" — in which a penitent 18th century Cuban landowner reenacts Christ's final meal with 12 of his black slaves as "apostles," then finds himself faced with a plebian uprising — is the kind that might have set Luis Bunuel's anti-seminarian eyes a-twinkling, at least from the ecclesiastic ironies that cry out from the basic plotline.

As a prime example of New Cuban Cinema, however, and helmed by Tomas Gutierrez Alea director of "Memories of Underdevelopment," revolutionary consciousness reigns supreme, with typical effects on the net result. Though finely acted and streaked with moments of wry perception, the pic doesn't know when its cards are fully stacked and overemphasizes its political barbs to an ultimate point of redundancy and longwindedness. Specialized urban and college bookings in U.S. are probable best chances.

The pity of it is that the film's concept — and much of its content — is intelligent and workable. Dubbing itself "an allegory of Christian liberalism," pic scores in observing the scions of wealth and aristocracy using church dogma to reinforce their own power. Basic rationalization employed by the landowners is historically a familiar one: the vain assumption that slaves and peasantry would always be content with their lot in life, no matter how brutal or inhumane, as long as they could be persuaded that their reward would be even greater than their masters' when they died and made it to heaven.

Centerpiece of the film, which opens with the sadistic recapture of a perpetually escaping slave, is the brainstorm of plantation owner Nelson Villagra to demonstrate his Holy Week humility by replaying the Last Supper with 12 slaves as apostles. Urging them to momentarily forget their shackles and think of him as a brother, Villagra adopts the guise of wine-induced humanity and liberalism, a self-congratulatory "treat" that successfully convinces the slaves of their master's warm Christian spirit.

Next morning, though, their glee proves short-lived; confronted with a large sugar-quota, Villagra decides he's done enough.

A brutal revolt ensues, terminating in a hunt for the "apostles," all of whom are beheaded except for the one rebellious spirit who finally manages to escape at fadeout.

Script, which Alea co-wrote with Maria Eugenia Haya and Tomas Gonzalez, makes canny capital of the twisted catechism Villagra uses to sell slaves on hopes of a better after-life, also casting the fine black cast as witty, occasionally razor-edged mouthpieces for the underlying spirit of would-be freedom and dignity that, frustrated, eventually fires them into violence.

But it all does tend to go on and the film's prime message — that there is no such thing as "a little bit" of freedom or "temporary" liberty — has been made and remade at least a half-hour before the film grinds to its predictable ending.

Technical credits are good.
—*Step.*

FM
(COLOR)

Flawed look at life at an FM radio station. Hazy outlook outside big cities.

Hollywood, April 18.

Universal Pictures release, produced by Rand Holston; co-producer, Robert Larson. Directed by John A. Alonzo. Features entire cast. Screenplay, Ezra Sacks; camera (Technicolor), David Myers; editor, Jeff Gourson; production design, Lawrence G. Paull; sound (Dolby), Bruce Bisenz; assistant director, Bert Gold; costume design, Kent Warner. Reviewed at Universal Studios, L.A., April 18, '78. (MPAA Rating: PG.) Running time: **104 MINS.**
Jeff Dugan . . . . Michael Brandon
Mother . . . . Eileen Brennan
Doc Holiday . . . . Alex Karras
Prince . . . . Cleavon Little
Eric Swan . . . . Martin Mull
Laura Coe . . . . Cassie Yates
Carl Billings . . . . Norman Lloyd
Bobby Douglas . . . . Jay Fenichel
Lt. Reach . . . . James Keach
Albert Driscoll . . . . Joe Smith
Regis Lamar . . . . Tom Tarpey
Special concert appearances by Linda Ronstadt and Jimmy Buffet.

"FM" is the modern equivalent of the 1930s newspaper film, all break-neck dialog, quirky happenstances and behind-the-scenes drama transposed to a 1970s rock radio station.

Unlike such classics as the original "Front Page," however, this Universal release goes nowhere with a potentially-fascinating set of plot elements. Despite star-studded soundtrack, outlook is hazy outside of major metropolitan centers.

Controversy has surrounded this production ever since its inception, with former exec producer Irving Azoff asking his name be removed from screen credits, and Universal complying. There have also been public skirmishes between creative personnel from both film and music areas over which influence should dominate in "FM". The end result: a seriously flawed picture.

Ezra Sacks' script presents station WSKY and its staff of deejays, under station manager Michael Brandon's stewardship, as a group of hardworking, funloving staffers who just want to play their form of beautiful music. Enter ad salesman Tom Tarpey, who on orders from broadcast v.p. Joe Smith, is out to sell WSKY's rate card to the highest commercial bidder, in this case, the U.S. Army, as represented by recruiter James Keach.

Brandon puts his foot down and quits in protest, sparking the rest of the staff to barricade themselves in the station and broadcast "the music you really want to hear." A riot develops outside the station, until corporate bigwig Norman Lloyd arrives on the scene, and pardons the frivolous, but gutsy, youngsters.

The strength of Sacks' script, as is obvious, lies not in the situation, but in the characters with which he peoples the radio station. Among the deejays, Cleavon Little, Eileen Brennan, Alex Karras or Martin Mull could each merit a film in his or her own right. But in John A. Alonzo's directorial debut, these personalities get swept under the rug, replaced by drawn-out concert sequences featuring Linda Ronstadt and Jimmy Buffet.

Both musicians will probably add marquee value to "FM," but they don't make it a better film. Shoehorning of current musical hits into an otherwise dramatically-valid pic may help in the short run, but film will be dated that much sooner, and appeal will be strictly limited to those already addicted to the kind of rock showcased here.

Brandon does his best to hold the film together with a strong and resonant performance, but it's a lost cause. Brennan, Karras and Little are reduced to little more than walk-on cameos, a tremendous waste of talent.

Making his film and dramatic debut, **Martin Mull comes as close to walking away with the pic as any-** one. As cosmic deejay Eric Swan, Mull is the apotheosis of hip FM gibberish, complete with on-air chimes.

Adding excellent support are Casie Yates, Jay Fenichel, a would-be jock, Tom Tarpey as the earnest salesman and Robert Patten as Mull's sleazy agent.

Elektra/Asylum Records chairman Joe Smith is okay as corporate heavy, but James Keach overdoes his bit as the pot-smoking recruiter. Rest of casting is solid.

Lawrence Paull's FM radio set perfectly imparts an L.A. slickness without overdoing the effect, and action surrounding it is beautifully lensed by David Meyers. Alonzo's background as a top cinematographer certainly helps the visual look of "FM," but dramatically, the pic lacks punch.

List of soundtrack artists resembles a who's who of popular music biz. Disk sales should help cross-pollinate pic's appeal, but in this case, the album's better than the film. —*Poll.*

Hot Tomorrows

Meditation on death. Martin Brest's first.

Hollywood, April 22.

An American Film Institute production, produced, directed, written and edited by Martin Brest. Stars Ken Lerner, Ray Sharkey, Herve Villechaize, Victor Argo, George Memdli. Camera (black & white)-associate producer, Joacques Haitkin; choreographer, Lloyd Gordon; production manager-line producer, Fredic Shore; sound, Mark Bovos. Reviewed at the Royal Theatre, West L.A., April 21, '78. (No MPAA rating.) Running time: **73 MINS.**
Michael . . . . Ken Lerner
Louis . . . . Ray Sharkey
Alberict . . . . Herve Villechaize
Tony . . . . Victor Argo
Man in Mortuary . . . . George Memmoli
Night Embalmer . . . . Donne Daniels
Tante Ethel . . . . Dr. Rose Marshall
Lecturer . . . . Paul Schumacher

It's an accomplishment to produce a full-length feature for $30,000, but to turn out a sensitive, funny and entertaining one on that budget is a miracle. That's what Martin Brest has done with his first feature, "Hot Tomorrows."

It's a simple film with a slight plot. A transplanted New Yorker is living in LA. trying to make it as a writer. He's obsessed by death and is writing a series of short stories about an elderly aunt. A childhood friend is out on the coast visiting him and they spend Christmas Eve wandering around Hollywood. They visit his apartment, a mortuary, the Paradise Ballroom, a coffee shop and later to an old people's home. A tragedy at the end of the evening ties everything together.

The film is about the writer's obsession and in many ways this is a meditation on death. There are funny moments, but the picture is mostly downbeat, shot in black and white and only 73 minutes long, so the commercial possibilities are limited. But the cult audiences are out there and the film would connect with students and college markets.

Like Martin Scorsese's early films — "Who's That Knocking At My Door" and "Mean Streets"— this is a difficult work to describe. Not much happens. The two friends meet an odd duo early ih the evening and they have a weird encounter at the mortuary. They watch a Laurel & Hardy film. They drive around Hollywood.

Ken Lerner plays the writer and Ray Sharkey the friend, kind of a jerk, but likable and loyal. The acting has a sponteneous, effortless quality. Brest wrote, edited, produced and directed and Jacques Haitkin photographed the film in appropriately moody tones. The film was backed by the American Film Institute. — *Hege.*

Les Routes Du Sud
(The Roads Of The South)
(FRENCH-COLOR)

Paris, May 2.
Parafrance release of Trinacra Films-FR3-Profilmes production. Stars Yves Montand, Miou-Miou. Directed by Joseph Losey. Screenplay, Jorge Semprun, Losey, Patricia Losey; camera (Eastmancolor), Gerry Fisher; editor, Reginald Beck; art director, Alexandre Trauner; producer, Yves Rousset-Rouard; music, Michel Legrande. Reviewed at Antegor, Paris, April 25, '78. Running time: **97 MINS.**
Larrea .... Yves Montand
Julia .... Miou-Miou
Laurent .... Laurent Malet
Eve .... France Lambiotte
Miguel .... Jose Luis Gomez
Metayer .... Jean Bouise
Garcia .... Maurice Benichou

Joseph Losey's second film in French, after "Mr. Klein," is a film which deals with a political activist who seems to be losing his faith in his long fight against the Spain of Franco, which intrudes upon his personal life.

Yves Montand lends his intense presence to this figure who feels the past is necessary to understand the present and begins to live too much with his memories. Film seems to be a followup to Alain Resnais's "The War Is Over," also with Montand, also scripted by Jorge Semprun and about an anti-Franco leftist militant.

Fact is, pic appears to be a fictionalized aspect of Semprun's political life. But Resnais's more hermetic, probing of memory and time is here given a spacious feel by Losey's fairly subtle and perceptive direction. His usual punchy visuals only perk up this quietly flowing film, as when Montand suddenly plays Russian roulette before his son who then grabs the pistol to

have it deflected by someone, go off and break a mirror.

Otherwise, the film has a tendency to be a sort of lament for lost political causes with the characters more mouthpieces than fully developed personages. This may be the result of their beliefs and vacillations. Montand has a strained relation with his 23-year-old son, played with effective tension by Laurent Malet, and even his wife who is perhaps more militant than he is.

The film takes place during the year of Franco's death. Montand has left Spain as a young boy, become involved iñ the anti-Franco leftist cause and been a resistant in France during the Occupation. Now he is a film scriptwriter and still militant but less wholeheartedly. As his wife puts it, they may have lost some of their certainty, but not their illusions.

Montand's wife goes on a mission which leads to her having an accident and dying. The son, already estranged from Montand, and who is against all political sentiment, can hardly forgive him. But a friend of the son, a free living girl played with pert shrewdness by Miou-Miou, has a brief affair with Montand and leads to his finding out his wife had a liaison with a Spanish contact when she finds her diary.

Splintered through it, in reflecting his thoughts, is an idea Montand is working on for a film about the German private who tried to warn the Russians of the impending German invasion in the last war only to be shot as a provocateur on Stalin's orders. This recurring image is a leit motif that might mirror Montand's growing disillusionment with the Spanish underground left and his own actions.

The death of Franco leaves the dissidents somewhat baffled, but still feeling their past will make them effective in a coming democratized Spain. Perhaps too elegant at times for its theme, pic still holds interest and builds a web of emotional, political and human motives that may help this at the wickets. albeit needing care in its handling. Festival outings should also help. Fine production and technical aspects are added assets.
—Mosk.

L'Etat Sauvage
(The Savage State)
(FRENCH-COLOR)

Paris, April 18.
Gaumont release of Films 66-Gaumont production. Stars Marie-Christine Barrault, Michel Piccoli, Claude Brasseur, Jacques Dutronc. Directed by Francis Girod. Screenplay, Georges Conchon, Girod from book by Conchon; camera (Eastmancolor), Pierre Lhomme; editor, Genevieve Winding; music, Pierre Jensen. Reviewed at Salle Ponthieu, Paris, April 12, -'78. Running time, **111 MINS.**

Laurence .... Marie-Christine Barrault
Gravenoire .... Claude Brasseur
Orlaville .... Michel Piccoli
Avit .... Jacques Dutronc
Doumbe .... Doura Mane
Modimbo .... Baaron
Tristan .... Rudiger Vogler

Based on a prizewinning novel, film is a highly dramatic look at a new African state in the 1960s. It zeroes in on the racism of both whites and blacks. A French woman is living with a "progressive" Minister of the state.

A blonde, good looking, heavyset French woman had left her plodding civil servant husband to run off to this new mythical Afro nation with a ruthless adventurer. There she leaves the adventurer to take up with the local Minister of Health. The spurned man, who has made money photographing the natives, is also involved in deals to get France a first crack at handling the country's uranium.

The Minister is for giving Russia and many other countries a chance to bid. The Frenchman, for revenge and for his commission, decides to try to get the Minister. Some murky machinations appear as the woman's husband, now with UNESCO, is sent on a culture mission through the French company opting for the uranium.

Arriving in the country, he is soon involved in a series of political and amorous adventures.

Some characters skirt stereotypes of the literature and films of the white man and colonies, in this case Africa. Jacques Dutronc, however, as the weak, meandering husband who finally shows some grit, has a presence that overcomes his worm-turning personage and raises it. Michel Piccoli, as a grizzled police chief who cannot stop these manifestations, is also effective.

Marie-Christine Barrault is somewhat too placid as a woman who has opted to go her own way due to her boredom with her husband and hatred of the man she ran off with. Claude Brasseur has the rabid vulgarity for this role. Director Francis Girod, who was more fervid and punchy in his previous pix, here is more reserved and misses a needed final epiphany of force.

Pic finale is somewhat mismanaged, with some inept dialog also distracting from its needed force. Film's theme, rare these days, about a Continent now in the news, could make for good local chances. Production and technical aspects are good. —*Mosk.*

In Alle Stilte
(In All Intimacy)
(BELGIAN-COLOR)

Brussels, April 25.
Promofilm production and release. Produced by Renaat Rombouts. Directed by Ralf Boumans. Stars Mark Bober, Johan Leysen, Peggy De Landtsheer. Screenplay, Ralf Boumans, Ria Aerts; camera (Eastmancolor), Willem Baeckelmans; editor, Henri Erismann; art direction, Philippe Graff; sound, Koen Pee; music, Franz Schubert with arrangements by Pieter Verlinden. Reviewed at Cinema Marivaux, Brussels, April 24, '78. Running time, **93 MINS.**
Fred .... Mark Bober
Peter .... Johan Leysen
Isabel .... Peggy De Landtsheer
Mother .... Yvonne Mertens
Liza .... Paula Sleyp
Priest .... Nolle Verzijp
Suzy .... Beatrice Janssens
Gerda .... Netty Vangheel
Ellie .... Sien Eggers
Mrs. Lea .... Mieke Verheyden
Mrs. Persu .... Line Geysen
Neighbor .... Blanca Heirman
Alex .... Peter Strynckx
Washerwoman .... Lia Lee
Servant .... Magda De Winter
Fred, 8 yrs. ...... Ludo Van Fraeyenhoven
Peter, 8 yrs. .... Ronny Van de Loop
Usabel, 8 yrs. .... Ise Arnould

A love story? In a way. Film about a true friendship? There is something of this, too, in Ralf Boumans' first fiction film. Drawback is a frail storyline that almost constantly strays from two main themes losing dramatic impact through too many irrelevant details. Flashbacks don't serve clarity either.

Still, in spite of many flaws typical of filmmakers in search of a definite style, "In All Intimacy" is not devoid of assets, main one being the use of natural settings, in this instance a picturesque village in the Belgian Ardennes.

For its genuine bucolic charm, well-captured by Willem Baeckelmans' attentive camera, some dull stretches have a chance of being overlooked. In fact this is typical of the school of young Belgian film directors: they have an eye for nature but seem unable to limit themselves to the essentials.

Fred, a 28-year-old woodcutter acting occasionally as gravedigger, has always been in love with Isabel. But he is shy and social differences exist. One day, an old friend, Peter, reappears. Latter has just separated from his wife, he is in need of companionship and Fred takes him in. During that stay he discovers Fred's secret love for Isabel. The love-starved girl literally throws herself into Peter's arms but he refuses her. Desperate, she loses control of her car and is killed. For three days Fred stays by the body but, finally, with Peter's help, is restored to reality.

Script won a state prize, but seems to have been watered down in the making. One feels seldom moved, nor concerned, even though playing by three principals is not without merit. Tighter editing might have improved some languid passages. —*Flor*.

The Greek Tycoon
(COLOR)

Thinly disguised, lush-trashy biopic of Jackie Kennedy and Aristotle Onassis. Big B.O. outlook.

Hollywood, May 5.

A Universal Pictures release of an Abkco Films production, produced by Allen Klein and Ely Landau; executive producers, Mort Abrahams, Peter Howard and Les Landau. Stars Anthony Quinn and Jacqueline Bisset. Directed by J. Lee Thompson. Screenplay, Mort Fine from a story by Nico Mastorakis, Win Wells and Fine; camera (Technicolor), Tony Richmond; production design, Michael Stringer; editor, Alan Strachan; music, Stanley Myers; art director, Tony Readin, Gene Gurlitz, Mel Bourne; set decorator, Vernon Dixon; sound, Robin Gregory; assistant director, Ariel Levy; co-producers, Nico Mastorakis, Lawrence Myers; associate producer, Eric Rattray. Reviewed at Universal Studios, L.A., May 5, '78. (MPAA rating: R.) Running time: **106 MINS.**

Theo Tomasis	Anthony Quinn
Liz Cassidy	Jacqueline Bisset
Spyros Tomasis	Raf Vallone
Nico Tomasis	Edward Albert
James Cassidy	James Franciscus
Simi Tomasis	Camilla Sparv
Sophia Matalas	Marilu Tolo
Michael Russel	Charles Durning
Paola Scotti	Luciana Paluzzi
John Cassidy	Robin Clarke
Nancy Cassidy	Kathryn Leigh Scott

As a thinly disguised biopic of Aristotle Onassis and Jacqueline Kennedy Onassis — accent on thinly disguised — "The Greek Tycoon" has the conviction of its subject. It's a trashy, opulent, vulgar, racy picture. The originals sold more tabloids than Cher, Cheryl Ladd and Farrah Fawcett-Majors combined and made the novels of Harold Robbins seem like documentaries. You've watched the headlines, now you can read the movie.

Plenty of people will — the film has ingredients. It's got Anthony Quinn and Jacqueline Bisset starring as the jetsetters; a $6,500,000 budget with production values to match; glamorous locations; and a tale of love, tragedy, divorce, politics and sex. How can it miss? Outlook is strong across the board for the Universal pickup.

Mort Fine's script begins with Quinn as Theo Tomasis returning from a business trip. He greets his wife, wades through the guests at his island manor searching for his son and quickly spots Jackie B. with her husband Senator James Cassidy.

Part of the charm of this film is how closely the actors resemble the real life celebrities Universal will swear they're not portraying. Bisset is a dead ringer for Jackie Kennedy as is Quinn for Onassis.

The story moves quickly onto Quinn's yacht, actually a $20,000,000 cruiser lent to the producers by American millionaire William Levitt. The Cassidys are persuaded to join the affair and while the senator is immersed in conversation with a former British prime minister, Quinn lays the seeds for his own affair.

Meanwhile, Quinn multiplies his millions by buying a fleet of tankers and an airline. He gives his handsome, daredevil son a start in business with advice that blackmail is part of commerce, needles his brother, and tortures his wife by sleeping around.

Finally, Bissett, who's now the president's wife, takes a cruise with the magnetic magnate. After her husband is assassinated and a complicated marriage contract drawn up, the knot is tied.

The film is lush with scenery, schmaltzy dialog and plot. We're to believe that money can't buy happiness, although it can make people ridiculously comfortable. This is supposed to be fiction. Quinn is most comfortable, however, with peasants. Two of the picture's best scenes show him dancing at a modest restaurant and at the end of the film, after he's a broken man following his son's death, with humble fisherman.

Quinn is fabulous as Tomasis, a charming, wealthy, conniving and influential tycoon. He's the center of the film and his shoulders capably support the production. Raf Vallone as Quinn's brother, James Franciscus as President Cassidy, Edward Albert as Quinn's son and the always reliable Charles Durning as Quinn's lawyer and later attorney general, all turn in good performances. As Liz Cassidy, Bisset capitalizes on her looks, but her accent seems off for the part and much of the acting is just posing.

All production values are handsome and some of Tony Richmond's photography stunning. J. Lee Thompson capably directed Fine's script from a story by Nico Mastorakis, Win Wells and Fine.
— *Hege*.

It Lives Again
(COLOR)

Murderous babies back again. For them what responds, previously numerous.

Burbank, May 4.

A Warner Bros. release, produced, directed and written by Larry Cohen. Camera (Technicolor), Fenton Hamilton; editors, Curt Burch, Louis Friedman, Carol O'Blath; assistant director, Reid Freeman; sound, Ken Scrivener; music, Bernard Herrmann, with additional music by Laurie Johnson. Reviewed at The Burbank Studios, May 4, '78. (MPAA Rating: R.) Running time: **91 MINS.**

Eugene Scott	Frederic Forrest
Jody Scott	Kathleen Lloyd
Frank Davis	John P. Ryan
Mallory	John Marley
Dr. Perry	Andrew Duggan
Dr. Forest	Eddie Constantine
Det. Perkins	James Dixon

In his sequel to "It's Alive," which has racked up a surprising $6,800,000 in rentals to date, Larry Cohen aims squarely at the same audience, which should be attracted back for more of the murderous babies.

As in the original, producer-director-writer Cohen does not show a lot of the demonic infants nor explain what they really are. But whatever got into the blood of the first mom is now rampant through the country and they're aborning everywhere, threatening the survival of humanity.

Though this is all so much silliness, Cohen effectively uses a good cast topped by Frederic Forrest and Kathleen Lloyd to build up suspense for the slashing, growling attacks by the terrible tykes.

John P. Ryan reappears as the father of the first little killer, now gone a bit goofy by the whole experience. Guilty at the destruction of his own son, Ryan has joined with scientists Andrew Duggan (also in the original) and Eddie Constantine to save the kids and tame them.

Equally determined to wipe them all out is John Marley, a cop whose own wife was torn asunder at the nascent stage.

Caught between are Forrest and his expectant wife, Lloyd. Like Ryan, they wish their kid was better-behaved but really don't want to join forces with the 10 jillion cops out to chop them down with machine guns.

Since the babies are fairly defenseless except at close range, Cohen must go to ridiculous lengths to get his well-armed characters into vulnerable positions, wrapping up with a totally absurd police siege. When the kids are about to bite, though, it's good horror-house fun and that's apparently what the initial fans came for. —*Har*.

Newsfront
(AUSTRALIAN-COLOR, B&W)

Sydney, April 14.

A Roadshow release of a Palm Beach Pictures Production. Produced by David Elfick. Features entire cast. Directed by Phillip Noyce. Screenplay, Noyce, based on a concept by Elfick; camera (Panavision-color/b&w), Vince Monton; sound, Tim Lloyd; production design, Lissa Coote; art direction, Larry Eastwood; graphic design, Lee Whitmore; special effects, Kim Hilder; editor, John Scott; music, William Motzing. (Censorship rating undetermined). Reviewed at United Sound Theatrette, Sydney, April 13, '78. Running time: **110 MINS.**

Len Maguire	Bill Hunter
Frank Maguire	Gerard Kennedy
Fay Maguire	Angela Punch
Amy McKenzie	Wendy Hughes
Chris Hewett	Chris Hayward
Charlie	John Ewart
A.G. Marawood	Don Crosby
Ken	John Dease
Cliff	John Clayton
Geoff	Bryan Brown
Greasy	Tony Barry

Bruce .... Drew Forsythe
Ellie .... Lorna Leslie

———

Set in an historically turbulent period for Australia, "Newsfront" deals with the lives of movie newsreel cameraman and uses the events in which they are involved as a sort of microcosmic view of how, in a very short period of time, the country underwent remarkable socio-political change.

In the years 1949-56, Australia was being continuously buffeted by recurrent shock waves of one sort or another, be they cultural, social, political or technological; and the narrative intermingles actual events and fictional plot-lines in a movie version of the literary style of John Dos Passos.

The approach is interesting and the film benefits greatly from two central strengths: history and Hunter (as Len Maguire). The actor turns in a strong performance as the self-effacing, unassertive brother and paradoxically dominates the film. In his feature film debut, director Phillip Noyce demonstrates his ability to deal with actors, narrative, and choreograph . background activity: he shows remarkable skill and is clearly a talent to watch.

By clever merging of b&w newsreel footage and scenario-inspired monochromatic sequences, he moves his film into and out of actuality and fiction in such a way as often to blur the edges so well that it frequently takes a conscious effort to detect the blend-point. his is especially true in one of his major setpieces re-creating the disastrous floods in the Maitland area in the early 50s; here he effectively uses directed drama and newsreel intercuts to create a cinematic synergism that comes off superbly.

Whether what is on screen is color or black & white seems to depend on the mood of the film at the time — not, albeit, an innovative technique, necessarily, but one used most effectively in this particular context and its success lifts the film immeasurably.

Plot concerns the rivalry between two competing newsreel companies: Len works for the plodding, traditionally-valued, Aussie-owned Cinetone, and ambitious brother Frank has left them to run the go-ahead, pushy, Yank-owned Newsco. (It's no great exercise to discern that the two and their approach to their business are based on real-life rivals, Cinesound and Movietone; the former operated by Greater Union here, the latter by Fox).

Events and technology (in the form of television) overtake the movie newsreels: just as Frank moves on to Hollywood and higher aspirations while Len remains to observe and log Australia's future shock as and when it happens.

Important contemporaneous events such as the 1951 referendum on banning the Communist Party have their effect on the characters personal lives, fomenting family crises and profound clashes. In this case, religio-political differences between Len and his wife Fay, a devout Catholic, are triggered by his pro-Labor stance and serve to exacerbate the already nagging sexual disillusionment within the marriage.

Acting performances are all fine, particularly Angela Punch as the embittered wife, John Dease as the voice-over man, and Chris Hayward as the brash Britisher who gets a job as a camera assistant.

You don't have to be Australian to get the most out of "Newsfront" because the storyline is about humans, but the historical scaffolding on which it is pinned is, all the same, perhaps more easily comprehended Down Under.

Tech' credits are uniformly excellent with a particular nod to cinematographer Vince Monton, who has done a monumental job of matching shots and lighting, and editor John Scott who has here a remarkable achievement. Mention must also be made of the music, by ex-patriate Yank Bill Motzing, which underpins the whole production subtly but superbly in helping set period.

Coote's production design gives an over-all good look to the film; production values are enormous. Commercial prospects for the film look set in domestic play-offs which, if it catches, could easily refund the pic's $A500,000 budget to the investors, among them the Australian Film Commission, the New South Wales Film Corp. and Roadshow Distributors. Chances elsewhere could be good contingent upon careful and devoted marketing. —Miha.

———

Blue Fire Lady
(AUSTRALIAN-COLOR)

———

Melbourne, May 6.
A Blue Fire Productions Pty. Ltd. Picture for Australian International Film Corp. Produced by Antony I. Ginnane. Stars Cathryn Harrison, Mark Holden, Peter Cummins. Directed by Ross Dimsey. Screenplay, Bob Manumil; camera (Eastmán), Vincent Monton; editor, Tony Patterson; art director, John Powditch; sound, Gary Wilkins; wardrobe, Terry Ryan; assistant director, Geoff Morrow. Previewed at Mayfair Cinema; May 6, '78. Running time: 95 MINS.
Jenny .... Cathryn Harrison
Hbarry .... Mark Holden
McIntyre .... Peter Cummins
Mrs. Gianni .... Marion Edward
Mr. Grey .... Lloyd Cunnington
Mrs. Bartlett .... Anne Sutherland
Charlie .... Gary Waddell
Gus .... John Wood
Mr. Peters .... John Ewart
Reporter .... Rollo Roylance

Vet .... John Murphy
Chief Steward .... Telford Jackson

There is nothing confusing about the formula adopted by writer Bob Maumill and the producers of "Blue Fire Lady." This sort of thing has been done before, notably in "National Velvet," but this is no reason to assume that it can't be done again.

Film deals with the relationship between a girl (Cathryn Harrison) and a horse that captures her heart. The ingredients for a good sob are there: a vicious horse-trainer, McIntyre (Peter Cummins), does the heavy work — and there is a satisfactory love interest between Harrison and young pop-star Mark Holden.

The Jenny Grey character, at 18, could be too old for the young kids to identify with. However, the film is cleverly made.

Introduction of well-known local racing characters is a shrewd ploy that has invested the product with a necessary touch of authenticity.

Harrison is effective as Jenny, the only person the race horse will trust, and as Barry, the romantic hero, Mark Holden makes an auspicious debut.

"Blue Fire Lady," with all the ingredients to appeal to a wide audience, should do well. — Hind.

———

La Mazzetta
(The Payoff)
(ITALIAN-COLOR)

———

Rome, May 1.
A United Artists release of a Filmauro Production. Produced by Luigi and Aurelio De Laurentiis. Features entire cast. Directed by Sergio Corbucci. Screenplay, Dino Maiuri, Massimo De Rita, Luciano De Crescenzo, Elvio Porta, based on book by Attilio Veraldi; camera (color), Luigi Kuveiller; music, Pino Daniele; set designer, Giantito Burchiellaro. Reviewed at the Adriano Theatre, Rome, April 21, '78. Running time: 120 MINS.
Sasa Iovine .... Nino Manfredi
Police commissioner
  Assenza .... Ugo Tognazzi
Don Michele Miletti .... Paolo Stoppa
Luisella .... Marisa Laurito
Nicola Casali .... Gennaro Di Napoli
Giulia Miletti .... Imma Piro
Elena Milette .... Marisa Merlini
The twin Tonino .... Salvatore Borgese
The twin Pasquale .... Giovanni Borgese

———

After his success in the '60s with the Italian-style western, Sergio Corbucci, with 'Payoff,' may very well be on to another trend: the Italian-style thriller. Like the western all'Italiana, 'Payoff' exaggerates the macabre, one is bumping into corpses at every turn, but here he gives the extra bonus of high comic relief.

Combining the talents of Nino Manfredi and Ugo Tognazzi (in the cameo role of philosophical police commissioner Assenza), Corbucci has assured himself of boxoffice success in Italy and a possible winner abroad.

Manfredi plays a small-time Neopolitan operator, Saso Iovine, who suddenly finds himself in the thick of a multi-murder mystery. Don Michele, a Neapolitan building contractor involved in a number of housing scandals, hires Iovine to find his daughter, Giulia, who has stolen some incriminating documents and run off with her boyfriend. Instead, the hapless Iovine finds the nude bodies of Michele's third wife and the daughter's boyfriend. He is then abducted by Michele's rival, Don Nicola, who applies Neapolitan gut pressures to get the compromising documents. Finally convinced he didn't have them, Nicola released Iovine promising him an even bigger payoff if he uncovered the infamous papers.

Iovine's troubles, however, have only just begun. He is harassed by his girl friend who has been leaving him for the past 10 years, pursued (in the classic car chase and over rooftops) by killer twins who were hired by Don Nicola, and shadowed by Commissioner Assenza who always manages to arrive after another body has been discovered. Seven bodies later, including that of Michele himself, Iovine finally recovers the documents and heroically decides to hand them over to the police. But it is too late. Don Michele's mafioso rival has already bribed the police and Assenza has been demoted.

The plot is, of course, secondary to the action and the fun. 'Payoff' combines the Italian tradition of the political 'giallo' or thriller and the best of Italian comedy. The ending is marked by political cynicism where the good guys always finish last.

As for Italian comedy, Manfredi and Tognazzi prove that those who have been sounding its death knell have been a bit premature. In addition to the Manfredi-Tognazzi tandem, particularly noteworthy are the performances of Marisa Laurito who played Iovine's long-suffering Neapolitan fiancee and Paolo Stoppa who gives us a convincing portrait of the aging mobster Michele. Mix these ingredients with a panoramic view of Naples and the surrounding countryside and you have the entertainment recipe for a thriller guaranteed to please. —Hurfim.

———

Fantasm Comes Again
(AUSTRALIAN-COLOR)

———

Melbourne, May 5.
A First Film Finance Picture for Australian International Film Corp. Executive producers, Robert F. Ward and Mark Josem. Produced by Antony I. Ginnane. Features entire cast. Directed by Colin Eggles-

ton; screenplay, Ross Dimsey; camera (color), Vincent Monton; editor, Tony Patterson; art director, Antony Brockliss (in Los Angeles); art director, Antony Brockliss (in Los Angeles); sound recordists, Neil Rozensky (in L.A.); assistant director, Tom Jacobsen (in L.A.); sound editor, Tony Patterson. Previewed in Melbourne, May 5, '78. Running time: 94 MINS.

With Rick Cassidy, Mary Gacin, Con Covert, Bill Margold, Uschi Digart, Serena, Dee Dee Levitt, Rainbeaux Smith, Clive Hearne, John C. Holmes, Angela Menzies-Willis, Tom Thumb, Liz Wolfe, Rosemarie Bern, Urias S. Cambridge, Peter Kurzon, Lois Owens, Mike Stapp, Michael Barton, Suzy A. Star, Amanda Smith, Herb Layen.

"Fantasm Comes Again" is the first sequel to the successful "Fantasm," which ran for some eight months last year. It is an unabashed soft-porn movie that has been filmed mainly in Los Angeles.

The script offers the unlikely and rather labored premise that a young femme reporter has just taken over the "lonely hearts" column of a metro daily from an older cynical male journalist. She attempts to answer some of the weird letters that have been sent in, thereby creating an opportunity for the enactment of several salacious sequences.

This script attempts to be whimsical, but fails. However, it is likely people will not go to this film hoping for spiritual uplift or for any revelations on the subject of art.

Films that are long on soft-porn and short on wit do well in Australia, and "Fantasm Comes Again" can probably look forward to considerable success. The budget, of $94,000, would seem not to be at risk.
— Hind.

Girlfriends
(COLOR)

Claudia Weill's first feature excellent. Fine acting.

Hollywood, April 30.

A Warner Bros. release of a Cyclops Film, produced by Claudia Weill and Jan Sanders. Directed by Claudia Weill. Screenplay, Vicki Polon from a story by Weill and Polon; camera (Du Art Color), Fred Murphy; editor, Suzanne Pettit; music, Michael Small; art director, Patrizia von Brandenstein; sound, Ed Rothkowitz, Hanna Wajshonig, Emily Paine. No other credits available. Reviewed at the Academy of Motion Picture Arts & Sciences Little Theatre, April 30, 1978. (No MPAA rating.) Running time: 86 MINS.

Susan Weinblatt . . . . Melanie Mayron
Rabbi Gold . . . . Eli Wallach
Anne Munroe . . . . Anita Skinner
Martin . . . . Bob Balaban
Eric . . . . Christopher Guest
Julie . . . . Gena Rojak
Ceil . . . . Amy Wright
Beatrice . . . . Viveca Lindfors
Abe . . . . Mike Kellin
Photo editor . . . . Russell Horton

This is a warm, emotional and at times wire picture about friendship, a film deserving of a wide audience. It's documentary filmmaker Claudia Weill's first feature, although there's no reason to apologetically pigeonhole this movie as a "promising first feature." It's the work of a technically skilled and assured director.

For her debut Weill chose mostly unseasoned actors. Financial considerations were probably a major factor — with deferments the picture was budgeted at less than $500,000 and funded through various grants. The director's casting abilities are keen.

Melanie Mayron is outstanding as a photographer fresh out of college maturing under the strains of professional insecurity and loneliness. Previously, Mayron has scored modestly in "Harry & Tonto," "Carwash" and "You Light Up My Life." By far this is her most developed and complex role.

Down the line Weill has extracted first-rate performances. Anita Skinner is Mayron's best friend and until she suddenly marries Christopher Guest, her roommate. Eli Wallach portrays a rabbi and almost paramount for whom Mayron sometimes photographs Bar Mitzvahs and weddings. Bob Balaban is Mayron's slightly off-center boy friend and Viveca Lindfors is Beatrice, owner of a Greenwich Village gallery who believes in Mayron and gives her a big break.

Each performance is a little gem and so are the characters developed by Vicki Polon from a story by her and Weill. They look and act like people, which is a relief. There are no false touches of glamour.

Mayron as Susan Weinblatt is not beautiful; she's a bit chubby and suburban. Her emotional insecurities are understandable and sparked when she's "abandoned" by her friend. More important, her triumphs and recovery are modest.

She has doubts about her boyfriend — he's not exactly a substitute, he's got foibles and problems and he's not mushy and pretty. He stays home one night to watch a football game. They don't take a walk along the beach or have a pillow fight. Her professional triumph is equally mild and credible, a showing at a small gallery for young photographers. That's enough to keep the audience rooting and believing.

Warner Bros. picked up the film about a month ago. Slow sell should turn it into a modest success, especially in urban markets. —Hege.

Rembrandt — Fecit 1669
(Rembrandt—1669)
(NETHERLANDS-COLOR)

Los Angeles, April 27.

A Jos Stelling Film Produkties Film. Produced and directed by Jos Stelling. Features entire cast. Screenplay, Stelling, Wil Hildebrand, Chlem van Houweninge; camera (color), Ernest Bresser; editor, Jan Overweg, Floris Hazemeijer, Marcel Bayer, Ate de Jong; music, Laurens van Rooyen. No other credits available. Reviewed at the Plitt Theatres, Century City, April 27, '78. Running time: 114 MINS.

Cast: Frans Stelling, Ton de Koff, Aya Fil, Lucie Singeling, Hanneke van der Velden.

Technically, "Rembrandt — Fecit 1669" is a fascinating film. It is a near perfect union of form and content. Dutch producer-director Jos Stelling has set out to paint a cinematic portrait of Rembrandt and the result looks like a Rembrandt painting. That's quite an accomplishment and much of the credit for the film's look — its lighting and camerawork — rightly goes to director of photography Ernest Bresser.

The story, however, is clubfooted — portrait of an artist as a soap opera character. Stelling, along with Wil Hildebrand and Chlem van Houweninge, wrote the screenplay and have concentrated only on the painter as a profligate, not the painter as artist.

The plot opens with Rembrandt's move to Amsterdam, which is also his first step towards moral decay. After the death of his wife and the birth of his son, Rembrandt's life degenerates into an exercise in irresponsibility. He spends too much and controls his sexual passion too little.

All of this may be factual, and Stelling has gone to great lengths to research and cast the film. But the relationship between the person and his art is barely explored. Surely it had an impact — that's the reason for the film — but the association is only hinted at.

All of the production values are handsome, the acting is confident, and at 114-minutes the picture is well paced. Commercial outlook for the U.S. is limited, although museums and other festivals certainly should take a look. —Hege.

The Irishman
(AUSTRALIAN-COLOR)

Sydney, March 24.

A Greater Union Organization release of a Forest Home Film Production, produced by Anthony Buckley. Features entire cast. Directed by Donald Crombie. Screenplay, Crombie from novel by Elizabeth O'Conner; camera (Agfacolor), Peter James; production design, Owen Williams; art direction, Graham Walker; 1st asst. dir. Mark Egerton; wardrobe design, Judith Dorsman; editor, Tim Wellburn; music, Charles Marawood. Reviewed at Pitt Center, Sydney, March 23, '78 (Rated NRC by Commonwealth Censor). Running time: 108 MINS.

Paddy Doolan . . . . Michael Craig
Michael Doolan . . . . Simon Burke
Jenny Doolan . . . . Robin Nevin
Will Doolan . . . . Lou Brown
Granny Doolan . . . . Tui Lorraine Bow
Grandpa Doolan . . . . Andrew Maguire
Robert Dalgliesh . . . . Tony Barry
Mrs. Dalgliesh . . . . Marcella Burgoyne
Bailey Clark . . . . Vincent Ball
Mrs. Clark . . . . Roberta Grant
Chad Logan . . . . Gerard Kennedy
Eric Haywood . . . . Bryan Brown
Kevin Quilty . . . . Roger Ward
Hotel Missus . . . . Babette Stevens

The north of Queensland in the 1920s must have been much like west Texas at the turn of the century if we can believe the movies. A hard land populated by hard men and women working hard in hard conditions.

But times are a-changing, and whenever that happens there's usually a rugged but dogged individual who praises the candle and cries out against the light of progress. One such is Paddy Doolan, the eponymous migrated Celt.

Paddy the teamster, with his team of 20 giant Clydesdale draught horses crossing the great wide river, open the film and immediately create awe and admiration. They are such superb beasts that it is made that much easier to accept Paddy's stubbornness later when he refuses to see that his team is being superseded by the internal combustion engine in the shape and sound of Haywood's bone-rattling, brand-new truck.

Aesthetics aside, the theme of the film is Doolan's refusal to give in and the effect it has on those around him. His wife is sensible, yet acquiescent; his older son, Will, defiant; the youngest, and most sensitive — and ultimately therefore the most affected — is bewildered, but devotedly and hopelessly goes with Paddy. And his "My father, right or wrong" feelings are inevitably eroded. In any event Paddy's recalcitrance demolishes the family, eventually destroys his self esteem and ultimately himself.

The film has great moments of emotional triumph, and at times is unabashedly sentimental, but it never descends to mawkishness.

It's a highly accessible film for most audiences because it deals in very human emotional terms; the characters are basically likeable people, and in their humanity, their personalities are varying shades of grey; but it may just be that the shifting realities of the people on screen could leave audiences with too few points of identification.

Paddy is positive but wrongheaded; Michael has such a true-to-life adolescent lability that he is sometimes exasperating. Jenny is cursed by her unemancipated times. Only Will appears to have a spark — but that's all, and in his shallowness it burns out.

The script draws the character carefully and fully, and director Donald Crombie has an evident empathy for this kind of human area (his previous film "Caddie," had a similar understanding warmth about it). The performances he gets from his players are excellent, and he uses the full scope of the terrain and a marvelously evocative location town to create mood and sense of period.

The use of Agfacolor stock gives another dimension to Australian light, and gives a marvelously warm look to the film. Cinematographer Peter James puts on the screen the lush greens and rich browns that make the countryside look tropically lush one minute and dryly-defeating the next.

As noted, Crombie's control is sure, and his use of Marawood's music adds another aspect to the overall excellence of the picture. Tech credits are all great, with the period recreation by Williams and Walker deserving a kudo or two for their part in creating the right visual feel. —*Miha.*

Weekend of Shadows
(AUSTRALIAN-COLOR)

Sydney, April 17.

Roadshow (Australia) release of a Samson-South Australian Film Corporation Production, produced by Tom Jeffrey and Matt Carroll. Directed by Tom Jeffrey. Features entire cast. Screenplay,˙ Peter Yeldham, from a novel by Hugh Atkinson; camera (Eastman colour), Richard Wallace; editor, Rod Adamson; music, Charles Marawood; sound, Ken Hammond; art director, Christopher Webster. Reviewed at Film Australia Screening Room, Sydney, April 16, '78. Running time, 94 MINS.

Rabbit .... John Waters
Vi .... Melissa Jaffer
Sergeant Caxton .... Wyn Roberts
Helen Caxton .... Barbara West
Ab Nolan .... Graham Rouse
Bernie Collins .... Graeme Blundell
Bosun .... Bill Hunter
David Wayne .... Keith Lee
Badger .... Les Foxcroft
Ryan .... Kit Taylor
The Pole .... Mark Gaweda

"Weekend of Shadows" has a good story to tell, and tells it well. Set in a small Australian town in the '30s, it opens with the discovery of the murdered wife of a small property owner (rancher). Suspicion immediately falls on a Polish immigrant who was working on the farm and who has disappeared. The local policeman, Caxton, seizes the opportunity to reestablish himself with his superiors in the city; he'd been sent to this out of the way town after an earlier incident when two youths had been shot dead in a city fracas for which Caxton was responsible.

Egged on by his snobbish wife, Caxton sees the chance to gain some easy glory. He assembles a motley posse of locals, including the town bully, Bosun, and the simpleminded, slightly sub-normal Rabbit. The latter is also urged by his wife, Vi, to join in the manhunt as she's tired of her husband being treated as a laughing stock.

As the weekend wears on the members of the posse become more and more drunk, Caxton is in less and less control of the situation, and

Rabbit becomes more and more identified with the (it turns out innocent) fugitive.

The pic has echoes of Hollywood classics from "They Won't Forget" to "The Ox-Bow Incident," but Tom Jeffrey has made it a typically Australian situation. For once, flashbacks filling in details of Rabbit's relationship with his wife, who was formerly the town's easy-to-love barmaid, don't hold up the action because they're so well handled and provide such an essential core to the film.

Acting is tops right down the line, and Jeffrey (whose previous effort was the film version of David Williamson's play "The Removalists") makes excellent use of South Australian locations, finely lensed by Richard Wallace.

Ending is abrupt, downbeat, but logical and dramatically satisfying. One can quibble only with Charles Marawood's over-insistent and repetitive music score. Otherwise, this is another excellent Australian feature which could find audiences overseas on its timeless theme, its knowing direction and its highly satisfactory performances. Technically tops in all departments. —*Strat.*

Il Messia
(The Messiah)
(ITALIAN-COLOR)

Hollywood, April 29.

An Orizzonte 2000 production, produced by Silvia d'Amico Bendico. Directed by Roberto Rossellini. Features entire cast. Screenplay, Rossellini, Bendico; camera (color), Mario Montuori; editor, Yolanda Benvenuti, Laurent Quaglio; music, Mario Nascimbene. No other credits available. Reviewed at the Suncrest Cinema screening room, Century City, Calif., April 28, '78. (No MPAA rating.) Running time: 150 MINS.

Cast: Pier Maria Rossi, Mita Ungaro, Antonella Fasano, Tony Ucci, Flora Carabella, Carlos de Carvalho, Luis Suarez.

Before his death last June, Roberto Rossellini had turned away from theatrical features to television. His series on great world figures — Socrates, Saint Augustine, Descartes, and Louis XIV — all had been produced for European television. "The Messiah" was one of only two departures from the video route taken by Rossellini after 1964 and this two-and-a-half hour examination of the most influential figure in the history of western civilization is as ambitious as its subject was important.

The film opens in the 11th century B.C. with the Israelites wandering in the desert trying to find Palestine. In less than 30 minutes it jumps ahead more than 1,000 years with the establishment of the state of Israel, the subsequent rise to power of kings and the corruptive abuse of that power.

This is one section of the work. The second movement begins during the year of Christ's birth with other portions moving ahead to the 12th year A.D., 28, 32 and the year's of Christ's crucifixion. A narrator ties the parts together.

This is a long film, but of course Rossellini and producer and co-scripter Silvia d'Amico Bendico could extract only portions out of Jesus' life. He is shown as a child, entering the temple and presenting his first sacrifice, with his disciples, at the Last Supper, accepting his fate, crucified and buried at Golgotha.

It is an inspiring work, a film by a religious man, and at times visually stunning as well as shocking. There are the elaborate camera movements and zooms so much a part of Rossellini's work which had been criticized in later years as distracting. It works elegantly here. The acting is by non-professionals including those playing Mary, Jesus, his disciples and the Roman officials and they are well directed by Rossellini who had often worked with non-professionals.

The film had been picked up and partially financed by De Rance Inc., through the Family Theatre before Rossellini's death. The religious and charitable foundation has stated that it plans to alter the film from the version premiered at the L.A. Film Exposition. The film's producer has also stated that this is the version Rossellini had personally supervised and wanted shown.

Whether that is to be the case will be decided in future months. As previously reported, De Rance did not want this film screened in its present form, but could not prevent the unspooling through court action. What is shaping up is another battle between filmmaker and distributor, similar to the one fought by director Bernardo Bertolucci over his five and a half hour version of "1900."

Regardless of the running time, the commercial outlook for "The Messiah" is limited to selected art theatres, the college market and religious groups. It'll make little difference in the overall b.o. if the film runs 90 minutes or 145 minutes. In fact, shortening the film, altering it from Rossellini's intentions, is liable to cut into the art circuit grosses. —*Hege.*

Youngblood
(COLOR)

Lawrence Hilton-Jacobs in solid black street meller. Depending on ad campaign, could crossover.

Hollywood, May 4.

American International Pictures release of an Aion production. Produced by Nick Grillo, Alan Riche. Directed by Noel Nosseck. Features entire cast. Screenplay, Paul Carter Harrison; camera (CFI-Color), Robbie Greenberg; editor, Frank Morriss; music, WAR; art director, James Dultz; sound, Jan Schulti; wardrobe, Adrianne Levesque; assistant director, Bill Kerr; stunt coordinator, Eddie Smith. Reviewed at the BevHills Hotel Screening Room, Beverly Hills, Calif. May 3, '78. (MPAA Rating: R.). Running time: 90 MINS.

Rommel .... Lawrence-Hilton Jacobs
Youngblood .... Bryan O'Dell
Sybil .... Ren Woods
Hustler .... Tony Allen
Corelli .... Vince Cannon
Junkie .... Art Evans
Basketball pusher .... Jeff Hollis
Reggie .... Dave Pendleton
Bummie .... Ron Trice
Joan .... Sheila Wills
Mrs. Gordon .... Ann Weldon

"Youngblood" is a taut, well-plotted street melodrama that swerves around the usual black exploitation script cliches to arrive at a solidly dramatic conclusion. The American International Pictures release has already piled up healthy grosses in an initial Chicago run, success that should be duplicated in other urban milieus.

Marquee value will rest primarily with Lawrence-Hilton Jacobs, showcased here in a significant departure from his "Welcome Back, Kotter" comedy role. He plays a returned Vietnam vet still fighting a private war, this time on the gang level in the L.A. ghetto.

Portraying a character oddly named Rommel, Jacobs takes young Bryan O'Dell, in the title role, under his wing and instructs him in the realities of street fighting. O'Dell, who is careful not to overplay the character, has troubles at home (an errant mama, well-limned by Ann Weldon) and school, where he gets suspended.

That places the teenager right out on the avenue, where he wastes no time in hooking up with Rommel's gang, the Kingsmen, along with friend Bummie (Ron Trice). A la "West Side Story," there is the inevitable neighborhood rumble, where Youngblood gets his bloody initiation, prelude to future gang wars.

But scripter Paul Carter Harrison has added a unique plot twist to the standard story. Angered by the overdose death of a gang buddy, the Kingsmen attempt to wipe out the local drug traffic, which is controlled by white bankroller Vince Cannon and black entrepreneur Dave Pendleton, who just happens to be Youngblood's older brother. With nary a cop in sight, the anti-drug vendetta becomes a sanguine affair, related personally to Youngblood by the heroin addiction of his young girlfriend (Ren Woods, in an unappealing perf). Noel Nosseck keeps the momentum going with tight direction, and Frank Morriss' cross-cutting is exemplary. Finale just manages to avoid the pre-ordained tragedy, and is effective on both actioner and emotional levels. Original score by rock group WAR adds strongly to impact.

Jacobs offers a well-rounded comprehension of his character (scenes with lonely wife Sheila Wills add an extra dimension), one that goes beyond the black militant type-casting. O'Dell likewise offers shadings to what could be a one-dimensional part. Good support is offered by Jeff Hollis as a basketball-playing junkie, and Tony Allen as a drug pick-up man. Pendleton isn't quite right as the brother, however, and Cannon plays the financier as a typical heavie.

Tech credits are very polished, especially Robbie Greenberg's lensing, which is sharp and makes excellent use of L.A. street locations. Only criticism would be low mike levels for Jan Schulti's sound.

"Youngblood" has some white crossover potential thanks to Jacobs, but this is a film that could appeal to all audiences, if AIP structures its campaign accordingly.
—*Poll.*

Mouth to Mouth
(AUSTRALIAN-COLOR)

Sydney, April 21.

A Vega Film Productions presentation. Produced by Jon Sainken and John Duigan. Features entire cast. Directed by John Duigan. Screenplay, Duigan; art direction, Tracy Watt; camera (Eastman), Tom Cowan; sound, Lloyd Carrick; music, Roy Ritchie; editing, Tony Paterson. Reviewed at Hoyts Theatrette, April 20, '78. (Unclassified by censor). Running time: **93 MINS.**

Carrie	Kim Krejus
Jeannie	Sonia Peat
Tim	Ian Gilmour
Serge	Sergio Frazzetto
Fred	Walter Pym
Tony	Michael Carman

Young filmmaker John Duigan's second feature, "Mouth to Mouth," is an indication that here is another nascent Aussie talent who could blossom, given correct handling and larger budgets. He has a nice feel for character interaction and a good grasp of pace and timing. From young and relatively untried actors, he has extracted excellent performances, placing them carefully against a contemporary urban backdrop to create an environmental entity in such a way as to establish an unassailable veracity.

Two tough young femme delinquents (Kim Krejus and Sonia Peat) escape from a Home and hit the city. They get jobs in a food bar and augment their incomes by a sideline in shoplifting. Two young unsettled males meet them and a menage a quatre is set up in a derelict warehouse which the girls have fitted out. The old wino who crashes there becomes a sort of mascot. The establishment of the arrangement is handled deftly and with some wit.

Duigan lets events enlarge and mold his quartet's characters; when there is a cash crisis, and one of the "clean" guys starts shoplifting, his girl (Krejus) bad-mouths him for descending to her standards. When she and her girlfriend are forced by finances to start hooking, it's Krejus who balks and can't go through with it.

Throughout the film Duigan rings some subtle changes, and one's conceptions are constantly being re-arranged as the character develops and deepens his or her personality. Storywise, it is a fine piece of structure, and the characters are translatable into almost any Western urban locale. They're nice kids, somehow off the tracks, who in ten years' time will either be solid middle class or dead from an o.d. And you care.

Camerawork by Tom Cowan is excellent providing a good sense of locale and ambience; he's fluid without being showy, and it helps give the pic a subdued, docu feel that aids the reality. Music hits the right balance between self-drama and don't-give-a-damn demon- ‐trated by the attitudes depicted. Other tech' credits fine.

Pic looks good despite its small ($175,000) budget, largely because of its visual immediacy and pace. Commercial playoffs Down Under will require careful nurturing; pretty much the same way the better importers would treat a similar film made, say, in France. As for overseas, the story is virtually universal, as are the characters: it will depend on the eye of the beholder whether or not it all applies in his market. —*Miha.*

Le Dernier Amant Romantique
(The Last Romantic Lover)
(FRENCH-COLOR)

Paris, May 9.

WB-Col release of Film & Co.-French Movie-PECF production. Stars Dayle Haddon, Gerard Tybalt, Fernando Rey. Directed by Just Jaeckin. Screenplay, Ennio De Concini, Jaeckin; camera (Eastmancolor), Robert Fraisse; editor, Francoise Bonnot; music, Pierre Bachelet. Reviewed at Marignan-Pathe, Paris; April 26, '78. Running time: **100 MINS.**

Woman	Dayle Haddon
Man	Gerard Tybalt
Max	Fernando Rey

Just Jaeckin is the ex-photographer who directed that worldwide hit exotic, "Emmanuelle." Now he insists he wants to make more personal films, starting with this one. Result is a mixture of familiar small circus capers, an inane, somewhat overindulged, contest to find the world's last romantic lover and a romantic comedy of the sophisticate tamed by the simple but romantic lover.

American actress Dayle Haddon has brittle good looks as the editor of a woman's mag that runs a contest to ferret out the world's last heart throb. A liontamer in a circus whose lion has died, is coerced into entering by his colorful boss, hammily played by Fernando Rey, for the prize money.

The contest runs long but has its moments as the men must compete in all sorts of tasks. The circus man wins second place, which entitles him to 10 days with a girl supplied by the mag. He insists on it being Haddon and she finally accepts.

The usual contretemps ensue, until true love finds her giving up her giddy mag life and lover for the circus man, latter played by new thesp Gerard Tybalt. — *Mosk.*

Egy Erkolcsos Ejszaka
(A Very Moral Night)
(HUNGARIAN-COLOR)

Budapest, April 21.

A Hungarofilm Production. Dialog Studio, Budapest; world distribution, Hungarofilm, Budapest. Features entire cast. Directed by Karoly Makk. Screenplay, Istvan Orkeny, Peter Bacso, based on the short story, "The House with the Red Light," by Sandor Hunyady; camera (Eastmancolor), Janos Toth. Reviewed at Hungarofilm Screening Room, Budapest, April 20, '78. Running time: **103 MINS.**

Madame	Iren Psota
Mother	Margit Makay
Kelepey	Gyoryg Cserhalmi
Darinka	Gyorgyi Tarjan
Bella	Carla Romanelli

"A Very Moral Night" is an easygoing, atmospheric tale drawn from a short story, "The House with the Red Light," by Sandor Hunyady, whose original title would give some of the fun away. It focuses on a one-night incident in a bordello of a small university town somewhere in Hungary early in this century.

Helmer Karoly Makk is best remembered for his moving Cannes entry a few years back, "Love," which also hit a goldmine in a simple tale that ran a mile deep in emotional, human, psychological truth.

Pic opens with a sketch of the principal characters in contrasting light on a typical night in the bordello. The madam returns home with the girls from an evening out at the theatre, a treat, during which they dressed like "ladies" and behaved even better. They change into their working clothes, the red light is turned on, the customers gather at the door, and the piano player plinks away in a smoke-filled reception room.

One of the regulars is a medical student, the girls' favorite, always low on cash but welcomed all the same and complimented as "Doctor" in deference to his studies. He spends the night due to a sudden downpour and is invited to stay in the spare room to save on his al- lowance from home sent by his widowed mother. He, of couse, accepts.

Some days alter his mother arrives for a visit, unannounced, and the madam swiftly converts the premises into a boarding house for respectable ladies and gentlemen. At this point the pic takes off: it belongs to the madam (Iren Psota) and the mother (Margit Makay), two veteran legit-and-film thesps who know a ripe role when they see one. The girls put on their best duds, smoking is forbidden, and dinner is served — in hopes that the son, out on a spree for the night, will return home soon to pack his mother off to the station. He does arrive — but in company with town officials ready to crown an evening of cards with a romp with the girls.

"A Very Moral Night" thrives on this double-standard role-playing: laughs mingle with tears, propriety with a lust for life, the human with the moral. Before she leaves at dawn for the station, the mother has comforted one of the girls with a yen for an admiring journalist fearful of declaring his love, and she notes as a whole that her son is a sincere and clever young man — so "the rest doesn't matter."' The game of pretense had its saving moral lessons.

Karloy Makk has a way with actors and situations that require few if any words. Pic will score on fest circuit (it's slated for Cannes) and has solid off-shore chances if handled properly. One of those memorable stories that Yank scribes from Stephen Crane to Damon Runyon, as well as helmers in velvet-pants Hollywood, handled on occasion with grace and distinction. The Europeans often do it better. —*Holl.*

Leidenschaftliche Bluemchen
(Passion Flower Hotel)
(W. GERMAN-COLOR)

Munich, April 28.

A CCC-Film (Artur Brauner production). Directed by Andre Farwagi. Screenplay, Paul Nicolas, based on Rosalind Erskine's novel, "The Passion Flower Hotel"; camera (color), Richard Suzuki; music, Francis Lai; original music "See You Later Alligator," "Rock A Beatin' Boogie," "Shake Rattle And Roll" played by Bill Haley and his Comets; lyrics for "Debbie's Song," "My Baby Blue," "The First Kiss" by Andre Farwagi; World sales, Cine Export, Paris. Reviewed at Neue Constantin screening room, Munich, April 27, '78. Running time: **94 MINS.**

Cast: Nastassja Kinski, Carolin Ohrner, Marion Kracht, Veronique Delbourg, Fabiana Udenio, Gerry Sundquist, Nigel Greaves, Sean Chapman, Stefano d'Amato.
(English Soundtrack)

Based on the bestselling novel, "The Passion Flower Hotel," by Rosalind Erskine this internationall concepted pic is mainly aimed at worldwide young audiences. With its rich decor, beautiful actors and photography (the latter distinctly leaned on David Hamilton's "Bilitis" art) and music by Francis Lai, it tells the romantic love story between an American girl Debbie (Nastassja Kinski) and a British boy, Fibs (Gerry Sundquist).

Both are in neighboring boarding schools and are the respective leaders of rather harmless early youth sex clubs that are more given to wishful thinking than getting results. All the depicted pranks and the joyful nonsense the youngsters undertake border on the erotic but it is always in good taste and the scarcely shown nudity is beautiful.

The actors are excellent, full of the required naivete and blitheness and Nastassja Kinski, (daughter of actor Klaus Kinski) in her looks reminding of a very young Ingrid Bergman, has visible star quality. Even if the film seems a trifle too long, it should reach the teenage audience. A nice, frothy bubble that offers itself for quick, entertaining consumption. —*Koci.*

S Lyubov I Nezhnost
(With Love And Tenderness)
(BULGARIAN-COLOR)

Sofia, April 14.

A Bulgarofilm Production, Meadost Creative Group, Sofia; world rights, Bulgarofilm, Sofia. Features entire cast. Directed by Rangel Vulchanov. Screenplay, Valeri Petrov; camera (color), Dimko Minov; art direction, Maria Ivanova; music, Kiril Donchev. Reviewed at Bulgarofilm Screening Room, Sofia, April 13, '78. Running time: **100 MINS.**
Sasho .... Alexander Dyakov
Lotte .... Tsvetana Eneva
Patricia .... Gergana Gerassimova
The Architect .... Yossif Surchadjiev
The Artist .... Theodor Youroukov

A fruitful teaming of two exceptional Bulgarian talents — helmer Rangel Vulchanov and writer-poet Valeri Petrov — "With Love and Tenderness" is slated for the Cannes Fest and should capture the critical attention of those who have followed with interest the steady development of a national cinema to one of the most important and creative in East Europe.

Vulchanov, a director of the "older" generation, put Bulgaria on the world film map more than a decade ago with "A Small Island": the script was written by Petrov, who became nationally famous for his Shakespeare translations into the native tongue. That pic set standards for the generation to follow, who now are scoring regularly at international fests and at well-calculated, representative film weeks in Western cultural capitals. "With Love and Tenderness" crowns this development with a mature, balanced, sophisticated view of the artist and his world.

It's like the Fellini-Antonioni confrontation with an established, hypocritical, somewhat decaying milieu, the "in" crowd among the hip well-to-do. On the Black Sea within a stone's throw of the tourist center lives Sasho, a sculptor, who retired to this idyllic paradise years ago to rivet together a pile of junk into the final "masterpiece" of his life. His studio-shack with the mountain of concrete and iron before the door has enchanted the fisherman and villagers in the area, who give the eccentric artist and German-born, long-suffering wife cash and compliments to keep him going over the years.

One day an architect and an artist arrive from the big city with news that his masterpiece has been chosen for an exhibition, and a large sum of money is offered for the purchase (regulated by fixed state prices for such a sculpture). With this money Sasho can pay off his debts, but he feels he hasn't quite completed the work of art and these conformist, cliched-parroting bores disturb his sensibilities. Only the architect's lovely, fashionable wife and the couple's innocent-minded, pre-teenager daughter capture his heart. He decides to make the compromise and sell the dubious masterpiece.

During the night's celebration, during which his friends and acquaintances join to speak their minds about art and life, Sasho grows more and more depressed under the influence of alcohol and truth of the situation. He quarrels with nearly everyone and decides in the morning to end it all at sea in his fishing boat — but the little girl has secretly stowed away and thwarts even this gesture.

"With Love and Tenderness" is finely acted (Alexander Dyakov as Sasho) and subtly directed in presenting an accurate cross-section of Bulgarian society.

Credits are tops and b.o. possibilities strong. —*Holl.*

The Sealed Soil
(IRAN-COLOR-16m)

Hollywood, April 26.

A Nabili Films production. Produced, directed, written and edited by Marva Nabili. Camera (color-16m), Barbod Taheri. Features entire cast. No other credits available. Reviewed at the Royal Theatre, West L.A., April 26, '77. Running time: **90 MINS.**
Cast: Flora Shabaviz and the villagers of Noo-Asquar Village.

"The Sealed Soil" is a painfully boring film. It is the kind of picture which turns up at "international" film festivals as part of an overall effort by fest program committees and directors to showcase "world cinema." This entry is from Iran. It's 90-minutes long, and is recommended viewing for those inter-

ested in the ability of motion pictures to extend reel time.

Marva Nabili produced, wrote, directed and edited on a $17,000 budget this work about a peasant girl living in a poor backward village who rejects her traditional role; that is, she refuses to get married, so everyone thinks she's crazy.

Everything about this film is static. Little happens, the camera never moves, there's almost no dialogue and except for a railroad crossing in the center of the village, there's nothing of interest to look at. —*Hege.*

122 Rue De Provence
(One Two Two)
(FRENCH-COLOR)

Paris, May 9.

WB-Col release of Orphee Arts production. Features entire cast. Directed by Christian Gion. Screenplay, Albert Kantoff, Christian Watton; camera (Eastmancolor), Robert Fraisse; editor, Natalie Lafaurie; music, Ennio Morricone. Reviewed at Publicis, Paris, April 26, '78. Running time: **98 MINS.**
Fabienne .... Nicole Calfan
Paul .... Francis Huster
Crevel .... Jacques Francois
Jamet .... Henri Guybet
Judith .... Anicee Alvina
Countess .... Catherine Alric
Clarisse .... Sophie Deschamps
Doriane .... Nicole Seguin

The title is the address of a famed Paris bordello of the '30s, renowned for its girls as well as its club-like atmosphere and frequented by politicos who use it to entertain visiting heads of state and diplomats. The history of France is those years of upheavals and war is seen through the frills of this lush lounge.

Film has the usual love story; this time a young, ambitious prostie who leaves Marseilles to push her way into the One Two Two and a young man trying to break into politics. They meet at the station in Paris and of course she lies to him about herself and destination. His following about a governmental Minister with a letter of introduction gets him into the one where the girl has succeeded in getting a job.

Pic is glossy rather than insightful into the life of the house or the times. Director Christian Gion, who has come from ad films, seems to be trying to sell the house rather than create a drama or build an ironic parallel between the world of the house and that outside.

Nicole Calfan apparently is in the business to get to the top and be called Madam. She makes it. Francis Huster plays the rising young diplomat singularly without charm.

The house has a smart restaurant where the top girls go but Calfan breaks in and gets the boss's eye. She helps Huster get to the Minister. But he finally marries the Minister's daughter and she be-

comes the head girl under the boss when her predecessor runs off with a rich Latino.

The Stavisky scandal, the Spanish Civil War, the rise of Naziism, the French Popular Front and the last war are background to the running of the house. Not much sex, but glimpses of the rooms that had a stable for those liking milkmaids, a mock-up railroad carriage, etc. Lensing has that sparkling look of commercials. Recreation is acceptable.

It may have legs at home, but for foreign climes looms mainly playoff. — *Mosk.*

Un Papillon Sur L'Epaule
(A Butterfly on the Shoulder)
(FRENCH-COLOR)

Paris, May 9.

Gaumont release of Action Films-Gaumont, Citel Films production. Stars Lino Ventura. Directed by Jacques Deray. Screenplay, Jean-Claude Carriere, Tonino Guerra from book by Jean Gearon, "The Velvet Well;" camera (Eastmancolor), Jean Boffety, Jean Charvein; editor, Henri Lanoe. Reviewed at Salle Ponthieu, Paris, April 26, '78. Running time, **95 MINS.**
Roland .... Lino Ventura
Woman .... Claudine Auger
Raphael .... Paul Crauchet
Doctor .... Jean Bouise
Sonia .... Nicole Garcia
Carrabo .... Laura Betti
Miguel .... Xavier Depraz

Director Jacques Deray has adequately handled this psychological suspenser about an ordinary man caught up in skullduggery in the world's undercover activities. But it lacks the fillip of visual excitement and playing. Result is an okay entertainment of its type, auguring good chances at home with playoff mainly indicated abroad on its theme.

Plot has Lino Ventura, a solid actor, playing a seemingly simple middleaged man who jumps ship in Barcelona. He soon becomes involved in an intricate string of story twists including murders, kidnappings and mysterious appearances and disappearances. Tale of a man caught up in things beyond him ends with Ventura's being gunned down.

Spanish locales help the atmosphere and other players are good. Technically savvy, it just needed more vigor and drive to raise it above the stolid but watchable film it is. —*Mosk.*

Unsichtbare Gegner
(Invisible Adversaries)
(AUSTRIAN-COLOR)

Hollywood, May 1.

Produced and directed by Valie Export. Features entire cast. Screenplay, Peter Weibel; camera (color), Wolfgang Simon; editor, Juno Sylva Englander; music, Hartl-Kalchauser. No other credits available. Reviewed at the Academy of Motion Picture Arts & Sciences Little Theatre, Beverly Hills, Calif. April 30,; '78. Running time: **112 MINS.**

Anna.....................Susann Widl
Peter.....................Peter Weibel

───

Like so many other "experimental" films, "Invisible Adversaries" begins as tongue in cheek and ends as foot in mouth. It's a dense 112-minute exercise more accessible through the program notes than by viewing. Austrian avant-gardist Valie Export directed — her first feature film — and Peter Weibel scripted and costarred with Susann Widl. Only potential outlets for the item are film societies which specialize in this kind of fare.

For the record, "Invisible Adversaries" is some type of science fiction film. A mysterious force known as Hyksos is invading and taking over the earth. Those it has penetrated don't necessarily know that the invisible adversaries are in control. But an impartial observer can look at the goings-on in the streets of Vienna and surmise that all is not kosher.

In this case, the audience is the impartial, and unwitting, observer, mostly of the effect of the unseen devils on a photographer and her boyfriend. The film is rife with dense images and multi-media experiments, none of which ease the boredom or annoyance of this work.
— *Hege.*

───

La Escopeta Nacional
(The National Shotgun)
(SPANISH-COLOR)

───

Madrid, May 5.

An Incine production, presented by Alfredo Matas. Directed by Luis G. Berlanga. Screenplay, Luis Berlanga, Rafael Azcona; camera (Eastmancolor), Carlos Suarez; sets, Rafael Palmero; editor, Jose L. Matesanz. Reviewed at Incine screening room, Madrid, May 4, '78. Running time: **88 MINS.**

Cast: Jose Sazatornil, Antonio Ferrandis, Jose Luis Lopez Vazquez, Rafael Alonso, Luis Escobar, Agustin Gonzalez, Andres Mejuto, Conchita Montes, Monica Randall, Barbara Rey, Laly Soldevila, Amparo Soler Leal, Rossanna Yanni.

───

Speak of "new Spanish cinema" and here's a good example of it. Luis Berlanga, who was battling the Frankist censors for decades, has now let down his hair and launched with merry gusto into an attack on the whole corrupt structure of Spain, then and now. Carlos Saura has handled the subject with brooding symbolism; Berlanga now gives it a light, almost farcical touch as he parades out a mocking sideshow of the powers that have ruled the country: priests, venal politicians, aristocrats, prostitutes, businessmen. His fling is more subdued than, say, Luis Buneul's "Viridiana" but equally incisive and sometimes very funny.

What Berlanga and Rafael Azcona have done is assemble Spain's "finest" at one of those almost legendary hunting weekends so beloved of aristocrats and politicians. The characters range from the depraved and idiotic to the scheming and ruthless. Though at first sight some of the antics may seem a bit exaggerated, they are probably as authentic as the fact of Franco's daughter recently getting caught smuggling 20 gold coins out of Spain.

The anti-hero of the shenanigans is a Catalan businessman (Catalans are famous for their business sense and dislike of Castilian centralism) who, in fact, is paying the impecunious marquis for the hunting, who brings in tow his "secretary" and tries to butter up influential ministers and bankers for them to invest in a housedoor intercom scheme to replace Spain's *porteras*. The characters at the lodge include a crippled old marquis who collects female pubic hair in little bottles, his moronic son who snatches a pretty model and holes up with her in a barn threatening to shoot anyone coming near, a self-righteous priest who condemns the surrounding immorality but takes umbrage under the doddering aristocrats, a sinister Latin American ex-dictator (Peron?) living it up in Spanish exile, a government minister and his concubine and other assorted symbols of "upper class" Spain.

There isn't much of a plot to the film, but it keeps a fairly brisk pace throughout as the Catalan and his girl alternately curse (in Catalan, with Spanish subtitles) or try to ingratiate themselves to the big shots, who are too busy wheeling and dealing or womanizing to pay much attention to him. Finally, the Catalan must quickly change his strategy as it is rumored a cabinet change is in the offing, with the Opus Dei slated to take over. In a final effort, the Catalan plays up to the priest and he prim minister-elect, but the latter drives off hurriedly after morning mass in his official limousine declining even to tip the shooting-party peons.

Jose Sazatornil puts in a delightful performance as the favor-currying Catalan, Jose Luis Lopez Vazquez plays the part of the overwrought marquis's son to perfection, and all others are equally proficient and convincing in this well-lensed production. Pic will certainly mean more to Spaniards themselves, who can pick out some of the prototypes, but item is broad enough to score in other countries as well. Though the antics sometimes verge on the grotesqueness of opera buffa, Berlanga has spiced them with enough humor and pointed dialogs to maintain interest. Some offshore sales might be generated on Berlanga's name and as an expose pic repping the newest in Spanish cinema from an old master.
— *Besa.*

───

Long Weekend
(AUSTRALIAN-COLOR)

───

Sydney, April 12.

A Dugong Films presentation. Produced by Richard Brennan. Directed by Colin Eggleston. Features entire cast. Screenplay, Everett De Roche; music, Michael Carlos; camera (Panavision-Eastmancolor), Vincent Monton; editor, Brian Kavanagh; art direction, Larry Eastwood; costumes, Kevin Reagan; sound John Phillips; set decoration, Tony Hunt. Reviewed at the Hoyts Theatrette, April 11, '78. (Unclassified by Commonwealth Censor). Running time: **100 MINS.**

Peter....................John Hargreaves
Marcia....................Briony Behets
Truck Driver.............Mike McEwen
Bartender...............Michael Aitkins
Old Man.......................Roy Day
City girl................Sue Kiss von Soly

───

"Long Weekend" is director Colin Eggleston's second feature and he's taken on an ambitious concept with which to prove his ability to control drama. (His first, semi-softcore, "Fantasm Comes Again," hardly qualifies as a serious test of his handling of histronics). Basically, this pic is a two-hander: John Hargreaves and Briony Behets, a young married couple whose marriage is foundering, take to the hills for the weekend in an attempt to air things out.

Eggleston's manipulation of his players and De Roche's script is subtle enough that though you're aware that the pair isn't going to have it easy (their relationship precludes that), you're not entirely ready for the way all outdoors closes in — it's the claustrophobia of nature that is the threat. Not that this in that sense is a horror film, to the contrary; it's just that sometimes it gets scary out.

The whole film was shot on location, and Eggleston has made impressive use of Vincent Monton's Panavision cameras to reinforce the oppression inherent in his exteriors; in that, the film is a tour de force.

Hargreaves and Behets carry the film thespically, and it's a measure of both their control and that of the director that it isn't alarmingly noticible that there are really only two parts in the picture. The pair's performances are kept tautly within character, and despite Peter's inherent (and not so inherent) nastiness, one can appreciate what a nice girl like Marcia is doing in a place like that.

The film could work equally well in another medium (indeed, it could be absolutely superb radio); but it really does need the big screen to make its points. It will be interesting to watch when eventually it is shown on tv, because it will most probably work well there, too, if the tv print is carefully made, because for all the vistas, there is some striking use of close-up shooting.

The ecological overtones aren't heavy, but they're there, and if the measure of retributive action is severe, it's all too plausible none the less. And the finale is a shocker.

Tech credits are all top notch; in addition to Monton's fine lensing, the sound and music heighten the action marvelously. As noted, Behets and Hargreaves are excellent: it's only nature that overacts.

Commercial prospects seem good at home with Hoyts Theatres taking up the release. Elsewhere, it could have ready acceptance because apart from the flora and fauna, the story could have happened anywhere. —*Miha.*

───

Licao de Amor
(Love Lesson)
(BRAZIL-COLOR)

───

Los Angeles, May 1.

An Embra film release of a Corisco Filmes Ltd. production, produced by Luiz Carlos Barreto and Eduardo Escorel. Directed by Eduardo Escorel. Screenplay, Escorel and Eduardo Coutinho from the novel "Love Intransitive Verb" by Mario de Andrade; camera (color), Murillo Salles; editor, Gilberto Santeiro; music, Frances Hime. No other credits available. Reviewed at the Royal Theatre, West L.A., May 1, '78. (No MPAA rating.) Running time: **75 MINS.**

Fraulein..............Lilian Lemmertz
Felisberta Souza Costa.....Rogerio Froes
Da. Laura.................Irene Racache
Carlos................Marcos Taquechel
Maria Luisa.........Maria Claudia Costa
Laurita..................Magali Lemoine
Aldinha..................Mariana Veloso
Celeste.....................Marie Claude
Tanaka.....................William Wu
Matilde....................Deia Pereira

───

One of two Brazilian entries at recent L.A. Filmex, "Love Lesson" tells the story of a young man's sexual initiation. That's usually a subject for self-discovery, but in this 75-minute item Marcos Taquechel as Carlos is schooled by a German governess, Lilian Lemmertz, in the secrets of love. Subject is handled with restraint and sensitivity by Eduardo Escorel.

The film is set in the 1920s and opens with Carlos' father, a somewhat stuffy and wealthy Brazilian land baron, employing Lemmertz. She's a hard-edged German expatriate, trying to raise enough money to return to her country.

Relating — and illustrating — the facts of life is now her profession. She's actually a cultured and educated woman, very definitely, not a whore. Lemmertz is hired by wealthy fathers so that their sons will not learn of love from prostitutes.

Observing Carlos' growing attraction to his governess and

teacher is what's interesting about this work. The film's conclusion is known — the relationship will be consummated and the teacher will be sent away. It's the gradual discovery and controlled performances which hold the attention.

—*Hege.*

The Buddy Holly Story
(COLOR)

Excellent musical bio of early rocker. Outlook is formidable.

Hollywood, May 12.

Columbia Pictures release of an Innovisions-ECA production. Produced by Fred Bauer. Exec producers, Edward H. Cohen, Fred T. Kuehnert. Directed by Steve Rash. Features entire cast. Screenplay, Robert Gittler, based on story by Alan Swyer; camera (color), Stevan Larner; editor, David Blewitt; music director, Joe Renzetti; director of special audio, Joel Fein; production design, Joel Schiller; assistant director, Carol Himes; sound, Willie Burton. Reviewed at MGM Theatre, Culver City, May 11, '78. (MPAA Rating: PG.) Running time: **113 MINS.**

Buddy Holly	Gary Busey
Jesse	Don Stroud
Ray Bob	Charles Martin Smith
Riley Randolph	Bill Jordan
Maria Elena Holly	Maria Richwine
Ross Turner	Conrad Janis
Eddie Foster	Albert Popwell
Jenny Lou	Amy Johnston
Madman Mancuso	Fred Travalena
Sol Zuckerman	Dick O'Neil
Mrs. Santiago	Gloria Irricari

Given the tepid b.o. performance of Paramount's "American Hot Wax," the market for recycled 1950s rock 'n' roll seems questionable. But if any film can succeed in revitalizing that era, it's "The Buddy Holly Story." The Columbia Pictures release packs solid dramatic and musical punch. Outlook is very strong if proper marketing approach can be worked out.

There have been several abortive attempts to get the life of pioneer rocker Holly on celluloid, most notably 20th Century'Fox' "Not Fade Away." Contractual agreements with Holly's widow remained a perennial snag until producers Edward H. Cohen and Fred Bauer convinced her of this project's sincerity.

It was a wise choice. "The Buddy Holly Story" smacks of realism in almost every respect, from the dramaturgy involving Holly and his back-up band, The Crickets, to the verisimiltitude of the musical numbers. Latter were recorded live, using 24 tracks, and there was no studio rerecording. It was a gamble that pays off in full, and the Holly repertoire (an extensive one) gives the pic its underlying structure.

Casting by Joyce Selznick was also letter-perfect. Gary Busey not only imparts the driven, perfectionist side of Holly's character, but his vocal work is excellent, as is his instrumentation. While Busey has a background as a pro- musician, cohorts Don Stroud and Charles Martin Smith do no, a fact well disguised in the realistic song stylings.

Since pic represents maiden effort by both director Steve Rash and scripter Robert Gittler, some nervousness may have been evinced on Col's part when picking up the indie production. All fears should be allayed by the final product.

Gittler's screenplay takes Holly from his early days in Lubbock, Texas, where he churns out be-bop for the roller rink crowd, through his disastrous recording career (he punches out a Nashville producer), and up through national recognition on the heels of his big hit, "That'll Be The Day."

Along the way, Rash zeroes in on the growing conflict between Busey, drummer Stroud (who has his best part in years) and bassist Smith, and the love relationship of Busey and Maria Richwine as his Puerto Rican bride. All principals register strongly.

Supporting cast is likewise excellent, especially Bill Jordan as Busey's first supporter, Conrad Janis as an honest record producer, Fred Tavalena as a manic deejay and Dick O'Neil as the stunned booker of the Apollo Theatre, presented with a white act.

The Apollo scene and the pic's final concert, which precedes the title card announcing Holly's death in a 1959 plane crash, are galvanizing in their immediacy. Joel Fein, who masterminded the live recording setup, and music director Joe Renzetti both turn in superb work.

Tech credits, especially David Blewitt's editing, are strong. Stevan Larner's lensing was murky in some places, but backstage shots are notoriously hard to light. Only other criticism would be running time, which seems about 20 minutes too long. In every other respect, however, "The Buddy Holly Story" is firstrate filmmaking.

—*Poll.*

Thank God It's Friday
(COLOR)

Corny script alternates with songs. Fast playoff in teenybopper markets.

Hollywood, April 26.

Columbia Pictures release, produced by Rob Cohen; executive producer, Neil Bogart. Directed by Robert Klane. Features entire cast. Screenplay, Barry Armyan Bernstein; camera (Metrocolor), James Crabe; aerial photography, Frank Holgate; editor, Richard Halsey; production design, Tom H. John; set decoration, Jeff Haley; sound, Arthur Piantadosi, Les Fresholtz, Michael Minkler, Al Overton Jr.; costumes-wardrobe, Betsy Jones, Michael Kaplan, Jack Angel, Kathy O'Rear, Paula Cain; asst. director, Charles Ziarko; second unit director, Jim Gavin; stunt coordinator, Phil Adams. Reviewed at The Burbank Studios, April 26, '78. (MPAA Rating: PG). Running time, **89 MINS.**

Nicole Sims	Donna Summer
Frannie	Valerie Landsburg
Jeannie	Terri Nunn
Marv Gomez	Chick Vennera
Bobby Speed	Ray Vitte
Dave	Mark Lonow
Sue	Andrea Howard
Tony	Jeff Goldblum
Maddy	Robin Menken
Jennifer	Debra Winger
Ken	John Freidrich
Carl	Paul Jabara
Jackie	Marya Small
Gus	Chuck Sacci
Shirley	Hilary Beane
Floyd	DeWayne Jessie
Themselves	The Commodores

The disaster film genre of a few years back has been succeeded by the 45 rpm Ark picture, populated by pre-fab human stereotypes competing for attention with dozens of golden oldies and golden newies supplied by the music biz entrepreneurs whose perception of film-as-trailer may in time boomerang. Talk about your screen advertising. "Thank God It's Friday," an 89-minute rock revue from Otown and Casablanca, focusses on one night at a disco where pairs of people cavort in corny playlets. The Columbia release looks like a fair pre-summer flash.

Donna Summer makes her film debut in a comparatively charming role of an aspiring singer who cons her way to the disco stage and instant stardom. Fact that she is not known as an actress makes the thesping believable. Rest of cast, however, includes many with strong prior credits who are shot down by the Barry Armyan Bernstein script and Robert Klane's direction. Players are shoehorned between as many as 32 different songs, a few, including "Last Dance," new and pleasant.

Producer Bob Cohen and exec producer Neil Bogart have invested most effort in the colorful disco physical environment; the related production credits are all strong.

With this and other rock revues in abundance, some smart exhibitors will in time be able to plan all-night film concerts for off-season periods. Flat rentals of course will be in order, but, not to worry, since most of the pix will be flat within weeks.

—*Murf.*

Metamorphoses
(ANIMATED-COLOR)

Hollywood, May 4.

A Sanrio release, produced by Terry Ogisu, Hiro Tsugawa. Exec producer, Shintaro Tsuji. Written, produced and directed by Takashi, based on material from Ovid's "Metamorphoses." Camera (Technicolor), Bill Millar; animation editor, Barbara Ottinger; music coordinator, Bob Randles; sound effects, Sound Arts; scene planner, Ruth Tompson. Reviewed at Village Theatre, Westwood, May 4, '78. (MPAA Rating: PG.) Running time: **89 MINS.**

Animation Credits: Sequence directors, Jerry Eisenberg, Richard Huebner, Sadao Miyamoto, Amby Paliwoda, Ray Patterson, Manny Perez, George Singer, Stan Walsh; production designers, Paul Julian, Ray Aragon, Kuni Fukai, Rebecca Ortega Mills, Akira Uno; animation, Edwin Aardal, John Ahern, Mikiharu Akabori, Robert Carlson, Brad Case, Marija Dail, Edward DeMattia, Joan Drake, Edgar Friedman, Edwardo Fuentes, Morris Gollub, Fred Grable, Masami Hata, Fred Hellmich, Ernesto Lopez, Daniel Noonan, Ken O'Brian, Jack Ozark, William Pratt, Thomas Ray, Virgil Ross, Glenn Schmitz, Martha Swanson, Reuben Timmins, James Walker, John Walker, Shigeru Yamamoto, Rudolfo Zamora; layout, Nino Carbe, Oscar Dufaux, Don Morgan, Lew Ott, Mike

Ploog, Jose Rivera, Ed Verraux; background, Yukio Abe, Ron Dias, Alison Julian, Phil Lewis, Eric Semones, Gloria Wood.

———

In its first major production and release, Sanrio Films may have overextended itself. "Metamorphoses," based on five tales of classical mythology by Ovid, presents so many differing styles of animation, coupled with a score that ranges from rock to atonal electronic music, that audiences may be more confused than enthused by the finished product.

Three years in the making, "Metamorphoses" was screened last fall, then pulled back for more tinkering. End product seems abbreviated in some sections, overlong in others. Primary selling point would seem to be as a "head" film, attracting 18-25 age group. Since many scenes will be terrifying to children (thus the PG rating), family appeal seems negligible. Rock soundtrack should add marquee value.

Writer-producer-director Takashi has utilized five of the most familiar Greek and Roman myths: creation, the hunter Actaeon turned into a stag by the goddess Diana, Orpheus and Eurydice, Mercury, and the House of Envy, Perseus and Medusa, along with the final tale of Phaeton driving the sun chariot.

Differing storylines are integrated via having a running animated character portray each of the heroes and/or victims. But unless audiences are up on their Greek and Roman mythology, much of the film will be incomprehensible. Either subtitled prologue, or some voice-over explanation, could help immensely in clearing up the confusion.

As in any animated feature, the power of "Metamorphoses" lies in its drawings. And there is some superb animation on display here, efforts that can rival anything that Disney has turned out. A snake, representing evil, writhes with envy; the hounds that turn on Actaeon are completely terrifying; the devil in the Orpheus tale is immensely foreboding, and a scene where his backbone turns into a giant stairway to Hades is positively brilliant.

All too often, however, Takashi's vision seems a personal one, especially given the relationship between pictures and score. Disney influence seems strong, but never consistent, and there is the appearance of economizing in the texturing of both landscape and characters, and the supplemental drawings (such as Diana's griffin) are often brilliant. .

With exception of the Pointer Singers number in third fable, the Orpheus story, soundtrack is basically a dud. Even the Dolby sound encoding system can't help the washed-out tone of Joan Baez, and the otherwise-modern score

will be a turnoff to most viewers.

Other tech credits, especially MGM lab work, are superior. Outlook seems limited, however, to art houses and double-billings with items like "Fantasia." (Double-billing with a Disney release is not very likely. — Ed.) Word of mouth will probably not help. — *Poll.*

If Ever I See You Again
(COLOR)

———

Musical treacle. Strong teenybopper outlook.

———

Hollywood, May 3.
Columbia Pictures release, written (with Martin Davidson), scored, produced and directed by Joe Brooks. Features entire cast. Camera (Technicolor), Adam Holender, Don Sweeney; editor, Rick Shaine; art direction, Don Gilman; sound, Richard Dior, Roger Pietschman; asst. directors, Jim Maniolas, David Whorf. Reviewed at The Burbank Studios, May 3, '78. (MPAA Rating: PG.) Running time, 105 MINS.
Bob Morrison . . . . Joe Brooks
Jennifer Corly . . . . Shelley Hack
Mario . . . . Jimmy Breslin
Steve Warner . . . . Jerry Keller
David Miller . . . . Kenny Karen
Lawrence . . . . George Plimpton
Young Morrison . . . . Michael Decker
Young Corly . . . . Julie Ann Gordon
Morrison Children . . . . Danielle Brisebois,
Branch Emerson
Housekeeper . . . . Shannon Bolin
Laura Miller . . . . Caroline Mignini
Producers . . . . Joe Leon, Ed Kovins

Joe Brooks' "If Ever I See You Again" is another high-calorie teenybopper fairy tale in which a successful-but-lonely romantic is reunited with an old, college flame. Overripe as the hairspray, soft drink and airline commercials it resembles, the film features in its 105 minutes several plays of five songs, including the title tune which is saturation plugged. There's no reason at all to believe that the Columbia release will not find its target audience.

Brooks, whose "You Light Up My Life" was a surprise hit last fall, this time heads the cast as the romantic teleblurb composer who has never forgotten Shelley Hack from college days. His partner, Jerry Keller, and their associate, Jimmy Breslin (in an offbeat but effective casting), are prominent in the overlong sequences devoted to the boredom and idiocy of Madison Avenue. This is odd, since the film, when taking itself seriously and self-consciously, is a series of meller playlets direct from the same place. And the product plugola — besides the songs — is hardly discreet.

Suffice it to say that the two lovers, after predictable reunion, flashback, intimacy and talk (lots of that, and statically directed), finally come together forever and ever. There's nothing wrong with such a story; it's one of drama's staples. But when the telling is clumsy, the form becomes banal.

Unintentionally amusing is the film's anachronistic cliches about

California living. Particularly ludicrous is part of a song lyric (you get to know the words after so many reprises) about "*** the winds called Santa Ana (making) you feel like you belong." Poetic license aside, the death and destruction those winds usually bring makes the sentiment as gauche as a love song to Manhattan talking about a garbage strike there. The melody, however, is lush enough, and familiar enough, to pass.

Brooks is not to be denied a certain sensitivity to the more maudlin facets of the mass ticket-buying (and record-buying) market. There's a strident sincerity in this contrived hoke that can put it over. Audiences, of couse, will recognize the film for what it is and enjoy it as such. The only danger is that somebody might just consider this first class filmmaking —*Murf.*

Our Winning Season
(COLOR)

———

Tepid imitation of "One on Onw." Action seems limited to ozoners. ———

Hollywood, May 5.
American International Pictures release, produced by Joe Roth. Exec producer, Samuel Z. Arkoff; exec in charge of production, Louis S. Arkoff. Features entire cast. Directed by Joseph Ruben. Screenplay by Nick Niciphor; camera (Movielab Color), Stephen Katz; editor, Bill Butler; music, Charles Fox; art director, Angelo Graham; sound, Larry Jost; costumes, Jimmy George; stunt coordinator, Mickey Gilbert; assistant director, Ed Markley. Reviewed at Samuel Goldwyn Theatre, BevHills, May 5, '78. (MPAA Rating: PG.) Running time: 92 MINS.
David Wakefield . . . . Scott Jacoby
Alice Barker . . . . Deborah Benson
Paul Morelli . . . . Dennis Quaid
Jerry McDuffy . . . . Randy Herman
Dean Berger . . . . Joe Penny
Cathy Wakefield . . . . Jan Smithers
Cindy Hawkins . . . . P.J. Soles
Burton Fleishaur . . . . Robert Wahler
Susie Wilson . . . . Wendy Rastatter
Miller . . . . Damon Douglas
Sheila . . . . Joanna Cassidy

"Our Winning Season" is a lacklustre little film that goes nowhere with a story of a young athlete struggling against life's hard knocks. Despite a fresh young cast, and some flashy, if ultimately ineffectual, direction, outlook seems confined to ozoner circuit, where the audience doesn't much care what's happening on the screen.

Despite all sorts of coy, imitative gestures, "One On One" this is not. AIP would have been smarter to avoid the pallid mimicry of the Warner Bros. sleeper hit that has returned some $13,000,000 in rentals, and set out on a more original tack.

But script by Nick Niciphor leaves director Joseph Ruben and his cast of virtual unknowns very little room in which to work. Basically a one-note story, plot has high school track man Scott Jacoby hungry for the taste of victory, but unable to best rival Robert Wahler,

who also heads up an opposing school gang.

Enter Vietnam draftee Joe Penny, former track star who returns home to woo Jacoby's sister, Jan Smithers, and drop a few pearls of wisdom before heading overseas to his death. Funeral of Penny snaps Jacoby and buddies Dennis Quaid and Randy Herman out of their immature hijinks, and propels Jacoby to win not only the big race, but a girl who believes in him (Deborah Benson).

Thanks to Ruben's inventive visual plotting, "Our Winning Season" just avoids the treacle inherent in Niciphor's screenplay. The introductory high school scene is a masterful one-camera tracking shot, and there are other signs of intelligent direction not evident in Ruben's previous hit, "The Pom-Pom Girls." Bill Butler's editing also helps immensely, but Stephen Katz' lensing was often out of focus.

What appeal "Our Winning Season" does impart comes through its casting. Jacoby is sympathetic but not especially interesting in the lead role, but acting kudos go to Dennis Quaid as Jacoby's manic buddy. In one of the few non-stereotyped potsmoking scenes of recent films, Quaid is outstanding. Joanna Cassidy also turns in a gem as a matronly prostitute Jacoby visits on his 18th birthday.

Solid support is offered by Herman, Smithers and Benson, but "Our Winning Season" never goes far enough in developing any of these characters into a believable personage. Reality is also forfeit by the total absence of adults in the cast, other than a few cardboard coaches.

Georgia locations serve film well. "Our Winning Season" features lotsa smooching, which should be attractive to drive-in crowds, who often like to see their own actions mirrored on the screen. —*Poll.*

The Wild Geese
(BRITISH-COLOR)

Playable if flawed action meller with good marquee value.

London, May 10.

A Rank Organization release of a Euan Lloyd production. Directed by Andrew V. McLaglen. Associate producer, Chris Chrisafis; Stars Richard Burton, Roger Moore, Richard Harris, Hardy Kruger. Screenplay, Reginald Rose, based on book by Daniel Carney; camera (Panavision-Color), Jack Hildyard; editor, John Glen; music, Roy Budd; sound, Gordon Everett; assistant director, Derek Cracknell. Reviewed at Century Theatre, London, May 9, '78. Running time: **132 MINS.**

Colonel Allen Faulkner ... Richard Burton
Shawn Fynn .... Roger Moore
Rafer Janders .... Richard Harris
Pieter Coetzee .... Hardy Kruger
Sir Edward Matherson .. Stewart Granger
R.S.M. Sandy Young .... Jack Watson
President Limbani ...... Winston Ntshona
Jesse .... John Kani
Witty .... Kenneth Griffith
The Priest .... Frank Finlay
Balfour .... Barry Foster
Mr. Martin .... Jeff Corey
Jock .... Ronald Fraser
Tosh .... Ian Yule
Samuels .... Brook Williams
Keith .... Percy Herbert
Rushton .... Patrick Allen
Esposito .... Glyn Baker
Heather .... Rosalind Lloyd
Mrs. Young .... Jane Hylton
Sonny .... David Ladd
Emile .... Paul Spurrier

Euan Lloyd's uppercase actioner, centered on a caper by mercenaries in Africa, attempts to be a cornucopia of tried boxoffice hooks but ultimately fails to meld its comedy, adventure, pathos, violence, heroics — or even its political message — into a credible whole.

It tries to provide within its rip-'em-up adventureneering something for every escapist but despite a strong lineup of marketable stars and a technically well-produced package it falls between several stools.

It's also overlong and could be improved by tightening.

Marquee name value, expensive look and topical hardboiled action should see it okay in general playoff but its heterogeneous story ingredients make it an ungainly hybrid. That may affect word-of-mouth trade.

Reginald Rose's adaptation of Daniel Carney's story — about mercenary toughguys who parachute into the African bush to snatch a deposed African president for reinstatement to suit British business interests — is routinely predictable and, in the end, cornily incredible.

First 42 minutes of the 132-minute pic deals with a "Magnificent Seven"-type recruiting drive (for Yul Brynner read Richard Burton) in London, to enlist mercenaries enduring various mundane civilian fates apparently worse than the death they might otherwise expect in the jungle.

Combat training sessions, re-astically supervised by Jack Watson as a veteran NCO, gives Jack Hildyard's camerawork first of numerous well-grabbed chances to shine during action sequences. And Dick Hillard's aerial shots of the mercenaries freefalling into Africa are a highlight in a generally well photographed feature.

Andrew V. McLaglen's direction, in attempting to achieve the multifaceted result demanded by the script, often appears fickle.

Roger Moore's shootouts with the Mafia in London and Hardy Kruger's neat killing of three sentries with cyanide-tipped arrows is good "traditional" escapism. Then, as if to contemporize the film, Peckinpah-fashion, the screen's suddenly filled with bloody graphics and four-letter words. (Interestingly, of the four leaders, script demands only one, Harris, to use a single serious expletive).

Winston Ntshona is well cast as the deposed president Limbani though much of his "message" dialog is unnecessarily and unpalatably heavy for what's presumably designed as a riproaring blood and guts actioner.

Aforementioned potpourri of styles may well have confused the direction of Roy Budd's music which is on occasion over-jolly at the least jolly of times. Joan Armatrading's theme song is suitable, if unspectacular. —*Swan.*

Malibu Beach
(COLOR)

Typical Crown summer exploitationer. Nothing new under the sun.

Hollywood, May 8.

A Crown International Pictures release of a Marimark production. Produced by Marilyn J. Tenser; exec producer, Newton P. Jacobs. Directed by Robert J. Rosenthal. Screenplay, Celia Susan Cotelo, Rosenthal; camera (Deluxe) Jamie Anderson; editor, Robert Barrere; sound, Don A. Sanders; art director, Fred Chriss; costumes, Diana Daniels; stunt coordinator Von Deming; assistant director, Gerald T. Olson. Reviewed at UA Theatre, Marina Del Rey, May 7, '78. (MPAA Rating: R.) Running time: **93 MINS.**

Dina .... Kim Lankford
Bobby .... James Daughton
Sally .... Susan Player Jarreau
Dugan .... Stephen Oliver
Paul .... Michael Luther
Ms. Plickett .... Flora Plumb
Claude .... Roger Lawrence Pierce

Not much has changed with the beach bunny picture since its inception in the late 1950s. Bikini-clad girls, bronzed musclemen, hot cars, surf and sand still predominate. The only new wrinkle Crown International's "Malibu Beach" introduces is the shift from beer guzzling to pot smoking. Otherwise, this summer exploitation item repeats the excesses of American International's interminable string of "beach blanket" epics.

Following in the path of its own success, Crown encores the format that paid off so handsomely in "Pom Pom Girls": a string of unrelated vignettes (in this case, beach-oriented) linked together by characters who interact, usually in the romantic sense of the term.

Kim Lankford is the new femme lifeguard at Malibu, where she's quickly importuned by body builder Stephen Oliver, and beach bums James Daughton and Michael Luther. There's some partner swapping involving Lankford and friend Susan Player Jarreau, but eventually the blond couple ends up together, as do the brunettes, and Oliver is left out in the cold.

That leads to some macho rivalry between Oliver and Daughton, culminating in a vehicle wipe-out and a very silly (and overdone) bit involving a phony "Jaws" scare. In the end, the youngsters manage to establish, of all things, a "relationship," while Oliver stomps off with a priggish schoolteacher turned beach beauty.

"Malibu Beach" is California living with an "as told to Hollywood" approach. The pangs and hardship of young love, the pleasures (and surprising rewards) of cruising, and the new emphasis on marijuana as a social pleasure should find lots of empathy from ozoner patrons.

All of this was done 15 years ago, and even Oliver's character of Dugan evokes memories of Harvey Lembeck and "Eric Von Zipper."

Robert J. Rosenthal keeps the pace as lively as can be expected, and sound effects were especially well-handled. Other tech credits are okay, and film has a surprisingly clean gloss.

"Malibu Beach" should have no trouble finding its niche on drive-in screens in the coming months. Only hope is this won't start another run on beach pix, or we might be facing "Malibu Beach Bingo" in the future. —*Poll.*

Corvette Summer
(COLOR)

Excellent comedy-drama with wide audience potential.

Hollywood, May 4.

United Artists release of a Metro-Goldwyn-Mayer picture, produced by Hal Barwood. Stars Mark Hamill, Annie Potts, Eugene Roche. Directed by Matthew Robbins. Screenplay, Barwood, Robbins; camera (Metrocolor), Frank Stanley; second unit camera, Rexford Metz; editor, Amy Jones; music, Craig Safan; art direction, James Schoppe; set decoration, Richard Spero; sound, Willie D. Burton, William McCaughey, Aaron Rochin, Michael J. Kohut; costumes-wardrobe, Aggie Guerard Rodgers; asst. director, Jim Bloom; second unit director, Buddy Joe Hooker; stunt coordinator, Bobby Bass. Reviewed at MGM Studios, Culver City, May 4, '78. (MPAA Rating: PG.) Running time: **105 MINS.**

Ken Dantley .... Mark Hamill
Vanessa .... Annie Potts
Ed McGrath .... Eugene Roche
Wayne Lowry .... Kim Milford
Principal .... Richard McKenzie
Police P.R. .... William Bryant
Gil .... Philip Bruns
Kootz .... Danny Bonaduce
Mrs. Dantley .... Jane A. Johnston
Ricci .... Albert Insinnia
Tico .... Isaac Ruiz Jr.
Con Man .... Stanely Kamel
Tony .... Jason Ronard
Jeff .... Brion James

Like an oasis in the current Sahara of youth-themed films, "Corvette Summer" is a most delightful comedy about a three-way romance: Mark Hamill, the sports car he and his school class lovingly restored, and Annie Potts, a trainee hooker (and a bright new performer in the Judy Holliday style). Matthew Robbins' directorial debut is excellent in a firstrate screenplay which he wrote with Hal Barwood, whose production is very strong. The Metro-Goldwyn-Mayer picture, originally titled "Stingray," has lots of inherent commercial potential for United Artists release in the months ahead. Adults as well as kids can laugh their heads off.

The foundation of the film's success is the screenplay about young people which neither talks down to them nor plays up to them. Eugene Roche's auto shop class has rebuilt a sports car, only to have it stolen. Hamill (right off his "Star Wars" success) wanders to Las Vegas where the car is spotted. En route, he is given a ride by Potts, out to make the big time in her water-bed van as an aspiring though nervous Strip prostie.

The plot nicely keeps several major story lines in prominence: Hamill's goofy escapades which segue into young maturity; Potts' laughable attempts at promiscuity: their budding romance; the gradual emergence of Roche as an inflation-whipped middle class teacher who has been drawn into car theft to support his family. Kim Milford, a former pupil, heads a hot car ring in Las Vegas into which Hamill is briefly inducted. The interplay of these story lines produces smiles and laughs, with a substantive base with which young and older audiences can identify.

Robbins' direction is assured and the performances are all super. Second unit director Buddy Joe Hooker and the stunt crew (coordinated by Bobby Bass) assist in contributing some flashy action sequences, nicely restrained and not overdone. Craig Safan's music is very effective. All production credits are tops and, as usual, the entire film has the smart MGM polish which makes them all consistently the best "looking" motion pictures made in Hollywood.

Considering the story locale in Las Vegas, let nobody accuse Metro of plugging its Grand Hotel there. Apart from one brief shot, the locations are those of competitors.

—*Murf.*

Midnight Express
(BRITISH-COLOR)

Grim story of prison life in Turkey. Muddled plot makes empathy hard. Outlook mixed.

Hollywood, May 16.
Columbia Pictures release of a Casablanca Filmworks production, produced by David Puttnam, Alan Marshall; executive producer, Peter Guber. Directed by Alan Parker. Features entire cast. Screenplay, Oliver Stone, based on he book by William Hayes with William Hoffer; camera (Eastmancolor), Michael Seresin; editor, Gerry Hambling; music, Giorgio Moroder; production design, Geoffrey Kirkland; art direction, Evan Hercules; sound, Clive Winter; costumes-wardrobe, Milena Canonero, Bobby Lavender; asst. director, Ray Corbett. Reviewed at The Burbank Studios, May 16, '78. (Not yet rated by MPAA.) Running time, 120 MINS.
Billy Hayes .... Brad Davis
Jimmy .... Randy Quaid
Max .... John Hurt
Tex .... Bo Hopkins
Hamidou .... Paul Smith
Mr. Hayes .... Mike Kellin
Erich .... Norbert Wiesser
Susan .... Irene Miracle

"Midnight Express," based on the book, is a sordid and ostensibly true story about a young American busted for smuggling hash in Turkey and his subsequent harsh imprisonment and later escape. Cast, direction and production are all very good, but it's difficult to sort out the proper empathies from the muddled and moralizing screenplay which, in true Anglo-American fashion, wrings hands over alien cultures as though our civilization is absolutely perfect. The Columbia release may aim for the "Papillon" trade. Global reception may be very mixed. Film is in this year's Cannes Film Fest.

Oliver Stone is credited for adapting the book by Billy Hayes (who wrote it with William Hoffer), young tourist who, in the midst of airline terrorism and world pressure on Turkey over drug farming, is discovered wearing a not-insignificant amount of hash strapped to his body. Brad Davis plays Hayes in a strong performance.

Acceptance of the film depends a lot on forgetting several things: He was smuggling hash; Turkey is entitled to its laws, and is no more guilty of penal corruption and brutality than, say, the U.S., U.K., France, Germany, etc.; a world tourist can't assume that a helpful father (played well by Mike Kellin)

is going to have the same clout as with some midwestern politicians; nor can an American expect to be treated with kid gloves everywhere.

However, the script loads up sympathy for Davis, also fellow convicts Randy Quaid (a psycho character), John Hurt (a hard doper) and Norbert Weisser (playing the obligatory gay inmate), by making the prison authorities even worse. Paul Smith, chief guard and official torturer, exemplifies the characterization.

Irene Miracle does well as Davis' girlfriend, and Bo Hopkins disappears too soon as an investigator who wants to help Davis; in return, Davis tries to escape.

Alan Parker's direction and other credits are also admirable, once you swallow the specious and hypocritical story. Davis escapes, by the way, after 120 minutes of running time, for a happy still montage reunion. So what.

Project was sponsored by Casablance Filmworks, whose chairman Peter Guber was exec producer. David Puttnam and Alan Marshall produced well on European locations. Giorgio Moroder's music is extremely good. —*Murf.*

Jennifer
(COLOR)

For the young in head.

American International Pictures release of a Steve Krantz production. Features entire cast. Directed by Brice Mack. Screenplay, Kay Cousins Johnson, from story by Krantz; camera (CFI color), Irv Goodnoff; film editor, Duane Hartzell; music supervisor, Jerry Styne; title son, Porter Jordan. Reviewed at Forum Theatre, New York, May 19, '78. (MPAA Rating: PG). Running time: 90 MINS.
Jennifer Baylor .... Lisa Pelikan
Jeff Reed .... Bert Convy
Mrs. Calley .... Nina Foch
Sandra Tremayne .... Amy Johnston
Senator Tremayne .... John Gavin
Luke Baylor .... Jeff Corey
Jane Delano .... Louise Hoven
Dayton Powell .... Ray Underwood
Pit Lassiter .... Wesley Eure
Miss Tooker .... Florida Friebus
Deedee Martin .... Georganne La Piere

This imitation of "Carrie" differs from that earlier, more deservedly successful effort, in one respect. This schoolgirl doesn't go in for hyperkenesis; she digs snakes. At any rate, she's able to conjure up an assortment of vipers at will to wreak vengeance for some mistreatment she receives at school.

It's the old routine. Plain, poor girl (with a religious fanatic father instead of a Piper Laurie mother) is in a posh girls school on a scholarship (evidently the only one), without a single friend. One especially bitchy blonde (who's supposed to be the best looking gal in school but, based on what's on the screen, is

outclassed by most of the other students) keeps needling her until the expected, but late in happening, bit of revenge. The cast plays like everyone is on drugs and some cast members (such as John Gavin) are in and out so fast a blink of the eye will miss them.

Technically, things are good (especially the snake handling) but histrionically it's a loser. —*Robe.*

Lulu
(COLOR)

Cinematic opera. Fests and film society may be interested.

Los Angeles, May 3.
Produced, directed, photographed and edited by Ronald Chase. Screenplay, Frank Wedehind; music, Alban Berg; co-editors, Jay Miracle, Todd Boekelheide, Bonnie Koehler; art director, Vance Martin, Donald Eastman. No other credits available. Reviewed at the Royal Theatre, West L.A., May 3, '78. (No MPAA rating.) Running time: 94 MINS.
Ludwig Schon .... Paul Shenar
Lulu .... Elisa Leonelli
Alwa Schon .... John Roberdeau
Countess Geschwitz ...... Norma Leistiko
Walter .... Stephen Ashbrook
Dr. Goll .... Warren Pierce
Prince Escerny .... Michael Anderson
Jack the Ripper .... Thomas Roberdeau

"Lulu," Ronald Chase's second feature, is a series of visual shocks set to music. Based on two Frank Wedekind plays, "Earth Spirit" and "Pandora's Box," and best known as an opera by Alban Berg, "Lulu," tells the story of a loose living woman's rise in society through a succession of marriages and her ultimate fate at the hands of London's 19th century Jack the Ripper.

The ending is violent. The opening sections are also fairly explicit.

Except for one of the film's half dozen parts, all divided by title cards introducing a new chapter in Lulu's life, this is a silent film. The narrative is told through visuals, with an emphasis on close-ups and tight close ups, and by the same kind of title cards used in silent films.

"Lulu" will be of interest to film societies and the non-theatrical market. Its commercial potential, even on the art circuit seems limited. — *Hege.*

Towing
(COLOR)

Chicago, May 16.
A United International Release of Sibling Productions. Produced by Frederick A Smith. Executive producers, Alan Gelband and Bob Greenberg; Directed and written by Maura Smith; Features entire cast. Camera (color) Hal Schullman; music, Martin Rubinstein; editing, Bernard F.

Caputo; sound, Art Ziemke, Kurt Kreutz. Reviewed at the Village Theater, Chicago, Ill. May 4, -78. (MPAA Rating: PG). Running time: 85 MINS.
Jean .... Jenniffer Ashley
Lynn .... Sue Lyon
Tony .... Bobby DiCicco
Chris .... Joe Mantegna
Putch .... J.J. Johnston
Irate Lady .... Audry Neenan
Irate Man .... Steve Kampman
Pizza Man .... Don DePollo
Nan .... Nan Mason
Phil .... Mike Nusbaum
Lois .... Susanne Smith
Tow Truck Driver .... Jake Stockwell
Mayor .... Lee Stein
Waitress .... Sandy Halpin
News Reporter .... Bob Wallace

When a relatively inexperienced group of Hollywood outsiders manage to bring in a feature for under $1,000,000 and get bookings in a number of large markets credit must be given for perseverance.

Unfortunately, that hustling talent is misplaced on "Towing," a tasteless comedy with bad camera work, poor sound and a disjointed plot. Outlook is thin for any extended play but pic might do okay in big city bookings where towing is a universal problem.

Center of script involves two bar maids' attempts to break up an illegal towing ring that scours the streets of Chicago for cars and charges owners $60 in cash to get their vehicles back. In opening sequence the pic scores points with a disco theme by Martin Rubinstein and some funny bits where everything from an ambulance to a Channel 2 news truck is hauled away.

But as the film progresses emphasis shifts to the personalities of the bar maids, Sue Lyon and Jennifer Ashley, neither of whom is intriguing enough to sustain interest. The shift is the pic's downfall, with the actresses playing the characters as morons who can't hold onto their jobs, much less have the smarts to break up an illegal towing operation.

Supporting players are okay but poor dialog limits any standouts. Script makes Joe Mantegna look ridiculous as Lyon's love interest who just happens by on a busy street every time the girls need him. Bobby DiCicco and other members of the cast are hindered by blaring music and sound problems that muffle much dialog.

Shot entirely in Chicago, the pic has a big city look that years ago seemed limited to New York or Hollywood. But several out-of-focus scenes ruin that plus.

A number of crude sexual jokes in the film as well as a tacky ad campaign featuring sexy cartoon figures of Ashley and Lyon give pic the look and feel of low-budget, R-rated exploitation. Too bad since its PG rating could have attracted a wider potential audience. —*Berg.*

Olyan Mint Otthon
(Just Like at Home)
(HUNGARIAN-COLOR)

Budapest, April 21.

An Hungarofilm Production, Dialog Studio, Budapest; world rights, Hungarofilm, Budapest. Features entire cast. Written and directed by Marta Meszaros. Camera (Eastmancolor), Lajos Koltai. Reviewed at Hungarofilm Screening Room, Budapest, April 20, '78. Running time: 95 MINS.
Cast: Anna Karina, Zsuzsa Czinkoczy, Jan Nowicki.

Another in Marta Meszaros's committed line of pix dealing with women's problems (Women's Lib just doesn't seem to fit her style), this one is a bit more improvisational than the others and has a lighter, fresher appeal. There were indications already in "The Two of Them" (1977) that she had exhausted the "emancipation-message" in "Nine Months" (1976): the former relies on personalities rather than theme, as in the latter, dominating the action.

In "Just Like at Home" Mezsaros wanders all over the place, so much so that the figure of Anna Karina, the emancipation thread, is lost to sight after stating her case as a woman who shouldn't take back the "big baby" (again Jan Nowicki, the Polish actor in all three of her last pix) just because he got tired of America and returned home to Hungary to pick up the pieces. The lad's arrogance, however, is conquered by another young lady, a pre-teenager (Zsuzsa Czinkoczy, the waif in Lazslo Ranody's "No-Man's Daughter," a winner at the 1976 Karlovy Vary fest), who needs a father "like she dreamed of" but would never get in a family with seven children.

The "adopted" father-and-daughter team grow to know each other — and that's where pic gets interesting — shades of Margaret O'Brien and Hollywood kid pix.

"Just Like at Home" may appeal neither to Meszaros's strongest admirers nor fiercest critics, but it's a human story without the pitfalls of stereotypes and pat solutions. This femme helmer gets better with each film, and now improves with a light hand with thesps who instinctively give what is required. — *Holl.*

La Raison D'Etat
(State Reasons)
(FRENCH-ITALO-COLOR)

Paris, May 23.

Silenes Distribution — Lugo Film release of Paris Cannes Production — Alpes Cinema — Mida Produzione Cinematografiche production. Stars Jean Yanne, Monica Vitti. Directed by Andre Cayatte. Screenplay, Cayatte, Jean Curtelin, Jean-Marie Guillaume; camera (Eastmancolor), Armando Nannuzzi; editor, Paul Cayatte; music, Vladimir Cosma. Reviewed at Normandie, Paris, May 12, '78. Running time, 110 MINS.
Leroi .... Jean Yanne
Angela .... Monica Vitti
Marrot .... Francois Perier
Jobin .... Michel Bouquet
Bernanrd .... Jean-Claude Bouillon

Andre Cayatte, who usually deals didactically with miscarriages of justice, here tries for a polemical attack on the corrupt practices of the French government in its arms sales, with the American CIA also thrown in. Fuzzy direction, lacklustre playing and a lack of true welding of character and a more defined political force make this a tract rather than a drama, more a mediocre lawyer's brief than a penetrating revelation on an important theme.

Monica Vitti is miscast as a good-natured Italo biologist who becomes involved when a friend hands her secret political documents to keep. These show that France sold arms illegally through Italy to a rebel African force that killed a group of children in a Red Cross plane.

Only governments, the film seems to suggest can now sell arms acting even more ruthlessly than the old private dealers. But all becomes predictable as Jean Yanne, French arms chief, has his corrupt secret service chief kill off Vitti's friend and then frame Vitti, eventually killing her.

Yanne is ill at east as a man who realizes his dejection but who uses the cover of reasons of state for his dirty work. Lacking the force of Constantine Costa Gavras's politico thrillers or Francesco Rosi's socially dramatic films, this looks mainly aimed at quick playoff on its names and a subject that deserved better treatment. —*Mosk.*

Magyarok
(The Hungarians)
(HUNGARIAN-COLOR)

Budapest, April 22.

An Hungarofilm Production, Dialog Studio, Budapest; world rights, Hungarofilm, Budapest. Features entire cast. Written and directed by Zoltan Fabri, based on a novel by Jozsef Balazs. Camera (Eastmandolor), Gyorgy Illes; music, Gyorgy Vukan. Reviewed at Hungarofilm Screening Room, Budapest, April 21, '78. Running time: 110 MINS.
Andras Fabian .... Gabor Koncz
Mrs. Fabian .... Eva Pap
Janos Szabo .... Bertalan Solti
Mrs. Szabo .... Noemi Apor
Elek Tar .... Gellert Raksanyi
Mrs. Tar .... Erzsi Papai
Daniel Kis .... Andras Muszte
Mrs. Kis .... Anna Muszte
Daniel Gaspar .... Tibor Molnar
Abris Kondor .... Istvan O. Szabo
Brainer .... Zoltan Gera
Anton, a Driver .... Istvan Holl
Farmer .... Sandor Szabo
Priest .... Janos Koltai

"The Hungarians" is the best Zoltan Fabri film of his last extremely productive phase that has included "The Last Sentence" (1975) and "The Fifth Seal" (1976), both literary adaptations (like "The Hungarians") which have won prizes at the last two Moscow Film Fests. This vet helmer seems to wax stronger in his old age as many Hollywood directors did: he is particularly adept at the handling of actors, a virtue many young helmers unfortunately look upon as superfluous today.

Jozsef Balazs's novel, upon which the film is based, is not large and expansive in the vein of most war stories. This one takes place entirely behind the scenes, and for that reason its moments of truth are little more than unforgettable vignettes. There are no heroes to speak of, but this is just about how life was far behind the front lines during the last war, and pic could be a sleeper on the fest circuit and in art houses.

Like a pastoral symphony, pic is divided into four movements corresponding to the seasons with an extra "Winter" thrown in to underscore the tragic side of the story. It's about a small group of Hungarian peasant-farmers and their wives coming from a remote corner of Hungary to Germany in the middle of the War (the year is not stated, but it's probably 1942-43 from certain clues); they go to work for a farmer on his large estate (mostly growing potatoes) near the Baltic Sea. Working here brings more money than at home, and wives are permitted in the work-crew. The leader of the group, Andras Fabian, is quiet and only slightly educated, but he has a strong moral character and reacts openly to the wartime events he observes around him.

"Winter" depicts the farm-hands (all landless peasants) coming to Northern Germany; they notice a POW camp, heavily guarded, next to the barracks they live in but surrounded by sentries and walled fence. "Spring" brings more troubling suspicions as the Hungarians see Polish women and children herded along the road and into their barracks (no fraternization allowed), then Soviet POWs and the killing of a German soldier who refuses to execute a straggler. "Summer" is a trifle idyllic as the pause waiting for the harvest brings a visit to the neighboring town to see the sea and buy a bicycle for Andras's son back home; the group, however, stumbles on a dead man as they take cover from a rain storm. "Autumn" finds them all picking potatoes, together with POWs, and a quarrel breaks out between the hired-hands and their Hungarian-born, Germany-employed foreman over such moral questions as fairness and humanity; the death of the youngest, constantly ill farmhand in poor health leads to the burial in foreign land, the funeral rites performed by a French POW priest and attended by the German landowner, who also lost a son in the war who was the same young age.

"Winter" forces a decision: either to stay in Germany and accept land of their own (for the first time in their lives) or to return to Hungary with the spare wages they have earned and saved. The group chooses the latter alternative to a man — but the younger members of the group are immediately drafted for the war on the very evening of their arrival. The next day they leave for the front — Andras will never return, and his wife's memories include a departing photograph and a house blessing she brought back with her from the year in Germany. — *Holl.*

Norng Mia
(The Sister-in-law)
(THAI-COLOR)

Bangkok, May 11.

A Saha Mongkol Films release. Written, produced and directed by Prince Chatri Chalerm Yukol. Features entire cast. Story, Prince Anusorn Yukol; camera (color), Prince Chatri Chalerm; music, Keow Achariyakul, Sanga Arampi, Preecha Metrai and Prachamitr; sound, Kasem Militachinda. Reviewed at Chalerm Thai theatre, Bangkok, May 10, '78. Running time: 110 MINS.
Saeng .... Sorapong Chatri
Prang .... Viyda Umarin
Tabtim .... Lalana Sulawan
Khun Nai .... Choosri Misomon
Taxi Driver .... Adul Green
Night Club Customer ..... Chinadit Bunnag

Opening with a houseboat at the tail end of a long line of rice barges moving up Chao Phya river, "Norng Mia" makes the river trip terminate in a drab-looking floating market, a Thailand tourist attraction. The inhabitants are a husband and wife (Sorapong Chatri and Viyada Umarin), the wife's sister (Lalana Sulawan) and an infant child.

This is the first film that Viyada, real-life wife of filmmaker Prince Chatri, has made since she won the Asian Fest best actress prize for her performance in Chatri's "Tong-peun Kokpoh" (The Citizen). One would expect that she would be assigned a challenging, dramatic new role, if only to give the public additional proof of her talent.

Sorapong's protracted search for his wife takes up much of the film. He turns his attention to his sister-in-law afterwards, so that it appears as though he was seized by lust rather than any real romantic interest in her. —*Cano.*

The Stick Up
(BRITISH-COLOR)

London, May 17.

Trident-Barber release of an Elliott Kastner and Danny O'Donovan presentation, produced by George Pappas; Stars David Soul. Written and directed by Jeffrey Bloom. Features entire cast. Camera (color) Michael Reed; music, Michael J. Lewis; sound, Ron Butcher; assistant director, Frank Ernst; wardrobe, Mike Jarvis. Reviewed at the Columbia Theatre, London, May 16, 1978. Running time, 101 MINS.

Duke Turnbeau	David Soul
Rosie McCratchit	Pamela McMyler
Smiley	Johnny Wade
Tall Cop	Tony Melody
Short Cop	Norman Jones
Older Cop	Glynn Edwards
Younger Cop	Robert Longden
George	Pat Durkin
Ritchie	Alan Tilern
Amazon Lady	Cyd Child
Sam	Michael Balfour

"The Stick Up" is a slow to medium-paced meller about a Yank fortune seeker's misadventures in 1930s England. It combines the boxoffice appeal of tv's David Soul, herein star-billed, with a passable romantic comedy plot, written and directed by Jeffrey Bloom. Lush green England countryside where it was shot is impressively captured by Michael Reed's camera. Entry should do okay in fast dualer playoff.

Lensed in the style of a "Bonnie & Clyde" or "Paper Moon," the opus relies heavily on the chemistry of Soul and Pamela McMyler, who plays an Irish serving wench who originally sees the American as her passport to greater things.

"Greater things" manifest in a million-pound armored truck robbery but not before a series of sometimes amusing situations which the couple experiences on their way to London.

Originally titled "Mud" the two most impressive scenes involve Soul's attempts to lasso a recalcitrant cow and McMyler's muddy tussle with a femme wrestler known as the Amazon Lady.

By way of frustrating compromise, Bloom's direction divides between Keystone Kops at one extreme and something much more sophisticated at the other. It resultantly succeeds well in neither and apart from its sometimes exceptional photography, and an excellent score by Michael J. Lewis, it's bereft of distinction. —Swan.

Legato
(HUNGARIAN-COLOR)

Budapest, April 22.

An Hungarofilm Production, Budapest Studio, Budapest; world rights, Hungarofilm, Budapest. Features entire cast. Directed by Istvan Gaal. Screenplay, Gaal, Imre Szasz, based on a play by Imre Szasz; camera (Eastmancolor), Gyorgy Illes; music, Andras Szollosy. Reviewed at Hungarofilm Screening Room, Budapest, April 21, '78. Running time: 96 MINS.

Andras Gajzago	Geza D. Hegedus
Mari, His Wife	Nora Kovacs
Rossika	Klari Tolnay
Amalka	Margit Dayka
Franciska	Lujza Orosz
Schoolmaster Gallo	Sandor Szabo

"Legato" is Istvan Gaal's first feature in seven years, after scoring earlier at the Cannes Fest with "The Falcons" and with "Dead Landscape" at Karlovy Vary, both of which won prizes and critical recognition. His new pic will also do well on the summer fest circuit by virtue of its narrative style and the helmer's remarkable talent for blending symbols and metaphors — title could mean either "a messenger" or "something received" from its Latin roots (a typical Gaal teaser) — into a tale that already stands on its own feet.

Pic treats only a day and a night in the lives of a newly married couple, but it's less about them than a journey into the past to discover some loose facts about the boy's father, a physician who died a martyr's death as a resistance fighter in the last war. The young medical student and his wife live under the shadow of a memory in the home of the boy's mother, where one room is set aside to honor the dead father and husband while the couple, expecting a baby, have to get along in cramped servant's quarters. When they are asked by the mother at the beginning of their summer vacation to visit the village where the father died to push for the unveiling of a commemorative plaque, they agree with reluctance as they are sick of the father's memory and it has become a bone of contention between them.

Arriving in the village, they meet a number of people who knew the partisan doctor, and their memories of the past hint that maybe it's better to leave everything untouched and don't dig too deep for the truth. An elderly schoolmaster eventually brings the couple to the home of the aged Zorkoczy sisters and a third woman, a nurse who served the doctor, at whose residence the father hid out as a Communist resistance fighter. In the course of the evening, it becomes clear that the two sisters were in love with the doctor, one (now an invalid) even being his mistress, and that the nurse eventually forced the father out of the house lest more misfortune come their way.

The past is thus revealed as a thorny path of painful memories, of treacherous inhumanity as well as heroic deeds, and of mixed feelings as to what was really right or wrong at that time. The boy, the spitting image of his father, comes also to grips with the relics of a by-gone day, and, in the end, the cloud over their marriage has just about vanished. But not before a suspenseful adventure involving a stolen fake Toulouse-Lautrec painting, a menacing encounter with the sisters' con-man nephew, and a chance, uncomprehended meeting with the widow of a man the father mysteriously shot (thus the delay with the hero's plaque). The trick is to tell two stories in one — and Gaal does it perfectly.

Story is based on a play, but as a film it has its own merits to lift the tale above the simple line of development. Wordy passages perhaps minimize off-shore chances, although acting is on the plus side (the three elderly ladies are veteran stage thesps who know a good role when they see one, and the young couple are talented newcomers fresh from the film-and-theatre acting school with a future to look forward to). Lensing is also polished, as are all the credits. What Gaal seems to be saying in the long run is that the old-style partisan theme of great heroes can now be peacefully, and reverently, laid to rest. — Holl.

Koo Rak
(The Lovers)
(THAI-COLOR)

Bangkok, May 2.

A Chao Poj Films release. Produced and directed by Pornpoj Kanitkasen. Features entire cast. Story and screenplay, Banjerd Tavee; camera (color), Sophon Jaenphanit; music, Prachin Songpow; editor, Pravit Lilawai; sound editor, Montri Ongiam; production designer, Prasobchai Kanitsen; costumes, Rasaniwan Kanitsen. Reviewed at Siam theatre, Bangkok, May 1, '78. Running time: 120 MINS.

Young lovers are the new rage in Thai movies. For years, such roles were monopolized by Sombat Metanee and Aranya Mamwong. Even if they were no longer teenagers, they had to pretend to be lovestruck young ones countless times.

Things have changed. Following the success of the "Wai Olawon" (Only Sixteen) series, young new stars became very much in demand.

After debuting in "Wai Olawon," Pairoj Sangvoributr has appeared in one hit after another. None of his films have flopped and producers are happy to pay him top salary of 100,000 baht (about $5,000) per pic.

His talent lies mainly in his comic rapport with the audience. His secret seems to lie in letting other players try harder at getting laughs than he does.

Campus romance is pic's main subject. Not a classroom scene is included, but there are plenty of other student activities shot on location at Chiang Mai University, in Northern Thailand.

The lovers, Pairoj and Nawarat, are at odds rather than in love with one another most of the time. Their silly quarrels give their fans plenty to be delighted about. —Cano.

Kihajolni Veszelyes
(Don't Lean Out the Window)
(HUNGARIAN-COLOR)

Budapest, April 22.

An Hungarofilm Production, Dialog Studio, Budapest; world rights, Hungarofilm, Budapest. Features entire cast. Directed by Janos Zsombolyai. Screenplay, Andras Simonffy; camera (Eastmancolor), Elemer Ragalyi; music, Gabor Presser and Locomotiv GT Group. Reviewed at Hungarofilm Screening Room, Budapest, April 21, '78. Running time: 81 MINS.

Jozsef Kerek, Station Master	Nandor Tomanek
Tobi	Gyula Bodrogi
Klarika	Mari Kiss
Young Man	Janos Szikora
Ferke	Ferenc Bencze
Tamas	Robert Koltai

"Don't Lean Out the Window" introduces a new talent, Janos Zsombolyai, who makes an auspicious debut with this tale of a railroad station as a microcosm of humanity. It's like a brief short story, a vignette, which holds the attention from beginning to end in compressed brevity.

The station master gets reluctantly stuck with a young student who is thrown off a passing train because he hasn't a ticket and not enough identification papers to erase suspicions. He is kept under house arrest, so to speak, for the night and observes what is going on in this lonely, isolated neck of the woods: the station master is thriving on illegal trade, abetted by two cronies who maintain the station with him. A girl who cooks and sells tickets flirts with passing Lotharios, the student included, who might be the man of her dreams to take her away from nowhere. As for the student, he asks too many questions to be allowed to stay on for long, and besides he's in a hurry to get to Budapest.

Nothing much happens, save for the passing of a mysterious train early in the morning, which the station-hand sees but not the boss, and he doesn't believe it. Throughout the day, the station master thinks only of flirting with the girl and getting rid of the student. When, due to another mishap, the student must stay overnight again, it is he who sees the mysterious train early in the morning — heading in the direction of a scheduled and on-time train on the same track. To avert an accident, he tries to convince the station master, who shrugs off belief and responsibility. The film's end reveals a crash and an evening telecast that the student is being held by the police in the inquiry into the case.

Save for the tied-on ending, "Don't Lean Out the Window" is a neat allegory in a Hitchcock-like story that could appeal to both commercial and hip auds. It could be a sleeper in the art houses, as lensing and acting are plusses, while only drawback is that it barely makes feature length. —*Holl.*

Rak Kam Lok
(September Love)
(THAI-COLOR)

Bangkok, April 28.

A Bangkok Films release. Produced and directed by P. Chalong. Story and screenplay, So Asanachinda; camera (color), Visit Saengtavee; music, Prachin Songpao; editor, Dachanee; sound editor, Maitree Janjarasskul; production designer, Sumol Pakdivijit. Reviewed at Siam Pattana Screening Room, Bangkok, April 27, '78. Running time: 100 MINS.

Tony .... Krung Srivilai
Chanond ......᠈......... Vitoon Karuna
Nitra .... Nawarat Yukthanan
Noon .... Lalana Sulawan
Anong .... Piathip Kumvongse
Pai .... Somchai Samipak
Carol .... Carol Green
Mike ....᠇........... Michael Theros
Cazal "Mad Dog" ... William R. Barbridge
Joe .... Federico Coburn
Steve .... Eddie Coburn

Meant to conform with audience preference for love stories and comedies at the moment, "Rak Kam Lok" (September Love) is promoted as a film in the romantic comedy genre. But the producer-director, P. Chalong, has carved a name as an action director. His latest pic may present an equal mix of action and romance, but obviously the action scenes are better executed than the love scenes.

To say that the romance between the young lovers here, Vitoon Karuna and Nawarat Yukthanan, is "love on the wing" is putting it precisely. The entire film is a series of chases almost from start to finish.

Vitoon, a young artist and Nawarat, a musician, are being pursued by members of a drug syndicate. Thus, it would appear that they would be too busy trying to escape rather than start falling in love with each other.

This is Vitoon's first film and his performance has already earned him a number of other film offers, while Nawarat has become the most sought after love interest in Thai movies.

"Rak Kam Lok" is supposed to focus attention on Krung Srivilai as an Interpol police detective, but the younger players keep stealing scenes from him, especially Lalana Sulawan, who is paired with him.

As producer-director of this pic, first to be shot on location in the U.S. by a Thai filmmaker, Chalong can take credit for taking continually bigger risks in film production budgets, mainly in an effort to make films that can also sell abroad. Indeed he could proudly claim that he has consistently enjoyed the support and patronage of Thai filmgoers. —*Cano.*

---

80 Huszar
(80 Hussars)
(HUNGARIAN-COLOR)

Budapest, April 22.

An Hungarofilm Production, Objektiv Studio, Budapest; world rights, Hungarofilm, Budapest. Features entire cast. Directed and photographed (Eastmancolor) by Sandor Sara. Screenplay, Sara, Sandor Csoori; music, Andras Szollosy. Reviewed at Hungarofilm Screening Room, Budapest, April 21, '78. Running time: 137 MINS.
Hussars:
Andras Korsos .... Jozsef Madaras
Istvan Czordas ....Gyorgy Cserhalmi
Mozes Biro .... Gesa Polgar
Marton Csuha ....Gabor Csikos
Peter Acs .... Jacint Junasz
Sargeant Janos Bakos ..... Tibor Patassy
Old Hussar .... Zoltan Vadasz
Priest .... Piotr Wysocki
Captain Vyss .... Stefan Szmidt
General Leopold Krueger ... Sandor Szabo

Based on a true incident that occurred in the revolutionary year of 1848, this is the story of "80 Hussars" who refuse to obey military orders to fire on the civilian population in the university town of Cracow (it's not named but scenes seem to indicate so). The regiment of Hungarian hussars enlisted in the Imperial Austrian Army have served their required time, know about the uprising at home, and decide as a group to pick their way across the border and through the Austrian lines. They never make it — all along the way they are ambushed and encountered resistance until an open-field military tribunal condemns every tenth man in the regiment, dead or alive, to be shot as an example of insubordination.

Such a story allows for a lot of pomp-and-ceremony, and even stunt tricks, as the calvary group crosses terrain as though Indians were lurking in the forest and behind rocks. It also offers some insights into the times, for the regiment is a mixture of educated and simple people, sensitive and brave men, who learned useless code-of-honor gestures in a dying, decaying tradition of places-and-kings. Even the pledge the hussars make among themselves to die "one for all, all for one" seems archaic and hopelessly tragic in the face of overwhelming odds.

For this gallant gesture Hungary's gifted cameraman, Sandor Sara, renders the event in pictures of captivating beauty. His third feature pic on his own, Sara places too much emphasis on images — the final execution roll-call, for instance, goes right down the line, man for man — but there's so much to delight the eye that such story-lapses seem fortuitous.

A natural for Hungarian film weeks and art houses specializing in unusual East European Cinema.
—*Holl.*

Big Wednesday
(COLOR)

Pretentious surfing film from John Milius. Outlook: shaky ride.

Hollywood, May 13.

Warner Bros. release of an A-Team production, produced by Buzz Feitshans; executive producers, Alex Rose and Tamara Asseyev. Stars Jan-Michael Vincent, William Katt, Gary Busey. Directed by John Milius. Screen-play, Milius, Dennis Aaberg; camera (Metrocolor), Bruce Surtees; production designer, Charles Rosen; editor, Robert L. Wolfe, Tim O'Meara; music, Basil Poledouris; second unit director, Terry Leonard; assistant director, Richard Hashimoto; sound, Harlan Riggs; set decorator, Ira Bates; art director, Dean Mitzner; special effects, Joe Unsinn; surfing sequences produced by Greg MacGillivray. Reviewed at the National Theatre, L.A., May 12, '78. (MPAA rating: PG.) Running time: 126 MINS.
Matt .... Jan-Michael Vincent
Jack .... William Katt
Leroy ....Gary Busey
Sally .... Patti D'Arbanville
Peggy Gordon .... Lee Purcell
Bear ....Sam Melville
Fly .... Robert Englund
Mrs. Barlow .... Barbara Hale
Lucy .... Fran Ryan
Enforcer .... Reb Brown

A rubber stamp wouldn't do for John Milius. So he took a sledgehammer and pounded Important all over "Big Wednesday." This film about three Malibu surfers in the 1960s has been branded major statement and it's got Big Ideas about adolescence, friendship and the 1960s. Milius is here to deliver his message to the great unwashed, but his intentions come out muddled and precious. Commercial outlook for the Warner Bros. release of the A-Team production appears slim indeed.

"Big Wednesday" has a character named Bear, a combination John Milius-Ernest Hemingway, played by Sam Melville. He is described this way: "He knew where the waves came from and why." Really. Even the Melville character grows tired of philosophizing, so he opens up a surfboard shop and later turns into a bum, proof that pretentiousness doesn't pay. Milius might take a tip.

But Melville is a secondary character. The film revolves around three friends, Jan-Michael Vincent, William Katt and Gary Busey. Each is a noted surfer with Vincent something of a legend. Their life is surfing, but man — not even boy — can not live by salt water alone. So they grow up, awkwardly.

The movie is divided into four movements with each section moving ahead a few years. It climaxes at the final segment, Big Wednesday, when the surf has swelled to unknown proportions and the three reunite as men to again conquer the ocean.

Each movement is introduced by a narrator. Listen closely — as the words take on significance the sentences shorten.

The beach and the surf are the film's main locations and there are a number of surfing sequences, produced by Greg MacGillivray. They are exciting and attempts at innovation are made; the camera is placed almost inside the waves. However, surfing sequences on the Sunday sports shows also are exciting and don't suffer much compared to those in "Big Wednesday."

Milius co-scripted with Dennis Aaberg. The screenplay has its moments — for example, Busey at his Army physical exam — but they stand alone, like tv skits. Technical credits are okay. The editing is choppy.

Vincent, a capable actor, still hasn't found a part to showcase his potential. Busey has an unusual, nasty quality. Katt's part, like Melville's, is too dumb as written

Buzz Feitshans produced and Alex Rose and Tamara Asseyev were the executive producers.
—*Hege.*

Cannes Festival

L'Albero Degli Zoccoli
(The Tree of Wooden Clogs)
(ITALIAN-COLOR)

Cannes, May 17.

An Italnoleggio-RAI release of a G.P.C. (Milan) production for RAI 1 and Italnoleggio. Cast: non-professionals from rural countryside of Bergamo. Written and directed by Ermanno Olmi. Camera (Gevacolor), Ermanno Olmi; art director, Eurico Tovaglieri; editor Ermanno Olmi; music, J.S. Bach, folk and choral. Reviewed at Cannes, May 16, '78. Running time: 175 MINS.

"A Tree of Wooden Clogs" is Ermanno Olmi's most ambitious mosaic to date, patiently and lovingly created on a budget of $400,-000 as a lyric paean to the Italian peasant. Pages could be filled in comparing it to Bernardo Bertolucci's "1900" but it suffices to note Olmi's serene attribution of peasant survival, late last century, to age-old fundamentals of family and religious faith in a region traditionally conservative while Bertolucci led his peasants to revolt and radicalized masses in what has become the Red central region of Italy.

Both filmmakers went back to origins in the bleak countryside — one to trace rural life and strife as a forerunner to revolutionary class conflict; the other, to re-assert faith in the Catholic religion and to counsel gradualism in social change. From a common vision of life in the fields as a daily burden of cruel existence and social inequities, the two filmmakers end up at opposite roles — a new order on earth and existence as a sombre sojourn en route to eternity.

Around his basic concept, Olmi assumes auteur status with a vengeance as producer, scripter, director, cinematographer and editor and fulfills prodigiously in all departments for a work essentially patterned as a three-part television series. In the developing cross-cut of cinema and tv, "Wooden Clogs" preemed as a theatrical feature and seemed overlength at 180 mins. But even through 180 mins. of theatrical feature, Olmi's filmmaker talent rarely falters.

His minute recreation of place and time, without plot or substantial narrative, brings to life five families in a tiny farm community. Early sharp, fast montage brings people, problems and surroundings into focus blending into the seasonal cycle of man and nature. Daily routines give way to events and anecdotes transcending nature for Olmi's overview of man in the sight of God.

To achieve this design without sacrificing the authenticity of peasants on the land, Olmi selected a full cast in the countryside where for months he rolled exteriors and natural interiors. He has filmed with non-pros in all his films but never on such a challenging scale and with such brilliant results.

His decision to go with local dialect gives each word its just cadence but it will estrange Italo audiences. Sub-titled version at Cannes saved the day, though confirming need to dub for both tv and cinemas.

Feel for the land and people on it, is enhanced by Olmi's cinematography and almost raises doubts that one man could be that creative.

In most of his films to date, Olmi attains his spiritual goals through purity and simplicity. In "Clogs" he sets out for the first time to situate his people in terms of religious faith. Undoubtedly a true picture of the times in Bergamo environs though exasperated by Olmi's surprising intrusion to elaborate and accent his religious mystic.

"Wooden Clogs" is a worthy RAI successor to 1977's "Padre Padrone" and should likewise follow last year's Golden Palm winner to dual exposure in cinemas and on the tube in world markets.
—*Werb.*

Bye Bye Monkey
(ITALIAN-FRENCH-COLOR)

Cannes, May 23.
Gaumont release of 18 Dicembre-Prospectacle-Action Film production. Stars Gerard Depardieu, Marcello Mastroianni, James Coco. Directed by Marco Ferreri. Screenplay, Ferreri, Gerard Brach, Rafael Azcona; camera (Eastmancolor), Luciano Tavoli; editor, Ruggero Mastroianni; music, Philipe Sarde. Reviewed at Cannes Film Fest (Competing), May 18, '78. Running time: **114 MINS.**
Lafayette . . . . Gerard Depardieu
Nocello . . . . Marcello Mastroianni
Flaxman . . . . James Coco
Angelica . . . . Gail Lawrence
Toland . . . . Geraldine Fitzgerald
Miko . . . . Avon Long
(In English)

Marco Ferreri has been a sharp, incisive social critic in his pix of attitudes to old age, sexual taboos, family life and macho men and woman's new consciousness. He has usually used black humor and with his "La Grande Bouffe" caused polemics in his depiction of four men literally eating themselves to death. Now he has come up with a sort of fable on man's transient state today which he intimates has about destroyed all the old standards, without much to replace it yet.

Ferreri has chosen to place his tale of fringe characters in New York as seen by two foreigners, a Frenchman and a middleaged Italian. Set in a section where old buildings are falling into decay, backed by skyscrapers and big residential buildings, their good friends are an old woman living alone, a black musician and an aging white man.

Gerard Depardieu, the Frenchman, seems to prefer using a whistle to talk and Marcello Mastroianni, the Italian, feels his knowledge and humanity are just overlooked by youth and older people alike. This strange tale may turn some off but intrigue others in its blend of humor, the bizarre and an apocalyptic look at childish young manhood and older people who have lost touch.

James Coco appears as a man who keeps a Roman Museum as a bastion against what he feels to be a new barbarian age. And, in fact, rats are all over the ruined houses in which Depardieu and Mastroianni live. Depardieu works at Coco's museum and also at a femme consciouness-raising theatre group. At the latter, he is raped one day when the distaff group decides to find out what the feelings would be.

He and the girl who does it, while others hold him, start a liaison. One day, a giant carcass of a sort of King Kong mannequin is found on the beach that fronts this part of N.Y. A little baby chimp is found and Depardieu adopts it to Coco's disgust. The monkey is even made "human" when Mastroianni secures false papers and the monkey gets civil status. Mastroianni commits suicide, leaving his goods to the monkey and one day Depardieu finds the monkey devoured by rats.

He cannot face the girl's pregnancy and finds Coco playacting in his Roman Museum. Coco cannot accept Depardieu's anguish at the loss of a monkey and sets off a fire that destroys both. The survivor is the girl, shown at the end playing with her daughter. Women, Ferreri seems to imply, now seem more resilient and adaptable than men.

Depardeiu is effective as the youth unable to cope with any true emotion. Mastroianni is excellent in a character role. There are some witty passages but film does not always have the more fluid illumination and comic force that helped Ferreri's other pix. Film does not flinch from a scene of the old woman, played by Geraldine Fitzgerald, still attractive and talking of the need for love and indulging in some passionate embraces with Depardieu. A specialized pic at best, with not all of Ferreri's ideas coming through this uneven but sometimes jolting and entertaining tale. —*Mosk.*

The Shout
(BRITISH-COLOR)

Cannes, May 23.
The Rank Organization release of a Recorded Picture Company production. Stars Alan Bates, Susannah York, John Hurt. Directed by Jerzy Skolimovsky. Screenplay, Michael Austin, Skolimovsky from a story by Robert Graves; camera (color), Mike Molloy; editor, Barrie Vince; art director, Simon Holland; music, Rupert Hine, Anthony Banks, Michael Rutherford; produced by Jeremy Thomas. Reviewed at Cannes Film Festival (Competing), May 19, '78. Running time, **87 MINS.**
Crossley . . . . Alan Bates
Rachel . . . . Susannah York
Anthony . . . . John Hurt
Medical Man . . . . Robert Stephens
Robert . . . . Tim Curry
Vicar . . . . Julian Hough
Wife . . . . Carol Drinkwater
Cobbler . . . . Nick Stringer
Inspector . . . . John Rees
Harriet . . . . Susan Woolridge

Polish director Jerzy Skolimovsky is no stranger to English-language films. He did a previous one in Britain, "Deep End," and an adventure opus for UA in Italy called "The Adventures of Gerard." Now he again comes from Poland to make this occult-tinged drama of a tale possibly told by a madman and definitely full of sound and shrewd narrative fury, to twist an old quotation, and signifying something.

The director has been able to create a gripping film that holds attention most of the way through its economical length. It probes a couple beset by a catalyst that breaks their seemingly surface contentment. Film is told by Alan Bates during a cricket match in an asylum. The game, mainly for the British and ex-British colonials, seems placid on the surface but has a tension in its posing, batting, wickets, etc. that has an effect even if not understood or explained. Like the pic.

A couple, obviously not at ease, drives up at the beginning. The man goes to play cricket, one of the few so-called normal ones to play, while the woman is a nurse at the institution. On the field, the asylum chief introduces a young normal-acting writer-visitor to Bates, a man he considers one of the most unusual he has ever met and whose soul seems to have been broken into four pieces.

The latter two are ushered into a little cabin on wheels which is the scoring room. Bates, bearded, imposing, and slightly disturbing, decides to tell the other a tale. It seems there is time in th is slowly paced game. The couple at the beginning and Bates figure in it.

Bates, a tramp-like figure, accosts the man, John Hurt, outside a church one day. It is a small town and he, Bates, gets invited to dinner and stays. He tells strange tales of how he lived with Australian aborigines and killed his own children when he left and how he learned how to cast various spells, especially a shout (title of the pic) that can kill.

Flash forwards indicate Bates will disrupt the couple with one problem of the man apparently dallying with the wife of the local shoemaker. Bates weaves a spell that makes the wife his sexual subservient which Hurt does not know about yet. Bates also invites the husband out one morning and performs the shout which kills sheep and a shepherd. Hurt is saved by covering his ears.

Hurt is an electronic music composer and his work counterpoints Bates's shout in a way. The story builds as the listener becomes apprehensive. It crescendos as Bates, in the tale, reduces the wife to his whims before Hurt who has found a certain pebble represents Bates's soul and which he manages to break. Bates is then arrested and committed to the asylum.

The cricket game becomes difficult when some inmates go into tantrums and when the director tries to call the game Bates in a paroxysm gets ready to show his shout as the writer flees and the director, in the hut, is killed either by the shout or a bolt of lightning along with Bates.

Susannah York, playing the wife with a mixture of elegance and repressed desire, looks at Bates's body when it is brought in. Film leaves things up in the air as Bates's tale shows scenes he might not have seen but heard about. But it could be a part of his powers. In all, it is a well-told, offbeat tale that could well find its way with general and more selective audiences on its name players, good thesping and generally absorbing treatment.

—*Mosk.*

Who'll Stop The Rain?
(U.S.-COLOR)

Cannes, May 23.

United Artists release of a UA, Herb Jaffe and Gabriel Katzka production. Stars Nick Nolte, Tuesday Weld, Michael Moriarty. Directed by Karel Reisz. Screenplay, Judith Roscoe, Robert Stone from the book by Stone; camera (Color), Richard H. Kline; editor, John Bloom; music, Laurence Rosenthal. Reviewed at Cannes Film Fest, May 21, '78. Running time, **125 MINS.**

Ray .... Nick Nolte
Marge .... Tuesday Weld
John .... Michael Moriarty
Antheil .... Anthony Zerbe
Danskin .... Richard Masur
Smitty .... Ray Sharkey
Chairman .... Gail Strickland
Eddy .... Charles Haid
Bender .... David Opatoshu

British filmmaker Karel Reisz for his second American film has come up with a corking couple-on-the-run adventure pic, given depth in its focus on the personal disarray, the growing governmental corruption and the effects of that most unpopular, divisive Vietnam war on America.

With some evidence that the public is now showing some interest in that traumatic event, pic might cash in on its insight, visual drive and hardbitten treatment, not forgetting its action aspects. Savvy handling is indicated, however.

Michael Moriarty, a journalist and photog during the Vietnam War, suffers a trauma under a deadly enemy barrage and the mayhem around him. Perhaps weak, intellectual but unfocused, and seemingly wishing to pay for this in some sort of destructive act, he decides to try to smuggle heroin to the U.S.

The woman he goes to seems to have some connections with U.S. governmental offices. Moriarty rings in an old Marine buddy, Nick Nolte, who is now in the Merchant Marine. Moriarty had turned Nolte on to books and philosophers. Nolte, a natural rebel against what he feels is too much unearned authority around him, has only smuggled grass but soon gives in.

Nolte is to get in touch with Moriarty's wife, Tuesday Weld, and wait for him, Moriarty, to get back. But back in the U.S. Nolte is followed. He overcomes two gunmen and he and Weld go on the lam after sending Weld's little girl off to relatives for safekeeping.

Anthony Zerbe, a corrupted government narcotics man, uses two eerily comic and threatening hoods for his dirty work. He is after the dope. Moriarty gets back only to be tortured and sequestered by the two hood-type Zerbe men. Meanwhile, Nolte and Weld are trying to get rid of the stuff in California.

The Zerbe crew, with Moriarty in tow, find their whereabouts and Nolte and Weld hole up in an old hippie-cum-religioso retreat for the final gunplay.

Based on a bestseller, it has a hardnose progression and solidity in its characterizations. Nolte earns his star stripes here, displaying presence and perceptiveness in socking home his character, while Weld and Moriarty are also effective.

Reisz shows a fine adaptation to the American scene, with technical credits also effective. Title change saw switch to "Who'll Stop the Rain," from a soundtrack song backing working title, "Dog Soldiers." —*Mosk.*

A Dream Of Passion
(GREEK-COLOR)

Cannes, May 23.

SNC-Coline release of Brenfilm-Melina Film production. Stars Melina Mercouri, Ellen Burstyn. Directed, produced and written by Jules Dassin. Camera (Eastmancolor), George Arvanitis; editor, George Klotz; art director, Dionysis Fotopoulos; music, Iannis Markpopoulos. Reviewed at Cannes Film Fest (Competing), May 21, '78. Running time: **110 MINS.**

Maya .... Melina Mercouri
Brenda .... Ellen Burstyn
Kostas .... Andreas Voutsinas
Maria .... Despo Diamantidou
Dimitris .... Dimitris Papamicahel
Edward .... Yannis Voglis
Ronny .... Phedon Georgitsis
Margaret .... Betty Valassi
(In English and Greek)

Jules Dassin, that longtime European resident who after being blacklisted in the U.S., made films in Britain, France, Italy, and Greece before making his first film in 20 years in the U.S. in 1969, the updated, all-black version of "The Informer" as "Up Tight." Now he has a Greek film in English and Greek featuring Melina Mercouri and Ellen Burstyn.

Two older women are caught up in a strange parallel. One, Mercouri, is a film star who returns to her native Greece to do the Greek tragedy, "Medea," on stage. The other, Burstyn, is an American living in Greece who has killed her three children "just as Medea did" due to her husband's flaunting of her love and needs.

A misguided public relations idea, having Burstyn talk to Mercouri after seeing no one for a long time, backfires when photogs and press burst in. While Burstyn screams invectives, Mercouri feels cheapened, guilty and decides to take an interest in the case. She sees Burstyn again and gets her story.

Pic alternates two stories, as Mercouri's life and work are intertwined with her growing interest in Burstyn. Is it to help her understand Medea's motives, or is she being affected as a woman? Film is not always clear on that, and prefers a duality, a blending of the two which Dassin underlines with a scene showing the legit company looking at Ingmar Bergman's "Persona" about two women who are made to be parts of the same one.

In the background, the theatrical spats, work dramatic incidents continue as Mercouri also has problems with her director with whom she has had a relationship. She keeps seeing Burstyn, who finally does talk of how she killed her children. Murder scenes are shown, but without going in for gory details.

Burstyn is shattering as a religious, partially-educated woman caught up in a foreing land. At the end, Burstyn bursts into hysterical tears, which are intercut with Mercouri's dramatic finale in which she kills Medea's children in the Play.

Though sometimes fastidious in the rehearsal scenes, there are insights into growing tensions and explosive releases and some effective scenes from the play itself as it progresses. Andreas Voutsinas is the director who wants only sacred passion and not human compassion in his version of Greek tragedy. He will not let Mercouri play it on a subdued level.

The pairing of the women fits new pic currents but needs careful and specialized handling for best results on its sometimes ambiguous aspects.

Dassin made a simple comedic romp with Mercouri in "Never On Sunday," but here uses her dramatic side and her temperament, obviously influenced by their life together. (They have been married since 1966). An uneven but often effective drama. —*Mosk.*

Moi Laskoviy I Niejnie Zver
(A Hunting Accident)
(SOVIET-COLOR)

Cannes, May 23.

Sovexport film release of Mosfilm production. Features entire cast. Directed and written by Emil Lotianu from a story by Anton Chekhov. Camera (Sovcolor), A. Petritzki; music, Yevgueni Doga. Reviewed at Cannes Film Fest (Competing), May 16, '78. Running time, **107 MINS.**

Cast: Galina Belaieva, Oleg Yankovski, Kirill Lavrov, Svetlana Toma, Grigori Grigouiou.

The Russians might one day go through all their classics for film use, and especially the works of Anton Chekhov. Then they could start over again. But until there are more potent contemporary pix, Chekhov does lend his pathetic characters to film very well.

This one perhaps strives too hard to add a lyric element but this tale of the creaking culture and class system of the early part of the century still has some fine characters and a rousing recreation of the times in poetic rather than realistic form.

A nobleman, who thinks he is dying of a bad liver, and whose domain is run down, throws a party for a friend, a magistrate, featuring gypsy singers and musicians. A lovely, innocent-seeming 16-year-old, daughter of a gamekeeper who is committed to an asylum, runs about the place and entices all the men.

The Count's foreman, an older man with two children, loves her madly and the magistrate is smitten as is the supposedly dying count. All this leads to different approaches to this girl who still wants to get out of her poor situation. She first marries the foreman, swears her love to the magistrate and dallies with the Count.

The husband leaves the estate, and, at a picnic, the girl is shot in what is first thought a hunting accident. But the magistrate pins it on the husband. Years later he brings a book to a publisher which is about their lives and the publisher, after reading it, knows the writer was really responsible.

The magistrate, attended by the Count, now ruined, lets himself die of tuberculosis without care to pay for his crime against this girl who loved him, but despite her innocence, was corrupted by life around her.

Elegantly shot, the uneven wedding of director Emil Lotianu's lyrical scenes of festivity and the theme's more pertinent look at lives caught up in a society nearing decadence sometimes lose this the dramatic edge it needs. But the expert acting, Soviet actors do take well to the past, beautiful lensing and the human insights, despite its sometimes overheated treatment, could give this some specialized, school and especially festival legs but is not, as yet, the Russo film to break through in more commercial and demanding areas abroad. —*Mosk.*

Ai No Borei
(Phantom Love)
(JAPANESE-FRENCH-COLOR)

Cannes, May 23.

Argos Films release of Oshima Productions Ltd.-Argos Films production. Features entire cast. Directed by Nagisa Oshima. Screenplay, Oshima from the book by Itoko Nakamura; camera (Eastmancolor), Yoshio Miyajima; editor, Keiichu Uraoka; art director, Jusho Toda; music, Toru Takemitsu; production coordination, Shibata Org. Inc. Reviewed at Cannes Film Fest (Competing), May 20, '78. Running time: **108 MINS.**

Seki .... Kazuko Yoshiyuki
Toyoji .... Tatsuya Fuji
Gisaburo .... Takahiro Tamura
Hotta .... Takuzo Kawatani

Nagisa Oshima's previous pic, "In the Realm of the Senses," called "Corrida of Love" in Japanese, created polemics, seizures and law suits and was judged both pornographic or, depending on one's viewpoint, one of the great erotic films in its depiction of two lovers destroying themselves by their own creation of a world of sex. This new one is more about the destructive forces of passion in a more rigid world where the supernatural seems a part of everyday life.

Oshima has not opted for planted psycholological symbols in this tale where a married woman and her younger lover murder her husband. They are not afflicted by remorse and conscience but more by an acceptance of a time when phantoms existed, later to be replaced by learned studies in human behaviour.

Film thus remains fantastic but diversified in character and treatment, giving deeper insights into this doomed couple. The woman is still lovely at 40 and married to an older rickshaw driver. A young man, half her age, is in love with her. But he comes to her as a child as well as a suitor, bringing cakes and demanding complete passion and even protectiveness.

Oshima has only simulated sexual adhesion which is often oral and sometimes child-like with the man insisting she shave her private parts. Now he tells her they must kill her husband for he will suspect something. Latter is given to drinking. She gets him drunk and she and the lover strangle him together, each pulling on the end of a cord.

Then they dump him into a deep, abandoned well. She tells people he has gone to work in Tokyo. Story takes place in a rural village and is based on a real event in 1895. Not to arouse suspicion, they cannot see each other often. The dead man begins to appear to the wife and even invades the dreams of two villagers, especially the murdered man's grown daughter.

Another murder brings a police inspector to the village and the wife and the lover are finally found in an embrace in her house as the police arrest them. Hung from trees and brutally whipped by bamboo poles until they confess, they are hustled off for payment of their crimes.

The late Kenji Mizoguchi used ghosts in his "Ugetsu" and in "The Crucified Lovers." But his was a lyrical, poetic treatment while Oshima's is cool and finely observed, creating a climate where the fantastic and the tragic exist side by side.

Like its predecessor film was made with French coproducer Anatole Dauman who has world rights except for Japan. It was shot in Japan but all rushes were done in France as were the editing, scoring and finishing of the pic.

"Senses" played in the Director Fortnight at Cannes in '76 and emerged the most projected film of the event. Now the new one is competing at the Cannes Film Fest. It does not have the polemic drive of "Senses" yet is likely to create similar critical pros and cons. Its brilliant, visual drive, its fine playing, its haunting overtones should have this a specialized film that could find selective audiences everywhere with the right handling.

French title, and world title outside Japan, is "The Empire of Passion." It marks Oshima as one of the more unusual directors on world scene today. —*Mosk.*

Ecce Bombo
(ITALIAN-COLOR)

Rome, May 24.
A CIDIF release, produced by Mario Gallo for Alphabeta Film and Filmalpha. Features Nanni Moretti, Luisa Rossi, Fabio Traversa, Lina Sastri, Glauco Mari. Written and directed by Nanni Moretti. Camera (Kodak), Giuseppe Pinori; art director, Massimo Razzi; editor, Enzo Meniconi; music, Franco Piersanti. Reviewed in Rome, May 23, '78. Running time, 100 MINS.

Nanni Moretti is a one-man phenomenon who has achieved "auteur" status in Italian cinema on the strength of two features — one in super-8, "I Can Do It Alone," and now with "Ecce Bombo," his first color pic in 16m.

Irreverent, iconoclastic, ooozing with self-confidence, Moretti with "Ecce Bombo" has been hailed as a young Fellini. At 22, he is a contestant for the Cannes' Golden Palm.

"Ecce Bombo" is the handiwork of a versatile filmmaker in all departments — script, direction, performance and editing. He is also a showman with a sense of entertainment that cuts through his own personal brand of elitism exhibitionism and self-indulgence to attract mass audiences.

The film is plotless. It is a kind of low-key "Hellzapoppin" though behind the inventive word gags and sketch sitcoms Moretti marks the transition of a youth generation from political militancy to a limbo of impotent detachment. Between the delusion with active campus and nabe leftism and the wasteland of preoccupied parenthood, Moretti half-heartedly wreathes the irrational hopelessness of his own age group in grey humor. The bitter and sweet play off each other smartly.

Moretti is particularly convincing in his illustration of present day youth — with all the new tics, postures, irrationality and hangups. This feat takes the curse off some "Bombo" shortcomings — the awkward attempt to dethrone people (Andreotti, Alberto Sordi, etc.) and politics in straightout commentary or annotations, a small glut of repetition, surprisingly few and technical limitations of inexperience and budget.

"Ecce Bombo" need not be translated. It is Moretti's cry of despair of today's young people his age flaked out on bright new worlds and scared stiff of the idiot adult world they will one day have to join. Trapped, Moretti and his cronies use "Ecce Bombo" as a war cry to smash and shatter when existential futility becomes too much to bear. But before the cry is raised, his sketch view of youth today is mainly hard and lively entertainment.

Film introduces a castful of bright young thesps at a time when Italian cinema needs new performing talent badly. Camera work leaves little to be desired while editing is almost Americanized. Rapid pace is an important factor in this non-plot feature.

In the music department, Franco Piersanti has turned in a clever, biting score. Producer Mario Gallo ended up with a lot more quality than his $350,000 budget (roughly) could be expected to achieve.

This mix of talent and quality will open doors for specialized handling in many markets. The film, will also spend a year at least turning up at world film fests. —*Werb.*

Violette Noziere
(FRENCH-COLOR)

Cannes, May 23.
Gaumont release of Filmel-FR3-Cine Video production. Stars Isabelle Huppert, Stephane Audran, Jean Carmet. Directed by Claude Chabrol. Screenplay, Odile Barski from book by Jean-Marie Fitere; camera (Eastmancolor), Jean Rabier; editor, Yves Langlois. Reviewed at Cannes Film Fest (Competing), May 20, '78. Running time, 122 MINS.
Violette .... Isabelle Huppert
Mother .... Stephane Audran
Father .... Jean Carmet
Lover .... Jean-Francois Garreaud

Claude Chabrol has skirted the clinical in this tale based on a real-life case dating back to 1934 in which an 18-year-old girl killed her father by poison while giving her mother a less than fatal dose. However, his cynical insights give this an abrasive, liberating quality that score points in revealing human behavior without any sentimentaltiy or censure and add a dramatic side to this tale of a girl leading a double life.

Isabelle Huppert, who played the introverted working-class girl in "The Lacemaker," here is more extroverted. In the evening, or even during the day when she can, she sneaks off, dressed up in imitation of the elegant ladies of the day. At home, she is a scrubbed school girl.

She has affairs nonchalantly and gets paid by some though she does not ask for money. She seems able to convince herself she is not a prostitute or even a thief, though she steals money constantly from her mother's savings. She also has an older man who helps her whenever she needs money and invents tales for her parents.

This mythomaniacal activity is cannily mined by Chabrol against a background of growing Nazism, and its French variants at the time. The small apartment and her hearing and seeing her parents making love seems to have killed pleasure for her. But she does meet a young man on whom she showers her money.

Her sudden decision to kill seems brought on by overhearing her parents say they will not give her any more money until she marries. She is arrested, faces her mother who survived, and is condemned to death. Later, she is pardoned and eventually rehabilitated to lead a normal life and have several children. Chabrol has a feel for the period and shrewdly does not try to pin guilt on either side.

Perhaps somewhat one-toned, with some repetitive sections, film still keeps interest in its look at a strange escape from a petty family through an aping of lowlife and highlife women that eventually leads to an emotionless murder. Film should find home legs and might be the first Chabrol film to make its way abroad in some time.
—*Mosk.*

Despair
(WEST GERMAN-COLOR)

Cannes, May 23.
Swan-Diffusion release of Bavaria Atelier-SFP-Geria production. Stars Dirk Bogarde. Directed by Rainer Werner Fassbinder. Screenplay, Tom Stoppard from novel by Vladimir Nabokov; camera (Eastmancolor), Michael Ballhaus; editor, Juliane Lorenz, Franz Walsch; music, Peer Raben; art director, Rolf Zehetbauer. Reviewed at Cannes Film Fest (Competing), May 20, '78. Running time, 119 MINS.
Herman .... Dirk Bogarde
Lydia .... Andrea Ferreol
Ardalion .... Volker Spengler
Felix .... Klaus Lowitsch
(In English)

That prolific German director, Rainer Werner Fassbinder, with this his 32d pic at 31, comes up with his first pic in English. Trying to get the spirited linguistic innovations, wit and penetrating insights of the late writer Vladimir Nabokov defeated Polski filmmaker Jerzy Skolimovski with "King, Queen, Knave" and Tony Richardson with "Laughter in the Dark," not to forget Stanley Kubrick's pallid "Lolita."

Despite a witty, albeit theatrical, script by Tom Stoppard, Fassbinder does not quite bring it off but it is a good try. It emerges overlong, over-indulged in this tale of an exiled Russian in Germany in the late 1920s, who is driven to a weird murder.

Dirk Bogarde, using a generally satisfactory Russo accent, though it slips at times, has a pulpy, dim-witted, sensual wife, played in campy period style by French actress Andrea Ferreol. He runs a chocolate factory that is going on the rocks as the Depression hits the world. He has strange delusions of seeing himself outside of himself watching himself.

That is, he sees another replica of himself watching his carryings-on with his wife or even imagining himself dressed as a budding Nazi of the times going in for macho sadistic sexual actions. His wife is having an affair with her cousin, a bad painter, which Bogarde seems to ignore.

He insures himself and then, on a business trip where a needed merger is refused because he intimates he is Jewish, he meets a down-and-out whom, he thinks, looks just like him. He decides to use this man in a trumped-up action that may be a holdup but is aimed at killing the man, passing him off as himself and collecting his insurance.

But all goes awry and Bogarde is finally cornered by the police as his delusions give way to a sort of madness and he insists he is a film actor who is coming out to the police. Period garishness, the background of the rise of Nazism and the plight of exile are tied up with this handsome looking but finally repetitive, drawn out and tedious exercise.

Bogarde brings off a tour-de-force thesp stint and Fassbinder, who has long talked of leaving Germany for the U.S., or other climes, shows he can handle the English lingo and not show any strain in rhythm or delivery though many of the thesps are dubbed. A film that has its place at a fest despite its over-literary flavor with mainly specialized chances abroad.

— *Mosk.*

Alicia En La Espana De Las Maravillas
(Alice in Spanish Wonderland)
(SPANISH-COLOR)

Barcelona, May 13.

Roda Films (Barcelona) production. Directed by Jorge Feliu. Features entire cast. Screenplay, Jordi Feliu, Jesus Borras, Antoni Colomer; sets, Elisa Ruiz; music, Juan Pineda; editor, Teresa Alcocer, Guillermo Maldonado; camera, (Eastmancolor) Raul Perez Cubero; exec producer, Isabel Fabra. Reviewed at Salvador Serra screening room (Barcelona), May 12, '78. Running time: **86 MINS.**
First Alice .... Mireia Ros
Second Alice .... Silvia Aguilar
Third Alice .... Montserrat Mostoles
Grown-up Alice .... Concha Bardem

Guardian Angel .... Pau Bizarro
Swindler .... Alfredo Lucchetti

Strange, visually powerful but sometimes long winded takeoff on the Alice in Wonderland story, turned by Jorge Feliu (whose first serious pic this is) into a ferocious critique of the Franco years in Spain.

Using four different Alices, Feliu puts them through a hallucinatory maze, sometimes grotesquely symbolical, often harrowingly realistic as he lashes out at the Spanish ills of 40 years ranging over film censorship, anti-feminism, suppression of regional freedoms, ecclesiastical abuses, the raping of Alice by the multinationals (some rather naive anti-Americanism crops up, too) and dozens of other misadventures, some of them easy to grasp, other requiring a knowledge of Spain and her history.

Alicia is a film hard to define. It is professionally directed, photographed and acted; its varied images are often visually stunning and its liberal thrust is poignant, though sometimes it becomes redundant and labors the obvious. Still, "Alicia" is perhaps the most direct frontal attack so far on Franco Spain. Despite some of its shortcomings, it is a film well worth seeing for all interested in modern Spanish cinema. Item might do some biz in art and university circuits abroad.

— *Besa.*

The Mafu Cage
(U.S.-COLOR)

Cannes, May 23.

Clouds Production release and production. Stars Lee Grant, Carol Kane. Directed by Karen Arthur. Screenplay, Don Chastain from French play by Eric Wesphal; camera (color), John Bailey; editor, Carol Littleton; music, Roger Kellaway. Reviewed at Director Fortnight, Cannes (non-competing), May 18, '78. Running time, **102 MINS.**
Ellen .... Lee Grant
Cissy .... Carol Kane
Zom .... Will Geer
David .... James Olson

Karen Arthur, for her second pic, also an indie, has cooked up a hothouse tale of two strange sisters in a kind of interdependent lesbo, physical, spiritual, emotional state. Sometimes uneven in conception, film still has a strange, almost hypnotic quality that could give this good playoff chances with the makings of a cultist film. It was chosen to kick off the sidebar Director Fortnight at the unspooling Cannes Film Fest.

Lee Grant is the cool, well-tailored older sister, who is a noted solar astronomist, while Carol Kane is a sort of flower child with a bent towards killing higher type monkeys and apes usually kept in a cage, the Mafu Cage of the title, in their house. It seems their father

was an anthropologist specializing in anthropoids and the house also has tropical foliage inside, Afro artifacts and jungle sounds and Afro music in the background.

Kane is kept by her sister and seems a bit insane though possessed of a talent for drawing and seemingly indispensable to the sister with hints of more than sisterly love between them.

Grant's co-worker, James Olson, seems more interested in sex than the love he professes and finally gets to her. Meanwhile Kane gets disgruntled by an orangutang who tries to hug her and puts him in the cage in arm irons and batters him to death. Grant again covers up and they profess their need for each other.

Pic's last phase has a man visiting when Grant is away. Kane works him into the cage and gets him chained to the wall, kills him and buries him in the garden. Grant's return and realization of what happened, by a picture Kane had drawn, leads to her, Grant, being chained as well and finally dying. Kane buries her and locks herself in the cage after she has informed all they are off on a trip.

Kane's accent is a bit strident but she is physically effective. Offbeat item indeed, but Arthur shows a flair for atmosphere and refrains from explaining too much to give this an ambiguous quality despite its sometimes strained proceedings. Pic is technically fine.

— *Mosk.*

Bilbao
(SPANISH-COLOR)

Barcelona, May 13.

A Figaro-Ona Films (Barcelona) coproduction. Written and directed by J.J. Bigas Luna. Features entire cast. Camera (Eastmancolor), Pedro Aznar; editor, Anastasio Rinos; sets, Carlos Riart; music, Iceberg; exec producer, Pepon Coromina. Reviewed at Universal Films (Barcelona), May 12, '78. Running time: **90 MINS.**
Leo .... Angel Jove
Maria .... Maria Martin
Bilbao .... Isabel Pisano
Pimp .... Francisco Falcon
Aunt .... Pepita Llunell
Uncle .... Jordi Torras

Bilbao is the name of a Barcelona hooker who obsesses an introverted misfit whose other occupations include cruising crowded subways and department stores just for the pleasure of being there. Though he rarely mumbles a word, his inchoate thoughts are provided by a monotonous "off."

A nasty vein of suppressed violence runs through the film, though its taciturn anti-hero rarely does little more than follow the girl about at a distance and paste anything related to "Bilbao" (the Basque City, the Lotte Lenya song, the hooker)

into his scrapbook. He makes inscrutable sketches and wraps pieces of tape around his wrist.

Overly delayed climax comes when the silent one chloroforms the girl (in two different versions), takes her to a converted barn, strings her up unconscious on two ropes. Two scenes later she mysteriously dies from a nail wound as she sits nude strapped to a chair beside her captor, who's watching home porno pix. Her fate is to be transmogrified into countless sausages at his uncle's pork factory, and that's all.

At times kinky and disturbing, pic keeps up a plodding suspense which, however, is never fulfilled. Direction by Bigas Luna and thesping by Isabel Pisano as the volumptuous hooker and dancer are good, but Angel Jove's deadpan performance as the fetishist slows down pacing considerably. Some commercial interest might be generated on basis of some of the masosadistic sex scenes. Item is probably more for grind circuits than art house outlets. — *Besa.*

Insiang
(FILIPINO-COLOR)

Cannes, May 18.

A Mariposa Production, produced by Ruby Tiong Tan. Directed by Lino Brock. Screenplay, Mario O'Hara and Lamberto Antonio, from story by Mario O'Hara. Editor, Augusto Salvado; music, Minda Azarcon; camera (color), Conrado Baltzar. Reviewed at Cannes Festival (non-competing) May 18, '78. Running time: **95 MINS.**
Features Hilda Koronel, Mona Lisa, Ruel Vernal, Marlon Ramirez.
(Tagalog soundtrack)

"Insiang" has the unique distinction of being the first Filipino or Tagalog movie to be officially shown in Cannes in the Director's Fortnight section.

It is a trailblazer for a film industry that primarily gears its feature films to an undemanding market.

Directed by socially conscious Lino Brocka, who belongs to a new breed of Filipino directors, pic made its Continental debut during the third day of the festival.

The title refers to a lovely but withdrawn 17-year-old girl who lives with her nagging mother. Insiang works as a laundry maid while her mother is a fish vendor in the slum area of Tondo, Manila. They are typical examples of provincial folk who venture into the concrete jungle seeking a better life. Instead of progress they face disintegration of the human spirit brought about by a sub-human existence.

The hand-to-mouth theme of slum struggling is universally apparent as poverty is a condition that exists throughout the world. In the process of growing up, Insiang suffers the humiliation and final degradation of being raped by her mother's burly and greasy gigolo lover.

Later, Insiang plots a cunning and intricate scheme of revenge and the film ends tragically, with a minor twist.

There is a slow build-up to establish local color and the teeming tapestry of a dirty city slum. Brocka's direction and Conrado Baltzar's cinematography truly capture the atmosphere of the environment of an impoverished community.

Made on a mini-budget in only 14 days, "Insiang" is a deeply moving work in the cinema verite genre. The flaws of the shrill soundtrack, uneven color prints, rough editing and some overly melodramatic episodes are however overshadowed by the well-intentioned and carefully thought out direction and general presentation.

For instance, the nattering antics of the tigress of a mother (Mona Lisa) is beautifully contrasted by the gentle reaction of Insiang, played with unusual subtlety by charming Hilda Koronel who has expansive and expressive eyes. This is specially evident as the mother fights her daughter for the lover. The dialogue, in Tagalog, is natural and not at all contrived.

Koronel may seem too beautiful to be a slum girl but she nevertheless manages to project realism in her role and thus becomes believable. Her natural beauty and charm creates audience empathy and is nowhere distracting.

The film also succeeds because of Brocka who is one of the few Filipinos to bring raw realism, professionalism, and depth to his work. A graduate of the University of the Philippines, he is socially conscious — and it shows.

His style is a departure from the usual escapist entertainment in its social message and value as well as its presentation.

Film is definitely a departure from the norm of Filipino fare. The emotion-ridden sequences and searing encounters are almost reminiscent of Loren's and Magnani's early Italian classics. —Mel.

Die Frau Gegenuber
(The Woman Across The Way)
(WEST GERMAN-B&W)

Cannes, May 23.

DNS Munich films release and production. Features entire cast. Directed by Hans Noever. Screenplay, Noever, Elvira Del Boca; camera (black and white), Walter Lassally; editor, Crista Wernicke, music, Robert Eliscu. Reviewed at Cannes Critic Week (Non-competing), May 20, '78. Running time, 90 MINS.

Cast: Petra Maria Gruhn, Franciszek Piecza, Jody Buchmann, Agnes Dunneis-

en, Brigitte Mira, Herbert Weihbach, Madeleine Kristl, Horst Nowack.

A gray and sometimes grim film about obsession that explores a middleaged man's thirst for the absolute. Married to a younger woman from the country, he begins to feel she may not love him. Film solidly, sometimes stolidly, spins an elaborate scheme he compiles to spy on his wife while he is supposedly away on a business trip.

In the process it explores that German psyche familiar from silent and Thirties films except it is done up with modern frills as he bugs his house, gets an apartment from which he can peer into his and finally manages to convince himself his doubt is right by pushing a colleague into her life.

When they become lovers, he shoots the man with a high-powered rifle and goes home to await the police. Hans Noever uses black and white which is appropriate for this strange tale and is helped by Walter Lassally's astute camera work. The wide windows of the apartment they live in take in the outside life and peering people that can only be shut out by drawing the curtains.

Expressionism is avoided, but there are hints the husband may be of foreign or even Jewish background though completely assimilated.

The playing is reserved and right and this emerges an odd tale of human hangups that is right for fest sidebar outings, but perhaps too steeped in ferreting out guilts, motives and obsessiveness for more dramatic bite. Directorial knowhow is evident.

It's mainly a local item due to its many allusions as to German guilt, stodgy life and some inside bits, as a game the couple play on making up faces from different pieces. —Mosk.

Alambrista
(The Illegal)
(US-COLOR)

Cannes, May 23.

Film Hans — Bobwin Prod. — Michael Hausman and Irwin Young release and production. Features entire cast. Written, directed and lensed (color) by Robert Young. Editor, Paul Jaeger. Reviewed at Cannes Film Festival (Critic Week-Non-Competing), May 23, '78. Running time, 90 MINS.
Roberto . . . . Domingo Ambriz
Joe . . . . Trinidad Silva
Sharon . . . . Linda Gillin
Wife . . . . Ludevina Salazar
Passer . . . . Ned Beatty

A perceptive tale of an alien illegal Mexican worker in the U.S., a wetback, known as an alambrista, film follows him in his adventures until a growing anger and a sudden coincidence of being present at his long missing father's death has him head homeward.

Director Robert Young does not

force violence and allows the film to develop slowly and in an observant manner seeing the U.S., mostly western towns and farms, through the Mexican's eyes. He is first seen on his own farm in Mexico. When his wife has a child he decides they need more than his farm can give.

The only solution is going to work in the U.S. and sending back money. He expects to be gone six months, but his mother warns him his father left the same way and never came back. He sneaks across the border, a wire fence, and manages to avoid U.S. police and immigration people and makes it to the U.S.

He wanders about, sees a farm and is set on by a dog. He gets his first offer of a job and meets other Mexicans. One cocky character takes him under his wing and in a trip to town, riding under the train on makeshift boards placed on iron supports, the man is killed.

The alambrista gets to town and hangs about and gets other jobs. Worked hard and paid little, he falls asleep at a counter in a coffee shop out of sheer fatigue and is deposited on the sidewalk. A waitress stops a man from stealing his money and takes him home. Though they cannot communicate, they take to each other and live together as he works and sends money home, but still becomes her lover.

Caught in an immigration raid, he is sent back but at the border recruited for a strike-breaking job, unknown to him and others, and smuggled back to the U.S. It is there, after a scene of anger at their treatment, that he is witness to his father's death and sees that he had married an American woman and sent money to her instead of back to Mexico. Film is not preachy and has insights into its ordinary but taking characters.

Reportedly made for tv, it probably is more suitable for that media. Theatrical outings could also be possible on its ample progression, insights into its characters and the theme. Young shows a surefooted directorial tact and handling of actors. —Mosk.

Jarha Fi Lhaite
(A Hole in the Wall)
(MOROCCAN-COLOR)

Cannes, May 23.

Farida Benlyazid - Kamar Film - Centre Cinematographique Morocain - Izza Gennini release and production. Features entire cast. Written and directed by Jillali Ferhati. Camera (Eastmancolor), Ahmed El Maanouni; editor, Amelie Cabral; music, Jil Jilala. Reviewed at Cannes Critic Week (Non-competing), May 19, '78. Running time, 87 MINS.
Cast: Jillali Ferhati, Ahmed Ferhati, Bachir Skiredj, Ahmed Boudaoudi, Ghita Ben Abdeslam.

A slice-of-life film about socalled little people that displays directorial insight and avoids tedium or

preachiness via a fine visual tone. Pic has an insight into everyday life in a big Moroccan city as well as the hangovers of colonial days in a country that is still relatively new in its independence.

The film may be limited to film festivals and some specialized outings offshore, though a promising lingo entry, but it does show the beginning of an assimilation of film techniques and adjustment to worthy themes that may eventually go beyond Moroccan borders.

Jillali Ferhati uses the flashback theme of a man leaving prison and thinking back over his life. He handles a zoom lens subtly to backtrack in time. He also plays the man with reserve and feeling.

A public scribe who types letters for people in the streets, usually to relatives abroad and mainly asking for money, lives alone alongside his deaf mute brother. He has two good friends, a middleaged tourist guide living off his mother, and one who has an okay civil service job and is trying to find a way of marrying his childhood girlfriend.

The scribe one day, in need of money, tries to wrest a woman's purse and she is killed when he pushes her. He runs off when police begin to pick up his friends for the woman had worked in a hotel they all frequented. He comes back and is imprisoned.

There are some excesses in hallucinations as the man is revealed as both a victim of some social inequality as well as being guilty. But the rich flair for friendship, the colorful feel of city life and unforced looks at changing mores indicate Ferhati is a man to be watched and perhaps more Moroccan weight at future fests is in store. —Mosk.

Ocana, Retrat Intermitent
(Ocana, an Intermittent Portrait)
(SPANISH-COLOR)

Barcelona, May 13.

A Teide-Prozesa production (Barcelona). Written and directed by Ventura Pons. Producer, Jose Maria Forn. Features entire cast. Camera (Eastmancolor), Lucho Poirot; editors, Emlio Rodriguez and Valeria Sarmiento. Reviewed at Universal Films (Barcelona), May 12, '78. Running time: 80 MINS.
Cast: Jose Perez Ocana and friends.

Documentary on one of the transvestite characters living off Barcelona's Ramblas. Pic consists mostly of Ocana speaking to the camera, though a few cinema-verite inserts of gay demonstrations, Holy Week processions with Ocana singing a *saeta* and theatrics are interspliced.

In simple, conversational fashion, sometimes spiced with wit, Ocana tells of his Andalusian childhood, how he came to live in Barcelona, his views on society, religion, art, sex, etc.

Most interesting are shots of his paintings and some street scenes with his male lover. But the monolog becomes tedious . —Besa.

Here Come The Tigers
(COLOR)

'Bad News Bears' ripoff.

Hollywood, May 26.

An American International Pictures release. Produced by Sean S. Cunningham and Stephen Miner. Features entire cast. Directed by Sean S. Cunningham. Screenplay, Arch McCoy; camera (Movielab color), Barry Abrams; music, Harry Manfredini; editor, Stephen Miner; art director Susan E. Cunningham; assistant producer, Cindy Veazey; assistant director, Nancy Hart; sound, Max Kalmanowicz. Reviewed at the Culver City Theatre, Hollywood, May 25, 1978. (MPAA rating: PG.) Running time: **90 MINS.**

Eddie Burke	Richard Lincoln
Burt Honneger	James Zvanut
Bette Burke	Samantha Grey
Felix the Umpire	Manny Lieberman
Kreeger	William Caldwell
Aesop	Fred Lincoln
Buster Rivers	Xavier Rodrigo
Patty O'Malley	Kathy Bell
Noel Cady	Noel John Cunningham ningham
Art Bullfinch	Sean P. Griffin
Mike "The Bod" Karpel	Max McClellan
"Eaglescout" Terwilliger	Kevin Moore

"Here Come The Tigers" is a smudged carbon copy of Michael Ritchie's "Bad News Bears." Object of this AIP pickup is to cash in on the success of the Paramount release and its sequel, "The Bad News Bears· In Breaking Training." To date the original has collected film rentals of more than $24,000,000, and Paramount has a third version scheduled for summer release. If "Tigers" takes in but a tenth of the original's audience, the low budget item will be a smash. AIP is booking the film wide for short stops market by market and should achieve its objective — success by imitation.

Of course, independent filmmaking is rife with derivatives. Just count the number of "Jaws," "Exorcist" and "Carrie" carbons. It's somewhat unusual, however, to take the lead from a comedy.

Arch McCoy's script makes few alterations on the original. The bumbling Little League baseball team is called the Tigers, its new coach is a rookie policeman, not a swimming pool scrubber, and he's got an assistant. That's about it. The team is bad and everyone laughs at its incompetence; it's a racially mixed collection and its counterpart in the championship is overly disciplined and zealous. Of course, there's a juvenille delinquent. The one slightly original twist is a Bruce Lee-like cleanup hitter.

Stylistically, "Tigers" attempts to imitate the original, even employing bogus symphonic music tuned by Harry Manfredini. Sean Cunningham's direction is dull. Acting is dreadful. Barry Abrams outdoor photography is okay. — Hege.

Fire In The Middle
(DOCU-COLOR-16m)

Muddled docu on pyramid power. Non-existent commercial outlook.

Hollywood, May 21.

A Virgin Earth Inc. production. Written, produced and directed by William Word and Joan Kasich. Camera (CFI Color), Word and Kasich; editors, Word, Kasich, Brad Thompson; sound, Thompson, Kasich, Sue Burkland; music, William Harkleroad; narrator, Bob Barnett. Reviewed at Brentwood Theatre, Santa Monica, May 21, 1978. (No MPAA Rating.) Running time: **90 MINS.**

"Fire In The Middle" is an earnest, yet ultimately boring, documentary touting the beneficial effects of "pyramid power." Although much of the 90 minute, 16m effort concentrates on the mysterious conception and execution in ancient Egypt of the Great Pyramid at Cheops, final section turns to irritating plugola of various pyramid schemes and products.

·Begun as a master's thesis at Humboldt State College in California by filmmakers William Word and Joan Kasich, docu was four years in the making, and includes location footage shot in Egypt.

Lotsa statistics are offered to explain the various dimensions of the Great Pyramid, with scholars still unable to determine whether structure was a tomb, an astronomy lab or some obscure symbol.

The dry historical narration jumps between long discourses on mathematical equations, and intonations of "the greatest monument built on earth," etc. But there's no mention of the incredible human suffering it must have taken thousands of men to build the huge edifice — only its classical beauty is extolled.

Film picks up a bit when various pyramid experts participate. These include a few legitimate scientists (from such groves of academe as the Stanford Research Institute), plus some nutty thinkers, including followers of Atlantis, and a "catacylsmologist" from L.A. Docu also gives a group called the "Ancient Research Soceity" a lot of free time to explore their skeptical theories, and resultant belief that it must have been visitors from outer space who constructed the pyramids.

"Fire In The Middle" avoids most of the excesses of the "Chariots Of The Gods"-type farcical docus, but adds little of interest instead. We see the Toronto Maple Leafs hockey team benefitting from sitting under a pyramid, but then a "pyramid guide" hustler appears on screen, and we're back to P.T. Barnum.

Actuality interviews break up the diagrams, stills and phony historical recreations, with lensing by Word and Kasich a bit muddy.

Sound quality is good, and other tech credits (including graphics) are as well done as can be expected, given 16m format.

Commercial outlook seems nonexistent, however, Syndication sales (via cable and cassette) might appeal to those already converted, but "Fire In The Middle" could have used some of the energy reportedly imparted by the pyramids. —Poll.

Kru Ban Nok
(The Rural Teacher)
(THAI-COLOR)

Bangkok, May 17.

A Duangkamol Entertainment release. Produced by Kamol Kuntangwattana. Directed by Surasee Bhatham. Executive producer, Boonlert Setthamongkol. Features entire cast; Story, Kamnan Khonkhai; screenplay, Senyanupap Saengkawannij; camera (color) and editor, Niwat Sinlapasomsak; asst. camera, Somwong Manivongse; music, Phet Pingtong and Titsoh Lampreun; sound editor, Porng Asavinikul; art director, Krisanapong Nakathon; asst. director, Issara Lookhong. Reviewed at Scala Theatre, Bangkok, May 16, '78. Running time: **133 MINS.**

Puya	Piya Trakulrat
Duangdao	Vasana Sitiwet
Pisit	Somchart Prachatai
Kammao	Nopadol Duangphorn
Sieng	Kanya Mothong
Jankaen	Ton Tomol

The Thai Motion Picture Producers Assn. gave "Kru Ban Nok" the official nod as Thai entry to the Tashkent Fest this year. Pic is a refreshing departure from all the love stories glutting the Thai film market at present.

No attempt is made to glamorize this film through use of pretty people in a pretty rural setting. It is highly realistic, with a great deal of emphasis on what is ordinary rather than what is special. Material is a combination of several provincial teachers' true stories put into one single neophyte teacher's tale. As the teacher, Piya Trakulrat has more than enough to keep him busy.

The finale is crudely contrived and undermines the simple and honest work that the hero is supposed to achieve. Nonetheless, much of what transpires before it is absorbing. —Cano.

Los Ojos Vendados
(Blindfolded Eyes)
(SPANISH-COLOR)

Madrid, May 19.

Elias Querejeta production. Written and directed by Carlos Saura; associate producers Claude Pierson and Tony Moliere. Features entire cast. Editor, Pablo G. Del Amo; camera (color), Teo Escamilla; sets, Antonio Belizon. Reviewed at Cine Penalver (Madrid), May 18, '78. Running time: **109 MINS.**

Emilia	Geraldine Chaplin
Luis	Jose Luis Gomez
Manuel	Xabier Elorriaga

Also with Lolola Cardona, Andre Falcon, Carmen Maura.

For those fond of unravelling filmic conundrums, tracking down symbols and setting juggled time sequences aright, there'll be plenty to do in this newest Carlos Saura opus, which offers no surprises and follows in the introspective vein of earlier of his works. Like its fore-runners, pic is challenging and in-telligent, but also ambiguous and confusing.

In the Franco years this vague-ness might have had its explana-tion in official censorship; but now it can be laid to nothing else but a per-sonal quirk or an artistic penchant for abstraction per se.

The subject this time is torture, certainly one that lends itself to elo-quence, forthrightness and pointed statements. Instead we are once again immersed into the director's own world of symbols and, as in "Elisa, Vida Mia," are hard-pressed to know what is fact and what is fiction. There are flash-backs, sequences which may be dreams of reality, and an awful lot of sotto voce talking suggesting that momentous issues are being dis-cussed. Straining one's ears doesn't help to clarify much.

The astute may come away with a notion of what it's all about, but to the average filmgoer it is all a rather longwinded Saurian mono-log with the culprits vaguely left as "totalitarian dictatorships."

Pic opens at an Amnesty International-type conference in which torture is condemned and surviving victims come on stage in disguise to tell of their experiences. On the board is a theatrical di-rector, a kind of Saura alter-ego, who decides to produce a play on the same subject, using for his main thesp the blah wife of his dentist. As the free-acting sessions continue, the wife breaks with hubby and moves in with the director; each starts digging assiduously into his/her past. The dentist has slap-ped his wife, and, of course, being a dentist, provides symbolical grist as a torturer. Meanwhile the director recalls his boyhood days working in a coal shop where the owner tormented him by sending him down into the cellar with the roaches.

Pic's denouement comes when Emilia decides to finally break with her husband; when she returns to the director's digs, he has been beaten up in his house by rightwing thugs (off stage — no flashbacks) who have been sending him threat-ening notes throughout the film. He is taken to a hospital, but she goes on stage to do the play. Final con-trived scene (or is it all in his imagi-nation?) has gunmen shooting down the thesps as they're doing the anti-torture bit.

Film might generate some in-terest on Chaplin's and Saura's names and for its human rights stand. But item is lacking the strength and production values of earlier Saura works such as "Cria" and "Cousin Angelica." Though Saura has touched upon an up-to-date problem, he handles it in a highly personalized style so that those looking for an anti-dicta-torship truncheon like "Z" will be disappointed.

Photography and direct sound are not quite up to crack. Geraldine Chaplin's thesping is identical to that of earlier Saura pix — you can love it or hate it, while Jose Luis Gomez is very subdued. —Besa.

Chui Petela
(Hark to the Cock)
(BULGARIAN-COLOR)

Sofia, April 16.

A BulgaroFilm Production, Sredets Group, Sofia; world rights, BulgaroFilm, Sofia. Features entire cast. Directed by Stefan Dimitrov. Screenplay, Konstantin Pavlov; camera (color), Emil Wagen-stein; art direction, Nikolai Surchadjiev; music, Georgi Genkov. Reviewed at BulgaroFilm Screening Room, Sofia, April 15, '78. Running time: 90 MINS.
Cast: Nikolai Binev (Granddad Toshe), Nevena Kokanova (Grandma Petrounka) Ivan Tsvetarski (Lyuben), Elena Kuneva (Pepa).

An actors' film, Stefan Dimi-trov's "Listen to the Cock" features two top legit and film thesps, Nevena Kokanova and Nikolai Binev, in character roles of people much older than they. And the story is a heart-tugging, sentimental melodrama that somehow works — perhaps because the script fits the situation to a tee.

Setting is an abandoned village where old people congregate to spin tales of the past for nothing better to do (the young people are off to work in cities). One braggart repeats his exploits in the First World War for the nth time, and brawls with a crony who doesn't believe him anymore. His comeuppance occurs when his wife on her deathbed asks his forgiveness for an indiscretion with the "Cock's" olf buddy.

But the old man can't find it in his heart to forgive. He reviews the past detail in painful detail, including his neglect for a son whoom he never quite found the time to understand, although loved in return. In the end the old man dies, the widow rises from her bed to bury him, and the old guard mourns his absence.

A gentle film with subtle strains of irony and wit. One of those tour-de-force thesp pix for Bulgarian Film Weeks. —Holl.

Talisman
(BULGARIAN-COLOR)

Sofia, April 15.

A BulgaroFilm Production, Hemus Group, Sofia, world rights, BulgaroFilm, Sofia. Features entire cast. Directed by Rashko Ouzounov. Screenplay, Pravda Kirova; camera (color), Tsvetan Cho-banski; art direction, Milko Marinov; music, Alexander Yossifov. Reviewed at BulgaroFilm Screening Room, Sofia, April 14, '78. Running time: 89 MINS.
Cast: Daniella Boyanova (Iskra), Lilyana Yovanovich (Isabella), Emilia Radeva (the Mother), Lyubomir Kirilov (the Father).

Children's pix are as much a part of Bulgarian production as they are in the Soviet Union — both coun-tries often watch Western product in the category of psychological real-ism and social import. "Talisman" is a good example: it deals with the problems of a sensitive fifth-grade student who depends on the powers of her talisman, a multicolored stone given by her father (a geolo-gist) as a present, to prove her right in an unlucky confrontation with school officials and her classmates.

The girl believes in the truth to the extreme and expects her school friends to back her in putting down a classmate, the arrogant son of a schoolteacher, when it proves necessary to do so. At home the par-ents are kind, but the contact is to the father rather than the mother, who has enough on her hands as it is. The introvert view of outside life makes it difficult to change or roll with the punches — until the mo-ment comes when she must help a younger, similarly stubborn six-year-old boy climb down from the perilous side of a building by fan-tasizing with the truth as he sees it. She now realizes the full con-sequences of holding to a principle without budging. —Holl.

Badi Blagoslovena
(Be Blessed)
(BULGARIAN-COLOR)

Sofia, April 15.

A BulgaroFilm Production, Mladost Group, Sofia; world rights, BulgaroFilm, Sofia. Features entire cast. Directed by Alexander Obreshkov. Screenplay, Kiril Topalov; camera (color), Kroum Krou-mov; art direction, Konstantin Rous-sakov; music, Dimiter Griva. Reviewed at BulgaroFilm Screening Room, Sofia, April 14, '78. Running time: 90 MINS.
Cast: Marianna Dimitrova (Elena), Dorothea Toncheva (Little Mother), Ev-genia Barakova (Gena), Maria Statoulova (Annie).

This is a strong theme for Social-ist countries: the problem of unwed mothers and illegitimate children. The treatment in Alexander Ob-reshkov's "Be Blessed" is more documentary than feature film, but some scenes are worth waiting for after long stretches of heavy-hand-ed direction of plain, unimagina-tive dialog (even the title sounds a

bit too pretentious, referring to a mock wedding ceremony for new-comers to a state institution).

Pic doesn't try to pull any punch-es and lead thesp, the talented Mari-anna Dimitrova, carries pic over many of the lumpy spots. It's about a young girl who comes to the "home" to have her baby away from parents and acquaintances (they often don't know a thing), who faces problems as they come so far as lover, parents, and child are con-cerned. She also sees how others have tried to make a go of it as un-wed mothers, as well as the pains of giving a first-born up for adoption. In fact, just about everything relev-ant to the theme is dropped into the script for some reflection. Only few if any answers are offered, and the drama inherent in the situation vanishes midway through the pic.

What's significant is that such socially engaged themes have become the bread-and-butter of many East European cinemas. Pix like "Be Blessed!" compare well with social pix in Hollywood of the 1930s. For native auds they quite new and challenging, although of minor b.o. interest to the West out-side of a relevant New Bulgarian Cinema retro. —Holl.

Muzhki Vremena
(Manly Times)
(BULGARIAN-COLOR)

Sofia, April 14.

A BulgaroFilm Production, Haemus Group, Sofia; world rights, BulgaroFilm, Sofia. Features entire cast. Directed by Eduard Zahariev. Screenplay, Nikolai Haitov; camera (Eastmancolor), Rado-slav Spassov; art direction, Anghel Ahbra-nov; music, Kiril Donchev. Reviewed at BuglaroFilm Screening Room, Sofia, April 13, '78. Running time: 100 MINS.
Cast: Grigor Vachkov (Banko), Mar-ianna Dimitrova (Elitsa), Nikola Todev (Kara Kolya), Trayan Yankov (Ilcho), Georgi Georgiev (Petko), Velko Kunev (Velko), Teofil Badelov (Gelyo).

A prizewinner at the last Teheran Film Fest (thesp awards to Mar-ianna Dimitrova and Grigor Vach-kov), Eduard Zahariev's "Manly Times" has been hailed as one of the break-through pics in New Bul-garian Cinema. With this film three top professionals established them-selves in addition to the above men-tioned actors: helmer Zahariev, scripter Nikola Haitov, and ace cameraman Radoslav Spassov. The combination worked to per-fection: a Bulgarian feature with both commercial and artistic possi-bilities.

The story runs like an ancient Greek tragedy. It comes from one of the writer's own collection from the Rhodope Mountains, a series of folktales that have made Haitov famous beyond the borders of his country. In brief, it deals with a paid kidnapping of a pretty young girl, already betrothed, by a rich boy from the neighboring village — the twist comes when the kidnapper-chief falls in love with his captive, and she with him.

The young lady is a she-cat who doesn't give up the fight easily, and the tragic hero (fittingly named "Banko") begins to suffer after the initial enjoyment of foiling escape-attempt after escape-attempt — one of which he in fact loses, for the girl's threat to hurl herself from a cliff was thwarted in the end only by sleep. Banko, a man of honor, decides to return his prize in the end, but he receives a bad shoulder wound in return for his troubles; it leads to a feverish illness on the sad day of the unexpected wedding celebration. Then the girl leaves her bridegroom and declares mutely her love for her captor, which leads to further, inevitable complications. The girl is later "claimed" again by one of Banko's own relatives, but it's clear she just wants to be near the man she really loves, who has not lost an arm (in the fight with the girl's family) and is too much a cripple to maintain his dignity as a man.

Story moves at a swift, narrative pace, strongly abetted by a stylistically observant camera free of tricks or overkill. This is the first adventure for Zahariev with Haitov — his usual script-partner is Georgi Mishev, who specializes in homespun humor and satire — and he demonstrates a relish for a tale rich in psychological nuance and tragicomic situations. A must for Bulgarian Film Weeks and this summer's non-laurel fest circuit.

—Holl.

Pantelei
(BULGARIAN-COLOR)

Sofia, April 16.

A BulgaroFilm Production, Sredets Group, Sofia; world rights, BulgaroFilm, Sofia. Features entire cast. Directed by Georgi Stoyanov. Screenplay, Vassil Akyov; camera (color), Radoslav Spassov; art direction, Georgi Todorov; music, Bozhidar Petkov. Reviewed at BulgaroFilm Screening Room, Sofia, April 15, '78. Running time: 100 MINS.

Cast: Pavel Poppandov (Panteley), Dobrinka Stankova (the Girl), Velko Kunev (the Eccentric), Nikoa Anastassov (Marko), Nikolai Nikolaev (Vicho).

"Pantelei" (or "Panteley" in English) refers to the hero, rather anti-hero, of this comedy, set, surprisingly enough, during the Resistance in 1944 as the country was in upheaval. Helmer Georgi Stoyanov and lenser Radoslav Spassov combine talents in this absurd spoof, which could find its way into art houses if the gods on the summer fest circuit are kind and proper handling pushes it gently in the right direction.

Consider a Harry Langdon type wearing a Beckett-Godot derby and rim glasses perched on slim frame with an elongated visage. This chump of the streets thinks a girl-agent in the Resistance is flirting with him when she only needs momentary cover on a train, hands over his ID card to a hospital administrator checking in a typhoid patient (who mysteriously handed our chump a gun and a piece of paper as he drops dead in his apartment), and thereafter flees from the police into the arms of the partisans and back into the arms of the police — until, after many adventures, the Reds march into Sofia with a new Revolutionary Government. Guess what: a policeman asks Panteley for his ID card.

"Panteley" has been a b.o. hit at home: the gags are fresh and the situations believable. All the main characters play their roles with relish in a tongue-in-cheek, dead-pan manner. If this was Hollywood, a sequel would already be on the way.

—Holl.

Zvezdi V Kossite, Salzi V Ochiete
(Stars in the Hair, Tears in the Eyes)
(BULGARIAN-COLOR)

Sofia, April 15.

A BulgaroFilm Production, Hemus Group, Sofia; world rights, BulgaroFilm, Sofia. Features entire cast. Directed by Ivan Nichev. Screenplay, Anghel Wagenstein; camera (color), Tsvetan Chobanski; art direction, Anghel Ahryanov; music, Kiril Tsiboulka. Reviewed at BulgaroFilm Screening Room, April 14, '78. Running time: 100 MINS.

Cast: Katya Paskaleva (Elissaveta Strzova), Peter Slabakov (Pierre Stomanyakov), Tatyana Lolova (Soultana Syarova), Nikolai Binev (Dinko Syarov), Ivan Dervishev (Benediktov), Leda Taseva (Mitsa), Antony Ghenov (Kalaidjiev), Ivan Tsvetarski (Rachev), Nikolai Nachkov (Vitlehem).

"Stars in the Hair, Tears in the Eyes" is a slight film, but it's fun and doesn't try to be pretentious in dealing with the turn of the century in Bulgaria as seen through the eyes of a wandering acting troupe. The backroads of a recently freed nation (from the Turks) beckon these pioneers of Bulgarian theatre, who bring such unknown classics as Shakespeare's "Othello," Ibsen's "A Doll's House," and Gorky's "The Lower Depths" to a culturally deprived people. This is the kind of fiction docu that instructs in an amusing and entertaining manner.

Ivan Nichev is the helmer, but much credit goes to scripter Anghel (Jackie) Wagenstein, a veteran who helped put his country's cinema on the map two decades ago with the screenplay for Konrad Wolf's "Stars" (1959), an East German-Bulgarian coprod. The idea is a deceptively simple one: the troupe tries to present art to the unspoiled masses, but the rich gentry demand pap and entertainment. A schoolteacher type who knows many of the classics by heart joins the troupe's ranks as a naive amateur, develops into a first-rate professional, and eventually takes over the group when the leader gives in to the offer of his own theatre provided he plays for the gentry. The beginning thus refers to the young actress's "stars in her hair," and the ending to the "tears in her eyes."

Wagenstein also intended many of the drama excerpts presented in legit performances to reflect back on the private lives and thoughts of the chief protagonists. —Holl.

Matriarhat
(Matriarchy)
(BULGARIAN-COLOR)

Sofia, April 14.

A BulgaroFilm Production, Savremennik Group, Sofia; world rights, BulgaroFilm, Sofia. Features entire cast. Directed by Lyudmil Kirkov. Screenplay, Georgi Mishev; camera (color), Georgi Roussinov; art direction, Bogoya Sapoundjiev, Assya Popova; music, Boris Karadimchev. Reviewed at BulgaroFilm Screening Room, April 13, '78. Running time: 90 MINS.

Katya Paskaleva (Tana), Nevena Kokanova (Ganetta), Emilia Radeva (Jella), Katia Tchoukova (Schtipana Bona), Georgi Georgiev-Getz (Milor), Georgi Roussev (Dim Boy).

"Matriarchy" consists of a series of loose sketches written by Georgi Mishev, one of Bulgaria's talented story-tellers who specializes in folk humor, light satire, and human touches in the profoundly moral sense. Mishev works with either Lyudmil Kirkov, as in this case, or Eduard Zahariev, both of whom are able helmer partners in handling material that is more mood and atmosphere than words and action.

Picture a semi-abandoned village where the women tend to household chores and fields, while their men are working long or permanent stretches in city factories or on-the-road construction and skilled-labor jobs. Since the fields are collective farms and family plots need day-to-day care, the women are both lonely and chained to seasonal crops. The exodus from the village is, of course, tragic, for Bulgarian industrialization has shifted the emphasis from peasant culture and agrarian life to something socially and psychologically inhuman (although perhaps necessary on the thorny path of progress).

Pic focuses on six different women working on the collective farm; the only males are the agronom, another man waiting for a job in the city, and a couple of travelling-salesmen types who tend to have other things on their mind in addition to business. The tragic moments involve the death of a household ox, the arrest of one woman's husband (the crooked manager of a coop warehouse) followed by a degrading roll in the hay during a visit to a farm-prison, and the death of an old woman suffering from an incurable desease.

An honest film worthy of attention for those who follow life and customs in East European countries. —Holl.

Pokriv
(A Roof)
(BULGARIAN-COLOR)

Sofia, April 15.

A BulgaroFilm Production, Hemus Group, Sofia; world rights, BulgaroFilm, Sofia. Features entire cast. Directed by Ivan Andonov. Screenplay, Kuncho Atanassov; camera (color), Victor Chichov; art direction, Juliana Boshkova; music, Georgi Genkov. Reviewed at BulgaroFilm Screening Room, Sofia, April 14, '78. Running time: 93 MINS.

Cast: Peter Slabakov (Kiril), Pepa Nikolova (the Woman), Katya Paskaleva (Maria), Velko Kunev (the Dark-Skinned Fellow), Maria Stazlova (Dimitrina), Nadia Todorova (Dena).

Helmer Ivan Andonov is better known to Bulgarian auds as a stage and film thesp, but he also wrote some skits for satirical shows and gradually via this route worked his way up to film direction. "A Roof" will guarantee enough fans at home and abroad to keep him in the director's seat, for this is a delightful satire in the mold of Italian neo-realist Vittorio De Sica's humorous odes to human foibles (who made a pic with the same title and much the same theme). It's a must in New Bulgarian Cinema retros and could score at one of the summer film fests.

This is a fast-moving, salty story of a construction worker in an industrial town who is trying, by fair means or foul, to build his own home for his wife and kids. At the moment the couple are living with a glib-tongue, warm-hearted neighbor, and it's the give-and-take between these two that sets the pace at the beginning — until our hero meets a red-blooded gypsy girl who matches wits with him in such a manner as to carry the film through to the end. The love affair can't go too far due to circumstances—"the woman," as she's referred to in the film, has been "bought" from the girl's parents by another, the "dark-skinned fellow," and that's next to law according to traditional rules.

Thus the construction driver has to find ways to venture off the given path to meet the girl who bedevils him. The physical attraction for another can't be hid very well at home: the wife comes to expect the worse, but the needs of buildings the house constantly detract — usually in a very funny manner — from facing the full truth. And the gags emanating from the girl's fate (she has to be locked up by her first suitor and finds multiple ways to duck sweaty armpit labor) adds to the earthy merriment.

This is an unusual and delightful Bulgarian pic, well-acted by the two principals (Peter Slabakov and Pepa Kinolova), which has solid commercial chances on the art house circuit. Another trump card in NBC's impressive production year. All credits are plus. —*Holl.*

Hirourzi
(Surgeons)
(BULGARIAN-COLOR)

Sofia, April 14.
A BulgaroFilm Production, Mladost Group, Sofia; world rights, BulgaroFilm, Sofia. Features entire cast. Directed by Ivanka Grubcheva. Screenplay, Georgi Danailov; camera (color), Yatsek Todorov; art direction, Konstantin Roussakev; music, Kiril Tsiboulka. Reviewed at BulgaroFilm Screening Room, Sofia, April 13, '78. Running time: **103 MINS.**
Cast: Vassil Mihailov (Dr. Panov), Mihail Mihailov (Dr. Dimitrov), Anton Radichev (Dr. Anghelov), Anghel Lambev (Chief Doctor), Iskra Radeva (Dr. Simeonova), Tsvetana Maneva (Dr. Panova), Stoycho Mazgalov (Stefanov), Lyudmilla Cheshmedjieva (wife of Dr. Dimitrov).

One of two talented femme helmers in Bulgaria (tops is Binka Zhelyaskova), Ivanka Grubcheva has come up fast through psychologically sound children's pics, like the prizewinning "Exams at Any Time" and "With Nobody." This is her first adult treatment, but the line of human observation is the same. It could have been a b.o. winner abroad, save for a rather heavy script which too often gets in the way just when one character or another gets interesting.

"Surgeons" is a moral tale: the hero is a sharp-tongued surgeon in a provincial clinic who hasn't the patience to combat stupidity among the people or in higher places. To save a young girl's life, he operates without the permission of the parents — she dies through no fault of his own, but the indiscretion brings an investigation and perhaps will cost him his career.

It's the character studies that surmount the rather predictable outcome. One doctor follows the old line of conformist thinking — "don't take risks" — and the others haven't quite enough guts to take sides when the chips are down. One surgeon sleeps with another surgeon's wife when the latter is on duty, another has never thought seriously of his profession in the first place, and so on. The climactic moment occurs when another little girl, the daughter of a high public official, must be operated on after an accident — this time successfully, but with the rub that the girl is not really the father's child after all.

"Surgeons" is worth critics' o.o. at Bulgarian Film Weeks and festival sidebars. —*Holl.*

Los Restos Del Naufragio
(The Remains of the Shipwreck)
(SPANISH-COLOR)

An Icine-Televisa-Promociones Aura-Mon-Vel production. Written and directed by Ricardo Franco. Features entire cast. Camera (Eastmancolor), Cecilio Paniagua; editor, Guillermo Sanchez Maldonado; music, David Thomas; sets, Joes Antonio de la Guerra; Exec producer, Jose Maria Pascual; production director, Jose Maria Cunilles. Reviewed at Cine Azul (Madrid), May 19, '78. Running time: **98 MINS.**
Maestro . . . . Fernando Fernan Gomez
Adelaida/Maria . . . . Angela Molina
Mateo . . . . Ricardo Franco
Don Emilio . . . . Alfredo Mayo
Dona Elsa . . . . Felicidad Blanc
Don Jorge . . . . Luis Ciges

Thoroughly delightful, offbeat, idiosyncratic film with an acting performance by Fernando Fernan Gomez which should win him kudos and prizes wherever pic unspools. Franco, whose previous film "Pascual Duarte" drew critical praise at Cannes a few years ago, here mixes whimsy and introspection as he plays off his own deadpan performance against the ebullient forays of Fernan Gomez. Blending in touches of wry humor prevents the film from becoming too ponderous and self-conscious.

Plot revolves around a young man with a cello who shows up at an old-age home run by nuns and asks to be admitted. The interviewing nun misunderstands and he gets a job as gardener. Soon he strikes up a friendship with a recalcitrant old-timer who smokes in secret, is preparing a play he has written, called "The Remains of the Shipwreck," and who has a secret chest in which he has kept mementoes of yore, most of them related to a love affair he had in a tropical seaport and a buried pirate's treasure in the Caribbean. The girl in the old man's romance and in the young man's present-day liaison are both played by Angela Molina.

Through some droll flashbacks and amusing dream sequences we learn of the imagined history of the Maestro, a title given him by the inmates of the home, who are alternately entertained and scandalized by his histrionic ways. The play is finally put on with grandiloquent eclat to the accompaniment of a cello solo; then the two friends tear up the mementoes and part.

Item is shot in direct sound, which often makes it hard to follow, but other technical credits are fine. Supports by Angela Molina, Alfredo Mayo and others are topnotch. In all, pic will probably be a top contender on the fest circuits this year and could do biz commercially on

the art circuits and in select Latin American and European playoffs as a top example of "new Spanish cinema." —*Besa.*

Cannes Festival

The Chant Of Jimmie Blacksmith
(AUSTRALIAN-COLOR)

Cannes, May 30.
Filmhouse, Australia Party Ltd. release and production. Features entire cast. Written, directed and produced by Fred Schepisi from the book by Thomas Keneally. Camera (Eastmancolor-C'Scope), Ian Baker; editor, Brian Kavanaugh. Reviewed at Cannes Film Fest (Competing), May 26, '78. Running time: **122 MINS.**
Jimmie . . . . .Tommy Lewis
Mort . . . . Freddy Reynolds
Farrell . . . . Ray Barrett
Neville . . . . Jack Thompson
McReady . . . . .Peter Carroll
Graff . . . . Elizabeth Alexander

The Australian film has been building up festival recognition for some time now. Government economic aid and a burst of new talents have made the Down Under films not only fest regulars but recipients of film weeks in various countries. They are at the beginnings of commercial incursions.

Now Australia has finally come from sidebar showings at the Cannes Festival and into competition. This, as other films seen, show a surge of interest in the past of the sprawling sub-continent.

Fred Schepisi, for his second film, reveals a sure hand, a dynamic thrust in using a true turn-of-the-century happening to delve into the racism of the times against aborigines and the beginnings of governmental federation of its many regions.

The tale of a mulatto aborigine, raised by a Methodist minister, and torn between his people and his Christian teachings, has sweep and interesting insights into the loss of the aborigine culture and the life of a man who does not belong to either culture anymore.

Tommy Lewis, a non-actor, is well utilized as Jimmie Blacksmith. His childhood has him learning ancient lore from his uncle and Christian ethics from a minister who sees some hope for him for he is half white. He grows up and is able to read and write.

He decides to leave the white family and his relatives for the squalor of native life — which is characterized by drinking, squalid shanty towns and exploitation after heavy decimation by the colonizing whites.

He gets various jobs where he is tolerated, exploited and usually

cheated on rightful earnings. The stirrings of revolt are shown by his standing up to many oppressors.

He has an affair with a servant white girl and when she becomes pregnant sends for her and is allowed to marry her. He works for a white family who allow him to build a hut for his family. The child turns out to be all white and not his. But he accepts it. Then slowly the family begins to refuse him rightful pay and they object to a visit by his brother and uncle.

When there is no food and no pay, after an altercation with the owner, he and his uncle go to the house, where the men are absent. Each has hidden an axe under his coat just for protection since the woman always comes to the door armed.

The refusal of food leads to a sudden explosion of all the smoldering resentments and they slaughter the wife, two teenage daughters, a school teacher living with them and a young boy. A child is mercifully spared.

The violence is instinctive, harrowing but not exploited. It is masterfully handled by Schepisi. Jimmie and his brother leave the old uncle and the wife and child and go on the lam as a great manhunt begins. They are tracked down but not before further killings. Eventually they die.

Reminiscent of other tales of outlaws driven to it by racism or injustice, this has the fine feel of the land, the revelation of the loss of an ancient culture. Treatment and playing are sound.

An Aussie pic that could find foreign chances on its dramatic, colorful, violent and insightful look at a period of the creation and problems of a new country. Schepisi sometimes is too leisurely but has an boservation, punch and dynamism that bode well for the new Aussie film movement and this pic in particular. —*Mosk.*

Moliere
(FRENCH-COLOR)

Cannes, May 30.
United Artists release of Films 13-Films Du Soleil et la Nuit-Antenne 2-RAI production. Features entire cast. Written and directed by Ariane Mnouchkine. Camera (Eastmancolor), Bernard Zitzerman; editor, Francoise Javet, Georges Klotz; art director, Guy-Claude Francois; music, Rene Clemencie. Reviewed at Cannes Film Fest (Competing), May 29, '78. Running time: **255 MINS.**
Moliere . . . . .Philippe Caubere
Forest . . . . Marie-France Audollent
La Grange . . . . Jonathon Sutton
Moliere as kid . . . . Frederic Ladonne
Mother . . . . Odile Cointepas
Father . . . . Armand Delcampe
Cesse . . . . .Jean Daste
Genevieve . . . . Francoise Jamet
Louis XIV . . . . .Jean-Claude Penchenat

A rather cumbersome, richly-textured, sprawling film about the life and times in the 17th century of the great iconoclastic French playwright Moliere. Made by a creative director of a legit company, Ariane Mnouchkine, its good points and flaws come from the theatrical approach to film rhythm, drama and spectacle.

The big scale scenes of a mardi gras that ends in the tar-and-feathering of three tax collectors and the reprisals of the king's police is mostly pageant. It's repetitive agitation rather than revealing of more forceful visual insights. It is is here that the young Moliere, a student, stumbles on a theatrical troupe that is to set his vocation and break with his family.

Pic is divided into two parts. First is his childhood, his break with the family tradition of rugmaking and his schooling to the point where he joins a travelling group of actors. Second recounts the adventures of the troupe around a starving France and their final acceptance of patronage of the nobleman and finally King Louis XIV himself and Moliere's rise to eminence.

There are some solid scenes of early theatrical lore, the mergence of Moliere's wit, social insights and his feel for the hypocrisies of the times. The actual plays are mainly glossed over in a montage of posters or book titles of his many plays.

There is a fine feel for the period and the actors, mostly unknown, help this overdone film. It neatly counterpoints a time of poverty with the splendor of the court of the King.

Philippe Caubere displays perceptive limning of the young and subsequently old and ailing playwright who falls on court approbration but is still backed by the King.

The last scene of his attack on stage doing "The Imaginary Invalid" has him rushed to his home and up a seemingly endless flight of stairs as he gushes blood from his mouth and his life flashes before him.

It sums up the film's overdoing of good visual ideas that are just bludgeoned too much and repeated too often to be effective.

With a great deal of pruning and tightening this could emerge as a film with fine chances for school and non-commercial usage. It should appeal theatrically on its home grounds but needs careful cutting for specialized chances in other climes.

Too often, Moliere's plays are glossed over and pic presupposes knowledge of them. But its inventive period flair, its dovetailing of court fastness and robust ordinary life show director Mnouchkine, a resourceful filmmaker who should be even more effective with more roadwork and understanding of film narrative.

It is at its best in its theatrical scenes. It commands respect and has backing from both French and Italo tv. It should be a good video series. —*Mosk.*

El Recurso Del Metedo
(The Recourse to the Method)
(MEXICAN-CUBAN-FRENCH-COLOR)

Cannes, May 30.

Conacine-ICAIC-K.G. Productions-FR3 production. Features entire cast. Directed by Miguel Littin. Screenplay, Littin, Jaime Augusto Shilley, Regis Debray from the book by Alejo Carpentier; camera (Eastmancolor), Ricardo Aronovich; editor, Ramon Aupart; music, Leo Brouver; art director, Pedro Garcia Espinosa, Edith Verpirini. Reviewed at Cannes Film Fest (Competing), May 24, '78. Running time, **190 MINS.**

First Magistrate	Nelson Villagra
Mayorala	Katy Jurado
Academician	Alain Cuny
Ofelia	Marta Adelina Vera
Peralta	Salvador Sanchez
Hoffmann	Reynaldo Miravalle
Student	Gabriel Retes

Chilean filmmaker Miguel Littin has given this Cuban-Mexican-French coproduction a cohesive feel and treatment as it delves into a historical probing of political power in general and in Latin America in particular. It is in the person of a colorful head of a Latin state who is the Center of this unusual historic pic that avoids didactics, has a sense of humor and demonstrates rather than getting shrill about tyranny, despotism and economic imperialism.

Nelson Villagra is effective as this head of a Latin agricultural state in the early 1900s. He likes to spend time in Paris where French logic and culture, completely at odds with the needs and outlooks of his own country, fascinate him. He wenches, drinks, spoils his grown daughter and allows her to wallow in European culture and pays off venal French politicos for their recognition and even cultural aid.

But a series of successive attempts to overthrow his dictatorial regime see him easily overcoming new strong-men and their bids for power. The U.S. backs him due to trade concessions.

There is an adventurous sweep to his battles. His mixture of urbanity, religious superstition, ruthlessness and an occasional streak of understanding of the changing times give this rambling, historic spree a sort of absorbing flair.

The First World War brings prosperity but when falling prices again imperil him, he becomes more cruel. He wipes out people revelling in the false rumor of his death (whcih he started himself) and stamps out student uprisings.

Not abreast of the changing times, he is finally forced to flee. Back in Paris, he lives out his life with his daughter, one loyal man and his mistress. He is finally buried in Paris with only them in the funeral procession.

Over three hours, it may be somewhat too discursive for general audiences but will have a following in Latin spots. Specialized spotting looms mainly for this unusual attempt to try to personalize the ambiguous theme of power.

Here it is in the person of one man, sprung from the people, who guides them with an iron fist. Many past historical and leadership figures are part of this anti-hero.

It does not try to force any parallels. with current situations. But they are there, as in most historical opuses.

An estimable work that is still perhaps somewhat too insidey, oblique and elusive for many general audiences but is a worthy fest entry and something for more demanding audiences. Technically excellent down the line. —*Mosk.*

Spirala
(Spiral)
(POLISH-COLOR)

Cannes, May 30.

Film Polski release of TOR production. Features entire cast. Written and directed by Krzysztof Zanussi. Camera (Eastmancolor), Edward Klosinski; music, Wojiech Kilar. Reviewed at Cannes Film Fest (Competing), May 25, '78. Running time, **90 MINS.**

Man	Jan Nowicki
Woman	Maja Komorowska
Old Man	Aleksander Bardini

Krzysztof Zanussi has already dealt with those basic universal problems of facing life and death in his school film about a dying priest. After a series of pix on moral and ethical problems, he comes back to a man and his death in a poignant, probing film that avoids being depressing by its insights into human reactions. It has visual solidity and pace plus fine acting.

Not an easy film commercially but a worthy one that had its place at the Cannes Fest and added to the Polish standing of films with penetrating themes.

A man comes to a ski resort and throws away the keys to his car before entering the hotel.

He tries to communicate with people but is mainly too direct, truthful, insulting and slightly hysterical to make much contact. He is repulsed by a comely widow, insults and probably high central party figure who gets privileges and finally goes off into the mountains.

Those people he had come across, however, banded together and, with help, found him badly frozen but alive.

The final drama is played out in a sanatorium. It appears the man, played with impressive presence and feeling by Jan Nowicki, had an incurable disease and had been a successful man but was now in a psychotic phase as he faces up to his position.

People he had met at the ski center came to see him and try to help. They profess to accept their deaths, some going through religious dogmas. Nowicki finally gets on a window ledge and hesitates before falling to his death.

A film that should have resonance everywhere despite its downbeat theme. Zanussi has caught the time of facing up to the fact of approaching death with insight, a balance of observation and dramatic reactions, to make this a film that needs careful handling and placement but should find selective audiences on its sheer rightness in tone, approach and treatment.

The only flaw in this otherwise touching film is a lack of empathy with the characters. — *Mosk.*

Die Linkshandige Frau
(The Left Handed Woman)
(WEST GERMAN-COLOR)

Cannes, May 23.

MK2 release of Road Movies Filmproduktion. Features entire cast. Written and and directed by Peter Handke. Camera (Eastmancolor), Robby Muller; editor, Peter Przygodda. Reviewed at Cannes Film Fest (Competing), May 20, '78. Running time, **119 MINS.**

Woman	Edith Clever
Stefan	Markus Muhleisen
Bruno	Bruno Ganz
Waiter	Michel Lonsdale
Fransziska	Angela Winkler
Publisher	Bernhard Wicki
Actor	Rudiger Vogler
Father	Bernhard Minetti

Peter Handke is a German playwright and novelist who has also penned scripts for rising German filmmaker Wim Wenders. Now Handke adapts his book about a woman breaking with her husband as director-writer to make a literary, visually pretty but indulgent opus.

It will find its place at festivals but is more a throwback to the days of alienation films rather than the more permissive probing of female consciousness-raising prevalent today.

Edith Clever, a theatre actress, has presence as the woman whose husband leaves her as she tries to find a way to cope with her young son and make a living since her husband has cut her allowance. There are walks, characters intruding on her solitude, a visit from her robust father and finally her still alone with her own plight.

Not as dry as some other opuses on this theme, and having a fine visual look, film has Clever more trance-like than facing up to or revealing the gnawing but admittedly hard-to-pin-down needs that have led to her separation from her husband. Bruno Ganz is effective as the sorely pressed husband.

A German exercise of style that is somewhat old hat in treatment, it is still arresting enough with its insights into couple and child parent relations. It has a sort of hypnotic litany that keeps this indulgent pic on the rails despite its repititious ness. It should feature at other festivals, too, and has possibilities for New York playoff. —*Mosk.*

Miris Poljs Kog Cveca
(The Smell of Wild Flowers)
(YUGOSLAV-COLOR)

Cannes, May 30.

Yugoslavia Film release of Centar Film production. Features entire cast. Directed by Srdjan Karanovic. Screenplay, Karanovic, Rajko Grlic; camera (Eastmancolor), Zivko Zalar; editor, Branka Ceperac; music, Zoran Simjanovic. Reviewed at Cannes Film Fest (Critic Week-Non-competing), May 20, '78. Running time: **99 MINS.**

Cast: Ljuba Tadic, Aleksander Bercek, Olga Spirironovic, Sonja Divac, Mrgud Radovanic, Branko Cvejic.

The festival circuit has shown Yugoslavia beginning to perk in more contemporary, more accessible films this past year. This airy comedy, that still deals in the age old problem of people getting fed up with their lives, displays wit, irreverence and a breezy insight that continue Yugoslav promise.

A second film, it tries to get too much anecdotal material into its tale and, sometimes, does not quite dovetail its various plot strands. But it has wry wit and disarming candor.

Not the film to break into world markets, but one for the fests and perhaps some specialized, selected spots abroad on its sheer good spirits and at times devastating insights into human comportment.

It seems many people are just fed up with things in general. A known, middleaged actor one day just walks out on a play and goes off with a friend, a barge captain. But a tv team making a film on him follows and when they dock in a little hamlet, with a small restaurant, many people fed up with life begin to appear and the actor is almost forgotten as all try to get a place in the papers or in the tv film which continues.

Laced in is a woman found dead in the river in a wedding dress, the only one who gave in to her depression.

Film maliciously twits those existentialist factors of world weariness that now seem to be infecting the socialist countries. A director to be watched in Srdjan Karanovic. A tingling, catchy musical score, fine thesping and good technical aspects are also assets. —*Mosk.*

I Miss You, Hugs & Kisses
(CANADIAN-COLOR)

Cannes, May 21.

An Astral release of a Paradise Films Limited production. Produced by Murray and Charles Markowitz. Features entire cast. Written and directed by Murray Markowitz. Camera (color), Don Wilder; music, Howard Shore; editing, Don Ginsburg; sound, Ingrid Cusiel. Screened at the Vox Theatre, Cannes, May 20, '78. Running Time: **90 MINS.**

Magadalene Kruschen ..... Elke Sommer
Charles Kruschen .... Donald Pilon
Gershen Isen .... Chuck Shamata
Pauline Corte .... Cindy Girling

For people who like their violence peppered with sex, "I Miss You, Hugs and Kisses" should run well on the exploitation market. It is based on one of the more notorious crimes in recent Canadian history.

Peter Demeter, a Toronto real-estate developer, was accused and convicted of killing his wife through the intermediary of 'persons unknown' in 1975. Although this unresolved murder and the controversial activities leading to the conviction are brought to the screen in fictionalized version, the film retains the essential form of the actual event.

Through the use of flashbacks, Markowitz fills the audience in on the background of the crime (husband's escape from Hungary, his rise from poverty, subsequent marriage and unfaithfulness). Fantasy scenes also introduces alternative hypothesis about the wife's death and a veritable rogue's gallery of possible murderers.

The result is a violent film in which the victim, played by Elke Sommer, is killed repeatedly but not without giving her husband due cause.

Markowitz is an intelligent and able filmmaker, and although "I Miss You" is heavy on action and rather short on psychology, it continues to promise that he will soon make a more substantial film.
— *Tadr.*

Koko Le Gorille
Qui Parle
(Koko, The Talking Gorilla)
(FRENCH-COLOR-DOCU)

Cannes, May 23.

Films De Losange - INA release and production. Conceived and directed by Barbet Schroeder. Camera (Eastmancolor), Nestor Almendros; editor, Dominique Auvray, Denise De Casabianca. Reviewed at Cannes Film Fest (Non-competing), May 20, '78. Running time, **82 MINS.**
(In English)

A documentary on American psychology student Penny Patterson's experiments with a seven-year-old gorilla, Koko, loaned to her by the San Francisco zoo. She has taught it over 350 words in sign language and film mainly looks at them at play and work.

This carries a certain fascination as this powerful gorilla shows itself to be mainly affectionate if capable of sudden bad spirits which could be dangerous due to its strength.

Film's main aspect is just watching the animal living with its teacher and friend. But it raises many questions that cannot really be answered. Can Koko really talk, or is it a reflex conditioned by rewards? Is it analagous to the early learning of humans?

The zoo wants the gorilla back because the keepers feel it is dangerous and wrong to "humanize" it. Is the gorilla now a person, does it have civil rights, is it taking on the WASP outlooks of its teacher?

All sides are repped but the result is in conclusive.

Film is a natural for tv and school usage. But it has a solid flair for observation, and, with the right handling, could find possible theatrical chances. —*Mosk.*

A Dama Do Lotacao
(The Lady On the Bus)
(BRAZILIAN-COLOR)

Cannes, May 28.

An Embrafilme — Regina Filmes production. Directed by Neville d'Almeida. Features entire cast. Associate producers, Luiz Carlos Barreto, Newton Rique. Screenplay, Nelson Rodriguez; camera (Eastmancolor), Edson Santos; sets, Gilberto Loureiro; editor, Raimundo Higiono; music, Caetano Veloso. Reviewed at Salle B, Palais des Festival (Cannes), May 28, '78. Running time: **104 MINS.**

Cast: Sonia Braga, Nuno Leal Maia, Jorge Doria, Paulo Cesar Pereio, Paulo Villaca, Claudio Marzo, Marcia Rodrigues, Iara Amaral, Roberto Bonfim, Liege Monteiro, Ney Santana, Ivan Setta, Washington Fernandes, Waldir Onofre.

"The Lady in the Bus" could be one of the hottest international softcore films in a long time. A kind of Brazilian "Emmanuelle," the film has a weak plot and runs a bit long, but the sex scenes and suggestive background are of the sort that could make the film click in all markets having no tough censorship restrictions.

Item has been a runaway success in its native Brazil, following the trajectory of "Dona Flor and Her Two Husbands." Judging from the success of that film in areas like Lisbon, Paris and New York, it is more than likely that "Lady on the Bus" will follow suit.

Carrying the whole film is Sonia Braga, a bewitching mixture a coyness and voluptuosity, who in a sense does a repeat of her performance in "Dona Flor," though here she lets down her dress rather more often. The director has her trying different men in different locales ranging from a nuptial bedroom to under a waterfall. The sex situations are all the more tantalizing for not being explicit, and Braga will keep audiences on the edges of their

seats with her shenanigans wherever pic plays.

Story, which is sometimes interlaced with touches of sly humor, concerns a young bride who is frigid on her wedding night. While the upper class husband is being slowly driven mad by his wife's lack of response, she starts trying out other men, ranging from the husband's best friend to his father, to see what her sexual potential is.

She then starts to ride buses and pick up men there, discarding each after he has served his male function. There isn't much to think about behind it all, but the writing, direction and thesping all have a light and often charming touch, so that the film never drags and at the end proves to be winsome.

Location shooting in and around Rio de Janeiro may give an added "exotic" touch to the film, just as the Bahia background helped "Dona Flor" score outside Brazil. Technical credits on the whole are okay, and the music score is catchy and appropriate, though lab work is not as good as it should be. — *Besa.*

Oka Oorie Katha
(The Marginal Ones)
(INDIAN-COLOR)

Cannes, May 30.

Parandhma Reddy release and production. Features entire cast. Directed by Mrinal Sen. Screenplay, Mohit Chattopadhyaya, Sen; camera (Eastmancolor), K.K. Mahajan; editor, Gangadhar Naskar; music, Vijay Raghava Rao. Reviewed at Cannes Film Fest (Director Fortnight-Noncompeting), May 23, '78. Running time, **116 MINS.**

Father .... Vaseduva Rao
Son ....Mamata Shankar
Wife .... Narayana Rao

Mrinal Sen is known mainly among film buffs and festgoers. But this bristlingly humane, provocative, funny and yet disturbing look at India's marginal myriads of the poor, through a father and son, should boost wider interest in Sen's work. Fellow Bengalese Satyajit Ray has a worthy colleague in Sen.

Sen does not have Ray's tranquility but does possess a quirky sense of humor that makes the characters alive and resonant. He does not overdo the grim poverty.

The father, played with gusto by Vaseduva Rao, is an extraordinary character. He rants against the system that reduces his kind to practically slaves exploited by rich owners.

He is also shrewd, devious, half mad but engaging in his evasion of work, a mixture of obsequiousness and revolt, of his earthy wit and garrulousness.

They live in a sagging mud hut, which collapses at times, and work in the field. To stave off hunger they sometimes rob branches and even steal food from the owners.

But the son decides to marry a lovely girl from a neighboring town. The father is moved to sleeping on a makeshift arrangement in the roof and resents the intruder.

The wife has charm, beauty and freshness which adds a poetic twist to this both funny and poetic tale. She has to work hard, is left alone too often and dies in child birth.

Begging for money to bury her, they get more than they have ever seen. It leads to the father making vows of the need for food, shelter and help to him and his impoverished kind.

Film may not have the moving pitch and insights of Ray's pix, but has an added balance of iconoclastic rage and an anarchic comedic edge to give this specialized and institutional chances abroad.

Pic should finally focus attention on this prolific filmmaker who deserves more chances outside his own country. —*Mosk.*

Alyam Alyam
(Oh The Days)
(MOROCCAN-COLOR)

Cannes, May 30.
Izza Genini release of Centre Cinematographique Marocain Rabii Films production. Features entire cast. Written, directed and lensed by Ahmed El Maanouni. Editor, Martine Chicot; music, Nass El Ghiwane. Reviewed at Cannes Film Fest (Certain Look Section-non-competing), May 23, '78. Running time, 90 MINS.
Cast: Addelwahad, Tobi, Afandi Redouane, Ben Brahim.

Morocco gets recognition at this year's Cannes event with two pix in official sections. This one looks at everyday life and poverty in a fragmented, sometimes heavy-handed manner as a young man decides to go to France to make money and escape the poverty and misery of his lot.

Film is a sort of litany that shows the barren conditions, stories of emigrant workers affecting those left behind, and does give a more realistic picture of one aspect of life among the more disinherited in this country.

New director Ahmed El Maanouni needs to add a more visual approach to his fine handling of non-actors and pros.

Film is slow and repetitious but does keep interest in its sharp insight into its characters and their needs.

Mainly for school, fest and seminar usage, but showing a promising reflection of life in that country that could add more potently phrased and executed films to future fests. —*Mosk.*

Blackout
(CANADIAN-FRENCH-COLOR)

A Cinepix release of a Dal-Agora-Maki co-production of a Sommerhill House film. Producers, Nicole Boisvert, Eddy Matalon, John Dunning. Executive producers: Andre Link, Ivan Reitman, John Vidette. Directed by Eddy Matalon. Screenplay, John C. Saxton; camera (color), J.J. Tarbes; music by Didier Vasseur; editors; Debbie Karen, Michael Karen; sound Henri Blondeau.Screened at the Vox Theatre at Cannes, May 18, 1978. Running time: 89 MINS.
Dan the cop . . . . Jim Mitchum
Christie . . . . Robert Carradine
Annie . . . . Belinda Montgomery
Mrs. Grant . . . . June Allyson
Henry Lee . . . . .Jean-Pierre Aumont
Mr. Stafford . . . . Ray Milland

A neat combination of comedy and terror make "Blackout" a refreshing and sturdy pic for audiences looking for a quick escape. Should do especially well in drive-ins.

The scene is New York, July, 1977, the night of the big blackout. As the electricity fails, four psychotic criminals take over a Manhatten high-rise and terrorize the residents, apartment by apartment, warming to their task as they go. The good cop puts a stop to all the carnage, but not until most of the harm is done.

The film's strucutre is standard for the disaster genre. Excellent performances by June Allyson and Ray Milland lend depth to the pithy interpretations of Belinda Montgomery and Jim Mitchum.

"Blackout" is technically solid and marks progress for both producer and director. Especially well-done are the aerial shots of the darkened city.

Although the pace is stronger in the first half of the film, audiences should leave giggling, and just a little afraid. —*Tadr.*

92 minutter af i gaar
(92 Minutes Of Yesterday)
(DANISH-COLOR)

Cannes, May 22.
A Partner & Kompagnon ApS production and release. Written by Carsten Brandt and Mogens Elkow. Executive producer, Elkow. Directed and edited by Brandt. Features entire cast. Camera (Eastmancolor Widescreen); music, Henrik Blichmann. Reviewed at Cinema Le Star 3, Cannes Festival, May 22, '78. Running time, 110 MINS.
The Woman . . . . Tine Blichmann
The Man . . . . Roland Blanche

The man is a Parisian businessman en route to Stockholm with a 92-minute stopover and a change of trains in Copenhagen. He sells transistor radios that also serve as shavers, lighters and can openers. He is middleaged and balding and he keeps running into mishaps like jammed doors and out-of-order telephone booths.

He is played with understated humor and sensitivity by French actor Roland Blanche. He carries a parcel that he tries to deliver to a Danish acquaintance who turns out to have left his address for good.

The woman who has taken over the apartment (the moving people are still at work) was not supposed to have come back at all. It is Midsummer's Eve with bonfires and parties, but a younger girl had a bad fight with her boyfriend during one such garden party and is taken to her home by the woman and put to bed. After that the woman goes home, too, and finds the Frenchman with his parcel.

The two communicate haltingly, neither understanding one word of the other's language. But silent laughter and a certain tenderness spring up between them. The telephone rings. The young girl has attempted suicide. The man and the woman embrace briefly and then he is back on his train to Stockholm.

Carsten Brandt tells his now-story with a compassion that is never overdone and with a very special sense of quiet farce. Film's photography is brilliant (Dirk Burle is not, like Brandt, a newcomer to films), and the very slow pulsebeat of the entire film is as calculated as it is just right for the mood. Tine Blichmann is not an actress of Blanche's stature, but she serves well in the context.

"92 Minutes Of Yesterday" could be a sleeper hit on the art circuit and possibly even in more commercial situations everywhere. Since few words are spoken, and those spoken phrased so as to be understood only through the aid of sign language, film will need no subtitles. —*Kell.*

In Search Of Anna
(AUSTRALIAN-COLOR)

Cannes, May 21.
A Storm Production, produced, written and directed by Esben Storm. Features entire cast. Assoc. prod. Natalie Miller. Camera (color) Mike Edols; editing, Dusan Werner; prod. mgr, Jane Scott; sound, Laurie Fitzgerald; make-up, Anne Pospischil. Reviewed, Paris Cinema, Cannes, May 20, '77. Running time: 94 MINS.
Tony . . . . Richard Moir
Sam . . . . .Judy Morris
Jerry . . . . .Chris Hayward
Peter . . . . .Bill Hunter
Maxie . . . . Garry Waddell
Buzz . . . . Ian Nimmo
Bert . . . . Maurie Fields
Tony's father . . . . Alex Taifer
Undertaker . . . . Richard Murphett

Esben Storm's "In Search of Anna" spent a long time in post-production and looks it. The director, who indicated such promise with his debut film, "27a" (about an iniquitous Catch 22 in Queensland's mental health laws, and which subsequently prompted a change) has had too much time to brood about his latest subject: the common catalytic effect of a young ex-con and a mixed-up model.

The central problem with the script is the superficiality of the values demonstrated by the central characters. Their essential shallowness denies from the outset any real character development, and the film's heavy reliance on flashback retards what might have been discernable growth.

It is a confused and confusing film with an overbearing soundtrack that detracts from the good-looking images — though even these at times are marred by a self-consciousness that jars.

The "Look-Ma! No-Hands" technique is especially evident near the end where a mish-mash of cutting creates a semi-cigarette commercial of Tony actually in search of Sam: a monotonous montage of freezeframes that extends, but fails to make any sense of, the boy's transference to the Judy Morris character. But that's not the only off-the-wall, evidently unmotivated, episode.

The narrative as set out is that Tony (Moir) gets out of prison and, after a brief period of attempting to re-establish a home life, is rejoined by former associates who want to know where the money they stole (for which Tony took the rap) is some six years later.

They beat him up: he wreaks his revenge and sets off in search of a former girlfriend, the eponymous Anna, only to be picked up by a feckless and footloose neurotic model played with a constant air of embarrassment by Judy Morris.

Together with his dog, they drive in her 1938 sedan 3200 kilometers in search of his ex-lady, only to find each other.

However, it doesn't all happen in that order even if it does happen to the frequent intrusion of loud rock music (an aspect evidently designed to appeal to an audience undistracted by irrelevant, melodic insistence).

Unexplained is whether his fight with his former criminal colleagues fomented his fugue, or whether it was a pre-determined effort to find his previous paramour: the sentimental voice-overs reading their prison correspondence would suggest the latter, however the on-screen events indicate otherwise.

Either motivation could be a rationalization, but upon closer examination could equally be sloppy plotting. Given the film's overall unevenness, it would seem to be a constructional flaw rather than a subtle development.

Hayward is particularly good as Jerry, the upstart hood, and Moir's performance has a nicely underplayed restraint — though this is often eroded by what he and others have to do; things that seem outside the experience or inclination of the character. Frequently these aberrations are demonstrably the product of actors' improvisations — always a dangerous practice in the hands of a tyro director, and one which only rarely can be brought off by even the most experienced.

A good-looking film, but one that tends to be arty rather than artful, and often tries to be a bit cleverer than it is capable of achieving.

—*Miha.*

Black Sun
(SWEDISH-YUGOSLAV-COLOR)

Cannes, May 22.

A Stockholm Film production in collaboration with Jadran Film, Zagreb. Script by Wahloo and Arne Mattson, based on Per Wahloo's novel "The Lorry" (U.S. title "A Necessary Action"). Directed by Mattson. Executive producer Jorn Donner. Features entire cast. Editor, John Trumper; music, Wilfred Josephs; camera (Eastmancolor) Tony Forsberg. Reviewed at Cannes Festival at Cinema Le Regent, May 22, '78. Running time: 100 MINS.

Willi Nohr	Helmut Griem
Santiago	Slobodan Dimitrijevic
Dan	John Hamill
Siglinde	Gunnel Fred
Police Sergeant	Richard Warwick

(English Soundtrack)

This political thriller bid for an immediate world market is an almost total failure. This in spite of star and thesp presence of high quality (Helmut Griem, Richard Warwick), lavish production dress, English dialog and a story concocted by much-lauded writer Per Wahloo. Director Arne Mattson, a veteran of solid accomplishment, has very evidently. worked from a script devoid of plot logic that fails to establish participating characters who, reasonably enough, don't seem to know what is going on.

It would seem that Willi Nohr, a German painter and permanent resident of a Spanish fishing village during the latter France years (film was shot on Yugoslav locations) kills a local fisherman to revenge the rape and murder of his lodger, a young Scandinavian woman (Gunnel Fred) who has been flaunting her nudity all over the place.

But are we to believe that Willi himself has lusted for the woman? Well, the murderer had an accomplice, who turns out to be engaged in arms smuggling to workers planning a strike in a nearby factory town. The arms smuggler (Slobodan Dimitrijevic) and the German now join forces to help the workers and defy the local police and especially a couple of sadistic secret agents.

Everything goes wrong. Only the bad guys survive. And in the plaza of the factory town, police soldiers kill about 20 women, undress them and use flame throwers on their genitals.

And that is the end of the film, set to the heightened effect of flamenco guitar playing.

Even if there is a market somewhere for outright screen sadism, this "moment of truth" only arrives after 95 minutes of confusion and boredom. —*Kell.*

Le Dossier 51
(The 51 File)
(FRENCH-COLOR)

Cannes, May 30.

Gaumont release of Elefilm-SFP-Maran Film production. Features entire cast. Directed by Michel Deville. Screenplay, Gilles Perrault. Deville; camera (Eastmancolor), Claude Lecomte; editor, Raymonde Guyot; music, Jean Schwarz. Reviewed at Cannes Film Fest (Certain Look Section-Non-competing), May 21, '78. Running time. 108 MINS.

Dominique	Francois Marthouret
Liliane	Claude Mercault
Philippe	Philippe Rouleau
Marguerite	Nathalie Juvet
Esculape	Roger Planchon
Mother	Francoise Lugagne

A sleek, familiar tale of undercover agents and their creation of a file on a young French diplomat by bugging, studying his life and trying to find something to give them a hold on him. The only original aspect is telling the whole thing through the mysterious outfit setting up the file, unknown to the man being studied.

Actually, it is a tale of a closet queen who builds up a psychological defence which is finally shattered by the work of the group setting up his file. It leads to a predictable suicide. Bugging, intrusion on privacy, etc., has been better treated before and this essentially obvious character study — a bit old hat in these days of permissiveness — looms more potent for tv than more demanding theatrical slotting abroad.

Michel Deville has directed with efficiency but the gimmick of seeing this drama only through the eyes and work of this mysterious organization is finally over-indulged. It adds little to the dramatic edge of the unknowing man's forthcoming destruction.

— *Mosk.*

The Cheap Detective
(COLOR)

Outstanding Neil Simon comedy takeoff on "Casablanca," et al. Terrific cast and b.o. potential to match.

Hollywood, June 1.

Columbia Pictures release, produced by Ray Stark. Directed by Robert Moore. Features entire cast. Screenplay, Neil Simon; camera (Metrocolor), John A. Alonzo; editors, Sidney Levin, Michael A. Stevenson; music, Patrick Williams; production design, Robert Luthardt; art direction, Phillip Bennett; set decoration, Charles Pierce; sound, Bill McCaughey, Mike Kohut, Lyle Burbridge, Al Overton Jr.; costumes-wardrobe, Theoni V. Aldredge, John A. Anderson, Agnes G. Henry; asst. director, John C. Chulay. Reviewed at The Burbank Studios, May 31, '78. (MPAA Rating: PG). Running time, 92 MINS.

Lou Peckinpaugh	Peter Falk
Jezebel Dezire	Ann-Margret
Betty DeBoop	Eileen Brennan
Ezra Dezire	Sid Caesar
Bess	Stockard Channing
Marcel	James Coco
Pepe Damascus	Dom DeLuise
Marlene DuChard	Louise Fletcher
Jasper Blubber	John Houseman
Mrs. Montenegro	Madeline Kahn
Paul DuChard	Fernando Lamas
Georgia Merkle	Marsha Mason
Hoppy	Phil Silvers
Sgt. Rizzuto	Abe Vigoda
Boy	Paul Williams
Col. Schlissel	Nicol Williamson
Butler	Emory Bass
Sgt. Crosseti	Carmine Caridi
Tinker	Scatman Crothers
Lt. DiMaggio	Vic Tayback

"The Cheap Detective," which might also be called "Son Of Casablanca," is a hilarious and loving takeoff on all '40s Warner Bros. private eye and foreign intrigue mellers. Neil Simon's outstanding screenplay, Robert Moore's superb direction and Ray Stark's handsome and deliberately evocative soundstage production expertly reunite the "Murder By Death" team of two summers ago. Peter Falk, in the Bogart-esque title role, heads a terrific cast of top names, all of whom make the Columbia/EMI/Rastar project a sure big b.o. winner across many general audience age groups.

Once again, Simon's sure writing touch is evident in a fully-developed plot which is loaded with humor of the Bob (Elliott) & Ray (Goulding) school of deadpan malaprop and satire. The time is 1940, San Francisco, where clumsy gumshoe Falk is accused of murdering his partner, whose wife Marsha Mason (in early Janet Leigh curls) has been Falk's mistress. Detective Vic Tayback and assistants regularly blunder into matters.

Madeline Kahn, with as many smart clothes changes as aliases, appears in Falk's office. She's in league with John Houseman (Sydney Greenstreet to the core), Paul Williams (Elisha Cook Jr. was never like this) and Dom DeLuise (a fat

Peter Lorre) in search of ancient treasure — a dozen diamond eggs.

But wait! Enter Louise Fletcher and Fernando Lamas (Ingrid Bergman and Paul Henreid), loyal French citizens in desperate need of passage to Oakland where James Coco can operate a Free French restaurant in which the partisans can listen to World War II on the radio. Fletcher was once Falk's fiance, and "their song" — "Jeepers Creepers" — recurs frequently in the contrivedly lush Patrick Williams score. Scatman Crothers is the Dooley Wilson update on the piano.

Nicol Williamson is stalking Lamas and Fletcher; he's head of the Nazi party in Cincinnati. Eileen Brennan is a slinky cafe chanteuse of the Bacall school who falls for Falk. Ann-Margret plays the sexy young wife of senile millionaire Sid Caesar, whose secret identity is unraveled from an anagram by Stockard Channing, Falk's faithful secretary.

Amidst the confusing threads of mystery, Falk is regularly affronted by the overly explicit descriptions of sexual torture inflicted on all the dames. But at fadeout he's got a lot more going for him than Bogart did in the final dissolve.

Robert Luthardt's outstanding production design and John Alonzo's cinematography perfectly recreate the period of the spoof. Wayne Fitzgerald's titles get the film off to a fine start — names painted on all manner of furniture and street hardware as the mysterioso camera tracks the crawl through gutter and alley. The very smart 92-minute running time matches the length of the original film being sent up; it also will help the turnover of laughing audiences.

Two years ago, "Murder By Death" opened without fanfare to its rewarding public response. "The Cheap Detective" deserves a fanfare which will not disappoint. This one rates a Bravo! to all concerned. — *Murf.*

High-ballin'
(COLOR)

Trucking pic. Okay rural-drive-in outlook.

Hollywood, May 30.

An American International Pictures release of a Stanley Chase/Pando Co. production, produced by Jon Slan; executive producers, Stanley Chase, William Hayward. Stars Peter Fonda, Jerry Reed. Directed by Peter Carter. Screenplay, Paul Edwards from a story by Richard Robinson and Stephen Schneck; camera (Movielab color), Rene Verzier; art director, Claude Bonniere; editor, Eric Wrate; music, Paul Hoffert; assistant director, Tony Thatcher; sound, Douglas Ganton; stunt coordinators, Gary Davis, Bud George Davis; special effects, Richard Helmer. Reviewed at the AIP Screening

Room, Beverly Hills, May 30, '78. (MPAA Rating: PG.) Runningtime: 100 MINS.

Rane . . . . Peter Fonda
Duke . . . . Jerry Reed
Pickup . . . . Helen Shaver
King Carroll . . . . Chris Wiggins
Harvey . . . . David Ferry
Tanker . . . . Chris Langevin

With hijackers on the loose and a large trucking firm bent on destroying the independent, Peter Fonda and Jerry Reed battle corruption on the highway atop the cab of an 18-wheeler in "High-ballin'." Plenty of CB talking, some moonshine running, a modest love story, efficiently staged stunts and car crashes plus assorted brawls should assure good business in rural markets and at the drive-in circuit. Urban areas, even those where Universal's "Smokey & The Bandit" clicked will not respond because of the film's serious tone and basically downer ending.

Reed, again natural and freewheeling as an indie trucker, doesn't want to surrender his freedom and work for King Carroll (Chris Wiggins). But he's scared and he's got a wife, son and farm to consider.

Fonda, again reticent and mysterious as a motorcycle riding freespirit, is an old friend of Reed's. He's there to help his old buddy fight the evil forces, led by David Ferry and Wiggins. The two good guys soon ally themselves with another freespirit, Helen Shaver, herself a trucker and Fonda's love interest.

First half of the picture is light and has some nice moments with Reed whooping it up while Fonda fends off the hijackers by throwing a load of old cars the two are transporting at the pursuing bandits. Why the two are transporting such old cars is never explained. Probably to keep the film's budget down.

Second half becomes ominous. Tech credits are okay. Ditto for Peter Carter's direction and the stunts coordinated by Gary Davis and Bud Geroge Davis. —Hege.

Jaws 2
(COLOR)

Excellent sequel with more emphasis on teenage appeal. Torrid summer outlook.

Hollywood, June 2.

Universal Pictures release, produced by Richard D. Zanuck, David Brown. Stars Roy Scheider, Lorraine Gary, Murray Hamilton. Directed by Jeannot Szwarc. Screenplay, Carl Gottlieb, Howard Sackler, based on characters created by Peter Benchley; camera (Technicolor), Michael Butler; second unit camera, David Butler, Michael McGowan; underwater camera, Michael Dugan; live shark camera, Ron and Valerie Brown; editor, Neil Travis; music, John Williams; production design, Joe Alves; art direction, Gene Johnson, Stu Campbell; set decoration, Philip Abramson; sound, Robert L. Hoyt, Jim Alex-

ander; costumes-wardrobe, Laurann Cordero, Gil Loe; asst. directors; Scott Maitland, Don Zepfel; second unit director, Joe Alves; stunt coordinator, Ted Grossman. Reviewed at Universal Studios, L.A., June 1, '78 (MPAA Rating: PG.) Running time, 117 MINS.

Brody . . . . Roy Scheider
Ellen Brody . . . . Lorraine Gary
Mayor Vaughn . . . . Murray Hamilton
Peterson . . . . Joseph Mascolo
Hendricks . . . . Jeffrey Kramer
Dr. Elkins . . . . Collin Wilcox
Tina . . . . Ann Dusenberry
Mike . . . . Mark Gruner
Andrews . . . . Barry Coe
Old Lady . . . . Susan French
Andy . . . . Gary Springer
Jackie . . . . Donna Wilkes
Sean . . . . Marc Gilpin
Larry . . . . David Elliott
Ed . . . . Gary Dubin
Brooke . . . . Gigi Vorgan
Timmy . . . . G. Thomas Dunlop
Helicopter Pilot . . . . Jerry M. Baxter

Despite a notable but effective change in story emphasis, "Jaws 2" is a worthy successor in horror, suspense and terror to its 1975 smash progenitor. Producers Richard D. Zanuck and David Brown encored both the sequel and the manifold production logistical complications. Director Jeannot Szwarc, who replaced John Hancock, scores most effectively in his second feature assignment. The Universal release should be a major summer b.o. performer. How big? Who can say, but, certainly, big enough.

The Peter Benchley characters of offshore island police chief Roy Scheider, loyal spouse Lorraine Gary, temporizing mayor Murray Hamilton and gee-whiz deputy Jeffrey Kramer are used as the adult pegs for the very good screenplay by Carl Gottlieb and Howard Sackler. The targets of terror, and the principal focus of audience empathy, are socres of happy teenagers.

So strong is the emphasis on adolescent adrenalin that "Jaws 2" might well be described as the most expensive film that American International Pictures never made. However, there's enough intelligence for audiences across the age spectrum, though popcorn escapism is the obvious market here.

Special shark model effects by Robert A. Mattey and Roy Arbogast, combined with perfectly intercut photography and another outstanding John Williams score (which nicely gives the sea its periodic moments of peaceful magnificence), create and sustain dramatic tension for the film's 117 minutes. Interim dramatic pauses are most adroitly spaced, and most welcome; audiences are likely to feel thoroughly but satisfyingly wasted when the film concludes.

Suffice to say that the story again pits Scheider's concern for safety against the indifference of the town elders as evidence mounts that there's another great white shark out there in the shallow waters.

Ever-more complicated teenage jeopardy leads to the climactic showdown with a buried cable.

The $10,000,000 planned budget area for "Jaws 2" was the overage of the original; its $20,000,000 final cost area is 25% accounted for by mere dollar inflation, plus the Szwarc-Hancock segue delay and new production kinks. Project should be off its nut by $35-40,000,-000 in world rentals, which is still comfortably shy of the estimated worst-case situation of "only" $60,65,000,000 in global distrib rentals, that doomsday minimum being one-third of the original's $200,-000,000 world rental haul from theatres alone.

In all respects, the production lives up to its tagline, "all new."
—Murf.

Harper Valley P.T.A.
(COLOR)

Pop tune into comedy film, visually successful.

Chicago, June 6.

An April Fools Production. Executive producer, Phil Borack. Produced by George Edwards. Features entire cast. Directed by Richard Bennett. Screenplay, George Edwards, Barry Schneider, based on song "Harper Valley PTA," words and music by Tom T. Hall, sung by Jeannie C. Riley; music, Nelson Riddle; camera (Deluxe), Willy Kurant; editing, Michael Economu; art direction, costumes, Tom Rasmussen; set decoration, Bob Breen. Reviewed at Norridge Theatre, Chicago, June 1, '78. (MPAA Rating: PG) Running time: 93 MINS.

Stella Johnson . . . . Barbara Eden
Willis Newton . . . . Ronny Cox
Alice Finely . . . . Nannette Fabray
Dee Johnson . . . . Susan Swift
Kirby Baker . . . . Louis Nye
Otis Harper, Jr. . . . . Pat Paulsen
Bobby Taylor . . . . John Fiedler
Flora Simpson Reilly . . . . . Audrey Christie
Holly Taylor . . . . DeVera Marcus
Myrna Wong . . . . Irene Yah Ling Sun
Mavis Schroeder . . . . Louise Foley
Corley . . . . Clint Howard
Reilly Twins . . . . Jan & Laura Teige
Henry Reilly . . . . Pitt Hervert
Willa Mae Jones . . . . Faye Dewitt
Olive Glover . . . . Molly Dodd
Herbie Maddox . . . . Ron Masak
Shirley Thompson . . . . . . Amzie Strickland
Carlyle Ridley . . . . Brian Cook
Barney . . . . Tobias Anderson
Skeeter . . . . Bob Hastings
Bertha . . . . Arlene Stuart
Nolan . . . . JJ Barry
Dutch . . . . Royce D. Applegate
Stunt Man . . . . Whitey Hughes

Based on the 1960's hit song of the same name, "Harper Valley PTA" is typical drive-in fare — it gives the audience little to think about but is good enough for laughs. Pic should enjoy popularity at outdoor screens across the country, particularly in smaller markets where some of the "good ole girl" humor is bound to be appreciated.

In this case the good ole girl is Barbara Eden as sexy Stella Johnson, mother of the "teenage daughter attending Harper Valley Junior High." A sorry assortment of smalltown PTA board members have

been aiming to run Stella out of the county because of her short skirts and finally threaten to expel daughter Dee from school unless Mom shapes up. Undaunted, Eden and best friend Nanette Fabray set out to get even and expose the foibles of "upstanding" board members. Revenge is basis for rest of the plot which has Eden doing everything from taking bedroom pictures of a stuffy sex education teacher to letting loose three pink elephants on unsuspecting town drunk, Pat Paulsen.

Film is loaded with lotsa fine character players as PTAers, each spotlighted in the scene where Eden gets revenge. Paulsen, Louis Nye, John Fiedler, Audrey Christie and an assortment of others are good enough foils for Stella's wrath, which is overplayed after a while.

But key to film is its broad comedy — thin on believability but heavy on visuals — and on this score it succeeds. Scripters George Edwards and Barry Schneider were forced to build around the song for marketing's sake and seemed to have come up with what was intended even if the tune is a decade old.

Direction, camera and sets are all okay making the picture easy to watch although difficult to follow. But in the end this doesn't matter.
—Beta.

Capricorn One
(COLOR)

Thriller about a bogus Mars landing. Poor script, exciting finale. Moderate outlook.

Hollywood, May 19.

Warner Bros. release of an Associated General Films production, produced by Paul N. Lazarus 3d. Stars Elliott Gould, James Brolin, Brenda Vaccaro, Sam Waterston, O.J. Simpson, Hal Holbrook. Written and directed by Peter Hyams. Camera (CFI Color), Bill Butler; music, Jerry Goldsmith; editor, James Mitchell; production designer, Albert Brenner; art director, David M. Haber; set decorator, Rick Simpson; costume designer, Patricia Norris; associated producer, Michael Rachmil; assistant director, Irby Smith; sound, Jerry Jost. Reviewed at the National Theatre, L.A., May 19, '78. (MPAA rating: PG.) Running time: 127 MINS.

Robert Caulfield . . . . Elliott Gould
Charles Brubaker . . . . James Brolin
Kay Brubaker . . . . Brenda Vaccaro
Peter Willis . . . . Sam Waterston
John Walker . . . . O.J. Simpson
Dr. James Kelloway . . . . Hal Holbrook
Hollis Peaker . . . . David Huddleston
Walter Loughlin . . . . David Doyle
Betty Walker . . . . Denise Nicholas
Elliot Whitter . . . . Robert Walden
Sharon Willis . . . . Lee Bryant
Capsule Communicator . . . . . . Alan Fudge
Judy Drinkwater . . . . Karen Black
Albain . . . . Telly Savalas

"Capricorn One" begins with a workable, if cynical cinematic premise: The first manned space flight to Mars was a hoax and the American public was fooled through Hollywood gimmickry into believing that the phony landing happened. But after establishing the concept, Peter Hyams' script asks another audience — the one in the theatre — to accept something far more illogical, the uncovering of the hoax by reporter Elliott Gould.

An essentially down, slap-in-the-face, thriller like "Capricorn One" is a hard b.o. sell to the American public. However, the exciting, campy 15-minute dogfight finale — everything the previous 112 minutes should have been — will leave audiences talking and spread word-of-mouth for at least a few weeks of business.

Like the previous Lew Grade-Associated General films, this one suffers from an underdeveloped script. It's got spectacle, but little logic. And it shares another malady with the other Grade items — scattershot casting.

The astronaut trio of James Brolin, Sam Waterston and O.J. Simpson individually may entice ticket buying in various foreign markets. But together they add up to nothing; there's no group chemistry.

Still, scattershot means once in a while you hit and in the final scene Gould and Telly Savalas are teamed. The duo is a bullseye. Savalas, in a delightful cameo as a crop duster hired to help rescue Brolin in the desert and uncover the plot, is a marvelous complement to Gould.

By themselves the performances are okay. But again you must return to the script. Hal Holbrook plays the mission commander who calls off the Mars shot and engineers the dupe. He's fine and his character must change from sincere — he believes he's doing the right thing by fooling the public — to menacing. But too early he delivers a painfully silly speech explaining why he's called off the flight. It ruins the character.

In general, it is a script of conveniences. Conveniently, the three trapped astronauts walk out of a locked room and steal a jet. But conveniently, for the plot the jet is low on fuel and the trio crash lands in the desert. A technician suspects that something is awry in the flight plan. So conveniently he disappears. Audiences are willing to suspend disbelief, but not for the cause of paranoia.

This is all the more unfortunate because of the high level of the technical credits. Bill Butler's photography and lighting are first-rate. Albert Brenner's production design masterfully recreates mission control and the fake Mars set from which the bogus trans-

missions are relayed. And when his script doesn't get in the way, Hyams direction is fluid. — *Hege.*

Damien — Omen II
(COLOR)

More deaths in the family of devilish Damien, ghastly enough for good boxoffice.

Hollywood, May 31.

Twentieth Century-Fox release, produced by Harvey Bernhard; coproducer, Charles Orme. Features entire cast. Directed by Don Taylor. Screenplay, Stanley Mann, Michael Hodges; camera (DeLuxe Color), Bill Butler; editor, Robert Brown, Jr.; music, Jerry Goldsmith; production design, Philip M. Jefferies, Fred Harpman; sound, Al Overton; assistant directors, Al Nicholson, Jerry Ballew. Reviewed at 20th-Fox Studios, May 31, '78. (MPAA Rating: R.) Running time, 109 MINS.

Richard Thorn	William Holden
Ann Thorn	Lee Grant
Damien Thorn	Jonathan Scott-Taylor
Paul Buher	Robert Foxworth
Mark Thorn	Lucas Donat
Charles Warren	Nicholas Pryor
Bill Atherton	Lew Ayres
Aunt Marion	Sylvia Sidney
Sgt. Neff	Lance Henriksen
Joan Hart	Elizabeth Shepherd
Pasarian	Alan Arbus
Murray	Fritz Ford
Dr. Kane	Meshach Taylor

Alas, Little Orphan Damien, lucky enough to be taken in by a rich uncle after bumping off his first pair of foster parents, can't resist killing the second set, too, along with assorted friends of the family. Damien is obviously wearing out his welcome, but presold interest and a couple of gruesome, ghastly death scenes should shore up business for the summer.

Recalling a bit of biographical background, Damien is the anti-Christ, born unto a jackal and switched into the unsuspecting Thorn family. When last seen, Damien was six years old and, having dispatched everyone in his original household, holding hands with the President of the U.S. at his parents' funeral.

When met again in the sequel, Damien is 13 and has a double personality problem, being both an anti-Christ and a rather obnoxious teenager. Stoically played by Jonathan Scott-Taylor, Damien has apparently been behaving himself for the past seven years, since his uncle (William Holden) and aunt (Lee Grant) suspect nothing and love him very much as does his cousin (Lucas Donat.)

Only cranky old Aunt Marion (Sylvia Sidney) knows something is wrong with the boy, but a raven gets rid of her early in the picture. Then the pesky reporter (Elizabeth Shepherd) shows up and she knows all about the boy's background. So the raven pecks her eyes out and she stumbles in front of a truck. "It was so strange for her to get hit by a

truck on a deserted highway," somebody comments, but nobody says anything about the ravishings of raven.

By the time kindly Lew Ayres slips beneath the ice while the raven sits overhead in a tree, it seem fairly obvious that the bird is Damien's real protector, hanging around to make sure he grows up properly. Ayres was an executive with Holden in Thorn Industries and with him out of the way, ambitious Robert Foxworth also shows a special interest in young Damien.

Damien himself doesn't seem to find anything unusual about his life, except for an inordinate number of funerals in the family. Until one day his platoon sergeant at the military school — a friend of Foxworth's — suggests he read the Book of Revelations and find out why he's special.

As the school band comes marching through the hallways — a rather strange place to drill — Damien gets a Bible and finds out about himself. Apparently upset, he runs and runs until he reaches the end of the pier and cries, "Why? Why me?".

Whatever the answer, he soon gets the knack of killing people himself, with spectacular touches that top the decapitations of his tender years.

So far as the story goes, however, the evil acts of the little kid were easier to accept than those of his teenage years. Producer Harvey Bernhard and director Don Taylor, who took over the helm from Michael Hodges (who retains partial script credit despite "artistic differences"), are obviously struggling this time to keep the plot straight.

But a third sequel is planned, at age 28. —*Har.*

Grease
(COLOR)

Slick as a ducktail hairdo. An easy winner.

Hollywood, June 6.

Paramount Pictures release of a Robert Stigwood and Allan Carr production. Directed by Randal Kleiser. Stars John Travolta, Olivia Newton-John, Stockard Channing. Screenplay, Bronte Woodard; adaptation, Allan Carr, based on original music by Jim Jacobs and Warren Casey; camera (color), Bill Butler; dances and musical sequences staged and choreographed by Patricia Birch; music supervision, Bill Oakes; film editor, John F. Burnett; production designer, Phillip Jefferies; costumes, Albert Wolsky; set decorator, James Berkey; unit publicist, Gary Kalkin. Reviewed in Hollywood, June 5, '78. (MPAA Rating - PG). Running time: 110 MINS.

Danny	John Travolta
Sandy	Olivia Newton-John
Rizzo	Stockard Channing
Kenickie	Jeff Conaway
Frency	Didi Conn
Jan	Jamie Donnelly

Marty	Dinah Manoff
Doody	Barry Pearl
Sonny	Michael Tucci
Putzie	Kelly Ward
Patty Simcox	Susan Buckner
Eugene	Eddie Deezen
Tom Chisum	Lorenzo Lamas
Leo	Dennis C. Stewart
Cha Cha	Annette Charles
Mr. Rudie	Dick Patterson
Nurse Wilkins	Fannie Flagg
Mr. Lynch	Darrell Zwerling
Waitress	Ellen Travolta

Guest appearances: Eve Arden, Frankie Avalon, Joan Blondell, Edd Byrnes, Sid Caesar, Alice Ghostley, Dody Goodman, Sha Na Na.

"Grease" has got it, from the outstanding animated titles of John Wilson all the way through the rousing finale as John Travolta and Olivia Newton-John ride off into pre-Vietnam era teenage happiness.

The Robert Stigwood-Allan Carr production values complement superbly the broad comedy-drama, zesty choreography and very excellent new plus revived music. The Paramount release has more than enough appeal for the teenage market, as well as solid entertainment values for slightly elder audiences, too.

Carr is credited with adapting the 50's style legituner of Jim Jacobs and Warren Casey, which Bronte Woodward then fashioned into an excellent screenplay that moves smartly throughout its 110 minutes. Director Randal Kleiser and Choreographer Patricia Birch stage the sequences with aplomb, providing as necessary the hoke, hand or heart appropriate to the specific moment. Bill Butler's super cinematography and Phil Jefferies' sharp production design are major assets.

Plot tracks the bumpy romantic road of Travolta and Newton-John, whose summer beach idyll sours when he feels he must revert to finger-snapping cool in the atmosphere of the high school they both wind up attending. Stockard Channing, third featured under title and impressing anew in this latest screen attempt, provides a nice contrast to Newton-John in a hard but really nice characterization. Jeff Conaway is very good as the type guy for whom Travolta is a natural leader.

Travolta has more to do here than in "Saturday Night Fever," and he is excellent. A wider range of talent is on good display in this film. Newton-John registers very impressively — far better than the usual personality casting one has come to expect — and they play together quite well.

Supporting roles by Eve Arden, Frankie Avalon (in a teenager's dream sequence), Joan Blondell, Edd Byrnes ("Kookie" looks just fine in the Dick Clark type role here), Sid Caesar, Alice Ghostley and Dody Goodman all work nicely.

Sha-na-na, appearing as a fictional group, gets much opportunity to show their stuff. The featured songs, inserted just as predictably as you'll want them to be, are uniformly effective. Bill Cakes and Louis St. Louis deserve their separate credits, both of which suggest major contributions to the impact of the song selections.

The Dolby sound is terrific. This is another film that exhibitors might well play at higher sound levels for greater audience involvement.
—*Murf.*

Bravo Maestro
(YUGOSLAV-COLOR)

Cannes, May 30.

Yugoslavia Film release of Jadran Film production. Features entire cast. Directed by Rajko Grlic. Screenplay, Grlic, Srdan Karanovic; camera (Eastmancolor), Zivko Zalar; editor, Zivka Toplak; music, Branislav Zivkobvic. Reviewed at Cannes Film Fest (Competing), May 29, '78. Running time, 99 MINS.
Cast: Rade Serbezija, Aleksander Bercek, Bozidar Boban, Mladen Budiscak, Koraljka Krs, Zvonko Lepetic.

Yugoslavia, after some years in the doldrums, showed new promise by getting this film in competition plus another in the sidebar Critics Week.

A group of filmmakers trained at the Prague Film School in Czechoslovakia seems to have assimilated that wry, probing, human comedy insight into personal and bureaucratic life that marked the Czech renaissance from 1963-68 before the Warsaw Pact invasion turned off the Prague Springtime.

This tale of a composer who manages to get a name by family pull, bureaucratic coverup and finally by plagiarism is never shrill or preachy. The hero (or anti-hero) writes what he feels is a new kind of music but is turned down by the local music reps.

He marries a rich girl and gets involved with his stepfather's foreign trade shenanigans. The stepfather lands in jail but the composer still manages to keep up this trade and is heralded for a work that has never been played.

Journalist friend keeps up his reputation and finally money from the worker funds of the town is voted to put on one of his works which he has not yet finished.

The composer cannot work and finally makes up a sort of operatic-dance oratorio gleaned from many others and especially a friend's work. The latter finds out and threatens to expose him but is overridden by the many bureaucrats now involved in this cultural event.

Ironically, it is a hit. He is left by his friends and his wife, falls into self hatred and even tries to stop the show. He is restrained and takes his bewildered bows. It is played adroitly and director Rajko Grlic has given this film insights without overdoing the heroics. It is a bit hermetic at times in its many allusions to bureaucratic corruption.

Pic is an unlikely commercial bet and may be more for the fest circuit, and film weeks. But it indicates a robust new generation of filmmakers in Yugoslavia. —*Mosk.*

The Scenic Route
(COLOR)

Cannes, May 30.

Written, directed and produced by Mark Rappaport. Camera (color), Fred Murphy; art director, Lilly Kilvert; sound, Samantha Heilweil; editor, Mark Rappaport. Reviewed at Cannes Film Fest (Director's Fortnight), May 29, '78. Running time, 76 MINS.
Estelle .... Randy Danson
Lena .... Marilyn Jones
Paul .... Kevin Wade

Mark Rappaport's fourth narrative feature film stubbornly resists the tinge of the commercial slickness, yet this effort is his most entertaining to date, even in the stalwart context of the avant-garde. Story is set in New York, told in various stylized tableaux through monolog and dialog of three characters whose relationships rebound against contemporary trends.

Estelle, recently divorced, suffers from a life of outdated myths and random violence. She studies the Orpheus legend faithfully without inspiration, while murders occur in the streets and buildings around her. During one such stabbing, she meets Paul who says little but seems to be carnally insatiable. Estelle's sister, Lena, moves in and complicates the affair, and the rest of the pic has the three in perpetual tryst.

Rappaport's script is wry, intelligent, but wordy, often aiming for an easy target of urban apartment dwellers' ennui. Estelle's preoccupation with art creates an immediate identification for the museum and university market toward which "Scenic Route" is firstmost aimed. Beyond the subtext of art's banality, "Scenic Route" peppers its texture with some quick turns of action: a spontaneous disco session at home, the visual acting out of art works, a silly and aborted drive in the country, and an hilarious reversal in street hassling.

Most of all, the extremely minimal and flat sets juxtapose physically in highly artificial combinations of back-projection, mirrors, and rising backdrops, reducing the possibility of pretentiousness. Estelle's haughty commiseration is drained of its potential weightiness by Rappaport's malleable mise-en-scene. There are no real conclusions in the plot, but getting there is what it's all about.

Technical credits (shot in 16m) are fine, if exemplary only in the staging, and the pace is easily the most creditable aspect. For the art circuit and any accidental cross-over crowd, "Scenic Route" is a refreshing and alert entry. —*Pege.*

Love And The Midnight Auto Supply
(COLOR)

Muddled .youth exploitation item. Will have trouble finding market.

Hollywood, May 21.

Producers Capital Corp. release of a James Polakof film. Exec producer, Beverley Johnson. Produced, directed and written by James Polakof; camera (Movielab Color), Lawrence Raimond; editor, Irving Rosenblum; art director, Perry Ferguson II; sound, Keith Wester; music, Ed Bogas; stunt coordinator, Richard Butler. Reviewed at the Culver Theatre, Culver City, May 21, '78. (MPAA Rating: PG.) Running time: 93 MINS.
Duke .... Michael Parks
Annie .... Linda Cristal
Justin .... Scott Jacoby
Ramon .... Bill Adler
Billie Jean .... Colleen Camp
Kathy .... Monica Gayle
Violet .... Sedena Spivey
Peter Santore .... George McCalister
Tony Santore .... John Ireland
Len Thompson .... Rory Calhoun
Sheriff Dawson .... Rod Cameron
Mayor John Randolph .... Burt Freed

"Love And The Midnight Auto Supply" is a film in search of the right audience. Present ad campaign drops the first three words of the title, leading one to believe this is a standard crime and chase caper. It isn't. Plot line involves prostitutes aiding a car theft ring, suggesting some amorous adventures. There aren't any. Thrust of this PG-rated low-budgeter seems geared for the youth market, but teens have no way of knowing, this, severely limiting outlook.

Writer-producer-director James Polakof seems as muddled in his goals as Producers Capital Corporation is in their handling of the film. What emerges has some charm, a number of effective performances and surprisingly good technical credits. But what do you call it?

Precisely because it can't be easily pigeonholed, "Midnight Auto Supply" succeeds where many genre films fail. Michael Parks leads a gang adept at stripping automobiles in seconds flat, thus leading to the abbreviated title, slang for hot car parts.

Out of nowhere comes student radical Scott Jacoby and buddy George McCalister, who convince Parks and company to donate half their pickings to the cause of displaced farmworkers. The fact that Mc-Calister's daddy (John Ireland) is about to be the next mayor of the corrupt town only adds to the excitement, so Parks, Jacoby and the helpful hookers at the Friendship Farm go into action.

While Jacoby gets himself busted, McCalister is being seduced by prostie Colleen Camp, who is berated by madame Linda Cristal for not being sufficiently motivated in her work. To satisfy those teen urges, Polakof tosses in some horseback rides and woodland romps in the midst of jail breaks and farmworker demonstrations. The whole jumble is kept moving only by the infectious spirits of the cast, with Parks, Cristal and Camp especially good, as is Bill Adler as Parks' manic sidekick.

Because of the wildly differing approaches, "Midnight Auto Supply" has more than its share of jarring moments, although Ed Bogas' score does its best to center the film on at least one consistent track. Polakoff does pull off a neat trick ending to keep the finale honest, but those in the front row may still be shaking their heads, wondering what it was they just saw.

Contra Costa County locations are used to good effect, although Lawrence Raimond's camerawork is a bit jerky. Other tech credits are solid, but they won't help the film find its intended market. Of the differing groups being pitched by the ads, somebody's bound to be disappointed. — *Poll.*

Go Tell The Spartans

Vietnam war pic starring Burt Lancaster. Slim outlook.

Hollywood, June 7.

An Avco Embassy Pictures release of a Spartan Co. production, produced by Allan F. Bodoh and Mitchell Cannold; executive producer, Michael Leone. Stars Burt Lancaster. Directed by Ted Post. Screenplay, Wendell Mayes, based on "Incident At Muc Wa" by Daniel Ford; camera (CFI Color), Harry Stradling, Jr.; art director, Jack Senter; editor, Millie Moore; music, Dick Halligan; associate producer, Jesse Corallo; costumes, Ron Dawson; sound, Bill Randall. Reviewed at the DGA Theatre, Hollywood, June 7, '78. (MPAA rating: R.) Running time: **114 MINS.**

Major Asa Barker	Burt Lancaster
Cpl. Stephen Courcey	Craig Wasson
Sgt. Oleonowski	Jonathan Goldsmith
Capt. Al Olivetti	Marc Singer
Lt. Raymond Hamilton	Joe Unger
Cpt. Abraham Lincoln	Dennis Howard
Lt. Finley Wattsberg	David Clennon
Cowboy	Evan Kim

A good war film needs heroes. But Vietnam, the most unpopular war in U.S. history, had no heroes in the eyes of most Americans. Commercially then, all Vietnam War films must overcome a handicap, and perhaps it's a losing battle from the start. Even a reasonably well-made and well-acted earnest effort like "Go Tell The Spartans," set in 1964 when the U.S. involvement was limited to "military advisors," can't overcome that disadvantage. Therefore b.o. outlook for the Avco Embassy pickup appears limited.

Based on Daniel Ford's novel, "Incident At Muc Wa," Wendell Mayes script follows a detachment of Americans and Vietnamese mercenaries as they occupy an outpost abandoned by the French a decade ago. Lancaster is the commander of an advisory group at Penang who must order the raw detachment into the jungle. When the Vietcong move in on the soldiers, Lancaster arranges for their evacuation.

However, there is room only for the American soldiers in the helicopter which brings them out. The Vietnamese are to be abandoned and only Craig Wasson objects staying behind to help in their rescue. So too, does Lancaster, making he and Wasson the film's heroes.

The film was shot in Southern California and art director Jack Senter, director of photography Harry Stradling, Jr., and director Ted Post have done a credible job creating the Vietnam jungle. It's a two location picture — the Muc Wa outpost and the headquarters for the U.S. advisors — but audiences will believe they're watching southeast Asia.

Lancaster leads a mostly untried cast, including Marc Singer as his assistant, Jonathan Goldsmith playing a burned out veteran, Joe Unger as a naive over-zealous lieutenant on his first mission and Evan Kim as the tough leader of the Vietnam mercenaries. All turn in fine performances which represent a cross-section of the kind of soldiers who fought that war.

—*Hege.*

Cu Minile Curate
(With Clean Hands)
(RUMANIAN-COLOR)

Bucharest, April 18.

A Rumaniafilm Production, Bucharest; world rights, Rumaniafilm, Bucharest. Features entire cast. Directed by Sergiu Nicolaescu. Screenplay, Titus Popovici, Petre Salcudeanu; camera (color), Alexandru David; music, Richard Oschanitzky. Reviewed at Rumaniafilm Screening Room, April 17, '78. Running time: **95 MINS.**
Cast: Ilarion Ciobanu (Nihai Roman), Sergiu Nicolaescu (Miclovan), Alexandru Dobrescu (Patulea), Gheroghe Dinica (Lascarica), George Constantin (Semaca), Sebastian Papaiani (Oarca).

The kingpin of Rumanian helmers, Sergiu Nicolaescu specializes in thrillers in the Western vein and historical melodramas, both guaranteed to bring in the customers at the home boxoffice. He's well known beyond the borders of his own country as both a thesp and a helmer of repute, who started his career as a cameraman.

Nicolaescu's camera separates him from other action directors in East European cinema: it's always "moving" in its mode of expression, much like the Roger Corman school. Stories, however, are something else. "With Clean Hands" (perhaps his hottest pic today for home auds) opens as the last war comes to an end, the streets of Bucharest plagued by Capone-type hoodlums who shoot the town up.

A new police chief arrives on the scene who believes in doing everything "with clean hands" — one of his lieutenants (played by our helmer), however, prefers tough tactics, and thus the two come in conflict but respect each other. It's the tough guy who proves he's right in the end as he dies in a gun-fight with the unknown leader of the gangs.

Plenty of action, cars and costumes appropriately match the period (although a bit on the 1920s side), and all this violence doesn't necessarily have to be taken seriously. This is the Eastern as opposed to the Western — instead of partisans fighting the fascists, it's good old law-and-order. —*Holl.*

Cursa
(The Long Drive)
(RUMANIAN-COLOR)

Bucharest, April 18.

A Rumaniafilm Production, Group One, Bucharest; world rights, Rumaniafilm, Bucharest. Features entire cast. Directed by Mircea Daneliuc. Screenplay, Timotei Ursu, from an idea by Petru Vintila; camera (color), Florin Mihailescu; music, Lucian Metianu; sets and costumes, Dumitru Georgescu. Reviewed at Rumaniafilm Screening Room, Bucharest, April 17, '78. Running time: **90 MINS.**
Cast: Mircea Ablulescu (Savu), Tora Vasilescu (Maria), Constantin Diplan (Panait), Olga Bucataru, Paul Lavric, Angela Costache, Teofil Caliman, Constanta Comanoiu, Mircea Daneliuc.

"The Long Drive," Mircea Daneliuc's first feature pic in 1975, broke new ground and helped establish New Rumanian Cinema. The young helmer worked his way up the ranks as assistant to Mircea Dragan after graduating from the Bucharest Theatre & Film School. Pic bares a resemblance to Soviet helmer Vassili Shukshin's "Once There Was a Lad" and a recent East German pic about truckers and their adventures, all three pix being "road" films slanted toward unexpected adventure and unveiling of character.

A veteran trucker is hauling a huge construction element on an oversize trailer to a dam site; his companion is a friendly chap just out of army service, who, on a layover, meets a girl in need who must get to a nearby town to see her fiance again. Reluctantly, the femme passenger is taken along although the arrangement is a bit out of the ordinary, which of course leads to conflicts between the two drivers due mostly to vet trucker's disbelief in the girl's story.

The older man gradually becomes the key figure as it becomes clear that his wife (who left him for another) died at a certain curve in the road in a car accident; he hasn't paid a visit back to his home town in 17 years. The girl's story about a boyfriend waiting for her turns out to be a straw in the wind; she calls instead on a young couple with child rather unexpectedly in the middle of the night. The fate of these two "misfits" draws the two together in the end, while the young trucker saves the vehicle from dropping off a cliff by a swift decision at the last minute.

Pic is ripe for New Bulgarian Cinema weeks. — *Holl.*

The Last Survivor
(ITALIAN-COLOR)

Not so grand bouffe.

Hollywood, June 7.

An American International Pictures release of a United Producers film. Produced by Giorgio Carlo Rossi. Features entire cast. Directed by Ruggero Deodato. Screenplay, Tito Cardi, Giafranco Clerici, Renzo Genta; camera (Movielab Color), uncredited; editor, Danielle Alabiso; dubbing editor, Nick Alexander; special effects, Paolo Ricci; assistant director, Stefano Rilla. Reviewed at the World Theatre, Hollywood, June 6, '78. (MPAA Rating: R.) Running time: **83 MINS.**
Cast: Massimo Foschi, Me-Me Lai, Ivan Rassimov, Sheik Renal Shker, Judy Rosly, Suleiman, Sanshe.
(*Dubbed English Soundtrack*)

Massimo Foschi and Ivan Rassimov play two explorers who, for some unexplained reason, venture onto a verdant jungle island to find some friends camping in the wilderness. The campers, of course, are long gone, and director Ruggero Deodato (who has also helmed Italo westerns under the monicker of Roger Rockefeller) wastes no time in showing why.

The reason is a large tribe of mudcaked cannibals, who are early on seen ingesting, with much lip smacking and gurgling, the still-warm body of one of the campers. A title card proudly points out that this footage is the real thing, which hardly makes it more attractive.

Foschi and Rassimov are soon separated (Rassimov apparently being drowned) and Foschi is taken prisoner by the natives, who keep him in a cistern with a lot of birds. The birds are used as crocodile bait, a fate Foschi realizes awaits him, too, until he gets Me-Me Lai, beautiful jungle girl, to aid him in his escape. Miraculously, he meets up with Rassimov again (no explanation of how) and the pair manage to find their plane and take off.

Without the lurid sound effects, which include everything from the standard jungle noises to the wrenching sound of bones being cracked and sucked, "The Last Survivor" could be considered relatively harmless, except to one's digestion. But the unwarranted killing of several animals, including the garrotting of a still-live crocodile, is defenseless, and should have animal decency groups up in arms.

Deodato has done a good job of meshing documentary footage with live-action filming, and the jungle locations are intimidating. But each disaster is clearly foreshadowed through ridiculous editing, and the scenes of the natives resemble a National Geographic special gone mad.

American International refused to supply credits for this film. It's not hard to see why. —*Poll.*

Raba lubvi
(Slave Of Love)
(RUSSIAN-COLOR)

Cinema 5 release of a Sovexport production. Features entire cast. Directed by Nikita Mikhalkov. Screenplay, Friedrich Gorenstein, Andrei Mikhalkov-Konchalovsky; camera (Color), Pavel Lebeshev; set designers, A. Adabashyan, A. Samulekin; sound, V. Bobrovsky; music, Eduard Artemiev. Reviewed at Magno Screening Room, N.Y., June 9, '78. Running time: **94 MINS.**

Olga	Elena Solovey
Victor	Rodion Nakhapetov
Kalyagin	Alexander Kaliagin

Yuzhakov . . . . Oleg Basilashivili
Fedotov . . . . Konstantin Grigoryev
(English subtitles)

The actual translation of this Russian import is "Bondage of Love," but Cinema 5 evidently feels that its version has more boxoffice appeal. Neither title conveys the film's real attraction — a wonderfully colorful look, with many laughs amidst its eventually tragic tale, of filmmaking somewhere in the Crimea during the 1917 Revolution. Superbly cast with a wonderful assortment of human types, "Slave Of Love" clearly foretells the talent that director Nikita Mikhalkov later brought to his principal work to date, "Unfinished Piece For Player Piano," internationally landed but still to be seen in the U.S.

This is a tiny make-believe world make up of eccentrics, trying bravely to finish a film before the real holocaust of the Bolshevik Revolution breaks around them. Besides the logistical problems of impending war, there are all sorts of emotional problems beseting the little group — the promised leading man does not show up, the supply of precious film stock runs out, there's a sadistic Czarist officer breathing down their necks, kept at arm's length only because he has a crush on the company's leading lady.

There are three important roles in the film, — the ethereal Elena Solovy as actress Olga Voznesenskaya who changes from a scatterbrained, vain "movie star" into a wonderful human being as she's drawn unwilingly into the snares of revolution. Rodion Nakhapetov (himself a well-known director) as Victor, the cameraman who both loves and uses the leading lady and brings about the tragic ending and, best of all, character actor Alexander Kaliagin as Kalyagin, the overweight, worrisome director who is a spiritually lazy person, aware of the limitations of his talent but a wonderful human being. He's the best thing in the film and evidently Mikhalkov considers him his favorite actor as he's used Kaliagin in all three of his major films, in increasingly important roles (he's the lead in "Player Piano"). He'll be a character actor to watch as his talent grows (he's only 35).

All the supporting roles are cast beautifully, down to the smallest role. A very funny, very moving Russian film in which even the expected propaganda seems to have dramatic importance. —*Robe.*

Doctor Poenaru
(RUMANIAN-COLOR)

Bucharest, April 19.

A Rumaniafilm Production, Group One, Bucharest; world rights, Rumaniafilm, Bucharest. Features entire cast. Written and directed by Dinu Tanase. Camera (color), Mihai Popescu; music, Adrian Enescu; sets, Florin Gabrea; costumes, Ileana Mirea. Reviewed at Rumaniafilm Screening Room, Bucharest, April 18, '78. Running time: **107 MINS.**
Cast: Victor Rebengiuc, Stefan Iordache, Elena Dacian, Vasile Nitulescu, Gheorghe Dinica, Gheorghe Metzenrath, Dionisie Vitcu, Victor Strengaru, Adrian Georgescu, Ion Vilcu.

This is the type of pic East European cinema thrives on: a doctor comes to an isolated village (in the Baragan Plain, in this case) to run a clinic at a crucial time (1919-1939), fighting for justice and moral rights of the individual against political and social odds that seem overwhelming. The result is an awakening of conscience to the needs of the people by a once-dubious population gradually taking the hero's side to fight for the same cause.

Dinu Tanase drew his story from a novel by Paul Georgescu of the same name. The center of the moral conflict is the doctor's relationship with an old school chum who has worked his way up (like the doctor) from poverty to a political candidate in this district for the Liberal Party. Doctor Poenaru supports his friend with some reluctance, but later comes to regret it. With this breakdown of trust the villagers seem about to return to their old ways — the doctor, however, has been awakened to the revolutionary movement and looks hopefully towards a better future.

Credits are on the merit side, save for a script that drags in parts as many literary adaptations do. Dinu Tanase is obviously a helmer with talent, who can both write and direct. —*Holl.*

Rock 'n' Roll Wolf
(RUMANIAN-RUSSIAN-FRENCH COLOR)

Bucharest, April 18.

A Rumanian, Soviet & French Coproduction, Group Three, Bucharest Features entire cast. Directed by Elisabeta Bostan. Screenplay, Vasilica Istrate; camera (color), Ion Marinescu, Konstantin Petricenco; music, Temistocle Popa, Gerald Bourgeois. Reviewed at Rumaniafilm Screening Room, Bucharest, April 17, '78. Running time: **90 MINS.**
Cast: Ludmila Gurcenco, Florian Pittis, Mihail Boiarski, George Mihaita, Violeta Andrei, Oleg Popov, Saveli Kremerov, Valentin Manohin, Paula Radulescu, Vasile Mentzel, Vera Ivleva, Liliana Petrescu, Evgheni Ghercikov, Marina Poliak, Natalia Kracikovskaia, Lulu Mihaiescu, Matei Opris, Timur Asaliev, Adtian Cristea, Petia Dektiarev.

Tops in the children's film category, Elisabeta Bostan has outdone herself with "Rock 'n' Roll Wolf," a coprod with the Soviet Union (the main actors) and France (some technical credits). This could be a winner on the commercial side in the English version, expertly synched by the French partner in songs and dialogue.

Like a Disney musical, "Rock 'n Roll Wolf" uses a fairyland set and characters wearing face-masks: the baddies are a wolf and his jackass friend, while those threatened aren't a family of pigs but a mommy-cat and her four children. Main line of the story evolves around Mommy's departure for town (where there's a fair) and the kids' decision on whether to open to door to the right-sounding singing voice (the rub is that Mommy catches a cold and sounds like the wolf on her return).

One youngster runs off to have a bit of fun on his own, which leads to a snatching of two of the kids — the wolf wants gold, but ends up falling into an ice pond for his troubles.

Plenty of good fun and delightful songs and dances, although not as peppy as western auds are used to. Could be an amusing twist for tv auds comprised of kids and grownups. — *Holl.*

Zidul
(The Wall)
(RUMANIAN-B&W)

Bucharest, April 18.

A Rumaniafilm Production, Group Three, Bucharest; world rights, Rumaniafilm, Bucharest. Features entire cast. Directed by Constantin Vaeni. Screenplay, Dumitru Carabat, Costache Ciubotaru; camera, (black and white), Iosif Demian; music, Cornelia Tautu; sets, Vittorio Holtier. Reviewed at Romaniafilm Screening Room, Bucharest, April 17, '78. Running time: **95 MINS.**
Cast: Gabriel Oseciuc (Victor), Gheorghe Dinica, Victor Rebengiuc, Cornelia Pavlovici, Mitica Popescu, Nicolae Radu, George Mihaita, Constantin Vaeni, Theo Partisch.

Tight, well-told psycho-drama about a young man who freely walls himself in for months during the Resistance period at the end of the Second World War, Constantin Vaeni's "The Wall" holds up well over a long stretch and is among the best of New Rumanian Cinema. Helmer comes from the documentary film, this being his feature debut in 1974 and an impressive one.

"The Wall" deals with the difficult decision of a sensitive lad to isolate himself from society for over a year with an underground radio. Meanwhile, the police-inspector is searching angrily in vain for both radio and sender, once coming close by arresting the contact but never reaching his man until the city is liberated. Then, as the boy leaves cover, he is shot by his pursuer on the streets.

Gabriel Oseciuc as the boy wrestling with his fears and fantasies carries the pic with ease. Much is revealed about his personality during the hermetic self-exile, his remembrance about the death of his father during a strike in particular.
—*Holl.*

The Bad News Bears Go To Japan
(COLOR)

Third strike and out.

Hollywood, June 9.

Paramount Picture release of a Michael Ritchie production. Produced by Michael Ritchie. Directed by John Berry. Features entire cast. Written by Bill Lancaster; camera (Movielab color), Gene Polito (USA), Kozo Okazaki (Japan); editor, Richard A. Harris; production design, Walter Scott Herndon; sound, Gene Cantamesa; music, Paul Chihara; wardrobe, Tommy Welsh, Nancy Martinelli; assistant director, Jerry Ziesmer. Reviewed at Paramount Studio Theatre, Hollywood, June 8, '78. (MPAA Rating: PG.) Running time: **91 MINS.**
Marvin Lazar . . . . Tony Curtis
Kelly Leak . . . . Jackie Earle Haley
Coach Shimizu . . . Tomisaburo Wakayama
Arika . . . . Hatsune Ishihara
Network Director . . . . George Wyner
Louis The Gambler . . . . . . Lonny Chapman
E.R.W. Tillyard III . . . . Matthew
Douglas Anton
Ahmad Rahim . . . . Erin Blunt
Miguel Agilar . . . . George Gonzales
Jimmy Feldman . . . . Brett Marx
Rudy Stein . . . . David Pollock
Toby Whitewood . . . . David Stambaugh
Mike Engelberg . . . . . . Jeffrey Louis Starr
Mustapha Rahim . . . . Scoody Thornton

The dangers inherent in sequelmaking are clearly apparent in "The Bad News Bears Go To Japan," third in the series of junior baseball antics that began with the smash "Bad News Bears" original in 1976. Latest version is more successful than the middle outing, but the situation and characters are getting tired. Paramount should be able to extract healthy summer revenues from this edition, but it's a property that will be milked dry in short order.

Producer Michael Ritchie (who directed the first installment) and writer-creator Bill Lancaster encore with "Japan," resulting in a more vigorous film than the sodden "Bad New Bears In Breaking Training" of last year.

By now, most audiences are familiar with the bumbling bunch of peewee sluggers, who can't seem to do anything right on or off the field. In keeping with tradition, the boys are taken in by yet another hustler (following in the steps of Walter Matthau and William Devane), this time Tony Curtis as a Hollywood agent out for big bucks via promoting a game between the Bears and the Japanese all-star Little Leaguers.

Formula is strictly standard, with Curtis inviting the enmity of the kids, with exception of moppet Scoody Thornton, only to be reformed before the final game which, of course, the Bears win. Japanese locations at least add a different look, and there is much joking about language and cultural customs, humor that went out of style with "Sayonara."

There's also a silly exhibition wrestling match with Antonio Inoki, a superfluous love story between Bear slugger Jackie Earle Haley and budding geisha girl Hatsune Ishihara. George Wyner plays a put-upon tv sports director trying to capture the mishmash for the folks back home.

Director John Berry ignores the kids, for the most part, dwelling instead on the friendship between Curtis and rival Japanese coach Tomisaburo Wakayama, a relationship weakened by the fact that Wakayama speaks little or no English, and subtitles aren't employed. In fact, a good portion of the dialog is in Japanese, which should make the pic a natural for that market, but won't help out too much domestically.

Basic problem is that characters and their relationships have been spun out once too often, leaving little room for exploration. What was once fresh and original is now very familiar, and even Curtis' energetic performance can't help turn the tide.

New additions Thornton and Matthew Douglas Anton as a sharp young cookie are helpful, and returning Bears Haley, Erin Blunt, George Gonzales, Brett Marx, David Pollock, David Stambaugh, and Jeffrey Louis Starr all do what's expected of them. Wakayama is a good foil for Curtis, if he could only be understood.

Gene Polito's camerawork is quite good, as is Japanese counterpart Kozo Okazaki's. Other tech credits are admirable, and running time is wisely kept short. Fast playoff would seem to be the rule here — and then Paramount will hopefully put the "Bad News Bears" down for a well-deserved rest. —*Poll.*

Filip Cel Bun
(Filip the Good)
(RUMANIAN-COLOR)

Bucharest, April 18.
A Rumaniafilm Production, Bucharest Group Three, world rights, Rumaniafilm, Bucharest. Features entire cast. Directed by Dan Pita. Screenplay, Constantin Stoiciu; camera (color), Florin Mihailescu; only credits available. Reviewed at Rumaniafilm Screening Room, Bucharest, April 17, '78. Running time: 92 MINS.
Cast: Mircea Diaconu (Filip), Vasile Nitulescu, Ica Matache, Lazar Vrabie, Ileana Popovici, Nunuta Hodos, Draga Olteanu, Georgi Dinica, George Mihaita.

A new Rumanian Cinema in the making arrived with Dan Pita's "Filip the Good" (1974), the young helmer's first solo feature after working together with Mircea Veroiu, on docus and features at the beginning of the 1970s. The reason these young helmers are not too well known outside of their own country

is due to home-breeding at their own Bucharest Film School (rather than studying abroad), which helps to determine the gradual maturing direction of NRC on the basis of avid audience response.

"Filip the Good" focuses on a willing member of the younger generation who doesn't fit in anywhere, mostly because the example at home is not all that good (the father took the blame long ago for a factory misdemeanor that wasn't altogether his fault) and corruption in the jobs he's offered after leaving secondary school dispirits his searching for the vocation that inspires him. Filip is just too good for a world that is mostly dog-eat-dog or catch-as-catch-can.

Gradually, however, he comes to make some decisions for himself. He turns from his mother's wishes to go to the university and look for the easy way out. He searches back into his father's past for the truth via mysterious friends in higher places who offer him jobs of a crooked nature. He indirectly helps his sister break off with a good-for-nothing husband who mostly lays around the family's overcrowded apartment. His girlfriend seems at first worth fighting a hoodlum for, but she's too flighty to roost anywhere for a length of time. And a girl on the street-corner appears to be interested in him, and he in her, but the courage to meet her never really surfaces. In the end, Filip is just about where he was in the beginning, save for redeeming visit to his father's former factory and a talk with grandpa in the village his family left in disgrace that open his eyes to the truth. —*Holl.*

The Cat From Outer Space
(COLOR)

Purrfect Disney light comedy.

Hollywood, June 10.
Buena Vista release of a Walt Disney Production, produced by Ron Miller. Directed and coproduced by Norman Tokar. Screenplay, Ted Key; camera (Technicolor), Charles F. Wheeler; editor, Cotton Warburton; sound, Bud Maffett; music, Lalo Schifrin; art direction, John B. Mansridge, Preston Ames; assistant director, Gene Sultan; stunt coordinator, Richard Warlock; special effects, Eustace Lycett, Art Cruickshank, Danny Lee. Reviewed at Goldwyn Theatre, Beverly Hills, June 9, '78. (MPAA Rating: G.) Running time: 103 MINS.
Frank .... Ken Berry
Liz .... Sandy Duncan
Gen. Stilton .... Harry Morgan
Stallwood .... Roddy McDowall
Link .... McLean Stevenson
Ernie .... Jesse White
Wenger .... Alan Young
Heffel .... Hans Conried
Sgt. Duffy .... Ronnie Schell
Capt. Anderson .... James Hampton
Col. Woodruff .... Howard T. Platt
Olympus .... William Prince

Though lacking the sheen of a Disney classic, "The Cat From Outer Space" has three good undercoatings of craft and should wear well in the family market.

Cartoonist Ted Key, who previously scripted "Gus" the mule and "$1,000,000 Duck" for the studio, now turns to noodling over a spaceship commanded by a cat, forced to land on earth for emergency repairs. For help, the cat turns to a likable physicist, Ken Berry, to help him get $120,000 in gold needed to repair his saucer in time to rendevous with the space fleet.

Before long, Berry's girlfriend Sandy Duncan and buddy McLean Stevenson are in on the problem and planning to parlay the cat's extraterrestial powers into a series of winning bets with bookie Jesse White. But veterinarian Alan Young mistakenly puts pussy to sleep in the middle of the wagering.

In the meantime, General Harry Morgan and soldiers are comicly searching for the spaceman, not knowing it's a cat. And the villains, Roddy McDowall and William Prince, are trying to lay hands on the cat's collar, the source of its power.

That's the framework. The fun, as usual with Disney pix, comes in the believable sight gags provided along the way. Also as usual, it's a good cast of veterans and nothing to tax them beyond their abilities, all ably kept in pace by director Norman Tokar. The aerial climax is especially good. —*Har.*

The Virgin Witch
(BRITISH-COLOR)

Tired British retread along for the ride.

Hollywood, June 13.
Joseph Brenner Associates release. Produced by Ralph Solomons. Directed by Ray Austin. Screenplay, Klaus Vogel; camera (uncredited color), Gerald Moss; editor, Philip Barknel; music, Ted Dicks; sound, Derek Ball; assistant director, Garth Haines. Reviewed at Vine Theatre, Hollywood, June 12, '78. (MPAA Raing: R.) Running time: 90 MINS.
Christine .... Ann Michelle
Sybil .... Patricia Haines
Betty .... Vicki Michelle
Johnny .... Keith Buckley
Peter .... James Chase
Gerald .... Neal Hallett

"The Virgin Witch" is a dated, British-made occult film that should have been allowed to rest in whatever vault in which it was entombed. Joseph Brenner unwisely dug up this item to accompany the reissue of "The Devil's Rain," another supernatural clunker.

Apparently made in the post-"Exorcist" era, when devilish situations and characters were lurking around every corner, "The Virgin Witch" takes a soft-core pornography approach to covens, sacrifices, and voodoo. Exposed flesh may temporarily distract from the inane goings-on, but titillation without delivering the real goods eventually becomes boring, too.

For the record, sisters Ann and Vicki Michelle head to London to become famous models, only to be hoodwinked by lesbian procuress Patricia Haines into being newest initiates for a coven led by country gentleman Neal Hallett, who is only into "good" witchcraft. Keith Buckley and James Chase are bewildered males in tow.

Script by Klaus Vogel is not worth commenting upon, and other credits range from poor to miserable. Only Ann Michelle projects any presence — she manages a full-bodied eroticism, if nothing else. But since cinematographer Gerald Moss keeps zooming in on her eyes trying to capture a (baleful glance), her other charms receive short shrift.

"The Virgin Witch" can be dated by the prevalence of those short-short miniskirts that flourished in the late 1960s. —*Poll.*

Joe And Maxi
(U.S.-COLOR-DOCU-16M)

West Berlin, May 31.
A Maxi Cohen Production. Directed and sound by Joel Gold and Maxi Cohen. Camera (color), Joel Gold; editing, Pat Powell, Marion Kraft, Maxi Cohen. Reviewed at Arsenal-Kino, West Berlin, May 30, '78. Running time: 78 MINS.

Some Yank docus travel well in Europe. Joel Gold and Maxi

Cohen's "Joe and Maxi" is one of them: it preemed at the international film fest in Rotterdam, was spotted by the Internal Forum of Young Cinema in Berlin, and was a hit here with critics and public.

And since this is one of those pix supported by a number of benevolent art and film associations stateside-to wit: National Endowment for the Arts, Women's Fund-Joint Foundation Support, Jerome Foundation, New Jersey State Council on the Arts, Creative Artists Public Service Program (CAPS), Lucius and Eva Eastman Fund, Burroughs Corporation, Video Repetorie Ltd., Assn. of Independent Video and Filmmakers Urban Corp., N.Y. State Council on the Arts, Strang Clinic, Pandora Films, and Media Equipment Resource Center — it also makes for good p.r. abroad in light of usual befuddled USIA programming.

Docu tells the story of Maxi's (the filmmaker's) relationship to her father who's dying of cancer, and everyone in the family — two sons and a daughter (mother already dead of cancer) — knows it as well. Cohen is the sound girl and Joel Gold the cameraman, both appearing on the spot wherever the time seems ripe to talk with all concerned, particularly Joe, the father. Since summer is coming on, the two boys must make a decision whether to stay at home to be close to the father, as well as decide whether or not to give up college.

All of which sounds rather busy body, but the honesty of the search into life and its meaning cannot be doubted. Nor can the filmers' sincerity in the long run: there's nothing mawkish, sentimental, or voyeuristic about the father's illness and his attitude to it.

Indeed, just when the film tends to go overboard in its self-conscious mission, the line is drawn by somebody to put things back on an even keel.

Despite many hitches in technical quality and the lack of an overriding concept to put film into a more objective focus than just personal reasons, "Joe and Maxi" deserves a look-see by any who have faced with some reservations the realities of dying. —*Holl.*

The Billion Dollar Hobo
(COLOR)

Slow paced comedy starring Tim Conway. Juve market only.

Hollywood, June 14.

International Picture Show Company release. Produced by Lang Elliott; exec producers, Lloyd N. Adams Jr., Dorrell McGowan. Directed by Stuart E. McGowan. Screenplay, McGowan, Tim Conway, Roger Beatty; camera (Deluxe color), Irv Goodnoff; music, Michael Leonard. No other credits available. Reviewed at Loyola Theatre, Westchester, June 14, 1978. (MPAA Rating: G.) Running time: **96 MINS.**

Vernon Praiseworthy	Tim Conway
Choo Choo Trayne	Will Geer
Steve	Eric Weston
Mitchell	Sydney Lassick
Leonard Cox	John Myhers
Ernie	Frank Sivero
Jen	Sharon Weber
Rita	Sheela Tessler
Barbara Henderson	Victoria Carroll

If "Billion Dollar Hobo" had lived up to the promise in its title, this G-rated comedy toplining tv star Tim Conway might have taken off. As it stands, however, the International Picture Show production elicits more yawns than chortles. Prospects are strictly limited to the juvenile market.

Tim Conway limns the title character in a refashioned image of his vid persona from the "Carol Burnett Show," that of the helpless klutz who bumbles his way through a disaster-pocked life. Unable to hold a steady job, he is suddenly informed he is the only remaining relative of multi-millionaire Will Geer, whose predilection is demonstrated by his name, Choo Choo Trayne.

In order to take over the Trayne fortune, Conway has to duplicate Geer's early experiences as a hobo during the Depression, with the aid of Bo, a super-smart canine who is the direct descendant of Geer's original pooch.

Had the action continued in this vein, the same sort of fun that emerged from Preston Sturges' 1941 comedy, "Sullivan's Travels" (about a Hollywood producer ineptly trying his hand at riding the rails) could have followed suit here. But director and screenwriter (with Conway and Roger Beatty) Stuart McGowan opt instead for the standard heist angle, this time involving the theft of a rare Chinese dog by toughs Eric Weston and Frank Sivero. Conway and Bo, of course, are caught in the middle as unwitting accomplices, until the crooks are captured and the heroes vindicated.

Even for a moppet pic, "Billion Dollar Hobo" is ho-hum all the way. Conway is given no one of substance against which to play off, other than the dog. This was the late Will Geer's final feature performance.

McGowan seems to have encouraged over-emoting, with John Myhers as a State Department official the worst culprit. Weston and Sivero are okay as the thugs, ditto for the rest of the cast. Lensing by Irv Goodnoff is pleasing, but Michael Leonard's overly-bouncy score is irritating from the opening titles on. —*Poll.*

The Punk Rock Movie
(BRITISH-DOCU-COLOR)

Cinematic Releasing release of a Punk Rock Films presentation. Features Johnny Rotten & The Sex Pistols, The Clash, The Slits, Siouxsie & The Banshees, X-Ray Spex, Slaughter & The Dogs, Generation X, Subway Sect, Shane, Wayne County, Eater, Johnny Thunders & The Heartbreakers, Alternative T.V. Produced by Peter Clifton & Notting Hill Studios. Directed and photographed (color) by Don Letts; associate producer, Andrew Czezdwski, Franz Schneider, Serafim Karalexis; editor, John Hackney; still photography by Nurry & Sheila Rock. Reviewed Embassy I, N.Y., June 14, '78. (MPAA rating: R) Running time: **86 MINS.**

"The Punk Rock Movie" from England, is an attempt to capitalize on interest in the punk rock scene, an interest which is limited at best. Filmed in a large part at the Roxy, London, in 8m, the pic has been transformed to 35m, with little success. Prints are hazy. Even worse, the sound is deplorable. Many performers, such as Wayne County, one of the two U.S. acts shown, are virtually inaudible. Even interviews are unclear, although backstage scenes are often the most interesting, ranging from kidding around to serious preparation of material.

Bus tours also have some interest with the Clash, Siouxsie & The Banshees, the Slits, a femme combo and Johnny Thunders & The Heartbreakers, the other American group, in fun interplay. Only the headlined Sex Pistols, with Johnny Rotten featured, who close the live performance shots, come off well, but this hardly compensates for the visual and aural defects.—*Kirb.*

Dracula's Dog
(COLOR)

Two-extra teeth cause diet difficulty for family pet. Limited outlook.

Hollywood, June 8.

Crown International Pictures release, produced by Albert Band and Frank Ray Perilli. Features entire cast. Directed by Band. Screenplay, Perilli; camera (DeLuxe Color), Bruce Logan; editor, Harry Keramidas; music, Andrew Belling. Reviewed at Joe Shore Screening Room, L.A., June 7, '78. (MPAA Rating: R.) Running time: **90 MINS.**

Michael Drake	Michael Pataki
Veidt-Smit	Reggie Nalder
Inspector Branco	Jose Ferrer
Marla Drake	Jan Shutan
Linda Drake	Libbie Chase
Steve Drake	John Levin
Mrs. Parks	Cleo Harrington
Fisherman	Simmy Bow
Fisherman	JoJo D'Amore

Over in Transylvania, the soldiers stumble upon the tomb of the Dracula family, buried with their faithful pet, Zoltan. The earth rumbles and the canine coffin falls out. A soldier opens it and removes the stake and from then on it's just one big romp. Instead of getting wrapped up in the lamp cord and pulling it over the sofa, Zoltan chases people and sucks their blood.

The earth rumbles again and Reggie Nalder falls out. He's one of these half-vampires who can work days and was long in the employ of the Count himself. Though the two extra teeth make the job difficult, Zoltan gets a grip on Nalder's stake and brings him to life. You might then expect that Nalder and the dog would arouse the rest of the family, including their former master.

But no. They go off to America looking for the last member of the Dracula clan. Enter Ferrer, a Transylvanian inspector specializing in vampires. He sets off in pursuit.

The last surviving member of the Dracula family is Michael Pataki who has no idea of his heritage except for a puzzling picture of granddad in a cape with the dog. Pataki now has a wife, two kids and four dogs of his own who are incredible boring for the first hour of the picture.

The family goes camping, followed by Zoltan and Nalder, followed by Ferrer, carrying the stakes. Nalder tells Zoltan to go bit Pataki so they can have a new master, but the dog is put off by the cross around Pataki's neck, a bit of canine theology that isn't fully explained.

Pataki and Ferrer send the family home and hole up in a cabin. The dogs attack and Zoltan chews through the roof, but sunlight saves the pair. With their cabin full of holes, the two guys go out the next night, looking for the dogs in a convertible with the top down.

After that, it gets funnier and funnier.—*Har.*

Matilda
(COLOR)

Boxing kangaroo gets a title shot. Could score.

Hollywood, June 13.

An American International Pictures release of an Albert S. Ruddy Production, produced by Albert Ruddy; executive producer, Richard R. St. Johns. Stars Elliott Gould. Directed by Daniel Mann. Screenplay, Ruddy and Timothy Galfas based on the book by Paul Gallico; camera (Movielab Color), Jack Woolf; production designer, Boris Leven; editor, Allan A. Jacobs; costumer, Jack Martell, Donna Roberts Orme; associate producer, Paul Sapounakis; special effects, Jerry Endler. Reviewed at the AIP Screening Room, Beverly Hills, June 12, '78. (MPAA Rating: G.) Running time: **105 MINS.**

Bernie Bonnelli	Elliott Gould
Duke Parkhurst	Robert Mitchum
Uncle Nono	Harry Guardino
Billy Baker	Clive Revill
Kathleen Smith	Karen Carlson
Wild Bill Wildman	Roy Clark
Pinky Schwab	Lionel Stander
Gordon Baum	Art Metrano
Lee Dockerty	Larry Pennell
Tanya Six	Roberta Collins

"Matilda" is a pleasant, oldfashioned rags to riches story about a theatrical agent and the boxing kangaroo that hops into his life. Albert Ruddy's comedy, which he produced and scripted with Timothy Galfas, is such an off-the-wall idea that the AIP pickup has a shot. It's wonderfully cast and lovingly directed by Daniel Mann without the bland harmlessness of so many G-rated films. "Matilda" has nothing weightier on its mind than the screenplay's final thought, "Life is grand, isn't it," but that's a nice sentiment, if not a particularly heady one.

It's a show biz success story. Clive Revill, former welterweight champ, is down on his luck. So is Elliott Gould, a small-time promoter, who shares office space with his brother-in-law, Lionel Stander, manager of heavyweight champ Larry Pennell. Stander is just a front for Harry Guardino, who's Uncle Nono, Mafioso boss. Robert Mitchum is Duke Parkhurst, influential sports solumnist, itching for a crack at Guardino. And so on.

Matilda will bring joy to everyone's heart, even Karen Carlson, an animal lover who wants to protect the kangaroo from exploitation. Everyone comes out a winner in this picture.

No one seems to surprised to find a kangaroo in the world of prizefighting. In fact, no one seems much surprised to find a kangaroo walking around in New York City, until he scarfs some ices from a street vendor. That's the world in which this film operates. If you'll accept a boxing kangaroo fighting in Lake Tahoe for the heavyweight championship, or a guy in a kangaroo's suit fighting for the title — and you will — then you'll accept the conventions of the plot.

Ruddy has assembled a bunch of Mr. Reliables for the cast — Mitchum, Clive Revill and the wonderful Lionel Stander. A couple of scenes don't work — for instance, one in which Roy Clark plays a boxing commissioner, easily manipulated by Gould. It has the feel of an unrehearsed skit on a tv variety show, but it's forgotten quickly.

However, what won't be forgotten quickly by audiences, are the blatant on-screen ads. Ruddy has gotten lotsa push behind his picture through tie-ins, but he's paid a high price. The spots for MacDonald's, Saks Fifth Avenue, American Airlines and Harrah's lack subtlety and may offend some. Which is a shame, because everything else about this picture is so endearing.
—Hege.

Das Andere Laecheln
(The Other Smile)
(WEST GERMAN-COLOR)

Berlin, May 31.

A Robert Van Ackeren Film, Berlin, in coproduction with Bavaria Atelier, Munich, Peter Maerthesheimer, producer; released by Luxmeta. Features entire cast. Directed by Robert Van Ackeren. Screenplay, Van Ackeren, Joy Markert, Peter Stripp; camera (color), Janken Janssen; editing, Hannes Nikel. Reviewed at Arsenal-Kino, Berlin, May 30, '78. Running time: **115 MINS.**

Irma	Katja Rupe
Ellen	Elisabeth Trissenaar
Paul	Heinz Ehrenfreund
Carola	Anja Muessiggang

Robert Van Ackeren's past reputation centered on the amazing success of "Harlis" (1973), which exposed the tender underbelly of the Berlin erotic scene in a style that recalled Ufa's weaker moments. Another interesting pic was the adaptation of Heinrich Mann's "Belcanto," starring Berlin transvestite Romy Haag and indirectly highlighting the city's gay scene. Now he's made "The Other Smile," an intimate study of women and sexual relations that signals a mature talent on the rise.

"The Other Smile" works on several levels. As a narrative story, it's about a housewife with a daughter who invites a girlfriend to live at home because of time on her hands. The husband, a liquor salesman, has put her in a pumpkin shell and prefers his ambitions and order. Gradually she and the girlfriend unconsciously, or perhaps consciously, change roles, the latter even duplicating the other's appearances and manners — until the husband accepts the girlfriend, now a carbon copy of his wife but more malleable and submissive, to be his partner instead of the resisting woman, who can't stand conformity and is now dissolving into madness.

The other level is the socalled "vampire theme," which Carl Th. Dreyer and F.W. Murnau exploited to perfection rising out of Swedish Naturalism and German Expressionism in the silent film. The only difference is that Van Ackeren is fascinated by the social consequences that result from a society that allows such extreme forms of personality suppression and absurd role-playing for the sake of an image or a position — in short, social standing.

In one probable interpetation, the wife refuses to conform to the hubby's picture of her as a model housewife and mother, as in cigaret and kitchen ads; instead, she recedes into herself and eventually seems to be living peacefully in a passive world where she is "completely happy."

The girlfriend, a druggist apprentice, becomes more and more the dominant figure in the household, taking on some of the traits of the wife but also adhering completely to the husband's standards of life and living.

The husband, for his part, doesn't even seem to notice the change in the two, which is an amazing feat of directing to watch — two opposites, at the beginning, gradually converge on each other heading in different, bypassing directions. This changing in roles, in fact, is what makes the film so unusual.

She also rejects the "stranger" in the household who eventually takes over mother's image and position. In fact, she looks upon the transference as a sham, a horrifying distortion in society that not even the principal characters are aware of.

This is an intelligent statement on "emancipation;; and "self-consciousness" (terms too often heard in film circles today), in addition to providing a classic case for sociologists and psychologists, behaviorists and psychiatrists, as well as making an entertaining film.

Thesp performances are tops, lensing is by one of the ace cameramen in New German Cinema (Juergen Juerges), and Van Ackeren will be a NGC helmer to watch after this. Some possibilities for the art houses provided pic is handled properly. —Holl.

Drevo Jelania
(The Miracle Tree)
(SOVIET-COLOR)

Cannes, May 20.

A Grusiafilm Production, Tbilisi. Features entire cast. Directed by Tengiz Abuladze. Screenplay, Revas Inanishvili, Abuladze, based on a story by Georgi Leonidze; camera (color) Lomer Ahvlediani; sets, Revas Mirashvili; costumes, Achab Abakarov; music, Bidsina Kvernadze, Jakov Bobochidze; editing, G. Omadso, sound, T. Naobachvili. Reviewed at Cannes Film Fest (Film Market), May 19, '78. Running time: **108 MINS.**

Marita	Lika Davtaradze
Gedia	Sosso Dchatchvliani
Cheta	Sasa Kolelichvili
Zizikore	Kote Dauchvili
Fufala	Sofiko Chiaureli
Joram	Kachi Kawsadze
Bumbula	Erosi Mandchgaladze
Elios	Otar Megvinetuchuzesi
Ochrochine	Ramas Chikwadze
Chatchika	Georgi Gegetchkori
Maradia	Cecilia Takaichvili
Batula	Georgi Chobua
Tagria	Dchemal Gaganidze
Koria	Boris Zipuria
Ninuza	Ija Chobua
Ninore	Msia Machviladze
Nargisa	Termina Tuajeva
Boy Beaten on Ear	Dato Abachidze
Cheta's Mother	Tina Burbutachvili
Shepherd	Chota Chirtladze

One of the loveliest feature pix to come out of the Soviet Union of late, Tengiz Abuladze's "The Miracle Tree" (also translated "Tree of Dreams" or "Tree of Wishes") first appeared in the Film Market at last summer's Moscow Film Fest, then at Berlin (in Forum of Young Cinema) and now at Cannes (Film Market), and is slated for the summer fest circuit. It's a Georgian pic, made by the same helmer who won international recognition with the tradition-oriented "Grandmother, Iliko, Illarion and Me" (1963) and "The Appeal." (1968).

This is a tale full of allegory, symbolism, and mystic nuance, rooted in the soil of Georgia and drawing its strength not from a single narrative but a series of 22 individual episodes loosely bound together as in a photo scrapbook. It's the turn-of-the-century in Georgi Leonidze's story (written in poetic blank-verse); the village is Kachetien, the same place the famous primitive painter Niko Pirosmani was born (who died in 1918); and the tree in the title has relevance in that the individual episodes "branch" out from the same source-of-inspiration (tree is shown majestically on a meadow towards the end of the film).

The main story concerns a lovely village maiden, who cannot marry the man she loves because she's promised to another. When the lovers after her wedding meet on their own, the rendezvous is discovered and the girl is shamefully paraded by the villages on a rainy day to suffer mud splattered on her continence. The opening shots of the film forecast the tragic end: a white horse lies dying in a meadow filled with red summer poppies, with a sorrowing lad leaning over him to offer affection in a last fruitless gesture. Life and death, dream and reality, good and evil blend into a whole like a Shakespearean tragedy of divided love.

Scenes are rich in colors and composition, sometimes drawing on Pirosmani's vision and sometimes resembling the Flemish painter Breughel. "The Miracle Tree" has all the qualities of a Georgian epic based on traditions and legends. A must for Soviet film weeks and art houses catering to national cinemas. —Holl.

The Sailor's Return
(BRITISH-COLOR)

Cannes, May 27.

A Euston Films Production made by Ariel Productions Ltd. in association with NFFC; world rights, Osprey Film Distribution, London; produced by Otto Plaschkes, executive producer, Verity Lambert. Stars Tom Bell, Shope Shodeinde. Directed by Jack Gold. Screenplay, James Saunders, based on the novel by David Garnett; cameraman not available; music, Carl Davis. Reviewed at Cannes Film Fest (Film Market), May 26, '78. Running time: **112 MINS.**

William Targett	Tom Bell
Tulip	Shope Shodeinde
Tom	Mick Ford
Lucy	Paola Dionisotti
Harry	George Costigan
The Rev. Pottock	Clive Swift

Fred Leake .... Ray Smith
Molten .... Ivor Roberts
Carter .... Bernard Hill
Jack Sait .... Anthony Langdon

Following the success of "The Naked Civil Servant" for Thames Television, helmer Jack Gold teamed again with exec prod Verity Lambert on "The Sailor's Return," an adaptation of David Garnett's novel.

Garnett is the last surviving member of the famous Bloomsbury Group, a group of Cambridge-schooled London writers who flourished in the pre-World War I days and included such distinguished names as E.M. Forster, Virginia Woolf, Lytton Strachey, Clive Bell, and Roger Fry, among others.

For the record and to put "Sailor's Return" in literary focus, the Bloomsbury Group were influenced by G.E. Moore's ethical and esthetic "Principa Ethica" (1903), but only insofar as they were in favor of passionately striving towards honesty and clarity in their writing and a certain perception of real, though passing, beauty in the world. These insights seem to spill over into Gold's film concept of Garnett's novel via the gentle ease with which he tells his story. But the quiet pace may be only fruited for tv exposure, and "Sailor's Return" will not return b.o. coin as did his zany, satirical "National Health," "Man Friday," and even "Naked Civil Servant."

Set in the early reign of Queen Victoria (1819-1901), story is about a sailor who returns home to England with a bride from the black Kingdom of Dahomey in West Africa. It's her dowry, a treasure of pearls, that sets them up in business with an inn for thirsty passersby in a lush English countryside. But her color and the presence of a black son set them off from intolerant neighbors, despite some support from friends in the area.

Conflicts with the sailor's sister, the local pastor (who preaches hell fire), and prejudiced visitors to the inn lead to slow alienation in a foreign land. The light in Tulip's eyes gradually goes out, although her love for William Targett and her innate African faith in the goodness of man sustain her through thick and thin.

The day comes when the money runs low and the customers stop coming, then her newly-born child dies, and finally the sailor is killed after a fight he fairly fought and won. Tulip finds a way to send her son back to Africa on a ship, but when she herself is not allowed passage, she returns to the inn to grow old as a quaint cleaning woman.

Tom Bell scores as the sailor Targett, and Shope Shodeinde (a native Nigerian) as the African princess bring credibility but hardly sparkle to Tulip, a lively flower that must slowly wither in a foreign climate with the accumulation of disappointments and unawaited hostility. Further, the story seems too fragile to carry anywhere else save on paper. Credits are tops. Pic could get legs for solid offshore chances, if properly handled or boosted by a fest kudo for art house circuit. —Holl.

Das Zweite Erwachen Der Christa Klages
(The Second Awakening of Christa Klages)
(WEST GERMAN-COLOR)

Cannes, May 26.

A Bioskop-Film, Munich, production in collaboration with Westdeutscher Rundfunk, Cologne; world rights, Filmverlag der Autoren. Features entire cast. Directed by Margarethe von Trotta. Screenplay, von Trotta, Luisa Francia; camera (color), Franz Rath; sound, Vladimir Vizner; music, Klaus Doldinger; editing, Anette Dorn; executive producer, Eberhard Junkersdorf. Reviewed at Cannes Film Fest (Film Market), May 25, '78. Running time: 93 MINS.

Cast: Tina Engel (Christa), Silvia Reize (Ingrid), Katharina Thalbach (Lena), Marius Muller-Westernhagen (Werner), Peter Schneider (Hans).

After its initial unspooling at the Forum of the Berlin Film Fest, Margarethe von Trotta's debut pic has found its way into the German string of studio cinemas and may get legs for off-shore climes due to fem angle in theme and credits. Based on a true incident, "The Second Awakening of Christa Klages" is a meller on how three women awake to the social consciousness needed to go their own ways.

Trotta, scripter wife of Volker Schloendorff, is best known for her screenplay to Schloendorff's "Katharina Blum," based on a Heinrich Boell story and the top b.o. winner in New German Cinema annals. She's also tried her hand at thesping, starring in hubby's "Coup de Grace." For "Christa Klages" the fem angle not only includes three leads in the pic, but also coscripter Luisa Francia.

Christa needs money to keep her day care center going, a storefront for children (like her own daughter) in a nonauthoritarian atmosphere. So she, together with the trustful, uncomplicated Werner, steals it from a bank and asks a Reverend friend to cover the grab by passing it off as a free contribution of church funds to the center.

The Reverend nixes the idea, and things get hotter for our heroine when the femme bank teller noses around the center and could put the finger on her. Christa and Werner go underground.

A friend, Ingrid, puts them up for a while because she's mostly bored with her drab existence in a condominium. The husband returns home only on weekends and of course doesn't cater to his suspicious-looking guests. Then Werner is fatally shot by cops for running away from a routine identification check after making what appears to be a fumbling effort at car theft. So Christa is off to Portugal to work picking vegetables in a farm coop, and Ingrid (who loaned a passport) joins her there later.

Christa discovers she can't speak Portugese well enough to discuss fem problems and is rather unsuited for the job; the co-op also discovers the truth about her, and she's asked to leave. Back in Germany, loneliness creeps in and she visits old friends—only to be arrested. The climactic moment is the confrontation with the bankteller, who, rather predictably, doesn't recognize her after all.

Tina Engel as Christa is convincing as a socially engaged but emotionally muddled tragic heroine, although the narrative ball takes too many bounces off the wall to draw the best from her. Credits are a good cut above average.

—Holl.

Picassos aeventyr
(The Adventures of Picasso)
(SWEDISH-COLOR)

Stockholm, June 9.

An AB Svenska Ord/AB Svensk Filmindustri production, AB Svensk Filmindustri release. Features entire cast. Original story and script, Hans Alfredson and Tage Danielsson with additional ideas by Goesta Ekman. Directed by Tage Danielsson. Camera (Eastmancolor) Tony Forsberg, Roland Sterner; production design, Hans Alfredson, Per Ahlin, Stig Boquist; executive producer, Staffan Hedquist; editor, Jan Persson; music, Gunnar Svensson with quotes from Eric Satie, Puccini, etc. Reviewed at Roeda Kvarn, Stockholm, June 9,'78. Running time: 110 MINS.
Picasso .... Goesta Ekman
His father .... Hans Alfredson
His mother .... Margretha Krook
Mrs. Ingrid Svensson-
Guggenheim .... Birgitta Andersson
Gertrude Stein .... Bernard Cribbins
Alice B. Toklas .... Wilfrid Brambell

"Picasso's Adventures" is no ordinary film. It makes do without conventional plot contrivances. It is stagey and uses its characters as human puppets. Still, it is a world of lovely madness unto itself and will, with careful sales handling, eventually capture world audiences.

Carrying the subtitle, "A Thousand Loving Lies," film is an affectionate tribute, an homage in gentle madcap comedy style, to the spirit and also to the very human presence of the late great painter, to his work and to his sense of humor, his approach to women and to his political fairmindedness.

The writer-actor team of Hans (Hasse) Alfredson and Tage Danielsson (the latter taking director's credit alone this time) constitute a mighty force on stage and screen at home and have also made their mark in some off-shore territories with such mildly politically tinged, lyrical crazy comedies as "The Apple War" (anti-EEC) and "Release The Prisoners, It's Spring" (anti the Swedish penal system).

With "Picasso's Adventures," which uses a narrator sparingly and otherwise relies on a dialog of heavily accented jokester's ideas of French, Spanish and English plus a few snippets of Swedish and otherwise mostly on sight gags, mime and music. Alfredson and Danielsson by now deserve their worldwide audience.

If not the Mel Brooksians, then such related folks will enjoy a chuckle feast as much as a laugh riot.

Imaginary events in Picasso's life are told in comedy sketches about his birth in Malaga (where the heavily breathing woman in the bed turns out not to be Picasso's mother at all, thus supplying story's only outright erotic joke) to his death at his own hand (he vanishes into the blue, escaping all those who exploited his art).

In between, Picasso is seen (forever wearing white, loose shorts and too big striped t-shirts) painting a lot, loving quite some, but mostly being thrown into all kinds of absurd situations by his avaricious entrepreneur-father.

Some episodes are gentle in their happy abandon (Picasso's costume party thrown in honor of fellow painter Rousseau), some are unashamedly vulgar and some are wittily served through animation supplied by Per Ahlin (of the cartoon feature "Dunderklumpen" fame). Ahlin also did all the loyally invented Picasso paintings seen throughout the film.

Goesta Ekman creates a mild-mannered, bemused Picasso, sometimes indulging in intense and successful pratfalls, but never, alas, exuding much the real Picasso's sexual charm. Hans Alfredson is the fool with the iron will to succeed as the father.

From England, Bernard Cribbins and Wilfrid Brambell have been called in to do marvellous take offs on Gertrude Stein and Alice B. Toklas. Denmark's Jytte Abildstroem has a truly hilarious face making exchange with Ekman, and Norway's chubby comedy fumbler Rolv Wesenlund goes through his fumbling as an electrician trying to make the electric chair work when Picasso is sitting strapped to it, having been framed, so to speak, during an art raid in New York in the years of The Great Art Prohibition.

Sweden's own Brigitta Andersson comes on and off as Mrs. Ingrid Svensson-Guggenheim, an art patroness hot on Picasso's tail and trail, with much of the film's otherwise lacking sensual gusto.

As Picasso's mother, Margretha Krook does her celebrated Grand Old Warhose bit, and Per Oscarsson is back in fine, nervous shape as the poet Appollinaire, while tiny Lena Nyman is out to murder practically everyone as Sirrka, the Finnish soprano.

"Picasso's Adventures" is a typical see it twice film which can be explored endlessly for more nuggets of wit. But as it stands now, it is decidedly overlong and often too much in love with its own jokes to pack the comic wallop that really lies within both performances, script and production.

Also, a few episodes such as a senile Dr. Albert Schweitzer operating on a bound Picasso really do not belong to this particular film. Which does not detract from the fact that Hans Alfredson and Tage Danielsson with this feature have really secured their own niche among the greats of movie comedy. — *Kell.*

Sayat Nova
((SOVIET-COLOR)

Cannes, May 28.
An Armenian, Georgian, and Azerbaijan Production, Soviet Union; world rights, Goskino, Moscow. Directed by Sergei Paradjanov. No other credits available. Reviewed at Cannes Film Fest (Film Market), May 27, '78. Running time: **90 MINS.**
Cast unavailable.

The legend surrounding Sergei Paradjanov's "Sayat Nova" makes better copy for some crits than the film itself. Also known as "Color of the Pomegranate," pic was produced in a common effort by the Armenian, Georgian, and Azerbaijan studios in the Soviet Union, although it deals distinctly with Armenian national history and heritage. It takes the form of an epic poem with images heavily laden with symbolic and metaphoric meaning, tracing the life of the 18th-century Armenian poet and monk Sayat Nova through his writings.

Paradjanov burst on the international scene in 1965 when his "Shadows of Our Forgotten Ancestors" won some 16 international kudos around the world, including the Grand Prix at Mar del Plata fest and exposure at San Francisco and Montreal. Shortly thereafter, upon completing "Sayat Nova" (1970), he fell into disgrace and was imprisoned for a criminal offense. The circumstances of the trial and imprisonment quickly became a bone of contention, resolved only recently by Paradjanov's release.

Meanwhile, an apparently pirated print has made the rounds of film clubs in Paris, with an introduction attached by Amnesty International on Armenia's historical background and with some

comments on the film and director. According to the badly scratched and partially cut version (some 16 minutes were taken out) shown in the Cannes film market, the issue of genocide plays a major role in the film, as the Armenian people suffered severely under Turkish persecution (1894-1915) as well as from recurrent invasions from Persia.

This is only a partial element in the film, however. "Sayat Nova" seems to be a national epic in verse, neatly divided into episodes with still-life tableux as though a series of icons were being paraded before the viewer's eyes. In this regard, it should be mentioned that the film was shown in the Soviet Union — but more than likely is only completely understandable to the Armenian nation and people (not only in the Soviet Union, but scattered throughout Turkey and Iran as well).

To capture the essence of "Sayat Nova," the viewer should be aware that Armenia was the first country to adopt Christianity as a state religion (303). The Armenian Church became autonomous about 500 and flourished culturally in the 10th and 11th centuries under independent-minded native rulers, after which it fell under Byzantine and later Turkish domination. The persecutions by the Ottoman Empire often verged on genocide, resulting in a vast migration to the Russian section obtained in an agreement with Turkey and Persia in 1828. After the October Revolution, Armenia regained its independence briefly until 1920.

These nationalist threads and cultural heritage buried in beliefs and traditions course thorugh "Sayat Nova" like a rushing river from beginning to end. The images of a monastic ruins, the emphasis on ritual and ceremony, the architectural decorations drawn from the bible, the sacrificial elements reflected in herds of sheep and the color of the pomegranate, and the icon-like portraits of angelic faces and priestly ministers (to say nothing of traces of the Passion) — all these blend into a visual book of prayer, a hymn to a people. It's both an exotic and mystical mosaic, all the more sensual and relevant because the poet-monk Sayat Nova was killed during one of the Persian invasions.

A film that has to be seen more than once to gather its full meaning, "Sayat Nova" deserves proper exposure in light of current circumstances. Pic has been known to be seen legitimately outside of the Soviet Union on occasion via Armenian Film Weeks. — *Holl.*

Kruta Lubost
(Cruel Love)
(CZECHOSLOVAK-COLOR)

Prague, June 2.
A Czechoslovak Film Production, Koliba Studios, Bratislava; world rights, Czechoslovensky Film, Prague. Features entire cast. Written and directed by Martin Tapak. Camera (color), Vincent Rosinec; music, Svetozar Stracina. Reviewed at Czechoslovensky Film Screening Room, Prague, June 1, '78. Running time: **87 MINS.**
Cast: Maria Macakova, Juraj Kukura, Magda Vasarypva, Jozef Majercik, Viliam Polonyi, Kveta Lukoskova, Beata Znakova, Maria Hajkova, Juraj Kovac, Zdenka Nererova, Frantisek Desset.

A two-episode pic set in the Slovak Tatra mountains near the Polish border, Martin Tapak's "Cruel Love" features two women named Kristka who fight for their love, each in their own way. In both instances, their victories are bittersweet ones and tinged with tragedy. The stories are drawn from folk legends common to this area, the darker side to the popular "Heimat-Film" or "homeland" pix which only romanticize love against mountain-greenery settings.

The first episode, "Grey Eyes," is about a singing milk-maid who falls in love with a rowdy robber, a Robin Hood figure who not only steals from the rich to give to the poor, but has an eye for the girls as well. One day, our heroine helps him to escape from the Austrian-Hungarian police (these are pre-World War I times), and she accepts his advances in return as a fitting reward. Later, however, she realizes that his true love is another, and, in an act of vengeance, she brands her competitor with a torch in the face.

The second story, "The Infected Heart," deals with a shy Krista who is married to an untamed ruffian she, in truth, loves with unfailing loyalty and trust. He, however, returns her tenderness with rebuke — all the more so when she becomes pregnant against his will. The ending at least leans towards a tragic beating, as he lashes out blindly to rid himself of his softer feelings — then he changes his mind and accepts his destiny as a responsible father.

Both stories are inseparably intertwined. The raw, impulsive emotions of the first Krista win her nothing, while the shy, fragile sensibilities of the second lead to a partial but evident victory. Both men are similar personalities, the second an apparent extension in storyline of the first. As for a moral, there really isn't any: this is home-spun philosophy, a picture of life as it is (and is related) in the mountains.

A musical introduction frames both stories to bring us into the present. Also, there're folkloric dances and singing numbers that stand up very well by themselves as well as being effectively integrated into the

whole. Acting is unpretentious and natural.

A lovely pic from Slovakia, an independent state in Czechoslovakia with its own production facilities and aim. Tapak, pic's helmer, is also in charge of the Koliba Studios in Bratislava. A natural for Slovak and Czechoslovak film weeks and the art house circuit. — *Holl.*

Muenchhausen
(The Adventures of
Baron Muenchhausen)
(WEST GERMAN-COLOR)

Cannes, May 24.
A Ufa Production, Berlin, restored by the Friedrich-Wilhelm-Murnau released by Neue Constantin; world rights, Atlas International, Munich. Foundation. Stars Hans Albers, Brigitte Horney. Directed by Josef von Baky. Screenplay, Erich Kaestner (under Pseudonym Berthold Buerger); camera (color), Werner Krien; special effects, Konstantin Irmen-Tschet; art direction, Emil Hasler, Otto Guelstorff; music, Georg Haentzschel; producer, Eberhard Schmidt. Reviewed at Cannes Film Fest (Film Market), May 23, '78. Running time: **100 MINS.**
Baron Muenchhausen ....Hans Albers
Catherine the Great ...... Brigitte Horney
The Man in the Moon .... Wilhelm Bendow
Prince Karl of
Brunswick ....·....... Michael Bohnen
Frederick von
Hartenfeld ....Hans Brausewetter
Sophie von Riedesel ... Marina von Ditmar
Prince Potemkin .... Andrews Engelmann
Baroness Muenchhausen ...Kaethe Haack
Christian
Kuchenreutter ...... Herman Speelmanns
Runner .... Walter Lieck
Count Cagliostro ....Ferdinand Marian
Sultan Abd-ul-Hamid ....:.... Leo Slezak
Casanova ....Gustav Waldau
Princess Isabella d'Este ...... Ilse Werner

After the lengthy, informative report on "Muenchhausen" in *Variety*, May 17, the German weekly mag, Der Spiegel, did another feature on the Nazi Ufa pic adding further info and commentary. Here's a critic's wrap-up on the salient aspects of this German classic now released in German, French, and English.

Pic was planned for the 25th anniversary of the founding of Ufa in 1943. Josef Goebbels wanted an international success and chose the Hungarian-born Josef von Baky, with a slight-of-hand genius for musicals and romance oaters, to direct an epic worthy of the studio's technical facilities (he thus superseded the heavy-handed Teutonic propaganda helmer Veit Harlan). Baky went to Erich Kaestner, a friend who was on the Nazi blacklist, to script "Muenchhausen" under the pseudonym Berthold Buerger.

For the Agfacolor process to make this an extravaganza worthy of Hollywood, pix like "Gone with the Wind" were studied in detail. Special effects by Konstantin Irmen-Tschet easily equals anything Hollywood was doing at the time. Sets were carbon copies of the rococo period: European palaces where the ageless Baron Muenchhausen cavorted under magic spells and guises, including the opulent court of Catherine the Great, the harem of a Turkish sultan, and the 18th-century hang-outs of Casanova and Cagliostro, as well as lovely princesses longing to be taken into the Baron's arms for a night of bliss.

For the exteriors, Baky shot in Venetian gardens and allowed Albers (an actor Goebbels couldn't stand) a free rein ham it up as he pleased. The result is a German highpoint in comedy, action and witty dialog; it's a relaxed, easy-flowing thespian tour-de-force for both Albers and Brigitte Horney, as Catherine the Great. Another major plus is the Agfacolor tint: Baky used Rembrandt and Renaissance painting for the Italian scenes, winter blues for Russia, gold for Constantinople, and autumn colors for the Baron's fading days in his Braunschweig residence.

Atlas International reports having had to comb archives for remaining prints to restore the colors and find missing pieces, although a pristine print has long been said to exist somewhere (either in the East German film archive or among American contraband prints reportedly stored in Dayton, Ohio).

The main problem seems to be the question of rights, as with so many 'Old masterpieces' which can't be shown publicly because of conflicting claims. The Murnau Foundation got off the hook with a personal transfer-of-rights by Kaestner himself before his death.
—*Holl*

Tanczacy Jastrzab
(The Dancing Hawk)
(POLISH-COLOR)

Cannes, May 26.

A Film Polski Production, Profil Unit, Warsaw; world rights, Film Polski, Warsaw. Features entire cast. Written and directed by Grzegorz Krolikiewicz, based on the novel by Julian Kawalec. Camera (color), Zbigniew Rybczynski. No other credits. Reviewed at Cannes Film Fest (Film Market), May 25, '78. Running time: **100 MINS.**

Cast: Franciszek Trzeciak, Beata Wedrychowicz, Beata Tyskiewicz.

A film with good intentions and a strong theme, Grzegorz Krolikiewicz's "The Dancing Hawk" won a national film prize at last autumn's Gdansk Film Festival. But it will have trouble in foreign climes due to the experimental style of putting the message over. Images and narrative are too self-conscious for this political portrait of an opportunist in the postwar era up to present.

"The Dancing Hawk" refers to the son of a peasant who senses he can climb to the job in troubled

times by playing his cards right. His slavery to work match his ambitions, and gradually he reaches the social position he desires. But the costs have included a dehumanized soul and a loss of moral conscience. People have had to pay for his advancement, including those nearest him.

The downfall is equally painful. Either imprisonment or the easy way out are offered as alternative, the latter more appealing in nature of the offences and the humiliation.

Franciszek Trzeciak is convincing as a peasant who has not lost any of his bad manners and carries the pic when given room to show his thespian skills. A straight narrative might have put the film over. —*Holl.*

Die Glaeserne Zelle
(The Glass Cell)
(WEST GERMAN-COLOR)

Cannes, May 26.

A Roxy/Solaris Film Production, Munich, in collaboration with Bayerischer Rundfunk; world rights, Filmverlag der Autoren, Munich. Stars Helmut Griem, Brigitte Fossey. Directed by Hans C. Geissendoerfer. Screenplay, Geissendoerfer, Klaus Baedekerl, based on novel of the same name by Patricia Highsmith; camera (Eastmancolor), Robby Mueller; music, Niels Walen, sets, Heidi Luedi, editing, Peter Przygodda; production manager, Bernd Eichinger, Luggi Waldleitner. Reviewed at Cannes fest (film market), May 25 '78. Running time: **100 MINS.**

Phillip Braun	Helmut Griem
Lisa Braun	Brigitte Fossey
David Reinalt	Dieter Laser
Lasky	Walter Kohut
Timmie	Claudius Kracht
Goller	Guenther Strack
Guard	Klaus Muenster
States Attorney	Hans Guenther Martens
Sales Girl	Christa-Maria Netsch
Little Girl	Gerlinde Egger
Police Commissioner	Bernhard Wicki

This is the third Patricia Highsmith adaptation in two years: Claude Miller's French prod "Tell Him I Love Him," based on "This Sweet Sickness," was shot in 1976 and released in 1977; Wim Wenders' German version of "Ripley's Game" was lensed at almost identically the same time; and Hans C. Geissendoerfer's "The Glass Cell," another Teutonic feature, was finished only a few months later than the prior two in the spring of this year. Miller and Wenders were paired at the London Fest (after Wenders competed at Cannes), then all three pix narrowly missed unspooling at the Berlin fest in February-March at sidebars, where Highsmith was serving on the international jury as the Yank rep.

Highsmith will be best remembered for Hitchcock's adaptation of her "Strangers on a Train," today a cult pic widely acclaimed as one of the master's master thrillers. Geissendoerfer's "The Glass Cell" may

not go down in film history as vintage Highsmith, but it did win the top kudo of this year's German Film Prizes. It should get good exposure on the summer fest circuit and might get an attractive art-house playoff, if handled properly with nod to current fad for detective writing.

As with the main stream of Highsmith's writing, murder itself takes a back seat — it's the motivation that interests her and the circumstances that trigger a crime. Helmut Griem plays a respectable architect who is ultimately held responsible for faulty construction materials that result in a school cave-in and death and injury to innocent children. During the appeal to his sentence he goes to jail, only to discover later that his wife, Brigitte Fossey, has had a brief affair with his lawyer.

The lawyer claims to have unearthed new evidence to pin the deed on the real culprit just as Griem leaves prison to start a new life, again with the help of the lawyer-friend who still loves his wife. The infidelity is used as a blackmail threat by the bad guy, who feels the lawyer is getting too close for comfort — and the sensitive, moody, distraut Griem kills his lawyer-friend one evening in a rage of jealousy. Then he is driven to an intentional crime when the blackmailer-culprit produces a tape-recording of a tell-tale telephone conversation. The wife backs Griem with an alibi when the police commissioner is sure he has caught his man.

Story is fascinating in itself, but drags in the scenes that count the most: the development of an innocent into a killer. Griem practices one face, and although he's right for the role, he doesn't carry the pic over the long stretch.

Technical credits are a major plus. —*Holl.*

Chaussette Surprise
(Surprise Sock)
(FRENCH-COLOR)

Paris.

GEF-CCFC release of Clap 7, SFP, Peby Guisez production. Features entire cast. Produced and directed by Jean-Francois Davy. Screenplay, Davy, Jean-Claude Carriere; camera (Eastmancolor), Jacques Guerin; editor, Thierry Derocles; music, Marie-Paule Belle. Reviewed at Salle Ponthieu, Paris, June 8, '78. Running time: **95 MINS.**

Bernadette	Bernadette Lafont
Nathalie	Anna Karina
Juliette	Christine Pascal
TV Man	Michel Galabru
Bernard	Bernard Haller
Antoine	Rufus
Doctor	Claude Pieplu

This is an attempt at screwball comedy that goes awry. Aimed mainly at home grounds, it could find its audiences here, but appears a chancey item abroad.

Director Jean-Francois Davy scored with a pseudo sociological docu about a porno actress, "Exhibition," which got to the New York Film Fest. He ran into some bad luck with a docu on "Prostitution" and then a banned pic, "Exhibition 2," which put his company in receivership. Now, with a new company, he has made this satirical look at femme lib, high prices, tv madness and other foibles.

Four men in a mass auto accident meet in a hospital. One sells old furniture but usually refuses to part with them, another is a star in tv commercials, a third an inventor of a device to save people in high rise buildings in case of fire, and the last has ingested his tv set literally.

Their wives meet and taste liberty, but all is right in the end. There are a few good ideas and gags but it is mostly obvious. Technically fair. —*Mosk.*

Adela Jeste Nevecerela
(Adele Hasn't Had Her Supper Yet)
(CZECHOSLOVAK-COLOR)

Prague, June 2.

A Czechoslovak Film Production, Barrandov Studios, Prague; world rights, Czechoslovak Film, Prague. Features entire cast. Directed by Oldrich Lipsky. Screenplay, Jiri Brdecka; camera (Eastmancolor), Jaroslav Kucera; sets, Vladimir Labsky, Milan Nejedly; special effects, Jan Svankmaier; music, Lubos Fiser. Reviewed at Czechoslovensky Film Screening Room, Prague, June 1, '78. Running time: **100 MINS.**

Nick Carter	Michal Docolomansky
Josef Ledvina	Rudolf Hrusinsky
Baron Kratzman	Milos Kopecky
Professor Bocek	Ladislav Pesek
Kvetusa	Nada Konvalinkova
Police Inspector Kauntiz	Martin Ruzek
Hotel servant	Vaclav Lohnisky
Irma, Gizela	Olga Schoberova
Countess Thun	Kveta Fialova

"Adele Hasn't Had Her supper Yet" might have had "Nick Carter" in its title, had not a President with the same name been in office, and an offense could hardly be aimed in this direction. Oldrich Lipsky's spoof on the turn-of-the-century detective paperbacks recalls his earlier merry satire on the Western, "Lemonade Joe," which got a hefty run in art houses around the world a decade ago. This one is just as good and needs only a boost on the fest circuit to get legs for solid off-shore chances.

The parody on Nick Carter draws directly on a collection of paperbacks in Prague in Jiri Brdicka's possession. Brdicka is a gifted animation filmmaker, as well as a master storyteller of old Prague and Czech legends with that peculiar blend of fantasy and imagination, some adapted to feature pix under his own direction. Lipsky was a cofounder of the famous Satirical Theatre in Prague, where "Lemonade Joe" first saw the light of day and thereafter went on to a top kudo at the San Sebastian fest as a film.

Nick Carter (Michal Docolomansky) is seen in his New York office fending off attacks on his life like swatting flies, when the call from Prague comes to find a missing person (actually a dog). Off he goes and arrives in Prague, dressed in a disguise (an outlandish Czech outfit) that is easily seen through by friend and foe. His side-kick on the case is a sausage-and-beer detective played by Rudolf Hrusinsky, and his arch enemy is a mad baron with a man-eating (and dog-eating) plant named Adele. One crazy scene follows another as Nick courts a local beauty and the baron (an international criminal) tracks Nick.

In his detective work Carter uses dozens of gimmicks and odd-ball inventions, which makes "Adele" a visual feast for antique and memorabilia collectors.

The hotel he's staying at is art nouveau deluxe; costumes are accurate down to the last frill and hatpin; and old Prague has seldom been shown in a better light, inclusive of restaurants serving Pilsen beer and Czech sausages.

The high-point is when Carter disguises Hrusinsky (a face every Czech on the street knows as a veteran of stage and screen) as his man escaping across Prague in his getaway balloon. There's also the animated special effect to make the man-eating plant move and slurp when supper is in sight, ingeniously devised by Jan Svankmaier.

The treats don't stop there. Any film buff worth his salt will recognize "Fantomas" in the Nick Carter figure amid the running series of inside jokes recalling both the Louis Feuillade serial (1913-1914), on the master of disguises, and Georges Franju's "Judex" (1962), based on the exploits of the pulp hero (a "Fantomas" on the side of the law).

Credits are tops. A pic that is festival bait and augurs well for Czechoslovakia. With proper handling this could be an art house winner. —Holl.

Pe Aici Nu Se Trece
(No Trespassing)
(RUMANIAN-COLOR)

Bucharest, April 19.

A Rumaniafilm Production, Group Five, Bucharest; world rights, Rumaniafilm, Bucharest. Features entire cast. Directed by Doru Nastase. Screenplay, Titus Popovici; camera (color, cinemascope), Aurel Kostrakiewicz; music, Tiberiu Olah; sets, Guta Stirbu. Reviewed at Rumaniafilm Screening Room, Bucharest, April 18, '78. Running time: 150 MINS.
Cast: Silviu Stanculescu, Vlad Radescu, Ana Szeles, Vladimir Gaitan, George Motoi, Mihai Mereuta, Victor Mavrodineanu, Eugenia Bosinceanu, Cornel Coman, Sorin Kepa, Stefan Velniciuc, Ovidiu Moldovan, Ilarion Ciobanu.

A vet of some 20 feature pix, Doru Nastase has made adaptations of the "Leatherstocking Tales" as well as national epics. His specialty is the wide-screen and larger-than-life action stories that wed well to landscapes or battlegrounds. "No Trespassing" deals with a cadets' academy in Rumania at the end of the last war; the heroes are young lads who must momentarily halt the retreating German forces (as the country joins the Resistance) in a noble sacrificial gesture.

Although the suspense builds rather slowly, helmer Nastase does present the life of a military academy in a favorable light. The boys are nearly all friends and feel prepared to face the tragedy of war, including a sensitive master of the organ who has a great career ahead of himself and is particularly liked by the German military commander of the school. Since the boy is relieved from time to time to play Bach for the German officer-in-charge, it is assumed that he will not arise to the occasion with the others — he proves instead to be the sacrificial lamb who ties the entire story together.

There are some overexaggerated scenes towards the end, but in general this is a film with polish. —Holl.

Arriba Hazana
(Long Live Hazana)
(SPANISH-COLOR)

Madrid, June 8.

Sabre Films production. Features entire cast. Directed by Jose Maria Gutierrez; screenplay, Jose Samano and Jose Maria Gutierrez based on novel by Jose Maria Vaz de Soto, "El Infierno y la Brisa"; exec producer, Jose Samano; camera (Eastmancolor) Magi Torruella; music, Eduardo Aute; editor, Rosa Salgado. Reviewed at Cine Gran Via, Madrid, June 7, '78. Running time: 97 MINS.
Cast: Fernando Fernan Gomez, Hector Alterio, Jose Sacristan, Gabriel Llopart, Lola Herrera, Andres Isbert, Jose Luis Perez, Emilio Siefrist, Quique San Francisco, Agustin Navarro, Inaki Marimon, Hans Isbert.

The "Hazana" of the title is a schoolboy's mistake for Azana, the president of the Spanish Republic before the Civil War, one of the bogeymen of the Franco regime. Though the children in the parochial school where the action is set, presumably during the last years of Franco's dictatorship, don't really know who Azana was, his name is taken as a rallying call against the oppressive educational system they live under.

The subject of the medieval kind of education given to most children till recently in Spain could certainly have provided plenty of subject matter for a skilled writer. Unfortunately, the script for "Hazana" never quite decides where it's go-

ing; at times it veers towards adolescent humor and smart-aleck pranks from the boys as they fight the school system; at other times dramatic situations (and even homosexuality on the part of the principal) are touched upon but never developed.

Nor are we ever shown how the children really suffer from the system; and the mini-revolt they kick up in the second half of pic is also not terribly convincing. Otherwise, item is well-paced and thesping by Hector Alterio as the principal, Fernando Fernan Gomez as the hardline teacher and the children are topnotch. Other technical credits are good. Limited outlook commercially, though some interest might be aroused in secondary foreign circuits based on the laffs and anti-establishmentism in the film. — Besa.

Stin Letajiciho Ptacka
(Shadow of a Flying Bird)
(CZECH-COLOR)

Prague, June 2.

A Czechoslovak Film Production, Barradov Studios, Prague; world rights, Czeschoslovensky Film, Prague. Features entire cast. Directed by Jaroslav Balik. Screenplay, Jan Otcenasek. Only credits available. Reviewed at Czeschoslovensky Film Screening Room, Prague, June 1, '78. Running time: 90 MINS.
Cast unavailable.

Helmer Jaroslav Balik scored at the last Karlovy Vary fest with "One Gold Piece," a tale of lumberjacks in the Tatra mountains during the last war; the style was strongly realist and stamped with the helmer's psychological soundness. His "Shadow of a Flying Bird" moves in the same direction, this time exploring the pain and adjustment a family goes through in suffering the loss of a son, the only child the parents have.

Pic opens with a pair of lovers in a forest. After an idyllic affair together, they head for home on a motorbike and run headlong into an accident, killing the boy. The bereaved father arrives one day at the hospital to visit the girl, whom he is meeting for the first time and never heard about from his son before. The girl treats him rudely but obviously feels both loss and guilt.

Later the girl comes to stay with the family, as she is apparently without home, family, or profession. The mother gradually comes to the realization that the girl fills the vacuum left by the son's painful absence, but it later becomes clear that she hasn't been telling the whole truth about the affair and what really happened just before the accident.

One probing question, for instance, is whether the son was actually on his way home to present the

girlfirend to the parents — or travelling with her in exactly the opposite direction . . (as he apparently was, in the father's study of the accident on the road).

The upshot is a showdown and the girl's inclination to leave rather than stay. All of the principal characters, however, have changed in the process of examining themselves and their motives. The girl has also become familiar with the good qualities the boy possessed and seems to be convinced that the love she briefly shared was genuine.

Thesps and lensing are on the plus side. Script drags too much to carry the film in the long run, and there are too many open questions that need at least a hint of an answer to be taken at face value.

This is the kind of problem film Socialist countries delve into with moral lessons as an aim. Too pat for Western auds, but Balik deserves exposure on fest circuit and at Czech film weeks abroad. —Holl.

Gamin
(COLOMBIAN-FRENCH-COLOR-DOCU)

Cannes, May 22.

A Clause Antoine (for S.N.D.) Production, in collaboration with the Institut National de l'Audiovisuel et UNO, Bogota. Written and directed by Ciro Diran. Camera (color), Luis Cuesta; music, Francisco Zumaque; editing, Ciro and Joyce Duran. Reviewed at Cannes Film Fest (Directors' Fortnight), May 26, '78. Running time: 110 MINS.

This docu on children who run the streets of Bogota (and other large cities in Colombia and South America) — known as "Los Gaminos" — echoes news stories on the same in European magazines (a recent report appeared in the West German "Stern," for example). It also recalls Luis Bunuel's savagely true "Los Olvidados," which won a top prize at Cannes two decades ago.

"Gamin" uses hidden camera tricks and direct-cinema techniques to explore the world of children who beg, steal, and stoop to prostitution just to stay alive. The police can do nothing to stop the wave of crimes perpetrated by the poorly dressed and homeless kids, simply because they are the direct result of shanty-town slums: to do away with one means to correct the conditions that cause the slums in the first place. Helmer Diran doesn't polemicize on a better world — he doesn't have to, as the bare facts are chilling enough.

Docu shows all the tricks of the trade. A snatch of groceries from a woman's hands is shown on a busy downtown street. A boy places a nail on a railroad track to be hammered by a passing train into something close enough to a key for opening autos in residence areas and stealing radios. A girl barely in her teens paints her face before stepping onto the streets to solicit customers. A jar of gasoline is bought at a service station for sniffing: it deadens hunger pains in the stomach. These are just a few of a score of documentary and reenacted scenes on survival at its elementary and most frightening level.

If "Gamin" does nothing else, it pleas for justice in terms any social critic will readily understand. It's the kind of film that awakens the hard-heartened and politically naive to the complex problems of political revolution, social welfare programs, and the dignity of life itself. A must for docu fests and film conferences leaning toward the socially, engaged, documentary.
—*Holl*.

La Tortue Sur Le Dos
(As a Turtle on Its Back)
(FRENCH-COLOR)

Cannes, May 20.

A Filmoblic Production, Paris produced by Hubert Niogret; world rights, World Marketing Film, Paris. Stars Bernadette Lafont, Jean-Francois Stevenic. Directed by Luc Beraud. Screenplay, Beraud, Claude Miller; camera (color), Bruno Nuytten; sound, Joele van Effenterre; editor, Beraud. Reviewed at Cannes Film Fest (Film Market), May 19, '78. Running time: **110 MINS.**

Camille	Bernadette Lafont
Paul	Jean-Francois Stevenin
Nathalie	Virginie Thevenet
Madame Beuve	Veronique Silver
Pierre	Claude Miller
Sylvie	Marion Game
Nietzsche Student	Valerie Quenessen
The Arrogant Girl	Veronique Dancigers
Bad-Tempered Invalid	Jean Daste
Jean-Louis 1	Francois Lafarge
Jean-Louis 2	Etienne Chicot
Reveller Who Reads Manuscript	Michel Blanc
Prokosh	Sandy Withelaw
The Black	Souare Bhime
The Usherette	Jo Perque
Ava	Florence Lafuma

A debut pic, Luc Beraud's "As a Turtle on Its Back" quickly became a hot tip for film buffs scouring the Rue d'Antibes at the Cannes fest for something fresh by a new name. Beraud has directed a number of shorts and assisted such distinguished French helmers as Jacques Rivette, Marguerite Duras, Jean Eustache, and Claude Miller before branching out on his own. He coscripted Claude Miller's "Tell Him I Love Him" (based on Patricia Highsmith's "Sweet Sickness") and received help from Miller in return for "Turtle on Its Back," who also plays a part in the film.

This is an hilarious story of a writer who was a success with his first book, "Portraits," stemming from heady revolutionary days a decade ago, but hasn't written anything since. This literary impotence matches a fear of sexual impotence at the same time, plus a grown aggression against the woman he has been living with, a post-graduate student who supports him with an honest job on the side.

The would-be writer hangs around the house and cafes trying to get the juices going again, but it's no use no matter what means are tried — and they are some of the funniest inspiration tricks imaginable (stealing from other authors, loud marching music, seeking new sexual contacts, etc.). Gradually, his girl friend sees through him and he gets thrown out of bed and board — which proves to be a severe blow to his pride.

After seeking a reconciliation with little hope in sight, he takes a job as a ghost-writer to pay for hotels on the seamy side. A benefactress recognizes his plight and offers him the family villa; he accepts, but is trapped again — pencils are laying all over the guest room to prompt inspiration, from wherever it may come (even in the bathroom).

Now down on his luck and wandering the streets, our writer is picked up by a pair of hoodlums who threaten to beat him unless he shells out cash by any means possible. An accident lands him in a hospital, where he suddenly begins to write for the first time — only to be disturbed by a loud-mouth in the next bed. Slowly the muse returns as he writes down all the crazy things that are happening to him.

A comedy about a writer and writing, "Turtle on Its Back" is carried magnificently by thesp Jean-Francois Stevenin as Paul and Bernadette Lafont as his long-suffering girlfriend. Technical credits are another plus, although some of the gags are predictable and a bit worn. Beraud is a helmer to watch, and pic could score on fest circuit and art house cinemas with proper handling. —*Holl*.

Heaven Can Wait
(COLOR)

Outstanding comedy-drama. Big money.

Hollywood, June 23.

Paramount Pictures release, written (with Elaine May), produced and directed (with Buck Henry) by Warren Beatty; executive producers, Howard W. Koch Jr., Charles H. Maguire. Features entire cast. Based on the play by Harry Segall; camera (Movielab Color), William A. Fraker; editors, Robert C. Jones, Don Zimmerman; music, Dave Grusin; production design, Paul Sylbert; art direction, Edwin O'Donovan; set decoration, George Gaines; sound, John K. Wilkinson, Tommy Overton; costumes-wardrobe, Theadora Van Runkle, Richard Bruno, Mike Hoffman, Arlene Encell; asst. director, Koch. Reviewed at Paramount Studios, L.A., June 23, '78. (MPAA Rating: PG.) Running time, **100 MINS.**

Joe Pendleton	Warren Beatty
Betty Logan	Julie Christie
Mr. Jordan	James Mason
Max Corkle	Jack Warden
Tony Abbott	Charles Grodin
Julia Farnsworth	Dyan Cannon
The Escort	Buck Henry
Det. Krim	Vincent Gardenia
Sisk	Joseph Maher
Head Coach	Dolph Sweet
Team Manager	R.G. Armstrong
Former Team Owner	John Randolph
Nuclear Reporter	William Sylvester
Oppenheim	Keene Curtis
Bentley	Hamilton Camp
Lavinia	Jeannie Linero
Everett	Arthur Malet
Corinne	Stephanie Faracy

"Heaven Can Wait" is an outstanding film. Harry Segall's fantasy comedy-drama, made in 1941 by Columbia as "Here Comes Mr. Jordan," returns in an updated, slightly more macabre treatment. Elaine May and Warren Beatty scripted, Buck Henry and Beatty directed, and Beatty heads the below-title cast in his own sharp production. Exec producers Howard W. Koch Jr. and Charles H. McGuire also must share credit for the superb results. This looks like another big winner for Paramount.

The years have been good to Beatty in that there is now a bedrock of maturity in his screen charisma without any loss of the quiet exuberance that has endured. He plays an aging footbal star, prematurely summoned to judgment after a traffic accident because celestial messenger (played by co-director Henry) jumped the gun. This embarrasses James Mason into permitting Beatty to inhabit temporarily another body. The only available one is that of a wealthy industrialist whose death is plotted by floozy wife Dyan Cannon and Charles Grodin, the tycoon's nerd secretary.

Julie Christie falls for the rich guy, whose main ambition is to resume his football career in which coach Jack Warden plays an important part. Beatty eventually switches characters again, Christie somehow makes the connection and all ends well. Entire cast is excellent. Warden, one of whose screen highlights is remembered in Beatty's "Shampoo," again hits a new peak as the loyal friend.

Script and direction are very strong, providing a rich mix of visual and verbal humor that is controlled and avoids the extremes of cheap vulgarity and overly esoteric whimsy. Production credits are all tops.

In the earlier version, Robert Montgomery handled the Beatty character, and other pairings are: Christie-Evelyn Keyes; Mason-Claude Rains; Cannon-Rita Johnson; Grodin — John Emery; Warden-James Gleason; Henry-Edward Everett Horton; butler Joseph Maher-Halliwell Hobbes; detective Vincent Gardenia-Donald MacBride in 1941; Alexander Hall directed and Everett Riskin produced.

This remake is not to be confused with a 1943 20th-Fox pic of Ernst Lubitsch (with a different story) which used the original Segall play title. —*Murf*.

International Velvet
(BRITISH-COLOR)

Excellent family entertainment. Tatum O'Neal heads fine cast. Promising outlook.

Hollywood, June 20.

United Artists release of a Metro-Goldwyn-Mayer picture. Written, produced and directed by Bryan Forbes. Stars Tatum O'Neal, Christopher Plummer, Anthony Hopkins, Nanette Newman. Adapted from the novel, "National Velvet," by Enid Bagnold; camera (Metrocolor), Tony Imi; aerial camera, Geoff Mulligan; U.S.A. race sequence camera, Edward R. Brown; editor, Timothy Gee; music, Francis Lai; production design, Keith Wilson; set decoration, Ian Whittaker; sound, Ken Barker, Gus Lloyd; costumes-wardrobe, John Furness, Dorothy Edwards, John Hilling; asst. director, Philip Shaw; stunt coordinator, Richard Graydon; U.S.A. racing sequence coordinator, Don Boyd. Reviewed at MGM Studios, Culver City, June 20, '78. (MPAA Rating: PG.) Running time, **125 MINS.**

Sarah Brown	Tatum O'Neal
John Seaton	Christopher Plummer
Capt. Johnson	Anthony Hopkins
Velvet Brown	Nanette Newman
Pilot	Peter Barkworth
Mr. Curtis	Dinsdale Landen
Beth	Sarah Bullen
Scott Saunders	Jeffrey Byron
Tim	Richard Warwick
Wilson	Daniel Abineri
Roger	Jason White
Mike	Martin Neil
Howard	Douglas Reith

"International Velvet" is an extremely fine film for (in the best sense) family audiences. Bryan Forbes wrote, produced and directed the sequel to "National Velvet" in such a way as to provide sentiment, excitement and dual-level drama that shoud ring true with its target audience. Tatum O'Neal heads a strong cast as an orphaned teenager whose attachment to a horse leads to her own adjustment and maturity. The warmly pastoral Metro-Goldwyn-Mayer picture, handsomely produced at Pinewood Studios plus many excellent locations, should make a very good commercial complement to the hyper-action film competition during the summer and fall months.

Most sequels pick up the story quite soon after the original, but here Forbes, in expanding on Enid Bagnold's original "Velvet" novel, wisely jumps a quarter century, in the process creating viable contemporary situations and conflict. "National Velvet," made in 1944 by Pandro S. Berman and Clarence Brown, made a new star of Elizabeth Taylor as the kid whose love for an unruly horse led to her winning a major race, though later she was disqualified for being an underage girl.

In the new script, the original Velvet Brown is now nearing middle age as a childless divorcee though happy in a relationship with Christopher Plummer, an author who provides her much emotional support. Taylor at one time was discussed to take this part, and it would have been a superb vehicle for her. But it's Nanette Newman's good fortune to play the role, and she does so excellently. Newman's periodic voiceovers help bridge the past and present, and the Plummer-Newman interplay provides a most effective interwoven dramatic plot line which lends a grownup tone.

All this is to the good while O'Neal evolves from a hostile alien orphan to a high degree of adolescent maturity. O'Neal has grown some, and the precocious antics of "Paper Moon" and "The Bad News Bears" are long behind her — as they should be. What is sometimes known as the awkward age is upon her, but far from being a handicap, this is a very propitious transition vehicle that few moppet stars have ever had the advantage of getting. Fact that she has not been over-exposed in a slew of pre-teen roles is fortuitous, and the occasional stumbles in characterization are handily covered by the film's plotting and pacing.

Speaking of which, the pic's 125-minute length is precisely that of "National Velvet" in its Christmas, 1944, preem dates. Forbes' use of brief sequences and rapid dissolves keeps everything moving smartly along. Tony Imi's cinematography and Keith Wilson's production design provide a fine canvas for the story. Francis Lai's music is also a good asset.

Also starred above title with O'Neal, Plummer and Newman is Anthony Hopkins, excellent as the equestrian team trainer whose dedication to the sport will give con-

temporary audiences a graceful exposition of what is going on. Jeffrey Byron, the young American Olympics opponent with whom O'Neal falls in love, and Sarah Bullen, an older British teammate, are very good in key support.

The final 30 minutes of the film are quite effective in depicting the climactic Olympic events. The scenes move in a natural time and not the freeze-frame type of hyping which in this film would destroy the gracefulness that has preceded.

As usual, it's got the superb Metro production polish. Rank's lab did the fine processing, and MGM's domestic lab the prints. —Murf.

Ottokar Der Weltverbesserer
(Ottokar, The World Reformer)
(EAST GERMAN-COLOR)

Berlin, June 7.
A DEFA Film Production, Group Roter Kreis, Berlin; world rights, DEFA Aussenhandel, Berlin. Features entire cast. Directed by Hans Kratzert. Screenplay, Gudrun Duebener; camera (color), Wolfgang Braumann; sets, Joachim Otto; music, Guenther Fischer. Reviewed at DEFA Aussenhandel Screening Room, Berlin, June 6, '78. Running time: 85 MINS.
Cast: Lars Herrmann (Ottokar), Steffen Bannischka (Harald), Steffen Endert (Pillenheini), Guenter Junghans (Father Domma), Micaela Kriessler (Mother Dimma), Kurt Boewe (School Master Burschelmann), Wolfgang Winkler (Father Kugler), Walfriede Schmitt (Mother Kugler), Fred Artur Geppert (School Master Luschmihl), Simone von Zglinicki (Miss Kinzel), Karin Gregorek (Miss Pittuhn), Dieter Wien (School Master Kurz), Marianne Wuenscher (School Mistress Seidenschnur).

A children's pic with some lively twists, Hans Kratzert's "Ottokar, The World Reformer" focuses on the adventures of a young lad who can't help butting in where he's not wanted. The trouble is that Ottokar, 10, is usually right, and the teachers at school can put him down only with difficulty when the cards are on the table.

Ottokar's sense of decency and justice particularly flares up whenever his nemesis in the classroom picks on the girls or resorts to mean tricks, but he also intervenes in the world of older students and grownups if the occasion demands.

It's when Ottokar meddles too strongly that the story gets particularly interesting: he climbs trees next to the school to overhear a teachers' meeting; he releases a lot of energy in his Pioneer group when he campaigns against his classroom opponent; and he gets into trouble trying to cover up for an older student's foolish drinking bout (to prove his manhood, apparently). Occasionally, he gets a black eye or swollen lip, falls into a mud puddle, and so on.

Pic is delightfully carried by Lars Herrmann as Ottokar, a young

acting find who is just right for this film with a intuitive flair for fun and nonsense. Good bet at a children's fest for some kind of kudo, even with a light social message slipped in on the side. —Holl.

Die Flucht
(The Flight)
(EAST GERMAN-COLOR)

Berlin, June 7.
A DEFA Film Production, Roter Kreis Group, Berlin, world rights, DEFA Aussenhandel, Berlin. Features entire cast. Directed by Roland Graef. Screenplay, Hannes Huettner, Braef; camera (color), Claus Neumann; sets: Georg Wratsch; music, Guenther Fischer; editing, Monika Schindler. Reviewed at DEFA Aussenhandel Screening Room, Berlin, June 6, '78. Running time: 90 MINS.
Dr. Volkmar Schmidt . . . . Armin Mueller-Stahl
Katharina . . . . Jenny Groellmann
Mittenzwei . . . . Erika Pelikowsky
Meissner . . . . Wilhelm Koch-Hooge
Gudrun . . . . Karin Gregorek
Mrs. Seebohm . . . . Simone von Zglinicki
The Fat Man . . . . Rolf Hoppe
Zeiske . . . . Wilfried Glatzeder
Schmith's Father . . . . Gerhard Bienert

Roland Graef's "The Flight" is worth a critical look-see if only because of its red-hot theme: the question of "body-brokers" peddling people from East to West Germany for a price.

In the case of a dissatisfied East German physician who feels he is being discriminated against at home, the price turns out to be high as he can't quite make up his mind which side he prefers and dies on a roadside after the escape attempt falls to pieces because of his own indecision.

Pic is not strong enough to be taken seriously. There are plenty of holes in this one-sided view of the situation, but even more controversial are the illusions about what goes on in the West, where some of the scenes take place.

"The Flight" deals with an individual who is both ambitious and in love with a young specialist under his care in a clinic where infantile mortality in premature birth is studied. Since his research is not properly recognized at the clinic, he signs a contract with a mysterious "fat man" from the West who can arrange for his flight to West Germany, where he could conceivably take over a children's clinic of his own. Then, as he prepares to make good his flight, the word comes that he can do his research in the German Democratic Republic after all, although under conditions that still don't please him.

Meanwhile, a colleague has tried to flee to the West while on vacation in the Balkans (or some such point where false passports can be effectively used) and is caught; it surfaces that the idea was his wife's

and the escape was on impulse rather than entirely intentional.

In any case, pic points out that doctors are rather prone to escapes to the West — a reality rather openly handled in the story, which to the GDR's credit (considering that the admittance of the presence of the Wall as a primary measure to stop brain-drain is p.r. dynamite).

In the end, the doctor decides to go anyway but wants to take his newly found girl friend with him. He makes the mistake, however, of not telling her until the last minute, just when he fears that, due to the signed contract, there's now no way back to his old status — he would lose all privileges when the cat is out of the bag. While waiting for the pick-up on the highway, the girl balks; he gets slugged fatally on the head for his moral indecision.

Despite a lot of loose ends in the story, a pic to be seen nonetheless. Credits and thesps are not up to standard GDR fare. — Holl.

National Lampoon's Animal House
(COLOR)

Okay maiden screen transplant of famed magazine's humor. Pleasant outlook, if uneven.

Hollywood, June 16.
Universal Pictures release. Produced by Matty Simmons, Ivan Reitman. Directed by John Landis. Features entire cast. Screenplay, Harold Ramis, Douglas Kenney, Chris Miller; camera (Technicolor), Charles Correll; editor, George Folsey Jr.; music, Elmer Bernstein; art direction, John J. Lloyd; set decoration, Hal Gausman; sound, Bill Varney. Howard Wollman, Alan Holly, William B. Kaplan; costumes-wardrobe, Deborah Nadoolman, Dan Chichester, Gene Deardorff; asst. director, Cliff Coleman; second unit director and stunt coordinator, Gary R. McLarty. Reviewed at Universal Studios, L.A., June 16, '78. (MPAA Rating: R) Running time, 109 MINS.
John Blutarsky (Bluto) . . . . . . John Belushi
Eric Stratton (Otter) . . . . . . Tom Matheson
Dean Wormer . . . : . . . . John Vernon
Marion Wormer . . . . Verna Bloom
Larry Kroger (Pinto) . . . . . Thomas Hulce
Mayor Carmine DePasto . . Cesare Danova
Mandy Pepperidge . . . . Mary Louise Weller
Kent Dorfman (Flounder) . . . Stephen Furst
Greg Marmalard . . . . James Daughton
Daniel Day (D-Day) . . . . Bruce McGill
Doug Neidermeyer . . . . Mark Metcalf
Otis Day . . . . DeWayne Jessie
Katy . . . . Karen Allen
Robert Hoover . . . . James Widdoes
Babs Jensen . . . . Martha Smith
Clorette DePasto . . . . Sarah Holcomb
Shelly . . . . Lisa Baur
Chip Diller . . . . Kevin Bacon
Donald Schoenstein (Boon) . Peter Riegert
Stork . . . . Douglas Kenney
Hardbar . . . . Christian Miller
Mothball . . . . Joshua Daniel
B.B. . . . . Bruce Bonnheim
Prof. Jennings . . . . Donald Sutherland

Steady readers of the National Lampoon may find "National Lampoon's Animal House" a somewhat soft-pedalled, punches-pulled parody of college campus life circa

1962. However, there's enough bite and bawdiness in the Matty Simmon-Ivan Reitman production to provide lots of smiles and several broad guffaws. John Landis' direction and a cast of relative newcomers are good elements in what shapes as a promising, if not spectacular, b.o. prospect for Universal release. In any case, it's worth developing another Lampoon film project.

Writers Harold Ramis, Goudlas Kenney and Chris Miller have concocted a pre-Vietnam college confrontation (allegedly based on Miller's experiences at Dartmouth) between a scruffy fraternity and the high-elegant campus society. Interspersed in the new faces are the more familiar John Vernon, projecting well his meany charisma here as a corrupt dean; Verna Bloom, Vernon's swinging wife; Cesare Danova, the Mafioso-type mayor of the college town; Donald Sutherland as the super-hip young professor in the days when squares were still saying "hep."

Of no small and subtle artistic help is the score by Elmer Bernstein which blithely wafts "Gaudeamus Igitur" themes amidst the tumult of beer "orgies," neo-Nazi ROTC drills, cafeteria food fights and a climactic disruption of a traditional Homecoming street parade. (Second unit director and stunt coordinator Gary R. McLarty plus the special effects by Hal and Henry Millar are in strong evidence. Film was shot in 35 days on Oregon locations.)

Among the younger players, John Belushi and Tim Matheson are very good as leaders of the unruly fraternity, while James Daughton and Mark Metcalf are prominent as the snotty fratmen, all of whom, quite deliberately, look like Nixon White House aides. (The now-required epilog of character destinies in fact notes that one of them, a Nixon aide, was "raped n prison, 1974.")

Martha Smith, as a plastic hostess type, gets the final big laughs in the 109-minute film: Her ultimate fate is "Tour Guide, Universal Studios," and scrawled on the usually-blanked off Universal tour plug is the exhortation to "Ask for Babs" (her character name). Hopefully the film cans will alert projectionists to this funny fadeout fillip.

Although rated R, film is what could loosely be considered a "soft" R. Lampoon magazine fanatics might have wished for more pungent material on the theory that if you're gonna get an R, you might as well get a strong one. But some Lampoon on the screen is better than none. —*Murf.*

Convoy
(COLOR)

Formula Sam Peckinpah fodder for fast summer playoff.

Hollywood, June 21.

United Artists release, produced by Robert M. Sherman; executive producers for EMI, Michael Deeley, Barry Spikings. Stars Kris Kristofferson, Ali MacGraw. Directed by Sam Peckinpah. Screenplay, B.W.L. Norton, based on the song by C.W. McCall; camera (DeLuxe Color), Harry Stradling Jr.; second unit camera, Richard Kelley; editors, Graeme Clifford, John Wright, Garth Craven; music, Chip Davis; song lyrics, Bill Fries; production design, Fernando Carrere; art direction, J. Dennis Washington, Francis Lombardo; sound, Don Mitchell, Bob Litt, Steve Maslow, Bill Randall; costumes-wardrobe, Kent James, Carol James; asst. directors, Tom Shaw, Richard Wells, Pepi Lenzi, John Poer, Cliff Coleman, Newton Arnold; second unit directors, Walter Kelley, James Coburn. Reviewed at MGM Studios, Culver City, June 21, '78. (MPAA Rating: PG.) Running time: 110 MINS.

Rubber Duck . . . . Kris Kristofferson
Melissa . . . . Ali MacGraw
Lyle Wallace . . . . Ernest Borgnine
Pig Pen . . . . Burt Young
Widow Woman . . . . Madge Sinclair
Spider Mike . . . . Franklyn Ajaye
Chuck Arnoldi . . . . Brian Davies
Gov. Haskins . . . . Seymour Cassel
Violet . . . . Cassie Yates
Hamilton . . . . Walter Kelley

Sam Peckinpah's "Convoy" starts out as "Smokey And The Bandit," segues into either "Moby Dick" or "Les Miserables," and ends in the usual script confusion and disarray, the whole stew peppered with the vulgar excess of random truck crashes and miscellaneous destruction. Kris Kristofferson stars as a likeable roustabout who accidentally becomes a folk hero, while Ali MacGraw recycles about three formula reactions throughout her nothing part. Lots of people worked before and behind the cameras in this United Artists-EMI project, produced on southwest freeway locations by Robert Sherman. It's strictly a summer-popcorn picture for the nondiscriminating.

B.W.L. Norton gets writing credit using C.W. McCall's c&w poptune lyric as a basis. No matter. Peckinpah's films display common elements and clumsy analogies, overwhelmed with logistical fireworks and drunken changes of dramatic emphasis.

This time around, Kristofferson (who, miraculously, seems to survive these banalities) is a trucker whose longtime nemesis, speed-trap-blackmailer cop Ernest Borgnine, pursues him with a vengeance through what appears to be three states. Burt Young, Franklyn Ajaye and Madge Sinclair head, literally, a mile of sign-on rebels whose collective presence then attracts media and political attention. Every few minutes there's some new roadblock to run, alternating with pithy comments on The

Meaning Of It All. There's a whole lot of nothing going on here.

Since Peckinpah's films no longer kill lots of people in slow-motion ballet, this job, with its major concentration on property destruction, gets by with a PG rating. Scores of craft personnel assisted in setting up the unmotivated crashes and such; it's not their fault there's nothing in the story to really justify such a cynical waste of time and money. —*Murf.*

Pastorale
(SOVIET-COLOR)

Moscow, June 8.

A Gruzia-Film Production, Georgia; world rights, Goskino, Moscow. Written and directed by Otar Yoseliani. Only credits available. Reviewed at Goskino, Moscow, June 7, '78. Running time: 90 MINS.

Some Western critics have rated Georgian helmer Otar Yoseliani second only to Andrei Tarkovsky in the cadre of New Soviet Cinema directors. And this despite only three known feature pix: "When Leaves Fall" (1967), unspooled in Cannes in the Week of the Critics, "Once There Was a Song-Thrush" (1970), and "Pastorale" (1976). The three films can be looked upon as a unit or trilogy, but there is a fourth feature, "April" (1961), which, never released, also apparently bears the marks of his central theme.

Yoseliani defends the spiritual in life. His style is quiet and meditative, manifesting a feeling for music and beauty while highlighting such abstract realities as friendship, fantasy, and passion for its own sake.

"Pastorale," with barely a narrative story, is anchored to a recurring motif: the presence of a string quartet in a Georgian village on summer holidays. Once this esthetic peg is taken into consideration, the film unfolds like a flower in springtime to put everything in lyrical, "pastoral" focus.

"Pastorale" is a modest film. It doesn't preach or moralize, hasn't a story in the strict sense to tell, and doesn't fall into the prejudicial "documentary" category in painting an accurate portrait of village life. The film takes life's pulse as the filmmaker sees it. Yoseliani seeks to record the everyday in its more poetic moments, to underscore man's taste for living in a hurry-up, industrialized civilization. Undoubtedly, pic will find support on the fest circuit.

Yoseliani has a distinct gift for observation. Trained first as a painter and musician in Tbilisi, he went to Moscow to study engineering before switching over to the film school. He worked as a common laborer and once went to sea. As a filmmaker, he is Georgian to the bone in that he stays close to the theme and doesn't embellish the facts. All he adds is a respect for the

traditional, with its regard for fantasy and dreams, and an understanding of the vulnerable in man.

"Pastorale" moves like a symphony. Music stemming from the rehearsals of the string quartet in a village house blends into the life of the family renting the group (two boys, two girls) rooms, thereby fascinating the children and a young girl in particular. Cattle, goats, and pigs pass along the street, and workers are shown going to and from the fields. Rain comes at night and beats on the roof: the contact with nature — the musicians picking berries, the agronom illegally dynamiting a river to "catch" fish, an air plane chemically sprays the fields — remains constantly in the foreground. Wine is drunk with gusto, and a feast in typical Georgian fashion is prepared.

On rainy days piano lessons are given and a chess game commences; charades and record albums and painting while the time away. More practice by the string quartet. Meanwhile, a house is being built next to the property with a window pointing in the direction of the neighbors; a quarrel ensues. The differences are patched up at the banquet. There the village politicians also show up, party bosses who earlier scolded offenders for illegal delivery of building materials or farm supplies and goods.

A slight touch of romance between two young people is thrown in on the side. The departure of the musicians brings a tinge of sadness. Sometimes the viewer is nudged to laugh or smile by a person or object on the screen after they become indispensable figures in the landscape. Once, the face of Yoseliani himself can be seen impishly staring from the back of a passing bus.

"Pastorale" is a filmic composition of images and sounds. Little or no dialog is necessary to understand what's going on (the version seen was in Georgian dialect with a talk-over in Russian, translated into English when an occasion demanded it). It is the work of a unique, individual talent. —*Holl.*

Good Guys Wear Black
(COLOR)

Chicago, June 27.

A Mar Vista Production of a Ted Post Film. Directed by Ted Post. Produced by Allan F. Bodoh; exec producer, Michael Leone. Features entire cast. Screenplay, Bruce Cohn, Mark Medoff from story by Joseph Fraley; music composed and conducted by Craig Safan. No other credits available. Reviewed at the United Artists Theatre, Chicago. June 14, 1978. (MPAA Rating: PG). Running Time: 96 MINS.

John T. Booker . . . . Chuck Norris
Margaret . . . . Anne Archer
Murray . . . . Lloyd Haynes
Conrad Morgan . . . . James Franciscus
Government Man . . . . Dana Andrews
Doorman . . . . Jim Backus

A late-in-the-cycle attempt to cash in on the audience appeal for karate champion and former Bruce Lee film star Chuck T. Norris would seem the major reason for "Good Guys Wear Black." But in actuality the film is a well-made although somewhat unrealistic yarn of government corruption with enough action to swell boxoffice receipts for indie distrib American Cinema.

Although film has some validity as a tale of political corruption selling point is action sequences which are abundant. Norris plays John T. Booker, former head of a top Vietnam Army commando unit that used to rescue American POW's behind enemy lines. The role is much like the Clint Eastwood/Charles Bronson one-man vigilante, and Norris possesses the good looks, strength and agility needed to carry it off.

Settled into a quiet post-war life as a teacher, Booker's military past is dredged up by a woman investigating his unit's last mission (done for the CIA) where the men were left stranded in a Vietnamese jungle waiting for American rescue helicopters that never showed. Question to be answered becomes whether Booker and his group were set up by the government and if so why.

As story progresses, the remaining members of Booker's unit are systematically killed leaving Booker to unravel the mystery. He receives some help from CIA agent Lloyd Haynes, government man Dana Andrews and sharp lawyer lady friend Ann Archer. All are believable but focus is on the indestructable Booker as he takes revenge against the corrupt politician (James Franciscus) he ultimately discovers sold him out.

Although script creates suspenseful moments it's at times thin on believability, especially when each of Booker's buddies are killed precisely when they are to learn of the government's evil deeds. Technical credits and stunts are superior although latter are also overplayed as audience is asked to believe Norris can karate kick an enemy through the windshield of a speeding car and come out without a scratch. But this is the stuff that makes action films and no doubt will be exciting fare for its aficionados. —Berg.

Hiev Up
(Heave Up)
(EAST GERMAN-COLOR)

Berlin, June 7.
A DEFA Film Production, in collaboration with GDR Television, Berlin; world rights, DEFA Aussenhandel, Berlin. Features entire cast. Written and directed by Joachim Hasler. Camera (color), Peter Krause; sets, Georg Wratsch; music, Gert Natschinski; editing, Annelise Hinze-Soko-

lowa. Reviewed at DEFA Aussenhandel Screening Room, Berlin, June 6, '78. Running time: 90 MINS.
Cast: Alfred Mueller, Regina Beyer, Juergen Heirich, Solveig Mueller, Dietmar Richter-Reineck, Madeleine Lierck, Fred Delmare, Renate Mallon, Ruediger Joswig, Erik S. Klein, Ostara Koerner, Frank Strobel, Peter Friedrichson, Arnim Muehlstaedt.

A comedy about sailors and their lives on board and in port, Joachim Hasler's "Heave Up" relies mostly on the merchant-ship crew's necessity to settle down and spend freetime with each other and with a woman of their choice, instead of wasting opportunities by running off singly whenever a port looms in sight. The humor is too local to win favor abroad, but the pic does have a few episodes that draw a laugh because of the tangles in the plot.

One of the crew happens to be courting the captain's daughter — which means, of course, that matters will now be too intimate, and the ship's captain is against that. Besides, the lad is question does more running around than staying put. Another nice gag is built around a sailor who uses the crew's celebration party as the occasion for his wedding reception, because it's cheaper in the long run.

Credits are commendable, but story lags badly in the middle. And a song, "All Together," lacks a good song-and-dance team. — Holl.

The Fox In The Chicken Coop
(ISRAELI-COLOR)

Tel Aviv, May 21.
Forum Films release of Hashualim Production. Produced by Itzhak Kol and Ephraim Kishon. Written and directed by Ephraim Kishon. Camera (color), David Gurfinkel. Music: Nurit Hirsch. Edited by Hadassa Shani. Reviewed May 20, '78 in Tel Aviv. Running time: 90 MINS.
Cast: Shai K. Ophir, Shoshana Shani, Mosko Alkalay, Gideon Singer, Mordechai Ben-Zeev, Shlomo Vishinsky, Yoseph Bashi.

This may well be the first outright casualty in the otherwise extremely successful career of Ephraim Kishon. For years now, he has been a best-selling humorist of international reputation, particularly in German-speaking countries. And his films, while not always favorably reviewed, have scored heavily at the boxoffice in Israel. This time around, it seems that critics and public agree and they have turned their backs on it.

An old-time labor activist and political figure, who has to retire for his health to a remote mountain village, finds to his utter dismay, that no one has ever heard about him and nobody cares for politics, right or left. The story saw light some years ago as a novel. The plot elaborates how in a few weeks the whole village turns from an idyllic para-

dise to a political cauldron, thanks to the politician's effort to raise public spirit and responsibility. Concept may have been timely, when it was first published, as it contained numerous, if transparent, barbs, at some prominent political leaders in Israel. Yet, even then, the heavy handed satire seemed suspicious and this was not one of Kishon's bigger literary successes.

But since that time many things have changed. Its contents will have a hard time finding the right audience, as it may seem too highbrow for amateurs of broad comedies and too pedestrian for the sophisticated public. And for the first time, the film isn't funny

Shai K. Ophir, in the lead, is far too young for the character he plays, supposed to be somewhere in his 70s. Usually a fine cinema actor, Ophir has to rely heavily on make-up and tends to overplay. The rest of the cast look out of their depth, going for heavy mimicry, and even old-time Kishon veterans from previous pix and plays, such as Shoshana Shani, Zaharira Harifai and others, find it hard to make the shallow-jokes work.

While technical credits are okay and special efforts have been made, the commercial outlook here seems pretty grim as film is in only one cinema, in Tel Aviv, after a country-wide release only three weeks ago. But since film has been sold, on Kishon's reputation, to some territories, it may still recover most of its original cost. —Edna.

Brandstellen
(Scenes Of Fires)
(EAST GERMAN-COLOR)

Berlin, June 6.
A DEFA Film Production, Group "Berlin," world rights, DEFA Aussenhandel, Berlin. Features entire cast. Directed by Horst E. Brandt. Screenplay, Gerhard Bengsch; based on novel of same name by Franz Josef Degenhardt; camera (color), Rolf Sohre; sets, Christoph Schneider; music, Peter Gotthardt, Reiner Gaebler; theme music, Lokomotive Kreuzberg; editing, Karisch Kusche. Reviewed at DEFA Aussenhandel Screening Room, Berlin, June 5, '78. Running time: 90 MINS.
Bruno Kappel .... Dieter Mann
Maria Ronsdorf ....Heidemarie Wenzel
Herbert Ronsdorf .... Wolfgang Dehler
Tom Strathmann .... Eduard Haussmann
Doris Strathmann .... Petra Hinze
Heinz Spormann Dietmar Richter-Reinick
Pacco .... Berko Acker
Schiebeck ....Thomas Wolf
Martin Baller .... Dieter Wien
Thea .... Annekathrin Buerger

Occasionally a West German writer has the distinction of seeing his novels and stories filmed in East Germany: one is the "proletarian" storyteller Max von der Gruen; another is the song-writer and novelist Franz Josef Degenhardt.

Degenhardt's "Scenes of Fires" under the direction of Horst E.

Brandt is the latest to raise eyebrows across the border, for it deals with anarchy, terrorists, political sympathizers, and the constitutionally legal German Communist Party in West Germany — all neatly thrown together into an action thriller.

The story runs at a quick pace, holding close to the original with a variety of sub-plots beneath the main narrative. It seems a famous Hamburg lawyer once knew, on rather intimate terms, a now notorious woman anarchist, who is in hiding after a shoot out with the police and needs his legal help. The lawyer used to belong to the enlightened Left, as did the city's public prosecutor (a convenient coincidence), which can be particularly embarrassing to the latter. The anarchist needs money, but she's also wounded and hanging around with petty thieves and conmen for the most part. The lawyer drops his boring business and goes off to meet his former love to test his emotions and beliefs.

Along the way he meets a woman teacher who, as a card-carrying member of the German Communist Party, has lost her job under the sting of "Berufsverbot" (a legal tactic whereby Left-leaning Communists and Social Democrats can, be discriminated against as "dangerous to the country"). The girl belongs to a citizens' group fighting to stop a forest preserve and nature-park from being turned into a NATO site. There's the inevitable confrontation with the police.

The lawyer finds himself standing between the causes of two women, also facing the question of his career for the first time. Further, he meets foreign workers and average citizens with problems of their own. His experiences in the socalled "Underground" where the anarchist goes for help (a doctor for the wound), also demands a final realization of which way the former 1968 student revolt is now heading — towards violence and terrorism. In the end, the hero shelves his job and joins the school teacher, leaving anarchy to its own

Degenhardt obviously meant to portray the thinking behind the Baader-Meinhof phenomenon in West Germany. Brandt's pic, on the other hand, only skims the surface of main political events over the past few years, and leaves out a lot of historical and current truths on the matter. Still, this is an East German pic on West Germany and reveals a line of thinking thereby. A must for East German film weeks.
—Holl

A Santa Alianca
(The Holy Alliance)
(PORTUGUESE-COLOR)

———

Cannes, May 22.

A Portuguese Cinema Institute Production, Lisbon. Features entire cast. Written, directed, and edited by Eduardo Geada. Camera (color), Manuel Costa e Silva; music, Pedro Osorio. Reviewed at Cannes Film Fest (Directors' Fortnight), May 21, '78. Running time: 110 MINS.

Cast: Io Apollini, Lia Gama, Henrique Viana, Helena Isabel, Paulo Duarte, Jose De Castro, David Silva.

———

Like other Portuguese feature pix today, Eduardo Geada's "the Holy Alliance" reviews the political events in his country since the April 1974 military coup. It seeks with talky narrative and heavy symbolism to show how the Left and Right both laid claim to the future of Portugal and then reduced revolutionary fervor to staid ideology.

But at the same time it's a film about the awakening of the social consciousness to change and political action. "The Holy Alliance" is the most interesting pic to emerge from Portugal over the past three years, offering evidence that the Portuguese Cinema Institute has matured into a social force to reckon with. A strong national cinema may be on the horizon.

The main figure of pic is a rich middle class bourgeoise businessman who despises Socialism in its extreme "Red" form. He visits an enchanting theatre actress on the side (who supports the Left), while maintaining a fiercely authoritarian household in his domestic life.

The wife and son are treated like his property, the former dying when she attempts a secret abortion at home, and the latter awakening to sex when the father drops him one evening in the arms of a lady-of-leisure. The burial scene comes across particularly as a cold, stifling ceremony reflecting the past puritan suppression of the country's spirit.

The Left is not spared criticism either. A revolutionary theatre group prepares an agitprop production for the masses. But when the performance takes place, they play to empty seats — in the end, it was the learning process among the actors that counted the most.

"Holy Alliance" moves slowly and could have said everything in half the time. Undoubtedly, it holds major interest for native auds via nuances in dialogue and could be of some interest to political science buffs abroad. Boxoffice outlook is slim. —Holl.

Fah Larng Fon
(After the Rain)
(THAI-COLOR)

———

Bangkok, May 13.

A Jirabunterng Films release. Produced by Jirawan Kampana Senyakorn. Features entire cast. Written, edited and directed by Pisan Akaraseni. Story, Maj. Gen. Bunterng Kampana Senyakorn; camera (color), Boonseng Sitti; music, Movala Vorakit; sound recording, Maitree Janjarasskul; art direction, Pisan Akaraseni; asst. director, Jaran. Reviewed at Coliseum Theatre, Bangkok, May 12, '78. Running time: 120 MINS

Garand	Vitoon Karuna
Phanes	Ampha Pusit
Darat	Nawarat Yukthanan
Wan	Piathip Kumvongse
Opoh	Dek Chai Apirat
Cheng	Jamroon Huajun

———

In a two handkerchief film, Ampha Pusit becomes an overnight sensation here via her role as an ever suffering wife and mother, forsaken by her husband (Vitoon Karuna), who falls prey to the feminine wiles of a spoiled rich girl (Nawarat Yukthanan).

Things might have been different, if only Ampha and Vitoon had a chance to talk about their problem. But that might lead to a possible reconciliation, and that is not what the story is after. It seeks to reunite another newcomer, Dek Chai Apirat, who plays Vitoon and Ampha's son, about eight years or so after Ampha's death for the tear-jerking finale.

Ampha's self-sacrifice involving running away from Vitoon and working at a construction site to support herself and her young son is rendered vaguely. More emphasis is on child actor Dek Chai Apirat. Ampha makes her own bid at stardom by having the first portion focussed almost entirely on her, since she dies before halfway through the film and her subsequent reappearances occur only as flashbacks.

Director Pisan Akaraseni includes several nice touches, and the overall result may seem longwinded and sentimental, but the people behind this film are laughing all the way to the bank. —Cano.

Robert Et Robert
(FRENCH-COLOR)

———

Paris, June 27.

AMLF release of Films 13 production. Stars Jacques Villeret, Charles Denner. Written and directed by Claude Lelouch. Camera (Eastmancolor), Jacques Lefrancois; editor, Sophie Bhaud; music, Francis Lai, J.C. Nachon. Reviewed at Colisee-Gaumont, Paris, June 16, '78. Running time, 105 MINS.

Robert	Charles Denner
Robert	Jacques Villeret
Manager	Jean-Claude Brialy
Agathe	Macha Meril
Mother	Regine

———

Claude Lelouch recently came-a-cropper on both side of the pond with his hybrid oater-cum-epic love story, made in the U.S. and France, "Another Man, Another Chance" (UA). Now he returns to a film geared for local tastes, which should do well at home, with some foreign possibilities on its simplistic, anecdotal tale of an odd couple of friends, both named Robert.

Lelouch's often hand-held camera, sometimes overdone, zeroes in on two bachelors living with their mothers. One, Jacques Villeret, is a classic timid soul and the other (Charles Denner) is a fussy Jewish taxidriver. They meet in a matrimonial agency and become pals.

Film manages to avoid exploiting solitude and mediocrity and opts for the happy ending. Denner's sympathetic tic-laden character, who can face up to anti-Semitism, but is a victim of superstition, is a help with Villeret, an acceptable bumbling but likable self-effacing character, to the point of neurosis, with a demanding mother.

Film just gets tangled up with a bit too much attitudinizing about how life can be wonderful if one just tries, leading to some bouts of sentimentality. But it skirts bathos and even gets smug with Lelouch working in the music of his great hit, "A Man and a Woman," at a windup wedding ceremony of two lonely hearts from the marital agency.

It lacks a comic edge and it opts for a sudden discovery of Villeret having a comic mimic talent at the wedding. Denner immediately gets an idea for him to go pro and Villeret becomes a big star and even gets married before he comes home to his friend Denner, now living with Villeret's mother. The new wife just preferred another artistic character.

With Lelouch's three-year-old, overstuffed detective yarn, "Cat and Mouse," reportedly doing okay Stateside, this too might find its way though its callow plotting will call for careful handling. Lensing and editing are not up to par for a Lelouch item. But has has set out to please and does so a part of the way. —Mosk.

Les Vautours
(The Vultures)
(FR. CANADIAN-B&W)

———

Produced with the financial assistance of the Canadian Film Development Corp. Produced by Louise Ranger. Directed by Jean-Claude Labreque. Features entire cast. Screenplay, Robert Gurik, assisted by Jacques Jacob; camera (black and white), Alain Dostie; art director, Normand Sarrazin; music director, Tony Roman; music composed by Dominique Tremblay; sound, Serge Beauchemin. Reviewed at Museum of Modern Art, N.Y., Cinema Quebecois retrospective, June 1, '78. Running time: 91 MINS.

Louis Pelletier	Gilbert Sicotte
Yvette Laflamme	Monique Mercure
Marie Roberge	Carmen Tremblay
Adele McKenzie	Amulette Garneau
Sister Ste.-Germaine	Denise Proulx
Maurice Duplessis	Jean Duceppe
Doctor Loiselle	Gilles Pelletier
Joseph Beriault	Guy L'Ecuyer

Also: Gabriel Arcand, Paule Baillargeon, Jacques Bilodeau, Raymond Cloutier, Robert Gravel, George Groulx, Rita Lafontaine, Robert Lebel, Nicole Leblanc, Gilbert Lepage, Claude Maher, Jean Mathieu, Anne-Marie Provencher, Phillippe Robert, Yolande Roy, Jean-Pierre Saulnier.

(French with English titles)

This French-Canadian effort by Jean-Claude Lebrecque, made in 1975, is intended by its director as a political allegory. Actually what it is, and what it comes across as, is a study in greed. On that level, it is rather successful. A better-than-average cast with a single exception, gives dramatic depth to this rather slight screenplay by Robert Gurik.

Lebrecque's political allusions, while possibly apparent to les Quebecois, remain generally hidden to outsiders and limit this film's international appeal. In some ways, the story is not too unlike Lillian Hellman's "The Little Foxes." When a young man's mother dies, her three sisters come to Quebec City to arrange her funeral and settle the estate. They're immediately set up as being "vultures," only interested in what they can get out of the sorry business. The son is left with almost nothing, and even the job he has been promised disappears with the death of his supposed benefactor, the Prime Minister.

The three vultures are beautifully played by Carmen Tremblay, Amulette Garneau and Monique Mercure. (latter is even better in "J.A. Martin, Photographe." Other small parts are generally well handled, particularly Gilles Pelletier, Guy L'Ecuyer and Denise Proulx. The biggest drawback to the film is the way the central role of the son is written and the manner in which it is played. He's completely unsympathetic, a lazy lout with no redeeming qualities. As Gilbert Sicotte plays him, there's no way to sympathize with him or his plight. You don't really care what happens to him.

Filmed in black and white and, for some unexplained reason, given a blueish tint, the film's technical qualities are generally excellent. The use of a small-roomed, many-hallway house for an actual location provides a claustrophic quality that is in keeping with the story. For another unexplained reason, there's a lengthy and unnecessary rock music sequence interpolated into the plot. Possibly the running time needed padding. This one is all right on the retrospective or museum circuit but has little to offer commercial theatres. — Robe.

Il Regno Di Napoli
(The Kingdom of Naples)
(WEST GERMAN-ITALIAN-COLOR)

Cannes, May 25.
A Geissler Film Production, Munich, in collaboration with Zweites Deutsches Fernsehen, Wiesbaden, and PBC, Rome. Features entire cast. Writtena nd directed by Werner Schroeter. Camera (color), Thomas Mauch; music, M. Tregadio; editing, Ursula West, Schroeter. Reviewed at Cannes Film Fest (Directors' Fortnight), May 25, '78. Running time: 125 MINS.

Cast: Romeo Giro, Antonio Orlando, Tiziana Ambretti, Maria Antonietta Riegel, Christina Donadio, Dino Mele, Renata Zamengo.

Werner Schroeter's main contribution to New German Cinema has been art experimental pix of an unusual nature, blending images of faraway, fantasized places with equally dream-like musical background scores.

"The Kingdom of Naples" is his first feature pic attempt to tell a story without resorting to stylization. It deals with postwar Naples from 1944 to 1976 and the contrasting fates of a brother and sister who go different ways. A new beginning for Schroeter — this is his best pic to date and a sure bet for New German Cinema programs.

The story is told in 16 sequences with a commentary filling in missing years. He's influenced by neorealism and the Rossellini-Germi-Olmi personal portraits of individuals and families. The brother and sister, born in the closing years of the last war, grow up in misery and hunger in a Naples ghetto. The boy seeks a way out via the Communist Party, works for the cause instead of studying for the future, is jailed as a youth for participating in a demonstration, and then feels himself betrayed in the end as his only job through the Party is menial labor.

The girl, on the other hand, maintains her dignity as a cleaning woman, learns English, and becomes an airline stewardess, thus escaping from the misery of the ghetto but into a fate just as depressing and dehumanizing in the long run.

Schroeter's remarkable feel for atmosphere and docu realism stems from a long-term knowledge of the city and the people. He studied in Naples and has had a running acquaintance with events there over the past 15 years. Friends and acquaintances in Italy joined in the project, to such an extent that this could be called more an Italian film for Italians than a German one shot in Italy.

Although too simplistic and somewhat repetitive in theme, personalities come and go in such a fashion as to enliven the action and even save certain scenes. A Negro sailor (shades of Rossellini's "Paisa") attempts to communicate his wishes to a young girl with chocolate and gestured English words. A prostitute plies her trade against a red curtain, as the Communist Party struggles for power against the Christian Democrats. The Michelangelo statue of the Pieta embarks majestically for the New York World's Fair from the Naples docks, not far from the misery-laden ghettos. A Communist oratory leader is shot by a disgruntled, driven-to-madness aunt in the family. Love and betrayal constantly interweave in a mosaic of faces and feelings, each episode explored for nuance or subtly accented with a musical background of an ironic or supportive nature.

Pic has chance for fest and art house circuit. Credits are tops, particularly Thomas Mauch's lensing, but it's the thesps who ultimately put the film over. A Teutonic sideglance at Italy, nonetheless. —Holl.

Anton Der Zauberer
(Anton the Magician)
(EAST GERMAN-COLOR)

Berlin, June 6.
A DEFA Film Production, Group Johannisthal, Berlin; world rights, DEFA Aussenhandel, Berlin. Features entire cast. Directed by Guenter Reisch. Screenplay, Karl Georg Egel; camera (color), Guenter Haubold; sets, Hans Jorg Mirr; music, Wolfram Heicking; editing, Baerbel Weigel. Reviewed at DEFA Aussenhandel Screening Room, Berlin, June 5, '78. Running time: 95 MINS.

Anton	Ulrich Thein
Liesel	Anna Dymna
Father Grubske	Erwin Geschonneck
Sabine	Barbara Dittus
Ille	Marina Krogull
Schroeder	Eric S. Klein
Lawyer	Marianne Wuenscher
Mayor	Jessy Rameik
Prison Director	Ralph Borgwardt
Guard	Gerry Wolf
Franz Rostig	Werner Godemann
Sergeant	Grigori Grigoriu
Istvan	Dezso Garas
Max Kettler	Leon Niemczyk
Bank Representative	Alfred Struwe

One of the most interesting talents working in the German Democratic Republic, Guenter Reisch has also made one of the best pix to come out of his country in the postwar period. "Anton the Magician" should get a slot on the summer fest circuit, where its commercial as well as critical chances could be tested for Western auds. It's a winner at home.

This is the story of a con-man, a "magician" in the black-market days that immediately followed the last war when a Wall did not separate the two Berlins and Germanys. The story picks up the hero returning home in his army uniform, conning a lift from a Soviet truck to take him where he wants to go. His ready smile and clever hands with motors of every type win him friends by the score — plus customers, when he opens his junk shop specializing in turning auto wrecks into shiny new cars.

The business goes so well that soon Anton has collected a heap of illegal marks on the side. He's also good at charming the girls, one being his long-suffering and trusting wife, and the other the proprietor of a way-side pub who has a yen for business as well as a few moments of tender affection. One day, Anton and his accomplice, Sabine, sneak their bundle into West Berlin and open up an account at a Western bank; he's now a rich man by Socialist standards with hopes and plans for the future.

Anton's comeuppance occurs when he is betrayed by an envious snake-in-the-grass. Although the anti-hero has been improving the town's image and adding to the country's economic growth due to his genius for turning wartime junk into needed tractors, he is being paid on the side for his initiative by farmers (during "collective farming") and public officials for extra preferences of an illegal nature. Taken to court, he pleads guilty and goes to prison, where he again stands out as an expert for factory improvement and is, of course, loved and respected by all. His girlfriend, meanwhile, has departed for Switzerland with the bank loot — there to die in an accident.

Leaving prison, Anton goes to work for the State and proves himself adept at exchanging goods under the counter to meet the required goals; the only difference now is that he is working for society, rather than himself. Growing older, his forceful nature pushes him to overwork and exhaustion, then he briefly confronts his past when he discovers that his girlfriend in the West bequeathed him a luxury automobile — which he destroys, and afterwards, in an intentional drinking bout, does the same to himself. He is mourned by scores of friends and acquaintances as "one of us."

A pic that says more abqut Socialism and the German Democratic Republic than dry books written on the subject. It's also a fresh wind from the East: more satirical, humorous, warm-hearted comedies of this sort would find recognition on the Western art-house circuit. Thesps are tops, particularly Ulrich Thein as Anton, and credits are good cut above the average.
—Holl.

Sieben Sommersprossen
(Seven Freckles)
(EAST GERMAN-COLOR)

Berlin, June 7.
A DEFA Film Production, Johannisthal Group, Berlin; world rights, DEFA Aussenhandel, Berlin. Features entire cast. Directed by Herrmann Zschoche. Screenplay, Christa Kozik; camera (color), Guenter Jaeuthe; sets, Harry Leupold; music, Guenter Erdmann; editing, Rita Hiller. Reviewed at DEFA Aussenhandel Screening Room, Berlin, June 6, '78. Running time: 90 MINS.

Cast: Kareen Schroeter (Karoline), Harald Rathmann (Robbi), Christa Loeser, Evelyn Opocynski, Jan Bereska, Barbara Dittus, Hilmar Baumann, Janine Beilfuss, Carola Spindler, Sabine Schmich, Michael Boettcher, Rene Rudolph.

A story of first love set in a summer camp where a production of Shakespeare's "Romeo and Juliet" is performed on the side, Herrmann Zschoche's "Seven Freckles" is another in his line of children's and youth pix that have merited critical attention at home and abroad. Zschoche scored first with "Wide Streets, Quiet Love" (1969), an Ulrich Plenzdorf script about two truck-drivers crossing the country, and has been a GDR helmer to watch ever since.

"Seven Freckles" deals with 14-year-olds who are awakening to life and its accompanying responsibilities and crises. But the age-old tale goes deeper than expected due to the atmosphere in the summer camp: a prudish directress doesn't like mixing of the sexes and enforces a strict discipline, while two younger counselors are for open expressions of tenderness among teenagers so long as it's genuine. The two pedagogical principles clash all along the way, until the latter pair take responsibility on their own shoulders — they produce an amateur production of "Romeo and Juliet" with kids taking parts.
ing parts.

The twist is that a real-life Romeo-and-Juliet story unfolds on the side. The boy and girl who meet at the camp have known each other from childhood, then were separated when one of the families moved; moreover, the girl has an extra responsibility at the camp of looking after her younger sister and is aware that she must grow up without some of the pleasures of youth as her mother works and supports the family alone.

Then there's a bit of jealousy, in that another girl has a crush on the boyfriend and writes a letter with a false signature to cause complications with the camp directress: our Juliet must be sent home. In the end, everything is put right and the performance proves a success at the camp's closing ceremony. It's obvious, too, that the young lovers are no longer children after a night's adventure together during which their clothes were stolen while swimming bare in a brook. •

Story doesn't always hold up and the Shakespearean touch is too far-fetched to cover scenes with insight or wisdom when matters get sticky. But pic offers a more than interesting portrait of a society not much different from our own in the West.
—*Holl.*

Servus Bayern!
(Bye-Bye Bavaria!)
(WEST GERMAN-COLOR)

Cannes, May 28.

A Herbert Achternbusch Production, Buchendorf; world rights, Filmverlag der Autoren, Munich. Features entire cast. Written and directed by Herbert Achternbusch. Camera (Eastmancolor), Joerg Schmidt-Reitwein; sound, Peter van Anft; editor, Cristl Layrer; production manager, Walter Saxer. Reviewed at Cannes Film Fest (Film Market), May 27, '78. Running time: 84 MINS.

Cast: Annamiri Bierbichler, Herbert Achternbusch, Sepp Bierbichler, Heinz Braun, Barbara Gass, Karolina Herbig, Gunter Freyse, Gerda Achternbusch.

A cult figure who has risen very quickly to the top of New German Cinema as of late, Herbert Achternbusch is a poet-novelist-dramatist-filmmaker who singlehanded restored "Bavarian Cinema" to the heights it enjoyed in the merry heyday of Karl Valentin. Valentin was the Munich cabaretist-filmmaker in the Roarin' Twenties, who not only made Bertolt Brecht laugh but coached him into theatre and film-making himself. Achternbusch is an original talent — and if the viewer is not insulted into a couple of good bellylaughs in watching his mapcap pix, then he's probably never been to Bavaria.

Achternbusch's books thus far include "The Power of the Lion's Roar," "The Alexander Battle," "The Day Will Come," "The Hour of Death," and "Land in Sight" — each autobiographical and chaotically springing from films he's seen and experiences he's had.

. The Bavarian has also written intelligently on Charlie Chaplin before leaping headlong into film-making: "The Andechs Feeling," "The Atlantic Swimmers," "Beer Battle," and now "Bye-Bye Bavaria!" As some of the titles seem to indicate, Achternbusch specializes in the every-day and the possibility of the banal threatening a catastrophe tantamount to Judgment Day. His one play, "Ella," reflects on the decay of human life.

Like all of his films, "Bye-Bye Bavaria'." doesn't have a story line to speak of. A self-styled "poet-poacher," played by Achternbusch, kisses goodbye to Bavaria (where he refuses even to die) because the people and politics there are enough to turn a good man's stomach. Off he goes to Greenland in distress: he can't write any-

more, the reporters are hot on his trail, his girlfriend loves a hunter. They confront each other in this visually beautiful exile and, in the end, the poet dies amid icebergs, but not before he catches a glimpse of his wife through a telescope — in Sicily.

The remarkable power of this film, Achternbusch's best to date, is the put-down of so many sacred cows and art-blisters on the German cultural scene. In an hilarious opening scene, he parodies the current wave of sloppy tv talk-shows and the ever-witty interviewers who practice one-upmanship as a defense for their ignorance. He lays into the Bavarian cultural scene without mercy, and backed the project with his own producing company (no tv backer in sight, apparently). He satirizes his own literary style by presenting a woman scolding the camera for stealing the lines of others for his autobriographical binges. The end effect is a feeling for tragi-comedy: an author reduced to an art-object who can't live anymore at home.

It's a film for insiders. But anyone who has sensed the ego-worship in New German Cinema among its leading king-pins will enjoy this Teutonic Marx Brother on the loose. Lensing is exceptional (Joerg Schmidt-Reitwein is Werner Herzog's cameraman), and technical credits are big improvement over early Achternbusch. A chance for the art house circuit. —*Holl.*

Ich Zwing Dich Zu Leben
(I'll Force You to Live)
(EAST GERMAN-COLOR)

Berlin, June 6.

A DEFA Film Production, "Babelsberg" Group, Berlin; world rights, DEFA Aussenhandel, Berlin. Features cast. Written and directed by Ralf Kirsten. Camera (color), Juergen Brauer; sets, Dieter Adam; music, Siegfried Mattus; editing, Ursula Zweig. Reviewed at DEFA Aussenhandel Screening Room, June 5, '78. Running time: 90 MINS.

School Master Gruebler ......Rolf Ludwig
Helga Gruebler ...... Anne-Else Paetzold
Wolfgang......................Peter Welz
Wulf ....Horst Kotterba
Heschke ....Robert Pfeiffer
SS-Officer ....Eberhard Kirchberg
Landser .... Dieter Bellmann
Kuhnert ....Erich Mirek
Mrs. Kuhnert ....Elsa Grube-Deister

Ralf Kirsten's "I'll Force You to Live" is one of those pix that was a long time in coming: it deals with the last days of the war and the tragedy of a father who tries to save his son's life by refusing to let the 14-year-old youth go to the front lines.

Film focuses on the determination of a father to knock some sense into his son, who is a patriotic "Hitler-Youth" with dreams of glory on the battle-front in his head. On the night before the boy is to leave home, the father literally kidnaps him out of his bed and, bound-and-

tied, bears him away on a cart into the nearby forest (in the Orc Mountains). There he tries to hide out until the Russians come and convince his son that he is doing the best for him, rather than playing the role of a coward. The son, a close friend of the young, patriotic leader in charge of the local Hitler-Youth group, doesn't believe a word his father says — even when, in the woods, the two encounter refugee women and children streaming along a road and an army deserter who tells the boy the truth about the war.

The upshot is that the boy tries repeatedly to run away, then melts a bit as he notes the sacrifices his father is making for him. Since the father had also faithfully served the Nazi cause as a school teacher, the ensuing explanation for the change-over is what makes the film interesting.

Gradually, a psychological shift in the boy's thinking is evident, matching in turn the physical needs on the two as they live rather unprotected in the forest. One day, the father returns to the village to visit the wife and mother, is noticed by the Hitler-Youth watch-guard, and trailed back to the hiding place.

In the climax, the over-zealous Hitler-Youth back home is finally in possession of the gun he has long dreamed of. The militant-minded kids surround their victims, and as the father attempts to save his son by calling attention to himself — he is shot.

Thesps are tops and more than believable for a story that calls for truth in a kind of Shakespearean self-admittance showdown. Pic should get exposure at fests and East German film weeks. — *Holl.*

Die Allseitig Reduzierte Persoenlichkeit — Redupers
(The All-Around Reduced Personality — Outtakes)
(WEST GERMAN-B&W)

Berlin, June 19.

A Helke Sander Film, Berlin, produced by Basis-Film Verleih, Berlin, in coproduction with Zweites Deutsches Fernsehen, Wiesbaden. Features entire cast. Written and directed by Helke Sander. Camera (black and white), Katia Forbert; editing Ursula Hoef; photos, Abisag Tuellmann; sound, Gunther Kortwich; production manager, Clara Burckner. Reviewed at Cinema-Kino, West Berlin, June 18, '78. Running time: 98 MINS.

Cast: Helke Sander (Edda Chiemnyjewski), Joachim Baumann, Frank Burckner, Eva Gagel, Ulrich Gressieker, Beate Kopp, Andrea Nabakowski, Helga Storck, Gesine Strempel, Ronny Tanner, Abisag Tuellmann, Ulla Ziemann, Gisela Zies.

Helke Sander (not to be confused with another femme helmer, Helma Sanders) is best known as a leading figure in the Women's Lib movement in Berlin, editing through Rotbuch Verlag the only

European feminist film quarterly, "Frauen und Film." "The All-Around Reduced Personality — Outtakes" is her debut pic, although she is a grad of the Berlin Film & TV Academy and has done a number of shorts on femme and political themes.

It's a film rich in nuance and perceptive judgment on the Berlin scene as a whole, which deserves to be seen and studied by both femme lib followers and polit-pic pushers, as well as by any who like the bittersweet, honest-to-a-fault bio-portrait. The title itself is a teaser: anyone who listens to radio broadcasts from East Berlin will catch the sardonic fun poked at the oft-heard, politically numbing phrase: "the all-around realized Socialist personality." Sander goes meaningfully in the opposite direction: she looks upon herself as "an all-around reduced personality" — a candid way of saying "I'm not much good at anything."

Edda — Sander's alter ego in the film — is a photographer who must hustle the entire day taking pictures commissioned by official agencies and for sale to newspapers and magazines. She can barely make ends meet, has a school-age daughter who hangs on for more attention, and realizes that she's only half-good at everything although totally committed to several causes. A chance comes when a women's group receive a commission from the Berlin Senat to photograph and present the city through their eyes and, by extension, through the eyes of the Women's Lib movement.

What she comes up with, as both a photographer and a filmmaker, is a depressing, tragic, realistic, but intimate portrait of a city cut in two and surrounded by a wall "with holes in it." Her comments on the international status of West Berlin are both informative and pungent, and this is surely what makes this pic a long-running hit in West Berlin since its release at the Berlin Fest's Forum last spring. When her own commentary fails her (it's not very often), she reaches into a bag filled with quotes from former and current East German writers (Thomas Braasch, Christa Wolf) or uses film clips from pix by femme helmers (Yvonne Rainer's "Film About a Woman Who ...," Valie Export's "Invisible Opponent," Ursula Reuter-Christiansen's "The Executioner") to put a point across.

But it's the film's easy-going style that makes it a stand-out. These "outtakes" from the everyday duties and determination of a working photographer" with both feet on the ground but the head in the clouds" are lensed and cut together with a feel for a camera's eye and with a refined ear for sound. Photos and scenes of the Berlin Wall harmonize in such a way as to juxtapose reality with illusion. Many in-jokes — like the carrying of a huge photo to a segment of the Wall photographed — comment on both the fact and the silliness of making a photo-exhib about it. Sander runs around in convenient black like a spider seeking prey, then switches to white clothing suddenly to reveal (in a b-&-w pic) a sensitive human being after all. When the group's photo-exhib proves a let-down, it's still a minor victory in light of Sander's encounter with cliched phrases and puppet-figures in the establishment.

An engaging pic about Berlin — and women. Art house chances are good. —Holl.

Exploszia
(Explosion)
(RUMANIAN-COLOR)

Bucharest, April 19.

A Rumaniafilm Production, Bucharest; world rights, Rumaniafilm, Bucharest. Features entire cast. Directed by Mircea Dragan. Screenplay, Ioan Grigorescu; camera (color), Nicolae Margineanu; music, Theodor Grigoriu; art direction, Constantine Simionescu. Reviewed at Rumaniafilm Screening Room, Bucharest, April 18, '78. Running time: 103 MINS.

Cast: George Danica (Salamandra), Toma Caragiu (Party District Secretary), Radu Beligan (chemistry professor), Jean Constantin (Tilica), Dem Radulescu (sailor), George Mottoi (commander), Florin Piersic (foreign sailor), Colea Rautu (port commander), Draga Olteanu (Salamandra's wife), Mircea Basta (fire brigade commander), Mircea Diaconu (a sailor), Cezaro Dafinescu (stowaway), Aurel Cioranu (wedding party guest).

A big b.o. winner at home, Mir-.cea Dragan's "Explosion" is an action pic by vet helmer noted for his historical epics. Pic is based on a true incident: in 1971 a Panama freighter, the Poseidon, was abandoned by its crew at the mouth of the Danube where it flows into the Black Sea resort area. Its cargo of ammonium nitrate, a chemical fertilizer, could result in a dreadful explosion when heated to a certain high temperature — the ship had caught on fire and apparently had been abandoned by the crew in a fog.

Like the recent run of Yank catastrophe pix (which "Explosion," oddly enough, preceded), the thriller never lets up for a second as the fire spreads. Plans for handling the situation depend on split-second decisions. Besides the harbor crew, there's an explosion expert — an oil-well fire extinguisher named Salamandra or Catastrophe — on a wedding feast who becomes the hero of the day as well as providing with his companions a bit of down-to-earth comedy. In the end the explosion occurs far enough away from the densely populated area without the innocent vacationers

being the wiser as to the initial danger.

All credits are tops. Pic is a must for overall view of New Rumanian Cinema. —Holl.

Roger Corman: Hollywood's 'Wild Angel'
(U.S.-COLOR-DOCU-16m)

Berlin, June 16.

A Christian Blackwood Production, in collaboration with Michael Blackwood. Only credits available. Reviewed at Berlin Tonfilm Studio, Berlin, June 15, '78. Running time: 58 MINS.

German helmers have been fascinated at the strength and prestige of New American Cinema, particularly since the latter has stolen most of the thunder from the natives on their home grounds and are the favorites of the young crowd frequenting the studio art houses here in growing numbers. When "Roger Corman: Hollywood's 'Wild Angel'" unspooled at the recent Berlin Film Fest in the Info Show, every German helmer in sight streamed into the theatre.

Christian Blackwood's docu features the "king" of the Hollywood Independents in easy-going conversation, charting the history of the low budget pix for mostly drive-ins in the late 1950s, when the bottom had fallen out of Old Hollywood. He tells the stories of the Edgar Allan Poe production ("The Fall of the House of Usher") with Vincent Price and the origin of the wild-angel "road" pix. He was then a film director, for the most part.

The meat of this docu on Hollywood is Corman's role as producer, however. He backed Martin Scorsese's "Box Car Bertha" as the young helmer was leaving behind his film courses at NYU, boosted David Carradine, Peter Fonda, Jack Nicholson, Dennis Hopper, and scores of others in his self-styled "training college." Corman's formula, per one of his young working helmers today, is reduced to (1) comedy, (2) action, (3) sex, and (4) a trifle of social comment, in that order. One season, most of the Oscars went to Corman graduates with exception of one — the next year Nicholson picked it up.

Docu is interspersed with relevant clips from his "school's" pix. Each point is aptly illustrated. Nifty pic worth praise, although too many bows to one of the key figures in New American Cinema. —Holl.

Editie Speciala
(Special Edition)
(RUMANIAN-COLOR)

Bucharest, April 18.

A Rumaniafilm Production, Group One, Bucharest; world rights, Rumaniafilm,

Bucharest. Features entire cast. Directed by Mircea Daneliuc. Screenplay, Beno Merovici, Daneliuc; camera (color), Florin Mihailescu; music, Lucian Metianu; sets, Filip Dumitru, Florin Gabrea. Reviewed at Rumaniafilm Screening Room, Bucharest, April 17, '78. Running time: 103 MINS.

Cast: Stefan Irodache (Matei Olaru), Ioana Craciunescu, Costel Constantin, Mircea Albulescu, Paul Lavric, Mircea Daneliuc, Zaharia Volbea, Constantin Dinulescu, Dem Niculescu, Elena Bog, Dinu Ianculescu.

An action thriller with political overtones, Mircea Daneliuc's "Special Edition" focuses on the troublesome days of 1939, when newspaper journalism was not exactly a profession to be desired. Events and milieu make for a fiction document of the times, although it would be difficult for an outsider to grasp everything that's going on. Daneliuc is a hot young helmer to keep an eye on and this is a step in the right direction, which should win him more favor among his supporters at home and abroad.

It's a "street" film. An honest but politically naive journalist is stopped by a scene on a corner that troubles him — the mistreatment of a woman by a ruffian — and he foolishly steps in to help, whereby the girl escapes. It turns out the girl is suspected of being a Communist agent, the bullies are policemen in the employ of the reactionary government, and he is told to find her again or forfeit his own freedom. Half susptected by the Bucharest police of belonging to the Communist Underground, his political conscience gradually awakens in the dangerous process of ducking parties on both sides of the fence.

The cops-and-robbers games through the streets of Bucharest are entertaining and enough to carry the film, but an added touch is the hero's battle-scarred face (police brutality) and segs possibly inspired by Yank thrillers. The main character, Matei, is comical in tracking down the missing girl with a femme companion who seems to go along just for the fun. The destruction of the liberal newspaper office by the Iron Guard (Rumanian fascists) underscores the perils of dissent even further: from this point midway in the film the story takes off. The end leads to a lonely death on the outskirts of town as pursuing forces close in on the enlightened reporter who now knows too much.

Lensing and thesps are plus factors to boost pic's chances on fest circuit. With "Special Edition" and "The Long Drive," Daneliuc has quickly risen to the top ranks of New Rumanian Cinema. —Holl.

Nachtvorstellungen
(Late Show)
(WEST GERMAN-COLOR-16M)

West Berlin, May 30.

A Lothar Lambert Production, West Berlin. Features entire cast. Produced, written, directed, and edited by Lothar Lambert. Camera (color), Reza Dabui. With excerpts taken from an incompleted film by Harry Puhlmann. Reviewed at Balin-Kino, West Berlin, May 29, '78. Running time: 89 MINS.

Cast: Cihan Anasai, Dagmar Beiersdorf, Beate Hasenau, Sylvia Heidemann, Mustafa Iskandarani, Lothar Lambert, Dorothea Moritz, Ethel Reschke, Erika Wilde.

Another of those low-budget but delightfully thrown-together Berlin pix with charm and fun stamped all over it, Lothar Lambert's "Late Show" is already a winner with home auds and even made it to the Rotterdam Film Fest.

Lambert earns his living as a film critic for Berlin's Abend, but likes to shoot films as a hobby. They run about $20,000 as a rule and thus have every right to be taken seriously within their own genre.

Moreover, Berlin thesps belonging to legit, cabaret and underground like this kind of light, spontaneous fare and lend their services to Lambert & Co. free of charge. There's charm, esprit, and humor in Lambert's "Ex und Hopp," "Sein Kampf" (a play on "Mein Kampf," meaning here "His Struggle"), "1 Berlin-Harlem," and "Faux Pas de Deux," starring Lambert and his friends and dealing with the seamy, gay, erotic side of Berlin.

"Late Show" is a take-off on femme emancipation — a man tries to liberate himself from a puritan-minded sister as well as his mother and lover (a girlfriend) to find his way to his true self. He does this mostly by going to a late show at a cinema, where a similar fate — starring himself (in a fragmented, incomplete film started but not finished by Harry Puhlmann) — awakens his fantasies and, by mixing dreams with reality, helps him to solve his problem. Lambert in a double role, his best to date and well worth a peep for followers of the Berlin School. —Holl.

Filming 'Othello'
(U.S.-COLOR-DOCU-16m)

Berlin, June 15.

Only credits available: camera (color), Gary Graver; music, Francesco Lavagnino, Alberto Barbaris. Reviewed at Berlin Tonfilm Studio, Berlin, June 14, '78. Running time: 120 MINS.

This exceptional docu on a film director, Orson Welles, popped up unexpectedly at last spring's Berlin fest. The facts on the pic are about as mysterious as "Filming Othello" in reality was.

What happened here is the following: the decision of German Television to run an Orson Welles series required some kind of introduction featuring the filmmaker or some legendary aspect of his past. This docu interview with Welles fit the bill perfectly in featuring his reminiscences on the film that won the Golden Palm at the 1952 Cannes Film Festival. The docu could very well have been made by Welles himself, as everything is too neatly anchored to his deft talent for telling a story well.

And the story is a magnificent tall-tale. Welles began filming "Othello" in 1948, and over the next four years he shot sporadically in Morocco, Viterbo, Rome and the island of Torcello, as the story goes. In between he worked as a film actor for Carol Reed in "The Third Man" (1949) and for Henry Hathaway in "The Black Rose" (1950), while acting in and directing "Othello" on a London stage. Earlier, Welles had done "Macbeth" (1948) on a tight 21-day schedule for Republic. He seems to have had somewhat the same plans for "Othello," sinking all his own ready cash into the project, but it lasted years instead. The amazing fact, however, that name actors dropped everything to work for him at the literal drop of a dime made "Othello" the great adventure that it is.

Welles tells everything with a dry wit and a wink in the eye. One of the funniest stories is the murder of Cassio in a Turkish bath, a stroke of genius prompted when the ordered costumes didn't arrive in time.

Another is the awarding of the Golden Palm to Welles at Cannes — for a film without a country or a national anthem to speak of. It must have been great fun, "filming 'Othello'." —Holl.

Ein Irrer Duft Von Frischem Heu
(A Terrific Scent of Fresh Hay)
(EAST GERMAN-COLOR)

Berlin, June 6.
.A DEFA Film Production, Berlin Group, Berlin; world rights, DEFA Aussenhandel, Berlin. Features entire cast. Directed by Roland Oehme. Screenplay, Rudi Strahl, Oehme; based on theatre play of same title by Stahl; camera (color), Juergen Lenz; sets, Dieter Adam; music, Guenther Fischer; editing, Helga Teichmann. Reviewed at DEFA Aussenhandel Screening Room, Berlin, June 5, '78. Running time: **90 MINS.**
Mattes ....Peter Reusse
Angelika ....Ursula Werner
Himmelsknecht ....Martin Hellberg
Aventuro ....Jan Triska
Lydia ....Ursula Staack

Based on his popular legit prod of the same title, Rudi Stahl wrote the film script for Roland Oehme's film

version of "A Terrific Scent of Fresh Hay." It's a light comedy in the vein of the Don Camillo stories of the 1950s.

The jokes are already in the names of the people involved: a scientific Marxist researcher named Angelika Unglaube (Angela Unbelief, in other words), a village party secretary named Himmelsknecht and a Monsignor from the Vatican named Romeo Aventuro. It's a case of a party leader who is believed to be able to work miracles; indeed, strange things do seem to happen in the small town of Trutzlaff, but it could just as well be the scent of fresh hay in summer, as the story goes.

Our Marxist may be an imperfect angel in disguise, but as an eligible bachelor he also has two girls running after him. The winner is eventually the city-girl researcher, hardly dressed for country ways but soon growing to love it. The result: a union between "Belief" and "Unbelief."

Pic is stagy with several talkative long sequences. —Holl.

The Norseman
(COLOR)

Bionic man retrogresses.

Hollywood, June 30.
An American International Pictures release of a Charles B. Pierce/Fawcett-Majors Production. Written, produced and directed by Charles B. Pierce. Stars Lee Majors. Camera (Movielab color), Robert Bethard; music, Jaime Mendoza-Nava; editors, Stephen Dunn, Shirak Kojayan, Aladar Klein, Sarah Legor, Robert Bell; associate producer, Tom Moore; assistant director, Dave Woody;' sound, Ken King; costumes, Bonney Langfitt; set designers, John Ball, Henry Peterson. Reviewed at the AIP Screening room, Beverly Hills, June 30, '78. (MPAA rating: PG). Running time: **90 MINS.**
Thorvald ....Lee Majors
Ragnar ....Cornel Wilde
King Eurich ....Mel Ferrer
Death Dreamer ....Jack Elam
Rolf...................ᴄ Chris Connelly
Indian woman .... Ḳathleen Freeman
Rauric ....Danny Miller
Gunnar ....Seaman Glass
Olaf ....Jimmy Clem
Winnetta ....Susie Coelho
Kiwonga ....Jerry Daniels
Thrall....................Deacon Jones

. If the Leif Erikson Society decides this year to start handing out film awards, Charles B. Pierce would be well advised to begin polishing his acceptance speech. Having already tackled more recent legends of Americana, in his latest for AIP, "The Norseman," writer-director-producer Pierce goes back to near the beginning. Item is sure to be a big hit in the Scandinavian nabes; other commercial outlook appears shaky.

Lee Majors, apparently the first Viking to hot comb his hair every morning, leads a troupe of Norse hulks across the ocean to find his father the King, played by Mel Ferrer. Ferrer and his expedition have been lost for over a year now and are in the hands of Indian savages.

On board with Majors is his second in command, Cornel Wilde, and some tough customers outfitted with armor plates, those nifty Viking horned hats and assorted weaponry. They look like 10th Century Hell's Angels. Thanks to a sympathetic and beautiful Indian maiden (Susie Coelho) they find the King and his party, who have since had their eyes gouged out, fight a couple of battles with the Indians and head back to Greenland.

This is Pierce's seventh film and he's got it all down to an efficient formula. He writes a script calling for handsome outdoor locations and some fighting. There's always one offbeat character for comedy relief, in this case a wizard, Jack Elam, who keeps his face half covered and makes dire predictions.

The lead is played by an actor with boxoffice appeal who can lend some dignity to the hokum, in this case Majors, and possibly Wilde as well. Everything else is low bud-

get, including the staging of the action scenes, always for some reason shot in slow motion.

Except for Majors and Wilde, acting requirements are minimal. Majors has to appear earnest and Wilde loyal, both of which are accomplished competently. The Indians just whoop, the captured all are blind and the Norsemen with Majors just have to look big.

Nonetheless, besides Majors' neat hairdo, there are two oddities. Aren't Vikings supposed to be blonde giants? Except for Chuck Pierce Jr., who plays Majors' younger brother, just about everyone is dark-haired and dark-skinned. And Pierce, the young Viking, has picked up a thick southern accept. For once, Pierce Sr., doesn't act. — Hege.

El Tango Cuenta su Historia
(The Tango Tells Its Story)
(ARGENTINE-DOCU-B&W/COLOR)

Santiago, June 25.
An Aries Cinematografica Argentina production. Produced and directed by Fernando Ayala, Hector Olivera. Screenplay, Julio Marbiz; camera, (black & white/color), Victor Hugo Caula; editor, Carlos Julio Piaggio. Reviewed June 23 '78 at Cine Windsor, Santiago. Running time: **82 MINS.**

For tango lovers it will no doubt come as a pleasure to see some 30 of their favorite singers and musicians — past and present — come to life, but filmwise, "The Tango Tells Its Story" is only a loose and not particularly interesting anthology.

There is no attempt to introduce ideas or historical analysis, but only an accumulation of old film clips. Wherever possible, there are "then and now" contrasts, with specially shot footage of aged artists, but no attempt is made to conduct telling interviews with them, and these items are basically used as linking footage. Among those shown in the past and present tense are Tita Merello, Hugo del Carril and Alberto Castillo.

Carlos Gardel is unfortunately represented by only one item. On a contemporary level, there are three pieces by Astor Piazzolla, including his hit, "Diary of a Madman" (sung by Amelita Baltar). The ending, with a revue production number, danced by Nelida Lobato and her ballet, is weak.

This is a pic that should do quite well wherever there are plenty of tango aficionados, for whom it would be a welcome nostalgia trip. It has no particular interest for other audiences. —Amig.

The Wedding Of Zein
(KUWAITI-COLOR)

Beirut, June 20.
Produced, directed and written by Khaled Siddik, based on Altayeb Saleh's novel. Features entire cast. Camera (color), Towsik Amir, Siddik; editor, Mohyee A. Jawad; sound, M. Breima; production designer, Ebrahim Ebid; music, Siddik and Souleiman Jamil. Reviewed in Beirut, June 20, '78. Running time: 110 MINS.

"The Wedding of Zein" is the second film of Khaled Siddik, Kuwait's foremost producer, director and winner of several awards. His first film, the 1973 "The Cruel Sea," a story of an illfated love in Kuwait of the 1930s, won him nine international awards.

"Zein," completed in early 1976, has been shown at film festivals in Cannes, Montreal and Paris. It is a combination of Kuwaiti and Sudanese expertise which has produced a moving and gripping film, which should appeal to Arab and Western audiences alike.

The story portrays the development of Zein, a Sudanese village boy, from childbirth to marriage. He becomes the village buffoon, with his hoarse laughter and angular erratic gestures. The child is deceptively simple, for one senses an inner intelligence and religious devotion which far outshines that of the other villagers and is first recognized by the wandering holy man, Haneen, and by the pious beauty, Nima.

Zein is attracted to the village girls, whose love he declares to the whole community. Time after time these girls find suitable suitors, and the two-toothed Zein glows in the light of the admiration and attention he receives from the girls and their hopeful mothers, but is subdued by the perceptive severe glances of Nima.

The plot is deceptively simple, as a myriad facets of life are depicted. Strong images are helped by excellent photography. Siddik gives us a story that enables us to see into the heart of the culture he is portraying.

Ali Mahdi plays Zein and is well supported by Tahiya Zaroug as role in Nima and Ibrahim Salahi as Haneen, the holy man.

The film not only tells the story of Zein but depicts the strong impact of Islam on the community, a religion tempered by local beliefs, in holy teachers, in saints and the haunting and power of ancient gods and evil spirits. The theme is of the contrast of man against nature with religion as the apex of the triangle of life.
—Abbo.

Istoriya As: Klyachimol
(Asya's Happiness)
(SOVIET-B&W)

Moscow, June 8.
A Mosfilm Production, Moscow; world rights, Goskino, Moscow. Features entire cast. Directed by Andrei Mikhalkov-Konchalovsky. Screenplay, Yuri Klepikov; camera, G. Rerberg; sets, M. Romadin; music, V. Ovchinnikov. Reviewed in a Private Screening Room, Moscow, June 7, '78. Running time: 90 MINS.
Cast: Iya Savina, nonprofessionals.

Shortly after collaborating with Andrei Tarkovsky on "Andrei Rublov" (1966) (he wrote the script), Andrei Mikhalkov-Konchalovsky made a much discussed but seldom seen film about the dreary side of Siberian village life, "Asya's Happiness" (1966), which finally saw the light of day at last year's Moscow fest in a sidebar screening arranged by the helmer himself. Although now ten years old, pic is still worth a critical once-over and gives vital clues to the giant steps forward Soviet cinema took a decade ago at the instigation of a young group of talented directors, writers, and actors.

The raw energy alone deposited in "Asya's Happiness" is striking. Yuri Klepikov, the writer who later collaborated on Larissa Shepitko's "The Ascent" (Grand Prix at Berlin in 1977), reportedly waited three years to work with Konchalovsky on a script he tentatively titled "Asya the Lame One." It's the story of a crippled girl badly mistreated by a young boy she is in love with, who gets her pregnant but refuses to marry her. Life is extremely hard in the village she lives in (like an Alaskan mining camp), but she grits her teeth and shows backbone in spite of the daily miseries. She is a kind of symbol for the Russian pioneer spirit dedicated to opening "New Land" in the Wilderness.

Nothing much happens in the film, save for the daily routines of peasants (who play themselves) and occasional contacts with the outside world. Then, an acquaintance offers to marry her despite the lameness and pregnancy, but he is older and hope for her true love still springs eternal. It proves her one chance to leave the rigors of village life behind to go to the city. In the end, she refuses even the late change-of-mind of her lover, faces the fatal birth alone, and resigns herself to her destiny. A realist film with a powerful social message.

Lead is played by Iya Savina, one of the few professional actresses in the film, who is better known as "The Lady with a Dog" (1960) in the Josef Heifitz film. At this time Konchalovsky was influenced by the Polish director Andrzej Wajda, but even more significant is the tradition of Soviet realism going back to such early sound pix as Nikolai

Ekk's "Road to Life" (1931) and Boris Barnet's "Outskirts" (1933).
A must for Soviet retros at international film fests and a solid contender for Western art houses.
—Holl.

Dobro Poshalovat
(Welcome)
(SOVIET - B&W)

Moscow, June 10.
A Mosfilm Production, Moscow; world rights, Goskino, Moscow. Features entire cast. Directed by Elem Klimov. Screenplay, Semyon Lunghin, Ilya Nussinov; camera, Anatoli Kuznetsov; sets, V. Kamsky, B. Blank; music, M. Tariverdiev. Reviewed at Goskino, June 9, '78. Running time: 85 MINS.
Cast: Arina Aleynikova, Lydia Smirnova, Yevgheni Yevstigneyev, Vitya Kosykh, I. Rutberg.

The full title of Elem Klimov's (debut pic) "Welcome" (1964), is "Welcome — No Trespassing" and refers to a sign on the entrance to a summer camp for young pioneers (the equivalent of America's Boy-Girl Scouts). It's on the surface a richly entertaining children's pic, which has made the rounds of a number of international fests and Soviet film weeks. But it's also a hilarious satire, in the vein of similar shots in his student days at the Moscow Film School (VGIK): "The Fiancee," "Careful — Banality," and "Look — the Sky." All of these made Klimov known a decade ago as "the Soviet Milos Forman" — or, vice-versa, Forman as "the Czech Elem Klimov."

Klimov is the unheralded backbone of New Soviet Cinema, a moralist who takes stands no matter how unpopular they may be. His first two pix were comedies, "Welcome" and "Adventures of a Dentist" (1967), in both instances with something extra in the way of sharp wit added. He has also made two compilation-docus: "Sport, Sport, Sport" (1971), and the last part of Mikhail Romm's incompleted "Ordinary Fascism" (1965), the latter a statement on the Personality Cult as well as an historical overview of the rise of Fascism in Europe. Klimov's keen analytical mind in these docus prepared him for the still unreleased "Agonia" (1975), an historical portrait of the Revolutionary Year of 1917 which several Socialist helmers and observers have praised as a milestone in contemporary Soviety cinema. (Klimov was given access to the files on Rasputin and Czar Nicholas II for this epic film, apparently commissioned to commemorate the 60th anniversary of the October Revolution.)

"Welcome" is meant for grownups as well as children. The "forbidden" signs placed all over the camp by the narrow-minded director reach to the extreme, a contradiction to the atmosphere of such a holiday resort. Here is zany absurdity worthy of Yank screwball comedies: plastic statues of youths spoofing staid, imitation-like, Socialist Realism sculpture; a grandmother who looks like Krushchev; inept, bureaucratic camp leaders trying in vain, to find a boy hiding "underground" in their midst; and pungent, visual gags tumbling one upon another. "Welcome has already become a kind of classic in-joke, and pic is as popular today as when it was made.

Of particular note is the pic's technical quality. The camp is lensed in light tones to accent its fairytale, fantastic character. Trick shots are used, one in which the rebellious boy's grandmother flies through the air, as in Vittorio De Sica's "Miracle in Milan." Worthy of Charlie Chaplin and Rene Clair, pic is also solidly in the tradition of Soviet satire, as Yakov Protossanov's "The Feast of St. Jurgen" (1930) or Georgian comedies of late.
A must for Soviet Film Weeks.
— Holl.

Shiwjot Takoj Paren
(There Was A Lad)
(SOVIET-B&W)

Moscow, June 9.
A Gorky Studios Production, Moscow; world rights, Goskino, Moscow. Features entire cast. Written and directed by Vassili Shukshin, based on his own short stories. Camera (black and white), Valeri Ginsburg; music, Pavel Chekalov; sets, A. Vagichev; sound, V. Vhlobynin. Reviewed at Goskino, Moscow, June 8, '78. Running time: 101 MINS.
Leonid Kuravlev (Pashka Kolokolnikov), Lidia Alexandrova (Nastya), Larissa Burkova (Karia), Boris Kalakin (Uncle Kondrat), Bella Achmadulina (Journalist), Rodion Nachapetov, N. Sazonova, R. Grigoryeva, A. Suyeva, J. Teterin.

Of all the talented directors in New Soviet Cinema, Vassili Shukshin was the most loved by his countrymen. His premature death in 1974 at the height of his fame as a writer-actor-filmmaker was a great blow to the Soviet film industry, although before his death few of his films were shown in the West and only recently have full retros of his pix been unspooled at fests: Karlovy Vary in 1976 and the International Forum of Young Cinema at the Berlin fest this spring. He played in 19 Soviet films and was a very popular actor, but lines collect before any Moscow cinema featuring pix in which he himself starred, wrote, and directed. His grave in a Moscow cemetery draws visitors like pilgrims, people who have both read his stories and loved his movies — a rare manifestation, indeed, of a man's greatness.

The Shukshin features in the forum retro include "There Was a

Lad'' (1964), ''Your Son and Brother'' (1969), ''Strange People'' (1969), ''Travelling Companions'' (1973), and ''The Red Snow-Ball Tree'' (1974). In addition, there's a Shukshin screenplay filmed by friends and starring his wife Lidia Fedoseeva in a role apparently written for her: Stanislav Ljubshin and German Lavrov's ''Call Me from Afar'' (1977), unspooled at last year's Mannheim Film Festival where it copped the top kudo.

Shukshin the actor does not appear in ''There Was a Lad,'' but the young hero Pashka is an alter ago and relives many of the writer-director's own experiences as a youth who, born in Siberia, worked on construction projects and farms, was a truckdriver, served in the military, and went to night schools to become a self-taught storyteller and afterwards enter the Moscow Film School. There, at VGIK, with the simultaneous appearance of his stories in print and the acceptance of his screenplays, he became famous overnight with the appearance of ''There Was a Lad'' in 1964. The film has proven so popular that two similar East European pix bear remarkable resemblances to the original and were equally successful: Herrmann Zschoche's ''Wide Roads, Quiet Love'' (1969) in the German Democratic Republic, and Mircea Daneliu's ''The Long Drive'' (1975) in Rumania.

The young hero is a free spirit travelling across country (a common theme in Shukshin films, in the same manner as John Ford's characters are continually on the move in search of something). His car breaks down and he gets a lift from a truckdriver, lending a hand wherever needed along the way but sometimes mixing too much into business that really doesn't concern him, save that the situation seems to demand it. He dances with a girl at a town gathering, plays checkers in a library, and makes a laughing play for a girl who has her eyes really on attracting another. Back on the road with the truckdriver, they pick up a woman passenger and, upon noticing that both his companions have led hard, lonely lives, he attempts to play cupid; another acquaintance on the road, an elderly woman, tells a humorous story about a naked woman. And so on, one encounter after another.

The upshot is a brave deed by Pashka, driving a burning oil truck over a cliff but breaking a leg in the process. In the hospital his good humor and love of life still captivate others ''so we can go on living,'' as one says. Warm tale of a kind of Huck Finn or Jack London, Soviet style. Credits are tops. A natural for Soviet Film Weeks and a possible for art houses. —Holl.

Krylya
(Wings)
(SOVIET-B&W)

Moscow, June 9.

A Mosfilm Production, Moscow; world rights, Goskino, Moscow. Features entire cast. Directed by Larissa Shepitko. Screenplay, Valentin Yezhov, Natalia Ryantseva; camera, Igor Slabnevich; sets, Ivan Plastinkin; music, Roman Ledenov. Reviewed at Goskino, Moscow, June 8, '78. Running time: 90 MINS.

Cast: Maya Bulgakova (Nadezhda Petrovna), Zhanna Bulatova, Panteleimon Krymov, Leonid Djjatshkov, Sergei Nikonenko, Nikolai Grabbe.

Recently the Soviet ''middle-generation'' helmers have become known in the West via retros at international film fests. Two years ago, the late Vassili Shukshin was featured at the Karlovy Vary film fest, followed by a similar honor to the prematurely deceased director at the Forum of Young Cinema at the Berlin fest this spring. Another Soviet helmer with a retro at Berlin this year was Larissa Shepitko, considered by many critics to be one of the world's leading femme filmers.

The retro included her four feature pix: ''Heat'' (1963), ''Wings'' (1966), ''You and I'' (1971), and ''The Ascent'' (1976). ''The Ascent'' won the Grand Prix at Berlin last year, and this time around Shepitko served on the international jury. ''Wings'' had never been shown before in the West (the same with Shukshin's ''Your Son and Brother,'' also made in 1966 and unspooled in the Forum). This made the event all the more attractive, particularly as an impromptu symposium with the helmer crowned the retro.

Pic offers a human portrait of a once-famous fighter-pilot in the Second World War, aviatrix Nadezhda Petrovna (modelled after a real person from an actual wartime woman's fighter squadron). She now finds it difficult to fit into the routine of a commonplace job in the postwar years; she's 42, unmarried (her one great love died in the war), and the director of a secondary school in the provinces. Unable to find herself emotionally and returning often in thoughts to the heroic fighting days when she had a surer identity, she covers her misgivings with an authoritative manner and loses contact with the school's students and her own adopted daughter. The students, in fact, despise her.

A conflict inevitably arises between the older and younger generation, complicated all the more by the admiration and respect the citizens of the town and the members of the school board hold for her. Somewhat like Monica Vitti in ''Eclipse,'' she wanders from place to place recalling the past while searching for some answers to what has gone wrong in the present.

Shepitko's strength lies in the power of her images and the total commitment to a central theme — in this case, an affirmation-of-life without resolving the immediate problem of identity. Many scenes stick to the memory: the heroine in a cafe with a friend which normally serves only men customers; the casual loops of a plane in mid-air that trigger a remembrance of helplessness as, in the war, she followed her wounded lover's plane to a fatal crash; the awkward meeting with the daughter's choice of husband after she has left home for good; and the final scene at the airport as she jokingly enters a cockpit once more to unexpectedly take off into the freedom of the skies.

Maya Bulgakova is outstanding as the disoriented aviatrix (playing the role of an older woman with finesse and nuance). Pic has interweaving touches of humor and sombreness: one in particular matches the school directress's inability to make peace with a rebellious youth, and a girl who defends him, together with a children's play, in which she must carry a prop of a wooden doll (a Russian souvenir-figure) comically across a stage surrounded by a bunch of marching little dolls. Shepitko is a master of rhythmic blending of reality and fantasy.

''Wings'' is a milestone in the development of New Soviet Cinema. A must for fest retros and film weeks, as well as art houses. —Holl.

Sport, Sport, Sport
(SOVIET-DOCU-B&W/COLOR)

Moscow, June 10.

A Mosfilm Production, Moscow; world rights, Goskino, Moscow. Directed by Elem Klimov. Screenplay, H. Klimov; camera, B. Brozhovsky, O. Zguridi; sets, N. Serebryakov, A. Speshneva; music, A. Shnitke. Reviewed at Goskino, Moscow, June 9, '78. Running time: 90 MINS.

Cast: G. Svetlani, L. Novozhilova, B. Andreev, V. Lyakhov, V. Brumel, H. Klimov, Nikita Mikhalkov, Larissa Shepitko.

Elem Klimov's fiction-docu on the history of sports and the trials and travails of champions offers much critical food for thought as the glorification of sports keep escalating year by year. Klimov doesn't polemicize nor investigate into what makes an athlete tick — but he does show the hard facts through multiple film clips and dramatized sequences taken from real life. ''Sport, Sport, Sport'' (1971) is a sometimes humorous, brilliantly compiled reportage on the glories and agonies of the world's chief pastime. With the 1980 Olympic Games in Moscow approaching, pic deserves exposure in Western theatres (it was a prize-winner at the Oberhausen Sports Festival a couple years back).

''Sport, Sport, Sport'' opens with a lone figure on a track and mounts to the excitement of a light-athletic racing contest in a large stadium. Sports events featuring exertion of various kinds follows: horses falling, skiers tumbling, muscles being messaged. The scene switches to a sports-training camp for children: a young girl swimmer is shown near exhaustion and later unable to sleep properly as drams force her body to twitch fretfully. Shots of old people exercising and visiting saunas to conserve life's fading energies are matched with people trying to take off weight. The brutality of boxing and contact sports is examiend in sharp detail. Shots of accidents, crowded city life, and the physical strain to break records follow.

Two high points put this unusual docu in a class by itself. One is the death of a runner in a Philadelphia meet on a scorching, hot summer day: water and salt in his body simply dried up under the circumstances, and the man was running simply on self-will — to his death. Another is a hilarious staged combat between gladiators in a fictitious early Soviet Sports Event, replete with a costumed Oriental audience like at Western medieval joust between knights.

A human document. It should be seen by both the committed sports fan and the critical nay-sayer. Credits and editing techniques are top grade. —Holl.

Posowi Mnja W Dal Swjet Luju
(Call Me from Afar)
(SOVIET-COLOR)

Moscow, June 8.

A Mosfilm Production, Moscow; world rights, Moscow. Features entire cast. Directed by Stanislav Lyubshin and German Lavrov. Screenplay, Vassili Shukshin; camera (color), Yuri Ardeev; music, Yuri Butcko. Reviewed at Goskino, Moscow, June 7, '78. Running time: 90 MINS.

Cast: Lidia Fedosseva-Shukshina, Stanislav Lyubshin, Mihail Uilanov, Ivan Ryjov.

The Grand Prix winner at last year's Mannheim Film Fest, this last screenplay by the talented Soviet actor-writer-filmmaker Vassili Shukshin was posthumously filmed by two thesps, Stanislav Lyubshin and German Lavrov. It features Lyubshin in one of the lead roles, together with the widowed wife (Shukshin died in 1974) of the author, Lidia Fedoseeva, who starred with her husband in the memorable ''Travelling Companions'' (1973) made but a year before his death.

The relationship between ''Travelling Companions'' and ''Call Me from Afar,'' Shukshin's last screenplay, is significant. Both carry, practically speaking, untranslatable titles: the first, ''Petschki-Lawotschki" in the original Russian, should be rendered "Cracker-Barrel Chatter" instead of "Travelling Companions" (its foreign title); and the film here in question, "Posowi Mnja w Dal Swjet Luju" in Russian, should run something like "Call Me in the Distance Bright" instead of the simpler "Call Me from Afar" (which has more force considering the filmmaker is deceased).

Also, both pix are autobiographical and consist almost entirely of conversation between friends and new and old acquaintances about life in general, its meaning and pleasures, pains and surprises. In "Travelling Companions" Shukshin travels with his wife across the Soviet Union from Siberia to Moscow and then down to Yalta, leaving two daughters behind because he has an ailment that can only be treated in a cure center at Yalta. The pair meet three key individuals along the way: an insulting city-slicker type, a kindhearted con-man and petty-thief, and a knowledgeable, generous professor of folklore. Shukshin perceptively, lovingly analyzes the failings in man amid the accompanying pitfalls in society.

In "Call Me from Afar" Shukshin is writing about a widow (did he perhaps suspect that his alter ego's illness in "Travelling Companions" was fatal?), who must now make an adjustment to life and start over from the beginning. And the film in between these two — "The Red Snow-Ball Tree" (1974) — depicts the hero, an ex-prisoner trying to start over again (played by Shukshin, together with Lidia Fedoseeva), as marked for death in a fatal chain of circumstances. Put all three pix together and it immediately becomes clear why Shukshin films starring his wife and himself draw mass audiences whenever unspooled in Moscow.

"Call Me from Afar" opens with the mother and son together, followed by a talk with a kindly brother who hints she should marry again. He has even found a candidate in the village, a bachelor so shy he nearly botches the first meeting between the two. Two problems arise thereafter: the eligible bachelor admits to a past alcohol problem, a failing that comes to the surface again under stress; and the son is, given to pranks and a general distrust of intruders in the house. At a reception to celebrate the match, the new man in the family suddenly falls to pieces and makes a scene that indicates he is also perhaps a bit touched in the head. The widow is back where she started.

Finely sketched thesp performances in two-shot lensing reminiscent of John Ford (the

helmer Shukshin seems most to resemble in the West) make "Call Me from Afar" a strong contender for art house circuit, particularly if matched with an equivalent, earlier Shukshin pic. —Holl.

Adventures of a Dentist
(SOVIET-B&W)

Moscow, June 10.

A Mosfilm Production, Moscow; world rights, Goskino, Moscow. Features entire cast. Directed by Elem Klimov. Screenplay, Alexander Volodin; camera (black & white) S. Rubashkin; sets, V. Kamsky, B. Blank; music, A. Shnitke. Reviewed at Goskino, Moscow, June 9, '78. Running time: 90 MINS.

Cast: Andrei Miagkov, B. Vasilyeva, A. Freyndlikh, P. Krymov, I. Kvasha.

"Adventures of a Dentist" combined two leading Soviet talents for original comedy and critical satire: filmmaker Elem Klimov and playwright-scripter Alexander Volodin (pseudonym for Alexander Lifshits). The film reportedly took a while in coming — perhaps due to Klimov's prior film-satire, "Welcome" (1964), and Volodin's play, "The Factory Girl" (1957), both of which produced a wave of pro-and-contra controversy in the Soviet Union.

Problems of ethics and morality concern both artists. They take strong stances against conformity, routine, dehumanizing aspects of contemporary society, which deaden spiritual forces in life. The script was not immediately approved, and pic seems to be a truncated version of the original.

"Adventures of a Dentist" concerns an exceptionally gifted dentist: coming directly from his graduating class to a provincial town, he suddenly discovers he can pull teeth painlessly, indeed miraculously, and is a success overnight. This, of course, creates problems. Everyone wants to go to the painless dentist, and his colleague, a lady dentist, is without work altogether. The day comes when an investigating commission arrives on the scene — our hero refuses to pull a tooth because he decides he doesn't want to rock the boat.

His miraculous powers also get him into trouble. Besides the notoriety, our shy hero is in love — he resolves to seek a new profession. A friend, however, comments, "The most important thing is not to be dependent on other people's opinions." As a dental teacher now, his new colleagues urge him to practice again. The showdown comes when a dental-school student under his direction ends up pulling a tooth exactly in the way he did. The main thing in life apparently, is to believe strongly in something after all.

Pic as light entertainment has plenty of visual gags to carry the story on its own terms. The allegorical aspects apply to Western auds as well as in the Soviety Union. Andrei Miagkov (a Klimov discovery) is a find as the dentist credits are top grade, and pic is ripe for Soviet Film Weeks. —Holl.

Thursdays Never Again
(SOVIET-COLOR)

Moscow, June 8.

A Mosfilm Production, Moscow; world rights, Goskino, Moscow. Directed by Anatoli Efros. Only credits available. Reviewed at Goskino, Moscow, June 7, '78. Running time: 100 MINS.

Anatoli Efros is best known abroad for his theatrical productions, but as a teacher at the State Theatre Institue (GITIS) in Moscow, he also has worked and directed in the cinema. This is his second feature pic and is strongly stamped by his legit experiences — in fact, "Thursdays Never Again" appears to be a tour-de-force for thesps and related to contemporary dramatic themes known to Moscow auds. Pic is rumored for an international fest.

In the tradition of Chekhov and Gorky, "Thursdays Never Again" — also known as "Forest Preserve" — takes place in the country and features a family reunion at a summer dacha with a lot of aimless but revealing talking. There is one central figure, the mother, who at an elderly age suddenly dies and forces the rest to reflect on the meaning of life and their own attitudes to each other. By contrast, the father is revealed as a foolish old man with delusions, and the son as a complacent egoist.

The setting is a forest preserve near Moscow, a paradise of landscaping with a flowing river, plus bears, dogs, and wild animals of various sorts — including a deer killed by a poacher. A laboratory is on the grounds, a kind of museum for scientific study and research. A girl in white wanders into the scene. Talk of a concert on the morrow sets the stage for the son's reflection on the past and his present immersion in city life. There's a familiar touch of Antonioni's ennui and self-searching running through the theme, save this is Chekhov country.

A fascinating pic, out of the usual mold of the Soviety School of Realism today. Credits and thesp performances are tops, and a director's sure hand is felt throughout. Good chances for art houses with proper handling. — Holl.

Beli Bim-Chornoye Ukho
(White Bim With Black Ear)
(SOVIET-COLOR)

Moscow, June 10.

A Gorky Film Studios Production, Moscow; world rights, Goskino, Moscow. Features entire cast. Directed by Stanislas Rosototzki. Screenplay based on novel by Gavril Troepolsky. Only credits available. Reviewed at Goskino, Moscow, June 9, '78. Running time: 90 MINS.

Cast: Viatcheslav Tikhonov (Ivan Ivanovich).

The Gorky Film Studios in Moscow specialize in children's and youth pix, although many productions are meant for old as well as young. And once a director finds a footing there, he is liable to remain and make thereafter what he chooses. It was this way with the late Vasili Shukshin, whose first pic, "There Was a Lad," starred a youth journeying across the country as a truck-driver's assistant; afterwards, he went on to make films that spoke directly to his own generation in no uncertain terms.

Stanislas Rostotzki's "White Bim with Black Ear" is a family pic. It features an elderly Army veteran whose health is no longer the best; some of his neighbors, however, are only half the man he is, as the story goes. His one close friend is a pup named Bim, a white dog with a black ear who grows up to be a faithful companion within a couple years. The companionship sometimes makes it difficult for the master (bus rides into the country, for instance, don't allow animals on board), but the dog saves the day by alerting citizens in a housing project in Kalouga to some illegal goings-on by hypoctitical neighbors.

Story spills over into sentimentality: this is, after all, a children's pic with a moral. Film offers an interesting portrait of life in a small town, nonetheless, which makes it worth a look-see. Viatcheslav Tikhonov in the lead is a popular Soviet character actor.

—Holl.

Foul Play
(COLOR)

Excellent crime-suspense-romance a la Hitchcock. Big outlook.

Hollywood, July 7.

Paramount Pictures release, produced by Thomas L. Miller, Edward K. Milkis. Stars Goldie Hawn, Chevy Chase. Written and directed by Colin Higgins. Camera (Movielab Color), David M. Walsh; second unit camera, Rexford Metz; editor, Pembroke J. Herring; music, Charles Fox; production design, Alfred Sweeney; set decoration, Robert R. Benton; sound, Jay Harding, Jeff Wexler; asst. director, Gary D. Daigler; second unit director, M. James Arnett. Reviewed at Paramount Studios, L.A., July 6, '78. (MPAA Rating: PG.) Running time. 116 MINS. -

Gloria Mundy .... Goldie Hawn
Det. Tony Carlson . . .. Chevy Chase
Landlord Hennesey .... Burgess Meredith
Gerda Casswell .... Rachel Roberts
Archbishop .... Eugene Roche
Stanley Tibbets .... Dudley Moore
Det. Scott .... Bruce Solomon
Stella .... Marilyn Sokol
Det. Fergie .... Brian Dennehy
Theatre Manager .... Chuck McCann
Religious Bookseller .... Billy Barty
Scarface .... Don Calfa
Stiltskin .... Marc Lawrence
Sandy .... Cooper Huckabee
Albino .... William Frankfather
Turk .... Ion Teodorescu
Massage Parlor Madame .... Pat Ast
Coleman .... John Hancock
Elsie .... Queenie Smith
Ethel .... Hope Summers
Mrs. Monk .... Irene Tedrow
Pope Pius XIII .... Cyril Magnin
Newscaster .... Chuck Walsh

"Foul Play," an excellent film, revives a relatively dormant film genre — the crime-suspense-romantic comedy in which low-key leading players get involved with themselves while also caught up in monumental intrigue. The name missing from the credits is Alfred Hitchcock, whose film tricks and artistry hang over much of the Thomas L. Miller-Edward K. Milkis production. Writer Colin Higgins makes a good directorial bow. Goldie Hawn is superb in a strong return to pictures, and Chevy Chase, also above title, works well as a screen partner. The Paramount release spells big money and long legs.

If you think you've been through the plot before, you have: Hawn, likable librarian, picks up undercover agent Bruce Solomon who passes her film evidence of how Rachel Roberts, Eugene Roche and other heavies are going to assassinate visiting Pope Pius XIII (played by S.F. socialite Cyril Magnin) at a performance of "The Mikado" in the Opera House. Chase, a detective, eventually believes Hawn's stories about attempts on her life. Car chases and theatre shootout climax the film's 116 minutes.

The charm, humor and excitement of this type film are more than enough to excuse some flaws: The rather sumptuous apartments of the stars though their plot professions are modestly-salaried; the severe slowdowns in pacing when the stars evolve their romance (Hitch usually interleaved such material more smoothly); the cumulatively sick taste of sidebar incidents which in themselves are merely vulgar.

Ironic in light of current taxpayer revolt is the reason for the assassination — Roberts, Roche, Marc Lawrence, William Frankfather, Don Calfa and Ion Teodorescu want to end tax-exempt status of religious property.

Entire cast comes off very well. In prominent support are Burgess Meredith as Hawn's landlord; Dudley Moore, a dedicated swinger who turns out to be the opera conductor; Marilyn Sokol, Hawn's girlfriend who carries anti-rapist tools in her handbag; Chuck McCann, lecherous theatre manager (and in a retrospective cinema, too); Billy Barty, a religious bookseller who knocks on the wrong door.

San Francisco is a beautiful enough film locale without the obligatory car chases up and down hills, but second unit director M. James Arnett and his cinematographer Rexford Metz do an excellent job in the assignment. This action intercuts with the opera performance, done by the N.Y. City Opera conducted by Julius Rudel and staged by Jack Eddleman. Since Hawn doesn't warble pluggable film songs — yet, anyway — Barry Manilow sings a good original by Charles Fox and Norman Gimbel.)

David Walsh's excellent camera work and Albert Sweeney's handsome production design highlight the technical credits. From time to time, the pacing suggests a certain pre-cut for tv story-telling quality, even to some sidebar cheap humor that could easily be removed later on.

This is easily Hawn's best film to date. Instead of the prior roles in which her character was kooky enough (and often shallow enough) to recall her initial "Laugh-In" smash on tv some years ago, here she is showcased as a normal, "everyday" (film-style) girl who might live next door. This toned-down, vulnerable image is just right and broadens extensively her future theatrical dramatic spectrum. For this alone, "Foul Play" is meritorious. —Murf.

Portret S Dojdem
(Portrait in the Rain)
(SOVIET-COLOR)

Moscow, June 11.

A Mosfilm Production. Moscow: world rights, Goskino, Moscow. Features entire cast. Directed by Grigori Egiazarov. Screenplay, Alexander Volodin; camera (color) Valeri Shuvalov; sets, Anatoli Kuznezov; music, Alexei Mashukov. Reviewed at Goskino, Moscow, June 10, '78. Running time: 90 MINS.

Cast: Galina Polskich (Klava), Igor Ledogorov, Alexei Petrenko, Valentina Talysina.

Grigori Egiazarov's bitter-sweet tale of a woman over forty, titled appropriately "Portrait in the Rain," is penned by dramatist-scripter Alexander Volodin, one of the Soviet Union's better writing talents. It's a human story, but with a few unexpected twists to dig below the surface of the story and raise pic to something out of the ordinary.

Setting is a port-city in the South, probably Yalta or somewhere nearby. Our heroine has already had two disappointing love affairs behind her: she left her first husband, taking her son with her (now a teenager); and the man she next fell in love with was inconveniently married to an ailing wife, thereby leaving her with a daughter and still very much alone. Now she meets a sailor, whose mother has just died and is being buried; as a good-hearted acquaintance, she steps in to help with the arrangements, as he now has no contacts at home at all.

The upshot is the sailor returns to see her again, and a relationship grows between the two in a quiet, sometimes awkward manner. Her friends however, advise her to keep a strong hold on her emotions, while her son is having his first love affair with a girl who works an honest but ordinary job as a waitress — and the daughter needs to be looked after. She decides, momentarily, to put an end to the meetings.

When the sailor departs for his ship, however, her feelings for the dark stranger in her life grow stronger. She runs to see him off — only to be interrupted along the way by a sudden down-pour of rain and the necessity to cover a small, soaked girl with her umbrella. She arrives too late at the docks and stands in the rain.

Pic reflects current characteristics of Socialist society and Soviet middle-class standards of living. It's well told and acted, with credits a good cut above average. A portrait of a city. — Holl.

Goodbye Emmanuelle
(FRENCH-COLOR)

Paris, July 11.

Parafrance release of Trinacra Films, Parafrance production. Stars Sylvia Kristel. Directed by Francois Leterrier. Screenplay, Leterrier, Monique Lange based on the characters of Emmanuelle Astier; camera (Eastmancolor), Jean Badal; editor, Marie-Josephe Yoyotte; music, Serge Gainsbourg. Reviewed at Publicis-Matignon, Paris, July 2, '78. Running time: 95 MINS.

Emmanuelle .... Sylvia Kristel
Husband .... Umberto Orsini
Dorothee .... Alexandra Stewart
Lover .... Jean-Pierre Bouvier
Woman .... Olga Georges Picot

Pic is the third installment in the life of the free-living, sexually-feverish "Emmanuelle." This release, made by a more ambitious director, suffers from some pretentious dialog pertaining to the erotic patterns of a group of swingers now living in the Seychelle Islands, off Africa, after Bangkok and Hong Kong.

There have been various imitations of the first "Emmanuelle," picture, which is in its fifth year of firstrun in Paris with over $6,000,000 taken in ticket sales, "Emmanuelle 2," was shown this season though producer Yves Rousset-Rouard fought France's X-label, which he felt unjust, and won.

The second feature did over $1,000,000 in its Paris firstrun. But the third try seems somewhat tame in these permissive times. Emmanuelle, played with her usual languor by Sylvia Kristel, is still married to a husband who allows all her affairs and even joins in them until it seems affectional love, though it appears only mechanical sex, comes to Emmanuelle in the person of a rather stuffy young film director who is to shoot in the Seychelles.

There are the expected coupling scenes between hetero pairs, or two women and a man plus the standard Emmanuelle exotico background of compliant servants and tropical bliss. This time Emmanuelle is piqued when the film director treats her like a joy girl. So that is "love." Her husband is worried for the first time and prevents her going off with the young filmer but she finally leaves to join him in Paris.

Husband is a hypocritical type who prefers not to know if his wife cheats and will not tell her if he does.

Plot this time implies a followup but producer Rousset-Rouard has said it is the last. And Emmanuelle should be left to her middle age. She is getting a bit dull.

A playoff in France seems fair plus some fast possibilities abroad on the past rep of the early "Emmanuelles."

Director Francois Letterier does not exhibit the pictorial flair for this sort of exotico-erotic stuff and his attempt to give these pithy characters some substance does not come off. —Mosk.

Viva Italia
(ITALIAN-COLOR)

Cinema 5 release of a Dean Films production. Produced by Pio Angeletti and Adriano De Micheli. Directed by Mario Monicelli, Dino Risi and Ettore Scola. Stars Vittorio Gassman, Ornella Muti, Alberto Sordi, Ugo Tognazzi. Screenplay, Age, Scarpelli, Ruggero Maccari, Bernardino Zapponi; camera (Technispes Color), Tonino Delli Colli; editor, Alberto Gallitti; music, Armando Trovajoli; set design, Luciano Ricceri. Reviewed at Paris Theatre, N.Y., July 10, 1978 (No MPAA rating.) Running time: 90 MINS.

Cast: Vittorio Gassman, Ornella Muti, Alberto Sordi, Ugo Tognazzi, Orietta Berti, Luigi Diberti, Eros Pagni, Fiona Florence, Emilia Fabi, Yorgo Voyagis.

(English subtitles)

Released in its native Italy to resounding commercial success last year, this nine-episode black comedy anthology opened there as "I Nuovi Mostri" or "The New Monsters," a sequel to director Dino Risi's 1962 pic, "I Mostri." Here, Risi shares directorial chores with Mario Monicelli and Ettore Scola, although their individual contributions aren't parceled out in the credits.

Present package, like its predecessor, is keyed to the proposition that Italian males are essentially vain, manipulative, egocentric and sometimes murderously cruel. Putting that theme into a comedic framework is hard at the best of times, and only three or four of these segments manage to shine without being overly silly or overly ugly. Fortunately, the perpetual presence of Alberto Sordi, Ugo Tognazzi and Vittorio Gassman — whether alone or in tandem — dignifies even the dregs. Expect fair to good results in urban art spots, though long legs are unlikely.

Basic structure of the tales, which range in length from three to 14 minutes, is to set up a mildly amusing stock situation, then build it to an increasingly bitter final twist or punchline. Highlights include Gassman as a smooth-talking Cardinal who stumbles on a left-wing suburban parish and uses a flowery sermon to sway a group of angry peasants back to the church and away from social justice; Tognazzi as the husband of a popular singer who contrives to "accidentally" have her legs broken when her voice fails before a lucrative concert tour, hoping audience sympathy will keep her career going; and Sordi's broadly played turn as a decadent aristocrat who picks up a bleeding accident victim in his Rolls, can't get the man admitted to a hospital, and finally dumps the victim back where he found him.

With time out for some coarsely played slapstick — a disgusting food fight in a provincial kitchen, the funeral of a comedian which turns into a festive song-and-dance routine — film's emphasis is distinctly on human cruelty. Two episodes in particular (one in which Sordi uses a string of desperate deceptions to force his elderly mother into a nightmarish nursing home; another in which a silent romance between an airline stewardess and a young man results in his gifting her with a terrorist bomb) are more likely to make audiences writhe with discomfort than anything else. Here, comedy is entirely sacrificed to blackness.

Film's stateside title should not be confused with Roberto Rossellini's similarly titled "Viva l'Italia," made in 1960. —*Step*.

Hot Lead And Cold Feet
(COLOR)

Cold idea and cool prospects.

Hollywood, July 1.

Buena Vista Distribution Co. release of a Walt Disney production. Produced by Ron Miller. Directed by Robert Butler. Screenplay, Joe McEveety, Arthur Alsberg, Don Nelson; camera (Technicolor), Frank Phillips; editor, Ray de Leuw; art direction, John B. Mansbridge, Frank T. Smith; costume design, Ron Talsky; sound, Gregory Valtierra; music, Buddy Baker; special effects, Eustace Lycett, Art Cruickshank, Danny Lee, Hal Bigger, Billy Lee; stunt coordinator, Buddy Joe Hooker; assistant director, Paul "Tiny" Nicholas. Reviewed at Walt Disney Studios, Burbank, June 30, '78. (MPAA Rating: G.) Running time: **90 MINS.**

Eli, Wild Billy,
Jasper Bloodshy .... Jim Dale
Jenny .... Karen Valentine
Denver Kid .... Don Knotts
Rattlesnake .... Jack Elam
Mansfield .... John Williams
Mayor Ragsdale .... Darren McGavin
Boss Snead .... Warren Vanders
Roxanne .... Debbie Lytton
Marcus .... Michael Sharrett

Through years of cinematic conditioning, the Walt Disney organization has groomed its audience to expect the predictable: a clean, fun type of picture that will not embarrass any member of the audience and may even amuse the folks, as well as the toddlers.

Always doing the predictable leads to a rut, however, and "Hot Lead And Cold Feet" is mired in just such a groove. Antiseptic enough to pass hospital muster, it lampoons a genre most moppets aren't even aware of. For a generation growing up on "Star Wars," the humor in "Hot Lead" is about as potent as the blank bullets being fired every other moment on screen.

Jim Dale, a vastly talented British actor, is wasted in this constricted vehicle. He plays three characters, a grizzled old father who has set up a cowboy town named after himself, Bloodshy, and his two sons, one a mild-mannered salvationist, the other a crazed outlaw-type.

With a decent script, and the solid supporting cast around him (Don Knotts, Jack Elam and Darren McGavin), Dale might have been able to make something of the tripartite role. But the story by Joe McEveety, Arthur Alsberg and Don Nelson (an elaborate race between the brothers to win the family fortune) never manages to create much suspense or humor.

Director Robert Butler relies on expansive double-takes to fill the numerous holes in the script, and Dale's romantic interest, Karen Valentine, is allowed to smile, encouragingly, and nothing more. Dragged into the film as the typical "cute" youngsters are Debbie Lytton and Michael Sharrett, whose roles are more one-dimensional than the usual Disney tykes.

Knotts and Elam, given star billing, are actually relegated to cameo appearances as two bumbling gunfighters, and McGavin is given absolutely nothing to do.

Only bright spots are Ron Talsky's authentic costume designs and the excellent stunt work coordinated by Buddy Joe Hooker. Much of the realism contributed by the stuntmen is obviated by the phony process work that increasingly acts as an impediment to Disney films. Even children are sophisticated enough in this era of special-effects to spot back projection, and such shots in "Hot Lead" aren't well-masked.

So while the Disney logo may act as a Pavlovian cue to the family film crowd, "Hot Lead And Cold Feet" is pedestrian enough to alter the traditional response. Outlook is spotty. —*Poll*.

Sgt. Pepper's Lonely Hearts Club Band
(COLOR)

Beatles music in a garish fantasy setting. Teenbopper the target audience.

Hollywood, July 11.

Universal Pictures release, produced by Robert Stigwood; executive producer, Dee Anthony. Stars Peter Frampton, The Bee Gees. Directed by Michael Schultz. Screenplay, Henry Edwards; camera (Technicolor), Owen Roizman; editor, Christopher Holmes; music, John Lennon, Paul McCartney, George Harrison; production design, Brian Eatwell; set decoration, Marvin March; sound, Arthur Piantadosi, Les Fresholtz, Michael Minkler, Charles M. Wilborn; costumes-wardrobe, May Routh, Jennifer Parsons, Anthony Faso; asst. director, L. Andrew Stone. Reviewed at Universal Studios, L.A., July 11, '78. (MPAA Rating: PG.) Running time, 111 MINS.

Billy Shears .... Peter Frampton
Mark .... Barry Gibb
Dave .... Robin Gibb
Bob .... Maurice Gibb
Mr. Mustard .... Frankie Howerd
Dougie .... Paul Nicholas
B.D. Brockhurst .... Donald Pleasence
Strawberry Fields .... Sandy Farina
Lucy .... Dianne Seinberg
Mr. Maxwell Edison .... Steve Martin
Future Villain .... Aerosmith
Father Sun .... Alice Cooper
Sgt. Pepper Reincarnation ... Billy Preston
The Diamonds .... Stargard
Benefit Act .... Earth Wind & Fire
Mayor Kite .... George Burns

"Sgt. Pepper's Lonely Hearts Club Band" will, in its first days of release, attract some grown-up flower children of the 1960s who will soon find the Michael Schultz film to be a totally bubblegum and cotton candy melange of garish fantasy and narcissism. The Robert Stigwood production crams nearly 30 songs, largely by The Beatles, into newly-recorded versions tailored for stars Peter Frampton and The Bee Gees. The Universal release has enough summer flash to draw, but this seems another one of those films which serve as feature-length screen advertising for an album.

Henry Edwards is credited for the script which attempts to construct a story out of the famed "Sgt. Pepper" album of more than 10 years ago. Suffice it to say that showmanly-cast George Burns, supplying enough voiceover exposition for a documentary, is testimony to the writing achievement. Plot has Frampton as the grandson of the earlier Sgt. Pepper who carries on the family band tradition with a modern-sound in partnership with The Bee Gees.

Story introduces a lot of freakish characters out to steal the band's instruments which, somehow, make Heartland, U.S.A., a dream of a small town. They don't succeed, though there's enough teeny-bopper-teasing naughtiness to amuse and thrill the target audience. Donald Pleasence, one of the heavies, plays a music biz wizard whose fictional trademark is that of the real-life Stigwood organization.

Near the end of the 111-minute film, when all wrongs have been righted, there's a celebrity olio in which many familiar names appear to be singing happily. The sound of this isn't any more lifelike than much of the preceding singing.

Roger M. Rothstein gets credit as exec in charge of production. Patricia Burch choreographed. The film's visual look is that of the musical theme park atmosphere apparently sought by the filmmakers. Electronic visual effects are appropriate; Ron Hays was in charge of that particular crew. Stigwood' involvement with "Saturday Night Fever" and "Grease" have a lot of people wondering if he can make three in a row; we'll soon know. —Murf.

The Swarm
(COLOR)

A fast visit with killer bees. Short life on screen.

Hollywood, July 18.

Warner Bros. Release, produced and directed by Irwin Allen. Features entire cast. Screenplay, Stirling Silliphant, based on a novel by Arthur Herzog; camera (Technicolor), Fred J. Koenekamp; special photographic effects. L.B. Abbott; editor, Harold F. Kress; music, Jerry Goldsmith; production design, Stan Jolley; set decoration, Stuart Reiss; sound, Arthur Piantadosi, Les Fresholtz, Michael Minkler, Herman Lewis; cosutmes-wardrobe, Paul Zastupnevich; assistant director, Mike Salamunovich; stunt coordinator, Paul Stader. Reviewed at The Burbank Studios. June 22, 1978. (MPAA Rating: PG.) Running time: 116 MINS.
Brad Crane . . . . Michael Caine
Helena . . . . Katharine Ross
Gen. Slater . . . . Richard Widmark
Dr. Hubbard . . . . Richard Chamberlain
Maureen . . . . Olivia de Havilland
Felix . . . . Ben Johnson
Anne MacGregor . . . . Lee Grant
Dr. Andrews . . . . Jose Ferrer
Rita . . . . Patty Duke Astin
Jud Hawkins . . . . Slim Pickens
Major Baker . . . . Bradford Dillman
Clarence . . . . Fred MacMurray
Dr. Krim . . . . Henry Fonda
Gen. Thompson . . . . Cameron Mitchell
Paul Durant . . . . Christian Juttner
Dr. Newman . . . . Morgan Paull
Dr. Martinez . . . . Alejandro Rey
Pete Harris . . . . Don (Red) Barry

"The Swarm" currently is in more than 1,200 theatres. It should, before word of mouth catches up with Irwin Allen's disappointing and tired non-thriller. Killer bees periodically interrupt the arch writing, stilted direction and ludicrous acting. But the Warner Bros. release will get its money quickly.

Stirling Silliphant gets writing credit, based on an Arthur Herzog novel. It's the kind of screenplay where characters who supposedly are familiar with certain technical work spend most of their time explaining it to each other. Such corny exposition is but one lowlight. Then there's the sub-plot romance be-

tween schoolmarm Olivia de Havilland (with the worst phony southern accent imaginable) and either Fred MacMurray or Ben Johnson.

Michael Caine heads the cast as a scientist who must contend with killer bees as well as with Richard Widmark, once again playing one of those cardboard military officers. Lots of other familiar names crop up.

Pic's 116 minutes only occasionally bring excitement; too much time is given over to gab and one-two-three-kick directorial tedium. Allen was smarter on "The Towering Inferno" to have a partner handling the dramatic sequences. By the time the bees get to Houston, and the city is torched, few will care.

Production credits are routine.
— Murf.

It's A Funny, Funny World
(ISRAELI)

Tel Aviv, July 5.

Noah Films release of a Golan-Globus Production. Produced by Menahem Golan, Yoram Globus. Features entire cast. Directed by Zvi Shissel. Screenplay, Boaz Davidson, Shissel; camera, Adam Greenberg. Amnon Salomon, editor, Alain Jacubowicz; songs, composed and sung by Ariel Zilber. Reviewed in Tel Aviv, July 5, '78. Running time: 90 MINS.
Cast: Boaz Davidson, Zvi Shissel, Izik Albalak, Ophelia Shtrall, Uri Gross.

Touted as a hit, preceded by an enormous press campaign, helped along by two incidents with the law (with cases still pending in court) and with feature stories following up every move of its creators, this candid camera comedy may face trouble as audiences will expect much more than film is capable of delivering.

Inspired by the relative success of Allan Funt's "Candid Camera" series, aired here last year, and by the impressive results of the South-African feature, "Funny People," Golan-Globus Productions (who, incidentally, distributed "Funny People") gave free rein to Boaz Davidson, of "Lemon Popsicle" fame, and to Zvi Shissel, who has been involved in the past, as writer, producer and actor in some of Uri Zohar's movies.

From the results, it is obvious that the two enjoyed themselves while making the picture, often appearing on camera. But what probably looked great on set is much less enticing on screen, and this for several reasons.

First, the main attraction of "Candid Camera" is the sophistication in contriving and presenting the practical jokes, springing the gags subtly on unsuspecting victims, in order to convince them that surrealistic situations are indeed real. But there is very little subtlety here

as jokes tend to astonish and too often elicit shrungs of incomprehension.

The naked lady in the back of a passenger car or the fake policewoman checking private parts of a male audience entering a cinema, the two scenes which provoked the police into arresting filmmakers, were much funnier when told by those who were present on location, than as they appear on screen.

The gimmick which is successful involves a recording of a passing train, played by a concealed speaker at a crossing, with stunned drivers watching barriers go down, hearing a train rush by, but seeing nothing.

Davidson and Shissel, engineering many of the practical jokes themselves on camera, look pleased with themselves, but show is stolen by pokerfaced Izik Alabalak, a tv prop man, whose reputation as art director for a very successful satirical tv series is equalled only by his fame as a prankster.

The print shown at the press screening being a faulty one, it would not be fair to criticize quality of either image or sound, which were below par but may have been corrected in later prints. —Edna.

Millionaire In Trouble
(ISRAELI)

Tel Aviv, July 5.

Shapira Film Ltd. release of a Roll Film production. Produced by Israel Ringel, Yair Pradelsky. Stars Yehuda Barkan, Yaakov Bodo. Written and directed by Yoel Silberg. Camera, Nisim (Nitcho) Leon; production designer, Kuli Sander; editor, Tova Neeman; music, Dox Selzer; lyrics, Uriel Offek. Reviewed July 1, '78 in Tel Aviv. Running time: 85 MINS.
Cast: Yehuda Barkan, Yaakov Bodo, Edna Flidel, Gideon Singer, Hannah Laslow, Uriela White, Mandy Rice-Davies.

The mistaken identity plot has been old since the days of Roman drama, and here it is again, in one of its least memorable versions.

Yoel Silberg won't gather any laurels with this tired idea of a millionaire and his driver changing identities in order to prove that character is worthier than money and charm has nothing to do with a fat bank account. The switch is made in New York, the homeland of millionaires, but plot moves to Israel, where rich man and poor man arrive incognito to check the many properties owned by the magnate.

Dramatic development is carefully avoided, the script doing its best to pile jokes on jokes. There is no story and nobody is surprised at final curtain, as pretty girl weds millionaire, while driver rates only a chambermaid.

Heading the cast are Yehuda Barkan, one of the few bankable stars in Israeli cinema (a status that may be endangered by the present

opus) and Yaakov Bodo, who repeats his broad, low-brow style of clowning. —Edna.

Revenge Of The Pink Panther
(COLOR)

Cluttered plot dissipates latest in series, but still good outlook.

Hollywood, July 12.

United Artists release, produced and directed by Blake Edwards; executive producer, Tony Adams. Stars Peter Sellers. Screenpay, Frank Waldman, Ron Clark, Edwards, based on an Edwards story; camera (Technicolor), Ernie Day; editor, Alan Jones; music, Henry Mancini; production design, Peter Mulllins; art direction, John Siddall; sound, Roy Charman; costumes-wardrobe, Tiny Nichols; asst. director, Terry Marcel; second unit director, Anthony Squire; stunt coordinators, Joe Dunne, Dick Crockett. Reviewed at MGM Studios, Culver City, July 12, '78. (MPAA Rating: PG). Running time: 98 MINS.
Clouseau . . . . Peter Sellers
Dreyfus . . . . Herbert Lom
Simone Legree . . . . Dyan Cannon
Douvier . . . . Robert Webber
Cato . . . . Burk Kwouk
Scallini . . . . Paul Stewart
Marchione . . . . Robert Loggia
Auguste Balls . . . . Graham Stark
Claude Russo . . . . Sue Lloyd
Guy Algo . . . . Tony Beckley
Tanya . . . . Valerie Leon

"Revenge Of The Pink Panther" isn't the best of the continuing film series, but Blake Edwards and Peter Sellers on a slow day are still well ahead of most other comedic filmmakers.

This time out, Sellers tracks down an international drug ring. Herbert Lom also encores as Sellers' nemesis and Dyan Cannon is delightful as the resourceful discarded mistress of dope smuggler industrialist Robert Webber. The United Artists release should do okay in summer release.

Frank Waldman, Ron Clark and producer-director Edwards wrote the screenplay from an Edwards story, and what seems to have gone wrong is a paradoxical embarrassment of riches: Sellers, faithful servant Burt Kwouk, Lom, Cannon, etc., each alone and also in various combinations, are too much for a simple story line. The result is that the plot roams all over the map, trying to cover all the bases but in totality adding up to less than the parts. This has affected the acting and direction as well.

The "Pink Panther" series is the film art's only continuing textbook in both contemporary and classic screen comedy. The reunion of Sellers and Edwards three years ago, after the span of a decade since the first "Panther" pix, yielded an astonishing partnership of mature film talents which shines through the stumble in this latest effort. But aduiences won't mind too much, knowing that the next one should be on track again.

Production credits are all very good, including the animated titles, a looked-for regular feature of these films. —*Murf.*

Noche De Curas
(Priests' Night)
(SPANISH-COLOR-DOCU)

Madrid, July 9.

Loxos Film production, directed by Carlos Morales Mengotti. Camera (Eastmancolor), Augusto Fernandez Balbuena; editor, Gloria Carrion. Features five ex-priests identified only as Jesus, Arturo, Julian, Miguel and Jeronimo. Reviewed at Cine Penalver (Madrid), July 8, '78. Running time: 75 MINS.

Shot in only two days and two nights by novice helmer Carlos Morales Mengotti, this pic, despite its cinema-verite format, complete with shaky camera and poor direct sound, has enough going for it to maintain interest of audiences.

In essence, film is the edited verbatim dinner conversation of five youngish ex-priests who familiarly discuss and reminisce about their days in the seminary. Over their plates of roast lamb, wine, country bread and coffee in a rustic house in an abandoned village in Zamora province, they talk about what induced them to prepare for the priesthood, what life in the seminaries was like, and ultimately their reasons for throwing off their cassocks.

The conversation for the most part is lively and spontaneous. Though not overly anti-Catholic nor anti-religious in intent, the gist of the dialogs and some of the conclusions drawn are certainly a condemnation of the Catholic church and its suppressive role in education and politics, especially during the post-Civil War years, when the five priests in question were in seminaries.

Cut into the dialog occasionally are scenes in which the five are seen singing around the table with a guitar, or playing an organ, or mimicking a lecture on religion and morality.

But though none of it is militant, the incisiveness of such bits as "They castrated us with the seminary system," or, "In villages the only way out for a poor boy was to become a gendarme or a priest," or "Woman was considered as the Devil" and "We weren't allowed to read newspapers or even the Bible; once someone sent me a sandwich wrapped in a paper and I read it secretly in the toilet," are evident and might give pic some commercial chances in art and university circuits. — *Besa.*

Sluzhebni Roman
(Romance During Office Hours)
(SOVIET-COLOR)

Mosców, June 11.

A Mosfilm Production, Moscow; world rights, Goskino, Moscow. Features entire cast. Directed by Eldar Ryazanov. Screenplay, Emil Braginsky, based on his play; camera (color), Vladimir Nakhabtsev; sets, Alexander Borisov; music, Andrei Petrov. Reviewed at Goskino, Moscow, June 10, '78. Running time: 150 MINS.

Cast: Andrei Miagkov, Alicia Freindikh, Svetlana Nemolyaeva, Oleg Basilashvili, Lia Akhedzhakova, Lyudmila Ivanova.

One of the funniest comedies to emerge from the Soviet Union in recent years, Eldar Ryazanov's "Romance during Office Hours" has the winning flavor of a Tracy-Hepburn war-of-the-sexes made famous during the heyday of Hollywood. Pic has already proven a hit in Moscow cinemas, and with the boost of a convenient international film fest or appropriate Soviet Film Week it could get legs for art house circuit or tv exposure.

Pic matches two well known comic thesps, Andrei Miagkov and Alicia Freindikh, who work in the same office — she's the boss and he's a clerk. There's also a number of hilarious individuals who pass to and from: a slick talker who travels abroad and a receptionist with a hundred other things on her mind, to name but two. The pivotal joke is the boss's hard, unfeminine nature matched with the warm, unassuming character of the employee. Our hero is also a recent widower with two children to take care of, an eligible bachelor who really could use a woman around the house.

The two wage war, so to speak, during office hours due to differences of opinion. But a decisive moment comes when she invites him home for dinner and blossoms into a woman for the occasion.

The dinner and table talk turns out to be an uncomfortable mess for both of them, but a howl for the audience. Later, a showdown occurs at the office as, in a quarrel, the underling tries to hand in his resignation — it proves unacceptable, so he insults her and a fight ensues, which carries out of the office, into the streets, and finally inside a cab. The walls of resistance then crumble and the two are paired for life.

Story is too long and builds up slowly in the beginning. But once off the ground, "Romance During Office Hours" has some snappy dialogue that carries through to the end. Many hardy laughs at both the system and the social mores of the day. Ryazanov is a longtime vet of satirical comedies. —*Holl.*

Hooper
(COLOR)

Terrific stunts and effective ensemble acting. Big outlook.

Hollywood, July 20.

A Warner Bros. release of a Burt Reynolds-Lawrence Gordon production, produced by Hank Moonjean; executive producer, Lawrence Gordon. Stars Burt Reynolds. Directed by Hal Needham. Screenplay, Thomas Rickman and Bill Kerby from a story by Walt Green and Walter S. Herndon; camera (Metro Color), Bobby Byrne; art director, Hilyard Brown; editor, Donn Cambern; music, Bill Justis; sound, Jack Solomon; set decorator, Ira Bates; costume supervisor, Norman Salling; stunt coordinator, Bobby Bass; assistant director, David Hamburger. Reviewed at the Directors Guild of America Theatre, Hollywood, July 20, '78. (MPAA Rating: PG.) Running time: 99 MINS.

Sonny Hooper	Burt Reynolds
Ski	Jan-Michael Vincent
Gwen	Sally Field
Jocko	Brian Keith
Max Berns	John Marley
Cully	James Best
Adam	Adam West
Tony	Alfie West
Roger Deal	Robert Klein

It's been too long since actors have projected as much on-screen chemistry as Burt Reynolds, Jan-Michael Vincent, Sally Field and Brian Keith do in Warner Brothers' "Hooper." Individually, the performances in this story of three generations of Hollywood stuntmen are a delight. And Hal Needham's direction and stunt staging are wonderfully crafted. But it's the ensemble work of this quartet, with an able assist from Robert Klein, which boosts an otherwise pedestrian story with lots of crashes and daredevil antics into a touching and likable piece.

Reynolds, in a further extension of his brash, off-handed wise guy screen persona, plays the world's greatest stuntman. He took over that position 20 years back from Brian Keith. His status is being challenged by a newcomer, Jan-Michael Vincent.

To cement a place in the stuntman's record books, Reynolds must perform one last stunt, in this case a 325-foot jump in a jet powered car over a collapsed bridge. He'll watch the gauges with Vincent behind the wheel. It'll be his final feat, and presumably afterwards, he'll hand over the reigns to the next generation.

All this is to take place in a film, "The Spy Who Laughed At Danger," some sort of a disaster James Bond type picture being directed by the deliciously obnoxious Robert Klein.

The plot's elements have been dramatized before. Think of Sam Peckinpah's pictures about an aging hero performing one last heroic act to confirm his masculinity. But Needham, himself a former stuntman, and screenwriters Thomas Rickman and Bill Kerby have a

sympathy for their characters — even Klein — rarely found in Peckinpah's pictures. And each of the performers displays an understanding and empathy not only for his own character, but also for each other's.

Sally Fields plays Reynolds' girlfriend and roommate. This is her third picture opposite Reynolds and she proves again one of the most reliable double threats working today — a capable comedienne who can switch mid-scene to serious drama.

Besides the final jump over the bridge, Needham and stunt coordinator Bobby Bass have arranged a smorgasbord of stunts — car crashes, barroom brawls, chariot races, helicopter jumps and motorcycle slides. All are skillfully executed.

The question, of course, is, can Reynolds and Needham repeat the enormous success they enjoyed with "Smokey & The Bandit?" Because of the more serious overtones of "Hooper" and the film within a film element, which has never been a big boxoffice draw, probably not. Still, outlook is big. The film will draw and please the action seekers as well as filmgoers looking for something more serious. And Reynolds continues to be one of maybe a half dozen dependable b.o. actors working today. His fans will flock to this one and not be disappointed. —*Hege.*

Warlords Of Atlantis
(BRITISH-COLOR)

The city that won't stay lost. Okay for the popcorn munchers.

London, July 17.

EMI Films presentation (Columbia Pictures release in U.S.), produced by John Dark. Stars Doug McClure. Directed by Kevin Connor. Screenplay, Brian Hayles; camera (Technicolor), Alan Hume; editor, Bill Blunden; art director, Jack Maxsted; production designer, Elliot Scott; music, Mike Vickers; sound, George Stephenson, Ken Barker; monster sequences, Roger Dicken; special effects supervisor, John Richardson. Reviewed at Warner West End Theatre, London, July 17, '78. Running time, 96 MINS.

Greg Collinson	Doug McClure
Charles Aitken	Peter Gilmore
Captain Daniels	Shane Rimmer
Delphine	Lea Brodie
Atmir	Michael Gothard
Grogan	Hal Galili
Fenn	John Ratzenberger
Jacko	Derry Power
Prof. Aitken	Donald Bisset
Sandy	Ashley Knight
Briggs	Robert Brown
Atsil	Cyd Charisse
Atraxon	Daniel Massey

In "Warlords of Atlantis," Doug McClure and several other earthlings suffer a close encounter with Cyd Charisse and Daniel Massey who rule over the legendary lost city. More terrifying are their brushes with various species of marine monsters on periodic rampages.

And a good thing, too, in an otherwise skimpy reworking of the hoary Atlantis legend. The John Dark production is one of those okay optical sprees for the program market whose only justification is the special effects. Storywise, this one's on a par with the old Saturday matinee serials.

Columbia has been playing the EMI entry for some weeks in the U.S., but apparently neglected to invite trade appraisal.

Donald Bisset and Peter Gilmore are appealing as a British father-son scientific team in quest of Atlantis. McClure, solo above title, is the Yank who made the diving bell that plumbs the sea and implausibly manages to resurface.

Between establishing sequence and final escape from the clutches of a giant octopus, the adventurers encounter almost nonstop jeopardy between the rulers of Atlantis and those monsters, not to mention greedy crew hands aboard their square rigger.

The one not inconsiderable virtue of the Brian Hayles script is that it keeps the pot boiling. Direction by Kevin Connor and the editing keep the eye-filling pace brisk. The cliched characters are played in workmanlike fashion by all hands, but with no distinction for anyone. Except Roger Dicken, in charge of the very good monster sequences, and John Richardson, who supervised the busy special effects. The kids will like. —*Pit.*

Patrick
(AUSTRALIAN-COLOR)

Sydney, July 12.

A Filmways release of an Australian International Fim Corporation production. Produced by Antony I. Ginnane and Richard Franklin. Features entire cast. Exec. prod. Bill Fayman. Directed by Richard Franklin. Screenplay, Everett De Roche; camera, (Agfacolor), Don McAlpine; art direction, Leslie Binns; special effects, Conrad Rothman; asst. directors, Tom Burstall, James Parker; sound, Paul Clarke; wardrobe, Kevin Regan; editing, Edward Queen-Mason; music, Brian May. Reviewed at Hoyts Theatrette, Sydney, July 11, '78. (Commonwealth censorship rating: For Mature Audiences). Running time: 110 MINS.
Kathy Jacquard .... Susan Penhaligon
Dr. Roget .... Robert Helpmann
Ed Jacquard ....Rod Mullinar
Dr. Wright .... Bruce Barry
Matron Cassidy .... Julia Blake
Sister Williams ....Helen Heminway
Nurse Panicale ....Maria Mercedes
Detective Sgt. Grant .... Frank Wilson
Grant's Assistant ....Peter Culpan
Day Desk Nurse .... Marilyn Rodgers
Night Desk Nurse ....Peggy Nichols
Patrick's Mother ......Carole-Ann Aylett
Captain Fraser ....Walter Pym

Psychokinesis is a subject that can usually be relied upon to create some spectacular effects on screen, and as a result, occasionally the story and characters become sub-

ordinated to cinematic magic tricks. Not so with "Patrick" which is more a study in character reactions: and the growing potential menace is all the better reinforced because of it.

Effects man Conrad Rothman doesn't really pull out all the stops until the last few minutes of the picture — only to be upstaged by the final few frames in which the camera concentrates on the denominative "Patrick."

He is introduced as a matricide who, after having done away with mom and her lover, is next seen in the intensive care section in a state of chronic, advanced — and, we're told — irreversible catatonic reaction: "160 pounds of limp meat hanging off a comatosed brain," says Dr. Roget (Robert Helpmann) who is head of the clinic where this medical mile post is lodged. Apart from the electronic gadgetry that monitors Patrick's tentative connection with itself, there is no manifestation in support of his being thought of as alive — save that he has a tendency to spit occasionally.

Kathy Jacquard (Susan Penhaligon) is a recently estranged wife who returns to nursing to support herself. At Roget's clinic, as the newest member of the staff, she's given Patrick to watch over, but far from perceiving this as a chore, she accepts it as a challenge, and it is her insistence that the patient can communicate that creates the shift that foments the final confrontation. The developments to that stage are aided by the fact that (as is traditional) the patient falls in love with his nurse, which would be okay if he only had tonsilitis and was normal: Patrick is polyplegic and homicidal and possessed of this really terrific sixth sense which he uses spitefully.

The inert (and uncredited) lead, with help from Richard Franklin's shrewd direction, creates an incredible menace while the other thesps surrounding him go through their action. It's not the first time that a plot has given the audience the edge over the actors, but it's handled nicely here by Franklin and de Roche's scripting.

While lacking the fury of "Carrie" the picture falls well within the genre, borne aloft on the production values obtained, the playing and the overall style of the direction which doesn't always take the subject totally seriously. This latter aspect comes in especially useful when circumstances force characters into uttering cliches because it undermines the audience's natural disbelief; keeping the whole thing just plausible enough to amuse and vice-versa.

In a longer version, "Patrick" racked up impressive sales at Cannes and after, with Cinema Shares

handling the foreign sales. The version reviewed here is the final cut for overseas sales and the local market. Film was financed between A.I.F.C. , the Australian Film Commission and the Victorian Film Commission. —*Miha.*

The Driver
(COLOR)

Bleak film of a wreck.

Hollywood, July 25.

A 20th Century-Fox release of a Lawrence Gordon production. Produced by Lawrence Gordon. Stars Ryan O'Neal, Bruce Dern, Isabelle Adjani. Written and directed by Walter Hill; camera (DeLuxe color), Philip Lathrop; production designer, Harry Horner; music, Michael Small; editor, Tina Hirsch, Robert K. Lambert; stunt coordinator, Everett Creach; art director, David Haber; set decorator, Darrell Silvera; special effects, Charley Spurgeon; associate producer, Frank Marshall; assistant director, Pat Kehoe; sound, Richard Wagner. Reviewed at 20th Century Fox, Century City, July 11, '78. (MPAA rating: R.) Running time: 91 Mins.
The Driver .... Ryan O'Neal
The Detective .... Bruce Dern
The Player ....Isabelle Adjani
The Connection .... Ronee Blakley
Red Plainclothesman ....Matt Clark
Gold Plainclothesman .....Felice Orlandi
Glasses .... Joseph Walsh
Teeth .... Rudy Ramos
Exchange Man .... Denny Macko
The Kid .... Frank Bruno
Fingers .... Will Walker

By the end of "The Driver" you can almost smell rubber burning, there are so many screeching tires. This may be the first film where the star of the show isn't an actor or even a machine but a sound effect. The 20th Century-Fox-EMI presentation of Walter Hill's second film as a director should bring cheers from a convention of tire salesmen, but everywhere else outlook is bleak, even with Ryan O'Neal, Bruce Dern and Isabelle Adjani as the co-stars.

O'Neal, who hasn't been seen since "A Bridge Too Far," plays a master getaway driver who does most of his talking with his accelerator toe. Bruce Dern, departing only slightly from his maniac roles, plays an obsessed detective out to nab O'Neal. Adjani is another reticent character, a gambler hired as an alibi for O'Neal, in a supporting role, Ronee Blakley, portrays O'Neal's connection; she sets up the jobs.

There's not much more to the plot than that. O'Neal is a great driver and Dern is a detective. They're enemies and one of them is going to win the game.

Hill and stunt coordinator Everett Creach have engineered a number of car chases and they are fabulous, if you like car chases. One scene in a deserted parking garage — the screeching tires echo during this one — has O'Neal prove his driving abilities by systematically crushing and dismantling the body

of a Mercedes, which is kind of funny if you enjoy watching a Mercedes being dismantled.

Because of the quiet and mysterious mood of this picture, it has a pretentious quality to it. Whenever someone does speak, the dialogue seems precious, as if the last sentence of each speech were edited out.

Technical credits — and maybe production mixer Richard Wagner should be singled out — are fine, but the end product is a muddled disappointment. — *Hege.*

Nightmare In Blood
(COLOR)

Modest, hip horror spoof.

San Francisco, July 25.

PFE release of a Xeromega production. Written and produced by John Stanley and Kenn Davis. Directed by Stanley. Features entire cast. Camera (Techniscope), Charles Rudnick; editor, Alfred Katzman; sound, Robert Gravenor, John Brumbaugh; asst. director, Julie Staheli. Reviewed at York Theater, San Francisco, July 14, '78. (M-PAA Rating: R.) Running time: 90 Mins.
Prince Zaroff .... Kerwin Mathews
Malakai .... Jerry Walter
Prof. Seabrook .... Dan Caldwell
Cindy O'Flaherty .....Barrie Youngfellow
Scotty ....John J. Cochran
B.B. .... Ray K. Goman
Harris .... Hy Pyke
Ben-Halik .... Irving Israel
Arlington ....Drew Eshelman
George Wilson .... Morgan Upton
Dr. Unworth .... Justin Bishop
Marsdon ....Stan Ritchie
Flannery ....Charles Murphy
Barbara .... Yvonne Young
Lt. Driscoll .... Mike Hitchcock
Girl in Graveyard .... Erika Stanley

This is a low-budget, but not cheap-appearing, first feature effort by two of the most devoted followers of the horror film, producer-director-writer John Stanley and co-producer-writer and cameraman Kenn Davis. Both work full-time in Frisco for the Chronicle, Stanley as an entertainment writer and Davis as an artist. They've collaborated previously in 16m shorts and detective fiction.

Their current effort, shot entirely in Frisco with local SAG members, shows sufficient competence and is frequently quite amusing. Via PFE, they've managed a 10-situation booking in the Bay Area with-in the next two weeks and have playdates elsewhere, although not in such saturation.

Commercially, the outlook is probably bleak because, save for a "Young Frankenstein," the satiric horror genre is so untested.

Still, there's sufficient gore in "Nightmare in Blood" to please the followers of fright flicks who may not dig the flip, hip writing. Thus, the film looms as an old-fashioned "B" venture, apt for pairing with a more exploitation product.

Strength of the picture is in its writing. Scenario is build around a horror film festival featuring a vet star of vampire films protrayed by Jerry Walter. But there's a twist — Walter really is a vampire. And his two FR men (Ray K. Goman and Hy Pyke, who give the best performances) are a couple of old-time slaughterers who are kept alive by their boss with massive blood transfusions every decade or so. Naturally, the blood must be fresh, and so murders abound.

Stanley keeps the action moving, but there's really not enough of it to fill 90 minutes. The technical work throughout is quite professional.

— *Herb.*

La Mujer De La Tierra Caliente
(Woman From the Torrid Land)
(SPANISH-ITALIAN-COLOR)

Madrid, July 11.

Orfeo PSCA (Madrid) and I.I.F. SRL (Rome) coproduction. Directed by Jose Maria Forque. Features entire cast. Exec producer, J.M. Forque. Screenplay, Hermogenes Sainz, Forque; camera (Eastmancolor), Alejandro Ulloa; editor, Mercedes Alonso; music (CAM), Carlo Savina; sets, Rafael Richart. Reviewed at Cine Torre de Madrid (Madrid), July 10, '78. Running time: 80 MINS.
Cast: Stuart Whitman, Laura Gemser, Pilar Velazquez, Enrique Alzucaray, Antonio Gamero, Francisco Algora, Javier Loyola.

Some exotic backdrops from locations in Colombia and the presence of Laura ("Black Emmanuelle") Gemser will be the chief selling points in this pic with a wandering story. A few, rather mild, sex scenes have been thrown in, but the kinkiest it ever gets is when the nameless heroine moves in with a one-legged fruit vendor.

Story, told mostly in flashbacks, concerns a village girl who dreams of breaking away from the rudimentary farm life she is leading and going to the big city, where, she hopes, elegance and luxury await her. After working her way through several beaus, and deciding that prostitution is no solution either, she hitches a ride in a trailer to return to the village.

Thrust into the trailer with her is an equally unhappy American engineer, whose marriage quite literally went on the rocks when his highfalutin' wife went over Angel Falls in a rowboat. The flashbacks are broken by the antics of the two truck drivers and ultimately the lovemaking of the couple. When they reach their destination, he gets out to buy a beer, realizes he should have stuck to the native charmer, but finds only an empty trailer.

Thesping throughout is of the middling level, and some of the dialog is too self-conscious and banal. Otherwise, Forque's direction is professional, though it fails to bring out the potentials of the exotic scenery and erotic imagery. —*Besa.*

L'Ordre Et La Securite Du Monde
(Order and Security of the World)
(FRENCH-COLOR)

Paris, July 25.

CIE release of Dedalus-Seul Audiovisuel-FR3 production in association with the American Sign Company. Stars Bruno Cremer, Donald Pleasence, Laure Dechasnel, Dennis Hopper. Directed by Claude D'Anna. Screenplay, D'Anna, Francoise Bonin; camera (Eastmancolor), Eddy Van Der Enden; editor, Kenout Peltier; music, Claude Nougaro, Maurice Vander; producers, Henry Lange, Francois Lesterlin. Reviewed at Ariane, Paris, July 17, '78. Running time, 105 MINS.
Lucas .... Bruno Cremer
Rothko .... Donald Pleasence
Helen .... Laure Dechasnel
Medford .... Dennis Hopper
Johnson .... Joseph Cotten
Herzog .... Gabriele Ferzetti
Muller .... Michel Bouquet
Kauffer .... Pierre Santini
Massonier .... Henri Serre

Director Claude D'Anna has stressed atmosphere and mood too heavily in this tale of an innocent caught up in and destroyed by big scale multinational company intrigue. Underneath all the broody lensing of posh offices and rainy streets is a familiar tale of a couple on the run.

Action only explodes near the end with a savage fight outside a moving train. Characters are mainly silhouettes in this chase story done up with notations of the impersonal underpinnings of violence in so-called economic imperialism which may be abetted by national secret service orgs.

Film is not quite an actioner due to its insistence on repetition and slowness in exposition. But it still might find outlets in this vein with a bit of tightening and some international playoff on its overall theme which has some timely aspects these days.

Pic has a number of known thesps playing small parts, such as Joseph Cotten as the harsh head of the U.S. company, Michel Bouquet as the opponent and Donald Pleasence as the gobetween. Dennis Hopper is effective as the vicious killer with Cremer and Deschasnel world weary as the pawns in this deadly international game. Technical and production values are tops. —*Mosk.*

Passe Montagne
(Mountain Pass)
(FRENCH-COLOR)

La Rochelle, July 18.

Pari Films release of Les Films Du Losange production. Features entire cast. Directed by Jean-Francois Stevenin. Screenplay, Stevenin, Babou Rappeneau Stephanie Granel, Michel Delahaye; camera (Eastmancolor), Lionel Legros Jean Yves Escoffier; editor, Yann Dedet; music, Philippe Sarde. Reviewed at La Rochelle Film Fest. June 30, '78. Running time 110 MINS.

Georges .... Jacques Villeret
Serge .... Jean-Francois Stevenin
Friend .... Texandre Barberat
Sppeer .... Yves Lemoign'
Cook .... Andre Riva

Film is a first by actor-director Jean Francois Stevenin. Touted as a needed new talent and film, it unfortunately appears too indulgent, private and, finally, heavyhanded to indicate a new movement of more accessible films to bolster the crisis that currently faces the French; namely poor quality, falling b.o. and lacklustre foreign take.

"Passe Montagne" is a sort of road film as two fortyish men meet at a rest center on a superhighway. One is from the provinces and has a garage, while the other is a Parisian, presently the owner of a disabled car. The former offers to tow the latter's car away, while the latter's friends leave, conveniently allowing the two to take off on a strange sort of ambiguous adventure and tale of friendship.

Stevenin plays the provincial who is apparently married but denies it. He is secretive and unpredictable. Jacques Villeret plays the city man drifting along with this so-called adventure. They end up in the mountains and eventually fall in with locals who stay up all night drinking and dancing.

There is a trip into the mountains and some near fights as Stevenin cuts down a big tree with a chainsaw. There is also a strange sort of unfinished house with bird-like wings where Stevenin ends up as Villeret departs.

Granted that a film can depend on atmosphere, ambiguous human relationships and indications of themes, but this one is just bouncing about in a void.

Is it a tale of an unavowed friendship between the two? That remains unclear as they gad about, talk of the internal mechanics of the Parisian's car while it is being repaired and knock about in the strange night world of mountain inns and carousing peoples.

Stevenin has presence as an actor and, as a director, a feel for space. But he as yet can not clarify his intentions and this tale ends up being too mannered, and evinces the need for more coherent scripting that is often the problem with French films as most directors insist on scripting their pix as well.

Technically, film is handled effectively. —*Mosk.*

Lam Ah Chun
(HONG KONG-COLOR)

Hong Kong, July 8.

Golden Harvest release of a High Pitch production. Executive producer, Siao Fong Fong. Features entire cast. Directed by Rikkie Chan. Screenplay, Rikkie Chan; songs, Siao Fong Fong. No other credits provided. Reviewed in Hong Kong, July 8, '78. Running time: 94 MINS.
Cast: Siao Fong Fong, Yi Lui.
(Cantonese dialog with English subtitles)

The demise of kung-fu in the international mart brought forth the re-birth of Cantonese comedies for home use and other Asian countries. Riding the crest is "Lam Ah Chun," the comedy produced by the newly-formed company, High Pitch Productions. It has already passed the HK$1 million B.O. mark on its second week of release.

Lam Ah Chun is the name of a young scatter-brained Chinese girl with an M.A. degree from America. She's a cross between Lucille Ball and Mary Poppins, Hong Kong style. It's a television character conceived, popularized then expanded to the big screen by Josephine Siao Fong Fong, the darling of Cantonese tearjerkers many moons ago.

Fong Fong, now a full grown movie actress is also a popular tv personality. She tries her hand in low comedy. However, it is obvious that she is most suited for playing suffering heroines in romantic mellers than comic characters.

However, "Lam" is a fine example of a contemporary Cantonese comedy that sells in Asia. It has the look of a film made in a hurry, there is no story line and the tight budget (H.K.$800,000) shows in the crude photography and editing. Production is marred by high handed amateurism.

Film is disjointed and relies heavily on one liners, its verbal humour geared to the lower taste levels of the general public. It is perhaps for this reason that the mumbling, fumbling and bubbling Miss Lam is doing great business.

The plus point of the prod is the frenetic pacing or non-stop whirlwind physical slapstick that begins in chaos and ends in chaos. The film is at least consistent in presenting chaotic situations in the style of Mel Brooks. Versatile and enterprising Fong Fong who acts as exec producer also sings the two soundtrack songs which are now top in the local pop charts. The film is currently being dubbed in Mandarin for release in Taiwan.

The success of Lam Ah Chun should set the trend of forthcoming Hong Kong films, and may inspire budding filmmakers here to attempt to join the "fun" bandwagon, in the usual instant chop suey style.
—*Mel.*

Netepichnaja Istoria
(An Untypical Story)
(SOVIET-COLOR)

Moscow, June 9.

A Mosfilm Production, Moscow; world rights, Goskino, Moscow. Features entire cast. Directed by Grigori Chukhrai. Screenplay, Chukhrai, V. Merejko; camera (color). P. Sokal. M. Demurov: music. M. Ziv. Reviewed at Goskino, Moscow, June 8, '78. Running time: **95 MINS.**

Cast: Nona Mirdjukova, Valentina Telichkina, Vadim Spiridonov, Andrei Nikonaev.

———

In more than a quarter-century of activity on the Soviet postwar film scene, Grigori Chukhrai has made some of the most significant films to emerge from his country in cultural trades with the West. His "The Forty-First" (1956), "Ballad of a Soldier" (1959), and "Clear Skies" (1961), the last of particular interest because it dealt with the post-Stalin years, are known to both fest and art house auds. Now a late-flowering pic of remarkable thematic daring, **"An Untypical Story,"** should be added to that list.

"An Untypical Story" deals with the war years in a manner never before attempted in Soviet cinema. A young man, a widow's only son, has to leave for military service. It is winter, and the mother takes him to the train-station in a snow-cart. At the last minute she changes her mind and, making use of a fortunate accident, brings her son home to live secretly in her house. This is a kind of Anne Frank story in reverse.

But it's more than that. The mother and son proceed to play psychological games with each other, conversational give-and-takes which provide first one and then the other with the upper hand. Meanwhile, the life of the village goes on: the mother is treated as a strange recluse who refuses to see anyone as she recedes further into herself. At times it is not clear whether the events are going on entirely inside her mind — in any case, the son degenerates into a shabby, thin, long-haired Rip van Winkle type as the seasons and years past. When the war is apparently long over, the mother suffers a heart attack and the boy is suddenly left alone. He emerges bewilderedly into the summer sun, pale and blinded.

Pic is well acted by a handful of thesps who carry the film with ease. Credits are also tops. Here's a film of strong psychological realism in a Chekhovian vein (his short stories, not the plays) to quiet any critic's remaining fears that the outmoded form of Socialist Realism still rules the roost in the Soviet Union. Pic could win recognition easily on the summer fest circuit. —*Holl.*

———

Lebanon ... Why?
(LEBANESE-DOCU-COLOR)

———

London, July 12.

A Camera 9, Group 4 production, produced and directed by Georges Chamchoum. Collaboration of Yuna Haikel, Gino Arigoni; camera (color) Vassilis Christomoglou; music, Hussein Nazek; editor, Marwan Akkawi. Reviewed at CIC Pre-

view Theatre, London, July 11, '78. Running time: **100 MINS.**
(English subtitles)

———

"Lebanon...Why?" is a seriously-intentioned newsreel-type documentary concerning the bloody two-year civil war which in that time reportedly cost the lives of some 120,000 Lebanese from both Christian and Moslem fronts. It features excerpts from 35 hours of live interviews that represented a good cross section of the peoples

The "why" in the title refers to a question posed by producer-director Georges Chamchoum as to the reason for such a terrible war. But it could equally refer to why the producers believe that anyone, other than the most directly involved, should want to pay to see such a long (100 minutes), harrowing piece of reporting.

Its marquee value must be minimal even to the morbidly curious. Boxoffice potential will not be helped by Vassilis Christomoglou's camerawork which is hazy, dull and depressing, even in shots unhampered by battle action.

The Lebanese docu's biggest failing, from an English language viewpoint, is in the quickfire subtitles which are often impossible to read in the time given and are difficult to comprehend at such a pace. Mostly the film comprises interviews.

Chamchoum has chosen to leave atrocity scenes until near the end rather than using them as punctuation marks between interviews (which might have worked better in conveying the point).

That Chamchoum and his six-man crew should have risked their necks to deliver this footage is commendable. Commercial exploitation, however, is questionable.
—*Swan.*

———

Akibiori
(End of Autumn)
(JAPANESE-COLOR)

———

La Rochelle, July 18.

Pari Films release of Shochiku production. Features entire cast. Directed by Yasujiro Ozu. Screenplay, Kogo Noda, Ozu; camera (Agfacolor), Yuji Atsuda; music, Kojun Saito. Reviewed at La Rochelle Film Fest, July 7, '78. Running time: **131 MINS.**

Cast: Chishu Ryu, Nobuo Nakamura, Teruo Oshida.

———

A still-beautiful widow becomes the focus of three friends of her late husband, each of whom loved her at one time. It is a typical theme of the late Japanese filmmaker Yasujiro Ozu. This 1960 item is part of a small salute to Ozu.

The widow's attractive daughter refuses to marry at present, though she plans to eventually. She admires her mother's devotion to the memory of her late father. But the three suitors decide that marrying

off the mother might incite the daughter to marry.

They decide one of them, a widower, will be the lucky man. But one, sent to talk to the mother, never mentions it though the daughter learns of the plan. At first she is angry with her mother and decides to marry out of spite. But the mother tells her she had no intention of marrying and calmly starts a new life alone as the three friends have their usual dinners sans women and discuss the matter.

Ozu's use of brief elliptical scenes without fades between major scenes transmit a feeling of life going on, and blend with the doings of the characters as they try to resolve the changing aspects of their lives. The men are simple but resolved in their attempts to help an old friend's family, despite the hangups of their love for the mother.

Ozu built a stock cast, and the actors were thus at ease in many of his films. The men depicted eating together in restaurants without their wives is a Japanese characteristic, but not unlike men's clubs in other climes.

Slow, but always effective and insightful into human actions, Ozu's film needs careful handling. There is no heavy dramatic treatment, no violence, no permissiveness but rather a poetic flair that makes it warm and moving. "Akibiori" finally comments on the human condition within the basic social unit, the family.

Ozu has long been a buff fave, but it may now be time to get his films more general outings because their true feeling for basic human relationships can still make them effective despite the social changes and permissiveness marking the last decades. —*Mosk.*

———

Interiors
(COLOR)

———

Woody Allen's first serious drama looks like an American version of Ingmar Bergman. Limited commercial outlook.

———

Hollywood, July 27.

A United Artists release of a Jack Rollins-Charles H. Joffe production, produced by Charles H. Joffe; executive producer, Robert Greenhut. Written and directed by Woody Allen. Camera (Technicolor), Gordon Willis; editor, Ralph Rosenblum; production design, Mel Bourne costume design, Joel Schumacher; assistant director, Martin Berman. No other credits available. Reviewed at the MGM studios, Culver City, July 27, '78. (MPAA rating: PG). Running time: **93 MINS.**

Flyn	Kristin Griffith
Joey	Marybeth Hurt
Frederick	Richard Jordan
Renata	Diane Keaton
Arthur	E.G. Marshall
Eve	Geraldine Page
Pearl	Maureen Stapleton
Mike	Sam Waterston

———

Nothing could prepare Woody Allen fans for "Interiors." This is the serious film he has long promised to make. Since Allen has often expressed his admiration for Ingmar Bergman, "Interiors" is no mere homage to the Swedish master, but a direct adaptation of his techniques and even his themes and concerns. Commercial outlook appears questionable.

Regardless of how United Artists handles the advertising and promotion of this picture, audiences will "read" Woody Allen and "think" comedy, or at a minimum, light drama. But this is stonefaced straight drama about death, art and the human condition. It is full of pain, angst and psychic suffering. There isn't a single joke in the script; not one scene is played for laughs. Except for two or three minutes when source music is heard in the background, the film use no music. The opening credits, in plain typeface, come on screen over silence.

Watching this picture a question keeps recurring: What would Woody Allen think of all this? Then you remember he wrote and directed it.

The film is populated by characters reacting to situations Allen has satirized so brilliantly in other pictures. Diane Keaton is a suffering poet married to Richard Jordan, a novelist overshadowed by Keaton's accomplishments and talents. Keaton has two sisters — Kristin Griffith, a television actress, and Marybeth Hurt, the most gifted of the three, but the least directed.

What would be called the film's action — like Bergman's pictures, the movement is interior, in the mind — revolves around the relationship among the sisters and their parents, E.G. Marshall and Geraldine Page.

Marshall, apparently, is a very wealthy man. His wife, (Geraldine Page), an artist of some sort, is a meticulous and disturbed woman. Suddenly, over breakfast one morning, Marshall announces that he is leaving her in a trial separation. Page falls apart and emotionally destructs after Marshall announces that he plans to marry another woman, Maureen Stapleton. The daughters, each involved in a personal crisis of their own, must then react to their mother's torment.

Because of the nature of the characters and their intelligence, the reactions are complex and cerebral and the film deals with Big Issues. Again, Bergman's themes — death, the possibilities of communication between people, the role of the artist.

"Interiors" also looks like a Bergman film. Characters are photographed against blank walls, Keaton's discussions with her analyst appear almost to be a confession into the camera. And the final third of "Interiors" was shot near the ocean in Long Island and looks like the Swedish island on which Bergman has photographed so many of his films.

Keaton's role is the most difficult, but her performance the least believable of the eight principals in the picture. Maureen Stapleton as the woman Marshall marries after divorcing Geraldine Page, is the only character who reacts more from the heart than the head. She is wonderful. That is not to underplay the other performances, all of which are complex and well managed.

"Annie Hall" proved how far Allen had progressed as a director since "Take The Money And Run." And this very deliberate and controlled film reinforces that proof.

Commercially, "Interiors" appears to be a very iffy prospect. There will be some curiosity about the project among urban sophisticates, especially with Keaton, so a certain likely market is out there. But the film is such a sombre, downbeat work — think again of Bergman — that the possibilities in the general market appear to be nonexistent. —*Hege.*

Eyes Of Laura Mars
(COLOR)

Stylish, classy, haunting thriller.

Hollywood, July 25.

A Columbia Pictures release of a Jon Peters Production, produced by Jon Peters; executive producer, Jack H. Harris. Stars Faye Dunaway, Tommy Lee Jones. Directed by Irvin Kershner. Screenplay, John Carpenter and David Zelag Goodman from a story by Carpenter; camera (Metrocolor), Victor J. Kemper; music, Artɩ Kane; editor, Michael Kahn; production designer, Gene Callahan; costume designer, Theoni V. Aldredge; art director, Robert Gundlach;

associate producer, Laura Ziskin; set decorator, John Godfrey; assistant director, Louis A. Stroller. Mel Howard; sound, Les Lazarowitz; love theme words and music, Karen Lawrence. John Desautels; gallery photographs, Helmut Newton; Eyes of Laura Mars photographs, Rebecca Blake; stunt coordinator, Alex Stevens. Reviewed at The Burbank Studios, Burbank, July 25, 1978. (MPAA rating: R.) Running time: **104 MIN.**

Laura Mars .... Faye Dunaway
John Neville .... Tommy Lee Jones
Tommy Ludlow .... Brad Dourif
Donald Phelps .... Rene Auberjonois
Michael Reisler .... Raul Julia
Sal Volpe .... Frank Adonis
Michele .... Lisa Taylor
Lulu .... Darlanne Fluegel
Elaine Cassel .... Rose Gregorio
Bill Boggs .... Bill Boggs
Robert .... Steve Marachuk

"Eyes of Laura Mars" is a very stylish thriller in search of a better ending. In his first film since "A Star is Born," producer Jon Peters has carefully chosen the right technical talent to complement a first rate cast. The result, a haunting whodunit, should perform well and benefit from almost certain critical acclaim. Probably outlook would have been brightened even further if the John Carpenter-David Zelag Goodman script had one of those clever twists that holds audience's minds long after leaving the theatre.

Faye Dunaway stars as a chic fashion photographer with mysterious and accurate premonitions about a series of murders. All of the victims are either friends or associates. Tommy Lee Jones, in an inspired bit of casting, plays a police lieutenant assigned to the case and an integral element in the mystery. Brad Dourif as Dunaway's driver, Rene Auberjonois as her trendy and obnoxious manager and Raul Julia as her ex-husband, add marvelous supporting performances.

In too many of his previous films, Irvin Kershner's direction has been marked by an excess of artifice. With "Eyes," however, Kershner's style fits splendidly and Peters can be complemented for his choice. All of the technical credits, especially Victor Kemper's camerawork and production designer Michael Kahn's realization of the world and aura of New York's beautiful people culture, are of the highest quality. Again, the word is stylish.

Especially well handled are the screen realizations of Dunaway's premonitions. They look like a blurred videotape, as she explains to Jones at one point, a conception which works well on screen. It is at the same time real enough to be frightening and mysterious enough to be inexplicable as a psychic phenomenon.

The relationships among the characters, Dunaway's portrayal of a chic and haggard photographer-artist and even the choice of Helmut Newton and Rebecca Blake's violent and stark photos as the work of the fictional Dunaway character are satisfying and engaging.

Even the ending is satisfying. But that's not enough. It would be unfair to analyze the particulars of what's insufficient without giving away the ending and the identity of the killer. To reveal, however, that his (or her) identity is predictable points to the fact that the writers could have done better. —*Hege.*

Interno D'Un Convento
(Interior Of A Convent)
(ITALIAN-COLOR)

Paris, Aug. 1.

Parafrance release of Trust International Films production. Features entire cast. Written and directed by Walerian Borowczyk, loosely based on Stendhal's "Promenade in Rome." Camera (Eastmancolor), Luciano Tovoli; art director, Luciano Spadoni; music, Sergio Montori. Reviewed at Paramount-Elysees, Paris, July 28, '78. Running time, **95 MINS.**

Clara .... Ligia Branice
Veronica .... Marina Pierro
L'Abbesse .... Gabriella Giacobbe
Martina .... Loredano Martinez
Confessor .... Mario Maranzana

Polish director Walerian Borowczyk has been a resident in France for almost 20 years though he went back to make a feature in his native country three years ago. He started as a noted animator and then graduated to features in France going from politico metaphorical themes to the middle ages to costume and modern erotic films. Now he has made one in Italy loosely based on a tale of French novelist Stendhal.

Borowczyk gives a crucible look at an early 19th century convent beset by an outbreak of sexuality among the many comely young nuns who seem to react against the repression and hypocrisy of their overseer and a male confessor. Most are there because their families force them in to use their inheritances for themselves.

The fine-fitting gowns and white starched head-pieces make colorful uniforms as these women cavort under the eyes of the head mistress. Latter carries a sword cane which she uses to prod mattresses to find any letters or hidden forbidden things. Coming on one nun copulating with a man, who has sneaked into the convent, she punishes her and also lets her know this man is being sent away to America by his family.

It is this frustrated girl who leads to a rash of poisoning in this way-out nunnery. The main character is a lovely girl who seems to be dedicated but actually has a sort of sensual relationship to religion. She exercises nude before a mirror, and finally falls for the nephew of the confessor allowed to study in the convent library.

One day she makes love with the young man while another lets in a lover. Both have been aided by the nun who has poisoned the superior

and now they too are poisoned as the whole affair is hushed up by the Church. Though there is masturbation with a wooden dildo and simulated cunnilingus and copulation there is a plastic and textural beauty to the film, a robust, healthy attitude that makes this more forthright than pornographic or blasphemous.

The line between religious ecstacy and sexual elan has been explored by Borowczyk before. The players are effective, and, though this may raise hackles in some spots, it has not run into censor problems here or in other parts of Europe. Playoff is there worldwide for this tale of convent sexuality. —*Mosk.*

Agent 69 Jensen i Skyttens Tegn
(Agent 69 Jensen In The Sign Of Sagittarius)
(DANISH-COLOR)

Copenhagen, July 19.

A Happy Film (Anders Sandberg) production, A/S Europa Film release. Features entire cast. Story by Edmondt Jensen. Script and directed by Werner Hedmann. Camera (Eastmancolor) Rolf Roenne, Gerhard Petersen; music, Bent Fabricius-Bjerre; editor, Maj Soya; production design, Erling Joergensen; costumes, Keld Rex Holm. Reviewed at Saga, Copenhagen, July 19, '78. Running time, **90 MINS.**

Matty Harry .... Gina Janssen
Penny .... Anna Bergman
Agent 69 Jensen .... Ole Soeltoft
Madame KomPhur ...... Lee Fong Wong
K.B. .... Andre Chazel
Arnold .... Soeren Stroemberg

In producer Anders Sandberg's and writer-director Werner Hedmann's Astrological Sign, internationally top-selling series of porno spoofs, this latest item, "Agent 69 Jensen In The Sign Of Sagittarius," is by far the funniest. Its porno sequences are cleanly executed and dramatically well motivated, the participating women (notably Germany's Gina Janssen) have wit as well as good looks, the men are all first-rate comedians, the camerawork and the editing would serve any firstrate feature, serious or otherwise, the comedy sequences are madcappy but somehow logically controlled, and the dialogue is adequately zany.

Impossible to go into detail about the plot which involves secret agents from Denmark, Albania, Russia and Kong Kong, all in quest of five powder compacts, one of which contains a microfilm, othe others explosives. The hunt goes through Tangiers nightclubs, Copenhagen fashion shows and a slim-down clinic with erotic gymnastics as its chief cure. All spy film cliches are nailed down in a happy off-hand way and underscored wittily by Bent Fabricius-Bjerre's James Bond theme music parodies.

Distributors from several countries converged in Copenhagen even ahead of film's opening with checkbooks at the ready. —*Kell.*

El Monosabio
(The Wise Monkey)
(SPANISH-COLOR)

Madrid, July 22.

An El Iman (Madrid) production. Directed by Ray Rivas. Features entire cast. Screenplay, Pedro Beltran, based on story by Rivas; camera (Eastmancolor), Fernando Arribas; music, Jose Nieto; editor, Jose Salcedo; sets, Adolfo Cofino. Reviewed at Cine Palafox (Madrid), July 21, '78. Running time: 88 MINS.
Juanito .... Jose Luis Lopez Vazquez
Rafa .... Curro Fajardo
Amparito .... Manuela Camacho
Antonita .... Antonita Linares
Clara .... Chus Lampreave
Manene .... Alberto Fernandez
Paca .... Mercedes Barranco

This is Yank helmer Ray Rivas's first feature, shot in Spain for Jose Luis Borau's El Iman banner. Curiously enough, pic is reminiscent of some of the local product of the 1950s with its simplistic story and Jose Luis Lopez Vazquez hamming it up. "El Monosabio" is almost a nostalgia trip for Spaniards. It steers a wobbly line between drama and comedy, and its ultimate weakness is that it never quite decides which it's opting for.

Story is about a bullring helper, or Monosabio, the lowliest two-legged form of the taurine world, whose dream it is to find glory in the arena, partly through his own business dealings and the promotion of a young boy in the neighborhood who, he feels, has the makings of a great matador.

Most of pic involves the monosabio's wheeling and dealings to try to raise the coin for a village bullfight. After snapping up a pile of cash intended for his daughter's abortion (the culprit, of course, is the fledgling torero), he finally manages to get the young bulls and rent the suits and trappings needed for the fight.

Final sequence has the boy\shying out in fear of the bulls, and the monosabio, after being thrown a couple of times, mastering the bull in a moment of apotheosis. It all ends happily when boy gets girl and family and neighbors frolic at the baptism. Rivas' direction is okay for a first effort, and technical credits are on the whole satisfactory. Strictly for the Hispano market, with possibly some sales prospects in Latin America. —*Besa.*

Ils Sont Fous Ces Sorciers
(These Sorcerers Are Mad)
(FRENCH-COLOR)

Paris, Aug. 1.

AMLF release of Lira Films production. Features entire cast. Directed by Georges Lautner. Screenplay, Norbert Carbonneaux, Robert Kantof, Claude Mulot; camera (Eastmancolor), Henri Decae; editor, Michele David. Reviewed at Ambassade-Gaumont, Paris, July 17, '78. Running time: 90 MINS.
With: Jean Lefebvre, Henri Guybet, Renee St. Cyr, Julien Guiomar, Catherine Lachens, Jean-Jacques Moreau.

In these days of brilliant film special effects, the small scale occult comedic attempts in this fairly flaccid pic are a letdown. Two rather dim Parisians on a tropical isle urinate on a sacred totem to become the plaything of the native Gods. Repetitious, and with only a few yocks, this could have local legs but appears more for some playoff in Latino and Asian marts rather than more demanding ones.

Two second string local comics, Jean Lefebvre and Hanry Guybet are the bewitched ones. Former has a combo vacation-biz trip to the Maurice Islands off Africa and latter is on holiday. After their run-in with the Gods, they cannot see themselves in mirrors, levitate against their will, can guide things telepathically, etc.

They finally use their new gifts to straighten out their problems. A slim warm weather item that is directed somewhat loosely though given okay production dress.
—*Mosk.*

Antalya Fest

Maden
(The Mine)
(TURKISH-COLOR)

Antalya, July 5.

A Maden Film Production, Istanbul. Features entire cast. Directed by Yavuz Ozkan. Screenplay, Yavuz Ozkan; camera (color), Izzat Akay; music, O. Zulfu Livaneli. Reviewed at Antalya Film Fest, July 4, '78. Running time: 95 MINS.
Cast: Cuneyt Arkim, Tarik Akan, Hale Soygazi, Meral Orhansoy.

A socially engaged film with a strong political undertone, Yavuz Ozkan's "The Mine" merits praise as a breakthrough in Turkish cinema in that both theme and style carry weight, enough to make it the Grand Prix winner in Antalya in the first international competition sweepstakes. It also won the top kudo in the national film fest (Antalya's 15th).

Now that the pic scored in both fests to broad critical acclaim, chances are better than even that it will pop up again at other fests on the circuit before the year is out.

"The Mine" works well on two levels. It's the story of mining, that precarious profession offering high movie drama when the expected cave-in takes place. But this is also the chronicle of a strike, a necessary measure a group of committed miners take to prevent such disasters from happening again after a series of accidents point to the worst if matters continue as they are. The leader of the strikers is, apparently, a politically motivated individual feared by the big bosses because of his ability to collect signatures and persuade workers by his moral courage.

Particularly interesting in the story is the attention to humanistic detail, rather than pic getting embedded in dry polemics. One of the workers in this provincial mining town is attracted to a girl working in a passing carnival troupe, who in turn is longing for something lasting rather than being pawed by the usual local clientele. The story of this married man's indecision to face reality mirrors the social conditions in the country.

Pic provides excitement in a climactic sequence down in the mine. As Turkish cinema works largely without studio facilities and mostly out-of-doors, the mine sequence required extra expense. It's a solid piece of documentary footage in the vein of Joris Ivens and G.W. Pabst (to name but two who have handled similar themes). Helmer Ozkan, from television, apparently spent a good deal of the time researching his subject.

Pic's only drawback is the script. Little motivation is given for the hero's political and social engagement, nor is there a clear definition of the conflict between the miner-strikers and the mine-owners. The hiring of thugs to break up meetings (the leader and his group are gunned down in one action scene) is strong stuff, but, again, more information on background is desirable so far as unions and such organizations are concerned. These are minor points, however, when one considers the general impact of the film on the typical Turk audience and the overall lack of such committed pix amid light entertainment and sex comedies (the country's normal film fare).

"The Mine" demonstrates that there's something progressive going on in Turkey. Thesps and credits are a good cut above the average.
—*Holl.*

Urgia
(Calamity)
(RUMANIAN-COLOR)

Antalya, July 7.

A Rumaniafilm Production, Bucharest; world rights, Rumaniafilm. Features entire cast. Directed by Josif Demian, Andrei Blaier. Screenplay, Fl. N. Nastase; camera (color), Gheorghe Voicu; music, Adrian Enescu; sets, Stefan Antonescu. Reviewed at Antalya Film Fest (International Competition), July 6, '78. Running time: 90 MINS.
Cast: Gheorghe Cozorici, Luiza Orosz, Nicolae Praida, Dana Dogaru, Ica Matache, Costel Constantinescu, Jean Sandulescu, Dan Condurache, Mihai Cafrita, Gelu Birau, Ion Musca.

A kind of epic portrait of a Rumanian village via a deathbed flashback of an elderly farmer, Josif Demian and Andrei Blaier's "Calamity" relies mostly on poetic images rather than a narrative style to tell its story. Demian is a former cameraman and Blaier at vet helmer of dramatic action pix, the two combining their talents to make this pic one of the more interesting stylistic experiments to emerge from Rumania in recent years.

"Calamity" is not a light entertainment pic; it seeks to be critical and straightforward in its review of recent history. The prewar years are shown in an idyllic light, a kind of pastoral backdrop against which the fate of a people is mirrored in minute detail. The central character has a son and a daughter, the latter engaged to another youth and a lively girl when the war comes and he is called to the front. Like so many others the son dies — but the father insists that his heir was survived and will return home one day. Meanwhile, the daughter commits suicide when her lover returns home without legs from the war. Then the Germans advance into the village as the country changes allegiance, causing a mass exodus of the population.

Amid all the excitement, the father returns to his farm and (it's revealed at the end) kills a Nazi officer who is stationed there. During the war, he has become a recluse, and afterwards refused to emerge from his hiding place as he and his wife grow old. The times change and progress comes to the village; the old man, however, still hides away and awaits his son's arrival. The mystery of his madness is unravelled at the end through the compassion of a relative.

"Calamity" is perhaps too national in its theme to be understood completely abroad, but Demian and Blaier have constructed an impressive historical portrait of the times.
— *Holl.*

Firatin Cinleri
(The Bad Spirits of the Euphrates)
(TURKISH-COLOR)

Antalya, July 3.

A Korhan Film production, Istanbul. Features entire cast. Directed by Korhan Yurtsever. Screenplay, Ihsan Yuce; camera (color), Salih Dikisci; music, Cahit Barkay. Reviewed at Antalya Film Fest, July 2, '78. Running time: 78 MINS.
Cast: Aytac Arman, Betul Ascioglu, Tugay Toksoz.

A sleeper at the recent San Remo fest, Korhan Yurtsever's "The Bad Spirits of the Euphrates" also caught critic attention at the new Antalya Fest of Turkish cinema as one of the best pix made here in recent years. It's a personal "auteur" pic made on a small budget by a young helmer who worked for some years in the commercial side of the industry, saved his money, and lensed this striking tale of poverty and superstition with a team of friends. A good bet for more international fests on the summer circuit (an invitation was extended by Locarno), pic should be included in Turkish Film Weeks as evidence that a strong national cinema is rapidly developing in Asia Minor.

In southeastern Turkey (near the Syrian border), the Euphrates River flows from its mountainous source through lovely gorges where the original Seljuk Turks settled and ancient history was written by warring Romans, Byzantines, and Persians in efforts to control the gateway between East and West. Today this rusty-red landscape is inhabited mostly by shepherds and tenant farmers, who are in bondage to landowners who control the destinies of entire villages. A living is made by the sweat of the brow, depending to a great extent on the generosity of the Euphrates River as it begins its low winding journey down to the Persian Gulf.

A farmer and his wife resist the pressures of a greedy landlord to take over their plot of land. In flashbacks, it becomes clear that the landowner has a yen for the lady in question, which hasn't quite abated despite her marriage, a child, and another pregnancy. Further, two attempts were made to kidnap or molest her — once amid the spectacular ruins of the Commagene sanctuary of Nemrut Dagi (with the toppled heads of collossal statues of gods stemming back into antiquity), and another time which resulted in the killing of the woman's "bandit" uncle (a feared champion for the rights of the downtrodden).

Pic opens with the husband being beaten by the landowner's hired thugs after the former tries to stop poaching on his land (situated across the swift-moving Euphrates). The wife and villagers witness the attack from afar and can do nothing to help — further, the oppressor has a gun and is not afraid to use it whenever someone gets in his way. The young farmer has debts, but decides to sell his cow at a distant marketplace to buy a gun. The landowner offers to make a deal instead, provided the farmer kisses his hand publicly before the villagers.

But the bad spirits of the Euphrates take possession of the wife, who has epileptic fits and goes into forced labor to have her child. Later the bleeding doesn't stop, and various remedies of a superstitious nature are tried. She is finally "condemned" by the villagers and thrown bodily into the Euphrates. The husband also goes mad at this point, kills the tyrant, and leaps into the river after wife.

Pic is astonishing for the beauty of many shots and the general atmosphere supporting a whisp of a story. But even more remarkable are the documentary aspects of the film: the portrait of village and mountain life in a rugged part of Turkey that has changed little over the centuries. A film for both the art house and the docu circuit by a young helmer to watch in the future. —Holl.

Selvi Boylum Al Yazmalim
(The Girl With The Red Scarf)
(TURKISH-COLOR)

Antalya, July 5.

A Yesilcam Filmcilik Production, Istanbul. Features entire cast. Directed by Atif Yilmaz. Screenplay, Ali Habib Ozgenturk, based on book of same title by Gengiz Aytmatov; camera (color), Cetin Tunca; music, Cahit Berkay. Reviewed at Antalya Film Fest, July 4, '78. Running time: 90 MINS.
Cast: Turkan Soray, Kadir Inanir, Ahmet Mekin, Hulya Tuglu.

One of Turkey's better-known helmers, Atif Yilmaz is a leader in the "realist" tradition stemming from the 1950s, a student of Lutfi Akad and an associate of Yilmaz Guney. This time he has adapted a popular story by Soviet-Kirghizian author Gengiz Aytmatov, "The Girl (or the Slender One) with the Red Scarf," a Central Asian Soviet writer from that area of the country where the Turks mark their ancestral own descendancy.

Aytmatov, it should be noted, inspired such New Soviet Cinema helmers as Larissa Shepitko ("Heat"), Andrei Mikhalkov-Konchalovsky ("The First Teacher"), and Bolot Shamsheiv ("The White Ship") as far back as the beginning of the last decade, long before he was "discovered" by Hedrick Smith in his politically-oriented survey, "The Russians." His writings are both entertaining and socially critical, full of rich symbolism and motifs taken from national traditions and everyday life.

"The Girl with the Red Scarf" works its magic, first, as a story about a girl rescued from a life of poverty by a passing truck driver, who, in love, names his truck after her and her bright red head-scarf. But after the birth of a son, he loses his driver's job and is reduced to a mechanic, due to illegally using the company's truck to transport people in a rainstorm. Taking to drink, he loses his wife's love and returns to his former flame; thereupon, the "slender one" sets off on her own and is helped along the way by a gentle worker who also falls in love with her. Now faced with two men in her life, after the return of her former drunken husband asking for forgiveness after intervening years, she is torn apart inside and finally settles for her own son's choice of father (of course, the gentle worker).

The original Aytmatov story runs a couple miles deeper than this lightly rendered melodrama. His critique on the industrial destroying of past mores and traditions, as well as dehumanizing working conditions, is felt rather than defined. Principal actors are popular stars, smiling, tear-drenched, matinee idols, while the original story calls for stronger stuff. The second thesp in her life attempts reserved understatement, but still a less sturdy and moral figure is called for to give the story its proper depth.

"The Girl with the Red Scarf" deserved its third-place kudo in the national section of the Antalya Film Fest by virtue of outdoor settings and rugged trucking-and-construction milieu to keep the story moving. Good bet for Turkish Film Weeks. —Holl.

Dugun
(The Wedding)
(TURKISH-COLOR)

Antalya, July 8.

An Erman Film Production, Istanbul. Features entire cast. Written and directed by Lutfi Akad. Camera (color), Gani Turanh. Only creidts available. Reviewed at Antalya Film Fest (Retro), July 7, '78. Running time: 90 MINS.
Cast: Hulya Hocyigit, Ahmet Mekin, Kamuran Usluer.

An important pic when it won the top kudo at the 1974 Antalya Film Fest, Lutfi Akad's "The Wedding" is a semi-docu on the plight of villagers who migrate to the city — in this case, Istanbul — to work odd jobs as street-salesmen and housepeddlers. (Akad and Atif Yilmaz were the two vet helmers who first gave Yilmaz Guney, Turkey's most famous director, jobs as a screenplay writer and movie actor two decades ago.)

"The Wedding" focuses on the greed of the head of an exvillage clan, who mistreats the girls in the family in particular, one sister of whom has sacrificed herself to raise the younger members of the family (two other sisters and a brother) after the death of the parents. Having started out with little to peddle on the streets and intent on the younger boy getting a school education, the family head tries to better his luck by marrying off the younger sisters for money to expand in the business. One is "sold" to buy a vendor-truck, which later results in a fight over a corner and the unintentional slaying of a competitor; the younger brother (for apparent reasons of family honor) takes the blame for a weak uncle and goes to prison.

The next move is to put another sister on the block and marry her off to an underhanded goods-supplier. It's here that the older woman in the family rebels and puts things straight on the wedding day. Docu angle is pic's strong side, while dialog and story line runs too much along its predictable way to merit further attention. A statement against out moded tribal traditions. —Holl.

Hidir
(TURKISH-COLOR)

Antalya, July 4.

A Bizim Film Production, Cengiz Nacaroglu, Istanbul. Features entire cast. Directed by Yavuz Figenli. Screenplay, Ahmet Undag, Ihsan Yuce; camera (color), Rafet Siriner. Reviewed at Antalya Film Fest, July 3, '78. Running time: 81 MINS.
Cast: Behcet Nacar, Menderes Samancilar, Gonul Eren, Kazim Kartal.

An action pic with plenty of Italo-Western pop-punches on a regular 20-minute scale, Yavuz Figenli's "Hidir" adds a dash of social comment in this story of village revenge that carries to union organizations in Istanbul. There are faint echoes of "On the Waterfront" in the awakening of a tough ex-prisoner (he killed one of the men who killed his father and is now searching for the son of the other) to the social and political realities about him. Pic is titled on hero's name: Hidir.

The opening sequence points the direction of the film thereafter. In Eastern Turkey villagers carry on bloody feuds. A young boy's father is killed before his eyes; he himself only narrowly escapes and remembers the shiny gun in the hand of the killer. Later, after being told to kill by the clan's elderly leader, he shoots the accomplice who didn't pull the trigger and is sentenced to a long jail term. Emerging from prison now as a tough individualist, he is hounded by his village laws and his relatives to still kill the son of his father's killer. Since the man is now organizing unions in Istanbul, but no one knows exactly what he looks like, he must go from place to place in search of him.

The twist is that he sides with the union leader without recognizing who he is, takes the side of the workers against thugs trying to stop a strike, and makes friends in the end with the man he's supposed to kill. The latter, meanwhile, accepts the fate his father was responsible for, although he has a girlfriend he soon plans to marry. A few more punches, and everything comes to a happy end. —Holl.

Arkadas
(The Friend)
(TURKISH-COLOR)

Antalya, July 7.

A Guney Film Production, Istanbul. Stars Yilmaz Guney. Written and directed by Yilmaz Guney. Camera (color). Cetin Tunca. Only credits available. Reviewed at Antalya Film Fest (Retro), July 6, '78. Running time: **90 MINS.**

Cast: Yilmaz Guney, Melike Demirag, Kerim Afsar, Azra Balkan, Ahu Tugbay.

This is perhaps the high point in Yilmaz Guney's career. Turkey's leading director and one of the most mature talents to be found in Arab and so-called Third World Cinema. Guney produced, directed, wrote and acted in "The Friend" (1974). But that's not the important factor — the pic appeared after Ecevit came to power at the head of a new coalition government.

Oddly enough, "The Friend," mirrors the controversial atmosphere which surrounds Guney himself. Born in 1937 in Adana in Southern Turkey, he began writing in student days in Adana, Ankara, and Istanbul, turning to script-writing at the age of 20 for films he also acted in. The publication of a story in 1961 brought him recognition, then the popularity of "Hope" (1970) and "Elegy" (1971), in which he took sides with the downtrodden, raised him in the eyes of the public to a kind of national hero.

"The Friend" is characterized by an astute social analysis and warm sensibility for his subject. It became an instant b.o. hit and has remained so (if the resort crowds at Antalya are any indication).

"The Friend" hints that Guney has ripened into a talent of world-class rank, although his sociopolitical position is anything but clearly defined. Like writer-director Zika Pavlovic in Yugoslavia (Serbia) and writer-director-actor Vassili Shukshin in Russia (born in Siberia), as well as Salah Abu Seif in Egypt, Guney takes his impulse from precise observation of everyday life and the plight of the common man. He does little more than render the facts as he sees them, letting the audience sort out the social forces and political realities behind them. He analyzes without preaching.

As a mysterious friend who comes to the home of a rich man living in the exclusive section of Istanbul, Guney does not have very much to say but it's his presence that commands. Jimmie, a companion in youth, has changed from an idealist to a cold commercial businessman living on this barricaded island of sensual pleasures and moral indifference (the street leading into the colony is guarded in the fashion of an exclusive country club). The "friend," on the other hand, has kept his ideals intact.

A conflict arises between the friend and the wife, who wants to keep Jimmie just the way he is, although she too is taken by the stranger invited to live in the house. It's the daughter who watches closely, longing for something other than sunning the day through in a bathing suit. Her discussions with the stranger reveal, first, the moral character of the friend and, second, add a note of mysticism to his presence in the house. Also, a long-haired youth in the neighborhood is taking out his frustrations by cutting the tires of affluent autos secretly, only to be discoverd by "the friend" who doesn't say a word. (Finally, Jimmie journeys with the stranger to a peasant community and sees life again with his old eyes; upon returning home, he confronts his wife (who slaps Guney in anger) and then shoots himself. The youth and daughter make changes for the better.)

A remarkable pic reminiscent of Pier Paolo Pasolini's "Teorema," Guney has mingled technical elements — sharp camera work, sounds and music on the soundtrack — to top thesp performances. A must for Turkish Film Weeks and any interested in the quality and strength of Anatolian cinema.

— Holl.

Umut
(Hope)
(TURKISH-B&W)

Antalya, July 8.

A Guney Film, Abudrrahman Heshine, Production, Istanbul. Stars Yilmaz Guney. Directed by Yilmaz Guney. Screenplay. Guney, Serif Goren; camera, Kaya Ererez, music, Arif Erkin; editing, Celal Kose. Reviewed at Antalya Film Fest (Retro), July 7, '78. Running time: **105 MINS.**

Cabbar	Yilmaz Guney
Fatma, his Wife	Gulsen Alniacik
Hasan	Tuncel Kurtiz
The Holy Man	Osman Alyanak
Cemilee	Sema Engin
Hatice	Sevgi Tatli
Mehmet Emin	Kursat Alniacik
Hieret	Hicret Gursen
Nizam	Nizam Erguder
Pickpocket	Enver Donmez
Salesman	Lutti Engin
Commissioner	Kemal Tatli
Hand Worker	Almet Koc

One of the best Turkish films made, Yilmaz Guney's "Hope" (1970) unspooled to a large resort crowd at Antalya on this East Mediterranean Riviera. Pic put helmer Guney and Turkish cinema on the map when it appeared at Cannes in the Directors' Fortnight in 1971, but the real critical breakthrough came when a Guney retro-arrived at San Remo fest last year, followed by another at the Berlin Forum of Young Cinema. His films are more popular than ever at home and gain constant recognition from foreign critics.

"Hope" (long forbidden in Tur-key until the present Ecevit government came to power) is an auto-biographical work. It's about a coachman, a horse-drawn taxi-driver, in the city of Adana on the Mediterranean coast in Southern Turkey. The time of the horse-carriage is passing, as automobiles supply the principal taxi transportation; nevertheless, Cabbar is illiterate and knows no other trade. Besides, he is obsessed with the illusion of hope, the dream of wining a pot-of-gold in a lottery, for which he sinks his hard-won pennies and then depends on others to read the printed results.

One day, his carriage is rammed by a car and one of his horses is killed. The court decision goes to the car-driver simply because of his status, and Cabbar has to look for a loan to pay another horse. Meanwhile, his creditors come and take everything he has at home, leaving only the abandoned coach with wife and children on the verge of starving. He pawns what he has for a gun and makes a feeble attempt at robbery, while a pickpocket seeks him out as likely prey. As the driver's circumstances worsen, he takes to blindly imitating his greedy-minded oppressors, striking those under him (including the children) with the back of his hand.

The day comes when Cabbar and his crony-friend (equally ignorant) are persuaded by a limping "holy man" that there is a buried treasure in the desert wastes waiting to be dug up by anyone able to interpret the secret signs of nature. The three set out in search of the treasure; after days under the hot sun, a barren tree on a bluff next to a stream is recognized as the key landmark to the treasure. After digging for a time, nothing materializes, and Cabbar gradually goes mad and begins walking blindfolded in a circle.

"Hope" recalls "Bicycle Thief" and other neorealist pix in the first half, then draws attention to "The Treasure of Sierra Madre" in the second. But in the long run this is an original Turkish pic, having much more in common with films in Egypt and other Arab countries. It's become a modern, minor classic, strongly directed and acted. —Holl.

Copculer Krali
(The King of the Street Cleaners)
(TURKISH-COLOR)

Antalya, July 5.

An Arzu Film Production, Istanbul. Features entire cast. Directed by Zeki Okten. Screenplay, Umor Bugay; camera (color). Erdogan Engin. Only credits available. Reviewed at Antalya Film Fest, July 4, '78. Running time: **88 MINS.**

Cast: Kemal Sunal, Sener Sen, Aysen Gruda.

Arzu Film specializes in comedies and has a group of regular thesps, cabaret style, to put them over. One is Kemal Sunal, who in Zeki Okten's "The King of the Street Cleaners" plays a Jerry Lewis-like character, cleaning Istanbul streets and yodelling on the side. He also has an eye for the girls, and believes a servant girl working for his boss is making eyes at him.

The upshot is that two comic characters, employer and employee, are chasing the same skirt, while the boss's mother is preventing her son from becoming a bridegroom because she believes her son is marrying below his uniform. Meanwhile, our street cleaner visits the girl's family and is suddenly accepted as a good prospect — after he is pursued onto a nightclub stage with his broom in his hand and his singing makes him a hit. The club's mid-day audience, composed of women, love his grinning antics. Later, before a sophisticated evening audience, his slapstick antics only make for havoc. Our hero is sent back to street cleaning, and the boss gets the girl (who turns out to be a nagging wife).

Some comic scenes of usual merit, but the emphasis is mostly on verbal puns which a foreign aud can't catch. Thesps and credits in this whacky comedy are on the plus side. —Holl.

Hodina Pravdy
(The Hour of Truth)
(CZECHOSLOVAK-COLOR)

Antalya, July 7.

A Czeschoslovensky Film Production, Studio Barrandov, Prague: world rights, Czechoslovak Film Export, Prague. Features entire cast. Written and directed by Vaclav Matejka, based on a radio play by Natasha Tanska; camera (color), Jaromir Sofr. Only credits available. Reviewed at Antalya Film Fest (International Competition), July 6, '78. Running time: **90 MINS.**

Cast: Svatopluk Matyas (Dr. Slezak), Ruzena Merunkova (his wife), Hana Maciuchova (Petra), Eliska Sirova (Tereza), Jana Gyrova (Tereza's teacher), Vladimir Brodsky (Grandpa), Jiri Pieskot, Rudolf Jelinek.

"The Hour of Truth" was originally a radio play titled "English Lesson," whose author Natasha Tanska wove a tale of varied psychological relations within an hour's school lesson given to a young girl. The play won first prize in a Czechoslovak Radio competition, thereafter being adapted to the screen by helmer Vaclav Matejka in a version that covers one day instead of a single hour. It doesn't quite work, but the story does command respect by way of theme.

It's about a man's relationship to his wife in the screen version, rather than just a girl's remembrance of details about a family relationship and the mother's pending suicide due to an incurable illness. The husband is a doctor whose wife's long-term illness has driven him to the arms of a young nurse, who spends time with him whenever possible at his country dacha. On the day in question, the mother sends the daughter off to stay with the teacher, writes a note of farewell to her husband (off for the weekend), and waits for the right moment to take her pills (after the nurse's usual injection and departure).

At about the same time, the hospital (where the doctor-husband works) is reviewing the wife's case and a decision is made to reach the doctor at his villa. As though by coincidence, the doctor becomes uneasy in the course of the day with his mistress and makes plans to return home. And the teacher, in talking with the daughter, comes to suspect the truth of the situation at home, as the girl prefers the mistress's company to her own mother's. Pic ends on a still-frame shot of the girl in her mother's dress and the daughter's echoing voice calling "Mama."

Not much chance for off-shore interest, but psychological dimension does carry the pic for a good part of the way until the audience has enough hints as to how it will end. — *Holl.*

Kara Carsafli Gelin
(The Dark-Veiled Bride)
(TURKISH-COLOR)

Antalya, July 8.
A Murat Film Production, Istanbul. Features entire cast. Directed by Sureyya Duru. Screenplay, Vedat Turkali, based on short stories by Bekir Yildiz; camera (color), Ali Ugur. Only credits available. Reviewed at Antalya Film Fest (Retro), July 7, '78. Running time: **90 MINS.**
Cast: Hakan Balamir, Semra Ozdamar, Aytac Arman, Aliya Rona, Huseyin Peyda.

Sureyya Duru is known as a comparatively strong helmer who adds a social message to dramatic material that can stand by itself. His "The Dark-Veiled Bride" copped two honors at last year's Antalya Fest of Turkish cinema, and his "Sun over the Swamp" unspooled as the Turkish entry at this year's Karlovy Vary fest.

"The Dark-Veiled Bride" deals with suppression of the peasants on the dry, mountainous plains of Eastern Turkey near the Syrian border. Here, rich landowners exploit the villagers by playing them off one against another, resorting to murder if necessary. In this case, a poor farmer is paid a sum of money by the landowner's strong-arm foreman to kill a man; because he needs the money for his starving family, he commits the murder but is captured by the police. He goes to prison and his own daughter must go to work in the home of the slain man, due to the unwritten laws and ancient customs.

When she grows up, she's still mistreated by the dead man's wife — although the son falls in love with her. Another son, recently home from army service, decides to stand up to the landowner's injustice and investigates the crime by going to the prison to talk with the murderer. In panic, the foreman engineers another death, is discovered after the deed is committed (on the day of son's wedding to the girl in the house), and is shot in vengeance by the young couple in turn. The landowner, looking on, realizes now that the villagers have united to resist his power.

Another episode in the story deals with smuggling across the border and the death of the girl's brother when Turkish border soldiers fire upon the group crossing the mine fields. As he lays dying, the boy stuffs a gold piece into his mouth, the ransom money needed to win back his sister to a free, rather than slave, status in the house of another.

Pic is well acted and has some docu twists of interest on the life of the nomad farmer. — *Holl.*

Hababam Sinifi Tatilde
(The Dunce Class on Vacation)
(TURKISH-COLOR)

Antalya, July 5.
An Arzu Film Production, Istanbul. Features entire cast. Directed by Ertem Egilmez. Screenplay, Sadik Sendil; camera (color), Erdogan Engin; music, Melih Kibar. Reviewed at Antalya Film Fest, July 4, '78. Running time: **100 MINS.**
Cast: Munir Ozkul, Kemal Sunal, Sener Sen, Adile Nasit.

A popular film series has been built on the crazy antics of the "Dunce Class," a group of dumb students played by grown-up cabaret-type thesps in short pants. The boys' school has teachers equally as eccentric, so the fun hardly ever lets up in a series of episodes loosely strung together to provide one gag after another.

Ertem Egilmez's "The Dunce Class on Vacation" opens with a new young teacher mistaken for a student when he joins in an impromptu soccer game. Later, when he shows up at class, they don't take him seriously as the man-in-charge, but neither do the other teachers in the faculty room. Another running gag is the presence of four girls in the class (the school needs money), who have a make-shift dormitory of their own; both sides play tricks on the other in and out of class.

The sports teacher is learning karate and is the biggest buffoon of all in imitating kung-fu (presently a tv rage in Turkey). The Dance Class goes off on an outing like a bunch of inexperienced boy/girl scouts, thus providing more rough-and-tumble slapstick. Meanwhile, the school director is faced with bankruptcy and the school has to be abandoned for desks in the woods. An ex-student, now a government official, comes to the rescue to save the school — so the Dunce Class can keep on working its magic. — *Holl.*

Gunes Ne Zaman Dogacak
(When the Sun Rises)
(TURKISH-COLOR)

Antalya, July 4.
An Orhun Filmcilik Production, Istanbul. Features entire cast. Directed by Mehmet Kilinc. Screenplay, Tugan Guner; camera (color), Abdullah Gurek; music, Tum Ata Grubu. Reviewed at Antalya Film Fest, July 3, '78. Running time: **98 MINS.**
Cast: Cuneyt Arkin, Oya Aydogan, Baki Tamer, Turgut Ozatay.

Mehmet Kilinc's "When the Sun Rises" deals with a minority group in Turkey and across the border who don't belong or fit in either society. From the garb of the central characters, the minority group appear to be Kurds or Caucasians, a people without a country of their own whose population is scattered along the Eastern frontier.

The story opens in a "foreign country" where religious beliefs are persecuted. Two men escape over the border to seek political asylum in Turkey: one is allowed to stay but the other has to go back, which means certain death. Also, a political agent is pursuing the two, who decide to go into the Underground in Istanbul rather than to part ways. A trail of blood follows them: first a friend is killed, then one of the two is shot by the agent, who is also eventually gunned down by Turkish police. Finally, the lone man must return over the border and is shot while crossing the bridge. All of which is the product of an action-packed imagination.

There's also the inevitable love story. Our hero meets a young girl who has exchanged Western ways for her national traditions; she gradually sees the errors of her way in confronting his moral courage. The two men-on-the-run are not too happy with the sex films on display in easy-going Istanbul either. Credits and production values are sub par. — *Holl.*

Karlovy Fest

Pasja
(Passion)
(POLISH-COLOR)

Karlovy Vary, July 12.
A Film Polski Production, Warsaw; world rights, Film Polski, Warsaw. Features entire cast. Directed by Stanislaw Rozewicz. Screenplay, Andrzej Kijowski, Edward Zebrowski; camera (color), Jerzy Wojcik; music, Piotr Mosy. Reviewed at Karlovy Vary Film Fest (Competition), July 11, '78. Running time: **120 MINS.**
Cast: Piotr Garlicki (Edward Dembowski), Zbigniew Zapasiewicz (Tyssowski), Boguslav Smela (Szela), Wojciech Alaborski (Wiesiolowski), Henryk Machalica (Smolka), Mieczyslaw Hryniewicz, Stanislaw Ignar.

Dull, overdrawn historical epic based on the Polish uprising in 1846, shortly before (1848-49) all of Central Europe was in turmoil. Stanislaw Rozewicz also made "Romantics" about the same period. This one is about writer-revolutionary Edward Dembowski in the form of a personal "Passion," as the title indicates.

It's a free interpretation of the events surrounding his last days, as apparently little is known about his death as he kept his activities underground after founding a political journal and worked for the Union of the Polish Nation movement (Poland was then divided among Russia, Prussia, and Austria).

Pic opens with the Austrian army exhuming a mass grave after the putdown of the Cracow Uprising in 1846 in an attempt to identify Dembowski's body. Thereafter, a chronicle of his efforts to win the support of the peasants to the cause throughout Galicia follows, tracing his path from Lwov to Cracow as an emissary of the Polish Democratic Association. In Cracow he forces his way into membership in the hesitant National Council, later leaving the city with his followers in a semi-religious procession to meet his death like a Christ during the Passion Week, hoping to win over the peasants. — *Holl.*

Autopsie D'Un Complot
(Autopsy of a Conspiracy)
(ALGERIAN-COLOR)

Karlovy Vary, July 12.
An Algerian Film Production. Features entire cast. Directed by Mohamed Slim Riad. Screenplay, Etienne Rolo; camera (color), Dahn Bukersh. Only credits available. Reviewed at Karlovy Vary Film Fest (Competition), July 11, '78. Running time: **90 MINS.**

A kudo winner at Karlovy Vary, this Algerian prod with a French title and thesps (everything about it seems to be French) takes place partially in a "foreign country, where an Arab consulate or embassy is bombed and people are killed on the street by secret agents. These acts of violence and terror underscore the thriller genre, whereas the political message stays in the background and is muddled as to aim and treatment. The "Autopsy of a Conspiracy" hints that bad Capitalists are out to fully destroy Algerian freedom in a plot that reaches to high political leadership in the West.

A terrorist organization is masterminded by a professional disguising himself as a respected businessman. His identity is uncovered by an inquisitive young reporter who recognizes his face in a current newspaper photograph from a previous picture revealing his full identity. Thereafter, it's only a question of time before he can prove to a few interested parties that a big-time conspiracy is underway. In the end, both he and the terror-organizer are considered dispensable, and wiped out. — *Holl.*

Stiny Horkeho Leta
(Shadows of a Hot Summer)
(CZECHOSLOVAK-COLOR)

Karlovy Vary, July 10.

A Czechoslovak, Studio Barrandov, Film Production, Prague; world rights, Czechoslovak Filmexport, Prague. Features entire cast. Directed by Frantisek Vlacil. Screenplay, Jiri Krizan; camera (color), Ivan Slapeta; music, Zdenek Liska. Reviewed at Karlovy Vary Film Fest, (competition), July 9, '78. Running time: **90 MINS.**

Cast: Juraj Kukura (Andrew Baran), Marta Vancurova (Theresa Baran), Gustav Valach (the Doctor), Karel Chromik (the Lieutenant), Zdenek Kutil (the Old Man), Jiri Bartoska (the Albino), Augustin Kuban (the Bald Man), Gustav Opocensky (the Wounded Man).

Frantisek Vlacil has carved out a distinguished career in Czech cinema as a helmer with the eye of a painter. He made "Marketa Lazarova" (1967) and "The Valley of the Bees" (1968), two Medieval tales fitted to a large canvas, as well as the recent "Smoke on the Potato Fields" (1977), about a doctor facing an identity crisis. "Shadows of a Hot Summer" seems to be somewhere in between, a story set in the lovely Moravian hills with touches of adventure to carry it through.

Plot bears a faint resemblance to Sam Peckinpah's "Straw Dogs," relating how a gentle farmer living in isolation above a village in the valley is surprised in the summer of 1947 by a five-man band of the Bender Gang, that is, Ukrainians and other nationalities who fought on the side of the Germans during the last war. The band is trying to make it to the Austrian border just as Czechoslovakia is making the decision to accept Communist rule, a political backdrop also noticeable in the story's opening sequences. The farmer, to protect his wife and children, accepts his fate meekly in the beginning and kidnaps the town doctor to save a wounded man's life.

Then he realizes he must take matters into his own hands and overpowers his enemies one by one, dying finally when the wounded man uses a gun hidden under his pillow as a last resort. He is buried as a kind of village hero.

Script lags badly after a good beginning and strong action-packed ending. But lensing is tops and pic has a professional polish throughout. "Shadows of a Hot Summer" shared Grand Prix at Karlovy Vary fest. — *Holl.*

Zrcadleni
(Reflections)
(CZECHOSLOVAK-COLOR)

Karlovy Vary, July 13.

A Czechoslovak Film Production, Barrandov Studios, Prague; world rights, Czechoslavak Filmexport, Prague. Features entire cast. Directed by Jaroslav Balik. Screenplay, Vladimir Kalina, Balik. Only credits available. Reviewed at Karlovy Vary Film Fest (out-of-competition), July 12, '78. Running time: **90 MINS.**

Cast: Stanislaw Zaczyk, Eva Sitteova.

Jaroslav Balik scored at the last Karlovy Vary fest in 1976 with "One Silver Piece," a partisan tale with psychological depth set in the Slovak mountains. Afterwards, he made two pix starring newcomer Eva Sitteova in the lead, "Shadows of a Flying Bird" and "Reflections." Both are sub-par for Balik in that the stories and dialogue texts tend to give everything away within the first half-hour and his ability to move an audience psychologically is thereby wasted.

"Reflections" deals with a successful business executive who has forgotten most of his past ideals and gets buried in his ambitions instead, to the detriment of his wife and daughter. The wife now refuses to accompany him abroad on trips, and the daughter has her heart set on a young man whom the father thinks is below her station despite a pregnancy (he wants a university student for a son-in-law). While visiting the Brno Trade Fair on business, he meets a young girl who looks just like the love of his youth — the encounter triggers reflections (Sitteova plays both parts) and the man faces an identity crisis never quite resolved at the end.

Script is heavy going and not very believable, although Polish thesp Stanislaw Zaczyk in the lead holds his own. Credits as a whole are on par with Czech proficiency and know-how. Slim chances off-shore.
— *Holl.*

Una Mujer, Un Hombre, Une Ciudad
(Woman, Man, City)
(CUBAN-COLOR)

Karlovy Vary, July 12.

A Cuban Film Production. Features cast. Directed by Manuel Octavio Gomez. Features entire cast. Screenplay, Gomez, Antonio Benites Rojo; camera (color), Pablo Martinez; music, Sergio Vitier. Reviewed at Karlovy Film Fest (Competition), July 11, '78. Running time: **100 MINS.**

Cast: Idalia Anreus (Marisa Sanchez), Mario Balmaseda (Miguel Mauri), Raul Pomarez, Omar Valdes, Alden Knight, Raquel Gonzalez.

Manuel Octavio Gomez is one of the leading helmers in Cuban cinema, the center figure in a retro of six pix unspooled in the Info Show last spring at the Berlin Fest (three of his films were shown). Together with Tomas Gutierrez Alea ("Memories of Underdevelopment," 1969), Humberto Solas ("Lucia") and docu-filmer Santiago Alvarez, he has helped put Cuban cinema on the map.

Gomez began his career as a journalist and film critic, then made docu pix and continued to exercise the function fo a journalist-documentarist in his feature pix, beginning with "History of a Battle" (1962). Large auds attended screenings of his "The Days of Waters" (1971), "Now It's Up to You" (1973), and "The Earth and the Sky" (1977) in Berlin. The attraction is essentially because one can learn a great deal about Cuban people — their customs, traditions, problems, working conditions, etc. — from a Gomez pic: they tend to be more honest and straightforward than many emerging from Socialist lands.

"Woman, Man, City" bears a parallel relationship to his earlier "Now It's Up to You": both docu-style reconstruction-interview pix about society, this one about the growing port of Nuevitas in the province of Camaguey. In the past, it was an export-center for sugarcane and surrounded by slum-dwellings for workers who could barely eke out a living on the docks. Today, due to the organizational skill of a fictional Marisa Sanchez, the working and living conditions have improved and the area is being settled by people migrating here from other areas. It's a reconstructed story of how a woman devoted her full time to the new life of the city, sacrificing her marriage and home life while setting an example for workers and women in factories and offices.

The story is pieced together by a research sociologist, an intellectual trained in Havana but coming from this district (with, apparently, memories of childhood). He doesn't want to take over the woman's half-finished task after her sudden death in a car crash, but he is temporarily the man for the job and doesn't have much choice. Gradually, as he comes to reason out the woman's unheralded success in the city among the workers despite unorthodox methods, he becomes the new "man" in the title obsessed by the town's future potential.

A fascinating pic, put together like a film mosaic of remembrances and experiences. Actors and mass scenes are well handled and dialogue flows easily in a complicated framework. A portrait of Cuban life today. — *Holl.*

Marie-Ann
(CANADIAN-COLOR)

Karlovy Vary, July 13.

A Canadian Film Production. Features entire cast. Directed by R. Martin Walters. Screenplay, Majorie Morgan; camera (color), Reginald Morris; music, Maurice Marshall. Reviewed at Karlovy Vary Film Fest (Competition), July 12, '78. Running time: **90 MINS.**

Cast: Andrea Pelletier (Marie-Ann), John Juliani (Jean Baptiste), Tantoo Martin (Tantoo), Gordon Tootoosie (Chief of the Indian Tribe), Bill Dowson (Steward), David Schurman, Linda Kupecek (Luise).

Slanted for the femme lib aud in telling the story of the "first woman to settle the Canadian West" via woman scripter's eyes (Marjorie Morgan), Martin Walters's "Marie-Ann" was a favorite at Karlovy Vary due to lush outdoor scenes of the Canadian West in changing seasons. Story is rather simplified (the West was surely tougher than as described), but there's a nice twist in having the girl adopted by an Indian tribe in order to calm both sides and keep her from being sent back to the farm in the East.

Jean-Baptiste Lagimodier is a trapper for the Hudson Bay Company at the beginning of the last century, who can't settle down although he now has a young wife of 25 he rather likes living with. But he also has a red-skinned girlfriend back at Fort Edmonton, who of course has a fit of jealousy when the white woman sets foot on her territory. Since all the other trappers have half-breeds for children, even the presence of a new-born son complicates things: it means settlers are coming. The Indian chief in the area also wants "White Cloud" in trade for a herd of horses. Marie-Ann solves everything by saying her god forbids bigamy, while her courage gets her adopted into the tribe.

Dialogue limps lamely in too many scenes to keep story interesting, and direction as a whole is unimaginative. But pic has charm and humor to make Walters a helmer to watch in the future.
— *Holl.*

Advokatka
(The Lawyer)
(CZECHOSLOVAK-COLOR)

Karlovy Vary, July 12.

A Czechoslovak Film Production, Koliba Studios, Bratislava; world rights, Czechoslovak Filmexport, Prague. Features entire cast. Directed by Andrej Lettrich. Screenplay, J.A. Tallo, Lettrich, based on a story by Tallo; camera (color), Alojz Hanusek; music, Svetozar Stracina. Reviewed at Karlovy Vary Film Fest (Competition), July 12, '78. Running time: **90 MINS.**

Cast: Emilia Vasaryova-Horska (Javorska), Svatopluk Matyas (Javorsky), Hana Packertova, Julius Vasek (Demin), Jaroslava Obermayerova (Police Officer), Lubo Roman, Lotar Radvanyi (Witness), Viliam Zaborsky, Dana Medricka (Deminova), Anton Korenci, Frantisek Filipovsky, Jozef Adamovic, Igor Hrabinsky.

Slovak cinema has traits and characteristics of its own, producing a half-dozen pix annually of critical merit. Andrej Lettrich's "The Lawyer" picks up a theme rather popular in Socialist countries: the questions of duty, conscience, and moral courage among women lawyers who must handle difficult cases as well as care for the needs of their family.

The young woman lawyer wants to throw in the chips at the beginning of the pic, as she has just finished defending a young woman sentenced for murder. Her superior gives her a different type case to save her career: this time an investigation into dishonest labor practices, which ironically involves her own husband's malfeasance. She defends the innocent party with renewed vigor, although her own marraige ends in divorce and the moral decisions are painful. In the end, the husband takes the stand in her favor and her confidence in humanity is restored.

Heavy going dialog and type acting doesn't gibe pic much room to breathe. Off-shore chances are slim. — *Holl.*

La Rochelle Fest

Yukinojo Henge
(Yukinojo's Revenge)
(JAPANESE-COLOR)

La Rochelle, July 18.
Pari Films release of Nagata production. Features entire cast. Directed by Kon Ichikawa. Screenplay, Natto Wada; camera (Eastmancolor), Setsuo Koba; music, Yasushi Akutgawa. Reviewed at La Rochelle Film Fest, July 3, '78. Running time: **110 MINS.**
Yukinojo
Yamitaro .... Kasuo Hasegawa
Ohatsu .... Fujiko Yamamato
Namiji .... Ayako Wakao
Hirutaro .... Raizo Ichikawa
Hoin .... Shintaro Katsu

Made in 1963, this period tale of vengeance has had an underground reputation. First shown by the late Henri Langlois at the Cinematheque Francaise, pic has at last made the La Rochelle Film Festival and will be released shortly in France by Parifilm.

A stylized film, "Yukinojo Henge" mixes Kabuki theatre with ritual, action, humor and derring-do that jell into an entertaining opus. The hero is an actor who impersonates females, for there are no women in Kabuki. But he carries his female impersonations into real life, too.

The actor has sworn vengeance on those who ruined his father's business and drove him to suicide.

The daughter of one of the "runists" falls for the actor, and he decides to use her to get to the others. There is also a Robin Hood-ish character who spies the goings-on and decides to help the actor.

Outdoor shots are staged on sets which add to the ambiguity but visual delight of the film. Kasuo Hasegawa is extraordinary as the actor, and he finally gets his revenge by setting the avid merchants against each other and ruining them, which also leads to the destruction of the innocent daughter.

Director Kon Ichikawa has done a sort of play-within-a-play pic that effectively sets up harsh dramatic decisions as the actor, also proficient in the martial arts, goes about his business of revenge. This also hurts him and evinces the coldness of his actions as the innocent suffer with the guilty.

No didactics or posturing here, but a shrewd mixture of styles, historical references and fable that make this almost a sort of pop legend. With the right handling, there should be good specialized chances for this long-neglected film in other climes.

Hasegawa began his career as an Oyama (i.e. actors who played female roles in the classic Japanese theatre), and actually played the same role in an earlier pic version of this tale 30 years ago. —*Mosk.*

The Magic of Lassie
(COLOR)

Contrived, weepy kid's pic with Sherman Brothers score. Name Collie provides key to family b.o. magic.

An International Picture Show release of a Jack Wrather presentation. Produced by Bonita Granville Wrather and William Beaudine Jr. Directed by Don Chaffey. Features entire cast. Screenplay, Jean Holloway, Robert M. Sherman, Richard B. Sherman; music and lyrics, Sherman & Sherman; orchestrations, Irwin Kostal; other credits not available. Reviewed at Radio City Music Hall, Aug. 4, '78 (MPAA Rating: G). Running time: **99 MINS.**
Cast: James Stewart, Mickey Rooney, Pernell Roberts, Stephanie Zimbalist, Michael Sharrett, Alice Faye, Gene Vans, The Mike Curb Congregation, Lassie.

Its title alone may ensure a hefty family turnout for "The Magic of Lassie," although this heavy-handed attempted throwback to the tradition that began with Metro's "Lassie Come Home" in 1943 has less substance, imagination or honest emotion than a typical half-hour episode of the longrunning tv series.

A sugary Richard and Robert Sherman score gives this go-around some surface novelty and the presence of Jimmy Stewart, Mickey Rooney and Alice Faye may provide marquee lure for parents shepherding the kids. Otherwise the only thing this film has going for it is the kiddy product shortage.

The storyline, also penned by the brothers Sherman (with Jean Holloway) is one of those stacked-deck jeopardy situations that may pull a happy ending out of the film's final moments, but forces the youngsters to sob their way through a mounting progression of tragedies (including the apparent death of Lassie after she has saved a kitten from a burning barn) before letting them off the hook.

In this case Pernell Roberts, after failing to convince Stewart to sell his prize-winning California grape orchards, takes a vindictive liking to grandson Michael Sharrett's collie (which he was given when his parents died in a highway crash), fakes papers establishing himself as the true owner and drags the dog away to Colorado. Next morning Sharrett begins the trek to the Rockies, Lassie escapes and heads back home and paths continually fail to cross until Lassie limps back home in time for Thanksgiving. So much for the laughs.

Produced by veteran tv Lassie producers Jack and Bonita Granville Wrather (with William Beaudine Jr.), the film manipulates young heart-strings with a lack of logic that verges on outright dishonesty, relying on a wellspring of knee-jerk emotionalism (or mundane musical lyricism between tragedies) to prevent anyone from sitting back and taking honest stock of things. Nor does the film compensate with anything approaching a sense of humor. Instead, it has music, lushly orchestrated by Irwin Kostal and usually sung over the action by the Mike Curb Congregation or Debby Boone (who even sings for the collie). Rooney has one number of his own; so does Stewart; Faye croaks along with a Pat Boone jukebox number.

With the exception of Stewart's engergetic blustering, acting is as one-dimensional and contrived as the script. Don Chaffey's direction does what it's supposed to do. Production credits are excellent.
—*Step.*

Piranha
(COLOR)

Little fish, little b.o. bite.

Hollywood, Aug. 4.
A New World Pictures release. Exec producers, Roger Corman and Jeff Schechtman. Produced by Jon Davison. Directed by Joe Dante. Features entire cast. Screenplay, John Sayles, based on a story by Richard Robinson and Sayles; camera (Metrocolor), Jamie Anderson; editors, Mark Goldblatt, Dante; art direction, Bill and Kerry Mellin; music, Pino Donaggio; special effects, Jon Berg; stunt coordinator, Conrad Palmisano; second unit director, Dick Lowry. Reviewed at Aidikoff Screening Room, BevHills, Aug. 4, '78. (MPAA Rating: R.) Running time: **92 MINS.**
Paul Grogan .... Bradford Dillman
Maggie McKeown ...... Heather Menzies
Dr. Robert Hoak .... Kevin McCarthy
Jack .... Keenan Wynn
Buck Gardner .... Dick Miller
Dr. Mengers .... Barbara Steele

If there hadn't been a "Jaws," a "Jaws 2," a "Sharks' Treasure" and a "Tintorera," then New World Pictures' "Piranha" might have had more going for it. Given its timing, however, summer action seems limited to ozoners and nabes.

Since the title characters in "Piranha" are never actually seen (there's lots of speeded-up nibbling, but no closeups of the deadly Brazilian river munchers), the pic utilizes a lot of red dye in the water, and an auditory effect for the gnawing that sounds like an air-conditioner on the fritz.

What is different about "Piranha" is the unusual number of victims. Not only is the requisite slew of cameo performers dispatched quickly (Keenan Wynn, Kevin McCarthy, Bruce Gordon), but an entire camp full of school children, and a holiday crowd at a lakeside resort get chomped. This is one film where the fish win.

Jon Davison, who produced, and Joe Dante, who directed, are the same team that made the delightful New World spoof, "Hollywood Boulevard," and a similar jesting tone predominates here. The characters take themselves very seriously, but a number of film buff in-jokes are evident, adding another dimension to a routine potboiler.

Heather Menzies plays an aggressive femme searching for missing persons, who enlists backwoods recluse Bradford Dillman in her cause. When they stumble on mad doctor Kevin McCarthy's mountain-top lab, they unwittingly release a generation of super-hardy piranhas McCarthy was breeding for use in the Mekong Delta during the Vietnam war.

As one of the few pix in which the heroes unleash the destruction to come, "Piranah" is not without its exciting moments, such as a raft trip down a river with the hungry fish doing their best to scuttle the voyage. It seems Menzies and Dillman get everywhere just a little bit too late, and the sequences of the piranhas gorging themselves on cute moppets aren't going to help anyone's digestion.

Barbara Steele turns up as a government scientist who hints the piranhas may be back for a sequel, but after the damage done to Dick Miller's resort, it's doubtful anyone will go near the water again.

Menzies is attractively competent, and Dillman does what he's supposed to, which isn't much. Steele and Miller distinguish themselves in bit parts, and one yearns to have seen more of McCarthy and his lab, where a scaly homunculus is seen lurking about, but never explained.

Tech credits are good, especially Jamie Anderson's atmospheric lensing, and Dick Lowry's second unit footage. The MGM lab work gives this New World release a surprising gloss. —*Poll.*

L'Arma
(The Gun)
(ITALIAN-COLOR)

Taormina, Aug. 8.
A CIDIF release produced by Maratea Film. Stars Stefano Satta Flores, Claudia Cardinale. Written and directed by Pasquale Squittieri. Camera, (Eastman-color) Giulio Albonico; Art Director, Luciana Vedovelli, Renato Ventura; editor, Pasquale Squittieri; music, Tullio De Piscopo. Reviewed at Taormina. Running time: 90 MINS.
Luigi Campagna . . . . . Stefano Satta Flores
Marta Campagna . . . . . . Claudia Cardinale
Rossana Campagna . . . . Benedetta Fantoli

Pasquale Squittieri and his two stars Claudia Cardinale and Stefano Satta Flores, formed a producer team to rush this film into production to fill gap before Squittieri started "Father of the Godfathers" for Capital and Rizzoli. His oversimplification of life in Italy's urban society, reduces the psycho stress and violence to cliche melodrama in a vehicle Squittieri designed to express in part his own mea culpa for

gun in hand law transgressions in private life.

CIDIF entry will find its market in Italy in general context of star names and extensive press and media coverage on Squittieri's peccadilloes. But in foreign markets, Squittieri is unknown.

In setting a social climate justifying the use of a gun for defense of person, family and property, Squittieri attempts to illustrate the dangers this form of self defense entails. Unfortunately, the victim on screen who falls into the gun-toting trap is a wholly negative member of society with all the banal extremities — less than adequate father-husband who has for years lost touch with his teenage daughter and abandoned any sexual contact with his patient and suffering spouse.

His rigid mannerisms, played with a melodramatic stance by Satta Flores for full volume mainly identifies this film as a fast commercial spinoff at home.

Cardinale alone lends some dignity as a long suffering but loyal wife but even her final breakout in a sudden burst of feminist inspiration puts "The Gun" back on the cliche track, confusing a serious problem of weapons in private hands and private justice to fight widespread crime.

Quality in all technical departments is above average. —*Werb.*

The Contract
(HONG KONG-COLOR)

Hong Kong, July 26.
A Golden Harvest Release. Produced by Raymond Chow. Directed and written by Michael Hui. Features entire cast. Camera (color), Tom Lau; art designs, David Chan; editor, Chang Yao Chung; music, Samuel Hui. Reviewed at Golden Harvest Preview theatre, Hong Kong, July 24, '78. Running Time: 90 MINS.
Cast: Michael Hui, Sam Hui, Ricky Hui, Tiffany Bao, Ellen Lau, Yeung Wei, Cheng Fu Hsiung, Russell Cawthorne, Chan King Chang, Chen Sau Ping, Louis Kwong.
(English Subtitles)

"The Contract" is the fourth film of Michael Hui and a guaranteed blockbuster. His two talented brothers, Sam and Ricky, also star in this very funny contemporary Cantonese comedy. "The Contract," in this case, is a blank piece of paper by which a tv station binds all its employes to eight years continuous service. Michael portrays Chi-Man, an aspiring but frustrated performer. With the help of inventor Ricky and magician Sam, he tries to steal his contract, locked in a safe guarded by meanies.

The plot is thin, but this is not the main ingredient in a Hui Bros. film. It serves as framework for Mel Brooks-type hilarious confusion. It is a combination of colloquial slapstick and madcap physical humor.

The production is excellent and

fueled with fresh ideas, confidence, finesse and well-thought-out sequences. The forced situations and stale jokes are few, with the many successful ones helping to cover up the weak points. Standouts include Hui as host of a quiz show, as dancer-singer in an audition, as a spaceman in a dance number and as a sexy lady in disguise. Hui executes his action scenes in a frisky fashion and the meticulous execution shows that the Hui family takes their humor seriously.

In "The Contract," the principals' paths intertwine only towards the middle part when a safe has to be opened. There's really a lot of things going for this film, and since the skits are physical and not verbal, the fun quality becomes universal and can easily be appreciated even by non-Asians.

This latest production may yet break the historic 1977 Hui comedy, "The Private Eyes," which grossed more money than any other film in Hong Kong's history by raking in HK$9,000,000 and the new film may find more legs abroad if dubbed properly in Japanese, English etc. Golden Harvest has something to be happy about with the release of "The Contract." —*Mel.*

Karlovy Fest

Aika Hyva Ihmiseksi
(Pretty Good for a Human)
(FINNISH-COLOR)

Karlovy Vary, July 10.
A Finnish Film Production. Features entire cast. Directed by Rauni Mollberg. Screenplay, Mollberg, Veikko Korpala, Seppo Heinonen; camera (color), Hannu Peltomaa; music, Harri Tuominen. Reviewed at Karlovy Vary Film Fest (Competition), July 9, '78. Running time: 100 MINS.
Cast: Martti Kainulainen, Raili Veivo, Toivo Makela, Asko Sarkola, Sirkka Metsasaariova, Gustav Wiklund.

Unspooled in "A Certain Look" section at this year's Cannes fest and now in competition at Karlovy Vary, Rauni Mollberg's "Pretty Good for a Human" is a period piece set in 1918 and the '20s to follow. Pic evokes life in a Finnish village and the surrounding countryside as it was then: it was a time of prohibition and smuggling, black market activities matched family squabbles. Film is based on the writings of popular Finnish novelist Sino Puuponen (his pen-name was "Aspeli") and other stories by different authors treating this period.

Among the many striking vignettes in this canvas of Finnish life is the story of a woman who comes to take care of a young boy in the household of a widower with little interest now in family affairs. Her presence (about midway through

the pic) gives the film depth and direction: she is a kind of homely, angelic messenger, whose blunt but compassionate ways bring order into the house and a measure of love and understanding to the boy. More episodes of this sort and pic could have been a winner.

As it is, "Pretty Good for a Human" was one of better pix at Karlovy Vary and should find its way as Finland's best of the year thus far. Credits are plus in nearly every category. —*Holl.*

Siawase No Cakusoku
Hankeci
(A Yellow Handkerchief of Happiness)
(JAPANESE-COLOR)

Karlovy Vary, July 12.
A Shochiku Film Production, Japan. Features entire cast. Directed by Yoji Yamada. Screenplay, Yamada, Yoshitaka Asama; camera (color), Tecuo Takaba; music, Masaru Sato. Reviewed at Karlovy Vary Film Fest (Competition), July 11, '78. Running time: 90 MINS.
Cast: Ken Takakura (Yusaku Sima), Chieko Baisho (his wife), Tecuya Takeda (Kinya), Kaori Mamoio (Akemi), Kiyoshi Acumi (Police Chief).

One of the three pix dealing with youth (Rumanian and Vietnamese entries were the other two) at Karlovy Vary, Yoji Yamada's "A Yellow Handkerchief of Happiness" bears a strong relationship to the other two (both love stories, with the Japanese and Rumanian pix using "happiness' in the titles). It's a moral tale dealing with youth's awakening to life and responsibility after encounters with disappointment and disillusionment.

A young lad gets a goodbye letter from his girl friend. He's upset enough to quit his job, buy a small car, and hit the road for the island of Hokkaido in the North.

Along the way he meets a girl on the beach, who joins him on the trip, and then an ex-prisoner who is returning home. The boy makes fumbling approaches to the girl and there is a spat between the two. Later, the young couple learns the truth about their extra passenger, a man who killed out of blind love for his wife and upon hearing the truth about her past; now he hopes to be reconciled with her after his time in prison. He wrote her a letter, and the sign of acceptance will be a yellow handkerchief flying from the window. It's there (a dozen yellow handkerchiefs greet him); the young couple are impressed.

Lensing and technical credits good, and "road" atmosphere keeps pic moving at a steady pace, despite lags in story line. —*Holl.*

Moi Tinh Dau
(First Love)
(VIETNAM-B&W)

Karlovy Vary, July 11.

A Vietnamese Film Production. Features entire cast. Directed by Nguyen Hai Ninh. Camera, Nguyen guang Tuan. Only credits available. Reviewed at Karlovy Vary Fest (Competition), July 10, '78. Running time: **90 MINS.**

Cast: Tra Giang (Hai Lan), Nhu Quynh (Diem Huong), Hong Lien (Mother).

Two years ago, Vietnam was present at Karlovy Vary with "When Shall We Meet Again?" This year, it's "First Love" set in South Vietnam during the war. The Yank presence is only shown on the side, but the South Vietnamese police are only too visible in this tale of disillusionment and rededication to a cause. Amateurishly made and acted, pic is evidence that Vietnam still has a long way to go before a truly national cinema is fostered and developed.

A young boy is in love with a Vietnamese girl who marries an American doctor. A second disappointment occurs at the university, when his friend is killed in a protest demonstration against the government. The boy leaves home, takes to drinking and hanging around with bad companions, and is well on his way to ruin in a degrading society.

Then his older sister returns home to Saigon from the North, where she has been trained in the liberation movement. She is here to help organize resistance in the city, has a strong political stand, and shows enough moral courage to awaken her brother to the changing of the times. Our young hero joins the movement.

Anti-Imperialist propaganda over weights the story. It's contended, for instance, that a planeload of orphan children to the States is not meant for adoption, but the training of future spies to return one day to Vietnam in the service of the Imperialists. —Holl.

El Cantor
(The Singer)
(EAST GERMAN-COLOR)

Karlovy Vary, July 14.

A German Democratic Republic Television Film, Berlin; world rights, Fernsehen der DDR Export/Import, Berlin. Stars Dean Reed. Written and directed by Dean Reed. Camera (color), Hans Heinrich; art direction, Heinz Roske; artistic advisor, Margit Schaumaeker; collaborator, Eolfgang Ebeling; music, Karel Svoboda; editor, Ruth Ebel. Reviewed at Karlovy Vary Film Fest (Market), July 13, '78. Running time: **90 MINS.**

El Cantor (Victor Jara) . . . . Dean Reed
Janet . . . . Friederlike Aust
Henry . . . . Gerry Wolf
Roberto . . . . Frank Bey
Manuel . . . . Thomas Wolf
Jose . . . . George Rositsch
Chorus Director . . . . Isabel Oregana

Mayor . . . . Dimitrina Sawowa
Colonel Baker . . . . Nikolai Dadon

Dean Reed is one of two Yanks who live and work in Socialist countires: Reed is a folk-singer in Berlin and the other, Gene Deitch, makes animated cartoons for the West in Prague. "El Cantor," made for East German television, was written and directed by Reed and stars him as a singer-actor in the role of Victor Jara, Chile's renown folksinger (and friend) who died after the military take-over.

Pic is one of three made in Socialist countries (the others are the French-Bulgarian coprod 'It Rains over Satiago" and the Soviet prod "Night over Chile" with Chilean cohelmer, thesps, and crew) about the downfall of President Allende in September 1973. In some ways, Reed's film, lensed in Bulgaria (the terrain looks the same), is the best of the three so far as a flesh-and-blood approach is concerned.

Reed attempts little more than to describe the last week of Jara's life in a fictional account that leans heavily on the singer's relationship with his wife and family (stemming from interviews with Joan Turner-Jara, living today in London). The songs are Jara's, sung in Spanish by Reed — he lived for a time in Chile and Argentina upon becoming in the mid-'60s the most popular singer on the hit parade in South America. The helmer was also a close friend of the Chilean singer.

Story moves at a smooth pace in opening scenes, although dialogue has a distinct programmed accent familiar to "engaged" pix where the gravy is poured on heavy so that the audience doesn't miss the point. Jara is shown with his wife rolling on the grass and romping with his daughters and dog; when he gets serious, he talks about the day when the Unidad Popular will win a full majority in the next election. Meanwhile, people are out to get Jara — his car is fired upon by pursuing gunmen (a boy among the passengers is killed) and a truck attempts to dump a pile of rocks into his lap.

It's when concerts are given and Reed-Jara sings that the film takes shape as a meaningful biographical docufiction account. Reed has a presence with a guitar in his hand that makes story and dialogue fall into place. Details on Jara's last hours at the barricaded university, followed by the arrest and murder in the sports stadium, give the closing sequences a human dimension to put pic over the top.

Credits and thesp performances (particularly Chileans in natural roles) are top grade. Reed as helmer still has a way to go, but as

debut tv film this one deserves cinema exposure by virtue of theme alone. —Holl.

E Atit De Aproape Fericirea
(Happiness Is So Near)
(RUMANIAN-COLOR)

Karlovy Vary, July 11.

A RumaniaFilm Production, Bucharest; world rights, RumaniaFilm, Bucharest. Features entire cast. Directed by Andrei-Catalin Baleanu. Screenplay, Constantin Stoicu; camera (color), Florin Paraschiv, Valentin Popescu; music, Radu Goldis. Reviewed at Karlovy Vary Film Fest (Competition), July 10, '78. Running time: **90 MINS.**

Cast: Diana Lupescova (Cristina), Albert Kitzi (Paul), Margareta Pogonatova, Constantin Diplan, Petre Gheorghiu, Alexandru Georgescu.

One of Rumania's youngest helmers (born in 1947), Andrei-Catalin Baleanu concerns himself with problems of youth in "Happiness Is So Near," a story about a girl meeting a boy. Script is by a writer, Constantin Stoicu, who is known for his preoccupation with contemporary society. Put them together and a portrait of Rumanian life today and the problems of the younger generation emerges: school, ideals, future.

Students at a Technical University leave theory behind in the classroom to encounter labor practices in a large Bucharest factory. One of them is Paul, who has a girl friend, Cristina, still not in the university as she flunked her entrance exams. Her parents are distraught because life only has meaning when status is attached to it.

After experiencing the boredom of a vacant social standard at home, the girl decides to study hard with aims to do something with her life in the future. The young couple, encountering challenges about them, know now that life is not only play but requires some work and commitment to have any meaning at all.

Interesting pic for cataloging levels in Rumanian society today. Technical quality of pic has merit. —Holl.

Dr. Vlimmen
(DUTCH-COLOR)

Karlovy Vary, July 11.

A Netherlands Film Production. Features entire cast. Directed by Guido Pieters. Screenplay based on a novel by A. Roothaerts; caemra (color), Theo van de Sande; music, Pim Koopman. Reviewed at Karlovy Vary Film Fest (Competition), July 10, '78. Running time: **90 MINS.**

Cast: Peter Faber (Dr. Vlimmen), Roger van Hool (Dacko) Chris Lomme (Truus), Brigitte de Man (Mientje), Jolanda Bertsch (Tilly), Wrad de Ravet, Monique van de Ven (Leonike), Manfred de Graaf.

Based on a popular bestseller, Guido Pieters's "Dr. Vlimmen" stays close to its literary source to

move slowly through a tale about a vetinarian living in the South of Holland. Docu style footage and a certain feel for the people and milieu keep pic interesting when action bogs down.

Dr. Vlimmen is a lonely man. His wife has left him and the villagers look upon his profession with distrust, particularly as he has to knock heads with stubborn farmers who think they and the "old ways" know better. The veterinarian places his trust more in animals than people, which isolates him all the more.

His sister and her husband come to live with him, but then a scandal takes place when the house maid spreads the rumor that she's pregnant by the doctor. Later, he's able to prove it's all a lie and thus saves his job, but the sister decides to migrate to America. The doctor's only consolation now is the daily rounds and a last friend, who one day marries.

Lensing is top grade, thesps are realistic enough, but story needs a dramatic spark and thesp finesse to put it over. —Holl.

Slnchev Udar
(Sunstroke)
(BULGARIAN-COLOR)

Karlovy Vary, July 10.

A Bulgarian Film Production, Sofia; world rights, BulgaroFilm, Sofia. Features cast. Written and directed by Christo Piskov and Irena Aktasheva, based on Georgi Dzhagarov's story "This Little Earth." Camera (color), Leonik Kalashnikov; music, Kiril Donchev; art direction, Assen Milev, Borislav Borisov. Reviewed at Karlovy Vary Film Fest (Competition), July 9, '78. Running time: **120 MINS.**

Cast: Armen Djigarhanian (Prof. Radev), Itzhak Fintsi (Dragiev), Nikolai Binev (Lazarov), Rashko Mladenov (Balchev), Katya Paskaleva (Snezha), Bella Tsoneva (Burzashka), Ivan Kondov (Prof. Dimov), Nevena Kokonova (Nevena), Konstantin Kotsev (Slavov).

The directorial team of Irena Aktasheva and Christo Piskov began back in 1960 with "The Poor Street," an antifascist theme in which Aktasheva was helmer Piskov's assistant. They then made together "There Is No Death" (1963), a contemporary story about the construction of a power plant. Later, a third party was added to the group, writer-playwright Georgi Dzhagarov, whose play, "Like a Song," was adapted by the helmer team in 1972. "Sunstroke" is also adapted from a Dzhagarov's play, "This Small Earth."

It deals again with the construction of a large factory, which in the process endangers the environment and renders the soil useless in the area. The director of an ecological institute is called in to help make the decision whether or not to build the plant; he decides against the project, much to the disagreement of a party functionary. Pressures mount against him to change his mind, coming from home and his own conscience as well as outside forces. In the end, he get helps from an unexpected quarter, a young scientist who had earlier disappointed him, and he wins the day for human existence. —*Holl.*

Yugoslav Festival

Okupacija U 26 Slika
(Occupation in 26 Pictures)
(YUGOSLAV-COLOR)

Pula, Aug. 8.

Yugoslavia Film release of Jadran Film-Croatia Film production. Features entire cast. Directed by Lordan Zafronovic. Screenplay, Mirko Kovac, Zafronovic; camera (Eastmancolor), Karpo Acimovic-Godina; editor, Josip Premenar; music, Alfi Kabilho. Reviewed at Pula Film Fest, July 27, '78. Running time, **116 MINS.**
With: Frano Lasic, Boris Kralj, Milvan Strljic, Stevo Zigon, Zvonko Pepetic, Tatjana Roberznik, Gordana Pavlov.

A remarkable film that deals in fascism, racism, occupation during World War II, resistance and revolution in the form of a family saga. It consecrates a director, Lordan Zafronovic, and adds to growing chances for Yugoslavian pix to achieve wider recognition after years of neglect, with such exceptions as Dusan Makavejev's "W.R.," and Alexandre Petrovic's "I Even Met A Happy Gypsy."

Zafronovic made two promising pix that were marred by some pretention and overblown symbolism, "Sunday" and "Matthew's Passion." But here he shows possession of a clear narrative style that easily blends romantics, baroque underpinnings and an unflinching, sudden burst of horrendous violence to make his film one that should spark interest everywhere.

Festival chances abound for the film and it has the earmarks for fine foreign chances. Film starts with an engaging romantic look at the peaceful port town of Dubrovnik before the last war, Germano-Italo occupation and the setting up of a fascist Croatian puppet state that unleashes the local fascists.

Threaded throughout is a tale of a friendship of three young men. One is from a well-off shipping family, one a Jew whose father has a successful antique shop and one from a local minority Italian family who is in love with the sister of the shipping family scion. They are first seen cavorting at a carnival and then at a private fencing club where the elitist headmaster shows signs of anti-semitism spurred by the times. It is the late 1930s.

There is a romantic dash to these scenes sans any slips or forced camaraderie. It is a sort of postcardish aspect of the richer class in this pearly city of Venice-like architecture and grace. But into this comes war and the arrival of advance Germans and the Italians.

The pompous entrance of the Italians is capped by an ostentatious speech by the Italian General and a general acceptance by the populace. But a victory march by the Italians has them slipping about in their own earth. Soon the Croatian state is formed and the girl's fiance, the Italian-origined youth, becomes a fascist.

The girl's brother goes against what he sees about him and at grotesque parties, and joins a group of young communist worker resistants while the Jewish boy is persecuted. Suddenly the Croatian oustashi, the local fascists taking Jews and other prisoners to jail stop the bus and go into an orgy of horrible murder on the pretext that Nazi rules give them the right.

Hammering nails into men's heads, knifings, cutting out tongues, rape slicing of a woman's breast and even a beheading take place while the Jewish youth escapes. It is done in a dramatic, almost ritualistic manner which displays the pompousness of fascism giving way to the horror of full power and what it can create in many. One of the worst butchers is also a pigeon fancier who asks help from a local priest when his wife is ill.

Church complicity is also there. The denouement has the father of the shipping family killed for joining with his leftist workers, not as a revolutionary, but due to a faith in man's dignity. The son finally kills the fascist who has since married his sister. The latter is left alone, pregnant, in their house as the brother and the surviving Jewish friend go underground.

Director Zafronovic displays a fine visual flair in his pacing, sensitive handling of actors and a sureness in bringing this tale to a dramatic epiphany. The social elements are handled with insight and there are brilliant scenes in the setting up of a local bordello. The aforementioned scene of carnage, the eventual dispersion of the shipping family and the taking of sides in an historic context that transcends it to make a statement on the differing degrees of man's reactions to historic demands.

Perhaps there are some influences of Italo and even Czech pix, for Zafronovic studied in Prague, but all assimilated to mark a director of international status.
—*Mosk.*

Stici Pre Svitanja
(Arrive Before Daybreak)
(YUGOSLAV-COLOR)

Pula, Aug. 8.

Yugoslavia Film release of Neoplanata production. Features entire cast. Directed by Aleksander Dordevic. Screenplay, Vlasta Radovanovic, from the books by Paasko Romac and Stanka Veselinov; camera (Eastmancolor), Dusan Ninkov; music, Mladen and Predrag Vranesevic. Reviewed at Pula Film Fest, July 26, '78. Running time, **94 MINS.**
With: Bata Zivojinovic, Ljubisa Samardzic, Stevan Gardinovacki, Pater Carsten.

This one is a sort of jailbreak story that is predictable and repetitious despite framing it in wartime circumstances. The jailbirds are noted Communists, imprisoned by local collaborators and the Germans. It is the tale of their breakout and joining with the growing Partisan movement.

There is the inevitable squealer who is dealt with, communications from the outside and the final breakout through a tunnel. It is based on real events, but cannot break with figures who appear stereotyped. There are the usual problems and aid from prison sources as well as brutal prison authorities and treatment.

Pic may have some local viability on its allusions. Though acting is effective within the scope of the now-familiar figures, it remains primarily a local item if it presages the move away from the actionful Partisan pix to other aspects of the last war. —*Mosk.*

Posljednji Podvig Diverzanta Oblaka
(The Last Mission of Demolitions Man Cloud)
(YUGOSLAV-COLOR)

Pula, Aug. 8.

Yugoslavia Film release of Jadran Film, Croatia Film production. Features entire cast. Written and directed by Vatroslav Mimica. Camera (Eastmancolor), Bozidar Nikolic; music, Marijan Makar. Reviewed at Pula Film Fest, July 29, '78. Running time, **113 MINS.**
With: Pavle Vuisic, Slavica Jukic, Predrag Manojilovic, Ivica Pajer.

Vatroslov Mimica, an ex-animator, has had an eclectic series of pix. From a whimsical look at an ordinary man to life in a concentration camp to a strange incident of awesome justice and a peasant rebellion in the middle ages, he now goes contemporary but with echoes of the past struggles against fascism.

Here a crusty old veteran of battles on the loyalist's side during the Spanish Civil War, and the later war against local, German and Italo fascists as a demolition man, he becomes involved with some technological and industrial corruption as well as confronting a tarnishing of his lifelong ideals.

Director-scripter Mimica has this a bit talky but never verbose. Pavle Vujisic adds life, humor, warmth and dedication as the old man. Fluid direction has the man mapped up by a tv show being done on him. His house is now a sort of museum on his exploits, but he is simple and not even worried about the probability of his house being torn down as large buildings spring up around him.

For a while his house has been spared but a run-in with a hot-headed football star starts trouble. The footballer may be benched and his club backers try to force the old man not to press charges. But this gets up his dander and his belief in the moral rights of the individual. He encounters corruption as pressures now again have his house up for demolition.

The old man is helped by an old war buddy in high position, but will not accept his house being spared amidst what he feels is corruption around him. There is a telling scene with his old friend who notes changing times and compromises as distinct from the clearer times of battle.

But the old chap destroys his house and apparently dies of a heart attack as he goes off pulling a boat he has built for his grandchild appropriately called Don Quixote. A warm moral fable but perhaps a bit too insidey and verbalized for much foreign playoff.

It does display a freer climate of subject matter in Yugoslavia. Pic has perceptive direction and ends on a poignant note sans bathos as the old demolitions man pulls off his last mission as far as his attitude and life are concerned. A gentle but never mawkish pic, it would uphold Mimica's record if it used a bit more punch. —*Mosk.*

Olly, Olly, Oxen Free
(COLOR)

———

For devout Hepburn fans only.

———

Hollywood, Aug. 11.

A Sanrio Film Distribution release of a Rico Lion Production. Stars Katharine Hepburn. Produced and directed by Richard A. Colla; exec producer, Don Henderson. Screenplay, Eugene Poinc, based on story by Maria L. de Ossio, Poinc and R. Colla; camera (Metrocolor) Gayne Rescher; editor, Lee Burch; production design, Peter Wooley; music, Bob Alcivar. Reviewed at RGB Screening Room, Hollywood, Aug. 10, '78. (MPAA Rating: G.) Running time: **83 MINS.**

Miss Pudd . . . . Katharine Hepburn
Alby . . . . Kevin McKenzie
Chris . . . . Dennis Dimster
Mailman . . . . Peter Kilman

———

"Olly, Olly, Oxen Free" is a modest independent film aimed squarely for the family market, an audience it should find thanks to the marquee lure of star Katharine Hepburn, in her first feature film role since "Rooster Cogburn." B.o. success is likely to be dependent on the clout indie distrib Sanrio can muster in terms of playdates. Pic has already been released in midwest test markets, including Kansas City.

Pic suffers from title-itis, for while the title phrase bespeaks childhood, it is unrelated to anything in the story and gives little idea what type of picture a prospective customer could expect.

By no means up to the standards of the giant in this genre, Walt Disney Studios, Richard Colla's production does feature a marvelous performance by Hepburn as an eccentric junkyard proprietress and some breathtaking hot air balloon footage.

The major handicap is Eugene Poinc's one-dimensional script, which gives the pic a choppy, unreal feeling that works directly against the ingratiating subject matter. The dialog, other than Hepburn's well-oiled soliloquies, is particularly trite, and only when the balloon is aloft does the film literally soar.

Hepburn befriends two youngsters, limned by newcomers Kevin McKenzie and Dennis Dimster, who dream of launching a decrepit balloon once the property of McKenzie's grandfather, who piloted the contraption at turn-of-the-century fairs and carnivals under the name of The Great Sandusky.

Throwing herself wholeheartedly into the challenge, Hepburn marshals her charges and gets the apparatus hooked up until, accidentally, the boys are aloft, with Hepburn soon to join them. It's an inspiring scene, one that lifts the film's, as well as the characters' spirits, but it comes two-thirds of the way into the picture. Before the airborne sequences, "Olly, Olly,

Oxen Free" may elicit mostly yawns.

Colla has a wonderful visual sense and an acute eye for detail that is revealed as the balloon floats above the Napa Valley, carefully tracked by Gayne Rescher's topnotch camerawork. Process shots are transparent, but obviously a necessity, and are kept to a minimum.

Pic's finale has Hepburn and company descending on a Hollywood Bowl concert during a rendition of the "1812 Overture," an effective closing that is marred by a tacked-on ending suggesting a sequel. Best leave well enough alone.

Hepburn is a joy to behold, and of the youngsters, Dimster is particularly engaging. A sheepdog is along for the ride, but it's Hepburn's show, and she makes the most of it. Other production credits are excellent. —*Poll.*

———

Una Settimana Come Un'altra
(Week In, Week Out)
(ITALIAN-COLOR)

———

Taormina, Aug. 8.

An Arsnova Co-op production. Features entire cast. Directed by Daniele Costantini. Screenplay, Daniele Costantini, Sergio Marconi, Domenico Calandruccio; camera (Eastmancolor), Antonio Maccoppi. No other credits available. Reviewed at Taormina Festival, Aug. 15, '78. Running time: **90 MINS.**

Cast: Leonardo Treviglio, Marcella Michelangeli, Nicoletta, Amadio, Donato Sanniti, Roberto Tortorella.

———

"Week In, Week Out" is a first film by Daniele Costantini, presented in the New Cinema section of the Taormina Film Festival. It is significant in pointing up a sentiment of disarray among young people in their 20's. This was also the theme of Nanni Moretti's "Ecce Bombo" — a much more professional view of the same problem with a skilled, convincing attempt to distill forlorn humor from a postteenage generation that had lost its idealistic vitality.

Emphasis in Costantini's film is on futility and his humorless approach centers on generalized youth inertia as an off-shoot of current economic crisis. Costantini makes an honest effort to reflect loss of faith and day-to-day listlessness stemming from it. The young characters go through the same motions of radical group activity that recently seemed like a formidable bid for youth power. In "Week In, Week Out," the continuity from recent years becomes only a mechanical simulation that quickly runs its individual course and ends in an unemotional void.

Coming after "Ecce Bombo," which struck a very sympathetic chord with youth audiences and made a bundle of money, "Week In, Week Out" at best lends confirma-

tion to the dilemma of youth in Italy today — with the ultimate choice lying between extremist terrorism or total non-engagement — the latter, ringed only with a daily dose of nothingness.

Young lead Leonardo Treviglio lives up to the young film author's thesis in true nebbish style. The girls around him are in the same empty rut.

As an indicative comment on Italy's college grads and post-grads, this first effort should get further exposure on the film fest circuit, but not much more. —*Werb.*

———

O Moravske Zemi
(The Moravian Land)
(CZECHOSLOVAK-COLOR)

———

Karlovy Vary, July 10.

A Czechoslovak Film Production, Barrandov Studio, Prague; world rights, Czechoslovak Filmexport, Prague. Features entire cast. Directed by Antonin Kachlik. Screenplay, Josef Vaculik, Kachlik, based on a story, "Slogan on the Gates," by Fanek Jilik; camera (color), Josef Illik. Reviewed at Karlovy Vary Film Fest (Market), July 9, '78. Running time: **100 MINS.**

Cast: Radoslav Brzobohaty (Jagos), Jana Vyslouzilova (Jagos's wife), Karel Kabicek (Chairman of the Cooperative), Bohus Pastorek, Karel Kolousek, Helena Ruzickova.

———

Antonin Kachlik, Jaroslav Balik and Frantisek Vlacil, are Czech directors of moral tales and reinterpreted history, whose pix echo at the same time a contemporary concern for social problems. All three have influenced the direction of current Czechoslovak cinema with a certain narrative style.

Kachlik's recent interest has been farm cooperatives in Moravia during the postwar years of development, first "Our Old Man Joe" and now "The Moravian Land."

"The Moravian Land" covers 10 years, from winter 1957 to summer 1966. This epic portrait of a community is told from the standpoint of a single individual, Jagos, who decides in the beginning to have nothing to do with the collective farm because of mismanagement — and then, when he finds the going alone is too tough, he joins the collective to stubbornly work for its improvement according to his own way of viewing things. Naturally, he is a rather unpopular individual by speaking his mind, but his enthusiastic drive wins out in the end.

Story moves slowly, but the change of seasons and lensing of nature, plus village customs and traditions, make it worth a look-see.

—*Holl.*

———

Chajrchan Ondor Chaana Bajna
(Discover Turquoise Mountain)
(MONGOLIAN-CZECH-COLOR)

———

Karlovy Vary, July 10.

A Mongolian-Czechoslovak Coproduction. Features entire cast. Directed by Najdangin Hjamdava and Ivo Toman. Screenplay, S. Dashdorov, based on a story by Zdenek Braunschlaeger; camera (color), Josef Illik, D. Batulga; music, L. Mordordzh. Reviewed at Karlovy Vary Film Fest (Competition), July 9, '78. Running time: **90 MINS.**

Cast: Josef Langmiler (Prof. Pudil), D. Elbegsajchan (Dr. Tomor), Karel Hlusicka (Mares), D. Dzanabadzar (Davasuren), S. Ceceg (Dulma), Slavka Budinova (Horakova), Josef Vetrovec (Vrutsky), Jan Kanyza (Machacek).

———

The first Mongolian-Czechoslovak coproduction, Najdangin Hjamdava and Ivo Toman's "Discover Turquoise Mountain" deals with an historical event many years ago, the discovery in Mongolia of copper deposits by a team of Mongolian and Czech geologists. Tale is told via the perspective and remembrances of a Czech geologist, whose fantasy-obsessed colleague left Prague to propose a searching plan based on legends about a mountain known as Turquoise Mountain.

Pic moves across the countryside like pioneers going west to look for gold. The expedition is divided into two groups, one searching for the mountains, the other staying close to camp to make research experiments. The scientist with the hunch goes on a plane search of the area, gets lost in a fog and crashlands — right in the area of Turquoise Mountain. There, not only copper is discovered, but also a deposit of turquoise.

Quaint story, but overladen with an impulse to drift all over the place in a naive rendering of facts. —*Holl.*

———

Aller Retour
(Round Trip)
(YUGOSLAV-COLOR)

———

Pula, Aug. 10.

Yugoslavia Film release of Danas Film production. Features entire cast. Directed by Aleksandar Petkovic. Screenplay, Dragoslav Mihailovic; camera (Eastmancolor), Tomislav Pinter; music, Kornelije Kovac. Reviewed at Pula Film Fest, July 29, '78. Running time: **93 MINS.**

With: Dusan Janicijevic, Milena Dravic, Slavko Simac, Ljubisa Samardzic.

———

Pic deal with a recurring theme in Yugoslav films people going abroad to work. After several about Germany, this deals with a farming family that goes to Paris. Exploited by their own people, the difficulty of finding work and the father's harsh character finally lead to tragedy.

Director Aleksander Petkovic is a talented cameraman but for his first film as a director he fails to put any dramatics and lifesize characters into this skimpily scripted film. Coming to Paris, they are taken to a house where Yugoslavs live that is under police siege, for it is condemned and they will not leave.

The father tries all sorts of work, is bilked by a Yugoslav promising work and finally wounds a man while drunk.

Arrested, he is to be deported but the family leaves to live with an old friend in the provinces. Here things are going well until an attempted robbery of them has the polic coming. The father's fear of being deported leads to drinking, no beating his wife and his sudden death.

Not really able to probe the problems of foreign workers, the film is predictable and finally flat despite a bevy of good actors and examination of the proud but brutal father's character. A proud man who cannot cope, he is finally done in by twists of fate. Mainly a local item.
—*Mosk*.

Ljubica
(Violet)
(YUGOSLAV-COLOR)

Pula, Aug. 15.

Yugoslavia Film release of Croatia Film production. Features entire cast. Directed by Kreso Golik. Screenplay, Goran Massot; camera (Eastmancolor), Zivko Zaler; editor, Katja Majer; music, Antonio Vivaldi. Reviewed at Pula Film Fest, July 30, '78. Running time, **92 MINS.**
With: Bozidarka Frait, Ivan Stancic, Relja Basic, Miodrag Krivokapic.

Ljubica is a thirtyish, still very attractive who works with deaf children. She is separated from her husband who works abroad, and her little son lives with her in-laws. She is lonely and has often been so for she was an orphan. Into her life comes a much younger man for a brief, needed love affair. But it ends with her living with her son and doing her work.

Film is helped by the fine acting and effective presence of Bozidarka Frait as a woman trying to find her own way in a still often macho-oriented society. But pic is slight and shows the lack of a script that would have brought out the tensions, drama and human relations more effectively.

Direction is competent but not deft or insightful enough to keep pic from being somewhat predictable, soft and sentimental. Its simple progression and close quarter work, plus intercut scenes of her with an analyst, tag this more viable for tv abroad than for theatrical datings. But its theme and generally efficacious if obvious narrative style could have this okay on its home grounds. —*Mosk*.

Cunesli Bataklik
(Sun Over the Swamp)
(TURKISH-COLOR)

Antalya, July 4.

A Murat Film Production, Sureyya Duru, Istanbul. Features entire cast. Directed by Sureyya Duru. Screenplay, Vedat Turkali; camera (color), Orhan Kapki; music, Hursit Yenigun. Reviewed at Antalya Film Fest, July 3, '78. Running time: **94 MINS.**
Cast: Semra Ozdamar, Hakan Balamir, Aytac Arman, Cagaloglu, Ihsan Yuce.

A socially engaged pic whose title, "Sun over the Swamp," hints at a metaphorical meaning, this is the story of a girl's awakening to the workers' cause after wavering between a choice of riches or decency. Sureyya Duru is a veteran of numerous action-melodramas with a social or political twist, but this time he gets lost in a muddled script.

The girl works as a secretary to the big boss and comes to recognize the dirty play for what it is in the hiring of gunmen to stop the workers from organizing in the factory. After a couple good guys are killed, a hero steps to the fore and challenges the bullies to a showdown. Meanwhile, the boss is killed by the girl's ex-lover who has played the slick between-man and pretty-boy gigolo. In the end, right seems to have triumphed over wrong.

The unlikely plot, however, of two young clerks who become ploys of the factory owner, one doing his dirty work and the other becoming his mistress, and later splitting to go separate ways, doesn't add up to a committed social consciousness.
—*Holl.*

Yugoslav Festival

Praznovanje Pomladi
(The Call of Spring)
(YUGOSLAV-COLOR)

Pula, Aug. 15.

Yugoslavia Film release of Viba Film production. Features entire cast. Directed by France Stiglic. Screenplay, Francek Rudolf; camera (Eastmancolor), Rudi Vavpotic; art director, Niko Matul; music, Alojz Srebotnjak. Reviewed at Pula Film Fest, July 31, '78. Running time: **94 MINS.**
With: Zonve Agrez, Relja Basic, Zvone Hribar, Angela Hlebec, Andrej Kurent.

France Stiglic is one of the deans of Yugoslav film directors from the Slovenian part of the country. He brought some early recognition to Yugoslav pix at fests with his pacifistic war pic "Valley of Peace" and a poignant tale of concentration camps "The Ninth Circle."

But this is a fairly academic film about star-crossed tragic lovers on a background of eradication of early pagan rituals still alive in the country, despite its being made Catholic as part of the Austro-Hungarian Empire in the early 18th century.

A young man had been practically sold off to the Austrian Army by a village chief so that his own son could court a girl in love with the other youth. Years later, the man comes back to see his girl being married off. The army is told to prevent a spring rite in the dead of winter which has the men donning grotesque masks to pose as wood demons to augur a good spring.

The girl has seen the youth and will not give in to her husband unless he dons one of the masks and goes dancing through the fields. Soldiers chase them. The young man saves the girl from attempted rape and they love again. She wants him to kill her husband. He rebels but finally dons a mask and fights with the man.

But when he doffs it, the husband's brother dons it and is killed by his own brother by mistake.

The young man goes off with the army to be killed, stripped and left naked and dead in the cold by the men he had kept from raping his loved one.

Stiglic has given this a fine mood and period atmosphere. But it remains stolid and literary in its treatment with rather stiff acting. The freedom, exhiliration and liberating aspects of the spring rites are more discussed than visually caught. But the masks are impressive and this film might have some **school and archive usage if too staid and lifeless for offshore theatricals.**
—*Mosk.*

Ljubav I Bijes
(Love and Rage)
(YUGOSLAV-COLOR)

Pula, Aug. 15.

Yugoslavia Film release of Sutjeska Film production. Features entire cast. Written and directed by Bakir Tanovic from story by Novak Simie. Camera (Eastmancolor), Danijal Sukalo; art director, Kemal Hrustanovic; music, Zoran Hristic. Reviewed at Pula Film Fest, July 28, '78. Running time: **92 MINS.**
With: Viktor Starcic, Merima Isakovic, Adem Cejvan, Dragomir Bojanic-Gidra.

A sort of oriental morality play with a superficial resemblance to that renowned Japanese film "Rashomon." But there comparison ends for this film is somewhat naively made and unevenly played.

An old, rich merchant buys a beauteous young girl from her poor father in early 19th century Sarajevo. This was and is the Muslim part of the country and the costumes, customs and ways are Arabic in look, lending it an exotic air.

Simply told, it does manage to have a certain charm despite its flaws for local consumption. The old man returns home from a trip one day to find the wife possessed. She claims the old man came home in the guise of a demon. He takes her to Catholic, Orthodox and Muslim priests but none can perform an exorcism.

Finally a disillusioned ex-soldier, who people brand a healer, for he lives alone, is consulted and he gets the real story of the girl's affair with a Frenchman. She also comes to him. All this is told by the participants as tales within tales when the healer and old man are captured by brigands. All the differing viewpoints are told.

The chief brigand finds that his view of the abjectness of humanity is correct after news of the wife's suicide is heard. The old man has sold everything and sent his wife off with their money on another caravan, and only he falls into the brigand's hands as well as the healer.
—*Mosk.*

Nije Nego
(Tit For Tat)
(YUGOSLAV-COLOR)

Pula, Aug. 15.

Yugoslavia Film release of Central Film Studio-Avala Films production. Features entire cast. Directed by Mica Milosevic. Screenplay, Ljuba Radicevic, Miloscevic; camera (Eastmancolor), Predrag Popovic; music, Korenlje Kovac. Reviewed at Pula Film Fest, Aug. 1, '78. Running time, **92 MINS.**
With: Bata Zivojinovic, Marko Taodrovic, Ruzica Sokic, Nikola Simic.

Mica Milosevic is a noted documentary maker and his first feature is flawed by a docu approach that leaves motivations skimpy with talk replacing a more visual approach to this tale of students getting a chance to give their side of things during a tv show being made on their school.

Students are a surface lot of pretty self absorbed girls and boys more interested in sports or girls. The one script invention is a blackboard drawing of a teacher accusing him of being a classroom lothario and lusting after students. There is a search for the culprit which brings in parents until the guilty party confesses.

The film underlines a lack of more penetrating scripting in Yugoslav pix. Moloseciv documents student escapades and does not quite achieve a balance between caricature and more deft probing of the rifts between pedagogues and students it aims at. Mainly a local item.
—*Mosk.*

Tigar
(The Tiger)
(YUGOSLAV-COLOR)

Pula, Aug. 15.

Yugoslavia Film release of Central Film Studio-Avala Film production. Features entire cast. Directed by Milan Jelic. Screenplay, Gordan Milic; camera (Eastmancolor), Predrag Popovic; editor, Lana Vukobratovic; music, Vojislav Kostic. Reviewed at Pula Film Fest, July 31, '78. Running time, **90 MINS.**
With: Ljubisa Samardzic, Slavko Simac, Vera Cukic, Bata Zivojinovic, Pavle Vujisic.

Actor Milan Jelic made his bow as a director some eight years ago with a wry comedy about an adolescent on the loose, "The Bug Eater." That one had a comic flair and ironic reflection of ordinary life. His new one seems a bit dated and lacks the more potent feeling for the serio-comic texture of life his first pic had.

A good-natured, thirtyish, second rate boxer is constantly nagged by his wife for his lack of earning power, his helping of others rather than themselves and his native honesty. He decides to quit after one more fight and the manager of his boxing club helps him win by siccing a woman on his opponent. She drains the man and helps the hero win.

When he gets a series of odd jobs his wife leaves him for a rich man. The boxer, played with good-natured innocence and charm by popular local actor Ljubisa Samardzic, one evening collars a young thief while a night watchman in a department store. But he lets him go after a hard luck story.

Later as a truck driver, Samardzic helps the young thief again and gets him a job as his assistant. Though thinking he is helping the boy, he finds himself sinking into small time crime when the boy devises a way of stealing meat they deliver by having himself weighed with the truck and keeping the extra meat to sell on the black market.

They began to save money, live better and even put a downpayment on a house. But Samardzic, when he finds out how he won his last fight, decides to spill all on the meat stealing as does the boy. Together in prison, they are forming a boxing team.

Gently played but all somewhat lightweight, and its reflection of lowlife and higher up corruption does not quite get the free-wheeling, zesty drive it had in earlier days.
— *Mosk.*

Miris Zemlje
(The Scent of Earth)
(YUGOSLAV-COLOR)

———

Pula, Aug. 15.
Yugoslavia Film release of Central Film Studio-Avala Film. Zespoly Filmowe Profil production. Features entire cast. Written and directed by Dragovan Jovanovic. Camera (Eastmancolor), Waclaw Dybowski; music, Szeslaw Nieman. Reviewed at Pula Film Fest, July 28, '78. Running time, **86 MINS.**
With: Kazimierz Borowiec, Neda Spasojevic, Ana Krasojevic, Ferdinand Wojcik, Crazyna Szapolawska.

———

A tale of peasant life in the 30s and its tribulations finally overshadowed by the destructiveness of war. Film is rather stolid and literary, and, though with some flair for the feeling of country life, is somewhat marred by overdone dramatic loss to really give life, ardor and depth to this tale of man who finds and loses two families.

A peasant labors hard. His wife is sick and one day his son allows the only cow to wander into the clover, leading to its death. The boy hides in the fields and is killed by lightning. The wife dies and the man turns to drink but is saved by love of a beautiful girl. He raises another family but war takes him away and he comes back to a destroyed farm, his family gone.

It is told in flashbacks. Polski-Yugosalv coproduction is aided by fine camerawork but is somewhat too static to make for any but local and possibly Polish chances. Peasant dramas seem as numerous as the partisan films in local production. —*Mosk.*

Sudbine
(Destinies)
(YUGOSLAV-COLOR)

———

Pula, Aug. 15.
Yugoslavia Film release of Dunav Film production. Features entire cast. Written and directed by Predrag Golubovic. Camera (Eastmancolor), Milivoje Milivojevic. No other credits available. Reviewed at Pula Film Fest, Aug. 2, '78. Running time, **70 MINS.**
With: Bert Sotlar, Faruk Begoli, Miroljub Leso, Mirceta Vukcic.

———

Director Predrag Golubovic astutely spliced four of his shorts about incidents in the last war by adding a few connecting shots of Germans advancing. There is almost no dialog and this is a general statement on man at war with both his humanistic and selfish and cruel sides brought out by it.

It is more general than particular but has a poetic feel for underlining its generalities. The particular in characterization is avoided and this remains more a lyrical look at war and its effects. First, advancing Germans are seen burning and killing inhabitants of villages. Perhaps as reprisals against Partisans.

One man escapes through a cornfield but rather than be caught has a cart drag him to his death when he puts a rope around his neck. In another a young German soldier suddenly puts down his gun when called to a firing squad to kill a group of blindfolded peasants.

He strips off his gear and takes his place with the Partisans as they join hands. The squad kills the Yugoslavs and the German. This is the only part with dialog as names are called out for the squad and the youth is admonished by his officer.

Then it is snowing and ill clad Yugoslav scavengers strip dead Germans of their clothes. One German is alive and two of them decide to take him to the village. They encounter Partisans and one runs off. The other continues to drag the German. He comes to the village and sees his fellow villagers slaughtered. Grabbing a discarded rifle, he clubs the German he has saved to death.

Then a Partisan comes back to his house which is stripped. He goes from house to house getting back his belongings which he lovingly puts back in place. He then smashes everything and torches them as he goes off. An old peasant, the only one he has greeted, stands up and doffs his hat.

Director Golubovic has a flair for making statements on human actions with taut and economical insights. However it is still a pasteup job and remains arresting but superficial in its skimming of man's humanity and inhumanity in war. It may not have the qualities for more demanding theatrical usage abroad but should surface at festivals and for archive and specialized usage on its fine imagery, insights and visual efficacity. —*Mosk.*

Trener
(The Coach)
(YUGOSLAV-COLOR)

———

Pula, Aug. 15.
Yugoslavia Film release of Central Film Studio-Avala Film production. Features entire cast. Written and directed by Purisa Dordevic. Camera (Eastmancolor), Zika Milic; editor, Mira Mitic; music, Milomir. Reviewed at Pula Film Fest, July 31, '78. Running time: **90 MINS.**
With: Tansije Uzonovic, Ljuba Tadic, Peter Karsten, Drago Cuma, Dorde Nenadovic, Dijana Sporcic.

———

Purisa Dordevic has written and scripted a quartet of war pix that broke with overdone partisan pix of derring-do and patriotics for a more poetic, insightful comment on those times. Mixing surrealistic touches, such pix as "The Girl," "Dawn," "Noon" and "The Cyclists" brought him local and outside renown. Now he uses this approach for more uneven results as he looks at that national pastime, football (soccer), and its internal workings, personal vendettas and corruption.

Its impressionistic approach makes this somewhat splintered and fragmented and perhaps too specialized in allusions to bring it off. However it does have some unusual moments of probing into player hazards and hangups not to forget the use as a national catharsis and for publicity by big companies.

A trainer gets his big chance at heading up a top team. He has recruited a small boy from his own home town on a visit to his father's grave who died in a concentration camp. The boy begins to make good but runs into enmity and envy. The trainer tells one star to keep away from his wife to conserve strength, but dallies himself.

Jealous of the new boy he discovered, he gets into difficulties with the manager and quits to go to a German team. He loses a first game to his old team but wins the second. But he feels he has somehow betrayed his father. An uneven mainly local film which might find some foreign outlets due to its subject matter. —*Mosk.*

Lude Godina
(Foolish Years)
(YUGOSLAV-COLOR)

———

Pula, Aug. 15.
Yugoslavia Film release of Zvezda Film production. Features entie cast. Written and directed by Zoran Calic. Camera (Eastmancolor), Milivoje Milivojevic; music, Kornelije Kovac. Reviewed at Pula Film Fest, July 27, '78. Running time: **85 MINS.**
With: Rialda Kadric, Vladimir Petrovic, Bata Zivojinovic, Ljubisa Samardzic.

———

A 15-year old girl is put in a family way by a 16 or 17-year old boy. Their innocence and a lack of parental rapport almost leads to tragedy at the hands of a quack abortionist. Somewhat didactic, it might serve some purpose in local schools but is too naive in these permissive days with flaccid direction not helping.

They meet in a dancehall. The girl is a good student and the boy is more a drifter with a harsh father who often works abroad. Their love affair is done with helicopter shots finding them atop buildings and running across bridges. Friends get wind of their trouble and try to help while they feel they cannot go to their parents who, if not guilty of the acts of their children, are blind to their problems.

The playing is somewhat arch with some solid older actors unable to do much with their stereotyped characters. —*Mosk.*

Dvoboj Za Juznu Prugu
(Battle For The Railway)
(YUGOSLAV-COLOR)

———

Pula, Aug. 15.
Yugoslavia Film release of Central Film Studio, Avala Film production. Features entire cast. Directed by Zdravko Velimirovic. Screenplay, Purisa Dordevic, Velimirovic; camera (Eastmancolor), Steva Radovic; editor, Miodrag Petrovic-Sarlo; music, Zoran Hristic. Reviewed at Pula Film Fest, July 26, '78. Running time, **105 MINS.**
With: Dragomir Bojanic-Gidra, Vojislav Miric, Nada Vojinovic, Neda Spasojevic.

———

A partisan film about attempts to block the railways used by Germans to ship important material to their Balkan strongholds and even Africa during the last war. Some okay battle scenes, though somewhat unclear in the many internal partisan splits and renegades and even the action itself.

Time was when these pix were the main staples of Yugoslav film. There were many heroic, well done, simple battle sagas, some with more depth and insight into the times and others with even comic and satirical elements. They are on the wane, a good thing as more contemporary or more ambitious historical subjects take over.

But they still remain popular and the yearly production could stand a couple. But this one is not the kind to get action fans or even more discerning audiences. The partisan group is run by a sterling, brave commissar whose sister is a nun and helps him hide people or obtain information.

Yugoslav collaborators, the local fascist terrorists, and the Chetniks fight with the Germans. There are numerous skirmishes and battles plus the partisans' hijacking a train which they soon lose, though it is not clear why. However, there is an ominous armored German train that is visually effective until the partisans destroy it.

Pic is too declamatory, sentimental and confused to add to the ranks of better pix of this ilk that have been mainstays of local production.'—*Mosk.*

Sono Stato Un Agente Cia
(Covert Action)
(ITALIAN-COLOR)

Rome, Aug. 17.

A Capitol release, produced by Gibi Milesi for Mires Cinematografico. Stars David Janssen, Corinne Clery, Maurizio Merli. Directed by Romolo Guerrieri. Screenplay, Vittorio Schiraldi, Mino Roti, Nico Ducci; camera (Technicolor), Erico Menczer; art director, Eugenio Leverani; editor, Antonio Siciliano; music, Stelvio Cipriani. Reviewed at Cinema Cola Di Rienzo, Rome, Aug. 17, -78. Running time: **100 MINS.**

Lester Horton	David Janssen
Anne Florio	Corinne Clery
John Florio	Maurizio Merli
Athens CIA Head	Arthur Kennedy
Greek Inspector	Philippe Leroy

Chances are "Covert Action" will be ultimately changed to something closer to the Italian title — "I Was a CIA Agent" — since the Mires production has more standard crime action in it than the shadowy suspense of gray counterespionage thrillers. Though action and dialogue have time-worn familiarity, "Covert Action" is sustained as a market item by David Janssen, a beauteous Corinne Clery, Arthur Kennedy and the effective support of Philippe Leroy, as well as a sage integration of the Greek backdrop with many-colored splendors for the fast-moving but commonplace yarn.

It rates dualler spot in the U.S. though how red-blooded Americans will react to Romolo Guerrieri's outspoken critique of the CIA, mostly flimsy caricature, is hard to predict even in these times when the Agency is often under fire.

Janssen plays an ex-spook investigating the death of his friend in the service by the service. Threatened by head counter-spy in Athens, Arthur Kennedy, for getting close to naked toes, Janssen continues his personal mission through modern brimstone and fury that Kennedy can throw at him in 99 mins. — including internment in the CIA's own psycho lager.

Tortured most of the way, except for brief romantic stopovers in paradise on the Island of Lindos with his ex-girlfriend, Corinne Clery (who becomes a widow when another spook (Maurizio Merli) gets eliminated by CIA killers looking more like smalltime Neapolitan thugs), Janssen finally gets away with the tape for his next novel with the help of a Greek police inspector — played by Philippe Leroy. Leroy sums up his attitude as Janssen's guardian angel on more than one occasion with his closing line: "The CIA is rich and potent; we are poor but honest."

Janssen is convincing as the do-good prober, but age tells in heavy action. Corinne Clery is a big romantic spark and Kennedy knows how to shrink the odds on Janssen's flight for life. But what stands out amid the spookery and violence is the wealth of well-selected backdrops — only a few of which fail to register the right measure of integration with story. Expertly lensed by Erico Menczer and edited for chase-suspense rhythm, the film, at times, looks bigger and brighter than most Italo undercover pix.

—*Werb.*

Love Of The White Snake
(HONG KONG-COLOR)

Hong Kong, Aug. 10.

A First Films Organization production and release. C.H. Wong, Executive Producer. Directed by Szu-Ma Ke. Camera (color), Chen Ching Chu; screenplay, Szu-Ma Ke' speccial effects, Tadashi Nishimoto. Reviewed at IFD Preview Theater, Hong Kong, Aug. 10, '78. Running Time: **98 MINS.**

Cast: Lin Ching Hsia, Charles Chi, Chin Chih Min, Li Kun.

(English Subtitles)

"Love Of The White Snake" is a well-known Chinese legend. Recreated on film, Cinderella-style, by First Films, it could prove a bonanza in its homeland. Might have chances in overseas markets if properly packaged and English dubbed for the Disney trade, thought snakes are not so acceptable to western entertainment.

The romantic plot tells about Hi Hsin (Charles Chin), a handsome pharmacist who gets involved with Pao (Lin Ching Hsia) and Shao (Chin Chin Min), lovely ladies who are really friendly snakes from another world. They all get caught in a storm and are forced to share a boat. Pao sees Hui as a prospective husband and is eventually lured to a hasty marriage. A colorful Chinese ceremony follows, complete with traditional nuptial costumes.

A Taoist priest later reveals their secret to the newly-married man. Hui gives Pao a strong drink that puts her into a trance. She reverts to her original form and Hui faints from shock. Pao then forces herself to be human again to get a potent fern from Heaven to cure her ailing husband. Meanwhile, Hui is kidnapped by another meddling monk whose mission is to fight evil spirits.

With the help of the God of Black Wing, the hero is saved. A teary confrontation and confession follow and true love wins despite countless barriers.

Beautifully photographed on location in Kora and Taiwan, the HK$2,500,000 production has exotic appeal. Though the general presentation resembles a stylized Cantonese opera, especially in the acting department, it has enough audio-visual tricks to keep everyone from getting restless.

The Chinese tale, if taken seriously, has the subtle message that true love can conquer and survive everything, including death, good and bad spirits and time. It is an ambitious project for First Films and its broad appeal succeeds on many levels. — *Mel.*

Lin Tse-hsu
(The Opium War)
(RED CHINESE-COLOR)

Sino-American Corp. release of a Haiyen Film Studio (Shanghai) production. Directed by Chen Chun-li. Features entire cast. No other credits provided. Reviewed at the Guild Theatre, New York, Aug. 14, '78. (No MPAA Rating). Running time: **90 MINS.**

Lin Tse-hsu, Imperial Commisioner	Chao Tan
Emperor Tao Kuang	Kao Chen
Mu Chabg-o, Chief Minister	Haiao Tien
Teng Ting-chen	Li Yung
Kuan Tien-pei	Teng Nan
Yu Kun, Customs Inspector	Lian Shan
Charles Elliot, British consul	Otto Williams
Leslie Dent, British Merchant	Gerald Tannenbaum
Kuang Tung-shan	Chien Chien-li
Mai Kuang	Wen Hsi-ying
Mrs. Mai	Ching Yin

(English Subtitles)

This Red Chinese theatrical film, purportedly the first to be released in the U.S., opens an exclusive engagement at New York's Guild Theatre next month.

It has a certain amount of theatrical value in that it offers the "other side" of an historical event usually explained from the British point-of-view — the opium wars in which the British tried to flood Indian-grown opium into China. Whatever their reason — some say to undermine the Chinese moral fibre to lay the way for wholesale invasion — it is dealt with in this film as completely the handiwork of the British. Indeed the arch villains of the piece are the British consul and a British merchant who connive with some Chinese court officials.

When this is brought to the attention of the Emperor, he dispatches his ablest (and most moral) official, Imperial Commissioner Lin Tse-hsu, to clear things up. He does and he doesn't. Actually, he is only able to defeat the opium merchants with the aid of the peasant class, headed by boatman Mai Kuang and village leader Kuang Tung-shen (this is the closest to present-day Chinese politics the film comes).

There are lots of battles, lots of killing and lots of the hammiest acting (by Western standards) yet seen on the screen. It would be interesting to know where the Red Chinese located the many Occidentals seen in the film — all non-professionals, judging by their acting.

A cinematic curiosity, worth viewing at least once. —*Robe.*

Locarno Fest

Fedora
(W. GERMAN-FRENCH-COLOR)

Locarno, Aug. 22.

Rialto Films release of Geria Film-Bavaria Studios, SFP production. Stars William Holden, Marthe Keller. Produced and directed by Billy Wilder. Screenplay, I.A.L. Diamond, Wilder from book by Tom Tryon; camera (Eastmancolor), Gerry Fisher; editor, Stefan Arsten; music, Miklos Rosza. Reviewed at Locarno Film Fest (non-competing), Aug. 9, '78. Running time, 110 MINS.

Barry	William Holden
Fedora	Marthe Keller
Vando	Jose Ferrer
Countess	Hildegard Knef
Balforu	Frances Sternhagen
Manager	Mario Adorf
Count	Hans Jaray
Kirtos	Gottfried John
Michael York	Himself
Henry Fonda	Himself

(English Soundtrack)

With "Fedora," based on a tale from Tom Tryon's bestseller, "Crowned Heads," Billy Wilder goes serenely back to Hollywood treatment of itself as legend, illusion and dreams rather than reality.

Wilder displays a seamless flair for welding the threads of this outsize tale together. However, allowing it to be told from two points of view blunts it. Well acted, but sans the true star faces to give an ironic tang to its acceptance of Hollywood star myths.

In his more successful, acerbic look at an over-the-hill star, "Sunset Boulevard," the star was a real oldtimer, Gloria Swanson. Neither Marthe Keller, as the once great star Fedora, or Hildegard Knef as a crusty Polish countess and the star's keeper, have that allusive, self absorbed but camera-loving look that stars possessed, though they are good.

William Holden tells most of the tale as he did in "Boulevard." But here he is an indie producer down on his luck trying desperately to get a script to the amazingly still youthful star, at 67, Fedora, in a hideaway on a Greek island. It appears she is being held captive by a quack doctor, once famed for keeping personalities youthful, well mimed by Jose Ferrer.

His attempts to help her fail and he then hears she has thrown herself under a train as Leo Tolstoy's "Anna Karenina" did. It happened in France and Holden was trying to get her to do a new version of "Karenina."

But then comes the gimmick as Knef takes over to tell remainder of the tale. Readers of the book know it and perhaps it may be unfair to give it away. But the real Fedora is the thing in point and the dramatic, beguiling, campy aspect of the pic is upset by the welter of new facts unveiling the truth of Fedora's youth.

European critics liked it at the Cannes Fest though Yank appraisers sneered. It may have more potency abroad than stateside, but it shoudl not be counted out. Wilder's directorial flair, the fine production dress, Holden's solid presence and Michael York playing himself as a narcissistic actor and Henry Fona, also as himself as head of the Academy who delivers a belated Oscar to Fedora, add some flavor to this bittersweet bow to the old star system.

It might have been more effective in leaving the gimmick to the last or unfurling it earlier for more audience impact. There are many inside allusions to old stars and cracks about tax shelter money and old Hollywood ways. But they are in character and Mario Adorf adds a neat comedic relief as a Greek hotel keeper who once played a bit part in "Zorba" and aids and abets Holden in his quest.

Pic can be summed up as a well made but flawed tale. The growing interest in the film media itself might help this pic stateside with adroit placement and fast playoff indicated. Missing are needed hints at Fedora's true star quality, which are not there from past clips or inherent in Keller's performance or that of Knef as her ruthless mentor, and which mar pic with disbelief.
—*Mosk.*

Maisons Dans Cette Ruelle
(Houses in This Alley)
(IRANIAN-COLOR)

Locarno, Aug. 22.

CTGE release of Dia Al Baytai production. Features entire cast. Written and directed by Kassem Hawl. Camera (Eastmancolor), Hatem Hussein; editor, Ahmed Metwalli; music, Abdel Amir Alsarraf. Reviewed at Locarno Film Fest (competing), Aug. 5, '78. Running time: 90 MINS.

Cast: Saadie Al-Zyde, Nizar Assamourai Suad Abdallah, Abdel Jabbar Kazem, Hana Mouhamed, Makki Badri.

A social-themed film that deals with exploitation of the people by businessmen and shady building operators. This is before the '68 revolution which supposedly has coped with these problems. Mainly for home consumption, as the film is too simplistic, technically faulty and surface for anything but curio interest abroad.

A building falls in but not much is done about it. Poor people wrap candy, fill perfume bottles and do other home industries for crass, opportunistic bosses until the revolution explodes. Surprisingly, film was picked for competition but would have served better in an informative sidebar section for a sampling of films from this little known production area in the Near East. — *Mosk.*

China 9, Liberty 37
(ITALO-COLOR)

Locarno, Aug. 22.

Titanus release of CEA production. Stars Fabio Testi, Warren Oates, Jenny Agutter. Produced by Gianni Bozzacchi, Valerio de Paolis. Directed by Monte Hellman. No other credits available. Reviewed at Locarno Film Fest (non-competing), Aug. 13, '78. Running time, 94 MINS.

Shaw	Fabio Testi
Sebanek	Warren Oates
Catherine	Jenny Agutter

An oater made in Spain with Italo backing in English and Italian, American and English thesps in the main roles. Though the director, Monte Hellman, is American, this is a strange western that eschews Italo pasta violence and camp, Hispano romantics or more robust Yank counterparts.

It adds a permissive note with explicit if soft love scenes between a gunslinger sent to kill another one, now owning a farm, by railroad reps who want the land, and the latter's wife.

There is the background of corrupt rail people a la Jesse James, the gunmen respecting each other and then the final shootouts as the two work together despite the problem of the wife.

Fabio Testi is sometimes hard to understand but he is supposed to come from Europe and it was a melting pot those days. He is the gunman who runs off after having the wife. But she follows him thinking she has killed her husband when he realizes what has happened and beats her up.

There is love until railroad men are sent after the gunslinger and the husband reappears with his brothers. Warren Oates is gruff as the husband, Jenny Agutter pliant as the torn wife who finally ends up again with her husband when the gunman will not kill him. It could play off in these days when thataways are in short supply. Pic misses the mixture of keen acting, psychological insight and sureness in tone to give it cult chances.

The old west looks a bit flat. One cameo scene is done by Sam Peckinpah, who gave the western a more stylized violent charge in "The Wild Bunch." He is a writer selling the legend rather than the reality of the west and who offers his services to the woman in the gunfighters' life but is refused.

Film has okay production dress and is worth playoff on its unusual balance of foreign and U.S. talents in an attempt to make a more outspoken oater that finally falls into conventions without transcending them. — *Mosk.*

La Morte Al Lavoro
(Death at Work)
(ITALO-B&W)

Locarno, Aug. 22.

SACIS release of RAI-Napoli, Gaetano Stucci production. Features entire cast. Directed by Gianni Amelio. Screenplay, Mimmo Rafele, Amelio from a story by Hanns H. Ewers; camera (B&W from Video), Mario Selo; music, Bernard Herrmann. Reviewed at Locarno Film Fest (competing), Aug. 13, '78. Running time, 85 MINS.

Cast: Federico Pacifici, Clara Colosimo, Fautas Avelli, Eva Axen, Giovannella Grifeo.

Shot on tape, then put to film, this black and white atmospheric tale of obsession is somewhat slight in scripting and stretches its tale to full length when it would have fared better as a short.

Probably originally intended for tv, it would fare better there on its setting in one room and slow but effective progression. A young man takes a room in an old town house, which was formerly occupied by an actor who killed himself.

The youth is surrounded by memorabilia of the actor, especially stills from films, a revolver and clothes. Across the way he notices a lovely girl one night and becomes obsessed. He stops work, ignores his girlfriend and talks to the girl in pantomime, affected by all the film artifacts surrounding him.

Director Gianni Amelio displays a solid feel for rhythm and mood, handling his actors well. A little girl seems to be involved with this strange obsession until the boy, too, kills himself, egged on by the mysterious beauty across the way. His girl goes to the mystery girl's apartment when she hears a tape made by the boy. But it is empty.

Video looks like a faded old b&w print which helps the mood in this muted, overstretched pic that still shows a promising talent in Amelio when he gets his technique more controlled for revealing character rather than just for effects.

A pot-pourri of the late Bernard Herrmann's film music helps the mood of this effete but well-made tale that sacrifices motivation to artifice. —*Mosk.*

Roberte
(FRENCH-COLOR)

Locarno, Aug. 22.

World Marketing Film release of Filmoblic production. Features entire cast. Directed by Pierre Zucca. Screenplay, Pierre Klossowski, Zucca from a book by Klossowski; camera (Eastmancolor), Paul Bonis; editor, Nicole Lubtchansky; music, Eric Demarsan. Reviewed at Locarno Film Fest (non-competing), Aug. 4, '78. Running time, 100 MINS.

Roberte	Denise Morin Sinclaire
Octave	Pierre Klossowski
Antoine	Martin Loeb
Vittorio	Barbet Schroeder
Little F	Juliet Berto

Von A . . . . Jean-Francois Stevenin
Bank Clerk . . . . Frederic Mitterand

Roberte is a fiftyish woman with a stern face but who retains her fine body. She seems to accept living her husband's fantasies of giving her to other men. Many young U.S. filmmakers have been going back to '30s and '40s films for inspiration, while here, director Pierre Zucca, for his second film, appears to be retreading the pre-war avant-garde films for this literary film full of abstruse conceits and old men's fancies.

The author of the book and coscripter from which the pic is taken plays the husband. He is decadent with seemingly fascistic desires of a world made up of old men, women and children. He apparently follows his wife about or has her photographed or sets up some of her sexual adventures in the streets, or with men who come to the house.

She has a nephew she wants to bring up right but who spies on her. There are also two strange friends of the boy, played by actresses, who indulge in blackmailing since they seem to be part of the affair. Also involved are flashbacks to Roberte's wartime experiences as a nurse in Italy where she gets mixed up with an SS man.

Her husband hires a tutor for her nephew. The tutor had humiliated and raped her as a young woman. There are layers of symbolism and perversions, as the husband's voyeurism finally ends in his death when he thinks he has won his way.

Lacking a true insight into repressiveness, or clarifying its erotic game, make this pic something that may turn up at specialized fests, archives and perhaps some cultist probing, if more open commercial chances appear chancey indeed. Writer Pierre Klossowski is sharp, hawlike and right as the instigator of this weird game.

Others are adequate and though Zucca has some flair for visual suggestiveness, the film is too vague, indulged and pretentious to achieve its look at aging perverseness. The woman is becoming important as a government censor during all her sex play and is planning to do away with her husband before he dies in apparent happiness at having turned her into what he wanted her to be. — *Mosk.*

Cseplo Gyuri
(HUNGARIAN-COLOR)

Locarno, Aug. 22.

Hungarofilm release of Hunnia-Bela Balasz Studio production. Features entire cast (non-pros). Directed by Pal Schiffer. Screenplay, Istvan Kameny, Schiffer; camera (Eastmancolor), Tamas Andro. Reviewed at Locarno Film Fest (competing), Aug. 7, '78. Running time: **96 MINS.**

Film is a sort of enacted documentary about gypsy life in present-day Hungary. Not the whining or exciting violins and palm reading, but in some cases, people relegated to small farming ghettos with bad facilities. This is the tale of a young man who decides to try for work in the big city.

Pic is astute and offers a view of the life of a people who have not as yet been assimilated by their socialist state. There are many dialog scenes that sometimes touch on old racist aspects of gypsies felt as thieves, indolent and ignorant.

But this is not forced or dramatized. The protagonist comes to the city and two others who return home. But he stays to do hard work, faces loneliness but finds other gypsies who are integrating and helping each other. Perhaps somewhat didactic in its choice of scenes, it still offers a revealing and just portrait sans falling into excess.

Yet its mixture of documentary and fiction lose this dramatic edge and it appears a film worth fest interest and school use plus specialized ethnographic events if more limited for theatrical ventures abroad. —*Mosk.*

Two Solitudes
(CANADIAN-COLOR)

Locarno, Aug. 22.

Compass Film Sales release of Two Solitudes Film Corp. production. Stars Jean-Pierre Aumont, Stacy Keach, Gloria Carlin. Directed and written by Lionel Chetwynd from the book by Hugh McLennan. Camera (COLOR), Rene Verzier; editor, Ralph Brunjes; Music, Maurice Jarre. Reviewed at Locarno Film Fest (competing). Aug. 13, '78. Running time, **116 MINS.**
Tallard . . . . Jean-Pierre Aumont
McQueen . . . . Stacy Keach
Kathleen . . . . Gloria Carlin
Yardley . . . . Christopher Wiggins
Beaubien . . . . Claude Jutra
Marius . . . . Raymond Cloutier
Cardinal . . . . Jean-Louis Roux

A solidly carpentered tale of Canada during and after World War I. Its theme of the clashes between French and English-speaking Canadians is still relevant but is treated in too stolid a manner to bring a needed breath of life into this literary tale of a seignurial French family destroyed by the war and differing attitudes towards the problems of the French-speaking minority.

Using English, though most of the characters are French, is sometimes awkward but finally acceptable since it was made by English-speaking filmmakers.

The still nominal head of a small French town in Quebec goes goes along with governmental decrees of conscription of French-speaking people during the war though many, including the man's nationalistic son, are against it.

Jean-Pierre Aumont is effective as the aging squire who wants to bring industry to his city as well as make a profit. Stacy Keach is a ruthless English-speaking businessman who finally ruins Aumont by going into business with the Church. Aumont's son is also against him and damages him by revealing his father's heretical outlook to the Church.

Film should spark interest at home but is somewhat too cold and mannered to get a dramatic edge into this saga about a family in a time of change. Direction is workmanlike, acting good but not effective enough for a needed dramatic charge to lift it out of an academic treatment. Technically fine.
—*Mosk.*

Susetz
(Rockinghorse)
(ISRAEL-COLOR/B&W)

Locarno, Aug. 22.

Susetz Ltd. release and production. Features entire cast. Directed by Yaki Yosha. Screenplay Yosha, Yoram Kaniuk from a book by Kaniuk; camera (Color/B&W), Ilan Rosenberg; editor, Yosha. Reviewed at Locarno Film Fest (non-competing), Aug. 12, '78. Running time: **85 MINS.**
Cast: Schmuel Kraus, Gedalia Besser, Arik Lavi, Jozi Katz, Miriam Bernstein-Cohen.

A rare personalized film from Israel that reveals a director of promise in Yaki Yosha who can go from the particular to a general blending of character and incident to make a statement on growing up in Israel and the feel and texture of life there.

It uses a film-within-a-film treatment that avoids fastidious refinement and has that feel of grace which dovetails everything to a revealing, charming look at Israel, warts and all. A young painter comes home after years in the U.S. where his first exposition had been marred by a burning of his paintings. It is never quite clear if he did it himself or not.

At home, he finds his father dying, plus a need to come to grips with himself and his country. He wanders about and meets a colorful character who spends his time making statistics about growing prostitution as well as servicing married women in the mornings whose husbands are too involved with work to care for them.

There is also a woman who felt he would grow up to be a good and just man, the kind needed in this country, when he gave back stolen apples as a kid. He denies he is other than ordinary but feels he must make a film even if he knows nothing about it. His film begins to develop, using these people he has met.

The film within is in color and the rest in b&w, which works in capturing the feeling of memory. The father's refusal to keep to his violin due to his lack of hope in humanity in general is evoked, as well as the painter's birth on the day the first talking film "The Jazz Singer" is shown in Israel.

His film completed, due to an old friend who is now a bombastic-type film producer, he returns to his father's picture framing shop. The film's unique blending of memory and life today, plus its fluid handling, should make this a pic that could find some specialized showings abroad besides the usual archive, museum, school and fest outings it will get. A director to be watched. — *Mosk.*

Diamante Bruto
(Rough Diamond)
(BRAZILIAN-COLOR)

Locarno, Aug. 22.

Embrafilme release of Pilar Films production. Features entire cast. Written and directed by Orlando Senna from the novel by Afranio Pexioto. Camera (Eastmancolor), Joao Carlos Horta; editor, Roberto Pires. Reviewed at Locarno Film Fest (competing), Aug. 8, '78. Running time: **114 MINS.**
Cast: Jose Wilker, Gilda, Conceicao Senna, Wilson Melo, Ademario Rufino, Flora, Filma Natalia.

Orlando Senna is a journalist who also makes films. Here he tries to squeeze in too much legend, local color and explanations, making this love story between a tv thesp star and a black girl back home too uneven, surface and padded by irrelevancies to bring it off.

But there are some good atmospheric qualities and the unaffected black and white love story, though there are indications of continued racism despite the integrated look of the country. This could make pic effective in Latino countries but sans the polish and insight for other offshore possibilities.

The man comes back to his old home in the diamond district of Chapada. Diamonds are practically extinct but miners go doggedly on with it. There are explanations of the miners' refusals to opt for raising cattle or industry. But the man has really come back to see a childhood sweetheart, now a lovely black girl, daughter of a miner.

Once friends, it now blossoms into love but she insists marriage can not be possible for them. She lies about having men before when they become lovers. He, however, hears from a white that she is only a prostie. Untrue but he believes it. He takes up with the older wife of his father's ranch foreman.

been seen going through a whole castration scene with a bull.

When the foreman goes looking for his wife, off with a man, the black girl warns them away but is killed by the irate husband. There are tales of legends about diamonds, showing up exploitation of the miners and the problems of the area. But Senna appears more newsman than being able to weld this into a drama that destroys one of its star-crossed lovers due to the social barriers and memories of legends.

He makes his points in a documentary fashion that waters down the film's impact. But when the theme fuses with his outlooks, as in his "Iricema," about the odyssey of a black girl around a developing Brazil, it can be effective. Here it misses despite fine playing, especially the piquant presence of a true rough diamond, Gilda, who plays the doomed girl back home who can only give herself and asks nothing in return. —*Mosk.*

The Little Town of Anara
(SOVIET-COLOR)

Locarno, Aug. 22.

Sovexport release of Grouzia Film production. Features entire cast. Written and directed by Irakly Kvirikadze. Camera (Sovcolor), Youi Kikabidze; music, T. Bakourdaze. Reviewed at Locarno Film Fest (competing), Aug. 10, '78. Running time: **90 MINS.**

Cast: Revaz Essadze, Cecile Takaicvili, Ramaz Tchkhikvadze, Henriette Lejava.

Georgian films have usually been the spice, the wine of Soviet film output. The Latin temperament, extroverted nature and forthrightness have added a comic element to the usually more serious pix from around this massive country. But it is not only comic relief, for some Georgian films have run into censor troubles in their looks at bureaucracy or themes of the individual out of step with the accepted ways.

This one, however, is a broad folk comedy that plays outrageously for laughs and succeeds often despite a heavy theatrical treatment. It also twists tradition. A fine looking old man is the top drinker in his town. He has the prize of an enormous decorated horn which only he can drain of several liters of wine.

There have been many who tried but it has stayed in the family for decades. One morning the old man is dressed by his adoring family to officiate at a local function, for his position makes him a top town figure. He is killed by a basket of feathers dropped on his head from a balcony.

His small, gentle son, only happy taking care of weather forecasting, finds himself beset by contenders for the horn. Actor Revaz Essadze is a true comic in his timing, double takes and gentle dealing with the eccentrics who come to empty the horn.

One is afraid of bears and shoots up the house after the preliminary toasts when he thinks they are all bears. Biggest yocks come from a man who, when frightened, can fall asleep for months. He does and the man of the house has to cart him about and deal with his snoring until his wife arrives to wake him.

Finally some cheaters, who siphon the wine off to hot water bottles hidden on the man, win the drinking horn. But the women find out and the son must recoup the horn. He goes and finds the man has the same problems with drunks and the sleeper. He retrieves the horn without needing to drink it. But on the way back it is broken by irate towns people after the man has remarked how nice the people were.

Freed from this unwanted tradition, the man is back to his amateur theatrics, some funny scenes here, and sending up rockets to stave off frosts which could endanger the vines, and, naturally, the wine crop. Perhaps too heavy-handed at times for much chances abroad, but a film that should get more fest and archive coverage on its sheer bombastic human insights and a welcome comedy from the Soviet film setup. —*Mosk.*

Hoshizora No Marionette
(Puppets Under Starry Skies)
(JAPANESE-COLOR)

Locarno, Aug. 22.

Hiroko Govaers release of Tokyo Video Center production. Features entire cast. Directed by Hojin Hashiura. Screenplay, Atuhsi Yamatoya, Hashiura from the book by Yushi Kita; camera (Eastmancolor), Yuji Pokumura; music, Ryoichi Kuniyoshi. Reviewed at Locarno Film Fest (competing), Aug. 6, '78. Running time: **99 MINS.**

Cast: Yoichi Miura, Kazuhito Takei, Ako, Teizo Muta, Haruko Mabuchi, Mocko Ezawa.

With the exception of Nagisa Oshima's unique erotic exploration, "In the Realm of the Senses," and oldtimer Akira Kurosawa's poetic tale of ecology, "Dersu Uzala," the Japanese film has not made much festival or commercial splash abroad since its key-days of films by Kenji Mizoguchi, Kurosawa, Yasujiro Ozu and Kon Ichikawa. This one will not help but does display a trend in films by young filmmakers.

That is, dealing more with young people and their disillusion with their society and families and a growing move towards revolt or suicide. This one has overtones of the noted James Dean pic "Rebel Without a Cause." There is a knife fight and the hero thrown together with a girl and a strange, lonely boy. But it is "Rebel" in a much more permissive scope.

The friend is effeminate and gay, the girl a tramp with many abortions behind her and now pregnant again. There are scenes of the three in an old house. All are turned on by drugs and the gay boy, after a futile pass at the hero and staving off the girl's advances, drowns himself.

The main character likes his motorcycle, works hard in a junk yard and dreams of his dead mother whom he felt was maligned by his father. Beaten badly by a gang of thugs, his father reappears after a long absence and they move in together when he is cured. He brings along the girl but she finally decides to stay with the father who will bring up her child.

The boy finally rams his motorcycle into a truck as his will to love is completely obliberated by memories of his mother, the suicidal boy and his distaste for society plus a gnawing romantic hangover of Japanese ritual, rites and ways.

Film is sharply made but dramatically flawed by too many cliches about wayward youth. More for home spots. Some playoff chances loom abroad on theme and sleek treatment though it exploits rather than gives insights into its drama. —*Mosk.*

On Efface Tout!
(We Forget Everything!)
(FRENCH-COLOR)

Locarno, Aug. 22.

Ideal Film release of Les Films Du Sioux production. Features entire cast. Directed by Pascal Vidal. Screenplay, Pierre Philippe; camera (Eastmancolor), Jacques Boumendil; editor, Arnaud Peit. Reviewed at Locarno Film Fest (competing), Aug. 5, '78. Running time: **110 MINS.**

Reporter	Yves Beneyton
Girl	Christine Pascal
Editor	Christine Murillo
Publisher	Bruno Cremer
Inspector	Bernard Fresson
Shopkeeper	Micheline Presle
Director	J.M. Thibault
Editor	Gerard Lartigau
Lawyer	Guy Trjan

A rare attempt by a new director to delve into politics, in this case underground terrorist organizations. But it is defeated by a vague script and a flaccid approach to such a theme. It will probably have more resonance at home than abroad.

A young journalist on a leftist newspaper gets involved with police and terrorist orgs when a girlfriend, who sometimes put up a young terrorist sought by the police, is traced to him.

He has a police shadow and the girl disappears after being picked up by what appears to be another group who may be in cahoots with the government. Somehow the newsman finds her dancing in a sex theatre and then she is killed, as is her terrorist friend.

The journalist finds his paper does not want to get mixed up in things to protect itself. All is compromise around him. One underground group is shown training at a chateau and it is not clear which group it is.

Pascal Vidal may evolve when he can clarify his intentions. Here it is somewhat too obtuse and tatty, with the characters fairly routine and allusions too unclear to give this a more coherent drive and insight into a worthy theme. —*Mosk.*

Non Contate Su Di Noi
(Don't Count On Us)
(ITALIAN-COLOR)

Locarno, Aug. 22.

VIS release of Manfredi Marzano-Istlan Film production. Features entire cast. Directed by Sergio Nuti. Screenplay, Francesca Ferrari, Nuti, Gianloreto Carbone; camera (Color), Renato Tufari; music, Maurizio Rota. Reviewed at Locarno Film Fest (competing), Aug. 11, '78. Running time, **90 MINS.**

Cast: Francesca Ferrari, Maurizio Rota, Sergio Nuti, Francesco Scalco.

Youth and drugs are now becoming European themes long after the many U.S. films on the subject. This one concerns a group who run into problems with police and the local pushers before the hero swears off the stuff. He then parts with the heroine, who has turned him on after he picked her up in a drugged state in the streets.

Film is rather flatly told and acted. However, it is matter-of-fact in its depiction of the drug scene and might evoke some interest on home grounds though too familiar, pedestrian and uneven for any foreign chances at this date. —*Mosk.*

Kleine Frieren Auch Im Sommer
(Young Ones Are Even Cold in the Summer)
(SWISS-COLOR)

Locarno, Aug. 22.

Rialto Film release of Cinov Producktion production. Features entire cast. Directed by Peter Von Gunten. Screenplay, Von Gunten, Herbert Meier; camera (Eastmancolor), Fritz E. Maeder; editor, Alexander Rupp, Marianne Pfister. Reviewed at Locarno Film Fest (competing), Aug. 10, '78. Running time: **100 MINS.**

Juliette	Verena Reichhardt
Max	Lorenz Hugener
Patricia	Esther Christinat
Gerard	Heinz Sommer
Rose	Silvia Jost

It appears that besides their hard currency Switzerland has hard drugs among its youth. This tale of four maladjusted teenagers has them on the run after some capers to raise money for drugs and to find some freedom. It falls into the usual cliche model and is too simplistic in its plot to make a more probing comment on delinquent Swiss-German youth.

A girl returns from abroad and is treated to a humiliating personal search for drugs on getting to

Switzerland. She looks up an old friend, a drug addict who rarely works, and goes to work to supply food for them. Into this comes a rich boy whose father cuts him off from money and a girl who's escaped from prison.

The boys take money the working girl has hidden in her clothes and buy a car to go off on a joy ride. The decent girl balks at the attempts at robberies when they run out of money and they go back. Here they are finally caught by the law.
Mainly local chances for this rather naive tale of delinquency and drugs.
—*Mosk.*

I Tembelides Tis Eforis Kiladas
(The Slothful Ones of the Fertile Valley)
(GREEK-COLOR)

Locarno, Aug. 22.

Alix Film Productions release and production. Features entire cast. Written and directed by Nicos Panayotopoulos from the book by Albert Cossery. Camera (Eastmancolor), Andreas Bellis; editor, Yorgos Triantafylou; music, Mahler. Reviewed at Locarno Film Fest (competing), Aug. 11, '78. Running time: 115 MINS.
Cast: Olga Karlatos, Yorgos Dialegmenos, Dimitris Poulikakos, Nikitas Tsakirglouu, Vassilis Diamtopolous.

A film on human sloth but laced with piquant black humor to make a tart comment on the human condition. It may have some shrewdly imbedded symbolism but sans insistence or didactics.

With echoes of Luis Bunuel's "The Exterminating Angel," it is not a copy but an homage. Bunuel had people strangely trapped in a rich house after a dinner while here it's a way of life forced by the father on his three grown sons. They have inherited a country house and the means to live in it without working from a rich, deceased relative. They retire there with a lovely maid.

Early euphoric life soon becomes a sort of enclosure that breeds a brief revolt or acquiesence. The father takes to his bed with a bad hernia. One son has a village lover whom he refuses to marry. Another seduces the maid and one also tries the maid but is already too lazy and out of condition to do much about it.

The maid's lover wants to break out and finally does with her. But he is tired and lays down to sleep in her arms after they have gone a way from the house. The maid's connivance with their ways, making up the bed around the son who only sleeps, letting the father play with her breasts, can be looked at as a class comment of the workers too frequently giving in to near slavery for the masters' pleasures.

Interpretations can be made and are there. But the film does not need them, for it is unusual, black humored and absorbing in its own right. A sort of permissive Chekhovian look at members of the upper classes who decide to cut themselves off from everything and its consequences, in collusion with a dedicated worker who is emotionally caught up in this decadence.

Definite specialized chances abroad for this offbeat pic, which unveils a disturbing new talent in director Nicos Panayotopoulos, who should be heard from again and who will give the Greek film another name outside the country besides Michael Cacoyannis. It is well played and technically good.
—*Mosk.*

Baara
(The Porter)
(MALI-COLOR)

Locarno, Aug. 22.

OCINAM release of Suleyman Cisse production. Features entire cast. Written and directed by Suleyman Cisse. Camera (Eastmancolor), Etienne Carton De Grammont, Abdoulaye Sidibe; editor, Andree Devanture; music, Lamin Konte. Reviewed at Locarno Film Fest (competing), Aug. 6, '78. Running time: 90 MINS.
Cast: Balla Moussa Keita, Bana Naire, Boubacar Keita, Oumou Diarra, Oumou Kone, Ismalia Sarr.

Up to now, Senegal has dominated the films from black African nations, especially the work of the gifted Ousmane Sembene using his ability to delve into African themes with assimilated film knowhow. Now Mali shows perking abilities in this dramatic tale of corruption and awakening social awareness.

A porter threads this tale together. Many young men leave their villages for the city and end up pulling little carts for deliveries of goods. Sans papers, they are usually picked up by the police. The one in the film sees families disrupted around him as a Muslim throws out one of his wives, is present at colorful market talk and petty fights and one day helps a young manager of a local textile factory deliver some things to his home.

The manager finds the porter is from his old part of the country. He decides to help him. His boss is a corrupt man attached to a younger wife who despises him and has a young lover and stands up to him despite the male-dominated society.

Director Suleyman Cisse blocks out his characters knowingly as well as the underlying social problems. He apparently has a good film background but does not ape, absorbing techniques to spin his tale of the terrible vengeance and fall of the boss. The boss has the young manager killed for taking too much interest in the workers and also kills his wife when he discovers the truth about her lover and she taunts him about his dishonesty.

A film that may still be too didatic in wrapping up its tale but still reveals a fine narrative sense, a feel for problems and human values. More suited for fests than for commercial chances abroad as yet, it still is another shaft of talent from Africa. —*Mosk.*

Bako, L'Autre Rive
(Bako, The Other Shore)
(SENEGALESE-FRENCH-COLOR)

Locarno, Aug. 22.

Release and production by Orpham Productions. Features entire cast. Directed by Jacques Champreux. Screenplay, Champreux, Cheik Doukoure; camera (Eastmancolor), Jacques Ledoux; editor, Andree Devanture. Reviewed at Locarno Film Fest (competing). Aug. 8, '78. Running time, 105 MINS.
Cast: Sidiki Bakaba, Doura Mane, Cheik Doukoure, Guilaume Korrea, Martin Trevieres.

Films about emigrant workers, wetbacks, Yugoslavs, Greeks, etc., have become familiar film fare. Here is still another about the tragic odyssey of an African from his native Mali across much of Africa, then Spain and finally Paris, where he was headed after much exploitation by whites and blacks alike.

French director Jacques Champreux has elicited good performances from his mostly black cast but has not been able to imbue this with a more probing and dramatic pitch to lift it out of the ordinary. It is a well meaning tale which should find some specialized, ethnographical and fest outlets without the more binding, revealing treatment to raise it above the many other pix of this kind.

The youth is sent from his poor, drought-ridden home to join his brother in Paris and send back money. He is given money by the others of the village and leaves his girl, promising to be back. But an uncle he stays with in Senegal throws him out after a few weeks. He is fleeced by some crooked French but helped by another man trying to find his way to France.

They band together and after many adventures find a man to get them across the mountains into France from Spain. But the friend dies, he gets ill from the mountain crossing and finally dies in Paris after trying to find his brother.
—*Mosk.*

Pokoj Z Widkiem Na Morze
(A Room With a View on the Sea)
(POLISH-COLOR)

Locarno, Aug. 22.

Polski Film release and production. Features entire cast. Directed by Janusz Zaor-

ski. Screenplay, Maciej Karpinski, Zaorski; camera (Eastmancolor), Edward Klossinski; music, Adam Stawinski. Reviewed at Locarno Film Fest (competing). Aug. 8, '78. Running time: 94MINS.
Cast: Marek Bargielowski, Piotr Franczewski, Gustav Holoubek.

Film is a crisply made yarn using that familiar literary and film device of a man on a ledge in a high building and the attempts to get him back in. Neatly played, it still does not add any depth to its characters or the generally good effect this would-be suicide's actions have on them.

The shots from the man's viewpoint are practically non-existent except out to the sea beyond him. The gaping passersby are there, an irate police inspector, and people whose work is disturbed by the man's actions as well as others who are mistakenly called in as parents or fiancee of the man on the ledge.

But main tale is about a retired psychology professor who is in conflict with a brilliant ex-student also trying to help. The old man is the only one who can get to the man on the ledge and finally talks him in after confessing a suicide attempt. It also thaws the too cocksure ex-student who at first tries to override the more humane approach of his old teacher.

Everything is predictable, but the pic does refrain from ever explaining the man's motives or the mistaken identity bit as it brings those who thought it was their son, fiancee or fellow worker to understand him and themselves better. Its close quarter work, thin characterizations and lack of transcending a familiar dramatic ploy make this more accessible for tv than theatrical offshore usage. — *Mosk.*

An Enemy Of The People
(COLOR)

Hollywood, Aug. 25.

Warner Bros. release of a First Artists (Solar) Production, produced and directed by George Schaefer; exec producer, Steve McQueen. Stars McQueen. Screenplay, Alexander Jacobs, based on adaptation of the Henrik Ibsen play by Arthur Miller; camera (Metrocolor), Paul Lohmann; editor, Sheldon Kahn; music, Leonard Rosenman; production design, Eugene Lourie; set decorator, Anthony Mondello; costumes, Noel Taylor; sound, Michael J. Kohut; assistant director, Jack Aldworth. Reviewed at The Burbank Studioes, Burbank, Aug. 25, '78. (MPAA Rating: G.) Running time: 103 MINS.

Dr. Thomas Stockmann ...Steve McQueen
Peter Stockmann ....Charles Durning
Catherine Stockmann .....Bibi Andersson
Morten Kiil ....Eric Christmas
Hovstad ....Michael Cristofer
Aslaksen ....Richard A. Dysart
Billing ....Michael Higgins
Captain Forster ....Richard Bradford
Morten Stockmann ....Ham Larsen
Ejlif Stockmann ....John Levin
Petra Stockmann ....Robin Pearson Rose

Transferring stage works to the screen has always been a procedure fraught with peril, and "An Enemy Of The People" fails to avoid the obvious pitfalls. With the unusual casting of Steve McQueen in the title role, the First Artists production faces a rocky commercial road. Warner Bros. has kept this film under wraps for more than a year-and-a-half until its World Film Festival preem last weekend in Montreal. The reasons are apparent.

The Henrik Ibsen drama, which was first performed in 1883, concerns a smalltown doctor who discovers that his village's new hot springs spa is contaminated by tannery waste. Over the objections of the town leaders (particularly his brother, the mayor), he attempts to publicize the scandal, only to be declared a social outcast, his family and career ruined.

McQueen wanted to do the Ibsen work itself, and that was his undoing. While "Enemy Of The People" has much relevance to current ecological dilemmas, Alexander Jacobs' script, based on an Arthur Miller adaptation, isn't content to simply raise the issues. They are proclaimed in ringing tones, intensifying the preachiness of a work that is already condescending to its audience.

Director George Schaefer does his best to eliminate the usual dull blocking of filmed plays, but he's hamstrung by the obvious miscasting of McQueen himself. The problem has nothing to do with the abandonment of a successful action adventure image, but rather the unsuitability of this particular actor to this particular role.

The imbalance wouldn't be so pronounced were Charles Durning not so magnificent in the role of the harshly realistic brother. Without an adequate presence to balance Durning's domination of the proceedings, "Enemy" founders in a sea of verbiage.

The other fatal miscasting comes with Michael Cristofer, as a supposedly radical newspaperman who quickly recants and joins those arrayed against McQueen. Cristofer projects a jarring '70s presence into a film that is otherwise true to its period, a further setback "Enemy" can ill afford.

Bibi Andersson is highly effective in the small part of Stockmann's wife, and of the other cast members, Eric Christmas as her miserly father, and Robin Pearson Rose as her liberated daughter, excel.

Eugene Lourie's production design is masterful, as is Anthony Mondello's set decoration. Paul Lohmann's photography, done with a sole 29m lens, is extraordinarily effective.

Schaefer has kept the film tightly paced, but it sags badly in the middle. As a "Hallmark Hall Of Fame" vidspec, a format Schaefer has almost pioneered, "Enemy" might be more effective. In feature form, however, it seems destined for art houses, college bookings and a generally academic audience, far, far from the paying crowds. —*Poll.*

The Uranium Conspiracy
(ISRAEL-COLOR)

Tel Aviv, Aug. 24.

A Noah Films release of a Golan-Globus-Dunamis production. Features Fabio Testi, Janet Agren and Assaf Dayan. Produced by Francesco Corti and Menahem Golan. Directed by Menahem Golan. Screenplay by David Paulsen based on story by Y. Ben Porath. Camera: Adam Greenberg. Editor: Dov Henig. Released Aug. 20, '78, Tel Aviv. Running time: 105 MINS.

With: Siegfried Rauch, Oded Kotler, Gianni Rizzo, Rolf Eden, Herbert Fux, Jay Koller.

Menahem Golan has acquired a reputation for transposing front page events to fiction films. His most successful venture in this direction has been "Operation Thunderbolt," the most ambitious Israeli production until now, which has been, on the whole, favorably received abroad.

When the story about a uranium-carrying ship which disappeared broke last year, Golan rushed to turn the factual mystery into screen adventure, in an international production to be shot entirely in Europe.

The problem is that facts, in this case, are pretty thin and none of the parties involved is willing to confirm or deny any information on the subject. Unfortunately, David Paulsen, relying on the documentary book by journalist Yeshayahu Ben Porath, has concocted a yarn that is not believable.

Trying to sell everything with a bang, he presents Israel's Mossad, usually considered one of the top secret services in the world, as a gang of irresponsible whiz kids, long on brawn and short on brains, killing indiscriminately first and deliberating later. If they succeed, it is only because police and intelligence in Western Europe is presented as totally incompetent.

Direction is mostly on the noisy side, with plenty of special effects and monotonous tough dialog. It is not always clear who chases whom, and where. Believability is diminished even more here when secret agents discuss secret matters among themselves, in English, as though it were the official language of superspies.

Fabio Testi, as the mercenary who turns volunteer for the cause, and swings the Uranium to Israel and Assaf Dayan, his Israeli sidekick, both credited above the title, have little character to sink their teeth into. Janet Agren disappears early in the story, a most unnecessary waste for the fledging star, who gets a credit much bigger than her role.

The distributor's attempt to cash in on a possible conflict with the censors turned sour after the film was released to all ages, with no restrictions, and the Censorship Board slapped the production with a suit for advertising a censorship fight which never existed.

Local commercial outlook seems to be below par, for Golan-Globus, who have enjoyed a healthy string of hits here lately. — *Edna.*

Un Second Souffle
(A Second Wind)
(FRENCH-COLOR)

Paris, Aug. 24.

Gaumont release of Cinepole, Film Produktion Janus, TF1 production. Stars Robert Stack; features, Anicee Alvina, Sophie Desmarets. Directed by Gerard Blain. Screenplay, Blain, Michel Perez; camera (Eastmancolor); Emmanuel Machuel; editor, Jean-Phillippe Berger; music, Jean-Pierre Stora. Reviewed at Salle Ponthieu, Paris, Aug. 18, '78. Running time, 101 MINS.

Francois ....Robert Stack
Catherine ....Anicee Alvina
Helene ....Sophie Desmarets
Sophie ....Marieke Carriere
Marc ....Frederic Meisner

Gerard Blain, one of the popular actors during the New Wave days, has since turned to direction. This is his fourth film, dealing with a man in his 50s, a successful dentist, who wants to stay young and leaves his wife and family for a mistress in her 20s. Robert Stack plays the man taking stock of himself. His French acceptable.

The main drawback of this carefully made pic is a dispirited quality in the characters. Film expands ideas rather than penetrating feeling into this potent theme.

As pic begins Stack has already left his home and is coming to grips with his mistress who also has a lover of her own age.

Stack tries to be youthful in accepting her lover. He even buys a motorcycle to keep up. It does have filmic ideas such as Stack's sudden race with a young cyclist in the street leading to a broken foot. It is the beginning of his break with his mistress but he is rejected by his wife who has found a new way of life.

Stack is left as the film found him, jogging. Sophie Desmarets, a fine comic actress, is handed a sticky assignment as the wife who makes little speeches. Anicee Alvina shows listless acceptance of her older and younger lovers.

Film pars things down to essentials but does not achieve the probing fusion of this theme into a dramatic focus. Film's deliberate slowness could slant this for tv. There are plus values on its theme and the Stack name. —*Mosk.*

Honning Maane
(Honeymoon)
(DANISH-COLOR)

Copenhagen, Aug. 29.

A Honning Maane production, Obel Film release. Original story, direction by Bille August; Camera (Eastmancolor) Dirk Bruel; production manager, Vibeke Windeloew; assistant director, Birthe Frost; productin designer, Erling Joergensen; costumes, Lissen Dirckinck-Holmfeld; music, Fuzzy; editor, Janus Billeskov Jansen. Reviewed at Grand, Copenhagen, Aug. 17, 1978. Running time: 99 MINS.

Jens ....Claus Strandberg
Kirsten ....Kirsten Olesen
Bjarne ....Jens Okking
The Mother ....Grethe Holmer
The Father ....Poul Bundgaard

Bille August is a cinematographer who steps out as a writer-director with a truly impressive love story, a tragedy rich in characters and events. The drama is underplayed but never reaches the point of having the audience lose interest.

Jens (Claus Strandberg) is a thoroughly nice, slightly naive young factory worker who marries a lively library assistant, daughter of a rather narrowminded, middle class family. The wedding and the honeymoon are followed by a short period of marital bliss. Then the bride drifts into a deep depression, attempts suicide and is hidden in her parents' house, while bewildered young Jens seeks solace in a friendship with an elderly fellow worker (Jens Okking in another strong but nuanced portrait) and later tries a little boozing and whoring but that is not really suitable to his character. He bids Kirsten a tactful goodbye that may help her back to normalcy while he himself opts for a new life in another country.

"Honeymoon" is a softspoken film with beautifully muted playing by everybody involved, and both Strandberg and Kirsten Olesen are among the most promising new talents on stage and screen in Denmark. — *Kell.*

Vas Y Maman
(Go On Mama)
(FRENCH-COLOR)
Paris, Aug. 24.

AML release of Renn Productions, Les Films Montfort, SFP, Les Films 21 production. Stars Annie Girardot; features, Pierre Mondy, Henri Garcin, Eleonore Klarwein, Richard Constantini. Directed by Nicole De Buron. Screenplay, De Buron, Pierre Sisser, Mathilde Pean; camera (Eastman-color), Etienne Becker; editor, Jacques Vitta; music Marie-Paule Belle. Reviewed at Colisee-Gaumont, Paris, Aug. 17, '78. Running time, 95 MINS.
Annie .... Annie Girardot
Jean-Pierre .... Pierre Mondy
Olivia .... Eleonore Klarwein
Julien .... Richard Constantini
Vincent .... Henri Garcin
Karin .... Nicole Calfan

A sitcom about feminist problems, played for laughs with the gags somewhat slight, often forced, this film has local draw Annie Girardot as a harassed mother of two teenagers, a self absorbed husband whose company makes sunglasses and recalcitrant kitchen machines.

All this is milked by director and scripter Nicole De Buron. She has penned some pix for successful comedies and this is her first directorial effort.

Girardot writes a sexy book which becomes a bestseller and almost breaks up her marriage. A happy ending however to this mainly local offering whose naive and strained comedics are more on the video level than theatrical possibilities. —*Mosk.*

Montreal Festival

Power Play
(COLOR-CANADIAN-BRITISH)

Military plot for sudden take-over of corrupt government, yields only death and worse tyranny. Plenty of gore for the action trade.

Montreal, Aug. 26.

Robert Cooper presentation of Canada United Kingdom production produced by Magnum International Inc. and Cowry Ltd. U.K. coproducer David Hemmings. Exec producers Robert Cooper and Ronald I. Cohen. Produced by Christopher Dalton. Associate producer John M. Eckert. Written and directed by Martyn Burke. Editor, John Victor-Smith. Stars Peter O'Toole, David Hemmings, Donald Pleasence. Photo-graphy by Ousama Rawi. Reviewed at World Film Festival, Montreal Aug. 25. Running time: 109 MINS.
Colonel Zeller .... Peter O'Toole
Colonel Narriman ...... David Hemmings
Blair .... Donald Pleasence
Jean Rousseau .... Barry Morse
Raymond Kasai .... Jon Granik
Mrs. Rousseau .... Marcella Saint-Amant
Barrientos .... George Touliatos
Hillsman .... Chuck Shamata
Aramco .... Gary Reineke
Anwar .... Harvey Atkin
Minh .... August Schellenberg
Dominique .... Eli Rill
Dick Cavett .... Dick Cavett

"Power Play," which emerges primarily as an action film with lots of violence, rides on the sardonic underlying thesis that "sincere" or "idealistic" reformers of corrupt governments may instead create a bloodbath leading to an even worse dictatorship.

The film was shot in 1977, partly in Toronto, partly in Germany, uses Canadian soldiers and military equipment (tanks rented at $163 an hour with driver; other rolling equipment at 57¢ a gallon). The government cooperation, Canadian style, also included the still availabile tax deferral advantages.

The appeal of "Power Play" is presumably to the action crowd. Distribution deals have been closed in various European markets and are being negotiated in the U.S. via ICM.

Intellectually, if that counts, the occasionally incoherent story line of the conspiracy will leave many minds puzzled. The screenplay shows signs of much re-editing and its character motivation clutter is of television flavor. The tube tie is stressed by the use of Dick Cavett as himself in beginning the recall of the failed plot.

Peter O'Toole photographed unevenly from scene to scene but despite the aging and health factors, he's still projecting some of his old-time charisma as the tank commander who joins only to double-cross the coup d'etat. He later slaughters his confreres by firing squad, notably the wholesome-looking colonel played by David Hemmings, who had instead expected to be the next president of the mythical country whose streets are partly German and whose government structures are of mixed location.

Donald Pleasance as the cold-blooded chef de torture of the old regime is also tied to a post and mowed down by a firing squad. From first to last there is a recurring obbligato of sudden death — at lawn parties, offices, road-blocks and airports. A girl conspirator, after agonizing electric shock, is ostensibly released to go home only to be shot in the back as she staggers away from the automobile.

These brutalities are the stock in trade of the film's commercial possibilities. "Power Play" is for the gore trade, not for the discriminating, although the moral of the screenplay written by director Burke after Edward N. Luttwak's novel could well inspire interest, even debate. Apparently certain South American dictatorships have already declined to license the film. No lessons in coup d'etat are wanted. — *Land.*

The Steppe
(COLOR-SOVIET RUSSIA)

Epic-like cinematic poetry from Bondartchouk. Ideal for festivals and colleges.

Montreal, Aug. 26.

Mosfilm production written and directed by Sergei Bondartchouk. Photography, Leonid Kalashnikov. Music, V. Ovtchinikov. Sound, Y. Michailov. Reviewed Aug. 25, 1978 at Montreal Film Festival. Running time: 113 MINS.
Players: Oleg Kuznetzov, Ivan Lapikov, Georgy Burkov, Stanislav Liubshin, Sergei Bondartchouk.

Sergei Bondartchouk, the Soviet director and actor who was at the previous Montreal Film Fest in 1967 with his three-part "War and Peace" is back again with "The Steppe." The 113 minute film is shown out of competition since Bondartchouk is also on the 1978 jury. It might well have rated a prize on its sheer narrative sweep of the Russian prairies which Chekhov described as "space yearning to become an object of human activity."

Commercially there must be doubts on the playoff of this slow, character and scenery starring vehicle. It has the feeling of both realism and heart in the remote peasant country before World War I. The players are mostly splendid, including Bondartchouk in a minor role as a choire singer who lost his voice from a chill swim in a Russian river years before.

The action involves the progress of a wagon train of wool and other produce to a distant market. There is also a carriage bearing a quaint Orthodox priest, a middle class trader and his nephew, an attractive boy of 10 being escorted to the town to be enrolled in a secondary school, in order that he may become a "gentleman." There's lots of class consciousness per the ancient regime, doffing of caps, and one future radical, a lackey at an inn who deliberately burned his inheritance in a stove, all of which spouts much against the evils of money and greed.

The tale is anecdotal, engrossing, simple, believable and tells the viewer much about the czaristic days. The boy encounters and later fantasizes about a beautiful countess, rather lovingly photographed, it might be supposed, partly because she is Madame Bondartchouk.

Such a splendid picture ought to be seen by more filmgoers of the west than will probably get a chance to do. — *Land.*

Avalanche
(COLOR)

Mother Nature seeks revenge again. Good outlook, if any disaster biz remains.

New World Pictures release, produced by Roger Corman. Directed by Corey Allen. Exec producer, Paul Rapp; screenplay, Claude Pola, Allen; camera (Metrocolor), Pierre-William Glenn; editors, Stuart Schoolnik, Larry Bock; sound, David Schneiderman; music, William Kraft; production design, Sharon Compton; art direction, Phillip Thomas; assistant director, Russell Vreeland; avalanche sequences (direction and editing), Lewis Teague; stunt coordination, Robert Bralver. Reviewed at Charles Aidikoff screen room, L.A., Aug. 29, '78 (MPAA Rating: PG.) Running time: **91 MINS.**

David Shelby	Rock Hudson
Caroline Brace	Mia Farrow
Nick Thorne	Robert Forster
Florence Shelby	Jeanette Nolan
Bruce Scott	Rick Moses
Henry McDade	Steve Franken
Mark Elliott	Barry Primus
Tina Elliott	Cathey Paine
Annette Rivers	Peggy Browne

Despite its undeviating devotion to the disaster-film formula, "Avalanche" combines all the familiar ingredients into a rolling, rushing thriller that will quickly capture its intended audience and finally come quietly to rest.

This time, Rock Hudson and Mia Farrow head the cast of characters gathered at a ski lodge beneath an uneasy cornice of snow. They warned Hudson not to build the lodge on this particular spot, but he went ahead with the same stubbornness that cost him the wife he still loves.

Farrow, that's the ex-wife, is on hand for the grand opening and quickly beds down with Robert Forster, the naturalist photographer who keeps complaining about the trees Hudson is cutting down. Hudson, in turn, is having a steam-room fling with his secretary.

Several other girls are romancing handsome heart-breaker Olympic ski champion Rick Moses, who gets out of bed long enough to have the first brush with danger as a small avalanche lets loose above him on the slopes. But he escapes by skiing into the top branches of a tree. And without a scratch.

Eventually, the whole mountain top comes down on the crowd of skaters, skiers and sledders. Using a lot of archive footage of an actual massive avalanche, director Corey Allen and crew have done a very good job of creating realistic scenes, especially with process photography and quick cutting that makes the heavy snow seem to crash over the actors. Unfortunately, much of the archive footage is badly scratched so some of the big boulders look like they're sliding down on wires.

Next, of course, comes the job of rescuing survivors and counting the dead, which includes the requisite number of villains and good folks, plus an assortment of faces that go by so fast you can't be sure who they are — or were.

Overall, the performances are fine. Hudson and Farrow are good enough to walk through their parts, while Forster gives his a little extra. As Hudson's feisty mother, Jeannette Nolan is a lot of fun, and has some good trapped-beneath-the-snow scenes with Steve Franken.

In the end, Hudson regrets he tampered with Mother Nature, whose forces are powerful. And Mia leaves the wreckage in a taxi, which apparently heard her whistle over the roar of the snow and the scream of the sirens. —*Har.*

A Wedding
(COLOR)

Robert Altman films a wedding with 48 forgettable characters. Even Altman fans will be disappointed.

A 20th Century-Fox release of a Lion's Gate Films Production, produced and directed by Robert Altman; executive producer, Tommy Thompson. Screenplay, John Considine, Patricia Resnick, Allan Nicholls, Altman from a story by Altman and Considine; camera (DeLuxe color), Charles Rosher,; editor, Tony Lombardo; sound, Jim Webb, Chris McLaughlin, Jim Bourgeois, Jim Stuebe; re-recording, Richard Portman; associate producers, Robert Eggenweiler, Scott Bushell; assistant director, Tommy Thompson; music supervisor, Tom Walls. Reviewed at the Director's Guild of America Theatre, Hollywood, Aug. 29, '78. (MPAA rating: PG.) Running time: **125 MINS.**

Tulip Brenner	Carol Burnett
Snooks Brenner	Paul Dooley
Muffin Brenner	Amy Stryker
Buzzy Brenner	Mia Farrow
Hughie Brenner	Dennis Christopher
Rev. David Ruteledge	Gerald Busby
Candice Ruteledge	Peggy Ann Garner
Nettie Sloan	Lillian Gish
Regina Corelli	Nina Van Pallandt
Luigi Corelli	Vittorio Gassman
Dino Corelli	Desi Arnaz, Jr.
Antoinette Goddard	Dina Merrill
Mackenzie Goodard	Pat McCormick
Dr. Jules Meecham	Howard Duff
Bishop Martin	John Cromwell
Rita Billingsley	Geraldine Chaplin
Jeff Kuykendall	John Considine
Florence Farmer	Lauren Hutton
Ingrid Hellstrom	Viveca Lindfors
Jim Habor	Robert Fortier
William Williamson	Bert Remsen
Gypsy Violinist	Ellie Albers

If "Nashville" is ensemble Altman at its best — and it is — then "A Wedding" is the other extreme. Altman's loose, seemingly unstructured style backfires in this comedy-drama. Even the innovative director-producer's legion of fans will be disappointed. Those already not a member of his cult will find this work tedious.

The title is self-descriptive; the picture is a day in the life of a wedding between the daughter of a nouveau rich southern family and the son of old midwestern money.

The setting is rife with conventions — marriage, religion, wealth. Altman along with John Considine, Patricia Resnick and Allan Nicholls who share script credit, prop up straw men targets as the butt of their satire and quickly knock them down.

Four dozen characters are part of the plot. Most are forgettable. Even Altman must have agreed that the plot was overpopulated because a number of the characters have been virtually edited out.

Unlike "Nashville," the film lacks a core. Nothing builds; the characters, except for Lillian Gish as the old money matriarch and Mia Farrow as the silent sister of the bride, are uninteresting and unsympathetic. They pop in and out of the film and when they pop out, who cares if they return?

Altman's idea of humor comes off as puerile and dated. John Cromwell plays a senile bishop who performs the wedding ceremony. He forgets how to conduct the service and is too near sighted to know that at one point he's talking to a corpse. That's hardly sharp edged satire.

The general level of the acting, including performances by Carol Burnett, Paul Dooley, Amy Stryker, Vittorio Gassman, Desi Arnaz, Jr., Howard Duff, Geraldine Chaplin, John Considine, Lauren Hutton and Bert Remsen, is acceptable, as are the technical credits.

But in the end, the idea was at best mediocre. —*Hege.*

Stevie
(BRITISH-COLOR)

An intelligent biopic of the life of British writer Stevie Smith. Too much talk, not enough drama. Slim outlook.

A First Artists release of a Bowden Production, produced and directed by Robert Enders. Stars Glenda Jackson. Screenplay, Hugh Whitemore, based on his play and the works of Stevie Smith; camera (Technicolor), Freddie Young; music, Patrick Young; editor, Peter Tanner; art director, Bob Jones; assistant director, Ken Baker; sound, Claude Hitchcock. Reviewed at the Aidikoff Screening Room, Beverly Hills, Aug. 30, '78. (No MPAA rating). Running time: **102 MINS.**

Stevie Smith	Glenda Jackson
Aunt	Mona Washbourne
Freddy	Alec McCowen
The Man	Trevor Howard

"Stevie" is a well-acted and literate, but also talky and claustrophobic screen biography of British poet and novelist Stevie Smith. Glenda Jackson stars in the title role and her performance — in fact, the entire style of the film — seems better suited to the stage than the big screen. The film has a theatrical look which shouldn't draw well in this country, especially since Smith is not generally known or appreciated in the U.S.

Robert Enders, who directed and produced from Hugh Whitemore's screenplay, has adopted a visual style better suited to a telefilm than a theatrical feature. Most of the picture's 102 minutes takes place inside a suburban residence Smith shared with her aunt, portrayed by Mona Washbourne in a charming and sympathetic performance.

By limiting the action to that one setting the film becomes stifling. Too much of Smith's life is described by Jackson in reminiscences to her aunt, confessions into the camera, or recitations of her poetry, rather than re-enacted.

Only other characters are Alec McCowen as a boyfriend of Jackson and Trevor Howard as companion who also comments on the poet's life and work.

Technical credits, including Freddie Young's photography and Patrick Young's editing, are above average. This feature would make a big splash on television, but holds little appeal for the theatrical market. —*Hege.*

Born Again
(COLOR)

Version of recent history is a turnoff in the screen version of Charles Colson's Watergate undoing and later religious commitment. Slim outlook.

An Avco Embassy release of a Robert L. Munger Production, produced by Frank Capra, Jr.; executive producer, Robert L. Munger. Directed by Irving Rapper. Screenplay, Walter Bloch; camera (Technicolor), Harry Stradling, Jr.; editor, Axel Hubert; music, Lex Baxter; associate producer, Paul Temple; production designer, William J. Kenney; set designer, Mark Poll; sound, Berg Hallberg; set decorator, Rick Gentz; assistant director, Bob Bender. Reviewed at CFI, Hollywood, Sept. 1, '78. (MPAA rating: PG.) Running time: **110 MINS.**

Charles Colson	Dean Jones
Patti Colson	Anne Francis
David Shapiro	Jay Robinson
Tom Phillips	Dana Andrews
Jimmy Newsome	Raymond St. Jacques
Judge Gerhard Gesell	George Brent
Sen. Hughes	Sen. Harold Hughes
Richard M. Nixon	Harry Spillman
Chris Colson	Christopher Conrad
Wendell Colson	Stuart Lee
Emily Colson	Alicia Fleer
E. Howard Hunt	William Zuckert

"Born Again" is an earnest if awkward screen version of former White House advisor Charles Colson's Watergate undoing and later commitment to Christianity. Dean Jones, himself a born again Christian, turns in a credible performance as Colson, whenever the action revolves around religious commitment rather than politics. It's the reworking of the all too recent history which makes the outlook for Avco Embassy's pickup of the Robert L. Munger production at best iffy.

Audiences are too familiar with the Watergate affair and Colson's part in it to sit still for the kind of historical sweetening found in Walter Bloch's script. It begins with Colson entering prison and flashes back to his recruitment to the Nixon White house, his role as a hatchet man in the first administration, later return to private law practice and indictment and sentencing over the Daniel Ellsberg affair. All true, but all painted in a light to make Colson as a constant victim rather than active participant.

Those historical remembrances take up almost half of the film's 110-minute running time and waiver somewhere between irritating and silly. Harry Spillman does a fair Nixon imitation, but there's something unintentionally funny about any reenactment when it includes Nixon. Compound that with H.R. Haldeman, John Ehrlichman and Henry Kissinger lookalikes seated around the same room and it becomes absurd.

Far more interesting is the story of Colson's turning to Jesus Christ during his darkest hours when the press and the grand jury were putting great pressure on him and his family. Colson's friend and business associate, Raytheon president Tom Phillips, portrayed by Dana Andrews, is credited as the greatest single influence in the conversion. His former enemy, Sen. Harold Hughes, embraces him as a brother in Christianity in a moving scene.

In prison Colson must overcome his name and publicity. He does more than that, beginning a Bible class and helping other inmates find belief and the strength to endure their imprisonment. Raymond St. Jacques, as the prison leader among the other inmates, turns in the film's best performance.

Colson's family, played by Anne Francis as his wife and Christopher Conrad, Stuart Lee and Alicia Fleer as his children, are other sources of strength. All are acceptable.

A number of the characterizations, however, especially William Zuckert as the off-handedly conspiratorial E. Howard Hunt and Jay Robinson as Colson's liberal, loyal and wise-cracking law partner, are obnoxiously cardboard and stereotypical.

Irving Rapper directed and like the other technical credits, his work is functional —*Hege.*

Montreal Festival

Double Suicide Of Sonezaki
(COLOR-JAPANESE)

Powerhouse Japanese (1703) period drama climaxing with lovers in joint bloody ritual taking of own lives. Strong word-of-mouth.

Montreal, Aug. 31.
Kodosha-Kimura-ATG Co-production. Produced by Hiroaki Fiujii, Motoyasu, Takahei Nishimura. Directed by Yasuzo Masumura. Script, Yoshio Shirasaka and Masumura, based on original story by Monzaemon Chikamatsu. Camera (color), Setsuo Kobayashi; sound, Rokubin Ota, Mitsutake Miyashita; art direction, Shigeo Mano, editor, Tatsuji Nakano, costumes, Toshiaki Makl; music, Ryudo Uzaki, played by Down Town Boogie Woogie Band. Reviewed at Parisien Theatre, Montreal Film Festival, Aug. 31, 1978. Running time: 112 MINS.
Ohatsu . . . . Meiko Kaji
Tokubei . . . . Ryudo Uzaki
Kyuemon . . . . Hiashi Igawa
Osai . . . . Sachiko Hidari
Kuheiji . . . . Isao Hashimoto
Kichibei . . . . Gen Kimura
(French subtitles)

The Japanese tradition of killing one's self to dramatize or repudiate dishonor, and/or hopelessly abused dignity, flairs anew and vividly, and many will no doubt feel shockingly, in this film based on a classic incident of 1703. What emerges on screen is a strong story of injustice told in the Japanese style of pictorial closeups, hypertensive speech and artistic scene composition. The big social and commercial question, and boxoffice value, comes at the end when the exploited and humiliated lovers, he a clerk, she a prostitute, fulfill their pact to seek paradise together.

Suicide as a bloody ritualistic protest is graphic and truesome, the positioned corpses striking an ultimate "picture" saturated in caked blood. Of this climax it may be said that there may be a morbid appeal, apart from the possible aversion. Something more may be remarked: most filmgoers cannot possibly have heretofore viewed such a scene. The audience at the Montreal Film Festival, a mixture of the French Canadian public, film buffs, festival visitors and the local Japanese colony, applauded at the religioso-philosophic overtone which closes out the double suicide.

The delicately beautiful Meiko Kaji and the man played by Ryudo Uzaki (who interestingly also provided the haunting special music) convincingly symbolize the hapless victims of a transitional period as the mercantile class takes over from the old samurai warriors (or hired killers, if one prefers) and the

resultant concepts of obligation, gratitude and fair play.

The merchant who takes his clerk's money, renders a false I.O.U. which he later disavows vents his fury on the clerk who takes a terrifying beating from the merchant and his three bodyguards. The audience has to welcome the later scene in a brothel when the girl's uncle, belatedly aware of the cheating heart of the merchant, inflicts a beating in kind upon this villain.

The plot detailing, the sense of long ago, the fine photography of Setsuo Kobayashi against the art design of Shigeo Mano and the lighting of Matsukiko Sato all qualify as first class professionalism.

The story is direct and substantially lucid, if some questions might go unanswered for western minds. It's a bit amusing to notice a screen credit for the orchestra namely, the Down Town Boogey Woogie Band.

Plainly the auspices must take great care with the English subtitles. For Montreal the print carried French titles which often seemed "hurried." On the whole the production is capable of international playoff. The Kabuki-like acting is, of course, a bit strident by present day western standards. The story is heavy with "action" (or translate violence) which will probably be more asset than otherwise. —*Land.*

Obratinaya Sviaz
(Feedback)
(SOVIET UNION)

Montreal, Sept. 1.
Lenfilm production directed by Victor Tregoubovitch. Screenplay, Aleksandr Gelman. Camera (color), Eduard Rozovsky; sound, N. Levitina; music, A. Rybnikov. Reviewed at Montreal Film Festival, Sept. 1, 1978. Running Time: 93 MINS.
Cast: Oleg Yankovsky, Mikhail Oulianov, Kirill Lavrov, Liudmila Gourtchenko, Natalya Gundareva, Igor Vladimirov.

This is a "message" film, a clever, convincing expose of careerism as the rock on which was expensively delayed a gigantic new production complex in the Soviet Union. The film's potential audience in the U.S. might well include, say, the Harvard Business School and all imitations thereof. While the complications in the tale are socialistic echelons, layer on layer of yes men, there are parallels to be recognized in capitalistic societies, too.

It strikes an outsider as somewhat remarkable that such a film was conceived and approved in the Soviet but as sheer filmmaking, if perhaps in need of some "light touches," and not western "entertainment" by definition, "Feedback" is engrossingly laden with insights. It might, of course, be argued, as an irony, that in the end everybody was wrong, and duly re-

primanded, but Moscow bureaucrats were, though taken by unpleasant surprise, themselves free of fault or responsibility.

No need to dwell on the acting save to say it's completely believable. A fine script, good photography, able, straightforward socialist realism direction. The one tidbit of humor had one bored bureaucrat, seated at a table of sombre colleagues, roll his agenda into a telescope and stare at a woman member of the party. —*Land.*

La Petite Fille En Velours Bleu
(The Little Girl in Blue Velvet)
(FRENCH-COLOR)

Paris, Sept. 1.
WB-Col release of Orphee Arts, Columbia Pictures production. Stars Michel Piccoli, Claudia Cardinale; features Lara Wendel, Marius Goring, Denholm Elliot, Alexandra Stewart. Directed by Alan Bridges. Screenplay, Christian Watton, Bridges; camera (Eastmancolor), Usama Rawi; music, Georges Delerue. Reviewed at UGC-Biarritz, Paris, Aug. 25, '78. Running time, 110 MINS.
Konrad . . . . Michel Piccoli
Countess . . . . Claudia Cardinale
Laura . . . . Lara Wendel
Man . . . . Denholm Elliot
Count . . . . Marius Goring
Rosario . . . . Alexandra Stewart

This film tries to capture the dangerous living of uprooted Europeans gathered on the French Riviera during the early part of the last war. It is a "dancing on a volcano" routine as sex and politics swirl around these refugees from Nazism and Fascism.

Embedded in all this rather stagey atmosphere is a fiftyish surgeon's platonic love affair with a girl of 13. She is no Lolita type but a rather severe, scrubbed girl who realizes the love before the man will admit it to himself. She even offers herself but he is able to pack her off.

Michel Piccoli is the man who fights this love and manages to remain incisive in a fairly ill-defined role. Director Alan Bridges cannot get the true reflection of the times or his mixed crew of characters to make this more than a rather routine drama.

Piccoli is an Austrian surgeon who has fled the Nazis and the girl the daughter of a Countess, played with over-intense mannerisms by Claudia Cardinale, who has fled Italo Fascism with a pianist-lover. The lover is wounded on their escape but Piccoli saves him at the hospital and takes all three to a villa given him by a domineering, hypocritical rich man whose life he once saved. Latter is played in true martinet style by Marius Goring.

There is the familiar character of a liberal who sells himself and others, played with petulance by Denholm Elliot. There are also decent and mean police who help or herd the refugees into camps, acting a bit like the Germans.

Locally acceptable, but without the dramatic insight for much chances abroad except for some specialized possibilities. Film has an English version but only the French one is being shown here.
—*Mosk.*

L'Argent Des Autres
(Other Peoples' Money)
(FRENCH-COLOR)

Paris, Sept. 1.

Planfilm release of Fildebroc, FR3, SFP, Films De La Tour production. Stars Jean-Louis Trintignant, Claude Brasseur, Michel Serrault, Catherine Deneuve; features Umberto Orsini, Francois Perrot, Juliet Berto. Directed by Christian De Chalonge. Screenplay, De Chalonge, Pierre Dumayet from a book by Nancy Markham; camera (Eastmancolor), Jean-Louis Picavet; editor, Jean Ravel; music, Patrice Mestral. Reviewed at Club 13, Paris, Aug. 22, '78. Running time: 105 MINS.
Rainier .... Jean-Louis Trintignant
Chevalier .... Claude Brasseur
Miremant .... Michel Serrault
Cecile .... Catherine Deneuve
Vincent .... Francois Perrot
Arlette .... Juliet Berto
Blue .... Umberto Orsini

This is a heavyhanded attempt to deal with banking corruption. It tries too hard for symbolism and moody treatment to give it enough human scale. Home chances appear good though offshore possibilities depend on careful handling.

Jean-Louis Trintignant is a bank exec who is fired when one of his clients is accused of fraud. But he fights back since he feels all the money loaned to the man with way out schemes was actually given by the director of his venerable bank.

Trintignant, looking lean and a bit sinister, is miscast as a man who cries when he burns his credit cards that served for business luncheons. Catherine Deneuve is his faithful spouse but does not have much to do. In fact, none of the characters have much depth. This scandal was based on a real event.

Director Christian De Chalonge has scenes in a high powered employment center which spies on its clients rather than placing them in jobs. Trintignant gets himself exonerated but the bank, despite its obvious connivance in a swindle, gets off free.

Operatic music, lush lensing of polished interiors and overblown acting cannot quite get this into a proper focus. —*Mosk.*

Chuen Chulamoon
(Happy Confusion)
(THAI-COLOR)

Bangkok, Aug. 31.

A New Five Star Productions release. Produced by Kiat Iampungporn. Directed and edited by Piac Poster. Story, Boonyarat; screenplay Vitsanusit; camera, Chone Bunnag; sound, Maitree Janjarasskul; music, Chairat Tiaptiam. Reviewed at Athens theatre, Bangkok, Aug. 29, '78. Running time: 110 MINS.
Tam .... Pairoj Sangborivutr
Oj .... Lalana Sulawan
Somjai .... Chandra Napaporn
Metr .... Somkuan Krajamsart
Jamsri .... Somkid Sapsamluay
Ad ...... Jirasak Issarangkul Na Ayudhya
Seah Pracha .... Prasert Srisomsak

Gone is the spontaneity from the once enjoyable "Wai Olawon" (Only Sixteen) series. The first picture in the series was the best, both part two and part three being a letdown. "Chuen Chulamoon," which director Piac Poster says will be the last and final chapter of "Wai Olawon," is nevertheless another hit.

What was once an entertaining idea for a film — the courtship and early married life of a young Thai couple whose lifestyle constantly see-saws between local and western cultural values, now gets bogged down in "a serious theme."

The storyline is not focused on the life of the young couple. Instead it deals with the issue of whether or not their maid deserves to receive compensation to the tune of 200,000 baht (about $10,000) for being bitten in the face by the dog of a wealthy old man in the neighborhood.

As the maid's lawyer, Pairoj masterminds what ultimately proves a victorious lawsuit, not forgetting to resort to such tricks as manufacturing evidence and telling white lies to win the case.

The maid does win about $7,500 in damages. When last seen, she's on her way to a plastic surgeon.

Such a minor-sounding lawsuit provides a "heavy subject matter" for local films. Piac said that the only way to get it past the censors was to do a comic treatment that nobody would find the least bit controversial.

This theme, however, is completely alien to the story of Tam and Oj, the young lovers of the series. It's the maid's story instead.

Despite this, the film is predicted to gross at least in its Bangkok run alone. —*Cano.*

Je Suis Timide; Mais Je Me Soigne
(I'm Timid But I'm Treating It)
(FRENCH-COLOR)

Paris, Sept. 1.

CCFC, EFC release of Albina Productions production. Stars Pierre Richard, Aldo Maccione; features, Mimi Coutelier, Robert Castel, Catherine Lachens, Jacques Francois. Directed by Pierre Richard. Screenplay, Richard, Alain Godard, Jean-Jacques Annaud; camera (Eastmancolor), Claude Agostini; editor, Pierre Gillette. Reviewed at Normandie-UGC, Paris, Aug. 24, '78. Running time: 90 MINS.
Pierre .... Pierre Richard
Aldo .... Aldo Maccione
Agnes .... Mimi Coutelier
Player .... Robert Castel
Trucker .... Catherine Lachens
Manager .... Jacques Francois

Pierre Richard is a local comic who usually essays absentmindedness or timidity as the basis for his routines and bits of business around a very loose narrative. Here he adds a chase aspect to fill out this sketchy item. It does have some laughs and is a rare local comedy that works hard to develop its few yocks, with most springing from character and situation.

It appears aimed for good returns at home though somewhat slight and one-note for abroad. But its easygoing aspects could snag this some interest with right handling, and peg Richard a man to watch. In the film, Richard is a timid soul who falls for what appears to be a rich heiress or model in the hotel he works at.

He takes a crash course from a con-man psychologist to cure his timidity and starts chasing the girl around France, but always balking though the psychologist is along to push him. There are several variations on the timidity but an uneven rhythm mars the overall comic structure.

Aldo Maccione is properly brash and yet likeable as the sidekick with Mimi Coutelier properly bland as the quarry, who turns out to be a shop girl who won a prize in a contest, allowing her to live like a rich girl. Richard's direction is workmanlike and production values good. — *Mosk.*

Saen Saeb
(Saen Saeb Canal)
(THAI-COLOR)

Bangkok, Aug. 30.

A Saha Mongkol Films release produced by Nitra Kasiwat. Directed and edited by Pairat Kasiwat. Story, Pai Muangderm; screenplay and production design, Tosapon Nakphorn; camera, Sophon Melintasai; sound and color processing, Tokyo Laboratories; music, Seksan Sominsart; costumes and makeup, Niran Sangkaroj; production manager, Karom Sangborivutr. Reviewed at President Theatre, Aug. 29, '78. Running time: 120 MINS.
Pleng .... Pairoj Sangborivutr
Choy .... Yuwathida Phonprasert
Ploy .... Nirachara Rachakul

Made in 70m and processed at Tokyo Laboratories, this has the minimum requirement of a Cinemascope screen. No matter how good a film is, if it's done in 35m, theatre owners shy away from it.

Key plot twist in "Saen Saeb" is a triangle in which two women are in love with the same man.

"Saen Saeb" has two climactic episodes. The first concerns the hero and the water buffalo he buys at an auction, at a time (early 20th Century) when one can purchase a buffalo for only $3. The animal becomes Pairoj's pet. Their reunion after being forcibly separated is overdramatized.

The other climax comes with one of the women's decision to become a Buddhist nun, entailing shaving her head. Going bald has become a bestselling gimmick, easily boosting a picture's b.o. potential.
—*Cano.*

Days Of Heaven
(COLOR)

Terrence Malick's second directorial effort is excellent. Slow buildup could yield okay results.

Hollywood, Aug. 7.

A Paramount Pictures release of an O.P. Production, produced by Bert and Harold Schneider; executive producer, Jacob Brackman. Written and directed by Terrence Malick. Features entire cast. Camera (Metrocolor), Nestor Almendros; additional photography, Haskell Wexler; art director, Jack Fisk; editor, Billy Weber; music, Ennio Morricone; costumes, Patricia Norris; additional music, Leo Kottke; sound mixers, George Ronconi, Barry Thomas; Dolby consultants, Steve Katz, Philip Boole, Clyde McKinney; special sound effects, James Cox; special effects, John Thomas, Mel Merrells; second unit director, Jacob Brackman; second unit photography, Paul Ryan; set dcorator, Robert Gould; assistant director, Skip Cosper. Reviewed at the MGM Main Theatre, Culver City, Aug. 5, '78. (MPAA rating: PG.) Running time: **95 MINS.**

Bill	Richard Gere
Abby	Brooke Adams
The farmer	Sam Shepard
Linda	Linda Manz
Farm foreman	Robert Wilke
Linda's friend	Jackie Shultis
Mill foreman	Stuart Margolin
Harvest hand	Tim Scott
dancer	Gene Bell
Fiddler	Doug Kershaw

"Days Of Heaven" is a dramatically moving and technically breathtaking American art film, one of the great cinematic achievements of the last decade. Told through the eyes and words of an innocent but wise teenage migrant worker, it traces a trio of nomads as their lives intersect with a wealthy wheat farmer. Even though the dialog is English and the dialect distinctly American, this is still an art film. And so, while it is a stunning work, it is also a demanding one. Even with careful and slow buildup. Paramount can expect no more than modest success from the Bert and Harold Schneider production. That's simply the reality of the marketplace.

The story, style and theme is reminiscent of Malick's earlier "Badlands." As with the previous film, where Sissy Spacek read from a diary which sounded like prose from a teenage romance magazine, there is a narrator — Linda Manz speaking in a heavy Chicago accent both narrating the action and commenting on it.

Malick's screenplay is more than a shooting script — it's literature. His ear and his ability to readjust to the mind of a naive, poverty stricken young girl at the turn of the century is uncanny. In context, many of the phrases and word choices spoken by Manz approach poetry.

The story opens in Chicago with Richard Gere shoveling coal in a steel mill. After an altercation with a foreman he's fired. He, his sister (Manz) and girlfriend (Brooke Adams), hit the road to find work in the fields, traveling as brother and sisters.

They find employment on a farm owned by a young, wealthy Sam Shepard, the playwright who makes his acting debut. Like the other performances Shepard's is quiet — this isn't from the tour de force school — but it is a marvel nonetheless. Without a single lapse, the entire cast assembled by Malick, the Schneiders and executive producer Jacob Brackman is equally inspired.

The trio become entangled with Shepard when he falls in love with Adams and marries her. Suddenly the threesome — once so poor they travelled in freight cars like cattle — are rich. And it seems that the days of heaven have arrived. But with wealth, they learn, also comes idleness. And with idleness boredom. The days of heaven are gone almost as quickly as they arrived. Locusts invade the land, destroy the crops. Following a violent crime the **three again are on the road, except that this time their road is a river, not a railroad track, and the vehicle a raft, rather than a train car.**

Told in 95 minutes, it is an efficient, meaningful story filled with some offbeat touches, literary references and beautifully developed characters. If audiences can only be persuaded to take the time they'll find an accessible story about innocence, greed and dreams.

Equal to the drama are the technical credits. Nestor Almendros' cinematography is at times so startling you wish the projectionist would roll the film back a few feet so the footage could be enjoyed again. Haskell Wexler is credited with "additional photography." It's difficult to say what scenes he shot, although it was probably a nighttime fire towards the middle of the film, a fire set by Shepard and his workers to eliminate an invasion of locusts. (He took over when Almendros had to depart for a previously-committed Francois Truffant film —Ed.)

Patricia Norris period costumes, Ennio Morricone's outstanding score and Jack Fisk's art direction should also be singled out for praise.

Worthy of special note is the film's sound. It is apparent from the details included in the Dolby encoded soundtrack, that not just the words and look of this picture were planned long ago, but the sound as well. Sounds such as the biting of an apple, crickets and the din of a city factory have been heard before on films, but never with the sense of reality found on this soundtrack.
—Hege.

The Class of Miss Mac-Michael
(BRITISH-U.S.-COLOR)

Paris, Sept. 6.

George Barrie-Brut Pictures release of a Kettledrum-Brut production. Stars Glenda Jackson, Oliver Reed, Michael Murphy, Rosalind Cash; features, John Standing. Directed by Silvio Narizzano. Screenplay, Judd Bernard from the book by Sandy Hutson; camera (Technicolor), Alex Thomason; editor, Max Benedict; music, Stanley Myers; producer, Bernard; executive producer, George Barrie. Reviewed at Brut Screening Room, Paris, Aug. 31, '78. Running time: **100 MINS.**

Miss MacMichael	Glenda Jackson
Sutton	Oliver Reed
Martin	Michael Murphy
Una	Rosalind Cash
Fairbrother	John Standing
Gaylord	Riba Akabusi
Stewart	Phil Daniels
Boysie	Patrick Murray
Marie	Silvia O'Donnel

This pic is about dippy doings at a special school for unruly teenagers whose next steps may be reformatories. Treading the usual characterizations and situations, film adds a more permissive tone in language and freewheeling sex of the students not to forget the harassed teachers and a scheming head master.

Though predictable, and the script serviceable for this oft-treated theme, with direction average, it has Glenda Jackson adding her presence to the part of a dedicated teacher who eschews a second marriage to stay with her impossible charges.

It appears to have a possible hook for youth audiences where the money is these days. Brut Productions, the Yank indie, made this as a British entry.

Jackson's dedicated but world weary air gives an edge to her character as she is the rare teacher who gets through to her charges. Michael Murphy's nice guy playing, but with hints of stodginess, make his boyfriend of Jackson role acceptable.

Oliver Reed overcharges his role of the martinet, hypocritical, mean principal who uses a false front to visitors and a mailed fist at the school. But the general antics of this pic could give Brut a good general market entry internationally.
— Mosk.

Paradise Alley
(COLOR)

Promising slum film of wrestling

Hollywood, Sept. 10.

A Universal Pictures release of a Force Ten Production, produced by John F. Roach and Ronald A. Suppa; executive producer, Edward Pressman. Stars Sylvester Stallone. Written and directed by Stallone. Camera (Technicolor), Laszlo Kovacs; production designer, John W. Corso; Editor, Eve Newman; Music, Bill Conti; Art Director, Deborah Beaudet; Set Decoration, Jerry Adams; Costumers, Sandra Berke, Lambert Marks; Sound, Charles Wilborn; Wrestling Choreography, Terry Funk; associate producer, Arthur Chobanian; assistant director, Cliff Coleman; unit production manager, Michael S. Glick. Reviewed at the Hollywood Pacific I Theatre, Hollywood, Sept. 8, 1978. (MPAA Rating: PG.) Running time: **107 MINS.**

Cosmo Carboni	Sylvester Stallone
Stich	Kevin Conway
Annie	Anne Archer
Burp	Joe Spinell
Lenny	Armand Assante
Victor	Lee Canalito
Susan Chow	Aimee Eccles
Frankie The Thumper	Terry Funk
Bunchie	Joyce Ingalls
Big Glory	Frank McRae
Mumbles	Tom Waits

"Paradise Alley" is "Rocky" rewritten by Damon Runyon. Set in New York's Hell's Kitchen area during the 1940's, it tells the uplifting tale of three brothers, played by Sylvester Stallone, Armand Assante, and Lee Canalito, and how they literally wrestle their way out of the ghetto.

it's an upbeat, funny, nostalgic film populated by colorful characters, memorable more for their individual moments than for their parts in the larger story. The Universal release of Stallone's very impressive directorial debut, which he also scripted, looks like a brawny boxoffice contender.

Stallone proves a number of points with this film. First that he's a very capable director with a keen eye for casting. Following "Rocky," Stallone promised to give new actors a show and "Paradise Alley" introduces some big screen novices such as Assante, Canalito and Joyce Ingalls, all of whom are fine under Stallone's confident direction.

While Stallone must venture outside street drama to truly prove his range as an actor, this picture shows a new dimension. He has a charming comic presence.

"Paradise Alley" shows off, once again, Stallone's ability as a writer. His sense of plot is old-fashioned — maybe it asks too much of a suspension of disbelief — but it's also very commercial. The basic element is a hopeful loser who wants desperately to be a winner and triumphs. That may be an old-fashioned idea, but it's one to which audiences continue to respond.

The plot of this film is almost a throwaway. Three brothers, a dumb, beefy ice man (Canalito), a bitter crippled war veteran (Assante) and Stallone, the conman, all want to escape the slums. Stallone decides that Canalito's muscles in a wrestling ring is their ticket uptown.

The brothers' nemesis is a small time hood, Kevin Conway, who manages Frankly the Thumper, a wrestler Canalito eventually takes on in the picture's finale. He's big money, the last match.

Each of the brothers has a girl friend, of course, Aimee Eccles is Canalito's. She's trying to teach him that he has a mind in addition to a set of muscles. Anne Archer is a dime a dance floozie. She's the girl Stallone wants but his brother, Assante, has. Stallone meanwhile hangs around with a heart of gold whore, Joyce Ingalls.

The relationship between the men and their women is never explored and is the one unsatisfying element in the film. The women have no life beyond their men; they are types who exist only as companions.

That is not to say that Stallone can't create character. He can. The three brothers are fully drawn and often complex personalities, each of whom grows and changes.

And there are some marvelous minor characters. Frank McRae is fabulous as Big Glory, an over-the-hill wrestler who lives in a rat-infested cellar below Paradise Alley, the club where he fights. Terry Funk is Franky The Thumper, a mean and vicious wrestler. — *Hege*.

La Portentosa Vida Del Padre Vincent
(The Prodigious Life of Father Vincent)
(SPANISH-COLOR)

———

Madrid, Sept. 2.
Ascle Films production. Written and directed by Carles Mira. Features entire cast. Camera (Eastmancolor), Teo Escamilla; sets, Alejandro Soler; editor, Pablo G. del Amo. Exec producer, Antonio Alguero Garceran. Reviewed at Cine Luchana, Madrid, Sept. 1, '78. Running time: **82 MINS.**
Father Vincent .... Albert Boadella
Milon .... Ovidi Montllor
Maria .... Angela Molina
Also: Quico Carbonell, Rafa Miro, Cuca Avino, Fernando Mira, Toni Mira, Carmen Platero, Maria Rey and Paula Molina.

———

This spoof of the life and tribulations of the 15th century Valencia Saint Vincent Ferrer has already raised storms of protest from ecclesiastical quarters in that province. This was to be expected, because director Carlos Mira, a newcomer on the Spanish scene, and actor Albert Boadella have clearly set out to ridicule the very concept of sainthood and the trappings that go with it.

Boadella, whose first film this is, gives a topnotch performance as the tormented priest trying to resist the temptations of the flesh and soul. Though he plays it straight, his face is so whimsical that it reminds one of Danny Kaye. The thread of irreverent humor, some of it "black," threads through the film, and crops out sometimes unexpectedly after serious spells in which Father Vincent preaches fire and brimstone sermons and rails against the dissipated lives of his fellows.

The humor, however, is spread a bit thin and the pacing sometimes becomes ponderous. The story, what there is of it, has Vincent traveling about the villages during the time of the Catholic Monarchs, nonchalantly performing miracles and resisting temptations. The latter include a gargantuan meal in a monastery, and a pretty girl (Angela Molina in a nude cameo) who tried to seduce him in his cell. Just when we think he's about to give in to the "devil," he knocks over a brazier and lies down on its embers, inviting the girl to join him. She, instead, flees. Another droll episode shows an orgiastic scene with hellfire burning before it, which Vincent witnesses, but ultimately resists.

Pic is well limned technically, with beautiful crisp lensing by cameraman Teo Escamilla. Item will offend religious-minded audiences, and is sure to run into trouble in most countries with censorship. Humor is too wry for mass appeal, but could click in art circuits.
— *Besa*.

Autumn Sonata
(SWEDISH-COLOR)

———

Bergman directs Bergman with interesting but pedestrian results.

———

New World Pictures release of a Lord Lew Grade (ITC) and Martin Starger presentation of a Personafilm GmbH (Munich) production. Stars Ingrid Bergman, Liv Ullmann. No writing credits (but probably Bergman). Camera (color), Sven Nykvist; set designer, Anna Asp; sound, Owe Svensson; editor, Sylvia Ingmarsdotter, asst. director, Peder Langenskiold. Review in New York screening room, New York, Sept. 12, '78. (No MPAA rating). Running time: **97 MINS.**
Charlotte .... Ingrid Bergman
Eva .... Liv Ullmann
Helena .... Lena Nyman
Viktor .... Halvar Bjork
Leonardo .... Georg Lokkeberg
The Professor .... Knut Wigert
The Nurse .... Eva Von Hanno
Josef .... Erland Josephson
Eva (as a child) .... Linn Ullmann
Uncle Otto .... Arne Bang-Hansen
Paul .... Gunnar Bjornstrand
Plus: Marianne Aminoff, Mimi Pollak.

(Swedish and English soundtrack; English subtitles)

The most interesting particular about Ingmar Bergman's "Autumn Sonata," and the principal factor in its evident boxoffice success, is the fact that this is the first time the Swedish director has directed Swedish actress Ingrid Bergman. It makes one wish that they had teamed up a long time ago. The film, which is Swedish, despite the fact that it was shot in Norway by Bergman's Munich-based company and financed by the British, is a return to the world of complex human relationships which he abandoned briefly for the ill-fated Munich-made "Serpent's Egg." A fascinating study, "Autumn Sonata" requires the full attention of the viewer and, for that reason, is not likely to win any new converts to the Bergman cult.

Ingrid Bergman is a famous concert pianist who finds herself emotionally alone when her lover of many years dies. She is invited to visit her daughter, Liv Ullmann, the wife of a country parson in Norway, whom she has not seen for seven years. The film deals with their reunion and the ultimate disclosure of their feelings for each other. It isn't all love and sunshine, by any means. Arriving at the parsonage, Bergman finds that a second daughter, Helena, who is wasting away from some undisclosed disease that renders her inarticulate, has been brought out of a state hospital to which she has been confined to be cared for by the seemingly charitable Eva (Ullmann).

Like the title the film is autumnal in tone. One feels that the belated confrontation, whatever its little solaces and comforts and ultimate baring of two souls, comes too late in the lives of both women to cure the feeling of abandonment on the one hand and to alleviate the apologetic ministrations of the mother. They meet, they find that both are capable of a mixture of love and hatred, they part.

One might expect Bergman, the director, to stack the cards a bit in favor of Ullmann but he has made Ingrid the much more colorful and interesting of the ill-matched pair. The camerawork, by Sven Nykvist, which one now takes for granted as superb, devotes much of its exposure to the close-ups of the two women and they are a lesson in facial histrionics. Of course, the heavy use of close-ups (much as used in "Scenes From A Marriage") makes the ultimate sale to television all that much easier. Other than the three women (and Lena Nyman only can make sounds as the bedridden Helena), the only principal male role is that of Halvar Bjork as Ullmann's parson husband.

Bergman buffs will, however, be able to spot some of his better-known males in silent cameos, including Erland Josephson as Josef, Bergman's husband and Ullmann's father, and Gunnar Bjornstrand as Paul, Bergman's agent. Her conversations with him, on the phone and on a train trip, are in English. Incidentally, sharp-eyed viewers can spot a copy of *Variety* during the train sequence. Ullmann (and Ingmar Bergman's) daughter, Linn, plays her mother as a child. She is fetching but not yet an actress.

Boxoffice interest would appear assured on this good but not great experiment. — *Robe*.

Up In Smoke
(COLOR)

———

Marijuana comedy probably has built-in audience, if conservatives probably will oppose subject.

———

Hollywood, Sept. 8.
A Paramount release of a Lou Adler Production, produced by Lou Adler, Lou Lombardo. Stars Tommy Chong, Cheech Marin. Directed by Adler. Screenplay, Chong, Cheech; camera (Metrocolor), Gene Polito; supervising editor, Lou Lombardo; editor, Scott Conrad; art director, Leon Ericksen; asst. director, Mike Moder; sound, Pat Mitchell; wardrobe, Ernie Misko. Reviewed at Paramount Studios, Hollywood, Sept. 7, '78. (MPAA Rating: R.) Running time: **86 MINS.**
Pedro .... Cheech Marin
Man .... Tommy Chong
Sergeant Stedenko .... Stacy Keach
Mr. Stoner .... Edie Adams
Strawberry .... Tom Skerritt
Jade East .... Zane Buzby
Debbie .... Anne Wharton
Gloria .... Louisa Moritz
Ajax Lady .... June Fairchild

Here is a possibly first major studio release of a comedy based on marijauna. Since several millions of Americans are by estimate addicted to the weed, there's presumably a large potential audience. Fire marshalls may have trouble with "no smoking regulations" when this pic unreels. The conservative elements of population may be opposed.

"Up In Smoke" is essentially a drawn-out version of the drug-oriented comedy routines of Tommy Chong and Cheech Marin, who have become identified with this genre via some successful comedy disks.

The Lou Adler production went through several title changes until arriving at present monicker, which is sufficiently suggestive to draw in the intended customers.

Script by the two comedians has hippie rich kid Chong teaming up with barrio boy Cheech in a confused search for some pot to puff on, presumably to aid them in putting together a rock band. Pursuit takes them to Tijuana, where they end up driving back a van constructed out of treated marijuana called "fibreweed."

In diligent pursuit is narcotics detective Stacy Keach, saddled with the usual crew of incompetent assistants. The trail eventually leads to popular L.A. nitery, The Roxy, (in which Adler is partnered) where the dopers' band engages in a punk rock marathon. They take top prize when the high-grade van, catching on fire, inundates the club with potent smoke.

What's lacking in "Up In Smoke" is a cohesiveness in both humor and characterization. Pic gets off to a great start, with Cheech's life in a crowded apartment, and the meeting of the two potheads, a comedic gem.

Large expository chunks seem to be missing, however, and once the more obvious drug jokes are exhausted, Adler lets the film degenerate into a mixture of fitful slapstick and toilet humor. Footage on the cutting room floor might explain what happened to top-featured roles of Strother Martin and Edie Adams, for instance — they occupy all of 40 seconds screen time.

Pic comes alive in final minutes when Cheech and Chong pick up hitchhiker Zane Busby, the craziest rider since Helena Kallianiotes in "Five Easy Pieces." But plot structure of "Up In Smoke" has lived up to its title by that time, although to this segment of the filmgoing public, dramaturgy is of small importance.

Tom Skerritt is wasted in a small role as a crazed Vietnam vet, and Keach keeps his narc captain on the cardboard cop level established by "Smokey And The Bandit." Louisa Mortiz and June Fairchild are effective in small bits. Tech credits are all pro.

Now that the pro forma routines have been used up, it will be interesting to see in what direction Cheech and Chong will go. They display a sharp sense of comic timing, and winning personalities that can be stretched a little further than Adler has done here. —*Poll.*

Perceval Le Gallois
(FRENCH-COLOR)

Paris, Sept. 6.
Gaumont release of Les Films DuLosange, FR3, ARD, RAI, Gaumont production. Written and directed by Eric Rohmer from the book by Chretien De Troyes. Camera (Eastmancolor), Nestor Almendros; editor, Cecile Ducugis; music, Guy Robert; art director, J. Pierre Kohut-Svelk; producers, Margaret Menegoz; costumes, Jacques Schmidt. Reviewed at Gaumont screening room, Paris, Aug. 31, '78. Running time: **140 MINS.**
Perceval .... Fabrice Luchini
Gauvain .... Andre Dussolier
Blanchefleur .....Ariel Dussolier Dombas
Arthur .... Marc Eyraud
Guinevere ....Marie Christine Barrault
Pucelle ....Clementine Amouroux

Eric Rohmer, who wound his so-called cycle of "moral tales" with "Claire's Knee," and then segued into an adaptation of H. Von Kleist's tale, "The Marquise D'O," here adapts a medieval tale, supposedly the first French novel.

Perceval Le Gallois is a youth living with his widowed mother who is awed by passing Knights and decides to set forth and become one. Film is mainly the story of his quest with an aside in an adventure of one of King Arthur's knights. Film uses stylized settings with painted backdrops, small scale chateaus and the use of troubadors to comment on the tale as a sort of Greek chorus.

Perceval is a high strung, intense do-gooder who leaves betrayed virgins and slain knights behind him across a girl in a tent and forces himself on her for his mother had told him to take a woman and multiply. She is disgraced when her suitor returns.

He comes to King Arthur's Court and is told he can take the armor of a knight who has just left. Perceval puts his lance into the man's eye and is helped into his armor as he sallies forth again to succor damsels in distress and disarm Arthur's enemies.

Rohmer adapted the ancient French into a charmingly archaic syntax and kept it in metered rhyme. Subtitling must be careful, but the imagery and the ironic tang carry this slow but graceful quest along. It has the dignity and elegance of a medieval painting.

It is a sort of parable on innocence. When Perceval begins to brood on his exploits there is a Passion Play interlude as he plays the Christ figure betrayed, flayed and crucified. The section with the Knight of Arthur's Court also reflects some aspects of the chinks in the armor of chivalry in catering to vanity and senseless battles.

Perceval is played with the right gaucheness and intensity by Fabrice Luchini. Others fit well into this languid but always eyefilling tale.

Film should find its audiences with the right handling. It will world preem at the coming New York Film Festival. Pic should find selective filmgoers. —*Mosk.*

Bloodbrothers
(COLOR)

Excellent cast in uneven family melodrama. Iffy outlook.

Hollywood, Sept. 13.
Warner Bros. release of a Stephen Friedman-Kings Road production. Produced by Stephen Friedman. Directed by Robert Mulligan; Features entire cast. Screenplay, Walter Newman, based on the novel by Richard Price; camera (Technicolor), Robert Surtees; editor, Shelly Kahn; music, Elmer Bernstein; production design, Gene Callahan; sound, Charles Knight; production manager, John Coonan; assistant directors, Howard Roessel, Robert Hargrove. Reviewed at The Burbank Studios, Sept. 11, '78. (MPAA Rating: R). Running time: 16 MINS.
Chubby De Coco .... Paul Sorvino
Tommy De Coco .... Tony Lo Bianco
Stony De Coco .... Richard Gere
Marie ....Lelia Goldoni
Phyllis .... Yvonne Wilder
Banion ....Kenneth McMillan
Dr. Harris .... Floyd Levine
Annette ... .; Marilu Henner
Albert ....Michael Hershewe

"Bloodbrothers" is an ambitious, if uneven, probe into the disintegration of an Italian-American family. Under Robert Mulligan's forceful direction, sharply-drawn characters clash, scream and argue, but fail to resolve any of their or the film's conflicts. Because of its shrill tone and abundance of foul epithets, commercial prospects are uncertain, and careful promotional handling is in order.

"Bloodbrothers" delves into the steamy emotional mess known as the De Coco clan, headed by construction worker father Tony Lo Bianco, his brother Paul Sorvino, wife Lelia Goldoni, and sons Richard Gere and Michael Hershewe.

Although the focus of the film isn't clear until about half-way through its 116 minutes, "Bloodbrothers" is concerned primarily with the plight of Gere, who is trying to make one of those crucial life decisions about whether he wants to join the men on the construction girders or opt for the job that gives him real pleasure, working with small children.

Mulligan and scripter Walter Newman have placed this pedestrian tale against a background of vibrant machoism, with numerous scenes of boozing, whoring and fighting set in the Bronx. Lo Bianco and Sorvino are basically pictured as perpetual juveniles in the bodies of grown men, still hung up on their past exploits and sexual conquests.

Lo Bianco gives wife Goldoni short shrift, and in her frustration she terrorizes younger brother Hershewe, for whom Gere has a special affection. Sorvino is around to try and smooth over the bumps, but it's a lost cause, a conclusion Gere eventually comes to when he exits at film's end with sibling in tow.

"Bloodbrothers" features superb acting from all parties, but

nagging questions continually undercut the film's effectiveness. The age span between Gere (supposedly playing an 18-year-old) and Lo Bianco lacks credibility and the relationships between the blustering characters are never defined satisfactorily. Perhaps this is a paean to "real life," but why should filmgoers pay to see what they already can hear in the next apartment.

Gere displays perhaps his best acting to date in "Bloodbrothers," and despite and through the Brando-esque mannerisms an exciting performer can be perceived. Sorvino, who has finally hit his cinematic stride, and Lo Bianco are excellent, as are Goldoni and Hershewe. Kenneth McMillan as the crippled neighborhood barkeep and Marilu Henner as a loose disco waitress who tries to help clear Gere's head are superb in support.

As always Mulligan's features are a visual accomplishment. Robert Surtees' photography is sombre, but glowing, and Gene Callahan's production design perfectly recreates a claustrophobic urban environment. Elmer Bernstein departs from his usual scoring techniques to come up with a driving, r&b-based soundtrack that adds immensely to the film's power. While flawed "Bloodbrothers" still represents a mostly intelligent bit of filmmaking in a season dominated by lighter, more entertaining fare.
— *Poll.*

Speed Fever
(ITALIAN-COLOR)

Rome, Sept. 12.
An Impegno release in Italy (Titanus, worldwide) of the Alessandro Fracassi production for Racing Pictures. Stars Sydne Rome. Directed by Mario Morra, Oscar Orefici. Screenplay, Pietro Rizzo; camera (Technicolor) Ottavio Fabbri; music, Guido and Maurizio De Angelis. Reviewed at Supercinema, Rome, Sept. 12. '78. Running time. 105 MINS.

Also: Niki Lauda, James Hunt. Mario Andretti, Emerson Fittipaldi; Carlos Reutemann.

The wedding of stock footage and live action camera work in "Speed Fever," together turned up moments of acute tension in an overview of car racing emphasizing the underdog chances of survival in a sport loaded with mortality statistics.

Properly promoted to reach the legion of racing fans, "Speed Fever" should find its way in all markets — including a dualler spot in the U.S.

The main spotlight — with a strong human touch — is on Niki Lauda who came out of his devastating crash on the German Nurburgring track from the utter brink with almost an entirely new plastic face.

Stock footage, including the disintegration of a track assistant during the Formula I race in South Africa, the mortal accident at Sandvoort in Holland, and Craig Breedlove's miraculous survival after attempting the world record on the Bonneville Flats are all high temperature moments in the film's favor. The celebrity watchers will also have a ball as Mario Morra and Oscar Orefici shift from the track stars to a number of film stars — all individually quizzed by Sydne Rome. Some of the queries are a letdown and some of the celebs are fleeting but the total appearances add up to a strong docu cast with many household names in it.

"Speed Fever" is as close as anyone has yet gotten to Grand Prix Formula I racing. Amplitude of human contact removes the solid docu structure, providing insights more often than not illustrating, defining and in the case of Lauda, personalizing dramatically the aftermath of his terrible accident.

It wasn't necessary to open up peak volume for the Guido and Maurizio De Angelis score, nor was it necessary to amp grinding gears from back of the stereo speakers, but on the other hand, the camerawork of Ottavio Fabbri is tensely encompassing. Color is expectedly uneven with intercuts of stock material though action reduces flaw to minimum. —*Werb.*

Brigade Mondaine
(Vice Squad)
(FRENCH-COLOR)

Paris, Sept. 6.
Planfilm release of FranCos Films production. Features entire cast. Directed by Jacques Scandelari. Screenplay, Jacques Robert from a book by Gerard De Villiers; camera (Eastmancolor), Francois About; editor, Catherine Snopko; music, Cerrone. Reviewed at UGC-Opera, Paris, Sept. 2. '78. Running time, 90 MINS.
Cast: Patrice Valota, Odile Michel, Florence Cayrol, J.P. Brissart, Jacques Berthier, Patrick Oliver.

A cagey mixture of exploitation ideas with soft porn, sadomasochism, drugs and an unorthodox policeman dressed up a la Serpico. However, this mixes into a fairly flat treatment, and woolly characters to give this okay home potential, but strictly quickie playoffs abroad.

There is also the use of disco music done in a thumping manner by Cerrone. The cop has a stripper girlfriend and they are constantly interrupted in their dallying by a case which concerns a flashy pimp who sets up girls for a rich, decadent pervert who likes to have them killed when he is through with them.

Direction is merely serviceable though not being penalized by an X-rating since any porno stuff is part of the theme, plus those wanting kinkier sex aspects and the action auds. It is doing okay locally.
—*Mosk.*

Hoer, var der ikke en, som lo?
(Did Somebody Laugh?)
(DANISH-COLOR)

Copenhagen, Aug. 18.
A Dagmar (for SAM Films) production. Warner/Constantin release. Features entire cast, based freely on novel by Eigil Jensen. Written and directed by Henning Carlsen. Camera (Eastmancolor) Henning Kristiansen; music, Corelli, Smetana, Krystof Komeda; editor, Henning Carlsen (with Christian Hartkopp); executive producer, Nina Crone. Reviewed at Dagmar Bio, Copenhagen, Aug. 18 '78. Running time: 100 MINS.
Anonymous storyteller and main character .... Jesper Christensen
Elizabeth .... Kirsten Olesen
Gravedigger .... Otto Brandenburg
The Acne Louse .... Jessper Klein
Elderly Sissy Bachelor ...... Karl Stegger
The Weight Lifter .... Jens Okking

Eigil Jensen wrote his very autobiographical short novel, "Did Somebody Laugh," as a sadly humorous story in 1940 and later dropped entirely out of literature. The book is about an unemployed young man's experiences in bread lines and worse during the Depression in the Copenhagen of the '30s. He is mild-mannered to the point of naivete. He keeps hoping for snow so that he can get a shovelling job. He has a few friends, one of them (Jens Okking) a cynic who steals books that the nameless protagonists gets some joy out of reading. He also has a brief love affair with an evidently sexually hungry, frustrated, beautiful young woman who is stuck with a dying aunt, but to her he is only a ship passing in the night.

The book-stealing cynic, known as "The Weightlifter," and other fellow unemployed members of the mercy crews also let him down and finally, he is turned out of his unpaid rented room, goes to sleep on a park bench and dreams that a Godlike Unemployment agency official condemns him to a hell for the superfluous. Then he wakes up, having heard heavenly laughter in his dream. And he is covered with snow. He gets up, heading, we must think, for the line for a shovelling job.

And that is it. No big dramatic scenes, no regular action sequences, only poignant episodes, nobly photographed, played with controlled abandon by all hands, production-designed so that it does never look like anything but the real thing. Henning Carlsen made "Happy Divorce," a Danish-French coproduction that opened the official Cannes competition program three years ago. His "Hunger" secured a Golden Palm for actor Per Oscarsson. But Carlsen is like veteran New Orleans trumpeter Bunk Johnson who was once complimented for his playing of a certain number. He said: "Oh, that, I got seven other styles."

Carlsen has made near masterpieces, but he has also made straight junk. He is erratic but always interesting to follow. "Did Somebody Laugh" stresses the real tragedy of the Depression through concentration on the minor details of just general sadness. Any mature audience would appreciate this movie. As a festival item it is sure to arouse interest. As a moneymaker, it would seem a riskier affair.
— *Kell.*

Oro Rojo
(Red Gold)
(SPANISH-MEXICAN-COLOR)

Madrid, Sept. 8.
Izaro Films (Madrid) and Esme Producciones (Mexico) production. Written and directed by Alberto Vazquez Figueroa. Camera (Eastmancolor), Jose Luis Alcaine; editor, Enrique Alarcon; exec producer, J. Estelrich; sets, R.G. Salgado; music, Carmelo Bernaola. Reviewed at Cine Callao, Madrid, Sept. 7, '78. Running time: 95 MINS.
Cast: Jose Sacristan, Isela Vega, Hugo Stiglitz, Patricia Adriani, Jorge Luque, Alfredo Mayo, Monica Randall.

Well-known novelist and now helmer-scripter of this pic Alberto Vazquez Figueroa had a fascinating subject to work with — the trafficking of blood and plasma — but, considering how sensationalist a subject it is, pic comes across too talky and contrived. Thesps Hugo Stiglitz and Jose Sacristan are terribly miscast and the dialogs are often stilted and awkward.

Story line has a mysterious sailor landing on a Latin American island ruled by a dictator (he's given a Portuguese name to throw us off track). He befriends a bum on the beach who lives (and dies) by donating blood, and flashes around his cash. Not surprisingly he's soon relieved of his billfold and misses his ship.

Various non-adventures and romantic involvements follow (some female nudity but nothing erotic) as he's sent off to a salt mine and escapes, but we never really get into the unbelievable characters and the little action there is in the film isn't properly developed to make it exciting. The rebellion to the dictatorship never materializes, and the stranded sailor and recalcitrant bum never accomplish anything. Even the sailor's final escape is left hanging in the air in the wishy-washy ending.

Technical credits are good, especially Jose Luis Alcaine's lensing, though editing is shaky. As a first effort, Vazquez Figueroa's direction is satisfactory, but the script is weak and the whole story two-dimensional. Item nonetheless might do some biz in some sophisticated Hispano circuits. —*Besa.*

Chez Nous
(SWEDISH-COLOR)

Malmoe, Sept. 6.
A Swedish Film Institute (production head Bengt Forslund)/HB Three Leaf Clover production, AB Sandrews release. Features entire cast. Directed by Jan Halldoff. Story and script, based on thier own stage play, by Anders Ehnmark, P.O. Enquist; camera (Eastmancolor) Jack Churchill; production design, Anders Barreus; music, quotes from the classics; editor, Wic Kjellin; executive producer, Jutta Ekman. Reviewed at Sandrews 1-2-3, Malmoe, Sweden, Sept. 5 '78. Running time, 95 MINS.
Maria .... Ewa Froling
Melin .... Ernst Gunther
Wiren .... Sven Lindberg
Chez Nous manager Ernst-Hugo Jaeregard
Elmgren .... Ingvar Kjellson
Eva-Lisa .... Lis Nilheim

Incredibly, young but veteran director Jan Halldoff has turned Anders Ehnmark's and P.O. Enquist's political tract-cum-crime and corruption thriller stage play into a dull, talkative feature film that will stand scant chances anywhere but on the dedicated political left-wing Little Theatre circuit.

This in spite of obvious possibilities for reaching larger audiences with the story of an investigative newspaperwoman (Ewa Froeling of severely dark, but very young and handsome mien), thwarted by behind the scenes political-economical powerplays in her attempt to discover the real motives behind the seemingly simple jealousy murder of a porno club's aquatic star (she performs in a hugh glass tank with a giant eel. The club's name is "Chez Nous," title indicating the overall idea that this might take place or is taking place in present-day Sweden).

Jack Churchill's cinematography would serve a Hitchcock or a Chabrol. The production design (big city tabloid's newsroom, porno club interiors) is both realistic and witty, and if a Columbo or some female counterpart had stepped in to speed things up, "Chez Nous" might at least have reached tv audiences worldwide. But Halldoff is too loyal to the authors' cardboard characters.

As the city room editor, Ernst Gunther, and as the porno club manager, Ernst-Hugo Jaeregard, put at least a little life to proceedings, but the rest of the film quietly dies. — *Kell.*

Schwarz Und Weiss Wie Tage Und Naechte
(Black and White Like Days and Nights)
(WEST GERMAN-COLOR)

Berlin, Aug. 31.

A Monaco-Film and Radiant-Film Co-production with ORF and WDR, Cologne. Georg Althammer, producer; Gunther Witte, WDT-TV producer. Features entire cast. Directed by Wolfgang Petersen. Screenplay, Karl-Heinz Willschrei, Jochen Wedegaertner, Petersen; camera (color), Joerg-Michael Baldenius; art direction, O. Jochen Schmidt; music, Klaus Doldinger; editor, Johannes Nickel; production manager, Michael Bittins. Reviewed at Sender Freies Berlin Screening Room, Berlin, Aug. 30, '78. Running time: **103 MINS.**

Thomas Rosenmund	Bruno Ganz
Marie	Gila von Weitershauen
Lindford	Rene Deltgen
Koruga	Ljubo Tadic
Gruenfeld	Joachim Wichmann
Doctor	Annemarie Wendl
Wilke	Alexis von Hagemeister
Father Rosenmund	Alexander Hegarth
Mother Rosenmund	Gudrun Vaupel
Thomas as a Boy	Markus Helis
Marie as a Girl	Elke Schuessler
Moderator	Eberhard Stanjek

After 20-odd original television films and two successful theatrical films — "One of Us Both" (1973), for Roxy-Film, and "The Consequences" (1977), slated for upcoming Toronto, San Francisco, and Chicago fests — Wolfgang Petersen has founded a company, Radiant-Film, for theatrical release of all his pix, including his latest tv-film, "Black and White Like Days and Nights."

This is arguably his best pic and has solid chances for more than just the art house circuit at home after its tv run this month, plus possible offshore prospects should it get legs via the Petersen retro at the San Francisco fest.

Petersen has a solid rep as West Germany's best action helmer (he made detective thrillers for tv here), but also scored with an adaptation of writer Max van der Gruen's "Danger Slippery Ice" (1974) for Cologne Television (WDR), the same backer of "Black and White" and equally packed with psychological tension and several surprise twists to keep the story moving at a fast clip.

Hero Thomas Rosenmund (a Bobby Fischer type, but country of his origin is unnamed) is introduced as a precocious young man who learns to play chess simply by watching his father's mistakes in matches with a neighbor. He can't bear to lose, and an early breakdown develops — he swears never to play again, and grows up instead with computers. The computer company supports a programmed match with the world champion, Stefan Koruga (also from an unnamed country, but played by Yugoslav actor Ljubo Tadic): the machine loses and Thomas is again humiliated. Not even childhood sweetheart Marie, now his wife, can stay him from going back to the chessboard to beat the world champion.

He does — in a match that's the high point of the film. The styles of the two men, one full of tension and the other relaxed, make for suspenseful moments during the world-match at Opatija, a former Austrian resort-town on the Adriatic. Rosenmund (Bruno Ganz in his best role) wins, then proceeds to go downhill into paranoia as he pushes his mental powers to the limits and another breakdown. The rematch with Koruga leads to a final twist of fate.

Chess matches make for high drama, even for neophytes to the game. But pic's plusses are the technical credits and thesp performances. Lenser Joerg Michael Baldenius has worked with Petersen on nearly every project since student days at the Berlin Film Academy. Scripter Karl-Heinz Willschrei worked with Petersen and Jochen Wedegaertner to pare text down to the minimum and construct the film on rhythm and mood rather than dialog.

Tadic nearly steals the show as the suave East European champ who enjoys life as much as he does chess, in contrast to the cramped, inarticulate Ganz. And vet German thesp Rene Deltgen, as the teacher of the new champion, brings a sense of reserved dignity into the proceedings.

Pic can be blown up to 35m with little loss, and this one deserves a run at the sweepstakes. One of the best German pix this season. —*Holl.*

Vinterboern
(Winterborn)
(DANISH-COLOR)

Copenhagen, Aug. 30.

A Panorama (Just Betzer) production and release in economic collaboration with the Danish Film Institute (Frits Raben). Based on novel by Dea Trie Moerch. Screenplay, Astrid Henning-Jensen, directed by Astrid Henning-Jensen. Editor, Astrid Henning-Jensen, Grete Moeldrup; camera (Eastmancolor) Lars Bjoerne; music, Hans Erik Phillip. Reviewed at Palads, Copenhagen, Aug. 30, '78. Running time, **90 MINS.**

Marie	Ann-Mari Max Hansen
Signe	Helle Hertz
Olivia	Lone Keller
Linda	Lea Risum Broegger

"Vinterboern" is on its way to bestseller status as Dea Trie Moerch's starkly realistic, yet warmly human and often humorous series of vignettes, each springing forth from the pages as clearly as characters in a full-length novel.

The Danish title "Vinterboern" actually means "Winter Children." They are the ones who will survive by a last chance of being placed in the Neonatal Dept.

Astrid Henning-Jensen has transferred the book into a film that should attain similar impact and status. It gives a precious insight into the miracle, for better or for worse, of pregnancy and birth. The actual birth is shown with realism combined with artistic tact.

The camaraderie, fears, hopes, little conspiracies and richly varied group of women suddenly stripped of their outside-the-hospital securities of apparel and possessions are shown with imagination and finesse and by (with a few exception) good actors directed by a superior director. Henning-Jensen also understands, like author Moerch, to make the vignettes work together into a dramatic whole.

Ann-Mari Max Hansen, striking of looks, and too often used by male directors for her looks alone, emerges as an actress of extraordinary skill and nuance. She is well supported by the controlled and warm talent of Helle Hertz, by jazz/rock singer Lone Kellerman (a debut away from the pop mike) and young Lea Risum Broegger, a student at the State Drama School. While a few men are sketched somewhat on the square side by Henning-Jensen (they were never square in the novel), most are shown without vogueish women's contempt.

"Vinterboern" is not a film classic nor innovative in any other way that showing the classical "group" in surroundings that will be new and astounding to all audiences. Sympathy and good boxoffice will meet it everywhere. Lars Bjoerne's camerawork is a wonder of discreet realism. —*Kell.*

Outside Chance
(U.S.-COLOR)

Deauville, Sept. 19.

Miller, Begun TV, Roger Cormon release and production. Stars Yvette Mimieux. Directed by Michael Miller. Screenplay, Ralph Gaby Wilson, Miller; camera (Color), Willy Kurant; music, Murphy Dunne, Lou Levy. No other credits available. Reviewed at Deauville Film Fest, Sept. 9, '78. Running time: **94 MINS.**

Dinah	Yvette Mimieux

Michael Miller made a sharply edged tale of a woman caught up in middle America violence in "Jackson County Jail" last year. It drew some critical fancy and focused attention on Miller, one of the young directors given a chance by Roger Corman's company.

Here is a spinoff using the same story with a twist. In the original, a svelte thirtyish woman driving to N.Y. from L.A. has her car stolen, ends up in prison, where she is raped by a degenerate guard, whom she kills, and she then escapes with a young delinquent.

But the film uses the "what if" gimmick in the man running off and she held for murder of the guard. She is railroaded by an ambitious district attorney who will not accept the rape story and escapes from prison during a fire and goes on the run.

This film is as adept as the first one, and a well made programmer that could find okay playoff. Yvette Mimieux is fine as she faces up to her victimization by police and the criminals she runs into as she escapes with a pregnant girl who was with the man who stole her car.

Film ends with her still on the run and other versions keep up the "what if" aspects indefinitely. Miller should try some other subjects to prove his directorial talent can work on subtler themes and subjects. —*Mosk.*

Deauville Fest

The Children of Sanchez
(U.S.-MEXICAN-COLOR)

Deauville, Sept. 19.

Hall Bartlett Films release and production. Stars Anthony Quinn, Lupita Ferrer, Dolores Del Rio. Directed by Hall Bartlett. Screenplay, Cesare Zavattini, Bartlett from the book by Oscar Lewis; camera (color), Gabriel Figueroa; music, Chick Mangione. Reviewed at Deauville Film Fest, Sept. 8, '78. Running time, **126 MINS.**

Sanchez	Anthony Quinn
Consuelo	Lupita Ferrer
Grandma	Dolores Del Rio
Roberto	Stathis Giallelis
Marta	Lucia Mendez
Manuel	Duncan Quinn
Chata	Katy Jurado
(In English)	

"The Children of Sanchez" is an earnest but flawed attempt to flesh out Oscar Lewis's well known book on a Mexican lower class family. It revolves around an earthy, sensual, inarticulate but harsh father figure played with his usual personality strength and acting vigor by Anthony Quinn. (Bartlett owned the property for years but was not allowed to film in Mexico by the government until last year.—ed.)

Quinn is surrounded by daughters, sons, grandchildren, an aunt and a new concubine in an overcrowded one room dwelling. The closeness breeds friction and Quinn's macho ways are opposed by one daughter whose dream is to become an air hostess to get out of the poverty.

Film goes in for a series of crises as one daughter leaves when Quinn will not allow her to see a young man and another son goes off to America after his wife dies. The hardheaded, would-be stewardess, the one who stands up to Quinn, also leaves after a fight with him.

The girl tries to do too many jobs to pay for her stewardess lessons and has a breakdown. Quinn wins a lottery and goes ahead and builds a house. A son comes back, another in the army deserts and he gets back his daughters. It ends with a party at the new house and another run-in with the headstrong daughter who is like him.

Lupita Ferrer is intense as the daughter who is seemingly most like him. But she appears too well bred to spring from this tawdry environment though she apparently was the rare one with some schooling.

Dolores Del Rio is still lovely as the middle class grandmother who helps the rebellious Sanchez children. Film is more illustrative than really delving deeply into the family ties. Mexican poverty is somewhat softened by the lush lensing. Quinn's earthy father is both resigned and haughty, knowing and brutal, an enigmatic Mexican.

Film will need careful handling to find it its audiences. —Mosk.

The Boss' Son
(U.S.-COLOR)

Deauville, Sept. 19.

The Boss' Son Productions, New American Cinema Ltd release and production. Features entire cast. Written and directed by Bobby Roth. Camera (Metrocolor), Alfonso Beato; editor, John Carnochan; music, Richard Markowitz; exec producer, Robert Estrin; producer, Jeffrey White. Reviewed at Deauville Film Fest, Sept. 8, '78. Running time: **101 MINS.**

Bobby . . . . Asher Brauner
Joseph . . . . Rudy Solari
Esther . . . . Rita Moreno
Charles . . . . Henry G. Sanders
Buddy . . . . James Darren
Albert . . . . Richie Havens
Cleo . . . . Michelle Davison
Bea . . . . Gammy Burdett

Boss' Son" is a personal film. It's never over-indulged. Has fine feel of character. Timeless theme concerns a youth going his own way.

Bobby Rose, played with feeling by Asher Brauner, has finished college, expecting to go into the family business, a big carpet company. But his still youthful father, a self made man, wants him to start in the delivery vans and learn the business all the way.

The son accepts at a time when business is off and carpet thefts are also a headache. He is paired with a free wheeling black driver whom he first suspects of being in on it. But friendship develops, deftly blocked out at a dinner somewhat disturbed by the man's bitter wife and other incidents.

The film builds as an investigative agency is brought in to find out about the thefts. The boss' son finds himself taking his father's side and turning in those who had indulged in theft, including his friend. But he also breaks with his father for he knows he cannot be a boss.

Rita Moreno is effective in the offbeat casting as the boy's mother, a

still lovely Jewish mama taken to drink. The film's start has her belting out a song in her room, perhaps indicating a certain frustration.

Henry G. Sanders is effective as the friend and technical facilities are okay as is unobtrusive thesping down the line. —Mosk.

Chameleon
(U.S.-COLOR)

Deauville, Sept. 19.

Jon Jost, Rising Sun Productions release and production. Features entire cast. Directed by Jon Jost. Screenplay, Bob Glaudini, Jost; camera (Color), Jost. Reviewed at Deauville Film Fest, Sept. 7, '78. Running time, **90 MINS.**

Chameleon . . . . Bob Glaudini
Woman . . . . Kathleen McKay
Girl . . . . Ellen Blake
Friend . . . . Lee Kissman

Jon Jost has been noticed at specialized film festivals with his personalized films on the U.S. subculture. Now he makes a more clearcut film that delves into personality of a drug pusher. Bob Glandini is thin and personable but with an underlying drive who seems to change with the people he encounters. Included are his musings on himself and experiences.

Jost made this for $35,000 which is a feat these days. It is mainly for the specialized routes but reveals an unusual visual talent. — Mosk.

The Last Campaign
(U.S.-DOCU-COLOR)

Deauville, Sept. 19.

Barbara Frank release and production. Conceived and directed by Barbara Frank. Camera (Color), Joan Churchill, Robert Eberlein, Eli Hollander, James Joannides, Eric Saarinen; editor, Jean-Claude Lubtchancsky; associate producer, Stephen Rohde. Reviewed at Deauville Film Fest, Sept. 4, '78. Running time: **85 MINS.**

This documentary follows Robert Kennedy during his fateful Presidential campaign in California 10 years ago. Apparently, filmmaker Barbara Frank waited all this time perhaps to give the film a more distanced study of an era, a personality and the political pulse.

Film does not add much as to Kennedy's outlook and attitudes. The passage of time and the viewers' foreknowledge of the impending assassination are values. Kennedy emerges a developing, politically astute figure as his campaign builds to his California win and, at its height, murder. —Mosk.

Who Is Killing The Great Chefs Of Europe?
(U.S.-WEST GERMAN-COLOR)

Makes "The Grand Bouffe" look like a peanut butter-and-jelly sandwich. Big boxoffice prospects.

Toronto, Sept. 16.

Warner Bros. release of a Lorimar presentation of an Aldrich Company-Lorimar production. Executive producers, Merv Adelson, Lee Rich. Produced by William Aldrich. Directed by Ted Kotcheff. Stars George Segal, Jacqueline Bisset. Screenplay, Peter Stone, based on the Nan and Ivan Lyons' novel, "Someone Is Killing The Great Chefs Of Europe;" camera (color), John Alcott; in association with Geria Productions-Bavaria Films (Munich); asst. director, Wolfgang Gattes; art director, Werner Achmann; costumes, Judy Moorcroft; music, Henry Mancini. Reviewed at Toronto Festival of Festivals, Sept. 16, '78. (MPAA Rating: PG). Running time: **112 MINS.**

Robby . . . . George Segal
Natasha . . . . Jacqueline Bisset
Max . . . . Robert Morley
Kohner . . . . Jean-Pierre Cassel
Moulineau . . . . Philippe Noiret
Grandvilliers . . . . Jean Rochefort
Ravello . . . . Luigi Proietti
Fausto Zoppi . . . . Stefano Satta Flores
Beecham . . . . Madge Ryan
Blodgett . . . . Frank Windsor
St. Claire . . . . Peter Sallis
Doyle . . . . Tim Barlow
Dr. Deere . . . . John LeMesurier
Cantrell . . . . Joss Ackland
Salpetre . . . . Jean Gaven
Saint-Juste . . . . Daniel Emilfork
Massenet . . . . Jacques Marin
Chappemain . . . . Jacques Balutin
Brissac . . . . Jean Paredes
Director . . . . Kenneth Fortescue

"Who Is Killing The Great Chefs of Europe?," is as happy a combination of the macabre and the merry as the screen has seen in a long, long time. It's a fast-moving, witty film, beautifully cast with a large group of international professionals who give full justice to Peter Stone's adaptation of Nan and Ivan Lyons' novel, "Someone Is Killing The Great Chefs of Europe." Producer William Aldrich has provided the very expensive mounting such a project requires and director Ted Kotcheff as handled it all with a firm but light touch.

While George Segal and Jacqueline Bisset carry star billing and, indeed, provide the romantic and plot evolution, it is Robert Morley, in his finest screen role in years, as a massive, dedicated gourmet, who provides the film's finest moments. Stone's dialog ripples off him with an ease that is always beguiling and often hilarious.

The series of murders which give the film both its mystery and its title is made the responsibility of some of France and Italy's most outstanding character actors. It's

touch and go who excels but Philippe Noiret underplays in a manner that gives him a slight edge over the more voluble Italians although Stefano Satta Flores' unabashed description of how he'll romance Bisset, given the opportunity, is Italian macho comedy at its finest.

The other endangered chef is Jean-Pierre Cassel, while Jean Rochefort is a red herring who'll fool no one. These are the principal roles but Madge Ryan as Morley's dedicated secretary is also a key figure. A multitude of small parts are handled efficiently, some of them almost throwaways, such as Joss Ackland as the Buckingham Palace master chef and Kenneth Fortescue as an egocentric television director.

Besides the excellent writing, Kotcheff has also provided some superb visual delights, including Noiret's funeral, in which the chief usher is his restaurant's maitre d', who handles the sympathizers in the same high-handed manner as he does in the restaurant.

Technically, the film is first-class throughout. Lorimar's cooperation with Germany's Geria Productions called for an impressive budget and every dollar, pound, mark, franc and lira shows on the screen. Shot principally on locations in London, Paris and Venice, the use of actual famous restaurants makes the film a stunning brochure for international gourmets as well as filmgoers. John Alcott has photographed food, scenery and actors with equal attention and Henry Mancini's romantic score properly underlines "each meal and murder," as well as Segals' pursuit of Bisset. One does occasionally wonder how a fast food entrepreneur ever won over the "world's greatest dessert chef" in the first place.

Stone has taken liberties with the Lyons novel, including a change in villains, but his major contribution has been to provide smart, fast dialog that such a practiced farceur as Segal and a jaded sophisticate like Morley would have spoken. It's a funny film and, at the same time, an engrossing one. It should find success quickly in the general market and its international flair makes it a natural for export. — Robe.

In Praise Of Older Women
(CANADIAN-COLOR)

Toronto, Sept. 16.

Astral Films (Canada) release of an Astral Bellevue Pathe and R.S.L. production. Executive producers, Stephen Roth, Harold Greenberg. Produced by Robert Lantos, Claude Heroux. Directed by George Kaczender. Stars Karen Black, Tom Berenger, Susan Strasberg. Screenplay, Paul Gottlieb from novel, "In Praise Of Older Women" by Stephen Vizinczey; camera (color), Miklos Lente; music, Tibor Polgar; editors, Kaczender, Peter Wintonick; art director, Wolf Kroeger; costumes, Olga

Dimitrov. Reviewed at the Elgin Film House, Toronto, Sept. 14, '78. Running time, 165 MINS.

Andras Vayda .... Tom Berenger
Maya .... Karen Black
Bobbie .... Susan Strasberg
Ann MacDonald .... Helen Shaver
Klari .... Marilyn Lightstone
Paula .... Alexandra Stewart
Julika .... Marianne McIsaac
Mitzi .... Alberta Watson
Andras Vayda Jr .... Ian Tracey
The Countess .... Monique LePage

"In Praise of Older Women" is a flashy exhibition of bare breasts, expert direction, Canadian female acting talent, solid camerawork, music, and art direction, and little else.

It promises far more than is delivered, falling down chiefly in development of the key character — a Hungarian "boy" who at 12 years of age is corrupted by World War II, pimping for prostitutes, and is later unsatisfied with anything but older women.

Two major faults: The boy, said to be 16½ years of age in postwar Budapest, is played by Tom Berenger who looks and acts at least twice that age. Paul Gottlieb's script gives him nothing to do except be a sex machine in episodes with seven women.

And the actresses concerned, except for Susan Strasberg and Alexandra Stewart, are plainly his own age and not older.

Berenger, in scenes with his other women (Karen Black, Marilyn Lightstone, Helen Shaver, Marianne McIsaac, and Alberta Watson) comes off blankly and without characterization. Shot from the waist up and with bare breasts regularly in plain view, the sex scenes pile up without erotic tone or dramatic excitement.

Director George Kaczender rides above it all, making this what should be his ticket to bigger and better features.

Strasberg, as an anti-Communist musician just before the Hungarian Revolution in the mid 1950s, bursts into her scenes with panache and dead-on effect. She is the best of the older women. Stewart, a magazine journalist who is frigid (a condition he cures), is positively world-worn and delicious.

Shaver, McIsaac, Watson, and Lightstone (a comic matronly tart-tongued) all rate highly in their best screen work to date.

All period stuff, this film has a rich look, splendid music (composed by Tibor Polgar, a musician of the time), and excellent camerawork by Miklos Lente.

Overall though, "In Praise Of Older Women is softcore all dressed up to play uptown. — *Adil.*

Blood And Guts
(CANADIAN)

Toronto, Sept. 16.

Ambassador Films (Canada) release of a Quadrant Films presentation of a Peter O'Brian Independent Pictures production. Executive producer, David Perlmutter. Produced by Peter O'Brian. Co-producer, John Hunter. Directed by Paul Lynch. Features entire cast. Screenplay, Joseph McBride, William Gray, John Hunter from original story by McBridge; camera, Mark Irwin; editor, William Gray; music, Milton Barnes; art director, Reuben Freed; costume, Delphine White; casting, Karen Hazzard Ltd.; wrestling supervisor, Reg Love. Reviewed at the New Yorker Film House, Toronto, Sept. 12 '78. Running time, 92 MINS.

Dan O'Neil .... William Smith
Lucky Brown .... Micheline Lanctot
Red Henkel .... Henry Beckman
Jim Davenport ...... Brian Patrick Clark
Jake McCann .... John McFadyen
Harry Brown .... Ken James

"Blood and Guts" is a snappy action picture about the trials and tribulations of a shabby professional wrestling troupe touring tank towns.

It's got all the elements for good playoff on the action circuit: a plot about a love triangle involving aging wrestler and a handsome and much younger newcomer, a battle for control of the young man's wrestling talents, some violence, and mainly robust acting.

Micheline Lanctot delivers a sustained, radiant and yet understated performance as the woman between the two wrestlers. And Henry Beckman as the troupe's tenacious, seen-it-all, done-it-all owner, trainer, and manager is terrific. Secondary roles are weak.

Direction by Paul Lynch is tops for a pic of this kind. The script is clean and without clutter, and production values are commendable. However, the pace is just a shade too slow.

William Smith's older wrestler has punch, but Brian Patrick Clark as the young man falls flat. The title, too, is an asset. — *Adil.*

The Third Walker
(CANADIAN-COLOR)

Toronto, Sept. 16.

A Melvin Simon-Quadrant Films-Wychwood production (no distrib). Produced and directed by Teri McLuhan. Features entire cast. Co-produced by Brian Winston. Screenplay, Robert Thom from an original story by Teri McLuhan; camera (color), Robert Fiore; music, Paul Hoffert; editor, Ulla Ryghe; art director; William McCrow; production consultant, Patrick Watson; wardrobe, Julie Ganton. Reviewed at Warner Bros. screening room, Toronto Sept. 14 '78. Running time, 83 MINS.

Kate MacLean .... Colleen Dewhurst
Munro MacLean .... William Shatner
James MacLean .... Frank Moore
Marie Blanchard ...... Monique Mercure
Etienne Blanchard .... Tony Meyer
Andrew MacLean .... David Meyer
Laura .... Andree Pelletier
Etienne as a boy .... Simon Rankin
Andrew as a boy .... Andrew Rankin
James as a boy .... Darren DiFonzo

The Nun .... Diane LeBlanc
Voice of the Judge .... Marshall McLuhan

Murky and stilted, "The Third Walker" does offer an unusually absorbing plot of which far more should have been made.

A first feature by director Teri McLuhan (daughter of communications expert Marshall McLuhan), it's the story of identical twins mixed up in hospital at birth. One mother gets her twin child and another one and raises both as her own. Another woman gets the other twin and does the same.

The film's main action takes place when the three children are 28 years of age and meet for the first time at their father's funeral. The twins become fast friends and plot their future together, leaving the non-twin an outsider.

The family backgrounds and the discovery of the twins by a convent teacher are told in flashback. If it all sounds confusing, the film is even more so. Not once do the three children discuss their maternal feelings or their predicament with each other. Questions are left all over the place. Accents of the twins and their parents clash.

William Shatner is effective and hardly recognizable as the father, tormented and turned to drink and finally suicide by his wife's determination to get her own twin back.

Colleen Dewhurst, the harsh, domineering mother, is bright and steely as usual but there isn't anything in the script to explain her dislike for the non-twin which she has reared as her own.

What works is the twins, at 28 years of age, played by British actor-twins Tony and David Meyer and as 8 year-olds by twins Simon and Andrew Rankin. Frank Moore as the older non-twin comes off wooden and cardboard but always of pure heart, a good worker and money earner.

Monique Mercure as the mother of the other real twin, a hard-working French-Canadian landlady and then a restaurant owner, does her role with customary passion and intelligence. And for buffs, there's McLuhan's father off camera as the voice of the judge who legally settles the real identities. Direction is pokey and the script tells too much too fast and without enough staples to keep it together. But the idea behind the film (director McLuhan is an identical twin herself) is compelling — mother-son love and identity. — *Adil.*

Three Card Monte
(CANADIAN-COLOR)

Toronto, Sept. 16.

Saguenay Films (Canada) release of a Regenthall Films production. Directed by Les Rose. Features entire cast. Screenplay, Richard Gabourie; camera (color),

Henry Fiks; editor, Ron Wisman; music, Jim Caverhill, Paul Zaza; sound, Peter Burgess, Paul Coombe. Reviewed at the Towne Cinema, Toronto, Sept. 15, '78. Running time, 91 MINS.

Busher .... Richard Gabourie
Toby .... Chris Langevin
Nicki .... Lynne Cavanagh
Clorissa .... Valerie Waburton
Walker .... John Rutter
Ryan .... Tony Sheer
Car Salesman .... Sean McCann

"Three Card Monte" is yet another downbeat Canadian feature about a desperate loser (this time a pool and card shark drifter) who comes to a violent end.

Because it's a first film for director Les Rose and because its performers are non professionals, making their screen debut, it's difficult and perhaps unfair to blame one and all concerned for the amateur acting, the plodding script and the generally meagre production values.

The drifter, played by Richard Gabourie, unwillingly lets a parentless 12-year-old boy tag along with him while he's being traced by hoods whom he beat in a pool game. Man and boy scam their way from city to city in tawdry surroundings. Along comes a girl. But she is sent away to be picked up later. Rose's direction shows signs that he has some talent and might do better the next time.

For the most part, the script abounds with cliches that come so quickly after one another that it's hard to take the whole thing seriously. Everyone involved obviously tried and "Three Card Monte" did receive 11 Canadian Film Award nominations but it's unworkable as it is. —*Adil.*

Marie-Anne
(CANADIAN)

Toronto, Sept. 16.

A Motion Picture Corporation of Alberta presentation. Produced by Fil Fraser. Directed by R. Martin Walters. Features entire cast. Screenplay, Marjorie Morgan and adaptation by George Salverson; camera, Reginald Morris; editor, Stanley Frazen; music, Maurice Marshall; art director, Phillip Silver; associate producer, Bill Davidson. Reviewed at the New Yorker film house, Toronto, Sept. 13 '78. Running time, 91 MINS.

John Baptiste .... John Juliani
Marie-Anne .... Andree Pelletier
Tantoo .... Tantoo Martin
Delacroix .... Paul Jolicoeur
John Rowland .... David Schurmann
Muldoon .... Patrick Hughes

Rigidly Canadian and tv documentary-ish in approach, "Marie-Anne" deals with the first white woman to settle in the Canadian west, in 1808.

It does give pert, gamine-esque Quebec actress Andree Pelletier a chance to shine and her co-headliner, film newcomer John Juliani, moments to flash his long-haired swashbuckling style. They play husband and wife.

And it provides character actress Tantoo Martin, another screen newcomer, a dandy debut as a jilted Indian maid. She is fiery, eyes blazing, and certainly worth seeing more often.

Director R. Martin Walters had to work with an inadequately developed script and more than a handful of dull actors. But Pelletier and Martin overcome most of what's surrounding them. Producer Fil Fraser does off-camera narration to set time and place. But the juice, the reasons for most of Pelletier's bull-headed actions in resisting attempts to ship her out of the British white womanless fort, are missing.

"Marie-Anne" is most suitable for less discriminating small towns. —Adil.

I, Maureen
(CANADIAN)

Toronto, Sept. 16.

New Cinema (Canada) release of a Jandu production in association with P.W.S. Associates. Executive Producers, Philip Speller, Duane Hanson. Produced by Duane Hanson. Directed by Janine Manatis. Features entire cast. Screenplay; Janine Manatis based on a short story by Elizabeth Spencer; camera, Marc Champion; editor, Kirk Jones; music, Hagood Hardy; art director, Nadia Salnick. Reviewed at the Warner Bros. screening room, Toronto, Sept. 14 '78. Running time, 85 MINS.

Maureen . . . . Colleen Collins
Diana . . . . Diane Bigelow
Vinnie . . . . Donna Preece
Charlie. Robert Crone
Dr. Paul Johnson . . . . Michael Ironside
Dennis . . . . Brian Damude

"I, Maureen," a first feature effort for director-scripter Janine Manatis, is a could-have-been entry.

A film that only ardent militant feminists could love, it's got a steadily interesting but slow, confusing starting plot about a married woman who, because of a premonition, leaves her wealthy husband and children and strikes out on her own with some success and some failures (the latter in love) but who persevers.

However, except for the central character well played by film newcomer Colleen Collins, the acting is amateurish in the extreme and there is self indulgence all over the place.

What raises this on the production side is the first-rate camerawork of Marc Champion who has shot several other Canadian features always lushly and in topnotch style. —Adil.

Death On The Nile
(BRITISH-COLOR)

Peter Ustinov creates one of the great screen detectives with a portrayal of Hercule Poirot. Big outlook.

Hollywood, Sept. 18.

A Paramount Pictures release of a John Brabourne and Richard Goodwin production. Stars Peter Ustinov, Jane Birkin, Lois Chiles, Bette Davis, Mia Farrow, Jon Finch, Olivia Hussey, George Kennedy, Angela Lansbury, Simon MacCorkindale, David Niven, Maggie Smith, Jack Warden. Directed by John Guillermin. Screenplay, Anthony Shaffer; (Camera (color), Jack Cardiff; production designer, Peter Murton; editor, Malcolm Cooke" costumes, Anthony Powell; music, Nino Rota; associate producer, Norton Knatchbull; assistant director, Ted Sturgis. Reviewed at the Academy of Motion Picture Arts and Sciences Theatre, Bev Hills Sept. 18, '78. (MPAA Rating: PG.) Running time: 140 MINS.

Hercule Poirot . . . . Peter Ustinov
Louise Bourget . . . . Jane Birkin
Linnet Ridgeway . . . . Lois Chiles
Mrs. Van Schuyler . . . . Bette Davis
Jacqueline De Bellefort . . . . . . Mia Farrow
Mr. Ferguson . . . . Jon Finch
Rosalie Otterbourne . . . . Olivia Hussey
Andrew Pennington . . . . . George Kennedy
Salome Otterbourne . . . . . Angela Lansbury
Simon Doyle . . . . Simon MacCorkindale
Colonel Race . . . . David Niven
Miss Bowers . . . . Maggie Smith
Dr. Bessner . . . . Jack Warden
Barnstable . . . . Harry Andrews
Manager of The Karnak . . . . I.S. Johar

"Death On The Nile" is a clever, witty, well-plotted, beautifully-produced and splendidly acted screen version of Agatha Christie's mystery. It's old-fashioned stylized entertainment with a big cast and lush locations. Peter Ustinov, the fourth actor to play Hercule Poirot, has created one of the great film detectives with his characterization of Christie's logical Belgian sleuth. The Paramount release of the EMI presentation, produced by John Brabourne and Richard Goodwin, can look forward to a long and steady run across the country. Outlook worldwide is equally optimistic.

A film such as this one begins with plot and Anthony Shaffer's adaptation of Christie's novel doesn't have a hole. When Ustinov reveals the killer in the final drawing room scene it comes as a complete surprise. Every one of the dozen characters floating down the Nile is a suspect. Every one on board could have and might have murdered Lois Chiles, the arrogant millionairess who has stolen her best friend's fiance.

In a time when so many pictures are carelessly plotted it's a pleasure to see one where the pieces fit together so well. Shaffer deserves high marks here.

Shaffer has also created a number of purposely exaggerated characters to complement Ustinov. There's Angela Lansbury's tipsy portrayal of a romantic novelist; Bette Davis as a stuffy and overbearing Washington socialite and Maggie Smith as her bitter companion; Jack Warden as an hysterical Swiss physician; I.S. Johar in a marvelously offbeat performance as the manager of the ship on which the murders take place; David Niven as Poirot's sidekick Colonel Race; and Jon Finch as a Marxist spouting rebel.

But the star is Ustinov and the penetrating mind of his character, Hercule Poirot. As played by Ustinov, Poirot is a gentleman with an urbane sense of humor and an inquisitive mind that misses nothing and remembers all. He is kind, thoughtful and learned. When presented with a case, however, add the qualities relentless, unerring and obsessed. His role is richly conceived and masterfully executed.

John Guillermin's conception of the mystery and his handling of this big production must also be applauded. All through the picture's 140 minutes, Guillermin and his producers have made sound choices.

First, by filming on location and letting the cameras roam on lush Egyptian settings. Also, especially when you consider how infrequently in "big budget" (especially disaster) films stars are seen in crowds or in long shots, it's refreshing to find the actual players against real backgrounds dressing up a larger scene.

Guillermin, in conjunction with Shaffer, has also developed a clever visual device to show how and why each of the suspects might be guilty. That is, by re-enacting the initial crime with the suspect committing it over Ustinov's narration. It works.

Other technical credits — and other performances, including Mia Farrow as the jilted lover, Olivia Hussey as Lansbury's daughter and Simon MacCorkindale as Farrow's fiance — are all first rate. At present time, Hollywood is rampant with sequels and remakes. Finally with "Death On The Nile," which is a followup to EMI's "Murder On The Orient Express," there's a sequel that's even better than the original. —Hege.

The Silent Witness
(COLOR)

Hollywood, Sept. 18.

An Independents International Films, Inc. release of a Screenpro Films production. Produced and directed by David W. Wolfe. Exec producers, Adam J. Otterbein, Peter M. Rinaldi. Screenplay, Ian Wilson, Henry Lincoln, David W. Rolfe; camera (color) Bahram Monocheri; editor, Peter Hollywood; sound, Wally Plummer. Reviewed at Aidikoff Screening Room, Los Angeles, Sept. 18, '78. (MPAA Rating: PG.) Running time: 55 MINS.

"The Silent Witness" is an interesting, intelligent — and almost persuasive — argument for the authenticity of the famed Holy Shroud of Turin, proclaimed for centuries as the linen in which Christ's body was wrapped when taken from the cross. But length and subject matter are problems for commercial release, unless paired with religious features or one of those other films purporting to prove strange things.

The issue, accepting by thousands on faith, is whether the faint visage and outline of a body on the cloth are actually the likeness of Jesus or an incredibly sophisticated hoax concocted in the Middle Ages by persons unknown.

At the start, producer-director David W. Rolfe examines both possibilities as he traces the history of the cloth from its first public display in France to its present resting place in Turin. Increasingly, though, Wolfe drops the objectivity to argue it's the real thing, based on latest examinations by highly trained scientists and historians of today.

He marshals his experts well. A former L.A. County pathologist, Dr. Robert Bucklin, examines the "body" and details the wounds, from sharp objects on the head (thorns?) to punctures of the wrists and feet (nails?), a stab wound in the side (spear?) and abrasions across the back (the cross?)

Another scientist traces pollen found in the cloth back to Jerusalem and two physicists fromt he U.S. Air Force Academy apply computerized techniques to study the image more closely while historians, some admittedly skeptical, discuss the possible history of the material and how it affected artistic renderings of Christ's likeness through history (i.e., Christ was usually drawn beardless before the sixth century when the shroud turned up in Constantinople. After that, he was generally shown with the beard evident in the cloth.)
— Har.

Somebody Killed Her Husband
(COLOR)

Farrah fares well, but her vehicle could use some repairs.

Hollywood, Sept. 21.

Columbia Pictures release of a Martin Poll production, in association with Melvin Simon. Stars Farrah Fawcett-Majors, Jeff Bridges. Directed by Lamont Johnson. Screenplay, Reginald Rose; camera (color-Panavision), Andrew Laszlo; editor, Barry Malkin; music, composed and adapted by Alex North; song, "Love Keeps Getting Stronger Every Day," music Neil Sedaka, lyrics Howard Greenfield, sung by Sadaka; production designer, Ted Haworth; art director, David Chapman, set decoration, Leslie Bloom; asst. director, Alex Hapsas; unit publicist, Ann Guerin. Reviewed at Burbank Studios, Burbank, Calif., Sept. 21, '78. (MPAA Rating: PG). Running time: **96 MINS.**

Jenny Moore	Farrah Fawcett-Majors
Jerry Green	Jeff Bridges
Ernest Van Santen	John Wood
Audrey Van Santen	Tammy Grimes
Hubert Little	John Glover
Helene	Patricia Elliott
Flora	Mary McCarty
Preston Moore	Laurence Guittard
Benjamin	Vincent Robert Santa Lucia
Frank Danziger	Beeson Carroll
Neighbor	Eddie Lawrence
Customer	Arthur Rhytis
Man in beret	Jean-Pierre Stewart
Lulu's mother	Terri DuHaime
Girl typist	Sands Hall
Night doorman	Joseph Culliton
Day Doorman	Dave Johnson
Employee	Melissa Ferris
Odd couple husband	Jeremiah Sullivan
Odd couple wife	Sloan Shelton
Indignant woman	Mary Alan Hokanson
Macy's night watchman	John Corcoran
Elf	Mark Haber

To get the most obvious question mark out of the way, Farrah Fawcett-Majors acquits herself admirably in the Martin Poll production of "Somebody Killed Her Husband," proving to be an adept actress who can range across comedy and drama. Unfortunately, more attention was paid to Fawcett-Majors' performance than to Lamont Johnson's turgid direction, turning a potentially enjoyable suspenser into a slow-paced non-mystery. With Majors on the marquee, boxoffice prospects are lucrative, but word of mouth should be a downer.

Reginald Rose has concocted a clever story about a Macy's toy department clerk (Jeff Bridges) who spots a leggy blonde customer (Fawcett-Majors) with child in tow. Out of this unlikely meeting emerges a quick-blossoming love affair, stemming from Fawcett-Majors' unhappy marriage to insurance exec Laurence Guittard.

The plot thickens when the lovers discover Guittard in the couple's fancy East Side apartment with a kitchen knife stuck in his back, a fate that soon befalls neighbors John Wood and Tammy Grimes, and phony detective Beeson Carroll. Bridges and Fawcett-Majors, the likeliest suspects, decide to solve the murders themselves, a painstaking process that occupies most of the film's 96 minutes, and seems much longer.

Since the actual culprit is obvious half way through the picture, director Johnson's task was to build as much excitement as possible about the climactic showdown. He doesn't do it. A scene with a body in a freezer, for example, is chillingly intriguing. But Johnson glosses over it with a quick cover shot. A hurried sense predominates, leaving Bridges and Fawcett-Majors rushing through the final chase scene involving giant Macy's thanksgiving parade figures as if the end titles were in pursuit.

Bridges fits comfortably into the role of the toy clerk who would rather be a children's book author, although at times he seems to be covering for Fawcett-Majors. But she needs no help — immensely attractive, she handles both the light and darker moments with ease. Together, they project a winning presence that gives "Somebody Killed Her Husband" most of its charm, a quality the film is long on.

Supporting cast is likewise top notch, especially Grimes and Wood as the nosy neighbors who are involved in the insurance-jewelry scheme that leads to their demise. Patricia Elliot excels as a sharp-tongued salesgirl with the hots for Bridges, but John Glover is much too unctuous as the private secretary with more secrets than he's willing to tell. Guittard is quite good in a small bit as the stuffed-shirt husband.

Ted Haworth's production design, structured completely around New York City locations, gives the film a velvety gloss, complemented by David Chapman's superb art direction, right down to the leopard skin steps in FFM's apartment. Alex North's score is more threatening than the on-screen action, and Andrew Laszlo's camerawork makes Fawcett-Majors look absolutely stunning.

When the design, players, script and technical credits all work in a production, but the film doesn't, the blame usually falls on the director.

—*Poll.*

Mon Premier Amour
(My First Love)
(FRENCH-COLOR)

Paris, Sept. 21.

Gaumont release of 7 Films-Gaumont-FR3 production. Stars Anouk Aimee. Written and directed by Elie Chouraqui, from the book by Jack Alain Leger. Camera (Eastmancolor). Bernard Zitzermann; editor, Marie-Josephe Yoyotte. Reviewed at Concorde, Paris, Sept. 16, '78. Running time. **100 MINS.**

Mother	Anouk Aimee
Son	Richard Berry
Father	Gabriele Ferzetti
Friend	Jacques Villeret
Girl	Nathalie Baye

Anouk Aimee, after a few years absence from the local scene, returned last year with a part in a Claude Lelouch pic and now in the first film of Lelouch's ex-assistant and present companion of Aimee. She believed in him, the property, and even produced as well as starred in this fairly glossy tearjerker by Elie Chouraqui.

Chouraqui is more reserved than his mentor, Lelouch, but this is still a series of impressions and rarely probes the theme of a 20-year-old son finally getting to know and love his still beautiful fortyish mother when she is dying of leukemia.

Richard Berry is an intense heavy-featured actor who may emerge effective with a less indulged role as the pampered son. Aimee is lively, lithe and she etches an acceptable character of a woman with few resources but her looks and her final realization of her love for her son.

impending death, and the son from a doctor, the two embark on a "getting-to-know you" series of dinners breaking the barriers of coldness by reminiscing. But the film too often sends them off on trips, hoked-up dinners and the final demise as she is mercifully released, or did she kill herself?, from her fear of losing her looks.

The needed dramatic probing, the sense of loss are not always there. However, director Chouraqui does show a fairly solid grasp of technique and with firmer scripts and more care in delineating the dramatic conflicts could be a needed more commercially-slanted filmmaker on the local scene.

There are some sacrificed characters, such as the flighty father who had left them long ago, played with incisiveness by Gabriele Ferzetti, and the boy's girl friend and best friend. Chances locally look acceptable with foreign outings possible for playoff on the theme and Aimee name. It just lacks the emotional pitch to make this sad tale more moving and poignant.

—*Mosk.*

The Boys From Brazil
(COLOR)

**Good, but not to the last drop.
B.O. uncertain.**

Hollywood, Sept. 13.

A 20th Century-Fox release of a Producer Circle Production, produced by Martin Richards and Stanley O'Toole. Exec producer, Robert Fryer. Directed by Franklin J. Schaffner. Features entire cast. Screenplay, Heywood Gould, based on novel by Ira Levin; camera (color), Henri Decae; editor, Robert E. Swink; sound, Derek Ball; music, Jerry Goldsmith; production design, Gil Parrondo; art direction, Peter Lamont; assistant director, Jose Lopez Rodero; costumes, Anthony Mendleson. Reviewed at the Samuel Goldwyn Theatre, Beverly Hills, Sept. 13, '78. (MPAA Rating: R.) Running time: **123 MINS.**

Josef Mengele	Gregory Peck
Ezra Lieberman	Laurence Olivier
Eduard Siebert	James Mason
Esther Lieberman	Lilli Palmer
Frieda Maloney	Uta Hagen
Barry Kohler	Steven Guttenberg
Sidney Beynon	Denholm Elliott
Mrs. Doring	Rosemary Harris
Henry Wheelock	John Dehner
David Bennett	John Rubinstein
Mrs. Curry	Anne Meara
Jack/Simon/Bobby	Jeremy Black
Strasser	David Hurst
Bruckner	Bruno Ganz
Harrington	Michael Gough

With two excellent antagonists in Gregory Peck and Lord Laurence Olivier, "The Boys From Brazil" presents a gripping, suspenseful drama for nearly all of its two hours — then lets go at the end and falls into a heap. Cast and interest in the Ira Levin novel from which it was adapted could spur boxoffice, but it could also meet the fate of most of these international intrigue pix of late.

In a fine shift from his usual roles, Peck plays the evil Josef Mengele, a real-life character who murdered thousands of Jews, including many children, carrying out bizarre genetic experiments at Auschwitz in Poland. Olivier, slipping completely into the role of an elderly Jewish gentleman, is the Nazi hunter who brings him to bay. (The real Mengele, if living has never been found.)

With the aid of James Mason, Peck is out to assassinate 94 fathers around the world. In a brief but lively part, Steven Guttenberg discovers the plot and tips Olivier, who sets out to find how the killings fit together. His search turns up three identical lads, all played menacingly by Jeremy Black, who are more than triplets.

What they are and whence they came are plausibly developed in Haywood Gould's script and director Franklin J. Schaffner builds the threatening menace well.

Eventually, Peck and Olivier come face to face, however, in a bloody sequence that turns silly as Peck keeps pouring bullets into the old man, who still manages to carry on a conversation. It's the best use of the flesh wound since the cowboy films of the '40s.

Worse still, though, is the last scene in the hospital, where Olivier totally loses his determined concerns and Schaffner and Gould lose the whole point of Levin's book.

Technical credits are all solid in the far ranging film, shot in several countries. Cast, too, is fie throughout, with limited appearances by Lilli Palmer as Olivier's sister and Uta Hagen as a Nazi war criminal.

— *Har.*

La Ballade Des Daltons
(The Ballad of the Daltons)
(FRENCH-ANIMATION-COLOR)

Paris, Sept. 26.

UA release of Dargaud Productions Films, Les Productions Rene Goscinny, Les Studios Idefix production. Written and directed by Rene Goscinny, Morris with directorial supervision by Henri Gruel, Pierre Watrin and script additions by Pierre Tchernia. Camera (Eastmancolor), Claude Poinis; editor, Gruel; music, Claude Bolling. Reviewed at Club 13, Paris, Sept. 15 '78. Running time: **82 MINS.**

Voices by Daniel Ceccaldi, Pierre Trabaud, Jacques Balutin, Bernard Haller, Roger Carel, Jacques Fabbri, Jacques Deschamps, Jacques Morel.

In this second film based on an oater comic strip, "Lucky Luke" is just passable and the ideas a bit repetitive. But with the shortage of sagers, it should be an okay moppet draw.

Lucky Luke is here involved with

the dastardly Dalton brothers who escape from prison to kill off the judge and jury who hung their uncle. They stand to inherit the uncle's money. Lucky has been stipulated to go along to verify the deaths.

Lucky had put them in prison in the first place. He manages to fake all the deaths and the Daltons end back in prison condemned by the judge and jury they tried to knock off. There are some good gags, but a dream sequence musical number is somewhat belabored. Pic is technically adequate.

Creator Rene Goscinny died during production and his company, Idefix, a big scale animation studio, has since closed down. He also made the successful "Asterix" animated entries about an ancient Gaul, the ancestors of the French, who defeated Roman invaders Popeye-style.

For a while contenders to the animation supremacy of the Walt Disney cartoons, Idefix is now out of the runnigg unless it is taken over and reopened. But Goscinny was the creative talent behind it. — *Mosk.*

Het Verloren Paradise
(Lost Paradise)
(BELGIAN-COLOR)

Brussels, Sept. 10.

Elan release of a Pierre Films Production. Produced by Jacqueline Pierreux. Stars Willeke Van Ammelrooy, Hugo Van den Berghe, Bert Andre. Directed by Harry Kumel. Screenplay, Harry Kumel, Kees Sengers; camera (Eastmancolor), Kenneth Hodges; editor, Suzanna Rosberg; art director, Philippe Graff; music, Roger Mores; sound, Henri Morelle; asst. directors, Dominique Janne, Maurice Noben. Reviewed at Cinema Marivaux, Brussels, Sept. 9, '78. Running time: **95 MINS.**
Pascale . . . . Willeke Van Ammelrooy
Benjamin Rolus . . . . Hugo Van den Berghe
Benjamin (child) . . . . Hans De Waegeneer
Jan Boel . . . . Bert Andre
Adeline . . . . Gella Allaert
Peterke . . . . Stephen Windros
Marie-Louise . . . . Blanka Heirman
Surveyor . . . . Jos Kennis
De Cat . . . . Serge Henri Valcke
Nora De Cat . . . . Nora Barten
Roelofs . . . . Alfred Van Kuyck
Sus . . . . Carlos Van Lanckere
Zulma . . . . Martha Woumans
Rural policeman . . . . Willy De Swaef
Minister . . . . Raf Reymen
Secretary . . . . Gerda Lindekens
Man in waiting room . . . . Nolle Versyp

Harry Kumel calls his new film a love story with a political twist. Perhaps it is both, having ingredients of two genres, but, above all, it is a story of village bickerings and intrigues, not always believable because director-script writer was never noted for subtlety and he is here as heavy-handed as usual, hence a lack of dramatic flair which hampers dramatic impact. He projects his conflict against an interesting background but, in underlining every intention twice, situations are too often deprived of credibility. One has an impression

of artificiality, of people being puppets instead of human beings. The finale is almost a caricature of what it depicts. In fact, here is a film where every move, every turn is predictable a mile in advance.

It concerns projected construction of a secondary highway from which a little Flemish village might profit. Shortest way would be through the vast domain inhabited by the mayor who has established there sort of a bird sanctuary. Quite naturally he has nixed this plan and having the right connections at the Ministry, everything seems in his favor. Instead, some houses inhabited by modest families will be demolished to make way for said highway.

The village has a loud-mouthed heavy whose ambition is to become burgomaster in turn and he leads the revolt. But, officially, he seems due to be defeated. He then brings in a Brussels prostitute with whom he has been having an affair and who happens to be the burgomaster's cousin, and the plot succeeds too well, heading to a showdown in which two corpses attest the vanity of wordly things. Peace returns to the village, which now has a new mayor.

Main flaw is that there seems to be too much of everyting: the hero is too incredibly naive, heavy too sneering, strumpet of a too novelettish conception, housekeeper too conniving. Stilted dialog helps neither. —*Flor.*

Trocadero Bleu Citron
(Trocadero Blue and Yellow)
(FRENCH-COLOR)

Paris, Sept. 21.

WB-Col release of Madeleine Films, SFP, Films De Gueville production. Features entire cast. Written and directed by Michael Schock. Camera (Eastmancolor), Bernard Laug; editor, Georges Klotz; music, Alec Costadinos. Reviewed at Colisee, Paris, Sept. 15, '78. Running time, **90 MINS.**
Mother . . . . Anny Duperey
Phil . . . . Lionel Melet
Caroline . . . . Berangere De Lagatineau
Politician . . . . Henri Garcin

France is light on moppet-slanted pix and this tale of a little boy smitten with a girl of his age, 10, on a background of skateboarding and adult nearness or misunderstanding, might find smooth playoff at home. Foreign chances are mainly for kid appeal.

A liberated mother bringing up her little boy alone is also a photographer and most understanding. When the boy tells her of his love for a little girl it is the mother who concocts a plan for breaking down the girl's imperious, politically-active parents and get the two together.

Kids avoid preciosity, but cannot quite give this the comic and even poignant balance aimed at. Killing

off the boy's dog is more an interlude than dramatically necessary. There are some refreshing skateboard scenes. Title is the place where most of the skateboarding takes place in Paris.

Adults play foils for the kids, which is right, and there are enough skateboard segs and moppet shenanigans for the kids. It is the kind of film that adults can sit through too which is a plus for its playoff future. —*Mosk.*

Shraga Katan
(Little Man)
(ISRAEL-COLOR)

Tel Aviv, Sept. 13.

Erez Films production. Produced by Baruch Ellah, Executive producer, Mirha Sharpstein. Stars Zeev Revach, Niza Shaul. Directed by Zeev Revach. Screenplay, Hillel Mittelpunkt and Zeev Revach; camera (color) Gad Danzig; editor, Zion Avramian; music; Shem-tov Levi; production designer; Sara Vinner; sound: Itamar Ben Yaakov. Reviewed Tel Aviv, Sept. 16, '78. Running time: **90 MINS.**
Cast: Zeev Revach, Niza Shaul, Zahi Noy, Yossi Karmon, Izhak Hizkia, Hille Mittelpunkt, Rafael Klatchtkin, Liora Tikozky, Lia Dulitzkaya, Ilan Dar.

Zeev Revach, whose reputation until now has been mostly as a lightweight comic relying on facial distortions, loud jokes and obvious gags in films directed by himself or by others, is changing wavelength. This time, he goes out of his way to make a personal statement about a subject close to his heart: interrelations between Western and Oriental Jews in Israel.

Moroccan-born Ruach says his story is based on facts, which happened to coincide with a play performed some time ago by the Haifa Municipal Theatre. The actor-director combined between fact and fiction, with Hillel Mittelpunkt assisting in the script and taking a lead in the film itself. Film recounts the story of an easy girl, a sometime singer, who goes on one night to entertain a unit of reserve soldiers. She begins to sing pitifully and ends up, far more successfully, with all five members of the unit. A couple of months later the five are called back to account for the girl's pregnancy and are ordered to select the one who will shoulder the responsibility. But the girl doesn't like the chosen fall guy, she runs away, comes to town and tries to infiltrate the life of the one who seemed most sympathetic to her cause. Because of her he misses a chance to marry a wealthy girl and having of a career. But, finally, he realizes that the rich bride and the fancy job wouldn't have suited him anyway, and he marries the pregnant girl.

Revach, playing the only member of the unit who is prepared to stand up like a man a take his medicine, is seconded by Izhak Hizkia

and author Mittelpunkt, as his partners in guilt. Niza Shaul, who has to deal with the more complex character of a floozy turned victim of society seems rather awkward and doesn't get too much help from the script.

Commercial prospects are chancy here, as Revach admirers expect him to be funny, which he certainly isn't, this time. If it will overcome initial dismay, it may find favor with the local public, who has shown in the past his appreciation for sobstories with ethnical overtones. —*Edna.*

The Wiz
(COLOR)

For the young in heart and deaf of ear. Should be a big one.

Universal Pictures release of a Motown Production. Executive producer, Ken Harper. Producer, Rob Cohen. Stars Diana Ross. Directed by Sidney Lumet. Screenplay, Joel Schumacher, based on play, "The Wiz," book by William F. Brown, and book, "The Wonderful Wizard of Oz," by L. Frank Baum; editor, Dede Allen; camera (Technicolor), Oswald Morris; special visual effects, Albert Whitlock; production design and costumes, Tony Walton; songs, Charlie Smalls; music adapted and supervised by Quincy Jones. Reviewed at Loews State II, New York, Sept. 29, '78. (MPAA Rating: G.) Running time: **133 MINS.**

Dorothy . . . . Diana Ross
Scarecrow . . . . Michael Jackson
Tin Man . . . . Nipsey Russell
Glinda . . . . Lena Horne
The Wiz . . . . Richard Pryor
Cowardly Lion . . . . Ted Ross
Evillene . . . . Mabel King

Universal can stop worrying. It looks as if they are in the enviable position of having a big, rousing, juicy hit on their hands that should enthrall the young in heart (albeit deafening them at the same time). Frank Baum would never recognize his simple little story in this fantastically blown-up version, but the heart of his tale — that a person must find what he's searching for within himself — is still there.

Whether this noisiest of all filmusicals will encompass every type of market remains to be seen, but certainly the overflow crowds at the special New York preview which necessitated a second showing included every age group and it roared, stamped, applauded and otherwise demonstrably showed approval after every one of the numerous production numbers and at the lengthy picture's end. The cast is virtually flawless but, when all is said and done, it's the combination of Oswald Morris's cinematography, the special visual effects of Albert Whitlock and Tony Walton's production design and costumes that linger longest in the memory.

Director Sidney Lumet has created what amounts to a love letter to the city of New York, which he equates with Oz. Even his frequent jibes at the Big Apple's shortcomings (off-duty cabs, uncollected garbage, even seamy 8th Avenue) are done with a sense of humor rather than caustic social comment. Settings include stylized versions of the New York Public Library (from which the Cowardly Lion evolves), the Chrysler Building (or Buildings as there are many of them), the Emerald City, surprisingly like the World Trade Center Plaza, the afore-said 8th Avenue, and even the sun comes up as a Big Apple.

The real-life sequences, from the beginning Thanksgiving dinner in Harlem, melt easily into the splendidly designed production numbers, as the dialog equally blends smoothly with the numerous tunes. Charlie Small's songs have been augmented with several by music supervisory Quincy Jones but all the familiar airs are there, especially "Ease On Down The Road" and "Don't Bring Me No Bad News."

Diana Ross, believable as a 24-year-old Harlem school teacher, is always in key with the mood, whether it calls for shyness, gaiety, courage or simply cutting up. Vocally, she's superb but, surprise, 'she also dances with all the abandon of an Alvin Ailey protege. One of the loudest receptions occurred when Lena Horne, looking young enough to play Dorothy, finally appears for her single but important song.

Of the supporting players and, despite their billing, that's what they amount to — Richard Pryor's Wiz (very briefly seen), Ted Ross's Lion and Mabel King's Evillene make the heaviest impressions. Nipsey Russell is fun as the Tin Man but Michael Jackson, though vocally great, needs more acting exposure. He appears to be over conscious of the camera all of the time but moves beautifully and should be seen more.

The entire production is also a tribute to the ability of New York production to handle any size future project. The Astoria Studios would seem to be the equal of anything outside Gotham, especially when the first-class technicians used for "The Wiz" are turned loose there.

The only reservation is that older people may be repelled by the turned-up volume, enhanced by the brilliantly clear Dolby Stereo sound, not just in major numbers, but throughout the film. It has to be the highest decibel film ever made and some of the more senior members of the preview audience were seen holding their fingers in their ears. Maybe, after all the initial furor has died down, something closer to Muzak might be found for more sensitive ears. —*Robe.*

Bully

Filmed stageshow done well, but for limited audience.

Hollywood, Sept. 28.

A Maturo, Image Corp. presentation, produced by Sam Maturo and Mel Marshall. Directed by Peter H. Hunt. Written by Jerome Alden. Camera (Color), Ken Pailus; editor, Terry Green; sound, Larry Stevens; set and costume design, John Conklin. Reviewed at The Hollywood Screening Room, Hollywood, Sept. 28, '78. (MPAA Rating: PG.) Running time: **120 MINS.**

Theodore Roosevelt . . . . . James Whitmore

As before with Will Rogers and Harry Truman, James Whitmore puts on an extraordinary one-man stage show as Theodore Roosevelt in "Bully," taped at the Ahmanson Theatre and transferred to film. But it's still a stage show and that will limit it's appeal to a specialized film audience.

From the moment Whitmore first appears running down the center aisle, "Bully" makes no attempt to be more than a film record of a legit evening. (Though the advertising showing Whitmore outdoors wielding pistol and saber suggests a broader scope.) And all of the drawbacks reflect the format rather than the performer.

Though the physical resemblance is artificial, Whitmore envelopes Roosevelt's blustering personality well, capturing his love of the outdoors, political roughhousing and devotion to duty and manliness.

Since Roosevelt was not as humorous as Rogers or Truman, Whitmore has fewer laughs here to pace the dramatic stretches and there's a bit of sameness that wears down after two hours. But there are some beautiful scenes, nonetheless, all the more remarkable because of the rigorous conditions of the extended dialog, captured in two days of taping.

Technically, there are many flaws, mainly because the equipment is picking up that which a legit audience is rarely aware of. Whitmore's breathing, for example, naturally becomes labored in sections after some vigorous stage business and the mike catches every wheeze, spoiling the effect of some of what he's saying. Closeups also magnify the physical differences at times.

Overall, though, film successfully presents a long visit on film with Theodore Roosevelt, one of our most interesting presidents. And that's what it intends to do. —*Har.*

Goin' South
(COLOR)

Except for Nicholson's name value, 'Goin' South' is gone.

Hollywood, Sept. 26.

A Paramount Pictures release. Produced by Harry Gittes and Harold Schneider. Features entire cast. Directed by Jack Nicholson. Screenplay, John Herman Shaner, Al Ramus, Charles Shyer, Alan Mandel; camera (color), Nestor Almendros; editors, Richard Chew, John Fitzgerald Beck; sound, Arthur Rochester; assistant director, Michael Daves; production design, Toby Carr Rafelson; costumes, William Ware Theiss; music, Van Dyke Parks, Perry Botkin, Jr. Reviewed at Paramount Studios, Sept. 26, '78. (MPAA Rating: PG.) Running time: **101 MINS.**

Henry Moon . . . . Jack Nicholson
Julia Tate . . . . Mary Steenburgen
Towfield . . . . Christopher Lloyd
Hector . . . . John Belushi
Hermine . . . . Veronica Cartwright
Sheriff Kyle . . . . Richard Bradford
Big Abe . . . . Jeff Morris
Hog . . . . Danny DeVito
Coogan . . . . Tracey Walter
Polty . . . . Gerald H. Reynolds
Mrs. Anderson . . . . Luana Anders
Anderson . . . . George W. Smith
Mrs. Haber . . . . Lucy Lee Flippin
Haber . . . . Ed Begley Jr.
Mrs. Warren . . . . Maureen Byrnes
Warren . . . . B.J. Merholz
Parson Weems . . . . Britt Leach
Florence . . . . Georgia Schmidt

Jack Nicholson playing Gabby Hayes is interesting, even amusing at times, but Hayes was never a leading man, which "Goin' South" desperately needs. Nicholson's name as both star and director will attract some business. But after that, "Goin' South" will probably be gone.

Picture starts off promisingly enough with Nicholson as a hapless outlaw who makes it across the border but the posse cheats and comes across after him, causing his horse to faint. Taken back to hang, Nicholson still has full control of the film in front and behind the camera. His old gang drops in to say goodbye and his girlfriend, beautifully played throughout by Veronica Cartwright, whispers tearfully, "You was the best I ever had, except for maybe that circus fella."

On his way to the gallows, Nicholson discovers an unordinary county ordinance that would allow him to go free if picked for marriage by a maiden lady in town. Despite his hurried-up courtships, nobody in the crowd wants him until an old lady (Georgia Schmidt) calls out at the last moment. But she drops dead before the vows and Nicholson is heading for the rope again.

Up to now, "Goin' South" is still going strong. But here it stops as lovely young Mary Steenburgen steps out of the crowd and agrees to marry the bearded, dirty horse-thief, though she could obviously have her pick of the town's finest.

Why she should do this is never satisfactorily established in the script carrying the names of four writers. Ostensibly, it's to get the manpower to help her mine her property for gold before the railroad takes over. But a simple hired hand could have done that, not to mention a boyfriend or husband with better credentials for hardwork than the outlaw. Even this slim premise could have been accepted, though, if the Nicholson-Steenburgen marriage had maintained the fanciful flair of the film's initial moments. But it never jells, as Nicholson continues to sputter and chomp, acting more like her grandfather than a handsome roue out to overcome her virginity.

He does that, of course, but again her reason for weakening is unclear and a subsequent husbandly rape scene confuses the tone further. (Later, Steenburgen wants to be tied up again, which today's feminists may have something to say about.) This largely uninteresting marital contest goes on against the interruptions of a jealous deputy sheriff, well-played by Christopher Lloyd, and his sidekick John Belushi, whose role is briefer than his billing might suggest, and the greed of the old gang.

·Cameraman Nestor Almendros' work is excellent, as are other tech credits generally. The cast is good and Steenburgen's film debut shows much promise.

But Nicholson directing Nicholson is the ultimate downfall. —*Har.*

Autopsy
((ITALIAN-COLOR))

A couple of cuts below average.

A Joseph Brenner presentation, produced by Leonardo Pescarolo. Directed by Armando Crispini. No writing credits. Features entire cast. (Color). Carlo Carlini. Stars Mimsy Farmer, Barry Primus, Ray Lovelock, Angela Goodwin. (No other credits available). Reviewed at Pix Theatre, Hollywood, Sept. 26, '78. (MPAA rating: R.) Running time: 125 MINS.

Before the first title in "Autopsy," (American distrib did not know original Italian title-Ed.) a fellow burns himself alive; a man puts a plastic bag over his head and jumps into the river; a father sits with two murdered babies and then turns a machine gun on himself; and a girl slashes her wrist.

Then it starts getting good.

Mimsy Farmer works in a morgue, surrounded by bodies and parts of bodies. But she's tired and thinks the naked fellow getting his skull sawed open is smiling at her and the beautiful naked girl is doing dirty deeds with another corpse.

But she also has a home life, surrounded by pictures of bodies and parts of bodies. Since she's more relaxed, however, these bodies do not do dirty deeds. However, the beautiful redhead from upstairs drops down to borrow an envelope and she's kind of sexy herself. But the phone rings and she rushes off mysteriously.

But she turns up soon at Mimsy's work, with an eye hanging out, a lot of teeth missing and other signs of a self-inflicted gunshot wound. But the redhead's brother, the priest, believes she was murdered and that Mimsi's dad did it. But Farmer finds the small injection mark below the body's breast and says, "I'm sure dad didn't do it. He hates needles."

For some reason, perhaps a busman's holiday, Mimsy goes to a horror museum, where there are more pictures of bodies and parts of bodies — even worse than those at home — and gets herself locked in a room with a wax dummy that blows its head off with a shotgun.

Oh, yes, Mimsy has a boyfriend who's a photographer and he shows her pictures of bodies, too. But these are bodies really doing dirty deeds. And Mimsy gets turned on, but keeps thinking of corpses while cuddling and this interferes with their love life.

The caretaker who saw the redhead that fateful night gets hung in the toilet and Mimsy finds the body, which upsets her because she is not used to bodies that are still in one piece with their clothes on.

Then dad falls — or was he thrown? — from the balcony and suspicion shifts. Is it the priest? The boyfriend? The business partner? That other lady who draws pictures of bodies and parts of bodies who loved father? Or is it Mimsy herself?

No, it is not Mimsy, who looks on in horror as the killer and the hero wrestle atop the cathedral. That was after she and the hero got their clothes back on after she was left to die in the bathroom.

No wonder her love life is lousy. —*Har.*

The Big Fix
(COLOR)

Richard Dreyfuss a fine contemporary gumshoe in a comedy-thriller with big outlook.

Hollywood, Sept. 27.

A Universal Pictures release, produced by Carl Borack and Richard Dreyfuss. Stars Richard Dreyfuss. Directed by Jeremy Paul Kagan. Screenplay, Roger L. Simon, based on his novel; camera (color), Frank Stanley; production designer, Robert F. Boyle; editor, Patrick Kennedy; costumes, Edith Head; music, Bill Conti; art director, Raymond Brandt; set decorator, Mary Ann Biddle; sound, David Ronne; assistant director, Jon C. Andersen. Reviewed at Universal Studios, Universal City, Sept. 27, '78. (MPAA Rating: PG). Running time: 108 MINS.

Moses Wine	Richard Dreyfuss
Lila	Susan Anspach
Suzanne	Bonnie Bedelia
Sam Sebastian	John Lithgow
Alora	Ofelia Medina
Spitzler	Nicolas Coster
Eppis	F. Murray Abraham
Oscar Procari, Sr.	Fritz Weaver
Jorge	Jorge Cervera, Jr.
Jacob	Michael Hershewe
Aunt Sonya	Rita Karlin

In "The Big Fix" Richard Dreyfuss delivers what is for him a particularly relaxed and confident performance as Moses Wine, the 1970's answer to Philip Marlowe, Lew Archer and Sam Spade. The marquee value of Dreyfuss, coupled with the real costar of the film, Roger Simon's clever, funny and convoluted screenplay, makes the Universal release a surefire b.o. bet.

Simply as a detective thriller, "The Big Fix" has strong appeal. Like any good piece of private-eye fiction, Simon's construction is so multi-layered it practically requires charts and scorecard to track. The studio's plot synopsis runs seven single-spaced pages, and as a centerpiece it has a tough, cynical, intelligent detective — an independent man with a rathole for an apartment, a personal life in need of some investigating and a full supply of wisecracks.

So far this could be Philip Marlowe. But Moses Wine's character has a very contemporary twist. A former Berkeley radical who left his idealism behind on the college campus, he now scrapes out a living and supports himself, two children and makes alimony payments to a wife involved in the latest self-help therapies, by spying on others for small fees.

Better than any recent film, "The Big Fix" captures the feeling of what it was like to grow up in the turbulent '60s. And no wonder — Dreyfuss, director Jeremy Paul Kagan, Simon and Carl Borack, who coproduced with Dreyfuss, all are products of that era. They are a group of young and very talented craftsmen and artists and their look at the '60s from a contemporary vantagepoint is engaging because it has a sense of humor about it.

Briefly, the film finds Dreyfuss employed by Susan Anspach, like Dreyfuss a former campus activist, gone straight as a campaign worker for a gubernatorial candidate. Someone is trying to sabotage the election by distributing leaflets linking the middle of the road candidate with radical elements.

Dreyfuss is a natural for the case because he knew people in the radical movement. He takes it only because of the money — like any good private eye he has no use for politicians or idealogues — and because he still has a soft spot for Anspach. The trail leads through Los Angeles — from the Beverly Hills mansions and social clubs to the Mexican barrios. There are murders, a reunion with an Abbie Hoffman-type radical and a resolution with oedipal overtones.

Kagan's direction is nicely paced, starting off slow with the development of Dreyfuss' character and then speeding up as the plot complications mount and the picture moves towards a resolution. Kagan has also elicited good supporting performances from a mostly young cast.

The Dreyfuss-Borack production benefits from the combination of youthful bravura and old line experienced technical talent provided by Frank Stanley's camera work, Edith Head's costumes and Robert F. Boyle's production design. It has a good feel for the location and the picture is well cast.

With Hollywood very quietly exploding with thrillers for the Christmas season, "The Big Fix" figures as one of the best, and Moses Wine as one of the more memorable sleuths. Simon has written other Wine novels and his next," "Peking Duck," is in the talking stages for Dreyfuss and Borack. It would be a reunion to look forward to. —*Hege.*

No Longer Alone
(COLOR)

Sincere religion drama that tells a touching story & never preaches. Could find an audience outside the religious market.

Hollywood, Sept. 22.

A World Wide Pictures release and production. Produced by Frank R. Jacobson; executive producer, William F. Brown. Directed by Nicholas Webster. Features entire cast. Screenplay, Lawrence Holben, based on Joan Winmill Brown's autobiography; camera (color), Michael Reed; editor, J. Michael Hooser; production design, John Lageu; costumes, Klara Kerpin; music, Tedd Smith; assistant director, Ed Harper; sound, Michael Strong. Reviewed at the Samuel Goldwyn Studios, Los Angeles, Sept. 22, '78. (MPAA rating: PG). Running time: 99 MINS.

Joan Winmill	Belinda Carroll
A.E. Matthews	Roland Culver
Alan Richards	James Fox
Lord Home	Wilfrid Hyde-White
William Douglas Home	Simon Williams
Miss Godfrey	Helen Cherry
Joan, age 12	Samantha Gates
Joan, age 6	Karen Dines
Robert Kennedy	Gordon Devol
Producer	Reginald Marsh
Bruce	John Alkin
Lady Home	Mary Kerridge
Joan's father	Robert Rietty
Elaine	Helen Cotterill
Basil	John Clive
Grandmother	Vivienne Burgess

"No Longer Alone" is a sincere account of the psychic sufferings of a British actress on the brink of suicide who finds relief by turning to God. While the film has a religious theme, it avoids preaching. It has a dramatic story to tell of a troubled woman, British actress Joan Winmill, honestly and effectively portrayed by Belinda Carroll, and it tells it well. The World Wide Picture release produced by Frank J. Jacobson and directed by Nicholas Webster should find a modest audience outside the religious market.

The script was adapted by Lawrence Holben from Winmill's autobiography. Before attaining some fame in the theatre Winmill suffered an unhappy childhood and numerous disappointments — the early death of her mother, her grandmother's breakdown, the death of a close cousin and a brief romance with the late Robert Kennedy.

Much of the story is told through flashbacks. Besides the scenes with Kennedy which suffer froom the usual problems of trying to depict a recent famous historical figure, the recollections are well drawn and often moving. Especially good performances are elicited from the two child actresses, Samantha Gates and Karen Dines, who play Winmill as a girl.

Technical credits are strong with Michael Reed's photography deserving of special praise.

World Wide is planning a national release of this film later in the month accompanied by a big tv campaign. It's too bad that those ads attempt to cash in on Winmill's association with Kennedy, which according to this film, was just one part of her life. The picture has a lot more to offer than a short romance with a Kennedy. —*Hege.*

The Dragon Lives
(HONG KONG-COLOR)

(Bruce Lee, or is it Li?)

Hollywood, Sept. 19.

A Film Ventures International release of a Herman Cohen presentation. Produced by C.H. Wong. Directed by Singloy Wang. Features entire cast. Screenplay, Wang, Yi Kwan; camera (color), Chen Wing, Li Wom Chung; editor, Mike Harris. No other credits available. Reviewd at Vine Theatre, Hollywood, Sept. 18, '78. (MPAA Rating: R). Running time: **90 MINS.**
Cast: Bruce Li, Caryn White, Betty Chen, Ernest Curtis.

To clear themselves of apparent legal liability, the producers of "The Dragon Lives" place the usual fictional disclaimer right under the main title card on the film. But **pic goes on to reveal a hammed-up version of Bruce Lee's life in almost every detail, right down to a wife named Linda and an (unnamed) job as a chauffeur on a popular American vidseries.**

Lawyers for widow Linda Lee may thus take more interest in the film than audiences, who seem to have lost their taste for such kung fu exercises. But "The Dragon Lives" does feature some well-staged martial arts activities amidst the worst dubbing seen this side of the China Sea.

For the most part, "Dragon" is laughable, especially in its depiction of so-called American locales, obviously set in Hong Kong. Long Beach, for instance, is represented by a Hong Kong gym with lots of Coca Cola signs plastered up, and a couple of rows of American teenagers. It doesn't seem to matter that all the rest of the participants are Chinese, or that most of the dubbed dialog is in British accents — Coke is all-American, right?

It's in Long Beach that Lee (played by look-alike Bruce Li) gets his big break by knocking out heavyweight champ Ernest Curtis, a hulking guy who looks genuinely mean. But his career kind of fizzles, as director and co-scripter Singloy Wang get hung up in showing how prejudicial Hollywood film-makers are about Chinese.

With all these sociological comments, the kung fu action gets pushed in the background, although there are a couple of dramatic battles well into the pic. Sound effects appear to have been made with the aid of a big piece of tin and a couple of two-by-fours — the cracking noises regularly precede the blows themselves.

There are a plethora of shots that don't match, characters appear in consecutive frames dressed differently, and flashbacks are in black and white, but then the audience for these pix is among the least discriminating, a fact of which producers are obviously well aware.

Less bloody and gory than many of its ilk (a factor that could hurt at the boxoffice), "The Dragon Lives" is destined for quick playoff. — *Poll.*

Skin Deep
(NEW ZEALAND-COLOR)

Auckland, Sept. 20.

Phase Three Films (John Maynard) production. Stars Ken Blackburn, Grant Tilly, Deryn Cooper, Alan Jervis. Directed by Geoff Steven. Screenplay, Piers Davies, Roger Horrocks, Steven; camera (Gevacolor) Leon Narby; sound, Graham Morris. Reviewed at Amalgamated Theatrette, Auckland, Sept. 19, '78. Running time, 103 MINS.
Boxing Manager . . . . Jim Macfarlane
Bob Warner . . . . Ken Blackburn
Vic Shaw . . . . Alan Jervis
Phil Barrett . . . . Grant Tilly
Mike Campbell . . . . Bill Johnson
Les Simpson . . . . Arthur Wright
Policeman . . . . Kevin J. Wilson
Alice Barrett . . . . Glenis Leverstam
Sandra Ray . . . . Deryn Cooper
Motel Manageress . . . . Wendy Macfarlane
Stephen Douglas . . . . Bob Harvey

Though world boxoffice cannot be predicted, "Skin Deep" looks a lively commercial entry for any market. Certainly, as a work of art it is New Zealand's long-awaited breakthrough film.

It is a soberly-paced but absorbing tale of a small country town which is making its bid, via a publicity campaign, to attract tourists and industry. When a masseuse is imported from the nearest big city and Vic's Gym becomes a massage parlor and sauna the inevitable happens. Many local males are anxious to try the parlor-style sex that previously they had only read about, and the respectable matrons pressure the police to shutter the den of vice.

An excellent script and three-dimensional characters flesh out this skeleton. Central to the theme and payoff is Sandra Ray (Deryn Cooper), the masseuse who, though she still emits plenty of erotic voltage, has had enough of the sex side of the business. She takes the job in the small town because she thought that there men would only be interested in straight massage. Helped by a script that drops the right sympathetic hints about the lady's private life, tactfully getting the audience on her side. Cooper turns in a near-flawless performance as a disillusioned woman who learns that even hicks expect more than a health-giving rubdown.

Leading the parade of straying husbands on the prowl for parlor extras is Bob Warner, (Ken Blackburn) chairman of the fund-raising group, the town's leading businessman and the first to run for cover when the squeeze comes on the massage establishment. Blackburn is winningly smooth in the role, and it is one of the film's many authentic strokes that he, displaying the crazy values of a man hellbent for extra-marital thrills, is given a wife who is younger and sexier than the lady at the parlor.

Grant Tilly is convincing as an upright accountant who runs amuk and sparks the final showdown. Here, too, the essential domestic details are economically sketched in. A few scenes with his wife, some lines of a dialog and his actions become only too humanly credible.

"Skin Deep" was brought in on a tiny budget (a reported NZ$180,-000) but no cost-cutting is visible in any department, least of all in the highly professional production detail. Almost half the coin was put up by the new Film Commission, its first investment. No better launch for a fledgling film industry can be imagined. —*Dub.*

New York Fest

Gates Of Heaven
(COLOR)

Produced and directed by Errol Morris. Camera (color), Ned Burgess; supervising editor, Charles Laurence Silver; editor, Morris; sound, Jay Miracle; production manager, George Csicsery. No other credits provided. Reviewed at the N.Y. Film Festival, Sept. 29, '78. Running Time: **82 MINS.**

Ostensibly a documentary about the establishment of a pet cemetery in California, "Gates of Heaven" only takes that as a jumping off point to underscore a number of subjects. It's about American small business, the rise of the technocrats, the fall of the patriarchs and families. Or, as Errol Morris told a N.Y. film fest press conference, "It's about desperation."

Pic, which was booked on an all-animal program almost as comic relief, is anything but silly. It skates across the twin poodles of craziness. Either we render animals into glop and fail to recognize the atrocity. Or we give them the last rites of life in a kind of pet theology that satirizes custom and religion to an embarrassing degree.

This docu, the last three cans of which were rushed into the projection booth after the first reel had already begun, is peopled by American types. It begins with the overall-clad humanist who dreams of starting a pet cemetery to reward man's most faithful friends. He fails and is forgotten. Morris also introduces a tallow manufacturer who sees himself in the forefront of the recycling business.

Nobody says "die." All the critters "pass on," as in the case of an unfortunate cat that snuck into the clothes dryer and stepped into oblivion. Morris employs almost Diane Arbus-like closeups of simple people explaining how it is they came to bury Caesar, which in this case, is a dog, as well as to praise him.

The film passes on, so to speak, from the sentimentalist to the Harberts family that finally establishes the cemetery for the loved ones in the California hills. Here Morris shifts focus. It doesn't matter what the business, no enterprise could withstand this kind of scrutiny without revealing the illogic that makes it go. It's simply easier to achieve irony by forcing on pet cemeteries.

The mind is assaulted with images of the burlesque of values. A neo-American gothic couple blubbers over photos of Trooper, their departed shepherd, opening its presents on Christmas morning. A funeral director comforts the bereaved. Finally, the epitaph "God is Love — Backwards It's Dog" inscribed on one of the many photo-bearing tombstones overwhelms all reason.

Morris nicely limns the development of the American family and its role in business by studying the Harberts. Cal Harbert, the father, is soldier-like in marshaling his pride in establishing an institution that will live on for hundreds of years. The older son is a burnt-out insurance salesman who sits in front of his pool and spouts more junk thought than McDonald's makes hamburgers. He is a devotee of W. Clement Stone, whose pic he keeps on his desk. And the younger son is a mystic running from his feelings, turning himself into a technocrat.

While Morris goaded the press with the assertion that people form relationships with other people because they can't form relationships with pets, it's plain that there is a despair running through this docu. It's despair turned into humor and anger.

"Gates" is pretty unsparing in letting its people reveal their stupidity. It allows them to ramble on, disgorging their impossibly warped theology which meets the Little Goodie Two Shoes & Adolph Eichman spectrum test for the banality of evil.

While Morris undoubtedly showed them the camera, it's clear that his subjects are his victims. As in the cast of the Maysles Brothers' look at the Beales, the victims may not agree, but the signature of a cuckoo may not be worth much on a release. Quite possibly no journalist, whether print or photo, can capture truth without betraying the subject.

And while "Gates" may have lots of grave matters on its mind, it doesn't make it as a boxoffice draw. Pic might jump to tv, where, like New York City's domestic critters, it should clean up in late night time periods. —*Jac.*

Affinita Elettive
(Elective Affinities)
(ITALIAN-COLOR)

An RAI-Instituto Luce production. Directed by Gianni Amico. Screenplay, by Amico, Marco Melani and I. Alighiero Chiusano, from the novel by Johann Wolfgang von Goethe; camera (color), Tonino Nardi; editing, Roberto Perpignani; sound, Claudio Maielli, Mario Bramonti, Remo Ugolinelli; music, Nicola Samale, Giuseppe Mazzuca; art direction, Giorgio Bertolini; costumes, Lina Nerli Taviani. Features entire cast. Reviewed at the N.Y. Film Festival, Sept. 29, '78. Running time: **135 MINS.**
Ottilia . . . . Francesca Archibugi
Edoardo . . . . Paolo Graziosi
The Captain . . . . Nino Castelnuovo
Charlotte . . . . Veronica Lazar
Mittler . . . . Edoardo Torricella
Architect . . . . Federic Pacifici
Teacher . . . . Ellis Dona
Nanny . . . . Luana Potrich
Baronness . . . . Lucia Poli
The doctor . . . . Bruno Cattaneo

Not destined for easy commercial playoff Stateside, Gianni Amico's "Elective Affinities" is based on Goethe's novel of the late 18th Century. It's an overlong, obvious exercise that has an operatic plot without the mitigation of music. Much sturm und drang, chest-beating, and rolling clouds in a failed fairy tale.

Costume dramas as a rule are useful in sneaking up on the audience which has lowered its defenses due to the lack of current social cues. Amico found in the Goethe work a chance to address questions of family, sex, and morality in the house of an aristocrat.

The model for the action is contained in the parlor-room explanation of then-current physics, with elective affinities being the final refinement on the push and pull of forces that affect the combination of elements. So too with relationships.

There are many people, some of whom are hard to keep track of until well into the film, wandering thorugh the woods, or setting up a new domicile, that combine and chafe. Veronica Lazar as the older woman who tries to hold fast against the forces of love is quite striking onscreen, but no one can really overcome the pained enterprise of the story or direction.

Overall production work is good, with some singularly nice visuals, occasionally marred by uncalled for hand-held camera work or seemingly intentional muddied colors. While the press audience accorded it applause at its conclusion, the pic drew a few snickers for its howling winds, blowing leaves and the like, all of which underscore the failure of presentation.

Not much to look forward to at the doemstic boxoffice, "Elective Affinities" is for opera-goers a little on the deaf side. —*Jac.*

San Sebastian Fest

Smyateniye chuvstv
(Confused Feelings)
(RUSSIAN-COLOR)

San Sebastian, Sept. 19.
M. Gorki Central Studios production. Directed by Pavel Arsenov. Screenplay, Alexander Volodin; camera, (color), Mijail Yakovich. Reviewed at Cine Victoria Eugina (San Sebastian), Sept. 19, '78. Running time: **79 MINS.**
Cast: Elena Proklova, Serguei Nagorni, Ia Savina, Alexander Kaliaguin, Inna Maguer, Arina Aleinikova.

Director Pavel Arsenov seems to have tried to make a Russo youth-oriented pic, but after an hour into the film he still hasn't made his point. The plot, the little there is of it, concerns a student and his romance with a girl living unhappily with her parents. There's a good deal of rather pointless conversation, numerous shots of the youngsters walking about the streets, family quarrels.

After playing hard-to-get, the girl finally falls into the boy's arms when she realizes that her family life is crumbling and her mother seems to be dying of some disease. The film is thoroughly inconsequential and unstructured. —*Besa.*

El Lugar Sin Limites
(The Place Without Limits)
(MEXICAN-COLOR)

San Sebastian, Sept. 18.
Conacite Dos production. Written and directed by Arturo Ripstein. Features entire cast. Story, Jose Donoso; camera (Eastmancolor panoramic), Miguel Garzon; editor, Francisco Chiu; music, Joaquin Gutierrez Heras. Reviewed at Cine Victoria Eugenia, San Sebastian, Sept. 18, '78. Running time: **110 MINS.**
Cast: Lucha Villa, Ana Martin, Gonzalo Vega, Julian Pastor, Carmen Salinas, Fernando Soler, Roberto Cobo.

This may be a daring film for Mexico, with its putting down of "machismo" and its humanization of a transvestite in a small village, but the script is so slow, the direction so clumsy and the camerawork so static that it becomes an ordeal to watch, though part of the audience in San Sebastian seemed to like the film.

Story revolves about a house of prostitution in a Mexican village, with its old-time cacique, who's here cast in godfatherly terms, a transvestite "entertainer" who never sings a song, his daughter and a he-man truck driver, a good-for-nothing sort who frequents the brothel and at the end kicks the transvestite to death. Most of the film is tedious and unsavory. Perhaps it could chalk up some sales in yahoo circuits in some other Latin American countries. —*Besa.*

Rekolekcje
(Recollections)
(POLISH-COLOR)

San Sebastian, Sept. 13.
Polish Corporation for Film Production, PROFIL Unit. Written and directed by Witold Leszczynski. Features entire cast. Camera (Eastmancolor) Maciej Kijowski; music, Helmut Nadolski; sets, Bogdan Kobierski; editor, Zofia Dworank. Reviewed at Cine Victoria Eugenia, San Sebastian, Sept. 13, '78. Running time: **80 MINS.**
Adam . . . . Ryszard Cieslak
Marek . . . . Wojciech Pszoniak
Also Ewa Pokas, Hanna Skarzanka, Andrzej Precigs, Gabriela Kownacka, Zdzislaw Maklakiewicz, Zdzislaw Wardejn et al.

Confused and confusing story of the mental and emotional crisis of a washed-up film director, reduced to doing video commercials and an occasional short. Adam, the director, has never been exactly lovable; his wife has left him, most of his friends have deserted him, and at mid-life he doesn't have much to look forward to. He has a way-out musician friend who makes strange noises with his bass, plays modern atonal music, and that sort of thing. The two men converse about life and death and the meaning of existence.

Helmer Witold Leszczynski jumbles about the time sequences and zeroes in with dead earnestness on the two men. There is really no plot, only a variety of scenes in Warsaw and Lodz and a lot of dialog, some rather pretentious. At the end Adam kills himself with sleeping pills and the musician listens to all his old tapes. Though thesping by Ryszard Cieslak and Wojciech Pszoniak is excellent, and technical credits and direction otherwise good, even treatment and subject commercial outlook is nil. —*Besa.*

Utopia
(FRENCH-COLOR)

San Sebastian, Sept. 11.
Utopia Productions and FR3 production Written and directed by Iradj Azimi Camera, (Eastmancolor) Etienne Becker; music, Henri Raschle and Patrice Holiner; editor, Anita Fernandez; production director, Marcel Mossotti. Reviewed at Cine Victoria Eugenia (San Sebastian), Sept. 11, '78 Running time: **92 MINS.**

Cast: Laurent Terzieff, Dominique Sanda, Jean Daste, Gerard Blain, Anne Marie Descotte, Catherine Gauvreu.

This plotless, snail-paced, surreal pic defies any kind of coherent description. Iranian helmer Iradj Azimi has succumbed to the worst kind of Gallic intellectual pretentiousness and the result is a collage of ineffable "truths" about the eternities of mankind and the world.

The camera labors slowly from one disjointed scene to another as the poet suffers and strikes poignant poses. What the snippets and dialogs mean can only be guessed at. It is poetic narcissim of a high order.

There is something about a poet remembering episodes of his past, teaching in a school, crying out for justice, uttering monologs as though in a daze, and finally walking into the sea, but all of it is scrambled together and, at least to this critic, thoroughly unintelligible. Perhaps sharp-witted Left Bank aesthetes will be able to make something of it, but lesser mortals will stop trying after ten minutes into the film.
— *Besa.*

Jaque A La Dama
(Check to the Queen)
(SPANISH-COLOR)

San Sebastian, Sept. 14.
Gregor Films S.A., Duna Films P.C., Cinema 2000 S.A. and Llama Films production. Directed by Francisco Rodriguez. Features entire cast. Screenplay, Francisco Rodriguez, Montserrat Julio, Rene Palacios; camera (Eastmancolor), Andres Berenguer; sets, Jose Maria Alarcon; editor, Eduardo Biurrun; music, Harmony. Reviewed at Cine Victoria Eugenia, San Sebastian, Sept. 14, '78. Running time: **87 MINS.**
Ana . . . . Conchita Velasco
Paula . . . . Ana Belen
Alberto . . . . Pedro Diez del Corral
Antonio . . . . Henry Gregor
Also: Olvido Lorente, Eduardo Mac Gregor, Miguel Angel Rellan, Carmen Gran, Mary Leyva, Beatriz Elorrieta, Manuel Gijon et al.

Incredibly inane and banal film with dialog so outrageously pretentious that audience broke out laughing at all the "deep" parts. How this item was chosen to be in competition at the Basque fest is a mystery.

Yarn concerns a latently lesbian relationship between an amateur thesp and a bored housewife. The thesp marries a famous novelist who with his intellectual friends endlessly palavers about art and philosophy, dropping names of literati and theorists. Wifey becomes disenchanted with what she feels to be her phony husband, while her long-standing friend, the housewife, also grumbles about an unhappy marriage.

At the end the thesp commits suicide. The sequences are jumbled up by the film editor, but no amount of jumbling can hide the thinness of the jejune script. Purely for the local market, if even that. —Besa.

Un Hombre Llamado Flor De Otono
(A Man Called Autumn Flower)
(SPANISH-COLOR)

San Sebastian, Sept. 11.
A Jose Frade production. Directed by Pedro Olea. Features entire cast. Screenplay, Pedro Olea, Rafael Azcona, based on story by Jose Maria Rodriguez Mendez; camera (Eastmancolor Panoramic), Fernando Arribas; editor, Jose Antonio Rojo; sets, Antonio Cortes; music, Carmelo Bernaola. Reviewed at Cine Victoria Eugenia (San Sebastian) Sept. 11, '78. Running time: 102 MINS.

Lluis	Jose Sacristan
Surroca	Paco Algora
Dona Nuria	Carmen Carbonell
Armengol	Roberto Camardiel
La Coquinera	Antonio Corencia
Bataclan Owner	Jose Franco
Police Chief	Felix Dafauca

Also Carlos Pineiro, Paco Espana and Mimi Munoz.

This latest film by Pedro Olea is the best thing he's done since "Tormento." Though pic progresses on a rather even, emotionless level the story elements of transvestitism and anarchism in the Barcelona of the 1920s are snappy enough to prevent interest from flagging. Given the limited production means for this kind of a period yarn, Olea has done very nicely in evoking the feel of the past and in reconstructing the case history of an upper-class transvestite singer who leads a double life and tries to blow up dictator Primo de Rivera.

In the story, Lluis is a militant anarchist whose one great love is his mother. At night he slips out to a garish dive in the waterfront region of Barcelona and performs as a transvestite singer. The mood of the period is well caught as we're served up three songs performed by thesp Jose Sacristan, who doesn't have much of a voice, but still comes across well.

Homosexual intrigues are rife in the tawdry club and one of the "girls" is murdered off scene.

Meanwhile Lluis has decided to dynamite the dictator's train and confess his transvestitism to his mother. The latter he succeeds in doing, but the former is thwarted by the police and Civil Guards who capture him and his two accomplices. Pic ends with the three of them being led off to a firing squad.

Sacristan puts in a fine performance as the transvestite, though he's a bit too intellectual for the role. Supporting cast is good and all technical credits up to crack. Pic should do good biz in Spain, and perhaps in some offshore areas, though the subjects of transvestitism and anarchism might close doors to it in conservative countries. —Besa.

Al Servicio De La Mujer Espanola
(At the Service of Spanish Womanhood)
(SPANISH-COLOR)

San Sebastian, Sept. 19.
Exclusivas Molpeceres S.A. production. Written and directed by Jaime de Arminan. Features entire cast. Camera (Eastmancolor), Domingo Solano; exec producer, Miguel Gomez; editor, J. Luis Matesanz; music, Mari Carmen Santoja; sets, Eduardo de la Torre. Reviewed at Cine Victoria Eugenia (San Sebastian), Sept. 19, '78. Running time: 109 MINS.
Cast: Marilina Ross, Adolfo Marsillach, Mari Carrillo, Amparo Baro, Emilio Gutierrez Caba.

This pic by Jaime de Arminan, who scored with "My Dearest Senorita" and "The Love of Captain Brando," has some interesting twists, but Arminan hasn't followed through on script development and leaves potentially powerful ideas hanging in the air. Even so, film is worth seeing and might do okay biz in Spain, though sales abroad will be very limited.

Story is set in Pontevedra, in the northwestern province of Galicia. A lonely-hearts radio program has been on the air for years, giving the conservative kind of counselling typical of the Franco years. The girl on the program lives with her pious sister in a large house. One day an admirer wheedles his way into her life. In fact, however, he hates everything she and the program stand for. But gradually she falls in love. After bedding down with him, however, he rejects her. She, nonetheless, has come to see things in a different light and is unable to continue her broadcasts.

Thesping by Marilina Ross, Mari Carrillo, Adolfo Marsillach and Emilio Gutierrez Caba is excellent, and the script is intelligent and literate.

Item is well paced, but several tacks are never developed, such as the admirer being a homosexual or transvestite, or a scene when he almost cuts her throat with a razor after declaring his hatred, or her initial rebelliousness. There are, of course, many implicit political overtones. Flashbacks to the admirer's childhood in a parochial school are well done, and there are many other good things in the film. More's the pity that Arminan hasn't taken proper advantage of them. —Besa.

La Vieja Memoria
(The Old Memory)
(SPANISH-DOCU-B&W)

San Sebastian, Sept. 16.
Profilmes S.A. production (Barcelona). Directed by Jaime Camino. Exec producers, Ricardo Munoz Suay, Jose Antonio Perez Giner. Camerawork, (black & white) Jose Luis Claine, Teo Escamilla, Roberto Gomez, Tomas Pladevall, Francisco Sanchez, Magi Torruella; editor, Teresa Alcocer. Interviews with Abad de Santillan, Federico Escofet, Raimundo Fernandez Cuesta, Jose Maria Gil Robles, Julian Gorkin, Eduardo de Guzman, Dolores Ibarruri, David Jato, Enrique Lister, Jaume Miratvilles, Federica Montseny, POUM group, Ricardo Sanz, Josep Tarradellas, Jose Luis de Villalonga. Reviewed at Cine Miramar (San Sebastian), Sept. 15, '78. Running time: 165 MINS.

Helmer Jaime Camino has assembled interviews and some vintage footage of the period from 1931-39 in Spain for a film whose importance as a historical document is beyond question, though its interest will be largely limited to those already well versed in the subject. For nearly three hours Camino interviews the survivors of those years — many of them still prominent in modern Spanish politics — and each recalls the events of the time.

Unfortunately those not very familiar with the historical background of the period, and especially that of Cataluna, which constitutes about 80% of the film, will be lost as such abbreviations as CNT, UGT, POUM and others are thrown at them. Camino takes for granted that audiences are thoroughly knowledgeable in the period, and he is simply setting some of the details straight. Even those fairly conversant in the subject will find much of it hard going.

Though, of course, the film is overtly Republican in its sympathies, Camino has also interviewed surviving right-wingers such as Gil Robles, Fernandez Cuesta, Falangist leaders as well as Communists like "La Pasionaria," Enrique Lister, anarchists and others. The film only touches briefly on activities outside Cataluna, but the subject is so vast that any way one slices it there will be more omissions than inclusions. The docu footage helps to break up the torpor of the interviews, but three hours is rather too long a run. Theatrical outlook very limited, though some video interest may be generated. —Besa.

Il Ritorno Di Casanova
(The Return of Casanova)
(ITALO-COLOR)

San Sebastian, Sept. 14.
A RAI-Radiotelevisione Italiana presentation of RAI Channel 1, produced by Monica Venturini for Filmes S.p.A, adapted by Paolo Battistuzzio. Director, Pasquale Festa Campanile. Features entire cast. Screenplay, Piero Chiara, based on a novel by Arthur Schnitzler; camera (color), Giuseppe Ruzzolini; music, Riz Ortolani; editor, Gian Maria Messeri. Reviewed at Cine Victoria Eugenia (San Sebastian) Sept. 14, '78. Running time: 124 MINS.
Cast: Giulio Bosetti, Mirella D'Angelo, Piero Vida, Grazia Maria Spina, Francesca Marciano, Pietro Tordi, Enzo Robutti, Bianca Toccafondi, Carlo Simoni, Ettore Carloni, Dino Emanuelli.

Beautiful production values, excellent thesping and a sensitive and intelligent script are counterbalanced by often excruciatingly slow pacing in this sensitive but overlong film on an aging Casanova. Scripters and director provide us with plenty of the famous lover's introspective, brooding doubts about himself and the world, and these, to a great extent, are the theme of the film. But viewers are apt to become impatient with the slow development and may yearn for the film to get on with the story.

Yarn starts with Casanova awaiting a letter from Venetian authorities who would tell him whether he could finally return to his native city after years in exile and spend the remainder of his days in peace and quiet. But as he's waiting, an old friend sees the by now impecunious lover and insists that he visit him in his estate. Casanova agrees. The friend's wife had formerly been one of his conquests, but his eye falls rather on a young girl who adamantly refuses his advances. He ultimately sleeps with her, only by bailing her lover out of a gambling debt and substituting for him in the dark. But upon revealing his identity, he draws only her hate. Her paramour is waiting to challenge him to a duel after the tryst, but Casanova kills him, lamenting that he had rather it were he (Casanova) who had died, since he dreads dragging on his life in poverty and old age.

Pic is far too long and talky for theatrical release, but might do some biz in video sales for special art circuits who'd have the patience to sit through it. —Besa.

Pablo
(CUBAN-DOCU-COLOR)

San Sebastian, Sept. 15.
Cuban Film Institute (ICAIC) production. Directed by Victor Casaus. Screenplay, Victor Casaus and Mario Crespo; camera (color), Raul Rodriguez; music, Silvio Rodriguez; editor, Roberto Bravo. Reviewed at Cine Victoria Eugenia (San Sebastian), Sept. 15, '78. Running time: 95 MINS.

Documentary on Pablo de la Torriente Brau, student leader, revolutionary and journalist, done via interviews with those who personally knew him. Helmer Victor Casaus uses a technique in which he blends the interviews with some period reconstructions filmed in sepia color. Interest will be limited to those already familiar with the Cuban revolutionary; others will leave after ten minutes, as was case in San Sebastian. —Besa.

Comes A Horseman
(COLOR)

Beautiful locations, lugubrious Alan Pakula western. So-so outlook.

Hollywood, Oct. 4.

A United Artists release of Robert-Chartoff-Irwin Winkler production, produced by Gene Kirkwood and Dan Paulson; executive producers, Robert Chartoff, Irwin Winkler. Stars James Caan, Jane Fonda, Jason Robards. Directed by Alan J. Pakula. Screenplay, Dennis Lynton Clark; camera (color), Gordon Willis; production designer, George Jenkins; editor, Marion Rothman; music, Michael Small; set decorator, Arthur Jeph Parker; sound, Chris Newman; costumes, Luster Bayless; stunt coordinator, Walter Scott; associate producer, Ronald Caan; assistant director, Paul Helmick. Reviewed at the Academy of Motion Picture Arts & Sciences Theatre, Beverly Hills, Oct. 4, '78. (MPAA Rating: PG). Running time: **118 MINS.**

Frank .... James Caan
Ella .... Jane Fonda
Ewing .... Jason Robards
Neil Atkinson .... George Grizzard
Dodger .... Richard Farnsworth
Julie Blocker .... Jim Davis
Billy Joe Meynert .... Mark Harmon
Hoverton .... Macon McCalman
George Bascomb .... Basil Hoffman
Ralph Cole .... James Kline
Kroegh .... James Keach
Cattle Buyer .... Clifford A. Pellow

Alan Pakula's "Comes a Horseman" is so lethargic not even Jane Fonda, James Caan and Jason Robards can bring excitement to this artificially dramatic story of a stubborn rancher who won't surrender to the local land baron. Those three names should be enough to assure this handsome United Artists release moderate business, but word of mouth will hurt and commercial outlook is not what might be expected from such high-powered casting.

The real star of the film doesn't get billing. It's a stretch of verdant land in Colorado known as the Wet Mountain Valley. Gordon Willis photographs this location with so much love and awe that talk by oil explorers about ripping it up is both moving and repulsive. It's nothing short of rape.

Whenever the picture stays close to the land — really whenever it stays outdoors — it transcends the pedestrian script by Dennis Lynton Clark. It's a pleasure to look at. The story of the violation of the earth has been told before, frequently within the context of the western. Still, it's rare to be emotionally affected by the non-human.

The heart of any drama, however, is people and it's here that "Comes A Horseman" fails. Robards' part is the most troublesome. He's the land baron who wants both Fonda and Caan to sell their parcels to complete his empire. Every one of Robard's lines is shaded by a black hat. He is Evil in the most convenient way. The same can be said of Fonda as the deter-

mined rancher, except her failing is a cold heart. The chill was brought on by Robards who she slept with as a girl.

Those two parts are contrived and the story always remains less than engaging because of it. It's difficult to become engrossed in a story, no matter how convincing the performances, when the premise rings false.

James Caan, also an independent rancher who recently returned from serving in World War II, teams up with Fonda after his partner is killed (presumably on orders from Robards). When Fonda realizes what an accomplished cowboy Caan is and how much she needs him their relationship warms.

The only really good part in the film is Richard Farnsworth's Dodger, Fonda's aging hand. He's an altogether sympathetic character, close to the land and one of the few who really understands Fonda.

Fonda and Caan, of all the performers, seem most comfortable in a western. They work naturally around horses and cattle and perform many of their own stunts, which benefits their performances. Some of the scenes where the two roundup cattle, ride together or just meander in the outdoors work extremely well. You almost forget the film's shaky premise.

But the indoor scenes are hard to accept. It's here that the plot is unraveled and regardless of how well the scenes are acted they're either dull or difficult to accept.

Inside also Willis' photography seem inappropriate. No one wants to argue against beauty, but Hollywood pictures are becoming too artful. The gloss is too high. In "Comes A Horseman" the exteriors should appear as lush as possible. But the interiors look too perfect. The shadows angle too carefully off the actor's faces. There's no grit.

The remainder of the tech credits are of very high quality and Pakula continues to be one of the few directors working today who experiments with sound. One complaint, however, is Michael Small's overly majestic score. —*Hege.*

Sonambulos
(Somnambulists)
(SPANISH-COLOR)

San Sebastian, Sept. 16.

Profilmes S.A. production. Written and directed by Manuel Gutierrez Aragon; Exec producer, Jose A. Perez Giner. Features entire cast. Camera (Eastmancolor), Teo Escamilla; sets Miguel Narros; editor, Jose Salcedo; music, Jose Nieto. Reviewed at Cine Victoria Eugenia (San Sebastian), Sept. 16, '78. Running time: **93 MINS.**

Ana .... Ana Belen
Norman .... Norman Brisky
Maria Rosa .... Maria Rosa Salgado
Javier (child) .... Javier Delgado

Fatima .... Lola Gaos
Javier .... Ricardo Franco
Pepe .... Felix Rotaeta
Pepe 2nd .... Jose Manuel Cervino
Doctor .... Eduardo Mac Gregor
Library Director .... Jose Luis Borau
Theatre Director .... Miguel Narros
Policeman .... Fernando Chinarro
Laly Soldevila .... Laly Soldevila
Juan .... Jose Luis Gomez

Helmer Manuel Gutierrez's former film, "Black Litter," was a fairly straightforward and comprehensible film, whether you liked it or not. Now Gutierrez has plunged into something that will leave virtually all audiences in a state of puzzlement. It is so intricate and complex, so laden with symbols, so confusing in its time sequences as to make Carlos Saura's pix simplistic by comparison. It's the sort of film critics will argue about, and general audiences will be turned away by. Maybe it's a "brilliant" film, but one even its admirers will have difficulty in explaining.

Scene is set in Madrid in 1960, the year of the Burgos trials when six persons were tried and executed for having killed a police inspector. Pic (like "Black Litter") starts spectacularly enough, with Burgos trial protesters rioting with police, and mounted officers crashing through a huge window pane of the Public Library. One girl, Ana, is injured in the scuffle. We shortly discover she is doomed to die of cancer. Other scenes are intercut — a modern play in English, part of an avant-garde theatre week, presumably. There's a quack doctor who says he can cure her by usurping her mind, a sinister maid, a secret book which contains all the answers to all the questions in the world, a queen that is the symbol of death and a magician who represents madness.

Production credits are excellent, crisp photography by Teo Escamilla, beautiful sets, intriguing moods, fine thesping throughout. Commercial outlook limited, though specialized art circuits might do some biz. —*Besa.*

Goin' Coconuts
(COLOR)

The Donny & Marie tv show, taken outdoors.

Hollywood, Oct. 10.

An Osmond Distribution Co. release, in association with Inter Planetary Pictures. Produced by John Cutts. Features entire cast. Directed by Howard Morris. Screenplay, Raymond Harvey; camera (Deluxe Color), Frank Phillips; editor, Frank Bracht; sound, Herman Lewis; assistant director, Bob Huddleston. Reviewed at Vine Theatre, Hollywood, Oct. 4, '78. (MPAA Rating: PG). Running time: **93 MINS.**

Donny .... Donny Osmond
Marie .... Marie Osmond
Sid .... Herbert Edelman
Kruse .... Kenneth Mars
Tricia .... Chrystin Sinclaire
Mickey .... Ted Cassidy

Webster .... Marc Lawrence
Wong .... Khigh Dhiegh
Ito .... Harold Sakata
Jake .... Charles Walker
Al .... Danny Wells
Charlie .... Jack Collins
Alecki .... Tommy Fujiwara

Extending their tv careers into motion pictures, Donny and Marie Osmond have come up with exactly that — an extended film version of their tv show, no better and no worse. But their fans, especially the younger ones, will probably be pleased.

Playing themselves, Donny and Marie are pretty and pleasant, bantering and teasing each other exactly as they do for the tv cameras. They also sing a lot. The only difference here is that one slim skit is extended to feature length, with added outdoor action.

Ancient plot brings Marie into innocent possession of a necklace which the bad men are after. Led by Kenneth Mars, the buffoon goons include Ted Cassidy, Khigh Dhiegh, Harold Sakata and Charles Walker, whose only high moments come when they get their pistols mixed up.

Herbert Edelman is okay as the Osmonds' manager and Chrystin Sinclair is fetchingly useful as a mysterious beauty who's also in pursuit of the necklace.

Absolutely nothing about the story is believable or interesting. But the Hawaiian backdrop is nice and there's one good nightclub production number, featuring the Osmond pair with typical island tourist performers.

And, naturally, it has a happy ending. —*Har.*

Le Temoin
(The Witness)
(FRENCH-ITALO-COLOR)

Paris, Sept. 26.

CIC release of Belstar Productions-M Films, PAC production. Stars Philippe Noiret, Alberto Sordi. Directed by Jean-Pierre Mocky. Screenplay, Rodolfo Sonego, Augusto Caminito, Sergio Amidei, Mocky, Jacques Dreux from a book by Harrison Judd; camera (Eastmancolor), Sergio D'Offizi; editor, Michel Lewin; producer, Jacques Dorfmann; music, Piero Piccioni. Reviewed at CIC screening room, Paris, Sept. 11, '78. Running time, **95 MINS.**

Antonio .... Alberto Sordi
Robert .... Philippe Noiret
Inspector .... Roland Dubillard
Wife .... Giselle Preville
Father .... Paul Crauchet
Cathy .... Sandra Dobrigna
Helene .... Consuelo Ferrara

Director Jean-Pierre Mocky's caustic wit and gritty satiric penchants jive in this tale of small town repressiveness and perversity that lead to murder and the execution of an innocent man. It could have sleeper potential with the right handling and placement in most climes.

It is blessed with two fine thesps, Alberto Sordi as a middleaged, good-natured bachelor who comes to a small town in France to restore church paintings. He has a good friend there, Philippe Noiret, who has married a rich woman for her money and runs a bank.

Sordi is done up with a crew-cut wig and his bonhommie, with an underlying sexual bravado, give his character panache and a certain charm. Noiret is warm on the surface, but with a hung-up intensity that belies his suavity.

Into this setting comes a local nymphette, a truly alarming girl-woman who grotesquely apes a mature woman and makes passes at Sordi who repels them. But she is raped and killed in the abandoned house of Noiret's mother. Sordi had thought he had seen Noiret leaving it when going by in his car.

A homosexual inspector, who hates rich people and foreigners, is on the track and traces the girl's demise to the house when she is found strangled. She had been thrown into a canal running in front of the place. Sordi tries to help his friend, but gets involved and finally is pinned with the murder when Noiret is killed by mistake by the girl's father when he is mistaken for Sordi.

Sordi is not helped by Noiret's wife, who covers things up, and is beheaded after a trial and years in prison. Sharply laid out, with a bevy of unsavory people, this still retains shrewd reflections of the darker side of small town life without becoming grotesque.

It does lack any relieving, more human personnages, but its fine, brisk pacing, its understanding of the two men trapped by general smugness and hypocrisy give this a balanced serio-comic progression. The nymphette is truly warped which might create some pressure group outcries though she is a mirror of her elders.

Mocky gets back into form for this one after some lacklustre pix where his barbed black humor did not come off. Sordi and Noiret make a fine team, as the former's good-natured humanity is balanced by the latter's tense mixture of worldiness and despair.

An offbeat drama which needs plenty of care but could catch audiences on its effective treatment.
—*Mosk.*

Koonche Rak
(The Key to Love)
(THAI-COLOR)

Bangkok, Sept. 20.

A Krung Keow Films release. Produced by Opart Rangchaikul. Features entire cast. Directed and edited by Charthep Chantanimit. Story and screenplay, Spa & Co.; camera (color), Pipat Payak; sound, Ram Inthra; music, Jonrak Jankanna; asst. director, Lek Chantanimit; production designer and art director, Rang Sant. Reviewed at Paris Theatre, Bangkok, Sept. 20, '78. Running time: 115 MINS.

Sompong	Sorapong Chatri
Wallaya	Nantana Ngaokracharg
Supranee	Suphan Titiang
Dee	Padee Jatrikat
Kitti	Kitti Daskorn
Chamnong	Somsak Chaisongkram
Sompong's father	Sokuan Krajangsart
Wallaya's parents	Surachart Traipong, Marasi Issarangkul Na Ayudhya

The most successful love team in the country, Sorapong Chatri and Nantana Ngaokrachang, who together made "Pae Kao" (The Scar), top-grossing Thai movie of all time, are reunited in "Koonche Rak," and the best reason for it, of course, is to cash in on their popularity.

Nantana tries in vain to rise above the material she is forced to work on. She is okay, though, in the earlier scenes when she plays pranks on Sorapong, trying to test his suitability as a husband-to-be. Parents on both sides are busy matching them up. In this kind of situation, we expect the parents to be either disappointed or gratified by their children's decision on the matter.

Film relies almost entirely on the numerous Sorapong and Nantana love team followers. They are bound to buy any kind of roles that these two top stars get assigned to do. —*Cano.*

Remember My Name
(COLOR)

Alan Rudolph forgets to remember the audience. Shaky b.o. prospects.

Hollywood, Oct. 10.

Columbia Pictures release of a Lion's Gate Films production. Produced by Robert Altman. Written and directed by Alan Rudolph; exec in charge of production, Tommy Thompson; camera (Deluxe Color), Tak Fujimoto; editor, Thomas Walls, William A. Sawyer; sound, Bob Gravenor, Chris McLaughlin; music, Alberta Hunter; costumes, J. Allen Highfill; assistant director, Thompson; sound by Dolby Sound Systems. Reviewed at Columbia Pictures, The Burbank Studios, Sept. 28, '78. (MPAA Rating: R.) Running time: 95 MINS.

Emily	Geraldine Chaplin
Neil Curry	Anthony Perkins
Pike	Moses Gunn
Barbara Curry	Berry Berenson
Mr. Nudd	Jeff Goldblum
Jeff	Timothy Thomerson
Rita	Alfre Woodard

Were Alan Rudolph a European director, he might be safe in the highly self-conscious, precious style he has demonstrated in his two films, "Welcome to L.A.," and now, "Remember My Name." As an American, however, Rudolph will be measured against a certain commercial standard. On the evidence of his work to date, he invariably falls short.

"Remember My Name" is an attempt to make what Rudolph calls a "contemporary blues fable." Whatever the generic goal, the end product is an incomprehensible melange of striking imagery, obscure dialog, a powerful score, and a script that doesn't know how to go from A to B.

A plot synopsis should really accompany each ticket purchase in this pic's release, because for at least the first half-hour, hardly anything makes sense. Anthony Perkins is a construction worker married to Berry Berenson. Geraldine Chaplin arrives on the scene and begins a petty harassment of the couple, which gradually turns more sinister.

It develops that Chaplin is an ex-convict, recently sprung from a 12-year sentence for murder. She got a job in a nearby five-and-dime store managed by Jeff Goldblum (whose mother is still doing time), where she terrorizes store clerk Alfre Woodard and Goldblum. Chaplin also gets a room in a rundown apartment building managed by Moses Gunn, with whom she has a brief liaison.

If done on a traditional, linear level, "Remember My Name" might have induced some interest as a moderate chiller with emotional undertones. In Rudolph's infuriatingly oblique style, however, it becomes an irritating and puzzling affair that insults, rather than teases, the viewer.

All the exposition is saved for one talky jail-house scene, but once the secret is out of the bag, Rudolph seems to lose all interest, and abruptly ends the film.

The performers wander around in a dazed state, as if unable to figure out what they're supposed to be doing. Chaplin is dementedly intense, while Perkins is his usually tightly-coiled self. Berenson is quite good in her screen debut as the wife who understands no more than the audience (and that's not much), and Moses Gunn scores as the stolid building super.

Best part of the film is the rich, honeyed voice of 83-year-old blues singer Alberta Hunter, whose Southern laments are used as aural counterpoint to Tak Fujimoto's extraordinary imagery. It's an unusual technique that doesn't quite succeed, but not because of any technical failures.

"Remember My Name" has the sheen of a beautiful film, but the hollow, empty core of an intellectual exercise. —*Poll.*

La Chanson De Roland
(The Song of Roland)
(FRENCH-COLOR)

Paris, Oct. 3.

Gaumont release of Z Productions-FR3 production. Features entire cast. Directed by Frank Cassenti. Screenplay, Michele Mercier, Thierry Joly, Cassenti; camera (Eastmancolor), Jean-Jacques Flori, editor, Michele Mercier; music, Antoine Duhamel; art director, Renaud Sanson; costumes, Galiane; producer, Jean-Serge Breton. Reviewed at Gaumont screening room, Paris, Sept. 28, '78. Running time, 110 MINS.

Roland	Klaus Kinski
Anne	Dominique Sanda
Turpin	Alain Cluny
Olivier	Pierre Clementi
Turold	Jean-Pierre Kalfon
Marie	Monique Mercure
Dealer	Niels Arestrup
Thierry	Serge Merlin
Duc Naimes	Laszlo Szabo

The Middle Ages seem to be appealing to local filmmakers these days. After Eric Rohmer's exquisite fable, "Perceval La Gallois," comes this more ponderous probing of the times, made before "Perceval." Told as a legend of the 10th century seen through the eyes of a group of 12-century pilgrims, pic does not quite bring off the attempt to penetrate a historical legend with a more realistic aspect of the problems of the times.

Film is also a bit cumbersome in segueing from the past to the deeper past. Pilgrims have a troupe who play the ancient and one of the earliest legendary poems "The Song of Roland." The same people play the characters in the legend.

Klaus Kinski is one of the players who is also the heroic Roland whose defeat in battle against Arabs in Spain is turned into glorious legend to take the sting from defeat. The few battle scenes are adequately clanking and effective.

The times are mainly served up as familiar pageantry of religious frenzy and some early stirrings against the beginnings of exploitation of peasants and workers by the growth of capitalism in the 13th century. This aspect makes it rather posey and affected.

Dominique Sanda is a stalwart early emancipated woman leading peasants and workers rising up against the violent oppression of the times. They are wiped out by marauding pillagers from another part of the country as are many of the pilgrims. But the Kinski player-Roland character lives to spread the need to react to poverty and exploitation.

Too much is forced on this historical opus which robs it of a true feeling for the times. All the points about social and physical oppression could have been implicit in treatment rather than in talk.

But there is a good technical and production backing to this film. Foreign chances are mainly specialized on its surface historical feelings. But it lacks the grace of entering either of the periods it treats with the right flair to make them revealing, human and inspired rather than surface lip service to human progress and adversity. —*Mosk.*

Zwischengleis
(Yesterday's Tomorrow)
(W. GERMAN-COLOR)

Munich, Sept. 2.

A Warner-Columbia release (in Germany) of an Artus Film/Bayerischer Rundfunk tv production. Features entire cast. Screenplay, Dorothee Dhan; camera (color). Igor Luther; music, Eugen Illin; producer, Dr. Harald Mueller; directed by Wolfgang Staudte. Reviewed at Warner-Columbia screening room, Munich, Sept. 1, '78. Running time: **106 MINS.**

Colonel Stone	Mel Ferrer
Anna Eichmayr	Pola Kinski
Alfons Eichmayr	Martin Luettge
Frau Almany	Hannelore Schroth
Hubert Almany	Volker Kraeft

Wolfgang Staudte, one of Germany's important directors, has not made a theatrical pic for some years, having devoted most of his time to television. The higher therefore the expectations for his first film after the hiatus. The verdict, however, is that Staudte isn't what he used to be.

The tragic story of the German girl Anna (Pola Kinski), who suffers from a traumatic postwar experience, falls in love with a German born U.S. colonel (Mel Ferrer), later marries a narrow-minded German salesman (Martin Luettge) and finally commits suicide, is just too superficial. Moreover, the film has the typical form of a German tv play which, these days, is not a compliment. There are a few atmospheric winter shots but too many talking heads. Adjacent to some touching scenes there are wooden and static ones. The adapted way of telling the story in back and forth jumps is confusing. Even after one gets used to that, the editing technique is very crude.

Many problems of the immediate German postwar history are touched on in this film and may wake memories in people — Americans and Germans alike — who lived through the period. But the story is superficial and lame, without a touch of humor, drive or charm. The beautiful Chopin music used lends the pic some audible quality.

Ferrer's and Luettge's performances are nevertheless outstanding, taking into consideration that Ferrer's colorless part was especially hard to enliven. Kinski in her first film (she is the sister of Nastassia and daughter of Klaus) is a rewarding discovery. —*Koci.*

Vamonos, Barbara
(Let's Go, Barbara)
(SPANISH-COLOR)

San Sebastian, Sept. 10.

Incine S.A. and Jet Films production, presented by Alfredo Matas. Directed by Cecilia Bartolome. Features entire cast. Screenplay Cecilia Bartolome, Concha Romero and Sara de Azcarate; camera (Eastmancolor), Jose Luis Alcaine; editor, Jose Luis Matesanz; music, Carlos Laporta. Reviewed at Cine Savoy (San Sebastian), Sept. 10, '78. Running time: **98 MINS.**

Ana	Amparo Soler Leal
Barbara	Cristina Alvarez
Ivan	Ivan Tubau
Paula	Julieta Serrano
Andreu	Jose Ruiz Lifante
Tia Remedios	Josefina Tapias

Neophyte femme helmer Cecilia Bartolome tries to broach some of the local women's lib pet peeves in this pic, but the few points she makes are diluted by a wobbly script. The touches of humor mostly fall flat or are too slight to follow through on. Overlong and ultimately wearisome, pic rambles on from one undramatic scene to another in the undeveloped and indecisive plot.

Story concerns the wife of a wealthy Barcelona business man who, after her first affair, at age 40, decides she's had enough of marriage and is going her own way. Taking her daughter Barbara in tow, she drives off in a Mercedes to a beach resort, meets some old-time girlfriends and has a fling with a not very attractive tourist guide. Meanwhile hubby has blocked her checking account and sent out his legal minion to serve a writ and obtain evidence of adultery. At the end she ditches the new male-chauvinist beau and drives back to Barcelona to face the music.

There's certainly a crying need to draw Spaniards' attention to women's rights, but this film hasn't come even remotely close to doing it. Acting all around is self-conscious and unconvincing, editing and music are clumsy and the script terrible. Item was reportedly a flop when released in Barcelona.

— *Besa.*

Aus Der Ferne Sehe Ich Dieses Land
(I See This Land from Afar)
(WEST GERMAN-COLOR)

Berlin, Sept. 17.

A Basis-Film Verleih Production, Berlin, in collaboration with WDR-TV, Cologne. Clara Burckner and Joachim von Mengershausen, production managers; world rights, Basis-Film Verleih, Berlin. Features entire cast. Dircted by Christian Ziewer. Screenplay, Antonio Skarmeta, Ziewer, based on Skarmeta's story, "Nix passiert"; camera (color), Gerard Vandenberg; music, Andariegos, Dance Group "Victor Jara," Omero Caro; art direction, Juergen Herze; editing, Stefanie Wilke. Reviewed at Studio am Kudam, Berlin, Sept. 16, '78. Running time: **98 MINS.**

Cast: Pablo Lira (Lucho), Anibal Reyna (Araya), Valeria Villarroel (Beatriz), Raul Becerra (Grandfather), Daniel (Daniel).

Christian Ziewer made a rep as the leading helmer in the Berlin School of Proletarian Cinema — pix dealing with the working class and their problems at home and in factories, often starring real hard hats in bit roles. "I See This Land from Afar" shifts the emphasis to the foreign worker, particularly the Chilean immigrant, whose fate is played out against job discrimination and an uncertain future in a land of plenty.

Inspiration for pic came from the writings of Antonio Skarmeta, who also collaborated with Peter Lilienthal on "The Country Is Calm," top kudo in the German Film Sweepstakes a few years back when several docu and feature pix appeared on the Chilean putsch and aftermath. Scribe Skarmeta has since settled in West Berlin, along with other refugees and committed artists who fled the country (same is true for East Berlin).

Ziewer, meanwhile, developed from a socially engaged, docu-oriented filmmaker to a rather fine storyteller, whose last worker pic, "Walking Tall" (1976), centered on the problems of an individualist in a factory trying to go his own way despite the restricting rules of union strikes. He is a moralist, somewhat like writer Max von der Gruen, an ex-coal-miner from Dortmund who is on the rise in the literary world at present. "I See This Land from Afar" marks Ziewer as a helmer to watch, although story is in debt to the slow-moving, heavy, sociocritical format of the proletariat pic.

It's about a young lad awakening to girls and a mind of his own in a family stuck in a social-housing settlement in the north of the divided city. The father works in an airline kitchen, but because he's a Socialist by conviction and a Chilean to boot, he gets bounced one day as a "security risk" in these precarious days of terrorist activities on airplanes. His honesty, however, wins him friends among fellow-workers, and there's a bit of worker compensation to fall back on. The son sees the difficulties ahead for the family with several mouths to feed and secretly quits school to work as stock boy in a store, bringing home extra money on the side.

He meets a German girl and has to fight for his honor and hers (she's the "property" of a local tough), and makes friends with a Greek lad, also of Socialist bent, about to return to his homeland as democracy surfaces again. To add another touch of dramatic realism, the boy's uncle (his mother's brother) has been arrested back in Santiago by the police and murdered. Pic ends with the father taking over the stockroom job, sending the lad back to school to learn for the future.

Lensing by Gerard Vandenberg is plus, while thesps are appropriately real people suffering the fate of the immigrant far from home. But dialogue is stiff and packed with messages, too many to win a commercial aud beyond the "in" crowd. —*Holl.*

Les Ringards
(The Small Timers)
(FRENCH-COLOR)

Paris, Oct. 10.

UGC-CFDC release of Les Films De L'Alma production. Features entire cast. Directed by Robert Pouret. Screenplay, Jean Lacroix; camera (Eastmancolor), Guy Dourdan; music, Francis Lai. Reviewed at Le Paris, Paris, Sept. 28, '78. Running time, **95 MINS.**

Anna	Mireille Darc
Aldo	Aldo Maccione
Charlot	Charles Gerard
Vilar	Julien Guiomar
Inspector	Georges Wilson
Friend	Genevieve Fontanel

A picaresque comedy about three inept thieves hounded by a dim-witted police inspector who thinks they are big time criminals. Overdoing the whimsical characters of the three bachelor crooks, uneven pacing and telegraphed gags make this one of those loyal pix slanted mainly for playoff at home.

The wife of the inspector gets interested in the crooks when the husbands jails them for something they did not commit. When they get out, she even joins them in their one successful caper that allows them to escape to tropical climes.

Players are personable but Robert Pouret's flaccid direction never gives this pic the needed blend of satire and action to keep up interest in this group of amiable stereotyped characters. Technically good. —*Mosk.*

El Asesino De Pedralbes
(The Pedralbes Murderer)
(SPANISH-DOCU-COLOR)

San Sebastian, Sept. 12.

A Figaro Films (Barcelona) production. Directed by Gonzalo Herralde. Exec producer, Pepon Coromina. Features entire cast. Camera (Eastmancolor) Jaume Peracaula; editor, Teresa Alcocer. Reviewed at Cine Victoria Eugenia, San Sebastian, Sept. 12, '78. Running time: **86 MINS.**

Cast: Jose Luis Cerveto, Fernando Chamorro, Antonio Garcia, Rafael Gavilan, Jose Marti Gomez, Francisco Mas, Antonio Membrilla, Juan Merelo.

Altogether fascinating documentary on a man who in 1974 murdered his employer and his wife and is now serving a jail sentence in Spain. Director Gonzalo Herralde, who last year helmed "Raza, the Spirit of Franco," has a film that will be of universal interest and, as a documentary, is especially apt for video sales. The interviews with Jose Luis Cerveto, the murderer, touch upon problems of homosexuality, the reasons for crime, social injustices and a critique of prison systems and especially the questionable usefulness of institutionalized psychiatry.

Herralde has shot about 12 hours of interviews, which he has skillfully cut down to 86 minutes. He tells the story more or less chronologically, and there is rarely a moment when interest flags. Cerveto, no matter how heinous his crime was, comes across as a sharp, articulate, analytical and intelligent being; as the story of his life and crimes unfold from his very lips, it is sometimes difficult to remember that this is not some actor mouthing lines that have been written for him, but the man himself who is talking.

As the tale unfolds we learn that Cerveto grew up in an orphanage and early on felt a sexual attraction for other children; this propensity got him into trouble as he grew older. He drifted from one job to another as a loner. Finally he took on a job as a handyman with a wealthy couple and one night in 1974 crept into their bedroom and killed them by stabbing them over and over again. He was caught almost immediately and given two death sentences. However the death of Franco and the advent of a new government enabled him to get a commutation of the sentences, but he'll be in prison till 2004.

This is the sort of film that could do brisk biz if properly distributed. Pic is unique and its implications transcend those of a mere murderer confessing to his crime. Herralde has come up with a truly mesmerizing film. —*Besa.*

New York Fest

Sado
(Third Base)
(JAPANESE-COLOR)

A Gentosha and ATG production. Directed by Yoichi Higashi. Features entire cast. Screenplay, Shuji Terayama, based on novel "September Town" by Haka Kenjo; camera (color), Koichi Kawakami; music, Michi Tanaka; art direction, Ikuro Ayabe; no other credits provided. Reviewed at the N.Y. Film Festival, Oct. 3, '78. Running time: **102 MINS.**
Third .... Toshiyuki Nagashima
His Mother .... Chiyoko Shimagura
(English subtitles)

"Third Base" is one of five films appearing in the Japanese sidebar section of the New York Festival, and one of two in which Shuji Terayama has a credit, this one for scripting. Film focuses on the relationship of one man to the world around him, variously his mother, the urban landscape of Japanese youth, and ultimately those incarcerated in a corrective school, after

he is involved in a murder stemming from his procuring ways.

Narrative is moved along back and forth between time frames, now in the reform school, then at home or in the streets of the city. It's an interesting way to tell a story, as director Yoichi Higashi develops it, and is part of the independent cinema scene in Japan. It was filmed by Gentosha and distributed via the Art Theatre Guild in that country.

Toshiyuki Nagashima is effective as the young man who seems to aimlessly fall into pimping for his two female friends, who go about prostituting themselves out of boredom and as a lark. When he sells one of them to a tough guy — all decked out in warrior decals — that situation leads to a fight wherein the young tough is killed.

Film opens with Nagashima in prison, lamenting his lack of a home base as he runs around a baseball diamond. His prison experience is made rougher by having separated himself from the group. That means a few cuffs on the head followed by periods of solitude nicely underscored in small touches caught by Higashi. It is a world within a world, all of them ungiving.

Perhaps the film serves at some deeper level to address the experience of postwar Japan, coming to terms with its chance encounter with exploitative strangers. Perhaps not. The emphasis on teamwork to retrain for entrance into the outside community certainly suggests the model by which Japan has chosen to play the game.

The time frame dynamic of moving backwards while moving forwards also suggests something to that effect, stripping away the associations from the labels to demonstrate the aimlessness of the act that starts the process — presumably leading to a better life.

Commercial prospects here are not the brightest, but the film might play in selected art film programs. —*Jac.*

Matsuri No Junbi
(Preparation For The Festival)
(JAPANESE-COLOR)

Japan Art Theatre Guild and Soeisha Ltd. production and release. Exec producer, Eiga Dojinsha. Feature entire cast. Directed by Kazuo Kuroki. Screenplay, Takehiro Nakajima; camera (color) Tatsuo Suzuki; art directors, Takeo Kimura, Yuji Maruyama; music, Teizo Matsumura. Reviewed at New York Film Festival, Oct. 5, '78. Running time: **116 MINS.**
Tateo .... Jun Eto
Ryoko .... Keiko Takeshita
Toshihiro .... Yoshio Harada
(English subtitles)

The Japanese love to make films about village life. But the villagers of Kazuo Kuroki's "Preparation For The Festival" have about as much relationship with Yoji

Yamada's highly popular "Torasan" types as the Hardy family has with Peyton Place. The neuroses carried about by Kuroki's characters are not little ones.

Kuroki, one of Japan's top young directors, started making short films in 1954, fresh out of college, including the brilliant 1962 "Hakkaido, My Love." When he went free-lance to make documentaries, his 1964 "The Document of a Marathon Runner" was one of the year's best films. "Preparations," made in 1975, is considered a "youth film," but the story by Takehiro Nakajima deals with many of the villagers, of all ages, centering on Tateo, a mother-dominated, confused youngster who wants to break away from home and village but lacks the courage.

His fellow villagers, besides a neurotic but loving mother and a father who lives across town with his mistress, include a grandfather who's convinced that he's fathered a child by a young girl who's slept with almost everyone in town, a drunken chum of the boy, and numerous other characters.

The title is never fully explained nor is the significance of Kuroki's use of symbols (most outstanding, a recurring shot of a red cloth tied to a post and blowing in the wind). At once a fascinating and irritating film by a talented director and well-placed in this festival. — *Robe.*

Watership Down
(BRITISH-ANIMATED-COLOR)

Bloody bunnies are box-office bother.

Hollywood, Oct. 12.

An Avco Embassy Pictures release of a Nepenthe Productions, Ltd. picture. Produced, directed and written by (from Richard Adams novel) Martin Rosen. Animation director, Tony Guy; animation supervision, Philip Duncan; editor, Terry Rawlings; music, Angela Morley, Malcolm Williamson. Reviewed at Consolidated Film Industries, Hollywood, Oct. 12, '78. (MPAA Rating: PG). Running time: **92 MINS.**
Voices: John Hurt, Richard Briers, Michael Graham-Cox, John Bennett, Simon Cadell, Roy Kinnear, Richard O'Callaghan, Terence Rigby, Ralph Richardson, Denholm Elliott, Zero Mostel, Mary Maddox, Hannah Gordon, Lyn Farleigh, Harry Andrews, Nigel Hawthorne, Clifton Jones, Michael Hordern, Joss Ackland.

With its bloody bunnies and dark moods, "Watership Down" should frighten and delight small children. But you can't do that anymore and get a G rating and the pic's PG label may make for a marketing problem, despite international success of book by same name. For the public unfamiliar with the book, moreover, title could be an additional sales setback, sounding as it does like a sunken submarine.

Employing fair-to-excellent animation and an array of fine voices drawn heavily from the English stage and screen, "Watership" traces the odyssey of a brave band of rabbits in search of a peaceful new home.

But this is not Bugs Bunny househunting. Producer-director Martin Rosen has taken author Richard Adams' concept of real rabbits — doomed by nature to be victims of those they cannot escape or outwit — and projected them into a fearful ordeal.

Along the way, the cottontails are shotgunned, bitten, gnawed, scratched, hawked and torn apart by dogs and meaner rabbits, with no skimping on red ink. In one particularly gruesome scene, one of the heroes is snared around the neck by a wire, gushing and gurgling blood quite realistically.

This is too much, some would say, for tender eyes (if intended for them). Hooey. It's just what kids imagine their ghost stories and fairy tales would look like. Besides, it's got an overall positive theme with inspirational and ecological overtones to go with the suspense and excitement.

But commercial success will depend on how many parents or teenagers take the tykes to see it, since it's a little too unsophisticated to appeal to older ages alone. It's hard to make a cartoon that will, but Rosen has made a grand attempt. It's a shame the ratings aren't bent better in the bunnies behalf. —*Har.*

Judith Therpauve
(FRENCH-COLOR)

———

Paris, Oct. 10.

Gaumont release of Buffalo Films-Gaumont S.A. production. Stars Simone Signoret. Directed by Patrice Chereau. Screenplay, Georges Conchon, Chereau; camera (Eastmancolor), Pierre Lhomme; editor, Francoise Bonnot. Reviewed at Paris Film Festival (competing), Oct. 5, '78. Running time 125 MINS.
Judith .... Simone Signoret
Damien .... Marcel Imhoff
Maurier .... Philippe Leotard
Droz .... Robert Manuel
Hirsch .... Francois Simon
Lepage .... Laszlo Szabo

Simone Signoret is having a big year. After the Academy Award-winning "Madame Rosa," and her well-received memoirs, "Nostalgia Isn't What It Used to Be," here is another big screen role. This time it is in a rather portentously-treated tale about a provincial newspaper being threatened with take-over by big national interests from Paris. In the end might prevails.

Director Patrice Chereau has a name in legit and opera for some ingenious slants. He made one pic, a few years ago, a rather glossy gangster item, "Flesh Of The Orchid." His mainly theatrical flair turns the present film into a series of scenes primarily in medium or long shots that miss the visual grace, mounting drive and potency needed for a study of press corruption and public apathy.

Signoret, widow of a resistance leader and also a heroine in her own right, now lives alone in a big house and does not have much interest in life or her grown son and daughter whose families invade her house weekends. One day some old resistance friends arrive.

They insist she take over a newspaper they started after the war which is now failing and its director dying. She agrees, although knowing nothing about newspapers. She manages to keep things going but is finally defeated by the tactics of the Paris forces and renegades and the union reps from her own paper.

She had even mortgaged her home to keep the paper alive. It is here where a shot rings out after she gets home from the last meeting and the impending sale to the never-seen Paris newspaper tycoon. Her suicide is left to a final scene of people running towards the house after the shot.

Signoret has solid presence but the director's distance from the characters, relying on talkative proceedings and not enough revealing interplay between them, does not give her much chance.

Philippe Leotard is effective as a man she ups to editor but whose heart is not really in it. Francois Simon has a few sharply etched scenes as the dying director with the others all doing their bits in theatrical stage style. —Mosk.

Tiempos De Constitucion
(Times of the Constitution)
(SPANISH-COLOR)

———

San Sebastian, Sept. 16.

Produced, directed and written by Rafael Gordon. Camera (Eastmancolor), Miguel Angel Martin; music, Fernando Brunet, Luis Fernandez Soria; editor, Jesus Valdizan. Reviewed at Cine Principal (San Sebastian), Sept. 16, '78. Running time: 101 MINS.
Cast: Veronica Forque, Hector Alterio, Francisco Algora, Jose Bodalo, Victoria Hernan, David Thomson, Jose Calvo, Yelena Samarina, Alfonso del Real, Kiti Manver, Carmen Vazquez Vigo.

Young filmmakers often have the wrong idea that plotless films are of interest to audiences. Novice Rafael Gordon's "Times of the Constitution" is a case in point. Dull, rambling and pretentious, it flounders about from one disjointed dialog to the next. There is no continuity in the scenes and little sense.

Sometimes it looks like pic is heading for the youth market, then it veers to puerile "philosophy," only to sink under the weight of its own vacuous pessimism. Maybe it's all symptomatic of the present era in Spain and the ennui of those who lament the smooth change-over after Franco.

The talky plot concerns a limousine driver, his girlfriend and her brother, all of them seemingly unhappy, nihilistic and anti-social. They flop about the screen, yakking incessantly. The driver picks up two girl tourists, drives them to see the Goyas and snidely decides that they understand nothing. He then marries his girlfriend in a cemetery chapel, takes on a job as house help with an eccentric couple (enter Hector Alterio, the only mature part of the film) living in the country, leaves again, etc. without the director even making his point in the meaningless sequences. Slim sales outlook even in Spain. —Besa.

Money Movers
(AUSTRALIAN-COLOR)

———

Sydney, Oct. 9.

A Roadshow release of a South Australian Film Corp. production. Produced by Matt Carroll. Directed by Bruce Beresford. Stars Terry Donovan, Ed Devereaux, Tony Bonner. Screenplay, Beresford, from novel by Devon Minchin; camera (color), Don McAlpine; editing, William Anderson; stunt coordination, Alf Joint; art director, David Copping; technical advisor, Devon Minchin; sound, Don Connolly; production manager, Pat Clayton; asst. directors, Mark Egerton, Mark Turnbull, Scott Hicks; wardrobe, Anna Senior; special effects, Ian Jamieson. Reviewed at Commonwealth Government Centre theatrette, Sydney, Oct. 4, '78. (Censorship rating: R-over 18s). Running time: 94 MINS.
Eric Jackson .... Terence Donovan
Dick Martin .... Ed Devereaux
Leo Bassett .... Tony Bonner
Robert Conway .... Lucky Grills
Sammy Ross .... Alan Cassell
Lionel Darcy .... Frank Wilson
Mindel Seagers .... Candy Raymond
Brian Jackson .... Bryan Brown
Jack Henderson ... Charles 'Bud' Tingwell
Ernest Sainsbury .... Gary Files
Griffiths .... Hu Price
Ed Gallagher .... Ray Marshall
Dawn Jackson .... Jeanie Drynan
Dino .... Terry Camilleri
Nacker .... Ted Hodgeman
Bengal Lancer .... James Elliott
Dim Sims .... Max Fairchild
Geronimo .... Rick Hart
Tony Duggan .... Robert Essex
Janitor .... Alan Penney
Patterson .... Tom Farley
TV Reporter .... Stuart Littlemore
Brian's girl friend .... Jo-Anne Moore
Henderson's mother .... Mimi Mattin
Managing Director .... Brian Harrison
M.D.'s Secretary .... Kathy Dior

"Money Movers" is a contemporary action picture, about a $20,-000,000 heist from an assertedly unassailable vault — the Aussie equivalent of Brink's — in the tradition of "Rififi," "League of Gentlemen," "Great Train Robbery" and the rest. Nothing particularly remarkable, perhaps, but extremely well and convincingly done in terms of location, characterization and action.

The latter is violent enough to evoke an "over 18" rating from the local censor, and possibly a few minutes of trimming in the editing could ease that, but it would effectively diminish the thrust of the film which is about criminals and robbery in its most contemporary (and hence violent) sense. These days the bad guys are fairly ordinary fellows, and in the case of "Money Movers" the badder guys (as exemplified by Bud Tingwell's Henderson) are even more banal, even if living, so to speak, "up market."

The violence is inherent in the subject, of course, and since this is an action picture there's a fair amount of it, but not enough to get in the way of the well-defined characterization. Nobody's intellect is going to be exercised by what goes on, but that wasn't meant to happen. The central plot is simple without being simplistic — the robbery will take place: problem is how will it be foiled?

Acting performances are standout in the macho department, though the femmes have little to hang their talents onto. The lead villain's wife (Jeanie Drynan), for example, has so little to do that it would seem most of her part was left on the cutting room floor.

The producers brought in English stunt coordinator Alf Joint to handle the physical action scenes, and the result is to give the film more veracity in those sequences. The staging is fine and the editing enhances the 'choreography' to provide a realism rare in local product.

Tech credits are excellent and Bruce Beresford moves the narrative and the actors briskly through their required motions to the finale in which the robbery is foiled. While the tension is maintained and the pace is kept up, there is no opportunity for interest to flag, but there are moments when the cross-cutting creates the odd flat spot.

Play off potential Down Under is slightly marred by the censorship rating, but the pic should perform well in ozoners. —Mike.

L'Orfeo
(Orpheus)
(GERMAN-SWISS-COLOR)

———

Zurich, Sept. 18.

Unitel Film Munich production. Written and directed by Jean-Pierre Ponnelle, from the Claudio Monteverdi opera. Conductor, Nikolaus Harnoncourt; camera (Eastmancolor), Wolfgang Treu; sound, H. Muehle; costumes, Pet Halmen; artistic direction, Claus Helmut Drese. Features soloists and choir of the Zurich Opera House. Previewed at Apollo-Cinerama, Zurich, Sept. 18, '78, running time, 103 MINS.
La Musica/Speranza .. Trudeliese Schmidt
Orfeo .... Philippe Huttenlocher
Euridice .... Dietlinde Turban
(sung by Rachel Yakar)
Messaggera/Proserpina .... Glenys Linos
Caronte .... Hans Franzen
Plutone .... Werner Groeschel
Apollo .... Roland Hermann
Ninfa .... Suzanne Calabro
Pastor 1 .... Peter Keller
Pastor2/Spirito 1 .... Francisco Araiza
Pastor 3/Spirito 2 .... Christian Boesch
(sung by Rudolf A. Hartmann)
Pastor 4/Spirito 3 .... Jozsef Dene

With a cycle of 17th century baroque composer Claudio Monteverdi's three operas, "L'Orfeo" (Orpheus), "L'Incoronazione di Poppea" (The Coronation of Poppea) and "Il Ritorno d'Ulisse in Patria" (Ulysses' Homecoming), done over three seasons, the Zurich Opera House registered a major artistic, critical and boxoffice success. Following sellout houses and rave reviews, a number of European festivals invited the Zurich company. So far, the Monteverdi trio has been successfully touring festivals in Hamburg, Vienna and Edinburgh, with Berlin, Milan, Florence, Wiesbaden and Flanders, Belgium, to follow shortly.

In collaboration with the Zurich Opera, Unitel Film Munich is filming the three productions with original casts, not live onstage, but in a studio, with separate sound recording. For "L'Orfeo", the latter was done in Zurich in stereo and used for playback with the 35m color negative made at the Wien-film studio in Vienna.

Filming of "L'Orfeo," first opera of the cycle, lasted four weeks.

"Poppea" and "Ulysses" will follow in 1979 and 1980, respectively. As filmed documents of a major musical enterprise, these films are (and will be) invaluable, especially to music schools and students, musicologists and opera lovers generally. Imaginative direction and lavish sets by Jean-Pierre Ponnelle (who also write and directed the film version), Pet Halmen's eyefilling costumes and Nikolaus Harnoncourt's flawless musical direction are all there on the screen.

Original or authentically rebuilt baroque instruments, played by specially trained musicians, have been used, same as in the stage version. The handpicked cast of singers (all singing is in original Italian) is near-perfect. Philippe Huttenlocher as Orfeo, Trudeliese Schmidt doubling as La Musica and Speranaza, Glenys Linos as Messaggera and Proserpina, Dietlinde Turban (with the voice of Rachel Yakar) as Euridice and virtually all others involved combine magnificent voices with good looks (not to be taken for granted in opera).

"L'Orfeo" is first being shown on tv in Austria and Western Germany and has reportedly been sold to the U.S. for the "Great Performances" series, and to Japan. Several European countries have expressed interest. Chances for theatrical use are very limited, but for television and special cultural and/or educational outlets. It should serve a useful purpose. —*Mezo.*

Rockers
(COLOR)

San Francisco, Oct. 8.

Rockers Film Corp. release. Produced by Patrick Hulsey. Stars Leroy Wallace. Directed and written by Theodoros Bafaloukos. Camera (color), Peter Sova; sound, Nigel Noble; editor, Susan Steinberg; associate producer, Avrom Robin; art director, Lilly Kilvert; costume designer, Eugenie Bafaloukos; asst. director, Walter Rearick. Reviewed at San Francisco International Film Festival, San Francisco, Oct. 7, '78. (No MPAA rating.) Running time: **100 MINS.**

Horsemouth	Leroy Wallace
Dirty Harry	Richard Hall
Madgie	Monica Craig
Sunshine	Marjorie Norman
Jakes	Jacob Miller
Jah (cq) Tooth	Gregory Isaacs
Burning Spear	Winston Rodney
Kiddus I	Frank Dowding
Robbie	Robert Shakespeare
Big Youth	Manley Buchanan
Dillinger	Lester Bullocks
The Mighty Diamonds	Themselves
Higher	Ashley Harris
Leroy Smart	Himself
Honeyball	Peter Honiball
Jack Ruby	L. Lindo
Leggo Beast	Trevor Douglas
Bongo Herman	Herman Davis
Jeep Man	Raymond Hall
Natty Majesty	Junior Wilby
Knatty Garfield	Errol Brown
Jah Wise	Robert Van Campbell
Prince Hammer	Berris Simpson
Easy Snapping	Theophilus Beckford
John Dread	Phylip Richards

Outlook for this lushly-lensed, marvelously-scored first film by one time Minneapolis spot maker Theodoros Bafaloukos appears clouded, unless there are millions of underground reggae buffs out there. And maybe there are.

"Rockers" arrived at the Frisco Fest sans distrib and without a record deal. The latter is critical if the film is to enjoy any success, for the music is the picture's strength and must be pre-sold vigorously for decent b.o. returns.

The makers have to be banking on some fallout from "The Harder They Come." Only intense devotees of reggae will be familiar with the performers in "Rockers," who appear as themselves, but are labelled in the film with nicknames.

Leroy "Horsemouth" Walker is a leading reggae drummer. In the screenplay, burdened by sub-titling that will take a bit of time to get used to because of the Jamaican patois, he portrays a drummer who decides to become a record distrib. But his business is aborted when an organized burglary syndicate swipes his motorcycle. So Walker and his musician buddies decide to steal from the thieves and turn over all the goods to the island's poor.

The tale, and the people, have fetching qualities. But whether a large enough audience awaits this interesting piece of work is questionable. —*Herb.*

Further Adventures of the Wilderness Family—Part 2
(COLOR)

That family is back, still up-staged by the scenery.

Pacific International Enterprises release of an Arthur Dubs production. Features entire cast. Directed by Frank Zuniga. Screenplay, Arthur Dubs; camera (color), John Hora; music, Douglas Lackey, Gene Kauer; lyrics, Dennis Brockman; songs performed by Barry Williams. Reviewed in New York screening room Oct. 20, '78. (MPAA Rating-G). Running time: **105 MINS.**

Skip Robinson	Robert Logan
Pat Robinson	Susan D. Shaw
Jenny Robinson	Heather Rattray
Toby Robinson	Ham Larsen
Boomer	George (Buck) Flower
Doctor	Brian Cutler
Pilot	Kurt Grayson

Back in 1975 Arthur Dubs made an innocent little film which he dubbed "Adventures of the Wilderness Family." At the end of 1978 he reported rentals to date in the U.S. and Canada amounting to $13,363,269.

If its sequel, "Further Adventures of the Wilderness Family - Part 2," which hits the nation's screens during Christmas Week does half that much it will still be a highly successful effort. And this despite the claim that it cost three and a half times as much as the original. From what is on the screen, there's no reason why the sequel shouldn't have the same appeal as the first film.

While the cast, especially Robert Logan as the father and Heather Rattray as his daughter (they've also survived the Aleutians in Warners' "The Sea Gypsies"), are generally impressive and natural, it's evident from the opening shot that they're going to play support to the scenery. Filmed at Irwin Lake Lodge, Crested Butte, Colorado, John Hora's color camera provides sweeping scenes of some of the Rocky Mountains' most stunning landscapes. The film goes through most of the seasons and there isn't one fake snowflake to be found.

The human actors are also hard put to it to out-perform the animals used — one assumes that even the seemingly wild ones, such as wolves, are carefully trained as the entire cast has to work in very close proximity. There's no credit given for the animal trainer but there should be, as this involves a dog, a large bear, two small bears, four wolves, a raccoon and other assorted beasts.

Arthur Dubs' simple script fortunately keeps his cast out of doors for most of the film as their interior scenes tend to get a bit sticky. Susan D. Shaw as the mother is excellent in her one opportunity to convey the loneliness that attacks at times, especially when she develops pneumonia. Ham Larsen is natural as the small boy of the family and prin-cipal trouble-originator. George Flower, as an old trapper, chews the scenery a bit but there's plenty of that to spare.

Action highlights include the family being besieged by wolves, led by a particularly vicious looking member, a series of small accidents, avalanches and other nature-type hazards. If the viewer never worries about the family's income and who pays for those frequent trips to town via private plane and other expenditures, he'll be rewarded with one of the best arguments for ecology currently available. —*Robe.*

Halloween

For drive-ins and fast play-off. More tricks than treat.

Hollywood, Oct. 13.

A Compass International Pictures release of a Falcon International production. Produced by Debra Hill. Executive producer, Irwin Yablans. Stars Donald Pleasence. Directed by John Carpenter. Screenplay, Carpenter, Hill; camera (color), Dean Cundey; music, Carpenter; editor, Tomy Wallace, Charles Burnstein, set decoration, Craig Stearns; production design, Wallace, assistant director, Rick Wallace; sound, Tommy Causey. No other credits available. Reviewed at the Vine Theatre, Hollywood, Oct. 13, '78. (MPAA rating: R.). Running time: **93 MINS.**

Loomis	Donald Pleasence
Laurie	Jamie Lee Curtis
Annie	Nancy Loomis
Lynda	P.J. Soles
Brackett	Charles Cyphers
Lindsey	Kyle Richards
Tommy	Brian Andrews
Bob	John Michael Graham
Marion	Nancy Stephens

After a promising opening, "Halloween" becomes just another maniac-on-the-loose suspenser. However, despite the prosaic plot, director John Carpenter, who authored the script with producer Debra Hill, has timed the film's gore so that the 93-minute item is packed with enough thrills to assure the Compass International release strong business in drive-ins and fast playoff situations.

The picture opens 15 years earlier, on Halloween night in a small midwestern town. A young boy spies his sister necking with her boyfriend. As they mount the steps for her bedroom he slips on his Halloween mask, pulls out a butcher knife and does some cutting.

The opening sequence is very cleverly filmed from the point of view of the young killer, through the eyeholes in his mask. Carpenter's influence very obviously is Hitchcock, complete with a staircase and a camera moving up the steps.

For the rest of the thriller the Hitchcockian influence remains, but the plot ambles along to a predictable conclusion. It is now the present, also Halloween, Donald Pleasence, a psychiatrist who has been caring for the killer during the years, is on his way to the state hospital to make sure that the maniac is never freed.

Of course, the maniac escapes, returns to the scene of the original crime and searches for suitable victims, in this case a trio of babysitting friends.

A film like "Halloween" is judged by the number of screams it can raise from an audience and not by its logic and this one raises quite a few yelps, especially during the last 20 minutes, which should help word of mouth. Carpenter has a good feel for timing the thrills and occasionally adds an offbeat, almost perverse sense of humor, which works.

Picture is low budget, but looks handsome, much to producer Hill's credit. Pleasence's part is not as large or crucial as his above the title billing might indicate. Performances by Jamie Lee Curtis (daughter of Janet Leigh and Tony Curtis),Nancy Loomis and P.J. Soles as the nubile victims and would-be victims are fine. —*Hege*.

Un Cuore Semplice
(A Simple Heart)
(ITALIAN-COLOR)

Barcelona, Oct. 13.
Cooperative Nashira production. Directed by Giorgio Ferrara; Screenplay, Cesare Zavattini, based on a Gustave Flaubert story; camera (Eastmancolor), Arturo Zavattini; editor, Roberto Perpignani; music, Franco Mannino. Reviewed at screening room of Barcelona Fest, Oct. 12, '78. Running time: **94 MINS.**
Cast: Adriana Asti, Joe Dallessandro, Alida Valli, Tina Aumont.

This beautifully limned, porcelain-fine film based on a Flaubert story, though at times a bit too lachrymose for comfort, especially in its final sequence, is nonetheless a superb piece of filmmaking. Adriana Asti puts in a magnificent, touching performance as a simple-minded 19th century servant girl whose life transpires with bucolic simplicity in a rural area; Cesare Zavattini's moving and often very funny script, Arturo Zavattini's romantic lensing, plus topnotch direction, sets, music and supports by the rest of the cast make this a truly memorable film, a small jewel which, if judiciously released, could generate considerable word of mouth interest.

The simple story of a servant girl who is jilted by her lover, then taken into the household of a wealthy country widow, and who then suffers the grief of losing two beloved adolescents, thereupon to pour all her affections upon a parrot, is told with snappy succinctness. Pic never becomes maudlin (as it might very easily have) thanks to a thread of wry humor which counterbalances the often heartrending tale.

When the parrot upon which the maid dotes dies, the servant piously has the bird stuffed and converts it into a quasireligious shrine for her room. At the end, aged, alone and dispossessed, she dies after an eventless life, a "simple heart" who sought love but never found it.

The film seems simplicity itself, but this is attained thanks to the great talents of all involved, especially the excellent thesping of Adriana Asti, whose stellar performance buoys up the whole production.

Though films based on 19th century classics are usually hard sells, this one certainly merits and conceivably could garner an appreciative audience for itself as a sleeper despite its period backdrop and irrelevance to modern problems
—*Besa*.

The Voyage Of Emperor Chien Lung
(HONG KONG- COLOR)

Hong Kong, Oct. 9.
Shaw Bros. release of a Sir Run Run Shaw productions. Producer, Mona Fong. Written and directed by Li Han-hsiang. Features entire cast. Camera (color), Lin Chao; art director, Chen Ching-shen; editor, Chiang Hsing-lung; martial art instructors, Tang Chia, Huang Pei-chi. Reviewed at Jade Theatre, Hong Kong, Oct. 8, '78. Running time: **100 MINS.**
Emperor Chien Lung .... Liu Yung
Ngo Yung-an .... Chiang Nan
Liu ....Li Kun
Kung-fu instructor ....Chow Shen
Siao Fung .... Hui Ying-hung
Chang Ah-wu .... Wu Hang-sheng
Changah-wen .... Lun Chia-chun
Old Man...................... Ho Li-jen
(Cantonese/Mandarin soundtrack; English subtitles)

Li Han-hsiang is an important director in the history of Chinese films. After a series of artistic ventures that flopped, he returned to Shaw Bros. to churn out over a dozen erotic films and historical epics that were mostly set in the period after the 1911 Revolution, an era with which Li seems to be most familiar.

His latest excursion takes him to 1762 A.D. during the reign of Emperor Chien Lung. Despite the costumes galore, ambiance of the colourful southern province of Yang Chow recreated at the Shaw backlot at Clearwater Bay, the gabby semi-epic falters and shows the declining years of a once creative and compelling Hong Kong director.

The film is enhanced a bit by the magnetic presence of actor Liu Yung who makes an impressive and arresting portrayal of Emperor Chien.

The plot is simple. It is the so-called adventure (if one can call it that) or Voyage Part II of the Emperor as a private citizen in an effort to mingle with the common folks. Together with his two loyal officials Lord Kuo (Chiang Nam) and scholar Liu (Li Kun) the Emperor makes his second incognito visit to the province which has nothing spectacular to boast about, except a lacklustre restaurant fight, an encounter with a fortune teller and a kind of gambling called "Far Wui."

Dull is the only word to describe this unremarkable historical piece that can easily be forgotten as a minor Li. Yueh Hua, Chang Ying and Wang Sha, popular name actors make-up the guest star list.

The English subtitles do not help the film. Its appeal is definitely limited to Chinatown theaters, not art houses. Viewers must have a good command of Mandarin to truly appreciate this production that the domestic market may tolerate because of the director's international reputation as a prestigious filmmaker of merit. — *Mel*.

Eutanasia Di Un Amore
(Break Up)
(ITALIAN-COLOR)

Sorrento, Oct. 7.
A Rizzoli Film picture. Produced by Mario Cecchi Gori for Capital Film and Koral International. Directed by Enrico Maria Salerno. Stars Ornella Muti, Tony Musante. Screenplay, Arduino Maiuri, Massimo De Rita, from novel of same title by Giorgio Saviane; camera (Technospes), Marcello Gatti; music, Daniele Patucchi, set design, Dante Ferretti; costumes, Waine Finkelman; montage, Mario Morra; distributor, Cineriz. Reviewed at Sorrento Encounter with Scandinavian Films, Oct. 20, '78. No running time given.
Sena .... Ornella Muti
Paolo ....Tony Musante
Silva ....Monica Guerritore
The doctor .... Mario Scaccia
Patrizia .... Elsa Trotter

After 10 years of apparent bliss, Sena, a young university assistant, walks out on her middle-aged lover, Paolo, a university professor. Beside himself with anguish, Paolo (and the audinece) tries desperately to find out the reason for her unexpected departure. After a tedious series of reunions and break-ups and several heavy-handed clues (a dump truck crushing a baby doll, Free Abortion signs), Paolo (and the audience) finally learn the awful truth. She wanted one and he didn't. A baby, that is.

Paolo then has an affair with a sterile woman, the symbol obviously of the universal mother, and discovers that he seeks an absolute and not dependent love. In the final scene, he floats away in a small boat while Sena speeds away on the yacht along with the sterile woman. Alone at last.

"Euthanasia" has been mistitled: this is not a mercy killing, but a slow and painful torture. The film should find easy success in Italy, Spain and France where Ornella Muti has a considerable following and may even touch ground in those areas where Enrico Maria Salerno's "Anonimo Veneziano" left trails of wet hankies (although Salerno has already objected, who knows why, to the distributor's use of his most famous pic to date in publicity mats).

Muti, who for the first time in her film career has been dubbed with her own voice, has been finally given a role that, as she put it, "has something to say" rather than her usual decorative part. Unfortunately, it takes half the film for her to have her say: the rest is a lot of slamming of car doors and telephone receivers or languid and tearful hellos and goodbyes.

Salerno milks these departure scenes ad nauseam. In a train station rendezvous worthy of "A Man and A Woman," Salerno's panning back and forth between the estranged lovers heading for an embrace makes Lelouch look subtle. Subtlety is not, however, the film's strong point: scenes starring the new Fiat Ritmo 65 (including a close-up of the car's rear end name plate) looked like a misplaced car commercial.

The only beacons in an otherwise dim film (even Salerno admitted that the film's lighting was off, blaming, however, his distributor, Cineriz, for releasing bad prints) are the performances of Tony Musante as Paolo and Monica Guerritore as Silva, the sterile woman. Musante, an Italo-American who physically could easily pass for a Florentine professor, is obliged to plod through a series of totally disconnected scenes. he does it and with great dignity. Guerritore is obliged to deliver the "I'm sterile" line like she would say, "I've got corns." She pulls it off with disarming naturalness. —*Argo*.

Wai Tok Kra
(An Old Woman)
(THAI)

Bangkok, Sept. 20.
A Nakornping Films release. Produced, directed and edited by Chana Krapayun. Features entire cast. Story and screenplay, Siri Madda; camera, Thavee Kiatinan; sound and dubbing, Kasem Militachinda; music, Nopadol Busapaketr; costumes, Khun Too. Reviewed at Chalerm Thai theatre, Bangkok, Sept. 20, '78, Running time: **126 MINS.**
Khun Noo ....Suan Prakkard
Sompop ....Sorapong Chatri
Pimjai .... Tarika Taratit
Nixa ....Choosri Misomon
Niwat .... Sompop Benjatikul
Lek .... Kumalee Komarakoon Nanakorn
Chaiporn ....Somjin Tamatat
Khoy.................... Vivian Suksom

As the grandmama in this picture, Suan Prakkard's main challenge is being able to shed tears when one of her three children shouts at her. Two are married with children of their own. A third is constantly in fear of becoming an old maid. All live in a housing compound with three houses in it. Thus, the irony of the situation is that there are too many houses in which Suan may stay, but she does not feel at home in any of them.

There are many laughs, particularly sequences satirizing the use of relatives of a government official to get a disputed project approved. The funny thing here is that newcomer Kumalee gets more laughs than experienced comedienne, Choosri. Director Chana Krapayun claims it was entirely "accidental," since Kumalee is supposed to be playing a straight dramatic role. —*Cano.*

Paris Film Fest

Messer Im Kopf
(Knife in the Head)
(WEST GERMAN-COLOR)

Paris, Oct. 15.

Filmverlag Der Autoren release of Bioskop Film Hallelujah Film production. Features entire cast. Directed by Reinhard Hauff. Screenplay, Peter Schneider; camera (Eastmancolor), Frank Bruhne; editor, Peter Przygodda; music, Irmin Schmidt. Reviewed at Paris Film Fest (competing), Oct. 11, '78. Running time, **108 MINS.**

Hoffman	Bruno Ganz
Ann	Angela Winkler
Anleitner	Hans Christian Blech
Volker	Heinz Honig
Scholz	Hans Brenner
Schurig	Udo Samel
Groske	Eike Gallwitz

A film tackling some tantalizing ideas and themes that unfortunately does not quite clarify its outlooks due to a rather cluttered and finally evasive script. However, its playing and direction label it a festival film and one that could have specialized chances though needing most careful handling and placement.

And it is a pity, for director Reinhard Hauff has given the pic a crisp finish and some potent probing of that disturbing subject of political terrorism and the other side of the coin, police terrorism.

A distraught man working in a laboratory seems angry at what he feels are lies and corruption around him. He rushes off to see his estranged wife at a local club of political leftists, but not necessarily terrorists. The police are taking many in and he enters and is shot in the head by an overzealous policeman.

Is he or is he not a terrorist? The police say yes, the others that he only comes at times to see his wife. At first, it seems to be about police creation of a terrorist by unfounded insistence. But then it goes into an unusual, absorbing study of the shot man, played expertly by Bruno Ganz, being reeducated when he

loses some speech and arm and leg movement after a brain operation.

As he slowly gets better, police attempts to put him in a prison hospital are stymied. He finally runs away and goes home to await trial. He now takes up protests against his wife's lover and finds that interest has been lost in him and goes to see the man who shot him.

In the man's apartment, he gets the latter's gun and pic ends as he is deciding whether or not to shoot him in the head. Film raises ideas about social protest being driven to terrorism and the use of it as barren and fatal for both sides. But pic skirts rather than faces up to making a statement, except that familiar one about violence breeding violence. —*Mosk.*

Doramundo
(BRAZILIAN-COLOR)

Paris, Oct. 12.

Ere Films release and production. Features entire cast. Directed by Joao Batista De Andrade. Screen-play, De Andrade, David Jose, Alain Fresnot; camera (Eastmancolor), Antonio Meliande; editor, Glauco Mirko Laurelli; music, Alemdo Prado. Reviewed at Paris Film Fest (competing) Oct. 10, '78. Running time, **100 MINS.**

Cast with Rolando Boldrin, Antonio Fagundes, Armando Bogus, Irene Revache, Rodrigo Santiago, Oswaldo Camposana.

A harsh look at a small mining and railroad town in 1939 beset by a series of strange murders. Film obviously wants to reflect on a country with a restrictive government that can easily suspend civil liberties or is beset by foreign intervention or colonialism, in this case British ownership of the railroads.

Sharp, mostly handheld camerawork adds a grim look to the murders of mainly bachelors killed by a fanatic of some sort wielding an iron bar. This brings in a high-level policemen at the request of the company who wants to solve things fast. He uses illegal detainment and harassment to get the killer.

Killer is not important, and the attempt to make the film transcend its theme is not effective. Pic is a flawed but sometimes revealing probing of the temperament of the lower proletariat. This gives it some fest handles but not the legs for more potent commercial possibilities abroad. —*Mosk.*

Wodzirej
(Top Dog)
(POLISH-COLOR)

Paris, Oct. 11.

Film Polski release of Zespoly Filmowe X production. Features entire cast. Written and directed by Feliks Falk. Camera (Eastmancolor), Edward Klosinski; music, Jan Kanty-Pawluskiewicz. Reviewed at Paris Film Fest (competing), Oct. 9, '78. Running time: **115 MINS.**

Danielak	Jerzy Sthur
Mela	Slawa Kwasniewska
Lasota	Wiktor Sadecki
Romek	Michal Tarkowski
Iza	Ewa Kolasinska

Polish films have been treating the excesses of the Stalinist period, or the misuse of hieretical powers, (lately Andrzej Wajda's "The Man of Marble" and Krsysztof Zanussi's "Camouflage" respectively). Now this pic looks ironically at a climber who is not above doing dirt to his best friend to get a job he thinks will launch him to better things.

Since the job he fights for is a sort of emcee at the inauguration of a provincial hotel, it does seem a bit slight in matching the impact of the aforementioned films.

But role is played with a shrewd mixture of pugnacity, boorishness and some attractiveness by Jerzy Stuhr. Direction of Feliks Falk is serviceable, but not pungent enough to give this familiar tale a more punchy directness and flair to hit a more transcending note on the more personal aspects of misguided or deliberate corruption.

He gets his comeuppance when his betrayed friend slaps him after he scores as the new dance leader and is being congratulated by higherups. Perhaps it does indicate the covering up of this form of ambition.

Film appears more a home item though worth festival usage on its theme and overall good blend of pace and playing. But it is promising in indicating more outspoken themes in regular as well as more ambitious pix. —*Mosk.*

Les Rendez-Vous D'Anna
(The Meetings of Anna)
(BELGIAN-FRENCH-
W. GERMAN-COLOR)

Paris, Oct. 24.

Gaumont release of Helene Films (Paris) — Paradise Films (Brussels) — ZDF (Mainz) production. Features entire cast. Written and directed by Chantal Ackerman. Camera (Eastmancolor), Jean Penzer; editor, Francine Sandberg. Reviewed at Paris Film Fest (competing), Oct. 9, '78. Running time: **127 MINS.**

Anna	Aurore Clement
Heinrich	Helmut Griem
Ida	Magali Noel
Man	Hanns Zieschler
Mother	Lea Massari
Daniel	Jean-Pierre Cassel

Chantal Ackerman, a Belgian, has found a specialized following locally and has become a film fest regular. She usually uses an intense series of longish scenes to lay bare a sort of grim reality.

In this film, a femme filmmaker seems to float around Europe, from Germany to Belgium and onto her home base, France, while having a series of run-ins with several people, both strangers and intimate re-

lations, that reveal her as a catalyst but not ready for any kind of commitment.

Pic might be tagged minimal filmmaking. It refuses to animate its action by more perceptive comportment. The girl, played with pained intensity, but with indications of strength by Aurore Clement, arrives in Germany for a showing of her film. She meets a teacher who likes her work.

It leads to lovemaking but then a farewell. But not before he has told her, in a long monolog, about his life with his mother and small daughter after his wife left him and the glow she has brought for a time.

She next meets the mother of a boy she was once interested in at a Belgian station as she is about to leave. Here life in Brussels is revealed. Then her mother comes to see her and they find a closer tie. On the train, a young man trying to find a country where he can settle down talks to her, later she is picked up by a lover when arriving in Paris. After a disappointing stay with him, she goes home to listen to her tape recorder of all the calls she has missed and with more plans to go on the road with her mysterious film.

Human needs are evoked. The fears of inflation, sickness, the difficulties of human contact are all indicated during Clement's many meetings. The finely-hued lensing and the intensity of the talk and reactions do finally exert a hypnotic effect. Definitely a fest film and it could find specialized niches as more demanding films seem to be finding more selective audiences.

Playing is staid and in keeping with the refusal to allow any emotions to interfere with the need to express the very core of being in talk rather than in action or in a true relationship.

A difficult, sometimes irritating film that may have captured a certain modern permissiveness that has both freed and set people adrift in search of new ways of facing the eternal needs of self knowledge and social coping. —*Mosk.*

Ecoute Voir ...
(Look See ...)
(FRENCH-COLOR)

Paris, Oct. 24.

Prospectacle release and production. Stars Catherine Deneuve, Sami Frey. Directed by Hugo Santiago. Screenplay, Claude Ollier, Santiago; camera (Eastmancolor), Ricardo Aronovich; editor, Alberto Yaccelini; producer, Maurice Bernart. Reviewed at Paris Film Fest (competing), Oct. 7, '78. Running time, **125 MINS.**

Alphand	Catherine Deneuve
Arnaud	Sami Frey
Flora	Florence Delay
Chloe	Anne Parillaud
Secretary	Didier Haudepin
Sect Man	Antoine Vitez

The winsome idea here is to have the alabaster, inexpressive French star Catherine Deneuve play a distaff private eye in the mold of Sam Spade, Philip Marlowe or Lew Archer. Arty treatment and slowness defuse its possibilities of homage or of much positive addition to the genre.

Director Hugo Santiago and cinematographer Ricardo Aronovic, both of Argentine origin, compose some pretty pictures. Pic has some vagueness in motives which would be acceptable if there was the punch, drive and pungent characterizations to gloss over the coincidences and sometimes elusive plotting of these kind of films. But pic lacks these requisities.

Deneuve walks through this gamely if not displaying the spunk, acumen and bounce to give a leavening of humor to this tale of a man who seems to have devised a radiobeam that can reduce people to automatons while it is on and induce any influence wanted on the subconscious.

He, played with intensity by Sami Frey, calls in Deneuve when his girl is kidnapped by an Eastern religious sect which want this secret ray to probably get new converts or worse, finds out about the ray and even kills Frey, though it was intimated a feeling, if no love play, had grown between them, when he comes after her when she has destroyed his apparatus.

Apparently director Santiago wanted to imbue this with poetic allusions to some classics, as the tragic love tale "Tristan and Isolde." But the more mythical qualities of the private eye pix come from within and are rarely consciously imposed. Humor is inadvertent as Deneuve keeps zapping people with one karate chop and takes on several others until she finally gets knocked out.

Languid tale might have appeal locally and in other European situations though it is more of curio value for any stateside chances.

— *Mosk.*

Otietz Sergii
(Father Serge)
(RUSSIAN-COLOR)

Paris, Oct. 24.
Sovexport release of Mosfilm production. Features entire cast. Written and directed by Igor Talankin from the book by Leo Tolstoy. Camera (Sovcolor), Guerogui Rerberg; editor, M. Verevnikov; music, A. Chnitke. Reviewed at Paris Film Fest (competing), Oct. 10, '78. Running time: 95 MINS.
With: Sergei Bondarchuk, Irina Skopseva, Y. Bourbov, A. Demidova, T. Korotkova.

For the 150th anniversary of the birth of the great Russian writer Leo Tolstoy the Russians are evidently turning out more films than usual on his works. This one, based on one of his last tales, delves into a proud, almost fanatically nationalistic nobleman's attempt to find faith and meaning in life as well as coming to terms with his overwrought libido.

Sergei Bondarchuk, actor-director who made the massive pic version of Tolstoy's "War and Peace," here plays the title character. Taking place in turn-of-the-century Russia, it shows him as a grizzled traveller listening to people talk of faith on a ferryboat. Then flashbacks block out his life.

Attached to the omnipotence of the Czar as a young boy at military school, he even slaps a superior officer whom he feels remiss in duties. As a man he becomes troubled by his feelings and finally decides to become a monk and renounce a marriage. Film is divided into episodes of his life preceded by titles describing each one.

Posily acted, academically directed, though with fine art direction and period re-creation, pic emerges as illustrative rather than creating a more revealing depth to the torments of this man who one night cuts off a finger to resist temptation from a coquettish woman who enters his hermetic house, where he has been secluded for years, on a bet.

He finally feels he is not worthy of being considered almost a saint and cuts his beard and sets off on a trek to find peace. He looks up a childhood sweetheart but her woeful life adds nothing to his need to find solace or belief. Film finally tells, in a title, that he ends up in Siberia as a teacher and doctor for the peasants.

Russians do these films well, if often — as in this case — too stolidly. Mainly possible school usage for this only surface approximation of Tolstoy's tale of fall and redemption. —*Mosk.*

Magic
(COLOR)

William Goldman's successful book as a less-effective film. Re-telling of the prior decades treatment of a ventriloquist controlled by his own dummy. Good scenes but downhill after strong first half hour.

Hollywood, Oct. 25.
A 20th Century-Fox release of a Joseph E. Levine presentation. Exec producer, C.O. Erickson. Produced by Joseph E. Levine, Richard P. Levine. Directed by Richard Attenborough. Screenplay, William Goldman, based on his novel of the same name; camera (color), Victor J. Kemper; editor, John Bloom; production design, Terence Marsh; music, Jerry Goldsmith; art director, Richard Lawrence; costumes, Ruth Myers; sound, Larry Jost; assistant director, Arne Schmidt. Reviewed at Academy of Motion Picture Arts & Sciences Theatre, BevHills, Oct. 25, '78. (MPAA Rating: R.) Running time: 106 MINS.
Corky Fats .... Anthony Hopkins
Peggy Ann Snow .... Ann-Margret
Ben Greene .... Burgess Meredith
Duke........................ Ed Lauter
Merlin .... E.J. Andre
Cab Driver ....:........... Jerry Houser

The 20th Century-Fox release of Joseph E. Levine's presentation is an occasionally absorbing character study that never fulfills its promise as a suspense chiller, despite an extraordinary performance by Anthony Hopkins.

The premise of "Magic," that of a dummy slowly taking over the personality of its ventriloquist-master, is not a new one. Michael Redgrave delineated the part with harrowing intensity in the Alberto Cavalcanti sequence of the British "Dead Of Night," and a similar treatment was employed in another English low-budgeter, "Devil Doll." (Not to forget "The Great "Gabbo" of Erich Von Stroheim, 1927).

In adapting his own best-seller, William Goldman has opted for an atmospheric thriller, a mood director Richard Attenborough, designer Terence Marsh and cinematographer Victor J. Kemper flesh out to its fullest.

The dilemma of "Magic" is that the results never live up to the standards established in the film's opening half-hour. Through flashbacks and claustrophic editing by John Booth, the relationship between Hopkins and his eerily-realistic dummy, Fats, is well-documented. So is the introduction of Burgess Meredity, well cast as a Swifty Lazar-type of superagent.

When Hopkins declines a lucrative tv contract because of insecurity, and flees to his boyhood Catskills home, where a high school girl on whom he had a crush (Ann-Margret) is enmeshed in a disastrous marriage to redneck Ed Lauter, "Magic" becomes disappointingly transparent.

Goldman has Hopkins becoming involved in the standard love triangle that inevitably leads to disaster for all parties concerned. It's this stereotyped plotting and conclusion that robs "Magic" of its initial, special quality, substi ating instead the dramaturgy of "An American Tragedy."

Attenborough, who is noted for his work with actors, again displays a flair for eliciting strong performances, especially from Hopkins, Meredith and Lauter, who is supremely menacing as the jealous husband. Ann-Margret has difficulty with her underwritten role.

There are scenes in "Magic" that should have the audience literally jumping out of their seats, such as the attempted drowning of Meredith. Instead, these moments remain glossily pacific, and "Magic" settles into a routinish, and predictable, windup.

The ventriloquism and magic stunts are expertly done by Hopkins, with the aid of tech advisor Dennis Alwood. And Fats does emerge. as .a distinctive,. if. unlik-. able personality, whose final soliloquy is very moving.

Jerry Goldsmith's score is an immense aid to the film's moodiness, and other production credits are way above par.

But as the Meredith character notes early on, "Magic is misdirection." That sentiment applies equally to the film. — *Poll.*

La Carapate
(Out Of It)
(FRENCH-COLOR)

Paris, Oct. 24.
Gaumont release of Gaumont International production. Stars Pierre Richard, Victor Lanoux. Directed by Gerard Oury. Screenplay, Oury, Daniele Thompson; camera (Eastmancolor), Edmond Sechan; editor, Albert Jurgenson. Reviewed at Ambassades-Gaumont, Paris, Oct. 13, '78. Running time, 105 MINS.
Duroc.................... Pierre Richard
Marcial .... Victor Lanoux
Marcel .... Raymond Bussieres
Panivaux .... Jean-Pierre Darras
Giselle .... Yvonne Godeau
Bach Yen .... Claire Richard

Director Gerard Oury made a name with his expensive comedies usually revolving around some sort of chase with well-honed gags and shrewd pairings of comedians or actors. Many had more serious themes within the essentially comic treatment such as the occupation in "La Grande Vadrouille," racism in "The Adventures of Rabbi Jacob," and now the near revolutionary May 1968 events back-dropping this tale about two ill-assorted characters on the run.

Big budget shows in the top production values, expert action segs and overall high technical quality. Partnering fey comic Pierre Richard, as a bumbling leftist lawyer, and more heavyweight, solid thesp

Victor Lanoux, limning a good-natured reactionary type sentenced to death for a murder he may not have done, works and they complement each other.

Richard goes to see Lanoux on death row to tell him he is trying to get to then President Charles De Gaulle to commute him to life imprisonment. There is a jailbreak and Richard ends up with Lanoux as he is considered responsible for the break. They have a series of adventures on the way to Paris including stealing a Rolls full of contraband money and gold a rich man is trying to get to Switzerland illegally due to fears of the May Days.

Lanoux and Richard get involved in all sorts of imbroglios, including getting caught between students and police on the barricades, with Lanoux finally exonerating Richard from the break and then escaping again as his new friend, Richard, waves goodbye from the Seine River into which he has naturally fallen.

Easygoing treatment and wit have this a good cut above the usual French action comedy. There is some good-natured spoofing of the skeptical and mean characters as well as the more sympathetic ones without the overindulgence usually apparent in French comedies.

Pic is sometimes mechanical and gags, at times, telegraphed. But film's sharp pace and invention overcome this. Director Oury does not attempt to get into the confused atmosphere of the '68 events except as a backing to this essentially escapist romp. Probably more potent at home, it still could have playoff legs abroad on its comedic drive. Some tightening and pruning would help. —*Mosk.*

The Odd Job
(BRITISH-COLOR)

London, Oct. 17.
Columbia release of Tavlorda Ltd. production; executive producers, Tony Stratton Smith, Steve O'Rourke; producers, Mark Forstater, Graham Chapman. Stars Graham Chapman, David Jason, Diana Quick. Directed by Peter Medak. Screenplay, Bernard McKenna, Graham Chapman; camera (color), Ken Hodges; production designer, Tony Curtis; editor, Barrie Vince; music, Howard Blake; costume designer, Shuna Harwood; sound, Claude Hitchcock; production manager, John Wilcox; assistant director, Stephen P. Christian. Reviewed at Columbia Cinema, London, Oct. 16, 1978. (BBFC rating: A). Running time: **86 MINS.**
Arthur Harris .... Graham Chapman
The Odd Job Man .... David Jason
Fiona Harris .... Diana Quick
Tony Sloane .... Simon Williams
Inspector Black ....Edward Hardwicke
Sergeant Mull .... Bill Paterson
Raymonde .... Michael Elphick
Bernaard .... Stewart Harwood
Angie .... Carolyn Seymour
Head Waiter .... Joe Melia
Caretaker .... George Innes

Good old British stereotypes are the mainstays of every scene of "The Odd Job," like skeletons come to haunt from the cupboard of a '50s British studio. Basic tenet of the script is that everyone is a complete idiot, chief being Graham Chapman as Arthur Harris, insurance executive and idiotic member of the English upper class.

Picture needs careful handling to find a market which cherishes memories of "Kind Hearts And Coronets" and "The Ladykillers" and will respond to seeing the style re-run. Teens and pre-teens may laugh without the memories.

Chapman hires an odd job man to murder him, then wants to call the deal off, but has programmed the man to ignore any instructions contrary to the original one. The remaining hour or so of the film is spent with Chapman trying to get out of this bind.

En route, in a London which consists almost exclusively of Big Ben and Regent's Park, he encounters a host of supporting caricatures of a stock range that has long fallen out of fashion, though still served up from time to time, reheated, in tv sitcoms: a fanatically racist caretaker; an instant-seductress neighbor; a gay paternalistic underworld-king, and his hopelessly stammering side-kick brother; the wife's best friend who turns out to be a lecherous cad; a horde of British policemen, fascistic in intent but doomed in practice; and so on.

So far, in a sense, so good. As a piece of nostalgia for some great days of British comedy, and with Chapman, prominent member of the Monty Python team, heading the cast, "The Odd Job" has something going for it. Peter Medak's direction, if somewhat cold, is efficient beyond reproach, and there is no skimping on production values. Shuna Harwood's costumes in particular contribute to a glossy look.

But the film never really pulls together, never settles into a style, and the cast is left straining for the laughs. Chapman clowns and grimaces ferociously, as if to hide his discomfort at holding stage-center for longer than a revue sketch.

Much more watchable is David Jason, star of BBC's children's show, "A Sharp Intake Of Breath," who cuts an eccentric and amusing figure as The Odd Job Man. This performance, like the few good moments in the rest of the picture, will have a universal appeal to kids, and the younger audience is surely the film's safest market.

Even they will be bemused by the cop-out ending, however, which has Chapman and wife falling headlong from the terrace of their apartment, the handrail having been "fixed" by The Odd Job Man in an earlier attempt to carry out his assignment.

At this point, the film lurches irrationally from '50s territory into a '60s surrealism recalling the close of "Dr. Strangelove," as the couple plunge in slow-motion through a sky as radiant as their faces to swelling chords and a lyric which runs, "Too late to say I'm falling for you..."

Inspired insanity has paid off for the Monty Python team, but this byproduct suffers from a shaky grip on the lunacy involved. —*Simo.*

The Tempter
(L'Anti Cristo)
(ITALIAN-COLOR)

Unappetizing exorcism fare.

Hollywood, Oct. 22.
An Avco Embassy release. Produced by Edmondo Amati. Directed by Alberto de Martino. Screenplay, Martino, Vincenzo Mannino, Gianfranco Clerici; camera (color), Aristide Massaccesi; editor, Vincenzo Tomassi; art director, Umberto Bertacca; music, Ennio Morricone. No other credits available. Reviewed at Picwood Theatre, West L.A., Oct. 22, '78. (MPAA Rating: R.) Running time: **96 MINS.**
Ippolita .... Carla Gravina
Massimo .... Mel Ferrer
Bishop .... Arthur Kennedy
Father Mittner ....George Coulouris
Irene .... Alida Valli
Gretel .... Anita Strindberg
Faith Healer .... Mario Scaccia
Psychiatrist .... Umberto Orsini

Just when you thought the devil was down for the last count, along comes Avco Embassy with yet another "Exorcist"-inspired film, this time an Italian import made in 1974 under title of 'L'Anti Cristo" laden with American performers who have very little to do. "The Tempter" trouts out all the familiar plot elements: a possessed girl who spews vomit regularly, a tortured clergyman, a helpful psychiatrist, and a triumphant priest who subdues Satan once again. Since there's obviously a market for this claptrap in inner-city nabes and drive-ins, a fast, saturation playoff may guarantee moderate returns.

The only factor to bestow any distinction on "The Tempter" is the bravura performance of Clara Gravina as the put-on soul. Her writhings, foaming and hurlings of obscenities are so realistic as to be occasionally frightening.

Otherwise, it's a long, grueling ride over familiar terrain, not helped by poor dubbing of the Italo actors, consistently out of focus lensing by Aristide Massaccesi, and bewildering editing by Vincenzo Tomassi. In other words, a technical shambles.

For the record, Gravina is the paralyzed daughter of Italian nobleman Mel Ferrer, who is dallying with Anita Strindberg to his offspring's displeasure. Head shrinker Umbert Orsini is brought in for consultation, and discovers through hypnosis that Gravina has inherited the curse of an ancestress burned a the stake as a witch.

Once the devil drops his cover, things liven up, but "The Tempter" is most ingenious in concocting a sexual seduction accomplished via an incubus, or invisible spirit. It's the perfect solution for explicit sex in an R-rated film: Gravina goes through all the gyrations, but the other partner can't be seen.

Arthur Kennedy, Mel Ferrere, George Coulouris and Alida Valli are all wasted in this pointless exercise that, unfortunately, probably won't be the last of its kind. —*Poll.*

Banished
(Hanare Goze Orin)
(JAPANESE-COLOR)

Toho release of film produced by Kiyoshi Iwashita and Seikichi Iizumi. Directed by Masahiro Shinoda. Features entire cast, based on novel by Tsutomu Minagami, adapted by Keiji Hasebe and director; camera (color), Kazuo Miyagawa; art direction, Kiyoshi Awazu; lighting, Takeharu Sano, music, Toru Takemitsu; sound, Hideo Nishizaki. Reviewed Oct. 18, '78 at Japand House, N.Y. Running time: 109 MINS.
Orin .... Shima Iwashita
Big Man .... Yoshhio Harada
Teruyo .... Tomoko Naraoka
Mountain Man .... Taiji Tonoyama
Besho .... Toru Abe
Saito .... Jun Hamamura

"Banished" was the first of five films from Japan shown to special audiences in Manhattan in the wake of the recent N.Y. Film Festival. Actually "Banished" has been ongoing at a single San Francisco theatre, though not one included in the *Variety* boxoffice estimates from there. Caught at Japan House auditorium near the United Nations this film proved to be beautifully photographed (Kazuo Miyagawa) and imaginatively directed (Masahiro Shinoda) with special recognition due the performance of Shima Iwashita as the blind and orphaned wandering mandolin-playing girl singer.

The term "banished" refers to the penalty when a girl trained and indentured to the Goze, a commune of blind Geishas, fractures her vow of chastity. The heroine thereupon is literally alone in the world, making a precarious living as best she can. Eyes closed, smiling enigmatically, puzzled by the prohibition of sex the Iwashita performance cannot fail to evoke sympathy and compassion.

The pictorial effect of the single-file of blind girls trudging barren terrain up to their kimona hems in snow has a peculiarly Japanese beauty. There are glimpses of the parties, some genteel, some rough, where the abandoned child now grown up is part of the entertainment in homes and inns of remote northern country.

Director Shinoda in his earlier screen work, "The Double Suicide," recently reviewed by this *Variety* staffer at the Montreal Film Festival, had also addressed other victims of difficult existence among the underprivileged, and in both films, death is the inevitable denouement of hopeless harassment.

The paradox of the young blind woman in "Banished" is that she cannot reconcile her mind to the puritanical prohibition against sex which to her is warmth, human contact and pleasure contrasting with the lack of other satisfactions or security in her own meagre, itinerant existence. She is in her quiet way a "rebel" against the plight of all Japanese girls at the time. Unless protected by family or marriage they had few choices — masseuse, prostitute, entertainer. Some of the blind entertainers, like their sighted sisters, slipped into sideline prostitution.

Incidentally, the Japanese in this case present rape with all due sexplicity but avoiding pornography. This is plot — justified sex, not prurience.

It is all quite touching. The dramatic twist arises when a sincere young man loves and guards the heroine but has religious scruples against sleeping with her. For a time they pretend to be brother and sister. Finally he is questioned by local police and while he is absent the girl is raped by a peddler. The lover returns, and though the girl wishes him to overlook the episode, he goes in pursuit, overtakes and murders the rapist.

The closing in of destiny involves the revelation that the sincere young man is an army deserter (circa 1918) as well as now a murderer. The military unmercifully beat him for the shame to the army but allow him, just before his execution, to have one final glimpse of the girl. After he's gone the girl seeks out his mother, only to learn she is dead. And so the inevitable suicide.

However grim the tales chosen by Shinoda the resultant screen works are remarkably emotional. The Japanese do not flinch from suffering or brutality. But their disapproval of evil is evident. One imagines that discriminating film fans and buffs will be enthralled.

—*Land.*

Secrets
(COLOR)

A 1971 film with Jacqueline Bisset in a nude scene which should have been kept a secret.

Hollywood, Oct. 26.

A Lone Star Pictures International release, produced by John Hanson. Stars Jacqueline Bisset, Robert Powell, Shirley Knight Hopkins, Per Oscarsson. Directed by Philip Saville. Screenplay, Rosemary Davies from a story by Saville; camera (color), Nic Knowland, Harry Hart; editor, Tony Woollard; music, Mike Gibbs. No other credits available. Reviewed at the UA Cinema Center, L.A., Oct. 26, '78. (MPAA Rating: R.) Running time: **92 MINS.**
Jacky .... Jacqueline Bisset
Raoul .... Per Oscarsson
Beatrice .... Shirley Knight Hopkins
Allan .... Robert Powell
Josy .... Tarka Kings
Raymond .... Martin C. Thurley
Dominique .... Stephen Martin

"Secrets" is Jacqueline Bisset's 1971 B.T. film. That's "before t-shirt." The only reason for releasing this precious, amateurish item is to cash in on Bisset's name and a five-minute nude scene.

Technically, the picture looks like outtakes from the six o'clock news. Nic Knowland and Harry Hart photographed the film using handheld cameras, which one can only suppose, was an artistic statement of some sort.

Rosemary Davies wrote the screenplay from a story by director Philip Saville. It concerns a couple and their daughter all of whom are keeping secrets from the other. Each has had a sexual encounter that day.

About the nude scene, it's fairly explicit and Bisset, as always, looks lovely. — *Hege.*

La Cage Aux Folles
(The Mad Cage)
(FRENCH-ITALIAN-COLOR)

Paris, Oct. 31.

United Artists release of UA-France-Da Ma Produzione Sta. production. Stars Ugo Tognazzi, Michel Serrault. Directed by Edouard Molinaro. Screenplay, Francis Veber, Molinario, Marcello Danon, Jean Poiret from a play by Poiret; camera (Eastmancolor), Armando Mannuzzi; editor, Robert and Monique Isnardon; music, Ennio Morricone. Reviwed at Ariane, Paris, Oct. 20, '78. Running time, **103 MINS.**
Renato .... Ugo Tognazzi
Zaza .... Michel Serrault
Charrier .... Michel Galabru
Simone................. Claire Maurier
Laurent .... Reni Laurent
Jacob .... Bennie Luke

Jean Poiret's French play, "The Mad Cage," is now in its fifth year on the boards and still going strong. Tale of a middleaged gay couple, beset by problems when the 20-year-old son of one announces his marriage, gets uneven film treatment. Most of the characters appear stereotyped and the familiar plotting reveals the gay duo could have as easily been heterosexual or an odd couple.

Though predictable, the film has one solid trump in Michel Serrault who makes the more feminine member of the happy couple a very shrewd limning of outsize campy gay attributes that avoid tastelessness. Thesp manages to comment on the queenly, demanding char-acter to garner most of the laughs and the few insights into gay life.

Italo player Ugo Toganazzi is the one who at one time, the only time, was bisexual enough to father a child brought up by him and Serrault. He, too, shows a feel for the surface mannerisms and outlooks of the more male side of the two. The son's bride-to be has bluenose parents and the father heads a politico party devoted to moral outlooks.

So the pic revolves around fooling the parents, not letting them in on the sex of the boy's father or his running a transvestite nitery where Serrault is the drag star. The long estranged mother of the boy is invited to the family meeting which angers Serrault and leads to many imbroglios before the wedding can take place.

Solid playing of Serrault and Tognazzi avoid caricature but film does not add much to old time comedics on femme impersonation or insights into the gay life. But it does not exploit the situation and could fare okay on home grounds and Europe, helped by the hit play derivation, and should not annoy gay lib too much.

Serrault's drag star status and talent is not too apparent in the few snatches of his act that are seen. Thesp's uncanny flair sometimes reveals how the campy actions are used as a shield or for acceptance to give the pic its few fine moments.

Molinaro's uneven direction and the overall staginess make this mainly for playoff use abroad on its exploitable theme. —*Mosk.*

L'Amour En Question
(Love In Question)
(FRENCH-COLOR)

Paris, Oct. 31.

Silenes Distribution release of Paris-Cannes-Production Alpes Cinema production. Stars Annie Girardot. Directed by Andre Cayatte. Screenplay, Jean Laborde, Cayatte; camera (Eastmancolor), Jean Badal; editor, Paul Cayatte; music, Olivier Dassault. Reviewed at Paramount-Elysees, Paris, Oct. 18, '78. Running time: **100 MINS.**
Suzanne .... Annie Girardot
Catherine .... Bibi Andersson
Man .... Michel Galabru
Philippe .... Michel Auclair
Lachot .... Georges Geret
Rhune .... Dominique Paturel

Director Andre Cayatte, after a look at corruption and political chicanery in government arms sales, "Reasons of State," goes back to his favorite theme of the workings of justice. Here it is not the usual overwrought brief about the miscarriages of man's meting out justice, but an attempt to deal with its workings and the influences of personal quirks which afflict both the accused and accusers.

All this is somewhat demonstrative rather than getting a human, graceful understanding of the people caught up in murder on both sides of the law. Bibi Andersson is effective as the Swedish wife of an older French architect. Her husband is murdered as he drives up to their house one day.

French justice has a magistrate, called a judge, who studies the case and then decides whether to book any suspects. The judge is played knowingly by Annie Girardot. She delves into Andersson's life, her love affair with an Englishman, accepted by her husband suffering from impotence, and other aspects of her life. Girardot begins to think that Andersson and the lover plotted the killing.

There are enough twists to keep this of interest though its abundance of talk and dry illustration of the case slant it more for tv abroad than theatrical chances. It is a good cut over Cayatte's recent films as it ironically contrasts the British court system to the French, insisting that errors can take place in both systems.

There are the British theatrical flourishes and prodding of witnesses and the French collusion of the real judges and the jury. The Englishman is tried in his own country and acquitted but he then confesses he did the killing alone during Andersson's "French trial."

It does not help and she gets five years even if the magistrate, Girardot, has become convinced of her innocence and had even wanted to drop the charges but had been overruled by her boss. Direction is helpful in this convoluted tale of murder and justice but the legal proceedings are incisive or revealing enough to make up for the lack of depth in its principal personnages.

—*Mosk.*

Message From Space
(JAPANESE-COLOR)

The illegitimate son of "Star Wars."

United Artists release of a Toei Company Ltd.-Tohokushinsha Film Co. Ltd. production. Produced by Banjiro Uemura, Yoshinori Watanabe, Tan Takaiwa. Features entire cast. Directed by Kinji Fukasaku. Screenplay, Hiroo Matusda; camera (color), Toro Nakajima' created by Shotaro Ishimori, Masahiro Noda, Hiroo Matsuda, Kinji Fukasaku; music by Ken-Ichiro Morioka, performed by the Columbia Symphony Orchestra (Japan); special effects technical unit — science fiction supervisory, Masahiro Noda; space-flying objects, Shotaro Ishimori; special photography effects, Minoru Nakano; art director, Tetsuzo Osawa; director of photography, special effect sequences, Nobaru Takanashi; director, entire special effects, Nobuo Yajim.
Reviewed at Magno Screening Room, N.Y., Oct. 30, '78. (MPAA Rating - PG). Running time: **105 MINS.**
General Garuda .... Vic Morrow
Hans .... Sonny Chiba
Aaron .... Philip Casnoff
Meia .... Peggy Lee Brennan

Esmeralida ....Sue Shiomi
Noguchi ....Tetsuro Tamba
Rockseia XII ...✶........... Mikio Narita
Urocco .... Makoto Sato
Shiro ....Hiroyuki Sanada
Robot Beba 2 ....Isamu Shimuzu
Jack ....Masazumi Okabe
Kamesasa ....Noburo Mitani
Dark ....Hideyo Amamoto
Kido ....Junkichi Orimoto
Lazarl ....Harumi Sone
(English-dubbed Soundtrack)

If imitation is the sincerest form of flattery, then 20th's "Star Wars" should feel highly flattered by this Japanese acquisition of United Artists. With a mixed-nationality cast and an English-dubbed soundtrack, "Message From Space" borrows wholesale from the earlier space effort — even unto a miniature robot for laughs, chases down canyons for thrills, spaceships whose designs seem very familiar, strange and bizarre creatures, lots of fights and the ultimate triumph of good over evil.

Still and all, if the Japanese have not come up with something original, they have brought forth an illegitimate baby that is so good that it will not shame its unacknowledged parent. The special effects are spectacular and the action is everything one could wish.

The acting? That's something else again but it's never allowed to intrude on the lavish production effects. And, when one considers the Japanese were there first with "Godzilla" and other films of that ilk, maybe "Star Wars" has a small debt to them. Director Kenji Fukasaku is known in the U.S. for his work on Darryl Zanuck's "Tora Tora Tora" and, to horror buffs, for "The Green Slime." Nobuo Yajima headed the large and talented team of special effects craftsmen and artists.

The only familiar face in the cast is Vic Morrow, who has top billing, but makes only a small contribution. The four young people, with an assist from Sonny Chiba, do most of the work. *—Robe.*

Eyeball
(Gatti Rossi In Un Labirinto di Vetro)
(ITALIAN-COLOR)

Don't look.

Hollywood, Oct. 24.
Joseph Brenner release, directed by Umberto Lenzi. Exec producer, Joseph Brenner. Stars John Richardson, Martine Brochard, Ines Pellegrin, Silvia Solar, George Rigaud. (No other credits available). Reviewed at Pix Theatre, Hollywood, Oct. 24, '78. (MPAA rating: R.) Running time: **91 MINS.**

Title is derived from the bodily organ removed from various victims by an unknown murderer. As such, it is a more descriptive title than the original Italian "Gatti Ros-si in Un Labirinto di Vetro" (Red Cat in a Labyrinth of Glass.")

The dubbed English dialog is just as far removed from the original Italian lips. The photography is lousy and the bloody special effects, which are often the only saving grace in pix like these, look phony in every scene.

At the screening caught, one of the resident Hollywood psychotics whooped and cheered the first murder and mutilation. But even he grew quiet and disinterested long before the end. *—Har.*

Caravans
(U.S.-IRANIAN-COLOR)

"The Searchers," Persian-style.

Universal release of an Ibex Films — FIDCI production. Features entire cast. Produced by Elmo Williams. Directed by James Fargo. Screenplay, Nancy Voyles Crawford, Thomas A. McMahon, Lorraine Williams, based on the James Michener novel; camera (Technicolor), Douglas Slocombe; music, composed and conducted by Mike Batt; editor, Richard Marden; costumes, Renie Conley; set and technical supervisor, Fereydoun Razavi; asst. directors, Anthony Waye, Bozorgmehr Rafia; title song sung by Barbara Dickson; art directors, Ted Tester, Peter Williams, Peter James; second unit camera, Gordon Meagher; sound editor, Mike Le-Mare; special effects, Karli Baumgartner; stunt coordinator, John Sullivan. Reviewed at Universal screening room, N.Y., Nov. 1, '78. (MPAA Rating: PG). Running time: **127 MINS.**
Zulfigar ....Anthony Quinn
Mark Miller ....Michael Sarrazin
Ellen Jasper.............Jennifer O'Neill
Sardar Khan ....Christopher Lee
Crandall ....Joseph Cotten
Nazrullah ....Behrooz Vosoughi
Richardson ....Barry Sullivan
Dr. Smythe ....Jeremy Kemp
Moheb ....Duncan Quinn
Peasant boy ....Behrooz Gueramian
Shakkur.......Mohammad Ali Keshavarz
Nur Mohammad ...Parviz Gharib-Afshar
Mira ....Fahimeh Amouzandeh
Dancing boy ....Khosrow Tabatabai
Maftoon ....Mohammad Kahnemout
Racha ....Susan Vaziri
Capt. Majid ....Parviz Jafari
Mullah 1 ....Mohammad Poursattar
Mullah 2 ....Hamid Lighvani
Mullah 3 ....Djamshid Sadri
Karima ....Shahnaz Pakravan
Also: Parviz Shahinkhoo, Ahmad Kashani, Eskandar Rafii, Firooz Bahjat Mohamadi, Sami Tahasonee, Ali Zandi, Bozorgmeh Rafia.

Considering what's happening in Iran today, this tale of 1948 Persia is pretty tame stuff. However, the Elmo Williams screen version of James Michener's "Caravans," picked up for Christmas release by Universal, also has its own moments of violence with a little torture on the side. It bowed at Radio City Music Hall Thursday (2) along with that other Eastern tale, "The Nativity," and some Rockettes for kicks.

The main trouble with "Caravans" isn't the Iranians, it's Hollywood. Almost every fake moment in the film, and there are lots of them, has the touch of Hollywood laid on with a heavy coating. Take away the Americans, of course, and you wouldn't have such a slick film, but you might have a more honest one. Fortunately for the average viewer, the scenic scope of the film, shot entirely on locations in Iran, is so sweeping that the tale that is told is almost palatable. But barely.

What might have happened to Michener's epic story is probably explained by the screen writing credits. Nancy Voyles Crawford, Thomas A. McMahon and Lorraine Williams are given writing credits in a size that dwarfs the tiny credit, "based upon the book by James Michener."

Briefly, the film deals with the search of a minor American consular employee (Michael Sarrazin) for an American woman (Jennifer O'Neill) who has married an Iranian colonel (Behrooz Vosoughi) but deserted him for a Kochi chieftain (Anthony Quinn) and has disappeared. Sarrazin finds her in short order (although in the 10 months she has been missing, no one else has been that lucky). That's when the real trouble begins. She won't go back and he won't go back without her and off everyone goes into the desert.

Along the way, of course, there are all sorts of minor intrigues, murders, betrayals, torture, executions, festivals and a few encounters with nature. It's never made clear who's really in love with whom but there's no real sex in the film (often suggested but never fulfilled).

Sarrazin, Quinn and O'Neill carry most of the story. The other non-Persians — Christopher Lee, Barry Sullivan, Jeremy Kemp and Joseph Cotten — are seen so briefly they may have done their roles over a long weekend. Histrionically, only Quinn is believable, followed closely by Vosoughi, who's Iran's foremost character actor, Parvis Gharib-Afshar as the Persian version of a redneck sheriff, Khosrow Tabatabai as a bisexual dancing boy who, as the sheriff says, is "pure evil" and an assortment of fascinating faces who make up the tribesmen.

Long in the making, it's the first film for Williams since his participation in Darryl Zanuck's "Tora Tora Tora." His supervision has resulted in excellent technical work — the camerawork of Douglas Slocombe and Gordon Meagher's second unit photography being the major asset of the film. Mike Batt's thundering score is effective in the action scenes and he knows how to bring it down to lullaby level when it's called for.

James Fargo seems more at home directing action sequences than he does one-to-one confrontations and Richard Marden's editing (which must have been a formidable job considering the months of shooting) sometimes leaves bits of business dangling. The film could still be trimmed considerably.

Fortunately for the filmmakers, it's understood that most of the financing came from Iran's FIDCI Production Company as the overall market would appear limited to action fans. If the public is interested in the rights of a nomadic tribe to live "outside" civilization, it may go for "Caravans." But it's doubtful. *—Robe.*

The Lord of the Rings
(COLOR-ANIMATED)

Hobbits? What are Hobbits?

Hollywood, Nov. 3.

United Artists release of a Fantasy Films Saul Zaentz production. Directed by Ralph Bakshi. Screenplay, Chris Conkling, Peter S. Beagle, based on stories of J.R.R. Tolkien; camera (no credits); music, Leonard Rosenman. No other credits provided. Reviewed at Samuel Goldwyn Theatre, Beverly Hills, Nov. 3, '78. (MPAA Rating: PG). Running Time: 131 MINS.

Students of animated technique and Tolkien story-telling will find a lot to like in what Ralph Bakshi has done with "Lord Of The Rings." But animated fantasies have their "crossover" problems, too, and this one will face trouble appealing to a broad audience beyond the most devoted.

Unquestionably, Bakshi has perfected some outstanding pen-and-ink effects while translating faithfully a portion of J.R.R. Tolkien's trilogy (which has sold 20,000,000 copies to people who presumably will form the hard-core interest for the film). But in his concentration on craft and duty to the original story — both admirable in themselves — Bakshi overlooks the uninitiated completely.

Quite simply, those who do not know the characters of Middle Earth going in will not know them coming out. The introductory narration explaining the Rings is confusing, making the rest of the quest seem pointless in many places. Boring is an equally good word, especially toward the end of two hours.

Consequently, Bakshi and producer Saul Zaentz can expect a lot of bad word-of-mouth in the broad marketplace. But the payoff will come from those who find that the visual version of a favorite tale fulfills their expectations, presumably giving the picture considerable strength along the art and college circuits. —*Har.*

Slow Dancing In the Big City
(COLOR)

Boy meets girl story. Paul Sorvino is outstanding, but hokiness will hurt b.o.

Hollywood, Oct. 29.

A United Artists release. Produced by Michael Levee and John G. Avildsen. Stars Paul Sorvino, Anne Ditchburn. Directed and edited by Avildsen. Screenplay, Barra Grant; camera (color), Ralf Bode; music, Bill Conti; art director, Henry Shrady; set decorator, Charlie Truhan; costume designer, Ruth Morley; choreographer, Robert North; roof solo choreographed by Anne Ditchburn; associate producer, George Manasse; asst. director, Dwight Williams; sound, Dennis Maitland. Reviewed at the Samuel Goldwyn Theater, Beverly Hills, Oct. 23, '78. (MPAA rating: PG). Running time: 101 MINS.
Lou Freidlander .... Paul Sorvino
Sarah Gantz .... Anne Ditchburn
David .... Nicolas Coster
Franny .... Anita Dangler
Roger .... Hector Jaime Mercado
Christopher .... Thaao Penghlis
Barbara .... Linda Selman
Marty .... G. Adam Gifford
Diana .... Tara Mitton
George .... Dick Carballo
Dr. Foster .... Jack Ramage
T.C. .... Daniel Faraldo

"Slow Dancing In The Big City" has so much heart John Avildsen's aorta is showing. There is a limit to how far audiences will suspend disbelief for the cause of sentimentality and uplift and Avildsen's last picture, "Rocky," probably reached the limit. He's gone too far this time and it'll hurt the b.o. prospects for a film which otherwise has much to offer.

Barra Grant's story is a simple boy meets girl tale, or in this case, dancer meets columnist, or to be even more specific, dancer meets Jimmy Breslin clone. Anne Ditchburn, a lovely dancer and choreographer, meets Paul Sorvino, the columnist.

Sorvino, like Robert Duvall and Charles Durning, is one of the most dependable actors working in films today. He seems to do a good job in any picture under any conditions and he's just terrific here.

Ditchburn is promising, but it's difficult to make a full statement about her performance. The postproduction looping is downright dreadful and interferes not just with her performance but with the flow of the film. A number of dancing scenes featuring Ditchburn — performances, rehearsals and a solo on the roof of a Manhattan apartment — are among the production's high points.

A simple boy meets girl tale is an acceptable premise for a film, always has been. Avildsen's problem, along with Grant, was that they were reaching too far for the uplifting. When you tug that hard on heartstrings they break.

The film has two plots moving along side by side although the focus clearly is on the Ditchburn-Sorvino relationship. The second genuinely touching plot concerns a young ghetto kid Sorvino is writing about and his struggle to overcome the harsh city.

Sorvino is also writing a column about Ditchburn. His interest, however, didn't begin professionally. He was struck by her the moment she moved into the rat trap apartment down the hall from him. The audience is given a number of reasons to feel sympathy for the dancer. Not only does she live in a slum, but she's just broken up with a boyfriend (a smug, snobbish heir), and she's sick and shouldn't be dancing.

All that gives her the opportunity at the end of the film to dance her heart out for the journalist she really loves. While you know Sorvino is going to carry her on stage for her bow, you still can't believe it when it happens.

What's a shame about "Slow Dancing" is that somewhere on the cutting room floor probably is a fine film. The best thing about this picture is Sorvino and if Avildsen had switched the focus away from the relationship between the columnist and the dancer and made it more of a film about the columnist, he would have had something touching but genuine. —*Hege.*

Once In Paris
(COLOR)

Scripter's encounter with a chauffeur and a lover in the City of Light. Low-budget beauty and potential sleeper.

Frank D. Gilroy release of his own production. Coproducers, Manny Fuchs and Gerard Croce. Features entire cast. Presented by Mitch Leigh and the McLaughlins. Directed by Gilroy. Screenplay, Gilroy; camera (color-TVC Labs), Claude Saunier; editor, Robert Q. Lovett; score, Mitch Leigh; sound, Daniel Brisseau, Gerard de Lagarde. George Bowers, David B. Cohn; asst. director, Francois X. Moullin. Reviewed at Rizzoli Screening Room, N.Y., Nov. 2, '78. (No MPAA rating). Running time: 100 MINS.
Michael Moore .... Wayne Rogers
Susan Townsend .... Gayle Hunnicutt
Jean-Paul Barbet .... Jack Lenoir
Marcel Thery .... Phillippe March
Abe Wiley .... Clement Harari
Eve Carling .... Tanya Lopert
Jean-Paul's wife ...... Marthe Mercadier
First man at party ....Yves-Massard
Second man at party .... Sady Rebbot
Lars Brady .... Matt Carney
His ex-wife .... Doris Roberts
First Waiter .... Max Fournel
Monsieur Farny .... Gerard Croce
Madame Farny .... Victoria Ville
Young man at party ..... Frank Peyrinaud
His friend ....Jean Jacques Charriere
Woman in Restaurant ... Sylviane Charlet
Her friend .... Pierre Dupray
Desk clerk .... Patrick Aubree
Bell boy .... Stephane Delcher
Second waiter ....Jean Jacques Rousselet
First chauffeur .... Jacques Bouanich
Second chauffeur ....Henri Attal
Girl in car .... Beatrice Chatelier
Party guests ....Marta Andras, Chouky
                  Sergent, Manny Fuchs
Freddie .... Andre Fetet
Brady's assistant .... Caroline Carliez
                           Andre Fetet
Jean-Paul's children .... Caroline Carliez,
                  Edgar Croce, Nicole Teboul,
                          Michael Teboul

Writer-director Frank Gilroy, whose two previous directorial efforts have been interesting though b.o. clunkers, has come up with a highly personalized tale of a rough-around-the-edges Yank screenwriter's relationship with a worldly chauffeur and a beauteous British aristocrat. Gilroy's developed the triad in subtle, believable, intelligent and often humorous fashion, making "Once in Paris" a superb

film and a strong sleeper possibility.

The film is very much a Gilroy project since he's responsible for its creation, financing, production and even its distribution and initial sale. Shot entirely in Paris, with a French crew, the pic gets maximum mileage from its three principals: Wayne Rogers, formerly of the "Mash" tv series; Gayle Hunnicutt, an American actress who's flowered in various legit and pic projects abroad; and Jack Lenoir.

The latter, a genuine discovery, is an Algerian-born Frenchman who's been a kind of general factotum of the French film industry for some 20 years. At one point in a highly checkered career, Lenoir actually toiled as a chauffeur-for-hire by various film production companies. He has shuttled about various topliners (Elizabeth Taylor, Charles Bronson, Otto Preminger) including Gilroy, who worked in Paris during a less than propitious period some years ago when he scripted the disastrous "The Only Game In Town," with Elizabeth Taylor and Warren Beatty.

In any event, the relationship in "Once in Paris" between the American scripter and his driver is a direct, literal descendant of Gilroy's own friendship with Lenoir back in the "Only Game In Town" days.

A number of other plot developments parallel actual events but pursuing their origins is irrelevant to an examination of why "Paris" is such a good film, and why it should be warmly received in art house situations, at the very minimum. Enough said that Gilroy is treading the fact-fiction line very closely.

Michael Moore (Rogers) is a scenarist travelling to Paris for the first time to salvage a film script so abysmal, it threatens to shutter an entire film production. He is met at the airport by a production exec who almost immediately informs the writer that the chauffeur (Lenoir) is a bad egg (he has served time for manslaughter), not to be trusted, and will be replaced tout de suite.

The driver stays, of course, and develops a strong friendship with the writer. The liaison is a believable update of a familiar plot device — the introduction of the rube American to Paris by a street-wise but warm-hearted native.

The writer eventually has an affair with the British aristocrat (Hunnicutt) in Paris on business — she just happens to occupy the hotel suite adjoining the scripter's (a forgivable plot contrivance). Gilroy maintains the three-way relationship throughout the film in a number of intriguing ways.

Outside of the love relationship, which finally embraces all three principal characters, not much happens on the surface. The writer and driver dine together, go to the races, visit socially in various contexts and play a local variation of bocce.

Gilroy skillfully etches the writer-driver teaming and then gracefully incorporates the emotional and psychological shifts brought on by the presence of the British woman. He doesn't overload with information about each, but imparts enough to make them intelligent and enormously likable individuals deserving of interest and sympathy.

Rogers is excellent as the scenarist, combining a sense of detached awareness with wide-open vulnerability. Hunnicutt exercises crisp control as the aristocrat whose emotions gradually outdistance her sense of liberated propriety. Lenoir, who speaks nearly unaccented, colloquial English, seems molded in his part, and appears not to be acting at all — a real achievement.

Unlike many films shot in Paris, "Once" doesn't make a big deal about its backdrop. Cafes, streets, bars, as well as the familiar tourist spots, emerge as winsome as ever but unobtrusively so. A big plus is Claude Saunier's photography, which captures the natural colors of the pic's many attractive settings. Mention should also be made, surely, of a fine processing job by TVC Labs.

For a long time now, critics have been pining for an American film about believable contemporary figures interacting in a manner not informed by natural disasters, sexual obsessions, exaggerated power drives or extremely violent propensities. Gilroy has very quietly come up with a beauty of a film that should, for the moment at least, provide some balm to the aislesitters. "Once in Paris" is a marvelous pic. — Sege.

The Hound Of The Baskervilles
(BRITISH-COLOR)

London, Nov. 1.

Hemdale International Films release of a Michael White and Andrew Braunsberg presentation. Produced by John Goldstone. Executive producers, Michael White, Andrew Braunsberg. Stars Peter Cook, Dudley Moore. Directed by Paul Morrissey. Screenplay, Cook, Moore, Morrissey; camera (color), Dick Bush, John Wilcox; music, Dudley Moore; editors, Richard Marden, Glenn Hyde; production designer, Roy Smith; costume designer, Charles Knode; associate producer, Tim Hampton. Reviewed at Audley Square screening room, London, Nov. 1, '78. Running time: **84 MINS.**

Sherlock Holmes	Peter Cook
Dr. Watson	Dudley Moore
Stapleton	Denholm Elliott
Beryl Stapleton	Joan Greenwood
Dr. Mortimer	Terry-Thomas
Mr. Barrymore	Max Wall
Mrs. Barrymore	Irene Handl
Sir Henry Baskerville	Kenneth Williams
Frankland	Hugh Griffith
Mrs. Holmes, Mr. Spiggot	Dudley Moore
Mary	Dana Gillespie
Seldon	Roy Kinnear
Glynis	Prunella Scales
Massage Parlor Receptionist	Penelope Keith
Baskerville Police Force	Spike Milligan

Recent extensions of Sherlock Holmes (or his smarter brother, in one instance) have proved largely ineffective at the boxoffice. Peter Cook's absurdly degenerate version of Conan Doyle's master-sleuth is likely to continue this letdown trend.

Devoted fans of the comic performing partnership of Cook and Dudley Moore may be turned on by the idea of the pair as Holmes and his bungling assistant, Dr. Watson. But judged from this outing, Cook and Moore have deteriorated into almost complete reliance on puns, double-entendres and lavatory humor to get laughs.

Over-reverent helming of the pair by Paul Morrissey has left the plot empty of inspiration, and allowed Cook and Moore to dwell too long over everything. Production has an intentionally studio-bound look, with the narrative punctuated by chapter-heads in the style of a Victorian novel.

One very funny characterization emerges when Dudley Moore doubles as Holmes' Jewish mother, addressing him as "Sherl." There's a chuckle, too, in Cook engrossed in a volume by S. Freud, entitled "Guilt Without Sex." —Simo.

The Toolbox Murders
(COLOR)

Vile, inept. Killer takes eight lives.

Hollywood, Nov. 3.

A Cal-Am release of a Tony Didio production. Directed by Dennis Donnelly. Screenplay, Robert Easter, Ann N. Kindberg; camera (color), Gary Graver; editor, Skip Lusk; associate producers, Kenneth A. Yates, Jack Kindberg; sound, Robert Dietz; music, George Deaton. Reviewed at the Vine Theatre, Hollywood, Nov. 3, '78. (MPAA Rating: R.) Running time: **93 MINS.**

Kingsley	Cameron Mitchell
Laurie	Pamelyn Ferdin
Kent	Wesley Eure
Joey Ballard	Nicholas Beauvy
JoAnn Ballard	Aneta Corsaut
Det. Jamison	Tim Donnelly

"The Toolbox Murders" is a vile, inept and dull exploitation film. Unlike other pictures of its kind, this Cal-Am release produced by Tony Didio is without a redeeming moment, performance or element.

Eight people are killed during the 93-minute life of this film. Here's how they die: one in a car crash, two by stabbing (one with a butcher knife and a second with a scissor), one is burned to death in a fire and four are the victims of the toolbox murderer.

Dressed in a ski mask with holes for his eyes, nose and mouth, the toolbox murderer drills one of his subject, stabs another with a screwdriver, shoots a third with a nailgun and murders the fourth with a hammer. The film features a lot of blood.

The reason for the rampage? No, it's not that his Allen wrenches were stolen. The toolbox murderer is clearing away the filth which somehow were responsible for the death of his daughter.

Printed above are the credits. Those mentioned are responsible. —Hege.

Un Neveu Silencieux
(The Silent Nephew)
(FRENCH-COLOR-16m)

Excellently-filmed, often harrowing, story of a bourgeois French family with a mongoloid child. Who is the victim — the child or the family?

Produced and directed by Robert Enrico. Features entire cast. Screenplay, Paul Savatier, with adaptation and dialog by Savatier and Enrico. No other credits provided. Reviewed at Alliance Francais screening room, Nov. 3, '78. (No MPAA Rating). Running time: **97 MINS.**

Joel	Joel Dupuis
Henri	Sylvain Seyrig
Odile	Coralie Seyrig
Louis	Andrew Falcon
Virginie	Aline Bertrand
Alexandre	Jean Bouise
Marthe	Lucienne Hamon
Mme. Verriere	Renee Faure

(English subtitles)

While this intimate look at French family life has little appeal for the commercial market, it should be seen by all sociology students and teachers, especially those majoring in family relationships. The entire film transpires during the summer vacation of a family that consists of grandmother, son and his wife and three children, daughter and her husband and two sons. The youngest boy, Joel, is a mongoloid but has a charming smile and happy nature that wins the hearts of almost everyone.

The almost is important. Grandmother and son and his wife are appalled by the proximity of the child, its hopeless future and the possible effect on the chances of a happy marriage for their daughter. Sly remarks, cool receptions which eventually lead to an undeclared war, eventually decide the tot's parents to leave. The accidental death of the child finalizes their decision, encouraged by the loyal support of their other son, but the petty grandmother and other members of the family may have already taken their toll.

Aline Bertrand and Jean Bouise are excellent as the boy's parents and the tiny Joel Dupuis, a real-life mongoloid member of a family of 10 children, wanders through the film, completely innocent of his role as a catalyst in the building tragedy. Renee Faure slightly overdoes her role as the grandmother as it is never explained how she could have raised such a mixture of nice and obnoxious offspring.

The work began as a screenplay by Savatier, who turned it into a novel with success, and then supervised the adaptation back into a film. It's Enrico's attempt to make people look at handicapped children slightly differently when they see them. At this, he's most successful as it isn't likely that any intelligent viewer will go away unmoved.

The commercial future for this film apparently lies with schools and other institutions. —Robe.

Le Sucre
(The Sugar)
(FRENCH-COLOR)

Paris, Nov. 7.

Gaumont release of Cineproduction-SFP-Gaumont production. Stars Gerard Depardieu, Jean Carmet. Directed by Jacques Rouffio. Screenplay, Georges Conchon, Rouffio; camera (Eastmancolor), Rene Mathelin; editor, Genevieve Winding; music, Philippe Sarde. Reviewed at Publicis, Paris, Oct. 26, '78. Running time, **102 MINS.**

Raoul	Gerard Depardieu
Adrien	Jean Carmet
Grezillo	Michel Piccoli
Hilda	Nelly Borgeaud
Karbaoui	Roger Hanin
Berot	Claude Pieplu

The sugar in the film is that commodity on paper that can spread fortunes or ruin on the stock market. French films have of late been probing corruption in banks ("Other People's Money"), the building biz ("Part of the Fire") and multinational corporations ("The Accuser"). Now it's the turn of the stockbroker, and this film, as the others, tries to explain too much, teeters between the grotesque, satiric and comedic, too often blunting its points.

"The Sugar's" main tale is a sort of bizarre friendship between a man taken by a brokerage firm and the wheeler dealer who hooks him. Gerard Depardieu somewhat overcharges the part of the operator, where the balance, with Jean Carmet's little-man portrayal of a man who has used his wife's inheritance on the market, is also uneven.

It seems the cornering of sugar was engineered by a Mittel-European financier who decreed there was a sugar shortage despite an abundant crop. Rumors lead to a run on the sweet stuff by a nervous public and soaring prices for the stockpiled product. Carmet is hustled by Depardieu and buys a small load. But then he sees how much he has made and is talked into giving carte blanche to the firm.

When the financier releases the sugar the stock drop disastrously.

Carmet seeks out Depardieu who has also lost all and the two become friends. They manage to save Carmet from being the fall guy on taxes. Pic is too broad and not walways clear, but the bouncy, sardonic treatment could still find it local legs.

Offshore chances call for some pruning to clarify its theme. Jacques Rouffio's direction has been more urgent in other pix, notably "Seven Murders by Prescription," and "Horizons." This one is technically fine, with top production dress. —*Mosk.*

Chicago Film Fest

Chuquiago
(BOLIVIAN-B&W)

Chicago, Nov. 7.
An Ukamau Production. Directed by Antonio Eguino. Features entire cast. Screenplay, Oscar Soria; camera, Fuguino, Julio Lencina; editing Deborah Shaffer, Susane Fern. No other credits available. Reviewed at Chi Film Fest Screening Room Oct. 23, 1978. Running time: **87 MINS.**

Isko .... Nestor Yulra
Johnny .... Edmundo Villarreoi
Carlos .... David Santalla
Patricia .... Taliana Aponte

Director Antonio Eguino seems to be attempting to present a view of contemporary Bolivian society through separate scenarios on four different inhabitants of the country. Although each episode is well-acted by a combined amateur and professional cast, the stories tend to drag and there is no bridge between episodes to tie the whole thing together. Result is one of those slice-of-life films where one leaves the theatre never quite sure of what points, if any, the filmmaker was trying to get across.

The four characters presented are real enough to sustain moments of interest even if the script is not. There's an unhappy young boy who's been given to an old woman to use as an assistant in the food marketplace; an Indian teenager who's turned to thievery as a means of getting away from his country; a middle-aged working family man whose only enjoyment is his weekly night out with the boys; and a pseudo-radical girl who ends up marrying the man of her parent's dreams. Any one of these characters would have been fine as the center of a single feature. Separately contained in the same film they're not enough alike or substantially different to be very effective. The director seems to have taken the easy way out by letting them each stand alone instead of doing some clever editing to provide some continuity.

According to talk here, Bolivia is not a country that's often represented at festivals. If this item is an indication of early attempts at the commercial celluloid there is some good raw talent, most noticably acting, that's worth watching. But any commercial play on this particular project looks dim. — *Berg.*

Floor Show
(U.S.-B&W)

Chicago, Oct. 28.
An experimental film written, directed and photographed by Richard Myers. No other credits available. Reviewed at the Chicago Film Festival Screening Room, Oct. 20, '78. Running time: **85 MINS.**

Director Richard Myers, whose 1969 "Akran," received favorable reviews, has made a self-indulgent, confusing film with "Floor Show" — a work that deals in vague analogies and generalities concerning what goes through a filmmaker's mind during the creative process. On paper the idea would seem a natural as an instructive tool, but even the most devout film student will probably have trouble following this one.

Myers narrates throughout the 85-minute black-and-white piece and enjoys talking in theoretical terms about the obvious — the importance of images and motion in film. After each tidbit about the difficulty of bringing the above to his own works, Myers attempts to demonstrate with clips of famous and fictitious examples. Unfortunately, his theories are never explained clearly and the examples are so obscurely related to them that they only serve to muddle the matter further.

One recurrent statement seems to be that art speaks only of shadows, not of the thing itself. (Myers loves to package his own neat non-sequiturs). Examples are given such as a man who wants to fly watching himself on television. A clear connection is never made between the theory and example. Furthermore, even if one accepts Myers' hypothesis without example, there still must be a point where those artistic shadows relate some discernable message. Myers never reaches that point.

The film is labeled an experimental work, a term the director seems to be believes frees him from making something an audience will understand (e.g.-anyone who doesn't can't be very sophisticated and any criticisms can't be taken too seriously since, after all, this is an experimental film). Experimental is not an excuse for a badly-executed concept and sloppy technical work (there are several poorly-lit sequences). Myers' only success with this film is that it holds true to its title. There will be an en-

tertaining floor show on the faces of an audience who will no doubt be wondering what message they've overlooked for 85 minutes. —*Berg.*

Erika's Passions
(W. GERMAN-B&W)

Chicago, Nov. 7.
A Ula Stockl Production (Munich) Germany; written and directed by Ula Stockl. Stars Karin Baal, Vera Tschechowa. Camera (black & white), Thomas Mauch; art direction, Hartmut Rathmayer, Diasy Boutique; sound, Martin Muller. Reviewed at Chicago Film Festival Screening Room, Oct. 31, '78. Running time: **65 MINS.**

This 65-minute German entry is a slow-paced, sometimes effective reminiscence of a love relationship gone sour. What makes it somewhat different than most films of the genre is not the individual resentments or anxieties between the parties involved but the fact that the relationship took place between two young and beautiful women.

It seems that onscreen the homosexual relationship is always made more dramatic, intense and sterotypical than the heterosexual one. Filmmaker Ula Stockl has thankfully not fallen into that trap here, showing the same feelings of jealousy, loneliness and disappointment common to all human interaction. For that alone she deserves ample credit.

Yet problems in content and rhythm upset the realistic characterizations she has set up. Circumstance of the film — Franziska coming to Erika's (their) apartment unannounced four years after the breakup on the latter's birthday and using her same key to get in — seems a bit contrived. Ditto some of characters' interaction. The long pauses as they shuffle from room to room are too frequent and give the short film an annoying dragging quality.

Thankfully there are some comic moments to pick up the pace, the best being in the second half of the film when the two women get locked in the bathroom. The actresses, Karin Baal and Vera Tschechowa, are especially convincing here and in later scenes where the protective layers they've built against each other are stripped away.

Stockl has represented two real people with her script but disappoints because she had the framework for a top notch feature-length film. As a director she's adequate but has a lot to learn about pacing. —*Berg.*

Movie Movie
(COLOR/B & W)

'Movie Movie' is awful awful.

Warner Bros. release of a Stanley Donen production. Produced and directed by Stanley Donen. Stars George C. Scott. Screenplay, Larry Gelbart, Sheldon Keller; executive producer, Martin Starger; cameraman for "Dynamite Hands," Charles Rosher Jr.; cameraman for "Baxter's Beauties of 1933," Bruce Surtees; art director, Jack Fisk; film editor, George Hively; music, Ralph Burns; choreography for "Baxter's," Michael Kidd; costumes, Patty Norris; songs, lyrics by Larry Gelbart, Sheldon Keller; music, Ralph Burns, Buster Davis; asst. director, Jonathan Sanger; set designer, Chris Horner; set decorator, Jerry Wunderlich. Reviewed at Warner Bros. screening room, N.Y., Nov. 13, '78. (MPAA Rating - PG)1 Running time: **105 MINS.**

"Baxter's Beauties of 1933"
Spats Baxter .... George C. Scott
Trixie Lane .... Barbara Harris
Dick Cummings .... Barry Bostwick
Isobel Stuart .... Trish Van Devere
Jinks Murphy .... Red Buttons
Pop .... Eli Wallach
Kitty .... Rebecca York
Dr. Bowers .... Art Carney
Gussie .... Maidie Norman
Mrs. Updike .... Jocelyn Brando
Also Charles Lane, Barney Martin, Dick Winslow, John Hudkinds, Robert Herron, Sebastian Brook, Jerry Von Hoeltke, Paula Jones, John Henry.

"Dynamite Hands"
Gloves Malloy .... George C. Scott
Betsy McGuire .... Trish Van Devere
Peanuts .... Red Buttons
Vince Marlowe .... Eli Wallach
Joey Popchik .... Harry Hamlin
Troubles Moran .... Ann Reinking
Pop Popchik .... Michael Kidd
Angie Popchik .... Kathleen Beller
Johnny Danko .... Barry Bostwick
Dr. Blaine .... Art Carney
Also: Clay Hodges, George P. Wilbur, Peter T. Stader, James Lennon, John Hudkins, Robert Herron, Denver R. Mattson, James Nickerson, Harvey G. Parry, Wally Rose.

Stanley Donen's "Movie Movie" is a clumsy attempt to spoof the kind of film fare encountered in pic houses of the '30s and '40s. The idea was patronizing in its conception, is a flatout embarrassment in its execution, and weak vehicle for George C. Scott and other principal talents involved, notably Scott's wife, Trish Van Devere. Thin outlook looms.

What writers Larry Gelbart and Sheldon Keller, not to mention producer-director Donen himself, had in mind isn't clear. They've split his overlong, 105-minute feature into three parts: a shot in black-and-white sendup of those boxing sagas where the slum youth fueled by earnest ambition gets catapulted to fame and riches; a satire of a coming attractions trailer featuring the voiceover of Westbrook Van Voorhis vintage narrating a saga of World War I pilots; and finally, a shot-in-color takeoff of the making of a Flo Ziegfeld-type Broadway musical.

But instead of gently twitting the conventions of old Hollywood potboilers, "Movie Movie" tries to milk the cliches by observing and scorning them simultaneously. The conception is a mess, and it shows.

Things are so muddied that Donen tacked on, after the pic was shot, a prolog by George Burns telling the audience that, yes, "Movie Movie" is intended as fun. Too bad Burns didn't stick around for the rest of the film.

It's difficult to come up with another couple less suited to the featherlight satirical touch required by this venture than Scott and his wife. Each plays assigned parts so broadly that all semblance of believability — a touch of which is essential for effective satire — is lost.

Even Art Carney, who appears in the two main segs as a blowhard doctor, is defeated by Gelbart and Keller's lame material. Eli Wallach, Red Buttons, Ann Reinking, Barry Bostwick and Rebecca York find themselves in various unflattering parts of varying non-support.

Of mild interest is the Ralph Burns score, nicely arranged by Buster Davis, and Michael Kidd's dance numbers in the musical portion of this attempted spoof (titled, "Baxter's Beauties of 1933"). Movies spoofed range from Busby Berkeley tuners to "On the Waterfront" — efforts certainly worthy enough for satire but not by this feeble gesture of a movie. —Sege.

Northern Lights

Minneapolis, Nov. 9.
Cine Manifest release. Produced, directed, written & edited by John Hanson & Rob Nilsson. Features entire cast. Camera (black & white), Judy Irola; music, David Ozzie Ahlers; art direction, Richard Brown; production design, Marianne Astrom-DeFina; sound editor, Susan Slanhoff. Reviewed at Univ. of Minnesota Film Society, Minneapolis, Nov. 8, '78. (No MPAA rating.) Running time: **90 MINS.**
Ray Sorenson .... Robert Behling
Inga Olsness .... Susan Lynch
John Sorenson .... Joe Spano
Kari .... Marianne Astrom-De Fina
Henrik Sorenson .... Ray Ness
Jenny Sorenson .... Helen Ness
Thor .... Thorbjorn Rue
Sven .... Nick Eldridge
Howard .... Jon Ness
Charlie Forsythe .... Gary Hanisch
Ole Olsness .... Melvin Rodvold
Adelaide Olsness ...... Adelaide Thornveit
Grandma .... Mabel Rue
Krist .... Krist Toresen

Birth of the Nonpartisan League, obscure North Dakota political movement spawned in desperation in 1915, wouldn't appear to have sufficient interest or dramatic impact for commercial film treatment. Young filmmakers John Hanson and Rob Nilsson, however, have tied in early NPL success with the death of the family farm which has left much U.S. agriculture in the hands of conglomerates. Subject has been handled with sensitivity and compassion, drawing heavily on recollections of their grandfathers who lived in North Dakota. "Northern Lights" moves too leisurely and is slow to get into its subject, but it's a touching slice of life view of struggling America.

Battle of the individual farmer against foreclosing bankers, profiteers and callous politicians has echoes of "Grapes of Wrath." Immigrant farmers' struggle was a shadow fight, waged largely against remote human forces. Severe natural elements were a more omnipresent enemy. Farmers were beaten down.

Depicted fight for survival took place 65 years ago, 40 years after the nearby battle of the Little Big Horn. Much of the story is told through docu narrative, expository crawl and subtitles translating the Scandinavian immigrants' words. Photography, appropriately b&w, is starkly beautiful.

Three professional actors are featured. Robert Behling and Susan Lynch are excellent as a young couple trying to scratch out a living from the unfriendly land. Joe Spano is also fine as a brother who becomes disillusioned over setbacks. Rest of the cast consists of North Dakota rustics, and they're a hardy, indomitable lot. Judy Irola's camera has captured weathered faces and moments of quiet poignancy in a cinema verite style. Picture hasn't been submitted to MPAA but would clearly warrant a G rating.

"Lights" has already played about 25 North Dakota towns, producers claiming the $330,000 production may be the first picture to be both lensed and initially exhibited in rural areas. It's booked for a Minneapolis opening Nov. 15 and is an entry in the Chicago Film Festival. Boxoffice prospects elsewhere may be thin, but the pic is a solid artistic achievement which may find a future in art houses and metro areas with Scandinavian enclaves. —Rees.

The Promise

Super soap opera neatly packaged for promising results.

Hollywood, Nov. 14.
A Universal Pictures release, produced by Fred Weintraub and Paul Heller. Directed by Gilbert Cates; exec producer, Tully Friedman; screenplay, Garry Michael White; camera (Technicolor), Ralph Woolsey; editor, Peter E. Berger; sound, Michael Evje; art direction, William Sandell; assistant director, Thomas Lofaro; music, David Shire. Reviewed at Universal Studios, Nov. 8, 1978. MPAA rating: PG. Running time: **98 MINS.**
Nancy/Marie .... Kathleen Quinlan
Michael .... Stephen Collins
Marion .... Beatrice Straight
Gregson .... Laurence Luckinbill
George .... William Prince
Ben .... Michael O'Hare
Allison .... Bibi Besch
Wickfield .... Robin Gammell
Wendy .... Katherine DeHetre

To dismiss "The Promise" as a soap opera would belittle its accomplishment. It is a soap symphony, a soap circus, a soap saga, a veritable super-bowl of soap, all neatly packaged in 98 minutes instead of years of afternoons. Could be a sales plus.

First seen on the streets of Boston (which look suspiciously like Beverly Hills), Kathleen Quinlan and Stephen Collins are obviously much in love. At a carnival, he wins her a cheap necklace which they bury under rock near the ocean, between a cypress and a Monterey Pine, with a promise to love forever.

While she works on an unfinished painting, he goes to inform his ruthless mother (Beatrice Straight) of his wedding plans. She objects because it will interfere with Collin's obligation to run the family construction business, founded by his grandfather.

In defiance, Collins and Quinlan rush off to get married. A blare of headlights, a screech of brakes, the terrible shattering of metal — her face is crushed beyond recognition and he's in a coma.

If Quinlan will go away and promise never to be heard from again, Straight promises to buy her a new face. She then tells Collins that his love perished in the crash. He's distraught, but never asks to visit the grave.

Under the skilled surgical hands of handsome Laurence Luckinbill in San Francisco, Quinlan's beauty is restored. In gratitude, she gives the doctor the finished painting she started with Collins, whom she now hates because she thinks he never tried to find her because she was so ugly without a new face.

She takes up photography and changes her name. In the meantime, Collins has become a celibate construction tycoon, still suffering the loss of his love. He needs a photographer to decorate the walls of a building he's putting up in San Francisco.

His helpers tell him there's this one girl whose work is excellent but she refuses to work for Collins. He goes to her studio to convince her personally. She's there in the dark. They talk, but he does not recognize her voice. She turns on the light; there's a long pause as the music stings — but he knows her not, even though it's been but a year since the crash. (In retrospect, director Gilbert Cates should have used a blonde wig and an eyepatch to distinguish Quinlan I from the patrician brunette beauty of Quinlan II.)

Collins can't understand why this stranger hates him so. He pursues her. She flees to Boston to root this love from her life once and for all. Looking for her, Collins goes to the doctor's house, where he sees — the painting. He knows the truth.

Back on the steep Massachusetts cliff overlooking the Pacific, Quinlan digs for the necklace. It is gone. She looks around puzzled as Collins steps out of the woods. He apologizes for his poor memory for faces and she falls into his arms.

Up with the lush strings but no organ in the David Shire score and the haunting theme song sung by Melissa Manchester. —Har.

Blue Fin
(AUSTRALIAN-COLOR)

Sydney, Nov. 9.
A Roadshow Distributors' release of a South Australian Film Corp.-McElroy and McElroy Production. Produced by Hal McElroy. Directed by Carl Schultz. Executive proiducer, Matt Carroll. Stars Hardy Kruger, Greg Rowe. Screenplay, Sonia Borg, from novel, "Blue Fin," by Colin Theile; story editor Harold Lander; art direction, David Copping; camera (color), Geoff Burton, editing, Rod Adamson; music, Michael Carlos; asst. director, Pat Clayton; wardrobe, Annie Bleakley; sound, Don Connolly; special effects, Chris Murray. Previewed at Roadshow theatrette, Sydney, Nov. 8, '78. Running time: **90 MINS.**
Bill Pascoe .... Hardy Kruger
Steve "Snoek" Pascoe .... Greg Rowe
Mrs. Pascow .... Elspeth Ballantyne
Ruth Pascoe .... Liddy Clark
Sam Snell .... John Jarratt
Stan .... Hugh Keays-Byrne
Herbie .... Ralph Cotterill
Con .... George Spartels
Geordie .... Alfred Bell
Andy Nelson .... Wayne Rodda
Snitch .... John Thompson
Ockie .... John Godden
Pamela .... Kelly Aitken
Truckie .... Terry Camilieri
Bellamy .... Graham Rouse
Minister .... Peter Crossley
Sid Hanna .... Rob George
Governor .... John Frawley
Lady Oswald .... Anne Mullinar
Oil Company Man .... Brian Moore
Pensioner .... Max Cullen

Clearly the lessons learned by the South Australian Film Corp. on its previous foray into Disney's Land with its youth-adventure-actioner, "Storm Boy," have had a beneficial effect because, with "Blue Fin," production values and other departments have improved considerably over the former, which was a terrific success, anyway.

Greg Rowe is again the eager-to-please son on the eve of his adolescence, and this time Kruger is the bluff, rough, gruff father who can't communicate his love for the boy. Dad captains the eponymous tuna-fishing vessel and junior is intent on busting his braces to stop being thought of as 'the kid.'

The storyline is uncluttered and direct, with only a few moments of banality; oddly enough, that is when the film makes attempts at humor, which come-off very heavy. However, since the target market responds to exactly that kind of quasi-slap stick one can't really take offense.

The central character conflict is, as stated, between the boy and his father, but the script doesn't milk the schmaltz to cringe point. And there are some nice touches such as when the boy, in disappointment, goes off with his friend to fish. This not only gives us another aspect of the Rowe character, but also allows a sly reference to "Storm Boy" by allowing pelicans to intrude into the action. This sequence could have been contrived, but it falls naturally into the general scheme.

The boy wants more than anything to prove himself at sea and while members of the crew are sympathetic, father is a harder taskmaster. Problem with "Blue Fin" is that Kruger exudes so few moments of warmth that when the change comes, Rowe already has all the sympathy.

The sub-plot, wherein his daughter (Clark) loses her boyfriend (Jarratt) in an off screen nautical disaster, lacks the necessary paternal response to make any realistic shadings of even grey. It may be Kruger's persona, of course.

The film's appeal is unabashedly G.P. and on that level succeeds admirably. The formula of a Borg script based on a Theile book with young Rowe in the case of a film made by the S.A.F.C. is a proven one; and with the adolescent actor inked to the Corp., it looks very much as though this won't be the last of the type we see.

"Blue Fin" is terrific material for a kid-oriented picture and, tied with the kind of marketing strategy the S.A.F.C. has mounted, a red-carpet to fiscal success. Before the pic finishes its run, it will have been seen by over half the school-children in Australia; this because the marketing began with South Australia's Education Dept. investigating ways in which the book and the film can be used in school syllabi.

Tech credits are excellent and the atmospherics caught by Geoff Burton's cameras parallel the exact mood of the film throughout, underlining development and event most subtly. The film has a nice sense of locale, too, with a remote fishing town on the far south coast of Australia looking and behaving as though it is on another time scale — which in reality it is.

Excellent prospects for play off in Australia because of the structured marketing on which Roadshow Distribs are capitalizing, and the inevitable spinoff word of mouth. The factor will be increased by the film's launch just prior to the traditionally strong Christmas holiday season (longer Down Under since it's summer).

Beyond the home market, "Blue Fin" should also appeal in countries where basic human values still pertain in sufficient numbers to create a market. —Miha.

The Bees
(COLOR)
—
Lame disaster opus.
—
Hollywood, Nov. 14.

A New World release of a Bee One/Panorama Films Production, produced, directed and written by Alfredo Zacharias. Stars John Saxon, Angel Tompkins, John Carradine, Claudio Brook, Alicia Encinias. Camera (CFI Color), Leon Sanchez; editor, Sandy Nervis; art director, Jose Rodriguez Granada; special effects, Jack Rabin; associate producer, Teri Schwartz; assistant director, Joe B. Carles, Michael Moore. Reviewed at the Sherman Oaks Cinema, Sherman Oaks, Ca. Nov. 8, '78. (MPAA rating: PG.) Running time: **83 MINS.**
John Norman .... John Saxon
Sondra Miller .... Angel Tompkins
Dr. Sigmund Humel ...... John Carradine
Dr. Miller .... Claudio Brook
Alicia .... Alicia Encinias

A strain of killer bees similar to the one which caused so much mayhem earlier this year in Irwin Allen's "The Swarm" has ransacked South America and is threatening the rest of the world in Alfredo Zacharias' "The Bees," currently in realse by New World. The first attack was mostly ignored by filmgoers; the second probably will go unnoticed.

While the picture includes some photographs of bees, the real threat seems to be a dark brown cloud which periodically settles over a major American city. It resists chemical attacks and other forms of abuse devised by John Saxon and Angel Tompkins.

Tompkins' husband, played by Claudio Brook, is killed by the blotch early in the film. To revenge her husband's death and, incidentally, to save the world she travels to the U.S. to collaborate with her Uncle Ziggy (John Carradine), a famous bee scientist.

Along with Saxon, Tompkins discovers that the bees want to negotiate with world leaders about the fate of the environment. They take their case to what appears to be a United Nations meeting being conducted in somebody's basement.

It's all rather silly, although the film has its campy moments. It's never scary. Carradine seems to have some fun with his German accent. —Hege.

Run For The Roses
(COLOR)
—
Overly sentimental tale of a lame horse who wins the Derby. Modest outlook.
—
Hollywood, Nov. 14.

A Kodiak Films release of a Pan-American Films production, produced by Mario Crespo, Jr. and Wolf Schmidt; executive producer, Arnold Pessin. Directed by Henry Levin. Screenplay, Joseph G. Prieto, Mimi Avins; camera (Metrocolor), Raul Dominguez; music, Raul Lavista; editor, Alfredo Rosas Priego; stunt coordinator, Tom Sutton; sound, Paco Guerrero; associate producer, Richard A. Rivers. Reviewed at the Hollywood Screening Room, Hollywood, Nov. 9, '78. (MPAA rating: PG.) Running time: **93 MINS.**
Clarissa .... Vera Miles
Charlie .... Stuart Whitman
Jim .... Sam Groom
Juanito .... Panchito Gomez
Flash .... Theodore Wilson
Carol .... Lisa Eilbacher

"Run For The Roses" is the story of a domineering aunt, her nephew, a 12-year-old Puerto Rican boy and a lame colt. At the end of 93 minutes the horse wins the Kentucky Derby, the boy is rich and famous and the aunt and her nephew have reconciled their past differences. And that's only the beginning of the happy news this picture chronicles. The Kodiak Films release is another example of heartstring yanking. The picture is so calculatingly good and pleasant it'll probably be forgotten.

Panchito Gomez is the young boy living in Kentucky with his mother and step-father, manager of a thoroughbred horse farm owned by the temporarily wicked aunt, portrayed by Vera Miles in an okay performance. He loves horses, desperately wants one and gets his chance when a prize race horse gives birth to a colt with a deformed knee and Miles, in disgust, gives the horse to the boy.

Everyone in this picture wants something and gets it. Miles wants a Kentucky Derby winner. Stuart Whitman, the boy's stepfather, wants his stepson to be happy. Sam Groom, the nephew, wants his aunt's love. He also wants Lisa Eilbacher to marry him. And Eilbacher wants him.

Suffice it to say that the level of dramatic sophistication of this picture, scripted by Joseph G. Prieto and Mimi Avins and directed by Henry Levin, gives everyone what he wants.

The names associated with this film have minimal marquee value to overcome the overly saccharine story, so the film's b.o. prospects appear dim. Technical credits are at best fair. —Hege.

Une Histoire Simple
(A Simple Story)
(FRENCH-COLOR)
—
Paris, Nov. 14.

AMLF release of Renn Productions-Sara Films-FR3-Rialto Film-SFP production. Stars Romy Schneider, Claude Brasseur, Bruno Cremer. Directed by Claude Sautet. Screenplay, Sautet, Jean-Loup Dabadie; camera (Eastmancolor), Jean Boffety; editor, Jacquelin Thiedot; music, Philippe Sarde. Reviewed at Antegor, Paris, Nov. 7, '78. Running time 107 MINS.
Marie .... Romy Schneider
Georges .... Bruno Cremer
Serge .... Claude Brasseur
Gabrielle .... Arlette Bonnard
Esther .... Sophie Daumier
Anna .... Eva Darlan
Francine .... Francine Berge
Jerome .... Roger Pigaut
Mother .... Madeline Robinson

Director Claude Sautet seems to like the device of weekend country meetings of friends to lay bare their loves, work problems and human outlooks. Quintessentially French, with its series of petty piques, sudden dramas, macho male shenanigans and gathering femme lib, though latter is more personal than a concerted movement, pic benefits from homogeneous thesping and astute direction.

Main thread of the film is Romy Schneider. She is an attractive, fortyish woman who has decided to abort a child she is bearing and drop her lover. The affair is over for her. She has a 19-year-old son who lives with her.

Working as a draftsman, all her friends seem drawn mainly from her work. There are little sub-plots alongside Schneider's march towards freedom of her actions. The odyssey ends with her having an affair with her ex-husband and deciding to bear another child by him though he will nt leave a young mistress for her.

There is a friend with two kids who will not take back a husband who left her and admits to sometimes making money as an amateur joy girl, a shrewish woman, an easygoing unmarried girlfriend and a man at the end of his tether who is being fired though once a power in the company.

Latter commits suicide as one strand in this richly peopled tale. Though sometimes reminiscent of a tv mini-series, it avoids soapiness and has a surefooted rhythm despite its shifting emphasis on the various characters as it looks into the lives of the white collar set.

Schneider is radiant and effective as a woman reaching fulfillment and maturity with Claude Brasseur properly vindictive as her discarded lover and yet appealing and Bruno Cremer is right as the ex-husband who is more effective in business than in human relations.

Pic calls for hard sell abroad but has enough revealing insights into human behavior to transcend its fragmented treatment and sometimes arch dialog. — Mosk.

Yasei No Shomei
(Proof of the Wild)
(JAPANESE-COLOR)
—
Tokyo, Oct. 27.

Nippon Herald release of a Kadokawa Publishing Co. production. Executive producer, Haruki Kadokawa. Producers, Jun Sakagami, Masaya Endoh, Fumio Matsuda, Simon Tse. Features entire cast. Directed by Junya Satoh. Screenplay, Koji

Takada, based on book by Seiichi Morimuma; camera (color), Masahisa Himeda; editor, Jun Nabeshima; music, Kuji Ono; art director, Horoshi Tokuda; lighting, Hideo Kumagai. Reviewed at Shinjuku Roman, Tokyo, Oct. 27, '78. Running time: **143 MINS.**

Ajisawa	Ken Takakura
Ochi	Ryoko Nakano
Nagai	Horoko Yakushimaru
Kitano	Isao Natsuki
Oba	Rentaro Mikuni
Muranaga	Hajime Hana

Fall in Japan has come to mean time for another film from the Kadokawa Publishing Company: "Inugami-ke No Ichizoku" (The Inugami Family) in '76; "Ningen No. Shomei" (Prof. of the Man) in '77; and now "Yasei No Shomei" (Proof of the Wild).

Each financed by Kadokawa. Each an adaptation of a book published by Kadokawa. And each a domestic hit, thanks to extensive ad campaigns ballyhooing the films out of all proportion to their merits. Unless and until Kadokawa learns how to saturate non-Japanese media, the company can never hope to duplicate its success abroad.

"Yasei" is set in Japan 1980. Ken Takakura, a member of a super-secret paramilitary group, is overcome with exhaustion while on wilderness training and stumbles onto a group of thirteen rural types. When he leaves, twelve lie dead and one, teen-ager Hiroko Yakushimaru, is in shock.

A year later, Takakura is back near the scene of the crime, this time as a claims adjuster investigating the death by drowning of a reporter insured by his company. Ryoko Nakano, sister of one of the 12 massacred villagers and herself a reporter on the same paper as the drowned man, has a hunch her colleague was killed and his death made to look like a suicide because **he had dug up too much dirt on crime boss Rentaro Mikuni.**

Detective Isao Natsuki, meanwhile, finds it suspicious that Takakura has adopted Horoko, the sole survivor of that massacre. Eventually, Takakura is arrested and charged with murder. The paramilitary organization to which he once belonged, hearing of this, decides to eliminate him lest he spill any beans. The film climaxes with Takakura, Natsuki and little Horoko being pursued over hill and dale by combat-ready troops.

As was "Ningen No Shomei," "Yasei No Shomei" is based on a mystery by Seiichi Morimura.

The film, much too long, features commercial tie-ins with everything from coffee to running shoes, but is nonetheless competently directed, photographed and acted. The presence of Takakura — once again playing a noble and stoic character — gives the film a believability, not to mention dignity, it sorely needs. A major surprise is Ryoko Nakano,

only passable in the past, who, perhaps challenged by Takakura, rises to the occasion and turns in a sensitive, delicately shaded performance. —*Bail.*

The Night The Prowler
(AUSTRALIAN-COLOR)

New South Wales Film Corp. release of a Chariot Films (Anthony Buckley) production. Directed by Jim Sharman. Features entire cast. Screenplay, Patrick White, based on his short story; camera (color), David Sanderson; music, Cameron Alan. No other credits provided. Reviewed in New York screening room, Nov. 9, '78. (No MPAA rating). Running time: **90 MINS.**

Cast: Ruth Cracknell, John Frawley, Kerry Walker, John Derum, Maggie Kirkpatrick, Terry Camilleri.

Australian film director Jim Sharman has had a measure of success with midnight film goers with his "Rocky Horror Picture Show." His latest effort, despite the collaboration of "Caddie" producer Anthony Buckley and Nobel Prize-winning writer Patrick White, is even more confusing than that bizarre work. Sharman evidently thinks of himself as the Down Under Alejandro Jodorowsky and, certainly, his films have that touch of the unreal that mark "El Topo."

A hodge-podge of flash forwards, flashbacks, and even some flash sideways, it tells the story, as one pundit put it, of a female slob's search for self-identification. A young woman, played in her film debut by Kerry Walker, moves into adulthood as an overweight, sullen, neurotic and ill-mannered daughter of a couple of middleclass stereotypes. The mother is attractive and dimwitted; the father is dull.

With flashbacks to the various stages of her youth, including the usual father fixation and an engagement to a rather boring young diplomat with a promising future, she fakes (or misinterprets) a visit from a prowler — in her version, with rape in mind. This event, of course, lessens her chances at a marriage which she wasn't too eager about anyhow and she goes through a series of increasingly demoralizing changes, finally emerging as a leather-clad night prowler on her own. During some of her nocturnal jaunts she meets a series of derelicts who are, apparently, meant to humanize her.

Not that the audience cares about any of this. There's a good possibility that any American distrib will have to change the title as it never lives up to the "horror" it suggests. Included in the upcoming Australian Film Festival in New York, it might also wind up on the midnight circuit. —*Robe.*

Stony Island
(COLOR)
Chicago, Nov. 11.

A World-Northal release. Produced by Andrew Davis and Tamar Hoffs. Directed by Andrew Davis; writers, Andrew Davis and Tamar Hoffs; camera, Tak Fujimoto; editor, Dov Hoenig; music, David Matthews; performed by Stony Island Band; supervised by Gene Barge. Reviewed at the Biograph Theatre, Chicago, Nov. 4, '78. (M-PAA Rating: PG). Running time: **97 MINS.**

Richie Bloom	Richard Davis
Kevin Tucker	Edward Stoney Robinson
Harold Tate	George Englund
Percy Price	Gene Barge
Ronnie Roosevelt	Ronnie Barron
Tennyson	Tennyson Stephens
Larry	Larry Ball
Windy	Windy Barnes
Janetta	Rae Dawn Chong
Donnell	Donnell Hagen
Criss	Criss Johnson
Kenny	Kenneth Brass
Ed	Edwin William
Steele	Steele L. Seals
Lucie	Susanna Hoffs
Lewis Moss	Nathan Davis
Raymond Popitch	Tom Mula
Barry Cowan	Carmi Simon
Jerry Domino	Dennis Franz

"Stony Island" has some weak points but for a small, independently financed feature shot in Chicago's worst winter for under $400,000, it succeeds in achieving some measure of audience involvement. The message here is the young person's dream of forming a successful band and although the script mostly fails in bringing its point across, the music manages to take over and save the situation in part.

Setting is a neighborhood on Chi's rough south side where Richie and friend Kevin are forming a band. Through the course of the film they pick up a poor hillbilly practicing sax in the music store where Richie works, also a seasoned musician who is a caretaker at a funeral home and an assortment of backup singers, guitarists and percussionists. Together the band must battle the forces preventing their success — lack of funds, bookings, instruments and support from authority figures. In the end, of course, they manage to achieve a somewhat happy ending.

Major problem here is writing and execution of script. Aside from little character development, events seem either staged or stereotypical or confusing. But consolation is to be found from the kids in the band, most of whom are musicians, not professional actors. Aside from transmitting the wide-eyed quality of any novice looking to make it big, their music, a combination of r&b and jazz, is right on target.

The filmmakers managed to capture the inner city look of Chicago.

However, there was just not enough budget to explore the entire city without creating a choppy, home movie quality.

Film opens Nov. 17 in Chicago and is planned to be released slowly throughout the country. Because music is the one strong element here, simultaneous release of soundtrack album could help.
—*Berg.*

My Way Home
(BRITISH-B&W)

Chicago, Nov. 12.

A BFI production. Directed and written by Bill Douglas. Reviewed at the Chicago Festival Screening Room, Oct. 30, 1978. Running time: **78 MINS.**

"My Way Home," the third part of a trilogy concerning the dismal life of troubled Scottish boy Jamie, is a mostly boring and confusing account that never manages to provoke empathy for its characters. Rather than stressing dialog, director Bill Douglas lets the players express feelings through symbolic gestures with the result being a muddled conglomeration of crossed references.

Douglas has managed to capture the mood of Jamie's life with the use of black and white throughout. As the plot goes, boy is taken from a depressing youth home to the constant bickering at his father's abode (Dad presumably put him in the home in the first place). It's then the story seems to become solely dependent on the boy's long, meaningful stares into the lens and some heavy-handed symbolism (e.g. a copy of "David Copperfield" Jamie gets from his doddering grandfather is used as an implied parallel of lifestyles). The technique just doesn't work to explain Jamie suddenly appearing at the Salvation Army turning up his nose at a bowl of mush and even more suddenly appearing on the Egyptian desert, apparently drafted into the armed forces.

While serving his country the boy kindles his first friendship with an upper-class, educated youth who begins to bring him out of his shell. There's some comic relief and occasional snatches of good acting here as the two almost go batty talking about their boredom.

Much of the film is spoken by characters with thick accents that should make understanding difficult for American audiences. Because there are so many loose ends in this project, showing it with the other parts of the trilogy might hold some interest.

(Pic won a Bronze Hugo at the Fest.) — *Berg.*

On The Yard
(COLOR)

_____

Chicago, Nov. 11.

A Midwest Film Production. Produced by Joan Micklin Silver. Directed by Raphael D. Silver. Features entire cast. Screenplay, Malcolm Braly; music, Charles Grois. Reviewed at Chicago Film Festival Screening Room, Nov. 2, '78. (No MPAA Rating.) Running time: **103 MINS.**

Juleson	John Heard
Chilly	Tom Waites
Red	Mike Kellin
Nunn	Richard Bright
Morris	Joe Grifasi
Captain Blake	Lane Smith
Stick	Richard Hayes
Gasolino	Hector Troy
Lt. Carpenter	Richard Jamieson
Warden	Thomas Toner
Manning	Ron Faber
Psychiatrist	David Clennon
Tate	Don Blakely
Luther	JC Quinn
Mendoza	Dominic Chianese
Lt. Olsen	Eddie Jones
Clemmons	Ben Slack
Larson	James Remar
Redmond	Dave McCalley
Candy	Ludwick Villani

_____

There are a lot of good ideas and subplots contained in "On the Yard," but ultimately the film does not hang together as a convincing piece of drama. Its makers have tried too hard to capture the total picture of prison life and have ended up with a series of vignettes that never add up to much of a story.

On his first attempt, director Raphael D. Silver, produced by wife Joan Micklin Silver of "Hester Street," has set up a decent cast of characters. Chilly, unofficial head of prisoners, is noted for being fair; a middle-aged con who's been in and out his whole life is sympathetic; and a smart, pretty boy who's in the tank for murdering his wife seems close to emotional breakdown. There are also assorted crazies, addicts and burnouts along with some brutal guards and an unsympathetic warden to round out the scene.

Silver's failure is in not using one of his subplots for a primary story. There are just too many characters and situations to follow here.

Notwithstanding, are several fine scenes within. Credit for their effectiveness is due to actors John Heard, Tom Waites and Mike Kellin, standouts in a generally fine cast of non-stars.

Scripter Malcolm Braly disappoints on a number of occasions. For most part prisoners sound too literate. The physical look of the picture is convincing but "On the Yard" is too superficial to attract the intellectuals and too tame to appeal to the blood and guts crowd.
—_Berg._

Bhumika
(The Role)
(INDIAN-COLOR)

_____

Chicago, Nov. 12.

A Blaze Film Enterprises and P.V.T. Ltd. Production. Produced by Lalit M. Bijlani and Freni M. Variava. Directed by Shyam Benegal. Screenplay by Shyam Benegal; editor, Bhanudas; camera, Govind Nihalani; music, Vanraj Bhatia; lyrics, Majrooh Sultanpuri and Vasanth Dev; dialog by Pt. Staya Dev Dubey. Reviewed at Chicago Film Festival Screening Room, Nov. 1, 1978. No MPAA Rating. Running time: **160 MINS.**
Featuring Smita Patil, Anant Nag, Amrish Puri, Naseerudding Shah, Sulabha Deshpande, Kulbhushan Kharbanda, Baby Rukhshana and Amol Palekar.

_____

If you can imagine a cross between the Hindu versions of "A Star Is Born," "Valley of the Dolls" and "Funny Girl" you've come up with a pretty good plot summary of Benegal's "The Role." But the schmaltz that might normally attract viewers to this kind of venture plays second fiddle to a hopeless attempt at a character study that expects almost every stereotype of the struggling actress.

Film opens with a famous but discontented film star Usha coming home from a long day on the set to all the materialistic trappings of fame as well as an aging, nasty husband, cute daughter and aloof mother. It is clear Usha is about'to reach the breaking point. Director uses this as the pretext to flash back over Usha's entire life.

Being pretty she is forced to support her family with a show business career. After singing painfully off-key at an audition a benevolent filmmaker gives her a break. But fancy cars, sex, gigolos and an abortion only bring her unhappiness. She eventually becomes mistress to a rich male chauvinist Indian businessman who imprisons her in his mansion.

Everyone is guilty of overindulgence and overacting here, but the major blame should be placed on director Benegal who's obviously seen too many old Hollywood films.

Music borders on the tortuous, editing appears non-existent and sub-titles are badly lit. Camera work is okay along with some nice color and costumes. —_Berg._

Same Time, Next Year
(COLOR)

_____

Marvelous screen version of Bernard Slade's play, wonderful performing. Good outlook.

_____

Hollywood, Oct. 31.

A Universal Pictures release of a Walter Mirisch-Robert Mulligan Production, produced by Walter Mirisch and Morton Gottlieb. Stars Ellen Burstyn, Alan Alda. Directed by Robert Mulligan. Screenplay, Bernard Slade, based on his play; camera (color), Robert Surtees; music, Marvin Hamlisch; production designer, Henry Bumstead; editor, Sheldon Kahn; costume designer, Theadora Van Runkle; set decoration, Hal Guasman sound, Gene Cantamesa; montage sequences, Charles Braverman, Ken Rudolph, make-up, William Tuttle; sepcial effects, Tim Moran, assistant director, Donald Roberts. Reviewed. at Universal Studios, Universal City, Oct. 31, '78. (MPAA Rating: PG.) Running time: **119 MINS.**

Doris	Ellen Burstyn
George	Alan Alda
Chalmers	Ivan Bonar

_____

"Same Time, Next Year" is a textbook example of how to successfully transport a stage play to the big screen. The Walter Mirisch-Morton Gottlieb production of Bernard Slade's play, sensitively directed by Robert Mulligan, is everything you'd want from this kind of film: It's been pushed open just enough to maintain interest without altering the material; it's cleverly and efficiently divided into movements with montages of still photographs; and it features two first class performances by Ellen Burstyn and Alan Alda. The Universal release looks like a hearty Christmas contender, especially for the upper age bracket of filmgoers.

A retelling of the picture's premise makes it seem somewhat contrived, although thanks to the humor and good nature of Bernard Slade's fine screenplay it's never that. This is the type of genuinely heartwarming and engaging material for which audiences gladly suspend disbelief.

The picture opens in 1951 at a resort in northern California. Burstyn, a 24-year-old Oakland housewife, and Alda, a 27-year-old accountant from New Jersey, meet over dinner, get along and have a fling. The next morning they wake up in the same bed, talk about what's happened, realize that while they're both happily married with six children between them, they're in love.

They make a pact to meet at the same resort every year, which is just what they do and is just what the film is about. We see the two every five or six years as they adjust to the changes time brings.

Alda moves to Beverly Hills, becomes a business manager, politically conservative, a convert to self-help therapy and a lounge pianist. Burstyn finishes high

school, turns Berkeley hippie, then successful businesswoman and grandmother. What always remains through the years is the deep affection the two share. It's nice to see a film about two people who like each other this deeply.

Two or three of the scenes start off a bit awkwardly. For example, Burstyn's characterization of a Berkeley radical initially is too broad; Alda's psychoanalytic hip California at first is too much. But overall the characterizations by the two are so strong and so appealing that even in the lapses one wants to believe in them. And at the end, the scenes always work.

Mulligan's direction is strong and sure, as are the other technical credits. Henry Bumstead's production design, along with Hal Gausman's set decoration, ages the cottage at which the couple annually reunite in a realistic and fitting fashion. William Tuttle's make-up work should be singeld out, as should Marvin Hamlisch's score and title song. —_Hege._

Le Pion
(The Pawn)
(FRENCH-COLOR)

_____

Paris, Nov. 20.

Prodis/Oceanic release of Films 21 production. Features entire cast. Written and directed by Christian Gion. Camera (Eastmancolor), Lionel Legros. No other credits available. Reviewed at George V, Paris, Nov. 19, '78. Running time, **90 MINS.**
Cast: Henry Guybet, Claude Pieplu, Michel Galabru, Claude Jade.

_____

A predictable tale of a fey assistant school teacher who manages to get the girl, write a prizewinning bestseller book and even win the admiration of his generally unruly students. Too syrupy for much theatrical chances abroad, this could do okay locally. It might have youthslanted playoff legs, however, as well as tv usage on its good natured if sentimental treatment.

Henry Guybet, usually a brash comic, shows a flair for adding some depth to his timid character. Kids go in for practical jokes and make his class the most insubordinate as he scribbles his book while they fight, make noise and avoid study.

The principal tries to get him sacked by bringing along an inspector. But the students get wind of it and foul up the other classes and make his a model. There are the outsize practical jokes too.

Calling the school the Jean Vigo High School might ruffle buffs though others might let it go by. Vigo was the great filmmaker whose "Zero De Conduite," a poetic raging surrealistic look at schools and student revolt, has become a classic. "Pawn" is technically okay and youngsters are acceptable and not too overweening in their carryings-on and associations with the adults. —*Mosk.*

L'Enfant De La Nuit
(Child of the Night)
(FRENCH-ITALO-COLOR)

Paris, Nov. 21.

Silenes release of Paris-Cannes Production-Alpes Film-A.P.K. Cinematografica production. Stars Agostina Belli. Directed by Sergio Gobbi. Screenplay, Ugo Pirro, from the book by G. J. Arnaud; camera (Eastman-color), Ennio Guarnieri; editor, Ruggero Mastroianni; music, Stelvio Cipriani. Reviewed at Le Paris, Paris, Nov. 10, '78. Running time: **102 MINS.**
Claudia .... Agostina Belli
Andrea .... Stefano Satta Flores
Nino ....,............ Sergino
Doctor .... Jean-Claude Bouillon

Sergio Gobbi, of Italo origin, has made most of his films locally through his own company, Paris-Cannes Productions. He went back to Italy for this French-Italian coproduction shot in Italian and dubbed into French. It is a novelettish drama of a woman who has lost her nine or 10-year-old son.

She comes back to a mountain area where her son died in an auto accident, which her husband survived. After visiting the boy's grave she thinks she sees a boy her son's age in the snow. She begins to hunt and finally finds him. Film adds a sort of occult note as to whether the boy exists or has been created in her mind due to her trauma over her son's demise.

Nobody sees the boy though there are footprints seen by others. Does the boy poison the family dog and kill the husband, or is it her? Languid film does create a moody atmosphere but misses the probing and personal directorial style to give it an edge for offshore chances outside playoff and tv possibilities.

The boy appears suddenly seated near her as she leaves the town though he had not been there when she started out. So maybe he is hallucination, and maybe not. Pic lacks the penetrating treatment to make one care. Agostina Belli looks anguished throughout. A few French thesps do small parts in this occult psycho drama. At least there are no demons. -- *Mosk.*

Pero No Vas A Cambiar Nunca Margarita?
(But Aren't You Ever Going To Change Margarita?)
(SPANISH-COLOR)

Madrid, Nov. 3.

Paraguas Films S. A. production. Written and directed by Chumy Chumez. Features entire cast. Exec producer, Antonio Cuevas; camera (Eastmancolor), Carlos Suarez, editor, Pablo G. del Amo; sets, Wolfgang Burman; music, Carlos A. Vizziello. Reviewed at Sincronia (Madrid), Nov. 3, '78. Running time: **57 MINS.**

Margarita .... Silvia Aguilar
Fermin .... Antonio Garisa
Jorge .... Fernando Rubio
Pepa .... Josefina Calatayud
Young priest .... Francisco Vidal

Spanish humorist Chumy Chumez, whose second pic this is, has set himself the task of attacking the dubious morality of the middle classes by way of glorifying the freewheeling ways of a kind-hearted prostitute. The characters depicted are more caricatures than flesh and blood people and the hypocrisies that are the butts of Chumy Chumez's humor are rather too obvious.

Pic is shot almost entirely in interiors and the dialogs, though spontaneous, more often than not fall flat. Some of the dullness, perhaps, is due to the lack of any outstanding thesping talent in the film; Garisa and Rubio are fine in supporting roles, but newcomer Silvia Aguilar, who spends half the film running around topless, isn't good enough to carry along the feeble story.

Yarn concerns a girl living in Madrid who has an aged sugar daddy. On the side she performs in a transvestite club. Her elder brother comes to visit her from Avila, tries to reform her profligate ways, and winds up sleeping with her. Sister-in-law and a priestly cousin also come to Madrid to try to change her ways, but Margarita resists. "Freedom" triumphs over straitlaced bigotry.

Item might rack up some offshore sales as a sex comedy and on the basis of Silvia Aguilar's physique, which is amply flaunted throughout the film. —*Besa.*

Der Kleine Godard
(A Little Godard)
(WEST GERMAN-COLOR-16m)

Berlin, Oct. 23.

A Production of the Toulouse-Lautrec-Institute, Hellmuth Costard, Hamburg, in collaboration with "Das kleine Fernsehspiel" of Second German Television (ZDF), Eckhart Stein, production chief, Wiesbaden. Features Jean-Luc Godard, Rainer Werner Fassbinder, Hark Bohm. Directed by Hellmuth Costard. Camera (color), Bernd Upnmoor, Hans-Otto Walter, Hanno Hart, Costard; sound, Herbert Jeschke, Marcia Bronstein; editor, Susanne Paschen; blow-up advisors, Helmut Rings, Helmut Herbdt. Reviewed at Klick-Kino, Berlin, Oct. 23, '78. Running time: **81 MINS.**

For over a decade now, Hellmuth Costard has played the gifted, creative, controversial imp in New German Cinema. His "Particularly Recommended" (1967), an out of focus shot on masturbation aimed at a governmental rating of films, nearly tore the Oberhausen Short Film Festival apart in 1968, although it was only a short of a few minutes. A tv pic, "Football Like Never Before" (1971), filmed only the movements of George Best in a regulation soccer game. In between, he made chronicled household slavery by filming a male in woman's dress to illustrate that "The Suppression of Women Is Recognizable Above All in the Restrictions Placed Upon Them" (1969).

"A Little Godard" is dedicated to the Kuratorium (production board) of Young German Cinema, a subsidy arm of the federal states in West Germany handing out pennies to directors seeking to make their first films. It seeks to point out, on the one hand, how difficult it is to sell a piece of talented flesh to the powers that be in German television, and, on the other, how to work economically without subsidies with a home-made 8m camera-and-sound-pack of your very own.

Pic shows the insides of Hamburg's cultural politics by filming a committee meeting on the spot discussing the pros and cons of inviting Jean-Luc Godard to come to Hamburg as a foreign artist-in-residence: Costard did it (Lord knows how) with his itsy bitsy invention. He also catches Godard in talks with prominent tv managers in Hamburg, as well as filming Teutonic helmers Rainer Werner Fassbinder and Hark Bohm while lensing "Despair" and "Moritz, Dear Moritz" respectively. This footage alone is so revealing that the pic immediately found critic response in the German press, was invited to the Edinburgh and London fests, and was seen by Jean-Luc himself in a recent screening at the Pacific Film Archive in Berkeley.

The real joy of "A Little Godard," however, is the demonstration of how Costard's 8m unit works. followed by several examples (principally those noted above) of the home-made invention in action and the viewer's awareness that this pic has been blown up to 16m format to slip it into festivals and a late-night slot on the "Little TV-Play." If this tongue-in-cheek, masterfully made "document" can be unspooled on the same evening as Fassbinder's heavily subsidized "Despair," the rub in the joke will hit home all the quicker. —*Holl.*

Ket Elhatarozas
(A Quite Ordinary Life)
(HUNGARIAN-DOCU-B&W)

Chicago, Nov. 21.

A Pro Vobis Film for ZDF. Directed and written by Imre Gyongyossy and Barna Kabay. Camera (black and white), Gabor Szabo. No other credits available. Reviewed at the Varsity Theatre, Chicago, Nov. 12, '78. Running time: **75 MINS.**

This simple, unassuming film was one of the best entries at this year's Chi Film Fest mostly due to its subject — a charming 74-year-old Hungarian peasant woman who reminisces about her life in the remote village of Rimoc.

Rather than mere storytelling, film lets Veronika Kiss discuss her existence as she's going about everyday chores of working the fields of her farm, feeding her geese or caring for her orchids. She's all alone with the exception of a son in England who she's determined to make enough money to visit. Her fortitude in achieving this goal is one of the special aspects of the picture.

Kiss' life is also used to tell history. Her brother died in World War I, a son was killed in World War II and her father was tortured to death after the Hungarian Communist Republic fell. Yet it's the photographs of this woman talking to friends and doing chores most people couldn't do at 35 that make this a worth watching documentary.

No one in this film appeared to be bothered by cameras so the needed natural state of things was achieved. Photography was good as was subtitling. The picture is a must for specialized art houses, film fests and eventually non-theatrical release. —*Berg.*

Kneuss
(SWISS-GERMAN-COLOR)

Zurich, Nov. 3.

Rex-Film Zurich release of a Cine Groupe Zurich and Sator Film Hamburg co-production. Directed by Gaudenz Meili. Features entire cast. Screenplay, Beat Brechbuehl, Meili, based on novel by Brechbuehl; camera (color) Pio Corradi; music, Tangerine Dream; sound, Stanislav Hromadnik; editor, Edelgard Gielisch; art director, Rica Mattmueller; technical director, Werner Santschi. Reviewed at the Frosch-Studio, Zurich, Nov. 3, '78. Running time, **96 MINS.**
Kneuss .... Ingold Wildensauer
Cecile .... Renate Schroeter
Schnaffelmann .... Harald Leipnitz
Agnes .... Mascha Gonska
Monika .... Herlinde Latzko
Berger .... Adolph Spalinger
Glimpf .... Alex Freihart
Kutscher .... Mario Hindermann
Marinetti .... Ettore Cella
Buchbinder .... Hans Gaugler

Swiss director Gaudenz Meili's decision to film Beat Brechbuehl's "Kneuss," a Swiss bestselling novel of eight years ago, was admittedly motivated, among other reasons, by his own identification with the title character, a free-wheeling, free-living outsider amidst a saturated society. He is trapped by a now-successful former buddy into a mysterious deal involving drugs and gangsters disguised as Mormons, starts an affair with his friend's beautiful wife and ends up by murdering him.

The picture wavers uneasily between trivial realism and the poetic probing of an unorthodox character. Neither comes off very convincingly. Script by Meili and

Brechbuehl has too many loopholes. Dialog often sounds distressingly stilted, too.

Film's most recommendable aspects are Pio Corradi's atmospheric color photography, a softly melodic score by Tangerine Dream and fine performances by Ingold Wildenauer in the title role and Renate Schroeter, lovely and sensitive as his mistress. —*Mezo*.

Olsen-Banden gaar i krig

(The Olsen Gang Goes To War)
(DANISH-COLOR)

Copenhagen, Nov. 6.

A A/S Nordisk Film production and release. Directed by Erik Balling. Original story and script, Henning Bahs, Balling; production design and special effects, Bahs; camera (Eastmancolor) Jeppe Jeppesen; music, Bent Fabricius-Bjerre; editor, Ole Steen Nielsen. Reviewed at the Palads, Copenhagen, Nov. 5, 1978. Running time: **95 MINS.**

Egon Olsen . . . . Ove Sprogoe
Benny . . . . . .' . . . . Morten Grunwald
Kjeld . . . . Poul Bundgaard
Yvonne . . . . Kirsten Walther

"The Olsen Gang Goes To War" is Erik Balling's (and Henning Bahs') 10th installment in the saga of three little crooks going through a lot of first-rate farcical hoopla towards their ever optimistic goal of scoring millions and their equally constant failing through the petit-bourgeois amition of the wife of one of the gang's members.

As designed by Bahs and Balling and as played by Ove Sprogoe, Morten Grunwald, Poul Bundgaard and Kirsten Walther plus a solid supporting cast including Ove Werner Hansen, Edward Fleming and Axel Stoebye, the new "Olsen Gang" feature must rate among the best of modern slapstick-with-a-human-face fare anywhere as did all its predecessors. It is to be hoped that, finally, more foreign distribution follows. Post-synch jobs would be preferable, but even with subtitles, most of the precision work fun should be easily understandable. The production value is, as always, also of a high order.

Story this time has the Gang getting hold of a secret West German-Common Market plan to turn Denmark into "Daisyland" (Denmark's Queen Margrethe is nicknamed Daisy), a holiday area for the entire Europe, with the Danish population serving mostly as waiters, guides, folklore dancers, etc. The plan is worth millions to some sneaky Danish entrepreneurs, and the Olsen Gang wants it share. Until, unexpectedly, patriotism awakens in their hearts.— *Kell.*

Saxofone
(Saxophone)
(ITALIAN-COLOR)

Rome, Nov. 13.

A CIDIF release produced by Irrigazione Cinematografica release. Directed by Renato Pozzetto. Produced by Achille Manzotti. Stars Renato Pozzetto, Mariangela Melato. Screenplay, Enzo Jannacci, Renato Pozzetto, Cochi Ponzoni, Giuseppe Viola; camera (Eastmancolor), Roberto Seveso; editor, Sergio Montanari; music, Enzo Jannacci. Reviewed at Metropolitan Theater in Rome, Nov. 13, '78. Running time: **100 MINS.**

Also: Teo Teocoli, Cochi Ponzoni, Massimi Baldo, Felice Andreassi.

Italian comedian Renato Pozzetto — for the first time both behind and in front of the camera — has produced a series of sketches that are sometimes surrealistic and sometimes corny, but too often badly integrated into the film as a whole. Despite its unevenness, however, "Saxophone" has enough zany moments to merit a look.

The film tells the you've-heard-it-before story of the bored bourgeois woman (Mariangelo Melato) who seeks adventure by following the haunting tune of a down-and-out saxophone player (Renato Pozzetto). "Saxophone" gives, however, a new twist to this time-honored film theme: the poor little rich girl finds out that although money can't buy happiness, it needn't prevent it either. "Happiness is all in your head," moralizes the ragtag sax player who at the end of the film turns out to be a closet millionaire.

Pozzetto as "Sax" dishes up the kind of night club humor that launched his career: in a particularly funny sketch, he is trying desperately to find a place where he can take a leak and ends up in a shop selling bathroom equipment. Melato, who plays the straight man to Pozzetto and his up-side-down world, provides the only thin thread that holds together totally disconnected scenes.

The surrealistic touches are superb. While the bourgeois woman and her husband are arguing in their kitchen about their dull lives, for example, the camera backs up to show them on a theatre stage. Some of the characters are deliciously bizarre (a five-year-old garage mechanic), but too many are embarrassingly slapstick (a mad scientist doctor and his blonde assistant dressed in leopard skins, an over-zealous priest who baptizes "Sax" with a watering can).

—*Argo.*

Miami Film Fest

Art Of Killing
(JAPANESE—COLOR)

Miami, Nov. 14.

Arthur Davis Organization Japan Inc. presentation. Executive producer, Arthur Davis. Associate producer, Miyako Ejiri. Created and produced by Hisao Masudo. Written and directed by Masayoshi Nemoto. Camera (color), Ryo Yano, Yoshiaki Kato; score, Stomu Yamashta; sound, Tetuso Sagawa; editor, Koichi Atsumo; production manager, Hiroshi Sakano; narrator, Harry J. Quini. Reviewed at Beach Theatre, Miami Film Festival, Nov. 13, '78. (No MPAA rating). Running time: **90 MINS.**

Behind the cycle of martial arts hokum pictures (in *Variety* paraphrase, the "Chop Socky" genre) there lurks the incredible discipline, mystical philosophy and mind control of the real thing. The result in this Arthur Davis feature (his second venture outside distribution proper) is a powerful and frequently amazing insight into Japanese history, point of view and vocation.

"Art of Killing," but the counterpoint is less to slay than to stay (alive), took three years to make. The details, the timing of the various defense techniques must have required innumerable retakes. Swordplay is peculiarly subtle. (The film includes a sequence on the hand-crafting of the traditional Japanese swords.)

Since Japan is the veritable homeland of Judo, Budo and the intervening attack-and-defense systems it is true blackbelt country. Some 15,000,000 Japanese are enrolled, from small children to men in their 60s, and with a numerous and formidable women's auxiliary. The use of sticks, farm tools and antique weapons have their own expert practioners. "Expert," and the way to become such, is the nub.

This film drew a big Miami crowd at the Beach Theatre, some 710 admissions at $4, and was well received. The photography is superior, the editing and production values carefully organized and the impact of certain scenes (man breaking cement blocks with elbow, and/or forehead) stuns the beholder.

In a film of this nature (part documentary, part essay, part anthropology) the musical score is important and Davis and coproducer Miyako Ejiri (who was also introduced from the Beach Theatre stage) secured the right talent in Stomu Yamashta. It is never intrusive, always appropriate, swells dramatically where called for.

Men, women, children, Sumo wrestlers and Japan itself are the "cast." Arresting "types" abound, including quite elderly Ken-do (sword) heroes. The narration is strong on extolling strength as a guarantor of peace, the weapons and their effective employment as guardians of honor.

Plainly there are all sorts of potential merchandizing angles here. U.S. alone has some 13,000 schools of karate. The music score, the Japanese scenery as pictorial material, lend themselves to commercial re-production.

The title is a bit on the lurid side, of course, but good showmanship. The overall approach is balanced, intriguing, occasionally scholarly. The sweep of the Japanese scenics and the wild seacoast all "compose" the centuries-old way of life.

Constantly interesting, intermittently exciting, "Art of Killing" ought to do well, and world-wide.

—*Land.*

The Kirlian Witness
(COLOR)

Miami, Nov. 16.

Jonathan Sarno production. Stars Nancy Snyder, Joel Colodner, Nancy Boykin, Ted Leplat. Directed by Sarno. Screenplay, Sarno, Lamar Sanders, from a story by Sarno; camera, Joao Fernandes (Technicolor); editors, Len Dell 'Amico and Edward Salier; associate editor, Veronica Loza; music, Harry Mandredini. Review at Beach Theater, Miami, Nov. 15, '78. (MPAA Rating — PG.) Running time: **91 MINS.**

Rilla . . . . Nancy Snyder
Dusty . . . . Ted Laplat
Robert . . . . Joel Colodner
Laurie . . . . Nancy Boykin
Detective . . . . Lawrence Tierney
Claire . . . .'. . . Maia Danziger

Producer-director-writer Jonathan Sarno, according to his press bio, has "previously worked in shorts" — but judging from his first full-length film, "The Kirlian Witness," Sarno should be graduated to long pants.

"The Kirlian Witness" is an auspicious debut, exceptionally well-mounted for an independent production. It's a murder mystery with a bizarre twist: the witness to the killing, and the witness which communicates telepathically with the killer's next intended victim, is a household plant. Using Kirlian photography and monochromatic "visions," the plant's information is visually transmitted to the woman in danger.

Sarno's story is based on such a case, when an expert hooked a lie detector up to a plant that had "witnessed" the murder of a New Jersey woman (according to the test, the plant correctly "identified" the killer). And though the premise may sound ludicrous, Sarno concentrates on the whodunit aspect and emerges with a very interesting murder mystery.

As in "The Eyes of Laura Mars," the ESP visions are transmitted and received under stress and in small pieces, so that the girl (Nancy Snyder) — as well as the audience — is not really certain of the murderer's identity. Logic, though, narrows to two possibilities: Robert (Joel Colodner), the girl's husband, and Dusty (Ted Leplat), an ominous acquaintance of the girl's sister (Nancy Boykin), whose murder was witnessed by the plant.

Although a few of the early scenes have a slight greenish tint to them, as though they were undergoing photosynthesis, Sarno's gifts for style and composition soon make themselves apparent. The location photography by Joao Fernandes is inventive and atmospheric: a high-level view of a few city blocks, tracking the path of the suspicious Dusty, recalls a similarly photographed scene in "M." In another appropriate film reference, a tv screen displays a scene from "The Day of the Triffids," a 1963 film about man-eating plants.

Snyder, Colodner and Leplat deliver unusually good performances for an independent film; Colodner and Leplat are convincingly menacing, and Snyder is an empathetic and believable detective-victim. The editing (credited to Len Dell'Amico, Edward Salier and Veronica Loza) is especially good, using actual Kirlian photography & a colorful film process that recreates the "auras" around living things — and the monochromatic "messages" for fine dramatic effect. The visuals are sufficiently unfamiliar and interesting to allow for explanation of the phenomena without boring the audience with lengthy exposition.

"The Kirlian Witness" explores new territory while remaining completely faithful to the mystery genre; it has the potential of attracting the occult enthusiasts without alienating the mystery fans, and it builds to a surprising and frightening climax. "The Kirlian Witness" and director Sarno deserve an environment in which they can grow and produce. —*Bian.*

Brutes and Savages
(DOCUMENTARY-COLOR)

Miami, Nov. 15.

Arthur Davis Organization presentation. Produced and directed by Davis. Associate producer, Miyako Ejiri. Editor, Alan J. Cummer-Price; narration written by Jenny Craven; spoken by Richard Johnson. Camera (color) by Natives; music, composed and conducted by Riz Ortolani. Reviewed at Konover Hotel, Miami Film Festival, Nov. 13, '78. (No MPAA rating). Running time: 94 MINS.

Arthur Davis, the former Florida theatre operator who became a world film distributor, went to South America on a personal holiday, but toting a hand camera. The resultant scenes prompted him to later return to Bolivian, Peruvian and Amazonian terrain with regular stock, professional technicians and Japanese co-producer Miyako Ejiri. Their "Arthur Davis Expedition" production is "Brutes and Savages" in the tradition of Italy's "Mondo Cane." There will be censor opposition here and there, but for its designated types of audiences this one should do well.

A salient value is the mood score of Riz Ortalani. It does a lot for pic "Brutes and Savages" has actually played off in certain Asiatic markets but awaits deals elsewhere. The people are primitives of the uplands or jungles far from the tourist trails. Some are Inca descendants, nominally Christian but with pagan customs still prevailing. A llama is sacrificed, the hand and knife of the native dragging out the still-pulsating heart of the beast. Again at a turtle blood ritual, bride and groom drink of the life juice which is obtained by intricate and rather horrifying neck surgery on the helpless turtle. (Other than for nuptials, the turtles' flesh and blood is never touched, says the narration).

Bolivia is little known and the scenes there tend to be colorful, strange and intermittently brutal, though the true villainy is in the animal kingdom, notably the wicked, wily, relentless, crocodile, an animal it is easy to fear and impossible to like. Down the toothy voids go jaguars, human legs, 20-foot snakes, all sorts of fatally inattentive small animals.

A novelty sequence is a visit, announced as illegal, to an Inca Museum to close-up on the pornographic pottery. They were, to put it mildly, sex-crazy people. The filming in each of several countries was largely with different crews, as the authorities would not allow Davis' own technicians in.

There is an 104-minute version as well as this 94-minute print shown at the Konover Hotel during the Miami Film Festival. Finale focuses upon an annual spring mating of llamas, described as beasts too lazy to perform reproduction act unless forced to by mortal hands. Climax is a scene of natives in bestial acts, the narrator suggesting that this was "simulated." Be that as it may, Germany's market wants that scene in; other markets may recoil.

Photography is generally good, the scenery beautiful, the jungle scenes reek of he hazards of survival. The black tribe whose men paint their heads and faces in weird modernistic-seeming color patterns are not the least of the "exploitable" poster material. —*Land.*

Day of The Woman
(COLOR)

Miami, Nov. 22.

Cinemagic Pictures Inc., produced by Joseph Zbeda and Meir Zarchi. Stars Camille Keaton, Eron Tabor, Richard Pace, Anthony Nichols. Directed by Zarchi. Screenplay, Zarchi; camera (color). Yuri Haviv; editing, Zarchi. Reviewed at Konover Theater, Miami, Nov. 15, '78. (MPAA Rating — R.) Running time: 101 MINS.
Jennifer .... Camille Keaton
Johnny .... Eron Tabor
Matthew .... Richard Pace
Stanley .... Anthony Nichols

This ought to please the violence-hungry and sex-starved drive-in crowd: in "Day of the Woman," the title character (Camille Keaton) is raped four times by four different men the same day, but she survives to seduce and kill each of her attackers.

The rape scenes are often comical, with the men's motions and grimaces more akin to seizures than sex, but the "revenge" scenes are more believable. One in particular, in which the girl castrates a man in a bathtub with a butcher knife, sent two women running and gagging toward the exit at the screening viewed. The other men get it by hanging, by being split with an axe and by being devoured by an outboard motor.

Typical of the film's intentions is that one of the men, a virgin semi-retarded bagboy named Matthew (Richard Pace), is there for the other men, and the audience, to ridicule. His dialog doesn't help: when he learns that the lady is from New York, he says, "Oooooh, you come from an evil place."

One scene redeems "Day of the Woman" from being instantly discardable. After her first rape, Keaton is fighting her way through the woods as muted harmonica music plays on the soundtrack. The music gets louder and louder, and Keaton emerges at a clearing to find one of her attackers perched atop a rock — playing the harmonica. But one scene does not a movie make; as for the castration scene, its impact is as powerful as its taste is questionable. The rest of "Day of the Woman" isn't as powerful, but it's no less questionable. —*Bian.*

The Cat And The Canary
(BRITISH-COLOR)

Miami, Nov. 22.

Cinema Shares International release. Richard Gordon, producer. Stars Honor Blackman, Michael Callan, Edward Fox, Wendy Hiller, Olivia Hussey, Carol Lynley, Peter McEnery. Directed by Radley Metzger. Screenplay, Metzger, based on John Willard play; associate producer, Ray Corbett; camera (color), Alex Thompson; editor, Roger Harrison. Reviewed at Gusman Cultural Center, Miami, Nov. 16, '78. Running time: 90 MINS.

Susan Sillsby .... Honor Blackman
Paul Jones .... Michael Callan
Hendricks .... Edward Fox
Allison Crosby .... Wendy Hiller
Cicily Young .... Olivia Hussey
Annabelle West .... Carol Lynley
Charlie Wilder .... Peter McEnery
Cyrus West .... Wilfrid Hyde-White

John Willard's 1922 stage play "The Cat and the Canary" has been filmed three times — by Paul Leni in 1927, Rupert Julian in 1930 (a sound version of Leni's silent adaptation) and Elliott Nugent in 1939, with Bob Hope. Now comes the fourth, filmed by Radley Metzger.

This time around, "The Cat and the Canary" seems plagued by schizophrenia, as though it couldn't decide whether to emulate Neil Simon or William Castle. Because of this, audiences are always looking for the laughs, and that helps to make the "scary" scenes lose their punch.

Still, audiences looking for laughs will have little trouble finding them. Callan, as a possible recipient of a family fortune, has clever lines and delivers them well. But the biggest laughs come from Wilfrid Hyde-White, who steals the show with a small role as the deceased benefactor who (thanks to a cinematic "will" recorded before his death) delights in chastising and ridiculing his greedy relatives. Thanks to the freer censorial standards of 1978, Hyde-White is able to verbally abuse his family with no holds barred, and his dry but wickedly impish performance is delightful.

The rest of the cast, and the rest of the film, is not as delightful. The supporting performances are less than inspiring, and Willard's plot is pedestrian compared to the complicated machinations of modern-day mystery films. However, the success of the Agatha Christie releases of late may help draw audiences more interested in style than substance: Metzger's direction is faithful to the genre, and Alex Thompson's photography sports a lushness similar to and evocative of "Murder on the Orient Express" and "Death on the Nile." —*Bian.*

The Deer Hunter
(COLOR)

Ambitious and demanding look at the effects of the Vietnam experience on the U.S. Has great performances. At three hours, a tough sell.

Hollywood, Nov. 22.

A Universal release of a Universal-EMI Films production. Produced by Barry Spikings, Michael Deeley, Michael Cimino and John Peverall. Stars Robert De Niro. Directed by Cimino. Screenplay, Deric Washburn, from a story by Cimino, Washburn, Louis Garfinkle and Quinn K. Redeker; camera (Technicolor), Vilmos Zsigmond; art directors, Ron Hobbs, Kim Swados; editor, Peter Zinner; music, Stanley Myers; set decorator, Dick Goddard, Alan Hicks; associate producers, Marion Rosenberg, Joann Carelli; sound (Dolby), Darrin Knight; assistant director, Charles Okun. Reviewed at the Samuel Goldwyn Theatre, Beverly Hills, Nov. 21, '78. (MPAA rating: R.) Running time: **183 MINS.**

Michael	Robert De Niro
Stan	John Cazale
Steven	John Savage
Nick	Christopher Walken
Linda	Meryl Streep
John	George Dzundza
Axel	Chuck Aspegren
Steven's mother	Shirley Stoler
Angela	Rutanya Alda
Julien	Pierre Segul
Axel's Girl	Mady Kaplan

Among the considerable achievements of Michael Cimino's "The Deer Hunter" is the fact that the film remains intense, powerful and fascinating for more than three hours. Three hours, however, is a long time for the average filmgoer (or theatre) and the running time of the Universal-EMI coproduction is just one of the handicaps this ambitious and demanding work will have to overcome.

Another hurdle is its theme — the impact of the Vietnam experience on this country — and that's a topic other pictures have tackled during the last 12 months, although none with more than modest success. If Universal can create an "event" out of "The Deer Hunter," subsequent word of mouth could make it the Vietnam b.o. exception.

The picture is a long, sprawling epic-type in many ways more novel than motion picture. It employs literary references stylistically, forecasting events which will happen in the film. Events are foreshadowed by the way the camera moves and by epigrammatic hints made by characters — techniques more frequently related to book writing. Cimino's film is worthy of serious study and certainly will be treated to much analysis during the next year, and decade as well.

It is a brutal work. Robert De Niro, John Cazale, John Savage and Christopher Walken head cast as friends living in a small Pennsylvania town. They attend a Russian Orthodox wedding at the beginning of the film. Directly afterwards three of them go deer hunting and

soon afterwards they are to serve in Vietnam.

The film's opening hour chronicles the wedding and while what happens at the wedding is interesting — exploration of the customs and rituals attendant with the affair — Cimino might have better spent the time detailing the protagonists' outside of this single event. It would have further fleshed out their individual personalities.

While in Southeast Asia, the trio is reunited during a battle scene and later captured by the Vietcong. As POWs they are forced to play a form of Russian roulette. A revolver with one bullet is passed back and forth between two prisoners. Spectators bet on which of the prisoners will blow his brains out.

This game, apparently, was played in Saigon and other parts of Southeast Asia as well. It was a parlor sport of some sort. The contest is shown a number of times and the filmmakers spare the audience none of the bloody consequences.

Throughout the film various ceremonies and cultural rituals are explored, compared and juxtaposed — the wedding, the game and the deer hunt. It is up to the viewer to decide how these rituals fit together and it is a big comprehension demand.

On a more superficial level the picture looks at the impact of the war on a small town. Two of the town's boys return home, one in a wheel chair and the other (De Niro) as a disturbed hero. Walken remains behind.

The action, throughout, is outstanding. Walken's performance is a marvel and it should at last give him the widespread recognition he deserves. Technical credits, Vilmos Zsigmond's cinematography, the art direction by Ron Hobbs and Kim Swados and Peter Zinner's editing, are also first rate.

Many will wish that the screenplay by Deric Washburn were a bit more straightforward. It may be too literarily "dense" for a wide audience.

Still, the film is ambitious and it succeeds on a number of levels and it proves that Cimino is an important director who deserves to be watched carefully. —*Hege.*

Drunken Monkey In A Tiger's Eye
(HONG KONG-COLOR)

Hong Kong, Nov. 15.

Seasonal Films release of a Seasonal Films Co. production. Written and directed by Ng Si Yuen. Stars Jackie Chan (Sing Lung), Ng Siu Tin, Wong Ching Li. No other credits provided. Reviewed at Queen's Theatre, Hong Kong, Nov. 15, '78. Running time: **100 MINS.**
(Cantonese soundtrack-English subtitles)

This is the new trendmaker in current local kung-fu films. It made

nearly HK$7,000,000 in Hong Kong alone and imitations mushroomed immediately like Chinese restaurants. Variations and revival of old Jackie Chan movies are in the offing.

"Drunken Monkey" like its unique title is kung fu with a big difference in the sense that unusual drunken martial arts techniques were mixed with high Cantonese comedy. Lead star Jackie Chan (contract player of Lo Wei Prod.) found fame at last by freelancing outside where his talents were properly utilized and to great advantage by director Ng Si Yuen.

Chan, an excellent acrobat, has the stamina and movements of an experienced kung-fu specialist. His charming boyish appeal and talent for comedy routines help in captivating audiences. In fact, he makes a very human hero as he doesn't win all the fights, with the exception of the required finale battle. "Drunken Monkey" is actually Chan's second pic using animal antics.

Here is a film with lots of potential and legs abroad. Properly dubbed, reedited and appropriate original music added, it could easily revive the waning image of kung-fu. Highlights include the practice sessions with an eccentric teacher called Shao Hai Yi. Then, the idea of having a couple of drinks prior to fighting add an off-beat touch to the disciplined art of kung-fu.

The storyline as can be expected is practically nil but the humour is universal enough for consumption abroad. The fights are strung together and are displayed in a series of easily provoked encounters. Photography of outdoor segments adds scope and visual excitement.

Two major distribs are interested in dressing up the film for proper selling abroad as occasional filmmaker Seasonal Films has yet to learn a lot about the intricate and sophisticated art of distribution outside its provincial territory, and Chinatown mentality. —*Mel.*

The 39 Steps
(BRITISH-COLOR)

Second remake of classic chase yarn. Routine effort with modest prospects.

London, Nov. 22.

Rank Organization release, produced by Greg Smith. Directed by Don Sharp; exec producer, James Kenelm-Clarke; screenplay, Michael Robson (based on the novel by John Buchan); camera (color), John Coquillion; editor, Eric Boyd-Perkins; sound, Peter Sutton; production designer, Harry Pottle; music, Ed Welch; assistant director, Barry Langley; associate producer, Frank Bevis. Reviewed at Leicester Sq. Theatre, London, Nov. 21, '78. BBFC rating: A. Running time: **102 MINS.**

Hannay	Robert Powell
Appleton	David Warner
Lomas	Eric Porter
Alex	Karen Dotrice
Scudder	John Mills
Sir Walter Bullivant	George Baker
Bayliss	Ronald Pickup
Marshall	Donald Pickering
Porton	Timothy West
David	Miles Anderson
Lord Rohan	Andrew Keir
Magistrate	Robert Flemyng
Harkness	William Squire
McLean	Paul McDowell
Tillotson	David Collings
Fletcher	John Normington
Lord Belthane	John Welsh
Woodville	Edward De Souza
Admiral	Tony Steedman
P.C. Forbes	John Grieve
Stewart	Andrew Downie
Renfrew	Donald Bisset
Donald	Derek Anders
Martins	Oliver Maquire
Lady Nettleship	Joan Henley
Perryman	Prentis Hancock
Milkman	Leo Dolan
Miller	James Garbutt
The Scott	Artro Morris
Crombie	Robert Gillespie
Guide	Raymond Young
P.C. Scott	Paul Jerricho
Vicar	Michael Bilton

Whether odious or not, comparisons with the stylish original film version by Alfred Hitchcock (circa 1935) are probably irrelevant as well for today's general audience market. Suffice that this new "39 Steps" is okay period suspense, directed with a smooth but unremarkable touch by Don Sharp for producer Greg Smith. Fast saturation playoff is the obvious ticket.

The new edition, scripted by Michael Robson, is workmanlike and has some moments, but in general lacks flair or anything like the original's grip on the imagination. The period atmosphere also seems routine.

For the short of memory, "Steps" is the melodramatic tale of a man on the run from Prussian assassins plotting World War I. It was first a classic novel by John Buchan, than a classic film by Hitch, with Robert Donat as the elusive hero and Madeleine Carroll as the romantic interest. An undistinguished 1959 remake, also British, had Kenneth More and Taina Elg. This new one has attractive young Robert Powell and Karen Dotrice, but nothing like the Donat-Carroll chemistry or flourish. Powell's recent and appealing television exposure might just help biz, however.

Pic is studded-with, and benefits appreciably from, a cast of polished British familiars, some of whom, like John Mills, only linger long enough for cameo impact before eliminated by the Prussians.

Mills is very good as the British agent trying to persuade the government of the momentous plot and its dire consequences. Also effective are David Warner as the topmost villain, Eric Porter as a police official initially dubious re Powell's innocence, and Timothy West as a politico.

Ronald Pickup and Donald Pickering stand out as crafty lieutenants of Warner who pursue Powell across Scotland in the belief he has inherited the evidence of their plot from Mills. This chase across the Scottish Highlands constitutes a lengthy narrative in itself and one that provides camera director John Coquillion with gorgeous landscape sequences.

But as to suspense, the only sequence that comes remotely close to breath-taking is the climactic Harold Lloyd routine in which Powell dangles from the big hand of Big Ben in London to foil the device that otherwise is timed to blow up Parliament.

Overall, technical credits are professional, with Ed Welch's score an obviously fine mood contribution.
—*Pit.*

Long Shot
(BRITISH-B&W/COLOR)

London, Nov. 23.

A Mithras Films production. Produced & directed by Maurice Hatton. Features entire cast. Screenplay, Maurice Hatton, Eoin McCann, and cast; camera (color, b&w), Michael Davis, Michael Dodds, Ivan Strasburg, Maurice Hatton, Teo Davis; editor, Howard Sharp; music, Terry Dougherty; sound, Diana Ruston, Eoin McCann, Peter Rann. Reviewed at National Film Theatre, London, Nov. 22, '78. Running time: **85 MINS.**

Charlie . . . . Charles Gormley
Neville . . . . Neville Smith
Anne . . . . Ann Zelda
A Distributor . . . . David Stone
Sue . . . . Suzanne Danielle
American Director . . . . Ron Taylor
Another Director . . . . Wim Wnders
Biscuit Man . . . . Stephen Frears
Prof. of Sexual Politics . . . . Jim Haines
French-Canadian
Director . . . . Maurice Bulbulian
Bille . . . . William Forsyth
Gallery Owner . . . . Richard Demarco
Neville's Doctor . . . . Alan Bennett
TV Producer . . . . Sarah Boston
Cartoonist . . . . Mel Claman
An Actress . . . . Susannah York
An Agent . . . . Dennis Selinger
A Film Executive . . . . Sandy Lieberson
The Director . . . . John Boorman

"Long Shot" is a long look by a British director at himself, and at a film industry which forces him into behavior he mostly despises. Maurice Hatton's pic, crafted on a shoestring budget but displaying auteur style nonetheless, was made possible by free cooperation from like-minders who "knew the problems of trying to finance movies in Britain," and shared Hatton's desire to record them.

Story traces the progress (or otherwise) of a Scottish producer attempting to set up a quote-commercial-unquote movie called "Gulf & Western," which takes the oil-boom city of Aberdeen as background. Screenings at both Edinburgh and London fests sparked much knowing laughter, buff-audiences being the film's safest beat.

Presence of Susannah York, and cult-directors John Boorman and Wim Wenders in the cast could collateralize very selective arthouse exposure.

Hatton made most of "Long Shot" during the 1977 Edinburgh Festival, with an ad hoc approach involving part improvisation, part guideline-scripting. Producer-in-real-life Charles Gormley acquits himself particularly well in this loose format, and there are remarkably few performance-wrinkles from other non-thesps. What suffers is the plot, which wastes time early on in unconvincing domestic longueurs and romantic diversions.

Ultimate bleakness of the film's message disqualifies it as general entertainment, but may assure it archive status as a monument to British independent filmmakers' morale in the late '70s. Hatton's puritanical viewpoint vis-a-vis commercial considerations, glimpsed throughout, is fully revealed in the final sequence. Gormley, spurred by Boorman's so-so interest in directing into a belief that his formula movie, however rewritten, can reach the screen, visits Hollywood.

Here, accompanied by a switch from black-&-white to color, he revels in the pavement inlays and other standard kitsch attractions. The patronizing tone of the fairy-tale commentary leaves a regrettable after-taste of sour grapes.
— *Simo.*

Force 10 From Navarone
(BRITISH-COLOR)

Romanticized World War II melodrama; strong b.o. outlook.

Hollywood, Nov. 24.

American International Pictures release of a Guy Hamilton production, presented by Samuel Z. Arkoff, Oliver A. Unger. Produced by Unger. Directed by Hamilton. Features entire cast. Screenplay, Robin Chapman, based on a screen story by Carl Foreman and novel by Alistair MacLean, camera (color), Chris Challis; music, Ron Goodwin; production design, Geoffrey Drake; costume design, Emma Porteus; editor, Ray Poulton; special effects, Rene Albouze; stunt coordinator, Eddie Stacey; assistant director, Bert Batt. Reviewed at Paramount Theatre, Hollywood, Nov. 24, '78 (MPAA Rating: PG). Running time: **118 MINS.**

Mallory . . . . Robert Shaw
Barnsby . . . . Harrison Ford
Miller . . . . Edward Fox
Maritza . . . . Barbara Bach
Lescovar . . . . Franco Nero
Weaver . . . . Carl Weathers
Drazac . . . . Richard Kiel

There are three basic elements — high adventure, suspense and a touch of humor — running through "Force 10 From Navarone" that, when properly combined as they are in this instance, should satisfy the entertainment desires of a not too-discriminating mass audience and make for happy days at the boxoffice.

This is not a sequel to the 1961 hit, "Guns Of Navarone," although "Force 10" opens with the bangup conclusion of the earlier exercise in World War II commando heroics, the infiltration and explosive destruction of the radar-controlled giant guns of the Nazi fortress on Navarone.

Right off, director Guy Hamilton has the challenge of coming up with an even more spectacular finale to this story on the opposite side of the Mediterranean — a mission to destroy a vital bridge separating the Germans and the Partisans in Yugoslavia. Two survivors of the spiking of the guns of Navarone, British Major Mallory (now played by the late Robert Shaw) and demolitions expert Miller (Edward Fox) provide the link that gives some purpose to the title "Force 10," etc. group.

While he is not invulnerable to some awkward moments of dialog and also dallies over some tense sequences to a point which strains credibility, Hamilton manages over the course of almost two hours to keep his audience on edge. And he does succeed in topping in sustained tension and explosive fury the very effective ending of the first pic. This time he has a double whammy destruction of a giant dam which sets loose forces of nature that crumble a seemingly indestructible bridge.

Indeed, good as the actors are in "Force 10" at least equal recognition must be given the special effects credited to Rene Albouze as well as to stunt coordinator Eddie Stacey and cameraman Chris Challis. For this is a visual picture wherein pyrotechnics are an important part of the story development, and the moods of fear, brooding danger, soaring expectations, and also of sheer scenic beauty, are exquisitely portrayed by the camera work of Challis.

Carl Foreman, who adapted and produced "Guns Of Navarone" from the Alistair MacLean novel, also did the adaptation of the author's "Force 10" book upon which Robin Chapman based his screenplay. It is a script, which, while effective, treads a familiar line in that a Yank task force leader is saddled with two unwanted Britishers (the survivors of Navarone) and at times stretches credulity to the point where one wonders how the Nazis lasted as long as they did.

The weakness in Hamilton's direction is that he moves too slowly at times and gives viewers opportunity to think instead of being carried onward by the rush of events — and there are enough to have made the emotional involvement all consuming.

Although he has competent, and in some individual scenes very competitive colleagues indeed, this next-to-last film appearance of Robert Shaw is not, as one might wish, his glory farewell. He is very good in what he is called upon to do, but the role is not one that makes any particular demand upon an exceptionally talented person.

Harrison ("Star Wars") Ford does a creditable job as the American Colonel; Fox is excellent as the British demolitions expert; Carl Weathers gives a powerful performance as the unwanted black GI who proves himself in more ways than one (including a couple of obtrusive racial encounters). Barbara Bach, lone femme, does fine in a tragic, patriotic role as a Partisan. Franco Nero as a Nazi double agent who fools the Partisans is slickly nefarious, which is what the role requires him to be.

One of the weak dramatic points is that Shaw, who is assigned to kill Nero, an old foe from Navarone, plays a prolonged cat and mouse game with an enemy he knows but can't prove to be the man he is assigned to kill.

Richard Kiel as a towering — the man's physical size is awesomely impressive — Chetnik conspirator is impressive and has a brutal hand-to-hand death encounter with Weathers, whom he has racially taunted as "Blackie."

AIP and producer Oliver Unger should be able to sit back and watch the money roll in from "Force 10 From Navarone." —*Pry.*

Nighthawks
(BRITISH-16m-B&W)

Chicago, Nov. 21.

A Four Corner Films Production. Produced by Ron Peck and Paul Hallam. Directed by Ron Peck. Features entire cast. Screenplay, Peck, Paul Hallam; camera, (black and white) Joanna Davis; sound, Diana Ruston; editing, Richard Taylor, Mary Pat Leece; music, David Graham Ellis; lyrics, Stuart Craig Turton. Reviewed at the Biograph Theater, Chicago, Nov. 8, '78. Running time: **113 MINS.**

Jim . . . . Ken Robertson
Mike . . . . Tony Westrope
Judy . . . . Rachel Nicholas James
Pat . . . . Maureen Dolan
Neal . . . . Stuart Craig Turton
Peter . . . . Clive Peters
John . . . . Robert Merrick
American . . . . Frankl Dilbert
Artist . . . . Peter Radmall

"Nighthawks" is an amateurish attempt at a gay version of "Looking For Mr. Goodbar" without the violent ending. It is also a film that masquerades as an honest look at what it's like to be a homosexual bar cruiser, but for the most part is so stereotypically depressing and sleazy that it manages to set gay liberation back 25 years.

Script centers around Jim, a teacher of kids by day and a lonely homosexual, cruising gay discos, in the evening. For most of the two hours the audiences is given the displeasure of watching almost the same set of scenes — that is Jim at the disco, in his apartment with a pick-up, driving "friend" home the next morning and eventually winding up teaching class. The sequences are so dull and superficial that at this screening the audience began groaning about midway through the film.

Probably due to discrepancies in the script Ken Robertson's portrayal of Jim is not believable. In first half he's a sympathetic guy running into nasty pick-ups. But in the second half, when he begins to make contact with decent human beings, he takes on the baddie role. The only seemingly viable explanation, that he can't deal with his homosexuality, doesn't jell in light of a later scene where he thoughtfully explains being gay to members of his class.

Musical soundtrack is worse than awful in both technicals and content and is unfortunately present in a major portion of the film. Director Peck's technique of spending most of his time scanning the sleazy characters in the disco and eventually zeroing in on Jim's eyes for some inner meaning is tiresome.

This is one of at least five homosexual-themed films that seem to be quite popular at the Chicago Film Festival this year. Theatre was sold out for this one-time showing, suggesting there is a significant gay market in the country hungry for films relating to that lifestyle. However, this film is a poor example. —*Berg*.

Yim Sawasdi
(Smile Hello)
(THAI-COLOR)

Bangkok, Nov. 1.

A Chao Poj Films release. Produced, directed and edited by Pornpoj Kanitkasen. Features entire cast. Executive producer, Rachiniwan Kanitkasen. Story, Banjered Tawee; screenplay, Tanachai Chinothai; camera (color), Sophon Jaenphanit; music, Prachin Songpow-production designer Urai Srisombat; art director, Prasobchai Kanitkasen; sound, Montri Ong-iam. Reviewed at Oscar Theatre, Bangkok, Nov. 1, '78. Running time: 110 MINS.

Ehsana . . . . Pairoj Sangborivutr
Darakanit . . . . Nawarat Yukthanan
Dambanara . . . . Setta Sirachaiya
Naidang . . . . M.L. Rujira Issarangkul
Na Ayudhya
Police Chief . . . . Supravat Patamasoot
Darakanit's Governess . . . . . . Juree Osiree

Thai film titles for love stories are chosen for their potential boxoffice appeal; they do not have to mean anything, or have any connection with the story. Generally speaking, most of them have to use the word "rak," meaning love. "Yim Sawasdi" dispenses with "rak" in the title, since there is a close relation between it and the earlier hit from the same company, "Koo Rak" (The Lovers), with the same leads.

A rich girl (Nawarat) runs away from her domineering household and meets a young reporter-photographer (Pairoj), who becomes her companion for a tour of Southern Thailand, making good use of the beautiful countryside.

The main requisite is that nothing must be treated seriously. Comic touches are essential to local fans. When Nawarat returns home, Pairoj bills her father for what he has spent on her. Only original work is done by Setta Sirachaiya during a dream sequence, in which he plays a typical Thai student in the familiar white uniform, carrying a T-square and wearing dark glasses. His funny gait and accurate mimicry are hilarious.

The finale is unconvincing, and even Setta, who is made to parachute down on a landscaped lawn where a wedding party is gathered, couldn't make it work. Somehow this illustrates that good performers are much better off when improving roles on their own; once they are given something to do in a mediocre script, they cannot help looking silly and absurd. —*Cano*.

Die Schweizermacher
(The Swissmakers)
(SWISS-COLOR)

Zurich, Nov. 15.

Rex Film AG Zurich release of a T & C Film AG Zurich production. Written and directed by Rolf Lyssy. Stars Walo Luond, Emil Steinberger. Script collaboration, Christa Maerker, Georg Janett, Martin Schmassmann, Pierre Lachat. Producer, Marcel Hoehn; production manager, Rudolf Santschi; camera (Eastmancolor), Fritz E. Maeder; art direction, Edith Peier, Bernhard Sauter; costumes, Greta Roderer; sound, Hans Kuenzi; lighting, Max Isler, Andre Simmen; music, Jonas C. Haefeli; editor, Georg Janett; choreography, Juerg Burth. Reviewed at the Studio Nord-Sued, Zurcih, Nov. 15, '78; running time: 104 MINS.

Max Bodmer . . . . Walo Luond
Moritz Fischer . . . . Emil Steinberger
Milena Vakulic . . . . Beatrice Kessler
Dr. Helmut Starke . . . . . Wolfgang Stendar
Gertrud Starke . . . . Hilde Ziegler
Francesco Grimolli . . . . Silvia Jost
Sandra Grimolli . . . . Silvia Jost
Martha Grosz . . . . Bettina Lindtberg

The Swiss naturalization practice has long been a target for criticism. Although it is recognized that a tiny country with little over 6,000,-000 population is bound by certain limits, residing foreigners applying for Swiss citizenship are often scrutinized to an extent including prying into private lives.

Swiss filmmaker Rolf Lyssy (whose "Konfrontation" in 1974 was favorably received, but failed to click) has treated this theme, familiar to every Swiss resident, as a satirical comedy in "The Swissmakers." Central characters are two police officials whose job it is to interview, inquire about and "shadow" applicants for citizenship: a German psychiatrist and his wife, and Italian pastry cook and a Yugoslav ballet dancer.

While the former two end up with a Swiss passport, the ballerina is rejected. But she'll eventually become a Swiss just the same, as the younger of the two officials has fallen in love with her, follows her to a ballet engagement in Amsterdam and will marry her.

Lyssy wisely avoided falling into the trap of broad farce which the theme would have offered. He chose the more rewarding, but much more difficult possibility: light comedy with a serious background. Served by his own good script plus a handtailored cast, he has succeeded admirably. His direction has the necessary light touch, without neglecting the more serious aspects.

As the senior official, conservative, narrow-minded and humorless, Walo Luond, a vet Swiss character actor, is marvellously disciplined and restrained in a role which could have been played as broad caricature. As his junior assistant, Emil Steinberger, Switzerland's most popular cabaretist-comedian, is terrific. He, too, abandons his widely known cabaret style and surprises by a subtle, charming and most winning characterization.

Beatrice Kessler as the dancer impresses as an attractive new personality. Other parts are also well cast, notably Wolfgang Stendar and Hilde Ziegler as the German couple and Claudio Caramaschi as the wide-eyed, naive Italian.

Made on a shoestring budget of $480,000, "The Swissmakers" was privately financed, without state subsidies, as the Swiss government refused a grant, fearing maybe a picture too openly critical of "established" Swiss practices. They need not have feared. Lyssy is too intelligent a director to go beyond the bounds of good taste.

First openings here point to a boxoffice click, with excellent grosses and ditto reviews. Since the picture is in Swiss dialect and treats a theme familiar mostly to locals, it remains to be seen what the foreign chances are. As to its quality, "The Swissmakers" would deserve to be noticed abroad. — *Mezo*.

Uncle Joe Shannon
(COLOR)

Rocky b.o. trail for mawkish Burt Young script.

Hollywood, Nov. 24.

United Artists release of a Robert Chartoff-Irwin Winkler production. Stars Burt Young. Exec producer, Gene Kirk-wood. Produced by Irwin Winkler, Robert Chartoff. Directed by Joseph C. Hanwright. Screenplay, Young; camera (color), Bill Butler; editor, Don Zimmerman; music, Bill Conti; production design, Bill Kenney; costume design, Bobbie Mannix; sound, Michael Evje; exec in charge of production, Hal W. Polaire; assistant director, Brian E. Frankish. Reviewed at Samuel Goldwyn Theatre, Academy of Motion Picture Arts & Sciences, BevHills, Nov. 24, '78. (MPAA Rating: PG). Running time: 108 MINS.

Joe Shannon . . . . Burt Young
Robbie . . . . Doug McKeon
Margaret . . . . Madge Sinclair
Goose . . . . Jason Bernard
Braddock . . . . Bert Remsen
Dr. Clark . . . . Allan Rich

While the goal of turning out modestly-budgeted, "small" pictures amidst the welter of big-buck spectaculars remains admirable, "Uncle Joe Shannon" does not serve the cause well. Skedded to break in the midst of the Christmas onslaught, the United Artists release will face rough sledding at the boxoffice.

Burt Young, who stars and wrote the original script, has combined elements reminiscent of several films, including "The Champ," "The Five Pennies," and his own telefilm, "Daddy, I Don't Like It Like This," aired earlier this year with the same child actor featured here, Doug McKeon.

Some crucial errors in plotting and structure mar what could have been a sensitive and moving picture, however. Notable among these is Young's decision to portray a professional trumpet player, whose life turns from diamonds to ashes when his wife and child are killed in a fire.

Confronted with the same problem that faced Danny Kaye and Kirk Douglas in previous pix. Young fails miserably in attempts to tie his horn-blowing with Maynard Ferguson's soaring solos on the sound-track. "Shannon" loses all believability when even during a simple rendition of taps, Young doesn't move his fingers.

Also interfering with "Shannon's" credibility is a ludicrous prolog showing Young to be the happiest man on earth, with immense talent, a beautiful, cover-girl wife, and a precocious child. After the fire, however, it's next stop skid row, a transition that could have adequately been handled by flashbacks.

Given all this ground to make up, "Uncle Joe Shannon" manages to turn into an interesting film until Young pulls out all the dramatic stops. Introduction of McKeon as a crippled youngster abandoned by his floozy mother, and the budding relationship between him and Young, is handled well. Joseph Hanwright directs in straightforward fashion.

Also effective in a neat role reversal are Madge Sinclair and Jason Bernard as a black, middle-class couple who try to help Young but are put off by his wallowing in self-pity.

But it is Young's inarticulateness, a trait that has made him so powerful as a character actor, that ultimately sinks "Shannon." We see his character attempt suicide, reconsider, slide down again, rise up, and fall once more without ever understanding his real emotions. There are numerous holes in the exposition, too, especially in regards to police authorities.

The scenes played with McKeon are emotional and affecting, and the youngster proves himself an excellent actor. With all the bathos flooding around the characters, however, the results are mawkish and uncomfortable, especially the "Tiny Tim" ending.

What does distinguish "Uncle Joe Shannon" is the incadescence of Bill Butler's extraordinary cinematography. In a year of distinguished-looking pix, this release ranks among the top. Bill Kenney's production design, making excellent use of L.A. locations, is likewise superb. Special mention should also be made of Terry Liebling's excellent secondary casting. —*Poll.*

Seetha Kalyanam
(Sita's Wedding)
(INDIAN-COLOR)

Chicago, Nov. 14.

A Chitrakalpana Films Production of Ananda Lakshmi Art Movies. Produced by P. Ananda Rao. Features entire cast. Directed by Bapu. Screenplay, Mullapudi Venkata Ramana; camera (color), K. S. Prasad; special effects, Ravee Nagaich; music, K.V. Mahadevan; songs, Arudra, C. Narayana Reddy; art direction, K. Nageswara Rao. Reviewed at the Village Theatre, Chicago, Nov. 5, '78. (No MPAA Rating). Running time: **110 MINS.**

Rama/Vishnu .... Ravi Kumar
Seetha/Lakshmi .... Jaya Prada
Ravana .... Satyanarayana
Dasaratha .... Gummadi
Second Queen .... Jamuna
Viswamitra .... Mukkamala

"Sita's Wedding" is a beautifully photographed and costumed fantasy film that unfortunately has little commercial value since its plot is almost impossible to follow. Indian director Bapu has captured the magic needed for this kind of mthological presentation but without his being there to explain it, as he was at its showing at the Chi Film Festival, much of its meaning is indiscernable.

Plot involves evil king Ravana who is so nasty and powerful even the gods have trouble getting rid of him. Because of this they get together and appeal to Vishnu, protector of the universe, who decides to take human form and take care of the evil man himself. After that there is an incredibly large assortment of characters wandering in and out of the picture with names that are almost as long as their individual speeches.

Indian music takes a little getting used to but provides sufficient background for the picture. Technical credits are all good, especially the make-up which gives some of the characters a real out of this world quality.

This is decent festival fare but it's doubtful it could be much else.

—*Berg.*

They Went That-A-Way & That-A-Way
(COLOR)

Tim Conway in tired rehash of Laurel & Hardy routines.

Hollywood, Nov. 30.

An International Picture Show Release. Exec producer, Lloyd N. Adams Jr. Produced by Lang Elliott. Features entire cast. Directed by Edward Montagne, Stuart E. McGowan. Screenplay, Tim Conway; camera (color), Jacques Haitkin; music, Michael Leonard; associate producers, Eric Weston, Wanda Dell. No other credits available. Reviewed at Wilshire Theatre, Santa Monica, Calif. Nov. 30, '78. (MPAA Rating: PG.) Running time: **95 MINS.**

Dewey .... Tim Conway
Wallace .... Chuck McCann
Duke .... Richard Kiel
Warden Warden .... Dub Taylor
Billy Jo .... Reni Santoni
Brick .... Lenny Montana
Lugs ....Ben Jones
Margie Dell .... Timothy Blake
Butch .... Hank Worden

Had "They Went That-A-Way & That-A-Way" been made 40 years ago, it might have seemed fresh and original. Now it simply comes off as old hat, with Tim Conway and Chuck McCann doing a spotty impersonation of Laurel & Hardy and their classic funnymen routines. With yocks few and far between, this International Picture Show release won't be laughing all the way to the bank.

Conway's original script has the vet tv actor paired with the oversized McCann as two incompetent small-town cops sent into a prison to uncover the whereabouts of some stolen loot. If the material was sharper, the casting might have been inspired, since McCann and Conway play off each other extremely well.

But there's very little mileage in the numerous sight gags, most of which just sputter along. Sole exceptions are a marvelous bit by Conway as a would-be dentist disabled by Novocaine, and a final scene featuring Conway as a Japanese interpreter and McCann in drag as his Geisha girl wife.

Direction by Edward Montagne and Stuart E. McGowan is strictly routinish, unable to make effective use of a solid cast that includes Richard Kiel and Lenny Montana as two cons, Dub Taylor as a crotchety warden and Reni Santoni as his loyal assistant.

Buffoonery is kept on a low level, especially in the final scenes, when a mishmash of subplots is tossed together simply to bring the proceedings to a halt. Editing is particularly sloppy, with jump cuts numerous and very evident.

PG rating, unusual for product from Atlanta-based distributor, derives from some innocuous smooching between Santoni and Timothy Blake as Taylor's hot-blooded wife.

—*Poll.*

Les Bronzes
(The Suntanned Ones)
(FRENCH-COLOR)

Paris, Dec. 5.

CCFC release of Trinacra Films production. Features entire cast. Directed by Patrice Leconte. Screenplay by cast and Leconte; camera (Eastmancolor), Jean-Francois Robin; music, Serge Gainsbourg. Reviewed at Le Paris, Paris, Nov. 24, '78. Running time, **105 MINS.**

Producer Yves Rousset Rouard hired a Paris cabaret theatre group and set them loose in a specially constructed African vacation village for a takeoff on the local craze for vacation clubs.

Though of cabaret origin, script and treatment opt for the pathetic at times. The satire is not to barbed, but the boring aspects of these supervised vacations come through. Written by the group, the characters are fairly familiar, from the supposedly free and swinging couple still tinged with remorse to the misfit who latches on to everyone to the would-be Don Juans, the fat man who doggedly tries to ski to others, etc.

Item is a bit skimpy but easygoing, with probable okay local legs where these adventures have some resonance.

Yet it is universal enough for some playoff chances abroad and also tv usage on its disarming and sometimes witty probings into vacation activities. —*Mosk.*

La Femme Qui Pleure
(The Crying Woman)
(FRENCH-COLOR)

Paris, Dec. 5.

AMLF release of Les Productions De La Gueville-Lola Films-Renn Productions production. Features entire cast. Written and directed by Jacques Doillon. Camera (Eastmancolor), Yves Lafaye; editor, Isabelle Rathery. Reviewed at Club 13, Paris, Nov. 25, '78. Running time, **90 MINS.**

Dominique .... Dominique Laffin
Jacques .... Jacques Doillon
Haydee .... Haydee Politoff
Lola .... Lola Doillon

Jacques Doillon did a promising early film on a young baker's work and women problems, "The Fingers in the Head," and the acceptable if perhaps too impersonal version of a bestseller about two young boys on an odyssey across France during the last war to join their parents in the non-occupied zone, "A Bag of Marbles." Now, after three years, he is back with a personal but muted look at a love triangle.

Doillon plays the man himself and his own little daughter is also in the film. He says it is not autobiographical and decided to act in it himself when he could not get a desired thesp. Pic was also shot mainly in his own country home. Film deals with a domestic crisis when a philandering husband, whose peccadilloes have been accepted, now seems to be really in love.

It starts with the wife crying as Doillon comes home from a visit with his mistress. Dominique Laffin, the wife, remains in a pitch of hysteria practically throughout the film. She demands love and sex from him, both unsatisfactory. She begins to feel hatred for her own daughter and goes off on drunken fugues and pickups.

Doillon, the husband, is rather dry and evasive as he plies his love affair with a 30ish woman who is finally brought to his house. Before this, the mistress has a run-in with the wife who even offers sex to her as a means of not being excluded.

The wife comes back to be with her child and all three stay together but it finally cannot be contained due to the wife's inability to cope.

This is done sans music, with a series of scenes separated by dissolves that lay out this sexual and social impasse. Laffin is effective as the distraught wife who finally leaves the husband and takes her child. The mistress also leaves and is almost run down by the car of the wife.

There are some revealing reflections on the problems of a couple. Film has a rhythm that keeps up interest though the chemistry of the criss-crossed couples is not sharp enough and sometimes blunts a more dramatic and perceptive probing of the breaking point of a married couple with a child.

Pic should be heard from at festivals next year, with specialized chances locally. A title change may be in the offing, from "La Femme Qui Pleure" (The Crying Woman) to "Une Femme Dangereuse" (A Dangerous Woman."

Doillon still registers as more promising than accomplished but is an original filmmaker worth watching. —*Mosk.*

Nam Karng Yod Deo
(The Last Dewdrop)
(THAI-COLOR)

Bangkok, Dec. 5.
An Apex Productions release. Produced by Nanta Tansacha. Written and directed by Suchart Vuthivichai. Features entire cast. Original music score, Seksan Somimsart; camera (color) Choochart Tohprathip; sound, Prasert and Paeh of King Sound Studio, dubbing, Jaturong Studio; art director/production designer, Suthee Piboravudh; publicity, Suriya Rajitwattana; costumes, Charin Choochitr; make-up, Sam. Reviewed at Pyramid screening room, Bangkok, Nov. 15, '78. Running time: 103 MINS.
Prang .... Nit Alissa
Prote .... Suradej Srichoomsin
Ton .... Krit Wongyai
Krerk .... Sanok Suchima
Danai .... Somkid Bukoontot

Suchart Vuthivichai, 38, joins the ranks of new Thai writer-directors who go into local filmmaking with a strong determination to create a new kind of film. Prior to turning filmmaker, Suchart was an advertising creative director. With the existing prohibitive film import duty, resulting in sharp reduction of foreign films shown here, there is a large untapped market for quality films that young filmmakers like Suchart could fill.

Suchart picked a subject that he seems to know pretty well, the misery and suffering of a young married couple and their young son living in a tenement house for low-income people. Their daily activities are designed to comment on harsh realities of life in Bangkok for the poor in a highly satirical manner.

Pic closes with a double suicide that taxes the imagination, and leaves the viewer not so much stunned or depressed, but rather disappointed that the family shared only a very few happy moments together.

All-new cast acquit themselves and are surprisingly good, since none of them has any previous acting experience.

Interspersing of light satirical comedy with heavy melodrama is a very popular movie format in Thailand, but few such movies create any lasting impact. Perhaps "Nam Karng Yod Deo" will be one of the few exceptions, at least boxoffice wise. This picture has not yet opened here. —*Cano.*

Ligabue
(ITALIAN-COLOR)

Rome, Nov. 25.
A SACIS release of a RAI-TV production. Directed by Salvatore Nocita. Features entire cast. Screenplay, Cesare Zavattini, Arnaldo Bagnasco, based on a text by Zavattini; camera (color). Roberto Gerardi; music, Armando Trovaioli. Reviewed at Supercinema, Italian premiere, Rome, Nov. 24, '78. Running time: 126 MINS.
Cast: Flavio Bucci, Giuseppe Pambieri, Pamela Villoresi, Andrea Ferreol.

If you missed the book (a richly illustrated volume of Ligabue's works published in 1975 with text by Cesare Zavattini), if you missed the television production (a three-part series shown on RAI-TV year), by all means don't miss this extraordinary film.

The film, which took top honors at the Montreal Film Festival last August, is a shortened version of the television series which was based on the Zavattini text. Director Salvatore Nocita cut nearly 90-minutes from the original production for the film, sacrificing a number of effective scenes. The final product, however, is tighter, more intense and should have as much success as the tv version.

"Ligabue" is not the usual artist's biography, but then Ligabue was not the usual artist. A naif painter who felt more at home with the world's four-legged beasts than with two-legged creatures, he was a mysterious individual who was always treading the thin line between sanity and insanity, but who miraculously managed to translate his inner torments onto canvas.

The film, more descriptive than narrative, is slow moving at first. It begins with Ligabue's arrival in central Italy after 20 years of life in Switzerland where his Italian father had gone in search of work and where the artist was born. He speaks a mixture of Italian and German, a clever device that emphasizes his confusion and inability to communicate with others.

Wandering from job to job, he finally takes up residence in a hut on the banks of the Po where he lives virtually like a savage. The townspeople who have dubbed him "il tedesco" (The German) shun him as a wild man, but a local sculptor who has seen the fantastic animal poster he painted for a traveling circus and his scribblings on the town walls gives a reluctant Ligabue his first canvas to paint on. He sells his paintings (now worth millions) for 10 bowls of soup and swaps one for a red motorcycle, but despite an increasing success remains essentially a primitive and lonely soul.

Roberto Gerardi's photography cleverly juxtaposes the soft browns and greys of the Emilian countryside whose flat horizon is interrupted only by the straight lines of poplar trees with the explosive yellows and greens of Ligabue's tormented works underlining the artist's life as a misfit. Music by Armando Trovaioli sets the right mood for this character study.

The real credit for Ligabue's success, however, must go to Flavio Bucci who has managed to get under the skin of this enigmatic artist to the point of bearing an uncanny resemblance to his dozens of self-portraits. With his jaw firmly set, his Chaplinesque walk, his constant temper tantrums and his pleading eyes, Bucci as Ligabue has provided us with some clues to understanding a painter who is at the same time one with nature and at odds with man, a mixture of mental hospitals and museums, insanity and artistic genius. —*Argo.*

Carry On Emmannuelle
(BRITISH-COLOR)

London, Nov. 29.
A Hemdale International Films Limited release of a Thirtieth Film Productions Limited production. Produced by Peter Rogers. Features entire cast. Directed by Gerald Thomas. Screenplay, Lance Peters; camera (color), Alan Hume; editor, Peter Boita; art director, Jack Shampan; costumes, Courtenay Elliott; music, Eric Rogers; song, "Love Crazy," composed by Kenny Lynch, sung by Masterplan; production manager, Roy Goddard; asst. director. Gregory Dark; sound, Danny Daniel. Reviewed at Audley Square screening room, London, Nov. 28, 1978. (BBFC Rating: AA.) Running time: 88 MINS.
Emmannuelle .... Suzanne Danielle
Emile .... Kenneth Williams
Leyland .... Kenneth Connor
Lyons .... Jack Douglas
Mrs. Dangle .... Joan Sims
Richmond .... Peter Butterworth
Theodore .... Larry Dann
Mrs. Valentine .... Beryl Reid
Harold Hump .... Henry McGee
Harry Hernia .... Howard Nelson
Doctor .... Albert Moses

"Carry On" series now has 30 releases over 20 years. Formula is low budgets, low laughs. Which sums up "Carry On Emmannuelle."

Emmannuelle, English-style, is wife to the French ambassador. She sleeps with most of London, from key government officials to servants, until an immigrant doctor restores hubby's priapic power and all ends happily in the embassy bedroom.

Rude, rollicking fun, at a breathless pace, was the order of earlier "Carry On" days. This one is rude, certainly, but the relentless phallic innuendo is as labored as makers' determination to show nothing to worry the censor. Leaden comic timing compares poorly with tv sitcoms which pic otherwise resembles in production values. — *Simo.*

Corleone
(Father of the Godfathers)
(ITALIAN-COLOR)

Rome, Dec. 5.
A Cineriz release, produced by Mario Cecchi Gori for Capital Film. Stars Guiliano Gemma, Claudia Cardinale. Directed by Pasquale Squitieri. Screenplay, Barrese, De Rita, Maiuri, Squitieri; camera (Kodak) Eugenio Bentivoglio; art director, Umberto Turco; editor, Mauro Bonanni; music, Ennio Morricone. Reviewed at Metropolitan Cinema. Running time 111 MINS.
Vito Gargano .... Giuliano Gemma
Rosa Accordino .... Claudia Cardinale
Don Giusto .... Francisco Rabal
Natale Calia ...... Stefano Satta Flores
Michele Labruzzo .... Michele Placido

Pasquale Squitieri is an action director who goes a step beyond bloodletting to analyze social and political motivations behind it. After tackling the crime structure in Naples, where the "Guappi" are in control, he moved on to Sicily to put the Mafia in focus.

He scored last year with "Il Prefetto Di Ferro" (I Am The Law) covering the Mafia in Sicily from 1900 to 1930 and now picks up in 1952 with the death of the bandit Giuliano to explore the conflict between the old and new Dons. This conflict accounts for the heavy action in "Corleone" and filtrates comment to explore the Mafia-justice-state interdependence in a social phenomenon no longer confined to Sicily itself, but now national and international.

Inspired by real life Mafia leaders, past and present, "Corleone" is essentially a home market product, but action loaded conflicts, cast stars Giuliano Gemma, Claudia Cardinale and Francisco Rabal and a first act laid in the colorful Mafia-ridden Sicilian countryside around Palermo, could open many other markets including a dualler spot in the U.S.

Gemma provides the strong thread as the farm hand who sprouts criminal claws in a revolt against timeworn poverty of the countryside as a Mafia lieutenant at the outset. In the big city, he learns all the new tricks of the game — legal participation in real estate and land development, developing political support — locally and nationally. Along the way he climbs to the highest echelon by modernizing Mafia warfare and eliminating the traditional godfathers — only to end up a dead don as the political Mafia takes over.

The scripts and Gemma are more convincing in early reels, where the community drama comes to life under Mafia rule. His transition from peasant to trigger man is flash rapid and from there on eases into a one dimensional stance as the pic itself thins out.

Cardinale has little to do but keep the melodramatic scenes glued together — though effectively symbolizing the unchanging status of women in the new Mafia clans. Stefano Satta Flores as the young local lawyer with high political ambition and Rabal as the time honored mafioso Don neatly complement Gemma as the principal figure throughout. A few of the secondary clan roles rise above the cliche' distinguishing the Mafia from ordinary human beings.

Perhaps Squitieri tried to say too much too fast — thereby eliminating the human touches that provide credibility. Filmmaker's ambition to pinpoint 30 years of transition in Mafia crime, leaves the door open for ambiguity — compared for example, to a film like Damiano Damiani's "The Day of the Owl" and others in the long list of nationally produced Mafia films. But Squitieri is adept at staging action and timing it with razor edge pace. This, essentially is what makes "Corleone" a valid entry.

Music in Ennio Morricone's score is outstanding in itself, but too classically dignified for the subject matter it backgrounds. Lensing is mainly excellent — especially on exteriors. —Werb.

Count Dracula And His Vampire Bride
(BRITISH-COLOR)

The Count makes another comeback.

Hollywood, Nov. 24.

A Dynamic Entertainment release of a Hammer Film Production. Produced and directed by Alan Gibson. Screenplay, Don Houghton; camera (color), Brian Probyn; art director, Lionel Couch; editor, Chris Barnes; sound, Claude Hitchcock; music, John Cacavas; associate producer, Houghton; assistant director, Derek Whithurst. Reviewed at the World Theatre, Hollywood, Nov. 24, '78. (MPAA rating: R.) Running time: **87 MINS.**

Count Dracula	Christopher Lee
Van Helsing	Peter Cushing
Murray	Michael Coles
Torrence	William Franklyn
Professor Keeley	Freddie Jones
Jessica	Joanna Lumley
Mathews	Richard Vernon
Lord Carradine	Patrick Barr
Chin Yang	Barbara Yu Ling
Porter	Richard Mathews
Freeborne	Lockwood West
Hanson	Maurice O'Connell
Jane	Valerie Van Ost

"Count Dracula And His Vampire Bride" finds Christopher Lee as the 700-year-old vampire looking like a chairman of the board more interested in destroying mankind than finding a neck to sink his teeth into. Life, it seems, has become complicated even for the world's most famous bloodsucker. The Dynamite Entertainment release at 87 minutes is silly, dull and lacks a sense of humor. Commercially, a routine programmer.

The Count plans to annihilate human life through a new strain of bubonic plague. Peter Cushing, a professor who has gained his doctorate by studying evil, discovers the plot and along with a group from Scotland Yard attempts to put an end to it.

Alan Gibson, who wrote and produced from Don Houghton's screenplay, takes this Dracula business very seriously. He does know a lot about Dracula and his picture offers a few tips for those who someday may run into a vampire.

First, bring along a cross. That temporarily prevents a bite on the neck. Second, if you want to finish off the vampire, bring along a gun with a silver bullet. You can also kill a vampire with wooden stakes, although it's not necessary to carry any. As this film indicates, there are always spare wooden stakes lying around. —Hege.

Superman
(COLOR)

'Superman' is super movie.

Hollywood, Dec. 11.

Warner Bros. release of an Alexander and Ilya Salkind production. Produced by Pierre Spengler. Directed by Richard Donner. Stars Marlon Brando, Gene Hackman. Screenplay, Mario Puzo, David Newman, Leslie Newman, Robert Benton; story, Puzo; based on characters created by Jerry Siegel, Joel Shuster; executive producer, Ilya Salkind; music, John Williams; film editor, Stuart Baird; camera (color), Geoffrey Unsworth; production design, John Barry; additional script material, Norman Enfield; creative supervisor & director of special effects, Colin Chilvers; creative supervisor & director of optical visual effects, Roy Field; creative supervisor and director of mattes and composite, Les Bowie; creative dir. of process photography, Denys Coop; model sets directed and created by Derek Meddings. Reviewed at the Burbank Studios, Burbank, Dec. 11, '78. (MPAA Rating: PG). Running time: **143 MINS.**

Jor-El	Marlon Brando
Lex Luthor	Gene Hackman
Superman/Clark Kent	Christopher Reeve
Otis	Ned Beatty
Perry White	Jackie Cooper
Pa Kent	Glenn Ford
First Elder	Trevor Howard
Lois Lane	Margot Kidder
Non	Jack O'Halloran
Eve Teschmacher	Valerie Perrine
Bond-Ah	Maria Schell
General Zod	Terence Stamp
Ma Kent	Phyllis Baxter
Lara	Susannah York
Young Clark Kent	Jeff East
Jimmie Olsen	Marc McClure
Ursa	Sarah Douglas
Second Elder	Harry Andrews
Baby Kal-El	Lee Quigley
Baby Clark Kent	Aaron Smolinski

Magnify James Bond's extraordinary physical powers while curbing his sex drive and you have the essence of "Superman," a wonderful, chuckling, preposterously exciting fantasy guaranteed to challenge world boxoffice records this time round, and perhaps with sequels to come.

In sum, director Richard Donner and his large crews of British and American technical experts did it: they brought this cherished and durable comic book character to the screen, overcoming every challenge in presenting the man who leaps tall buildings in a single bound.

The risk, of course, was that the audience would refuse to believe and laugh in the wrong places. Thanks to the skill of process photography, however, it's easy to believe and the laughs present — and there are plenty — are cued directly to the script and the delightful performances of Christopher Reeve, Margot Kidder, Gene Hackman, Valerie Perrine and Ned Beatty.

Forget Marlon Brando who tops the credits. As Superman's father on the doomed planet Krypton, Brando is good but unremarkable and is gone for all practical purposes within the first 15 minutes. So

much for multi-million-dollar marquee value.

As both the wholesome man of steel and his bumbling secret identity Clark Kent, Reeve is excellent. As newswoman Lois Lane, Kidder plays perfectly off both of his personalities and her initial double-entendre interview with Superman is wickedly coy, dancing round the obvious question any red-blooded girl might ask herself about such a magnificent prospect.

In response, Reeve gives Superman a smidgen of sexual interest but nothing to sap his powers. When he takes her on a moonlight flight over Metropolis, however, the passions are far more romantic than a camera could ever capture in a bedroom. The women are going to love it.

Tracing the familiar cartoon genesis, film opens with spectacular outer-space effects and the presentation of life on Krypton where nobody believes Papa Brando's warnings of doom. So he and wife Susannah York ship their baby son on his way to Earth as the planet explodes in an exciting display of stunt and model work.

Striking terra firma, the baby is found by Glenn Ford and Phyllis Thaxter who take him for their own. As a teenager forced to hide his powers at Ford's wise insistence, the boy is nicely played by Jeff East.

But the time must ultimately come when Superman's powers for good are revealed to the world and his debut becomes a wild night, beginning with Lane's rescue from a skyscraper, the capture of assorted burglars and the salvation of the Presiden'ts airplane.

Lurking in wacky palatial splendor in the sewers beneath Park Ave., supercriminal Hackman views this caped arrival as a super-threat befitting his evil genius. Assisted by the bumbling Beatty and sensuous, yet almost innocent Perrine, Hackman is a charming jackanape with plans to make a real-estate killing on the new waterfront remaining east of the San Andreas Fault after causing everything west to sink into the ocean.

It's a big plot and the dastardly results are a dozen disaster films packaged in one. But Superman's ultimate triumph involves a lot more than super-feats of strength, exercising the heart muscles as well.

Naturally, most of the plot elements are completely absurd (not the least of which houses reporter Kidder in a glamorous penthouse apartment), but Donner and scripters Mario Puzo, David Newman, Leslie Newman and Robert Benton never let the silliness get out of control. It's easy enought to just enter their world and adjust to new realities.

With so many chores to be

handled expertly, it's impossible to cover all the accomplishments. Obviously, the cinematography by the late Geoffrey Unsworth (to whom the film is dedicated) is a major factor. Ditto John Williams' bold score and John Barry's production design.

But though the stars played brilliantly, the game here was won in the technical trenches by the long list of craftsmen. —Har.

Tattooed Tears
(COLOR)

London, Nov. 24.
Documentary funded by Corporation for Public Broadcasting and National Endowment for the Arts. Produced & directed by Nick Broomfield, Joan Churchill. Camera (color), editing & sound, Nick Broomfield, Joan Churchill. Reviewed at National Film Theatre, London, Nov. 23, '78. Running time: **85 MINS.**

"Tattooed Tears" is a 16m documentary which by virtue of controversial content and makers' proficiency could rate occasional theatrical play-off in arthouse situations where double-bill programming applies.

Most remarkable aspect of this inside-view of the California Youth Training School is that Broomfield and Churchill were permitted unrestricted access by the resigning Youth Authority director, whose statement in a sense the film is. He had become convinced during office that rehabilitation was impossible in the institution, which houses 2,000 juveniles convicted of violent crimes.

Pic stresses that these society-dubbed maniacs are warded and taught by hot-gospelers and yellow-peril fanatics just as maniacal as themselves. One prisoner, the only one featured to have gone straight since, observes to the school board that within an institutional set-up there is no way of judging whether a person has reformed sufficiently for the outside world. —Simo.

California Suite
(COLOR)

Strong commercial outlook.

Hollywood, Nov. 29.
A Columbia Pictures release of a Ray Stark production. Produced by Stark. Features entire cast. Directed by Herbert Ross. Screenplay, Neil Simon, based on his play; camera (color), David M. Walsh; editor, Michael A. Stevenson; supervising editor, Margaret Booth; production design, Albert Brenner; costume design, Patricia Norris; music, Claude Bolling; sound, Al Overton Jr.; associate producer, Ronald L. Schwary; assistant director, Jack Roe. Reviewed at Directors Guild of America, Hollywood, Nov. 29, '78 (MPAA Rating: PG). Running time: **103 MINS.**
Bill Warren .... Alan Alda
Sidney Cochran .... Michael Caine
Dr. Willis Panama .. .. Bill Cosby
Hannah Warren .... Jane Fonda

Marvin Michaels .... Walter Matthau
Mrs. Michaels .... Elaine May
Dr. Chauncy Gump .... Richard Pryor
Diana Barrie .... Maggie Smith
Lola Gump .... Gloria Gifford
Bettina Panama .... Sheila Frazier
Harry Michaels .... Herbert Edelman

Together, Ray Stark, Herbert Ross and Neil Simon make one of the most formidable producing-directing-writing teams in recent memory. The string of hits that began with "The Sunshine Boys" and "The Goodbye Girl" should continue with "California Suite," the most ambitious of the three in both scope and accomplishment. The Columbia Pictures release seems assured of a rich boxoffice harvest, thanks to both the Simon-Ross legacy and the marquee value of a top-heavy cast.

Simon and Ross have gambled in radically altering the successful format of "California Suite" as it appeared on stage. Instead of four separate playlets, there is now one semi-cohesive narrative revolving around visitors to the Beverly Hills Hotel, which is marvelously recreated in Albert Brenner's stunning production design.

Alan Alda and Jane Fonda portray a divorced couple wrangling over possession of their child, while Michael Caine and Maggie Smith play a showbiz couple with varying sexual tastes holed up at the Bev-Hills prior to the Academy Awards. Walter Matthau has to explain his unwitting infidelity to spouse Elaine May in a third segment, and Richard Pryor and Bill Cosby, accompanied by their wives, Gloria Gifford and Sheila Frazier, manage to turn a vacation into a series of disastrous mishaps.

The intercutting of the various relationships has been accomplished smoothly by Ross and editors Michael A. Stevenson and Margaret Booth, and the Simon "touch" is present everywhere. The results, however, differ significantly from the "laff-a-minute" style of both "The Sunshine Boys" and "The Goodbye Girl" — Simon here displays his serious bent for the first time to film audiences.

Ross and Simon have set up as counterpoint to the more tragic-omic episodes (those involved Alda and Fonda, and Caine and Smith) some farcical moments around Matthau and blitzed floozy Denise Galik, along with the Pryor-Cosby shenanigans. The technique is less than successful, veering from poignant emotionalism to broad slapstick in sudden shifts.

The satirical jabs at which Simon excels, and the uniformly strong cast manage to pull "California Suite" out of this mild form of schizophrenia. Bon mots are sprinkled through the script with delightful regularity, especially as delivered by the likes of Smith, May and Alda.

Fonda demonstrates yet another aspect of her amazing range, making her one of the most dynamic feminine screen stars in decades, although her brittle quips with Alda seem very stage-bound. Smith and Caine interplay wonderfully, as do Pryor and Cosby. The latter duo get the worst break, however, as their seg is chopped up, spread around and generally given short shrift. Matthau and May seem to be doing an encore of their work in "A New Leaf."

Much of the material is very showbiz-oriented, and it's questionable how a joke about "Hardy Canyon" will play in Peoria. But Ross has laid over Simon's barbs a blanket of compassion and humanity, and the results should appeal to a wide variety of audiences.

Claude Bolling's jazzy score is subtly effective, and special mention should be made of Wayne Fitzgerald's title design using David Hockney's paintings. The MGM lab and color work is, as always, superb.

For the record, the legit "California Suite" preemed April 25, 1976 at the Ahmanson Theatre in L.A. Cast included Tammy Grimes and George Grizzard in the combined Fonda-Alda, Smith-Caine roles, and Jack Weston and Barbara Barrie in the Matthau-May and Pryor-Gifford parts. Grizzard and Grimes also doubled in the Cosby-Frazier roles. —Poll.

The Brink's Job
(COLOR)

Weak on suspense. Excellent cast.

Hollywood, Dec. 5.
A Universal Pictures release of a Dino de Laurentiis presentation, produced by Ralph Serpe. Features entire cast. Directed by William Friedkin. Screenplay, Walon Green, based on book by Noel Behn; camera (color). A. Norman Leigh; editors, Bud Smith, Robert K. Lambert; sound, Jeff Wexler; production design, Dean Tavoularis; assistant director, Terence A. Donnelly, art direction, Angelo Graham; music, Richard Rodney Bennett. Reviewed at the Goldwyn Theatre, Beverly Hills, Dec. 5, '78 (MPAA Rating: PG). Running time: **103 MINS.**
Tony Pino .... Peter Falk
Joe McGinnis .... Peter Boyle
Vinnie Costa .... Allen Goorwitz
"Specs" O'Keefe .... Warren Oates
Mary Pino .... Gena Rowlands
Jazz Maffie .... Paul Sorvino
J. Edgar Hoover .... Sheldon Leonard
Sandy Richardson .... Gerard Murphy
Gus Gusciora .... Kevin O'Connor
Gladys .... Claudia Peluso

It was a bunch of low-level buffoons who masterminded the "crime of the century" in 1950, knocking off the Brink's vault in Boston for more than $2,000,000. Now director William Friedkin and writer Walon Green have chosen to flow with this notion with little concern for suspense or conflict or any-

thing else that might rivet the attention.

The picture may work for some, thanks to the expert clowning by the "gang." Peter Falk, Peter Boyle, Allen Goorwitz, Warren Oates, Paul Sorvino, Gerard Murphy and Kevin O'Connor. Falk is especially good, though he tends to play the role like Columbo gone bad, complete with long coat.

At every turn, though Friedkin and Green fail to enchance the rather mundane truths of the case. Individually, the gang members weren't that interesting, but a lot of time is spent bringing them together. Their decision to take on the supposedly impregnable Brink's vault isn't based on any brilliant strategy — they simply discover it's really a carelessly guarded crackerbox. Afterwards, there's no problem to the getaway or sitting on the loot while the statute of limitations ticks away.

There could have been some suspense built around Warren Oates' character, who winds up in prison after another robbery. It's made clear that his concern for a dying sister may prod him to spill the beans on the Brink's gang. But there's no will-he-or-won't-he before time runs out on the police. He just does, a couple of days before the statute tolls. And the gang goes to jail. —Har. .

Brass Target
(COLOR)

Boring recreation of Patton assassination attempt; misses the target.

Hollywood, Dec. 6.
A United Artists release of a Metro-Goldwyn-Mayer film. Exec producer, Berle Adams. Produced by Arthur Lewis. Features entire cast. Directed by John Hough. Screenplay, Alvin Boretz, based on the novel, "The Algonquin Project," by Frederick Nolan; camera (color), Tony Imi; editor, David Lane; production design, Rolf Zehetbauer; music, Laurence Rosenthal; costume design, Monika Bauert; sound, Peter Beil; special effects, Karl Baumgartner; assistant director, Bert Batt. Reviewed at MGM Theatre, Culver City, Dec. 6, '78. (MPAA Rating: PG.) Running time: **111 MINS.**
Mara .... Sophia Loren
Major Joe De Lucca ..... John Cassavetes
Gen. George S. Patton Jr. George Kennedy
Col. Donald Rogers .... Robert Vaughn
Col. Mike McCauley ... Patrick McGoohan
Col. Robert Dawson .... Bruce Davison
Col. Walter Gilchrist ... Edward Herrman
Shelley/Webber .... Max Von Sydow
Col. Elton F. Stewart .... Ed Bishop
Lucky Luciano .... Lee Montague

"Brass Target" is the second major feature in two years to speculate on what might have happened to an historical figure in World War II had a given set of circumstances taken place. The ITC production of "The Eagle Has Landed" found few takers in the domestic market, a fate that seems likely to befall "Brass Target." This talky, lugubrious MGM production might find some action overseas through its CIC release, but domestic distrib UA will probably be left holding the bag.

This time, instead of Winston Churchill getting bumped off, it's General George Patton's turn. Writer Alvin Boretz has turned Frederick Nolan's speculative novel, "The Algonquin Project," into a seemingly true-to-life revelation of how Patton actually died, not in a car accident, but at the hands of a clever paid assassin.

Unfortunately, "Brass Target" represents this imaginary scenario as reality by changing the fictional character in Nolan's book to Patton. Rewriting history is fine as long as the boundaries between truth and fantasy are kept clear — this film dangerously blurs them.

What's worse, it does so in boring and heavyhanded fashion. Robert Vaughn, Edward Herrman and Ed Bishop play three officers in occupied Germany who concoct a plan to steal the Third Reich's gold stores with the help of OSS head Patrick McGoohan, who supplies the m.o. for the heist.

Patton, as played by George Kennedy, gets into a snit when the Russian Allies taunt him about the theft, and personally supervises the investigation, joined by OSS vet John Cassavetes. Gradually, just about every cast member is eliminated by one side or the other, until only Cassavetes, assassin Max Von Sydow, and mutual lover Sophia Loren remain for the predictable finale.

Aside from the fact that the motivation for the robbery is never fully explained, "Brass Target" fails in a number of other areas. Its characters are one dimension and almost laughable in their cliched reactions to one another. Endless discussions about the crime fill up most of the long 111 minutes, leaving director John Hough little to do except reaction shots.

Hough manages to interject some excitement into the action scenes, but these come few and far between. A generally competent cast is hamstrung by the material at hand, although Cassavetes and Von Sydow are believable, when almost nothing else is. The Cassavetes-Loren-Von Sydow love triangle adds nothing to the plot other than a convenient resolution.

Kennedy's interpretation of Patton makes it clear why George C. Scott won an Oscar for his version. McGoohan offers a bizarre reading of the OSS head that doesn't click, and Vaughan's character is further burdened by a gratuitous hint of homosexuality. Lee Montague stands out in a brief bit as Lucky Luciano.

Rolf Zehetbauer's production design of war-torn Frankfurt at least gives the audience something creative to look at, but Laurence Rosenthal's score adds to the drowsy mood established by Boretz' script. Tony Imi's camerawork is quite good.

The World War II drama seems to have exhausted its appeal, a fact only reaffirmed by "Brass Target." —Poll.

King of The Gypsies
(COLOR)

Gypsy version of "The Godfather." Impressive debut for Eric Roberts. So-so outlook.

Hollywood, Dec. 1.

A Paramount Pictures release of a Dino De Laurentiis presentation, produced by Federico De Laurentiis; executive producer, Dino De Laurentiis. Features entire cast. Directed by Frank Pierson. Screenplay, Pierson, suggested by "King Of The Gypsies" by Peter Maas; camera (Technicolor) Sven Nykvist; production designer, Gene Callahan; editor, Paul Hirsch; music, David Grisman; costumes, Anna Hill Johnstone; associate producer, Anna Gross; set decorators, Robert Drumheller, John Godfrey; art director, Jay Moore; assistant director, J. Alan Hopkins; sound, Dennis Maitland; choreography, Julie Arenal. Reviewed at Paramount Studios, Hollywood, Dec. 1, '78. (MPAA rating: R.) Running time: **112 MINS.**

King Zharko Stepanowicz	Sterling Hayden
Queen Rachel	Shelley Winters
Rose	Susan Sarandon
Groffo	Judd Hirsch
Dave	Eric Roberts
Tita	Brooke Shields
Sharon	Annette O'Toole
Persa	Annie Potts
Spiro Giorgio	Michael V. Gazzo

Frank Pierson has seen "The Godfather" one time too many. His adaptation of Peter Maas' book takes a subject with a history, aura and richness all its own and transforms it into a clone. Eric Roberts' encouraging screen debut as the reluctant heir to the leadership of a gypsy family should create interest in the Dino De Laurentiis presentation to be distributed domestically by Paramount, but the otherwise uneven cast and unoriginal approach to a colorful topic will keep the pic's b.o. prospects far below expectations.

Pierson's screenplay spans three generations of the Stepanowicz family. The picture begins where it ends, with one family trying to break an arrangement for a daughter to marry into another family.

In the opening, Sterling Hayden, in a confident performance as the king of the clan, is called on to settle the dispute by kidnapping the girl. Roberts solves a similar problem near the end of the film by kidnapping his sister, played by Brooke Shields, who again reaffirms that she is badly in need of a series of acting lessons.

In between, Roberts' develop-

ment from a child attempting to escape his heritage for world of the gadjo, is chronicled often using his own words as voiceover narration.

What's most interesting about this film is its recreation of the world of the gypsy — the world of the scam, of fortune-telling and nightlong celebrations. Pierson as director, with a very capable assist from production designer Gene Callahan, as well as Paul Hirsch who wrote the music and Julie Arenal who choreographed the dancing, succeeds on this point handily.

But the film's storyline, Roberts' inevitable ascension to the role of leader in a world he wants desperately to repudiate and his reluctance to accept that role, is far less engaging. One could have hoped for a film that concentrated more on being an atmospheric examination that one tied to a plot, along the lines of Martin Scorsese's "Mean Streets."

Outside of Shields, Roberts and Hayden, performances by the remainder of the cast are either very good or very bad, with Michael Gazzo, Annette O'Toole, and Judd Hirsch on the positive side and Susan Sarandon, Shelley Winters and Annie Potts, terribly miscast, on the negative. —Hege.

The Secret Life Of Plants
(DOCUMENTARY-COLOR)

Lots of pretty pictures, but an iffy commercial future, unless the "head" crowd catches on.

Hollywood, Dec. 8.

A Paramount Pictures release of an Infinite Enterprises Film. Exec producers, Burt Kleiner, Paul Kantor. Produced by Michael Braun. Directed by Walon Green. Screenplay, Peter Tompkins, Green, Braun, based on the book "The Secret Life Of Plants" by Tompkins and Christopher Bird; camera (Metrocolor), Bob Bailin, Ghislain Cloquet, Mike Hoover, Ed Janss, Robin Lehman, Ian Masters, David Myers, Daniel Pearl, Robert Primes, Peter Smolker, Louis Schwartzberg; natural history cinematography, Ken Middleham; music, Stevie Wonder; editors, Christopher Lebenzon, Robert Lambert, Masters; sound, (Dolby) Jeff Wexler, Michael Vionnet, Jan Ross, David Ronnee, Bob Leighton, Larry Johnson; art direction, John Told; costumes, Jeanne Blackburn, Barbara Whitaker; narration, Tompkins, Elizabeth Vreeland, Ruby Crystal. Reviewed at Paramount Studios, Dec. 8, '78. (MPAA Rating: G.) Running time: **96 MINS.**

While "The Secret Life Of Plants" would seem an impossible subject to bring to film, this Paramount release produced by Michael Braun and directed by Walon Green does its best to establish a link between human and plant consciousness. How this topic will be received by a mass audience remains an iffy question, and nontheatrical markets may turn out to be "Plant's" best shot.

Braun and Green, using Peter Tompkins and Christopher Bird's book as a launching point, have devised a visually stunning documentary that thankfully dwells more on the looks, rather than the thoughts, of flora. The approach is similar to that employed by the 1971 release, "The Hellstrom Chronicle," (also directed by Green), but the message here is much more upbeat.

The use of microscopic lenses and time-lapse photography is extensively employed in "Plants," and on a certain level, there's not much difference between this pic and numerous "National Geographic" tv specials except the Dolby sound. But Green, Braun and Tompkins, who coauthored the screenplay, display a heavily scientific bent in their efforts to prove that plants, like most other living things, feel pain and joy, and are silently expressing these emotions.

Unfortunately, it turns "Plants" into more of a tract than an actual documentary. There are several scenes, both historical and current, of experiments proving plants say their own equivalent of "ouch" when pinched, but nary a word from the opposition, in this case, the majority of scientists.

Not helping matters is the BBC-like pretentious narration by author Tompkins, Elizabeth Vreeland and Ruby Crystal, who pounce on phrases like "the touchstone to a universal consciousness." And the spectre of "comrade" plants in the USSR, or a Japanese woman talking to her cactus, may inspire ridicule rather than converts.

"The Secret Life Of Plants" may find its greatest audience, ironically, from those who don't converse with plants, but smoke them. The extraordinary imagery, and excellent score by Stevie Wonder, should bring in the same audience that turned another sleeper, "Up In Smoke," into a b.o. smash. —Poll.

La Cle Sur La Porte
(The Key Is In The Door)
(FRENCH-COLOR)

Paris, Dec. 12.

CCFC release of Cineproduction, SFP production. Stars Annie Girardot, Patrick Dewaere. Directed by Yves Boisset. Screenplay, Andre Weinfeld, Boisset from book by Marie Cardinal; camera (Eastmancolor), Michel Carre; editor, Albert Jurgenson; music, Philippe Sarde. Reviewed at Salle Ponthieu, Paris, Dec. 1, '78. Running time: **102 MINS.**

Marie	Annie Girardot
Philippe	Patrick Dewaere
Jerome	Stephane Jobert
Charlotte	Eleonore Klarwein
Cathy	Barbara Steele
Alice	Malene Sveinbjornsson
Vincent	Mathieu Schiffman

Schooldays, fortyish women finding their own way without any femme lib lip and the generation gap are frequent subjects in French films lately. Director Yves Boisset mixes all three with a dollop of sentiment, nice ensemble acting with popular Annie Girardot effective as a more outgoing and liberal teacher and mother of three aged 18, 16 and 10.

Girardot teaches French lit at a high school but is ready to discuss drugs, sex and homosexuality to keep pace with her students. She also keeps the key in her door at home as friends of her children gather to talk, sing, dance and play and increase her contact and standing with the young and her students for her 16-year-old daughter is in her class.

But the idyll goes awry when an anarchic student enters her class and begins to score with her daughter. Girardot meanwhile has met a young doctor who goes around at night for medical calls in a car when one of her youthful visitors is found beaten up outside the house. The teacher's husband had left her five years ago and he is the first man in her life since then.

Her liberalism is challenged by her daughter as perhaps being too benevolent at the expense of the family. The mother is jolted, stays away from class a few days, has an affair with the doctor and comes back to find she has a place with her students and daughter but has to do it on a mature rather than sometimes condescending level of friendship.

Director Boisset keeps this fluid and avoids mawkishness despite a final party thrown for Girardot by her new beau, children and students. Pic just does not offer much new or perceptive insights into the theme and story.

Film should have legs at home on its perky playing and pacing with offshore chances there for playoff. Patrick Dewaere has charm as the medical suitor and youngsters are good, especially Eleonore Klarwein as the troubled teenage daughter. — *Mosk.*

L'Adoption
(The Adoption)
(FRENCH-COLOR)

Paris, Dec. 12.

Les Films Moliere release of Reggane Film-Arthur Cohn Productions-SFP-FR3 production. Stars Geraldine Chaplin, Jacques Perrin. Directed by Marc Grunebaum. Screenplay, Grunebaum, Bernard Stora, Peter Krall, Magdeleine Dailloux; camera (Eastmancolor), Luciano Tovoli; editor, Kenout Peltier; music, Michel Portal. Reviewed at Salle Ponthieu, Paris, Dec. 5, '78. Running time, **93 MINS.**
Wife .... Geraldine Chaplin
Husband .... Jacques Perrin
Etienne .... Patrick Norbert

Mark Marc Grunebaum as a new director to watch with this piercing, perceptive tale of a youth caught up with a childless couple that leads to violence and tragedy. Film is absorbing, chilling, and with an impact that stays well after it is over.

Geraldine Chaplin and Jacques Perrin are effective as a well-to-do, childless, thirtyish couple who one night awaken to a fire in their barn at their country home. They find a young man, about 18 or son, in the house having an epileptic fit.

It is never clear as to whether he set the fire. The boy, living with his grandmother and just out of an asylum, is taken in by the couple. Is it charity, human kindness, a need or are they just using him to break a barren time in their relations? The boy begins to paint, receive medical care, adjust and get shown off to their friends.

The husband even tolerates the wife's attraction to the boy and his love trysts with her. But then she is pregnant and they begin to lose interest in him. The boy neglects his medicine and feels he will be pushed out.

He attacks her, ostensibly against the coming baby, but, in a frenzy, kills her and then the husband. He goes off alone as he came. There's nothing gritty, forced or overwrought here. Film has tension and texture and avoids any forced symbolism. The dialog is terse and serviceable and film is exacting, revealing and morally persuasive in its probing of youthful attempts to cope and adjust to the adult world.

At last, here's a neophyte French director who is accessible and yet personal in plumbing the agonizing and rapturous times of youthful encounters with life and people. No judgments, but a revealing, forceful look at people in interaction and the dramatic forces that come into play.

Patrick Norbert is excellent in his limning of the youthful victim and victimizer. Music is a fine counterpoint without being intrusive with technical credits high. A film to be heard from at festivals and with the originality, bite and drive for promising chances in all climes.

Incidentally, there was a Hungarian film that played in France this year, and at various festivals in 1977, called "Adoption" by Marta Meszaros. This one is "L'Adoption" (The Adoption.) —*Mosk.*

Come Perdere Una Moglie E Trovare Un'Amante
(How To Lose A Wife and Find a Lover)
(ITALIAN-COLOR)

Rome, Nov. 30.

A Titanus release of a Cinematografica Alex production. Directed by Pasquale Festa Campanile. Stars Johnny Dorelli, Barbara Bouchet. Producer, Luigi Borghese; camera (Kodak), Giuseppe Ruzzolini; music, Gianni Ferrio. Reviewed at FonoRoma, Rome, November 30, '78. Running Time: **100 MINS.**
Also: Carlo Bagno, Elsa Vazzoler, Felice Andreassi.

For those less sophisticated filmgoers who want good clean fun, but don't, after all, mind a few breasts and bums here and there, Pasquale Festa Campanile's "How To Lose" is made to order. Using every old gag in the book and a Hollywood plot to boot, the Italian director has put together a mindless, but amusing comedy that obviously caters to breast worshippers.

The overexposure of the mammary gland is not completely gratuitous in this sitcom. Alberto (Johnny Dorelli), director of a milk company, not only has a professional interest in the female gland, but also has a psychological reason for his hang-up.

His American wife (caught under the shower with the plumber) has left for America, and he has suffered a sexual block which his psychiatrist (whose female patients strip before taking to the couch) has diagnosed as nostalgia for his mother's breast.

The other half of the sitcom is Eleonora who also has marital problems under probe by the same psychiatrist. Eleonora found her musician husband laying a bass violin concert on the nude back of the maid (an obvious allusion to Festa Campanile's successful film "The Male Crow") and has fallen into a deep depression.

Alberto and Eleonora constantly bump into each other (parking lots, hospitals, in the mountains) and after a series of mistaken identities and predictable gags the two are finally united.

Dorelli, an appealing character in the style of Jerry Lewis and Louis de Funes, stumbles his way through the film's improbable situations with great charm and humor. Bouchet, rigid — perhaps incapable of such silliness but content with playing Dorelli's straight person.

Although Festa Campanile cannot pretend to comic originality, he can be credited with resourcefulness in showing one more pair of breasts. In one of the final scenes, Alberto is called on to choose a model whose breasts can be used in an ad for the company's product. The parade of entries should saturate even the most ardent breastophile. —*Argo.*

Invasion Of The Body Snatchers
(COLOR)

Excellent sci-fi remake whose b.o. potential should be equally good.

Hollywood, Dec. 13.

A United Artist release, produced by Robert H. Solo. Directed by Philip Kaufman. Stars Donald Sutherland. Screenplay, W.D. Richter, based on the novel by Jack Finney; camera (Technicolor), Michael Chapman; editor, Douglas Stewart; production design, Charles Rosen; music, Denny Zeitlin; sound, Art Rochester; makeup effects, Thomas Burman, Edouard Henriques; special effects, Dell Rheaume, Russ Hessey; special sound effects, Ben Burtt; assistant director, Jim Bloom. Reviewed at MGM Studios, Dec. 13, '78. (MPAA Rating: PG.) Running time: **115 MINS.**
Matthew Bennell .... Donald Sutherland
Elizabeth Driscoll .... Brooke Adams
Dr. David Kibner .... Leonard Nimoy
Nancy Bellicec ...... Veronica Cartwright
Jack Bellicec .... Jeff Goldblum
Geoffrey .... Art Hindle
Katherine .... Leila Goldoni
Running Man .... Kevin McCarthy

"Invasion Of The Body Snatchers" validates the entire concept of remakes. This new version of Don Siegel's 1956 cult classic (originally released by Allied Artists) not only matches the original in horrific tone and effect, but exceeds it in both conception and execution. Given the increased interest in cinematic sci-fi, the United Artists release looks to have very strong b.o. potential.

W.D. Richter has updated and changed the locale of Jack Finney's serial story to contemporary San Francisco, where Donald Sutherland is a public health inspector, assisted by Brooke Adams. Following the blanketing of the city by spidery webs, Adams notices unusual and sudden changes in b.f. Art Hindle, who becomes emotionless and distant.

Similar transformations are happening all over the city, and while at first Sutherland doubts Adams' sanity, he is soon won over to her paranoia. He invokes the help of an est-type of psychiatrist played with wonderful shading by Leonard Nimoy.

The plot twists are well known to those familiar with the original, but the basic premise is that an alien race (shown in an amoebic state in a marvelous credit sequence by Ron Dexter and Howard Preston) has invaded earth, and is taking over human bodies through a reduplication process while the victims sleep.

Jeff Goldblum and Veronica Cartwright portray a couple who stumble on one of the blank pod bodies before Goldblum succumbs, and later Sutherland rescues Adams from a similar attempt. As the legions of zombies grows, these four remain about the only humans left, and the latter part of "Body

Snatchers" details with methodical ominousness their pursuit.

What makes the Robert H. Solo production so good is the startling veracity of the story. Philip Kaufman is finally given a chance to display the directorial talent suggested by his earlier "White Dawn," and he excels in every respect here: pacing, storytelling and eliciting fine performances from a uniformly superb cast.

Sutherland has his best role since "Klute," and his portrayal of the scientific mind confronted by an unspeakable horror is quite moving. He gets excellent support from Adams, who projects a touching vulnerability, and makes her budding romance with Sutherland a subtle counterpoint to the principal storyline.

Also very good are Goldblum and Cartwright, a dizzy couple who run a mud bath operation, and who are not taken in at all by Nimoy's smooth talking rationalizations. It's a credit to the latter actor, by the way, that his intentions are not revealed until well into the plot resolution.

Film buffs will have a delight in spotting Kevin McCarthy, who starred in the original version, picking up exactly where he left off at the first pic's finale. Also in for a cameo appearances are director Siegel, who limns a cab driver taking the fleeing Sutherland and Adams out of the city, and Bay Area Pacific Film Archives director Tom Luddy.

Tech credits are superior in every aspect, from Charles Rosen's tasteful production design, to the terrifying makeup effects created by Thomas Burman and Edouard Henriques. Also notable was Denny Zeitlin's electronic score, augmented by piercing sound effects by Ben Burtt that figure significantly in the pic's tremendous twist ending.

Pic could use some trimming, especially in the final chase sequences, but Michael Chapman's smooth camerawork effectively covers up most of the laggard moments.

In the 1956 version, which also derived from Finney's mag stories, McCarthy limned the Sutherland part, and Dana Wynters played the g.f., now essayed by Adams.

Industry observers may also note with humor the preponderance of shots featuring the Transamerica pyramid tower, home base of distrib UA, a sort of corporate plugola.
—*Poll.*

L'Affaire Suisse
(The Swiss Affair)
(SWISS-FRENCH-ITALIAN-COLOR)

Zurich, Dec. 7.

Monopole Pathe Films S.A. Geneva release of a Peter Ammann-Saba Cinematografica-Cromix coproduction. Directed by Peter Ammann. Features entire cast. Screenplay, Fabio de Agostini, Bernard Bengloan, John L. Huxley, Ammann; dialog, Huxley; camera (Eastmancolor), Aldo di Marcantonio; music, Giancarlo Chairamello; exec producer, Bruno Paolinelli. Reviewed at the Corso 3, Zurich, Dec. 7, '78. Running time: **93 MINS.**

Cast: Jean Sorel, Brigitte Fossey, Franco Fabrizi, Paul Muller, Colette Descombes, Guillaume Cheneviere, Michel Viala, Pierre Walker, Silvano Tranquilli, Guido Alberti.

"L'Affaire Suisse," Swiss director Peter Ammann's first feature film following three documentaries and a number of tv films, was rejected by the 1978 Locarno Festival's selection committee for allegedly lacking in artistic quality. This decision stirred up some dust here, as many interpreted it, perhaps rightly, as a political one. The film, in fact, is sharply critical of Swiss banks and their financing and speculation practices — a theme very much in the news for some time, both here and abroad.

In the course of an inquest about a Swiss journalist's accidental death in Italy, believed to be a murder, a Geneva police inspector uncovers a many-folded criminal transaction involving Swiss and Italian financiers, lawyers, speculators and banking experts. Bombs are placed in cars, innocent victims are killed, but at the end, established practices, described as being on the borderline of legality, remain more or less undaunted.

A bumpy script, flat direction and indifferent or stilted performances hamper the picture's credibility. Political thrillers with leftwing tendencies have been done before, and much better, by such directors as Francesco Rosi, Constantino Costa-Gavras, Elio Petri or Yves Boisset. Perhaps a new twist here is the denunciation of Switzerland as not quite so sheltered anymore. Original dialog changes from Italian to French, according to locale. —*Mezo.*

Oliver's Story
(COLOR)

Not as many tears, but lots of b.o. potential.

Hollywood, Dec. 11.

A Paramount Pictures release, produced by David V. Picker. Stars Ryan O'Neal, Candice Bergen. Directed by John Korty. Screenplay, Erich Segal, Korty, based on Segal's novel; camera (Color), Arthur Ornitz; editor, Stuart H. Pappe; music, Frances Lai, Lee Holdridge; art direction, Robert Gundlach; set decoration, Phil Smith; sound, Jack C. Jacobsen; assistant director, Mel Howard. Reviewed at Paramount Studio Theatre, Hollywood, Dec. 11, '78. (MPAA Rating: PG.) Running time: **92 MINS.**
Oliver Barrett .... Ryan O'Neal
Marcie Bonwit .... Candice Bergen
Joanna Stone .... Nicola Pagett
Phil Cavilleri .... Edward Binns
John Hsiang .... Benson Fong
Stephen Simpson .... Charles Haid
Jamie Francis .... Kenneth McMillan
Mr. Barrett .... Ray Milland
Dr. Dienhart .... Josef Sommer
Mr. Gentilano .... Sully Boyar
Gwen Simpson .... Swoosie Kurtz
Mrs. Barrett .... Meg Mundy

"Love Story," which has returned more than $50,000,000 in domestic rentals to its distributor, Paramount, is a tough act to follow, but "Oliver's Story" manages to hold its own. The continuation of Erich Segal's tale of fated lovers gets a sensitive and moving treatment from director and coscripter (with Segal) John Korty. The boxoffice returns may not be as dramatic, but the teaming of Ryan O'Neal with Candice Bergen provides romantic chemistry that should translate into heavy action at the wickets.

"Oliver's Story" begins with the burial of Jenny Cavalleri Barrett, whose death closed out the first pic. O'Neal, working as a lawyer in a prestigious New York firm, is burdened by a sense of despair and loneliness, along with a liberal dose of self-pity. His father-in-law, now played by Edward Binns, attempts to rouse him, as do friends Charles Haid and Swoosie Kurtz, but to little avail.

Enter Candice Bergen as the Bonwit heir in Bonwit Teller, the flip side in looks and disposition to the Jenny character created by Ali McGraw. Their meeting is one of those coincidences that only occur in films, but Korty and Segal plot the relationship with a sureness that proves to be highly endearing.

In contrast to the poor/rich dichotomy of the original script, "Oliver's Story" pits money against money, with both lovers up in the millionaire class. O'Neal still cherishes his 1960s notions of liberalism, working on tenant-landlord cases and bemoaning the fate of workers in Hong Kong, where he accompanies Bergen on a fashion factory expedition.

There is the usual Segal banter between the players, but the dialog is neither as smarmy nor as self-serving this time around. Korty has fleshed out this brief (92 minutes) story with a keen eye for detail and a compassionate sense of observation about how people fall in (and out of) love.

The most moving segments come, ironically, not out of the O'Neal-Bergen encounters, but from a few brief scenes between O'Neal and Ray Milland, who encores as his wealthy banker father. It's a tribute to both performances and Korty's direction that this most basic of conflicts is resolved here in a genuinely satisfying manner, sure to reprise the tears that flowed so abundantly in the original.

"Oliver's Story" is not without its defects, principal among which is the unlikable nature of O'Neal's character. Still inherently a spoiled child, Oliver Barrett doesn't seem to deserve the beautiful women, concerned friends and elevated circumstances that accrue to him. It's no wonder Bergen's Marcie Bonwit gives up in despair — if the film had continued much longer, so might the audience.

Still, O'Neal delivers a studied and rich performance, perfectly complemented by Bergen's classical beauty and quick wit. Milland is excellent in his few scenes, and Nicola Pagett has a very effective small part as a blind date for O'Neal. All the supporting players are competent in very small roles.

There are cast changes from "Love Story," with John Marley replaced by Binns as the father-in-law, and Meg Mundy taking over for Katherine Balfour as Milland's wife.

Tech credits, in particular Arthur Ornitz' lensing, are elegant. Stuart Pappe's editing is very sharp at the beginning, but the Hong Kong scenes seem somewhat choppy, and the film ends rather abruptly.
—*Poll.*

For Whom To Be Murdered
(HONG KONG-COLOR)

Hong Kong, Nov. 1.

A Safety Walk Motion Picture Co., released by Bang Bang Projections. World Sales: William Hay & Company, Hong Kong. Directed by Patrick Yuen. Features entire cast. Screenplay, Raymond Wond, Raymond Lai; camera (color), Chung Chi Man. No other credits provided. Reviewed at Isis Theatre, Hong Kong, Nov. 1, '78. Running time: **102 MINS.**
Fong Tin Yau .... Tony Wong
Helen Cheung .... Angie Chiu
Killer .... Chan Wai Man
Other Girl .... Lam Kin Ming
Liu Man (Journalist) ... Raymond Wong
Also: Lay Dan. Cheung Ying.

The title gives the impression that this Bang Bang release is a potential dud. A viewing during the first midnight showing confirms the impression. It could never be a "Jumping Ash," but it definitely is a poverty-stricken variation of the unhappy "Foxbat."

The lead stars are two unknowns — Tony Wong and Raymond Wong, who also coscripted. Tony can be likable, athletic and sympathetic, but no actor. The other Wong looks undernourished, a caricature of an underpaid journalist who makes up for the lack of weight with a loud mouth that heightens his charmlessness.

The two play overseas Chinese (from Singapore) who come to Hong Kong for a brief holiday. Instead, they get trapped in what is supposed to be a thriller-melodrama that simmers with nonsense.

The Wongs have an encounter with disbelieving local cops as they enjoy the sights (all overused tourist spots, naturally), then meet two giggly local girls — Angie Chiu and Lam Kin Ming. In the course of clowning Cantonese style, Tony Wong has a precognition (or is it plain premonition?) that a murder is about to be committed. Indeed, they later witness a murder at Repulse Bay (a popular beach resort) and get to fight Chan Wai-ming (typecast as a hired killer).

Sophistication and style are nowhere to be found in this production. The silly plot works dismally on the "man" alone theme. In this case, it is Tony Wong who suffers from a murder rap and from thuggery.

One would expect some suspense from the tension mounted on highly visual terms. But the mystery is a giveaway from the start and then finished off with touches of the unseem which is never developed, let alone explained.

It is regrettable that the company which was once expected to revive quality in Cantonese films has finally succumbed to releasing assembly line product for the mass Asian market. Still, "For Whom to be Murdered" might yet attract the local denim set whose tastes at the moment are quite predictable.

—*Mel*

Ice Castles
(COLOR)

Skating pic should glide to financial success.

Hollywood, Dec. 7.

A Columbia Pictures release, produced by John Kemeny. Executive producer, Rosilyn Heller. Directed by Donald Wrye. Screenplay, Wrye, Gary L. Bain, based on a story by Baim; camera (color), Bill Butler; editors, Michael Kahn, Maury Winetrobe, Melvin Shapiro; music, Marvin Hamlisch; production design, Joel Schiller; choreography, Brian Foley; sound, Glen Anderson, Richard Raguse; assistant director, Jerry Grandey. Reviewed at Columbia Pictures, Dec. 7, '78. (MPAA Rating: PG.) Running time: **113 mins.**

Alexis Winston	Lynn-Holly Johnson
Nick Peterson	Robby Benson
Beulah Smith	Collen Dewhurst
Marcus Winston	Tom Skerritt
Deborah Macland	Jennifer Warren
Brian Dockett	David Huffman
Sandy	Diane Reilly

"Ice Castles" is that rarity, a perfectly realized look at a specific theme (in this case, ice skating) that manages to surmount its specialized nature and touch a broad-based nerve. The Columbia Pictures release combines a touching love story with the excitement and intense pressure of Olympic competition skating. With the proper handling, "Ice Castles" can skim some big profits during the downbeat winter months. The pic is skedded for a wide break at the end of January, although some test engagements kick off this month.

It's a long way from the Sonja Henie musicals of the late 1930s to Donald Wrye and Gary L. Baim's probing look at the world on ice. Now skating is big business, and the Olympics the pot of gold at the end of the rainbow.

Screen newcomer Lynn-Holly Johnson portrays a farm girl from upstate Iowa who has the raw talent to be a great skater. Under the training and encouragement of local ice rink operator Colleen Dewhurst, she wins a regional competition, where she is spotted by Olympic coach Jennifer Warren.

With the aid of tv sports commentator David Huffman, Warren propels Johnson to instant stardom as a Cinderella figure who comes out of nowhere to win the hearts of the American people, much as real-life skaters Peggy Fleming and Dorothy Hamill did. All is progressing smoothly until Johnson has a freak accident, and is partially blinded. Robby Benson, who plays Johnson's boy friend, and Tom Skerritt, her father, bring the teenager out of her shell, leading up to the inspiring ending.

Director Wrye, making his theatrical feature debut, walks a fine line here between outright bathos and tender sentimentality, but always manages to stay on the right side. The characters are well developed, and most importantly, interesting. They invite audience empathy, an unusual quality in these days of cynical plotting.

"Ice Castles" is structured in three parts, the rise, fall and comeback of Johnson's career. The first segment is the most interesting, as it takes the small-town femme into the harsh and frenetic world of Olympic sponsors, back-biting among the skaters, and the inevitability of media manipulation.

Warren and Huffman, who perceive Johnson as their ticket to success, are excellent in support, with Warren particularly giving a studied, meticulous performance. Huffman also comes across strongly, becoming involved romantically with Johnson, but leaving the scene with a sense of dignity.

The core of the film, however, centers around Benson, Dewhurst and Skerritt, who together offer the warmth and support that keeps Johnson going. Dewhurst, who appears all too infrequently in pix, excels in her role as the hard-bitten ex-skater trying not to live out her failed dreams through Johnson. Skerritt gives another outstanding perf as the overly-protective father who also realizes his failings.

Top-billed Benson takes a back seat in this venture, but is a solidly complex character in his own right. The real kudos go to Johnson, who shows the potential of being an excellent actress, in addition to a top skater. She is consistently believable, even in the more maudlin moments, and makes Lexie a character to care about.

Locations in Minnesota and Colorado serve the pic well, especially with Bill Butler's expert lensing (MGM did the lab work) to illuminate them. Brian Foley's ice choreography is visually appealing, and editing by Michael Kahn, Maury Winetrobe and Melvin Shapiro keep the film well-paced at 113 minutes. The title theme, with music by Marvin Hamlisch and lyrics by Carole Bayer Sager, augments the mood, and is especially effective in the closing scenes.

In short, "Ice Castles" is a beguiling and affecting film. With the boom of interest in skating, it could launch a new wave of ice spectaculars. —*Poll.*

Every Which Way But Loose
(COLOR)

Clint and Clyde — for Laffs.

Hollywood, Dec. 7.

A Warner Bros. release of a Malpaso Company Film. Produced by Robert Daley. Stars Clint Eastwood. Directed by James Fargo. Screenplay, Jeremy Joe Kronsberg; camera (color), Rexford Metz; art director, Elayne Ceder; editor, Ferris Webster. Joel Cox; associate producer, Fritz Manes, Kronsberg; assistant director, Larry Powell; set decoration, Robert De Vestel; stunt coordinator, Wayne Van Horn; sound, Bert Hallberg; special effects, Chuck Gaspar; costumes, Glenn Wright. Reviewed at Plitt's Century Plaza Theatre. L.A., Dec. 7, '78. (MPAA rating: R.) Running time: **119 MINS.**

Phil Beddoe	Clint Eastwood
Lynn Halsey-Taylor	Sondra Locke
Orville	Geoffrey Lewis
Echo	Beverly D'Angelo
Ma	Ruth Gordon

As one of the half dozen stars in Hollywood with a long and not often broken history of b.o. successes, Clint Eastwood has the clout to arrange studio backing for just about any project. And he's proven his position with "Every Which Way But Loose." This film is way off the mark. If people will line up for this one — and they probably will — they'll line up for any Clint Eastwood picture.

Jeremy Joe Kronsberg's screenplay has Eastwood as a beer guzzling, country music-loving truck driver who picks up spare change as a barroom brawler. When Sondra Locke, an elusive singer Eastwood meets at The Palomino Club, takes off for Colorado, Eastwood packs his pickup truck in pursuit.

Behind him are a motorcycle gang and an L.A. cop. Both have been victims of Eastwood's fists. They want revenge. Traveling with Eastwood is Geoffrey Lewis and Beverly D'Angelo, whom the two meet on the road.

There's also an orangutan. His name is Clyde. Eastwood won him a few years back in a fight. He goes everywhere with Eastwood. He drinks beer, finds a one-night stand at a zoo in New Mexico and cheers, on his friend.

Watching the homestead while these four head east to find Locke is Ruth Gordon. In her latest version of the eccentric old lady, Gordon spends her time trying to get a driver's license. By now, the character has become stale.

For Eastwood fans, the essential elements are there. Lots of people get beat up, Eastwood walks tall and looks nasty, cars are crashed. It should be enough to assure the commercial success of "Every Which Way."

James Fargo directs limply. Whatever charm or humor the Kronsberg script may have contained, is lost under his hand. The action sequences are acceptably choreographed. But why Fargo chose to use so many closeups is a mystery. It's as though he were shooting a tv film and someone told him midway through production that the picture was for theatrical release.

Characterizations by Lewis, D'Angelo and Locke are okay, as are the remainder of the tech credits. What is disappointing about this, is why Eastwood and his producer, Robert Daley, would want to latch onto such third-rate material. The old complaint about the paucity of good material in Hollywood won't explain this film. Eastwood can do better —*Hege.*

Cosi Come Sei
(Stay As You Are)
(ITALIAN-COLOR)

Rome, Dec. 19.

A CEIAD release of San Francisco Film production. Produced by Giovanni Bertolucci. Directed by Alberto Lattuada. Stars Marcello Mastroianni, Nastassja Kinski. Screenplay, Enrico Oldoini, Alberto Lattuada; camera (color), Luis Alcaine; music, Ennio Morricone. Reviewed at the Astor, Rome, Dec. 12, '78. Running time: **118 MINS.**
Also: Francisco Rabal, Anja Pieroni, Giuliana Calandra.

Billed as a film on incest, "Just As You Are" never really confronts fully that taboo, but does provide an interesting twist to the May-December romance theme so popular this season on the peninsula ("First Love," "Break-up").

With headliners Marcello Mastroianni and Nastassja Kinski (in her first stab at serious acting) couple with lovely backgrounds in Florence and Spain, the film should have no trouble finding takers.

The story line, written by director Alberto Lattuada and Enrico Oldoini, is simple. After a night of lovemaking with Francesca, an 18-year old student, Giulio, a 50-year old architect, is warned that his new-found young lover may be his own daughter. He had had an affair with Francesca's mother, Fosca, exactly 18 years before: she had slipped away unnoticed while they were at the movies and he had never heard from her since.

Was Fosca pregnant when she walked out of Giulio's life? We never know the truth (even Francesca doesn't know the true identity of her father and now Fosca is dead), but Giulio's agonizing over such a possibility raises some interesting questions about the nature of fatherhood. Back on the home front, Giulio's known daughter (played admirably by Giuliana Calandra, a young actress to watch) tells her father that she is pregnant, has decided to keep the child, but leave the baby's Spanish father — underscoring again the theme of fatherhood as a choice and not a biological fact.

This theme, however, is unfortunately only a backdrop to the more traditional story of a middle-aged man vainly seeking the fountain of youth. The contrast between the calm, mature figure of Mastroianni and the exuberant childishness of Kinski is well exploited by Lattuada especially in the Spanish hotel room where the 18-year-old is filled with sexual energy and playfulness, while the older man tries to interest her in Goya.

The final scene is predictable, but artfully done: Francesca leaves Giulio alone in a Florentine theatre during a screening of Carl Dreyer's "Vampire."

While the sensuous photography of Luis Alcaine and the suggestive music of Ennio Moricone create a necessary atmosphere of eroticism, several nude scenes seemed forced: the youthful orgy at Francesca's Florentine apartment, and the series of still shots of Mastroianni and Kinski in various erotic (and not particularly comfortable) positions after they decide (incest or no incest) to continue their affair.

The character of Giulio's wife also seems forced. Although her sternness and lack of compassion certainly provide a reason for Giulio's flight, her character is needlessly stereotyped. Mastroianni, looking as attractive as ever, plays his role with just the right amount of irony: one could easily imagine him 20 years from now having an affair with an 18-year-old who could be his granddaughter. —Argo.

Moment By Moment
(COLOR)

Seems like hours and hours.

Hollywood, Dec. 12.
A Universal Pictures Release of a Robert Stigwood prouction. Stars Lily Tomlin, John Travolta. Exec producer, Kevin McCormick. Produced by Stigwood. Written and directed by Jane Wagner. Camera (color), Phillip Lathrop; editor, John F. Burnett; production design, Harry Horner; music, Lee Holdridge; costume design, Albert Wolsky; sound, Charles M. Wilborn; assistant director, Michael Grillo. Reviewed at Samuel Goldwyn Theatre, Academy Of Motion Picture Arts & Sciences, Dec. 12, '78. (MPAA Rating: R.) Running time: **105 MINS.**

Trisha .... Lily Tomlin
Strip .... John Travolta
Naomi .... Andra Akers
Stu .... Bert Kramer
Peg .... Shelley R. Bonus
Stacie .... Debra Feuer
Dan Santini .... James Luisi

"Moment By Moment" has to rate as one of the major disappointments of 1978. What seemed like inspired casting on paper, the teaming of John Travolta and Lily Tomlin, fails badly in execution. While initial returns may be strong based on curiosity about the star teaming, the Universal release seems sure to sputter once word-of-mouth gets out.

It's not easy to ascertain just where the difficulties began, but by the time "Moment By Moment" reaches the end of its very long 105 minutes, there have been so many problems, it really doesn't matter.

The lion's share of the blame must go to writer-director (and long-time Tomlin collaborator) Jane Wagner, who concocted this improbable story of a Beverly Hills chic housewife whose marriage has gone sour, and who meets up with an insecure young drifter, with whom she has an affair. A story about the attraction between older women and younger men deserves to be told (it's certainly been done enough from the opposite angle), but Wagner was apparently not the right choice to tell it.

Given the stilted and forced nature of the dialog, the contrived situations, and the humdrum pacing, it's a wonder "Moment To Moment" has even a few good moments. Most of these are supplied by Travolta, who reaffirms that he is a major screen presence in his first overtly dramatic role.

Insouciant and likable from the outset, Travolta pursues the distant Tomlin like a determined puppy dog — once he latches on, she can't shake him loose. The first half hour of the pic, with this unusual courtship, is appealing, and only makes what follows more of a letdown.

As approachable as Travolta is, Tomlin goes overboard in the other direction. Approaching Trisha as if she was one of her stable theatrical creations, Tomlin never varies her nasal monotone, nor her imperturbable exterior. It's a one-note performance that frustrates the entire picture.

Not helping matters is Wagner's banal script, which has cliche piled atop cliche, and dialog that evokes embarrassing laughter. Unfortunately naming the Travolta character Strip (after Sunset), Wagner has Tomlin lovingly call out the name time and again. Since Travolta seems to be constantly getting in and out of his clothes (a reversal of the standard cheesecake footage), the appellation becomes an unintentional joke.

The supporting cast is virtually non-existent, another miscalculation, since neither Tomlin nor Travolta have anyone else with whom to interact. Andra Akers is briefly effective as Tomlin's bosom buddy, but Bert Kramer is a cardboard cutout as the errant husband.

The waste of time and talent is compounded given the beauty of Phillip Lathrop's camerawork, and Harry Horner's sharp production design of Malibu, BevHills and L.A. locations.

The only way "Moment By Moment" might work is with the soundtrack off. And since silent films were phased out some 50 years ago, that hardly seems a likely possibly. —Poll.

The Hills Have Eyes
(COLOR)

London, Nov. 27.
A Blood Relations Co. production, produced by Peter Locke. Features entire cast. Directed by Wes Craven. Screenplay, Craven; camera (color), Eric Sadrinen; editor, Craven; art director, Robert Burns; music, Don Peake. Reviewed at the National Film Theatre, London, Nov. 24, '78. Running time: **89 MINS.**

Brenda Carter .... Susan Lanier
Bobby Carter .... Robert Houston
Ethel Carter .... Virginia Vincent
Bob Carter .... Russ Grieve
Lynne Wood .... Dee Wallace
Doug Wood .... Martin Speer
Katie Wood .... Brenda Marinoff
Beauty .... Flora
The Beast .... Stricker
Jupiter .... James Whitworth
Mama .... Cordy Clark
Ruby .... Janus Blythe
Pluto .... Michael Berryman
Mars .... Lance Gordon
Mercury .... Arthur King
Fred .... John Steadman

Wes Craven's blood-and-bone frightener about an all-American family at the mercy of cannibal mutants is a satisfying piece of pulp with good drive-in and latenight prospects.

Reputedly based on genuine 17th century Scottish cave-dwellers, these savages terrorize a strip of Californian desert in which the Carters are stranded by a snapped axle. Hollywood movie-dog tradition is put to use in the forms of Beauty and the Beast, Carters' protective pets, which play their part in final outwitting of the marauders. But there's plenty of death before then, survivors of the symbolic struggle being the teenagers on both sides, one dog and a baby, on whose future (in the world or in the pot) much of the rival hysterias have centered.

Gratifying aspects are Craven's businesslike plotting and pacy cutting, and a script which takes more trouble over the stock characters than it needs. There are plenty of laughs, in the dialog and in the story's disarming twists.

The savages, bizarrely equipped with CB radio, are a grotesque-featured bunch with more extravagance than credibility. Janus Blythe hits a touching note as the defecting urchin who saves the WASP infant. —Simo.

Charleston
(ITALIAN-COLOR)

An Analysis Films release produced by Elio Scardamaglia. Directed by Marcello Fondato. Features entire cast. Screenplay, Scardamaglia, Fondato; music, Guido & Maurizio De Angelis; U.S. sound, Fred De Croce. No other technical credits provided. Reviewed at 5th Ave. Screening Room, New York Dec. 18, '78. (No MPAA Rating). Running time: **77 MINS.**

Charleston .... Bud Spencer
Inspector Watkins .... Herbert Lom
Texan .... James Coco

There are a couple of things Charleston could mean. It could refer to a dance in the 1920's jazz era, or it could mean Charleston, South Carolina. But in "Charleston," an Italian import shot in England and English, it is simply a convenient title to use for a picture, because pictures have to have titles, and it gives a bunch of stage extras a dance to perform to begin and end the film. The publicity release explains that it is an underground buzz-word for a murphy game — which is useful to know, because the picture itself doesn't impart that information. It's a tawdry 77 minutes.

The plot is still lodged in producer Elio Scardamaglia's and director Marcello Fondato's notebooks somewhere, because it hardly made it to the screen. Somebody steals a Gauguin from Inspector Watkins, played by Herbert Lom, who pinches Bud Spencer, a.k.a. Charleston, an international crook of wider girth than renown. In exchange for his freedom, Spencer will buy and or sell a yacht from James Coco.

Somehow or other — via a faked television show for Coco's benefit — Spencer gets his freedom and a lot of money, Lom gets his painting back, Coco gets the can.

Soundtrack proves interesting, since the visual is in English and the film has been optically dubbed in English. That makes for great fun in hearing the word before the actor gets to say it. —Jac.

Sammy Stops The World
(COLOR)

Reworked for Sammy Davis Jr. It's a bore.

Hollywood, Dec. 19.

A Special Event Entertainment release of an Ed Rood, Sr. production, produced by Mark Travis and Del Jack. Executive producers, Saul Barnett, Hillard Elkins. Stars Sammy Davis Jr. Directed by Mel Shapiro. Book, music and lyrics by Leslie Bricusse and Anthony Newley; choreography, Billy Wilson; camera (Deluxe color), David Myers; editor, William H. Yahraus; sound, Thomas W. Morse; associate producer, Robert Becker; assistant director, Jonathan Haze; set designer and costumes, Santo Loquasto; lighting, Pat Collins. Reviewed at the Music Hall, Beverly Hills, Dec. 19, 1978. (No MPAA rating). Running time: 105 MINS.

Littlechap . . . . Sammy Davis, Jr.
Baton Twirler . . . . Dennis Daniels
Schoolgirl . . . . Donna Lowe
Evie . . . . Marian Mercer

"Stop The World — I Want To Get Off," the Leslie Bricusse-Anthony Newley musical, has one or two memorable numbers, but it's mostly a poorly integrated, mediocre stage vehicle. Transforming it into a Sammy Davis Jr. vanity production and changing the name to "Sammy Stops The World" brought it down a further notch. And moving it out of the legit theatre onto the big screen with a quickie version makes it almost unbearably trite and boring. Commercial outlook for this Ed Rood Sr. production, being released by Special Event Entertainment appears to be nil. The 105-minute film could find a market via cable television, but for hungry CATV only.

The show tells the rags to riches story of a coffee vendor who marries the boss' daughter, or is forced to marry her after she becomes pregnant, and rises through the ranks as a commerce bigshot and later successful politician. He loves his wife, but fools around in his many travels only to realize that the perfect woman for him all along has been his wife.

Besides an off-key, clumsy chorus, "Sammy Stops the World," features Davis as the fortune seeker and Marian Mercer as his wife. For some reason, which only turns into confusion for the viewer, Mercer also plays Davis paramours.

By this point in his career, Davis' charades as the sterotypical hip black character have become so irritating, but withal, the man is a big talent, and he can deliver tunes with power. Unfortunately there are only brief moments where that talent emerges in this film. Emphasis, however, is brief.

Mel Shapiro directed the stage production as well as the film. His direction consists of placing a few cameras in front of the stage and one or two on the audience for reaction shots. To remind the film audience of how much fun they should be having, Shapiro has included a number of shots showing the theatre crowd enjoying themselves. They won't fool many.
—*Hege.*

Ballet Gayane
(COLOR)

Flat-footed.

Hollywood, Dec. 15.

Special Event Entertainment release, produced by Victor Stoloff. Directed by Horace King. Exec producers, Ed Rood, Sr., Saul Barnett. Camera (color), Paul Beeson; editor. H.G. Ink; sound (Dolby Stereo). Ray Prickett; costumes, Biruta Gage. Reviewed at Music Hall Theatre, Beverly Hills, Dec. 15, '78. (No MPAA rating) Running time: 110 MINS. (including two 10-minute intermissions.)

Gayane . . . . Larisa Tuisova
Giko . . . . Alexander Rumyantsev
Armen . . . . Genadi Barbanyov
Machak . . . . Maris Koristin

If technically and artistically perfect, "Ballet Gayane" would face enough boxoffice problems as a film of a stage presentation, especially a hard sell ballet. But it is neither technically nor artistically perfect.

Poorly lit and lacking depth and other cinematic support, the film constantly distracts from the beauty of this classic Aram Khachaturian ballet (in a new version created and choreographed by Boris Eifman), performed by the Ballet Company of Riga, Latvia, USSR.

Under such conditions, it's hard to judge the dancing itself. In the supporting roles, Genadi Barbanyov is especially good and Maris Koristin is powerful. But the leads, Larisa Tuisova and Alexander Rumyantsev seem uneven, except for a beautiful pas de deux at the end of Act II.

The company performs a rousing "Sabre Dance," the most familiar number from the work, but their shield-slapping triple encore is a bit hammy. There is, in fact, a lot happening on stage that appears terribly camera-conscious and conductor Alexander Vilumanis gets absolutely carried away when the lens is on him. —*Har.*

Confidences Pour Confidences
(Confidences For Confidences)
(FRENCH-COLOR)

Paris, Dec. 26.

GEF/CCFC release of Albina Production TF1 production. Features entire cast. Directed by Pascal Thomas. Screenplay, Thomas, Jacques Lourcelles; camera (Eastmancolor), Renan Polles; editor, Nathalie Lafaurie; music, Vladimir Cosma. Reviewed at Salle Ponthieu, Paris, Dec. 14, '78. Running time, 110 MINS.

Emile . . . . Daniel Ceccaldi
Mother . . . . Laurence Ligneres
Gabriel . . . . Michel Galabru
Brigitte . . . . Anne Caudry
Pierrette . . . . Carole Jacquinot
Florence . . . . Elisa Servier
Francois . . . . Ogor Lafaurie

Pascal Thomas displayed a sure-footed feel for youthful adaptation in his early films, be it teenage boys in "The Zozo's" or a precocious country girl in "Don't Cry With Your Mouth Full." After these promising films he embarked on two disastrous satirical pix, "Chef's Soup" and "Sea Urchin In the Pocket." Now he goes back to his early bent in this saga of the life of a lower middle class shopkeeping family.

It covers 15 years as one of three daughters looks back on her family and personal life. This memory format allows for shifting back and forth in time from her days from about five to seven and then from about 17 to 25. Film also avoids sentimentality and mainly shows the family unit in action and its effects on the girls and theirs on the parents and the eventual breakaway of the children to their own lives.

Non-pro Anne Caudry should be heard from on the local film scene. She is fresh, dauntless and effective as a girl who goes ahead to have a baby and refuses to marry the father. One sister marries when she is pregnant but ends with a nervous breakdown and the other is content to marry too after pregnancy and just go on having kids.

Thomas keeps this from falling into genre family comedy and geneeration gap pitches. But it lacks some of the edge, unpredictability and good spirits of his first two film son youthful adaptation. Film should find audiences at home and also rates foreign playoff on its accumulation of insights into the evergreen subject of family ways and adaptability.

There is an understanding grandfather who helps the storytelling heroine understand herself a bit more. There are several anecdotal aspects that often enhance characterization but sometimes are too forced as the sister with the breakdown doing a frowzy housewife scene when her husband brings a mistress to dinner.

Daniel Ceccaldi gives a warm, knowing performance as the weak but loving father and others are also effective in this generally winning look at large slices of ordinary family life. If theatrical chances abroad are more for general playoff, tv possibilities are also there in this sometimes slow but always revealing film about the family as social crucible. There are some extraneous characters but most fit into this odyssey of a girl's way to maturity. —*Mosk.*

Martin Et Lea
(Martin and Lea)
(FRENCH-COLOR)

Paris, Dec. 26.

MK2 Diffusion release of Les Productions De La Gueville production. Features entire cast. Directed by Alain Cavalier. Screenplay, Cavalier, Isabelle Ho, Xavier Saint-Macary; camera (Eastmancolor), Jean-Francois Robin; editor, Joelle Hache. Reviewed at Celtec, Paris, Dec. 12, '78. Running time, 92 MINS.

Lea . . . . Isabelle Ho
Martin . . . . Xavier Saint Macary
Lucien . . . . Richard Bohringer
Viviane . . . . Cecile La Bailly
Wolf . . . . Louis Navarre
Father . . . . Pham Q' Tri
Leila . . . . Zina Delouange
Inspector . . . . Francois Berlean

It may be coincidence, but a few films lately, including this one, are concentrating on couples, blending pro and non-pro thesps and going in more for a series of vignettes, usually separated by dissolves, than a tighter narrative structure. The relations are probed and commented on.

"Martin and Lea" appears more a psycho drama than a fulfilling film. Pic deals with an ill assorted couple that finally gets over moral and personal problems to end up a real couple with a baby on the way Director Alain Cavalier and the people playing the couple, Isabelle Ho, non-pro, and Xavier Saint Macary, a pro, wrote the script together.

Trio limn the girl as a sort of procurer for a mysterious man with plenty of money. She sets up teenagers for love trysts with him. Her apartment is taken care of, as well as money, by the man, but she never touches anything the girls get from him. A form of evasiveness. She is Vietnamese but brought up in France. Her lover is a worker studying to be a classical singer.

They first have a one night stand and he leaves. But he comes back and finally moves in. They spat when he criticizes her life after love has bloomed. She goes back to her father. Meanwhile a 16-year-old girl, realizing she is just a prostie and this is not a game, for she is the favorite of the man who keeps the Vietnamese girl, commits suicide to jolt all to reality.

Too much of the film is illustrative of ideas. For example, the suicide as a catalyst is somewhat too sketchy. The unlucky girl is only lightly filled in as a foil rather than in depth. However, it is true teenage suicide is growing in the Western world and she, of Arab origin, may be aware of racism and her previous refusal to admit her actions.

It makes the film ambivalent but it does have good playing, especially by Ho as the woman who finally faces up to her wooly morality after going back to her Vietnamese origins. Xavier Saint Macary is acceptable as the good natured would-be singer. But it is not clear if he is supposed to be as bad a singer as he seems.

At any rate, there is unobtrusive but observant direction from Cavalier for his seventh film. Pic could find festival outings and specialized interest at home. It is somewhat diffuse for foreign climes where it would need most careful handling to find selective youthful audiences on its refusal to moralize in indicating the drifting mores of the times. —*Mosk.*

The Extras
(HONG KONG-COLOR)

Hong Kong, Dec. 13.
A Bang Bang Films release of a Film Force Productions. Directed by Yim Ho. Screenplay, Yim Ho, Philip Chan, Ronny Yu; music, Joseph Koo, James Wong; editor, Wong Yee Shin; camera (color), Johnny Ko. Reviewed at Queen's Theatre, Hong Kong, Dec. 10, '78. Running Time: **87** MINS.
Cast: James Yi Lui, Idi Chan, Ken Cheng, Tsang Kong.

"The Extras" was made for HK$650,000 in 40 days but the production looks like a million dollars. It's the third attempt of Bang Bang Productions, the first directional debut of tv man Yim Ho on the big screen and another contemporary Cantonese comedy in the Michael Hui style, mainly made for the Asian market and Chinatown circuits abroad.

It's a good example of ensemble work by Film Force and is more than just a one joke comedy. The film strives to show the hardships of a simple movie extra and in the process wins the underdog compassion of the audience. The storyline revolves around accident-prone James Yi Lui who dreams of being a movie star but has to start from the "extra" category. Lui's movie career is marred by a series of mishaps and accidents that are meant to be funny.

As can be expected of a local commercial venture, it mixes zany humor with old fashioned slapstick mechanics that go primarily after the amplified guffaw. But the film sparkles with drive, imagination and style, the type that masterfully orchestrates both laughter and empathy for the hero.

Liu gives a sensitive and memorable performance. Supporting him in a romantic sub plot is tv starlet Idi Chan who makes a charming heroine.

"The Extras" is lighthearted, and the jokes are in good taste. There's sentiment, warmth, verbal and visual humor but most important is that it has "heart." "The Extras" may have limited legs in foreign countries but the film is unique in the sense that though basically a Cantonese comedy, the approach, the direction and feel can be labelled as western. "The Extras" is being released for the Christmas season and the local film industry is watching closely to see whether this style of comedy is acceptable to locals used to just physical humor. —*Mel.*

Les Chemins de L'Exil, ou Les Dernieres Annees de Jean Jacques Rousseau
(The Roads Of Exile)
(FRENCH-COLOR)

London, Nov. 30.
A TFI-SSR-Telecip-BBC-RTB- SRC-TV60 production. Directed by Claude Goretta. Features entire cast. Screenplay, Georges Haldas, Claude Goretta; camera (color), Philippe Rousselot; editor, Joele van Effenterre; art directors, Jacques Bufnoir, Enrique Sonois; costumes, Jean-Yves Tavernier; sound, Daniel Ollivier, Pierre Gamet. Reviewed at the National Film Theatre, London, Nov. 29, '78. Running time: **200 MINS.**
Jean Jacques Rousseau .. Francois Simon
Therese .... Dominique Labourier
Bernardin Saint-Pierre ..... Roland Bertin
Diderot .... Michel Berto
Prince de Conti .... Garbiel Cattand
Madame d'Houdetot .. Martine Chevallier
Wintzenreid ....Sylvain Clement
Lord Keith .... William Fox

Claude Goretta's account of the last years of Rousseau, which ran well over three hours at its premiere screening, is shaped more like a dissertation than a narrative. Made for tv, "The Roads Of Exile" will appeal more to students of philosophy and literature than to film buffs, and nontheatrical earnings are pic's steadiest prospects.

Rousseau is forced to leave France in 1762 when his latest book, "Emile," is denounced and burnt. He ekes out his exile successively in Switzerland, Prussia and England, hounded by the church for his alleged anti-Christian writings, and by the neighbors on account of his non-espoused companion, Therese, and his habit of dressing like an old woman.

As years go by, Rousseau's naive insistence that his rectitude will triumph over politics turns to querulous persecution mania. Dramatic development is slow, and his stages of deterioration predictable as the tale unwinds in concentric circles.

Goretta's special filmmaking qualities, evident in his last feature, "The Lacemaker," make "The Roads of Exile" similarly watchable: clear, unpretentious composition, uncluttered dialog, and a painstaking eye for naturalistic detail in settings and performances. Devotees of the earlier pic, however, will find this long haul unrewarding, since the self-ponderings of a finally tiresome old man are less moving than the sight of a young girl declining into madness. Appreciation of the lengthy voice-overs depends on viewer's desire to learn more about Rousseau's pre-Marxist socialism. For those with such appetite, the film delivers handsomely.—*Simo.*

Just Crazy About Horses
(DOCU-COLOR)

Horses as honorific ritual of rich. Nicely done but play-dates highly selective.

A Fred Baker Films Release, produced and written by Tim Lovejoy and Joe Wemple. Directed by Lovejoy, Wemple and Victor Kanefsky; camera (color), Peter Stein; additional photography, Cotter Watt, Ted Churchill, Mike Lerme; editor, Samuel D. Pollard; music, Sam Waymon. Narrated by Tammy Grimes. Reviewed at Guild Theatre, N.Y., Dec. 24, '78. (MPAA Rating: PG). Running time: 105 MINS.

A lively documentary look at mankind's obsession with thoroughbred horseflesh, "Just Crazy About Horses" confines itself exclusively to one human breed — the uppercrust racing and husbandry set that alternately views horse riding as (1) an aristocratic social ritual, and (2) as a million-dollar investment business-cum-hobby.

Considering this narrow focus, it could have been a lot more incisive, never going beyond a kind of gentle irony to show the quirks and ultimate irrelevance of the socialite horse crowd. In balance though, it does a good job of documenting a little known way of life and leisure and — in the case of a look at the workings of a stud farm — the intimate workings of assembly-line equine sex. Commercial prospects are specialized at best, and will be maximized at the non-theatrical level.

The film, produced and written by Tim Lovejoy and Joe Wemple (both codirecting with Victor Kanefsky), begins with a high stakes auction (a mare credited with great "residual values in her ovaries") that shows the kind of money involved, then follows through with glimpses of the Saratoga race circuit, manorial fox hunts, equitation competitions and the matings, births and occasional tragedies that horseflesh is heir to.

The focus is decidedly less on the animals, though, than it is on the rituals that surround them. Net impression, via casual conversation with legions of women who look like Katharine Hepburn and men who cultivate the affectations of British squires, is one of a society dedicated to isolating itself from the present and spending limitless cash to do so. Where the film does fall down is in not considering the socialite set's "non-horse" everyday existence, implying by default that this obsession is the guiding force in their lives.

What the film chooses to show — accompanied by a gloriously mocking narration by Tammy Grimes — does make a pretty case for obses-sion. Thus there's virtual ostracism for any foxhunter caught referring to "hounds" as "dogs," banishment for anyone talking about a "bark" (hounds "speak" in these circles), and a fair sampling of society matrons willing to spend the off-season on crutches, waiting for their next chance to break another pelvis the following year (one woman, paralyzed in a fall, strapped herself to a horse for one final ride).

Most eye-opening segment is the aforementioned tour of a stud-farm, where a stallion's one-time services cost a mare's owner $33,000 and the entire mating is choreographed by a half-dozen human assistants. Not for the squeamish, the scene is a powerful look at the extremes business will go to in harnessing nature for its own profit, and it effectively underscores one of the major points of the film. Technical aspects are okay, although the 35m blowup is often overly grainy and a mock-Bacharach soundtrack score frequently makes the pic sound like an institutional short subject. —*Step.*

1979

Martin
(COLOR)

Gruesome vampire pic now takes route of midnight shows.

Hollywood, Dec. 27.

A Libra Films release of a Laurel Group presentation. Produced by Richard Rubinstein. Features entire cast. Written and directed by George A. Romero. Camera (color). Michael Gornick; editor, Romero; music. Donald Rubinstein; sound, Tony Buba; special effects and make-up, Tom Savini. No other credits available. Reviewed at Royal Theatre, West L.A., Dec. 27, '78. (MPAA Rating: R.) Running time: **95 MINS.**

Martin . . . . John Amplas
Cuda . . . . Lincoln Maazel
Christina . . . . Christine Forrest
Mrs. Santini . . . . Elayne Nadeau
Arthur . . . . Tom Savini
Housewife victim . . . . Sarah Venable
Train victim . . . . Fran Middleton
Lewis . . . . Al Levitsky

It seems reasonable to guess that there has never been a vampire-themed film quite like "Martin." George A. Romero, who turned over a lot of boxoffice dollars along with audience stomachs with his 1968 release, "Night Of The Living Dead," returns here with an alternately absorbing and repelling study of a teen-aged bloodsucker on the prowl in rural Pennyslvania. "Martin" bowed earlier this year in midnight bookings in Gotham, a pattern that will be repeated in L.A., and worked extremely well for "Night." Given the clientele that frequents such unspoolings, b.o. prospects seem lucrative, although it will be a slow accretion.

A Pittsburgh-based auteur who wrote, directed, edited and appeared in "Martin," Romero is more than a simple purveyor of graphic blood-and-guts footage. He is dealing with some stimulating themes, from teenage sexual angst to the cajoleries of radio talk-show hosts, in a manner significantly more sophisticated than his earlier pic.

Title character in "Martin" is a supposed 84-year-old vampire (played with disturbing realism by John Amplas) whose youthful visage has survived his escape from Rumania through his contemporary journey to Braddock, Pa., where grandfather Lincoln Maazel is determined to drive out "Nosferatu," with Martin as the last remaining relative afflicted with the family curse.

This urban vampire kills not with his teeth, but with prepackaged razor blades, neatly slicing veins and arteries for his mealtime pleasure. Martin's predilection is for older, dark-haired femmes, but he also makes do with a couple of winos, or the boyfriend he discovers seducing one of his would-be victims.

Voice-over explanation is supplied by Martin's on-air chats with a local radio gabfest, whose host dubs him "The Count" and sees in him a way to hypo ratings. It's a sly comment on this form of ersatz pop psychology, as Martin explains his inability to handle the "sexy stuff" with girls.

An affair with neighbor Elayne Nadeau doesn't help straighten him out, and Martin continues in his sanguinary ways until Maazel puts an end to his grandson and the film with the familiar stake through the heart.

Romero is still limited by apparently low budgets, as the over-miked sound, generally poor lab work and extensive use of nonpros suggest. But he has inserted some sepia-toned flashback scenes of Martin in Rumania that are extraordinarily evocative, and his direction of the victimization scenes shows a definite flair for suspense.

The insistence on bloody and dramatic closeups remains, however, and "Martin" contains scenes that make "The Deer Hunter" look like a G-rated picture. Romero's following will probably eat this up (no pun intended), but it's a limiting factor on what would otherwise be a mass-market chiller.—*Poll.*

Les Heros N'Ont Pas Froid Aux Oreilles
(Heroes Are Not Wet Behind the Ears)
(FRENCH-COLOR)

Paris, Jan. 9.

SND release of Atya Productions-International Film Promotion, Terminus production. Features entire cast. Directed by Charles Nemes. Screenplay, Gerard Jugnot. Nemes; camera (Eastmancolor), Etienne Faudet; editor, Marie-Sophie Dubus; music, Jacques Delaporte. Reviewed at Club 13, Paris, Dec. 28, '78. Running time: **83 MINS.**
Jean . . . . Daniel Auteuil
Pierre . . . . Gerard Jugnot
Karine . . . . Anne Jousset
Jacqueline . . . . Patricia Karim
Berthier . . . . Henri Guybet

A flock of new directors with more personal, small-budgeted films, brought off by advance aid and tv backing, added to the over 200 pix made in France this past year. Not too many unusual talents were unearthed, though a couple drew attention, as will Charles Nemes for "Heroes Are Not Wet Behind The Ears."

Luc Beraud showed a free-wheeling invention in a tale of a hungup writer, albeit somewhat indulgent, while Marc Grunebaum displayed a solid flair for detailing adolescent pains and exploitation in "Like a Turtle on Its Back" and "The Adoption" respectively. Now Nemes enters the promising category though none as yet can rate New New Wave tags or cries of a local pic renaissance.

"Heroes" delves into a certain petty side of French middleclass character. Two near thirtyish provincial cousins working in a bank together and living in an inherited apartment in Paris are a tatty duo indeed.

They make snide passes at a woman teller, insult the man she lunches with, display cowardice and cynicism. Nemes may lack a sure hand as yet for more pointed satire or comic impertinence but he manages to stretch this essentially sketchy material to an acceptable 83 minutes.

There are some human sides to this odd couple though survival and self protection are uppermost. After a scare, when the bank alarm does not work and a sinister character comes in, they take to testing the alarm, when fixed, until the boss gives them a weekend off.

They leave for the country in a battered rented car and manage to get a comely girl hitchiker away from another motorist with mean means. They head back to Paris, end up seducing her and finally taking her home when they see an ad in a paper and realize she is a minor. They get a reward adn even want to be nice and spend some of it on the girl. But she tells them off.

Gerard Jugnot and Daniel Auteil are effective as the creepy cousins with Anne Jousset adding a human, generous note as the girl. Film just misses a needed comic punch and repeats effects after its characters are established.

It might tickle local fancies, for the French like to laugh at rather than with characters, and even find some playoff abroad on its limning of simple types who yet comment on a certain aspect of French character. However it lacks the bite and revelation for more demanding attention. It copped a press prize at the Trouville Young French Cinema Fest in France last summer.
—*Mosk.*

Dove Vai In Vacanza?
(Where Are You Going On Holiday?)
(ITALIAN-COLOR)

Rome, Dec. 23.

A Cineriz release of a Rizzoli film. Produced by Gianni Hecht Lucari. Directed by Mauro Bolognini, Luciano Salce, Alberto Sordi. Stars Ugo Tognazzi, Stefania Sandrelli, Paolo Villaggio, Anna Maria Rizzoli, Alberto Sordi, Anna Longhi. Screenplays, Ruggero Maccari and Jaja Fiastri; Furio Scarpelli and Sandro Continenza; Roberto Sonego and Alberto Sordi; camera (Eastmancolor), Luciano Tovoli, Danilo Desideri, Sergio D'Offizi. Reviewed at Adriano Theatre, Rome, Dec. 23, '78. Running Time: **167 MINS.**

"Saro tutta per te"
(I Will Be All Yours)
Enrico . . . . Ugo Tognazzi
Giuliana . . . . Stefania Sandrelli
"Sì buana"
(Yes, Buana)
Wilson . . . . Paolo Villaggio
Margherita . . . . Anna Maria Rizzoli

"Le vacanze intelligenti"
(Intelligent Vacation)
Remo . . . . Alberto Sordi
Agostina . . . . Anna Longhi

Released in Italy in time for the holiday trade, "Where Are You Going On Vacation?" offers three films for the price of one. All three segments are related more or less with vacations and are more or less funny, but each distinctly reflects the special brand of humor of its main star: Tognazzi, Villaggio and Sordi.

The film should touch ground in those countries where Italian comedy is popular. Unfortunately audiences will have to wade through the first two stories to get to the real gem of this troika.

The first "mini" film directed by Mauro Bolognini — "I Will Be All Yours" — is a sex comedy starring Ugo Tognazzi once again in the role of a frustrated Latin lover. Enrico (Tognazzi), a 50-year old dentist, decides to spend his vacation with his now emancipated young ex-wife in her present lover's villa. Arriving for the sole purpose of taking her to bed, he is continually thwarted by the arrival of house guests, Giuliana's disinterest and finally his own failure to perform.

Intended to be a wry comment on the Latin lover's plight after feminism, opening seg never really scores despite the valiant attempts by Tognazzi and Stefania Sandrelli.

In Paolo Villaggio's "Yes, Buana," a slapstick comedy, the vacation scene shifts to Kenya where Villaggio is in charge of a safari trip. Lured into illegally bagging a lion for a well-developed client (Anna Maria Rizzoli), who is really only interested in knocking off her husband in a "hunting accident" to collect the insurance, Villaggio romps through the corny scenes with great charm.

Especially comical is Villaggio's "native" aide who in reality is a black man born and raised in Rome. He not only speaks with a heavy Roman accent, but is struck with nostalgia for the Eternal City and sings Roman folk songs around the campfire (gas-operated, of course).

The best of the threesome is saved for last with Alberto Sordi's "Intelligent Vacation." Sordi—this time directing himself — plays the kind of character in this comedy of manners that has made him famous: Remo, the Italian greengrocer and his plump signora (delightfully played by Anna Longhi) are sent off on an "intellectual" vacation prepared by their three college-age kids who think their parents need some culture.

The image of Sordi in pointed brown and white shoes that even immigrants don't wear anymore and Longhi, an Italian mama worthy of the name, traipsing thorugh the Etruscan tombs, painfully listening to a modern music concert in Florence and wandering wide-eyed through the preposterous modern art exhibits at the Venice Biennale (a pen of sheep with purple spots on their backs) is **not only side-splitting but a wonderful comment on the world of "Kultur" so completely out of touch with the common man.** —*Argo.*

Primo Amore
(First Love)
(ITALIAN-COLOR)

Rome, Dec. 26.

A United Artists Europa release, produced by Pio Angeletti and Adriano de Micheli for Dean Films. Stars Ugo Tognazzi, Ornella Muti. Directed by Dino Risi. Screenplay by Ruggero Maccari; camera (Technospes). Tonino delli Colli; art director. Luciano Ricceri; editor, Alberto Gallitti; music, Riz Ortolani. Reviewed at Cinema Gioiello, Rome, Dec. 26, '78. Running time: **112 MINS.**

Picchio .... Ugo Tognaazi
Renata .... Ornella Muti
Lucia .... Caterina Boratto
Director .... Mario del Monaco

The twilight years of a live entertainer and his last fling with a young beauty have been a recurrent theme on film for years. As the title suggests, Dino Risi goes one step further to make it a first-time love affair for the hale and hearty vaud vet entering the show biz rest home Villa Serena.

Basic end-of-the-road theme has been cropping up with increasing frequency in Italian cinema as a generation or more of top stars and career helmers come to grips morosely with the shattering possibility of moving offstage as their names come off the marquees for all times.

Risi's direction and Ugo Tognazzi's thesping give "First Love" more than a bittersweet tone. Tognazzi as the newcomer to Villa Serena portrays the retired vaud comedy star with such energy and self-confidence that his fling with Renata (Ornella Muti) and their elopement to the big city give the first 70 minutes of the Dean production a good dose of heart and entertainment. The inmates of Villa Serena, most of whom are ex-legit and vaude retirees, coupled with scripter Ruggero Maccari's rich vein of sit-coms, in which the futility of show biz comeback hopes is always prominent, shower promise on this latest Dino Risi pic — until the elopement is consummated.

From there on the script goes out with the tide as Tognazzi bumbles pathetically and unconvincingly through his last big separation check without a chance to revive a long-extinct live revue or plus marry the pretty resthome attendant thirsting for sex, romance and fame.

Second act is patched together with irrevelancies, no longer funny or genuinely sentimental. Perhaps Risi should have confined the entire script within the four walls of

the rest home, where the director (Mario del Monaco) attempts to temper Belle Epoque fantasies with rigid discipline.

Muti is merely a foil for Tognazzi's slick comedy role and the foil snaps with her quickly acquired elegance and inevitable infidelity — to end up as a strip act on late night tv. In Act II, Risi overplays the obvious and timeworn, in a over-length ploy before bringing his exvaud star back to the resthome — alone.

As undone in the second half, the UA Europa release will find its natural markets in the Mediterranean Basin, Latin America and some Far Eastern situations. All technical credits are plus factors. —*Werb.*

Dante, akta're foer Hajen
(Dante, Mind The Shark)
(SWEDISH-COLOR)

Malmoe, Dec. 20.

A Gunnar Hoglund Film Productions AB/AB Europa Film production, Europa Film release. Features entire cast. Script Linder and Gunnar Hoglund, based on Bengt Linder novel. Directed by Hoglund. Camera (Eastmancolor), Kalle Bergholm; music, Bjoern Jason Lind, Lasse Berghagen; executive producer, Stig Skoglund; production manager, Michael Hoglund; editor, Gunnar Hoglund. Reviewed at Rio, Malmoe, Dec. 20, '78. Running time, **100 MINS.**

Dante .... Jan Ohlsson
Tvaersan .... Ulf Hasseltorp
Police Sergeant .... John Harrison
The Shark .... Carli Tornehave
Annika .... Lillemor Ohlsson

The "Dante" books are popular juvenile reading in Sweden, all dealing with young teenager Dante and his friend Tvaersan's local Crime Busters' Society, always solving crimes that frustrate the ridiculous police.

Film could be rated JG (for Juvenile Guidance) although the parent generations might tire a little of director Hoglund's failure at editing his own work into a faster narrative style and at tuning his two otherwise charming juvenile leads (Jan Ohlsson and Ulf Hasseltorp) down from the loudness of their vocal exuberance.

John Harrison has funny moments as the police sergeant and Carli Tornehave is comically mean as the jewel thief who runs afoul of the smarter boys.

In cameos as Dante's parents, Boerje Ahlsted and Christina Schollin drop out of the action all too soon. Film has a few scenes of violence not consistent with an otherwise humorously told story, but they could easily be cut to make "Dante" a fair sales item internationally on the juvenile cinema circuit. —*Kell.*

Da Lang Tao Sha
(Great Waves Purify The Sand)
(CHINESE-B&W)

Berlin, Dec. 18.

A Pearl River Studio Film Production, Canton. Features entire cast. Directed by Yi Lin. Screenplay, Chu Tao-Nan, Yu Pin Kuen, Yi Lin; camera, Liu Tsin-Tang; sets, Tiang Tsin; editing, Tan King-Long; music, Che Ming; sound, Li Lie-Hung. Reviewed at Berlin Cine-Center Screening Room, Dec. 18, '78. Running time: **120 MINS.**
With Tsin Kung Cho, Yu Yang, Ku Ta-Ming, Tien Jui Chao, Yang Ju-Kuan.

Shortly after Yi Lin's "Great Waves Purify the Sand" (1963-64) was completed, it disappeared into the vaults until 1977 when it could be released. The reason was the subject matter: it presented "intellectuals" fighting for the liberation of China in 1925 in Jinan, the capital of Shandong Province. This was helmer Yi Lin's own story, he himself one of the "intellectuals" who joined the Red Army early in fighting for liberation and social change. The pic was refused release in 1964 due to the hot discussion then about the nature of a cinematic theme and the kind of individual standing in the middle of the story.

In the mid-1920s four "intellectuals" meet on a boat and form a pact of friendship. In Canton the revolution has already begun under a new government, and the Northern Campaign under the motto "Against Imperialism and Feudalism" is being prepared; the Revolutionary Government consists of The Kuomintang and the Communists. The four youths have joined the revolution after witnessing oppression under the War Lords at home.

In the course of their studies the youth come in contact with two contrasting revolutionary leaders. Also, two of them support the revolutionary principles of Sun Yat-Sen, while the third sides with the masses in a more direct contact, and the fourth hopes to help form a national elite circle. The historical events as depicted actually took place.

Gradually the "intellectuals" go different ways, following such key historical events as the Shanghai Massacre, Chiang Kai-Shek's move to the Right, and the betrayal of Wang Jin-Wei and the radical Left. Then, after the Wuchan Incident, the youths find themselves fighting each other on different ideological fronts — the pact is broken with little hope of reconciliation.

The upshot is that one of the youths simply becomes a painter, an artist minus the drive to work for social change and a self-determined future. Another attempts to assassinate a former teacher in a counter-revolutionary movement, and is killed. The two remaining youths, supported by Mao's writings (particularly "Class Analysis of Chinese

Society"), join the revolutionary Peasants Army and head out for the Jing-Gang mountains, the corner of China from which the "Long March" is to begin many years later.

"Great Waves Purify the Sand" (in the West German cinema release it's simply referred to as "Gold and Sand") presents a valuable chronological record in fiction form of the Communist revolutionary movement of the 1920s, made by a film director who was an eye-witness to the events depicted. Well acted and staged, it is a convincing portrait of the times with subtleties in the narrative and characterizations. Credits are good cut above the average. A pic for both Chinese history and film society buffs.
—*Holl.*

Red Blossoms in the
Tian Mountains
(CHINESE-COLOR)

Berlin, Dec. 18.

A Sian Film Studio Production, Sian. Directed by Tsu Wei. Screenplay, Ou Lin. Only credits available. Reviewed at Berlin Cine-Center Screening Room, Dec. 18 '78. Running time: **100 MINS.**

Made in 1964, Tsu Wei's "Red Blossoms in the Tian Mountains" focuses on the fate of a woman elected to lead a workers' brigade in Sian in Northwest China, the autonomous region of the Uigur. A shepherdess named Ashal, a former serf, finds herself in the difficult position of responsibility for an agricultural collective — the communal effort is not only unacceptable to the independent, richer herdsmen, but also frowned upon by her husband, Aikuli.

The conflict on the family side rises quickly to the surface. Ashal wants to better herself and the community, while Aikuli prefers a nonpolitical housewife and eventually a self-sufficient business of his own. During the election for the brigade-leader he refuses to vote, and accuses Ashal of voting for herself. The envious and richer shepherds, meanwhile, plot through Aikuli to destroy the collective by influencing him to sell community-owned grass on the black market for private gain — when the crime is revealed, the emancipated wife leaves her husband's tent in protest.

Another enemy of the brigade schemes with the local veterinarian to wipe out their success overnight during a wintry cold spell. The lives of the sheep are endangered when the shed is left open to the elements, followed by falsely administered injections to the sick animals by the vet — all of which the brigade-leader gradually sees through. After unmasking the culprits, she is shot by the fleeing culprit and wounded — but wins the confidence of her husband in the end.

A pic more for Women's Lib groups than film buffs, but entertaining all the same and worth a look-see. —*Holl.*

Slaegten
(The Heritage)
(DANISH-COLOR)

Copenhagen, Dec. 21.

A Just Betzer, A/S Panorama production, A/S Panorama released. Features entire cast. Script by Anders Refn, Flemming Quist Moeller, based on Gustav Wild novel. Directed by Anders Refn. Camera (Eastmancolor, Panavision) Mikael Salomon; art director, Helge Refn; music, Kasper Winding; editors, Anders Refn, Kasper Schyberg; production manager, Lars Kolvig; costumes, Gitte Kolvig. Reviewed at the Saga, Copenhagen, Dec. 21, '78. Running time, **117 MINS.**
Baron Helmuth . . . . .Jens Okking
Baroness Alvilda . . . . Helle Hertz
Dowager Baroness . . . . Bodil Udsen
The Vicar . . . . .Poul Reichhardt
Count Scheele . . . . .Stefan Ekman

Towards the end of the 19th century, faint stirrings of social revolt hardly creased the surface of law and order calm on Baron Helmuth's estate, while the Baron's personal life in itself could cause the most violent outbreaks of ugliness and disaster. The vulgar bull of a baron has just taken a bride to ensure the heritage, but undoubtedly he loves her truly and is impressed by her elegant manners.

She holds no love for her new husband, however. She has married him for the security and respectability he could provide for herself, a divorcee, and her 12-year-old daughter.

She drifts into a love affair with a house guest, her cousin who as a count stands well above the baron both socially and in manners. The dowager baroness nurses strong suspicions and when she finally makes her son recognize that he is being cuckolded, the baron runs amuck and takes murderous revenge. A subplot has to do with the local vicar, who without any luck at all fights the demon of erotic passion within himself.

Director Anders Refn is probably the technically most skillful of all Danish filmmakers and his "The Heritage" is an obvious fest item plus a fairly good bet on the international commercial circuit. His film has it share of Bertolucci inspirations, but stands on its own in its insistence on seeing all its characters as frail subjects of a dark fate well beyond divine or social redemption.

In fact, Refn believes so much in the duality of everybody that audiences might find it hard to care very much about any of the leading men or women. Good playing, tightly reined by Refn, is however pro-

vided by Jens Okking as the baron, Helle Hertz as the baroness, Bodil Udsen as the rock solid, icy-hearted dowager baroness and Poul Reichhardt as the conscience-tormented vicar.

The epic sweep and suspense eludes Refn and his and Mikael Salomon's Panavision-shot frames often see without the inner connection dramatic coherence depends on. "The Heritage" remains, however, an impressive work, well worth the big money spent on its making by private investor Just Betzer and the State Film Institute. Handled carefully in the distribution outlets, the investment ought to pay off handsomely. —*Kell.*

Belfer
(ISRAELI-COLOR)

Tel Aviv, Dec. 23.

A Nachshon Films release. Produced by Izkah Shani, Josef Dimant. Directed by Igal Burstein. Stars Gadi Yagil. Screenplay, Igal Burstein, based on original story by Yossi Birstein; camera (color), Adam Greenberg; editors, Alain Jakobowitz; sets, Eytan Levy; music, Roni Weiss; title song performed by Sherri. Released in Tel Aviv, Dec. 23, '78. Running time: **87 MINS.**
Cast: Talia Shapira, Avner Hizkiahu, Hana Laszlo, Rafael Klatchkin, Jacques Cohen.

This unfunny comedy, released after compromises and conflicts which took over two years to settle, is one of the less successful achievements of the Israeli film industry. More so, since scripter-director Igal Burstein has been considered in the past, on the strength of a number of shorts he has directed, one of the promising talents here.

Script was awarded a hefty prize a couple of years ago, but continuous disputes over casting and nature of the film, culminating in warnings to the producer that prize may be denied if final product does not bear the stamp of the winning script, have plagued the production all along the way, leaving their marks in the film itself.

The story was supposed to pit against each other, in the context of modern Israel, life in kibbutz and life in the city. The leading character, Shlomo Belfer, born and raised in a kibbutz, dreams of wealth and riches outside, hoping to emulate his father's example and become an international playboy. As plot unravels, it should become apparent that kibbutz life, nowadays, isn't that idealistic any more, while capitalist success in town is acquired at the price of happiness.

The film falls for all the possible cliches in the book, with people falling in and out of love on first glance, and behaving in general at the level of a music-hall sketch. Hardly any direction is felt all through the story, and actors seem, in general, to grope in the dark, looking for the

right note to strike. A pity since at least some of them, such as Talia Shapira and Avner Hizkiahu, have the potential to offer much more.

Choice of camera angles and editing are erratic, and on the whole, the film fails to involve in any sense. It's not funny and it's not sad, the general feeling being that somehow, this is something one will want to forget in a hurry. —*Edna.*

Rock 'n' Roll
(ITALIAN-COLOR)

Rome, Dec. 24.

A Medusa release of a Cinemaster Production. Produced by Galliano Juso. Stars Rodolfo Banchelli, Rosaria Biccica, Macha Meril, Carlo Monni. Written and directed by Vittorio De Sisti. Camera (Eastman Color), Giovanni Ciarlo; music, Little Richard, Bill Haley, B.C. Corporation and the Darts. Reviewed at Supercinema, Rome, Dec. 24, '78. Running time: **97 MINS.**

Rock 'n' roll is alive and well and living in — of all places — Florence, Italy. Producer Galliano Juso has cashed in on both the popularity of "Saturday Night Fever" and the rock 'n' roll revival (Italy has just won the world r 'n' r crown for the fifth year in a row) with a film that stars Italy's rock 'n' roll darlings, Rosaria Biccica and Rodolfo Banchelli.

Although mainly a home-grown product, "Rock 'n' Roll" could find audiences outside Italy as well, especially in countries where the specialty was once firmly rooted.

"Rock 'n' Roll" deals with the present and includes footage from current dancing competitions, held regularly in central Italy. Following Biccica and Banchelli through the city, regional, national and international championships, the film was shot on location in discotheques and ballrooms from Florence to Ravenna.

Rock today is a far cry from the past. The bobby socks are gone. The dance has become a display of rhythmic acrobatics performed with a high degree of professionalism.

Camera work of couples in action is generally slick, with effective double image and slow motion shots. The rhythm — and the steps — are, however, repetitious. Long dance sequences needed more variation to check monotony.

The dances are 90 percent of the film, spliced by a feeble story line closely resembling "Saturday Night Fever." Banchelli (who plays himself) is fed up with his work in a clothes factory and takes refuge in dancing. He has troubles with his family, his girlfriend and his dance partner, Biccica, and near troubles with the law, but out on that dance floor, he's all smiles.

The scenes with Banchelli's family — a sister, mother, widowed aunt and hard-of-hearing grandmother

— are real comic relief, but the others seem like an after thought, pasted together as a prop for the dancing. Director Vittorio De Sisti had some veteran actors working for him (Macha Meril and Carlo Monni) but above all he had a promising newcomer in Banchelli. With a strong script, he might have uncovered a local Travolta. —*Argo.*

Angel Mine
(NEW ZEALAND-COLOR)

Wellington, N.Z., Dec. 20.

An ILA Film Productions release. Produced by David Blyth and Warren Sellers. Features entire cast. Written and directed by David Blyth. Camera (color), John Earnshaw; sound, Mike Westgate; editor, Phillip Howe; music, Mark Nicholas, played by Auckland Youth Orchestra, Charisma, Urban Road and Suburban Reptiles. Reviewed at Lido Cinema, Wellington, Dec. 20, '78. (NZCC rating R.18). Running time: **72 MINS.**
Cast: Derek Ward, Jennifer Redford.

No locally made film has caused more hullabaloo since the advent of the State-sponsored NZ Film Commission than David Blyth's "Angel Mine," which premiered in Auckland in November, and has since moved to other of the country's main cities.

It has been the cause of renewed urgings to the Minister of Internal Affairs Allan Highet to tighten censorship law, and to the Government in general to carefully watch how the taxpayers money is being spent in the new surge towards a developed local film industry.

Porn watchdog Patricia Bartlett, in particular, has been assiduous in penning letters to Government leaders and newspapers about what she sees as the degrading content of the film and the use of public money for such enterprises.

In fact, "Angel Mine," which has been made on a miniscule budget of about $30,000 and blown into 35m from original 16m footage, is much more than all the "put down" ballyhoo suggests.

Sensitively perceived and realized, if somewhat short in some areas on technical expertise, it is clearly a director's piece.

What it does is make a particularly strong statement about urban materialism and the corrosive nature of visual advertising in the context of the relationship — sexual and otherwise — of a suburban couple.

Highly amusing as well as thought provoking, Blyth has extracted good performances from his actors, Derek Ward and Jennifer Redford, who finally are unable to separate their fantasy lives from reality.

Despite the relative youth of 22-year-old Blyth, "Angel Mine" is as mature and entertaining an analysis on this theme as has emerged in film here, and could do well on film festival circuits — if not in commercial cinemas.

It also joins "State of Siege," another shortish film made by the younger generation of NZ filmmakers, and which won the Golden Hugo award at the recent Chicago Film Festival, as one of the most important movies yet made under the film Commission's banner.

—*Nic.*

Alpenbaringen
(The Revelation)
(NORWEGIAN-COLOR)

Berlin, Dec. 14.

A Norsk Film Production, Oslo. Features entire cast. Directed by Vibeke Loekkeberg. Screenplay, Loekkeberg, Terje Kristiansen; camera (color), Paul Rene Roestad. Reviewed at Arsenal-Kino, Berlin, Dec. 14, '78. Running time: **81 MINS.**
With Marie Rakvam, Wilfred Briestrand, Bonne Gauguin, Wilhelm Lunds, Vibeke Loekkeberg, Terje Kristiansen.

Vibeke Loekkeberg's "The Revelation" won respect and attention at the last Berlin Forum of Young Cinema as one of the best "women's pix" of the year. It was also unspooled at the Film Market in Cannes, then made another appearance in Luebeck at the recent Northern Film Days in November.

It's about a woman, a housewife, who has reached the end of her usefulness — after raising a son, she sits at home alone because her husband is busy at work and she can't hold a job with any feeling of self-assurance. Pic opens with an embarrassing moment as a saleswoman peddling some odd piece of consumer junk and her subsequent dismissal; the husband then suggests that she take a holiday on her own, which she does but still can't fit in with the social life around her (she's fat and a bit too self-conscious). But she does talk with an emancipated woman at the resort hotel, who puts a few new thoughts in her head.

Upon returning home prematurely, she finds her husband "romancing the secretary" (another lonely type, it appears) and she pulls up roots completely. Paying a visit home to her elderly parents, she sees where the future is leading — the father is bedridden and senile, the mother worn down — then makes a stab at emancipation by partying with an old chum and her boyfriends. Again, it ends in disaster — the husband comes and takes her home.

The final embarrassment is a clumsy attempt by the husband to get her back into bed. Thereafter, she takes to cleaning the house out of a certain empty, unfulfilling desperation. This final scene has been forecast by surreal mental flights of fantasy throughout the film. She has slipped into psychological passivity.

Highly recommended pic for Femme Helmer's Weeks. —*Holl.*

En vandring i solen
(A Walk In The Sun)
(SWEDISH-COLOR)

Malmoe, Dec. 20.

A Swedish Film Institute/HB Three Leaf Clover production, AB Europa Film release. Features entire cast. Script, based on Stig Claesson's novel, Bibi Edlund. Directed by Hans Dahlberg. Camera (Eastmancolor. 35m) Roland Lundin, Bertil Rosengren; production design, Mona Forssen; editor, Wic Kjellin; music, no credits; production planning, Bo Jonsson/Viking Film; in charge of production, Bengt Forslund; Greek locations supervisor, Francis Carabott. Reviewed at Rio, Malmoe, Dec. 20, '78. Running time: **96 MINS.**
Tore .... Goesta Ekman
Marion .... Inger Lise Rypdal
Ellen .... Margaretha Krook
Siv .... Sif Ruud
Vera .... Irma Christensson
George .... Kenneth Haigh

Something went sadly wrong here. Stig Claesson wrote a charming, funny-sad little novel about a young sports writer who seeks refuge from a washed-up love affair and from the Swedish winter by joining an ordinary charter tour to Cyprus where he starts out by drinking himself into a stupor, then into a spot of nude swimming on a public beach and through that into jail and on to a private asylum.

When he is returned to his hotel, the young woman tour guide is mad at him, some of his co-tourists are scandalized, others, notably three older women and a lazy Irishman befriend him. He now drinks only mineral water, renders his new friends various favors like taking long walks in their locally purchased shoes (new shoes cannot be brought into Sweden), falls in love with the guide, a reciprocated love instantly ended by the guide's accidental death by drowning.

The novel was written in a slightly off-beat style, highly humorous without losing touch with the essential everyday tragedy of the young man's predicaments.

In transferring this story into moving pictures, director Hans Dahlberg wants to parallel Stig Claesson's writing style, but winds up telling the story without any style, not even a conventional narrative style that might have worked.

Even though he gets wonderful help from Goesta Ekman who is perfect in the lead, Margaretha Krook as an amorously vigorous middle-aged lady and Sif Ruud and Irma Christensson as the goodhearted, rather helpless elderly ladies, Dahlberg fumbles every scene, serving flat and lukewarm champagne all the way. Norway's Inger Lise Rypdal, another pop songstress attempting the acting game, has neither looks, warmth nor talent for her role.

Commercial. prospects even at home would seem slight even though Ekman at present is an actor all Sweden has a love affair with.
—*Kell.*

Udhetim Ne Pranvere
(A Journey Into Spring)
(ALBANIAN-COLOR)

Berlin, Dec. 20.

An Albfilm Production, Tirana; world rights, Albania Film, Tirana. Features entire cast. Directed by Qerim Mata. Screenplay, Gjergj Zheji; camera (color), Pellumb Kallfa; art direction, Kleo Nini. Reviewed at Berlin Cine-Center Screening Room, Dec. 20, '78. Running time: **80 MINS.**
With Minella Borova, Liliana Kondakci, Nikolin Xhoja.

An Albanian musical comedy featuring a romance to boot, Qerim Mata's "A Journey into Spring" (1975) is a luscious color travelog through villages and country regions of Albania in springtime. The story is only a frame for the settings. and the various folkloric groups are mostly non-professional artists performing traditional dances and musical numbers.

A young femme member of the "Eagle" artistic ensemble is making her first journey through the country; her driver is a handsome young man, and the two fall innocently in love as they set out to join the ensemble already on tour. Along the way the couple meet the working people and farm-hands on the job and learn through experience how the population feel about their country, even to the point of defending it on the spot against possible invaders. Some disappointments in life and duty are also to be expected, and the film covers both sides of Socialist endeavor.

Pic is neatly lensed with several attractive landscape and nature shots, and the amateur folk groups are well worth a look-see. —*Holl.*

Waga Koi Wa Moenu
(My Love Has Been Burning)
(JAPANESE-B&W)

New Yorker Films release of a Shochiku production. Features entire cast. Directed by Kenji Mizoguchi. Screenplay, Yoshikata Yoda, Kaneto Shindo, based on story by Kogo Noda; camera (black and white), Kohei Sugiyama, Tomotaro Nashiki; music, Senji Ito; sound, Taro Takahashi, Takeo Kawakita; art direction, Hiroshi Mizutani, Dai Arakama, Jun'ichi Osumi; historical research, Sunao Kai; producers, Hisao Itoya, Kiyoshi Shimazu. Reviewed at New York screening room, Jan. 2, '79. (No MPAA rating). Running time: **84 MINS.**
Eiko Hirayama .... Kinuyo Tanaka
Kentaro Omoi .... Ichiro Sugai
Chiyo .... Mitsuko Mito
Ryuzo Hayase .... Eitaro Ozawa
Tochiko Kishida .... Kuniko Miyake
Prime Minister Inagaki .... Koreya Senda
State Councillor Ito .... Eijiro Tono

Although the feminist movement first made itself felt in Japan in 1884, which is the subject of Kenji Mizoguchi's 1949 film, "My Love Has Been Burning," it is little wonder that it made no headway immediately as Japan, itself, was just emerging from the feudalistic government of the shogunate and beginning to adopt some Western ideas. Mizoguchi's film, therefore, is as much about shifting political ideas as it is about the emergence of independent womanhood.

The heroine, a schoolteacher who has been influenced by a leading feminist, leaves home and goes to Tokyo to work with the newly-formed Liberal Party. When she realizes that the young man who heads the party, and with whom she has fallen in love, has male chauvinist ideas in his own personal approach to the male-female problem, she leaves him, to return home and promote women's rights through education. During her period in Tokyo she is falsely imprisoned for helping a female millhand who is raped and tries to burn down the mill. The servant becomes her companion in the final struggle for female rights.

As in all Mizoguchi films, the art direction is excellent with the historical research highlighting some of the absurdities of too-eager Japanese who can't wait to be Westernized. —*Robe.*

The North Avenue Irregulars
(COLOR)

Breezy Disney comedy that seems assured of potent b.o.

Hollywood, Jan. 3.

A Buena Vista release of a Walt Disney Production, produced by Ron Miller and Tom Leetch. Directed by Bruce Bilson. Features entire cast. Screenplay, Don Tait from book by Rev. Albert Fay Hill; camera (Technicolor), Leonard J. South; music, Robert F. Brunner; songs, Al Kasha and Joel Hirschhorn; editor, Gordon D. Brenner; art directors, John B. Mansbridge and Jack T. Collis; associate producer, Kevin Corcoran; set decorator, Norman Rockett; special effects, Eustance Lycett, Art Cruickshank, Danny Lee; stunt coordinator, Eddy Donno; titles, Art Stevens and Joe Hale; assistant director, Christopher Seiter; costumes, Chuck Keehne, Emily Sundby; sound, Bub Maffett. Reviewed at the Disney Studios, Burbank, Jan. 2, '79. (MPAA Rating: G.) Running time: **99 MINS.**

Michael Hill . . . . Edward Herrmann
Vickie . . . . Barbara Harris
Anne . . . . Susan Clark
Jane . . . . Karen Valentine
Marv . . . . Michael Constantine
Claire . . . . Cloris Leachman
Rose . . . . Patsy Kelly
Delaney . . . . Douglas V. Fowley
Cleo . . . . Virginia Capers
Tom . . . . Steve Franken
Mrs. Carlisle . . . . Dena Dietrich
Howard . . . . Dick Fuchs
Dr. Fulton . . . . Herb Voland
Harry the Hat . . . . Alan Hale
Carmel . . . . Melora Hardin
Dean . . . . Bobby Rolofson
Max . . . . Frank Campanella
Rev. Wainright . . . . Ivor Francis
Mrs. Gossin . . . . Louisa Mortiz
Mother Thurber . . . . Marjorie Bennett
Dr. Rheems . . . . Ruth Buzzi

"The North Avenue Irregulars" is one of the liveliest, most inventive live action comedies to come out of the Walt Disney Studios in years. Although the film begins with an altogether ordinary Disney premise — naive minister fights organized crime with the help of spunky femme parishioners — thanks to good casting, neat characterizations and spunky direction, it rises far above the normally innocuous level of the recent Disney comedies. Outlook for the standard G-rated Disney market appears secure. With proper marketing, "The North Avenue Irregulars" could attract substantial crossover audience. At the very least, there shouldn't be quite so many squirming adults in neighborhood theatres during matinees next month.

Edward Herrman is the Rev. Michael Hill, a young priest on his first assignment. With his horn-rimmed glasses, groomed appearance and "golly gee" demeanor, Herrman is a fitting Disney hero. He's also lanky and therefore a bit of a clutz and overly optimistic, all of which doesn't hurt.

Herrmann arrives at the North Avenue Church with plans: He's going to give his parish responsibility. But as his secretary (Susan Clark) warns, the members are a bunch of irresponsible misfits. Beware.

When Herrmann hands over a church fund to Patsy Kelly and she invests the cash in a horserace, he's tempted to agree. Ever the optimist, however, Herrmann tries to recover the money from the bookie, discovers a deep layer of evil in his town and becomes determined to save his adopted city.

That's how the picture begins. And with enough forgiving, suspension of disbelief, it works. However, other elements make the film endearing and special.

Herrmann, in a sympathetic performance, is a very likable Disney hero. So too are his cohorts against crime, especially Barbara Harris as a frazzled housewife stalking the mob from a stationwagon loaded with kids in the back seat along with Virginia Capers, Cloris Leachman and Patsy Kelly. Ruth Buzzi adds a spirited cameo.

Don Tait's script is filled with clever sight gags, genuinely amusing lines and funny situations. And Bruce Bilson, a television director making his theatrical debut, has kept the pacing crisp. The final chase scene, involving about a dozen cars, is terrific.

Other tech credits fine.—*Hege.*

The First Great Train Robbery
(BRITISH-COLOR)

Victorian period thriller, periodically victorious.

London, Jan. 9.

United Artists release of a Dino De Laurentiis presentation. Produced by John Foreman. Directed by Michael Crichton. Stars Sean Connery, Donald Sutherland, Lesley-Anne Down. Screenplay, Michael Crichton, based on his novel; Starling Productions executive, Stanley Sopel; camera (color), Goeffrey Unsworth; music, Jerry Goldsmith; editor, David Bretherton; production designer, Maurice Carter; costumes, Anthony Mendleson; sound, Liam Saurin, Derek Ball; asst. director, Anthony Waye. Reviewed at Leicester Square Theatre, London, Jan. 8, '79. (BBFC Rating: AA). Running time: **110 MINS.**

Edward Pierce . . . . Sean Connery
Agar . . . . Donald Sutherland
Miriam . . . . Lesley-Anne Down
Edgar Trent . . . . Alan Webb
Henry Fowler . . . . Malcolm Terris
Sharp . . . . Robert Lang
Clean Willy . . . . Wayne Sleep
Burges . . . . Michael Elphick
Emily Trent . . . . Pamela Salem
Elizabeth Trent . . . . Gabrielle Lloyd
Harranby . . . . James Cossins
Station Despatcher . . . . Peter Benson
Maggie . . . . Janine Duvitski

Two recurring elements of British entertainment are combined here, namely, historical settings and elegant, upperclass humor. Both have proved exportable. Period romances have wowed on the tube, and James Bond's witticisms have always enhanced his stunts. Featuring creditably authentic recreation of 19th century England, and splendid wickedness from Sean Connery, b.o. prospects for Yank auteur Michael Crichton's British outing look okay.

Based on fact, the story concerns the first recorded heist from a moving train. Suave arch-criminal Connery enlists master-picker of locks and pickets, Donald Sutherland, and death-defying scaler of buildings, Wayne Sleep, in a bid to lift a payroll of gold bars destined for the Crimea in 1855. A vital part, or rather series of parts, in the plan is played by Lesley-Anne Down as Connery's versatile yet reliable mistress. She it is who, by a neat ruse, contrives his ultimate escape after capture and trial.

On the plot side, the best is kept till last. Early scenes proceed at a measured pace. This allows time for the odd hole to show up, not always papered over by jokes of variable luster.

The actual theft is ingenious, however. The film's highpoint comes when Connery, with no cheating via stuntman or backprojection, clambers from car roof to car roof as the steam train speeds smokily under low bridges.

Unexpectedly from so accomplished a writer, Crichton's films drags in dialog bouts, but triumphs when action takes over. This is due in great part to technical achievement. The full and inventive soundtrack, Dolby-treated and mixed by Oscar-winner Derek Ball, includes an outstanding score by Jerry Goldsmith. The prevailing use of Ireland locations, both rural and architectural, in place of studio sets strikes a worthwhile blow for realism. With only one exception, the few glass-shot backgrounds are convincing.

Handling of the train sequence by recently-deceased cinematographer Geoffrey Unsworth, is a lesson in the superior effectiveness of a well-placed camera over fancy tricks. A final caption dedicates the film to his memory, stating: "His friends miss him." So will his audiences. Pic will be released in the U.S. under the title, "The Great Train Robbery." — *Simo.*

The Bermuda Triangle
(COLOR)

Bits and pieces of folklore for tv blurb campaign.

Hollywood, Jan. 3.

A Sunn Classic Pictures release of a Charles E. Sellier Jr. and James L. Conway production. Directed By Richard Friedenberg. Screenplay, Stephen Lord, from book by Charles Berlitz; camera (Technicolor), Henning Schellerup; editor, John Link; art director, Charles Bennett; music, John Cameron; stunt coordinator, Alan Gibbs; asst. director, Jeff Richard; sound (Dolby Stereo), Robert Eber; special effects, Doug Hubbard; set decorator, Freddie Mullis; narrated by Brad Crandall. Reviewed at Vine Theatre, Hollywood, Jan. 3, '70. (MPAA rating — G). Running time: **93 MINS.**

Buried within just about all of Sunn Classic's feature documentaries are 60-second gems. No one knows that better than the people who put together the television teasers for the company's films. They've created an artform out of the tv ad. Or maybe it's a new kind of brainwashing. How else does one explain thousands of people flocking to pictures like "In Search Of Noah's Ark" and "Beyond And Back"? Following this week's run of "The Bermuda Triangle," an amateurish 93-minute look at the mysterious goings-on in that triangle in the Atlantic Ocean, another title might be added to the question.

Similar to the style of other Sunn Films, "The Bermuda Triangle" takes a look at a fairly well-known exploitable pseudo-scientific phenomenon. Charles Berlitz' book of the same title provides the background for Stephen Lord's screenplay. This time, however, the film ends with a plea to world leaders to investigate this "shocking and important" phenomenon. (No kidding.)

As with the other Sunn films, recollections from people, both living and dead, who have experienced the phenomenon in question are reenacted in a silly, unconvincing fashion. So-called experts with degrees and credentials are carted out in front of the camera to add weight to the arguments. Brad Crandall narrates, tying together the bits and pieces.

But "The Bermuda Triangle," again like the other Sunn efforts, is so bad it's beyond criticism.

Charles Sellier Jr. and James L. Conway, who produced, probably know that. The film itself isn't important. It's the tv campaign and the booking pattern which count. If any company has transformed commerce into art it's the people at Sunn Classics. To repeat the adjectives so frequently used by Crandall in these films, that's an "incredible and staggering" achievement.

—*Hege.*

Billy In The Lowlands
(COLOR)

A Theatre Company of Boston-FTF Inc. production and release. Executive producer, Rikk Larsen. Produced by Nick Egleson. Written and directed by Jan Egleson. Features entire cast. Camera (color), D'Arcy Marsh; editors, Jan Egleson, D'Arcy Marsh; sound, Adrienne Linden; music, The Nighthawks. Reviewed at New York screening room, Jan. 10, '79. (No MPAA rating). Running time: **88 MINS.**

Billy Shaughnessy . . . Henry Tomaszewski
Father . . . . Paul Benedict
Joey . . . . David Morton
Social worker . . . . David Clennon
Officer Duncan . . . . Ernie Loew
Liz . . . . Genevieve Reale
Mother . . . . Bronia Wheeler
Uncle . . . . Robert Owczarek

Jan Egleson's "Billy In The Lowlands," which is the first film being shown in the American Mavericks Festival of Independent American Films, is another tale of a "lost" youth trying to find himself. What saves it from being run-of-the-mill is Henry Tomaszewski's performance in the title role. One of those chronic in-trouble kids, when he finds that his estranged father has come east for a family funeral, he breaks out of jail and the rest of the film deals with his journey to the site of their reunion, predictably disastrous.

The ending may be considered upbeat by parents when the boy returns to take his medicine and seek employment; the kid's peers will probably consider it downbeat as he resigns himself to an unimaginative future of borderline security. From his language and associates, he's obviously a school dropout.

The script is unimaginative but the camerawork of D'Arcy Marsh makes the film seem better than it is. Other than Tomaszewski, performances are cliche as most of the characters are stereotypes. Paul Benedict overacts atrociously as the drinking, shiftless father.

The language alone would rate this one an "R" if it ever gets submitted to the MPAA. Other than the chance fest showing, this one has little commercial appeal. —Robe.

Soldados
(Soldiers)
(SPANISH-COLOR)

Madrid, Jan. 2.

An Antonio Gregori P.C. production. Directed by Alfonso Ungria. Features entire cast. Screenplay, Alfonso Ungria, Antonio Gregori, based on Max Aub novel "Las Buenas Intenciones"; camera (Eastmancolor), Jose Luis Alcaine; editor, Javier Moran; sets, Antonio Cortes. Reviewed at Cine Conde Duque, Madrid, Jan. 2, '79. Running time: 124 MINS.
Cast: Marilina Ross, Ovidi Monllo, Francisco Algora, Claudia Gravy, Jose Calvo, Julieta Serrano, Lautaro Murua, Jose Maria Munoz.

Absorbing, beautifully-directed and photographed film set during the last months of the Spanish Civil War with excellent production values, topnotch acting and snappy enough pacing to keep audience attention, despite the overlong two hour-plus running time.

At times "Soldados" seems to be biting off more than it can chew as it leaps about from one flashback to another endeavoring to tell the stories of those caught up in the final retreat of the Republican Army in 1939; and some of the scenes are a bit too sketchy and histrionic, but these are minor points and the overall level is so high that the story comes across beautifully. The recreation of the feel and ambience of the period is masterfully done, thanks largely to magnificent lensing by Jose Luis Alcaine and

imaginative direction by Alfonso Ungria. The sets and costumes are wonderfully evocative.

Yarn concerns the lives of a half dozen persons who are fleeing towards Alicante on the Mediterranean coast as Franco's troops push on for the final victories of the war. Each person's bio is briefly told in flashbacks, as the soldiers and civilians drag themselves along the roads towards the south, occasionally meeting Nationalist resistance. There are a good many action scenes and shootings and also some well-done period scenes with brothels, night clubs, village dances, etc. The sex scenes are done with discretion and good taste, never flaunted needlessly.

The grab-bag of fleeing characters includes a former prostitute, a soldier who before was a gangster, another who had been a militant revolutionary, a couple who had embarked on a marriage of convenience before the war, but then separated each to lead his and her own adventures, who finally meet up again, and several others all of them well portrayed in the film. The hopelessness and confusion of the routed army is vividly captured and blends easily with the dramas of each of the characters. "Soldados" is one of the best films to come out of Spain for a long time and might do okay biz in art houses and on the festival circuits. —Besa.

Soldier Of Orange
(DUTCH-COLOR)

Seattle, Jan. 6.

A Rank Film Organization-Stage Fright, Inc. release of a Rob Houwer Production. Directed by Paul Verhoeven. Features entire cast. Screenplay, Gerard Soeteman, Kees Holierhoek, Paul Verhoeven, based on a novel by Erik Hazelhoff Roelfzema, camera (color), Jost Vacano, Peter De Bont; music, Rogier Van Otterloo; editor, Jane Speer. In Dutch (with English subtitles) and English. Reviewed at Moore-Egyptian Theatre, Seattle, Jan. 6, '79. Running time, 165 MINS.
Erik .... Rutger Hauer
Gus .... Jeroen Krabbe
John .... Peter Faber
Alec .... Derek De Lint
Robby .... Eddy Habbema
Jacques .... Lex Van Delden
Colonel Rafelli .... Edward Fox
Esther .... Belinda Meuldijk
Susan .... Susan Penhaligon
Queen Wilhelmina ......Andrea Domburh
(English Subtitles)

A rousing World II story, with plenty of action and suspense, although emphasis is on the effect of the war and the Nazi takeover of Hollan upon six young Dutch university students rather than just the war's violence and injustice. Director Paul Verhoeven has deftly fashioned the film on both levels, both absorbing, so long running time works for rather than against audience involvement and interest. (There's an intermission at the Moore).

Rutger Hauer as Erik, the rather reluctant joiner of resistance efforts after the Nazi takeover, does a great job in his leading role; hesitantly joining in first attempts at escape to England when effort is similar to a college prank, living through other failures and finally making it to England (along with Gus) where he becomes involved with supplying resistance groups with materials and aid, and winding up as liaison to Dutch Queen Wilhelmina's government in exile.

Closely pushing Hauer for acting honors is Jeroen Krabbe as Gus, debonair university leader, who joins (also reluctantly) resistance operations and dies at the hands of Nazis after revenging the group by killing Robby, a member of the student group who has become a Nazi agent, partly to protect his Jewish girl friend (Esther) by such treachery. John, the boxer and Jewish member of the group, meets early death at the hands of the oppressors; Derek De Lint is properly hateful, although understandable, as a student volunteer to fight the Russians.

When the war is over and the Queen, played excellently by Andrea Domburg, returns to Holland with aide Erik he finds that the remaining student of the original six — Lex Van Delden as Jacques, has finished his university work and seemingly has not been involved or bothered by war or oppression.

Edward Fox is fine as Colonel Rafelli, the imperturbable head of the British Secret Service who works with the Dutch partisans. Susan Penhaligon as Susan, a complaisant British WREN, has some good sex scenes with both Erik and Gus, handled nicely to supply romantic interest. Belinda Meuldijk as Esther, is appealing as the lover of both Robby and Erik, and doomed to injustice.

Film's viewpoint and treatment is reminiscent of U.S. war films of the late 1940s and 1950s, with contest clearly between the good guys and the bad guys, but is more sophisticated and not so overtly sentimental as those past films, and, as noted, while there is sufficient action and gore, the change in major characters from early, youthful optimism to grim determination makes film work at both levels.

Camera work by Jost Vacano and Peter De Bont is excellent; jaunty music by Rogier Van Otterloo nicely supports the adventurous theme, and all other technical aspects are first class. This film should find ready acceptance if sold properly, both in art houses and commercial venues; only quibble is long runnign length for turnover, but the length certainly doesn't detract; it all speeds by at a good clip. —Reed.

Always For Pleasure
(DOCUMENTARY-COLOR)

A Les Blank Film production and release. Produced and directed by Les Blank. Camera (color), Les Blank, Maureen Gosling; editors, Les Blank, Maureen Gosling; sound, Maureen Gosling; paintings, Bruce Brice. Reviewed at a New York screening room, Jan. 19, '79. (No MPAA rating). Running time: 58 MINS.

Guest appearances: "Blue Lu" Barker, Professor Longhair, Kid Thomas Valentine, Irma Thomas, Allen Toussaint, The Wild Tchoupitoulas with the Neville Brothers.

One of the entries in the American Mavericks Festival of Independent American Films, this Les Blank reprise of one area of the New Orleans ethnic picture is a joyous occasion, so lighthearted, in fact, that the viewer would never suppose the black citizens of the Louisiana city ever did anything but prepare for carnival — Mardi Gras. saints days, lodge meetings, or whatever. Interlaced with some great folk music performers, it starts with the traditional New Orleans jazz funeral march — a slow beat to the graveyard, fast high-stepping all the way home — and goes through most of the traditional music forms.

Concentrating on one major group, the Wild Tchoupitoulas, Blank paints a colorful tribute to one of our few remaining sub-cultures. The craziest Indian chief, in his zaniest battle dress, never came close to the costumes dreamed up by these imaginative citizens. It's an interesting fact that most of the more elaborate getups are worn by large, physically-imposing gentlemen as it must take a strong torso to keep all that gear in operation.

Along the way, Blank also introduces the viewer to some of the food that goes along with these celebrations and it's regional cooking at its most tempting. A musical and visual treat which should be a natural for the public broadcasting channels.

On the same bill with "Always for Pleasure," and equally charming in its way, is Blank's earlier 41-minute "Spend It All," which does for the Louisiana Cajuns what the longer film does for the New Orleans blacks. He and Skip Gerson have put on film one of the best records of that strangely romantic sect which still retains many of the customs of their French-speaking Acadian ancestors. Their music leans toward the country and western genre but their foods are enticing originals. —Robe.

Tobi
(SPANISH-COLOR)

Madrid, Jan. 4.

Blau Films producton (Madrid). Exec producer, Antonio Martin. Directed by Antonio Mercero. Features entire cast. Screenplay, Horacio Valcarcel, Antonio Mercero; camera (Eastmancolor), Manuel Rojas; sets, Wolfgang Burmann; editor, Javier Moran. Reviewed at Roxy A (Madrid), Jan. 4, '79. Running time: **91 MINS.**

Cast: Lolo Garcia, Maria Casanova, Antonio Ferrandis, Francisco Vidal, Silvia Tortosa, Jose Ruiz Lifante, Andres Mejuto, Walter Vidarte, Joaquin Prats, Manuel Martin Ferrand, Norma Aleandro.

Director Antonio Mercero likes to take an everyday subject, add a disconcerting touch of anomaly to it, and then develop a plot, imbuing it with a parable. In his half-hour video program, "The Phone Booth," it was a man locked into a public booth when no one could open; in "The Gioconda Is Sad" it was the famous Leonardo Da Vinci painting appearing one morning with a frown. In "Tobi" it's a young boy who sprouts angelic wings.

But the parable this time is tissue thin and the humorous situations rather too slight to keep up audience interest. In fact the subject matter would have sufficed for a half-hour to program, but creaks and strains when drawn out into a full-length feature. Even at 90 minutes "Tobi" seems to run far too long.

Helping the film along is a delightful performance by Lolo Garcia (who had already scored in "Daddy's War") as the alternately cherubic and devilish moppet, crisp lensing, good direction and some droll situations as Tobi is examined by specialists and wooed by the media and ad agencies. Meanwhile Tobi's working class parents are driven nearly to distraction as the presence of wings on their child brings on more and more complications, among them the animosity of Tobi's schoolmates.

The parents finally decide to have the wings taken off by surgery; but they grow back again, and the difficulties are compounded. Pic ends with Tobi climbing to the top of a tower in Madrid's amusement park and flying off towards some birds (the camera zooms away), the point presumably being that earthlings with wings cannot live in the stifling atmosphere of our world. —Besa.

Snap-Shot
(AUSTRALIAN-COLOR)

Sydney, Jan. 5.

A Filmways Australasian Distributors release of an Australian International Film Corp. production. Produced by Anthony I. Ginnane. Exec. prod. William Fayman. Directed by Simon Wincer. Stars Chantal Contouri, Robert Bruning, Sigrid Thornton. Screenplay; Chris and Everett De Roche; camera (Eastmancolor); Vincent Monton; art direction, Jon Dowding, Jill Eden; sound, Paul Clark; editing, Phil Reid; music, Brian May; special effects, Chris Murray; fire stunts, Grant Page. Previewed at A.T.A. Leisuretime Theatrette, North Sydney, Jan. 5, '78. (Commonwealth Censorship classification: M.). Running time: **92 MINS.**

Madeline .... Chantal Contouri
Angela .... Sigrid Thornton
Elmer .... Robert Bruning
Linsey .... Hugh Keays-Byrne
Daryl ....Vincent Gil
Lilly ....Denise Drysdale
Becky .... Jacqui Gordon
Roger .... Peter Stratford
Wendy .... Lulu Pinkus
Peter .... Stewart Faichney
Mrs. Bailey .... Julia Blake
Mr. Pluckett .... Jon Sidney
Paula ....Christine Amor
Bachelor .... Chris Milne
Boris .... Peter Flemingham
Captain Rock .... Bob Brown

A taut little thriller set in the glamorous demi-monde of the fashion photography scene in Melbourne, "Snap-Shot" is the tale of a pretty young hairdresser's assistant who hits the big time and how her success affects those around her, and their reactions. Central is a fine performance by Sigrid Thornton as Angela and some casually-nice playing by Robert Bruning as the menace. Hugh Keays-Byrne, usually reliable, is cast against physical character and at times his Linsey seems camped-up, rather than just far-out.

Director Simon Wincer appears more sure of things cinematic than the people he's dealing with and this especially shows in his non-control over Chantal Contouri as Madeline whose Sapphic designs on young Angela are telegraphed so heavily that any other novice would have shied away long before the eventual rift. The result is that there is at times a preponderance of heavies, which tends to make the film Angela-against-the-world, and throws off what balance could have been achieved.

But between them, Wincer and cameraman Vincent Monton have achieved a handsome-looking film with excellent production values. The action keeps on the move at sufficient a pace that what plot and motivation lacunae there are don't immediately snag your consciousness. And there is only enough discreet nudity to be titilating without being sexy or even erotic: so little in fact that the Aussie censors deemed it suitable only for "mature audiences" which under the Act means anyone from two upwards.

In fact, right up until its convoluted and contrived payoff, "Snap-Shot" is a good, brisk pot boiler of modest ambitions. But the De Roches' screenplay's flaws shoudl have been tagged earlier than post production which even Phil Reid's pacy editing can't entirely gloss over.

Tech credits are fine, as is the minor role playing. But there seems a lack of master shots that might have, if used, created a visual flow and smoothed down the overall abrupt look of the product. Brian May's good and evocative score seems therefore to get over-used in an effort to punch up the action. Admittedly made on a tight, low budget, the film only just escapes looking cheap by dint of the aforementioned high production values.

Pic should do okay in outdoor situations and in carefully-placed hardtops; likewise, it ought to perform well in markets where action takes precedence over content, especially when flavored by some exploitable semi-nudity. —Miha.

Albert — Warum?
(Albert — Why?)
(WEST GERMAN-B&W-16m)

Hof, Oct. 28.

A Munich Film & Television Academy diploma film. Features entire cast. Written and directed by Josef Roedl. Camera, Karlheinz Gschwind; sound, Hans Roedl; assistant, Angela Kifmann. Reviewed at Hof Film Fest, Oct. 28, '78. Running time: **115 MINS.**

Albert...................... Fritz Binner
His Father .... Michael Eichenseer
Hans .... Georg Schiessl
Eva ....Elfriede Bleisteiner

The highlight of the Hof Film Festival, Josef Roedl's "Albert — Why?" is a 16m diploma pic financed on a low budget by the Munich Film & Television Academy and lensed in the small village of Darshofen/Oberpfalz in Bavaria near Regensburg, where the young helmer was born and raised. Roedl worked two years on the two-hour pic, using lay-actors from the village playing themselves and a small, intimate team of friends forming the production crew.

The title refers to a hulking giant of a man, a gentle soul who stutters when he speaks and can barely control the movements of his gangling body — he may or may not be slightly retarded, but in any case he is treated like an outsider, one who has spent some time in a "nuthouse." Strangely enough, he has the movements and countenance of a Boris Karloff, but in fact he symbolically stands for the typical dim-wit common to village life and city neighborhoods. This is a true story.

Pic begins with Albert released from a mental asylum and picked up at the railroad station by his father with the farm tractor and trailer; his problem was drinking rather than "madness," caused principally by being an outsider in a cold, indifferent world. The main thread of the story deals with Albert's relationship to his family, relatives, and villagers, some detailed more than others in viewing him as a social misfit. Albert, however, is not too dumb to know that his gestures of kindness are returned with mockery and pranks, particularly by the young to whose company he gravitates for some kind of companionship and understanding.

He also understands that, during his absence in the asylum, his aging father has signed over the farm to a family relative — and his cared-for pets are no longer there. In protest Albert refuses to live at home, taking quarters instead in a kind of chicken-coop where he keeps rabbits. Now more of an outsider than before, he become the village clown although some relief comes with "playing house" with small children. He takes to drinking again, is tantalized one day by a girl who bares her breasts to him, becomes more and more isolated — then hangs himself with a rope to the church bell which tolls his merciful passing from this world.

This is a document, not a fiction film nor a documentary. It tells the true story of Fritz Binner who plays the lead role himself and, indeed, died shortly after completing the film by drinking himself to death. Helmer Roedl was one of his few friends (thus the title), who shared a desk with him in his youth at the village school. The idea for the film came naturally and was developed slowly over a period of time (the dubbing of Binner's voice was necessary at the film's completion). It's as though often the camera just happens to be "there" as a scene takes place with little or no cuts or editing.

"Albert" deserves some kind of festival or forum to launch it, but it's so well done that it could find its way into a German Film Week and thereafter get recognition by film buffs nourished on Bresson and Dreyer, as well as the Flaherty tradition of the story-documentary. Here, too, is solid evidence that shortly the young directors in West Germany will be crowding Werner Herzog and others for a share of the spotlight. —Holl.

Di Dao Chan
(Tunnel Warfare)
(CHINESE-B&W)

Berlin, Dec. 20.

A Peking Film Studio Production. Produced by the Army Propaganda Unit Only credits available. Reviewed at Cine-Center, Berlin, Dec. 20, '78. Running time: **90 MINS.**

This 1965 Chinese Army film production, "Tunnel Warfare," even has a comic book to recommend it. Every school-child reads about how Mao's troops stymied the Japanese invaders in 1942 via a resistance known as "tunnel warfare." And this accompanying film was not only a great success at home, it was unspooled on West German television and drew huge crowds again at the Info Show of last year's Berlin Film Festival in a Chinese Film Series.

The historical background for "Tunnel Warfare" goes back to 1933, when the Japanese occupied Northeast China and established a new government in Manchuria. Then, in 1937, war broke out between Japan and China on a full scale, and the quarrelling Nationalist and Communist troops joined to form a united front. The Japanese occupied large cities — Shanghai, Nanking, Wuhan — but the control of the countryside always slipped through their grasp.

The reason was that the peasants cleverly instigated an obstinate, underground form of partisan warfare. Supported in the Resistance by the people, tunnels were dug underground for surprise attacks and guerrilla warfare. For this particular battle, an ingenious set of passage-ways and shafts led from house to house in a village, thus allowing the Chinese "underground" to surface, attack, and disappear at will — even the enemy lines were mined via the caves and passage-ways.

Pic is comically entertaining as the Japanese, like in a comic-strip, are caricatured for the delight of a young, unsophisticated audience.

— *Holl.*

Die Anstalt
(The Institution)
(WEST GERMAN-B&W)

Hof, Oct. 28.

A Common Film Production, distributed by Basis-Film Verleih, Berlin. Features entire cast. Written and directed by Hans-Ruediger Minow. Camera, Bernd Fiedler; music, Andi Brauer; editing, Hanne Huxoll; sound, Heiko von Swieykowski; sets, Renate Pfab; production manager, Helmut Wietz. Reviewed at Hof Film Festival, Oct. 28, '78. Running time: **90 MINS.**

Anna Theyn	Susanne Ganzler
Dr. Reincke	Wolfgang Preiss
Dr. Steinhausen	Gerd Baltus
Dr. Bongartz	Wolfgang Ransmayr
Mrs. Hillger	Ursula Roche
Attendant Godau	Hans-Peter Korff
Attendant Langenfeld	Dieter Prochnow
Mrs. Huelfrich	Christiane Bruhn
Mrs. Draeger	Eva Dreyer-Eschenbach
Mrs. Peters	Carin Braun
Selbmann	Rolf Beuckert
Old Man	Walter Ladengast
Mr. Krueger	Peter Petran
Mother Theyn	Gertrud Hinz
Father Theyn	Friedrich W. Rasch
Court Judge	Guenter Keutemeyer
Notary	Til Kiwe

"The Institution" has had a phenomenal success in West Germany upon its appearance at the Hof Film Festival and the Studio am Kudam in West Berlin, in the backyard of the enterprising Basis-Film Verleih — who have also backed the successful Helke Sander fem pic, "The All-Around Reduced Personality — Outtakes," and Christian Ziewer's Chilean tale set in West Berlin, "I See This Land From Afar." All three pix speak of the growing importance of the Berlin "school" on the German film scene today.

"The Institution" introduces helmer Hans-Ruediger Minow, a grad of the Berlin Film & Television Academy whose metier is the fully researched documentary and (in this case) fiction-documentary of a sociopolitical nature. He began working on the project in 1975, shortly after articles appeared in German and American newspapers about psychiatrists voluntarily disguising themselves as patients to enter mental institutions (in California and Illinois) to uncover ·evidence that several schizophrenic patients were in fact sane and healthy but medically mistreated by doctors and attendants. Then, in February 1978, a scandal hit the headlines about a mental clinic near Cologne where two young woman patients died from maltreatment.

Pic takes it from there, offering several factual scenes of how schizos are treated in mental asylums. Story focuses on a young female psychologist just out of the university, who freely admits herself to a clinic, makes human contact with other patients, and is gradually "terrorized" by psychiatrists, doctors, and attendants — to the extent that even her visiting parents (particularly the father) believe the doctrinaire, spiteful statements of the director of the institution rather than the pleas of their own daughter to voluntarily leave as she came.

Finally, the mess is unveiled for what it is — oddly enough, through a doctor whose behavior unmasks himself as the real nut in the clinic. All of which appears to be a deus ex machina ending, but it's amusing and delights audiences who are partial to anti-clinic pix. Here is a story similar to Edgar Allan Poe's "Dr. Tar and Mr. Feathers" and Kenneth Loach's feature pic, "Family Life," on schizophrenia. "The Institution," appropriately lensed in black-and-white, is ripe for Film & Psychiatry seminars, as well as art houses special-programming docus of this genre. —*Holl.*

Der Junge Moench
(The Young Monk)
(WEST GERMAN-COLOR)

Hof, Oct. 27.

A Herbert Achternbusch Production, Munich. Features entire cast. Produced, written, and directed by Herbert Achternbusch. Camera (color), Joerg Jeshel; sound, Peter van Anft; editor, Christl Leyrer; production manager, Dietmar Schneider. Reviewed at Hof Film Festival, Oct. 27, '78. Running times: **84 MINS.**

Heinz	Heinz Braun
Branko	Branko Samarovski
Karolina	Karolina Herbig
Herbert	Herbert Achternbusch

Helmer Herbert Achternbusch might be taken as an amateur filmer, were he not an author and playwright of some repute and

Bavaria's best humorist-satirist since the days of Karl Valentin, another filmmaker-cabaretist-satirist whose reputation in the 1930s was as sacrosanct as that of W.C. Fields. Achternbusch had made five pix in a row — "The Andechs Feeling" (1975), "The Atlantic Swimmers" (1976), "Beer Fight" (1977), "Bye-Bye Bavaria" (1977), and now "The Young Monk" — for an amused, faithful audience, plus one play — "Ella" (1978) — that has proved he can be as deadly serious as he is absurdly comical.

"The Young Monk" appeared on the scene at about the time one pope died and another was elected — while there was Herbert the actor garbed in white robes to have a go at the Church and a few of its myths, legends, and credos. In fact, "The Young Monk" reworks the catalogue of Biblical beliefs to present a new saviour longing to redeem something, then working his way up to become Pope whose God is the Easter Bunny.

All of which sounds wickedly sacrilegious — and it is, to some extent. But Achternbusch the director is always stealing the thunder from someone in authority (in "Beer Chase" he impersonated a policeman), and the skits come across like night-club scenes on Lenny Bruce night. Some of the gags work to perfection as the tall, gangling Bavarian is adept at timing and the put-down — and a routine about a simple country boy following his visions to Rome as a revolutionary, new-born Christ seeking converts and working wonders rights deserves our attention today. —*Holl.*

Liebe Und Abenteuer
(Love And Adventure)
(WEST GERMAN-COLOR)

Hof, Oct. 28.

A Stelly-Film Production, Hamburg, in collaboration with Zweites Deutsches Fernsehen (ZDF), Wiesbaden-Mainz. Features entire cast. Written and directed by Gisela Stelly. Camera (Color), David Slama; sound, Heiko von Sweiykowski; art direction, MAT-Peter Braun; editing, Heidi Handorf; production manager, Chris Sievernich. Reviewed at Hof Film Festival, Oct. 28, '78. Running time: **88 MINS.**

Lara	Brigitt Hoffmeister
Robert	Hub Martin
Hans	Harold Vogl
Leo	Leo Bardischewski

The latest in a line of femme helmers on the West German film scene, Gisela Stelly apparently reached back into her own adolescence for this abstract tale of a 16-year-old girl's loneliness, titled "Love and Adventure" (without much of either in the story). It will get a late-evening tv-run on "Das kleine Fernsehspiel" — the Second Channel (ZDF) supporter of small-budget feature pix by debut helmers.

Almost totally without narrative, "Love and Adventure" tries to communicate with images and fragmented scenes, reminiscent of Agnes Varda's "stream of consciousness" style heralding the French New Wave of the late-1950s. But neither the four characters — two boyfriends and a grand-dad, plus the girl — say very much about what the problem is, and the narrative doesn't give away any secrets either. Worst of all, pic is badly lensed and clumsily cut.

Pic could make it to a femme fest somewhere, but even there the ladies today are fast becoming critically conscious of style and theme. —*Holl.*

Kalte Heimat
(Cold Homeland)
(WEST GERMAN-B&W)

Berlin, Nov. 22.

A Triangel Film, Cologne-Berlin, in coproduction with Westdeutscher Rundfunk (WDR), Joachim Von Mengershausen. Features entire cast. Directed by W. Werner Schaefer. Screenplay, Peter Steinbach, Schaefer; camera, Gerard Vandenberg; music, Juergen Knieper; costumes, Uschi Welker; sets, Edwin Wengobowski, Norbert Scherer; sound, Rainer Wicker. Reviewed at Studio am Kudam, West Berlin, Nov. 22, '78. Running time: **120 MINS.**

Helmut	Nikolaus Cohen
Julia	Dietlinde Turban
Hilde	Barbara Adolph
Robert	Nikolas Lansky
Frau Lukaschewski	Margit Carstensen
Old Man	Dudolf Schindler
Frau Feuerlein	Brigitte Bottrich

With only one other pic to his name (not a feature), newcomer W. Werner Schaefer took a ripe script by Peter Steinbach (highly praised for his last screenplay, "Zero Hour," directed by Edgar Reitz) and fashioned it into one of the best New German Cinema pix of the year. In many aspects pic parallels Steinbach's earlier "Zero Hour," set in a small town near Leipzig in 1945 at the end of the war when Americans and Russians criss-crossed each other's military paths in a kind of No Man's Land.

"Cold Homeland" is also autobiographical, the story of Steinbach's short stay in a Cologne mansion as a youth among refugees leaving their "cold homeland" in East Germany to settle in the West in the early 1950s, during the Adenauer Years just before the Berlin Wall was built and the country split in half by a guarded border. In 1951 some 5-10,000 Germans left the German Democratic Republic each day for the Federal Republic of Germany; by 1954 the sum was up to 20,000 a day, the majority crossing over at Berlin; between 1949 and 1961 the total reached 2.7 million refugees.

The primary reasons for the stream of refugees, per historians and case-histories, were the loss of private businesses and collectivization of farms by decree in the GDR in 1952 and the belief that the "Golden West" offered a higher standard of living. Among the families living in the Cologne villa, one of several abandoned mansions belonging to Jews before Hitler's rise to power, are the Zeitlers — a farmer who summarizes West Germany as "big autos, eating, drinking."

"Cold Homeland" does, in fact, refer metaphorically to both Germanys: the one left behind by the typically ill-prepared, hasily departing refugee, and the new home where a German citizen could even be looked upon as a foreigner. It is a film about experiences, personal, bittersweet experiences, about people assigned abitrarily to live together in a villa until jobs and homes could be found for them. Into this villa comes the Zeitler family (father, mother, teenage son), an old gentleman who will probably die there, a man who tires quickly of the Golden West and returns back to East Germany, a woman, with her daughter, who simply got off a train on impulse as it passed through West Berlin, and others who left simply for personal reasons.

The film begins with newsreel shots of the migration at its peak at the beginning of the 1950s, the camera catching the drama of the moment like the March of Time — then, imperceptibly, the black-and-white lensing of a fiction-documentary sweeps the viewer into the real situation via a long tracking shot through a crowded railway depot, picking out faces and baggage and the aura of the "displaced person."

The scene shifts to the Cologne villa, and a new life, of sorts, begins for 20 or 30 stray people in the land of freedom. Newspapers on a lending-library system are pedalled from door to door; a gawky, clumsy teenage innocent is introduced (Helmut Zeitler), who is too sensitive to mix with girls (he misses his Pioneer pals back East) and can't quite hold a job as a delivery boy at a photoshop; the father begins to wonder why he can't get a farm like the one he left behind, instead of working as a watchman at a factory; and a minor tragedy unfolds as a mentally disturbed, impulsive woman buries herself in the household and, one day, simply commits suicide. In the end, buses come to take the group away for a day in the country with Konrad Adenauer — we are back to actual newsreels again on a chilly day in the Friedland camp with its historical "be us of freedom."

"Cold Homeland" is a chapter in modern German history, an astonishing recapturing of a period by a young helmer who never really experienced it himself, but studied the 1950s intensely and had screenplay writer Steinbach's eye-witness account to go by. Costumes, dialogue, life-styles, the atmosphere of the times — all contribute to a portrait of (West) Germany now nearly forgotten but only a generation ago.

Thesps are all new faces, save for Margit Carstensen as the woman-with the psychological problems, who carry each vignette with ease in a film without a clearly cut narrative line. Lensing is also tops, as are the credits in general. An unpretentious pic for film and history buffs. —Holl.

Bao Feng Chou Yu
(Hurricane)
(CHINESE-B&W)

Berlin, Dec. 18.

A Peking Film Studio Production. Features entire cast. Directed by Hsie Tie-Li. Screenplay, Lin Lan, based on the novel with the same name by Chou Li-Po; camera, Wu Shen-Han; music, Li Huan-Chi; sound, Shen Jie-Hsi. Reviewed at Berlin Cine-Center Screening Room, Dec. 18, '78. Running time: **130 MINS.**
With You Yank, Yu Ping, Li Bai-Wan, Wu Su-Chin, Liu Chi-Yun.

Made in 1961 and one of the finest films to emerge from China in the early 1960s, Hsie Tie-Li's "Hurricane" was based on an important novel and was the young director's first film, as well as the cameraman's debut, per Jay Leyda's "Dianying." Script was by the helmer's wife, which hardly departs from the essence of the book's narrative, but character development within the limitations of the script was generously allowed — the film was a b.o. success.

Story is set in Northeast China (Manchuria in 1944-1947). A "land-reform working-committee" of the People's Liberation Army comes to a village where the landowner (and his lackies) are still in power, while the small landowners are fearful of taking sides in unison against him. The peasants without land are also distrustful of "liberation" after having been subjugated for centuries.

But the leader of the working-committee can speak the language of the people and sees through the wily tricks of the village-despots; he is determined to overthrow the feudal system. This requires, however, that the peasants themselves fight for their freedom. The landowner, meanwhile, sabotages the land-reform through bribes, enlisting the aid of a pseudo-revolutionary, and spreading the rumor that the anti-Communist Kuomintang troops are about to recapture the village and that the People's Liberation Army is only interested in the fruits of the coming harvest.

In the end the Kuomintang troops do return from their hide-away in the mountains, but the Communists and the villagers join forces to defeat the common enemy. A showdown between the Kuomintang leader and the village peasant leader results in death for both, but not before the revolutionary leader, mortally wounded, admonishes his followers that "we must defend the power of the poor." The landowner must stand public trial, confesses to a murder he committed, and is condemned to death.

Credits are tops, particularly thesps and lensing. Pic is a natural for Chinese Film Weeks and film clubs, and could also find its way into specialized art houses. —Holl.

Dimri I Fundit
(The Last Winter)
(ALBANIAN-B&W)

Berlin, Dec. 21.

An Albfilm Production, Tirana; world rights, Albania Film, Tirana. Features entire cast. Directed by Ibrahim Mucaj and Kristaq Mitro. Screenplay, based on motifs in A. Kondo's story, "The Women of My Village;" Nexhat Tafa, camera, Ilia Terpini; art direction, Shyqyri Sako; music, Aleksander Lalo. Reviewed at Berlin Cine-Center Screening Room, Dec. 21, '78. Running time: **90 MINS.**
With Liza Laska, Margarita Xhepa, Agim Qirjaqi, Gulielm Radoja, Rajmonda Bulku.

A partisan pic which introduces the Germans as the enemy instead of the usual Italians (who occupied the country since 1939), Ibrahim Mucaj and Kristaq Mitro's "The Last Winter" (1976) is set at the peak of fighting in 1943-44 when villages were the center of combat. This tale deals with the heroism of women aiding the partisan fighters — their sons, husbands, and relatives — under the noses of the Nazi troops searching for the enemy.

Several Yugoslav and East European "Easterns" follow this same story line, but pic does come across as convincing due to contributions by thesps in the main roles. The winter landscapes in grey, black-and-white tones add to the realism of the story.

Helmers Mucaj and Mitro collaborated again the same year on "Blood-Soaked Land" (1976), a drama of peasant life before, during, and after the Second World War in which class injustice (landowner versus peasant) is dealt with under the impact of the new Communist regime. —Holl.

Der Erste Walzer
(The First Waltz)
(WEST GERMAN-COLOR-16M)

Hof, Oct. 27.

A Doris Doerrie Film, Munich, in collaboration with the Munich Film School and Bavarian TV. Features entire cast. Directed by Doris Doerrie. Screenplay, Doerrie, W.A. Reimann; camera (color), Peter Fauhe; sound, Jan Christian Martens; editor, Raimund Barthelmes; production manager, Franz X. Gernstl. Reviewed at Hof Film Fest, Oct. 27, '78. Running time: **58 MINS.**
Max ....Christopher Thomas
Sandy ....Katharina Hembus
Max's Mother ....Jutta Mueller-Schwarz
Sandy's Mother ....Louise Francia
Sandy's Father ....Sepp Bierbichler

"The First Waltz" is one of several West German pix aimed for the young crowd and dealing with problems of youth, particularly in finding a job and keeping a girlfriend or boyfriend. This one by Doris Doerrie, shot in 16m for Bavarian Television and the Munich Academy for Film and Television, is the best to come along in the genre primarily because it doesn't preach a dubious social message of "solidarity" or protest against an indifferent society.

Max can't find anything he really likes to do now that he's grown up. His mother lends him money when he needs it, and the mechanic's apprentice doesn't quite appeal to him — but his good looks and easy charm help to relieve the stress, and he falls in love with Sandy, a barber-and-beautician's assistant. They spend free time together, once borrowing a flashy car for a drive in the country where they, somewhat conveniently, run out-of-gas. Both seem to be finding their way in the end, although no solutions are offered.

An unassuming, attractive pic with amateur actors playing out their own destinies, somewhat like the vogue of plays-musicals ("The Runaways") and fiction-documentaries (Max Willutzki's "Fist in the Pocket" is another West German feature pic on teenage unemployment) dotting the landscape today in America and Europe. Fem helmer Doerrie has now earned her stripes as a film director (she also made the docu, "Whether Rain or Shine," on the death of movie houses in the provinces), but she could use a little help turning a promising script into realistic, spontaneous dialogue. —Holl.

Murder By Decree
(BRITISH-COLOR)

Holmes meets Jack The Ripper for handsome b.o. results.

Hollywood, Jan. 19.

An Avco Embassy Pictures release of an Ambassador Films production, produced in cooperation with Canadian Film Development Corp. and Famous Players Ltd. Exec producer, Len Herberman. Coproduced by Rene Dupont, Bob Clark. Features entire cast. Directed by Clark. Screenplay, John Hopkins; camera (Metrocolor) Reg Morris; editor, Stan Cole; production design, Harry Pottle; costume design, Judy Moorcroft; sound, John Mitchell; assistant director, Ariel Levy. Reviewed at Regent Theatre, Westwood, Jan. 19, '78. (MPAA Rating: PG.) Running time: **120 MINS.**

Sherlock Holmes ... Christopher Plummer
Dr. Watson .... James Mason
Robert Lees .... Donald Sutherland
Annie Crook .... Genevieve Bujold
Inspector Foxborough .. David Hemmings
Mary Kelly .... Susan Clark
Sir Charles Warren ...... Anthony Quayle
Lord Salisbury .... John Gielgud
Inspector Lestrade .... Frank Finlay

"Murder By Decree" is probably the best Sherlock Holmes film since the inimitable pairing of Basil Rathbone and Nigel Bruce in the 1940s series at Universal. Unfortunately, it also shares some of the defects of those films, i.e. slow pacing, an improbable story line, and an undue emphasis on odd characters. Despite its flaws, the Avco Embassy release of this Anglo-Canadian production should please both Baker Street buffs and the general public to good boxoffice effect.

The film's charm derives mainly from John Hopkins' literal, deadpan script that makes no attempt to either mock or contemporize Sir Arthur Conan Doyle's literary creation. This being the 134th screen version (going back to 1903 one-reelers) of the famed sleuth's career, there's a rich tradition to mine, and Hopkins and director Bob Clark make effective use of the stock-in-trade Holmesiana, including swirling fog, rattling carriages, and the familiar hat and pipe.

Ironically, Christopher Plummer works against this recreation by presenting a Holmes who looks as if he's just returned from a Caribbean vacation. Next to James Mason, who may be the most delightful Watson to ever appear on celluloid, Plummer's blonde handsomeness seems especially foreign.

But the two performers click together, and Plummer's Holmes is just as shrewd, logical and surprisingly emotional as necessary. They are the core of an involved plot blending freemasonry, royal marital indiscretions, religious prejudice, Jack The Ripper, English revolutionary socialism, and other Victorian story artifacts into a visual stew that is both engrossing and entertaining.

Clark covers the dangling plot threads with particularly sharp editing by Stan Cole, a massive period recreation job by Harry Pottle and Ken Pattenden, and expressive costuming by Judy Moorcraft. All the British-based tech credits are strong, although the dialects seemed particularly atrocious, given the proximity of the locales.

There's little sense in trying to untangle the dense story line, but suffice it to say that Holmes and Watson are not called into help solve a series of murders eventually linked to Jack The Ripper. Anthony Quayle, as the new topper at Scotland Yard, has his reasons for excluding them, as does Inspector David Hemmings. Donald Sutherland has an excellent cameo as a psychic who receives intimations of the involvement of a dissipated court physician, played with extreme horror by Roy Lansford.

The plot comes to hinge on Genevieve Bujold as the discarded mistress of a prominent personage, and thanks to the aid of Susan Clark (highly effective in another small role), Plummer manages to track her down in a faithful recreation of a Victorian lunatic asylum.

An exciting dockside battle between Plummer and Peter Jonfield as the Ripper character should provide the pic's denouement, but Clark and Hopkins unwisely feel the need to recap the entire series of events, and stretch the film out by 20 unnecessary minutes.

Mason almost steals the pic with his harrumphing Watson, and a digression with a squashed pea is the film's comic highlight. Bujold, Quayle, Hemmings and John Gielgud are all employed to good effect,
— Poll.

The Sweet Creek County War

Amateurish Western due for lean b.o. grazing.

Hollywood, Jan. 12.

A Key International Film release of an Imagery Films production. Exec producers, Ray Cardi, Marie Cardi. Produced by Ken Byrnes, J. Frank James. Features entire cast. Written and directed by James; camera (color), Gregory von Berblinger; editor, Ronald Sinclair; production design, Allen H. Jones; music, Richard Bowden; costume design, Peggy Sjulstad; sound, Kenneth Isley; assistant director, John Hockridge. Reviewed at UA Cinema Center, Westwood, Jan. 12, '78 (MPAA Rating: PG). Running time: **99 MINS.**

Judd Firman .... Richard Egan
George W. Breakworth ...... Albert Salmi
Firetop Alice Dewey .... Nita Talbot
Jitters Pippin .... Slim Pickens
Lucas K. Derring .... Robert J. Wilke
Lyle Derring .... Joe Orton
Rowdy Derring .... Ray Cardi
Virgil Harper .... Tom Jackman

"The Sweet Creek County War" is a good example of why westerns aren't being made in great quantity any more. All of the oater cliches are trotted out, and then some, in amateurish and heavy-handed form. Lacking a stellar cast, and featuring almost no exploitable angles, this Key International Film release is facing a particularly bleak future at the boxoffice.

J. Frank James, whose acumen is handling this genre does nt live up to his namesake, wrote and directed the tale of a lawman and an outlaw who band together to fight off the advances of a land-hungry rancher. The same story has been told time and again, most recently in the United Artists release, "Comes A Horseman," and James adds nothing of interest to the stock plot turns.

The script is so loaded with hoary and pretentious lines that the (presumably) unintentional result makes "Sweet Creek County" into a semi-comedy. Those scenes with humorous intent come off as puerile, with an especially disgusting emphasis on jokes involving genital areas.

Richard Egan plays the sheriff who rescues desperado Albert Salmi from a hanging, and then inexplicably turns in his badge to turn to the ranching life. He settles on a spread owned by Robert J. Wilke, and his two oafish sons, played with embarrassing ineptitude by Joe Orton and co-exec producer Ray Cardi. Tom Jackman strolls in as a representative of foreign money interests, out to control the ranch, and instigator of the "war" against Egan and Salmi, who are joined by prostie Nita Talbot.

The kindest thing that can be said about Egan's performance is that his age works against him in this casting. Salmi and Talbot struggle with the material, but it's a losing cause. Fine character actors such as Slim Pickens and Wilke are wasted.

Wyoming locations are well utilized, and Gregory von Berblinger's lensing is the sole tech standout.
—Poll.

The Young Cycle Girls
(COLOR)

Naked riders.

Hollywood, Jan. 16.

A Peter Perry Pictures release, produced and directed by Perry. Executive producer, Sue Perry. Features entire cast. Screenplay, John Arnoldy; camera (no color credited), Ron Garcia; editor, Marco Perri. No other credits available. Reviewed at Pacific II Theatre, Hollywood, Jan. 16, '78. (MPAA rating: R.) Running time: **80 MINS.**

Cast: Loraine Ferris, Daphne Lawrence, Deborah Marcus, Lonnie Pense, Kevin O'Neill, Bee Lechat, Billy Bullet.

In "The Young Cycle Girls," three tender beauties from Colorado set out to see the Pacific Ocean, stopping along the way for laughs and dancing and rape and drugs and other perils of the open road. From the scratches on the film screened, it seems they dragged the print behind them.

The girls, Loraine Ferris, Daphne Lawrence, Deborah Marcus, show no serious probability of becoming actresses, but they ride okay and skinny dip superbly. Producer-director Peter Perry fills in with lots and lots of highway shots, catching some really good trucks and road signs tracing the trip to California which the script says the girls "will really love ... surfing is far out."

Along the way, the girls call a fellow in a pickup truck a "dirty pervert" and he drives by the camera to reveal an ominous skull painted on the door.

The girls love the outdoors, even though people tie them up at night and do disgusting things. So when they get to the California border, they praise nature by spray painting their names on a rock.

Suddenly, over the dune — the Pacific Ocean. The girls are ecstatic. Then bang, blood. Bang. blood. Bang, blood. The poor girls are dead and there's that skull on the door again.

It's a sad ending. But it saves the audience the trip home to Colorado.
—Har.

Take Down
(COLOR)

Lighthearted look at high-school wrestling.

Buena Vista Distribution release of an American Film Consortium production of a Kieth Merrill Film. Stars Edward Herrmann, Kathleen Lloyd. Executive producer, David B. Johnston. Produced and directed by Kieth Merrill. Screenplay, Merrill, Eric Hendershot, based on a story idea by Hendershot; camera (DeLuxe), Reed Smoot; film editor, Richard Fetterman; music, composed and conducted by Merrill B. Jenson; art director, Douglas G. Johnson; technical advisory, Eric Hendershot; sound, Robert E. Sheridan; musical score performed by The National Symphony, London. Reviewed at National Theatre, New York, Jan. 18, '79. (MPAA Rating: PG). Running time: **107 MINS.**

Ed Branish .... Edward Herrman
Jill Branish .... Kathleen Lloyd
Nick Kilvitus .... Lorenzo Lamas
Brooke Cooper ...... Maureen McCormick
Jimmy Kier .... Nick Beauvy
Randy Jensen .... Stephen Furst
Jasper MacGruder .... Kevin Hooks
Bobby Cooper .... Vincent Roberts
Ted Yacabobich .... Darryl Peterson
Chauncey Washington .... "T"Oney Smith
Tom Palumbo .... Salvador Feliciano
Jack Gross .... Boyd Silversmith
Robert Stankovich .... Scott Burgi
Doc Talada .... Lynn Baird
Warren Overpeck ...... Ron Bartholomew
Zeno Chicarelli .... Kip Otanez
LeRoy Barron .... Larry Miller
Thad Lardner .... Gary Petersen
Mr. Kilvitus .... Oscar Roland
Principal .... Hyde Clayton
Referee .... Prentiss Rowe

Mrs. Kilvitus . . . . .Elizabeth Grand
Suzette Smith . . . . Christy Neal
Rockville coach . . . . Bob Kawa

Kieth Merrill didn't exactly set the cinematic world on fire a couple of years ago with his American Indian pic, "Three Warriors," but this time around he has come up with a handsome, well-constructed and admirably played item, dealing with the adventures of a high school wrestling team that could find a big welcome in the family film market. This may be the reason why Buena Vista, which gives a heavy look at product it expects to distribute, has picked up the independent production.

Comedy-drama topbills Edward Herrmann, who more than deserves the star billing, and Kathleen Lloyd, who doesn't but is still quite good. Herrmann is an English teacher in a small town high school (location isn't specified but it looks like northern California), sweating out a teaching assignment to Harvard (the most unbelievable part of Merrill and Eric Hendershot's script). He's given the undesirable extra job of coaching the school's wrestling team. As this school's athletic record is the pits, it figures that nothing is expected of the grunt-and-groan kids.

The key turn in the plot is the team's need for a wrestler in the 185-pound bracket and the only one in school (and who couldn't care less) is Lorenzo Lamas (son of Fernando Lamas), who's built like a teenage Arnold Schwarzenegger. He was seen rather briefly in "Grease" and is a handsome but, so far, rather expressionless young actor. Here he does an excellent job of the poor kid, behind in his grades, but responsive to Herrmann's appeal to him on behalf of the team and the school.

Other parts are frequently colorful especially Darryl Peterson as the cherubic but gigantic leader of the team, Kevin Hooks as the team clown, Vincent Roberts as the tiniest member, and Kip Otanez as an Italian-American team member who only responds when he hears music (which leads to some funny byplay on the part of the other students). Maureen McCormick is decorative as Lamas' girl (and Roberts' sister).

All technical credits are excellent, especially Reed Smoot's crisp camerawork and Richard Fetterman's sharp editing. — Robe.

Horizonte Te Hapura
(Clear Horizons)
(ALBANIAN-B&W)

Berlin, Dec. 20.
An Albfilm Production, Tirana; world rights, Albania Film, Tirana. Features entire cast. Directed and photographed by Viktor Gjika. Screenplay, Dritero Agolli; art direction, Shyqyri Sako; music, Limos Dizdari. Reviewed at Berlin Cine-Center screening room, Dec. 20, '78. Running time: **90 MINS.**
With Dhimiter Orgocka, Sander Prosi, Robert Ndrenika, Gaqo Spiro, Pandi Raidhi, Mirketa Cobani, Nikolin Xhoja.

Viktor Gjika, together with helmers Dhimiter Anagnosti, Husen Habani, and Kirstaq Dhamo, is one of the founders of Albanian cinema so far as directors go. He is proficient in the action pic and often works as cameraman on his own films, as in this case; he did, in fact, begin his professional career as a lenser and works in this capacity for other helmers. He also makes documentary films, as "Four Songs of the Party" (unspooled in the Info Show at the 1978 Berlin fest).

"Clear Horizons" in 1968 was a breakthrough in Albanian cinema. It treated a contemporary issue, rather than dealing with an historical or heroic partisan theme. Pic presented real people in real working conditions — the shipyards of Tirana — but the main attraction is the true story of a worker who sacrificed his life to save a crane vital to the docks during a severe storm. There's also a parallel romance story, which illustrates life as it is among various social types.

Albania's first major step forward after a decade of experimenting and raising its output from one feature pic a year to double that — with assurance of solid b.o. backing among native aud. — Holl.

Circle Of Iron
(COLOR)

Carradine opens new chopping center.

Hollywood, Jan. 16.
An Avco Embassy Pictures release of a Sandy Howard/Richard St. Johns production. Stars David Carradine. Exec producer, St. Johns. Produced by Paul Maslansky, Howard. Directed by Richard Moore. Screenplay, Stirling Silliphant, Stanley Mann, based on a story by Bruce Lee, James Coburn, Silliphant; camera (CFI Color), Ronnie Taylor; editor, Ernie Walter; production design, Johannes Larsen; costume design, Lilly Fenichel; sound, Cyril Collick; technical advisor, Kam Yuen; assistant director, Nissim Levy. Reviewed at CFI Screening Room, Hollywood, Jan. 16, '78. (MPAA Rating: ¾.) Running time: **102 MINS.**

Chang-Sha . . . . David Carradine
The Blind Man . . . .   ''
The Monkey Man . . . . . .   ''
Death . . . .   ''
Cord . . . .'. . . . . Jeff Cooper
White Robe . . . . .Roddy McDowall
Man In Oil . . . . Eli Wallach
Tara . . . . Erica Creer
Zetan . . . . .Christopher Lee
Morthond . . . . Anthony De Longis
Black Giant . . . . .Earl Maynard

Despite all the philosophical trappings, impressive locales, and quality technical credits, "Circle Of Iron" is basically just another chop socky film, albeit a highly-polished one. Made under the title, "The Silent Flute," and deriving from an idea by the late kung-fu great Bruce Lee and actor James Coburn, the Zen-oriented "fable" may not satisfy either the action or the art crowd. Boxoffice results, therefore, will be closely tied to how the film is sold by Avco Embassy, which picked it up last fall.

David Carradine, billed above the title here, assumes the role originally written for Lee, and he again demonstrates he's a forceful screen presence, playing four distinct parts with flair and acumen.

As both goad and guide to a knowledge-seeking martial artist played by Jeff Cooper, Carradine gives "Circle" a core that it needs, since the script by Stirling Silliphant and Stanley Mann dwells mostly on Zen platitudes, variations on the "What is the sound of one hand clapping?" theme.

Since neither time nor place is ever identified (the setting seems to be fantasy world where everyone is well instructed in Eastern martial arts), "Circle Of Iron" founders along, with various trials in store for Cooper until he reaches a version of Shangri-La, governed by an impatient Christopher Lee who would just love to turn his robes over the new newcomer.

Along the way, there are monkey people, demons, bandits and a beautiful woman (played by the stunning Erica Creer) to be vanquished, and director Richard Moore, with the aid of kung fu tech advisor Kam Yuen, stages the various battle scenes with a sensibility foreign to most Hong Kong-based chop socky efforts. But there are still the familiar post-synched grunts, groans and heavy breathing associated with this genre, and enough violence to earn a picture with minimum dialog an R rating.

Carradine is masterful in all his roles, especially as the blind teacher and the desert warrior, Chang-Sha. Cooper projects a distinctly American presence in a clearly non-Western world, but his fighting abilities carry his performance. Roddy McDowall, Eli Wallach and Lee fill cameo roles.

Visually "Circle Of Iron" is exceptional, thanks to the well-chosen Israeli locations. Ronnie Taylor's camerawork is superb, as is Johannes Larsen's impressive production design, and Lilly Fenichel's imaginative costuming. Pic is an excellent plug for Israeli lensing. —Poll.

L'Amour En Fuite
(Love on the Run)
(FRENCH-COLOR)

Paris, Jan. 23.
AMLF release of a Films du Carrosse production. Directed by Francois Truffaut. Features entire cast. Screenplay, Truffaut, Pisier, Jean Aurel, Suzanne Schiffman; camera (color), Nestor Almendros; editor, Martine Barraque-Curie; music, Georges Delerue; set decoration, Jean-Pierre Kohut-Svelko; title song sung by Alain Souchon. Reviewed at Salle Ponthieu, Paris, Jan. 10, '79. Running time: **94 MINS.**
Antoine Doinel . . . . Jean-Pierre Leaud
Colette . . . . .Marie-France Pisier
Christine . . . . .Claude Jade
Liliane . . . . .Dani
Sabine . . . . Dorothee
Colette's mother . . . . Rosy Varte
Monsieur Lucien . . . . Julien Bertheau
The Librarian . . . . Daniel Mesguich
Divorce judge . . . . ,. . . . . . . Marie Henriau
Christine's lawyer . . . . Jean-Pierre Ducos
Maitre Renard . . . . Pierre Dios
Judge in Aix . . . . Alain Ollivier
Madame Ida . . . . .Monique Dury
Antoine's friend . . . . Emmanuel Clot
Train wolf . . . . Christian Lentretien
Angry telephonist . . . . Roland Thenot
Alphonse Doinel . . . . Julien Dubois
Restaurant car child . . . . Alexandre
Janssen

Francois Truffaut has made it a habit to announce after every new installment in his semi-autobiographical Antoine Doinel series (which so far contains "The 400 Blows," "Love at Twenty," "Stolen Kisses" and "Bed and Board") that the latest would undoubtedly be the last. But inevitably a new Doinel always seems to come along.

Although Truffaut has said much the same about "L'Amour en fuite" (Love on the Run), this one is such a gem that more Doinels should be sure to follow.

Sure to follow because "L'Amour en fuite" should gain back for Truffaut much of the audience he lost with the generally lacklustre performances of his last two films, "The Green Room" and "The Man Who Loved Women."

This one has Antoine Doinel, played by Jean-Pierre Leaud, now 34 (he was only 14 when he first portrayed Antoine in "400 Blows"), finally divorcing Claude Jade, the woman he had courted in "Stolen Kisses" and married and cheated on in "Bed and Board."

Using a framework very much like that adopted by Ingmar Bergman in "Summer Interlude," a film Truffaut admires, Truffaut has Doinel making unsuccessful attempts to recapture and conserve the beautiful moments of the past. Finally, he realizes that love is perpetually on the run and that one must simply accept what the present makes available which in Doinel's case is an off-and-on relationship with Sabine, a comely brunette who repairs clocks (played by Dorothee, who bears an uncanny resemblance to actress Francoise Dorleac, who starred in Truffaut's 1964 "The Soft Skin," and who died three years later in an automobile crash).

But for a surprisingly clumsy pre-credit sequence, the film is constructed with clockwork precision, which is helpful because fully half of "L'amour en fuite" is composed of excerpts and outtakes from several previous Truffaut films. These include bits from other pictures in the Doinel series as well as "The Man Who Loved Women" and "Two English Girls."

In spite of the ostensible heterogeneous nature of the film's constitutent parts, "L'Amour en Fuite" is assembled so smoothly that one is not conscious of the flashbacks and other inserts.

In this picture, unlike the others, Doinel seems to have realized that first kiss and first love are just beautiful memories, and should be left that way. One's reaction to glimpses of his earlier life is one of nostalgia for the better moments of something which has inevitably grown worse.

Some exceptional performances are given in "L'amour en fuite:" by Jade, Leaud, whose last film was "Les Lolos de Lola" in 1974, Dani, Marie-France Pisier, Julien Bertheau, Rosy Varte and Dorothee, a children's television program announcer who is here making her first motion picture appearance.
—*Mich.*

Escape To Athena
(BRITISH-COLOR)

London, Jan. 17.

ITC Film Distributors (Associated Film Distributors in U.S.-Canada) release of a Lew Grade presentation. Produced by Jack Wiener, David Niven Jr. Stars Roger Moore, Telly Savalas, David Niven, Stefanie Powers, Claudia Cardinale, Elliott Gould, Richard Roundtree, Sonny Bono. Directed by George P. Cosmatos. Screenplay, Richard S. Lochte and Edward Anhalt, based on original story by Lochte and George P. Cosmatos. Camera (color), Gil Taylor; editor, Ralph Kemplen; art direction, John Graysmark; music, Lalo Schifrin; sound, Derek Ball; assistant director, Derek Cracknell. Reviewed at Audley Square Preview Theatre, London, Jan. 16, '79. Running time: **125 MINS.**

Maj. Otto Hecht	Roger Moore
Zeno	Telly Savalas
Prof. Blake	David Niven
Eleana	Claudia Cardinale
Nat	Richard Roundtree
Dottie	Stefanie Powers
Rotelli	Sonny Bono
Charlie	Elliott Gould
Volkmann	Anthony Valentine
Braun	Sigi Rauch
Mann	Michael Sheard
Reistoffer	Richard Wren
Vogel	Philip Locke
Lantz	Steve Ubels
Brotel girl	Elena Secota

"Escape to Athena" not only has the unabashed look of a cynical "package" but also plays like one as well. It's a joke up wartime action retread, feeble as to both humor and suspense, in which a group of Anglo-American prisoners of the Germans scramble to liberate (a) themselves and (b) some Greek art treasures.

The David Niven Jr.-Jack Wiener production for Lord Lew Grade's ITC banner is another name-laden entry with a throwaway script, routine direction and

performances. Fast mass playoff is advisable. Outlook in some foreign markets is more hopeful than in U.S.-Canada, where the new Associated Film Distributors will release pic.

Of those billed above the title, Roger Moore as the Nazi camp commander, Elliott Gould, David Niven, Sonny Bono, Stefanie Powers and Richard Roundtree as POWs (how's that for a motley bunch?) Telly Savalas as a Greek resistance leader, and Claudia Cardinale as a brothel madam, none have much scope to register with any dimension and most are as implausible as the hammy action.

The screenplay is credited to Richard S. Lochte and Edward Anhalt, from a story by Lochte and the film's director, George Pan Cosmatos. Style and wit have bailed out many an implausible plot, but this one has neither. With a bit of both, one could maybe forgive the fact pic also has no sense of time and period, in dialog, military hardware, etc. Under the circumstances, Cosmatos' direction is professionally accomplished.

Moore is only seemingly cast against heroic type, since his character is obviously sympathetic (no Nazi — good German) and winds up collaborating with the prisoners.

Pic was shot on the Greek island of Rhodes, and of the few affirmative elements, one can cite the ravishing landscapes (often via swirling helicopter shots — a cliche already but still effective) and the sharp lensing of Gil Taylor, also a smart job of cutting. Lalo Schifrin's score is an appealing mix of martial airs and hymns.

What little gripping action there is climaxes with some lusty fireworks. —*Pit.*

Le Cavaleur
(The Skirt Chaser)
(FRENCH-COLOR)

Paris, Jan. 23.

A Films Ariane - Mondex Film - FR3 Production. Produced by Georges Danciger, Alexandre Mnouchkine. Stars Jean Rochefort. Directed by Philippe de Broca. Screenplay, Michel Audiard, Philippe de Broca; camera (color), Jean-Paul Schwatz; editor; Henri Lanoe; music, Georges Delerue. Reviewed at Films Ariane Screening Room, Paris, Jan. 11, '79. Running time: **104 MIN.**

Edouard Choiseul	Jean Rochefort
Marie-Frances	Nicole GAERCIA
Murielle Picoche	Catherine Alric
Valentine	Catherine Leprince
Olga	Lila Kedrova
Suzanne Taylor	Danielle Darrieux
Charles-Edmond	Jean Desailly
Pompom	Carole Lixon

Though it may not have been intended as such, Philippe de Broca's new film has the earmarks of an old-fashioned star vehicle: to wit, a screenplay lacking in imagination,

underwritten supporting roles and a general lack of directorial effort.

The star is Jean Rochefort who rose to prominence a few years ago with Bertrand Tavernier's "The Clockmaker" and "Let Joy Reign Supreme" (Que la Fete Commence). Since then he has consolidated a reputation as one of the leading male actors in the French film industry. Remarked for his urbanity, subtlety and Frenchness, Rochefort seemed destined to take the role of an irresistible Gallic lady-killer. Well, here he is.

Rochefort plays Edouard Choiseul, a celebrated classical pianist with a short memory span and a long history of amorous side-activities. He has a beautiful wife and three children (not to mention a teenage daughter who lives with his first wife) and, of course, an incredibly perserving beauty whom he continually manages to stand up, not out of malice — he has none, which is perhaps one of his problems — but simply out of forgetfulness.

And then, in the midst of this tangle of concerts, recordings, rendezvous and phoned excuses to his wife, Choiseul is smitten by the beautiful young daughter of an old flame; but the girl definitely belongs to a new age, one that suddenly jolts Choiseul into the realization that time is sharing his piano bench. On top of this, his wife finally decides enough is enough and walks out on him. Deprived of the company of all the women in his life, he gradually discovers new roles, such as coaching the gifted son of an old companion and becoming a grandfather. With this new-found peace Choiseul also restores his marriage.

The screenplay, by de Broca and Michel Audiard, skips lightly along the beaten track, abdictating any real contact with the theme of the compulsive seducer, adding nothing of substance to the innumerable films, plays and novels that have already dealt with this personage. That Choiseul is a great artist seems ultimately to have little bearing on the proceedings. And the theme of the sudden awareness of time passing is trite.

At its worst de Broca's direction is perfunctory — you can almost hear the cliches agonize at times, as in the shot in which Rochefort stares uncomprehendingly at his reflection in a filmy, dirt-specked mirror. But, as one would expect of this master practitioner of light comedy, he can still charm in many of the purely comic moments. Still, the film is another example of how a fine comic filmmaker falls into the traps of facility.

Again, the film is Rochefort's, and he steers it with professional ease, taste and appeal, though he does not succeed in dredging up the

poignancy that the script so obviously makes a dull stab at in the second half. Actors of Rochefort's **talents deserve a picture, not a frame.**

The women fare less well; they are required not so much to act their parts as to occupy them physically. Beautiful blanks. This is particularly unfortunate in the case of Nicole Garcia, who seems to have something more to off as Rochefort's current wife. Annie Girardot contributes a brief note of distanced tenderness as the first wife and Danielle Darrieux still radiates star quality as the oldtime conquest. Catherine Alric and Catherine Leprince have grace and loveliness as two of the protagonist's pursuits. —*Len.*

Was Ich Bin, Sind Meine Filme
(I Am What My Films Are)
(WEST GERMAN-COLOR-16m)

Hof, Oct. 29.

A Nanuk-Film Production, Munich; world rights, Filmwelt Munich. A Werner Herzog Portrait, directed by Christian Weisenborn and Erwin Keusch. Camera (color), Rene Perraudin, Martin Schaefer; interviewer, Laurens Straub. Reviewed at Hof Film Fest, Oct. 29, '79. Running time: **93 MINS.**

The Werner Herzog-Portrait, "I Am What My Films Are," is another in a wave of docus on film directors — in the last year have appeared similar portraits of Roger Corman and Martin Scorsese, while Hamburg critic Hans C. Blumenberg has made a career with films about Hollywood and Hollywood directors (coming up shortly is one on Budd Boetticher).

Docu on Herzog was made by Christian Weisenborn and Edwin Keusch, the latter the young helmer who caused more than a splash on the New German Cinema scene with the b.o. success, "The Baker's Bread" (1977). Weisenborn and Keusch started out with six hours of film conversation with Herzog, helped along by interviewer Laurens Straub, long-time friend of the director with a far-reaching knowledge of his past and film projects.

Talk centers on Herzog's childhood, his self-taught approach to filmmaking, the several adolescent experiences until he "came of age" with "Signs of Life" (1968), his first feature pic — then it shifts over to the films with clips and photos as the director discusses the making of "Even Dwarfs Start Out Small" (1969), "Fata Morgana" (1970), "Land of Silence and Darkness" (1972), "Aguirre" (1973), "Sky Flyer" (1974), "Kaspar Hauser" (1975), "Heart of Glass" (1976), "Stroszek" (1977), a work in progress which is filmed on the set in Berlin, and others.

All of Herzog's themes are

touched in the hour-and-a-half docu, but of particular interest is the man himself and his surrealist visions. —Holl.

Einer Von Uns Beiden
(One or the Other)
(WEST GERMAN-COLOR)

Berlin, Dec. 13.

A Wolfgang Petersen Film, produced by Roxy-Film, Munich, Luggi Waldleitner; world rights, Transocean International. Features entire cast. Directed by Wolfgang Petersen. Screenplay, Manfred Purzer, based on a thriller by Ky; camera (color), Charley Steinberger. Reviewed at Deutsche Werbung Screening Room, Berlin, Dec. 13, '78. Running time: 90 MINS.

With Elke Sommer, Juergen Prochnow, Klaus Schwartzkopf, Klaus Theo Goertner, Otto Sander.

After some 20 tv pix, many of them detective stories, Wolfgang Petersen is recognized as West Germany's leading action director in the Hollywood vein. Shortly he is to film Robert Neeley's thriller, "The Plastic Nightmare," in San Francisco with an American crew and cast — and may get Roger Corman's backing to boot in addition to making his own first indie investment in his own future.

"One or the Other" (1973) was his first feature for the cinema theatre circuit, produced by vet Luggi Waldleitner for Roxy-Film in Munich, which is now back in a re-release (and picked up by Lufthansa for cross-Atlantic flights). It stars Elke Sommer in a brief walk-on as a prostie who gets herself murdered by a jealous lover as she gets ready to drop the trade with a nest-egg of savings to fall back on. Another of her friends earns his living writing term papers for lazy university students, and thus he stumbles on a plagiarized dissertation by a famous sociology professor living in a villa in Berlin.

Blackmail leads to falling in love with the professor's daughter, a thrilling auto chase and reckoning with Sommer's killer, and a twist at the end involving the two adversaries as split personalities always trying to get the better of each other — even in death. Credits are tops. —Holl.

Nosferatu: Phantom Der Nacht
(Nosferatu, The Vampire)
(FRENCH-GERMAN-COLOR)

Paris, Jan. 18.

A Gaumont release of a Werner Herzog Filmproduktion-Gaumont co-production. Produced by Werner Herzog. Features entire cast. Written and directed by Werner Herzog. Camera (color), Jorg Schmidt-Reitwein; editor, Beate Mainka-Jellinghaus; music, Popol Vuh, Florian Fricke; make-up, Reiko Kruk; sound, Harald Maury; special effects, Cornelius Siegel; art direction, Henning Von Gierke. Reviewed at Gaumont Champs-Elysees, 66

Champs-Elysees, Paris, Jan. 17, '79. Running time: 106 MINS.
Count Dracula .... Klaus Kinski
Lucy Harker ....Isabelle Adjani
Jonathan Harker .... Bruno Ganz
Captain .... Jacques Dufilho
Renfield .... Roland Topor
Dr. Van Helsing ...... Walter Ladengast

(German-language soundtrack)

There's already been a lot of nit-picking — apparently started by Werner Herzog himself — about whether his "Nosferatu" is a "remake" of F.W. Murnau's celebrated 1922 classic, or an entirely new version. Comparisons are certainly inevitable, for Herzog has not only retained most of the silent film's narrative structure but has also quoted and paraphrased shots and sequences from it. But comparisons are unnecessary in sizing up this new Dracula tale as a major disappointment, often pictorially striking but singularly unengrossing.

The story is familiar, though it varies in many respects from Tod Browning's 1930 sound version with Bela Lugosi. Jonathan Harker, a young real estate clerk, is dispatched to Count Dracula's castle in Transylvania to seal an agreement for the purchase of a house in Harker's home town of Weimar. Preyed upon by the vampire, Harker is locked in the castle, helplessly looking on as the Count departs for Germany with his earth-filled coffins. Realizing that his lovely young wife, Lucy — whose portrait Dracula has seen — is in mortal danger, he manages to escape and make his way back to Weimar. Too late — Dracula has already disembarked with an army of plague-infested rats. Learning of the vampire's weaknesses, Lucy sacrifices her life by luring Dracula to her bedside and keeping him there with her until the sun rises to destroy him.

Herzog has registered some telling alterations on the tale. Whereas Murnau's clerk never suffers from Dracula's bite, Herzog's character arrives home feverish and amnesiac. Upon Dracula's death he becomes the new vampire.

These changes only suggest the moral ambiguity that is Herzog's major innovation. Dracula is rendered more human and sympathetic. By contrast, Lucy is stuffy and pallid, bordering on morbidity. These disturbing currents merge in the final scenes when Dracula comes to claim Lucy, who expires shortly after the vampire with an oddly satisfied expression. Subsequently Harker bares his new fangs and rides off into the distance to the accompaniment of a Gounod mass on the soundtrack.

But Herzog's execution is bloodless, without accent. Understandably Herzog wants to avoid the overfamiliar cliches of the horror

film, but it is less understandable why he completely rejects any recourse to terror and horror. Herzog flattens and distances. His images, evoked through Jorg Schmidt-Reitwein's masterly color photography, only intermittently create a climate of otherworldly mystery. The Weimar scenes, with the invasion of rats, are particularly flat, and Herzog again displays a lack of skill in directing actors and their movements.

In this general monotony there are isolated moments of power and beauty, notably in the climactic scene between Dracula and Lucy. With the help of his cameraman and cast, Herzog gives these moments an incomparably unsettling eroticism and sense of moral irony.

Klaus Kinski is a pleasure to watch as the vampire, anguishing over the curse of eternity and longing for love. Bruno Ganz is fine as Jonathan Harker and Isabelle Adjani is disturbingly equivocal as Lucy. Roland Topor, however is disappointing in the unwisely truncated role of Renfield, the Count's man in the Baltic.

The renewed vogue for Dracula vehicles will give Herzog's film a certain commercial success, though there will undoubtedly be many disappointed spectators. Herzog is being true only to himself, which will continue to delight his followers and further alienate his detractors. It should be exhausted by the time the Frank Langella-Laurence Olivier version is ready for the market. —Len.

Lulekoqet Mbi Mure
(Red Poppies on the Wall)
(ALBANIAN-B&W)

Berlin, Dec. 21.

An Albfilm Production, Tirana; world rights, Albania Film, Tirana. Features entire cast. Directed by Dhimiter Anagnosti. Screenplay, Petraq Quafzezi; Anagnosti; camera, Pellumb Kallfa; art direction, Namik Prizreni; music, Kujtim Laro. Reviewed at Berlin Cine-Center Screening Room, Dec. 21, '78. Running time: 100 MINS.

With Timo Flloko, Agim Qirjaqi, Kadri Roshi, Alfrd Kote, Liza Laska, Anastas Kristofori, Luan Qerimi, Enver Dauti, Strazimir Zaimi, Enea Zeku, Artur Huxholli.

Albania's top helmer, Dhimiter Anagnosti (also spelled Anagosti) has worked on nine feature pix to date, roughly a fifth of the national production since the Albanian industry got started in 1958. In the beginning he was a cameraman (Hysen Hakani's "Debatic" in 1961 and "Our Land" in 1964), together with Viktor Gjika, another of the country's top directorial talent who developed similarly along professional lines. Then he and Gjika directed and photographed as a team "Commissar of Light" (1966), after which he branched off as a director on his own.

Other Anagnosti pix follow in the mold of the former: heroic stories of partisans or brave men under stress and trial. "A Silent Duel" (1967) salutes the history of the Albanian navy; "Old Wounds" (1969) (script and direction) is set in a mine and a surgery ward; "The Girl of the Mountains" (1974) introduced color in a ballet film, followed by another color spectacular, "When the Masks Are Down" (1975), on the Tirana Variety Show Theatre.

"Red Poppies on the Wall" (1976) is set in an orphanage during the Italian Occupation. The fascist director uses the boys to clear the streets and walls of painted Communist slogans and posters, but a resistance group is formed secretly to aid the guerrilla unit in town — until finally the director himself is targeted in slogans by the boys. Thesps and credits are plus. —Holl.

Zonja Nga Qyteti
(The Lady from the Town)
(ALBANIAN-COLOR)

Berlin, Dec. 21.

An Albfilm Production, Tirana; world rights, Albania Films, Tirana. Features entire cast. Directed by Piro Milkani. Screenplay, Ruzhdi Pulaha, based on Pulaha's play with the same name; camera (color), Lionel Konomi; art direction, Arben Basha; music, Agim Krajka. Reviewed at Berlin Cine-Center Screening Room, Dec. 21, '78. Running time: 105 MINS.

With Violeta Manushi, Rajmonda Bulku, Stavri Shkurti, Pandi Raidhi, Yilka Mujo, Petraq Kita.

A popular play turned into a film, Piro Milkani's "The Lady from the Town" (1976) stays close to the theatrical lines of the play without venturing off on its own into filmic gags to boost its attractiveness. Malkani is one of the busier helmers in the second line of directorial talent appearing on the scene in the 1970s. Other pix are the partisan tales, "Once at Dawn" (1971) and "War Paths" (1974), and the folk-drama "The Happy Couple" (1975)

The "lady" in the story is an over protective mother living in the town, whose daughter, a medical assistant, has been assigned to a post in the country, despite the mother's efforts to keep her close to home through various connections. The mother is also interested in finding a "good match" for her daughter in the city, and this aim-in-life contrasts with the ready warmth and open-mindedness of the towns-folk. Gradually, after several comic situations involving misunderstandings and the like, mother and daughter hit it off and the handsome school-teacher is accepted as a promising bridegroom — and who knows, they might just settle here.

Well acted an credits a good notch above average. An animation sequence accompanies the unspooling of the pic's titles to set the mood. —Holl.

Ne Fillim Te Veres
(At The Beginning Of Summer)
(ALBANIAN-COLOR)

Berlin, Dec. 20.

An Albfilm Production, Tirana; world rights, Albania Film, Tirana. Features entire cast. Directed by Gezim Erebara. Screenplay, Peci Dado; camera (color), Faruk Basha; art direction, Astrit Tota; music, Kujtim Laro. Reviewed at Berlin Cine-Center Screening Room, Dec. 20, '78. Running time: 105 MINS.

With Astrit Cerma, Sander Prosi, Demir Hyskja, Agim Shuke, Albert Verria, Elida Cangonji, Ndrek Luca.

Shortly after Albania Film made a giant step forward in 1974 with five feature productions, two of which were filmed in color, Gezim Erebara directed the successful "At the Beginning of Summer" (1975), a partisan pic in color dealing with key events in the summer of 1942, shortly after the Communist Party organized a guerrilla resistance movement against the Italian Occupation forces. His previous feature, "The Brave" (1970), was set in the mountains and dealt with the coming-of-age of a young boy. Later, Erebara made the first widescreen, color pic, "Trees of Freedom" (1976).

"At the Beginning of Summer" tells the story of the beginnings of partisan resistance in the summer of 1942. The National Liberation Front had been formed under the leadership of Enver Hoxha, a French-educated Moslem Tosk, who obtained military aid from Tito in Yugoslavia and united the people later in a general armed uprising. Pic shows how all walks of life — intellectuals, peasants, workers, patriots — were united in planning sabotage strikes against the enemy.
—Holl.

The Glacier Fox
(JAPANESE-DOCU-COLOR)

Well-done nature docu. Should hunt up some b.o.

Hollywood, Jan. 25.

A Sanrio Film Distribution release of a Sanrio Film. Exec producer, Shintaro Tsuji. Produced by Hiromu Tsugawa. English version co-produced by Mark L. Rosen; written and directed by Koreyoshi Kurahara; English narration by Walter Bloch, camera (color), Masao Tochizawa, Akira Shiizuka, Seizo Sengen, Tsuguzo Matsumae, Hideo Omura, Keisuke Tateishi, Yoshio Mamiya; editor, Kurahara, Akira Suzuki; Terry Anderson; sound, Kazumi Inamura; music, Masaru Sato; assistant director, Junichi Mimura. Narrated by Arthur Hill. Reviewed at Director's Guild, Hollywood, Jan. 24, '78. (MPAA Rating: G.) Running time: 90 MINS.
(Dubbed English Soundtrack)

"The Glacier Fox" is the most impressive cinematic study of animals in their natural setting since the Disney "Nature Life" series in the mid-1950s. This Japanese documentary, five years in the making, is both stirring and affecting. It should do extremely well in the depleted family film market, if fledgling Sanrio Films can muster the proper ad campaign and bookings.

Actually, "The Glacier Fox" far exceeds any of the Disney films (which ran about 30 minutes shorter) in terms of conception and accomplishment. Writer-director Koreyoshi Kurahara set out to fit a fictional story line of the life cycle of these small, distinctive foxes into some 600,000 feet of raw footage shot on the isolated Japanese island of Hokkaido.

The result is a technical masterpiece, and a strong emotional statement about survival of the fittest, and how that evolutionary process has been altered and warped by the encroachment of man.

A big b.o. click in Japan, the docu has been re-edited for American release, and new lyrics and an English narration by Arthur Hill added. There revisions hardly seem necessary, and at times detract from the purity and beauty of the imagery, which again demonstrates that film by itself is an international language.

Kurahara's cameras begin with the courtship of the male and female foxes, following with the birth of a litter of pups, the death of the mother at the hands of a cruel snare trap, the expulsion of the young foxes by the male at the time of their adolescence, and the ultimate fate that befalls this "family."

"Foxes" is not without the anthropomorphic qualities that marred the Disney pix (such as having the foxes cavort to the strains of "I Think I'm Falling In Love"), but the animal subjects are treated with the dignity they deserve. It's a docu made with respect, not cuteness.

Despite several fights with dogs, the trapping of the female, and

other bloody disasters, the editing is extremely discreet, and the pic is well designed for the moppet trade. Sanrio has announced its intention to appeal the G rating, and that would seem to be a mistake, since there's nothing in the film to warrant a more restrictive tag.

Adults will be fascinated by the breathtaking tech accomplishments, in particular the p.o.v. shots from the foxes' angle, and the incredible close-up work via telephoto lenses.

Only drawbacks are the syrupy, MOR score, and the croaky narration by Hill, supposed to represent the encompassing viewpoint of an old oak tree. The device doesn't work, and it might have been more interesting to hear the original Japanese score on the soundtrack.

As a rare species in its own right, "The Glacier Fox" may have a hard time finding its audience. But if patrons can be lured into the theatre, it's doubtful they'll leave disappointed. —Poll.

Attack Of The Killer Tomatoes
(COLOR)

Spoiled fruit.

Hollywood, Jan. 22.

An NAI Entertainment release of a Four Square production. Produced by Steve Peace, John De Bello. Directed by De Bello. Features entire cast. Screenplay, Costa Dillon, Peace, De Bello; camera (color), John K. Culley; editor, De Bello; sound, Paul Wear; music, Gordon Goodwin, Paul Sundfor; Special effects, Greg Auer. No other credits available. Reviewed at Hollywood Pacific Theatre, Hollywood, Jan. 22, '78. (MPAA Rating: PG.) Running time: 87 MINS.

Mason Dixon .... David Miller
Jim Richardson .... George Wilson
Lois Fairchild ....Sharon Taylor
Agriculture Official ....Jack Riley
Wilbur Finletter .... Rock Peace
Senator Polk ....Eric Christmas
Ted Swan .... Al Sklar
President .... Ernie Meyers
Major Milis .... Jerry Anderson
Newspaper Editor ....Ron Shapiro

"Attack Of The Killer Tomatoes" could offer conclusive proof of a product shortage. If this item can make it to the screen, the exhibitors must be more desperate than anyone supposes. The low-budget indie production, made by a group of young San Diego filmmakers, isn't even worhty of sarcasm. There may be some boxoffice sell in the title, but after the word gets out, biz is bound to be wanting.

Only saving grace is the satire pic's opening titles, a clever lampoon of theatre trailers and advertising pitches, including a midcredit title card that boasts, "This space for rent." There's also a tongue-in-cheek parody of disaster pic music, sung in a deep basso voice, but that's over in about two minutes.

Thereafter it's all downhill, rapid-

ly. "No one is laughing now," the final credits warns, and the prophesy comes true. Whatever sight gags there are, such as a tiny conference room for 10 generals, are played out to boring tedium.

Plot, if it can be called that, concerns sudden growth spurt of tomatoes and their rampage —Poll.

L'Ange Gardien
(The Guardian Angel)
(CANADIAN-FRENCH-COLOR)

Paris, Jan. 18.

An A.M.L.F. release of Promedifilm (Marseille) — Les Films Prospec Inc. (Montreal) co-production. Stars Margaret Trudeau, Francis Lemaire. Written and directed by Jacques Fournier. Camera (color), Yves Pouffary; editor, Frederic de Chateaubriant; music, Marcel Napoleoni. Reviewed at the Cinema Berlitz, Paris, Jan. 17, '79. Running time: 90 MINS.

Annie .... Margaret Trudeau
Aldô .... Francis Lemaire
Andre Roussel .... Andre Falcon
Miss Pickwick ....Jacqueline Jefford

"L'Ange Gardien" is a slight and tired comedy about a bumbling Clouseau-like private detective who is hired by a Canadian executive to keep a watchful eye on his attractive young wife as she vacations alone on the Riviera. After secretly helping her stave off the onslaught of admiring males, he himself falls for her charms — she reciprocates. As it turns out, the "husband" is not her husband at all, merely a jealous boyfriend, allowing the two lovers to drive off free and easy.

Jacques Fournier's screenplay and direction rehash stock situations and old sight gags. He at least has the sense not to get in the way of his actors: the young woman. is played by Margaret Trudeau, whose previous "credits" need no mention here. She displays no acting ability but manages to get through the film with a repertory of three or four expressions. She is exceedingly easy on the eyes. The detective is played by Francis Lemaire, who is a warm and engaging comedian — with better material he could make a firm impression. —Len.

New Delhi Fest

Chitegu Chinte
(The Restless Corpse)
(INDIAN-COLOR)

New Delhi, Jan. 15.

G.N. Lakshipathy, Sawan Movies release and production. Features entire cast. Directed by M.S. Sathyu. Screenplay, Javed Siddiqui; camera (Eastmancolor), Ashok Gunjal; editor, Chakraborty; music, G.K. Venkstesh. Reviewed at New Delhi Film Fest, Jan. 14, '79. Running time: 129 MINS.

With: C.R. Simha, Manjula, Ram Prakash.

A rare Indian attempt at a satirical film that sends up crooked politics and the Indian corn-laden song and dance films. It does have some shrewd comedic insights but finally degenerates into a mixture of action film and comedy jape which loses its essential early wit and satirical shafts.

A big shot gangster type rules the town from his bed in a home for the blind which is a charity coverup for his activities. A popular, hammy actor is to be done away with for he has too big a following but he leads a charmed life. The politico decides to make him president of the mythical island of the film and lives to regret it.

Mainly a local item, but showing enough ease in comedic invention and action interludes, plus added Bondian gadgets, to tag M.S. Sathyu a man to watch when he can balance his satirical thrusts and visual and verbal comedics. Offshore possibilities are limited.

—*Mosk.*

Ondanondu Kaladalli
(Once Upon A Time)
(INDIAN-COLOR)

New Delhi, Jan. 9.
Lakshmipathy-Narayan release and production. Features entire cast. Directed by Girish Karnad. Screenplay, Karnad, Krishan Basrur; camera (Eastmancolor), Apurba Kishore Bir; editor, P. Bhaktavatsalam; music, Bhaskar Chandvarkar. Reviewed at New Delhi Film Fest, Jan. 8, '79. Running time, 160 MINS.
With: Shankar Nag, Sundar Krishna Urs, Akshata Rao, Sushilendra Joshi, Sundar Rajan, V. Ramamurthy.

A fine, warm, perky bow to action films in general and to work of noted Japanese filmmaker Akira Kurosawa in particular. It is an homage with the influences well worked into medieval India without copying, sending up or aping but assimilating it to a robust, perhaps overlong adventure opus laced with a comic assurance and full blooded characters who are familiar but not stereotyped.

Shankar Nag, looking a bit like Toshiro Mifune in many of Kurosawa's period films, is a mercenary who is set on by some men of a village chief. He bests them and helps two men they were chasing. The head men are brothers who did in their older brother and are vying for his place.

The dead man's son is allowed to live with the brother whose men Nag has helped. The mercenary goes into the chief's employ pitted against an old warrior representing the other. There are scenes of Nag training the men and, secretly, the real heir, to whom he takes a fancy and who is kept out since he is a relative but who is not allowed to learn an of the martial arts.

Latter are mainly sword play and

leg work with none of the supernatural boundings of kung fu. It finally leads to the chiefs' betraying their own military leads who band together to fight them. It is a titanic battle ending with the death of the mercenary and the other military man sparing the son of the real chief who may presumably become a just leader.

Director Girish Karnad, an actor, scripter and theatre man, shows a fine directorial feel for pace, mood and derring-do as well as showing the nobility of a mercenary who had become on through corrupt things around him. An antihero with cravings of justice and feeling it right to get paid for a just cause.

Reminders of Kurosawa's "Seven Samurai" and especially "Yojimto" are there but winningly utilized in a more serene film. The sword fights are well done, especially one with so-called belt swords of thin flailing long blades. Pic could be tightened but is an entertainment that might find playoff abroad on its sheer good spirits and adherence to a genre type without in any way degrading it and keeping intact its sentiments about duty and justice. —*Mosk.*

Kodiyettom
(The Ascent)
(INDIAN-B&W)

New Delhi, Jan. 16.
Trivandrum release of Chitralekha Film Cooperative production. Features entire cast. Written and directed by Adoor Gopalakrishnan; camera (B&W), Ravi Varma; editor, M. Moni. Reviewed at New Delhi Film Fest, Jan. 15, '79. Running time, 130 MINS.
With: Gopi, Lalita Azeez, Kaviyoor Ponnamma, Adoor Bhavani, Vilasini Suseela.

A remarkable film from the Southern part of India, Malayalam, where a spurt of unusual filmmakers was revealed at the recent New Delhi Film Festival. This one looks at a drifter who lives off his sister's earnings, plus a few odd jobs, and helps about the village and has time to pay with children, sell his vote and attend religious festivals.

He is not exactly simple-minded but uninformed. He admires a kindly widow who has an attachment to a rich man, unknown to him, and he finally gets married at his sister's insistence. But he is unable to change and goes about his old ways neglecting his wife who leaves him when she is pregnant.

He then gets a job with a harsh truckdriver and slowly begins to change as he first sees life outside his village. He is profoundly hurt by the suicide of the widow he had always admired. He begins to try to see his child and take things to his wife.

Film is full of fine observation that transcends its Indian setting to make a statement on that evergreen theme of a man finding identity and possibly maturity. Pic is slow but always revealing and full of poetic insights into the characters, place and time giveing it universal impact that should reveal the director, Adoor Gopalakrishnan, at European film fests. —*Mosk.*

Agraharathil Kazhuthai
(Donkey in a Brahmin Village)
(INDIAN-B&W)

New Delhi, Jan. 16.
Nirmithi Films release and production. Features entire cast. Written and directed by John Abraham. Camera (black and white), Ramachandrabub; music, M.B. Srinivasan. Reviewed at New Delhi Film Fest, Jan. 15, '79. Running time, 95 MINS.
With: Swathi, Veeraraghavan, Krishnaraj.

Simple, seemingly crudely made film, this still distills into a telling look at religious excess. There is an unassuming directorial touch, but pic adds up to a most disarming proving of village life with its charms undercut by taboos and repressions.

In the city, a good-natured teacher finds a baby donkey on his doorstep. Its mother had been killed by an angry mob when it kicked a boy chasing it with a stick. The man takes in the donkey. Soon students are mocking him and the school director forces him to get rid of the animal.

The donkey is taken to the teacher's village where a deaf-mute girl is hired to take care of it. But the donkey just does not fit in and a local joker keeps pushing it into meetings, temples, marriages to build up resentment towards it.

The mute is seduced by a local and she gives birth to a dead baby. The shocked midwife fears a curse and leaves it near the temple. It is discovered as the donkey goes by and the temple dignitaries insist the animal is an evil omen and stone it to death.

But later somebody thinks he saw the donkey and it becomes a revered memory and miracle worker to add a neat ironic stroke to this uneven but incisive film on human vaguaries and outlooks. Black and white treatment and deceptively slow but revealing unfoldment slant this for mainly specialized and fest chances in most climes. However it marks John Abraham, a director to watch from the Tamil section of the country, and adds to the unusual films and talents emerging in the lesser known filmmaking sections of the nation. —*Mosk.*

Anugraham
(The Boon)
(INDIAN-COLOR)

New Delhi, Jan. 10.
Raviraj International release and production. Features entire cast. Directed by Shyam Benegal. Screenplay, Satyadev Dubey; camera (Eastmancolor), Govind Nihalani; music, Vanraj Bhatia. Reviewed at New Delhi Fest, Jan. 9, '79. Running time: 132 MINS.
With: Vanishree, Anant Nag, Smita Patil, N.T. Rama Rao, Amrish Puri.

Here is a fable, a morality play, a sort of occult parable on human reactions to divine intervention. However, tale is told with asperity and does not fall into didactics or pretention. It's an offbeat film that could find some specialized interest abroad.

A man, seething with anger at his bad treatment by an older brother, also meted out to his new wife, strides along the beach and meets an ancient mythological Indian God who promises him power if he will live in chastity. He is also given a root that can abort a pregnant woman.

At first, the wife and family are distraught by his new ways and decision to abide by the way of the Gods. His wife, too, goes along despite the vow of chastity. He slowly becomes the town holy man and even gets a rich, lubricious man to underwrite the restoration of the town church.

But his new powers begin to have him trying to control lives and leads to a mistake as he administers the abortive root to the rich man's daughter-in-law who he thought had been impregnated by the former. The holy man had also lusted for this woman in dreams.

It ends in his realization of his mistake when the rich man reveals he is sterile and the son is his brother's. Film is well acted and keeps from falling into overblown dramatics as it peels off the layers of vanity, the overuse of power and the misuse of religious precepts that lead to tragedy for the protagonist as his wife falls into a pit, maybe she leaped, after he destroys her faith in him by forcing himself on her and breaking his holy vow of chastity.

Shyam Benegal is a most eclectic and prolific director who makes about two pix a year. He made this one in two versions, Hindi and Telegu. There is added postcriptum to the regional Telegu version with a voice demanding the audience think about what this man has done and whether he was a victim or victimizer. This can be excised easily. Perhaps a bit exotic, but having a universal theme about religion and corruption. Technically excellent.

—*Mosk.*

Thampu
(The Circus Tent)
(INDIAN-B&W)

New Delhi, Jan. 15.
Production Company-General Pictures release and production. Features entire cast. Written and directed by G. Aravindan. Camera (black and white), Shaji; editor, Ramesh; music, M.G. Radakrishnan. Reviewed at New Delhi Film Fest, Jan. 14, '79. Running time, **130 MINS.**
With: Gopi, Venu, Sheeraman, Jalaja and artists of the Great Chitra Circus.

On the surface, this film seems to be a documentary on the setting up of a small circus in a small town. But sharp visual flair and an emerging melding of the circus with the various town stratas begins to give the film a crucible insight into rural India.

It is a real circus with some young and some older tired performers. The tent goes up, people gawk and there is some license trouble, smoothed out when a rich town resident is talked into helping the circus on its first night.

The show and the audience reactions are extraordinarily caught. The people react well and even make the ordinary acrobatics, animal turn with a leopard and a knockabout clown routine seem better as they assuage a need for wonder by both farmers and townspeople.

Film does have a tendency to repeat the give and take of show and onlookers, but there is always some revelation of character to keep up interest. There is an inspired crosscutting between making up an old clown of the show and a monkey. It is also used on a town festival created by the rich man for a coming political vote which cuts into the circus.

The circus has a party during which the irate owner, who has lost biz, strikes the old clown who then talks of being in the circus all his life and now playing dead in a comic slapstick scene to keep alive.

The circus goes off in its truck after striking the tent. It has left some joy even if the circus people themselves are exhausted and exploited. It reveals a director of extraordinary visual drive. Film needs pruning and looks to have doubtful commercial chances abroad but could find festival outings. —*Mosk.*

Gaman
(Going)
(INDIAN-COLOR)

New Delhi, Jan. 7.
Integrated Films release and production. Features entire cast. Written and directed by Muzaffar Ali. Camera (Eastmancolor), Nadeem Khan; editor, Jethu Mundul; music, Jaidev. Reviewed at New Delhi Film Fest, Jan. 6, '79. Running time, **135 MINS.**

With: Farooque Shaikh, Smita Patil, Gita Siddharth, Jabal Agha.

A well-meaning but pedestrian treatment of a young man's attempt to make money in the city when he has to leave his rural town due to lack of work and land takeovers by monied people. It just spends too much time setting up the theme, and the script is too rambling to give a more potent insight into the problems and characters of the protagonist and his family and friends.

The young man joins a friend who drives a taxi in Bombay. He sends back money and finds that it is never enough and gets letters about his wife's loneliness and his old mother's accident.

His friend, a more robust character, has a girl he wants to marry. Her brother and uncle plan to make money by selling her into servant work. She refuses and they attack her boyfriend and kill him in the fight.

The friend decides to go back but film ends as he stands at the train gate uncertain about going back. Director Muzaffar Ali, for a first film, has some narrative flair but needs more help on scripting. Acting is acceptable. —*Mosk.*

Junoon
(Obsession)
(INDIAN-COLOR)

New Delhi, Jan. 4.
Film-Valas release and production. Stars Shashi Kapoor. Directed and written by Shyam Benegal. Camera (Eastmancolor), Govind Nihalni; editor, Bhanudas; music, Vanraj Bhatia. Reviewed at New Delhi Film Fest, Jan. 3, '79. Running time: **144 MINS.**
Javed .... Shashi Kapoor
Ruth .... Nafisa Ali
Wife .... Shabana Azmi
Mariam .... Jennifer Kendal

Shashi Kapoor, one of the top stars in the Hindi region of Indian filmmaking, where the main commercial films are made, turned producer-star for this tale of a love obsession on the background of an Indian uprising against the British in the last century.

Eclectic and prolific filmmaker Shyam Benegal, who has made more demanding films on the caste system, attempts at rural co-ops and some feudal hangovers in remote areas, gives this film a romantic gloss, but it remains predictable.

A group of Indian soldiers in the British Army revolt in a small garrison town. They massacre the English in a church. An Anglo-Indian family of mother, daughter and grandmother are the only ones to escape when hidden by a friendly Indian.

But a Muslim, Shashi Kapoor, who is enamored of the daughter, kidnaps her and her family. He wants to marry her but his wife objects. To her they are enemies even if he has the right to other wives. Meanwhile the fights go on and film deals in some well-limned skirmishes as the English get the upper hand.

There are some interesting subtle revelations of the girl's fear of Kapoor beginning to turn to interest. But Kapoor, who finally goes off to fight when a cousin is killed, comes back to find the English have the upper hand and the people are fleeing. He goes back to try to see the girl. She and her mother are locked in the church. The girl comes out to watch him go off when her mother refuses to allow him to see her.

Film has fine production dress for a reported $200,000 budget. Kapoor has grace and the relentless insistence of a man with obsession while others are acceptable in this historical film that remains surface rather than achieving a truly obsessive flair in delineating the wild love that transcends the revolt around him to Kapoor. The girl in question does not have much to do but cry and whimper but does have a near-sex dream of rape one night.

Should find its way on home grounds and with possible playoff abroad on its exotic tale, robust action and colorful period background. —*Mosk.*

Parasuram
(Man With the Axe)
(INDIAN-COLOR)

New Delhi, Jan. 13.
Production Co. Dept. of Information release and production. Features entire cast. Directed by Mrinal Sen. Screenplay, Sen. Mohit; camera (Eastmancolor), Ranjit Roy; editor, Gangadhar Mashkar; music, B.V. Karanth. Reviewed at New Delhi Fest, Jan. 12, '79. Running time: **99 MINS.**
With: Arum Mukherjee, Bisvas Chakraborty, Nirmal Ghosh, Sreela Majumdar.

A rare film on the street people who live in hovels against walls or the very street itself in many Indian cities. Bengali director Mrinal Sen, who has touched on social, political, colonial, village poverty themes, sometimes in satiric, comedic or even revolutionary manner, here takes a distance from this potent theme by treating it more subjectively.

The people usually come from rural areas and band together from the same place or accept others. The title character is a strange type given to hallucinations who flees to the city when the man he is a servant for beats him for a theft he did not commit.

He has an axe, with which he says he once killed a tiger, but more in reflex than valor. In town, he finds a group of street dwellers who at first do not accept him. But he is given a mythical name of a God who carried an axe. He is accepted but holes up in a nearby cemetery culvert where he meets an old beggar.

Film deals with police raids and destructions of hovels, soon rebuilt, runaway girls and the very problem of existence seemingly on handouts, begging and odd jobs. The axe man somehow seems able to exist and dream in this lowly life and even finds a woman. But his old friend dies, the girl leaves and he, working on a high building one day, falls to his death.

The hovel people insist on getting his body for burial. Director Sen creates a sort of nether world with its own outlooks. This gives the film a sort of irreality which might intimate an inkling that abject poverty can only be coped with this way if there is no way out by government help, changing economic aspects or revolt. It might be one way of treating this difficult subject.

It is ably handled despite its ambivalent look at these street people. Another Indian entry that may find interest sparked for it at festivals later this year though its sometimes evasive treatment may slant this for seminars, school and archive showings. —*Mosk.*

Chuvanna Vithukal
(Red Seedlings)
(INDIAN-B&W)

New Delhi, Jan. 8.
Production Company release and production. Features entire cast. Written and directed by P.A. Backer. Camera (black and white), Vipin Das; editor, Ravi; music, Devera Jan. Reviewed at New Delhi Fest, Jan. 7, '79. Running time: **88 MINS.**
● With: Rehamn, Shanta Kumari, Zeenath, Nilambur Ayesha.

A simple story of two sisters that takes on dimension by observant direction and a revealing welding of personal and social dimensions. It could find its way onto the film festival route this year.

A comely young woman takes care of a teenage sister. The former is a prostitute and has only love for her sister whom she wants to integrate in society. But a raid on the house has the older one locked up and the younger sister goes off with a young man who had often followed her but had been kept at bay by her sister.

Out of prison, she wanders about and plies her trade in thee streets with frightened or mean clients who often desert her without paying. Picked up by a truckdriver one day, he takes her home. Finding she has fever he rushes her to a doctor.

For once someone has cared. A relationship springs up which is blocked out without any sentimentality. The driver feels he has not been such a good man and the woman appeals to him and he will not judge.

It goes on well but one day the younger sister is standing before the door with a child. A brilliant epiphany has a sudden jangle of music as the older sister's hand clutches and slowly drops kernels of rice she has been working on. It may be the end of her chance at her own life.

P.A. Backer is a director from a Southern region of India, Malayalam, which is beginning to show an unusual growth of new directors and films with more potent themes and treatment. He is certainly one to be watched who may find recognition abroad for this finely wrought look at the woman's drama that remains human and revealing on both personal and social planes. —*Mosk.*

Dooratwa
(Distance)
(INDIAN-B&W)

New Delhi, Jan. 10.

Buddadeb Dasgupta release and production. Features entire cast. Written and directed by Buddhadeb Dasgupta. Camera (black and white), Ranjit Roy; editor, Mrinmoy Chakabarty; music, Ain Rasheed. Reviewed at New Delhi Film Fest, Jan. 9, '79. Running time: **96 MINS.**

With: Mamata Shankar, Pradip Mukherjee, Bijon Bhattacharya, Niranjan Roy, Singdha Bannerjee.

Buddhadeb Dasgupta emerges a promising filmmaker from the Bengali part of India which spawned the one internationally known Indian director, Satyajit Ray. Dasgupta, as yet, may intimate rather than reveal more amply the ambitious theme he undertakes of probing the emotional and political impasse of a young middle-class professor.

The young man is called in by a friend to possibly help a young woman who needs work. They begin to see each other and he proposes. She accepts but then after marriage has to tell him she had been pregnant by another man.

He does not understand that she had decided to have the child as a sort of revolt against a certain sterility she felt in the life around her. He, himself, supposedly a liberal, had left his party, refused to help hide a man on the run, and now decides to leave his wife.

He tries a liaison with another woman, attempts to pick up things with his wife and party but does not seem to be able to do it though his wife can accept him as a friend and he may be on his way to a more knowing commitment.

Dasgupta has elicited fine performances and used the city and other characters subtly as counterpoint to the professor's attempt to find a means of assuaging his loneliness as well as taking a stand on his values and actions that he has too often refused to do.

Film has good rhythm, and a theme that may try to be a bit too reflective. Yet it still holds interest and should find its way to festivals abroad and certain specialized situations. —*Mosk.*

L'Adolescente
(The Adolescent)
(FRENCH-W. GERMAN-COLOR)

Paris, Jan. 20.

A Parafrance release of a Carthago Films (Paris) — Janus Films and SWF (West Germany) co-production. Produced by Philippe Dussart. Directed by Jeanne Moreau. Stars Edith Clever, Francis Huster, Jacques Weber, Laetitia Chauveau, Simone Signoret. Screenplay, Henriette Jelinek, Jeanne Moreau; camera (Eastmancolor), Pierre Gautard; editing, Albert Jurgenson, Colette Leloup; art direction, Noele Galland; sound, Dominique Dalmasso; music, Philippe Sarde. Reviewed at Club 13, Paris, Jan. 15, '79. Running time: **90 MINS.**

Marie . . . . Laetitia Chauveau
Mamie . . . . Simone Signoret
Eva . . . . Edith Clever
Jean . . . . Jacques Weber
Alexandre . . . . Francis Huster
Romain . . . . Roger Blin

As an actress Jeanne Moreau has strongly marked the French cinema of the last two decades. In 1975 she brought the fruits of her rich career to bear in her first directing effort, "Lumieres," which sharply divided opinion. Her second film, "L'Adolescente," will create the same division, for though she has poured her love into the project, it fails to etch itself on the viewer's heart or mind.

"L'Adolescente" tells of the passage from childhood to adolescence of 12-year-old Marie who, in the weeks before World War II, leaves the military clamour of Paris with her parents to spend the summer in a picturesque village lost in the heart of France. Here in the sensuousness of the countryside, Marie becomes aware of herself physically and emotionally — she falls in love with a newcomer to the community, a young Jewish doctor. She experiences her first heartache as well when she discovers that, in a temporary separation from her father, her mother has embroiled herself in an affair with the doctor. Her parents are eventually reconciled, despite a last attempt on the part of the doctor to claim her. Marie and her parents return to Paris on the very day war is declared.

The screenplay by Moreau and Henriette Jelinek is unremarkable in its treatment of themes and characters that are overfamiliar and in need of deeper probing. In particular the character of Marie's affectionate and mystically wise grandmother strikes one with the dismay of recognition. The screenplay's unfortunate veering towards the conventional is typified by the narrative development that sep-

arates Marie's parents — bound together in a sometimes disquieting sexual passion — to make way for the less interesting development of the mother's first infidelity.

Moreau's direction only emphasizes the weakness of the script by immersing the action in an old-fashioned atmosphere of tender lyricism — there is even a pair of young lovers who drown in each other's gaze while avowing their passion. The entire film passes like the pictures in a beautiful family album, arranged so as to tell a story. Worse, Miss Moreau often insists on lingering over a scene that could have been tightly edited to more effect. In the end, the director's love excludes our own.

Moreau is on surer ground with her choice of actors. Simone Signoret blocks out the role of the grandmother with her usual integrity and bearing. Jacques Weber and Edith Clever ignite some sparks as Marie's passionate parents. Francis Huster is fine as the young Jew. As Marie, Miss Moreau has cast a remarkable young girl named Laetitia Chauveau and gets from her all the confusion, impatience and innocent callousness that the role requires.

—*Len.*

When You Comin' Back, Red Ryder?
(COLOR)

Misfired translation from stage to screen. B.o. prospects seem dim.

Hollywood, Jan. 31.

A Columbia Pictures release of a Melvin Simon production. Exec producer, Melvin Simon. Stars Marjoe Gortner, Hal Linden, Peter Firth, Lee Grant. Produced by Gortner. Co-produced by Paul Maslansky. Directed by Milton Katselas. Screenplay, Mark Medoff, based on his play of the same title; camera (color), Jules Brenner; editor, Richard Chew; music, Jack Nitzsche; production design, Ted Haworth; costume design, Joe J. Thompkins; sound, Don Johnson; assistant director, David Whorf. Reviewed at Columbia Pictures Screening Room, Jan. 30, '79. (MPAA Rating: R.) Running time: **118 MINS.**

Cheryl . . . . Candy Clark
Teddy . . . . Marjoe Gortner
Angel Childress . . . . Stephanie Faracy
Clarisse Ethridge . . . . Lee Grant
Richard Ethridge . . . . Hal Linden
Stephen Ryder . . . . Peter Firth
Lyle Striker . . . . Pat Hingle
Tommy Clark . . . . Bill McKinney
Ceil Ryder . . . . Audra Lindley

'When You Comin' Back, Red Ryder" does not make the transition from legit melodrama to film very easily. The factors that won Mark Medoff's stage version acclaim are dissipated in this Melvin Simon production, being released through Columbia Pictures. Despite a brace of very strong performances by Marjoe Gortner (who also produces) and Peter Firth, the film's downbeat ending and theatrical mannerisms do not bode well for boxoffice success.

"Red Ryder" employed a technique common to other stage works, that of imprisoning the audience in the same dilemma the characters face. In this instance, that's in a dusty Southwest diner being temporarily ruled by a homicidal Vietnam vet, g.f. in tow, who torments and terrorizes the workers in the restaurant, a visiting concert violinist and hubby, and a neighboring gas station owner.

Onstage, "Ryder" works because the audience is included in this claustrophobic intensity. But in adapting his own play for the screen, Medoff has expanded both the setting and his characters, and the result is to let out all of the suspenses too.

Gortner plays the vet, hot off a drug deal and customs search at the Mexican border, who pulls into the roadside eatery, accompanied by frazzled hippie Candy Clark. There he confronts a plump waitress (played with moving fragility by newcomer Stephanie Faracy), a frustrated punk and the Red Ryder of the title, limned by Peter Firth, and Hal Linden and Lee Grant as the rich city folk passing through.

What ensues are a series of psychological games that are supposed to be revealing, but on film, come off as theatrically excessive. There are also various Peyton Place-like subplots thrown in, including Linden and Grant's marital problems, and the plight of Firth's all-too-accessible mother, Audra Lindley.

Without an intermission, the verbal harangues get to be a bit much, and director Milton Katselas doesn't help things with his close-in, tight direction. Jules Brenner's camerawork seems to follow the stage directions, rather than a cinematic flow, as does Richard Chew's editing.

Gortner's performance packs a lot of power, although gleams of his "Marjoe" proselytizer keep peeking through. Despite his English accent, Firth shines in the role of the misunderstood hash slinger who wants out badly, and he and Faracy give "Red Ryder" its best moments.

In almost two hours, unfortunately, these aren't quite enough, and a tacked-on retributive-ending just makes the finale more unsatisfying. Hingle, Lindley and Bill McKinney are solid in support, but Clark had best beware of any more roles in which she plays an imbecilic character. After this and "The Big Sleep," she runs the risk of being typecast.

With more and more works being imported from Broadway, and film companies getting into the act early via financing legiters, there are some lessons to be learned from "Red Ryder" on how not to transfer a work from stage to screen.
— *Poll.*

Quintet
(COLOR)

For Altman's inner circle.

Hollywood, Feb. 6.

20th Century-Fox release of a Robert Altman production. Produced and directed by Robert Altman. Features entire cast. Screenplay, Frank Barhydt and Robert Altman, and Patricia Resnick, based on story by Altman, Lionel Chetwynd, Resnick; camera (DeLuxe), Jean Boffety; exec producer, Tommy Thompson; music, composed and conducted by Tom Pierson; production designer, Leon Ericksen; art director, Wolf Kroeger; editor, Dennis M. Hill; asst. director, Tommy Thompson; costumes, Scott Bushnell; music performed by the London Symphony Orchestra; sound, Robert Gravenor; sound effects, David Horton; special effects, Tom Fisher, John Thomas. Reviewed at 20th Century-Fox Studios, L.A. Feb. 1, '79. (MPAA Rating: R). Running time: **100 MINS.**
Essex .... Paul Newman
St. Christopher .... Vittorio Gassman
Grigor .... Fernando Rey
Ambrosia .... Bibi Andersson
Vivia .... Brigitte Fossey
Deuca .... Nina Van Pallandt
Goldstar .... David Langton
Francha .... Tom Hill
Redstone's mate .... Monique Mercure
Redstone .... Craig Richard Nelson
Jaspera .... Maruska Stankova
Aeon .... Anne Gerety

Obelus .... Michael Maillot
Wood supplier .... Max Fleck
Charity house woman .... Francoise Berd

Toward the end of "Quintet," Robert Altman's latest impenetrable exercise in self-indulgence, a character asks, "Understand? Is that important now?" Well, it would have helped make the time go faster. But it's too late to do anything about that, meaning here's another one for Altman's inner circle.

In one of the few obvious points about the picture, the title refers to a game popular in some future city (Montreal?) that's slowly dying in a new Ice Age. Though the finer details are anybody's guess, the game involves five players trying to eliminate each other, plus a sixth who comes late to the board.

Paul Newman arrives in the city with his young pregnant bride, Brigitte Fossey, and finds some of the citizens playing the game for real, with Fernando Rey as referee. After losing his bride to a bomb, Newman is drawn into the game with Vittorio Gassman, Bibi Andersson, Nina Van Pallandt, Craig Richard Nelson and David Langton.

Before it's over, there have been two bloody throat slashings, a hand bursting open in a fire and one vigorous stabbing. Oh yes, Van Pallandt winds up with an arrow through her head and sits there dead as others carry on a conversation. This is supposed to be grim and gruesome, but she looks too much like a Steve Martin routine for it to really be. The audience applauded, nonetheless, when someone threw a cloak over her head.

They should have thrown the cloak over the camera. — *Har.*

Revenge
(ITALIAN-COLOR)

Rome, Feb. 6.

A Titanus release of a Liberty production. Stars Sophia Loren, Marcello Mastroianni, Giancarlo Giannini. Written and directed by Lina Wertmuller. Camera (Eastmancolor), Tonino Delli Colli; production supervisor, Enrico Job; editor, Franco Fraticelli; music, Dangio and Nando De Luca. Reviewed at Cinema Barberini, Feb. 5, '79. Running time: **112 MINS.**
Titina Paterno .... Sophia Loren
Lawyer Spallone .... Marcello Mastroianni
Nick .... Giancarlo Giannini
Sicilian Baron .... Turi Ferro

"Revenge" had many things going for it — a prime cast for a strong imaginative director, in turn backed by technicians of high order. Yet in filming this love story of two contrasting machos in love with a Sicilian-based Neapolitan widow (reciprocally in love with both), filmmaker Lina Wertmuller falls short of the grotesque comedy-fantasy equation, achieved to such good advantage in earlier films.

Grotesque situations abound but

the comic irony is missing. The characters are bigger than life but comedy is sacrificed under Wertmuller's baton, for a undimensional melodramatic stance. And the dialog, at least in the original Italian version (reportedly, the many close-ups were shot in English), is smothered in obscurity by three variations on the Sicilian accent.

Marcello Mastroianni, a socialist lawyer, speaks pure Sicilian of sorts. Giannini speaks snatches of Sicilian with a smattering of pigeon English, while Sophia butchers her delivery with fragments of Neapolitan dialect.

Overabundance of unclear dialog, underdeveloped character vignettes, overemphasis on Greek ruins and paysage in Sicily (film's major location) and brittle story diminish essential vitality of "Revenge" and keep spectators at a standoff.

Yarn is triangular. The Sicilian Mafia leaves Titina (Sophia Loren) a widow and no one in the small island community will help her to justice. Spallone (Marcello Mastroianni), returning to his Sicilian homestead to organize resistance against Mussolini's impending march on Rome, wants her to reopen the murder case, falls in love, and ends up with her in the marital four-poster.

Enter cousin Nick (Giancarlo Giannini) — an up and coming Yank gangster who goes berserk at the sight of her beauty and, ignoring bloodlines, wants to take her back with him. Having succumbed to both, Titina is forced to live on a split-second time schedule for her encounters and beddings. Nick and Spallone shoot up the local Fascists after Mussolini's triumph in Rome and escape with Titina. The men are gunned down at dockside and Sophia, now with child, embraces them both.

The love affair provides the big moments, particularly those of Sophia yielding under body pressures to the flamboyant Yank gangster and the idealistic barrister. It is not enough, though, to sustain the politically-slanted period melodrama that should have been another of Lina Wertmuller's grotesque comedies.

In Italy, "Revenge" lost the young audience, becoming a precarious market item, but the heavyweight cast and positive technical aspects in all departments should land "Revenge" a berth in many territories. A carefully edited subtitle version could play with profit in the big U.S. cities — the filmmaker's best market.

Loren delivers another majestic performance, Giannini's cigar-chewing gangster style must have been an ordeal for the actor but will chill Yank audiences as a cardboard character. Mastroianni's

romantic splurges in intimate scenes with Loren stand out. Enrico Job's eye-filling Sicilian backgrounds never really integrate into the Wertmuller script. Lensing is superior. Dangio and Nando De Luca's score is a calculated dosage of lyric, folk and film music hopefully composed to tie together the disparate elements in the filmmaker's fragmented concept.

There is no mistaking Wertmuller's talent and it shines through frequently even in "Revenge," but she apparently refuses to bridle inspiration or temper creative self-indulgence. — *Werb.*

The Golden Lady
(BRITISH-COLOR)

London, Jan. 30.

Target International Pictures release of a Jean Ubaud-Keith Cavele production. Executive producers, Jean Ubaud, Keith Cavele. Produced by Paul Cowan. Features entire cast. Directed by Jose Larraz. Screenplay, Joshua Sinclair; camera (color), David Griffiths; music, Georges Garvarentz; editor, David Campling; art director, Norris Spencer; costumes, Sandy Moss; sound, Trevor Carliss; asst. director, Paul Fisher. Reviewed at Bijour screening room, London, Jan. 29, '79. (BBFC rating: X). Running time: **96 MINS.**
Julia Hemmingway ...... Christina World
Dahlia .... Suzanne Danielle
Lucy .... June Chadwick
Carol .... Anika Pavel
Max Rowlands .... Stephan Chase
Yorgo Praxis .... Edward De Souza
Dietmar Schuster .... David King
Charles Whitlock .... Patrick Newell
Wayne Bentley .... Richard Oldfield

Hard to see much appeal in this cheapie, which features Danish newcomer Christina World as a distaff James Bond, but which will leave audiences neither shaken nor stirred. Action is underpowered, while sex, ever-expected, is under-exploited.

Script by Joshua Sinclair gets enmeshed in a pretentious plot about rival bidders for a strip of Mideast oil territory, each of whom is fronting for a world power. The golden lady of the title, aided by three femme accomplices and a private computer, is hired by the undercover KGB rep to eliminate the others. When the girls discover the global stakes involved, they switch to protecting the Arab king from elimination.

Theme begs some kind of outlandish treatment to provide pizzazz, doesn't get it, and ends up tame. Minor pluses are David Griffiths' photography, which lends a cliched gloss, and some fine helicopter stuntwork. — *Simo.*

Objasnenie W Lubwi
(Confession of Love)
(SOVIET-COLOR)

Moscow, Jan. 4.

A Lenfilm Production, Leningrad; world rights, Goskino, Moscow. Features entire

cast. Directed by Ilya Averbach. Screenplay. Yevgeni Gabrilovich. Only credits available. Reviewed at Goskino, Moscow, Jan. 3, '79. Running time: **120 MINS.**
With Yuri Bogatirojov, Eva Shikulska.

One of the best features of the new season in the Soviet Union, Ilya Averbach's "Confession of Love" is based on a screenplay by Yevgeni Gabrilovich, one of the most talented, and uncompromising writers whose personal experiences reach back to the silent cinema. Little doubt, Averbach is also a coming helmer, perhaps the best working presently in the Lenfilm Studios of Leningrad. This pic deserves a fest invitation on the merits of the theme alone.

Averbach first drew critical attention with his "Monologue" (1972), a review of the past with sociocritical observations, and "Strange Letters" (1976), a psychological tale about the life of a teacher in the provinces and a teenager who sees the truth only through her own eyes.

As for Gabrilovich, he was a friend of Meyerhold and an acquaintance of Eisenstein, whose deep love for the cinema drew him away from writing novels and adapting works for the theatre to become the Soviet Union's leading scenarist.

Gabrilovich has written a script for Averbach, another swift comer on the Soviet film scene. It appears to be autobiographical: the story of a fumbling, soft hearted writer and his love for a woman whom he meets during the Revolution-Civil War years, loses for a time to another man (or men), and is reunited with at the end of the Second World War. A frame-like story-within-a-story opens and closes the pic with the now elderly husband visiting his wife at a clinic and presenting her with a small volume of newly written stories. The writer's mind wanders off into flashbacks (are these the stories in the book?) to relive their years together once more.

The first part recounts the young writer's personal experiences during the Civil War, when he meets his wife and her infant son while looking for a room — she takes this comical eccentric under her wing and falls half in love with him. He goes through some harrowing experiences as a revolutionary writer (once faced with certain death in a shoot out affair, he actually faints and this apparently save his life), who via his travelling assignments learns what the Revolution meant to many people during the poverty-striken hunger years of the 1920s and early 1930s.

In the second part, comes World War II and an assignment to the war front, where he meets again a publisher who once had a yen for his wife and knows the truth about her unfaithfulness. At this time, the woman has left the writer, due perhaps to the loss of her pre-teenage son in an unfortunate street accident, for which she holds herself responsible and thus tries to forget the past together. The two comrades on the front run into an airplane attack on their jeep, the strafing wounding the publisher-friend in the leg, who later dies of internal bleeding. When the writer returns home after the war — now a greying man-of-experience and achieving renown from his books — his wife is mutely waiting for him in the same darkened attick apartment they formerly occupied together.

This is a film of psychological nuance, one in which the characters are more important than the story line. Several scenes stick to the memory due to care for thesp performances and subtle lighting — the two-hour playing time doesn't fall into dullsville if the viewer has any inkling at all of the times presented on the screen.

Thesps Yuri Bogatirojov as the writer, and Polish actress Eva Shikulska as his attractive wife — are pluses, but so are most of the technical credits. Averbach could move into the forefront of the New Generation with this pic. A natural for Soviet Film Weeks and a must in Gabrilovich retros. —*Holl.*

Ashanti
(COLOR)

Routine adventure with African slave trade backdrop. Okay prospects.

London, Feb. 1.

Columbia Pictures release of a Georges-Alain Vuille production. Exec producer, Luciano Sacripanti. Producer, Georges-Alain Vuille. Directed by Richard Fleischer. Features entire cast. Screenplay, Stephen Geller (based on a novel, "Ebano," by Alberto Vasquez-Figueroa); camera (color), Aldo Tonti; production designer, Aurelio Crugnola; art director, Kuli Sander; sound, David Hildyard; associate producer, John C. Vuille. Reviewed at Odeon Leicester Sq. Theatre, London, Jan. 31, '79. (BBFC rating: AA). Running time: **117 MINS.**

Dr. David Linderby .... Michael Caine
Suleiman .... Peter Ustinov
Anansa Linderby .... Beverly Johnson
Malik .... Kabir Bedi
The Prince .... Omar Sharif
Brian Walker .... Rex Harrison
Jim Sandell .... William Holden
Djamel .... Zia Mohyeddin
Ansok .... Winston Ntshona
Faid .... Tariq Yunus
Dongaro .... Tyrone Jackson
Marcel .... Jean-Luc Bideau
Capt. Bradford .... Johnny Sekka

"Ashanti" is nominally concerned with contemporary slave trading in Africa, with the foreground plot tracking doctor Michael Caine in pursuit of his kidnapped beautiful black wife, Beverly Johnson. The outcome is polished but lacklustre adventure entertainment.

Independently produced by Swiss exhib turned producer Georges-Alain Vuille, and directed with competence if not much verve by Richard Fleischer, pic is obviously exploitable, well-baited with names, and should prove useful for exhibs in the general market. Columbia has it for most foreign territories, and Warners has just made a pickup for U.S.-Canada, with an Eastertime spread in some 450 houses planned.

Caine and Johnson are World Health Organization medics on a visit to an African tribe when the lady becomes a prize catch of Arabian slave trader Peter Ustinov. Caine's retrieval odyssey thereafter is variously aided by Rex Harrison as an ambiguous go-between, William Holden as a mercenary helicopter pilot, and Indian actor Kabir Bedi as a Bedouin with his own score to settle with Ustinov. All acquit with professional grace but unremarkable impact.

Portraying a royal client of Ustinov is Omar Sharif, looking and sounding as if filling time between bridge tournaments. But, in fairness, he, too, has little room for expressive maneuver.

At 117 minutes, "Ashanti" is bloated with expendable narrative in Stephen Geller's script based on a novel by Alberto Vasquez-Figueroa. Action elements are slight or modest, the characterization superficial, and a potentially arresting subplot, the story of slave trading itself, only perfuntorily touched.

No help to the film's grip on interest is Fleischer's minuet pacing. He seems, for one thing, to have come under the spell of those Saharan sand dunes lavishly and lengthily dwelled on as Caine and Bedi pick up Ustinov's trail.

There is a moderately amusing bit in the desert when Caine is introduced to the tricks of camel travel, and some climactic slambang aboard Sharif's yacht, but these are incidental pleasures in an otherwise long, languid, uninspired feature.

All technical credits, including Aldo Tonti's lensing, are fine. No big b.o. bang in sight from this one, just okay business. —*Pit.*

New Generation
(FRENCH-COLOR)

Paris, Jan. 18.

A Silem release of a French Lollipop production. Produced, written and directed by Jean-Pierre Lowf Legoff. Features entire cast. Musical conception; Robert Bonnaire, Iser, Jean-Pierre Lowf Legoff, Dominique Rousseau; music and lyrics, too many to be cited here; camera (color), Serge Halsdorf; sound, Gerard Barra; editing, Pauline Leroy; choreography, Amadeo. Reviewed at Club 13, Paris, Jan. 17, '79. Running time: not provided.
Jeff .... Jeff Manzetti
Lagaffe .... Eric Rawson
Lollie .... Lollie Serres
Also: Wilson Lambert, Serge Malik, Caroline Tabourin, Jean-Luc Autret, Nathalie Boutigny, Jackie Sardou, Henri-Jacques Huet.

The "Disco" musical is still a young phenomenon, but its children are already being spawned. "New Generation" is notable only because it is a French product and the French — with the possible exception of Jacques Demy — have never been craftsmen of musical cinema.

Written and directed by Jean-Pierre Lowf Legoff, this would-be "new" musical is nothing of the sort: the music is imitative and nondescript, the choreography nonexistent. The young performers are vaguely appealing, but they badly need direction, which they don't get. The whole thing smacks of an amateurishness that smothers any energy the actors manage to generate. It's Saturday Night without the Fever.

Legoff promises more to come. The least one could ask of him is that he learn more about the technical aspects of cinema before embarking on a sequel. Of all film genres, the musical requires the most proficient craftsmanship.

Needless to say, the film will probably do well anyway with young audiences. —*Len.*

Baara
(MALI-COLOR)

Saint Vincent, Jan. 31.

Produced and directed by Souleymane Cisse. Stars Balla Moussa Keita, Oumou Kone, Baba Niare, Boubakar Keita, Oumou Diarra, Fanta Diabate. Screenplay, Souleymane Cisse; camera (color), Etienne de Grammont, Abdoulaye Sidibe; sound, Assimoye Keita; music, Lamine Konte; editor, Huchee Davanture. Reviewed at UNESCO Encounter with Francophone Cinema, Saint Vincent, Jan. 30, '79. Running time: **95 MINS.**

Factory owner .... Balla Moussa Keita
Wife of factory owner .... Oumou Kone
Engineer .... Boubakar Keita
Wife of engineer .... Oumou Diarra
Street worker .... Baba Niare
Saleswoman .... Fanta Diabate

Souleymane Cisse's "Baara" proves that African films need not look like a Margaret Mead documentary to be "authentic." Set in Bamako, the capital of Mali, "Baara" leaves behind the folklore and tribal customs — so often the subject of films by and about Africans — and focuses on the problems of the city and of an Africa just beginning to industrialize.

Cisse already has seven film prizes under his belt for "Baara," including kudos from the Carthage Film Festival. Some critics have lamented, however, that the Malien director has made a film that is too "European."

The story line — the murder of an engineer who encourages union activities in a local factory — may make "Baara" seem more European than many other African films that concentrate on the provincial problems of the Black continent, but it is precisely the choice of exposing the problems of urban Africa that makes this film interesting. While it is a world that still affects only a minority (the large majority of Maliens still live in traditional rural areas), it is obviously the world in which the real changes on the continent are taking place. The problems of industrialization can no longer be considered a Western filmmaker's monopoly.

If by "European," on the other hand, is meant technical excellence, than "Baara" is by all means a European film. While unraveling the narrative of the young engineer, Cisse skillfully provides a mosaic of African city life and the world of work which in the language of Mali translates as "baara." The rhythms, colors and noises of this film are, however, all African. Music by Lamine Konte is particularly well integrated.

Especially well-done are the market and street scenes and the interior shots of family life and family tensions. The film also provides a series of glimpses at the status of women in Africa (the saleswoman who never pays her bills, the engineer's wife who is educated but forced to stay at home, the factory owner's spouse who takes up a lover).

All other credits are commendable. Special mention goes to Baba Niare, the street worker who in entering the factory bridges the gap between the old and new Africa. Niare, a natural on the screen, is an amateur actor who has never left Bamako in his life — not even to go to the nearby city of Kati. —*Argo.*

Eduardo The Healer
(DOCU-COLOR-16m)

Produced and written by Douglas G. Sharon and Richard Cowan. Directed by Richard Cowan. Camera (color), Robert Primes, editing, Lee Rhoads; research, Douglas G. Sharon; music, Centro Folklorico de Machu Picchu; Rafael Amaranto y son conjunto. Distributed by Serious Business. Reviewed at New York Film Expo, Brooklyn Museum, Jan. 16, '79. Running time: **55 MINS.**
(Spanish and English, with English subtitles)

On the surface, "Eduardo the Healer" might seem the type of film able to attract anthropologists only, but this fascinating and provocative character has already proven itself in several West Coast theatrical bookings. The popular connection is, of course, the use of drugs in this South American's healing ritual. (The film was, in fact, financed by the Drug Abuse Council of the Dept. of Health, Education and Welfare.) Eduardo's practice involves the use of an hallucinogenic cactus — the San Pedro plant — which patient and practitioner imbibe alike. The climax of the film is a nighttime ritual preserved by the camera, involving a man's economic and domestic "de-hexing."

What saves "Eduardo" from being a mere distant curiosity about strange practices is the man's articulateness and intelligence. His bookshelf contains art history, Jung, Edgar Allan Poe and Gandhi. His education as a sculptor and fisherman helps augment his income, while he performs his healing largely out of conviction. The film begins with a brief "test" for illness, which involves the death of a guinea pig and the spewing of scented water. Eduardo's past is then detailed, with his many children and admirers surrounding him in a poor neighborhood near Trujillo.

Since Eduardo's cures seem effective, and his religious beliefs sound remarkably similar to a Judeo-Christian doctrine, the question is rightly raised about the prejudices and superstitions of our own "civilized" culture.

Distribution is obviously limited, but coupled with another like title, the possibility remains for "Eduardo the Healer" to raise itself out of the festival, museum, and library market. —*Pege.*

Beauty And The Beast
(CZECHOSLOVAK-COLOR)

Prague, Jan. 12.

A Czechoslovak Film Production, Studio Barrandov, Prague; world rights, Czechoslovak Film, Prague. Features entire cast. Directed by Juraj Herz. Screenplay, Ota Hofmann. Only credits available. Reviewed at Czechoslovak Film Export Screening Room, Prague, Jan. 11, '79. Running time: **90 MINS.**
Cast: Zdena Studenkova (Beauty), Vlastimil Harapes (Beast), Vaclav Vosko (Beauty's Father), Jana Brejchova (Gabina, Beauty's Sister), Zuzana Kocurikova (Malinka, Beauty's Sister).

Juraj Herz is a master of baroque-cinema in Prague, city of shadows which gave the film world "The Golem" and the inspiration for "The Cabinet of Dr. Caligari" among other legendary fantastic pix. The helmer is best remembered abroad for "The Crematorium" (1969) "The Petroleum Lamps" (1971), which revealed a liking for the theme of decadence and moral decay.

Another side of Herz's talent — a love for the French costume pic and the Gothic tale — surfaced in "Morgiana" (1972), featuring Good and Evil in conflict within the Self, and found completion in his two fairytales dealing with evil spells and macabre, mysterious danger: "Beauty and the Beast" (1978) and "The Ninth Heart" (1978).

"Beauty and the Beast" will recall immediately Jean Cocteau's "La Belle et la Bete" (1945), with Jean Marais and the bewitched prince in the French fairy-tale. For the record, there's also a Soviet feature-length cartoon on the subject.

This "Beauty and the Beast" is a horror pic, a kind of "Golem" monster wrestling with Evil within and hoping-against-hope to rescue his soul from immortal damnation through a free act of love. In other words, the "Faust and Gretchen" legend of Middle European tradition has been mixed freely into the French formula.

Most striking are the baroque sets: the enchanted castle in ruins, and Beauty's splendid manor-house (her father is a merchant who benefits from the Beast's generosity in return for the free-willing hand of a daughter). Lensing of the enchanted forest and its menacing atmosphere is meant to be chilling from the beginning, in as much as this beast feeds on raw meat (stags and animals as well as human flesh) but suffers, because his human conscience plagues him and allows him to fall fatally in love with a victim.

Once the Beast and Beauty are alone in the castle, the story takes on a softer lyrical tone and is then carried neatly to the end by the two main actors: the lovely Zdena Studenkova and the featurd ballet-dancer at the National Theatre in Prague, Vlastimil Harapes, who moves with grace in his hawk-like mask and half-bird outfit and has that required countenance of a fairy prince when the curse is lifted.

A film for both young and old, but as a counterpart to Cocteau's film classic it can also stand on its own feet. In fact, with plus credits in every category, "Beauty and the Beast" could get legs for art-house chances after fest exposure. —*Holl.*

Boomerang
(BULGARIAN-COLOR)

Sofia, Jan. 16.

A Bulgarian Film Production, Sofia; world rights, Bulgarofilm, Sofia. Features entire cast. Directed by Ivan Nichev. Screenplay, Svoboda Bucharova, Jenny Radeva, Nichev; camera (color), Victor Chichov; art direction, Anghel Ahryanov; music, Kiril Tsiboulka. Reviewed at Bulgarian Film Screening Room, Sofia, Jan. 15, '79. Running time: **90 MINS.**
Mihail . . . . Lyuben Chatalov
Peter . . . . Yavor Spassov
Boris Krustev . . . . Nikolai Binev
Nina . . . . Katya Paskaleva
Sylvia . . . . Krassimira Damyanova
Roumyana . . . . Anzhela Atanassova
Editor-in-Chief . . . . Velya Goranov

Ivan Nichev's "Boomerang" will put to rest doubts that Bulgarian Cinema is deserving of only fringe benefits on the international festival circuit. This is a strongly written, fast-paced and directed pic, which would put to shame similar efforts in Socialist countries because it refused to pull a single punch. Exposure at a key fest on the spring or summer circuit could launch "Boomerang" and New Bulgarian Cinema into the big city art houses.

Like similar Polish pix on generally the same subject, Nichev's "Boomerang" takes a critical view of Socialist society but does so in a positive, constructive manner by making the characters flesh-and-blood humans. The ploys a young graduate from the Sofia University's School of Journalism (Michael, or "Mihail" in Bulgarian) use to crash the upper crust and avoid being sent out to the provinces for the usual writing apprenticeship are dishonest, but the manner of demonstrating how the young, arrogant, good-looking, woman-chasing boy gets slowly entangled in his own intrigues makes for a moral message in the best tradition of Hollywood's (particularly Warner Brothers) socially engaged cinema and England's "Angry" Theatre.

Michael never commits a crime to get the winds of fate to blow in his direction. He merely senses a ripe opportunity and uses it — his looks and measure of talent, plus on occasion a warm heart, help to do the rest. Further, he knows that others in higher positions need him to satisfy some deep-felt need of their own.

One of these is an opera singer, whom Michael has met while working partime as a lighting assistant backstage and started an affair with. Another is a worn-out writer of "old-fashioned" stories who needs Michael and his young company for "inspiration" and, in his villa on the edge of the city, offers the young writer a nook of his own to weave his webs of one-upmanship. The old writer in return helps Michael, under false pretences, to get a story printed with his own name on it (written by guess-who) in a literary magazine — thereby upping the latter's chances to stay put in Sofia and get a top-flight job with a publication editor.

However, the compromises hint of a Mephisto pact, for the young writer begins to barter both his conscience and his young friends to get ahead. A girlfriend leaves him after being invited up to the villa, where Michael now lives with the old writer, for "an evening" — and his best friend, Peter, in the midst of his own first disappointing love-affair with a femme fatale, wakes up to the whole mess and goes off on his own difficult but honest way in the end.

Meanwhile, the roof caves in on Michael's schemes: everything has "boomeranged" back on him and he's doomed in the end to the provinces. Even the old writer, who has been using these intimate experiences as material to write a new novel, decides to burn the manuscript.

Tale is anchored to a story written by two femme writers in collaboration with helmer Nichev, and it takes a good long look at the Sofia academic scene and the culturally privileged "in" crowd, common to every European capital or large city. Thesp performances — Nichev's strong suit in all his films — are tops down to the bit-roles. Lensing is also a plus. "Boomerang" has solid chances for a fest on the circuit this season, and should win favor at Bulgarian film weeks.

—Holl.

Gziekolwiek Jestes, Panie Prezydencie
(Wherever You Are, Mr. President)
(POLISH-B&W)

Warsaw, Jan. 9.
A Film Polski Próduciton, Warsaw, Film Unit "TOR." Features entire cast. Directed by Andrzej Trzos-Rastawiecki. Screenplay, Wladislaw Terlecki, Trzos-Rastawiecki; camera (black and white), Zygmunt Samosiuk; sets, Zenon Rozewicz, Andrzej Kowalczyk; music, Jerzy Maksymiuk; production manager, Wielislawa Piotrowska. Reviewed at Film Polski Screening Room, Warsaw, Jan. 8, '79. Running time: 90 MINS.
With Henryk Czyz (Mayor Stefan Starzynski), Wanda Elbinska, Jozef Konieczny, Waldislaw Kozlow, Rudolf Golebiowski, Halina Labonarska, Andrzej Polkowski, Ryszard Sobolewski.

"Wherever You Are, Mr. President" is documentary footage filled out with reenacted scenes about the invasion of Poland and the air raids on Warsaw as shown through the day-to-day experiences of Warsaw's mayor, Stefan Starzynski, during the month of September 1939. The documentary footage is excellent and worth the price of admission alone, but even more impressive is the manner in which cameraman Zygmund Samosiuk and helmer Andrzej Trzos-Rastawiecki gave the re-enacted scenes an authentic documentary touch. Sometimes it's difficult to separate documentary from fiction.

Like Jerzy Kawalerowicz's earlier "Death of a President," this is a kind of "You Are There" historical tv-documentary, which will find response with film and history buffs. Newsreel footage comes primarily from Polish archives, but some obviously draw upon Nazi film sources. Wladyslaw Terlecki as the Warsaw mayor brings dignity and depth to his impersonation of a well known national hero who refused to capitulate although the President of Poland had fled to Rumania — until the lack of water and medicine ended any further chances of resistance. Starzynski remained at his

post in radio contact with the city's beleagured citizens until the Gestapo came and took him away — his grave has never been found.

Even the most passive viewer will be impressed at the valor and courage demonstrated by the Polish people as a whole in this moment of catastrophe. The Poles in the defense of their city and homeland in this single month of September left an example behind that has been almost unparalleled in modern European history — not only did the day-by-day resistance rally foreign diplomatic support to their cause, but the fall of the better equipped and fully mobilized French army a year later proved beyond a shadow of a doubt that the Poles as a fighting nation had nothing to be ashamed of. The underground resistance movement throughout the war and later reconstruction of Warsaw out of ruins is also due entirely to national pride and a will for self-determination.

"Wherever You Are, Mr. President" is more than just a film — it is a testament — it should be included in every Polish Film Week abroad.

—Holl.

Sentados Al Borde Del La Manana Con Los Pies Colgando
(Sitting on the Edge of Tomorrow With the Feet Hanging)
(SPANISH-COLOR)

Madrid, Jan. 26.
Incine-Impala S.A.-Ofelia S.A. production. Produced by Carlos Escobedo. Directed by Antonio Jose Betancor. Screenplay, Javier Moro; music, Carlos Vizziello; sets, Christian Boyer; editor, Eduardo Biurrun; camera (Eastmancolor), Hans Burman. Reviewed at Cine Capitol (Madrid), Jan. 25, '79. Running time: 98 MINS.
Miguel .... Miguel Bose
Marta .... Beatriz Elorrieta
Chiki .... Bettina Bose
Alicia .... Esther Farre
Also: Concha Gregori, Josema Yuste, Fernando Conde, Millan Salcedo, Quique Sanfrancisco, Saturno Cerra, Fernando Colomo, Luis Ciges, Alberto de Mendoza, Carlos Otero, Fojo, Eva Lesmes, Manuel Ayuso, Francisco Betancor.

Amateurish, inconsequential and pretentious pic, of the sort that long-suffering Spanish audiences have to see these days due to the film quota. If the title of this rambling non-film seems bad, it is still infinitely better than the contents.

About the only thing that prevents item from being a complete disaster is presence of Miguel Bose, who at least provides a touch of professionalism to it, though his part is purely "dramatic" and he doesn't sing a single song.

The moronic story is about a group of teenagers who set up a commune in an abandoned house, each one doing his own thing, which of course includes free love, the set-

ting up of a free nursery for the neighborhood locals, free plays, though, inexplicably, no pot smoking. Eventually the baddies, who are never seen or identified, throw rocks through the windows and beat up one of the idealists and City Hall evicts them from their motley Parnassus. The plea for youthful freedom is put forth solemnly, though frolicking and pranks are added through a telescopic lens, which seems to be one of the director's weaknesses.

It's never explained who pays for the upkeep of the groupies. Maybe those same people foolish enough to pay the b.o. admission for the film.

—Besa.

Bajecni Muzi S Klikou
(Those Wonderful Men with a Crank)
(CZECHOSLOVAK-COLOR)

Prague, Jan. 12.
A Czechoslovak Film Production, Studio Barrandov, Prague. Stars Rudolf Hrusinsky, Jiri Menzel. Directed by Jiri Menzel. Screenplay, Oldrich Vlcek, Menzel, based on a story by Vlcek; camera (color), Jaromir Sofr; sets, Zbynek Holoch; music, Jiri Sust. Reviewed at Czechoslovak Film-Export Screening Room, Prague, Jan. 11, '79. Running time: 90 MINS.
Pasparte .... Rudolf Hrusinsky
Kolenaty .... Jiri Menzel
Evzenie .... Blazena Holisova
Emilie Kolarova-Mlada Vlasta Fabianova
Slapeta .... Vladimir Mensik
Pepicka .... Jaromira Milova
Aloisie .... Hana Buresova
Berousek .... Oldrich Vlcek
Benjamin .... Josef Kemr

In the splurge of feature pix made recently on the dawn of films, Jiri Menzel's "Those Wonderful Men with a Crank" will find an honored place and is far and away the best of the lot. It should easily get legs for a lusty jaunt through the Yank art houses and elsewhere. Slated presently for the Berlin Fest, pic now only needs critical recognition.

"Those Wonderful Men" was made to commemorate the 80th anniversary of the Czechoslovak film industry in 1978. Menzel's film is set in 1907, the year the travelling road-shows settled into a family-oriented "nickelodeon."

This is a warm, affectionate, technically perfect salute to the beginnings of filmmaking in Prague. In fact, there is enough evidence in the Czech film archives to prove that (a) a Prague film pioneer improved on the Lumiere camera at the very turn of the century; (b) filmmaking got on its feet here commercially four or five years before Berlin and (c) Czech cinema drew on its own traditions and national traits to become a genuine film capital in the prewar years.

That's the film-history background to "Those Wonderful Men with a Crank." The charm of the pic lies in the story, the thesp per-

formances (all first-class and supportive of each other), and that hard-to-define but ever-so-mirthful "Czech humor."

Oldrich Vlcek wrote the original story on which Menzel's pic is based, and he also plays one of those mad-men obsessed with the dream-box entrusted to their care and the only source of visible income.

Pic draws its inspiration and liveliness from the period itself, which Menzel studied in detail and meticulously reproduced with creative wit and gags of his own. Old Prague is lensed in its art-nouveau quaintness and charm at the turn-of-the-century; the tones of the photography (Jaromir Sofr) is a tinted-brown, sepia-hued copy of early photographs; the historical one-reelers are "reenacted" rather than shown as they were; and, best of all, a handful of "dream-sequences" springing from the impresario Hrsinsky's own imagination demonstrates how those movie-crazed madmen functioned with an entertainment toy still depending completely their creative inspiration.

More jokes are developed from the first audiences' reactions to on-rushing trains or comic scenes projected on the bed-sheet screen common to the movie circuit. It's these jokes that will mesmerize film buffs. —Holl.

Der Sturz
(The Fall)
(WEST GERMAN-COLOR)

Berlin, Jan. 23.
An Independent Film Heinz Angermeyer Production, Munich, in collaboration with ABS/Maran/von Vietinghoff Film, Munich; world rights, Filmverlag der Autoren, Munich. Features entire cast. Directed by Alf Brustellin. Screenplay, Brustellin, Bernhard Sinkel, based on the novel of same name by Martin Walser; camera (color), Dietrich Lohmann; sets, Winfried Hennig; music, Klaus Doldinger. Reviewed at Studio am Kudam, Berlin, Jan. 22, '79. Running time: 101 MINS.

Anself Kristlein .... Franz Buchrieser
Alissa Kristlein .... Hannelore Elsner
Edmund Gabriel .... Wolfgang Kieling
Rosa Blomich .... Eva Maria Meineke
Elmar Glatthaar .... Klaus Pohl
Theophont Dirlewanger Carl Fox-Duering
Frau Eltron .... Mady Rahl

Alf Brustellin's adaptation of Martin Walser's novel, "The Fall," is one of these stories that's better off read than seen on a screen — it's another of those boresome literary adaptations that pass through film-subsidy committees without a hitch because no one likes to turn down an important author's novel in the process. Martin Walser's book is a social allegory featuring a hero named "Kristlein" ("Little Christ") who takes the world's suffering on his shoulders as he scolds the establishment and defends the outcasts in the classy vacation area around Lake Constance. Book (part of a trilogy) is bestseller.

Brustellin was scripter on Bernhard Sinkel projects (sharing equal billing), where he learned the ins and out outs of the literay pic trade, save how to direct a film with a measure of competence. A dud in every category. —*Holl.*

Bez Znieczulenia
(Without Anaesthetic)
(POLISH-COLOR)

Warsaw, Jan. 9.

A Film Polski Production, Warsaw, Film Unit X. Stars Zbigniew Zapasiewicz. Directed by Andrzej Wajda. Screenplay, Agnieszka Holland, Wajda; camera (color), Edward Klosinski; music, Jerzy Derfel, Wojciech Mlynarski; sets, Allan Starski; production manager, Barbara Pec-Slesicka. Reviewed at Film Polski Screening Room, Warsaw, Jan. 8, '79. Running time: **131 MINS.**
Cast: Zbigniew Zapasiewicz (Jerzy Michalowski), Ewa Dalkowska, Andrzej Seweryn, Krystyna Janda, Roman Wilhelmi, Emilia Krakowska, Kazimierz Kaczor, Magda Teresa Wojcik, Jerzy Stuhr.

Like his earlier "Man of Marble" (1977), Andrzej Wajda's "Without Anaesthetic" deals with actual people and authentic events which took place in Poland during the postwar period. This one, set in the 1960s, chronicles the fate of a "personality" who is readily recognizable to the intellectual class in Warsaw, where the film is set but transplanted to a contemporary time and place for dramaturgical reasons. Chances are ripe for fest exposure somewhere this season, probably Cannes.

"Without Anaesthetic," due to its length (more than two hours), needs cutting to find legs for a commercial run abroad, but as the strong material is up front and the latter part melodrama, it shouldn't be too hard to zero in on the politthriller for its own sake. Pic's fast pace is a strong plus, but another is the thesp performances.

A famous Polish journalist — played superbly by Zbigniew Zapasiewicz (a Krzysztof Zanussi discovery) — presents a problem for the powers-that-be when he displays his full political skill and knowledge on a television show featuring questions-and answers on a world conference by a panel of journalists. Since our stigmatized hero is a globe-trotting journalist, the counter-move by his enemies is simply to take away his privileges one by one without offering explanation.

The shock of being suddenly "unwanted" parallels a deeper disappointment in his private life: his wife is having an affair with a jealous young rival and, after 15 years of marriage and two daughters, wants a divorce. His wife offers no explanations, and the journalist-husband has to sort out the mystery for himself.

For a while, the two stories run parallel — the hero feels he merely has to "get on top" of things to know what to do and solve both situations. But each move turns out to be a wrong one, both in bucking the "higher-ups" and facing-down his wife's lover. He takes to drinking heavily one evening with students eager to attend his next university seminar, after he discovers the course has been cancelled for no reason. Then a female student moves into his apartment.

This in turn offers more dynamite for a publicized divorce case, at which point the pic bogs down in sentiments. The journalist, once suave and commanding in appearance, is reduced to tight-lipped 'silence. Shortly after leaving the courtroom in a refusal to contest the obvious lies and calumny in the case, he dies mysteriously in his apartment when the gas heater in the bathroom explodes and tears the room apart.

Agnieszka Holland's script is sharp and well-written — she's a coming light in Polish cinema. Wajda's helming is again up to par, and he is presently demonstrating in "Man of Marble" and "Without Anaesthetic" how the news media in Poland works from the inside. Pic, as a cross between polit-thrillers and social commentaries could fin a corner of the action on the arthouse circuit. — Holl.

Kratko Sluntze
(A Ray of Sunlight)
(BULGARIAN-COLOR)

Sofia, Jan. 16.

A Bulgarian Film Production, Sofia; world rights, BulgaroFilm, Sofia. Features entire cast. Directed by Lyudmil Kirkov. Screenplay, Stanislav Stratiev, based on his own story; camera (color), Georgi Roussimov; music, Boris Karadimchev; art direction, Assaya Poppova. Reviewed at Bulgarian Film Screening Room, Sofia, Jan. 15, '79. Running time: **90 MINS.**
Sashko .... Vihur Stoychev
His Girlfriend .... Rossitsa Petrovna
Anton .... Anton Gorchev
Vankata .... Pavel Poppandov
Old Lambo .... Nikola Todev
Kroumov .... Georgi Kishkilov
Worker .... Kiril Gospodinov

One of the best of the new season of Bulgarian pix, Lyudmil Kirkov's "A Ray of Sunlight" tells a straight story that has a few mystery twists in it to hold the audience's attention to the very end. It's also a socially critical pic with the extra irony that an "accidental" yet premeditated murder can rise out a simple difference of opinion and moral failings.

The youth Sashko, in love, wants to spend the summer vacation months earning some side money instead of working on a collective farm (normal summer employment for university students); so he gets a doctor to excuse him for medical reasons and goes to work for a well-drilling team. Their present job is to find well-water on the property of a conniving official in a mountainous area near Sofia tagged a "villa zone," where a new breed of consumer-minded uppercrust try to "keep up with the Joneses."

Sashko takes notice of the manner in which the well to do can buy or get their hands on anything they need, and some even use the villas as a rendezvous with girlfriends during the day. It is hot and the work for the team is hard, but he and a bulldozer driver get rid of some of their frustrations by piling sand around the car of one of the afternoon visitors.

In digging the well the boy hits on the bones of a buried corpse: either this was an isolated killing (perhaps a horse-thief of long ago) or a Bulgarian freedom-fighter who was executed in the "white terror" of 1923-25, when a dictatorship replaced a democratically elected parliament. In any case, the discovery of the bones requires an investigation by the authorities, which would result in a costly delay in the completion of the well. The owner, therefore, tries to cover up the incident by bribing the workers to say nothing about the remains of a dead man.

All the workers finally agree to shut up save for the youth, who is guided by his emotions (he is in love with his girlfriend and doesn't want to sully that relationship with a lie) and his reason (what if more bones are to be found, and just who was this man?). The others beat him up, and the villa owner decides in panic to arrange for an accident by cutting the rope bringing a heavy bucket of earth from the bottom of the hole. The next morning the boy returns to the bottom of the well, finds more bones while digging, and then dies in the prepared accident. The other workers realize their mistake too late and turn in rage on the villa owner.

A quietly told and thoroughly convincing pic with psychological nuance and fine thesp performances by all. Kirkov's best film to date and attractive for fests and film weeks because the ending is left opn — the audience decides just who the guilty parties are. —Holl.

Na Boca do Mundo
(In the Mouth of the World)
(BRAZILIAN-COLOR)

Rio de Janeiro, Jan. 26.

A Lente Films — Embrafilme (Brazilian National Film Industry) - Antonio Pitanga production. Produced by Morris Israel, Zakhia Elias, Noilton, Cezar Antonio Elias. Directed by Antonio Pitanga. Features entire cast. Screenplay, Leopold Serran, from the book by Carlos Diegues and Antonio Pitanga; camera (color), Fernando Duarte; scenic design, Regis Monteiro; editing, Sergio Sanz; assistant director, Jorge Fernando Duran Parra; music, Jorge Ben; title song sung by Caetano Veloso. Reviewed at Cinema Pax Ipanema, Jan. 25, '79. (Brazilian rating: 18 yrs. and over). Running time: **108 MINS.**
Clarisse .... Norma Bengell
Antonio .... Antonio Pitanga
Terezinha .... Sibele Rubia
Cardoso .... Angelito Mello
Tourist .... Milton Goncalves

Set in exotic Atafona, fishing village in the north of Rio de Janeiro state, this film has many of the same ingredients which made "Dona Flor" a success outside of Brazil. Meaning: a native story with roots in literature's classics, an attractive duo of actresses and a versatile leading man, a unique tropical setting and pulsating music from Latin America's richest musical culture.

The title tune, "Lover Beloved," says it all: "I want that you catch me, embrace me, kiss me and love me and then send me away." And this exactly is what Clarisse (Norma Bengell), symbolizing the power and money of the upper classes in Rio de Janeiro, does with gas station attendant Antonio (Antonio Pitanga).

In the seductive process of "acquiring" her rude, naive lover Antonio, Clarisse takes him away from the natural flow of his life and away from his fiancee Terezinha (Sibele Rubia), who sells crabs to tourists to earn her keep. The results of Antonio's metamorphosis is fatal, destroying him mentally and eventually physically.

The simple plot hits at a profounder one in Brazilian life and society, if not in other "third world" cultures: the eternal struggle between the "haves" and "havenots."

Antonio Pitanga, if any comparison can be made, is Brazil's Sidney Poitier. He and Norma Bengell are veterans of Brazil's theatre and novels, or tv melodrama mart. The white woman-black man love scenes won't be everyone's cup of tea, but the simple plot, exoticism and pop singer Caetano Veloso chiming Jorge Ben's bouncing tune is something different from a promising young film industry just opening up internationally.

While the color and photography run parallel with international standards, the editing, while better than local piz, is imperfect as compared to American and European standards.

Sibele Rubia (Terezinha) is particularly lovely to watch, in all her natural, unsophisticated beauty. A film headed for more success in an American art house than in general cinemas. —*Emrt.*

El Diputado
(The Congressman)
(SPANISH-COLOR)

Madrid, Jan. 19.

Figaro Films — Producciones Zeta — UFESA production. Directed by Eloy de la Iglesia. Features entire cast. Screenplay, Gonzalo Goicochea, Eloy de la Iglesia; exec producer, J.A. Perez Giner; camera (Eastmancolor) Antonio Cuevas; editor, Julio Pena; sets, Gumer. Reviewed at Real Cinema, Madrid, Jan. 19, '79. Running time: 111 MINS.

Roberto Orbea	Jose Sacristan
Carmen	Maria Luisa San Jose
Juanito	Jose L. Alonso
Nes	Angel Pardo
Carres	Agustin Gonzalez
Bardem	J.A. Bardem
Mother	Queta Claver
Moreno Pastrana	Enrique Vivo

"El Diputado" is probably the most challenging and controversial film to come out of Spain over the past year. It will doubtlessly rub a lot of people the wrong way because of its special focus on homosexuals, but even more so due to its militant Marxist-mongering and its glorification of Spain's Socialist Party. Others will exalt its axgrinding and deem it a powerful statement against fascism and everything the Franco era stood for.

A powerful film it certainly is. It is also a film that is too talky and often deadpan and poorly acted. But aside from all the red-flagwaving propagandistic devices and some pretty explicit homosexual sex scenes which earned it here the "S" classification (enter at your own risk since "sensibilities" may be offended) it is a film that is often exciting and moving and should do extremely well in the local market, and possibly in the more sophisticated offshore situations.

Director Eloy de la Iglesia, who coscripted the film, and whose best film this is to date, has availed himself of the political turmoil in Spain over the past three years and, often using well-known incidents of that period in which the country was struggling to free itself of Frankist infrastructures and heretofore outlawed political parties such as the Communists and Socialist strove to legalize themselves, has interwoven the story of a homosexual Socialist leader. Yarn is told as one long flashback in which the now-Congressman Roberto recalls the early student days of his political clandestinity and his first homosexual contacts while serving a prison term.

Subsequently married to a pretty comrade, Roberto nonetheless is drawn back to his homosexual proclivities, first through his former cellmate and then through an adolescent hood who's working for the fascists. But Roberto and his indulgent wife set up a *menage a trois*, and get the kid interested in the "higher" things of life, meaning museums, Socialism and protest songs. But the fascists exact their due, having grown suspicious of the boy, Juanito.

De la Iglesia enlivens the story by citing many familiar (to anyone who knows Madrid) places and names, just barely concealed. Everything from the Fuerza Nueva cafeteria hangout on Calle Goya, to the smash-up of left-wing stands in the Rastro, to a prison scene with director Juan Antonio Bardem. These devices give the film an air of authenticity and cinema-verite and make it more convincing. In all, "El Diputado" is certainly the most commercial film to come out of Spain in a long time and could generate considerable biz if properly released abroad. —*Besa.*

Brussels Fest

Des Morts
(Of Death and Deàds)
(BELGO-FRENCH-COLOR)

Brussels, Jan. 23.

Documentary release of Zeno Films (Brussels) and Films du Losange (Paris) production. Directed by Jean-Pol Ferbus, Dominique Garny, Thierry Zeno. Camera (Eastmancolor) Terry Stegner, Thierry Zeno; sound, Jean-Pol Ferbus, Dominique Garny; editors: Thierry Zeno, Roland Grillon; mixing, Dominique Hennequin; music, Alain Pierre. Reviewed at Passage 44, Brussels Jan. 22, '79. Running time: 106 MINS.

Here is a truly repulsive film. One might have come to the conclusion that Jacopetti, when he so complacently showed the monstrosities of the universe in his "Mondo Cane," had reached the bottom, that it was almost impossible to get further by way of degradation of the human race. Not so: three Belgian filmmakers have taken still another step down the ladder. No wonder some people fainted at the premiere at the Brussels Film Festival and others fled the unbearable images. Horror films, even the most gory, can be viewed unperturbed because, at the back of the mind, one knows it is just fiction. But here it is reality from beginning to end, without remission.

The three authors perhaps struck on a good idea when they plotted their work: they set out to film funerary customs (orig title was "Les Rites des Morts") all the world over. But this requires visual flair, talent, imagination and the good sense to stop when the offensive rears its ugly head. One looks in vain for these assets in a film that is over-provocative.

The smell of death and decay is all over this gory product. There is unnecessary cruelty of animals killed in full view of the camera. One is treated to a seance of embalming with the corpse slit open from head to foot. A rotting corpse is complaisantly covered from all angles. Scenes in a Mexican hospital are nightmarish.

Makers went to the United States, Nepal, South Korea, Thailand to add spicy bits to their dissertation, even stopping in Belgium for a couple of totally insignificant funeral scenes.

Degrading is perhaps the very word to describe this descent into the bowels of a most deplorable lack of taste. Unimaginatively filmed with sequences just stuck together and stretched beyond patience. Editing is equally poor. Definitely not for the squeamish! This bloodbath was in part financed by the Ministry of French Culture. —*Flor.*

Mysteries
(DUTCH-COLOR)

Brussels, Jan. 23.

A Cine-Vog release of Sigma Film (Amsterdam). Produced by Matthijs Van Heyningen, Yannick Bernard. Stars Rutger Hauer, Sylvia Kristel. Directed by Paul De Lussanet. Screenplay, Paul De Lussanet, from novel by Knut Hamsun; camera (color), Robby Muller; music, Laurens Van Rooyen; editor, Jane Sperr. Reviewed at Passage 44, Jan. 21, '79. Running time: 100 MINS.

Johan Nagel	Rutger Hauer
Dany Kielland	Sylvia Kristel
Minuut	David Rappaport
Martha Gude	Rita Tushingham
Kamma	Andrea Ferreol
Dr. Stenerson	Kees Brusse
Mrs. Stenerson	Liesbeth List
Commissioner	Fons Rademakers
Innkeeper	Adrian Brine
Karlsen	Peter Faber

"Mysteries" lives up to its title. This story is riddled with question marks. What makes the people tick? Where do they come from and what are they driving at? No answer! Director Paul De Lussanet drives his people through a maze of artificial situations and, when they finally vanish, one still wonders what it was all really about. What remains is an album of rather pretty cliches but of dubious interest.

The Knut Hamsun novel seems to have been twisted and what survives is of debatable interest. Action has been moved from a Scandinavian country to the Isle of Man. An international cast was assembled, the "foreigners" dubbed in Dutch, which adds another touch of artificiality.

Where a "Wuthering Heights" atmosphere might have helped, there is only shallowness. One has the impression of viewing a pre-war film and not a very good one.

Main character Johan Nagel arrives in a little coastal town and starts to antagonize some of the natives by his bizarre ways. Where does he come from and what are his motives? Was he a friend of a man who, only a few days previously, died in mysterious circumstances? Is he seeking revenge and, if so, on whom? What is obvious is that Nagel falls in love with a local beauty who teases and repulses him in turn. Why does this man suddenly wants to marry a fading local spinster who perhaps played part in his earlier life for he seems to be a local boy after all? He finally commits suicide but is there any reason for it?

If all this created suspense one could only applaud, but there is a total lack of this element. With no motives explained, hollowness runs riot, the novelettish dialog unable to make these vacuous individuals absorbing in any way.

Rutger Hauer seems ill at ease. No wonder Sylvia Kristel, of "Emmanuelle," woodenly walks through her part. Rita Tushingham fights valiantly against the odds of an impossible part. Andrea Ferreol adds an incongruous cameo, totally out of place. Only midget David Rappaport succeeds in getting away with a couple of scenes. Pleasant location adds a certain sheen. Commercial values nevertheless appear restricted.
—*Flor.*

Kasper in De Onderwereld
(Kasper in the Underworld)
(BELGIAN-COLOR)

Brussels, Jan. 19.

CIC release of Van de Velde Films production. Stars Jos Houben, Annelies Vaes. Directed by Jef Van der Heyden. Screenplay, Hubert Lampo, based on his novel, Jef Van der Heyden; camera (Gevacolor), Fernand Tack, Theo Van der Sande; music, Francois Glorieux; lighting, Claude Decibber, Jacques Borremans; sound, Frans Van der Laan, Haane Reichardt, Wim De Clercq; editor, Jan Dop. Reviewed at Passage 44, Brussels, Jan. 18, '79. Running Time: 93 MINS.

Kasper	Jos Houben
Prostitute	Lieve Berens
Woman in yellow	Rosemary Bergmans
Surveyor	Rik Bravenboer
Eurydice	Annelies Vaes
Simon	Charles Janssens
Benedictus	Gaston Vandermeulen
Priest	Loet Hanekroot
Ferryman	Hubert De Stobbeleer
Chairman's wife	Ann Petersen
Prostitute	Monica De Vos
Jonathan	Manu Verreth
Dr. Molenaar	Leo Haelterman
Helene	Anita Koninck
Strikers	Max Schnur, Johan Van Lierde, Joris Collet, Bernard Verheyen
Lecturer	Bouk Martens
Chairman	Piet Bergers

Orpheus is definitely no newcomer to the screen, he has been seen in black and white, in color, and has gone in search of his Eurydice in all sorts of attire. Now he has been roaming the plains of Flanders and has died tragically in an Antwerp street during a strike. But the symbolism of the tale has worn very thin and what is perhaps even worse is that director Jef Van der Heyden appears still too green in the business to give conviction to a story which requires deeper insight and experience. This "Kasper" is not a total mishap for it has a few interesting moments and cameramen Fernand Tack and Theo Van der Sande make good use of the Flemish landscape. But it remains too incoherent, too far fetched to mobilize permanent attention.

Slightly mentally deranged, Kasper, former concert pianist, leaves his retreat in Geel in order to find a woman he loved and whom he thinks is now in hell. But hell is a city and so he finally reaches Antwerp where, in a cemetery, he meets a strange keeper. By this man he is taken to a few strange places, apparently discovers his beloved, but is mortally wounded and dies in the gutter.

Director fails to infuse much life in situations which are far fetched. There are reminiscences of Hieronymus Bosch, Brueghel, even Ensor but ropes are far too apparent, pulled by clumsy hands.

Jos Houben is rather wooden in the name part and with the possible exception of a couple of cameos, general acting adds to the artificality of the plot. Visual effects create some impact, as already mentioned.

Actually, this film was finished in 1973 but only edited five years later. Tastes have apparently changed in the meantime and "Kasper" already looks old hat. —*Flor.*

Agatha
(BRITISH-COLOR)

Stylish mystery that would do Agatha Christie proud. Strong b.o. outlook.

Hollywood, Feb. 8.

Warner Bros.-First Artists release of a Sweetwal production in association with Casablanca FilmWorks. Stars Dustin Hoffman and Vanessa Redgrave. Produced by Jarvis Astaire, Gavrik Losey. Directed by Michael Apted. Screenplay, Kathleen Tynan, Arthur Hopcraft, based on a story by Tynan; camera (Technicolor), Vittorio Storaro; editor, Jim Clark; music, Johnny Mandel; production design, Shirley Russell; art direction, Simon Holland; sound, Christian Wangler; assistant director, Jonathan Benson. Reviewed at The Burbank Studios, Feb. 7, 1979. MPAA Rating: PG. Running time: **98 MINS.**

Wally Stanton	Dustin Hoffman
Agatha Christie	Vanessa Redgrave
Archie Christie	Timothy Dalton
Evelyn	Helen Morse
Nancy Neele	Celia Gregory
John Foster	Paul Brooke
Mrs. Braithwaite	Yvonne Gilan
Sgt. Jarvis	David Hargreaves

For all the acrimony and disputation that has surrounded it, "Agatha" is an engaging and stylish film mystery. The film lives up to the legacy of its subject matter, author Agatha Christie, in every respect. The Warner Bros. release of the First Artists presentation should score at the wickets, thanks to the ingenious plot and the stellar performances by Dustin Hoffman and Vanessa Redgrave, both billed above the title.

With a cloud of litigation hanging over this production, it would seem wasteful for the film itself to be obscured in the haze of legalese. Billed as "an imaginary solution to an authentic mystery," Kathleen Tynan's original story fills in the gaps of Agatha Christie's well-publicized disappearance in 1926, and does so with just the right dash of reality.

Christie, as portrayed by Redgrave in superlative fashion, is confronted with the breakdown of her marriage to war hero Timothy Dalton, who is prepared to marry his secretary, played by Celia Gregory. She flees to a remote health spa, where she sets in motion a unique form of revenge, while thousands scour the British countryside for some sign of her.

Enter Hoffman as a celebrated American journalist writing a Yank's-p.o.v. column for one of the British tabloids. He, too, joins the search, at first with the idea of a story, and then pursuing more romantic notions.

Director Michael Apted, with the aid of production designer Shirley Russell and art director Simon Holland, has perfectly recaptured the mood of post-war Britain, and the film is gorgeously photographed in soft, muted imagery by Italian cinematographer Vittorio Storaro, who accomplished similar miraculous work for Bernardo Bertolucci.

But it is Hoffman and Redgrave, both separately and in tandem, who carry the weight of the film in effortless fashion. A mismatched couple physically (she towers over him in several scenes), they strike the proper emotional chords to make the love story subplot an almost viable one.

Almost is the key here, since the romantic underpinnings are the weakest link in "Agatha." Hoffman's motivation for pursuing Redgrave with such single-minded devotion is never adequately explained, and the film's ending seems to raise more issues than it resolves.

On the whole, however, "Agatha" is one of the smartest-looking films of this year, and packs a surprise twist that the real Agatha Christie might have envied. Also bolstering the production is a superb supporting cast, especially Dalton, Helen Morse as Redgrave's sensual friend and Paul Brooke as a provincial reporter whom Hoffman befriends. Johnny Mandel's score is also a decided asset, although a dreamy love ballad over the closing credits seems misplaced.

Casablanca FilmWorks is given a production credit, incidentally, because of the early involvement of producer David Puttnam, and some financial backing. But the company is not involved in the court battles that lie ahead, and which seem certain to keep "Agatha" in the headlines. —*Poll.*

Travels With Anita
(ITALIAN-COLOR)

Rome, Feb. 3.

A United Artists release of a PEA production. Stars Goldie Hawn, Giancarlo Giannini. Directed by Mario Monicelli. Screenplay, Leo Benvenuti, Piero De Bernardi, Tullio Pinelli, Paul Zimmerman and Mario Monicelli; camera (Eastmancolor), Tonino Delli Colli; editor, Ruggero Mastroianni; art director, Lorenzo Baraldi; music, Ennio Morricone. Reviewed at Fono Roma, Feb. 2, '79. Running time: **125 MINS.**

Anita	Goldie Hawn
Guido	Giancarlo Giannini
Elisa	Claudine Auger
Cora	Aurore Clement
Omero	Renzo Montagnani

Mario Monicelli has never fully dominated the American elements in his pictures. He was at a loss in "Mortadella" in a story bringing Sophia Loren from the deli factory in Bologna to New York and now still finds himself on unfamiliar ground with Goldie Hawn as Anita. With a weak, improbable story teaming Hawn and Giancarlo Giannini, the UA Europa release will have hard sledding in foreign markets including the U.S., but skilled re-editing for Yank audiences could improve chances to some extent.

"Travels With Anita" is the type of film hand-fashioned for Monicelli. Conceived as a black comedy — a Monicelli specialty — both the comedy and irony are subverted for most of the film to give Giannini and Hawn at least a full hour in which to develop and untie a hot romance. But even here, Giannini's character as a loutish bank exec and his partner's bewildered naivete take the bloom off the rose — leaving a pair of caricatures — one of a lame Latin lover; the other an incomplete portrait of an autonomous young 'Americana' who takes a long time to see the light.

Heart of the Monicelli pic is the basis for the Rome-Pisa journey—death in a Tuscan working-class family. Giannini could have reached his father's bedside before the old man passed away, but fleshdabbling with Anita delays him until after rigor mortis. Death re-unites family and family scenes are skillfully filmed to (expose) each and everyone's skeletons. After Anita finally opens her eyes and leaves, black comedy takes over as the family components, lined up in funeral procession, hurl family scandals back and forth ad nauseam.

Sidebar components, such as the last goodbye by the father's longtime mistress, as the family prepares for burial rites, is sarcastically heart-warming. Several others like it indicate hope for a doctored version re-scrambling the choice cuts and hacking away at the unlikely romantic escapade that throws the film out of focus.

All of the technical departments combine to give the PEA production a rich look in sight and sound. —*Werb.*

The Warriors
(COLOR)

Stay out of the subways.

Hollywood, Feb. 13.

Paramount Pictures release of a Lawrence Gordon production. Exec producer, Frank Marshall. Produced by Lawrence Gordon. Directed by Walter Hill. Screenplay, David Shaber, Hill, based on novel by Sol Yurick; camera (color), Andrew Laszlo; editor, David Holden; art direction, Don Swanagan, Bob Wightman; music, Barry DeVorzon; costume design, Bobbie Mannix; set decoration, Fred Weiler; sound, Jack Jacobsen, Al Mian; stunt coordinator, Craig Baxley; assistant director, David Sosna. Reviewed at Paramount Studio Theatre, Feb. 9, '79. (MPAA Rating: R.). Running time: **90 MINS.**

Swan	Michael Beck
Ajax	James Remar
Fox	Thomas Waites
Cleon	Dorsey Wright
Snow	Brian Tyler
Cochise	David Harris
Cowboy	Tom McKitterick
Rembrandt	Marcelino Sanchez
Vermin	Terry Michos
Mercy	Deborah Van Valkenburgh
Luther	David Patrick Kelly
Cyrus	Roger Hill

As the first of the upcoming "gang" pictures cycle, "The Warriors" offers audiences a taste of what's to come: bone-cracking violence, dialog consisting mostly of expletives, and an emphasis on the more degrading aspects of human nature. under Walter Hill's forceful direction, the Paramount release should do well with the bare-knuckle crowd, along with those curious about this subculture.

Theme of the pic, based on Sol Yurick's 1965 novel, is a variation on countless westerns and war films. A group of men (in this case, boys) are trapped behind enemy lines, and must make a run for their own turf, and hoped-for safety.

Update the setting to modern-day New York, and the avenues of escape to graffiti-emblazoned subway cars, and that's "The Warriors." In this instance, a charismatic hood (Roger Hill) is gunned down as he attempts to wield a multitude of gangs into one powerful army that will outnumber Gotham's finest.

The slaying is pinned on a Coney Island gang, the Warriors of the title, by the reel perpetrators, and the word soon goes out that the group's members are to be eliminated. It's a long subway ride to Coney Island, so for at least 70 of the film's 90 minutes, the boys in this band experience a variety of macho passage rites.

As with his previous pix, "Hard Times" and "The Driver," Hill demonstrates an outstanding visual sense here, with the gaudy "colors" of the gang members, the desolation of nighttime N.Y., and the cavernous subway platforms where much of the action takes place.

The minute one of Hills' characters opens his mouth, however, "The Warriors" goes from the sublime to the ridiculous. Hill has apparently not abandoned the existential bent he demonstrated with "The Driver," and his script (with David Shaber) is tolerable only in the action sequences.

The cast of unknowns is remarkably strong, if somewhat faceless, since Hill allows only one or two clearly-defined personalities to emerge. These include Michael Beck as the gang leader, and James Remar as a looney cohort, along with David Patrick Kelly as the psychotic killer. Deborah Van Valkenburgh is the love interest for Beck, an apparent afterthought, since her character has no clear purpose.

Tech credits are highly polished, especially Andrew Laszlo's vivid lensing and David Holden's deft editing. Barry DeVorzon's score plays an integral part in setting the mood of the pic, but it seems highly reminiscent of a similar electronic soundtrack on William Friedkin's "Sorcerer."

There was no pre-release trade-screening of "The Warriors," ostensibly due to last-minute editing and an unavailability of prints. That explanation doesn't hold up, however, since Paramount opened the film in 670 venues last Friday, and it takes at least two weeks for that many prints to be struck.

More likely explanation is fear of a repeat of the critical drubbing Hill and producer Lawrence Gordon took on their previous pic, "The Driver." Ironically, the strategy may have backfired, since "The Warriors" is far more impressive, and should gain some critical, as well as boxoffice, success. —Poll.

The Late Great Planet Earth
(COLOR)

Not so great.

Hollywood, Feb. 13.

A Pacific International Enterprises release of an RCR production. Exec producer, Michael F. Leone. Produced by Robert Amram, Alan Belkin. Written and directed by Amram, based on the book by Hal Lindsey with C.C. Carlson; biblical sequences written and directed by Rolf Forsberg; music, Dana Kaproff. Narrated by Orson Welles and Hal Lindsey. No other credits available. Reviewed at Culver Theatre, Culver City, Feb. 6, '79. (MPAA Rating: PG.) Running time: **90 MINS.**

"The Late Great Planet Earth" is simply a more sophisticated version of the fellow who used to parade around streetcorners, wearing sackcloth and ashes, and holding a sign proclaiming the end of the world to be imminent. Pacific International Enterprises should flush out most of the true believers through its market saturation approach, but otherwise, its appeal will be extremely limited.

Hal Lindsey's book, on which this semi-documentary is fashioned, has reportedly sold some 12,000,000 copies, meaning there are a lot of people who believe, in Lindsey's words, that we're "racing on a countdown to the end of history."

This film won't reassure them. Writer-director Robert Amram offers a different explanation for all the natural phenomena explained elsewhere by UFOs, ancient visitors or Bermuda triangles, but the litany of impending destruction sounds awfully familiar.

Orson Welles is around to pronounce services over the planet in suitably ominous fashion, and he performs his chores with the same facility that he sells wine in various vidblurbs. Author Lindsey also makes several on-screen appearances that are less successful.

Remainder of the film is taken up with Biblical re-enactments, in which every prophet has a long, white beard, and is never believed by his contemporaries. But Lindsey, backed by quick clips of academics and scientists, knows better, or so this film purports.

"The Late Great Planet Earth" is really a kind of big-screen picture book, with visual accompaniment to Welles' soothing narration. There's clearly an audience for this kind of fare, but if "The Late Great Planet Earth" is to be believed, there won't be for long. —Poll.

Hardcore
(COLOR)

Solid stuff.

Hollywood, Feb. 13.

A Columbia Picture release of an A-Team Production, produced by Buzz Feitshans. Written and directed by Paul Schrader. Features entire cast. Executive producer, John Milius. Camera (color), Michael Chapman; editor, Tom Rolf; sound, Bud Maffett; production design, Paul Sylbert; art direction, Ed O'Donovan; assistant director, Richard Hashimoto; set decoration, Bruce Weintraub; music, Jack Nitzsche. Reviewed at Columbia Studios, Jan. 25, '79. (MPAA Rating: R.) Running time: **105 MINS.**

Jake VanDorn	George C. Scott
Andy Mast	Peter Boyle
Niki	Season Hubley
Wes DeJong	Dick Sargent
Ramada	Leonard Gaines
Kurt	David Nichols
Tod	Gary Rand Graham
Detective Burrows	Larry Block
Ratan	Marc Alaimo
Felice	Leslie Ackerman
Beatrice	Charlotte McGinnis
Kristen VanDorn	Ilah Davis
Jis'm Jim	Will Walker

Paul Schrader's "Hardcore" is rough stuff, calculated to bring a broad audience as close to the cold world of hot pornography as a major studio will stand for. But what isn't shown — and that's not much — is generally talked about in explicit terms, a highly exploitable combination boosted by the fact that this is also a very good film.

Title, of course, reflects the modern slang for what used to be called smut. But it's also a word for unwavering religious faith, anchoring old-fashioned values. Without moralizing on either side. Schrader brings these two meanings into conflict through George C. Scott, giving as fin a performance as he's ever done.

An unventuring Calvinist, Scott lives a contented small-town Michigan life until his daughter, Ilah Davis, disappears on a trip to L.A. He hires seedy private-eye Peter Boyle who eventually finds her on film in a porno movie. Forced to watch, Scott's anguish at the sight bespeaks a clash of values still haunting the country.

From this emotional peak, film settles into the numbed netherworld of commercialized sex as Scott goes searching for Davis. Inevitably, Schrader sees this world through the same eyes through which he witnessed the harsh surroundings of his "Taxi Driver" and there are likenesses. But it's even more fascinating this time, in its own tawdry fashion.

For many, even those who patronize porno films, this will be the first up-close look at the world behind the scenes, including nude-conversation encounters, massage parlors, bondage joints and the lowest degradation — "snuff" films.

To aide in his search, Scott enlists the help of a porno actress, beautifully played by Season Hubley, and they develop a friendship that's neither fatherly nor sexual. After discovering his long-time celibacy since his wife ran away, she sums up their attitudes. "You think sex is so unimportant, you don't even do it. I think it's so unimportant, I don't care who I do it with."

Though dialog like that is somewhat contrived, it keeps the point of the picture in focus, a necessity lest Scott's quest sink into expose.

The easily shocked may want an expose, or more a condemnation. Equally so, the more sophisticated may grow tired of Scott's morality. And the in-between will find fault with some of the film's lapses in storyline and momentary artifacts. But shocked, cynical or dissatisfied, nobody's going to be bored. —Har.

Just a Gigolo
(W. GERMAN-COLOR)

Engrossing, bitter-funny recall of pre-Hitler Germany, with Dietrich and Kim Novak to help prospects.

London, Feb. 12.

Tedderwick Ltd. release (in U.K.) of a Leguan Film presentation. Stars David Bowie, Sydne Rome. Produced by Rolf Thiele. Directed by David Hemmings. Screenplay, Joshua Sinclair, Ennio de Concini; camera (color), Charly Steinberger; art director, Peter Rothe; original music, Gunther Fischer; costume design, Ingrid Zore; editors, Susan Jaeger, Fred Srp, Maxine Julius; no other credits available. Reviewed at Columbia Theatre, London, Feb. 12, '79. Running time: **105 MINS.**

Paul	David Bowie
Cilly	Sydne Rome
Helga	Kim Novak
Capt. Kraft	David Hemmings
Mutti	Maria Schell
Prince	Curt Jurgens
Baroness	Marlene Dietrich
Eva	Erika Pluhar
Gustav	Rudolf Schundler
Aunt Hilda	Hilde Weissner
Otto	Werner Pochath
Von Lipzig	Bela Erny
Von Muller	Friedhelm Lehmann
Lothar	Rainer Hunold
Frau Aeckerle	Evelyn Kunneke
Frau Uexkull	Karin Hardt
Frau von Putzdorf	Gudrun Genest
Greta	Ursula Heyer
Gilda	Christiane Maybach
Director	Martin Hirthe
Agent	Rene Killdehoff
Drunken worker	Gunter Meisner
First man in bath	Peter Schlesinger

Those who dug "Cabaret" probably will also admire "Just a Gigolo," possibly more so, as a kindred harkback to the post World War I Germany of lost souls and rising aryan nationalism. No less romanticized, perhaps, but with an added, effective edge of satire, though whether that will widen its urban appeal is less certain.

The Rolf Thiele production, handsomely photographed in Berlin and directed with finesse by David Hemmings, has David Bowie as a Prussian war vet back from the dead who drifts from one demeaning job to another and finally into employment as a gigolo. In this case Webster-defined as "a professional dancing partner or male escort."

The fascinating, and obviously exploitable, casting includes Marlene Dietrich as a kind of gigolo den mother, and the return of Kim Novak portraying a libidinous widow. Sydne Rome, who shares above-title billing with Bowie, is an appealing revelation as his ambitious childhood sweetheart, notably in a cabaret turn sequence.

Dietrich, so long away from the screen, is perforce hypnotic in what amounts to a cameo (she also touchingly croons the evergreen title song), in which she adds Bowie to her gigolo stable. Novak, another longtime-no-see name, also makes a strong impression, with commanding presence as well as mature beauty. The role suits her and vice-versa, which adds up to clever rather than mere gimmick casting.

Bowie goes through his tumbleweed paces with engaging appeal, meeting violent albeit innocent death at the end. The role may be said to call for tentative conviction, or possibly non-heroic impact, and the result is appropriate.

"Just a Gigolo" provides an evocative and sometimes pungent account of the despair, militarism, sexual puritanism, hedonism and bourgeois appearances that marked between-the-wars Germany. The script by Joshua Sinclair and Ennio de Concini, often has a nice line in crisp wit and cutting irony.

On the other hand, bitter, provocative Brecht it isn't. Those incipient Nazi hoodlums depicted in "Gigolo" are too clownish and thick to provide a proper chill factor. And some will surely note the curious neglect of the preposterous inflation, circa 1923, that reduced Germany to pathos and bathos and ultimately delivered the Weimar Republic into Hitler's hands.

But the film still delivers a lot of bittersweet entertainment and is never less than engrossing. Period mood is a great strength, with an effective visual mixture of sepia and soft color tints, and a music track of period ballads and jolly ragtime tunes.

Hemmings also appears, and stylishly, as a rabble-rouser. But it's in the role of director that he really shines, handling his material and cast with authority and dexterity, filling many of his scenes with a compulsive look and energy. At 105 minutes, the film paces well in the version caught, which is said to be an extensive recut of the original one that flopped in West German release.

A lot of other responsive performances dot the narrative — Maria Schell as Bowie's bewildered mother, reduced to postwar employment in a Turkish bath; Erika Pluhar as a classy prostitute; Curt Jurgens as a rich aristocrat whom Rome marries after Bowie spurns her carnal advances; and an exemplary lineup of German names in bits-and-pieces support.

• On the technical side, Charly Steinberger's photography is first-rate; likewise the costumes of Ingrid Zore, Peter Rothe's production design, and the editing of Maxine Julius, credited with the recut herein appraised. —*Pit.*

Samba Da Criacao Do Mundo
(Samba of the Creation of the World)
(BRAZILIAN-COLOR)

Rio de Janeiro, Feb. 6.

A Circofilm Beija-Flori Livio Bruni production. Features the samba school Beija-Flor is Nilopolis, state of Rio de Janeiro. Directed by Vera Figueiredo. Sound editor, Walter Goulart; sound and film technicians: Victor Rasposeiro, Jorge Saldanha, Mario da Silva, Antonio Cesar, Helio Vicente, Jose Sette and Didi Guper. Reviewed at Cinema Bruni-Copacabana, Rio, Feb. 6, '79. Running time: **90 MINS.**

Here is one of those documentary type of pics which will either bore you to death or make you go "wow." There's no in-between for the viewer. The idea is a front-row seat to the Carnival — in fact this pic is better than the most expensive seat in the stands in downtown Rio during this famous event.

Actually filmed during last year's Carnival, "Creation" zooms in on not only the action and events in the kingdom of Momo but most important, the words. One hesitates to guess that if the Portuguese legends would be translated and the film shortened there might be an international market.

For Samba and Carnival are two Brazilian events which take on a profundity and even a complexity when examined close-up. Here's an opportunity to observe, through the looking glass, the marchers, singers, dances and masqueraders who descend from the favelas or slums of Rio and march onto Avenida Central with all the alegria, or happiness, they can display to the world.

The legends explain exactly what is being sung to those pulsating rhythms and in this case it is the "world's creation" according to the beautiful African legends which the slaves brought to Brazil and planted into the cultural soil.

But again, the pic might either bring a yawn or an open-eyed thankfulness to a viewer introduced to a culture well fictionalized but not always as well documented on the screen. —*Emrt.*

The Promise
(COLOR)

Soap opera, without the commercials.

Universal Pictures release of a Gilbert Cates Film. Produced by Fred Weintraub, Paul Heller. Stars Kathleen Quinlan, Stephen Collins, Beatrice Straight. Directed by Gilbert Cates. Screenplay, Garry Michael White, based on a story by Weintraub and Heller; exec producer, Tully Friedman; camera (color), Ralph Woolsey; editor, Peter E. Berger; art director, William Sandell; set decoration, Jeff Haley; sound, Michael Evje; music, David Shire; title song, lyrics, Marilyn and Alan Bergman, music, David Shire; special effects, Greg Auer. Reviewed at Universal homeoffice, N.Y., Feb. 14, '79. (MPAA Rating: PG). Running time: **97 MINS.**

Nancy/Marie	Kathleen Quinlan
Michael	Stephen Collins
Marion	Beatrice Straight
Dr. Gregson	Laurence Luckinbill
George Calloway	William Prince
Ben Avery	Michael O'Hare
Dr. Allison	Bibi Besch
Dr. Wickfield	Robin Gammell
Wendy Lester	Katherine DeHetre
Dr. Fenton	Paul Ryan
Painter	Tom O'Neill
Nurse	Kirchy Prescott
1st Cab Driver	John Allen Vick
2nd Cab Driver	Dan Leegant
Cal	Jerry Walter
Dr. Sidney Meisner	Bob Hirschfeld
Barker	Alan Newman
Truck driver	Carey Loftin
Truck driver	Max Balchowsky
Truck driver	Mickey Gilbert

The title of this romantic melodrama, which has been booked into Radio City Music Hall as the Easter attraction, has to do with a buried necklace and the promise of undying love and faith in each other made by a young architectural student and a girl student, So much ceremony is made about burying the necklace under a stone by the seashore that one counts the minutes before the plot returns to the scene. Which it does, of course.

The girl is severely injured in an auto accident and the boy is unconscious for some time, during which his mother — a female building tycoon — persuades the girl to undergo some very expensive plastic surgery and seek a new life elsewhere. She tells her son the girl is dead.

The scene changes to California. The girl, a promising artist, has for reasons known only to herself, switched to photography — maybe, it could be her new face and new name. She's an overnight success and is sought by — guess who — the young architect who's building a medical center. Does he recognize her? Well, not hardly, this early in the film. Does he ever recognize her? Remember that necklace and "the promise?"

If the film didn't have such a slick production it might get pretty sticky as there's at least three handkerchiefs worth of happy tears before the lovers are finally reunited.

Kathleen Quinlan, after a brief period of obvious makeup in the early stages, is pretty convincing as the painter/photographer and a new, very handsome, young leading man is added to the Hollywood scene (and could they ever use him!) with Stephen Collins as the architect.

Overshadowing both of them in most of her scenes and, easily, the best performance in the film, is Beatrice Straight as Collins' mother. She is protective and manipulating but avoids being the monster this type of role usually calls for. Had she been given the type of dialog Paddy Chayefsky provided in "Network," she'd be on her way to another Oscar.

Also excellent in considerably lesser roles are Laurence Luckin bill as the plastic surgeon who gives Quinlan a new, beautiful face (to believe this one takes absolute faith on the part of the viewer), William Prince as Straight's business partner, Michael O'Hare as Collins' closest friend and Bibi Besch as a femme psychiatrist who helps Quinlan adjust ("don't worry, honey, you'll just have to get used to looking like Hedy Lamarr") to her new situation.

The production design looks expensive so, if the Massachusetts shoreline looks suspiciously like the sun-kissed California coast, it isn't important enough to worry about.

Gilbert Cates comes very close to making out-and-out soap opera not only endurable but believable. David Shire's handsome score is a great help. With the present trend towards superviolence on the nation's screens, this one could help swing the pendulum back in the other direction. —*Robe.*

En rig mand
(A Rich Man)
(DANISH-DOCU-COLOR)

Copenhagen, Feb. 3.

A Statens Filmcentral/Denmark's Radio production, Statens Filmcentral release. Written and directed by Jon Bang Carlsen. Camera (16mm Eastmancolor) Alexander Gruszynski. Starring Hans and Cardy Smith as themselves. Music, Ida Klemann, Torben Andersen. In charge of production, Vibeke Windeloev. Reviewed at Delta Bio, Copenhagen, Feb. 2, '79. Running time, 67 MINS.

Danish multimillionaire Hans Smith, inventor and license-holder of the plant food, Substral, steps in front of his white Rolls or of his pop art originals or of his minor palaces in Beverly Hills and Monte Carlo or of the Copenhagen slum backyards where he was born 58 years ago to make certain statements directly to the camera that has otherwise followed him through his days of luxury eating, swimming or bubble-bathing naked with his young wife Cardy, giving his many servants softly modulated orders or hopping elegantly around on the crutches polio inflicted upon him as a teenager.

The statements Smith makes are grand platitudes about the few who dare grasp at Luck's outstretched hand, about money securing him total freedom, about the envy of the have-nots, about reaching in vain for things in dreams, but not giving his dreams any thought since awake, he has always obtained what he set out to obtain, etc. Smith and his wife collaborated with filmmaker Jon Carl Bang on this extraordinary documentary all the way and approved of it in its entirety before its release.

So nobody can accuse writer-director Bang Carlsen of finger pointing or moralizing or stacking the cards against his subject. "A Rich Man" tells it like the rich man wants it to look and sound. His life, to most audiences, will seem curiously devoid of any real life or suspense.

Film transcends the ordinary docu on several levels. It also contains a sequence describing the fulfilment of Smith's wish for his burial rites: he is to be placed in an open coffin aboard his yacht which will then be brought into the open sea and then blown-up at the exact hour of Smith's birth back in the Copenhagen slum.

"A Rich Man" could make an attractive item at any festival and specialized theatres as well as tv stations everywhere will be sure to queue up to purchase Bang Carlsen's work. Special production honors go to cinematographer Alexander Gruszynski, production manager Vibeke Windeloev and to Ida Klemann and Torben Andersen who wrote the gently suggestive soundtrack music. —*Kell.*

Fast Break
(COLOR)

Basketball comedy has some prospects in major cities, before running out of gas.

Hollywood, Feb. 13.

Columbia Pictures release of a Stephen Freidman/Kings Road production. Exec producer, Jerry Frankel, Stars Gabriel Kaplan. Directed by Jack Smight. Screenplay, Sandor Stern, based on a story by Marc Kaplan; camera (color), Charles Correll; editor, Frank J. Urioste; music, David Shire, James di Pasquale; art direction, Norman Baron; sound, Lee Alexander; assistant director, Carl Olsen. Reviewed at Directors Guild Of America, Feb. 13, '79. (MPAA Rating: PG.) Running time, 107 MINS.
David Greene ....Gabriel Kaplan
D.C. .... Harold Sylvester
Preacher ....Mike Warren
Hustler .... Bernard King
Bull.........................Reb Brown
Swish ....Mavis Washington
Bo Winnegar ....Bert Remsen
Jan ....Randee Heller
Alton Gutkas ....John Chappell
Enid Cadwallader-Gutkas .. Rhonda Bates
Ms. Tidwell................... K. Callan
Howard .... Richard Brestoff

"Fast Break" appears to be a telefilm that has wandered into the wrong arena. Likable in a rather harmless fashion, the Columbia Pictures release seems certain to turn up on the tube soon, after quickly exhausting the potential of major markets where its basketball theme could click. Otherwide, boxoffice potential seems limited.

The Stephen Friedman production takes a familiar, mocking approach to a popular sport, much as "The Bad News Bears" series of pix lampooned baseball. Gabriel Kaplan, in an expansion of his vid character in "Welcome Back Kotter," abandons his wife and work to take a basketball coaching job at an obscure Nevada college, where his salary is dependent on taking a rag-tag team to victory.

To assure his efforts of some credibility, Kaplan recruits his players from New York street games, and imports them to Cadwallader University, where, lo and behold, they turn into a UCLA-calibre team.

The big game looms, of course, with Bert Remsen's top-ranked basketball five, and the Cadwallader bunch comes out on top in the cliffhanger. "Fast Break" evokes more pix than it's comfortable to mention, while failing to establish a firm identity of its own.

The comedy aspects derive primarily from a femme player (Mavis Washington) forced into reverse drag, and her budding relationship with teammate Harold Sylvester, who can't figure out why "Swish" never showers with the rest of the guys. Each player has a personal peccadillo, but Kaplan manages to straighten eveyrone out by the final credits.

"Fast Break" is well cast, although Kaplan may have made a major error career-wise by choosing to make his screen debut with a character virtually identical to his tv image. Newcomer Washington is very effective, as are Sylvester and basketball star-turned-actor Mike Warren. Pro forward Bernard King should stick to his chosen profession. Bert Remsen, John Chappell and Richard Brestoff are all solid in support.

Major problem in both Sandor Stern's screenplay and Jack Smight's direction, aside from slow pacing and untoward attention to frivolous detail, is the absence of that vitality and spark which distinguishes a feature film from its television counterpart. "Fast Break" leaves one waiting for a commercial, and a chance to go get another beer. —*Poll.*

Voices
(COLOR)

Love conquers everything but boxoffice resistance.

Hollywood, Feb. 14.

A United Artists release of a Metro-Goldwyn-Mayer picture, produced by Joe Wizan. Directed by Robert Markowitz. Screenplay, John Herzfeld; camera (Metrocolor), Alan Metzger; editor, Danford B. Green; sound, Les Lazarowitz, Gustave E. Mortensen; art direction, Richard Bianchi; assistant director, Michael Rauch; set decoration, Fred Weiler; associate producer, Betty Gumm; music, Jimmy Webb. Reviewed at MGM Studios, Culver City, Feb. 14, 1979. (MPAA Rating: PG.) Running time: 106 MIN.
Drew Rothman .... Michael Ontkean
Rosemarie Lemon .... Amy Irving
Frank Rothman .... Alex Rocco
Raymond Rothman .... Barry Miller
Nathan Rothman ....Herbert Berghof
Mrs. Lemon .... Viveca Lindfors

The triumph of love, courage and determination over affliction, as seen recently in "Ice Castles" and "Slow Dancing In The Big City," is again the theme in "Voices," a nice enough little film with likable characters, acted well. But its weak title and underwhelming reception for those similar pictures are big odds against it.

Michael Ontkean and Amy Irving pick up a couple of superior credits as the loving young couple. He's a rough-edged Hoboken truck driver who wants to sing, she a deaf girl who wants to dance. They're an unlikely couple, but that's the story.

Both have family problems. Her's is an overly protective mother, well played by Viveca Lindfors. His is a boisterous but affectionate brood, consisting of a gambling father, Alex Rocco, delinquent young brother, Barry Miller, and kindly grandfather, Herbert Berghof.

The males are all good, especially Rocco, and the best scene of the picture takes place when Ontkean brings Irving home for the first time.

John Herzfeld's script is straightforward but full of contrivances and overly obvious tugs at the heartstrings. Robert Markowitz' direction reflects the tv career that launched him into this film.

For all its faults, though, "Voices" never gets silly as it rounds up its sympathies and proceeds to its happy ending. —*Har.*

Les Enfants de L'Oubli
(The Children of Oblivion)
(BELGIAN-COLOR-B&W-16m)

Brussels, Jan. 25.

Camera release of a Joao Correa — Jules Brunin production. Directed by Joao Correa. Feature entire cast. Screenplay, Alain Verdier, Dominque Hanssens; camera (black and white), Jacques Duesberg, Jean-Paul Kesnier; editors, Bob Van Hammee, Luc Bourgeois, Maria Joao Tiago; music, G. Soccio. Reviewed at Passage 44, Brussels, Jan. 24, '79. Running time: 90 MINS.

A film? Pamphlet seems a more appropriate word for this documentary that shook the Brussels Festival crowd. Not because it is outstandingly made — it is not in fact — but here is a theme that drives an arrow into heart and conscience.

Implicated are the 35,000 Belgian children depending on the Youth Protection, living from public charity in homes, loveless and unwanted. The state looks after them, but they may be scarred for the rest of their lives, physically and morally exposed to many dangers, ill prepared to grow into useful citizens: the flotsam of society so to speak. A courageous man, himself a former "lost child," Jules Brunin has devoted his time and efforts to draw attention to try and rehabilitate these socalled "children of the Judge." Ten years have passed and there is still no solution.

This is what this independently produced, without financial support (but some film professionals came to the rescue), is all about. It is doubtful that it will find its way into the commercial circuit, but it might, with some luck, get into circles where social aspects constitute a leading motive. Lack of shading can be deplored. Brunin does not always use the right words in his denunciation of people, cited by name. In a scene he exhibits a little girl bearing cigarette burns, a heart-breaking moment perhaps but the words underlining this diminish the impact.

During nine months, Joao Correa and Jules Brunin went in search of filmic material, greatly hampered in more than one way, one of them being the 1965 law strictly forbidding under sixteens to be photographed, so the minors bringing testimony of their sad plight wore Ku Klux Klan hoods. Quite naturally, access to homes concerned was simply out of the question. But what appears on the screen nevertheless is hard hitting at times. And what comes to the foreground is lack of love and pity, corrupt practices of people at the top. Some of these pariahs could well be adopted by couples in search of children they could not produce themselves but here again obstacles are created in every possible way. The more inmates the more profits for homes and institutions! So they are over-crowded.

Injustice and cruelty exposed are the leading motives of this social pamphlet which made a deep impression here. Will it serve the purpose pursued by the makers? This remains to be seen. —Flor.

40 Anos Sin Sexo
(40 Years Without Sex)
(SPANISH-COLOR)

Madrid, Feb. 13.
Producciones Zeta S.A. production. Directed by Juan Bosch. Camera (Eastmancolor), Tomas Pladevall; screenplay, Juanjo Puigcorbe, Francisco Bellmunt and Enrique Josa; editor, Emilio Rodriguez; music, Maestro Soto; sets, Ramon Pou. Reviewed at Cine Velazquez, Madrid, Feb. 12, '79. Running time: 87 MINS.
Cast: Marta Angelat, Antonio Ceinos, Carlos Lucena, Alfredo Luchetti, Alicia Orozco, Maria Rubio, Taida Urruzola, Maria Rey.

The 40 years of the title of this film refers to the Franco era when Spain was a bulwark of conservatism, especially in the first 20 years following the war. The conservatism was especially noticeable in all matters regarding sex. This film basically consists of a half dozen skits which tell, in a humorous fashion and with

enough softcore situations to make it titillating, some of the more outlandish incidents of the period.

Generally well directed and acted and with good production values, the film nonetheless seems too inconsequential, especially the first half, with some of the skits trailing off pointlessly or terminating abruptly, though in the second half the stories get livelier.

Episodes concern boys masturbating in a camp under the sheets; a contest to pick the most "macho" man, who is coupled with a beauty queen, but fails to perform; a woman raped by a German shepherd dog; a couple who fondle each other in an Andalusian theatre; an almost classic tale of infidelity in a provincial wife who is seduced by her house doctor; and the story of a fascist blue shirt whose young son turns out to be homosexual.

Pic generally keeps up a good pace, and some of the stories, though very slight, are nonetheless entertaining. Item could rack up some offshore sales thanks to its risque themes and touches of wry humor. —Besa.

Eclair au Chocolat
(Chocolate Eclair)
(FRENCH CANADIAN-COLOR)

Montreal, Feb. 13.
A Films Mutuels release of a Jean-Claude Lord film. Produced by Pierre David and Robert Menard for Les Productions Mutuelles Ltd. and Les Productions Videofilms Ltd. Stars Lise Thouin, Jean Belzil-Gascon, Jean-Louis Roux, Colin Fox. Directed by Jean-Claude Lord. Screenplay, Jean Salvy, Jean-Claude Lord, based on Jean Santacroce novel; camera (color), Francois Portat; editor, Jean-Claude Lord; music, Richard Gregoire; sound, Henri Blondeau; executive producer, Robert Menard. Reviewed at National Film Board of Canada, Montreal, Jan. 30, '79. Running time: 105 MINS.
Cast: Lise Thouin, Jean Belzil-Gascon, Jean-Louis Roux, Colin Fox, Danielle Panneton, Aubert Pallascio, Olivier Fillion, Valerie Deltour.

The steadiest French-Canadian director of the '70s has been Jean-Claude Lord. Quebec audiences for homegrown movies have shrunk in recent years and so has demand for the services of many native directors. But Lord has bucked this and other trends (particularly the one toward foreign co-production) and he has continued to find both funds and audiences for such films as "The Doves," "Bingo," "Panic" and "Parlez-nous d'amour."

The hallmark of Lord's work until now has been its topicality. "Panic," "Bingo" and "Parlez-nous d'amour" were all inspired by what the French call "actualites" (i.e. headlines) and they have avoided esthetic niceties in favor of hard-hitting, television-type, dramatic exposes.

For whatever reason, Lord has

decided to change that pace in his newest feature, "Eclair au chocolat," and the result is mildly disappointing.

"Eclair" is the soap-operatic story of a teenage girl from small-town Quebec who is raped by her uncle and shamefully covers-up the deed by running away to the city and pretending to everyone, especially to her illegitimate son, that his father was a poetic young boyfriend who died in a road accident.

The young mother (Lise Thouin, Mrs. Lord off-screen) makes a brave go of it alone in Montreal, first as a bank clerk and then as a hostess-cum-guide for visiting American conventioneers. As her son (Jean Belzil-Gascon) matures, his curiosity grows and so does his skepticism. The poems of his "father" begin to seem quite banal and he can't understand why his mother is so reluctant to visit her family in the country.

Neither, quite frankly, can the audience. The script that Lord and Jean Salvy (his regular collaborator) have adapted from Jean Santacroce's French novel, is not very strong on logic or character motivation and several important scenes end up being carried entirely on the wavering shoulders of the cast.

This weakness becomes glaringly apparent in the film's soppy finale — a long sequence in the mansion of a bachelor American businessman (Colin Fox) who had met the mournful heroine in Montreal and invited her and her son to spend Christmas with him in San Francisco.

Francois Portat's misty color photography and Richard Gregoire's lush musical score help to distract our attention from these faults, but the cast is not always up to the large task and Lord's film remains little more than a Quebec-style "Unmarried Woman," heavily overlaid with gothic romance. —Mali.

Itchy Fingers
(HONG KONG-COLOR)

Hong Kong, Feb. 11.
Advance Films Ltd. and Golden Harvest Production-coproduction. Features entire cast. Directed by Po Chi-leung, Screenplay, Richard Ng, Po Chi Leung, Wong Ching; camera (color) Cheung Yiu Jo; special effects photography, Arthur Lavis; editor, Cheung Yiu Chung; music; Frankie Chan, Ricky Fung. Reviewed at State Theatre, Hong Kong, Feb. 10, '79. Running time: 94 MINS.
With: Richard Ng, Roy Chao, Cora Miao.
(English subtitles)

This Hong Kong-made comedy is slick and sparkles with smoothness. It has the professional look and touch which distinguishes it from routine Cantonese comedies. Though its marketability in the

West looks dim, the Asian outlook is bright. Made for only HK$1,200,000 by Advance Films in association with Raymond Chow's Golden Harvest, the classy packaging and presentation paid off with nearly HK$4,000,000 business during the Chinese New Year holiday run and is still going strong at the b.o.

Acting is good, especially Richard Ng who delivers excellent verbal and visual gags with ease and is nicely complemented by his butterball side-kick, Roy Chiao. They execute firstrate clowning without the excessive use of insane slapstick. But the best sequence is when Ng searches desperately for the bathroom after a beer drinking contest bout.

Meanwhile, Po Chi-leung's direction has few very flaws and flimsy moments. The frenetic pace created by Po and the glossy special effects of Englishman Arthur Lavis are fine tributes to the unrelenting imaginative energies of everyone involved in the production. It's the unforced type of Cantonese comedy that needs few itchy fingers to tickle Chinese viewers to laughter.

The film begins in sepia flashbacks to introduce the young principals, Biggie (Roy Chiao) and Tiny (Richard Ng) who sort of grew up together in the slums. Biggie is honest and straight forward as a cop while Tiny is resourceful and tricky as a con-man.

Color filters in as they grow-up and as they become pros in their respective trade. Biggie is now a detective and Tiny a professional thief. A friendly rivalry links the two together.

In one episode, Tiny is approached by underground groups to steal the world famous diamond "Star of the South Seas." The store is under the custody of glamorous Tina (Cora Miao), supposedly the daughter of the jeweler.

But Tiny decides to get the jewel himself. But before Tiny can steal anything, the diamond and other gems disappear mysteriously and he becomes the scapegoat. Biggie smells a rat. He makes secret investigations and is convinced that the Hong Kong honored (O.B.E.) jeweler is involved. Biggie makes a proposal to Tiny, to steal the diamonds back and then split the reward. Posing as Arab sheiks, they crash the jeweler's high society party. As the diamonds are in the gadget laden vault, they have to do some incredible things to steal them and this is one of the highlights. Things went wary at th start of the robbery but everything ends happily as the heroes and heroine fly off to France.

"Itchy Fingers" is a production that can easily compete with any of the Hui comedies in terms of quality though the Ng-Chiao team is not as established as the three Hui brothers. Hopefully, there will be another teamwork for "Fingers Number Two." —*Mel.*

Norma Rae
(COLOR)

Martin Ritt, aided by top performance by Sally Field, creates a superb look at American life.

Hollywood, Feb. 16.

Twentieth-Century-Fox release of a Martin Ritt/Rose and Asseyev production. Produced by Tamara Asseyev, Alex Rose. Directed by Martin Ritt. Features entire cast. Screenplay, Irving Ravetch, Harriet Frank Jr.; camera (Deluxe Color), John A. Alonzo; production design, Walter Scott Herndon; music, David Shire; editor, Sidney Levin; art direction, Tracy Bousman; set decoration, Gregory Garrison; sound, Bruce Bisenz; assistant director, James Nicholson. Reviewed at 20th Century-Fox Studio Theatre, Feb. 16, (MPAA Rating: PG). Running time: **113 MINS.**

Norma Rae . . . . Sally Field
Sonny . . . . Beau Bridges
Reuben . . . . Ron Leibman
Vernon . . . . Pat Hingle
Leona . . . . Barbara Baxley
Bonnie Mae . . . . Gail Strickland
Wayne Billings . . . . Morgan Paull

"Norma Rae" is a superb film. Paced by Sally Field's best performance to date in a rapidly accelerating career, and under Martin Ritt's firm but sensitive direction, the 20th Century-Fox release is that rare entity, an intelligent film with heart. With union organizing as its theme, "Norma Rae" may be a hard sell at first, but it's doubtful audiences will resist its warmth and appeal.

Films about unions haven't always fared well at the boxoffice, but that didn't deter Ritt and screenwriters. Harriet Frank Jr. and Irving Ravetch from updating the traditional management-labor struggles to a sharp contemporary setting. Now the battle is being waged in Southern textile mills, where the din of the machinery is virtually unbearable, and workers either go deaf or suffer the consumptive effects of "brown lung" disease.

Ron Leibman arrives on the scene as a New York-based labor organizer, who picks Field as his most likely convert. She's divorced, mother of two children (one of them illegitimate), and deeply dissatisfied with her life without knowing quite why, although her mindless job at the local mill provides her with specific gripes.

This unlikely pairing of Jewish radicalism and Southern miasma is the core of "Norma Rae," and is made real and touching by the individual performances of Leibman and Field. Their relationship is platonic, but only on the surface. Underneath is a smoldering mass of emotions, which Field manages to communicate with the sensitivity and grace that only great actresses possess.

It is to Ravetch and Frank's credit that "Norma Rae" is con-

cerned with more than just a subdued love story. The thrust of the film, and one that can't be ignored by Fox in their selling of the pic, is the union, and the struggle (never a pleasant one) to unify workers around a common goal.

"Norma Rae" also fleshes out its characters to an unusual depth. Field's parents, as portrayed by Pat Hingle (in one of his best performances in a long career) and Barbara Baxley, are more than cardboard cutouts, as is Field's g.f., Gail Strickland, whose stolid presence is unobtrusively effective.

The only problem comes in the Beau Bridges, character who marries Field about one-third of the way into the pic. While Bridges does his best to round him out, the husband is too gracious and understanding to be anything but a foil for Leibman's boisterous aggressiveness. It's one of the few flaws in the script, although not disastrous.

By surrounding himself with what amounts to a stock creative company (Frank and Ravetch, cinematographer John A. Alonzo, designer Walter Scott Herndon and editor Sidney Levin have all worked together many times before), Ritt has mounted a smooth and cohesive cinematic vision. The pacing, at 113 minutes, is fresh and never laggard, and "Norma Rae" virtually hums right along.

Ritt's greatest triumph, however, is with his performers. Fields now ranks among the finest contemporary actresses, and Leibman is finally given the opportunity to open up his range on the screen. His is a major talent, and Leibman provides the counterpoint required by Field's tour-de-force job in the title role.

All tech credits are accomplished, right down to the small details. Special mention should go to David Shire's music, in particular Jennifer Warner's vocal work over opening and closing credits. —*Poll.*

Messidor
(FRENCH-SWISS-COLOR)

Paris, Feb. 16.

A Gaumont release of a Citel Film-SSR Geneva-Action Films-Gaumont co-production. Written and directed by Alain Tanner. Stars Clementine Amouroux, Catherine Retore. Camera (Eastmancolor), Renato Berta; music, Arie Dzierlatka; editing, Brigitte Sousselier; sound, Pierre Gamet; production manager, Bernard Lorain. Reviewed at Salles Ponthieu, Paris; Feb. 14, '79. Running time: **120 MINS.**
Jeanne . . . . Clementine Amouroux
Marie . . . . Catherine Retore

After a two-year hiatus from commercial filmmaking, Alain Tanner returns with "Messidor." His previous film, "Jonah Who Will Be 25 in the Year 2000," disconcerted some admirers who thought it a step in the wrong direction. This

film should dissipate anxieties — it is a remarkable and harrowing filmic scanning of Tanner's own heart of darkness, Switzerland.

With lucid objectivity and insight Tanner presents the frightening and, at times, strangely exhilirating disintegration of two ordinary girls at odds with themselves and a prosperous but vacuously nondescript society. "Messidor" is the name given to the harvest period in the old French Revolutionary calendar; at one point the student lies to a policeman that she and her friend are the "Messidor sisters." They are, in effect, the children of prosperity, but the joke is to take on cruelly ironic significance.

Tanner shot the film with no fixed script, all the more reason to admire its fluid but unlinear progressions, its inexorable feeling of deepening anxiety. The film runs two hours and it would be hard to find a single scene that could be excised, as oblique as it might seem to the film's concerns. Few directors are as good as Tanner at creating such loose-limbed but sinewy textures.

Every scene is marked by Tanner's tact and intelligence. Incidents like a rape attempt are rightly horrible and devoid of the voyeurism that seems to titillate too many male directors. And canny good judgment dictates how far to take a scene in which the girls give expression to sudden homosexual impulses. In all of this Tanner's camera manner is limpid and his editing spare and unemphatic. He is finely served by Renato Berta's photography and Arie Dzierlatka's musical score.

The girls are played with unerring truth by Clementine Amouroux and Catherine Retore, both making their film debut. They are as much responsible for the film's impact as Tanner's technical expertise. —*Len.*

The Passage
(BRITISH-COLOR)

Nazis pursue international cast through Pyrenees. Rough going all the way.

United Artists release of a Hemdale and United Artists Theatre Circuit Inc. presentation of The General Film Co. Ltd. production. Stars Anthony Quinn, James Mason, Malcolm McDowell. Produced by John Quested in association with Maurice Binder and Lester Goldsmith. Directed by J. Lee Thompson. Screenplay, Bruce Nicolaysen, based on his book "Perilous Passage;" camera (color), Mike Reed; score, Michael J. Lewis; sound, Norman Bolland; editor, Alan Strachan; exec producers, John Daly and Derek Dawson; associate producer, Geoffrey Helman. Reviewed at United Artists screening room, N.Y., Feb. 26, '79. (MPAA Rating: R.) Running Time: **99 MINS.**
The Basque . . . . Anthony Quinn
Professor Bergson . . . . James Mason
Von Berkow . . . . Malcolm McDowell

Ariel Bergson . . . . Patricia Neal
Leah Bergson . . . . Kay Lenz
Head Gypsy . . . . Christopher Lee
Renoudot . . . . Michael Lonsdale
Perea . . . . Marcel Bozzuffi
Paul Bergson . . . . Paul Clemens
Madame . . . . Rose Alba
Lt. Reincke . . . . Neville Jason
Son of the Gypsy . . . . Robert Rhys
German Soldier . . . . James Broadbent
French Guide . . . . Peter Arne
German Major . . . . Frederick Jaeger
1st German Sentry . . . . Terence York
2nd German Sentry . . . Terence Maidment

With this J. Lee Thompson clunker, the international production community has once again mined World War II for those demented Nazis, valiant resistance fighters and other stalwarts who lend themselves to myriad program actioners peppered with international casts. All this may sell in Uruguay, but "The Passage" may have trouble rousing even middling b.o. domestically.

This one has Anthony Quinn doing another of his salt-of-the-earth peasant turns leading an American scientist (James Mason), his wife (Patricia Neal), and children (Paul Clemens and Kay Lenz) through the Pyrenees Mountains from occupied France to Spain and freedom.

Why Mason is so valuable and why he's in flight from the Nazis isn't explained very clearly (we're not even told his specialty) but no matter. Bruce Nicolaysen's script (based on his own novel, "Perilous Passage") doesn't linger on such niceties but rather sets up the stereotypes and proceeds with the chase and the shooting.

In what appears to be a nod to Nazi-camp, Visconti · style ("The Damned"), Malcolm McDowell turns up as a milk-drinking SS captain who is, in no particular order, amenable to gourmet cooking, wears a swastika on his jock strap and has inventive methods of dispatching Gypsies. Perhaps because Thompson and the script leave little choice, McDowell hams it up providing the picture's few intended laughs.

Quinn as a Basque shepherd is reduced to a series of solemn, meaningful stares broken by sentence fragments in fractured English. This pic is an all-English effort, sparing audiences all those tedious German accents affected by American and British actors. Small favor.

This is Neal's first pic in some years, and she's suitably self-serving as the wife whose ill-health prevents her passage through the mountains. The character kills herself off early in the pic, but it's not clear just how. One morning she turns up frozen on a wintry slope.

Mason is thoroughly wasted as the scientist, a role that calls for brief, statesmanlike observations about killing and war.

Lenz is perhaps best in an awkward scene in which she's raped by McDowell while pretending to be a member of a Gypsy camp. The scene of sexual violation accounts for the pic's R grading, and very nearly throws "The Passage" completely off-balance with its gratuitous realism.

Marcel Bozzuffi ("The French Connection") and Michael Lonsdale ("The Day of the Jackal") augment the international flavor of this outing in one-dimensional parts as selfless resistance fighters. Lonsdale's finest moment comes when that sadistic SS officer removes his finger tips in the cause of haut cuisine.

Technical credits are all just fine. Mike Reed's photography provides a slick, travelog look at the Pyrenees, where the pic was lensed, and Norman Bolland's sound delivers each cliche with resounding fidelity. Director Thompson stage manages the action with efficiency but displays his lack of invention with this material by relying far too heavily on Michael Lewis' loud and intrusive score. —Sege.

Szpital Przemienienia
(Hospital of the Transfiguration)
(POLISH-COLOR)

Warsaw, Jan. 10.
A Film Polski Production, Warsaw; world rights, Film Polski, Warsaw. Feature entire cast. Directed by Edward Zebrowski. Screenplay, Zebrowski, Michal Komar; camera (color), Witold Sobocinski. Reviewed at Film Polski Screening Room, Warsaw, Jan. 9, '79. Running time: **90 MINS.**

Cast: Gustav Holoubek, Zbigniew Zapasiewicz.

One of the most interesting prods of the new season, Edward Zebrowski's "Hospital of the Transfiguration" introduces a directorial talent (born 1935) who has always been in the background for some reason or other since his impressive "Deliverance" (1972), also set in a hospital.

Remarkable in "Deliverance" and "Hospital of Transfiguration" is the use of the hospital as a spiritual metaphor — these are pix dealing with the inner person, the question of identity, psychological problems, and the soul. Death, too, plays an important role in what takes place. All of which makes Zebrowski a helmer to watch as a complement to such strong Polish directors as Krzysztof Zanussi and Antoni Krauze.

"Hospital of Transfiguration" is set in 1943 at a mental asylum in the country. But this is an unusual hospital, for not only are several patients incurable schizophrenic and paranoid cases (so it seems), but also the staff is a bit buggy and a writer has voluntarily entered the clinic because he is "peculiar" and a drug addict. Obviously, these character portraits are meant to be a cross-section of Polish life and the cultural, educated class during and before the war.

Then the German Gestapo arrives to charge the pic with a harsh reality. The Commandant asks for the list of patients, sorts out the "Aryan" doctors from the others on a return trip, and herds everyone into trucks for evacuation to the extermination camps. The pic's key figure, a young doctor who views everything at the hospital with a critical eye, momentarily escapes by covering himself, and one of the patients he looks after, under a pile of laundry in the basement and then disappearing into the woods — just as Nazi soldiers appear.

This is a well acted and directed pic, with top thesps Gustav Holoubek and Zbigniew Zapasiewicz turning in plus performances as the writer and one of the doctors, both playing mental cases. Lensing is also top grade. Pic's only drawback is that the allegorical dimension can be sorted out after the first couple reels, and the final pick-up by the Gestapo is predictable. Such "parables" were made before in Poland: this one says nothing new. —Holl.

Coco La Fleur, Candidat
(Coco-the-Flower, Candidate)
(FRENCH-COLOR)

Paris, Feb. 14.
A Rush Production release of a Rush Production-Claude Guedj production. Produced by Claude Guedj. Written and directed by Christian Lara. Features entire cast. Camera (Panavision-Eastmancolor), Jean-Claude Couty music, (written and performed by) Experience 7; editor, Gerard Kikoine; sound, Jack Jullian; art director, Traute Sigel. Reviewed at Studio La Boetie, Paris, Feb. 12, '79. Running time: **85 MINS.**
Coco la Fleur . . . . Robert Liensol
Marie Ange . . . . Jennifer
Gaston Monbin . . . . Greg Germain
Embuscade . . . . Guy Pierre Mineur
Denis Pauvert . . . . Felix Marten
Delbois . . . . Jean-Jacques Moreau
Manel . . . . Lucrece Saintol
Ti-Dolphe . . . . Lucien Gerville-Reache

More and more French films continue to illuminate the tragic situation of Third World peoples, particularly of the African immigrant on French soil. Now West Indian-born writer-director Christian Lara proposes a widening of focus in this evocation of the social and economic realities of his native Guadeloupe.

Lara traces the stirrings of consciousness in the person of Coco-La-Fleur, a simple (but not simple-minded) islander whose mother works for the well-to-do, Europeanized Monbin family.

The younger Monbin brother returns home to the island after making a name for himself in Paris — now he seeks a major political post on his home soil. His French advisers suggest the setting up of a dummy third candidate to draw votes away from the opposition. Coco, popular with the poor community through his raconteur talents, is chosen and tutored for the role. But Coco learns only too well as he is unwittingly pushed into an awareness of the unidyllic realities he has always taken for granted. Coco wins the first ballot, as foreseen, but then refuses to bow out in favor of Monbin. In desperation a French advisor engineers his assassination.

Lara skimps Coco's development and leaves too much to take for granted. Lara catches the little climaxes along the road to the great awareness, but omits the intervening distances.

Lara has cast an excellent West Indian stage actor named Robert Liensol. Though there are no nooks and crannies to explore, Liensol fills his personage with luminous generosity of spirit and intimations of unmined resources. Thus Coco's death produces a sense of loss, but not of tragedy because he never becomes aware that his actions risk a mortal penalty.

Lara's direction is sometimes hesitant and the camerawork and editing reflect this slackness. He best asserts himself in the casual documenting of island manners and mores and idiosyncratic local types, like Ambush, the unvocal "cowboy" who hails a bus by drawing his pistols on it. Lara elicits quiet and sincere performances from the rest of his cast.

The film, a great success in the West Indies, may have difficulty making a bid for attention elsewhere. Lara needs bolder dramatic contours in his scripts and firmer technical control. —Len.

Trampa
(Swap)
(BULGARIAN-COLOR)

Sofia, Jan. 17.
A Bulgarofilm Production, Sofia; world rights, Bulgarofilm, Sofia. Features entire cast. Directed by Georgi Dyulgerov. Screenplay, Vladimir Ganev, Dyulgerov, based on Ivailo Petrov's story "Three Meetings"; camera (color), Radoslav Spassov. Only credits available. Reviewed at Bulgarofilm Screening Room, Sofia, Jan. 16, '79. Running time: **100 MINS.**

Cast: Iliya Dobrev (Dobrin Iliev), Margarita Pehlivanova (Nassya), Maria Karel (Madarliyeska), Jeanna Marcheva (Katya), Vulcho Kamarashev (Old Stamen), Tanya Shahova (Maya), Petya Doubarova (Petya).

Georgi Dyulgerov's "Swap" deserves to be seen in relation to his former prizewinning pic, "Advantage" (1978) (Best Director Prize at the 1978 Berlin Film Festival): both deal with the troublesome 1950s when the Stalinist Personality Cult prevailed in the Socialist countries in every phase of life and culture. Dyulgerov has handled the theme in his own country, a factor that has placed Bulgarian cinema in the forefront of international festivals for the simple reason that his "Advantage" appeared on the scene before Wajda's "Man of Marble," Kovacs' "Stud Farm" (Berlin entry this year), and Tarkovsky's "The Mirror."

"Swap" is there for further study by historians and film buffs. It's not as strong as "Advantage," but more is said indirectly and openly about the troublesome past than before — and thus still deserves a fest bow somewhere on the summer circuit to open the way for discussion on theme.

"Swap" refers to the trading of morals — the Bulgarian word, "Trampa," is a Turkish word of Italian origin, meaning of course a simple trade like kids do on street corners. In this case, a Sofia radio correspondent during the present looks back on his role as a budding journalist in the 1950s as farms in Bulgaria were being collectivized.

Upon returning to his village as a jury member on a amateur art-and-poetry contest in a high school, he meets a girl who reminds him of a relationship he had with a girl he loved and lost in this same place two decades before — in fact, this young girl is the daughter of woman he loved and could very well (if circumstances then had been different) be his own daughter.

What happened in the past was a "swap" of a true love for a brief fling with another woman. The same "trade" has also taken place in the present: the young student has also swapped her bumbling writing with the poetic verses of a talented girlfriend in order to impress the visiting journalist.

This double-swap triggers flashbacks to the 1950s, which then makes the pic very interesting as well as complicated in its dramatic structure. There were excerpts from old Socialist Realist films praising the heroics of the shock-worker and the labors of the collective-farm leaders, paired with the pain in reviewing (through flashbacks) some of the tragic moments in this particular village. Scenes of heated meetings and discussions, as well as personal inner anguished by the principle protagonist, make this pic well worth seeing for the wealth of information and impressions it leaves.

Thesps — particularly Iliya Dobrev (a Sofia legit actor) and the two women in his life: Jeanna Marcheva as Katya of the 1950s, and Tanya Shahova as Maya of the present — are big pluses, and it's a pity they didn't have more room to fatten out their roles. Lensing by Radoslav Spassov is again up to international standards. The weakness of "Swap" is that the helmer himself has traded too much dialog for visual effects. —Holl.

Stopar
(The Hitchhiker)
(CZECHOSLOVAK-COLOR)

Prague, Jan. 13.

A Czechoslovak Film Production, Gottwaldov Film Studio; world rights, Czechoslovak Film-Export, Prague. Features entire cast. Written and directed by Petr Tucek. Camera (color), Jiri Kolin; music, Ferdinand Havlik. Reviewed at Czechoslovak Film-Export Screening Room, Prague, Jan. 12, '79. Running time: 90 MINS.
Cast: Josef Vinklar (Jiri Duek), Ivanka Devata (Jaruska), Julie Juristava (Marta), Oldrich Navratil (Fanda).

"The Hitchhiker" is one of the first features to emerge from the Gottwaldov Film Studio, now third in Czech importance after Barrandov in Prague and Koliba in Bratislava. Helmer Petr Tucek has made a light, engaging comedy, a sure hit for the home aud and possibly also abroad at Czechoslovak Film Weeks and some fests.

It's one of those neat four cornered husband-wife-mistress-boyfriend tales with sitcom gags to pull it through to the end. The two-timing hero runs a fashions section at the Brno Trade Fair with an assortment of dress models under his wing, one of whom is his girl on the side. After a particularly trying day at the Fair — at which his mistress takes a shine to a visiting Italian salesman — the two are off to a country villa, picking up a male hitchhiker along the way.

He's a mechanic by profession and is soon needed to repair the car's engine after a breakdown upon reaching the villa. The wife and daughter, meanwhile, arrive on the scene unexpectedly — and the hitchhiker plays the role of the mistress's boyfriend to save the day for the husband. Boy and girl like each other in the end — but the mannekin still has her career on her mind when she returns to Brno and her other admirer. —Holl.

Neskolko Interwju Po Litschnym Woprosam
(Some Interviews on Personal Questions)
(SOVIET-COLOR)

Moscow, Jan. 6.

A Grusiafilm Studios Production, Tbilisi (Georgia); world rights, Goskino, Moscow. Features Sofiko Chiaureli. Directed by Lana Gogoberidze. Only credits available. Reviewed at Goskino Screening Room, Moscow, Jan. 5, '79. Running time: 90 MINS.

Lana Gogoberidze, the leading femme helmer in the Soviet Republic of Georgia, attracted attention in 1965 with "I See the Sun," and won an avid following with the more recent "When the Almond Trees Were in Bloom" (1972) and "Tumult" (1977), the latter a genuine, homemade musical comedy, Georgian-style. The star of "Tumult" was thesp Sofiko Chiaureli and she's teamed with Gogoberidze again in "Some Interviews on Personal Questions."

"Interviews" was clearly shot in the current femme-pic vein of sympathy for the career-minded housewife and shame on the unfaithful husband who simply wants his wife to stay at home where she belongs.

Pic focuses on the travails of a newspaper interviewer, who follows up on inquiries sent in by readers together with a photog. At home she has the teenage kids and a husband and an aged mother to look after on the side, all of which adds to further complications when the man of the house (unfaithful with a younger woman) forces her to decide between the house and the career. She chooses the career and thus finds herself the center of her own "enquiry" — a discarded lady, with the friendly, adoring photog on her neck.

Interviews, however, make for strong social comment. —Holl.

Was Oshidajet Grashdanka Nikanorova
(Comrade Nikanorova Awaits You)
(SOVIET-COLOR)

Moscow, Jan. 7.

A Mosfilm Production, Moscow; world rights, Goskino, Moscow. Features Natalya Gundareva. Directed by Leonid Marjagin. Only credits available. Reviewed at Goskino Screening Room, Moscow, Jan. 6, '79. Running time: 90 MINS.

A warm comedy about a chubby, temperamental woman who always picks the wrong man to run off with from the village he doesn't particularly find satisfying — each time the rendezvous at the railroad station (thus the title: a loud-speaker announcement) turns out to be a bitter personal disappointment.

"Comrade Nikanorova Awaits You" opens with the leading lady left holding her travelling bag at the station, after which she must return home embarrassing to the cutting remarks of her neighbors at the collective farm where she has been living and working for much too long. Only this time her abandoned cottage has been rented to a veterinarian, a lonesome chap with a similar fate hanging over his shoulder. She collects her recently dispensed belongings from irate neighbors (only one friend sticks to her side), and sets about evicting the male interloper from her quarters.

But it turns out the two must live in the same house until other housing can be found for the veterinarian — and on top of that he has invited a friend to come and stay for a short weekend visit.

Of course, the friends throws a pass at the heroine, who falls again for the same line of promises as before. This time, however, the friendly vet intervenes after the letdown, admits in so many stumbling phrases to be in love, and then goes freely on his way to leave her in peace. She discovers suddenly her own heart and chases after him — frantically trying to reach him over the station's loud-speaker before the train pulls out.

Helmer Leonid Marjagin has a light hand for comedy. Nataly Gundareva is at her best in portraying a typical maid at a crossroads.
—Holl.

Pyat' Vecherov
(Five Evenings)
(SOVIET-B&W/COLOR)

Moscow, Jan. 7.

A Mosfilm Production, Moscow; world rights, Goskino, Moscow. Directed by Nikita Mikhalkov. Screenplay based on play of same name by Alexander Volodin (pseudonym for Alexander Lifshitz). Only credits available. Reviewed at Goskino Screening Room, Moscow, Jan. 6, '79. Running time: 100 MINS.

Nikita Mikhalkov, the younger brother of Andrei Mikhalkov-Konchalovski and a well known thesp as well as helmer, rose to prominence quickly with "Slave of Love" (1976) and "Unfinished Piece for a Player Piano" (1977) — the former getting legs for a run in Yank art houses recently, and the latter bowing at the Cannes Film Festival a couple seasons ago to good press. Now he's back for the third year in a row with "Five Evenings," his most demanding pic to date for a critic and quite possibly one of the important Soviet pix of the present season.

"Five Evenings" is based on the play with the same title by Alexander Volodin, the pseudonym for Alexander Moiseivich Lifshitz (born 1919). Volodin began writing in the postwar years and caused a stir with his first play, "The Factory Girl" (1957), which divided the critics and public in a pro-and-contra dispute. Then came the equally important "Five Evenings" (1959), which preemed at Tovstonogov's Leningrad theatre, followed by "On a Visit and at Home" (1960), "My Big Sister" (1961), and "The Appointment" (1963), a tragicomedy. In each of these plays he showed a remarkable talent for describing the ethical and moral problems of the everyday, as well as presenting characters with psychological depth while criticizing the behavior of the petit bourgeois class.

"Five Evenings," like many pix based on plays, is drowned in lengthy conversation and relies heavily on the tour de force of the thesps to get its message across. A middle-aged man with a hat arrives in the big city (Moscow or Leningrad), meets four or five individuals in a large apartment, who talks endlessly, and causes a scene in a railroad-station restaurant upon departing. Credits are tops.
— *Holl.*

Soldiers Never Cry
(ROMANIAN-COLOR)

Bucharest, Jan. 14.

A Romaniafilm Production, Film Group One, Bucharest; world rights, Romaniafilm, Bucharest. Directed by Dinu Cocea. Features entire cast. Screenplay, Mihai Opris, Vasile Chirita; camera (color), Marian Stanciu; sets, Mara Cuculas; music, Stefan Zorzor; editing, Magda Ghise Ghincioiu. Reviewed at Romaniafilm Screening Room, Bucharest, Jan. 13, '79. Running time: **108 MINS.**

An epic production with a cast of hundreds and an enormous outlay of war machinery, Dinu Cocea's "Soldiers Never Cry" tells the story of the first woman-officer in the front lines of the First World War. This modern Joan of Arc (known as the "heroine from the Jiu") started as a nurse on the front in the autumn of 1916, as fighting was hot and heavy between Romanian troops and the German and Austrian-Hungarian forces. She eventually is driven to taking up arms herself out of national ferver, wins honors for her bravery (she's once severely wounded), and eventually dies on a charge against the enemy lines.

Script is quite heavy, but lensing and action scenes are worth a look-see. —*Holl.*

Toplo
(Warmth)
(BULGARIAN-COLOR)

Sofia, Jan. 17.

A Bulgarofilm Production, Sofia; world rights, Bulgarofilm, Sofia. Features entire cast. Directed by Vladimir Yanchev. Only credits available. Reviewed at Bulgarofilm Screening Room, Sofia, Jan. 16, '79. Running time: **90 MINS.**

Cast: Grigor Vachkov, Stefan Danailov, Todor Kolev.

Vladimir Yanchev's "Warmth" aims to be nothing more than a light comedy on middle-class manners, the type of pic that is appearing in greater numbers these days in Socialist countries. It's about a large apartment building that may have to wait many months and possibly years before central heating is installed in the building — due to city planning at the moment.

The apartment dwellers — a cross-section of Sofia's (or another large city's) population — decide on their own to hire a private heating-installation concern to do the job for them. These workers are, however, bandits with a left hand for any kind of household chores. They take the money, bore several holes in the walls of the building, then scram with the dough. But they get caught in the end, and then the apartment owners decide to hire them out of prison to finish the job they started.

Plenty of gangs are built around the various silly personalities in the apartment house — a Customs Officer with whisky and such stashed in the basement, a sex-bomb, a bookworm academic type, a journalist, an irate pensioner, a student, and so forth. The main fun, however, is wondering in which room the blundering trio are going to crash into next. —*Holl.*

At Ziji Duchove!
(Long Live Ghosts!)
(CZECHOSLOVAK-COLOR)

Prague, Feb. 13.

A Czechoslovak Film Production, Studio Barrandov, Prague; world rights, Czechoslovak Film-Export, Prague. Features entire cast. Directed by Oldrich Lipsky. Screenplay, Zdenek Sverak, from a story by Jiri Melisek; camera (color), Jan Nemecek; music, Jaroslav Uhlir; sets, Vladimir Labsky. Reviewed at Czechoslovak Film-Export Screening Room, Prague, Feb. 12, '79. Running time: **92 MINS.**

Cast: Jiri Sovak (the knight Brtnik), Dana Vavarova (Leonine), Jiri Prochazka (Jeannot), David Vlcek (Adamek), Tomas Holly (Vendelin), Igor Broz, Petr Stary, Igor Nachtigal Vladimir Brodsky (director Vavra), Lubomir Lipsky (Jouza).

"Long Live Ghosts!" is a children's pic made by the prolific Oldrich Lipsky, who scored a hit last season with his detective-pic parody, "Adele Hasn't Had Her Supper Yet" — or, as it's sometimes known, "Nick Carter in Prague." As usual, "Ghosts" is full of the Lipsky line of visual gags, enough to please an older aud as well as the kids.

A twists on the "Canterfield Ghost" pic of yore (with Charles Laughton as the ghost afraid of his own shadow), the Lipsky version has a bunch of boys exploring a ruins of a "haunted castle" at night, where of course an old Prague knight pays his respects to frighten the daylights out of the intruders. Later, however, the boys rescue the bumbling knight from a trap he set for other trespassers, and they all become friends in a common fight again local authorities who want to use the castle ruins for the growing of mushrooms. In the end, the knight even enlists the help of friendly elves from the forest to put

things right and add a bit more flavor to the tale.

There's also the medieval knight's 11-year-old daughter, another ghost, who is rescued by an adoring youth to enter the world of humans. Cheery stuff. — *Holl.*

Before Silence Came
(ROMANIAN-COLOR)

Bucharest, Jan. 14.

A Romaniafilm Production, Film Group One, Bucharest; world rights, Romaniafilm, Bucharest. Features entire cast. Written and directed by Aleka Visarion, based on Ion Luca Caragiale's short story, "In Time of War"; camera (color), Nicu Stan; sets, Vittorio Holtier, Sava Cuzmin; editing, Maria Neagu. Reviewed at Romaniafilm Screening Room, Bucharest, Jan. 13, '79. Running time: **103 MINS.**

Cast: Liviu Ronovea, Valeria Seciu, Ion Caramitru, Mircea Diaconu, Florin Zamfirescu, Gilda Marinescu, Vasile Muresan, Nicolas Praida, Cornel Dumitras, Elisabeta Jar-Rozovea, Constantin Petrican, Adriana Trandafir.

Aleka Visarion's "Before Silence Came" scores as one of the most important Romanian pix of the season on the reputation of the literary source alone: Ion Luca Caragiale (1852-1912) is recognized today as the father of Romanian literature and drama, upon whose short story, "In Time of War," the film is based.

Caragiale himself came from a poverty-striken background, and he never achieved success until he was in his thirties — about the time he wrote this tale of two brothers and one woman they both loved set during the 1877 War of Independence, as the yoke of Turkish rule was thrown off for good but the peasants were still suppressed under the yoke of rich landowners. Helmer Visarion tries to present a panorama of historical impulses coursing through levels of society at that time — to a great extent he succeeds.

On the social level this is a portrait of the rich and poor classes, about people with too much to eat and those with nothing at all. The narrative thread focuses on an innkeeper, who thinks mostly of his possessions — among which is his wife, who has an affair on the side with his more handsome brother, a kind of Robin Hood in Orthodox priest clothing who also goes to war to fight for his country. The innkeeper is tortured by fears and in the end causes his wife's death as he goes slowly mad. Lensing a plus.
—*Holl.*

Nechci Nic Slyset
(Leave Me Alone)
(CZECHOSLOVAK-COLOR)

Prague, Jan. 13.

A Czechoslovak Film Production, Studio Barrandov, Prague; world rights, Czechoslovak Film-Export, Prague. Features entire cast. Written and directed by Ota Koval.

Only credits available. Reviewed at Czechoslovak Film-Export Screening Room, Prague, Jan. 12, '79. Running time: **90 MINS.**

Cast: Vladimir Brodsky, Jana Brejchova.

A children's pic on the serious side, Ota Koval's "Leave Me Alone" follows in the same vein as his previous "Jakob" in treating the trials of a boy doesn't fit in anywhere. In "Jakob" the story was about a young boy in an institution for children, whose father spent some time in prison and mother was absent as well. This time it's about a boy who loses both parents in an automobile accident and thereafter refuses to speak to anyone.

"Leave Me Alone" recaps the boy's happiness before the accident by showing the family's relationship on the day it happened. Now the lad is given over to a child psychologist, a motherly type who hopes the ice will be broken by sharing a room with her slightly older son. It happens too that a traveling children's theatre troupe happens on the scene, which of course hints what the end will be — as the troupe leaves and a balloon attached to the caravan rises in the air, the boy manages to speak again.

A bit sentimental, but an interesting tale for its child psychology dimensions. Also well acted with credits, save for script, a good cut above the average. —*Holl.*

Hungarian Fest

Magyar Rapszodia and Allegro Barbaro
(Hungarian Rhapsody and Allegro Barbaro)
(HUNGARIAN-COLOR)

Budapest, Feb. 27.

Hungarofilm release of Mafilm, Diolog Studio production. Features entire cast. Directed by Miklos Jancso. Screenplay, Jancso, Gyula Hernadi; camera (Eastmancolor), Janos Kende. Reviewed at Magyar Film Fest, Budapest, Feb. 12, '79. Running time, Magyar Rapszodia, **101 MINS.** Allegro Barbaro, **74 MINS.**, together **175 MINS.**

Istvan	Gyorgy Cserhalmi
Gabor	Lajos Balazsovits
Szeles	Gabor Koncz
Bankos	Bartalan Solti
Barsa	Joszef Madaras
Mari	Gyorgi Tarjan
Karoly	Istvan Bujtor

Miklos Jancso is one of the best-known Magyar filmmakers. His visionary, historical films have made impacts at many festivals and have gotten some commercial outlets abroad though the results have usually not been up to his critical acclaim. Now he has completed two parts of an ambitious trilogy delving into Hungarian history from the turn-of-the-century to the Second World War.

The two parts, which will compete at the coming Cannes Film Fest as one film, are here reviewed together. Jancso again uses a subjective technique to comment on events, time and the upheavals of the era. It is told through one man, actor Gyorgy Cserhalmi, son of a big landowner who is first a hotheaded feudal type who slowly is won over to the peasant cause and finally the anti-fascist movements as well as the leftists.

There is an interesting ambiguity for his change, due more to personal affiliations, one with a Communist girl, and the feel for a need for justice and against the unfounded powers of his class, than an actual political ideology. This aspect gets extraordinary treatment in the first section, "Hungarian Rhapsody."

It begins with much pomp as there are parades, dances and feasting to celebrate Cserhalmi and his brother's commissions in the army. The peasants join the dances, parades and excitement. Cserhalmi is an actor with extraordinary dynamism and personal attraction.

His father is busy running the stumping for an election to keep the landowning and rich interests in power to the detriment of exploited peasants. They are hosed down by some peasants and the haughty sons go to chastise the latter with gendarmes that leads to torture and the sons' killing the head of the peasant socialist group.

The protagonist is then off to World War I where he tries to put down a mutiny of soldiers by mass executions which are not followed out though many are killed. After the war he throws in his lot with those wiping out the remnants of the short-lived Communist Commune.

But he begins to see he is not one of them, is tortured by guilts, and turns away from his own brother and others. He finally fights it out with the peasant son of the man he killed and this saga ends on a note of uncertainty as he realizes the oppressiveness of his group and begins to revolt against it.

This part is rich in form, subjective scenes of Russian roulette games that symbolize the overwrought romanticism of a class beginning to lose ground. (With "Deer Hunter," this seems to be the year of Russian roulette).

There is a scene of his ordering a peasant from his land to shoot his own horse, one the man has brought up, when they are in the army together, that sums up the strange rites and rituals that bind these disparate men together. There is the death of his girl in the roulette game and her burial. The film may seem hermetic to some but is an unusually exciting visual testament to the class struggle which is not didactic but poetic and ritualized.

The second part, "Allegro Barbaro," has Cserhalmi home and slowly joining forces with the peasants, the people of the man he killed, and with whose son he had fought. He turns against his own brother and the politicos of the time and there are foreshadowings of his death when the country goes over to the Nazis in World War II.

There are unusual dances of revelry, nude women underlining the various phases of his break with his old life as a symbol of a new attitude in all things, men soaring on kites to create the vision of a new and more demanding life that will fight against oppression.

Some might find it overwrought but most should be taken by the inventiveness of this poetic paean to liberty and change. Janos Kende's lensing and extraordinary camera movements, that go from indoors, with a plane flashing by to revels or battles or discussions outside in one shot, are still assets to Jancso's unusual techniques that have as yet not fallen into mannerisms.

Specialized and festival outings loom for this film of symbols, ritual and poetic drive but more demanding audiences might be found with the right handling and placement. Ostensibly based on the life of a real man, Jancso has taken his usual liberties to give a bombbastic, subjective, balletic look at the changing times and people. —*Mosk.*

Angi Vera
(Vera's Training)
(HUNGARIAN-COLOR)

Budapest, Feb. 17.

Hungarofilm release of Mafilm Objectiv Studio production. Features entire cast. Written and directed by Pal Gabor from a book by Endre Veszi; camera (Eastmancolor), Lajos Koltai; music, Gyorgy Selmeczi. Reviewed at Magyar Film Fest, Budapest, Feb. 13, '79. Running time, 96 MINS.
Vera .... Veronika Papp
Anna .... Erszi Pasztor
Istvan .... Tamas Dunai
Maria .... Eva Szabo

A cool treatment of early Communist Party training of selected people to fit into various areas of the new socialist regime at its beginnings in 1948. It is mainly about an innocent 18-year-old girl and her corruption by the hardline, puritanical, Stalinist outlooks of the day.

Perhaps a bit more directorial punch might have made this film more unusual, but, as is, it is an engrossing look at this period though not too new on the Eastern European scene as far as castigating Stalinist excesses in thought and behavior are concerned.

The girl, played with intensity by Veronika Papp, attacks the rundown methods of a hospital she works at during a party meeting. She is singled out and sent off to a

party school. Here she gets tied up with a rather hardlining older woman who has her even turning in an old worker who has confided to them why he took part in a strike.

She is enamored of a married teacher and finally goes to his room for an idyllic love scene. But thinking her mentor has seen her, she renounces what she did in a self-confession scene before the school. It leads to his ousting and her graduating with honors and seemingly off to a life of Party power even if she has sacrificed a certain honesty and integrity she once had.

The good playing, the perceptive direction, despite its lack of more dramatic sweep, and its theme might well find this audiences in various climes. The still more earthy women in her life, who may later be toned down by the party or disowned by them, are not able to get the main character to adhere to her early forthrightness as the Party trappings lose the possibilities at the time for that coveted socialism with a more human face.

A film that may no longer be daring but still comments on a subject that is contemporary from the vantage point of the near past. Presumably things are better in Hungary now, and belonging to the Party is not as weighty for careers as it once was. —*Mosk.*

Buek
(Happy New Year)
(HUNGARIAN-COLOR)

Budapest, Feb. 17.

Hungarofilm release of Mafilm Objectiv Studio production. Features entire cast. Directed by Rezso Szoreny. Screenplay, Peter Modos, Szoreny; camera (Eastmancolor), Janos Zsombolyai. Reviewed at Magyar Film Fest, Budapest, Feb. 16, '79. Running time: 84 MINS.
Laci .... Istvan Bujtor
Kati .... Erika Bodnar
Gyula .... Andras Balint
Eva .... Cecilia Esztergalyos
Reka .... Judit Meszieri
Erszi .... Erika Horineczi

Three friends (two men and a woman), who have worked together in a chemistry lab are letting off steam after months of hard work. It is the day before New Year and then they go their ways to meet up later for a night on the town for the coming year. But it leads to a night that brings up some usually buried personal hurts, rancors and animosities among themselves despite their friendships.

They are joined by a pickup, one's wife and a couple of other women friends. In this slim envelope director Reszo Szoreny has created a sharply observed comedy that slowly builds to a denouement of a truth game that goes sour with too many gripes and insults let out of the bag.

One has a quick sex play with the wife of his friend and they find out a

new man has been appointed to head their section though he knows nothing about their work. One of them had even joined the Party recently but it did not help.

Film keeps up a lively pace and does not get solemn about the problems facing these people who may set things right when one finds a better rapport with his wife and the others accept some responsibility. It is light but has a right feel for its well limned characters and should enhance Magyar fest inroads plus displaying a director who can say things about life in Hungary today without rhetoric. — *Mosk.*

A Kedves Somszed
(The Nice Neighbor)
(HUNGARIAN-COLOR)

Budapest, Feb. 17.

Hungarofilm release of Mafilm Objectiv Studio production. Features entire cast. Directed by Zsolt Kezdi-Kovacs; screenplay, Geza Beremenyi, Kezdi-Kovacs; camera (Eastmancolor), Janos Zsombolyai. Reviewed at Magyar Film Fest, Budapest, Feb. 16, '79. Running time, 102 MINS.
Dibusz .... Laszlo Szabo
Okolicsni .... Lajos Szabo
Ide .... Margit Dayka
Hajdu .... Agi Margittay
Bea .... Gyongi Vigh
Teacher .... Bertanal Solti
Erszi .... Agi Kakasi

Housing shortages are endemic in Eastern European countries but not limited to them. Film uses an old house ready for demolition as a crucible to show ordinary, mainly harried people trying to find better shelter. Into this comes a shrewd operator who plays the nice guy trying to help his neighbors but is really out for himself.

Laszlo Szabo, an actor-director who has lived in Paris, returns for the part of the wheeler-dealer and gives this fairly contrived film a deeper insight as he manages to be apathetic but yet likable as he fights to enlarge a one-room, no-bath cubby hole he lives in so he can have a bigger new apartment when the house is torn down and the tenants are allotted commensurate space in new houses.

He teams with a man who has a large family in one room after a hassle when he tries to keep the former from breaking into the room of an old woman who had just died. He tries to woo a spinster who lives with another woman, and they may be lesbos, to marry her for joining his room and hers. It does not work.

He makes it with the wife of another man who joins up with him and then a paranoid girl whose room he gets to extend his own plus that of the two women who leave theirs. He also attempts to get an old professor, who has young boys visiting him, to share and creates a sort of family feeling in the house.

But when they have to leave they are scattered around town and only one old woman refuses to leave. She had been there when it was a famous bordello. Director Zsolt Kedzi Kovacs keeps this from slipping into sentimentality and creates a shrewd human comedy that might find attention in other climes besides the inevitable archive, fest and film week usage it will be getting. —*Mosk.*

Gsaladi Tuzfezek
(Family Nest)
(HUNGARIAN-B&W)

———

Budapest, Feb. 18.

Hungarofilm release of Bela Balasz Studio production. Features entire cast. Written and directed by Bela Tarr. Camera, Ferenc Pap, Barna Mihok; music, Janos Brody. Reviewed at Magyar Film Fest, Budapest Feb. 17, '79. Running time, 115 MINS.

Iren .... L. Horvath
Laci .... Laszlo Horvath
Father .... Gabor Kun
Mother .... G. Kun
Gabi .... Gabor Kun
Friend .... Iren Racz

———

A fictionalized cinema verite type of film. The main subject is the effects of overcrowding in a one room apartment containing a family of four and a son's wife and child. A real family in this situation has reportedly been used but the conflicts fictionalized.

It leads to some arresting scenes that amply reveal character, outlooks and the frictions that amplify their problems of living together. The husband-son comes back from military service and is chastised by the father. If he had re-enlisted it might have given them a better chance for a larger apartment.

The wife has a fight for bringing home a friend. The proximity breeds contempt at times and a sort of moral laxity exemplified by the returned soldier and a friend forcing themselves on the wife's friend when they walk her home.

Another fight has the father telling his son his wife had been out with men. She is also trying to get an apartment but is too far down the list. She finally, leaves with her daughter when the father will not give her money to bribe the housing official.

It ends with the soldier saying he might have been wrong to side with the father and an apartment would solve everything reiterated by the wife now squatting precariously in an abandoned house.

Pic does have some arresting human scenes, ably limned by these non-pros. But it degenerates into talk, uneven progression and finally repetition and too much lingering on scenes that have already made their points. It is thus for ethnic fests, archives and school and specialized use primarily.

It also underlines the treatment of workers and others in Magyar films not to forget the unselfconscious use of nudity and love scenes, rarely exploited but justified, cropping up in many local pix of late. —*Mosk.*

A Kis Valentino
(The Little Valentino)
(HUNGARIAN-B&W)

———

Budapest, Feb. 16.

Hungarofilm release of Mafilm Hunnia Studios production. Features entire cast. Written and directed by Andras Jeles. Camera (black and white), Sandor Kardos; music of Schubert arranged by M. Miklos. Reviewed at Magyar Film Fest, Budapest, Feb. 15, '79. Running time, 92 MINS.

Laszlo .... Janos Opoczki
Amal .... Mrs. Sekacs
Iren .... Mrs. Levai
Jozsi .... Istvan Ivanyi
Taxi Driver .... Jozsef Farkas

———

A tale of an aimless day in the life of a young man who has gotten a sum of money and is just drifting rather than going off to work. At first full of sharp observation, film finally drifts into aimlessness, perhaps mirroring the boy's outlook but not adding any punch, cohesion or true insight into this odyssey.

He floats about in a cab, flirts, goes home to a hysterial grandmother or aunt and is then off again to eat at a fancy restaurant and finally pay a girl for himself and a friend. The title of "The Little Valentino" may be ironic, and, finally, he is seen losing money betting on a pinball machine.

New director Andras Lanyi needs more coherent scripting before he can emerge a possible talent worth watching. He does have a way with actors and getting insights into a young man's outlooks in some of the scenes though there is propensity to indulge the character and finally turn the film into a rather turgid affair rather than probing the personal and social aspects of his milieu and life. —*Mosk.*

A Trombitas
(The Trumpeter)
(HUNGARIAN-COLOR)

———

Budapest, Feb. 15.

Hungarofilm release of Mafilm Objectiv Studio, Hunnia Studio, Magyar TV production. Features entire cast. Directed by Janos Rosza. Screenplay, Istvan Kardos; camera (Eastmancolor), Elemer Ragalyi; music, Levente Szorenyi. Reviewed at Magyar Film Fest, Budapest, Feb. 14, '79. Running time, 102 MINS.

Trumpeter .... Zoltan Czoma
Havran .... Ferenc Fabian
Bajusz .... Ferenc Bencze
Janko .... Robert Koltai
Lieutenant .... Ferenc Baks

———

Hungary, freed from Turkish domination by the Austrian Empire in the late 17th century, is now exploited by the latter. Former fighters become outlaws and film details a young man's attachment to three rogues for a violent action pic that touches on the twisting of humans by historic conditions.

But film does not go beyond its rugged violence to humanize it enough to make a more potent statement on its theme of picaresque answers to a disgruntlement with the times and its hardships.

It has an earthy trio of hoods who stop a group on their way to a wedding and slaughter them. A young trumpet player, a slave to the group, is spared for amusement. But he is convinced the trio really want money to buy arms for a new uprising in which his father is engaged.

Disillusion sets in as he sees them rape and pillage though he kills for them when a corrupt soldier who shields them takes their plunder. He gets back the loot for the supposed arms. He finally sees they always lie and turns them in only to again think they are would-be freedom fighters as they react well when they are rounded up along with actual rebels.

But one is killed for singing a song of revolt and the other two are impaled on sharp stakes and drawn and quartered respectively for a bloody end to this nicely acted, well handled but essentially playoff actioner. —*Mosk.*

Rosszemberek
(The Bad Guys)
(HUNGARIAN-COLOR)

———

Budapest, Feb. 16.

Hungarofilm release of Mafilm Hunnia Studio production. Features entire cast. Directed by Gyorgy Szomjas. Screenplay, Peter Dobai, Szomjas; camera (Eastmancolor), Mihaly Halasz; music, Ferenc Sebo. Reviewed at Magyar Film Fest, Budapest, Feb. 15, '79. Running time: 93 MINS.

Chief .... Djoko Rosic
Joska .... Janos Derzsi
Soromfai .... Gyorgy Dorner
Wife .... Mari Kiss
Lord .... Miklos Benedek

———

A sort of goulash oater as a band of highwaymen, at one time freedom fighters in the revolt against Austria, are tracked down by Austrians and local railroad men whose expansion they threaten. Okay action, and imbuing the outlaws with some dignity though they finally get their comeuppance.

Film deals with one gang led by a charismatic leader who becomes the man the so-called law really wants. His right hand man has a wife who wants him home and the man finally informs. But as the group is decimated and he and the leader are led off the man decides to name all accomplices for a full pardon. His wife shoots him for going too far as an informer.

It has the predictable derring-do and appears an actioner for local usage though neatly directed and hueing to the tenets of socalled good outlaws finally being outmoded and destroying themselves in the last throes of aimless banditry. —*Mosk.*

Szabadits Meg A Gonosztol
(Deliver Us From Evil)
(HUNGARIAN-COLOR)

———

Budapest, Feb. 15.

Hungarofilm release of Mafilm Hunnia Studio production. Features entire cast. Directed by Pal Sandor. Screenplay, Zsuzsa Toth from the play by Ivan Mandy; camera (Eastmancolor), Elemer Ragalyi; music, Gabor Presser. Reviewed at Magyar Film Fest, Budapest, Feb. 14, '79. Running time, 94 MINS.

Mother .... Iren Opsota
Zsuzsa .... Erzebet Kutvolgyi
Andras .... Andras Kern
Brother .... Deszo Andorai
Man .... Otto Stetner

———

An offbeat comedy-drama about a lowlife milieu that tries to symbolize the time, 1944, when Hungary was ready to be taken over by its ally, Germany. People were being hunted by local Nazis and life was topsy turvy. Reminiscent of Bertolt Brecht's didactic forays into this sort of expressionism, it lacks the cohesion, drive and insight to humanize its grotesques and make a more potent statement on the times.

Director Pal Sandor is inventive but finally overdoes this tale of a search for a coat from the cloak room of a seedy dancing emporium. Owned by a family, the mother insists it must be found to keep face and integrity. Actually, a half-witted son had stolen it to get some money to procure a girl.

The chase is on. A man carrying a sack is thought guilty and is killed in the chase. They cart him to a sleazy bathhouse to get rid of him in a big bass fiddle case. But the man is alive and the chase goes on as the daughter's fiancee, a soldier, is killed for deserting and the others get embroiled in police roundups, with a female duo who run a fence clothing shop and others in these strange times.

Well-made, but too forced and oblique to make its points, the film looks mainly for some fest outings on its creation of milieu and time albeit finally too indulgent to make it effective. —*Mosk.*

Az Erod
(The Fortress)
(HUNGARIAN-COLOR)

———

Budapest, Feb. 17.

Hungarofilm release of Mafilm Budapest Studio production. Features entire cast. Directed by Miklos Szinetar. Screenplay, Gyula Hernadi, Szinetar; camera (Eastmancolor), Miklos Biro. Reviewed at Magyar Film Fest, Budapest, Feb. 16, '79. Running time: 119 MINS.

Director .... Bella Tanai
Gregor .... Sandor Oszter
Guest .... Adam Rajhona
Ranger .... Ferenc Bencze

———

A sleek tale of simulated war games by a sort of specialized company in an imaginary state. They do the games for bored, unhappy or thrill seeking types with the clients fighting company mercenaries. Somewhat familiar since "Westworld" and the Swedish "The Gladiators" of Peter Watkins, this one adds nothing new and gets a bit too convoluted and steeped in dialectics about the games after a racy beginning.

Several deaths occur though only two are allowed to get by the government. The customers come close to winning in this and the ending has the company now being signed by the government to train mercenaries as the deaths are hushed up.

Smartly made though repetitive and more likely for tv playoff where its obvious characters and action might be more acceptable with some theatrical playoff in Latin or Asian climes after some pruning.

It was to have been made at one time by that protean director of historical epics Miklos Jancso. Coming before the others, and with more dynamic visual sweep, it might have made a way for itself. It is now a bit late. — *Mosk.*

Manesgazda
(The Stud Farm)
(HUNGARIAN-COLOR)

Budapest, Feb. 14.

Hungarofilm release of Objectiv, Dialog Studios. Features entire cast. Written and directed by Andras Kovacs from a book by Istvan Gaal. Camera (Eastmancolor), Lajos Koltai. Reviewed at Magyar Film Fest, Budapest, Feb. 13, '79. Running time, 100 MINS.
Janos .... Joszef Madaras
Matyas .... Ferenc Fabian
Kristof .... Sandor Horvath
Schobert .... Karoly Sinka
Baszi .... Ferenc Baks

Another film dealing with the early, painful days of the changeover to the new socialist regime. It is 1950 and a stud farm for horses serves as the symbolical grounds for this tale of still resentful people and how it destroys a new young head of the farm.

Somewhat discursive, the film is a bit laborious but does delve into the difficult adaptation of men to new ways. The new chief does not know much about the farm and tries to read and get help from the mainly taciturn men around him.

He gets beaten up one day, but by some friends of the owner of a local bar, a woman, whom he had treated as a slattern. The men are still against him even more so when police arrive. Action takes place on a border, probably Austria, where the police shoot a bunch of dogs who set off mines.

The men get into an argument with the director and one knifes him as they run off towards the border and perhaps death from the mines. It does probe the lack of help from the leaders of the times but finally appears more didactic but fully coming to grips with its timeless and timely theme of adaptation to changing times. Film has fest chances, but appears a bit too didactic for more commercial chances abroad. —*Mosk.*

Berlin Festival

Die Ehe Der Maria Braun
(The Marriage of Maria Braun)
(WEST GERMAN-COLOR)

Berlin, Feb. 27.

United Artists release of Albatros Film (M. Fengler) - Trio Film - WDR - Filmerlog Der Autoren production. Stars Hanna Schygulla. Directed by Rainer Werner Fassbinder. Screenplay, Peter Marthesheimer, Pia Frolich; dialog, Fassbinder; camera (Fujicolor), Michael Ballhaus; editor, Juliane Lorenz. Reviewed at Berlin Film Fest (competing), Feb. 20, '79. Running time: 120 MINS.
Maria .... Hanna Schygulla
Hermann .... Klaus Lowitsch
Oswald .... Ivan Desny
Willi .... Gottfried John
Mother .... Gisela Uhlen
Bill .... George Byrd
Betti .... Elisabeth Trissenaar

Rainer Werner Fassbinder has now racked up over 40 films. He may be one of the most prolific western filmmakers and is only in his mid-thirties. With a buff following, probably more appreciated abroad than at home, here he has accepted a rare outside script, (though he reportedly made many revisions) and has seemingly opted for a more accessible drama built around a love-obsessed woman in the last years of World War II and up to the early 1950s.

What starts as promising finally becomes somewhat tedious. For a change, there is a look at a near defeated Germany starting in '43 as people scrounged for food. A woman, Hanna Schygulla, had a delirious day and a night with her husband; they were married during a bombardment. Now she is waiting for him as she tries to help her mother and an old man who had aided them.

She parades with a sandwich sign before returning soldiers hoping to find news of her husband who seems to have disappeared in Russia. She finally gives this up but is sure he is alive. She takes a black American lover, whom she likes but does not love and gets food and help for the family, after the war.

But the husband, pronounced dead by a friend, shows up while she is with the American. He hits her and while the Yank tries to subdue him the wife hits the American over the head and kills him while only trying to save her beloved from humiliation. The husband insists he did it and is imprisoned.

The wife, undaunted, insists she is his man and comes to see him often as she takes up with a rich manufacturer and becomes his lover but refuses to be his mistress. Fassbinder has often gone on record as being influenced by Douglas Sirk, the Yank maker of pungent, bustling tearjerking melodramas who was born in Denmark and worked in Germany before going Stateside.

Fassbinder treats this too morosely and loses the needed humanity. Schygulla is hard and with only fair looks manages to seem enticing. But the film lacks a true sensuality and the brio and more engaging human warmth to give this sociological look at a woman who seems above her times, due to a love that thinks anything is acceptable, a more incisive treatment and insight.

There are a few twists as her husband is freed and goes off until he can care for her. She is now rich and important in her lover's firm. The husband does come back finally after the rich man's death. But it seems he had made a deal with the man, who had found out about him, to get a controlling interest in the firm but give it over to her. An explosion, maybe chance or deliberate, for she had left the gas on, marks the end of this starcrossed couple.

Maybe pic wanted to underline the inability to cope with the new dynamic Germany which demanded more collective rather than personal deportment. Fassbinder does give this some unusual moments in underlining the materialistic outlooks foisted by wartime suffering that maybe led to the economic boom but destroyed some more human change in the process.

This is belied by his ambivalent treatment of the woman who lacks a human comportment and charm. Her obsessive character is not humanized to perk up this otherwise heavyhanded melodrama. Fassbinder buffs should take to it and it might have some playoff chances though not incisive enough in its probing of the times and its people, or more flamboyantly touching in its drama, for more demanding placement abroad. Local chances also seem ambivalent but the Fassbinder name should help in other climes. —*Mosk.*

Prova D'Orchestra
(Orchestra Rehearsal)
(ITALIAN-FRENCH-W. GERMAN COLOR)

Rome, March 2.

Released worldwide by Gaumont (Paris) and SACIS (Rome). A RAI Channel I presentation produced by Daimo Cinematografica (Rome) and Albatross Productions (Munich). Stars Balduin Baas. Written and directed by Federico Fellini with script collaboration by Brunello Rondi. Camera (Eastman Color), Giuseppe Rotunno; art director, Dante Ferretti; editor, Ruggero Mastroianni; music, Nino Rota. Reviewed at Rivoli Cinema, Rome, March 1, '79. Running time: 70 MINS.
Orchestra conductor .... Balduin Baas

Federico Fellini originally conceived "Orchestra Rehearsal" as a tv divertissement to keep active during delays on his upcoming feature, "The City of Women." Between original conception and release print, "Orchestra Rehearsal" grew to a 70-minute feature and developed into a highly creative social metaphor, unlike anything the maestro has done in the past.

Release of this very special, nonnarrative, explosive overview of the film director's judgment on the anarchy and violence of modern times can be counted on to whip up interest for the Gaumont-SACIS entry in all markets, but very special handling is a basic requirement in bringing the RAI-I production to world masses. It is not circuit fare and has little in common with standard film entertainment, but it constitutes an intriguing tribute to visual audacity as Fellini abandons, for the first time, his perpetual revocation of times past and looks melancholically at the world around him.

A symphony orchestra is certainly a valid symbol of the complex variance in society itself. In its details an orchestra offers the elements to demonstrate, instrument by instrument, the loss of harmony and the eruption of violent discord in the social texture of today.

Regardless of the many details illustrating Fellini's civic irks and social fears, he really takes over the podium for a long view, with the help of Nino Rota's ironic score, to issue a solemn warning over the masses' heads that democracy and violent discord are incompatible, leaving society a helpless prey to dictatorship.

Sustained development meticulously identifies and situates the orchestral components musically and metaphorically — reaching climax during general mayhem when a demolition ball shatters one side of the rehearsal hall inside a century-old church to set the stage amid shock and disarray for the contested conductor to regain the podium and reassert authority with jargon expressions reminiscent of the Hitlerian bark.

While Fellini's social posture is open to debate and the ending subject to individual interpretation, there can be little or no quibbling with the creative depth of this exercise — intensified, if anything, but Giuseppe Rotunno's ingenious lensing, the stark pace — once the orchestra is fully assembled — of Ruggero Mastroianni, and the sardonic notes of Nino Rota's score — an integral part of the Fellini pic in which an unknown German actor, Balduin Baas, and a score of hand-selected Fellini characters (aided only by a few professional musicians) constantly keep the metaphor alive. —*Werb.*

The China Syndrome
(COLOR)

Tale of nuclear hanky-pank could be either a big bang or a big dud at the b.o.

Hollywood, March 1.

Columbia Pictures release of a Michael Douglas/IPC Films production. Stars Jane Fonda, Jack Lemmon, Michael Douglas. Exec producer, Bruce Gilbert. Produced by Michael Douglas. Directed by James Bridges. Screenplay, Mike Gray, T.S. Cook, Bridges; camera (Metrocolor), James Crabe; production design, George Jenkins; editor, David Rawlins; set decoration, Arthur Jeph Parker; sound, Willie Burton; costumes, Donfeld; special effects, Henry Millar Jr.; assistant director, Kim Kurumada. Reviewed at Columbia Pictures, The Burbank Studios, March 1, 1979. (MPAA Rating: PG.) Running time: **122 MINS.**

Kimberly Wells .... Jane Fonda
Jack Godell .... Jack Lemmon
Richard Adams .... Michael Douglas
Herman DeYoung .... Scott Brady
Bill Gibson .... James Hampton
Don Jacovich .... Peter Donat
Ted Spindler .... Wilford Brimley
Evan McCormack .... Richard Herd
Hector Salas .... Daniel Valdez
Pete Martin .... Stan Bohrman
Mac Churchill .... James Karen

"The China Syndrome" is a moderately compelling thriller about the potential perils of nuclear energy, whose major fault is an overweening sense of its own self-importance. Superior performances by Jack Lemmon, Jane Fonda and Michael Douglas (who also produced) in the lead roles, accentuated by ultra-realistic production values should propel the Columbia Pictures release to some b.o. success, but the message "overload" is going to scare off other patrons.

There's a tendency when socalled escapist fare is dominating theatre screens for some filmmakers to take to the other extreme, and attempt "important," socially-conscious pix.

Jane Fonda and exec producer Bruce Gilbert have been in the forefront of this movement with their IPC Films banner, which adds "China Syndrome" to "Coming Home." Unlike the latter pic, however, issues rather than characters

dominate "China," and the result is sometimes unbearable self-righteousness.

There are so many flags that director James Bridges tries to wave that he almost obscures the film's strongest asset, its casting. Fonda limns a tv anchorwoman stuck in a "happy news" rut, who hires freelance cameraman Douglas for a series on energy that she hopes will break her into the world of hard news.

While filming at a nuclear energy plant, they witness a control room crisis involving supervisor Lemmon, which is surreptitiously lensed by Douglas. The resulting footage becomes a political hot potato, as station manager Peter Donat buckles under pressure from power company exec Richard Herd, Douglas allies himself with the anti-nuclear forces, and Fonda battles the tentacles of newsroom sexism.

It's not until the final half-hour of "China Syndrome" that its promise catches up to its punch, and the wind-up packs a solid wallop. But a cop-out feeling predominates, since the pro-nuclear corporate heavies, tarred with a bad-guy brush for 99% of the pic, are ultimately vindicated.

Screenplay by Mike Gray, T.S. Cook and director Bridges is well-paced but littered with excessive nuclear terminology. Other than the title translation (a meltdown of the core radiation material), it's difficult to understand just what Lemmon and the others are discussing, a problem marvelously explicated in Lemmon's swan song before a live tv audience.

Fonda plays a modern-day Brenda Starr, complete with flaming red locks, and her character has other cartoonish aspects. Douglas is solid in support, as are Donat, Herd, and especially Wilford Brimley as one of Lemmon's co-workers, one of the best delineated character roles in recent memory.

Tech credits are strong, in particular George Jenkin's production design, using facilities of the L.A. Department of Water & Power, James Crabe's muted photography and Richard Edlund and Matthew Yuricich's miniature and matte work.

"China Syndrome" really belongs to Lemmon, however, since his character galvanizes the film's resolution. It's a remarkably well-rounded perf, wrenching in its final moments, and makes use of all the actor's considerable skills.

Had "China Syndome" possessed the depth and shading of Lemmon's delivery, it might have surmounted these stumbling blocks. But it remains a political tract, and film audiences are rarely in the mood for a lecture. —*Poll.*

Au Nom Du Fuhrer
(In the Name of the Fuhrer)
(BELGIAN-DOCU-B&W)

Paris, Feb. 26.

An ADITEC release of a Films Lyda production. Screenplay, Frans Buyen, Lydia Chagoll. Directed and edited by Lydia Chagoll. Camera (black and white), Fernand Tack, Andre Geoffers; music, Arsene Souffriau; voice-over, Marcel Dossogne, Anne Marev. Reviewed at Cinema La Clef, Paris, Feb. 26, '79. Running time: **87 MINS.**

One of the dismaying conclusions to be drawn from reactions to German and French broadcasting of the American tv film, "Holocaust" is that there has been an overall failure to effectively burn into the collective conscience the unprecedented horror of the Nazi genocide against the Jews. Yet even amid the current flurry of emotion and debate it is shameful to note that a film called "In the Name of the Fuhrer" has received only perfunctory comment from most of the Paris press. This documentary by Lydia Chagoll does in 90 minutes what "Holocaust" cannot do in several heavy-breathing hours.

It is an especially horrible 90 minutes because its focus is on the Nazi attitude towards children, their own as well as those of Jewish birth. For their own it meant the inculcation of belief in the Aryan myth and the intense hatred of all who were not German. For the Jewish children it meant a fate no different from that of the adults.

Chagoll has not written a commentary, she has found it: in Nazi edicts, directives, pedagogical manuals, war diaries, quotations, etc. Two voices cite these texts in simultaneity with the presentation of Nazi newsreels, photographs and other documents; scenes of proudly triumphant, clean-cut German youth are intercut with grisly images of the consequences. Unfathomably horrible as it is to see images of murdered children, it becomes even more atrocious to hear over these pictures the smugly euphemistic, pseudo-scientific diagnosis: "Unfit for Germanization!" (How much more chilling it would have been to hear these texts in the original German.)

"In the Name of the Fuhrer" is valuable precisely because it has set itself a reasonable field of investigation. In trying to embrace everything as "Holocaust" strains to do one ends up by capturing nothing of profound import. Films like Chagoll's and Alain Resnais' "Night and Fog" should be shown in television not merely confined to pedagogical circuits. —*Len.*

Phantasm
(COLOR)

Hollywood, March 4.

An Avco Embassy release. Produced by D.A. Coscarelli. Written and directed by Don Coscarelli. Features entire cast. Co-produced by Paul Pepperman. Camera (Technicolor), Coscarelli; editor, Coscarelli; sound, Michael Gross; production design, S. Tyer; art director, David Gavin Brown; visual consultant, Roberto Quezada; music, Fred Myrow, Malcolm Seagrave; special effects, Paul Pepperman. Reviewed at UA Westwood, Westwood, March 3, '79. (MPAA Rating: R.) Running time **90 MINS.**

Mike .... Michael Baldwin
Jody .... Bill Thornbury
Reggie .... Reggie Bannister
Lady In Lavender .... Kathy Lester
The Tall Man .... Angus Scrimm

"Phantasm" is a fine example of what can be done with a little cinematic ingenuity and a lot of red and yellow blood. Although this old-fashioned type horror film does suffer from the customary gaps in plot, taken as a whole it will probably fulfill its purpose to alternately scare, delight and generally gross out its unsuspecting audience.

Pic opens with 13-year-old Mike Pearson, who foolishly disobeys his older brother's orders not to attend the funeral of a close friend who, unbeknownst to everyone, was really stabbed by a woman after the two made love in a cemetery. Being the precocious lad he is, Mike hides in the bushes during the ceremony and later happens to eye the villainous tall man loading the casket into a car after everyone else has left thinking the body is safely six feet under.

Mike decides to leave and tell his brother of the strange goings-on, which also includes several endearing brown gnomes sneaking behind select tombstones. Of course, brother Jody doesn't beleive Mike, forcing the lad to bravely investigate the dank mausoleum near the cemetery for clues all by his lonesome.

Once inside, the fun begins, with Mike treated to a quite grisly murder courtesy of a futuristic flying silver sphere and the wrath of the tall man, who doesn't cotton to the kid's curiosity. Film the follows Mike, Jody and company as the attempt to unravel exactly what is going on.

Strong point of the feature is that it's played for both horror and laughs. Don Coscarelli, who deserves most of the credit as producer, director, writer, and cinematographer, uses both suspense and gore to frighten his audience, thankfully not going too overboard on the latter. But more importantly, there's also a nice tongue-in-cheek feeling to the whole thing, with the actors every so often breaking the tension with understatements like "something weird is going on."

Michael Baldwin and Bill Thornburry are fine as Mike and Jody, as are rest of the cast in lesser roles. Angus Scrimms' intermittent appearance as the tall man is delightfully frightening. Coscarelli directs all with ease and excels as cinematographer, avoiding the cheap, grade B quality. Several special effects by Paul Pepperman work well.

Coscarelli's plot line could have been a little bit more succinct, particularly at the conclusion, which tends to leave things a bit clouded and unexplained. But pic seems a natural for fine drive-in play, and judging from popularity of other recent horror items like "Halloween," could have some hardtop potential, too. —Berg.

Real Life
(COLOR)

Spoof on social-minded Film Documentaries and their makers. Mostly fun.

A Paramount Pictures release. Produced by Penelope Spheeris. Directed by Albert Brooks. Exec producers, Norman Epstein, Jonathan Kovler. Features entire cast. Screenplay, Brooks, Monica Johnson, Harry Shearer; camera (color), Eric Saarinen; editor, David Finfer; music, Mort Lindsey; art direction, Linda Spheeris, Linda Marder. Reviewed at Cinema II, N.Y., March 2, '79. (MPAA rating: PG) Running time: 99 MINS.
Warren Yeager . . . . Charles Grodin
Jeannette Yeager . . . . Frances Lee McCain
Dr. Ted Cleary . . . . J.A. Preston
Dr. Howard Hill . . . . Matthew Tobin
Albert Brooks . . . . Albert Brooks
Lisa Yeager . . . . Lisa Urette
Eric Yeager . . . . Robert Stirrat
Dr. Jeremy Nolan . . . . David Spielberg
Martin Brand . . . . Jennings Lang
Isaac Steven Hayward . . . Norman Bartold

Expanding on the deadpan satiric tone of the short parodies and pseudo-documentaries he's filmed in the past for NBC's "Saturday Night Live" into his first feature, Albert Brooks has come up with a mostly very funny (though uneven) take-off on social-minded docu filmmaking that stands to draw boxoffice support from the young adult, primarily college crowd that's made the late-night tv show the success it is.

The film, which Brooks directed, co-wrote and toplines — playing himself — chronicles his mock efforts to move in with a "typical American family" (Charles Grodin, Frances Lee McCain and two kids) and film every detail of their day-to-day life, with the joint backing of a mythical behavioral research institute and a Hollywood studio.

Under the callous scrutiny of Brooks's crew, the family quickly disintegrates into near-breakdowns, and eventually the institute and studio both withdraw from the project under media pressure, leaving Brooks as mad as a hatter by fadeout. "Real Life," like the film-

within-a-film, eventually disintegrates itself, but not before it's done a cruelly effective job of parodying both the Pat Loud "American Family" public tv docu-series that inspired the takeoff, and Hollywood filmmaking in general.

The film is best in its individual set pieces, not surprising considering that Brooks formerly confined his efforts to pithy two- and three-minute shorts seen on the home tube. Standouts include jargon-laden parodies of the "scientific" testing to initially select the ideal family; a visit to McCain's gynecologist, who ejects the film crew only because he was badly maligned in a "60 Minutes" expose on black market babies a few months earlier; and Grodin (who plays a veterinarian) bungling an emergency operation on a prize horse, the malpractice captured for posterity on celluloid.

Pic also has its share of Hollywood in-jokes, ranging from a union-demanded 20-member film crew that Brooks dismisses (at full pay) on the first morning of shooting ("see you guys at the premiere," he cheerily shouts), to his telephone confrontations with the crassly commercial studio topper (the voice of real-life producer Jennings Lang), who suggests the pic might have a better shot at the turnstiles if James Caan is hired to play a next-door neighbor, and eventually turns off the cash.

Grodin and McCain are excellent as the put-upon but well-meaning targets, and Brooks holds the whole thing together with a tone of over-rehearsed sincerity and calculated innocence. Technical credits are tops. — Step.

Coup de Tete
(Hot-Head)
(FRENCH-COLOR)

Paris, Feb. 14.

A Gaumont release of a Gaumont-S.F.P. production. Produced by Alain Poire. Directed by Jean-Jacques Annaud. Stars Patrick Dewaere. Screenplay, Francis Veber, from an original idea by Alain Godard; camera, (color), Claude Agostini; sound, Francois Soler; music, Pierre Bachelet; editor, Noelle Boisson; art director, Alain Maunoury. Reviewed at Films Ariane, Paris, Feb. 14, '79. Running time: 90 MINS.
vided.
Francois Perrin . . . . Patrick Dewaere
Stephanie . . . . France Dougnac
President Sivardiere . . . . Jean Bouise
Brochard . . . . Michel Aumont
Lozerand . . . . Paul Le Person
Langlumey . . . . Michel Fortin
Marie . . . . Dorothee Jemma
Berthier . . . . Patrick Floersheim

"Coup de Tete" is a gleefully blunt; frontal assault on the inverted moral values in a provincial French city whose soccer team precedes all else in importance. Director Jean-Jacques Annaud has ridden the American success of his first feature "La Victoire En Chan-

tant," back to more receptive critical attention in France, which greeted that film with indifference.

Francis Veber's scenario follows the fortunes of Francois, a young ne'er-do-well, dumped from the soccer team for intractability and subsequently fired from the factory for the same reasons by the same individual, Sivardiere, president of both the factory and soccer club.

Cut off from social anchorage; Francois drifts aimlessly about the city until he is arrested for an attempted rape, actually committed by the star of the soccer team. But the scapegoat becomes the saviour when a road accident incapacitates several team members just before the National Cup playoffs: Sivardiere and cohorts spring Francois temporarily to play. He wins the game and becomes an untouchable hero, which allows him leeway to plan a campaign of vengeance. Everyone prepares for the worst which never comes, because Francois' rage has burnt itself out.

Veber covers much-travelled terrain but with caustic efficiency in a well-structured scenario. His talents are particularly evident in the often brashly funny dialog. Annaud displays the workmanlike skill of his first film and gets well-judged performances from the entire cast.

Patrick Dewaere is eminently believable as the human pinball rebounding off the pillars of a small-minded society that condemend him to insignificance. —Len.

Amo non amo
(I Love You I Love You Not)
(ITALIAN-COLOR)

Rome, Feb. 20.

A Titanus release. Produced by Valerio De Paolis and Gianni Bozzacchi for Compagnia Europea Cinematografica. Directed by Armenia Balducci. Stars Jacqueline Bisset, Maximilian Schell, Terence Stamp. Screenplay, Armenia Balducci, Ennio De Concini; camera (Technicolor), Carlo Di Palma; art director, Maria Paola Maino; music Goblin Bixio-Cemsa. Reviewed at Titanus, Rome, Feb. 19, -79. Running time: 100 MINS.
Louise . . . . Jacqueline Bisset
John . . . . Maximilian Schell
Henry . . . . Terence Stamp
Giulia . . . . Monica Guerritore

At last a film on feminism that has the courage to admit that leaving husbands, acquiring and discarding lovers and/or keeping them is not all that easy. Director Armenia Balducci, in her first attempt behind the camera, refrains from making a heavy statement about women's liberation · and simply shows just how trying the whole business can be.

On the surface, "I Love You" appears to be another romantic beach film: in a lovely resort town near Rome beautiful people make love in the sunkissed waters of the Medi-

terranean and in a sauna listening to opera music. These scenes — plus boxoffice draws like Jacqueline Bisset, Maximilian Schell and Terence Stamp — should attract a healthy crowd, but unfortunately they might scare away many who could appreciate the film beneath these trappings.

Balducci — who has done her own scripting — is describing the ambiguity created by women's newly acquired independence. Louise — played with aplomb by Jacqueline Bisset — has left her husband, launched a career as a dress designer and with her 10-year-old son Roby by her first marriage has moved in with John, a lawyer. Despite this emancipated exterior, however, she is still constantly bumping into the same old knotty problems: a son who demands her attention, a lover who has not completely shaken off his macho ways and good old-fashioned jealousy.

In a particularly effective scene, Louise and Giulia, a woman who has just spent the afternoon on the beach with John, compare notes and conclude that women are still "in a mess." Louise' own affair with Henry (played unconvincingly by Terence Stamp), her alternate dreams of John's suicide and her murder of him, and finally her return to the beach house to watch John and Roby together sailing out to sea underscore the doubts and insecurities (already reflected in the film's title) that plague women in their relationships with men.

Schell plays a sullen type who never shows even a modicum of sensitivity to Louise's plight, a fact that adds a note of pessimism to the film. Monica Guerritore as Giulia earns the right to land a meaty lead instead of her usual roles. All other credits commendable.

"I Love You," originally shot in English, was the film that touched off the actors' protest against the granting of national subsidies to foreign-language Italian films.
—Argo.

Berlin Film Fest

David
(WEST GERMAN-COLOR)

Berlin, Feb. 28.

Filmverlag Der Autoren release of Vietinghof Filmproduktion, Pro-Ject Film Produktion, Filmverlag Der Autoren, ZDF, Dedra Pictures production. Features entire cast. Directed by Peter Lilienthal. Screenplay, Jurek Becker, Ulla Zieman, Lilienthal from the book by Joel Konig; camera (Eastmancolor), Al Ruban; editor, Siegrun Jager; music, Wojiech Kilar. Reviewed at Berlin Film Fest (competing), Feb. 27, '79. Running time: 125 MINS.
Rabbi Singer . . . . Walter Taub
Wife . . . . Irena Vrkljan
Toni . . . . Eva Mattes

David .... Mario Fische
Leo ...., ... Dominique Horwitz

"David" comes on the heels of the unusual impact of the American tv mini-series, "Holocaust," on German consciousness about the liquidation of the Jews during the last war. Local filmmakers have rarely been able to approach its sheer emotional reactions.

Peter Lilienthal's David is a teenage Jewish boy caught in Nazi Germany with his sister after his parents and brother have tried to get out. He is resourceful and receives help from a German official who gets him false papers. He is finally able to get to Israel.

The early Nazi days are neatly etched as David as a boy is attacked by Nazi youths. Then with the war comes acceleration of attacks on Jewish people and the burning of the synagogue headed by David's father, Rabbi Singer.

The film has a convoluted mosaic as David gets odd jobs, hides out in a concealed room, lives in a small shack in a railroad station where he gets work and his final chance to escape. Meanwhile, a shoemaker hides his sister but exacts payment in taking belongings from their apartment.

Walter Taub is especially effective as the Rabbi who tries to convince himself they can go on even after his temple is burned before his eyes and a Nazi swastika is carved in his bald pate. But he tries to get away with papers to Latin America with his wife and may or may not have succeeded.

Direction is serviceable but rarely manages a true epic or deeply emotional insight into this tor-'tuous era. Mario Fischel is acceptable as David as he just goes about trying to save himself in his contacts with decent, fanatic or just ordinary people also caught up in this nightmarish time.

On its theme and feel for the times pic might find specialized outings abroad and have impact on its home base. Film does not add a more incisive insight into the Holocaust which has now become a timely subject. "David" is just a small addition to the more penetrating films that have already been made on this subject. —Mosk.

Kassbach
(AUSTRIAN-COLOR)

Berlin, Feb. 26.

Patzak-Satel Film release and production. Features entire cast. Directed by Peter Patzak. Screenplay Patzak, Helmut Zenker from a book by Zenker; camera (Agfacolor), Dietrich Lohmann, Attila Szabo; editor, Trude Gruber; Daniela Padalewski; music, Peter Zwetkoff. Reviewed at Berlin Film Fest (competing), Feb. 25, '79. Running time, 95 MINS.
Kassbach .... Walter Kohut
Wife .... Immy Schell

Mother .... Maria Engelstorfer
Son .... Konrad Becker

A glum but often penetrating portrait of a neo-Nazi type. Film relentlessly illustrates Hannah Arendt's by-now well-known statement about the banality of evil in referring to the Nazi types who appeared before the war crimes commissions after World War II.

Kassbach, played with chilling directness by Walter Kohut, is a grocer who has alienated his wife and son, bucks supermarkets by giving credit and cleverly cheating gullible customers. He has joined a neo-Nazi group as an outlet for his own seeming discontent with his life, though he covers it up by bravado and boasts.

He faces his son when some leftist crowds try to break up a meeting of the fascist group. He and some henchmen begin to use violence as a means of making themselves felt, by knifing a Yugoslav worker. Then Kassbach shoots a man who might have recognized him when they are breaking up the meeting of a leftist organization.

Film ends with a confrontation with his son in which he pulls a gun on him as the frame freezes. Somewhat talky, it still paints a grim picture of Kassbach's preying on people around him, including a backward teenage girl who works for him, before his final acceleration to violence. Film avoids didactics but does stay a bit surface. A timely subject in Germanic countries today with tv legs there on its simple progression while theatrical chances remain more difficult.
—Mosk.

Kejsaren
(The Emperor)
(SWEDISH-COLOR)

Berlin, Feb. 24.

Svenska Filminstitutet release of Treklovern, Svenska Film Institutet production. Features entire cast. Directed by Josta Hagelback. Screenplay, Hagelback, Sten Holmberg from the book by Birgitta Trotzig; camera (Eastman-color), Sten Holmberg; editor, Peter Falack; music, Ragnar Grippe. Reviewed at Berlin Film Fest (competing), Feb. 26, '79. Running time: 95 MINS.
Elje .... Anders Aberg
Albin .... Bo Lindstrom
Pig Girl .... Anna Lindroth
Foreman .... Runp Ek
Polish Girl .... Katarina Strandmark

A resolutely determined attempt to renew with the lyrical, ballad-like Swedish films that tried to delve into internal human effects of repression. Here it is the racism that was stirred towards any Swedes of foreign origins or any foreigners in the country, due to the use of foreign workers on the land in the '30s, plus the turn-of-the-century use of Poles as strikebreakers.

Film takes place in '38 on the eve

of the World War II. A young man whose mother had been Polish is discriminated against but seems to have a sort of holy mission (or psychotic obsession) to find out about his mother who has left to go back to Poland.

Film has a dense, well-lensed observance of this rugged land beset by almost feudal patrons. The boy lusts for a Polish girl but finds many men have had her and rejects her. He goes off, only to be thrown in jail in Poland when he goes with a prostitute (perhaps an image of his mother) but has no money. Here he begins to crack and ends up in an asylum back in Sweden.

Another story is evoked of a Polish pig keeper and village whore who gives birth to a dead baby and ends up as a nurse at the asylum with the boy. She is finally killed by the boy, who thinks of himself as some sort of emperor as he escapes. Film is somewhat diffuse and edges into pretentiousness after a firm, earthy beginning with poetic insights.

More a domestic item, but perhaps worth some foreign attention on its sometimes effusive, poetic treatment of an earthy, elemental people caught up in racism and poverty on the eve of the war.

Josta Hagelback should be a new director to contend with when he can control his sometimes overdone visual elan. —Mosk.

L'Hypothese Du Tableau Vole
(Hypothesis of the Stolen Painting)
(FRENCH-B&W)

Berlin, Feb. 24.

INA release and production. Features entire cast. Written and directed by Raul Ruiz from an idea by Pierre Klossowski. Camera (black and white) Sacha Vierny, Maurice Pejimond; music, 'Jose Arriagada. Reviewed at Berlin Fest Youth Forum (noncompeting), Feb. 23, '79. Running time: 67 MINS.

With: Jean Rougeul, Anne Debois, Chantal Palay, Alix Comte, Jean Narboni, Stephane Shandor

---

An intriguing idea that is still somewhat hermetic, open to interpretations and finally too mannered for other than the festival, archive and school usage it should attract. An imaginary painter's series of pictures are probed by a collector in his home and paintings come alive as posed by unmoving tableaus.

The old collector slowly forges an idea that a story lies behind these paintings which seem to have some similar characterial and figurative links, though taking place in different eras.

The paintings begin to intermingle as the narrator delves into them. Chilean director Raul Ruiz may have wanted to show how

didactics can be forced on art or images but have to grow out of them, or perhaps he wanted to say something about criticism in general.

With all its evasive aspects, pic still exerts a sort of hypnotic effect. Ruiz has gone from more naturalistic films to meditations on aspects of human behavior or art. By now a highly specialized filmmaker, but mainly for buffs.
— Mosk.

Ernesto
(ITALIAN-COLOR)

Berlin, Feb. 27.

Clesi Cinematografica release of Clesi Cinematografica-Jose Frade Prod.-Albatros Produktion 'production. Features entire cast. Directed by Salvatore Samperi. Screenplay, Barbara Alberti, Amadeo Paganini, Samperi; camera (Technicolor), Camillo Bazzoni; music, Carmelo Bernaola. Reviewed at Berlin Film Fest (competing), Feb. 26, '79. Running time, 98 MINS.
Ernesto .... Martin Halm
Ilio ...., ... Michele Placido
Mother .... Virna Lisi

A part of Italy, Trieste, under the Austro-Hungarian Empire in pre World War I days serves as a classic backdrop for this tale of a handsome young man's initation to life, sex and class ways of the times. Despite the possible use of sex as a subversive element, pic remains somewhat posey rather than able to make a comment on the times or, for that matter on sexual patterns.

Title character comes from a Jewish family. His mother had been abandoned by her Christian father and they are kept by an irascible uncle. The boy, (Martin Halm), plays at socialism to annoy his uncle and has a job in a warehouse employing itinerant workers. Ernesto has a first affair with a homosexual worker whom he finally subjugates and discards and then finds he is also heterosexually inclined when he visits a prostitute.

He meets some rich twins and is drawn to both boy and girl, for they are mixed. Finally, the families arrange a wedding with the girl as Ernesto accepts his role.

Mainly playoff is indicated on its colorful era and sexual imbroglios though the scenes are done with tact. It just lacks a more discerning probe of the times to lift this out of the picturesque. —Mosk.

In Einem Jahr Mit 13 Monden
(In a Year of 13 Months)
(WEST GERMAN-COLOR)

Berlin, Feb. 24.

Filmproduktion Im Filmberlag Der Autoren, Tango Film (Rainer Werner Fassbinder) release and production. Features entire cast. Written, directed, lensed and edited by Rainer Werner Fassbinder (in

Eastmancolor). Reviewed at Berlin Film Fest Youth Forum (non-competing), Feb. 23, '79. Running time: **129 MINS.**

Elvira	Volker Spengler
Rote	Ingrid Caven
Anton	Gottfried John
Irene	Elisabeth Trissenaar
Marie	Eva Mattes

Rainer Werner Fassbinder displayed his eclectic, prolific aspects with an accessible melodrama (The Marriage of Eva Braun) in the competing section of the Berlin Fest. Now this more familiar tale of fringe characters displays gritty humor and attempted pathos about the last days of a transexual in its non-competing slot in tests sidebar Youth Forum.

Reportedly a sort of homage to a friend who committed suicide, pic might have been painful to make for Fassbinder. But it is also a little painful to take due to a heavy-handed treatment and an inability to humanize this man by splitting the film into diatribes, forced metaphors and rancorous humor alongside meditations on the meaning of suicide.

The transsexual was once a happy worker in a slaughterhouse which he revisits with a friend for a long scene of efficient, industrial killing and preparing of animals. He had gone for his sex operation because he loved a man though married and with a child. And he may not even have been gay.

He is now getting fat, hirsute and ugly and is losing boyfriends, though his wife, a local tart, is still loyal. Well played by Fassbinder's stock company, especially by Volker Spengler as the hapless new woman, film appears more slanted for Fassbinder addicts and a sure fest bet, with commercial outlets more problematical.

As usual, with Fassbinder, it is technically sound and full of allusions that will get to those who know his work. —*Mosk.*

Hair
(COLOR)

Broadway event of 1960s. As screen tuner poses questions re today's youth and box-office problems.

Hollywood, March 13.

United Artists release of a Lester Persky and Michael Butler production. Features entire cast. Directed by Milos Forman. Screenplay, Michael Weller, based on Gerome Ragni, James Rado and Galt MacDermot's musical play; camera (color), Miroslav Ondricek; choreography, Twyla Tharp; music, adapted and conducted by Galt MacDermot; lyrics, Gerome Ragni, James Rado; costumes, Ann Roth; production designer, Stuart Wurtzel; film editor, Lynzee Klingman; second unit director, Gerald Cotts; unit publicist, Larry Kaplan; set decorator, George De Titta' special effects, Al Griswold. Reviewed at Cinerama Dome, Hollywood, March 9, '79. (MPAA Rating: PG). Running time: **118 MINS.**

Claude	John Savage
Berger	Great Williams
Sheila	Beverly D'Angelo
Jeannie	Annie Golden
Hud	Dorsey Wright
Woof	Don Dacus
Hud's fiancee	Cheryl Barnes
Fenton	Richard Bright
The General	Nicholas Ray
Party guest	Charlotte Rae
Steve	Miles Chapin
Sheila's mother	Fern Tailer
Sheila's father	Charles Deney
Sheila's uncle	Herman Meckler
Sheila's aunt	Agness Breen
Berger's mother	Antonia Rey
Berger's father	George Manos
Vietnamese girl	Linda Surh
Debutante 1	Jane Booke
Debutante 2	Suki Love
Claude's father	Joe Acord
Sheldon	Michael Jeter
Prison psychiatrist	Janet York
Lafayette Jr	Rahsaan Curry
The Judge	Harry Gittleson
The M.P.	Donald Alsdurf
A barracks officer	Steve Massicotte
A barracks officer	Mario Nelson
"Aquarius" soloist	Ben Woods

Hollywood, March 13.

When first staged at the New York Shakespeare Fest in 1967, "Hair" was more than just a Broadway-bound tuner — it was an event, mirroring the joyful liberation of a generation giving full rein to its passions. Now, 12 years' later, with Milos Forman's cinematic adaptation, "Hair" is less of an event and more of a muddle. United Artists will have to maximize the response from those who grew up in the late-60s, because the older audience will continue to be turned off by the pic's PG-rated frankness, and today's teenagers will find little relevance in the film version.

Forman, together with a talented coterie of associates, has still wrought considerable wonders. There are moments in "Hair" that are vibrant and innovative, in ways that no musical has succeeded in the late 1970s.

The Lester Persky-Michael Butler production attempts to satisfy all quarters of the filmgoing public, and may succeed in pleasing but a few. Michael Weller has imposed a rough storyline on the original book by Gerome Ragni and James Rado, but there are large expository gaps. These are accentuated by Forman's determination to have free-form musical numbers evolve out of the tale of a draftee adopted by a bunch of New York hippies, who tune him into their uninhibited lifestyles.

John Savage plays the inductee, fascinated by the group he stumbles upon at a Central Park be-in, composed of Treat Williams, Annie Golden, Dorsey Wright and Don Dacus. They get him stoned, urge him on in his quest for debutante Beverly D'Angelo, and pursue him to his basic training camp in Nevada and a bittersweet finale.

On the surface, "Hair" seems a radical departure from its antecedents, but Weller's screenplay is a return to the outline of Joseph Papp's original production, rather than the Broadway and road show versions it spawned. The spirit and elan that captivated the Vietnam protest era are long gone, and what **Forman tries to make up with splash and verve fails to evoke potent nostalgia.**

Twyla Tharp's choreography, more muted than perhaps intended, is forthright in its semi-erotic writhings, but the staging of scenes such as the title song in Gotham's Tombs Prison defy comprehension. Otherwise, the high camp of the commingled "Black Boys/-White Boys" number, and the extraordinary psychedelic church wedding sequence, are visual and aural highlights.

"Hair" incorporates themes from earlier Forman pix, most notably his first American film, "Taking Off," but the input of a foreign sensibility to an essentially native theme has not provided the creative spark one might have expected. "Hair" still seems like a film that has come 10 years too late — a failed Broadway revival, mounted in the fall of 1977, tends to validate this impression.

The casting is one of the strongest elements of "Hair," with Savage the perfect choice for the naive Oklahoma cowboy, who for some inexplicable reason, journeys to Gotham for his induction. Williams leads the longhairs with gusto, and Golden may be the only player who truly captures the "flower power" feeling. D'Angelo does quite well as the mixed-up deb, and Dorsey Wright, Don Dacus, Richard Bright and Miles Chapin are suitable in support. Cheryl Barnes makes a strong impression in her solo rendition of "Easy To Be Hard," but the full close-up number seems out of synch with the rest of mayhem.

Tech work is top-level, especially Miroslav Ondricek's fluid camerawork, Ann Roth's snazzy costumes, and Stuart Wurtzel's well-heeled production design. Special mention should be made of the re-recording work done by Bill Varney, Steve Maslow and Bob Minker — "Hair" has one of the finest post-synch jobs in recent memory.

Even with most of the film's budget on the screen, "Hair" is a triumph of technical craftsmanship over conceptual artistry. At a time when filmusicals have a rough go of it without John Travolta in a lead role, "Hair" is in for some close shaves at the boxoffice.

"Hair" preemed at the N.Y. Shakespeare Fest in October, 1977, moving over to the off-Broadway Cheetah before arriving at the Biltmore on April 29, 1968, where it ran for 1,759 performances, making it the ninth-longest-run musical in Broadway history. —*Poll.*

Jacob Two-Two Meets the Hooded Fang
(CANADIAN-COLOR)

Montreal, March 2.

A Gulkin Productions release. Produced by Harry Gulkin. Exec producer, John Flaxman. Written and directed by Theodore J. Flicker, based on novel by Mordecai Richler. Stars Stephen Rosenberg, Alex Karras. Camera (color), Francois Protat; editor, Stan Cole; art director, Seamus Flannery; music composed and sung by Lewis Furey; costumes, Francois Barbeau. Reviewed at the Snowdon Theatre, Montreal, Mar. 2, '79. Running time: **80 MINS.**

Jacob Two-Two	Stephen Rosenberg
The Hooded Fang	Alex Karras
Master Fish	Guy L'Ecuyer
Mistress Fowl	Joy Coghill
Mr. Cooper/Judge	Earl Pennington
Mister Fox	Claude Gai
Emma/Shapiro	Marfa Richler
Noah/O'Toole	Thor Bishopric
Louis Loser	Victor Desy

This children's novel is nicely translated to the screen in a film written and directed by Theodore J. Flicker, who shot the film on locations in Montreal in 1976 but when 1977 tests by its U.S. distributor (Cinema Shares) proved disappointing, the film was temporarily shelved. Producer Harry Gulkin then instigated a major re-editing of the film and has now undertaken to market it himself in Canada.

The film's strength remains its content; its weaknesses are mainly technical. The story recounts the nightmarish adventures of a small boy who must constantly repeat himself because adults never listen to him the first time.

Little Jacob (winningly played by Montreal schoolboy Stephen Rosenberg) dreams he is arrested for insulting adults and sentenced by a clearly prejudiced judge of the "children's court" (Earl Pennington in one of two very funny roles) to two years, two months, two weeks, two days, two hours and two minutes in the deepest, darkest dungeons of the children's prison on Slimer's Island, a smog-ridden concentration camp which is presided over by the Hooded Fang (ex-footballer Alex Karras turning in a delightfully hammy performance), a former wrestler who hates kids because they think he is, ugh, cute.

The script, especially parts which have been taken directly from Richler's book, is excellent, a funny and often quite sharp, kid's-level look at relationships between children and adults. And the acting is up to the same standard.

But the film's production values are uneven. Visually (the color photography, interior lighting, some sets and costumes) and aurally (fuzzy sound recording) the movie is no match for the slickness of Disney's productions or those by similar specialists., Lewis Furey's musical score is fine in itself but the grownup lyrics of his songs are often inappropriate.

Despite its faults, "Jacob Two-Two" is redeemed by its pertinence and some very witty scenes — one, in children's court, is worthy of Alice in Wonderland.

Plurielles
(Plurals)
(FRENCH-B&W-16m)

Paris, March 3.

A Films Arquebuse-Maison de la Culture de la Seine Saint-Denis co-production. Produced by Michelle Plaa and Rene Fere. Written and directed by Jean-Patrick Lebel. Features entire cast. Camera, (black and white), Jean Monsigny; editing, Christine Lack; sound, Rene Levert and Auguste Galli. Theatre extracts from the play, "Jacotte or The Pleasures of Daily Life," by Jacques Kramer. Reviewed at Club 13, Paris, Feb. 23, '79. Running time: 90 MINS.

With: Christine Murillo, Jacques Denis, Monique Melinand, Jenny Cleve, Michel Amphoux, Judith Comets, Guillaume Lebel.

"Plurielles" is a multiform look at the conditions of women today and the progress they have made in the professional world. Jean-Patrick Lebel's first feature — shot in 16m and co-produced by the Seine Saint-Denis Cultural Centre for which he directs an audio-visual division—affords some intelligent comment and humorous insight on vital issues, though its very diffuseness curtails the depth of its inquiry.

The film casually interweaves fiction, documentary, video-taped interviews, filmed theatre, illustrations. The video segment records the faces and words of three women who talk about their own experiences and ideas; scenes from a stage production follow the seriocomic plight of a young girl growing up in a bewildering world; images from real life present some working women — truck-driver, phone company employee, waitress, judo expert, film editor (shown working on this film); some old historical illustrations are scanned for depictions of women's roles; a fictional portion presents an apparently balanced marriage.

Much of this is interesting to watch. The interviewed women are worth hearing out and the stage production is sprightly and well-played. But the juxtaposition of all these modes of presentation is tentative and merely tantalizing.

In its perky efficiency and sly humor the fiction sequences work best, confirming Lebel's brisk intelligence. The couple look like an ideal, liberated pair sharing housework and shopping alike. What comes out of their mouths though is not idle chit-chat but lengthy citations from Friedrich Engels' "Family, Private Property and the State."

Yet these Godardian eccentrics, delightfully played by Jacques Denis and Christine Murillo, are far from a perfect state of Marxist, marital bliss; she still maintains benign tyranny in supermarket affairs and he clings to certain cliches of masculinity. In the end he is still spouting Engels —*Len.*

Marian
(SPANISH-COLOR)

Madrid, March 3.

Iruna P.C. and Cinema 2000 production. Directed by Luis Cortes. Features entire cast. Screenplay, Juan Antonio Porto, Luis Cortes; camera (Eastmancolor) Jose Luis Alcaine; editor, Guillermo Maldonado; sets, Jose Antonio de la Guerra. Reviewed at Cine Azul, Madrid, March 2, '79. Running time: 87 MINS.

Marian	Isabel Mestres
Marcos Salazar	Javier Escriva
Jaime	Jabier Elorriaga
Ana	Maria Asquerino
Alfredo	Hector Alterio
Irene Sierra	Lina Canalejas
Mariana (child)	Susana Prados
Jaime (child)	Alberto Belmonte

Honest but very slight item by neophyte helmer Luis Cortes about a girl who's unresponsive to a loving but overworked husband and several lovers she picks up at miscellaneous places. Trouble stems from an almost classical Oedipus complex when as a young girl living in a village Marian caught her mother and the family doctor in bed after the father who doted on her, had died.

Story moves along jerkily, and it seems that every few minutes the grown Marian chances upon some momento or scene that immediately evokes a childhood incident related to her father or her mother's new fling. Most of pic Isabel Mestres plods along expressionlessly, and not until she meets her father-image in the person of a novelist, does she crack a smile. Many of the dialogs are embarassingly flat, though occasionally pic does capture a moment of tenderness.

There are a few sex scenes, but nothing explicit or in bad taste.

Film, however, has no punch and hops about lackadaisically, never really developing the mundane theme. Sales prospects very dim.
—*Besa.*

Mais Ou Et Donc Ornicar
(FRENCH-COLOR)

Paris, Feb. 25.

A Mallia Films release of a Mallia Films-Bertrand van Effenterre-Herbert de Zaltza production. Stars Geraldine Chaplin, Brigitte Fossey. Directed by Bertrand van Effenterre. Screenplay by Bertrand van Effenterre and Dominique Woldon; camera (color) Nurith Aviv, Jean-Louis Melun, Thierry Jault; sound, Pierre Gamet, Alain Lachassagne, Bernard Chaumeil, Patrice Noia; editing, Joele van Effenterre; art direction, Max Berto; music, Antoine Duhamel. Reviewed at Salle CELTEC, Paris, Feb. 22, '79. Running time: 110 MINS.

Isabelle	Geraldine Chaplin
Anne	Brigitte Fossey
Michel	Jean-Francois Stevenin
Philippe	Didier Flamand
Vincent	Jean-Jacques Biraud

In its concern with the problems of the couple, Bertrand van Effenterre's "Mais Ou Et Donc Ornicar" is part of the recent trend in French films toward intimate examination of sexual and emotional relationships. But unlike the huis clos of films like Jacques Doillon's "La Femme Qui Pleure" this is a private film that opens onto public vistas, exploring human bonds and the difficulties of communication.

In the story's foreground: two women, both eager to assert themselves in responsible professional posts. Isabelle, having decided upon a separation from the man she still loves in order to have her own life, directs a video unit for sociological research, seeking to communicate and help her subjects, the tenants of a large apartment block. Anne still lives with husband and children but has little time for them: she has broken a professional barrier by landing a job as head mechanic in a garage. Their exultation is short-lived; they meet with incomprehension and isolation. Isabelle cannot understand the reticence of her interviewees before the video cameras; Anne finds a chasm between her and her unhappy husband as well as new lines of demarcation in her work.

Around them move other characters and silhouettes in counterpoint, particularly Anne's husband, lonely and bewildered by the new self-assertion of women that has alienated him from his wife and children.

Van Effenterre and his co-scenarist, sociologist Dominique Wolton, have made an intelligent and affecting film that avoids being a dry social tract thanks to the generally fine quality of observation of script and direction. Their stance is neither pro- or anti-feminist; they try only to take stock of the emotional damage that is an unavoidable consequence of any major social change.

The curious title is a mnemonic device used by French schoolchildren to recall grammatical conjunctions. This student gimmick obliquely touches on the film's themes: the difficulty of connecting with others, the ineffectuality of rote emotional responses to new situations. Title may also refer to film's framing incident: the mute, inexplicable bond of affection between a child and the strange teenager who has carried her off. Based on an actual event, this silent, tantalizing bond is posited against the futile efforts of the main characters to articulate their feelings.

Van Effenterre asserts a fine sensibility with this, his second film. (His first, "Erica Minor," dates back to 1973). He is a particularly able director of actors — the film is rich in its performances. Brigitte Fossey, Geraldine Chaplin and Jean-Francois Stevenin give their roles sober vitality and secondary roles are excellently filled. —*Len.*

Prisonniers de Mao
(Prisoners of Mao)
(FRENCH-COLOR)

Paris, March 8.

A C.C.F.C. release of a Stephan-Films production. Scenario (uncredited) based on "Prisoner of Mao" by Jean Pasqualini in collaboration with Rudolph Chelminski. Directed by Vera Belmont. Features entire cast. Camera (color), Jean-Marie Esteve, Pierre Boffety, Daniel Bernard, Wang Sheng; sound, Pierre Befve, Dominique Hennequin; art direction, Ku Ching Tjen; editing, Anne-Marie Deshayes; Annick Breuil, Elisabeth Graine; historical advisor, Jean Pasqualini. Reviewed at Quintette cinema, Paris, March 5, '79. Running time: 110 MINS.

Cast: Liu Tsung Hui, Hung Liu, Chang Feng, Hu Pao Hsiang, Ching Yung Hsiang, Meng Yuan, Lee Ying, Wang Yu, Pao Jo Wang.

Vera Belmont's "Prisoners of Mao" is based on the actual experiences of Jean Pasqualini, a French citizen father Corsican, mother Chinese living in China at the time of of the Communist takeover in 1957. Uneasy in the new Communist society, Pasqualini was arrested as a counter-revolutionary and condemned to 12 years of, not imprisonment, but work-enforced "reeducation." In 1964 the establishment of diplomatic relations between France and China won Pasqualini curtailment of his sentence. He was escorted to the borders and expelled, leaving behind him his family. Pasqualini recorded his ordeal in a book, "Prisoner of Mao," first published in English in 1973. It is the immediate basis for the film.

Belmont's film appositely dedicated to George Orwell has the virtues of careful dedication and filmic intelligence. Shot in Taiwan and Hong Kong with a cast of non-professionals, the film blocks out the major stages of Pasqualini's (here named Perrini) descent through the several circles of Maoist hell and his abrupt re-emergence into the air of physical and psychological freedom.

Film is especially viable in its documentation of Maoist prison methods. The Chinese incarceration is particularly insidious in the way it reduces camaraderie among prisoners by turning them against each other, making each man the guardian and "educator" for his neighbor. The horrible irony is unmistakable: Chinese penal life is merely a claustrophobic extension of the workers' paradise, with less options. Each milieu is a metaphor for the other.

Well-shot and edited, the film is not without serious shortcomings. The necessity of encompassing the entire period of Pasqualini's imprisonment sacrifices indepth probing of the protagonist's psychological vicissitudes he remains at best a sort of pathetic guide, eyes wide open on this absurd microcosm of Chinese totalitarianism. And the obvious limitation of means and acting ability now and then vitiates the visceral impact of scenes that should make us cringe. One comes away from the film dismayed but not profoundly shaken. "Prisonniers of Mao" is a good film that falls short of being an excellent one.

Some notes of interest: Pasqualini himself appears briefly in the film in the role of the arresting officer: And the Chinese Embassy in Paris has requested withdrawal of the film from French cinemas. Nothing doing. —Len.

Oscar, Kina Y El Laser
(Oscar, Kina and the Laser)
(SPANISH-COLOR)

Madrid, Feb. 17.

Signo P.C. production. Exec producer, Salvador Porqueras. Directed by Jose Maria Blanco. Features entire cast. Screenplay, Jose Maria Blanco, Salvador Porqueras, based on story by Carmen Kurtz; camera (Eastmancolor), Juan Gelpi; music, Castro Dario; editor, Ramon Cuadreny; special effects, Juan Palleja. Reviewed at Cine Cartago, Madrid, Feb. 16, '79. Running time: 92 MINS.
Oscar . . . . Jose Manuel Alonso
Oscar . . . . Manuel Alberto
Tony . . . . Carlos Castellanos
Maruxina . . . . Monica Garcia
Felisa . . . . Dora Santacreu
Jim . . . . Jose Ballester
Tadeo . . . . Cesar Ojinaga

Oscar is a little boy from Barcelona who builds a home-made laser ray machine, and together with his friend, a goose, Kina, sets off to rainy Galicia province to rescue a little boy who has been kidnapped by a mob of baddies. The

laser machine, which he keeps in a wooden box, has a personality of its own and not only talks to Oscar, but enables him to become invisible at the crucial moments when he's escaping from the bumbling thugs or needs to get a free meal or a gratis ride on a plane.

Some of the younger matinee moppet audiences may go for the shenanigans, which become brisker in the second half after a rather slow start. Thesping, direction and technical credits are okay. —Besa.

Berlin Film Fest

Meetings With Remarkable Men
(BRITISH-COLOR)

Berlin, March 13.

Remar Productions (Stuart Lyons) release and production. Features entire cast. Directed by Peter Brook. Screenplay, Jeanne Salzmann, Brook from the book by G.I. Gurdjieff; camera (Eastmancolor), Gilbert Taylor; editor, John Jympson; music, Thomas De Hartman, Laurence Rosenthan. Reviewed at Berlin Film Fest (competing), March 1, '79. Running time, 110 MINS.
Gurdjieff . . . . Dragan Maksimovic
Prince . . . . Terence Stamp
Skridlov . . . . Athol Fugard
Father . . . . Gerry Sundquist
Pogassian . . . . Donald Sumpter
Giovanni . . . . Tom Fleming

Film is theatre director and experimentalist Peter Brook's seventh film. He has tried to give a visual reflection of mysticism, which is hard indeed. For here is a film that starts with a narrative flair but then tapers off to a more pedestrian level as the protagonist ends his search for teachers who can give him the balance of religion, science and insight into human nature he is seeking.

Pic is based on the memoirs of George Gurdjieff who in the 20s formed a sort of sector school where he tried to pass on his knowledge to people. But pic is mainly concerned with his quest. As a young boy in some part of Russia he decides he must find out what man's real nature is.

He sets out over Asia and meets people also wanting to find out about the essence of life. They track down ancient schools and he finally, after losing many friends, founds a school where dance and study have seemingly been able to balance man's mixed nature of good and evil and rational and religious outlooks.

The beginning has some interesting revelations on Gurdjieff's feeling about the illusive aspects of life he finds hidden by convention and his first brush of mortality, where, with a rival, he does a sort of Russian roulette bit as they hide in craters in a cannon-firing range.

But trying to pin down his search, and eventual finding of solace in

dance and meditation, is finally picturesque, repetitive and unrevealing. Brook still remains essentially a theatrical talent and here his use of ritual dancing, cursory plot angles and talk are rarely given a truly visual insight and dramatic pitch to keep film from falling into tedious stretches.

Acting is acceptable though a bit posey with fine lensing and good technical quality for a film made entirely on location in Asian and Eastern locales. Film calls for specialized handling but its theme of a search for absolutes and a meaning to life might find this some youthful audiences with proper placement.

Actually, the life of Gurdjieff in Europe applying his teaching might have made a more viable vehicle. Maybe that can emerge as "Meetings With Remarkable Men 2" though this pic needs careful work indeed to find a commercial niche for itself. — Mosk.

Genese D'Un Repas
(Origins of a Meal)
(FRENCH-DOCU-B&W)

Berlin, March 1.

Luc Moullet Productions release and production. Written and directed by Luc Moullet. Camera (black and white), Richard Copans, Patrick Frederich. Reviewed at Berlin Film Fest Youth Forum (noncompeting), Feb. 28, '79. Running time, 117 MINS.

What starts out as a tongue-in-cheek idea turns into an unusual probing of the exploitation of the third world in re foodstuffs by France, and, it is implied, other more advanced nations. Ex-critic Luc Moullet is eating tunafish and bananas with a friend and then begins to talk about how these foods finally reach the consumers.

Moullet interviews tunafish canners who have very French labels on their cans but admit much of it comes from Senegal. Moullet is then in Africa and interviews exploited workers and fisherman who get a small part of the pay given over to French fishermen working there.

Old cliches are trotted out about white supremacy. He also looks into the big banana republic, Ecuador, and the way bananas get various different labels of origins to suit the markets. Film may be overlong, dirgelike, but Moullet ably makes his points and also notes he managed to get advance aid for this film but getting it to the public may be more difficult.

It should make fine tv fodder, show up at special economic meetings and symposiums and make its dent at festivals. Theatrical outlets are difficult but pic could possibly find specialized and school outlets on its clear if drawn out look at food distribution. Viewers might think twice about what

they are eating after this film, especially if it is tunafish and bananas. —Mosk.

Die Erste Polka
(The First Polka)
(WEST GERMAN-COLOR)

Berlin, March 6.

Bavaria Atelier release of NDF/Bavaria Atelier production. Features entire cast. Directed by Klaus Emmerich. Screenplay, Helmut Krapp from the book by Von Horst Bienek; camera (Eastmancolor), Michael Ballhaus; editor, Hannes Nikel; music, Edward Aniol. Reviewed at Berlin Film Fest (competing), Feb. 28, '79. Running time: 105 MINS.
Valeska . . . . Maria Schell
Leo Maria . . . . Erland Josephson
Montag . . . . Guido Wieland
Wondrak . . . . Ernst Stankovski
Josel . . . . Marco Kruger
Ulla . . . . Miriam Geissler
Tante Lucie . . . . Eva Maria Bauer
Heiko . . . . Marcus Stolberg

Why did it take a well wrought but melodramatic tv series, "Holocaust," to make such a drastic impression on Germany and other countries about the horrific concentration camp system after so many more probing films and documentaries on this sorry subject? Apparently, it was time for both older and younger people to face up to and cope with this past.

Also, it was evident that West German filmmakers were also trying to make films about the war, anti-Semitism and guilts of the era though they often seemed a bit too introspective, pussyfooting and even a evasive. Now this film deals with the part of Germany that was on the Polish border, with part of it full of German-speaking people within Poland itself.

It is a town on the German side, albeit also affected by Polish culture and people, where this literary period piece takes place. It uses a stolid middle class family as its focal point a few days before the German invasion of Poland and the beginning of World War II.

Maria Schell is the imperious, cold mother of the family with a sickly, bedridden husband. Her teenage son is getting mixed up with Hitler youth, but still respects a man the family is allowing to stay in cabin on their land who is Jewish though he had converted. Nazi law made him so.

The boy ends up killing a soldier who is attacking his girlfriend by hitting him on the head. The Jew gives him money to go off and then commits suicide when a German soldier comes to his door. But the soldier was looking for the dead soldier who had been billeted with the family.

There is a wedding of the daughter of the house to a soldier where the Pole mixes with German dances and the local priest makes a speech that Polish and

German cultures are inextricably bound together. There is the Nazi trumped-up attack on the local radio station blamed on the Polish and one of the reasons for the invasion.

It is a solidly-made but finally cold film that adds nothing new to that period. Pic is lacking in true emotional insights into the early days before the last World War in a border area torn between two ways of life. Local chances appear more indicated. —*Mosk.*

Eine Frau Mit Verantwortung
(A Woman With Responsibilities)
(WEST GERMAN-COLOR-16m)

Berlin, Feb. 26.

Eikon Film, ZDF release and production. Features entire cast. Written and directed by Ula Stockl. Camera (Color), Mario Masini; editor, Beate Levertow. Reviewed at Berlin Film Fest (non-competing), Feb. 25. '79. Running time, 72 MINS.
Helga .... Christina Scholz
Father .... Nikolaus Dutsch
Husband .... Erwin Keusch
Friend .... Philippe Nahoun

At first, this film offers a simple, surface look at a teenage girl who runs the family for her father after the mother has left them. But then, astute observation leads to the girl's breakdown. She simply can not cope on her own, having avoided true acceptance of her own responsibilities, due to her father's well meaning but overly protective ways.

She is allowed to go to work in Paris where she has her first affair. Then she returns home due to her father's insistence, meets a young man and marries him. A child is soon born and then she is too quickly pregnant again.

Unable to cope, she slowly begins to slip into a sort of schizophrenic state as she tries to keep some semblance of balance by insisting on cleanliness. However, she can not seem to get anything clean, almost allows her child to drown and finally needs psychiatric help.

Film's deceptively slow treatment finally pays off as the insights into her predicament and inability to mature grow as she slips into mental illness.

Directed with ease, film lacks a dramatic edge. It could still find its way at fests and other specialized outlets. —*Mosk.*

They Are Their Own Gifts
(U.S.-DOCU-COLOR-16M)

Berlin, March 2.

Rhodes-Murphy Venture release and production. Directed and conceived by Lucille Rhodes, Margaret Murphy. Camera (Eastmancolor), Babete Mangolte; editor, Susan Fanshel, Rhodes, Murphy; music, Susanna Nason. Reviewed at Berlin Film Fest (non-competing), March 1, '79. Running time, 52 MINS.

A perceptive look at three artists whose works have spanned a good part of this century. Film adroitly intersperses still pictures, footage of the times and interviews with poet Muriel Rukeyser, choreographer Anna Sokolow and painter Alice Neel.

Rukeyser is a gusty woman who fought for civil rights in the '30s. Her poems exalt life but touch on the horror of war and political assassination. She is still fighting to help persecuted people and recites her poems with force and tells of her life with disarming lightness.

Anna Sokolow imbued her dance work with reflections on the Spanish Civil War as well as Jewish persecution and ghetto loneliness. Alice Neel is a perky portrait painter whose work touched on many important labor leaders and pictured events over her long life. Like the others, she has a fine presence. —*Mosk.*

El Corazon Del Bosque
(Heart of the Forest)
(SPANISH-COLOR)

Berlin, March 13.

Arandano S.A. release and production. Features entire cast. Directed by Manuel Gutierrez Aragon. Screenplay, Luis Megino, Aragon; camera (Eastman-color), Teo Escamilla; editor, Jose Salcedo. Reviewed at Berlin Film Fest (competing), March 2, '79. Running time, 105 MINS.
Juan .... Norman Briski
Amparo .... Angela Molina
Andarin .... Luis Politti
Suso .... Victor Valverde
Atilano .... Santiago Ramos

The Civil War and its aftermath are a natural Spanish film theme since the death of Franco and the democratization of the country. Treated with symbolical and hermetic methods during Franco's lifetime, this film has not shaken off that approach.

It is a rather murky tale of a holdout loyalist who is still up in the hills 10 years after the war. He is helped by the people in the valley and constant police hounding cannot stop him. A young man from these surroundings, who had left the country after the war, returns to try to get the rebel down.

He sees his sister who, unknown to him, has been the man's mistress. His attempts to reach him are frustrated as lashing rains often come down as he tries to get to this outmoded symbol. New ways of external resistance to Franco are now on.

The film does prove that the rain in Spain is not only on the plains. The man finally gets to the almost mythical rebel who is infested with vermin and disease and considers everybody traitors to the lost cause.

He is shot down by the man who had come to get him out of pity or duty. But the killer is picked up by the police, probably turned in by his sister though she now hated the anarchic rebel and was going to be married.

But after prison the man comes back to his old home which had again gotten to him during his obsessive hunt for the last holdout of the war. Direction is florid and somewhat pretentious. There may be more meaning for locals in this film, than for offshore audiences, on its allusions. —*Mosk.*

The Bell Jar
(COLOR)

Did you always hate your mother?

Avco Embassy Release of a Larry Peerce/Robert A. Goldston production. Produced by Jerrold Brandt, Jr. and Michael Todd Jr. Directed by Larry Peerce. Stars Marilyn Hassett, Julie Harris, Anne Jackson, Barbara Barrie, Robert Klein. Screenplay, Marjorie Kellogg, based on the novel by Sylvia Plath; camera (color), Gerald Hirschfeld; production design, John Robert Lloyd; costumes, Donald Brooks; music, Gerald Fried; editor, Marvin Wallowitz; set decoration, Don Holtzman and Paul Heffernan; assistant director, Steve Barnett. Reviewed at Cinema I, N.Y., March 12, '79. Running time: 107 MINS.
Esther .... Marilyn Hassett
Mrs. Greenwood .... Julie Harris
Dr. Nolan .... Anne Jackson
Jay Cee .... Barbara Barrie
Lenny .... Robert Klein
Joan .... Donna Mitchell
Doreen .... Mary Louise Weller
Mr. Gilling .... Scott McKay
Buddy .... Jameson Parker
Marco .... Thaao Penghlis
Hilda .... Carlo Monferdini
Betsy .... Debbie McLeod
Bea Ramsey .... Meg Mundy
Vikki St. John .... Elizabeth Hubbard
Toni LaBouchere .... Karen Howard

Despite some decent performances, "The Bell Jar," based on the late poet Sylvia Plath's autobiographical novel, evokes neither understanding or sympathy for the plight of its heroine, Esther Greenwood, the epitome of a straight-A, golden-girl-overachiever, who is mentally "coming apart at the seams." As played by Marilyn Hassett, who has a cool, "Seventeen" magazine kind of prettiness, Esther emerges as a selfish, morbid little prig. She eventually confesses to hating her mother, admirably played by the admirable Julie Harris, presumably because her mother refuses to wallow in the details of her father's death with her.

Marjorie Kellogg's screenplay seems fairly faithful to the novel's spirit, though there are some silly bits of dialogue. For example, when Esther's boyfriend Buddy, played as a slightly bright, all-American clod by Jameson Parker, tells her she was stupid for taking an overdose of barbiturates, she might have died, the whole scene echoes Robert Benchley's comment to Dorothy Parker on one of her many suicide attempts, "Dotti, you've got to stop this or you're going to make yourself sick." Esther informs Buddy that she was not stupid but sick and uses her sickness on him as if it were a badge of honor.

Larry Peerce's direction too often plods and fifteen minutes into the film provides a sense of headachey dullness. Things perk up when Barbara Barrie comes on as a bitchy magazine editor who has worked her way up through the ranks. Mary Louise Weller nicely limns a Southern belle with hopeless dreams and

Donna Mitchell is properly spaced out as one of Esther's fellow sufferers who has lesbian tendencies. Anne Jackson has little more to do than look sympathetic and motherly while Robert Klein as a cowboy-styled disc jockey is mostly silly.

Donald Brooks' costumes are the perfect evocation of 50's style, the film's time period, and the color of Gerald Hirschfeld's camera, especially in the outdoor scenes, is almost too pretty.

Mental illness is neither a pleasant or a romantic subject. Too many healthy people find it difficult to sympathize with physical sickness let alone mental. "The Bell Jar" doesn't help the cause by exploiting the symptoms and making them almost glamorous. The causes of mental illness are cumulative and many and not the simplistic one the screenwriter and Plath's critics are ramming down throats: that she felt abandoned by her father and wanted to join him in death. —*Lee*.

Boulevard Nights
(COLOR)

Far cry from "The Warriors," which fact may help or not at the b.o.

Hollywood, March 6.

Warner Bros. release of a Tony Bill-Bill Benenson production. Exec producer, Tony Bill. Produced by Bill Benenson. Directed by Michael Pressman. Features entire cast. Screenplay, Desmond Nakano; camera (color), John Bailey; editor, Richard Halsey; music, Lalo Schifrin; production design, Jackson DeGovia; sound, Robert Gravenor, Kenneth Isley; assistant director, Ramiro Jaloma. Reviewed at Market Street screening room, Venice, Calif., March 5, '79. (MPAA Rating: R). Running time: 102 MINS.
Raymond Avila .... Richard Yniguez
Chuco Avila ....Danny De La Paz
Shady Landeros .... Marta Du Bois
Gil Moreno .... James Victor
Mrs. Avila ....Betty Carvalho
Mrs. Landeros .... Carmen Zapata
Big Happy .... Gary Cervantes
Mr. Landeros ....Victor Millan
Toby .... Roberto Covarrubias

To label "Boulevard Nights" simply another gang picture because its milieu is the streets of East Los Angeles would be doing the Tony Bill-Bill Benenson production a disservice. Unfortunately, the film fails to carve out a separate identity of its own, rehashing a familiar story about inter-family conflicts. Given the adverse publicity that has accompanied previous gang pix, "Boulevard Nights" has an uphill ballyhoo struggle ahead of it, though the publicity itself may well draw helpful notice.

The decision to film "Boulevard Nights" on location in the barrios, using a largely Hispanic cast, is admirable, but does not automatically provide a raison d'etre for the pic. Desmond Nakano's original screenplay has to prove itself on dramatic, as well as sociological, grounds, a goal only partially realized.

Authenticity is the key here, and director Michael Pressman has accurately captured the sense of despair in this community, when the only alternative to sniffing paint fumes is a job reupholstering custom car interiors. Richard Yniguez plays a graduate of the VGV gang, who still maintains his ties with the group because of his younger brother, Danny De La Paz.

Yniguez' g.f., Marta du Bois, has dreams of upward social mobility, but is unable to shake him loose from his ties to the machismo competition of "hopping" hydraulic car lifts. De La Paz, meanwhile, becomes heavily involved in a gang war, until a pat dramatic crisis wraps up the film in a depressing and inconclusive fashion.

While the acting throughout "Boulevard Nights" is first-rate, especially from Yniguez, du Bois and screen newcomer De La Paz, there simply isn't enough to distinguish the pic from a number of previous ethnic-set mellers. Realism is no substitution for dramatic complexity, and for all its good intentions, "Boulevard Nights" never manages to touch on the extraordinary, rather than mundane, emotions.

Supporting cast is highly effective, with James Victor noteworthy as an employer who tries to help De La Paz, and Gary Cervantes excelling as a gang member immersed in revenge. John Bailey has shot the film in day-glo colors reflective of the every-present "low-rider" cars, and other tech credits are fine. —*Poll*.

Cristo si e fermato a Eboli
(Christ Stopped at Eboli)
(ITALIAN-FRENCH-COLOR)

Rome, March 17.

A Titanus release in Italy. Produced by Franco Cristaldi and Nicola Carraro for RAI-TV 2 and Vides Cinematografica (Rome)-Action Films (Paris). Directed by Francesco Rosi. Stars Gian Maria Volonte. Written by Francesco Rosi, Tonino Guerra, Raffaele La Capria, from a novel by Carlo Levi; camera (color), Pasqualino De Santis; art director, Andrea Crisanti; editor, Ruggero Mastroianni; music, Piero Piccioni.

Reviewed at Flamma Theatre, Rome, March 7, '79. Running time: 150 MINS.
Carlo Levi ....Gian Maria Volonte
Don Luigi Magalone...... Paolo Bonacelli
Baron Rotundo ....Alain Cuny
Luisa Levi .... Lea Massari
Giulia ....Irene Papas
Don Traiella .... Francois Simon

Francesco Rosi's "Christ Stopped at Eboli," a film adaptation of the autobiographical novel of the same title by writer-painter Carlo Levi, paints a stunning portrait of the life of Lucanian peasants in Mussolini's Italy, but it unfortunately remains a portrait that never really fleshes out.

The shadows and textures of the rude countryside in southern Italy provide the backdrop for "Christ Stopped" which is more an anthropological document than a narrative film. The superstitions, work rhythms, living conditions and religious practices of the villagers are superbly illustrated (Pasqualino De Santis' photography often takes your breath away), but the audience never really gets under the skin of these people who live out their miserable lives like their ancestors did thousands of years before them.

The film should have considerable success in specialized cinemas if only on the strength of Levi's extraordinary book.

The film's (and book's) title comes from a popular saying that insists Christ never went beyond Eboli, a city on the edge of the Lucania region south of Naples. Modern civilization never pentrated the mountainous areas of Italy's poorest region. "Christ never came," wrote Levi, "nor did individual spirit, nor hope, nor the link between cause and effect, reason and history."

The film begins with these reflections of Levi in his Turin studio, then follows a younger Levi from the train station in Eboli, over rough terrain to a small village in Lucania. Levi was sent there by Mussolini in 1935 as a "confinato," or political exile, for his anti-fascist activities during the Ethiopian War.

Alone except for the company of a dog who befriended him at the Eboli station, Levi — an intellectual from the north — marvels at this strange southern world. A visit from his sister (played admirably by Lea Massari) and a confrontation with the local fascist chief (the latter scene, dominated by Paolo Bonacelli, is one of the best of the film) allow Levi's own reflections to be exposed, but happily Gian Maria Volonte underplays his role leaving center stage to the peasants themselves.

Presented in a series of often choppy and confusing scenes, the villagers — a drunken priest (Francois Simon), a crazy gravedigger, a returning emigrant who dreams of New York, the old men who pass their time in the village square and especially Giulia (played brilliantly by Greek actress Irene Papas), Levi's superstitious cleanig woman — appear too briefly, however, to elicit the empathy that is the stuff of real drama. The peasants remain instead flattened portraits on a mysterious canvas. — *Argo*.

Breakthrough
(Sergeant Steiner)
(WEST GERMAN-COLOR)

Munich, March 10.

A Palladium (Hubert Lukowski)-Rapid Film Production, Munich. (No U.S. distrib yet). Directed by Andrew V. McLaglen. Stars Richard Burton, Rod Steiger, Helmuth Griem, Curt Jurgens, Robert Mitchum, Michael Parks. Exec producers Wolf C. Hartwig, Ted Richmond. Produced by Achim Sellus, Alex Winitzky. Screenplay, Tony Williamson; camera, (Eastmancolor, Panavision), Tony Imi; music, Peter Thomas; sound, David Hildyard, Peter Horrocks; editor Raymond Poulton; asst. director, Burt Batt; special effects, Sass Bedig; production designer, Gerhard Janda; military advisers, Maj. Gen. Bernadiner and Lt. Col. (ret.) Sam Magill. Reviewed at Mathaeser Filmpalast, Munich, March 9, '79. Running time: 115 MINS.
Sgt. Steiner .... Richard Burton
General Webster .... Rod Steiger
Colonel Rogers .... Robert Mitchum
General Hoffmann ....Curt Jurgens
Major Stransky .... Helmuth Griem
Sgt. Anderson .... Michael Parks
Corp. Krueger ....Klaus Loewitsch
Yvette ....Veronique Vendell
Capt. Kirstner .... Joachim Hansen

Hoping for the b.o. breakthrough in the U.S., producer Wolf C. Hartwig had the action in his sequel to "Cross of Iron" shifted to the Western front and adorned it with a good look at the American side. The second part tells the story of Sergeant Steiner (Richard Burton) as it continues after the Russian front. Steiner is transferred to the West, is embroiled in the German July 20 anti-Hitler conspiracy. His friend Stransky (Helmuth Griem) is killed. Steiner saves U.S. Colonel Robert Mitchum's life and survives himself.

The screenplay serves less here as the base for spectacular fireworks (as it was in the Peckinpah pic) but moves more into human fields of tension. There is still enough tough action though to satisfy patrons who are lookigg for it. The story line spreads good and evil, loveworthy and less loveworthy characters adroitly on both sides so that everybody finds something to his taste.

It would, however, be unjust to call the film speculative. Just the contrary: the story is credible and the pic is definitely not a western clad in World War II uniforms. Although the film simplifies, it does not distort and with the help of expertly used simplification it both entertains and gives a pretty objective history lesson. Just in passing and embedded in good suspense it shows that not all German soldiers were fanatic Nazis but human beings, at the same time conveying the feeling of the ever present evil power of the regime.

Andrew McLaglen led his stars and cast (especially outstanding Burton, Mitchum, Steiger, Griem, Loewitsch, Parks) so subtle that the strived-for human emotions really become captivating. Curt Jurgens as a German general, who committs suicide after his participation in the plot to kill Hitler is uncovered, has not been so good in a long time.

Considering the top credits, the gripping story and the entertaining value, pic should do as good as any high budget American war film in the U.S. and certainly better than part one. —*Koci.*

Old Boyfriends
(COLOR)

Offbeat and perceptive look at long-lost love needs careful nurturing.

Hollywood, March 29.

Avco Embassy release of an Edward R. Pressman Production. Produced by Edward R. Pressman, Michele Rappaport. Executive producer, Paul Schrader. Stars Talia Shire, Richard Jordan, John Belushi, Keith Carradine. Directed by Joan Tewkesbury. Written by Paul Schrader, Leonard Schrader; camera (color), William A. Fraker; film editor, Bill Reynolds; art director, Peter Jamison; asst. director, Tony Bishop; sound, Bill Kaplan; costumes, Tony Faso, Suzanne Grace; unit publicist, Wally Beene.
Reviewed at Television City Studios, Hollywood, March 16, '79. (MPAA Rating: R) Running Time: **103 MINS.**

Diane Cruise ....Talia Shire
Jeff Turrin ....Richard Jordan
Wayne Van Til ....Keith Carradine
Eric Katz ....John Belushi
Dr. Hoffman..............John Houseman
Art Kopple ....Buck Henry
Dylan Turrin ....Nina Jordan
Sam The Fisherman .....Gerritt Graham
Sandy.........................P.J. Soles
Mrs. Van Til ....Bethel Leslie
Pamela Shaw ....Joan Hotchkis
David Brinks ....William Bassett

The premise of "Old Boyfriends" is an intriguing and universal one, the fantasy of revisiting lovers out of an individual's past. Despite dramatic promise, and some weighty marquee names, the Avco Embassy pickup of the Edward R. Pressman production will need special handling to find its desired audience. Word-of-mouth will be a critical factor here.

A similar plot hook was employed in Julien Duvivier's 1937 French film, "Carnet De Bal" (Life Dances On), in which a widow seeks out her old dance hall suitors, and discovers them in various stages of dissipation.

Script by Paul Schrader, who exec produced, and his brother, Leonard, is contemporary and grounded in realism, right down to the shifting morals which have marked male-female relationships in the last 25 years. In this case, the femme' (Talia Shire) is a clinical psychologist who roots into her past after a failed suicide attempt.

Shire's odyssey takes her across America to old beaux including her college sweetheart (Richard Jordan), high school romance (John

Belushi) and first adolescent love (Keith Carradine). The experience proves to be disquieting. While Shire's motivation for the journey into her past remains murky, the consequences provide ample ammunition for the Schraders and novice director Joan Tewkesbury.

A protege of Robert Altman, Tewkesbury, who scripted his "Nashville," employs similar loosely narrative techniques, with the Shire character holding together the series of set pieces. She finds unexpected companionship from Jordan, now a docu filmmaker, wreaks a suitably adolescent revenge on Belushi, who humiliated her in high school, and seduces Carradine, brother of her now-dead childhood crush.

What's missing, in both the Schraders' script and Tewkesbury's direction, is a strong sense of just why Shire is trying to recapture her past, other than idle curiosity. As in other Schrader pix, the characters are carefully distanced, and only Jordan projects any real warmth. The overwhelming sense of alienation may prove the pic's biggest drawback.

Performances are uniformly high-grade, especially Shire, a model of feminine complexity, Carradine, perfect as the addled brother, and Jordan. Casting of Belushi, ironically, works against the thrust of "Old Boyfriends." As leader of a rock band once called Ricky & The Red eyes, and now dubbed Bloodshot ("just keeping up with the times," he notes), Belushi is so comical as to throw his scenes out of whack, and his segment becomes the weakest of the three.

Buck Henry, John Houseman, Gerritt Graham and Bethel Leslie sparkle in cameo roles. Tech credits are uneven, with Bill Reynolds' editing a bit abrupt, and William Fraker's lensing inconsistent — a scene shot by candlelight is maddening to watch. David Shire contributed a score that sounds like a paean to 1950s exploitation pix.
—*Poll.*

Poitin
(IRISH-COLOR-16m)

Hollywood, March 1.

A Cinegael production. Produced, directed, edited by Bob Quinn. Features entire cast. Screenplay, Colm Bairead; camera (color), Seamus Deasy; art direction, Frankie MacDonncha. Reviewed at Universal Studios, March 1, '79. Running time: **65 MINS.**
A poteen-maker ....Cyril Cusack
His agent ....Niall Toibin
Another agent ....Donal McCann
Daughter of
 the poteen-maker .Mairead Ni Conghaile
Garda ....MacDara O Fatharta
A publican ....Sean O Coisdealbha

If nothing else, "Poitin" deserves a nook in film history as

allegedly the first fictional feature ever shot in Gaelic. In its scope and methods, picture resembles nothing so much as the early efforts of the burgeoning film industries of various Third World nations, but since the landscape is more familiar and the situation less overtly politicized, it's going to be an uphill battle even to be received in quarters normally receptive to minority viewpoints.

For years lip service has been paid to the idea of a native Irish film industry. Over the years John Ford and John Huston locationed there when possible, and in 1957 Ford made "The Rising of the Moon" for Lord Michael Killanin with an all-Irish cast in an attempt to inspire local production. More recently, John Boorman, among big international filmmakers, has championed the cause, but, as has so often happened in the other arts, Irish talents with cinematic aspirations have invariably moved on to England or the U.S. to pursue the muse.

Ironically, director Bob Quinn of County Connemara made "Poitin" with the announced aim of belatedly rectifying some of the sentimental falsifications perpetrated by Ford in "The Quiet Man," set in the same coastal neighborhood, and pointedly cast Cyril Cusack, one of the stars of "The Rising of the Moon," in the lead.

As might be expected, the film fails to match the awesome challenge of "The Quiet Man," but it does offer a contrasting, considerably more bitter view of the impoverished society in the wilds of Western Ireland.

"Poitin" means "moonshine" in Gaelic and Cusack brews the stuff in a remote corner of a bay on which he lives with his daughter. The story, which really unfolds more like a long anecdote, proceeds deliberately and with a characteristic lack of urgency, as two local no-goods run afoul of both the law and the old moonshiner himself in their attempts to dispose of the sack.

Unfortunate aspect of the tale is that, in depicting the frankly stupid, derelict characters at center stage, film insists upon the Irish national tragedy: that they can't help themselves from the temptation of the bottle, that they're hopelessly small-minded and limited in their aims and imagination. That this thesis holds some truth is undeniable, but it can hardly be held up as a satisfactorilly complete rebuttal to the romanticism of "The Quiet Man."

Director Quinn vacillates from scene to scene between a pleasingly light touch and a bitter social view. One scene, in which one of the bumbling thugs steals into the local constabulary to retrieve some brew a policeman has confiscated and then passing out from drinking, is

delightfully whimsical in the classical Irish tradition. On the other hand, Cusack's extraordinarily severe final revenge on his hapless henchmen is unbelievable in the slickness with which it is executed.

Ultimately, the mere existence of "Poitin" is more admirable than the result itself, since it suggests that Ireland may try again to establish a voice in the world cinema. —*Cart.*

It's Me
(DUTCH-COLOR)

Hollywood, Feb. 21.

A Nico Crama production. Produced by Nico Crama. Directed, written by Frans Zwartjes, Camera (color) Zwartjes, Mat van Hensbergen; music, Lodewijk de Boer, Zwartjes; editor, Wouter Snip; decor, Zwartjes, Trix Zwartjes, Floor Peters, Reviewed at 20th Century-Fox Studios Theatre, L.A., Feb. 21, '79. Running time: **68 MINS.**
Woman .... Willeke van Ammelrooy

Beautiful women have served as both the pretext and excuse for countless films since the invention of motion pictures, but rarely has a camera subject come under such close scrutiny as Willeke van Ammelrooy does in "It's Me." A statuesque beauty whose looks conjure up a cross between Isabelle Adjani and Linda Carter and who holds the screen alone for the entire 68-minutes running time, she bathes, talks on the phone, smokes, meditates on her body, dresses up, gets mad, paces around, composes herself, straightens up her room, then cries and laughs after making a climactic phone call. In short, nothing happens in the usual narrative sense, but one is never really bored or tempted to look away for fear of missing yet another astonishing, revealing perspective on van Ammelrooy, such is the perceptiveness with which she is lit and shot.

This is Frans Zwartjes' first feature, after having made over 30 shorts in the Netherlands, and markets for the film are definitely limited to specialized outlets, as it's more an objet d'art than anything else. With a possible nod in the direction of Chantal Ackerman's 1975 avant-garde groundbreaker "Jeanne Dielman," Zwartjes is interested in documenting real time and the minute fluctuations of mood in a relentlessly examined woman. His objectives, however, are not ideological but rather textural, as he experiments with light, shadow and fabrics in a manner occasionally reminiscent of Josef von Sternberg's visual meditations in his septet of films with Marlene Dietrich.

Van Ammelrooy is playing an actress, evidently trying to make up her mind whether or not to accept a proposed role, which provides an acceptable rationale for her extensive posturing and brooding. One says "evidently" because what dialog there is has been purposely garbled and distorted. A moody electronic score by Lodewijk de Boer and Zwartjes covers most of the running time.

On its own terms, "It's Me" is a beautifully realized piece of work, but the bottom line here is really the luminous Willeke van Ammelrooy, who acquits herself more impressively than have many other "directors' discoveries." — *Cart.*

Theatre Girls
(BRITISH-DOCU-B&W-16m)

Hollywood, March 6.

National Film School of London production. Directed, edited by Kimona Longinotto, Claire Pollack; camera (black and white), Longinotto. No other credits available. Reviewed at Paramount Studio Theatre, L.A., March 6, '79. Running time: 82 MINS.

Though the rough sound, grainy b&w printing and occasionally thick Cockney accents will be enough to put off many viewers at first, emotional impact gradually generated by "Theatre Girls" finally overcomes the technical handicaps. Shot at the Theatre Girls Club in Soho, London, this docu on destitute women is necessarily limited in potential by its very nature, but could find outlets on the specialized college circuit and with sociologically and feminist-inclined orgs.

Without explicit editorial comment, portraits are forged of a variety of women, mostly old, many alcoholic, some on the verge of genuine lunacy, who are shunned by society and without personal resources. At the Theatre Club they wait out the remainder of their sad existences in a run-down townhouse under the minimal supervision of welfare workers and an imposing black cook. Latter resents the intrusion of the camera crew more than any of the inmates, at one point throwing potatoes at the inquisitive lens. General frame of mind of the women is summed up by one who plaintively admits, "I've had no luck for over 20 years. I have no happiness."

Nonetheless, some of the subjects reveal themselves and their life histories to an extent that supersedes the inherently depressing nature of the enterprise. One with a distinctly upper-class accent who resembles an aged Lauren Bacall tells of her losing battle with the bottle in deeply moving terms, a chronic shoplifter insists that, "All I want is one silver tea service and I'll be finished," and an emaciated youngster who looks 16 going on 60 gets her legal drug fix while endlessly repeating that she's "registered ... registered."

It's harrowing but unavoidably human stuff, filmed unsparingly by a young female team that stayed at

the hostel for two-and-a-half months. Approach is austere and technical aspects make it demanding, but once it's gotten used to it seems appropriate to the overall aims. Pic was made under the auspices of the National Film School of London. —*Cart.*

Iskindiria ... Leh?
(Alexandria ... Why?)
(EGYPTIAN-ALGERIAN-COLOR)

Hollywood, Feb. 21.

A Misr International Films production. Produced, directed by Youssef Chahine. Features entire cast. Screenplay, Chahine, Mohsen Zayed; camera (color), Mohsen Nasr; music, Fouad El Zaheri; editor, Rashida Abdel Salam. Reviewed at 20th Century-Fox Studio Theatre, Los Angeles, February 21, '79. Running time: 133 MINS.
Sarah ....Naglaa Fathi
The Pasha.................Farid Shawki
Morsi ....Ezzat El Alayli
Tommy ....Gerry Sundquist
Yehia .... Mohsen Mohiedine

Cultures converge like assorted zoo animals thrown together into the same cage in "Alexandria ... Why?" by veteran Egyptian filmmaker Youssef Chahine. Well-crafted but erratically constructed, film should prove much more accessible to western viewers than many other Middle Eastern features due to characters' fanatical obsession with things American, but markets will nonetheless probably remain limited to film festivals and other outlets catering to the intelligensia.

Set in the upper classes of society in the historical port city of the title, the story is framed between 1942 and 1945, understandably a highly volatile period in Egypt's history. The British occupation force was already there (and actively disliked), Rommel was closing in from the West, the Italians were not far off and the spectre of a future Palestinian-Jewish conflict was already on the horizon. From the film's perspective, only the Americans, largely because of their movies and in part because they hadn't yet appeared in the area in person, could be idolized, and that they were.

Yehia, a teenager oblivious the prevailing political climate, sits transfixed at the beginning watching MGM musicals (one of the numbers, "I'll Build a Stairway to Paradise," comes from "American in Paris," not made until 1951, but perhaps poetic license can be granted by virtue of the fact that featured singer Georges Guetary is of Egyptian extraction). After a dramatic display of histrionic talent at school and learning that the Pasadena Playhouse offers the best training to be had, Yehia single-mindedly sets his sights on engineering a move to California, which he manages after war's end.

At the same time, a more politically concerned young man continually plots subversive acts against the hated British, even Churchill himself, a homosexual picks up Anglo soldiers for the thrill of threatening them with death, and a beautiful Jewess, pregnant by an Arab, flees with her aristocratic father to South Africa to wait out the Nazi threat.

Coloring all the action is the pervasive influence of American culture, especially its music and movies. Chahine has found inspiration in many of the same sources that Martin Scorsese did for "New York, New York" and though his context is much more distant, a similar attitude of affectionate revisionism applies. Yehia stages a disastrous musical which threatens to put an end to his theatrical ambitions and is bailed out only by the strenuously Capra-esque efforts of his family to raise sufficient funds for his trip to Pasadena within 48 hours.

Cahine's energized, constantly roving camera, as well as the tense, unusual setting, sustain interest through at least the first hour, but as Yehia's efforts to find passage to the States become increasingly frantic, the foregone conclusion is awaited well before it arrives.

Though the film fails to stir the emotions as the best emigrant sagas always have, "Alexandria ... Why?" still offers an unusual kaleidoscopic look at a time and place hitherto unexplored onscreen. —*Cart.*

No Maps On My Taps
(DOCU-COLOR-16m)

Hollywood, March 15.

A GTN production. Produced, directed by George T. Nierenberg; camera (color), Robert Achs, Phil Parmet, Robert Elfstrom, Vic Losic, Ted Churchill, George T. Nierenberg, Paul Goldsmith; music director, Lionel Hampton; musical arrangements, Dick Vance; editor, Paul Barnes; sound, Larry Loewinger, Nigel Nobel, Mike Scott Goldbaum, Peter Hliddal, Chat Gunter. Reviewed at the American Film Institute, March 15, '79. Running time: 58 MINS.
Cast: Sandman Sims, Bunny Briggs, Chuck Green, Lionel Hampton, John Bubbles.

With evident love for its subject and sense of the form's general neglect, "No Maps On My Taps" explores the heritage of tap dancing by focusing on three oldtime Harlem hoofers who carry on in the immortal footsteps of Bill Robinson and John Bubbles. Slickly produced docu is a natural for fests and schools and has already been set for airing on PBS, one of its many backers.

Gotham-based producer-director George T. Nierenberg has brought together three of the best remaining dancers — Sandman Sims, Bunny Briggs and Chuck

Green — and framed their reminiscences around a "competition" amongst the three at Small's Paradise in Harlem. Backed by Lionel Hampton's band, the display of talent here is awesome. As long as these men survive, tap lives.

Their recollections are also of considerable interest, notably those concerning the towering figures of Robinson and Bubbles (who appears in pic talking on the phone with Green from his L.A. home but who can no longer dance due to a recent stroke) and the explanations of how, during the Depression, blacks learned to tap on the street, constantly challenging other sidewalk dancers in an effort to be the best. In a couple of scenes in an open-air bandstand and by the stage door of the Apollo Theatre, Sims delightedly teaches his young son a few steps.

Sandman sums up performers' attitude when he guesses that, "the three of us is probably the last parade," and points out that it still can be hard for them to find many gigs. Unmentioned is racism they may have encountered over the years and the taint of Uncle Tomism that has sometimes been associated with tap, but these gentlemen speak like pure artists existing in space and time somehow apart from temporal considerations. For them tap is the greatest form of dancing. "No Maps On My Taps" happily preserves three of its foremost exemplars. —*Cart.*

Itim
(The Rites Of May)
(FILIPINO-COLOR)

Hollywood, Feb. 24.

Produced and directed by Mike de Leon. Features entire cast. Screenplay, Doy del Mundo, Gil Quito; camera (color), Ely Cruz, Rody Lacap; editor, Ike Jarlego Jr.; music, Max Jocson. No other credits available. Reviewed at Paramount Studio screening room, Feb. 23, 1979. Running time: 116 MINS.
Jun ....Tommy Abuel
Teresa ....Charo Santos
Dr. Torres ....Mario Montenegro
Aling Bebeng ....Moody Diaz
Aling Pining .... Mona Lisa
Rosa ....Susan Valdez

Trying to capture spiritualism on film is like trying to bottle air — it's what you can't see that counts. That fact seems to have been lost on Filipino filmmaker Mike de Leon, whose "The Rites Of May" was released in Asian markets in 1976.

Tale of a young photog whose g.f. keeps getting strange flashes of her missing sister has some potential for suspense, but director de Leon keeps his cast talking about the problem, rather than showing it. Result is a tedious, somnambulent film wrought with religious symbolism that will be meaningless to those unfamiliar with the celebration of Lent in the Near East.

Tommy Abuel plays the lenser, who returns to the family estate out in the sticks, where his paralyzed father's condition is worsening. He develops an attraction for Charo Santos, who immediately picks up bad vibes from Papa, until a seance at the pic's end clues in the father's long-ago dalliance with Santos' sister, and the subsequent abortion that precipitated the girl's death.

Paucity of subtitles doesn't help in clarifying the mysterious goings-on, but the final seance sequence, using sepia-toned flashbacks, is highly effective, and makes all that preceded it look boring in comparison.

Santos, who copped the Asian Film Fest's top actress award, is powerful in the closing moments of "The Rites Of May," but rest of the cast is strictly pro forma. —*Poll.*

Not Everything That Flies Is a Bird
(WEST GERMAN-COLOR-ANIMATED)

Hollywood, Feb. 27.
A Francis J. Stockman production. Produced by Stockman. Directed and written by Borislav Sajtinac. Animator, Branco Ilic; music, special effects, Rolf Adrian. Reviewed at The Burbank Studios, Burbank, Feb. 27, '79. Running time: **80 MINS.**

Second feature-length effort by Yugoslavian animator Borislav Sajtinac is a repetitive, obviously padded hodgepodge which, even at 80 minutes, proves way overlong. Film is comprised of several of Sajtinac's shorts stitched together with some new material, and the seams show. This may initially attract the usual hardcore animation fans worldwide, but can hardly be counted a major effort.

Framing device establishes a cowering, dominated little man experiencing assorted dreams, often featuring an aggressive black bird, and then trying to convince his avicular wife of their validity. Device quickly becomes wearying, as does the similarly ominous nature of what are largely absurdist nightmares. Since anything goes in the realm of dreams, Sajtinac could try to justify his dark flights of fancy by the theory that dreams need not follow any logic but their own. But while the little reveries of the meek man conjuring up Don Quixote and Sancho Panza or imagining a cat magician who has a specialty act with mice might have been diverting as individual short cartoons, it was ill-advised to try to create a coherent whole out of the collection.

Animation style is unmistakably of the stylized, modernistic Eastern European school and is at times eye-catching in individual compositions but lacks the truly fantastic elements necessary to sustain interest at feature length. American accents in the English-language dubbing are slightly at odds with the insistently middle-European self-persecution complex betrayed in the material. —*Cart.*

Armee der Liebenden Oder Aufstand der Perversen
(Army Of Lovers Or Revolt Of The Perverts)
(W. GERMAN-COLOR-DOCU)

Hollywood, March 12.
Produced, directed, written and edited by Rosa von Praunheim, assisted by Mike Shephard. Camera (color), Von Praunheim, Lloyd Williams, Juliana Wang, Michael Oblovitz, Ben van Meter, Nickolai Ursin, John Rome, Bob Schub, Werner Schroter. No other credits available. Reviewed at the American Film Institute, March 12, '79. (No MPAA rating.) Running time: **107 Mins.**

If gays have rights, as indeed they do, then they must also have wrongs — and this film is certainly one of them.

Though his purpose is to protest discrimination against homosexuals in the U.S. and urge them to fight back, German documentarian Rosa von Praunheim does his cause no good with this clumsy, amateurish and underfinanced venture, whose slim hope of appeal beyond the gay audience is virtually eliminated by gratuitious hard-core homosexual sequences.

Von Praunheim's sincerity doesn't make up for the disservice he does his cause by presenting endless parades of flaming exhibitionists who mince and whine about their lot in life. Except for a few more sober reflections, he captures only one segment of the homosexual population — and the least popular and most controversial. So what's the point?

When he stumbles upon something interesting — like lesbian outrage at the appearance of disco queen (and male gay favorite) Grace Jones at a rally — he lets it slip by without probing deeper.

Von Praunheim does introduce the outsider to some new angles, like a gay Nazi blathering an incredible collection of nonsense. But it hardly makes up for the boring hand-holding and kissing in public, which may or may not be a Constitutional right but certainly less important than the right to be left alone in private.

The boredom, though, is unwelcomely relieved at first by a quick flash of hardcore sex, followed by an extended exhibition of male love by Von Praunheim himself. Hired by the S.F. Art Institute to teach a cinema class, the director decided it would be a good project for his students to film him making love to a male porno star.

Which is just the sort of thing the rednecks on the right are frothing about in trying to chase gays out of the schools. Von Praunheim's exhibition, of course, doesn't prove the rightwing point, but it's hard to see how it helps defend his movement. — *Har.*

Begging the Ring
(BRITISH-COLOR-16m)

Hollywood, March 1.
A Colin Gregg Films production. Produced, directed, edited by Colin Gregg. Features entire cast. Screenplay, Gregg, Hugh Stoddart; camera (color), John Metcalfe. No other credits available. Reviewed at Universal Studios, March 1, '79. Running time: **55 MINS.**

Jack Bryant	Danny Simpson
George Bryant	Jon Croft
Deidre Bryant	Janette Legge
Mr. Merrith	Kenneth Midwood
Arthur Collins	Terence Conoley
Captain James	Alan Penn
Private	Brian Capron

With a persistent streak of underlying irony, "Begging the Ring" shows the world closing in on a remote community in North Cornwall in the fall of 1916. Achieving great pictorial effects on a budget of under $20,000, docu filmmaker Colin Gregg here shows promise in the fictional vein. Due to running time and inherent modesty of the production, horizons would seem limited to fests and possibly tv.

In 1916 conscription laws were put into effect in the U.K. for the first time due to the demands of World War I. Pic introduces a young worker in the employ of a local factory owner who's preparing for a wrestling match he thinks he can win. Despite the call of duty, locals urge the youth to put off his service long enough to claim his belt. Needless to say, consequences of such a delay are considerable, but this takes a long time to dawn on the provincials for whom the war seems so remote and meaningless.

Character types are fairly broadly drawn, from the self-important local industrialist to the neighborhood philosopher, but the drama itself is nicely underplayed to allow very gradual buildup of tensions. Particularly impressive is Jon Croft as the youth's rugged father who teaches him wrestling on a stunning stretch of beach. Indeed, the wild beauty of the landscape virtually dominates the film and Gregg has been lucky with the turbulent weather which backdrops much of the exterior action.

Basic thrust of the story is to illustrate the process by which an increasingly international-minded state swallows up its helpless citizens, a large theme treated here in the most minute of terms. It's effectively done withal, carefully structured, even if without any particular dynamism. —*Cart.*

The Tourist Trap
(COLOR)

Wooden plot for live dummies.

Hollywood, March 14.
Compass International/Manson International release of a Charles Band production. Exec Producer, Charles Band. Produced by J. Larry Carroll. Directed by David Schmoeller. Features entire cast. Screenplay, David Schmoeller, J. Larry Carroll; camera (Metrocolor), Nicholas Von Sternberg; music, Pino Donaggio; editor, Ted Nicoloau; sound mixer, Courtney Goodin; special sound effects, Joel Goldsmith; special effects, Rich Helmer; art direction, Robert Burns; set decoration, Amanda Flick; assistant directors, Ron Underwood, David Wyler. Reviewed at Pix Theatre, L.A., March 14, '79. (MPAA Rating: PG). Running time: **85 MINS.**

Slausen	Chuck Connors
Jerry	Jon Van Ness
Molly	Jocelyn Jones
Eileen	Robin Sherwood
Becky	Tanya Roberts
Woody	Keith McDermott
Tina	Dawn Jeffory

Irwin Yablans' Compass International Pictures, which most recently scored heavily at the boxoffice with the thriller "Halloween," delivers another of the genre with "The Tourist Trap." Although pic has some appropriately menacing music and occasionally employs some decent special effects, the plot is too loaded with cliches, from the concept to individual bits of dialog to be taken seriously and not silly enough to be regarded as delightfully bad. Item's outlook appears dim overall, especially with lack of blood and guts that will probably prevent it from catching on as good drive-in fare.

Life-like dummies are the supposed horror-provoking element here, with Chuck Connors serving as their menacing master. Armed with a southern accent, a limp, dressed in overalls and carrying a shotgun, Connors portrays Mr. Slausen, proprietor of "Slausen's Lost Oasis," an endearing country museum that houses some amazingly life-like mannequins. A band of teenagers stumble on Slausen's tucked-away retreat in search of their friend Woody who has wandered off to fix his flat tire.

Aside from the life-like dummy theme being slightly unoriginal, everyone but the kids in the film will early on recognize the similarities between Mr. Slausen and the dummy-like creature terrorizing everything in sight. Rich Helmer has done a nice job with the special effects, but numberous parts of the pic are poorly lit, diminishing that plus. Music by Pino Donaggio is superior but large gaps in the script (like exactly how those dummies are so life-like) by J. Larry Carroll and David Schmoeller, the latter also at the helm, subdue its effectiveness. —*Berg.*

Beethoven 'Fidelio'
(FRENCH-COLOR/B&W)

Paris, March 8.

A Gaumont release of a Sunchild - F.R.3. - Radio France - OCAV - Dept. of Culture and Communication co-production. Produced by Stephane Tchalgadjieff. Directed by Pierre Jourdan. Features entire cast. Israeli Philharmonic Orchestra and the London New-Philharmonic Choir under the direction of Zubin Mehta. No other technical credits provided. Reviewed at Club Publicis, Paris, March 8, '79. Running time: 130 MINS.

Leonore-Fidelio	Gundula Janovitz
Florestan	Jon Vickers
Pizarro	Theo Adams
Rocco	William Wildermann
Marceline	Stella Richmond
Jaquino	Misha Raitzin

(Opera performed in German)

Opera, which often proves indigestible on stage, is almost always unbearable on film. Pierre Jourdan's cinematic rendering of a Beethoven opera bears this out. (Ingmar Bergman's "Magic Flute" is the great exception -Ed.)

Beethoven worked on his "Fidelio" between 1805 and 1814. It grew from his dismayed reaction to Napoleon's crowning himself Emperor of France in 1804. To the composer it was an unforgivable betrayal of the people's trust.

Jourdan's film begins interestingly. As the overture plays magnificently on the soundtrack, we are presented with a montage of sequences from Abel Gance's "Napoleon," one of the most extraordinary achievements of the silent cinema. (The original 5-hour plus version — long thought irretrievably multilated — has been recently restored by English critic-historian Kevin Brownlow.) This fest for the eyes and the ears gives us the necessary context in which Beethoven wrote the opera.

Then everything goes wrong. We are whisked to the chipped splendor of the Roman theatre at Orange. Our expectation is that we are going to get a staid recording of a stage production of the work. No such luck. Jourdan wants to make *cinema* and, to this end, he shoves much of the action into the recesses of the stage and brutalizes it with his camera, which incessantly tracks, plans and zooms. The irritation this produces is aggravated by the nervous editing, dictated by neither dramatic nor cinematic logic. The result is neither a theatrical event nor a cinematic experience.

The actor-singers, who might be theatrically effective in the circumstances of a normal stage version, are made to look ungainly in this new proximity. And the direct sound recording does not do justice to their singing.

Best to stay home and listen to a recording of the opera made under ideal studio conditions. —*Len.*

Dirt
(COLOR)

Will probably bite the dust.

Hollywood, March 14.

American Cinema Releasing Inc. release of a Pacific Films-Sports VIP production. Exec Producers, Michael F. Leone, Roger Riddell. Produced by Allan F. Bodoh, John Patrick Graham. Directed by Eric Karson, Cal Naylor. Written by S.S. Schweitzer, Bud Freidgen, Tom Madigan, music, Dick Halligan; editor; associate producer, Skeeter McKitterick. Reviewed at Director's Guild of American Screening Room. March 14. '79. (MPAA Rating: PG). Running time: 95 MINS.

Cast: R.R. Young, camera, Parnelli Jones, Rick Mears, Mickey Thompson, Bobby Ferro, Malcolm Smith.

As a theatrical release, "Dirt" will undoubtedly have problems since it is essentially a documentary covering the sport of off-road racing, and not even a superior one at that. Outdoor screens appear the only outlet for the American Cinema release, and even those theatres should have problems since "Dirt" doesn't really have the daredevil races that has almost ensure audience involvement.

Overall success of pic seems entirely dependent on how many staunch racing afficionados there are who will pay to see 95 minutes of competition shot in various parts of the country.

Pic takes audience everywhere from Pike's Peak to Pismo Beach in search of different types of racing. Vehicles range from cycles to tractors and terrain can be anything from snow to swampland. There's a narrator who sets the scene for what's to come as the camera crew moves around the United States in an attempt to educate viewer to just how much the term off road racing encompasses.

Some of the footage is very good, including one race that gives the driver's view of the road. And for those who like to watch pretty girls (it seems that's most of what car drivers do besides race) there are more than a few shots zeroing in on unsuspecting female spectators during the competitions. There are also several conversations with some racing greats, including Parnelli Jones, that are somewhat endaring.

"Dirt's" failing is that it never takes the time to explore the reason why so many people are so hooked on racing or the personalities of some of the drivers that are featured. —*Berg.*

Roveh Huliot
(The Wooden Gun)
(ISRAELI-COLOR)

Tel Aviv, March 7.

A Makor Films/Hardy & Saunders Motion Pictures release, produced by Eitan Even, Richard Sanders, John Hardy. Features entire cast. Written and directed by Ilan Moshenson, camera (color), Gadi Danzig; production designer, Eytan Levy. Running time: 91 MINS.

Cast: Judith Sole, Leo Yung, Ophelia Strahl, Louis Rosenberg, Michael Kfir and Eric Rosen.

Ilan Moshenson's first film, recently presented in the Information Section of the Berlin Film Festival, is a serious attempt, one of the very few, by a young Israeli filmmaker, to assess certain moods, values and attitudes which came into being during the short years since the inception of this young State.

In the frame of what might seem, at first glance, a kid story, Moshenson pits two groups of children against each other, in a confrontation which gains particular significance, as it is unfolded during the early years of the State of Israel. The children's behavior, their interpretations of terms such as heroism, honor, nationalism and friendship, their search for better weapons (one of them being the wooden gun which lent its name to the film) and tricks to defeat the opponents, and their opinions of what is permitted or not in times of war, reflect many of the adult ideas at the time, and will naturally lead to close associations, for whoever has followed the history of the Middle East in the last 40 years.

Moshenson's attitude toward the entrenched set of values accepted by the Israeli society, as reflected in these children, is often critical, but at the same time he is trying to supply the background necessary in order to understand the origins of these values, the difficult first days of independence, dire economic problems and people who break down and leave shamefacedly to go back to Diaspora, teachers proud of newly acquired victory and educating their pupils to grow up chauvinist bigots, parents still unable to overcome the Holocaust trauma and searching for remnants of a family which disappeared long ago, or struggling against language and culture barriers they did not expect to encounter.

These are facts which are crying out to be told and Moshenson has his heart in the right place. But as this is his first film and as it was made on a shoestring budget, the result is not always on the par with its intentions.

Both in writing and directing, Moshenson doesn't get his audience involved in his story, his characters being too sketchy, dramatic points being forced in and their symbolic meaning driven home sometimes on the obvious side.

Financial pressures forced the film into an early release, not always in the best locations, which may turn out to spoil some of its chances. But as this is an unusual treatment of a topical subject, there may be interest from TV abroad (early contacts have been already established in Berlin) and venture may still prove to be solvent, not just worthwhile. —*Edna.*

The Champ
(COLOR)

Is the world ready for another Jackie Cooper? Re-make mostly promising.

Hollywood, March 28.

United Artists release of a Metro-Goldwyn-Mayer film. Produced by Dyson Lovell. Directed by Franco Zeffirelli. Features entire cast. Screenplay, Walter Newman, based on a story by Frances Marion; camera (Metrocolor), Fred J. Koenekamp; editor, Michael J. Sheridan; production design, Theoni V. Aldredge; sound, Jerry Jost, William McCaughey, Aaron Rochin, Michael J. Kohut; music, Dave Grusin; assistant director, David Silver. Reviewed at MGM Studio Theatre, Culver City, March 21, '79. (MPAA Rating: PG.) Running time: **121 MINS.**

Billy	Jon Voight
Annie	Faye Dunaway
T.J.	Ricky Schroder
Jackie	Jack Warden
Mike	Arthur Hill
Riley	Strother Martin
Dolly Kenyon	Joan Blondell
Josie	Mary Jo Catlett
Georgie	Elisha Cook

Hardly anyone can resist a cute kid, and with Ricky Schroder, "The Champ" has the most irresistible moppet seen on the screen in decades. Franco Zeffirelli makes an auspicious debut on these shores with his first American film, bolstered by earnest performances from Jon Voight and Faye Dunaway. Key question remains whether film audiences today are willing to empty their tear ducts, much as their counterparts did 48 years ago with the original Metro version. If so, "The Champ" could be crying all the way to the bank.

Walter Newman's script adroitly updates Frances Marion's original scenario (she is screen credited for the story idea), placing down-and-out boxer Voight as a horse handler in Florida, accompanied by sprig Schroder. An inveterate gambler and drinker, Voight doesn't hit the comeback trail until ex-wife Faye Dunaway, now a society matron, reappears to threaten his and Schroder's buddy-buddy relationship.

Even those unfamiliar with the 1931 pic will feel resonances in the current "Champ." The original launched Jackie Cooper as a major moppet star (helped the same year by "Skippy" and a lot of experience in shorts-Ed.) and this edition promises to do the same for Schroder, who projects a comparable emotional range and depth.

Most debatable, and in some respects unsettling, aspects of the update concern the Voight-Dunaway characters and relationships. Unlike Wallace Beery, Voight is believable in his grab for his former boxing fame, and his physical resemblance to young Schroder is uncanny.

But Voight, under the Italian director, has adopted a Joe Palooka accent and outlook that seems at odds with the contempo setting, and seriously weakens the credibility of a relationship between him and the cool, elegant Dunaway. Latter has apparently found her metier in this slightly bitchy characterization, peeled away at film's end to reveal a warm and loving mother.

Zeffirelli, using a maximum number of close-ups and tight shots, wrings considerable bathos out of the maudlin plotting, and between Schroder, Voight and Dunaway, enough real tears are shed on screen to put the glycerine suppliers out of business.

"The Champ" has the amber glow of Zeffirelli's European pix, and Theoni V. Aldredge's pink and pastel costumes perfectly complement Herman A. Blumenthal's lush production design and Fred Koenekamp's subdued lensing.

Slow pacing (Zeffirelli seems to work out of a visual longhand, never cutting a scene succinctly if it can be stretched out) and an over-abundance of sentimentality may turn off some segments of the audience, but it's doubtful there'll be a dry eye in the house at the closing credits.

The 1931 version was directed by King Vidor, with dialog by Leonard Praskins from Marion's story. Beery played the Champ, Cooper the kid, and Irene Rich the estranged wife. As an example of how film times have lengthened, running time of the original was only 85 minutes. —*Poll.*

Due Pezzi Di Pane
(Two Pieces Of Bread)
(ITALIAN-FRENCH-COLOR)

Rome, March 21.

A United Artist release, produced by Gianfranco Piccioli and Mauro Berardi. Stars Vittorio Gassman, Philippe Noiret. Directed by Sergio Citti. Screenplay, Sergio Citti, Giulio Pardizi; camera (Eastmancolor), Giuseppe Ruzzolini; editor, Nino Baragli; art director, Luciano Ricceri; music, Alessandro Alessandroni. Reviewed at Barberini Theatre, Rome, March 21, '79. Running time **105 MINS.**

Pippo	Vittorio Gassman
Peppe	Philippe Noiret
Restaurant Owner	Luigi Proietti

A nostalgic trip back into the Rome of yesteryear with its traveling minstrels and neighborhood trattorias, "Two Pieces" never really comes alive too often succumbing to the ridiculous. What could have been an utterly charming film — some scenes actually generate the kind of excitement found in the works of Citti's mentor Pier Paolo Pasolini — becomes instead an overplayed stereotype of both past and present Rome.

"Two Pieces" could have a certain success abroad where such stereotypes are often appreciated, but audiences will be necessarily baffled by the film's oscillation between sheer silliness and moments of delicious irony.

The story line is clever; Pippo and Peppe (Vittorio Gassman and Philippe Noiret) who sing for their supper with guitar and flute discover that both have been the lovers of the same woman who has just died giving birth to a baby boy. After a judicial fight to establish paternity that divides the whole neighborhood into pro-Peppe and pro-Pippo factions, the two old friends reunite and decide to raise the child — whom they call Piripicchio — together. They teach him the old ways, but he eventually grows up, leaves them and becomes a part of a harsh and modern Rome with its fears, noise and concrete.

Disregarding any pretense of realism — the trattoria, whose owner (Luigi Proietti) sings old Roman ballads with tears streaking down his face, is clearly a set—Citti has created a theatrical atmosphere — reinforced by flat, straight on camera shots — that gives the impression of an old Roman state play.

Unfortunately this mise-en-scene only works occasionally. When a group of Romans — including a carbinieri on horseback — enter the voting headquarters and begin to dance, when prison inmates begin to sing old Roman songs in four-part harmony and when a centenarian expires blowing out his birthday candles, one gets a glimpse of just how sublime this film could have been. The rest is simply corny.

The choice of using heavyweights Noiret and Gassman may have been made with an eye on the French and U.S. markets, but it unfortunately has deprived the film of its chance to charm (Gassman in particular looks frightfully uncomfortable in his role as a singing bum). —*Argo.*

Achilleshaelen er mit vaaben
(The Achilles Heel Is My Weapon)
(DANISH-COLOR)

Copenhagen, March 16.

A Danish Film Studio/Danish Film Institute production. Dagmar Distribution release. Written and directed by Jytte Rex. Features entire cast. Camera (Eastmancolor) Dirk Bruel, Alexander Gruszynski, Jytte Rex; music, quotes from classical and traditional recordings; editor, Grethe Moldrup; production manager, Nina Crone. Reviewed at Ankerstjerne Film Laboratories, Copenhagen, March 16, '79. Running time: **92 MINS.**

Clemens	Clemens Hildebrandt
Maria	Helle Ryslinge

In her second feature film, writer-director Jytte Rex remains an exponent of loosely-structured, impressionistic film story telling that will hardly appeal to larger audiences, but she demonstrates with "The Achilles Heel Is My Weapon" that she is a true cinematic talent.

The non-story has young Clemens (Clemens Hildebrandt) escaping from prison and seeking refuge with his former girl-friend Maria (Helle Ryslinge), who keeps on loving him in spite of his repeated outbursts of temper, doubts, etc., plus his equally repeated outings into territories away from her.

The two main characters meet other characters on their way, most of them not very clearly defined, all of them having kissed an intellectual Blarney Stone but still hopelessly naive in their handling of words, ideas and themsevles. As depicted by Rex and her excellent cinematographer Alexander Gruszinsky, all shape up real lifelike, however. —*Kell.*

Love And Bullets
(BRITISH-COLOR)

A plot full of lead.

London, March 22.

ITC Film Distributors release of a Lew Grade presentation. Produced by Pancho Kohner. Directed by Stuart Rosenberg. Stars Charles Bronson, Jill Ireland, Rod Steiger. Screenplay, Wendell Mayes, John Melson; camera (color), Fred Koenekamp (U.S.), Anthony Richmond (Switzerland); music, Lalo Schifrin; production designer, John De Cuir; editor, Michael Anderson; sound, Gene Garvin, John Bramall; costumes, Dorothy Jeakins; asst. director, Jack Aldworth. Reviewed at London Pavilion theatre, London, March 21, '79. (BBFC Rating: A.) Running Time: **95 MINS.**

Charlie Congers	Charles Bronson
Joe Bomposa	Rod Steiger
Jackie Pruit	Jill Ireland
Louis Monk	Strother Martin
Brickman	Bradford Dillman
Vittorio Farroni	Henry silva
Huntz	Paul Koslo
Cook	Sam Chew
Lobo	Michael Gazzo
Caruso	Val Avery
Mike Durant	Bill Gray
FBI Agent Marty	Andy Romano
FBI Agent George	Robin Clarke
Police Captain	Cliff Pellow
Vittorio's Girlfriend	Lorraine Chase

Charles Bronson's presence in this routine yarn about a lone cop on an assignment in Switzerland is the pic's only firm selling point. In a traditional role, pitched against a succession of hitmen, he's perfectly assured. Fast playoff with heavy promotion should yield adequate business in action-happy markets.

Slowly and predictably, Wendell Mayes and John Melson's script plots Bronson's mission, on behalf of the FBI, to pick up a mobster's moll who's got separated from her paramour and is presumed to be a mine of incriminating information.

Bronson's personal obsession with bringing down the gangland king is accentuated when he discovers the girl knows nothing after all, and then falls for her. When the mob, equally convinced she'll shop them, have her killed, he takes private revenge.

There are hints throughout of sharper characterizations and less superficial relationships, but these are hampered by unambitious dialog and repeatedly trite situations. Rod Steiger's performance as the effete Mafia boss is tantalizing in this respect. So too is the emergent love affair between Bronson and Jill Ireland, her comic talent largely starved for lack of material.

Refreshing to report, this essentially family thriller refrains from gratuitous sadism and nudity, often seemingly employed to distract attention from a poor script, or regarded as the modern route to the public's wallet. At worst, "Love And Bullets" is bland and fails to thrill. But it's never offensive.

(The British censor removed shots which show, in detail, Bronson constructing a lethal blowpipe from items available in his hotel, for fear the device could easily be copied. This sequence may, of course, remain intact for other territories.)

Also on the upside, Anthony Richmond's Swiss location photography is pleasing, and Lalo Schifrin's score at times stylish. For youthful transportation-freaks, the mobile hardware, besides the obligatory helicopter, includes an aerial tramcar, electric taxis, a paddlesteamer, railroad auto carriers and European trains of all descriptions.

But the lingering pace and contrived backgrounds belong more to a travelog than an adventure picture. Director Stuart Rosenberg could have glossed over the plot's less believable twists with a brisker style and a lot more attack.

(Pic was originally worktitled "Love And Bullets, Charlie.")
—Simo.

Un Si Joli Village ...
(Such A Lovely Town ...)
(FRENCH-COLOR)

Paris, Feb. 22.

A Planfilm release of a Planfilm-Films de la Tour-Jacques Roitfield-Films de la Drouette co-production. Screenplay, Andre' G. Brunelin, Etienne Perier, based on the novel "The Lesser Evil," by Jean Laborde. Stars Victor Lanoux, Jean Carmet, Valerie Mairesse. Directed by Etinne Perier. Camera, Jean Charvein; sound, Michel Desrois; music, Paul Misraki; art direction, Jean-Jacques Caziot; production manager, Roland Thenot; asst. director, Olivier Gerard. Reviewed at Salles Ponthieu, Pairs, Feb. 21, '79. Running time: 116 MINS.
Stephan Bertin ....Victor Lanoux
Judge Noblet ....Jean Carmet
Muriel Olivier ....Valerie Mairesse
Gaspard ....Michel Robin
Maurois ....Jacques Richard
Freval ....Gerard Jugnot
Demaison ....Francis Lemaire

Pierre Bertin, owner of a tannery that assures the economic sustenance of a picturesque provincial town, accidently kills his wife in a dispute. But lulled by his self-importance he chooses to dissimulate his wife's disappearance by simply stating that she has walked out on him. A plausible explanation, since Bertin has been shamelessly carrying on an affair with the town's schoolmistress who is now pregnant with his child, a child he wants very much — a boy, he is sure, who will carry on the economic dynasty.

The arrival of an examining magistrate fails to perturb him, but the judge's dogged investigation turns up the corpse and Bertin gets slapped with a murder indictment. With the complicity of the townfolk, whose terror before the impending unemployment outweighs any moral considerations, Bertin mounts a campaign of economic blackmail that ends in his acquittal. Bertin wins his freedom but loses his mistress — and son — when she decides she cannot live with a man whose monstrous ego is ready to sacrifice even those most faithful to him.

There is a good film to be made with his material, but director Etienne Perier has not made it. The screenplay that he and co-scripter Andre Brunelin have drawn from a novel by Jean Laborde is politically glib and psychologically unconvincing. Nor has Perier done much to cultivate the seeds of an analogy planted in the script: that of Bertin as feudal lord to a township of faithful vassals. The remnants of medievalism inherent in the town's economic structure and social nature are not sufficiently explored and the idea of Bertin as a sort of a throwback to a feudal mentality is impeded by the miscasting of Victor Lanoux — the huskily charming lover of "Cousin, Cousine" — in the main role. Lanoux has physical authority, but fails to do justice to the character's brutal megalomania.

Perier shoves the narrative along at a good clip but with a dull literalness that denies any resonance in his images. A more stylized treatment might have better suited the script's ideas.

Jean Carmet is fine as the unassuming but persistent magistrate whose mediocre life has not swayed his professional efficiency. Valerie Mairesse, the plump and pretty blonde of "One Sings, the Other Doesn't," is okay in the sketchy role of the mistress who finally says no. —Len.

Starcrash
(COLOR)

Out of orbit.

Hollywood, March 7.

New World release. Produced by Nat and Patrick Wachsberger. Directed by Lewis Coates, (Luigi Cozzi). Features entire cast. Screenplay, Coates, Wachsberger; camera (Metrocolor), Paul Beeson, Roberto D'Ettore; editor, Sergio Montanari; Dolby consultant, Don Digirolamo; music, John Barry; production design, Aurelio Crugnolla; special effects directors, Armando Valcuda, Germano Natali, Electronic visual effects supervisor, Ron Hays. Reviewed at Vine, Hollywood, March 7, '79. (MPAA rating: PG.) Running time: 92 MINS.
Akton ....Marjoe Gortner
Stella Star ....Caroline Munro
The Emperor ......Christopher Plummer
Simon ....David Hasselhoff
Thor ....Robert Tessier
Count Zarth Arn ....Joe Spinnell
Queen of the Amazon.......Nadia Cassini
Elle.....................Judd Hamilton
Voice of Elle ....Hamilton Camp

Script traces the adventures of Akton and Stella Star (yes, that's her name), the best navigator and pilot in the galaxy, respectively. Starting out as mere smugglers the two are eventually recruited by Emperor of the Universe, because of their supreme skills, to save everyone from the evil deeds of Count Zarth Arn. Among their feats over the next 92 minutes are escaping from a band of skimpy-clothed Amazons, beating to death a seemingly spastic group of cavemen and destroying two mammoth metal men with a laser-like rod.

Marjoe Gortner and Caroline Munro portraying Akton and Stella. Although the characterizations are little bit more than cardboard cutouts, it's hard to fault actors when they're given lines like "I'll fix you" or "I hope they're (creatures) friendly" to say.

Weak screenplay is by director Lewis Coates and producer Nat Wachsberger. Coates' direction seemed to have no apparent plan. What is surprising for a picture of this genre, however, is the lackluster photography by Paul Beeson and Roberto D'Ettore and special effects by Armando Valcauda and Germano Natali. Photography almost never convinces that this is actually taking place anywhere but on the movie screen and special effects seem little more than poor imitations of what's been done before.
—Berg.

Janiksen Vuosi
(The Year of the Hare)
(FINNISH-COLOR)

Hollywood, March 3.

A Filminor production. Produced by Kullervo Kukkasjarvix. Directed by Risto Jarva. Features entire cast. Screenplay, Arto Paasilinna, Risto Jarva, Kullervo Kukkasjarvi; camera (color), Antti Peippo, Erkki Peltomaa, Juha-Veli Akras; editor, Risto Jarva, Matti Kuortti; music, Markku Kopisto. Reviewed at Universal Studios, Univ. City, March 3, '79. Running time: 105 MINS.

Although uneven in spots, "The Year of the Hare" is an often delightful, occasionally thought-provoking account of what happens when a middle-class, middle-aged man decides to drop out of society with only a hare to keep him company. Directed by the late Risto Jarva, who was killed in a car accident after film's premiere in 1977, item has big potential at commercial art houses across the country. Its light tone makes it palatable to broad audience and with proper care in distribution, film could find its public.

Upfront credit should be given to Antti Litja who as discontented advertising executive Vatanen virtually carries the film along with the hare (unbilled in cast credits) he finds on a country road. Litja portrays Vatanen's discontent with the competitiveness of the civilized world effectively, and manages to project a warm, loving relationship with an animal that does little more than wrinkle its nose every so often.

It takes a while to set up Vatanen's situation at home and work and consequently the film is a slow starter. But once the hare is introduced and Vatanen decides to spend the foreseeable future with it there are some irresistable scenes as he feeds it, talks to it, takes it to the veterinarian, and puts it to bed. The animal even proves to be of help when Vatanen is arrested and policemen begin crawling around the floor trying to attract the hare's attention.

Where the picture runs into problems is when the animal is not on-screen. There is a long unexplained section in the middle where the hare is nowhere in evidence that breaks the light mood established. And when the bunny does return there is a tendency to get caught up in some rather heavy-handed messages about the rat race of contemporary society that had been quite clear by implication earlier on.

Editing by Matti Kuortti and Jarva seems to have been a bit haphazard, giving the film a choppy effect at points. But Jarva's decision to leave the end up in the air works well and Antti Peippo, Erkki Peltomaa and Juha-Veli Akras come up with some beautiful shots of the European countryside.
—Berg.

Amada Amante
(Beloved Lover)
(BRAZILIAN-COLOR)

Hollywood, March 17.

Produced by Luis Carlos Barreto. Directed by Bruno Barreto. Features entire cast. Screenplay, Jose Louzeiro, Leopoldo Serran; camera (color), Lauro Escorel Filho; editor, Raimundo Higino; music Guto Graca Mello. Reviewed at the Samuel Goldwyn Studios, Hollywood, March 17, '79. Running time: 98 MINS.
Galvao ....Paulo Gracindo
Sandra ....Cristina Ache
Toninho ....Paulo Guarnieri
Solange ....Ligia Diniz
Darcy................Flavio Sao Thiago

Brazilian director Bruno Barreto has marvelously captured the seedy side of life with "Beloved Lover." Film is a brutal account of what goes on when one turns to sex us a means of making money as well as a compelling drama focusing on love relationship between prostitute and hustler in a city being terrorized by a murderer. There seems to be a significant commercial market for item, although a number of American pics with alike themes, most recently "Hardcore," could dissuade audiences from attending foreign version of something they could see in English. Still, word of mouth should give boost and usual art crowd will undoubtedly lend strong support.

Barreto has a fine eye for detail throughout, capturing the grittiness of the city and degenerate nature of people more through surroundings and action than dialogue. Technique is evident from beginning, with chilling opening scene where detective Galvao (Paulo Gracindo) views daughter Sandra (Cristina Ache) in a strip show, and later returns to his empty apartment. The de-emphasis on words should particularly draw in viewers who are somewhat uncomfortable with sub-titles.

Story slowly builds as its discovered Sandra's transvestite roommate has committed suicide and his ex-lover Toninho comes looking for a photograph of the two in Sandra's apartment, Chemistry between Cristina Ache and Paulo Guarnieri as Sandra and Toninho is instant and electrifying, as the two go from love to hate and back again during ensuing scenes. The desperate distrustful natures of two people on the streets as well as the carnal passion of a pair of lovers who sense their time together is limited are thoroughly fleshed out by Ache and Guarnieri and their performances ultimately make the film.

There is also fine support from Paulo Gracindo as the detective who meanwhile is investigating a killer given to murdering cab drivers at night and leaving them locked in their cars with the radio on. Gracindo plays off well against Ache in some father-daughter scenes that could have easily appeared overly sentimental.

Screenplay by Jose Louzeiro and Leopoldo Serran is on-target with exception of several "coincidences" that manage to weave everything together at a somewhat abrupt ending. Particularly intriguing is Toninho and his unapologetic manner for a lifestyle that he ably illustrates is his because society left him no other choice.

Music by Guto Graca Mello is appropriate, Raimundo Higino's editing is smooth and Lauro Escorel Filho does an outstanding job on camera.

Although there are those who will probably be put off by some rather graphic sex scenes (a small amount of editing may be needed to achieve an "R" rating), pic mostly succeeds in combining both a believable character study with contemporary drama. And few films made in any country today can claim that.
—*Berg.*

Feedback
(U.S.-COLOR)

Hollywood, Feb. 28.

A Feedback Company production. Produced, directed, written by Bill Doukas. Camera (Movielab color), Oliver Wood; music, Jake Stern; editor, Carol Hayward. Reviewed at the Goldwyn Studios, Hollywood, Feb. 28. '79. Running time: **90 MINS.**
Rick Dawson .... Bill Doukas
Gabrielle .... Myriam Gibril
Eve .... Denise Gordon
Judge .... Taylor Mead
Jerry .... Louis Walden

In its hysterical, close-up look at New York criminal low-life, "Feedback" forces comparison to Martin Scorsese's "Mean Streets," which is too bad for the new indie feature. Producer-director-writer-star Bill Doukas has bitten off more than he can chew in trying to portray the anguished dilemma of a loser caught in the web of underworld and governmental intrigue. Outlook is dim.

Actually, Doukas, who received partial funding from the American Film Institute, seems to have "bigger" things in mind than Scorsese did, like existential guilt and Kafkaesque manipulation of the individual by a conspiratorial State. Unfortunately, his style is inexpressive and, while some of the intent may come across, it's not enough to lend any credibility to the proceedings.

Premise has Doukas, living comfortably but tentatively with two highly unsympathetic women, receive a criminal indictment in the mail. He spends the next hour-and-a-half trying to dodge the consequences, consulting with double-talking lawyers, visiting a priest, seeing a shrink who gives him a hallucinogen and getting his finger cut off by hoods.

In its last 10 minutes, pic takes a wild turn toward comedy with the entrance of Warhol thesp Taylor Mead as a demented judge who hears Doukas' case. If "Feedback" held any aspirations to realism or believability, they all fall by the wayside in the climactic courtroom scene. Intentionally or not, this sequence is hilarious.

Another liability is the acting which, particularly in the cases of the two women, Myriam Gibril and Denise Gordon, is blatantly amateurish. Doukas himself muddles through, while another former Warhol regular, Louis Walden, pops up in a supporting role.

Program notes indicate that Doukas wrote the original version of this script while imprisoned in Syria for four years, without indictment or trial, on suspicion of espionage. In this light, his paranoia is understandable, but he hasn't been able to make very meaningful use of his experiences in "Feedback."—*Cart.*

Punk in London
(W. GERMAN-COLOR-DOCU-16m)

Hollywood, March 17.

An HFF Munich) production. Directed and written by Wolfgang Buld. Camera (color), Helge Weindler, Willy Brunner; music, The Stranglers, X-Ray Spex, The Lurkers, Anonymous Chaos, Subway Sect, The Adverts, Kill Joys, Wayne County and The Electric Chairs, Chelsea, The Jam, Boom Town Rats, Rough Trade, Jolt, The Clash. Reviewed at the Century Plaza Theatre, Hollywood, March 17, '79. Running time: **111 MINS.**

Unlike the few other punk docus that have come before, "Punk in London" is a sharp, professionally made effort whose main defect of overlength is both caused and mitigated by its being as thorough an examination of its subject as could possibly be desired. If the punk phenomenon hangs around long enough, pic might find toeholds at specialty outlets and midnight shows. Good non-theatrical prospects would seem to exist.

German-made look at the London punk scene (unsubtitled German narration would have to be recorded in English for commercial release) shows many of the major groups playing in their natural habitat, the small clubs, with fans pogoing madly. Sound recording is quite satisfactory, only drawback being that such unabatedly loud music can be hard to take over 111 minutes.

Fortunately, helmer Wolfgang Buld has interspersed performance footage with some informative talk with musicians, punk adherents, managers and sociologically-oriented observers. Main point of both the talk and songs' lyrics is that punk movement sprang directly from the dire social and economic problems of Britain's lower class youth, and a couple of the more articulate interviewees claim that the intentions of the movement have already been betrayed by the music biz and a certain snobbery within punk, one remarking that, "Punk hasn't fulfilled a lot of its original aims."

One particularly intriguing sequence features interviews with aging Teddy Boys, Britons who grew up in the 1950s, still grease their hair back, listen exclusively to Buddy Holly and contemporaries and have nothing but contempt for the punks. An expression of the current generation wariness of outsiders is vividly caught when a band member refuses to be filmed by the crew because it's German, therefore automatically suspect.

As one rocker admits, punk is just another musical fad. "It's just a couple of bands ... the rest will just fade away and die." Filming in summer 1977, Buld caught the scene a little late but still with sufficient relevance and precision to make his film a good historical document of one more wave in the ocean of popular culture. —*Cart.*

Diary Of A Moonlighter
(U.S.-DOCU-COLOR)

Hollywood, March 21.

Produced, directed and edited by Gar LaSalle. Camera (color), Kris Malkiewics. No other credits available. Reviewed at Century Plaza 2 Theatre, Century City, March 21, 1979. Running time: **70 MINS.**

"Diary Of A Moonlighter" is an interesting, but extremely amateurish, effort by an emergency-room specialist to film himself at work among the ill and injured.

Obviously, an emergency room offers plenty of drama and humor and Dr. Gar LaSalle knows his domain well. He's a good, caring doctor who's able to express himself verbally very well. But he's not a very good filmmaker and his docu has more faults than would be fair to cite of a nonprofessional.

Much of what's on film, though, compels attention, but not unless you can take the sight of blood. LaSalle also tells a number of good emergency-room yarns not seen on camera. And, yes, a full moon does increase the casualties. —*Har.*

Blacks Britannica
(BRITISH-COLOR-DOCU-16m)

Hollywood, March 20.

A David Koff/Musindo Mwinyipembe production. Produced by Koff, Mwinyipembe. Directed by Koff. Camera (color), William Brayne, Mike Davis, Charles Stewart; editor, Tom Scott Robson; music, Steel Pulse. Reviewed at Century Plaza Theatre, Hollywood, March 19, 1979. Running time: **57 MINS.**

Shades of the United States a decade ago loom large in "Blacks Britannica," a startling look at the growing politicization of blacks in Britain and an unsettling portrait of an England in transition. Already the cause of controversy when re-edited by its original backer, WGBH, a Boston public tv station, and labeled "dangerous" by the British Information Service, film should cause talk wherever it's shown and will find ready audiences among those concerned with pressing contemporary social issues.

L.A.-based filmmaker David Koff has previously made "People of the Wind," nominated for 1977 best feature docu Oscar, as well as a trilogy on colonialism and nationalism in East Africa. By way of concise historical reportage and highly articulate spokesmen, he here reveals how racism and government domestic policy have contributed to increasing discontent and political consciousness among the country's two million blacks.

Koff focuses mainly on West Indians and uses reggae music for his score, but the problem encompasses not only the Islanders but those from Pakistan, India and other former colonies from which people could freely emigrate by virtue of their British passports. Though there were blacks in the U.K. before and during World War II, the first big wave hit in the 1950s. Naturally, "we did the dirty jobs, the uncomfortable jobs, for low pay," as one points out.

In 1962, the first in a series of restrictive immigration laws was passed, so-called ghettoes (or "Brown Towns") were razed and replaced with high-rises specifically designed to restrict access to two entrances to facilitate police supervision, and, in the words of one of the speakers, the major political parties began "closing ranks" not only against blacks but the entire working class. Estimate is made that 80% of black youths from ages 16-19 can't find jobs and, naturally, crime has increased, alarming the populace at large and providing grist for the propaganda mills of the National Front, Britain's fascist party.

As a result, blacks have begun to become more organized. Despite the differences of accent, proportionally smaller representation in the society, and fact that most blacks are recent immigrants rather than longtime residents, it all conjures up very recent (indeed, continuing) American memories, and it remains to be seen how the more rigidly class-structured English society copes in the near future.

Koff makes little effort to represent the undoubtedly varying white points of view, but it's clear that for him there's no more time for debate, only action to improve the situation. "Blacks Britannica" explicitly bares the reasons for the struggle and refuses to pretend that there are any easy answers. —Cart.

Ileksen
(AUSTRALIAN-PAPUAN-DOCU-COLOR-16m)

Hollywood, March 21.
Produced by Dennis O'Rourke. Directed by Dennis O'Rourke, Gary Kildea. Camera (color), Dennis O'Rourke' editor, Peter Berry. No other credits available. Reviewed at Century Plaza II Theatre, Century City, March 21, 1979. Running time: 59 MINS.

The ethnographic film enjoyed some vogue a few years ago, with anthropologists all ready to drop their notebooks and pencils and pick up an Arriflex. But if "Ileksen" is any example, it should be back to the bush for would-be ethnographers, since this docu is a prime example of cultural bias.

Made by Aussie filmmakers Gary Kildea and Dennis O'Rourke, "Ileksen" surveys the political scene in Papua New Guinea after the island won its independence from Australia in 1975. Occasion is the first general elections, with the party in power facing a rash of opponents, including headhunters, a femme separatist and the usual opposition leaders.

Weak on background, the docu never clearly identifies the combatants, or their respective political philosophies. Absence of narration further confuses things, although clever inclusion of an Aussie propaganda film shows the pitfalls of that route.

Whatever insights "Ileksen" provides are invalidated by the docu's closing title card, which reveals the film was commissioned and paid for by the party in power, a classic no-no for both anthropologists and indie filmmakers. If the on-camera subject is also the financier, the result isn't a docu — it's a paid advertisement.

American Nitro
(U.S.-COLOR-DOCU-16m)

Hollywood, March 2.
A K.B. production. Produced by Jim Kimberlin, Tim Geideman. Directed, edited by Bill Kimberlin. Camera (color), Kimberlin, Geideman; music, Art Twain. Reviewed at Universal Studios, March 2, 1979. Running time: 75 MINS.

Though "American Nitro" provides a full meal for drag racing aficionados, non-fans are likely to find their patience taxed to unwanted lengths. Competently made, inoffensive and at time pleasantly humorous, docu about the California funny car scene offers more than most probably ever wanted to know about the subject. If, as is claimed, drag racing is one of the nation's most popular spectator sports, film, like surfing pix, might have a shot in specialized situations. For general audiences, it's all a bit lightweight and esoteric.

Shot at the Fremont Dragstrip with top drivers Don Prudhomme and Tom McEwen taking part and a large crowd on hand, "American Nitro" starts out ingratiatingly by refusing to take itself too seriously. A wonderful montage of cars as they shimmy, shake, blow off steam and go nowhere makes the subject look quite ridiculous and partially breaks down one's resistance to obsessive doting on souped up, psychedelically painted vehicles.

After the light opening, pic begins spreading its informational and sociological wings, telling us that sport is in danger because of dwindling oil supplies (6½ gallons of nitro methane are expended in a normal quarter-mile run), that it costs up to $200,000 per year to compete seriously and that drag racing is losing some of its purity by being transformed from a sport into show biz.

Some explosive accidents are documented, the U.S. Army is seen recruiting at the track by rolling out dragsters dressed as tanks, buxom babes in t-shirts parade around for an ogling camera and a truly spectacular motorcycle jump-cum-hangglider flight over a long row of trunks tops things off.

It's slickly done by director-editor Bill Kimberlin, but hardly compelling stuff. As one deadly serious fan remarks, "Funny cars like this, there's really nothing funny about it." —Cart.

El Super
(CUBAN-U.S.-COLOR)

Hollywood, March 3.
A Max Mambru Films Ltd. release. Produced by Manuel Arce, Leon Ichaso. Directed by Leon Ichaso, Orlando Jimenez-Leal. Features entire cast. Screenplay, Manuel Arce, Leon Ichaso, based on the play by Ivan Acosta; camera (color), Orlando Jimenez-Leal; editor, Gloria Pineyro; music, Enrique Ubieta; no other credits available. Reviewed at Universal Screening Room 3, March 3, '79. Running time: 90 MINS.
El Super .... Raymundo Hidalgo-Gato
Aurelia .... Zully Montero
Pancho ....: .... Reynaldo Medina
Bobby .... Efrain Lopez-Neri
Ofelia ... Ana Margarita Martinez-Casado
Aurelita .... Elizabeth Pena
Cuco .... Juan Granda

Creation of a new film genre in this era of international cinema seems unlikely, but "El Super" does launch a new sub-group, the Cuban-American film, made by exiles who fled the Caribbean island after Communistic takeover. A witty and affectionate portrait of a Cuban building superintendent in New York, the modestly-budgeted indie production has definite crossover appeal from the Spanish market to art and retro houses, where it will also pick up curiosity value.

Story is deceptively simple, slice-of-life look at El Super (Raymond Hidalgo-Gato), his long-suffering wife (Zully Montero), and Americanized daughter (Elizabeth Pena). Trapped in the "land of cold and work," Hidalgo-Gato and his chums (Reynaldo Medina, Efrain Lopez-Neri and Juan Granda) recall the balmy days in Havana, elaborate on their wartime experiences during the Bay Of Pigs fiasco, and try to cope in an essentially foreign world.

Without an active plot (pic is keyed to the family's eventual decision to relocate south to Miami), "El Super" drags at times, and some scenes, such as a rooftop jaunt by Hidalgo-Gato, are unclear. What the film lacks in pacing, it makes up in verve, and there are delightful moments, such as three-way conversation between a Gotham building inspector, Hidalgo-Gato, and Granda, whose fractured English confirms what can be lost in a translation.

Directors Leon Ichaso and Orlando Jimenez-Leal have modeled script by Ichaso and co-producer Manuel Arce into a deft and subtle twist on the melancholy of strangers in a strange land. These are not bufoons played for laughs — they are victims caught in a political struggle beyond their control, a dilemma tastefully explicated in "El Super."

Thesping is effective across the board, with Hidalgo-Gato limning the lead role with moody sensitivity, and Montero, Medina, Lopez-Neri and Granda all superior in supporting roles.

Given the apparent financial limitations, tech work is fine, particularly Orlando Jimenez-Leal's lensing, and smooth editing by Gloria Pineyro. Cuban dialect may provide some problems in sales to other Latin markets, but "El Super" should find a viable U.S. future in specialized bookings.
—Poll.

Song of the Canary
(U.S.-DOCU-COLOR-16m)

Hollywood, March 19.
A "Song of the Canary" production. Produced, directed by Josh Hanig, David Davis, camera (color), John Else, Michael Anderson; music, Doug McKechnie, Si Kahn; editors, Davis, Hanig, Stephen Stept. Reviewed at Century Plaza Theatre, Hollywood, March 19, '79. Running time: 58 MIN.

"Song of the Canary" could virtually be used as a definition of an activist documentary. Not only did the filmmakers expose a literally cancerous situation, but they appear also to have opened workers' eyes and provoked some actual change through the course of their efforts. Results like this provide the inspiration even diehard idealists sometimes need to carry on, and the film has a bright outlook on the docu marketplace.

Title refers to the canary coal miners used to take with them down into the mines; if the bird collapsed or died, workers were tipped off to otherwise undetectable presence of carbon monoxide gas.

Setting in question is no longer a coal mine but the Ag Chem Department of the Occidental Chemical Company's plant in California's San Joaquin Valley where, in the absence of their own canary, workers have served as their own guinea pigs while mixing 200 varieties of pesticides. Skin disease, respiratory difficulties and shortened lifespans have always been taken for granted, but the men interviewed admit that, until questioned by the film crew, they rarely discussed these matters among themselves and found it best not to think about them too much.

Eventually, producer-directors Josh Hanig and David Davis got seven Oxy employees working with the pesticide DBCP to take sterility tests. The results showed all seven to be sterile, prompting media interest, further tests and, ultimately, the removal of DBCP from the market. The process is thoroughly shown from all sides (although, predictably, management comes off badly) and, as in "Harlan County, U.S.A.," the human factor is never forsaken in the face of statistics and rhetorical outrage.

The second half of the film focuses upon a non-union textile plant much like the one currently on view in the fictional "Norma Rae." The history of unions vis-a-vis this massive southern industry is neatly drawn, while the issue of the moment, brown lung disease caused by cotton dust in the mills, is brought home through interviews with victims and a presentation of the efforts of the Carolina Brown Lung Association to improve plant conditions.

In both sections, workers clearly articulate the relative lack of choice they have in where they live and toil and embrace the opportunity given them by the filmmakers to have their eyes opened to possibilities for change. Movingly, many of the older ones admit it's already too late for them, but, acknowledging that their descendants will undoubtedly work in the same field, want better conditions for future generations.

Admirably assembled and obviously committed, "Song of the Canary" has already served its purpose just in being made. It will prove even more valuable if it can reach audiences the equivalent of the people it discusses, not just the readily convinced urban liberals. —*Cart.*

A Little Romance
(U.S.-FRENCH-COLOR)

New Orion Pictures firm debuts in classy fashion. Careful marketing will bear out b.o. potential.

Hollywood, March 30.

Orion Pictures release through Warner Bros. of a Pan Arts (George Roy Hill)-Trinacra (Yves Rousset-Rouard) coproduction. Executive producer, Patrick Kelley. Produced by Yves Rousset-Rouard, Robert L. Crawford. Features entire cast. Directed by Hill. Screenplay, Allan Burns; camera (color), Pierre William Glenn; editor, William Reynolds; production design, Henry Bumstead; art direction, Francois De Lamthoe; wardrobe design, Rosine Delamare; sound, Michel Desrois, asst. director, Carlo Lastricati. Reviewed at Century Plaza I Theatre, Century City, Calif., March 30, 1979. (MPAA Rating: PG). Running time: **108 MINS.**

Julius . . . . Laurence Olivier
Richard King . . . . Arthur Hill
Kay King . . . . Sally Kellerman
Lauren . . . . Diane Lane
Daniel . . . . Thelonious Bernard
Brod . . . . Broderick Crawford
George de Marco . . . . David Dukes
Bob Duryea . . . . Andrew Duncan
Janet Duryea . . . . Claudette Sutherland
Londet . . . . Graham Fletcher-Cook
Natalie . . . . Ashby Semple
Nichel Michon . . . . Claude Brosset

The first film out of Orion Pictures' stable, "A Little Romance" emerges as a classy winner. A charming blend of youthful innocence and guile, though the George Roy Hill film will need careful marketing to find its desired audience, which is larger than many may suppose. Only drawback for Orion is that "Romance" will prove a tough act for it to follow.

History is littered with failed attempts to deal with adolescent love in a straightforward and humorous fashion — among the bleached bones is Hill's own "The World Of Henry Orient." But in adapting Patrick Cauvin's French novel, "E Equals MC Squared, Mon Amour," Allan Burns has craftily kept the point of view of the youngsters, screen newcomers Diane Lane and Thelonious Bernard while the adults, with certain exceptions, are seen as suitably grotesque and ridiculous, giving "Romance" a crest of humor on which to ride.

Lane is the offspring of flighty jet-setter Sally Kellerman, who spends the film mooning over auteur director David Dukes, rather than hubby Arthur Hill. Bernard takes refuge in film theatres from his ill-humored cab driver father. The teenagers (both 14 when filming started) are drawn to one another, persevere in the face of family pressure, and eventually take off in pursuit of a romantic ideal.

Fulcrum in Burns' script is the beneficent boulevardier, limned by Laurence Olivier in a modern refashioning of the old Maurice Chevalier role. The prototypical

lovable scoundrel, Olivier hams it up unmercifully, the latest of his recent dialectician roles. It's his 60th screen role, and the well-rounded nature of his characterization still astounds.

After getting off to a great start, thanks to Hill's adroit handling of his young leads, and William Reynolds' droll editing, "Romance" falters briefly during the episodes with Olivier, and then arrives at the finish line with a poignant conclusion.

Lane is remarkable in her feature debut, a fully mature but still girlish personality. As her looks and talent develop, she will undoubtedly be seen more. Bernard, forced to rely more on charm than skill, manages to be quite effective.

Supporting cast is excellent, especially Hill as the one understanding adult, Kellerman (perhaps her best role and performance since "Mash"), and Ashby Semple, a complete delight as Lane's gangly girl chum.

Broderick Crawford also shows up, and Hollywood gets a lancing with the David Dukes character, which has shadings of unnamed cult directors. Burns and Hill only falter with the lampoon on American tourists, personified by Andrew Duncan and Claudette Sutherland, a stereotype that was tired 10 years ago.

Technical work by the combined French-American crew was up to the superior standards of "Romance." Yves Rousset-Rouard and Robert L. Crawford, latter longtime Hill assistant now getting his producer stripes, have managed to deliver the kind of light, touching comedy that has almost gone out of style. It's a worthy start for Orion, and hopefully a harbinger of what's to come.

World preem at Filmex, incidentally, was somewhat historic for the unveiling of a new major studio logo. —*Poll.*

Buck Rogers
(COLOR)

Buck has come a long way since 1939, but not far enough.

Hollywood, March 27.

A Universal release of a Glen A. Larson Production, produced by Richard Caffey. Executive producer, Glen A. Larson. Directed by Daniel Haller. Features entire cast. Screenplay, Larson and Leslie Stevens; camera (Technicolor), Frank Beascoechea; editor, John J. Dumas; sound, Andy Gilmore, John Carter, Clyde Sorenson. art direction, Paul Peters; set decoration. Richard Reams; assistant directors, Phil Bowles; Jerry Sobul; costumes, Jean-Pierre Dorleac; special effects. Bud Ewing, Jack Faggard; music, Stu Phillips. Reviewed at the Directors Guild of America theatre, L.A., March 27, '79. (MPAA Rating: PG). Running time: **89 MINS.**

Buck Rogers . . . . Gil Gerard
Princess Ardala . . . . Pamela Hensley
Wilma Deering . . . . Erin Gray

Kane . . . . Henry Silva
Dr. Huer . . . . Tim O'Connor
Draco . . . . Joseph Wiseman
Tigerman . . . . Duke Butler
Twiki . . . . Felix Silla
Twiki's voice . . . . Mel Blanc

"Buck Rogers," the telefilm whose ambition to be a feature exceeds its abilities, should nonetheless cash in on its tackiness because it's not so awful that it can't be watched with some fun, especially by younger people.

With a little more care, it might actually have succeeded in what it attempts to be: A camp excursion into the 25th Century, a bit of a satire on "Star Wars" and "Battlestar Galactica," (the latter a sci-fi stablemate in Glen A. Larsons Prods.)

Instead, it only hits that peak in brief moments, thanks to the fey attitude of Gil Gerard in the title role. Gerard gets some help from Pamela Hensley as the evil Princess Ardala, but not much, and none at all from wooden Erin Gray. Too much, it all looks like an acting class for Universal contract players, against a background of expensive special effects.

Unfortunately, the effects aren't expensive enough. Though impressive by the standards of U's "Buck Rogers" serial of 1939, they pale beside the capabilities of 1979. All the familiar elements are present, the mother ship, the streaking fighters, the mid-space explosion, the futuristic city — and not for a moment can you clear the mind of models and mattes. Oh yes, there is a tiny robot, too.

Among the nice touches are a futuristic minuet to electronic music and some wacky costumes by Jean-Pierre Dorleac. Script by Larson and Leslie Stevens makes it hard to tell whether the laughs are intentional or just dumb lines. Given the initial goals, Daniel Heller's direction seems competent and obviously clock-conscious.

A picture like this, however, doesn't deserve too much judgment. After all, "Buck Rogers" began as a comic strip in 1929. —*Har.*

Hurricane
(COLOR-70M)

Hurricane blows hard, but faces a stiff wind on its way to recouping $22,000,000 negative cost. Outlook maybe better overseas.

Hollywood, April 2.

Paramount Pictures release of a Dino De Laurentiis presentation of a Famous Films, N.V. production. Exec producer, Lorenzo Semple, Jr. Stars Jason Robards, Mia Farrow, Max Von Sydow, Trevor Howard, Timothy Bottoms, Dayton Ka'ne. Produced by Dino De Laurentiis. Directed by Jan Troell. Screenplay, Lorenzo Semple, Jr., based on the novel by Charles Nordhoff and James Norman Hall; camera, (Technicolor, Todd-AO) Sven Nykvist, editor, Sam O'Steen; production, costumes, set design, Danilo Donati; music, Nino Rota; second unit director, Frank Clark; special effects, Glen Robinson, Aldo Puccini, Joe Day; assistant director, Jose' Lopez Rodero.

Reviewed at Royal Theatre, San Francisco. March 23, 1979, and Paramount Studio screening room, April 2, '79. (MPAA Ratings: PG.) Running time: **119 MINS.**

Captain Bruckner	Jason Robards
Charlotte Bruckner	Mia Farrow
Dr. Bascomb	Max Von Sydow
Father Malone	Trevor Howard
Matangi	Dayton Ka'ne
Jack Sanford	Timothy Bottoms
Sargeant Strang	James Keach
Lieutenant Howard	Richard Sarcione
Moana	Ariirau Tekurarere
Corporal Morrah	Willie Myers
Commander Blair	Nick Rutgers
Mrs. Blair	Nancy Hall Rutgers
Samolo	Manu Tupou
Velage	Simplet Tefane
Running Man	Piero Bushin
Tano	Noel Teparii
Faleiva	John Taea
Elder	Taeve Tetuamia

The storm blows fiercely but the love story doesn't match its power in "Hurricane," Dino De Laurentiis' latest epic, reportedly delivered for Paramount release with a $22,000,-000 negative cost. There could be rough seas ahead in the long voyage toward profit, although prospects overseas might be brighter than domestically.

Charles Nordhoff and James Norman Hall's novel, "The Hurricane," was filmed relatively faithfully in 1937 by John Ford for producer Samuel Goldwyn, with Dorothy Lamour and Jon Hall then playing native lovers in conflict with French ruling authorities led by Raymond Massey.

The context and conflicts in the new production, which was originally to have been directed by Roman Polanski, have been altered significantly. Scripter (and exec producer) Lorenzo Semple Jr. has set the tale in Eastern Samoa, circa 1920, with Jason Robards lording it over the natives on behalf of the U.S. Navy. Instead of a native girl, the female love interest is now a white woman, with Mia Farrow sailing in from Boston to see her commander father, but gradually becoming involved with the young chieftain of a near by island, Dayton Ka'ne.

With no code restrictions now standing in the way, the dramatic, sociological and erotic possibilities offered by this tabu romance in such an exotic setting were substantial, but they remain dormant. No strong vision is applied to the material, little point of view is evident except for the standard attitude that the white man only brought trouble and tragedy to the societies he tried to teach and control.

While the raison d'etre of the production is the climactic storm, which is effectively foreshadowed at various points, more important dramatically is the central love

story, which encompasses three-fourths of the running time. Unfortunately, it just doesn't take. To compensate for the romance's implausibility, some emotional history or psychological background was needed for Mia Farrow's character, which is never forthcoming.

The obvious age difference between her and Ka'ne is never commented upon, it's never suggested that she might be giving up something in her previous life to throw it over and defy her father by taking up with the native boy. Though Farrow tries earnestly, her character seems like a silly little girl playing with love rather than a woman torn between two worlds, a dimension needed to justify the devastation of two societies by the cataclysmic tempest.

Jan Troell, who did exquisitely detailed work in "The Emigrants," "The New Land" and his last Swedish film, "Bang!," but who tripped over an impossible script in "Zandy's Bride," his only other American picture, never finds a handle on this material. The dramatic timing seems a little off in many of the scenes, and romantic interplay doesn't seem to be his forte.

The hurricane itself, which runs 25 minutes and was created entirely on location in Bora Bora by a special effects team led by Glen Robinson, who performed the same function on the 1937 production, Aldo Puccini and Joe Day, is impressive enough. However, it remains to be seen whether the spectacle of a raging ocean can engage the interest and terror of domestic audiences. Sven Nykvist's camerawork is solid, but doesn't rival what Conrad Hall (son of "The Hurricane" co-author James Norman Hall) did on a similar tropical isle in "Hell In The Pacific."

Ending is unfortunate. After the storm has subsided, Farrow and Ka'ne are found clinging, unbruised, to a tree. As they stumble upon the sand, it becomes clear that they are the only survivors.

Of the principals, newcomer Ka'ne comes off best. Robards' character must carry the weight of all the villany in the picture and remains one-dimensional, Trevor Howard's priest is strictly comic relief, Max Von Sydow's doctor is a sympathetic bystander.

Nino Rota's score is not one of his major achievements, as it consists basically of one tune, the first few notes of which faintly recall the "Godfather" theme, repeated in assorted arrangements.

Only the production, costume and set designs of Danilo Donati can truly be called top-flight. —*Cart.*

It's Not the Size That Counts
(BRITISH-COLOR)

Hollywood, March 30.

Joseph Brenner Associates release of a Betty E. Box/Ralph Thomas production. Produced by Betty E. Box. Executive producer, Larry Gordon. Directed by Ralph Thomas. Screenplay by Sid Colin, from a story by Harry Corbett; additional dialogue, Ian La Frenais; camera (Eastmancolor), Tony Imi; editor, Ray Watts; music, Tony Macaulay. Reviewed at the Vine Theatre, Hollywood, March 30, '79. (MPAA Rating: R). Running time: **90 MINS.**

Percy	Leigh Lawson
Clarissa	Elke Sommer
Emmanuel Whitebread	Denholm Elliott
Dr. Fairweather	Judy Geeson
Dr. Klein	Milo O'Shea
Stavos Mammonian	Vincent Price
Miss Hanson	Julie Ege
Professor	George Coulouris

"It's Not the Size That Counts!" is the kind of dirty old man's sex comedy that it was thought time had passed by. Indeed, five years have passed since it was made as "Percy's Progress," a sequel to the 1971 "Percy" by the same team. Joseph Brenner has now picked it up for the States, but only potential audience is the raincoat brigade.

Journeyman helmer Ralph Thomas, late of the "Doctor" series, directed shamelessly, and a cast of not-bad actors seems to take it all in stride. Demands on the distaff cast members amount to panting a lot and raising their eyebrows as high as possible when examining the evidence under the sheets. —*Cart.*

A Perfect Couple

An imperfect film, which could spell more trouble for Altman at the b.o.

Hollywood, March 15.

Twentieth Century-Fox release of a Lion's Gate film. Exec producer, Tommy Thompson. Produced and directed by Robert Altman. Features entire cast. Screenplay, Robert Altman, Allan Nicholls; camera (color), Edmond L. Koons; editor, Tony Lombardo; sound, Robert Gravenor, Don Merritt; music production, Allan Nicholls; assistant director, Tommy Thompson. Reviewed at Doheny Plaza Theatre, BevHills, March 15, '79. (MPAA Rating: PG.) Running time: **110 MINS.**

Alex Theodopoulos	Paul Dooley
Sheila Shea	Marta Heflin
Panos	Titos Vandis
Eleousa	Belita Moreno
Fred Bott	Henry Gibson
Athena	Dimitra Arliss
Dana 115	Allan Nicholls
Skye 147	Ann Ryerson
Mona	Mona Golabek
Teddy	Ted Neeley
Mary	Heather MacRae
Sydney-Ray	Tomi-Lee Bradley
Bobbi	Steven Sharp

Despite the lukewarm-to-disastrous boxoffice reception that has greeted his previous two pix, "A Wedding" and "Quintet," Robert Altman has persevered in making another offbeat film, "A Perfect

Couple," that will again appeal to only the fringes of the mass audience. Immensely likeable in some parts, and a complete turn-off in others, "Perfect Couple" reaffirms both Altman's intelligence and his inaccessibility.

The same theme that has characterized earlier Altman pix turns up again here: the struggle of individuals to deal with forces and circumstances beyond their control.

In this instance, it's two different family structures. The linear family has Alex Theodopoulos (Paul Dooley) imprisoned in a suffocating, old-world Greek clan, dominated by patriarch Titos Vandis. Flip side is Sheila Shea (Marta Heflin), an elfin singer locked into a rock group/commune under the iron hand of Ted Neeley.

The couple meets through a videotape dating service (the kind of institution Altman loves to poke fun at), have an on-again, off-again relationship complicated by both families, until true love prevails by the closing credits.

Altman is attempting something much more ambitious than just a love story, of course, or it wouldn't bean Altman film. He and co-scripter Allan Nicholls have tried to integrate the musical score to a degree that it becomes another character.

That attempt proves the downfall of "Perfect Couple," since the musical numbers by Keepin' 'Em Off The Streets (consisting of Neeley, Heflin, Heather MacRae, Tomi-Lee Bradley and Steven Sharp) are frequent and repetitive. There is also little counterbalancing from the classical music favored by the Theodopoulos clan, and the L.A. Philharmonic is employed as a giant prop.

Otherwise, "Perfect Couple" has its sly and charming moments, especially when Dooley abandons his pursuit of Heflin, and takes up with a randy veterinarian, played with lusty delight by Ann Ryerson. Scripter Nicholls also makes an effective appearance as a competing suitor for Heflin's attentions who provokes a domestic brawl. The hospital scene that follows, with love emanating from the operating table, is Altman at his conversation best.

But these random moments don't sustain a whole picture, and "A Perfect Couple" ultimately disappoints those who favor either the music or the characters. No one else is making films like this any more, and while that used to be a plus in Altman's favor, it's now turned into a liability.

Cast is generally efficient, if not spectacular, with Dooley often seeming out of place, and Heflin apparently Altman's realization of his quest for an actress skinnier than

Shelley Duvall. Some other fine performers, such as Dimitra Arliss and Henry Gibson, are wasted in cameo roles, but Tomi-Lee Bradley, Steven Sharp and Heather Mac-Rae excel as the happy-go-lucky band members.

As always, Altman delivers a clean, professional film, with Edmond L. Koons' lensing a definite plus, and the vaunted Lion's Gate eight-track sound system again proving it's the best in the business for this kind of picture. —Poll.

The Silent Partner
(CANADIAN-COLOR)

Cast should help this suspenser a lot.

Atlanta, March 22.
EMC Film Corp. release of a Mario Kassar and Andrew Vajna presentation. Executive producer, Garth H. Drabinsky. Produced by Joel B. Michaels, Stephen Young. Features entire cast. Directed by Daryl Duke. Screenplay, Curtis Hanson, based on Anders Bodelson novel, "Think of a Number;" camera (color), Billy Williams; production designer, Trevor Williams; original music, Oscar Peterson. No other credits available. Reviewed at Tower Place Omni 6, Atlanta, March 21, 1979. (MPAA Rating: R) Running time: 103 MINS.

Julie Carver	Susannah York
Harry Reikle	Christopher Plummer
Miles Cullen	Elliott Gould
Elaine	Celine Lomez
Packard	Michael Kirby
Detective	Ken Pogue
Simonson	John Candy
Louise	Gail Dahms
Berg	Michael Donaghue
Fogelman	Jack Duffy
Girl in sauna	Nancy Simmonds
Mrs. Skinner	Nuala Fitzgerald
Locksmith	Guy Sanvido
Mrs. Evanchuck	Aino Pirskanen
Young woman in bank	Michele Rosen
Newsboy	Ben Williams
Detective No. 2	Sandy Crawley
Little boy's mother	Jan Campbell
Little boy	Jimmy Davidson
Girl at party	Eve Norman
Detective No. 3	John Kerr
Tv newswoman	Sue Lumsden
Bank assistant	Candace O'Connor
Freddie	Stephen Levy

"The Silent Partner," showing at eight locations in metropolitan Atlanta, without having held N.Y. or Hollywood trade screenings, is one of the films that run the gamut from intrigue to violence. The excellent cast is headed by Susannah York, Christopher Plummer and Elliott Gould. It is entertaining.

Plummer plays the villain in for a change — a bank robber. Gould is a bank clerk who finds out that Plummer, dressed in a Santa Claus suit, plans a robbery. York is a bank employee under pressure from Plummer and newcomer Celine Lomez is a cohort of Plummer. The story has Gould, a teller in a branch office, get suspicious when it is the Christmas season and the bank is filled with shoppers. The robber hits and Gould's alertness inspires him to

hide $50,000 in a lunch box with the police believing that the robber has all the loot.

Plummer harasses Gould with such tactics as phone calls, breaking into his apartment, etc. As a result Gould loses the key to the safety deposit box where he has concealed the money and takes Lopez into his confidence to get a key made while box guardian York is at lunch. Plummer's brutality could have been lessened without hurting the film but the shock value should be talked about by viewers.

Filmed entirely in Toronto, it's an independently financed film which won six Canadian Film Awards. EMC Film Corp. picked up the film for the U.S. —Lucc.

Le Gendarme et les Extra-Terrestres
(The Gendarme and the Creatures From Outer Space)
(FRENCH-COLOR)

Paris, March 20.
An SNC production and release. Produced by Gerard Beytout. Directed by Jean Giranet. Stars Louis de Funes, Michel Galabru. Screenplay, Jacques Vilfrid, based on characters created by Richard Balducci; camera (Eastmancolor), Marcel Grignon, Didier Tarot; sound, Paul Laine; art direction, Sydney Bettex; music, Raymond Lefevre; editor, Michel Lewin. Reviewed at Cinema France-Elysees, Paris, March 19, '79. Running time: 92 MINS.

Cruchot	Louis de Funes
Gerber	Michel Galabru
Beaupied	Maurice Risch
Taupin	J.P. Rambal
Tricard	Guy Grosso

This is the fifth film in a series of comic vehicles in which Louis de Funes plays a Saint-Tropez gendarme, dedicated to enforcing the law and his own monumental stupidity. In this current adventure De Funes and his cronies tangle with some metalloid space creatures who have landed in Saint-Tropez (to study human mores (in Saint-Tropez?). Complications arise from the fact that the aliens can assume any human form though their disguises are continually belied by the clang produced when one strikes them and their continual need for lubricating oil. Of course, the gendarmes find the clue to their destruction and come out triumphant.

Given the quality of script, direction and performance, it is hard to call this a happy ending. There is not one genuinely funny gag in this whole listless affair and even De Funes, who can be an effective low comedian in the hands of a comic director like Gerard Oury, doesn't make much of an effort to exploit his repertoire of grimaces and contortions. Nevertheless the film is currently a boxoffice leader in France and Belgium, confirming De Funes as the successor to Fer-

nandel as France's reigning popular film comic.

Once again it is sad to see that excellent actor Michel Galabru wasting away in yet another dismal comedy that takes no note of his true mettle. —Len.

California Dreaming
(COLOR)

Mindless surfers and their bikini girls.

Hollywood, March 29.
American International Pictures release of a Taft Organization-Whittaker Production. Exec producer, Louis S. Arkoff. Produced by Christian Whittaker. Directed by John Hancock. Screenplay, Ned Wynn; camera (Movielab) Bobby Byrne; editors, Sid Leven, Herb Dow, Roy Peterson; music, Fred Karlin; production design, Bill Hiney; sound, Howard Steele. Reviewed at American International Pictures Screening Room, Beverly Hills, Calif. March 29, '79. (MPAA Rating: R) Running time: 92 MINS.

Corky	Glynnis O'Connor
Duke	Seymour Cassel
Fay	Dorothy Tristan
T.T.	Dennis Christopher
Rick	John Calvin
Stephanie	Tanya Roberts
Mike	Jimmy Van Patten
Jordy	Todd Susman
Corrine	Alice Playten
Earl	Ned Wynn
Tenner	John Fain
Ruben	Marshall Efron

Although American International Pictures' "California Dreaming" shares its title with the monster 60s hit by the Mama's and the Papa's, it's hard to imagine the ever in their wildest Coast fantasies the group envisioned this as the film counterpart to their record. While the disk was a celebration of the west coast lifestyle the film, either intentionally or unintentionally, does everything in its power to prove to the rest of the world that California consists primarily of brainless, beach bums whose major concern is how thick they can get the wax on their surfboards.

Fortunately, for the distrib, there is some nice camera work of surfers and a bright soundtrack, including the title tune by America, that might enable some decent one or two week playdates at outdoor screens. But chance for anything more than that is remote at best.

Pic falls victim to almost every stereotype concerning the California beach world that's ever been bandied about. There's the mindless sufers, their bikinied women, aging beach people living in the past and the vestal virgin who won't go in for the cheap sex that seems to be going on everywhere she turns. Enter, of course, the Midwest kid via bus, who acts and dresses like he comes from another planet (in this case it's that hick town, Chicago).

Will he fall victim to the superficial ways around him? Can he fit in

if he doesn't learn how to surf or play volleyball? Will he ever bed the vestal virgin? That's the basic plot line.

In terms of acting, Glynnis O'Connor, Dennis Christopher, Seymour Cassel and Dorothy Tristan do the best possible in lead roles. But Ned Wynn's script gives them so few believable lines that they more often than not come across as laughable. Director John Hancock doesn't help much by switching story's emphasis scene by scene and thus confusing an already weak screenplay. —Berg.

Ils Sont Grands Ces Petits
(These Kids Are Grown-Ups)
(FRENCH-COLOR)

Paris, March 27.
A United Artists release of a Cathala Films United Artists-FR3 co-production. Directed by Joel Santoni. Stars Catherine Deneuve, Claude Brasson. Produced by Norbert Saada. Script: Daniel Boulanger, Jean-Claude Carriere, Joel Santoni, from an original scenario by Jean Jabely; camera, (Eastmancolor) Walter Bal; art direction, Tony Roman; sound, Georges Prat and Luc Perini; editing, Ava Zora. Reviewed at Cinema Paramount-Orleans, Paris, March 26, 1979. Running time: 95 MINS.

Louise	Catherine Deneuve
Leo	Claude Brasseur
Arthur Palanque	Claude Pieplu
Monestier	Jean Francois Balmer

Catherine Deneuve and Claude Brasseur give some needed-luminosity to this generally lackluster comedy about two children who grow up in a world of gadgets and inventions. When an unscrupulous banker tries to push them out of their homes to make way for some typically ungainly building developments the platonic couple declare electronic war on the trresspassers. In the course of their struggles the two electronic wizards fall in love. Despite their victory they end up retiring to a small Arab kingdom where their idiosyncratic interests find indulgent benefactors.

The script's comic ideas are trite and the promise of outlandish mechanical warfare is not kept, leaving the story to fizzle out rather than peak. Nor does the Deneuve-Brasseur love realtionship have anything particularly unusual about it that makes it a functional part of the action. There are some gently amusing moments in the scenes in which the two pull off a bank robbery with a bugged box of chocolates and their little arsenal of motorized toys. Other than that, the only other compensation is watching Deneuve and Brasseur enjoy themselves. One could do worse. —Len.

Love At First Bite
(COLOR)

Bat-ting average looks good.

Hollywood, March 16.
American International Pictures release of a Melvin Simon production. Executive producers, George Hamilton, Robert Kaufman. Produced by Joel Freeman. Directed by Stan Dragoti. Features entire cast. Written by Robert Kaufman; camera (CFI color), Edward Rosson; editors, Mort Fallick, Allan Jacobs; sound, Don Bassman; production design, Serge Krizman; associate producer, Harold L. Vanarnum; choreography, Alex Romero; music, Charles Bernstein. Reviewed at The Directors Guild of America theatre, L.A., March 16, '79. (MPAA Rating: PG.) Running time: **96 MINS.**

Count Dracula	George Hamilton
Cindy Sondheim	Susan Saint James
Dr. Jeff Rosenberg	Richard Benjamin
Lt. Ferguson	Richard Benjamin
Lt. Ferguson	Dick Shawn
Renfield	Arte Johnson
Rev. Mike	Sherman Hemsley
Judge	Isabel Sanford

"Love At First Bite" is a kick for those who resist being too critical of sometimes uneven comedy. Outlook should be enhanced by all-out personal-appearance push by exec producer-star George Hamilton, anxious to prove a light heart beats beneath that handsome leading-man image of 48 previous films.

In truth, Hamilton is known privately as quite a good mimic and the film was born beside a swimming pool with the actor regaling writer Robert Kaufman with Bela Lugosi imitations, thoughts turning to "what would happen if " Dracula was victimized by life in modern New York City.

It's a fun notion and Hamilton makes it work. In the first place, he's funny just to watch. Veteran make-up artist William Tuttle, who created Lugosi's Dracula look in 1934, retains the grey, drained visage while adding a nutty quality that Hamilton accents with the arch of an eyebrow.

When Hamilton starts to talk, the familiar accent is there, but the stresses are amusingly in the wrong place. Most importantly, Hamilton always takes himself seriously as a monster, no matter how misunderstood at the moment by the ingrates of Gotham.

Story — which some will undoubtedly say is silly, and may be right — evicts Dracula from his Transylvania castle and takes him in pursuit of Susan Saint James, a fashion model he loves from an old photo. In the care of his bumbling manservant, slightly overplayed by Arte Johnson, Hamilton's coffin is naturally misrouted by the airline, winding up in a black funeral home. He next gets drunk and hungover on the blood of a skidrow wino, encounters muggers, etc.

But he meets the girl of his day-light dreams in a disco, where they waltz in film's best scene, choreographed by Alex Romero. After this night of romance, she wakes up with a "dynamite hickey," yet smitten with the count, despite boyfriend psychiatrist Richard Benjamin's warnings that three bites and she's a goner.

With his familiar squarely frantic style, Benjamin sets out to save her, with the dubious help of Dick Shawn as a cop. There's a great scene when Hamilton and Benjamin hypnotize each other while Saint James leaves in a bored, feminine huff. Another when Benjamin pumps three silver bullets into the vampire, who blithely reminds, "Silver bullets are for werewolves."

Despite a tendency to lurch from joke to joke, director Stan Dragoti keeps the chuckles coming, spaced by a few good guffaws. He, Kaufman and the cast, though, are less successful in an attempt to provide a genuine romantic love story beneath it all, though it's there in part. But you can't always have everything and what's here in a nice, compact 96 minutes is good enough. —*Har.*

Firepower
(BRITISH-COLOR)

Shady outlook for sunglass saga.

Hollywood, April 3.
Associated Film Distribution release of a Scimitar Films Production. Produced and directed by Michael Winner. Features entire cast. Screenplay, Gerald Wilson; camera (Technicolor), Robert Paynter, Dick Kratina, editor, Arnold Crust; sound, Jim Willis, Newton Avrutis; production design, John Stoll, John Blezard, Robert Gundlach; assistant directors, Ted Moreley, Alex Hapsis, Francois Moullin; music, Gato Barbieri. Reviewed at Mann's Westwood Theatre, L.A., April 3, '79. (MPAA Rating: R). Running time: **104 MINS.**

Adele Tasca	Sophia Loren
Jerry Fanon/Eddie	James Coburn
Catlett	O.J. Simpson
Sal Hyman	Eli Wallach
Dr. Felix	Anthony Franciosa
Gelhorn	George Grizzard
Frank Hull	Vincent Gardenia
Halpin	Fred Stuthman
Calman	Richard Caldicot
Manley Reckford	Frank Singuineau
Stegner	George Touliatos
Cooper	Andrew Duncan
Oscar	Hank Garrett
Dominic Carbone	Billy Barty
Lestor	Conrad Roberts
Harold Everett	Victor Mature

"Firepower" is one of those international action thrillers designed to combine a top-name cast with lots of shooting and explosions so the story can be followed regardless of whether you understand the language, includ-ing English.

Though competent with chases and gunfire, producer-director Michael Winner handles the dialog scenes as if the most significant thing in the world were sun-glasses. When people are mad and about to kill each other, they whip off their sun-glasses. When they're sultry and seductive, they whip off their sun-glasses. If they are just evil extras in the background, they keep their sun-glasses on.

According to Gerald Wilson's script, beautiful Sophia Loren believes her chemist husband was murdered at the order of Stegner, a wealthy, seclusive industrialist similar to you-know-who. She persuades the Justice Department, who also wants Stegner, to put the pressure on mobster Eli Wallach to entice retired hitman James Coburn to — get Stegner.

Coburn enlists O.J. Simpson (who is rapidly becoming a likable screen personality) to help him. And off they go, ashooting, aburning and abombing. Naturally, the intrigue all becomes more complicated and nothing is as it first seems. Coburn has a double who makes no difference and Loren is up to no good herself, not to mention Anthony Franciosa's hidden secret.

If the story becomes too tough or too tiresome to follow, or the action grows tepid and repetitive, there's always the beautiful scenery of the glamorous Caribbean locales. Or, as one preview lady was heard to remark to her mate during the climactic shootout between helicopter and boat, "Isn't the water a beautiful blue? Let's go there this summer." —*Har.*

An Almost Perfect Affair
(COLOR)

Cannes-themed satire should be boffo for buffs, but otherwise uncertain elsewhere.

Hollywood, April 10.
A Paramount Pictures release. Stars Keith Carradine, Monica Vitti. Produced by Terry Carr. Directed by Michael Ritchie. Screenplay, Walter Bernstein, Don Peterson, based on a story by Ritchie and Peterson; camera (Deluxe Color), Henri Decae; editor, Richard A. Harris; art direction, Willy Holt; music, Georges Delerue; sound, Bernard Bats; assistant director, Marc Monnet. Reviewed at Paramount Studio Theatre, April 3, '79. (MPAA Rating: PG.) Running time: **93 MINS.**

Hal	Keith Carradine
Maria	Monica Vitti
Freddie	Raf Vallone
Carlo	Christian De Sica
Jackson	Dick Anthony Williams
Lt. Montand	Henri Garcin
Amy Zon	Anna Maria Horsford

By setting "An Almost Perfect Affair" smack in the middle of the Cannes Film Festival, and peopling his romantic satire with directors, producers, producers' wives and producers' reps, Michael Ritchie has already won over the film industry segment of his audience. How the uninitiated will respond to these wheelings and dealings is uncertain, and could slow down the Paramount release at the box-office.

The emotions Ritchie is parlaying in this slim fable, which revolve around tender egos and unlimited ambition, are universal, and that's a plus for the film's potential. But the details are so specific, and so grounded in industry reality, that the larger implications in Walter Bernstein and Don Petersen's script may be lost.

In contrast to his most recent pix, which unleashed wicked jabs to beauty contests, tyro baseball and football ("Smile," "The Bad News Bears" and "Semi-Tough"), Ritchie returns to a more contemplative nature here, exhibited earlier in "Downhill Racer" and "The Candidate."

Keith Carradine is the young filmmaker, who wraps up two years of devotion to a film about executed murderer Gary Gilmore, "Choice Of Ending," by sinking all his remaining funds into a trip to Cannes. His film is seized at French customs until the censor can see it, an unlikely possibility until Monica Vitti, spouse of producer Raf Vallone, intercedes on his behalf.

The cinematic innocent abroad, Carradine mirrors lotsa nouveau helmers adrift in their initial dealings with industry salesmanship. Black hustler Dick Anthony Williams quickly latches onto Carradine and his film, changes the title to "Shoot Me Before I Kill Again," and lines up the Cannes ballyhoo with beauties in tightfitting t-shirts displaying bullseyes.

Focus of "An Almost Perfect Affair" is the intriguing relationship between Vitti and Carradine, which starts out as a one-nighter, and turns into a brief, but ill-fated romance. The affair ends when Vitti confides she really didn't care for Carradine's pic, followed by the inevitable dialog that people mean more than films, etc.

Unfortunately, the love story never commands as much interest as its background, which displays all the dizzy hoopla that makes Cannes more than just another fest. Industryites will have a lot of fun spotting familiar faces, since footage was shot at last year's edition.

Vitti, appearing in her first English-language film since "Modesty Blaise" in 1966, provides a warm counterpoint to Carradine's spoiled child character, and she emerges the more endearing of the pair thanks to a fine, meticulous performance. Vallone, in a not-so-subtle takeoff on Dino de Laurentiis, is quietly effective as the producer, and Christian de Sica, sprig of the late Italian director, is excellent as Vallone's officious son.

French locales, which have proved attractive to American directors as of late, are well utilized by lenser Henri Decae, and other tech credits, primarily from French craftsmen, are all superior.

Had "An Almost Perfect Affair" been an out-and-out comedy, Par might have a hit on its hands. With serious overtones against a trivialized backdrop, pic emerges as a curiosity item, and little more.

—*Poll.*

Frihetens murar
(The Walls Of Freedom)
(SWEDISH-COLOR)

Malmoe, March 28.

A Swedish Film Institute (Executive producer Joern Donner) - Three Leaf Clover HB production, AB Svensk Filmindustri release. Directed and edited by Marianne Ahrne. Written by Marianne Ahrne, Renzo Casali; camera (Eastmancolor) Hans Welin and Solveig Warner; no music credit. Reviewed at Camera, Malmoe, Sweden, March 28, '79. Running time: **100 MINS.**
Sergio . . . . Renzo Casali
Karin . . . . Marianne Stjernqvist
Anita . . . . Annicka Kronberg
Katja . . . . Christine Kronberg

"The Walls Of Freedom" has young Sergio, an Argentine would-be actor who found political conditions at home intolerable, arriving in a cold, remote, modern Stockholm. He had hoped to find paradise here, but soon discovers that even the city's own citizens hardly recognize the place as anything like their given home.

Sergio is a man of beatific disposition, the milk of human kindness fairly oozes out of his pores, so very soon he wins over Karin (an intelligent, underplayed performance by Marianne Stjernqvist), his elderly translator-landlady, Karin's younger friend Anita, who works as a switchboard operator at day and sings in a jazz club at night thus having not much time for her nineyear-old daughter, Katja, who, of course, is also befriended by bighearted Sergio.

Sergio finds work as a waiter in an elegant restaurant where he helps a customer rid herself of a nervous tic and in general helps generate a feeling of camaraderie among the kitchen staff that is otherwise tyrannized

Acute jealousy develops between Karin, Anita and Katja over Sergio's favors. Still, he suppresses his own immigrant's unhappiness most of the time. Until, one day, he decides to move back to supposedly warmer climates close to his Latin roots.

For no good reason, "Walls Of Freedom" (a perfect title) will be marketed abroad as "Roots Of Grief."

Whatever the title, this feature should not be hard to market in situations catering to mature foreign fare even though writer-director Ahrne is terrible when she gets into a philosophical mood. She comes off much better as a director of actors and creator of beautiful, naturally moving frames. She operates, unfortunately, very much with shopworn cliches, but her people and her action comes alive in both a humorous and truly affecting way by the leading actresses and by rotund Renzo Casali (actually an Italian who also worked with Ahrne on the script).

Hans Welin's and Solveig Warner's camera work has fine fluency and Marianne Ahrne edits her own work without any self indulgence. All production credits rate top marks. And as Anita, Annicka Kronberg has a deep, dark, mature beauty and a remarkable talent that might well add her name to the ever growing roster of international Swedish star players. —*Kell.*

Tilt
(COLOR)

For pinball freaks only.

Hollywood, March 30.

Warner Bros. release of a Melvin Simon production. Exec producer, Ron Joy. Produced and directed by Rudy Durand. Features entire cast. Screenplay, Rudy Durand, Donald Cammell, based on story by Durand; camera (Technicolor), Richard Kline; editor, Bob Wyman, Don Guidice, production design, Ned Parsons; music, Lee Holdridge; sound, Dean Salmon; assistant director, Pat Kehoe. Reviewed at The Burbank Studios screening room, March 30, 1979 (MPAA Rating: PG). Running time: **111 MINS.**
Tilt . . . . Brooke Shields
Neil Gallagher . . . . Ken Marshall
The Whale . . . . Charles Durning
Mickey . . . . John Crawford
Henry Bertolino . . . . Harvey Lewis
Replay . . . . Robert Brian Berger
Truck Driver . . . . Geoffrey Lewis
Mr. Davenport . . . . Gregory Walcott
Mrs. Davenport . . . . Helen Boll

Pinball fans should love "Tilt," but it's doubtful who else will. Rudy Durand, who waited more than 10 years for the opportunity to produce and direct this story, perhaps unwisely meshed the game action with a 1930s' style melodramatic plot. There are a lot of pinball players in the world, and their support will fan some interest in the Melvin Simon production, but otherwise, the Warner Bros. release seems unlikely to rack up any bonus points.

Not since "Tommy" in 1975 has pinball had a major screen showcasing, and it's easy to see why. The game is a one-on-one experience, between the player and the board, and the camera acts almost as an intruding agent. With the aid of tech advisor Michael "Pinball" Sehnert, Durand takes the audience inside the plexiglass top, and right onto the brightly lit game board, marking "Tilt's" major accomplishment.

Pinball sequences are few and far between, and the rest of "Tilt" is a disappointment. Brooke Shields, whose acting has shown no significant progression since "Pretty Baby," is a teen-age pinball hustler adopted by Ken Marshall, making film debut as a would-be rock star.

The two set out on a cross-country odyssey, ostensibly to launch Marshall's musical career. Real motivation is a grudge match between Marshall and Charles Durning, who plays a bloated bar owner with a reputation as a pinball champ.

Had "Tilt" gradually marshaled its forces until the climactic showdown between Shields and Durning, as "The Hustler" did for the game of pool, the pic's other defects would not seem so glaring.

But Durand dawdles through his story, relying on endless filler shots of bridges, freeways and pedestrians, along with various vignettes, rather than pacing to a solid finale. And when the big match does arrive, well into the night at a deserted bar, Durand interrupts the tension with a meal and chit-chat between the big man and little girl.

Segues are noticeably absent, and may reflect severe editing reportedly done on the pic. And while teenagers are certainly nonplussed by rough language (which did "Saturday Night Fever" little harm), screenplay by Durand and Donald Cammell seems overburdened by gratuitious vulgarisms.

Lee Holdridge's score is adequate, although hopelessly inappropriate to scenes like Durning shooting pinball to a disco beat. Much of Richard Kline's photography is overly dark, and ruins the effect of Ned Parsons' masterful production design. Other tech work is good.

The pinball sequences are what will sell "Tilt," and final montage, using angles from the ball's p.o.v., are impressive. —*Poll.*

Et La Tendresse?...
Bordel!
(Tenderness, My Fanny!)
(FRENCH-COLOR)

Paris, April 1.

A Gaumont release of a Chole Production — Foch Production co-production. Produced by Jean-Pierre Fougea. Features entire cast. Written and directed by Patrick Schulmann. Camera (color), Jacques Assuerus; editor, Aline Freess; music, Schulmann; sound, Pierre Lorrain; sound editor, Michel Patient; make-up, Yatzu. Reviewed at Cinema Gaumont Colisee, Paris, March 30, 1979. Running time: **90 MINS.**
Francois . . . . Jean-Luc Bideau
Eva . . . . Evelyne Dress
Luc . . . . Bernard Girardeau
Julie . . . . Anne-Marie Philipe
Leo . . . . Regis Porte
Carole . . . . Marie-Catherine Conti

Sex rears its ugly head in "Et la tendresse? ... Bordel" a first feature written and directed by 30-year old Patrick Schulmann, who composed the score as well. This sex comedy, which may prove to be the French sleeper of the year, is more promising than accomplished, a volatile mixture of caricatural and idealized portraiture, banality and fancifulness. Despite several funny scenes, it leaves an unpleasant aftertaste.

Against the background of a sexually intemperate society Schulmann interweaves the story of three couple-types. The "Phallocratic couple" is represented by Francois (ably played by Jean-Luc Bideau) a libidinous businessman who maintains his after-hours mistress, Carole, in a comfortable apartment while continuing to sweet-talk other women (in rhymed couplets, no less) into his bed. Carole has renounced her independence for an easy but affectionless life.

Regis and Julie are the "romantic couple" in love with each other even before they formally meet. Their relationship is characterized by clumsiness, naivete and confused ideals. They end up in listless wedlock.

Luc and Eva, on the other hand, are unselfconscious and direct, their love functioning on tenderness and understanding. Their relationship is strengthened by the world around them: Eva works in a psychological hospital peopled with victims of sexual overkill and Luc conducts door-to-door polls on people's life styles. Eventually they decide to retire to the country to have their baby.

Schulmann directs with the kind of punchy assurance that can goad the audience to laughter even when the humor is questionable, which it often is. The frequently trite script has no real insights to offer on phallocratic impulses (though there is a very funny scene involving a club where young men are instructed in how to pick up women in the most underhand way) and the gags scored off the romantic couple are increasingly distasteful and gratuitous) — Schulmann never gets beyond the cliche of naive romantics as near-sighted, clumsy dolts and his disdain is ill-disguised.

Schulmann does better with the tender couple and some of the minor characters where his sense of humor is coupled with genuine liking. Nor can one underestimate the genuine contribution of Bernard Girardeau as gentle Luc, who is a walking endorsement for the joy of living. The other actors are fine.

Some viewers may be turned off by Schulmann's tacit moral smugness: the phallocrat is literally castrated by a former mental patient (queazy reminders of Marco Ferreri's "The Last Woman" and Nagisa Oshima's "In the Realm of the Senses") and the romantic pair marry after the girl is hit by a car; husband then assumes Bideau's former functions and takes a mistress.

Only the tender couple and some minor characters get a kind of moral okay. Strange how asexual this couple is, as if pure carnal pleasure has no place in the film's scheme of things. It smacks of prudishness. —Len.

L'Homme En Colere
(The Angry Man)
(FRENCH-CANADIAN-COLOR)

Paris, March 30.

A United Artists release of a Films Ariane - F.R. 3. (Paris) — Cinevideo (Montreal) co-production. Produced by Alexandre Mnouchkine, Georges Dancigers, Denis Heroux. Stars Lino Ventura, Angie Dickinson. Directed by Claude Pinoteau. Written by Jean-Claude Carriere, Pinoteau: co-adaptor, Charles Israel; camera (Eastmancolor), Jean Boffety; editor, Marie-Josee Yoyotte; art direction, Earl Preston; music, Claude Bolling. Reviewed at Cinema Marignan-Concorde Pathe, Paris, March 27, 1979. Running time: 105 MINS.
Romain . . . . Lino Ventura
Karen . . . . Angie Dickinson
Julien . . . . Laurent Malet
Nancy . . . . Hollis McLaren
Pumpelmayer . . . . Donald Pleasence
MacKenzie . . . . Chris Wiggins

Claude Pinoteau's "L'Homme en colere" is a competent but conventional psychological thriller with the kind of story and craftsmanship that shows up fairly frequently on tv these days. Pinoteau has spoken of his interest in the problem of young, illegal French immigrants in Canada who are sucked into unhealthy environments and dubious jobs. This film, however, is not an enquiry into the situation, which is simply a pretext for the film. With a minimum of rewriting, story could take place in any other country.

Lino Ventura plays a widower who flies to Canada to identify the body of his son, killed in a shoot-out with police. But the corpse is that of a stranger and Ventura decides to find his son himself and convince him to surrender to the police, who suspect him of theft and murder. Their relationship has been poor for years, ever since the death of Ventura's wife in a forest fire. Son holds his father indirectly responsible for the tragedy.

Ventura makes his way through the urban maze frequented by his son, finding some companionship and aid in the person of a waitress

(Angie Dickinson) with a prison past. She helps him make contact with his son in face of police surveillance. Underworld is also looking for the young man, who plans to head for California with booty that has fallen into his hands. All the parties converge at the U.S. border where father and son are finally reconciled. A new wife and mother awaits to restore a family environment.

Script is neatly constructed but, wholly predictable. One knows reels in advance that Ventura is going to bloody and be bloodied and one suspects (rightfully) that the stubborn father and equally stubborn son will try to resolve the impasse of their relationship with blows. Bertrand Tavernier made a superior film on a similar theme in his fine first feature, "The Clockmaker."

Still, film is moderately interesting with some fine taut moments and scenes. And, of course, there is Lino Ventura, who in action or immobility is an always fascinating camera subject. He is ably supported by Angie Dickinson, Laurent Malet as the son and Donald Pleasence in one of his typically unpleasant roles.

Film was shot in French and English versions. —Len.

The Runner Stumbles
(COLOR)

With proper handling could set good pace at boxoffice.

Hollywood, April 4.

A Stanley Kramer Production. Exec producer, Melvin Simon. Produced and directed by Stanley Kramer. Features entire cast. Written by Milan Stitt, based on his Broadway play; camera (CFI) Laszlo Kovacs, A.S.C.; sound, James H. Pilcher; production design, Al Sweeney Jr.; editor, Pembroke J. Herring; music, Ernest Gold; assistant director, Craig Huston. Reviewed at MGM Studios Screening Room A, Culver City, Calif., April 4, '79. (MPAA Rating: PG). Running time: 99 MINS.
Father Rivard . . . . Dick Van Dyke
Sister Rita . . . . Kathleen Quinlan
Mrs. Shandig . . . . Maureen Stapleton
Monsignor Nicholson . . . . Ray Bolger
Erna . . . . Tammy Grimes
Toby . . . . Beau Bridges
Prosecutor . . . . Allen Nause
Amos . . . . John Procaccino
James . . . . Billy J. Jacoby
Sister Immaculata
. . . . Sister Marguerite Morrissey
Sister Martha . . . . Zoaunne LeRoy
Maurice . . . . Don Riley
Sheriff . . . . Ted D'Arms
Louise . . . . Kendall Kay Munsey
Marie . . . . Casey Kramer
Matt Webber . . . . Jim Doyle
Sophie . . . . Katherine Kramer
Judge . . . . Bill Dore
Dr. McNabb . . . . Jock Dove
Fire Chief . . . . Larry Buck

"The Runner Stumbles" is a powerful, thought-provoking film that manages to relate a simple love story and at the same time raise some severe moral questions.

Based on an actual murder case in 1927 where a priest is accused of killing a nun he was in love with, subject matter is on the surface, not one with much mass appeal, and might very well offend some. But as is often the case the impending controversy could very well work to pic's advantage at the boxoffice and, coupled with good word of mouth, might produce the kind of top notch "class" picture distribs like to brag about.

Director Stanley Kramer has, over the years, become known for dealing with moral questions like racism, gratuitous violence and the danger of nuclear power with such pictures as "Guess Who's Coming to Dinner," "Bless the Beasts and the Children" and "On the Beach." With "Runner" he has taken a basically uncommercial subject, celibacy in the Catholic church, and presented it in such a way that, at times, it appears like the best of the old-fashioned 1940's tear jerkers, complete with overly lush soundtrack. Yet "Runner" ultimately emerges as more than melodrama because Kramer puts equal emphasis on the priest and how he grapples with his love for God and this woman in his life.

Picture opens with staid Father Rivard in jail accused of murdering Sister Rita, a young attractive nun who was assigned to teach at the parish school when two ailing and aging sisters became ill. Instead of simply relating the entire story in flashback, Kramer skillfully recreates it by going back and forth on three levels — that is, the priest in jail, the story of his relationship with Sister Rita and the ensuing trial for murder. The technique is not the least bit confusing and, in fact, works quite well in capturing the different emotions in each time period.

Throughout, the film is paced by fine performances, especially Dick Van Dyke as Father Rivard, Kathleen Quinlan as Sister Rita and Maureen Stapleton as Van Dyke's housekeeper, Van Dyke appears a little too stiff in the beginning, but more than makes up for it as he slowly strips away the protective layers the once fun-loving priest has built around himself over the years. Quinlan is charming as Sister Rita, the obvious female version of the Father in his younger days. But it's **Maureen Stapleton who almost walks away with the picture as Van Dyke's confused housekeeper, the only person who's been privy to exactly what went on between the priest and nun. Stapleton's role is key to the development of the plot and it's because she's so convincing throughout that the film manages, in the end, to hold together so well.**

In supporting roles, Tammy Grimes, Ray Bolger, and Beau Bridges are also strong, with Grimes particularly good in one scene where Van Dyke and Quinlan try to comfort her when her father dies.

Film was originally a Broadway play, but there isn't a hint of it in the screen adaption by Milan Stitt, who was also responsible for the stage version. Laszlo Kovacs' camera work is clear and original, with he and Kramer devising a number of interesting dissolves that will probably cause even the untrained eye to be intrigued. Ernest Gold's music gets too overpowering at times, but thankfully does not hurt a number of highly emotional scenes.

Distrib deal has not yet been set on picture, entirely financed by Mel Simon productions. Because of subject matter, distrib's handling of release will probably play a bigger than usual role in b.o. performance. —Berg.

Suite California, Stops and Passes
(COLOR/B&W)

Champaign, Ill., April 1.

Produced, written, and directed by Robert Nelson. Sound and technical assistance, Diane and Steve Nelson; music, Mike Henderson, Chuck Wiley, Hobert Nelson, Gil Turner, Steve Nelson; camera (color), Robert Nelson. Reviewed at Picture Start screening room, Champaign, Ill., April 1, '79. Running time: 90 MINS.
Francisco . . . . Pete Maccan
Luz . . . . Diane Nelson
Ike . . . . Mike Henderson
Beatrice . . . . Mertis Schecaloff
Ted . . . . Robert Nelson

Robert Nelson's first film in a long time reflects two recent trends in the avant-garde; autobiography and feature-length films. Subtitled "a travelog," "Suite California" rambles, bumbles affectionately, stumbles and speeds across the West Coast, employing all the qualities of the '60s underground, and, as one of its creators, Nelson is entitled to that style. A hand-held camera which stares at tourists in Hollywood, overexposed film ends, a mock border escape in subtitled Spanish, old footage of orange pickers from Edison, and the landmarks of Death Valley punctuate the first half of the film, which is undoubtedly obsessed with the illusionistic power of Tinsel Town. The camera watches the city awake from a vantage point under the Hollywood sign in the Hills

Second half of film moves to San Francisco, to the personal space of family and friends, including a funny history of Golden Gate Bridge, yodeling deer hunters in the wilderness, the family opening gifts at Christmas, and the crumbling values and properties in the Bay Area. Although any attempt at narrative dissolves early in the picture, Nelson keeps a close watch on the human beings in his film, giving it an accessible humanity usually lacking in independent film.

Similarly, there is a sinewy humor throughout, reminding one that Nelson's classic "O Dem Watermelons" brands him as the true underground humorist. There is feeling in his footage, as well as striking images (of a sleeping cat, the Bay Skyline, endless highways in the desert, etc.), and that makes this independent feature (financed in part by National Endowment for the Arts) extremely watchable, even when the laid-back connectives aren't clear. —*Pege.*

The 5th Musketeer
(AUSTRIAN-COLOR)

Sharp swords, dull film.

Hollywood, April 4.
Columbia Pictures release of a Sascha-Film-Ted Richmond production. Exec producer, Heinz Lazek. Produced by Ted Richmond. Directed by Ken Annakin. Features entire cast. Screenplay, David Ambrose, based upon novel by Alexandre Dumas and screenplay by George Bruce; camera (color), Jack Cardiff; editor, Malcolm Cooke; music, Riz Ortolani; sound, Simon Kaye, Jim Willis; production design, Elliot Scott; art direction, Theo Harisch; costume design, Tony Pueo; assistant director, David Anderson. Reviewed at Columbia Pictures screening room, Burbank, April 4, '79. (MPAA Rating: PG.) Running time: **103 MINS.**
King Louis XIV/Philippe ... Beau Bridges
Marie-Therese .... Sylvia Kristel
Madame de la Valliere ... Ursula Andress
D'Artagnan .... Cornel Wilde
Fouquet .... Ian McShane
Aramis .... Lloyd Bridges
Porthos .... Alan Hale Jr.
Althos .... Jose Ferrer
Spanish Ambassador ..... Helmut Dantine
Colbert .... Rex Harrison
Queen Anne .... Olivia De Havilland

"The 5th Musketeer" is the third feature version to be made of Alexandre Dumas' 19th century political-adventure novel, "The Man In The Iron Mask." This Austrian-made production, featuring an international cast, adds nothing new to the genre, deriving its inspiration totally from the 1939 United Artists release written by George Bruce, who is credited here along with Dumas. Fast playoff domestically seems the best bet for the Columbia Pictures pick-up, which may score better overseas based on the cast's marquee value.

Made under the title of "Behind The Iron Mask," the Ted Richmond production was financed by the Sascha-Wien Co. as its second English-language feature. Retitling is an apparent attempt to cash in on the success of Richard Lester's simultaneously-filmed "Three" and "Four Musketeers," but the similarity ends after the opening credit.

Lester treated the swashbucklers

as ripe for satirization, and filled his pix with visual sight gags tweaking the usual solemnity of costume dramas. Ken Annakin, on the other hand, stifles "The 5th Musketeer" with ornate production values, deadly earnest swordplay and dialog as moth-eaten as the peasant costumes. The result? Yawnsville.

Beau Bridges fills the dual roles of King Louis XIV and his twin brother Philippe, who contests France's crown , aided, respectively, by scoundrels (Ian McShane, Ursula Andress) and heroes (Cornel Wilde, Lloyd Bridges, Alan Hale Jr. and Jose Ferrer as the Four Musketeers, along with Rex Harrison).

While the idea of casting the feisty quartet as aging swordsmen is a good one, there's no follow-through in terms of comic or dramatic potential. Wilde and company wield their blades with the same vigor as men 20 years younger, and they slay countless soldiers with little more than wrist action.

Sylvia Kristel, whose previous exposure has been in sofe-core sex films, proves an attractive Infanta of Spain, although hardly virginal. A deshabille scene with Bridges seems to have been excised here to preserve a PG rating, but will probably be restored in foreign térritones where Kristel has b.o. clout.

Amakin manages no suspense in his tale, and the chief rewards are Jack Cardiff's lush photographic work, Elliot Scott and Theo Harisch's lavish use of Austrian palaces and locales, and Tony Pueo's rich costumes. David Ambrose's script has only updated Bruce's dialog, and Riz Ortolani has contributed an uneven score, overdone in some scenes and totally absent from others.

Louis Hayward filled the title roles in the 1939 version, which James Whale directed for producer Edward Small. Joan Bennett had the Kristel role, and Warren William, Miles Mander and Bert Roach created the parts now filled by Wilde, Bridges and Ferrer. Alan Hale Jr. supplants his father, who portrayed Porthos in the UA release, while Walter Kingsford, Marian Martin, Montague Love and Doris Kenyon preceded Harrison, Andress, Helmut Dantine and Olivia De Havilland in their respective castings.

An earlier, silent version was made in 1929 with Douglas Fairbanks in the title role, Allan Dwan directing. There was also a tele-version with Richard Chamberlain. —*Poll.*

The Lovers' Wind
(IRANIAN-COLOR-DOCU)

Hollywood, March 28.
An Iran National Film Center production. Produced, directed by Albert Lamorisse. Re-edited by Mehrdad Azarmi; Text by Roger Glachant; camera (color) Guy Tabary, Raymond Letouzey; editors, Denise de Casabianca, Claude Lamorisse; music, Hosein Dehlavi. Reviewed at the Century Plaza Theatre, L.A., March 28, '79. Running time: **74 MINS.**

The late Albert Lamorisse, director of the Children's classic, "The Red Balloon," went aloft one last time to shoot "The Lovers' Wind," a visually stunning helicopter tour of Iran. Nominated for the Best Feature Documentary Oscar this year, film would seem to have lots of potential on the non-theatrical market with travel, cultural, historical and educational groups and is a good bet for tv.

Lamorisse continually searched for improved methods of filming flight throughout his career and died in a 1971 copter crash just as he was completing work on this picture, which has been re-edited by Mehrdad Azarmi for current release. Some of Lamorisse's effects would seem to be unparalleled, as one fabulous shot manages to accompany an airborne eagle for a long period. Virtually the entire film is from an aerial perspective, accompanied by poetically omniscient narration from the point of view of the wind of the title.

Focus is primarily on the history of Iran, with startling views of ancient cities backdropped by commentary on how civilization after civilization has come and gone in the region. The temporal nature of politics is thus contrasted with the eternal qualities of the land, so that when we finally arrive over Teheran, the overall effect could even be construed as ironically subversive in that, since docu was made, yet another seemingly unshakable regime has fallen. As the "wind" points out, only the roving gypsies of the land stay the same; all else passes.

Much of the terrain observed uncannily resembles the American West, even a section which looks like Monument Valley, although some of the sights, such as peasants herding water buffalo in the foreground while mammoth oil refineries smoke away in the background, could only be seen in a land where industrial development has exploded at a pace unequal to the historical progress of the country as a whole.

Though the philosophical attitude of the picture — "The more things change, the more they remain the same" — is valid, "The Lovers' Wind" is one of those rare films which is sustained on visual beauty alone. — *Cart.*

Kaleidoskop: Valeska Gert, Nur zum Spass-nur zum Spiel
(Kaleidoscope: Valeska Gert, For Fun-For Play)
(W. GERMAN-COLOR-DOCU-16m)

Hollywood, April 3.
A Bioskop-Film Production. Produced, directed, written by Volker Schlondorff. Features entire cast. Camera (color), Michael Ballhaus; editor, Gisela Haller; music, Friedrich Meyer. Reviewed at the Century Plaza Theatre, L.A., March 15, 1979. Running time: **41 MINS.**
Cast: Valeska Gert, Pola Kinski.

Valeska Gert is an eccentric Bohemian actress best known to modern audiences for her roles in Renoir's "Nana" and opposite Garbo in Pabst's "The Joyless Street." Two years ago German helmer Volker Schlondorff cast her in one of his pix, "Coup de Grace," and was so taken with her stories of 1920s Berlin and Paris that he decided to make this docu on her. It's of specialized interest, a minor but worthwhile footnote to the era's cultural history.

Gert, now in her 70s but still very spry, was a sensation in her day not so much for her acting but for her "expressionist" or "athletic" dancing.

Insisting in his narration that it's impossible to convey the effect Gert had on auds in her heyday, Schlondorff, visiting her at home on the island of Sylt, has her recreate some of her dances with the help of young actress/dancer Pola Kinski. The results of this experiment are mixed but, along with some rare clips of Gert in her prime, do give an idea of what she was getting at in her art.

With the impudence of a teenager, Gert goes over the old days, puncturing holes in the whole idea of Expressionism, calling Murnau a "kitsch" artist and ridiculing the exalted reputations of the likes of Marlene Dietrich and Conrad Veidt.

A completely intuitive artist, Gert must leave most of the theorizing to the director. She does point out, however, that, whether in film or dance, she always portrayed character types who were exploited by the bourgeoisie, and her iconoclastic personality is what comes through most strongly in Schlondorff's little portrait. —*Cart.*

Alzire oder der neue Kontinent
(Alzire or the New Continent)
(SWISS-COLOR-16m)

Hollywood, March 12.
A Filmkollektiv Zurich/Thomas Koerfer Film production. Directed by Thomas Koerfer. Features entire cast. Screenplay, Dieter Feldhausen; camera (color), Renato Berta; editor, Georg Janett. Reviewed at the Samuel Goldwyn Studios, March 11, 1979. Running time: **108 MINS.**
Voltaire .... Francois Simon

Rousseau .... Roger Jendly
Leo ....Rudiger Vogler

"Alzire" is a play by Voltaire and this film with the same title is about a little theatre troupe in modern Switzerland trying to stage it. This third feature by Thomas Koerfer, who made a small splash with his first film, "The Death of the Flea Circus Director, or Ottocaro Weiss Reform's His Firm," has its humorous and provocative moments, but in the long haul proves too dry and abstract for any strong impact. Prospects outside the fest circuit would appear to be marginal.

Rudiger Vogler, known locally for numerous leading performances in Wim Wenders' films, stars as a stage director with the idea of mounting Voltaire's little-produced drama to commemorate the 200th anniversary of the author's death. Unable to secure municipal funding, the rag-tag company retreats to the country where the members attempt to establish a theatrical commune with church backing. Failing again, the actors disperse and "real life" intrudes in a way which reflects back upon the theatrical version of history they were trying to present.

Framing this slowly paced action are five fanciful and amusing scenes featuring Voltaire and Jean-Jacques Rousseau in a verdant paradise, discussing their lives' work, jousting sarcastically with each other and commenting upon the futile efforts of the theatrical group to keep Voltaire's name alive. Since in 1978 not even the government is willing to back a staging of Voltaire with money, Rousseau has a field day with the satirist, though Voltaire scores points as well. Adding to the enjoyment of these scenes is the evident pleasure Francois Simon and Roger Jendly take in playing them.

Unfortunately, Dieter Feldhausen's dialog for his contemporary players isn't up to what he created for the two eminences gris. Bickering among the players in the troupe drags on and on, digs at Swiss authorities lose their effectiveness through repetition and the ineffectuality of the characters eventually rubs off on the film itself.

A rather sour disenchantment with contemporary society appears to be a recurrent theme in Swiss pix, but others have found more pertinent ways of expressing it than Koerfer has here. The Voltaire/Rousseau dialog is a marvelous conceit, but it's ultimately smothered by the dourness of the playwright's modern adherents.
—Cart.

With Babies And Banners: Story of the Women's Emergency Brigade
(COLOR-DOCU-16m)

Hollywood, March 17.
Produced by Anne Bohlen, Lyn Goldfarb, Lorraine Gray. Directed by Lorraine Gray. Camera (color), Ting Barrow, Max Reid, Lorraine Gray; editors, Mary Lampson, Melanie Maholick; sound, Samantha Heilweill, Carol Polakoff, Anne Bohlen. Reviewed at the Academy of Motion Picture Arts and Sciences Screening Room. March 17, '70. Running time: 45 MINS.

"With Babies and Banners: Story Of The Women's Emergency Brigade" is not only a fine documentary, but a touching story of real people who fought for and achieved a goal that, to some, changed the direction of this country.

Lorraine Gray, who directed and coproduced, succeeds in capturing on film the story of the women's role in the General Motors sit-down strike of the 1930's in Flint, Mich. (which eventually established the power of the United Auto Workers) without a hint of the usual preachiness or lethargy many documentaries fall victim to.

This is achieved mainly because she tells the story through the reminiscences of a group of women (now in their 60s and 70s) who were actual participants in the strike.

As members of the Women's Emergency Brigade, women marched in front of factories while men sat down inside in an effort to get management to agree to better conditions on the job.

Film points out that although past publicity focused on men who were actually inside factor during the strike, women marched and had added burden of managing the home on little or no money during the month and one-half period.

Picture alternates between interviews with women and footage of the actual strike. Editing by Mary Lampson and Melanie Maholick is done skillfully, capturing the growing enthusiasm of the women as they get further into their story.

What works out particularly well in the project is documakers' decision to film recent 40th anniversary of the strike in Flint, where women were not allowed a speaker during the proceedings despite having filed requests beforehand.
—Berg.

Il Mammasantissima
(Big Mamma)
(ITALIAN-COLOR)

Rome, Feb. 15.
A P.A.C. release of a Ciro Ippolito production for Orsa Maggiore Cinematografica. Stars Mario Merola. Directed by Alfonso Brescia. Written by Piero Regnoli, Ciro Ippolito, from story suggestion by Ippolito; camera (color), Silvio Fraschetti; editor, Carlo Broglio; art director, Romeo Costantini; music, Eduardo Alfieri. Reviewed at Fonoroma, Rome, Feb. 14, 1979. Running time: 89 MINS.
Cast: Mario Merola, Malisa Longo, Elio Zamuto, Biagio Pelligra.

"Big Mamma" is a fast-paced, action-packed kitsch pic that jams the magic, pathos, rhythm and mystery of a city like Naples, the setting of the film, into 89 minutes of sheer entertainment. With the right advance publicity and careful subtitling, "Big Mamma's" prospects, especially stateside, are excellent.

An ex-longshoreman who literally knows how to throw his weight around, Mario Merola has already won fame in Italian theatrical circles starring in revivals of Neapolitan sceneggiata, a musical genre that was wildly popular not only in Naples, but among Italian immigrants in the '20s. Merola — a husky, a bull-faced man — has been brought to the screen by producer Ciro Ippolito along with the character that made the sceneggiatta so successful: the tough guy — the guappo or "Big Marama" — with a heart of gold who tries to defend the little people from a sea of injustices.

In "Big Mamma" and other films starring Merola ("The Last Tough Guy," "The Caliber 9 Serenade") Ippolito has cleverly combined elements of the old sceneggiata with the more modern techniques of the western or gangster film. Cowboys and Indians riding across the plains have been replaced by cigarette smugglers — here the good guys — on their blue motorboats speeding across the Bay of Naples.

The film is peopled with delicious characters: a street-wise scugnizzo or Neapolitan urchin, a Pugliese who comes to Naples and loses his shirt (and his pants) in a roadside betting match, and Maria — Big Mamma's raven-haired daughter who dies of shame after being raped by her father's enemy. The death scene is appropriately mawkish and Merola's cry for vengeance appropriately chilling.

These characters — the innocent victim, the dastardly villains and the well-dressed Big Mamma himself — come right out of the Neapolitan theatrical tradition as does the melodrama (which may be a bit much for some) with its themes of honor and revenge. The setting, however, has been updated and like a Neapolitan "West Side Story" "Big Mamma" has combined explosive street scenes (including a marching band of Pucinellas) with a captivating language that is used like a musical score to tell the real-life drama of a remarkable city.
—Arço

Dawn of the Dead
(COLOR)

Return of Romero's zombies. For the light of head and strong of stomach.

United Film Distributing Co. release of a Laurel Group-Alfredo Cuomo and Claudio Argento production, presented by Herbert Steinmann and Billy Baxter. Produced by Richard Rubinstein. Directed by George Romero. Features entire cast. Screenplay, Romero; camera (Technicolor), Michael Gornick; script consultant, Dario Argento; editor, Romero and Kenneth Davidow; makeup and special effects, Tom Savini; sound, Tony Buba; lighting, Carl Augenstein; costumes, Josie Caruso; assistant director, Christine Forrest. Reviewed at United Artists Eastside Cinema, N.Y., April 11, '79. (No MPAA rating.) Running time: 125 MINS.
Stephen .... David Emge
Peter .... Ken Foree
Roger ....Scott Reiniger
Francine .... Gaylen Ross

George Romero, the Russ Meyer of the horror-gore genre, has come up with a continuation of his 1968 "Night of the Living Dead" click that, while lacking in redeeming esthetic value, leaps for the viscera at every turn. "Dawn of the Dead" stacks up as a slickly-made Grand Guignol outing that promises swift b.o. from sensation-bent and less squeamish audiences.

While it lacks the genuinely scarifying wallop of "Night," "Dawn" pummels the viewer with a series of ever-more-grisly events — decapitations, shootings, knifings, flesh tearings and even an occasional evisceration — that make Romero's special effects man, Tom Savini, the real "star" of the film.

That's fortunate since the actors are as woodenly uninteresting as the characters they play. Romero's strong suit is pacing and technical fluidity. His film has a keen visual sense that tersely extracts the maximum from all the bloodletting.

Romero's script, however, is banal when not incoherent — those who haven't seen "Night" may have some difficulty deciphering exactly what's going on at the outset of "Dawn." There's virtually no plot or character development.

But the audience for which "Dawn" is best designed is not likely to dwell on such niceties. To his credit, Romero professes no pretention to "art" on his film's behalf. He declares he set out to make a "straight-ahead" horror outing.

On that less lofty scale, "Dawn of the Dead" is for the most part successful. Romero introduces the mayhem at key points when the story line and dialog threaten tedium. His sense of visual balance — which directors of more heralded films could well use — salvages the pic.

The plot isn't worth detailed description. Enough said those carnivorous corpses that stalked through "Night" return in sufficient numbers to threaten extinction of the entire U.S. population.

The four main characters — two ex-National Guardsmen (Scott Reiniger and Ken Foree) plus a tv technician (Gaylen Ross) and her live-in boyfriend (David Emge) — take refuge in a shopping mall near Pittsburgh to escape the cannibalistic zombies. In between dispatching latter with skull-shattering rifle shots, the quartet tries to figure out how to cope with the technicians' pregnancy and various zombie-inflicted wounds.

There's a predictable denouement with two of the four characters escaping — via helicopter — unscathed. Romero uses the shopping center confinement to make semi-telling points about materialistic drives amidst life-threatening chaos. Point is made indirectly; mayhem is center stage throughout.

Pic was shot for under $1,500,000 in the Pittsburgh area, Romero's professional base. Non-union operation permitted the slick look for little money, although Michael Gornick's photography warrants a special nod.

Pic, which is going out without a rating, will doubtlessly stir complaints about its violent content. Complaints won't be unjustified but Romero has made his principals and zombies — portrayed by Pittsburgh locals in ashen facial makeup — lacking in humanity that their fates will evoke little sympathy.
—*Sege.*

Al Tish'ali Im Ani Ohev
(Don't Ever Ask Me If I Love)
(ISRAELI-COLOR)

Tel Aviv, April 8.

A Forum Films Presentation of a K.R. A.K. Production. Produced by Amos Kolek, Rafi Reibenbach. Directed by Barbara Noble. Screenplay, Kolek, Mark Dickerman, based on novel by Kolek; camera (color), David Gurfinkel; editor, Alain Jakobowitz; music, Niruth Hirsch. Songs performed by David Broza, Sherri and Josy Katz. Reviewed in Tel Aviv, April 7, 1979. Running time: **94 MINS.**

Cast: Amos Kolek, Shelby Leverington, Joe Cortez, Yossi Yadin, Shraga Harpaz, Lya Koenig, Yossi Polak, Lea Orsher, Gidi Gov.

This is basically a one-man-show, Amos Kolek, whose novel served as basis for the story. He also worked on the adaptation, was partner in the production and plays the lead.

Kolek's family interests everybody here, his father, Teddy, being the mayor of Jerusalem, and one of the most active political figures in Israel. The father-son relations, which tend to show that the charming, out-going personality of the

parent looked at differently in the eyes of his progeny, who felt often neglected, is only part of the story, centered mostly round the romance between the playboy son, living in an exotic pad without any visible means of existence, comfortably writing a novel which nobody seems anxious to read, and an American girl, lodging in the middle of the Arab quarter in the Old City, and working at archeological excavations. The background is everyday life in Jerusalem, Kolek style.

There may be a message about violence, but it is hidden under mountains of mumbled statements.

The truth is that Kolek, who bought the filming rights back from an editor, in order to have complete control on the project, is simply not up to doing everything at the same time. His script is amateurish, his characters diffuse and unclear, his dialog crammed with platitudes. He is a very poor actor, delivering his lines in a monotonous singsong, and wearing always the same expression of anxiety which might have been intended to arouse sympathy but doesn't.

No less a mystery is the presence of American actor Joe Cortez, given a starring credit, in a supporting role as Kolek's best friend. He has to play an Israeli officer and all he is required to do, is look nice and hardly open his mouth, a trick probably devised to hide the many out-of-sync sequences dubbed. For Shelby Leverington, playing Kolek's love, there is at least a reason to be American, and she is certainly the most believable character in the whole set-up, struggling valiantly with lines who sound often unbelievable.

While no exact figures on the investment were released there were some hints that half a million tickets would have to be sold in order to recoup the costs. Judging by initial reaction by critics this seems an almost impossible mission, locally at least. —*Edna.*

Beneath the Valley of the Ultravixens
(COLOR)

A hot Russ Meyer time in the old town tonight.

RM Films International, Inc. release of a Russ Meyer production. Produced, directed, photographed and edited by Meyer. Features entire cast. Written by R. Hyde and B. Callum from a story by Meyer. Reviewed at the Westside Screening Room, N.Y., April 12, '79 (No MPAA Rating). Running time: **93 MINS.**

Lavonia .... Francesca (Kitten) Natividad
Eufaula Roop .... Anne Marie
Lamar Shedd .... Ken Kerr
Junk Yard Sal .... June Mack
The Stripper .... Lola Langusta

Mr. Peterbuilt .... Pat Wright
Semper Fidelis .... Michael Finn
Rhett .... Steve Tracy
Flovilla Thatch .... Sharon Hill
Martin Bormann .... Henry Rowland
Dr. Asa Lavender ..... Robert E. Pearson
Zebulon .... De Forest Covan
Beau Badger .... Don Scarbrough
Tyrone .... Aram Katcher
Supersoul .... Uschi Digard
The Very Big Blonde .... Mary Gavin
The Man From Small
Town U.S.A. .... Stuart Lancaster

For the fanciers of pneumatic pulchritude. Russ Meyer is back with "Beneath the Valley of the Ultravixens," which as the on-screen narrator says "is a very simple story," presumably for very simple people.

Briefly, the strand of plot concerns Lavonia, whose only fault is "enthusiasm" and her unsatisfactory sex relationship with her man Lamar, who has an I.Q. of 37 and is part Greek, but not by birth. In the course of curing Lamar so that he will straighten up (no, he's not gay) and satisfy, Lavonia has a hot time with everybody in town, from a traveling lingerie salesman to the local garbageman to a lesbian encounter with a nurse.

Finally Lamar is saved by Eufaula Roop, an evangelist of the air, who takes him into her "tub of joy" and immerses him in more ways than one. How does this cure him? Strange are the ways.

This is the umpteenth in Meyer's vixen series and as long as they're profitable, there are doubtless more to come — "The Jaws of Ultravixen" is next. But are they satire, as Meyer would have one believe, or fantasy, or both? If anything, they are funny — in a dirty joke way — and though a bit too long, Meyer, who does everything: directs, edits, photographs and produces, keeps the action fast and furious and obviously gives his customers their money's worth. —*Lee.*

The Evictors
(COLOR)

Good try, poor results.

Hollywood, April 12.

American International Pictures release. Produced and directed by Charles B. Pierce. Features entire cast. Written by Charles B. Pierce, Garry Rusoff, Paul Fisk; camera (Movielab Color), Chuck Bryant; editor, Shirak Khojayan; music, Jaime Mendoza-Nava. Reviewed at Charles Aidikoff screening room, L.A., April 12, '79. (MPAA rating: PG). Running time: **92 MINS.**

Ben Watkins .... Michael Parks
Ruth Watkins .... Jessica Harper
Jake Rudd .... Vic Morrow
Olie Gibson .... Sue Ane Langdon
Bumford .... Dennis Fimple
Preacher Higgins .... Bill Thurman
Buckner .... Jimmy Clem
Wheeler .... Harry Thomasson
Mrs. Bumford .... Twyla Taylor
Dwayne Monroe .... Glen Roberts

Producer-director Charles B.

Pierce made an early reputation for turning out some rather interesting pictures with very little money. Now, for the second time since "The Norseman," he has the money and very little picture. Weak title won't help attract even the limited axe-murder fans the pic might appeal to.

Pierce, cameraman Chuck Bryant and generally good cast ably create a smalltown southern atmosphere of the 1930s and 1940s, maintaining a mood and authenticity within which something interesting might happen. But it never does.

Familiar centerpiece is an old house with a horrid history. Arrive the likable young couple, Michael Parks and Jessica Harper, soon to be perturbed by the strange goings-on and whispered stories about their dreamhouse.

Vic Morrow plays the realtor — not to be trusted — who sold them the house without telling its background. And Sue Ane Langdon is the friendly neighbor — not to be trusted either, obviously — who is happy to tell the bloody history, detailed on screen in flashbacks.

Nothing comes as a shock, since all the murders are well-telegraphed in advance and not that exciting when they happen. And it all climaxes in a triple-surprise ending.

By then, if you're surprised at all, that'll be the surprise. —*Har.*

En kaerleks sommar
(A Summer Of Love)
(SWEDISH-COLOR)

Malmoe, March 27.

A Nordisk Tonfilm (Ingemar Ejve) production, AB Svensk Film release. Stars Goesta Ekman, Maria Andersson, Anita Ekstroem. Directed by Mats Arehn. Written by Jonas Cornell, based on novel by Ivan Klima; camera (Eastmancolor) Lars Bjoerne, Bertil Rosengren; music, Terje Rypdal; no editor's credit; executive producer, Peter Kropenin. Reviewed at Scania, Malmoe, Sweden, March 27, 1979. Running time. **98 MINS.**

David Jernberg .... Goesta Ekman Jr.
Eva .... Maria Andersson
Ingrid Jernberg .... Anita Ekstroem

Mats Arehn, in an edgeway manner established as a modern director with a firm grasp of fluency in film story telling, shows rather wanton courage in serving up once more the oft-told tale of the mature, yet still youngish intellectual (a scientist dealing with the problems of old age), solid family man caught in the turmoil of sudden sexual infatuation with a naive, socially inferior, obviously self-dramatizing and only defiantly happy (her wrists show suicide scars), occasionally vicious and moody, physically alluring yet not really very attractive younger girl.

Arehn succeeds in keeping audiences (and audiences practically everywhere will buy, however reluctantly, this morose love story) interested through the strength and guts of his portraiture of one such victim of sexual circumstance and also with the aid of Goesta Ekman's finely honed, neurotic yet intellectually controlled performance in the lead role.

Maria Andersson as the object of Ekman's passion, appears to be delivered, gift-wrapped, from the socially doomed, brashly defiant disco/bohemian background of haphazard life in undefined slum suburbia. She has genuine intuition for showing antagonism towards her lover's bourgeois behaviour patterns and her total abandonment in moments of erotic passion seem relaxed in a way glorious enough to explain the essential idiocy of her confused lover.

Terje Rypdal, a Norwegian jazz-rocker of considerable fluency, adds dramatic impact without ever intruding on the essentials of the story, and appears to be an ideal movie score writer. He works along with the uncredited film editor (Arehn himself?) and cinematographer Lars Bjoerne towards a natural build of a conventional story into an unexpected experience of joys and sorrows to be commonly shared by larger audiences of all ages. Added soft-focus flashbacks supply spice but are largely just pretentious and as unnecessary as footnotes in a novel. —*Kell.*

Der Pfingstausflug
(The Pentecost Outing)
(WEST GERMAN-COLOR)

West Berlin, April 2.
An Ottokar Runze Film Production. Hamburg, in collaboration with Second German Television (ZDF) and SRG. Features entire cast. Written and directed by Michael Guenther, based on an idea by Peter Albrechtsen. Camera (color), Michael Epp; music, Hans-Martin Majewski. Reviewed at Cinema Paris, West Berlin, April 1, '79. Running time: 90 MINS.
With Elisabeth Bergner, Martin Held, Brigitte Groohum, Edda Seippel, Gaby Gasser, Dagmar Biener, Simone Rethel, Ewald Wenck, Otto Czarski, Horst Poenichen, Friedhelm Ptok, Klaus Sonnenschein.

Elisabeth Bergner, one of the great stars theatre and cinema of the 1920s and 1930s, returned to Germany and Berlin after three decades to make this light comedy about an elderly couple escaping from an Old People's Home for a day's outing. Not only did she win the Berlin Critics' Ernst-Lubitsch-Prize for her part in Michael Guenther's "The Pentecost Outing," but the pic has been a b.o. winner in the city where her name once was an institution.

"The Pentecost Outing" works its magic as a vignette: two lovable innocents venture out into a world of past memories amid confusing streets in the wooded Grunewald "villa" area of West Berlin. Everyone about them — the Home's manager, the bus driver, even people on the street — appear to be the "baddies," while our elderly couple charms the audience with witty remarks, pratfalls, cane-shaking, and all-around joking about the foibles of life and modern living. Somehow, it works — for most of the time.

A must for Bergner and Held fans — don't be surprised if a sequel is on the way for grateful Berliners who are nostalgically rooted in Berlin's golden past. Credits are minor, and direction is often embarrassingly fumbling. —*Holl.*

Nacionalna Klasa Do 785 CM3
(National Class)
(YUGOSLAV-COLOR)

Belgrade, April 6.
A Centar Film Production, Belgrade; world rights, Yugoslavia Film, Belgrade. Features entire cast. Written and directed by Goran Markovic. Camera (color), Zivko Zalar; sets, Miodrag Miric; music, Zoran Simjanovic. Reviewed at Yugoslavia Film, Belgrade, April 5, '79. Running time: 90 MINS.
With Dragan Nikolic, Bogdan Diklic, Gorica Popovic, Danilo Stojkovic, Olivera Markovic, Aleksandar Bercek.

Goran Markovic had a b.o. winner on his first outing as a helmer with "Special Education" (1977), which copped a kudo at the Mannheim fest for first and second features. This tale of juveniles on the run won him a young following at home — for whom he apparently made "National Class."

"National Class" in its full title (add on the figures "Do 785 CM3") refers to the brand name of a Fiat car, whose little size and fast build allows it to squirm through traffic and into parking places with some ease. Its driver (Dragan Nikolic) is a lazy lout, with girls on his mind and excuses for not getting a job. Everything he gets he gets by conning others, but he does have his heart set on winning a drag race on a rain-soaked, mud-splattering race course. The race is a riot, the high point of this comedy.

Pic's only drawback is that most of the humor is local, and thus the comic lines can't be translated into an equivalent idiom. As for the visual jokes, most of them are generated by gags minutely executed around the presence of the flivver on and off camera.

"National Class" is worth a look-see. —*Holl.*

Roberte
(FRENCH-COLOR)

Paris, March 22.
A Seine Distribution release of a Filmobic production. Produced by Hubert Niogret. Directed by Pierre Zucca. Features entire cast. Screenplay, Pierre Klossowski, Pierre Zucca from the novel, "Le Revocation de l'Edit de Nantes," by Pierre Klossowski; camera (Eastmancolor), Paul Bonis; sound, Michel Vionnet; art direction, Max Berto; costumes, Christian Gasc, Renee Renard; editing, Nicole Lubtchansky. Music, Eric Demarsan. Reviewed at Seine Cinema, Paris, Feb. 15, 1979. Running time: 100 MINS.
Roberte .... Denise Morin Sinclaire
Octave .... Pierre Klossowski
Antoine .... Martin Loeb
Vittorio .... Barbet Schroeder
Little F .... Juliet Berto
Justin .... Michel Berto

As far as overly intellectual films go, "Roberte" is a notch above the rest. Pierre Zucca and Pierre Klossowski have adapted the latter's novel to the screen with an often kinky sense of humor.

Action revolves around the figure of Roberte, a priggish Calvinist woman with an ascendant political career. Out of a sense of sacrifice she has married Octave, a voyeuristic Catholic aesthete who collects obscure paintings and prostitutes his wife to other men, an activity to which she submits. Oppressed by the present, menaced by her past involvements during the war, Roberte finally decides to act and poison Octave. But Octave dies of his own overheated passions during one of the tableau vivant in which he makes Roberte take part.

Film toys with themes of sexual and religious repression and marriage. Though the goings-on remain inscrutable some of the scenes are intriguing and often witty in the use of symbolism and space. Film owes it sustained interest to Zucca's technical skill and Klossowski's well-knit dialog. Still, the film remains an item for the art house circuit and intellectual fodder for the more specialized film journals.

The perverse couple are effectively played by Klossowski and his wife, Denise Morin Sinclaire, whose poise is admirable. One hopes that film is not composed of coded scenes from personal life, which would be disagreeable. —*Len.*

The American Game
(DOCU-COLOR)

A World-Northal release. Produced by Anthony Jones. Written and directed by Jay Freund and David Wolf. Camera (color) and location direction, Robert Elfstrom, Peter Powell; coproducers, Powell, Robby Kenner; associate producer, Grania Gurievitch; editors, Freund, Nancy Baker; contributing editors, Michael Steinfeld, Kenneth Eluto, Judith Guerra; sound editor, Al Nahmias. Reviewed at Rizzoli Screening Room, N.Y., March 29, '79. (No MPAA rating.) Running Time: 85 MINS.

Intercutting the separate stories of two high school basketball aces — one a stolidly middle class Indiana town kid, the other a black Brooklyn ghetto youth — "The American Game" is a well-conceived and generally involving feature documentary that charts the parallel but widely different paths that lead to their eventual escape from dead-ended community to college scholarships.

For all its virtues, however, not the least of them a strong dramatic flow, the film's low-budget origins — especially an imperfect blow-up from 16m to 35m format — and basketball-themed environment probably make it too rough-hewn and specialized to penetrate the commercial market (film's Gotham bow is at an eastside art house). Careful booking, capitalizing on educational and athletic group tie-ins, could maximize its point-spread.

In charting the two kids' final high school season, writer-directors Jay Freund and David Wolf have succeeded admirably in detailing the gut importance of the game itself, along with the disparate social pressures that propel the two youths into seeing their on-court ability and the sole key to self-realization.

The filmmakers' selection of their two subjects provides an acute study in contrasts, ranging from the tight-knit family and smalltown Indiana community that sees Brian Walker as their local great white hope, to the parentless and depressed situation of Brooklyn's Stretch Graham, who looks on his team and coach as the breadth of his family.

With the camera intimately sitting in on team and family discussions, high-pressure college recruitment pitches, locker-room tensions and on-court battles, the film is at its best when it gets down to the stark emotions of a lost game or, in the case of Walker, the constant pressure from a family that can't find glory anywhere but in their son's prowess.

Those moments, though searing, unfortunately are too few and far between. And though the film is wisely structured to parallel the intensity of two key playoff games with the final deadline for the two kids to make their first major life-decision, not enough emotion is generated overall to keep "American Game" from being much more than a straightforward documentary. Though interest rarely flags, it's the kind of interest that could just as easily be served by the home tube as theatrically.

Graham and Walker, though their paths are interesting to watch, don't have much in the way of presence or articulateness. Most blatant measure of that is the fact that Graham's coach, whose hard-edged concern and love for his team generate the film's strongest emotional moments, has the face audiences will carry away with them. —*Step.*

Tally Brown, N.Y.
(WEST GERMAN-COLOR-16m-DOCU)

A Rosa von Praunheim production. Stars Tally Brown. Directed by Rosa von Praunheim, with the assistance of Mike Shephard. Camera (color), Juliana Wang, Ed Lieber, Michael Oblowicz, von Praunheim; other assistance, Reno Sweeney's, Hans Dudelheim, Anja Philipps. Reviewed at Millenium, New York, March 30, '79. Running time: **110 MINS.**

With Tally Brown, Taylor Mead, Holly Woodlawn, Divine, Ching, Elisabeth and Robert Kashy, Edward Caton.

Winner of a German Film Prize, Rosa von Praunheim's "Tally Brown, N.Y." follows in the same vein as his earlier "I'm an Anti-Star" about Teutonic Underground star Evelyn Kuenneke. This time the subject is Tally Brown, who was the outrageous star of several Gotham Underground pix of the 1960s, when Andy Warhol, Ken Jacobs, Taylor Mead, Jack Smith, and Ron Rice ruled the roost in a patented anti-moralist approach to sexuality.

Von Praunheim became acquainted with the fading New York Underground scene in 1974, when he made "Underground and Immigrants" for the SoHo — Downtown Manhattan program at the 1976 Berliner Festwochen (a Berlin salute to the Yank Bicentennial).

This nostalgic review of Tally's career — from opera training and Tanglewood outings to blues singer and star in Underground pix and strip joints — is remarkable for its loving recollection of a bygone era through the stories of the star's closest friends, particularly Taylor Mead, Holly Woodlawn, and Divine. What's missing are some appropriate clips from her pix to add to the fun, but docu already gives considerate space to let Tally, in grand style, tell her own story.

Credits are plus, and docu is worth a look-see. —*Holl.*

H.C. Andersen I Italien
(Hans Andersen In Italy)
(DANISH-ITALIAN-COLOR-DOCU)

Copenhagen, April 3.
An IDA production (Rome) and release. Written by Ulla Kampmann and Fernando Cavaterra. Directed by Cavaterra. Features entire cast. Camera (blown-up 16m, color) Roberto Nappar, Gregers Nielsen, Tue Ruetzow; editor, Riccardo Parmigiano; music, Steven Schlacks, Lars Fjeldmose. Reviewed at Hans Andersen's Fairy Tale Restaurant, Copenhagen, April 2, 1979. Running time. **70 MINS.**

Hans Andersen (adult) ...... Jesper Klein
Hans Andersen (child) ..... Sune Schmidt
Andersen's mother ..... Jytte Abildstroem

Rome society lady ..... Maude Berthelsen
Sculptor Thorvaldsen .. Henrik Stangerup
A street juggler .... Palle Schmidt

A lot of non-professional Danish writers, singers, artists, etc. gathered around artist Ulla Kampmann and her Italian husband Fernando Cavaterra to help her scrape together private funds for this fantasy-docu. Jesper Klein was chosen for the role of the famous fairytale writer. "H.C. Andersen In Italy" is based on the chapter, "Journey in Italy," from Andersen's autobiographical "A Poet's Bazaar."

Film has all the earmarks of an outright amateurish work, but still contains flashes of charm and wit congenial with Andersen's own special brand of cunning naivite. Some tv sales are to be expected when various technical mishaps, especially on the soundtrack, have been righted.

Andersen is said (on the soundtrack) to have been deeply impressed both by the Italian landscapes and by the Italian people, but what is on the screen is mostly an enthusiasm for outright folklore. Audiences would have to be almost Andersen scholars to appreciate the allusions to his shyness in relation to women, his (possible) homosexuality, etc.

One of Andersen's tales is retold in the film and there are several moments of either maudlin or comical flashbacks to his poor childhood. Klein, always an amazing talent of madcap wit and soft-focused inner warmth, hardly has more than the outward melancholy, none of the deeper aspects of tragedy in Andersen's life. Sune Schmidt is a ray of pure sunshine as Andersen, the small child, and Maude Berthelsen is witty and sensually strong in her attempts to seduce the sexually repressed poet. —*Kell.*

Ett anstaendigt liv
(A Decent Life)
(SWEDISH-DOCU-COLOR)

Gothenburg, March 28.
A Stefan Jarl production, AB Svensk Filmindustri (domestic), Folkets Bio (foreign) distribution. Written and directed by Stefan Jarl. Features entire cast. Camera (Eastman-color, 16m blown up to 35m) Per Kaellberg, Staffan Lidqvist, Roland Lundin; editors, Anette Lykke-Lundberg, Jan Persson, Badis Andersson; music, Ulf Dageby, Johannes Leyman, Nacksving, Kenta Gustafsson, Eva Blondin, Stoffe Svensson. Reviewed at Cosmorama, Gothenburg, Sweden, March 28, 1979. Running time, **102 MINS.**

Eleven years ago, Stefan Jarl (with Jan Lindqvist) documented the young beer swilling dropouts of Welfare Stockholm in "They Call Us Mods," part 1 in a planned trilogy of which "A Decent Life" is part 2, describing what happened 10 years later when the "Mods," boys and

girls, had been turned into more or less hopeless drug addicts — at least, those boys and girls who have remained alive at all.

Actually, one of the young men in "A Decent Life" O.D. during the filming. Others, if only a minority, give small signs of coming to grips with the demands of society.

Film is rough, technically and in general attitude. No attempts are made at snaking the message through via aesthetic trickery or conventional entertainment and plot maneuvering.

Jarl opens his long documentary with a Breughel painting of the Great European Plague, then takes us literally underground into today's Plague Playground, the haunts in and around subway toilets of downtown Stockholm's heavy dopers.

The camaraderie between the dopers is not sentimentalized. A few characters are followed more closely than others, but it is the overall picture of a life of degradation that has Jarl's greater interest.

Among the "players," Stoffe Svensson "performs" with animal directness. He is the one who died of a heroin overdose during the filming. Kenta Gustafsson is a faintly shining light (he is a country boy with a built-in resistance and he even gets around to start building a family life) in a darkness that becomes total in the description of "Bettan" (Elizabeth Backe), the toothless, teenage heroin addict prostitute who is kicked almost to death by a "socially upright" customer.

"A Decent Life" (possibly to be marketed as "A Respectable Life") should be assured wide interest through all less traditional outlet. —*Kell.*

Oginsaga
(Love and Faith; Lady Ogin)
(JAPANESE-COLOR)

Hollywood, March 29.
Toho Co. Ltd. release. Produced by Tsuneyasu Matsumoto, Kyoko Oshima, Muneo Shimojo. Directed by Kei Kumai. Features entire cast. Screenplay, Yoshitaka Yorita, based on a story by Toko Kon; camera (color), Kozo Okazaki; music, Akira Ikufube; art direction, Takeo Kimura; editor, Tatsuji Nakashizu. Reviewed at Kokusai Theatre, Los Angeles, March 29, '79. Running time: **150 MINS.**

Sen Rikyu .... Takashi Shimura
Ogin .... Ryoko Nakano
Tajko Hideyoshi .... Toshiro Mifune
Mozuya .... Daijiro Harada
Soji Yamagami .... Atsuo Nakamura
Takayama Ukon ... Kichiemon Nakamura
Ankokuji .... Eji Okada
Sojin Kamiya .... Akira Nishimura

Young Japanese director Kei Kumai made a big impression Stateside with his last film, "Sandakan No. 8," nominated for the Best Foreign Film Oscar in 1975. As his lat-

est production for Toho, he's chosen to do the umpteenth remake of the perennial Japanese epic soap opera, "Love Under the Crucifix," and the results are disappointingly laborious. Despite its name cast, little chance is held out for this one to break out of the normal limited Japanese distribution circuit.

"Oginsaga" (title has been translated locally both as "Love and Faith" and "Lady Ogin") is the tale of a grand amour bedevilled by the influx of Christianity into Japan in the late sixteenth century. Lady Ogin can never marry her converted beloved, who himself is being hounded into exile by the marauding consolidator of Japan, Hideyoshi.

Kumai has cast this saga of tragic inevitability impeccably but has paced it ploddingly, bringing little that's sufficiently original or different to justify the lavish production values and excessive running time. Overall effect is similar to that of a Shakespearean tragedy presented reverentially and without outs in the text, resulting in tedium and lack of relevance.

Mitigating against Kumai's foot-dragging is the cast. Ryoko Nakano is radiantly lovely as the long suffering Lady Ogin. Takashi Shimura, who essayed the lead in Akira Kurosawa's "Ikiru" is dignity itself as her protector and a representative of the old ways finally destroyed by the conqueror Hideyoshi, played with stern violence by Toshiro Mifune. —*Cart.*

Mijn Vriend
(The Judge's Friend)
(DUTCH-BELGIAN-COLOR)

Brussels, March 30.
An Elan Film release of a Fons Rademakers (Amsterdam) — Cinemagna (Brussels) production. Produced by Jos Van der Linden. Directed by Fons Rademakers. Stars Peter Faber, Andre Van den Heuvel. Screenplay, Gerard Soeteman; camera (Eastmancolor) Theo Van de Sande; music, Georges Delerue; production design, Philippe Graff; sound, Frank Struys; asst. director, Lili Rademakers. Reviewed at Cinema Eldorado, Brussels, March 29, '79. Running time: **128 MINS.**

Jules Depraeter ....Peter Faber
John Jensen ....Andre Van Den Heuvel
Ondine Van Aelst ....Magda Cnudde
Henri Vannoote ....Dirk De Batist
Helene Te Winckel ....Pleuni Touw
Mrs. Jensens .... Florence Jamin
Cecile .... Kees Ter Bruggen
Floorke Vannoote ......Camilia Blereau
Hektor Morgenhand ...Paul Cammermans
Brederode .... Frans Vercammen
Dr. Te Winckel ....Idwig Stephane
Andre .... Frank Aendenboom
Verstegen .... Dirk Celis
Lt. Tille ....Herbert Flack
Policeman .... Herman Coessens
Mrs. Lebelle ....Germaine Pascal
Mulder .... Frank Bravenboer
Vermessen ....Piet Marchie
Lebelle .... Alexis Sachnovsky

This being a good film, solidly built, reception on the home front will probably prove profitable. It is based on a court case that created quite a stir here, and it is easy to see why Dutch filmmaker Fons Rademakers felt fascinated by the dramatic possibilities.

Considering the impact this trial created, the publicity that surrounded it, "My Friend" should do extremely well, especially in the Flemish-speaking part of Belgiums as well as in Holland, and it might have a chance abroad. Not only by virtue of all the mud slung about during what has been called here "the court case of the century," but simply because it is an extremely well handled film. Story is not always easy to follow: it appears slightly melodramatic at times, but Rademakers definitely excels in story-telling while bringing to the foreground, in real cinematographic style, details on which he never insists. Only from time to time do the cameras venture inside the four walls of the Ghent Court of Justice. The different characters emerge from their often attractive background with clarity, the impudent real-life rogue, here called Depraeter, getting more space to move in than the others.

Once or twice film tends to slow down a little and perhaps too much footage is devoted to the coupling of two horses, everything shown in full detail and an insistence on close-ups: sheer sensationalism which adds nothing to the dramatic impact. But lapses of this sort nevertheless remain unimportant as tension never ceases to build up very nicely all through. The ultimate court scene is very moving: to watch the world of an apparently decent if indiscreet man crumble down so miserably might well bring a lump in the throat of many.

Peter Faber, already an excellent "Dr. Vlimmen," delivers a virtuoso performance. Only here and there does he tend to overdo slightly — but perhaps things really happened that way in real life? — but his machiavellian approach to the character is otherwise impressive. As is in perfect contrast the sober playing of Andre Van den Heuvel as Jensers, in reality Jespers: a perfectly controlled performance that never ceases to be convincing. All the others do well and technical credits are faultless, the atmospheric score by George Delerue included.
—*Flor.*

Manhattan
(BLACK & WHITE)

A winner from Woody.

Hollywood, April 21.

United Artists release of a Jack Rollins-Charles H. Joffe production. Features entire cast. Executive producer, Robert Greenhut. Produced by Charles H. Joffe. Directed by Woody Allen. Written by Woody Allen, Marshall Brickman; camera (black and white), Gordon Willis; production designer, Mel Bourne; costumes, Albert Wolsky; film editor, Susan E. Morse; music, George Gershwin, performed by the New York Philharmonic, conducted by Zubin Mehta and the Buffalo Philharmonic, conducted by Michael Tilson Thomas; music, adapted and arranged by Tom Pierson; asst. director, Frederic B. Blankfein; set decorator, Robert Drumheller; unit publicist, Scott MacDonough. Reviewed in Hollywood, April 20, 1979. (MPAA Rating-R). Running time: **96 MINS.**

Isaac Davis	Woody Allen
Mary Wilke	Diane Keaton
Yale	Michael Murphy
Tracy	Mariel Hemingway
Jill	Meryl Streep
Emily	Anne Byrne
Connie	Karen Ludwig
Dennis	Michael O'Donahue
Party guest	Victor Truro
Party guest	Tisa Farrow
Party guest	Helen Hanft
Guest of honor	Bella Abzug
Television director	Gary Weiss
Television producer	Kenny Vance
Television actor No. 1	Charles Levin
Television actor No. 2	Karen Allen
Television actor No. 3	David Rasche
Willie	Damion Sheller
Jeremiah	Wallace Shawn
Shakespearean actor	Mark Linn Baker
Shakespearean actress	Frances Conroy
Porsche owner No. 1	Bill Anthony
Porsche owner No. 2	John Doumanian
Pizzeria waiter	Ray Serra

Woody Allen never seems to tire of topping himself. With his latest film, "Manhattan," he has created an irresistible yarn of personal relationships that draws skillfully on the best comic moments of "Annie Hall" and the raw emotions he portrayed in his last picture, "Interiors."

There doesn't seem to be anyone around who can create more real and easily identifiable characters than Allen in the course of just 96 minutes, and it is this talent, combined with the first onscreen pairing of him and Diane Keaton since last year's Oscar sweep, that is certain to make the United Artists release an instant winner at the ticket window.

Allen uses New York City as a backdrop for the familiar story of the successful but neurotic urban over-achievers whose relationships always seem to end prematurely. The film is just as much about how wonderful a place the city is to live in as it is about the elusive search for love. With some extraordinary lensing from cinematographer Gordon Willis, Allen has, in black and white, captured the inner beauty that lurks behind the outer layer of dirt and grime in Manhattan. But what makes Allen's message especially effective is that it is presented ever so subtly through the sunrise shots of he and Keaton on a park bench or in walks through the Museum of Modern Art.

Allen's most saleable strength has always been is comedy but it seems now more than ever he has found a way to use the snappy one-liners and insults for something other than just their comedic value. He has foresaken the broad visual humor and quick asides to the viewing audience in favor of characters well-defined enough to incorporate Allen's wit within their dialog to each other. It's a far more effective tool as suggests Allen's considerable growth as a filmmaker.

The core of the story revolves around Allen as Isaac Davis, an unfulfilled television writer and his best friends, Yale and Emily, an upper-middle class, educated Manhattan couple. Isaac has lately taken up with Tracy, a gorgeous 17-year-old who can more than hold her own with the adults on all levels, but the age difference is becoming too much of an obstacle for him. That's especially the case when he meets Yale's girlfriend, Mary, a fast-talking, pseudo-intellectual Radcliffe graduate, expertly played by Diane Keaton, to whom Isaac is instantly attracted. Mary is, on the surface, everything Isaac can't stand in a person, but as both characters strip away their protective layers it becomes apparent they have more in common than he thought.

This sets up the rest of the film for Isaac to go back and forth between any number of relationships. Fine editing by Susan E. Morse convincingly shows his affair with both Mary and Tracy, his friendship with Yale and Emily, and feelings for an ex-wife and son. In particular, there's one scene at a concert where Isaac, Mary, Yale and Emily alternately stare at each other that probably tells more about relationships than any one line in the picture.

Although Allen is the prime mover in all of his films, his cast in this one is excellent. Michael Murphy and Anne Byrne are perfect as the married couple, Meryl Streep is honest in a small role as Allen's ex-wife and Mariel Hemingway shows lots of promise for other major roles as Tracy. But it is Diane Keaton who's most convincing as both Isaac and Yale's object of affection. Her appearances with Allen couldn't be more endearing and the bantering between them is one of the pic's highlights.

Allen has wisely reteamed with "Annie Hall" collaborator Marshall Brickman on the script to excellent results. Ditto his choice of Tom Pierson to adapt George Gershwin's music, which suggests the proper New York flavor as played by both the New York Philharmonic and Buffalo Philharmonic orchestras.

All other credits are also top-notch.

The film's "R" rating has been unsuccessfully appealed by producers Jack Rollins and Charles H. Joffe. Theme and content suggest a more mature audience, especially with Allen and his relationship with the 17-year-old, which might turn off a few. But overall, it looks like a boxoffice winner. —*Berg.*

Fen
(Sweetheart)
(THAI-COLOR)

Bangkok, April 12.

A Hollywood Films release. Produced and directed by Lek Kitiparaporn. Executive producer, Chalie Amartyakul. Features entire cast. Story and cast. Story and screenplay, Too Satabot; camera (color), Saravuth Vuthichai; music, Prasert Choorakit; sound, Jaturong Studio. Reviewed at Siam Theatre, Bangkok, April 11, '79. Running time: **105 MINS.**

Wit	Pairoj Sangvoributr
Kip	Nawarat Yukthanan
Leung	Jamroon Nuatchim
Kip's parents	Somkuan Kajangsart and Pong Ladda Pimolphan
Maid	Choosri Misomon

When producer-director Lek Kitiparaporn cast Pairoj Sangvoributr and Nawarat Yukthanan in "Fen," they were the most popular love team here, but due to overexposure the love team lost a lot of their following by the time "Fen" was completed.

Lek, in fact, tried to test three different endings using various student groups, before making his final choice on the last scene.

Pairoj and Nawarat are put through an artificial ordeal that does not for a moment endanger their chances of coming out of it alive and none the worse for the experience, blithesome as ever.
—*Cano.*

The Odd Angry Shot
(AUSTRALIAN-COLOR)

Sydney, Feb. 2.

A Roadshow release of a Samson Productions Film. Produced by Tom Jeffrey and Sue Milliken. Directed by Tom Jeffrey. Features entire cast. Camera (color), Don McAlpine (Eastmancolor); production design, Bernard Hides; editor, Brian Kavanagh; music, Michael Carlos; sound, Don Connolly; asst. dir., Mark Egerton; special effects, Brett Nolen; fight coordinator, Buddy Joe Hooker; stunts, Grant Page. Previewed at Roadshow Theatrette, Sydney, Feb. 1, 1979. Running time: **90 MINS.**

Harry	Graham Kennedy
Bung	John Hargreaves
Bill	John Jarratt
Rogers	Bryan Brown
Dawson	Graeme Blundell
Medic	Richard Moir
Scott	Ian Gilmour
Lt. Golonka	John Allen

Isaacs	Brandon Burke
Cook	Graham Rouse
Black Ronnie	Tony Barry
Warrant Officer	Max Cullen
Intelligence Corporal	John Fitzgerald
Padre	Johnny Garfield
Range Corporal	Ray Meagher
Spotted Soldier	Frankie J. Holden
Clifford	Roger Newcombe
Mayberry	Brian Evis
Nurse	Rose Ricketts
1st Marine	Chuck McKinney
2nd Marine	Freddie Paris
Bill's Mum	Joy Westmore
Bill's Dad	Brian Wenzel
Bill's Girl	Sharon Higgins
Bar Girl	Sarah Lee
Barman	Brian Anderson

Australia's involvement in the Vietnamese war created a political and moral dichotomy in the country such as hadn't been seen since the question of sonscription at the time of World War I. Sufficient time has passed for the subject no longer to be taboo, and, if anything, Tom Jeffrey's "The Odd Angry Shot" could be said to be cathartic. Certainly, it takes a humanitarian view of the people it portrays in that highly technological and inhumane conflict.

The film concentrates on a group of Aussie volunteers. Special Air Service troops, militarily as elite as the Yanks' Special Forces, but in this view, at least, rather more bawdy than the Americans as depicted in "The Deer Hunter." It is the same futile war, but what Jeffrey has expressed faithfully in the pragmatism and essential hope-of-survival of the troops on the groun — former civilians all — who want nothing more than to get back, and away from the shooting.

Professionals by signature on a form only, basically the Aussies in the S.A.S., were essentially amateurs; a peculiarity of the Australian persona and national attitude that pervades social and business life and extends into other aspects of life.

Jeffrey's humanizing of his soldiers makes their activities totally understandable. What comes over is the inherent character of Aussies at war: they treat it pretty much like a sporting fixture — until the shooting gets serious.

Jeffrey has been helped immeasurably by his cameraman, Don McAlpine, who worked as a news cameraman in Vietnam. Together they have created an immediacy in the fire fights that has a chilling verisimilitude, and equally the back-at-base scenes have an air of truth that makes one almost smell the sweat and damp canvas of the tents. What is also well conveyed is the claustrophobic atmosphere created by living in close proximity to other men and in grave danger.

There is no agonising political or moral message because essentially the film is a comedy, and Jeffrey maintains the basic good humor of the guys who just happen to be there at a very believable pitch.

Performances are excellent with Kennedy great as the jaded two-time loser; the regular army soldier self-trapped by the system, institutionalized by familiarity of military routine which he found to be an adequate (but only occasionally unsatisfying) substitution for real life. Also standout are John Jarratt, John Hargreaves and Bryan Brown.

Cooperation by the Dept. of Defense gives the film all the hardware needed to recreate Vietnam in the late 1960s, and excellent special effects do the rest. Tech credits are of high standard over all.

Film should perform well commercially if pitched right. What might appeal most is its honesty and humanity because whatever the larger reasons for Australian troops being sent to Vietnam, they were there and they were not going to stop being Aussies just because of that. —Miha.

Dreamer
(COLOR)

'Rocky' Goes Bowling.

Hollywood, April 18.

Twentieth Century-Fox release of a Michael Lobell production. Produced by Michael Lobell. Directed by Noel Nosseck. Screenplay, James Proctor, Larry Bischof; camera (DeLuxe color), Bruce Surtees; editor, Fred Chulack; music, Bill Conti; art direction, Archie Sharp; set decoration, Bruce Kay; costumes, Guy Verhille; associate producer, James Herbert; assistant director, William Hole. Reviewed at the Samuel Goldwyn Theatre, Beverly Hills, April 18, '79. (MPAA rating: PG.) Running time: **90 MINS.**

Dreamer	Tim Matheson
Karen	Susan Blakely
Harry	Jack Warden
Taylor	Richard B. Shull
Angie	Barbara Stuart
The Fan	Owen Bush
Elaine	Marya Small
Spider	Matt Clark
Riverboat Captain	John Crawford
Chris Schenkel	Himself
Color Man	Nelson Burton Jr.
Old Timer	Morgan Farley
Too	Pedro Gonzalez Gonzalez
Juan	Speedy Zapata
Patterson	Jobe Cerny
Lady	Azizi Johari
Johnny Watkin	Dick Weber

Shamelessly attempting to be a "Rocky" of the bowling world, "Dreamer" is a preposterous, colorless down-home fantasy about a youth who makes the jump from unknown bushleaguer to national champion in three easy lessons. Lacking in any b.o. assets aside from the story's similarity to the "Rocky" blueprint, this looks like another spring gutter ball from Fox.

Nicest scene in the film is the title montage, which employs vintage sepia stills of by-gone bowling alleys and sportsmen. Despite unusual locations in Alton, Ill. and St. Louis and the relative rarity of the milieu as a screen subject, a deja vu feeling hits as soon as the film proper begins, due to the hackneyed script and Noel Nosseck's obvious direction.

At the outset, "Dreamer" Tim Matheson wins a local contest, but has to bully his way into professional status. He also has to deal with the incessant griping of g.f. Susan Blakely, who doesn't like playing second fiddle to his career aspirations. After winning a regional tourney, the next step for the boy wonder is the national championships, in which he cooly defeats the veteran ace, played by real-life pro Dick Weber. It's as simple as that.

The whole picture is unalloyed confection, served up with little charm or distinction. Matheson is earnest but bland and Blakely, deglamorized to play a small-town type, acts mostly with her teeth. Jack Warden is in to play Dreamer's coach, who missed his own chance for greatness but puts his faith in the lad. Peripheral characters around the bowling alley are all cartoon figures.

Whole enterprise might look a bit better on the tube. —Cart.

A Portrait of the Artist As a Young Man
(COLOR)

James Joyce autobiog novel faithfully filmed. Heavy reliance on dialog. Falters toward end.

A Howard Mahler Films release of a Ulysses Film Company Ltd. production. Directed by Joseph Strick. Associate producers, Richard Hallinan, Betty Botley. Features entire cast. Screenplay, Judith Rascoe. Based on the novel by James Joyce; camera (color), Stuart Hetherington; editor, Lesley Walker; music, Stanley Myers; sound, Pat Hayes; costumes, Judy Nolan. Reviewed at the Guild Theatre, N.Y., April 23, '79. (No MPAA rating.) Running time: **98 MINS.**

Stephen Dedalus	Bosco Hogan
Simon Dedalus	T.P. McKenna
Preacher	Sir John Gielgud
May Dedalus	Rosaleen Linihan
Dante	Maureen Potter
Uncle Charles	Cecil Sheehan
Davin	Niall Buggy
Lynch	Brian Murray
Stephen (age 3)	Terence Strick
Stephen (age 10)	Luke Johnston

Beautifully lensed on Irish locations and impeccably acted by a cast largely unknown beyond the emerald isle, Joseph Strick's screen version of James Joyce's "A Portrait of the Artist as a Young Man" succeeds almost completely in translating Joyce's largely autobiographical first novel to the screen. That fact accounts not only for its many virtues, but also ultimately weighs against it as a film.

Strick, who tackled an ambitious version of Joyce's "Ulysses" in 1969 by attempting to capture the stream of consciousness nature of that later tome, wisely opted for cinematic simplicity on "Portrait." The result, though it eventually becomes unavoidably bogged down in a virtual recitation of Joyce's highly charged language, is a finely wrought, appropriately "small" film that should draw a respectable audience in strict art house berths.

Chronicling the gradual lapse in his Catholic faith as its protagonist, Stephen Dedalus, wends his way through adolescence to young manhood, the film's first two-thirds succeed in honing a tight narrative. Following Dedalus from his clergy-dominated childhood through his battles with flesh and spirit at a Jesuit college in turn-of-century Dublin, Judith Rascoe's screenplay allows Joyce's politics, religious ideologies and artistic musings to unfold comfortably within her well-tune dialog.

Once the narrative halts, however, and the final portion of the film is given over to the protagonist's purely interior thoughts, this "Portrait" virtually falls into the over-rich mire of Joyce's language. At this point, the film becomes little more than a nicely photographed catechism, as Dedalus (staunchly played by Bosco Hogan) responds to a series of questions on God, beauty, art and life with a string of monologs.

Fortunately, there's enough in the film's earlier vignettes — which also conjure a lively portrait of Dedalus's increasingly destitute family and his academic surroundings — to make the net effect distinctly positive. These are finely acted throughout, with T.P. McKenna (as Hogan's politically passionate father) and Sir John Gielgud (as a hellfire and damnation priest whose graphic sermon on the fires of hell sends Hogan racing to the confessional) standing in sharp relief.

Technical aspects are excellent. —Step.

The Water Babies
(BRITISH-COLOR)

Do-gooding can be fun.

London, April 11.

Pethurst International release in association with Productions Associates (U.K.) of an Ariadne Films production. Produced by Peter Shaw. Directed by Lionel Jeffries. Stars James Mason, Billie Whitelaw, Bernard Cribbins, Joan Greenwood. Screenplay, Michael Robson, based on Charles Kingsley's novel; camera (color), Ted Scaife; editor, Peter Weatherley; art director, Herbert Westbrook; costumes, Phyllis Dalton; sound, Cyril Collick; in charge of production U.K., Ben Arbeid; production supervisor, Bruce Sharman; songs, Phil Coulter, Bill Martin; animation, Miroslaw Kijowicz (Film Polski), J. Stokes and Cuthbert Cartoons; assistant director, Ray Frift. Reviewed at 20th Fox screening room, London, April 10, '79. (B-BFC Rating: U). Running time: **93 MINS.**

Grimes	James Mason
Mrs. Doasyouwouldbedoneby	Billie Whitelaw
Masterman	Bernard Cribbins
Lady Harriet	Joan Greenwood
Sir John	David Tomlinson
Sladd	Paul Luty
Tom	Tommy Pender
Ellie	Samantha Gates

The musical screen version of "The Water Babies" leaves out most of the Victorian moralizing of Charles Kingsley's children's novel and tells the story of innocence-versus-evil more or less straight. It combines live action footage and — for the underwater sequences — animation. It started production in October, 1976.

It's directed by Lionel Jeffries with a pleasing lack of "talking down" to the very young kids who constitute its safest market. With careful promotion and release-timing, prospects in both English-speaking and foreign language territories look reasonable in relation to the slim $2,000,000 production budget.

Michael Robson's screenplay, which pays restrained lip-service to period dialect, plots the adventures of a 12-year-old apprentice chimneysweep, wrongly accused of theft, who dives into a pool to escape his pursuers. Trapped below the surface, he meets a succession of human stereotypes, jokily animated as underwater creatures.

After a battle to free the water babies, who normally inhabit an eternal playground in mid-ocean but have been captured by a shark and an electric eel, the boy's wish to return to the dry world is granted. His name has been cleared in the meantime, and he's reunited with the little girl, orphaned like himself, whom he met before the trouble started.

The boy's fairy godmother, Mrs. Doasyouwouldbedoneby, who crops up in various disguises, is the one potentially unappealing homily element retained as part of the general message that selflessness is rewarded. But Billie Whitelaw brings enough mysteriousness to the role to avoid being sugary.

James Mason as the drunken mastersweep, and Bernard Cribbins as his weasel-faced sidekick (a character invented for the film), form a duo of villains more laughable than frightening. Tommy Pender is agreeably natural as the boy. Samantha Gates, with a mass of crimped golden hair, does okay

as his fantasy-object — like a Victorian portrait brought to life.

The animated sequences, where the creators have opted for garish colors and some crudely-conceived characters, score by maintaining a strong pace. Original drawings were done by Cuthbert Cartoons in London, then the movement was synchronized by Miroslaw Kijowicz in Poland to a pre-recorded soundtrack. The join doesn't show. The Poles would probably have created subtler caricatures had they handled the whole job, though this wouldn't necessarily have paid off commercially. **The tv spot style of humor quite successfully matches the story-book characters of the live action, despite the implied clash of periods.**

The songs by Phil Coulter and Bill Martin are simple and catchy. The rigors of Victorian England are acceptably conveyed by Herbert Westbrook's interior designs and location dressings, photographed with an eye for detail by Ted Scaife. Production values are higher on the whole than the cost would suggest, with only some low-light exterior shots as evidence of a tight schedue. —*Simo.*

Petualang Cinta
(The Playboy)
(INDONESIAN-COLOR)

Jakarta, March 18.
A Sarinande Films release. Produced and directed by Turino Junaidy. Features entire cast. Written by David R. Manan; camera (color), Sutardjo; editor, Alex Hassan; music, T. Junaidy; sound and lighting, Kemal; productin designer, Winarto; asst. director, M. Yusof. Color processing by Color Film Australia. Reviewed at Sarinande Films Studio, Jakarta, March 17, 1979. Running time: **110 MINS.**

Budi	Robby Sugara
Ona/Laila	Paula Romokoy
Sutini	Nenny Triana
Mansur	Mansursia
Laila's adopted father	Rendra Karno

This film and "Salangit Mesra" (Sky-High Love) represent last year's annual film production output of Sarinande Films, which belongs to leading Indonesian filmmaker, Turino Junaidy. Storyline is of the sort often employed by Junaidy, about an erring playboy (Sugara) who forsakes his young sweetheart (Romokoy) when he is separated from her due to a job transfer.

Sugara gets a new assignment from the navy. He is sent to Surabaya, which is supposedly distant enough from Jakarta to make communication between the lovers difficult. The main obstacle, of course, is another young woman (Triana) in Surabaya. Triana is the producer-director's daughter in real life.

Romokoy, a poor nobody from the provinces, turns to Sugara following an accidental first meeting

when all of her money and belongings get stolen by a young thug at the train station.

The girl does not forget, however. She is pregnant by Surara, and waits patiently to exact sweet revenge upon him later on. It helps that she becomes a successful fashion model, then a movie star. Subsequently, she is adopted by a rich childless couple. They look after her and her child, and let her know that she could have everything she wants.

Prevalence of story loopholes does not stop the players from acting to the hilt, as though the pic were completely realistic. Such performances receive no negative criticism. On the contrary, the public loves it.

Local producers would rather play it safe than risk their investment on something different. This may sound like a contradiction of the fact that moviegoing in Indonesia has actually dropped and most films were flops, because of most producers' insistence in using the same old plots. At this point, however, Juniady still believes that he is much better off sticking to his familiar style, instead of going in a new direction. —*Cano.*

Dawn
(AUSTRALIAN-COLOR)

Sydney, Feb. 14.
A Hoyts Distribution Company release of the Aquataurus Film Productions presentation in association with the South Australian Film Corporation. Stars Bunney Brooke, Ron Haddrick, John Diedrich, Tom Richards, Gabrielle Hartley, Bronwyn Mackay-Payne. Producer Joy Cavill. Director, Ken Hannam. Screenplay, Cavill; camera (color), Russell Boyd; editor, Max Lemon; sound, Ken Hammond; art direction, Ross Major; asst. directors, Mark Egerton, Penny Chapman, Scott Hicks. Previewed Hoyts Theatrette, Sydney, Feb. 13, '79. (Commonwealth censorship rating for Mature audiences). Running time: **111 MINS.**

Dawn	Bronwyn Mackay-Payne
Harry	Tom Richards
Gary	John Diedrich
Mum	Bunney Brooke
Pop	Ron Haddrick
Kate	Gabrielle Hartley
Len	Ivar Kantz
Joe	David Cameron
Bippy	Kevin Wilson
Edie	Lyndall Barbour
Syd	John Clayton
Louise	Margaret Gerard
Doctor	Don Barkham
Vivian	Joan Evatt
Japanese police inspector	Go Mikami
Dawn (age 6)	Carmelina Caterina

The eponymous central character is the legendary Aussie swimming champion Dawn Fraser whose extraordinary aquatic feats won her four Olympic gold medals in three Olympic Games: Melbourne '56, Rome '60 and Tokyo '64. The film covers the 15 years around that trio of main events, and her adventures out of the water have been

drawn together to create the narrative fabric.

Despite the plethora of incident, the plot is thin and while the film is in no way an apologia for the tempestuous and willful swimmer, stern officialdom and society come in for their share of whacks for being so stiff and staid when confronted with adolescent ebullience. Maybe Dawn would have got-t-en away with more if she had been Dave, but the fact is, back in the days of the last decade girls didn't behave like that: or shouldn't have been caught at it, anyway.

Fraser still lives in the Sydney harborside suburb in which she was born and brought up, and in fact, was technical adviser on the film. She's evidently exercised scant editorial control on her own story because while sympathy is elicited for the character, it isn't dragged out of the viewer. The 10-year ban for stealing a flag at the Tokyo Games, for example, seems draconian reaction by Australian officials compared with the relative nature of the offense. But throughout the script has been making the point that Dawn is mischievous at best and downright unruly at worst.

Fraser's story is a lively one, and it has its moments of pathos and hilarity, but as seen on screen it doesn't add up to a satisfactory total. This seems largely due to the self-destructive nature of the main character and the lack of any real human warmth in the characters that surround her. Exacerbating this is a rather mono-emotional performance by Bronwyn Mackay-Payne in her debut. Like the subject, she's impressive in the water, but on dry land something more is required than sheer physical presence — and she is no Esther Williams in the looks department sad to say.

But then neither was Dawn Fraser, which inevitably brings one back to the veracity of the piece which is, save a few lacunae, incontrovertible: the problem is that truth is not necessarily rivetingly interesting, especially if it is presented unintriguingly.

And that, disappointingly, is the flaw in "Dawn." The drama appears applied, rather than being organic to the story. In a feature film that doesn't purport to be essentially a documentary, some dramatic license is surely some sort of requirement: such as is here is insufficient. When viewed impartially from a non-Aussie viewpoint, simply the film falls flat on its facts.

Potentially, the story of Dawn Fraser could have been in other hands an aquatic Aussie "Rocky:" the potential hasn't been fulfilled because of Cavill's determination not to memorialize her heroine. Or even fictionalize her — wherein "fictionalize" is not meant to equate with "distort," but to enhance dramatically. The result is purely parochial drama.

The main problem with "Dawn!" is that it is probably too true.

—*Miha.*

Salangit Mesra
(Sky-High Love)
(INDONESIAN-COLOR)

Jakarta, March 18.

A Sarinande Films release. Produced, written and directed by Turino Junaidy. Features entire cast. Co-writer, Mutingo Busye; camera (color), Sutardjo; sound and lighting, Kemal; editing, Alex Hassan; music, Benjamin; production designer, Winarto; asst. director, M. Yusof. Color processing by Color Film Australia. Reviewed at Sarinande Films Studio, Jakarta, March 17, 1979. Running time: 110 MINS.

Alex .... Benjamin
Emy .... Amalia
Emy's Parents .... Ade Irawan and Bambang Irawan
Alex's Parents .... Bambang Siswando and Chandra Devi

In lieu of a salary, top Indonesian comedian Benjamin asked Turino Junaidy for a brand-new Mercedes Benz ($37,000) for toplining in two of Junaidy's films and got it. Pic was only modestly successful at the b.o. when released recently. Junaidy admits that Benjamin is miscast. The actor is supposed to play a teenaged student when he's already in his mid-thirties.

Amalia makes a lovely teenage heroine, though. She also has a comic rapport with Benjamin, so that in most of their scenes together they are quite successful as a comedy team. She is less effective when allowed to emote alone, as in a number of scenes where she is supposed to pine away for him.

Sex scenes must be handled astutely, if they are to pass the local censors. To avoid any possible infringement of taboos when it comes to sex in local movies, Junaidy never shows the young couple in bed together. He more than makes up for it, however, in one hilarious scene when the mother of the girl suddenly bursts into her room, almost catching the lovers together, but instead discovering his underwear on the bedroom floor.

—*Cano.*

Min aelskade
(My Beloved)
(SWEDISH-COLOR)

Malmoe, March 27.

A AB Svensk Film/Cinematograph AB (Ingmar Bergman executive producer), Swedish Film Institute with the 3 Leaf Clover Associates production, AB Svensk Film release. Features entire cast. Written and directed by Kjell Grede. Camera (Eastmancolor) Tony Forsberg (with 16m additions by Lasse Karlsson); editor, Lasse Hagstroem; production designer, Anna Asp; costumes, Inger Pehrsson. Film Institute producer, Mans Reuytersvaerd; music (no credits). Reviewed at Camera, Malmoe, March 27, 1979. Running time, 108 MINS.

John .... Bjoern Skagestad
Sonja .... Lena Nyman
Disa .... Agneta Ekmanner
Bernhard .... Keve Hjelm

Writer-director Kjell Grede's extreme sensitivity and grasp of visual impressions of inner conflicts play maudlin tricks on him in the case of this (partly) Ingmar Bergman-produced wasteland of emotional junk title "My Beloved" (just appearing simple does not guarantee depth).

It is a feature to dull the senses with excesses of morose deep-think thunder in the story of a young man (played with an attempt at lovable idiocy by handsome Bjoern Skagestad who may be an innocent director's victim) who refuses to come to grips with realities, loses a solid job along with a more straight-minded wife (Agneta Ekmanner, once again proving herself a contender for superior Scandinavian acting honors) only to drift into a nondescript love affair with a tiny woman of poor and diffuse, yet still comparatively well-ordered life style (women are sacrosanct in latterday men's films and thus generally uninteresting).

Lena Nyman, otherwise a superior actress, comes off moon-faced and sloppily sentimental in the role of the young man's new inspiration. Keve Hjelm has the part of the young man's Evil Spirit, a man of means and power, yet, of course, powerless in the face of what may be meant as the True Love Of The Truly Innocent.

The film is poor from start to finish, a clear indication that good will, previous output and forehead frowns are not enough to keep audiences awake even if the Bergman banner flies from the production masthead. —*Kell.*

Rock 'n' Roll High School
(COLOR)

High school's a blast.

Hollywood, April 19.

New World Pictures release. Exec producer, Roger Corman. Produced by Michael Finnell. Directed by Allan Arkush. Features cast. Screenplay, Richard Whitley, Russ Dvonch, Joseph McBride, based on a story by Arkush, Joe Dante; camera (color), Dean Cundey; editor, Larry Bock, Gail Werbin; art direction, Marie Kordus; set decoration, Linda Pearl; sound, Michael Moore' music, The Ramones; assistant director, Gerald T. Olson. Reviewed at Joe Shore Screening Room, L.A., April 19, '79. (MPAA Rating: PG.) Running time: 93 MINS.

Riff Randell .... P.J. Soles
Tom Roberts .... Vincent Van Patten
Eaglebauer .... Clint Howard
Kate Rambeau .... Dey Young
Miss Togar .... Mary Woronov
Mr. McGree .... Paul Bartel
Fritz Hansel .... Loren Lester
Fritz Gretel .... Daniel Davies
Coach Steroid .... Alix Elias
Screamin' Steve Stevens ...... Don Steele
Angle Dust .... Lynn Farrell

In the early '60s, when final credits for youth exploitation pix came up, they were usually set against a beach or highschool gym scene, with the kids twisting away in sedate fashion. In "Rock 'n' Roll High School," the finale is capped by the students blowing up the high school, and dancing in front of the flames. Times change, but the youth market is still there, and should respond in force to this New World Pictures release. Only problem may come from exhibs nervous about their customers following the on-screen example, and turning schools into ozoners.

The tongue-in-cheek humor more and more evident in New World pix is in full flower here, as director Allan Arkush, and scripters Richard Whitley, Russ Dvonch and Joseph McBride live out all their repressed fantasies about high-school existence.

Mary Woronov plays a tough-minded principal who arrives at Vince Lombardi H.S. with the goal of straightening out a dizzy student body, led by rock fanatic P.J. Soles. Intertwined in the slapdash script is Soles' obsession with the New Wave rockers, the Ramones, and a love angle between Soles' g.f., Dey Young, and her hearthrob, jock Vincent Van Patten, egged on by teenage entrepreneur Clint Howard.

What ensues is alternately silly and inciteful, but never boring. Arkush isn't dealing with characters, but caricatures. Intended audience shouldn't mind, since in addition to the Ramones, there's a pulsating soundtrack of other rock hits, and the pace, like the music, never lets up.

Soles has been in enough of these films to graduate to something better, and Young makes an impressive debut as a wallflower turned rocker. Van Pattan should stick to the tennis court. Rest of the cast is eager, and not much else.

New World has clearly filled the niche vacated by American International, when it moved up to bigger budgets, if not bigger returns. And as long as Roger Corman keeps finding young directors, writers and performers who have a clear grasp on what their peers want to see, it'll be a financially comfortable perch.

"Rock 'n' Roll High School" is also of interest in terms of what can be presented on film while still achieving a PG rating. Thanks to drugs, sex and rock 'n' roll, high school just isn't what it used to be, which won't come as any surprise to this film's audience. —*Poll.*

Suru
(The Flock)
(TURKISH-COLOR)

West Berlin, April 8.

A Gueney Film Production, Istanbul; world rights, Gueney Film, Istanbul. Features entire cast. Directed by Zeki Okten. Screenplay, Yilmaz Gueney. Only credits available. Photographed in Eastmancolor. Reviewed at Klick Kino, West Berlin, April 7 '79. Running time: 129 MINS.

"The Flock" is obviously a Turkish pic with a message. Scripted by the imprisoned Yilmaz Gueney, it's both a tribute to his stature as Turkey's leading filmmaker and a plea for his pardon and release. Helmer Zeki Okten, otherwise a maker of comedies ("The King of the Street Cleaners"), copied Gueney's style to the camera angle, and everyone involved apparently did the same in their respective departments. Pic came out a winner: it copped the Catholic and Protestant Film Prizes at the Berlin Fest's Forum of Young Cinema. It will do just as well at other fests on the summer and autumn circuit.

This is the story of a family of nomadic sheepherders in southern Turkey — apparently they are Khurds, judging by their dress. The customs among this tribe are centuries-old, and the father-patriarch is an uncompromising tyrant. He has three sons, each married to the daughter of an enemy tribe to prevent revengeful blood-letting on both sides. One son wants to leave his father's tent; he is meek and knows the world has changed, but he also has a sick wife he loves who is in need of medical care to stop internal bleeding. The son challenges the father as the film opens.

A deal is made whereby the son may take his sick wife with him on the trek to Ankara to sell the flock of sheep — after which he is free to go his own way. But as the transport to Ankara begins, the group encounters nothing but trouble. Bribes must be paid with money or sheep to officials or merchants all along the way; on occasion, the sheep are stolen via one ruse or another by bandits.

The train ride, in particular, is striking in capturing the crowds and calamity of such a transport. It soon becomes evident that the patriarchal father has not reckoned with this strange new world of trading, and he blames all his misfortunes on the presence of his sick daughter-in-law. One of the sons gets seduced by a train-station whore while he's supposed to be keeping watch over the valuable sheep. And so on — until the teeming city of Ankara is reached.

There the son demands the agreed-upon sum from his father to pay for his wife's medical care. The father, meanwhile, doesn't get the agreed-upon price for his sheep from the merchants in the stockyards of Ankara. And the younger son runs off as soon as he gets a chance.

This powerful, realist film doesn't end here. The son carries his wife on his shoulders through the city streets to a doctor, but she herself won't allow her body to be inspected because of religious and traditional reasons. A bottle of medicine only leads to further intestinal complications, and the woman dies. The crazed husband feels compelled to bear her burden on his back further, now completely lost as for what he should do.

Helmer Okten, a vet of some 25 pix in his own right, has handled this story so well that it appears only government permission has to be granted to witness a renaissance of Turkish cinema (some 300 pix are produced here annually). Thesps and lensing are outstanding, although pic gets off to a slow start in describing, in sound docu fashion, the rituals of nomadic sheepmen.
—*Holl.*

Les Egouts du Paradis
(The Sewers of Paradise)
(FRENCH-COLOR)

Paris, April 17.

A CFDC release of an Alexia Films production. Produced by Jean-Pierre Rawson, Anne-Marie Toursky. Directed by Jose Giovanni. Stars Francis Huster. Screenplay, Jose Giovanni; dialog, Michel Audiard; based on novel by Albert Spaggiari; camera (color), Walter Bal; editors, Jacqueline Thiedot and Marie-Therese Boiche; sound, Jean-Francois Anger; music, Jean-Pierre Doering; art direction, Georges Petitot. Reviewed at Cinema U.G.C. Danton, Paris, April 10, 1979. Running time: 115 MINS.

Albert Spaggiari .... Francis Huster
"68" .... Jean-Francois Balmer
Charlotte .... Lila Kedrova
The Egyptian .... Clement Harari
Biki .... Michel Subor

"The Sewers of Paradise" purports to recreate the famous Nice bank heist of July 1976 in which a band of burglars entered the city's sewer system, burrowed their way into the basement strong room of the Societe Generale and, over the space of a weekend, pillaged the safe-deposit vault of an estimated $10-$15,000,000.

The brains behind this audacious coup, Albert Spaggiari, was arrested some months later only to make a spectacular escape from the Court House where he was consulting with judge and lawyer. His own account of the break-in was

published last year, inspiring this film.

Scenarist-director Jose Giovanni botches what could have been an engrossing film. The quasi-documentary impulse to film in the very sewers traversed by Spaggiari's band is continually ridiculed by a script — slick, decorative dialog courtesy of Michel Audiard—bloated by a romanticized presentation of criminal genius and underworld camaraderie. One might counter that Giovanni is being faithful to Spaggiari's book — in that case, chalk up gullibility as another of film's misdemeanors.

But faithful Giovanni is not. Evoking dramatic license the director presents dumb interpolations like the scenes in which Spaggiari, in mid-robbery, resurfaces to visit an old cohort (Lila Kedrova) who has the bad judgment to die just then. Spaggiari gets roaring drunk but arrives back at the bank already pretty sober, ready for action. Although the real Spaggiari writes in his book that he surfaced for four hours to establish an alibi by dining in a restaurant, Giovanni's dramatic embroidery leaves one incredulous.

It's bad enough that the script fudges Spaggiari's shady past and allegedly fascistic leanings, but the coup de grace is the casting of cute Francis Huster as the veteran brawler and arms-smuggling mastermind, and the director aggravates the miscast by repeatedly framing him in larger-than-life contemplations over dreamy French hillsides. And to think that Giovanni ruled out Charles Bronson and Jean-Paul Belmondo as inappropriate!

The actual robbery, scenes don't save things, possibly because the caper is based not on ingenious convolutions of plot but on the prodigious physical effort and endurance needed to dig a hole and force open safe-deposit boxes. And how exciting is that to watch?

By the way, British independent tv recently produced a tv film on this very same "great drain robbery" (as one journalist dubbed it). Titled "Dirty Money" it starred Ian McShane as a pointedly fascist Spaggiari. His wife is said to have denounced the soiling of her husband's good name! —*Len.*

Huadjai Ti Jom Din
(Heartbreak People)
(THAI-COLOR)

Bangkok, April 12.

A Saha Mongkol Films release. Produced by Somsak Techaratanaprasert. Directed by Chao Mikunsoot. Features entire cast. Story and screenplay, Torn Kosol; camera (color), Sanit Rujiratakul; music, Chintanart Wacharasathien, Pisanu Sri-

vonand; sound, Sngar Wacharasathien; production designer, art director, Anant Chantanakorn. Reviewed at Coliseum Theatre, Bangkok, April 11, '79. Running time: 115 MINS.

Perk .... Pisan Akaraseni
Tuanjai .... Pisamai Wilaisak
Wanwipha .... Yuwathida Pornprasert
Seksan .... Uthen Boonyong
Tuanjai's sister ..... Marasi Nabangchang

Together with his two brothers, Piac and Chai, Chao Mikunsoot has specialized in action pictures in the past. Now he tries his hand at drama, local b.o. grosses have indicated that audiences here prefer dramatic pictures.

Coincidences play a major role. Two leading characters, Uthen Boonyong and Yuwathida Pornprasert, are brother and sister here; he pimps for Pisamai, while she happens to be Pisan's girl friend.

Uthen finds out about Pisan's real identity through Pisamai herself. She often goes to her son's school and once Uthen goes with her. He then becomes the villain by trying to stop Pisan from seeing his sister.

The conclusion suggests "Oedipus Rex." Pisan nearly commits incest with Pisamai during a drunken night with friends in a brothel.

There continues to be a "good enough" local market potential for a sad movie with a shocking ending, which local filmmakers never seem to forget. —*Cano.*

Nicht Alles Was Fliegt, Ist Ein Vogel
(Not Everything That Flies Is a Bird)
(WEST GERMAN-COLOR-ANIMATION)

Hollywood, March 19.

A Franz/Stockmann Film Production. Written, directed and designed by Borislav Sajtinac. Animation, Branko Illic; editor, Rolf Adrian. Reviewed at Filmex, Los Angeles, March 18, '79. Running time: 80 MINS.

This feature-length animated film grew out of a series of grotesque, strikingly visual cartoons made in Yugoslavia and West Germany by Borislav Sajtinac. He strung them all together into a macabre, bizarre portrait of mankind in a manner that could be described as "Kafka's Nightmare" or "Freud's Horror-Chamber" — instead he choose as a title "Not Everything That Flies Is a Bird," the title of one of the short cartoons. (Not to be confused with Dusan Makavejev's similarly titled "A Man Is Not a Bird" —Ed).

The link is a little man in an abandoned house trying to catch a few winks of sleep. He has a wife, Martha, and a different nightmare each evening in his new quarters. The film opens with a quote from

Edgar Allan Poe's "The Raven," and one dream sequence features a giant crow suppressing everything around him with his giant, menacing hulk.

All of which might appear confusing to the average spectator. The key may be the added reality of living in a divided Europe torn between two contradicting ideologies: a corner of the world like Yugoslavia, from which Sajtinac emigrated to live in the West. Should the viewer choose to read recent postwar European history into this string of "parables" or "metaphors," he will probably emerge from the cinema a bit wiser and fresher than otherwise.

At least, that's how the Sajtinac cartoons were received at the Oberhausen Short Film Festival over recent years, where the separate segments first appeared — and were applauded by a knowledgeable aud.
—*Holl.*

Bach: H-Moll Messe
(Bach: B-Minor Mass)
(WEST GERMAN-B&W)

Hollywood, March 19.

An Artfilm Pitt Koch Production, Munich, in collaboration with Second German Television (ZDF), Wiesbaden; world rights, Eginhart Hillenbrand, Munich. Features performance of Bach's "B-Minor Mass" and Ana Torrent. Written and directed by Klaus Kirschner. Camera, Dietrich Lohmann (one scene is in color); music, Johann Sebastian Bach's "B-Minor Mass," musical production, CBS Records, producer, Hans Joachim Daub, sound engineer, Richard Hauck. Reviewed at Filmex, Los Angeles, March 18, '79. Running time: 150 MINS.

Ana .... Ana Torrent
Soprano .... Arleen Auger
Contralto .... Julia Hamari
Tenor .... Adalbert Kraus
Bass .... Siegmund Nimsgern
Beritone .... Wolfgang Schoene
Conductor ...:.......... Helmuth Rilling
Gaechinger Kantorei Stuttgart, Bach-Kollegium, Stuttgart, and extras from Montbard.

Klaus Kirschner's film adaptation of Johann Sebastian Bach's "B-Minor Mass" drew a healthy crowd one Sunday morning at Filmex despite (or perhaps because of) its 150 minute length. This is an interpretation of a musical classic which will draw paying customers long into the future, provided it's presented as a kind of musical religious experience (as it was in Los Angeles) in a theatre, or properly handled as a television attraction.

German "music films" have done considerably well at home when presented as confrontations with both the music and the composer — in fact, the subtitle of Kirschner's pic is "Ana's Encounter with the Music of Johann Sebastian Bach." Earlier, in 1976, he made "Mozart: A Childhood Chronicle," which preemed at the

Berlin Film Festival in a pristine four-hour-plus version; that one used family diaries and letters to study the composer intimately at ages 8, 12, and 20, and it runs regularly (often, too, on Sunday mornings) in cinemas across Germany.

Kirschner's location for "B-Minor Mass" is the ruins of the Cistercian Fontenay Abbey in Burgundy, France, and his 12-year-old girl encountering Bach's music for the first time is Ana Torrent, the young Spanish actress who appeared in Victor Erice's "The Spirit of the Beehive" (1974), and Carlos Saura's "Cria Cuervos" (1975) and "Elisa, My Life" (1977). The music is a recording by Helmuth Rilling, whose interpretation (the filmmaker felt) corresponded with the "sacred theatre" performance in the film. The "religious experience" dimension thus lifted one of the most celebrated choral Masses in music history out of its baroque "museum" setting (composed between 1733 and 1738, first performed 1834-35) into a more appropriate "church" atmosphere.

A film for both music and film-art lovers. —Holl.

Kvar
(Breakdown)
(YUGOSLAV-COLOR)

Belgrade, April 6.
A Film Danas Production, Belgrade; world rights, Yugoslavia Film, Belgrade. Features entire cast. Directed by Milos Radivojevic. Screenplay, Svetozar Vlajkovic, Radivojevic; camera (color), Aleksander Petkovic. Reviewed at Yugoslavia Film Screening Room, Belgrade, April 5, '79. Running time: **90 MINS.**
Cast: Aleksandar Bercek, Neda Arneric, Milena Dravic, Ljuba Tadic, Dusko Janicijevic, Olga Spiridonovic, Danila Stojkovic, Irfan Mensur, Rada Zivkovic, Djordje Jelisic.

One of the best pix to emerge from Yugoslavia in the present decade, Milos Radivojevic's "Breakdown" marks a high point in the still young career of a talented filmer who, until now, has had nothing but trouble getting his films seen and distributed at home and abroad. Radivojevic has made three other feature pix; "Bats in the Belfry" (1970), about a young man going crazy; "Film Without Title" (1972), another "mental discourse" stringing together a series of sequences; and "Testament" (1975), with only one character imagining someone is "out to get him."

Each of those pix featured some of Belgrade's finest thesp talent — Dragan Nikolic, Milja Vuljanovic, Neda Arneric, and Danilo-Bata Stojkovic — and each was a kind of "experiment" in analyzing mental breakdowns. Now, in "Breakdown," Radivojevic had tied all the pieces together in a story that runs smoothly along a sure narrative line from start to finish. Pic only needs a fest boost to find its way to the art house market abroad.

A young man who works as a kind of tv reporter awakes one morning to find an irritating rash on a sensitive private part. He lives comfortably in a villa with a pretty young thing for a wife, supported to a great extent by his father in law (whose professional line and access to ready wealth is left open). Most of the day amounts to idle words and a mishmash of half baked phrases and worn out cliches — particularly at the tv station. That gnawing rash, in other words, corresponds to a meaningless mental routine heightened by day-to-day imbecilities.

Once the viewer catches this message early in the game, the rest is smooth sailing and a delight every inch of the way. Our hero starts to drift without really knowing where he's going or why. He quarrels with the tv staff over some inane project, hits the road in his shiny car and picks up a lady in another shiny car for a night in a motel, has it out with his wife (a mannikin-type who, in her own way, loves him) and father in law, and then quits everything in the end.

One thing, however, he doesn't get rid of is the rash. He visits a doctor-friend and gets some cream to rub on a couple times a day — there's a hilarious scene in a public toilet where he performs the administrations with his back entirely to the audience. That microscopic spot on his skin proves to be his Achilles' Heel.

Lensing and other credits are all tops. Aleksandar Bercek as the young man is a thesp find, while Neda Arneric and Milena Dravic as the two women in his life, and Ljuba Tadic as his tv superior, offer strong supporitng roles. Most striking of all, pic maintains a cool, distant, unengaged atmosphere throughout to fashion moments that are often appropriately chilling in psychological depth. —Holl.

Legend Of The Mountain
(HONG KONG-COLOR)

Hong Kong, April 10.
A King Hu-Prosperity Film Company Ltd. release. Directed by King Hu. Features entire cast. Screenplay, Ling Chung; camera (color), Henry Chen; music, Ng Tai Kong; martial arts supervisor, Wu Ming-tsai; costume and art design, King Hu; editor, King Hu. Reviewed at IFD Preview Theatre, Hong Kong, April 7, '79. Running time: **Approx 190 MINS.**
Cast: Hsu Feng, Sylvia Chang, Shih Chun, Tung Lin, Tien Feng, Wu Ming-tsai, Rainbow Hsu, Chen Hui-lon, Sun Yueh, Wu Chia-hsiang.
(Mandarin soundtrack with English and French sub-titles.)

"I've been there in a dream ... and I'm going there in real life," could very well be the theme of King Hu's latest, "Legend of the Mountain." Basically an old-fashioned legend, foreigners may relish in unraveling hidden metaphors and symbolisms that are sandwiched between shots of well-composed on location scenes re-creating the Sung dynasty period during the 11th century in old China.

The film took two years to finish and cost over HK$3,000,000 to produce. The storyline deals with a romance that transcends time and human existence, the clash of physical and spiritual forces and the relationship of dreams with reality. The mysticism and opaqueness of "Legend" is thus open to provocative interpretations.

Hampered by the rather common material, Hu still manages to salvage the fable with his dramatic and professional flair-for pictorial grandeur.

The hero is a young scholar, Ho, given the task to copy in final form a Tantric sutra. It is intended to guide wandering souls to their next incarnation or destination. A monk warns him that evil spirits may attempt to steal the completed sutra.

The second half begins one autumn day when Ho encounters Lady Chuan who also has a daughter, Cloud. Ho is appalled to learn that he has been consorting with ghosts.

"Legend," which runs for more than 3 hours, could be more effective and riveting in a shorter version.

The ensemble cast act their roles with enthusiasm though they can't give much substance to the cliche people who inhabit a typical Chinese ghost story. Shih Chun gives subtlety and resourcefulness to his one-dimensional character of Ho. The role really requires narrow emotional range.

King Hu can be criticized on two major points. He repeats himself. Present once again are the repetitive somersaults and acrobatic leaps of "Touch of Zen" and "The Valiant Ones." Hu is a major talent who needs more powerful material. He could have tackled a more comtemporary subject or simply transport the old myth to a modern setting. "Legend" is from a short story of the Sung Dynasty, setting. "Legend" is from a short story of the Sung Dynasty, entitled "A Cave Full of Ghosts In the West Mountain."

Technically, "Legend" is a massive and superlative effort. And foreigners not exposed to the ordinary Oriental lore will find it fascinating and enchanting. An elegant plus to the production is the soundtrack music, played on a unique Chinese musical instrument. It blends beautifully with the stunning visuals and at the same time effectively accelerate some of the plodding parts. —Mel.

Saint Jack
(COLOR)

Bogdanovich in Singapore. Finely crafted film of "iffy" outlook.

New World Pictures release of a Playboy — Shoals Creek — Copa de Oro Picture. Directed by Peter Bogdanovich. Produced by Roger Corman. Stars Ben Gazzara. Screenplay, Howard Sackler, Paul Theroux; Bogdanovich, based on novel by Theroux. Exec prods., Hugh M. Hefner, Edward L. Rissien. Camera (color), Robby Muller; editor, William Carruth; sound, Jean-Pierre Ruh; art direction, David Ng. Reviewed at Magno Theatre, N.Y., April 24, '79. (MPAA Rating: R). Running time: 112 MINS.
Jack Flowers .... Ben Gazzara
William Leigh .... Denholm Elliott
Frogget .... James Villiers
Yardley .... Joss Ackland
Smale .... Rodney Bewes
Yates .... Mark Kingston
Mrs. Yates .... Lisa Lu
Monika .... Monika Subramaniam
Judy .... Judy Lim
Senator .... George Lazenby
Eddie Schuman .... Peter Bogdanovich
Gopi .... Joseph Noel
Hing .... Ong Kian Bee
Little Hing .... Tan Yan Meng

Edging away from the string of big-budgeted major studio box-office disappointments that last saw "Nickelodeon" surface briefly in 1976, director Peter Bogdanovich has gotten considerably closer to earth, if not broad-based commercial potential, with "Saint Jack."

Shot entirely on location in Singapore, the film (produced by Roger Corman, who gave Bogdanovich his start of "The Wild Angels" in 1964) is extremely well crafted, finely acted, and conjures up a positively intriguing milieu.

At bottom line, though, it's essentially a character study — Ben Gazzara excels as a pimp with a heart of gold — told in a mood that begins with a twinkling-eyed bawdiness, but becomes progressively more sombre and even nihilistic as the sparse story wends its way. For all its exotic locale, it winds up going nowhere.

Based on Paul Theroux's novel (Theroux co-scripted with Bogdanovich and Howard Sackler), the film is laid in 1971, putting its exclusive focus on Gazzara, an expatriate U.S. hustler-type who jumps ship and uses the cover of a local provision broker to operate a freelance prostitution ring.

His dream is to establish his own pleasure palace, which he manages to do despite the ominous threats and strong-arm tactics of the local underworld within a year, they succeed in literally destroying his operation. Taken under the wing of an ambiguous American mobster type (played by Bogdanovich), Gazzara sets up another operation designed to service Vietnam-bound and returning U.S. soldiers with local flesh.

Throughout the pic there are hints that Gazzara's character runs deeper and more sensitively than his wisecracking exterior will admit. Already cynical about "fattening up" the young soldiers for the Vietnam slaughter ahead, his conscience peaks when Bogdanovich offers him $25,000 to photograph an influential Senator in flagrante with a young male prostitute. Conscience wins at fadeout. That's the story.

The script is a good one, gutsy and sometime very funny, and largely keyed to the pic's basically interesting characters. Unfortunately, the details don't add up to much, although the cast — which includes Denholm Elliott in a finely tuned and moving portrait of a decent British accountant at odds with his smarmy environment — Joss Ackland and James Villiers — is uniformly fine.

Bogdanovich has made "Saint Jack" an object lesson in seamless, effortlessly fluid piece of work, reeking with atmosphere but in need of a stronger narrative core. Technical credits, particularly Robby Muller's lensing and William Carruth's editing, are excellent.

Pic was partially bankrolled by Playboy Productions (a gratuitous lesbian striptease seems designed for a pic-hyping magazine spread) with Hugh Heffner exec producing with Edward L. Rissien. —*Step.*

Les Chiens
(The Dogs)
(FRENCH-COLOR)

Paris, April 20.
A G.E.F.-C.C.F.C. release of an A.J. Films — A.M.S. Productions — Films de la Drouette (Paris) — Pacific Films (Tahiti) co-production. Produced by Laurent Mayniel. Stars Gerard Depardieu, Victor Lanoux, Nicole Calfan. Directed by Alain Jessua. Screenplay. Andre Ruellan, Jessua, based on an original idea by Jessua; camera (Eastmancolor), Etienne Becker; editor, Helene Plemmianikov; music, Rene Koering; sound,; Harald Maury; art director, Jean-Louis Poveda; dog trainer, Andre Noel. Reviewed at Cinema Gaumont Colisee, Paris, April 16, 1979. Running time: 100 MINS.

Morel .... Gerard Depardieu
Dr. Ferret .... Victor Lanoux
Elisabeth .... Nicole Calfan

Alain Jessua's "The Dogs" does not bite. In trying to fashion an admonitory parable of modern France, through the very real problem of the increased use by private citizens of trained guard dogs for self-defense, Jessua fails to make either a satisfying thriller or a convincing social analysis.

Set in one of those hideously impersonal new French towns, film concerns a young doctor, his practice newly set up, who quickly becomes aware of citizen reaction to juvenile delinquency, rape and the presence of an immigrant working community. Everybody is buying dogs, including the young rape victim whom the doctor treats and subsequently becomes involved with.

When the mayor is murdered by a guard dog there becomes evident a complicity between some of the townspeople and Morel, the dog-trainer who provides the animals. The town's disaffected youth declare war on the fascistic citizens responsible for some "accidental" attacks on Africans and young people — violence erupts. Morel is killed and his kennels burned. The doctor and his girl-friend escape to another locality — a picturesque village — only to wake up next morning and find a neighbor out walking his growling German shepherd.

Script is shrill and downright conventional, a patchwork of dramatic elements and character types inherited from horror melodramas and films like Don Siegel's "Invasion of the Body Snatchers" (whose hero is also a doctor). Emotional involvement in minimal, leaving one free to watch the director overwork certain effects, such as the ironically idyllic scene, where the dog-trainer frolics, in slow-motion, with his favorite dog on the river bank.

Jessua doesn't seem to have worked enough with his actors, who lack force and conviction. Much of the direction went to the dogs.

Film is not to be confused with Burt Brinckerhoff's "Dogs," an American nature-gone-mad horror film made in 1976, or Antonio Isasi's 1977 "El Perro" (The Dog). —*Len.*

Quadrophenia
(BRITISH-COLOR)

Youth-cult drama with better-than-cult prospects.

London, April 27.
A Curbishley-Baird production for The Who Films Ltd. Produced by Roy Baird, Bill Curbishley. Executive producers, The Who. Directed by Franc Roddam. Features entire cast. Screenplay, Dave Humphries, Martin Stellman, Franc Roddam, based on the album, "Quadrophenia," by Pete Townshend; camera (color), Brian Tufano; editor, Mike Taylor; musical directors, John Entwistle, Pete Townshend; sound, Chris Wranger; designer, Simon Holland; choreographer, Gillian Gregory; asst. director, Ray Corbett. Reviewed at the British Academy of Film & Television Arts screening room, London, April 26, '79. Running time: 120 MINS.
Jimmy .... Phil Daniels
Dave .... Mark Wingett
Chalky .... Philip Davis
Steph .... Leslie Ash
Pete .... Garry Cooper
Monkey .... Toyah Wilcox
Ace .... Sting (Gordon Sumner)
Ferdy .... Trevor Laird
Jimmy's Mother .... Kate Williams
Jimmy's Father .... Michael Elphick
Yvonne .... Kim Neve
Kevin .... Raymond Winstone
Spider .... Gary Shail

"Quadrophenia," as the first British film for some years to have the courage of its ethnic convictions, could give the lie to the notion that for a picture to be internationally marketable it must involve star names, uppercase production values and an American-style theme.

Without any of these usual pluses — though with a fine soundtrack by The Who which plays a strong integral part in the storytelling, since the film's based on composer-guitarist Pete Townshend's songs for the band's 1973 same-title album — "Quadrophenia" looks set to score both as an authentic piece of nostalgia and as a youth-drama which hits home for a wider-than-average age group. Hefty promotion shoudl pay off via strong world-of-mouth, so prospects in most markets look bright.

Set in 1963, when rival image-cults among young Britishers led to a wave of crowd-fights in normally staid seaside resorts, the picture plots the plight of one pill-popping, fashion-mad "Mod" who abandons himself completely to the gang-identity. After fighting the enemy "Rockers" (denoted by black leather, motorbikes and beer) in a disorderly clash on Brighton beach, and being arrested for the cause, he swiftly discovers the hollowness of the whole image thing when he realizes his girl only went for him in the heat of the moment, and until his nattily-equipped motorscooter — the ultimate Mod status symbol — is wrecked.

It's a tribute to helmer Franc Roddam's simple, restrained direction that the downbeat ending, when the jobless, exhausted kid is left in the advanced state of schizophrenia implied by the title, succeeds in being climactic, since the film gets better as it goes along. Whereas some earlier sequences lack drive, often because the script seems to strain to convey a sense of period when more dramatic push is needed, the closing scenes are economically written and movingly played.

Phil Daniels, with the right pinched features and a naturally sympathetic manner, makes out well as the anti-hero in search of somewhere to belong. Sting, as the weekend super-Mod whose image collapses when he's revealed to work as a bellhop, cuts a slick dash in the dancehall sequences.

Leslie Ash is well cast for the role of the skin-deep dolly-girl, and makes her switch to rejecting Daniels both chilling and believable. Among the other unknowns, Raymond Winstone is standout as the kid's buddy-turned-Rocker.

The fight scenes, involving hundreds of extras, are competently handled by Roddam and the cinematographer, Brian Tufano, whose lighting for the London night-locations is also creditable. Considerable trouble has been taken with most period details — there are very few studio settings — with the exception of uniformly modern railroad stock. —*Simo.*

The Dark
(COLOR)

Werewolf in blue jeans from outer space should pocket some change.

Hollywood, April 25.

A Film Ventures International release of an Edward L. Montoro-Dick Clark presentation. Executive produced by Derek Power. Produced by Dick Clark and Edward L. Montoro. Associate produced by Igo Kantor. Features entire cast. Directed by John (Bud) Cardos. Screenplay, Stanford Whitmore; camera (DeLuxe Color/-Panavision), John Morrill; editor, Martin Dreffke; music, Roger Kellaway; art direction, Rusty Rosene; sound, Robert Dietz. Reviewed at the Vine Theatre, L.A., April 25, '79. (MPAA Rating: R.) Running time: **92 MINS.**

Roy Warner	William Devane
Zoe Owens	Cathy Lee Crosby
Dave Mooney	Richard Jaeckel
Sherman Mossberg	Keenan Wynn
De Renzy	Jacquelyn Hyde
Captain Speer	Warren Kemmerling
Detective Bressler	Biff Elliot
Courtney Floyd	Vivian Blaine
Pathologist	Casey Kasem

Produced and cast with a bit more seriousness than the standard creature from outer space exploitationer, "The Dark" gets by for part of its running time on decent craftsmanship in all departments. However, once the beast is seen in all its gruesomeness, pic quickly deteriorates, falling back on 1950s-style monster film cliches. Item should be able to find a niche in the action-horror market.

After a narrator intones the premise that all alien encounters will "not necessarily be friendly," intercutting between the creature's nightly killing sprees around Santa Monica and characters affected by the crimes takes over. Murders, which alternately take the form of decapitations and zappings by the alien's laser-type eyes, create some chills the first couple of times, but eventually diminish in effectiveness through repetitive handling of the stalking sequences and the gradually revealed appearance of the fiend, which resembles nothing so much as a werewolf in blue jeans.

Unlike so many pictures in the genre, "The Dark" doesn't bog down completely in the dialog interludes. William Devane and Cathy

Lee Crosby as, respectively, an author and a tv newscaster who, for their own reasons, become involved in the case, manage to bring somewhat off-beat qualities to what are essentially thankless roles. The pressure the police feel to solve the crime wave is given unusual and realistic play in Stanford Whitmore's screenplay, given the circumstances, and, as a harassed cop, Richard Jaeckel is terrific in a part that had no right to deserve him.

Unfortunately, pic ends as so many others have, with the demon cornering the lovers in a dark, deserted house, the cops ineffectually blasting it with all the conventional ammo they've got, and the beast finally self-destructing into thin air to leave open the option for a sequel.

John (Bud) Cardos, who took over from Tobe Hooper just before shooting began, directed fluidly, and John Morrill's camerawork is very fine. Roger Kellaway's score purposely telegraphs each apparition of the alien. —*Cart.*

Cathy's Child
(AUSTRALIAN-COLOR)

Sydney, Jan. 25.

A Roadshow release of a C.B. Films production. Producers, Pom Oliver, Errol Sullivan. Features entire cast. Director, Donald Crombie. Screenplay, Ken Quinnell from a book by Dick Wordley; camera (color), Gary Hansen; production design Ross Major; sound, Tim Lloyd; editor, Tim Wellburn; asst. directors, Mark Egerton, Mark Turnbull. Previewed at the Roadshow Theatrette, Sydney, Jan. 24, '79. Running time: **89 MINS.**

Cathy Baikas	Michelle Fawdon
Dick Wordley	Alan Cassell
Nicko	Bryan Brown
Peter	Harry Michael
Donna	Anna Hruby
Mike	Bob Hughes
Angelina	Sophia Haskas
Young Nun	Sarah McKenzie
Lil	Judy Stevenson
Barmaid	Bobbie Ward
Smedley	Gerry Gallagher
Perilli	Annibale Migliucci
Minister	Arthur Dignam
Athens Consul	Willie Fennell

"Cathy's Child" is based on a true story in which a young Greek mother living in Sydney had her three-year-old daughter abducted by the child's father who returned to Greece with it. The incident was made into a cause celebre by one of the local afternoon newspapers whose reporters turned the spotlight on bureaucracy's mishandling of the situation.

Michelle Fawdon turns in a super performance as the young migrant mother, evoking terrific sympathy in those anguished moments when she can't comprehend what is going on around her due to language gap. Donald Crombie helps her create in the character exactly the right kind of pathos and help-

lessness, tempered with the determination to get her baby back.

To her aid comes a battered old pro' journalist, Dick Wordley, (Alan Cassell), who with the help of his tough young city editor forces the story out of the advice columns and onto the front page. The storyline follows the events as they happened and some nice acting moments and good structuring by Ken Quinnell give Crombie the kind of atmospherics and incident that help develop character alongside the plot. Bryan Brown is standout as the embittered editor who some years before had been through a similar experience to Cathy; the exposition of this is deftly and subtley handled.

Production values are excellent for the budget of less than $800,000 with shooting on location in Greece and in the Sydney area. Tech credits are excellent also, with Gary Hansen's cameras matching moods and utilizing lighting contrasts to underline location.

Pic has an undeniable aura of soap opera about it if for no other reason than its subject; but that is no put down in this case since Crombie and the players keep interest up even though it's clear there'll be a happy ending come fade-out.

Commercial prospects could be good if the right marketing approach is taken. Outside Australia, the film might have an appeal it could lack here in so far as with their in-built temptation to apathy, Australians are oft prone to dismiss a picture because they think they know the story.

If so, it's their loss because "Cathy's Child" is a very human tale of maternal determination and sidelights an often overlooked grey area of international indolence on a bureaucratic level. And says it all without being "preaching," what's more. —*Miha.*

Last Embrace
(COLOR)

First-rate suspenser evokes Hitchcock favorably.

Hollywood, April 19.

United Artists release of a Taylor/Wigutow production. Produced by Michael Taylor, Dan Wigutow. Directed by Jonathan Demme. Features entire cast. Screenplay, David Shaber, based on novel "The Thirteenth Man" by Murray Teigh Bloom; camera (color), Tak Fujimoto; editor, Barry Malkin; music, Miklos Rosza; production design, Charles Rosen; costume design, Jane Greenwood; sound, Les Lazarowitz; assistant director, Michael Rauch. Reviewed at MGM Screening Room, Culver City, Apirl 19, '79. (MPAA Rating: R.) Running time: **103 MINS.**

Harry Hannan	Roy Scheider
Ellie Fabian	Janet Margolin
Richard Peabody	John Glover
Sam Urdell	Sam Levene
Dave Quittle	Charles Napier
Eckart	Christopher Walken
Dr. Coppersmith	Jacqueline Brooks
Rabbi Drexel	David Margulies
Bernie Meckler	Andrew Duncan
Adrian	Marcia Rodd

Of the numerous filmic homages to Alfred Hitchcock in the last few years, among them pix by Francois Truffaut and Brian DePalma, "Last Embrace" ranks among the best, both for its subtlety and suspenseful pacing. Director Jonathan Demme now proves conclusively that he can handle a strictly commercial assignment, while embellishing it with the creative touches that mark a first-rate filmmaker. Boxoffice prognosis for the United Artists release is healthy, although the mystery genre seems to be in temporary eclipse.

"Last Embrace" is the maiden producing effort by former UA execs Michael Taylor and Dan Wigutow, and offers Demme the chance to validate the favorable critical reaction to his first big-budgeter, "Citizens Band" ("Handle With Care"), which went down the b.o. drain.

The team has picked an interesting subject, that of a government agent being phased out after a nervous breakdown, triggered by his wife's murder. Roy Scheider is the paranoid subject of more attention than he'd prefer, especially when it comes from Janet Margolin, a wigged-out grad student.

Scheider's fears turn out to be well-grounded, with Margolin as the lynchpin to his worries. David Shaber's screen adaptation of Murray Teigh Bloom's novel, "The Thirteenth Man," is complex, but rarely dull, and Demme brings to it a menacing, wholly cinematic style.

The Hitchcock's references are frequent (a shower curtain suddenly pulled back, a sea of yellow raincoats that recalls the plethora of umbrellas in "Foreign Correspondent," a genuine MacGuffin in the form of an ancient Hebrew death threat) but never intrusive, and Demme accomplishes what every cineaste dreams of — to elaborate upon, and not simply mimic, the gifts of a master.

Scheider is on-screen almost constantly, and he delivers a convincing, nerve-tingling perf that should break out of the "Jaws" rut, and reaffirm he can handle a romantic lead. Margolin is highly appealing as the revenge-minded femme, whose moral ambivalence gives a shading to her character rarely seen in either thrillers or love stories.

Christopher Walken is seen briefly in a cameo performance as Scheider's boss, and the rest of the supporting cast, especially Sam Levene as a Jewish investigator and

John Glover as a frazzled academic, is essential to the film's effectiveness. Demme himself makes a brief appearance as, what else, a stranger on the train.

One of strongest virtues of "Last Embrace" is its clean, fresh look, due in great measure to Tak Fujimoto, who co-photographed Terrence Malick's "Badlands" and did the solo work on Alan Rudolph's visually stuning "Remember My Name," is one of the most underrated cinematographers around. Also top-notch was Charles Rosen's imaginative use of New York and Niagara Falls locales, and Barry Malkin's smart editing.

Miklos Rosza, who scored Hitchcock's "Spellbound" 34 years ago, contributes a similarly eerie soundtrack here. While "Last Embrace" isn't up to the standard of that and other Hitchcock classics, it stands head and shoulders above most of its contemporary competition. —Poll.

The Riddle of the Sands
(BRITISH-COLOR)

Plodding period spy adventure. Soft b.o. outlook.

London, April 23.
Rank Film Distributors release, produced by Drummond Challis. Directed by Tony Maylam. Stars Michael York, Jenny Agutter, Simon MacCorkindale. Screenplay, Tony Maylam, John Bailey (based on novel of same title by Erskine Childers); camera (color), Christopher Challis; editor, Peter Hollywood; music, Howard Blake; art direction, Terry Pritchard; sound, Rene Borisewitz; second unit camera, Arthur Wooster, assistant director, Neill Vine-Miller. Reviewed at Rank screening room, London, April 23, '79. (B-BFC rating: U). Running time: 102 MINS.

Charles Carruthers .... Michael York
Clara .... Jenny Agutter
Arthur Davies ..... Simon MacCorkindale
Dollmann .... Alan Badel
Von Bruning .... Jurgen Andersen
Frau Dollmann .... Olga Lowe
Grimm .... Hans Meyer
Bohme .... Michael Sheard
The Kaiser .... Wolf Kahler
Withers .... Ronald Markham

In "The Riddle of the Sands," Michael York and Simon MacCorkindale portray pip-pip chaps who intercept and foil a German plot, circa 1901, to invade England by transporting troops on a flotilla of barges. The lackdustre Rank release looms as dual-bill fodder for general situations with a gap in playing time to plug. Boxoffice prospects are modest.

As a solo yachtsman cruising the coastal waters off Germany, MacCorkindale has a provocative encounter with Alan Badel, playing a renegade English naval officer involved in the Kaiser's plot. Thus aroused, MacCorkindale summons York, a longtime-no-see chum from college days at Oxford,

and the two pit wits against Badel and cohorts.

The Tony Maylam-John Bailey screenplay shifts back and forth from North Sea to German coast with predictable monotony and moody atmospherics that only accentuate the wide-spaced action under Maylam's languid direction. What little suspense film generates is easily bearable.

York and MacCorkindale are satisfactory in a yarn rife with cliched characterization and implausible situations, but Jenny Agutter as Badel's inscrutable daughter, fancied by MacCorkindale and vice-versa, is wasted in a part that hardly matters. Other performances are professionally routine.

Christopher Challis' photography and Howard Blake's dramatic score are both okay, ditto other technical credits. A lot of the Dutch and German locations were either nocturnal or shot tight. Hence, for all their non-impact, the British crew might just as well have stayed home. —Pit.

Serie Noire
(Thriller Story)
(FRENCH-COLOR)

Paris, April 26.
A Gaumont release of a Gaumont-Prospectacle co-production. Produced by Maurice Bernart. Stars Patrick Dewaere, Myriam Boyer, Marie Trintignant, Bernard Blier. Directed by Alain Corneau. Screenplay, Corneau, Georges Perec, based on the novel "A Hell Of A Woman," by Jim Thompson; camera (Fujicolor-Panavision), Pierre-William Glenn; editor Thierry Derocles; sound, Michel Desrois. No original score. Reviewed at Antegor screening room, Paris, April 13, 1979. Running time: 110 MINS.
Frank Poupart .... Patrick Dewaere
Jeanne .... Myriam Boyer
Mona .... Marie Trintignant
Staplin .... Bernard Blier
Andreas Tikides .... Andreas Katsulas

French admiration for American film and literary thriller finds its consummate expression in Alain Corneau's "Serie Noire." Neither an intellectual puzzle that uses the detective story as a pretext, nor a slavish homage, this striking film is a brutally visceral distillation of a genre not taken seriously until French intellectuals and artists began to analyse it and draw inspiration from its vision and conventions.

Corneau and Georges Perec have adapted an American thriller, "A Hell Of A Woman" by American writer Jim Thompson, pruning it of its cumbersome plot machinery and transplanting the action to France. In giving his film the title "Serie Noire," (literally, "Black Series") Corneau makes direct reference to the reputable crime fiction series — in which Thompson's novel appeared in its

French translation — founded and edited after the war by writer and detective fiction connoisseur Marcel Duhamel.

Set in one of those hideous Par suburbs where life flushes its human waste, the sordid tale concerns Frank Poupart, a pathetic, fantasy-drugged salesman whose equally lamentable wife decides to leave him in order to think things over.

When Poupart meets sleepy-eyed, withdrawn Mona (a haunting Marie Trintignant) and learns that her dreadful aunt, who prostitutes the girl to Poupart in exchange for a sweater, is hiding a fortune in the house he sees a way out of this environment. Using as scapegoat a stupid Greek boxer, (an excellent Andreas Katsulas) in debt to Poupart, the salesman murders both old woman and Greek. He and Mona then arrange to make their getaway.

But Poupart's wife comes back suddenly, eager to start again — he kills her in mad despair. Then his unscrupulous employer (Bernard Blier, effectively repulsive), who has figured out what is going on, blackmails Poupart into handing over the entire hoard. He is left with Mona, without money, having exchanged one void for another.

The film is an extraordinary tour de force, creating an atmosphere of such palpitating nightmare that one is drained by its insistent odiousness. From first to last frame we wallow in a vision so dark that even the slightest apparently decent impulse seems grotesque and excessive. Undoubtedly many will find the entire film an exercise in gratuitousness. But what an exercise:

Corneau's direction is razor-sharp (even though there is some technical sloppiness, like a large bloodstain that disappears a few shots later) and he has the invaluable aid of Pierre-William Glenn's brooding color photography, which imparts to places and objects an identity of oppressive menace, Thierry Derocles' editing and Michel Desrois' sound (superb use is made of source music, emphasizing the emotional emptiness).

But film's motor is Patrick Dewaere's febrile performance as the vertiginously hollow Poupart, shifting with impressive skill between near-catatonic astonishment and manic activity. This role may be an acme for Dewaere, whose work in the training ground of cafe-theatre improvisation finds eloquent purpose here.

Promoted as a thriller "Serie Noire" has good chances abroad. It will probably be snatched up quickly at the Cannes fest, where pic is competing for France. The title,

"Serie Noire," was used in 1955 for an Erich van Stroheim vehicle.
—Len.

7 Dias De Enero
(7 Days in January)
(SPANISH-COLOR)

Madrid, April 11.
A Goya Films and Les Films des Deux Mondes production. Directed by Juan Antonio Bardem. Exec producer, Serafin Garcia Trueba. Features entire cast. Screenplay, Bardem, Gregorio Moron; camera (Eastmancolor), Leopoldo Villasenor; music, Nicolas Peyrac; editor, Guillermo Maldonado; sets, Antonio de Miguel.
Reviewed at Cine Tivoli, Madrid, April 10, 1979. Running time: 130 MINS.
Cast: Manuel Egea Martinez, Fernando Sanchez Pollack, Virginia Gonzalez Mataix, Madeleine Robinson, Jack Francois, Alberto Alonso Lopez.

Over the past year or so some Spanish filmmakers have been raking back over the country's recent political past and extracting the more exicting events for film themes. Juan Antonio Bradem has done this with the shooting of a group of Communist lawyers by right wing militants in Madrid in 1977. The trouble with the film, however, is that aside from ther eenactment of the actual shooting in the Calle Atocha, there's no plot or story.

Bardem uses the major Spanish political events leading up to and following the shooting (the "seven days" of the title is misleading), mixing in some docu footage for the sake of authenticity, but never succeeds in penetrating any of the characters or developing any kind of a story. Instead, he serves up the shooting on three different occasions in the film: first from outside the lawyer's office, secondly by panning the blood stains, and third by showing the gunning-down in slow motion, a la Sam Peckinpah.

Thesping throughout is truly terrible, with most of it stilted and amateurish. The only actor who comes through convincingly is the one who plays the police chief. The script and dialogs are insubstantial and flat and the helming sparkless. The film drags on far too long, but even if it were cut there is little to salvage.

From an ideological standpoint, item is a gung-ho Communist tract, with the then-outlawed Reds depicted as hardworking idealists and blameless libertarians and the baddies a conglomerate of pious fascists. The lines are drawn too black and red, though in real life they may be blacker and redder than depicted.

There's also an embryo of a love story between one of the young fascists and a prudish girl, but it never really develops into anything. Sales will probably be very limited, except perhaps in East Bloc lands where Bardem's Party standing will be of avail. In Madrid item is playing to virtually empty houses. —*Besa.*

CS Blues
(DOCU-16m-COLOR/B&W)

Hollywood, April 21.

A Rolling Stones presentation. Produced by Marshall Chess. Directed by Robert Frank, Daniel Seymour. Editors, Susan Steinberg, Paul Justman. No other credits available. Reviewed at Fox Venice Theatre, Venice, Calif., April 21, '79. No MPAA Rating. Running time: **95 MINS.**

Features: The Rolling Stones, Marshall Chess, Stevie Wonder, Andy Warhol, Truman Capote, Dick Cavett, Terry Southern, Lee Radziwill, Tina Turner, Bianca Jagger, Bobby Keyes, Jim Price, Nicky Hopkins.

Filmed during the Rolling Stones' 1972 American tour, "CS Blues" has remained largely unseen since then, as the band's displeasure with the pic resulted in a court order limiting it to four public screenings per year. Controversy is clearly the docu's biggest selling point and while it does contain a few eyebrowraising moments, they are rather outweighed by dullness and lack of sharp artistic focus.

Made by photographer Robert Frank, with a codirecting credit also going to cameraman Daniel Seymour, pic struggles with a problem that has confronted and defeated many before, that of how to portray tedium (in this case, of a long concert tour) without lapsing into tedium oneself.

Because the subjects here are the Stones, film has the advantage of a certain glamor and Mick Jagger's charisma, as well as the group's exciting music. Performances of several tunes, either whole or in part, are included, although sound recording quality is way below state of the art in this area and film can't be considered a "performance" film along the lines of "Gimme Shelter" or "Ladies and Gentlemen, the Rolling Stones," the latter also having been lensed during the 1972 tour.

Rather, Frank seems to be pursuing a portrait of the behind-the-scenes phenomenon of a major rock tour, with the inevitable cast of roadies, groupies, musicians, journalists and celebrity hangers-on. Some incidents, such as roadies horsing around with a couple of girls on the tour plane while the leering Stones beat out a throbbing musical accompaniment, or Keith Richards and Bobby Keyes tossing a tv set out of a hotel window, are the kinds of things one reads about happening on tour but haven't been shown before.

On the other hand, music rehearsals and dressing room make-up sessions are a drag whether it's the Stones or a high school folk trio, and Frank has done little to alleviate the boredom here, except to catch Richards passing out at one point and, in an extraordinary sequence, to follow the group as it proceeds from its cubicles backstage through hallways and finally out onto the stage.

Film also raises the perennial cinema-verite question of how much of what we see is "real" and how much happens because of, or for, the camera. A ludicrous disclaimer at the outset insists that all the events depicted except the musical numbers are "fictional," but suspicion persists that many of the more outrageous events on view were staged, or at least happened because the presence of the camera encouraged individuals' exhibitionistic tendancies. It's somehow hard to imagine that the camera just happened to be there when some of the roadies and their girls were shooting up or taking cocaine, rather easier to believe that something in them wanted their activities to be documented.

If ever cleared from its legal entanglements, film would probably prove too ragged and lethargic for most audiences aside from hardcore Stones fans. Otherwise, it's more of sociological than artistic interest and not quite the sensational shocker that rumors over the years have suggested.
—*Cart.*

The Chicago Maternity Center Story
(DOCU-B&W-16m)

West Berlin, April 18.

A Kartemquin Collective Production, Chicago, world rights, Kartemquin Films, Chicago. Screenplay, direction, and editing by Jerry Blumenthal, Suzanne Davenport, Sharon Karp, Jennifer Rohrer, Gordon Quinn; camera (black and white), Quinn, Rohrer, Davenport; commentator, Rohrer. Reviewed at Arsenal-Kino, West Berlin, April 17, '79. Running time: **60 MINS.**

With Beatrice Tucker and the personnel of the Chicago Maternity Center, members of WATCH (Women Act to Control Healthcare), Scharene Miller and her family and friends.

"The Chicago Maternity Center Story" bowed at the International Forum of Young Cinema in Berlin shortly after it preemed in Chicago in 1977. It's a docu on childbirth and Healthcare, a timely subject which gave a sense of urgency and ring of integrity to what be otherwise classified as another of those "message" films.

Proof of the pic's integrity has been its history in both of the Germanys over the past months. "The Chicago Maternity Center Story," together with the group's "Trick Bag" (1975), was unspooled at the Leipzig Festival of engaged docus in East Germany first, went on to West Berlin's Forum, and "Trick Bag" was even picked up by West German television recently for a program of international shorts.

The filmmakers, known as the Kartemquin Collective, stem from a socially and politically engaged documentary tradition in the Chicago area. The team of Gerald Temaner and Gordon Quinn founded Kartemquin Films in the mid-1960s; their purpose then was to make fiction-like docus in a cinema-verite style that would provoke lengthy discussion, as well as "confront," among the socalled "experts" in various social-minded fields. Their best known pix are "Home for Life" (1967), about new occupants in an Old Age Home (Edinburgh Film Festival), and "Thumbs Down" (1968), about suburban teenagers rebelling against parents and society in general (Florence Festival dei Popoli).

In the 1970s the production company broadened to include docus on ethnic peoples in the Chicago area and the new feminist film movement. Kartemquin Films became a collective reflecting varying interests, some say the best Yank docu group handling feminist themes in a social context.

"The Chicago Maternity Center Story" tells what happens when modern medicine decides childbirth at home is now out of the question, and thus a venerable institution with a low infant mortality rate (in a city with the country's highest such rate) servicing large blacks and Latins in the poor areas is in danger of closing down.

Docu records the facts as they are in the Center today, focusing after a while on a pregnant woman, who wants her child born at home, and an elderly woman doctor, who has dedicated her life to making the Chicago Maternity Center what it is. The feminist group, WATCH (Woman Act to Control Healthcare), acts to try and save the Center at the last minute. A birth takes place on screen at the end to prove (if such proof is necessary) that natural childbirth at home is not only acceptable, but also (in this case) preferable.

A clip out of Pare Lorentz's rather melodramatic "Fight for Life" (the docu was incompleted) about this same Center gives docu a timeless quality. Lensing and commentary are first-class. Docus such as these don't pass easily into oblivion as so many period-pieces do.
—*Holl.*

Le Coup de Sirocco
(The Sirocco Blow)
(FRENCH-COLOR)

Paris, April 22.

A Gaumont release of an Alma Films — Alexandre Films coproduction. Produced by Serge Laski. Features entire cast. Directed by Alexandre Arcady. Screenplay, Daniel Saint-Hamon, Jan Saint-Hamon, Arcady, from novel by Saint-Hamon; camera (Eastmancolor), Jean-Francois Robin; sound, Guillaume Sciama; music, Serge Franklin; editor, Joelle Van Effenterre. Reviewed at Salles Ponthieu, Paris, April 13, 1979. Running time: **100 MINS.**

Albert Narboni	Roger Hanin
Marguerite Narboni	Marthe Villalonga
Lucien Bonheur	Michel Auclair
Paulo Narboni	Patrick Bruel
Jacob	Lucien Layani

This first feature by Alexandre Arcady is the first film to take a look at the situation of the "Pieds-Noir" (literally, "Black Feet"; i.e. those Algerians of French, not Arabic, origin) who were repatriated to France following Algerian independence in 1962. Arcady, himself a "Pied-Noir," has opted for comic treatment "in the Italian manner" and has adapted a novel by Daniel Saint-Hamon (who collaborated on the script), taking the liberty to insert elements from his own experiences.

"Coup de Sirocco" considers one family, the Narbonis; we first meet them in 1945 reopening their grocery store and falling into raptures over their new-born son. As the years pass they lend little import to the political tremors around them, going on with their modest lives, watching their son grow. They never do realize the full significance of events even when they are obliged to sell their grocery and make for France like a million other "Algerians."

Second part of film deals with their problems of insertion into French society, which is alien to them. Though bewildered and hurt, they maintain their generosity of spirit and high-decibel garrulousness. Albert Narboni finds a job in a supermarket and befriends a quiet-voiced Parisian businessman who tries to talk the Narbonis into marketing their own preparation of couscous, a traditional Arabic dish. But this friend proves hollow and the Narbonis return to their difficult adaptation with humble modesty.

Anxious to avoid what he calls "the tragic, the vindictive and the tear-jerking" Arcady bathes the film in the bittersweet haze of reminiscence (story is narrated by the son looking back on past) and therefore attenuates abrasive emotion and harsh realities. Thus the film has genuine warmth and humor but fails to communicate with immediacy the pain of dislocation and adjustment. Unlike the best Italian comedies, "Coup de Sirocco" dilutes its theme more than it distills. Spectators abroad, not familiar with the problems evoked in the film, may underestimate their gravity.

The true pleasures of the film lie in the acting, particularly Roger Hanin and Marthe Villalonga who are poignant and vibrantly funny as Mr. and Mrs. Narboni, characters worthy of Pagnol. Michael Auclair is insidiously smooth as the phlegmatic Parisian, a superb foil to the Mediterranean temperaments of "Pied-Noirs." — *Len.*

Repmanad
(The Call-Up)
(SWEDISH-COLOR)

———

Malmoe, April 21.

A Bo Jonsson-Viking Film with RiFilm and Europa Film production, Europa Film release. Story by Lasse Aberg. Written by Aberg and Bo Jonsson. Features entire cast. Directed by Aberg. Camera (Eastmancolor), Hanno-Heinz-Fuchs; editor, Sylvia Ingemarsson; music, Janne Schaffer; production design, Rolf Larsson. Reviewed at Rio Bio, Malmoe, Sweden, April 20, 1979. Running time, **84 MINS.**

Helge Jonsson . . . . Lasse Aberg
Oscar Loefgren . . . . .Janne Carlsson
Bea . . . . . . Lena-Maria Gardenaes-Lawton

Sweden has an enduring tradition for strong neutrality, strong military power, and strong slapstick service entertainment. The latter has, however, lain dormant in films for some time until producer Bo Jonsson and writer-director-actor Lasse Aberg came up with the idea for "Repmanad" (The Call-Up), which actually refers to the annual period of military retraining old Swedish conscription veterans still must go through.

These old guys are now thoroughly established in civilian life and manners and thus obvious fodder for farcical fare when put back in uniform. Aberg operates with practically no plot, mostly sitcom sequences, but he has scored one of several years' biggest boxoffice hits at home by having his actors amuse themselves as much as the audiences by remaining truly human throughout. All pratfalls are stopped short just before becoming heirs to old cliches.

Will such a film be of interest outside its home country? Financially, it will not have to, but it might, if handled carefully, amuse some selected territories because of the enjoyment and the talent of its players in universal situations.

Aberg himself is charmingly clumsy as the shy bachelor who falls into the tender trap of the woman "war correspondent" Bea (played by newcomer Lena-Maria Gardenaes-Lawton who may emerge as Sweden's answer to Lily Tomlin, and is already signed for several major roles). Similarly, there is s bit of a controlled Swedish John Belushi madness in the playing of Janne Carlsson as the enlisted man nicknamed The Chairman. It should be noted also, that Aberg has avoided all the easy anti-military cliches. Actually, the company commander, turns out to be the most mild-mannered civilian of the whole bunch. —*Kell.*

La Drolesse
(The Hussy)
(FRENCH-COLOR)

———

Paris, April 30.

A La Gueville Productions — Lola Films coproduction. Produced by Daniele Del-orme and Yves Robert. Features entire cast. Written and directed by Jacques Doillon. Script collaborator, Denis Ferraris; camera (Eastmancolor), Philippe Rousselot; art director, Jean-Denis Robert; editor, Laurent Quaglio; sound, Michel Kharat. Reviewed at Club 13, Paris, April 26, '79. Running time : **90 MINS.**

Mado . . . . Madeleine Desdevises
Francois . . . . .Claude Hebert

The intimacy of Jacques Doillon's films shouldn't fool anyone into misjudging them as minor. For all his cautiousness Doillon makes bad mistakes, but his new film, "La Drolesse," should dispel any doubts as to his abilities and importance in the French cinema. It is a French competing film at the Cannes Fest.

His last film, "La Femme Qui Pleure," was a lopsided examination of a couple torn by the husband's callous infidelities. Doillon made a bad mistake in playing the male lead himself; he is not an actor, at least not under his own direction. But the film made a deep impression thanks to the raw truth of Dominique Laffin's performance as the suffering wife. She is sure to astonish us even more in the future.

With his new film, Doillon corrects the imbalance. This is the tale of a 20-year-old country boy who kidnaps an 11-year-old girl and sequesters her in the garret of the farmhouse where he lives with his boorish mother and step-father. Doillon documents the young people's mercurial relationship up to the time when the boy is arrested for kidnapping.

Film's immediate reference is not to William Wyler's "The Collector" but to a recent French film, "Mais Ou Et Donc Ornicar," in which director Bertrand Van Effenterre used, as a framing device, the true incident of a young man who kidnapped a young girl: their wordless, unperverse bond of love baffled police and psychologists.

Doillon's main characters are both misfits: unloved, gawky in appearance. The boy makes his living by collecting boxes and bottles and selling them to local merchants. The girl is an indifferent student whose mother rejects her odd expressions of affection. In drawing her portrait, Doillon seems to make reference to Robert Bresson's tormented "Mouchette."

The poignancy and originality of the film is in the very progression of their rapport. These are not two beings seeking love; they are full of it, yet their timidity, awkwardness & lack of experience prevent them from finding the form. Throughout their time together they shop for roles — teacher-student, doctor-patient, warden-prisoner, husband-wife — trying them on for size, then putting them back on the rack of social convention. When the policemen finally get to them, in a remarkable final scene, they impose their own interpretation of the boy's actions.

Doillon superbly directs his own script, avoiding the traps of facile schematism he could have fallen into.

The main roles are acted by two unknowns: Madeleine Desdevises and Claude Hebert, both remarkable as two misfits propelled by their groping mutability. —*Len.*

Good Luck, Miss Wyckoff
(COLOR)

Poor overall, salacious angles may help Black-rape-of-White spinster.

———

Hollywood, April 30.

A Bel Air-Gradison Productions presentation of a Raymond Stross production. Produced by Raymond Stross. Associate Producer, Robert Lecky. Directed by Marvin J. Chomsky. Screenplay, Polly Platt, based on the novel by William Inge; camera (Metrocolor), Alex Phillips Jr.; editor, Rita Roland; music, Ernest Gold; art direction, Jim Bissell; set decoration, Roy Stennard; costumes, Tom Rasmussen. Reviewed at the Aidikoff Screening Room, L.A., April 30, '79. (MPAA Rating: R.) Running time : **105 MINS.**

Evelyn Wyckoff . . . . Anne Heywood
Dr. Steiner . . . . Donald Pleasence
Dr. Neal . . . . .Robert Vaughn
Beth .Carolyn Jones
Mildred . . . . Dorothy Malone
Betsy . . . . Ronee Blakely
Mr. Havermeyer . . . . Dana Elcar
Rene . . . . Doris Roberts
Rafe . . . . John Lafayette
Ed Eckles . . . . .Earl Holliman
Lisa Hemmings . . . . Jocelyn Brando

———

The late William Inge had mostly good luck with the films he was associated with during his lifetime, particularly "Splendor in the Grass" and "Picnic," but what's been done now to his only novel is something else. The slight story of a Midwestern spinster who experiences a sexual awakening at the hands of a "black buck," "Good Luck, Miss Wyckoff" has been made into a lamentable film. Not having made a sale, the producers are testing the distribution waters themselves, and while the picture could never make it on quality, salacious elements could make it exploitable in a "Diary of a Raped Virgin" vein.

Polly Platt's screenplay hews closely to the novel which, while no masterpiece, at least managed some plausible insights into a cloistered mind. Effect of the film, however, is that of a clinical case study, devoid of believable motivations or emotional effectiveness. Adaptation also alters the schoolteacher's first sexual encounter, making it into a rape by the young black school janitor rather than a somewhat mutual act, thereby raising some unpleasant racial overtones.

Director Marvin J. Chomsky brings nothing to the material, composing virtually every shot in tv-like close-ups, cross cutting academically and failing to create the mood or texture of a small Kansas town, circa 1954. Nor does Alex Phillips Jr.'s muddy, grainy photography help in establishing an ambiance. Alex North's score is solid in the traditional manner.

Anne Heywood, her English accent occasionally popping up, still looks good but claiming her age as 35 in the script, even if this was the case in the novel, is stretching things just a bit.

Carolyn Jones manages to break through the somber proceedings with a humorous characterization as Heywood's old maid friend, Jocelyn Brando has a funny moment when she refers to her real life brother's tremendous magnetism in "A Streetcar Named Desire" and Earl Holliman projects some legitimate emotion as a bus driver on the make. The rest of the cast can't do anything to counteract Chomsky's obvious direction of them.

Pic is a fairly hot "R," with an even steamier version reportedly having been prepared for Japan.

—Cart.

Apocalypse Now
(COLOR)

Powerful war drama. Coppola reconfirmed as a film creator though latter portion of film goes fuzzily 'literary' and may hamper audience appeal.

Hollywood, May 12.

United Artists release of a Francis Coppola production. Produced and directed by Francis Coppola. Features entire cast. Coproduced by Fred Roos, Gray Frederickson. Screenplay, John Milius, Francis Coppola, based on Joseph Conrad's "Heart of Darkness"; camera (Technicolor), Vittorio Storaro; editor, Barry Malkin; production design, Dean Tavoularis; art direction, Angelo Graham; set decoration, Bob Nelson; sound, Jacob Jacobsen; asst. director, Tony Brandt. No other credits available. Reviewed at Bruin Theatre, Westwood, Cal., May 11, 1979. (No MPAA Rating). Running time: **139 MINS.**

Col. Kurtz	Marlon Brando
Captain Willard	Martin Sheen
Lt. Col. Kilgore	Robert Duvall
Chef	Fred Forrest
Lance	Sam Bottoms
Chief	Albert Hall
Clean	Larry Fishborne
Photo-journalist	Dennis Hopper

Also: Harrison Ford, G.D. Spradlin, Bill Graham, Cynthia Wood, Francis Coppola.

"Apocalypse Now" was worth the wait. Alternately a brilliant and bizarre film, Francis Coppola's four-year "work in progress" offers the definitive validation to the old saw, "war is hell." Coppola's vision of Hell-on-Earth hews closely to Joseph Conrad's novella, "Heart Of Darkness," and therein lies the film's principal commercial defect. An exhilarating action-adventure exercise for two-thirds of its 139 minutes, "Apocalypse" abruptly shifts to surrealistic symbolism for its denouement. Result will be many spectators left in the lurch, a factor that won't help in recouping the $50,000,000 or more necessary for break-even by distrib United Artists, Coppola and the worldwide territorial distribs involved.

"Apocalypse Now" will also have trouble avoiding political pigeonholing, since it's the first film to directly excoriate U.S. involvement in the Indochina war. To be sure, inhumane attitudes surfaced on both sides as inevitable consequences of a misunderstood conflict, but Coppola wields a wide tabrush in painting Americans as either "conspiratorial" or "homicidal," with no one in between.

Thus, it seems ironic that the most widely heralded production of the last 10 years may find its niche co-opted by a pic dealing with a common subject, the effect of the Vietnam conflict on its participants, "The Deer Hunter" and "Apocalypse Now" are widely differing treatments in tone and viewpoint, but in the eyes of the film-going public, if you've seen one Vietnam war pic, you might have seen them all.

Which possible reaction would be a shame, because Coppola here reaffirms his stature as a top filmmaker. "Apocalypse Now" takes realistic cinema to a new extreme — Coppola virtually creates World War III onscreen.

There are no models or miniatures, no tank work, nor process screens for the airborne sequences. The resulting footage outclasses any war pic made to date. Coppola's wisest decision was to narrow his focus on the members of the patrol boat crew entrusted with taking Intelligence assassin Martin Sheen on a hazardous mission upriver into Cambodia. There Sheen hopes to track down and "terminate with extreme prejudice" Marlon Brando, a megalomoniac officer whose methods and motives have become, in Pentagonese, "unsound," as he leads an army of Montagnard tribesmen on **random genocide missions.**

Interaction of Sheen and the two black (Albert Hall, Larry Fishborne) and two white (Fred Forrest and Sam Bottoms) seamen gives "Apocalypse" a narrative flow when, in fact, there's very little narrative (Sheen has a sporadic voice-over commentary done in groggy sotto-voce that does little to explicate the action).

Robert Duvall appears mid-way as an expansive screen character, an air cavalry helicopter commander who's a surfing nut, and has his boys riding the waves in the midst of flak attacks. These and some other-worldly, nighttime river excursions seem the principal contributions of original scenarist John Milius (who now shares screenwriting credit with Coppola), and they contain a wacky, manic energy that serves "Apocalypse" well.

It's when the ghost of novelist Joseph Conrad enters the picture, and when Milius and Coppola in effect take a back seat to a literary homage, that "Apocalypse Now" runs aground. Despite Vittorio Storaro's haunting imagery, Barry Malkin's explosive editing, and Dean Tavoularis' eerie production design, final third of the pic fails to jell.

Experience is almost a psychedelic one — unfortunately, it's someone else's psyche, and without a copy of crib notes for the Conrad novel, today's mass audience may be hard put to understand just what is going on, or intended.

Marlon Brando's intimidating but inscrutable performance as the bald-headed Colonel Kurtz (named after Conrad's character in "Heart Of Darkness") doesn't clarify anything.

Rest of the cast is extraordinary, with Sheen extremely effective in laconic style, and Forrest, Hall, Fishburne and Bottoms superb in their respective delineations.

Coppola himself show up in a brief cameo as a combat director, and Bill Graham, Harrison Ford and G.D. Spradlin have minor roles. Duvall gives one of the best characterizations of his career as the surfer commander, and Dennis Hopper is effectively "weird" as Brando's official photographer.

"Apocalypse Now" is emblazoned with firsts: a 70m presentation without credits, a director putting himself personally on the hook for the film's $18,000,000 cost overrun, and then obtaining rights to the pic in perpetuity, and a revolutionary sound system that adds immeasurably to the film's impact.

Even if Coppola isn't haunted by the spectre of financial fiascos like "Cleopatra," there's no assured future for "Apocalypse." It's a complex, demanding, highly intelligent piece of work, coming into a marketplace that does not always embrace those qualities.

That doesn't lessen its impact as film or art, but it may give the next filmmaker who plans a $40,000,000 war epic a few second thoughts.

—Poll.

Walk Proud
(COLOR)

Well done, but another ethnic gang war plot, of kind lately trouble-prone.

Hollywood, May 15.

A Universal Picture release, produced by Lawrence Turman. Directed by Robert Collins. Screenplay, Evan Hunter; camera (Technicolor), Bobby Byrne; editor, Douglas Stewart; sound, Jim Alexander; art direction, William L. Campbell; assistant director, Ronald J. Martinez; music, Robby Benson. Reviewed at Universal Studios, May 10, '79. (MPAA Rating: PG). Running time: **102 MINS.**

Emilio	Robby Benson
Sarah	Sarah Holcomb
Mike	Henry Darrow
Cesar	Pepe Serna
Dagger	Trinidad Silva
Gannett	Ji-Tu Cumbuka
Lassiter	Lawrence Pressman
Cowboy	Domingo Ambriz
Kelsey	Brad Sullivan
Mrs. Mendez	Irene De Bari
Carlos	Gary Cervantes
Hugo	Eloy Phil Casados
Paco	Tony Alvarenga
El Tigre	Daniel Faraldo
Manuel	Panchito Gomez
Store owner	Joe D. Jacobs

Originally titled "Gang," this film presents an obvious problem for Universal Pictures which would like to steer clear of the unpleasant publicity from similar pix, selling it as a love story set against a barrior background. But, love story or not, it's still a gang picture and exhibs best be braced for that.

Unlike "Warriors" and "Boulevard Nights,' moreover, "Walk Proud" has the added problem of Robby Benson in the role of a Chicano gang member, a sore point already complained about in some ethnic quarters and likely to generate more talk after release.

Actually, Benson acquits himself quite well in the part, exploring the sensitivity and vulnerability beneath the machismo surface needed for survival in the Los Aztecas gang led by Pepe Serna, who turns in a fine performance.

(For all their trouble, these pictures are showcasing some excellent minority actors — in this case, Trinidad Silva, Domingo Ambriz, Eloy Phil Casados, Daniel Faraldo, Tony Alvarenga and Gary Cervantes as gang members, Irene De Bari as Benson's mother and Ji-Tu Cumbuke, outstanding as the gangwise black cop).

Benson's love is Sarah Holcomb, who is solid as upper middleclass Anglo girl he meets at school. She's opposed to his being in a gang, as are his mother and social worker Henry Darrow. But he holds on to his macho stance until a trip back to Mexico for a grandmother's funeral where his mother introduces him to the father he's never seen.

The barroom scene with his drunken, bigoted — and Anglo — father (well played by Brad Sullivan) is one of the strongest in the picture. Yet it's also one of the major collapses in an otherwise straightforward construction by writer Evan Hunter and director Robert Collins. There's no indication why the mother would introduce him to his father after all these years — or how such a thoroughly dislikable and insulting person would himself have survived so long among the "greasers," as he calls them.

At any rate, the self-doubt resulting from learning his true genes and the pull of Holcomb put Benson in a confused state when the action starts with a rival gang, culminating in a brutal beating in a ritual by his own Los Aztecas. Though the same rite earlier left a member **near-death in a hospital with broken bones and missing teeth, Benson survives still on his feet, proving that manhood is within the individual not in numbers. All in all, a** rather sappy way to prove a serious point.

In truth, if the message is able to be heard over the hubbub, "Walk Proud" is an anti-gang picture with more soft moments than hard. As the PG rating suggests, there's very little bloodshed and one crucial gang fight is never seen. But some films just aren't lucky and this could be one of them. —*Har.*

Julio comienza en Julio
(Jules Starts With Jules)
(CHILEAN)

Santiago, April 20.
An Alberto Celery-Silvio Ciaozzi-Nelson Fuentes production. Executive producer, Alberto Celery. Directed by Silvio Giaozzi. Camera, Nelson Fuentes; screenplay, Gustavo Frias; music Luis Advis. Reviewed at Theatro U. Catolica, April 19, 1979. Running Time: **115 MINS.**
Cast: Elsa Alarcon, Jorge Alvarez, Luis Alarcon, Magdalena Aguirre, Rafael Benavwnte. Shlomit Beytelman, Jose Cabello, Maria Castiglione, Tennyson Ferrada, Ana Gonzalez, Delfina Guzman, Pedro Gaete. Alfonso Luco, Gloria Munchmeyer, Juan Cristobal Meza, Maria Elena Montero, Ana Maria Palma, Felipe Rabat, Aquiles Sepulvede, Fritz Stein, J.M. Salcedo, Lucy Salgado, Marion Soto, Nissim Sharim, Victor Sepulveda, Vincente Santamaria, Sergio Urrutia, Jaime Vadell, Jorge Yanez.

Technically, this is the best film to come out of Chile but, in spite of already being sold to German TV, and a likelihood of good local b.o., it is unlikely to create a stir abroad. The screenplay, although not uninteresting, lacks adequate development, which may partly be due to the sidestepping of its implicit social implications, which could have proved troublesome with the censors.

The story takes place in 1917 and the film's sepia tinting was chosen to help the period atmosphere. Julio Garcia Castano is an aristocratic and powerful landowner, who slowly forges his only son, also called Julio, in his own image. On his 15th birthday he organizes a party to which he invites the whores of a nearby town "to make a man of him." The plan misfires because the son falls in love with one of them, a liaison which is ruthlessly squashed by Garcia Castano.

The latter is also involved in a long legal squabble with a neighboring Franciscan monastery over some land which he badly needs as feeding ground for his cattle. Although he and his family are very religious, business comes first and, at night, he proceeds to move the fences.

Garcia Castano, well played by non-actor (and restaurant owner) Felipe Rabat is the closest the film has to a fully developed character. Juan Cristobal Meza is much weaker as his son, to a large extent because he plays a rather passive role in the proceedings.

On the other hand, there are many strong types among the landowners' friends, family, servants and peasants and these are the film's forte and contribute very successfully to the overall atmosphere. In many cases they are only small roles but, well acted by some of Chile's best known legit thesps,

make an important contribution to the film. The editing could have been tighter, but otherwise technical credits are good, including the blowup from 16 to 35m "Julio comienza en Julio" was selected from the Directors' For-t-night at Cannes and, a first for Chile, a novelization of the screenplay was published simultaneously with the pic's opening. — *Amig.*

Hanover Street
(BRITISH-COLOR)

More action, less tears, would have made a better film.

Hollywood, May 7.
Columbia Pictures release of a Lazarus/Hymas production. Stars Harrison Ford, Lesley-Anne Down, Christopher Plummer. Produced by Paul N. Lazarus III. Written and directed by Peter Hyams. Camera (color), David Watkin; editor, James Mitchell; production design, Philip Harrison; music John Barry; art direction. Malcolm Middleton, Robert Cartwright; sound (Dolby) Robin Gregory; costume design, Joan Bridge; special effects, Martin Gutteridge. Reviewed at MGM Studios, Culver City, May 7 '79. (MPAA Rating: PG). Running time: **109 MINS.**

David Halloran	Harrison Ford
Margaret Sellinger	Lesley-Anne Down
Paul Sellinger	Christopher Plummer
Major Trumbo	Alec McCowen
Jerry Cimino	Richard Masur
Martin Hyer	Michael Sacks
Sarah Sellinger	Patsy Kensit
Harry Pike	Max Wall
Col. Ronald Bart	Shane Rimmer

"Hanover Street" is reasonably effective as a war film with a love story background. Unfortunately for Columbia Pictures, it's meant to be a love story set against a war background. Resulting confusion won't help Col in selling the Paul N. Lazarus 3d-Peter Hyams production, and commercial forecast is bleak.

There seems to be a prevalent feeling that out and out romantic stories don't play well in a contemporary setting. Drawing his inspiration from MGM's 1940 release, "Waterloo Bridge," and other pix of that ilk, writer-director Hyams has moved this tale of starcrossed lovers up to World War II England, where American flying ace Harrison Ford and British hospital nurse Lesley Anne-Down meet during an air raid, and fall hopelessly in love.

But "Hanover Street" demonstrates that sugary dialog doesn't work any better in the 1940s than in the '70s. Hyams has proven himself an adroit action-adventure director with "Capricorn One," but his writing lags behind his other skills, and "Hanover Street" is filled with the kind of limp lines that test a performer's mettle.

Only when Down takes a back seat, and Ford is thrown together with her cuckolded husband, British secret service topper Christopher Plummer, does "Hanover Street" manifest any vital life signs. The last third of the picture becomes a model of efficient war filmmaking, but then it's back to tears and stiff upper lips, and a finale that makes "Mrs. Miniver" look perceptive.

Down again distinguishes herself in a role that doesn't seem up to her standards, while Ford back in the pilot's seat again projects an earnest, if dull, presence. Rest of the cast, including Plummer, Alec McCowen, and Richard Masur and Michael Sacks as part of Ford's bomber crew, is under-utilized. Masur is particularly wasted as a wisecracking flyer, whose dialog is neither wise nor cracking.

Philip Harrison's production design seems stage-bound, and there are numerous questionable period details, such as Down's hair style and clothing, and the luxury of Plummer's wartime existence. David Watkin's lensing is smooth, although he and Hyams seem overinfatuated with the Panaglide camera system. James Mitchell's editing is distracting in its emphasis on short scenes and a cinematic tendency to flip back and forth between the two storylines.

John Barry, has contributed a score that evokes Douglas Sirk's glossy tearjerkers of the 1950s, and indeed, title sequence for "Hanover Street" could have come right out of one of Sirk's pix for Universal 20 years ago.

This is 1979, however, and with the exception of "The Deer Hunter," war films with any kind of background are having trouble gaining boxoffice ground. "Hanover Street" doesn't seem the film to turn that trend around. —*Poll.*

Winter Kills

Presidential assassination top confusingly assembled but with fine photography

Hollywood, May 2.
Avco Embassy release of a Leonard J. Goldberg-Robert Sterling production. Exec producers, Leonard J. Goldberg, Robert Sterling Produced by Fred Caruso. Features entire cast. Written and directed by William Richert, based on novel of same title by Richard Condon; camera (color), Vilmos Zsigmond; editor, David Bretherton; music, Maurice Jarre; costumes, Robert De Mora; production design, Robert Boyle; art direction, Norman Newberry; sound, Chris Newman. Reviewed at American Film Institute, BevHills, May 2, '79. (MPAA Rating: R.) Running time: **97 MINS.**

Nick Kegan	Jeff Bridges
Pa Kegan	John Huston
John Ceruti	Anthony Perkins
Z.K. Dawson	Sterling Hayden
Joe Diamond	Eli Wallach
Emma Kegan	Dorothy Malone
Frank Mayo	Tomas Milian
Yvette Malone	Belinda Bauer
Gameboy Baker	Ralph Meeker

Keith . . . . Toshiro Mifune
Keifetz . . . . Richard Boone

If there's a decent film lurking somewhere in "Winter Kills," writer-director William Richert doesn't want anyone to see it. His Byzantine version of a presidential assassination conspiracy makes the lingering questions about the John F. Kennedy slaying look like a connect-the-dots puzzle. Theatrical runs look to be brief for the Avco Embassy release.

"Winter Kills" has a lot of ground to gain just to break-even mark. A conservative tally of outstanding debts comes to around $6,300,000, not including the salaries of Richert and producer Dan Blatt, who resuscitated the production with the aid of Gotham lawyer and former MGM counsel Benjamin Melniker and Frisco moneyman Frank Aries after original producers Robert Sterling and the late Leonard Goldberg declared bankruptcy.

Tale of wealthy family patriarch John Huston, whose elder son was a President slain 19 years before the pic's beginning, and younger sibling Jeff Bridges, now after his brother's killer(s), is an exercise in methodical obfuscation.

Since the story's outcome is apparent within the first 10 minutes, Richert spends the next 87 minutes peopling a series of breathtaking locales with star names who should have known better.

There's Anthony Perkins, doing yet another variation on Norman Bates with his portrayal of Huston's meglomaniacal intelligence chief; Dorothy Malone as Bridges' alcoholic mother; Sterling Hayden as a militaristic multimillionaire; Eli Wallach, Ralph Meeker and Tomas Milian in brief glimpses as Mafioso; Toshiro Mifune as the faithful Oriental retainer, and Richard Boone, who is brought in periodically to explain the story is, after all, "a conundrum, a riddle within a riddle."

Most of the action centers on Bridges' curious relationship with Belinda Bauer, an Australian actress inexplicably saddled with a French accent for this role. Most of their dialog is via a phone answering machine, an expository device that seems to have been abandoned after the film's lengthy hiatus. Pair also participate in one of the more crude sex scenes viewed recently — if there was more flesh, Avemb might have a sexploitation angle, but Richert abandons this dimension, too.

"Winter Kills" has two chief virtues: an exceptionally clean look, thanks to Vilmos Zsigmond's sparkling camerawork, and a fine supporting cast in the bit parts, particularly Brad Dexter as a spaced-out cop, Irving Selbst as a gangster

heavy, and Joe Ragno, superb as a psychotic Gotham doorman.

Huston gives a powerhouse performance, and Bridges, always likeable, runs through his repertoire of facial expressions and grimaces, but it's a lost cause, since Richert has revised Richard Condon's novel for unintentional comic effect, in particular a pseudo-patriotic ending.

Elizabeth Taylor has a worldless cameo as a procuress for the late President, but contractual provisions prevent her name from being used in connection with "Winter Kills." The rest of the cast should have been so Lucky. —Poll.

Van Nuys Blvd.
(COLOR)

More cars and teen sex should pay off for Crown.

Hollywood, May 7.
A Crown International Pictures release of a Marimark Production. Executive producer, Newton P. Jacobs. Produced by Marilyn J. Tenser. Written and directed by William Sachs. Features entire cast. Camera (DeLuxe color). Joseph Mangine; editor, George Bowers; music, Ron Wright, Ken Mansfield; sound, Don A. LSanders, Ove H. Sehested; art director, Kenneth H. Hergenroeder; costumes, Diana Daniels. Reviewed at the Aidikoff Screening Room, L.A., May 7.; '79. (MPAA Rating: R). Running time: **93 MINS.**
Bobby . . . . Bill Adler
Moon . . . . Cynthia Wood
Greg . . . . Dennis Bowen
Cameille . . . . Melissa Prophet
Chooch . . . . David Hayward
Wanda . . . . Tara Strohmeier
Al Zass . . . . Dana Gladstone
Motorcycle Girl . . . . Di Ann Monaco
Jason . . . . Don Sawyer
Frankie . . . . Jim Kester
Nurse Bradley . . . . Minnie E. Lindsey

"Van Nuys Blvd." is a very slick, attractive exploitationer which is chock full of teen sex and less obsessed with cars and vans than similar fare from the last couple of summers. Crown International should do well in its usual markets with this one, which amounts to a veritable catelog of things Southern California kids do for kicks.

Country boy Bill Adler complains at the outset that, if he stays in the boondocks, "I'm never going to amount to anything," so where else does he head for but Van Nuys Blvd., the Champs-Elysees of the San Fernando Valley where "cruise nights" of youths strutting their mobilized stuff have made their special contribution to the gasoline shortage.

Bill gets molested by a hot number at the local hamburger stand, drag races with the strip's sharpest chick, lands in jail, rides the rollercoaster at Magic Mountain, checks out the disco scene, plays pinball, visits the Malibu Grand Prix and then starts maturing when his drag racing foe falls hard for him, real-

izing that vans and low riders with lifts are for kids, while love is for grown-ups.

In its distance from, and ultimate rejection of, the whole cruising scene, "Van Nuys Blvd." is just a bit more serious than most pix of this ilk, and some of the action has a curiously mirthless quality. Having run out of tourist attractions half-way through, latter stretches bog down in a couple of laborious comic set-pieces, such as a cop being handcuffed to his car and a kid experiencing lockjaw after trying to eat a submarine sandwich.

But the bottom line with such fare lies in attractive cast members and a zippy style, and here "Van Nuys Blvd." has what it takes. Adler is appealing and, among the femmes, former Playmate Cynthia Wood is exceedingly fetching as the hot-shot driver for whom Adler finally throws over his motorized playthings.

William Sachs' writing and direction fulfilled the demands of the genre, and Joseph Mangine's cinematography is pro. Pic also has a full-bodied disco soundtrack which is not limited to the extended, choreographed dance club sequence.
— Cart.

Mad Max
(AUSTRALIAN-COLOR)

Sydney, May 4.
Roadshow release of a Mad Max Pty. Ltd. production. Produced by Byron Kennedy. Directed by George Miller. Features entire cast. Screenplay, George Miller, James McCausland, from story by Miller and Kennedy; camera (Todd-AO 35, color), David Eggby; editors, Tony Paterson, Cliff Hayes; music, Brian May; sound, Gary Wilkens; art director, Jon Dowding; stunt co-ordinator, Grant Page. Reviewed at Village Theatre, Double Bay, Sydney, April 3, '79. Running time: **90 MINS.**
Mad Max . . . . Mel Gibson
Jess . . . . Joanne Samuel
The Toecutter . . . . Hugh Keays-Byrne
Jim Goose . . . . Steve Bisley
Fifi . . . . Roger Ward
Nightrider . . . . Vince Gil
Plus Tim Burns, Lulu Pinkus, Nick Lathouris, John Ley, Steve Millichamp, Sheila Florance, Max Fairchild, Steven Clark, George Novak.

"Mad Max" is something of a new departure for Australian films, an all-stops-out, fast-moving exploitation pic in the tradition of New World / American International productions. The plot is extremely simple. A few years from now (opening title), the Australian countryside is terrorized by marauders who create mayhem on the roads. A crack police force, using souped-up cars, black leather outfits, and plenty of weaponry, opposes the villains — these are the Pursuit and Interceptor patrols.

Mad Max is one of the fastest and most ruthless of these cops of the future, who operate out of a seedy, rundown, prison-like Hall of Jus-

tice. When one of Max's friends, Jim Goose, is killed by The Toecutter and his motor-bike gang, Max quits the force to take a vacation with his wife and baby — he's disgusted with his life and the violence around him. But when The Toecutter's gang kills his wife and child, he dons his leather uniform again to hunt them down.

As will be seen from the above, the plot is by no means original, and it's really just a peg on which to hang some simple moralizing ("Only a badge makes us different from them" Max tells his superior officer on quitting) and plenty of action and stuntwork. The stunts, coordinated by experienced local practitioner Grant Page, are among the best seen outside an American picture: a car is driven through a trailer and into an oil tanker (which explodes); motorbikes fly over the parapet of a bridge, and one ends up (with rider) under a heavy truck. All the stunts are electrifying and very convincing, and the stunt team deserves full marks.

Stunts themselves would be nothing without a filmmaker behind the camera and Miller, a lawyer and film buff making his first feature, shows he knows what cinema is all about. This is the most audience-involving film since "Halloween" (in fact Miller's work is reminiscent of John Carpenter's and also of the Canadian David Cronenburg); the camera is always on the move, tracking and craning every which way, while the audience is never sure where the menace will come from next.

Nor does he dwell on the violence, despite the fact that some local commentator have made hysterical cries for the film to be banned. Much violence is done to cars and motor-bikes, but Miller is restrained when it comes to mayhem on people — plenty of horror is implied, but very little seen, and though it's shocking to see the savage way the bike gang destroys a car with a cowering couple inside, or the way a trapped cop reacts when he realizes he's about to be burnt alive, Miller doesn't dwell on these scenes and prefers to stay at a discreet distance (the death of Max's wife and baby is shot in a particularly distanced way).

The film belongs to the director, cameraman and stunt artists; it's not an actors piece, though the leads are all effective. It looks like being a winner down under, and has already chalked up overseas sales of $1,000,000 via Warners and American-International. —Strat.

La Rabia
(Rage)
(SPANISH-16m-B&W)

Barcelona, May 4.
Producciones Teide film. Directed by Eugeni Anglada. Exec producer, Joseph Maria Forn. Screenplay, Anglada, Miguel Porter Moix, Miguel Hernan; camera (black and white), Tomas Pladavall, Anglada; music, J. Vidal; editor, Anglada. M. Glizancos. Reviewed at Club de Cine (Barcelona), May 3, '79. Running time: **98 MINS.**
Cast: Marta May, Maria Asuncion Sancho, F. Jarque Zurbano, Alfred Luchetti, Manuel Sanchez, Ramon Corominas, Carme Casanovas, Darius, Mariangels.

Simple, sometimes touching documentary-type film chronicling the life of a small village near Barcelona during the first years of the Franco government. Eugeni Anglada, who has written, directed, filmed and edited the film, is clearly drawing heavily on autobiographical material. The idea is to present village life as seen by an insider, and in this he succeeds.

Some of the scenes may turn off spectators, especially those involving animals, and often the hand-carried jerky camera technique is too much, but other segments come across well, such as a local dance, the ruthless teaching methods in an elementary school, the background of political fear, the children's first contacts with sex. From a technical standpoint, quality of photography, sound, editing etc. is largely on an amateurish level. Outlet will be largely limited to film club circuits, though in pic's release in Barcelona it did surprisingly well commercially.— *Besa.*

The Lady Vanishes
(BRITISH-COLOR)

Remake of a Hitchcock classic. So-so outlook. Moderately amusing but sans cohesive directorial style.

London, May 9.
Rank Organization presentation of a Hammer Film produced by Tom Sachs. Executive producers, Michael Carreras, Arlene Sellers, Alex Winitsky. Stars Elliott Gould, Cybill Shepherd, Angela Lansbury, Herbert Lom. Directed by Anthony Page. Screenplay, George Axelrod, based on novel by Ethel Lina White; camera (color), Douglas Slocombe; editor, Russell Lloyd; music, Richard Hartley; production design, Wilfred Shingleton; art direction, Bill Alexander, George von Kieseritzky; costumes, Emma Porteous; assistant directors, Michael Dryhurst, Michael Mertineit. Reviewed at Leicester Sq. Theatre, London, May 8, '79. (BBFC rating: A). Running time: **99 MINS.**
Robert Condon . . . . Elliott Gould
Amanda Kelly . . . . Cybill Shepherd
Miss Froy . . . . Angela Lansbury
Dr. Hartz . . . . Herbert Lom
Charters . . . . Arthur Lowe
Caldicott . . . . Ian Carmichael
Mr. Todhunter . . . . Gerald Harper
Baroness Kisling . . . . Jean Anderson
Mrs. Todhunter . . . . Jenny Runacre
Trainmaster . . . . Vladek Sheybal
Nun . . . . Madlena Nedeva
Helmut . . . . Wolf Kahler
Rose Flood-Porter . . . . Madge Ryan
Mrs. Barnes . . . . Rosalind Knight
Waiter . . . . : Jonathan Hackett
Madame Kummer . . . . Barbara Markham
Maid's daughter . . . . Hillevi
Manservant . . . . Garry McDermott
Maid . . . . Jacki Harding

"The Lady Vanishes" is the latest golden oldie of sainted buff memory to be recycled by Britain's Rank Organization. The result is a midatlantic mish-mash with some moderately amusing moments but no cohesive style. Boxoffice outlook is chancy.

The Tom Sachs production, directed to flat effect by Anthony Page, has Cybill Shepherd as a madcap Yank heiress and Elliott Gould as a Life mag photographer foiling a political conspiracy aboard a train outbound from prewar Germany. Slapstick hokum, bland suspense and mystery elements that will fool almost no one add up to a heavy-handed affair. The George Axelrod script from an Ethel Lina White novel is best when dwelling on English eccentricity, which permits Angela Lansbury as a British nanny, and the lady who seemingly disappears, to make the film's most endearing impression.

Shepherd, dressed throughout in one costume, a slinky evening gown, and Gould, doing his all-to-familiar jokey number, stack up as contrived cliches, characters that jar rather than complement. What the former lacks in this context is light comedy insouciance, a neglected art in the modern era. Herbert Lom, on the other hand, is dependably effective as a not-so-innocent surgeon, but it's a no-strain effort he could have phoned in.

Alfred Hitchcock's original version, circa 1938, had pretty much everything the remake doesn't in the way of breezy comic thrill packaged with nimble touch. It also had Michael Redgrave, Margaret Lockwood, Paul Lukas, Dame May Whitty, et al. Style was the net result.

By contrast, the new edition invokes location picture-postcard gloss, including a lovely old steam train and ravishing Austrian landscapes posing as the Bavarian Alps, all smashingly captured by Douglas Slocombe's Panavision photography. Decor often seems the film's major asset, but audiences with no basis for comparison may glean a chuckle or two from the plot antics.

Arthur Lowe and Ian Carmichael function appealingly as eccentric Englishmen with cricket on the brain, and there are polished efforts by Gerald Harper, Jean Anderson, Jenny Runacre and Vladek Sheybal, among others.

Axelrod's scenario gives a "based-on" credit to the Frank Launder-Sidney Gilliat original screenplay. The pair lives on, and may either cringe or gloat if, as and when they catch up with the remake.

The appropriate music is by Richard Hartley, and all technical credits are pro.— *Pit.*

Les Belles Manieres
(Fine Manners)
(FRENCH-COLOR)

Paris, May 8.
A Gaumont Distribution release of a Diagonale production. Produced by Paul Vecchiali. Features entire cast. Directed by Jean-Claude Guiguet. Script, Guiguet and Gerard Frot-Coutaz; Camera, Georges Strouve; editors, Paul Vecchiali and Frank Mathieu; sound, Jean-Francois Chevalier; make-up, Ronaldo Abreu; costumes (for Helene Surgere), Nina Ricci. Musical extracts from Berlioz, Beethoven, Brukner, Mozart and J. Strauss. Reviewed at Cinema Quintette, Paris, May 2, 1979. Running time: **90 MINS.**
Helene Courtray . . . . Helene Surgere
Camille . . . . Emmanuel Lemoine
Domino . . . . Martine Simonet

First presented in the Directors Fortnight and Perspectives in French Cinema sidebar events at last year's Cannes festival, this fine first film by Jean-Claude Guiguet has at last surfaced after a year of distribution limbo.

Former critic and assistant to director Paul Vecchiali (who produced and coedited this film), Guiguet also had the opportunity of working as art director and costume designer for "Theatre des Matieres" in 1977, a first film by another critic turned director, Jean-Claude Biette.

These experiences feed into "Les Belles Manieres." Not only does he display a firm, telling camera manner, but he also has a fine plastic sense and a feeling for space and color. Script concerns a young itinerant worker, Camille, who comes to Paris in response to an ad from Helene Courtray, a well-heeled, attractive middle-aged woman separated from her husband. Camille's sole task is to take meals up to the woman's son, who lives in seclusion in a maid's room, nursing his fear of life and hatred for his mother.

During this period the young provincial discovers Paris and finds his own sister, who has taken up prostitution.

Camille's new life in the Courtray apartment continues until the time his employer leaves for a few weeks. The day of her return, the young man buys some flowers, arranges the apartment and, in the same series of gestures, sets fire to the apartment.

Camille is imprisoned, yet Helene refuses to press charges, determined instead to help him. But Camille remains impassive to her restrained solicitousness. He returns to his cell only to later be the victim of homosexual rape. Camille hangs himself.

Without recourse to psychological conventions, Guiguet etches a disturbing picture of two essentially incompatible natures which circumstances have thrown together in a falsely harmonious rapport.

Helene Surgere is superb as the woman whose refined maternal instincts, taste and poise imperceptibly drive an unpretentious young man to a tragic fate. As Camille the director has shrewdly cast a non-professional actor, Emmanuel Lemoine, whose ingenuousness and lack of actor's mannerisms give the role its proper coloring.

Film's subtlety of expression and muted performances may prevent it from finding other than a specialized audience here and abroad.
—*Len.*

Dimboola
(AUSTRALIAN-COLOR)

Sydney, May 4.
Greater Union Distributors release of a Pram Factory Pictures Production, with the Victorian Film Corporation and the New South Wales Film Corporation. Produced by John Weiley. Directed by John Duigan. Features entire cast. Screenplay, Jack Hibberd, from his play; camera (Panavision and Eastmancolor), Tom Cowan; editor, Tony Paterson; music, George Dreyfus; sound, Lloyd Carrick; art/director, Larry Eastwood. Reviewed at Greater Union Theatrette, Sydney, April 3, '79. Running time: **89 MINS.**
Morrie McAdam . . . . Bruce Spence
Maureen Delaney . . . . Natalie Bate
Vivien Wooster-Jones . . . . Max Gillies
Dangle . . . . Bill Garner
Vivien's girl . . . . Kerry Dwyer
Bayonet . . . . Chad Morgan
Father O'Shea . . . . Tim Robertson
Priest . . . . Barry Barkla
M.C. . . . . Jack Perry
Stripper . . . . Claire Binney
Doctor . . . . John Murphy
Plus Max Cullen, Helen Sky, Dick May, Irene Hewitt, Alan Rowe, Esme Melville, Terry McDermott, Paul Hampton, Evelyn Krape, Val Jellay, Sue Ingleton, Laurel Frank, Claire Dobbin, John Murphy, Fay Mokotow, Max Fairchild, Phil Motherwell, Matt Burns, Frankie Raymond, Sandra Evans; Matchbox.

In adapting Jack Hibberd's popular play, "Dimboola," for the screen the makers decided to open it out, shoot in Panavision and locate the action in the small Victorian town of Dimboola itself. Most of the strengths and weaknesses of the film flow from this decision.

On the plus side, Tom Cowan's inventive camerawork creates one of the best-ever impressions of a small town, reminiscent of the very best sections of Peter Weir's first feature, "The Cars That Ate Paris." The townspeople of Dimboola mix with the professional actors to create a delightful feeling for a rural community, and the highly professional visuals bring them to vibrant life.

Story covers a period of three days during which the town is visited by a journalist from the London Times writing an article on Australia. He picks a weekend when Morrie McAdam will marry Maureen Delaney, and is able to observe not only the 'kitchen tea' (all-female party for the bride), which he attends somewhat incongrously in drag, but also the 'bucks party' for the groom, an event of uninhibited horror which inevitably involves much boozing and the participation of a stripper imported from the city for the purpose.

The film takes in a lot of characters involved around the fringes of these cheerful nuptials, including the groom's parents who are undergoing a crisis as the mother reveals that, owing to a pre-marital affair, the groom may be more closely related to the bride than anyone would care to think about; the best man, jealous of the bride and determined to upset the wedding if he can; the tipsy priest, who collapses at the wedding reception; and three girls from the milk bar who are rehearsing a musical play.

Director John Duigan has a considerable reputation for his previous films, "The Trespassers" (1976) and "Mouth to Mouth" (1978), both realistic studies of contemporary Australians. On the evidence of "Dimboola," comedy may not be his forte: he handles most of the actors well, and choreographs the characters in a relaxed style, but the timing is sometimes off and some jokes tend to fall flat. The script could have been beefed up a bit too.

Of the players, it's worth noting the talented comedian Bruce Spence finally has a juicy part again: he was in one of the first films of the New Australian Cinema, Tim Burstall's "Stork" (1971), and his tall lanky body and rubbery face made a hit with audiences then; he's played bit parts in films since, but should score again with his role as the groom here. In fact all the players are good, though Max Gillies as the visiting Englishman is altogether too arch and too much of a caricature.

Technical credits are tops. "Dimboola" should be a success where the play is well known and especially in Victoria from whence most of the actors hail. —*Strat.*

The Psychic
(Sette Note in Nero)
(ITALIAN-COLOR)

Few holdovers for this dubbed Italian job.

Hollywood, May 2.
A Group 1 release of a Brandon Chase presentation. Produced by Cinecompany. Features entire cast. Directed by Lucio Fulci. Camera (DeLuxe color), Sergio Salvati. No other credits available. Reviewed at the Hollywood Theatre, L.A., May 2, 1979. (M-PAA Rating: R). Running time: **89 MINS.**
Cast: Jennifer O'Neill, Gabriele Ferzetti, Marc Porel, Gianni Garko, Evelyn Stewwart, Jenny Tamburi, Fabrizio Jovine, Riccardo Parisio Perrotti, Vito Passeri, Luigi Diberti.
(Dubbed English Soundtrack)

"The Psychic" is an overpoweringly dull and incompetent pseudo thriller. Filmed in Italy under the title "Sette Note in Nero," pic features at least two dozen zooms into Jennifer O'Neill's pretty eyes as she experiences psychic visions of people's deaths, but the chills are nowhere to be found. One-week runs loom likely.

Only remotely effective scene in terms of audience impact is the opening, in which O'Neill as a little girl "sees" her mother's suicide, as the latter jumps off what looks like the white cliffs of Dover and bangs her head on the way down in rather grisly close-ups.

Rest of the film is largely devoted to O'Neill nervously pacing around rooms in her villa, trying to convince unbelieving authorities of the veracity of her visions and her efforts to escape her own death when that seems like a possibility.

She speaks with her own voice but the rest of the cast is dubbed, which is not of undue concern since much of the film is done without dialog. Ominous uncredited music fills in the blanks.

Aside from opening presentation credit, 'O'Neill's card and title, pic bears no credits at all in the American version, not even a director credit. It's just as well for all concerned. —*Cart.*

Ciao, Les Mecs
(Ciao, You Guys)
(FRENCH-COLOR)

Paris, May 2.
A Silenes presentation of an Alpes-Cinema - Paris-Cannes Production - Ginis Film production. Features entire cast. Directed by Sergio Gobbi. Screenplay, Enrico Oldoini. Camera (Eastmancolor), Jean Badal; sound, Paul Habans; editor, Gabriel Rongier; music, Paul-Jean Borowsky. Reviewed at Salles Ponthieu, Paris, April 26, 1979. Running time: **100 MINS.**
Roberto .... Gerard Herold
Nicole .... Anne Lonnberg
Charles .... Charles Aznavour
Lawyer .... Jean Piat
Annie .... Dany Saval
Peasant .... Michel Galabru
Doctor .... Roland Dubillard

That this film underwent a title change from "Love Comedy" to "Ciao, You Guys!" gives some inkling as to one of its problems. Sergio Gobbi's comedy doesn't know whether it's about love or friendship, although it seems to want to be all things to all men and all women.

Enrico Oldoni's script starts off as a love story about an Italian immigrant in Paris searching for the woman who has walked out on him and then takes a sharp detour into the joys of buddy-buddy hob-nobbing (with a bunch of Italian males yocking it up in the worst stock Italian tradition), and then jumps back on the track for a feeble finish. Along the way there are a series of comic and pseudo-philoso-phical asides in the persons of Charles Aznavour, Roland Dubillard and Michel Galabru. What starts out as a simple comedy degenerates into muddled pretentious statements about Life.

The lumbering script is not helped by Gobbi's pedestrian direction and the generally poor technical quality. The two leads, Gerard Herold and Anne Lonnberg, aren't asked to do much except look warm and attractive, which they have no problem doing. But then those loutish Italian males keep coming back for more jocularity. —*Len.*

Caniche
(Poodle)
(SPANISH-COLOR)

Barcelona, May 4.
A Figaro Films production. Written and directed by Bigas Luna. Features entire cast. Exec producer, Pepon Coromina; camera (Eastmancolor), Predro Aznar; eidtor, Anastasi Rinos; sets, Carlos Riart. Reviewed at Club de Cine (Barcelona), May 3, '79. Running time: **90 MINS.**
Bernardo .... Angel Jove
Eloisa .... Consol Tura
Dani .... Linda Perez Gallardo
Alberto .... Cruz Tobar
Aunt Lina .... Sara Grey
"Can" .... Marta Molins

Bigas Luna's "Bilbao," which ran in last year's Cannes sidebar event, is now followed by "Caniche," similarly chosen by Cannes for the Directors Fortnight section. There is great similarity between the two films, and the considerable success of "Bilbao" may indicate a similar windfall for "Caniche," though the sex angle is played down and the voluptuous Isabel Pisano is substituted by Consol Tura in the part of a bitchy, abrasive sister to the expressionless Angel Jove.

The Catalan director-writer has a flair for creating moods by serving up unpleasant scenes. The viewer is assaulted with close-ups of snails, a dead dog, a meat grinder, a dead rat fished out of a pool, eyes, nails being cut, a dentist at work, raw meat fed to the poodle and so on. It's all seemingly leading up to something, but, as in "Bilbao," the ambiguous ending is a disappointment and nothing violent is ever seen to really happen, leaving the

spectator irked at all the gratuitous false leads.

The feeling throughout the film is decidedly kinky and sick. A brother and sister live in an old country mansion and seem to spend the day quarreling. Each has his own sexual hang-ups, with Sis clearly ruthlessly dominating the brother. She, it is suggested, buys puppies and sticks them in the meat grinder, though this is never actually shown and there is nothing specific for the ASPCA to latch on to.

They are both found dead, seemingly clawed and bitten to death. Who did it is left a mystery, though, farfetched as it is, presumably each has killed the other in canine ecstasy. —*Besa.*

Droemme stoejer ikke, naar de doer
(Dreams Make No Noise When They Die)
(DANISH-COLOR)

Copenhagen, March 27.
A Det Danske Filmstudio 1979 production. A/S Dagmar Film release. Written and directed by Christian Braad Thomsen. Features entire cast, camera (Eastmancolor alternating with black and white) Dirk Bruel; editor, Grete Moeldrup; music, various recording by Bob Wills & The Texas Playboys, Albert Ayler, Ivan Leth and others; production manager, Per Arman. State Film Institute production aid granted by Councelor Frits Raben. Reviewed at Dagmar Bio, Copenhagen, April 27, 1979. Running time: **80 MINS.**
The dying man .... Kaj Holm
His wife .... Asta Esper Andersen
The son .... Jon Bang Carlsen
The son's wife .... Irm Hermann

Writer-director Christian Braad Thomsen has long been a film activist combining left wing opinions with pragmatic viewpoints and much technical skill as a filmmaker. In a previous feature film, "Children Of Pain," he proved a keen ear and a clear eye for the landscapes and people of his own rural childhood.

The same sensitivities are tapped for all they are worth in "Dream Make No Noise When They Die," but Braad Thomsen has wanted to prove that good, popular dramatic feature films could be made on a small budget, and this, unfortuntately, is no such proof.

Around the deathbed of an old, morose farmer there is the farmer's embittered wife, their young left wing politician son and the son's German wife. It seems that the father collaborated, if only half-heartedly, with the German occupation forces in the years of World War II. While waiting for Death to come, the young German woman is raped by the village idiot. She receives scant comfort from her husband who has his psycho-political axe to grind first: he seeks out motives in a deprived childhood for the rapist's act.

There is too much sermonizing on the part of the son, but it is not clear whether Braad Thomsen means to sympathize with him or to depict a political intellectual bereft of real feeling in a moment of personal crisis.

Anyway the son's role is poorly played by Jon Bang Carlsen, while Irm Hermann of Rainer Werner Fassbinder's regular troupe never displays any other feeling than sheer sourfaced irritability.

As the odd couple, Kaj Holm and Asta Esper Andersen give creditable performances. Frame compositions and camerawork is excellent, and the miscellany of music on the soundtrack is used with great effect and originality.

But the blend of Claude Chabrol's psycho-sex-thrills with flashbacks to the family's earlier years plus the insistence on making political statements via the dialog will make "Dreams ..." a hard film to market outside of very specialized situations, where Braad Thomsen's previous features are already known and appreciated.—*Kell.*

Companys, Proces A Catalunya

(Companys, Catalonia On Trial) (SPANISH-COLOR)

Barcelona, May 4.
Produccions Zeta S.A., La Llanterna Films and P.C. Teide coproduction. Directed by Josep Maria Forn. Features entire cast. Exec producer, J.A. Perez Giner; screenplay, Josep Maria Forn, Antoni Freixas; camera (Eastmancolor), Cecilio Paniagua; sets, Josep Maria Espada, Josep Maria Segarr; editor, Emilio Rodriguez. Reviewed at Sonoblok Studios, Barcelona, May 3, '79. Running time: **103 MINS.**
Lluis Companys i Jover ......Luis Iriondo
Angela .... Marta Angelat
Ramona Companys ... Montserrat Carulla
Fortuny .... Xabier Elorriaga
Miquel .... Pau Garsaball
Military Consul .... Agustin Gonzalez
Commandant Urrutia ..... Alfred Luchetti
President of Military Council Carlos Lucena
Carme Ballester .... Marta May
Urraca Pastor .... Biel Moll
Jordi .... Ovidi Montllor
Capita Colubi .... Jordi Serrat

(Soundtrack in Catalan and Castilian)

Stirring, often touching account of the last year in the life of Lluis Companys, the President of Catalonia, his escape to France at the end of the Spanish Civil War, his capture and return to Franco Spain by the Vichy government, and his final court martial and execution in Barcelona in 1940.

Topnotch thesping by Luis Iriondo as Companys (ironically a Basque actor, whose first major role this is), fine period production values, magnificent lensing by the late Cecilio Paniagua and a generally literate and sitrring script all add up to distinguished film on all levels

which certainly is a natural for a film festival. It is hard to understand why it was rejected for competition in Cannes, and put into the "A Certain Look" sidebar section.

Though at times a bit talky and perhaps running a little too long, pic should do well in sophisticated circuits, and especially in regions where local autonomies are still being fought for. Perhaps Companys is presented a trifle too much the perfect political hero, too much the disinterested patriot, but he nonetheless comes across as a believable leader. The film happily does not get bogged down in allusions to local politics, and where explanations are needed they are handled by an occasional flashback, sometimes using documentary footage.

The story starts out during the last hours of the Catalan government, just before the entry of Franco's troops into Barcelona. Companys and the Basque leader Aguirre flee to the safety of France. But after the Nazi invasion, Companys is caught and driven back to the Spanish border at Irun.

After interrogation and torture in Madrid (for Franco is trying to find out where the Catalans have stashed their gold), he is ultimately sent back to his native Barcelona and incarcerated in the Montjuich prison. —*Besa.*

Cannes Festival

Die Blechtrommel

(The Tin Drum) (W. GERMAN-FRENCH-YUGOSLAV-POLISH-COLOR)

Berlin, May 4.
A Franz Seitz Film/Bioskop-Film/Artemis Film/Hallelujah-Film/GGB 14.KG/Argos Films Paris production in collaboration with Jadran Film Zagreb and Film Polski Warsaw. Franz Seitz, producer; world rights, United Artists. Features entire cast. Directed by Volker Schloendorff. Screenplay, Jean-Claude Carriere, Schloendorff, Franz Seitz; extra dialogue, Guenter Grass; based on the Guenter Grass novel of the same name; camera (Eastmancolor), Igor Luther; art direction, Nicos Perakis; editing, Suzanne Baron; music, Friedrich Meyer; production manager, Eberhard Junkersdorf. Reviewed at Gloriette cinema, Berlin, May 3, '79. Running times: **150 MINS.**
Matzerath .... Mario Adorf
Agnes .... Angela Winkler
Oskar .... David Bennent
Jan Bronski .... Daniel Olbrychski
Maria .... Katharina Thalbach
Greff .... Heinz Bennent
Bebra .... Fritz Hakl
Roswitha .... Mariella Oliveri
Anna Koljaiczek .... Tina Engel
Oma Anna .... Berta Drews
Joseph Koljaiczek .... Roland Teubner
Loetsack .... Ernst Jacobi
Scheffler ...., ... Werner Rehm
Gretchen Scheffler .... Ilse Page
Musican Meyn .... Otto Sander
With Andrea Ferreol and Charles Aznavour.

Slated for entry at Cannes, this two-and-a-half-hour adaptation of Guenter Grass's world renown novel, "The Tin Drum," was made by the best craftsman on the Grman film scene today, Volker Schloendorff, and produced at a circa \$4,000,000 budget by vet producer Franz Seitz. It was lensed partially in Poland (also in France and Yugoslavia, as well as West Germay) to fit the novel's Danzig character (Grass's origin) and adheres to the book more than enough not to disappoint avid readers of the bestseller, but it is at the same time hampered by the "literary" tag and may have trouble getting legs due to the over-length. But it's worth the o.o. by art-house distribs, and needs only a push at Cannes to put it over elsewhere than the German public, where it should be a hit.

"The Tin Drum" (published 1959) is as hard to break your teeth on in book form as Heinrich Boell's related historical metaphor, "Group Portrait with Lady" (Cannes entry, 1977), directed by Yugo helmer Aleksandar Petrovic (whose only mistake then was getting bogged down in the dense German taxshelter scene). This is a complex, "free association" novel, strongly anti-religious and (in a positive sense) anti-political; it is also humorous and absurd, as well as being historical and metaphoric. In short, it is a parody of German society, a mud-sling at the beloved "Bildungsroman" in classic German literature.

Now, 20 years later, the film has appeared — although there was never a want of offers at Grass's door. The chance, however, to work closely with Schloendorff and Seitz on a project of a large-scale (the biggest budget ever in modern German film history) proved irresistible. Grass assisted on the dialog and provided hints along the way. The film, in general, covers more than half of the novel's contents.

This is the tale of a Tiny Tim who is a Jack the Giant Killer at the same time. Even before his birth Oskar Matzerath in his mother's womb realizes he has special gifts and will use them at will, but not to raise suspicion among his family and acquaintances. One of his gifts is breaking glass with his voice; another is the decision at three years of age not to grow another centimeter. His parents think it is the result of a bad fall down the cellar stairs, but Oskar has arranged this accident as well. The important aspect the viewer must keep in mind is that this is a chron-

icle on the history of Germany from the beginning of this century (the film's introductory part before Oskar is born) up to nearly the present day, i.e. 1959 (the final chapters of the book are excluded), with a special emphasis on the city of Danzig where Poles and Germans were constantly in strive. Most of all, it's about that social and political phenomenon known as Nazism.

Oskar is a rather blasphemous character. He knows that his mother, married to the German Matzerath, is carrying on a weekly affair with the Pole Bronski, whom the boy suspects to be his real father. Because of his stunted growth, he can crawl under tables and skirts to watch, with a sardonic eye, the lies and hypocrisies about him.

In a sense, he narrates the film in giving his views of these misdemeanors; but he is also directly responsible for the death of several key individuals: Matzerath, Bronski, and even (to a degree) his own mother. But each spurious act reflects also the doom hanging over Danzig, as, first, the Germans in 1939 take out their hate of Poles and Jews as the war begins, and, second, the closing days of a losing fight leads to more destruction. Finally, at the grave of his father (killed by a Russian Mongol), Oskar decides it is high time to "grow up" and conveniently falls into the grave for another advantageous blow on the head. At that point in the novel, the film ends.

Several scenes in "Tin Drum" are eye-catchers. The attack on the Danzig Post Office where Polish Resistance fighters have banded together is expertly handled, as well as other crowd scenes, particularly one about a Nazi Party Day during which Oskar's drum puts everything out-of-step in what is the best parody in the film. Also, Oskar's meetings with the midget Bebra, a prophecizing figure throughout, are very well written and quite convincing in conveying the ignominy of the times. David Bennent as Oskar (a boy of 12 hindered in his own growth, so that he appears to be about five years old) has the eyes and the acting talent to carry some scenes remarkably well, but he is not the insatiable wallower in sex and religious mysticism that Grass intended.

All literary misgivings aside, however, this is an entertaining pic. —*Holl.*

L'Ingorgo

(Bottleneck) (ITALIAN-FRENCH-SPANISH-W. GER.-COLOR)

Cannes, May 11.
A Titanus release (Italy) produced by Sil-

vio Clementelli for Clesi (Rome) — Greenwich Film (Paris) — Jose Frades (Madrid) and Albatross (Munich). Directed by Luigi Comencini. Stars in order of appearance Alberto Sordi, Orazio Orlando, Annie Girardot, Fernando Rey, Miou Miou, Gerard Depardieu, Ugo Tognazzi, Marcello Mastroianni, Gianni Cavina, Stefania Sandrelli, Harry Baer, Ciccio Ingrassia and Patrick Dewaere. Screenplay, Luigi Comencini, Ruggero Maccari and Bernardino Zapponi. Camera (Eastmancolor) Ennio Guarnieri; art director, Mario Chiari; editor, Nino Baragli; music, Fiorenzo Carpi. Reviewed at Cannes Film Festival, May 10, 1979. Running time: **116 MINS.**

Luigi Comencini, a keen observer of Italian life, and one of the highly regarded filmmakers of Italian cinema, has poured a lot of his sardonic humor and spleen into "Bottleneck." So much so that it just misses as a big allegoric black comedy — promisingly developed in the first 60 minutes of the two hour Clesi entry. As it spins off, this fracted multi-part pic still has something for everyone in all markets. Above all, it has a wealth of workable vignettes, gags, visual comedy and a number of great performances from a big European cast. Skilled doctoring could make it a salable 90-95 mins. pic in the U.S. market.

To lense his vision of a human contemporary crosscut in a black comedy format that evolves in the second half as an equally somber drama, Comencini falls back on a ploy of a monster traffic jam when all road access to Rome is clogged. Bumper to bumper affinities from late afternoon to dawn provide the mechanism to see humanity at its worst.

All the foibles of class, power, infirmity, age and mass psychotics are pinpointed relentlessly to validate Marcello Mastroianni's crack in closing reels: "Humanity is disgusting." Unrelenting vivisection of human condition in all its zero points is also a buildup for a close to finish extremeunction delivered by an unfrocked priest access in an exortation against social evils and a plea for a return to "nature, life and love."

Seen in comedy satire, the film is sprightly and dotted with laughs. When it turns serious, "Bottleneck" slowly becomes sinister, malicious, violent (all favoring box-office ingredients these days) but loses tempo along the way and overshoots what might have been a sustaining cutoff.

Like Fellini in "Orchestra Rehearsal," Comencini veers into drama to speak up about the threat of violent anarchy as industrial technologies erode civic balance and restraints. He achieves a touch of sci-fi disaster-horror in closing reels but in sharp damaging contrast with hearty social satire initially.

Outstanding performances of many cameo stars must include Alberto Sordi as a big business potentate wedged into a stalled mass of four-wheeled humanity, Fernando Rey and Annie Girardot — depicting gut hatreds of a middle aged couple, Angela Molina — a youth spirit shattered by rape. Marcello Mastroianni (playing himself) and Stefania Sandrelli as a poor, pregnant suburbanite, shine in an overnight seduction routine abetted by her conniving husband. Splintered sequence with Gerard Depardieu, Ugo Tognazzi and Miou-Miou valiantly attempt to highlight infidelity inside a Fiat but gets nowhere.

Fine performances by supporting actors are lushly sprinkled through the film, contributing to credibility of massive existential view. Harry Baer, who befriends the raped girl, and Ciccio Ingrassia, as the ambulance case more worried about how much accident money he can get from the bus company than with survival, are two of many supports.

Art director Mario Chiari built a convincing 'roadway set on the backlot of Cinecitta' and kept it filled with hundreds of hard vehicles through most of the film.

Lenser Enrico Guarnieri effectively trailed Comencini on the comedy-drama curve. So did composer Fiorenzo Carpi and editor, Nino Baragli.

(Writer-filmmaker Fabio De Agostini is taking legal steps to prevent use of title which he says he's used twice before for non-film projects but nothing has been resolved-Ed). — *Werb.*

Woyzeck
(WEST GERMAN-COLOR)

Cannes, May 15.
Gaumont release of Werner Herzog-Munich-ZDF production. Features entire cast. Written and directed by Werner Herzog from the play by Georg Buchner. Camera (Eastmancolor), Jorg Schmidt-Reitwein; editor, Beate Mahka-Jellinghaus. Reviewed at Cannes Film Fest (Competing), May 14, '79. Running time: **82 MINS.**
Cast: Klaus Kinski, Eve Mattes, Wolfgang Reichman, Willy Semmerlbrogge, Josef Bierbichler, Paul Burian.

Werner Herzog seems to be getting as prolific as his fellow countryman director Rainer Werner Fassbinder. He made this one back to back with "Nosferatu." However, "Woyzeck" shows him in more sanguine form than with the bloodless vampire tale.

Based on Georg Buchner's mid-19th century play about a lowly man, the lowest of the low, an orderly in the German Army, film is given a probing, chilling force by Klaus Kinski's tense, desperate playing and Herzog's relentless direction.

Kinski is the orderly Woyzeck who is first seen being worked to exhaustion by an officer. Kinski is forever running fast, seen shaving a wouldbe benign officer too quickly. The latter insists Kinski is a good man and knows his place as Kinski, in a difficult, inarticulate way, tries to show himself as a natural man who has had a child by a prostitute he lives with.

A sinister doctor uses him for experiments before his students as he notes the symptons brought on by undernourishment that have reduced Kinski to a sort of group of reflexes like a cat dropped into Kinski's arms from a first floor window.

A handsome, brutish, overbearing officer takes over Kinski's woman and humiliates him in a tavern. Kinski's rage finally turns to murder. But it is the woman he murders as he stabs her many times before a stream in an explosive ritual.

Herzog seems to want to resurrect the great German Expressionist film period, but has not used the excessive acting of the earlier players who exteriorized their inner disarray by overdone facial contortions, clawed hands and twisted body postures.

The film benefits from strong but not overstressed acting and a fine use of an old city of Germanic architecture found in Czechoslovakia. The prostitute is also a victim who yearns for some meaning and tenderness but is defeated by poverty and the harsh caste system of the times. — *Mosk.*

Een Vrouw Tussen Hond En Wolf
(A Woman Between Dog and Wolf)
(BELGIAN-FRENCH-COLOR)

Cannes, May 15.
Gaumont release of NIM, Productions De La Gueville, Gaumont production. Features entire cast. Directed by Andre Delvaux. Screenplay, Ivo Michiels, Delvaux; camera (Eastmancolor), Charlie Van Damme; editor, Nicole Berckmans; music, Etienne Verschueren. Reviewed at Cannes Film Fest (competing), May 14, '79. Running time: **108 MINS.**
Lieve .... Marie-Christine Barrault
Francois .... Roger Van Hool
Driann .... Rutger Hauer
Butcher .... Bert Andre
Georges .... Rol Reymen
Priest .... Senne Rouffaer

Andre Delvaux is one of the few Belgian filmmakers with a critical and buff following. However, his moody films, some with touches of surrealism or clairvoyance, were highly specialized items commercially. His first feature in five years, this one is more accessible though somewhat mannered and predictable in its tale of a woman coming of age during the trauma of World War II.

French thesp Marie-Christine Barrault, dubbed into Flemish, is the center of this tale of the effect of war on a middle-class woman. She is adequate as this heavyset, self-effacing woman whose tribulations lead to her break with her accepted past after the incursion of love, politics and violence into her sheltered life.

She marries in 1940 when Belgium was still neutral. Then the Germans invade and her husband is off to war. He is back after the short-lived war convinced that the Flemish people should throw in their lot with the Germans. He goes off with some others to fight with the Germans against the Russians.

Barrault happens to find a resistant hiding in her doorway one night and hides him though worried and scared. She has been ostracized because of her husband but love blooms with the more relaxed, more outgoing resistant.

The war is over, the husband comes back and is imprisoned. The resistant helps him for her, but she decides to stay with her husband when he is freed. Film then goes into her break with her husband, after they have a child, when he still goes on trying to excuse and justify his wartime actions.

When she assails him about the war horrors he can only cringe. She also breaks with the resistant who sees her at times, but is now busy in politics' and goes off with her child after 12 years of a life of self deception.

Film is well-meaning but somewhat labored with a script that telegraphs reactions and does not smooth out the coincidences with more insight into the characters. The period is effectively conveyed, opting for intimacy rather than epic proportions.

The pettiness of her own relatives during the war, who live high off their farm but do not help her, is outlined. She is only helped by a fascist butcher who kills his children and himself after the war.

With attention on World War II after the "Holocaust" tv airings, and reappraisals of past guilts, this film might find its way in European theatres with cogent hard sell called for in other climes. Film is technically fine. — *Mosk.*

The Europeans
(BRITISH-COLOR)

Cannes, May 15.
Merchant-Ivory Productions Ltd. release and production. Stars Lee Remick, Robin Ellis. Directed by James Ivory. Screenplay, Ruth Prawer Jhabvala; camera (color), Larry Pizer; editor, Jeremiah Rusconi; music, Richard Robbins. Reviewed at Cannes Film Fest (competing), May 15, '79. Running time: **90 MINS.**

"The Europeans" are Americans who grew up in Europe. They come back to the U.S. to visit rich cousins they have never met before. Perhaps a bit down on their luck, the arrival leads to a mingling and interaction of cultures, rather than a clash, that ends up with the more innocent, unimaginative even hardheaded Yankee outlooks holding their own with the more cultured, worldly wiles of the European ways.

The European cousins are Lee Remick as a mid-thirtyish Baroness now estranged from her Austrian nobleman husband and her younger brother, a more brash, free living portrait painter with bohemian attitudes. They were brought up abroad as their mother, from a wealthy Protestant family, had married a European Catholic and broke with the family to go live in Europe. It is the mid-19th century.

Shot in the U.S., New England is a lovely backdrop with its autumnal hues, languid, genteel ways and, above all, extraordinary houses (mostly Salem, Mass.) that are a mixture of European and local influences. The newcomers are grudgingly accepted and given a smaller house to live in on the big estate.

Remick takes on the sentimental education of the twentyish son and heir and is also courted by an older rich second cousin. She cures the younger man of excessive drinking, but alienates the older one by her seeming desire to set up both as possibilities. The period is delicately recreated. Remick's brother falls for one of his cousins, a headstrong, romantic girl thirsting for adventure.

Her beau, an ardent clergyman, transfers his attentions to her sister. The Baroness goes back emptyhanded. Remick is excellent as the capricious, worldly woman who outsmarts herself up against the more hidebound Americans.

Director James Ivory handles this roundelay with subtlety and comes up with an engaging drama, that, besides festivals, should find its way in world markets. It is a change from the violent fare these days. A period film that reveals a past with more cogent moral precepts and human relations that reflects on today as well as being true to its period.

Acting is fine with all worth a nod and it is technically tops. Though shot in the U.S., 75% of the financing was British and it is the official British entry at the Cannes Festival despite some early squawks from official British film sources. It is a feather in any country's hat. —*Mosk.*

Les Soeurs Bronte
(The Bronte Sisters)
(FRENCH-COLOR)

Cannes, May 14.
Gaumont release of Action Films-Gaumont-FR3 production. Stars Isabelle Adjani, Marie-France Pisier, Isabelle Huppert. Directed by Andre Techine. Screenplay, Techine, Pascal Bonitzer, Jean Gruault; camera (Eastmancolor), Bruno Nuytten; editor, Claudine Merlin; art direction, Jean-Pierre Kohut-Svelco; music, Philippe Sarde. Reviewed at Cannes Film Fest (competing), May 13, '79. Running time: **115 MINS.**

Emily . . . . Isabelle Adjani
Charlotte . . . . Marie-France Pisier
Anne . . . . Isabelle Huppert
Branwell . . . . Pascal Greggory
Father . . . . Patrick Magee
Mrs. Robinson . . . . Helen Surgere
Nicholls . . . . Roland Bertin

Pretty pictures, but this pic does not come to grips with the apparently tormented and repressive lives of that trio of British writers, "The Bronte Sisters," not to forget their promising but doomed brother. It is set in 19th century Britain, in a stark, remote countryside where the father is a priest in the local church, is the background for this anecdotal film.

Apparently, director Andre Techine was more interested in their lives than their work. But if they were sterile, the film rarely illuminates this or creates a needed narrative drive. The father is just a grimacing presence at times and there is a sort of caricatural Dickensian aunt who replaced their mother.

Their work is still read and "Wuthering Heights" and "Jane Eyre" have been filmed several times. But that is not important. The relations of sisters are rarely delved into though they are seen reading one of the books together at one time.

The brunt of the rare romantic aspects of the film is used in detailing the brother's love for a woman 17 years older than him whose children he tutored. She does not come to him when her husband dies and he turns to drink and drugs and an early death at 31.

The main players are French and it is a Gallicized view of these siblings. There is a lack of austerity and sharpness in their characters but acceptable since all are tempered this way. Isabelle Adjani is Emily who wrote "Wuthering Heights" and is given to roaming the moors in men's clothes.

Marie-France Pisier is the more determined Charlotte whose "Jane Eyre" was successful while Isabelle Huppert is the most subdued and self effacing of them. Pascal Greggory plays the brother in a self-pitying manner that fits a promising but essentially deluded would-be artist.

No excessive symbolism is used. There is a scene when the brother's oil lamp is knocked over and a fire seethes around his bed. But he is too drugged to awake or be purged of anything. The sisters put it out, for once acting together.

The Britain of the time is well recreated. Specialized audiences are growing and may be found for this sometimes appealing but too often heavy-footed tale of a trio of girls brought up in poverty but maintaining original spirits that turned into books rather than revolt.

Emily died at 30, Anne at 29 from tuberculosis. Charlotte lived to 39 and even got married. —*Mosk.*

Saiehaieh Bolan De Bad
(Tall Shadows of the Wind)
(IRANIAN-COLOR)

Cannes, May 16.
Farmanara release and production. Features entire cast. Directed by Bahman Farmanara. Screenplay, Houshang Golshiri, Farmanaara from the book by Golshiri; music, Ahmad Pejamn. No other credits available. Reviewed at Cannes Film Fest (Critic week-Non-competing), May 15, '79. Running time: **104 MINS.**

With: Faramarz Gharibian, Said Nikpour, Hossein Kasbian, Atash Khaeyer.

Iran is still in the news and this film, made under the regime of the deposed Shah, is an unusual fable about fear and oppression that might reflect the past and even new governments, but stands in its own right as a parable on how people can turn something seemingly innocuous into a symbol of power and repression.

The driver of a bus gets mired down outside his town one day. A scarecrow has been raised nearby. The driver is upset and goes down to take a drink from his bottle of brandy in the field. He feels some sort of premonition and a stone falls in a stream near him. He retrieves what looks like a tiny monolith.

He watches the scarecrow, which, on a cross, has a head bound in cloth and is swathed in a greatcoat. It has its center stake in the ground. He approaches and draws a nose on the cloth head. Back in town he talks of what happened.

He at first does not take it seriously for he had had a few drinks, but others do and it begins to spread. A woman apparently has a miscarriage because of the scarecrow and buries the dead fetus under it. An hysteria spreads and the driver decides to face this now malevolent power figure which even seems to stomp around town at night as the noise of a thumping stake is heard.

He is found with his toes lopped off and dies of gangrene. Dreams and the growing fear are well handled in this slow, gripping film. Measured pacing helps add to this taking sombre study of irrational forces.

Bahman Farmanara emerges a director with flair for atmosphere and never falls into the picturesque or hermetic. Fine lensing also helps and this an Iranian entry to put Farmanara on the promising list among such other Iranian filmmakers, already known by fest exposure as, Sohrab Saless and Daryoush Mehrjoui. —*Mosk.*

Jun
(JAPANESE-COLOR)

Cannes, May 13.
Kogei-Sha release and production. Features entire cast. Written and directed by Hiroto Yokoyama from the book by So Kuramoto. Camera (Fuji-color), Akira Takada; editor, Keiichi Uraoka; music, Toshi Ichiyanagi. Reviewed at Cannes Film Fest (Critic Week-Non-competing), May 12, '79. Running time: **90 MINS.**

Jun . . . . Jun Eto
Yoko . . . . Yoko Kizima
Woman . . . . Koko Enami
Mother . . . . Chiyoko Akaza

A rare Japanese film to find a niche in a major film festival lately, albeit in the non-competing Cannes Critic Week. It is a tale of obsession, a strange one indeed, groping women in subways. Despite probably evoking nervous laughter, indignation or disbelief, at first, in Western audiences, film still carries an erotic punch.

A young man from a strange island shaped like a ship is in Tokyo where he works in a machine shop but also aspires to be a comic strip cartoonist. His frequent trips on the usually crowded subway have him indulging in a bizarre sexual practice. He feels up women who get excited, disturbed, moan but never make a scene.

They give in and accept the indignities even if some seem shamed by it. But one, a lovely woman in a kimono with a child, even croons a song of love during the violating of her body under her kimono. The strange hero, Jun, has a girl who sees him doing this one day and his getting caught by the police.

But the woman whose body he kneaded insists it is not so and nobody's business and the boy gets off but his girl will not see him. There is a strident but effective musical backing to this strange odyssey maybe due to his isolated childhood on the island or his relations with his girl.

He goes back to honor his father's grave but cannot find it and sees the island now practically deserted and falling to ruin. Film sums up the sickly practice of female molestation in a scene when several men paw a woman and the young man is one of the male onlookers who do not interfere.

It might reflect the ambivalent social outlooks as past macho ways linger on with an intimation that freer relations, as the boy's final reunion and love with his girl, could begin to alleviate this seemingly banal sex activity.

Film is kinky but still captures this sexually strange side of Japanese society and the sometimes crippling effect it has on youth. Film could find its way as a cult entry abroad on its unusual treatment of what seems like weird sexual activity, but is saved from exhibitionism by sharp direction, good play and a canny insight into the residue of restrictive mores in an as yet evolving society. —Mosk.

Fremd Bin Ich Eigezogah
(I Came As a Stranger)
(AUSTRIAN-W.GERMAN-COLOR-16m)

Cannes, May 14.
Titus Leber Vienne-Clasart Munich production. Features entire cast. Written, directed and edited by Titus Leber. Camera (Color), Ditter Witich, Leber, Wittigo; music, Franz Schubert. Reviewed at Cannes Film Fest (Critic Week-Non-competing). May 13, '79. Running time: 70 MINS.

Schubert . . . . Axel Shanda
Child . . . . August Schnigg
Mother . . . . Alicia Meyer-Stauffen
Father .Enrst Dungl
Caroline . . . . .Angenlika Berlage

Titus Leber has experimented with superimposition of images in shorts and now adapts it with effectiveness to a first feature. Composer Franz Schubert hallucinates on his deathbed and evokes scenes of his childhood and life for a pretty sometimes portentious melding of the times and music of the composer.

Schubert twists in his bed and images multiply as he walks down long deserted country roads, scenes from his operas are evoked as well as his overbearing mother, understanding father, and his feeling of insecurity in the shadow of Beethoven's music plus others in his life. Schubert's music counterpoints the cascade of images.

Film seems indicated for music and film fests with a visual beauty that might also find it some commercial outlets with careful handling. Its blending of overlapped images may not always be revealing of Schubert's life and music, and it sometimes lapses into pretentiousness. But the film remains a treat for the eye, plus the ears for Schubert lovers. —Mosk.

Les Servantes Du Bon Dieu
(The Servants of the Good Lord)
(CANADIAN-DOCU-COLOR-16m)

Cannes, May 15.
Les Productions Prisma-SDICC-Radio-Quebec-OTEO release and production. Conceived and directed by Diane Letourneau. Camera (Color), Jean-Charles Tremblay; editor, Josee Beaudet. Reviewed at Cannes Film Fest (Critic Week-Non-competing). May 14, '79. Running time: 90 MINS.

A perceptive, somewhat overlong documentary on a Catholic nun's order in Canada, Les Petites Soeurs De La Sainte-Famille, created literally to do housework for priests and lay people attached to the Church. It does not attempt to be subversive or take sides and displays all aspects of the lives and standing of the Order.

Unfortunately, the material seems somewhat repetitive as a feature and would have made a better medium-length film. Serving may be a church tenet, but here it mirrors a sort of religioso symbol of outmoded ideas of women's place in the home for cleaning, kitchen, waiting on tables, albeit no children here, that have become anathema to feminists.

These nuns, aged from 40 to 96, with about 300 or so, may be slowly fading away as lay workers replace them for many chores, and, seemingly, not many younger women join up as they pass away at an average of about three a month. All seem dedicated and happy and have found a release from ordinary life. One dies during the film, suddenly pointing up, perhaps, the aimlessness but also dedication of such an Order.

There are also interviews with doctors, priests, the nuns themselves and Church higher-ups. One shot of priests eating and ignoring the serving nuns adequately sums up the subservient place of these cheerful women not to overlook exploitation. Public service tv seems the place for this well shot and carefully edited film with theatrical outlooks limited.

It is the sort of film the Critic Week likes to latch onto. One that is open to conjecture or individual reactions rather than having a more forceful viewpoint. Trying to be objective is hard indeed. Shots are selected after all and thus create an outlook. Entry is a fest film, however, and could be used at seminars, religious and lay, too. —Mosk.

Moments
(ISRAELI-FRENCH-COLOR)

Cannes, May 15.
Rosa Productions-Mica Films-Bein Hashurot release and production. Features entire cast. Written and directed by Michal Bat-Adam. Camera (Eastmancolor), Yves Lafaye; music, Hubert Rostaign. Reviewed at Cannes Film Fest (Certain Regard Section-Non-Competing), May 13, '79. Running time: 90 MINS.

Yola . . . . Michal Bat-Adam
Anne . . . . Brigitte Catillon
Avi . . . . Assaf Dayan
Guard . . . . Avi Pnini

Israeli actress Michal Bat-Adam, who has appeared in some films in Israel and France directed by Moshe Mizrahi ("Madame Rosa" among others), makes her directorial bow as well as doing one of the lead roles in this engaging albeit slightly lightweight Israeli-French coproduction on a friendly lesbianic relationship.

A young Israeli woman, director Bat-Adam, meets a French woman, Brigitte Catillon, a tourist, on a train in Israel. They decide to stay at the same hotel in a town. A friendship springs up as they confide, find common outlooks and a more sensual attraction.

The French woman has been married and is now living with a married man who would probably never divorce his wife for her. The Israeli wants to write a book as a sort of attempt at self-fulfillment, but does not seem up to it. They have an affair and the French woman also has one with the hotel security guard.

Bat-Adam's boyfriend, Assaf Dayan, comes down and the three end up making love together. But then the couple goes away for Bat-Adam fears losing her lover to the other woman. The French woman comes to visit some years later. Bat-Adam and Dayan are now married with a child. —Mosk.

Twee Vrouwen
(Twice A Woman)
(DUTCH-COLOR)

Cannes, May 12.
An Actueel Film releaseof a William Howerd/M.G.S. Production. Produced by William Howerd, Anne Lordon. Directed by George Sluizer. Features entire cast. Screenplay, George Sluizer, Jurrien Rood, based on the novel, "Twee Vrouwen," by Harry Mulisch; camera (color), Mat van Hensbergen; music, Willem Breuker; sound, Pjotr van Dijk; art director, Michel Bodt; cutting, Leo de Boer; asst. director, Jurrien Rood. Reviewed at the Ambassades, Cannes, May 11, -79. Running time: 113 MINS.

Laura . . . . Bibi Andersson
Alfred . . . . Anthony Perkins
Sylvia . . . . Sandra Dumas
Laura's mother . Tilly Perin Bouwmeester
Sylvia's mother . . . . Kitty Courbeois
Karin . . . . Astrid Weyman
Mr. Rublyov . . . . Georg Frenkel Frank
Playwright . . . . Charles Gormley
Alan Denderman . . . . Adrian Brine
Francois . . . . Arnold Gelderman
(English Soundtrack)

"Twice A Woman" (Dutch title "Twee Vrouwen" means "Two Women," already used in the past for another film) is based on a local bestseller by Harry Mulisch, but not available in translation. Film was shot in English and will be released in Holland in the original version with Dutch subtitles. Initially, it was to be produced by Matthijs van Heyningen, but he sold the rights to George Sluizer, and then made a film with a similar plot, though less sophisticated, "A Woman Like Eve," with Maria Schneider.

A 41-year-old woman, divorced and a curator of an icon museum, is lonely and on the spur of the moment starts talking to a girl in the street and invites her home. This initial premise is hard to believe, but film and performances by Bibi Andersson and Sandra Dumas, are strong enough to overcome it.

The girl, Sylvia, proposes to go to bed with her, though neither has done so before. Laura asks the girl to stay and an earnest love affair begins, and though they keep their friendship secret, it's their respective mothers who see through the pretence and suspect the truth. After a while gossip starts and Alfred, a cocky theatre critic who was married to Laura for seven years, confronts her and warns her of the consequences.

After pledging her love, Sylvia leaves Laura, apparently for a stay with her parents, but after a few days, it appears she is living with Alfred in a decrepit little hotel. Alfred wants to divorce his wife and goes to Paris with Sylvia. Coming back to Laura, Sylvia confesses she is still in love with her and only wanted to get pregnant, so that she and Laura could raise a child of their own. But Alfred being jealous does not accept this new development.

"Twice A Woman" is directed in good taste by George Sluizer, who also scripted, with Jurrien Rood, especially fleshing out the part of Alfred, making him more understandable and human. Film has three love scenes, one between Sandra Dumas and Bibi Andersson, two with Dumas and Anthony Perkins, all very chaste. The three main actors are convincing and good. Bibi Andersson in a difficult role comes off best. Cast of secondary characters is fine, Charles Gormley standing out in two scenes as a Scottish writer-friend of Laura's.

Framework of "Twice A Woman," with its flashbacks, may be unclear or even confusing to some, though Bibi Andersson's long hair or short hair indicates in which part of the action of the film she is. Director Sluizer was interested in the characters and the symbolism of the story, and wittingly ignored the clash of accents of all actors, that without explanation, is somewhat bewildering, especially when a memory flash to childhood has a young Laura speak high English. All technical credits good. —Saal.

Something's Rotten
(CANADIAN)

Cannes, May 11.

Dabara Films (Toronto) release of a Hazelton Motion Pictures Inc. presentation. Produced by David F. Eustace, Nancy E. Stewart. Features entire cast. Directed by F. Harvey Frost. Screenplay, Norman Fox; camera, Brian R.R. Hebb; music, John Kuipers; sound, Peter Shewchuk; editor, Brian Ravok. Reviewed at the Vox Theatre, Cannes, France. May 11, '79. Running time: **90 MINS.**

The Queen	Charlotte Blunt
Prince Calvin	Geoffrey Bowes
Marina Falk	Trudy Weiss
Prince George	Christopher Barry
Alexis Alexander	Cec Linder
Dr. Burns	Jean-Peter Linton

The title of this low budget Canadian feature, a first effort for most hands concerned, couldn't be more apt. Only it's not just something but almost everything.

It's supposed to be a mystery thriller in which a central European Queen's twin sons are rivals for succession to the throne. But the script and direction come off so half baked that it could be a failed comedy of how not to bring off a feature.

It's supposed to be a mystery thriller in which a central European Queen's twin sons are rivals for succession to the throne. But the script and direction come off so half baked that it could be a failed comedy of how not to bring off a feature.

Some talent does peek through, such as a striking Charlotte Blunt who deserves better and Geoffrey Bowes and Christopher Barry as her two mean-streaked sons. Both are left-handed and if this film is meat to say left handers are heavies anyone who is should sue.

In the end, evil triumphs but, despite some neat ventriloquist sequences, this effort fails on most counts. It's difficult to spot any market for it. —Adil.

Samuel Fuller & The Big Red One
(DUTCH-DOCU-COLOR-B-W)

Cannes, May 12.

Produced by Thijs Ockersen and Tom Burghard. Directed and written by Thijs Ockersen. Camera (color 16m), Hans den Bezemer and Steve Posey; sound, Bert Steeman and Travor Black; editor, Ot Louw; production in U.S.A., Paula Reiskin. Narrator, Aldo Ray. With Samuel Fuller, Lee Marvin, Mark Hammill, Kelly Ward, Robert Carradine, Bobby Dicicco. Reviewed in the Marche du Film, Cannes, May 11, '79. Running time: **72 MINS.**

Dutch critic and filmmaker Thijs Ockersen last year saw a dream come true, when he made a docu-mentary of his favorite (together with Don Siegel, subject of his next film) director Samuel Fuller.

While 66-year-old Fuller made "The Big Red One," Ockersen observed him filming in Israel. Fuller was so occupied directing his first film in many years, on an $8,000,000 budget, that it was hard for him to reflect on his past work. Sequence of interview with Sam Fuller in his study at home in California was shot later.

Fuller may be best known for his words, "Film is like a battlefield ... love, hate, violence, action, death ... in one word: emotion," uttered in Jean-Luc Godard's "Pierrot le Fou," at a time when Fuller was in **Paris to set up his film "Fleurs Du Mal,"** one of many abortive projects. Fuller comes across as an uncompromising filmmaker, a writer of a series of screenplays never made into films and which he will not let others make either.

His interest in assassins resulted in a film about Bob Ford, "The Man Who Shot Jesse James," filmed in 10 days. Originally a journalist, his films many times centered on newspapers ("Park Row") and reporters ("Shock Corridor"). "The Big Red One" represents many years of work and reflects all his ideas on war and heroism.

"The Big Red One" is the story of the first division of the American infantry, during World War II, from the first shot to the last, taking place in seven countries. About five men who think they are fighting all wars by themselves, it is epic and spectacular. Fuller was in the Big Red One during the war and already at that time wanted to write a book and make a film about its history.

Pic gives good over-all view on Fuller (though clips from his films are limited) and is excellent for festival showings and tv slots.—Saal.

Summer's Children
(CANADIAN)

Cannes, May 11.

Produced by Julius Kohanyi and Don Haig. No distributor. Director, Kohanyi; screenplay, Jim Osborne; camera, Joe Seckeresh; wardrobe, Elinor Galbraith; editor, M.C. Manne. Reviewed at the Vox Theatre, Cannes, France. May 11, '79. Running time: **95 MINS.**

Steve	Tom Hauff
Jennie	Paully Jardine
Albert	Don Francks
Kathy	Kate Lynch
Elaine	Patricia Collins
Tony	Ken James

A first feature for director Julius Kohanyi, "Summer's Children" is a serious but undernourished story of brother-sister incest.

It boasts some bright, competent performance by the central players, Tom Hauff and Paully Jardine and, in key support roles by Don Francks, Kate Lynch, Patricia Collins, and Ken James. But much of the real stuff is submerged and the screenplay by Jim Osborne ultimately lies flat.

After an off-camera sexual encounter with his sister, the brother leaves for the big city and lives with another woman. He learns that his sister is in the same city, carrying on a life of low repute. He hunts for her, meets up with a racing tout, expertly carried off by Francks, a lesbian, portrayed with dash by Collins, and he works in a car repair garage overlorded by James.

Finally, brother and sister reunite and decided to live together. No sex scenes are shown between them.

The storyline has more possibilities than realized success, but Kohanyi's direction and the actors keep it going. Despite its current concentration on international efforts, the Canadian Film Development Corp. has an investment in this low-budget piece. It required more work but there could be a student market and play in some offbeat centres. Nothing more the way it is. —Adil.

Alien
(COLOR)

Another hot summer at the Fox-office.

Hollywood, May 17.

A 20th Century-Fox release of a Brandywine-Ronald Shusett Production, produced by Gordon Carroll, David Giler and Walter Hill. Directed by Ridley Scott. Exec producer, Ronald Shusett. Screenplay, Dan O'Bannon. Camera (Eastman Color), Derek Vanlint; editor, Terry Rawlings; sound (Dolby), Derrick Leather; production design, Michael Seymour; art direction, Les Dilley, Roger Christian; special effects, Brian Johnson, Nick Allder; costumes, John Mollo; assistant director, Paul Ibbetson; music, Jerry Goldsmith. Reviewed at Samuel Goldwyn Theatre, Beverly Hills, Calif., May 16, 1979. (MPAA Rating: R.) Running time: **124 MINS.**

Dallas	Tom Skerritt
Ripley	Sigourney Weaver
Lambert	Veronica Cartwright
Brett	Harry Dean Stanton
Kane	John Hurt
Ash	Ian Holm
Parker	Yaphet Kott

Twentieth Century-Fox has another goodie for the summer. Or as they say in the world of science, when your Celsius is soaring, your Celsius is soaring.

Plainly put, "Alien" is an old-fashioned scary movie set in a highly realistic sci-fi future, made all the more believable by the expert technical craftmanship that the industry just gets better and better at. Picture isn't quite good enough to be a combination of "The Exorcist" and "Star Wars," but both titles are likely to come to mind as word-of-mouth spreads rapidly.

Dan O'Bannon's script has more loose ends than the Pittsburgh Steelers but that doesn't matter as director Ridley Scott, cameraman Derek Vanlint and composer Jerry Goldsmith propel the emotions relentlessly from one visual surprise — and horror — to the next.

The price paid for the excitement, and it's a small one, is very little involvement with the characters themselves. Often, in fact, it's hard to tell what they're doing or why. But it really doesn't matter when the screaming starts.

In contrast to the glamorous adventurous outer-space life often depicted in sci-fi, "Alien" initially presents a mundane commercial spacecraft with crew members like Yaphet Kotto bitching and moaning about wages and working conditions.

The tedium is shared by captain Tom Skerritt, his aide Sigourney Weaver and the rest of the crew, Veronica Cartwright, Harry Dean Stanton, John Hurt and Ian Holm, a generally good cast in the concededly cardboard roles. Eventually, it will be Weaver who gets the biggest chance in her film debut and she carries it off well.

Since they were doomed to get an R rating for gore, anyway, the filmmakers have thrown in some 20th century swearing for Weaver, which seems odd and awkward in he context, plus a bit of a skin show that's fetching but a little far-fetched. —Har.

The Prisoner Of Zenda
(COLOR)

Tame Sellers comedy. Middling b.o. likely.

Hollywood, May 17.
A Universal release of a Walter Mirisch production. Produced by Walter Mirisch. Stars Peter Sellers. Directed by Richard Quine. Screenplay, Dick Clement, Ian La Frenais, based on the novel by Anthony Hope, as dramatized by Edward Rose; camera (Technicolor), Arthur Ibbetson; editor, Byron "Buzz" Brandt; music, Henry Mancini; production design, John J. Lloyd; special visual effects, Albert Witlock; costumes, Susan Yelland; set decoration, Joe Chevalier, Marc Meyer; art direction, Herwig Libowitzky; sound, Brian Marshall, Lowell Harris; associate producer, Peter MacGregor-Scott; assistant directors, Ted Morley, Victor Tourjansky, David Menteer. Reviewed at the Samuel Goldwyn Theatre, Beverly Hills, May 17, '79. (MPAA rating: PG). Running time: **108 MINS.**

Rudolf IV/Rudolf V/Syd	Peter Sellers
Princess Flavia	Lynne Frederick
General Sapt	Lionel Jeffries
The Countess	Elke Sommer
The Count	Gregory Sierra
Duke Michael	Jeremy Kemp
Antoinette	Catherine Schell
Fritz	Simon Williams
Rupert of Hentzau	Stuart Wilson
Bruno	Norman Rossington
Archbishop	John Laurie
Erik	Graham Stark
Luger	Michael Balfour
Deacon	Arthur Howard
Johann	Ian Abercrombie
Conductor	Michael Segal

Latest remake of "The Prisoner Of Zenda" is a tame comic vehicle for another exercise in multiple role-playing by Peter Sellers. The untiring efforts of the star squeeze more laughs out of the material than reside in the script, and Walter Mirisch's production for Universal may appeal in some measure to kids and perhaps to older generations, but the approach is too genteel to tickle the funnybones of those weaned on Mel Brooks and "Animal House."

This is at least the fourth version of the classic tale of royal masquerade to be filmed under the original title, although buffs will recall that a major section of Blake Edwards' "The Great Race" traded heavily on the same plot in a flamboyantly comic vein.

Current edition, on which budget reportedly soared to over $10,000,-000 opens with the elderly king of Puritania, played by Sellers, meeting his end after a balloon accident. Next in line of succession is the fey Rudolf, whose trouble pronouncing his Rs allows Sellers a field day to mangle the language a la Inspector Clouseau.

Rudolf's brother Michael, an im-posing Jeremy Kemp, will stop at nothing to secure the crown for himself and, as a decoy, a Cockney hansom driver (Sellers again) is recruited to pose as Rudolf until the way can be cleared for a safe coronation.

The script by Dick Clement and Ian Le Frenais strains for wackiness without producing many results and Richard Quine, making his first pic in five years, directs in rather subdued fashion. Some of the comic set-pieces seem strangely over-cut and awkwardly matched, resulting in muted impact.

More than anything, pic resembles some of Danny Kaye's comic romps of decades past, such as "The Court Jester," but with a lot fewer laughs. What yocks do arise come mostly from inventiveness of the players. Sellers is in good form, especially as the English imposter who falls for the Princess Flavia, appealingly played by the lovely Lynne Frederick. Gregory Sierra scores as a pompous count forever challenging Sellers to duels, Stuart Wilson is properly obnoxious as a hyena-like mercenary and Lionel Jeffries and Elke Sommer have a couple of moments each as relatively peripheral figures.

Henry Mancini's score is exceedingly graceful, a perfect example of active but unobtrusive music buttressing less than inspired screen action. Arthur Ibbetson's lensing is straightforward, Susan Yelland's costumes look extraordinarily lush, and heavy reliance is put upon Albert Witlock's matte paintings to lend the pic an even broader canvas than could be obtained by location shooting in Austria (some secondary work was done at Universal in Hollywood).

Rex Ingram directed a silent version of the story in 1927 with Lewis Stone and Ramon Novarro. Best-known telling was Selznick's in 1937, with John Cromwell directing Ronald Colman and Douglas Fairbanks Jr., with a 1952 edition directed by Richard Thorpe starring Stewart Granger and James Mason making less of an impression. — Cart.

Over The Edge
(COLOR)

Orion besmirches its new image with crass youth pic.

Hollywood, May 17.
Orion Pictures release, thru Warner Bros., of a George Litto production. Produced by George Litto. Directed by Jonathan Kaplan. Features entire cast. Screenplay, Charlie Hass, Tim Hunter; camera (color), Andrew Davis; editor, Robert Barrere; music, Sol Kaplan; production design, Jim Newport; set decoration, A.C. Montenaro; sound, William Kaplan; special effects, Richard Johnson; assistant director, Ed Ledding. Reviewed at The Burbank Studios, May 17, '79. (MPAA Rating: PG). Running time: **95 MINS.**

Carl	Michael Kramer
Cory	Pamela Ludwig
Richie	Matt Dillon
Mark	Vincent Spano
Claude	Tom Fergus
Doberman	Harry Northup
Fred Willat	Andy Romano
Sandra Willat	Ellen Geer
Cole	Richard Jamison
Julia	Julia Pomeroy
Johnny	Tiger Thompson

"Over the Edge" hammers one more nail into the coffin of the current youth pix cycle. The Orion Pictures release, its second through Warner Bros., is a realistically downbeat tale of suburban youth on the rampage, a subject that won't soothe nervous theatre operators whose seats are still in tatters from "The Warriors" bookings. Orion is quietly releasing the George Litto production today in the Southwest, with good cause, but a longshot possibility exists for some boxoffice sparks if the youth market responds.

Jonathan Kaplan, who has long labored in the B picture vineyards, delivers another bottle of that vintage with "Over The Edge." Pic is well-cast in its youthful provocateurs, and competently directed, but there's little to set it off from the recent spate of similarly-themed films.

The aimless generation pictured in "Rebel Without A Cause" 20 some years ago has grown up, but their kids aren't much better off, hellbent on getting stoned or drunk in pursuit of the elusive "good time."

Screenplay by Charlie Haas and Tim Hunter captures these self-destructive tendencies with glum accuracy, with results that tend to reduce audience empathy. There's too much of a message for the kids, while adults will no doubt see glorification of anarchic behavior.

Fringe benefit of the new youth exploitation pix is the showcasing of some fine young talent, and "Over The Edge" boasts some promising newcomers, particularly Matt Dillon, Vincent Spano and Tom Fergus as three punks, leading good-boy-going-bad Michael Kramer down the primrose path.

Andy Romano and Ellen Geer are quite credible as Kramer's distraught parents, but Harry Northup as an overbearing cop, and Richard Jamison as a neighborhood leader revert right back to 1950s stereotypes.

"Over The Edge" closes with the teens laying waste to the local high school, second such film to end like this in the last month. If this keeps up, it won't be long before th P.T.A. stops scolding television, and begins pointing a finger at the neighborhood theatre. —Poll.

Les Heroines du Mal
(The Heroines of Evil)
(FRENCH-COLOR)

Paris, May 3.
An Argos Films presentation of a Films du Jeudi production. Produced by Pierre Braunberger. Features entire cast. Directed by Walerian Borowczyk. Screenplay, Borowczyk; camera (Fujicolor), Bernard Caillencourt; art direction, Jacques D'Ovidio; costumes, Piet Bolscher; music, Olivier Dassault, Philippe D'Aram. Reviewed at Cinema Balzac Elysees, Paris, May 2, 1979. Running time: **109 MINS.**

Margherita	Marina Pierro
Raphael	Francois Guetary
Bini the banker	Jean-Claude Dreyfus
Marceline	Gaelle Legrand
Petrus	Assan Fall
Marie	Pascale Christophe
Gangster	Gerard Ismael

Walerian Borowczyk, high priest of perverse eroticism, is at it again, but his latest hymn to amoral womankind is monotonous and finally loathsome.

"Heroines of Evil" (the title is a pretentious nod to Baudelaire) is a triptych of portraits: Margherita, inspiration for the great Italian painter, Raphael, poisons both the artist and an important banker after seducing them both; Marceline, a young French girl who slaughters her parents in their sleep to avenge the death of her pet rabbit, a cute little thing whose nose may have led to the invention of the vibrator; and Marie, wife of a successful art gallery owner who is kidnapped and saved by her faithful dog, whose castrating jaws not only do in the criminal, but the woman's husband as well.

These three tales are badly written, indifferently acted and sloppily directed and edited. The erotic interludes have little groin appeal and Borowczyk's obsession with the secret communion between woman and beast is here given perfunctory and thus repulsive treatment. Even those partial to director's interests will be ovettaken by boredom.
—Len.

Between Men
(DOCU-COLOR)

Athens, Ohio, April 25.
Distributed by Ohio River Films. Produced and directed by Will Roberts. Camera (color), Steogehen Lighthill, Josh Hanig, Robert Ellis; sound, Nelson, Stoll, Marie Ashton, Peter Entell; editors, Will Roberts, Joe Gray, Charles Miller, Matt Hausle. Reviewed at Athens Cinema, Athens, Ohio, April 25, '79. Running time: **57 MINS.**

Will Roberts' first time out was Academy Award winning documentary, "Men's Lives," a study of male role in society which is used as center for consciousness-raising groups. The royalties from "Men's Lives" financed most of "Between Men," a look at masculinity and the military.

Using interview and compilation footage, Roberts poses a valid proposition for a sociological query: Why are men traditionally involved in war, and is fighting an inherently masuline trait? Soldiers from every war of this century are given a chance to theorize, with World War I vets proclaiming the object was winning and current recruits claiming that it's the money and school and jobs which make them go military.

Children, when questioned, seem to assimilate a sex segregation early, with boys claiming to be tougher and girls professing to be more "mellow." A racist anti-Japanese newsreel from World War II is used to demonstrate the dehumanization society approves in times of conflict. Vietnam veterans explain the tacit rape approval that goes with the military program, intense "buddy" relationships are mentioned, and Roberts managed to film basic training at Fort Bliss when the brass wrongly assumed National Endowment for the Arts funding implied he was making an army training film.

With an angry Viet vet expressing rage, and a mercenary of five wars coldly describing murder, "Between Men" hovers on imprecise ground from time to time without ever becoming a polemic in any direction. By toning down any position of his own, Roberts has delivered a sincere, but unsensational, delving into the broad area of war's reasons. He concludes that "the time has come to discover new directions," but he only hints at what some alternatives might be. tives might be.

The film is essentially to be used with other tools, conferences and men's groups, as a staring point for discussion. "Between Men," copremiered at Filmex and Athens International Film Festival, is a clean collection of elements which never really firms up into a defined whole, which is admittedly what Roberts intended. —*Pege.*

Dao Ruang
(The Yellow Flower)
(THAI-COLOR)

Bangkok, May 2.

A Saha Mongkol Films release. Produced by Somsak Techaratanaprasert. Executive Producer, Primprapai Galashimee. Features entire cast. Directed by Neramitr. Screenplay, Tomayanti, Tananya Prapasalobon; camera (color), Anant Inlaord; music, Universal Lab (Hong Kong); sound, Kasem Militachinda; editor and lighting, Piyakul Sudpranond; production designer, Sa-ard Guptarak; continuity, Chaluay Sriratana. Reviewed at Coliseum Theatre, Bangkok, May 1, '79. Runing time: 120 Mins.

Ruang	Lalana Sulawan
Jintawat	Tirayuth Silapirat
Pooyay Tan	Jamroon Nuatjim
Rungta	Adinan Singhilan
Panchoon	Suphan Buranaphim
Suwan	Cheng Chomaduah
Kamjorn	Sayant Chantrawiboon
Police Officer	Bu Vibulnan

The pleasure of watching "Dao Ruang" comes mainly from the uniquely Thai values in it, built around a rural love story that manages to involve just about everybody living in its small Thai village setting.

Storyline depicts how Tirayuth subdues and wins the love of a young shrew played by Lalana, who's confused whether or not she should give up her bossy, cheeky ways. "Dao Ruang" differs from the spate of love stories that have been produced during the past year in its particular emphasis on local customs and tradition in a humorous vein.

Nor are action scenes forgotten. They surface inevitably. Again the evil-doers are a bunch of illegal loggers, giving Tirayuth his opportunity to fulfill the obligatory heroic deed.

Filmmaker Neramitr (pseudonym of Amnuay Galasnimee) is an old hand in this film genre. His confident and smooth direction is evident all throughout the pic. His excellent work with the players, especially Lalana who gives an uncommonly good performance, certainly makes the movie more fun to watch than most of the other filmed love stories here that do not have a fraction of the local color in this socially and culturally enlightening pastiche. —*Cano.*

Space Coast
(COLOR)

Athens, Ohio, April 24.

Produced and distributed by Ross McElwee and Michel Negroponte. All technical credits by McElwee and Negroponte. No other credits provided. Reviewed at Athena Cinema, Athens, Ohio, April 24, '79. Running time: 90 MINS.

Ostensibly a documentary, "Space Coast" doesn't really resemble any known form. Its subject is equally unique: the sad remnants surviving near Cape Canaveral five years after the phasing out of the Apollo Moon Landing Program.

By observing the routines of three characters in the area, McElwee's and Negroponte's camera indirectly implicate the expensive and disposable aspects of society at large. Papa John, a fiftyish motorcycle gang leader is shown at home, subjugating his wife and daughter with sadistic teasing. Mary is a reporter who follows every minor rocket test and pampers her poodles. Willy, an oversize area businessman, spouts obscene and racist remarks as he takes his sons turtle hunting.

Through developing parallel glimpses, the three situations become progressively weirder. We no sooner are convinced that we have pegged these individuals than the footage will reveal some new bizarre facet. Papa John spouts theology and plays piano at church, Mary gets involved with a scheme to market dismantled rocket iron, Willy doubles as a clown on a children's tv show, and so forth.

All technical credits are smooth, and one wonders how the filmmakers managed to find such eccentrics and film them in casual intimacy. The temptation is resisted to display the people as metaphors for decaying civilization, but even the subtlety can't make marketing possibilities better than iffy due to length (although pace is painless) and one-of-kind nature of film. "Space Coast" won a Special Merit award at Athens International Film Festival in Features category this year. —*Pege.*

Cannes Festival

My Brilliant Career
(AUSTRALIAN-COLOR)

Cannes, May 17.

New South Wales Corp., GUO release and production. Features entire cast. Directed by Gill Armstrong. Screenplay, Eleanor Witcombe from the book by Miles Franklin; camera (Eastmancolor-Panavision), Don McAlpine; editor, Nick Beauman; music, Nathan Waks. Reviewed at Cannes Film Fest (competing May 16, '79.) Running time, 98 MINS.

Sybylla	Judy Davis
Harry	Sam Neill
Helen	Wendy Hughes
Frank	Robert Grubb
Gussie	Pat Kennedy
McSwart	Max Cullen

Australia is becoming a regular competer at the prestigious Cannes Film Fest as it unveils a film in the running for the second year in a row. Film is a charming look at 19th-century rural days in general and the stirrings of self realization and feminine liberation in the persona of a headstrong young girl who wants to go her own way.

Judy Davis is fine as an ugly duckling who blossoms into an independent writer and refuses to give into the ritual and place reserved for women at the time which was, namely, marriage.

She is from the poor arm of a fairly wealthy, landed family. She gets to stay with her rich grandmother where her independent ways are always admonished but where she gets the attention of a boorish British visitor and a nearby well-to-do landowner.

But she will give in to neither though a relation grows with the richer man. The latter runs into financial difficulties. The girl is shipped off to tutor and rather raffish brood of poor farm children to make up for a debt incurred by her father.

She resists marriage with the landowner, who regains his fortune, to write her book and go on with her own life. Perhaps the last part of her servitude with the farmer and his family is forced. But there is a rightness in tone in delving into the hidebound society and early flaunting of its taboos by an engaging girl. She fights off pressures and even love to find her own way thereby indicating the beginnings of an evolving female place in down under society.

Gill Armstrong can be tagged a promising new filmmaker on the Aussie scene. Film may be a bit familiar but could find some outlets abroad on its charm and neat acting down the line. —*Mosk.*

Caro Papa
(Dear Papa)
(ITALIAN-COLOR)

Cannes, May 14.

AMLF release of Dean Film, AMLF, Prospect Films release. Stars Vittorio Gassman. Directed by Dino Risi. Screenplay, Bernardino Zapponi, Marco Risi. Risi; camera (Color), Tonino Delli Colli; music, Manuel De Sica. Reviewed at Cannes Film Fest (competing), May 13, '79. Running time: 110 MINS.

Albino	Vittorio Gassman
Margot	Aurore Clement
Julia	Andre Lachapelle
Mario	Stefano Madia
Parrella	Julien Guiomar

Vittorio Gassman has built up a persona of an overbearing, self-serving type, rich or poor, exploited by director Dino Risi in this film. Latter's usual social comedies are subverted toward a more serious and timely look at political terrorism as experienced in one family.

The generation gap is clouded by the personal life styles of a rich father, head of a multinational company, and his eldest son, a member of what appears to be the Red Brigade who execute businessmen, bureaucrats, police, politicos, etc., as political moves. Father and son have a tenuous relationship at best.

Gassman is the business magnate who is not above taking business from a man he feels in his way, though a friend, leading to that man's suicide. Gassman's wife has been reduced to a mental case and he has a mistress, the wife of a friend driven overboard by the fear of terrorists.

The son seems weak but does stand up to Gassman at times and refuses to confide in him. Gassmann takes a belated interest in his son and runs across his diary poking through the boy's room. He finds a sort of code in re names and anarchic slogans and indications that his son's group, some sort of cell, is planning to kill someone whose name starts with the letter P.

Gassman thinks it might be a colleague but the P turns out to stand for papa as Gassman is gunned down. That life force is now paralyzed in a wheelchair and in a state of shock keeping him from talking. At home it is his son who wheels him to his room in a wheelchair as both cry.

Timely, yest, but somewhat reduced by near stereotyped characters and a glossy, evasive approach to such a dramatic theme. True probing of character eludes the film. It finally has a sentimental surface approach to the issues rather than probing the situation more revealingly.

Gassman does etch, a larger-than-life portrait that makes his vulgarity and lack of contact with his family a reflection of his business ethics which seem acceptable in his milieu. On its theme, and sometimes prodding reflections of the mixed social and political outlooks these days, the film should find good reactions at home with some playoff abroad despite its predictable aspects. —Mosk.

Arven
(The Heritage)
(NORWEGIAN-COLOR)

Cannes, May 14.
A Norsk Film A/S production and release. Original story and script by Anja Breien, Oddvar Bull Tuhus and Lasse Glomm. Directed by Anja Breien. Features entire cast. Camera (Eastmancolor) Erling Thurmann-Andersen; editors, Henning Carlsen, Christian Hartkopp; executive producer, Harald Ohrvik; production managers, Laila Mikkelsen, Hans Lindgren; production design, Lubos, Madla Hruza; costumes, Siri Bryhni; music, Mozart and other recordings. Reviewed (official competition entry) at Le Palais de Festival, Cannes, May 14, 1979. Running time: **90 MINS.**

Jon .... Espen Skjoenberg
Marthe .... Anita Bjoerk
Hanna .... Haege Juve
Jonas .... Jan Haarstad
Gard .... Eva Opaker

Anja Breien was born in 1940 in Norway, got her filmmaking education at the National French Film School, has worked closely with Danish director Henning Carlsen ("Hunger," a Golden Palms winner in 1966), stepped in two years ago and salvaged a major Swedish feature ("Games Of Love And Loneliness") when it found itself without a director and turned it into an accomplished work of high production and artistic value.

Having made several earlier, sharply-focused little features of her own at home in Norway, she

now, with "The Heritage" (possibly to be marketed as "Next of Kin") represents her Nordic kingdom with a woman's film that should appeal to world-wide audiences as an adult comedy. It is bitter but not black and deals with behavior patterns recognizable to everyone who has been even remotely corralled by the sudden-inheritance syndrome.

An immensely rich shipowner and head of family dies in his early fifties, leaving his survivors with company command, all the shares, all the properties, houses, valuable paintings, etc. on one condition only: they must all obey the dictates of the will (and those dictates all seem very fair), otherwise the entire estate will be turned over to a Cancer Research.

Everybody seemed satisfied until cracks in the family unity begin to show. At first over valuables not listed in the will, later over more serious matters, involving the generaton gap, marital squabbles, etc. But things get really bad (while regular suspense mounts) when the older inheritor-brother decides that he does want to receive his share at all. Meaning that everything goes to Cancer Research.

Breien plays her theme for intelligent laughs, but also probes some depths and she gives her fine cast (headed by Espen Skjoenberg in a marvelously muted performance as the older brother) good lines to speak and makes all actors speak same lines with realistic conviction, generally controlled even in their shriller moments.

The director has been handsomely served by her cinematographer (Erling Thurmann-Andersen), and her Danish editors, Henning Carlsen and Christian Hartkopp.

Every obvious trap in the film's theme is avoided by everybody involved, and "The Heritage" should prove solid entertainment of artistic merit on the commercial circuit everywhere. In a year, when Norwegian film making seems to be coming of age after many lean years, Anja Breien is surely headed for an international career. —Kell.

Spirit of the Wind
(U.S.-COLOR)

Cannes, May 17.
Raven Pictures, Doyon Ltd. release and production. Features entire cast. Directed by Ralph Liddle. Screenplay, Liddle, John Logue; camera (color), John Logue; editor, Mark Goldblatt; music, composed by, and with original songs sung by, Buffy Sainte-Marie. Reviewed at Cannes Film Fest (A Certain Look Sect.-non-competing), May 16, '79. Running time: **98 MINS.**
George .... Pius Savage
Moses .... Chief Dan George
Obie .... Slim Pickens
Father .... George Clutesi

A natural four waller. A simple

tale of Indian life in a remote part of Alaska tracing the times of a young man who became the top dog sled racer in the state.

Based on a true character, film stays surface and good intentioned as the hero becomes a winner despite a game leg which had him hospitalized for eight years.

There is a disarming quality to this film. It has a dedicated father with patriarchal dignity and natural wisdom as well as the old story-teller played with zest by Chief Dan George already known from "Little Big Man" and other films.

The life of a family living in a lovely but harsh wilderness is depicted with charm. It makes one root for the young man, when, after finding it hard to readjust to his life at home after his eight year absence, he finds a way of dedication in turning a too domesticated huskie dog into a top lead sled runner and makes himself a champion at the same time.

The life of trapping, fishing and feel of the seasons is an asset. There is a freshness in the film despite a fairly routine treatment and picturesqueness rather than more discerning insights into its theme of Indian life and its changes.

Indian problems of adjustments are touched on indirectly in scenes of drunken Indians in town. But their rural life seems well adjusted and they can stand up to a trader for payments for their furs and sometimes wonder at the ways of the whites.

Not patronizing, but a film mainly for fast playoff with tv possibilities also there on its colorful background. It is technically efficient. —Mosk

---

Les Petites Fugues
(Little Escapes)
(SWISS-FRENCH-COLOR)

Cannes, May 14.
Cactus Film, MKA Diffusion release of Film Et Video Collectif, Filmkollektiv Zuerich-Television SSR Geneve-Television FR3 Paris-Les Films 2001 production. Features entire cast. Directed by Yves Yersin. Screenplay, Yersin, Claude Muret; camera (Eastmancolor), Robert Alazraki; editor, Yersin; music, Leon Francioli. Reviewed at Cannes Film Fest (Non-competing), May 13, '79. Running time: **140 MINS.**
Pipe .... Michel Robin
Josiane .... Fabienne Barraud
Luigi .... Dore De Rosa
John .... Fred Personne
Rose .... Mista Prehac
Alain .... Laurent Sandoz
Marianne .... Nicole Vatier
Stephane .... Leo Maillard

A bucolic film about a crusty, lovable old farmhand that soars over its seemingly familiar theme in making it a tale of the spiritual realization and freedom of an old man. The sleeper of the festival which graced the official non-

competing A Certain Look auxiliary section.

Film is a bit long and could use some tightening. But this is incidental for under the seemingly minute observation of farm life, patronizing bosses and changing ways lies the universal theme of human autonomy. Michel Robin, as a crusty 66-year-old farm laborer, on the same farm for 40 years, etches an unusual character whose fanciful late life rebelliousness influences people around him.

With his old age pension he buys a motorbike. There are hilarious scenes of his learning to drive it, helped by an Italian itinerant laborer on the farm. But then Robin is off discovering the land and people around him for the first time.

After mastering the bike he one day is going down a lane when the camera, subjectively from his viewpoint, seems to soar up over the land. He has always hankered to see the Alps, too, and seems to have a spiritual trip when he follows a glider on his bike.

The daughter of his boss has an illegitimate child and Robin's attempt to free himself from the semi-slavery he has always lived in affects her. She decides to have an affair with the Italian worker and go off on her own. The farmer's son is ready to try to convert the farm to modern ways.

Robin's simplistic, stubborn growth of independence is extremely well worked out as he becomes involved in all sorts of adventures on his bike forays. He even wins a Polaroid camera. But people are not too generous and he gest into scrapes, drinks too much and finally loses his bike after a drunken accident.

But the camera allows him to study things around him. A helicopter trip around his adored Alps shows him they are just rocks after all and he has to find a way to blend his new sense of freedom with ordinary earth-bound life.

Director Yves Yersin has made only documentaries before this first fiction film. His background serves him well in observing the land and its ways. He also shows a sure-footed feel for natural human comedy sans excess and a poetic elan that might make this tale of freedom a film that could emerge a commercial as well as film fest sleeper.

Yersin can take his place with such other Swiss filmmakers known outside their borders as Alain Tanner, Claude Goretta, Daniel Schmidt and others. An intensely Swiss film with the sharp human insights and avoidance of sentimentality that could make it palatable anywhere. —Mosk.

Chrissomaloussa
(The Girl With Golden Hair)
(GREEK-COLOR)

Cannes, May 18.
Lycouressis release and production. Features entire cast. Directed by Tony Lycouressis. Screenplay, Stratis Karras. Lycouressis: camera (Eastmancolor), Andreas Bellis, editor, George Triandafillou. Reviewed at Cannes Film (Director's Fortnight-non-competing), May 17, '79.
Running time: 98 MINS.

Tassis	Anotonis Katsaris
Eleni	Vera Krouska
Guard	Vangelis Kazan
Count	T.A. Velloudios

A perceptive tale of atavistic class hangovers and repressiveness in a rural part of Greece today. A natural romantic liaison, a natural freer outlook turn into tragedy in this promising first film.

A widow, whose husband died when they were living in Germany, returns to live with her father-in-law who takes care of the grounds of the fairly impoverished old nobleman of the region.

The woman has a liaison with the local schoolteacher. The latter is more progressive and innocently tries to comment on some of the more backward aspects of the life of this area in a folk play he is doing for the region which is an annual event for the tourists.

But the woman's father-in-law secretly desires his daughter-in-law and the old nobleman and others resent the liberties and criticism the school-teacher brings to the play.

He gets into the trouble with the authorities and the woman leaves for Germany again. The father-in-law, out of ignorance, his feeling for the woman and the old codes of honor, shoots the school-teacher who mocks him.

Direction is perceptive, acting right and this reveals a promising new director in Tony Lycouressis though it might be a bit too national in its allusions for commercial chances abroad. It should get festival and non-commercial attention. —Mosk.

The Onion Field
(U.S.-COLOR)

Cannes, May 17.
An Avco Embassy release of a Black Marble Production. Screenplay, Joseph Wambaugh from his book. Produced by Walter Coblenz. Directed by Harold Becker. Stars John Savage, James Woods. Franklyn Seales, Ronny Cox. Music, Eumir Deodato: production design by Brian Eatwell: editor, John W. Wheeler; camera (color), Charles Rosher, asst. director. Tom Mack; sound editor, Keith Stafford; set decoration. Dick Goddard: set design, Joe Hubbard: technical advisors courtroom, Phillip Halpin, Dino Fulgoni, technical advisor police procedure. Richard Falk. Reviewed at Le Rex, Cannes, May 17 '79. Running time: 122 MINS.

Karl Hettinger	John Savage
Greg Powell	James Woods
Jimmy Smith	Franklyn Seales
Ian Campbell	Ted Danson
Pierce Brooks	Ronny Cox
District Attorney Phil Halpin	David Huffman
Jailhouse Lawyer	Christopher Lloyd
Helen Hettinger	Diane Hull
Chrissie Campbell	Priscilla Pointer
Greg's Woman	Beege Barkett
Beat Cop	Richard Herd
Emmanuel McFadden	Le Tari
Glenn Bates	Richard Venture
Billy	Lee Weaver
District Attorney Marshall Schulman	Phillip R. Allen
Jimmy's Lawyer No. 2	Pat Corley
Mrs. Powell	K. Callan
Mr. Powell	Sandy McPeak
Nana	Lillian Randolph
LAPD Captain	Ned Wilson
IAD Captain	Jack Rader
Judge No. 2	Raleigh Bond
Red Haired Cop	Brad English
Greg's Lawyer No. 2	Stanley Grover
District Attorney Dino Fulgoni	Michael Pataki

A highly-detailed dramatization of a true case, "The Onion Field" deals in its two hours with death and guilt; and the manipulation of the judicial system to pervert justice. As is to be expected, the subject is viewed from the standpoint of the victim, in this case a policeman whose partner was murdered by two petty criminals. That he escaped alive is his burden, and his entire life is affected by the incident.

In so far as the story's originator was a working policeman when he wrote it, it is understandable that the eventual screenplay should depict the two killers as seen from in back of the badge. On the evidence presented it is very difficult for the viewer to make out a sympathetic case for the pair — which is clearly the writer's intention. They seem to represent how American justice has been redefined as to tip the scales against society.

Set in 1963, two plainclothes cops on patrol in Hollywood stop a couple of suspicious-looking punks in a car. In a swift moment one of the bad guys pulls a gun and the cops are disarmed and kidnapped. They are taken to an onion field miles away and one is brutally murdered. The second makes his escape. The two killers are quickly arrested, they each agree to cooperate, but each claims the other did the killing.

On this confusion, the prosecution's case flounders and the trials and re-trials drag on for years. Concurrently the survivor goes through bouts of self-tortuous guilt and is forced to resign from the force. The clear thesis of the film is that it is often the innocent who pay while the guilty escape without payment.

The picture's strength is in the superb performances of its leading actors. Woods as the near-psychotic Powell is chillingly effective, creating a flakiness in the character that exudes the danger of a live wire near a puddle.

Savage, as the guilt-ridden Hettinger, finely draws a complex human being whose character undergoes a hideous trauma. And Seales is excellent as Smith, the punk out of his depth and dragged along by events he helped create.

Standout in a supporting role is Lee Weaver as Billy, the black, street-wise, petty criminal who brings Powell and Smith together.

Wambaugh's script dots all the "i's" and crosses all the "t's" as thoroughly as if he were preparing evidence — which in a sense he is. If anything, the film could have gained from a tightening in its expositional episodes.

Becker directs with a sure hand and Rosher provides him with some marvellous visual atmospherics, capturing equally well the seediness of the street scenes and the abject horror of senseless and sudden death in an open field at night. All other tech credits uniformly high.

Commercial chances are "iffy" without intense educational campaign to convince the consumer that this isn't just another cops and killers story. Good use could be made of Savage who since making this has come to fame in "The Deer Hunter." Also, the best-seller aspects of Wambaugh's book could help, though the time passed between publication (in 1973) and now could have eroded public enthusiasms. —Miha.

Zulu Dawn
(BRITISH-COLOR)

Cannes, May 16.
An Orion Pictures release (Warners in U.S.) of a Lamitas presentation of a Samarkand Production. Producer, Nate Kohn; executive producer, Barrie Saint Claire: co-producer, James Faulkner. Stars Burt Lancaster, Peter O'Toole. Simon Ward. Directed by Douglas Hickox. Original story and scenario, Cy Enfield: screenplay Cy Enfield, Anthony Storey; music, Elmer Bernstein; asst. director John O'Connor; camera (Technicolor), Ousama Rawi; sound mixer, Robin Gregory; editor, Malcolm Cook: production designer, John Rosewarne: art director, Peter Williams: action sequences/stunt coordinator, Bob Simmons: second unit director David Tomblin. Previewed at L'Olympia, Cannes, May 15, '79. Running Time: 117 MINS.

Colonel Durnford	Burt Lancaster
Lord Chelmsford	Peter O'Toole
William Vereker	Simon Ward
Sir Bartle Frere	John Mills
Colonel Hamilton-Brown	Nigel Davenport
Colonel Crealock	Michael Jayston
Norris Newman	Ronald Lacey
Lt. Col. Pulleine	Denholm Elliott
Bishop Colenso	Freddie Jones
Lt. Coghill	Christopher Cazenove
Lt. Harford	Ronald Pickup
Major Russell	Donald Pickering
Fanny Colenso	Anna Calder-Marshall
Lt. Melvill	James Faulkner
Quartermaster Sgt.	Peter Vaughn
Capt. Shepstone	Graham Armitage
Company Sg.	
Maj. Williams	Bob Hoskins
Pvt. Williams	Dai Bradley
Pvt. Storey	Paul Copley
Lt. Milne, Royal Navy	Christ Chittell
Lt. Raw	Nicholas Clay
Maj. Harness	Patrick Mynhardt
Maj. Smith	Brian O'Shaughnessy
Cetshwayo	Simon Sabela
Lt. Cavaye	Midge Carter
Boy Soldier Pullen	Phil Daniels
Sgt. Murphy	Raymond Davies
C.S.M. Kambula	Ken Gampu

Somehow throughout the country's history the British have managed to turn their major military defeats into moral victories; not least the subject of "Zulu Dawn," the Battle of Islandlhwana wherein some 1,500 redcoats were slaughtered by 16 times their number of Zulu warriors led by legendary chief Cetshwayo.

The film is, in fact, a sort of "prequel" to the 1964 picture "Zulu," which dealt with an heroic stand at Rorke's Drift by a small band of British soldiers in January, 1879. Islandlhwana took place hours before that action, which is alluded to in passing in the current film. Small wonder: Cy Enfield wrote and directed "Zulu" and is the main scripting source for "Zulu Dawn." It's almost as though he couldn't bear to waste his original research.

The later film, however, deals more with the strategy of the politico-military situation in Natal, even if in order to make it readily palatable to mass audiences, it treats a complex power play in a somewhat simplistic manner. It would be difficult for the script not to take that approach because the film is a wide-vista'd spectacle and little else than a gigantic set battle piece.

The action sequences are superbly handled, as are the scenes in which the men and material are assembled and manoeuvered. For sheer scope and numbers of people being manipulated for the cameras, "Zulu Dawn" is positively De Mill-esque in scale.

Characterization is dealt with in cinematic shorthand, with Sir Henry Bartle Frere (John Mills) as he sends in the troops, delivering lines such as, "Let us hope, gentlemen, that this will be in the Final Solution (sic) to the Zulu problem."

Such banality as there is is, thankfully, confined to the expositional sequences which are quickly gotten out of the way to allow the army to get on the march. It is a matter of historical fact that the British were ineptly led and brilliantly out-generaled by the native chief (played by the outstanding South African actor Simon Sabela). In all it was a sorry moment for British soldiery.

Given the subject and events, it is hard to see how Enfield and Hickox could have made a more intimate film — and one of the original film's greatest assets was the way in which it dealt with the microcosmic relationships within the texture of a spectacle. Maybe it is just that the ordinary soldier in these affairs is more interesting than his leaders. Other films which take great battles as their subject would tend to bear out that opinion.

Quite where a film like "Zulu Dawn" fits in a contemporary international release structure is a problem Orion and Warners will have to solve: the film will have to recoup an enormous amount of money before it shows a profit. And it is a question as to whether there is a market for expensive period war films that revisit an area of such memorable success.

Technical credits are faultless with much praise due to some superb sound mixing by Robin Gregory. He orchestrates his effects to create a chilling menace as the natives gather. Bernstein's music is also evocative, drawing on contemporaneous hymns as passing lietmotifs within his major theme, and driving the drama on.

Thesping talent is there in abundance —*Miha.*

A Very Big Withdrawal
(CANADIAN-COLOR)

Cannes, May 14.
Avco Embassy release of a Bennett Films in association with McNichol presentation. Stars Donald Sutherland, Brooke Adams, Paul Mazursky. Executive Producer, Frederick W. Field. Producers, Peter Samuelson and John B. Bennett. Directed by Noel Black. Screenplay, Raynold Gideon, Bruce A. Evans, from a story by Gideon and Evans; camera (color), Jack Cardiff; editor, Carl Kress. Reviewed at the Regent Theatre, Cannes, May 14, 1979. Running time: **100 MINS.**
Reese .... Donald Sutherland
Stacey .... Brooke Adams
Norman .... Paul Mazursky
Peter .... Allan Magicovsky
Marie .... Leigh Hamilton
Gino .... Nick Rice

Donald Sutherland, Brooke Adams, and Paul Mazursky team up for what should be the comedy pic of the season. It's a terrific, fast-paced, smoothly-acted story of two computer experts who plug into a bank under construction and then take out millions without being caught.

Adams is along for the love interest, unaware fo the caper until far along. By that time, she's hooked to Sutherland and free of a schnook played crisply by Allan Magicovsky. She won't tell and the three escape happily on a plane to Macao where the money is being stashed.

Filmed in Vancouver and in Hong Kong and Macao, this one's bright, breezy, well directed by Noel Black, smartly edited by Carl Kress, and shot handsomely by Jack Cardiff. Sutherland's loose and Mazursky reads his lines as if they were improvised on the spot. Adams is dandy. Together, they make a delightful trio and they should be reunited soon. A perfect crime and a perfectly good time in this one for adults of any age. —*Adil.*

The Kids Are Alright
(BRITISH-COLOR/B&W)

Cannes, May 14.
A Rock Films presentation. Produced by Bill Curbishley, Tony Klinger. Executive producer, Sydney Rose. Directed by Jeff Stein. Stars Pete Townshend, Roger Daltrey, John Entwistle, Keith Moon (The Who). Camera (color), Peter Nevard, Norman Wexler, Tony Richmond; editor, Ed Rothkowitz; music, Peter Townshend; musical director, John Entwistle; production managers, Tim Van Rellim, Peter Price. Reviewed at the Olympia Cinema, Cannes, May 13, '79. Running time: **96 MINS.**

As a full length, compilation documentary feature on the British rock group, The Who, "The Kids Are Alright" (title is a track from a '60s album, "My Generation") is jumbled, inadequately informative and bereft of an angle, but still lovely enough to reap okay returns from fast theatrical playoff in hardtop and drive-in situations.

The film is saved, in fact, by the band members' own talents to entertain, whether with their music or via the many mercilessly irreverent interviews they've given during their 15-year career. The largely arbitrary assemblage of old media material (some black-and-white, and a good deal transferred from videotape) and new footage of two recent, specially-staged concerts scores little through the efforts of the filmmaker, Jeff Stein.

It's watchable because The Who is as good a combo to see as to hear; because guitarist-composer Pete Townshend has always possessed a gift — unusual among rock artists — for articulating his own shifting frustrations and aspirations, and those of a generation; and because drummer Keith Moon, who died last year, was, in Townshend's words, "different from anyone else I'd ever met."

With some poignancy, Moon — who during a famous British tv chatshow describes himself to host Russel Harty as a "rust repairer and fulltime survivor" — dominates the interview clips. The film thus comes across more as a retrospective tribute than a promotion exercise, at odds with the band's current keenness to establish an ongoing identity with Moon's replacement, Kenney Jones, now confirmed in the lineup.

Best by far are the onstage sequences, and the older the footage, the more intriguing. Numbers from the recent concerts are performed at full strength, well lit, and well recorded. Scattered through the film, they suffer only from lack of a sense of time and place, chiefly because there are no shots of the venues

(London's Shepperton film studios and a suburban theatre), nor of the invited audiences.

By not arranging the offstage material chronologically, nor — perhaps advisedly — adding a commentary, Stein's aim seems to have been to build a general picture of The Who as relentless flouters of convention, and leave it at that. Commercially, the concentration on frivolities is hardly damaging.

But there's room for more inventive images like the set up scene where John Entwistle machine-guns gold disks tossed in the air like clay pigeons. Room, too, for more thoughtful (if dated) verbalizings such as Townshend's extant interview with Tony Palmer in a 1968 telefilm, "All My Loving," of which only a fraction is used. —*Simo.*

Das Fuenfte Gebot
(The Fifth Commandment)
(WEST GERMAN-COLOR)

Cannes, May 12.
An Oase-Film Production, Jelka Naber-Le..., producer; distributed by Neue Constantin Film; world rights, Mike Freudenstein. Filmgroup, Rome. Features entire cast. Directed by Duccio Tessari. Screenplay, Michael Lentz, Tessari; camera (color), Jost Vacano; editing, Eugenio Alabiso; sets, Bernhard Sauter; music, Armando Trovaioli. Reviewed at Cannes Film Festival (Market), May 11, '79. Running time: **113 MINS.**

Cast: Helmut Berger (Bernhard Redder), Peter Hooten (Leo Redder), Udo Kier (Peter Duemmel), Heinrich Giskes (Linnemann).

"The Fifth Commandment" drew attention in Germany due to efforts of a well-known film critic Michael Lentz to write and produce his own pic, helmed by Italowestern director Duccio Tessari. The result is a cross between an Italian action pic and Bonnie-and-Clyde theme (some scenes apparently adapted for original). All of which adds up to a formula pic without much of a personal touch.

The scene is the industrial Ruhr section in western Germany during the inflationary Twenties, when two brothers from Essen, the Redder Boys, became wanted criminals for armed robbery and murder. Pic shows at outset how both were badly treated at home as youngsters by a tyrannical father, against whom they rebelled, and later how they were duped into joining a pack of Nazi stormtroopers on weekend bully excusions. Film is a portrait of Nazi "Stahlhelm" and "Freikorps" movement as well, which makes it worth a looksee.

Credits are a good cut above average, and thesp performances okay. —*Holl.*

Fast Company
(CANADIAN-COLOR)

Cannes, May 16.
Danton Films (Canada) presentation of a Quadrant Films production. Executive producer, David Perlmutter. Producers, Michael Lebowitz, Peter O'Brian, Courtney Smith. Directed by David Cronenberg. Features entire cast. Screenplay, Phil Savath, Courtney Smith, David Cronenberg, from original story by Alan Treen; camera (color), Mark Irwin; editor, Ron Sanders; art director, Carol Spier. Reviewed at Les Ambassadeurs, Cannes, May 16, '79. Running time: **90 MINS.**
Lonnie "Lucky Man"
Johnson .... William Smith
Phil Adamson .... John Saxon
Sammy .... Claudia Jennings
Billy "The Kid"
Brooker .... Nicholas Campbell
Elder .... Don Francks
Gary "The Blacksmith"
Black .... Cedric Smith
Candy .... Judy Foster
Meatball .... George Buza

A snappy, showy, no nonsense dragstrip racing pic, "Fast Company" should do well in drive-ins, non-classy urban centres, and with people who follow stripped down cars.

The plot hinges on a champion driver who runs afoul of the motor oil company for whom he races. It picks a younger guy and he and cohorts steal their car back and race it. William Smith acquits himself well as the fading star as does Claudia Jennings as his long distance lover.

There's hunkered down direction by David Cronenberg but what's missing is a focus on car groupies. Only one scene has car bunnies getting motor oil poured down their naked breasts. John Saxon comes off nicely as the oil company bad guy and there are competent performances by Nicholas Campbell, Cedric Smith, Judy Foster, and Don Francks. —*Adil.*

Palm Beach
(AUSTRALIAN-COLOR)

Cannes, May 12.
An Albie Thoms Production. Produced and directed by Albie Thoms. Features entire cast. Screenplay, Thoms; camera (color), Oscar Scherl; location sound, Michael Moore; production manager, Bob Hill; asst. director, Jan Chapman; editing, Thoms; a helicopter photography, Keith Lamber, Terry Lee; music, Terry Hannigan. Reviewed at Les Ambassadeurs VII, Cannes, May 11, 1979. Running time: **88 MINS.**
Nick Naylor .... Nat Young
Joe Ryan .... Ken Brown
Leilani Adams .... Amanda Berry
Paul Kite .... Bryan Brown
Kate O'Brien .... Julie McGregor
Larry Kent .... John Flaus
Wendy Naylor .... Bronwyn Stevens-Jones
Zane Green .... David Lourie
Rupert Roberts .... Peter Wright
Eric Tailor .... John Clayton
Mrs. Adams .... Lyn Collingwood
David Litvinoff .... Adrian Rawlins
Det. Sgt. Robinson .... P.J. Jones
Magazine editor .... Mick Eyre
Art School Dean .... Jim Roberts

Art School Student .... Cathy Power
Board Polisher .... Mick Winter
Boardshop Owner .... Tony Hardwick
Projectionist .... David Elfick

"Palm Beach" marks the feature film debut of Albie Thoms who is Australia's leading avant-gardiste — or at any rate was, because this film is a fast-paced thriller of the most commercial kind, and well in the mainstream. Plot concerns four main story lines that converge on the eponymous locale, Sydney's equivalent of Malibu.

Tightly edited, though with long takes, the film derives much of its pace from Thoms's use of overlapping sound. It is in the pic's audio track that the director's filmmaking background is most evident.

Julian Ellingworth's sound mix deserves kudos because — at least to Aussie-orientated ears — there is no confusion other than what was clearly intended. However, subtitling would pose nearly insurmountable problems, and dubbing perhaps would be only slightly easier.

Shot originally in 16m and blown-up to 35m, the picture if anything is visually-enhanced by the resulting grain gain. The effect creates a "newsier" style, underlining the storyline's immediacy.

The four interwoven tales concern a desperate unemployed (Bryan Brown) who eventually resorts to sticking-up a supermarket (with a gun he stole at a party) and who takes it on the lam and ends up in a cave; a promiscuous teenage runaway, (Amanda Berry) being trailed by a private eye (John Flaus); and a petty criminal (Ken Brown) who is seeking a drug deal.

Gradually over the 88 minutes, the stories counter-cross and culminate at the resort, none entirely satisfactorily for the characters. Flaus, an amateur thesp who is otherwise a lecturer on film, turns in a fine performance as Larry Kent, whose underlying seediness is neatly summed-up at the end when, at an ironic moment (the cops solved his case), he wearily takes off his toupee.

Bryan Brown is one of the recent crop of young local actors, and one currently very active and thus in danger of over-exposure, (he is in four of the 16 Aussie films at Cannes). Luckily, Brown turns in consistently good performances, though, conveying the coiled-spring, potential violence that often marks an emerging major talent.

Tech credits are all commendable, but standout is Terry Hannigan's music which provides a pacemaking sub-pattern and at the same time makes for smooth elides between the various elements.

Such in-jokes that Thoms includes are bonuses for the knowledgeable, but happen so fast that the non-cognescenti would fail to notice, and thus miss without offense. In all it is what it set out to be: a quick, slick flick. And one that asks of its audience very little for what they get back. Thoms has a difficult picture to market outside Australia, but should have little or no trouble recouping his investment domestically. —Miha.

The Magician Of Lublin
(ISRAELI-W. GERMAN-COLOR)

Cannes, May 19.
A Golan-Globus Presentation of a N.F. Geria III Production. Produced by Menahem Golan, Yoram Globus. Executive Producer, Harry N. Blum. Star Alan Arkin. Directed by Menahem Golan. Written by Irving S. White, Menahem Golan, based on novel by Isaac Bashevis Singer; camera (color). David Gurfinkel; editor, Dov Henig; music; Maurice Jarre; art-direction; Yurgent Kibach. Viewed at the Club Cinema, Cannes, May 18, '79. Running time: 115 MINS.

Yasha Mazur .... Alan Arkin
Emilia .... Louise Fletcher
Zeftel .... Valerie Perrine
Elizabeta .... Shelley Winters
Magda .... Maia Danziger
Esther .... Linda Bernstein
Wolsky .... Lou Jacobi
Shmul .... Shai K. Ophir
Bolek .... Lachi Nov

No effort has been spared to make this production of Isaac Bashevis Singer's novel as lush and colorful as possible. Shot in Berlin and profiting from a substantial subvention accorded by the municipality to encourage filmmaking there, the film is one of the more ambitious projects of Menahem Golan, who had planned for a very long time to film this specific story.

Indeed, there is much to attract any filmmaker to this story of a wandering Jewish magician, endowed with many unusual talents, including an irresistible charm to women and an unending urge to improve himself in every way, from making love to the perfection of his trade, symbolized by his dream of performing one day the impossible feat of flying.

As Bashevis Singer wrote it, this could be a treatise on the relationship between artist and society, this could also be the saga away from and then back to faith, for a Jew from Eastern Europe, and finally, and probably most importantly, this is once again, as in most of Singer's work, a nostalgic reminiscence of Jewish life in that part of the world, with a mixture of mysticism and metaphysics giving it a particularly wondrous aspect.

As far as production values go, Golan has made a fair job, but of course, there is much more than a string of events to be told here. Selecting from the story some of the juicier parts and making use of the ample endowments of Valerie Perrine, the feline build of Maya Danziger and asking even Shelley Winters to bare her bosom, he is pretty efficient in interpolating the different love interests in the life of Yasha Mazur.

But, as this is done, he rests his case, missing all of the real inner struggles of the character, and the overwhelming charm he can turn on at will.

The camera work of David Gurfinkel is directed toward the picturesque, shooting often against the sun, using filters to diffuse light and trying to get as many warm hues as possible on the screen, but it passes all the mystery by and the implications which should be derived from the action, if the spirit of Singer was to be kept alive.

Golan, who in his better films can keep a story rolling at a nice pace, does it again here but his direction lacks subtlety and insight. What may seem particularly disturbing is the fact that Jewish traditions and Jewish thought, which are basic for anyone wishing to cope with Singer, are sadly missing.

While much thought and planning seems to have gone into the background, the foreground is rather less successful, mostly because all the leads are giving rather lackluster and pedestrian performances. Alan Arkin tries to get by in fits of hysteria, and such experienced performers as Louise Fletcher and Winters are just reading their lines and hamming it up every time the situation gets out of hand. One laudable exception is Lou Jacobi, playing Yasha's impresario with all the warmth and understanding that all the other characters lack.

Still, the film may find its audience on the strength of its international cast, and it is quite possible that for a public which will consider it simply as a picturesque historical yarn, with plenty of action and breastbaring, there will be no complaints. —Edna.

Felicite
(FRENCH-COLOR)

Cannes, May 15.
Gaumont release of Les Films 2001 — Gaumont production. Features entire cast. Written and directed by Christine Pascal. Camera (Eastmancolor), Yves Lafaye; editor, Thierry Derocles; music, Antoine Duhamel. Reviewed at Cannes Film Fest (Non-competing). May 14. '79. Running time: 96 MINS.
Felicite .... Christine Pascal
Girl .... Dominique Laffin
Mother .... Monique Chaumette
Father .... Paul Crauchet
Boyfriend .... Chil Marx

Sister .... Judith Founry
Doctor .... Jean Champior

Christine Pascal lets it hang way out in this intense personal pic she wrote, directed and acted in. There is a strip tease, masturbation, vivid explorations of the past, dreams of love without rational basis or true human relations as a young woman goes through a night of jealousy that has triggered her drinking and a fragmented, hallucinatory exploration of her life.

Pascal, a thin, intense dark thesp with off-beat good looks, shows a flair for visual ideas, pacing and an obvious intensity that allay somewhat the faults of a first time that is too indulgent in re personal ideas and tics that are not always clear.

Pascal goes to a film with her current lover. She runs off when he runs into an old friend and he invites her to join them after the film. At home she drinks heavily and flashes back to a childhood with a mother who stifled her children by an overbearing attitude towards them.

Pascal as child is shamed when the mother insists she is getting too heavy and develops a fear of eating. A mitten covers a hand whose thumb she sucks. But she goes against these constraints.

There are dream patterns of the mother coming back to haunt her and walks in sordid streets where she finds a sleazy club for her strip-tease and is followed by a man for a love bout in a strange period decorated room. There are intimations of bestiality with a large slavering dog to boot.

The boy friend finally comes home and she insists on knowing all the details of his lovemaking in a rather provocative indication of perversity or exorcism of her jealousy.

Though often too private, film does have moments of revelations into the facing of parental death and attempts at self realization and understanding. Just somewhat too indulgent and finally exhibitionistic. But it marks Pascal an interesting directorial debutant, who, with help on a script, might add a new director to the French film scenes. Exploitation handles are there, plus some cultist possibilities, for offshore spotting.
—Mosk.

Die Faust In Der Tasche
(Fist in the Pocket)
(WEST GERMAN-COLOR)

Cannes, May 14.
A Basis Film Production, West Berlin. Features entire cast. Written and directed by Max Willutzki. Camera (color), Mario Masini; editing, Ola Hoef; sets, Goetz Heymann; music, Satin Whale; asst. director, Claudia Holldack. Reviewed at Cannes Film Festival (Market), May 13, '79. Run-

ning time: **106 MINS.**

Cast: Ernst Hannawald (Wolle), Ursela Monn (Elke), Manfred Krug (Brother Lukas), Jakobeit Benz (Eddie), Tommi Piper (Archie), Inge Wolffberg, Gerd Holtenau, Albet Venohr, Friedhelm Lehmann, Horst Pinnow, Isolde Chalpek.

———

One of those committed message pix about the social problems in West Germany, Max Willutzki's "Fist in the Pocket" leaves nothing to the imagination in a rundown on the unemployment headaches among the youth of West Berlin. Everybody takes a bow: good and bad neighborhood toughs, a religious "Boys' Town" cleric fighting for his kids, lame-brain public officials and religious leaders, and so on. The climax, of course, takes place at a Youth Club the pet project of the Catholic Brother in danger of being shut down due to the shenanigans going on there.

Thesp Manfred Krug (recently a starliner in East Germany) makes his first pic in the West and nearly saves "Fist in the Pocket" from a very inept script, although he isn't given more than cliches to work with in the first place. Ernst Hannawald (his debut was recently in Wolfgang Petersen's "The Consequence") plays the painter's apprentice without a job, but too hotheaded to figure out where to go from there. Lesing and credits so-so. —*Holl.*

La Nona
(The Grandmother)
(ARGENTINIAN-COLOR)

———

Cannes, May 13.

An Aries Cinematografica Argentina S.A. production. Directed by Hector Olivera. Features entire cast. Screenplay, Roberto Cossa, Hector Olivera, based on play of same name by Roberto Cossa; exec producers, Fernando Ayala and Luis Osvaldo Repetto; camera (Eastmancolor), Victor Hugo Caula; sets, Oscar Piruzanto; music, Oscar Cardozo Ocampo; editor, Carlos Julio Piaggio. Reviewed at Les Ambassadeurs (Cannes) May 12, '79. Running time: **74 MINS.**
La Nona .... Pepe Soriano
Chicho .... Juan Carlos Altavista
Carmelo .... Osvaldo Terranova
Marta .... Graciela Alfano
Anyula .... Eva Franco
Don Francisco ...... Guillermo Francisco
Maria .... Nya Quesada

———

"La Nona" is "black humor," at times with Italo overtones, with some very funny episodes. But what makes pic click, even more than a lively, down-to-earth script is the magnificent performance by Pepe Soriano in the part of the ancient "grandma." Though at times pic moves along too much on an even emotional plane, it nonetheless provides ample entertainment value to assure off-shore sales in Latin American as well as other world markets.

Yarn revolves around a 100-year-old parasitic grandmother living in the midst of a humble Argentinian family. Problem is that the decrepit old lady never stops eating and is literally devouring the family out of house and home. Various plans are developed by the hard-working son and his shiftless brother to solve the unappeasable appetite of the grandmother. First they try to send the lazy, song-composing brother out to work, so as to help with the family income. La Nona is then deposited on the doorstep of an old-age home; she's married off to an aged candy-store owner, and finally, in desperation, the family tries to poison her. But all to no avail. She outlives them all. Pic ends with her innocently shuffling off and being invited into the house of a wealthy family "for a piece of birthday cake."

Olivera, who together with partner Fernando Ayala, is one of Argentina's top directors, writers and producers, does include some very oblique critiques of life in Argentina. But it would be foolish to look for political overtones in what is clearly a straightforward comedy. Olivera and Soriano's backgrounds notwithstanding. Supporting cast is excellent and all technical credits up to crack. Basically this is a wry and funny film that should appeal to a broad base of audiences. —*Besa.*

Tim
(AUSTRALIAN-COLOR)
Cannes, May 12.

A Pisces Production of a Michael Pate film. Produced and directed by Michael Pate. Stars Piper Laurie, Mel Gibson. Screenplay, Pate from novel by Colleen McCullough; camera (color), Paul Onorato; editor, David Stiven; art direction, John Carroll; sound, Bob Cogger, Les McKenzie; asst. director, Michael Midlam. Reviewed at Les Ambassadeurs VII, Cannes, May 11, '79. Running time: **108 MINS.**
Mary Horton .... Piper Laurie
Tim Melville .... Mel Gibson
Ron Melville .... Alwyn Kurts
Emily Melville .... Pat Evison
Tom Ainsley .... Peter Gwynne
Dawn Melville .... Deborah Kennedy
Mick Harrington .... David Foster
Mrs. Harrington .... Margo Lee
Mr. Harrington .... James Condon
John Martinson .... Michael Caulfield
Mrs. Parker .... Brenda Senders
Dr. Perkins .... Brian Barrie
Curly Campbell .... Kevin Leslie
Secretary .... Louise Pago
Ambulance Attendant ..... Arthur Faynes
Minister .... Geoff Usher
Marriage
Celebrant .... Sheila McGuire-Taylor
Mr. Thompson .... Alan Penny
Mrs. Martinson .... Catherine Bray
Maudie .... Doris Goddard

———

Michael Pate's first feature is a film deliberately kept small, focussing as it does on the growing relationship between a woman in her mid-forties (Piper Laurie) and the denominative Tim (Mel Gibson), who is a functioning 24-year old illiterate with an I.Q. in the mid-80s: clinically a moron.

What initially attracts her to him is his sheer physical beauty, though she's too-up-tight a character to admit it to herself. She hires him as her part-time gardener, a neat psychological displacement, and eventually plies him with tea and chocolate cake. Her growing — sexually disinterested — interest in the boy takes shape in the form of her teaching him to read. Concurrently, the boy's parents come to trust the older woman and appreciate her interest in their son.

It is possible to view "Tim" on any number of levels, ascribing it a sub-text that conveys how ill-served the mentally retarded are by society. One can equally apply a super-structure to the characters, giving them life and motivations that aren't spelled out on the screen. The film can also be viewed as unadulterated schmaltz.

This last opinion would be supported by the audio track which has Eric Jupp's lushly romantic score underlining every emotional moment. At times it is in danger of turning the pathos into bathos, and it wouldn't take more than a couple of rowdies in the audience to tip the scales.

Pate's script from Colleen McCulloch's first novel (she since went on to write "The Thorn Birds") varies from the book, but in no way is unfaithful to its theme. Some changes were necessary because of the period change — Pate up-dates it from the 1950's — and some were required by the difficulty in making them conform to screen terms.

What he has done is strip away a sub-plot which has Tim relating to other retardees at a school for the mentally handicapped. This hasn't hurt the flow or created problems in understanding the problems involved, however. What it has done possibly is to lighten the potential oppressiveness of the subject.

There is no denying that for a lot of the time Pate is going for the moist-eye, and Gibson's performance is frequently very affecting. But as the pair's affection grows, though Laurie gradually loses her initial stiffness, at no time does she really seem to be relaxed.

Onorato's camerawork is rich, endowing the visuals with an aura seen rarely even in Australian films, which are noted for their consistent good looks. Other technical credits are excellent, as are the main supporting actors with the nod going especially to Kurts as Tim's gruff but loving father.

Production values are tops giving the film a much more expensive look than you'd see in the budget sheets. Funding came from the Australian Film Commission, the New South Wales Film Corp., GUO Film Distributors (who thus get the rights Down Under) and the Nine Network. —*Miha.*

City On Fire
(CANADIAN-COLOR)

———

Cannes, May 14.

Astral Films (Canada) release of an Astral Bellevue Pathe production. Executive producers, Sandy Howard, Harold Greenberg. Producer, Claude Heroux. Features entire cast. Directed by Alvin Rakoff. Screenplay, Jack Hill, David P. Lewis, Celine LaFreniere; camera (color), Rene Verzier; music, William McCauley, Matthew McCauley; editor, Jean-Pol Passet, Jacques Clairoux; sound, Patrick Rousseau. Reviewed at the Rex Theatre, Cannes, May 14, '79. Running time: **104 MINS.**
Dr. Frank Whitman ...... Barry Newman
Diana Brockhurst-Lautrec ...Susan Clark
Nurse Andrea Harper .... Shelley Winters
Mayor William Dudley ..... Leslie Nielsen
Jimbo .... James Franciscus
Maggie Grayson .... Ava Gardner
Fire Chief Risley .... Henry Fonda
Herman Stover .... Jonathan Welsh

———

An oil refinery explodes in a city affected by a long hot summer of drought. Good idea for a disaster pic? You bet. But this one never delivers the goods. It's potted by chronically slow direction, near comatose acting from most of the leading actors, and punk effects.

At best, it's an aneasthetized disaster effort, at worst an unintended comedy send-up of what could have been. What makes matter worse is that a newly opened hospital is the pivotal location and patients all look so sunny and healthy that one wonders if they're in the right film.

Henry Fonda is an amazingly slow fire chief; Ava Gardner, back on the screen after some absence, a drink-happy tv news anchor personality who seems to be on the air all day even before the disaster; and Shelley Winters, a mouthy head nurse who's wrongly cast.

Coming out of this one with some charm are Susan Clark as a wealthy widow and Jonathan Welsh as a disgruntled refinery mechanic who sets up the blaze.

Snails pace editing, ridiculous scripting that has no one really in a panic state, and a couple of suggestions of love and sex interest are all a part of this package, too. Pre-sold to CBS, "City On Fire" fails on most counts. It's plain dull and badly done. —*Adil.*

Les Fabuleuses Aventures du Legendaire Baron de Munchausen
(The Fabulous Adventures of the Legendary Baron Munchausen)
(FRENCH-ANIMATED-COLOR)

———

Cannes, May 17.

Produced by Les Films Jean Image. Directed by Jean Image. Screenplay, Image and France Image; dialog, France Image and Serge Nadaud; animation, Olivier Bonnet. Denis Boutin. Jean-Pierre Jacquet; music. Michel Legrand; decors. Enrique Gonzalez; camera (color), Per Ofal Csongovai. Reviewed at Les Ambassades Theatre. Cannes, May 16, '79. Running time: **78 MINS.**

A new animated cartoon for children by veteran artisan Jean Image, with a distinctly European flavor, but which could click with kids worldwide, through probably mainly via television.

The film's strong points are its well-defined characters, which will be simple for young audiences to understand, led by the cheerful, moustache-twirling Baron, and use of bright, paintbox colors that will help youngsters get close to the picture. The animation is more basic than the smooth flowing output of the Disney studio, but is not lacking in jerky charm.

Baron Munchausen loves to tell his dinner guests stories of his far-fetched exploits, and here recounts the adventures that came his way when the king asked him to deliver a gift to an Oriental pasha.

Story line holds up in the main, though is not always strong is some of the situations, which need more bite and wit. Though the laughs do not come thick and fast, there is absence of unpleasant violence and frights. —*Ted.*

Trilogie Des Wiedersehens
(Trilogy of Wiedersehens)
(WEST GERMAN-COLOR)

Cannes, May 14.
A Regina Ziegler Film Production, West Berlin. Features cast. Directed by Peter Stein. Features entire cast. Screenplay, Botho Strauss based on his drama; camera (color), Michael Ballhaus; sets, Karl-Ernst Herrmann; editing, Clarissa Ambach; sound, Peter Kellerhals. Reviewed at Cannes Film Festival (Market), May 13, '79. Running time: **128 MINS.**
Cast: Lipgart Schwartz (Susanne), Peter Fritz (Moritz), Otto Maechtlinger (Fçanz), Gerd Wameling (Answald), Elke Petri (Elfriede), Ben Becker (Klaeschen), Werner Rehm (Lothar), Edith Clever (Ruth), Tina Engel (Marlies), Roland Schaefer (Felix), Sabine Andreas Johanna), Otto Sander (Richard), Hans Madin (Martin), Christine Oesterlein (Viviane), Paul Burian (Peter), Guenter Mayer (Kiepert).

Peter Stein, the play director who made the Schaubuehne am Halleschen Ufer an institution in itself, adapted for the second time one of his own legit prods, Botho Strauss's "Trilogy of Wiedersehens." The formula is simple: the play is staged, in the first place, with plenty of breathing space for a roving camera, which then picks out pertinent details for a knowledgeable film public.

"Trilogy" is set in the West German provinces on a hot summer day. Moritz, the director of the local Art Society, is preparing to open his exhibition on "Capitalist Realism," which, unfortunately, includes a painting that insults a leading town banking official. Each member, of the Society represents a peculiar type of the German bourgeoisie, none of whom is very exemplary as a connoisseur of art, life, or anything else for that matter.

The group haggles over the mutual problem of the exhibit, grateful too for the opportunity to talk about themselves. There's the ex-wife of the offended banker, a father-and-son set of actors, a doctor, a pharmacist and his wife, a would-be painter, a writer, a printer, and several friends and relatives, down to a brat who takes everybody's picture with his Polaroid. Make no mistake: this is a biting portrait of contemporary upper-crust German society.

One humorous scene stands out amid several satirical caricatures. The printer (Otto Sander) attempts to explain the plot of a detective story he has just read to the painter's boyfriend (Roland Schaefer), who's busy trying to gulp down a gooey canape — which drips its way down his shirt. It's a side-splitting scene, the only one that really works throughout a long evening of talking and crying over spilled beans.

Stein, nevertheless, is a coming cinema talent, should he ever take note of the fundamental difference between acting on the stage and before the screen. At the moment, he's mostly getting his kicks out of editing fragments of dialogue and action in a formalistic vein. Lensing by Michael Ballhaus is good cut above the average. A fest treat on the summer circut for the legit and film buff. — *Holl.*

Die Abfahrer
(On the Move)
(WEST GERMAN-COLOR)

Cannes, May 15.
An Adolf Winkelmann Film Production. Dortmund, in collaboration with Westdeutsche Rundfunk (WDR). Cologne; world rights. Filmverlag der Autoren. Munich. Features entire cast. Directed by Adolf Winkelmann. Screenplay. Winkelmann, Gerd Weiss; camera (color). David Slama; editing. Helga Schnurre; sets. Gerlinde Feddeler. Bernd Twardy; music. "Die Schmetterlinge." Reviewed at Cannes Film Festival (Market). May 14, '79. Running time: **94 MINS.**
Cast: Detlev 'Quandt (Atzi). Ludger Schnieder (Lutz). Anastasios Avgerlis (Sulli). Beate Brockstedt (Sved). Josefine Carree. Manfred Doenicke. Martha Dors. Betti Eiermann. Freddy Garber. Harald Hampe. Gerd Hohmann. Hermann Lause. Gertrud von Linteln. Regina Mueller. Edzard Obendiek. Eduard Schalow. Tana Schanzara. Otto Schnelling. Dagmar Schulz. Wolf Sesemann. Irmgard Thielebeule. Willi Wagener. Gerd Weiss.

The sleeper of the new season, Adolf Winkelmann's "On the Move" (in German the title is "Die Abfahrer") popped up in the German series of the Berlin Film Festival, went on to bag good boxoffice among the country's young audience and will find a place on the summer fest circuit (probably Locarno) to win broader critical attention.

It's the tale of three unemployed youths laid off a specialized job in a factory around Dortmund, where pic was mostly lensed. They then steal a moving van (with a faulty brake system) and set off across country with no particular goal in mind, picking up a girl hitchhiker along the way who's not too set on returning home. The rest is laughs — in fact, one of the best comedies made this year on the Teutonic scene.

This is a kind of comic "Two Lane Blacktop," the Monte Hellman pic that has become a cult film in West Germany of late. The story line makes little or no sense, nor does the audience know where the wacky group is headed and how it comes out in the end. They're just "on the move" because there's no reason for them to stop anywhere for any particular length of time. Further, the society around them is shown to be no better off for having settled down into dreadful routine.

Helmer Adolf Winkelmann has made a reputation for a number of shorts at the Oberhausen festival. This is his first feature pic on a small budget. Thesps (nearly all amateurs) are the big plus, but general narrative style and ease with dialogue points to a promising directorial talent. Worth everyone's looksee. — *Holl.*

Der Durchdreher
(It Can Only Get Worse)
(WEST GERMAN-COLOR)

Cannes, May 17.
A Helmut Dietl Film Production. produced by Balance Film. Munich; world rights. Atlas International Film. Munich. Features entire cast. Written and directed by Helmut Dietl. Camera (color). Fred Tammes. Hermann Fahr. Lothar-Elias Stickelbrucks; sound. Ed Parente; sets. Jochen O. Schmidt. Peter Grundke; costumes. Bernd Stockinger; editing. Thea Exmess. Reviewed at Cannes Film Festival (Market). May 16. '79. Running time: **95 MINS.**
Cast: Towje Kleiner (Maximilian) Mo Schwarz (Gloria). Helmut Fischer. Ilse Neubauer. Herb Andress. Dieter Augustin. Toni Berger. Lambert Hamel. Kurt Huebner. Christine Kaufmann. Karl Lieffen. Alexander May. Richard Muench. Rolf Olsen. Barbara Valentin. Helen Vita.

Okay comedy that won a German Film Prize this year. Helmut Dietl's "It Can Only Get Worse" features a would-be writer and boulevard journalist who, on the day of his divorce, gets mixed up with another divorcee and shacks up with her.

Meanwhile, his friend tries to set him straight on the facts of life, just as he is about to be fired from the newspaper, and the only publisher interested in his book wants erotic material added to the potential best-seller.

The new girlfriend moves into his two-room apartment with all her furniture, then puts the already shaky relationship on the rocks by deciding the two should move to the country. The writer's plight only gets worse and worse — he can't even run off to an exotic island to get away from it all, but ends up in a body-beautiful sauna.

Some scenes have sharp satirical edge, but pic needs better book despite solid performances from thesps. —*Holl.*

Schluchtenflitzer
(Whizzer)
(WEST GERMAN-COLOR)

Cannes, May 14.
A Monika Neuchtern Film Production. Munich; world rights. Cine-International Filmvertrieb. Munich. Features entire cast. Written and directed by Ruediger Neuchtern. Camera (color). Juergen Juerges; music. Joerg Evers; editing. Manja Rock; sound. Kurt Huettl. Reviewed at Cannes Film Festival (Market). May 13. '79. Running time: **112 MINS.**
Cast: Hans Kollmannsberger (Andy). Hans Brenner (his father). Ruth Drexel (his mother). Eva Mattes (salesgirl). Renard Hatzke. Verena Disch. Anette Juenger. Rudolf Plommer. Anton Teintinger. Peter Scharrer.

A prominent example of the Second Line pix in New German Cinema, Ruediger Nuechtern's "Whizzer" is aimed squarely at the young filmgoing public and doesn't miss a bet in showing life in Bavarian small towns just as it is today - kids with little else on their mind except motor-bikes and dating after the work on the farm is over.

Ruediger Nuechtern scored a hit at the Hof Film Festival a year ago with "Anschi and Michael" (1977), about a young couple from different sides of the tracks living in Munich. Now he's back with much the same story set in the Bavarian hills and centering on the first affairs of a gangling rebellious youth named Andy. It's fun, and pic is doing well at the box office.

"Whizzer" moves at a fast pace with several comical scenes dealing with pursuit of the opposite sex, capped by the unexpected death of the lad's father in a farm accident (during the construction of a silo).
—*Holl.*

Wild Horse Hank
(CANADIAN-COLOR)

Cannes, May 15.
A Film Consortium of Canada production (no distributor). Executive Producers. Jerry Leider. Dan Wilson. Producers, Bill Marshall. Henk Van Der Kolk. Stars Linda Blair. Directed by Eric Till. Screenplay. James Lee Barrett from novel. "The Wild

Horse Killers," by Mel Ellis; music, Paul and Brenda Hoffert; camera (color), Richard Leiterman; editor, George Appelby. Reviewed at the Olympia One, Cannes, May 15 '79. Running time: **94 MINS.**

Hank Bradford .... Linda Blair
Charlie Connors .... Michael Wincott
Jay Conors .... Al Waxman
Richard Crenna .... Pace Bradford

A gentle family adventure, "Wild Horse Hank" centres on a college girl determined to save wild horses from the clutches of nasties who want to sell them for dog food.

Rebelling against her father, she rides them across the plain, over the mountains, onto a public highway, and into a Federal game reserve where they will be safe.

Generally, the pic works except in unnecessarily long sequences of her alone with the horses where nothing but moving along takes up all the action. Linda Blair, however, looks stunned most of the time and comes off without too much drive. Music by Brenda and Paul Hoffert is catchy and should play on radio.

As the nasty leader, Al Waxman overextends himself in loutish behavior but makes his mark. The same clean acting is delivered from newcomer Michael Wincott as his good brother who is attracted but never touches the girl. Richard Crenna is smooth as her father. In the end, everything works out neatly and director Eric Till and cameraman Richard Leiterman have added another pro job to their list of credits. "Wild Horse Hank" should do alright and better on tv. —*Adil.*

Die Dritte Generation
(The Third Generation)
(WEST GERMAN-COLOR)

Cannes, May 14.
Filmverlag Der Autoren release of Tango Film-Filmverlag Der Autoren production. Features entire cast. Written, directed and lensed (Eastmancolor), by Rainer Werner Fassbinder. Editor, Juliane Lorenz; music, Peer Raben. Reviewed at Cannes Film Fest (non-competing), May 13, '79. Running time: **111 MINS.**

Harry .... Rudolf Mann
Petra .... Margit Carstensen
Lenz .... Eddie Constantine
Susanne .... Hanna Schygulla
August .... Volker Spengler
Hark .... Gerhard Gast
Edgar .... Udo Kier

Rainer Werner Fasbinder is undoubtedly the most prolific filmmaker on the European, and possibly world, film scene. He had two films at the Berlin Film Fest this year and now another at Cannes. That extreme filmic fecundity may be the problem as he gets repetitious, too full of inside gags and even careless in the construction and aims of his films.

Fassbinder, for his 34th or 35th pic, looks at terrorism in treating a group of inept, scared young people

whose actual ties, outlooks and reasons are never explained. Perhaps Fassbinder wants to reflect on the previous generations that formed this reaction in an admittedly small part of the present generation.

The group meets in various houses and plots the kidnapping of a multi-national company chief. But a police inspector, whose son-in-law is part of the group, is tracking them down and wiping them out.

There are ironic insights and the usual fine visual ideas of Fassbinder. But they are only decorative aspects of this highly confused, arbitrary attempt to use black comedy to comment on government harshness in dealing with the terrorists who seem in it more for adventure than dedication.

Fassbinder is now also his own photographer and shows a good aptitude for it. Film is mainly for Fassbinder fanatics and the usual cultist and non-commercial changes that are the fate of many of the films of this talented but uneven filmmaker.

However there's no counting Fassbinder out. But perhaps a bit more gestation of ideas and intentions before films might send him off on another streak of unusual films treating racism, politics and the Nazi past that found him a name among film buss though only intermittently with the general public. —*Mosk.*

Willi Und Die Kameraden
(Willi and the Comrades)
(WEST GERMAN-COLOR)

Cannes, May 14.
A Regina Ziegler Film Production, West Berlin, in collaboration with Second German Television (ZDF), Wiesbaden. Christoph Holch. Features entire cast. Written and directed by Helmut Kopetzky. Camera (color). David Slama; sets. Juergen Henze; make-up. costumes, Barbara Naujok. Cornelia Leitner; sound. Heiko von Swieykowski; editing. Susanne Busse-Lahaye; music, Rio Raiser. Reviewed at Cannes Film Festival (Market), May 13, '79. Running time: **78 MINS.**

Cast: Thomas Vahl (Willi Klein). Dorothea Moritz (Frau Klein). Horst Pinnow (Herr Klein). Peter Schiff (Krueger). Arnfried Lerche (Schoolteacher Gebhardt). Heinz Hoenig (Baldur). Jako Benz (Wolf). Silvia Bommert (Marion).

One of the first German pix to deal with Neo-Nazis. Berlin critic and filmer Helmut Kopetzky did a lot of solid research in the making of his "Willi and the Comrades." It's the story of young boys dropping out of school with little hope for jobs, and are thus ripe prey for rejuvenated Nazi exploiters. Despite small budget, pic got a life from the recent "Holocaust" tv-series broadcast, but apparently underwent unnecessary last-minute changes to make it even more relevant at the cost of story-line.

Willi is 15 years old and a nut for

building model tanks: in fact, he knows all about the war and lives in a kind of dream-world of his own. School opportunities and job-finding agencies don't relate to him, but a garage mechanic knows how to recruit kids for his Hitler-Youth-style outings and exploit them without paying wages at his garage at the same time. Well worth a looksee, despite overkill with extra docu footage. —*Holl.*

Aufwind
(Up Wind)
(WEST GERMAN-COLOR)

Cannes, May 16.
A Rudolf Steiner Film Production: world rights, Cine International, Munich. Features entire cast. Directed by Rudolf Steiner. Screenplay, Renate Cesar; camera (color), H.-V. Moennling; music, Charles Orieux. Reviewed at Cannes Film Festival (Market). May 15, '79. Running time: **90 MINS.**

Cast: Ingolf Gorges, Uschi Bour, Tatjana Blacher.

One of those pix slapped together according to cliched formulas, Rudolf Steiner's "Up-Wind" tells the story of a sky-flier who has a bad accident one day and is then left a paralyzed cripple from the wasit down.

Not caring much for a life without legs, he contributes a spare kidney to save another man's life — and the reward is an invitation to live with his newly found friend and sister, who (natch) falls in love with him.

This generosity leads, eventually, to a suicide attempt on his birthday, followed by lots of tears and everyone facing the sober truth.

Worth a looksee to note how film subsidies get thrown away in West Germany on scripts with a heart of gold. Credits are subpar. —*Holl.*

Was Heisst'n Hier Liebe
(This Is Love, Isn't It?)
(WEST GERMAN-COLOR)

Cannes, May 16.
A Project Film Production in Filmverlag der Autoren, a DENKmal-Film; world rights. Filmverlag der Autoren. Munich. Features entire cast. Directed by Walter Harrich. Claus Strigel, Bertram Verhaag. Screenplay, camera (color), and editing, Harrich, Strigel, Verhaag, based on a play with the same title by Holger Franke, Helma Fehrmann, Juergen Fluegge, with the cooperation of Guenter Brombacher and Alfred Cybulska; music. Heiner Goebbels. Reviewed at Cannes Film Festival (Market), May 15, '79. Running time: **133 MINS.**

Cast: Helma Fehrmann, Guenter Brombacher, Ulli Radhoefer, Holger Franke, Alfred Cybulska, Juergen Fluegge, and the "Rote Gruetze" ensemble.

A prime example of whychildren's and youth-oriented legit theatre ensembles are enjoying a renaissance today in West Germany,

"This Is Love, Isn't It?" developed from the ideas and mutual cooperation of the Rote Gruetz ensemble in Munich. The play has been such a hit that the Filmverlag der Autoren backed the film project to get the play around to even more audiences in Germany and elsewhere.

"This Is Love, Isn't It?" is full of laughs and good fun, about a pair of teenagers just awakening to their emotions and a first love affair. Plays like these have indirectly prompted such new pix like Adolf Winkelmann's "On the Move" for a vast new audience in West Germany. The younger generation of German filmmakers is here to stay and this pic definitely deserves a look.—*Holl.*

Nues Vom Raeuber Hotzenplotz
(The Latest on Robber Hotzenplotz)
(WEST GERMAN-COLOR)

Cannes, May 14.
A Gustav Ehmck Film Production. Munich; world rights, Transocean International, Munich. Features entire cast. Directed by Gustav Ehmck. Screenplay, Karl U. Nastvogel. Andy Hoetzel; camera (color). Hubs Hagen. Reviewed at Cannes Film Festival (Market). May 13, '79. Running time: **90 MINS.**

Cast: Peter Kern (Robber Hotzenplotz). Muckenstruntz and Bamschabl (Kasperl and Seppl). Barbara Valentin (Mrs. Schlotterbeck). Wal Davis, Hans Richter, Karl U. Nastvogel, Carsta Loeck.

Dull and predictable children's pic featuring a "dangerous" (read "tame" here) robber, Gustav Ehmck's "The Latest on Robber Hotzenplotz" takes up where his earlier "Robber Hotzenplotz" (1973) left off: our big, bad brigand is in jail, escapes in a constable's stolen uniform, and terrorizes an old grandmother just for kicks.

Naturally, no one in the young audience is to taken in by any of these shenanigans, and there's also a string of worn and tired gags played with little verve or conviction. Peter Kern as the baddy, and Barbara Valentin as the good witch in town are wasted on an inept script and even worse dialogue.

—*Holl.*

The Muppet Movie
(COLOR)

Muppets should march to boxoffice success in first big-screen effort.

Hollywood, May 25.

Associated Film Distribution release of an ITC Entertainment film and a Jim Henson production. Exec producer, Martin Starger. Produced by Jim Henson. Co-produced by David Lazer. Directed by James Frawley. Features entire cast. Screenplay, Jerry Juhl, Jack Burns; camera (CFI Color), Isidore Mankofsky; editor, Chris Greenbury; production design, Joel Schiller; music, Paul Williams; art direction, Les Gobruegge; sound (Dolby), Charles Lewis; costumes (Muppets), Calista Hendrickson; costume design, Gwen Capetanos; assistant director, Ron Wright. Reviewed at CBS Studio Centre, Studio City, May 25, '79. (MPAA Rating: G.) Running time: **98 MINS.**

Kermit the Frog, Rowlf.
Dr. Teeth, Waldorf .... Jim Henson
Miss Piggy, Fozzie Bear, Animal.
Sam The Eagle .... Frank Oz
Floyd Pepper, Crazy Harry, Robin the Frog, Lew Zealand .... Jerry Nelson
Scooter, Statler, Janice.
Sweetums, Beaker .... Richard Hunt
The Great Gonzo, Zoot.
Dr. Bunsen Honeydew ...... Dave Goelz
Doc Hopper .... Charles Durning
Max .... Austin Pendleton
Frog Killer .... Scott Walker
Also featuring: Edgar Bergen, Milton Berle, Mel Brooks, James Coburn, Dom DeLuise, Elliott Gould, Bob Hope, Madeline Kahn, Carol Kane, Cloris Leachman, Steve Martin, Richard Pryor, Telly Savalas, Orson Welles, Paul Williams.

"The Muppet Movie" is a winner. Appeal of the G-rated release from Associated Film Distribution will encompass not only the sizable moppet crowd weaned on the syndicated "Muppet" vidseries, but many young and middle-aged adults. Despite some laggard moments, this translation from small to big screen looks to be a champ contender at the boxoffice. AFD's biggest danger lies in overselling the already-popular characters.

Two stumbling blocks that previously tripped up pix like this should no longer prove insurmountable. The onetime stranglehold Disney held on the family film market has been broken frequently and successfully, by pix from "Benji" to the "Wilderness Family." And the theory that people won't pay for something they can see free on the tube has also been dented by recent success of telefilms transformed into features.

But Jim Henson, Muppet originator, and Frank Oz, who gets creative consultant credit on the pic, took the one necessary step to virtually assure success. They abandoned, for the most part, the successful format of their vidshow, and inserted thier creations into a well-crafted combo of musical comedy and fantasy-adventure.

Result is a muppet update of "The Wizard Of Oz," with Kermit the Frog leading a motley Muppet troupe on the asphalt road to Hollywood. Script by Jerry Juhl and Jack Burns incorporates the zingy one-liners and bad puns that have become the teleseries' trade mark, but also develops the Muppets themselves as thinking, feeling characters.

Director James Frawley, is espanding the entire focus on the Muppets, has a lot of fun with cinematic sleight-of-hand, including shots of Kermit pedalling a bicycle, the Muppets driving an assortment of cars and trucks, and additional full-body camerawork, accomplished via radio controls and other electronic gimmickry.

Fortunately, the special effects never intrude on the cogent storyline, which runs Kermit thorugh a gamut of emotions, from self-doubt and bashful love (via Miss Piggy) to a moral showdown with the pic's villain, Charles Durning, on the old "High Noon" set. A love of films and showbiz is apparent in every frame, and gives "The Muppet Movie" an extra touch of class.

While Durning and Austin Pendelton are the two stet characters who pursue Kermit to plug their fried frog legs franchise, there are 15 guest shot cameos by a variety of performers, with Mel Brooks and Steve Martin the most effective of the lot.

Real stars, though, are the unseen Henson, Oz, Jerry Nelson, Richard Hunt and Dave Goelz, who do an astonishing range of vocal characterizations. The key to Henson's success on tv is an extraordinary lifelike sense to his creations in both vocalisms and actions, and these transfer intact to the feature screen.

Frawley does let the middle of the film sag somewhat, and the cameos tend to destroy the continuity, as to several plot recaps. But the music and lyrics by Paul Williams and Kenny Ascher propel the action along, and Kermit, Miss Piggy, Fozzie Bear, the Great Gonzo, Rowlf, and a dynamic rock group named Dr. Teeth and Electric Mayhem, prove highly attractive.—*Poll.*

Behinderte Liebe
(Handicapped Love)
(SWISS-COLOR)

Zurich, May 13.

Filmkollektiv Zurich AG release of a Marlies Graf production. Written and directed by Graf, in collaboration with a group of handicapped and non-handicapped persons. Camera (Kodacolor), Werner Zuber; sound, Florian Eidenbenz, Urs Kohler; music, Hugo Sigrist; editor, Graf; music (recordings), Keith Jarrett, Fly Orchestra Zurich, Sero-Sextett Oberhofen. Features Therese Zemp, Jules Burgener, Christoph Eggli, Ursual Eggli, Paolo Poloni, Wolfgang Suttner. Reviewed at the Studio 4, Zurich, May 12, '79; Running time: **120 MINS.**

The title of this Swiss documentary film must be taken in its grimly literal sense. It is a frank, honest and unsentimental account about a taboo subject usually passed over in silence or believed to be non-existent: the need for (and right to) physical satisfaction and sexual fulfillment of the physically handicapped. This worthwhile film is also a plea for their right to have sex and for the understanding of the non-handicapped.

Swiss director Marlies Graf collaborated on the script with a group of severely handicapped young men and women, including paraplegics, muscular dystrophy victims, etc., as well as some non-handicapped social workers and sympathizers. The result is a deeply moving film on a delicate subject, completely natural and tastefully handled. Main assets are its authenticity and simplicity. There are no voyeuristic aspects, just interviews, group discussions and especially four most impressive and very frank monolog-type self-accounts.

Of course, the subject matter, considered by many to be "unsavory," limits the film's commercial possibilities. Furthermore, it is filmed in 16m Kodacolor, although blowing up to 35m would be no problem. School and tv use appears indicated in any case. The Zurich release in a regular outlet, the Studio 4, caught on much better than expected and even registered some sellout performances. —*Mezo.*

Beyond The Poseidon Adventure
(COLOR)

Irwin Allen goes overboard in soggy remake of "Poseidon Adventure."

Hollywood, May 23.

A Warner Bros. release of an Irwin Allen production. Features entire cast. Produced and directed by Irwin Allen. Screenplay, Nelson Gidding, based on the novel by Paul Gallico; camera (color), Joseph Biroc; editor, Bill Brame; production design, Preston Ames; music, Jerry Fielding; costume design, Paul Zastupnevich; special photographic effects, Harold Wellman; sound, Herman Lewis; assistant director, Mike Salamunovich. Reviewed at The Burbank Studios, May 23, '79. (MPAA Rating: PG.) Running time: 122 MINS.

Mike Turner .... Michael Caine
Celeste Whitman .... Sally Field
Capt. Stefan Svevo .... Tally Savalas
Frank Mazzetti .... Peter Boyle
Harold Meredith ....Jack Warden
Hannah Meredith .... Shirley Knight
Gina Rowe ....Shirley Jones
Wilbur .... Karl Malden
Tex ....Slim Pickens
Suzanne ....Veronica Hamel
Theresa Mazzetti ......Angela Cartwright
Larry Simpson ....Mark Harmon

Maybe Warner Bros. and Irwin Allen thought they were making a sequel to "The Poseidon Adventure." 20th-Fox release that returned $42,000,000 in domestic film rentals, but film-goers will soon know better. "Beyond The Poseidon Adventure" (whatever that means) comes off as a virtual remake of the 1972 original, without that film's mounting suspense and excitement. Boxoffice results won't carbon Fox' success, although initial wicket interest may be strong. Foreign and tv sales loom as the pic's financial salvation.

Since different distribs are involved (due to Allen's moveover to Warners), there's no mention of the first version, and recap of original premise, a luxury liner turned upside down by gigantic tidal wave, is accomplished in a few seconds.

New plot turn pits salvage tug operators Michael Caine, Karl Malden and Sally Field against evil-doer Telly Savalas for looting rights to the big boat. Caine and company are after hard cash, while Savalas, posing as a medico, is searching out a cargo of valuable plutonium.

Shortly after the scavengers arrive, however, an explosion seals off their entrance, and scenarist Nelson Giddings begins a replay of the first film's premise, which derived from Paul Gallico's novel. What once seemed novel and purposeful has now become tired and derivative, awash in cliches.

To flesh out the story, Giddings and producer-director Allen have the newcomers stumble on an unlikely group of survivors, including Jersey bartender Peter Boyle and daughter Angela Cartwright, blindman Jack Warden and wife Shirley Knight, ship nurse Shirley Jones, Slim Pickens as a drunk imposter, Mark Harmon as Cartwright's savior, and Veronica Hamel, apparently one of Savalas' minions.

The only change, then, in this group's struggle to reach the top (really, the bottom) of the boat is a set of different faces. Caine takes over the Gene Hackman role as the group leader, exhorting his charges ever upward, while Boyle becomes his nemesis, just as Ernest Borgnine goaded Hackman in the original. Instead of Shelley Winters and Jack Albertson, Warden and Knight supply the pathos, with sightlessness provoking the same crisis excess weight did in the 1972 version.

Because the outcome is so predictable, the defects in Gidding's script take on greater magnitude. There are annoying and unresolved hints that Savalas precipitated the original accident to obtain the nuclear material, which doesn't seem the usual cargo for a passenger liner. And unless the Poseidon was on its maiden voyage, its hull should have at least a few barnacles.

Although none of the original tech staff repeated on the second version, Preston Ames' realistic design of the crippled ship is the real star of "Beyond." But the special effects, despite Howard Jensen's best efforts, just don't equal the impact of those in "Poseidon Adventure," and are confined to heavy objects falling through several decks. Matte work and other visuals by Harold Wellman are good. Exterior footage was lensed off of Catalina Island, while complicated interior sets were constructed at The Burbank Studios.

Caine comes off as best as can be expected, given the banal dialog, and Field elicits some laughs as a wisecracking gamine. Knight adds the only other touch of class, with Savalas strictly cardboard as the villain, and Boyle pure ham as the bully. Jones, Malden, Warden stay as much in the background as possible, and wisely so.

Allen's adventure spectaculars seem better off in directorial hands other than his own, although not even D.W. Griffith could have done much with this script. With its tame dialog, and total lack of violence and sex, "Beyond The Poseidon Adventure" seems perfectly suited for the home screen. Unfortunately for exhibs, that's where most people will wait to see it. —*Poll.*

Vlad Tepes
(The True Life of Dracula)
(RUMANIAN-COLOR)

Cannes, May 18.

A Romaniafilm Production, Bucharest; world rights, Romaniafilm, Bucharest. Features entire cast. Directed by Doru Nastase. Screenplay, Mircea Mohor; camera (color), Aurel Kostrakiewicz; music, Tiberiu Olah; sets, Guta Stirbu; editing, Adina Georgescu Obrocea. Reviewed at Cannes Film Festival (Market), May 17, '79. Running time: **100 MINS.**

Cast: Stefan Sileanu, Ernest Maftei, Emanoil Petrut, Alexandra Repan, George Constantin, Teofil Vilcu, Constantin Codrescu, Constantin Barbulescu, Vasile Cosman, Ion Marinescu, Kovacs Gyorgy, Vadasz Zoltan, Petre Gheorghiu-Dolj, Mihai Paladescu.

This Rumanian pic on "The True Life of Dracula" (the original title is correctly translated "Vlad the Impaler") deals with the historical character who apparently inspired the Gothic novel and the horror genre Universal made famous in Hollywood. Vlad Tepes, or Dracula (meaning in Rumanian "son of the devil"), defended his country, Wallachia, in 1457 against the Turks under Mohammed II (who conquered Constantinople and brought to an end the Byzantine Empire). He was a soldier, a captain who gathered an army under his name just at the time when Turkish expansion meant a counter-crusade against Christendom under the Hungarian king, Mathias Corvin. A picture of Dracula was found in Ambras Castle, and legends about him range from a man of cruelty to a courageous leader.

Helmer Doru Nastase, whose metier is the historical action pic, prefers the heroics. He previously made "Michael the Brave" (1970), about another national hero. Lots of costumes and battle scenes. — *Holl.*

Wanda Nevada
(COLOR)

A 1950s western of spotty outlook.

Hollywood, May 23.

A United Artists release Executive producer, William Hayward. Produced by Neal Dobrofsky. Dennis Hackin. Stars Peter Fonda, Brooke Shields. Directed by Peter Fonda. Screenplay, Dennis Hackin; camera (color), Michael Butler; editor, Scott Conrad; music, Ken Lauber; associate producers, Hilary Holden, Thomas Perry; art director, Lynda Paradise; assistant director, Ric Rondell. Reviewed at MGM Studios, Culver City, May 23, '79. (MPAA rating: PG.) Running time: **105 MINS.**

Beaudray Demerille	Peter Fonda
Wanda Nevada	Brooke Shields
Dorothy Deerfield	Fiona Lewis
Ruby Muldoon	Luke Askew
Strap Pangburn	Ted Markland
Merlin Bitterstix	Severn Darden
Texas Curly	Paul Fix
Old Prospector	Henry Fonda
Card Hustler	Larry Golden
Gas Station Greaser	John Denos
Sherman Krupp	Bert Williams

"Wanda Nevada" is a serio-comic romance which is unconvincing on virtually every level. What sharm it has stems from the quirky convergence of several different genres, but Peter Fonda's third directorial outing is all but sunk by Brooke Shields' critically deficient performance. B.O. outlook is spotty.

Pic, which is set in the West circa 1950, opens with gambling man Fonda winning orphan Shields in a poker game, the two then hitting the road and later searching for gold they learn is hidden in the Grand Canyon. Their pursuit by two comic baddies and the introduction of unexplained elements of Indian mysticism provide only a smidgen of dramatic urgency, rendering the pair's odyssey through the beautiful landscapes placid and leisurely in the extreme.

Lightly combining aspects of the western, couple-on-the-run gangster sagas, wispy fables and gold prospecting dramas, "Wanda Nevada" scrupulously avoids the "Lolita"-ish possibilities inherent in the relationship between a man and a girl more than 20 years his junior, Dennis Hackin's script striving instead for the touching, intangible emotionalism, derived from oddball couplings, that made successes of films like "Paper Moon" and "The African Queen."

Whatever their other qualities, those films wouldn't have made it without their inspired casting. In cases where the leading couple is in constant focus, chemistry is all, and the duo here just doesn't have it. Fonda performs in his usual relaxed fashion, but Shields is frequently embarrassing, unpleasantly overdoing grimaces and insolent line readings to convey the character's initial childishness, then failing to mature and blossom into the "woman" demanded by the script's final sections.

Ending is particularly aggravating, as one of the characters is apparently killed, only to inexplicably spring to life again in the final moments. Even granting that both premise and intent of pic are fanciful, only probably audience reaction to the denouement is a gaping, "What?"

For a film set in 1950, characters have a heavily contemporary, hip look, with most of the men sporting beards or moustaches and longish hair. Most supporting perfs are on the order of loopy cameos turns, with Severn Darden at home as a desert misfit and Paul Fix notably effective as a drunk who's struck it rich. An eighth-billed Henry Fonda, virtually unrecognizable behind thick goggles and beard, makes a dramatic appearance late in the proceedings as another oldtime prospector. This marks the first time father and son have worked together on a picture.

Peter Fonda showed real directorial promise in "The Hired Hand" eight years ago and here helms with an eye for the eccentric. Tech qualities are pro, with Michael Butler's photography nicely drawing out the warm, golden qualities in both the landscapes and Shields' skin. On the other hand, whoever was in charge of washing and pressing Shields' shirts and jeans was working overtime. —*Cart.*

O Coronel e O Lobisomem
(The Colonel And The Werewolf)
(BRAZILIAN-COLOR)

Rio de Janeiro, May 16.

Alcino Diniz Filmes Lda. and Embrafilme production. Directed by Alcino Diniz. Features entire cast. Screenplay, Alcino Diniz; dialogs, Jose Candido de Carvalho, based on his novel of same title. camera (color), Antonio Goncalves; editing, Giuseppe Baldacconi; executive director, Maria Santo Cristo; music, Helvius Vilela, Marco Versiani. Reviewed at Hotel Meredien Cineclub, Copacabana, May 15, 1979. Running time: **118 MINS.**

Coronel Furtado	Mauricio do Valle
Dona Esmeraldina	Nogueira Maria Claudia
Dona Francisquinha	Clea Simoes
Velho (Grandpa) Simeao	Jofre Soares
Pernambuco Nogueira	Nildo Parente
Dona Isabel Pimenta	Selma Egrei
Dona Bebel de Melo	Louise Cardoso
Dona Celeste	Izabel Ribeiro
Juquinha Quintanilha	Luthero Luiz
Fontainha	Fernando Reski
The Werewolf	Tonico Pereira
Joao Fonseca	Wilson Grey
Engineer Balthazar	Otavio Augusto
Narrator	Oscar Polidoro

Alcino Diniz is correct when he calls his Colonel "the Don Quixote of the Third World." But instead of having windmills to fight, this Brazilian Colonel is battling his inner world which is a conflict of reality with masturbatory phantasy.

"Colonel" could only have been filmed in South America and specifically Brazil as it mixes the unlikeliest of elements into a unique, often charming and innocent but occasionally tiresome epic.

In Dinize's blender then mix a little bit of local light porno with art film, highly imaginative and creative scenes with crass commercialism and the supernatural with Brazil's wild natural setting.

Mauricio do Valle is the one-man show in this pic. Dialog, word and action are centered around his complex character of a spiritually-haunted military man in a bygone Brazil bygone. His is an existence caught between dream and reality, between dreams of sexpots and werewolves.

None of the pic's other characters emerge as more than cardboard characters. The picmaker may have planned it this way in order to focus on the "Colonel," but pic resultingly lacks a dimension of depth and exploration this viewer at least might had expected.

This is what Diniz wants and that's what we get: a flavored, colorful pic with one foot in the quicksand of b.o. entertainment for the masses and another foot climbing the ladder towards a work of art.

—*Emrt.*

Brot und Steine
(Bread and Stones)
(SWISS-COLOR)

Zurich, May 16.

Majestic Films S.A. Lausanne release of a Logos-Film Zurich (Claude M. Beck) production stars Liselotte Pulver, Henrik Rhyn. Directed by Mark M. Rissi. Screenplay, Walther Kauer, from an idea by Otto Locher; (color). Edwin Horak; editor. Evelyne von Rabenau; music, Martin Boettcher. Veronique Muller. Trio Eugster; lyrics, Muller. Max Rueger. Reviewed at Capitol Theatre, Zurich, May 15, '79; running time: 95 MINS.

Widimatthauerin .... Liselotte Pulver
Hans .... Henrik Rhyn
Ursula .... Beatrice Kessler
Bodenbauer .... Walo Luond
Dr. Steiner .... Sigfrit Steiner
Ruedu .... Hans Gaugler
Fridu .... Peter Leu

The struggle for survival of Swiss farmers against expanding industrial and speculative groups is an acute problem in Switzerland. Animal breeding bordering on cruelty to assure higher rentals is another topical subject here. Mark M. Rissi, Swiss director, and scripter Walther Kauer used this and other topics on the Swiss agricultural scene as the basis for "Brot und Steine" (Bread and Stones).

A young farmer refuses to give in to a project agreed upon between the community and a financially powerful industrial group, which would rob him of his farmland. With the help of another farmer's son, he finally has his way and even wins a bride in the person of a pretty veterinarian student from the city.

If this sounds hackneyed and simplistic, it is. Rissi's attempt at social engagement is a feeble one and fails to convince. The film is too conventional to evoke more than passing interest. It is best suited for rural Swiss regions. Some camera shots look like picture postcards. Two songs by Veronique Muller and the Trio Eugster are slightly better than Martin Boettcher's lush background music, completely unsuitable for the subject.

The cast is the film's main asset. With the exception of Liselotte Pulver, too young as the farmer's mother, it is well chosen. Henrik Rhyn as the belligerent young farmer is a personable newcomer. As the student he falls in love with,

Beatrice Kessler confirms the favorable impression on her debut in "The Swissmakers," the season's local smash hit. Walo Luond as a rival farmer and Sigfrit Steiner as the old village veterinarian offer fine characterizations beyond script limitations. —*Mezo.*

Plern
(Dr. Plern)
(THAI-COLOR)

Bangkok, May 15.

An Apex Productions release. Produced by Nanta Tansacha. Written and directed by Prince Tipayachatr Chartchai. Features entire cast. Executive producer, Orasri Chartchai. Camera (color). Sanit Rujiratrakul; music, Prasit Payomyong; sound, Maitree Janjarasskul; editor, Sngar Janjarasskul; production design, M. R. Rapipat Patanachatr; costumes, Poon Pansomboon; make-up and hairstyle, Kiat Syarm; asst. director, Tiow Karna. Reviewed at Siam Theatre, Bangkok, May 14, '79. Running time: 110 MINS.
Dr. Plern ...... Choompoonuj Yukthanan
Khunying .... Nawarat Yukthanan
Piac .... Pisan Akaraseni
Tih .... Aporn Tonnawanij
Thom .... Mathurot Ratana
Uan .... Needa Suksawat
Jum .... Acharee Chaisiri
Doo .... Cherd Tansacha
Sea .... Dekying Orachaiya

"Plern," the sequel to "Rak Oy" (The Lovers) marks acting debut of Choompoonuj Yukthanan, elder sister of Thai actress Nawarat Yukthanan. It promises to be an even bigger hit than the original, thanks to a gimmick that worked — two real sisters teaming for the first time.

The plot and background music are strongly reminiscent of the original, which came up with no less than five hit songs. Only the heroine's theme song is new this time, however. The rest of the music consists of reprises from the previous hit.

If the film's grosses are any indication (over 1,000,000 baht (about $50,000) in three days' showing in five situations), Choompoonuj has made it. The familiar pattern for successful new stars like her is to go on working with the filmmaker who discovered them, since other filmmakers are too busy trying to find their own new stars. —*Cano.*

Der Schneider Von Ulm
(The Tailor From Ulm)
(WEST GERMAN-COLOR)

Cannes, May 13.

An Edgar Reitz/Peter Genee Film Production, in collaboration with Second German Television (ZDF), Wiesbaden; world rights. Filmverlag der Autoren, Munich. Features entire cast. Directed by Edgar Reitz. Screenplay, Petra Kiener, Reitz; camera (Eastmancolor), Dietrich Lohmann; music, Nikos Mamangakis; editing. Siegrun Jaeger; sets, Winfried Hennig. Reviewed at Cannes Film Festival (Market), May 12, '79. Running time: 115 MINS.

Cast: Tilo Prueckner (Berblinger), Vadim Glowna (Fesslen), Harald Kuhlmann (Degen), Dieter Schidor (Schlumberger), Rudolf Wessely (Pointet), Herbert Prikopa (Kratzky), Marie Colbin (Irma), Otto Kackovic (Moretti), Michael Hoffbauer (Fritz), Ivan Vyskocil (Herr von Besserer), Karel Augusta (King Friedrich), Bronislav Poloczek (Duke Heinrich), Hannelore Elsner (Anna).

Conceive a costly New German Cinema historical production without the basic requirements of a flowing narrative and dialogue, nor thesps who realize movies require a different set of rules to legit theatre, and you have Edgar Reitz's "Tailor From Ulm." There's so much that's praiseworthy in this film — sets, costumes, aerial lensing, general story — that one wishes this was only the first cut and the pic could still be saved (it probably can!).

At the end of the 18th century, an apprentice tailor in Ulm, Albrecht Berblinger, contrives with friends to build a sailing contraption to fly from steep hills through the air with the greatest of ease.

The twist is that these are also revolutionary times, and German lords are fearful that the French Revolution will sprea.. in their direction. Our tailor finds himself politically in the middle.

Lensing is tops, and pic is worth a look.—*Holl.*

Arabian Adventure
(BRITISH-COLOR)

Enough flying carpets to dazzle space-age kids. Lively b.o. outlook.

London, May 24.

EMI Films (Orion-WB in U.S.) presentation of a John Dark production. Directed by Kevin Connor. Features entire cast. Screenplay. Brian Hayles; camera (color). Alan Hume; music, Ken Thorne; editor. Barry Peters; production design, Elliot Scott; art-director, Jack Maxsted; special effects. George Gibbs (supervisor). Richard Conway, David Harris; sound, Jim Atkinson. Reviewed at Bijou Preview Theatre, London, May 23, '79. Running time: 98 MINS.

Alquazar .... Christopher Lee
Khasim .... Milo O'Shea
Prince Hasan .... Oliver Tobias
Princess Zuleira .... Emma Samms
Majeed .... Puneet Sira
Wazir Al Wuzara .... Peter Cushing
Vahishta .... Capucine
Daad El Shur .... Mickey Rooney
Bahloul .... John Wyman
Abu .... Shane Rimmer
Achmed .... John Ratzenberger
Beggarwoman .... Elizabeth Welch
Fruitseller .... Michael Watkins

"Star Wars" with flying carpets in lieu of space ships — that's "Arabian Adventure," brisk, action-packed costume fantasy. The John Dark production for EMI and Orion Pictures (via Warner Bros.) should

prove a lively family trade performer.

Christopher Lee, heading an all-featured cast, plays a power-mad caliph with the gift of sorcery who's vanquished by the greater power of a magical rose. The Brian Hayles screenplay is properly pure hokum, shrewdly studded with special-effect action, smartly edited and paced under Kevin Connor's direction.

Mickey Rooney, Peter Cushing, Capucine and Milo O'Shea are also deployed, but scene-stealing honors go to little Puneet Sira and a companion monkey, the former as a waif of the streets who's the key to Lee's undoing. Oliver Tobias as a manly hero prince, and bosomy Emma Samms as a princess in bondage to the caliph, both function with okay appeal.

One and all, however, play no more than second fiddle to the special effects of George Gibbs (supervisor), Richard Conway and David Harris, whose bag of tricks ranges from magic dust to a magic precious stone, also a cave right out of Rube Goldberg, loaded with mechanical monsters (of which Rooney is the laughing mad custodian). And not least, those squadrons of flying carpets flown by libertarian revolutionaries against the caliph's forces that climaxes the tight 98-minute narrative.

The action is strictly stagebound and looks it, but the kids will lap up the gaudy settings of production designer Elliot Scott and art director Jack Maxsted. —*Pit.*

Claude Francois: Le Film De Sa Vie
(Claude Francois: The Film of His Life)
(BELGO-FRENCH-B&W/ COLOR)

Brussels, May 12.

Elan Film release of Elan Films (Brussels) - S.N.D. (Saint Ouen) co-production. Written and directed by Samy Pavel. Assistant director, Alain Cohen; camera (Eastmancolor). Ramon Suarez; editors, Pierre Didier, Eloise Cohen; sound, Pierre Daventure. Reviewed at Cinema Eldorado, Brussels, May 11, '79. Running time: 90 MINS.

A true story, this illustrates the life and times of French singer Claude Francois who died accidentally March 11, '78, in his bathroom by touching an electric bulb. He has been mourned since by thousands of his devoted fans whose money contributions have paid towards the erection of his life-size image in the cemetery where he was buried.

Patient research has permitted filmmaker Samy Pavel to film a life devoted to show business. First half of his film succeeds in spite of flaws to string together sufficient material, mostly drawn from TV sources, to explain the impact of Francois' grip on the crowds. Real asset here is the fact that his mother proved available, a charming old lady, not a bit camera shy, giving credibility and a certain human interest to events which might otherwise have fallen rather flat. There are also short interviews of Charles Aznavour, Michel Sardou, Gerard Lenorman and repetitious bits by Gilbert Becaud and Demis Roussos while testimonies by singer's first two wives also make their point.

Second half, unfortunately, in spite and perhaps because of superfluous adornments often too far fetched, simply drags. Had Pavel resisted the impulse to make a long feature, and 90 minutes is quite taxing, he might have made a much more entertaining film. Even the confession of Kathleen, the American friend who shared Claude Francois' last months, moving as it should have been, turns into a tear jerker, thus losing much impact, spoiled on the other hand by "artistic" improvements.

Strictly for Claude Francois fans; film will have to rely mainly on their active support to overcome the pitfalls of a total lack of dramatic suspense. —*Flor*.

Fast Charlie ... The Moonbeam Rider
(COLOR)

Should trail field in race for b.o. receipts.

Hollywood, May 24.
A Universal release. Produced by Roger Corman and Saul Krugman. Directed by Steve Carver. Features entire cast. Screenplay, Michael Gleason based on a story by Ed Spielman and Howard Friedlander; camera (color), William Birch; editors, Tony Redman and Eric Orner; music, Stu Phillips; art direction, Bill Sandell and Michael Riva; set decoration, Margie Fritz; sound, Glenn Williams; special effects, Roger George; assistant director, David McGiffert. Reviewed at Universal Studios, May 24, '79. (MPAA Rating: PG.) Running time: **99 MINS.**

Charlie Swattle	David Carradine
Grace Wolf	Brenda Vaccaro
Floyd Bevins	L.Q. Jones
Al Barber	R.G. Armstrong
Lester Neal	Terry Kiser
Calvin Hawk	Jesse Vint
Pop Bauer	Noble Willingham
Wesley Wolf III	Whit Clay
Sheriff	Ralph James
Young Man	Bill Hartman
Cannonball McCall	Stephen Ferry

"Fast Charlie ... The Moonbeam Rider" is a predictable but harmless bit of fluff about an essentially unlikable motorcycle rider in the 1920's who fulfills his dream of win-

ning the First Transcontinental Motorcycle Race (which actually runs only from St. Louis to San Francisco). Unfortunately, there doesn't seem to be too much of a market for post-World War I motorcycle pictures, especially those that look like they're taking place somewhere on the wagon trails of the 1800's.

Distrib Universal has apparently recognized this and is breaking the film in spotty bookings, most often as the bottom half of a drive-in double bill. That's good since it won't ruin the picture for the somewhat larger television audience it should attract in short order.

David Carradine, with a 1960's haircut and WW I flying ace garb, limns the title role of a war veteran who left his army buddies via his motorcycle just as the Germans were about to attack (the troop apparently seved as some sort of motorized messengers during the war).

Feeling a bit guilty and in search of a pit crew for the big race, Carradine rounds up the now down-on-their-luck guys (who've all managed to survive the Germans) and gives them the cash to meet him in St. Louis. While trying to bilk the rest of the money needed for the trip, he's double-crossed by clever waitress Brenda Vaccaro, who forces Carradine to take her and her son on the road with him in hopes of some money. By the time they get there, Carradine and Vaccaro are more than friends and Carradine begins to like playing daddy.

Latter portion of the picture centers on the race and Carradine's attempts to thwart some dirty trickster cyclists and emerge victorious with the trophy, the prize money and the girl.

There's something inappropriately old west about the picture, especially when Carradine goes whizzing by groups of people traveling by horse-drawn wagons to the tune of Stu Phillips' cattle ranch music.

In addition, a significant portion of the race footage is poorly photographed, making it difficult to tell whether Carradine or one of his competitors has made it to the next pit stop until the racer takes off his headgear.

Steve Carver's direction moves the story along somewhat but there's an overall choppy quality in the finished product edited by Tony Redman and Eric Orner. The actors do what they can with the surface characters, which ultimately **take second place to the race.**

Basically, the story is inoffen-

sive, and if one overlooks some of the mindless dialog, Carradine's mythical attraction as the "Hero" and the fact that Vaccaro loses more and more of her midwestern twang as the picture goes along, the film occasionally emerges as passable excapism.

But it'll take more than that to bring people out to theatres to see it.
—*Berg*.

Retour a la Bien-Aimee
(Return to the Beloved)
(FRENCH-COLOR)

Paris, May 9.
A Prodis release of an ATC 3000 - F.R. 3 - Prodis co-production. Produced by Benjamin Simon. Stars Isabelle Huppert, Jacques Dutronc, Bruno Ganz. Directed by Jean-Francois Adam. Screenplay, Adam, Georges Perec. Jean-Claude Carriere, Benoit Jacquot; camera (color), Pierre Lhomme; sound, Pierre Lenoir; music, Antoine Duhamel; editor, Eric Pluet; art directors, Yves Bernard and Nicole Bertrand; costumes, Christian Gasc. Reviewed at Cinema U.G.C. Odeon, Paris, May 7, 1979. Running time: **98 MINS.**

Jeanne	Isabelle Huppert
Julien	Jacques Dutronc
Kern	Bruno Ganz

This is Jean-Francois Adam's third film in nine years. Unsatisfied with his two previous efforts ("M As In Mathieu" and "Game of Solitaire"), which he scripted alone, this stage director and former assistant to Truffaut, Godard and Chabrol has enlisted the talents of scenarists George Perec (Alain Corneau's "Thriller Story") and Jean-Claude Carriere and director Benoit Jacquot for the script of this haunting moral thriller.

Film is about Julien, a pianist, who ruthlessly plots to regain possession of ex-wife, Jeanne, and child and the country house, his childhood home, in which she currently lives with her new husband, a doctor.

Julien stages a fake burglary of their property and then lures to the grounds a man who has done some detective work for him. Julien shoots him with a gun taken from the doctor's study.

Following the discovery of the corpse Jeanne asks Julien to come and stay for a time, presumably for the child's sake. Thus within the house he can watch his scheme follow its course: the doctor is arrested for the crime, leaving the musician to lure his wife back into his emotional grasp. Despite her efforts to keep him off, she ends by surrendering to him even as the police close in on the house where they are lost in a timeless, dreamlike embrace.

It's a cool, adult fairy tale of implacable perversity and moral enigma, beautifully contrived by Adam and his co-writers and elegantly executed by the director,

with the immeasurable aid of Pierre Lhomme's indelible images and stealthy camera work, Eric Pluet's subtle editing and Antoine Duhamel's music. The principal roles are held by Jacques Dutronc and Isabelle Huppert, two fine actors who command the eye with restraint and professional ease. Bruno Ganz is also capably on hand as Huppert's new husband, passively watching his whole life being taken from him.

Adam is clearly a director of ability with a style that appears to owe much to the hieratic quality of some of the best Japanese filmmakers. Indeed the memorable final sequence, with the camera stealing across the hall of the country house to reveal Dutronc and Huppert on the staircase, oblivious to the immobile policemen in the open doorway through which an impenetrable mist can be seen lurking, evokes Mizoguchi. —*Len*.

Ravagers
(COLOR)

A ramble among assorted weirdos. Hard going probable.

Hollywood, May 22.
A Columbia Pictures release, produced by John W. Hyde. Exec producer, Saul David. Features entire cast. Directed by Richard Compton. Screenplay, Donald S. Sanford, based on novel, "Path To Savagery," by Robert Edmond Alter; camera (Metrocolor), Vincent Saizis; editor, Maury Winetrobe; sound, Garry Cunningham; production design, Ronald E. Hobbs; costumes, Ron Talsky; assistant director, Pat Kehoe; Fred Karlin. Reviewed at Columbia Studios, May 22, '79. (MPAA rating: PG.) Running time: **91 MINS.**

Falk	Richard Harris
Faina	Ann Turkel
Sergeant	Art Carney
Rann	Ernest Borgnine
Leader	Anthony James
Brown	Woody Strode
Miriam	Alana Hamilton
Blindman	Seymour Cassel

This film's failure is too bad because it obviously isn't a shoddy exploitation effort. Much of it has been made with care and with a good cast and visually, it is constantly interesting. Production designer Ronald E. Hobbs and cameraman Vincent Saizis have done an excellent job in transferring Alabama locations into a desolate landscape of the future after some kind of disaster — the film never says what — has destroyed the country and poisoned the sea.

Richard Harris is first seen carrying a rifle down a deserted city street. Suddenly, someone shoots at him. Does he take cover? Shoot back? No, he pauses a moment and continues on down the street and there are no more shots. He reaches a deserted steel mill, where he lives with his young wife, Alana Hamilton, who looks remarkably healthy since they're supposed to be near-starvation.

A gang of raggedy "Ravagers," led by Anthony James, attacks and murders Hamilton. That night Harris murders one of them in revenge, then runs off. James doesn't know which way in the world Harris went but manages to lead the gang after him anyway. On the road, Harris, encounters a blind man, Seymour Cassel, who's been turned out by his tribe. Harris takes him back and the tribe rains large stones down on their head from high above. But the rocks only hit Cassel and Harris is on the road again.

Next he comes upon an old missile base watched over by daffy Art Carney. Apparently the ravagers or anyone else have never stumbled over the base before because it's full of food and machine guns and the ravagers are still fighting with sticks and bones. Carney takes Harris to visit a nearby tribe who live in tents inside a cave, though it's not explained why they would rather live there than at Carney's cozy missile base.

Harris meets another young beauty, Ann Turkel, though it isn't clear where all these foxes are coming from since it's been established that the disaster took place 50 years before and there are no children anywhere around.

After bedding with Turkel, Harris goes back on the road with Carney and run across Turkel the following night in the woods. "I've been following you since yesterday," she says. "What the hell for?" he asks. "Why the hell do you think," she responds, but unfortunately the questions are never answered. And there are lots of scenes like that.

The trio ends up in a deserted farmhouse and the ravagers attack again. Though Harris and Carney have a machine gun and a repeating rifle and seem to be doing a handy job blowing away the guys with sticks and knives, Harris and Turkel retreat to the woods and Carney is captured.

By now, nobody should be surprised to learn that there's another bunch of people in this desolate land who've been able to survive in relatively luxury on an old navy ship And they allow Harris to come aboard with his machine gun. Thereupon he discovers that some of the residents don't like living under the benevolent dictatorship of Ernest Borgnine and would rather be out scrounging for food and living in rags like everybody else.

In the meantime, the ravagers have let Carney go so he would lead them to Harris. And they attack the ship. (Somehow, though about two-

thirds of the gang were shot up back at the farmhouse, the ravagers have now increased in number about four-fold.) There's a big battle and the ship blows up.

Harris, Turkel, Carney and some of the ship's dissidents end up on the beach with no food, but they seem happy. And the whole thing says something about man's will to survive and be free and rejuvenate the earth. But certainly doesn't say much. —*Har.*

Cronica De Um Industrial
(Chronicle Of An Industrialist)
(BRAZIL-COLOR)

Cannes, May 20.
Produced by Luis Rosemberg Filho and Renator Coutinho. Directed by Rosemberg. Features entire cast. Screenplay. Rosemberg; camera (color), Luis; edited by Ricardo Miranda. Reviewed at Cannes Film Festival. Directors' Fortnight, May 19, 1979. Running time: **100 MINS.**
Cast: Renato Coutinho, Ana Maria Miranda and Wilson Grey.

There could be some dispute whether the leading influence on Luis Rosemberg is Straub, Schroeter or Daniel Schmid, but its mixture of sex, violence, political discourse, Bach, and occasionally striking imagery is certainly not in the mainstream of Brazilian cinema, and, in spite of its search for originality, it tends to be derivative.

Equally damaging is the lack of clarity in its political ideas. "Chronicle Of An Industrialist" has been prohibited on its home territory. This would definitely appear a case of overzealousness; left to its own devices, it would be unlikely to have either audience or even much festival impact. —*Amig.*

Wsrod Nocnej Ciszy
(Quiet Is The Night)
(POLISH-COLOR)

Cannes, May 18.
A Film Polski Production. Film Unit "X." Warsaw; world rights. Film Polski, Warsaw. Features entire cast. Directed by Tadeusz Chmielewski. Screenplay, based on novel by Ladislav Fuks. "Inspector Heumann"; camera (color). Jerzy Sawicki; music. Jerzy Matuszkiewicz; sets. Teresa Smus-Barska. Reviewed at Cannes Film Festival (market). May 17. '79. Running time: **128 MINS.**
Cast: Tomasz Zaliwski, Piotr Lysak. Antonina Barczewska. Halina Kowalska. Zygmunt Maciejewski. Czeslaw Lipowska. Tadeusz Teodorczyk.

A psychological detective story about a police hunt for the murderer of young boys between 8 and 10. Tadeusz Chmielewski's "Quiet Is the Night" has the necessary

twists to put it a cut above the average crime pix emerging from Socialist countries in ever more frequency of late. What's unusual about it is that the police commissioner ends up tracing the clues to his own home: there he has an unusual adolescent son he has not been able to communicate with due to divergences of opinion on everything from dreams and hobbies to hiding and helping a foreign-born psychopath on a river barge. All three die in the final shoot-out just as the public is about ready to guess who the real killer is.

Lensing and thesp performances are above par, but story and dialog lacks a sharp edge to give the central figures depth and motivation. Still, this genre has come a long way in East Europe, and one waits for the day when a b.o. winner with legs will emerge — particularly from Poland where novelties and filmmakers often collaborate on projects. —*Holl.*

Yotz'Im Kavua
(Going Steady)
(ISRAEL-W. GERMAN-COLOR)

Cannes, May 25.
A Noah Film Distribution of a Golan-Globus Production. Produced by Sam Weinberg. Menahem Golan and Yoram Globus. Features entire cast. Directed by Boaz Davidson. Screenplay. Boaz Davidson. Eli Tavor; camera (Color). Adam Greenberg; editor, by Alain Jacubowicz; art director. Eytan Levi. Reviewed in Olympia Cinema. Cannes. May 24. 1979. Running time: **100 MINS.**
Benjie .... Yiftach Katzur
Bobby ....Jonathan Segal
Huey......................Zachi Noy
Tammy .... Yvonne Michaeli
Shelly .... Daphna Armoni
Martha .... Rachel Steiner

Since puppy love in the "Lemon Popsicle" formula has proven such a success the first time around, a sequel was only to be expected. And indeed, director Boaz Davidson is returning to the high school types who made his fortune in his previous film, sending them on more typicaly adolescent adventures.

This time, he abandoned any pretense of supplying a credible background, either as to location of period. Unless one is very familiar with Tel Aviv, it is very difficult to say where it is taking place, and looking at the jeans everybody wears, there is no indication that the whole story doesn't happen right in the Seventies. The only indication which hints more accurately at the fact that Davidson is again talking about the late Fifties, are the string of hits on the soundtrack, compiled in "American Graffiti" style to follow the characters around and

give the necessary amplification to their feelings (for instance, the old weepy "Tell Laura I Love Her" is used in moments of distress).

The story is even thinner than in the first opus, with the nice boy. Yiftach Katzur, the ladykiller, Jonathan Segal, and fatty Zachi Noy, being concerned with one problem only: how to find sex.

While this may seem extraordinary for a country in which youth has to face so many problems so early in life, it seems, at least from experience, that it is exactly what the doctor ordered for the boxoffice.

Humor is on the broad side, big laughs being elicited when Katzur, giving vent to loud complaints, or Noy hiding under the bed while a couple is using it, or the same Zachi Noy getting caught in a bathroom window by a group of hoodlums.

Yet, the film lacks some of the more riotous scenes which turned into showstoppers in "Lemon Popsicle."

Acting, on the whole, is natural, being an advantage for this kind of story which could be killed by too much self-consciousness. Katzur is cockier than he ever was in "Lemon Popsicle," and his new screen heartbeat, Yvonne Michaeli, comes out quite convincingly, in spite of many personal problems she had during production.

Indeed, the ground has been laid for a very successful initial release in Israel, with public relations promising the public lots of daring jokes, and with the reputation of the first success attracting crowds. But after hitting the market, it will have to rely mostly on word-of-mouth, as the critics are unlikely to give it much assistance. —*Edna.*

La Empresa Perdona Un Momento De Locura
(The Management Forgives A Moment of Madness)
(VENEZUELAN-COLOR)

Cannes, May 20.
A Proa C.A., production. Directed by Mauricio Walerstein. Screenplay. Walerstein; camera. (color). Hector Rios; music. Alberto Slewynger; art director. Tony Sanchez; editor. Alberto Torija. Reviewed at Cannes Film Festival. May 19. 1979. Directors' Fortnight. Running Time: **90 MINS.**
Cast: Simon Dias. Eva Mondolfi. Rafael Briceno. Maria Escalona. Arturo Calderon. Rafael Gomez. Fausto Verdial.

The development of workers' social consciousness and the problems of unions are shown in this Venezuelan film, parallel to management's evolution from oldtime use of physical violence to more modern methods of repression.

The story is centered on Mariano,

a foreman who worked 20 of his 48 years in the same factory. The idea of social change is unattractive to him and, in spite of the tensions that surround him, at the factory and in the working class district where he lives, he simply does not question prevailing conditions. Until one day Mariano goes berserk because a youngster, against his advice, was put to work at a machine with insufficient training and his hands are maimed. Instead of fining him, the management sends Mariano to a psychiatrist where, under guise of treatment, he is reconditioned (i.e., brainwashed) into docility. Thus, a potential union leader is neutralized.

The screenplay, contains some interesting ideas but wavers towards the end, meandering excessively before it reaches its otherwise effective ending.

The film's most serious problem is inadequate craftsmanship. Mexican director Mauricio Walerstein does not handle actors well and the crowd scenes, although they may have used authentic workers, appear too artificial. Editing should have been much tighter and there is an all round amateurishness that limits the pic's interest. —Amig.

Los Sobrevivientes
(Survivors)
(CUBAN-COLOR)

Cannes, May 23.

An I.C.A.I.C. production. Directed by Thomas Gutierrez Alea. Features entire cast. Screenplay, Antonio Benitez, Gutierrez Alea; camera, (color), Mario Garcia Joya; music, Leo Brouwer.

Cast: Enrique Santisteban, Reinaldo Miravalles, German Pinelli, Ana Vinas, Vicente Revuelta, Carlos Ruiz de la Tejera, Leonor Borrero. Reviewed at Cannes Film Festival, in competition, May 22, '79. Running time: 116 MINS.

The film's opening credit dedication to Luis Bunuel is no idle "hommage," for the development of Tomas Gutierrez Alea's film is close to Bunuel's idiosyncrasy and specifically linked to his "Exterminating Angel."

The story begins shortly after Castro's revolution (1959): the members of the aristocratic Orozco family are shocked at the turn of events, but hopefully believe they can't last. So they decide to isolate themselves, in order to remain uncontaminated by what-to them-is a crumbling outside world. At first their actions reflect what actually happened among the bourgeoisie at the time; they hoard food and withdraw their money from bank accounts in case these are blocked.

But soon events take an ever more grotesque turn, with plentiful moments of black humour. The Orozcos still wear black tie for dinner, for within their scale of values appearances are paramount. In their isolated little world they strive to maintain "Orden y progredo" (approximately, "law and order") but, left to their own devices, the inbuilt decadence of the upper classes expresses itself: there is what psychologists would call a mechanism of regression, as they revert to ever more rudimentary forms of personal and economic relationships. When there are signs of rebellion from their servants, these are reduced to slavery and, when the servants flee, the crisis becomes really serious.

"Survivors" is a carefully thought out metaphor in which nothing is left to chance. Some viewers at Cannes felt that the symbolism was less subtle and ambiguous than is the case in Bunuel's films and they are right; but Gutierrez Alea's objectives are also different and, behind the imaginative direction and humor, there clearly is a mind at work. Guitierrez Alea is one of his country's leading filmmakers; his point of view towards society is Marxist and this will obviously lead to disagreements with his approach by some viewers.

But, at the same time, his satire of the traditional Cuban aristocracy is pretty true to life. On the other hand, in spite of the film's good technical level and acting it is too drawn out. A parable of this sort has to flow continuously; it cannot afford to stand still and, towards the end, (around the cat-hunting scene), "Survivors" loses its rhythm. A little tightening could go a long way. —Amig.

Zmory
(Nightmares)
(POLISH-COLOR)

Cannes, May 21.

A Film Polski Production, Warsaw, Tor Unit; world rights, Film Polski, Warsaw. Features entire cast. Directed by Wojciech Marczewski. Screenplay, Pawel Jajny, Marczewski, based on a novel by Emil Zegadlowicz; camera (color), Wieslaw Zdort, editing, Irena Chorynska; music, Zigmunt Konieczny. Reviewed at Cannes Film Festival (Directors' Fortnight), May 20, '79. Running time: 111 MINS.

Cast: Tomasz Hudziec, Piotr Lysak, Hanna Skarzanka, Maria Chwalibog, Teresa Marczewski, Bronislaw Pawlik, Janusz Michalowski.

Wojciech Marczewski's "Nightmares" scores as a period piece dealing with the Austrian occupation of Polish territory before the First World War. The main figure is a boy of primary school age, who later grows up to be a rebellious, poetic-minded teenager in the same school at the very moment when a national movement towards revolt is underway. In short, this is a parableo of historical proportions which can fit several countries today where church and state, or similar weddings of social ideologies, work together to suppress the human spirit. At times, particularly in the first part, Jean Vigo's "Zero for Conduct" comes to mind as a closely related sardonic metaphor on school days.

Marczewski, a young helmer with tv experience, handles thesps with a sure hand and draws excellent performances from all the school boys, who suffer in different ways from the daily tyranny dished out by a pro-Austria school director (the boy is Polish-bred), a fanatical religion teacher (the boy's leaning is towards atheism), and a cruel-minded prof who demands the kids laugh while he tortures them mentally and physically. No wonder our young hero cannot separate harsh reality from recurring nightmares.

But he's also separated from his parents: the father was, in fact, a respected professor, and the mother has to put him in a boarding house for lack of funds in supporting his education. There is thus little chance for the boy to rebel save in his poetry and silent resistances. Further, the boarding house is also a bordello on the side, and the boy gets into fights with fellow students on occasion due to his frailty and sensitivity. Some fellow students get picked up by police.

This is an unrelenting, pessimistic tale, but one that holds the acquainted viewer's attention from start to finish. Everything dealing with social classes and sacred institutions is held up to ridicule and analysis, while the main thread of the story quietly blends into the main character's daily experienced nightmares until the lines of reality are wiped out.

Though not a commercial pic, "Nightmares" was one of the best entries in the Directors' Fortnight at Cannes. It deserves further exposure on the summer fest circuit and in Polish Film Weeks. Credits are good notch over average, particularly lensing. — Holl.

Die Schattengrenze
(Frontiers Of Darkness)
(WEST GERMAN-COLOR)

Cannes, May 19.

A CCC-Television Production, West Berlin, for Second German Television (ZDF), Wiesbaden; world rights, Wolf Gremm-CCC-Television Berlin. Features entire cast. Directed by wolf Gremm. Screenplay, Dieter Wellershoff, based on his novel of the same title; camera, (color), Juergen Wagner; sets, Herbert Schaefer; costumes, Uschi Welter; tv editor, Willi Segler. Reviewed at Cannes Film Festival (Market), May 18, '79. Running time 105 MINS.

Cast: Guenter Lamprecht (Matthias Berger), Antje Hagen (Hilde), Friedrich W. Bauschulte, Dieter B. Gerlach, Ulli Kinalzik, Carlos M. Bravo, Roman A.N. Gonzales, Ayten Erten, Dorothea Moritz, Andreas Mannkopf, Engelbert von Nordhausen.

A tv prod slated also in the "German Series" of the recent Berlin Film Festival, Wolf Gremm's "Frontiers of Darkness" is another Teutonic shot at the popular "cine noir" genre (sometimes referred to as the "existentialist thriller") that traces its roots back to Hammett-Chandler pix in Hollywood. Not very much needs to make sense in this make-shift copy of mysterious cops-and-robbers, so long as it's tightly edited and carried by a strong leading actor (as in Hawks-Bogart's "The Big Sleep").

Gremm's "Frontiers of Darkness" focuses on a loser in his late forties, mysteriously handed a car repair shop to manage, then finding himself duped by the girlfriend who helped him get the job (he met her, of course, on a train taking him nowhere in particular) and a gang of car-thieves (foreign accents for more mystery) who need the garage for shady international deals involving broken-down cars and false papers. Our hero also stupidly takes to embezzling company funds. He gets caught in the middle, taken for a ride by the gang, and shot in a dumpyard.

Poor dialog and inept handling of story and thesps lead to a dud in category, although the makings of a successful thriller are in the story.
—Holl.

The World Is Full Of Married Men
(BRITISH-COLOR)

Good outlook for sex-meller with a message.

London, May 30.
New Realm presentation of a Married Men Production. Executive producer, Adrienne Fancey. Produced by Malcolm Fancey, Oscar Lerman. Features entire cast. Directed by Robert Young. Screenplay, Jackie Collins (with additional dialog by Terry Howard), based on her novel; camera (color), Ray Parslow; editor, David Campling; music, Frank Musker, Dominic Bugatti; art director, Tony Curtis; sound, Claude Hitchcock, Trevor Pyke; asst. director, David Anderson; score features Hot Gossip, title song sung by Mick Jackson, Bonnie Tyler, and various disco tracks. Reviewed at the Classic theatre, Haymarket, London, May 29, '79. (BBFC Rating: X.). Running time: **107 MINS.**

David Cooper . . . . Anthony Franciosa
Linda Cooper . . . . Carroll Baker
Claudia Parker . . . . Sherrie Cronn
Gem Gemini . . . . Paul Nicholas
Jay Grossman . . . . Gareth Hunt
Lori Grossman . . . . Georgina Hale
Conrad Lee . . . . Anthony Steel
Joe . . . . John Nolan
Miss Field . . . . Jean Gilpin
Gerda . . . . Moira Downie
Sharon . . . . Alison Elliott
Mercedes Benz . . . . Eva Louise

Jackie Collins, regularly described as Britain's answer to Jacqueline Susann, differs from her American counterpart in that — in her first (1968) novel at least, "The World Is Full Of Married Men," and now in her own screen adaptation of it — she's more honestly desirous on behalf of her sex for sweet revenge on the ubiquitous, double-standard male. Her fervently opportunistic feminism claims an equal right not just to the fruits of ordinary labor, but to the forbidden fruit as well — the sexual supergoodies.

Set in a glossy world of penthouses and charge accounts, the medium for her message is sexploitation melodrama which, cunningly, will titillate both sexes. Efficiently acted, snappily edited and adequately directed, the picture is a good deal better than the long line of limp-core cheapies which have served as the bottom line of British film production through flush times and lean. As socalled sizzling fare, it should be consumed while hot, and fast playoff should show a decent return.

Locally it's aimed at speedy nationwide coverage via producer New Realm's own distribution arm and EMI theatres, with tv spots tied to release of the disco soundtrack album by Ronco Records, a socalled tv merchandiser. Deals for the U.S. and other territories are not yet settled.

Anthony Franciosa brings a mercifully light touch to the central antihero, an errant advertising executive who trips over one floozie too many and falls in love. Obsessed with an ambitious model who proves a lot tougher than himself, and stumbling helplessly from one wrong move to the next, he successively forfeits his marriage, the affair, his cool and — Collins' most vengeful stroke — his potency. In a final sensationalist twist, he vents a new-found insanity on his wife's popstar lover, and shoots him dead onstage.

Notwithstanding the strictly escapist, midatlantic neverneverland in which it all takes place, the script contains enough dialog to demand slightly more of the actors than posturing as mere foreground-dressing. All the same Collins' manipulative technique does not allow for in-depth characterization, so cameos tend to come off best. Georgina Hale is routine (for her) but effective as a laconic wife who's come to terms with the sexcess scene.

Carroll Baker works creditably hard as Franciosa's oft-betrayed spouse who — in a suspiciously convenient dramatic move — finds affection in the back of a limousine with a teen-idol some 15 years her junior. Paul Nicholas in that role is uncharismatic, but renders some hard-to-stomach romantic sequences made plausible by committed playing. Sherrie Cronn as the doll with the heart of plastic is more successful flouncing around half-dressed than making an essentially superficial character believable.

With okay production values, the film's main credit goes to director Robert Young and editor David Campling, who have done a professional job of keeping up the pace through the more laughably lurid moments. — *Simo.*

Hot Stuff
(COLOR)

Could Live Up To Its Title.

Miami, June 1.
Columbia Pictures release of a Rastar-Mort Engelberg production. Executive producer, Paul Maslansky. Produced by Mort Engelberg. Directed by Dom DeLuise. Stars DeLuise, Suzanne Pleshette, Jerry Reed. Screenplay, Michael Kane, Donald E. Westlake; camera (color), credit not provided; music, Patrick Williams. Reviewed at the Dadeland Twin theatre, Miami, May 25, '79. (MPAA Rating - PG). Running time: **103 MINS.**
Ernie Fortunato . . . . Dom DeLuise
Doug Van Horne . . . . Jerry Reed
Louise Webster . . . . Suzanne Pleshette
Eduardo . . . . Louis Avalof
Capt. Geibarger . . . . Ossie Davis

Dom DeLuise's directorial bow, filmed entirely on Miami locations, may break the "made in Miami" hex. "Hot Stuff," in which he also stars, is funny stuff. It's pratfall, slapstick stuff handled in a manner that makes audiences laugh the way good comedies used to.

Joining DeLuise are Jerry Reed and Suzanne Pleshette, the latter making her first feature film in a number of years. Reed wrote the title song, which sounds as if it will be a seller. Pleshette doesn't have much to do. DeLuise and the characters he has rounded up take up most of the footage.

Plot is a basic wacky theme. Pleshette, DeLuise and Reed portray officers on a Burglary Task Force. They decide the best way to get convictions is to go into the fencing business themselves, with Pleshette stationed behind a two-way mirror to film all the "customers" (and they're a motley bunch).

If there's anything seriously wrong with "Hot Stuff," it's DeLuise's obsession with the people he discovered and cast in offbeat roles. At times, their parade into the fence shop seems endless.

Otherwise film is sly and satirical at times, though most of its energy is poured into the visual comedy that is a DeLuise forte. The preview audience at a screening here howled for most of the film's two hours. — *Von.*

Butch And Sundance
(COLOR)

Not enuf horsing around in placid "Butch Cassidy" prequel.

Hollywood, May 30.
20th Century-Fox release of a Pantheon-William Goldman production. Produced by Gabriel Katzka, Steven Bach. Directed by Richard Lester. Features entire cast. Screenplay, Allan Burns, based on characters created by William Goldman; camera (color), Laszlo Kovacs; editors, Antony Gibbs, George Trirogoff; music, Patrick Williams; production design, Brian Eatwell; art direction, Jack DeGovia; costume design, William Theiss; sound, David Ronne; stunt coordinator, Loren Janes; assistant director, Jack Frost Sanders. Reviewed at 20th Century-Fox, May 30, '79. (MPAA Rating: PG.) Running time: **110 MINS.**
Sundance Kid . . . . William Katt
Butch Cassidy . . . . Tom Berenger
Ray Bledsoe . . . . Jeff Corey
Harvey Logan . . . . John Schuck
Mike Cassidy . . . . Michael C. Gwynne
Joe LeFors . . . . Peter Weller
O.C. Hanks . . . . Brian Dennehy
Bill Carver . . . . Chris Lloyd
Mary . . . . Jill Eikenberry
Wyoming Governor . . . : . . . . Arthur Hill
Guard . . . . Vincent Schiavelli

With so many sequels being churned out these days, 20th Century-Fox decided to go the other way with their 1969 smash, "Butch Cassidy And The Sundance Kid." But the prequel, "Butch And Sundance: The Early Days" doesn't match its progenitor in either casting or style, and boxoffice grazing looks to be lean.

This isn't the first time a story line has catapulted backwards in time. Paramount tried a similar feat in 1966, when "Nevada Smith" picked up on the early career of the Steve McQueen character first introduced (voa Alan Ladd) in the 1964 release of "The Carpetbaggers." Lillian Hellman did the same with "Another Part of the Forest," the earlier days of "The Little Foxes."

Without Paul Newman or Robert Redford in the title roles, however, it doesn't matter whether "Butch" dwells on the pair's infancy or senility — there's no star chemistry, nor any marquee value. Tom Berenger and William Katt acquit themselves admirably, but they simply can't compete with the ghosts of two superstars.

"Butch" is also disappointing given the creative elements involved. Richard Lester had distinguished himself as of late by setting up realistic period pieces, and then puncturing historical myths with highly visual comedy, as in "Robin And Marian" and "The Three Musketeers." There's some of that in "Butch," but considering scripter Allan Burns' background as a tv comedy scribe, not nearly enough.

For most of its 110 minutes, "Butch" is standard sagebrush material, with few of the comic misadventures that characterized original screenplay by William Goldman and spritely direction by George Roy Hill. There are some patented Lester hijinks in the first half-hour of the prequel, but these peter out surprisingly soon.

What's left is a mishmash of effective stuntwork and visuals, and a story line that moseys along with little suspense or excitement. Scene in which Berenger dreams up Katt's Sundance monicker, for instance, has all the excitement of seeing Edison invent the electric light bulb — you know whats going to happen.

Pic's best element is its secondary casting, with Mike Fenton and Jane Feinberg picking all the right faces for the smaller roles. Jeff Corey is the sole returning cast member from the original, but he gets good help from Brian Dennehy as a vengeful outlaw, John Schuck and Chris Lloyd as incompetent accomplices, and Michael C. Gwynne, Peter Weller and Vincent Schiavelli in assorted minor roles.

But they don't make up for the loose ends resulting from Burns' raggedy plotting, and after the initial curiosity interest is satisfied, "Butch And Sundance: The Early Days" faces a long, hard boxoffice trail. — *Poll.*

The Brood
(CANADIAN-COLOR)

Slick shocker with killer kids looks exploitable in usual market.

Hollywood, June 1.
New World Pictures release. Executive producers, Pierre David, and Victor Solnicki. Produced by Claude Heroux. Stars Oliver Reed, Samantha Eggar. Directed by David Cronenberg. Camera (color), Mark Irwin; editor, Alan Collins; and written music, Howard Shore; art direction, Carol Spier; sound, Bryan Day. Reviewed at the Aidikoff Screening Room, L.A., June 1, '79. (MPAA Rating: R.) Running time: **91 MINS.**

Dr. Raglan	Oliver Reed
Nola Carveth	Samantha Eggar
Frank Carveth	Art Hindle
Candice Carveth	Cindy Hinds
Julianna	Nuala Fitzgerald
Barton Kelly	Henry Beckerman
Ruth	Susan Hogan
Inspector Mrazek	Michael McGhee
Mike Trellan	Gary McKeehan
Jan Hartog	Bob Silverman
Dr. Desborough	Joseph Shaw
The Child	Felix Silla
Resnikoff	Larry Solway
Birkin	Rainer Schwartz
Chris	Nicholas Campbell

Yet another horror entry which casts children in the role of malevolent little monsters, "The Brood" is an extremely well made, if essentially unpleasant, shocker which trades freely in elements found in other pics such as "Village Of The Damned," "Night Of The Living Dead" and even the current "Alien." Canadian-made effort errs in its talkiness but is eminently exploitable and should do well in its intended market.

Writer-director David Cronenberg developed a cult following on the basis of "They Came From Within" and "Rabid" and continues to show marked technical development. Though not yet up to the level of John Carpenter, who works in a similar vein, Cronenberg's helming is skillful enough to command attention even through his script's needlessly long stretches of dialog and in the last 15 minutes he makes it all pay off, even if his intentions are rather base, even repugnant.

Cronenberg keeps the audience as well as his characters in the dark as to what's going on until the last possible minute. Much of the surface action is relatively plodding stuff, with young parent Art Hindle trying to keep his daughter away from mother Samantha Eggar, who's supposedly in psychotherapy at the posh forested retreat of analyst Oliver Reed. Action is spiked with the mysterious murders of Eggar's parents as well as some effective psycho-drama scenes conducted by Reed.

Reed registers forcefully as the egotistical doctor and Eggar is appropriately flipped out but, unfor-

tunately, most of the running time is spent with Hindle center stage and the actor is just too morose to enlist much sympathy, despite his plight.

Technically the film is outstanding. Mark Irwin, a young Canadian cinematographer with only a few pictures behind him, turns in a terrific job which bears favorable comparison with any lensing being done on this level of filmmaking in either Canada or the States. Howard Shore's music is properly tense and the locations, particularly Reed's modernistic compound.

Pic is copyrighted by the Montreal Trust Co. of Canada and was backed by the Canadian Film Development Corp. —*Cart.*

Sunnyside
(COLOR)

Joey Travolta's no John in another dud gang saga. Time to get off the streets.

Hollywood, May 31.
American International release of a Robert Schaffel production. Produced by Robert L. Schaffel. Directed by Timothy Galfas. Features entire cast. Screenplay, Timothy Galfas, Jeff King, from story by Jeff King, Robert L. Schaffel; camera (Movielab color), Gary Graver; editor, Herbert H. Dow; supervising editor, Eric Albertson; Alan Douglas, Harold Wheeler; assistant director, Ramiro Jaloma. Reviewed at AIP Screening Room, Beverly Hills, May 31, 1979. (MPAA Rating: R.) Running time: **100 MINS.**

Nick Martin	Joey Travolta
Denny Martin	John Lansing
Donna Rosario	Stacey Pickren
Eddie Reaper	Andrew Rubin
Harry Cimoli	Michael Tucci
Ann Rosario	Talia Balsam
Reggie Flynn	Chris Mulkey
Mrs. Martin	Joan Darling
Hector	Richard Beauchamp
Ice	Heshimu Cumbuka
Wild Child	Jonathan Gries
Rage	E. Lamont Johnson

AIP will probably go to great lengths to disguise the fact, but the company's got a full-blown gang picture on its hands in the innocuously titled "Sunnyside," with a downer ending to boot. John Travolta's brother Joey is okay in his pic debut, but the role's so bland and the film's so bad that lightning won't strike twice, at least this time out. B.O. prospects look shaky.

Joey plays a kid who should have left the gang life behind a long time ago but who, like Tony in "West Side Story," can't quite shake his roots. He thinks he can do some good for the "community" by staying on the streets and knocking off a rival gang called the Savage Warlocks, after which he'll move to Manhattan for the good life with g.f. Stacey Pickren. As he says, in the manner of so many headstrong heroes before him, "I gotta do what I gotta do." But like Tony, he pays the price for stretching his luck.

Unfortunately, Joey's role is so much the good, sweet guy, almost a mediator-missionary among all the other punks and louts on the block, that the character generates no dramatic tension or excitement. He's got John's swagger, accent and smile, but he actually looks as much like Joe Namath as he resembles his brother, with his present acting talent seeming to lie somewhere in between.

Desultory script by director Timothy Galfas and Jeff King, from King's and producer Robert L. Schaffel's story, flops awkwardly from one hackneyed scene to another, never developing any dramatic plausibility or insight into lower-class life. For a film centering on supposedly economically oppressed characters, money never seems to be a problem for anyone, with Joey's upwardly mobile brother scouting a new apartment on an extremely ritzy Gotham street. Clinker lines abound, best of which may be, "I saw some of your graffiti today. It keeps getting better."

Galfas, a still photographer and commercial and tv director, shows surprisingly little adeptness with the camera, often shooting scenes from high angles which cover all the action but dissipate visual force. Gary Graver's photography is good, with a bit of New York lensing establishing the locale and L.A. doubling in most scenes. The score by Alan Douglas and Harold Wheeler seems an attempt to create enough contemporary music to fill out an album (to be distributed by Casablanca), but nothing leaps off the track as an obvious hit.

Most of the characterizations are in the earnest vein, with John Lansing as the brother constantly imploring Joey to get off the streets and Stacey Pickren spending most of her time throwing her arms around Joey and looking sweet. Most effective, despite the stock part, is Andrew Rubin as the slick Latino rival gang leader. Joan Darling is in briefly as the boys' mother. —*Cart.*

Summer Camp
(COLOR)

For teenage drive-in crowds only.

Hollywood, June 1.
Seymour Borde & Associates release of a Borson production. Exec producers, Seymour Borde, Dan Sonney. Produced by Mark Borde. Directed by Chuck Vincent. Features entire cast. Screenplay, Avrumie Schnitzer, based on a story by Mark Borde and Schnitzer; camera (color), Ken Gibb; editor, Mark Ubell; music, Sparky Sugarman; sound, Trevor Black; choreography, Dino Joseph Giannetta. No other credits available. Reviewed at Vine Theatre, Holly-

wood, June 1, '79. (MPAA Rating: R.) Running time: **85 MINS.**
Cast: Michael Abrams, Jake Barnes, Bud Bogart, Louise Carmona, Verkina Flower, Brenda Fogarty, Barbara Gold, Shelly Hart, Walt Hill, Ray Holland, Peter Lovett, Debra Marx, John C. McLaughlin, Matt Michaels, George Mills, Collene O'Neil, Dustin Pacino Jr., Harry Reardon, Alexis Schreiner, Valdesta, Ralph Von Albertson, Robert Wald, Bonnie Werchan.

It's a good thing summer comes along every year for playoff of pix of this ilk — even drive-in operators would turn this one down if they had an advance look. Given the realities of the market, however, "Summer Camp" will get some fast reruns before being consigned to double-bill oblivion.

Not even a pale imitation of "National Lampoon's Animal House," the Borson production is set at failing Camp Malibu, which invites long-ago campers back for a "funfilled" weekend in the hopes their parents will cough up the needed cash.

Only ones coughing up with "Summer Camp" will be its audience, however. Pic is ridiculously plotted, atrociously shot, and features a cast whose primary attributes are between their necks and their knees.

Primary appeal will be the preponderance of softcore footage, dwelling exclusively on the femme players. But even that loses its interest, especially given the poor technical quality of the lensing and editing. Chuck Vincent's direction is not apparent.

"Summer Camp" marks first foray into production by indie distrib Seymour Borde & Associates, with a screenplay by United Artists Theatre Circuit's Southern California film buyer, Avrumie Schnitzer. All parties concerned should have known better. —*Poll.*

Cannes Festival

Siberiade
(RUSSIAN-70M-COLOR)

Cannes, May 21.
Sovexport release of Mosfilm production. Features entire cast. Director Andrei Mikhalkov-Konchalovsky. Screenplay, Valentin Ejov, Mikhalkov-Konchalovsky; camera (Sovcolor), Levan Paatashvili; editor, Valentina Koulaguine; music, Edouard Artemiev. Reviewed at Cannes Film Fest (competing), May 20. Running time: **210 MINS.**

Afanassi	Vladimir Smailov
Nikolai	Vitale Solomina
Anastassia	Nathalia Andreitchenko
Evofei	Erqueni Petrov
Radian	Mikhail Knonov
Alexei	Nikita Mikhalkov

Taia . . . . Ludmila Gourtchenko
Spiridou . . . . Sergei Shakourov

"Siberiade" is a lumbering Soviet epic spanning three generations of two families in a Siberian hamlet from 1900, through 1917, the Russian Revolution, to the '60s. Familiar, often academic, film displays lavish treatment, fine craftsmanship, poetic shafts for festival interest, though it's somewhat long-winded and diffuse for other than specialized, careful placement outside the Socialist bloc.

The saga seems telescoped in spots and it has reportedly been cut down from an original six-hour version. The momentous historical events are indicated by montages of old newsreel and feature footage before they seep slowly down to this backwater town.

A rich family with overbearing children and a poor family with a more humane child are first etched. The poor boy helps an escaped political prisoner who brings some social consciousness to the town before he is apprehended by the police.

The boy is mistreated by the rich girl and the latter even has him run naked in the snow for a little food he wants. Then they grow up and fall in love, but her family refuses to let them marry and he is beaten and set adrift in a small boat.

The revolution comes and the girl runs off to join him. He comes back with a teenage son years later and learns that the girl had been killed.

Murder and revenge follow, and the boy becomes an engineer and looks for oil in his old town. He is finally killed helping people in an oil fire.

Film is visually rich, there are some ecological aspects in the poor boy's father's building a wooden road for communication to somewhere and feeling for the forest. For a Soviet film, there is also a freer treatment of sex and the remnants of the old mystical Russia.

Director Andrei Mikhalkov-Konchalovsky keeps this massive fresco coherent and gets some good performances, especially from half brother Nikita who is last in the line of the poor family, but may have impregnated a woman before his death.

Color goes from more garish hues at the beginning to more metallic ones for the more modern segs. A prestige item that won Russia a special jury prize at the Cannes Fest. —*Mosk.*

Victoria
(SWEDISH-W. GERMAN-COLOR)

Cannes, May 22.
Widerberg-Corona Film release and production. Features entire cast. Written and directed by Bo Widerberg from the novel by Knut Hamsun. Camera (Eastmancolor). Hanno H. Fuchs; music, Verdi. Reviewed at Cannes Film Fest (competing), May 21, '79. Running time: 107 MINS.
With: Michaela Jolin, Stephan Schwartz, Pia Skagermark, Erik Eriksson.

Both the Cannes Film Festival and Swedish director Bo Widerberg would have been better off if "Victoria" had not been shown in competition. Practically a work print, which Widerberg wrested from the German coproducer and worked on up to projection, film also suffers from a badly-dubbed English track.

An unsuccessful example of an attempt to make an international film, this tale of star-crossed lovers in the late 19th century destroyed by society and also disease might have been a bit more palatable in Swedish.

Widerberg returns to the style of his noted romantic tale "Elvira Madigan" where lovers were also done in by social repressiveness. This one, based on a novel by Nobel-prized Norwegian writer Knut Hamsun, lacks a romantic edge, has simplistic dialog and fairly puerile plotting.

A miller's son in love with the daughter of the local rich man becomes a writer so as to be invited to her home. But despite their declared love, her father, now in debt, needs a rich marriage to help him.

This plan fails when the intended groom is killed in a hunting accident. But tuberculosis is not to let the love be. The writer takes up with a girl he loses and the beloved dies from her malady leaving the writer only his art.

It is prettily shot but a true dramatic aura eludes it. Mainly for home consumption. —*Mosk.*

Wise Blood
(U.S.-WEST GERMAN-COLOR)

Cannes, May 25.
Ithaca-Anthea Coproduction release and production. Features entire cast. Directed by John Huston. Screenplay, Benedict Fitzgerald, based on Flannery O'Connor story; camera (color)k Gerald Fisher. Reviewed at Cannes Film Fest (non-competing), May 24, '79. Running time: 108 MINS.
Hazel . . . . Brad Dourif
Hoover . . . . Ned Beatty
Asa . . . . Harry Dean Stanton
Enoch . . . . Daniel Shor
Sabbath . . . . Amy Wright
Landlady . . . . Mary Nell Santacroce
Grandfather . . . . John Huston

John Huston, with uncluttered direction and expert handling of actors, has fashioned a disturbing tale of the fringe side of overzealous religious preachers in the deep South. These evangelistic off-shoots of organized religion run the gamut from the dedicated to the false to the almost maniacally obsessed.

Taken from a short novel by the late noted southern writer Flannery O'Connor, film is grim and Gothic in feeling, but balanced by an underlying tenderness for these fringe people. Film received accolades from foreign critics but divided many American appraisers at the recent Cannes Film Fest where the film was shown as a noncompeter in an homage to Huston.

Brad Dourif is effective as a young man home from the wars, probably World War II. He visits his now boarded-up house in the country and then doffs his uniform to buy clothes making him look like a preacher.

He goes to a city where he is attracted by a blind preacher with a teenage daughter who gives him lubricious looks. Flashbacks reveal Dourif as the grandson of a fire and brimstone preacher, played by Huston himself.

The blind man supposedly destroyed his own sight which attracts the preachers. He is also followed about by a backward youth who shows him monkeys in the zoo and a shrunken Indian mummy in a museum which he steals to present to Dourif as a symbol of a God figure. Dourif is driven to preach for a church without Christ since there is no sin and no need of a redeemer, but a trust in one's own instincts. But he finds the blind man is not blind, the girl is corrupt and he is used by another guitar-playing preacher to extort money from crowds.

Dourif finally blinds himself to learn the truth, but is made the prisoner of a landlady who wants to care for him and marry him. He runs off, is brought back by police to die or be the prisoner of the older landlady.

Film is downbeat, though the girl cradling the ignoble mummy creates an eerie tenderness and feel for these pathetic people. It misses a needed excessiveness to add a blend of black humor that these driven people evoke here only intermittently.

Well-acted, shot on U.S. Southern location, a good part of the backing is from German tax shelter money. A film needing hard sell due to its ambivalent treatment of the kinky religious scene, though it does give some insight into the extension of these loner fanatics into sects. —*Mosk.*

Fad, Jal
(Grandfather)
(SENEGALESE-DOCU-COLOR-16m)

Cannes, May 21.
Senegal Film release and production. Conceived and directed by Safi Faye. Camera (color), Patrick Fabry, Jean Monod; Papa Moctar Ndoye; editor, Andree Davanture. Reviewed at Cannes Film Fest (non-competing), May 20, '79. Running time, 108 MINS.

Mainly an ethnic documentary on a small African village facing the loss of old values and land reforms and progress begin to be felt in remote areas. Without a narrative thread, and more ritualistic than clarifying the various issues of old and young outlooks and changing mores, film seems intended more for school and seminar outlets than as a theatrical entry.

Director Safi Faye does, however, have an eye for revealing daily village life. She should be an addition to the African film scene with either a more decisive fictional try or documentary pix with more clarity. But "Fad, Jal" does give a fine surface picture of village life through it's sometimes repetitive, using local color for the picturesque rather than more revealing insights. —*Mosk.*

Le Musee Du Louvre
(The Louvre Museum)
(JAPANESE-DOCU-COLOR)

Cannes, May 20.
Fuji Telecasting Co. production and release. Directed by Toshio Uruta. Screenplay, Shuntaro Tanikawa; camera (Fuji-color), Kozo Okazaki; music, Tohru Takemitsu. Reviewed at Cannes Film Fest (non-competing), May 19, '79. Running time: 119 MINS.

A strikingly photographed documentary shot in the Paris Louvre Museum by the Japanese tv company Fuji Telecasting Co. for its 20th anniversary. A bit didactic, a dry commentary, some unnecessary connecting links (a French actress playing a restorer) still do not detract from the unusual beauty of the art objects chosen to represent this massive museum.

Film goes from antique art up to impressionism. At the beginning the ancient artifacts and objects are intercut with scenes in Egypt today and the Near East. There is a fine visual scanning of the objects. There are interesting looks at the inside of the Louvre in re-restoration, research and other rooms and enlightening interviews.

A part with the French thesp coming and going to the museum is used mainly for some shots of Paris today. It could be excised. The choice of 60 paintings and about 100 statues and other works of art from 250,000 seems adequate and balanced though they could be challenged.

As documentary, it should show well on tv, be a fine school film and perhaps have some commercial outings. —*Mosk.*

Threshold of Spring
(CHINESE-COLOR)

Cannes, May 22.
A Peking Film Production. Features cast. Written and directed by Hsie Tie-li, based on the novel by Jou Shih. Camera (color), Li Wung-hu. Reviewed at Cannes Film Festival (Market), May 21, '79. Running time: **90 MINS.**
Cast: Sun Tao-lin, Hsieh Fang.

One of the classics of modern Chinese cinema, Hsie Tie-li's "Threshold of Spring" (1963) — also known as "Second Lunar Month" and "Spring in February" (its French title) — finally showed up at the Cannes fest as a latecommer in the Certain Regard section.

Two years earlier, Hsie Tie-li's other masterpiece, "Hurricane" (1961) — adapted from Chou Li-po's novel with the same name — drew SRO crowds at its unspooling in Berlin as part of the fest's Info Show.

Hsie-Tie-li (other spellings are Xie Tie'Li's and Hsieh Tieh-li) began his career at the Peking Studio after directing theatre. His first film, "Hurricane" (book adapted for the screen by his wife, Lin Lan), was made at the age of 40 and dealt with land reform in Northeast China after the defeat of the Japanese in 1945. His handling of actors and departure from conventional dictates of direction made for an alive treatment of a humanist theme. It was a critical and boxoffice success.

The director then embarked on an adaptation of Jou Shih's novel at a time when the book's sentimental character was considered by officials in the Film Bureau as undesirable for movie audiences. The writer, however, was a national hero — he was 30-years-old in 1931 when the Kuomintang government arrested him with other artists and executed him. Jay Leyda reports that when "Threshold of Spring" (Sidney Shapiro's English translation of title and book in 1963) appeared in the cinemas in 1964, it was an immediate success despite open hostility in the press and attacks against the pic's "escapism" and "bourgeois humanitarianism." It was the director's last film just before the Cultural Revolution.

Today, "Threshold of Spring" holds up due to those humanist qualities in the story and direction. Story is set in the 1920s, a period of corruption and intellectual darkness in China. A teacher leaves the city to find refuge of sorts in a primary school in Lotus Town. There, while teaching, he meets a proud widow with two children who is unable to make ends meet and faces starvation. He supports her with his meagre income (her dead husband was a former friend), arranges that the daughter board at his school,

and suffers with the woman when her tiny son dies of a fever.

His good-will then leads him to propose marriage, although he is in love with a colleague teaching at the same school. The widow commits suicide rather than complicate matters for her benefactor any more.

Not only is this story out of the mold of current Red Chinese pix of the day, but there is a scene in which propaganda for its own sake is criticized in the script. Needless to say, none of the film's crew found work afterwards, and helmer Tie-li disappeared from sight following the Cultural Revolution of 1965-66.

A natural for Chinese Film Weeks, but pic should also find its way to other fests on the summer circuit. Credits are tops, particularly lensing and thesp performances. —Holl.

A Nous Deux
(Us Two)
(FRENCH-COLOR)

Cannes, May 24.
AMLF release of Les Films 13-Cinevideo production. Stars Catherine Deneuve, Jacques Dutronc. Written and directed by Claude Lelouch. Camera (Eastmancolor), Bernard Zitzermann; editor, Sophie Bhaud, Hugues Darmois; music, Francis Lai. Reviewed at Cannes Film Fest (non-competing), May 23, '79. Running time, **110 MIN.**

Francoise .... Catherine Deneuve
Simon .... Jacques Dutronc
Tonton .... Jacques Villeret
Mimile .... Paul Preboist
Inspector .... Bernard Crommbey

Claude Lelouch is one of the most prolific filmmakers. For his 23d film he is still a do-it-yourself filmmaker, here coproducing, writing, directing and even shooting a good bit of the tale. He still could use a scriptwriter to set his free wheeling mixture of romance and adventure into a more coherent whole.

The maker of the much-prized hit, "A Man and a Woman," hues here again to the use of a couple. They are a second generation gangster and a raped middle-class woman who has gone into seducing men for wives wanting divorces when police break in on them and also blackmailing politicians she has affairs with.

They meet when both are on the lam and holed up in a professional hideout run by an older couple. Police soon have them on the run together in a series of holdups, eluding police and finally falling in love despite their different backgrounds.

Lelouch again uses synthetic situations, but does keep this bowling along with some inventive scenes. There is the old keeper of the hideout giving a macho talk on woman as the weaker sex and

breaking out of a police trap by insisting they have two hostages but going off together when they demand two cars for each to take out a hostage.

Catherine Deneuve is properly uptight until love thaws as the girl and Jacques Dutronc has a wry, fey presence that counterpoints his violence and shrewd criminal ways.

Their adventures take them to Canada and finally the U.S. where indications are they may turn straight. But Lelouch insists, in dialog, that, after all, America is a country of gangsters, a throwback to the many gangster films about sympathetic people turned bad by society.

Lelouch should have a good run for this picaresque pic at home in spite of its inconsistencies. —Mosk.

Flamme Empor
(Torch High)
(WEST GERMAN-COLOR)

Cannes, May 25.
A Telefilm Saar Film Production. Features entire cast. Written and directed by Eberhard Schubert. Camera (color), Atze Glanert; music, Gaby Mueller-Blattau. Reviewed at Cannes Film Festival (Market), May 24, '79. Running time: **98 MINS.**
Cast: Mareike Carriere, Hans-Juergen Schatz, Michael Schories, Ulrich Gebauer.

Since Eberhard Fechner's "Tadelloeser & Wolff" (1975), a tv production based on Walter Kempowski's family saga and dealing with the author's youth during the Third Reich, a number of excellent, informative pix have covered those same Hitler years with growing honesty and critical interest: Theodor Kotulla's "Death Is My Trade" (original title was "From a German Life") (1976), based on the Auschwitz Commandant's diary; Peter Lilienthal's "David" (1979), based on a ture story about a Jewish boy living in Berlin throughout the 1930s (Grand Prix at Berlin Fest); and even Volker Schloendorff's "The Tin Drum" (1979), the Golden Palm winner at Cannes based on Gunter Grass's best-seller.

"Flamme Empor" belongs to this series. The title of a nationalist song (roughly translated as "Torch High"), this tv show found its way into the International Forum of Young Cinema last February and immediately won attention and respect. This is the story of the Saarland, a segment of Germany on the French border placed under a League of Nations mandate World War I but returned when the population voted in a plebiscite for Fatherland 15 years later — in 1934, shortly after Hitler came to power.

Pic describes the political thinking and leanings of various youths

on a summer outing in this area in 1932. Two young men and two young women are the key figures: one with romantic ideals, another an intellectual liberal, still another with a French upbringing, and a fourth torn between beliefs as a confrontation comes. This confrontation occurs when opposing Hitler Youth and Communist youngsters happen upon the same youth hostel in a wooded area run by a director (a "Wandervogel," or hiker-type), who is not sure where he stands on national issues. Further, a choral-and-dance group, devoted to traditional songs and the like, regularly perform in the background, and even a former aviation hero from World War I happens on the scene with leater cap and goggles.

The meat of the story is when the leader of the Hitler Youth company trades opinions and, occasionally, insults with the young liberal in contending for leadership at the hostel after a pile of wood burns down mysteriously (did the Communists do it?). And, as things turn out, the girl one lad is romantically attracted to likes his best friend instead, which adds to the complications as described above.

All in all, this is a fascinating portrait of the times. The issues are clearly drawn, but the neophyte audience will have to review his German history beforehand. A quality low-budget pic well worth the o.o. by New German Cinema buffs. —Holl.

Running
(CANADIAN-COLOR)

Cannes, May 21.
A Universal release of a Robert Cooper-Ronald Cohen production. Executive Producer, Michael Douglas. Produced by Robert Cooper, Ronald Cohen; line producer, John Eckert. Written and directed by Steven Stern. Stars Michael Douglas, Susan Anspach. Camera (color), Lazlo George; music, Andre Gagnon; editor, Kurt Hirschler. Reviewed at the Vox Theatre, Cannes, May 21 '79. Running time: **102 MINS.**
Michael Andropolis ..... Michael Douglas
Janet .... Susan Anspach
Coach Walker .... Larry Dane
Howard .... Charles Shamata
Ritchie Rosenberg .... Eugene Levy

With the Canadian-produced "Running," Universal has a dandy on-track effort about a marathon runner who like "Rocky" must go the distance to prove himself worthwhile.

Handsomely photographed by Lazlo George and backed by the sweet, middle-of-the-road musical score by Quebec's Andre Gagnon, the pic gives Michael Douglas another star turn after his recent outings in "Coma" and "The China Syndrome."

Here, he is a vulnerable 34-year-old, separated from his wife and children, a failure at everything and this time determined to make the American marathon Olympics team. He is further challenged because he failed to show up 10 years previously for an all-important Pan-American Games race and gotten nowhere since.

Douglas shines but Anspach, as the loving wife, smiles too much and in a scene where she must slam him for suspecting she's been sleeping with a used car salesman, she can't quite overcome her silly expression and a suggestion that maybe she's not all bright in the head.

Douglas trains all by himself, overcomes a hardbitten coach (played by Larry Dane who is given little to do but bark) and a used car salesman, Charles Shamata, and gets injured in the Olympics marathon in Montreal.

Everyone else finishes the race and he picks himself up and runs into an empty stadium. However, what could have been a resounding finish falls short because other athletes rally around and it's not quite clear whether he gets over the finish line or not. Sportscaster Jim McKay is on hand to tell everything except that piece of information.

What's missing in this pic is the sweat (something "Rocky" had in spades) and any talk between runners of their time and of their sore limbs and injuries. If anything, "Running" is too clean and tidy. But as a straight beat-the-odds effort, it's in stride.

Scriptwriter Steven Stern, who directed, never really capitalizes on the sport of running which has become so popular, but Douglas overcomes to deliver a polished performance. If it's taken as a modern fairy tale, "Running" should do well.—*Adil.*

Dr. Norman Bethune
(CHINESE-COLOR)

West Berlin, May 30.
A Peking Film Production. Features cast. Written and directed by Chang Chun-hsiang. Features entire cast. Camera (Color), Ma Li-fa; art direction, Hang San-yi; editing. Chu Chao-seng; music, Liu Qi-ming; sound, Wu Chang-hai. Reviewed at Berlin Werbung Screening Room, West Berlin, May 29, '79. Running time: 115 MINS.
Cast: Tain Nin-pang (Norman Bethune), Chun Li (Fang Chao-yiuan), Yin Ruo-cheng (Secretary Tong), Wu Shiu (Commander).

When this Chinese pic, Chang Chun-hsiang's "Dr. Norman Bethune" (1964/1977), showed up at Berlin for viewing by the Selection Committee for possible inclusion in the fest's Info Show, it was evident that the long-awaited Chinese film biography of the famous Canadian surgeon had finally found its way

Westward after many years of suppression. Production was underway in 1963 with Gerry Tannebaum in the title role (Tain Nin-pang?), according to film historian Jay Leyda — then suddenly stopped in 1964 as the Great Cultural Revolution was getting underway and foreigners were asked abruptly to leave the country. A new version of pic was finally completed in 1977.

The print screened in Berlin appears to be almost entirely the original 1964 version (perhaps parts have been cut out to shorten the length). It's an English-spoken version too, and the likeness to Bethune in face and other characteristics of the man is astonishing.

Undoubtedly, the 1939 docu footage lensed by cameraman Wu Yin-hsien, as well as the resurfacing of the same in 1961 in an historical compilation of the war years, helped considerably to get the Bethune project off the ground in the early 1960s. The Canadian doctor's heroism with guerrilla fighters in Yenan and the Border Region during the last nine months of his life in 1939 was also legendary.

Per Leyda's reports, xenophobia was the cause of the film's shelving. Even though Norman Bethune was the only Westerner ever accorded a state burial and ceremonial honors, it was impossible to present a "white man" on the screen. Whether or not it's accidental, the actor in the film appears to be half-Chinese and may not be the original actor Tannebaum at all. In any case, the story behind this pic is as interesting as the film itself.

Story as told is a trifle too melodramatic for Western auds to be successful, but it's worth a look-see in view of the current Yank-Canadian prods underway to film Bethune's life again. Further, the facts on the surgeon's last months and the events leading to his death carry the pic with ease over the two hour stretch. There's also touches of quaint humor to lighten the tale. Credits are above average. — *Holl.*

Mourir a Tue-Tete
(A Scream from Silence)
(CANADIAN-COLOR)

Cannes, May 20.
Office National Du Film Du Canada release and production. Features entire cast. Directed by Anne Claire Poirier. Screenplay, Marthe Blackburn, Poirier; camera (Color), Michel Brault; editor, Andre Corriveau; music, Maurice Blackburn. Reviewed at Cannes Film Fest (non-competing), May 19, '79. Running time, 95 MINS.

Suzanne . . . . Julie Vincent
Rapist . . . . Germain Houde
Philippe . . . . Paul Savoie
Director . . . . Monique Miller
Editor . . . . Micheline Lanctot

A hard, polemical, didactic film on the feminist theme of rape, which has become a familiar subject in films of late. Using a format of a film within a film, it looks more slanted for seminars, tv and festival outings, with theatrical outlets chancier on its fragmented approach.

A woman is making a film on the rape of a woman after a study involving interviews with many women who have undergone that traumatic experience. She and another woman discuss the scenes running through an editing machine.

This allows for a narrative about one woman who is raped. It is acted out but there are documentary sections involved as well as a symbolical courtroom scene underlining that rape still shames and often accuses the woman.

The film wants to exorcise the shame that seems to plague most victims as well as the misunderstanding of those around them. The rape makes up the first part of the film as an aggressive, practically subjectively-made, scene that is disturbing in its lack of sexuality and the hatred directed at all women by the rapist.

There is a rugged scene of ritual clitoridectomy of young girls in an African tribe. This may still go on but underlines director Anne Claire Poirier's harsh, no-nonsense approach to this subject.

The woman is finally driven to possible suicide by her inability to face up to the shame and bewilderment of her position afterwards. It is a film that should stir up pro and con reactions. It does insist there is an atavistic vein in most men that is too often activated towards women and denies the latter the liberty of their own bodies and selves.

It is a warning, a visually loaded but still effective representation of this touchy and always timely situation though perhaps somewhat one-sided in its treatment of males. Poirier is a forceful director but needs a more rounded feature or straight documentary to make the impact more dramatically viable.

Technically excellent, with Julie Vincent adding a more human note to the more sweeping generalisations as the hapless and finally defeated victim.

The rapist is played with hysterical, disturbing efficiency by Germain Houde who also, in quick shots, represents the rapist of other women who testify. —*Mosk.*

Ein Komischer Heiliger
(Some Kind of Saint)
(WEST GERMAN-COLOR)

Cannes, May 24.
A Coproduction of Albatros Munich- and

Popular-Film, Berlin; world rights, Munic Films, Munich. Features entire cast. Written and directed by Klaus Lemke. Camera (color), Ruediger Meichsner, Erik Riechardt, Wolf Bachmann; editing, Ines Regnier, Caya Piper; music, Lothar Meid, "Follow Me," sung by Amanda Lear. Reviewed at Cannes Film Festival (Market), May 23, '79. Running time: 90 MINS.
Cast: Cleo Kretschmer, Wolfgang Fierek, Luitpold Roever, Horatius Haeberle, Peter Emmer, Arno Mathes.

Several German productions of late take their cues from American commercial pix: Woody Allen's "Annie Hall" showed up in a different version in Helmut Dietl's "Things Can Only Get Worse"; Monte Hellman's "Two Lane Blacktop" (1971) (a popular cult pic in Germany) went through a metamorphosis in Adolf Winkelmann's "On the Move"; and the tv sitcom winner, "Bewitched," is only a heartbeat away from Klaus Lemke's "Some Kind of Saint."

Lemke is a master of improvisational, low budget cinema. He never runs to subsidy wells for free presents of one kind or another — instead, his crew enjoys the fun of working with loose scripts and taking their chances on a modest return at the boxoffice, after or before a tv run. His biggest winner to date was "The Sweethearts" (1976), in which a group of girls played pretty much themselves in rendering a string of vocals in hilarious, unassuming fashion. One of them was Ingeborg Maria Kretschmer, now back as "Cleo" Kretschmer playing a cuddling witch to Wolfgang Fierek's naive clergyman in the wicked quarter of Munich.

Story is made up along the way. The young clergyman feels he is called to save souls but can't convince anyone that he's even very serious in his profession — save for B-Girl Baby (Cleo), who takes a liking to him, enough to attempt a seduction in between reading fortunes and dropping curses on people. They fall in love when both end up in a hospital after a missionary squeeze on a cellar-bar's clientele fails.

Her sort of protection, however, only gets them both into more trouble with the police. The upshot is that our "comical saint" (direct translation of the original title) figures it's best to leave town for good — only to hitch up with Baby in the end despite his religious calling.

Lots of good fun, and a winner among the new story-telling helmers gradually moving to the forefront of New German Cinema via modest, low budget productions for the younger generation. —*Holl.*

Rocky II
(COLOR)

Despite some sagging sections, Stallone and company punch through with box-office winner.

Hollywood, June 10.
United Artists release of an Irwin Winkler and Robert Chartoff production. Written and directed by Sylvester Stallone. Stars Stallone. Camera (Panavision-Technicolor), Bill Butler; music, Bill Conti; film editor, Danford B. Greene; art director, Richard Berger; asst. director, Jerry Zeismer; fight sequence edited by James D. Mitchell, Christopher V. Holmes; sound effects editor, Frank Warner; "Street Scat," "Two Kinds of Love," words and music, Frank Stallone; set decorator, Ed Baer; boxing technical advisor, Al Silvani; publicist, Stanley Brossette. Reviewed at MGM screening room, Culver City, June 9, '79. (MPAA Rating: PG). Running time: **119 MINS.**

Rocky Balboa ....Sylvester Stallone
Adrian ....Talia Shire
Paulie ....Burt Young
Apollo Creed ....Carl Weathers
Mickey..............Burgess Meredith
Apollo's trainer ....Tony Burton
Gazzo........,.............Joe Spinell
Agent ....Leonard Gaines
Mary Anne Creed ....Sylvia Meals
Meat foreman ....Frank McRae
Cutman ....Al Silvani
Director ....John Pleshette
Announcer ....Stu Nahan
Commentator ....Bill Baldwin
Salesman ....Jerry Ziesmer
Father Carmine ....Paul J. Micale

There's an old saying that one shouldn't tamper with a winning formula and apparently the makers of "Rocky II" have recognized it. The sequel follows much the same theme as its predecessor — that is fighter Rocky Balboa's path to a stab at the heavyweight crown. In its boxing and training scenes "Rocky II" packs much of the punch the original did, complete with an exciting pugilistic finale that's even better than its predecessor.

However, in an attempt to tell the new story — that of Rocky's adjustment to near-success and an attempt to lead a non-boxing life — the plot tends to drag and the picture takes on a murky quality.

Luckily, director, actor and scripter Sylvester Stallone and producers Irwin Winkler and Robert Chartoff know from experience audiences love to root for the underdog and have concocted an irresistible final 30 minutes that should ensure strong boxoffice. Coupled with all the built-in interest in a sequel, the United Artists release looks to be a big moneymaker.

Stallone continues his portrait of the lovable dumbbell who follows a dream that takes him to the top with enough wit and charm to last through a dozen sequels. But as a writer, he's given little more than a surface indication of what life is for a fighter who has just missed the brass ring.

Picture opens with immediate energy with a good 10-minutes from the final fight scene of "Rocky." New footage lands Stallone in the hospital, eventually receiving confirmation from his competitor Carl Weathers that the champion had indeed given him "his best shot." Several months later Stallone is released with advice from his doctors not to fight again because of an eye injury and the comfort of a healthy bankroll to spend.

Film then concentrates on life after the big fight — the overspending, hangers-on, married life, and failed attempts to get a "regular" job. This could have been a better illustrated story had filmmakers not felt compelled to stick to the original formula and build everything to the same climactic fight scene. Because everything is done to accommodate Stallone's second shot at the heavyweight crown the importance of what leads him there is diminished.

Although audience is shown all of Stallone's difficulties, the problems just seem to get in the way of what promises to be the real audience pleaser in "Rocky II" — the re-match.

When that point is finally achieved the picture tends to take on a new life. And when wife Talia Shire gives her blessing to the fight (she'd been against it because of Stallone's eye), it's as if someone has taken an electric plug and lit up the picture. To the strains of Bill Conti's chilling "Gonna Fly Now," Stallone and the film take on a renewed strength that thus far had only been evident in scenes from the original.

In a somewhat unusual occurrence, all of the original main characters from "Rocky" have returned. Shire creates an effective sensitivity as Stallone's wife and Burt Young, although not seen as often as in the original, is convincing as Stallone's brother-in-law. But because neither are given enough dramatic scenes their impact is severly lessened.

Characters involved in the boxing story fare better. Burgess Meredith tends to be a bit too grizzly to accept without a chuckle or two but provides good balance to Stallone as his trainer. Weathers is expert as Stallone's boxing nemesis as is Tony Burton as Weathers' trainer.

Stallone has taken over directing chores from "Rocky's" John Avildsen and just doesn't move the film along as well as he should. Photography from Bill Butler is okay throughout but not exceptional until the climax. There's an annoying sameness during most of the picture and although the sequel is ex-

actly the same 119-minute length as the original it seems much longer.

The real stars of "Rocky II" are the fight scenes, which Stallone choreographed with technical advice from Al Silvani. So convincing are Stallone and Weathers in the ring that whatever faults the picture has seem small by its conclusion. Audiences will undoubtedly be cheering by the finale which more than leaves room for "Rocky III." And with $54,000,000 in domestic rentals collected from the original, audiences will probably see a lot more of Stallone in the ring. —Berg.

The In-Laws
(COLOR)

Lotsa yocks in comic marriage between Peter Falk and Alan Arkin.

Hollywood, May 30.
A Warner Bros. release. Produced by Arthur Hiller, William Sackheim. Exec producer, Alan Arkin; stars Peter Falk, Alan Arkin; directed by Hiller. Screenplay, Andrew Bergman; camera (color), David M. Walsh; editor, Robert E. Swink; music, John Morris; production design, Pato Guzman; sound, Larry Jost; assistant director, Jack Roe. Reviewed at Academy of Motion Picture Arts & Sciences, BevHills, May 30, '79 (MPAA Rating: PG). Running time: **103 MINS.**

Vince Ricardo ....*........ Peter Falk
Sheldon Kornpett .... Alan Arkin
General Garcia ....Richard Libertini
Carol Kornpett .... Nancy Dussault
Barbara Kornpett .... Penny Peyser
Jean Ricardo ....Arlene Golonka
Tommy Ricardo ....Michael Lembeck
Mo ....Paul Lawrence Smith
Angie ....Carmine Caridi
Barry Lutz ....Ed Begley Jr.
Mr. Hirschorn ....Sammy Smith
Bing Wong ....James Hong

With "The In-Laws," Warner Bros. should have a first certifiable comedy hit of the summer. The Arthur Hiller-William Sackheim production brims over with laughs, but brand of screenwriter Andrew Bergman's humor (previously seen in "Blazing Saddles") may be too wacky for mainstream audiences. Chief appeal will be to teenagers and young adults, although the title and star billing of Peter Falk and Alan Arkin (also exec producer) would seem to solicit an older crowd. WB will therefore have to be careful in its ad campaign, and word-of-mouth will be essential.

Falk and Arkin were the perfect choices to play an addled CIA agent and a Gotham dentist, respectively. Brought together by the impending marriage of their individual offspring (Michael Lembeck and Penny Peyser), they're quickly at one another's throats, as Falk lures Arkin into a neverending series of improbable adventures.

Bergman's script elements include stolen U.S. treasury plates (lifted in a slick heist that gets the

pic off to a great start), underworld thugs, a South American banana republic and its deranged leader, and as many misspent bullets as were fired in "The Deer Hunter."

Under Arthur Hiller's fast-paced and engaging direction, everything keeps moving quickly enough to stymie audience qualms about plotting, character developments and a rapidly-compressed time frame. Unfortunately, that haste shows up in the finished film itself. "In-Laws" is beset by a plethora of continuity problems and other cinematic lapses.

A scene with Falk and cabbie in a bar, for instance, has the pair switching places in cutaway shots, while some of the car chase footage is repeated two or three times. And in the film's finale, when Falk and Arkin descend from a helicopter for the climactic wedding, the seat belts keeping them in the hoist have magically disappeared by the time they reach the ground.

Those quirks aside, Bergman and Hiller, along with their cast, seem to be having a great time, a feeling that should be communicated to audiences. While borrowing liberally from Woody Allen's "Bananas" and "Take The Money And Run," Bergman's creation of Richard Libertini as a dictator with an impressive collection of vulgar velvet paintings is a comic gem, even if Libertini gets carried away with a venerable Senor Wencas routine.

Supporting cast is quite effective, especially Nancy Dussault and Arlene Golonka as Arkin and Falk's respective spouses, Paul Lawrence Smith and Carmine Caridi as ineffectual hoods, and Ed Begley Jr. as a bland CIA agent. James Hong turns in a delightful bit as a Chinese airline steward, and Lembeck and Peyser are fine as the kids.

David Walsh's lensing is suitable, as are other creative elements, and John Morris' score adds to the pic's bounce. But "The In-Laws" belongs to Falk, simply tremendous as the expansive, crazy hero, and Arkin, superb as the stuffy suburban dentist who first hates, then comes to respect, his familial counterpart. Comic chemistry works so well, in fact, it might make sense to pair Falk and Arkin together in a vehicle a little more on the beam. —Poll.

Die Farbe Des Himmels
(Milk War in Bavaria)
(WEST GERMAN-COLOR-16M)

Berlin, May 30.
An Infafilm Manfred Korytowski, Berlin/Munich, Film Production, in collaboration with Second Channel Television (ZDF), Mainz. Features Hans Brenner and Ruth Drexel. Written and directed by

Thomas Hartwig. Camera (color). Horst Schlier: editing. Elfriede Boettrich; music, Birger Heymann; sound, Peter Beil; sets. Ingo Toegel; assistant, Anke Becker; production manager. Manfred Korytowski. Reviewed at Studio am Kudam. West Berlin, May 29. '79. Running time: **110 MINS.**

Cast: Hans Brenner (Thomas Preissinger). Ruth Drexel (Maria Preissinger). Peter Kaufmann (Josef Stressl), Guenther Ziessler (Wilhelm Fuenfer), Gustl Weishappel (Attorney Ehlicher), Anton Rattinger (Sascha Mehringer), Helmut Fischer (Secretary Ascher), Elisabeth Karg (Franziska Stressl). Rudolf Lenz (Baron Truchsess), Nino Korda (Director Zehnt), Robert Fackler (Director Biedermann). Peter Boehlke (Administrator Luegerer).

———

One of the pix in a recent german Series slated for fest exposure and German Film Weeks abroad, Thomas Hartwig's "Milk War in Bavaria" follows on the heels of such social-comment features as Erwin Keusch's "The Baker's Bread" (1976) and the tv adaptation of a Max von der Gruen novel, Wolfgang Petersen's "Danger: Slippery Ice" (1975).

All of these pix, and several others made by Christian Ziewer and the Berlin School of the Proletarian Film, aim at one result: to present the worker's problems in as clear and dramatic a way as possible to convince the viewer of a just cause with moral/ethical rights. As such, pix are somewhat limited in scope, but well worth a look-see all the same.

"Milk War in Bavaria" deals with a price rise in the sale of milk by a large dairy concern in Bavaria, but the dairy farmers don't get a penny of the profit. So they start their own company (or threaten to) and finally get a small share — but the price of feed then goes up, and they thus don't win a penny. .

Helmer Hartwig, a grad of the Berlin Film & Television Academy, made this debut feature film after working as cameraman for docu filmer Klaus Wildenhahn (the best in West Germany) and serving an apprenticeship with television on shorts. He lensed "Milk War" in 1977 on a low budget. Other young filmers who have done the same and won a supportive audience amoung the younger, moviegoing generation are Josef Roedl, Adolf Winkelmann, Erwin Keusch, and Ruediger Nuechtern, with such pix, respectively, as "Albert — Why," "On the Move," "The Baker's Bread," and "Whizzer."

"Milk War in Bavaria" scores due to two factors: the dialog and story line is carried with ease by two ace thesps, Hans Brenner and Ruth Drexel (the stars also of Nuechtern's "Whizzer"), and the lensing is first class. Although filmed in 16m. —*Holl.*

The Double McGuffin
(COLOR)

Kids save the day for Mulberry Square while Benji's away. Okay summer fodder.

———

Hollywood, June 7.
A Mulberry Square release and production. Stars Ernest Borgnine, George Kennedy. Elke Sommer. Produced, directed, written by Joe Camp. Story by Camp, Richard Baker; camera (color), Don Reddy; editor. Leon Seith; music, Euel Box; production designer, Harland Wright; art director, Ed Richardson; associate producer, Dan Witt; assistant director, Terence A. Donnelly; sound, Jim Sabat. Reviewed CFI Laboratories, L.A., June 6, '79. (MPAA Rating: PG). Running time: **101 MINS.**

Firat	Ernest Borgnine
Chief Talasek	George Kennedy
Prime Minister Kura	Elke Sommer
Assassin No. 1	Ed (Too Tall) Jones
Assassin No. 2	Lyle Alzado
Moras	Rod Browning
Specks	Dion Pride
Jody	Lisa Whelchel
Billy Ray	Jeff Nicholson
Arthur	Michael Gerard
Homer	Greg Hodges
Foster	Vinnie Spano

For Mulberry Square's first PG-rated release and second non-Benji feature, Joe Camp has concocted an innocuous, mildly diverting mystery about a bunch of teens cracking a plot to assassinate a beauteous Middle Eastern prime minister. Plausible it ain't, but it's been assembled with a modicum of professionalism and is reasonably playable summer fare.

Despite the above-title billing of the three stars, most of the running time is spent with the bright, aggressive kids who stumble upon clues left by the mysterious presence of sinister Ernest Borgnine in their affluent southern town. A money-laden attache case, a dead body and a trunk of arms lead the youngsters to suspect something's up, although the evidence always disappears when they bring local police chief George Kennedy in to take a look.

When it becomes apparent that Elke Sommer (who speaks German and is supposed to preside over a small Middle Eastern country — no explanation of that one) and her daughter are in grave danger of being bumped off at a school assembly and that the authorities aren't going to do anything about it, the kids take it upon themselves to foil the plot.

Since the basic situation is so unreal and no one is ever in any immediate jeopardy, little suspense is generated, but the youths' thinking is so hyperactive and the pace so speedy that sheer movement, rather than logic, carries the day.

The generally attractive kids display little emotion other than determination and at times border on the obnoxious in their fast-talking.

Standing out a bit from the rest are Michael Gerard, quite believable as a prissy computer expert, and country singer Charley Pride's son Dion, who seems comfortable in front of the camera.

Among the adults, Borgnine for once plays a suave, urbane type, Kennedy is good as the low-key cop and Sommer pops in intermittently, even offering a quick flash of nudity in an early scene, certainly a first for Mulberry Square. Nothing is asked of pro footballers Ed "Too Tall" Jones and Lyle Alzado except to look menacing, which they do very convincingly.

Camp's direction is nothing if not energetic, and tech credits are strong. An uncredited Orson Welles provides some explanation upfront as to what a McGuffin is (impressive as Welles' voice is, it's too bad Camp couldn't engage Hitchcock for this little chore) and Charleston, S.C. provides an unusually rich backdrop for the proceedings. —*Cart.*

Players
(COLOR)

Tennis tale double-faulted by script and MacGraw.

———

Hollywood, June 5.
Paramount Pictures release of a Robert Evans production. Stars Ali MacGraw, Dean-Paul Martin. Exec producer, Arnold Schulman. Produced by Robert Evans. Directed by Anthony Harvey. Screenplay, Arnold Schulman; camera (Metrocolor) James Crabe; editor, Randy Roberts; production design, Richard Sylbert; music, Jerry Goldsmith; set decoration, Robert Gould; costume design, Richard Bruno, Calvin Klein; second unit director, Rimas Vainorius; sound, Rene Borisewitz; assistant director, Jack Sanders. Reviewed at Academy of Motion Picture Arts & Sciences. BevHills, June 4, '79. (MPAA Rating: PG). Running time: **120 MINS.**

Nicole	Ali MacGraw
Chris	Dean-Paul Martin
Marco	Maximilian Schell
Pancho	Pancho Gonzalez
Rusty	Steven Guttenberg
Ann	Melissa Prophet

Producer Robert Evans certainly knows how to deliver a beautiful looking film, but looks alone won't help "Players." Another love story in disguise, this time backgrounded against the tennis world, "Players" is disqualified by exec producer Arnold Schulman's wobbly script, a simpering performance by Ali MacGraw, and a preponderance of tennis footage.

Like so many other pix trying to cash in on contempo crazes, "Players" is possibly two years too late in tapping into tennis mania.

Schulman's original screenplay uses an initially-confusing flashback technique to highlight the rise of racket hustler Dean-Paul Martin, who at the film's beginning is pitted against Guillermo Vilas in

the Wimbledon championships. Via backward glances, it's explained that Martin rescues socialite Ali MacGraw from a car accident, is adopted by her when he and pal Steven Guttenberg are roughed up by some sore betting losers, and eventually falls in love with her.

Some basic problems emerge under Anthony Harvey's direction, however, mostly concerning the MacGraw character, who periodically deserts Martin at the beck and call of yacht-bound Maximilian Schell. There's no background on MacGraw or her life at all, save a cheap revelatory scene with Schell near the film's end, and thus the blossoming love affair has little credibility. Actress' one-note performance is no help.

Harvey doesn't aid matters by inserting the standard love and sex montages, all carefully edited to preserve the PG rating. Periodic returns to the Wimbledon match, interspersed with flashbacks of Martin's spiraling career, may satisfy tennis buffs, but will leave mass audiences out in the cold.

Only ace in "Players" is casting of Martin, who, in his first film role proves highly believable in both his tennis and dramatic scenes. Excellent support is offered by Pancho Gonzalez in a re-creation of his real-life role as a pro-turned-teacher, and numerous tennis stars make cameo appearances likewise as themselves. Most of the secondary roles seem to have ended up on the cutting room floor.

Dramatic content aside, "Players" is one of the most visually entertaining films of 1979; James Crabe's lucid photography is topnotch, as is Richard Sylbert's handsome production design using Cuernavaca, Monte Carlo and British locales. Jerry Goldsmith's score is one of the few subtle and effective touches in the film, a perfect complement to the lovely gloss MGM consistently delivers with its Metrocolor lab work.

With the exception of boxing, sports films haven't really scored well at the boxoffice lately. "Players" makes a game effort. —*Poll.*

Dizengoff 99
(ISRAEL-COLOR)

Tel Aviv, June 2.
A Shapira Films Presentation of an Arnon Milchan, David Shapira and Roni Yaakov Production. Written and directed by Avi Nesher. Features entire cast. Camera (color): Jean Boffety; editor, Izhak Zhayek; art direction, Dita Ahayov, Ben Lam; sound, Eli Yarkoni; music, Koby Oshrath, Yorik Ben-David, Dori Ben-Zeev, David Broza, Igal Bashan, Rikki Gal, Beny Nagari, Eric Sinai, Dany Litani, Gali Attari, Rami Fortis, Zvika Pik, Izhak (Churchill) Klefter, Judith Ravitz, Yoni Rechter and Eric Rudich. Reviewed in Tel Aviv, June, 1, 1979. Running time: **110 MINS.**

Natti	Gidi Gov
Ossi	Anath Azmon
Miri	Gali Attari
Moshon	Meir Suissa
Ilana	Heli Goldberg

Avi Nesher's first film, "Sing Your Heart Out," made quite a dent on the domestic market on the strength of a successful mixture of broad humor ranging on slapstick, hit songs, and hectic pace. As the result did sell more than 500,000 tickets, Nesher got his second chance soon enough.

Nesher, still in his 20s, had some trouble during production, as United Studios dropped out of the project, maintaining that pic was too costly to recuperate at home, their share being picked up by Arnon Milchan's and Roni Yaakov's Milron Productions. Final print was rushed as film is scheduled for summer release. The print screened fr the press was an early and somewaht faulty one, as far as color balance is concerned.

No one could ever doubt the intentions of this venture. It aims to hit its public below the belt, and it does so as often and as accurately as censorship will allow, here. The story of two boys and a girl, employees in an insurance company, who decide to live and work together, producing commercials, is flimsy and unbelievable. it is hard to understand now Nesher, can imagine that the public will swallow the face that an insurance clerk become a lighting cameraman, overnight another one a director, and they can produce a movie with stolen equipment which incidentally they forget to return. As for the story, it has a flock of girls going crazy for the charms of pop star Gidi Gov, whose charms may be less than obvious to a non-Israeli audience. His powers over the weaker sex are intense, that if a girl can't get him by herself she is only too happy to share him with a friend, and doesn't mind.

Lots of sexual innuendo, bare breasts, and dialog in which it is hinted that the only point of interest the characters may have lies below the belt, could turn this into another domestic hit for Nesher. The throwaway lines are handled easily by cast which performs naturally on the whole, except for those moments when they have to ponder on the meaning of life. In that situation they get self conscious.

Soundtrack is crammed with songs by some successful tunesters, but not all are in top form.

As the domestic market is still impressed by home-made sex jokes and summer is the right itme for light entertainment, the film will probably have a bright run here. Whether it will be sufficient to cover its relatively considerable budget, remains to be seen. On the foreign market, it will try to court the same customers who went for "Lemon Popsicle" (it even has the same girl, Anat Axmon, as one romantic lead) but lacks the cuteness and touch of innocence which gave that one its charm. —Edna.

La Memoire Courte
(Short Memory)
(FRENCH-COLOR)

Cannes, May 20.
Unite Trois — Paradise Films release and production. Features entire cast. Directed by Eduardo De Gregorio. Screenplay, Edgardo Cozarinsky, De Gregorio; camera (Eastmancolor), Willy Lubtchansky; music, Eric Simon. Reviewed at Cannes Film Fest (Non-Competing), May 19, '79. Running time: 105 MINS.

Judith	Nathalie Baye
Frank	Philippe Leotard
Genevieve	Bulle Ogier
Husband	Xavier St.-Macary
Mann	Andrian Brine

Argentine scripter-director Eduardo De Gregorio's second film in France delves into an international group still helping Nazis in hiding Nazis in hiding as well as other political criminals on the run regain Europe. Its theme gives this timeliness.

Done more as a thriller, with an underlying study of the morality of those who get caught up with the knowledge of this traffic and the actual lack of interest, cover-up even, by governmental officials, the film does not reach more inventive insights and treatment to make it a more penetrating statement on a still vital issue.

A translator working in UNESCO, a young woman who has broken with her husband, is given a job doing a study on a writer who died in an accident. Seemingly routine, she finds he was on the trail of a network smuggling Nazis to Europe from Latin America. A young man she meets when picking up the writer's papers appears suspicious and in her mind takes the place of the mysterious ringleader as she piles up information.

But he works with her and they eventually find that the leader is a prosperous businessman against whom they can do nothing. The man is looking for him, because his parents, fleeing after being politically on the wrong side during a colonial war, had been done in to rob them of their fortune.

An attempt at a poetic aside, as the girl keeps putting the man who helps her into the roles of the possible guilty ones, is too oblique. The adept thriller treatment makes this a well-made film that lacks the spark to bring it out of the ordinary . —Mosk.

Ikarus
(EAST GERMAN-COLOR)

Berlin, June 1.
A DEFA Film Production, Gruppe Babelsberg; world rights, DEFA Aussenhandel, East Berlin. Features entire cast. Directed by Heiner Carow. Screenplay, Klaus Schlesinger; camera (color), Juergen Brauer; music, Peter Gotthardt; sets, Dieter Adam. Reviewed at Studio am Kudam, West Berlin, May 31, '79. Running time: 85 MINS.
Cast: Peter Welz (Mathias), Karin Gregorek (Mother), Peter Aust (Father), Hermann Beyer (Jochen Keller).

One of the best children's pix to emerge for the German Democratic Republic, Heiner Carow's "Ikarus" reaches far beyond its immediate theme to show life on a sociological plane in East Germany today. It was Carow's good fortune to have a script written by a coming GDR author, Klaus Schlesinger, to lean on, and he makes the most of it.

Story focuses on an eight-year-old boy, whose parents were recently divorced, due perhaps to too little time together — the mother works as the leader of a factory brigade, and the father is a journalist. The boy is exactly at that age when he needs his father's company, and the fact that he is missing hurts. Further, his mother has a new "uncle" visiting on occasion.

One day, the boy uses a free hour at school to run off and see his father, who lives not too far away. His father has an "auntie" visiting him during the afternoon break — another disappointment. The father tries to set things right by telling the story of Daedalus and Icarus (a picture hangs on the apartment wall depicting the ancient Greek myth), and promising a flight in an airplane over Berlin on the boy's coming ninth birthday.

The day comes, and the father is not there. Young Mathias visits every place where his father could be, even the airport, but he is apparently on a news trip. Back home, he finds an electric train from his father for his birthday — the airplane ride has been completely forgotten.

As for his new uncle, he flies model airplanes for a hobby — which, as the boy witnesses, also tend to crash on occasion. On the point of despair, he now realizes that, if he is to survive in the world of adults, he must learn to carve out his own future.

"Ikarus" is a kind of thesis film, with plenty of information about East German life for the informed insider. It is, arguably, Carow's best pic, but it deserves to be seen together wtih his earlier "Legend of Paul and Paula" (1972) (script by Ulrich Plenzdorf) and his recent "Until Death Does Us Part" (1979) (script by Guenther Ruecker) — which form a kind of Carow "trilogy" on social problems in the German Democratic Republic.

(For the record, Carow also made a classic children's pic — "They Called Him Amigo" (1958), from a script by Wera and Claus Kuechenmeister — set in the Nazi period: it dealt with group of kids in Berlin's back-lots who hide a political prisoner and suffer the consequences. It established the director as a talented helmer with nonprofessional kids in lead roles.)

"Ikarus" handles such universal concerns as parent-children relationships, divorce rates (one out of three in East Germany), and authoritarian teaching methods, in addition to that metaphorical, but down-to-earth, concept of why people in a closed society dream, in the first place, of the possibility of flying. Most of all, it argues for a moral responsibility towards children in this Year of the Child. —Holl.

Prophecy
(COLOR)

From CIA to See-I-didn't.

Hollywood, June 7.
Paramount Pictures release, produced by Robert L. Rosen. Directed by John Frankenheimer. Features entire cast. Screenplay, David Seltzer; camera (Color), Harry Stradling, Jr.; editor, Tom Rolf; sound (Dolby), Gene Cantamesa; production design, William Craig Smith; set decoration, George Gaines; special make-up and artifacts, Thomas R. Burman; special effects, Robert Dawson; assistant director, Andy Stone; music, Leonard Rosenman. Reviewed at the Chinese Theatre III, Hollywood, June 7, '79. (MPAA Rating: PG.) Running time: 102 MINS.

Maggie	Talia Shire
Rob	Robert Foxworth
Hawks	Armand Assante
Isley	Richard Dysart
Ramona	Victoria Racimo
M'Rai	George Clutesi
Pilot	Tom McFadden

"Prophecy" is the picture that had an ex-CIA agent in charge of security so the plot wouldn't be ripped off by television. Well, he must have slipped up because the same film, or variations of it, have been on after midnight for 30 years or more. Quite simply, director John Frankenheimer has made a frightening monster movie that people could laugh at for generations to come, complete with your basic big scary thing, cardboard characters and a story so stupid it's irresistable. If audience appreciates these left-handed virtues, it may do some business; if not ...

Once again, the real villain is Careless Mankind. Only this time, it isn't Atomic Fallout that's creating giant ants and killer cockroaches but Industrial Pollution.

Government agent Robert Foxworth goes to Maine to do an

environmental study in hopes of settling a dispute between the local Indians and the paper mill. Wife Talia Shire tags along, carrying a cello and an unborn baby. Before they arrive, several people have disappeared mysteriously in the woods but nobody seems very concerned. Lumber exec Richard Dysart figures it's probably the Indians on the warpath, but hasn't called for the calvary.

The couple take up residence in a cabin by the river, which turns out to be full of giant fish and tadpoles, which seems harmless compared to the rampant raccoon that attacks by night. Even before he hears the giant panting in the forest, Foxworth figures something is amiss and, thanks to Shire's shoe, comes up with the answer: Mercury poisoning.

Three more campers are fiendishly murdered in the forest and this is too much for Dysart, who wants Indian leader Armand Assante arrested, figuring he's responsible for the smashed bodies and deep scratches 20 feet up in he trees. Inevitably, the couple, Assante and his wife Victoria Racimo, Dysart, George Clutesi and Tom McFadden are stranded deep in the forest.

Shire finds a baby monster that's just too awful to look at and reminds her what her own kid might be like since she's been eating some of the same fish. Then the big monster attacks and it's twice as ugly. Now the environmental problem is getting out of the woods before the monster gobbles them up.

Minus most of the original band, the two couples make it to the river, swimming across to the dock by their cottage. The monster follows, sinking beneath the surface. "He's drowned," Foxworth cheers as Assante continues to dangle his own body from the dock.

But reports of the monster's demise were premature and he finally tears the house down and wreaks more havoc. This makes Foxworth really mad.

At last, this mild-mannered government doctor is fed up with the big fellow going around smashing bodies, biting heads off and tearing the roof from the cabin. So when the monster foolishly grabs him, Foxworth picks up an Indian arrow and teaches that bully a lesson, toppling him into the river.

Foxworth is so mad in fact that he jumps in after him, which should be a lesson to monsters the world over that you don't fool around with Foxworth.

Frankenheimer guides all this goofiness with sincerity, if not pomposity. Technically, pic looks like what it is: A professional, quality package whose budget exceeds its bounty. Among the performers, only Assante gets half-a-chance to show his talent and Shire is reduced to a whining wimp, cradling the baby monster in the most amazing way. Leonard Rosenman's score cheats constantly, building to frightening moments that don't happen.

And just when there's almost a happy ending, up comes the final cliche, faithful to many a monster movie that came before. Its last secret revealed, "Prophecy" predicts more gloom and doom, not least for itself. —Har.

Game Of Death
(COLOR)

Last of late Bruce Lee?

Hollywood, June 5.
Columbia Pictures release of a Raymond Chow production. Produced by Raymond Chow. Directed by Robert Clouse. Features entire cast. Screenplay, Jan Spears; camera (color), Godfrey A. Godar; editor, Alan Pattillo; music, John Barry; sound, William Stevenson; production manager, David Chan; special effects, Far East Effects; martial arts direction, Hung Kim Po; assistant director, Mike Gowans. Reviewed at Burbank Studios, Burbank. June 5, '79. (MPAA Rating: R.) Running time: 102 MINS.
Billy Lo ....Bruce Lee
Jim Marshall .... Gig Young
Dr. Land .... Dean Jagger
Steiner .... Hugh O'Brian
Ann Morris .... Colleen Camp
Carl Miller .... Robert Wall
Stick .... Mel Novak
Hakim .... Kareem Abdul-Jabbar
Fighter .... Chuck Norris
Pasqual ....Danny Inosanto
John .... Billy McGill
Lo Chen ....Hung Kim Po
Henry Lo .... Roy Chaio

"Game of Death" is attempt to capitalize on some of the last film footage of martial arts idol Bruce Lee. Early on it becomes obvious that some enterprising individuals couldn't bear to pass up the chance to make a buck on Lee's unfinished film and thus constructed a ludicrous plot to surround the action scenes (which on several occasions are obviously not Lee but an uncredited stand-in). Initial outlook for pic is okay for the intended market, but there could be a backlash once fans realize what's going on.

Lee (and his "double") limn a kung-fu film star who's being threatened by an evil syndicate out to own him. Being the good guy he is, Lee spends the initial part of the picture beating up his adversaries and swearing he'll never compromise. Finally, the no-gooders shoot him and he ends up in the hospital where extensive plastic surgery must be done on his face in order to make him look normal and have a way of continuing the picture. As the action builds, Lee (or whoever he is) gets the chance to give his enemies their just desserts.

A gaggle of names are assembled in supporting roles, presumably for the sake of marketability since there was not enough of Lee to carry the picture. Dean Jagger and Hugh O'Brian are members of the syndicate, and Gig Young (who, reportedly committed suicide last October) appears as Lee's newspaper reporter confidant. It's a good bet that none have ever appeared more ridiculous on screen.

Kareem Abdul-Jabbar is featured in a fight scene and luckily gets away with only a line or two of dialog. Coleen Camp overacts as Lee's girlfriend but sounds okay singing the pic's theme song. Others turn in forgettable perfs in supporting roles.

John Barry has written some good music that might work if Jan Spears' script or Robert Clouse's direction could compensate for the fact that Bruce Lee was simply not alive to complete the picture. Unfortunately Lee died back in 1973 in the midst of making the film and no amount of doctoring could hide it. Obviously, there were a number of people who thought they could.
— Berg.

Salak Jitr
(Miss Salak Jitr)
(THAI-COLOR)

Bangkok, May 23.
A Kiattisak Film Productions release. Produced by Kanchana Metanee. Directed by Sombat Metanee. Features entire cast. Story, Vuth Piyamatr; screenplay, Pan Kam; camera (color), Niyom Srisuphan; sound, Pong Asvinikul; music, Piac; production manager, Niyom Panpreecha. Reviewed at Paramount Theatre, Bangkok. May 22, '79. Running time: 110 MINS.
Adio .... Sombat Metanee
Salak Jitr ....Jarunee Suksawat
Khun Poo ....?.. So Asanachinda
Khun Ah .... Supranee Jitiang
Chandra .... Marasri Nabangchang
Salak Jitr's Uncle .....Manop Assawathep

A young actress, Jarunee Suksawat, is responsible for much of the success of "Salak Jitr," partly filmed in England. As a protege of local filmmaker Promsin Sibunruang, Jarunee became a film star a few years ago via the school dramas of Pan Kam (Promsin's pseudonym).

Though Jarunee projects a wholesome rather than sexy image, it's understood that her innocent charm is what makes her irresistible. Her performance is supposed both to create a certain freshness and unity in the picture, as well as help make it very popular. She succeeds on both counts.

The camerawork keeps up with a growing concern among local filmmakers to exploit new camera angles and techniques. In comparison to it, the music is much less creative. Though this type of romance needs at least one good, hummable tune, there is none. The theme song can best be described as soothing, but so are scores of other Thai love story background music.

Scenes shot in England are mostly limited to sightseeing and picture-taking. Invariably that's precisely what local audiences get from pix partly made abroad. Hand-held cameras are employed in these particular scenes with what appears to be very little or no preparation.

With more time on his hands now that there's a lot more competition from new stars, Sombat Metanee managed both to star in and direct this vehicle. His performance could have passed unnoticed, except for the fact that he plays a man of indeterminate age here. In any case, Sombat has been known to play a teenager or an elderly uncle before, and apparently the local audience is given a choice as to what to imagine him to be. As a film director, Sombat simply lets his large cast of experienced supporting and character actors completely take over in most cases.

Making "Salak Jitr" a b.o. smash and Jarunee a bigger young star than ever turned out to be as simple as putting Jarunee in a film in which people fall over each other trying to be the first to tell her how pretty she looks. —Cano.

Shtigje Te Luftes
(Paths of War)
(ALBANIAN-B&W)

Berlin, June 1.
An Albanian Film Production, Tirana; world rights, Albania Film, Tirana. Features entire cast. Directed by Piro Milkani. Screenplay, Safet Kurti, Skender Plasari; camera (black and white), Faruk Basha; sets, M. Fushekati; music, Kujtim Laro. Reviewed at Cine-Center Screening Room, West Berlin, May 31, '79. Running time: 90 MINS.
Cast: Timo Flloko, Robert Ndrenika, Perike Gjezi, Sander Prosi, Pandi Raidhi, Ndrek Luca, Albert Verria, Liza Laska.

Made in 1974, Piro Milkani's "Paths of War" comes across as one of the top epic war pix made in Albania. It's set in the Peza region of Central Albania, the place where the partisan fighters and resistance-movement gathered in 1942 to win the Albanian people to their side in the fight against the Italian fascists. The foundations of the Albanian Communist Party were laid here as well.

Because the Peza region was a hotbed for partisan activity, the Italian occupation troops try to hunt down the leaders or destroy the movement by suppressing the people. Terror, violence, and infiltration are used as the primary means, while the main hope of the Italians is at least to split the resistance movement in half, and thus stifle the Communists altogether.

Lots of bang-up battle scenes, heroic action, and the like keep pic moving at a fast pace. Thesps are vets to this kind of role, and several are honored as the country's top film actors. Credits are up to the standards of the typical "Eastern" emerging regularly from the Socialist countries, which seems to be the model for this enterprise.
— *Holl.*

Michael Kohlhaas
(WEST GERMAN-COLOR)

Munich, June 7.
Produced by Horst Film GmbH & Co. KG, Berlin-Munich for Westdeutsches Werbefernsehen. Directed and written by Wolf Vollmar. Features entire cast. Camera (color), Wolfgang Hannemann; music, Peter Sandloff. Reviewed at Herzog Film 7screening room, Munich, June 6, '79. Running time: 95 MINS.
Cast: Rolf Boysen, Alfred Schieske, Wilhelm Borchert, Wolfgang Buettner, Irene Marhold, Kaspar Brueninghaus, Hans Elwenspoek, Alexander Allerson.

German playwright Heinrich von Kleist's (1777-1811) story "Michael Kohlhaas," first published in 1810, is based on a historical incident and belongs to the best-known and best-regarded German literary works. In the German language the nickname Kohlhaas still stands for someone who wants to achieve things by going headfirst. This exciting tale was first made into a picture by Volker Schloendorff in 1968. But unlike his current "Tin Drum" click, the pic, financed by Columbia Picture's German production arm Oceanic Film with DM 2,-500.000 (then worth some $1,000,-000) was a b.o. disappointment.

This newer version, originally constructed as a tv series but never broadcast for legal reasons, has been reedited by helmer Wolf Vollmar into a feature film, thereby eliminating most of the longeurs dictated by tv-oriented serial thinking.

The outcome is very filmic, splendidly photographed and excellently acted (cast is part of the creme de la creme of German stage), with beautiful locations.

The story tells of Michael Kohlhaas (his historical model, Hans Kohlhasen, lived in Coelln on the Spree river in the 16th century) who is held up wrongfully by a county squire, deprived of his horses and later finds himself in a web of legal niceties and hairsplitting.

After one year of that, he channels all his wrath into terror. Kohlhaas becomes a feared rebel and guerrilla fighter, taking his due by force. Finally he is captured and executed but shortly before his decapitation, he experiences justice — at least according to the books.

Besides timeless political and human truths, this German story is the nearest thing to such American legends as Billy the Kid or Jesse James, with a dash of Robin Hood thrown in. —*Koci.*

Tachi and Her Fathers
(CHINESE-COLOR)

Berlin, May 31.
An Omei Film Studio and Changhun Film Studio coproduction, China. Features entire cast. Directed by Wang Chia-yi. Screenplay, Kao Ying; camera (color), Wang Chun-chuan, Chang Hui; music, Lei Chen-pang, Ya Hsin, art direction, Li Chun-chieh. Reviewed at Cine-Center Screening Room, West Berlin, May 30, '79. Running time: 110 MINS.
Cast: Chen Hsueh-chieh (Tachi), Liu Lien-chih (Jen Ping-ching), Chu Tan-nan (Maho), Niu Chien (Mooka), Hsuan Hai-chih (Wu Chih-hung), Chou Shu (Ka-komu) Hsu Shih (Kuhah), Hamailo (Tar-mu), Wang Chun-ying (Erpoo), Yu Chung-lien (Hsiao Wang), Jung Jo-pei (Hsiao Ma).

Wang Chia-yi, first an actor and then a director, worked out of the Changchun Film Studio in northeast China and made three entertaining feature pix in the late 1950s and early 1960s: "Five Golden Flowers" (1959), "Chin Yu-chi" (1960), and "Tachi and Her Fathers" (1961). The best of these, per film historian Jay Leyda, was "Chin Yu-chi" with the renown femme thesp, Pai Yang, in the lead — she fell into disfavor during the Cultural Revolution, and even those associated with her also fell under suspicion. Thus, Wang Chia-yi's "Tachi and Her Fathers" was apparently his last registered pic, which surfaced recently.

"Tachi and Her Fathers" comes across today as rather innocent, sentimental fluff. It's about an orphan girl raised by a friendly family without knowing her real father is still alive. That secret slowly emerges when Tachi's "two fathers" settle some friendly affairs and piece the past together. Tachi, now a teenage girl, is then left with the decision what to do, and her real father nearly sacrifices himself for his daughter. Then everything works out for everyone. She keeps her two fathers.

Thesp performances and credits are top, save for dialogue and story line, which are far too creamy and sentimental. —*Holl.*

Nje Udhetimi I Veshtire
(A Difficult Transport)
(ALBANIAN-B&W)

Berlin, June 1.
An Albanian Film Production, Studio New Albania, Tirana; world rights, Albania Film, Tirana. Features entire cast. Directed by P. Llanaj and Xhezair Dafa. Screenplay, P. Llanaj, B. Hexha, H. Rama; camera (black and white), J. Kandsci, J. Kenemi; sets, A. Basha; music, Sh. Kosha. Reviewed at Cine-Center Screening Room, West Berlin, May 21, '79. Running time: 90 MINS.
Cast: Demir Hyskja, Pandi Siku, Sotlrog Cill.

The story of a pair of truckdrivers transporting a huge, over-length piece of factory equipment (it resembles a tower) from the harbor-city Tirana to a place in the mountains, P. Llanaj and Xhezair Dafa's "A Difficult Transport" draws on the same theme that made other East European pix commercial hits: Vasili Shukshin's "Once There Was a Lad" (1964) in the Soviet Union, Herrmann Zschoche's "Broad Roads, Quiet Love" (1969) in East Germany, and Mircea Daneliuc's "The Long Drive" (1975) in Rumania. Made in 1977, "A Difficult Transport" can easily rep Albania abroad without bowing too much to the pat formula.

The trick is how to get the precious load to its destination despite narrow road and dangerous curves. The two chosen drivers, one elder and the other younger, must learn on the trip to rely on each other absolutely without losing their nerves. The younger one nearly blows the works, then comes through in the end as a hero. Both thesps give solid performances, and pic has polish and psychological depth.

Well worth a look-see for Albanian Film Weeks and the like. Credits are a good cut above average. —*Holl.*

Goldengirl
(COLOR)

Olympic girl runner brain-washed to win. Tv version comes in 1980.

Hollywood, June 11.
Avco Embassy release of a Backstage production. Produced by Danny O'Donovan. Exec producer, Elliot Kastner. Directed by Joseph Sargent. Features entire cast. Screenplay, John Kohn; based on novel by Peter Lear; camera (Eastmancolor), Stevan Larner; editor, George Nicholson; sound (Dolby), Don Sharpless; music, Bill Conti; art direction, Syd Litwack; set decoration, Gerald Adams; asst. director, Bill Martin. Reviewed at the Directors Guild, Los Angeles, June 11, '79. (MPAA Rating: PG.) Running time: 104 MINS.

Goldengirl	Susan Anton
Dryden	James Coburn
Serafin	Curt Jurgens
Dr. Lee	Leslie Caron
Esselton	Robert Culp
Winters	James A. Watson, Jr.
Valenti	Harry Guardino
Cobb	Ward Costello
Sternberg	Michael Lerner
Armitage	John Newcombe
Ingrid	Julianna Fjeld
Debbie Jackson	Sheila DeWindt
Teammate	Andrea Brown
Krull	Anette Tannander
Dr. Dalton	Nicolas Coster

"Goldengirl" is amusingly poor. It masquerades as a psychological drama concerning a female track star who's been programmed by a bunch of lecherous hangers-on to become Goldengirl — Queen of the 1980 Moscow Olympics. Devoid of any believable flow of events and few convincing characterizations, picture looks to jog into theatrical oblivion after curiosity seekers get their fill of Susan Anton in a track suit tight enough to stop the circulation of even the most nimble-footed runner.

"Goldengirl" has been financed in large part by advance television, cable and syndication deals. Part of the agreement is that a longer version will be shown as a two-part telefilm on NBC next year. Perhaps the additional footage will fill in the large story gaps for those few viewers who decide to sit through it again on the tube.

Film opens with Anton, clad in snug white leotard and looking like a Playboy model furiously running back and forth in an effort to beat the electrical shock her trainer gives her when he thinks she's not running fast enough. Just as one begins to ponder why she's subjecting herself to this unpleasantness it's revealed that over the last few years she's been brainwashed by a psychiatrist, a trainer and a slightly maniacal adopted-father into believing that the only way she'll ever receive true love is to be the darling of the 1980 Olympics and win three Gold medals.

Anton's doctor dad has assembled a consortium of investors to finance the training with the agreement the businessmen will reap the tremendous merchandising benefits once Anton achieves Olympic fame. James Coburn is brought in to act as Anton's agent and although he initially appears to be only concerned with money, he softens when he sees the poor girl manipulated. His concern is enough to persuade Anton into bedding him and together they set their sights on the games.

In what must be record time, several months later Anton is at the Olympics as the United States' best hope. Meanwhile, it's learned over the years she's been given injections of a dangerous drug to promote growth and is coming down with curious symptoms of leg pains, schizophrenia and blackouts. All this builds to a somewhat confusing climax that's not really worth figuring out.

Central fault to film is Anton's character, who seems to alternate between robot, country girl and schizophrenic. Her screen debut is at best, forgettable, with Anton doing little to clear up the mystifying script. The fact that she sports enough hair to slow down the entire men's relay team also doesn't do much for realism.

Curt Jurgens is just plain silly as her father, whose German accent seems to be enough of a signal for scripter John Kohn to indicate Jurgens' conducted some kind of crazy experiments under Hitler. James Coburn is too slick as the agent to convince he really loves Anton and Robert Culp is a little too mean and overambitious as a tv reporter who wants to expose the goings on.

Leslie Caron, Harry Guardino, Ward Costello and Michael Lerner are not much better as the psychiatrist and members of the consortium. James Watson Jr. provides some measure of intelligence as Anton's trainer.

Lion's share of the blame seems to lie with scripter Kohn and director Joseph Sargent. Both seem to be involved in a conspiracy to keep countless loose ends in the picture intact. They receive ample help from George Nicholson's editing but are hampered somewhat but Bill Conti's effectively haunting music.

The premise of an Olympic competitor being brainwashed is an interesting one. It also would seem highly marketable in light of next year's Olympic games. Perhaps by then someone will come up with coherent picture that illustrates the premise. —*Berg*.

Sib Tamruat Toh Buntung
(Sgt. Buntung)
(THAI-COLOR)

Bangkok, May 31.
An Amolrat Films release. Produced by Kittipong Wetpooyant. Written and directed by Pote Siriphan, based on the novel by Sangphet Senibaddin. Camera (color), Niyom Srisuwan; sound, Sanan Aroonrat; music, Montri Ong-iam; art director, Narong Patpreow. Reviewed at Petchrama Theatre, Bangkok, May 30, '79. Running time: **125 MINS**.
Buntung .... Piya Trakulrat
Apple .... Jarunee Suksawat
Japhon .... Suwin Swangrat
Poom .... Poom Patanayuth
Dr. Toon .... Tosapon Srisai
Klae .... Uap Tomchat

Becoming successful in a certain performance and creating a popular screen image is one of the surest ways of becoming typecast. Piya Trakulrat became an overnight success as the dedicated teacher in "Kru Ban Nok" (Rural Teachers). He does a similar role in another guise, an uncorruptible cop, in "Sib Tamruat Toh Buntung."

On the whole, there seems to be far too many protracted sermons on being a good cop and what it takes to be one in "Sib Tamruat Toh Buntung." The main theme is that if you're going to be a real good cop, you musn't let your emotions get the better of you.

Suwin Swangrat, as the police chief, plays a few comic scenes with Piya, in which the former tries to teach the latter how to catch criminals. Piya proves much more adept at it on his own, and the quick cuts on his one-man clean-up campaign of gambling places proved some of the funniest bits.

The stereo sound system employed often succeeds in bringing a whole countryside to life. Overlapping sounds and lialog do not make one lose the story's thread. Northeastern Thailand's folk songs are also pleasantly exploited as background music. Nothing was shot inside a studio, all the filming done on location. — *Cano*.

Escape From Alcatraz
(COLOR)

Superior Eastwood prison pic should get away with lotsa b.o. loot.

Hollywood, June 13.
A Paramount Pictures release. Produced and directed by Donald Siegel. Stars Clint Eastwood. Exec producer, Robert Daley. Screenplay, Richard Tuggle, based on the book by J. Campbell Bruce; camera (color), Bruce Surtees; production design, Allen Smith; editor, Ferris Webster; set decoration, Edward J. McDonald; sound, Bert Hallberg; assistant director, Luigi Alfano. Reviewed at Motion Picture Academy of Arts & Sciences, June 13, '79. (MPAA Rating: PG.) Running time: **112 MINS**.
Frank Morris .... Clint Eastwood
Warden .... Patrick McGoohan
Doc .... Roberts Blossom
Clarence Anglin .... Jack Thibeau
John Anglin .... Fred Ward
English .... Paul Benjamin
Charley Butts .... Larry Hankin
Wolf .... Bruce M. Fischer
Litmus .... Frank Ronzio

"Escape From Alcatraz" reunites Clint Eastwood with producer-director Don Siegel in one of the finest prison films ever made. An expert combination of brutal realism and spine-tingling suspense, "Escape" returns both Eastwood and Siegel to their prime form. Thanks to a PG rating, with a minimum of explicit violence, box-office returns look to be gargantuan, with not only the action-adventure crowd certain to respond, but also the more diverse audience Eastwood successfully captured in "Every Which Way But Loose."

Considering that the escape itself from rock-bound Alcatraz prison consumes only the film's final half-hour, screenwriter Richard Tuggle and Siegel provide a model of super-efficient filmmaking. From the moment Eastwood walks onto The Rock, until the final title card explaining the three escapees were never heard from again, "Escape From Alcatraz" is relentless in establishing a mood and pace of unrelieved tension.

Pic's only fault may be an ambiguous ending, tied, of course, to the historical reality of the 1962 escape, only successful one in Alcatraz' 29-year history as America's most repressive penal institution. So much empathy is built up with Eastwood and his cohorts that audiences may resent not being able to savor a proven victory.

No matter. Eastwood returns here to the taciturn, hard-edged persona that first brought him fame, with an added human dimension that has the audience rooting for him from the time the first cell door slams shut.

Siegel has grouped around him the perfect rogue's gallery, including an oversized killer (Bruce M. Fisher) whose sexual advances Eastwood spurns, a likable con inseparable from his pet mouse (Frank Ronzio), an aged prisoner-artist (Roberts Blossom), a bitter black inmate (Paul Benjamin), and a nervous nellie unable to make the prison break (Larry Hankin).

It's a tribute to first-time scripter Tuggle that these characters are not only believable, but that they mesh so well with the inevitable plot conclusion, each playing a pivotal, if unobtrusive, role.

Key counterpoint to Eastwood's character comes from Patrick McGoohan as the megalomaniacal warden. Wisely underplaying (and successfully hiding his British ac-

cent), McGoohan avoids the excesses of character that often bedevil pic prison toppers.

Production designer Allen Smith and set decorator Edward J. McDonald have done an astonishing job of camouflaging the currently decrepit condition of Alcatraz, and blending studio interiors with location work. Bruce Surtees has shot "Escape" with a soft and grainy realism that seems to have incorporated the San Francisco Bay fog within his lens. Ferris Webster's editing is a central element in the pic's effectiveness, and is worthy of the highest praise.

Fischer, Benjamin, Ronzio Blossom and Hankin excel in their respective delineations, and Jack Thibeau and Fred Ward are well cast as Eastwood's accomplices in the final escape. Both prison inmates and guards project a realism unusual for a film using this many extras.

When all is said and done, "Escape From Alcatraz" belongs to Eastwood and Siegel, in their fifth teaming, and their most successful since "Dirty Harry" in 1971. Rugged and imperturbable, Eastwood proves himself the king of the one-liners — with his dialog pruned to a minimum, there's simply no one better for this type of role.

Siegel has been on prison turf before, most notably in 1954 with "Riot In Cell Block 11," with "Escape From Alcatraz," he reaffirms his reputation as not only a master technician, but a consummate filmmaker. By successfully evoking the classic prison pix such as "White Heat," "Each Dawn I Die" and "Brute Force," the Paramount release demonstrates that old genres don't have to fade away, but can only better. —*Poll*.

Rak Ri Sayar
(Jealousy)
(THAI-COLOR)

Bangkok, May 31.
A G.P. Film Promotions release. Produced by Opas Rangchaikul. Directed by Patravadee Sritrairat. Story and screenplay. Thavorn Suwan; camera (color), Chome Bunnag; lighting, Patrick Govain; music, Menrat Srikanond; sound, Kasem Militachinda; art director, Vorachon Yuchinda. Reviewed at Washington Theatre, Bangkok, May 30, '79. Running time: **120 MINS**.
Pathama .... Titima Sangkapitak
Cherd .... Chalit Fuang-arome
Monchan .... Duangjai Hataikan
Prajak .... Kamthorn Suwanpiyasiri
Rick .... Jakarat Virasant
Samorn .... Juree Osiree

Almost one year in the making, Patravadee Sritrairat's "Rak Ri Sayar" opened recently with a Royal Command Performance. It's Patravadee's first film directing effort, although she has produced, directed and toplined several Thai tv serials. She also produced a film, "Games," several years ago.

This pic has all the plusses compared to the majority of Thai films — well-chosen locations, carefully motivated acting styles, fine photography and lighting. In fact, the too familiar material gets much better treatment than it deserves. But Patravadee's direction may well serve as a model for other local directors.

The storyline dealing with problems between widows and widowers on the one hand, and the effect of remarriage on their children, on the other, always verges on sentimentality, if not downright soap operatic scenes. Making her film acting debut in this pic, Titima is terrific.

Others in the cast give very fine support. Duangchai Hataikan displays an astonishingly good talent for comedy as a provincial lass who aspires to become as sophisticated as Titima. Both Chalit Fuang-arome and Kamthorn Suwanpiya-siri avoid overacting in roles where that's the main danger. Jakarat Virasant gives some depth to the only villainous part. And Juree Osi-ree, who thought people would laugh at her even in a serious role, reveals her dramatic acting ability onscreen (she has played hundreds of tragic heroines as a film dubber). —*Cano.*

The Music Machine
(BRITISH-COLOR)

Disco spinoff sans fever.

London, June 12.

A Norfolk International Pictures presentation. Exec producer, James Kenelm Clarke. Produced by Brian Smedley-Aston. Directed by Ian Sharp. Features entire cast. Screenplay, Kenelm Clarke; camera (color), Phil Meheux; editors, Alan Patillo, Smedley-Aston; art director, Roger King; sound, Mickey Hickey; music composed and performed by The Music Machine, with guest singer Patti Boulaye; asst. director, Vic Priggs. Reviewed at the Rialto theatre, London, June 11, '79. (BBFC Rating: A). Running time: **90 MINS.**
Gerry .... Gerry Sundquist
Clare .... Patti Boulaye
Laurie .... Clarke Peters
Howard .... David Easter
Candy .... Mandy Perryment
Mark .... Billy McColl
Sue .... Chrissy Wickham
Joe .... Ray Burdis
Sharon .... Frances Lowe
Aldo .... Garry Shail
Nick .... Mickey Feast

In relocating the elements of "Saturday Night Fever" virtually intact to London, but with an added dollop of downbeat British realism, "The Music Machine" aspires to tell the scene like it is, instead of like it was packaged. Plot, characters and production values, however, stand considerably less scrutiny than those of the original, and the comparison, albeit invited, ends up invidious.

With some appeal nonetheless to fans of disco at any cost — however low — the film could cut the odd caper at boxoffices close to home, if promoted via its strong soundtrack to the very young-in-mind, and preferably young-in-fact. Prospects beyond these shores, besides possibly in the traditional British Commonwealth markets, look shaky.

James Kenelm Clarke's script tilts directly at unseating the "Saturday Night Fever" myth. It plots an unemployed youth's finally successful attempts to win a dance competition against the local champ, played by David Easter, who not only looks like John Travolta, but dances and dresses like him as well. Raw, likeable talent defeats smooth, arrogant image.

The prize for the victorious couple (attractive but insubstantial Gerry Sundquist is partnered by Patti Boulaye, seemingly more assured as a cabaret artist than as an actress) is leading roles in a feature film planned by the contest's sponsors. One of the story's bigger holes is that in order to portray the poor-man's movie-moguls as suitably villainous, it's made clear in an early scene that the winners will more than likely be exploited anyway. This makes it hard to feel victory is worth much.

Standout among the young cast is Clarke Peters, who alone projects some screen charisma as the disco deejay and general mentor. He and Chrissy Wickham, Sundquist's partner until boyfriend trouble causes her to drop out — a decided loss to the film, take credit as the only convincing dancers.

Ian Sharp, debuting as a feature director, and cinematographer Phil Meheux both come off respectably enough, but the predictable material and evidently tight economics leave little room for distinction, beyond an effective, twice-used craneshot of a highrise building staircase. —*Simo.*

Raices De Sangre
(Roots Of Blood)
(MEXICAN-COLOR)

Hollywood, June 12.

An Azteca release of a Conacine production. Directed, story and screenplay by Jesus Salvador Trevino; camera (Eastmancolor), Rosalio Solano; editor, Joaquin Ceballos; music, Sergio Guerrero; sound, Sigfrido Garcia. Reviewed at Azteca Screening Room, L.A., June 12, '79. No MPAA rating. Running time: **100 MINS.**
Carlos Rivera .... Richard Yniguez
Roman Carvajal .... Ernesto Gomez Cruz
Hilda Gutierrez .... Malena Doria
Juan Vallejo .... Pepe Serna
Rosamaria Mejia .... Adriana Rojo
Lupe Carrillo ...... Roxana Bonila-Gianini

Shot in 1976 and released in a handful of U.S. Spanish-language theatres over the last few months, this Mexican production received its English-subtitled preem at the Golden Gate Theatre in L.A. May 30 and will shortly enter general release in this country. A solidly made call to political activism which effectively points up the problems of Mexicans on the border in very human terms, "Raices De Sangre" is a refreshingly honest antidote to Hollywood's recent dalliance with Chicano problem pictures. Already a hit in Mexico, pic could be carefully nurtured to good results stateside with both Latino and Anglo audiences.

Rather like "Norma Rae," this film deals with the oppression of female garment industry workers in an American-owned plant just south of the Texas-Mexico line. Situation is considerably more complex, however, since two governments and languages are involved, along with the dilemmas of illegal aliens, drug trafficking and racial pride.

In no way more subtle than many other Third World-type agit-prop works, pic delineates the growing political awareness of a sharp young man who has escaped his roots, obtained a Harvard law degree and established a good life in San Francisco. Back on the border to work for the community action Barrio Unido over a summer, he's reluctantly dragged into commitment to the cause of his people.

Film particularly excels in its depiction of divisiveness within the movement, showing the temptation American bucks provide to Mexican workers to betray their own people, the skirmishing of more radical youths to attain community position, the reluctance of others, particularly parents, to become tinged by politics, and the general sense of uncertainty as to how and where to organize confrontations and influence the various power structures. Also implicit in the film's point of view is the acknowledgment that things have improved over the last 10 to 20 years.

Writer-director Jesus Salvador Trevino stages the action simply and forcefully, blundering just once when he leaves a group of illegal aliens, which includes two major characters, locked up in a truck with no resolution offered at picture's end. Mix of Spanish and English dialog is very effective, although the subtitles are a bit simplified and too concise.

Richard Yniguez is significantly more effective here than he was earlier this year in "Boulevard Nights," though his emotional depth could still be in question. Roxanna Bonilla-Gianini appealingly renders a longtime organizer who, politically and romantically, helps sway Yniguez over to the cause.

Neo-realist and Third World cinema often seems somewhat remote from American concerns, but "Raices De Sangre," through its even-handedly considered polemics, brings another culture's problems a lot close to home.
—*Cart.*

The Apple Dumpling Gang Rides Again
(COLOR)

Half-baked Disney western should sit well with kiddie crowd.

Hollywood, June 9.

Buena Vista Distribution Co. release of a Walt Disney production. Produced by Ron Miller, Tom Leetch. Directed by Vincent McEveety. Features entire cast. Screenplay, Don Tait, based on characters created by Jack M. Bickham; camera (Technicolor), Frank Phillips; editor, Gordon D. Brenner; art direction, Norman Rockett; special effects, Art Cruickshank, Danny Lee; sound, Henry A. Maffett; assistant director, Robert W. Webb. Reviewed at Academy of Motion Picture Arts & Sciences, BevHills, June 8, '79 (MPAA Rating: G.) Running time: **88 MINS.**
'79 (MPAA Rating: G.) Running time: **88 MINS.**
Amos .... Tim Conway
Theodore .... Don Knotts
Private Jeff Reid .... Tim Matheson
Marshal Woolly Bill Hitchock ....
.... Kenneth Mars
Millie Gaskill .... Elyssa Davalos
Big Mac .... Jack Elam
Lt. Jim Ravencroft .... Robert Pine
Major Gaskill .... Harry Morgan
Tough Kate .... Ruth Buzzi
Martha Osten .... Audrey Totter
Sgt. Slaughter .... Richard X. Slattery
Sherick .... Joan Crawford
Wes Hardin .... Cliff Osmond
Frank Starrett .... Ted Gehring
Corporal No. 1 .... Morgan Paull

It seems ironic that the one studio turning out westerns with any frequency is Walt Disney, aiming for the moppet sagebrush crowd once again with "The Apple Dumpling Gang Rides Again," sequel to its successful ($16,500,000 in domestic film rentals) 1975 release, "The Apple Dumpling Gang." While sequel bears little relation to its predecessor, there's always a new generation of tots, and matinee biz should be profitable. The G-rated Buena Vista release won't disappoint any of the diehard Disney fans.

Tim Conway and Don Knotts, who supplied comic relief in the 1975 original, now take center stage as two outlaw misfits. Subplot involves Robert Pine as a crooked soldier trying to unseat fort commander Harry Morgan, whose daughter, Elyssa Davalos, is engaged to Pine. Tim Matheson plays an Army spy who eventually straightens out the whole mess. Kenneth Mars plays a revenge-minded sheriff.

Don Tait, who also scripted first "Apple Dumpling Gang" (title has even less relevance in this version), relies solely on the sort of physical humor, pratfalls and sight gags that has worked in previous genre pix, including last summer's "Hot Lead And Cold Feet," which also featured Knotts.

Under Disney vet Vincent McEveety's direction, "Apple Dumpling Gang Rides Again" lurches from one set piece to another, in a fashion that makes its 88-minute running time seem much longer. Conway and Knotts have perfected their bumbling routines to a very minor art form, but principal laughs are supplied by drunk jokes, and character names such as Jack Elam's Big Mac. When hamburger trademarks become chief yock-suppliers, time has come to look elsewhere.

Supporting cast is varied, with Ruth Buzzi doing a manic job of a meddling old lady, and Mars predictably weird as the unlucky lawman. Harry Morgan (who also appeared in the original), Elam, Audrey Totter, Richard X. Slattery and Cliff Osmond escaping unscathed, but Tim Matheson and Elyssa Davalos are ill-suited for the romantic roles. It's a good thing the small fry has few standards of comparison.

Other tech credits are okay, with special effects particularly good from Disney regulars Art Cruickshank and Danny Lee. Paired with the original, "Apple Dumpling Gang Rides Again" should provide Buena Vista with reissue fodder for years to come. —*Poll.*

The Main Event
(COLOR)

Healthy prospects.

Hollywood, June 19.
Warner Bros. release of a First Artists presentation of a Barwood (Jon Peters) Film production. Stars Barbra Streisand, Ryan O'Neal. Executive producers, Howard Rosenman, Renee Missel. Produced by Jon Peters, Barbra Streisand. Directed by Howard Zieff. Screenplay, Gail Parent, Andrew Smith; camera (color), Mario Tosi; editor, Edward Warschilka; production designer, Charles Rosen; asst. directors, Gary Daigler, Pat Kehoe; technical consultants, Hedgemon Lewis, Jose Torres; stunt co-ordinator, Denver Mattson; set decorator, James Payne; music, supervised by Gary Le Mel; publicist, Vic Heutschy; songs, "The Main Event," Paul Jabara, Bruce Roberts, "Fight," Jabara, Bob Esty; "Angry Eyes," Loggins & Messina; "The Body Shop," Michalski & Oosterveen. Reviewed at National Theatre, Westwood, June 19, 1979. (MPAA Rating: PG). Running time: 112 MINS.
Hillary Kramer .... Barbra Streisand
Eddie (Kid Natural) Scanlon ....
.... Ryan O'Neal
David .... Paul Sand
Percy .... Whitman Mayo
Donna .... Patti D'Arbanville
Luis .... Chu Chu Malave
Hector Mantilla .... Richard Lawson
Gough .... James Gregory

Tour guide .... Richard Altman
Stunt double kid .... Joe Amsler
Newsman .... Seth Banks
Girl in bed .... Lindsay Bloom
Kline .... Earl Boen
Owner Sinthia Cosmetics ... Roger Bowen
Heavyweight in gym .. Badja Medu Djola
Fighter in Kid's camp ..... Rory Calhoun
Brenda .... Sue Casey
Man in gym .... Alvin Childress
Lucy .... Kristine De Bell
Gomez .... Al Denava

Since 1979 seems to be the year for pugilistic pix, the timing of "The Main Event" seems well chosen, given the need for a boxing spoof to set the other canvas tearjerkers in perspective. Instead of a comic knockout, however, the Warner Bros.-First Artists release is more of a cream puff. Given the proven audience for coproducer-star Barbra Streisand, biz prospects are healthy, although it's doubtful "Main Event" will go the distance to boxoffice blockbuster status.

Problem is not that the premise and script by Gail Parent and Andrew Smith lacks humor. Situation of a bankrupt perfume queen left with a sore-handed fighter (picked up as a tax shelter loss) as her only asset has comic potential, but producers Streisand and Jon Peters, and director Howard Zieff, pad the story unmercifully. Result is like watching a 15-round match in which the combatants slug it out only fitfully, and spend the rest of their time sparring.

Matched up against each other again (first pairing was in the successful 1972 release, "What's Up, Doc?"), Streisand and O'Neal fail to live up to their earlier effort, although the parts are virtual carbons. Streisand is the garrulous yenta, after the passive and resistant O'Neal to resume his championship form and win her back the $60,000 she unknowingly wasted on him in her plush days.

Zieff, at whomever's instigation, has chosen to emphasize sexual innudendo above any of the other comic elements, and result is a low-blow effort that evokes more titters than guffaws.

Romantic aspects, which should be chief draw of "Main Event," are also blunted, until a final seduction scene instigated by Streisand that gives the pic its only resonance. Even that's spoiled, however, by a ridiculous finale that caps the unreal marriage between the boxing backdrop and the Streisand-O'Neal antics.

In a film whose sum is way less than its parts, some of the lesser names walk away with most of the laughs. Patti D'Arbanville is a delight as O'Neal's sleazy girlfriend — when her character evokes the biggest yocks with a hacking cough, something's gone awry.

Whitman Mayo is solidly human

as O'Neal's manager, and James Gregory as a promoter, Denver Mattson as a referee and Tim Rossovich as an animalistic fighter offer good support. Tech credits are pro, although Technicolor Lab work seems to have emphasized the fleshy tones in Mario Tosi's camerawork.

Putting aside all of the ridiculous aspects of "Main Event" (Streisand's glamorous wardrobe on a nickel-and-dime budget, the complete disregard for boxing rules and tradition, and the highly improbable ending), major disappointment is Streisand's apparent contentment to stay with a character she has now exhausted on the screen.

And since "Main Event" is a production of three companies either she or Peters are involved in, there's nowhere else to shift the blame. —*Poll.*

Imi Hageneralit
(My Mother, The General)
(ISRAELI-COLOR)

Tel Aviv, June 11.
A Noah Films Presentation of a Golan-Globus Production. Produced by Menahem Golan, Yoram Globus. Stars Gila Almagor, Zachi Noy. Executive Producer, Dan Dimburt. Directed by Yoel Zilberg. Screenplay, Eli Tavor, Yoel Zilberg, based on the play by Eli Saghi; camera (color), David Gurfinkel; editor, Irit Paz; art director, Yossi Azmon; music, Nurith Hirsch. Reviewed in Tel Aviv, June 10, 1979. Running time: 84 MINS.
Cast: Gideon Singer, Gilat Ankori, Uri Sali, Avi Pnini, Eyal Geffen, Makhram Khouri, Marlen Bejali, Haim Polani, Ariel Fourman.

Describing this as a vulgar comedy may not be as much of a criticism as it looks at first sight. Based on a comedy which was absolutely hated by the critics, it turns into a feature film to share the same fate. But, as it broke boxoffice records on the stage, it could repeat its performance on the domestic screen. What's more, the filmization adds an epilog to the play, which gives it the distinction of being the first film to deal with the Israeli-Egyptian entente cordiale, another feather in the public relations cap of the Golan-Globus productions.

The stage version told about a typical Jewish mother, hitting the road to the Suez Canal post, to find her darling son and take care of him. The son happens to be the commander of the post, which changes with the appearance of his authoritative parent, who naturally takes charge, turning the military discipline on its head. The film moves the border post inside Sinai, as according to the disengagement agreements, the epilog adds an Egyptian mother, identical to the Jewish one, visiting

her own son on the other side of the border.

Aiming directly at the gut, the writing and the direction rely mostly on coarse military slang and on obvious visual gimmicks, such as the rotundities of Zachi Noy.

Cast conforms to the general atmosphere, and if there is any complaint to be raised against Gila Almagor, in the lead, it is that she looks and acts too refined, despite her dedicated efforts. Other names, such as Gideon Singer, ham their way through, but many of the younger newcomers just sham. Surprisingly enough, the more restrained and natural are West Bank actress Marlen Bejali, playing the Egyptian mother, and Israeli-Arab theatre actor Makhram Khouri, as her son.

Mostly shot on location, and produced at top speed, final copies were still expected from the Rank laboratories, as late as four days before the official opening, the press saw a working copy, making technical appraisal impossible. —*Edna.*

(Pic may be first Israeli film invited to the Cairo Film Fest-Ed.)

Moonraker
(BRITISH-COLOR)

High-interest Bond, due now.

Hollywood, June 26.

United Artists release of an Albert R. Broccoli production. Stars Roger Moore. Directed by Lewis Gilbert. Executive producer, Michael G. Wilson. Screenplay, Christopher Wood, based on Ian Fleming novel; camera (Panavision-color), Jean Tournier; music, John Barry, lyrics, Hal David; production designer, Ken Adam; film editor, John Glen; visual effects supervisor, Derek Meddings; production managers — France, Jean-Pierre Spiri-Mercanton; U.K., Terence Churcher; second unit directors, Ernie Day, John Glen; asst. director, Michael Cheyko; art directors, Max Douy. Charles Bishop; set decorator, Peter Howitt; sound mixer, Daniel Brisseau; special effects, John Evans, John Richardson; publicists, Steve Swan, Gilles Durieux; title song sung by Shirley Bassey. Reviewed at Samuel Goldwyn Theatre, Beverly Hills, June 22, 1979. (MPAA Rating - PG). Running time: **126 MINS.**

James Bond	Roger Moore
Holly Goodhead	Lois Chiles
Drax	Michael Lonsdale
Jaws	Richard Kiel
Corinne Dufour	Corinne Clery
"M"	Bernard Lee
Frederick Gray	Geoffrey Keen
"Q"	Desmond Llewelyn
Moneypenny	Lois Maxwell
Manuela	Emily Bolton
Chang	Toshiro Suga
Dolly	Blanche Ravalec

Also Jean-Pierre Castaldi, Leila Shenna, Walter Gotell, Arthur Howard, Irka Bochenko, Michael Marshall, Douglas Lambert, Alfie Bass, Anne Lonnberg, Brian Keith, George Birt, Kim Fortune, Chris Dillinger, Georges Beller, Johnny Traber, Lizzie Warville, Chichinou Kaeppler, Francoise Gayat, Catherine Serre, Christina Hui, Nicaise Jean-Louis, Beatrice Libert.

When a Bond comes due, as it does every two years now, there's nothing to do but cash it and "Moonraker" will pay plenty as it offers up sufficient fun for fantasy fans. But more than ever producer Albert R. Broccoli and director Lewis Gilbert seem to be strapped for fresh thrills, falling back on formulas that worked in the past.

As usual, however, they've come up with a wowzer for an opening, but deja vu sets in quickly after that, as Roger Moore goes after a missing spaceship. Predictably, this will lead to the discovery of another mad plot to take over the world, masterminded this time by Michael Lonsdale.

Lois Chiles is the beauty with the gigglesome name and Corinne Clery is the one-night stand who will soon be dead, etc. Richard Kiel returns as the towering steel-toothed "Jaws," whose wacky villainy is twisted further with a romance with tiny Blanche Ravelec and a touch of goodness at the end.

Christopher Wood's script takes these characters exactly where they always go in a James Bond pic and the only question is whether the stunts and gadgets will live up to expectations. They do. But like a familiar meal, you wish there was something on the menu besides more dart shooters, boat chases and another underwater battle with a denizen.

The main problem this time is the outer-space setting which somehow dilutes the mammoth monstrosity that 007 must save the world from. By comparison, the theft of Fort Knox or the hiding of three nuclear subs in a supertanker have dimensions that the mind can scale to. But one more big mothership hovering over earth becomes just another model intercut with elaborate interiors, no matter how imaginatively conceived by production designer Ken Adam.

The visual effects, stuntwork and other technical contributions all work together expertly to make the most preposterous notions believable. And Moore, though still compared to Sean Connery, clearly has adapted the James Bond character to himself and serves well as the wise-cracking, incredibly daring and irresistible hero.

More so than usual, sex is suggested instead of seen. But Moore's last floating embrace with Chiles is enough to encourage more rapid development of space flight.

All in all, a solid chapter — the 11th — in what must now be one of the longest successful runs with a single character in feature history. This is clearly an accomplishment and it can't be all that easy to come up with toppers for a full two-hours. Even when they repeat themselves, the results are effective. But just not as much fun the second, third and fourth times around.

—Har.

Up From The Depths
(FILIPINO-COLOR)

Goofball big fish satire unlike to rise from b.o. depths.

Hollywood, June 26.

A New World Pictures release. Executive Producer, Jack Atienza. Produced by Cirio H. Santiago. Directed by Charles B. Griffith. Features entire cast. Screenplay, Alfred Sweeney; camera (Metrocolor), Rick Remington; editor, G.V. Bass; music, Russell O'Malley; asst. directors, Jill Griffith, Manny Norman. Reviewed at the Fox Theatre, Hollywood, June 22, 1979. (No MPAA rating.) Running time: **75 MINS.**

Greg Oliver	Sam Bottoms
Rachel McNamara	Susanne Reed
Earl Sheridan	Virgil Frye
Oscar Forbes	Kedric Wolfe
David Whiting	Charles Howerton
Iris Lee	Denise Hayes
Ed	Charles Doherty
Louellen	Helen McNelly

With its flipped-out sense of humor and dubbing that must have been done blindfolded, "Up From The Depths" plays just about like Woody Allen's first pic, "What's Up, Tiger Lily?". It might even be said that, rather than leeching off "Jaws" yet again, New World is beating Universal (now planning "Jaws 3, People0") to the punch with a goofball satire of the big fish mini-genre. As in Mel Brooks' "The Producers," preview audience members came expecting one thing and stayed to laugh their heads off, which is the only response this Filipino-made programmer will ever elicit. Murky b.o. is in store.

Helmer Charles B. Griffith was responsible for the scripts for most of Roger Corman's wackier efforts of the late 1950s, such as "A Bucket Of Blood" and "The Little Shop Of Horrors," and his bent comic sense comes through here as the only factor which sustains pic's meager 75 minutes. It's not nearly enough, however, as operative sensibility seems to know how bad film is but is unable to do anything about it.

It's the same old story again, with a ravaging monster wreaking havoc on visitors to a seaside resort. Switch this time is that the hotel manager (in a funny performance by Kedric Wolfe) stages a contest for guests to kill the beast. which one member of the audience derisively likened to a surfboard with teeth.

Climax is particularly hilarious, as a couple of seafarers tie the corpse of a former comrade to the back of their boat and string it along behind them as bait for the ravenous creature. "He'd a wanted it like this," insist the men, as the audience goes up for grabs.

Sense of humor involved is indicated in the opening titles, which feature lead Sam Bottoms' name superimposed over two frantically undulating derrieres. Dubbing (presumably necessitated by faulty on-location sound recording, as pic was shot in English) is on a par with the worst Italian-Yugoslavian co-production imports of the 1960s, and camerawork is at times astoundingly jerky. *—Cart.*

Meatballs
(CANADIAN-COLOR)

Lotsa b.o. sauce in Par's summer sleeper hit from Canada.

Hollywood, June 26.

Paramount Pictures release of an Ivan Reitman production. Produced by Dan Goldberg. Directed by Ivan Reitman. Features entire cast. Screenplay, Len Blum, Don Goldberg, Janis Allen, Harold Ramis; music, Elmer Bernstein; editor; Debra Karen; art director, David Charles; camera (color), Don Wilder, Songs, Norman Gimbel, Elmer Bernstein. Reviewed at National Theatre, Westwood, June 16, 1979. (MPAA Rating: PG) Running time: **92 MINS.**

Tripper	Bill Murray
Morty	Harvey Atkin
Roxanne	Kate Lynch
Crockett	Russ Banham
A.L.	Kristine DeBell
Candace	Sarah Torgov
Spaz	Jack Blum
Fink	Keith Knight
Wendy	Cindy Girling
Wheels	Todd Hoffman
Jackie	Margot Pinwidic
Hardware	Matt Cravenn
Brenda	Norma Dell'Agnese
Rudy	Chris Makepeace
Eddy	Michael Kirby

Also Greg Swangon, Ron Barry, Paul Boyle, Vince Guerriero, James McLarty, Heather Preece, Ruth Rennie, Alison Diver, Valerie Fersht, Allan Levson, Patrick Hynes, Hadley Kay, Bill Kishonti, Peter Hume.

Record of tv stars making the transition to feature films is spotty overall, but Bill Murray proves a welcome exception to the rule. The "Saturday Night Live" regular manages to sock over "Meatballs," with amazing vitality and elan. With summer camp as its topical theme, and the setting and cast to back up its premise, the Paramount release looks to be the sleeper hit of the summer, with excellent boxoffice prospects in all markets.

"Meatballs," which originally carried the "Summer Camp" title before it was taken by another feature, should also demonstrate that a Canadian-financed and produced pic, featuring a largely Canadian cast, can match its American counterparts, and probably out-perform them as well.

It's difficult to come up with a more cliche situation for a summer pic than a summer camp, where all the characters and plot turns are readily imaginable. That makes producer Dan Goldberg and director Ivan Reitman's accomplishment all the more noteworthy.

Murray limns a head counselor in charge of a group of misfit counselors-in-training. The usual types predominate: the myopic klutz, the obese kid who wins the pig-out contest, the smooth-talking lothario, and a bevy of comely lasses.

Scripters Len Blum, Goldberg, Janis Allen and Harold Ramis have managed to gloss over the stereotypes and come up with a smooth-running narrative that makes the camp hijinks part of an overall human mosaic. No one is unduly belittled or mocked, and "Meatballs" is without the usual grossness and cynicism of many contempo comedy pix.

Without Murray, however, "Meatballs" might have faltered more than once. His character, all bluff and bravado, is immensely likable. Without ever demeaning himself or the film, Murray has a flip, cool style that transfers astonishingly well from videotape to film.

Most of the secondary players are unrecognizable in name and face to American audiences, but are uniformly well chosen for their roles. Harvey Atkin is fine as the camp director, ditto Kate Lynch as Murray's femme counterpart and romantic interest. Russ Banham, Kristine DeBell, and especially Sarah Torgov, Jack Blum, Keith Knight and Margot Pinvidic, are unusually competent as the unruly counselor trainees.

One sign of pic's class is in relationship between Murray and Chris Makepeace as a troubled young camper. In a fashion that's never hokey, and with surprising directness, Murray takes the moppet under his wing, and enables him to build up some self-respect.

That dimension is totally absent from most summer programmers, and is one more measure of success of "Meatballs." Reitman, who previously produced Universal's blockbuster, "National Lampoon's Animal House," has obviously learned some lessons since his last directorial effort, the Canadian low-budgeter, "Cannibal Girls." Tech work from the Canadian crew is pro, as is Elmer Bernstein's score.

"Meatballs" has a way to go until it equals "Animal House," but the same audience will respond, no doubt in force. — Poll.

Khon Krang Detr
(Slum People In The Sun)
(THAI-COLOR)

Bangkok, June 6.
A Saha Mongkol Films release. Produced by Somsak Techaratanaprasert. Features entire cast. Written and directed by Kidd Suwannasorn. Camera (color), Pornitti Virayasiri; music, Prat Suwannasorn; sound, Maitree Janjarasskul; production designer, Somneuk Gohasuwan; costumes, Suchada Takeesit. Reviewed at Paris theatre, Bangkok, June 5, '79. Running time: 130 MINS.
Pleow .... Ron Rittichai
Paeh .... Benjawan Boonyakart
Samrerng .... Nopadoe Duangphorn
Meow .... Sasithorn Pantoorat
Paporng .... Manat Putikiat

Artistic directors often run the risk of going over the heads of average filmgoers. Kidd Suwannasorn's "Khon Krang Detr" opened at the same time as another release from the same production company, Saha Mongkol Films. The other pic is crudely made, full of the sort of crassness that Kidd tries to avoid, and yet it clicks.

Maybe Kidd's passive hero of the slums, played by Ron Rittichai, could have been more accessible to a larger audience, if only Ron had been a bigger-than-life character. According to Kidd, making Ron a truck driver is an intentional device. Ron is a bystander forced to take arms against evil forces operating in his slum district.

Kidd's choice of the main protagonist works against his film. The audiences want somebody to

root and cheer for — a genuine champion of the masses. Not just an average fellow.

A fine supporting cast command more of the viewer's attention than the central character. Sasithorn Pantoorat is a sickly, sensitive child who idolizes Ron. Benjawan Boonyakart might well have provided the usual love interest, but that's again superseded by another brother-sister relationship. As Ron's partner, Nopadol Duangphorn is a natural character actor, convincing and funny as the good-natured sidekick.

Sasithorn's essay, shedding light on the deteriorating aspects of life in Bangkok, in both the physical and spiritual sense, is the film's parting message — perhaps a bit too esoteric a summing up of the rather mundane clash between good and evil that goes on before it.

In the face of the rising cost of living and other present-day realities, the majority of Thai filmgoers continue to prefer nonsensical, escapist comedies. Most local film producers consider so-called "relevant" social dramas as low priority projects. —Cano.

Lost And Found
(COLOR)

Okay comedy should find its audience.

Hollywood, June 12.
A Columbia Pictures release. Produced and directed by Melvin Frank. Stars George Segal, Glenda Jackson. Exec producer, Arnold Kopelson. Screenplay, Melvin Frank, Jack Rose; camera (color) Douglas Slocombe; editor, Bill Butler; production design, Trevor Williams; set decoration, Gerry Holmes; art direction, Ted Tester; sound, John Mitchell; music, John Cameron; assistant director, Tony Lucibello. Reviewed at Burbank Studios, Burbank, June 12, '79. (MPAA rating: PG.) Running time: 106 MINS.
Adam .... George Segal
Tricia .... Glenda Jackson
Jemmy .... Maureen Stapleton
Eden .... Hollis McLaren
Lenny .... John Cunningham
Reilly .... Paul Sorvino
Julian .... Kenneth Pogue
Zelda .... Janie Sell
Ellie .... Diana Barrington

"Lost and Found" is a pleasant enough romantic comedy that manages to evoke laughter more often than not. First onscreen pairing of George Segal and Glenda Jackson since the highly successful 1973 film, "A Touch of Class," the picture is nowhere near the tour de force for both performers its predecessor was although the roles are uncomfortably similar.

In addition, despite the fact that most principals involved in "Touch" return to "Lost and Found" five years later, the new picture has neither the charm or style of 1973 picture, depending too

much on forced physical comedy. Still, the laughs are there and summer boxoffice for the Columbia release looks to bloom as the weeks go on.

Segal and Jackson come close to carboning "Touch" characterizations of the sardonic British lady and the clumsy, lovable but married American man who meet on a tropical vacation and carry on a bittersweet love affair. Only this time Jackson and Segal both unattached get acquainted at a French ski resort (where they've broken each others' legs), and instead of a continuing affair, decide to wed. Events leading up to matrimony, which comprise the first third of the picture, are among the best as Segal and Jackson go through a number of enchantingly caustic verbal exchanges and physical arguments both have become expert at projecting.

Film then takes a turn downward as the newlyweds return to the United States and settle in the small New England town where Segal is a college professor at the local university competing for tenure against his best friend John Cunningham. Despite several outstanding scenes, including one where Jackson gets drunk at a faculty party, picture begins to lose its momentum in both dialog and visuals.

Slapstick scenes, which never match the biting lines, become tiresome. As for dialog, Segal and Jackson did better early on in the pic and even better than that in "Touch."

Still, when "Lost and Found" works it does so extremely well. Jackson has a way of twisting a line with sarcasm enough to counter 10 pratfalls. Segal is her perfect foil, occasionally getting back a one-liner but more often than not playing the infuriated fool to the hilt. Melvin Frank and Jack Rose, who teamed on script for "Touch," have done similar chores on "Lost and Found." Although there's a likable story here, it seems to never quite live up to its comedic potential. Segal and Jackson are so good in their roles that when they don't get laughs weaknesses in the script are even more apparent.

Supporting players are effective, particularly Cunningham as Segal's friend and Maureen Stapleton as his archetypal Jewish mother. Cunningham makes his presence known in a not-so-big role and Stapleton, as usual, lends an endearing uniqueness to a character type that has been overdone. Hollis McLaren as Segal's assistant and Paul Sorvino (who was around in "Touch") as a wiseacre cabdriver, are also okay.

Frank, who produced and directed both pictures, has made this

film a little too much like a telefilm with scene changes so frequent that one almost expects a commercial break. However, he does know how to direct movements of Segal and Jackson effectively, especially in some slapstick scenes where he's helped by Douglas Slocombe's fine camera work. Other tech credits are all superior.

With "Lost and Found" Frank and company have created a picture so similar to "A Touch of Class" that comparisons are unavoidable. Unfortunately, the former never quite matches the latter in any departments. Fortunately, it features two highly skilled performers who can play the material for more than it's worth. — Berg.

Je Te Tiens Tu Me Tiens Par La Barbichette
(I've Got You You've Got Me By The Hairs Of My Chinny Chin Chin)
(FRENCH-COLOR)

Paris, June 20.
An SNC release of a Yanne Productions/SNC/Tele-Hachette coproduction. Produced and directed by Jean Yanne. Features entire cast. Screenplay, Yanne and Gerard Sire; camera (color), Bernard Lutic; editor, Anne-Marie Cotret; sound, Michel Vionnet; music,, Jacques Morali; art director, Theo Meurisse; choreographer, Marylin Corwin. Reviewed at the Elysees Point Show cinema, Paris, June 13, 1979. Running time: 100 MINS.
Cast: Mimi Coutelier, Micheline Presle, Georges Beller, Claude Brosset, Carlos, Jean-Pierre Cassel, Jean Desailly, Michel Duchaussoy, Jacques Francois, Jean Le Poulain, Jean Pierre Moulin, Marco Perrin, Francois Perrot, Daniel Prevost, Lawrence Riesner, Mort Shuman, Bernard Tiphaine, Jean Yanne, Les Clodettes, Ritchie Family and Village People.

Actor Jean Yanne has cowritten, directed and performed in this satire, yet another futile spoof of the television industry and its attendant imbecilities. The film's curious title is the name of a children's game in which two players engage in a staring contest while holding each other by the chin; the first to laugh loses.

In Yanne's satire this kiddie bout has become a tv game show rage with Yanne, as an impassive police detective investigating the kidnapping of a tv station's popular disco program host, ending up as a triumphant contestant. It's pretty limp ribbing since one can switch on the tv and find actual game shows that outstrip this one for infantilism.

But the film's major problem is that it has no shape or point. Yanne's camera meanders through the studio offices and sound stages, exposing for the nth time the greed, egoism and rabid stupidity of industry chiefs and underlings, stopping every once in a while for some faintly amusing parodies of French tv commercials or for the staging of a disco number.

When it comes to the latter, Yanne is all eager spectator and it's ironic that the straightforwardly presented musical numbers — such as the one featuring the hunkering male disco group, Village People — are among the film's few highlights.

Most of the cast is wasted, but there are a few high spots with Jean-Pierre Cassel as the tv host presumably kidnapped by a terrorist group. When Cassel concludes a blubbering plea to viewers during a pirate tv broadcast and suddenly regains his professional composure to wish everyone goodnight on behalf of himself and the terrorist tv crew, you know you're watching a consummate comic artist. —*Len.*

Flic ou Voyou
(Cop or Hood)
(FRENCH-COLOR)

Paris, June 20.

A Gaumont release of a Gaumont International/Cerito Films co-production. Produced by Alain Poire. Stars Jean-Paul Belmondo. Directed by Georges Lautner. Screenplay, Jean Herman, based on novel, "L' Inspecteur De La Mer," by Michel Grisolia, dialogue by Michel Audiard; camera (Eastmancolor), Henri Decae; sound, Alain Sempe; editor, Michelle David; art director, Tony Roman; music, Philippe Sarde. Reviewed at the Marignan-Concorde Pathe cinema, Paris, June 20, 1979. Running time: **110 MINS.**

Stan Borowitz ......Jean-Paul Belmondo
Musard ....Georges Geret
Grimaud ....Michel Galabru
Edmonde .... Marie Laforet

The new Jean-Paul Belmondo vehicle, "Flic ou Voyou" will leave breathless only those who rush to the cinema to see him. Others will find a trite action thriller lacking action and thrills, indulging in the violence is-fun syndrome propagated by Clint Eastwood and Charles Bronson. Film, however, found wide popularity here and led the b.o. list for a time.

In this one Belmondo plays a Paris police inspector who goes slumming as a sports car driving hood in order to break the gangland stranglehold on a southern French city (Nice, of course, Marseilles being passe of late). The role playing doesn't give the story any real impetus but it does allow Belmondo to change outfits, cars and nonchalant grins every few scenes.

The film is distasteful, for Belmondo lends his charm and ease to a personage who is nothing less than a scoundrel, sticking his thick-barrelled pistol in people's faces, bombing casinos and cars, engaging in coercion and violence with a smile, all in the name of law and order. It's more insidious than East-

wood or Bronson's heroes, who act with taciturn resoluteness.

After some opening-scene pretentiousness, Georges Lautner's direction is competent and unremarkable, the script offering him no action set pieces to flex his muscles on. The slick dialog is once again the work of Michel Audiard. Technical credits are sound. —*Len.*

Dracula
(COLOR)

Drac's back for big biz.

Hollywood, July 3.
A Universal Pictures release, produced by Walter Mirisch. Directed by John Badham. Features entire cast. Executive producer, Marvin E. Mirisch. Screenplay, W.D. Richter, based on stage play by Hamilton Deane, John L. Balderston from novel by Bram Stoker; camera (Technicolor), Gilbert Taylor; editor, John Bloom; sound (Dolby Stereo), Robin Gregory; production design, Peter Murton; art direction, Brian Ackland-Snow; costumes, Julie Harris; special visual Albert Whitlock; assistant director, Anthony Waye; associate producer, Tom Pevsner; special effects, Roy Arbogast; models, Brian Smithies; music, John Williams. Reviewed at the Samuel Goldwyn Theatre, Beverly Hills, June 28, 1979 (MPAA Rating: R). Running time: **109 MINS.**
Dracula ....Frank Langella
Van Helsing .... Laurence Olivier
Seward ....Donald Pleasence
Lucy .... Kate Nelligan
Harker ....Trevor Eve
Mina .... Jan Francis
Annie ....Janine Duvitski
Renfield .... Tony Haygarth
Swales .... Teddy Turner

With this lavish retelling of an oft-told tale. "Dracula" puts the male vamp back in vampire. Traditionalists may find fault, but director John Badham and Frank Langella pull off a handsome, moody rendition, more romantic than menacing, while tossing in enough gore for an R rating. At any rate, Universal probably has another big hit launched from the cape.

Oddly enough, "Dracula," is one of those pictures that's never really as good as it seems to be at any given moment and when it's over is a lot worse the more you think about it. But that's to Badham's credit, proving he has the audience in his grip throughout.

As he was on stage, Langella is the key in coming up with one more interpretation of the vampire out of hundreds previously presented. More humanly seductive, he's terrific with the ladies and the men would like him well-enough if he weren't so good-looking and arrogant. All in all, a swell chap who happens to drink too much.

Film gets under way much too slowly, bringing the count to the somber English countryside where he's introduced to Donald Pleasence, his daughter Kate Nelligan, her fiance Trevor Eve and a visiting friend, Jan Francis.

Finally, Francis is drained dry and the action starts to pick up. Her father, Laurence Olivier, arrives to investigate and Badham begins to bring the more traditional elements into play — garlic, crosses, mirrors and stakes — coming the closest he ever gets to terror when Pleasence and Olivier encounter the risen Francis beneath her grave.

Nelligan will naturally be the next victim and the center of this story really is her willingness to go along. She's a sexy, excellent actress and a couple of her blood-sucking scenes with Langella go beyond the need for nourishment.

Can Pleasence, Olivier and Eve rescue Nelligan from herself and dispatch the count? Of course they can. But the ending is far from satisfactory, with Langella seeming to die an agonizing death one moment and flitting away into the skies the next, presumably more interested in setting up the sequel than returning to the fray and keeping Nelligan for himself.

There are, in fact, lots of oddities throughout, like why Langella keeps climbing up the sides of houses when he can fly. Also, though it certainly isn't Badham's fault, the picture is haunted throughout by recollections of the Dracula satire that's currently in release.

(Not only do Langella and George Hamilton look a bit alike, it's impossible to watch Eve vainly shoot silver bullets into Langella without recalling Hamilton's line that "bullets are for werewolves" when Richard Benjamin tried the same trick on him.)

All of the photography, effects and setwork are excellent throughout, except for some psychedelic nonsense that doesn't fit in. John Williams' score is excellent as usual. Producer Walter Mirisch tackled a big project, a risky challenge that couldn't psosibly please everyone. The result is a commercial triumph that won't replace Universal's 1931 version in the hearts of Dracula fans. But they won't dare miss it. —*Har.*

A Force Of One
(COLOR)

More karate action equals more Chuck Norris b.o. action.

Hollywood, July 2.
An American Cinema Releasing release. Executive producer, Michael F. Leone. Produced by Alan Belkin. Stars Jennifer O'Neill, Chuck Norris. Directed by Paul Aaron. Screenplay, Ernest Tidyman, from a story by Pat Johnson, Ernest Tidyman; camera (CFI color), Roger Shearman; editor, Bert Lovitt; music, Dick Halligan; associate producer, Jonathan Sanger; art director, Norman Baron; assistant director, Jerald Sobul; sound, Marty Bolger. Reviewed at CFI Laboratories, L.A., June 28, 1979. (MPAA rating: PG.) Running time: **90 MINS.**
Detective Mandy Rust ... Jennifer O'Neill
Matt Logan ....Chuck Norris
Dunne ....Clu Gulager
Rollins ....Ron O'Neal
Moskowitz ....James Whitmore Jr.
Melrose ....Clint Ritchie
Orlando ....Pepe Serna
Newton .... Ray Vitte

Bishop .... Taylor Lacher
Pimp .... Chu Chu Malave
Johnson .... Kevin Geer
Murphy .... Eugene Butler
Moss .... James Hall
Dr. Eppls .... Charles Cyphers
Jerry Sparks .... Bill Wallace
Charlie Logan .... Eric Laneuville

With "Good Guys Wear Black" still playing off around the country, former world karate champ Chuck Norris and American Cinema Releasing are back to collect more coin on the PG action circuit with "A Force Of One." Though plot is far-fetched and production values aren't much superior to tv fare, likable protagonists and strong karate sequences will carry the day with the intended audience. B.O. results in initial playdates, backed by heavy ad buys, have been very good, so ACR looks to have winner.

Again playing a Vietnam Special Forces vet, Norris this time is recruited by a small town California narcotics squad to instruct its members in the finer points of martial arts, as several officers have been bumped off just as the town has become a center for drug dealing.

Despite the fact that Norris has a championship match coming up, he finds the time to pitch in for the community's sake. When his adopted son is killed after having spotted the drug kingpin, however, Norris' mission takes the form of a personal vendetta.

Paul Aaron's direction is uninspired but allows the basic good guy-bad guy dimensions of the plot to emerge in clear-cut fashion. Unaffected naturalness is the keynote among the performers, with Norris and Jennifer O-Neill, as a femme undercover cop, easy to take as the leading duo who only strike romantic sparks at fadeout, Eric Laneuville engaging as Norris' knockabout black "son" and current world karate champion Bill Wallace very effective as Norris' nemesis in and out of the ring. Clu Gulager and Ron O'Neal play it straight as other narcotics agents.
—Cart.

The Frisco Kid
(COLOR)

A Jewish western. Guess is better urban than non-urban audience appeal.

Hollywood, June 30.
Warner Bros. release of a Mace Neufeld production. Produced by Neufeld. Exec producer, Howard W. Koch Jr. Stars Gene Wilder, Harrison Ford. Directed by Robert Aldrich. Screenplay, Michael Elias, Frank Shaw: camera (color), Robert B. Hauser: editors, Maury Winetrobe, Irving Rosenblum, Jack Horger: music, Frank DeVol: production design, Terence Marsh; set decoration, Marvin March; sound, Jack

Solomon: assistant director, Mel Dellar. Reviewed at Avco III Theatre, Westwood, June 29, '79. (MPAA Rating: PG.) Running time: **122 MINS.**
Avram .... Gene Wilder
Tommy .... Harrison Ford
Mr. Jones .... Ramon Bieri
Chief Gray Cloud .... Val Bisoglio
Darryl Diggs ..... George Ralph DiCenzo
Chief Rabbi .... Leo Fuchs
Rosalie .... Penny Peyser
Matt Diggs .... Wiliam Smith
Samuel Bender .... Jack Somack
Sarah Mindl .... Beege Barkett
O'Leary .... Shay Duffin

Casting about for a means to snap the recent string of unsuccessful oaters, producer Mace Neufeld and Warner Bros. came up with a unique concept. "The Frisco Kid" may not be the first Jewish western, but its overtly religious appeal will be confined to broad-minded audiences. Gene Wilder and Harrison Ford, both billed above the title, are strong marquee lures, but this is one pic the stix may well nix.

"Blazing Saddles" proved that ethnic humor can ride the range, of course, but "Frisco Kid" (formerly titled "No Knife") is a different kettle of herring. Director Robert Aldrich has always adroitly mixed comedic and dramatic aspects in his films, and "Frisco Kid" is no exception. For audiences expecting Mel Brooks belly-laughs amidst the Yiddishisms, however, there's bound to be disappointment.

As Avram Belinsky, Yeshiva flunky packed off to an American rendezvous with a leaderless 1850s San Francisco congregation, Wilder has his best role in years. The manic gleam featured in the early Wilder pix has now turned into a mature twinkle, and this performance is particularly impressive in accumulation of small character details.

Excellent counterpoint is provided by Ford, who finally lives up to the potential displayed in "Star Wars" and earlier George Lucas pix. As the cowboy who reluctantly adopts the greenhorn for their westward journey, Ford proves the perfect foil for Wilder's gaffes, and their scenes play wonderfully.

"Frisco Kid" remains a series of set pieces, however, and not a cohesive film. The two-hour-plus running time has several laggard moments, and for all his skills, Wilder is given too many solo shots. As is his practice, Aldrich has also inserted some action sequences that are jarring in their sadistic intensity, particularly an early episode, in which Wilder is fleeced by bad guys William Smith, George Ralph Dicenzo and Ramon Bieri.

Latter characters provide a running motif of harassment that is expertly used by Aldrich to flesh out his two leads, although Smith and his cohorts are surprisingly in-

genuous for 19th-century criminal types.

Another distressing interlude that breaks the pattern of historical realism comes with Wilder and Ford's capture by Indians, headed by Val Bisoglio. His tribe seems to have relocated directly from the Catskills, although the situation, which involves a near martyrdom, is not all that funny.

Otherwise, Terence Marsh's classy production design, Robert B. Hauser's superb lensing, and editing by Maury Winetrobe, Irving Rosenblum and Jack Horger, all contribute to the pretty picture. Frank Devol's music blends in a lot of Americana, and Jack Solomon's sound mixing is firstrate.

For all its plusses, "The Frisco Kid" still has considerable hurdles ahead of it. Warner Bros. will have to nurse this one along, in the hopes of ecumenical boxoffice.
—Poll.

Driller Killer
(COLOR)

What listening to punk rock will do to you.

Rochelle Films release of a Navaron Film production. Executive producer, Rochelle Weisberg. Features entire cast. Directed by Abel Ferrara. Screenplay, Nicholas St. John; camera (color), Ken Kelsch; sound, J.P. MacIntyre; music, Joseph Delia. Reviewed at Entermedia Theatre, New York, June 29, 1979. (No MPAA Rating). Running time: **90 MINS.**
Cast: Carolyn Marz, Jimmy Laine, Baybi Day, Bob De Frank, Peter Yellen, Harry Schultz, Tony Coca Cola and the Roosters.

This bit of gore was undoubtedly inspired by "The Texas Chainsaw Massacres" but, as a filmmaker, director Abel Ferrara makes Tobe Hooper look like Federico Fellini by comparison. A hastily-shot, technically inept in every department operation, its only outlet appears to be those houses which find midnight showings a good source of income.

An artist, living in a tenement near Union Square with two girlfriends who're not reluctant to turn to each other when Leonardo da Vinci's attentions are elsewhere, find it increasingly difficult to keep the wolf from the door (especially with one of the chicks making frequent and lengthy phone calls to California). Things couldn't get worse, but they do. A punk rock band moves into the floor below him and the noise pushes him over the edge (but not as soon as it does the audience).

The most stupid thing about the film is why, when he turns into a murderer with an electric drill, he doesn't go downstairs and eliminate the band, which would have

improved the tone of the film by at least a thousand per cent. No, he picks winos in doorways as his victims before turning to other targets — his girlfriends.

The photography seems to have been done during the night hours only, with most interiors so dark that it causes eyestrain within a matter of minutes (although the preview audience at the Entermedia, properly juiced beforehand, cheered every reappearance of the drill).

In all technical departments, a washout. —Robe.

Nightwing
(COLOR)

Vampire bats in the reservation.

Hollywood, July 2.
Columbia Pictures release of a Martin Ransohoff production. Produced by Ransohoff. Exec producer, Richard St. Johns. Directed by Arthur Hiller. Screenplay, Steve Shagan, Bud Shrake, Martin Cruz Smith, based on novel by Smith; camera (color), Charles Rosher; editor, John C. Howaard; music, Henry Mancini; production design, James Vance; set decoration, Richard Kent; sound, Larry Jost; special visual effects, Carlo Rambaldi; assistant director, Gary Daigler. Reviewed at Directors Guild, Hollywood, June 25, '79. (MPAA Rating: PG). Running time: **103 MINS.**
Youngman Duran .... Nick Mancuso
Phillip Payne .... David Warner
Anne Dillon .... Kathryn Harrold
Walker Chee .... Stephen Macht
Selwyn .... Strother Martin
Abner Tasupi .... George Clutesi
Roger Piggott .... Ben Piazza
John Franklin .... Donald Hotton
Henry .... Charles Hallahan
Judy .... Judith Novgrod
Claire Franklin .... Alice Hirson

Bats are such thoroughly repulsive little creatures that it's not hard to make them seem frightening on a big screen. It's much tougher to make them seem funny, although the accomplishments of "Nightwing" in this regard won't win Columbia Pictures any praise. The Martin Ransohoff production may ingest some initial business, but after that, audience torpor will set in.

Clearly, Ransohoff and director Arthur Hiller intended "Nightwing" to be the kind of scary suspenser that prompts filmgoers to look nervously around as they exit a theatre. But this mixture of Indian occultism, native rights, pseudoscience and romance will evoke those nervous twitches long before the final credits.

Flat results are no fault of the cast, but rather the characters they're asked to portray. In his feature debut, Canadian actor Nick Mancuso projects strongly as a reservaiton cop who doesn't quite believe in his tribe's religious rituals, and dallies with Anglo nurse Kathryn Harrold (also a film novice).

But the screenplay by Steve Shagan, Bud Shrake and "Nightwing" author Martin Cruz Smith gives the players lots of gorgeous scenery to chew, and little else. Aside from the attack of the vampire bats, there's a subplot about rival Indian honcho Stephen Macht dickering with oil interests, but that's soon obscured by all the bat talk.

While the close-ups of the sharptoothed flying rodents are competently handled, the other special effects by Carlo Rambaldi and Van Der Veer Photo Effects don't hold a candle to the National Geographic specs, for instance.

Long-shots of the swirling bats resemble electro-static pieces of charcoal, while Sam Shaw's sound effects contradict the cast's keen ears, due to frequent allusions to high-pitched noise which just aren't audible.

Strangest element is David Warner's character, a bat exterminator with a ready supply of quips to explain his single-minded mission. The more Warner's on the screen, the less believable "Nightwing" becomes, meaning the last 60 of the film's 103 minutes are pretty much a total loss.

Hiller seems better suited to urban-themed stories, although Charles Rosher's lensing makes the most of the Southwestern locations. Other tech credits are okay, and supporting cast does its best under the circumstances.

By unfavorably invoking comparisons to Alfred Hitchcock's "The Birds," however, "Nightwing" bites off more than it can chew.
—Poll.

Bloodline
(COLOR)

Some initial wicket action likely, but stamina wobbly.

Hollywood, July 2.
A Paramount release of a Geria production. Produced by David V. Picker. Sidney Beckerman. Stars Audrey Hepburn, Ben Gazzara, James Mason, Claudia Mori, Irene Papas, Michelle Phillips, Maurice Ronet, Romy Schneider, Omar Sharif, Beatrice Straight, Gert Frobe. Directed by Terence Young. Screenplay by Laird Koenig, based on the novel by Sidney Sheldon; camera (Movielab color), Freddie Young; editor, Bud Molin; music, Ennio Morricone; production design, Ted Haworth; associate producer, Richard McWhorter; costume design, Enrico Sabbatini; assistant directors, John Longmuir, Gianni Cozzo; sound, Gordon Everett. Reviewed at Paramount Studios, L.A., June 26, 1979. (MPAA Rating: R). Running time: 116 MINS.

Elizabeth Roffe ....Audrey Hepburn
Rhys Williams .... Ben Gazzara
Sir Alec Nichols .... James Mason
Donatella .... Claudia Mori
Simonetta Palazzi..........Irene Papas

Vivian Nichols ....Michelle Phillips
Charles Martin .... Maurice Ronet
Helene Martin ....Romy Schneider
Ivo Palazzi ....Omar Sharif
Kate Erling .... Beatrice Straight
Inspector Max Hornung ......Gert Frobe
Julius Prager ....Wolfgang Preiss
Man in Black ....Marcel Bozzuffi
Dr. Wal .... Pinkas Braun
Young Sam Roffe .... Wulf Kessler

"Bloodline" is bloodless. With a plot that becomes more ludicrous the more one thinks about it, this Geria production for Par release plays woodenly. Interest in the Sidney Sheldon and Audrey Hepburn names could spell some initial ticket sale, but drop-off may be quick in coming.

Like Federico Fellini, Russ Meyer and Jacqueline Susann before him. Sheldon gets his name above the title this time, although he didn't even pen the screenplay. Laird Koenig must take the rap for the clumsy introduction of the 10 leading characters within the first 10 minutes and for the dialog.

Even for the never-never land of high chic melodrama the film inhabits, the tale of a woman who, unprepared, inherits control of her father's vast pharmaceutical empire contains wild implausibilities. Flashback reveal papa's medical genius in a Jewish Polish slum. Audience is then asked to swallow premise that, 40-odd years later, his family, making up the company's scheming board of directors, contains Italian and French uppercrusters as well as a member of the British Parliament.

Other lapses include mixed-up time frame, identifying a Munich office building as being in Zurich, and leaving some of the leads up in the air with no resolution to their stories, not to mention ignoring such matters as motivation for the villain and explaining the place of offensive snuff movies in an otherwise relatively decorous and sedate melodrama.

This is Terence Young's first completed film since "The Klansman" in 1974 and he's clearly out of practice, as his performers range unevenly in tone from the comic (Omar Sharif, Irene Papas, Gert Frobe) to the merely drab (James Mason, Michelle Phillips, Maurice Ronet).

Using an inordinate amount of very high key lighting and occasional filters, Freddie Young's camera mostly stays at a respectful distance from Audrey Hepburn, whose prim, unflamboyant character sets exceedingly narrow emotional parameters for the story. Though it would take several pictures on the level of "Bloodline" to seriously damage her stature, it's a shame she picks something like this now that she works so seldom.

Finale, with Hepburn trapped in a house as the lights go out, conjures up a happier collaboration with Young 12 years ago on "Wait Until Dark." Ben Gazzara at least manages to provoke the proper ambivalence his character's intended to do, and Ennio Morricone's score creates a mood of exalted romanticism the images don't begin to approach. —Cart.

Dolphin
(DOCU-COLOR)

Pretentious 'expedition.' Murky outlook.

San Francisco, July 3.
Michael Wiese Film Productions presentation. Produced by Wiese. Directed by Hardy Jones, Wiese. Written by Jones. Camera, (color), John Knoop; editing, John V. Fanto; music, Basil Poledouris. Reviewed at Palace of Fine Arts, San Francisco, June 26, '79. (No MPAA rating.) Running time: 75 MINS.

Only first-rate lensing and sound work keep this docu from slipping into dolphin depths. Its story line is so contrived, affected, pretentious and self-indulgent that it's often embarrassing — and particularly rude to the dolphins it seeks to embrace.

The picture had a one-week Frisco run at the 1,000-seat Palace of Fine Arts theatre, site of the annual filmfest here, on a four-wall deal; there's an L.A. booking in the works under the aegis of Northern California exhib Gary Meyer. Otherwise, there's no distrib and no release plans. Nor should any be anticipated.

Filmmakers Michael Wiese and Hardy Jones wrap the storyline in their expedition to see how dolphins react to a guy playing a piano underwater. The reaction can best be described as polite. Wiese and Jones are so intent on portraying themselves and their friends, via clearly hoked-up verite gabfests over beer, that they dilute their stated intent of "influencing legislation leading to the protection of dolphins and whales."

With cutting, there's enough footage for a half hour public TV dolphin assemblage, thanks to the principal cinematography of John Knoop and the underwater lensing of James Hudnall and Jack McKenney, the cutting of John V. Fanto and the sound team. —Herb.

Hometown USA
(COLOR)

"American Graffiti" fans will love this funny variation on theme.

Chicago, June 28.
Film Ventures International release of a Baer/Camras production. Produced by Roger Camras and Jesse Vint. Directed by Max Baer. Features entire cast. Story and screenplay, Jesse Vint; no camera credit (CFI color); editor, Frank Morris; music coordinator, Marshall Leib. Reviewed at Oriental Theatre, Chicago, June 28, '79. (MPAA Rating: R). Running time: 93 MINS.

Rodney C. Duckworth .....Gary Springer
Recil Calhoun .... David Wilson
T.J. Swackhammer ....Brian Kerwin
Marilyn .... Pat Delaney
Andrea....................Julie Parsons

In "Hometown USA" director Max Baer has drawn liberally from material used in original "American Graffiti," but that shouldn't bother those who see "Hometown USA," because, although made on modest scale, it still contains generous amount of earthy wit that flows naturally from pic's characters and action.

Baer has obviously put some effort into establishing proper, circa 1957, atmosphere for story of adolescents fixated on hot rods, necking and cruising hometown boulevards all night. Two of male stars, David Wilson and Brian Kerwin, were cast for resemblance to late Elvis Presley. For numerous sequences where cars are an integral part of action, Baer has rounded up a number of vintage models. Also "Hometown USA's" soundtrack is filled with '50s pop favorites by likes of Richie Valens, Jimmy Clanton and Little Richard. In short genuine attempt has been made to recreate feel of 1950s in "Hometown USA," and it shows.

Pic's screenplay by Jesse Vint is simply an excuse for series of funny set pieces, most of them dealing with a meek, sexually naive teenager, Gary Springer, and his cronies, Wilson and Kerwin, who supposedly want to fix him up with a date, but who always seem to end up with the girls themselves. In one sequence, Springer has an ill-fated fling with one of the looser lasses in town, while the girl's crazed parents wait up with a shotgun.

There are some great scenes at a local drive-in, which Baer has captured in all its garish neon splendor. While waitresses in red satin shorts sail around on roller skates, mating games go on midst much innocent flirting. Throughout "Hometown USA" Baer doesn't hesitate to poke fun at kids whose story he's telling. This satiric touch adds an unexpected bit of depth to what is basically a piece of entertainment.

Despite short stretches of leaden dialog and little action, Baer moves the pic along well.

"Hometown's" acting chores by Springer, et al are competently handled. At least everyone mouths the '50s lingo convincingly, and knows when to exploit screenplay's humor for all its worth.

Editor Frank Morriss has some effective crosscutting between cars.

"Hometown USA" was made with teenage summer filmgoers in mind, and it should appeal to such sensibilities. Nothing sophisticated here, just reasonably good. —*Zaro.*

Las Verdes Praderas
(The Green Pastures)
(SPANISH-COLOR)

Madrid, June 12.
A Jose Luis Tafur P.C. production. Directed by Jose Luis Garci. Ceatures entire cast. Screenplay, Jose Maria Gonzalez Sinde, Jose Luis Garci; exec producer, Jose Maria Gonzalez Sinde; camera (Eastmancolor), Fernando Arribas; sets, Francisco Prosper; editor, Miguel Gonzalez Sinde. Reviewed at Cine Conde Duque, Madrid, June 11, 1979. Running time: **95 MINS.**

Jose ...:................Alfredo Landa
Conchi ....Maria Casanova
Ricardo ....Carlos Larranaga
Don Enrique...............Angel Picazo
Dona Marita........Irene Gutierrez Caba
Alberto ....Pedro del Corral

Jose Maria Gonzalez Sinde and Jose Luis Garci, who in the past made the excellent and apposite "Asignatura Pendiente" and "Solos en la Madrugada," have now turned their attention to the quiet desperation of an ad executive who, for all intents and purposes, has succeeded in life. He is happily married, has a couple of children (the inevitable boy and girl), a good job and his house in the country for weekends.

Story traces one of these weekends, complete with nagging mother-in-law, condescending in-laws, a lawn mower that doesn't start, a soccer game he walks away limp from and endless other mishaps and minor annoyances. Jose realizes he has forged his own golden cage, and the wife, in sympathy, sets the model house in its characterless development area on fire Sunday night. Both watch it burn, with no regrets, before driving back to Madrid.

The subject, certainly no newcomer to films, is treated largely in a whimsical fashion as the antihero bumbles through his onerous routine. Alfredo Landa, famous in Spain for his facile comic parts, comes across very nicely as Mr. Average Spaniard, and Maria Casanova as the indulgent wife puts in a fine performance which will doubtless enable her to get further work in the future.

Notwithstanding its merits, pic is rather too slight and plods along at the same emotional level throughout. The final blaze is not really believable, given the kind of upper-middle class people depicted. At the end, the dull ad exec is just a bit too familiar and dull. Pic however is doing okay at local wickets. —*Besa.*

That Summer
(BRITISH-COLOR)

London, June 26.
A Columbia Pictures release. Produced by Davina Belling, Clive Parsons. Directed by Harley Cokliss. Features entire cast. Screenplay, Janey Preger, based on a story by Tony Attard; camera (color), David Watkin; editor, Michael Bradsell; art director, Tim Hutchinson; sound, Peter Sutton, Archie Ludski; original music, Ray Russell; asst. director, Selwyn Roberts. Reviewed at the Rank preview theatre, London, June 25, '79. (BBFC Rating: AA). Running time: **94 MINS.**

Steve ....Ray Winstone
Jimmy ....Tony London
Carole ....Emily Moore
Angie ....Julie Shipley
Tam ....Jon Morrison
Georgie ....Andrew Byatt
Stu ....Ewan Stewart
Pub Landlord ....David Daker
Pub Landlady ....Jo Rowbottom
Swimming Coach ....John Judd
Mr. Swales ....John Junkin
Mrs. Mainwaring ....Stephanie Cole
Detective ....Nick Donnelly

Columbia's latest British outing, a lowbudgeter cofinanced with the state-funded National Film Finance Corp., is respectable if less than enthralling. Its appeal stems chiefly from excellent performances by the cast of unknowns. Its main drawback is a script that needed sharpening up, compounded by direction which tends to linger on insignificances.

Seeming longer than its 94 minutes, "That Summer" will rate enthusiastic word-of-mouth only from very indulgent audiences, but could be promoted around some English-speaking and European markets to fair acceptance by the holiday trade.

Janey Preger's screenplay, from Tony Attard's story, takes much from the '60s British Tom Courtenay-starrer, "The Loneliness Of The Long-Distance Runner," but this time the sport is swimming, and the emphasis firmly on fun rather than social comment. Cute and predictable, it plots the adventures of four teenagers — one, the swimmer, just out of youth penitentiary — at large for the summer in an English seaside resort. Naturally the baddies (all Scotsmen, by an oldfashioned, nationalistic stroke of characterization), end up in the hands of the police, while the London delinquent-made-good wins the race and gets the girl.

Two elements dignify the proceedings. One is cinematographer David Watkin's experienced yet fresh eye for light and composition. The other is Ray Winstone's compelling performance in the lead role. He seems, in fact, a natural screen actor, with the rare gift of making even banal lines believable.

Of the others, Julie Shipley and Emily Moore ring true with some well-observed dialog as two factory girls to whom the English south coast is practically Florida. Tony London, in the least rewarding part of the four, still manages to be memorable; and there's an equally understated and successful cameo by Stephanie Cole as the disciplinarian manageress of the hotel where the girls find jobs as chambermaids.

Harley Cokliss, debuting as a feature director after some acclaimed work on children's films, proves stronger on bringing out the reality in individual scenes than on pacing the film as a whole. Where the action does liven up, it's generally due to the well-chosen New Wave hits that make up most of the music track. —*Simo.*

The Wanderers
(COLOR)

Blend of comedy and nostalgia may beat off gang typecasting.

Hollywood, June 21.
An Orion Pictures release thru Warner Bros. of a Martin Ransohoff production. Produced by Ransohoff. Exec producer, Richard R. St. Johns. Directed by Philip Kaufman. Features entire cast. Screenplay, Rose Kaufman, Philip Kaufman, based on the novel by Richard Price; camera (color), Michael Chapman; editors, Ronald Roose, Stuart H. Pappe; costume design, Robert de Mora; art direction, Jay Moore; sound, Nat Boxer; assistant director, Alan Hopkins. Reviewed at The Burbank Studios, June 21, '79. (MPAA Rating: R.) Running time: **113 MINS.**

Richie ....Ken Wahl
Joey ....John Friedrich
Nina ....Karen Allen
Despie Galasso ....-........Toni Kalem
Turkey ....Alan Rosenberg
Buddy ....Jim Youngs
Perry ....Tony Ganios
Peewee ....Linda Manz
Emilio ....William Andrews
Terror ....Erland Van Lidth de Jeude
Mr. Sharp ....Val Avery
Chubby Galasso ....Dolph Sweet
Clinton ....Michael Wright

"The Wanderers" is a good example of a film unable to escape its genre. When producer Martin Ransohoff and director Phil Kaufman set out to translate Richard Price's novel about youth gangs coming of age in the Bronx in 1963, they probably didn't anticipate that five or six gang-themed pix would immediately precede them. That's what happened, and the legacy of "The Warriors," et al., seems likely to cloud the boxoffice future of the Orion Pictures release through Warner Bros.

It's a shame, because despite an uneasy blend of nostalgia and violence, "The Wanderers" is a well-made and impressive film. Kaufman, who also co-scripted with his wife, Rose, has accurately captured the urban angst of growing up in the 1960s. Question remains, however, just who will relate to this era, since the contemporaries of this film's cast are at the upper end of the filmgoing audience.

As in "American Graffiti," the California-set equivalent in terms of peer group, "The Wanderers" makes extensive use of early rock 'n roll tunes, to excellent effect. Patrons may come out humming the ditties, however, rather than remembering the plot.

Latter is deceptively simple, with Ken Wahl, John Friedrich, Jim Youngs, Alan Rosenberg and Tony Ganios as youthful members of a non-violent gang, the Wanderers. About to graduate high-school, they prowl the Bronx with the desperate feeling that something's slipping away from them.

The Kaufmans' script relies on vignettes to sock the message across that two eras are about to collide, the gang-ridden '50s acceding to the socially-relevant '60s, with the Kennedy assassination as the demarcation point. Plot resolution(s) remain unformed, and "The Wanderers" ends not with a bang, but a fizzle.

Thesping is first-rate from the largely unknown cast, with Wahl, Friedrich and especially Ganios delivering well-rounded and believable characterizations. Also outstanding are Toni Kalem as a gum-popping flirt, and Karen Allen as her more serious, soulful counterpart. It's a credit to the screenplay and film that femmes are not used as targets for cheap shots, but instead are fully integrated into the story.

Disturbing elements in "The Wanderers" crop up in the explicitly violent episodes, including those involving the symbolic Ducky Boys, a murderous pint-sized gang, and the Fordham Baldies, bald behemoths. It's in this arena, with petty sadism, family beatings, murder and torture, that "Wanderers" evokes unpleasant memories of its predecessors, and may well prove a turn-off to audiences.

Kaufman has also left some of his best comedy ploys up in the air, particularly in the relationship between tiny Linda Manz and Baldies leader Erland Van Lidth de Jeude. A scene in which the drunken Baldies enlist in the Marines is never given a follow-up, a short coming of the other story lines, too.

Michael Chapman has shot "Wanderers" in dark, moody colors that seem inappropriate to the pic's general tone, although other production credits are fine. In his last two films (the other being remake of "Invasion Of The Body Snatchers"), Kaufman has proved himself a stylish and innovative director who sometimes forsakes content for form. Results may look good on the screen, but fail to leave an impression of much more than technical expertise. —*Poll*.

A surfeit of whimsy and cuddly characterizations quickly renders trivial this comedy about Jews and Jewishness. Peter Kassovitz's first feature aims to celebrate the life force in four generations of Jewish males gathered together to fete the 90th birthday of the family patriarch.

A series of facilely endearing domestic scenes ensue, during which Ben, a Parisian Jew, tries to smooth the strained relationship between him and his wife while looking after his ten-year old son, his father, Elie, an orthodox rabbi now living in Israel, and his grandfather from southern France, Isaac, whose advanced age has not put the damper on his need for female companionship. When the old man receives a letter of rejection from a younger woman he has been courting, he commits suicide.

Kassovitz evokes 20th century Jewish history — the pogroms, the Holocaust, the founding of the state of Israel — as a backdrop to this superficial hymn to the Jewish will to live rather than survive. But this idealized portrait gallery lacks insight and conviction and the emphasis on continuity rather than generation conflict reduces dramatic interest. What with its orthodox rabbi, who won't say no to a joint nor shrink before the sight of a naked woman, and its horde of cute children the film sinks under its load of saccharine effects. Kassovitz makes things even worse by indulging in a propensity for portentous and coy symbolism that sits heavily in the film.

As a nice film about nice Jewish characters in a nice middle-class environment film could have good chances abroad, particularly after the international success of Moshe Misrahi's "Madame Rosa" (La Vie Devant Soi). Politeness continues to be the hallmark and the tombstone of anything that can be distantly referred to as the "Jewish cinema." —*Len*.

---

saf Dayan seems to have abandoned any pretense he might have had in the past, when his first independent feature "Saint Cohen," received an award in San Remo, and gone all the way into commercial cinema of the cruder kind.

Here he tries to send up "Saturday Night Fever," "Grease," "Rocky" and most everything else, using the enormous popularity of HaGashash HaHiver (The Pale Pathfinder), Israel's top entertainment group. But even compared to the previous joint effort of Dayan and trio, this looks primitive in story line, camera, sets, music, costumes and most of all dialog, which tries very hard to be funny but is never more than loud.

Initial release in big houses and natural curiosity of the stars' many fans, may help make the first days very lucrative and as film was relatively inexpensive (reputed less than $200,000) it may recover its costs and prove the commercial point of the venture. But it is doubtful whether it holds any interest for foreign markets, and it is certainly no feather in anybody's cap.
—*Edna*.

Breaking Away
(COLOR)

Nice comedy. Hard sell.

Hollywood, June 29.
20th Century-Fox release. Produced and directed by Peter Yates. Features entire cast. Screenplay, Steve Tesich, camera (DeLuxe Color), Matthew F. Leonetti; editor, Cynthia Scheider; sound, Bud Alper; art direction, Patrizia von Brandenstein; assistant director, Mike Grillo; music, Patrick Williams. Reviewed at 20th Century Fox studios, L.A., June 29, 1979. (MPAA rating: PG.) Running time: 100 MINS.

Dave	Dennis Christopher
Mike	Dennis Quaid
Cyril	Daniel Stern
Moocher	Jackie Earle Haley
Mom	Barbara Barrie
Dad	Paul Dooley
Katherine	Robyn Douglass
Rod	Hart Bochner
Nancy	Amy Wright

Though its plot wins no points for originality, "Breaking Away" is a thoroughly delightful light comedy, lifted by fine performances from Dennis Christopher and Paul Dooley. But its weak title and lack of big box-office name could keep "Breaking Away" from breaking through unless sales effort is super sharp.

Once again, the story is nothing more than a triumph for the underdog through sports, this time cycle racing. Christopher, Dennis Quaid, Daniel Stern and Jackie Earle Haley are four recent high-school graduates with no particular educational ambitions, yet stuck in

a small college town — and a fairly snooty college at that.

But Christopher is a heck of a bike rider and such an adulator of Italian champions that he pretends to be Italian himself, even at home. His Mediterranean manners around the house bring him into hilarious conflict with father Dooley, a used-car salesman and former stone cutter who figures he got a clunker for a kid.

Warmly between the two is mom Barbara Barrie and whatever the fate of the film, any tv producer would be lucky to have this family trio in a weekly series. In addition to the humor, producer-director Peter Yates generates a lot of love among the three, though Dooley and Christopher obviously have difficulty expressing theirs.

The relationship among the four youths is also warm and funny, yet full of different kinds of conflicts. Quaid is very good as the ex-quarterback facing a life with no more cheers; Haley is good as a sawed-off romantic and Stern is superb as a gangly, wise-cracking mediator.

Pretending to be an Italian exchange student, Christopher meets pretty coed Robyn Douglass (an able film debut for her) and this ultimately brings the boys into conflict with the big men on campus that must finally be resolved in a big bike race.

Though pic sometimes seems padded with too much cycle footage, the climax is exciting, even though predictable. And the ego boost for the quartet and their friends and family looking on all add up to your basic happy ending.

Incidentally, Christopher loses his love for the Italians along the way after they cheat him in an earlier race, setting up a fine scene as Dooley awkwardly tries to soothe the lad's hurt. Ultimately, though, Christopher meets a French girl and it's worth a trip to the theatre just to see Dooley's double-take when he first hears "bon jour, papa." —*Har*.

Rai Saneh Ha
(The Megalomaniac)
(THAI-COLOR)

Bangkok, June 28.
A Nakornping Films release. Produced by Wannapha Krapayun. Directed Chana Krapayun. Features entire cast. Story, Woh Vinitchaikul; screenplay, Pratin Puangsamri; camera (color) and lighting, Thavee Kiatinan; music, Seksan Sominsart; sound, Kasem Militachinda. Reviewed at Siam Theatre, Bangkok, June 27, '79. Running time: 115 MINS.

Rongram	Pisamai Wilaisak
Anuphon	Sorapong Chatri
Mep	Nipaporn Nongnuj
Naiyana	Tarika Tidatit
Danoo	Niroot Sirichanya
Pra-on	Hansa Jariyaporn
Pimjai	Choosri Misomon

Au Bout Du Bout Du Banc
(At the Brink of the Brink of the Bench)
(FRENCH-COLOR)

Paris, June 30.
A Planfilm release of a Films de la Drouette/Films de la Tour co-production. Produced by Victor Lanoux. Stars Lanoux, Jane Birkin, Georges Wilson, Henri Cremieux. Directed by Peter Kassovitz. Screenplay, Kassovitz, Elie Pressman, Chantal Remy; camera (Eastmancolor-Panavision), Etienne Szabo; music, Georges Moustaki; editor, Chantal Remy. Reviewed at the Normandie Cinema, Paris, June 28, 1979. Running time: 105 MINS.

Ben	Victor Lanoux
Peggy	Jane Birkin
Elie	Georges Wilson
Isaac	Henri Cremieux
Mathias	Matthieu Kassovitz

Schlager
(Hit Song)
(ISRAEL-COLOR)

Tel Aviv, July 1.
A AKA Films Production. Produced by Yaakov Kozky. Stars: HaGashash HaHiver. Written and directed by Assaf Dayan. Camera (color): Danny Schneur; editor, Tal Shuval; sets, Yaron Turel; music, Zvika Pik; lyrics, Assaf Dayan. Released Tel Aviv, June 30, 1979. Running time: 94 MINS.

Cast: HaGashash HaHiver (Israel Poliakov), Shayke Levi, (Gavri Banai), Ofra Haza, Shula Revach, Menahem Zilberman.

A quickie made for local consumption in a hurry, the less said about this film, the better. As-

Dr. Payah . . . . Sompop Benjatikul

Some film actors may go through a lifetime just trying to prove that they can really act, which is understood as an outstanding performance in a dramatic picture. That seems to sum up the career of Pisamai Wilaisak.

She plays a spinster with an unhappy childhood in Chana Krapayun's "Rai Saneh Ha." The fact that her mother always punished her for the slightest mistake as a child, and that she received less of everything than her pretty younger sister, hounds her all her life. She then tries to get even by imposing her will on everyone around her.

The story could have sidestepped the unintentionally comic sequences, if it had been told from another person's point of view. Pisamai's role needs a great deal of subtlety, and the pic is wide off the mark.

Nipaporn Nongnuj and Hansa Jariyaporn are two pretty lasses confused as to why Pisamai should want to compete with them. Choosri Misomon is a snobbish wealthy woman — a role she invariably does to perfection.

Technical credits suggest the constant efforts of local film technicians to improve their work. Beautiful photography complements the scenic locations. Original musical background themes by Seksan Sominsart are very fine.
—Cano.

Collections Privees
(Private Collections)
(FRANCO-JAPANESE-COLOR)

Paris, June 29.
A UGC release of a Films du Jeudi-French Movies (Paris)-Toei Company (Tokyo) coproduction. Produced by Pierre Braunberger. Features entire cast. Directed by Just Jaeckin, Shuji Terrayama, Walerian Borowczyk. Reviewed at Publicis'screening room, Paris, June 26, 1979. Running time: 105 MINS.
"L'Ile Aux Sirenes" (Jaeckin). Script, Jean-Michel Ribes; camera, (color), Robert Fraisse; editor, Michelle Boehm, Michelle Ansellem; music, Pierre Bachelet. With Robert Blanche, Laura Gemser, Catherine Gadois, Marpessa Dawn, Edwige Thabouis.
"Le Labyrinthe d'Herbes" (Terayama). Script, Terayama & Rio Kishida, based on the novel by Kyoka Izumi; camera (color), Tatsuo Suzuki; sound, Katsuhide Kamura; editor, Tomoyo Oshima; art director, Isao Yamada; music, J.A. Seazer. With Hiroshi Mikami, Takeshi Wakamatsu, Keiko Niitaka, Juzo Itami.
"L'Armoire" (Borowczyk). Script, Borowczyk, from story by Guy de Maupassant; camera (color), Noel Very; editor, Khadicha Bariha; sound, Jean-Charles Ruault; costumes, Piet Bolscher. With Marie-Catherine Conti, Yves Marie.

Pierre Braunberger produced this Franco-Japanese "sketch film" which does little to enhance a genre that has been a specialty of the Italians. Perhaps the most interesting thing about the film is that it exists at all at a time when France's film short industry is mired in deep crisis, with films besign produced but denied viable commercial outlets.

Just Jaeckin, of "Emmanuelle" fame, directed the first entry in which a crass yachtsman is swept overboard and washed onto an island where he discovers four island nymphs who provide him unimagined sexual joy until the day he discovers that for these beauties "pleasures of the flesh" has a chiefly gastronomic meaning. The film, which takes the notion of woman as a predatory animal to its logical conclusion, sits heavily on the stomach — it's vulgar, predictable and panderingly misogynistic.

Japanese director Shuji Terayama offers a heavily symbolic and confusingly convoluted tale of a young man in search of the words to a childhood song his prostitute mother used to sing to him. The quest coincides with his passage into adulthood during which he is time and again being swallowed up in the Oedipal labyrinth of his mind. Photographed in the kinds of striking color one associates with Japanese cinema, Terayama's film plays too heavily on effects and is often too derivative of earlier filmmakers like Kobayashi, whose sketch film of the supernatural, "Kwaidan," this film seems to evoke.

The Polish-born director Walerian Borowczyk directed the final work, based on a short story by Guy de Maupassant, about a jaded Parisian who buys the company of a Folies-Bergere chorus-girl for the night. She takes him back to her dreary lodgings where they make love. Afterwards he discovers that the young woman has locked her child in the closet in order to accommodate her guest. Borowczyk's direction is spiritless and the use of de Maupassant's words for the voice-over narrative only emphasizes the poverty of the images. One yearns for the artistry of Max Ophuls.
—Len.

Just You And Me, Kid
(COLOR)

A laff-an-hour non-comedy, despite George Burns.

Hollywood, July 11.
A Columbia Pictures release of an Irving Fein/Jerome M. Zeitman production. Produced by Fein and Zeitman. Stars George Burns, Brooke Shields. Directed by Leonard Stern. Screenplay, Oliver Hailey, Stern, from a story by Tom Lazarus; camera (color), David Walsh; editor, John W. Holmes; music, Jack Elliott; production design, Ron Hobbs; art direction, Sig Tinglof; set decoration, Rick Simpson; sound, Don Johnson; assistant director, Pat Kehoe. Reviewed at The Burbank Studios, July 11, '79. (MPAA Rating: PG.) Running time: 93 MINS.

Bill	George Burns
Kate	Brooke Shields
Max	Burl Ives
Shirl	Lorraine Gary
Harris	Nicolas Coster
Dr. Device	Keye Luke
Reinhoff the Remarkable	Carl Ballantine
Manduke the Magnificent	Leon Ames
Tom	Ray Bolger
Stan	John Schuck
Sue	Andrea Howard
Roy	Christopher Knight
Demesta	William Russ

George Burns' career rejuvenation has been nothing short of remarkable. At 83, he might be considered to have some tired blood, but that's an affliction of his latest vehicle, and not of him. "Just You And Me, Kid" is an unfunny comedy that sputters and expires in spite of Burns' most earnest efforts. The Columbia Pictures release may open to good numbers, but word-of-mouth will not be good.

Seeing Burns spout vaudeville one-liners that make him seem young in comparison is always a delight, but stretched over 93 minutes, even that pleasure wears thin. Director Leonard Stern, who cowrote the screenplay with Oliver Hailey from Tom Lazarus' ingenious story idea, has to take most of the blame for the uninspired goings-on, along with producers Irving Fein and Jerome M. Zeitman.

Awakened daily to the sound of taped applause, Burns putters around a very ritzy abode until a naked Brooke Shields turns up one day in the trunk of his vintage car. It develops that she's hiding from a dope pusher (William Russ) whom she burned for $20,000, and with uncaring foster parents, has nowhere else to go.

Nosy neighbors John Schuck and Andrea Howard observe her trying to escape from Burns' manse, and notify the comic's daughter, Lorraine Gary, who is trying to have her father committed for his generous allegiance to his old showbiz pals.

While the situation seems ripe for some comedic growth, Stern develops it along purely sitcom lines, and the results wouldn't even produce decent Nielsen ratings. Doors are forever being opened and closed, the action is virtually confined to Burns' house, and most glaringly, the yocks are few and far between.

Chief disappointment is Brooke Shields, who affords Burns the equivalent of playing off a blank wall. Ever since "Pretty Baby," Shields' talent has been in an inverse ratio to the increasing importance of her roles.

In contrast, Gary is fine as the scolding daughter, and her scenes with Burns provide as many sparks as Shields' work lacks. Otherwise, cast ranged from ok to poor, with Burl Ives, Schuck, Howard and Nicolas Coster misused, and villain Russ making a particularly inauspicious film debut.

Pic's dilemma is best expressed in the manner Stern and company throw away one of the film's chief casting assets, the grouping of vet principles Keye Luke, Carl Ballantine, Leon Ames and Ray Bolger as Burns' card-playing cronies. Together for the first, and probably last time, the quartet is allowed to do nothing but scurry around in one brief scene, after which they're never heard from again.

The same may be said of "Just You And Me, Kid." No one else can come close to Burns in doing what he does best. But even the venerable performer can't pick up a deflated concept and run with it when there's nowhere to go.

Tech credits are all passable, although Don Johnson's sound mixing seems to be missing one critical ingredient — a laugh track.
—Poll.

Raining In The Mountain
(HONG KONG-COLOR)

Hong Kong, July 8.
Lo and Hu Co-Production Ltd. film and release. Directed by King Hu. Producers, Lo Kai-muk, Wu Sau-Yee, Ling Chung. Features entire cast. Screenplay, King Hu; camera (color), Henry Chen; editor, King Hu; music, Ng Tai King. Reviewed at Queen's Theatre, July 7, '79. Running time: 125 MINS.
Cast: Hsu Feng, Sun Yuek, Shik Chun.

In a place like Hong Kong where films are simply made for money, a scholarly director like King Hu is likely to be overpraised if not overrated. Hu's films are analyzed and dissected, then interpreted to convey more than what they actually mean. His "A Touch of Zen" had the opportunity of taking on a Cannes Film Festival aura and his latest two films, that he did simultaneously in Korea and Taiwan ("Raining" and "Legend of the Mountain") both suffer from weak storylines, self-conscious directional technique, repetitive sequences, prolonged picture post-card scenery and a tiring ensemble cast.

"Raining In The Mountain" is an unfullfilled cinematic promise. Firstly, the rain promised in the title never comes and secondly it is a distinct deja vu. If you've never seen a King Hu film, then the film may intrigue but on the other hand, you've been there. And while the production values are handsome and ornate the characterizations of the people are merely skin deep. It has more splendour than message and it produces boredom ... a film that tells an old story that should be given a rest.

The setting of "Raining" takes place during the Ming Dynasty in a Buddhist monastery. There's the problem of appointing a new abbot which is further complicated when some of the invited guests try to steal a precious scroll of the Mahayana Sutra. In the other new Hu picture it was also a Sutra and the only difference is that the ghosts wanted it instead of human beings.

"Raining" languishes so much on visual virtuosity that foreigners seeing this King Hu film will likely rant and rave in ecstasy. The exotic oriental mysticism, aesthetic elements and opaqueness are open to various interpretations which are expected. There are some bits and pieces that merit attention but huge chunks are needed to make a totally memorable movie.

Several of the characters meet various fates, the others learn the difference between material values and spiritual existence, while the lead characters Buddhist enlightenment. But the audience is left behind with the hope that something climactic will emerge. There is none ... what's left is a balladic nostalgia for the dying cinema style of King Hu.

Pic was premiered at the Third Hong Kong International Film Fest. —*Mel.*

Sai Thip
(THAI-COLOR)

Bangkok, June 14.
A Sayawan Motion Picture Co., Ltd. release. Written, produced and directed by Uthai Wongwaisayawan. Features entire cast. Based on a story by Pochana Kiatchinda; camera (color, Athee Wong; music, Panthip Virayaphanit, Asvinikul; production design and costumes, Kanokorm Kanakornkhan; asst. director, Gan Boonchoo. Reviewed at Paramount theatre, Bangkok, June 13, 1979. Running time: **125 MINS.**
Sai Thip . . . . Nantana Ngaokrachang
Prasarn . . . . .Patompong Singha
Jarunee . . . . Sidemi Aoki
Porng . . . . .Piathip Kumvong
Lert . . . . .Sompop Benjatikul
Chansom . . . . Suphan Buranaphim
Mopeung . . . . Wallaya Tonnawannij
Keow . . . . .Pailin Chindanoot
Tamsen . . . . Prachon Chindanoot

In less than two years following her successful debut in "Pae Kao" (The Scar), Nantana Ngaokrachang has died at least three or four times in her films. It's getting to be a habit.

In spite of the fact that she has done almost nothing but repeat herself on screen, for obvious commercial reasons, none of the films she has made has come anywhere near the b.o. success of "Pae Kao."

Costarring is Patompong Singha, a new male actor. Local audiences now expect a new lead star in every other Thai picture.

Japanese actress Sidemi Aoki, received 500,000 baht (about $25,-000), or more than six times what Thai leading actresses get per pic. Her name is used extensively to promote "Sai Thip."

Both Piathip Kumvong and Sompop Benjatikul are defeated by their obtuse roles. As the madwoman of the village, Piathip is supposed to provide a counterpoint to the general sadness of the story, but her part has been written to make her a laughingstock. Sompop could have been an effective villain, but one witty remark from Nantana is enough to eliminate him.

Most of the time there are only two people on screen — Nantana and Patompong. Main obstacle to their romance is the fact that she is older than him.

Technical credits are above average, particularly the music score, a collaboration among three leading Thai musicians. Production design and costumes also impressive in recreating the '20s in Bangkok.

—*Cano.*

Middle Age Spread
(NEW ZEALAND-COLOR)

Wellington, N.Z., June 28.
Endeavour Productions and N.Z. Film Commission release. Produced by John Barnett. Directed by John Reid. Features entire cast. Screenplay, Keith Aberdein from play by Roger Hall; camera (color), Alun Bollinger; sound, Craig McLeod; editor, Michael Horton; music, Stephen McCurdy. Reviewed at Lido Cinema, Wellington, June 28, '79 (NZCC rating R13). Running time: **94 MINS.**
Colin .Grant Tilly
Elizabeth . . . . .Dorothy McKegg
Reg .Peter Sumner
Isobel . . . . .Bridget Armstrong
Judy . . . . .Donna Akersten
Robert . . . . .Bevan Wilson

There is nothing more inevitable than middle age spread — that time in life when living patterns start running amok and all that one has taken for granted begins to sag and hang limp.

Keith Aberdein's fine screenplay from the Roger Hall stage hit, which has played to more than 80,000 New Zealanders, keeps in place all the wry humour, and gen-

tle sadness, of the original.

Indeed, this film adaptation of the middle life crisis of a collection of middle class couples proves to contain the most satisfying content of any NZ feature film made during the current production upsurge.

Made on low budget, but crisp in appearance and offering top drawer performances, it is a distinguished first-up presentation from the production stable of John Barnett.

"Middle Age Spread" centres on Colin (Grant Tilly), a college teacher whose promotion to principal coincides with a number of personal crises.

Not least are a widening girth, which has him jogging round the streets at night, and a tentative first-and-last affair with a much younger teaching colleague, Judy (Donna Akersten).

At a dinner party he hosts, with his increasingly sexually disinterested wife, Elizabeth (Dorothy McKegg), the morality and values of their tight-knit circle of friends are played out with deadly accuracy.

To his credit, director Reid, one of the actors in the original stage presentation, has created a film that is not just a pale adaptation of the play. The dinner party denouement is neatly balanced with events linking the main characters in the immediate past, and he has a keen eye for the visual gag. Only rarely is the central flow of the piece disrupted.

But it will be the performances that are remembered, particularly that of Tilly in the main role. Physically unprepossessing, he captures completely the gentle susceptibility and momentarily disturbed soundheadedness of Colin in the manner of an antipodean Woody Allen. With his expertise, the film cannot fail.

Akersten, rapidly gaining a reputation as the moist-lipped femme fatale of NZ movies, has the necessary attack and vulnerability as Judy, and McKegg has some splendid moments as the unwittingly, often acid, Elizabeth. Australian import Sumner, as a randy aging teachers' college lecturer with a taste for nubile liberal arts students, hangs in well as Reg.

But "Middle Age Spread" is no mere parading of middle class morality. Wit and thoughtfulness are judiciously mixed. And there is a bonus in the excellent original music of Stephen McCurdy. —*Nic.*

Bedniyat Louka
(Poor Lucas)
(BULGARIAN-COLOR)

Sofia, July 7.
A Bulgarian Film Production. Mladost Unit, Sofia; world rights, Film Bulgaria, Sofia. Features entire cast. Directed by Yakim Yakimov. Screenplay, Ivan Stanev, based on novella with same title by Dobri Nemirov; camera (color), Ivan Velchev; art direction, Bogoya Sapoundjiev; music, Kiril Tsiboulka. Reviewed at Film Bulgaria Screening Room, Sofia, July 6, '79. Running time: **90 MINS.**
Cast: Naoum Shopov (Lucas), Katya Paskaleva (Militsa).

Set in the 1920s, Yakim Yakimov's "Poor Lucas" is a film adaptation of a novel bearing the same title. It's the story of a poor photographer who can't quite make ends meet, he's also burdened by a wife who feels that matters will go from bad to worse now that a new photographer has moved into the neighborhood to win over to his studio whatever customers are left.

Then a rebel on the run stops by with a suitcase full of money for the resistance cause against the dictatorship government. Because he and Lucas had been in the First World War together and Lucas had saved his life, the friendship is renewed and our poor hero is trusted with the suitcase of money, which will be picked up at a later time when the heat is off. Lucas is also known for his honesty and integrity.

Poverty, however, is beating at the door. — *Holl.*

Spodelena Lyubov
(With Shared Love)*
(BULGARIAN-SOVIET-COLOR)

Sofia, July 5.
A Bulgarian and Soviet Film Coproduction, Sofia and Moscow, Sredets Film Unit, Sofia. Features entire cast. Directed by Sergei Mikaelian. Screenplay, Rustam Ibrahimbekov, Katya Goumnerova, Sergei Mikalien; camera (color), Leonid Kalashnikov; art direction, Yuri Fomenko; music, Kiril Tsiboulka. Reviewed at Film Bulgaria Screening Room, Sofia, July 4, '79. Running time: **90 MINS.**
Cast: Velko Kunev (Petko), Simeon Morozov (Kostya), Rossitsa Petrova (milena), Veronica Isotova (Tamara), Georgi Roussev (Kolev), Bogomil Simeonov (Modev).

A coproduction between the Soviet Union and Bulgaria, "Shared Love" is by a Soviet director but tells the story of a Bulgarian youth who goes to the Soviet Union to help build the Drouzhba gas pipeline, which is to supply the Socialist countries in East Europe when completed. Sergei Mikaelian's direction is a bit flat and unimaginative, but there are some informative and comical scenes that say a good deal about youth problems and living-and-working conditions in the Soviet Union, plus insights into how a gigantic gas line (like the Alaskan Pipe Line) is built nowadays.

Two chums, the Bulgarian Petko and the Russian Kostya, become fast friends on the construction site. Both are in love with girlfriends, Petko carrying on his romance per telephone, and Kostya needing help to make contact with a girl in a nearby youth camp. Since it's summer and the landscape is lovely, the boys also get involved in fighting for an environmental cause — the needless abuse of fertile land in building the pipe.

Thesp performances hold this youth pic together. — Holl.

The Villain
(COLOR)

When horses steal the show from the cast, there's trouble afoot.

Hollywood, July 13.

A Columbia Pictures release of a Rastar-Mort Engelberg production. Produced by Mort Engelberg. Exec producer, Paul Maslansky. Stars Kirk Douglas, Ann-Margret, Arnold Schwarzenegger. Directed by Hal Needham. Screenplay, Robert G. Kane; camera (color), Bobby Byrne; editor, Walter Hannemann; art direction, Carl Anderson; music, Bill Justis; sound John V. Speak; stunt coordinator, Gary Combs; assistant director, David Shamrov Hamburger. Reviewed at The Burbank Studios, Burbank, July 13, '79. (MPAA Rating: PG.) Running time: **93 MINS.**

Cactus Jack	Kirk Douglas
Charming Jones Handsome	Ann-Margret
Stranger	Arnold Schwarzenegger
Nervous Elk	Paul Lynde
Bank Clerk	Foster Brooks
Damsel In Distress	Ruth Buzzi
Avery Simpson	Jack Elam
Parody Jones	Strother Martin
Mashing Finger	Robert Tessier
Telegraph Agent	Mel Tillis
Working Girl	Laura Lizer Sommers

Columbia Pictures, Rastar and producer Mort Engelberg had better prepare for a major media buy in the Saturday ayem tv ghetto, because the moppet trade is going to be crucial to the success of "The Villain." Other than tykes trained on Roadrunner cartoons, there will be little audience enthusiasm for this broad, only intermittently funny western spoof.

Idea for the satire, at least in Robert G. Kane's script, must have looked great on paper. Why not take all the standard sagebrush types — the handsome stranger, the decollete femme, the evil outlaw, etc. — and put them through a parody of their usual paces?

The answer no one came up with was that without any depth of characterization, and only the flimsiest plot structure, a take-off has nowhere to go. Hal Needham, whose stunt background has been employed to excellent effect in both "Smokey And The Bandit" and

"Hooper," again dazzles audiences with some eye-popping feats, but the film gets lost in the dust.

With Kirk Douglas in the title role, Arnold Schwarzenegger as the good guy, and Ann-Margret as the lascivious girl who loves being fought over, "The Villain" becomes even more of a disappointment. Rarely has so much talent been used to so little purpose.

Real Star(s) of the film turn out to be the eight identical black horses used in the role of Whiskey, Douglas' canny mount, who steals every scene (they're) in. Mel Tillis, Foster Brooks, and especially Paul Lynde as a fey Indian chief, add some chuckles, but they're like droplets of water in a parched desert.

Douglas and Ann-Margret seem to be enjoying themselves, and both display excellent physical form in their respective roles, but they're called on to do little more than grin or grimace. Schwarzenegger show little development as an actor since his last part in "Stay Hungry," while such other veterans as Jack Elam and Strother Martin are relegated to cameo roles, as is Ruth Buzzi.

Gary Combs' stunt coordination, and wrangler Stevie Myers' work with the nags are principal contributors to what success "The Villain" enjoys. Bobby Byrne's lensing of Arizona locales, including Monument Valley, is pleasant to the eyes, altho Needham overuses helicopter aerial shots.

Bill Justis' score is not above lifting music directly from the Roadrunner cartoons, which points to a major failing of "The Villain." When feature films are forced to rely on tv for inspiration, there isn't much cause for laughter. —Poll.

The Unidentified Flying Oddball
(BRITISH-COLOR)

Disney treatment of Twain's Arthurian legend heavy with sci-fi effects and laffs.

London, July 17.

Buena Vista release of a Walt Disney production. Features entire cast. Produced by Ron Miller. Directed by Russ Mayberry. Screenplay, Don Tait, based on Mark Twain's "A Connecticut Yankee In King Arthur's Court;" camera (Technicolor), Paul Beeson; art director, Albert Witherick; editor, Peter Boita; special photographic effects, Cliff Culley; music, composed and conducted by Ron Goodwin. Reviewed in London, July 16, '79. (BBFC Rating: U). Running time: **93 MINS.**

Tom Trimble	Dennis Dugan
Sir Mordred	Jim Dale
Merlin	Ron Moody
King Arthur	Kenneth More
Sir Gawain	John Le Mesurier
Clarence	Rodney Bewes
Alisande	Sheila White
Senator Milburn	Robert Beatty
Dr. Zimmerman	Cyril Shaps
Winston	Kevin Brennan
Watkins	Ewen Solon
Oaf	Pat Roach
Prisoner	Reg Lye

Past and present collide with pleasing comicality in "The Unidentified Flying Oddball," Disney's latest made-in-England fantasy, wherein Yankee space-age technology saves King Arthur's Camelot from a palace coup. The Ron Miller production is good fun for both kids and grownups and merits lively b.o. action. Pic will play Blighty and other territories as "The Spaceman And King Arthur."

Dennis Dugan is appealing as a NASA whizkid who, with a look-alike robot, is inadvertently lofted into space at time-warping velocity and deposited in pastoral sixty-century England. Thereafter, either Dugan or the humanoid are subjected to stake-burning by Ron Moody as Merlin and Jim Dale as Mordred, before the climactic battle in which the latter two are routed.

Most of the laughs in Don Tait's disarming script dwell on whether Dugan is vegetable, animal or mineral, with a sprinkling of 'in' history jokes that will fly over the kids but provide adults with a few chuckles.

Pic has some good slapstick touches and offers a generous serving of visual tricks and space hardware, though on a par with "Star Wars" in that department it ain't.

Dugan's boyish all-American appeal meshes well in the polished company of Britons, including cutie-pie Sheila White, who lose their hearts to each other. Kenneth More is agreeably tongue-in-cheek as King Arthur, and there's good support from, among others, Rodney Bewes as a court page, Cyril Shaps as a space scientist, and Robert Beatty as a claghorn U.S. lawmaker.

Pic runs a brisk 93 minutes under Russ Mayberry's proficient direction, with an unobtrusive score by Ron Goodwin and fine photographic sweeps of merrie olde England by Paul Beeson. Other technical credits are pro. —Pit.

Barierata
(Barrier)
(BULGARIAN-COLOR)

Sofia, July 5.

A Bulgarian Film Production, Mladost Film Group, Sofia; world rights, Film Bulgaria, Sofia. Features entire cast. Directed by Christo Christov. Screenplay, Pavel Vezhinov, based on Pavel Vezhinov's novella of the same title; camera (color), Atanas Tassev; art direction, Stefan Savov; music, Kiril Tsiboulka. Reviewed at Film Bulgaria Screening Room,

Sofia, July 4, '79. Running time: **90 MINS.**

Cast: Innokenti Smoktunovsky (Anthony), Venya Tsvetkova (Dorethea), Maria Dimcheva (Dr. Youroukova).

The presence of the famous Soviet actor, Innokenti Smoktunovsky (he played Hamlet in Grigori Kozintsev's adaptation back in 1964), in Christo Christov's "Barrier" marked this psychological pic for critical attention from the very beginning. But it also happens to be one of the best Bulgarian pix of the present season and, upon its official release at the Moscow Film Fest in August, will probably be a commercial hit at home and possibly on the art house circuti abroad as well.

Nothing much occurs in "Barrier," but those who like psychological dramas and literature will appreciate the mental breakdown of a burnt-out composer played superbly by the Leningrad thesp. At the start it is fairly evident that the aging artist, now divorced and living alone, cannot create as he used to and is living on his laurels. Then a young woman with mysterious powers enters his life who can read his mind — is she real, or is she only a figment of his imagination? Finally, at the end, the breakdown is complete: schizophrenia and a psycho ward are only a step away.

How Christov tells the story makes "Barrier" both attractive and something stylistically new in Bulgarian cinema. The helmer (with an extra degree in psychology) has previously made "The Last Summer" (1974) and "Cyclops" (1976), both of which deal with similar individuals who can't match reality with what's going on in their minds. In "Last Summer" a villager resists moving from his land although a new dam will soon leave everything he owns under water, and he has surrealist hallucinations in combating his imagined enemies. In "Cyclops" a submarine captain on a mysterious journey also fashions a similar fantastic world of his own through the periscope.

In both cases man is proven to be a weak, perishable individual when clashing with the gods of nature or technology. In other words, they run up against a barrier of their own making. Now, in the film "Barrier," Christov expresses his thesis on less metaphysical or revolutionary grounds, but maintains the fantasy and mystical side in a tightly filmed and lensed "kammerspiel" context. The girl, Dorothea (meaning "Gift of God" in Greek), enters the composer's life mysteriously one evening in his car as he drives home from nightclub bar in Sofia. She tells him of her powers to fly after taking up residence in her home.

The composer falls in love with the girl, visits her psychiatrist in a hospital ward (he learns she is an incurable schizophrenic), and gives in one evening to her invitation to teach him to fly. Both are frightened from the experience, and the girl regrets letting Anthony, the composer, in on her secret too early in the game. She tells him the story of her mistreated youth, which is recounted in flashbacks and is a tale of poverty and child-abuse. One day the composer returns home and discovers the girl is dead in an automobile graveyard a distance from the apartment — and when Anthony tries to explain to investigators her ability to fly, he has also obviously crossed the barrier.

Well acted and lensed pic, and a sure bet for the fest circuit after bowing at Moscow. —*Holl.*

Rust Never Sleeps
(COLOR)

Should open big on Neil Young music fans.

Hollywood, July 13.

An International Harmony release. Produced by L.A. Johnson. Exec producer, Elliot Rabinowtiz. Directed by Beranrd Shakey, camera (DeLuxe Color), Paul Goldsmith, Jon Else, Robby Greenberg, Hiro Narita, Richard Pearce, Daniel Pearl; editor, Bernard Shakey; sound (Dolby Stereo), David Briggs, Tim Mulligan. Reviewed at MGM Studios Main Theatre, Culver City, July 13, '79. (MPAA Raing: PG). Running time: 103 MINS.

Features: Neil Young, Billy Talbot, Ralph Molina, Frank "Pancho" Sampedro.

Neil Young fans will undoubtedly frequent theatres unspooling "Rust Never Sleeps," filmed concert that complements Young well veteran band, Crazy Horse. Feature gives devotees a front-row seat for the Young concert they might not have caught last year — a concert that compliments Young well musically as he performs a mixed bag of his old and new music. Boxoffice outlook is good for initial flurry of interest.

Uninspired camera work and muddled series of messages that appear to be going on throughout the concert will fail to do much for the vastly larger filmgoing public. The excitement of the live perf is never generated here and for those who are not enamored of Young and his music, film will begin to drag unmercifully before the halfway point.

Young's music is hauntingly effective, but he seems determined to translate some kind of message about rock 'n' roll during his performance that is never made clear. Film opens with Young's roadies, dressed in monk outfits and lights on their faces which resemble little Orphan Annie eyes, setting up the stage with mammoth versions of a microphone and a glass of water. After about 10 minutes Young is unveiled from inside a stage prop made to look like an instrument case. He launches into some fine acoustic guitar numbers, especially listenable due to the film's top notch Dolby sound.

But as perf progresses a number of strange things happen. Technicians with coneheads wander across the stage in what seems like magicians' garb,' the monk roadies scurry about, dancing and at one point lifting Young offstage while he's "sleeping;" tapes of Chip Monck emceeing the Woodstock festival are played between sets; and a man lowered onstage via a rope from the ceiling and is quickly whisked away.

Strangest of all is when another man takes centerstage and tells the concert audience to put on their "Rust-O-Vision" glasses in order to view Young and his group "rust" before their eyes. Theatre audience needn't be concerned if glasses are not provided at their local deluxer as it is never quite clear what, if anything, the glasses are supposed to do.

Because the antics are inexplicable they dull the effectiveness of Young's music and the film in general. Not helping matters is the uninventive camera work throughout. Most shots are simply frontal views of Young and the ones that deviate seem to do so for no apparent reason other than to provide cameramen with a change of scenery.

There are only one or two quick shots of the audience during the entire feature, one reason why much of the excitement of the live performance is lost. During most of the film it seemed as if Young could have been performing to a cassette tape of cheering.

But despite mentioned drawbacks and the fact that there's an unprofessional graininess to much of the film, Young has his loyal aficionados who'll no doubt be bowled over by what they see. It's too bad they'll have to settle for a concert film that is so far below what Young and his music seem capable of. —*Berg.*

Avalanche Express
(COLOR)

Slow-paced 'thriller.'

London, July 20.

20th Fox release of a Lorimar production. Produced and directed by Mark Robson. Stars Lee Marvin, Robert Shaw. Screenplay, Abraham Polonsky, based on the novel by Colin Forbes; camera (color), Jack Cardiff; editor, Garth Craven; production designer, Fred Tuch; sound, George Stevenson; costumes, Mickey Shirrard; associate producer, Lynn Guthrie; in charge of production, Harry Caplan; Bavaria production exec, Willy Egger; special effects (miniatures) director, John Dykstra, camera (miniatures), Bruce Logan; boat battle sequence director, Allan Gibbs; special effects (boat), Ross Hahn; music, Allyn Ferguson; asst. director, Wieland Liebske. Reviewed at Classic Theatre, Haymarket, London, July 19, '79. (BBFC Rating: A). Running time: 88 MINS.

Marenkov	Robert Shaw
Wargrave	Lee Marvin
Elsa Lang	Linda Evans
Bunin	Maximilian Schell
Haller	Mike Connors
Leroy	Joe Namath
Scholten	Horst Buchholz
Geiger	David Hess
Neckermann	Arthur Brauss
Helga Mann	Kristine Nel
Olga	Sylva Langover

Well-stocked with veteran topliners, this slow-paced, routine thriller will likely do moderate business via hit-and-run playoff in most markets. Beyond some okay avalanche effects — which are not kept till the end, but provide a midway climax after which little action of note occurs — it has few significantly saleable production values.

Plot concerns the defection of a high-ranking Soviet played by the late Robert Shaw (creditably Slavic in appearance), and a concurrent maneuver to eliminate Maximilian Schell, another Russian heavy who's masterminding a biological warfare program.

A train, the Atlantic Express, is the all-too-contrived choice of transportation across Europe for Shaw and his CIA escorts, as a means of flushing out Schell's agents along the route. The plan is devised by maverick agent Lee Marvin, who is thus improbably permitted by superiors to use America's hottest property as bait for repeated attacks on the train.

With most dialog as flatfooted as the tale, and a marked lack of technical distinction despite cinematographer Jack Cardiff's involvement, "Avalanche Express" depends for relief on the performers' charismatic qualities. These, however, have small chance to survive through the generally banal actioning. Even Schell's normal originality is fettered by dull direction, intractable situations and, for much of the time, an absurd disguise.

It should be stated that production was beset with unusual problems, not least that producer-director Mark Robson died during shooting, and "postproduction services" are credited to Monte Hellman and Gene Corman. Actor Shaw also died, reportedly before completion of the soundtrack, which presumably partly explains the instances of mediocre postsync work. —*Simo.*

More American Graffiti
(COLOR)

Ambitious sequel overreaches itself, to boxoffice detriment.

Hollywood, July 19.

A Universal Pictures release of a Lucasfilm Ltd. production. Produced by Howard Kazanjian. Exec producer, George Lucas. Directed by B.W.L. Norton. Features entire cast. Screenplay, Norton, based on characters created by Lucas, Gloria Katz, Willard Huyck; camera (Technicolor), Caleb Deschanel; editor, Tina Hirsch, art direction, Ray Storey; sound (Dolby Stereo), David McMillan; costume design, Agnes Rodgers; set decoration, Doug Van Koss; assistant director, Thomas Lofaro. Reviewed at Goldwyn Theatre, Bev Hills, July 19, '79. (MPAA Rating: PG). Running time: 111 MINS.

Debbie Dunham	Candy Clark
Little Joe	Bo Hopkins
Steve Bolander	Ron Howard
John Milner	Paul Le Mat
Carol/Rainbow	Mackenzie Phillips
Terry The Toad	Charles Martin Smith
Laurie Bolander	Cindy Williams

Eva	Anna Bjorn
Major Creech	Richard Bradford
Ralph	John Brent
Newt	Scott Glenn
Sinclair	James Houghton
Lance	John Lansing
Beckwith	Ken Place
Teensa	Mary Kay Place
Andy Henderson	Will Seltzer
Felix	Ralph Wilcox

"More American Graffiti" may be one of the most innovative and ambitious films of the last five years, but by no means is it one of the most successful. In trying to follow the success of George Lucas' immensely popular 1973 hit, writer-director B.W.L. Norton overloads the sequel with four wholly different cinematic styles to carry forward the lives of "American Graffiti's" original cast. Initial returns should be very strong, on title lure alone, but repeat biz looks to be shallow.

While dazzling to the eye, the flirtation with split-screen, anamorphic, 16m and 1:85 screen sizes does not justify itself in terms of the film's content. What Norton and producer Howard Kazanjian are attempting, and what a variety of technicians pull of flawlessly, is daring, but ultimately pointless.

There's a lot going on in "More American Graffiti," as Norton takes the characters (minus a few exceptions) created by Lucas, Gloria Katz and Willard Huyck, and advances them two, three, four and five years into their future.

Paul Le Mat's still rooted in the early '60s, drag-racing and pursuing an Icelandic beauty (Anna Bjorn) with whom he's no more successful in communicating than he was in the original with Mackenzie Phillips. Charles Martin Smith and Bo Hopkins are assigned to a helicopter unit in Vietnam, while Candy Clark and Phillips have gone the flower power route in San Francisco. As expected, Ron Howard and Cindy Williams have married

Part of Norton's presumed goal, of course, is to show how the 1960s fractured and split apart, and that the cohesiveness that marked Lucas' (and the participants' lives) film is now dissipated, as characters branch out, and in some instances, are snuffed out.

But without a dramatic glue to hold the disparate story elements together, "Graffiti" is too disorganized for its own good, and the cross-cutting between different film styles only accentuates the problem.

Otherwise, Lucasfilm Ltd. has amassed an extraordinary cast an crew that succeeds in almost snatching victory from the jaws of defeat. The aural counterpoint via period recordings that virtually changed the conception of film soundtracks is again employed to excellent, if more downbeat, effect by music editor Gene Finley, supervising sound editor Ben Burt and re-recordists Bill Varney, Steve Maslow and Greg Landaker.

Work of cinematographer Caleb Deschanel, and optical coordinators Peter Donen, and Bill Lindemann, is extraordinary in meshing the four film sizes, which are beautifully handled in effortless segues. Especially noteworthy are the Vietnam sequences, filmed in Central California, and almost as impressive as some of the "Apocalypse Now" footage.

Smith tops the performers as the likable klutz, unable to get himself wounded and sent home even in the midst of the Vietnam War. Clark carries off her psychedelic scenes with panache, and Howard and Williams sparkle as the young marrieds forced to confront a changing society.

Bjorn is terrif as Le Mat's uncomprehending Venus, and Le Mat himself shows remarkable continuity in characterization, especially after a six-year layoff. Supporting players are uniformly well-chosen, with Scott Glenn and Ralph Wilcox very good as rock band members, Mary Kay Place as Bjorn's girlfriend, and Ralph Place as Le Mat's competitive buddy. Richard Dreyfuss, only cast principal not to return, is sorely missed, but Harrison Ford shows up in an unbilled cameo as a motorcycle cop. Phillips, one of the first film's most delightful characters, gets short shrift in this version.

Rest of thesping and tech work is all more than acceptable, but doesn't help "More American Graffiti" offers conclusive proof that in the case of sequels, less can be more. —Poll.

Royalut
(The Grand Piano)
(BULGARIAN-COLOR)

Sofia, July 8.
A Bulgarian Film Production. Sredets Unit, Sofia; world rights. Film Bulgarian, Sofia. Features entire cast. Directed by Borislav Pounchev. Screenplay, Nikola Roussev; camera (color), Georgi Mateyev; art direction, Peter Goranov; music, Simeon Pronkov. Reviewed at Film Bulgaria Screening Room, Sofia, July 7, '79. Running time: 90 MINS.

Cast: Georgi Kaloyanchev (Little Tooth), Ivan Grigorev (the Perch), Georgi Partsalev (the Candle), Naoum Shopov (the Director), Konstantin Kotsev (Genadiyi), Velko Kunev (the Shock-Worker), Madeleine Cholakova (Nadya).

A pic about the everyday concerns of the working class, Borislav Pounchev's "The Grand Piano" has a great deal of authenticity to recommend it. The script is by Nikola Roussev, one of the better dramatists working in Bulgaria's legit theatres who also specializes in comedies for the screen. Thesps too are well known legit actors, with whom the average moviegoer can relate and identify as types facing universal problems.

The story is built around an average happening in the course of a week, much in the vein of Yank sitcoms on television. A working crew on a construction site has to be tricked into finishing the job ahead of time by the Director (played by Naoum Shopov, a popular stage-and-legit thesp). He hits on the idea of celebrating the conclusion of the construction job with a concert by a bevy of top Bulgarian singers and musicians. But due to the artists' necessity to travel abroad, the workers are told they must finish the job by working overtime in order to have the big honorary concert. Then it's discovered that a grand piano is necessary for the big celebration, and off go a few comical members of the crew in search of an old-style, long-forgotten grand piano.

Plenty of humor and helmer has light hand with thesps. Credits also okay. —Holl.

North Dallas Forty
(COLOR)

A touchdown on every play. Yablans, Kotcheff, Nolte and Davis make for a winning team.

Hollywood, July 20.
A Paramount Pictures release of a Frank Yablans production. Produced by Frank Yablans. Exec producer, Jack B. Bernstein. Stars Nick Nolte. Directed by Ted Kotcheff. Screenplay by Yablans, Kotcheff, Peter Gent, based upon the novel by Gent; camera (Metrocolor), Paul Lohmann; editor, Jay Kamen; production design, Alfred Sweeney; music, John Scott; costume design, Dorothy Jeakins; set decoration, Art Parker; sound, Larry Jost; assistant director, Victor Hsu. Reviewed at Paramount Studio Theatre, Hollywood, July 20, '79. (MPAA Rating: R). Running time: 119 MINS.

Phillip Elliott	Nick Nolte
Maxwell	Mac Davis
Coach Johnson	Charles Durning
Charlotte	Dayle Haddon
Jo Bob Priddy	Bo Svenson
Conrad Hunter	Steve Forrest
B.A. Strothers	G.D. Spradlin
Emmett	Dabney Coleman
Joanne	Savannah Smith
Art Hartman	Marshall Colt
Eddie Rand	Guich Koock
O.W. Shaddock	John Matuszak

It's no surprise that the National Football League refused to cooperate in the making of "North Dallas Forty." The Frank Yablans production is the most realistic, hard-hitting and perceptive look at the seamy side of pro football to date. Despite a hard R rating for locker-room lingo, the Paramount Pictures release looks to score lots of boxoffice points.

What distinguishes this screen adaptation of Peter Gent's best-seller is the exploration of a human dimension almost never seen in sports pix. Most people understand that modern-day athletes are just cogs in a big business wheel, but getting that across on the screen is a whole different matter.

That's where director Ted Kotcheff, who also co-scripted with Yablans and Gent, is so successful. And in large measure, that success is due to a bravura performance in the lead role by Nick Nolte, who finally hits his stride as a premiere actor.

Gent's book has been cleaned up considerably, but enough rough edges protrude to give "North Dallas Forty" some real bite. Nolte is a wide receiver about to go over the hill, but still possessing "the best hands in the game."

Mac Davis is his quarterback-best buddy. Dayle Haddon and Savannah Smith are his love interests, and G.D. Spradlin, Charles Durning, Steve Forrest and Dabney Coleman the coaches and owners of the North Dallas Bulls, pitted against Nolte in a struggle no less elemental than the "game" of football itself.

Without NFL backing, the on-field action is kept in reserve for a powerful finale, but the real battles are raging within Nolte. The proverbial wiseacre, he's accused of immaturity not for agreeing to be doped up before every game, but because he has the nerve to think about it.

Nolte's disinclination to join "the family," as the football establishment is aptly named, is encouraged by his relationship with girlfriend Haddon, and by what he sees going on around him.

In his first film role, Davis is superb as the quick-talking survivor who appreciates Nolte's dilemma, but has already resolved his own qualms. It's a unique male relationship to discover in a football film, and Davis looks to have an unexpected acting career before him.

Even the villains have shading in "North Dallas Forty." Spradlin and Forrest, in particular, offer in-depth characterizations, with Durning relegated to the role of the more stereotyped, loud-mouthed coach. Bo Svenson is super as an over-sized lineman whose off-field appetites are as ravenous as his gametime play, and Oakland Raider John Matuszak adds a chilling touch of psyched-up insanity.

Kotcheff keeps the action flowing smoothly, and has perfectly captured the locker-room intensity, and post-game letdown that never shows up on the tube. A series of fade-outs after some subtle, piercing observations in the script manages to get the point across without having to hit the audience over the head.

Tech work is pro all the way, with Paul Lohmann's sharp images and Alfred Sweeney's adroit production design cleverly covering the fact that Los Angeles locations are doubling for Dallas. Jay Kamen's editing could be a little tighter, but that's a very minor fault in an otherwise superlative film.

"North Dallas Forty" may disillusion some fans, but it will enlighten many more as to the dramas behind modern-day Sunday gladiatorial battles. And for once, coarse and crude language seems fully integrated into its setting, band not just tossed in as a sop for jaded audiences.—*Poll.*

Corps a Coeur
(Body to Heart)
(FRENCH-COLOR)

Paris, July 20.

A Parafrance release of a Diagonale production. Produced, written and directed by Paul Vecchiali. Features entire cast. Camera (color). Georges Strouve; sound. J.-Francois Chevalier; editor. Vecchiali; music. Gabriel Faure. Reviewed at the Paramount City-Triomphe cinema, Paris, July 9, 1979. Running time: **126 MINS.**

Pierre . . . . Nicolas Silberg
Jeanne . . . . Helen Surgere
Mother . . . . Madeleine Robinson
Melinda . . . . Myriam Mezieres
Emma . . . . Beatrice Bruno
Anna . . . . Christine Murillo

Paul Vecchiali, an eclectic, independent "auteur," produced, wrote, directed and edited this curious contemporary love story about a lady-killing 35-year-old suburban garage mechanic who is seized with an uncontrollable passion for a still-attractive 50-year old pharmacist. She firmly resists his increasingly desperate advances until she learns that she is stricken with an incurable disease. She decides then to spend her last days with him in happy seclusion.

Essentially it's the stuff innumerable mindless weepies are made of, but Vecchiali is no shameless tear-mongerer. He's deployed many of the conventions of literary and filmic romantic melodrama, altering, subverting or inverting them to find a new angle of vision on the subject of passion. Here the age difference is considerable, yet unimportant, since both lovers are adults and it is the man who sulks and suffers tearfully and waits anxiously next to the telephone for word from his beloved (But it's still the woman who dies prematurely at the summit of bliss).

As a cool analysis of excess emotions, the film is often valid and perceptive, sometimes comic in the way it exposes the ludicrousness of romantic gestures and attitudes. But Vecchiali seems to want things both ways: keep a distance and yet solicit the viewers' emotions as well. So many scenes teeter on this line of ambivalence that one ends up wondering how to react to a scene and to the characters. It's no wonder that local critical reception spans the spectrum from harsh derision to effusive admiration.

What flatly doesn't work in the film is the background involving picturesque and eccentric neighborhood types who spout sententious comments about life, indirectly commenting on the sufferings of the lovesick working class Romeo. Here the film buff instincts of the director go wildly astray as he tries to recreate the popular slices of poetic life created in the 1930's French cinema by Jacques Prevert.

Technically the film is excellent and the acting compliments go mostly to the women, particularly Helene Surgere, whose start in film at middle age has proven no hindrance to her playing roles of intense passion and sensuality. In smaller roles Christine Murillo, as the mechanic's old flame, and Madeleine Robinson, as his mentally unbalanced mother, give the film some of its true, unmediated pathos. The male lead is played by Nicolas Silberg, a member of the Comedie-Francaise, whose first major film role this is. Handsome and competent, he nevertheless pales before Surgere's luminosity. —*Len.*

Fatalnata Zapetaya
(The Fatal Comma)
(BULGARIAN-COLOR)

Sofia, July 8.

A Bulgarian Film Production. Savremenik Unit. Sofia; world rights. Film Bulgaria, Sofia. Features entire cast. Directed by Liliana Pencheva. Screenplay, Maxim Assenov; camera (color). Dimko Minev; art direction. Youlyana Boshkova; music. Bozhidar Petkov. Reviewed at Film Bulgarian Screening Room, Sofia. July 7, '79. Running time: **90 MINS.**

Cast: Tatyana Tsvetkova (Sylvia). Georgi Kadourin (Ventsi). Dimiter Marin (Misho). Nikolai Kolev (Zhivko). Katya Dineva (Sylvia's Mother). Yakim Mihov (Sylvia's Father).

Another youth film set in the classroom, where Bulgarian children's pix often take place. Liliana Pencheva's "The Fatal Comma" deals with the problem of honesty and class loyalty. A top student in her early adolescent years comes from a Professor's family and is therefore trusted by everyone more than the rest. Yet she is guilty of covering her own tracks on an absentee list for the mathematics class: she puts a comma between two numbers on the list and thus implicates two other students, and they both receive lower marks due to their apparent absences from class

The twist is that the students in jeopardy are usually guilty of skipping assignments, but in this case are innocent. The Professor's daughter decides to cover up the misdemeanor by rationalizing the proceedings in her own favor. But her classmates tend to suspect the wrongdoing, one of whom is her boyfriend. The upshot is that the girl learns slowly that it's better to face the music than complicate the situation any further than absolutely necessary. To reach this decision, however, requires plenty of dialogue. —*Holl.*

Porridge
(BRITISH-COLOR)

Tasty tv spinoff.

London, July 18.

ITC Film Distributors release of a Witzend production presented by Jack Gill for Black Lion Films. Produced by Allan McKeown, Ian La Frenais. Directed by Dick Clement. Features entire cast. Screenplay, Dick Clement, Ian La Frenais; camera (color). Bob Huke; editor, Alan Jones; sound, Clive Winter; art director, Tim Gleeson; asst. director, Richard Hoult. Reviewed at 2oth Fox preview theatre, London, July 17, '79. (BBFC Rating: A). Running time: **95 MINS.**

Fletcher . . . . Ronnie Barker
Godber . . . . Richard Beckinsale
Mackay . . . . Fulton Mackay
Barrowclough . . . . Brian Wilde
Grouty . . . . Peter Vaughan
Bainbridge . . . . Julian Holloway
Governor . . . . Geoffrey Bayldon
Beale . . . . .Christopher Godwin
Oakes . . . . .Barrie Rutter
Rudge . . . . .Daniel Peacock

Deftly directed by cowriter Dick Clement on a slimmer-than-slim budget, and thoroughly well acted, "Porridge," looks to do fine in all territories where the British tv sitcom series of which it's a spinoff has scored. In others, such as the U.S., its firmly parochial humor must limit its prospects to careful exposure as a curiosity.

With a real prison location ("porridge" is local slang for time spent in the pen) used instead of the studio sets of the series, a realism dimension has been added to the basically simple plot in which the lynchpin character — a perennial inmate played by Ronnie Barker — escapes more or less by mistake, then breaks back in to avoid trouble.

Scripters Clement and Ian La Frenais have penned a fair quota of gags, but in settings of real stone and peeling paint, lit by cinematographer Bob Huke with a moodiness unattained on the tube, the effect is often more bleak than belly-laughable. While this accords with the writers' generally laconic style — recurring digs at the British weather are stock-in-trade to a fault — it takes the edge off the film's sheer entertainment value, and suggests aspirations to social significance which fans of the series could find puzzling.

Overgrimaced comedy playing would have been insupportable in this context, so it's especially gratifying that characterizations, too, are securely rooted in reality, and all the funnier for that.

Barker's essentially subtle performance alternates expertly between poignancy and hilarity. And Fulton Mackay succeeds in making a perpetual fallguy prison officer an object of pity as well as lampoon.
—*Simo.*

Ken Murray Shooting Stars
(DOCUMENTARY-COLOR)

Home movies are still home movies, even in Hollywood.

Hollywood, July 11.

A Royal Oak Film Corporation release. Executive producer, Bud Cole. Produced and directed by Ken Murray. Screenplay, Bette Lou Murray, Helen Rackin; camera (color). Ken Murray; editors, Ken Murray, Paul Vitella; music, Richard LaSalle; associate producer, Steve Bushelman. Reviewed at Aidikoff Screening Room, L.A., July 10, '79. (MPAA rating: PG.) Running time: **95 MINS.**

Cast: **126** Hollywood notables.

Vaude, revue and screen comedian Ken Murray has been shooting home movies featuring Hollywood celebrities for over 50 years. Part of his stage show, at least recently, has consisted of the screening of selections from his personal library, and Murray has now assembled highlights into this feature-length documentary, "Ken Murray Shooting Stars." Result, even for buffs, is largely tedious, unilluminating and even depressing, as the majority of figures on view have passed on.

Pic's one haunting moment comes early on, as Murray takes Ann-Margret for a drive up to Pickfair. He then flashes back to footage he lensed at the estate in 1930. Mary Pickford comes out of the house and greets an automobile, out of which steps famed aviatrix Amelia Earhart.

The two engage in a stilted conversation about the flier's contributions to women's social advancement, whereupon Douglas Fairbanks and Earhart's husband George Putnam rush up and whisk them off to lunch. Despite its "staged" quality, the sequence is strangely moving, evocative of a whole era which is gone forever.

Nothing else Murray has to offer begins to approach this clip, however, as most of the shots predictably show stars smiling at the camera, goofing off or doing nothing at all. There's some amusement to be had in seeing John Wayne and Dick Powell, both then very young, playing ping pong, Cary Grant and Spencer Tracy playing tennis, Errol Flynn aboard a boat with Dolores Del Rio, or Mickey Rooney stepping to the plate in a celeb baseball game, but the pleasures don't go beyond those of seeing familiar faces in somewhat unfamiliar settings. —Cart.

Po Diryata Na Bezsledno Izcheznalite
(On the Tracks of the Missing)
(BULGARIAN-COLOR)

Sofia, July 6.

A Bulgarian Film Production. Hemus Unit, Sofia; world rights. Film Bulgaria, Sofia. Features entire cast. Directed by Margarit Nikolov. Screenplay, Nikolai Hristozov; camera (color), Ivan Samardjiev; art direction, Zahari Savov; music, Kiril Donchev. Reviewed at Film Bulgaria Screening Room, Sofia, July 5, '79. Running time: 200 MINS.

Cast: Naoum Shopov (General Vulkov), Boris Loukanov (Prof. Alexander Tsankov), Assen Milanov (President of the Court), Lyubomir Mladenov (Czar Boris), Dimiter Hadjianev (Yossif Herbst), Isaac Fintsi (Todor Strashimirov), Lyubomir Buchvarov (Geo Milev).

An historical document on the White Terror years (1923-25), Margarit Nikolov's "On the Traces of the Missing" ran in both the cinemas and on television as a two-part production. The best known of Bulgarian actors interpret historical personalities during this period, from the Bulgarian King Boris down to the country's leading intellectuals and political leaders of the time. All the historical speeches took place in the Sobranie (Parliament) as depicted, ad the film intends from the very beginning to make sure in the viewer's mind that neither persons or places are coincidental.

Following the death of Premier Alexander Stomboliski in 1923, the Agrarian Party found themselves without leadership, and the Communist Party rose in revolt against a dictatorship government under Alexander Tsankov. Several members of the intelligentsia and Parliament were shot on the street or were simply reported missing, among the latter the journalist Yossif Herbst; and brother of writer Anton Strashimirov, Todor Strashimirov; and the poets Geo Milev and Hristo Yassenov.

Pic recounts how an unmarked mass grave was discovered in 1953, whereby the guilty parties still living were put on trial and a chronological retro of events traces the past via several historical speeches and events. —Holl.

Migove U Kibritena Boutiyka
(Moments in a Matchbox)
(BULGARIAN-COLOR)

Sofia, July 6.

A Bulgarian Film Production. Mladost Group, Sofia; world rights. Film Bulgaria, Sofia. Features entire cast. Directed by Marianna Evstatiyeva. Screenplay, Olga Krusteva; camera (color), Emil Wagenstein; art direction, Eva Yordanova; music, Simeon Pironko. Reviewed at Film Bulgaria Screening Room, Sofia, July 5, '79. Running time: 90 MINS.

Cast: Dilyana Semeonova (Anetta), Vladimir Vasselev (Boy), Violetta Doneva (Anetta's Mother), Dossyo Dossev (Grandfather), Stefan Danailov (Boarder).

Marianna Evstatiyeva's "Moments in a Matchbox" gets off to a good start as two 12-year-old classmates, Anetta and Boy, living next door to each other, decide to take their puppy-love seriously and run off together. The girl has to visit her grandmother in the provinces, and the boy also has a similar date with his parents in much the same place — so they conspire to take different trains and both get off at a prearranged stop along the way to spend a day or so together on their own while still fulfilling family duties.

The adventure turns out other than expected, however. Both miss the designated stop and get off the train at the next station, then separately wind their way back to the arranged meeting place by hitchhiking. They both have to stay overnight somewhere in the meantime before they accidently find each other, which makes for meeting strangers and having both good and bad experiences. The girl keeps up her courage by following her sick grandfather's instructions — when in need or trouble, light a match and make your dreams come true in the flickering flame.

At the end, the favorite grandfather dies while she's away, which brings the summer vacation to an end with a sudden moment of feeling grown-up as well. Lensing and credits are above average, but story tends to drag toward end.
— Holl.

Belyazani Atomi
(Tagged Atoms)
(BULGARIAN-COLOR)

Sofia, July 7.

A Bulgarian Film Production, Sofia; world rights. Film Bulgaria, Sofia. Features entire cast. Directed by Grisha Ostrovsky. Screenplay, Assen Georgiev; camera (color), Boris Yanakiev. Reviewed at Film Bulgaria Screening Room, Sofia, July 6, '79. Running time: 90 MINS.

Cast: Nencho Hristov, Vanya Tsvetkova.

Helmer Grisha Ostrovsky, a theatre director in Sofia and Varna, made "Tagged Atoms" with students from the Theatre Art Institute in Sofia, where he teaches in his free time (as do several legit directors and filmmakers). He is best known for "Sidetrack" (1968), his debut pic made together with lenser Tudor Stoyanov.

"Tagged Atoms" comes across like a diploma film, and perhaps it was meant to be simply an exercise in acting and improvising a theme around young people in the age of crisis. The main figures are five boys leaving secondary school for induction into military service (a required draft in Bulgaria), one of whom is pronounced unfit due to a heart condition. The boy himself knows he's unfit, but his inseparable friends decide to train him into top physical condition by exercising on a bicycle racing course.

The lad soon equals his four colleagues in physical fitness, but the others demonstrate that they are far behind him in moral courage and self-knowledge. One boy's animosity towards a waiter in a restaurant who earlier betrayed his father during the politically difficult past years never finds proper release, and another gets entangled in silly affairs with older women. The boy with the heart condition, and a girl who loves him for his integrity and self-assurance, dies suddenly — and the truth of his sickness is out. It brings the others to a moment of self-realization.

So-so direction of a potentially good story. —Holl.

Delirium
(COLOR)

St. Louis, July 14.

An Odyssey Pictures release of a Worldwide Production (Delirium Associates). Produced by Sunny Vest, Peter Maris. Executive producer, Mark Cusumano. Directed by Peter Maris. Features entire cast. Screenplay, Richard Yalem; story, Yalem, Eddie Krell, Jim Loew; music, David Williams; camera (color), John Huston, Bill Mensch; editor, Dan Perry; special effects, Bob Shelly. Reviewed at Wehrenberg Screening Room, St. Louis, July 13, '79. (MPAA Rating: R). Running time: 90 MINS.

Susan Norcross	Debi Chaney
Paul Dollinger	Turk Cekovsky
Larry Mead	Terry Ten Broeck
Eric Stern	Barron Winchester
Charlie Gunther	Nick Panouzis
Donald Andrews	Bob Winters
Mark	Garrett Bergfeld
Captain Hearn	Harry Gorsuch
Det. Parker	Chris Chronopolis
Det. Simms	Lloyd Schattyn
Devlin	Jack Garvey
Specter	Mike Kalist
Wells	Myron Kozman

A lot of murder and blood, and an occasional touch of sex, for the unsophisticated drive-in crowd, are the features of "Delirium," third feature of St. Louis-based Worldwide Productions. Same group also filmed the softcore "Take Time to Smell the Flowers" and the auto-

actioner, "Stingray," in the area, for regional multi-screen distribution.

Tale involves an underground, vigilante-type organization, headed by Barron Winchester and backed by wealthy businessmen. Its aim is to capture, try and execute "criminals" who have been acquitted through usual channels of law. Things go awry, however, when one of the hit men goes berserk and starts a cross-country trail of killings, beginning with the roommate of Debi Chaney, a pretty local college girl with minimal acting ability.

Nick Panouzis, as the non-speaking killer, is fearsome and effective, though his victims are mostly women who make up in patience what they lack in sense.

Cekovsky and Ten Broeck are the detective team that begins with the first murder — a spear through a door — and finally gets to Winchester's organization. They get help from Cheney, who happens to work as the secretary to one of the group's backers.

Cekovsky, calm and low-keyed, is easily the acting standout, with Winchester nicely evil and crazed, though his role is necessarily one-dimensional. Ten Broeck is awkward and stilted, especially when he romances Chaney.

There is considerable use of flashbacks to Vietnam battle scenes to show where Winchester and Panouzis went wrong, and other flashbacks to the first murder.

Direction, by Peter Maris, and screenplay, by Richard Yalem, are predictable and trite, but on the proper level for the expected audience. Music by David Williams, adds little.

Screening print was excessively grainy in many scenes, probably due to the blowup from 16m to 35m, and one reel was poorly synchronized. Camera work is adequate, and final shootout cleans up all loose ends in a bath of blood.
—Jopo.

Der Uebergang
(The Border Crossing)
(EAST GERMAN-COLOR)

Berlin, July 17.

A DEFA Film Production, East Berlin. Features cast. Written and directed by Orlando Luebbert. Features entire cast. Camera (color), Juergen Brauer; music, Ivan Pequeno; artistic advisor, Tamara Trampe. Reviewed at DEFA Screening Room, East Berlin, July 16, '79. Running time: 80 MINS.

With Adelaida Arias, Oscar Castro, Hugo Medina, Anibal Reyna.

A DEFA pix directed by Chilean exile helmer, Orlando Luebbert. "The Border Crossing" is set in Chile at the time of the military putsch and features refugee thesps living in both East and West Germany, as well as other parts of Europe. Luebbert was formerly an assistant to Patricio Guzman and won a prize at the Karlovy Vary fest for "Fists Before the Cannon" in 1976.

This is the second pic this year dealing first-hand with the experiences of the Chilean exiles. Earlier, Christian Ziewer's West Berlin feature pic, "I See This Land From Afar," featured an ex-union leader with a family living in Berlin and having trouble keeping a job at Tegel airport due to security reasons. And Dean Reed's GDR-TV pic, "The Singer" (El Cantor), also completed this year, chronicled the last days of Chilean folk-singer and popular hero, Victor Jara. Both "The Singer" and "The Border Crossing" were lensed in Bulgaria, whose mountainous terrain resembles Chilean landscape.

The factor that makes "The Border Crossing" attractive for special audiences — Chilean Film Weeks, summer fest circuit, campus and art-house devotees — is the authenticity of the story and its true-adventure character. A party member of the Unidad Popular is fleeing with a young companion for the border and hoped-for safety in an unnamed Latin American country: they meet a third man also in flight and, in a comic scene, overcome their distrust and bicker among themselves as to electing a leader, per party regulations.

Later, the trio witness the killing of a defenseless peasant by border policemen as he returns home from a village after buying baby clothes for a child his wife is expecting — and they are delayed in their journey as they help the murdered peasant's wife by assisting at the birth. Then, after crossing the border, two of the group are turned back over to the sadistic policemen, and the young boy (who had escaped) is shot. This killing arouses the two captives to overpower a guard and wreak revenge.

Pic is simply and effectively told, and lensing is a plus. The ending has, of course, its preordained message, but this comes across as the natural consequence of the tale. With proper handling, pic could do well abroad where Chile is a byword for political and social engagement. —Holl.

Khon Pukao
(The Mountain Man)
(THAI-COLOR)

Bangkok, July 11.
A New Five Star Productions release. Produced by Kiat Iamphungporn. Written, edited and directed by Vichit Kounavudhi. Features entire cast. Camera (color). Preecha Subprawong: sound and music. Knit Kounavudhi: executive producer. Thongpond Kounavudhi. Reviewed at Athens Theatre. Bangkok. July 10. '79. Running time: 120 MINS.
Ar-Yo . . . . Montri Janeaksorn
Mei Fin . . . . Valaikorn Paovarat
Ar-Mee-Yo . . . . . . Suphavadee Tiensuwan
Am Liu . . . . Petchara Intarakamhang
Torn Ho . . . . Pisit Anutchitcharnchai
Missionary . . . . Robert Keith

This Thai film took a year to finish, and that's unusual. Thai producers do not want their capital tied up for longer than three months, otherwise they get nervous.

Vichit Kounavudhi also recruited the film's cast entirely from unknowns — another big gamble — and the majority are under 25.

The adventures of a rather unlucky E-kaw minority tribesman, played by Montri Janeaksorn, provide the main thread of the story, including tribal rituals from two other hilltribes. Yao and Musor. Montri's first wife (Suphavadee Tiensuwan) gives birth to twins. Their tribe have a superstitious belief that the birth of twins is a bad omen. The babies are killed, but the hero's misfortunes are just beginning. He and his wife are banished, according to tribal custom. At a river crossing, the wife drowns but Montri survives by grabbing just in time at a floating log.

Kounavudhi is a leading artistic director in Thailand. But his work in "Khon Pukao" makes it obvious that he worried in advance about its commercial prospects, and settled for a lot of cliches, including naked young girls bathing in a stream, robbery and rape, plus an often employed touch of local color consisting of an entire village helping to build a house for the hero in one day, etc.

None of the mountain people here think and feel any different from the lowlanders (Thais).

In the end, both the mountain people and the Thais come to the same conclusion: mountain people should stay where the belong.

"Mountain Man" did not get a public screening in Singapore during the Asian Fest, and yet it received one of two top prizes for promotion of international understanding. —Cano.

Chereshovata Gradina
(The Cherry Orchard)
(BULGARIAN-COLOR)

Sofia, July 7.
A Bulgarian Film Production. Sofia; world rights. Film Bulgaria. Sofia. Features entire cast. Directed by Ivan Andonov. Screenplay. Nikolai Haitov; camera (color). Plamen Wagenstein. Reviewed at Film Bulgaria Screening Room. Sofia. July 6. '79. Running time: 90 MINS.
Cast: Peter Slabakov (Party Secretary in the Village). Nikola Todev (Head of Branch Economy in Village's Agroindustrial Complex). Maria Statoulova (Secretary's Wife). Lydia Petrova (Schoolmistress). Georgi Cherkelov (Secretary's Friend). Domna Ganeva).

Actor-director Ivan Andonov scored a hit a season ago with his "The Roof" (1978), which impressed writer Nikola Haitov to such an extent that he wrote the screenplay of "The Cherry Orchard" (not to be confused with Chekhov's play) especially for him. This film is also one of the best in the current season of Bulgarian cinema, and will surely find its way to a festival sometime in the near future.

Like all of Haitov's stories, it takes place in the Rhodope Mountains and deals with village life in the same vein as Chengiz Aytmatov writes about his native Kirghizia in the south-central section of the Soviet Union. Both authors are known for the native flavor of their tales, which also carry a depth of philosophical truth amid metaphoric symbolism.

"The Cherry Orchard" is set in the autumn and depicts a head-on clash between a gentle, nature-loving Party Secretary in the village with the Head of a kind of collective farm (the "Agroindustrial Complex") who only has potatoes on his mind — in contrast to the former's care for a young orchard of cherry trees. The two are ideologically on different sides of the fence, and the fact that the gentle woodsman type is married to his opponent's sister doesn't help matters either.

The village's machinery and manpower are channelled entirely in the direction of the potato crop, while the woodsman-secretary has to enlist (in a warming scene) the school's children to help paint the trunks of the endangered cherry trees (a measure against rabbits eating away the bark). The wife begins to think her husband is having an affair with the young teacher, and rumors are then spread around to discredit the secretary at the next town meeting.

Meanwhile, friends have discovered that the Head of the Agro-industrial Complex has falsified records to increase government handouts, but they are afraid to interfere in local politics and so keep silent. Shortly, the school is closed down for a shortage of pupils, the secretary loses his job for incompetence and is reduced to a goatherd, and the cherry orchard is maliciously cut down. Then, when the honest hero dies in an explosion (to save animals under his care), the villagers stand up in his honor to confront the lies against him.

Well rendered by two natural storytellers. "The Cherry Orchard" stars the able Peter Slabakov (the lead in Andonov's previous "The Roof") as the good-hearted man, too gentle to do anything else but

---

follow his own instincts. Lensing and credits are also tops. —Holl.

Lachenite Obouvki Na Neznainiya Voin
(The Unknown Soldier's Patent Leather Shoes)
(BULGARIAN-COLOR)

Sofia, July 5.
A Bulgarian Film Production. Sredets Group. Sofia: world distribution. Film Bulgaria. Sofia. Features entire cast. Written and directed by Rangel Vulchanov. Camera (Eastmancolor). Radoslav Spassov: art direction. Georgi Todorov: music. Kiril Conchev. Reviewed at Film Bulgaria Screening Room. Sofia. July 4. '79. Running time: 88 MINS.
Cast: Borislav Tsankov (Mone. the boy). Slavka Ankova (Granny Slava). Ivan Stoichkov (Granddad Dobrin). Emilia Mirinska (the Bride and boy's Aunt). Nikolai Velichkov (the Black Uncle).

Rangel Vulchanov — as his latest pic. "The Unknown Soldier's Patent Leather Shoes" proves — is still a key man in New Bulgarian Cinema, a movement he started two decades ago with his pathbreaking "On a Small Island" (1958), followed by the equally impressive and personally earmarked "First Lesson" (1960) and "Sun and Shadow" (1962). These three pix were written by poet-playwright Valeri Petrov (he translated Shakespeare into modern Bulgarian), and the two were to collaborate again many years later on "With Love and Tenderness" (1978), another highwater mark in Bulgarian cinema.

About the same time as Vulchanov was experiencing his initial success in the first wave of a new national cinema, he wrote the script for "The Unknown Soldier's Patent Leather Shoes" — and then waited some 17 years for permission to film it. It's a collection of personal remembrances from childhood, loosely joined together as in a dream. Events are simply sparked by a filmmaker's (Vulchanov) lensing of the Changing-of-the-Guard ceremony at Buckingham Palace one day. The director then begins to comment on the past (it's Vulchanov's own voice on the soundtrack) with wit, warmth, and nostalgia.

A boy of about 10, Little Mone, steps into the foreground. This is Vulchanov's poignant, visionary account of his own childhood in a village, a chronicle of the 1930s about peasant life as a whole. Since he did not leave the village until he himself was 16-years-old, the people and places are clearly etched in his memory — so much so that he chose non-actors for all the roles, and was even convinced by colleagues to use his own voice (instead of a professional actor's) for the narration of the story.

The bittersweet, bucolic tale has a touch of Mark Twain throughout: there's Granny who bore 30 children (it's said), Granddad who fought gallantly in the First World War, the lovely White Aunt who marries the Black Uncle to give the pic its principal motif — a wedding. The boy's main interest, however, is nature and animals: the summer and harvest seasons are rendered in lush, embracing colors, and there's a dog who bites and other barnyard pets with dispositions of their own.

The boy's fantasy runs loose throughout the film. He imagines his grandfather returning home from war, to breed another member of the family. He envisions his grandmother, a bit touched in the head, wanting to set fire to the household at night or stealing things on the side. The Black Uncle is also a bit crazy, a retarded grownup always grinning and much too undersized to get married in the first place. The boy's love is reserved for his White Aunt, whom he relates to a beautiful white dove. The wedding day is complete with the ritual of the "First Night," plus a vengeful stabbing among the guests. And the harvest shows the boy wandering through the fields with a bandaged head ("the dog bit out my eyes") as he carries water to the workers. —*Holl.*

Byugai, Obicham Te
(Run Away, I Love You)
(BULGARIAN-COLOR)

Sofia, July 8.

A Bulgarian Film Production. Mladost Film Unit, Sofia; world rights. Film Bulgaria, Sofia. Features entire cast. Directed by Rashko Ouzounov. Screenplay, Kiril Topalov; camera (color), Tsvetan Chobanski; art direction, Moni Aladjemov; music, Peter Yossifov. Reviewed at Film Bulgarian Screening Room, Sofia, July 7, '79. Running time: **90 MINS.**
Cast: Stanimir Stoilov (Koki), Ventsislav Koulev (Anghel), Zoya Kircheva (Svetia).

Rashko Ouzounov scored a hit with a children's pic, "The Talisman" (1978), a year ago; it deals with the pains of growing up and the uncertainties of the pre-adolescent years. Now he's back with a film for youth, "Run Away, I Love You," a very fine film treating 16-year-olds and the problems of friendship. Both films are also set in the school classroom and focus on human failures in depicting how being right is not always the important thing in life.

Two sport chums do everything together from training for boxing matches to sharing a refreshing drink after exercises and bouts. Both come to know each other's strengths and weaknesses as boxers, but they are equally sure that they will never have to fight each other. Then the day comes when the sports commission matches the two as opponents. Since the usual winner of all his matches is not exactly in the best condition for the fight, the question is raised among the boys' classmates whether friendship will prevail as usual.

The audience is let in on one of the boy's determination to win at any cost. When the fight is over, and the tables are turned on the one who abused his friendship, the school bystanders feel that perhaps friendship had really prevailed after all and the match was thrown. The boys, however, know that things will never really be the same between them again.

Scenes are strongly directed and often strikingly lensed, but pic's main attraction is helmer's accurate feel for acting types. —*Holl.*

Snimki Za Spomen
(Snapshots as Souvenirs)
(BULGARIAN-COLOR)

Sofia, July 6.

A Bulgarian Film Production. Savremenik Unit, Sofia; world rights. Film Bulgaria, Sofia. Features entire cast. Directed by Roumen Sourdjilski. Screenplay, Atanas Tsenev, Dimiter Dimitrov; camera (color), Vyacheslav Anev; art direction, Ivan Apostolov; music, Bozhidar Petkov. Reviewed at Film Bulgaria Screening Room, Sofia, July 5, '78. Running time: **90 MINS.**
Cast: Elena Dimitrova (Saska), Svetlana Atanassova (Nikolina), Iskra Genkova (Rosa), Elizabeth Nahoumova (Iskra), Galina Gancheva (Steffa), Mihail Mihailov (Mihail), Alexander Ilindenov (Georgi), Svilen Stoyanov (Kivi), Slavka Slavova (Filena), Stefan Iliev (Todorov).

A youth pic by a debut helmer, Roumen Sourdjilski's "Snapshots as Souvenirs" gets its message across in straightforward terms. It's about that recurrent youth problem common to all countries: a teacher in a high school abuses his trust by reprimanding two students for an action they are innocent of. The boy and girl involved stand up for their principles, but their moral courage only gets them deeper into trouble and violates their conscience at the same time. In fact, the compromise that is made by the girl leads to her attempted suicide after it's clear that none of the grownups about her are ready to defend the truth in the matter.

Conflict begins over a basketball game that was interrupted by an arrogant bystander — when he charges onto the court, a youth pushes him away and, for this effort, gets reprimanded in a letter by the offended individual to the school principal. The physical education teacher (and vice-director) of the school knows the truth as a witness, but feels it's correct to punish the boy involved all the same. When a girl in the class, Sashka, stands up for the innocent youth, she's doubly punished and receives a bad behavior mark that would prevent entrance into the university. Parents are also brought into the conflict, but it proves that nothing can be done to prevent the teacher from having his way in spite of everything. Things to from bad to worse: the girl compromises her principles and finally apologizes to the teacher for contradicting him in public. But since she lives alone with her mother (who is having some kind of affair with another man), she still feels betrayed and decides to leave home and live with a painter friend (who loves her and wants to marry her) in his attic apartment. Then when she spends the night of her graduation party there (instead of joining her classmates), she gets scolded by the apartment building's manager. This leads to the overdose of pills and near death.

Pic's strong point is that it doesn't show a way out at the end. The teacher is still in charge, and the girl has just about ruined all chances to further her future although she is a gifted, moral, and decent individual. The film simply presents the problem and allows the viewer to decide for himself.

Dialog and thesp performances are above average, while direction and lensing hold their own. Youth fest potential winner, all the same. —*Holl.*

ASIAN FEST

Jiken
(The Incident)
(JAPANESE-COLOR)

Singapore, July 5.

A Shochiku Company Ltd. release. Produced by Yoshitaro Nomura, Akira Oda. Directed by Yoshitaro Nomura. Features entire cast. Story, Shohei Oaka; screenplay, Kaneto Shindo; camera (color), Hakashi Karamata; music, Yashushi Aktagawa; sound, Akagasko Yamamoto; editor, Kasua Ota. Reviewed at Jade Theatre, Singapore, July 4, '79. Running time: **105 MINS.**

Hiroshi	Toshiyuki Nagashima
Yoshiko	Keiko Matsuzaka
Hatsuko	Shinobu Ohtake
Ueda	Tsuneihiko Watase

Producer-director Yoshitaro Nomura's "The Incident" is another murder mystery, in the tradition of his meticulously plotted and delivered works in this genre. His film, "Village of Eight Graves," the immediate predecessor to "Incident," won the best art direction prize in the 1977 Asian Fest.

A classic whodunit, no less, is attempted by Nomura. There are many topnotch supporting performers, including the former teacher of the dead woman, an old woman fruit seller, an old woodkeeper and a grocery store owner — all of them are asked to take the witness' stand. They contribute important clues and a great deal of comic relief as well.

There are interesting subplots about the judge and his two associates, and the rivalry between the defense and prosecution lawyers, both inside and outside the courtroom. It's always interesting how Nomura interprets the role of the press in crime reporting, except that this time there is no leading journalist character as in his other thrillers. Journalists are present this time only as extras, milling outside the courtroom, waiting to interview witnesses.

The main crux of the story revolves around four main players: Toshiyuki Nagashima, the murder suspect; Keiko Matsuzaka, his wife and the younger sister of the dead woman; Shinoku Ohtake, the alleged murder victim; and Tsuneihiko Watase, Ohtake's bodyguard and lover.

The best performance in a film with plenty of exemplary performers is given by Ohtake, who, in her various relationships with the other players, is one woman and many different persona at the same time.

The best thing about Yashushi Aktagawa's musical scoring is his eschewing stingers, which others just could not resist in a thriller. The romantic themes are beautiful, more western than Japanese, in accordance with pop usage in majority of Asian movie romances. Editing by Kasua Ota plays a significant contribution, and it's highly impressive.

Nomura received the Asian Fest prize for most convincing performance of human emotion for "The Incident." —*Cano.*

Mool-Dori Village
(KOREAN-COLOR)

Singapore, July 6.

A Hap Dong Films release. Produced by Kwak Jung Hwan. Directed by Lee Doo Yong, Zee Doo Yong. Features entire cast. Story and screenplay, Yu Dong Fun; camera (color), lighting and special effects, Song Ung Cha; music, Choi Yon Dong; sound, Han So Jong of Hanang Studio (Seoul). Reviewed at Jade Theatre, Singapore, July 5, '79. Running time: **100 MINS.**
Cast: Kim Young-Ran, Han So Ryong, Hyung Kil Soo, Kim Jung Ah

---

Based on an old Korean legend concerning the origins of a mask festival, the brothers Lee Doo Yong and Zee Doo Yong's film, a horror fantasy romance, could have been transformed into something much more grand and exciting.

It is also very enlightening to know that simple peasants and priests in a small Korean village imagined God is a woman. God's presence is represented through a woman's voice, warning the hero of future calamities and how best to avert them — something similar to the story of Moses, with less miracles, and perhaps that's what's missing in this Korean effort.

A young priest, played by Han So Ryong, receives a divine message that he and his woman, Kim Young-Ran, will be thrown in purgatory unless he makes masks and sends the woman away while he is at work. Young-Ran becomes impatient and restless. Not without reason, because while she seems quite determined to spend the waiting period praying before a shrine, lascivious monks always come to force here away and try to rape her. She falls down a hill trying to escape from an evil monk who desires her. Later, sick and delirious, she has but one dying wish: to see her "darling" for the last time.

Intercutting of scenes between Young-Ran on her way to Ryong's tent, and the latter carving wooden masks fails to impress the hardships of mask-making, precisely because the dying woman seems to be having a much more difficult time just trying to reach the tent.

Young-Ran's very expressive lovely face makes an engrossing camera subject. She makes it seem as though it's not necessary to follow the story, there's more going on in her face. She might have turned into an old hag or a witch in her determination to oppose divine will, but the filmmakers seemed even more dead set on not making her look ugly.

The enactment of the curse on the lovers could also have been visualized as a far more splendid display of photographic and special effects than what the film contains. The filmmakers settle for something unsatisfactory, mainly because it starts the viewer thinking of other ways it could have been handled.

For her performance in "Mooldori Village," Kim Young-Ran received an award for outstanding actress in a costume drama.

—*Cano.*

He Never Gives Up
(TAIPEI-COLOR)

Singapore, July 5.

A Central Motion Picture Company release. Produced by Mei Chang-Ling. Directed by Lee Hsing. Executive producer, Koo Chen Fu. Features entire cast. Story, Cheng Feng Shih; screenplay, Chang Yung Hsiang; camera (color), Chen Kuen Howe; lighting, Lin Den Huang; sound, Lee Ya Tong; music, Tang Wong. Reviewed at Prince Theatre, Singapore, July 4, '79. Running time: 115 MINS.

Cast: Chin Han, Lin Feng-Chiao, Tsao Chien, Liu Meng Yuan, Ou Di.

The most talked about and most sensational b.o. attraction of the Asian Fest Silver Jubilee in Singpore, "He Never Gives Up" is based on the true story of a cripple, Cheng Feng Shih, who became one of Taiwan's 10 Most Outstanding Young Men two years ago, shortly before he died.

Born into a large family, Cheng, played by Ou Di as a child and Chin Han as an adult, had deformed feet. His family would have let him die but his uncle, who made a living performing shows with a trained monkey in marketplaces, intervened and offered to bring him up.

The little cripple's life is sorrowful. He loses his uncle at an early age and is forced to return to his family. His fifth brother is his closest ally against the other children in their village, but brother cannot always be around when needed. During one stormy night, little Cheng is left alone to cope with a rising flood, a collapsing shelter and a hundred ducks belonging to the family. His father and brothers arrive just in time to rescue him, providing one of the film's most dramatic moments.

Later, there's a repeat of the same situation with Cheng as a young man left by himself in an abandoned boarding house during a typhoon. This time his girl friend, played by Lin Feng-Chiao, comes to his assistance, saving him from drowning as well as promising never to leave him again, since she almost broke up with him because her father told her to do so.

Cheng's greatest achievement is the publication of his autobiography, which takes some time to win readers. When the book finally takes off, they can't print enough copies to satisfy the demand for it. Cheng then gives a series of inspirational talks to cripples. His acceptance speech during the 10 Outstanding Young Men ceremony is pic's major highlight, and though it seems a facile way of summing up the hero's existence in his own words, the emotional impact on viewers is undeniable.

The conclusion, which takes place during the appropriately melancholy Autumn Festival, deals with the last days of Cheng's life.

None of the films in this year's Asian Fest can vie with "He Never Gives Up" in popularity. It's a melodrama that lots of people feel they can like as well as believe, because it actually happened.

Pic won the most number of prizes for any single film entered in the Asian Fest — a total of four awards for best direction in a drama film to Lee Hsing, most moving performance by an actor in a tragic drama to Chin Han, most outstanding actress to Lin Feng-Chiao and the Organization Catholique International Du Cinema (OCIC) Award to the producer, Mei Chang Ling. —*Cano.*

November 1828
(INDONESIAN-COLOR)

Singapore, July 6.

An Inter Studio and Gemini Satria Films release. Produced by Nyoohansiang. Written and directed by Teguh Karya. Features entire cast. Camera (color), Tantra Suryadi; music, Frankie Raden; sound, S. Parman; editor, Tantra Suryadi; production designer, Benni Benhari. Reviewed at Jade Theatre, Singapore, July 5, '79. Running time: 135 MINS.

Capt. De Borst	Slamet Rahardjo
Laras	Jenny Rachman
Kromoludiro	Maruli Sitompul
Lt. Van Aken	El Manik
Baoa Demang	Rahmat Hidayat
Kromoludiro's Wife	Sumarti Rendra

Winner of five awards in the Indonesian Film Festival two months ago, including best picture, "November 1828," the most expensive Indonesian production released this year, deals with the events leading to Indonesia's fight for independence led by two war heroes, Sentot and Diponegoro.

The story, however, is not told from the viewpoints of the two major heroes. Sentot is often mentioned in awe and admiration but does not put in an appearance, and Diponegoro appears only briefly in the concluding portion.

Historical time and space are not all-encompassing but limited to events set in a small village during the early stages of the uprising.

A village patriot, Kromoludiro (Maruli Sitompul), is betrayed by his neighbor to the Dutch authorities, an army contingent led by a Capt. De Borst, played by Slamet Rahardjo. Topbilling goes to the villain, Rahardjo, bemoustached and bespectacled, whose ambition is to become a general. Rahardjo and another officer, Lt. Van Aken (El Manik), have mixed parentage, Dutch father and Indonesian mother.

The main difference between the two men, as suggested by two brief flashbacks into their childhoods is the fact that El Manik has always believed in the innate goodness of the Indonesian people, although raised to serve in the Dutch Army. On the other hand, Rahardjo is only interested in exercising power over the local people as a Dutch officer.

El Manik wishes to join the local people in their struggle for freedom, but it's too late. Rahardjo imprisons him, and by the time the villagers stage an uprising, Rahardjo sees to it that El Manik dies first.

Overdramatized is the misery and suffering of the village patriot's family. The patriot is also personally killed by Rahardjo when the former refuses to reveal the whereabouts of Sentot and Diponegoro. As the patriot's daughter, Jenny Rachman has the leading actress role, but she's given little to do.

The battle scenes feature hundreds of extras, but very similar to war pictures made earlier in the region — there's pandemonium, people shooting in all directions and clouds of dust and smoke veiling the proceedings more often than necessary.

The dilatory arrival of Diponegoro and his followers on horseback is shot in slow motion — an unfortunate choice.

By no means is the pic lacking in comic relief, however. The Judas figure is very funny, with quick darting eyes and a comical squint and gait that are perfectly in character, since he seems to be sneaking everywhere. And a regular comedian is also cast as a Dutch Army private, always saying and doing the wrong things.

"November 1828" leaves the viewer wondering what a picture with Sentot and Diponegoro as the actual central characters would have been like. Worshipful words from the villagers do not offer a clear picture of what these heroic men actually did for their country.

Predictably, "November 1828" was prized with the most outstanding historical presentation trophy. —*Cano.*

Death Has No Mercy
(FILIPINO-COLOR)

Singapore, July 6.

A Mairik Films release. Produced by Jesse Chua. Written and directed by Cesar Gallardo. Features entire cast. Camera (color), Rey Lapid; music, Ernanie Cuenco; sound, Rolly Rota; costumes and make-up, Rhoda Perez. Reviewed at Jade Theatre, Singapore, July 5, '79. Running time: 120 MINS.

Ben	Lito Lapid
Lisa	Marian de la Riva
Mando	Eddie Garcia
Pacita	Rosemarie Gil
Rodrigo	Nello Nayo

The only Filipino feature entry in this year's Asian Fest, "Death Has No Mercy" is an action drama about a young fighter (Lito Lapid) avenging the murder of his father by an army officer who coveted his mother for his wife, thus separating Lapid from his mother and younger sister. If that sounds rather complicated, it is not at all unfamiliar to Asian viewers, however.

Lapid is raised by an uncle, who teaches the former the art of "arnis," which employs a long stick in one hand and a short one in the other. From childhood the boy trains to become a highly skilled fighter.

His body is tied up with ropes and he twists and turns on the ground as the uncle pulls at the ropes. The same ropes are used to let Lapid perform high leaps. He is also required to clear a column of low bamboo archs, akin to limbo dancing.

The villain, played by Eddie Garcia, who has distinguished himself as a Filipino movie "contrabida" (bad guy) over the years, employs a lot of hooligans in his warehouse near the seaport — the same goons who were accomplices in the kidnapping of Lapid's mother and sister.

Garcia orders his men to kill Lapid's uncle, who happens to witness the massacre of labor union leaders opposing Garcia's will. This gives Lapid all the more reason to seek vengeance. In between fights, a close friendship develops between Lapid and his sister (Marian de la Riva), who, being unaware of their real relationships, falls in love with him.

Incest is quickly avoided with Lapid's decision to confront his mother with the truth in front of his sister. Between that and the final showdown between Lapid and Garcia are many more fights reiterating the same point: Lapid must go through the hired goons first before he could fight the big boss.

As a result, the fights become tiresome and unexciting after a while. To make the fights seem realistic, the hero takes on his enemies one at a time, man to man. But he seems to be pushing his luck too far, and nobody knows what's stopping his enemies from playing dirty and ganging up on him. Besides, with everybody, including the police, looking for him, the viewer assumes that he went into hiding, but then he is shown much later still working in the warehouse, which is a big strain on credibility.

As though to add to the confusion in the film, "Death Has No Mercy" received an Asian Fest prize as the best murder mystery. That certainly needs an explanation. While it is true that several murders occur in the pic, there is also no attempt whatsoever to hide the real identity of the mastermind. —*Cano.*

Tragedy Of Love
(SINGAPORE-COLOR)

Singapore, July 6.
A Shaw Bros. release. Producer, Runme Shaw. Written and directed by Chen Hung Lieh. Features entire cast. Camera (color). Chen Kuan Ho: music. Lua Ming Toh: sound. Tien Loo: executive producer. Mona Fong. Reviewed at Prince theatre, Singapore. July 5, '79. Running time: 110 MINS.

Cast: Liu Shang Chien. Chow Tan Wei.

Young love as a film theme is invariably destined to become a b.o.

hit. Especially if the love team featured happens to be two such popular teenage idols as Liu Shang Chien and Chow Tan Wei. Entered in the Asian Fest Silver Jubilee as a Singapore feature entry, "Tragedy of Love" was made and shot in Taipei and the stars also are from there.

The film is episodic, the leading players go through one crisis after another.

This young couple have all sorts of problems — all commonplace. Where does the sad part come in? In the final portion, when the couple's baby dies of neglect, because everybody's too busy with other problems. Wei, feeling guilty about her baby's death, jumps off a bridge and drowns herself.

For a film that's supposed to be a tragedy, this pic is still 90% comedy drama, which is more than enough reason for fans to forgive the filmmakers for letting Wei die in it.

Chow Tan Wei copped the most moving performance by an actress in a tragic drama for her performance in "Tragedy of Love," which, together with "He Never Gives Up," was the big b.o. hit of the fest. —*Cano.*

The First Error Step
(SINGAPORE-COLOR)

Singapore, July 5.
A Golden Star Berhad release. Produced by Yap Chin Hock. Directed by Au-Yang Chong. Features entire cast. Story and screenplay. Ma Sha: camera (color), Chin Hu: music. Ma Hwa: sound, Chin Hon. Reviewed at Jade Theatre. Singapore. July 4. '79. Running time: 100 MINS.
Cast: Ma Sha. Yang Hui San. Chin Po.

Another film version of a true story, "The First Error Step" is based on the autobiography of Ma Sha, who also wrote and stars. Left in the care of his grandmother from childhood, Ma Sha longs to be with his parents, but neither his father, a rich businessman, nor his mother, a prostitute, wants any further involvement with him apart from giving him money, which is of course not what he really wants — he wants love.

Ma Sha makes a living in the streets selling cigarettes as a child, then pimping at 18 in a brothel, where he gets into a fight and kills one of the customers — thereby committing the "first error step" of the title.

Then, he spends the next twelve years of his life in prison. He escapes. The police bring him back. He goes into solitary for fighting with another problem prisoner. Finally, he is taken to an isolated island used as a military reform school.

Paroled for good behavior, Ma Sha is in his early thirties and wants

a change — an honest living and a family he can call his own. Being an ex-con does not make things easy.

Looking for a publisher with his life's story, Ma Sha discovers nobody is interested. But his luck changes for the better at about the same time that his wife gives birth to a son. One night, he rescues a woman from some thugs and lands in a hospital. He makes front page news. The reporters learn he has written a book, and one of them offers to help Ma Sha find a publisher.

"Ma Sha" also copped the Asian Fest prize for outstanding screenplay depicting moral values.

—*Cano.*

Lantern Festival Adventure
(TAIPEI-COLOR)

Singapore, July 6.
A Central Motion Picture Company release. Produced by Hu Cheng Ting. Directed by Chang Pei Cheng. Executive producer, Ma Han Ying. Features entire cast. Story and screenplay. Szuma Ching Yuan: camera (color). Wang Chi Yang: lighting. Wu Chich: editor. Li Chich: music. Tony Wong: sound. Li Kuan U. Reviewed at Jade Theatre. Singapore. July 5. '79. Running time: 100 MINS.
Cast: Huang I-Lung. Liu Huan Kuo. Tang Chin. Chang Fu-Chine.

Like Chinese swordplay epics, kung fu films are here to stay. There was talk among Chinese film producers two years ago of coming up with something to replace kung fu as the main staple of Chinese pix, but they soon discovered that they have by no means exhausted its possibilities.

As popularized by Bruce Lee, kung fu had to be taken seriously. It wasn't until Chen Long achieved tremendous popularity through kung fu comedies over a year ago that a whole new series of kung fu pix was born.

"Lantern Festival Adventure" is a further extension of the comical kung fu genre, employing two child stars, a boy (Huang I-Lung) and a girl (Liu Huan Kuo) as its hero and heroine. With such new developments, it seems certain that the kung fu genre can go on indefinitely.

Owing to the often very violent and gory content of previous kung fu films, they were not accessible to children. Now, a lighthearted look at kung fu, "Lantern Festival Adventure" cannot be mistaken for anything but wholesome family fare.

Eventually, good triumphs over evil with all the villains promising to turn a new leaf. As an old storyteller sums up his story, the children promptly say they have heard the same message "eight hundred times," and yet they are all looking forward to the next story-

telling session.

Child actor Huang I-Lung copped the most outstanding child actor prize for his performance in "Lantern Festival Adventure" in this year's Asian Fest. —*Cano.*

Dendang Perantau
(Stranger's Melody)
(MALAYSIAN-COLOR)

Singapore, July 5.
A Varia Film Productions release. Produced by Mustafa Haji Ton. Written and directed by Jamil Sulong. Features entire cast. Camera (color). Abdul Rackman: lighting. Roger Idris: music. Kasem Masdoor: sound. Peter Lim of Perfima Studio. Kuala Lumpur: editor. Salehan: costumes and make-up. Yurni Mustafa. Reviewed at Jade Theatre. Singapore. July 4. '79. Running time: 100 MINS.
Des Iskandar . . . . Rathip Ibrahim
Emilia . . . . Uji Raschid
Farid . . . . Hali Amir
Farida . . . . Deh Farida
Adilah . . . . Urni Ka Isuk
Datu Arif . . . . Rurnaino

Asian actresses usually retain their popularity longer than Asian actors. Nowhere is this more evident at present in this region than in Malaysia, where film producers are frantically searching for new actors to play opposite top actresses, because former leading male actors have diminished b.o. appeal.

In this Malaysian Asian Fest entry, for instance, topbilled is actress Uji Raschid, opposite a new male star, Rathip Ibrahim. Raschid's former co-star, Hali Amir, now plays second lead. The story is a college campus romance, and the fact that Raschid is a bit older than her coed role calls for is just casually ignored.

Parents' attitudes, especially fathers who impose their will on their children, once again pose the major dilemma. Both Raschid's father and Amir's father, who are business partners, have made up their mind that their offspring should wed each other, turning a deaf ear to what their wives and children have to say.

Just at the point where a happy ending seems inevitable, tragedy strikes — something that seems to be gaining immense popularity in most recent Asian love tales.

Malaysia has been actively producing color pix only in the past few years. Until last year, the majority of the country's features were still being shot in black and white. This makes Abdul Rackman's highly professional camerawork quite an achievement and on a par with that of some Asian cameramen with much more experience.

"Dendang Perantau" copped the most outstanding sound recording prize, won by Peter Lim of Perfima Studio. Kuala Lumpur.

—*Cano.*

Shaolin Rescuers
(HONG KONG-COLOR)

Singapore, July 5.

A Shaw Bros. release. Produced by Run Run Shaw. Directed by Chang Cheh. Executive producer, Mona Fong. Features entire cast. Screenplay, Chang Cheh, Yi Kuang. Chei Nai-bin: camera (color). Tsao Hui-chi: editor, Chiang Hsing-lung and Li Yen-kai: art director, Johnson Tsao: music, Cheng Yung-yu: martial art instructors, Tai Chi-hsien, Lu Fung and Chiang Sheng. Reviewed at Jade theatre, Singapore, July 4, '79. Running time: 100 MINS.

Chen Ah-chin	Lo Meng
Liang Ta-Pao	Kuo Chue
Chu Tsai	Sun Chien
Han Chei	Chiang Sheng
Kao Chen-chung	Lu Feng
Hung Hsi-kuan	Pai Piao
Chien Shih-kon	Ku Kuan-chung
Feng Tan-chung	Yang Huan
Chen Szu	Tsao Tao-hua

As Chinese filmmakers keep going back to the Ming and Ching dynasties in search of new variants of kung fu, they never fail to come up with surprises. In "Shaolin Rescuers," it's something director Chang Cheh calls "Black Tiger kung fu."

The real charm of Cheh's new pic rests not with the novel fighting style, but with the choice of stars. There are four new action stars introduced here: Lo Meng, Kuo Chue, Sun Chien and Chiang Sheng.

Cheh's four heroes are young and poor, using all their spare time to practice and improve thier kung fu. Meng is an assistant in a beancurd shop, Chue, a restaurant waiter, Chien, a dyeing mill worker and Sheng, an actor with a traveling Chinese opera group. Since they happen to be all new actors, fans are curious to find out if these newcomers can compare with the top kung fu stars.

Always the inevitability of leaving too many dead bodies behind in the course of their fight for justice dictate that kung fu heroes perish themselves in the end — they live in a world of blood for blood. This rules out sequels, but no successful kung fu filmmaker ever worried about that, since there is always a way of bring back kung fu stars.

"Shaolin Rescuers" is cleaning up in the Far East, which means that the new Shaw Bros. action stars have bright careers ahead of them.

The main villain of the pic, Lu Feng, received the most outstanding supporting actor in an action film prize in this year's Asian Fest. —Cano.

La Rochelle Fest

Morte Di Un Operatore
(Death of a Cameraman)
(ITALIAN-COLOR-16m)

La Rochelle, July 17.
RAI-TV release of Ager Cinematografica, RAI production. Features entire cast. Written and directed by Faliero Rosati. Camera (Color), Angelo Bevilacqua. Reviewed at La Rochelle Film Fest, July 7, '79. Running time 65 MINS.
With: Daniele Griggio, Remo Remotti.

Faliero Rosati was reportedly an assistant of filmmaker Michelangelo Antonioni. Understandably, he could be influenced. Here a video strip on the killing of a cameraman during the Arab-Israeli War is as obsessive as the photo in Antonioni's "Blowup."

A reporter comes to the Sinai with the bit of tape and a portable video machine. The tape shows a man shot by a soldier and then dying in a room. He is trying to find that room. He cannot get a guide and finds a deserted town and finally the room. He has left on his video camera and it has picked up the face of a young girl — or was the image on the original tape?

The mystical side, accompanied by mirages, is well handled but film remains somewhat portentous. However, it does give an insight into audivisual hallucination and marks Rosati a director to watch when he can get off the track of artifice.

It is more an interesting idea than a film without the revelation or depth for any theatrical showings. However, it could win tv outings and, of course, festivals. —Mosk.

Kuldetes
(Portrait of a Champion)
(HUNGARIAN-B&W-DOCU)

La Rochelle, July 17.
Hungarofilm release of Studio Objectiv production. Conceived and directed by Ferenc Kosa. Camera (black and white), Janos Gulyas, Ferenc Kaplar. Reviewed at La Rochelle Film Fest, July 7, '79. Running time, 96 MINS.

It isn't even necessary to know what the pentathlon is in the Olympics to savor this documentary on a most unusual man. Andras Balczo won the pentathlon five times, probably a world record, but film is more about him as a man and coming to grips with his life after his sports career that is the crux of this outspoken, penetrating and absorbing Magyar documentary.

It is in black and white but not talking heads. For Balczo, besides being photogenic, which helps, is shrewdly interrogated and

emerges a decent man without being sanctimonious or self-aggrandizing. He quit at 34, refused lucrative offers to train people from many countries but found himself not used much in his own country where he elected to stay.

Never bitter for not being put in charge of choosing and training pentathlon athletes, he is seen at one time helping put up hurdles at a horse jumping demonstration.

Director Ferenc Kosa, a feature director who won a prize at Cannes for "10,000 Suns," gets a bit portentous in asking questions about the worth of Balczo's wins, whether he could change lives and what it was all worth.

This works well against Balczo's deceptively simple ways. The man felt people were with him and at one time saw hundreds running alongside a cross country race with him. It was something worth doing and could not change lives but could help give dignity and pleasure.

Balczo talks about his reading, his sudden need for human contact after years of solitary athletic dedication and his hopes for getting the Olympic choices based on ability and dedication without any red tape or pressures. His crying when a son is born springs from a humble character but he is never a self-pitying one.

He makes clear the differences between humble and humiliation when he insists his doing workman chores at athletic meets is useful. If a film could change things, it would be fine if Balczo did get the job he deserved. Maybe he has, but the important thing is a film that amply depicts a personality by fine observation. Film is a record of a truly unusual man worth tv and school use though perhaps not the stuff for theatrical needs. — Mosk.

Al Aswar
(The Walls)
(IRAKIAN-COLOR)

La Rochelle, July 17.
ETC release and production. Features entire cast. Directed by Muhammad Shoukri Jamil. Features entire cast. Screenplay, Sabry Moussa, Fawaz Mouaffar Khidr from a book by Abd-er Rahmane Rabi; camera (Eastmancolor), Rifate Abdelhamid; editor, Amer arakoushi, Jamil. Reviewed at La Rochelle Film Fest, July 5, '79. Running time, 94 MINS.
With: Ibrahim Jalal, Abdel Hamio, Saadiya Zobeydi, Tou'ma Tamini.

Iraq has not been heard from lately on the film festival circuits, nor have many other Arab countries. Film, about a revolt against an oppressive regime in the '50s, has some brio but flat and near stereotyped characters. There is some promising work by director Muhammad Shoukri Jamil who keeps this politico potboiler perking.

There is a good man, a barber, who serves as a rallying point for growing distrust of the corruption of the regime at the time. There is a conservative type for the regime and young students ready to stage demonstrations as the police repressiveness gets more severe.

Film has some personal bravura as a policeman's son is killed in a student parade or another's daughter refuses to be wed to a man she considers an informer. There is some knowhow in the mixture of drama, resistance and action, but, on the whole, film is a predictable, surface affair that is reviewed mainly for the record. More for home and informative fests or archive showings abroad than having the flair for any commercial possibilities. —Mosk.

Panny Z Wilka
(The Young Ladies of Wilko)
(POLISH-FRENCH-COLOR)

La Rochelle, July 17.
Film Polski-Films Moliere release of Ensemble X-Pierson Productions production. Features entire cast. Directed by Andrzej Wajda. Screenplay, Zbigniew Kaminski from the book by Jaroslav Iwaszkiewicz; camera (Eastmancolor), Edward Klosinski; editor, Halina Prugar; music, Karol Szymanowski. Reviewed at La Rochelle Film Fest, July 7, '79. Running time, 118 MINS.

Victor	Daniel Olbrychski
Jula	Anna Seniuk
Tunia	Christine Pascal
Jola	Maja Komorowska
Zosia	Stanislawa Celinska
Kazia	Krystyna Zachwatowicz

Noted Polish director Andrzej Wajda has been in fine form of late. After two political films that had problems at home but high popularity, as well as at film festivals and in some Western countries, "The Man of Marble," on Stalinism, and "Rough Treatment," on bureaucratic pressures, his latest is a romantic period piece and a truly successful change-of-pace.

Film takes place in the late 20s with a Chekhovian atmosphere of longing, an attempt to return to the past without undue sentimentality and revealing touches and characterization. The characters are human and touching rather than pathetic.

With the scare, war and violent pix so prevalent these days, this quiet, pensive but revealing look at people in stress and decision might find its audiences with the right placement. A Polski-French co-production, it still remains Polish in its panache and perception.

A thirtyish young man, who heads a small factory, faints at the funeral of a close friend. He decides to go home to his aunt and uncle for a while, but gets involved with a family of five women who had all been in love with him at one time though he had apparently loved only one, who, unknown to him, had died since his departure.

Wajda wisely uses no flashbacks except for two quick shots of the dead girl as the man, played with perception by Daniel Olbrychski, talks of a time he had seen her nude after a swim. The women are mainly disillusioned with life or estranged from husbands while the youngest has a crush on him.

Christine Pascal, a French thesp, is well dubbed and the right mixture of tenseness and shyness as the younger girl he also spurns. Before he can get trapped in this twilight life, he decides to leave again.

Wajda obviously felt and enjoyed this tale which is communicated in airy direction and perceptive progression. He has also again focused on an 85-year-old writer, Jaroslav Iwaszkiewicz. He adapted another book of his, "The Birch Forest," and now this reveals a writer of deft flair for the human comedy.

In fact, Iwaszkiewicz appears at the end in the same train as the hero after the latter leaves. It may be a bow to the writer, who is held in closeup, or a portent of the hero's old age. At any rate, an unusual film that deserves attention in world climes. It has opened in Paris to good reviews and fair early biz. Tony Moliere, who released Wajda's "The Man of Marble" successfully locally, was coproducer and local distrib of this excellent new Wajda film. —*Mosk.*

Ce Repondeur Ne Prend Pas De Message
(This Answering Service Takes No Messages)
(FRENCH-COLOR)

La Rochelle, July 17.
Xavier Saint-Macary release and production. Written and directed by Alain Cavalier. Features entire cast. Camera (Color), Jean-Francois Robin. No other credits available. Reviewed at La Rochelle Film Fest. May 6, '79. Running time. **80 MINS.**

Alain Cavalier started in '62 with some promising films on budding fascism, the touchy Algerian War and then went in for more commercial items before opting out for a few years and then surfacing with a so-so comedy and a more interesting love story involving two deluded people, "Martin and Lea."

Now he comes up with an extremely personal, small-budgeted (reportedly $40,000) film that seems a personal exorcism or a cry of loneliness and despair. A man comes to an apartment and proceeds to break up the chairs and paint himself in, including the windows, after a few attempts to scare up people in other apartments which are all deserted.

He then begins to burn the wood from the destroyed chairs. The hero has a bandaged head a la Claude Rains in "The Invisible Man" except that his eyes show. He had had an automobile accident and it seems a woman with him was killed.

The man talks of this woman and others as he blacks out the apartment and his past life which may be an act of renewal. Actually Cavalier's wife, promising actress Irene Tunc, was killed in an accident some years ago and her picture is seen during the solo character's talk of women.

But that is for insiders. The film has a strange hypnotic quality that could slant this for festival, archive and maybe even specialized cult showings but appears difficult for general commercial showings. Done in chronological order, film does display a growing tension as mixed talk of the past counterpoints the personage's physical cutting himself from life which might be a renewal or the end.

Now Cavalier may re-emerge on the film scene after his eclipse. He does display a solid craftsmanship, despite his diffuse theme, in this off-beater. —*Mosk.*

The Amityville Horror
(COLOR)

Film likely to have book's success, also its problems.

Hollywood, July 24.
An American International Pictures release. produced by Ronald Saland and Elliot Geisinger. Exec producer, Samuel Z. Arkoff. Directed by Stuart Rosenberg. Features entire cast. Screenplay, Sandor Stern, based on book by Jay Anson; camera (color), Fred J. Koenekamp; editor. Robert Brown: art direction, Kim Swados; visual effects design, William Cruse; special effects. Delwyn Rheaume; music. Lalo Schifrin. Reviewed at Goldwyn Studios. Hollywood, July 24, '79. (MPAA rating: R.) Running time: 117 MINS.

George Lutz	James Brolin
Kathleen Lutz	Margot Kidder
Father Delaney	Rod Steiger
Father Bolen	Don Stroud
Amy	Natasha Ryan
Greg	K.C. Martel
Matt	Meeno Peluce
Jeff	Michael Sacks
Carolyn	Helen Shaver
Sgt. Gionfriddo	Val Avery
Jackie	Amy Wright
Father Ryan	Murray Hamilton
Father Nuncio	John Larch
Aunt Helena	Irene Dailey

"The Amityville Horror" has all the tingles and terrors of a classic haunted-house story, plus an address familiar to all the millions who bought the book. Advance interest appeared keen as pic opened Friday on 810 screens. But the film may be more fun for those who haven't read the book.

Taken from the Jay Anson tome, Sandor Stern's script deals faithfully with the supposedly true (but since challenged) story of the Lutz family who move into a home in Amityville, N.Y. at a knocked-down price because of its bloody history. According to Anson's reporting, the Lutz' fled 28 days later in terror. (Original town didn't want film made there: Tom's River, New Jersey was substituted — Ed.)

Stepfather James Brolin, mother Margot Kidder and moppets Natasha Ryan, Meeno Peluce and K.C. Martel sympathetically play the happy innocent family and director Stuart Rosenberg — ably aided by efex specialists William Cruse and Delwyn Rheaume — have the house all ready for them.

Flies swarm where they shouldn't; pipes and walls ooze ick; doors fly open; and priests and psychic sensitives cringe and flee in panic. It's definitely a house that audiences will enjoy visiting, especially if unfamiliar with the ending.

But the problem with the film, as with the book, is the lack of resolvable conflict. Without doubt, this is as written, a terrifying domicile. but so overwhelming there's no way to fight back. Brolin and Kidder can only suffer, taking out their fears on each other.

As priests. Rod Steiger and Don Stroud are no match either for whatever inexplicable evil has gripped the home and Steiger finally overacts his defeat, as he has a tendency to do at the hands of a director who doesn't control him.

Family friends Michael Sacks and Helen Shaver are good, she especially in one psychically vibrating scene. And Val Avery, as the cop familiar with the house's deadly history, also must stand by.

Readers, to be sure, will know the weakness of the ending (made more so by post-Anson revelations that the next family to occupy the same house lived there happily ever after.) Nonreaders will at least have a visual buildup equal to the book.

Lalo Schifrin's score, employing unusual instruments, is properly spooky and Fred J. Koenekamp gets all out of his camera that's needed for a slick, professional ghost story. Or whatever it is that has that house in its frightening grip. And it is frightening. — *Har.*

The Concorde-Airport '79
(COLOR)

Another in-flight movie, with predictable results.

Hollywood, July 27.
A Universal Pictures release of a Jennings Lang production. Produced by Lang. Directed by David Lowell Rich. Features entire cast. Screenplay, Eric Roth, from a story by Lang, inspired by the film "Airport" based on the novel by Arthur Hailey; camera (color), Philip Lathrop; editor. Dorothy Spencer; production design. Henry Bumstead; music, Lalo Schifrin; costume design, Burton Miller; set decoration, Marry Ann Biddle, Mickey S. Michaels; sound. Jim Alexander; special photographic effects, Universal Hartland; special visual effects. Abe Milrad; stunt coordinator, George Sawaya; assistant director. Newton Arnold. Reviewed at Samuel Goldwyn Theatre, BevHills, July 27, 1979 (MPAA Rating: PG). Running time: **123 MINS.**

Metrand	Alain Delon
Maggie	Susan Blakely
Kevin Harrison	Robert Wagner
Isabelle	Sylvia Kristel
Patroni	George Kennedy
Eli	Eddie Albert
Francine	Bibi Andersson
Margarita	Charo
Robert Palmer	John Davidson
Alicia	Andrea Marcovicci
Loretta	Martha Raye
Elaine	Cicely Tyson
Boisie	Jimmie Walker
O'Neill	David Warner
Nelli	Mercedes McCambridge
Coach Markov	Avery Schreiber
Amy	Sybil Danning
Gretchen	Monica Lewis
Dr. Stone	Nicolas Coster
William Halpern	Robin Gammell
Froelich	Jon Cedar

Where else could producer Jennings Lang and Universal take their "Airport" series but further up in the air? Result is "The Concorde - Airport '79," fourth in the lucrative ($85,000,000-plus in cumulative domestic film rentals) series. This time the odd-shaped, supersonic jet takes center stage, a wise move that spares audiences most, if not all, the banalities that characterized the three previous pix. Unintentional comedy still seems the "Airport" series' forte, although excellent special effects work, and some decent dramatics should help "Concorde" take off to good boxoffice results. It's worth noting, however, that returns on each pic have dropped precipitously since the 1975 original, a trend latest entry will have to reverse.

Definitely not for sophisticates, "Concorde" is a throwback to the old popcorn genre, and rather enjoyable at that. The writing credit is suitably complicated (Eric Roth scripted from a story by Lang, in turn "inspired" by the original "Airport" and Arthur Hailey's novel), but plot turns will be familiar even to those not acquainted with the earlier pix.

This time out, the title entity is pursued by a dogged electronic missile, avoids an attack by a French fighter jet, barely makes a runway landing with no brakes, suffers a lost cargo door that rips open the bottom of the plane, manages a crash landing in an Alpine snow bank, and explodes just as its chic passengers disembark. That's all just part of a couple of days' work for pilots George Kennedy, Alain Delon and flight engineer David Warner.

Behind all these evil machines is billionaire industrialist Robert Wagner, who's trying to stop newshen and girlfriend Susan Blakely from spilling the beans on his illegal arm sales. Just why Blakely continues to tote this info halfway around the globe isn't too clear, but that's just one of plot contrivances lost somewhere in the jet stream.

Along for the ride is the usual cast of glossy characters, this time numbering stewardess Sylvia Kristel, who somnolently rekindles her affair with Delon; airlines head Eddie Albert and terrified spouse Sybil Danning; sportscaster John Davidson and Russian gymnast Andrea Marcovicci, sneaking kisses behind the back of coach Mercedes McCambridge; weightlifter Avery Schreiber and his deaf daughter, Cicely Tyson bearing a heart transplant for her dying son; and Monica Lewis, now on the other side of the aisle after a stint as a stewardess in "Airport '77," as a jazz singer accompanied by saxophonist Jimmie Walker.

Martha Raye provides overt comic relief as a restroom frequenter, although she gets stiff competition from much of Roth's dialog. Bibi Andersson is grounded as a Paris hooker matched up with Kennedy by Delon, and Charo has a

mercifully brief walk-on. Rest of cast is undistinguished, although Jon Cedar makes an impression as a shifty mechanic.

Real star, of course, is the Concorde itself, and Universal's various special effects wizards deliver in fine fashion. While some of the matte work lacks credibility, Cleo E. Baker's miniature sequences are outstanding, especially the two landing segments, and MCA's in-house Hartland group did a super job with the in-air footage. George Sawaya's stunt people are adroit, and Philip Lathrop photographs the entire jumble in suitably cheery colors. Lalo Schifrin's score leaves no diaster unnoticed.

While not a film that calls for acting honors, "Concorde" does feature some better-than-average thesping from Delon, who survives the transition to American pix surprisingly well, Warner and Kennedy, the one running character in the series. Blakely is okay as the media gal, and Wagner makes a most convincing villain. Everyone else seems along for the ride, and not much more.

Director David Lowell Rich does his best, but this is one example of a self-created genre with a life and mind of its own, much as the James Bond series has taken on super-real dimensions. In fact, that could be the pairing that could put a graceful end to both cycles: "James Bond Meets Concorde In Airport '81."
—Poll.

The Great American Bugs Bunny- Road-Runner Chase
(ANIMATED-COLOR)

Bugs and friends in vintage form, though careful sell needed.

Hollywood, July 25.
A Warner Bros. release of a Chuck Jones production. Produced, directed by Chuck Jones. Screenplay, Mike Maltese, Jones; production designer, Maurice Noble; music, Carl Stalling, Milt Franklyn; editor, Treg Brown; graphics, Don Foster; "Bugs Bunny At Home" co-director, Phil Monore; production designer, Ray Aragon; music, Dean Elliott; editor, Horta Editorial; voice characterization, Mel Blanc. Reviewed at the Burbank Studios, July 25, '79. (MPAA Raging: G). Running time: **97 MINS.**

"The Great American Bugs Bunny-Road-Runner Chase" is a nice 40th birthday present from Chuck Jones to the irrepressible rabbit which should make older audiences warm with nostalgia and provides younger viewers the chance to see some vintage cartoons on the big screen for the first time. Compilation film, with about 20 minutes of new footage, was first released in April in some test mar-

kets as "The Great American Chase," with Warners now planning to send it out as "The Bugs Bunny-Road-Runner Movie," although the title listed above is what appears on the screen. Given the format and preponderance of recycled material, b.o. prospects might appear questionable, although careful handling in specialized situations could pay off a la "Bugs Bunny Superstar" a few years back.

Fresh animation, spaced throughout pic, presents Bugs in retirement at his carrot palace in Beverly Hills looking back at some of the more memorable adventures he and cohorts such as Daffy Duck, Elmer Fudd and Porky Pig indulged in between 1939-62, while Jones was a member of the Warners animation department. A sort-of "That's Entertainment" in drawings, film features five complete Bugs Bunny shorts and scenes from 24 other cartoons, including the classic "Duck Amuck," a great laugh on, and illustration of, the art of animation.

In-jokes abound, and Bugs' home even includes a portrait gallery of others, besides Jones, who were so important to his development, such as Tex Avery, Friz Freleng, Robert McKimson, Mike Maltese and Mel Blanc. In line with the show biz inspiration of so many of the cartoons, new material features a humorous homage to the opening titles of "Star Wars," as well as another to "My Fair Lady."

The Road-Runner, which Jones created in 1948, makes its entrance after 75 minutes and a virtual montage of scenes featuring Wile E. Coyote's self-destructive attempts to intercept the bird, culled from 16 different cartoons, consumes pic's last 20 minutes.

Only off-key note is struck at the end, when Bugs uncharacteristically pontificates about the importance of laughter and chases in life. Otherwise, pic is undiluted vintage Chuck Jones which, whether they know his name or not, is good news for plenty of animation fans. —Cart.

The Lady In Red
(COLOR)

Corman returns to gangster folklore for another gundown. Okay prospects.

Hollywood, July 31.
A New World Pictures release of a Julie Corman production. Produced by Julie Corman. Co-producer, Steven Kovacs. Directed by Lewis Teague. Stars Pamela Sue Martin, Robert Conrad, Louise Fletcher. Screenplay, John Sayles; camera (color), Daniel Lacambre; editors, Larry Bock, Ron Medico, Lewis Teague; production design, Jac McAnelly; art direction, Philip

Thomas; set decoration, Keith Hein; music, James Horner; sound, Anthony Santa Croce; assistant director, Gerald T Olson; costumes, Danny Morgan, Pat Tonnema; second unit director, Pat Crowley. Reviewed at the Joe Shore Screening Room, L.A., July 27, '79. (MPAA Rating: R.) Running time **93 MINS.**

Polly Franklin	Pamela Sue Martin
John Dillinger	Robert Conrad
Anna Sage	Louise Fletcher
Jake Lingle	Robert Hogan
Rose Shimkus	Laurie Heineman
Eddie	Glenn Withrow
Pinetop	Rod Gist
Pops Geissler	Peter Hobbs
Frognose	Christopher Lloyd
Patek	Dick Miller
Tiny Alice	Nancy Anne Parsons
Melvin Purvis	Alan Vint

Ostensibly a return to the currently dormant gangster genre, "The Lady In Red" is in many ways a compendium of variations on the "woman in jeopardy" format New World has so thoroughly mined over the years. On her way to folklore immortality via her brief association with John Dillinger, the lady of the title gamely struggles through life as a tyrannized daughter, mistreated lover, ill-paid working girl, prisoner in a woman's ward, professional hooker and fullfledged gangster, among other roles. With proper exploitation handling, pic, which opened last week in Los Angeles and other western cities, should roll up satisfactory results in the usual Corman action market.

Having only begun shooting in late April, film bears no real traces of a rush job, although all-L.A. and under $1,000,000 budget minimized opportunities for much exterior recreation of 1930s Chicago and environs. By and large, production values are good, and while bloody shoot-ups punctuate the proceedings at regular intervals, primary emphasis, unsuually, is on characterization rather than action.

With her sights vaguely set on Hollywood, farm girl Pamela Sue Martin heads first for Chicago, where one mishap after another lands her in prison, then in the employ of classy madam Louise Fletcher. Bordello scenes provide director Lewis Teague with the opportunity to play some low-budget riffs on scenes from "The Damned" and "Pretty Baby."

After the bawdy house is closed down, Pamela Sue finally thinks she's found true love in Robert Conrad, but after he's gunned down outside the Biograph Theatre following a showing of "Manhattan Melodrama," she discovers that her man was really John Dillinger and that he'd been lying to her all along by saying that he really worked at the commodities exchange.

Though Fletcher was the real betrayer, Pamela Sue is branded by the press as the infamous "lady in red," so she turns to a life of crime and, at fadeout, finally heads for

Lotusland, albeit by a highly unlikely route.

Teague, a former second-unit director, guides his large cast reasonably well through John Sayles' craftsmanlike script, though neither brings anything new to the genre. Momentum is not as frantic as that in many former New World productions, and focus on character, rather than mayhem, is refreshing. Daniel Lacambre's lensing lends a clean, pro look to the proceedings.

Martin, looking quite modern and doing a few nude scenes, has definitely graduated from Nancy Drew, as she suffers life's injustices with plenty of grit. Conrad pops up briefly more than halfway through, and Fletcher is oke as the Rumanian backstabber, although her accent is impossible to pinpoint.

There's nothing terribly wrong with the film across the boards, and overall approach is much less exploitative than might have been expected under the circumstances, but there doesn't seem to be a whole lot of point to it either. —Cart.

Eagle's Wing
(BRITISH-COLOR)

The West, for art's sake.

London, July 25.
Rank Film Distributors release of a Peter Shaw production. Executive producer, Peter Shaw. Produced by Ben Arbeid. Directed by Anthony Harvey. Stars Martin Sheen, Sam Waterston. Screenplay, John Briley, based on an original story by Michael Syson; camera (color), Billy Williams; editor, Lesley Walker; music, Marc Wilkinson; sound, Simon Kaye; production designer, Herbert Westbrook; costumes, Tim Hutchinson; production supervisor, Bruce Sharman; asst. directors, Jake Wright, Manuel Munoz. Reviewed at the Prince Charles Theatre, London, July 24, '79. (BBFC Rating: A). Running Time: 104 MINS.

Pike	Martin Sheen
White Bull	Sam Waterston
Henry	Harvey Keitel
The Widow	Stephane Audran
Judith	Caroline Langrishe
The Priest	John Castle
Red Sky	Jorge Luke
Lame Wolf	Jose Carlos Ruiz
Miguel	Manuel Ojeda
Gonzalo	Jorge Russek
Jose	Pedro Damieari
Monk	Farnesio De Bernal
Girl	Cecilia Camacho
Sanchez	Cludio Brook
Don Luis	Julio Lucena
Shaman	Enrique Lucero

Claiming to evoke "the West, the way it really was, before the myths were born," British director Anthony Harvey's poised, loving linger in the 1830s badlands of New Mexico is primarily an art film — resolutely romantic, high on production values, low on grit.

Selective playoff with an eye to upmarket critical respect as a likely ally, must be the pattern, and re-

turns to cofinanciers the Rank Organization and Lamitas inevitably gradual. Where Sergio Leone's "spaghetti westerns" satisfied both buffs and action-seekers, the similarly-ritualized — but far gentler — "Eagle's Wing" holds little for the latter. But it could look to cult-status, and thus longevity, in some markets.

Ostensibly a tussle for possession of a uniquely fleet white horse (poetically described by the title), the distinctly allegorical plot pits Martin Sheen as a city-bred, novice trapper against a no-longer-so-young Indian brave, played with remarkable success by Sam Waterston. Wilier, and better equipped for survival on his own terrain, Waterston somewhat overstatedly embodies the independence keenly sought by Sheen, whose dogged attempts to reclaim the prize steed are really a pursuit of the Indian's soul.

Within that framework, other characters are merely dressing, though well enough conceived as such. Stephane Audran makes a tantalizing appearance as a sensual middle-aged widow, whose stagecoach is attacked and robbed by Waterston. He opts, however, to carry off an ordinarily nubile Irish cotraveller, unexceptionally played by Caroline Langrishe, with whom the resultant captor-captive interplay is less interesting than if, as initially expected, Audran had been the one.

Sheen, wild-eyed and vulnerable, is good casting and copes well with the central character's awkward soliloquizing. Harvey Keitel, lowkey but impressive as Sheen's companion and mentor, is lumbered with a lot of superfluous exposition dialog, then killed by Waterston before John Briley's screenplay (from Michael Syson's story) settles into a sparer and more effective style.

Once the verbiage has abated, Billy Williams' painstaking cinematography comes into its own, with fine exploitation of the anamorphic format. Dramatic skies, choice use of murkey halflight, and raw facial photography all contribute to an authentic sense of history-on-the-screen.

Tim Hutchinson's thoroughgoing costumes are equally helpful in that respect, as is the prevalence of untranslated Spanish (the drift is always clear) where appropriate.
— Simo.

The Servants
(HONG KONG-COLOR)

Hong Kong, June 20.
A Bang Bang Films Company Ltd. production. Produced by Jimmy Ip. Directed by Ronny Yu, Philip Chan. Stars Chu Kong, Hu Terry (Hu Yan Mou), Chan

Wai Man, Philip Chan, Melvin Wong, Lam Wai Kei. Camera (color), Henry Chan; editor, Wong Yee Shun; music, Joseph Koo; lyrics, James Wong; screenplay, Joyce Chan, Philip Chan, William Ho, Ronny Yu. Reviewed at Union Lab, June 19, 1979. Running Time: 90 MINS.
(English sub-titles with Cantonese soundtrack)

"The Servants" is another slam bang picture from Bang Bang's film factory unit. It is not "Jumping Ash II," as previously predicted. The literal translation of the Chinese title is "Inside and Outside the Cell Wall." Though still about cops and mobsters, young and westernized directors Ronny Yu and Philip Chan made the most of their under HK$1,000,000 budget, routine plot and 90-minutes running film time to create a super-glossy blood and gore pic that Hong Kong's contemporary mass audiences will love. They have succeeded in making an adequate and valid "now" film.

"The Servants" has all-action modern gimmicks and keeps going at a slick pace. There is also enough rough stuff to keep filmgoers awake.

The film begins with an influential Asian drug dealer in jail. Lau never forgets the fact that Inspector Chow is responsible for his being there. Chow (Chu Kong) is a good cop, perfect son and a drab, ordinary boy-next-door type. Lau plans in prison a two-pronged scheme, the first is to have Chow murdered and the other to stage a daring robbery of a diamond shipment from Italy.

However, an inside man is needed to complete the intricate plan and they require a policeman who heads the Blue Beret unit. That man is Pang (Philip Chan), an unconventional cop who loves gambling, cheap women and discos. Through a doctored card game, Pang is tricked to incur heavy debts and has not choice but to cooperate as an accomplice.

The film's high point is a sequence involving a train set that has been set to explode. A standard love song wails in the background which makes the situation ridiculously unreal.

Most viewers will marvel at the superior camerawork of Henry Chan. His cinematography helped a lot in elevating the tired story into something visually exciting. "The Servants" is a worthy effort of Bang Bang for the domestic market, though "Jumping Ash" remains a personal favorite. —Mel.

The Hong Kong Tycoon
(HONG KONG-COLOR)

Hong Kong, July 12.
Dragon One Films release. Directed by

Cecille Tang Shuen. Stars Michael Lai, Tina Ti, Linda Liu, Leung Shing Po. (No other screen credits available). Reviewed at Sunbeam Theater, July 10, 1979. Running Time: 100 MINS.
(With English sub-titles, Cantonese soundtrack).

Cecille Tang Shuen rose to prominence in the late '60s with "The Arch," widely acclaimed as a Chinese masterpiece. It had both artistry and sensitivity. Then, she made two Hong Kong-inspired films that facilitated her slow route to obscurity. One project was an effort to produce a commercially acceptable feature with disastrous results. "The Hong Kong Tycoon" is her latest work and looks like her last for a while. "Tycoon" shows Tang's decline as a individualistic and serious film director of merit. The film dismally fails to create a serio-comic examination of very realistic human situations and conditions in modern Hong Kong of the '70s.

The first image shows Hong Kong harbour and, like the City, projects great promise. Sad to say, "Tycoon" never took off and went bankrupt on two counts ... cinematic style and viewers. It is yet another film that explores the melodrama of a rags-to-riches story that's been presented with boring lethargy.

The minus points include the blaring non-stop soundtrack music that distracts and drowns dialog, irritating sound effects to punctuate body movements and emphasize basic human emotions. Made two years ago and only granted commercial release recently on a minor theater circuit, the contemporary gloss of the Hong Kong business scenes remain bu the colours like the presentation appear faded.

The dated direction of Tang lacks insight and imagination while the acting is stiff and self-conscious. All told, the rich possibilities of the subject matter did not get tapped fully. What Tang offered is the mere skeleton of her art instead of depth and deeper understanding about living and loving in a rat race city like Hong Kong. —Mel.

The Butterfly Murders
(HONG KONG-COLOR)

Hong Kong, July 23.
A Seasonal Film Production and Release. Directed by Hark Tsui. Features entire cast. Screenplay, Lum Chi-Ming; camera (color), Fan Ching-Yu; action director, Wong Shih-Tong; story, Hark Tsui. Reviewed at Ocean Theatre, Hong Kong, July 21, '79. Running Time: 100 MINS.

Fong	Lau Siu-Ming
Tien	Wong Shih-Tong
Green Shadow	Michelle Mee
Lady Shum	Jo Jo Chan
The Thousand Hands	Tino Wong

The Holy Fire .... Koh Hung
Master Shum .... Ching Kwok-Chu
(Cantonese soundtrack with English subtitles)

Innovative ... fantastic ... different ... stunning are some of the words to describe the work of young Hong Kong filmmaker Hark Tsui. He makes a strong debut as a feature-length moviemaker after a tv stint. "Butterfly Murders" creatively combines the moody elements of old Japa-Italian westerns. Out of that is born a most un-Chinese cinema that may stun and bewilder the ordinary patrons of stale Kung fu films.

The plot has Fong (Lau Siu-Ming) portraying a unique character in the martial arts genre. He does not know how to fight. Instead, he is a writer of sorts who travels in order to chronicle major battles in the world of martial arts. He is respected by all and he relates the strange Butterfly Murders.

One of the incidents that Fong witnesses when Tien (Wong Shih-Tong), who heads a clan of fighters, get invited to the castle of Master Shum. With the assistance of a female fighter called Green Shadow they encounter mysterious characters like the futuristic robot man and bizarre murders by a swarm of butterflies.

"Butterfly" attempts to explore new elements in costumed period kung fu films by adding environmental elements, novel twists, sci-fi and futuristic visions set in an old world. It is then topped with the belief in the weakness of the human body. Another interesting ingredient is the transposition of the harmless butterfly, which symbolizes an Oriental image of delicate beauty and happiness, into a dangerous insect that can kill. Enhancing it all is the superb camerawork and dazzling camera angels.

Though the plot is convoluted and not told in the most straight-forward fashion, the unique production is very professional. The special effects are done with the expertise of a modern-day American film.

Here is one of the most impressive Hong Kong productions of 1979 despite flaws in the story-telling department. Properly reedited and repackaged with foreign eyes and ears in mind, "Butterfly" has very high commercial potential abroad. The unique film will definitely set a trend here and will keep the Hong Kong major studios on their toes as a whole new wave of young talents is given opportunities to set the pace for the coming decade. —*Mel*

Sunburn
(COLOR)

No scorcher.

Hollywood, Aug. 7.
Pararmount Pictures release of a John Daly. Gerald Green production. Executive producers. Jay Bernstein. John Quested. in association with Philip A. Waxman. Features entire cast. Directed by Richard C. Sarafian. Screenplay, John Daly. Stephen Oliver. James Booth, based on book. "The Bind." by Stanley Ellin; camera (Technicolor), Alex Phillips Jr.; music. composed and arranged by John Cameron; production designer, Ted Tester; editor, Geoff Foot; asst. director, Steve Barnett; underwater sequences. Ramon Bravo; sound editor, Vernon Messenger; art director, Augustin Ituarte; set decorator, Dick Purdy; special effects. Laurencio Cordero, Jesus Duran. Reviewed at Paramount Studios. Hollywood. Aug. 6. 1979. (MPAA Rating-PG). Running time: 99 MINS.

Ellie .... Farrah Fawcett
Jake .... Charles Grodin
Marcus .... Art Carney
Nera .... Joan Collins
Crawford .... William Daniels
Webb .... John Hillerman
Mrs. Thoren .... Eleanor Parker
Mark Elmes .... Keenan Wynn
Karl .... Robin Clarke
Joanna .... Joan Goodfellow
Gela .... Jack Kruschen
Fons .... Alejandro Rey
Vasquez .... Jorge Luke
Dobbs .... Seymour Cassel
Mamie .... Joanna Lehmann
Kunz .... Alex Sharpe
Milan .... Bob Orrison
Dr. Kellogg .... Deloy White
Also: Christa Walters, Youigi Rogi, Miguel Burciaga. Steven Wilensky. George Belanger. Dick Subley. Ken Smith, Enrique Kahn. Delores Devine.

A perfect example of the type of modest, middle-range picture that has effectively been driven to extinction by television and increasing budgets, "Sunburn" exists for no other reason than to provide a vehicle for Farrah Fawcett. She's great to look at, natch, but that's the case on tv and in photos as well, so until someone can dream up a way to use her in plausible dramatic or comedic context, her screen career will remain in the starting gate. Pic's not an entire write-off due to Charles Grodin and Art Carney's delightful scene stealing, but b.o. prospects would seem limited.

Confection has Fawcett (married name Majors appears onscreen, but not in current ads or press material) as a Gotham model posing as Grodin's wife as he sleuths around chic Acapulco settings investigating the mysterious death of an industrialist on behalf of an insurance company stuck with a $5.000.000 claim. Scenes devoted to real plot movement are few and far between in script's first hour, since Fawcett's character is mostly irrelevant and has to be given something to do, like being scared by a lizard entering her bedroom or displaying a striking gown at a cocktail party.

Tone is kept light all the way, as it's obviously not the kind of film where any of the principals are going to be put in any serious danger. Grodin works overtime to carry the picture and does so marvelously. displaying a savvy low-key comedy style that's perfectly complemented by Carney as a sweaty but cheerful local dick. Grodin and Joan Collins share a farcial seduction scene that's a small comic gem.

Given that she's thrown in with several highly adept character actors. Fawcett acquits herself ably. but what she could use at this point are a few Howard Hawks-style lessons in voice lowering a la Lauren Bacall or Angie Dickenson to giver her more weight and authority of presence.

Richard C. Sarafian directs mainly with an eye to showing off the rather gaudy sets and lush backgrounds. Technically. film is below top professional standards in several departments. Photography by Alex Phillips Jr. Mexican house cinematographer on many American productions south of the border, is often fuzzy or washed out. with shadows looking murky and skin tones appearing overly red even before impact of the title has had a chance to affect characters.

Editing by Geoff Foot betrays a lack of judgment re most effective cutting for maximum impact, and the sound mix occasionally allows background noises to intrude unduly into dialog. Use of pop tunes, pointedly eminating from a tape player, is utterly nonsensical.
—*Cart.*

House of The Lute
(HONG KONG-COLOR)

Hong Kong, July 23.
A Hung Way Films Production. Produced by Chan Hok-Yan. Directed by Lau Shing-hon. Stars Yum Tat-Wah, Kwan Hoi-Shan. Chan Lap-Pun, Lok Bec-Kay. Screenplay. Lau Shing-hon; camera (color). Johnny Koo: art direction. David Chan: lute music. John Thompson. Reviewed at Union Lab. Hong Kong. July 20. '79. Running Time: 95 MINS.

(Cantonese soundtrack with English subtitles)

Lau Shing-hon belongs to a new breed of serious Hong Kong filmmakers. Independently produced, "House of the Lute" is his first full-length feature and ranks high in its ambitious pretensions and artistic qualities. It's a well-made conventional ghost story with a surprisingly effective love triangle that has been laced with black humor, explicit sex sequences and serious underlying messages about conflicts. Some of the conflicts deal with age-old traditions affected by a modern tv culture and conservative social mores tainted with sexual freedom.

"House of the Lute" may not break any local boxoffice records, but it has great possibilities for film buffs and cultists. An interesting coincidence is the fact that it has certain elements similar to Nagisa Oshima's "The Empire of Passion."

The story is set in an old and deserted Chinese country house. The four central characters include a young house boy, a paralyzed rich old man. his sensuous and sexual young wife, an irritating old servant and a chatty parrot. Playing an integral symbol in the story is the Chinese lute. the musical instrument continuously played by the old man. The old man in "Lute" is a traditional rich Chinese who is ruled by art and music. He is underplayed by actor Kwan Hoi-shan.

In an enclosed environment, the sex-starved wife is immediately attracted to the young house boy. Her suggestive looks lead to indiscretion, secret liaisons and uncontrolled sexual desires.

While the plot is relatively thin, Lau effectively uses it as the instrument to convey his personal comments about political, cultural, and social ills that ail Hong Kong.

The film can be criticized though for making a short story long. The weak acting of female star Lok Bec-Kay is noticeable yet she excels in the bold scenes. Meanwhile, young television actor Yum Tat-wah shows his hesitance to give all in the lovemaking sequences though he was successful in candidly showing his transition from a harmless innocent to a cocky and over-confident young man.

The Chinese calligraphy and art direction of David Chan evokes an interesting classical atmosphere, and the film is excitingly complemented with the distinctive lute music on the soundtrack. played by one of the rare lute players in the world. American John Thompson. In the film's original music. a real Ming Dynasty lute was used. Equally impressive is the moody cinematography of the mysterious villa and surrounding environs. with visuals ranging from fresh flowers to decaying plants.

"House of the Lute" is an unconventional Chinese film that deserves deep analysis for it says more than what it shows. The film is not a great one but it can be praised for its quiet eloquence, serious content, vivid portrayal of raw human passions and the unexpected horror that comes in the final reel. Lau as a director shows brio, flair and imagination. His first film may mark him as someone to watch on the generally lacklustre Hong Kong film scene. "House of the Lute" will also be shown at this year's Edinburgh International Film Festival.
—*Mel.*

Nutcracker Fantasy
(COLOR)

Animated puppets could mop up with moppets.

Hollywood, July 30.

A Sanrio Film Distribution release. Produced by Walt deFaria. Mark L. Rosen. Arthur Tomioka. Executive producer. Shintaro Tsuji. Directed by Takeo Nakamura. Screenplay adaptation. Thomas Joachim. Eugene Fournier: story. Shintaro Tsuji, based on "The Nutcracker And The Mouseking" by E.T.A. Hoffman: camera (color). Fumio Otani. Aguri Sugita. Ryoji Takamori: lighting. Toshikiyo Nakatani: editors. Jack Woods. Nobuo Ogawa: Takeo Nakamura: music. Peter Illych Tchaikovsky. adapted and arranged by Akihito Wakatsuki. Kentaro Haneda: set design. Mayasa Kaburagi. Hiroshi Yamashita: dialog supervisor. Jack Woods. Reviewed at the Samuel Goldwyn Theatre. Beverly Hills. July 30. '79. (MPAA Rating G) Running time: 82 MINS.

(Voices)

Narrator	Michele Lee
Clara	Melissa Gilbert
Aunt Gerda	Lurene Tuttle
Uncle Drosselmeyer Street Singer	
Puppeteer Watchmaker	Christopher Lee
Queen Morphia	Jo Anne Worley
Chamberlain Poet Wiseman	Ken Sansom
King Goodwin	Dick Van Patten
Franz Fritz	Roddy McDowall
Indian Wiseman Viking Wiseman	Mitchel Gardner
Chinese Wiseman Executioner	Jack Angel
Otto Von Atra French Wiseman Clovis	Gene Moss
Queen Of Time	Eva Gabor
Mice Voices	Joan Gerber
	Maxine Fisher
Princess Mary	Robin Haffner

The idea of an animated puppet musical is potentially enough to make many adults squirm even before they're in their seats. but Sanrio's new production. "Nutcracker Fantasy." which fits those specifications. should prove a delight for kids and is even palatable for their parents. This specially tailored English-language version of an otherwise Japanese venture should do good family business when released at the end of the year.

Story. which bears strong overtones of "The Wizard Of Oz." "Sleeping Beauty" and "Alice In Wonderland." is purest fantasy. with a young girl dreaming of romance and adventure in a world inhabited by a king whose daughter has been turned into a sleeping mouse which can only be transformed and reawakened by the rescue of her heart. which has been stolen by an army of evil mice. A heroic prince naturally accomplishes the task. falling in love with the young dreamer at the same time.

Tale is embellished by several tuneful songs. some lavish set pieces and plenty of comic relief characters. as well as two rather extraneous ballet sequences featuring live dancers. which will do nothing for tots except provide them with the opportunity to run out to the concessions stand.

Unusual technique employed involves sculpted dolls with moveable parts whose movements were filmed one frame at a time on miniature sets. Though this method imposes more limits than those encountered in normal animation. heavy use of opticals and special effects transports the characters from their surroundings and lends a magical patina to the proceedings.

Script adaptation by Thomas Joachim and Eugene Fournier. both of whom had a hand in the student-made "Fraternity Row" of two years ago. is literate and not condescending. content to work along classical fantasy guidelines and doing so handsomely.

Single element which puts pic across for over-10-year-olds is the consistent excellence of the readings by actors engaged to fill in the voices. Melissa Gilbert and Michele Lee do beautifully as the dreamer as girl and grown-up. respectively. Roddy McDowall is properly noble and dignified as the prince. but perhaps best is Christopher Lee in four parts. His vocalizations stand as a model of flavorful characterization. Other character parts are simarly brought to life by an array of good actors. some of whom double and triple up for small roles.

Technical work is fine. although occasional image fuzziness is caused by some individual frame enlargements and freeze framing. Pic also makes an attempt to humanize the puppet characters by including in the the story actual wind-up dolls and a puppeteer which are perceived as different from the "real" characters inhabiting the tale. —Cart.

Americathon
(COLOR)

Panders to youth; and with futuristic satire. Prospects poor.

Hollywood, Aug. 7.

A United Artists release of a Lorimar production. Produced by Joe Roth. Exec producer. Edward Rosen. Features entire cast. Directed by Neil Israel. Screenplay. Israel. Michael Mislove, Monica Johnson, from a story by Israel. Peter Bergman. Philip Proctor: camera (Technicolor). Gerald Hirschfield: editor. John C. Howard: production design, Stan Jolley: set design. Mark L. Fabus: costume design, Daniel Paredes: sound. Jim La Rue; assistant director. Jack Baran. Reviewed at Directors Guild of America. West Hollywood. Aug. 7. '79. (MPAA Rating: PG). Running time: 85 MINS.

Eric McMerkin	Peter Riegert
Monty Rushmore	Harvey Korman
Vanderhoof	Fred Willard
Mouling Jackson	Zane Buzby
Lucy Beth	Nancy Morgan
Chet Roosevelt	John Ritter
Jerry	Richard Schaal
Sam Birdwater	Chief Dan George
Oklahoma Roy Budnitz	Meat Loaf
Danny Olsen	Terry McGovern

"Americathon" represents the sorry results of pandering solely to the youth audience. Lorimar's initial release through United Artists of the Neil Israel film has a cheap, sleazy look to it. Coupled with the basically unfunny nature of the futuristic satire, the film's shoddy patina will present severe marketing problems for UA and boxoffice results look to be poor.

Israel mined this territory extensively with his 1976 indie winner, "Tunnelvision." but at least that film displayed some originality and wit. "Americathon," which involves many of the same creative people, including producer Joe Roth and co-scripter Michael Mislove, builds upon most of the same jokes, in a satirical style as broad as it is flat.

Setting supplied by Israel and "Firesign Theatre" alumnae Peter Bergman and Philip Proctor, along with Mislove and Monica Johnson, is a morally and financially bankrupt America circa 1998. To "save" the country from its debts being called due by an inexplicably wealthy Chief Dan George, media honcho Peter Riegert is called upon by president John Ritter to mount a national telethon.

Most of the film approximates the vignettes used in "Tunnelvision," but the complicated (and totally unnecessary) plotline intrudes at every turn. Fred Willard limns a presidentail aide conspiring with the United Hebrab Republic (combo of Arabs and Jews) who want to take over the U.S., via sabotaging the Americathon being hosted by Harvey Korman.

Simple assumption that cracks about tv and politics will be riotously funny to a mindless audience is the underlying premise of "Americathon," and a base one at that. Even the most escapist forms of entertainment need a focus to pull their elements together — "Americathon" scatters its potshots everywhere, in the hope at least some will hit the target.

"Americathon" apparently received extensive re-editing, as some players listed in the credits (such as Howard Hesseman) are nowhere to be seen in the film, ditto several plot turns. And those who do appear are generally wasted, especially Korman, who delivers an all-out perf. Zane Buzby as a Vietnamese punk star, and Nancy Morgan, an attractive actress who deserves some better parts. Riegert. Ritter. Richard Schaal and Willard do little more than embarass themselves. Several other listed cameos can be missed in the blink of an eye.

Israel's direction is non-existent, and other tech credits range from adequate to poor. With a slow 85 minutes of "Americathon" to endure. film audiences may go out and contribute to a fund to stop more pix like this from being made. —Poll.

Beschreibung Einer Insel
(Description of an Island)
(WEST GERMAN-COLOR-16m-DOCU)

Berlin, Aug. 5.

A Moana Film Production, West Berlin. Features entire cast. Directed by Rudolf Thome. Cynthia Beatt. No other credits provided. Reviewed at Kurbel Cinema, West Berlin. Aug. 4. '79. Running time: 192 MINS.

With Gabrielle Baur, Brian Beatt. Cynthia Beatt. Susanne Christmann. Otto Kayser. Edda Loechl. and inhabitants of the island of Ureparapara.

Rudolf Thome, Berlin critic and filmer, has specialized in original fiction-docus of an autobiographical nature, each with a preconceived structure and enough built-in humor to be called feature pix. "Germany and USA" (1974) described his trip to the States, and "Diary" (1975) recounted the breakup of his marriage utilizing Goethe's "Elective Affinities" as a literary inspiration.

"Description of an Island," made together with Cynthia Beatt and unspooled at last February's Forum of Young Cinema in its three-hours-plus version, chronicles an adventure for six months on the island of Ureparapara in the New Hebrides (southeast Pacific Ocean. about 500 miles from Fiji). This is where Cynthia Beatt grew up (the general area, that is), and since she can even communicate with the natives in island jabber, why not?

The "Moana Film" prod hints at

the direction taken by the crew and cast (a half-dozen adventurous souls) in making this docu. In the beginning, it's a Flaherty-like examination of native customs and rituals through the eyes of academic-minded Europeans. Midway through this film experiment, however, it becomes clear that the white visitors have to use most of their resources to survive infections, boredom, and outright rebellion amongst their own numbers (the cameraman quit or was fired, one member of the group ended up in a hospital far from the island, and people simply began to get on each other's nerves).

The wonder is that the film was finished at all. The delight is that it was completed with such honesty and attention to detail. Not only does the viewer appreciate the ways of the islanders in the first half (the chief commercial product on these volcanic strips of land is copra, a.k.a. coconut meat), but a friendship slowly grows up between natives and visitors, to such a point that native songs and stories are recorded before the camera in the island lingo.

Still, "Description of an Island" is not ethnological or anthropological. It is more the study of a scientific failure. Thome, as the prime director, never enters within camera-range; the others gradually use the opportunity to reveal their thoughts and feelings on the whole matter as the months wear on. The only one who seems to be entirely at home is the brother of the femme cohelmer, who wonders aloud at the start why everyone is living in a shack ("will I catch anything?") and then spends his free time ('there's not much else to do in these parts") skin-diving and chatting with the natives in their own tongue.

Perhaps that's what the crew should have done too, instead of planning such an impossible adventure for some kind of forthcoming published book — if ever! Credits are a plus in this odd but fascinating document. —*Holl.*

Scum
(BRITISH-COLOR)

Tough subject, tough viewing.

London, Aug. 7.
A Boyd's Co. production. Executive producers, Don Boyd, Michael Relph. Produced by Davina Belling. Clive Parsons. Directed by Alan Clarke. Features entire cast. Screenplay, Roy Minton; camera (color), Phil Meheux; editor, Mike Bradsell; sound, David John; art director, Mike Porter; associate producer, Martin Campbell; asst. director, Raymond Day. Reviewed at the Baronet preview theatre, London, August 6, '79. (BBFC Ratin: X). Running Time: **96 MINS.**

Carlin	Ray Winstone
Archer	Mick Ford
Sands	John Judd
Richards	Phil Daniels
Banks	John Blundell
Eckersley	Ray Burdis
Davis	Julian Firth
Angel	Alrick Riley
Woods	John Fowler
Taylor	Nigel Humphreys
Greaves	Philip Jackson
Governor Baildon	Peter Howell
Miss Biggs	Jo Kendall
Goodyear	John Grillo
Meakin	Alan Igpon

Given that "Scum," a relentlessly brutal slice of British reform school life, is strongly directed by Alan Clarke, and acted with admirable conviction, it is a pity as to the film's boxoffice prospects that Roy Minton's hard-hitting screenplay, on an important theme, is more passionate tract than powerful entertainment.

That is not to imply that the curse should have been taken off it. Rather that its appeal could have been wider with more dramatic light and shade, and its message more likely to find its mark if the basic point — that a youth penitentiary can kill, not cure — had been made through more investigative character-study, instead of via a catalog of horrific events.

Controversy value alone, however, should render the independent venture readily marketable in territories with lenient censorship, with returns okay but unspectacular.

Significantly, the plot of a "trainee" (young offender) whose means of survival in the corrupt reformatory is to become top dog by meeting violence with violence started life as a BBC-TV play. Although filmed, it was never aired on account of its alleged bias and unpalatability. It thus became more of a local cause celebre probably than if it had been transmitted.

In remaking it as a feature, Clarke (who directed the play) and producers Davina Belling and Clive Parsons have departed little from the original, and that's the root of the problem. Not that it needed enlarging for the bigger canvas, nor that an upbeat ending (for example) would have been appropriate. But unremitting bleakness is a likely effective recourse for a scripter in order to contrast the blandness of an evening's viewing on the tube, no-hope subjects seem to work best as theatrical fare. Minton's remorseless villains, victims or not, key only hate.

An exception to the one-dimensional characterizations is Mick Ford as an intelligent and insolent trainee who never breaks rules, but affects conscientious fads which the sadistic wardens are forced to accommodate — religious convictions, vegetarianism, and suchlike. Those scenes are both entertaining and telling.

Ray Winstone, although compelling here and there, never quite brings the central role to life, largely because the boy's early transformation into a vicious zombie deprives him of vulnerability, and so also of sympathy.

Technical credits are fine, and the production wears its slim cost and tight winter location schedule commendably. Absence of music is well-judged, and Mike Bradsell's seamless editing a notable plus. Pic may be entry in the N.Y. Film Festival. —*Simo.*

Easy Road
(GREECE-COLOR)

Athens, Aug. 14.
An Eleftheroudakis release. Produced by Mikalis Lefakis for Greca Film and Andreas Thomopoulos. Directed by Andreas Thomopoulos. Features entire cast. Screenplay, Andreas Thomopoulos; camera, (Eastmancolor) Dimitris Vernikos; art director, Maria Karayanopoulou; music, George and Mikis Theodorakis and other songs and lyrics by Andreas Thomopoulos. Reviewed at Apollon Cinema, Athens, Aug. 14, 1979. Running time: **110 MINS.**

Paul	Paul Sideropoulous
Ann	Betty Levanon
Anastasia	Elen Manyiati
Irene	Vera Kruzka
Father	Stavras Xenidis
Flu	Kostias Vrettos

In his second feature film that stamps him as a qualified member of the new filmmakers group, Andreas Thomopoulos manages to strike a balance between the sore spots of social reality and the inclination to capture as big a youth audience as possible rather than alienate it with a splash of arty techniques.

The young, British-trained filmmaker deeply probes the many generational problems of Greek youth but in relation to protagonist Paul (Paul Sideropoulous), a modern day composer of ballads and a sidewalk troubadour. Paul has kicked over his post-graduate studies in medicine to create a new life and new identity a la Bob Dylan. Most women want him integrated and he drifts away. When he finds the right woman, a divorced mother of two children, he assumes responsibilities of the family, completes post-grad studies and tries to enter the medical fraternity. It doesn't work; medical practices are polluted. The woman understands and together they go off, heads high, to a new, unknown future.

Sideropoulous, as the protagonist of "Easy Road," almost single-handedly gives the film its boxoffice potential. His singing and natural underplaying are easy on the eye and ear and give the film a heavy youth-oriented quality, including the entertainment factor.

Thomopoulous handles all thesps with flying colors, including Kostias Vrettos (a social fringe musician who strongly influences the protagonist). Songs with lyrics by the filmmaker himself, together with one tune by George and Mikis Theodorakis, plus latter's background music, should end up at the top of the Greek record charts. Music track is also a b.o. hypo.

Film slows at times with extended array of social ills. Digression in closing reels to compound youth problems with those of the medical profession, over-accents social reality. But fine debuting performance of singer-actor Sideropoulous and strong support from the talented legit cast gives the young filmmaker the elements to make "Easy Road" work.

Picture is also an interesting document of what young Greek filmmakers are thinking and where the targets are posted. The film should do solid biz in Greece and will find it markets outside Greece when the striding new Greek cinema makes it global impact in the next year or two. —*Werb.*

Den attonde dagen
(The Eight Day)
(SWEDISH-COLOR)

Malmoe, July 27.
An AB Svensk Filmindustri (SF) production and release. Based on novel by Rose Lagerkrantz. Features entire cast. Written and directed by Anders Groenros. Executive producer, Olle Hellbom. Camera (Eastmancolor), Joergen Persson, Rolf Lindstroem; editor, Yolanda Knobel; music, Keith Jarrett. Reviewed at Palladium, Malmoe, Sweden, July 26, 1979. Running time: **92 MINS.**

Anna	Susanna Radoe
Pejter	Benny Feher
Anna's kid brother	Bo-Patrik Gusterman
Mariette	Tin-Tin Andersson
Mariette's boyfriend	Per Leonstroem

"The Eight Day," a first time out for 25-year-old Anders Groenros as a director, has been helped considerably by its producer, Svensk Film veteran Olle Hellbom.

Groenros himself seems an accomplished filmmaker with this feature that must be a safe bet for foreign sales to theatrical as well as tv situations. All will be well served with this finely-honed psychological portrait of a pre-teen couple's tentative, scared, valiant, aggressive, confused and altogether lovely first groping towards love.

Swift, just-right editing by Yolanda Knobel, surefooted, energetic yet poetic cinematography by Joergen Persson ("Elvira Madigan"), a soft-spoken musical score for piano by Keith Jarrett all help to assure a film of the highest technical credits, but director-writer Gronroes, who hews very closely and carefully to his meticuously worked out script, deserves the main laurels for his insight and for his work with the amateur actors.

Story is about Anna, 12, who lives with her family on an island that is visited for seven days each summer by Pejter, also 12, son of a divorced father who lives on the island. For a year, Anna has been daydreaming about Pejter's next return. When the boy does arrive, Anna cannot express her feelings for him in other than such perverse ways as teasing, patronizing, standoffish, even vicious (she locks him in an old castle ruin during a thunder storm).

Anna is miserable and takes it out on her sweet and patient kid brother, when Pejter himself is not to be found or at hand. For all of his vacation's seven days, Anna cannot make headway with Pejter, himself an open-minded, imaginative, sensitive youngster, puzzled by Anna's rough approaches, but forgiving in the face of her small acts of desperation.

Both children yearn for a physical contact they are not yet up to fulfilling, so much less since they are being teased and bullied by a slightly older teenage couple.

However, Anna does succeed in persuading Pejter into staying an extra, the eighth, day, and film has an up-beat but not over-emphasized happy ending.

The camera is most of the time on the two main protagonists, as it should be. There is not a shred of psychological or socio-political finger-pointing here.

Susanna Radoe and Benny Feher are not only funny, warm and touching to look at and listen to, they are made to perform like highly accomplished actors without for a second losing their spontaneity.

The ending takes on a somewhat high-falutin' note and is easily expendable. Groenros seems reluctant to say goodbye to his two lovely creations. Audiences will understand and forgive. —*Kell.*

The Seduction Of Joe Tynan
(COLOR)

Wins on primary level. Political plot uphill.

Hollywood, Aug. 9.
A Universal Pictures release of a Martin Bregman production. Produced by Bregman. Exec producer, Louis A. Stroller. Directed by Jerry Schatzberg. Stars Alan Alda, Barbara Harris, Meryl Streep. Screenplay, Alda; camera (color), Adam Holender; editor, Evan Lottman; art direction, David Chapman; set decoration, Alan Hicks; music, Bill Conti; sound, Jim

Sabat; assistant director, Ralph Singleton. Reviewed at Samuel Goldwyn Theatre, BevHills, Aug. 9, '79. (MPAA Rating: R.) Running time: **107 MINS.**
Joe Tynan .... Alan Alda
Ellie .... Barbara Harris
Karen Traynor .... Meryl Streep
Senator Kittner .... Rip Torn
Senator Birney .... Melvyn Douglas
Francis .... Charles Kimbrough
Janet .... Blanche Baker
Paul Tynan ....Adam Ross
Aldena Kittner .... Carrie Nye
Jerry .... Chris Arnold
Edward Anderson .... Maurice Copeland
Arthur Briggs ....Robert Christian

Hanging over the release of "The Seduction Of Joe Tynan" is the familiar black cloud that palls most political films. The industry myth that pix about politics simply won't sell at the box office has doomed some fine films. And few are better than "Joe Tynan," which features a literate script, sensitive direction and a brace of fine performances by Alan Alda, Barbara Harris and Meryl Streep. But the Universal release faces an uphill struggle, and even title change and shift from back rooms to bedrooms may not help at the wickets.

Universal, along with producer Martin Bregman, writer-star Alda and director Jerry Schatzberg, should be commended for plowing ahead anyway. Adroitly combining humor and intimate drama, "Joe Tynan" joins that list of exemplary Washington-set pix, including "Advise And Consent" and "The Best Man."

In large part, the credit goes to Alda, whose portrayal in the title role is no less complex and multifaceted than his screenplay. Joe Tynan is a familiar political figure: the young, handsome liberal Senator who rides upward on the coattails of a few big media victories. Alda assumes the pasted-on smile, the hearty handshake and breezy confidence of a politico with immense ease. He seems to have been born for the role.

Less often explored is the price paid for such double-edged success, and this is where "Joe Tynan" excels. As Alda's intelligent and frustrated wife, Barbara Harris gives the performance of her career, one that certainly merits Academy Award consideration. With a few brief gestures and meaningful glances, Harris communicates a world of emotion, looking from inside the fishbowl, and hating what she sees. It's a breathtaking job of acting, fully in keeping with the pic's pace and rhythm.

Also outstanding is Meryl Streep as the labor lawyer with whom Alda dallies, and eventually abandons. Southern to her core, Streep avoids the gushy sentimentality that could have resulted, and underplays beautifully to both Alda and Harris.

The fine meshing of these characters is a tribute to Schatzberg's craftsmanship. The director has previously excelled in exploring human relationships, especially in "Panic In Needle Park" and "Scarecrow," and Alda's screenplay (his first for a feature) gives him malleable material aplenty.

Supporting cast is fine, particularly Rip Torn as a Roman-like Senator wallowing in the perquisites of his power, and Melvyn Douglas, who gives immense dignity to an aging politician losing his grip on reality. Blanche Baker is quite good as Alda's disaffected daughter, ditto Adam Ross as his son, Charles Kimbrough, Carrie Nye and Chris Arnold sparkle in lesser roles.

Technically, "Joe Tynan" is firstrate, especially Adam Holender's clear camerawork, David Chapman and Alan Hicks' realistic settings, and Jim Sabat's crisp sound. Only Bill Conti's cutesy score seems intrusive, and at odds with the subject matter.

Main weakness in Alda's script comes at its end, when he and Harris have it out at a Democratic National Convention that seems to be taking place in a time warp, with all candidates' names, affiliations, etc. carefully masked. Audiences may also feel disappointed in the lack of a clear-cut resolution to the characters' dilemma, but that tone of no-nonsense realism is fully in keeping with the rest of the film.

In a summer that has seen lesser films exceed their promise financially, however, "The Seduction Of Joe Tynan" may find itself in a one-way race to extinction. —*Poll.*

Now Or Never
(WEST GERMAN-B&W-16m)

Berlin, Aug. 6.
A Lothar Lambert Film Production, West Berlin. Features entire cast. Produced, written, directed, photographed, and edited by Lothar Lambert, in collaboration with Uwe Sange. Dedicated to the memory of Sylvia Heidemann. Reviewed at Helmut Arlt Screening Room, West Berlin, Aug. 5, '79. Running time: **81 Mins.**
With Sylvia Heidemann, Tally Brown, Ronald Perry, Dagmar Beiersdorf, Pat Evans, Exuma, Erskine Philip, Maryse Richter, Rufus Harper, Lothar Lambert.

Another of those unique, entertaining home movies by Lothar Lambert, Berlin crit and helmer, "Now or Never" was made on a budget of $5,000 with the generous support of thesps and friends in West Berlin and New York. Pic is dedicated to vet actress Sylvia Heidemann, who died tragically while the project was underway (her death becomes a part of the film and it was dedicated to her memory).

Lambert has made consistently

good fun of the demimonde scene in Berlin in past pix: "Ex and Hopp" (1972), "Sein Kampf" (1973) and "1 Berlin-Harlem" (1974) (these three made together with Wolfram Zobus), "Faux Pas de Deux" (1976) and "Night Show" (1977). For "Now or Never" he's off with his sidekick, Uwe Sange, to New York and the underground film tradition that supplied most of the inspiration for his own wacky experiments. This is a kind of docu on his travels, the fiction side being his own search for a lost identity amid the gay crowd and summer goings-on in Central Park, Harlem, and Brooklyn.

What makes Lambert's pix attractive is the humor and the adept ability to turn a joke on himself. As the lead in the pic (he also produced, directed, wrote, lensed, and cut the film), Lambert often gives the impression of a Harry Langdon lost in the Big City.

The "New York Experience" (pic's subtitle) does, however, bring him into contact with a typical cross section of Gotham humanity: a black on welfare, another studying at an academy, underground film star Tally Brown, and assorted lovelies from the gay scene. Since Lambert is very much a member of the team, the footage on transvestites proved easy to come by and forms the core of his experience. All in good taste and with tongue-in-cheek humor.

At the end, Lambert returns home free of his depressions. — *Holl.*

Rich Kids
(COLOR)

Kids pay price of parents divorce, promising with clever sell if forthcoming.

United Artists release of a Lion's Gate Film. A Robert Altman and George W. George presentation. Produced by George and Michael Hausman. Exec producer, Altman. Directed by Robert M. Young. Screenplay, Judith Ross. Camera, Ralf D. Bode; editor, Edward Beyer; art direction, David Mitchell; musical score, Craig Doerge; songs, Doerge, Allan Nichols. Reviewed at Coronet Theatre, N.Y., July 14, '79. MPAA rating: PG. Running time: **96 MINS.**
Franny Philips .... Trini Alvarado
Jamie Harris ....Jeremy Levy
Madeline Philips .... Kathryn Walker
Paul Philips ....John Lithgow
Ralph Harris .... Terry Kiser
Steve Sloan .... David Selby
Barbara Peterfreund ... Roberta Maxwell
Simon Peterfreund .... Paul Dooley
Stewardess .... Diane Stilwell
Ralph's secretary ....Dianne Kirksey
Madeleine's mother .... Irene Worth

Departing from the more off-beat and parochial fare that's been emerging at a rapid clip from exec producer Robert Altman's production stable, "Rich Kids" is a kids-eye-view of divorce that, at least in structure and intent, seems aimed at a broader, more commercial market than Lion's Gate has explored to date.

Whether the film — which is basically an ambitious situation comedy with a predictable core of seriousness — can maximize that audience at the bottom line is another question, and probably depends more on how the pic is sold than on the material itself. Prospects seem fair to good.

Directed by Robert M. Young ("Short Eyes") from a smooth-flowing script by Judith Ross, the film is mildly funny, mildly heart-tugging and extremely well acted. But with none of its creative elements as known quantities to most audiences, and wavering in treatment between humor and sentimentality, the material never catches enough fire to ensure an easy sell.

Set among the denizens of New York's upper income bracket, pic details the effects of her parents' crumbling marriage on a precocious 12-year old (Trini Alvarado) who knows the blow is coming, but is waiting for parents John Lithgow and Kathryn Walker to officially break the news. In the meantime, she takes up with a super-bright classmate (Jeremy Levy), who's been through the mill himself and proceeds to instruct her on how to deal with it.

That education, which includes a very funny double-date between the two kids, Levy's swinging father (Terry Kizer) and a dumb-dumb stewardess; several expert manipulations of parental guilt, and a clandestine weekend of puppy love in Kizer's vacant bachelor pad, is cannily contrived in Ross's script to counterpoint their innocence against the uglier realities of adult incompatibilities.

Most of those points, however, are scored at the adolescent level, and while younger viewers will likely identify with the kids' efforts to tightrope-walk between romanticized fun & games and the harsher facts of grown-up life. Adult audiences may find the maneuverings too sentimentalized to be genuinely involving.

Pic's ultimate message — that kids shouldn't pay the emotional price for their parents' domestic mistakes — is nicely developed, if obvious. But while a number of well-played scenes between Walker and Lithgow have considerable emotional impact — including settlement and custody discussions compounded by the fact that Walker's attorney (David Selby) is also her lover and Lithgow's best friend — the serious underpinnings are frequently undermined and diluted by sitcom contrivances.

Young has directed the light-weight affair at an appropriately rapid clip, with staunch focus on the generous thesping abilities of a cast drawn largely from the Gotham stage. Of the two newcomers, Alvarado scores as an exceptionally wide-ranged new talent, while Levy tends toward a self-consciousness that works against overall credibility. Ralf D. Bode's Manhattan location lensing is crisp and fluid, and technical credits are tops throughout. —*Step.*

Tirak Cong Norng Noo
(The Love of a Little Girl)
(THAI-COLOR)

Bangkok, July 26.
A Saha Mongkol Films release of a S.P. Productions film. Produced by Chart-chapong Suphan. Written and directed by Rungsiri Lim-aksorn. Features entire cast. Based on an idea by Wan Voravudhi. Camera (color), Sophon Jaenphanit; music, Prachin Songpao; sound, Johnny Wong's Cinelab Syarm; art director, Rungsiri Lim-aksorn; asst. director, Rayat Plaikeow. Theme song, "Rak Rong Tang" (Love Lost Its Way), music and arrangement by Prachin Songpao, lyrics by Chalie Intravijit. Reviewed at Siam theatre, Bangkok, July 25, '79. Running time: 120 MINS.
```
Boke . . . . . . . . . . . . . . . . . . . . Vitoon Karuna
Sandee . . . . . . . . . . . Kanang Damrongkat
Marithong . . . . . . . . . . . . . Piathip Kumvong
Pote . . . . . . . . . . . . . . . . . Pinyo Tongchua
Ern . . . . . . . . . . . . . . . . . . . Wan Voravudhi
Noo . . . . . . . . . Anyarat Suthat Na Ayudhya
Norng . . . . . . . . . . . . . . . . Pete Tongchua
Pikulthong . . . . Sutichit Viradejkamhaeng
Moh Detr . . . . . . . . . . . . . . Somjin Tamatat
Daengtoey . . . . . . . . . . . Malee Wetprasert
```

Restricted to making only low budget films, director Rungsiri Lim-aksorn decided to specialize in economical character sketches. And since he can write dialog that excels locally in wit and humor, his films are an enjoyable study of the latest Thai middle class society people's "problems of the heart.

In a single household in "Tirak Cong Norng Noo," everybody suffers from one persistent malady: the need to love and be loved. Two old maid sisters, Piathip Kumvong and Sutichit Viradejkamhaeng, are led to think that they both have one last chance each to get a husband.

Piathip, who's putting on weight, puts her excess avoirdupois to good use. She's funny and pathetic at the same time with her hair in curlers at the breakfast table. As she is seldom seen leaving her house, she wears awful clothes and no make-up. The most that Piathip is expected to do is look glamorous later on. Because she can very easily manage that, the audience is deprived of the thrill of anticipating her "new look."

Sutichit has a nose lift, with a psychological side effect. She starts speaking through her nose, causing her great embarrassment. She opts to speak at all until she recovers her

normal speaking voice. It may seem a forced comic device, but it's side-splitting slapstick, nevertheless.

A precocious young actress, 10-year-old Anyarat Scithat Na Ayuaha, brings to her role a compelling charm. In a scene where she complains in the nasal Sutichit about bieng "heartbroken," upon discovering that Wan is in love with another girl, Anyarat's complaint, which Sutichit takes for granted, seems at once the funniest and saddest emotional outpouring the film has to offer. Anyarat perhaps does it instinctively, and she's wonderful.

Sophon Jaenphanit's camerawork is fine, particularly in the disco sequence, some of the best footage inside a disco club that has been shot locally. Costumes are also very chic, an added incentive for Rungsiri's fans. —*Cano.*

The Man You Love To Hate
(DOCU-COLOR AND B/W)

Produced by Film Profiles, Inc. in association with B.B. Corp., Fremantle International, Killiam Shows, Norddeutscher Rundfunk. Produced and directed by Patrick Montgomery. Written and researched by Richard Koszarski. No camera credits; editor, William Loeffler; music, composed and conducted by Herbert Deutsch. Narration spoken by Edward Binns. Reviewed at Preview Theater, New York, Aug. 7, '79. (MPAA rating). Running time: 90 MINS.

Making "The Man You Love To Hate" must have been a lot of fun, as there is a lot of fun on the screen. The film deals with Hollywood's heyday and one of its most flamboyant showmen, Erich Von Stroheim. A career-biography of Von Stroheim necessarily must combine humor and sadness, triumph and defeat.

There is a final vindication for Von Stroheim — after his titanic wars with Irving Thalberg and Louis B. Mayer, who mutilated his masterpiece "Greed" — in his belated recognition as a major film artist, an authentic original surrounded by phonies, a true auteur with a special vision of the human mess.

The new Patrick Montgomery documentary on Von Stroheim has already been sold to the BBC and 12 nations. It reconstructs and humanizes the man behind the Von Stroheim legend, while also introducing him to new film generations.

Excerpts from 30 films directed by and/or starring Von Stroheim are well selected for key scenes to illustrate his range. These film clips, and the interviews, are bridged by a narration that is in-

telligent, wordly, ironic and leaving one wanting more. —*Hitch.*

SCI-FI FEST

Test Pilot Pirx
(POLISH-COLOR)

Trieste, Aug. 7.
A production of the Polish Corporation for Film, Production Zespoly Filmowe and Tallinnfilm. Directed by Marek Piestrak. Features entire cast. Screenplay, Piestrak, based on the book of same title by Stanislaw Lem; camera (color), Janusz Pawlowski; music, Arvo Part; set decoration, Jerzy Sniezawski, Wiktor Zilko. Reviewed at Trieste International Festival of Science Fantasy Films, San Giusto Castle, Trieste, July 10, '79. Running time: 104 MINS.
Cast: Sergei Desnitsky, Boleslaw Abart, Vladimir Ivashov, Aleksander Kajdanowski, Zbigniew Lesien.

At a time when cinematic creativity around the world is being unduly influenced by film auteurism — the idea that one man, the auteur, should be responsible for all the major creative steps in the making of a film, production, direction, screenplay, etc. — a film like "Test Pilot Pirx" comes along like a breath of fresh air.

For "Pirx" is the obvious outcome of the collaboration of a number of talented people: Piestrak the director, Lem the author of the original book and, with Piestrak, author of the film's screenplay, Janusz Pawlowski, the director of photography who is responsible for the sober but brilliant images, Arvo Part, the music composer, and Jerzy Sniwzawski and Wiktor Zilko, set decorators. Such films are also a tribute to educational systems like Poland's which require film school students to specialize in specific areas.

"Pirx" is about "finite non-linears," robots that closely resemble human beings but are even more perfect than humans; they are intended, eventually, to replace human beings in space flights. Somewhat apprehensive about their usefulness to man, the United Nations sets up a space flight to determine their reactions to outer-space and to the human beings who also make up the crew. Pirx is selected as the commander of the flight, although the identity of the robots is not revealed to him.

In the wake of films like "Star Wars" and television series like "Star Trek," "Test-Pilot Pirx" could prove a timely and successful entry into the American market. Moreover, "Pirx" is an intelligent film, examining an idea — the possible relationships, in the future, between humans and non-humans — that few other films have dared to do.

It's also a film that's beautifully done, so well made that whether one is on the ground (parts were shot in New York City and on the Champs-Elysees in Paris) or up on the spaceship on the way to Saturn (the special effects, also well handled, were done in the Soviet Union — Poland does not have its own special effect labs), one never becomes conscious for one moment that he is anywhere else but where, in the film, he is supposed to be.

—*Mich.*

Plutonium
(WEST GERMAN-COLOR)

Trieste, Aug. 1.

A Pentagramma film production GmbH & Co. production in cooperation with the ZDF (Second German Television). Written, produced and directed by Rainer Erler. Camera (color), Wolfgang Grasshoff; editor, Hilma von Boro; music, Eugen Thomass; scientific consultant, Karl Kompa. Reviewed at Trieste International Festival of Science Fantasy Films, San Giusto Castle, Trieste, July 11, '79. Running time: 90 MINS.

Cast: Charlotte Kerr, Wolf Roth, Werner Rundshagen, Bob Cunningham, Lester C. Muller.

Although Rainer Erler's "Plutonium" attempts to warn about dangers of nuclear proliferation, it may tell us a lot more about the dangers inherent in making films, like this one, which use fictional situations to attempt to convey a hidden message. The pretext — the risks of nuclear spread — of "Plutonium" hangs so heavily over the film's plot that what could have been a very credible and competently handled political thriller proves ultimately a bore.

The situation used by Erler to convey his message is the quest of an American woman tv newsreporter to track down terrorists who've stolen 100 pounds of plutonium from a West German plant and plan, it's assumed, to use the material to construct a nuclear bomb. Her investigation takes her ultimately to the Third World where she meets the culprits, but where she also is fated to die.

But one feels little sorrow for her, more compassion than for the people who undergo her very probing questions. Charlotte Kerr, the woman reporter, is so sure of herself, that any suspense her quest might have created is squelched from the start. And her manner of hammering away at all those persons she suspects of harboring the secret of her quest is so little developed as "Plutonium" evolves that she becomes utterly monotonous.

—*Mich.*

Yugoslav Festival

Era E Lisi
(The Wind and the Oak)
(YUGOSLAV-COLOR)

Pula, Aug. 14.

Yugoslavia Film release of Kosova Film-Televizija Pristina production. Features entire cast. Directed by Besim Sahatciu. Screenplay, Perit Imamai from the book by Sinana Hasanija; camera (Eastmancolor), Rudolf Sopi; music, Rexho Mulioi. Reviewed at Pula Film Fest, July 28, '79. Running time: 110 MINS.

With: Abdurrahman Shala, Faruk Begolli, Hazir Myftari, Istref Begolli, Shani Pallaska, Quemaji Pallaska, Qemaji Ajdini, Xhevat Qorraj.

A sprawling, disjointed tale of a renowned, illiterate, middleaged partisan who comes home after the war. He takes power of the town to overcome some leftover reactionary elements and is then elected president of the town council. But he is finally axed due to a lack of education and the police tactics employed.

Lensed in the Albanian area of the country, now the republic of Kosova, film denounces an early, seemingly Stalinist form of rule from above. But the film is too disjointed as episodes are telescoped and time goes by without sufficient insight into the changing political atmosphere.

It may be due to the fact this is a spinoff from a series made for tv. Mainly of interest for its political content, film remains a local item.

—*Mosk.*

Trofej
(Trophy)
(YUGOSLAV-COLOR)

Pula, Aug. 14.

Yugoslavia Film release of Neoplanta Film production. Features entire cast. Directed by Karolj Vicek. Screenplay, Ferenc Deak, Vicek; camera (Eastmancolor), Dusan Ninkov; music, Mladen and Pedrag Vranjesevic. Reviewed at Pula Film Fest, July 27, '79. Running time, 93 MINS.

With: Stole Arandelovic, Slobodan Dimitrijevic, Eva Ras, Jagoda Kaloper, Tanja Boskovic, Vojislav Miric, Mica Tomic, Velemir Zivotic.

A noted war veteran, now a gamekeeper, is put in as head of a commission to investigate the growing practice of illegal house building. Trying to do right, the group brings about a tragic burning of a house by a distraught man but loses its outlook and powers as some higher ups put on pressures to stop further probing.

Obviously well meaning, the film is somewhat slow paced and stays general rather than delving into the characters and the consequences of their work.

But it does show the more outspoken themes now more prevalent in local films. From the republic of Vojvodino, made up of ethnic Hungarians as well as Serbs, it could herald more unusual films coming from this area. —*Mosk.*

Usijanje
(Burning)
(YUGOSLAV-COLOR)

Pula, Aug. 14.

Yugoslavia Film release of Centar Film production. Features entire cast. Directed by Bosko Draskovic. Screenplay, Draskovic, Mirko Kovac; camera (Eastmancolor), Predrag Popovic; music, Arhivska. Reviewed at Pula Film Fest, July 30, '79. Running time, 93 MINS.

With: Dragan Maksomovic, Rade Serbedzija, Gordana Kosanovic, Ivo Gregurovic, Marko Todorovic, Fabijan Sovagovic.

Early pre-World War II days and the effects of the times, the war and its aftermath on three young people, two men and a girl, are graphically illustrated in this austere, measured film.

It takes place in a stoney, poor village that survives by growing tobacco. The people are exploited by local police plus the governmental monopoly's low pricing of their wares. Not even allowed to smoke their own crop, they depend on sale of black market tobacco to live.

The war prompts the young men to sell tobacco to the occupying Italians, in turn exploiting their own people. One marries the girl and has a child, but soon departs to join the Partisans. The other stays.

The Partisan comes back and is imbued with new socialist ideas and decides to turn the house they all owned into a school and give their tobacco to the nationalized state farms.

But the other, too warped by his early days under royal oppression and the war, kills his friend rather than give up the house and his tobacco. He wanders off aimlessly as the film ends. Director Bosko Draskovic has given this a dry, harsh treatment in keeping with the clime and lifestyle of these people.

An unusual film but one that is often too illustrative of the theme and the diverse effects changing times have on different people without adding a more incisive human insight into its otherwise effective look at these times of transition. Foreign chances seem more geared for festivals, but it is another step forward in treating the war and its effects in a more profound manner as opposed to the

romantic partisan films. Technical quality is top-rate.

—*Mosk.*

Drugarcine
(The Pals)
(YUGOSLAV-COLOR)

Pula, Aug. 14.

Yugoslavia Film release of Avala Film production. Features entire cast. Directed by Mica Milosevic. Screenplay, Vlasta Radonovic; camera (Eastmancolor), Bozidar Nikolic; music, Vojislav Kostic. Reviewed at Pula Film Fest, July 31, '79. Running time: 95 MINS.

With: Milan Gutovic, Beba Loncar, Erol Kadic, Ratko Miletic, Zeljka Basic, Pavle Vujisic.

A rare youthful comedy that unconvincingly turns to bloody drama at the end, film takes place after the last war. Pic's beginning is a good natured romp that the film exploits instead of providing any new twists to the traumatic era of Yugoslavia's changeover to socialism.

However, on its view of school life, as four young men and a girl, all war heroes, return to school with the resultant romantic imbroglios, fights, etc., the film might be okay on its home grounds though not of the stuff to enhance Yugoslav films abroad.

One returned youth is a big, good-natured type, another a born leader, one has a way with women and there is the comedy relief little fellow. The big one finds a girl and is ready to get married when he is shot in the woods one day by some holdout Chetniks, the royalist fascist Yugoslavs who fought alongside the Germans.

Film then details their hunting down and extermination by the victim's friends. The ladies man then makes it with one of the teachers played by lovely thirtyish Beba Loncar, who played in Yank films some years ago. She is much too well dressed and made up for a school teacher right after the war.

They all go off to find teaching jobs after graduation with the town relieved of their escapades by the exit. Director Mica Milosevic might turn into a good commercial helmer when he makes up his mind to allow the social and political comments to be a part of the events rather than foisting them upon what is essentially a youth comedy since they have emerged from the bloody war as they left it.

—*Mosk.*

Krc
(Cramp)
(YUGOSLAV-COLOR)

Pula, Aug. 14.

Yugoslavia Film release of Viba Film production. Features entire cast. Directed by Bozo Sprajc. Screenplay, Zeljko Kozinc; camera (Eastmancolor), Rado Likon; music, Tomaz Pengov. Reviewed at Pula Film Fest, July 29, '79. Running time, 95 MINS.

With: Mateja Glazar, Boris Cavazza, Milena Zupanic, Ivo Ban; Stojan Colja, Janez Starina.

———

A strangely convoluted look at smalltown repressiveness, film is often too portentous and obscure. It does create a certain fascination in the comportment of a group of intertwined characters, besides being quite free with nude love scenes and intimations of outside political obtuseness, when pic tries to help this agricultural town exist by both promising and then denying a needed factory to provide jobs.

Again a contemporary film treating touchy themes but not succinctly enough, or with the flair to bring it off. A politician with outside connections will hopefully get the factory built. He is having an affair with the town nurse. But his car is taken one night and runs down a local backward youth.

Homicide is done by a strange youth who covets the nurse. The man is exonerated, but his affair with the girl is weakened. She finds out who did it, but prefers to build a clandestine house outside town with a local who coveted her and was the lover of her roommate, a frustrated teacher. Very confusing, no doubt.

Film is uneven, but its sheer meldramatics are more for local chances where all its allusions will be clearer. —Mosk.

———

Zivi Bili Pa Vidjeli
(That's The Way The Cookie Crumbles)
(YUGOSLAV-COLOR)

———

Pula, Aug. 14.
Yugoslavia Film release of Zagreb Film production. Features entire cast. Written and directed by Bruno Gamulin, Milivoj Puhlovski. Camera (Eastmancolor), Zivko Zalar; music, Bulldozer Rock Group. Reviewed at Pula Film Festival, July 26, '79. Running time: 100 MINS.

With: Sanja Vejnovic, Boris Buzancic, Ana Karic, Zarko Potocnjak, Danko Ljustina.

———

A romantic comedy with an underlying theme of subtle corruption in architecture as a fey but seemingly honest, gifted and dedicated young student comes up against love and corporate machinations.

Film does not have a sharp enough tone and biting treatment to make it mesh. He meets a lovely young girl and they are soon lovers. Her father is manager of a big architectural concern and he takes on the youth to work on a housing project.

But as love grows, his disillusion with his future father-in-law explodes, and the youth sounds off

during a management meeting against the concessions made to other sectors for more gains and graft. He is fired but marries the girl and they have a child.

He takes a job as a wrecker. There are seemingly many illegal houses built and they are torn down by young men hired for this job by so-called regular builders acting under the law. He finds himself tearing down his own house where they had unknowingly rented a garret in an illegal house.

They are put on a tow truck with all their belongings but are refused sanctuary anywhere as they and their baby are propped on their bed and go gaily through the town. It ends on this comic note.

Played with charm by some new young actors, film is still somewhat indulgent and lacks the needed bite and romantic flair to bring it off. New directors Bruno Gamulin and Milivoj Puhlovski are worth watching, but more coherent scripting and more potent viewpoints are still needed. —Mosk.

———

Bosko Buha
(YUGOSLAV-COLOR)

———

Pula, Aug. 14.
Yugoslavia Film release of Centar Film production. Features entire cast. Directed by Branko Bauer. Screenplay, Bosko Matic, Dusan Perkovic; camera (Eastmancolor), Branko Bazina; music, Zoran Simjanovic. Reviewed at Pula Film Fest, July 26, '79. Running time, 120 MINS.

With: Marko Nicolic, Zarko Radic, Ljubisa Samardzic, Miroljub Leso, Milena Dapevic, Milan Strljic, Ljiljana Blagoljevic.

———

A genre, by now familiar, Yugoslavian partisan film. But this has a fillip in concentrating on the young partisans who range from as young as 12 to 17. The hero is about 13 and a top "bomber."

The bombers were small enough to slip in close to bunkers and armed houses to toss grenades and bombs inside. The friendships and even enmities among these youngsters exposed to the difficulties and excitement of war are well-limned though the adults remain stereotypes.

There is the tough but fair leader, the comic peasant partisan and others. The hero is a stalwart young man not afraid to fight youths bigger than himself and selfless in battle.

The battle scenes are neatly staged, as is hero Bosko Buha's brief romantic interlude with a young girl before he is killed in an ambush by Yugoslav Chetniks who fought with the Germans.

Pic should do well at home though somewhat too predictable for much foreign action and perhaps too violent for kid shows. Well played, within its limitations of

romanticizing its characters, and well made. —Mosk.

———

Povratak
(The Return)
(YUGOSLAV-COLOR)

———

Pula, Aug. 14.
Yugoslavia Film release of Jadran Film-Slavica Film-Croatia Film, FRZ production. Features entire cast. Directed and written by Antun Vrdoljak. Camera (Eastmancolor), Tomislav Pinter; music, Miljenko Prohaska. Reviewed at Pula Film Fest, Aug. 1, '79. Running time, 95 MINS.

With: Boris Dwornik, Fabijan Sovagovic, Boris Buzanic, Milena Dravic.

———

An austere tale of a wartime incident that brings up the moral aspect of whether action is worth the known reprisals it will lead to. Film is well made, the characters somewhat familiar, but it makes its comments on war and the need for commitment sans any excess heroics or preachiness.

Seven youthful communists are arrested by Yugoslav gendarmes who worked with the occupying Italians on a small Dalmatian island. Their friends decide to free them from the local jail when the Italian boat taking them to the mainland is held up by bad weather.

A respected local fisherman joins them as do some others, but their heroic attempts are in vain. However, the killing of some gendarmes leads to savage Italian reprisals of rape and murder in the island village.

Years later the man who had joined and led the attempt comes home after having served in the war. Some do not forgive him, but most do for his actions during those three days. Well directed by Antun Vrdoljak and played with insight by Boris Dwornik as the man forced into action, film should find its way at home and perhaps in some foreign locations on its solid treatment of a time when taking sides was difficult. —Mosk.

———

Covjek Koga Treba Ubiti
(The Man To Kill)
(YUGOSLAV-COLOR)

———

Pula, Aug. 14.
Yugoslavia Film release of Jadran Film-Croatia Film-Filmski Studio Titograd production. Features entire cast. Directed by Veljko Bulajic. Screenplay, Bruni Di Geronimo, Ratko Durovic, Bulajic; camera (Eastmancolor), Branko Ivatovic; art director, Veljko Despotovic; music, Jose Privsek. Reviewed at Pula Film Fest, Aug. 1, '79. Running time: 100 MINS.

With: Zvonimir Crnko, Vladimir Popovic, Charles Millot, Ranko Kovacevic, Tanja Boskovic, Dusica Zegarac, Tanasije Uzunovic, Mato Ergovic.

———

Veljko Bulajic directed one of the most expensive and biggest hits ever made in Yugoslavia with his

second World War II epic on Tito's breakthrough victory, "The Battle of Neretva," and one of the films that first revealed the country on the fest circuits, "Train Without a Timetable," on the shifting of ethnic groups to new territories after the war.

But his latest film lacks the budget it called for and its naivite does not help give this parable on love and power the disarming romanticism it aims at. The Devil and his domain, Hell, are involved in this too as Lucifer tries to right an 18th-century political incident that almost upsets the balance of power on earth between the Devil and the Church.

Hell is a sort of papier mache place with horned characters that are satirical facsimiles of people on earth. It is a cabaret vulgarization that makes Hell appear more comic than cosmic.

In the 18th century the Russian Czar is murdered to be replaced by his wife Catherine. The Devil feels this will give an edge to the Church and concocts an elaborate plot to send one of his minions, a schoolteacher double of the late Czar, to the earth over his abode.

The double, armed with magic weapons, is sent to Montenegro, a part of the future Yugoslavia, where there are soldiers loyal to the old Czar. Here he wins them over and they assume he is the Czar. But he falls in love, subsequently refuses to take his place on the Russian throne and has to be killed by the Devil's henchmen.

Bulajic does have his visual know-how but the balance of fantasy, romance and politics eludes him to make this mainly an item of local interest. —Mosk.

Life Of Brian
(BRITISH-COLOR)

Irreverent religioso spoof should top previous Monty Python pics. Probably will rile churches.

Hollywood, Aug. 14.
A Warner Brothers-Orion Pictures release. Produced by John Goldstone. Executive producers, George Harrison, Denis O'Brien. Directed by Terry Jones. Screenplay, Graham Chapman, John Cleese, Terry Gilliam, Eric Idle, Terry Jones, Michael Palin; design and animation, Terry Gilliam; camera (color), Peter Biziou; editor, Julian Doyle; music, Geoffrey Burgeon; art direction, Roger Christian; costume design, Hazel Pethig, Charles Knode; sound (Dolby Stereo) Garth Marshall; associate producer, Tim Hampton; assistant director, Jonathan Benson. Reviewed at the Bruin Theatre, W. Los Angeles, August 14, '79 (MPAA Rating: R.). Running time: **93 MINS.**
Cast: Terry Jones, Graham Chapman, Michael Palin, John Cleese, Ken Colley, Gwen Taylor, Eric Idle, Sue Jones-Davis, Spike Milligan, George Harrison, Terry Gilliam.

Monty Python's "Life Of Brian," utterly irreverent tale of a reluctant messiah whose impact proved somewhat less pervasive than that of his contemporary Jesus Christ, is just as wacky and imaginative as their previous film outings. As such, it should prove as appetizing to hardcore fans of the British comedy troupe as was "Monty Python And The Holy Grail," which Cinema V nurtured to over $5,000,000 in domestic rentals. With Orion and Warner Brothers handling it, this one could perform even better.

Pic gets off to a sock start as three wise men visit the manger of a newborn babe in Bethlehem and bestow gifts upon tot's crazed mother (played by director Terry Jones in drag), only to discover that the manger they're interested in is further down the street.

As an adult in Roman-occupied Palestine, Brian's life parallels that of Jesus, as he becomes involved in the terrorist Peoples Front of Judea, works as a vendor at the Colosseum, paints anti-Roman graffiti on palace walls, takes an unexpected trip thorough outer space in a wonderfully designed special effects sequence, unwittingly wins a following as a messiah and is ultimate condemned to the cross by a foppish Pontius Pilate.

Tone of the film, which will certainly earn the undying wrath of the many Christian believers, (see news stories this issue), is set by such scenes as a version of the sermon on the mount in which spectators shout out that they can't hear what's being said and start fighting amongst themselves, and the finale, in which a couple of dozen crucified men sing a chorus of "Bright Side Of Life."

One major sequence, in which two rival terrorist groups converge accidently in the sewer system on their respective ways to kidnap Pilate's wife, is a blatant lift from the bank robbery scene in Woody Allen's "Take The Money And Run."

Using stunning Tunisian locales, Peter Biziou's cinematography (with uncredited color processing or printing), gives film a great look, with all other creative aspects, such as music, costumes and art direction, adding significantly to the impression of lushness and verisimilitude.

Principal factor weighing against Monty Python breaking through with a truly mass audience is the frequent impenetrability of the English accents, difficult even for fairly accustomed American ears. Many also find that a little of this sort of humor goes a long way.

—*Cart.*

Le Divorcement
(FRENCH-COLOR)

Locarno, Aug. 21.
Gaumont release of Les Films De L'Alma-SFP production. Stars Michel Piccoli, Lea Massari. Directed by Pierre Barouh. Screenplay, Barouh, Marc Cadiot, from book by Cadiot; camera (Eastmancolor), Yves Lafaye; editor, Alain Leamitre-Mory; music, Barouh, Chris Rambault. Evelyne Dress. Reviewed at Locarno Fest, Aug. 11, '79. Running time: **115 MINS.**

Philippe	Michel Piccoli
Rosa	Lea Massari
Antoine	Jean-Claude Bouillon
Eva	Ann Lonnberg
Le Luthier	Maurice Baquet
Marianne	Christine Murillo
Mamam	Evelyne Dress

Pierre Barouh, songwriter, actor, singer, directed a sympathetic, loosely knitted film about two Algerian workers, "It Comes, It Goes," some years ago. Now he tries his hand at helming again and is still too apt to let his narrative meander and sprawl in this look at the effects of a divorce on a family of six.

Michel Piccoli, a seemingly successful pub rel man in his late forties, wants a divorce from Lea Massari, an emotional Italian woman who runs a shop. It is broached simply and it appears Piccoli is having an affair and she may have had one.

The children, ranging from 18 to seven, react in various ways as the time approaches for the final break. Barouh makes this all somewhat diffuse as Piccoli and his wife spend time with friends, who may be ex-lovers, talking about things that rarely reveal character or advance the narrative and with many cuttable to give more pace.

Piccoli has an aborted affair with a married woman, a final dramatic scene when his seemingly resigned wife suddenly gets hysterial and they end up making love for the last time. —*Mosk.*

Affairs
(HONG KONG-COLOR)

Hong Kong, Aug. 5.
A Sino-Great Wall Production. Produced by Fu Chi. Executive producer, Patrick Lui. Features entire cast. Directed by Stephen Shin. Screenplay, Mok Song; camera (color), Danny Tsang, Yeung Wor-Leung; editor, Li Yu-Huai, Koo Chi-Wai; music, Joseph Koo. Reviewed at Sunbeam Theatre, Hong Kong, Aug. 3, '79. Running Time: **112 MINS.**
Cast: Shih Hui, Fu Chi, Gigi Wong and Ivan Ho.
(Cantonese soundtrack with English subtitles.)

The closedown of a major television station (CTV) brought about the mass move of young directors from the small screen to the big one. One of these "new generation" talents is Stephen Shin who directs his first feature with Sino-Great Wall Prod.

Shin brings his light comedy situation tv style to "Affairs" and blend Oriental culture with the Western and the result is a passable pic about "now" Hong Kong.

"Affairs" is about love, marriage, adultery and related extra-marital activities in contemporary Hong Kong. The cast has been drawn from tv and their performances are just average. The film, though, establishes the refreshing entry of Shin in the field of commercial cinema.

The film is passable in practically every aspect. There are four episodes, namely In Love, Trial Love, Love and Broken Love.

In the first episode, a teacher called Zhu is a gambler and enjoys sex fantasies. His friends share his interests. Then Zhu gets smitten by a lovely new lady teacher and he changes his ways. This leads to marriage and after a series of humorous events, Zhu eventually returns to his old vices, but hides it from his wife and friends.

Trial Love is about Joe and Mary, who live together though not married which worries their conservative parents. Joe is jealous of Mary's exposure to other men because of her job as journalist. To hook her permanently, Joe proposes, but Mary refuses till she makes a fool of him first.

Love features a married man who leads a drab, stale life after many years of marriage. He tries to change his environment with disastrous marital results. The wife runs away but returns later and everything is the same. But nothing has changed and the prison-like life continues.

Broken Love is about a divorced couple trying to reunite with the help of a friend. The situation gets complex when the husband falls for the wife's best friend arranging for the reunion. But everything ends well when all the characters get their respective right partners.

Pic was shown at the third Hong Kong International Film Fest. "Affairs" has limited appeal for foreign viewers, but is just right for the Chinatown circuit as the film portrays Hong Kong of today which is the main selling point. —*Mel.*

The Proud Twins
(HONG KONG-COLOR)

Hong Kong, Aug. 4.
A Shaw Brothers production and release. Produced by Run Run Shaw. Directed by Chu Yuan. Features entire cast. Screenplay, Chin Yu, based on novel by Ku Lung; camera (color), Hung Chieh; music, Eddie Wang' martial art instructors, Tang Chia, Hunag Pei-chi. Reviewed at Jade Theatre, Hong Kong, Aug. 2, 1979. Running time: **100 MINS.**

Hsiao Yu Erh	Alexander Fu Sheng
Yen Nan Tien	Wang Yung
Trieh Sheng Lan	Wen Hsueh Erh
Mao Yung Ching	Ou Yang Pei San
Hua Wu Chueh	Wu Wei Ku
Princess Yi Hua	Meng Chiu
Priest Shen Hsi	Ai Fei
Hsiao Mi-mi	Liu Hui Ling

Chu Yuan was once an innovator in the field of martial arts movies. Now, he is merely a churner of standard Shaw Bros. costume epics. "The Proud Twins" is something he cannot be proud about though the film did well at the box-office mainly due to the material of writer Ku Lung. While a local crowd pleaser the pic was mainly produced for the majong playing clientele.

The plot is nothing new. Yen Nan Tien (Wang Yung), a known swordsman, departs for the Valley of the Villains with his dead friend's child, in search of the man responsible for the calamity. The other child was left with a rich woman. He is attacked by the villains and the child is taken away from him but finally rescued by a friendly magical doctor. The baby was kidnapped by the bizarre villains and raised to be a cynical and cunning person.

When he reaches the age of 18, Hsiao Yu Erh (Fu Sheng) is already a master martial artist. He gets rid of the people who raised him to seek evidence re his parent's death and his true identity. He meets Tieh Sheng Lan (Wen Hsueh Erh) who has a precious map leading to a treasure. Then he meets up with his twin brother without knowing it. The usual encounters and problems are faced by the hero but everything ends well in the end with the twin brothers joining forces to rid of all evil forces.

The film's best asset is the presence of action star Alexander Fu Sheng who is fast emerging as a capable comedian. He is cocky, handsome, exhuberant, refreshing and dashing as the poor twin. The sets though are laughable. The scenes shift from indoor studio sets to outdoor locations while the soundtrack music varies. —Mel.

Locarno Fest

Gli Anni Struggenti
(Th Burning Years)
(ITALIAN-COLOR)

Locarno, Aug. 21.
Filmalpha. Megavision release and production. Features entire cast. Directed by Vittorio Sindoni. Screenplay, Nicola Badalucco. Sindoni, Mario Gallo; camera (Color), Safai Teherani; editor, Angelo Curi. Reviewed at Locarno Film Fest, Aug. 6, '79. Running time: **90 MINS.**
Saverio .... Fabio Traversi
Andreina .... Laura Lenzi
Father .... Gabriele Ferzetti

Film harks back to the early sixties and is the tale of a young man's break from his oppressive father who wants him to follow in his footsteps as an educator in a small town. But it does not give any new twists or insights into the period and emerges a rote, unassuming but now slightly outmoded film.

Acting is somewhat disparate from Gabriele Ferzetti's florid, overplayed, demanding father to the introverted dreamy son of Fabrio Traversa and the wooden prettiness of Laura Lenzi who brings first love to the son and his first attempt to break with his demanding family.

He is brought back by his father when he misses his exam for a teaching post due to his affair with a girl he meets in Rome while waiting for his exam. But he finally realizes he has lost something and decides to leave home for good.

It is a predictable spinoff from more successful late fifties and early sixties pix, especially Ermanno Olmi's "The Job." Its sitcom surface gentleness could make this an okay playoff item at home though lacking any originality and more potent and pointed insights into youthful revolt to give this much foreign chances.

Technically average. —Mosk.

Fagyongyok
(Mistletoes)
(HUNGARIAN-B&W)

Locarno, Aug. 21.
Hungarofilm release of Hunnia Studio — Bela Balasz Studio production. Features entire cast. Written and directed by Judit Ember. Camera (black and white), Jan-os Illes; music. Zsolt Dome. Reviewed at Locarno Film Fest, Aug. 10, '79. Running time: **91 MINS.**
Jeno .... Jeno Sipos
Nora .... Nora Sipos
Mother .... Eleonora Lukasik
Grandmother .... Mrs. Lukasik

There seems to be a movement growing in the Hungarian film of fictionalized documentaries using real people and made in black and white for more authenticity. After "Family Nest," about overcrowding in worker homes and family adjustment, comes this slice-of-life of a young worker from the country who wants to build his own home and shape his own life within the system.

There is a charm in the interplay of the characters and enough incident and pertinent observation to overcome the lack of narrative thread. Film has a neat evocation of the hero's relationship with his soon-to-be wife who is soon to have his child and has two other children by other men.

Her mother is also well limned as a whimsical woman who sometimes annoys but yet charms her daughter, man with her ideas for the house they are building. He does his work but also picks mistletoe to sell at markets and finally buys an old car to ease things.

A film that may lead to more revealing, more probing films on the lives of workers, Judit Ember is a director to be watched as she gets a more rounded edge into her mixture of reworked reality into narrative form. —Mosk.

Staromodnaia Komedia
(The Old Comedy)
(RUSSIAN-COLOR)

Locarno, Aug. 21.
Sovexport release of Mosfilm production. Features entire cast. Directed by E. Savelieva, Tatyana Berezantseva. Screenplay, A. Abrouzov, V. Jelenzniakov from the play by Abrouzov; camera (Sovcolor), B. Kotcherov; editor, L. Boulgakova; music, M. Tariverdiev. Reviewed at Locarno Film Fest, Aug. 8, '79. Running time: **100 MINS.**

Lidia .... Alissa Freyndikh
Rodion .... Igor Validimirov

A stagebound film version of a two-character Russian play about two fiftyish people that fits that old formula of boy meets girl though in this case it is man meets woman. The play was a hit in Paris last season and played the U.S. two years ago as "Do You Do Somersaults?"

At a seaside health resort, a bright and pert woman of 50 or so comes late for a meeting with a more staid and simple doctor of about 60. Her fey ways bother the doctor and they part in anger. But they meet again and slowly begin to unburden themselves to each other as a common acceptance and, perhaps, love grow.

She finally decides to stay with him. The verbal battles and then revealing of past hurts and needs is somewhat static on film though they can be more acceptable on stage. Alissa Freyndikh is rightly lively and vulnerable as a woman who has lived with her heart on her sleeve while Igor Validimirov is properly reserved as he finally goes from exasperation to love.

Film is opened up a bit for walks, restaurants and other areas. But this remains essentially static though enlivened by two plucky players. The garish color, flat direction and sometimes arch and cloying characterizations keep this mainly a local item and a surprising one to be seen competing at an international film festival.
—Mosk.

Le Nouveau Venu
(The Newcomer)
(BENIN-COLOR)

Locarno, Aug. 21.
Iris Films, International Tropic Films release and production. Features entire cast. Directed by Richard De Meideros. Screenplay, De Meideros, Rene Ewagnion, Bouraima Lawani; camera (Eastmancolor), Maxime Lefevre, Bouraima Lawani; editor, Andree Davanture. Reviewed at Locarno Film Fest, Aug. 3, '79. Running time. **87 MINS.**
With: Michel Djondo, Sikirou Ogoujobi, Ages Capo-Cichi, Sebastien De Souza.

Films from black African nations only intermittently surface at film festivals, outside those of the Senegalese filmmaker Ousmane Sembene. But the Locarno Festival unveiled an interesting film from Mali last year, "The Porter," on changing ways, and this year from another country, Benin, also dealing with the conflict of old and new ways of thinking.

Benin is the new name for the independent country that was once an African colony, Dahomey. The language of business and government bureaus is French and colonial hangovers conflict with newer ways as life evolves in this country.

A serious young administrator takes over a government office. He comes into conflict with the old boss of the workers who is against any attempts for more efficiency and especially for more work for his staff or challenges to his standing.

There is a witty scene when he gets rid of a new man who is too efficient at the typewriter. When the new director insists on changes he puts an ancient hex on him and perhaps even poisons his drinks.

The director begins to feel ill and even a bit frightened as he has atavistic dreams of old spells. He has himself exorcised by his old tribal chief but has an auto accident that leaves him with a limp.

The old office chief suddenly has a change of mind as he admits to the limping director, on his return, that he has been wrong in his ways and will now work with him. This may be a naive, didactic addition for locals. But the film has assimilated accepted film grammar and yet invoked an insight into African ways, thinking and manners.

It may not be the film to break into more commercial or even specialized theatrical circuits abroad but appears worthy of fest, seminar and museum showings. More promising than completely successful in its probing of the problems of the emerging African nations as seen on a smaller scale in an office. The characters are types though they have a bit more depth than the often stereotyped personnages representing old and new ways in African films. —Mosk.

Letze Liebe
(Last Love)
(WEST GERMAN-COLOR)

Locarno, Aug. 21.
Thuering. Engstrom Filmproduktion release and production. Features entire cast. Written and directed by Ingemo Engstrom. Camera (Eastmancolor), Ingo Kratisch; editor, Gerhard Theuring. Reviewed at Locarno Film Fest, Aug. 9, '79. Running time: **125 MINS.**
With: Angela Winkler, Rudiger Vogler, Therese Affolter, Hildegarde Schmahl, Wolfgang Kinder, Geoffrey Layton.

A grim portentous tale of a doomed couple playing out their passionate but pointless love on the background of a world going neurotic and violent. But much is too symbolic and the death wishes of the protagonists more metaphorical than building up a more potent human basis to this essentially pretentious treatment of alienation.

A woman works in a psychiatric ward and uses video as a means of making contact with her patients as well as for her notes. One is a woman who wanted to commit suicide with her husband. She meets a mysterious man alongside the river and they become lovers in a small hotel that faces some nuclear reactors in the distance.

She had had children, now living in Paris, and he seems just adrift. When she is dismissed from her work she takes along some poison. She and her lover are seen lying alongside the river.

Directed with more solemnity than insight, the film has a certain in visual finesse but is finally too pedestrian to bring an enlightening and revealing touch to its theme of maladjustment and refusal to allow love to take the place of a saner world. Old German weltschmerz, world weariness, is not quite brought up to date.

Film is well played by Angela Winckler and Rudiger Vogler as the couple. It might be worth West German film week outings and festival and museum airings but is somewhat too nebulous and over-indulgent for more commercial use abroad. The West German film renaissance seems to be getting somewhat too personalized and losing touch with its ambitious themes. —*Mosk.*

Rallarblod
(Blood of the Railroad Workers)
(NORWEGIAN-COLOR)

Locarno, Aug. 22.

Norsk Film release and production. Features entire cast. Written and directed by Erik Solbakken. Camera (Eastmancolor), Bjorn Jegerstedt; editor, Edith Toreg. music, Gunnar Germeten. Reviewed at Locarno Film Fest, Aug. 7, '79. Running time, 112 MINS.

With: Nils Olle Oftebro, Ragnhild Hilt, Svein Tindberg, Katja Medboe, Espen Skjonberg.

This period tale of itinerant railroad builders at the turn-of-the-century does try to add salient social issues of repressiveness, snobbism and ostracism to its essentially familiar tale of macho line workers and their redblooded lives as brawlers and lovers. But it lacks insights into its characters and a more knowing blend of action and observation to bring it off.

There are too many cliches, as a love scene outdoors which leads to panning up a tree trunk, and the usual brawls and the manliness of the hero railroad lineman who finally ends up with the daughter of a rich land-owner near one of their building sites when they stand up to the mores of the times.

The period seems right and this does have some robust scenery. But it misses a more rounded approach to this basically familiar theme of breaking class barriers through love. Technically good and probably looking in for good chances on its home grounds.
—*Mosk.*

Grauzone
(Zones)
(SWISS-B&W)

Locarno, Aug. 21.

Cactus Film release of a Nemo Film production. Features entire cast. Written and directed by Fredi M. Murer. Camera (black and white), Hans Liechti; editor, Rainer Trinkler; music Mario Beretta. Reviewed at Locarno Film Fest, Aug. 8, '79. Running time: 103 MINS.

With Giovanni Fruh, Olga Piazza, Janet Huafler, Walo Luond.

Dark black-and-white lensing does not help this heavyhanded attempt at satirizing Swiss or any national human complacency. Trying to take a swipe at regimentation, consumer slavery and the growling lack of privacy, film is somewhat too bleak and unimaginative to give it a needed blend of comic and dramatic relevance.

The hero has been promoted to head of a system of electronic spying on all aspects of his company. But a clandestine radio station and newspaper ads talk of an epidemic of human dreariness and self negation that awakens the hero to a sudden decision to tell all the employees they are being spied on.

Film may have some more meaning and appeal to Swiss audiences on its allusions but it appears somewhat obtuse, over-indulged and finally repetitively dull to the uninitiated. Mainly a local item that may reveal some flaws in this rich, self-sufficient little country.
—*Mosk.*

Novinar
(Journalist)
(YUGOSLAV-COLOR)

Pula, Aug. 14.

Yugoslavia Film release of Jadran Film-Croatia Film-Radna Filma production. Features entire cast. Written and directed by Fadil Hadzic. Camera (Eastmancolor), Tomislav Pinter; music, Alfi Kabilgo. Reviewed at Pula Film Fest, July 31, '79. Running time: 105 MINS.

With: Rade Serbedjija, Fabijan Sovagovic, Mladen Budiscak, Milena Zupancic, Vera Zima, Tonko Lonza.

A good but hotheaded journalist on a political newspaper comes up against pressures that lead to his downfall when he bucks what he feels are unsound pressures from his editor and other "higher ups."

He has a fight with the editor who refused to print his story on a metal factory strike. He then gets arrested when he strews the papers from a newsstand while drunk one night, and is brought up before the self management council of the paper.

He is reprimanded for his actions but stays on. He has trouble at home as his wife is against his ways. She wants him to follow the management's dictates so they can have more money. But he goes his own way with more fallouts with the editors and loses a court case brought by a politician who claims he was misquoted in a story by the journalist.

Witnesses are coerced, and the newsman has a mild heart attack. His wife leaves him, taking their son. Even an obit he does on an old alcoholic, a once renowned newsman, in which he invokes the transient aspects of journalism and its meaning, is heavily cut. He ends up alone and perhaps will give in or go the way of the alcoholic newsman.

Film does bring up various attitudes concerning the meaning of a free press. But the film lacks personal feeling and human characters. The journalist is too intransigent and somewhat sanctimonious in his crusade.

But it does have a good visual flair as it presents the various sides of both journalist and management though finally more didactic than truly dramatic and effective in its handling of a familiar but potent theme. More interesting in its subject matter than treatment, film remains a respectable but mainly local item. —*Mosk.*

Supersonic Man
(SPANISH-COLOR)

Madrid, Aug. 14.

Almena Films S.A. production. Directed by Juan Piquer. Features entire cast. Screenplay, Sebastian Moi and Juan Piquer; camera (Eastmancolor-Supercolor and Dinavision), Juan Marine; editor, Pedro del Rey; special effects and sets. Emilio Ruiz and Francisco Prosper; optical effects, Jack Elkubi and Miguel Villa; music, Gino Peguri, Juan Luis Izaguirre, Carlos Attias. Reviewed at Cine Roxy B, Madrid, Aug. 13, '79. Running time: 85 MINS.

Cast: Michael Coby, Cameron Mitchell, Richard Yesteran, Diana Polakov, Jose Maria Caffarel, Frank Brana, Javier de Campos, Tito Garcia, Quique Camoiras, Luis Barboo, Angel Ter.

There is, admittedly, not a single original idea in "Supersonic Man." It is a conglomerate of "Superman," "Star Wars," James Bond and even an inconsequential touch of "Jaws." But given its comic strip level, and its low IQ dialogs, it nonetheless has enough excitement and convincing special effects to make it palatable to non-sophisticated audiences. Item could do well in commercial circuits around the world as filmic fodder for action-prone audiences.

"Supersonic Man" is a thinly-disguised Superman; instead of him being a newspaper reporter, he's a private eye. His costume is similar to Superman's (he wears a mask in addition); he has also come from a distant galaxy to save the world, and is gifted with the power of flight and superhuman strength. There is also a villain, Dr. Gulk, bent upon destroying the world, played by Cameron Mitchell, plus a rather unattractive take-off on Lois Lane, named Patricia.

What makes the film click are the special effects and some touches of moppet-level humor, both very well handled. Though the effects are not as slick as in "Superman" they are certainly well-enough done on the whole to be spectacular and convincing. We see Supersonic flying through the air over Manhattan (part of pic was lensed in New York on locations), space craft travelling interstellar distances, a Bondlike underground launching site; Supersonic lifts a steam roller to save his gal from crashing into it with her car; he defies bullets (by catching them and throwing them back), braves hell fires and ice, escapes in civvies from a bag under water with hands tied. And the effects are usually good enough to be believable.

To liven up the action a bit more, producer-director Juan Piquer, ("Voyage to the Centre of the Earth"), also throws in a robot, that shoots rockets at trucks and bullets at soldiers. There are some excessively talky parts, when Dr. Gulk argues morality with the heroine's captured father, Prof. Borgen, citing Caesar and Shakespeare. But generally film works well enough and is certainly in the international Grade-B level. —*Besa.*

At Taormina

La Giacca Verde
(The Green Jacket)
(ITALIAN-COLOR)

Taormina, July 23.

An Arturo La Pegna, CEP Production. Directed by Franco Giraldi. Written by Giraldi, Lucio Battistrada, Sandra Onofri, Cesare Garboli. Sets, Guido Josia; camera (color), Dario di Palma; music, Luis Bacalov; editor, Raimondo Crociani; costumes, Danda Ortona. Features Jean-Pierre Cassel, Renzo Montagnani, Senta Berger, Vittorio Senipoli. Reviewed at Taormina Festival, July 23, '79. Running time: 120 MINS.

Inspired by a story of Soldati, this film is a well-played, intense character study revolving around the aesthetics of the true-false side of one's artistic talents and impulses. The drama concerns a famous symphonic conductor, Salvini (Jean-Pierre Cassel), who suffers a mental crisis while rehearsing Verdi's "Otello."

The source of this neurosis seems to be his recognition of the orchestra's tympanist as someone from his past. There is a flashback, to the final days of World War II, when Salvini had taken a false identity in order to hide, for political reasons, in a rural convent. There he meets a rather pompous, well-meaning fellow, a person of some authority who fancies himself a musical genius. This character, Romualdi, clad in a bilious-green woolen jacket, is looked upon as an amusement for the real maestro, who encourages Romualdi's fumbling efforts as a choirmaster and concert pianist.

Salvini is also distracted by a beautiful film actress (Senta Berger) who is residing in her country retreat to escape the dangers of the not-too-distant battles. The conductor and the actress both have malicious fun with the dilettante-maestro, as well as indulge in a listless affair.

The cruelty towards the feckless but likable Romualdi backfires, because he becomes Salvini's tympanist, throwing into the story the entire moral responsibility of their friendship. Romualdi's humble acceptance of his mediocrity causes Salvini to question his own talents.

In the telling, the story is a slight one, and its tendency to drag here and there is lightened by the excellent performances of Cassel, Berger, and particularly Renzo Montagnani, who wins one's sympathies throughout. All technical credits ae fine, and Giraldi has wrought a subtle, worthy Italian drama here. —*Albe.*

Der Landvogt von Griefensee
(The Bailiff of Griefensee)
(SWISS-COLOR)

Taormina, July 28.
A Condor Film, Zurigo Production. Directed by Wilfried Bolliger Written by Bolliger and Gerold Spaeth from the novel by Gottfried Keller. Features entire cast. Sets, Mario Garbuglia; camera (color), Armando Nannuzzi, music, Arie Dzierlatka; editors, Johnny Dubach. Uschi Meier. Reviewed as Taormina Festival, July 26, '79 Running time: 100 MINS.

This very stylish adaptation of Gottfried Keller's 19th century novel is a thoroughly delightful comedy of manners, somewhat reminiscent of Eric Rohmer's "La Marquise von O." with its witty aphorisms, pastel color photography and a strong ironic twist to the plot.

The director, Wilfried Bolliger, is a newcomer who has worked independently in Switzerland and Germany, and in this, his second feature, proves to be a discovery to watch in the future.

The story concerns a handsome cavalier ("The Bailiff of Griefensee") named Salomon Landolt, who, in his later years, looks back upon his picaresque love life and decides to invite the five women who most dominated his affections to spend a weekend with him. Each woman has not seen Salomon for years and thinks that she alone has been invited. The film flashbacks to the five amorous interludes, then concludes with those brilliant sequences describing the encounter of Salomon and his lost loves.

The cast is a very attractive one, and acting is on a high level. Christian Quadflieg is a dashing hero, and among the women, Laura Trotter, Silvia Dionisio, Adelheid Arndt and Pauline Larrieu are standouts. Alida Valli as a roguish housekeeper is delightful, particularly in the denouement, in which Salomon asks his ladies (most of them married) to choose as his wife either a mature hausfrau or a virginal young maidservant.

Technically, the film is superb, with certain sequences reminiscent of paintings by Watteau. Pic is sure to turn up on the international market, via festivals.
—*Albe.*

Tsenu Smerti Sprosi u Miortvykh
(The Dead Pay the Price for Death)
(RUSSIAN-COLOR)

Taormina, July 25.
A Tallin Film production. Directed by Kalio Kiisk. Written by Mati Unt; sets, Tynu Virve; camera (color), Juri Sillart. Reviewed at Taormina Festival, July 26, '79, Running time: 75 MINS.

Cast: Juozas Kiselus, Gediminas Girdvainis, Kabjn Kommissarov, Maria Klens Kaya, Elle Kul.

A well-made, slightly confusing story of espionage, revolutionary activists and counter-revolutionary vendettas in 1925 Estonia. The heroes are well-defined, and young Juozas Kiselus as Anton, the major figure in this violent story, is one of those emblematic figures who is constantly interesting to watch, even if the political motivations remain obscure. It has all been seen before (chases, tortures, betrayals, ruthless tribunals and double-crosses) and it is only the novelty of seeing an Estonian film that gives this work much interest.

The direction by Kalio Kiisk is slick and technically proficient, and the acting ranges from mere attitudes to a sort of cynical hysteria. This is all melodrama, but cameraman Juri Sillart has produced some unusual visual effects in color-shading that catch one's attention more than the plot. —*Albe.*

Time After Time
(BRITISH-COLOR)

H.G. Wells as the Frisco Kid.

Hollywood, Aug. 22.
Warner Bros./Orion release of a Herb Jaffe production. Produced by Jaffe. Directed by Nicholas Meyer. Stars Malcolm McDowell, David Warner, Mary Steenburgen. Screenplay, Meyer, based on a story by Kearl Alexander, Steve Hayes; camera (color), Paul Lohmann; editor, Donn Cambern; music, Miklos Rozsa, production design, Edward C. Carfagno; sound, Jerry Jost; stunt coordinator, Everett Creach; special effects, Larry Fuentes, Jim Blount; assistant director, Michael Daves. Reviewed at Samuel Goldwyn Theatre, BevHills, Aug. 21, '79. (MPAA Rating: PG.) Running time: 112 MINS.

H.G. Wells	Malcolm McDowell
Stevenson	David Warner
Amy	Mary Steenburgen
Lt. Mitchell	Charles Cioffi
Mrs. Turner	Andonia Katsaros
Shirley	Patti D'Arbanville
Carol	Geraldine Baron

"Time After Time" is a delightful, entertaining trifle of a film that show both the possibilities and limitations of taking liberties with literature and history. Nicholas Meyer, who specializes in this sort of endeavor (he scripted "The Seven Percent Solution," and wrote and directed "Time"), has deftly juxtaposed Victorian England and contemporary America in a clever story, irresistible due to the competence of its cast. If word-of-mouth can be stimulated, Warner Bros. and Orion may have a minor hit on their hands.

In "Seven Percent Solution," Sherlock Holmes and Sigmund Freud were joined on cinematic ground. This time around, it's the turn of H.G. Wells and Jack The Ripper, who abandon London circa 1893 in Wells' famous time machine. Their arrival in 1979's San Francisco is played for all the enevitable anachronisms, with results that are both witty and pointed.

In lesser hands, "Time After Time" might have been hamstrung by the essentially thin plot line. After all, once Wells and Slashing Jack have acclimatized themselves to the Frisco fog, what's left?

Thanks to Meyers' astute scripting and direction, and superb performances by Malcolm McDowell as Welles, David Warner as the mythical killer, and Mary Steenburgen as the woman in between, there's plenty of mileage in "Time."

All that's lacking, in fact, is additional background on the friendship between Wells and the Warner character, a trusted physician associate of McDowell's before his nastier instincts are unveiled. Since the film dwells excessively on this relationship, especially with McDowell in pursuit of Warner, some further character development was in order.

Essence of the pic's appeal, however, centers not on the thriller aspects (which are in abundance), but on the very human qualities expressed by McDowell and Steenburgen. Former is excellent as the gullible Gulliver in a strange world, befuddled by the reality of his dreamed-of Utopian paradise.

It's Steenburgen, in only her second film role after a nice debut in "Goin' South," who gives "Time After Time" something special. With her loose delivery and natural style, Steenburgen resembles a laid-back Judy Holliday, and her comic timing is just as adroit. Together, she and McDowell make the love story aspects of "Time" affecting, not affected.

Warner is proving himself a highly versatile performer with a brace of recent and upcoming roles that differ widely in scope and character. His 19th century villain, who, in chortle, "I'm Home" among the pimps and sex shops of North Beach, may adjust a hint too quickly, but he plays the part to the hilt.

In his first directorial effort, Meyers has mounted a handsome, lithe production that falters in only one respect. The comedy-romance aspects are unwisely mixed with violence that becomes gruesome, rather than sanguinary, particularly in a concluding scene. The unsettling effect this will have on audiences remains to be seen, but it detracts from the appealing nature of the film.

"Time After Time" succeeds on almost every other level, including Paul Lohmann's clean, spare camerawork, Donn Cambern's facile editing, Miklos Rozsa's appropriate score, and Edward C. Carfagno's atmospheric production design.

There are also some special visual effects by Larry Fuentes and Jim Blount that are a welcome return to the twinkling opticals of yesteryear. These, and the reappearance of the retired WB logo, make "Time After Time" a welcome remembrance of things past, present and future. —*Poll.*

Nest Of Vipers
(Ritratto di Borghesia in Nero)
(ITALIAN-COLOR)

Hell hath no fury, etc.

Paramount Pictures release of a Mars Film production. Produced by Piero La Mantia. Directed by Tonino Cervi. Stars Ornella Muti, Senta Berger. Screenplay, Tonino Cervi, Cesare Frugoni, Goffredo Parise, based on short story, "The Piano Teacher," by Roger Peyrefitte; camera (color), Armando Nannuzzi; editor, Nino Baragli; music, Vincenzo Tempera. No other credits provided. Reviewed at Paramount Screening Room, Aug. 30, 1979. (M-PAA Rating-R). Running time: 105 MINS.
Elena Mazzarini . . . . Ornella Muti
Carla Richter . . . . Senta Berger
Mattio Morandi . . . . . . Christian Borromeo
Amaalia Mazzarani . . . . Capucine
Also: Giuliana Calandra, Stefano Patrizi, Giancarlo Sbragia, Paolo Bonacelli, Mattia Sbragia, Maria Monti, Eros Pagni, Antonia Cancellieri, Suxanne Creese Bates, Raffaele Di Mario, Giancarlo Marinaangeli, Giovanni Caenazzo.

This Paramount-financed Italian effort, going into the Trans-Lux East in New York this week in a fast booking, was originally called "Ritratto di Borghesia in Nero" (Portrait of a Bourgeois in Black), which is less meaningful than the "Nest of Vipers" label pinned on it for its American release. As all of the character range from weak and susceptible to vicious and vindictive it's an apt description.

The main thing going for it are the pulchritudinous ladies who share the top billing — the stunning Ornella Muti and the beautiful Senta Berger. The tale is simple — seduction by Berger of a young friend of her son. The boy in turn falls in love and plans to marry a maiden who's Berger's student. Jealousy and revenge. There's not a great deal of originality in the plot — filmgoers who remember Elizabeth Taylor and Susannah York in "X, Y and Zee," can easily see what's coming in one of the several seduction scenes.

The male members of the cast are colorless by comparison to the two females — no, make it three as Capucine is also stunning as Muti's mother. Aside from the acting, the main asset of the film is Armando Nannuzzi's gorgeous photography of Venice — without dwelling on the canals, he makes the various palazzi handsome and comfortable. There's a villa on an island in one scene that could be a tourist poster for the city.

Entertaining and lovely but not very exciting. —*Robe.*

Krigernes Boern
(Children Of The Warriors)
(DANISH-COLOR)

Copenhagen, Aug. 24.
A A 'S Panorama (Just Betzer) production and release. Features entire cast. Directed by Ernst Johansen. Screenplay, Hans Oversen, camera Ernst Johanson; (Eastmancolor) Peter Roos, editor and asst. director, Lizzi Weischenfeldt; music, Sebastian; production designer, Palle Arestrup; executive producer, Lars Kolvig. Reviewed at Palladium, Copenhagen. Aug. 24, 1979. Running time, 90 MINS.
Nelo . . . . Jannik Lesnaik
Alfo . . . . Soeren Hindborg
Kerama . . . . Lars Froehling
Ilni . . . . Susanne Storm
Nyla . . . . Charlotte Mortensen
My . . . . Jeanette Hultberg
Andante . . . . Ove Sprogoe
Neral . . . . Pierre Lindstedt

"Children of The Warriors" is an ambitious and costly (close to 3,000,000 Danish Kroner, some of money supplied by the State Film Institute) feature made for a too-limited market: the serious-minded teenagers.

Older children and adults will find plot dramatics and dialog far too schematic, and director Ernst Johansen's direction of actors is so weak that neither sweet faced children nor highly skilled professional actors like Ove Sprogoe succeed in mouthing their words convincingly. Cutting film up in three parts might, however, make it a good offshore sales item for tv.

Plot has five children run away from the tyranny of the warrior tribe (drawn rather like Stone Age People) they belong to. They hope to find a haven and a better life with the citizens, artisans and fishermen, on an island where life is lived to look rather like the 1920's, Scandinavian style. Their hopes are thwarted, however, when the islanders soon prove to be either exploiters or exploited in the worst kind of class-divided society, where life's conditions have made mean people out of most of them.

Violence and abuse pursue the children, but their optimism somehow leads a few of the islanders to both kinder ways and to social revolt.

Production design is handsome, but Peter Roos' cinematography and Lizzi Weischenfeldt's editing struggle in vain to put life into the story-line's messed up dramatics and a dialog always uncomfortably close to rhetoric. —*Kell.*

Au Revoir ... A Lundi
(Good-bye ... See You Monday)
(FRANCO-CANADIAN-COLOR)

Paris, Aug. 29.
An United Artists release of a Fildebroc — CAPAC (Paris)/Sommerville House (Montreal) coproduction. Stars Miou-Miou, Carole Laure, Claude Brasseur, David Birney. Directed by Maurice Dugowson. Screenplay, Jacques and Maurice Dugowson, Roger Fournier, from novel, "Moi, Mon Corps, Mon Ame, Montreal, etc." by Fournier; camera (color), Francois Protat; music, Lewis Furey, Jean-Daniel Mercier; editor, Jean-Bernard Bonis; art director, Michel Proulx; sound, Henri Blondeau. Reviewed at the U.G.C. Normandie cinema, Paris; Aug. 27, 1979. Running time: 110 MINS.
Lucie . . . . Carole Laure
Nicole . . . . Miou-Miou
Arnold . . . . Claude Brasseur
Frank . . . . David Birney
Robert . . . . Frank Moore
Jack . . . . Alain Montpetit

Contrived scripting seriously depreciates this sometimes poignant tale of two women — one French, the other Canadian — living in Montreal. It's a view of young, single women of ordinary intelligence and no real skills or professional ambitions who are looking for the "grand amour." Some local critics have come down hard on the film because its male authors have chosen personages who cannot function without men in their lives.

Carole Laure and Miou-Miou are fine as two roommates who seem locked into a trend of getting involved with married men who love them during the week and leave them on weekends to rejoin their families. Their latest affairs have proven as unfruitful as ever except that Laure is left pregnant. In defiant, rankling disappointment she decides to have the baby.

When Miou-Miou meets handsome David Birney, a doctor from Florida, she falls immediately. That he's single is an added attraction and she precipitously decides to go live with him in the States. Laure gets involved with another married man, Claude Brasseur. Both relationships founder and Miou-Miou returns to Montreal and her girlfriend.

Like Agnes Varda's "One Sings, the Other Doesn't," Maurice Dugowson's film is a paean to the enduring bond between women that functions even during separation. Through Dugowson's sensitive clear-eyed direction, the two actresses make their scenes together glowingly natural and touching.

This naturalness is marred by a rigidity in the shape of the story that gives the film an artificial, unconvincing veneer. In a neat play of events the two girl's fortunes run amazingly parallel: their relationships with men breaking up and forming — they meet Brasseur and Birney the very same day — with a synchronization that works better in a play. All of this is not helped by some weak scripting, as in the scenes of Miou-Miou's life in Florida.

The production is quite handsome, particularly Francois Protat's color photography, which captures the special appeal of snowbound Montreal. —*Len.*

When A Stranger Calls
(COLOR)

Don't answer the door.

Hollywood, Aug. 31.
Columbia Pictures release of a Melvin Simon production. Produced by Doug Chapin, Steve Feke. Exec producers, Melvin Simon, Barry Krost. Directed by Fred Walton. Stars Charles Durning, Carol Kane, Colleen Dewhurst. Screenplay, Feke, Walton; camera (color), Don Peterman; editor, Sam Vitale; music, Dana Kaproff; production design, Elayne Barbara Ceder; sound, Martin Bolger; assistant director, Ed Ledding. Reviewed at The Burbank Studios, Burbank, Aug. 31, '79. (MPAA Rating: R.) Running time: 97 MINS.
Jill Johnson . . . . Carol Kane
John Clifford . . . . Charles Durning
Tracy . . . . Colleen Dewhurst

Curt Duncan . . . . Tony Beckley
Dr. Monk . . . . Rachel Roberts
Mrs. Mandrakis . . . . Rutanya Alda
Dr. Mandrakis . . . . . . Carmen Argenziano
Lt. Charlie Garber . . . . Ron O'Neal
Stephen Lockart . . . . Steven Anderson

"When A Stranger Calls" has all the classic elements and devices of mystery-suspense films except one: plausibility. The Melvin Simon production, which represents the first feature for scripters-director Steve Feke and Fred Walton, should scare up some good business in the hinterlands. But true success may prove elusive without the essential grounding in reality this kind of pic needs. Still, with the proper hard sell, Columbia Pictures should reap more than adequate returns.

Thanks to a fine cast, a rich and atmospheric score by Dana Kaproff, and astute direction by co-writer Walton, "Stranger" is unquestionably a scary film. Bridging two distinct storylines, one the standard frightened babysitter alone in a dark house, and the other the subsequent manhunt for an escaped killer, script by Feke and Walton has chills a-plenty.

But something seems lacking overall. By the film's end, the deficiency seems clear — key actions and motivations just don't make sense. Questions that are glossed over in throwaway lines or hurried explanations come back to haunt "When A Stranger Calls."

Since thriller audiences aren't in theatres to exercise their minds, it may not make a difference. And "Stranger" delivers what it sets out to do, by inflicting a prickly sense of 'error in almost every shot.

Carol Kane, who disappears for almost 70 of the film's 97 minutes, is quite good as the terrified sitter who grows up to have the same chilling chain of events begin all over again. Colleen Dewhurst is also fine in the other principal femme role, a barfly who narrowly escapes from killer Tony Beckley.

It's Charles Durning, who excels in these low-key characterizations, who ends up giving the pic some class, along with Beckley, very frightening as the British killer. Rachel Roberts and Ron O'Neal are given little to do.

More than anything else, "When A Stranger Calls" resembles a good, old-fashioned grade B thriller. That's almost a dying breed, and "Stranger" serves its memory well. —Poll.

Kristoffers hus
(Kristoffer's House)
(SWEDISH-COLOR)

Malmoe, Aug. 27.
A Swedish Film Institute, HB Three Leaf Clover, AB Svensk Film production, AB Svensk Film release. Features entire cast. Screenplay, Lars Lennart Forsberg, Vilgot Sjoman, Thommy Berggren, based on Johan Bargum's novel, "Darkroom"; Directed and edited by Lars Lennart Forsberg. Camera (Fujicolor), Lennart Carlsson, Lasse Karlsson; production design, Ulf Axen; executive producer for Swedish Film Institute, Mans Reutersvaerd; music, Lars Dahlberg, Bjorn Isgaard. Reviewed at Camera, Malmoe, Sweden during Malmoe Film Days Aug. 27, 1979. Running time: **96 MINS.**
Kristoffer . . . . Thommy Berggren
Hanna . . . . Agneta Eckemyr
Grandmother . . . . Mimi Pollack
The mother . . . . Gunnel Brostroem
The editor . . . . Boerje Ahlsted
The half-mute girl . . . . Pia Garde
Little Frida . . . . Linda Megner

"Kristoffer's House" is an ambitious thriller in depth doomed to be spooked by its many resemblances to Michelangelo Antonioni's "Blow-Up" since it deals heavily in symbols and has as its chief protagonist a young photographer who reaches a crisis in his own life when contemplating photos he has taken on the sly of a lonely, elderly suicide in a Stockholm apartment.

Could the dead man be a distorted mirror image of Kristoffer's own eventual fate? Kristoffer lives with his grandmother and his small daughter (he has won custody and gets a monthly allowance for the child from the remarried mother) in a huge old house, whose owner Kristoffer's ever-absent mother, will surely sell it any day.

Kristoffer's way of life and work is also threatened by an increasing disgust with the more lurid aspects of his work although he is just abut to gain recognition as a serious pictorial artist.

Furthermore, his mistress claims that he loves only himself when he does not allow her to stay overnight in his house. She starts taking other lovers, mostly as a revenge, but it works on Kristoffer's nervous system.

Looking into the dead man's background, Kristoffer finds out that he is of rural stock and has only been transferred from rural family life to the lonesome, modern apartment when he was getfing to be a nuisance to his family. The socio-political analogy is obvious, but at the same time, though Forsberg tells his story as Everyman's Crisis, he points no moralistic fingers. This is a strength insofar as it allows audiences to fill Forsberg's frames with whatever meaning they want, but it is also a weakness because one might suspect that the same frames are empty.

Thommy Berggren is a marvel as an actor. Whether his face is still or in motion it exudes moods and psychological shadings far richer than anything implied in the script. Agneta Eckemyr is nicely eye-catching as the mistress and does some clean, subdued acting. So does Boerje Ahlsted as the cynical editor of a scandal weekly.

Everybody performs well, actually, the cinematography is handsome and so are all production values. Where Forsberg's film fails is in stating its theme andor its message strongly enough for many people to identify with Kristoffer's crisis.

With too muddy a psychology and too loose a suspense structure, "Kristoffer's House" will be a hard sale everywhere, but it will achieve a certain status at festivals and may eventually do well on the art house circuit. — Kell.

Nous Maigrirons Ensemble
(We'll Grow Thin Together)
(FRENCH-COLOR)

Paris, Aug. 22.
A Silenes release of an Alpes Cinema/Le Goff Production co-production. Produced by Jean-Pierre Le Moine, Sybil Le Goff. Stars Peter Ustinov. Written and directed by Michel Vocoret. Camera (color), Georges Barsky; sound, Georges Barra; editor, Claudio Ventura; music, Pierre Perret. Reviewed at the Gaumont Colisee cinema, Paris, Aug. 20, 1979. Running time: **100 MINS.**
Victor . . . . Peter Ustinov
Corinne . . . . Bernadette Lafont
Patricia . . . . Catherine Alric
Doctor . . . . Sylvie Joly

Peter Ustinov brings all of his weight and little of his talent to bear on this witless comedy about an obese, accident-prone film director who becomes aware of his excess fat and decides to do something about it, despite the fact that girl-friend Bernadette Lafont doesn't mind his taking up so much space in her life. After many weight-watching misadventures, Ustinov meets beautiful, rich Catherine Alric, who is hankering to share house and bed with him. He moves in with her.

It's dismaying to see a personality of Ustinov's talent lend himself to such a project, particularly one in which he is asked to lead with his belly instead of his ability. It's an embarrassment. —Len.

Aran
(FRENCH-DOCU-COLOR- 16M)

Paris, Aug. 1.
A Films du Plateau production and release. Directed by Georges Combe. Camera (color). Guy Marconnier; editor, Philipe Baudart; sound, Claude Joly; music, traditional airs specially recorded by Combe. Reviewed at the Saint Andre des Arts cinema, Paris, Aug. 1, 1979. Running time: **60 MINS.**
With: Maggie Dirranne and the inhabitants of the Aran Islands.

This 60-minute color documentary, shot over a five-year period by Lyon-based filmmaker Georges Combe, is a sort of filmic postscript to Robert Flaherty's famous "Man of Aran" (1934), a heroic account of Man vs. Nature on the wind-swept Aran Islands, which lie off the Irish coast.

Combe uses sequences from Flaherty's "narrative documentary" to punctuate his own footage and includes parts of an interview with islander Maggie Dirranne, who co-starred in "Man of Aran." These scenes recall Flaherty's glorification of a life lacking romantic aspects and material comforts. Flaherty's hyperbolic vision, we are reminded, exhilerated Hitler and Mussolini, who saw Aryan man in Aran man.

The director also cites passages from the Irish dramatist, John Millington Synge, whose dramatic and prose works were most responsible for the crystallization of the myth the Aran islanders have been burdened with.

Around this core of the past, Combe's camera records bleak images and realities of the present, an existence of uncompromising harshness threatened with tourist waves and possible extinction. Fledgling industry has made its incursions, not so much as a matter of progress but as a desperate attempt to keep the young girls of the Islands from fleeing to the mainland when they are old enough.

Combe's film is a bit too cursory, ending when it just seems to get started. But it admirably recaptures the primordial, austere beauty of the islands and the wind-ravaged faces of its inhabitants. In trying to undo the myth of Aran, Combe seems at times to succumb to the same sense of mystic beauty that inspired Flaherty. —Len.

Jaguar Lives!
(COLOR)

Karate doesn't, however.

Hollywood, Aug. 29.
An American International release. Produced by Derek Gibson. Executive producer, Sandy Howard. Directed by Ernest Pintoff. Features entire cast. Screenplay, Yabo Yablonsky; camera (Color), John Cabrera; editor, Angelo Ross; music, Robert O. Ragland; art director, Adolfo Cofino; costume design, Ron Talsky; sound, George Stephenson; associate rpoducer, Quinn Donoghue; assistant director, Kuki Lopez Rodero. Reviewed at AIP screening room, Beverly Hills, Aug. 29, '79. (MPAA Rating: PG.) Running time: **90 MINS.**
Jonathan Cross (Jaguar) . . . . . . Joe Lewis
Caine . . . . Christopher Lee
General Villanova . . . . . Donald Pleasence
Anna . . . . Barbara Bach
Zina . . . . Capucine
Ben Ashir . . . . Joseph Wiseman
Sensei . . . . Woody Strode
Ralph Richards . . . . John Huston
Ahmed . . . . Gabriel Melgar
Brett . . . . Anthony De Longis
Terry . . . . Sally Faulkner
Consuela . . . . Gail Grainger

Coblintz .... Anthony Heaton

In that fully 16 different world-wide locations, many of them complete with identifying label, pop up in the course of pic's 90 minutes, "Jaguar Lives!" might perform more effectively in travelog situations than in the action market. That all creative personnel perform as if they had permanent jetlag is therefore understandable under the circumstances.

Yabo Yablonsky's script might easily have been found by producer Derek Gibson and exec producer Sandy Howard in a drawer full of five-year-old submissions, as story is just the kind of thing everyone was rushing to make in the wake of the early 1970s kung fu craze. Undercover agent Joe Lewis, touted as former undefeated world heavyweight karate champ, is sent around the globe to run down international drug kingpins, all of whom have plenty of martial arts experts in their employ but can never bring themselves to use guns against Lewis, even in a pinch. Their motto seems to be, "Never shoot when kung fu will do."

Plot allows a number of weatherbeaten character actors to perform listless cameos on location. John Huston as a shipping magnate looks tired and constrained performing from a wheelchair, Donald Pleasence is ludicrous as a banana republic dictator and Christopher Lee strains for a sinister charm that the project won't allow, but Woody Strode, missed on screen of late, still looks to be in great shape.

Lewis bears a certain cool, blue-eyed resemblance to Steve McQueen, but the charisma normally required of action heroes isn't there and his thesping abilities are clearly limited to the physical. Karate champ also staged the action sequences, which are frewuent, redundant and not as outlandish as those previously seen in some Oriental exports.

Director Ernest Pintoff was probably lucky to remember what country he was in while shooting and was unable to bring my coherence or conviction to the project. Tech credits are somewhat substandard overall. Prospects overseas in undemanding situations might prove better than stateside. —Cart.

Moscow Film Fest

Que Viva Mexico
(U.S.-RUSSIAN-B&W)

Moscow, Aug. 28.
Sovexport release of Upton Sinclair & Assocs. production. Features non-pro cast. Written and directed by Sergei Eisenstein. Camera (black and white), Edward Tisse; editor, Grigori Alexandrov. Reviewed at Moscow Film Fest, Aug. 14, '79. Running time, 90 MINS.

The great Russian director Sergei Eisenstein's unfinished epic film on Mexico, "Que Viva Mexico!," which he made in 1931-'32, has been a lodestone for film specialists, archivists and buffs every since.

Though two films were made from the footage, Sol Lesser's "Thunder Over Mexico," reportedly with footage given him by producer Upton Sinclair, and Eisenstein biographer Marie Seaton's "Time in the Sun," film people could just conjecture what it might have been like if Eisenstein, maker of "Potemkin," "Alexander Nevski," "October," "Strike," "Ivan the Terrible," etc., had been able to finish it.

It appears that problems with his backers and lack of funds closed the film down and Eisenstein went back to Russia. The footage was used for the two aforementioned films, in part, and reportedly appeared as stock footage in some Hollywood films including the notable "Viva Villa" of Jack Conway.

Five hours of rushes were screened at the Museum of Modern Art in Gotham and the Cinematheque Francaise in Paris and other film centers. Still, the dream about its power, brilliance and greatness, offered in part by the films made from it and the rushes, remained only conjecture.

Then the Museum of Modern Art purportedly was able to present Russia with the footage. Grigori Alexandrov, friend and assistant of Eisenstein, who was along during all the shooting, has now edited it into a film.

Alexandrov is first seen discussing the shooting and noting he followed Eisenstein's own script, ideas and sketches for this now supposedly definitive version. Then the film unfolds. Rarely seen is the first actual sketch about the Mexican Indians at a time of supposed freedom in a story of a woman's marriage.

Before this are Eisenstein's shots of Aztec ruins studying the faces of the modern Indians at that time still resembling the figures in the carvings on the immense ruins. Then comes the familiar tale of the young peon whose girl is raped by a haughty landowner and an aborted revolt by the peasants.

There is the cruel bullfight tale centering on a young matador and then some sketches and stills from an idea for an episode about the women who followed the revolutionaries during the Mexican Revolution. It ends in a montage of Day of the Dead shots, a holiday in which candy is made up as skeletal death symbols. But it is a time of rejoicing and renewal and the mainstay of the Mexican people who have coped with misery and death.

Of course, films have since dealt with many of these themes and some even before Eisenstein. It is not that they are predictable or redundant, there is still the brilliant imagery of Edward Tisse and Eisenstein's compositions. It is just that, overall, the film is a letdown after all these years of discussions as to what it might have been.

Eisenstein might not have used the overdone Mexican-motifed music and perhaps cut it in a different way and shot more for some scenes besides the planned sketch that was never done. At any rate, it is interesting to have the footage in a coherent mixture of documentary and fictionalized sketches.

It should be a boon to scholars, archives and museums though commercial usage appears extremely limited. But it is here for film lore and study. —Mosk.

The Sky Is Clearing
(MONGOLIAN-COLOR)

Moscow, Aug. 24.

A Mongolian Film Production; world rights, Goskino, Moscow. Features entire cast. Directed by R. Dorzhpalam. Screenplay, S. Dashchdoorov. Only credits available. reviewed at Moscow Film Festival (Competition), Aug. 24, '79. Running time: 90 MINS.

Cast: Zh. Selengesuren, A. Ochirbat, B. Tsetsebalzhid.

A popular theme in Socialist cinema is the life-style working-man's "brigade," or union crew (to seek a Yank equivalent). The situation is common enought: differences of opinion arise on the job, people take sides, but eventually the conflict is resolved to the good of the working crew (although self sacrifice is often a legitimate part of the resolution). Several films and plays in the Soviet Union have also been critical in analyzing contemporary social problems that really don't offer ready answers.

The Mongolian entry in the Moscow fest, R. Dorzhpalam's "The Sky Is Clearing," follows the usual formula with little variation. A working brigade of young people in a rural area faces a conflict between two prevailing points of view. The work is hard, and there's both a romantic interest and round-table discussions by Party officials to find the proper answer. Outdoor nature scenes and native folk customs make this pic worth a once over.
— Holl.

Ija Ominira
(Fight For Freedom)
(NIGERIAN-COLOR)

Moscow, Aug. 28.
Friendship Motion Picture Co. release and production. Features entire cast. Written and directed by Ola Balogun from the book by Adebayo Faleti, music, Duro Ladipe. No other credits available. Reviewed at Moscow Film Fest, Aug. 18, '79. Running time, 101 MINS.

With: Ade Folayan, Duro Ladipo, Oyin Adejobi, Jimoli Alu.

African films are surfacing at all film festivals this year. At Moscow it was Nigeria's turn with a sprightly folk tale, replete with action, dancing and song, about people fighting for liberty from a tyrant. It is naive in allowing the actors to overplay and keeps this folk saga light hearted despite its violence.

The son of a king, who controls several villages, humiliates men by riding on their backs, rapes a bride-to-be and has any slow workers, who gather grass for the King's needs, ruthlessly beaten.

But one young man, son of a village patriarch, rebels, and finally causes the downfall of the cruel prince and his ruthless father. When his minions are defeated, the King demands what it is they want. And they all sing, it is freedom.

Film has charm and a true African folk spirit. Set in seemingly precolonial days, this colorful film is still mainly for home use, but is a disarming festival revelation. More film knowhow should make director a man to watch on the Afro film scene. —Mosk.

Amator
(Camera Buff)
(POLISH-COLOR)

Moscow, Aug. 17.
A Film Polski Production, Film Unit Tor, Warsaw; world rights, Film Polski, Warsaw. Stars Jerzy Stuhr. Directed by Krzysztof Kieslowski. Screenplay, Kieslowski, Stuhr; camera (color), Jacek Petrycki; music, Krzysztof Knittel; sets, Rafal Waltenburger; production manager, Wielislawa Piotrowska. Reviewed at Moscow Film Fest (Competition), Aug. 17, '79. Running time: 112 MINS.

Cast: Jerzy Stuhr, Malgorzata Zabkowska, Ewa Pokas, Stefan Czyzewski, Jerzy Nowak, Tadeusz Bladecki, Marek Litewka, Boguslaw Sobczuk.

Two of Poland's coming talents, helmer Krzysztof Kieslowski and thesp Jerzy Stuhr, worked together on "Camera Buff," an outstanding Polish comedy that will easily win more favor on the fest circuit after Moscow and could find its way into offshore art houses thereafter. Kieslowski made his rep with Polish television and at various fests.

This time, Stuhr worked with Kieslowski on the film's dialog and apparently created the character of the amateur camera buff on his own from a close observation of this odd-ball, vulnerably human specimen of mankind. Every move that Stuhr makes tickles the funny bone. But there's much more — this is a parable on Polish life made with feeling and compassion.

The camera buff, a young, married factory worker in a provincial town near Cracow, buys a Super-8 camera to photograph his newly-born daughter. But once this magic instrument is in his hands, he becomes obsessed with taking pictures of everything and everyone that moves. And what happens? The factory director has a small fund for "cultural affairs" — and the naive hero is asked to film a coming anniversary celebration.

The camera buff is now following people in and out of doors, to and from the toilet, and all over the dance floor. He shoots pigeons through the window, poses his wife with the baby in a dramatic sequence, and photographs his neighbors. Since he's a very popular fellow, everyone likes having him around, and he's given a basement room at the factory as his camera shop. The wife, however, realizes she's lost him when one success follows another.

The camera buff wins a third prize in an amateur film contest in Warsaw, to which he is pushed along by a pretty promoter in the Amateur Film Club with an eye for men. The hero now tastes the first fruits of glory — he's going to create art, or at least present "life as it really is." At this point the film is both hilarious and down to earth in depicting how film and culture, art and politics, reality and illusion get all mixed up in an amateur's swelled head. The parody on the film industry alone (not only in Poland, but in every country) will also bring gleeful tears to the eyes of anyone who know the insides of the business.

There are too many masterful touches to cite, but one film-within-the-film stands out. The camera buff in shooting the daily routine of a dwarf-worker at the factory, a faithful employee shows him to be a human being like the rest of us. The 16m film then gets shown on national television, much to the factory director's consternation. The upshot is that the camera buff's immediate superior and chief backer is relieved of his position. The camera buff's wife also leaves him. But the tv showing is another big success. Now commercial and political interests begin to put the lid on the buff's activities.

Credits are all tops. Kieslowski, somewhat of an "enfant terrible" among Polish helmers, now belongs to the company of Andrzej Wajda and Krzysztof Zanussi to form a top trio of Polish directors.

Zanussi, in fact, makes a personal appearance in "Camera Buff" — he visits the factory town to lecture at the buff's request. —*Holl.*

Tren
(Moment)
(YUGOSLAV-COLOR)

Moscow, Aug. 28.
Yugoslavia Film release of Avala Film production. Features entire cast. Directed by Stole Jankovic. Screenplay, Jankovic, Antonije Isakovic from the book by Isakovic; camera (Eastmancolor), Bozidar Miletic. No other credits available. Reviewed at Moscow Film Fest, Aug. 18, '79. Running time, **97 MINS.**
With: Velimir-Bata Zivojinovic, Pavle Vujistic, Radko Polic, Svjetlana Knezevic, Dragan Nikolic.

A partisan film, but filtered through memory as Yugoslav films return to this war genre in new ways. An old man looks back on his life, but it is dominated by his war years as a partisan officer.

He has not quite been able to console himself over the loss of friends, his family, the horrors of war that saw civilians massacred and the evil done to each other by Yugoslavs to preserve their own lives.

The film is somewhat muted and veiled as is the man's memory. The attempt at poetic evaluations of war are sometimes forced. Film does hold attention but is not revealing enough to transcend its self indulgence.

Primarily a festival and home film, but one that does have good performances and slow but knowing direction. —*Mosk.*

Godisnja Doba
(The Four Seasons)
(YUGOSLAV-COLOR)

Moscow, Aug. 22.
A Zagreb Film Production, Zagreb; world rights, Zagreb Film, Zagreb. Features entire cast. Written and directed by Petar Krelja. Camera (color), Ivica Rajkovic, Ante Verzotti; music, Arsen Dedic. Reviewed at Moscow Film Fest (Market), August 22, '79. Running time: **85 MINS.**
Cast: Slavko Stimac, Tatjana Ivko, Rajka Rusan, Marina Nemet, Sandra Langerholz, Boris Buzancic, Vanja Drach, Zvonko Torjaned, Lela Margetic.

Debut pic by a promising helmer, Petar Krelja's "The Four Seasons" is a composite of three shorts made for tv and cinemas about the problems of deserted children and delinquents kept in state institutions, all of whom are waiting for either adoption, or a foster family, or, at the age of 19, to go off on their own. Each of these stories bears an individual title and deals with sensitive girls.

"Adoption" tells the story of a five-year-old who has caught the eye of a well to do couple at the home. Zeljka, however, has given

up on communicating and is emotionally deprived. Slowly, however, she adjusts, but with some pain, to her new parents and surroundings.

"Holidays" features a 15-year-old girl, Visnja, on vacation at the home in winter. She spends her time trying to understand juvenile delinquents in this cell-like institution, and then falls in love with a young boy who has been mistreated by his father throughout his young life.

"Probation" recounts how a 19-year-old girl, Branka, has difficulty finding a decent job (although trained for a profession). She ends up washing dishes in a restaurant, and being exploited by a leering restaurant owner. Her future is uncertain, particularly as she's alone and attractive.

Pic is a natural for youth fests with credits a big plus. —*Holl.*

Fish Hawk
(CANADIAN-COLOR)

Moscow, Aug. 28.
The Fish Hawk Co., CFDC release and production. Features entire cast. Directed by Donald Shebib. Screenplay, Blanche Hanalis from the book by Mitchell Jayne; camera (color), Rene Verzier; editor, Ron Wisman. Reviewed at Moscow Film Fest, Aug. 22, '79. Running time: **97 MINS.**
Fish Hawk .... Will Sampson
Corby .... Charlie Fields
Charlie .... Geoffrey Bowes
Sarah .... Mary Pirie
Deut .... Don Francks
Marcus .... Chris Wiggins
Mary .... Kay Hawtrey
Joke .... Mavor Moore

"Fish Hawk" is an aging drunken Indian who lives alone among the white men who dispossessed his people at the turn-of-the-century. His liaison with a little white boy leads to his taking stock and finally going off to find his own people.

Will Sampson, who played in "One Flew Over the Cuckoo's Nest" (UA), is the tall, craggy Indian who is actually quite well educated and bears the white people's racism with stoicism and drinking. His family had been decimated by smallpox.

When he tracks down a bear that has been killing the livestock of a farmer, he is invited to stay with them and work. He has lost his dog during the bear hunt due to a hangover and swears off drinking.

His friendship with the boy, the farmer's son, grows as he reads to him and teaches him tolerance and understanding. But the little boy turns against him when he refuses to hunt a dangerous old boar, the only one still around, an anachronism like him, after the boar has killed the boy's dog as well as a backward village boy.

The animal work is superbly done, especially the fight between

the bear and the boar and a mountain lion grieving over a cub killed by the boar. The attempts to symbolize the relationships by the animals is forced and the film's pace is a bit sluggish.

Sampson has the right craggy looks and dignity but the boy is somewhat self conscious. The film looks good and might be a useful moppet entry though lacking the visual flair and potent characterizations for older audiences.
—*Mosk.*

Bandera Rota
(Broken Flag)
(MEXICAN-COLOR)

Moscow, Aug. 28.
Rio Mixcoac release and production. Features entire cast. Directed by Gabriel Retes. Screenplay, Retes, Ignacio Retes; camera (Eastmancolor), Genaro Hurtado; editor, Eufemio Rivera, music, Raoul Lavista. Reviewed at Moscow Film Fest, Aug. 16, '79. Running time: **95 MINS.**
Arizpe .... Manolo Fabregas
Hernan .... Luis Iriarte
Ana .... Tina Romero
Alberto .... Jorge Humberto Robles
Tono .... Jorge Santoyo
Ernesto .... Ignacio Retes
Arry .... Abel Woolrich

Moral responsibility, political and class excesses are explored in this basically well-meaning but melodramatic film. Having laudable intentions is not enough, a film has to have heart, clarity and persuasive characterization too. This cooperatively-made Mexican film is therefore somewhat lacking.

A young director, with only a cameraman and his girlfriend, is making a film on femme lib. By chance, they film an incident in a valley below a hill where they are shooting as a man chases a woman from an expensive car and shoots her several times and then drives off.

They rush off instead of investigating. When they develop the film it shows that the woman was probably killed, but the director will not get involved with the police while the others think it should be done.

The woman, from a rich family, is found and the film people find the murderer is a well-known rich businessman. They decide to blackmail him into giving more concessions to his workers and going into politics as a progressive.

But a friend of the filmers tries to blackmail on his own and leads henchmen of the killer to them and they are tortured and wiped out by these hired killers. The husband of the murdered woman has received a copy of the film, but will do nothing against the man who murdered his wife, she had been the man's mistress, because of business ties.

Perhaps the pic wants to show the dangerous ambivalence of progressives who sometimes cannot act out of fear and the corruption of a certain class. But it is all somewhat pat. It might have more possibilities at home than abroad, but its theme should get it fest outings. —*Mosk.*

Zemaljski Dani Teku
(The Days Are Passing)
(YUGOSLAV-COLOR)

Moscow, Aug. 20.
A Center Film Production, Belgrade, and Belgrade Television; world rights, Yugoslavia Film, Belgrade. Features entire cast. Written and directed by Goran Paskaljevic. Camera (color), Milan Spasic; sets, Dragoljub Ivkov; music, Zoran Simjanovic. Reviewed at Moscow Film Fest (Market), August 20, '79. Running time: 85 MINS.
Cast: Dimitrije Vujovic, Obren Helcer, Sarlota Pesic, Mila Keca.

Goran Paskaljevic has risen quickly on the Yugoslav scene. His "Beach Guard in Winter" (1976) won favor at the Berlin and Chicago fests, then "Dog Who Liked Trains" (1978) was unspooled at the Berlin and San Francisco fests with equal praise. Now he's written and directed a tv pic, "The Days Are Passing," which proved to be a sensation when unspooled at the Pula Film Festival this summer. It's arguably his best film to date.

"The Days Are Passing" takes its title from a folk song, but the reference is to an Old Peoples Home and focuses on human dignity as age takes its toll. It's the story of a retired sea captain who prefers taking care of himself (he draws portraits on the side to earn his keep), but now he knows he has to enter a state home because he can't manage it alone any more.

On his pension the human needs of the body are taken care of — this individual, however, is a man of the spirit, and he conveys a love for life to those about him by his talent for singing, laughing, drawing, and storytelling. The man's good humor is contagious, so much so that even the audience is infected.

Paskaljevic works with nonprofessionals in this film. On a low budget, he shot everything in 16m (for tv) and blew it up to 35m (for cinema). The script was developed out of the experiences of the personalities on the screen, the two lead actors — the captain and his dour roommate — providing a kind of human comedy to carry the pic with humor and tears.

Pic focuses on the relationship between the captain and his roommate, the latter an individual whose family has no need of him anymore — more than likely because of his constant bickering and sour disposition. He hardly speaks to anyone in the home. But now that New Year's Eve is approaching,

the captain and the house director agree on arranging a kind of amateur-hour entertainment show for occupants, relations, and friends. Everyone joins in the preparations, save for the roommate.

It's how this little idea catchs fire and animates the Old People's Home that makes "The Days Are Passing" worth seeing.

Since several in the film are actually in this situation, the whole comes across at times like a cinema-verite docu (to the director's credit, since he has "guided" his non-thesps through their parts). The high point is the New Year's Eve party: the captain suffers a heart attack, is taken to the hospital, and dies. But this occurs just after his lonely companion leaves his room to join the festivities and the singing.

It's the pace of the pic and the presence of the personalities on the screen that make "The Days Are Passing" memorable. One of the best pix on the aged made, it deserves a round on the fest circuit. Only drawback is poor quality of blow-up print. Credits otherwise tops. —*Holl.*

Companero De Viaje
(Travelling Companion)
(VENEZUELAN-COLOR)

Moscow, Aug. 28.
Betancourt, Quintana release and production. Features entire cast. Directed by Clemente De La Cerda. Screenplay, Rodolfo Santana, Orlando Abrauyo. No other credits available. Reviewed at Moscow Film Fest, Aug. 20, '79. Running time, 110 MINS.
With: Toco Gomez, Maria Escalona, Julio Motta.

Government grants have hyped Venezuelan film production of late. This is one of the first of the new crop that captures the mixture of surrealistic impishness, political posturing and moralistic metaphores appearing via the better Latin American writers.

It may lack polish and adept narrative skill, but it does evoke an amusing crucible of Latin life in the guise of a small town.

An old colonel rules the town with patronizing rigidity. There is someone who writes slogans against him and other important people on the town walls every night.

Accused is a bitter, limping man who is jailed often. Some sort of outside takeover of peasants puts the limping man in charge. But he becomes even more authoritative than his predecessor. And the writer of the wall protests turns out to be a supposed young illiterate.

Film has some definite qualities in its mixture of comic insight and resonant looks at the Latin American condition. Perhaps indulgent,

and wrapping things up too easily, film could still find some foreign outlets with the right handling. —*Mosk.*

Tieng Goi, Phiatruoc
(The Call of the Front)
(VIETNAMESE-B&W)

Moscow, Aug. 28.
Vietnam Feature Film Studio release and production. Features entire cast. Directed by Long Van. Screenplay, Phu Thang; camera, Nghien Phu My. No other credits available. Reviewed at Moscow Film Fest, Aug. 15, '79. Running time: 82 MINS.
Commander .... Huy Cong
Tom .... Doan Dung
Dana .... Dang Viet Bao
Kapo .... Nguyen Dang Khoa

A Vietnamese war film without any ugly Americans. It is mainly a drama about the stalwart Viet Cong army and the personal plight of a commander who hears his son has joined the South Vietnamese Army.

It is simply made and more a heroic tale for home consumption though geared for socialist festivals via its theme. The son happens to be a prisoner of his father's company though they do not know each other since the father had left to fight when his son was a little boy.

The father wants to try to make the prisoners realize they belong with the Viet Cong. He succeeds with his son, but the latter finds out it is his father but will not tell him until he has proved himself.

Narration is concise though visuals are uninspired. Film is mired in sentiment and is reviewed mainly for the record. —*Mosk.*

Nahla
(ALGERIAN-COLOR)

Moscow, Aug. 28.
RTA release and production. Features entire cast. Directed by Farouk Beloufa. Screenplay, Rachid Boudjedra, Beloufa; camera (Eastmancolor), Alell Yahiaoui; editor, Moufida Tlatli; music, Ziad Rahbani. Reviewed at Moscow Film Fest, Aug. 17, '79. Running time: 180 MINS.
Nahla .... Yasmine Khlat
Maha .... Lina Tebbara
Hind .... Nabila Zitouni
Larbi .... Youcef Saiah
Nasri .... Roger Assaf
Michel .... Ahmed Zine
Raouf .... Fayek Hamissi

A rather overambitious first film that works too many themes into the background of Palestine terrorism and the Lebanese Civil War. It gets bogged down in repetition and loses on most fronts.

However, Algerian director Farouk Beloufa does display some flair for handling players and narration in this convoluted tale of several people thrown together during a time of political instability.

A singer is losing her voice, seemingly due to some romantic and career traumas. She is thrown in with a divorced woman who works on a militant newspaper and meets a young Algerian reporter and others who fall for her.

Then comes the civil war and killings as they all take their stands. The singer may be finally going back to her interrupted career.

Cutting this three-hour film will not help much, it is just too overinvolved with its characters trying to work out their personal problems and hangups during a time that called for commitment.

More script care and easing up on highly personal ideas that are not always clear and coherent might possibly make director Beloufa a worthy newcomer on the Arab film scene. —*Mosk.*

Clipa
(The Moment)
(RUMANIAN-COLOR)

Moscow, Aug. 23.
A Rumaniafilm Production, Bucharest; world rights, Rumaniafilm, Bucharest. Features entire cast. Directed by Gheorghe Vitanidis. Screenplay, Dinu Sararu; camera (color), Nicu Stan; sound, Dan Ionescu; sets, Guta Stirbu; costumes, Gabriela Ricsan; editing, Maria Chise. Reviewed at Moscow Film Fest (Competition), Aug. 23, '79. Running time: 138 MINS.
Cast: Gheorghe Cozorici, Ion Dichiseanu, Octavian Andrei, Sebastian Papaiani, Emanoil Petrut, Mitica Popescu, Octavian Cotescu, Leopoldina Balanuta, Rodica Tapa.aga, Olga Tudorache, Margareta Pogonat, Valeria Seciu, Sandu Simionica, Amza Pellea, Vasile Nitulescu.

One of the best Rumanian pix made in the present decade, Gheorghe Vitanidis's "The Moment" is an historical review of the postwar period without pulling a single political punch.

In fact, this is a true-life incident and thus an encyclopedia of information on those troubled years, the 1950s, when farm collectivization and the personality cult brought out the best and worse in party leaders angling for position and power in a changing era.

"The Moment" refers both to the flashbacks from the current 1970s to the troubled time two decades earlier and to that instant when decisions must be made by a man of integrity. The main role is a party leader who recalls the past while visiting the places he lived and worked in during the 1950s, when he struggled with personal dignity to establish collective farming. The flashbacks reveal that he was betrayed by a friend in the party, falsely accused, and sentenced to imprisonment. But his unbending faith in his fellow man eventually led to exoneration, but not after some years of suffering.

Another lead figure in the story is a general manager of a chemical factory in the present day. He is under attack via anonymous letters and lies by people who want to see him removed from his post. The elderly party leader understands what's going on due to his own former experience, backs the younger man, and wins the day. Also, the femme architect of the new town center is simiarly under fire because she's the daughter of a former war criminal. She's also protected by the vet political figure's integrity.

All of which means that a lot of words spill over the dam as one dialog scene follows another in a two-hour-plus examination of an "hour of truth." Still, it's well worth sitting through for a number of reasons. One is the daring to lay all the cards on the table. Another is the openness of the Moscow fest to admitting the Rumanian pic into the festival.

Only real drawback is a lifeless style of direction and gratuitous camera movement and angles to "set up" dialog scenes and sequences. Otherwise, thesps carry story all along the way. "The Moment" shoudl find its way into Rumanian Film Weeks and perhaps score too on the fest circuit. —*Holl.*

Iskanja
(Search)
(YUGOSLAV-COLOR)

Moscow, Aug. 22.
A Viba Film, Ljubljana. Film Production: world rights. Viba Film, Ljubljana. Features entire cast. Directed by Matjaz Klopcic. Screenplay, Marko Slodnjak: camera (color), Tomislav Pinter: sets, Niko Matul. Reviewed at Moscow Film Fest (Market), August 22, '79. Running time: 90 MINS.

Cast: Boris Cavazza, Boris Juh, Milena Zupancic, Tanja Poberznik, Iva Zupancic.

Matjaz Klopcic has made eight feature pix at the Slovenian studio in Ljubljana, Viba Film, over the past decade. He has also shown a sure hand for historical dramas of a social and psychological nature.

"Search" explores human emotions. The time is just prior to World War I. Two travelling companions, an art historian (and a Catholic priest) and his German friend (who happens to be disenchanted with life), travel from Ljubljana to Venice to discuss their views on life and test their thories on art at the same time. The two could possibly be viewed as two sides of the same coin, a split-personality in intellectual dialog and conflict.

Nothing very much happens in this search for identity. The priest finds that his high-blown concepts on art and culture pale in the face of a flesh-and-blood creature, his friend's deserted fiancee, Ester, who embodies his visions of a madonna in Italian paintings. The German, on the other hand, loses his head over an emancipated beauty, who leads him astray. After these two inner conflicts in Ciril and Fritz have been established, the rest of the film slips into a lengthy dialog on the nature of life and existence.

For intellectuals, this is a nutcracker that provokes and fascinates. For the art lover, there's Titian's "Ascension" in a Venice church, among other art treasures, to delight the eye and weave an extra dimension into the story. For the film buff, "Search" is beautifully lensed and ups Klopcic's rep as a master craftsman in Yugo pix. Despite these top credits, however, "Search" is without a strong narrative line to guarantee offshore bids on the fest circuit and art houses. —*Holl.*

Mlady Muz A Bila Velryba
(The Young Man and Moby Dick)
(CZECHOSLOVAK-COLOR)

Moscow, Aug. 28.
Czech State Film release of Barrandov Studio production. Features entire cast. Directed by Jaromil Jires. Screenplay, Maria Rudlovcakova. Jires from the story by Vladimir Paral: camera (Eastmancolor), Emil Sirotek: music, Ladislav Staidl. Reviewed at Moscow Film Fest, Aug 22, '79. Running time. 92 MINS.

Vik	Eduard Cupak
Breta	Ivan Vyskocil
Edita	Jana Brejchova
Nada	Zlata Adamovska

Jaromil Jires's "The Cry," in 1963, heralded the burst of unusual Czech filmmakers that were to flourish until '68 and reap worldwide recognition of their comic insights into important themes.

Jires, along with Vera Chytilova and Jiri Menzel, has continued to work while others of the Czech film renaissance remain silent or emigrated. His new film seems a remote bow to his first film and also employs flashbacks and tries to delve into more profound psychological needs.

However, this film is somewhat too diffuse and remains cold in its tale of a young man's need for some absolute quest that would be a bit like the pursuit of Herman Melville's "Moby Dick" which he so admires and is stoked by an old fisherman who had once harpooned a whale.

The boy's roommate is an older, slightly cynical chemical engineer. The former's old mistress is due and the boy knows all about her ambition and selfishness from his friend. The woman, played with dramatic brio by Jana Brejchova, actually just wants to use her old lover's knowhow on an experiment she is not permitted to do in Prague. They live in a small town.

The older man tries not to help her, but finally gives in because the attempt to find a cheap way of making a needed base for most drugs intrigues him. The young boy, who works in the factory, is dragged into it when he suddenly falls for the older woman who seems more human with him.

This becomes his "Moby Dick." But his finding of a new way to clean the boilers in his factory leads to his death. He knows there is danger from the fumes and has installed two canaries as a warning. But he is so carried away with the project he does not see them drop and dies himself.

There may be an inkling of lost hopes and the sacrifice of youthful ideals in this convoluted tale that is finally unclear. The direction is sharp, but the focus of the theme is clouded. More for home use, but still showing promise of more unusual themes to come from the Czech cinema. It is technically tops as is usual in films from this country. —*Mosk.*

Bzlet
(The Takeoff)
(RUSSIAN-COLOR)

Moscow, Aug. 28.
Sovexport film release of Mosfilm production. Stars Yevgeny Yevtushenko. Directed by Savva Kulish. Screenplay, Oleg Osetinsky: camera (Sovcolor), Vladimir Klimov: art director, Vladimir Aronin: music. Oleg Karavaichuk. Reviewed at Moscow Film Fest, Aug. 23, '79. Running time. 148 MINS.

Tziolkovsky	Yevgeny Yevtushenko
Panin	Albert Filozov
Liuba	Elena Finogenova
Ignaty	Kiril Arbuzov
Tailor	Vadim Aleksandrov
Rokatov	Georgy Burkov

A rather bloated attempt at a lyrical film about a Russian scientist, reportedly of Polish origins, whose work, though not recognized in his lifetime, laid the foundation for future space travel and sources of energy from the sun. It also marks the acting debut of poet Yevgeny Yevtushenko as the scientist.

Film certainly had means at its disposal with unusual crane and helicopter shots, the use of the bug-eye lens and fine recreation of the times from 1880 to 1914. It brings to mind the renowned "Andrei Roublov" of Andrei Tarkovski, a film that had problems on its home grounds.

Yevtushenko rages at governmental obtuseness when he is always refused a grant for his experiments with lighter than air craft and rockets. When he hears of a zeppelin built in Germany, and the Russians bidding for it, he runs amuck and destroys his models.

But this pic lacks "Rublov's" true poetic flair about man's persistence and is a series of episodes concerning Yevtushenko's scientific experiments, hopes and his family life struck by tragedy when his favorite son, a nihilist, hills himself and his daughter is arrested for revolutionary activities and sent to Siberia.

No denying a sort of flashy showmanship in this sprawling saga which might make it a good item for Russian Film Weeks. But its academic, rambling progression tags this a more difficult commercial bet outside the socialist orbit.

Yevtushenko looks right, but cannot get depth into his character. But for a first time, and with such a large role, he is more than adequate. Director Savva Kulish piles on pathos, incident and historical sweep to cover a lack of narrative thread.

Probably geared to the 60th Anni of Soviet Cinema celebrations, the film is too heavy-footed to mix the human and the epic, the profane and the profound, and remains an overblown but showmanly biopic that celebrates a little known scientific cog in man's march to outer space. —*Mosk.*

Damned Be Those Who Cry
(IRANIAN-B&W)

Moscow, Aug. 15.
An Iranian Film Production, Teheran. Features entire cast. Directed by Mohammad-Ali Najafi. Screenplay, Najafi, Mahmud Ostad Mohamad. Only credits available. Reviewed at Moscow Film Fest (Competition). August 15. No other credits available. Running time: 90 MINS. (Competition). August 15, '79. Running time: 90 MINS.

Cast: F. Gharibian, R. Ale Payyam, G. Lotfi.

Now that Iranian cinema is in the doldrums, due to religious and political differences of opinion (the orthodox Moslems are in favor of closing the nation's cinemas), it's surprising that a feature film should be produced at all at this time. Mohammad-Ali Najafi as a filmmaker is also practically unknown, and his "Damned Be Those Who Cry" serves as a curiosity piece in these troubled times.

The title alone hints of sentimental political engagement. A teacher works with his students on an amateur play during the Shah's deteriorating rule: is this a political or religious theme that might be considered subversive? In any case, he is being closely watched. He takes a walk in the night to visit the home of one of the students, a young man who works late hours in a tea-room and has bad memories of mistreatment by his father in his youth. He wants to better himself, so he finally joins an underground printing group to be a part of the coming revolution. The teacher is later the victim of an intentional hit and run driver.

Muddled story, save for Iran film buffs. —*Holl.*

Usporeno Kretanje
(Slow Motion)
(YUGOSLAV-COLOR)

Moscow, Aug. 26.

A Jadran Film, Zagreb, Croatia Film, Zagreb, and Radna Zajednica Filma Film Production; world rights, Yugoslavia Film. Belgrade. Features entire cast. Directed by Vanca Kljakovic. Screenplay, Tomislav Sabljak; camera (color), Drago Novak; sets, Zeljko Senecic; music, Alfi Kabiljo. Reviewed at Moscow Film Fest (Market), Aug. 26, '79. Running time: **90 MINS.**

Cast: Vlatko Dulic, Ivica Vidovic, Mia Oremovic, Kostadinka Velkovska, Vanja Drach, Relja Basic, Boris Buzancic.

This is Zagreb helmer Vanca Kljakovic's fourth feature pic and arguably his best. It's the tale of an ex-football star, now a hotel receptionist, trying to find his way into a new life. The only trouble is that he never bothered much about people before — thus he's pretty much on his own in the hotel branch. "Slow Motion" is about a man's efforts to become the center of attraction again at 40, after a bum knee sidelined him from sports.

The ex-star seeks out old school chums in order to throw an anniversary class party at the hotel he works at. He visits people he hardly remembers anymore (the usual nonsense line on the past from both sides), tries to break off a messy affair with a lonely, aging woman-resident at the hotel (she commits suicide), and organizes another party for the bored and rich at the hotel (eating and drinking for the sake of eating and drinking). When his own party for his school shums is thrown, however, no one shows up and he celebrates alone.

Credits are standard, but story lacks depth. —*Holl.*

Retrato De Tersea
(Portrait of Teresa)
(CUBAN-COLOR)

Moscow, Aug. 28.

IDP release and production. Features entire cast. Directed by Pastor Vega. Screenplay, Ambrosio Fornet. Vega; camera (color), Livio Delgado; editor, Mirita Lores; music, Carlos Farinas. Reviewed at Moscow Film Fest. Aug. 21, '79. Running time: **103 MINS.**

Teresa .... Daysy Grandados

Husband .... Adolfo Llaurado
Girl .... Alina Sanchez
Foreman .... Raul Pomares

"Portrait of Teresa" has the earmarks of a tv sitcom in its evasiveness of the more dramatic sides of female liberation coming to the Cuba of today. The heroine wants more than housework though she tries valiantly to fulfil her outside work, home duties and dedication to a worker dance troupe.

All this gets too much for her rather macho husband, a rising tv repairman being offered a top job in a school in another town. After refusing to wait up for her, he starts an affair with another woman. **Some petty sides of his character are invoked.**

But Teresa is played in a too martyred way by Daysy Grandados and robs the film of a more discerning insight into this problem that now seems prevalent in socialist as well as capitalistic countries.

The family seems to live well. It is intimated that maybe Teresa, too, had an affair. She finally walks out but he comes after her and begs her to come back. He again makes a faux pas when he refuses to answer her question about what he would think if she had an affair as he did. She walks off as he tries to reach her in a crowd. Mainly for home use, but polished enough and by now universal enough for the lingo circuit usage abroad. —*Mosk.*

Golapi Ekhon Trainey
(The Endless Trail)
(BANGLADESH-COLOR)

Moscow, Aug. 22.

A Production of the Bangladesh Film Development Corporation and Amjad Hossain Film Production. Features entire cast. Written and directed by Amjad Hossain, based on his book with same title. Camera (color), Rafiqul Bari Chowdhury; music, Alauddin Ali; editing. Enamul Huq; sound Mustafe Kamal. Reviewed at Moscow Film Fest (Competition), August 22, '79. Running time: **140 MINS.**

Cast: Babita, Anwara, Roushan Jamil, Faruque, Rosy Samad, Anwar Hossain, A.T.M. Shamsuzzaman, Abdullah Al-Mamun.

"The Endless Trail" offers the chance to see the work of a popular writer-director, Amjad Hossain, in Bangladesh, together with the country's leading femme thesp, Babita. It's a singing drama about love and tragedy, much in the vein of Indian musicals made for weeping. This is apparently the first Bangledesh pic to reach an international fest, although a national cinema was begun in these parts 23 years ago.

Adapted from his own novel, Hossain's "The Endless Trail" tells the story of a girl named Gulapi (Babita), who leaves the country with a companion in times of pov-

erty to live and work in a nearby city, although this is against village customs. Then one of the village elders' young son falls in love with the girl and wants to marry her. He is punished by poisoning his food at a celebration. Left alone again, the girl must continue on her endless trail of suffering.

Too melodramatic for Western standards, pic is nevertheless a curiosity piece worth a once over by Bangladesh film buff. —*Holl.*

Kanal
(The Canal)
(TURKEY-COLOR)

Moscow, Aug. 20.

An Irmak Film Production. Erden Kiral, producer, Istanbul; world rights, Umut Sanat Urunleri, Istanbul. Features entire cast. Directed by Erden Kiral. Screenplay, Ihsan Yuce; camera (color), Salih Dikisci; music, Arif Erkin. Reviewed at Moscow Film Festival (Competition). Aug. 20, '79. Running time: **90 MINS.**

Cast: Tank Akan, Meral Orhonsay, Tuncel Kurtiz, Kamuran Usluer.

Debut pic by a tv vet, Erden Kiral's "The Canal" shows promise and deserves exposure at this international fest due to the timeliness of the subject matter. It's also an extremely popular pic in Turkey at present.

"The Canal" may appear to some as a tired western with good guys and bad guys fighting over water rights in the Adana district of South Turkey, where rice and cotton fields are plentiful. But the real situation is not much different than that depicted in this honest and forthright presentation of facts. The story, in fact, is based on a true to life incident.

A new magistrate (read lawman) comes to a poor village area with hopes of improving the roads, building schools, and the like. The rich landowners, however, want government irrigation water to grow more rice. A deal is made to rent the rights to the state canal, with the new lawman's knowledge that a village will thereby be flooded for a couple of months (thus allowing malaria to spread). A woman doctor opens his eyes to the mistake in time — he fights for justice and wins, but then is replaced to go to higher duties.

Although simplified, pic deserves once over. —*Holl.*

Osvajanje Slobode
(Winning of Freedom)
(YUGOSLAV-COLOR)

Moscow, Aug. 20.

An Avala Film, Belgrade, Production; world rights, Yugoslavia Film, Belgrade. Features entire cast. Directed by Zdravko Sotra. Screenplay, Gordon Michic; camera

(color), Dragoljub Mancic; sets, Bora Njezic; music, Vojkan Borisavljevic. Reviewed at Moscow Film Festival (Market), August 20, '79. Running time: **90 MINS.**

Cast: Radko Polic, Ivo Gregurevic, Radox Bajic, Gordana Kosanovic, Milan Puzic, Milivoj Tomic.

It would be difficult to imagine New Yugoslav Cinema without the name of scripter Gordon Mihic. He was a hot name in the 1960s as Yugoslav cinema was blooming, even codirected an earthy pic on outsiders ("Crows"), and was the author of Goran Paskaljevic's "Beach Guard in Winter" (1976) and "The Dog Who Liked Trains" (1978) as the young helmer was breaking in. Now he's writing for helmer Zdravko Sotra, whose "Winning of Freedom" is his debut pic. It's adapted from a popular tv series.

This is the story of two friends who try to bring some peace and order back into village life at the close of World War II. The difficulty is that the country is not safe from bandits and disgruntled citizens who sided with the enemy or collaborates during the war. In the tv series, every type of individual from freedom-fighting partisan on down to the ruthless traitor is depicted with a degree of compassion and understanding for the weaknesses in human nature.

The film version loses much of this edge, but focuses on the tragedies in the two men's lives with an emphasis on human dignity in fighting and dying for a cause.

Helmer Sotra and scripter Mihic are a team to watch in the future.
— *Holl.*

Genesis, Chapter X
(GHANA-COLOR)

Moscow, Aug. 23.

A Ghana Film Production. Features cast. Directed by Thomas Ribero. Screenplay, Ato Janney. Only credits available. Reviewed at Moscow Film Fest (Competition), Aug. 23, '79. Running time: **96 MINS.**

Cast: George Williams, Marilyn Meyer.

Ghana cinema has a long way to go to catch up with the French-speaking African film nations, particularly Senegal. But a recent African Cultural Festival (Horizons) in West Berlin revealed that music and dance ensembles are plentiful and world class in folkloric cultural concerts. For some reason, however, it's the Bible and not national traditions that form the plot and inspirational basis of Thomas Ribero's "Genesis, Chapter X." Pic was shot in English.

Story is about a Ghana surgeon in London who returns to his homeland to seek out his mother (as the tale unfolds in flashback). He goes to a shack off the beaten path and there asks for lodging for the night. The inhabitants, elderly people, recognize that he's wealthy and discuss a plan to kill him. In discussing the situation, their story as criminals is revealed in flashbacks: it turns out the doctor's mother (the lady of the house) was also to blame in the murder of his father and her husband, while the man she's living with committed the foul deed in a scuffle when the adulterating pair were surprised by the husband. In the end, the conversation between the two was overheard and the mother falls at her son's feet in a faint. Check Genesis, Chapter X for details.

This is an amusing tale, but it never makes it off the ground as a film. Thesps appear to be British or Yankee bred. Credits are sub-par. —Holl.

Runoilija Ja Muusa
(Poet and Muse)
(FINNISH-COLOR)

Moscow, Aug. 28.

Filmityo Oy release and production. Features entire cast. Directed by Jaakko Pakkasvirta. Screenplay, Titta Karakorpi, Pakkasvirta. No other credits available. Reviewed at Moscow Film Fest, Aug. 19, '79. Running time: 102 MINS.

Leino .... Esko Salminen
Mistress .... Elina Salo
Wife .... Katja Salminen

The biography of an early 20th-century lyric Finnish poet seen mainly through the more dramatic incidents in his life tempered by an area of carousing, sickness and decline. The film has a fine eye for the period and the outside events that are reflected in his work.

The editing helps keep the play of ideas coherent though this is mainly a film for festival, archive and school use outside its own land where the man's work is an integral part of this brooding portrait.

He gets married to a student. Early ardent love soon turns to jealousy and nagging on her part as his drinking increases and he infects her with syphilis caught during one of his nights on the town.

Unlike his brother, the disease is arrested somewhat. The days under Russia are invoked as he takes part in uprisings plus a liaison with an emancipated woman that ends up with an epic fight between her and his wife in the wine cellar of an epicurean nobleman as he bemoans the destruction of his vintage collection.

In short, an unusual mood piece that marks a plus for the rarely noted Finnish film on the world festival scene and a director to watch in Jaakko Pakkasvirta. Color is rightly muted, acting is ac-

ceptable and it is technically good down the line. —Mosk.

Habibeti-Ya Habba Atoot
(Sweet, Like Berries, My Love)
(SYRIAN-COLOR)

Moscow, Aug. 21.

A National Cinema Organization Production. Syria: world rights, National Cinema Organization of Syria, Damascus. Features entire cast. Written and directed by Marwan Haddad, based on Ahmed Dawood's novel of same title. Camera (color), George Loutfi El Khoury, Mounir Gebawi; editing, Marwan Akkowi; sets, Oussama Allash; production manager, Amid Horani; drama consultant, Hassas Sami Joussef; rural milieu consultant, Nazih Abou Afash; assistant director, Zouheir Daioub; sound, Emil Saade. Reviewed at Moscow Film Fest (Competition), Aug. 21, '79. Running time: 105 MINS.

Cast: Abdul Hadi Sabbagh Nadin, Asad Fadda, Ahmed Addas, Joussef Hanna, Adnan Barakat, Housein Idilbi, Ingrid Jabbour, Nahed Halabi, Hassan Sami Joussef, Nazih Abou Afash, Adnan Habbal, Mohamed Horani, Jihad Saad, Mohamed Tarakji, Quamar Mortada, Hani Sadi, Yoland Asmar, Nabila Karam, Amal Hanna, Tewfiq Morad, Ibrahim Kurdie.

A tale of social conflicts, Marwan Haddad's "Sweet, Like Berries, My Love" is based on a 1973 book by Ahmed Dawood, which uses a love story as a device to describe exploitation of the innocent and thus deliver a message on social change.

A young man marries a girl from the village and brings her to the city, where he in turn is seduced by wily business men in a night club affair. The girl also was suppressed in the village by poverty and oppression of the rich. Their love for each other amid misfortune and human weakness apparently inspired the title.

Weak direction and overacting mar an interesting story. Nevertheless, Syria is making an effort to enter the Arab film market with tales much in the vein of Egyptian entertainment cinema. — Holl.

Licne Stvari
(Personal Affairs)
(YUGOSLAV-COLOR-DOCU)

Moscow, Aug. 25.

A Centar Film, Belgrade. Film Production, in collaboration with Belgrade Television; world rights, Yugoslavia Film, Belgrade. Features entire cast. Written and directed by Aleksandar Mandic. Camera (color). Radoslav Vladic; sets, Mandic; music, Goran Bregovic. Reviewed at Moscow Film Festival (Market), Aug. 25, 1979. Running Time 85 MINS.

Cast: Maja Sabljic, Snezana Sabljic.

Tv helmer Aleksandar Mandic made his cinema debut with "Personal Affairs," a constructed cinema-verite pic that passes for a real-life story at the same time. The idea is an old and simple one: take a young girl on the verge of graduating from secondary school, who

has a yen to acting school, but has to pass the entrance exams first. Since Mandic only has to cover approximately four months (the summer vacation), his only problem is finding a likely candidate with some camera presence to carry the film on her personality alone. Helmer and pic almost succeeded.

The girl, Maja, is sensitive and emotional. She's constantly turned on by the pleasure of being a "star" already (for the tv portrait), but her lack of maturity and limited range of experiences in a well-to-do middleclass family only reveals an Achilles' heel at the very start & the viewer is aware she's not going to impress anyone with her talents at the acting school. She fails, and that's the end of it.

What's interesting, however, are the people the camera picks out on the side: the girl's family life, her shortterm affair with a macho type at the beach, and those stupid exams at the thesp school. —Holl.

Prijeki Sud
(Court Martial)
(YUGOSLAV-COLOR)

Moscow, Aug. 27.

An Adriafilm, Zagreb, Kinematografi, Zagreb, Zagreb Film, Zagreb, and Morava Film, Belgrade, Production; world rights, Yugoslavia Film, Belgrade. Features entire cast. Directed by Branko Ivanda. Screenplay, Zivko Jelicic, Ivanda; camera (color), Ivica Rajkovic; sets, Zeljko Senecic. Reviewed at Moscow Film Fest (Market), Aug. 27, '79. Running time: 90 MINS.

Cast: Pero Kvrgic, Zarko Potocnjak, Vlatko Dulic, Krunoslav Valentic, Ljubo Kaper, Tanja Knezic, Sanja Vejnovic.

A film critic who also studied direction, Branko Ivanda made an impressive debut with "Gravitations" (1968), then disappeared to work for television until his present "Court Martial." New pic leans heavily on metaphor and symbol to get the message across in a Beckettian line of dialog.

A court martial takes place in enclosed quarters of a military fortress: it's the middle of the last war just before the Italian capitulation. The intellectual figure is a Croatian middle Mediterranean-bred class lawyer, while the absolute judge in this phantom trial is an egotistical Italian military commander. There's also the lawyer's 14-year-old son and a giant dolt. All represent types and individuals of the human species. What happens is an existential, absurd game of one-upmanship throughout a long evening of play acting.

Although pic has some merits in thesp performances and comic scenes, the story drags on without saying much that's new or original. Still, this cross between Beckett, Pinter, Sartre and the Yugo-

slav Resistance movement deserves more exploring along these lines. —Holl.

Venice Films

Luna
(ITALIAN-COLOR)

Venice, Sept. 2.

A 20th Century-Fox release, produced by Fiction Film. Stars Jill Clayburgh. Directed by Bernardo Bertolucci. Script, Giuseppe and Bernardo Bertolucci, Clare Peploe; camera (Eastmancolor), Vittorio Storato; art director, Gianni Silvestri, Maria Paola Maino; editor, Gabriella Cristiani; music excerpts from Giuseppe Verdi. Reviewed at Venice Film Festival, Sept. 2, 1979. Running time: 145 MINS.

Caterina Silveri .... Jill Clayburgh
Joe .... Matthew Barry
Douglas .... Fred Gwynne
Marina .... Veronica Lazar
Communist .... Renato Salvatori
Giuseppe .... Tomas Milian

"Luna" (Moon) is a spectacle-sized melodrama filled with a variety of themes — plots and subplots that merge asymmetrically into a melodramaic mold. The saga of Jill Clayburgh as Yank lyric star afflicted with professional neuroses, fading pipes, a son on drugs and a close-to-incest mother-son development — falls neatly into the melodramatic world of Verdian opera and the unreal atmosphere behind the wings and offstage. The film also contains autobiog moments of Bertolucci's life from souvenirs of infancy to latter-day psychoanalysis.

This is Bertolucci's first non-political film, except for a sequence satirizing a Communist in the red belt of North Central Italy on the Parma-Bologna axis. Disengagement of the talented and controversial filmmaker leaves the impression that Bertolucci agreed to give 20th-Fox a better than average commercial vehicle for all markets.

The coupling of Clayburgh with Verdi in an ambience infrequently recreated in narrative fashion on screen, the stunning "Three Coins In the Fountain"-type settings reflecting the changed, now unromantic ways of the Eternal City life and the high tension relationship of mother and son — all seem tied to initial understanding between both parties when project was set.

World premiere at Venice does not really clarify what the Fox pickings will be. The task of sustaining melodramas for almost two and a half hours is only partially achieved. Moments of comedy relief are mainly local. Ambiguous and extraneous scenes (like Franco Citti's homosexual clinch with the young protagonist) or the opening scene after prolog, clarified two hours later.

Sudden death of singer's spouse and decision to resume singing in Italy with son Joe accompanying, moves the scene from Brooklyn Heights to Rome where the mother-son cleft takes over from Verdi appearances. Her battle to break down his detachment and drug habit is the core of the film — with her own career at stake as the voice gives under stress -- is not fully resolved until the main in the opening scene is identified as the real father and teenager sets out successfully to reunite the family unit. Emphasis is on the break-up and remending of family ties.

The father (Tomas Milian) willingly reasserts his role (with a slap in the kid's face) and the happy melodramatic finale comes through with vocie over as the singer grimaces back to form.

Clayburgh is hard pressed to sustain the melodramatic of "Luna." At moments she lapses into her own style for best results. Often she seems neutralized midway between America (by nationality) and Europe (by direction) - playing the role with dramatics somewhat alien to her natural talents.

Newcomer Matthew Barry as Joe is effectively strident on the road to self-destruction. The youngster is a promising newcomer after his impressive bow in a major role opposite an actress like Clayburgh. The big emotional mother-son scene — one that will create talk and b.o. is over strong, perhaps gamey, but in the meller framework and certainly short of the incest act.

The three male supports — Fred Gwynne as the U.S. father, Renato Salvatore as a Communist up in Parma and especially Milian as the boy's true father — add masculine strength to the cast in support of a tyke in the male lead.

Vittorio Storato has again given Bertolucci a splendid lensing input. Rome, Parma and the Red belt countryside never looked better. Art director team handled the many scene changes with great taste-sometimes leading Bertolucci into detailed insert shots that extend running time.

The editing pace is leisurely in keeping with sounds and stances of opera-melodrama. The scenes and music selections from Verdi are standout.

"Luna" is a big commercial entry. It provides entertainment and happy ending catharsis for teenagers and parents. Seeing the Bertolucci film together might help economize on analysis.—Werb.

Il Prato
(The Meadow)
(ITALIAN-COLOR)

Venice, Aug. 25.

A Sacis release produced by Giuliani De Negri for Filmtre and Rai-2. Features entire cast. Written and directed by Paolo and Vittorio Taviani. Camera (Eastmancolor), Franco Di Giacomo; editor, Roberto Perpignani; music, Ennio Morricone. Reviewed Venice Film Festival, Aug. 25, 1979. Running time: **120 MINS.**
Enzo .... Michele Placido
Giovanni .... Saverio Marconi
Eugenia .... Isabella Rossellini
Giovanni's Father .... Giulio Brogi

Attempt by established Italian filmmakers to come up with a plausible work on rebellious self-isolation of Italian youth within a society they see as hostile is taking on trend proportions.

The Taviani brothers, two years after their big hit with "Father Master" (Golden Palm at Cannes '77), have made a serious effort to probe smalltown youth in "The Meadow." For what it sets out to do, the film is generally disappointing — failing principally to attain a convincing essence in continuity, portrait and language.

Early footage carefully rolls out the Tuscan background and the mechanism of a three-way love affair. Giovanni (Saverio Marconi), down from Milan to sell off some Tuscan property. Eugenia, a local clerk, and Enzo, the militant see themselves as victims and misfits — unable to work in their chosen fields.

Emotional attachments add to social frustration as Eugenia wavers between Enzo and Giovanni, who become friends to further complicate relationships.

As the romantic ties slacken the Tavianis go on to undermine the common concept of nature as the ideal environment for human spirit and materia well being by paralleling the pangen recesses of the human condition with the worm-ridden seams of the meadow. A stylistic view of the world ending in Giovanni's games-ridden suicide offers youth one more hundred chance for love and happy fulfillment. Utopia is only a dream and the Tavianis stage a big dream sequence, showing Eugenia as the pied piper punishing the grownups and leading the kids to bountiful and beautiful pastoral community. Return to reality wipes it clean.

Between dreams and reality, the Tavianis miss on narrative structure and dialog. The film staggers from situation to situation. The words are inadequate, heavily enigmatic and often liltless. The spark, fight-back attitudes and caustic humor of youth today are totally missing.

The three young principals add little to breathe life into "The Mea-

dow." The daughter (Isabella Rossellini) looks like mother (Ingrid Bergman) but resemblance is a curio item, not much more in her first appearance. Cast shares responsibility with the director team for some of the heavier-handed moments of this beautifully made film.

In retrospect, the replacement of actor-director Nanni Moretti two weeks after shooting started by Saverio Marconi eliminated perhaps the one avenue to an authentic youth note in the film. Rossellini is young but still raw. Placido no longer has the youngish quality he had in "Till Marriage Do Us Part" some years back. Giulio Brogi, as Giovanni's father, gives the best characterization — that of a middle-ager, but his scenes are overstaged and his own conflict between self-fulfillment and fatherly anxieties are somewhat ambiguous.

Photography — aerial and terra firma — is a main asset. San Geminiano (an ancient Tuscan town) and surrounding meadows are brilliantly lensed. Poetic note of youth and nature seeps through only in Ennio Morricone's lyrical score. Editing is slow and could easily be tightened for a more realistic running time. Doctoring in this department would help the obvious commercial pitch for Rossellini's debut and the reputation of Paolo and Vittorio Taviani in world markets. —Werb.

I Giorni Cantati
(Swansong Days)
(ITALIAN-COLOR)

Venice, Sept. 4.

A Titanus release of a Co-op Lunga Gittata production. Features entire cast. Directed by Paolo Pietrangeli. Screenplay, Giovanna Marini, Francesco Massaro, Paolo Pietrangeli; camera (Technicolor), Dario Di Palma: art director, Elena Ricci Poccetto; editor, Ruggero Mastroianni; songs by Ivan Della Mea, Pasquale Malinconico. Giovanna Marini, Paolo Pietrangeli. Screened Sept. 4, 1979, at Venice Film Festival. Running time: **110 MINS.**
Cast: Roberto Benigni, Franco Bianchi, Ivan Della Mea, Francesco Guccini, Giovanna Marini, Mariangela Melato, Anna Nogara, Paolo Pietrangeli.

Paolo Pietrangeli's ambitious try to explain the rift between middle age and life and the abyss between grown-ups and youth in the world of political ballads and folk music is handled with such intensity that it almost becomes a parody of an expanding social problem.

Intensity of Pietrangeli's one-man effort as director, performer in the lead role, coscreenwriter and co-composer rises to obsessive heights — musically as well as dramatically (or melodramatically) and floats off into an irrational and ambiguous view of a generation gap so realistically a part of mod-

ern life though perhaps in a less generalized dimension than Pietrangeli presents.

Composer-ballad singer Marco (Paolo Pietrangeli) survives a suicide attempt and relapses into a psycho throwback to find out at what point his music and lyrics were lost on radical, political and fringe youth audiences. A rebel of '68 becomes a has-been a decade later as new idols come along with magic words and notes to enthrall youth in the thousands who turn out basically to be together. In his quest for the why fore, Marco holes up with a youth menage-a-trois next door but the incommunicability finally snaps his sanity and he kills the trio. Up to that high note finale, his wife, his ballad cronies and old friends are all trapped in the protagonist's over-exercised quandary.

Music, backgrounds and lensing come to the aid of "Swan Song Days" through the first half and more but when the director takes his cast indoors and relies on long silences for dramatic impact, the pace slows and plods, letting excess length slip into sequence after sequence.

But main letdown is Pietrangeli's obvious effort — both cerebral and emotional — to demonstrate impenatrability of youth lifestyles — perhaps at a time when strains of a youth reflux are starting to appear. This could date the film and limit audiences to the nostalgic. Pic, a co-op low-budget product, will get fest attention for its look at 1968 and beyond. Cast standout is ballad singer-composer Francesco Guccini for his voice and personable, simple stance on stage.

Dario Di Palma's lighting tops technical support. —Werb.

Ratataplan
(ITALIAN-COLOR)

Venice, Sept. 4.

Cineriz release. Produced by Franco Cristaldi and Nicola Carraro for Vides Productions. Features entire cast. Written and directed by Maurizio Nichetti; camera (Eastman Color), Mario Battistoni; art director, Maria Pia Angelini; editor, Giancarlo Rossi: music, Detto Mariano. Reviewed at Venice Festival Palace, Sept. 4, 1979. Running time: **90 MINS.**

Cast: Maurizio Nichetti, Angela Finocchiaro, Edy Angelillo, Lidia Biondi, Roland Topor.

Maurizio Nichetti's film debut with a nonsense comedy is filled with inventive sketch ideas, great lensing, sprightly thesping by a group of newcomers and barbed comment on youth and other humans in a rich-poor modern society. But the nonsense rarely translates into humor and "Ratataplan" remains an unfunny vehicle, at least for spectators from 25 and up who can no longer capture the spirit and fantasy of young high-jinks. Perhaps this is what young audiences are waiting for.

Nichetti comes off with a bigger share of brilliance as the lead actor in this mad prop-stacked series of sitcoms than he does for the pile of intellect he pours into his first pic to build for comedy that rarely gets off the ground.

"Ratataplan" is a very personal film embroidered with the unreal. the weird and the fantastic. It also leans heavily on slapstick and a strain of macabre farce. Styles clash wildly in a spirited pace — unaided by moments of flat banality and self-indulgence.

The Vides production is nevertheless a promising start for a new switch-hitting young filmmaker who for the moment shows more stance before the camera than he does behind it.

As Colombo, Nichetti delivers a resourceful performance of a lonely, timid youth who almost achieves happiness indirectly via a knack for modern gadgetry. The best scene in the picture is the electronic construction and manipulation of a Colombo double to make it finally with the girl downstairs. Most of the other performances are all high key delirium but to no avail.

Mario Battistoni's photography is perhaps the standout feature, followed effectively by Giancarlo Rossi's editing and sound effects and Maria Pia Angelini's art direction and costuming. Nichetti winds with three credits — as cast topper, writer and director. —*Werb.*

Il Y A Longtemps Que J'taime
(It's A Long Time I've Loved You)
(FRENCH-COLOR)

Montreal, Sept. 3.
A Films de la Tour presentation, written and directed by Jean-Charles Tacchella. Featuring Jean Carmet, Marie Dubois, Alain Doutey. Camera (color), George Lendi. Editing, Agnes Guillemot. Music, Gerard Anfosso. Reviewed at Montreal Film Festival, Sept. 3, 1979. Running time: 93 MINS.

Amusingly written and directed by Jean-Charles Tacchella this French film should be popular in the U.S.-Canada urban and campus markets where the Gallic way of laughing at sex, marriage and human nature generally is appreciated.

The photography of Georges Lendi, the editing of Agnes Guillemot and the often bouncy music of Gerard Anfosso are all values of

notable contribution to the entertaining 93 minutes. (The film was competitive at the Montreal Film Festival).

Briefly, a married pair announce, at their silver anniversary party, an intention to separate. Their children, now grown and married, protest. The screenplay then traces both partners, their efforts to enjoy their "independence," naturally frequently frustrating. Sentiment finally stages a comeback.

Full cast credits were not available at the Montreal film fest but the most prominent principals are Jean Carmet, Marie Dubois, Alain Doutey.

To summarize, an easy to enjoy "Idea" comedy based on a novel situation and observation of modern middle class Paris.

— *Land.*

Arthur Miller On Home Ground
(CANADIAN-COLOR-DOCU-16m)

A production of the Canadian Broadcasting Corp. Produced, directed and written by Harry Rasky. Camera (color-16m), Hideaki Kobayashi, Kenneth Gregg, Edmund Long; editor, Arla Saare. Reviewed at Screening Room, CBC, New York, Aug. 26, 1979. (No MPAA rating). Running time 90 MINS.
With Marilyn Monroe, Clark Gable, Burt Lancaster, Faye Dunaway, Lee J. Cobb, Colleen Dewhurst, George C. Scott, Maureen Stapleton, Raf Vallone, Mildred Dunnock, Christopher Plummer.

Prolific career of Arthur Miller continues unabated. Recent dispute concerns his made-for-tv movie "Playing For Time," scheduled for CBS-TV next season. Jewish groups are protesting the casting of Vanessa Redgrave (PLO champion) as an Auschwitz survivor.

A new full-length documentary by Harry Rasky makes an affectionate retrospective-tribute to the American playwright. It will have its television premiere on the CBC in Canada in mid-October on Miller's 64th birthday. Meanwhile, the film unreels Sept. 5 at the Montreal Film Festival.

"Arthur Miller On Home Ground" traces Miller childhood and youth in Harlem and Brooklyn, the Depression, and Miller's early writing at $22 weekly for the WPA arts projects. "The muscular aspiration" of New York City, with its dynamic center of U.S. theatre — "That was my time," says Miller. "I felt the form instantly." Miller's comments on drama generally, and on American theatre particularly, are right on target.

"On Home Ground" includes key scenes from film and tv adaptations of Miller dramas, with stars

that include the late Marilyn Monroe in "The Misfits." These excerpts are first rate and convey the range of Miller themes. Only faux pas among them is "I Don't Need You Anymore," a Miller short story dramatized by Rasky and narrated by Miller.

Recurrent Miller concerns to emerge include responsibility, identity and vocation, remembrance and yearning, waste of potential and spitirual values, and "the destruction of the hermetic seal around the family." Miller advocacy of ethical and humanistic values are not compromised, he hopes, by inadvertently slipping into propaganda.

Miller as president of PEN (Poets, Editors, Novelists) comments on the blacklisting and suppression of dissident artists. Miller comes by his credentials as PEN spokesman per his plays and his defiant testimony, albeit in measured reasonable discourse, before the House Un-American Activities Committee.

The Salem witchcraft trials of 1692 had interested Miller long before the McCarthy period. "I wanted to show in 'The Crucible' how terror can change people."

"On Home Ground" has a long brief tempestuous marriage was the stuff of Miller's "After The Fall," scene from which is enacted by Faye Dunaway and Christopher Plummer.

Faye Dunaway and Christopher Plummer.

"She was always playing with suicide," remembers Miller, after the excerpt, a harrowing scene. "She was always close to the edge ... What a monstrous waste that she should be gone that way."

A craftsman as playwright, Miller also makes his own furniture and is a serious farmer. Scenes in "On Home Ground" depict him at home in Connecticut with his family. His collaboration with wife-photographer Inge Monath on two books also figures in the film.

Miller's final words are of elusive and incomplete satisfaction, the wish someday "to do something really good." His lifetime, he summarizes, provides "a few moments of immense pleasure" that make the effort worthwhile. "Life is endless assertion ... We must renew our resolutions to the last minute." —*Hitch.*

Night-Flowers
(U.S.-COLOR)

Two Vietnam vets floundering toward adjustment. Along the way they commit two murders. Film is fairly interesting try, but pretty bleak.

Montreal, Sept. 3.
Willow Production Co. Ltd. presentation. Producer, Sally Faile. Distributor, Leonard Franklin Associates. Directed and edited by Luis San Andres. Featuring Jose Perez, Sabra Jones, Cabriel Walsh. Screenplay, Gabriel Walsh; camera (color), Larry Pizer; music, Harry Manfredini. Reviewed Sept. 3, 1979 at Montreal Film Festival. Running time 92 MINS.

One of 21 films in the prize-competitive sector of the Montreal Film Festival, this U.S. independent carries a crawl credit to the New Jersey Film Commission. The street scenes are around Hoboken, with the Staten Island Ferry identified. No information available as to the financing or the antecedents of the principal talents. A single descriptive word to cover the plot and the viewpoint would be "grim." that poses a doubt on playoff.

Narrative centers on a footloose friendship between a Hispanic and an Irish-American, both psychologically damaged by Vietnam. The Hispanic is sex-starved. He brutally corners, rapes and kills a girl who comes seeking to rent the pair's flat. Later, the other ex-soldier shoots a thief attempting to escape when his phoney alibi as a disco dancer is exposed.

What emerges is a film focussed on the seedy, sordid and psychotic aspects of urban society and the Veterans Hospital Spirit recalls "Midnight Cowboy," or "Taxi Driver," or you pick the analogy. The characters are believable and the direction reasonable. Not a great study of the under-side of America, but the story holds interest.

Gabriel Walsh who provided the script (apparently original) is the "haunted" G.I. His is a pretty effective joint contribution, if some quibbling could be filed. The vision is cynical and resentful though he speaks later of his happiness in having known the joy of falling in love, if only for an hour — since at that point of reminiscence he and his Hispanic chum are on a waterfront lam after the second murder in their existence.

The most interesting character perhaps is "Danny The Dancer," a slimey human being apparently a burglar by trade and/or a male-hustler. There are, however, a number of other nicely realized character vignettes.

Director San Andres and author-actor Walsh can be loged in the "probable better things later" pigeon-hole. —*Land.*

H.O.T.S.
(COLOR)

Lukewarm drive-in fare.

Hollywood, Sept. 6.
Derio Productions, Inc. release of a Great American Dream Machine Movie Company production. Produced by W. Terry Davis, Don Schain, Gerald Sindell. Exec producer, Davis. Directed by Gerald Sindell. Screenplay, Cheri Caffaro, Joan Buchanan; camera (Color), Harvey Genkins; editor, Barbara Pokras; music, David Davis; sound, Art Names; assistant directors, Gerald Olson, Michael Healy. Reviewed at the Aidikoff Screening Room, L.A., Sept. 6, '79. (MPAA Rating: R). Running time: **95 MINS.**

Honey .... Susan Kiger
O'Hara .... Lisa London
Teri Lynn .... Pamela Jean Bryant
Sam .... Kimberly Cameron
Clutz .... Mary Steelsmith
Boom-Boom .... Angela Aamers
Melody .... Lindsay Bloom
Cynthia .... K.C. Winkler
Doug .... Donald Petrie
Mad Dog .... Larry Gilman
Macho Man .... David Gibbs
Richie .... Danny Bonaduce
Dean Chase .... Ken Olfson
Charlie Ingels .... Dick Bakalyan
Bugs Benny .... Louis Guss

Following a long line of mindless but successful drive-in sex comedies, "H.O.T.S." should earn its proper place at outdoor screens across the country. The picture in the typical "youth film" — complete with lotsa sub-junior high school level humor, lecherous shots of breasts and buttocks and characters as ludicrous as the plot they seek to convey. Succeeding on that level, "H.O.T.S." should stir some initial interest in saturation bookings but will likely not stay around too long.

There's a formula for pictures like these — throw as many buxom coeds and dumb jocks as you can find into a college setting, show a generous amount of skin and keep the action moving. Chances are audiences will quickly put their brains aside and be caught up in a dreamland of bouncing mammeries and endless orgies.

Toss in some lame-brained adults for counterbalance and one might even be tempted to remain in the feigned nirvana.

That feeling doesn't last too long as "H.O.T.S." becomes tiresome less than halfway through. Once the stage is set for the rivalry between a mythical university's two top sororities "Pi" and "H.O.T.S.," and the girls play a few nasty practical jokes and shake their booties, audience interest will wane much the way it would if this were real life. Luckily, it's not.

Production values on the pic are good, with camera work by Harvey Genkins and color by DeLuxe quite sharp. Barbara Pokras' editing is adequate as is David Davis' score and Gerald Sindells director.

However, screenplay by Cheri Caffaro and Joan Buchanan can only be carried so far. Given all the demeaning uses of and references to females throughout the film, it seems surprising that two women banded to create the marshmallow-like story.

Actors do little more than appear overblown plasticized creations of what's on paper. There are some witty moments supplied by Larry Gilman as a campus cut-up and Louis Guss and Dick Bakalyan as two ex-cons. But these and any other entertaining spots are very, very occasional. —*Berg.*

French Postcards
(W. GERMAN-FRENCH) COLOR)

Cute, but nothing to write home about.

Hollywood, Sept. 7.
A Paramount Pictures release of a Geria production. Produced by Gloria Katz. Directed by Willard Huyck. Features entire cast. Screenplay, Huyck and Katz; camera (color), Bruno Nuytten; editor, Carol Littleton; music, Lee Holdridge; art direction, Jean-Pierre Kohut-Svelko; costume design, Catherine Letherrier, Joan Mocine; set decorator, Jacques Leguillon; sound, Bernard Bats; asst. director, Jean-Jacques Beineix. Reviewed at Paramount Studio Theatre, Hollywood, Sept. 7, '79. (MPAA Rating: PG.) Running time: **95 MINS.**

Joel .... Miles Chapin
Laura .... Blanche Baker
Alex .... David Marshall Grant
Toni .... Valerie Quennessen
Melanie .... Debra Winger
Sayyid .... Mandy Patinkin
Madame Tessier .... Marie-France Pisier
Monsieur Tessier .... Jean Rochefort
Mrs. Weber .... Lynn Carlin
Mr. Weber .... George Coe
Pascal .... Christophe Bourseiller
(English Soundtrack)

Innocents abroad are no longer so innocent, or so "French Postcards" would have us believe. Latest in a series of Francophile pictures, "Postcards" is a charming, delectable little film that seems certain to please a limited audience. Well-cast, scripted and directed by the team of Willard Huyck and Gloria Katz, longtime screenwriters just now gaining artistic control over their work, "Postcards" is not destined to set the world afire, but returns should certainly justify the effort.

As in "America Graffiti," greatest success of the Huyck-Katz team, emphasis is on that age group tottering between adolescence and adulthood. In this instance, the protagonists are students spending the proverbial college year abroad, and suffering the predictable loneliness, romantic interludes, and eye-openings that dislocation from familiar surroundings provokes.

In lesser hands, this might be cloying and precocious, but "Postcards" deals with its characters in a straightforward and refreshing fashion, dwelling on the warts as well as the dimples.

By concentrating on three principal characters, director Huyck and producer Katz wisely keep the focus of "Postcards" narrow, so audiences can develop emotional relationships with the screen personages. These include Miles Chapin as an indecisive suburbanite, David Marshall Grant as a would-be songwriter angling for some pseudo-Hemingway experiences, and Blanche Baker as a snobbish and lonely girl on a cultural binge.

Casting of Marie-France Pisier and Jean Rochefort as the husband and wife team running the Paris-based school was a stroke of genius. They give the film a solid bedrock of professionalism, and Pisier in particular develops an attractive and fascinating character. Rochefort is suave, as always, but his English is so fractured as to be almost unintelligible.

"French Postcards" works best when editor Carol Littleton is allowed to jump from one scene to another, weaving vignettes into an interesting and generally coherent story line. Chapin becomes enamored of worldly-wise Valerie Quennessen and Grant has a disastrous prelude to an affair with Pisier, before finding more common ground with Baker.

But in the last half-hour, the shifting relationships between a simple group of youngsters become as complex as multilayered French farce, and "Postcards" seems extenuated by the final whirl of partner-changing. Introduction of Chapin's parents also seems unnecessary, and a play put on by the students (with no advance warning) leads to continuity problems.

The cast is so suitable that the drawbacks may not matter. Chapin and Baker, with a couple of pix behind them, register strongly, and Grant is very likable in his film debut. Quennessen is one of the film's delights, an attractive and personable actress who should get more work in the future.

Supporting cast is especially good, particularly Mandy Patinkin as a lecherous Iranian, Debra Winger as another student, and Christophe Bourseiller as an anti-American French teenager.

Bruno Nuytten's cinematography is gorgeous, and Paris has rarely looked so well on film, quite a statement given the city's celluloid showcasing. Other tech credits, from a primarily French crew, are right up to Hollywood standards.

With "A Little Romance" acting as a dubious forerunner in the marketplace, "Postcards" may have difficulty in establishing itself against unusually heavy fall competition. Pic received funding from the German tax shelter group, Geria, and preemed at the Montreal Film Festival. —*Poll.*

From Hell To Victory
(FRENCH-ITALO-SPANISH-COLOR)

Madrid, Aug. 21.
New Film Production (Rome), Princess Films (Paris) and Jose Frade (Madrid) coproduction. Directed by Hank Milestone. Features entire cast. Screenplay, Umberto Lenzi, Jose Luis Martinez Molls, Gianfranco Clerici; camera (Eastmancolor) Jose Luis Alcaine; music, Riz Ortolani; sets, Giuseppe Bassan Rafael Ferry; editor, Vicenzo Tomasi. Reviewed at Cine Velazquez, Madrid, Aug. 20, '79. Running time: **100 MINS.**

Bret .... George Peppard
Maurice .... George Hamilton
Jurgen .... Horst Bucholz
Nicole .... Capucine
Ray .... Sam Wanamaker
Bick .... Jean Pierre Cassel
Fabienne .... Annie Duperey
Also Ray Lovelock, Angel Aranda, Antonio Mayans.

It is a pity that the many top-notch action scenes and showy production values of this costly film are never given the proper continuity to form a believable story. Some of the highlights of World War II are there: the Dunkirk disaster, bomber attacks on London, a Resistance shoot-out on the Eiffel Tower, a full scale tank battle, stirring dog fights and Commando raids into France.

But they add up to very little since they are disjointed and each episode is demarcated from the next by a date and place flashed on the screen, giving the film an almost documentary flavor at times. Ostensibly, the story is spun about a group of friends of diverse nationalities (French, German, English, American) who in pre-war Paris, when the world is on the brink of war, vow to meet each year on that date in the same place.

Yarn then unravels by following the activities of each of the principals, who keep on running into each other with fortuitous unbelievability. All, of course, are fighting vehemently on the Allied side. The German, becomes a tank division commander but remains as simpatico as at the beginning of the film. Some die along the way. The Resistance girl is saved at the 11th hour from the clutches of the SS when Paris is liberated, which happens to be the day of their yearly rendezvous in the cafe. She trudges off to meet two of the other survivors for a happy reunion.

Some attempts are made at character development, but fail to succeed; which wouldn't matter if there were a story to hold the action scenes together. But there isn't. Thesping is of a professional level throughout and all technical credits

up to crack, with some of the scenes, such as the retreat from Dunkirk, topnotch. Pic should do okay biz on the basis of the action sequences and good production values. Item managed to get an "all audience" classification in Spain.
—*Besa.*

Ga pa vattnet om du kan
(Walk On Water If You Can)
(SWEDISH-COLOR)

Malmoe, Aug. 29.
A Swedish Film Institute/Audio Investment/HB Three Leaf Clover/AB Europa Film production, Europa Film distribution. Features entire cast. Directed by Stig Bjorkman. Written by Sun Axelsson; camera (Eastmancolor), Petter Davidson; editor, Margit Nordquist; music, Berndt Eger; executive producer, Anna-Lena Wibom. Reviewed at private screening, Rio Bio, Malmoe, Aug. 29, 1979. Running time: **95 MINS.**
Orlanda . . . . Lena Nyman
Anders . . . . Tomas Ponten
Malin . . . . Claire Wikholm
Raul . . . . Norman Briski
Anna . . . . Annifrid Lyngstad
Jesus . . . . Toni Valente

"Walk On Water If You Can" may have a male, Stig Bjorkman, as its director, but this feature is very much a woman's film and will fare the better commercially abroad if marketed as such.

· Bjorkman has worked in close collaboration with several women, notably writer Sun Axelsson and lead player Lena Nyman who suggested several additions to dialog and script developments.

Result is a rather sluggish portrait of a youngish woman in revolt. Her name is Orlanda (mostly to justify a belated reference to her as Orlando Furiosa), she lives a hippie life style in Stockholm, works nights as an assistant nurse at a psychiatric ward and has for her best friend a neurotic, suicide-prone woman painter Claire Wikholm.

One day she involves herself in a happy love affair with a young diplomat, Anders (Tomas Ponten) on home leave from some unnamed Latin American dictator-ridden country.

The diplomat talks Orlando into following him to Latin America. Here (Spanish locations are used with discretion) she finds out that Anders is just recently divorced and that he, in spite of previous liberal attitudes, is really hopelessly mired in a career diplomat's conservative way of life.

Hospitalized briefly, Orlando makes friends with Raul (Norman Briski), a very humanitarian doctor. Strong socialist-sentimental bonds are established between the two. Orlanda moves away from the diplomat's villa and into a cheap pension, starts working with an un-

dergroundMarxist group, and gets arrested but avoids charges when the diplomat intervenes.

Back in the villa, Anders gets drunk and rapes Orlanda. When she regains consciousness, she appears to be a free woman, walking into the streets, smiling softly and holding her tiny, rotund body very erect.

In between, Orlanda has visions of a fattish, elderly Jesus having his feet washed by Anna (played by Annifrid Lyngstad of the ABBA group) and walking, rather reluctantly and much to his own surprise, on water. This Jesus later gives stones to starving people who throw them back at him when they do not turn into bread but remain rocks that break their teeth.

Film is rather schematic and dry, its editing lack rhythm, but the camerawork is nice and Bjorkman composes good frames and gets nice, natural performances from his actors. Lena Nyman is, as usual, a stand-out. — *Kell.*

Un Dramma Borghese
(Mimi)
(ITALIAN-COLOR)

Venice, Aug. 28.
A Variety Film release, produced by Gianni Minervini and Antonio Avati for A.M.A. Film and U.T.I. Productions. Stars Franco Nero. Directed by Florestano Vancini. Script Lucio Battistrada, Florestano Vancini, based on novel by Guido Morselli; camera (Eastmancolor), Alfio Contini; editor, Nino Baragli; music, Riz Ortolani. Reviewed at Venice Film Festival, Aug. 28, '79. Running time: **110 MINS.**
Guido . . . . Franco Nero
Therese . . . . Dalila Di Lazzaro
Mimmina . . . . Lara Wendel

Lara Wendel as a 15-year-old with aggressive incest in her eyes is the revelation of Florestano Vancini's loose adaptation of a Guido Morselli novel. But "Mimi" is essentially an exploitation melodrama, despite a culturally tinted prolog and epilog, and should hit the commercial trail in many markets.

Action takes place principally in a Swiss hotel suite. Foreign correspondent Guido (Franco Nero) has yanked his daughter (15) from boarding school and both are sharing the hotel suite after many years of separation. Most of the footage is given over to Mimi's play for her father (including a breast-stroking orgasm in bed at her father's side) and to Nero's sometimes awkward rebuffs, while attempting to understand how it all started and where it will end. Relationship becomes volatile when Mimi's schoolmate Therese (Dalila Di Lazzaro) suddenly visits — setting the groundwork for natural sex, (father and friend), the daughter's frustrated infatuation and her suicide attempt.

Incest is neither condoned nor

condemned. Psycho aspects of it are routine. With Therese's arrival, potential drama becomes melodrama and accent shifts to indiscriminate mass entertainment.

Nero's performance is balanced except for two or three embarrassing sequences staged by Vancini—one involving Nero's contortionist effort to give himself a suppository; the other where he faints flat on his face after daughter Mimi first gets him into her clutches.

Sultry Dalila Di Lazzaro is totally miscast. Her scenes with Nero strain credibility. On the other hand, Lara Wendel — the nymphette with incest in her heart — provides the emotional kick to the film. Vancini wisely contains incest theme within discreet limits and, more often than not, in low-key lighting. Act itself remains unconsumated despite daughter's wanton campaign.

The prolog-epilog gambit relating to novelist Morselli may be sluffed off for foreign sales. However, it provides a built-in promo angle for local release. Technical assists give "Mimi" a world market look and score. —*Werb.*

Edinburgh Festival

Black Jack
(BRITISH-COLOR)

Edinburgh, Aug. 24.
A Kestrel Films production in association with the National Film Finance Corp. Produced by Tony Garnett. Directed by Kenneth Loach. Features entire cast. Screenplay, Loach, from the novel by Leon Garfield; camera (color). Chris Menges; editor, Bill Shapter; designer, Martin Johnson; costumes, Sally Nieper; music, Bob Pegg; asst. director, Raymond Day. Reviewed at the Edinburgh International Film Festival, Claton Studios, Edinburgh. August 23, '79. Running Time: **106 MINS.**
Black Jack . . . . Jean Franval
Tolly . . . . Stephen Hirst
Belle . . . . Louise Cooper
Hatch . . . . Andrew Bennett
Dr. Carmody . . . . Packie Byrne
Mrs. Gorgandy . . . . Pat Wallis
Dr. Hunter . . . . John Young
Mr. Carter . . . . William Moore
Dr. Jones . . . . Russell Waters

Basically an adventure yarn set in northern England in 1750, the latest collaboration of writer-director Kenneth Loach and producer Tony Garnett tops their earlier work in features by adding firstrate period recreation to their already-established talents for sharp, telling realism. With less of an overtly social theme than "Kes," "Family Life" and most of the team's tv efforts, "Black Jack" scores as accessible entertainment, but is still stamped with something more than simple narrative.

Main problem the film faces

commercially is the lack of strong marketable elements, since it is bereft of boxoffice names and was financed (mainly by the British state-funded National Film Finance Corp.) largely on the strength of Loach's — albeit local — reputation. But it shapes to find a receptive, wide age-range audience in several European territories; and with careful promotion aimed primarily at public broadcast tv fans and younger kids, it could also dent the tougher U.S. market in time.

Loach's screenplay, adapted from Leon Garfield's same-title novel, suffers from a meandering plotline, but that hardly matters. Continuously engrossing, and enlivened with a wry wit, is his reconstruction of the class-ridden 18th century world, where self-deceiving rich folk are tricked, blackmailed and ultimately exposed by a bunch of gypsies — whose integrity stands more scrutiny despite their petty dishonesties.

The extraordinary authenticity attaching to that reconstruction stems not simply from the costumes and all-location settings, although design departments have contributed considerably more than could have been expected from the $1,000,000 budget. More importantly, under Loach's direction, the entire cast of unknowns convincingly conveys the impression that their raggedy dresses or fancy wigs are wholly familiar to them as everyday wear; that horse-drawn travel or repairing coaches is a natural part of their lives; in particular, that the casual violence and corruption of the times are so real to them as to be unremarkable.

The title-role is more catalyst than hero in the story. After miraculously surviving a hanging, Black Jack, a gigantic Frenchman with few words of English, endearingly played by Jean Franval, takes along a young boy (Stephen Hirst) with him on his escape, to "speak for him." The main plot concerns a girl (Louise Cooper) they encounter by chance, whose irrational behavior has caused her wealthy parents to commit her to a privately run madhouse for fear of possible scandal. She evades the profit-hungry quacks, and all three join up with a travelling band of fairground acts. Numerous intrigues ensue, as Hirst becomes convinced Cooper is in fact sane, and resolves to keep her with him.

The predictable happy ending entails the flowering of a romance between the pair — both only on the verge of puberty — which Loach handles with commendable lack of saccharin. Flawlessly natural performances by the children, and the generally laconic tone of Yorkshire speech, are two clear pluses in that respect.

Cinematographer Chris Menges has chiefly shot for bleached-out highspots and strong backlight, which create attractive effects without undermining Loach's realism. Bob Pegg's score, bright and unsentimental, reinforces the upbeat period flavor.

In view of the strong dialect spoken throughout, Garnett and Loach are reportedly prepared for substitution of a more intelligible dialog track for the U.S. release, which is so far not set. Pic is to be screened at the New York festival. —*Simo.*

The Tempest
(BRITISH-COLOR)

Edinburgh, Aug. 26.
A Boyd's Co. production. Executive producer, Don Boyd. Produced by Guy Ford, Mordecai Schreiber. Directed by Derek Jarman. Associate producer, Sarah Radclyffe. Features entire cast. Screenplay, Jarman, from Shakespeare's play; camera (color), Peter Middleton; editor, Leslie Walker; designer, Yolanda Sonnaband; music, Wavemaker; asst. director, Anthony Annis. Reviewed at the Edinburgh International Film Festival, Calton Studios, Edinburgh, Aug. 25, '79. Running Time: 96 MINS.

Prospero	Heathcote Williams
Ariel	Karl Johnson
Caliban	Jack Birkett
Miranda	Toyah Wilcox
Ferdinand	David Meyer
Alonso	Peter Bull
Sebastian	Richard Warwick
Gonzaolo	Ken Campbell
Antonio	Neil Cunningham
Stephano	Christopher Biggins
Trinculo	Peter Turner
Sycorax	Claire Davenport
Goddess	Elizabeth Welch

British helmer Derek Jarman's third feature, a film version of Shakespeare's most fanciful play, is definitely one of a kind. Its greatest strength is its "look," conceived by Jarman, and well executed by designer Yolanda Sonnaband and cinematographer Peter Middleton. That offsets the director-adaptor's generally limp control of the narrative.

Shot on location on a miniscule budget, "The Tempest" is rich in arty originality, and it's doubtful whether costlier casting, or a longer schedule, would have improved it. Jarman has achieved commendably lavish production values within the limitations.

Like his first feature, "Sebastiane," which combined high camp interpretation of a classical theme with memorable visuals (and Latin dialog), the latest is aimed squarely at upmarket arthouse playoff, with discerning gays the likeliest takers. The large amount of integral male nudity is bound to create censorship problems in some territories.

Although heavily cut and reorganized, the Bard's lines are used virtually throughout. The plot remains intact.

The play is no action-packed tale, and scores onstage through fantastical characters and resonant poetry. On film, Jarman has rendered it more static than ever, but packed his tableaux with a mass of convention-flouting — often surrealistic — visual ideas, so that the art department deserves top billing, and the players rank with the props. It's a feast for the eyes, but dramatically languid.

Heathcote Williams, younger than the magician is normally played, has presence, but throws away delivery of the colorful verbiage to the point of dullness. On the other hand, Karl Johnson as Ariel — a workmanlike sprite, dressed in white overalls — suggests a wealth of anguish and resentment at his enslavement to Williams by underplaying with compelling intensity.

Most successful innovation is Toyah Willcox's assault on the usually vacuous role of Miranda. Plump and punkish, her reaction to the first eligible male she has ever seen is more lusty than wide-eyed, and thoroughly believable. Disappointingly monotonous, however, is Jack Birkett as the grotesque house slave, Caliban, with a traditional line in theatrical grimaces.

Jarman's biggest liberty is the insertion of a wedding feast at the end, complete with dancing sailor boys, and blues singer Elizabeth Welch crooning "Stormy Weather" as a kind of diva ex machina. In the words of some other bard, for those who like that sort of thing, that's the sort of thing they'll like.

Use of a blue filter on all exterior scenes, notably the wreck sequence at the opening, contrasts helpfully with the warm colors and elaborate dressings of Williams' domain. That's the one acknowledgement Jarman has made of Shakespeare's repeated references to the elements in the imagery-ridden speeches. Filling out the sense that the castle's delapidated, candle-lit 18th century halls form a safe cell against the inhospitable world just outside, is the menacing score of music and effects created by Wavemaker, a London-based electronic workshop. —*Simo.*

Radio On
(BRITISH-W. GERMAN-B&W)

Edinburgh, Aug. 24.
A British Film Institute and Road Movies Film Produktion GmbH coproduction in association with the National Film Finance Corp. Executive producers, Renee Gundelach, Peter Sainsbury. Produced by Keith Griffiths. Directed by Christopher Petit. Associate producer, Wim Wenders. Features entire cast. Screenplay, Petit, Heidi Adolph; Camera (black & white), Martin Schafer; editor, Anthony Sloman; sound, Martin Muller; art director, Susannah Buxton; production supervisor, Patsy Nightingale; music, David Bowie, Sting, Kraftwerk, Eddie Cochran, Wreckless Eric and various Stiff Records artists. Reviewed at the Edinburgh International Film Festival, Calton Studios, Edinburgh, Aug. 23, '79. Running Time: 101 MINS.

Robert	David Beames
Ingrid	Lisa Kreuzer
Kathy	Sandy Ratcliff
Deserter	Andrew Byatt
Girl	Sue Jones-Davies
Just Like Eddie	Sting
Aunt	Sabina Michael
German Woman	Katja Kersten
Kid	Paul Hollywood

London critic Christopher Petit's directorial debut, a downbeat mystery tale set mainly on the road in damp midwinter, risks boredom by its lingering pace and head-on approach to its principal theme, the great British disease of apathy. But the chemistry, in this instance, of normally deadly ingredients produces an unexpectedly refreshing result.

Technically highly proficient on a peanut budget, "Radio On" will likely pick up praise at cultural-emphasis festivals, then could hold respectably in situations with a known audience for European art-films.

Promotion via the soundtrack, which includes music by David Bowie, the German band, Kraftwerk, and various New Wave acts, may be tempting in some territories, but could also lead to disappointed word-of-mouth. Although continually played out of cassette machines and juke boxes as well as radios, those numbers are used in the film in much the same way that media news reports, and the sounds of windshield wipers and an old automobile motor, are recurrently used — to create a background of despair.

Petit, who also scripted, has hinged his simple but ambiguous plot on a character seen as some kind of English archtype, a young, intelligent, middleclass fellow who teeters endlessly on the brink of involvement — emotional, political, professional — since he apparently sees no useful consequence to taking action. Ever polite and remote, the one gesture he makes towards solving the riddle of his brother's death is to drive unhurriedly to the city where it happened. Thereafter he systematically fails to follow up even the more tantalizing leads.

Oddly enough, his progress holds interest, even though — as played by David Beames — the role remains a cipher throughout. He's more symbolic than flesh-and-blood, from the moment early on when he lets his girlfriend move out without a vestige of a discussion, to the end, when he abandons his auto for a trivial reason and boards a train without knowing where it's heading.

What is intriguing about "Radio On" is Petit's fearsomely calm portrayal of a man — and a society — threatened with total, unproductive stagnation. In that exaggerated context, Beames' manipulated performance works okay, while Martin Schafer's elegantly contrived black-and-white cinematography is the real star. —*Simo.*

Moscow Film Fest

Sredi Ludei
(Among People)
(SOVIET-B&W)

Moscow, Aug. 25.
A Kirghizfilm Production, Kirghizia; world rights, Goskino, Moscow. Features entire cast. Directed by Bolotbek Shamshiev and Artyk Suyundukov. Screenplay, Talip Ibraimov, Shamshiev; camera (black & white), Manas Musayev; sets, Mikhail Scheglov; music, Rumil Vildanov. Reviewed at Moscow Film Fest (Market), Aug. 25, '79. Running time: 90 MINS.

Cast: Sabira Kumushalieva, Mir-Nurmakhanov, Ayturgan Temirova, Orozbek Kutmanaliev, Baidyla Kaltayev.

The Kirghizian director Bolotbek Shamshiev began his career by acting in Larissa Shepitko's "Heat" (1963) and making a short, "Manaschi" (1965), while studying at the Moscow Film School (VGIK); both pix were set in the steppes of this wild, rugged country and introduced Kirghizia as one of the more interesting filmmaking republics in the Soviet Union. He followed with the impressive "Shooting at the Karash Pass" (1968), set in pre-revolutionary Kazakhstan, and "The Red Poppies of Issyk-Kul" (1971).

Shamshiev then adapted a children's story by the noted Kirghizian writer, Chinghiz Aytmatov (he was also director of the republic's film studio for a time), "The White Ship" (1975) was the official Soviet entry at the Berlin Film Festival. Now he's collaborated with a young student at VGIK, Artyk Suyundukov, on "Among People," another pic dealing with ancient customs and honored traditions in his homeland.

It's the tale of a boy, Kanat, whose mother's suffering has included the loss of her husband and eight children. The young man feels compelled to continue a family tradition of sheep-herding, although he longs for the city and is the only youth left in this rural village set amid the mountains and the steppes. Another ancient tradition holding him back is the necessity to prove himself a man.

One day 20 sheep disappear from

the collective farm where he works. In keeping with an old custom, the villagers contribute a sheep apiece to make up for the loss, much to the shame of the mother.

The one really responsible for the farm disaster, however, rants on about the need to observe folk customs blindly. Then Kanat makes his manly decision, turns on the culprit's hypocrisy, and gives back the sheep. Afterwards, the villagers ostracize the hypocrite when the truth is out, but find it in their hearts to forgive when a second calamity befalls him.

Pic is worth a look on the basis of Kirghizian life and customs, although direction is flat and rooted to the script. Credits are a plus, particularly thesp performances.

—*Holl.*

Osenny Maraphon
(Autumn Marathon)
(SOVIET-COLOR)

Moscow, Aug. 28.
A Lenfilm Production, Leningrad; world rights, Goskino, Moscow. Features entire cast. Directed by Georgi Danelia. Only credits available. Reviewed at Moscow Film Fest (out-of-competition), Aug. 28, '79. Running time: **90 MINS.**

Soviet cinema's leading satirist, Georgi Danelia comes from Georgia, but made most of his films for Mosfilm in Moscow. He comes from a family of film people and the long tradition of Georgian cinema, where comedies are the spice in life. His films include "Seryozha" (1960), in collaboration with Igor Talankin, "The Way to the Harbor" (1962), "Walking the Streets of Moscow" (1963), "33" (1965), "Don't Grieve" (1969), "Hopelessly Lost" (1972), "Afonya" (1975), "Mimino" (1977) (First Prize winner in 1977 at the Moscow fest), and now "Autumn Marathon."

Danelia's pix are very popular with Soviet auds. For this reason, it was a tribute to the director to close the Moscow fest with "Autumn Marathon" after awarding of the juries' prizes. The howler was again a big success, some observers contending it is his best film to date (although Danelia also prefers his first one).

Story is about a gentle-souled English translator in Leningrad who can't keep his private affairs apart from his duties — that is, he has a mistress on the side and wife he loves. In addition, his Danish neighbor likes to go jogging each morning, and punctually rings his doorbell at dawn during this autumn season. Then there are his English-language students at the Institute where he teaches, a publisher hounding him for a translation into Russian of a new book, and a dumpy colleague needing his help to do her English-Russian translations.

The hours in the day are just too short for everything, particularly for his demanding mistress who's already taken over part of an attentive wife's duties.

The jokes derive from the situations and the fact that he's never on time for anything. The best deal with office and apartment ribs. One is when his colleague's translation (which the hero did as a favor) is considered better than his own work.

This is situation comedy to rock the seats in a Moscow cinema. The wife, of course, thinks that the hero's excuse to "bail out" a friend is just another excuse to leave the house to visit the girlfriend — just when the married daughter with her husband are in town for a short visit. At the end, nothing has really changed: the chump is still saying yes to both wife and girlfriend, the two loves in his life that he can't reconcile.

Credits are tops. This is a sure bet on further appearances on the fest circuit and at Soviet Film Weeks.

— *Holl.*

Strannaya Zhenshina
(A Strange Woman)
(SOVIET-COLOR)

Moscow.
A Mosfilm Production, Moscow; world rights, Goskino, Moscow. Features Irina Kupchenko. Directed by Yuli Raizman. Screenplay, Yevgeni Gabrilovich, Raizman. No other credits available. Reviewed at Moscow Film Festival (Market), Aug. 26, '79. Running time: **180 MINS.**
Cast: Irina Kupechenko in title role.

The director-scriptwriter combination of Yuli Raizman and Yevgeni Gabrilovich has produced some of the finest psychological dramas in modern Soviet film history.

The team first worked together on "The Last Night" (1936), followed by "Mashenka" (1942), "A Lesson in Life" (1955), "The Communist" (1957), "Your Contemporary" (1968), and now "A Strange Woman" (1977). Although "Strange Woman" has unspooled successfully in Moscow, the film has yet to find its way abroad but the market screening at the Moscow Fest might change that. This two part pic has solid offshore chances.

It's the story of a beautiful, successful, and prominent career-woman (wonderfully acted by Irina Kupchenko), married to a diplomat, and the mother of a teenage boy, who suddenly decides one day to leave her husband for a lover. All of which is rather ordinary as a contemporary theme in the West, and it's been treated before in Soviet and Socialist cinema, but never, however, in this fashion.

Gabrilovich's script presents a woman who dares to fight against her loneliness and unhappiness. As a lawyer in public administration, she has responsibility for others and does her job well. The opening scene, however, reveals that she has a lover in her middle age. The man in her life, a scientist, also has a teenage daughter and is apparently divorced. Her husband travels continually; their marriage has long since been over in spirit, and he is obviously interested only in his own career.

On a trip together to East Berlin and Paris (mixing business with pleasure), the womans spends an idle day visiting the sights in Berlin, then tells her husband that she wants to separate.

The usual scene takes place: the woman flies straight back home to her lover; she immediately moves in with him. But she fails to inform her relatives and friends, and doesn't even mention to her lover that she's left her husband for good. When this comes out (due to interfering friends), the lover finds it rather uncomfortable being in the middle of a strange relationship, loses interest in his prey, and treats her eventually much the same as her career-obsessed husband had. She leaves him and her job, this time departing for the provinces to visit her mother.

While far from Moscow, a young man, secretly in love with her, searches the woman out to reveal his love. Since he is considerably younger, this of course leads to further complications. Then her teenage son phones her to admit his loneliness (the father is on more trips). Mother and son find an apartment together. The film ends with the young admirer arriving again on the scene to try and prove his love.

Kupchenko is outstanding as a woman with a will of her own. A distant relative to Anna Karenina, the central character is completely credible and sympathetic. Raizman's handling of psychological scenes requiring little or no dialog is adept, the lensing and editing adding further depth to the story. Gabrilovich, one of the last of the Soviet film pioneers (he dates back to the Revolution), has written one of his finest scripts. A must for the Soviet film buff. —*Holl.*

La Coruna Fest

Tres En Raya
(Tic-Tac-Toe)
(SPANISH-COLOR)

La Coruna, Aug. 28.
Enrique Belloch - Togaport P.C. pro-

duction. Written and directed by Francisco Roma. Features entire cast. Camera (Eastmancolor) Miguel Mila; music, Pedro Luis Domingo; editor, Jose Luis Pelaez; sets, Carlos Marco. Reviewed at Cine Colon, La Coruna, Aug. 27, '79. Running time: **90 MINS.**
Cast: Pep Munne, Mireia Ros, Inaki Miramon, Hector Alterio, Irene Gutierrez Caba, Gemma Cuervo, Miguel Arribas, Mayrata O'Wisiedo, Antonio Gamero, Carmen Belloch.

Some funny moments in this local comedy-farce which is made by and slanted at Spanish youth audiences. If audience enthusiasm at preem here is any indication of acceptability, item should fare well at wickets around the country.

Basic premise is a "menage a trois" for three out-of-work drifters in their 20s, two boys and a girl. Pic consists chiefly of diverse situations they get embroiled in, all treated with a light hand by helmer Francisco Roma, accompanied by snappy dialogs, zany shenanigans and whimsical digs at the Establishment and the Spain of older generations.

Thus, the threesome decide to hold up a shop, only to find that the owner is one of the boys' aunt; an intended mugging turns into rout when the would-be victim attacks them instead; there's an encounter with a phony film director, a vamp who seduces one of the trio, and a wedding in which the girl is whisked off the alter by one of the triunvirate.

Most of it is fun, though at times the humor is thin and sophomoric. Though many of the credits are on an amateurish level, and pic has a shoestring budget look about it, thesping and script are kept lively enough to maintain interest.
— *Besa.*

Serenata A La Luz De La Luna
(Moonlight Serenade)
(SPANISH-COLOR)

La Coruna, Aug. 28.
Imatge Comunicacions, Producciones Cinematograficas Teide film. Directed by Josep A. Salgot and Carles Jover. Screenplay, Jover, Salgot, Albert Cruells, Jaume Sorribas; camera (Eastmancolor), Pedro Aznar; music, Joan Pineda and Albert Moraleda; editor, Emilio Rodriguez; exec producer Josep Maria Forn. Reviewed at Cine Colon, La Coruna, Aug. 28, '79. Running time: **81 MINS.**
Cast: Jaume Sorribas, Isabel Mestres, Rosa Morata, Hector Alterio, Felix Rotaeta, Pep Corominas, Carlota Marquina, Rosete Espinet, Carme Contreras, Fatima Sangareau.

Comedy of manners, a little bit in the vein of Robert Altman's "A Wedding," except that the occasion here is the betrothal of the scion of a very wealthy Catalan family.

Action is limited to one day and

provides some nice insights and touches of wry humor about the members of the moneyed class in Barcelona. Title refers to the song of the '40s played by a band hired for the occasion.

This first pic by two new Catalan helmers comes off very well indeed. It is a tasteful mixture focusing on social comment, the generation gap, family fidelity and personal integrity, all served up with some very droll scenes and two sex episodes, each funny in its way.

Scene is set in the sumptuous mansion of the Martis, whose daughter Fina is betrothed to the other family's eldest son. The atmosphere is strained and artificial as the father makes the usual speeches. The elder son shortly is taken by the family's piano teacher, who has been invited as a courtesy and is the only one who doesn't fit in with the Catalan high society, with its rich businessmen, ambassadors and generals. But the budding romance, after a sex scene in which the son agrees to run away with the piano teacher, is promptly halted when the father discovers the twosome and orders the girl out of the house. The son then submissively shuffles off to have a family group film portrait taken in which all appear as a happy family.

Though pic doesn't break any new ground, it is well directed and thesping is excellent. All technical credits are up to snuff. Especially fine performances by Hector Alterio, Isabel Mestres and Jaume Sorribas give the film a touch of distinction. Item is a good choice for fest circuits and might do okay biz in select playoffs. —Besa.

Con Mucho Carino
(With Lots Of Love)
(SPANISH-COLOR)

La Coruna, Aug. 29.
Z-Gora production, written and directed by Gerardo Garcia. Features entire cast. Camera (Eastmancolor), Roberto Gomez; editor, Rafael de la Cueva; music, Fermin Gurbindo; sets, Ignacio Inchaurbe. Reviewed at Cine Colon, La Coruna, Aug. 29, '79. Running time: 81 MINS.
Cast: Jose A. Garido, Ana Maria Simon, Almudena Cotos, Ana Maria Granda, Concha Gregori, Fernando Tejadas, Elvira Quintilla.

Inept and amateurish, this film is an affront to audiences. Dialog and situations seems to be made up while the talentless director was shooting. There is no script, no thesping, no composition, no lighting and no direction. The camera simply sits there and actors walk about and talk. To make matters worse the poor sound is direct and largely incomprehensible.

The non-plot revolves around Don Luis, the owner of a phar-

maceutical lab, his family and employees. It was vigorously booed by audience here. —Besa.

From Montreal

La Isla
(The Island)
(ARGENTINE-COLOR)

Montreal, Sept. 7.
MBC Productions presentation. Directed by Alejandro Doria. Features entire cast. Screenplay, Aida Bortnik; editing, Miguel Perez; camera (color), Miguel Rodriguez; music, Victor Pronchet. Reviewed Sept. 6, 1979 at Montreal Film Festival. Running time: 106 MINS.
Cast: Selva Alaman, Hugo Arana, Aldo Barbero, Hector Bodonde, Luisina Brando, Alicia Bruzzo, Graciela Dufau, Luisa Vehil, Sandra Mihanovich, Lizardo Laphitz.

Director Alejandro Doria and scenarist Aida Bortnik have taken what might be deemed a "trite" setting and situation — human misery, maladjustment, hope and hopelessness in a mental hospital — and managed to make it a convincing and tender study both of the patients and their families who come to visit. Even one scene of a pitched battle between two women in the hospital's hairdressing facility, which is rampant hysteria and could easily slide into unacceptable excess, is as believable as it is powerful.

There lurks a question of low strata fans who might see "The Island." Would they laugh to avoid the hard-to-tolerate agonizing?

Story is told with a symbolic recurring scene of first a young man, and later a flower-loving girl, being washed ashore on a barren reef. It asks the question: can the individual save himself or herself? None may be discharged back into society without working at recovery. Cure is not ever a medical miracle.

The types have been cleverly picked to suggest the various symptoms and stresses of dementia. It's all harrowing and thus the commercial prospects may seem dubious. Nor is there anything very "new" cinema-wise, about the drama and trauma of lunatic confinement. Nonetheless, Argentina is artistically impressive with this try. It ends on a tone of recovered sanity by the young man, but the girl with whom he has fallen in love is too frightened to leave her "island" of refuge. (Film was in the competition section of the Montreal Fest-1979). — Land.

Keiko
(JAPANESE-COLOR)

Montreal, Sept. 4.
Les Productions Yoshimura-Gagnon presentation. Producers, Yuri Yoshmura Gagnon, Claude Gagnon. Direction screenplay and editing by latter. Script, Aiko Hanada; camera, Andre Pelletier; art direction, Toshio Hashimoto; music, Jun Fukamachi. Reviewed at Montreal Film Festival, Sept. 4, 1979. Running time: 120 MINS.
Keiko .... Junko Wakashiba
Kazuyo .... Akiko Kitamura
Masaru .... Takuma Ikeuchi
Terayama .... Toshio Hashimoto
Noguchi .... Nobuo Nakanishi
Le Spectateur ....Ryu Nakano
(With French sub-titles)

This very modern Japanese tale of urban office working girl loneliness and sexual experiences has been expertly written, directed and edited by a Canadian, Claude Gagnon, and he sharing producership with his Japanese wife.

The photography is provided by another Canadian, Andre Pelletier. Hence the tendency at the Montreal Film Festival to speak of the feature as Japanese-Canadian. Either way, pride is justified.

Showing in the prize-competition sector at Montreal and running two hours, the film, though apparently made over four years ago under severe economic difficulties, is effectively executed and smartly edited, using short cuts and jumps where most artistic. The sexual scenes are explicit, erotic, but not pornographic.

A western viewer must be fascinated by the insights — street scenes, buses, small boites, small flats, motor bikes, outlying open land of modern Japan (near or in Kyoto and Nara). Much of the living environment per office life, vending machines, retail shops are Japanese varieties of the U.S.-Canada scene. The public bathing tubs are strictly Nipponese.

Presented at the festival with French subtitles, the suggestion is offered that when or if English subtitles are provided, the color of the type should sharply contrast with the color photography, so as to be readable. Many of the French sentences were smothered in the heavier palette.

Junko Wakashiba, who plays the title role, is described as a Japanese stage actress. She is totally compelling in her need for love and her disappointment in the males she romances. Plot-wise this prepares for a lesbian connection, idyllic in character because there is a "mating." It must and does end under Keiko's father's insistence that the girl wed, and his arranging for a husband. The film ends at the wedding reception line with a final, freeze shot of the girl, the obedient Japanese daughter and wife, but with her thoughts elsewehre.

The film has been cannily cast throughout, notably in the lesbian seductress role of Akiko Kitamura, who makes the situation understandable.

The lesbian twist to the narrative is achieved with imagination and considerable tenderness. No doubt this will be the selling point for world film rights. It will also offend many, perhaps seem unduly pro-lesbianism and yet Claude Gagnon has managed everything adroitly.
— Land.

...And Justice For All
(COLOR)

Pacino's name and talent turns muddle into money.

Hollywood, Sept. 12.

A Columbia Pictures release. Produced by Norman Jewison, Patrick Palmer. Directed by Jewison. Stars Al Pacino. Exec producer, Joe Wizan. Screenplay, Valerie Curtin, Barry Levinson; camera (Color), Victor J. Kemper; editor, John F. Burnett; music, Dave Grusin; production design, Richard MacDonald; sound, Robert Henderson; art direction, Peter Samish; assistant director, Win Phelps. Reviewed at Samuel Goldwyn Theatre, BevHills, Sept. 12, '79. (MPAA Rating: R.) Running time: **120 MINS.**

Arthur Kirkland	Al Pacino
Judge Rayford	Jack Warden
Judge Fleming	John Forsythe
Grandpa Sam	Lee Strasberg
Jay Porter	Jeffrey Tambor
Gail Packer	Christine Lahti
Arnie	Sam Levene
Ralph Agee	Robert Christian
Jeff McCullaugh	Thomas Waites
Warren Fresnell	Larry Bryggman
Frank Bowers	Craig T. Nelson
Carl Travers	Dominic Chianese
Leo Fauci	Victor Arnold

"...And Justice For All" is a film that attempts to alternate between comedy and drama, handling neither one incompetently, but also not excelling at either task. Centering on the impossible circumstances a sensitive lawyer encounters when dealing with the complexities and corruption of the American judicial system, which in itself can be both funny and tragic, pic is another good vehicle for Al Pacino to reveal his considerable acting powers. Pacino's name and talent, coupled with the rather soapy, idealistic tone, should cause the Columbia release to secure some solid, lasting b.o. action.

However, the lack of a central plot and the continuous mood changes will disappoint those looking for a serious statement on the country's legal system. But given what most theatregoers buy, not too many should leave this film unhappy.

It seems that director Norman Jewison has taken the easy way out by opting for a film that is more a "slice of life" rather than one consistently sticking to a primary story. Pic begins on a serious note with Pacino, jailed for contempt of court, witnessing jailers and inmates terrify a transvestite being locked up for robbery. Mood quickly changes to comedy with Pacino going off to the scene of a car accident to aid an overemotional client. It then becomes serious with the appearance of John Forsythe as a particularly villainous judge. It then retreats back to the lighthearted in a scene where Jack Warden, limning a suicidal, buffoon-like magistrate, decides to fire a pistol in his courtroom in order to obtain order.

Actress turned scripter Valerie Curtin, and Barry Levinson, coauthor of several Mel Brooks films, have concocted a screenplay that works best in several serious sub-plots. There are some fine moments where Pacino deals with clients, Robert Christian and Thomas Waites, latter particularly believable as an innocent young man sentenced to prison on a technicality.

On a more personal level, Christine Lahti is wonderful in her screen debut as Pacino's lawyer/girlfriend. Jeffrey Tambor shows impressive range as Pacino's jovial law partner who slowly goes off the deep end and Lee Strasberg lends an air of dignity as Pacino's sometimes senile grandfather.

Unfortunately, these instances never effectively come together to make a convincing cohesive statement. The story most explored, that of Forsythe's judge accused of brutally raping a young girl, is compelling but never fully fleshed out to satisfaction.

Even with all of the above, Pacino saves the film with a dynamite portrayal. Although he sometimes appears intolerably idealistic for an attorney who has been practicing for 12 years, his character is someone audiences will take to heart, if for no other reason than hope for the nation's moral future. When he gets on his soapbox for the overly melodramatic but hopeful ending, he's an irresistible hero.

Technically the film works well with Victor J. Kemper using the camera expertly to capture the proper moods, John F. Burnett demonstrating editing skill and Larry DeWaay's music. appropriate, albeit a little too television-like. —*Berg.*

Ogro
(ITALO-FRENCH-SPANISH-COLOR)

Venice, Sept. 4.

Vides release of a Vides (Rome)-Sabre Films (Madrid)-Action Films (Paris) coproduction. Produced by Franco Cristaldi and Nicola Carraro. Features entire cast. Directed by Gillo Pontecorvo. Screenplay, Pontecorvo, Ugo Pirro, Giorgio Arlorio; camera (Eastmancolor), Marcello Gatti; music. Ennio Morricone; editor Mario Morra. Reviewed at Venice Film Festival, Sept. 3, '79. Running time, **115 MINS.**

Ezarra	Gian Maria Volonte
Txabi	Eusebio Poncela
Amajur	Angela Molina
Luken	Saverio Marconi
Iker	Jose Sacristan
Txikia	Feodor Atkin
Gutierrez	George Stacquet
Dolores	Isabel Garcia

Disappointing new film by Gillo Pontecorvo ("Battle of Algiers," "Kapo"), this Venice contender nevertheless scores as a political thriller with a modicum of suspense and an authentic "feel." Except in certain territories (Spain, Italy, perhaps Germany), where its terrorist topicality could provide a b.o. tillip, it nevertheless looms mainly as specialized fare needing an appropriately selective sell.

Pontecorvo has chosen one of the most clamorous political assassinations of recent years, that of Spanish Admiral (and dictator Franco's heir apparent) Carrero Blanco, as the focal point of a suspenser pitting a small group of Basque separatists against the Fascist Spanish regime and its emerging figurehead. Plot which closely follows actual events has the subversive unit first planning to kidnap its target, then resorting to the killing — by literally blowing Blanco and his car into the Madrid sky — when his security coverage proves too tight.

Intertwined, but not sufficiently, are hints of internal friction about how violent the Basque campaign should be. In fact, one of the film's faults is the generally superficial handling of principal characters, whose motivations are only at times hinted at, and which seldom sufficiently involve the audience.

At its best, pic manages some tension in its graphic outline of the assassination plot (which involved digging a tunnel under a street, in which to plant the explosive charge which literally blew the official's car over the roof of an adjoining building), and the explosion itself is vividly rendered.

Some of the political messages, in which the film abounds, are instead proffered patly and flatly, and the drive and motivation behind the protagonists rarely grips or moves.

Acting, with some minor exceptions, is similarly wooden and uninvolving, while editing is crisp, music nicely attuned to action and setting, and location photography grimly evocative of actual times and settings. —*Hawk.*

Yanks
(COLOR)

Lovely, but listless.

Hollywood, Aug. 17.

A Universal Picture release. Produced by Joseph Janni and Lester Persky. Directed by John Schlesinger. Screenplay, Colin Welland, Walter Bernstein; camera (Technicolor), Dick Bush; editor, Jim Clar; sound, Simon Kaye; production design, Brian Morris; art direction, Milly Burns; costumes, Shirley Russell; associate producer, Teddy Joseph; assistant director, Simon Relph; music, Richard Rodney Bennett. Reviewed at Paramount Studios, L.A., Aug. 17, 1979. (MPAA Rating: R). Running time: **141 MINS.**

Matt	Richard Gere
Jean	Lisa Eichhorn
Helen	Vanessa Redgrave
John	William Devane
Danny	Chick Vennera
Mollie	Wendy Morgan
Mrs. Moreton	Rachel Roberts
Mr. Moreton	Tony Melody
Geoff	Martin Smith
Billy	Philip Whileman
Ken	Derek Thompson
Tim	Simon Harrison

Director John Schlesinger has done a beautiful job with both cast and craft in "Yanks," a multiple love story set in England in World War II. Yet little that's exciting ever happens in the picture, which could be a boxoffice handicap beyond those content with quality for its own sake.

The British director, working with his own and the personal recollections of writers Colin Welland and Walter Bernstein, vividly recreates the atmosphere in a small English village inundated by thousands of American troops prepping for the invasion of Europe. "The Yanks are overpaid, oversexed and over here," the English joked of their welcome allies, but not without real resentment.

The far differing cultures collide but also charm and captivate. And for the local ladies, it was only natural that the American soldiers would soon fill the romantic vacuum left by their own men away at war, forming localized alliances that ranged from lust to lofty love.

At one end of the extreme, Vanessa Redgrave and William Devane struggle to maintain a platonic friendship while both are deprived of their spouses. At the other, Chick Vennera and Wendy Morgan rush to bed immediately, with little initial concern for what lies beyond the war.

The more complicated and difficult middle path is taken by Richard Gere and Lisa Eichhorn, he a much more patient and sensitive sort than his buddy Vennera, she a model of English reticence under the hopes of her parents, Rachel Roberts and Tony Melody, that she will remain true to absent hometown sweetheart Derek Thompson.

The six lovers and both parents are played excellently and Schlesinger and crew have created an extravagantly authentic period setting. There's scarcely a mistake to note anywhere.

But each love story is haunted by predictability. The director comes up with no surprises and by the time the troops move on to war, as we know they must, there's something missing in the wake. Here and there, Schlesinger inserts a bit of action, a boxing match, some combat training and a particularly brutal, racist fight at a dance. But they only make more obvious the modest pace of the rest of the film.

Trade comparisons with "Hanover Street," this summer's other World War II romance, will probably be inevitable. But "Yanks" is a far superior job of story-telling. Whether the audiences re any more grateful remains to be seen. —*Har.*

Stalker
(RUSSIAN-W. GERMAN-COLOR)

Moscow, Sept. 17.

Mosfilm Production, Moscow, in coproduction with Zweites Deutsches Fernsehen (ZDF), Wiesbaden-Mainz. Features entire cast. Written, directed, and sets by Andrei Tarkovsky, based on motifs in book, "Picnic on the Road," by the Strugatsky Brothers. Camera (color), Alexander Knayzhinsky; music, Eduard Artemev; assistant director, Larissa Tarkovsky. (Credits taken from the screen.) Reviewed at Novorossiysk Cinema, Moscow, Sept. 17, '79. Running time: **140 MINS.**

Cast: Alexander Kaidanovsky (Stalker), Anatoly Solonitsyn (the writer), Nikolai Grinko (the scientist), Alisa Freindlich (Stalker's wife).

Andrei Tarkovsky's "Stalker," far and away the most important film at the Moscow Fest (barring Coppola's "Apocalypse Now," which preemed earlier at Cannes), was unspooled in a crowded, "barred-to-journalists" theatre of the film market with only a couple hundred seats.

Why this "Big Tease" at the Moscow Fest is still a bit of a mystery, particularly since "Stalker" will be aired shortly on West German television (it's a West German coproduction). Pic is two-hours-plus in length and demands viewer's complete attention to catch each and every nuance, but the experience is well worth the time.

Pic fits neatly into the helmer's recent pattern of science-fiction-like pix: "Solaris" (1972) and "Mirror" (1974), and "Stalker" forming a trilogy of sorts. There are also references to "Andrei Rublev" (1968) and "Ivan's Childhood" (1962) that any Tarkovsky fan will instantly recognize. In general, though, his films are deeply rooted in Russian tradition while remaining still highly original. Tarkovsky, in short, in a film poet who specializes in "confessions," meditative discourses on life, existence, suffering, and profound personal experience.

The son of a prominent Russian poet (Arseny Tarkovsky, whose family has long been associated with Moscow intellectual life), Andrei Tarkovsky pegs his films on conversations between central figures, which are usually poetic, abstruse and penetrating.

The "Stalker," to be understandable at all, must be linked to these former pix. There's even a key actor who has appeared in all of Tarkovsky's pix since "Andrei Rublev": Anatoly Solonitsyn, who played the icon painter Rublev, one of the space scientists (Sartorius) in "Solaris," and the man in the forest at the beginning of "Mirror." Solonitsyn thus appears to be an alter ego for Tarkovsky.

In "Stalker" Tarkovsky uses color tinting and sepia-like tones to bring out contrasts as the day breaks or still-life paintings begin to move in gentle rhythms. The soundtrack is esthetically important: an electronic-music composer, Eduard Artemev, has done the music for "Solaris," "Mirror" and "Stalker." (He's also worked for the Mikhalkov brothers on their films.)

"Stalker" begins with the sound of a train passing in the distance. A man (Stalker) rises from a sleepless night in a bleak room containing only a simple bed and table, on which a glass shakes to the rumble of the train. This is a kind of No Man's Land — a corner of the world where a meteor has recently fallen to destroy a lovely landscape. The first impressions, however, are of a dilapidated freight yard and a run-down shack. Stalker has already served a five year sentence for guiding people illegally through a "zone" into the forbidden meteor-area, to a place where wishes can be fulfilled. His wife fears he will make the same mistake again.

Stalker meets a writer and a scientist in a shack, who want to be guided to that secret place. The trio pass by a police guard (dressed in a futuristic uniform), then enter the zone where mines or the like prevent easy entrance — and come upon the ruins of a destroyed bus, which once tried to bring passengers to the secret place. As the dawn breaks (and the screen is splashed with light color tones), they sit down for a rest and begin to talk.

The scene is like out of Arrabal's "Automobile Graveyard," the conversation reminiscent of Beckett's "Waiting for Godot" and Pinter's "The Dumb Waiter." Only those without hope, it's hinted, can enter the zone.

The companions grow increasingly restless and irritable as they slowly advance along the route. The writer is secretly carrying a gun and the scientist a bomb, both forbidden by Stalker — who soon realizes that his leadership is being challenged and all may be lost.

The passage around filthy, oil-smeared, stagnating pools and discarded scrap-iron and through cesspool dungeons is like an Orphean descent into hell via an underground canal or sewer system — until the secret room of fulfilled wishes is reached. Each person speaks of his own convictions along the way: the writer of inspiration, the scientist of reason, Stalker of faith. But when the time comes, no one makes, or dares to make, a wish in the forbidden room. All return back to the shack. Another complex film metaphor in Tarkovsky's brilliant, head-spinning career. —*Holl.*

La Miel
(Honey)
(SPANISH-COLOR)

Madrid, Sept. 6.

Pedro Maso P.C. and Impala production. Directed by Pedro Maso. Features entire cast. Screenplay, Pedro Maso and Rafael Azcona; camera (Eastmancolor), Hans Burmann; exec producer, Francisco Hueva; editor, Alfonso Santana sets. Ramiro Gomez. Reviewed at Cine Coliseum, Madrid, Sept. 6, '79. Running time: **102 MINS.**

Ines .... Jane Birkin
Don Agustin .... Jose Luis Lopez Vazquez
Paco .... Jorge Sanz
Amelia .... Amelia de la Torre
Don Jaime .... Guillermo Marin
Tenant .... Agustin Gonzalez

"La Miel" is one of those irksome and brainless comedies geared directly at a special kind of middle-class Spanish audience, a respectable crowd that likes to be shocked in little things and who find it amusing to hear a small child using foul language or an absent-minded teacher being ribbed by his class.

Throughout the film Rafael Azcona and Pedro Maso use only stock characters and threadworm caricatures which include a bumbling Jose Luis Lopez Vazquez playing a conservative parochial school teacher, a streetwalker with a heart of gold, a right wing sister to the schoolteacher and a nasty little boy who spouts obscenities which are thought to be "cute."

Lopez Vazquez overacts, and Jane Birkin's two-dimensional performance is too flat for words. What is also irritating are the pat characterizations and a kind of moronic humor which plays to the lowest common denominator and is revolting in its glib choice of butts.

There are a few very mild sex scenes and a bit of nudity, but nothing that would draw crowds from the sex angle and that couldn't be easily cut for the more fastidious territories. Far more limiting is the local nature of the dialogs and situations, most of which don't transcend the Spanish border. —*Besa.*

Swap Meet
(COLOR)

Low-budget Americana good for a few laughs and a few bucks.

Hollywood, Sept. 9.

A Dimension Pictures release. Produced by Steve Krantz. Directed by Brice Mack. Features entire cast. Screenplay, Steve Krantz; music, Hemlock; art direction, Donald Harris; sound, Bill Nelson; asst. director, Thomas M. Hammel. No other credits available. Reviewed at the World Theatre, Hollywood, Sept. 9, '79. (MPAA Rating: R.) Running time: **84 MINS.**

Nancy .... Ruth Cox
Susan .... Debi Richter
Ziggy .... Danny Goldman
Annie .... Cheryl Rixon
Also: Jonathan Gries, Dan Spector, Loren Lester.

With its sights fixed resolutely on the exploitation market, "Swap Meet" trades in and ridicules the car culture, sleazy tough guys, skateboarders, dumb blondes, obnoxious kids and teenage lechery as it produces a few good laughs for undemanding audiences. Dimension's returns from this late-summer drive-in item should be okay.

On a much lower scale of ambition and pretention, writer-producer Steve Krantz has perhaps taken a cue from Robert Altman in setting his tale in a derisive sociologist's dreamland, where the foibles of middle-class America can be seen in close-up. The swap meet of the title is merely a pretext for car chases, youthful sexcapades and cheap thrills the likes of which have been seen in countless other exploitationers, but it's all here in one unholy stew.

As befits the genre, the principal femmes, Ruth Cox, Debi Richter and Cheryl Rixon, have plenty of s.a., although nudity is fleeting and sex scenes very tame. Entire cast performs with mucho energy and a prevailing sense of self-deprecating humor gives the ridiculous goings-on a needed lilt.

Director Brice Mack tidies up all the lose ends in a snappy 84 minutes. Technically, film is rudimentary, given even its low-budget origins. —*Cart.*

Der Comanche
(The Comanche)
(WEST GERMAN-COLOR)

Berlin, Sept. 18.

A Herbert Achternbusch Film Production, Munich, in collaboration with Second German Television (ZDF), Wiesbaden-Mainz. Features entire cast. Produced, written and directed by Herbert Achternbusch. Camera (color), Joerg Schmidt-Reitwein; editing, Heidi Handorf. Reviewed at Studio am Kuam, West Berlin, Sept. 18, '79. Running time: **90 MINS.**

Cast: Annamirl Bierbichler (Nurse), Barbara Gass (Doctor), Heinz Braun (Chief Doctor), Brigitte Kramer (Wife), Franz Baumgaretner (Policeman), Herbert Achternbusch (the Comanche), Sepp Bierbichler (another Comanche).

Trying to write a review about a Herbert Achternbusch film is like doing p.r. work for the Marx Brothers — there's no way to classify him save as a zany, witty writer (he won the prestigious Petrarca Prize for his novels, stories, and essays) who also writes, produces, and directs himself and his friends in his own creations that pass on the side for home movies. "The Comanche" follows such fresh odd-ball masterpieces as "The Young Monk" (Achternbusch plays the Pope), "Bye Bye Bavaria" (shot in Greenland or vicinity), "Beer Fight" (the October Fest in Munich), "The Atlantic Swimmers" (Herbert and Sepp swim a lake), and "The Andechser Feeling" (featuring filmers Margarethe von Trotta and Reinhard Hauff in bit roles).

"The Comanche" is great fun, if the viewer catches the humor and satire in the lines spoken with a rich Bavarian accent. Herbert is in a hospital, sitting in an incubator cage, where his dreams can be monitored on a tv screen via the wonders of modern science. A clip has him in Ceylon: he's speaking to elephants asking them if they're his wife and children. His dreams are so good that his wife sells them to television directly without editing or changing them — for Herbert believes he's a real-life Comanche Indian.

Later, the patient is released (the hospital is being abandoned, and the last, left-over patient simply has to go) and off he goes on an Indian raid to a Wiener Wald, a Vienna Woods restaurant where pale faces are congregated sloshing beer. There, a very witty and intellectual dialog takes place on the state of the world, which results in Death and Resurrection and what not.

Achternbusch is in good form, and this is an egghead teaser to attach on to German Film Weeks abroad. —Holl.

Lucie
(NORWEGIAN-COLOR)

Malmoe, Aug. 29.
An A/S Norsk Film production and release. Features entire cast. Written and directed by Jan Erik Duering, based on novel by Amalie Skram. Camera (Eastmancolor) Hans Nord; editor, Bente Kaas; music, Terje Rypdal; executive producer, Harld Ohrvik. Reviewed during Malmoe Film Days. Camera, Malmoe, Sweden, Aug. 29, 1979. Running time: **96 MINS.**

Lucie . . . . Inger Lise Rypdal
Gerner . . . . Goesta Ekman
Nilsa . . . . Kari Simonsen
Olsen . . . . Nils Sletta
Mrs. Reinertsen . . . . Rut Tellefsen
Doctor Moerk . . . . Alf Nordvang

Amalie Skram wrote her novels of downtrodden women and their budding revolt against male supression in the 1880's.

These days they are enjoying a publishing renaissance and, of course, seem to make good scenarios for feature films. Only they are far more subtle than the brick-throwing writer-director Jan Erik Duering employs in his handling of "Lucie," a story about a dance hall star (Inger Lise Rypdal) who is overjoyed with the prospect of landing herself a rich, though humorless lawyer-husband of good looks and fine standing in Oslo (then Kristianstad) high society.

The husband, Gerner (Goesta Ekman), soon turns out to be every cliche of a petty tyrant. The upper crust people around them reject the girl, too, except for an emancipation-minded matron (Rut Tellefsen) who spouts slogan-like sentences, urging Lucie towards revolt. Such revolt comes too late, however. Having been badly treated and/or ignored by her husband at a dinner party, Lucy runs away in fury.

In a park, she is raped by an elderly man with a huge mole on his cheek. Later, when Lucie finds herself pregnant, her husband seems to mellow a bit. Again, too late. A baby is born. With a mole on its cheek. And Lucie dies in as much emotional as physical pain.

The production design is of the highest order. Sweden's Goesta Ekman is an actor capable of the finer shadings, but here he has not much to do except look morose and angry.

Film's editing appear clumsy and abrupt but that may be due to shortcomings in the script. A subdued musical score and fine camerawork cannot obliterate the impression of overall squareness.

Rypdal (who teamed with Ekman to success in the Swedish "A Walk In The Sun" last year) mostly looks suffering; bewildered or artificially gay. She is best in a few moments of vulgar hysterics.

"Lucie" has already been acquired for Swedish distribution by AB Sandrews, but sales chances across other borders would seem severely limited except for situations uncritically devoted to Women's Lib items. —Kell.

Your Smiling Face
(TAIWAN-COLOR)

Bangkok, Aug. 28.
A Tsai Yu Wen Films release. Produced by Chou Lin Kang. Directed and edited by Larry C.H. Tu. Features entire cast. Executive producer, Shao Chi-Wu; story and screenplay, Sung Hsiang-lu; camera (color), Yu Chi Len; art direction, Chang Chi Ping; production consultants, Xi Fong Lu and Tang Chi. Reviewed at Rama theatre, Bangkok, Aug. 28, '79. Running time: **100 MINS.**

Ying Ying . . . . Hu Hui Chung
Huang . . . . Chang Hua Chu
Wang Su . . . . Jao Sao Thong

Story deals with two people whose lives closely parallel one another. Chang Hua Chu is mourning his departed wife, remembering the good times they shared together, while Hu Hui Chung is just beginning to fall in love with a young man, played by Jao Sao Thong, who later perishes in a motorcycle accident.

In the second half, both bereft, Chang and Hu find comfort in each other's arms. He has always thought she looked like his dead wife, while she has always sensed his presence, sitting alone at a corner table in the night club where she sings, even during the period of courtship between Hu and Jao.

A second major complication occurs when Hu discovers she's pregnant, and that the child's father is Jao. She wants an abortion, but changes her mind at the last minute, telling Chang that Jao was an orphan and if she gets rid of Jao's child, it would mean that Jao never existed, and she couldn't forgive herself for it for the rest of her life — the kind of impassioned speech which overwhelms viewers and make them burst into applause.

Beautifully photographed by Yu Chi Len, much of the pleasure comes from the way the scenes are lensed. Editing by director Larry C. H. Tu deftly combines flashbacks and dream sequences with the present.

Chang and Jao give okay performances — the former as a dignified businessman who's a stickler for personal discipline, the latter as a carefree fellow who prefers the mountains to the city.

"Your Smiling Face" was an official Taiwan entry in this year's Asian Fest Silver Jubilee, held in Singapore last July. Hu Hui Chung received the award for most promising new actress for her performance in it. —Cano.

Toronto Film Fest

Bastien, Bastienne
(FRENCH-COLOR)

Toronto, Sept. 18.
Les Films Moliere release of L'Agence D'Images. FR3 production. Features entire cast. Written and directed by Michel Andrieu. Camera (Eastmancolor), Rennan Plles; editor, Chantale Colomer. Reviewed at Toronto Film Fest, Sept. 10, '79. Running time: **106 MINS.**

Catherine . . . . Juliet Berto
Suzanne . . . . Anna Prucnal
Georgette . . . . Orane Demazis
Marie . . . . Beatrice Bruno
Eric . . . . Emmanuel Prat
Yves . . . . Serge Dambrine
Jean . . . . Mathieu Lacaille

"Bastien, Bastienne" is a muted period piece, visually rich, that tells its tale of wartime effects and family rituals with a fine economy of means and incisive touches that make newcomer director Michel Andrieu a man to watch.

It is 1916 and a woman and her two young sons, 12 and 13, her sister-in-law, a widow and her 12-year-old son, live in a big house with two servants. The war can be heard in the background.

Film slowly reveals that the haughty woman at the head of the house dislikes her sister-in-law, is overbearing in running the house, and hates her husband, away at war, who had allowed the estate to go to seed.

The boys decide to do an opera bouffe of Mozart which the composer wrote at their age, "Bastien, Bastienne." This touch of Mozart adds a lyrical epiphany to this subtle tale of emotional entanglements among the adults as they finally enact it for them before they have to flee the country house before the encroaching war.

Juliet Berto is effective as the embittered family head who is having an affair with an officer who visits the house at intervals and is later found dead by the boys in a field, killed by a possible stray war bullet or, perhaps, the sister-in-law, amply limned by Anna Prucnal.

The boys are effective and do the opera with charming innocence. Film is slow but never mannered. It has a fine rhythm despite its slight storyline with the subtle relations among the family and servants effective without undue dialog.

Film's measured telling and minimal action makes this a specialized item, but one that could get selected audiences with proper placement. It has a hy-notic effect and should also find more fest and archive attention.

It pays homage to the past French psychological, poetic, well-made literary tradition of filmmaking but erases the static qualities to make it a fluid, engaging but demanding film experience.
— Mosk.

Best Boy
(U.S.-COLOR-DOCU-16m)

Toronto, Sept. 18.
Written, produced, directed, conceived and edited by Ira Wohl. Camera (color). Tom McDonough. Reviewed at Toronto Film Fest, Sept. 7, '79. Running time: **110 MINS.**

Ira Wohl did not just aim his camera at his aunt, uncle, female cousin and especially his retarded cousin Philly, age 52, but with the comportment of a child of about five or six. It took him three years to make and it is a work of love.

The latter helps allay any accusations of exploitation or invasion of privacy that might be levelled at it. All those labels, cursory at best, of cinema verite, documentary, or cinema participation, in which the director is actually involved in an incident or process, and may even affect it, could be applied to the film.

But it is what is on the screen that counts. Film explores what happens to Philly when Wohl convinces his aging parents they must allow the man-child to try to advance and find a way of coping with life in anticipation of their eventual deaths.

Wohl is the catalyst. He wins over the parents and then follows the attempts at finding a special school for Philly and watching his evolution. There are no miracles, but Philly does get more self sufficient and he is allowed to leave home for an institution after the death of his father though still keeping in touch with his mother.

Philly is heavyset, his top front teeth are missing and he has the darting movements, short attention span and the unpredictability of a child. His father is a gaunt realist who realizes the boy must get a chance to begin to live some sort of life that is his own.

The mother has accepted her problems compounded by the death of another son. She really does not want to give up Philly, especially after the death of her husband, but finally does come around.

Film looks at a touchy subject with tact and intelligence which gives it a poignant but never sentimental charge. As well as revealing the problems of a retarded child, and that of his parents and family, it makes a statement on the time when a child must go his own way even if he is handicapped.

Film is well edited and apparently the three years of work finally made Wohl a familiar object around the family. Philly does at times peer into the camera or make remarks about it. But the scenes at home, the advancement of Philly, the schools, and Wohl's contributions all weld this into a most unusual film on a timely and timeless subject.

Film is a natural for seminars, institutions, school and public service usage. But its human insight into a subject of painful but human intractability, could get it theatrical outings.

It could easily be blown up to 35m from its present 16m format. Film will be at the coming New York Film Festival and should make an impact due to its uncompromising theme and intelligent treatment.
—*Mosk.*

Linus Eller Tegelhusets Hemlighet
(Linus And The Mysterious Red Brick House)
(SWEDISH-COLOR)

———

Toronto, Sept. 18.
Svenska Filminstitutet release of Svenska Filminstitutet, Trekovern production. Features entire cast. Written and directed by Vilgot Sjoman from his own book. Camera (Eastmancolor), Tony Forsberg, Roland Sterner; editor, Carl-Olav Skeepstedt; music, Bengt Ernyd. Reviewed at Toronto Film Fest, Sept. 9, '79. Running time, 113 MINS.

With: Harald Hamrell, Viveca Lindfors, Harriet Andersson, Pernilla Wallgren.

———

Vilgot Sjoman helped ease censorship restrictions in the U.S. with his outspoken politico-sex film "I Am Curious Yellow," in the '60s. Now he comes up with his best film, a dream approach to the coming-of-age of a 16-year-old boy in the '30s.

A brooding big red brick house takes on the symbol of the boy's world which leads to his first interludes with bought love, real love, Freudian destruction of his father and finally a seeming giving in to corruption around him by becoming corrupt himself.

But it is a tale of exorcism and enforced by brooding visuals, fine acting and absorbing flights of fancy in the boy's emotional, spiritual and human progress through this house. It is actually a bordello owned by a Countess who allows a brutish janitor and a cynical but generous madam to run it.

His father dallies with the wife of a friend as the brutal janitor and minions murder her socialist husband in the cellar. They put the body in the father's truck. He collects evidence to clear his father, but the janitor sees him and the chase is on.

He finally burns the evidence as a sort of break with his father and his own coming of age. He has found a relationship with the comely secretary of the Countess, but finally ends up with the Countess herself and winds up as manager of the affairs of the house after his father's arrest.

An unusual, absorbing film on the theme of achieving maturity that should travel well in other climes.
There is more than Bergman (Ingmar) on the Swedish film scene, albeit Sjoman was once a disciple and is already an old hand, with 13 pix under his belt. —*Mosk.*

Edinburgh Fest

———

Effects
(U.S.-COLOR)

———

Edinburgh, Aug. 28.
The Image Works production. Produced by John Harrison, Pasquale Buba. Directed by Dusty Nelson. Features entire cast. Screenplay, Nelson, from a novel by William H. Mooney; camera (color), Carl Augenstein; editor, Buba; art director, Ellen Hopkins; sound, Buba; special effects, Tom Savini. Reviewed at the Edinburgh International Film Festival, Calton Studios, Edinburgh, August 27, '79. Running time: 87 MINS.
Lacey	John Harrison
Celeste	Susan Chapek
Dom	Joseph Pilato
Barney	Bernard McKenna
Rita	Debra Gordon
Nicky	Tom Savini
Lobo	Chuck Hoyes
Scratch	Blay Bahnsen

———

"Effects" is a gory, salacious and unenjoyable piece of exploitation. Made with a certain gloss, it proves the Pittsburgh-based production company, The Image Works, which has specialized hitherto in commercials and documentaries, can meet technical standards of feature filmmaking. But the outfit's first excursion into full-length narrative is steeped in pretentiousness.

Likeliest ripples the picture will make are among younger buffs, who may tolerate the lack of tongue-in-cheek — usually employed to make bloodbaths entertaining fare, but entirely absent here. Campuses would seem the safest pitch.

Scripter-director Dusty Nelson's screenplay, adapted from William H. Mooney's novel, plays the turn-off trick of supposedly keeping an audience guessing, but never offering up enough information to guess with satisfactorily. The initially intriguing situation — cast and crew of a lowbudget horror-pic discover the voyeuristic, megalomaniac director is up to something more sinister, namely, a film-about-a-film in which the deaths are for real — becomes merely tiresome as confusions proliferate and reality is stylelessly abandoned.

Performances are convincing despite the humorless improbability of the characters, with Susan Chapek notably successful as the girl-gaffer who is conniving on several fronts. The main location, a folksy mansion buried in the countryside, is well-chosen for its chilling combination of luxury and discomfort. —*Simo.*

That Sinking Feeling
(SCOTTISH-COLOR)

———

Edinburgh, Aug. 30.
A Minor Miracle Film Cooperative production in association with the Glasgow Youth Theatre. Produced and directed by Bill Forsyth. Features entire cast. Screenplay, Forsyth; camera (color), Michael Coulter; editor, John Gow; designer, Adrienne Atkinson; sound, Alec Brown; music, Colin Tully. Reviewed at the Edinburgh International Film Festival, Calton Studios, Edinburgh, August 29, '79. Running Time: 80 MINS.
Ronnie	Robert Buchanan
Vic	John Hughes
Wal	Billy Greenlees
Simmy	Douglas Sannachan
Alec	Alan Love
Policeman	Danny Benson
Van Driver	Eddie Burt
Doctor	Tom Mannion

———

Aimed specifically at a local audience, and unlikely to see much commercial light of day beyond Celtic shores, the first wholly Scottish feature for many a year nonetheless proves debuting filmmaker Bill Forsyth an entertaining touch.

Since the Scots are natural talkers, most of the humor in "That Sinking Feeling" derives from the voluminous dialog. Unfortunately the heavy Glasgow dialect, near as arcane as Jamaican patois, defies comprehension by most, bar the natives. But for those in the know at least, there is much fun to be had from the traditional, deadpan style of self-abasement which the Glasgow Youth Theatre performers exploit with some skill.

Forsyth's screenplay, largely set in the city's dank demolition areas, plots a motley bunch of unemployed lads, amiably led by Robert Buchanan, who heist a hundred stainless steel sinks in a boisterous bid to embark on an essentially light-hearted life of crime.

The central joke — the absurdity of seeing sinks as likely hot sellers — is hardly strong enough to carry a full-length film. But Forsyth's incidental observations, and the generally high standard of playing by non-professionals, help to offset the fact that most scenes could be pruned to advantage.

Technical credits are remarkable considering the almost invisible production budget. But to judge from the nationalistic stir caused by the film in Edinburgh at festival time, that thrift could even mean profitability within a tiny home market. —*Simo.*

———

Home Movies
(U.S.-COLOR)

———

De Palma's pro-am outing is fun-packed.

———

Edinburgh, Aug. 29.
An S.L.C. Films production. Produced by Brian De Palma, Jack Temchin, Gil Ad-

ler. Directed by Brian De Palma. Features entire cast. Screenplay, Robert Harders, Gloria Norris, Kim Ambler, Dana Edelman, Stephen Le May, Charles Loventhal, from story by De Palma; camera (color), James L. Carter; editor, Corky Ohara; art director, Tom Surgal; Rachel Feldman; sound, Rick Wadell; music, Pino Donaggio. Reviewed at the Edinburgh International Film Festival, Calton Studios, Edinburgh, Aug. 28, '79. Running Time: **90 MINS.**

Dr. Tuttle (The Maestro) ... Kirk Douglas
Kristina .... Nancy Allen
Denis .... Keith Gordon
James .... Gerrit Graham
Dr. Byrd .... Vincent Gardenia
Mrs. Byrd .... Mary Davenport
Policeman .... Captain Haggerty
Bunny .... Himself

"Home Movies," which resulted from Brian De Palma's assignment to teach direction at Sarah Lawrence College, New York — he taught students there how to make films by making one with them — breaks his recent run of shock-horror vehicles, and instead recalls two earlier titles, "Greetings" and "Hi, Mom!" It carries the same marks of zany, episodic plotting, manic humor, and a steely thread of purpose tying it all together.

With familiar subjects like education and family life as the chief butts of its gaudy lampoon, this movie-within-a-movie-within-a-movie should do nicely enough at the wickets. Kirk Douglas' role is a genuine lead, not a cameo; and the production, mounted with a largely student crew and a tyro in the central part, looks in no way amateurish.

The story (by De Palma, though the script is credited to a group of students) has Kirk Douglas running a cult called Star Therapy. He exhorts each pupil to "put your name above the title" in life. Practicing what he preaches, he has his own life continuously filmed, with himself as director and star. The sessions, filmed with a mask reducing the frame, as if by Douglas' own 16m camera crew, are recurrently hilarious.

Singling out one pupil as an example of "an extra in his own life," Douglas spurs the boy — engagingly played by Keith Gordon — into an ego-quest which involves a successful pursuit of his elder brother's fiancee, exposure of his doctor-father's adulterous fumblings with a Swedish nurse, and some laughably inept attempts to film himself with a Swedish nurse, and some laughably inept attempts to film himself doing not-so-dramatic things like falling asleep.

The aforementioned brother is another teacher and cult-freak, whose obsession with body health — at the heavy expense of his own mental health — extends well beyond regular vegetarianism and exercise. His pupils are subjected to frenetic disciplines shakily based on the physical ideals of the ancient Greeks of Sparta.

Gerrit Graham, wild-eyed and strutting, plays him scary but splendidly idiotic; and is amusingly outstripped, per the plot, by Nancy Allen as his fluffy, but finally more knowing, girlfriend. Allen's character is the most colorfully developed in the film, since the others mostly just have their thing, and do it. She's fine and funny.

De Palma and coproducers Jack Temchin and Gil Adler have picked competent key technicians, and Pino Donaggio has contributed a neatly farcical score. —*Simo.*

Wege In Der Nacht
(Night Paths)
(WEST GERMAN-COLOR)

Edinburgh, Aug. 27.
A Westdeutscher Rundfunk production. Produced by Hartwig Schmidt. Directed by Krzysztof Zanussi. Features entire cast. Screenplay, Zanussi; camera (color), Witold Sobocinski; editor, Liesgret Schmitt-Klink; music, Wojciech Kilar; sound, Richard Kettelhake. Reviewed at the Edinburgh International Film Festival, The Filmhouse screening room, Edinburgh, Aug. 26, '79. Running Time: **97 MINS.**

Friedrich   Mathieu Carriere
Elzbieta   Maja Komorowska
Hans Albert   Horst Frank
Amadei   Zbigniew Zapasiewicz
Charlotte   Diana Korner

Made for West German tv, but with feature production values, Polish director Krzysztof Zanussi's latest full-length picture is at least as good as his much-praised 1976 feature, "Camouflage" (Barwy Ochronne), and deserves similar festival exposure and theatrical arthouse playoff.

Set in occupied Poland during World War II, Zanussi's cool, verbal (German language) screenplay traces a relationship — complex and brittle — between a young Nazi officer and an older Polish baroness whose estate has been commandeered. At first hostile to his dogged courtship, she progresses to exploiting it in order to further the aims of local resistance partisans. But the liaison becomes bitterly ambivalent when the officer's closest friend is killed in a skirmish.

Impressive alongside the many poised dialog scenes is Zanussi's seemingly effortless handling of the occasional, significant moments of action. Witold Sobocinski has photographed farmland and forest exteriors with an eye for evening light which conveys a strong sense of time stopped in the once-proud, benignly feudal community.

Maja Komorowska is superbly tough and impenetrable as the Polish aristocrat who bewitches Mathieu Carriere with something more than looks. He and Horst

Frank, as his soldier companion, conduct their puzzled discussions on the aesthetics of war with enough humor to leaven the lumps of philosophical analysis much-favored by the filmmaker. —*Simo.*

Venice Films

La Nouba Des Femmes Du Mont Chenoua
(Nouba)
(ALGERIAN-COLOR-16m)

Venice, Aug. 28.
Produced and released by Algerian Television. Written and directed by Assia Djebbar. Editor, Nicole Schlemmer. Feature documentary special. Reviewed at Venice Film Festival, Aug. 28, '79. Running time: **113 MINS.**

Produced by Algerian television, this film won one of the main critics' prizes at the festival. It is an unpretentious trip by a woman into her own past, except that this past is the period of Algeria's fight for independence.

Alain Resnais, with "Night and Fog," tried to express the horrors of the past by using only elements of the present, and showed the gruesome ruins of German concentration camps in the light of today's feelings concerning those horrors.

Assia Djebbar, in her first long film, attempts pretty much the same thing by showing the people and landscapes of Algeria today, once part of the war, without adding too much information, in excessive flashbacks or even documenting her facts. The film is simply the story of a woman's trip to see places and people from her own past.

Surprisingly, with such limited material — landscapes, encounters, a few conversations and many silences — the film succeeds in conveying a restrained intensity which goes beyond facts and becomes emotion. As Djebbar said in her press conference, the film helped her not only to understand her past but also to contact its survivors, and helped them meet and digest their horrible memories with a sense of realism. Also — and this may be the most important element of the film's success — it was seen on television by the people it is mostly about — the women in the Arab world who are always the victims of war and who are still often tied to the home as unequal members of Islamic society, even in Algeria's post-liberation culture.

"Nouba" also gives an image of a new society struggling to come to terms with its bloody past, and as such provides a wealth of information not usually accessible to moviegoers. Clearly, this film like the one

by Jean Rouch, will require special handling in its release, but even more than the Rouch it could have a chance in specialized situations because of its feature-length structure and partially dramatic construction. —*Gbac.*

Funerailles A Bongo:
Le Vieux Anai
(Funeral At Bongo: Old Anai)
(FRENCH-COLOR)

Venice, Aug. 30.
Produced by Les Films de l'Homme, Paris. Directed by Jean Rouch and Germaine Dieterlen. Editor, Daniele Tesier; sound, Moussa Hassidon Ibralirna Guirido. Feature documentary viewed at Venice Film Festival, Aug. 30, '79. Running time: **105 MINS.**

There were no official prizes at the Venice Film Festival this year, and thus the critics' prize assumed particular importance. Two of the three critics' prizes went to films from Arab and African countries, thus proving the upcoming importance of this cinema from the Third World. This film by Jean Rouch, in addition, won the special FIPRESCI jury prize in recognition of Rouch's continuing attempt, over the years, to carry his camera into areas of the globe (and of the soul) not usually invaded by the cinema.

Rouch is basically an anthropologist, but in the last 20 years he has become more and more important as a filmmaker, because audiences the world over have begun to be interested in films that go beyond entertainment.

Rouch has made features as well, but his main force are documentaries which tell stories taken from life and revealing elements of human strength and behavior. He is mainly known as the man who started the first African filmmakers on the road towards independence in producing films, by training an entire generation of young disciples in West Africa and particularly in Niger, where for years he was in charge of a film training program.

"Funeral at Bongo" is a film based on the death of a native of the Dongo tribe in Bandiagara, on the coast of West Africa, a man born in 1849, who died at the age of more than 120 years. The film follows the ritual that precedes, accompanies and follows this man's eventual demise and thus took a number of years to complete. The result of Rouch's repeated trips and continual filming is an extraordinary document which shows how a people meets and faces, but also accepts and lives, the presence of death in the tribe.

Obviously this will have to remain a film for festivals and special situations. With proper handling, a market for this unique product could be found. —*Gbac.*

Essakamat
(Death of the Water Carrier)
(EGYPTIAN-TUNISIAN-COLOR)

Venice, Aug. 29.
Produced by MISR International Film of Egypt and Societe Tunisienne de Cinematographie, Tunis. Written and directed by Salah Abu Saif. Camera (color), Mahmud Sabu; music, Fuad Az-Zahiri. Reviewed at Venice Film Festival. Running time: **110 MINS.**
Cast: Farid Shauqui, Ezzat al-Alayli, Shuyar, Amina Risq.

Again the melodramatic tradition of Eastern storytelling is at the base of this story set in the Egyptian past, carrying a lesson for the present.

In 1921, when Egypt was a not very independent part of the British Empire, but governed by local despots, the fate of the poor water carriers of the Cairo outskirts eking out a fragile living between hunger and humiliation, provided ample material for a symbolic tale of the underdog's comeuppance. Except that the story into which this lesson for the present is wrapped is so superficially dramatized and so puerile in its acting, lighting, delivery, and all other elements of cinematic construction, that whatever qualities the film might possess, remain hidden and defeat credence.

Egyptian audiences have admired rolling eyes, the fat, hennaed ladies, excellently made-up beggars and the rest of the arsenal of make-believe in their cinema for so many years, that even a serious filmmaker must utilize this banal film language to get his message across.

On the other hand, there is serious content here, inasmuch as Salah Abu Saif uses the metaphor of Death in a creative manner. The central character learns to overcome his fear of it and his son grows up in the process. The film teaches survival, and though the lesson may be as important for us as it is for the poor in Egypt to this day, it is questionable whether the film will have any sort of commercial career outside the Arab world. —*Gbac.*

The River
(IRAQI-COLOR)

Venice, Aug. 27.
Produced by General Establishment for Film and Stage, Baghdad. Written and directed by Faisal Yasini. Camera (color), Nuhad Ali; music, Faiq Hanna. Reviewed at Venice Film Festival, Aug. 27, '79. Running time. **100 MINS.**
Cast: Sami Kaftan, Kaid al Numani, Karim Awad.

"The River" is a strange mixture, not unusual for films from the Arab world, of superficial melodrama and important social issues. Essentially the film tells the story of a group of fishermen who slowly come to the realization that they are being maltreated and ruined financially by the mechanics of fish-selling which are imposed upon them by a rich and clever Shylock, who initially lends money to them and then exploits their labor unendingly since they can never quite repay the debt and the accumulating interest.

At the edge of tragedy, good wins out over bad, at least in the eye of the beholder, whose approach and reaction to the film are never in doubt, steered as they are by the clever manipulation of emotions employed by the director.

Basically it is a film made for those poor fishermen themselves, who under the old social system in Iraq were the eternal losers. Today, the film seems to say, things have changed, but in the new Iraq there may be other lurking social injustices which must be fought.

Therefore the film's form can afford to be naive and superficial, especially since the melodramatic form corresponds to an old tradition of storytelling and exaggeration in the Islamic world.

Excellent photography helps, but film seems destined for local consumption only. —*Gbac.*

10
(COLOR)

Blake Edwards scores high with his best pic in years.

Hollywood, Sept. 11.
An Orion Pictures release through Warner Bros. of a Geoffrey production. Produced by Blake Edwards, Tony Adams. Directed and written by Blake Edwards. Stars Dudley Moore, Julie Andrews. Camera (Technicolor, Panavision), Frank Stanley; editor, Ralph E. Winters; music, Henry Mancini; production design, Rodger Maus; set decorators, Reg Allen, Jack Stevens; costumes design, Pat Edwards; sound, Bruce Bisenz; assistant director, Mickey McCardle. Reviewed at Samuel Goldwyn Theatre, Beverly Hills, Sept. 11, '79. (MPAA Rating, R.) Running time: **122 MINS.**

George	Dudley Moore
Sam	Julie Andrews
Jenny	Bo Derek
Hugh	Robert Webber
Mary Lewis	Dee Wallace
David	Sam Jones
Bartender	Brian Dennehy
The Reverend	Max Showalter
Josh	Rad Daly
Mrs. Kissel	Nedra Volz
Fred Miles	James Noble
Ethel Miles	Virginia Kiser
Covington	John Hawker
Dental Assistant	Deborah Rush
Neighbor	Don Calfa
Larry	Walter George Alton
Redhead	Annette Martin
Dr. Croce	John Hancock
TV Director	Lorry Goldman

Blake Edwards' "10" is a shrewdly observed and beautifully executed comedy of manners and morals. Covering much the same geography and some of the same concerns as "Shampoo" with a similar serio-comic approach, film offers more than enough laughs and titilation to please mass audiences, but commercial fate will rest upon whether or not young viewers can warm up to Dudley Moore's decidedly middle-age problems, as well as to the Englishness of the two leading characters.

In any event, Edwards has come up with his best film in many years, and clearly one of his most personal. Since resuming the "Pink Panther" series in 1975, stylish writer-director has reestablished his clout in the marketplace, but it's been ages since one of his non-Peter Sellers ventures has scored heavily with critics or public. Even if "10" doesn't go all the way, it's bracing to see Edwards again dealing with material which obviously engages him strongly.

"10" is theoretically the top score on Dudley Moore's female ranking system, although he raves that his dream girl is an "11" after he first spots her. Frustrated in his songwriting collaboration with Robert Webber and in his edgy relationship with g.f. Julie Andrews, diminative Moore, forty-ish, owner of a Rolls-Royce and posh Bel Air digs and described as a four-time Oscar winner, decides to pursue the vision incarnated by Bo Derek despite fact that she's on her honeymoon with a jock type seemingly twice Moore's size.

Long build-up to Moore's big night with Derek, played out at the stunning Mexican resort Las Hadas, is spiced with plenty of physical comedy which displays both Moore and Edwards in top slapstick form, particularly in a scene on a beach where hot sand provides Moore with grilled feet and audience with blistering laughs. Pay-off ends with resolute seriousness as a moral stand-off between generations, with the star professing a philosophy of sex and life which Edwards undoubtedly worked out after much wrestling with the conflicts between libido and logic.

One of the easily overlooked miracles of the film is that Moore goes through it all utterly constipated, confused and often in physical distress, due to drink, dental work and an outrageous bee-sting on the nose, and still emerges as a relatively sympathetic character. Despite the abundance of sex all around him, as well as several chances, Moore doesn't really score throughout the entire two hours, writhing instead in a state of virtually continuous coitus interruptus.

Pic is less about conflict between desires for commitment versus swinging than about knowing what you want and why. Edwards also forthrightly acknowledges voyeuristic context for his tale of surface obsession and inner questioning, and suggests that what you like to see is not necessarily what you want to get.

Dialog-heavy scenes with Julie Andrews and Moore are well structured as essential counterbalance to latter's quest for the ultimate sexual experience, but Andrews seems rather miscast in a very cold, serious part and story resolution could be called into question since the pair seem basically incompatible.

A less central but more successful contrast to Moore's obsessive behavior is seen in Robert Webber's unhappy gay relationship with a macho beach bum. Both men are scrambling to hold onto youth and beauty in their different ways, neither with satisfactory results.

Moore deserves heavy credit for putting the film across, and his equal adeptness at comedy and more dramatic scenes marks him as a special talent. Derek more than measures up to any conventional standard of American beauty, is displayed to full advantage and comes off exceedingly well in her big scene toward the end, despite fact that Edwards is ultimately putting down her character.

Webber is superbly understated, Dee Wallace is affecting as a willing one-night-stand for Moore which doesn't come off, and Brian Dennehy is terrif as a bartender lending an ear and plenty of booze to the hapless hero. Remainder of cast, down to the smallest role, is similarly expert.

Longstanding collaboration of Edwards with Henry Mancini, which continues here, could lead some to imagine that composer has inspired some of the story and character elements in "10." Mancini's music is represented as Moore's own in film; and latter reacts badly when Derek at one point refers to his work as "elevator music," one more perception which separates the generations.

All credits, including Frank Stanley's camerawork, Ralph E. Winters' editing and Rodger Maus' lush production design, are of top pro standards. Film is dedicated to stunt coordinator Dick Crockett, who died during production.

—Cart.

Clair de Femme
(Womanlight)
(FRANCO-ITALO-GERMAN-COLOR)

Paris, Sept. 13.

A Gaumont release of a Films Gibe-Films Corona (Paris)/Parva Cinematografica (Rome)/Film Produktion Janus (Frankfurt) co-production. Produced by Georges-Alain Vuille. Stars Yves Montand, Romy Schneider. Written and directed by Constantine Costa-Gavras, based on the novel by Romain Gary. Camera (color), Ricardo Aranovich; art directors, Mario Chiari, Eric Simon; sound, Pierre Gamet; music, Jean Musy; editor, Francoise Bonnot. Reviewed at the Concorde cinema, Paris, Sept. 10, 1979. Running time: **105 MINS.**

Lydia .... Romy Schneider
Michel .... Yves Montand
Galba .... Romolo Valli
Sonia .... Lila Kedrova
Georges .... Heinz Bennent

"Clair de Femme," starring Yves Montand and Romy Schneider, is an example of a capable director not recognizing his artistic limitations Constantine Costa-Gavras has abandoned the well-defined precincts of the thriller mode for an expedition into the boggy terrain of poetic realism.

As early as his otherwise pulsating 1969 political thriller, "Z", Costa-Gavras showed what he couldn't handle: scenes of direct plangent emotion, like that in which Irene Papas reacted with unconcealed anguish to news of her political leader husband's assassination.

Imagine the Papas scene as a feature-length film and you'll have some idea of "Clair de Femme," which is based on a novel by Romain Gary. Montand plays a man crushed by the death of his wife; she commits suicide, with his complicity, to cut short the pain of a pro-

tracted terminal ailment. Rather than get on a plane and find a new life and love elsewhere he stays in the city and meets Romy Schneider, another grief-stricken soul. Her young daughter has perished in a car accident which left her husband brain-damaged.

The two try to offer one another solace and agree to take a plane together. Their shared solitude is disrupted by a small-time dog-act showman with a weak heart. He later succumbs, leaving behind his animals to enact a grotesque dance of death before his body.

Montand asks Schneider to accompany his dead wife. She then does an about-face and decides to get on that plane alone. Perhaps in a few months, when some of the wounds have healed, they can try again to form a real relationship.

Little rings true in this leadenly morbid affair. Costa-Gavras has hung himself from the start by using much of the novel's sententious dialog for his screenplay, which is forbiddingly pretentious.

Montand and Schneider, not to mention the rest of the cast, turn in sterile, self-conscious performances. Montand, who seems to acquire more presence with age, has not looked so ill-at-ease since he cut his actor's teeth on Jacques Prevert's romantic dialog in Marcel Carne's "Gates of Night," back in 1946.

Even the technical aspects suffer, with Ricardo Aranovich's unassertive color photography being somber without creating true mood. Editing is much too conventional to support the script's philosophical affectations.

Nevertheless, the names above the title are currently guaranteeing long lines at the local box-office. —Len.

Something Short Of Paradise
(COLOR)

Moderate comedy.

Hollywood, Sept. 9.

An American International release of a James C. Gutman/David Halpern Jr. production. Produced by Gutman, Lester Berman. Directed by Helpern. Exec producers, Michael Ingber, Herbert Swartz. Stars Susan Sarandon, David Steinberg. Screenplay, Fred Barron; camera (color), Walter Lassally; editor, Frank Bracht; music, Mark Snow; art direction, William De Seta; assistant director, Michael Kravitz; no other credits available. Reviewed at Samuel Goldwyn Theatre, BevHills, Sept. 9, '79. (MPAA Rating: PG). Running time: **91 MINS.**

Madeleine Ross .... Susan Sarandon
Harris Soane .... David Steinberg
Jean-Fidel Mileau .. Jean-Pierre Aumont
Ruthie Miller .... Marilyn Sokol
Barney Collins .... Joe Grifasi
Edgar Kent .... Robert Hitt

Both the virtues and handicaps of "Paradise" stem from Fred Barron's screenplay, which director David Helpern has transferred faithfully to the screen. Former film critic Barron's previous effort, "Between The Lines," was a devastating and underrated satire on underground newspapers, and the same fresh, pointed dialog emerges here, in the story of art house proprietor Steinberg falling hard for magazine scribbler Sarandon.

But Barron fails to give any depth to his central characters outside of their primary relationship (latter term, as befits the '70s, is overused throughout the pic). We never see Steinberg doing much of anything in his capacity as a theatre operator, and Sarandon's journalistic prowess is limited to asking some silly questions at a press conference for imported French star Jean-Pierre Aumont. Latter is brought in primarily to galvanize the off-again, on-again nature of the Steinberg-Sarandon coupling, a job he accomplishes by the end titles.

It's up to Steinberg, making his film debut, and the always-attractive Sarandon to carry off this bit of fluff on the strength of their personalities, a chore at which they almost succeed. Barron has given them some sharp scenes, especially in their courtship period, and Sarandon especially projects a winsome and appealing femme. Comic Steinberg still seems mired in his on-stage schtick, although he occasionally breaks through the comedian's trappings.

Rest of the cast is fine, although Marilyn Sokol is becoming obnoxious with her gallery of man-hating portrayals. Joe Grifasi is very good in support as Steinberg's partner, and Robert Hitt stays on the right side of the stereotype as a p.r. man for Aumont.

Helpern, who previously helmed the Oscar-nominated docu, "Hollywood On Trial," displays a confident use of the medium, although a flashback technique seems unnecessary and labored. Little imaginative use is made of the New York locations, however, and pacing lags throughout, leading to running-time estimates that far exceed the actual 91 minutes.

Other tech credits, particularly Walter Lassally's camerawork, are tops and opening titles, using color blow-ups of vintage film ads, are dazzling. But "Something Short Of Paradise" has too much of a tele-film mentality to go far on the theatrical circuit, no matter how gingerly AIP treats it. —Poll.

Only Once In A Lifetime
(U.S.-COLOR)

Deauville, Sept. 9.

A Movietime Films release of a Sierra Madre Motion Picture Company/Moctezuma Esparza Prods. production. Produced by Moctezuma Esparza and Alejandro Grattan. Features entire cast. Written and directed by Grattan. Camera (color), Turner Browne; music, Robert O. Ragland; editor, Esperanza Vasquez. Reviewed at the Deauville Festival, Sept. 5, 1979. Running time: **97 MINS.**

Dominguez .... Miguel Robelo
Counsuelo .... Estrellita Lopez
Sally .... Sheree North
Jimenez .... Claudio Brook

An unconvincing, bittersweet tale about a poor Mexican-American artist living with the memory of his dead wife and enjoying the companionship of an aging dog. Prohibited by a state zoning inspector from growing and selling produce on his property, unwilling to paint in the style that will get him some buyers, he drifts in quiet despair through L.A., refusing the assistance of an altruistic social worker and ignoring the warm gaze of an attractive Chicano schoolteacher. Finally, the artist snaps out of his passive state and accepts to start anew with the teacher.

Grattan is too busy expressing his warmth for the characters to be able to describe the harshness of the story's basic situations, but in Miguel Robelo, who plays the lead, he has an actor of warm presence who carries the picture for much of its length. However, even Robelo can do nothing for the protracted final part of the film in which all of the painter's acquaintances happen to show up at his doorstep within the same few hours.

Here Grattan's direction, for the most part competent but unremarkable, loses its control and the tale plods toward its predictable end. —Len.

Bete Mais Discipline
(Dumb But Disciplined)
(FRENCH-COLOR)

Paris, Sept. 10.

An AMLF release of a Christian Fechner Films production. Produced by Bernard Artigues. Stars Jacques Villeret. Written and directed by Claude Zidi. Camera (color), Jean-Paul Schwartz; art direction, Jacques Bufnoir; editor, Georges Klotz. Reviewed at the Marignan-Concorde Pathe cinema, Paris, Sept. 10, 1979. Running time: **95 MINS.**

Jacques .... Jacques Villeret
Sylvie .... Kelvine Dumour
Claudine .... Celeste Bollack
Stevenin .... Michel Aumont

Jacques Villeret, a pudgy, sad-eyed young comic whose one-man shows have earned him great critical and popular approval, stars in this mediocre Claude Zidi comedy about a soldier whose plan to propose marriage to his girl friend is threatened when his leave is revoked for the needs of a secret military mission.

Not as dumb as he seems, Villeret maneuvers the entire operation to the hotel in which his beloved works only to discover that she has eyes for the macho tennis champion who's playing up to her. Villeret does everything he can to keep the two from meeting, but his plotting only loses him his girl as well as his freedom when the authorities catch up with him.

Despite some clever plot turns and Zidi's competent direction the comedy fails to ignite. Part of the problem is due to the nature of Villeret's talent and appeal. Wistful and slow-moving, Villeret cannot ride a weak script in the same way that Fernandel, to whom Villeret is currently being touted as heir apparent, could get by with his exuberant mugging and broad doubletakes.

Zidi recognizes and respects Villeret's cautious, low-keyed style but doesn't know how to plumb the comic's subtler capacities for humour. What Villeret presents on the screen is a marvelous and promising outline waiting to be filled in.
—Len.

A Great Bunch of Girls
(U.S.-COLOR-16m)

Deauville, Sept. 9.

A Cowgirls Production. Produced and directed by Tracy Tynan and Mary Ann Braubach. Production supervisor, Karl Epstein. Camera (color), Eric Saarinen; editor, Anne Goursaud Epstein. Reviewed at the Deauville American Film Festival, Sept. 5, 1979. Running time: **58 MINS.**

Features the Dallas Cowboy Cheerleaders.

There's no irony in the title: the 36 member cheerleading squad of the Dallas Cowboy football team are indeed a great bunch of girls. This modest-hour-long docu makes that clear in its coverage of the selection process and the subsequent training period of one year's crop of these "clean kind of wholesome sexy" young ladies, as the cheerleading manager describes them.

A handful of these girls are interviewed by the directors, cautiously answering questions on sex, marriage and future aspirations.

The girls exude sweetness and vitality even if they have nothing of interest to say before the camera. The directors politely refrain from prodding them with more probing questions. It's an hour that's easy on the eyes, but of interest only to those who have some previous interest in so limited a subject. —Len.

Title Shot
(CANADIAN-COLOR)

Toronto, Sept. 8.

Ambassador of Canada release of a Regenthall Film presentation of a Title Shot production. Produced by Rob Iveson. Exec producer, Richard Gabourie. Directed by Les Rose. Stars Tony Curtis, Richard Gabourie. Screenplay, John Saxton from an original story by Richard Gabourie; camera, Henry Fiks; editor, Ronald Sanders; art director, Karen Bromley; music, Paul James Zaza. Produced in cooperation with the Canadian Film Development Corp. Reviewed at the Festival Theatre, Toronto, Sept. 8 '79. Running time: **96 MINS.**

Frank Renzetti	Tony Curtis
Blake	Richard Gabourie
Sylvia	Susan Hogan
Dunlop	Allan Royal
Rufus Taylor	Robert Delbert
Terry	Natsuko Ohama
Mr. Green	Jack Duffy
Lt. Grace	Sean McCann
Connie Rose	Taborah Johnson
Iggy	Robert O'Ree
Eddie	Dennis Strong

A downbeat feature with downbeat commercial possibilities, "Title Shot" deals with a Mafia deal to kill the heavyweight boxing champion of the world during a title bout.

But that description succeeds better than the film itself, bogged down by unclear explanation of who the principal players are (notably Tony Curtis, a ring owner who sells the attempted kill to a Mafia chieftan) and dialog that appears to border on outright comedy though unintentionally. Acting, except for Curtis, was slow.

Richard Gabourie is a violent cop, mean in his relationships with women and crooks with ridiculous lines such as "Pinball machines are like women. Sometimes you score big."

Of course, he thwarts Curtis but by that time, any interest that might have been there has dissipated. Direction by Les Rose is weakish and all other departments fail to come up to scratch.

Its preem in a new directors program at the Toronto Festival of Festivals was an unsuitable choice.

If this is a heavyweight boxing title shot, the sport is in big trouble. In all areas, "Title Shot" is bantam weight. —Adil.

Charles et Lucie
(FRENCH-COLOR)

Paris, Sept. 11.

A Cythere Films release of a Cythere Films/Films de la Chouette/Antenne 2/Tele Europe co-production. Produced by Claude Makovski. Stars Daniel Ceccaldi, Ginette Garcin. Directed by Nelly Kaplan. Screenplay by Kaplan, Jean Chapot and Makovski; camera (Eastmancolor), Gilbert Sandoz; editor, Gerard Le Du; sound, Guy Villette; music, Pierre Perret. Reviewed at Ponthieu screening room, Paris, Aug. 23, 1979. Running time: **97 MINS.**

Charles	Daniel Ceccaldi
Lucie	Ginette Garcin
Nostradama	Belen (Nelly Kaplan)

Leon	Jean-Marie Proslier

Nelly Kaplan directed this thin dramatic comedy about Charlie and Lucie, a washed-out middle-aged couple eking out an existence near the Paris Flea Market who are the victims of an elaborate con game that robs them of all their possessions.

Left to wander penniless in the south of France, pursued by the police for driving a stolen car, the two are swept away on misadventures that restore their taste for living and revive their long-dormant love. The apprehension of the con men and the discovery of an expensive painting among Lucie's sentimental belongings retrieve the couple from their perils, but the reborn lovers choose to stay on the road in a new vocation of travelling performers, using their adventures as dramatic material.

Daniel Ceccaldi and Ginette Garcin provide serio-comic vitality as the couple jolted out of their lethargy and self-deceiving habits and forced to confront the mediocrity of their life. But the scenario is unable to sustain the promise of the basic situation; instead of deepening, the characterization only becomes broader, leaving the actors to coast on their charm. Kaplan, who does well in a small role as an itinerant fortune-teller, is uncertain in her direction, never finding the right tone for the film.

Nothing comes near the one beautiful scene in which the camera passively looks on as dumpy, despairing Lucy, having lost everything that gave her life meaning, walks distractedly into the sea to drown herself. Her mate runs in to save her. As he carries her out of the waves the water gives Lucie's bare legs a virginal sheen. A marvelous image of rejuvenation in adversity. —Len.

Roy Likit
(Foretold by Fate)
(THAI-COLOR)

Bangkok, Aug. 28.

A New Five Star Productions release of a Jirabanterng Films production. Produced by Jirawan Kampana Senyakorn. Directed by Supravat Patamasoot. Features entire cast. Story, Tomayanti; screenplay, Busaba Dao Rueang; camera (color) Morojon; music, Pim Patiphan Poontamajitr; sound editor, Maitree Janjarasskul; art direction, Waroj; costumes, Jirawan Kampana Senyakorn; make-up, Kiat Syarm. Reviewed at Athens theatre, Bangkok, Aug. 28, '79. Running time: **105 MINS.**

Fan	Pisamai Wilaisak
Boke	Suphansa Nuangpirom
See Fah	Ampha Pusith
Bua/Barng	Metta Rungrath
Wee	Kamthorn Suwanpiyasiri
Niyom	Chamroon Nuatjim
Nangwin	Sutijitr Viradejkamhaeng
Athicorng	Pojetr Ganpetr
Dusadee	Suchart Kongcharoen
Seah	Bu Vibulnan

An old-fashioned tearjerker still remains the top choice of local producers when launching the career of new film actresses, and Jirabanterng Films does as expected by choosing "Roy Likit" to introduce Suphansa Nuangpirom.

The story is about the kidnapping and exchange of two little girls. Each girl is brought up not by her real mother. The culprit (Metta Rungrath) wants to avenge the killing of her outlaw husband by the policeman husband of the other mother (Pisamai Wilaisak).

Ampha Pusith, who made her debut two years ago with the same company, must give way to Suphansa, and let the latter steal most of the scenes. In fact, Ampha's intuitive awareness that she is an adopted child seems deliberately repetitious and boring.

Music by Pim Patiphan Poontamajitr benefits from extensive use of Thai traditional music, oddly bittersweet and developed to perfection for this type of movie. Photography by Morojon emphasizes the elegant surroundings of the affluent class as contrasted with the hard, albeit often hilarious, struggle to eke out a living among the lower class. —Cano.

San Sebastian Fest

Memorias De Leticia Valle
(Memoirs of Leticia Valle)
(SPANISH-COLOR)

San Sebastian, Sept. 10.

Produced and directed by Miguel Angel Rivas. Screenplay, based on Rosa Chacel novel of same name, by Marigel Alonso, Alberto Porlan and Miguel Angel Rivas; camera (Eastmancolor), Carlos Suarez; editor, Eduardo Biurrun; music, Alberto Bourbon; exec producer, Manuel F. Manchon. Reviewed at Cine Savoy (San Sebastian), Sept. 10, '79. Running time: 105 MINS.

Features Ramiro Oliveros, Jeannine Mestre, Fernando Rey, Hector Alterio, Emma Suarez, Queta Claver, Francisco Casares, Helga Line, Irina Kuberskaya, Maria Elena Flores and Esperanza Roy.

Longwinded, tedious tale set in a Spanish town near Valladolid in 1911 about a young girl, her infatuation with an unhappily married tutor and the melodramatically tragical denouement of their relationship. From beginning to end film is thesped and directed in a stilted way as the helmer tries to build up a mood for the final scenes. He dwells longishly on static scenes which contribute nothing to the very slight story, and never really explains many of the critical episodes in the yarn.

Story, told in one long flashback via the young girl's diary, concerns

Leticia's crush on a tutor, his sympathetic wife who gives her piano lessons, an ailing father and bitchy aunt. The tutor, whose marriage doesn't seem to be working out, though it is never explained why, finally is seen kissing the girl. It is unclear whether more than that is involved. The father somehow gets wind of it (again no explanation of how), goes over to the tutor to confront him with the dastardly facts, whatever they may be, and latter shoots himself offstage.

It's doubtful whether even in Spain this pic will manage to run more than a week after its possible release in Madrid. —Besa.

Aquella Larga Noche
(That Long Night)
(CUBAN-COLOR)

San Sebastian, Sept. 11.

Produced by the Instituto Cubano del Arte y la Industria Cinematografica. Directed by Enrique Pineda Barnet. Screenplay, Ambrosio Fornet, Enrique Pineda; camera, (color), Raul Rodriguez; music, Carlos Farinas; editor, Gloria Arguelles; producer, Rolindo Diaz Reyes; sets, Luis Lacosta. Reviewed at Cine Victoria Eugenia (San Sebastian), Sept. 11, '79. Running time: 100 MINS.

Features Raquel Revuelta, Maria Eugenia Garcia.

Political film set in 1958 Cuba about struggles of a group of pro-Castro revolutionaries. Story is told as one long flashback as the group waits out a long night in an apartment after assassinating a high police official and expecting to be caught themselves.

Story jumps around undramatically from scenes in Havana to guerrilla camps in the hills. At times, a Yank video-type music seems to lead the viewer to expect some decisive action, but it never takes place. Even the two action scenes in mid-film, when guerrillas attack a column of troops and another in which the Castro group is ambushed, are never followed through. Aside from the expected and simplistic political ax the film grinds, it is too disjointed and discursive to arouse much audience interest.

Thesping and direction are on the amateurish side. Item is okay as a propaganda piece and as an homage to those who are now the martyrs of the Castro revolution.
—Besa.

Prisoneros Desaparecidos
(Missing Prisoners)
(SWEDISH-CUBAN-COLOR)

San Sebastian, Sept. 9.

Svenska Filminstitutet and Instituto Cubano del Arte y la Industria Cinematografica coproduction. (Swedish title "De Forsvunna".) Directed by Sergio Castilla. Screenplay, Sergio and Patricio Castilla; exec producer, Sergio Castilla; camera (Eastmancolor), Patricio Castilla; music, Juanito Rodriguez and Chembo; sets, Betty Fischman; producer, Humberto Fernandez; editor, Roberto Bravo. Reviewed at Cine Victoria Eugenia (San Sebastian), Sept. 9, '79. Running time: 84 MINS.

Features Nelson Villagra, Lenardo Perucci, Elisabeth Menz, Hugo Medina.
(Spanish Soundtrack)

Simplistic non-story of three days in a clandestine jail in Chile under Pinochet's dictatorship. Most of pic is dedicated to showing prisoners being tortured and to the ranting of a police chief as he tries to wrangle information out of several men and women considered to be "Marxist" and who are suspected of being involved in anti-government activities.

Pic is not even a political tract, because at no time is any effort made to delve into the prisoners' or policemen's motivations or personal lives or political opinions. All that is presented on the scene is one grim torture scene after another in the jail, with no relief or character study or insight into the reasons for any of it.

Not for the squeamish. Hardline anti-Pinochet propagandists may be pleased at Chilean police brutality vividly depicted, but item is not bound to interest anyone beyond that. —Besa.

Im Feuer Bestanden
(Born of Fire)
(EAST GERMAN-COLOR/ B&W/DOCU)

San Sebastian, Sept. 10.

Produced and directed by Walter Heynowski and Gerhard Scheumann. Camera (color/black and white) Peter Hellmich; editor, Trante Wischnewski. No other credits available. Reviewed at Cine Victoria Eugenia (San Sebastian), Sept. 10, '79. Running time: 75 MINS.
(Spanish Soundtrack)

Documentary on the downfall of the Allende government in Chile in 1973 which claims to add some heretofore unused photographic and film material. In addition to the by-now familiar footage of the attack by rebel forces on the Moneda and Allende's last public speeches, pic adds interviews with a wide variety of persons involved in the Allende government and the coup.

Interviewed among others are Allende's widow, Augusto Pinochet, the squadron commander who bombed the presidential palace, survivors from the Allende side, and others. Though pic tries to give events a veneer of objectivity it is only a thinly disguised political tract, with innumerable plugs for Fidel Castro. Pinochet is never allowed to speak more than a few words before he is cut. Here's more fodder for the militants and left-wing historians. —Besa.

Starting Over
(COLOR)

Reynolds, Clayburgh and Bergen add up to boxoffice allure.

Hollywood, Sept. 25.

Paramount Pictures release of a James L. Brooks production. Produced by Alan J. Pakula, Brooks. Directed by Pakula. Stars Burt Reynolds, Jill Clayburgh, Candice Bergen. Screenplay, Brooks, based upon the novel by Dan Wakefield; camera (color), Sven Nykvist; editor, Marion Rothman; production design, George Jenkins; costume design, John Boxer; music, Marvin Hamlisch; sound, James Sabat; assistant director, Alex Hapsas. Reviewed at Samuel Goldwyn Theatre, BevHills, Sept. 25, '79. (MPAA Rating: R.) Running time: 106 MINS.

Phil Potter	Burt Reynolds
Marilyn Holmberg	Jill Clayburgh
Jessica Potter	Candice Bergen
Mickey Potter	Charles Durning
Marva Potter	Frances Sternhagen
Paul	Austin Pendleton
Marie	Mary Kay Place
Dan Ryan	MacIntyre Dixon
Larry	Jay Sanders
Everett	Richard Whiting
John Morganson	Sturgis Warner

"Starting Over" is a delight. Much more than the flip side of "An Unmarried Woman," to which it will inevitably be compared, the James L. Brook production takes on the subject of marital dissolution from a comic point of view, and succeeds admirably. Wryly directed by Alan J. Pakula, and featuring an outstanding cast headed by Burt Reynolds, Jill Clayburgh and Candice Bergen, the Paramount release looks to be a boxoffice giant. In this instance, all the lucre will be well-deserved.

Brooks is the latest screenwriter to graduate from television sitcoms (preceded by Alan Burns with "A Little Romance," among others), and the influence shows in some surprising ways. While there's a certain superficiality to "Starting Over," it's more than balanced by the warmth and wittiness with which Brooks invests his characters, qualities Pakula so skillfully draws out.

In fact, "Starting Over" favorably evokes the screwball comedies of the 1930s in more subtle fashion than other pix attempting to overtly mimic the heyday of American screen comedy.

Success in this regard stems from a cast and concept wholly integrated. Reynolds plays a mild-mannered writer unwillingly foisted into a "liberated" condition by spouse Bergen, feeling her feminine oats as a songwriter. Fleeing to Boston and the protection of relatives Charles Durning and Frances Sternhagen, he meets spinster schoolteacher Clayburgh, and the off-and-on romance begins.

What brings the story alive is not just the preponderance of snappy one-liners, nor the sly way Pakula couples and uncouples his principal characters. Whatever their defects, Reynolds, Clayburgh and Bergen, along with the rest of the cast, are fun to watch. Audiences may wince at Bergen's autobiographical ditties, or shudder at Reynolds' misguided love affairs, but the essential link between comedy and reality is never absent.

Without his ever-present moustache, Reynolds is appealingly vulnerable, and in "Starting Over," proves that he no longer has to prove anything. With unfailing comic timing, and a superb sense of reaction, Reynolds is the core of the film, and underplays marvellously. It's a performance that should get the critics off his back once and for all.

Bergen hits a career highlight as Reynolds' slinky ex-wife, and her caterwauling voice provides some of the film's comic peaks. A perfect contrast to Bergen's chic profile is supplied by Clayburgh, looking purposefully blowzy, as a woman afraid of emotional entanglement, yet simultaneously yearning for one. It's a well-developed character, right down to her apartment furnishings, and Clayburgh fleshes her out fully.

Pakula is assumed to be a more serious director than "Starting Over" would indicate, but one of the film's strengths is its lack of condescension toward its characters. Even Durning and Sternhagen, both superb as humanistic psychiatrists, are tweaked, rather than ridiculed. Ditto for Mary Kay Place, who is super as a man-hungry divorcee who literally attacks Reynolds.

Rest of the cast is likewise great, especially Austin Pendleton, MacIntyre Dixon, Jay Sanders, Richard Whiting, Alfie Wise and Wallace Shawn as members of Reynolds' divorced men's workshop. Pakula and Brooks are consistently able to turn stock situations, such as this men's group, into revealing and amusing insights, the true mark of a film that cares.

Cinematographer Sven Nykvist, lensing his first American screen comedy, has produced a warm, healthy glow well suited for "Starting Over," and George Jenkins, who previously worked with Pakula on "All The President's Men," has provided the optimum production settings. Rest of credits are all tops, and Marvin Hamlisch and Carole Bayer Sager have contributed material perfectly suited for Bergen's predatory singer.

"Starting Over" is not without its oversights, cliches and lapses, but on the whole, it's the most successful comedy to come out after a long mirthless drought. — *Poll.*

Night Creature
(COLOR)

A tame kitty.

Hollywood, Sept. 22.

A Dimension Pictures release of a Lee Madden Associates production. Produced by Ross Hagen. Directed by Lee Madden. Screenplay, Hubert Smith, based on a story by Lee Madden. Smith. Executive producer, Madden; camera (CFI color). Pemylot Cheydon; editor, Martin Draffke; music, Jim Helms; associate producer, Suzanne Jesse. Reviewed at the World Theatre, Hollywood, Sept. 21, '79. MPAA Rating: PG. Running time: **83 MINS.**

Axel MacGregor	Donald Pleasence
Leslie	Nancy Kwan
Ross	Ross Hagen
Peggy	Lesly Fine
Georgia	Jennifer Rhodes

Made in Thailand two years ago and just now being let out of its cage by Dimension, "Night Creature" is a tame and hokey man-vs.-beast tale with very little to offer the action-horror crowd, which will be the only one tempted by the "bloodbath" ad campaign. It's marginal fare even for drive-in situations.

Donald Pleasence, of all people, poses as a Hemingwayesque writer with his own island compound in Southeast Asia who becomes obsessed with a man-eating black leopard which has "made me afraid for the first time in my life," which is more than can be said for the audience. Two of his daughters, one with a boy friend, and a granddaughter turn up to share in the terror, which mainly consists of the big cat snarling a lot and stalking about in slow motion.

Waiting for the beast to make another appearance, Ross Hagen comments, "Funny how one day can seem like an eternity," which invites application to pic's running time. Strongly un-Hemingway-like climax has group giving up and fleeing in a boat, leaving the animal behind as solitary lord of the jungle island, as well as of Pleasence's fabulously appointed house. —*Cart.*

The Bitch
(BRITISH-COLOR)

London, Sept. 18.

Brent Walker production. Produced by John Quested. Executive producers, Edward D. Simons, Ronald S. Kass, Oscar S. Lerman. Directed by Gerry O'Hara. Stars Joan Collins. Screenplay, Gerry O'Hara, based on story by Jackie Collins; camera (color), Denis Lewiston; sound, David Crozier; art director, Malcolm Middleton; ass't directors, Redmond Morris, Terry Pearce, Michael Zimbrich. Reviewed at the Rialto Theatre, London, Sept. 18, '79. (BBFC rating: X). Running Time: **90 MINS.**

Fontaine Khaled	Joan Collins
Nico Cantafora	Michael Coby
Arnold Rinstead	Kenneth Haigh
Feather	Ian Hendry
Polly	Carolyn Seymour
Vanessa	Sue Lloyd
Leonard	Mark Burns
Hal	John Ratzenberger
Lynn	Pamela Salem
Luke	Anthony Heaton
John-Jo	Maurice O'Connell
Ricky	Peter Wight

"The Bitch" sequels "The Stud," a big hit last year around Blighty, in which jet-set disco operator Joan Collins, swatched in furs or peek-a-boo, demonstrated a boring itch to make it anytime, anywhere and with anyone.

There's more of the same in "Bitch," which offers more mock orgasm than plot as it oscillates between the disco floor and the sack — or the pool, shower, or wherever a couple can couple. Two lesbos, at one point, are glimpsed pawing each other in a sauna.

Not to mince about, the John Quested production, scripted and feverishly directed by Gerry O'Hara, is corny and coarse, but at least mercifully brief at 90 minutes. Pic has some laughs, but only one or two reasonable jokes. It should do well on the program circuits, at least in the British home market. ("Stud," the trailer, is due in 100 or so U.S. outlets this month via AIP. "Bitch" is still angling for pickup.)

Between all the sex and sybaritic palaver, there's some nuisance plotting involving Michael Coby as a debonair hustler in trouble with the mob. Pic's ending, ostensibly ironic, only seems confusing as to who done what to whom. But for disco freaks, there's plenty of their kind of action.

Collins does her spoiled nympho rich girl turn with assurance. Coby's adequate, and there's professional support from Kenneth Haigh, Ian Hendry, Carolyn Seymour, Sue Lloyd and Peter Wight, all proving that actors gotta work.

Technical credits are okay. —*Pit.*

Screams Of A Winter Night
(COLOR)

Amateur night at the house by the lake. No screams here.

Hollywood, Sept. 22.

A Dimension Pictures release of A Full Moon production. Produced by Richard H. Wadsack, James L. Wilson. Directed by James L. Wilson. Executive producer, S. Mark Lovell. Screenplay, Richard H. Wadsack; camera (PSI Color), Robert E. Rogers; editors, Gary Ganote, Craig Mayes; music, Don Zimmers; set, costume design, Mar'Sue Wilson. Reviewed at the World Theatre, Hollywood, Sept. 21, '79. MPAA Rating: PG. Running time: **91 MINS.**

John	Matt Borel
Sam	Gil Glascow
Carl	Patrick Byers
Elaine	Mary Agen Cox
Sally	Robin Bradley
Harper	Ray Gaspard
Jookie	Beverly Allen
Liz	Brandy Barrett
Alan	Charles Rucker
Lauri	Jan Norton

Mainly consisting of a bunch of kids sitting around telling stale spook stories, "Screams Of A Winter Night" characters all work themselves into a lather over nothing while viewers will hibernate during the running time, which seems as long as a winter in Lapland.

First reel is taken up by 10 college-age kids all going on about how scary the remote lake area they're headed to spend the weekend in is supposed to be. Indian legend has it that the devil wind in these parts doesn't like strangers, so naturally everyone waits around for the prophecy to come true.

In the meantime, youths take turns clumsily spinning scary yarns. Dramatized just as ineptly in flashbacks, first tale is about a Bigfoot type who hangs a young dude from a tree, second shows a group of guys spending the night in a haunted apartment, while third is about "Crazy Annie," a child-woman who kills anyone with a normal interest in sex. Each is about as terrifying as a "Little Orphan Annie" comic strip. —*Cart.*

Passe Ton Bac D'Abord
(Get Your Diploma First)
(FRENCH-COLOR)

Paris, Sept. 18.

An AMLF release of a Livardois Films/-Renn Productions/FR 3/I.N.A. co-production. Features entire cast. Written and directed by Maurice Pialat. Camera (color) Pierre-William Glenn and Jean-Paul Janssen; sound, Pierre Gamet, Michel Laurent; editors, Arlette Langmann, Sophie Coussein, Martine Giordano. Reviewed at Monte Carlo Cinema, Paris; Sept. 14, '78. Running time: **90 MINS.**

Elisabeth	Sabine Haudepin
Philippe	Philippe Marlaud
Valerie	Valerie Chassigneux
Mother	Annick Alane
Father	Michel Caron

Maurice Pialat's "Passe Ton Bac D'Abord" is a tonic contrast to the recent spate of soft-hued films about youth that seem designed to send the spectator from the theatre bathed in a warm glow of shared juvenescence. Its sober tone, and its contention that the lot of contemporary French teenagers is nothing to smile about, may stunt its commercial power, though it should draw the admiration of specialized audiences.

Pialat sets his camera down in a provincial French city in a northern mining region. It follows the peregrinations of some high school students, who see little reason to plod towards a baccalaureat that will probably qualify them for dead-end jobs or debilitating unemployment. They flounder about in this grey reality: drifting around town, meeting in the local bistro, making excursions to the coast, bickering with uncomprehending parents. Some engage in joyless sexual encounters, others drop into desperate marriage. A few pack up and head for the anonymous scramble of Paris life. In the meantime their unprovocative teachers drone on in futile dissertation.

Pialat records all this with an acute eye for detail, gesture and behavior and is admirably served by a cast remarkable for its naturalness and veracity. The director's omnipresent, discreet compassion never impedes his talent for social dissection.

Pialat's objectivity and veristic concern, already richly present in his first feature "Naked Childhood" (1967), has earned him the label of a "documentarist," which is telling, as far as the texture of his films is concerned, but misleading inasmuch as it fails to take into account his assiduous scripting. Certainly, Pialat is a proponent of a tendency towards renewed naturalism in the French cinema that includes, most notably, the films of Jacques Doillon.

The film is technically uneven, its shooting having been interrupted at one point and later resumed with a different crew. —*Len.*

Rend mig i traditionerne
(Traditions, My Behind)
(DANISH-COLOR)

Copenhagen, Sept. 15.

A Gunnar Obel (with Edward Fleming and The State Film Institute) production and release. Based on Leif Panduro's novel. Written and directed by Edward Fleming. Camera (Eastmancolor), Jan Wincke; editor, Maj Soya; music, Ole Hoyer and (title tune) Kim Larsen. Reviewed at Palads, Copenhagen, Sept. 14, '79. Running time: **90 MINS.**

David	Henrik Kofoed
Lis	Karin Wedel
David's mother	Bodil Kjer
Psychiatrist	Axel Stroeby
Traubert	Olaf Ussing
Lillian	Masja Dessau
Hubert	Jan Gustavsen
Fabby	Niels Hinrichsen

Leif Panduro's novel "Traditions, My Behind" has been a Danish youth classic, less poetic, but otherwise very similar to J.D. Salinger's "Catcher in The Rye" since its publication 21 years ago, but it took the acknowledged technical skill and artistic daring of director Edward Fleming to open up book's long stretches of inner dialog and straighten its multitude of flashbacks into a straight-forward, folksy yet genuine movie script and a feature to go with it.

As the film version of the story of young David, having a hard time coming to grips with the realities of sex, society, etc., now stands, it should be a saleable commodity in many youth-oriented situations worldwide. "Traditions, My Behind" is good, solid comedy of manners.

When David from the upper-crust milieu rebels by starting to bite the thighs of people who offend him or just to kick their behinds, his High Society caricature mother (Bodil Kjer, an actress of high achievement, here overplaying wildly) has him safely put away for some months at a private pscyhiatric nursing home.

He gets the usual mealy-mouthed hogwash from the psychiatrist, allies himself with a truly mad elderly gentleman (Olaf Ussing) who sees plots against his life in every flower, cake or bedpan around him, and together with young David, starts throwing around small bombs.

There is also a flirtation with a still youngish nurse (played with deft wit by Ghita Noerby) although David's real dream-girl Lis (Karin Wedel, muted, modern, funny) remains unapproached.

Actually, David (another modern, muted performance by Henrik Kofoed) is so sexually shy that, when a brash girl class mate (Masja Dessau) actually tugs off her featherweight underwear to accommodate him, he thinks it dropped by mistake and hands the garment back to her. An unthinkable situation today? Possibly, but played and put forward to ring true enough.

The true ring is maintained whereever the very young are portrayed and where they play. Cast's older, more professional members are generally (Ebbe Rode as a Latin Professor, Ove Sprogoe and the father of the young girl as notable exceptions) allowed to veer madly off into oldfashioned exaggerations. But it's the youth and the youth appeal of this picture that ultimately count. —Kell.

Parashat Winchell
(The Winchell Affair)
(ISRAELI-COLOR)

Tel Aviv, Sept. 16.
A KN Films Production, produced by Yaakov Kozky. Written and directed by Avraham Heffner. Camera (color) Daniel Schneur: Editor David Tor; art director, Yael Heffner; music Naomi Shemer. Reviewed in Tel Aviv, Sept. 15, '79. Running time: 91 MINS.
Ilana ....,.............Tal Nativ
Judy ....:.......Etty Zevko
Alex ....Oded Kotler
Baruch Wigotzky ....Dov Feigin
Irma ....Tova Firon

Yedidia Kogan ....Nathan Meisler
Zakkai ....Shimon Finkel
Illana's mother ....Nava Sh'an

———

Vaguely inspired by an unsolved political crime in the '30s, Avraham Heffner's third feature film combines a thriller-like investigation of an old mystery with the personal problems of the investigating journalist and her entourage.

Lord Winchell is a fictitious figure whose unexplained death created a political furor in the budding political establishment of the Jewish community. His case is slightly similar to the death of Haim Arlozoroff, leader of the labor movement at that period, and indeed local publicity has hinted as much, without being explicit about it, as many of the people involved in the Arlozoroff case are still alive and the dangers of a libel suit are quite realistic.

Heffner, probably the most serious Israeli filmmaker now active, uses the historical background, but his goal is not to supply a new version of the killing or suggest new solutions. He is much more interested in the psychological and political climate of that period, as it is seen through the eyes of 1979. Heffner intertwines the components of his story quite astutely, dealing at the same time with the two generations which have been the center of his previous films.

On the one hand, the generation of the founders, that is the first settlers in the renewed Israel, those who were born abroad and came here as adults, but somehow could never be entirely rid of the old habits of the old land, and tried to recreate the same conditions of life in their new home. On the other hand, the new generation, born in Israel, sons and daughters of the previous one, who have no nostalgia for a different world, but are still looking for their roots in their own land.

Heffner puts his points over intelligently, he catches the light, the mood and the language of the country just right, creating characters who look like real Israelis and talk as such, a feat not to be taken lightly in the Israeli cinema.

But his problem is his fear of overdramatization which partly hurt his previous "Aunt Clara." A hint is as strong a statement as he'll ever use here, holding back his actors to a point where there is some doubt whether the characters really care.

He uses a similar approach to visuals, trying as much as possible to avoid postcard color, or any brusque camera effect. Result puts much of the story-telling burden on the dialogue, not the best way to hold audience attention.

The cast, consisting of new faces and old experienced battle horses, acquits itself, very well on the whole. Particularly Tal Nativ, a journalist attacking her first dramatic part in a natural and remarkably controlled way, and the late Nathan Meisler, as a character who makes a career out of being a holocaust survivor. Daniel Schneur's photography fits in with Heffner's subdued style, and Naomi Shemer, Israel's leading tunesmith, supplies music in the same vein.

Altogether, a commendable effort, which has encountered many problems in distribution on the local market, used to a different kind of domestic products. It will require careful handling in order to help it find its own public. International festivals may be interested, for the different facet of Israeli life it presents. —Edna.

Seven
(COLOR)

———

Confusing spoof. OK for grinds.

———

Hollywood, Sept. 24.
American International Release of a Melvin Simon production. Produced and directed by Andy Sidaris. Exec producer, Melvin Simon. Stars William Smith. Screenplay, William Driskill, Robert Baird, from a story by Sidaris; set design, Sal Grasso; special effects, Joe Lombardi. No other credits available. Reviewed at Culver Theatre, Culver City, Sept. 23, '79. (MPAA Rating: R.) Running time: 100 MINS.
Drew ....William Smith
Alexa ....Barbara Leigh
Cowboy ....Guich Koock
Kinsella ....Art Metrano
Skip ....Martin Kove
Professor ....Richard Le Pore
T.K. ....Christopher Joy
Jennie ....Susan Kiger
Harris ....Robert Relyea
Malie ....Little Egypt
Kahyuna ....Lenny Montana
Hermit ....Reggie Nalder

———

"Seven" has a little more going for it than distrib American International apparently thinks, but not much. AIP is currently playing the Melvin Simon pickup in regional saturations, sans the usual trade screenings, or even complete credits. It's not difficult to see why, although the actioner is well-cast and should serve up good returns in double-bills and grind houses.

While AIP is billing the Andy Sidaris film as a tongue-in-cheek spoof, there are too many close-ups of bullet wounds to believe that line. Emphasis from producer-director Sidaris is strictly on violence, rather than sex, although Barbara Leigh and Susan Kiger offer pleasant alternatives to the preponderance of special effects blood.

Plot is as confusing as the title, since it's hard to understand whether latter refers to the number

of killers William Smith rounds up on government orders to wipe out a similar number of Hawaiian mobsters, or the payment, hinted at $7,000,000. Whatever the case, the murders are so numerous as to offer another possibility, that they've been inserted in multiples of seven.

Smith, who attracted quite a femme following in the "Rich Man, Poor Man" vidseries as Falconetti, breezes through the role with laidback assurance. Rest of the cast is more than adequate, with Guich Koock, Barbara Leigh, Art Metrano, Lenny Montana and especially Richard Le Pore doing all that's required of them.

Mel Simon exec Robert Relyea also makes his acting debut and rates an "introducing" credit. With his brief part as a government bureaucrat, Relyea validates that his talents lie behind the camera.

Uncredited lensing is good, but "Seven" is filled with stock Hawaiian footage, and not very good stuff at that. Pic lags continually, which won't pacify the action audience. Product plugs are also heavy-handed, and enumerated again with a final credit.

R rating of "Seven" is clearly deserved by the violence, which has three murders even before the opening titles. But the pic may have established a niche for itself by having the opening shot center on a cup, on which the verboten "F" word is prominently displayed. Now that's working fast. —Poll.

L'Associe
(The Associate)
(FRANCO-GERMAN-COLOR)

———

Paris, Sept. 18.
A Warner-Columbia release of a Magyar Productions/Fr 3/Maran Film (Stuttgart) co-production. Stars Michel Serrault. Directed by Rene Gainville. Written by Gainville and Jean-Claude Carriere, from the novel "My Partner, Mister Davis" by Jenaro Prieto. Camera (Fujicolor), Etienne Szabo; sound, Harrik Maury; art director, Sydney Bettex; music, Mort Shuman; editor, Raymonde Guyot. Reviewed at the Paramount Elysees, Paris; Sept. 17, '79. Running time: 94 MINS.
Julien Pardot ....Michel Serrault
Agnes ....Claudine Auger
Alice ....Catherine Alric
Mme Brezol ....Judith Magre
Louis ....Mathieu Carriere
Hellzer ....Bernard Haller

———

Rene Gainville's "The Associate" is a small oasis in the generally arid landscape of French film comedy. It's based on a 1927 satiric novel by the Chilean humorist Jenaro Prieto, which was first filmed in England in 1936 by French director Claude Autant-Lara under the title "My Partner, Mister Davis."

"The Associate" tells the story of unassuming, fiftyish Julien Pardot, a professional washout who is nevertheless convinced of his innate business sense. Since his own person fails to inspire confidence, he invents an imaginary business partner — a certain Mister Davis, an Englishman to whom he attributes all decisions.

The scheme works only too well: the financial counseling firm of "Pardot & Davis" skyrockets to international stature, but it is to see the mysterious Mister Davis that crowds of businessmen throng its offices. Pardot is, in the eyes of others, as mediocre as ever, but the unappreciated marketing wizard has his hands full just keeping up the charade — British-accented phone calls, cancelled appointments and long-distance telegrams assure the business world that Mister Davis' invisibility is merely the result of a profoundly misanthropic nature.

The matter of Davis' identity is forever the question of the day, but this doesn't prevent governments from decorating him, women from fantasizing about his sexual prowess (Pardot's mistress decides to become Mrs. Davis), and mothers from bursting into the offices clutching new-born babies and screaming that Mister Davis is the father.

Jealous, fed up with the crumbs of glory left behind by his imaginary creation, Pardot decides to kill off Davis. A faked kidnap note and a skeleton purchased from a medical supplier does the trick. But the trick backfires when Pardot is arrested for murder.

It would be unfair to disclose the rest of this consistently amusing tale. The script, which is the work of Gainville and long-time Bunuel collaborator Jean-Claude Carriere, glitters with broad ironies about the human propensity for mythmaking and bottomless capacity for self-deception.

Gainville's direction is competent, ably keeping pace with the screenplay's galloping absurdities. The pop music score by Mort Shuman, however, is inappropriate.

Michel Serrault, who last year won the French equivalent of the Oscar for his role in "La Cage Aux Folles," plays the mild-mannered, bemused Pardot with a perfect blend of comic gravity and subtle timing. The rest of the cast is good, with special mention for Judith Magre as Pardot's karate blackbelt secretary and comic Bernard Haller as a maniacal banker.

(Note: Autant-Lara's film version, which the director has disowned as his own work, was originally scripted by Jacques Prevert. The script was junked by the English producers. Autant-Lara told *Variety* recently that last year

he revised Prevert's scenario and sent it to a major production house. It was returned unread, he said.)
—*Len.*

Mr. Mike's Mondo Video
(COLOR)
An ugly sense of "humor." Questionable.

A New Line Cinema Release. Produced and directed by Michael O'Donoghue. Stars O'Donoghue. Exec producer, Lorne Michaels. Written by O'Donoghue, Mitchell Glazer, Emily Prager, Dirk Wittenborn; camera (video) Barry Rebo; editors, Bob Tischler, Alan Miller; production design, Eugene Lee, Franne Lee. Reviewed at 8th St. Playhouse, NYC, Sept. 29, '79. (MPAA Rating: R). Running time: **60 MINS.**
Cameo Cast includes: Dan Aykroyd, Jane Curtin, Carrie Fisher, Teri Garr, Joan Hackett, Deborah Harry, Margot Kidder, Bill Murray, Gilda Radner, Sid Vicious.

Originally bankrolled by NBC-TV as a latenight comedy special keyed to the wide "Saturday Night Live" audience, "Mr. Mike's Mondo Video" was dropped by NBC after production, its sick humor and aggressive offensiveness apparently deemed "unsuitable for network standards." Recently released to New Line Cinema for a stab at the theatrical market, the bottom-line product indicates that (a) even if NBC's censors hadn't axed the program, quality control probably would have dumped it, and (b) once word-of-mouth spreads, few patrons are going to shell out cash for something that wasn't good enough to be shown for free.

Using the parodic framework of an exploitative, "Mondo Cane"-type pseudo-documentary, "Mondo Video" pretty much confines itself to the sicker, more offensive end of the "Saturday Night Live" spectrum, though with far less humorous payoff than the latter regularly delivers. Limning of a world "where the bizarre is commonplace" begins with a report on a swimming school for cats, amounting to lovingly detailed shots of terrified felines being flung into a pool, then swimming — in tortured slow motion — to safety.

Other would-be highlights include a segment on "Celebrity Deformities" (Dan Aykroyd unveils his webbed toes), a report on a muu-muu draped religious cult that worships "Hawaii Five-O's" Jack Lord (get it?); a takeoff on classified Pentagon secret weapon footage (a laser-firing brassiere), appearances by punk rockers such as Sid Vicious, a string of female cameos (Margot Kidder, Teri Garr, Carrie Fisher, et al.) detailing which of their men's disgusting body habits turn them on, and other assorted juvenalia.

Directing acumen of producer Michael O'Donoghue, source of

"Saturday Night's" more black humored segments, is even more miniscule than his observable human compassion or sensitivity. Most segs are overlong, their peabrained punchlines obvious from the onset. Highlight of the pic — historically and aesthetically — turns out to be an uncredited 1928 nudie film loop, a "Cine-Art Featurette" entitled "Uncle Si and the Sirens."

Wearing its home tube origins on its soiled sleeve, pic includes "insert commercial" breaks in continuity, as well as mid-commercial lead-ins by O'Donoghue. Quality of the videotape to film transfer is terrible. As it turns out, it's also irrelevant. —*Step.*

The Legacy
(COLOR)

Satanic possession plot. Weak promise.

Universal Pictures release of an Arnold Kopelson presentation of a Turman-Foster Production. Produced by David Foster. Directed by Richard Marquand. Stars Katharine Ross, Sam Elliott. Exec producer, Arnold Kopelson. Screenplay, Jimmy Sanster, Patric Tilley, Paul Wheeler; Story, Sangster; camera (color), Dick Bush, Alan Hume; editor, Anne V. Coates; music, Michael J. Lewis; production design, Disley Jones; special effects, Ian Wingrove. Reviewed at Rivoli Theatre, N.Y.C. Sept. 28, '79. (MPAA rating: R.) Running time: **100 MINS.**
Maggie Walsh . . . . Katharine Ross
Pete Danner . . . . Sam Elliott
Jason Mountolive . . . . John Standing
Harry . . . . Ian Hogg
Nurse Adams . . . . Margaret Tyzack
Karl . . . . Charles Gray
Jacques . . . . Lee Montague
Barbara . . . . Hildegarde Neil
Maria . . . . Marianne Broome
Clive . . . . Roger Daltrey

Using the hoary convention of stranding a young couple in the mansion of a reclusive millionaire whose guests are progressively bumped off in an assortment of guresome ways, "The Legacy" tries for an added dimension of satanic possession, but winds up a tame, suspenseless victim of its own lack of imagination. Despite three or four grand guignol deaths and some pretty — though hollow — atmosphere, this glossy, soft-minded entry will have to capitalize on autumn product hunger, effective tv spots and its widely sold novelization to pick up some quick cash on the in-and-out showcase route.

Katharine Ross and Sam Elliott play the Yank couple, a pair of architects mysteriously summoned for an assignment in England and lured by a fat $50,000 advance. When they're accidentally forced off a country road by a chauffeured Rolls, owner John Standing invites them back for "tea," then disappears while they

find themselves trapped in the house for the weekend. Sharing the premises are an assortment of lurking cats, zombi-like servants and booby-trapped gadgets.

The film directed with an eye to prettiness, but no tension or suspenseful pacing by former tv director Richard Marquand, takes an eternity to get down to business. Temporary hope appears in the form of a contingent of well-heeled guests — onetime Nazi arms maker Charles Gray, publisher Hildegarde Neil, pop promoter Roger Daltrey, hotelier Lee Montague and ex-hooker Marianne Broome — who arrive for some preordained meeting, at which Ross apparently is the key figure.

But by the time three of the guests are gorily disposed of and the plot mechanations are made clear (the guests have sold their souls to satanic Standing and Ross is predestined to inherit the latter's diabolical powers) it's clear that Marquand can't even capitalize on the ample gore, let alone generate some needed suspense into the simplistic script. When all else fails, Marquand resorts to pouncing cats and suddenly opened doors to try for some shocks. He might as well have taken a tea break.

In spite of the sparse material, the predominantly British cast at least has some fun chewing up the polished oak scenery. Within all that oak, however, Ross and Elliott merely sway there unenergetically, as wooden as a pair of American elms. —*Step.*

San Sebastian Fest

Mama Cumple 100 Anos
(Mom's 100 Years Old)
(SPANISH-COLOR)

San Sebastian, Sept. 17.

Elias Querejeta production written and directed by Carlos Saura. Camera (Eastmancolor), Teo Escamilla; editor, Pablo G. del Amo; sets, Antonio Belizon; exec producer, Primitivo Alvaro. Reviewed at Cine Victoria Eugenia (San Sebastian), Sept. 16, '79. Running time: **98 MINS.**
Anna . . . . Geraldine Chaplin
Natalia . . . . Amparo Munoz
Mother . . . . Rafaela Aparicio
Fernando . . . . . . Fernando Fernan Gomez
Antonio . . . . Norman Brisky
Luchi . . . . Charo Soriano
Juan . . . . Jose Vivo
Carlota . . . . Angeles Torres
Victoria . . . . Elisa Nandi
Solange . . . . Rita Maiden
Anny . . . . Monique Ciron

For the first time in his career, Carlos Saura has turned to comedy. Pic is an updating of his sombre 1972 drama "Anna and the Wolves" which in its day was considered to be a virulent attack upon

Spain's Franco Establishment and prompted months of wrangling between the censors and its makers. Saura now claims to have completed the circle of his films and ended a phase of his filmmaking.

Pic serves up some droll scenes, which are mixed with others in which Saura seems to be veering back towards his symbols and serious dramatic situations. But he then stops short, as though remembering his original intention, and swings back to a wry humor which at its screening in San Sebastian amused some and left others cold.

Some of those who have watched Saura over the years, the combative, introspective, symbol-obsessed Saura, may feel the situations are too innocuous and inconsequential, the humor too flighty. In a sense Saura has here diluted, almost negated, what in its day was a frontal attack upon Spain's sacred cows: the Army, the Church and the upper bourgeoisie. Helmer has seemingly mellowed since those struggling years when he was the most famous and effective anti-Franco director in Spain.

This film instead is steeped in a kind of melancholy for the passing of the years and the death of some of "Anna and the Wolves" thesps, Jose Maria Prada. (In fact, Saura uses a clip from the former film to render homage to Prada. Otherwise, virtually the same cast is used. Anna is resuscitated from the former film (in which she was killed at the end), and exiled Argentinian actor Norman Brisky is added. The old, crazy mother is still there, though she certainly doesn't look a day over 65, as is Fernando, formerly a sort of anchorite who now disports with a huge glider which he never gets off the ground, plus all the other members of the family.

The story is very slight and rather pointlessly rambling. Saura simply lets his updated characters move about a bit on the stage, and even now can't resist some unexplained symbolisms, such as the sound of a helicopter flying over the house and seemingly working miracles.

Anna, an English girl who has lived in a family mansion in Spain years back, returns anew with her husband, apparently for no other reason than to relive old memories. She is warmly welcomed by the family. It is the day before grandma is to celebrate her 100th birthday. The husband soon falls into the clutches of the pretty young daughter, who seduces him. Anna finds out, reproaches him, and they make up again.

The family is meanwhile plotting grandma's death, to be effected by withholding her medicine the next time she has an attack. But Anna is forewarned by granny of their intentions and saves her life just as a cake with 100 candles on it is brought in. Pic ends with them all posing happily for a family portrait.

Thesping all around is good, with the possible exception of Norman Brisky, who seems out of place. All technical credits are up to par. Though pic fails to rise to the excellence of "Cria Cuervos" or "Prima Angelica" it might do okay biz in Spain, though its offshore chances seem more doubtful since humor travels only with great difficulty and those accustomed to the old Saura may not be ready to accept this whimsical transformation.

—Besa.

Gamin
(Waif)

(COLOMBIAN-COLOR-DOCU-16m)

San Sebastian, Sept. 16.

Claude Antoine S.N.D. and Instituto Nacional de la Audiovisual and UNO Ltda. production written and directed by Ciro Duran. Camera (color) Luis Cuesta; editors, Ciro and Joyce Duran; music, Francisco Zumaque. Reviewed at Cine Savoy (San Sebastian), Sept. 15, '79. Running time: **104 MINS.**

Generally absorbing and occasionally spellbinding documentary about street urchins in Bogota, their lives, entertainment, sleeping quarters and manner of surviving (or not).

Pic starts by showing the six and seven year olds and then works its way up to adolescents, also providing glimpses into the children's family backgrounds and the social and political shortcomings of the country.

Some of the footage is truly extraordinary as we see a cluster of street Arabs waking up on a sidewalk between two rows of traffic; or a scene of a little boy perilously playing with the plastic toy which he pushes and pulls away from under the wheels of moving cars. These are the best parts of the film, which starts to diminish in impact and interest about halfway through as we're shown how the adolescents have turned to prostitution and robbery to survive.

Nonetheless, item comes across effectively and could generate some interest, perhaps more in video than theatrical, though it might need some cutting. —Besa.

La Triple Mort Du Troisieme Personnage
(The Triple Death of
(The Third Personage)
(FRANCO-BELGIAN-SPANISH-COLOR)

San Sebastian, Sept. 18.

Babylone Films (Paris), 2000 Productions Belgium (Brussels), Producciones Zeta S.A. (Barcelona) coproduction written and directed by Helvio Soto. Exec producer, Guy Jacobs; Associate producers, J.A. Perez Giner and Ken Legaergeant; camera (Eastmancolor), José Luis Alcaine; editor, Rodolfo Wedeles; music, Juan Jose Mosalini; sets, Ramon Pou. Reviewed at Cine Victoria Eugenia (San Sebastian), Sept. 17, '79. Running time: **103 MINS.**

Latin American	Jose Sacristan
French girl	Brigitte Fossey
Marcel	Andre Dussolier
Carolina	Patricia Guzman
Music copier	Rafael Anglada
Andre	Marcel Dossogne
Invalid	Michel Lechat

For the first 10 minutes it seems this pic might turn into an upbeat thriller set against a background of European and Latin American intrigue. But that hope is soon dashed as writer-director Helvio Soto piles on one unexplained incident after another and juggles about his time sequences until halfway through pic, at which point even the most patient onlookers must throw in the towel and despair of ever understanding anything that's going on.

The unintelligible action sequences are interlarded with pompously talky interludes touching on a variety of "philosophical" and political subjects.

There are sinister French businessmen, people being photographed, others being killed; "dangerous" information passed on in a "Latin American" jail is mentioned and there's much talk of "the others," none of it ever explained.

Presumably, Helvio Soto being an exiled Chilean, the jail referred to is in Chile and his main character is supposed to be a Chilean. But all the rest of it is hopelessly murky. We never know who's getting killed by whom or why.

The explanation to it all supposedly is in a book the exile has published in Paris, which is to lead to the "third personage" who was held in the jail. There's some claptrap about a computer analyzing the book. Why the baddies themselves published the book is never made clear. Anyway, at the end they all get shot by somebody and the film is happily over.

Jose Sacristan is fine as the exile (though his thick Castilian accent is hardly convincing), and technical credits all along are okay.

Pic might have a limited appeal to audience who aren't concerned with cause and effect. —Besa.

El Proceso De Burgos
(The Burgos Trial)
(SPANISH-COLOR-DOCU)

San Sebastian, Sept. 15.

A Cobra Films and Irrintzi Zinema production, directed by Imanol Uribe. Camera (Eastmancolor), Javier Aguirresarobe; editor, Julio Pena; music, Hibai Rekondo; exec producer, Javier Vizcaino; production manager, Mischa Muller. Reviewed at Cine Victoria Eugenia (San Sebastian), Sept. 14, '79. Running time: **134 MINS.**

Cast: Josu Abrisketa, Itziar Aizpurua, Victor Arana, Julen Kalzada, Jose Antonio Karrera, Unai Dorronsoro, Jone Dorronsoro, Arantza Arruti, Eduardo Uriarte, Gregorio Lopez Irasuegi, Xabier Larena, Xabier Izko de la Iglesia, Jokin Gorostidi, Enrique Gesalaga, Jon Etxabe, Mario Onaindia.

"Burgos Trial" was unquestionably the most controversial film at the San Sebastian festival. Controversial not for the Basque audience which jammed the theatre and gave it a standing ovation, but for most non-Basques who consider the past the present activities of the Basque terrorist group ETA hardly something to be glorified in celluloid.

The pros and cons, rights and wrongs of ETA and other groups in other countries as terrorists by some and freedom fighters by others must be argued elsewhere. Suffice it to say that there were strong pressures here (especially from Suarez's UCD party) not to show the film, and it is very problematical whether pic will get released in the rest of Spain outside the Basque area where audiences may not cheer the ETA members, no matter how sympathetically they are portrayed.

It seems that the footage shown here is really only two-thirds of the film, dealing as it does with the origins of ETA and the 1960 Burgos trial.

The third part, not shown, apparently deals with the present activities of the ETA, which is even more controversial than what happened under the Franco regime.

Pic opens with a nervously pacing Letamendia, spokesman for the left-wing Basque group Herri Batasuna, giving some background info on the Basque nationalist movement and stating that the great enemy of the "people" are Madrid's centralistic government and local capitalists and industrialists.

Film then leads into lengthy interviews with many of those ETA members who stood trial and were sentenced to death at Burgos, all of them later to be reprieved by Franco under the internal and foreign pressures exerted at the time.

The interviewees for the most part come across most sympathetically and are convincing enough in their claims that they were fighting against fascism and for the rights of their people. They talk of how they became involved in ETA, means of raising money, their personal vicissitudes and difficulties as members of a clandestine organization, how they were tortured. There are touches of humor and at the end, as *persons,* they come across so well that it is hard not to feel sympathetic for their coverage and idealism. Even when they talk of bank robberies and kidnappings one tends to take it with the light-hearted grace of a Jesse James tale.

(Not so sympathetic perhaps will be those who, even if they can go along with the terrorist tactics of the Franco days, will nonetheless condemn their continued activities under the present freely-elected administration.

(Even during the course of the festival a bomb went off in a police car which critically injured two policemen, and there was a bomb scare in the casino of the Hotel Londres during which it had to be evacuated, and a prominent banker was assassinated — all of this accountable to ETA.)

As a historical document "Burgos Trial" is topnotch, and despite its long running time interest is maintained throughout. Some documentary footage of the trial, or at least scenes outside the courthouse, are shown. Also interviewed are lawyers and a priest who makes an apologia for armed violence.

It is all very "hot" material given the continued unrest in the Basque area. —*Besa.*

Il Piccolo Archimede
(The Little Archimedes)
(ITALO-COLOR)

San Sebastian, Sept. 19.
A RAI Italian Radio Television and TV2 production written and directed by Gianni Amelio based on book by Aldous Huxley. Camera (Eastmancolor), Guido Bertoni, shot in 16m and blown up to 35m. Sets, Ferdinando Ghelli; editor, Giorgio Pozzi; music, Roman Vlad. Reviewed at Cine Victoria Eugenia (San Sebastian) Sept. 18, '79. Running time: **83 MINS.**
Alfred . . . . John Steiner
Madame Bondi . . . . Laura Betti
Guido . . . . Aldo Salvi
Elizabeth . . . . Shirley Corrigan
Robin . . . . Mark Morganti
Mr. Bondi . . . . Graziano Giusti
Guido's Father . . . . Renato Moretti

Slow-paced, introspective but charmingly delightful version of a Huxley story about an English expatriate living in Italy in the 1930s who befriends an extraordinary peasant boy seven years old whose musical and mathematical talents are astounding.

Outstanding performance by John Steiner as he slowly discovers the latent abilities of the strange boy and starts giving him music lessons, while at same time feeling somewhat guilty about his own very average child. Pic is steeped in the mood and Huxlian ideas of the period, with the Englishman's inner thoughts narrated off screen.

Eventually, after the Englishman starts developing the boy's talents, the expatriate family is obliged to move to Switzerland and the boy is taken charge of by an overbearing landowner who pines at never having had her own son. The Englishman, who has come to love the "little Archimedes" more than his own son, receives one brief, plaintive letter form the boy, pleading to be rescued. When the expatriate arrives it is too late. The boy is dead. He has fallen out of the window of his captors.

Though this is a slight film, the story is told with such perfectly balanced sensitivity as to make it a jewel. Laura Betti, as Madame Bondi, comes across beautifully, and the background of classical music and the subtlety of portrayals could make this a favorite for the discriminating few, rather than fodder as a mass market vehicle.
— *Besa.*

Le Rose Di Danzica
(The Roses of Danzig)
(ITALIAN-COLOR)

San Sebastian, Sept. 15.
A RAI Italian Radio-Television production. Written and directed by Alberto Bevilacqua. Camera (Eastmancolor), Giuseppe Aquari; music, Luis Bacalov; sets, Mario Molli; editor, Raimondo Crociani; exec producer, Filiberto Bandini. Reviewed at Cine Victoria Eugenia (San Sebastian), Sept. 14, '79. Running time: **110 MINS.**

Konrad Von Der Berg . . . . . . Franco Nero
Erich Von Lehner . . . . Helmut Berger
Margarethe Von Lehner . . . Olga Karlatos
Elvira Von Lehner . . . . Macha Meril
Herbert Von Lehner . . . . Roberto Posse
Klaus Von Knobelsdorff Franco Javarone
Jutta . . . . Eleonora Vallone
Col. Wilhelm Hossbach Gianrico Tondinelli

Confused, talky, turgid and overlong drama with so many twists and turns that most spectators will be lost half way through unless they've carefully read the synopsis first. Though Franco Nero occasionally comes alive as one of the German officers, Helmut Berger as the aristocratic soldier wanders in a daze through his part. Bevilacqua's helming doesn't help us out of the muddle, nor does the helter-skelter cutting.

Story is set in 1919 Germany when two opposing German military units are deciding the fate of the country. There are allusions to the birth of Nazism, the class struggle and the dominance of the bourgeoisie, all of it rather vague.

Most of pic concerns the meeting in a deserted military camp of the two officers, who have a love-hate relationship going for them. They mope about, talk a lot and are shown in flashbacks in former times. At length, the aristocratic scion is obliged to shoot his adversary through the head, but then returns to his home to take vengeance on the capitalistic-neo-fascist evil-doers and is in turn himself put to death.

It is difficult to see who this nearly two-hour long pretentious muddle could appeal to. As a video vehicle Nero and Berger as names might help in sales. —*Besa.*

The Rose
(COLOR)

Late-blooming, but could be a winner.

Hollywood, Oct. 5.
Twentieth Century-Fox release of a Marvin Worth/Aaron Russo production. Produced by Worth, Russo. Directed by Mark Rydell. Exec producer, Tony Ray. Stars Bette Midler, Alan Bates. Screenplay, Bill Kerby, Bo Goldman, based on a story by Kerby; camera (Color), Vilmos Zsigmond; editor, Robert L. Wolfe; production design, Richard MacDonald; costume design, Theoni V. Aldredge; music arrangements, Paul A. Rothchild; choreography, Toni Basil; art direction, Jim Schoppe; sound, (Dolby Stereo) Jim Webb, Chris McLaughlin; assistant director, Larry Franco. Reviewed at 20th Century-Fox Main Theatre, Century City, Oct. 5, '79. (MPAA Rating: R.) Running time: 134 MINS.

Rose . . . . Bette Midler
Rudge . . . . Alan Bates
Dyer . . . . :. . Frederic Forrest
Billy Ray . . . . Harry Dean Stanton
Dennis . . . . Barry Primus
Mal . . . . David Keith
Sarah . . . . Sandra McCabe
Mr. Leonard . . . . Will Hare
Monty . . . . Rudy Bond
Don Frank . . . . Don Calfa
Dealer . . . . James Keane
Emcee . . . . Michael Greer
Rose's Mother . . . . Doris Roberts
Rose's Father . . . . Sandy Ward

"The Rose" should do for Bette Midler what "Lady Sings The Blues" did for Diana Ross seven years ago: establish her as a first-rate dramatic actress, as well as a potent songstress. The future of the 20th Century-Fox release does not look quite so bright, however, since the film is a downbeat elegy to a rock singer on her last legs. Director Mark Rydell has delivered a lengthy and impassioned expose of the dark side of the music biz, but it's questionable to what degree contemporary audiences wish to identify with the subject matter.

Producers Marvin Worth and Aaron Russo (latter, until recently, Midler's manager) haven't flinched from picking the scabs off the body of 1960s rock and roll. While there are certainly similarities to the tragic story of the late Janis Joplin, "The Rose" emerges as its own self-contained tale.

What's puzzling is that screenwriters Bill Kerby and Bo Goldman have chosen to dwell solely on the downward career spiral of Midler's character, known on and offstage as The Rose. Given the leisurely pacing, audiences may wait in vain for flashbacks showing how Midler reached the heights from which she so precipitously tumbles. Instead, pic opens with a stoned-drunk Midler barely able to disembark from her private jet, and closes with the singer's onstage death. So much for the joys of rock 'n-roll.

It's a tribute to the talent of Midler herself that she makes a basically unsympathetic and unlikeable character attractive at all. Rose is like a willful, spoiled child, furious when she doesn't get her own way, and burdened with few compunctions about achieving her goal.

Thankfully, Midler imbues her with a desperate, child-like longing to flee the pressures of concerts, recording sessions and interviews, and manages to blend the contradictory aspects of the character into a personage audiences may love to hate.

Revolving around the star are various satellites, including boyfriend Frederic Forrest (superb, almost to the point of stealing Midler's thunder), manager Alan Bates, road manager Barry Primus, and other characters brought in to establish dramatic points.

Result is an ultra-realistic look at the infusion of money, sex, drugs and booze into the simple process of singing a song, a chore Midler does faultlessly in several excellent concert sequences, each of which stands out. And while the look of "The Rose" is more '70s than '60s, the message remains the same as in older showbiz films, such as "A Star Is Born." The urge to create is separated from the urge to destroy by a very fine line, and on that line, stardom precariously rests, until the inevitable happens.

Goldman and Kerby have done their best work with the Forrest character, a hayseed chauffeur who takes off with Midler on a one-night stand that blossoms into the thrush's first full-fledged relationship. There's a core of down-home reality in Forrest's performance that's missing from the rest of the characters, to the point where he should win most of the audience empathy.

Bates, however, seems somewhat miscast as the English manager, constantly backing Midler into a corner, until the pic points the finger of guilt for her death directly at him. Primus is okay as the roadie, David Keith registers strongly as a soldier-cum-bodyguard for Midler, Harry Dean Stanton has a cameo as a country-western star, and Sandra McCabe seems out of place as a lesbian intruder on the Midler-Forrest relationship.

When all is said and done, "The Rose" is a supreme Midler vehicle, one that should turn on an entirely new audience for her. As adept at dramaturgy as comedy, she projects a presence so volatile as to almost throw heat off the screen. And when Midler belts out the powerful "Stay With Me" as her literal swan song, "The Rose" captures the magic moment of pure tragedy.

Technically, it's a beautiful film, thanks to Vilmos Zsigmond's con-trolled, desaturated photography, Robert L. Wolfe's fluid cutting, Richard MacDonald's studied production design, and Theoni V. Aldredge's fitting costumes for Midler. Paul A. Rothchild has staged the concert sequences with distinction, and these represent Dolby stereo's finest hour, at least in terms of musical re-creation, thanks to super crisp production sound work of Jim Webb and Chris McLaughlin, aided by Dolby's Stephen Katz. Rest of below-the-line work is uniformly excellent.

"The Rose" should act as career boost for Midler, Forrest and Rydell, and given what was attempted, the accomplishment is impressive. However, the nagging question remains: why do we enjoy seeing bigger-than-life symbols self-destruct on our behalf. "The Rose" shows us the wherefore, but never takes on the why.
—Poll.

Schwestern, Oder Die Balance Des Gluecks
(Sisters, or The Balance of Happiness)
(WEST GERMAN-COLOR)

Hamburg, Sept. 18.
A Bioskop Film Production, Munich, Eberhard Junkersdorff, producer, in collaboration with Westdeutscher Rundfunk (WDR), Cologne, Gunther Witte, tv-editor-in-chief; world rights, Filmverlag der Autoren, Munich. Features entire cast. Directed by Margarete von Trotta. Screenplay, Trotta, with additions by Luisa Francia. Martje Grohmann, Jutta Lampe; camera (color), Franz Fath; editing, Annette Dorn; sound, Vladimir Vizner, Stanislav Litera; music, Konstantin Wecker; sets, Winfried Hennig; costumes, Ingrid Zore; lighting, Jockel Stellmacher; asst. director, Helenka Hummel. Reviewed at Hamburg Film Fest, Sept. 18, '79. Running time: 92 MINS.

Maria	Jutta Lampe
Anna	Gudrun Gabriel
Miriam	Jessica Frueh
Robert	Konstantin Wecker
Maurice	Rainer Delventhal
Mother	Agnes Fink
Muenzinger, Maria's Boss	Heinz Bennent
Fritz	Fritz Lichtenhahn
Professor	Guenther Schuetz
Blind Woman	Ilse Bahrs
Maria as Child	Barbara Sauerbaum
Anna as Child	Marie-Helene Diekmann
Frau Eder	Liselotte Arnold
Sister of Blind Woman	Editha Horn
Nurse Fritz	Ellen Esser
Porter	Heinrich Marmann
Language Teacher	Edith Garten
Flutist	Kathie Thomsen
Robert's College	Volker Schwab
Student	Dionysos Kawathas

For those who prefer "women's themes" directed by femme helmers, Margarete von Trotta's "Sisters, or the Balance of Happiness" should please backers and partial on-lookers, and pack-'em'-in at Women Film Fests and those cinemas catering to the Fair Sex.

For those who prefer complex social themes with rich, probing dialog and a flowing narrative style with "something to say," Trotta's "Sisters" falls flat on its collective psychology.

"The Balance of Happiness," pic's subtitle, gives all the secrets away at the beginning. Maria, the older sister, is an efficient secretary, a Girl Friday whom the boss can't do without, and who takes pride in her job and position. Anna, the younger sister, is a university student about to obtain her degree in biology, a sensitive girl financed in her studies by her older sister's money and sacrifices. Trotta lets us know at the outset that one girl's happiness is the other sister's success.

There's also a third "sister" — a down-to-earth creature at the office with boys on her mind and joie de vivre as her credo for getting along in the world. Miriam likes Maria, but is surprised when the boss's secretary fails to take notice of the advances made by the boss's son (whom Miriam also has her eyes on). The two become friends.

Then the younger sister, Anna, commits suicide because she can't cope with life anymore, perhaps also due to her emotional dependence on Maria. Maria is shaken, but needs another "sister" to keep her own life in balance — and thus courts the attention and friendship of Miriam. Miriam, however, reads the dead sister's diary and guesses she's headed in the same direction — unless she breaks off the relationship. She does, and Maria is now left alone in the world — but she has learned something, how to laugh or dream, Hope springs eternal.

The plus side of pic is the professional handiwork, for all the technical credits are tops. The three thesps are new to the screen, although Jutta Lampe as the cold, calculating Maria has a distinguished stage career behind her at Berlin's Schaubuehne am Halleschen Ufer — her star is definitely on the rise, as is Trotta's.

The minus is the too slick show of "tenderness," as though femme helmers have a priority on the "feeling" in filmmaking. By contrast, what works well in "Sisters" are the office scenes, an area Trotta herself appears to know better than the moments of intimacy. —Holl.

Le Mouton Noir
(The Black Sheep)
(FRENCH-COLOR)

Paris, Sept. 19.
A Parafrance release of a Sofracima/Golden International Production co-production. Features entire cast. Directed by Jean-Pierre Moscardo. Screenplay, Moscardo and Jean-Claude Heberle; camera (Eastmancolor), Pierre Dupouey; sound, Raymond Adam; editor, Martine Barraque; music, Georges Delerue. Reviewed at Ponthieu screening room, Paris, Sept. 17, '79. Running time: 98 MINS.

Vincent	Jacques Dutronc
Alice	Helene Rolles
George	Arthur Wilkins
Martha	Tanya Lopert
De Brugeres	Jean Desailly

The nonchalant, melancholy charm of actor-singer Jacques Dutronc is the chief asset in this undisciplined first film by Jean-Pierre Moscardo, former photographic reporter and tv cameraman who has been directing for television for the last 10 years.

Dutronc plays an ex-lawyer who has dropped out of society after failing to save the neck of one of his clients. As the film opens he returns to Paris hoping to reclaim his daughter, who is now living with his ex-wife's parents. To pry her loose from his former father-in-law's tight grasp he concocts a plan with one of his two friends, (an American couple who are trying to hold on to their restaurant in central Paris), which involves gaining access to the computers of the father-in-law's bank. In possession of some secret information, he puts pressure on his daughter's guardians to give up custody of the child.

There's a little bit of everything here but coherence and credibility. First, it's about a father and daughter, then it's about the difficulties of being Americans in Paris (the couple is played appealingly by Arthur Wilkins and Tanya Lopert), then it's a picaresque caper cmedy. There's no center. And Dutronc's character, though attractive, is never believable.

Moscardo's direction is okay, but he should find himself a scriptwriter for his next venture. —Len.

Kiri-no-hata
(Sweet Revenge)
(JAPANESE-COLOR)

Bangkok, Sept. 16.
Toho Co., Ltd. production and release. Produced by Takeo Hori and Hideo Sasai. Directed by Katsumi Nishikawa. Features entire cast. Story, Seicho Matsumoto; screenplay, Kei Hattori; camera (color), Yonezo Maeda; editor, Ko Suzuki; music and sound, Nobumasa Fukushima; art director, Teruyoshi Satani; asst. director, Tomozo Yamaguchi. Reviewed at 3d Japanese Film Festival at Siri Hall theatre, Bangkok, Sept. 15, '79. Running time: 95 MINS.

Kiriko Yanagida	Momoe Yamaguchi
Keiichi Abe	Tomokazu Miura
Kinzo Otuka	Rentaro Mikuni
Michiko Kono	Akiko Koyama
Kenji Sugiura	Yusuke Natsu
Nobuko Ebara	Miyuki Kojima

A thriller more on the psychological rather than suspenseful side, "Sweet Revenge" examines the effects of the refusal of a top defense lawyer (Rentaro Mikuni) to help a young woman (Momoe Yamaguchi) whose elder brother has been falsely accused of homicide. The accused commits suicide in prison. Yamaguchi becomes a waitress and later a bar girl.

Yamaguchi is convinced her brother would have been found innocent, if only she were rich and could afford to hire Mikuni to handle the case.

Sometimes when least expected, an opportunity for revenge comes along. This is exactly what happens when Yamaguchi becomes the unwitting witness to a murder, in which Mikuni's mistress, in turn, happens to be the main suspect.

In a calm but relentlessly vindictive mood, Yamaguchi plants solid evidence against the mistress, lies to the police that she had earlier agreed to serve as a witness for the accused and refuses to surrender a lighter, which is major evidence that may well help exonerate the mistress.

It's suggested she must pay a heavy price for her conduct, and she does. She rejects a marriage offer from a young reporter (Tomokazu Miura), who has been following her through both murder cases and develops a deep concern for her.

This "tooth for a tooth" fable set in modern Japan underscores the fact that materialism largely affects decision-making, and that one's place in society very often depends on one's available cash.

Mikuni's profound regret over not having assisted the girl comes closest to a genuine moment, when he mutters to himself that he was a much better lawyer when he worked for almost nothing.

Acting by the older stars, Mikuni and Akiko Koyama as the mistress, are outstanding. As the main protagonist, Yamaguchi exudes too much class.

Photography is innovative, and editing, especially in the sequence where Yamaguchi and Koyama are interrogated by the police separately, is very impressive. Music is used sparingly, opting for natural sounds in its place, often to good advantage. —Cano.

Johnny Larsen
(Johnny Larsen)
(DANISH-COLOR)

Copenhagen, Sept. 22.
An A/S Panorama (Just Betzer) production (wtih the State Film Institute) and release. Based loosely on the novels of John Neghm. Features entire cast. Directed by Morten Arnfred. Screenplay, Joergen Melgaard, Morten Arnfred; camera (Eastmancolor), Dirk Bruel; Production design, Palle Nybo Arestrup; costumes, Gitte Kolvig, Manon Rasmussen; editor, Anders Refn; music, Toots Thielemans, Kaspar Winding, Ole Arnfred; executive producer, Lars Kolvig; production manager, Per Aaman. Reviewed at Ankerstjerne Film Laboratories, Copenhagen, Sept. 21, 1979. Running time: 105 MINS.
Johnny Larsen .... Allan Olsen
His father ....,.. Frits Helmuth
His mother .... Hanne Ribens
His grandmother ..... Berthe Quistgaard
His grandfather .... Karl Stegger
Britta .... Elsebeth Nielsen
The Blacksmith .... Sven Hansson
Hans .... Ole Meyer

"Johnny Larsen," without opting for the greater epic scale, in a friendly, easy-going, very Danish way succeeds in being an almost Ermanno Olmi-like period panorama with a clear yet never preachy workers' outlook.

Based by writer-director Morten Arnfred on John Nehm's suite of novels, story is centered on events during six months of 1952 in the life of the title's young man who is just venturing into a worker's adult life at a time of war or war-like stirrings abroad and of extreme insecurity on the labor market at home.

This young Johnny (played with sensitivity, humor and intelligence by Allan Olsen, a semi-pro who lives up beautifully to the cast's long list of pros who then tune down their offerings to rhyme with Olsen's more subdued ones) is a bit of a timid soul, it might seem, but soon he emerges as both tough and defiant when open injustice towards himself or others is committed.

Not much happens to Johnny. Except that we virtually see him grow up in this short span of time during which he experiences life as an unskilled worker, life as an unemployed laborer, the crumbling of socialist ideals within the older generations of his closest family, budding love and an inspiration to realize himself as a man of self-esteem. He even has a brief career as a volunteer in the Army and gets in trouble there.

There is no attempt at plot, but director Arnfred and his crew and cast manage to load each little sequence with solid dramatic impact and to connect them into a gliding, smooth, very musical rhythm. "Johnny Olsen" has about it much of the warm humanity and humor that once established young Czech feature films on the world market. Worldwide marketing of "Johnny Larsen" will not be the easiest of jobs, but via festival situations, sales could be expected wherever truly beautifully made features have a market at all.
—Kell.

Biarritz Fest

Pais Portatil
(Portable Country)
(VENEZUELAN-COLOR)

Biarritz, Sept. 27.
Ficciones C.A. production. Written and directed by Ivan Feo and Antonio Llerandi, based on novel by Adriano Gonzalez Leon. Camera (Eastmancolor), Hector Rios; sets, Tony Sanchez, Lesbia Hernandez, Alvaro Rodriguez, Miguel Corzo; music, Chuchito Sanoja; editors, Alberto Torija and Antonio Llerandi. Reviewed at Casino Cinema, Biarritz, Sept. 26, '79. Running time: 103 MINS.
Delia .... Alejandra Pinedo
Salvador Barazarte ... Hector Duvachelle
Andres Barazarte .... Ivan Feo
Leon Perfecto Barazarte .. Eliseo Perera
Ernestina Barazarte .... Silvia Santelices
Nicolasito Barazarte .... Eduardo Gil
Jose Eladio Barazarte .... Ibsen Martinez

This film has a lot going for it: fine thesping, good production values, exotic settings. But yarn is so jumbled that it becomes a temporal puzzle, with often bewildering flashbacks to the turn of the century, 1925, 1933, present, etc. It all comes together at the end, but some may not have patience to sit through lengthy monologs more apt for legit than cinema.

Pic traces three generations of a revolutionary family in the Venezuelan backlands, their sometime victories, political and personal failures and the final demise in what is presented as a hopeless long-term political situation.

In choppy flashbacks, the yarn tells of the last scion of the family who travels on a bus to his rendezvous and an ultimate shoot-out with the police. In final scenes his ancestors reappear with silent symbolism to pass him the ammunition.

Message seems to be that despite the futility of revolutionary efforts, one must carry on, or perhaps that the scion must avenge the failures of his forebears.

Story is too disjointed to effectively make its point. However, some interest may be generated at selected art house and campus circuits. —Besa.

Comedia Rota
(Broken Comedy)
(ARGENTINE-COLOR)

Biarritz, Sept. 29.
Nuevo Cine productores Cinematograficies Asociados film. Written and directed by Oscar Barney Finn, based on story by Julia Von Grolman. Camera (Eastmancolor), Alberto Basail; sets, Aldo Guglielmone; editor, Antonio Ripoli. Reviewed at Casino Cinema, Biarritz, Sept. 28, '79. Running time: 114 MINS.
Cast: Julia Von Grolman, Gianni Lunadei, Elsa Daniel, Ignacio Quiros, Darwin Sanchez, Elena Tasito, Monica Escudero.

Static meller with thesping and direction so stilted and script so pretentiously banal as to make it a veritable ordeal for public. At the screening here, during some of its many talky and embarrassingly self-conscious scenes, parts of audience broke into laughter.

Tale concerns the lives and loves of the bored Argentinian upper classes, their marital problems, always presented in a tragic key, and how they kill their time by talking and striking dramatic poses. The pouting and plangent poor little rich girl (played by Julia von Grolman who is also partly responsible for the script) has a psycho mother, a conservative father and a married lover. Enter Pablo, a "writer" and "intellectual" who, despite his rather affected mannerisms, opens a "new world of love and culture" to the girl.

He's working on the Great Argentinian Novel and perks his ears at classical hi-fi music. At the end of nearly two hours of melodrama and the striking of poses, the girl destroys his novel, he kills her dog and the mother attempts suicide. But there's a happy ending as the lovers make up and fly off to Rome together. Commercial outlook nil.
—Besa.

A Confederacao —
O Povo E Que Faz A
Historia
(The Confederation — The People Make History)
(PORTUGUESE-COLOR-16m)

Biarritz, Sept. 29.
Cinequanon production, financed by the Institut Portuges de Cinema and Calouste Gulbenkian. Directed by Luis Galvao Teles. Screenplay, Amadeu Lopes Sabibo, Luis Galvao Teles; camera (color-16m), Elso Roque; music, Sergio Godinho-Fausto, Jose Maria Branco; editor, Glara Diaz-Berrio. Reviewed at Cinema Casino, Biarritz, Sept. 28, '79. Running time: 105 MINS.
Cast: Margarida Carpinteiro, Carlos Cabral, Irene Ruivo, Jorge Cortes, Luis Santos, Jorge Vale, Artur Semedo, Santos Manuel, Ricardo Pais, Orlando Costa.

Even the otherwise patient French audiences at Biarritz were fleeing the theatre during this overlong, self-indulgent and amateurish pic. There's a good deal of talk about idealism and revolution and "the people," with the post-1975 armed forces cast as the heavies.

No story to speak of, only disjointed episodes, many of them supposedly symbolic; a few pointless sex scenes and lotsa talk, talk, talk. Anyone sitting through this should be given an endurance award. —Besa.

As Horas De Maria
(Maria's Hours)
(PORTUGUESE-COLOR)

Biarritz, Sept. 29.
Cinequanon production. Written and directed by Antonio de Macedo. Camera, (color-16m), Elso Roque. Reviewed at Casino Cinema, Biarritz, Sept. 28, '79. Running time: 105 MINS.
Cast: Cecilia Giumaraes, Eugenia Bettencourt, Joao d'Avila.

First half of this pic seems to show some promise. An empty clinic, seemingly in ruins, where one doctor holes up, a domineering nun and a blind girl who has passed through various unspeakable traumas are the ingredients for what might have been a good psychological drama with the shrink unraveling the girl's past. Some of the early scenes seem to point in that direction.

Unfortunately, however, helmer-scripter Antonio de Macedo goes off on a tangent and serves up seemingly pointless scenes of miracle-seekers in Fatima and the re creation of Biblical scenes illustrating the doctor's pet heretical theories in which Christ is cast as an anarchist subversive and revolutionary.

The girl's trauma is meanwhile never really explained. Her religious faith remains unshaken as she dies with sudden mysterious symbolism and for no obvious reason as the nun, who is also her aunt, reads a service for the dead. Thesping is good throughout, but technical quality often poor. Too slow and ultimately confused to generate any commercial interest. —Besa.

Meteor
(COLOR)

Horror on wholesale. Effects good. Characters wooden. B.o. promise strong.

Flagstaff, Oct. 13.

An American International release. Produced by Arnold Orgolini, Theodore Parvin. Exec producers, Sandy Howard, Gabriel Katzka. Directed by Ronald Neame. Stars Sean Connery, Natalie Wood, Karl Malden, Brian Keith. Screenplay, Stanley Mann, Edmund H. North, based on a story by North; camera (color), Paul Lohmann' editor, Carl Kress; production design, Edward Carfagno; art direction, David Constable; set decoration, Barbara Krieger; music, Laurence Rosenthal; sound, Jack Solomon; special effects, Glen Robinson, Robert Steaples; assistant director, Daniel J. McCauley. Reviewed at University Twin Theatre, Flagstaff, Ariz., Oct. 12, '79. (MPAA Rating: PG.) Running time: **103 MINS.**

Bradley	Sean Connery
Tatiana	Natalie Wood
Sherwood	Karl Malden
Dubov	Brian Keith
Adlon	Martin Landau
Sir Michael Hughes	Trevor Howard
Sec. of Defense	Richard Dysart
The President	Henry Fonda
Easton	Joseph Campanella

Since the disaster genre seems to have exhausted its earthly appeal, "Meteor" takes the next logical step and moves the action to outer space. Despite a story that stretches scientific credibility, and a lack of the emotional sub-plots that were a hallmark of previous "ark" pix, "Meteor" looks to have a glowing commercial future.

The special effects are frequent and impressive, the cast is distinguished and audiences should respond enthusiastically. Foreign biz should be especially good, and domestically, American International ought to continue its current hot streak.

"Meteor" really combines several disasters in one continuous cinematic bummer. Along with the threat of a five mile wide asteroid speeding towards earth, with smaller splinters preceding it, there's an avalanche, an earthquake, a tidal wave and a giant mud bath. All in all, special effects wizards Glen Robinson and Robert Staples, along with stunt coordinator Roger Greed, got a good workout.

Inevitably, topliners Sean Connery as an American scientist, Brian Keith as his Soviet counterpart, and Natalie Wood as the translator in between them, take a back seat to the effects. Director Ronald Neame has attempted to infuse as much life as possible into the characters created by coscripters Stanley Mann and Edmund H. North, but its a hopeless task.

While the acting is uniformly good (Keith, especially, adds sparkle to a caricatured role), and Mann and North have avoided the ludicrous dialog that characterized previous disaster films, something still seems missing from "Meteor." The Connery-Wood relationship, which holds much promise, is given short shift, and a romantic sub-plot between James Richardson and Katherine Dehetre is all but eliminated in the final version.

But cutting out the goo, Neame apparently failed to put anything in its place, and result is the principals mostly stand around waiting for the next calamity to happen. It's a waste of some talented (and well-paid) performers, since Connery's blunt and blustery character is rarely given a chance to open up. Ditto Wood's intelligent and attractive linguist.

What really matters to audiences for this kind of film, of course, is not the acting, but the visuals, and here, "Meteor" gets good, but not great, grades. The outer space machinations are characterized by excellent miniature work, as American and Soviet missiles on orbiting satellites are trained toward the approaching meteor, rather than their respective enemies.

Avalanche sequence is one of the best in memory, aided by the fact that producers Arnold Orgolini and Theodore Parvin were allowed to blow up a mountain in the Swiss Alps. But sloppy matte work undercuts the credibility of the tidal wave smashing Hong Kong, and the sequence where half of New York is sheared off (a development that may bring cheers in the Hinterlands) is quickly glossed over. Other tech credits are okay, although Laurence Rosenthal's score seems overdone.

Martin Landau is quite good in support as a paranoid, militaristic general, and Karl Malden adds some energy as a Washington bureaucrat on Connery's side. Trevor Howard and Henry Fonda add distinguished cameo appearances.

Complex financial history of "Meteor" has been well documented, and explains the plethora of presentation credits, with Gabriel Katzka having stimulated the Cannes financing, Run Run Shaw responsible for a portion of the budget, and Sandy Howard the overall tie up.

"Meteor" also boasts the "Star Wars" type crawl, de rigueur for any space-located feature, and a little pre-credits mini science lesson, which seems unduly academic.
—Poll.

Traellenes oproer
(Revolt of the Thralls)
(DANISH-COLOR)

Copenhagen, Oct. 9.

A Traellenes Boern (Ebbe Preisler) production and release. Based on Sven Wernstroem's novels. A cartoon feature with Jannik Hastrup as chief artist/animator. Voices, Berthe Quistgaard, Otto Brandenburg, Ove Sprogoe, Poul Thomsen, Birgit Bruel, Jesper Klein; music, Benny Holst, Anders Koppel, Peter Bastian; executive producer, Ebbe Preisler; editor, Jon Bille Brahe. Reviewed at Palads, Copenhagen, Oct. 5, 1979. Running time, **90 MINS.**

"Revolt of the Thralls" is part two of a cartoon feature trilogy to be completed during May, 1980. The technique employed by Jannik Hastrup has cardboard figures with movable parts moving over fixed backgrounds. This makes for slightly jerky movements, but generally the cartoon production values are of high standard.

Hastrup and his team have based their retelling of Scandinavian history of the Ancient and Middle Ages on Swedish author Sven Wernstroem's juvenile novels and totally retained the books' Marxist viewpoints in telling all events as seen from the tralls', the workers', the rural proletariat's point of view.

This makes for rather dogmatic entertainment, often quite preachy (with running commentaries spoken by an ever-present crow), but at the same time the episodes (three in each of the trilogy's films) brim with blood-curling violence and even some graphically described sex.

Trilogy, a Danish achievement made financially possible with the aid of the Danish Film Institute, The State Film Central of Denmark plus Sweden's Radio/TV Channel 2, will surely find its way across many borders either in locally subtitled or post-synched versions.

Television purchases seem more likely than theatrical releases, even though series' sequences of violence have made Swedish TV impose self-censorship by banning a work of which it is economic cosponsor. Film will, however, get a Swedish theatrical release through Folkets Bio —Kell.

Alison's Birthday
(AUSTRALIAN-COLOR)

Sydney, Oct. 3.

A Filmways-Australasian Distributors Release of an Australian Film Commission-Fontana Films presentation of the javid Hannay Production. Produced by David Hannay. Written and directed by Ian Coughlan. Stars Joanne Samuel and Lou Brown. Exec. producers, Ric Kabriel and John Sturzaker; camera (color), Kevan Lind; lighting director, Brian Bansgrove; editing, Timothy Street; sound, Phil Judd; music, Brian King, Alan Oloman; production design, Robert Hildritch; assistant director, Michael Falloon. Reviewed at Palm Beach Screening Room, Sydney, Sept. 20, '79. Running time: **95 MINS.**

Alison Findlay	Joanne Samuel
Chrissie Willis	Margie McCrae
Mr. Martin	Martin Vaughan
Maggie Carlyle	Rosalind Speirs
Helen McGill	Robyn Gibbes
Pete Healey	Lou Brown
Dave Ducker	Ian Coughlan

If writer-director-actor Ian Coughlan (who also wrote one of the musical themes) had sustained the chill and shock of his opening sequences in "Alison's Birthday," it would indeed have been a remarkable film. Sad to say he doesn't, and the resulting footage borders on a reasonably average possession-by-another-spirit film; an antipodeal reading of the "Rosemary's Baby" theme with the posessee coming of age at 19.

Kevan Lind's lensing relies a great deal on wide-angle optics, and when the effect is good it is very good, but when it's not you notice.

Coughlan needs to learn economy in the story-telling department; the immediate post credit sequences are highly expositional and tend toward the verbal. This is a scripting weakness shared by a number of other Aussie writer-directors, though it can't be construed as an excuse.

Flaws in structure and pace should have been ironed out before the camera rolled, but as is often the case Down Under, when budgets get trimmed it is invariably in the area of pre-production. Most often this is due to the anxiety of the Aussie filmmaker to get into production before something happens to thwart him or her yet again.

Performances have less of a cinematic presentation than that strange half-life that exists between stage and big screen which, together with the other production elements give an impression of big-screen tv to the interiors. However, the "Stonehenge" sequence, evidently shot at night, has an evocative eeriness about the light that is fine.

There are moments of the film in which the guignol elements are well handled, and could well elicit an audience's collective response that would carry over the troughs. In retrospect, there seems to be too few of them to retain the momentum, more's the pity.

Alison's aunt and uncle are too falsely nice, too anxious to please and look after her and cosset and protect her that even the most innocent 19-year-old would feel no reason to "stay for her birthday," however emotionally-black-mailing the entreaties. Alison's rejection of their effusive affection is the pivot on which the plot hangs and Coughlan muffs his chance by damping her ambivalence with drugs administered by a doctor in on their scheme and as anxious as

they are to set the eponymous heroine up as the next cult leader.

Pic's pacing and temp are admirably suited to television where the structured highs can be used to bridge the commercial breaks, and where the smaller dimension necessarily reduces such plot and production hang-nails that exist and snag the eye in a larger format. Nil nudity or other exploitation elements exist to make this anything other than fair home fare. —Miha.

The Black Stallion
(DRAMA-COLOR)

A beautiful picture. Big potential with all age groups.

Hollywood, Oct. 9.
A United Artists release. Produced by Fred Roos, Tom Sternberg. Directed by Carroll Ballard. Executive producer, Francis Coppola. Screenplay, Melissa Mathison, Jeanne Rosenberg, William D. Wittliff, based on the novel by Walter Farley; camera (Technicolor), Caleb Deschanel; editor, Robert Dalva; music, Carmine Coppola; art directors, Aurelio Crugnola, Earl Preston; assistant director, Doug Claybourne. Reviewed at Samuel Goldwyn Studios, Hollywood, Oct. 9, 1979. MPAA rating: G. Running time: 118 MINS.
Alec Ramsey . . . . Kelly Reno
Henry Dailey . . . . Mickey Rooney
Alec's Mother . . . . Teri Garr
Snoe . . . . Clarence Muse
Alec's Father . . . . Hoyt Axton
Neville . . . . Michael Higgins
Jake . . . . Ed McNamara
Arab . . . . Dogmi Larbi
Jockey No. 1 . . . . John Burton
Jockey No. 2 . . . . .John Buchanan
Becky . . . . Kristen Vigard
Rescue Captain . . . . Fausto Tozzi
The Black Stallion . . . . Cass-ole

"The Black Stallion" is a perfect gem — the beautiful craftsmanship alone makes it thrilling to behold. Based on Walter Farley's 1941 novel, which spawned 16 sequels, Carroll Ballard's feature debut is rich in adventure, suspense and mythical elements and marks the prize-winning short subjects director as a major talent. A considerable achievement for all concerned, film could emerge as a major attraction for all audiences with intelligent handling by UA.

Despite their perennial popularity throughout the world, Farley's "Black Stallion" books have never before been adapted for the screen. Marvel of the screenplay by Melissa Mathison, Jeanne Rosenberg and William D. Wittliff is that it does not for a moment descend to maudlin sentimentality or horsy hokum, emerging instead as one of the most rigorously intelligent scripts about a child and animals ever attempted.

Lion's share of the credit, however, must go to Ballard. He, like George Lucas, got his shot at feature directing through the sponsorship of his former UCLA classmate Francis Coppola, here serving as exec producer.

Most of his justly praised short pix, such as "Pigs," "The Perils of Priscilla," shot from a cat's p.o.v., and "Rodeo," have dealt with animals, and his sensitivity to the beautiful steed's grace of movement, nervous reactions to humans and even breathing rhythms is just one of the factors that lifts the picture far above standard works in this genre.

Ballard's camera eye and powers of sequence conceptualization are manifestly extraordinary.

Set in 1949, pic is divided into four basic sections, each memorable in its own right, although a consistent tone prevails throughout.

Opening sees the American boy Alec on a ship with his amiable father. Also on board is "the Black," stallion owned by a menacing Arab. A nocturnal shipwreck is created in shocking bursts of fire, movement and alarming sound, sequence in itself being a masterpiece of film editing.

After both end up overboard, Alec and the horse find sanctuary on a deserted Mediterranean island, filmed on unusual Sardinian locations. Ensuing half hour, in which the two gradually make contact, establish rapport and become horse and rider, is pulled off completely without dialog, backed instead by Carmine Coppola's richly complementary score.

After rescue, and almost an hour into pic, focus shifts Stateside. Alec's mother, played by Teri Garr, naturally doesn't understand her son's now nearly symbiotic relationship with Black. Horse escapes its backyard confinement, later to be found by the boy at farm of retired racehorse trainer Mickey Rooney.

Grooming of Alec into a jockey is solidly conveyed in an understated manner, while fourth act is consumed by Black's entry into a match race as a "mystery horse" against the two fastest horses of the day. Race itself is a stunner, full of suspense and marvelously covered by an array of moving cameras and subjective shots.

Ballard's occasional stressing of the mythical aspects of human-horse relationship is intrinsic and never pretentious, and even his penchant for nearly metaphysical lyricism in the Sardinian section never intervenes at the expense of narrative.

The power of nature and the elements are at times terrifyingly palpable, thanks not only to Caleb Deschanel's extraordinary camerawork but to the Dolby sound, use of which is subtle but powerful when needed.

Performances are all lowkeyed and right on pitch. As Alec, Kelly Reno's freckled face is offset by the toughness of a survivor and obstinance of a winner, which he con-

veys perfectly. Not only that, but the kid can really ride.

Rooney is excellent, notably when he confides certain tricks of the jockey's trade, and Clarence Muse and Hoyt Axton, as an elderly horse watcher and Alec's father, respectively, have some fine, warm moments.

Teri Garr is stuck with the least sympathetic role, as she for a while stands in the way of Alec achieving his dream of racing, but still hits the right notes.

Not enough can be said for the performance of the horse, Cass-ole, under the guidance of trainer Corky Randall and stunt coordinator Glenn (J.R.) Randall. If horses can still become stars, a la Trigger and Champion, this one belongs right up there with them.

Film went into production over two years ago and is said to have experienced numerous problems along the way. Whatever they might have been, they've all been ironed out, as resultant picture is one of the most exquisite and entirely satisfying to have come along in quite some time. —Cart.

Brasilia Fest

Contos Eroticos
(Erotic Stories)
(BRAZILIAN-COLOR)

Brasilia, Sept. 30.
Lynxfilm e Editora Tres production. Directed by Roberto Santos, Roberto Palmari, Eduardo Escorel, Joaquim Pedro de Andrade. Features entire cast. Screenplays, Sergio Toni, Yara Ramos Ribeiro, Aercio Flavio·Consolin, Pedro Maia Soares; camera (color), Marcelo Primavera, Geraldo Gabriel, Miguel Parente, Kimihiko Kato. Reviewed at the Brasilia Film Fest, Sept. 29, 1979. Running time: 100 MINS.
Cast: Joana Fomm, David Jose, Carmen Silva, Lima Duarte, Liza Vieira, Castro Gonzaga, Claudio Cavalcanti, Christina Ache, Carlos Galhardo.
(Portuguese Soundtrack)

Despite the suggestive title, the only section of this four sequence feature that is truly erotic is the final one. "O Arremate" does get a little rough, but even it could be tampered with a bit so that the entire film could be successfully exported. The first three stories range from sly to uproarious in their humorous approaches to would-be libidinous themes.

Roberto Santos' "Arroz E Feijao" (Rice and Beans) is Italian in style in its tale of an oversexed housewife (whose husband is more interested in his job than his marital duties) and her reaction to a young student who comes for lunch. The style is broad and uproarious. More subtle but with a surprising denouement is Roberto Palmari's "As 3 Virgens". (The Three Virgins), which has a young girl, who has been "naughty," sent to live with three virgin aunts. When they realize they can't convert her to spinsterhood they come up with a much better solution, to everyone's delight.

Joaquin Pedro de Andrade's "Vereda Tropical" could have been tasteless in less skilled hands but his funny story of a young student who makes love to vegetables because he can't afford girls has the best closing scene of the entire feature. Eduardo Escorel's "O Arremate" is pure exoticism with some rather graphic photography which may have accounted for the fact that the film is still banned in Brazil.

—*Robe.*

O Caso Claudia
(The Claudia Case)
(BRAZILIAN-COLOR)

Brasilia, Sept. 24.
Artenova Films Ltda. production. Directed by Miguel Borges. Features entire cast. Screenplay, Valerio Meinel, Jose Louzeiro, Miguel Borges, Alvaro Pacheco; camera (color), Renato Neumann; music, Remo Usai. Reviewed at the Brasilia Film Festival, Brasilia, Sept. 23, 1979. Running time: 110 MINS.
Cast: Katia D'Angelo, Carlos Eduardo Dollabela, Roberto Bonfim, Nuno Leal Maia, Jonas Bloch, Luiz Armando Queiroz, Claudio Correa e Castro.
(Portuguese Soundtrack)

Based on a real-life case, Miguel Borges' "The Claudia Case" was easily the most commercial film in the recent festival of Brazilian films held here and was, concurrently with the fest, showing at three Rio cinemas. This may be the reason why it did not fare well in the prize selections although, technically, it was superior to the other entries.

Using the authentic case of a girl murdered because of her knowledge (real or supposed?) of movements by high crime figures with whom she had become acquainted, Borges goes on and introduces other similar murders which are fictional. Shot against both the jet-set society and the working-class backgrounds of a Brazilian city (presumably Rio), the film is stunningly photographed by Renato Neumann and given a fast pace by the director.

With proper dubbing and promotion, it has sales possibilities outside the assured Brazilian market. Cast, generally unknown to foreign markets, is excellent in what really are stereotypes. Some scenes of violence could be shortened.

—*Robe.*

Jesus
(COLOR)

Somewhere between Jeff Hunter and Max von Sydow.

Hollywood, Oct. 3.
A Warner Bros. release of a Genesis Project production. Produced by John Heyman. Features entire cast. Directed by Peter Sykes, John Kirsh. Screenplay, Barnet Fishbein, based on the Gospel of Luke; associate producer, Richard Dalton; costumes, Rochelle Zaltzman. No other credits available. Reviewed at the Doheny Plaza Theatre, Beverly Hills, Oct. 2, 1979. (MPAA Rating: G.) Running time: 117 MINS.
Jesus	Brian Deacon
Mary	Rivka Noiman
Joseph	Yossef Shiloah
Simon Peter	Niko Nitai
Andrew	Gadi Rol
James	Itzhak Ne'eman
John	Shmuel Tal
Philip	Kobi Assaf
Bartholomew	Michael Varshaviak
Matthew	Mosko Alkalai
Thomas	Nisim Gerama
James,	
Son of Alphaeus	Leonid Weinstein
Simon Zelotes	Rafi Milo
Judas,	
Son of James	David Goldberg
Judas Iscariot	Eli Danker
John the Baptist	Eli Cohen
Mary Magdalene	Talia Shapira
Herod	Richard Peterson
Simon the Pharisee	Miki Mfir
Pontius Pilate	Peter Frye
Narrator	Alexander Scourby

"Jesus," clearly made by the devout principally for the already converted, is a Classic Comics version of the oft-told tale. Professionally made by individuals whose identities are nowhere to be seen on screen, film skims through the Saviour's life more quickly and superficially than most precious versions, hitting all the high spots, but leaving little time for contemplation or depth of character. Result will undoubtedly please those who have made up their minds to like it ahead of time. Warners and Inspirational Films are already tapping heavily into that crowd. Others will just stay away.

Produced by John Heyman, who founded The Genesis Project in 1974, and adapted faithfully from the Gospel of Luke, pic was lensed in Israel, with country's citizens filling nearly every role except the lead, on a $6,000,000 budget.

Tone is established immediately with a heavy dose of narration, reverential swells of music and "inspirational" shots of sunlight blessing the proceedings. Things settle down a bit once the adult Jesus is introduced.

As executed, it's a pageant of events more than anything else. Version intentionally walks a straight and narrow road, exploring neither the political nor social contexts a la Pasolini and Rossellini, not tempting to match the visual splendor Nicholas Ray's or George Stevens' versions, and fall-

ing far short of the emotional and religious power of the recent telling, Franco Zeffirelli's "Jesus Of Nazareth."

At the same time, it's not badly done. Production values and, crucially, sound recordings are professional, nothing craftsmen and technicians wouldn't want to have their names connected with. Although being kept under wraps for now, further credits will be revealed at the end of the year to meet requirements of the Academy.

Brian Deacon makes a good Jesus, not as charismatic as Robert Powell but strong, determined, sure of himself. His line readings, which betray a soft English accent, are crisp and clear and assertedly contain not a word not included in the Bible itself. Other roles amount to little more than walk-ons.

If this film is successful, The Genesis Project, which publishes the New Media Bible, plans to produce a whole slate of religious-themed pix.—*Cart.*

Killer Fish
(ITALIAN-BRAZILIAN-COLOR)

Exploits Brazilian river piranha. Late in mother nature horror cycle.

Hollywood, Oct. 12.
An Associated Film Distribution release of a Carlo Ponti/Filmar Do Brasil, Fawcett-Majors production. Produced by Alex Ponti. Executive producers, Olivier Perroy, Turi Vasile, Enzo Barone. Directed by Anthony M. Dawson (Antonio Margheriti). Features entire cast. Screenplay, Michael Rogers; camera (color), Alberto Spagnoli; editor, Roberto Sterbini; music, Guido, Maurizio De Angelis; art direction, Francesco Bronzi; costumes, Adriana Berselli; underwater sequences, Herbert V. Theiss; assistant directors, Michel Salliouti, Guiseppe Pollini. Reviewed at CBS Studio Center, Studio City, Oct. 17, '79. (MPAA Rating: PG). Running time: 101 MINS.
Robert Lasky	Lee Majors
Kate Neville	Karen Black
Paul Diller	James Franciscus
Gabrielle	Margaux Hemingway
Ann	Marisa Berenson
Tom	Gary Collins
Ollie	Roy Brocksmith
Hans	Dan Pastorini
Warren Bailey	Frank Pesce
Lloyd Bailey	Charlie Guardino
Max. Ship Captain	Anthony Steffen

(English Soundtrack)
Made in Brazil as "Treasure Of The Piranha" by Lew Grade's ITC, "Killer Fish" is a slap-dash actioner which casts its rod in water so overfished of late that it's amazing anything was still down there biting. But piranha apparently have inexhaustible appetites, and so does anyone who goes out of his way to see this after all the other nasty fish pictures of recent years. Prospects certainly look better overseas than domestically.

Pic is one of the most perfectly

cast in a long time: Lee Majors toplines as a macho tough guy, Karen Black plays an hysterical neurotic, Margaux Hemingway turns up as a fashion model and Marisa Berenson didn't have to take acting lessons to play a haughty aristocratic type. All seem eminently believable in their roles.

Assuredly hard pressed to come up with a new plot line involving underwater marauders and obliged as well to provide doses of action on cue, scripter Michael Rogers went back to one of the classics, "The Treasure Of The Sierra Madre," in concocting a tale of mutual suspicion among a group that's stolen a priceless collection of gems from a Latin American industrial concern.

Evil henchman James Franciscus' trick to bump off his collaborators is to dump the rocks in a lake he's populated with the hungry fishies. One by one, as the untrust-worthy gang members try to sneak down to recover the loot, they're eaten up, in increasingly gory fashion. Climax sees a whole boatload of the remaining stars stranded in the lake on a sinking ship, with the little buggers nipping away at their feet as the water level rises.

Direction of Anthony M. Dawson (aka Antonio Margheriti) is nothing if not energetic, and the special effects brigade has provided several spectacular explosions of an oil refinery, a bursting dam and even a tornado. Alberto Spagnoli's photography is very sharp and attractive, while Guido and Maurizio De Angelis' music is the loud sort one might expect to find in an Italian disco. — *Cart.*

Mountain Family Robinson
(COLOR)

Same mixture as before — and the same b.o.

Pacific International Enterprises release of an Arthur R. Dubs production. Executive producer, Fred R. Krug. Features entire cast. Written and produced by Arthur R. Dubs. Directed by John Cotter. Camera (CFI), James Roberson. No other technical credits provided. Music, Robert O. Ragland; lyrics, Carol Connors; songs performed by Dann Rogers. Reviewed at Columbia Pictures Screening Room, New York, Oct. 19, 1979. (MPAA Rating-G) Running time: 100 MINS.
Cast: Robert F. Logan, Susan Damante Shaw, William Bryant, Heather Rattray, Ham Larsen, George (Buck) Flower.

One wonders in how many more seasons Arthur R. Dubs can continue making the same picture over and over. If you saw "The Wilderness Family" you've seen the whole series, including this most recent version, "Mountain Family Robinson."

It still offers the same gorgeous scenery, most of it the Rockies in Colorado, the same excellent color photography, the same cast (with the only switch a new "villain" each time), and the same ridden-with-cliches script. Can a modern family, all disgustingly healthy, find happiness by returning to the bosom of nature? They've certainly been trying long enough.

The series has now reached the point where the regular filmgoer can predict the outcome of each new scene — Boomer will have a run-in with Samson, the bear; the wife (Susan Damante Shaw) will have her brief period of neuroticism and want to go home — she'll be back on the next plane, etc.

Still amazingly good, in addition to that stunning scenery, is the way the cast works with wild animals. Not since Bill Travers and Virginia McKenna domesticized Elsa and her brood of lion cubs has a group of professional actors seemed so at home with bears, mountain lions, bobcats and other denizens of the forest.

One touch of modernity, is an outdoor whirl-pool bath with everyone except old dad in there, au naturel. The editing is erratic with scenes unresolved, some nervous cutting that on occasion gets a bit irritating. But if nature is your bag, this picture will be, also. —Robe.

Stilleben
(Still Life)
(SWISS-B&W)
Zurich, Oct. 14.

Filmpool Zurich release of a Cinemonde Zurich production. Written and directed by Elisabeth Gujer. Features entire cast. Camera (black and white), Rob Gnant, Werner Zuber, editor. Uli Meier; sound. Hans Toni Aschwanden. Reviewed at the Studio Frosch, Zurich, Oct. 13. '79. Running time: 70 MINS.

Cast: Margrit Winter, Hans Heinz Moser, Elmar Schulte, Maja Stolle, Peter Oehme, Wolfram Berger. Ernst Baechi, Rodi Nater, Heinz Trudel, Robert Boner, Hedy Knorr, Lo de Fleury, Bouallala Riad, Johann Schaad.

"Still Life," the first feature film by a Swiss woman director, Elisabeth Gujer, concerns a fiftyish widow's efforts to remodel her life and change her bleak, meaningless existence. A temporary relationship with a middle-aged antique dealer, whose vitality seems to strike a responsive chord in her, soon tapers off due to mutual incompatibility.

Gujer's austere style, with mostly short, often chopped-off sequences, insert titles and a spoken commentary or "inner dialog," discourages any involvement. This — probably intentional — alienation effect leads to a chilling atmosphere. There is no place for human warmth or real sympathy—Mezo.

Courage Fuyons
(Courage, Let's Run For It)
(FRENCH-COLOR)

Paris, Oct. 10.

A Gaumont release of a La Gueville/Gaumont International coproduction. Produced by Alain Poire and Yves Robert. Stars Jean Rochefort, Catherine Deneuve. Directed by Yves Robert. Screenplay, Robert, Jean-Loup Dabadie; camera (color), Yves Lafaye; editor, Pierre Gillette; sound, Alain Sempe; art director, Jean-Pierre Gillette; sound, Alain Sempe; art director, Jean-Pierre Kohut Svelko; costumes, Christian Gasc; with artistic collaboration of Frantz Salieri and Laurent Petitgirard. Reviewed at Club 13, Paris; October 9, 1979. Running time: 98 MINS.

Martin Belhomme . . . . Jean Rochefort
Eva . . . . Catherine Deneuve
Eric de
Chalamond . . . Philippe Leroy-Beaulieu
Charley . . . . Robert Webber

Yves Robert's new comedy is about a man who gets into all kinds of tangles while running away from his own cowardice. The director, and his habitual coscenarist, Jean-Loup Dabadie, have taken a perennially rich comic premise, but unfortunately they failed to put together a credible story line to give plausibility to their amusing situations.

Jean Rochefort plays a bourgeois with a congenital yellow streak as long as the Seine river. He gets swept along in the May, 1968, student uprising in Paris to such an extent that he helps the mob destroy his own new automobile, watched by his wife and children from the windows of his home. So he turns tail and wakes up in a student commune where he first lays eyes on beautiful Catherine Deneuve, whom he follows to Amsterdam where she is a torch-singer in a night spot. They fall in love, but Deneuve has a violently jealous ex-boyfriend. Rochefort again runs away, back to Paris where he feigns amnesia to avoid explaining his long absence to his wife. She, in the meantime, has taken on another man.

News of the accidental death of Deneuve's ex-boyfriend sends the cowardly hero scurrying back to Amsterdam, where he is reunited with his love. Back in France, they marry, but there is a further twist, Deneuve suddenly produces another husband, a high-powered American businessman (Robert Webber), a home and kids. Rather than confront the chunky Yank and lay his claim, Rochefort, true to his craven spirit, reverts to subterfuge. He becomes Webber's chauffer, and benefits from his frequent business trips to carry on with Deneuve.

There are laughs along the way, but the film turns out to be a series of contrived contretemps through which Rochefort drives a wobbly yellow line. He navigates deftly through the plot's meanderings, which include those annoying unmapped stretches.

Deneuve has yet another role that is more decorative than demanding.

Some of Robert's previous comedies have been appreciated by audiences in the U.S. and other overseas markets. This popularity, added to Rochefort's growing reputation as a Gallic charmer with a wide range, may provide an adequate springboard for this film, yellow streaks and all. —Len.

The Wobblies
(DOCU-COLOR)

Pictorial recall of I.W.W. before World War I. Interesting for selected sites.

A documentary funded by National Endowment for the Humanities, The Film Fund, The Joint Foundation for Support and the United Auto Workers. Directed by Stewart Bird and Deborah Shaffer; camera, Sandi Sissel, Judy Irola, Peter Gessner, and Bonnie Friedman; sound, Dixie Beckham, Joe De Francesco, Shaffer; research, Perce Rafferty, Erika Gottfried and Peter Smallman; editors, Shaffer and Bird; associate editors, Gessner and Marilyn Frauenglass; sound editor, Joan Morris. Reviewed at the N.Y. Film Festival, Oct. 12 '79. (No MPAA Rating.) Running time: 88 MINS.

"Trust in the Lord and sleep in the street," recalls one of the surviving International Workers of the World in this slick documentary that recalls the pre-World War I era when "One Big Union" was the rallying cry for radicalized atheistic unskilled workers seeking bargaining parity with management and protection via union. Documakers Stewart Bird and Deborah Shaffer have performed a valuable service in marshalling the combination of interviews and original material ranging from pro-posters to scare-cartoons and old sepia-tone footage and stills.

Central exposition is via interviews with surviving Wobblies — so dubbed (per myth) after a striking Chinese in Vancouver told the press he was with the "I Wobble Wobble," or I.W.W. (International Workers of The World) to you. Considering the magnitude of the threat those initials spawned in their time, and the bloody strike at Laurence, Mass. in 1912, it is interesting for no other reason than to look at the last of the Wobblies to see the graying of radicals — the small comforts on the bureaus, the accumulated knickknacks of a lifetime somehow saying more than the text of their memories.

Film's strength really derives from these folks — the ex-loggers, dockworkers, silkworkers, miners, etc. — all of whom were then shunned by the American Federation of Labor, which "The Wobblies" still attribute primarily to racism. (one I.W.W. motto: "No Master, No God" was another cause).

There are shots of I.W.W. leaders Big Bill Haywood, Elizabeth Gurley Flynn and songs by Joe Hill, and footage of the Lawrence, Mass. textile strike, of 1912, the Paterson, N.J. strike of 1913 for wages and the 8-hour day, the Everett, Wash. loggers strike of 1916 that led to massacre.

In short, "The Wobblies" recalls a phase of U.S. history when European ideas failed to take root, namely, workers' ownership of the means of production.

What separates this film from greatness, however, is that it does not bring clarity to the complex question of unionism, today. —Jac.

Skatetown, U.S.A.
(COLOR)

First roller-skating pic out of the rink, should roll to good initial results.

Hollywood, Oct. 16.

A Columbia Pictures release of a Rastar production. Produced by William A. Levey and Lorin Dreyfuss. Exec producer, Peter E. Strauss. Directed by William A. Levey. Features entire cast. Screenplay, Nick Castle, based on a story by William A. Levey, Lorin Dreyfuss and Castle; camera (color), Donald M. Morgan; editor, Gene Fowler, Jr.; set decoration, George Gaines; art direction, Larry Wiemer; music, Miles Goodman; choreography, Bob Banas; stunt coordinator, Hank Hooker; sound, Al Overton, Jr.; costumes, Betsy Heimann, Bob Labansat; assistant director, Victor Hsu. Reviewed at The Burbank Studios, Oct. 16, 1979. MPAA Rating: PG. Running time: 98 MINS.

Richie . . . . Scott Baio
Harvey Ross . . . . Flip Wilson
Frankey . . . . Ron Palillo
Elvira . . . . Ruth Buzzi
Dave Mason . . . . Himself
Stan . . . . Greg Bradford
Susan . . . . Maureen McCormick
Ace . . . . Patrick Swayze
Jimmy . . . . Billy Barty
Allison . . . . Kelly Lang
Irwin . . . . David Landsberg
Alphonse . . . . Lenny Bari
The drunk . . . . Murray Langston
Skatetown doctor . . . . Bill Kirkchenbauer
Wizard . . . . Denny Johnston
Ripple . . . . Vic Dunlop

First picture to capitalize on the current roller disco craze, "Skatetown, U.S.A." won't disappoint the large number of roller skating aficionados across the country. Like the sport, film is a fun, escapist bit of fluff with lots of lights, color and action but little to think about. Well-paced by some fine skating, catchy music and silly comic bits, the Rastar film should do healthy biz for Columbia in its initial stages. Lasting b.o. action seems a bit more dubious, but the fact that "Skatetown" has beaten its competitors to the punch should help its staying power.

Pic takes place in a single evening at a mythical roller disco, where the filmmakers would have one believe anything is possible. That fantasy is realized in part as audience is introduced to an extensive cast of equally amusing and tiresome cardboard characters, none of whom are featured long enough to evoke much relating to reality.

Core of story centers on Greg Bradford as the handsome blond-haired street skater who has come to the roller disco to win a championship contest. Bradford's good guy is pitted against Patrick Swayze, long-reigning baddie champ who, as a gang leader dressed in black leather, will obviously do anything to keep Bradford from becoming number one on the roller rink.

Because it's doubtful even the most loyal fans could sit through 98 minutes of roller skating, a large cast of comic actors is assembled for relief until the big skate-off. Murray Langston, Bill Kirchenbauer, Vic Dunlop, David Landsberg and Gary Mule Deer are all appropriately zany diversions.

Flip Wilson is okay as proprietor of the rink, as is Billy Barty as his supposed "son," but both seem to be reprising bits they've done countless times before. Scott Baio is believable as Bradford's manager as is Ron Palillo as a member of Swayze's gang. Several name cameos provide necessary breaks from the action.

Ultimately the stars of the picture are the skating, atmosphere and music. Bradford and Swayze are both terrific skaters, and the latter, even manages to showcase some acting ability in what could have been surface portrayal. Choreography by Bob Banas and stunts by Hank Hooker are inventive. Lab work by Metrocolor helps bring into focus Larry Weimer's art work and George Gaines' sets. Music by Miles Goodman combines goodly amount of disco hits with some decent original tunes by Dave Mason.

With careful, fast-paced editing by Gene Fowler Jr. "Skatetown, U.S.A." rises above the somewhat surface script by Nick Castle. Hopelessly juvenile, it's still the kind of film fare people pay money to see. — *Berg.*

Hullabaloo Over Georgie And Bonnie's Pictures
(BRITISH-COLOR-16m)

London, Oct. 10.
Contemporary Films (U.K.) release of a Merchant/Ivory production in association with London Weekend Television. Produced by Ismail Merchant. Directed by James Ivory. Features entire cast. Screenplay, Ruth Prawer Jhabvala; camera (color, 16m), Walter Lassally; editor, Humphrey Dixon; music, Vic Flick; sound, Bob Bentley; art director, Bansi Chandragupta. Reviewed at the Rank preview theatre, London, Oct. 9, '79. (BBFC Rating: A). Running time: **82 MINS.**

Lady Gwyneth . . . . Peggy Ashcroft
Georgie . . . . Victor Bannerjee
Clark Haven . . . . Larry Pines
Bonnie . . . . Aparna Sen
Sri Narain . . . . Saeed Jaffrey
Lynn . . . . Jane Booker
Deaf Mute . . . . Shamsuddin
Servant . . . . Alladdin Langa
Governess . . . . Jenny Beavan

Theatrical release via Contemporary Films may be timely for this year-old, made for British tv feature, since the producer-director-writer team of Ismail Merchant, James Ivory and Ruth Prawer Jhabvala is currently hot in the art-film market, and "Hullabaloo" is as coolly entertaining fare as their latest, "The Europeans."

Treading familiar territory for them — post-colonial India — Ivory and Prawer Jhabvala have concocted a neat comedy of manners around the efforts of an oddly-assorted handful of bidders to get their hands on a private collection of Indian paintings. Reputedly unique and thus potentially priceless, the pictures are kept casually bundled up in his dusty palace storeroom by a young maharajah, who is more interested in his own photographs of western girls.

Of the various acquisitive contenders on his doorstep, Peggy Ashcroft, a doyenne of the British stage rarely seen on film, rings splendidly true as a penniless but dedicated English aristocrat bent on maintaining the tradition whereby India's finest treasures find their way into mother-country museums. Ashcroft's unexpected capacity for understatement on screen is far funnier than the caricaturing such roles tend to invite.

The names of the title roles — the maharajah and his sister (Aparna Sen, petulantly sexy) were apparently nicknamed by a Scottish governess back in colonial days — are among the many quaint touches with which writer and director have built up an authentically paradoxical portrait of British India and its aftermath. Predictability of the plot ending is outweighed by the character twists en route, as most of the leads turn out to have hidden depths. Larry Pine, for example, as a gangling American buyer, proves to be a genuinely passionate art enthusiast, not a walking checkbook as everyone had assumed. And Bannerjee, despite the playboy exterior, is no fool after all.

Available at present only on 16m gauge, the film's prospects are inevitably limited, though energetic promotion should ensure strong non theatrical outlook. Cinematographer Walter Lassally's no-risks lighting could be a plus, in that picture-definition throughout looks just capable of sustaining a blowup to 35m if the occasion arose.
—*Simo.*

Don Giovanni
(FRANCO-ITALO-GERMAN-COLOR)

Paris, Oct. 15.
A Gaumont release of a Gaumont-Camera One-Opera Film Produzione - Janus Film - Antenne 2 co-production. Produced by Michel Seydoux. Features entire cast. Directed by Joseph Losey. Based on the opera by W. A. Mozart and Lorenzo Da Ponte; cinematic conception by Rolf Liebermann; adaptation by Patricia and Joseph Losey, Frantz Salieri; camera (Color-Panavision), Gerry Fisher; art director, Alexandre Trauner; costumes, Marthe Mikon; sound, Jean-Louis Ducarme, Jacques Maumont, Michele Neny; editor, Reginald Beck; production manager, Pierre Saint-Blancat; orchestra and Choir of the Paris Opera under the direction of Lorin Maazel; musical advisor and harpsichordist, Janine Reiss. Reviewed at the Gaumont Champs-Elysees Theatre, Paris, Sept. 25, 1979. Running time: **184 MINS.**

Don Giovanni . . . . Ruggero Raimondi
The Commander . . . . John Macurdy
Donna Anna . . . . Edda Moser
Donna Elvira . . . . Kiri Te Kanawa
Don Ottavio . . . . Kenneth Riegel
Leporello . . . . Jose Van Dam
Zerlina . . . . Teresa Berganza
Masetto . . . . Malcolm King
Valet in Black . . . . Eric Adjani

Gaumont's film of Mozart's opera, "Don Giovanni," directed by Joseph Losey and toplining some of the greatest singers of the day, is free of the ponderousness too often associated with opera. The choice of setting, the director's masterly technical direction, Gerry Fisher's splendid color photography, Marthe Mikon's fine costumes and the magnetism of some of the performers, are positive aspects of this bid to bring Mozart's masterwork to a film-going public.

Two factors will limit commercial spread, however: the three-hour running time (not including intermission) and performance of the score in the original Italian, which means sub-titles in most territories. So, despite the film's visual and musical opulence, it may not completely fulfill the desire of Rolf Liebermann, administrator of the Paris Opera, and Gaumont's Daniel Toscan du Plantier, to "democratize" a traditionally elitist art.

The singing is uniformly superb. Soundtrack was recorded before shooting began, with the Paris Opera Orchestra and Choir under the direction of Lorin Maazel. This allowed Losey, who had to shoot on an unusually tight schedule, to give due attention to the plastic elements of the production.

Unfortunately, the shortage of rehearsal time, particularly crucial for artists who had no previous film experience, and Losey's unfamiliarity with opera, probably account for the weakness of dramatic credibility and interplay between the actor-singers.

But even though their roles remain dramatically unrealized, Ruggero Raimondi, Kiri Te Kanawa and Jose Van Dam meet the camera's gaze with poise, dignity and luminescent presence. The other great singers fare less well, with Teresa Berganza, alas, being shown up as much too old for the role of the young peasant girl.

Losey's other major failure is that he provides no guiding central concept as to what the opera is all about. His Don Giovanni has little of the cosmic braggadocio that is essential to the Don Juan theme, and without which the figure of the Commander, the Stone Guest, is meaningless. Raimondi provides the right self-obsessed drive, but there is little else in the interpretation that warrants all that magnificent Mozart.

The lack of a genuine vision and, possibly, the initial impulse to popularize opera, has led Losey to indulge in some heavy-handed directorial touches, such as the prop of a recumbent nude he provides for the exchange between the don and his servant, Leporello, in the beginning of Act Two, and the symbolic telegraphing of the protagonist's doom during the overture, with the don standing on a platform over a flaming cauldron in a glass-making factory.

Still, Losey's major shortcomings are sins of omission rather than commission, for which one can be grateful; Losey, the excellent film technician, does not try to compete cinematically with the opera, and the scenes that work best are those in which he preserves an essential theatricality.

The film's trump aesthetic decision was the filming of the opera in the neoclassic splendor of Palladio's villas in Vicenza, Italy, providing a real cinematic space that, at the same time, has imposing theatrical qualities. Too bad, then, that Losey sees the need to take some scenes out into the expanses of the surrounding countryside, in the naive tradition of "opening up" theatrical action. —*Len.*

Operasjon Cobra
(Operation Cobra)
(NORWEGIAN-COLOR)

Copenhagen, Oct. 9.
A Norsk Film A/S, Norway, production and release. Based on Anders Bodelsen's novel. Written and directed by Ola Solum. Features entire cast. Camera (Eastman-

color) Hans Nord. Cast: Roy Bjoernstad, Nils Ole Oftebro, Wencke Medboe. Reviewed at Palladium, Copenhagen, Oct. 8, 1979. Running time: **82 MINS.**

"Silent Partner," a Canadian-made feature, was the latest of Danish thriller writer Anders Bodelsen's many books to make the transition into a film.

Most Bodelsen books are adult fare, but he can write a good juvenile entertainment, too, and did so with "Operation Cobra," now a feature aimed at teen and just sub-teen audiences by Norway's Ola Solum, who is not too good at staging and editing overt action sequences, but who has a lucky hand with his young actors and who has retained most of Bodelsen's good dialog and witty characterizations.

Story has three schoolboys and one girl alerted to the fact of a U.S. Foreign Affairs Secretary's impending visit to Oslo by a teacher who tries to shake loose his pupils from their conditioned mental reflexes about the Arab-Israeli conflict.

Before the Kissinger-inspired statesman lands at Fornebu Airport, the children are by chance violently involved in a PLO plot to kill him.

One child is kidnaped by the terrorists, one of whom is a blond Norwegian political idealist who (like the teacher) tries to put the PLO viewpoints into words while setting the stage for the assassination.

The children, of course, find a way to thwart the PLO plot, but film is very open-minded in its telling the story, never resorting to gross propaganda, and the fact that the children are of variously Jewish, Arab and straight Nordic stock is a nice touch, never stressed too much. Film should fare well in situations catering to young audiences, but could be enjoyed by their parents, too. —*Kell.*

Head Over Heels
(COLOR)

Mild love story with mild results seen.

Hollywood, Oct. 10.

A United Artists release of a Triple Play production. Produced by Mark Metcalf, Amy Robinson, Griffin Dunne. Features entire cast. Directed and written by Joan Micklin Silver, based on the novel "Chilly Scenes Of Winter" by Ann Beattie. Camera (Color), Bobby Byrne; editor, Cynthia Schneider; music, Ken Lauber; production design, Peter Jamison; set decoration, Linda Spheeris; costume design, Rosanna Norton; sound, Ron Curfman; assistant director, Lorin B. Salob. Reviewed at MGM Studios, Culver City, Oct. 10, '79. (MPAA Rating: PG.) Running time: **97 MINS.**
Charles .... John Heard
Laura .... Mary Beth Hurt
Sam .... Peter Riegert
Pete .... Kenneth McMillan
Clara .... Gloria Grahame
Betty .... Nora Heflin
Patterson .... Jerry Hardin
Susan .... Tarah Nutter
Elise .... Alex Johnson
Ox .... Mark Metcalf
Rebecca .... Angela Phillips
Mark .... Griffin Dunne
Blind Man .... Allan Joseph

Success of Woody Allen's recent pictures seems to have opened studio minds to small "relationship" stories, which description certainly fits "Head Over Heels." Problem here is that, despite being based on a novel, situation, structure and desired tone is so similar to "Annie Hall" that it forces comparison, to the detriment of the newer film. Joan Micklin Silver's third directorial effort, and first for a major studio, possesses moderate charm and shows some of the talent she's exhibited before, but ultimately emerges as somewhat thin and one-dimensional. B.O. prospects would seem uneven.

Based on Ann Beattie's "Chilly Scenes Of Winter," a more poetic if less commercial title, Silver's screenplay has affable John Heard reflecting back on his happy past with Mary Beth Hurt from the wistful present. Thrust of pic has him trying, incessantly and obsessively, to win her back from the clutches of king-sized jock Mark Metcalf.

Paralleling of scenes, one strand showing his early successes, other thread detailing his depressed failures, results in a constant flip-flopping of tone from happy to sad. More critical difficulty, however, is the singularity of Heard's interest, which centers exclusively on Hurt. He's understandably not overly consumed by his unexciting job as a lower-echelon government office worker, he's got few friends, no ambition and seemingly no inclination toward other women over the entire year of their separation.

High degree of attention given over to Heard's extreme attitude toward their commitment puts a bit of strain on lead performers' charm, which is considerable to begin with. Early scenes of their meeting and courtship betray a delightful off-handed humor and sensitivity to the nice literary quality of the dialog, although lack of even a mention, much less visual evidence, of the importance or quality of their sexual relationship seems a bit odd today.

Ultimately, however, both characters rather wear out their welcome, Heard becoming almost oppressively absolutist in his feelings and Hurt seeming too confused and selfish to perhaps be worth all the trouble. After all the difficulties and anxieties that have preceded it, resolution comes off as a bit pat and conventional, wrap-ping up all the loose ends on Heard's demanding terms.

Pic makes a definite pitch for commitment in an easy-come, easy-go environment, but commitment is all Heard seems to have to offer, making Hurt's doubts increasingly plausible. Deep emotion is shown but not felt, which makes all the difference.

One-dimensionality strongly afflicts supporting cast. Peter Reigert is in strictly as a best friend sounding board and slovenly contrast to Heard, Gloria Grahame returns to the screen as his nutty mother who's constantly threatening suicide, and Kenneth McMillan, as his stepfather, is a good-hearted loser. Nora Heflin is excellent as a pathetic secretary who allows Heard to lead her on, with unfortunate results.

Salt Lake City, a seldom-used locale in pix, looks good in dead of winter in Bobby Byrne's pro cinematography. All other craft and tech work is solid.

End credits bear an unusual "special appreciation" credit to exec Claire Townsend, who succeeded in taking the project with her when she moved from 20th Century-Fox to United Artists.
—*Cart.*

The Watts Monster
(COLOR)

Black exploitation successor. Outlook poor.

Hollywood, Oct. 12.
Dimension Pictures release, produced by Charles Walker. Directed by William Crain. Features entire cast. Exec producer, Manfred Bernhard. Screenplay, Larry Le Bron; camera, Tak Fujimoto; music, Johnny Pate. (No other credits available). Reviewed at World Theatre, Hollywood, Oct. 12, '79. (MPAA Rating: R). Running time: **90 MINS.**
Cast: Bernie Casey, Rosalind Cash, Marie O'Henry.

With "The Watts Monster," black exploitation has now replaced Super-Fly with Super-Flake and it would be nice to say that the dramatic value of this picture rises above the title. It would be nice, but it would also be a lie. Grim outlook.

Bernie Casey plays a likable doctor, working late at night in the lab to find a cure for liver ailment. Alas, he comes up with a terrible potion that he uses upon himself, turning into the most dreaded of ghetto beasts — a White Guy.

Looking like a Hulk of a different hue, Casey starts murdering hookers, seeking them out in his fancy Rolls Royce. Though a big ugly white fellow driving the mean streets in such an elegant auto might ordinarily cause comment, the police have a dickens of a time figuring out who's behind the killings.

Rosalind Cash is a fellow doctor who loves Casey and stands around wishing he wouldn't take so much liver medicine. And Marie O'Henry is a prostitute with a heart of gold but no desire to turn white with the doctor.

Technical credits are not in evidence.—*Har.*

Natural Enemies
(COLOR)

A bizarre family relationship.

Cinema 5 release of a John E. Quill production. Stars Hal Brook, Louise Fletcher. Written, directed and edited by Jeff Kanew, based on a novel by Julius Horwitz. Camera (color), Richard E. Brooks; associate producers, Harry Daley, Robert Burke; music, Don Ellis; art director, Hank Aldrich; asst. director, Sol Fol. Reviewed at Rizzoli Screening Room, N.Y., Oct. 25, 1979. (MPAA Rating - R) Running time: **100 MINS.**

Paul Steward	Hal Holbrook
Miriam Steward	Louise Fletcher
Tony Steward	Peter Armstrong
Sheila Steward	Beth Berridge
Alex Steward	Steve Austin
Man on train	Jim Pappas
Secretary	Ellen Barber
Astronaut	John Bartholomew
Doctor	Charles Randall
Harry Rosenthal	Jose Ferrer
The madam	Lisa Carroll
Girls in brothel	June Berry, Alisha Fontaine, Pat Mauceri, Michele O'Brien, Claire Reilly
Dr. Baker	Viveca Lindfors
Cabdriver	Frank Bongiorno
Conductor	Harry Daley
Woman on train	Patricia Elliott
Newscaster	Robert Perry

This has been a good year for films about family relationships but this one veers off on a different tangent that takes a lot of suspension of doubt on the part of the viewer to accept. Hal Holbrook and Louise Fletcher, a pair of efficient but not very exciting actors, are perfect casting for the roles of Mr. and Mrs. John Q. Dullsville. They convey their boredom from the screen in a matter of minutes but during the entire running time of the film they never capture the minds of the audience.

Holbrook, a small but evidently very successful magazine publisher, finds that life, despite material success, no longer has meaning. Instead of seeking change via divorce or adultery or even suicide, he contemplates wiping out the entire family (in a manner of speaking, erasing his mistakes). Most of the film is given to his thinking (aloud) about this plan of action and getting the opinions of others on the subject (posing it as a possible magazine series for the future). Where the picture fails, with this viewer at least, is that you don't care what he does ... just get on with it.

The solution is ambiguous ... with the usual freeze frame ending and a voiceover of a radio commentator describing the crime as though it had actually happened. But did it? Tune in tomorrow for the answer.

The two short sequences when the film does show a few sparks are conversations of Holbrook, first with Jose Ferrer, who plays a former concentration camp inmate and now a writer, who per-

ceives Holbrook's homicidal bent; and another with Viveca Lindfors as an analyst (it is unclear whether she is speaking in a professional manner or just as a friend, but what she says and how she says it is fascinating). The children are in at the beginning of the film briefly and then dropped which could have been a budgetary solution rather than a plot incident. A sequence in which he engages the services of five, count 'em, five call girls at the same time borders on the ridiculous.

The technical credits are good. The picture, made on a small budget, looks rich on screen and even the limited settings (Holbrook's rather posh Manhattan offices and his West Redding, Conn. house) give a feeling of material success. Other sets are scattered but brief. Richard E. Brooks' handsome color photography is a big asset to the film's look.

The Great Santini

Terrif pic with title trouble.

Hollywood, Oct. 17.
An Orion Pictures release through Warner Bros., produced by Charles A. Pratt and Bing Crosby Prods. Features entire cast. Written and directed by Lewis John Carlino, based on novel by Pat Conroy. Camera (color), Ralph Woolsey; editor, Houseley Stevenson; sound, Lee Alexander; production design, Jack Poplin; assistant director, Edward Markley; set decoration, Jeff Haley, Don Sullivan; aerial sequences, Clay Lacey; music, Elmer Bernstein. Reviewed at The Burbank Studios, Oct. 17, '79. (MPAA rating: PG.) Running time: **115 MINS.**

Bull Meechum	Robert Duvall
Lillian Meechum	Blythe Danner
Ben Meechum	Michael O'Keefe
Mary Anne Meechum	Lisa Jane Persky
Karen Meechum	Julie Anne Haddock
Matthew Meechum	Brian Andrews
Toomer Smalls	Stan Shaw
Arrabelle Smalls	Theresea Merritt
Red Pettus	David Keith
Col. Hedgepath	Paul Mantee

It's been an exceptionally good year, both artistically and commercially, for the small, heartwarming picture so there's hope for "The Great Santini," a fine film which is gambling that the star pull of Robert Duvall can overcome a title that could confuse audiences into thinking picture is everything it isn't.

Once again, Duvall gives an excellent portrayal of a semi-psychotic, softened this time with a warmer side. But Duvall has to fight for every inch of footage against the overwhelming performances by several others in the cast — and that's the strength of "The Great Santini."

According to the production notes, director-writer Lewis John Carlino recognized that the title of Pat Conroy's autobiographical

novel might be mistaken on marquees for a circus or magician story, but decided to stick with it. But pre-release trade talk already demonstrates precisely that kind of confusion and Warner Bros. should spread the counterword fast.

Actually, title is a nickname Duvall picks up as the finest fighter pilot in the U.S. Marines. But this isn't a war picture either. Quite the contrary, it's the compellingly relevant story of a super-macho peacetime warrior with nobody to fight except himself and those who love him.

As Carlino showed before with his "The Sailor Who Fell From Grace With The Sea," he has a good feel for strong male relationships, graced by a lovely woman on the sidelines. As the sensitive son who strives to meet all of his father's supermasculine standards, Michael O'Keefe is terrific and emerges as the major star of the picture.

Blythe Danner is also strong as the wife who suffers Duvall's excesses while sharing her son's distress. Rounding out the family, Lisa Jane Persky is delightfully funny as a wiseacre younger sister and Julie Anne Haddock and Brian Andrews are also good in smaller parts.

Subplot showcases Stan Shaw in an outstanding performance as a poetic peddler who pretends to be dimwitted to avoid involvement with the town's rednecks. Shaw and O'Keefe turn in several fine scenes together and actually carry off the film's biggest excitements.

But none of it would work without Duvall, who seems in every sequence to bring out the best in the rest of the cast. Production credits are all first-rate and the town of Beaufort, S.C. provides a beautiful sleepy background for a taut drama. —*Har.*

Sufferloh
(WEST GERMAN-COLOR)

Hamburg, Oct. 24.
A Distelfilm Berlin Stenzel & Co. Production, with Werbedistel, Holzkirchen; distributor, Team-Film. Features entire cast. Directed by Hans-Christof Stenzel. Screenplay, Stenzel, Karl Guenther Hufnagel; camera (color), Paco Joan; editor, Rosemarie Stenzel-Quast. No other credits provided. Reviewed at Urania Kino, Hamburg. Oct. 22, '79. Running time: **84 MINS.**

Cast: Michael Langenbeck, Sandro Hauth, Martina Winkelbach, Susanne Baer, Herbert Berent, H.C. Artmann, Uli Kasten.

A lovely film about a corner of Bavaria (near Holzkirchen, Tegernsee, and Bad Toelz, not far from Munich), Hans-Christof Stenzel's "Sufferloh" is a tongue-in-cheek portrait of a small town. The same director made "C'est la Vie Rrose" (1977) from motifs based on

painter-dadaist Marcel Duchamps, and has a fine touch for the quaint and the oddball that makes life a good bit more cheerful than it sometimes is.

"Sufferloh" relies for effect on dialect speech patterns, some ribticklers in verbal expression alone. But the outsider also has enough to please the eye. For instance, there's an abandoned baroque chapel serving as a domicile for a gentleman soul of middle-age (the altar even has a chalice on display. There's also a young boy with a bulging beret cap serving as the foil for the "heavy," and a lass with and without clothes romping around the premises from time to time. Lastly, there's touches of the dadaist tradition, like cutting pieces out of a bra while chatting about the "Himmirater."

Stenzel's nod this time may be in the direction of Karl Valentin, that venerable W.C. Fields figure of Munich beer halls in the 1920s and 1930s (until the Third Reich put an end to this kind of merry madcap nonsense). —*Holl.*

Die Letzten Jahre Der Kindheit
(The Last Years of Childhood)
(WEST GERMAN-COLOR-16m)

Hamburg, Oct. 19.
A FEAT Film Production, Munich; world rights, Filmverlag der Autoren. Features entire cast. Written and directed by Norber Kueckelmann. Camera (color), Juergen Juerges; editor, Jane Sperr; music, Markus Urchs. Reviewed at Urania Kino, Hamburg. Oct. 19, '79. Running time: **110 MINS.**

Cast: Gerhard Gundel (Martin), Dieter Mustafoff (Hans), Lissy Zimmermann (Sonja), Leopoldine Schwankel (Frau Sontag), Thomas Wommer (Thomas Heine), Manfred Rendl (Roemer), Wilfried Klaus (Dr. Haering), Eggert Langmann (Pahlen).

One of the best pix made on youth problems and correction homes in West Germany, Norbert Kueckelmann's "The Last Years of Childhood" doesn't pull a punch while offering plenty for the average moviegoer in the way of dramatic realism. It was the big hit at the recent Hamburg Film Fest of Film Makers.

Helmer Kueckelmann, a lawyer and cofounder of the Curatorium for Young Cinema (subsidies for debut projects), writes books and makes films on the side as the occasion presents itself. His "The Experts" (1972), a debut pic unspooled at the Berlin Film Festival, dealt with the mistreatment of a psycho case; it was made under the pseudonym of Bernhard Guba. "Target Practice" (1974) and "Fear Is a Second Shadow" (1975) also kept to psychiatric cases.

"The Last Years of Childhood" examines how the law tends to mishandle delinquent children, and correction homes don't have answers either — in fact, the suicide at the end (suggested in the title) seems a logical consequence of society's inability to cope with the problem properly. This is the tale of a boy coming from impoverished family circumstances who steals, together with his brothers, whenever the opportunity presents itself (the first criminal offense is at age 7). He is shown to be a normal youth otherwise, but at 13 he's committed to a home and that spells the end of the line.

The boy, Martin, appears in the beginning to enjoy the fun of stealing, without overdoing it. His best friend is his older brother, who has a motorbike and substitutes as a parent for the most part. When Martin gets committed to a correction home, he is informed that his brother has died in an accident. Thereafter, he is passive in his relations to others, makes friends only with one older "protector" on his own terms, and runs away from the home at the first available opportunity.

The rest is a story of how Martin is picked up time and again after running away from a string of correction homes as, then, too, no one wants him because of his unwillingness to conform to any social environment. The single connection he maintains is to the older runaway, whom he meets from time to time on the road or in other penal institutions. Another contact is made with a psychologist in one of the homes, but this lifeline is broken by the other authorities in the institution. One day, the boy hangs himself.

Pic is well told with tight narrative line and should do well in a German Film Week or at a fest for youth pix. Kueckelmann has documented his case to the last pertinent detail, but the big pluses are sharp lensing (Juergen Juerges) and strong portraits from nonprofessional kids playing themselves. Although in 16m, a 35m blowup is planned and should help launch pic. —Holl.

Promises In The Dark
(COLOR)

Prognosis dim for cinematic downer.

Hollywood, Oct. 16.
An Orion Pictures release through Warner Bros. Produced by Jerome Hellman. Exec producer, Sheldon Schrager. Directed by Hellman. Features entire cast. Screenplay, Loring Mandel; camera (color), Adam Holender; editor, Bob Wyman; music, Leonard Rosenman; production design, Walter Scott Herndon; costume design, Ann Roth; sound, Darin Knight; assistant director, Kim Kuru-

mada. Reviewed at The Burbank Studios, Burbank, Oct. 16, '79. (MPAA Rating: PG.) Running time: 115 MINS.
Dr. Alexandra Kendall ... Marsha Mason
Bud Koenig .... Ned Beatty
Fran Koenig .... Susan Clark
Dr. Jim Sandman ...... Michael Brandon
Buffy Koenig .... Kathleen Beller
Gerry Hulin .... Paul Clemens
Dr. Walter McInterny .... Donald Moffat
Dr. Frucht .... Philip Sterling
Nurse Farber .... Bonnie Bartlett
Dr. Blankenship .... James Noble

Prognosis for most so-called 'downbeat' films is an unhealthy life at the boxoffice, but in the case of "Promises In The Dark," the diagnosis is fatal. Orion Pictures and producer-director Jerome Hellman have admirably attempted to focus attention on the death of a young cancer victim, a subject rarely, if ever, touched on in feature films. There's a reason why. "Promises" is so crushingly depressing that chances for survival in an escapist entertainment era seem dim.

Major problem remains not the promises physician Marcia Mason makes to her terminally-ill patient, Kathleen Beller, but the premise itself. No matter how well acted (and thesping here is superior) or mounted, a story that spends two hours watching a pretty young girl expire is just not most people's idea of a good time.

Lorin Mandel's screenplay pulls no punches, and medical realism is heightened to an extent that damages the film more than it helps. Beller injures her leg in the pic's opening sequence, and after that, it's an endless array of emergency rooms, surgery theatres and bed-ridden shots as the cancer spreads throughout her body.

Set up as counterpoint to the distress Beller, boyfriend Paul Clemens, and parents Ned Beatty and Susan Clark undergo is the courtship of divorced medico Mason by radiologist Michael Brandon. The humor seems forced, and almost in bad taste, as the effects of chemotherapy and other drugs waste Beller away.

Mason, who is given the central focus by Hellman's derivative direction, never really allows the audience to share in her conflicting emotions. Instead, her chin wrinkles frequently as the tears begin to flow, not quite a substitute for insight.

Rest of cast is first-rate, particularly Beller (whose 'why me' speech is heart-wrenching), Beatty, Brandon, Clemens and Bonnie Bartlett as a hawk-faced nurse who has made a career out of life support care, and knows a good thing when she sees it. Hellman's direction, however, seems to have been inspired by two colleagues he's frequently worked with, Hal Ashby and John Schlesinger. Adam

Holender's lensing is good, but Walter Scott Herndon's production design is ultra-realistic, and Leonard Rosenman's lugubrious score doesn't help matters.

Orion and Hellman will and should pat themselves on the back for tackling a subject like this, which ties in with the "death awareness" movement. But the film inevitably remains a downer, and audiences rarely line up for a pic out of a guilty conscience. —Poll.

Melancholy Baby
(FRANCO-BELGIAN-SWISS-COLOR)

Paris, Sept. 19.
A UGC release of a Dimage/Luna Films/Cine Vog Films/SSR-RTSI coproduction. Produced by Michele Dimitri. Stars Jane Birkin, Jean-Louis Trintignant, Jean-Luc Bideau. Directed by Clarisse Gabus. Screenplay, Gabus, Daniel Jouanisson, Andre Puig; camera (color), Charlie Van Damme; sound, Auguste Galli; music, Serge Gainsbourg; art director, Denis Martin-Sisteron; editors, Luciano Berini; Genevieve Letellier, Catherine Brasier-Snopko. Reviewed at the UGC Biarritz, Paris, Sept. 11, 1979. Running time: 100 MINS.
Olga .... Jane Birkin
Pierre ....Jean-Louis Trintignant
Claude .... Jean-Luc Bideau

The bad luck of this first feature by a 30-year old Swiss film editor, Clarisse Gabus, is to have come too late, lost at the tail end of a series of films that tell of women who grope their way out of blinkered security into unstable independence. Nevertheless "Melancholy Baby" shows signs of considerable directorial life.

Jane Birkin plays a bored young wife whose businessman hubby is frequently absent from their home in the luxurious countryside around Lugano. Languishing in her inactivity, she is prodded by a friend to see other people.

She visits one of her husband's friends (Jean-Louis Trintignant) who presents her to another visitor (Jean-Luc Bideau), a man worn down by the vicious circle of unemployment. The passivity of these men before their own solitude and social impotence slowly urges Birkin to tentative activity. She makes an advance at Trintignant, who rebuffs her. She accepts the company of a young restaurant waiter who would like to make a pass at her, but who is too spineless to try.

By the time her husband comes home, Birkin has made up her mind to live alone. He, uncomprehending, packs her off for a rest cure. When he comes to take her back, Birkin takes the wheel of the car and drives off alone.

The script is patchy, with some good scenes (Trintignant's rejection of Birkin, the young woman's exasperating encounter with a

stranger who sits near her on an empty lakeside terrace but who makes no attempt to pick her up even when Birkin speaks to him), and less good scenes (the obligatory confrontation scene between husband and wife). The acting is merely adequate.

The main interest here is the promise Gabus shows. She has sensibility, a fine eye for textures in image and editing (particularly in the way she evokes the environment as an insidious anaesthetic), a sense of poignant irony and an attentiveness to the "expressiveness" of her native Switzerland. —Len.

Sons For The Return Home
(NEW ZEALAND-COLOR)

Auckland, Oct. 20.
A New Zealand Film Commission presentation. Features entire cast. Directed by Paul Maunder. Screenplay, Maunder, from novel by Albert Wendt; exec. producer, Don Blakeney; camera (color), alun Bollinger; music, Malcolm Smith; sound, Don Reynolds. Reviewed at Westend (Kerridge-Odeon) Auckland Oct. 19, '79. (R 16.) Running time 115 MINS.
Sione .... Uelese Petaia
Sarah .... Fiona Lindsay
Sione's mother .... Moira Walker
Sione's father .... Lani Tupu
Sarah's father .... Alan Jervis
Sarah's mother .... Anne Flannery

The scenario of "Sons For The Return Home" is one of those for which there are two possible endings — the lovers will come together at the end, or they won't. (In this one they don't.) But the film is less concerned with what happens than with the whys, and the motivations and ethnic backgrounds of the lovers.

She is a white New Zealander, he is a brown Polynesian from Western Samoa. They meet when she picks him up in the library of the university in Wellington where they are students, and the film is about the impact on their affair of their contrasting cultures.

The proud tradition of the Samoan's family is well caught. When mention of marriage comes up the Polynesian elders display greater horror at the idea of miscegenation than do the girl's wealthy, conventional parents, which makes a nice switch on the usual racial prejudice theme. Subtitles are used for the Island segments and to judge from the delighted audience reaction at the session under review (it was a commercial screening in Auckland, where a generous sprinkling of patrons were Samoans) the native dialog and business is dead accurate. There was, however, some derisive laughter at a sequence where Sione, the Samoan youth, weeps over the loss of his native heritage.

Uelese Petaia is grim in a role that gives him no other options, but he captures a dignity and sadness that play off well against Fiona Lindsay's Sarah. Lindsay has the luminous animation of feature of the true screen natural, a face that tells it all without the need for dialog.

Production detail is okay and the neo-Chopin piano that is stock background for these idylls can be forgiven on the ground that it is easy on the ear. Camerawork and direction are relaxed enough to give the actors room to move.

For its theme and fresh locations alone "Sons For The Return Home" deserves a chance on foreign screens, and not just the college and festival circuits, where it should score. It is the first presentation by the NZ Film Commission, whose coin, whatever the commercial outcome, has not been wasted artistically. —*Dub.*

Die Hamburger Krankheit
(The Hamburg Syndrome)
(WEST GERMAN-FRENCH-COLOR)

Hamburg, Oct. 22.
A Hallelujah Film, Munich, Production, in collaboration with Michel Gast SND, Paris, ZDF, Mainz, Terra-Film, Coleidon Film, Munich; world rights, Filmverlag der Autorn, Munich. Features entire cast. Directed and edited by Peter Fleischmann. Screenplay, Fleischmann, Roland Topor, Otto Jaegersberg; camera (color), Colin Mounier; music, Erich Fersti, Die Gaichinger Pfeiffer, Esteban; sets, Luigi de Luca; tv-editor, Willi Segler. Reviewed at Urania Kino, Hamburg, Oct. 22, '79. Running time: 130 MINS.
Cast: Helmut Griem, Fernando Arrabal, Carline Selser, Tilo Pruechner, Ulrich Wildgruber, Rainer Langhans, Romy Haag, Evelyn Kuenneke, Peter von Zah.

Peter Fleischmann is best known for "Hunting Scenes in Bavaria" (1968) (based on Martin Sperr's play), a key film in the development of New German Cinema. He then made "Das Unheil" (The Unholy) (1970), a Cannes competitor; "Dorothea's Revenge" (1973), a Teutonic/Gallic spoof of porno prods.; "The Third Degree" (1975), set in a dictatorship (Greece?) with Michel Piccoli; and now "The Hamburg Syndrome."

His latest features Fernando Arrabal and Helmut Griem, but also a couple of German thesps on the nonprof side, Rainer Langhans and Romy Haag (who deftly steal the show), and the credits as a whole reflect the current "in" scene on at least the European intellectual circuit. This pic, in fact, only snuck in under the wire at the recent Hamburg fest, failed to show at last year's Cannes outing, and is surely slated for a major upcoming fest, if for no other reason because Arrabal plays one of the main roles.

The "syndrome" in the title — "Krankheit" could also, perhaps better, be translated "Sickness" — refers to a mysterious illness that surfaces during a physicians' conference in the port city in northern Germany. A doctor, one of the pic's protagonists (Helmut Griem), is aware of the plague in the city, but has different ideas on how to treat the spreading disease than the officials on hand. The question whether the plague (read "sickness" or "illness" or "syndrome" or whatever) is spiritual, moral, psychological, political, physical, or simply a filmic metaphor (read Bergman or Antonioni or whomever) is up to the audience to decide — the crit's view will probably not matter very much.

All along the way crazy things happen — the principles leave the city in a Volkswagen camper — and try (inexplicably) to head for the South. Several die in the process, either from the sickness, or plague, or from the syndrome that exists in this land. The jokers in the deck — Arrabal, Rainer Langhans (a former West German dissident, one side of the Langhans-Teufel duet fighting for a "reckoning with the past" in the 1968 Student Revolt), and Romy Haag (a famous Berlin transvestite, who strips to the essentials in the pic) — somehow keep going: they must constantly bypass roadblocks, withstand disenfection crews (are they really spreading the plague?), and, at the same time, maintain an appropriate innocence.

The doctor dies of the plague, the innocents are ruthlessly gunned down (Langhans' fate), and even the little people involved in the flight sell out, on occasion, to the demands of the consumer society. The last notes are in the direction of a Bavarian yodel, rather suitable in view of the coming elections in 1980 (one of the country's candidates, Franz Josef Strauss, hails from Bavaria).

Worth a fest bow, pic could also turn a neat coin at the box office at home. Offshore chances limited to lingo circuit. —*Holl.*

Die Patriotin
(The Patriot)
(WEST GERMAN-COLOR)

Hamburg, Oct. 20.
A Kairos-Film Production, Alexander Kluge, Munich. Features entire cast. Directed by Alexander Kluge. Screenplay, Willi Segler, Hans-Dieter Mueller, Dagmar Steurer, Christel Buschman, Helga Sander, Juergen Habermas, Oskar Negt, Karen and Bion Steinborn, among others. Camera (color), four independent teams, Guenter Hoermann, Werner Luering, Thomas Mauch, Joerg Schmidt-Reitwein; editing, Beate Mainka-Jellinghaus. Reviewed at Urania Cinema, Hamburg, Oct. 20, '79. Running time: 121 MINS.

Cast: Hannelore Hoger, Dieter Mainka, Alfred Edel, Alexander von Eschwege, Beate Holle, Kurt Juergens, Willi Muench, Mairus Mueller-Westernhagen, Guenther Keidel, Hans Heckel, Wolf Hanne, others.

Alexander Kluge's pix are admired, and rightly so, in West Germany for their provocative mixture of fiction and documentary.

"The Patriot" offers another complex metaphor on German history, past and present, which deserves a couple of viewings to crack its ascetic, esthetic shell. After two screenings (at the German Prizes ceremonies and the Hamburg fest), this reviewer has, hopefully, solved the major riddles, albeit with Kluge's help via a printed program. Not all will be as fortunate, though the helmer suggests three screenings.

"The Patriot" stems from "Germany in Autumn" (1978), an omnibus pic on terrorism and hysteria following the kidnapping and murder of Hanns Martin Schleyer and the death of three terrorists in prison at the same time. The questions this docu-fiction film raised, primarily through Kluge's editing of the pic, are partially answered in "The Patriot" — it's a frontal attack on German history, whether viewed politically, socially, economically, pedagogically, psychologically, or whatever. As in every nation's history, the present transcends the past depending on the state of current affairs.

In the case of West Germany in 1979, one has the feeling that Kluge is trying to dig up passages of German history to review events of past and present in a different light than usually given in history books. History teacher Gabi Teichert (Hannelore Hogar) sets out on a wintery day with a spade over her shoulder: the next 12 scenes vary in significance and complexity, drifting across the screen as though Luther were nailing his theses to the wall.

There's a knee that speaks (Kluge's voice) belonging to a fallen soldier at Leningrad: Teichert, the patriot, discovers the knee doesn't belong to any part of the body, a metaphor for history that cannot be properly researched since the essential core is invisible. Teichert also takes a telescope to peer into the distance for more clues. She goes to the Party Convention of the Social Democrats (SPD) on her quest, and is referred to a table with protocol material as an answer (this is docu footage).

Pic continues with interviews (a side-splitter with an expert on German fairy-tales), and several ironic statements along the line add to both the enjoyment and the mystery. Vintage Kluge. —*Holl.*

Tapage Nocturne
(Nocturnal Uproar)
(FRENCH-COLOR)

Paris, Oct. 22.
A Gaumont release of an Axe Films-French Production coproduction. Produced by Pierre Sayag. Features entire cast. Written and directed by Catherine Breillat. Camera (color), Jacques Boumendil; sound, Alain Curvelier; editors, Annie Charrier, Claudio Ventura; art director, Dominique Anthony; music, Serge Gainsbourg, performed by Bijou. Reviewed at the Gaumont Colisee Theatre, Paris, October 10, 1979. Running time: 95 MINS.
Solange .... Dominique Laffin
Emmanuelle ...... Marie-Helene Breillat
Bruno .... Bertrand Bonvoisin
Jim .... Joe Dallessandro

Catherine Breillat, 28, a novelist who earned early notoriety at age 17 with her first work, "L'Homme Facile," which raised brows with its precocious impudent sexual frankness, wrote and directed this willfully abrasive film about a contemporary young woman's uncentered erotic odysseys.

Dominique Laffin plays a female film director with a strong sexual appetite and a false sense of lucidity about her relationships with men. A female Don Juan, she nevertheless ends up falling for an impassive, distant young man with whom she carries on a draining, masochistic relationship that ends in an inevitable split. She has a good cry over him and then quickly forgets him.

Though the film strives for a kind of "Last Tango in Paris" bluntness and offers some sardonic comments on the sexual behavior of today's young generation, the film is singularly lacking in dramatic interest and characters who have a right to attention for 90 minutes; boredom sets in early. Although Breillat is no newcomer to film (she wrote and directed a previous feature and scripted photographer David Hamilton's first film, "Bilitis"), she has not been able to shape her literary talents into a workable screenplay. Her direction is undistinguished.

Laffin, remarkable as the suffering wife in Jacques Doillon's "La Femme Qui Pleure," proves once again her ability to act with her nerve ends, but here she seems to parody the powerful emoting she did in the Doillon film. Joe Dallesandro, a familiar sex object in Andy Warhol's iconography, makes a brief appearance as a familiar sex object. —*Len.*

Historien om en Moder
(The Story Of A Mother)
(DANISH-COLOR)

Copenhagen, Oct. 25.
A Claus Weeke/The Danish Film Studio production, Statens Filmcentral (Copen-

hagen) release. Production subsidized by Privatbanken (Copenhagen) and UNESCO (Paris). Features entire cast. Directed by Claus Weeke. Camera (Eastmancolor), Dirk Bruel; screenplay, Paul Gegauff, Claus Weeke, based on Hans Christian Andersen story; editor, Lars Brydesen; music, Mozart quotes; production manager, Jacob Eriksen. Reviewed at Statens Filmcentral screening room, Copenhagen, Oct. 25, 1979. Running time, **52 MINS.**

The Mother .... Anna Karina
Death .... Daniel Duvall
Kindergarden Teacher .... Tove Maes
Lady Janitor .... Bodil Udsen
The Child .... Gustaf Hagstroem

"The Story Of A Mother" was Denmark's official entry at the Nordic Film Days in Luebeck, West Germany. It is a brief item bearing the sometimes embarrassing earmarks of an ardent amateur's work, but should still be assured at least to sales in many territories since Claus Weeke's updating of one of Hans Christian Andersen's most somber tales also has some touching moments and occasional visual impact.

Denmark's Paris-based Claus Weeke has been a marginal assistant on some Claude Chabrol features. With Paul Gegauff, a Chabrol scripter-mainstay, he has concocted a script that has translated only uneastily into actual film. Protest marchers, drug addicts and abused porcelain painting workers are used to illustrate the ills of a world that Death frees the mother's little child from ever growing up to live in.

Having offered her embrace to a freezing man, her eyes to an angry protest marcher and her hair to the woman guardian of Death's Garden, the mother is finally allowed to confront death once more (he turned up first as a friendly social worker in the slum apartment where her son lay fatally ill), and she is finally unburdened of her grief and given faith's comfort.

Dirk Bruel's camerawork is fine in its Goya-esque shadings of the mother's nightly search for her lost child. Generally film works best where an actual fairy tale tone is reached for, while all the updating seem clumsy and dated. The production year would be guessed at as 1972 if the credits had not said otherwise.

France's Danish-born Anna Karina looks suitably haggard and grim as the mother with her hair swept away from what looks like a shaven hairline. She is, as always, more of a presence than an actual acting talent and she speaks her lines stiffly.

As death in a greay flannel suit, France's Daniel Duvall is a convincingly image of the Grim Reaper, and Bodil Udsen has a few grand moments when she, as the lady janitor, turns into a symbol of Night. —Kell.

Das Ende Des Regenbogens
(The End of the Rainbow)
(WEST GERMAN-COLOR)

Hamburg, Oct. 21.

A Basis-Film Production, Berlin, with Westdeutscher Rundfunk (WDR); world rights, Basis-Film, Berlin. Features entire cast. Written and directed by Uwe Friessner. Camera (color), Frank Bruehne; editor, Stefanie Wilke; music, Alexander Kraut, Klaus Krueger, Michael Nuschke, Matthias Kaebs; sets, Edwin, Wengoborski, Martin Mohr. Reviewed at Urania Kino, Hamburg, Oct. 21, '79. Running time: **107 MINS.**

Cast: Thomas Kufahl (Jimmi), Slavica Rankovic (Gabi), Henry Lutze (Bernie), Udo Samuel (Dieter), Heinz Hoenig (Joerg), Sabine Baruth (Monika).

Television film on youth meeting a sad end, Uwe Friessner's "The End of the Rainbow" has its heart in the right place but lacks polish to carry its weight in cinemas. Nevertheless, this is a well-researched document on the phases leading up to an 18-year-old boy's suicide, and will win critical attention upon tube airing.

Jimmi is a boy of the streets in West Berlin, who makes a few bucks to live from the homo trade and petty thievery. What he really wants, though, is a job and pride in self-achievement, but his hot-headed temperament and inability-to-function (why is not explained) leave him a constant outsider. He doesn't change clothes, constantly rants and raves against everything that displeases him, and is out to prove he has the worst manners in his territory.

When a student commune takes him in and applies nonauthoritarian methods for therapy, an attempt is even made to get him a job and teach him to read and write, in order to fill out an application. This doesn't work either, but helmer Friessner can get in a few slugs at unemployment problems and red tape in applying for a job. Further, the kid doesn't have a place to shack out with his girlfriend which, the film hints, might take the edge off his aggression.

Best scenes are those in which the director doesn't take himself too 'seriously and tries his hand at comedy. One of the students, for example, teaches Jimmi how to make a phone call to apply for a job, but since both are rather helpless individuals in their own way, the scene (and others between the two) is full of laughs. More of the same, and the pic's heavy social message would have gone down easier.

Credits are on the plus side. Cameraman Frank Bruehne is fast proving himself to be a top-flight lenser for exteriors. And while the amateurs sparkled as themselves, the real thesps only needed some dialogue to chew on to show their

---

stuff. Debut helmer Friessner is a comer. —Holl.

Thessaloniki Fest

O Asymvivastos
(An Uncompromising Man)
(GREEK-B&W)

Thessaloniki, Oct. 2.

A Michael-Lefakis, Greka Fil and Andreas Thomopoulos production. Written and directed by Andreas Thomopoulos. Features Pavlos Sidiropoulos, Vera Krouska, Betty Livanou. Camera (black & white), Demetris Vernicos; music, George Theodorakis; sets and costumes, Chris Protin; editing, George Triantafyllou; sound, Yannis Dermitzakis. Reviewed at the Thessaloniki Film Fest, Sept. 20, 1979. Running Time, **105 MINS.**

Writer-director Andreas Thomopoulos made good impression two years ago with his first pic, "Aldevaran," shown at that year's fest. This year he made his second film which, however, is not up to the quality level of his first one.

It is a character study of a man who does not want to live compromising with people and situations. A student of medicine, he gives up his studies to become a singer. Singing in the streets he contacts many people and, shares with them his thoughts and ideals until he meets a girl and marries her.

In order to be able to support his wife and children he resumes his studies at the University, gets his diploma and starts practicing in a hospital. There he realizes how the patients are cheated and exploited. Refusing to participate in such affairs he is fired. But when he opens his own office he gets a proposition to take part in another fraud. Not wishing again to compromise he leaves his job for good.

Director Andreas Thomopoulos knows how to handle his story, but this one based on an undeveloped script is very weak and the result is a modest effort. It is a well meaning, but uninspired tale without enough dramatic flair. Instead, it is full of naive philosophy and flat dialog which make commercial chances abrbad limited.

Worthy of mention is the performance of Betty Livanou who won the prize for best actress by the fest's jury, while Pavlos Sidiropoulos, who was supposed to carry most of the acting burden, failed. Other thesps are good, especially Costas Vrettos.

Technical credits are good in all aspects. —Rena.

To Mega Docoumento
(The Great Document)
(GREEK-B&W)

Thessaloniki, Oct. 2.

A George Filis and Katia Tsamati's production. Written by Katia Tsamati; directed and edited by George Filis. No other credits. Reviewed at the Thessaloniki Film Fest, Sept 20, 1979. Running Time: **120 MINS.**

George Filis is a Cypriot filmmaker who has turned out another film on the Cyprus drama. This time, after five years of work and intensive search, he has a picture that is an historical documentary covering the most important events of modern Greek history.

The pic got an honorary distinction at the fest. It consists of previous unknown material from old newsreels, films, stills and documents. A narration, though excessive and somewhat pompous, explains the events shown on the screen.

It is really a good rendering of the most dramatic and passionate periods of Greece's history, covering two Greek-Turkish wars, five civil revolutions and political upheavals.

It is apparent that this pic will have an impact on local audiences as well as to the Greek communities abroad showing them the events that they have lived and/or have heard of, but to those not familiar with the history of this period in Greece the pic will not have too much interest.

Editing is very good and all other technical credits are adequate.
—Rena.

Corpus
(GREEK-B&W)

Thessaloniki, Oct. 2.

A Stefi Film and Thanassis Retzis production. Directed by Thanassis Rentzis. Features entire cast. Screenplay, Gay Angueli, Thanassis Rentzis; camera (black & white), Vittorio Pietra, Elias Papageorgopoulos; music, George Kouroupos, Stefanos Vassilliades, Vaguelis Katsoulis, Demetris Lecas and Theodre Katelanos; editing, Thanassis Rentzis; narration Costa Tsoumas. Reviewed at the Thessaloniki Film Fest, Sept. 20, 1979. Running Time: **80 MINS.**

This is an advanced film, unique in conception and realization. Its theme is the human body as it was known from the beginning of civilization until today. Divided into seven chapters, each covers an historical era and the idea developed within it about the human body.

Thanassis Rentzis had made two films before which won prizes at Thessaloniki. This pic, made entirely by designs, is not a picture for general release, but is meant for art houses and or festivals.

It was the most noteworthy pic of this year's fest, a film full of harmony, color and designs, a peculiar and excellent achievement which honors not only its creator, but Greek film production as well.

Rentzis uses for each segment corresponding features of the era they belong. For the first chapter he used designs found in caves. For the Renaissance period paintings and wood engravings by famous artists, and so on. Each chapter is made by another style and a different music underscores it written by seven different composers.

This film deserved more than the honorary distinction it got at the Thessaloniki Film Fest. —*Rena.*

I Dadathes
(The Nurses)
(GREEK-B&W)

Thessaloniki, Oct. 2.
An Andreas and Nicos Zapatinas production. Directed by Nicos Zapatinas. Screenplay. George Skourtis, based on his own play; camera (black and white). Lefteris Papadopoulos; sets and costumes. Mikis Karapiperis. Tassos Diacomanolis; editor Takis Davlopoulos; sound. Argyris Lazaridis. Reviewed at the Thessaloniki Film Fest. Sept. 20, 1979. Running time: 110 MINS.
Cast: Vaguelis Kazan. Thymios Karakatsanis. Nikitas Tsakiroglou.

This pic is a theatrical piece transferred to the screen unsuccessfully. One gets the impression of watching a play on the stage. For this reason it is not likely to have an appeal to foreign audiences.

The story follows the adventure of two poor devils, Paul and Peter, who accept employment from a man as nurses to his wife. They have to live in a locked house with plenty of food, drinks, money, but the woman they are supposed to serve turns out to be a dead embalmed body. Their master believes that his wife is living and pretty and wants them to believe the same.

Paul, wishing to live well and have everything he was deprived of, accepts the situation, but Peter prefers freedom. Wishing to leave he is confronted by the master who wants to possess them both entirely. Finally, Paul, obeying orders of his master, kills his friend.

Director Nicos Zapatinas could not avoid the pitfalls which this theatrical piece offered. The static screenplay did not allow him to move the action further than the one room where the whole story takes place. The film is helped in large measure by its players, as the excellent performances distract the attention of the spectator from the confined settings and the excessive dialog.

Thymious Karakatsanis is ex-

cellent as Peter, Vaguelis Kazab very good as Paul and Nikitas Tsakiroglou firstrate as the master. The performances of these three thespians saves the picture.
—*Rena.*

Periplanissis
(Wandering)
(GREEK-B&W)

Thessaloniki, Oct. 2.
A Creativity Films Hellas production. Written and directed by Christoforos Christofis. Features entire cast. Camera. (black & white). Andreas Bellis; music. Eleni Karaendrou; sets and costumes. Christoforos Christofis. Georgette Themeli; editing. Depie-Danae Maroulakou; sound. Panss Panoussopoulos. Reviewed at the Thessaloniki Film Fest. Sept. 20, 1979. Running Time: 95 MINS.

This picture won the best picture prize at the fest plus two prizes for photography and sets. It was also the critics choice as the best picture.

It is the first directorial effort by young Christoforos Christofis who was considered the revelation of this year's fest.

It is a strange film and somewhat confusing for the average filmgoers and it would be a critics choice rather than a popular pacemaker. However, it might well attract limited international attention at art houses.

It is a film about Greeks emigrating to all parts of the world looking for a better way of life from the time of Alexander the Great, until the present. There is a poet who is heard but not seen, a lawyer, a boy, a clown, an old mariner, an impoverished noblewoman and a woman working in a railway station. Each one has his own story and drama which makes up the loosely-knit plot. In the end only the boy is left alone to symbolize the future.

The film is worth mentioning but uneven and without a dramatic structure to make it more comprehensible. The excellent photography by Andreas Bellis, who also did the sets, and the outstanding musical score by Eleni Karaendrou are definite assets.
— *Rena.*

Chicago Film Fest

Pavilion VI
(YUGOSLAVIA-COLOR)

Chicago, Oct. 30.
Centre Film (Belgrade) production. Directed by Lucian Pintilie. Screenplay, Pintilie; camera (color). Milorad Jaksic; no other credits provided. Reviewed at Chicago Film Festival screening room, Oct. 25, 1979. Running time: 92 MINS.
Cast: Slobodan Perovic. Zoran Radmilovic. Slavko Simic. Pavle Vujisic, Ljuba Tadic. Stevo Zigon. Drago Cuma.

Watching many of this sombre film's scenes unfold is like tracing the path of sludge through a drainpipe — slow going all the way. Director-scripter Lucian Pintilie's studied look at the mental unhinging of a Russian doctor at the turn of the century asks much patience in return for little reward. It's not a fair deal.

The apathetic doctor of middle years (Slobodan Perovic) is stuck in a remote rural Russian village sans family, friends and a lot of company. The medico seems to prefer it that way since he's a pensive chap given to such ruminations as, "happiness comes to a man only in solitude." In one long tracking shot after another, Pintilie shows his central character going to and from his home and office, walking amidst snow-covered woods, sometimes accompanies by a small child, a friendly character never developed.

The doctor's isolation is underscored by his slightly arrogant view that he's the intellectual superior of everyone around him — except for one person, a political prisoner detained in a local mental ward (the Pavilion 6 of the title).

The problem is that this character is a lunatic. Even so, exchanges with the rebel are so empathetic and intense, the doctor winds up questioning long-held values and going over the edge himself to a disastrous end.

"Pavilion VI" is loaded with metaphors of life under repressive governments, conformity versus individual expression, and so on. Production values are so-so and director Pintilie lingers with scenes long after specific points are made. A redeeming virtue is Slobodan Perovic's performance as the doctor. It's a subtle, intense and totally credible portrayal. —*Sege.*

The Last Tasmanian
(AUSTRALIA-DOCU-COLOR)

Chicago, Oct. 30.
An Artis production in association with the Australian Film Commission. Tasmanian Film Corp. and Societe Francaise de Production. Produced and directed by Tom Haydon. Written by Haydon. Rhys Jones; camera (color). Geoff Burton; score. William Davies; editor. Charles Rees; graphic design. Bernard Lodge; sound. Robert Wells. Mario Vinck. Edward Tise. Reviewed at Chicago Film Festival screening room. Oct. 22, 1979. Running time: 105 MINS.
Features Dr. Rhys Jones. Dr. Jim Allen. D.A. Lowe (Premier of Tasmania). Dr. Sir William Crowther. Andre Mary. Annette Mansell. Narrated by Leo McKern.

This earnest Aussie docu tells more than the viewer wants to know about the literal extermination of the Tasmanian aborigines who lived for some 1,200 years in

primitive isolation on an island south of Australia. How these "noble savages," as they struck Captain Cook, were wiped out by the forces of British colonialism in the late 19th century is the subject.

Produced, directed and co-authored by Tom Haydon, "The Last Tasmanian" grimly retells the particularly savage episode propelled by two dominant colonial forces — greed and the superiority of the Western white man. Pic isn't a racial tract but rather an informed, perhaps over-detailed, historical examination of what took place, where and why.

New information unearthed by anthropologist Dr. Rhys Jones is presented in reasonably coherent fashion, not an easy task since a host of social, historical, anthropological and archeological, not to mention moral, questions are tackled in 105 minutes. Filmmakers presumably wish to impart a sense of outrage to the viewer, but the response is likely to be a lot more controlled.

Briefly, although the aborigines on Tasmania were treated benevolently, enough by 18th century explorers, they became the wholesale victims of the British colonists between 1803 and 1876. Their numbers were reduced during that period from some 4,000 to one, literally. Latter is identified as Truganini, the last full-blooded Tasmanian, a key reference point in the pic.

The British were initially drawn to Tasmania to hunt seals. After establishing settlements and making off with some of the native tribeswomen, they set up permanent communities with the idea of eventually turning the island into a penal colony. British incursions were met by force from guerrilla bands of Tasmanians; retaliation was as brutal as it was comprehensive. A whole race of people was wiped out.

Through a number of visual devices, pic explains how it happened. Unfortunately, the manner of the telling seems forced — an unphotogenic Rhys pops up on camera much too often, reading from historical documents to underscore various points, and the pic's narrator, British actor, Leo McKern, seems on the verge of an anxiety attack.

Despite its expository flaws, "The Last Tasmanian" scores telling points about British and Australian scientific authorities, who defiled the Tasmanians even after death. In the name of anthropological research, hosts of Tasmanian corpses were exhumed, dismembered and otherwise mutilated. Even Truganini's grave was robbed, with her skeleton winding up on exhibit in a Tasmanian museum.

Technical values are almost as primitive as the pic's subjects, but the film's main points are delivered with some cogency. Commercial potential is extremely limited, although "The Last Tasmanian" would be a good bet in educational and museum forums.
—*Sege.*

Tess
(FRANCO-BRITISH-COLOR)

Paris, Nov. 1.

An AMLF release of a Renn Productions (Paris) Burrill Productions (London) co-production. Produced by Claude Berri. Features entire cast. Directed by Roman Polanski. Screenplay, Polanski, Gerard Brach and John Brownjohn, based on the novel "Tess of the D'Urbervilles" by Thomas Hardy; camera (color), Geoffrey Unsworth, Ghislain Cloquet; production designer, Pierre Guffroy; costume designer, Anthony Powell; music, Philippe Sarde; editor, Alastair McIntyre; art director, Jack Stephens; executive producer, Pierre Grunstein; co-producer, Timothy Burrill; associate producer, Jean-Pierre Rassam. Reviewed at the Elysees Lincoln cinema, Paris, Oct. 26, 1979. Running time: **180 MINS.**

Tess Durbeyfield	Nastassia Kinski
Alec d'Urberville	Leigh Lawson
Angel Clare	Peter Firth
John Durbeyfield	John Collin
Reverend Mr. Clare	David Markham
Mrs. Durbeyfield	Rosemary Martin
Vicar of Marlott	Richard Pearson
Marian	Carolyn Pickles
Mrs. Clare	Pascale de Boysson

"Tess" is a sensitive, intelligent screen treatment of a literary masterwork. Roman Polanski has practiced no betrayal in filming Thomas Hardy's 1891 novel, "Tess of the d'Urbervilles," and his adaptation often has that infrequent quality of combining fidelity and beauty.

The screenplay by Polanski, Gerard Brach and John Brownjohn judiciously blocks out the novel's action: Tess Durbeyfield is an uncommonly beautiful peasant girl whose derelict father learns of the family's descent from once noble Norman ancestry, the d'Urbervilles. Learning of the existence of a rich family bearing this name, Tess' parents induce the girl to present herself as a distant relation in the hope of reaping profit from the family tree.

The d'Urbervilles in question are not d'Urbervilles at all; they had merely bought the title. But the young rakish master of the house, Alec, gives her employment and succeeds in seducing her. Tess returns home and bears a child who dies after a short time.

The young girl again leaves home to live down her shame and misery on a dairy farm. She meets and falls in love with Angel Clare, the liberal-minded son of a pastor. They marry but on the wedding night, Tess reveals her past. Angel reacts horribly, leaves her the next day and goes abroad. Alone and wretched, Tess is reduced to a life of drudgery, sustained only by the hope of Angel's return.

The death of Tess' father and the subsequent penury of her family force Tess to accept Alec d'Urberville's renewed advances and aid (perhaps wisely, Polanski has omitted Alec's surprising conversion to evangelism). In the meantime, Angel returns to England remorseful and finds Tess living as Alec's mistress. In a paroxysm of desperation, Tess stabs Alec and joins her beloved. They share one night of happiness before the police overtake them in the Druid ruins of Stonehenge.

Beginning with the aesthetic premise that a three-hour screentime is essential in order to approximate Hardy's sublimation of well-worn melodramatic elements through its diffuse but richly textured narrative, Polanski gives breadth and filmic design to the heroine's tragic itinerary through rural 19th century English society.

Several scenes are exemplary for the way some of the novel's set-pieces are keenly transposed to the screen with delicacy and artfulness. The film's opening scenes, with the village maidens moving in procession along country roads to their May Day dance, their route crossing that of Tess' father, are particularly ample and splendid.

In the scrupulous recreation of Hardy's universe, Polanski has the sterling contributions of first-rate collaborators, especially the lambent color photography of Geoffrey Unsworth (who died during the shooting and was succeeded by Ghislain Cloquet, whose harmonious work is due homage to the late artist) and the superb production design of Pierre Guffroy. One recalls with astonishment that the film was entirely shot in France. Alastair McIntyre's editing, Anthony Powell's costumes and Philippe Sarde's music are excellent.

Despite all this excellence "Tess" falls short of total success in that it fails to achieve the accumulative emotional power of the book. Polanski falters in some crucial scenes.

The main insufficiency, however, is in the lead performance. Nastassia Kinski is a promising young actress endowed with fragrant beauty and grace, but she has only the beginnings of the technical and emotional register necessary to do justice to such a demanding role. Peter Firth is a good Angel Clare. The rest of the cast is impeccable, especially Leigh Lawson's excellent portrayal of Alec d'Urberville. —*Len.*

America Lost And Found
(DOCU-B&W)

A production of Media Study/Buffalo, American Portrait Unit. Project Director Dr. Gerald O'Grady. Produced by Tom Johnson. Directed by Lance Bird. Screenplay, John Crowley; narration by Pat Hingle; editor, Kate Hirson; music production, Arthur Gorson. Reviewed at Preview Theatre, New York, Oct. 26, 1979. **65 MINS.**

As if to celebrate, or to lament, the half-century since the onset of the Great Depression in October 1929, the new 65-minute documentary, "America Lost And Found," re-examines the consequences of the Wall Street Crash, that much-troubled decade of U.S. history prior to World War II. This is the tale of how we lost our confidence as our traditions went bankrupt, then regained faith as the unity and affirmation of war drew near.

"America Lost And Found" invokes many of the famous faces and voices of that period — F.D.R., Eleanor, Al Smith, Huey Long, Edison, Ford, a thousand others, even John Boles!

Perhaps in terms of new facts and insights, the film falls short for over-age viewers who are over-familiar with predictable stock-footage compilation documentaries. But the film succeeds anyhow. For one thing, much footage seems fresh although its topic is old. The selection and placement of a shot, juxtaposing it to another as irony, is intelligent. Pat Hingle's voice over the visuals is a voice weathered by the Depression.

Narration by John Crowley catches the contradictions of that decade, both the fun of it and its disastrous insanity. A half-dozen history professors were consultants to the film.

Producer Tom Johnson and director Lance Bird are both in their early 30s, but both have extensive experience in documentary and in public television.

"America Lost And Found" was funded by the National Endowment for The Humanities and WNET's Independent Documentary Fund. First seen at the Edinburgh festival last August, its U.S. premiere was at "Film at The Public" in New York.

Program kicks off a series of screenings, organized by Fabiano Canosa, on the Depression theme, entitled "1929-1939, From The Crash To The Fair." —*Hitch.*

The Fish That Saved Pittsburgh
(COLOR)

Not enuf hoopla in Pisces-ian basketball tale.

Hollywood, Oct. 30.

United Artists release of a Lorimar production. Produced by Gary Stromberg, David Dashev. Features entire cast. Directed by Gilbert Moses. Screenplay, Jaison Starkes, Edmond Stevens, from story by Stromberg and Dashev; camera (color), Frank Stanley; editor, Peter Zinner; art direction, Herbert Spencer Deverill; music, Thom Bell; choreography, Debra Allen; costumes, Patricia Norris; sound, Bud (Henry) Maffett; assistant director, Jerry Grandey. Reviewed at MGM Studios, Culver City, Oct.

30, '79, (MPAA Rating: PG.) Running time: 104 MINS.

Moses Guthrie . . . . Julius Erving
H.S. Harvey Tilson . . . . Jonathan Winters
Rev. Grady Jackson   Meadowlark Lemon
Setshot . . . . Jack Kehoe
Toby Millman . . . . Margaret Avery
Tyrone Millman . . . . James Bond III
Harry the Trainer . . . . . . Michael V. Gazzo
Driftwood . . . . Peter Isacksen
George Brockington . . . . . . Nicholas Pryor
Wally Cantrell . . . . M. Emmet Walsh
Mona Mondieu . . . . Stockard Channing
Malik Jamaal Truth . . . . Julius J. Carry III
Lucian Tucker . . . . Jerry Chambers
Jackhammer WashingtonJessie Lawrence
Ferguson
Bullet Haines . . . . . . Malek Abdul Mansour
Benny Rae . . . . Dwayne Mooney
Kenny Rae . . . . Daryl Mooney
Winston Running HawkBrancombe Richmond
Coach "Jock" Delaney . . . . Flip Wilson

Condensed down to the 15 minutes or so of actual storyline that's in the film, "The Fish That Saved Pittsburgh" might make a good half-time featurette for a telecast of a National Basketball Association game. As a full-length film, however, all it's got going for it is some fancy basketball footwork by the likes of Julius Erving, Meadowlark Lemon and a host of NBA players limning themselves. Commercial prospects are not outstanding for the Lorimar production; going out through United Artists, although a previous basketball pic, "Fast Break," did unexpected business.

Major problem facing producers Gary Stromberg and David Dashev was the absence of a real plot. The Pittsburgh NBA team is a washout, and eventually a walkout, as all the players ankle, leaving only million-dollar bonus baby Erving. Water boy James Bond III comes up with the idea of matching the astrological signs of the new players to jibe with Erving's (a Pisces), and with the aid of astrologer Stockard Channing, the team takes off on a winning streak that lands it in the championships.

While nobody's expecting an insightful study into sports psychology, "Fish" has trouble keeping even this superficial story line on keel. Director Gilbert Moses inserts court action at every conceivable juncture, destroying whatever dramatic continuity the film might have.

Scripters Jaison Starkes and Edmond Stevens fail to establish a solid grounding for Erving's lead character, although the athlete seems personable enough. Love interest with Toby Millman is negligible, and the rest of the plotting is even worse.

Biggest plus in "Fish" is that it gives several black thesps a rare opportunity for work outside of the exploitation arena, and Lemon, Julius J. Carry III, Jerry Chambers and Malek Abdul Mansour rise to the challenge with interesting performances. Jack Kehoe is good

as a pint-sized player, and Channing adds some sparkle as the stargazer. Jonathan Winters does his usual schtick, and actually cops some of the pic's rare humorous moments. Flip Wilson is in the film barely long enough to be noticed.

Tech credits range from adequate to poor with Thom Bell's music, supposedly an integral part of the story, failing to connect with the rest of the film. Lensing and editing are okay, but Bud Maffett's sound mixing is frequently off the mark, fading into incomprehensibility.

"The Fish That Save Pittsburgh" may enjoy some initial interest from basketball fans in the major cities and sports-hungry midwest, but is certain to lose its boxoffice bounce as the game progresses. Basketball has faced dwindling tv ratings, and its' unlikely paying audiences will respond to a sport they're disinclined to watch for free. —Poll.

Saraba Eiga No Tomo Yo
(So Long, Movie Friend)
(JAPANESE-COLOR)

Osaka, Oct. 29.

A Nippon Herald release of a Kitty Films production. Produced by Hideto Isoda. Features entire cast. Written and directed by Masato Harada. Camera (color), Masakichi Hasegawa; editor, Ko Suzuki; music, Ryudo Uzaki; art director, Yuji Maruyama; sound, Senichi Beniya. Reviewed at SBA Hall, Osaka, Oct. 29, 1979.

Cast: Naohiko Shigeta, Takuzo Kawatani, Atsuko Asano, Renji Ishibashi, Hiromitsu Suzuki, Miyako Yamaguchi, Toby Kadoguchi, Yuji Kosugi.

The directorial debut of film critic Masato Harada is a robust and energetic semiautobiographical work that envelops the viewer with its love of films.

Shuma (Naohiko Shigeta) is a "ronin" — a student looking for a university to admit him — in late 60s Tokyo. Whiling away an afternoon in a cinema, he strikes up an acquaintance with Dan (Takuzo Kawatani), a filmgoer whose addiction is even more pronounced than his own.

Problems ensue with the entrance of Minami (Atsuko Asano), a "bad girl" to whom Shuma is inexplicably drawn. His ardor turning to anger upon learning that she is little more than a gangster's moll, he asks Dan if the latter has ever wanted to kill anyone. While Shuma forgets this rhetorical question after going to Taiwan and losing his virginity, Dan — somewhat out of touch with reality and wanting to die like a film hero — remembers it all too well.

Harada's readily apparent proficiency as a director only serves to magnify his comparative short-

comings as a screenwriter. While his three major characters are fully three-dimensional people and while he has satisfactorily explained the friendship between Dan and Shuma, he has failed to proved a believable reason for the Minami-Shuma romance.

This failing aside, the film is a series of almost uninterrupted pleasures. The bond between Dan and Shuma is straight out of Howard Hawks and bits of everything from Dracula pics to "Singing in the Rain" are worked into the story.

A musical soundtrack of local hits from this particular era is an attraction. The camerawork of Masakichi Hasegawa is a perfect visual complement to the film's subtitle, "Indian Summer."

Where Harada really excels is in his handling of actors, with the performance he elicits from Kawatani, whom the director had in mind when he wrote the part of Dan, a standout. —Bail.

The Secret
(HONG KONG-COLOR)

Hong Kong, Oct. 30.

A Unique Films Production. Directed by Ann Hui. Stars Sylvia Chiang, Chiu Ah Chi, Tsui Siu Keung, Man Chi Leung, Li Hai Suk. Produced by Lo K.M., S.Y. Wu; screenplay, Joyce Chan; camera (color), C.M. Chung; editor, C.F. Yu; music composed by Violet Lam. Reviewed at Queen's Theatre, Golden Harvest, Oct. 25, 1979. Running time: 100 MINS.
Nurse and victim's
friend . . . . Sylvia Chiang
Female victim . . . . Chiu Ah Chi
The madman . . . . Tsui Siu Keung
Male victim . . . . Man Chi Leung
Male victim's mistress . . . . Li Hai Suk
(Cantonese soundtrack; English subtitles)

The abundant cinematic talents of tv-director Ann Hui is finally exposed with the release of "The Secret," her first for the big screen. It prominently displays the stylish technique of this femme Chinese director, a graduate of the London Film Institute. "The Secret" is loosely based on the authentic Lung Fu Shan murder case sometime in May 1970. It centers on the gruesome murder of a young couple tied to a tree with their faces smashed and clothes torn. The male victim is Yuen Shi-Cheuk (Man Chi Leung), medical student from the University, and an attractive girl (Chiu Ah Chi).

Hui combines exotic Oriental and Portuguese ingredients with Western influences, then spices her film with menacing moods of fear, environmental elements and close-up shots of suspicious but innocent-looking objects. The calculated suspense is tightened with a commendable original musical score composed by Violet Lam.

"Secrets" is out to scare the audi-

ence and the story is more or less of secondary importance in this chilling effort. The production can be lauded for its high style and universality in creating chic hysteria. On the other hand, it can be criticized for its shallow material and lack of content.

The story gets off to an intriguing start with dead bodies being discovered by young school children.

The general premise of "The Secret" is intriguing and hypnotic but the dark secret promised for the denouement is a disappointment. It ends up dramatic but limp and weak. The revelations are not stunning enough after being drawn by the mood, by the characters' outrageously strange actions and motivations. Then, the movie ends quite abruptly which is the second major weakness of the production. But overall, it achieves its objective of pleasurably scaring its viewers with generous helpings of suspense and what looks like "ghosts."

The persuasive production design shows sobriety, subdued fortissimo and intelligence. Sylvia Chiang shines in her role and is supported by a capable cast. As a film, it is basically cinema as visual art. It relies heavily on the weird murder and man-made supernatural imaginings that are later explained. The expressive cinematography is used to advantage in showing off Macao's environs.

"The Secret" has the tingles of a well-made, first-rate foreign mystery thriller and injects a classy image to the "made in Hong Kong" label. Unlike so many local pictures in the genre, it does not bog down till the very end.

Here is a contemporary Chinese suspenser that can exhibit both locally and abroad. It is a far cry from the assembly line movies of Shaw Bros., stale kung-fu features of the independents and the current low comedies of Golden Harvest. Hui is a major talent to watch and can be tabbed as a new Chinese master of suspense with quality. All in all, a most striking and memorable debut of a gifted and promising Hong Kong director. —Mel.

Chicago Film Fest

Gal Young Un
(U.S. COLOR)

Chicago, Nov. 6.

Nunez Films production. Produced and directed by Victor Nunez. Features entire cast. Screenplay, Victor Nunez based on a Marjorie Kinnan Rawlings short story; camera (color, TVC), Victor Nunez, Greg Garner; score, Charles Engstrom, performed by Azalea Blossom String Band and Lohman-Crozier Trio; editor, Victor Nunez; sound, Pat Garner, Bob Richter;

set decoration. Pat and Greg Garner. Reviewed at the Chicago Film Festival Screening Room, Oct. 30, 1979. Running time: **105 MINS.**
Matt .... Dana Preu
Trax .... David Peck
Elly .... J. Smith
Storekeeper .... Gene Densmore
Edna .... Jennie Stringfellow
    Also, Tim McCormack, Casey Donovan, Mike Garlington, Marshal New, Bruce Cornwell, John Pieters, Gii Lazier, Tina Moore, Marc Glick, Kerry McKenney, Sarah Drylie, Randy Ser, Bernie Cook, Fred Wood, Sissy Wood, Mr. and Mrs. Lewis Ivey, J.D. Henry, Billie Henry, Susan Holzer, Brian Lietz, Gus Holzer, Ross Sturlin, pat Garner.

Florida-based filmmaker Victor Nunez has come up with a slight, low-budget entry based on a Marjorie Kinnan Rawlings short story, set in Florida's rural back woods in the early thirties, about a lonely middle-aged widow who's victimized by a young, ne'er-do-well bootlegger.

Pic's tone is light, given the subject matter. The woman (Dana Preu) has almost a masculine homeliness that masks an intensely warm and giving nature she finds hard to express. The character as set up also has some cash, thus making her an attractive mark for the moonshine-making con man.

Witnessing the indignities heaped upon this woman is not pleasant, despite Nunez' attempts to maintain a light touch through snappy editing and a mock-country music score. It's grim going for the most part.

Once the con man (David Peck) woos and marries the woman, he sets about bilking her fortune to underwrite his burgeoning moonshine operation. Rather than losing the attentions of even a cruel companion, the woman is forced to work at the distillery against her will, to take all manner of verbal abuse, to feed and clothe him in demeaning fashion and, finally, to look the other way when he arrives home with his scatterbrained young mistress in tow (the gal young 'un of the title).

The woman's final revenge isn't sufficiently cathartic to cleanse the accumulated impact of the suffering viewed during the first nine-tenths of the film. The story is an unqualified downer, only slightly relieved by woman's friendship with the young mistress commenced at the finale.

The pic has its strong points, however. Technically, Nunez, who does everything here except go out for coffee, is a first-rate craftsman who extracts maximum visual mileage from modest settings. He is particularly skilled at positioning his camera to underscore plot points, and is a fine editor.

Nunez is much less successful working with actors. As the con man, Peck is particularly weak. His acting-school southern dialect

— plus a passing physical resemblance to actor Charles Grodin — lend unintentionally humorous aspects to his con-man characterization, much too broadly conceived in the first place. He's not believable in the part for a moment. ment.

Remainder of the cast — with the single exception of Preu — is adequate at best. **As the widow, Preu is a marvel. Her laconic yet** emotionally charged rendering of the victimized woman is completely right and a superb example of well-conceived under-acting. Preu's performance almost makes sitting through this dreary film worth it. —*Sege.*

Retrato De Teresa
(Portrait Of Teresa)
(CUBAN-COLOR)

Chicago, Nov. 6.
IDP Production. Directed by Pastor Vega. Features entire cast. Screenplay, Pastor Vega. Ambrosio Fornet: camera (color), Livio Delgado; editor, Mirita Lores; score, Carlos Farinas. No other credits provided. Reviewed at Chicago Film Festival screenig room, Oct. 29, 1979. Running time: **103 MINS.**
Teresa .... Daysy Grandados
Husband .... Adolfo Llaurado
Girl .... Alina Sanchez
Foreman .... : ...... Raul Pomares

Except for a handful of scenes of telling verisimilitude — laced with generous dollops of humor — it would be easy to dismiss Cuban director Pastor Vega's offering as soap-opera melodrama with a feminist slant. Too much of "Portrait of Teresa" is that but enough isn't.

In meticulously realistic detail, pic limns the daily challenges facing Teresa (Daysy Grandados) in trying to juggle her various roles as wife of a tv repairman (Adolfo Llaurado), mother of four, textile factory worker and costume designer for an amateur dance troupe.

Predictably, conflict ensues when the husband insists on the primacy of Teresa's domestic responsibilities. He wants her to stay at home, to be a mother and wifeservant. Teresa adamantly rejects such a limiting role and insists she wants more from marriage than her mother received.

The union founders, there's a separation during which the husband takes up with a full-thighed young beauty (portrayed with appealing zest by Alina Sanchez). Pic ends ambiguously after an attempted reconciliation doesn't hold — the husband agrees to share domestic chores but gags at giving his wife relief from the sexual double standard.

Director Vega and coscripter Ambrosio Fornet, unfortunately,

unfold the domestic scrapping in exhaustive detail and without a proper sense of pacing. Things aren't helped any by insertions of implicit and upfront agit-prop. One character, a factory foreman, presented as a benign family counselor, mouths lines like, "the revolution makes the impossible possible."

Even so, Vega has insinuated humor — the title character's mother observes, "men are men and women are women. Even Fidel can't change that." Vega is at his best when the pic focusses on scenes of specific marital conflict presented credibly, without a trace of sentimentality.

The cast principals are fine: Grandados beautifully combines a housewifely frumpishness with sullen sensuality; Llaurado is solid as a confused husband genuinely in love but without the slightest idea of what drives his mate. Other uncredited performers, portraying various family members and friends, turn in believable supporting performances. Less welcome are those from minor characters at plants, workshops and at the dance troupe, little more than propaganda puppets.

Production values are generally pedestrian as is Carlos Farinas' intrusive score, which sound like a large rhumba band recorded in a phone booth. —*Sege:*

---

1 + 1 = 3
(WEST GERMAN-COLOR)

Chicago, Nov. 6.
Genee & Von Furstenberg Filmproduktionsges M.B.H. and Heidi Genee Filmprodukt ion production. Features entire cast. Directed by Heidi Genee. Screenplay, Heidi Genee, Helga Kraus' camera (color), Gernot Roll; score, Andreas Kobner; editor, Helga Beyer; set design, Peter Grenz; costumes, Helga Beyer; asst. director, Robert Busch. Reviewed at Chicago Film Festival screening room, Oct. 31, 1979. Running time: **120 MINS.**
Katerina .... Adelheid Arndt
Bernhard .... Dominik Graf
Jurgen .... Christoph Quest
Anna .... Helga Storck
Robert .... Dietrich Leiding
Jurgen's Mother ..... Charlotte Witthauer
Bernhard's Father ... : ...... Kelle Riedl
Agent .... Helga Krauss
Lawyer .... Hark Bohm
Children .... Ina and Daniel Genee,
        Greta Kelwing, Karin Kussauer

This film, unspooled earlier this fall at the Montreal Film Festival is executed with the technical finesse of a tv blurb extolling the virtues of the Red Baron. "1 + 1 = 3" is a pleasantly scatterbrained drama about a pregnant young actress who decides to have her child minus the marital ministrations of either of two suitors, one of whom is the child's father.

German director and scripter

Heidi Genee has chosen to emphasize the lighter aspects of what promises to be — but never is in the film — a messy domestic situation. Larger social implications such as the disintegration of the family, child welfare and paternal rights are not tackled head on but always ironically by implication.

Trouble is, Genee's central idea — a woman cheerfully alone in a traditionally familial situation — hasn't been fully developed. Thus, "1 + 1 = 3" stretches lightweight material over a heavyweight, 120-minute running time. As likable as Genee's characters are (they behave with beguiling good humor in all manner of awkward situations) they can't sustain attention for the time the director dictates.

From the moment of first meeting with the actress (Adelheid Arndt), when she's three months pregnant to moments before birth at pic's end, the character doesn't change. She remains a pretty, fiercely-determined woman of quiet rationality, often the only cohesive force in the private dislocations facing those around her.

Her sister's marriage to an advertising manager cracks up. The father of one suitor, himself the father of her child, bumbles a marriage of 32 years standing and moves in with his sour-faced son. The other suitor, himself divorced, is a well-intentioned but slightly rattlebrained botanist who is also something of a mama's boy.

Genee deftly moves the characters and the settings around with welcome control; her editing and pacing are enviable. She extracts first-rate performances from a talented cast — Arndt is as lovely as she is gifted — and the principal and minor players are strong. Gernot **Roll's photography is lush to the** point of slickness, and Andreas Kobner's lilting score nicely complements the tone of the film.

For all its amiability, however, the pic is thin stuff stretched beyond the threshold of continued interest. Next time, Genee should hire another screenwriter. —*Sege.*

Boardwalk
(COLOR)

Touching character study. Jewish nabe under street hoodlum siege.

Atlantic Releasing Corp. release of a Gerrald T. Herrod production. Directed by Stephen Verona; screenplay, Verona and Leigh Chapman; exec producer, Gerry Herrod; producer, George Willoughby; camera (color), Billy Williams. No other credits provided. Reviewed at Rizzoli Screening Room, N.Y., Nov. 7, '79. No MPAA rating. Running time: **98 MINS.**

Becky Rosen	Ruth Gordon
David Rosen	Lee Strasberg
Florence	Janet Leigh
Leo	Joe Silver
Mr. Friedman	Eli Mintz
Eli	Eddie Barth
Charlie	Merwin Goldsmith
Strut	Kim Delgado
Peter	Michael Ayr
Marilyn	Forbesy Russell

At times genuinely affecting, at others patently manipulative, "Boardwalk" is a small, well-wrought feature that centers on the efforts of an elderly Jewish couple to survive the barrenness and dangers of their decaying Brooklyn neighborhood.

But although there's a strong emotional core (and ample talent) to its portrait of the stubbornly 'youthful' eldsters (Lee Strasberg and Ruth Gordon), it's the film's chronicle of their mounting terrorization at the hands of a black youth gang that overrides its tone, shading the pic into a "Death Wish" finale that ironically may be the peg for a wider audience.

Harnessing his generally superb cast against the impressively lensed backdrop of the depressed Coney Island beachfront environs, director and co-scripter Stephen Verona ("The Lords of Flatbush") quickly establishes his focal family as a tightknit, mostly loving unit struggling to keep its local cafeteria out of hock, while the Jewish and Italian middle-class families around them make their exodus to the safer suburbs.

Strasberg and Gordon, along with daughter Janet Leigh and middle-aged sons Joe Silver and Eddie Barth, refuse to budge, even when the old man's refusal to cower to local gang leader Kim Delgado prompts the gang to first steal from the cafeteria, later firebomb it, and eventually ravage their household.

Intercut with the family's mounting personal crises — Gordon's mid-film death from cancer, Leigh's estrangement from her musician son, the shuttering of the cafeteria — Verona gradually intensifies his coverage of the gang's vendetta, which includes the robbery and beating of close neighbors, a rampage through their own house and the eventual desecration of Strasberg's synagogue.

As charted here, the gang business is as contrived as the family details are moving, and while the victimization of the elderly (and the extra menacing edge of anti-Semitism) a headline-making fact of life in such areas, the cards are stacked so heavily that credibility eventually falls by the wayside. Whether the racist violence depicted might ignite the same kind of lower-case audience response that marred "The Warriors" and "Boulevard Nights" remains to be seen.

Verona's casting acumen and sensitivity to his actors is apparent throughout, most notably in Strasberg's tour de force as a decent, dignified and strong-willed 75-year old whose mounting grief lashes into "Death Wish" vindication at fadeout. The staccato gang episodes are disturbingly well handled, as are the family interrelationships, though the latter are sometimes overly mawkish in the writing, especially when Strasberg and Gordon aren't in exclusive focus.

Despite its schematized structure, "Boardwalk" succeeds in evoking a palpable and authentic sense of character and environment, aided to a major degree by British cinematographer Billy Williams' crisp, dynamic location lensing and lucid interior work. The film marks a major step ahead for Verona. —*Step.*

Parts The Clonus Horror
(COLOR)

None-too-horrifying sci-fi clone.

Hollywood, Nov. 8.
A Group 1 release of a Myrl A. Schreibman production. Produced by Myrl A. Schreibman, Robert S. Fiveson. Executive producer, Walter Fiveson. Directed by Robert S. Fiveson. Screenplay adaptation, Schreibman, Robert S. Fiveson; camera (Color), Max Beaufort; editor, Bob Gordon; music, Hod David Schudson; art director, Steve Nelson; costumes, Dorinda Rice Wood; sound, Ken Robinson; associate producer, Peter R.J. Deyell; assistant directors, Michael Lee, Paul Berkowitz. Reviewed at Joe Shore Screening Room, L.A., Nov. 8, '79. (MPAA Rating: R). Running time: **90 MINS.**

Richard	Tim Donnelly
Dr. Jameson	Dick Sargent
Jeff Knight	Peter Graves
Lena	Paulette Breen
Richard Knight	David Hooks
Jake Nobel	Keenan Wynn
Ricky	James Mantell
Dr. Nelson	Zale Kessler
George Walker	Frank Ashmore
Anna Noble	Lurene Tuttle
Senator	Boyd Holister

"Parts The Clonus Horror," being released by Group 1 simply as "The Clonus Horror," is a none-too-horrifying attempt to graft an Orwellian Big Brother conceit onto present-day American society. Execution simply isn't up to carrying off the idea, and biz looms flat as the picture.

Notion that clones would be virtually indistinguishable from normal inhabitants of suburban California is an intriguing one, and director Robert S. Fiveson has made do as best he could on his $250,000 budget by suggesting that an insidious menace lies present in a seemingly benign, comfortable environment.

Despite the contemporary setting, however, tale of a combined government - industrial - medical plot to clone the nation's populace without its knowlege seems many times warmed-over. Not only do echoes of "1984" and "Fahrenheit 451" reverberate strongly throughout, but pic's first half plays almost as a clone of George Lucas' "THX 1138."

Second act then evolves like a cheapie rerun of "The Parallax View," as rebel clone Tim Donnelly tries to expose plot to the real world in the face of omnipotent government authorities and hit men. Then, of all things, Donnelly decides he prefers life in the clone society to the world at large, since he at least feels at home there. Implausibilities abound throughout, robbing pic of any immediate or cumulative impact.

Seriousness of the effort indicates that Fiveson was at least trying hard, but direction hits a low during a lovemaking scene when camera rack focuses from Donnelly's hands caressing his g.f.'s posterior to a raging bonfire in the background. This is the kind of thing that ought to be left behind in film school.

Acting is uniformly rudimentary, and tech credits, while acceptable, are about a notch below standards normally found at main line indies. —*Cart.*

Can I Do It ... Til I Need Glasses?
(COLOR)

Shortsighted future.

Hollywood, Nov. 4.
A National-American Entertainment Corporation release of a Dauntless Production. Exec producers, Edward Colarik, Hal Wasserman. Directed by I. Robert Levy. Producer, Mike Callie. Screenplay, Mike Callie based on an original story by Callie and I. Robert Levy; Mike Price camera (color) Craig Green; editor, Steven Schoenberg; music, Bob Jung; art direction, Robert W. Zentis. Reviewed at the Hollywood Theatre, Nov. 4, '79. (MPAA Rating: R). Running time: **73 MINS.**

Features Roger & Roger, Jeff & Ernst, Victor Dunlap, Moose Carlson, Pat Wright, Joey Camen, Walter Oklewicz Saba, Ollie Prater, Ann Collier, Deborah Klose, Robin Williams, Ann Kellogg.

It doesn't take someone with 20-20 vision to figure out the motivation for the re-release of "Can I Do It ... Til I Need Glasses." Film is a juvenile, unfunny screen version of some of the oldest and worst sex jokes in comedy history. It has no plot, just a series of nonsensical vignettes masquerading as attempts at amusement.

In the usual set of circumstances, the picture probably would have been laid to rest after its limited distribution in 1977 and '78.

But because popular vidstar Robin Williams has a miniscule role (just three-and-one half minutes that were not even contained in the original version), the Mike Callie-I. Robert Levy film finds itself back at theatres boasting the screen debut of the tv actor. Latter will just not be reason enough for audiences to sit through this drivel and once the word is out picture should find itself back on the producer's shelf.

That is unless one of the many comedians featured happen to attain stardom in the future. —*Berg.*

Exoristos Stin Kentriki Leoforo
(Exiled In A Central Avenue)
(GREEK-B&W)

Athens, Oct. 25.

A Nicos Zervos and George Emirzas production. Directed by Nicos Zervos. Features Costas Ferris, Marilli Tsopanelli. Screenplay, Nicos Zervos, Costas Ferris; camera, (black & white), Sakis Maniatis; music, Nicos Zervos, Costas Ferris; sets and costumes, D. Fininis; editing Costas Ferris; sound, Panos Panoussopoulos. Reviewed in Athens, Oct. 23, '79. Running time: **90 MINS.**

This picture is about the generation gap between the generation that lived from 1950-1960 and the next decade. It is a noteworthy film because it describes the difference between these two generations in a true and direct way. However, it is too specialized for general release but should have a feature in the less commercial circuits and at festivals.

The story is about a man who is desperately wandering around Athens trying to adapt himself to the new social developments and with the "established" people and situations. He meets old friends but nothing can fill the emptiness he feels. His girlfriend is a girl of the seventies, full of enthusiasm and faith in the ideals of her generation. The man considers himself a "failure," a rebel against anything and the only solution, he thinks, that is left for him is to kill himself. However, things and events reverse towards the end of the picture.

Nicos Zervos narrates his story with constantly changing indoor sequences or with outdoor realistic scenes in which the people speak about their own problems and troubles. His camera explores the heroes of his picture, wishing to present their reactions.

All other production values are good. —Rena.

Chicago Film Fest

The Last Of The Blue Devils
(DOCUMENTARY-COLOR)

Chicago, Nov. 13.

Produced by the Last of the Blue Devils Film Co., John Kelly, Bruce Ricker and Edward Beyer. Directed by Bruce Ricker; written by Ricker and John Arnoldy; camera (color), Arnie Johnson, Eric Menn, Bob Gardener; editor, Thomas Henkel; sound, Rocky Rude and Wally Gaspar; executive producer, Mitchell Donian. Reviewed at the Chicago, International Film Festival screening room, Nov. 6, 1979. (No MPAA Rating). Running time: 91 MINS.

Cast: Count Basie and his orchestra, Big Joe Turner, Jay McShann, Buddy Anderson, Ernie Williams, Eddie Durham, Speedy Huggins, Budd Johnson, Baby Lovett, Charles McPherson, Paul Quinichette, Gene Ramey, Herman Walder, Jimmy Forrest, Crook Goodwin, Curtis Foster, Paul Gunther, Joe Jones, Sonny Kenner, Jesse Price, Buster Smith, Richard Smith, Calude Williams, Milton Morris. Also, film clips of Count Basie septet, Lester Young and the Charlie Parker-Dizzy Gillespie quintet.

Turning a straight-on documentary about musicians in performance — especially jazz musicians — into a visually interesting experience is an extremely tricky task. Whatever it takes, and it has been done brilliantly in the past, "The Last of the Blue Devils" just doesn't have it.

That's depressing to report since producer-director Bruce Ricker has the purest of intentions in attempting to revisit a fruitful place and period in jazz history — Kansas City during the late 1920s and early 1930s.

To his credit, Ricker hasn't inserted himself into the proceedings but has allowed the musicians themselves, in conversations and in performance, to recreate something of the flavor of the time this docu covers. In retrospect, he might have been better off being a bit more intrusive.

Ricker is a 36-year-old former New Yorker, who wound up practising law in Kansas City for a time before hitting on the idea of putting together a docu about Kansas City's enormous contributions to jazz history. He hit upon the idea of reuniting surviving members of a seminal KC group, Walter Page's Blue Devils, plus blues belter Joe Turner, and turning them loose in a contemporary club setting amidst a driving big band put together by tenor saxophonist Budd Johnson.

Ricker spiced up the proceedings by including footage of a recent Count Basie band perform-

ance, extensive chats with Basie himself and pianist-band-leader Jay McShann, and snippets of vintage footage showing Lester Young, Charlie Parker and Dizzy Gillespie in action.

Although hearing Basie's band in full flight is always a treat, the footage of the current orchestra's concert doesn't seem to have all that much to do with the period discussed. The Parker and Young footage, while technically crude, is marvelous stuff since anything visual or aural about these saxophone giants is inherently of interest.

Unfortunately, this footage is only a small part of the 91-minute running time. The Basie and McShann interviews are absorbing — the former is rarely this engagingly articulate in public — but run on too long. So too do the performances of Turner and other soloists with Johnson's big band, as aurally arresting as it is. One tires of watching musicians at work in a night club.

Perhaps most unfortunate of all, the pic fails to convey a cohesive picture of just who the Blue Devils were, and why they were so important. The Devils included Basie, singer Jimmy Rushing and Bassist Page and became the nucleus of Benny Moten's orchestra and finally Basie's big band.

The pic dwells too much in often inchoherent conversations with Ernie Williams, the Devil's drummer and a tangential figure. Even McShann's contributions — he hired Charlie Parker for his orchestra — aren't clearly discussed.

A brief interview with Milton Morris, a KC club owner active during the period discussed, is instructive not only about KC politics of the '30s under Boss Pendergast, but about Parker and saxophonist Ben Webster, another figure almost totally passed over.

Ricker would be wise to reedit the footage, add a informed narrative to cut down on superfluous reminisces by minor musicians, and make an effort to enliven the contemporary big-band footage. The Basie interviews, footage of his band, the conversations with McShann and the footage of Turner in vocal flight could well stand intact. Ricker has the makings of a fine music docu here. It's a shame he hadn't fully realized his project.

—Sege.

Caligula
(ITALO-U.S.-COLOR)

Rome, Nov. 16.

A PAC release produced by Bob Guccione and Franco Rossellini for Penthouse Films International and Felix Cinematografica. Stars Malcolm McDowell, Teresa Ann Savoy, Helen Mirren and Peter O'Toole; with John Steiner, Guido Mannari, Paolo Bonacelli, Giancarlo Badessi, Adriana Asti, John Gielgud and Leopoldo Trieste. Scenes directed by Giovanni Tinto Brass from an uncredited screenplay adapted from the story by Gore Vidal. Camera (Eastmancolor), Silvano Ippoliti; production designer, Danilo Donati; editing consultant, Nino Baragli; music, Paul Celmente. Reviewed at Holiday Cinema, Rome, Nov. 15, '79. Running time: 150 MINS.

Caligula	Malcolm McDowell
Drusilla	Teresa Ann Savoy
Cesonia	Helen Mirren
Tiberius	Peter O'Toole
Longino	John Steiner
Macrone	Guido Mannari
Cherea	Paolo Bonacelli
Claudio	Giancarlo Badessi
Ennia	Adriana Asti
Nerva	John Gielgud
Caricle	Leopoldo Trieste

There are two primary cases of mental sickness in this costly, litigation-ridden porno spectacle — one is the title character, Caligula; the other is Giovanni Tinto Brass, the creative spirit behind this moral holocaust.

With the biggest investment ever in porn to play with, Brass (and the anonymous editor who contributed a final 150 min. version from the three and a half hour edition seen at Cannes), in a creative fit of paranoic obsession, sifts through the pages of first century Rome under syphilitic Tiberius and epileptic Caligula to demonstrate with violence and horror the unlimited baseness of the human condition and to illustrate an anthology of sexual aberrations in which incest is the only face-saving relationship.

Any comment on political power is pure pretext for the basic dual design of degrading humanity and elongating ad nauseam his pocketbook illustrations of sexual fantasies. Brass tries wherever possible to make horror and lechery inseparable.

It is difficult to place a market evaluation on "Caligula." It violates censor scriptures in many countries. Nevertheless, "Caligula" cannot by any means be counted out as a commercial entry. It offers something for every appetite in pants or panties. It has a potential audience in flesh mag readerships and the Bob Guccione-Penthouse Films International presentation at the top of the credits is the link with millions of sex mag followers in America and elsewhere.

"Caligula" will also profit in release from the violent controversies it is bound to stir in all situations — capitalizing on con-

sequent curiosity to view the biggest genitalia costumer ever made.

What has Gore Vidal wrought? He is credited with basic story material though his original script for this project goes unmentioned. As a finished product, "Caligula" is far more Gore than Vidal.

Such established names as John Gielgud and Peter O'Toole will have to see to believe. Gielgud plays the only character worth saving and he dies by Caligula's hand before the young pretender is crowned. Malcolm McDowell as the sick and/or insane emperor (ruling four years from age 25) runs the gamut of cardboard emotions from grand guignol to hapless pathos. He comes off only when duplicating his wrathful, cruel stance in "Clockwork Orange."

Helen Mirren as Caligula's wife, gives the only performance of a developing character and brings it off with some stature. Teresa Ann Savoy as Caligula's sister-mistress maintains a uniform ambiguity about her inner feeings, but convinces as the stronger half of the couple appearing at the right time and place to protect her brother from taking the daily fatal step.

Effective supporting performances are delivered by John Steiner as the secretary-confidant, Giancarlo Badessi as Claudio — the retarded brother of Tiberius, Guido Mannari as the conspiring head of the pretorian guard and Adriana Asti, Mannari's wife and Caligula's mistress.

Paid off to yield final cut and end two years of film freeze litigation, Brass gets a kind of ambiguous director credit (scenes directed by). He filmed everything on screen; though some reports mention added porno inserts during the post-Brass completion period.

Deletions from the 210 minute version clandestinely screened at Cannes last May, would indicate the filmmaker's intention to stage a new "Fellatio Rise and Fall of the Roman Empire."

Style and obsessions go hand in hand. Brass is out to flaunt every last gruesome and lech detail in the spectator's face. He spares no one. Plebes, patricians, politicians — anything with human brain matter on two feet — are all associated in his mind with an eternal gut animalism in which human nature is only a vile or dirty joke.

This tarnished panorama of ancient Rome (equally valid for life and times before and after) is given a majestic mounting by veteran creative production designer Danilo Donati.

Sets, costumes and assortment of dressing and props give "Caligula" a background embellishment of singular fascination, lifting a tortured peep-show spectacle dimension.

Music by Paul Clemente attempts the same goal, but the score inexplicably reverts to vintage Hollywood schmaltz as a canopy idealizing true love from brother-sister-incest.

Et tu, Tinto. —*Werb.*

I Ora Tou Lykou
(The Hour of the Wolf)
(GREEK-B&W)

Athens, Oct. 25.
A Panayotis Anguelopoulos production. directed by Demetris Mavrikios. Features Costas Messaris, Maria Tsopanaki. Screenplay. George Mylonas: camera (black & white). Costas Papayannakis: music. Sakis Tsilikis: editing Panos Anguelopoulos: sound. George Michaelides. Reviewed in Athens, Oct. 24. '79. Running time: 92 MINS.

This film was shown at the Thessaloniki fest to the accompaniment of audience cat-calls. It is a disappointing waste of effort and money. Its commercial chances are slim even at local small situations with undemanding audiences.

It is the story of an actor who trying to avoid loneliness, strain and too much work, drinks heavily. He spends all his money on races and drinks and finally is fired by his producer. When he meets Eva accidentally, he falls in love. She tries to cure him but before his recovery, her father does everything to separate them. The hero kills himself, not knowing that Eva is carrying his child.

The film fails on most levels. The screenplay lacks imagination and the flat direction results in a picture which had no place in a festival. —*Rena.*

Sitting Ducks
(COLOR)

A sleeper which could spread wings for a long flight.

Hollywood, Nov. 20.
A Sunny Side Up production. Produced by Meira Attia Dor. Features entire cast. Directed, screenplay by Henry Jaglom. Camera (Metrocolor). Paul Glickman: music. Richard Romanus: sound, Jeffrey Hayes: assistant director. Jan Foster. No other credits available. Reviewed at Samuel Goldwyn Theatre. BevHills. July 27. '79. (MPAA Rating: R.) Running time: 90 MINS.
Simon . . . . Michael Emil
Sidney . . . . Zack Norman
Jenny . . . . Patrice Townsend
Leona . . . . Irene Forrest
Moose . . . . Richard Romanus
Jenny's friend . . . . Henry Jaglom

"Sitting Ducks" is the kind of picture that grows on viewers as it goes along and, as such, could mush-

room into a real sleeper success when word of mouth spreads. National marketplace has made room for a number of low-budget, off-beat personal pictures in the last couple of years, and given careful handling and intelligent sell, "Sitting Ducks," despite no-name cast and low advance profile, could spread its wings to enjoy a long flight.

Rather loopy story serves basically to provide a framework for several fabulous character riffs and to give a little momentum to any number of enjoyable crazy situations. Two small-time hustlers decide to make their stab at big money by making off with loot siphoned off from a gambling syndicate for which one works as a bookkeeper, and majority of the running time is devoted to their haphazard drive down the eastern seaboard to reach a plane that will carry them to a life of kings in Central America.

Along the way, hyped-up pair, acted in a marvel of improvisational style by Michael Emil and Zack Norman, meet up with two young ladies who hitch on for the wild ride. First, played by Patrice Townsend, gets a lot of mileage out of incessant innuendo and smiling sexual challenges, while second, Irene Forrest, seems to be stuck in a permanent crisis of self-confidence.

Interplay among the four constitutes the meat of the film, and every line and every scene springs spontaneously off the screen as if they're being played for the first time. Such a result can only be achieved through enormously careful casting and strategic catalyst work on the part of the director, so helmer Henry Jaglom deserves top marks for making his motley crew of characters, who are sometimes abrasive and patently foolish, come alive and completely engage audience sympahty.

Fact that Emil and Norman have been a team for some time is evident in their hilarious by-play, where nary a beat is missed. Emil's brash self-confidence is perfectly offset by Norman's relative reticence, and entry into their relationship of two equally disparate women makes for plenty of wacky opportunities, all of which are cashed in.

Townsend and Forrest are equally expert as the two tag-alongs, former projecting a teasing amorality which throws the men's relationship into a tizzy, the latter conveying an utterly convincing sense of vulnerability and uncertainty. Richard Romanus also scores as a show biz hopeful who strings along with the group for awhile.

Technical considerations clearly had second priority to work with ac-

tors, although pic is altogether acceptable and proficient in this area. Cinematographer Paul Glickman was often confined to cramped quarters such as cars and motel rooms, but claustrophobia never intrudes and performers keep every set-up hopping with energy.

Concluding reel introduces a melodramatic twist to the story, but resolution is in keeping with entire enterprise. A success at everything it sets out to accomplish, pic has qualities to win over many different types of audiences. —*Cart.*

Le Mors Aux Dents
(The Bit Between the Teeth)
(FRENCH-COLOR)

Paris, Nov. 16.
A UGC-CFDC release of a Sara Films UGC coproduction. Produced by Alain Sarde. Stars Jacques Dutronc, Michel Piccoli and Michel Galabru. Directed by Laurent Heynemann. Screenplay. Heynemann, Claude Veillot, Pierre Fabre. Camera. (Fujicolor) Alain Levent. Music. Antoine Duhamel. Editor. Armand Psenny. Art director. Jean-Baptiste Poirot. Sound. Michel Desrois. Reviewed at the Biarritz cinema. Paris, Nov. 5, '79. Running time: 99 MINS.

Loïc Le Guenn . . . . Jacques Dutronc
Pierre Chazerand . . . . Michel Piccoli
Charles Dreant . . . . Michel Galabru
Menard . . . . Charles Gerard

Laurent Heynemann, 31, made an excellent directorial debut in 1977 with the controversial "La Question," which had the courage to touch the still pulsating nerve of the Algerian War. In that true account of French paratroop's recourse to torture during the conflict, Heynemann displayed admirable restraint, keen analytical intelligence and a gift for directing actors.

These qualities are in full evidence in the director's second, more commercial, effort: "Le Mors aux dents," which treats a subject of great topicality: the race track. Every Sunday, 10,000,000 Frenchmen play the horses, into which they sink 25% of their leisure budget. Heynemann takes the viewer behind the scenes to spotlight the plotting and counterplotting that is called track-fixing.

The well-turfed script involves three pivotal figures: Chazerand (Michel Piccoli), a mathematical genius whose gifts are used in calculating the winning horses; Dreant (Michel Galabru), a rich scrap iron merchant with a file that compromises many high-ranking politicians and a desire to fix a racing event; and Le Guenn (Jacques Dutronc), a young political figure with a bright future which depends on his talents at dark machinations.

When Dreant "requests" a loan from Le Guenn's political party, Le Guenn is asked by his superiors to

find out what uses are planned with the cash. Learning of the businessman's plan to buy off a race, the politician leaks the information to Chazerand, who has his network of intermediary bettors play the expected winners. The resulting anormal concentration of winners in one area triggers an official investigation. Dreant (and Chazerand) are toppled, allowing Le Guenn's to retrieve the dangerous file.

For all its skillful but muted thriller aspects, which could provide a boost for overseas markets, "Le Mors Aux Dents" is most pleasurably an actor's film. Heynemann, who also directs for the stage, knows how to work with actors and it is the quality and fullness of the performances, right down to the minor roles, that gives the script a greater density and credibility. Piccoli is splendidly larger-than-life, Galabru shows once again his forcefulness in a straight dramatic role, and Dutronc is effectively lean and hungry-looking. —*Len.*

Stories From A Flying Trunk
(BRITISH-COLOR)

London, Nov. 13.
EMI Films release of a John Brabourne-Richard Goodwin production. Produced by John Brabourne. Richard Goodwin. Devised and directed by Christine Edzard. Features entire cast. Screenplay. Edzard, from three stories by Hans Christian Andersen: "The Kitchen," "The Little Match Girl," "Little Ida;" camera (color). Robin Browne. Brian West: editors, Rex Pyke. M.J. Knatchbull: music. Gioacchino Rossini, arranged by John Dalby. conducted by Philip Gammon: sound. Edgar Vetter, Hugh Strain: production manager. Jim Brennan: ballet settings. Irene Groudinsky: effects photography, Ken Worringham. Reviewed at EMI preview theatre. London, Nov. 12. '79. (BBFC Rating: U). Running time: 88 MINS.
Hans Christian Andersen . Murray Melvin
The Mother . . . . Ann Firbank
The Little Match Girl . . Tasneem Maqsood
The Tramp . . . . John Tordoff
Queen Victoria . . . . John Dalby
Little Ida . . . . Johanna Sonnex
Ballet Mistress . . . . Gerd Larsen
The Lettuce . . . . Patricia Napier
Prince Potato . . . . Graham Fletcher
The Princess . . . . Lesley Collier
Vegetables . . . . Dancers of the
Royal Ballet, London

Following on from their 1970 blend of fairytale and dance, "Tales Of Beatrix Potter," British producers John Brabourne and Richard Goodwin have come up with a more offbeat, but less beguiling, feature version of three stories by the classic children's author, Hans Christian Andersen.

Modern London locations replace the 19th century Danish settings of the original tales, but most kids will still be confused as to what's going on. The essential thread of each separate episode does not emerge strongly enough upfront to keep young minds interested in what develops. The third, too-long story is especially likely to prove bewildering, although there's some pleasing ballet at the end for fans who stay with it. Release calls for careful handling.

Stopframe animation is used extensively — to "bring alive" a range of kitchen items (chatting while the householders are out) in the first story, and various vegetables (ambitious to be dancers) in the third. Much of the confusion arises from a lack of strong vocal characterization given to the different objects. The second story, in which Andersen's Little Match Girl is portrayed as a poor Asian child in London's East End, suffers from a lack of clarity occasioned by night location shooting on limited resources.

Some of the effects, competently shot by Ken Worringham, will delight those still inclined to believe in magic, and a pas-de-deux by Royal Ballet dancers Lesley Collier and Graham Fletcher is good by any standard. But Christine Edzard, who devised and directed, could have kept a keener eye on the narratives, and not relied on individual ingredients to provide the appeal. Editor Rex Pyke deserves credit for imparting some fluency to the erratically-paced material, and achieving some seamless jumpcuts. —*Simo.*

Bobo, Jacco
(FRENCH-BELGIAN-TAHITIAN-COLOR)

Paris, Nov. 5.
A Planfilm release of a Belstar - AMS - Cathala - Tour Films - Pacific Business Group (Tahiti) - Sodep-Belga Films (Belgium) co-production. Produced by Jacques Dorfmann, Laurent Meyniel and Norbert Saada. Features entire cast. Written and directed by Walter Bal. Camera (Fujicolor), Pascal Gennesseau; sound, Alain Curnelier; editor, Michel Lewin. Music, Jacques Revaux. Reviewed at Studio 409, Paris, Oct. 23, 1979. Running time: **92 MIN.**
Jacco .... Laurent Malet
Magda .... Annie Girardot
Freddie .... Michel Montanary
Lise .... Evelyne Bouix
Guillaume .... Jean-Claude Brialy

Facile characterization and trite caricature are the earmarks of this first film by Walter Bal, a Dutch-born director of photography who works in France. Bal also wrote the script, which is a poor man's version of Bertrand Blier's "Going Places" (Les Valseuses) with moral safeguards installed.

Laurent Malet plays a callow young man who knocks about with a buddy (Michel Montanary), treating everyone and everything with utter crassness. Malet's surrogate mother-figure and indulgent mistress is Magda (Annie Girardot), who runs the bar in which the two youths hang out.

When Malet lays eyes on the beautiful daughter (Evelyne Bouix) of a woman who has picked him up at the bar, he drops both Girardot and Montanary to pursue her. His persistent advances finally break down her defensive impassivity, but the young girl is too weak-willed to ward off the hypocritical machinations of her mother, who maries her off to a businessman. His old pal having died in the meantime, the disillusioned Malet returns to Girardot a little sadder and, yes, a little wiser.

Bal's outlook is painfully simple-minded, with its over-30 middle class ogres and mummies (barring two or three indulgent, charitable sounds) and its shiftlessly abrasive, but basically good and sensitive, youth. The social and sexual rembles of the two companions are banal, missing the vigor and moral ambiguity that made "Going Places" so genuinely disquieting. Here the characters earn neither moral reprobation nor belated sympathy. —*Len.*

Geschichten Aus Dem Wiener Wald
(Tales from the Vienna Woods)
(W. GERMAN-AUSTRIAN-COLOR)

Berlin, Nov. 2.
A Coproduction of MFG-Film, Munich-Arabella-Film, Vienna-Franz Seitz Film, Munich-Solaris-Film, Munich, and Bayerischer Rundfunk, Munich; German distributor, Neue Constantin Film. Features entire cast. Produced and directed by Maximilian Schell. Screenplay, Christopher Hampton. Schell, based on folk play by Oedoen von Horvath with same title; camera (color), Klaus Koenig; sets, Ernst Wurzer; editing, Dagmar Hirtz. Reviewed at Gloriette Cinema, Berlin, Nov. 1, '79. Running time: 100 MINS.
Marianne .... Birgit Doll
Alfred .... Hanno Poeschl
Zauberkoenig .... Helmut Qualtinger
Valerie .... Jane Tilden
The Grandmother ..... Adrienne Gessner
Oskar .... Goetz Kauffmann
Hierlinger .... Andre Heller
Rittmeister .... Norbert Schiller
Mister .... Eric Pohlmann
Erich .... Robert Meyer
Master of Ceremonies ....
.... Wlater Schmiedinger
The Baroness .... Elisabeth Epp
Helene .... Lil Dagover
Beichtvater .... Vadim Glowna
Gnaedige Frau .... Vera Borek
Havlitschek .... Gerry Kronberger
Aunt .... Maria Englstorfer

Oedoen von Horvath, a contemporary of Bertolt Brecht who died tragically in Paris in 1938 (lightning struck a tree on the Champs Elysees under which he was standing during a rainstorm), experienced a renaissance on German stages recently when four of his Austrian-Bavarian folk-plays were rediscovered after long neglect under the Third Reich and during the postwar years. They included "Italian Night," "Kasimir and Karolina," "Faith, Love, Hope," and "Tales from the Vienna Woods" — "Tales" being his most complete and successful play.

Maximilian Schell, the actor-director, made "Tales from the Vienna Woods" with genuine Horvath thesps, Viennese actors who have played their respective roles several times on Austrian and German stages, so well in fact that their names on a movie marquee will guarantee a sizable home audience. Jane Tilden (Valerie), for instance, is known as a Horvath prototype, while others — Birgit Doll, Hanno Poeschl, Helmut Qualtinger, Eric Pohlmann — fit their roles like Strauss's music does the soundtrack.

"Tales from the Vienna Woods" is bittersweet, nostalgic, and laced with irony carried to its tragic dimensions. Horvath wrote his plays in cafes and beerhalls, mastering the dialect of the common people at the same time as linking his writing to the Austrian folk tradition, Marianne, his frail, romantic, tender-hearted heroine, is doomed from the start as a victim of the social conditions in a decaying Vienna of 1930, a city ripe for plucking by the equally vulgar National Socialism movement. The title of the play refers ironically to Johann Strauss and his operetta.

Our heroine from the Vienna Woods has been matched by her father to a butcher, but she is seduced by, and falls in love with, the good-for-nothing Alfred, with whom she has a child — and because of whom she is disowned by her father. When her lover abandons her, she sinks into the demimonde of Vienna to earn the pennies necessary to care for her child, and her father one day visits a striptease club with friends to find she is one of the performers. This descent into hell is echoed in other Austrian - Bavarian - Hungarian plays (Ferenc Molnar's "Liliom" offers a striking parallel) and is found in nearly all of Horvath's plays.

The figures in "Tales of the Vienna Woods" are much more than just flesh-and-blood, down-to-earth human beings — together, they offer a mosaic of society, revealing the good with the bad in humanity, but particularly the bad in times of depression and poverty. Thus it is that a kindly, but cruel, grandmother allows the child to catch a severe cold and die at the end. Also, Marianne has no way out of her misery and falls finally into the coarse hands of the butcher like another piece of flesh he can handle and abuse as he likes. The aging, sensuous Valerie, who lost Alfred to Marianne, comments with compassion on the rights of the girl to live her own life, but she too can do nothing to change the course of events.

Schell's direction is solid and geared to the literary and dramatic line of the story, relying on Horvath's rich dialog must of the way. The other pluses are tight editing and a easy hand with the actors. Pic may not be exactly festival fodder, but it's a sure bet for German films weeks and a windfall for Horvath fans abroad. —*Holl.*

Shaolin Abbot
(HONG KONG-COLOR)

Bangkok, Oct. 31.
A Shaw Bros. production and release. Produced by Run Run Shaw. Directed by Ho Meng-hua. Executive producer, Mona Fong. Features entire cast. Screenplay, Yi Kuang; camera (color) Yu Chi; art director,. Chen Chin-sam; editor, Chiang Hsing-lung; music, Chen Yung-yu. Reviewed at Warner theatre, Bangkok, Oct. 30, '79. Running time: 95 MINS.
Chih Shim .... David Chiang
Pai Mei .... Lo Lieh
Wu Mui .... Lily Li
Li Kam-lun .... Hsu Shao-chiang
Feng Dao-te .... Ku Kuan-chung
Yun Cheng .... Sze Wei
Chin Bao .... Pan Pin-chang
Yao Yin-chi .... Yu Yung
Hung Hsi-kuan .... Tang Yin-charn
Tung Chien-ching .... Wu Hang-sheng

There are at least three types of kung fu films. Bruce Lee started a serious look at kung fu as an intriguing Chinese martial art, using the body as a lethal weapon. Lee's director, Lo Wei, had an inspiration: kung fu follows hostile but dancelike techniques which, with some comical twists can elicit laughter instead of cheers.

Then, not to be outdone, Shaw Bros., largest producer of Chinese pictures, used both serious and comical patterns and what's in between besides — serio-comic kung fu. To this last-named format belongs director Ho Meng-hua's "Shaolin Abbot," toplining David Chiang in the title role.

"Shaolin Abbot" has the all-too-familiar story of crime and revenge. The crime is committed against Shaolin monks, executed en masse except for one survivor (David Chiang) by the Ching dynasty government. The monks violate an order against storing arms and are almost wiped out for it.

Chiang eliminates his enemies in the order of their fighting skill, that is, the climactic kung fu duel with archenemy Lo Lieh, is saved for the last.

Generally, kung fu films do not leave room for romance, and "Shaolin Abbot" is no exception. The leading femme, Lily Li, plays a nun. Any erotic scenes are out of the question and utilized only as a joke.

Acting is commendable, since the

main cast has had so much training in this genre. Main emphasis is lots of martial art techniques — old and new. —*Cano.*

Geheime Reichssache
(Top Secret - The History of German Resistance Against Hitler)
(W. GERMAN-DOCU-B&W)

Chronos Production, Berlin. Directed by Jochen Bauer. Written by Karl-Heinz Janszen; research, Lola Braxton; English adaptation, Esther and Albert Hemsing; producer, Bengt von zur Muhlen; asst. director, Manfred Helling; editor, Evelyn Mundin; music, Wolfgang De Gelmini; sound, Reiner Lorenz; optical work and effects, Studio Batoschek. Reviewed at Museum of Modern Art as part of "Recent Films From West Germany" series, Nov. 17, 1979. Running time: **100 MINS.**

(English narration and subtitles)

As part of a "Recent Films From West Germany" series at New York's Museum of Modern Art, in association with Goethe House New York and Export-Union der Deutschen Filmindustrie e.V. (Munich), this documentary, on screen, is more properly labeled "The History of the Trial of the July 20, 1944 Attempt to Assassinate Hitler." Footage of the trial is cross-cut with footage of Hitler's growth in power. That somewhat puts the lie to the film's title as the "resistance" shown is of a comparative handful of people, here and there, and much of it is not "resistance" which would mean that they were against him from the beginning but of their attempts to get rid of him once the evil work was done (and in many cases, with their willing cooperation).

Again, the other footage of literally thousands of people cheering with happy countenances and obvious approval overpowers the "resistance" claim. It doesn't really need this film, or similar ones, to negate the fact that Germany, for the most part, accepted and followed the Hitlerian philosophy.

Technically, the film is excellent with crisp footage, much of it not previously seen (where would documentarians be today if the Nazis hadn't had such fantastic egos that they carefully filmed all of their own activities?). The hidden cameras in the courtroom and the first-class sound bring the spectator right into the scene. Previous editing may be responsible for the fact that not one defendant is shown "speaking back" to the court.

An ambitious but not very revealing film, suitable for museum and school use but with little interest to the general public. —*Robe.*

Chicago Film Fest

The Last Word
(U.S.-COLOR)

Chicago, Nov. 20.
A Variety International Pictures Inc. release. Produced by Richard C. Abramson and Michael C. Varhol. Directed by Roy Boulting. Stars Richard Harris, Karen Black. Screenplay, Michael Varhol, Greg Smith, L.M. Kit Carson, based on a story by Horatius Haeberle; camera (color), Jules Brenner; editor, George Grenville; score, Carol Lees; production designer, Jack Collis; sound, Bill Marky and Dick Portman; set decorator, Dennis Peeples; special effects, Henry Millar; exec producers, A.J. Leydton, John Berglas, Reiner Walch. Reviewed at the Biograph Theatre, Chicago, Nov. 15, '79. (No MPAA rating.) Running time: **105 MINS.**

Danny Travis	Richard Harris
Paula Herbert	Karen Black
Captain Garrity	Martin Landau
Ben Travis	Dennis Christopher
Governor Davis	Biff McGuire
Roger	Christopher Guest
Denise Travis	Penelope Milford

Also, Bonnie Bartlett, Jorge Cervera, Nathan Cook, Linda Dangcil, Alex Henteloff, Pat McNamara, Michael Pataki, Natasha Ryan, Charles Siebert, James Staley and Richard Venture.

Despite its muddled conception and sometimes awkward execution, "The Last Word" (formerly titled "Danny Travis") is at heart an engaging film about a put-upon but amiable Irish inventor who fights City Hall — and after a good deal of melodramatic anguish — wins. Careful playoff could assure reasonably good b.o. results.

Set apparently in Los Angeles, the pic tells of Danny Travis' (Richard Harris) efforts to halt demolition of the ramshackle apartment house he and his three children (Dennis Christopher, Penelope Milford and Natasha Ryan) occupy along with a group of Chicano and other ethnic families.

Villain here is a smarmy governor (nicely portrayed by Biff McGuire) intent on urban renewal for private gain hypocritically masked as public good. All this is fairly familiar, if not predictable stuff, but "The Last Word" managed to score some solid comic and serious points about abuse of power by public officials and the potency of television news.

The film's fundamental weakness is its attempt to balance a kind of high-level tv sitcom comic sense with an earnest appraisal of a contemporary urban problem. The comedy, well-executed for the most part, often undercuts the pic's more serious underpinnings, sometimes vitiating the effect of both. Pic is based on a story by Horatius Haeberle, and had three writers (including Karen Black's husband,

L.M. Kit Carson) involved with the script. It shows.

A strong point is the generally good cast. Harris' portrayal of the inventor, complete with a brogue and crooked hat, starts off on a somewhat false note. He's not physically ideal for the part of the widowed, idealistic but genuinely talented inventor whose lack of basic business sense leaves his family on the brink of public assistance.

But as the pic develops, Harris informs his characterization with warmth and a coolly masked sense of outrage. Facing eviction, the inventor kidnaps a sheriff, holding him hostage in the apartment until the nefarious governor is exposed. Melodrama ensues as a company of police try to extricate the inventor from the apartment to alternately funny and grisly (the son is shot) results.

Karen Black is on hand as a happy-talk tv news reporter who has brains enough to realize that Travis' governmental skirmish is a solid story—"We may win a Pulitzer Prize for this," her boss advises. Black manages to crash the inventor's under-siege apartment for an exclusive, and from then on, any resemblance to Jane Fonda's role in "The China Syndrome" is purely intentional.

Dennis Christopher and Penelope Milford are two fine young performers, and both are wasted in their limited roles as Harris' older children. Martin Landau is very funny as a harassed police captain.

Director Ray Boulting has a nice sense of pacing, and sees his performers safely through the melodramatically arbitrary situations imposed via script-by-committee. Pic, incidentally, is being released by Variety International Pictures as this Los-Angeles-based indie's first big feature film entry. The company could have done a lot worse. —*Sege.*

Imposters
(U.S.-COLOR)

Chicago, Nov. 20.
Produced and directed by Mark Rappaport. Features entire cast. Screenplay, Rappaport; camera (color), Fred Murphy; set designer, Bob Edmonds; no other credits provided. Reviewed at the Chicago International Film Festival Screening Room, Nov. 13, 1979. Running time: **110 MINS.**

Chuckie	Charles Ludlam
Mikey	Michael Burg
Tina	Ellen McElduff
Gina	Lina Todd
Peter	Peter Evans

With "Imposters," Mark Rappaport's fifth feature, it's tough to decide whether he's just shucking or is simply untalented. Given his reputation in the hermetically-sealed world of non-commercial New York indie production — Rappaport's previous films, especially "Mozart in Love" and "Local Color," have their following and his "The Scenic Route" has been aired on public tv — it seems he's only pulling the viewers' collective leg.

To invest 110 minutes doing so is at best an futile exercise, and the result is tedious. It's hard to say exactly what Rappaport is up to in "Imposters," a tale of a pair of would-be murderous vaudeville magicians and their luscious lesbian assistant who takes up with a rich young man given to simpering and a little prevarication of his own.

The characters in deadpan fashion for the most part mouth banal lines in an intentionally unconvincing style. It's difficult to assess the import of Rappaport's put-on approach to the material but it's a bore to watch.

Charles Ludlam and Michael Burg do their best to inject some life into the magician characterizations, a low-camp set of twins who lean on film figures of the past, particularly the Marx Brothers and Peter Lorre. Burg, in particular, has a gift for comedy and would be worth seeing in another vehicle.

Ellen McElduff, a legit actress of earnest credentials, is easy to look at and would also be welcome in another film. Peter Evans plays the rich young dissembler.

Rappaport spent some $115,000 on this pic, shot in his SoHo studio in Manhattan and in other New York locations. (A well-timed $25,000 injection came from an unnamed Chicago investor). "Imposters" has a chintzy, claustrophobic look, and what's on the screen doesn't appear to justify even this modest outlay. —*Sege.*

Kramer Vs. Kramer
(COLOR)

Powerhouse drama of husband-wife conflict. Big money outlook.

Hollywood, Nov. 27.

A Columbia Pictures release of a Stanley Jaffe production. Produced by Stanley R. Jaffe. Written and directed by Robert Benton. Based on a novel by Avery Corman. Stars Dustin Hoffman; camera (color), Nestor Almendros; editor, Jerry Greenberg; music, Henry Purcell (adapted by John Kander), Antonio Vivaldi (adapted by Herb Harris); production designer, Paul Sylbert; costumes, Ruth Morley; associate producer, Richard C. Fischoff. Reviewed at Columbia Pictures, Burbank, Nov. 20, '79. (MPAA Rating: PG.) Running time: 105 MINS.

Ted Kramer . . . . Dustin Hoffman
Joanna Kramer . . . . Meryl Streep
Margaret Phelps . . . . Jane Alexander
Billy Kramer . . . . : Justin Henry
John Shaunessy . . . . Howard Duff
Jim O'Connor . . . . George Coe
Phyllis Bernard . . . . Jobeth Williams
Gressen . . . . Bill Moor
Judge Atkins . . . . . Howland Chamberlain
Spencer . . . . Jack Ramage
Ackerman . . . . Jess Osuna

Columbia Pictures has the perfect Christmas offering. "Kramer Vs. Kramer" is a perceptive, touching, intelligent film about one of the raw sores of contemporary America, the dissolution of the family unit. It's a tribute to writer-director Robert Benton, along with leads Dustin Hoffman, Meryl Streep and Justin Henry, that "Kramer" is about people, not abstract stereotypes. The Stanley Jaffe production should be greeted with warm boxoffice response from a wide variety of audiences.

Stories on screen about men leaving women, and women leaving men have been abundant as of late, but hardly any has grappled with the issue in such a forthright and honest fashion as "Kramer." In refashioning Avery Corman's novel for the screen, Benton has used a highly effective technique of short, poignant scenes to bring home the message that no one escapes unscarred from the trauma of separation, divorce and battles over child custody.

It is in the latter arena that "Kramer" takes place, as Meryl Streep breaks with up-and-coming ad exec Hoffman and tyke Henry to find her own role in life, "outside of being somebody's daughter, or wife or mother." Hoffman is thus left with a six-year-old son he barely knows, and begins a process of "parenting" that is both humorous and affecting.

Benton weaves his story so skillfully that the growing emotional impact of the relationship between Hoffman and Henry never becomes sentimental, nor does Streep's melodramatic reentry three-quarters into the film, when she comes to claim her first-born with the traditional mother's prerogative.

While a nasty court battle ensues, the human focus is never abandoned, and it's to the credit of not only Benton and Jaffe, but especially Hoffman and Streep, that both leading characters emerge as credible and sympathetic.

If Benton's direction was not so smooth and effortless, Hoffman could have "stolen" the picture with the force and dynamism of his performance, his best in years. Willing to abandon a bright future under the tutelage of ad agency topper George Coe, Hoffman runs the gamut of emotional responses while never losing contact with reality. Moppet Henry, a tyro performer, offers the perfect counterbalance to Hoffman, without descending into kiddie schtick.

Streep again shines in a "minor" role she manages to make "major," and rest of cast is likewise superior, especially Jane Alexander as a friend of the couple who switches allegiances, Howard Duff as Hoffman's realistic lawyer, and Jobeth Williams as a one-night stand for Hoffman.

Technically, "Kramer" is breathtaking, with Nestor Almendros' haunting imagery perfectly illuminating Paul Sylbert's rich settings. Special mention should also be made of Jerry Greenberg's smooth editing, and especially the musical choice of selection by Henry Purcell and Antonio Vivaldi. In a year when film music has sometimes overshadowed the screen action, the classical excerpts bestow an additional patina on a pic that already glows. —*Poll.*

Taxidi Toy Melitos
(Honeymoon)
(GREEK-B&W)

Athens, Oct. 25.

George Panoussopoulos-Movie Makers and Betty Livanou picture. Written and directed by George Panoussopoulos. Features Stavros Xenides, Aleca Paizi, Betty Livanou, Guely Mavropoulou, Marica Nezer, Koulis Stoliguas, Malena Anoussaki. Camera (black & white), Andreas Bellis; music, Manos Hatzidakis; sets and costumes, Thanassis Papayannacos, Yannis Kalaitzis; editing Yanna Spyropoulou, Panos Panoussopoulos. Reviewed in Athens, Oct. 22, '79. Running time: 112 MINS.

This is the first picture directed by George Panoussopoulos who, as a cameraman, had worked from 1965 till now on many Greek films.

His picture swept many prizes at the Thessaloniki fest, for best picture, best new director, best actor and actress. Commercially his picture has an adult appeal and will chalk up good b.o. results in discriminating situations with proper handling.

It is a film about people who, getting old, realize that very little time is left for them to live. The central characters are a couple in their sixties, Leon and Zaharoula, who are about to spend their vacation at their customary summer resort. But this time is different. Their only daughter has married and left for her honeymoon. Leon and Zaharoula feel lonely and, for the first time, realize that every day gets them nearer to the end. Leon especially is more anxious, almost panicky. One afternoon, walking with his wife by the beach, he is overwhelmed by a strong wish to do something crazy. He takes off his clothes and throws himself into the sea. Zaharoula follows him, but as she plays with the waves she is drowned.

Her death upsets other middle-aged vacationers. The tragic accident breaks up their everyday routine. Their dreams and passions come alive. Finally men and women start dancing in the garden of the hotel hysterically thinking they are young again. They are ready for their last journey.

Generally the picture shows the directorial know-how of its creator. However, the weakness of the script did not allow him to explore characters beneath their surface.

A great asset of the picture is the high level of acting. Stavros Xenides and Betty Livanou got prizes for their performances. Aleca Paezi, Guely Mavropoulou, Pericles Christoforides and all others in the cast turn in very good characterizations.

Other assets are the excellently balanced lensing by Andreas Bellis and the enchanting music by Manos Hatzidakis which underscores the scenes.

All other technical credits are above standard. —*Rena.*

The American Success Company
(COLOR)

Cynical point of view offsets visual values.

Hollywood, Nov. 20.

A Columbia Pictures release of an Edgard J. Scherick/Daniel H. Blatt production. Produced by Daniel H. Blatt, Edgar J. Scherick. Directed by William Richert. Screenplay, William Richert, Larry Cohen. Based on a story by Cohen. Stars Jeff Bridges, Belinda Bauer, Ned Beatty; camera (Color), Anthony Richmond; editor, Ralph E. Winters; music, Maurice Jarre; production design, Rolf Zehetbauer; art director, Werner Achmann; costume design, Robert De Mora, Helga Pinnow; sound, Gordon Everett; associate producer, Pia I. Arnold; assistant directors, Dietmar Siegert, Marijan Vajda. Reviewed at The Burbank Studios, Nov. 20, '79. (MPAA Rating: PG). Running time: 94

MINS.
Harry . . . . Jeff Bridges
Sarah . . . . Belinda Bauer
Mr. Elliot . . . . Ned Beatty
Rick Duprez . . . . Steven Keats
Corinne . . . . Bianca Jagger
Ernst . . . . John Glover
Greta . . . . Mascha Gonska
Herman . . . . Michael Durrell
Mrs. Heinemann . . . . Eva-Maria Meineke
Maitre D' . . . . Gunter Meisner
Gunter . . . . David Brooks
Landlady . . . . Marie Bardischewski

"The American Success Company" plays virtually like a continuation of William Richert's previous bizarre comedy, "Winter Kills," with an even greater sense of the absurd and much less coherence. Although almost everything that happens on screen is done with considerable style and a morbid sense of humor, lack of overall point to the proceedings ultimately sinks the picture, which represents a Pyrrhic victory of style over content. Film has already played several test engagements to nervous estimates.

Much as he portrayed the last remaining son of Big Daddy John Huston in "Winter Kills," Jeff Bridges here plays the mild-mannered son-in-law of international credit card tycoon Ned Beatty. Called a loser by his boss and under the thumb of gorgeous wife Belinda Bauer, youth decides to turn the tables on them by assuming the guise of a gangsterish tough-guy, then commencing to push them around to get his way in both professional and private life.

Only conceivable points being made are that it takes a crook to succeed in business today, and that women crave beasts, not gentlemen, cynical outlooks which prove, at least here, unable to sustain an argument of more than 90 minutes.

Undeniable, however, is Richert's visual flair and sometimes starling sense of the absurd. Helmer's view of global high finance as a Byzantine world populated by invidious schemers on the top and hapless victims underneath is beautifully represented in the gleaming locations and sets of Rolf Zehetbauer and Werner Achmann, and Anthony Richmond's fluid camera admirably shows off the brilliant surfaces in front of and within which the devious characters play out their charades.

Nary a sequence passes without a perverse touch or two. Representative of Richert's imagination is a running gag designed to convey Bridges' increasing sexual potency. After picking her up in a Munich transvestite club, Bridges instructs prostie Bianca Jagger to "teach me."

Following is a series of shots of a clock with second hand moving in stop-motion. Loud cry is heard after just a few seconds the first time, but staying power gradually increases, with about an hour passing in sequence's final shot before outburst is heard. Bridges thereupon returns to his wife, with expected knockout results.

All the same, pic seems tamer than it might have been, and suspicion persists that, to win a PG rating, at least two scenes which are naturally built up to but don't occur might have been excised.

Bridges, Beatty and Steven Keats, as a seedy detective, all have fun with their roles. Jagger is perfectly okay in her pic debut, although Bauer's odd accent marks her as a curious daughter for the all-American Beatty and renders her performance rather stilted. Mascha Gonska projects fabulous allure as an office associate of Bridges.

Billed as "A William Richert-Larry Cohen Film," pic was to have been helmed by Cohen, writer of the original story, and was known during production as "The Ringer." Munich's Geria Films was principal backer. —Cart.

Yesterday's Hero
(BRITISH-COLOR)

Soccer yarn with shaky legs.

London, Nov. 23.
EMI release of a Cinema Seven production. Executive producer, Elliott Kastner. Produced by Oscar S. Lerman, Ken Regan. Directed by Neil Leifer. Features entire cast. Screenplay, Jackie Collins; camera (color), Brian West; editor, Anthony Gibbs; songs, Bugatti and Musker; musical director, Stanley Myers; production designer, Keith Wilson; associate producer, Denis Holt; technical adviser (soccer), Frank McLintock. Reviewed at ABC Theatre, Fulham Road, London, Nov. 22, '79. (BBFC Rating: A). Running time: 95 MINS.
Rod Turner .... Ian McShane
Cloudy Martin .... Suzanne Somers
Jake .... Adam Faith
Clint .... Paul Nicholas
Sam Turner .... Sam Kydd
Susan .... Glynis Barber
Speed .... Trevor Thomas
Rita .... Sandy Ratcliffe
Georgie Moore .... Alan Lake
Mack Gill .... Matthew Long
TV Interviewer
  and Commentator ...... John Motsom
Marek .... Paul Medford

In departing from her well-trodden territory of penthouse frolics and highlife melodrama, and attempting a plotline where sex is merely incidental, writer Jackie Collins has come unstuck.

Apparently deserted by her normally keen market judgement, she's failed to enliven a banal but potentially adequate narrative with any of her customary edge. Local boxoffice prospects will likely suffer from disillusioned word-of-

mouth, and significant penetration elsewhere looks distinctly iffy.

Miscasting, too, bedevils "Yesterday's Hero," an independent production short on strong names but stocked with competent talent — unfortunately in ill-suited roles. In the case of Ian McShane, a good actor for whom the central part of a gone-to-seed soccer player given a comeback chance is well within his grasp, it's the routine and sentimental script that deprives him of credibility.

Adam Faith, another good and sympathetic actor, is wasted as the mean-minded manager of the team McShane joins on its way to (natch) winning the championship. Paul Nicholas makes all the right moves, but is too lightweight to convince as the team's Elton John-type popstar-owner.

Suzanne Somers alone overcomes Neil Leifer's paceless direction and some downright yesteryear musical numbers with surprisingly gutsy characterization of a basically vaporous role—Nicholas' costar, who becomes unhappily involved with McShane. But given the film's undistinguished technical credits, and passe concepts of glamor and emotional conflict, she can do little to offset the prevailing dullness. —Simo.

Der Willi-Busch Report
(The Willi Busch Report)
(WEST GERMAN-COLOR)

Hamburg, Nov. 5.
A Visual Film Production Elke Haltaufderheide, Munich. Features entire cast. Written and directed by Niklaus Schilling. Camera (color), Wolfgang Dickmann; sets, Christa Molitor; music, Patchwork, BSW-Combo, Fanfarenzug Wanfried; editing, Schilling. Reviewed at Esplanade Cinema, Hamburg, Nov. 4, '79. Running time: 118 MINS.
Willi Busch .... Tilo Prueckner
Adelheid Busch .... Dorothea Moritz
Rose-Marie Roth .... Kornelia Boje
Helga .... Karen Frey
Aenne .... Jenny Thelen
Sir Henry .... Hannes Kaetner
Arno Roesler .... Klaus Hoser
Aunt .... Hildegard Friese
Jupp Mueller ..... Wolfgang Groenebaum
Poradzki .... Christoph Lindert

A German helmer (born in Switzerland) with plenty of promise, Niklaus Schilling spends months planning and executing every meter of his feature from screenplay to editing.

A filmmaker's filmmaker, Schilling (a former cameraman for Klaus Lemke, May Spils, Rudolf Thome, and Jean-Marie Straub) uses every trick at his command to mix irony and satire, symbol and metaphor, into a banal story aimed to amuse as it embarrasses. The embarrassment has everything to do with what West Germany means for the stuffy upper middle class to-

day — in "Night Shade," the real estate broker; in "Expelled from Paradise," swindlers proliferating in the postwar "economic wonder" state (including the tax shelter film); and in "Rhinegold," the civil servant riding the comfortable TEE-Express train from Holland to Switzerland along the Rhine River.

If one looks closely at these films, one can peel back the first layer to get at something deeper that pertains directly to traditions like the Wagnerian cult, ancient mythology, and Love and Death in German Romanticism. Further, there are inside jokes referring to the New German Cinema community (a portrait of Rainer Werner Fassbinder in "Expelled from Paradise," for instance) that will tickle film buffs and observant critics at repeated viewings. A profounder helmer would be hard to find on the German landscape at present.

"The Willi Busch Report" is about a small-town brother-and-sister newspaper publishing duo, the family firm unluckily situated right on the W. German-E. German border in the middle of nowhere. A third of the customers have been lost to the partitioning fence, and our hero, Willi Busch has to scratch to find news to write about. His sister, Adelheid, watches in dismay as the Werra Post, the newspaper in question, slips downhill into financial ruin.

To save matters Willi takes to inventing news and discovers that Goebbels, to the town's embarrassment, was once saluted by the mayor as an honorary citizen. Then he hits upon a possible spy ring in the area at a class reunion of sorts. And a "saint with visions" turns Wanfried into a tourist attraction. For everything, naturally, Busch has an aphorism!

Shot with Steadicam lensing, pic should be a big winner. —Holl.

Just Out Of Reach
(AUSTRALIAN-COLOR)

Sydney, Nov. 11.
A Ross Matthews Production, made with the assistance of the Creative Development Branch of the Australian Film Comission. Produced by Ross Matthews. Directed by Linda Blagg. Screenplay by Blagg. Director photography, Russell Boyd; camera (Eastmancolor) Nixon Binney; sound Kevin Kearney; music, Bill Motzig; editing, Ted Otton; special effects, Bob McCarron; art direction, Grace Walker; production manager, Barbara Gibbs. Reviewed at the Palm Beach Screening Room, Sydney, Nov. 6, '79. (Unrated by Censor). Running time: 62 MINS.
Cath .... Lorna Lesley
Mike .... Sam Neill
Cath's Father .... Martin Vaughan
Cath's Mother .... Judi Farr
Steve .... Ian Gilmour
Cath's Sister .... Jackie Dalton
John .... Lou Brown

"Just Out of Reach" demonstrates an area of Australian filmmaking that is frequently overshadowed by the more commercial local product and consequently too often shoved aside when it comes time to select pictures to represent the country at overseas film fests. A low-budget — modest, even — but none-the-less highly personal film, it is far from inaccessible or in any way self-indulgent. It is a most interesting first feature by a female director of considerable promise.

Because Blagg establishes at the outset an obvious affinity for her leading actress, the adolescent Cath, it is difficult not to view the film as being at least partly autobiographical. Her treatment of Cath's initial suicide attempt and the ensuing flashbacks have an intensity that transcends fictional events and development.

Cath's story is one of a lifetime of personality conflicts, with father, mother, sister, boy-friend, lover and husband. But it is hard to say whether she is a natural victim or a neurotic perpetrator — in any case the result is the same: Cath's self-destruct button is constantly being pressed.

Actress Lorna Lesley is finely-attuned to the role of an ugly-but-beautifully young girl whose awkward adolescence creates a burden she carries into young womanhood. All her relationships are a reflection of her early life and Blagg's development of the character is helped immeasurably by some very sympathetic acting by Lesley. Cath gradually comes to echo her loud and overbearing father — she becomes what she most wants to escape eventually and drives away the ones she professes most to need.

Cath is as complex as any neurotic, but there is a "life" in the character that is recognizably true; and honestly depicted. Cath's retreat into an ill-advised, impulsive marriage with her former English teacher is just symptomatic of her basic inability to cope with human relationships on a domestic level. Clearly her family and social environment have failed to equip her to deal with the increasing strains of growing up with its concomitant emotional upheavals. Cath's temporary hormonal imbalance becomes a pattern.

The inescapable banality of marriage to Mike, an aspiring poet, only underlines her increasing frustration, self-induced though it is. It is Cath's inarticulation on an emotional level that is her real legacy from her past. The film says a great deal not only about problems unique to Australia, but variants on the same theme that exist in any culture.

It suits Blagg's thesis to have her male characters depicted as lacking many shades of grey. Everybody does, more or less, in the film because essentially the action is pivoted on Cath and her reactions to events: and she is quite incapable of objectivity in any degree. Anything that happens as far as she is concerned has happened *to* her; not because of her actions, but because of those of others. Her classic self-pity exacerbates her despair and the synergism results in the opening suicide sequence.

All the tech' credits are excellent, with particular kudos deserved by Russell Boyd for some superbly evocative lighting. Such criticisms as could be justified are plainly due to budget — or lack of it — and, in all, this could make an apt excuse for treating some of the Australian Film Commission's Creative Development Branch projects as "pilots" for features which ought later to be properly developed for wider distribution and made on proper feature film budgets.

—*Miha.*

Lamore
(GREEK-B&W)

Athens, Oct. 25.
An Ancora Film production. Written and directed by Denetris Mavrikios. Features Caterina Helmi, Anestis Vlahos. Camera (black & white) by Nicos Smaragdes; music. Loukianos Kaleidonis; sets and costumes. George Ziacas; edtiting, Yanna Spyropoulou. Reviewed in Athens, Oct. 25, 79. Running time: 110 MINS.

Demetris Mavrikios had presented in 1974 his first film, "Polemonta," at the Fest which was impressive. This film, however, disappointed everyone who believed in his talent.

It is well meaning but uninspired love story set in a small village with several political and social references. Unfortunately it turned out a halfway effort. Festival entry and only standard programming fare for Greek screens.

Anna lives with her step-daughter in a village now developed into a touristic summer resort. She is a widow.

She is in love with a young worker, Yannis, and in order to not lose him she marries him off to her step-daughter. Their neighbour Cosmas wants their house and the professor's next door to build a big hotel. The professor was exiled to this village by the junta. Cosmas finally succeeds, due to his political connections and the influence he has on Yannis.

Director Demetris Mavrikios was aiming to make a film on the life of people in provincial towns, and the position of the woman in social communities. But though his

directorial know-how is apparent, he failed to turn out a successful picture. The story line is poorly developed' with several details and scenes which had no place in his story, ruining its continuity.

Worthy of mention is the performance of Caterina Helmi while the rest of the cast turn in adequate performances. Other assets of the picture are the music by Louikianos Kelaidonis, sets by N. Ziacas and editing by Nicos Smaragdes.

—*Rena.*

Anatoliki Periferia
(Eastern Territory)
(GREEK-B&W)

Athens, Oct. 25.
A Vassilis Vafeas production. Written and directed by Vafeas. Featuring Menas Hatzisavas, Nelli Anguelidou, Yannis Goumas. Camera (black & white), George Kavayas; sets and costumes, Damianos Zarifis; editing George Korras; sound Thanassis Georgiades. Reviewed in Athens, Oct. 24, '79. Running time: 77 MINS.

This is a promising start of a new director, Vassilis Vafeas, who won one of the "best picture" prizes.

It is a well-aimed satire about people employed by private small enterprises and others working in big international concerns recently established in this country. The difference in work terms and the change in the way of life, character and behaviour of people which the new working conditions have introduced, are highlighted.

Vafeas directed it in a neat professional way. Commercially the picture will be a good specialized play-off item here and abroad.

The central character is a young villager who comes to the city and gets a job in a small factory run by a lady. He realizes soon that nothing is done systematically and professionally. Later he witnesses two accidents due to the negligence, bad maintenance and indifference of the people in charge. Victims are two of his fellow-workers. But when he is burned a little himself while on duty, he leaves his job disgusted and terrified.

In the second segment, the hero is employed by an international company where everything is under control and runs smoothly. He soon starts climbing until he is appointed assistant director. But he is not the same man any more. He becomes more inhuman and austere than the boss himself.

For a first picture, Vafeas shows a real flair for character and place, narrating his story in his own personal style. He directed the first segment in a quick pace satirizing the unprofessional but more human working conditions in small enterprises.

Acting is very good by Nelli Anguelidou, Menas Hatzisavas and Yannis Goumas delivering excellent performances supported by many other players in secondary roles. Editing and other production values are above standard. —*Rena.*

Ta Kourelia Tragoudoun Akoma
(The Thrushes Are Still Singing)
(GREEK-B&W)

Athens, Oct. 25.
A N. Nicolaides production. Written and directed by himself. Featuring Alkis Panayotides, Rita Bensousan, Constantine Tzoumas, Christos Valavanides, Olia Lazaridou. Camera (black & white), Stavros Hasapis; sets and costumes, Marie Louise Vartholomeou; editing, Andreas Andreadakis; sound, Marinos Athanassopoulos. Reviewed in Athens Oct. 23. Running time: 125 MINS.

Nicos Nicolaides is a Greek film director who four years ago had presented his first picture, "Evridiki," at the Thessaloniki fest. Though it had been screened in several other festivals it had not found its way as yet on to Greek screens. His second film, however, disappointed all those who had admired his first picture. Not because his directorial skill is inferior, as he has won the prize for best director, but because he based his film on a story which is unbelievable in several key areas and shored it up with exploitation values via sex, violence and loud music. The result is a film which could easily make money but is a doubtful critics' choice. Its chances in foreign markets are good.

The story is an unusual reflection of the generation of the fifties. Four old friends, aged 40 to 50 years old, meet after 20 years to spend some days together. Christos, an unsuccessful actor but a "good" family man; Constantine a cynical drifter; Alkis, an unsuccessful poet dreaming of an ideal woman and killing little girls at night; and Rita, a crazy woman just out of a sanitarium.

Though the main characters may seem incredible and the story line grim, Nicos Nicolaides narrates it with humour. In order to revive the atmosphere and background of the 1950's, he uses American music of that era.

The high level of acting carries the picture along. —*Rena.*

Chicago Fest

The Haunting of M
(U.S.-COLOR)

Chicago, Nov. 27.
Produced and directed by Anna Tho-

mas. Screenplay, Thomas; camera (color), Gregory Nava; editor, Michael Bockman, Trevor Black, Thomas; sound, Robert Yerington; associate producer, Gregory Nava, Robert Yerington. Reviewed at the Village Theatre, Chicago, Nov. 20, 1979. Running time: 98 MINS.
Marianna .... Sheelagh Gilbey
Halina .... Nini Pitt
Daria .... Evie Garratt
Karol .... Alan Hay
Aunt Teresa .... Jo Scott Matthews
Marion .... William Bryan
Stefan .... Peter Austin
Doctor .... Peter Stenson
Stahu .... Ernest Bale
Yola .... Isolde Cazelet
Irka .... Varvara Pepper

Although this pic doesn't achieve its gothic horror objectives — it tells of a young woman bedeviled by the ghostly return of an ancestor's lover — it intimates that its creator, Anna Thomas, is a director to watch. She may not show huge promise but she displays a strong knack in her first feature of creating a lush period atomosphere on a shoestring budget. The pic isn't a bad start.

Thomas, who directed, scripted, produced and had a big hand in editing "The Haunting of M," is a UCLA film school grad, worked as an assistant director on Gregory Nava's "The Confession of Amans" (1975), and lists among her credits a coscripting chore on "For Better or For Worse" for Twentieth Century-Fox.

She shot "Haunting" in Scotland using many local residents as extras, and working with a basic five-person crew. Her film belies the modest foundation in many respects: costumes appear to be highly-detailed replicas of 19th century aristocratic finery; the pic's basic set, a fine old brick and stone mansion, isn't visually confining in the least; pic is photographed well in good color stock; and its larger scenes of fancy costume balls and late-night soirees around an open fire are cleverly handled and look just right.

Thomas is much less successful with non-technical elements, such as scripting and handling actors. Too much of the film, especially the principal performances, have a stilted look one associates with a photographed stage play.

The initial in the title refers to Marianna (Sheelagh Gilbey), a long-nosed prospective spinster who finds herself beseiged by the spectre of a young, emaciated man who once impregnated Marianna's maiden aunt and met a grim end at the hands of the latter's aristocratic siblings.

Pic is a Victorian detective story, with Marianna's sister (Nini Pitt), an attractive actress and a family maverick, showing up to exhume the family's skeleton in the closet. The unraveling of the mystery isn't sufficiently taut to sustain interest.

What's worse, the denouement, Marianna's confrontation of the ghost (who resembles an anemic funeral director) has some unintentionally humorous aspects that undermine the suspense.

But those sidetracks into the family balls and dinners indicate Thomas can handle crowd scenes with entertaining dispatch. Too bad she didn't tie them a bit more tightly to the basic plot line.

Gilbey and Pitt seem like capable enough actresses but are defeated by the script's insistence that the chief characters declaim at rather than speak to each other. Pic's obvious concession to cost is the soundtrack, an assemblage of recorded works by Gustav Mahler, Leos Janacek and Frederic Chopin. The music is delightful, of course, but doesn't seem to be connected very much to what's going on up on the screen.

For "Haunting of M," Thomas deserves a pat for an ambitious first effort that leaves the viewer with positive expectations of her future work. She has accomplished quite a bit with very little. Pic, incidentally, was termed "the most asked for" by Chi Film Fest fans, and was brought back for an additional public screening. —*Sege.*

Cinema Cinema
(U.S.-FRENCH-COLOR)

Chicago, Nov. 27.

Shahab International Production Assoc. presentation. Produced by Shahab Ahmed. Directed by Krishna Shah. Features entire cast. Screenplay, Krishna Shah; Hindi script, Kamleshwar; camera (color), K.K. Mahajan; score, Vijay Raghav Rao; editor, Amit Bose; sound, Minoo Tampal; set designer, Ram Mohan; research consultants, B.D. Garga, P.K. Nair, Chindananda Das Gupta; executive producer, Bhupendra Shah. Reviewed at Chicago Film Festival screening room, Nov. 19, 1979. Running time: 102 MINS.
Cast: Dharmendra, Hema Malini, Amitabh Bachchan; Zeenat Aman, Kim, Mushtaque Merchant, Dinyar Contractor; Hoshidar Kambhatta, Kanchan Mattu, Sharad Bhagtani, Amar Sneh, Bishan Khanna, Hriday Lani, Momin Khan, Bobby Grewal, Phonsuk, Dharam Veer, Manmauji, Payal Parvez, Babu, Shyam Awasthe, Dev Sharma, Nandu.

With a weekly audience of some 70,000,000, a yearly production output of about 550 features add a $500,000,000 annual b.o. take, India is the most prolific film nation in the world. Whether U.S. audiences have missed much by rarely if ever getting a chance to see the bulk of this outpouring is very much an open question. But Krishna Shah's amusing docu-drama, "Cinema Cinema," indicates they may have been denied a few chuckles, at least.

Shah is well-known in the U.S. as a tv and feature helmer ("Rivals," "The River Niger" and, still unreleased, "Shalimar") who obviously has deep affection for a host of Indian pics that for esthetic and cultural reasons defy commercial export.

Shah spent some two years scouring world archives (including Eastman Kodak in Rochester and the late Henry Langlois' Paris Cinematheque) to compile clips from Indian pics dating from the turn of the century. But "Cinema Cinema" is no mere film historiography.

Shah balances the more scholarly portion of his work by assembling a group of actors in what appears to be a ramshackle Bombay theatre to illustrate the effects of Indian pics on local audiences.

Director's thesis is that Indian audiences are passionately involved with films and film stars, and are often more interesting to watch than what's on the screen. To anchor the planned audience response, Shah hired India's better known screen personalities — two men, Dharmendra and Amitabh Bachchan, and two women, Hema Malini and Zeenat Aman; all winsome enough but a mite overweight by U.S. glamor standards — to make screen appearances narrating the clips.

Shah's point about Indian patrons is borne out in "Cinema Cinema" because the audience of actors is easily more absorbing than most of the vintage footage, good deal of which was extracted from recent Indian comedies and musicals that are proof positive that the bulk of Indian films should remain in India.

Clips were actually extracted from a broad range of Indian pics, and some from Europe and the U.S. which played that country early on (Keystone Cops and Charlie Chaplin pics played cheek-by-jowl with "Kaliya Mardan" and "Bhakta Pralhad"). Various schools of Indian filmmaking are covered ranging from reasonably interesting neo-realist efforts "Humlog" and "Do bigha zamin" to contemporary song-and-dancers, termed "curry" movies.

Assembled audience of actors respond to each clip and star appearance in ways that make a Times Square action-house patrons look like models of decorum. Fistfights alternate with flirtations. There is raucous laughter, tears and, at the finale, an incompetent projectionist is pummeled until the misplaced concluding reel is located.

By combining all this good-humored mayhem with film scholarship, Shah has displayed a nice showmanly touch. "Cinema Cinema" never flags and is an extremely palatable introduction to a virtually unknown subject, the history of Indian pics.

Production values are fine, and although it's hard to immediately come up with a suggested commercial outlet for "Cinema Cinema" in the U.S., the Shah effort deserves the widest audience possible.—*Sege.*

The Electric Horseman
(COLOR)

Redford and Fonda short-circuit but 'Horseman' good for a few laps.

Hollywood, Dec. 1.
Columbia Pictures release of a Ray Stark production. Produced by Ray Stark. Directed by Sydney Pollack. Stars Robert Redford, Jane Fonda. Screenplay, Robert Garland from screen story by Paul Gaer. Garland, based on story by Shelly Burton; camera (Technicolor), Owen Roizman; production designer, Stephen Grimes; editor, Sheldon Kahn; music, Dave Gusin; song sung by Willie Nelson; asst. director, M. Michael Moore; art director, J. Dennis Washington; set decorator, Mary Swanson; unit publicist, Jack Hirshberg; special effects, Augie Lohman; sound editor, Gordon Davidson. Reviewed at Samuel Goldwyn Theatre, Beverly Hills, Nov. 29, 1979. (MPAA Rating: PG). Running time: 120 MINS.

Sonny	Robert Redford
Hallie	Jane Fonda
Charlotta	Valerie Perrine
Wendell	Willie Nelson
Hunt Sears	John Saxon
Fitzgerald	Nicolas Coster
Danny	Allan Arbus
Farmer	Wilford Brimley
Gus	Will Hare
Toland	Basil Hoffman
Leroy	Timothy Scott
Dietrich	James B. Sikking
Tommy	James Kline
Bernie	Frank Speiser
Bud Broderick	Quinn Redeker
Joanna Camden	Lois Areno

Also: Sarah Harris, Tasha Zemrus, James Novak, Debra L. Maxwell, Michelle Heyden, Robin Timm, Patricia Blair, Gary M. Fox, Richard Perlmutter, Carol Eileen Montgomery, Theresa Ann Dent, Perry Sheehan Adair, Sarge Allen, Sylvie Strauss, Richard Knoll, Angelo Giouzelis.

"The Electric Horseman" is a moderately entertaining film, which may not be enough to satisfy audiences expecting screen magic from the pairing of Robert Redford and Jane Fonda. The Ray Stark-Wildwood production is beautiful to look at and enjoyable to watch, but the sought-after star chemistry doesn't appear until near the film's conclusion. Boxoffice response should be intense for the opening weeks of the Columbia Pictures release domestically (Universal Pictures co-financed and has foreign rights), but a word-of-mouth may be less than electric.

Most of the "Horseman" problems derive from the unwieldy screenplay by Robert Garland, which in turn is based on a scenario he cowrote with Paul Gaer, which owes its inspiration to a story by Shelly Burton. The transmutations the property has apparently undergone are all too apparent on the screen, as the pic is overlong, talky and diffused.

Director Sydney Pollack doesn't help matters by adopting a leisurely pace through the film's first hour, and throwing away a climactic scene (Redford's well-publicized illuminated horsewalk through

Caesars Palace) without any build-up.

Even though Redford, as an ex-rodeo champ making big bucks on the breakfast cereal circuit, and Fonda, in a virtual carbon of her newshen role from "The China Syndrome," don't create the romantic sparks that might be expected, it's their dramatic professionalism that salvages "Horseman" and makes it a moving and effective film by the time the final credits roll by.

"Electric Horseman" represents Redford's first major screen role in almost four years, and reaffirms his maturity as an actor. Unfortunately, the cowboy mannerisms of his character sometimes intrude on his style, but on the whole, it's an impressive and winning performance.

Fonda takes a subordinate position in the film, one that almost sees her character lose its focus until her solitary journey with Redford and Mag in the film's final third. Then the actress' subtlety and persuasiveness is allowed to develop, enriching rather than detracting from the film's message.

What "Electric Horseman" is peddling, just as surely as Redford hawked kiddie cereal, is the virtue of "freedom," morally, economically and socially. Redford's attempt to liberate the prize-winning horse of the AMPCO conglomerate from an overabundance of steriods and pain-killing is presumably intended as an analogy for the way the American public is force-fed consumerism from today's corporate giants.

The deck is so stacked in Redford's favor, to borrow a Vegas metaphor from the film's early scenes, that it's all John Saxon can do as the corporate biggie to give his role some shading, rather than the simple black-and-white dichotomy the script suggests.

Saxon, who is perfectly cast as the sleek and heartless exec, gets excellent support from Basil Hoffman and Nicholas Coster as two of his corporate henchmen, while Redford's cause is immeasurably aided by singer-composer Willie Nelson, making a sparkling film debut, along with soundtrack warbling. Valerie Perrine is wasted in a silly bit part, but Alan Arbus, Wilford Brimley and Timothy Scott are good in supporting roles.

Owen Roizman's camerawork is a major asset, particularly the hard-to-light Vegas scenes along with the gorgeous Utah scenery. But Sheldon Kahn's editing is lackadaisical, Stephen Grimes' production design erratic, and J. Dennis Washington's art direction not particularly apparent. Ernie Pollack's work with Redford's

irridescent costume alone is worthy of praise.

Coming from filmmakers of lesser stature, "Electric Horseman" would be an achievement worthy of pride. But combining the talents of heavyweights such as Stark, Pollack, Redford, Fonda, etc. leads to heightened expectations, which are not fully realized. —*Poll.*

Fleisch
(Meat)
(WEST GERMAN-COLOR)

Munich, Nov. 8.
A Pentagramma Filmproduction. Written, produced and directed by Rainer Erler. Art director, Paul Winslow; camera, (color), Wolfgang Grasshoff; editing, Hilwa von Boro; music, Eugen Thomass. Cast: Reviewed at Atlas International screening room, Munich, Nov. 7, '79. Running time: **108 MINS.**
Cast: Jutta Speidel, Wolf Roth, Herbert Herrmann, Charlotte Kerr, Bob Cunningham, Ted Altice, Ben Zeller, Christoph Lindert.

Some would call this science fiction, but as a matter of (scientific) fact, the story is credible and, moreover, possible. Writer-director-producer Rainer Erler has projected possible abuse of human organ transplants into the near future (as in "Coma").

A young couple (Jutta Speidel, Wolf Roth) are kidnapped from a run down little motel outside Las Cruces, New Mexico with the help of the sinister old landlady. Two medics get hold of the man — the girl manages to escape — and disappear with him in an ambulance.

With the help of a trucker and his CB radio friends the girl finally exposes a ruthless, multi-national headhunting organization that kidnaps healthy young people for their livers, kidneys and other vital organs, selling them on a black market to organ banks.

Some eager German organizations mistook the film as being anti-transplant (which it is definitely not) and protested. An entertaining, expertly made shocker that foregoes tastelessness and draws its suspense from a well adapted will-they-get-them-or-won't-they-attitude. —*Koci.*

Heart Beat
(COLOR)

Kerouac tale suffers cardiac arrest.

Hollywood, Nov. 28.
An Orion Pictures release through Warner Bros. of an Edward R. Pressman production. Produced by Alan Greisman, Michael Shamberg. Written and directed by John Byrum. Exec producers, Edward R. Pressman, William Tepper. Stars Nick Nolte, Sissy Spacek, John Heard. Camera (Technicolor), Laszlo Kovacs; editor, Eric Jenkins; music, Jack Nitzsche; produc-

tion design, Jack Fisk; costumes Patricia Norris; sound, Bill Kaplan; second unit, Gary Kibbe; assistant director, Bill Scott. Reviewed at The Burbank Studios, Burbank, Nov. 28, '79. (MPAA Rating: R.) Running time: **109 MINS.**

Neal Cassady	Nick Nolte
Carolyn Cassady	Sissy Spacek
Jack Kerouac	John Heard
Ira Streiker	Ray Sharkey
Stevie	Anne Dusenberry
Mrs. Kerouac	Margaret Fairchild
Dick	Tony Bill
Odgen	Kent Williams
Bob Bendix	Stephen Davies
Betty Bendix	Jenny O'Hara
Tv Talk Show Host	John Larroquette
Undercover Agent	Ray Vitte

A strange time warp has enveloped Hollywood, in which films about the 1950s and '60s are suddenly presumed to have great relevance for the late '70s and '80s. "Heart Beat" is just the latest and most conspicuous failure in this regard, since the Edward R. Pressman production never manages to expand its loosely biographical tale of Jack Kerouac, Neal and Carolyn Cassady beyond a very narrow scope. Some curiosity value may attach itself to the Orion Pictures release through Warner Bros., but boxoffice potential looks to be selective and limited.

"Heart Beat" is not without its favorable aspects. Together, cinematographer Laszlo Kovacs and production designer Jack Fisk have wrought wonders, offering a detailed, lovely recreation of the late 1940s and the succeeding decade.

Nick Nolte and Sissy Spacek, as the Cassadys enmeshed in a love-hate relationship, are likewise standout in a film where performances dominate. Ditto Ray Sharkey, in a manic performance as a disguised Allen Ginsberg character.

Otherwise, "Heat Beat" fails to establish either a coherent story line, or a definitive treatment of the forces that shaped the literary and social explosion following publication of Kerouac's "On The Road" in 1957. Instead, writer-director John Byrum drops scenes into the film as if he were pitching pennies, with little dramatic impact and even less emotional resonance.

Apparently with the encouragement of producers Alan Greisman and Michael Shamberg, latter a veteran of "guerrilla" television, Byrum also uses "Heart Beat" to insert several episodes satirizing the '50s, in a style that is condescending to film audiences in its broad lampoons.

Above all, "Heart Beat," except for an exciting opening sequence and random moments elsewhere in the pic, misses out on the cool jazz pulse of the "beat" generation that provides the film's setting. And while there's no obligation for Byrum to adhere strictly to biogra-

phical detail, (credit says pic was "suggested by" Carolyn Cassady's memoir) the use of real people and their names demands a certain fidelity to spirit, if not fact.

Lack of dramatic force is a particular shame, given the excellent tech work involved, with Fisk's production design stunning in its visual impact, especially as lit and photographed by Kovacs. But their beautifully-composed shots remain just that, never coalescing into a cinematic flow.

John Heard struggles manfully with the Kerouac character, but Byrum has given him few compass points on which to base a reading. Diane Crittenden's casting is otherwise firstrate, with Stephen Davies and Jenny O'Hara perfect as a representative '50s couple, as are Kent Williams and John Larroquette as corruptive influences on Kerouac once he achieves literary fame. Ray Vitte has a small but excellent bit as an undercover agent who busts Nolte for marijuana possession.

Byrum's overemphasis on blackouts, and his single-minded portrayal of Kerouac as saint/Cassady as devil, roles which abruptly switch when Kerouac's star begins to rise, help slow "Heart Beat" to a murmur. The story of this domestic love and literary triangle is the stuff of excellent drama. The shame of it never shows up in "Heart Beat." — *Poll.*

The Prize Fighter
(COLOR)

Will have to be saved by the sell.

Hollywood, Nov. 30.
A New World Pictures release, produced by Lang Elliott and Wanda Dell. Directed by Michael Preece. Features entire cast. Screenplay, Tim Conway, John Myhers; camera (color), Jacques Haitkin; editor, Fabien Tordjmann; sound, Richard Goodman; assistant director, Pat Kehoe; costumes, Jane Jones; art director, Vincent Peranio; music, Peter Matz. Reviewed at Aidikoff Screening Room, Hollywood, Nov. 30, '79. (MPAA rating: PG.) Running time: **99 MINS.**

Bags	Tim Conway
Shake	Don Knotts
Pop Morgan	David Wayne
Mike	Robin Clarke
Polly	Cisse Cameron
Mama	Mary Ellen O'Neill
Butcher	Michael LaGuardia
Timmy	George Nutting
Flower	Irwin Keyes
Doyle	John Myhers
Announcer	Alfred E. Covington
Big John	Dan Fitzgerald

In their third picture together, Don Knotts and Tim Conway are getting more and more like Abbott & Costello, but unfortunately not as good. Still, the two comics have talent and, more importantly, a strong following in the hinterlands, where

"The Prize Fighter" has already played to respectable business.

What the pair need here is a script and the lame, predictable, hackneyed mess cooked up by Conway and John Myhers leaves them with nothing but schtick and aged sight gags, up to and including crashing into chicken truck.

Knotts plays the conceited lamebrain and Conway the lovable nicompoop, struggling along in the 1930s in the fight game. Penniless, they become foils for mobster Robin Clarke who fixes a series of fights so Conway can ultimately challenge the champion, played well by menacing Michael LaGuardia.

Clarke's plot is to cheat David Wayne out of the gymnasium he's holding onto as a nestegg for moppet George Nutting. Wayne, of course, bets all on Conway in the big match. Though Conway's talents as a boxer fit worse than his baggy trunks, it's no surprise who ultimately scores a knockout to save the gym.

The only saving moments are those Conway and Knotts struggle to come up with. But they are too few and all technical credits are minimal for pic, shot in Atlanta.

— *Har.*

The Outsider
(U.S.-COLOR)

Thoughtful terrorism drama, starring the IRA.

London, Nov. 27.
Paramount CIC release of a Cinematic Arts B.V. Production. Directed by Tony Luraschi. Features entire cast. Screenplay, Luraschi, based on the novel, "The Heritage Of Michael Flaherty," by Colin Leinster; camera (color), Ricardo Aronovitch; editor, Catherine Kelber; production supervisor (no producer credited), Philippe Modave; art director, Franco Fumagalli; costumes, Judy Dolan; music, Ken Thorne; asst. directors, Barry Blackmore, Bernard Farrel. Reviewed at Century screening room, London, Nov. 26, '79. (BBFC Rating: AA). Running time: **128 MINS.**
Michael .... Craig Wasson
Grandfather .... Sterling Hayden
Siobhan .... Patricia Quinn
Emmet .... Niall O'Brien
Russell .... T.P. McKenna
Farmer .... Niall Tobin
Tony Coyle .... Frank Grimes
Mrs. Cochran .... Elizabeth Begley
Finbar .... Bosco Hogan
Mac Whirter .... Ray Macanally
Mr. Tweeny .... Jimmy Devlin
Pat .... Joe Dowling
Hanlan .... Aiden Grennell

Ironic indeed for Britain and its film industry that the first feature to deal in depth with the troubles in Northern Ireland should (a) be made by a U.S. company, and (b) place the (outlawed) provisional Irish Republican Army at the center of the drama.

The 1975 AIP release, "Hennessy," which was a British production, used the troubles as springboard for a non-political suspenser set in London; but "The Outsider" represents the first attempt to get behind the incessant headlines and into the minds and motives at work on one of the longest-fought terrorist campaigns of the times — through an intelligent fictional story with an Irish setting.

Lack of concession on the part of director-scripter Tony Luraschi to conventional thriller pacing makes the Paramount-financed production no easy moneyspinner. But in relation to the under-$3,000,000 budget, selected playoff with an eye to critic-support should ensure a respectable return in time. London bow via CIC, to be closely followed by openings in Ireland, will act as first pointers in what Paramount reportedly sees as an extended, suck-it-and-see release pattern.

A measure of the effectiveness of Craig Wasson's performance, as a young Irish-American inflamed to join the IRA by his grandfather's (Sterling Hayden) tales of fighting the Brits in the religion-charged cause of Irish nationalism, is that by the time he finally leaves Ireland as a disillusioned fugitive he looks — without artifice — 10 years older.

What he's escaped is a neatly-plotted double trap; the IRA planned to shoot him with a British bullet, so his apparent martyrdom would boost fund-raising in the U.S.; the British army hoped to cover the identity of one of its informers by setting up the American as a target of IRA suspicion.

Some indulgent moments aside — notably the first and last sequences in Detroit, which provide a sentimental prolog and a facile final twist strangely out of key with the awesome realism of the rest of the film — the strength of Luraschi's features debut lies in its restraint. Excellent performances across the wide range of supporting roles justify the decision to build the narrative (based on Colin Leinster's novel, "The Heritage Of Michael Flaherty," due for publication next year) as much on character interplay as on plot development. That way, the oppressive complexity of the situation bears down on the viewer, as on the hero, with an insidiously tightening grip, and what certainly rings as truth proves far stronger than simplistic actioning.

Shot mainly on location in Dublin, serving as the Catholic backstreets of Belfast, the film uses telling images to reveal a way of life that's both dreadful and compelling. A "safe house" is guarded by an ancient crone with a revolver lodged in the couch beside her; a 12-year-old child helps make and throw incendiary bombs, then is shot dead by British soldiers as he flees the ensuing fracas; a long-serving IRS lad is so "used up" he's literally trigger-mad.

(Locally, the fact that "The Outsider" examines the IRA standpoint in infinitely greater historical and emotional detail than the British army's — and includes a scene in which a suspected IRA sympathizer is brutally tortured — is bound to raise political hackles, and could limit playdates. That's hardly likely elsewhere, however. The film in no way sensationalizes its terrorism theme.)

Of the consistently good cast, Frank Grimes, Niall O'Brien, Patricia Quinn, T.P. McKenna and Niall Tobin make standout contributions. The camera team under cinematographer Ricardo Aronovitch have made the most of the dank backgrounds and coped creditably with cramped interior locations. —*Simo.*

The War At Home
(DOCU-COLOR-&-B&W-16m)

Milwaukee, Nov. 29.
A Catalyst Film Production, in collaboration with the Wisconsin Educational Television Network. Produced and directed by Glenn Silber and Barry Alexander Brown. Associate producer, writer, Elizabeth Duncan; camera (color), Rick March, Bob Lerner; editor, Chuck France; director of film research, Jon Aleckson. Research, Ken Weiss, Bob Newton. Reviewed at Oriental Theatre, Milwaukee, Nov. 29, '79. Running time: **100 MINS.**

"The War at Home" scores as an all-embracing compilation docu on student revolts during the anti-Vietnam 1960s. Made by Glenn Silber and Barry Brown with support from friendly foundations, the Wisconsin Educational Television Network, and simply "scraping up cash" over a two-year stretch, this chronological account of what happened on the Univ. of Wisconsin campus in Madison (a prestige state institution referred to as "the Athens of the West") only a decade ago resurrects a critical page of recent American history also presents it in such a way as to win recognition on grounds of relevance alone.

No doubt, any tv special could have done as well in setting the period (mostly the late 1960s) in clear focus. The plus side of "War at Home," however, is the thorough research into forgotten archival sources — principally, a Madison tv station with film and tapes of exactly what happened on campus — and the guts of the two directors to offer a partial, but balanced, judgment, that is, a sound editorial opinion, on the material at hand.

Silber and Brown owe their documentary finesse to Emile de Antonio, who had an influence on both "War at Home" and the earlier "An Americanism: Joe McCarthy" (silber's first docu). The slant is, of course, on the political, liberal-Left side of the docu fence, but there are no visible political bones to pick and the audience is left pretty much on its own to form an ultimate opinion. In fact, it is the older generation, who experienced these years, that is hit the hardest — not Silber and Brown, who belong to the slower-footed 1970s.

Here is the Vietnam file laid open for a questioning review: President Kennedy's statements on the war (1961-63), Senator Ernest Gruening's lone position on the side of the rebellious students, Johnson and Humphrey on the war, Nixon and Ted Kennedy, Eugene McCarthy and Wayne Morse, and Defense Secretaries McNamara and Laird, to name just the primary political figures that should jolt even the indifferent viewer's memory of times past.

There's also — and that's the meat of the docu — the Madison activists who made the front pages together with their opponents: Paul Soglin (later Mayor of Madison, 1973-79), Karl Armstrong (activist presently in prison for the bombing of an Army information centre on the Madison campus, resulting in the death of a graduate student who was on the premises), the Madison Police Chief, a VFW Commander from the area, and the Chancellor of the Univ. of Wisconsin. What was said, and done, then and now poses a dialectical double-take on what that "war at home" was like just a few years ago — now something like a political light-year in the past.

The one problem with this docu is that a full decade is just too much to bite off in one film. A series would have been better to zero in on all the crucial facts and personalities. As it is, "The War at Home" has several tense dramatic moments to commend it even to a neophyte political viewer, while it's sheer dynamite to the committed and the film buff. Screenings in Madison and Milwaukee have broken house records; much the same has happened subsequently at picked cinemas in Chicago, Minneapolis, and Boston.

With good reason — there's footage here not to be found in "Hearts and Minds," and its emotional impact and immediacy is often far greater than "Coming Home," "The Deer Hunter" and "Apocalypse Now." Because this is Hometown America in revolt. Despite the poor quality of some scenes (tv footage transferred to 16m film, now about to be blown-up to 35m), it's a "document" not to be missed. —*Holl.*

Manoeuvre
(U.S.-DOCU-B&W)

London, Nov. 27.

A Zipporah Films production. Documentary on the U.S. Army. Produced and directed by Frederick Wiseman. Camera (b&w), John Davey; editor, Wiseman. Reviewed at the London Film Festival, National Film Theatre, London, Nov. 26, '79. Running time: **115 MINS.**

This year's production by documaker Frederick Wiseman — he's made one a year since 1967 — is a gently humorous but unnerving report of annual U.S. Army World War III rehearsals in West Germany. The footage speaks for itself, without commentary.

As with other Wiseman films, this one is destined for public tv airing in the U.S., wide 16m nontheatric distribution, and some theatrical exposure in the U.K. Unusually, world premiere of "Manoeuvre" was at the London Film Festival, predating the PBS telecast.

Early on, as troops leave Fort Polk, Louisiana, to simulate emergency movements into Europe in support of NATO, the point is made that the educational standard of military recruits has fallen significantly over the last 10 years. Suffice to say that during the forage which follows — described by a commanding officer as "the crucible of collective security" — nothing recorded by John Davey's camera serves to disprove the truth of that.

Producer-director Wiseman, working with customary black-and-white stock which he edited himself, repeatedly highlights quainter aspects of the alternately casual and frantic war game. One especially bizarre aspect of it all is that the "enemy" forces appear to be "played" by Germans, one of whom says at the end, with Teutonic formality: "Thanks. It's been very enjoyable. Goodbye, and happy war."

Overlength in places no doubt reproduces accurately enough the periodic dullness of actual participation in such an exercise, but it's hard to say if that's the intention, or if it results from misplaced zeal on Wiseman's part for some of the material to hand. Either way, the pace is often chancy.

In a world where SALT treaties would seem the paramount World War III consideration, and particularly by Britons currently pondering the placement of U.S. nuclear "cruise" missiles just north of London, conventional infantry defence may well be wryly regarded. That message emerges clearly from Wiseman's typical objectivity. —*Simo.*

La Guerre des Policiers
(The Police War)
(FRENCH-COLOR)

Paris, Nov. 5.

A UGC release of a Stephan Film production. Produced by Vera Belmont. Features entire cast. Directed by Robin Davis. Screenplay, Jean-Marie Guillaume and Jacques Labib; adaptation, Jean Patrick Manchette, Patrick Laurent, Guillaume, Labid, Davis; dialog, Laurent, Manchette and Davis. Camera (Eastmancolor), Ramon Saurez; editor, Jose Pinheiro; sound, Pierre Befve and Jean-Paul Mugel; Art director, Joey Fare; music, Jean Marie Senia. Reviewed at the Publicis screening room, Paris, Nov. 5, '79. Running time: **102 MINS.**
Fush . . . . Claude Brasseur
Marie . . . . Marlene Jobert
Ballestrat . . . . Claude Rich
Millard . . . . Francois Perier

The recent police ambush of France's Public Enemy Number One, Jacques Mesrine, and local headline splatters about police blunders give Robin Davis' "La Guerre des Police" firm anchorage in actualities, but they don't make this American-style thriller any less mediocre.

Claude Brasseur and Claude Rich play the heads of two competitive police investigative squads vying for the capture of a dangerous criminal. Both play dirty; interdepartmental hanky-panky is not out of bounds. Marlene Jobert is a bemused lady cop in Rich's outfit whose tentative amorous involvement with Brasseur only throws another wrench into the already disjointed works. Tensions are resolved only when Brasseur suicidally confronts the evasive gangster following a bungled ambush attempt.

The script, worked on by no less than five writers (including French thriller novelist Jean Patrick Manchette), has some brash humor and conventionally smart repartee, but is generally deficient in drawing pungent, credible characterizations and a narrative line that locks that viewer in, unquestioning. Davis directs the action scenes with textbook competence and the rest with unimaginative energy.

Brasseur's unquenchable charm deflects the reprehensibility of his actions. Jobert "acts" too hard to be acceptable. Francois Perier does a vigorous star turn as the police director who gives the detectives a good dressing down for not being good bedfellows. —*Len.*

Todesmagazin order Wie werde ich ein Blumentopf?
(Death Magazine or How To Become A Flowerpot)
(WEST GERMAN-DOCU-COLOR & B&W)

Munich, Nov. 10.

Filmwelt release of a Rosa Von Praunheim Production. Written, directed, produced and photographed by von Praunheim. Reviewed at Studio Isabella, Munich, Nov. 9, '79. Running time: **73 MINS.**

This docu was to be shown over the German ZDF tv network, but was dropped like a hot potato. Reason stated for the withdrawal was that an unprepared audience could not be burdened and shocked with the pic of this nature.

This brought about a furious campaign by filmmaker Rosa von Praunheim, accusing the tv brass of censorship and worse. A small distribbery (Filmwelt) picked the film up for theatrical release.

Would the mass of tv watchers consist of intelligent, psychologically healthy, educated, reposed, ethereal people, one could have broadcast the interesting, but ill-bred celluloid essay. As it is not so, the tv programmers did the right thing.

The film is anything but a masterpiece. It is rather an imposition. But whether or not the content of the footage shown in this is in good taste, is not the issue. Von Praunheim's aim is to shatter taboos and within this context does not deal with death in a nice, euphemistical, tasteful way. It is the style that defuses the would-be anti tabu bomb.

The photography is sometimes so bad that an 8m amateur would hide it from his family. This may be excused in some sequences where maybe the camera had to be hidden (like in some Chinese or Indian scenes). The rest is sheer sloppiness.

The film, in its chaotic formlessness, lacks creative power. It is a collage of often very gruesome pictures that would have had a much stronger impact were the underlaid with esprit and/or black humor.

The touch of sarcasm at the end, when von Praunheim and a friend briefly chat over ashes in flowerpots (a means of keeping the "loved ones" at home as advertised in America, that gives the pic its subtitle) is weak attempt at humor.

Interviews with two psychic figures in New York like the esoteric "poetess" Helen Adams ("I long for death") and the rock pop vampire woman Anja ("There's nothing more beautiful than getting killed by Sid Vicious") are much too long, and become vacant and boring. Not that they would not fit in the attempted over-all picture but more of such undead people could have added to the concept. Also the interview with the publisher of Death Magazine and Screw's Al Goldstein is too circumstantial.

The apparently psychicly ill singer of the punk rock group Con-tortions who, accompanied by an infernal noise, bellows an unintelligible song of death into the microphone, fits the macabre show. But to lay this overlong, terrible din at full blast over the images of corpses is disturbing and evidence of the absence of a feeling for impact. Not that the punk inferno as an audio commentary is wrong but only its length and volume.

It is a common experience for new German filmmakers (and their disciples among critics) to try to retouch inability with adjectives like "radical" or "honest."

The frames of Nazi concentration camps, the Vietnam war, of hanged, decapitated, burned, starved and half decayed human beings do certainly radiate that fascination that horror holds, the more so as one knows all these images to be real. They speak for themselves. They corroborate for the steadfast, intelligent viewer, even in the form of this crude and confused collage a fact he knows anyway, that our world has never been a paradise.

Whether the film is able to take away the fear of death from the not-so-intelligent, not-so-steadfast viewer, is doubtful. The contrary may occur.

Still, the pic has a much more appropriate place in a theatre than on the tube.

Biz could be quite good, considering the success of "Dawn Of The Dead," but of course not in the same proportions. With its inadequate conceptual and technical quality, "Death Magazine" has only chances in outsider threatres.
—*Koci.*

The Secret Policeman's Ball
(BRITISH-COLOR)

London, Nov. 29.

A Document Films production for Amnesty International. Produced by Roger Graef, Thomas Schwalm. Directed by Roger Graef. Features entire cast. Documentary of a live show presented in aid of Amnesty International, directed by John Cleese. Camera (color), Ernest Vincze, Clive Tickner, Pascoe MacFarlane; editor, Thomas Schwalm; sound, Judy Freeman, Simon Hayter. Reviewed at the London Film Festival, National Film Theatre, London, Nov. 28, '79. Running time: **91 MINS.**

Cast: John Cleese, Peter Cook, Clive James, Eleanor Bron, Pete Townshend, Rowan Atkinson, Michael Palin, Beetles and Buckman, John Williams, Ken Campbell, Sylveste McCoy, Billy Connolly, Terry Jones, Tom Robinson.

Roger Graef's film record of this year's Amnesty International benefit show at Her Majesty's Theatre, London, is primarily aimed at the tube, but is bound to rate occasional theatrical playoff — as did an earlier such venture, "Pleasure At

Her Majesty's" made three years ago — on the strength of the lineup of British comic talent involved.

John Cleese, Michael Palin and Terry Jones of the Monty Python team appear in various sketches; guitarist Pete Townshend plays acoustic versions of a couple of The Who's repertoire, joined on one by classical picker John Williams; Peter Cook (sans Dudley Moore) renders a takeoff of one of the local hits of the year — the judge's summing-up in the trial of Liberal politician Jeremy Thorpe; and Billy Connolly, Clive James and Eleanor Bron, among others, contribute solo spots. All gave their services free.

Newcomer Rowan Atkinson, who turns in a hilarious schoolmaster routine, looks set to carry on the British tradition of graduate comedians built by Cook, Cleese and others over the past 20 years. (At one point, Glaswegian Connolly remarks he's about the only performer onstage to "leave school before the age of 21.") New Wave singer-songwriter Tom Robinson scores in a serious vein with one of his edgier numbers in defense of being gay.

There is no backstage material in "The Secret Policeman's Ball," which is a disappointment. "Pleasure At Her Majesty's" included footage of hasty rehearsals and dressing-room neurosis, which leavened the laugh-lump with an extra dimension. A pity, too, that a spoof-rock act by Neil Innes and band had to be dropped from the film owing to a Musicians' Union wrinkle over fee-waivers. — *Simo.*

Star Trek
(COLOR)

Big openings assured. Outlook promising, but recoup needs staggers showmen's arithmetic.

Washington, Dec. 7.

A Paramount Pictures release. Produced by Gene Roddenberry. Directed by Robert Wise. Features entire cast. Screenplay. Harold Livingston, based on a story by Alan Dean Foster: camera (Metrocolor), Richard H. Kline: editor, Todd Ramsay: production design. Harold Michelson: music. Jerry Goldsmith: costume design. Robert Fletcher: special photographic effects. Douglas Trumbull, John Dykstra: art direction. Michelson, Leon Harris: make-up. Fred Phillips: no other credits available. Reviewed at MacArthur Theatre. Washington. D.C.. Dec. 6, 1979. (MPAA Rating: C.) Running time: 132 MINS.

Captain Kirk . . . . : William Shatner
Spock . . . . .Leonard Nimoy
Dr. McCoy . . . . DeForest Kelley
Scotty . . . . James Doohan
Sulu . . . . .George Takei
Dr. Chapel . . . . Majel Barrett
Chekov . . . . Walter Koenig
Uhura . . . . Nichelle Nichols
Ilia . . . . Persis Khambatta
Decker . . . . Stephen Collins
Klingon Captain . . . . Mark Lenard
Alien Boy . . . . Billy Van Zandt
Janice Rand . . . . Grace Lee Whitney
Commander Branch . . . David Gautreaux
Lt. Commander Sonak . Howard Itzkowitz
Chief Di Falco . . . . Marcy Lafferty
Chief Ross . . . . Terrence O'Connor
Lt. Cleary . . . . Michael Rougas

The U.S.S. Enterprise is off on its most elaborate fantasy, right on course for a threatening alien starship and b.o. success. Gene Roddenberry and director Robert Wise have corralled an enormous technical crew, and the result is state-of-the-art screen magic. Exploits of Capt. Kirk and company should thrill the legions of tv Trekkies while ensnaring a galaxy of new admirers.

Pic had its world preem Dec. 6 at the MacArthur Theatre at Kennedy Center as a benefit for the National Space Club, with openings scattered throughout the U.S. and Canada in 800-900 theatres starting the next day.

Harold Livingston's screenplay makes the most of its audience's familiarity with the longrunning tv series in this tale of people and gadgetry. The Enterprise has been completely reconditioned during a two-year drydock, but must be prematurely dispatched to intercept an Earth-bound attacker destroying everything in its wake. William Shatner's Kirk is told to lead the mission along with other show regulars such as DeForest Kelley (Dr. McCoy) and James Doohan (Scotty), and of course, Leonard Nimoy's emotionless Spock who joins en route.

Upshot is a search-and-destroy thriller that includes all of the ingredients the tv show's fans thrive on: the philosophical dilemma wrapped in a scenario of mind control, troubles with the space ship, the dependable and understanding Kirk, the ever logical Spock, and suspenseful take with twist ending. Touches of romance and corn also dot this voyage, natch.

The pic also benefits from two newcomers, Stephen Collins' determined young commander, and the fetching young navigator, Persis Khambatta. The latter's career will no doubt soar with this film, if in fact her completely shorn locks don't create hysteria within a hairdressing industry wary of a new fad.

But the expensive effects (under supervision of Douglas Trumbull) are the secret of this film, and the amazing wizardry throughout would appear to justify the whopping budget. The alien "planet," the mother ship, midair explosions, and an unseen foe with unbelievable electrical powers are among the predicted touches that would register as hackneyed if they weren't handled with so much class. The expert hand of director Wise is evident in the rising suspenseful tempo of the action and the deft blending of performances. All miniatures and models are firstrate, while Jerry Goldsmith's brassy score is the other necessary plus.

In short, the now-proven audience for this type of sci-fi caper — which cuts across all age groups — is not likely to eschew this item despite its "G" rating. The tv series, after all, would be similarly rated. —*Paul.*

Roller Boogie
(COLOR)

Mostly mindless exploiter of roller skating revival.

Hollywood, Dec. 6.

A United Artists release of Irwin Yablans production. Executive producer, Irwin Yablans. Produced by Bruce Cohn Curtis. Directed by Mark L. Lester. Stars Linda Blair. Screenplay, Barry Schneider, from an original story by Yablans: camera (Technicolor). Dean Cundey: supervising editor. Howard Kunin: film editors. Byron (Buzz) Brandt. Ediberto Cruz. Edward Salier: music. Bob Esty: musical numbers staged by, David Winters: art direction. Keith Michl: sound (Dolby). Anthony Santa Croce: asst. director, Dan Allingham. Reviewed at the Samuel Goldwyn Theatre. Beverly Hills. Dec. 6, 1979. (MPAA Rating: PG.) Running time: 103 MINS.

Terry Barkley . . . . .Linda Blair
Bobby James . . . . Jim Bray
Lillian Barkley . . . . .Beverly Garland
Roger Barkley . . . . .Roger Perry
Hoppy . . . . .Jimmy Van Patten
Lana . . . . , ...Kimberly Beck
Complete Control Conway . . Rick Sciacca
Jammer . . . . Sean McClory
Thatcher . . . . Mark Goddard
Gordo . . . . Albert Insinnia
Phones . . . . Stoney Jackson
J.D. . . . ., . . M.G. Kelly
Franklin . . . . Chris Nelson

After a slick opening which takes a great degree of interest in the mechanics and garb of roller disco, "Roller Boogie" grinds on as one of the more mindless, irrelevant concoctions churned out of late. Boxoffice prospects seem dim.

Plot unfolds on the Dobie Gillis level of social significance. Poor little rich girl Linda Blair runs away from her blank father and pill-popping mother to get into the Venice beach skating scene. Half-way through, the mob tries to muscle in on the disco rink, closing it down until the kids, "Babes In Arms"-style, rally together to route the baddies, reopen the hall and proceed with their roller boogie contest.

Director Mark L. Lester has done considerably better work in the past, as the furious editing in this one betrays a futile attempt to hype up the action in the cutting room. Barry Schneider's screenplay lacks any imagination, although exec producer Irwin Yablans' story admittedly didn't give him much to work with. Dean Cundey's photography is mobile and colorful, while the Dolby sound comes close to recreating the overbearing noise in discos everywhere.

Pic is overflowing with hot teenage bodies of all persuasions but of the principals, only Beverly Garland is on target in her caricature of a desperately with-it BevHills matron. Blair is simply miscast, and her skating competition in the finale is basically a cheat since it consists of her partner Jim Bray, who can really roll, hoisting and twirling her around in the air, thus deflecting any real demands on her to show her stuff.

Best that can be said for pic is that it should end the roller skate genre after a mere two films, for its predecessor faded quickly from the marketplace. —*Cart.*

Chapter Two
(COLOR)

Simon sez it's great and it is.

Hollywood, Dec. 8.

Columbia Pictures release of a Ray Stark production. Stars James Caan, Marsha Mason. Directed by Robert Moore. Screenplay, Neil Simon, based on his play; camera (color), David M. Walsh; executive producer, Roger M. Rothstein; music, Marvin Hamlisch; lyrics, Carole Bayer Sager; producer designer, Gene Callahan; editor, Michael A. Stevenson; asst. director, Jack Roe; sound effects editor, at Somerset; art director, Pete Smith; set decorator, Lee Poll; special effects, Sam Dockrey; unit publicist, Scott McDonough. Reviewed at Burbank Studios, Burbank, Calif., Dec. 8, 1979. (MPAA Rating -PG). Running time: 124 MINS.

George Schneider . . . . .James Caan
Jennie MacLaine . . . . Marsha Mason

Leo Schneider ....Joseph Bologna
Faye Medwick.......... Valerie Harper
Gwen Michaels .... Judy Farrell
Marilyn ....Debra Mooney
Custom's officer ....Isabel Cooley
Elderly lady ....Imogene Bliss
Maitre d' .... Larry Michlin
Gary........................Ray Young
Martin ....George Rondo
Electric girl .... Cheryl Bianchi
Also: Greg Zadikov, Paul Singh, Elizabeth Farley, Sunday Brennab, Danny Gellis, Carl Jones, Henry Sutton, D. Miller, Howard Jeffrey, Marie Reynolds.

"Chapter Two" represents Neil Simon at his big-screen best. Ray Stark's film version of Simon's successful and loosely autobiographical play is tender, compassionate and gently humorous all at once. Marsha Mason's tremendous performance under Robert Moore's sensitive direction gives the pic another boost, one that will undoubtedly pay off at the boxoffice for the Columbia Pictures release.

Simon, Stark and Moore, in their third film collaboration, have dared to alter the entire focus of the legit version of "Chapter Two," by subtly but inalterably concentrating on Jennie MacLaine, the actress being wooed by author George Schneider. rather than Schneider himself, who was the nexus of the play.

Result is to downplay the unusual casting of James Caan as Schneider (the choice still pays off richly), and affords Mason the opportunity for her best-realized film work to date. Rarely has an actress had the opportunity (or the strain) of having to mold a screen role based so closely on her own experiences.

From its inception, "Chapter Two" has been recognized as a literary transmutation of the manner in which playwright Simon met and married Mason after a brief courtship. In the legit version of the work, emphasis was clearly on Schneider and his guilt and frustration in his inability to shed himself of his emotional involvement with his late wife.

With the encouragement of author Simon and director Moore, Caan still plays Schneider with the puzzled outrage of one suddenly deprived of something very dear. It's a close-in, non-demonstrative performance that is clearly content to let Mason take center stage.

Mason is so appealing as the bright and vivacious Jennie that it's no wonder she wins audience sympathy when Caan, in effect, puts her on romantic hold. Role is taken far past that in a powerful monolog that catalyzes the pic's climax, in which Mason dramatizes not only the strengths of her character, but her skills as an actress.

Although Moore has successfully opened up the play both physically and emotionally, it basically remains a four-character comedy-drama. As the two subsidiary characters, Joseph Bologna (James Caan's brother) and Valerie Harper (Mason's girlfriend) are superbly cast and highly effective. Harper, in particular, takes Faye Medwick out of the cartoonish mannerisms with which she's been played on stage, and into a sharply-drawn, attractive and lonely woman who offers a perfect counterpoint to Mason's Jennie.

Bologna has the most difficult role in the pic, that of the loudmouthed brother, but plays it well, hitting all the right notes. Rest of cast, chosen well by Jennifer Shull, is properly supportive.

Gene Callahan's production design is rich and varied, and gives both Mason and Caan's separate residences a homey feel. "Chapter Two" may represent cinematographer David M. Walsh's best work to date, with New York and Bermuda locations stunningly photographed. Only tech flaws are some jumpy cuts from editors Michael A. Stevenson and Margaret Booth, and some indistinct dialog from sound mixer Tom Overton. Marvin Hamlisch contributes an opportune score.

"Chapter Two" may disappoint some Simon fans expecting the machine — gun bursts of one-liners and jokes. While Simon's unerring sense of humor is adroitly inserted periodically, "Chapter Two" does far more to illuminate the human experience than many of Simon's earlier, and funnier, works. Pic says a great deal about love, its discovery and loss, and effects of those twin movements on very real people.

For the record, Simon's play opened on Oct. 7, 1977, at the Ahmanson Theatre in L.A. with Judd Hirsch and Anita Gillette as the leads, and Cliff Gorman and Ann Wedgeworth in the supporting roles. Show opened on Broadway at the Imperial Theatre on Dec. 4, 1977, with same cast, and ran through 856 performances and 107 weeks.

One interesting footnote: the character played by Mason in the film is monickered Jennie MacLaine — in the play, Gillette limned Jennie Malone. No explanation was given for the name change. —Poll.

I Sing I Cry
(TAIWAN-COLOR)

Bangkok, Nov. 30.
A Chan Lin Kang Films production and release. Produced by Chan Lin Kang. Directed and edited by Sung Cheng Sheu. Executive producer, Tsai Yu Wen. Story and screenplay, Sung Hsiang Ju; camera (color), Liao Ching Sung; music and sound, Wu Meg Lin; production supervisor, Shaw Che Wu. Reviewed at Krung Kasem theatre. Bangkok, Nov. 29, '79. Running time: 100 MINS.
Cast: Hu Hwei Chung, Chang Ruo Chu.

Local viewers had to discover for themselves that "I Sing I Cry" is not a sequel to "Your Smiling Face," Taiwan actress Hu Hwei Chung's first movie, a smash hit. Nonetheless, people who enjoyed the earlier pic flocked to the new one.

The soundtrack album tapes from "Your Smiling Face" were still playing by the time "I Sing I Cry" bowed.

In both of her first two films, Hu plays a singer. That's where the songs come in. Her problem this time concerns her relationship with an alcoholic songwriter, played by Chang Ruo Chu (also her leading man in her film debut). He wants her to become a famous singer. Unsure of herself, she wants to give up. They argue in the rain.

It would have been another happy ending. But Chang, after successfully launching her career, lets her sign with another manager. He then goes back to the bottle.

As a hasty follow-up to Hu's first b.o. hit, "I Sing I Cry" amply proves that Hu may be a star now, but unless she's more careful about choosing her films, she may lose her popularity sooner than her film producer thinks. —Cano.

All That Jazz
(COLOR)

All that jazz and plenty of ego.

A 20th Century Fox and Columbia Pictures release. Produced by Robert Alan Aurthur. Directed by Bob Fosse. Screenplay. Fosse and Robert Alan Aurthur. Executive producer, Daniel Melnick. Features entire cast. Camera, (Technicolor), Giuseppe Rotunno; editor, Alan Heim; production design, Philip Rosenberg: costumes, Albert Wolsky; music, Ralph Burns; choreography, Bob Fosse. Screened at Cinema 1, New York, Dec. 10, 1979. (MPAA rating: R). Running time: 123 MINS.
Joe Gideon .... Roy Scheider
Angelique .... Jessica Lange
Kate Jagger ....Ann Reinking
Audrey Paris .... Leland Palmer
David Newman .... Cliff Gorman
O'Conner Flood .... Ben Vereen
Michelle ....Erzsebet Foldi
Dr. Ballinger .... Michael Tolan
Joshua Benn............... Max Wright
Jonesy Hecht .... William Le Massena
Leslie Perry ...._...... Chris Chase
Victoria ....Deborah Geffner
Kathryn .... Kathryn Doby
Paul Dann ....Anthony Holland
Ted Christopher ....Robert Hitt
Larry Goldie ....David Margulies
Stacy .... Sue Paul
Young Joe .... Keith Gordon
Comic .... Frankie Man
Eddie Lerner .... Alan Heim
Lucas Sergeant ....John Lithgow

"All That Jazz" is a self-important, ego maniacal, wonderfully choreographed, often compelling film which portrays the energetic life, and preoccupation with death, of a director-choreographer who ultimately suffers a heart attack and dies.

The picture, reportedly based heavily on aspects of the real life of its director, Bob Fosse, deals with the director-choreographer Joe Gideon's career and his involvements with women, particularly his ex-wife Audrey and his current girlfriend Kate, as well as his daughter Michelle. The film paints Gideon as an egocentric workaholic for whom a permanent relationship with one woman is constantly subsumed into his work and repeatedly jeopardized by his need to seduce others.

Eventually Gideon's workaholism, coupled with smoking, drugs and pills, results in his having a heart attack. Prompted by what can only be termed a death wish, Gideon disregards medical advice for this recuperation and ultimately dies.

Gideon's real obsession is his work and the film is most successful conveying his absorption with coregoraphy and directing to the exclusion of almost everything else: the tension which develops as he reves up for rehearsals, hyping himself each time with Dexedrine, cold showers and eye drops; the relentless demands he makes on dancers and finally, the dance sequences themselves, a number of stunning routines: choreographed, of course, by Fosse.

Roy Scheider gives a superb performance as Gideon, creating a character filled with nervous energy and seemingly motivated by the belief that to stop working or even slow down for a minute-risks failure. Running from project to project, the film portrays Gideon completing work on one film while working simultaneously on another project. Such was the case when Fosse worked on "Lenny" and the film in "All That Jazz" is clearly meant to be "Lenny," this time with Cliff Gorman playing the role.

Ironically Gideon's disciplined work life is in contrast to his personal life which seems out of control. Both his marriage and his current affair have been affected by his constant infidelities.

The film's major flaw lies in its lack of real explanation of what, beyond ego, really motivates Gideon. Although the script, coauthored by Foss and Robert Alan Aurthur has some strong dialog and a number of witty lines, Gideon does not appear to have much insight into his own behavior nor does the audience really ever learn enough about him to understand what motivates his obsessive behavior. While some viewers, absorbed by the behind the scenes life of a director, may be willing to chalk everything up to life in show business, others may find problems with a character whose egocentric behavior is never explained.

Because of so little explanation, the repeated confrontations between Gideon and his ex-wife and current girlfriend over his infidelities become predictable and repetitive, as do his selfish demands on other women.

By way of some attempt at explanation of what shapes Gideon, the pic provides the mysterious "Angelique" (Jessica Lange) who appears to represent, among other symbols, death. In several short intercuts, Gideon also discusses various periods and events in his life. However, the explanations are aborted and add little dimension to his character.

Given the limitations of a script which seems to imply simply that it is Gideon's brilliance (possibly coupled with their own masochistic streaks) which keeps both ex-wife Audrey and current girlfriend Kate tied to him. Both actresses, Leland Palmer as Audrey Paris and Ann Reinking as Kate Jagger turn in excellent performances.

Reinking, a former real-life girlfriend of Fosse's and the star of his Broadway show, "Dancin'," is convincing as the dancer who loves him, sees the good and for a time, excuses the faults. Palmer is stunning as the aging dancer loyal partly out of love and partly out of conviction that Gideon's artistic genius can halt her disappearance over the hill. As Michelle, Gideon's daughter, with whom he plays the tenderest and most human scenes in the film, Erzsebet Foldi is excellent.

Giuseppe Rotunno's camera work is first rate as is Alan Heim's editing particularly in the handling of the complex dance scenes. As was the case with "The Turning Point," "All That Jazz" affords dance aficionados the opportunity to see performances from angles which would be impossible at a live state performance. —Geri.

The Jerk
(COLOR)

Crude but funny enough.

Hollywood, Nov. 28.
A Universal release of an Aspen Film Society William E. McEuen-David V. Picker production. Produced by David V. Picker, William E. McEuen. Directed by Carl Reiner. Stars Steve Martin. Screenplay, Steve Martin, Carl Gottlieb, Michael Elias, from a story by Martin, Gottlieb; camera (Technicolor), Victor J. Kemper; editor, Bud Molin; music, Jack Elliott; production design, Jack To. Collis; set design, Joe Hubbard; set decoration, Richard Goddard; costume design, Theodora Van

Runkle; sound, Charles M. Wilborn; associate producer, Peter Macgregor-Scott; assistant director, Newton Arnold. Reviewed at Universal Studios, Universal City, Nov. 28, 1979. (MPAA Rating: R.) Running time: **104 MINS.**

Navin Johnson	Steve Martin
Marie	Bernadette Peters
Patty Bernstein	Catlin Adams
Mother	Mabel King
Father	Richard Ward
Taj	Dick Anthony Williams
Stan Fox	Bill Macy
Madman	M. Emmet Walsh
Frosty	Dick O'Neill
Hobart	Maruice Evans
Hester	Helena Carroll
Harry Hartounian	Jackie Mason
Carl Reiner	Himself

There hasn't been anything quite like "The Jerk" since Jerry Lewis went on his own back in the late 1950s. Goofy, dumb, innocent, loud, uncoordinated, bashful and quite dirty, Steve Martin's eager-beaver naif is almost continually remindful of Lewis and will likewise polarize viewers into camps of fanatic devotees and those who won't be able to stand him. But Martin fans will flock in abundance, and comedian might even make a few converts as well.

Pic is an artless, non-stop barrage of off-the-wall situations, funny and unfunny jokes, generally effective and sometimes hilarious sight gags and bawdy non sequiturs. As with many comedies, film loses steam in the last reel, but not before dozens of laughs have been chalked up.

Just as many of the situations in Woody Allen's first film, "Take The Money And Run," derived from his night club monologs, so the premise of "The Jerk" can be found in one of Martin's more famous routines. Upon receiving the stunning news that he's the adopted, not natural, son of black parents Mabel King and Richard Ward, Martin leaves home with his dog to make his way in the world. Opening sequences with the family are among the best, and nicely break down most prior resistance Martin non-fans might have had going in.

Martin's odyssey through contemporary America sees him taking odd jobs, such as a gas station attendent for proprietor Jackie Mason and as the driver of an amusement park train, and taking up with women, notably dominatrix Catlin Adams and pert Bernadette Peters. Again like Jerry Lewis, Martin's bumpkin innocence perturbs, but ultimately disarms, the ladies, and relationship with Peters moves film toward stabs at poignance.

But lunacy is never strayed from very far, as Martin strikes it rich as the inventor of a ridiculous nose support device for eyeglasses and moves into the famous (in L.A., anyway) sheik's house on Sunset Boulevard. Hilarity ebbs during his

decline and fall, and writers Martin, Carl Gottlieb and Michael Elias stumble over the age-old problem of ending comedies well, but final moments are sufficiently upbeat to allow auds to exit similing.

Martin's energy never lets up, his overbearing side being offset by constant wacky, if not ridiculous, inventiveness. Only Peters among the remainder of the cast has a substantial part, which she handles adroitly, although Mabel King stands out as Martin's mother and Adams scores as his s&m-oriented mistress.

Pic is big on cameo appearances.

Tech credits are all serviceable. Language is unusually vulgar for a mass-market comedy, but most of Martin's under-17 fans will undoubtedly find a way to get in, just as R rating didn't prevent many kids from seeing "National Lampoon's Animal House" and "Up In Smoke." —Cart.

La Derobade
(The Getaway)
(FRENCH-COLOR)

Paris, Nov. 26.
A Prodis release of an ATC 3000/Prodis coproduction. Produced by Benjamin Simon. Stars Miou-Miou. Directed by Daniel Duval. Screenplay, Duval, Christopher Frank, Jeanne Cordelier, based on "The Life" by Cordelier; camera (color), Michel Cenet; sound, Michel Vionnet; art director, Francois Chanut; editor, Jean-Bernard Bonis; music, Vladimir Kosma. Reviewed at Publicis cinema, Paris, Nov. 22, 1979. Running time: **1110 MINS.**

Marie	Miou-Miou
Maloup	Maria Schneider
Gerard	Daniel Duval
Andre	Neil Arestrup

"La Derobade" is a curiously antiseptic screen version of Jeanne Cordelier's autobiographical novel (published in English as "The Life") about her five years as a prostitute and her attempts, finally successful, to extricate herself from the profession.

Cordelier herself collaborated on the screenplay with director Daniel Duval and novelist Christopher Frank, but together they have not been able to come up with a functional equivalent to the book's gut-urgent first-person narrative. The film viewer winds up more voyeur than confidante.

After the briefest of expository scenes, in which are suggested the background and emotional make-up of Marie, a young girl of working-class upbringing, film jumps to her "love at first sight" encounter with Gerard, a taciturn, good-looking pimp with an expensive car and a broodingly violent disposition. They shack up together and he introduces her to her new vocation as his "girl." Film recounts her increasingly night-

marish ordeal and concludes with the day she splits definitively with Gerard and reasserts control over her mind, heart and body.

Film falls short primarily because it reduces the vicissitudes of Marie's brutal, despairing existence to a catalog of seamy dramatic high points, without the necessary psychological probing or social analysis that would make it genuinely engrossing and moving. The world's oldest profession is also one of the most threadbare of dramatic and literary topics and, deprived of Cordelier's own voice, film fails to overwhelm the viewer with pity and horror.

It's too bad because the film has sound qualities, not least of which is Miou-Miou's performance as Marie: fresh, impudent, touching, she often manages to anchor the skimpy screenplay in an emotional continuity.

Too, Duval's direction is generally intelligent, tactful and subtle and gives individual scenes dramatic credibility. He resists the temptations of the material to pander and vulgarize, laying "La Derobade" far clear of any pornographic labels.

Film is a major success locally, where book has been a bestseller. Given the unflagging fascination and internationality of the subject matter, "La Derobade" could find a ready audience in U.S. and other markets. In any case, it confirms Miou-Miou as an actress of growing talents. —Len.

Friday The 13th ...
The Orphan
(COLOR)

John Ballard's blood bank works overtime.

World Northal release of a Gilman-Westergaard Enterprises and Cinema Investments Co. in association with Trimedia Southwest Associates II production. Features entire cast. Written and directed by John Ballard. Camera (color), Beda F. Patka; art director, Sidney Ann MacKenzie; theme song, Janis Ian; musical score, Ted Macero. Reviewed at RKO-SW Cinerama II, New York, Nov. 29, 1979. (MPAA Rating - R). Running time: **80 MINS.**

Aunt Martha	Peggy Feury
David's mother	Joanna Miles
David's father	Donn Whyte
Dr. Thompson	Stanley Church
Mary	Eleanor Stewart
Akin	Afolabi Ajayi
Jean Ford	Jane House
Percy Ford	David Foreman
David	Mark Owens

Most first-time directors (who're also their own scripters) turn to autobiographical material for their plots because this is the area they know best but the most interesting sections of John Ballard's "Friday The 13th ... The Orphan" are when he fantasizes.

The best scene in the film is when David's aunt tells him that his behavior is beyond her control and she must send him to a boarding school. Instead of school, the boy's imagination converts the remark into a threat to put him in an orphanage (he's been taunted with the idea of being an "orphan" by other children although his parents apparently left him well fixed). The scene that follows (his imagined confinement to such a place) would scare the curl out of Orphan Annie's hair.

On the other hand, straight domestic scenes and much of the other violence is very familiar material and doesn't hold the viewer's attention. Part of the fault is the weak performance by Mark Owrens as the orphan in question.

There's another "Friday The 13th" being currently filmed in much the same area by Sean Cunningham which could lead to later title confusion. —*Robe.*

Le Pull-Over Rouge
(The Red Sweater)
(FRENCH-COLOR)

Paris, Nov. 16.
A Gaumont release of a Port Royal Films Gaumont coproduction. Features entire cast. Produced, written and directed by Michel Drach. Screenplay collaborator, Ariane Litaize, based on the book "The Red Sweater" by Gilles Perrault; camera (Panavision), Jean Boffety; sound, Bernard Ortion; editor, Andre Gaultier; music, Jean-Louis D'Onorio. Reviewed at the Marignan cinema, Paris, Nov. 13, '79. Running time: **120 MINS.**
Christian Ranucci . . . . Serge Avedikian
Mrs. Mathon . . . . Michelle Marquais
Examining magistrate . . . . .Claire Deluca
Commissioner Robiana . . . Roland Bertin
Inspector Coudert . . . . Roland Blanche
Ranucci's lawyers . . . . Regis Porte
Robert Rimbaud

Michel Drach's "The Red Sweater" is a forceful, harrowing denunciation of French justice, whose apparently summary methods condemned to death a man who may have been innocent of murder. Film reconstructs the series of events beginning with the kidnap-murder of a nine-year old girl near Marseilles in 1974. A young travelling salesman, Christian Ranucci, was arrested, tried and executed.

Subsequently, a novelist and investigative reporter, Gilles Perrault (author of "Dossier 51," filmed last year by Michel Deville), reexamined the entire two-year affair and presented the results of his inquiry in a well-documented book, "The Red Sweater." Thesis: Ranucci's guilt was far from certain, and the French court, possibly pressured by shrilly vengeful public opinion, suppressed all contradictory evidence and witnesses in its haste to supply a head for the guillotine. Drach's

film is a dramatic distillation of Perrault's findings.

Although the case against Ranucci was rather damning — among other facts, his knife was identified as the murder weapon and he confessed to the crime (though he later retracted, claiming he'd been brutalized into a confession) — some testimony and evidence worked for the defendant's innocent: to wit, the victim's little brother, who saw the kidnapper, failed several times to identify Ranucci in police lineups; and a red sweater found near the scene of the crime, supposedly worn by the kidnapper, proved to be several sizes too large for Ranucci. These and other facts were kicked under the carpet by the prosecution.

As argumentative document, "The Red Sweater" has the drawbacks inherent in this kind of cinema — it necessarily selects, condenses and arranges information, simplifying a welter of facts to satisfy the linear demands of a dramatic screenplay.

Drach also and unabashedly appeals to the emotions as well as to reason, which may alienate even those sympathetic to his thesis. At least, the director wisely retains the horrible unanswered questions that must haunt the mind of anyone who believes Ranucci a hapless victim of vicious chance.

As film it is dramatically full and compelling, directed with controlled anger and intelligence (barring some vapidly sentimental irrelevancies, as when Ranucci's mother sees her son as a little boy) and acted by a generally excellent cast, among whom must be singled out Serge Avedekian, deeply moving in the role of the accused.

Despite its harrowing content, the picture's controversial theme should raise interest in foreign markets where capital punishment is an issue of concern. —*Len.*

Le Toubib
(The Medic)
(FRENCH-COLOR)

Paris, Nov. 30.
A CIC release of an Adel Productions/-Antenne 2/Films 21 coproduction. Produced by and starring Alain Delon. Directed by Pierre Granier-Deferre. Screenplay, Granier-Deferre, Pascal Jardin, based on the novel, "Harmonie ou les horreurs de la guerre," by Jean Freustie; camera (color), Claude Renoir; art director, Maurice Sergent; editor, Jean Ravel; music, Philippe Sarde. Sound, Jean Labussiere. Reviewed at the Concorde cinema, Paris, Nov. 27, 1979. Running time: **90 MINS.**
Jean-Marie . . . . Alain Delon
Harmonie . . . . .Veronique Jannot
Francois . . . . Bernard Giraudeau
Marcia . . . . .Francine Berge

The new Alain Delon film, "Le Toubib," is so lacking in genuine

dramatic interest that even Delon followers may be hard-put to get excited about it. Film is pursuing a successful but far from extraordinary career locally; its chances in foreign markets will depend entirely on the star's stature.

The script is shot through with platitudes about war, innocence, hope and suffering and is transparent in its dramatic progression. Screenplay is an adaptation, by Pascal Jardin and director Pierre Granier-Deferre, of a well-regarded novel, "Harmony or the Horrors of War." Whatever the qualities of the book may be, they are not evident in the film (the banal title change is symptomatic of obvious dramatic reduction).

Delon plays a successful Paris surgeon, whose wife has just walked out. The time is 1983: an unidentified, local war is raging somewhere in Europe. Delon is assigned to a field army hospital. Here the embittered doc is irritated by the unwonted optimism of a pretty. young surgical assistant named Harmony. In trying to reject her he succeeds only in being drawn to her — his protective wall of indifference is worn down. His hope is shattered when he learns that she is doomed to an early death. Delon plans to insure Harmony's final months as happy ones, but she is killed by a mine.

The film functions on forced poignancy and facile horrors, like the sequence in which Delon and the girl are dropped into a combat area to search for survivors among the charred remains of tanks (good, grisly art direction here by Maurice Sergent). But with the characters so conventional and shallow, what is there new to say about war and its ravages?

Granier-Deferre's direction is infected by the script's banalities. Delon's performance is competently taciturn and laconic. As Harmony, newcomer Veronique Jannot has freshness and appeal, but her role is rarely credible.

Technical credits are fine, especially Claude Renoir's color photography. —*Len.*

London Fest

Shades of Silk
(CANADIAN-COLOR)

London, Dec. 5.
John and Mary Productions release and production. Features entire cast. Directed by Mary Stephen. Screenplay, Stephen, Ann Martin; camera (Color), John Cressy; editor, Stephen Martin; music, Alain Leroux. Reviewed at London Film Fest, Nov. 21, '79. Running time, **65 MINS.**
With: Alexandra Brouwer, Mary Stephen, John Cressey, Isabel Beers.

A very specialized, personal film

by a Chinese girl from Hong Kong, now Canadian, using a synthesis of haunting music, commentary and fleeting visuals to recapture memory. Obviously influenced by French filmmaker Marguerite Duras but not as insistent as its model.

Though shot in Paris, it nevertheless has an oriental look, much of the action is set in the Shanghai of the 30s. Two girls, friends and perhaps a bit more though never having admitted it, try to adjust to life. One does with a marriage of convenience. The other goes her own way.

Item is very special, but with a gripping quality that could try it for special festival usage. Commercial possibilities are more cultist. Director Mary Stephen does have visual flair but is yet too mannered and portentous. She plays one of the girls acceptably. —*Mosk.*

Joi Baba Felunath
(The Elephant God)
(INDIAN-COLOR)

London, Dec. 4.
R.D.B. & Company release and production. Features entire cast. Written and directed by Satyajit Ray. Camera (Eastmancolor), Soumendu Roy; editor, Dulal Dutt; music, Ray. Reviewed at London Film Fest, Nov. 22. Running time: **112 MINS.**
Felu . . . . Soumitra Chatterjee
Maganla . . . . Utpal Dutta
Lalmohon . . . . Santosh Dutta
Tapesh . . . . .Siddhartha Chatterjee
Ruku . . . . .Jit Bose
Umanath . . . . .Haradhan Banerjee

Satyajit Ray is still the best-known Indian filmmaker abroad despite the meager commercial outings of his 23 films outside his own country. His noted trilogy on growing up in India are world classics. His disarming historical tale of colonial days, "The Chess Players," was recently seen Stateside to more critical than business success.

Besides his human dramas, Ray has made some so-called children's films and also writes books of his kind and sci-fi and detective tales. Now he does another film aimed at young filmgoers that, on its deft scripting, felicity of mood and good humor (which do not obscure an engrossing film) could slant this for all ages.

The film might be Ray's bow to that Yank hardboiled private-eye classic, "The Maltese Falcon" by John Huston. However, it is less mordant and sophisticated as a benign detective unravels the theft of a highly valuable small statue of an elephant god in gold studded with precious stones.

Ray's shamus is played with restraint and perspicacity by Soumitra Chatterjee, who has been in several Ray films. On a vacation in Benares, Chatterjee is called in on the theft of the statue. There are some suspects and the film's main charms are the well knitted characterizations and inventive incidents.

Each suspect has his day and side characters, such as a body beautiful strongman, ready to flee town when he gets a warning intended for the detective by mistake, aid in character development of the others and as witty asides.

There is the son of the robbed old man who has business troubles, his little boy affected by it all and a local underworld character, as well as a disgruntled servant, not to forget a phony holy man who turns out to be a fence.

There are nice twists with Ray obviously enjoying making the film, which has his full attention, clever progression and also a comic edge still in keeping with the whodunit aspects. It remains engrossing to the end.

Though mainly for playoff abroad, as well as fest outings, film remains a fine genre item wrought by an unusual director. Ironically, it is reportedly doing better in India than Ray's "serious" films.

The Indian love of detective stories, adds a whimsical note to the film aided atmospherically by the colorful holy city of Benares. Ray's own music is an asset as well as sharp editing and finely hued lensing. —*Mosk.*

Poto and Cabengo
(U.S.-W. GERMAN-DOCU-COLOR)

London, Dec. 4.
J.P. Gorin, ZDF release and production. Conceived and directed by Jean-Pierre Gorin. Camera (Color), Les Blank; editor, Greg Durbin. Reviewed at London Film Fest, Nov. 21, '79. Running time, 75 MINS.

Jean-Pierre Gorin as Jean-Luc Godard's political mentor and co-director when that prolific New Wave French film innovator turned to political tract films during the 1968 near revolutionary days.

Godard then turned to video but is now again making a film in France. Gorin went off to teach film in California a few years ago and now surfaces with this engrossing documentary about the effect of parents and environment on children as well as probing the meaning of language itself.

Gorin went to see, and make a film on, identical twin girls, about 10 years old, who gained media notoriety when it was found they conversed in their own language. Gorin, with an atypical accent which is hard to pin down, narrates his meetings with the girls as well

as their family, therapists and specialists.

The father is an ex-G.I. who brought home a German bride and her mother. The grandmother speaks only German and the mother good but accented English. The father has had a series of jobs and they have moved around a bit.

Theme may involve the need for their own world, or standing up to changes and different languages. But Gorin wisely avoids didactics and focuses on the people around them who talk about themselves and allow viewers to make their own conclusions.

Director does have an opinion that children are often spoken through rather than to. Children, he seems to be saying, start with their ways of communication only to return eventually to regular language as they go to different schools.

Pic is a natural for seminars, festivals and schools but is absorbing enough to also warrant some theatrical outings, perhaps with another docu to make up a rounded program. —*Mosk.*

The Black Hole
(COLOR)

Superior Disney effort needs acceleration to catch "Star Trek" at the b.o.

Hollywood, Dec. 18.
Buena Vista release of a Walt Disney Productions film. Produced by Ron Miller. Directed by Gary Nelson. Features entire cast. Screenplay, Jeb Rosebrook, Gerry Day from a story by Rosebrook, Bob Barbash and Richard Landau; camera (Technicolor), Frank Phillips; music, composed and conducted by John Barry; production designer, Peter Ellenshaw; art directors, John B. Mansbridge, Al Roelofs, Peter Ellenshaw; set decorators, Frank R. McKelvy, Roger M. Shook; asst. director, Tom McCrory. Reviewed at Samuel Goldwyn Theatre, Bevhills, Dec. 14, 1979. (MPAA Rating: PG). Running time: 97 MINS.
Dr. Hans Reinhardt ... Maximilian Schell
Dr. Alex Durant ....Anthony Perkins
Capt. Dan Holland .... Robert Forster
Lt. Charles Pizer .... Joseph Bottoms
Dr. Kat McCraw .... Yvette Mimieux
Harry Booth ....Ernest Borgnine
Capt. S.T.A.R. ...... Tommy McLoughlin

Latest entry in Hollywood's race for space, "The Black Hole" may be the best yet in terms of sheer visual power. The most ambitious and expensive production ever mounted by Walt Disney Productions, and studio's first PG-rated film, "The Black Hole" uses traditional Disney story framework as a backdrop for Peter Ellenshaw's visionary designs of space travel.

Biggest obstacle the Buena Vista release may face is audience reluctance to sample more than one science-fiction spectacular, and since G-rated "Star Trek" bowed two weeks before release of "Black Hole" this Friday, pic will have to play catch-up. Consumer enjoyment seems assured, however, and boxoffice returns should be ample.

Above all, "Black Hole" reaffirms the Disney pre-eminence in special visual effects, whether they be miniatures, matte work or robots. A top technical staff led by vets Ellenshaw, Art Cruickshank, Eustace Lycett and Danny Lee have produced an overwhelming universe consisting of mammoth space ships, meteor showers and the strange title phenomenon.

The black hole itself gets short shrift in the screenplay by Jeb Rosebrook and Gerry Day, based on a story by Rosebrook, Bob Barbash and Richard Landau. Most of the pic's 97 minutes are devoted to setting up the story of mad scientist Maximilian Schell, poised on the brink of his voyage to the unknown, evoking memories of Disney's own "20,000 Leagues Under The Sea" from 1954. An exploration ship staffed by Robert Forster, Anthony Perkins, Joseph Bottoms, Yvette Mimieux and Ernest Borgnine,

stumbles on both Schell and the nearby black hole, with unpredictable results.

What ensues is sometimes talky and often simple-minded, but never dull. Director Gary Nelson has some difficulty maneuvering around the silly dialog, but his pacing and visual sense are right on target. The work of Disney's in-house staff is so brilliant as to overshadow many of the film's dramatic defects.

In typical Disney fashion, the most attractive and sympathetic characters are not human at all. George F. McGinnis has constructed a bevy of robots that draw inspiration from "Star Wars," but establish a mechanical world all their own. Companion to Forster and crew is Vincent, a free-floating mini-computer who displays a stiff British upper lip and a keen sense of humor. Pitted against him is leader of Schell's storm trooper robots, a hulking metal giant named Max who joins Disney ranks of truly sinister villians.

Since the robots get most of the best lines, all the flesh-and-blood performers can do is advance the juvenile story line, which has Schell keeping his captives so they can monitor his journey through the black hole, and Borgnine leading the escape attempt. Schell's performance has all the subtlety of a space station in transit and his philosophical ramblings provide the film's only slow moments. Rest of cast is adequate, with only psychically-endowed Mimieux establishing any characterization. Perkins and Borgnine look completely out of place.

John Barry's score makes everything seem properly dramatic, especially in Dolby stereo, but the real star is Ellenshaw's gargantuan, but oddly graceful, production design. "Black Hole" is the first film to present a truly artistic conception of space travel. Even though the film's ending, in which Mimieux, Bottoms, Forster and Perkins actually rebound through the black hole, remains unclear, the enormity of Ellenshaw's accomplishment cannot be denied.

Dialog redubbing is obvious, and a sound montage that accompanies descent into the black hole is confusing. But there are enough laser battles between robots to keep any moppet (and parents) on the edge of their seats. Disney goal has always been to entertain, and with "The Black Hole," that objective is splendidly achieved. —*Poll.*

The Search For Solutions
(DOCUMENTARY-COLOR)

Overlong but interesting look at science.

Playback Associates production, produced by James C. Crimmins. Directed by Michael Jackson. Co-producers, Michael Jackson, Kathy Mendoza. Narrator, Stacy Keach, (color), Mike Jackson. Camera, (color), editors, Ken Werner, Kris Liem, Kathryn Barnier, Arnold Briedman; writers, Jim Crimmins, Brad Darrach, L.L. Larison Cudmore, Gerald Jonas; music, Pat Metheny, Lyle Mayers; performed by Janet Forman, Ken Werner. Reviewed at Rizzoli Screening Room, N.Y., Dec. 12, 1979. (MPAA Rating - Not rated). Running time: **180 MINS** with intermission.

Despite its overall interesting look at science, this very lengthy (three hours) documentary seems strange fare for the holiday but it opens this week at the Cinema II, an eastside house. Divided into nine 20-minute sections, one could believe this film was made for public broadcasting exposure as each section unveils with the legend, "Narrated by Stacy Keach." Once, at the beginning of the film, would be more than sufficient.

For viewers who are willing to devote this much time to a film, it is most rewarding for those who come back after the intermission as the second part is the more interesting. The nine sections are "Trial and Error," "Evidence," "Context," "Modeling," "Adaptation," "Prediction," "Investigation," "Patterns" and "Theory." Most areas of science are covered, from chemistry to just plain guessing.

Excellent photography throughout, a dialog slanted at the layman, and generally interesting subjects make the documentary a rewarding treat. Whether the general public is going to endorse it remains to be seen but the film should be a natural for libraries and universities. Executive producer James C. Crimmins claims that the project took 14 months on 160 locations in 14 countries and has a "cast" of more than 200 scientists, artists, athletes and others. Some are fascinating; some are funny. None are dull. —*Robe.*

Cuba
(COLOR)

Unsympathetic types against finale of Batista reign. Rough outlook in Christmas rush.

Hollywood, Dec. 13.

A United Artists release of an Alex Winitsky-Arlene Sellers production. Produced by Sellers, Winitsky. Directed by Richard Lester. Screenplay, Charles Wood. Stars Sean Connery, Brooke Adams. Executive producer, Denis O'Dell; camera (Color), David Watkin; editor, John Victor Smith; music, Patrick Williams; production design, Gil Parrondo; art direction, Denis Gordon Orr; costume design, Shirley Russell; sound, Roy Charman; assistant director, David Tringham. Reviewed at the MGM Studios, Culver City, Dec. 13, '79. (MPAA Rating: R). Running time: **122 MINS.**
Robert Dapes . . . . Sean Connery

Alexandra Pulido . . . . Brooke Adams
Gutman . . . . Jack Weston
Raimirez . . . . Hector Elizondo
Skinner . . . . Denholm Elliott
General Bello . . . . Martin Balsam
Juan Pulido . . . . Chris Sarandon
Faustino . . . . Alejandro Rey
Therese . . . . Lonette McKee
Julio . . . . Danny De La Paz
Miss Wonderly . . . . Louisa Moritz

"Cuba" is a hollow, pointless non-drama. Cynical and evasive about politics, pic displays uniformly unsympathetic characters enacting a vague plot amidst a splendid recreation of Havana at the very end of the Batista regime. Winitsky-Sellers production would undoubtedly have had trouble even without heavy holiday competition, but to release it against the Christmas big guns seems like a commercial miscue.

Basic "Two Weeks In Another Town" situation has had all conventional melodrama calculatedly drained from it by director Richard Lester and scripter Charles Wood. Revolution is closing in on the upper crust types who serve as story focus, and Brooke Adams is torn between two men, but treatment deliberately goes against the grain of sentiments normally encountered in such potent dramatic set-ups, as if filmmakers felt above indulging in such commonplace motives. Approach leaves the audience with nothing to engage it.

Small points regarding rampant corruption of the dictator's regime are made in obvious ways — parking meter revenue is delivered directly to general Martin Balsam, workers are slapped around, everyone drinks a lot, payoffs guarantee instant privileges, and a "romantic" stroll is taken through muddy slums. But within the sourly negative context created here, even such reasonable pastimes as playing classical music and enjoying tennis take on, when indulged in by these characters, decidedly decadent aspects.

Of no help either is ineffectual interloper played, with unusually uncertain footing, by Sean Connery. A soldier of fortune in a business suit, he arrives in an attempt to promote British interests but ends by achieving nothing. That's undoubtedly the point, but as he agrees when told that he's come to Cuba too late, it's surprising he doesn't get out while the getting's good rather than waiting around in a futile attempt to convince old flame Adams to leave with him.

Given the worthless, motley crew seen to populate Havana — including gross American profiteer Jack Weston, cynical gentleman Denholm Elliott and Adams' philandering husband Chris Sarandon, as well as assorted military types and jaded aristocrats — political outlook would seem to be that things

couldn't get much worse, and maybe Castro will be a little bit better.

Cast, like the characters, seems trapped, although standout under the circumstances would have to be Danny De La Paz as a desperate youth bent on assassinating those he believes to be his oppressors and anxious to be taken as a good revolutionary.

In that U.S. filming in Cuba isn't yet a reality, team headed by production designer Gil Parrondo, art director Denis Gordon Orr, costume designer Shirley Russell and cinematographer David Watkin have done a marvelous job of creating a convincing sense of time and place. Lensed in various Spanish cities, pic has feeling of physical verisimilitude, even if story does not.

After success in a comic vein in the "Musketeer" pix, Richard Lester has yet to regain his footing on more serious ground. Lamentably, this one veers dangerously close to the meretricious cynicism of the territory the likes of Michael Winner have explored. There's no reward to be found there, either for filmmaker or audience. —*Cart.*

Going In Style
(COLOR)

Not-very-funny comedy of aging seen hard-go for young audiences.

Hollywood, Dec. 11.

A Warner Bros. release, produced by Tony Bill and Fred T. Gallo. Directed and written by Martin Brest. Exec producer, Leonard Gaines. Camera (color), Billy Williams; editors, Robert Swink, C. Timothy O'Meara; sound, James Sabat; production design, Stephen Hendrickson; art direction, Gary Weist, Fred C. Price; assistant director, Mike Rauch; music Michael Small. Reviewed at the Samuel Goldwyn Theatre, Beverly Hills, Dec. 11, '79. (MPAA rating: PG). Running time: **97 MINS.**
Joe . . . . George Burns
Al . . . . Art Carney
Willie . . . . Lee Strasberg
Pete . . . . Charles Hallahan
Kathy . . . . Pamela Payton Wright

Warner Bros. has already conceded publicly the difficulty of selling "Going In Style," planning to do its best to put it out as a comedy. But the picture isn't funny enough to qualify for that, though at times it is a sensitive look at the aged. Overall, very little appeal for today's young audiences.

Once again, George Burns turns in a good performance in a tailored role. Art Carney is also solid, but has done far better. Lee Strasberg is competent but out of place.

Wasting away as bored pensioners in N.Y., the trio decide they have little to lose in attempting a bank heist, an interesting premise and something of the same middle-class protest that Jane Fonda and

George Segal brought to "Fun With Dick and Jane." But this picture never makes as much use of the idea.

Working from his own script in a feature directing debut, Martin Brest constructs great moments and some feel for geriatric emptiness hypoed with hi-jinks for one last time. But other than a protest against a natural process — and perhaps some outrage that society has no better use for its elders — Brest fails to find any focal point in his script.

Consequently, pic moves from scene to scene with almost no dramatic conflict at all beyond the old men's individual emotions, especially Burns' as he loses first and then the other of his companions.

The bank job doesn't prove that difficult to pull off; a gambling spree to Las Vegas produces easy riches, topped by Burns' ultimate unexciting arrest. Along the way, Brest introduces off-screen threats — like the casino operators anger at their losses — but never pursues them.

Charles Hallahan especially and Pamela Payton Wright are good as the young couple who end up with the booty. And all tech credits are strong and Brest remains a director to watch. But not now.—*Har.*

Die Langen Ferien Der Lotte H. Eisner
(The Long Vacation of Lotte H. Eisner)
(WEST GERMAN-B&W-DOCU-16m)

Berkeley, Nov. 21.

Produced, directed, and written by Sohrab Shahid-Saless, in collaboration with Lotte H. Eisner. Reviewed at Pacific Film Archive, Berkeley, Nov. 21, '79. Running time: **60 MINS.**

Documentaries on famous people suffer a bit when fact is matched with legend. This one on Lotte H. Eisner, however, is both timely and long awaited, and it's finally been done by an Iranian director, in exile no less, Sohrab Shahid-Saless. Hopefully, more such interviews will be made with this grand lady in the not too distant future. Werner Herzog has been trying for years.

"The Long Vacation of Lotte H. Eisner" deals principally with her recollections: her childhood, her first years as a German critic — theatre critic, not a film reviewer — with Berlin papers and magazines, that wonderful period of German Expressionism in film, her long-standing relationships with Fritz Lang and F.W. Murnau, her decision to leave Germany in 1933 for Paris with a strong premonition of what was to come, the days and weeks in hiding in the south of

France during the Second World War, the warm, personal relationship with Henri Langlois and the French Cinematheque (she is today a curator there), and, finally, her straightforward, no-mixing-of-words views on the resurgence of New German Cinema.

All is rendered in clear, extraordinarily precise, and stylistic German, as though she were phrasing her autobiography as she goes along. The rapport with Saless is warm and intimate from the outset: obviously, from the tone of a letter written by her to the filmmaker at the film's opening, she respects both the man and admires his work. The docu also hints that she is the spiritual mentor of several other German helmers today.

Best of all, her views on German Expressionism in particular should fill in plenty of gaps left in classic and current film histories. For instance, she speaks with some authority on Fritz Kortner's "expressionistic" manner of speech as an actor — there was no place for his talent in the Hollywood film tradition, so he returned to Germany shortly after the war where he felt more at home.

Further, friends walk in the door from time to time, among them *Variety* correspondent Gene Moskowitz, and David Overbey, another Yank critic in Paris. She walks in a garden, comments on occasion on life and its quirks, blessings, and tragedies (the death of Langlois). Few at her age (somewhere in the eighties) have lived so fully and so well.

Saless combines photos with music and mood shots, as though chapters in Eisner's "long vacation" were unfolding in a leisurely manner to both delight and amuse the viewer-listener. The whole film, in fact, is done with such taste as to question why this critic-historian — author of "The Haunted Screen" and biographies on Lang and Murnau — has not been honored long, long ago with the highest literary awards conferred by the West German government. —*Holl.*

Being There
(COLOR)

A gem, with Sellers' best performance in years.

Hollywood, Dec. 13.
A United Artists release of an Andrew Braunsberg production for Lorimar. Produced by Andrew Braunsberg. Directed by Hal Ashby. Executive producer, Jack Schwartzman. Stars Peter Sellers, Shirley MacLaine. Screenplay, Jerzy Kosinski, based on his novel; camera (Technicolor), Caleb Deschanel; editor, Don Zimmerman; music, John Mandel; production design, Michael Haller; art direction, James Schoppe; set decoration, Robert Benton; costume design, May Routh; sound, Jeff Wexler; associate producer,

Charles Mulvehill; assistant director, David S. Hamburger. Reviewed at the MGM Studios, Culver City, Dec. 13, '79. MPAA Rating: PG.) Running time: **130 MINS.**
Chance .... Peter Sellers
Eve Rand .... Shirley MacLaine
Benjamin Rand .... Melvyn Douglas
President 'Bobby' .... Jack Warden
Dr. Robert Allenby ...... Richard Dysart
Vladimir Skrapinov ....Richard Basehart
Louise .... Ruth Attaway
Thomas Franklin .... Dave Clennon
Sally Hayes .... Fran Brill
Johanna Franklin .... Denise DuBarry

"Being There" is a highly unusual and an unusually fine film. A faithful but nonetheless imaginative adaptation of Jerzy Kosinski's quirky comic novel, pic marks a significant achievement for director Hal Ashby and represents Peter Sellers' most smashing work since the mid-1960s. Delicate, rarified quality of the material dictates a very careful sell by Lorimar and United Artists, but comic elements and Sellers' name should draw enough patrons initially to let word-of-mouth do the rest. Cross over from urban art crowd to mass market will be tricky but possible.

Kosinski's story is a quietly outrageous fable which takes Sellers from his position as a cloistered gardener to that of a valued advisor to an industrial giant and ultimately to the brink of a presidential nomination. Lead character is a childlike, unblinking naif who can't read or write and has never set foot outside his master's Washington, D.C. townhouse until he's ejected by lawyers upon the old man's death.

Injured by a limousine, he's taken by its owner Shirley MacLaine to the fabulous mansion she shares with financier and political kingmaker husband Melvyn Douglas. Immediately impressing the dying man by virtue of his surprising simplicity and seemingly wise aphorisms, all relating to gardening, the earth and the seasons, Sellers soon encounters President Jack Warden, who quotes the previously unknown sage in a speech.

This throws Capitol Hill into a tizzy, as journalists, the CIA, the FBI and foreign governments all try to discover the facts of this instant savant's past. While becoming a media celebrity and the rage of embassy parties, Sellers still spends most of his time at the mansion, passively resisting the infatuated MacLaine's advances and pursuing his favorite pastime, watching television.

Tale possesses political, religious and consumer society undertones, but by no means is an overly symbolic affair trying to impress with its deep meanings. As has been his habit lately, Ashby underscores most of the action with music, and in accordance with Sellers' obsession, effectively interpolates a con-

siderable amount of random tv footage into the picture, footage which, throughout the character's life, has represented his only means of acquiring knowledge of human behavior and the outside world.

Sellers' performance stands as the centerpiece of the film, and it's a beauty. Gray, drawn and utterly reserved, he evokes the necessary childlike quality to make the role work. As an actor, Sellers has excelled first and foremost on the mimic level, finding physical and vocal keys to his characters and elaborating upon them.

Here, without wigs, makeup, costumes or an outrageous accent, Sellers is performing nude, in a sense. Given that his unformed neuter of a gardener takes his behavioral cues from those around him, rather than from his own personality, role provides the opportunity to witness Sellers' own brand of genius in action, as he is continually adapting to the immediate situation in a way uninformed by previous experience.

On a more technical level, Sellers almost miraculously never breaks character and, in several scenes, reveals his comic timing to be in peak operating order. As usual when he's at his best, actor gets quite a few laughs that weren't in the script.

In a role more difficult than it may seem, Shirley MacLaine is subtle and winning, retaining her dignity despite several precarious opportunities to lose it. If such is possible in a picture dominated by Sellers, Melvyn Douglas almost steals the film with his spectacular performance as the dying financial titan. Avoiding all cliches, veteran actor movingly creates a crusty old character of full human dimensions. It's a heroic performance.

Supporting parts, from Jack Warden's president, Richard Dysart's suspicious doctor and Ruth Attaway's salty maid down to the many small bits, are strongly essayed. Particularly impressive is Dave Clennon's ambitious young attorney and John Harkins' frustrated newspaper reporter. Ashby's former producer Jerome Hellman smoothly handles the role of a talk show host.

Tech credits are all top drawer. Locations, particularly Douglas' castle-like abode, are fresh and gorgeous, and are abetted by Michael Haller's production design and James Schoppe's art direction. Caleb Deschanel confirms his standing as one of the top lensers now working, and John Mandel, presumably in collaboration with the director, has created an active, appropriate musical backdrop.
—*Cart.*

The Human Factor
(BRITISH-COLOR)

Preminger's first in five years impresses as a soft prospect.

Hollywood, Dec. 11.
A Metro-Goldwyn-Mayer release through United Artists. Produced, directed by Otto Preminger. Executive producer, Paul Crosfield. Screenplay, Tom Stoppard, based on the novel by Graham Greene; camera (color), Mike Molloy; editor, Richard Trevor; music, Richard and Gary Logan; art direction, Ken Ryan; costume design, Hope Bryce; associate producers, Chris Dillinger, Val Robins; assistant director, Kip Gowans. Reviewed at MGM Studios, Culver City, Dec. 11, '79. (MPAA Rating: R). Running time: **115 MINS.**
Colonel Daintry ... Richard Attenborough
Cornelius Muller ....Joop Doderer
Brigadier Tomlinson .... John Gielgud
Davis .... Derek Jacobi
Percival .... Robert Morley
Castle's Mother .... Ann Todd
Sir John Hargreaves .... Richard Vernon
Castle .... Nicol Williamson
Sarah .... Iman

Otto Preminger's "The Human Factor" is a gloss of Graham Greene's "The Human Factor." Vet director's first film since "Rosebud" five years ago was made independently and marks MGM's first pickup since dropping its distribution arm, but stands as a disappointingly minor entry from both parties. B.o. outlook is accordingly soft.

Greene's low-keyed, highly absorbing 1978 novel of an aging English double agent finding himself trapped into defecting to Moscow and leaving his family behind may have seemed like ideal material for Preminger's style of dispassionate ambiguity, but helmer doesn't seem up to the occasion, bringing little atmosphere or feeling to the delicate ticks of the story.

Playwright Tom Stoppard's screenplay covers the essential ground of the novel in shorthand fashion, adding a few clever lines for Robert Morley in the process. Unfortunately, Preminger stages it all as if he was just trying to get the actors through their line readings in under two hours, allowing no breathing room or time for character nuance in a tale which resolutely calls for quiet moments.

Nicol Williamson limns the lead role of a Secret Service desk man who, due not to political commitment but loyalty to a friend from his days in Africa, discreetly passes occasional information to the East. Basic theme evokes E.M. Forster's controversial remark that, forced to a choice, he would sooner betray his country than his friend.

When a leak in his department is discovered and office partner Derek Jacobi, mistakenly identified as the culprit, is eliminated, Williamson feels the walls closing in on him. Ultimately he's spirited off to the U.S.S.R., disconnected from his black South African wife and son and faced with a bleak future.

More a tale of character and contemplation than a rousing actioner, film scores only in its presentation of the elderly British espionage higher-ups who remain capable of utterly venal acts despite their genial, distinguished guises. Richard Attenborough does best in this line, although Robert Morley is highly effective as a callous physician and Richard Vernon is properly hardnosed as a security topper. John Gielgud is in for a few words in the opening scene.

Williamson tries hard but is uneven, although Preminger's lack of attention to modulation might be equally at fault. As lead's wife, Iman is woefully lacking in dramatic skills or ability to project emotion, which shortchanges the impact of the pair's separation. Jacobi, on the other hand, is excellent as the expendable paper pusher, and Frank Williams creates a stand-out cameo as a gay exile in Moscow.

Pic is erratic on technical level as well. Richard and Gary Logan's music is often imaginative and unusual for a film score, but Mike Molloy seemingly doesn't know how to light a scene in which lamps are supposed to be the major source of illumination. Unfortunately, most of the talk takes place indoors. Ken Ryan's set for the hero-victim's Moscow apartment is similarly artificial and unconvincing. —*Cart.*

The Shape Of Things To Come
(CANADIAN-COLOR)

Unexciting, skimpy remake of the 1936 sci-fi classic "Things to Come" with minimal b.o. prospects. Should have left Wells enough alone.

Film Ventures Intl. release of a CFI Investments presentation. Produced by William Davidson. Exec producer, Harry Alan Towers. Directed by George McCowan. Screenplay, Martin Lager. Remaining credits not available. Reviewed at Cinerama II Theatre, N.Y.C., Dec. 13, '79 (MPAA Rating: PG.) Running time: **95 MINS.**

Omus .... Jack Palance
Niki .... Carol Lynley
Senator Smedley .... John Ireland
Dr. John Caball .... Barry Morse
Jason Caball .... Nicholas Campbell
Kim Smedley .... Eddie Benton
"Sparks" (voice) .... Greg Swanson
"Sparks" (robot) .... Marc Parr

This Canadian updating of H.G. Wells' post-apocalyptic space yarn emerges as an inadvertent tribute to William Cameron Menzies' 1936 "Things To Come." In spite of all the technological breakthroughs in special effects that have intervened in the past 10 years or so, the

remake doesn't match for a moment the staggering visual imagery of the original. Muddily thought out, photographed and acted, the newer pic will have to rely on audience spillover from bigger-budgeted sci-fi entries to fill even a couple of rows.

Considering the shakiness and frequent silliness of the source material, more than mere updating with computer printouts, galactic miniature work and the spectre of nuclear radiation was required. The story takes place seven years after the earth was destroyed by nuclear "robot wars" with the moon now a glass-domed colony for the remaining earthlings who still rely on regular doses of a miracle drug to combat radiation.

Enter Jack Palance, a renegade who takes over control of a small planet where the drug is manufactured and tries blackmailing the moon into taking him back as dictator by cutting off their life-saving source. With the moon facing imminent destruction, hawkish scientist Barry Morse, son Nicholas Campbell, latter's girlfriend/scientist Eddie Benton, and a lovestruck robot, illegally rocket off to confront and finally destroy Palance.

Bulk of the film is confined to a few computer-strewn sets where a lot of talking goes on, with a side-trip to earth (where wild, post-holocaust children provide some would-be pathos), and a final portion on Palance's planet, where clumsy robots battle freedom-fighters led by Carol Lynley. Special effects are on the "Captain Video" level, although the miniature work is pretty good. Anything more ambitious, even simple matte-work, is subpar.

Pic originally was slated to be released via Allied Artists, that arrangement falling through when AA filed for Chapter XI, with domestic rights going to Film Ventures International. — *Step.*

1941
(COLOR)

Too many bombs, not enuf yocks in Spielberg's World War II spoof. Entertaining film carries some doubts.

Hollywood, Dec. 13.
Universal Pictures release of an A-Team production. Produced by Buzz Feitshans. Directed by Steven Spielberg. Exec producer, John Milius. Screenplay, Robert Zemeckis, Bob Gale from a story by Zemeckis, Gale, Milius; camera (color), William A. Fraker; editor, Michael Kahn; music, John Williams; production design, Dean Edward Mitzner; sound, Gene S. Cantamessa; special effects, A.D. Flowers; miniature supervisor, Gregory Jein; costumes, Deborah Nadoolman; art direction, William F. O'Brien; matte paintings, Matthew Yuricich; visual effects supervisor, Larry Robinson; production illustrator, George Jensen; set

decoration, John Austin; stunt coordinator, Terry Leonard; additional photography, Frank Stanley; choreography, Paul De Rolf; optical consultant, L.B. Abbott; optical effects, Van Der Veer Photo Effects; assistant directors, Jerry Ziesmer, Steve Perry. Reviewed at Directors Guild of America Hollywood, Dec. 11, '79. MPAA Rating: PG. Running time: **118 MINS.**

Sergeant Tree .... Dan Aykroyd
Ward Douglas .... Ned Beatty
Wild Bill Kelso .... John Belushi
Joan Douglas .... Lorraine Gary
Claude .... Murray Hamilton
Von Kleinschmidt .... Christopher Lee
Birkhead .... Tim Matheson
Commander Mitamura ... Toshiro Mifune
Maddox .... Warren Oates
General Stilwell .... Robert Stack
Sitarksi .... Treat Williams
Donna .... Nancy Allen
Herbie .... Eddie Deezen
Wally .... Bobby DiCicco
Betty .... Dianne Kay
Foley .... John Candy
Ogden Johnson Jones ..... Frank McRae
Dennis .... Perry Lang
Hollis Wood .... Slim Pickens
Maxine .... Wendie Jo Sperber
Scioli .... Lionel Stander
Meyer Mishkin ...... Ignatius Wolfington
U.S.O. M.C. .... Joseph P. Flaherty

Billed as a comedy spectacle, Steven Spielberg's "1941" is long on spectacle, but short on comedy. The Universal-Columbia Pictures co-production is an exceedingly entertaining, fast-moving revision of 1940s war hysteria in Los Angeles spawned by the bombing of Pearl Harbor, and boasts Hollywood's finest miniature and visual effects work seen to date. Due to the film's frenetic pacing and lack of empathetic characters, however, box-office prognosis is not as healthy as that of Spielberg's most recent pix, "Jaws" and "Close Encounters Of The Third Kind."

Another of this year's crop of oft-delayed, bloated-budget spectaculars, "1941" succeeds in many of the goals Spielberg apparently set for himself. It's filled with lavish sight gags, elaborate stunt work, lovely period settings and costumes and a brace of fine thesps. Fact that 82 cast members are specifically credited, along with more than 160 crew and tech personnel in a six minute end credits crawl, should be ultimate validation that film is a collaborative work.

When all is said and done, however, the vision on the screen is director Spielberg's, giving "1941" both its advantages and its drawbacks. There are few filmmakers who can demonstrate such technical mastery of the medium — Spielberg moves his actors, sets, props and cameras with the efficiency of a creative field marshal.

But "1941" suffers from Spielberg's infatuation with physical comedy, even when the gags involve tanks, planes and submarines, rather than the usual stuff of screen hijinks. Pic is so overloaded with visual humor of a rather monstrous nature that feeling emerges,

once you've seen 10 explosions, you've seen them all.

Screenwriters Robert Zemeckis and Bob Gale, who concocted the outlandish story line in conjunction with exec producer John Milius, are also daring in their attempt to intertwine five or six distinct storylines into one coherent tale. Largely, this works, thanks to Michael Kahn's fluid editing, John Williams' inspiring and unifying score, and Spielberg's incredible ability to juggle characters and plot turns.

Marquee value of the cast is so top-heavy that some fine performers get lost in the shuffle, through no fault of their own. Dan Aykroyd is very impressive in his feature debut as the serious army sergeant, but his former "Saturday Night Live" cohort John Belushi turns in a snarling, obnoxious performance that simply does not jibe with the rest of the pic.

Real cast standouts are Bobby DiCicco, who spends pic wresting pretty Dianne Kay away from horny soldier Treat Williams, Robert Stack as a bemused general, Nancy Allen as the airborne inamorata of Tim Matheson, Wendie Jo Sperber as a frustrated femme and Joseph P. Flaherty as a croony '40s emcee. Christopher Lee and Toshiro Mifune also excel as the bickering Axis powers determined to destroy the only thing of value in Los Angeles, Hollywood, while Ned Beatty, Lorraine Gary, Murray Hamilton and Eddie Deezen are quite good as U.S. citizens who come to their country's aid.

Spielberg also has the sense of humor to spoof his own work in pic's earliest minutes, and flashes of that humor continue intermittently throughout the pic. Main comic appeal, however, resides in whatever audience enjoyment will result from seeing Hollywood Boulevard trashed (in miniature scale), paint factories bulldozed, houses toppled into the sea, and a giant ferris wheel rolling to a watery demise.

Interspersed are some visual and aural delights, particularly a jitterbugging scene set at the Hollywood U.S.O. club, where DiCicco, Kaye and a host of hoofers go through a delightful routine choreographed by Paul De Rolf. There is also a madcap episode involving Warrent Oates and his troops expecting an invasion in Barstow, and a touching segment (another Spielberg perennial) in which Stack watches "Dumbo" while the skies of L.A. light up with ack-ack fire.

It hardly matters that the actual "Great Los Angeles Air Raid" took place on Feb. 26, 1942, and not Dec. 13, 1941, as pic's title and setting suggest, nor that some of the racist consequences of that night (along with concurrent Zoot Suit riots) are given short shrift in the film.

What is ultimately lacking from "1941" is that sense of cohesiveness and magic, for lack of a better word, that pulled "Jaws" and "Close Encounters" out of the realm of the ordinary and into the supernatural. No filmmaker should have to carry his previous successes around his neck like a celluloid albatross, of course, but Spielberg's talent is so manifest and dynamic, the pity is that it's not used to better effect here.

In any event, "1941" sets a new screen standard for special effects excellence, particularly with the work of cinematographer William A. Fraker, visual effects supervisor Larry Robinson, designer Dean Edward Mitzner, miniature supervisor Gregory Jein, special effects man A.D. Flowers, optical consultant L.B. Abbott and matte painter Matthew Yuricich.

Also worthy of the highest praise are Deborah Nadoolman's costumes, Gene S. Cantamessa's superior sound recording and Terry Leonard's disciplined stunt coordinating. —Poll.

Terror
(BRITISH-COLOR)

'Somewhat scary' sums up this release.

Hollywood, Dec. 3.
Crown International Pictures release. Produced by Les Young, Richard Crafter. Directed by Norman J. Warren. Features entire cast. Screenplay, David McGillivray, from a story by Young and Moira Young; camera (color) Les Young; editor, Jim Elderton; music, Ivor Slaney; art direction, Hayden Pearce' sound, Simon Okin; assistant director, Bryan Hirst. Reviewed at Culver Theatre Culver City, Dec. 3, '79. (MCAA Rating: R.) Running time: 86 MINS.
James .... John Nolan
Ann .... Carolyn Courage
Philip .... James Aubrey
Suzy .... Sarah Keller
Viv .., ... Tricia Walsh
Carol .... Glynis Barber
Gary .... Michael Craze
Diane .... Rosie Collins
Mad Dolly .... L.E. Mack

"Terror" opens with a meticulously recreated version of one of the Hammer witchcraft shockers from the 1960s, a film-within-the-film that goes on for almost 20 minutes. Unfortunately, what follows is never as good as the take-off, and Crown International, which is releasing the 1978 British production, should reap only moderate returns from the gasp-and-guts crowd.

Turns out the opening segment is part of a feature John Nolan is making about his ancestors and a familial curse handed down through the generations that doom all lineage members of royalty who had a vindictive witch (L.E. Mack in a genuinely terrifying portrayal) burned at the stake. Footage gets to Nolan's

cousin, played with conviction by Carolyn Courage, who begins slicing up friends and neighbors with apparent abandon.

While director Norman J. Warren has a clear ability to evoke suspense and accompanying tingles, scripter David McGillivray's dialog, and most of pic's thesping, are as medieval as the lingering curse. Selection of victims seems mystifyingly motivated, even by an out-of-touch spirit, and completely degenerates by pic's end, when the supposed protagonist also ends up neatly cleaved in half.

Warren emphasizes gore above all over elements (there are the usual decapitations, guillotinings and stabbings, along with some unusual numbers, such as limbs caught in bear traps), and chief attribute is co-producer Les Young's arty lensing. Rest of tech credits are murky to poor.

Usually, films that have to sell their genre in the title are best avoided. "Terror" succeeds better than most, although a more applicable monicker might have been "Somewhat Scary." —Poll.

Goodbye, Flickmania
(JAPANESE-COLOR)

Promising debut from buff-turned-director.

Hollywood, Dec. 12.
A Nippon Herald release of a Kitty Films production. Produced by Hideto Isoda. Directed, screenplay by Masato Harada; camera (color). Genkichi Hasegawa; editor, Ko Suzuki; music, Ryudo Uzaki; art direction, Yuji Maruyama; sound, Senichi Beniya. Reviewed at the Nuart Theatre, L.A., Dec. 14, 1979. No MPAA rating. Running time: 110 MINS.
Dan-san .... Takuzo Kawatani
Shuma .... Naohiko Shigeta
Minami .... Atsuko Asano
With: Renji Ishibashi, Hiromitsu Suzuki, Miyako Yamaguchi, Toby Kadoguchi, Yuji Kosugi.
(In Japanese with English subtitles)

"Goodbye, Flickmania" is literally a film buff's dream and a film buff's nightmare. First feature by 30-year-old Masato Harada, former L.A. correspondent for "Kinema Jumpo" film journal, brims over with ideas, energy and references to other pix to the extent that it seems that helmer almost too urgently wanted to flood the screen with his feelings. Obsessive work, on basis of subject matter alone, should find a good reception at fests and specialized houses patronized carbon copies of its characters.

Vividly recalling early efforts by Martin Scorsese such as "Who's That Knocking At My Door?" and "Mean Streets," "Goodbye, Flickmania" opens with a scene that will warm the hearts of film freaks everywhere, as celluloid addict

Takuzo Kawatani angrily silences noisy patrons and complains of out-of-focus projection to non-caring theatre staffers.

Willing himself into a Hawksian relationship with a similarly film-crazed youth, the frenetic Kawatani interferes in his pal's attempted relationship with a low-life girl. Core of the film centers on adolescent's dual pursuit of cinema and sex, and stems from premise that it's even getting hard to be a film buff these days.

Like Scorsese, Harada displays a proclivity for films, small-time gangsters, cheap cabarets, pop music and manic camera moves, which results in a work bubbling with cultural and emotional resonance.

On the downside, dramatic coherence is abandoned in favor of numerous digressions, making pic more a stew of impressions rather than a sharp, dynamic statement. The pleasures and usual excesses of highly personal cinema can be seen here in full flower.

Kawatani, a bit player known in Japan for having been killed in over 200 pictures, runs away with this one, at one point offering up a particularly hilarious Marlon Brando imitation. Naohiko Shigeta is the rather amorphous film buff, and Atsuko is effective as the spoiled young flower of his affections to whom Shigeta complains, "I'm tired of this G-rated relationship."

Bloodpath finale inevitably recalls that of another Scorsese film, "Taxi Driver," and it can be fairly said that pic overall is too insular for most tastes. But Harada shows promise and, now that he's gotten his obsessions out of his sytem, might be ready for other concerns. —Cart.

Lady Oscar
(JAPANESE-FRENCH-COLOR)

London, Dec. 4.
Toho release of Kitty Music Corporation production. Features entire cast. Directed by Jacques Demy. Screenplay, Patricia Louisiana Knop, Demy from the comic strip "Rose of Versailles" by Ryoko Ikeda; camera (Eastmancolor), Jean Penzer; art director, Bernard Evein; music, Michel Legrand. Reviewed at London Film Fest, Nov. 20, '79. Running time: 125 MINS.
Oscar .... Catriona Maccoll
Andre .... Barry Stokes
Marie Antoinette .... Christina Bohm
Fersen .... Jonas Bergstrom
(In English)

French filmmaker Jacques Demy, who has not made a film since 1973, as many projects fell through, is now back with a film made in English in France but backed mainly by Japanese coin.

He has given this international project, delving into French history, an opulent, posey, disarming naivete in keeping with its adapta-

tion from a very popular Japanese comic strip. It has also become a stage show in Japan.

The director does add his penchant for star-crossed lovers with which he succeeded so well in his all-singing, Cannes prizewinner, "The Umbrellas of Cherbourg," Demy uses a one dimensional but disarming mixture of real and fictional characters.

This imbues the film with a historical charm that recalls the innocence of early Hollywood epics. Story takes place in 19th century France where a girl is brought up like a boy by her noble martinet father fed up with a long line of girls.

She becomes the bodyguard of the flighty Queen of France, Marie Antoinette, and wears a man's uniform and is known as Oscar.

The girl had grown up with the family housekeeper's son. The latter loves her but she sees him only as a brother. This is to change as France heads for revolution brought on by abject poverty, cynical and debauched upper classes and a spendthrift royalty personified by the Queen's expenditures.

Demy has given this lightweight costumer an elegant look and some high visual points as the philandering Queen's tryst with Fersen in a glass enclosed garden house. The camera races around the house glimpsing them through the windows as they embrace.

History and fate allow Oscar to find love at last with her childhood friend, as class barriers break down, only to lose him during the storming of the Bastille that marks the beginning of the French Revolution.

The unknown British cast is acceptable and Demy can handle the language rhythms. he has already made two films in English, "Model Shop" and "The Pied Piper." Catriona Maccoll is worth further attention for her lovely limning of Oscar, a woman waiting to burst out of man's clothing.

Film has fine art direction, costuming, music and technical qualities. The actual attack on the Bastille is a bit pithy for the reported $4,000,000 outlay. Shooting on actual location in Versailles is an asset.

Now that Demy is back, and displays a sure hand in staving off mawkishness and silliness in this old fashioned outing, he should once again be ready for more demanding films.

He displays a fine film temperament with insights into that thing called love and the interaction of characters drawn together by fate, plus the social backgrounds and the effects on their actions. —Mosk.

Gas Pump Girls
(COLOR)

Flats Not Fixed.

Hollywood, Dec. 4.
A Cannon release, produced by David A. Davies. Exec producer, David Gil. Directed by Joel Bender. Features Entire cast. Screenplay, Davies, Bender, Isaac Blech; camera (Movielab color), Nicholas Von Sternberg; music, Leigh Crizoe. (No additional credits available). kReviewed at World Theatre, Hollywood, Dec. 3, 1979. (MPAA Rating: R). Running time: **90 MINS.**

Cast: Kirsten Baker, Dennis Bowen, Huntz Hall, Sandy Johnson, Leslie King, Linda Lawrence, Rikki Marin, Joe E. Ross, Mike Mazurski.

"Gas Pump Girls" brings a new perspective to the international petroleum crisis, suggesting that the ultimate solution lies not in topping off the tanks, but in taking off the tops. Lines at the boxoffice will be much shorter than at the stations.

When uncle Huntz Hall falls sick, sweet little Kirsten Baker and her well-endowed friends take over his rundown filling station, going broke in competition with the sleek facility across the street. With lots of hope, faith and very little clothes, the girls begin to attract plenty of customers.

They also learn a lot about the business, especially the amazing number of double-entendres that can be composed about nozzles, ball-joints and other trade terms.

When their boyfriends need to be encouraged to pitch in, the girls bare their bosoms. When the competition sends hoods Joe E. Ross and Mike Mazurski as a threat, the girls bare their bosoms. In fact, the only time the girls dress up is to disco in the garage by the grease rack.

There is, as a matter of fact, loads of discoing all the time in and around the cars in the driveway. But that at least keeps the vehicles in one place so there won't be any car chases, a saving grace for a film like this.

Finally, the competition manages to cut off their gas supply, but the girls strip to their bikinis and distract the attendants across the street while they steal all the gas from their tanks in broad daylight. They then change into harem outfits to take on the refinery tycoon.

Fortunately, during none of this did the scratches on the print ignite any fumes and set off excitement. —*Har.*

Rue du Pied-De-Grue
(Street of the Crane's Foot)
(FRANCO-BELGIAN-COLOR)

Paris, Nov. 19.
A CIC release of a Werlaine and Co./Little Bear/F3 SA co-production. Produced by Françoi Grand-Jouan. Stars Philippe Noiret, Pascale Audret, Guiliana De Sio, Jacques Dufilho. Written and directed by Grand-Jouan. Consulting scriptwriters, Philippe Dumarcay and Giorgio Bontempi; camera (color), Jean-Francois Robin; editors, Grand-Jouan, Francine Sandberg, Jacques Arhex; sound, Alix Comte, music, Andre Georget; executive producer, Jean-Serge Breton. Reviewed at the Ponthieu screening room, Paris, Oct. 29, 1979. Running time: **100 MINS.**
Father .... Philippe Noiret
Lulu .... Pascale Audret
Commissioner .... Jacques Dufilho
Tonton .... Jean Daste
Luisa .... Guiliana De Sio

"Rue de Pied-de-Grue" offers the saddening spectacle of a promising young writing talent who, infected with the "auteur" itch, insists on directing and editing as well, does so ineptly, and pretty much emasculates what should have been a genuinely funny film.

The vigorous imaginings of Grand-Jouan (he's pretentiously dropped Francois, his first name) have strong roots in the modern French theatre and the classic cinema of the '30's. Here he's taken the satiric absurdist elations that characterize the films of the Prevert brothers and the plays of Roger Vitrac, Eugene Ionesco and Roland Dubillard, and has mixed in elements of regional French myth (Nantes, the film's setting and the author's hometown, is darkly celebrated in French song).

Film is about a dippy bourgeois family dominated by a father who's a drunk and a novelist manque. His kid, 27, is utterly mediocre, sufficient grounds for Papa to consider him a new Mozart. When piano teachers fail to nurture his son's genius, Papa, with the aid of his aged uncle and sidekick, chucks them into the river. While the police commissioner pursues his inefifectual investigation, father and son prepare for the day of glory when their respective literary and musical gifts will bless the world. The world chooses to ignore the benediction. But the setback is only a temporary one.

As director, Grand-Jouan steamrollers flat the comic appeal of his zany gallery of middle-class misfits. He often doesn't know where to set up his camera, and how long to keep it there, and is unable to edit a scene for shape and effect. Intermittently, an idea or a scene suddenly lets loose and flies, but just as quickly drops back lifeless.

The feeling of avoidable waste weighs heavier when one considers a cast that boasts Philippe Noiret, Jean Daste, Jacques Dufilho and Pascale Audret, all sporadically savory, though unable to carry the script through the bog. —*Len.*

Bye Bye Brasil
(BRAZILIAN-COLOR)

Rio de Janeiro, Nov. 21.
Produced by Lucy Barreto. Presented by Luiz Carlos Barreto. Written and directed by Carlos Diegues. Features entire cast. Camera (color) Lauro Escorel Filho; editing and montage; Anisio Medeiros; musical direction, Roberto Menescal; musical themes by Dominguinho, Chico Buarque and Roberto Menescal; sound editor, Emanuelle Castro. Reviewed at screening room, Hotel Meredien, Rio de Janeiro, Nov. 21, 1979. Running time: **100 MINS.**
Lorde Cigano .... Jose Wilker
Salome .... Betty Faria
Cico .... Fabio Junior
Dasdo .... Zaira Zambelli
Andorinha .... Principe Nabor
Mayor .... Emanoel Cavalcanti
Ze da Luz .... Jofre Soares

This local version of "On the Road," a changing Brazil seen through the eyes of four wandering minstrels in the "Caravan Rolidei," has all the ingredients of an exportable pic. But perhaps it is so rich in "ingredients" and highly competent collaborators, it never fully realizes the vision and focus of one artist's viewpoint.

Pic has as its theme the Brasil (as the natives spell it) which is fading and disappearing as a new Brazil (as others spell it) rushes in to fill its place. Viewed through the eyes of four gypsy actors exploring the exotic and picturesque north of this paradoxical nation, this is often the exciting and revealing film which merits its dedication "to the Brazilian people of the 21st century."

Like Kerouac's travellers on the road to self discovery, the "Caravan Rollidei" meet dreamers, brigands, fellow wanderers, Indian chiefs and hustlers on the dusty path through "developing" Brasil. The nation they encounter then is a rich continent where jet planes fly above the heads of primitive tribesmen and where tv soap operas capture the imaginations and hypnotise the same isolated masses who used to delight in the entertainment of the visiting Carnival troupe.

The biggest enemy of the Caravan is the tv antenna and the imported culture and decadence which its repulsive sight implies. In this respect, there is one poignant scene where the Caravan tent with Salome, Rhumba Queen (Betty Faria) and Lord Gypsy — Emperor of the Magicians (Jose Wilker) goes empty while the unwashed masses huddle in front of the tube entranced by Sonia ("Dona Flor") Braga in "Dancin' Days." (The latter was a recent tv novela smash hit which brought a Rio discotheque into the living room of millions of Brazilians across the nation.)

The big star of ths pic is Brasil, meaning the unique nation forged by natives of colorful outlooks, personalities and different races. Competing with it is Brazil, the generality, Carmen Miranda, bananas, samba and Carnival, or the outsiders' distorted view of a nation of 120,000,000 people. Embratur, the national tourist agency, will therefore be delighted with this pic as a promotion device worldwide. For there are luscious scenes of the tempting beaches, palm trees, rivers where dangerous fish swim and an unsettled but beautiful no-man's land which will delight the eye.

Another eyeful is Brazilian bombshell Betty Farias, whose exotic lures are fully exploited by Carlos Diegues' omniscient camera. This pic could pin-up Faria to Braga fame, Jose Wolker, one of Braga's husbands in "Flor," is the leader of the gypsies and pro con mon and turns in a sharply focused and credible performance.

Supporting cast includes wide-eyed Cico (Fabio Junior), who plays an instrument we know as an accordion. He lusts for Salome, willing to forego his pregnant and faithful wife Dasdo (Zaira Zambelli) if Salome will give the green light. Andorinha, King of the Muscles, a silent black man ably portrayed by Principe Nabor, is a final addition to the attractive cast.

Within Diegues' work is nostalgia for a unique culture which is threatened with a loss of identity. He is a director and scripter of good taste and this pic is rare in the annals of local film making in that it neve stoops to light porn to conquer its audience. Diegues is also not an over-stater although the copy sometimes runs a bit slow and there are a few incoherent cuts which blot the total professionalism of the print.

The pic errs in following the same phobia which afflicts Brasil: looking outward and over its shoulder towards the hypothetical judgment of the outside "developed" world. The script for all its merits, seems more "developing" than fully developed. —*Emrt.*

Buone Notizie
(Good News)
(ITALIAN-COLOR)

Rome, Dec. 6.
A Medusa release. Produced by Elio Petri and Giancarlo Giannini. Stars Giancarlo Giannini, Angela Molina. Written and directed by Elio Petri. Camera (Eastmancolor), Antonio Nardi; art directors, Amadeo Fago, Franco Pellecchia; editor, Ruggero Mastroianni; music, Ennio Morricone. Reviewed at Fiamma Cinema, Rome, Dec. 6, 1979. Running time: **110 MINS.**
Husband .... Giancarlo Giannini
Wife .... Angela Molina
Ada .... Aurore Clement
Gualtiero .... Paolo Bonacelli

Girlfriend .... Ombretta Colli

"Good News" was heralded by coproducers Elio Petri and Giancarlo Giannini as an entertainment film divorced from ideologies, but the Medusa release slips somewhere between bitter irony and bold black humor — more a challenge for the engaged filmgoer than an entry qualifying as mass entertainment. Even the standard ingredients of four-letter grammar and a few flesh twists — normally a hypo to popularize serious film comment — cannot override Petri's puzzling approach to life.

Film develops on two levels — one in foreground in which Giannini, as a junior media exec, extravagantly caricatures his hangups with patient, frustrated wife Angela Molina. At some point Petri leaves the barren hearth and gets Giannini involved with a suspense situation tinged with alienation. Central element in the second act is Paolo Bonacelli, an old schoolmate, who appears from nowhere scared stiff of a threat on his life and pleading for Giannini's help. Between the two is Aurore Clement as Bonacelli's nympho wife.

Giannini's home life and embroilment with an obsessed friend are played out to surreal lengths. Second level is the realistic background — the six receivers in Giannini's office and the television screen at home providing the macabre reality of social torment. And the choice of pastoral urban backdrops are handpicked to accent ecological rot. Characters in background never connect but a few things happen — Giannini has an unconsummated fling with his friend's wife in a mental asylum where his friend is finally assassinated. In the only scene of Giannini and wife Molina outside the apartment — the finale — he finally gets to see a sunset and she will finally get to bear a child (from a weird "transfer" liaison with Bonacelli before he is killed). "Good News" is one of the gloomiest comedies in the realm of black humor. Carefully mounted, the pic is Petri's misanthropic testament of human triviality — a formidable barrier to human fulfillment.

The good news is that Giannini plays his role without a regional accent and even the caricature is softened to good advantage. Bigger-than-life comedy, however, is hard to sustain through 110 minutes. As a sex-repressed wife, Molina has the smoldering look without half trying and Ombretta Colli, who joins in for a brief menage a trois, is both fresh and luscious. Best performances are delivered by Bonacelli, a believable oddball, and his kinky spouse Clement. Credits in all departments are standout. —Werb.

Kamisama Naze Ai Ni Mo Kokkyo Ga Aru No
(God, Why Is There a Border In Love?)
(JAPANESE-COLOR)

Tokyo, Oct. 27.
A Toho release of a Toho Eiga production. Produced by Tsuneyasu Matsumoto, Kyoko Oshima, Michio Morioka. Directed by Yasuhiro Yoshimatsu. Features entire cast. Screenplay, Yoshimi Shinozaki, Yasuhiro Yoshimatsu, from original story by Hiroshi Kusaka; camera (color), Kazutami Hara; art director, Kazuo Takenaki; sound, Nobuyuki Tanaka; music, Michkie Yoshino. Reviewed at Toho Central, Tokyo, Oct. 23. 1979. Running time: 93 MINS.
Sho Hayami .... Tomiyuki Kunihiro
Liliane .... Carole Lizon
Goro Takio .... Takenori Murano
Kazu .... Yoshitaka Tanba
Gin .... Shohei Hino
Rosemarie .... Elvira Schalcher
Michael .... Franz Sauer
Weimar .... Conrad Von Bork
Anita .... Veronique Delbourg

Toho's latest release, which engages in the most relentless myth-mongering about Switzerland, may be regarded as an act of revenge.

The moment aspiring photographer Tomiyuki Kunihiro sets eyes on a Swiss Alp, he commences reeling off those items associated wiht Switzerland, including "chocolate" and "cuckoo clocks" and cowbells.

One kindly rustic, a grey-bearded, bespectacled type, gives Tomiyuki room and board in exchange for his performing unspecified chores. Tomiyuki's photos earn him folding money, though apparently not enough with which to open an account at a Swiss bank.

The love of Tomiyuki for Switzerland is surpassed only by his love for Swiss maiden Carole Lizon. Her parents however, do not share her affection for Tomiyuki.

Expelled from Switzerland on a trumped-up charge, Tomiyuki ekes out a meager existence as a factory worker in Germany, while Carole pines away. These modern-day lovers have a helpful cleric, an obnoxious Japanese priest, regretfully not bound by a vow of silence. Tomiyuki and Carole are reunited, her parents see how narrow-minded they've been and all ends well.

Although most dialog is in English, with smatterings of Japanese, German and Italian, an ability to read Japanese subtitles is advisable, since not one member of the cast is a native speaker. Indeed, so outrageous are some of the pronunciations that the viewer can close his eyes and, by listening alone, imagine that a far racier story is unfolding.

Production credits are fairly good, but location shots of Switzerland are strictly cliche. Michkie Yoshino of the group, Godiego, composed a relentlessly happy score. —Bail.

Taut Bamispar
(Wrong Number)
(ISRAELI-COLOR)

Tel Aviv, Nov. 18.
A Erez Films presentation of a Baruch Ellah and Zeev Revach Production. Stars Zeev Revach. Produced by Baruch Ellah. Directed by Zeev Revach. Screenplay, Zeev Revach, Shay K. Ophir; camera (color), Amnon Salomon; art direction, Arieh Halleh; editor, Tal Shuval; music, Yoel Sher. Reviewed at Tel Aviv Nov. 17, 1979. Running time: 90 MINS.
Cast: Zeev Revach, Shay K. Ophir, Shula Revach, Ophelia Strahl, Gideon Singer, Menashe Warshawsky, Miriam Fuchs.

Actor-director Zeev Revach is at the moment the most prolific filmmaker in Israel with five feature films to his credit in less than two years. Sold mostly on his reputation as a broad, lowbrow comic, they are systematically repeating time after time the same formula, with one notable exception, a film called "Little Man," released a year ago, which was a personal, non-comic statement by Revach, on a subject particularly close to his heart: the conflict between European and Oriental Jews. Predictably enough, the public which came to watch Revach being funny, went away disappointed and the film lost money.

Since that time, Revach went back to his old antics, using sketchy story lines and relying on his own wildly exaggerated facial expressions as the main asset of the venture. This time, the story is even thinner than usual, as it follows a businessman and his partner to a health resort, and having his wife and her friend pop up a few hours later. The whole thing develops into a comedy of errors. There is also a rabidly jealous police inspector, a distraught hotel manager and a fat redhead, all dragged in and out without much sense or logic.

To hide shortcomings, Revach tries to use slapstick extensively, going for mute gags, too similar, for comfort, to Keystone Cops and Chaplin.

The whole cast seems dumbfounded by the proceedings and all acting is overdone. Locations, mostly inside Tel Aviv's Laromme Hotel and Tiberias Health Spa, is short on production values, but Amnon Salomon's camera handling is a definite asset. Music improvised and recorded by pianist Yoel Sher tried to bring back some of the silents' feeling, not very successfully.

Revach fans have proved in the past to be particularly faithful, as long as he made them laugh.
—Edna.

Scavenger Hunt
(COLOR)

Heavy with names, light with humor. Poor outlook.

Hollywood, Dec. 19.

A 20th Century-Fox release of a Melvin Simon production. Produced by Steven A. Vail. Co-produced by Paul Maslansky. Exec producer, Simon. Features entire cast. Directed by Michael Schultz. Screenplay, Vail, Henry Harper from a story by Vail, adapted by, John Thompson, Gerry Woolery; camera (color), Ken Lamkin; editor, Christopher Holmes; art direction, Richard Berger; music, Billy Goldenberg; set decoration, Ed Baer; sound, Don Johnson; stunt coordinator, Jon Parker Ward; special effects, Phil Cory, Ray Svedin; asst. directors, Daniel J. McCauley, Benjamin Rosenberg. Reviewed at 20th Century-Fox Screening Room, Century City, Dec. 19, '79. (MPAA Rating: PG.) Running time: **116 MINS.**

Stuart Selsome	Richard Benjamin
Henri	James Coco
Sam	Scatman Crothers
Mildred Carruthers	Cloris Leachman
Jackson	Cleavon Little
Jenkins	Roddy McDowall
Bernstein	Robert Morley
Marvin Dummitz	Richard Mulligan
Henry Motley	Tony Randall
Jeff Stevens	Dirk Benedict
Kenny Stevens	Willie Aames
Babbette	Stephanie Faracy
Georgie Carruthers	Richard Masur
Zoo Keeper	Avery Schreiber
Duane	Stuart Pankin
Lisa	Maureen Teefy
Cornfield	Hal Landon Jr.
Milton Parker	Vincent Price

This 20th Century-Fox release is loud, obnoxious and above, all, unfunny. "Scavenger Hunt" had the potential for more humor than director Michael Schultz milks out of it. None of the characters are particularly engaging in terms of sympathy or laughter, and result is a 116-minute washout.

Game manufacturer Vincent Price, who appears only briefly at start, leaves an estate of $200,000,-000 that will go to the winner of a scavenger hunt, with various heirs and acquaintances the contestants.

Since the items being collected serve no comic purpose other than to get participants into embarrassing scrapes, pic is missing any coherency of purpose. Under Schultz' vapid direction, that same rootlessness affects the performances, which are so broad as to need widescreen space.

Cloris Leachman limns a screechy widow, joined by sleazy lawyer Richard Benjamin and enfant terrible Richard Masur. Opposing them are the household staff, consisting of James Coco, Roddy McDowall, Cleavon Little and Stephanie Faracy, with latter group providing most of the film's few laughs.

Richard Mulligan, who gives new meaning to the term daft, is also in on the chase, as are Dirk Benedict, William Aames and Maureen Teefy as the "nice" team. Tony Randall and his four children round out the competition, with assists from Scatman Crothers, Avery Schreiber, Liz Torres, Ruth Gordon, Meat Loaf, Pat McCormick and Arnold Schwarzenegger in the briefest of cameos.

Schultz seems unable to come up with any exciting visual gags, as most stunts revolve around people falling out of windows with their prizes. "Scavenger Hunt" also has the dubious distinction of insulting most minorities, along with those who are overweight, have speech impediments or other physical deformities.

Tech credits are okay, although Christopher Holmes' editing leaves many scenes without any dramatic or comic punch. —*Poll.*

Penitentiary
(COLOR)

Well-done, hard-hitting prison drama.

Hollywood, Dec. 17.

A Jerry Gross Organization release. Produced, directed, written by Jamaa Fanaka. Features entire cast. Camera (Color), Marty Ollstein; editor, Betsy Blankett; music, Frankie Gaye; art direction, Adel Mazen; no other credits available. Reviewed at Joe Shore's Screening Room, L.A., Dec. 17, '79. (MPAA Rating: R). Running time: **99 MINS.**

Too Sweet	Leon Isaac Kennedy
Eugene	Thommy Pollard
Linda	Hazel Spears
Wilson	Badja Djola
Inmate	Gloria Delaney
Lt. Arnsworth	Chuck Mitchell
Sweat Pea	Wilbur (Hi-Fi) White

A tough, distributing and relatively uncompromising look at contemporary prison life, "Penitentiary" is a solid third feature for Jamaa Fanaka and rates as one of the "blackest" pictures to come along since the blaxploitation trend waned a fewyears back. Pic is spiked with enough well-staged violence and inflammatory dramatics to possibly find its way on the action circuit, but is essentially serious-minded and might forge a double life in specialized slots and even at fests.

Fanaka attracted some attention with his first two films, "Welcome Home, Brother Charles" and "Emma Mae." Still working independently, he's here put together a film which, rough edges and all, delivers a potent punch.

Circumstantial evidence lands lanky, street-wise Leon Isaac Kennedy in prison. Balance of power in his cell block, largely inhabited by blacks, is dictated by brute force, with the meanest, toughest inmates lording it over the smaller (read sensitive) ones with their fists. Bottom line in prison relationships is sexual power, and Kennedy avoids the dreaded fate of being used as a "girl" only by beating up his monstrous, animalistic cellmate after rejecting the slave role suggested to him.

Kennedy's fighting skills lead him into competition in prison boxing tournaments, where victory offers the reward not only of a night of "connubial visitation" but, that of early parole. Even here, Darwin's principle applies, and those whose strengths lie elsewhere than their arms have to suffer the consequences.

Fanaka's greatest success comes in his delineation of the brutal realities of prison life. Rendered with extreme believability, and a welcome lack of preachiness or liberal posturing, incarceration is shown to be a supreme test of character strength, with some men growing, others going crazy, and a few simply going under.

Homoerotic aspects are shown with visual discretion, as elemental to much of the action. On the other hand, one of pic's highlights is a sort of running gag involving men and visiting women inmates who repair to the bathroom during boxing matches for quick satisfaction.

Dialog throughout snaps with highly colorful street jargon, and performers uniformly seem to know whereof they speak, lending significantly to the overall feeling of verisimilitude.

Kennedy is seen as a somewhat unformed wanderer with a steely resolve, and serves as a reasonably effective mirror off of which is seen the more turbulent action and emotions surrounding him. In addition, he "dances" beautifully in the boxing sense. Thommy Pollard draws sympathy as a relentlessly victimized "girl," and Chuck Mitchell is perfect as a fair-minded cop.

Tech achievements are elementary but appropriate, as the hard-edged style and fast ahead pace pace contribute to the dynamic energy of the film. —*Cart.*

Jag Aer Med Barn
(I'm Expecting)
(SWEDISH-COLOR)

Malmoe, Dec. 6.

An Olle Hellbom/Svensk Filmindustri production. AB Svensk Film release. Directed by Lasse Hallstroem. Original story and script. Lasse Hallstroem, Brasse Braennstroem, Olle Hellbom; camera (Eastmancolor), Roland Ludin; editor, Lasse Hallstroem; animated cartoon sequences, Per Ahlin; music, Bengt Palmers. Reviewed at the Royal, Malmoe, Sweden, Dec. 5, 1979. Running time, **103 MINS.**

Bosse	Magnus Haerenstam
Lena	Anki Liden
The Tough Guy	Mischa Gabay
The Secretary	Lis Nilheim

The title "I'm Expecting" actually has to have one of this feature's ads to go with it. A picture showing a man, not a woman. For this is the story of Bosse, in his 20s, who tires of his job in an ad agency, takes leave of absence to complete a novel, instead meets pretty and funny Lena, moves in with her, forgets about the novel in favor of begetting a child.

All this is followed by Bosse's working at being his woman's true partner all through the pregnancy. He reads all books available on baby and child care and he also joins Lena in gymnastics, etc. preparatory to childbirth. So far so funny. Lasse Hallstroem has a good contemporary comedy going, but he cannot leave good enough alone.

Hallstroem not only breaks his film in two by going on from the child's birth to Bosse's trials and tribulations as an active father, taking on more than a normal woman's share of day and night baby care. He also uses inserts involving a super male egoist, popping up in dream sequences in all kinds of disguises from western bandit to machine-gun toting gangster, always tempting Bosse to forget about being a parent in favor of returning to a bachelor's life.

These inserts do not merge with the natural flow of the comedy and soon become downright tiresome. Hallstroem has more luck with Per Ahlin's animated cartoon fantasies in other inserts about the as-yet unborn baby's future possibilities. But best of all is Magnus Haerenstam as the chubby, bewildered Bosse who is most convincing as a modern father, less so when he lets temptation lead him into a cute secretary's bed.

Haerenstam is forced, more by the plot than obvious desire, to leave home, woman and baby to concentrate on getting his novel written. He succeeds and calls the book, immediately accepted for publication. "The Male Piggy." This is the Swedish colloquial designation of "male chauvinist pig." Bosse is a thoroughly sweet guy, and of course finds his way back to Lena and the baby.

Hallstroem, as usual, is sure to have audiences with him on his home turf. Some foreign sales should be possible but not without strong effort. "I'm Expecting" fiddles with too many cinematic tricks to move as the universal comedy teaser of manners and morals around and about childbirth is should have been. —*Kell.*

Charlotte Loewenskoeld
(Charlotte Lionshield)
(SWEDISH-COLOR)

———

Malmoe, Dec. 6.

A Swedish TV Channel Goetenburg/AB Sandrew Film & Teater production, AB Sandrew release. Based on Selma Lagerloef's novels "Charlotte Lionshield" and "Anna Svaerd." Script, Bengt Bratt. Directed by Jackie Soederman. Camera (Eastmancolor), Rune Ericson: executive producer, Bo Berndtson; editor, Leif Gummesson; production design, Ingemar Wiberg; music, Eskil Hemberg. Reviewed at Sandrews 1-3, Malmoe, Dec. 5, 1979. Running time: **119 MINS.**

Charlotte	Ingrid Janbell
Karl-Artur	Lars Green
Karl-Artur's mother	Gunnel Brostroem
The Vicar	Gunnar Bjoernstrand
Vicar's wife	Sickan Carlssson
Schagerstroem	Sven Wollter
Anna Svaerd	Arja Saijonmaa
Thea Sundler	Christina Stenius

Jackie Soederman, a graduate of tv and the legit stage, comes out as a feature film director with a splendid work.

He has handled the late Nobel Prize-winning Selma Lagerloef's novel, "Charlotte Lionshield," in the grand tradition of romantic film story-telling. With good taste and dramatic sense he has lifted the essentials of conflict and visual inspiration from Lagerloef's rather long-winded writings. While respectful of the origin, Soederman has also managed to create a free-flowing cinematic style of his own.

Actually, plot does not pertain solely to the young woman of the title. Another pivotal figure is the young assistant vicar Karl-Artur, Charlotte's first and most ardent love, while all other characters come through as fully developed men and women audiences will care very much about.

Charlotte, all womanhood in one person, young, wise, impetuous, strong-willed, grimly determined, stubbron, fun-loving, all this and more, lives in rural Sweden in the early 1980's with her vicar uncle and aunt.

She attracts and is attracted by the recently appointed Karl-Artur, a religious zealot from the University of Uppsala.

The young people fall in love, but intrigue and misunderstanding plus possibly his own inclination make Karl-Artur spurn Charlotte in favor of "the first woman God leads me to." This turns out to be semi-gypsy Anna Svaerd who is not to Karl-Artur's mother's taste, which causes a break between the latter two, while Charlotte, on the rebound, agrees to marry Schagerstroem, the less romantic but solid and tactful country squire.

Karl-Artur has much of the political-religious zealot of any age and time in him, but it is to the director's and actor Lars Green's credit that we are spared seeing him as an outright monster or caricature of today's political redeemers of the world (as intended in script's first draft).

As his mother, Gunnel Brostroem radiates the aristocrat's haughty attitudes as convincingly as true human warmth when first Charlotte has won her over. Also Sven Wollter fleshes the Schagerstroem squire out to fit full dimensions. In fact, everybody in the large cast performs with both skill and happy confidence in the rightness of their roles.

As Charlotte, Ingrid Janbell is sure to join the ranks of international major actresses. She is petite and handsome like another Isabelle Adjani, but surely born to stardom of her own if she wants it.

So handsome are production design, choice of interiors and exteriors and cinematography that film rates superlatives in every department. —*Kell.*

———

La Sabina
(The Sabina)
(SPANISH-SWEDISH-COLOR)

———

Madrid, Dec. 12.

An El Iman (Madrid) and Svenska Film-institutet (Stockholm) production produced, written and directed by Jose Luis Borau. Features entire cast. Camera (Eastmancolor) Lars-Goran Bjorne; sets, Wolfgang Burmann; sound mixer, Lasse Summanen; editor, Jose Salcedo; music, Paco de Lucia. Reviewed at Cine Amaya, Madrid, Dec. 11, '79. Running time: **105 MINS.**

Daisy	Carol Kane
Michael	Jon Finch
Monica	Harriet Andersson
Philip	Simon Ward
Pepa	Angela Molina
Manolin	Ovidi Montllor
Felix	Fernando Sanchez Polac
Antonio	Francisco Sanchez

(English soundtrack version available)

It is now four years since helmer-producer-writer Jose Luis Borau scored with "Poachers." His new pic has been anticipated with high hopes. Despite some good thesping by Carol Kane, Angela Molina and Ovidi Montllor and an original story that could have made a fascinating film, "La Sabina" is a disappointment.

Pic goes awry on so many levels that it is hard to pinpoint the blame. Jon Finch moons through his part and never succeeds in generating any sympathy or interest. His role is that of a bibulous expatriate loser, and his drowsy performance fits in all too well with the tedium of the part. Lensing by Swedish cameramen is flat and static and never once captures the warmth and magic of Andalusia. Another major drawback is the film's Spanish soundtrack, which is largely incomprehensible, especially Angela Molina's Andalusian slang. Some touches of wry humor come across, but many are lost.

Far more serious is the choppy editing, which causes a lack of continuity in the unravelling of the rather complicated yearn, making much of it unintelligible. Some of the Paco de Lucia music is appropriate, but other parts are jarring, as though they were an afterthought thrown into the final mix.

Yarn, set in a modern Andalusian village, concerns an unsuccessful British writer (Michael) doing some literary sleuthing on a George Borrow-like traveler of the 19th century who, according to local legend, met his death in a cave supposedly haunted by a female dragon called La Sabina. Michael is shacking up with a wacky Yank called Daisy, but then falls for one of the village belles (Pepa), who bears some resemblance to the 19th century traveler's flame.

Enter Michael's literary crony and wife, fresh in from Albion, who further complicate the emotional and sexual relationships. There's also Pepa's deaf-mute brother, who supposedly was castrated by the dragon, but this is never made clear in the film. Everybody seems to be sleeping with everybody else, though Michael never makes it with Papa. Instead, in a fit of frustration, he lures his British chum and adversary Philip down to the cave and after killing him commits suicide.

Some offshore interest may be generated by the international cast and the exotic setting and yearn.

—*Besa.*

———

Charly og Steffen
(Charly and Steffen)
(DANISH-COLOR)

———

Copenhagen, Dec. 17.

A Merry production, A/S Europa Film release. Original story and script, Bent Rasmussen and Henning Kristiansen. Directed by Kristiansen. Features entire cast. Camera (Eastmancolor), Peter Klitgaard; production design, Sven Wickman; editors, Kristiansen, Sven Methling, Merete Brusendorff; music, Jacob Groth. Reviewed at ABCinema, Copenhagen, Dec. 17, 1979. Running time: **83 MINS.**

Steffen	Kim E. Larsen
Charly	Allan Olsen
Steffen's mother	Ghita Noerby
Janie	Pia Rosenbaum
Lilly	Lone Kellermann

Co-helmed by Henning Kristiansen and Morten Arnfred, "Me & Charly" brought home critical kudos and millions of boxoffice Kroners two years ago. Now Kristiansen goes it alone with "Steffen and Charly," bringing the restless bourgois teenager and his social misfit friend of both titles up to date. Sad to say, the boys and their surroundings have turned into a messy heap of cliches and faddish slogans.

Charly (again a magnificent performance by Allan Olsen) remains the happily independant misfit. Steffen is mired in a morose attitude of revolt against his own mother and milieu. Both youngsters seem to be seeing the light when they meet up with Janie (Pia Rosenbaum) who leads a music-theatre group that features every shopworn Leftish stance of the past two decades. Everybody else are, of course, outright morons.

Director Kristiansen, once a cinematographer of renown (with fine work for Carl Th. Dreyer on "Gertrud" and for Henning Carlsen on "Hunger"), obviously cannot handle actors, especially not the many semi-amateurs he employs. The script, for which he is co-responsible with Bent Rasmussen, is no great help either.

Although Allan Olsen confirms his already solid reputation as a very original talent, he alone, as Charly, cannot salvage this rudderless vessel on its stormy passage through a sea of left-over ideas and uninspired platitudes. —*Kell.*

———

Nissuim Nosach Tel Aviv
(Marriage, Tel Aviv Style)
(ISRAELI-COLOR)

———

Tel Aviv, Dec. 8.

A Noah Films Presentation of a Menahem Golan — Yoram Globus Production. Stars Tuvia Zafir. Written and directed by Yoel Zilberg, based on Moliere's "L'Avare." Camera (color), David Gurfinkel; music, Yannis Petritsis; editor, Irith Raz. Released in Tel Aviv Dec. 8, 1979. Running time: **90 MINS.**

Avigdor	Tuvia Zafir
Avram	Yossef Shiloah
Giora	Menahem Eyni
Pnina	Shosh Marciano
Rosa	Miri Aloni
Carmela	Gilath Ankori
Ronny	Sassi Kesheth

Even for the unsophisticated Israeli industry this film is an embarrassment. Badly directed, badly acted and loudly promoted, this kind of product will keep the Israeli cinema tied to the middle ages. The concept is simple: do everyting in a hurry, cut costs to the minimum, and try to hit the public quickly and recuperate the investment before it realizes what it has been really offered. Golan-Globus's Noah Films have done this kind of trick in the past with remarkable success, but it is nothing to be proud about.

Moliere's name is only a pretense to hide behind, as nothing of the spirit of his original play is to be found here. The main character is a repulsive loan shark, rather seedy and ungainly, looking for a young and attractive bride and at the same time trying to save every penny by destroying the line of his son and daughter. Typically enough, those two aren't exactly worth being saved, their only attributes being that they are not less unsavory than the rest of the characters.

In order to hide shortage of production values, most of the film is shot in close up or medium shots, with actors screaming their lines at the camera in what must be one of the loudest films in years.

Dialogs range between silly and crude, and with all due credit to David Gurfinkel's competent camera work, there is nothing much to be seen. Last but not least, there is a strong tinge of racism going through the film which isn't very pleasant to watch.

Critics here were pitiless, but wall-to-wall distribution and big advertising may keep the film in business. But as long as local industry will go on churning this kind of product, there is very little hope for progress. —*Edna*.

Olsen Banden overgiver sig aldrig

(The Olsen Gang Never Surrenders)
(DANISH-COLOR)

Copenhagen, Dec. 18.
A Nordisk Film Kompagni production and release. Original story and script, Henning Bahs, Erik Balling. Directed by Erik Balling. Features entire cast. Production design and special effects, Henning Bahs; camera (Eastmancolor), Claus Loof; production management, Bo Christensen, Christian Clausen, Lene Christiansen; editor, Finn Henriksen; music, Bent Fabricius-Bjerre. Reviewed at Nordisk Film screening room, Copenhagen, Dec. 13, 1979. Running time: 119 MINS.

Egon Olsen ....Ove Sprogøe
Benny ....Morten Grunwald
Keld ....Poul Bundgaard
Yvonne .... Kirsten Walther
Bang-Johansen ..... Bjoern Watt-Boolsen
Hallandsen ....Peter Steen
Police Lieutenant .... Axel Stroebye

"The Olsen Gang Never Surrenders" is Erik Balling (and close collaborator Henning Bahs) at their usual best the series has now reached installment number 11 in their comedy series about small-time crook Egon Olsen with even bigger plans towards the Big Score and his frustrations caused by his more or less hapless cohorts Keld and Benny and/or by Keld's sharp-tongued wife Yvonne with her petty bourgeois ideas about what, for her, constitutes The Good Life.

This time, Olsen & Gang tries to beat an international finance conspiracy towards nothing less than a multinational company's secret take-over of the Kingdom of Denmark. After a series of wildly contrived (and beautifully executed) bank vault break-ins, Olsen only succeeds in getting Denmark ex-

pelled from the European Community, an ending sure to be cheered by many, while others will not be able to help laughing anyway.

Production values are of the highest order. All actors, in their by-now accustomed roles, perform with a zest as if this was their first major career opportunity. The fun, visual and verbal as well as in plotting, is brilliant, but sly and mild satirical treatment of Danish manners and morals seems not to travel well. While Balling's films are constant hits in Eastern European countries and (in local cover versions) Norway, most other markets have so far refused taking a serious stab at the "Gang." It might be cheating somebody, however, not recommending giving the series another chance at off-shore launching.

For 10 consecutive years, Balling's comedies have been at the very top of Denmark's boxoffice and remain the only features to be made entirely without any state support.—*Kell*.

Baby Snakes
(COLOR)

Frank Zappa's three hours of numbers, horseplay, cartoonery. For cult following alone.

An Intercontinental Absurdities Presentation. Produced, directed and edited by Frank Zappa. Music, Zappa; camera (Deluxe), Robert Leacock, Richard Pearce, Phil Parmet; assistant editor, Laura Whipple. Reviewed at Victoria Theatre, N.Y.C., Dec. 24, '79. (MPAA Rating: R.) Running time: 166 MINS.
Cast: Frank Zappa, Adrian Belew, Tommy Mars, Terry Bozzio, Kerry McNabe, Ron Delsener, Bruce Bickford, Rob Leacock, Ed Mann, Warren Cucurullo, Chris Martin, Klaus Hundsbichler, French The Poodle, Ms. Pinky's Larger Sister, Roy Estrada, John Smothers, David Ditkowich, New York's Finest Crazy Persons, Bill Harrington, Patrick O'Hearn, Phil Parmet, Peter Wolf, Dick Pearce, Angel, Janet The Planet, Donna U. Wanna, Phil Kaufman, Tex Abel, Dale Bozzio, Diva, John, Chris, Nancy, Brian Rivera, Joey Psychotic.

Combine the absurdist Yippie mentality of the acid-soaked '60s with admittedly fine musicianship and you've got the essence of long time rock cult figure Frank Zappa, although "Baby Snakes" gives you a lot more than you want to know.

This amalgam of interminable in-concert song sessions, puerile backstage horseplay and dope-inspired animated fantasy interludes is fodder for cultists alone. At nearly three hours length, even that audience may be driven back to its home stereos. Commercial outlook seems very limited.

Zappa's professed goal was to frame 15 musical numbers within

the overall theme of "a tribute to people who do stuff that is not normal.". The band's music, which usually starts off melodic and fairly funny then veering into electronic garbling and bizarre vocal effects, is one way to do that. Presumably, playing with toy police cars and inflatable rubber sex dolls is another.

Concert segs are generally well shot (Zappa directed and supervised overall editing). The sound quality is louder than it is clear. Songs interspersed or overlaid with the elaborate animated clay-figure work by Bruce Bickford, grotesque stop-action panoramas of cannibalistic people, cars, discos, etc. Technically these are scrupulously done, but overkill makes them as boring as everything else here. —*Step*.

Kosu Den
(MALI)

Dakar, Dec. 18.
Directed by Sega Coulibaly. No other credits provided. Reviewed at Dakar Film Festival, Dakar, Senegal. Running time - not available.

The problem of the African cinema is simple: the burning issues are presented in the films which the public doesn't see because they are busy seeing westerns and kung-fu action thrillers. Over the years the African public has been fed pure entertainment by European, American and Far Eastern producers, and a movie-going habit has been established which practically precludes the possibility of introducing a different style of film making in the general African market.

Nevertheless, attempts at doing just that are constantly being made, and some of these have in fact succeeded to penetrate; such as Ousmane Sembene's "Xala" (Impotence), which has raked up the biggest grosses ever in its native Senegal. Here a "third way" has been used: Sembene made a film about important social issues in a comic style. That, it has been thought, was one of the solutions.

Now another African filmmaker, Sega Coulibaly, has chosen an even simpler way: he has clothed his important social message in a classic western formula. In "Kosu Den" a man is released from prison after spending only seven years at hard labor instead of the 15 he was sentenced to, and proceeds to cut down, one by one, the three profiteers whose libel had caused his sentencing in the first place.

There are classic stalking scenes in the high grass, shots of the booted hero's jean-clothed legs with only the butt of his rifle and the loop of his lasso showing, camera set-ups shot

into the sunset with body of one of the villains strung high from the branches of a Baobab tree, and then, for good measure, a car chase along the windy roads outside the city of Bamako, capital of Mali, where the film was made. No question but that African audiences will find a style of filmmaking here which they will recognize.

What makes the film particularly poignant is the fact that the hero, now dying in a hospital, intending to murder, as his last act, his wife who had shacked up with one of his opponents, realizes at the last moment that this woman had acted out of need: he had disappeared, justice had provided nothing for her or her child, and to go with the other man wa only an economic necessity.

This ending, which says a great deal about the situation of woman in Africa, and is perhaps, in the end, a true message of love, gives the film an uplift at the end that few had expected, and makes one realize that behind the violent facade a filmmker has tried to make a statement about his society with the only means that this society accepts — melodrama and violence. —*Gide*.

Chomps
(COLOR)

Family pic with limited b.o. bite.

Hollywood, Dec. 13.
American International Pictures release of a Hanna-Barbera/American International Production. Produced by Joseph Barbera. Directed by Don Chaffey. Features entire cast. exec producer, Samuel Z. Arkoff. Screenplay, Dick Robbins, Duane Poole, Joseph Barbera from a story by Barbera; camera (color), Charles F. Wheeler; editor, Waner Leighton, Dick Darling; music, Hoyt Curtin; set decoration, Tony Montenaro; sound, Keith Wester; assistant director, Al Nicholson. Reviewed at American International Pictures Screening Room, Beverly Hills. Dec. 13, '79. (MPAA Rating: G). Running time: 89 MINS.
Brian Foster .... Wesley Eure
Casey Norton .... Valerie Bertinelli
Ralph Norton ....Conrad Bain
Brooks .... Chuck McCann
Bracken ....'......Red Button
Ken Sharp ....Larry Bishop
Mrs. Fowler ....Hermione Baddeley
Mr. Gibbs .... Jim Backus
Merkle .... Robert Q. Lewis
Chief Patterson ....Regis Toomey

"Chomps" is a drawn-out G-rated comedy that had brief play this summer as a PG pic (without trade reviews) and was recut and re-rated in an effort to cash in on the family market this Christmas. Although it features a cute canine hero, a pair of do-gooding young people and a bevy of silly-minded adults, pic has little of the action or charm that lure audiences.

Wesley Eure limns a young mechanical genius who has created the canine home protection system, i.e.

a mechanical pooch that when activated has the viciousness of a saber-toothed tiger and the power of a 10-ton truck. Eure has lately fallen out of grace with Conrad Bain, prexy of the security systems company he works for but with the help of girlfriend Valerie Bertinelli, the boss' daughter, he is finally able to present his revolutionary invention that he promises will save Bain's ailing business.

Life is never usually that easy and this case is no exception. Rival corporation head Jim Backus wants the little dog for himself and uses Ken Sharp as a double agent to sabotage Bain's operation. Sharp in turn employs Red Buttons and Chuck McCann as a pair of bumbling Laurel and Hardy-type crooks to do his dirty work. Needless to say good triumphs over evil in the end.

Tech credits are all decent and director Don Chaffey has done what he can to keep the pic moving given what he has to work with. Actors are uniformly okay but there's really only one star in this picture, "Chomps." Benji he's not.

—*Berg.*

Ogon No Paatonaa
(Golden Partners)
(JAPANESE-COLOR)

Tokyo, Dec. 2.

A Toho release. Producer, Yorihiko Yamada; Directed by Kiyoshi Nishimura; Screenplay, Hiroshi Nagano; based on Ryotaro Nishimura's "Hasshinnin was Shisha" (The Sender Was Dead); camera (color), Yashushi Ichihara; underwater camera, Masao Nakamura; art, Kazuo Takenaka; sound, Toshiya Ban; lighting, Toshi Takashima. Reviewed at the Hachioji Toho, Tokyo, Dec. 1, 1979. Running Time: **98 MINS.**

Cast: Tomokazu Miura, Tatsuya Fuji, Misako Konno, Ruji Tonoyama, Shinsuke Ashida, Kai Sato, Noboru Nakamura, Kazuo Yoshiyaki.

"Golden Partners" is "Les Aventuriers" by way of "Butch Cassidy and the Sundance Kid," the whole adding up to far less than the sum of its parts.

Tomokazu Miura, a cameraman with his own yacht, sets sail for Saipan to clear up the mystery behind some mysterious SOS messages. Accompanying him are rogue cop Tatsuya Fuji and Misako Konno, whose papa, she fears, is in deep trouble. Scuba diving midst sunken World War II vessels, the three discover incriminating links between stolen gold and a powerful gangster.

The film is unfocused, its tone wavering uncertainly between adult mystery and Hardy Boys adventure. Kiyoshi Nishimura is a director who raises hopes only to dash them, setting up promising scenes that he then dissipates with annoying silliness. The camera work by Yashushi Ichihara is occasionally very eye-catching, while the music by Masayoshi Takanaka and Takao Raisho is intrusive.

While a dramatic contrast was presumably intended between the "light" character played by Miura and the "dark" one played by Fuji, the acting styles of these two is virtually undifferentiated, with the result that they spend their time bouncing off each others similar affections.

Miura and Fuji try for Redford-Newman palsy-walsiness, but come across instead like gentelmen who do their cruising not on ships, but in bars. Misako Konno, the "mascot girl" of a large Japanese corporation, is a very lively presence in this, her film debut.

Unfortunately, she is disposed of long before the final credits roll, leaving Miura and Fuji to continue throwing their arms around each other, pounding each other on the back and reciting, in chorus, their favorite catch word, "fantasuchikku" (fantastic), which "Ogon No Paatonaa" definitely is not. —*Bail.*

Thirst
(AUSTRALIAN-COLOR)

Sydney, Nov. 30.

A Greater Union Organization release of the F.G. Film Productions film, made in association with the New South Wales Film Corporation. Stars: Chantal Contouri, Henry Silva, Max Phipps, Shirley Cameron, Rod Mullinar, David Hemmings. Executive producer, William Fayman. Produced by Antony I. Ginnane. Directed by Rod Hardy. Screenplay, John Pinkney; camera (Panavision-Eastmancolor), Vincent Monton; art direction, Jon Dowding, Jill Eden; asst. director, Tom Burstall; sound, Stuart Beatty; wardrobe, Leo Reyes; music, Brian May; editor, Phil Reid; special effects, Conrad Rothman; stunts, Grant Page. Reviewed at the G.U.O. Theatrette, Sydney, Nov. 30, '79. Running time: **98 MINS.**

Kate Davis	Chantal Contouri
Dr. Fraser	David Hemmings
Dr. Gauss	Henry Silva
Hodge	Max Phipps
Mrs. Barker	Shirley Cameron
Derek	Rod Mullinar
Sean	Robert Thompson
Dichter	Walter Pym
Lori	Rosie Sturgess
Nurse	Lulu Pinkus
Martha	Amanda Muggleton

Described best, perhaps, as a "Dracu-thriller," the pic involves Chantal Contouri being absorbed against her best instincts into a contemporary blood-drinking cult. They believe that serum-supping is the ultimate aristocratic act, and for the convenience of cult members run a number of research units and keep highly-sanitary farms run on the lines of a modern commercial dairy operation. Here they "milk" their victims — kept docile with tranquilisers — and occasionally, if one of the "donors" particularly catches the eye of one of the elite group, he or she are chosen for their highest accolade: total exsanguination.

All of which might have been a sight easier to swallow, as it were, had there been the slightest irony in either the script, the playing or the direction. The result without that vital leavening leaves what is at best a thin tale and thinner characterization, virtually semi-permeable.

Performances are good given the material, however, and there are a number of scary moments of the kind usual in this sort of film, but director Rod Hardy has taken the whole thing too seriously — not that farce is indicated, but a touch of the old Hammer Productions-style "sense of non-reality" would have helped.

Screenplay by author-journalist John Pinkney is based on one of his "Instant Terror" series, and has many of the requisite gothic elements for such a tale, and the look of the film is aided greatly by some very atmospheric location choices. Brian May's music track is fine, especially in the ceremonial scenes in which he uses plainsong to good effect.

Production qualities are excellent, as are the technical credits. Special effects and stuntwork also are noteworthy. Presence of international thesps of the caliber of Silva and Hemmings enhance the on-screen values of course, while aiding in the promotional areas.

Pic is producer Antony Ginnane's seventh feature in nine years. Highly prolific, he has left no genre unturned in his quest for the big Aussie breakthrough picture. On this, overseas prospects are good. At home the Greater Union Organization is both distribbing and exhibiting. Should be good for ozoners. —*Miha.*

Skal vi danse foerst
(Do We Start Off With A Dance)
(DANISH-COLOR)

Copenhagen, Dec. 12.

A Kosmorama production, Cinema Film release. Original story and script, Marie Louise Lauridsen, Katai Forbert-Petersen, Annette Olsen. Features entire cast. Directed by Annette Olsen. Camera (Eastmancolor) Dan Laustsen; editor, Janus Billeskov Jansen; production design, Soeren Skjaer; executive producer, Katherine Nyholm; music, no credits. Reviewed at the Saga, Copenhagen, Dec. 11, 1979. Running time, **96 MINS.**

Susanne	Lene Gurtler
Her mother	Kirsten Rolffes
Her father	Frits Helmuth
Her girlfriend	Karen Berg
Her boyfriend	Benny Dahl
The silversmith	Erick Wedersoe

For rather murky deep-think reasons there is to be no question mark after the title's "Do We Start Off With A Dance." Most likely it has to do with a central scene in which the teenage girl Susanne is raped by the young but adult silversmith she visits, partially on a business errand and partly led on both by him and by her own, sensually tinged curiosity about him. Before throwing the girl over on his sofa, the man does put on a Dusty Springfield record to which they do a brief dance.

Plot is exceedingly commonplace: the girl gets pregnant, she dares not tell her well-meaning parents, a girlfriend shames her for planning to pass the baby off as her school boy-friend's offspring, but Nature comes to her rescue (along with a couple of rough rides on a motorcross track), and all ends well at the parents' silver anniversary where the father smiles benevolently while daughter and mother dance slowly together in a new - found mutual women's trust across the generation gap.

While this final scene is embarrassingly artificial, most of the film has a handsome ring of truth. The dramatic impetus starts lagging around the middle of a film that otherwise presents true to life characters, not one of them a caricature. Director Annette Olsen, who has done tv and feature film work in Poland before returning to Denmark, has a nice feel for adding perspective and illuminating points to moods, characters and milieus by dwelling briefly here and there on details of gesture that are not narrowly tied to plot development.

The second part's dramatic shortcomings will make film a slippery item across most borders even though it might do well in youth-specialized situations, and tv sales are quite likely, too. Lene Gurtler is very much alive as the typical teenager, clumsy and graceful as well as headstrong and bewildered at the same time.

Frits Helmuth is outstanding as always as the mild-tempered bus driver father, straight out of one of the best of the new-old Czechoslovak New Wave films, which Annette Olsen's feature at its best moments resemble very much. —*Kell.*

1980

Buffet Froid
(Cold Cuts)
(FRENCH-COLOR)

Paris, Dec. 28.

A Paralrance release of a Sara Films/-Antenne 2 co-production. Produced by Alain Sarde. Stars Gerard Depardieu, Bernard Blier, Jean Carmet. Written and directed by Bertrand Blier. Camera (Eastmancolor), Jean Penzer; editor, Claudine Merlin; art director, Theo Meurisse; costumes, Michele Cerf; sound, Jean-Pierre Ruh; music by Johannes Brahms. Reviewed at the Ponthieu screening room, Paris, Dec. 13, 1979. Running time: 95 MINS.
Alphonse Tram .... Gerard Depardieu
Inspector .... Bernard Blier
Murderer .... Jean Carmet
Widow .... Genevieve Page
  Also, Denise Gence, Carole Bouquet, Jean Benguigui.

Bertrand Blier, not content to rest on his Oscar and become respectable, has committed a marvelous new impertinence called "Buffet Froid." Like his other films, a comedy of bad manners, this one is darker, austere, less social and more absurdist, suggesting a new direction for Blier.

With its mordant surreal abstractions, film could prove more accessible to those previously put off by the director's truculent anti-feminism, despite the presence of Blier's usual thematic obsessions. However, its dry sense of offbeat humor and its unhurried, theatrically measured pace could limit commercial reach, although with Blier's foothold in the U.S., "Buffet Froid" should be going places, given the right promotion. With much of its comic effect dependent on dialog, film will demand first-rate subtitling.

With the inestimable contributions of Jean Penzer's excellent disquieting cinematography and Theo Meurisse's essential art direction, Blier shows himself in full control of his abilities as writer and director. The weaving of a texture of deepening nightmare, undergirded by a grimly funny sense of disconnected logic, is masterfully done and sustained.

Gerard Depardieu plays a bemused, unemployed young man who cannot figure out how his switchblade knife wound up in the belly of a stranger one night in a deserted subway station. He doesn't remember having put it there himself.

Bernard Blier (the director's father) is a dour-faced, phlegmatic police inspector who moves into the 30-story building whose only tenants are Depardieu and wife. A more cognizant murderer, Blier tells his new neighbor how he put an end to his wife's incessant musical habits by wiring her violin to an electrical outlet.

Jean Carmet is a difficult murderer who strangles Depardieu's wife in an empty lot and then visits him to confess his indiscretion. Depardieu is obliged to escort Carmet home because the little man is afraid to be out alone at night.

It's only the beginning of a series of bizarre, nocturnal misadventures that draw the hapless three together in an inescapable complicity of murder, treachery and paranoid flight. In the end, Depardieu, freed of his burdensome buddies, has the bad luck to run into the daughter of that first victim in the subway.

"Buffet Froid" is full of outlandish images and scenes, some of which could become classic moments of French film humor, such as the opening scene between Depardieu and Michel Serrault (making an uncredited appearance) on a deserted subway platform, or the sequence in an underground car park in which Depardieu, Carmet and Blier prepare to fulfill a contract killing.

Watching these three generations of French male actors play together to such splendidly incongruous effect is one of the most pleasurable film treats in quite some time.

This is not to downplay a faultless supporting cast, including the remarkable Genevieve Page as the quirky widow who moves in with Depardieu after he and his colleagues do away with her husband.

Also deserving special mention are Denise Gence, Carole Bouquet and Jean Benguigui. —Len.

Barnfoerbjudet
(Not For Children)
(SWEDISH-COLOR)

Stockholm, Dec. 20.

A Swedish Film Institute with HB Three Leaf Clover production/AB Sandrews release. Original story, script and directed by Marie-Louise de Geer Bergenstrahle. Features entire cast. Camera (Eastmancolor), Lars Svanberg, Ronald Sterner; executive producer, Anna-Lena Wibom; production management, Peter Hald, Britta Werkmaester; music, quotes from E. Kalman, F. Lehar; production design, Carl Johan de Geer. Reviewed at the Grand, Stockholm, Dec. 19, 1979. Running time, 76 MINS.
The little girl .... Ann Smith
Mommy .... Bibi Andersson
Daddy .... Rolf Skoglund
Granny .... Annalisa Ericson

"Barnfoerbjudet" is a word mostly used by censors to mark down films younger audiences must not see. This particular feature will be marketed abroad as "The Elephant Walk," a title indicating a child's attempt at walking in grown-ups' shoes; and again indicating the abyss between the heaven that, to quote Keats, lies about us in our infancy, and the hell we make out of our adult lives.

Marie-Louise de Geer Bergenstrahle is not being preachy about her message, however. She wants, in this fairytale of a film, to remind us that only by taking time out to love each other more can we hope to cross the aforementioned abyss.

Bergenstrahle is a multi-media artist of some renown and considerable talent (books, paintings, pop sculpture, etc.), but film-making seems to remain her unrequited love. With husband Johan Bergenstrahle as nominal director she did "Hello, Baby" a few years ago, a dismal attempt at a feminist answer to Fellini's "Amarcord."

This time, she both wrote and directed (but has refrained from acting as she did in an exhibitionist way in "Hello, Baby"). The result is at best curious, a stylized comedy operating with wind-up doll-like characters in settings of junk and vinyl decor.

A little girl (played with alert energy by Ann Smith) is being tossed around by her career and party-going nuts of a mom and dad. At home as well as in kindergarten, she seeks refuge in daydreaming, reality and dreams alike seen in sketches of pop-art tableaux. Bibi Andersson plays the mother and is expected to be shrill. She really means well (as does the father, played by Rolf Skoglund), but mannerisms drown out such intentions. Andersson, a superior actress, has lately been sorely in need of better roles and better directors. Annalisa Ericson as the youthful, babysitting grandmother, fares rather better.

"Not For Children"/"The Elephant Walk" is filmed as supposedly seen through the child's eyes. This ploy works only occasionally, and Bergenstrahle is no Lewis Carroll yet. Her film may appeal to programmers of children's video slots, but will most likely confuse young audiences as well as their parents. Some exposure at minor, specialized film festivals might help this elephant in hobbling along. —Kell.

Du aer inte klok, Madicken
(You're Out Of Your Mind, Maggie)
(SWEDISH-COLOR)

Stockholm, Dec. 20.

An SF Artfilm production, AB Svensk Filmindustri release. Story and script by Astrid Lindgren, based on her story collections, "Madicken" and "Madicken och Junibackens Pims." Directed by Goeran Graffman. Features entire cast. Executive producers, Olle Hellbom, Olle Nordemar; camera (Eastmancolor), Joergen Persson; music, Bengt Hallberg; editor, Jan Persson. Reviewed at the China, Stockholm, Dec. 19, 1979. Running time, 97 MINS.
Madicken .... Jonna Liljendahl
Lisabet .... Liv Alsterlund
Mamma .... Monica Nordquist
Pappa .... Bjoern Granath
Alva .... Lis Nilheim
Mr. Nilsson .... Allan Edwall
Mrs. Nilsson .... Birgitta Andersson
Abbe .... Sebastian Haakansson
Mayor's wife .... Yvonne Lombard

"You're Out Of Your Mind, Maggie" is a small-scale masterpiece in a genre not otherwise noted for superior efforts and results. Feature is also eminently marketable in almost any situation and territory. It is a picture sure to bring joy, laughter and an occasional moist eye to sub-teen audiences and adults in their company (togetherness highly recommended here) everywhere.

These glad tidings are already anticipated by many distributors and theatre managers plus tv programmers who have earlier profited with honor from producer-director Olle Hellbom's congenial tv and feature film versions of Astrid Lindgren's hilarious and wise children's books, "Pippi Longstocking" and "Emil of Loennaberga."

Coproducing with Olle Nordemar, Hellbom has yielded the helmer's chair to Goeran Graffman, a tv graduate of consummate technical skill, while Lindgren herself has scripted both a six half-hour tv series about "Madicken" and the simultaneously produced feature. In Sweden as in some other countries, the feature is released at the termination of the tv series' showing, while West German audiences will see the combined work as a 10-part series on the home screen.

Astrid Lindgren's Madicken stories contain less outright farce than "Pippi" and "Emil." Along with meticulous production design (a provincial town in the early 1920's) and costumes plus Joergen Persson's exquisite camerawork, this makes for a higher degree of reality, humor and lyricism smoothing reality's rougher edges without entirely blunting them. Lindgren, as always, remains the good humanistic socialist while she is first and foremost a story-teller of the first rank.

Madicken is a seven-year-old girl's self-invented pet name for Margaretha, but Maggie will have to do in an English translation. In episodes we follow her always curious, mostly joyous walk through family, school and community life in and around June Hill where she lives with her little sister Lisabet (a.k.a. Pims), her father (a well-to-do but socially very alert editor of The Workers' Herald) her mother (mild-mannered, firm, intelligent), and Alma, a young and warm-hearted housekeeper. In the Lindgren childrens' universe Good and Evil may do eternal combat, but the smile lurks in any shadow, the maudlin is always avoided, the sun eventually shines through.

Film is episodic but no less coherent for that. Characters are developed in the most natural ways. Only the mayor's scheming, pushy and snobbish wife is seen as straight caricature. Even she has a redeeming feature, however, in the fact that she is so obviously riding for a fall.

Acting throughout is of the highest order, not a note of condescension anywhere. Jonna Liljendahl as Maggie may be a little angel, but she is pretty tough, too. She is lovable without ever being cloying. Among the professional adults, Allan Edwall is superior. He does not make being drunk appear appealing, but he succeeds in making his condition a fact of life understandable, instead of too scary to Maggie and any other child. —*Kell.*

The Fog
(COLOR)

___

Carpenter builds another hit.

___

Hollywood, Jan. 4.

An Avco Embassy Pictures release. Produced by Debra Hill. Exec producer, Charles B. Bloch. Directed by John Carpenter. Features entire cast. Screenplay, Carpenter, Hill; camera (color), Dean Cundey; editors, Tommy Wallace, Charles Bornstein; production design, Wallace; music, Carpenter; sound, Craig Felburg; special effects, Dick Albain Jr.; costume design, Bill Whittens, Stephen Loomis; art director, Craig Stearns; assistant director, Larry Franco. Reviewed at Directors Guild of America Theatre, Hollywood, Jan. 3, '80. (MPAA Rating: R.) Running time: **91 MINS.**

Stevie Wayne	Adrienne Barbeau
Father Malone	Hal Holbrook
Kathy Williams	Janet Leigh
Elizabeth Solley	Jamie Lee Curtis
Machen	John Houseman
Nick Castle	Tommy Atkins
Sandy Fadel	Nancy Loomis
Dan O'Bannon	Charles Cyphers
Andy Wayne	Ty Mitchell

___

Alfred Hitchcock he isn't, but John Carpenter demonstrates he has a finger right on the pulse of today's filmgoing public with "The Fog." Well-made suspenser looks to be a good bet to equal or surpass the returns on Carpenter's sleeper hit, "Halloween," which should make distrib Avco Embassy happy.

Carpenter is anything but subtle in his approach to shocker material, laying out a series of carefully-orchestrated set pieces designed to scare the daylights out of the youthful filmgoers who are clearly the target audience here.

Premise is obvious from almost the first frame, as a grizzled John Houseman tells youngsters grouped around a campfire about a foggy curse that surrounds a coastal town where a horrible shipwreck took place 100 years ago. Analogy is blatant. Carpenter, the storyteller, simply presents a visual embellishment on the traditional ghost story.

It's a measure of the young director's ease with the medium that the story exposition and setting are well-established before the opening titles are over, and "The Fog" proceeds to layer one fright atop another until a strong denouement is reached (although an unnecessary voice-over ending spoils much of that effect).

Adrienne Barbeau (also Carpenter's wife) makes her film debut as the husky-voiced deejay of the town's sole radio station, perched atop a lighthouse from which the title phenomenon becomes increasingly apparent. Carpenter, with the aid of production designer Tommy Wallace and special effects supervisor Dick Albain Jr., has provided the pic with a fine brace of destructive effects for which contempo audiences are seemingly insatiable.

Cross-plotting has truck driver Tommy Atkins and hitchhiker Jamie Lee Curtis similarly afflicted by these strange occurrences, ditto priest Hal Holbrook and society matron Janet Leigh.

Screenplay by Carpenter and producer Debra Hill still short-circuits several of the plot synopses, but there's a big improvement evident since "Halloween," especially in the dialog and interjection of some actual humor via the Nancy Loomis character, an aide to Leigh.

Much of what happens really doesn't make logical sense, of course, but those who favor this type of fare don't give a hang for logic. The goal is to be scared half to death, and even if he wields a heavy hand at times, Carpenter delivers consistently.

Thesping is okay in all departments, although Leigh isn't given much to do, nor is daughter Curtis, who was so effective in "Halloween." Rugged Atkins is well-cast, as is Houseman, although the less said about Holbrook's performance, the better. Carpenter also has a lengthy cameo as a church maintenance worker, and in keeping with the numerous buff injokes, one character is named after Carpenter's former collaborator, screenwriter Dan O'Bannon.

Tech work from what has become Carpenter's stet crew is high on all levels, and musical score which director himself contributed adds immeasureably to the effect. Point Reyes locations provide the perfect atmosphere, although the special phosphorescent fog looks a bit like radioactive smoke.

While tendency is to compare Carpenter at this juncture in his career with the established masters of suspense, that judgment taking may be too premature. In every feature, Carpenter has gained a greater command of his medium, and furter growth is inevitable. After all Hitchcock didn't hit his cinematic stride until "The Man Who Knew Too Much," his 16th film. For Carpenter and his fans, the best is yet to come. —*Poll.*

Rien ne va plus
(Out Of Whack)
(FRENCH-COLOR)

___

Paris, Dec. 27.

A Gaumont release of a Renn Production Partners Production coproduction. Produced by Ariel Zeitoun. Stars Jacques Villeret. Directed by Jean-Michel Ribes. Screenplay, Ribes and Philippe Khorsand, with Laurent Heynemann; music, Michel Rivard; camera (Fujicolor), Bernard Zitzermann; editor, Jacques Witta; sound, Jean-Louis Ughetto; art director, Jacques Bufnoir. Reviewed at the Berlitz Cinema, Paris, Dec. 27, 1979. Running time: **92 MINS.**

Cast: Jacques Villeret, Eva Darlan, Roland Blanche, Philippe Khorsand, Tonie Marshall, Evelyne Bouix, Micheline Presle, Jacques Francois, Judith Magre, Daniel Prevost, Michel Blanc, Henri Cremieux.

___

Jean-Michel Ribes, a comic playwright of cafe-theatre background, makes a cautious but unsatisfying directorial debut in the cinema with this sketch film, headlining stand-up comic and actor Jacques Villeret and featuring an engaging group of supporting talents.

The skits zero in on French society — its traditions, pretentions, artist-intellectuals, deep-rooted fascism and daily rituals — and links them, rather arbitrarily, with interviews, both real and staged, about what the French think of this epoch.

Ribes' satiric barbs too often miss. It's not that he doesn't have good, corrosive ideas behind some sketches (one skit about three greasy motorcycle hoods who terrorize a Paris subway line at night is clearly calculated to make the spectator uneasy about laughing at it) but the writing lacks rigor and Ribes is not yet comfortable with the camera as an integral part of gag-making process.

Symptomatic of the film's inadequacies is the last sketch: a potential howler about oddball types in a local working-class cafe. The situations tick expectantly but fail to detonate as strived for, despite the deftly-performed caricatures.

If the film remains nonetheless agreeable it is thanks to the actors, led by Villeret, a pudgy, sad-eyed comic who has not yet found a workable screen image. Here he exhibits a good example of his mimic register in a number of widely varied impersonations (including the inevitable drag routine) and does so with charm and finesse. Among the other fine zanies must be singled out Roland Blanche, a dangerously funny man who's played some effectively slimy straight roles in film. —*Len.*

The Godsend
(COLOR)

___

"The Omen" without the scares.

___

Hollywood, Jan. 12.

A Cannon Films release. Produced, directed by Gabrielle Beaumont. Executive producers, Menahem Golan, Yoram Globus, Dennis Friedland. Stars Cyd Hayman, Malcolm Stoddard. Screenplay, Olaf Pooley, based on the novel by Bernard Taylor; camera (uncredited color), Norman Warwick; editor, Michael Ellis; music, Roger Webb; art direction, Tony Curtis; sound, Aubrey Lewis; associate producer, Christopher Toyne; asst. director, Derek Whitehurst. Reviewed at the Hollywood Pacific, Hollywood, Jan. 11, 1980. (MPAA Rating: R.) Running time: **90 MINS.**

Kate Marlowe .... Cyd Hayman
Alan Marlowe .... Malcolm Stoddard
Stranger .... Angela Pleasence
Dr. Collins .... Patrick Barr

———

Copy line for the print and tv campaigns of "The Godsend," "For God's sake, take it back," is really asking for it, since neither the modest pic nor the child of the title delivery the demonic thrills promised in the promo. Even so, strong sell could stir up some initial biz, although lack of suspense or violence in film itself will send customers away dissatisfied.

Opening reel sets up an "Omen"-like situation, as decidedly strange Angela Pleasence drops in on rural English couple Malcolm Stoddard and Cyd Hayman, has a baby girl, then disappears before dawn the next morning.

Over subsequent years, little albino Bonnie menacingly squints her blue eyes a lot and is seemingly responsible for the demise of the couple's four children. She also provokes a miscarriage by Hyman and gives the mumps to Stoddard, rendering him sterile.

All these dirty deeds occur offscreen and no motivation of even the flimsiest occult nature is offered up to explain them. Helmer Gabrielle Beaumont is clearly more interested in the domestic and psychological problems children's deaths have on the parents than in delivering shocks. Beaumont's style seems naturally delicate and intimate, and might be applied to better advantage on less artificial material.

Pic's one real plus is Hayman, a real beauty whose earnest, honest performance makes one take her seriously, even if the same can't be said of the film overall. Stoddard is decent as her hubbie, while little is asked of remainder of the cast.

Tech credits are okay. —*Cart.*

———

Chiedo Asilo
(My Asylum)
(ITALIAN-COLOR)

———

Rome, Dec. 24.

A Gaumont release, produced by 23 June - ASM Productions - Best Int'l Film. Stars Roberto Benigni, Dominique Laffin. Directed by Marco Ferreri. Screenplay, Gerard Brach; camera (Eastmancolor), Pasquale Rachini; art director, Enrico Mancelli; editor, Mauro Bonanni; music, Philippe Sarde. Reviewed at Quirinetta Cinema, Dec. 23, 1979. Running time: **105 MINS.**

Roberto .... Robert Benigni
Isabella .... Dominique Laffin

———

The latest Marco Ferreri film rates as a stronger boxoffice entry than many of the previous pix by this maverick filmmaker. "My Asylum" is as non-conformist as

any of Ferreri's previous credits, but it is carried leisurely to its unpredictable finale by virtuoso actor Roberto Benigni and a kindergarten-full of lovable brats.

Together they put the spectator at ease even through some of the slower sequences to enjoy the poetic and creative world of pre-school children as well as their unorthodox teacher.

Between one and the other, the Gaumont Italia release is an entertaining film about children in a society long alienated — a family film providing serious and comic insights. With stage handling, it should do more than skim-off biz in many markets and find a warm welcome at film festivals.

Ferreri took over a kindergarten on the outskirts of Bologna — a school symbolically ringed with fortress-like housing centers. Here Benigni joins the staff with a mind free of teaching doctrine, often leading his flock into strange pastures. His inventive methods amuse and stimulate. But in eliminating routine, he runs counter to some of the social nerve centers. His unannounced trip with the young ones to a nearby factory to visit their fathers at work almost rebounds. He skirts trouble with the police when he takes in a young runaway fiddle player, age five. His accordion is no match for a passing carnival float of a tv monster here.

Each skirmish with the world outside suggests that tots can only enjoy their innocence and fantasy at arm's length from society.

Benigni's love affair with the mother of one of his charges (Dominique Laffin) develops the one wholesome adult relationship of the film. And his concern for Gianluigi, another young charge who refuses to talk or eat, is the second link with an unexpected ending. After Laffin finds herself with child she goes off to her village in Sardegna to await the day. Benigni and a group of his children, including problem child Gianluigi, join her.

In an almost flash ending, childbirth in the village coincides with Gianluigi's vocal breakthrough on a nearby beach, as the kid requests Benigni to take him into the sea and back to the Great Mother. As they disappear into the Mediterranean, the pic ends on the wail of a newborn child in the village.

Each spectator will have to find his own meaning in this abrupt finale. Continuity of the life cycle is the least equivocal but stands alone, unrelated to the film's major emphasis on the contrast between society today and the purity of kids in kindergarten age.

Benigni emerges as a talented performer — disciplined when called for and cleverly spontaneous in many improvised mo-

ments. The children are natural thesps and blend with Benigni's style of acting to eliminate restraints. While Ferreri avoids probing for reasons behind Gianluigi's muted stance, the child's performance is revealing and convincing. Other adult performers, especially Laffin and teenager Luca Levi, add sensitivity and warmth.

Lensing and art work are high craft factors for mood and setting. Pace, could be tightened to eliminate momentary sag pockets.
—*Werb.*

———

The Shah of Iran
(BRITISH-DOCU-COLOR & B/W-16m)

Orson Welles speaks up for the deposed Shah in film made eight years ago, now a college circuit item.

———

Produced by Dean Maksor. Directed by Walter Ellaby. Narrated by Orson Welles; produced in cooperation with the Iranian Ministry of Culture and Arts. No other credits. Reviewed at C. W. Post College, Long Island University, New York. Running time: **60 MINS.**

———

As events in Iran escalate and as U.S. hostages there await their fate, a promotional film narrated by Orson Welles, "The Shah of Iran," is now getting lively exposure in the New York area, with screenings thus far at C. W. Post College, Pratt Institute, Millenium Film Workshop, The New School, and at Adelphi, Columbia, Hofstra and New York universities.

(Apparently none of the U.S. tv webs would buy this film and as far as known the negative rests on shelf awaiting possible future commercial use, or borrowing of certain scenes. The college print was a loan.)

"The Shah of Iran" is a skillful job, but not an objective neutral "documentary." Film cleverly builds a mutual identity and destiny of the Shah with the nation of Iran. The two are sensed as one. The Shah is father-monarch. He is shown repeatedly as both a private man and loving parent and as a benovolent ruler, thus by inference, the father of his countrymen. The Shah swims, skis, sprawls on the floor with his son, the Crown Prince. Such scenes are inter-cut with workaday duties as the Shah labors to solve Iran's problems.

With firmness, justice and love, states Welles as narrator, the Shah is reconciling Kurdish separatism, introducing land reform, mollifying ancient grudges and pioneering western-styled democracy and industrialization. Foreign esteem for the Shah is illustrated by hand-

shakes with Tito, De Gaulle and a covey of Soviet leaders.

"The Shah of Iran" begins informally, ingratiated by that familiar, friendly Welles voice. The Shah is first seen driving his limousine to work. "Come driving with a king," invites Welles, as the Shah waves happily to citizens thronging the curbs of Teheran. "A king — but a man, a husband, a father."

Welles' narration, although personal, even intimate in regard to the Shah's succession of wives, emphasizes Iran's political tranquility. There is non-stop praise for the "progress," "social reform" and "reforming zeal." Despite some "lingering corruption" and opposition by isolated soreheads to the Shah's modernizations, says Welles, "he has already left his mark on history."

Welles also does voice-over for visuals of old paintings reconstructing Iran's history from the conquest of Alexander The Great of Greece, thence to the recent past, with b/w newsreel footage of the Shah's father, an army colonel who founded the Pahlavi dynasty in the 1920s. He was deposed by the Allies as pro-Nazi, succeeded by his son, the current recent ex-Shah.

Business of Mossadegh and the CIA is disposed of neatly, as Welles calls that official a Marxist crank.

End of "The Shah of Iran" has director Walter Ellaby playing chess with the Shah, as Welles intones that the Shah must make the right moves to build Iran's future. Big final images of film are thrilling fireworks backed by appropriate sound symphonics, total combined to evoke celebration of Shah's perpetuity as Iran's revered monarch.

In contrast to new anti-Shah quickie documentaries being broadcast in recent months, and in production, the Welles "Shah of Iran" is a passionate love-song for the Shah. Produced eight years ago, it is a curio or artifact of a lost epoch of history, a unique pro-Shah portrait. The film belongs in universities for study by communications students being trained in skepticism, as the film illustrates the capacity of "news" and "documentary" footage to be edited and manipulated.

In this regard, the visuals for "The Shah of Iran" are oddly neutral. Without inherent meaning. Conceivably, the picture can be recut into an anti-Shah context, with a different voice-over reversing the pro-Shah theme to anti-Shah.

Welles's participation in "The Shah of Iran" connects to heavy Iranian investment in Welles's as yet incomplete "The Other Side of The Wind," semi-autobiographical feature starring John Huston.

Welles's "The Shah of Iran" connects also to an article in *Variety*, dated August 1, 1979, "Shah of Iran Biopic," date-lined Hollywood and describing biography-film on the Shah, being produced by Maurice Silverman and Durham Productions.

Windows
(COLOR)

Moody thriller.

Hollywood, Jan. 15.

A United Artists release of a Michael Lobell production. Produced by Michael Lobell. Directed by Gordon Willis. Features entire cast. Screenplay, Barry Siegel; camera (Technicolor), Willis; music, Ennio Morricone; editor, Barry Malkin; production design, Melvin Bourne; art direction, Richard Fuhrman; sound, Christopher Newman; set decoration, Les Bloom; assistant director, Robert Colesberry. Reviewed Jan. 15, 1980, at the MGM Studios, Culver City, Calif. (MPAA Rating: R.) Running time: **96 MINS.**

Emily Hollander	Talia Shire
Bob Luffrono	Joseph Cortese
Andrea Glassen	Elizabeth Ashley
Ida Marx	Kay Medford
Sam Marx	Michael Gorrin
Steven Hollander	Russell Horton
Dr. Marin	Michael Lipton

Reminiscent both thematically and stylistically of "Klute," "Windows" is a moody piece of urban female victimization which fails to synthesize the parallel psychological and thriller elements with which it grapples. Pic has already incurred the wrath of gay groups protesting the treatment of the frustrated lesbian villainess, but public-at-large will undoubtedly find tale too muted and far-fetched to swallow. Indifference, rather than fury, should dictate film's ultimate b.o. fate.

As another nervous, insecure heroine, Talia Shire finds herself assaulted by a hulking brute in the opening reel, forced at knifepoint to satisfy the demands of a tape-recorder-wielding assailant. Audience is soon tipped off that Shire's neighbor, svelte but obviously imbalanced Elizabeth Ashley, is secretly in love with her and has hired the man to record Shire's gasping protestations.

Shire moves out but Ashley follows her, spying on the meek woman's slowly blossoming affair with detective Joseph Cortese through a telescope. As in "Klute," confrontation between the two comes as surely as night settles upon the big city, and denouement pro provides little surprise.

Doubling as his own cinematographer, Gordon Willis creates a strong sense of urban isolation and desolation, even if most of the ideas are retreads. Somber and rather sad, pic is done in not so much by arty style as by unsound psychological underpinnings of Barry Siegel's script, which suggests that Ashley couldn't confront Shire honestly about her feelings, but instead was forced, through her "abnormality," to resort to extreme shock tactics to pursue her obsession.

It's the sort of film where everyone speaks haltingly and with grave seriousness, as if all humor and plain speaking had been banished from the world. Playing a shy, unassertive stutterer, Shire still manages to ingratiate herself to a degree, while Cortese is extremely low-key as her official and later personal protector. Ashley does well what she's asked, but what that is is another matter.

Tech credits are all strong, with Ennio Morricone's music providing excellent subdued support for the largely quiet scenes. Attention to background sounds is also exemplary. —*Cart.*

La Femme Flic
(The Woman Cop)
(FRENCH-COLOR)

Paris, Jan. 8.

An AMLF release of a Sara Films/Antenne 2/Societe Nouvelle Cinevog co-production. Produced by Alain Sarde. Stars Miou-Miou. Directed by Yves Boisset. Screenplay, Boisset, Claude Veillot, camera (color), Jacques Loiseleux; sound, Harald Maury, Jean Fontaine; editor, Albert Jurgenson; music, Philippe Sarde; art direction, Maurice Sergent, Jimmy Vanstennkiste. Reviewed at the Ponthieu screening room, Paris, Jan. 4, 1980. Running time: **103 MINS.**

Corinne Levasseur	Miou-Miou
Inspector Porel	Jean-Marc Thibault
Diego Cortez	Leny Escuder
Backmann	Jean-Pierre Kalfon
Dr. Godiveau	Francois Simon

A director of action films with strong socio-political topicality, Yves Boisset tried his hand with less sensational non-thriller material in his last two films, "A Purple Taxi" and "The Key In the Door," which were more concerned with character than incident.

"La Femme Flic" finds Boisset back in familiar territory, but the tone has changed. Conspicuously absent are the action setpieces. The film evolves as a soberly directed police procedural, in the feminine gender. But the plotting is still fitted with Boisset's usual spikey polemics.

Story concerns a female police inspector, Corinne Levasseur, young, intelligent, attractive, and profoundly serious about her work. When one of her investigations proves to be embarrassing to some figures in power, she is transferred out of Paris to a small, dreary city in the northern French mining region, where she comes up against incomprehension and loneliness.

After being confined to office labors, she is eventually permitted to work in the field, but is usually assigned to morals cases, (particularly those involving children) which prove discomfiting to her male colleagues. She handles these cases with tactful receptivity.

When the body of a little girl is found on the city outskirts, the young inspector kicks off an investigation that leads to the discovery of a wide-spread child pornography network that victimizes in particular children of working-class backgrounds.

Unfortunately the trail leads to members of the family that controls most of the city's industry and institutions. Unwilling to cut short her pursuit of the guilty party, the idealistic woman cop is discreetly obliged by her superiors to hand in her resignation.

Film suffers from an overall glibness in the writing and characterizations and often breaks down into much too simple oppositions (idealistic youth vs. corrupt establishment, etc.) with the script finally suggesting that women, by nature more ethical than men, have no effective place in the police force, crippled as it is by compromise manipulation and short-sightedness.

Still the film has impact through the harsh verities of individual scenes, well-directed by Boisset. Best are those sequences that deal with child abuse and the vulnerability of the young in working-class environments. Boisset deserves credit for confronting unflinchingly such grim realities.

Boisset is a fine director of actors and the excellent cast helps put meat on some of the script's bones. Miou-Miou seems an unlikely choice for the title role (originally intended for Isabelle Huppert) but provides the part with austere introspective intensity and a sense of quiet concern and dedication.

Funnyman Jean-Marc Thibault plays it straight and true with a fine composition as the police commissioner. Francois Simon turns out a memorable seconary role as a despised fascistic homosexual doctor suspected of murder. Biggest acting surprise is from gaunt pop-singer Leny Escudero as a young anarchist. He definitely has the stuff good actors are made of. Others are fine. —*Len.*

Il Malato Immaginario
(The Hypochondriac)
(ITALIAN-COLOR)

Rome, Dec. 26.

A CIC release, produced by Piero La Mantia for Mars Film Produzione. Stars Alberto Sordi, Laura Antonelli. Directed by Tonino Cervi. Screenplay, Cesare Frugoni, Tonino Cervi, Alberto Sordi, camera (Eastmancolor), Armando Nannuzzi; art director, Piero Tosi; editor, Nino Baragli; music, Piero Piccioni. Reviewed at Fiamma cinema, Rome, Dec. 26, 1979. Running time: **110 MINS.**

Argante	Alberto Sordi
Tonina	Laura Antonelli
Argante's Wife	Marina Vlady
Argante's Daughter	Giuliana De Sio
Doctor	Bernard Blier

Notary .... Stafano Satta Flores
Handyman .... Vittorio Ciprioli

Pairing Alberto Sordi and Laura Antonelli gives the CIC entry a brace of powerhouse boxoffice names in the Italo market, but this low-comedy burlesque of Moliere's "Le Malade Imaginaire" should have spotty results across the borders.

Where the 17th century French classic was a piquant study of French manners and a whipping satire on the medical profession, the Italian film version, transplanted to the Eternal City of the same period, is a tasteless hodgepodge of Moliere's basic ingredients, with an incredibly anachronistic injection of youth revolt (terrorism, bombs, et al.) and timeworn burlei skirts (many extended to over-indulgent lengths). In an addendum to Moliere, Argante — who suffers mainly from indigestion and purges — becomes a bourgeois hero. Even the right of public domain goes up in smoke as Argante, the ailing recluse (Alberto Sordi), gets rid of his medic quacks, exposes a treacherous and greedy wife (Marina Vlady) and her bedmate-notary (Stefano Satta Flores), makes peace with his estranged daughter (Giuliana De Sio) and her wounded rebel boyfriend — all with the aid of his well-stacked chambermaid (Laura Antonelli) — to end his long isolation, open wide his manor doors and return to life in the tortured times of papal Rome.

The main prop in "The Hypochondriac" is the portable toilet and the principal sound effect is the passage of air from below the belt. Both are complimented by an interminable enema sequence and ensuing bowel movement of legendary volume. The aim to please an indiscriminate audience is so elementary that the Mars production should prove to be gold, in this market at any rate, where the sound stopped the show time and time again.

If Sordi ever dreamed of getting the Legion d'Honneur, he can now forget it. One of filmdom's outstanding comedy talents, he hams through his title role, more often than not up to his knees in vulgar, trivial dialog and sitcoms. Antonelli, now a gracious lady of Italian cinema, romps in and out with heavy tread and early Renaissance cleavage as she wiles her way to lady of the house.

Remaining cast are largely costumed caricatures in cliche' roles. Film gets a lift from Armando Nannuzzi's lensing. Piero Tosi's dependable touch with sets and locales and Piero Piccioni's unintruding score (practically defaced by natural body noises). —*Werb.*

To Forget Venice
(Dimenticare Venezia)
(ITALIAN-FRENCH-COLOR)

Quartet Films release of a Robert A. McNeil presentation. A Rizzoli Film (Rome) - Action Films (Paris) coproduction. Features entire cast. Directed by Franco Brusati. Screenplay, Franco Brusati, Jaja Fiasti, based on a story by Brusati; camera (color), Romano Albani; music, Benedetto Ghighlia; art direction, Luigi Scaccianoce; costumes, Luca Sabatelli; editor, Ruggero Mastroianni. Reviewed at Rizzoli screening room, New York, Jan. 21, 1980. (NO MPAA rating). Running time: **110 MINS.**
Nicky .... Erland Josephson
Anna .... Mariangela Melato
Claudia .... Eleonora Giorgi
Picchio ....David Pontremoli
Marta .... Hella Petri
Rossino .... Fred Personne

(Italian with English subtitles)

With Franco Brusati's "Bread and Chocolate," American viewers discovered a very human film director. With his new film, "To Forget Venice," which is the Italian entry in the "best foreign language" category of the 1979 Academy Awards, they'll discover that Italy's writer-director is also a highly intellectual filmmaker. Familiarity with his earlier films would have told them that, but it was "B&C" that established him on the American market.

Brusati's tale of a family of highly-inhibited but basically nice people takes place during a visit to the country home of retired opera singer Marta (Hella Petri), with whom live two young women — referred to as nieces but whose actual relationship is never clarified — by her brother Nicky (Erland Josephson) and his companion-lover Picchio (David Pontremoli). They're there for the group to make an excursion to nearby Venice. This never materializes because of several dramatic incidents that end with the death of Marta and the "growing up" of her three "dependents," all of whom had conisdered her a mother replacement. The girls are also lovers (Mariangela Melato and Eleanora Giorgi) but for a film about two pairs of homosexuals, there's not one display of affection other than a fast embrace by the two males.

There is, however, a considerable amount of nudity, most of which is dramatically plausible, by the three younger principals. When the end finally comes and the girls and Josephson have to grow up overnight, it isn't made clear whether they're really up to it or not. The girls leave for Milan with Picchio, Nicky stays on in the house (he says to Picchio that he's "tired of being young" but one doubts that peace and contentment is really his goal).

The acting, like the writing and direction, is first class by every

member of the cast, including a scene-stealing bit by an uncredited ancient crone who's the cookhousekeeper for the strange menage. Fred Personne is also excellent as what is suggested as being a boyhood conquest of Nicky but who has gone the straight and married path with six children.

Romano Albani's color camera makes the country setting a lush, but peaceful spot that underscores the quiet underplaying of the cast. Although it is obvious that an Italian actor has dubbed Josephson's lines, the voice is compatible with the Swedish actor's performance and never interferes. Benedetto Ghighlia's score is bucolic and nonintrusive. —*Robe.*

Yomegaeru Kinro
(Resurrection of the Golden Wolf)
(JAPANESE-COLOR)

Tokyo, Dec. 30.
A Toei release of a Kadokawa Production. Executive producer, Haruki Kadokawa. Producer, Michiru Kurosawa, Gosukei Ito, Tatsuro Shigaki. Directed by Toru Murakawa. Features entire cast. Screenplay, Shuichi Nagahara, based on novel by Haruhiko Oyabu; camera (color), Seizo Sengen; music, Casey Rankin. Reviewed at Toei Bunka, Tokyo, Dec. 29, 1979. Running time: **131 MINS.**
Cast: Yusaku Matsuda, Jun Fubuki, Kei Ito, Mikio Marita, Shinichi Chiba, Joji Shin, Asao Koike.

The action in this action-filled release may be summarized by "And with a single bound, he is free."

Taken into a storeroom by ruffians, searched for concealed weapons, hero Yusaku Matsuda pulls out a gun his captors conveniently overlooked ... and with a single bound, he is free.

Matsuda is a loner dedicated to taking over a company controlled by a criminal syndicate. He kills, steals, deals in drugs and turns into a heroin addict a young woman from whom he solicits information and to whom he makes love, only to begin courting the company president's daughter. The former young woman, less angry at being made a junkie than being made a fool, stabs Matsuda, who nonetheless manages to make his way to a nearly deserted Narita International Airport, there to board a plane on which to expire. This is the beginning.

As the woman Matsuda does wrong, Jun Fubuki is a revelation, her performance multifaceted, at once sensual and naive.

Otherwise, "Yomigaeru Kinro" is a typical Haruki Kadokawa production. It is too long, based on pulp literature, with a plot as labyrinthine as it is illogical, directed by someone unable to resist the excessive tough. —*Bail.*

Bear Island
(BRITISH-CANADIAN-COLOR)

Corny meller, with script as stiff as the Arctic setting. So-so prospects.

London, Jan. 17.
Columbia Pictures release (in U.K.) of a Selkirk Films presentation. Produced by Peter Snell. Stars Donald Sutherland, Vanessa Redgrave, Richard Widmark, Christopher Lee, Barbara Parkins, Lloyd Bridges, Lawrence Dane. Directed by Don Sharp. Screenplay, Sharp, David Butler, Murray Smith (based on novel by Alistair MacLean); camera (color), Alan Hume; editor, Tony Lower; art direction, Kenneth Ryan, Peter Childs; Tony Lower; art direction, Kenneth Ryan, Peter Childs; special effects, David Harris, Thomas Clark, Paul Whybrow; stunt coordinator, Vic Armstrong; assistant directors, Stuart Freeman, Don Brough, Roy Stevens, Jerry Daly; associate producer, Bill Hill. Reviewed at Leicester Sq. Theatre, London, Jan. 16, '80. (BBFC rating: A.) Running time: **118 MINS.**
Frank Lansing .... Donald Sutherland
Hedi Lindquist .... Vanessa Redgrave
Otto Gerran .... Richard Widmark
Lechinski .... Christopher Lee
Judith Ruben .... Barbara Parkins
Smithy .... Lloyd Bridges
Paul Hartman ....Lawrence Dane
Inge Van Zipper .... Patricia Collins
Heyter ....Michael Reynolds
Jungbeck ....Nicholas Cortland
Marine technician ... August Schellenberg
Lab assistant .... Candace O'Conner
Meteorological ass't. ..... Joseph Golland
Technician ....Bruce Greenwood
Larsen .... Hagen Beggs
Ship's captain .... Michael Collins
Radio operator .... Terry Kelly
Helicopter pilot .... Terry Waterhouse

Don't be fooled by the title — a nature film it isn't. Neither is "Bear Island" a zippy suspense thriller. This time, in short, it's questionable whether author Alistair MacLean's usually bankable name will turn the trick.

The Anglo-Canaɔian production, produced by Peter Snell with routine direction by Don Sharp, teems with cliches about a multinational scientific expedition to the Arctic, gold bullion left over from the war, and the efforts of some Nazi types to wrest the precious metal from an old German U-boat.

Scripted by Sharp with David Butler and Murray Smith, the result is dull dialog and feeble characterization which leaves the actors with little chance, and it shows. Vanessa Redgrave and Donald Sutherland, as film's romantic pair, fare the worst, with maybe three expressions between them. But Richard Widmark, Barbara Parkins,* Lloyd Bridges, Christopher Lee and Lawrence Dane as other principals (all billed above title) come off little better. Some dialects — Redgrave's Norsk, Widmark's German, Lee's Slavic — flunk the test, not that it matters. But better they shouldn't have even tried.

The cutting and Alan Hume's camera direction are as conventional as the story. "Bear Island's" something to look at when the camera's panning trackless glacial mountainscapes (the far reaches of Alaska), and there's some acceptable stunting with snowmobiles in a pursuit sequence, but otherwise the action's too little too late. At nearly two hours, the slack shows and the triteness is magnified.

Withal, pic may prove a useful booking as and when the marketplace hits a dull patch.

Other technical credits, art direction, special effects, etc., are all pro. —Pit.

I Comme Icare
(I As In Icarus)
(FRENCH-COLOR)

Paris, Jan. 3.
An AMLF rlease of a V Films/ SFP/Antenne 2 co-production. Produced and directed by Henri Verneuil. Stars Yves Montand. Screenplay, Verneuil, Didier Decoin; camera (color, Jean-Louis Picavet; art director, Jacques Saulnier; editor, Henri Lanoe; music, Ennio Morricone; sound, Serge Deraison, Jacques Maumont. Reviewed at the Colisee cinema, Paris, Jan. 3, 1980. Running time: 120 MINS.
Henry Volney . . . . Yves Montand
Heininger . . . . Michel Etcheverry
Prof Nagarra . . . . Roger Planchon
Despaul . . . . Jacques Denis

Henri Verneuil's "I Comme Icare" was born of fascinating material: the Yale University experiments on "Submission to Authority," undertaken by professor Stanley Milgrim between 1960 and 1963, which demonstrated how an average person could be led to harm a complete stranger when acting under the sanction of an authority he or she respects.

Verneuil, a director of thrillers, was knocked out by the idea of a suspense tale that would incorporate Milgrim's findings into the fabric of the action. He reportedly spent an unusually long time (more than three years) working out a script with co-scenarist Didier Decoin, set up his own company to produce and got Yves Montand to play the lead.

The result is a dull, half-baked, pointless political thriller: poorly contirved, lumpily directed and indifferently acted, with mediocre technical credits and a torpid score by Ennio Morricone. Film is a soaring hit locally and ran off with this year's Grand Prix du Cinema (Louis Lumiere).

Plot takes the form of an investigation into a political assassination. Verneuil appropriates in outline the assassination of John F. Kennedy and thinly dresses it up. Action is set in a fictitious state, but the national flag sports a red-white-and blue design and the alleged killer is anagrammatically named Daslow.

Montand is a district attorney who rejects the official report findings that the president's death was the work of a solitary deranged individual. He launches his own investigation and comes across the existence of a wide-reaching conspiracy masterminded by the country's own secret service. Before he can act he is assasinated.

The script is ludicrous, with all kinds of plot holes. Among the many howlers is a scene in which Montand gets a call from the only surving witness to the identity of the true assassin (Daslow having been a duped decoy and the other witnesses having being eliminated). Montand tells him not to reveal his address but to go out and call from a public phone, so that they can trace his call and pick him up!

The real corker is that the Milgrim theories don't illuminate these clumsy mechanics in the least; most of the characters act out of fear, personal gain or warped political beliefs, but not out of regard for authority.

All Verneuil has done is to insert a 20-minute demonstration sequence in the heart of the action, its presence explained by the unlikely fact that Daslow once took part in the experiments. It's the most interesting part of the film, chiefly because the guinea pig is played by that most natural of actors, Jacques Denis, who gives the action its only true layer of emotion.

Montand, dignified in grey hair and spectacles, is all gravity and dedication, but the role is so pallid who cares. —Len.

Laura: les ombres de l'ete
(Laura: Shadows of Summer)
(FRENCH-COLOR)

Paris, Jan. 4.
An SNC release of a Alma Films-Cora coproduction. Produced by Alain Terzian. Features entire cast. Directed by David Hamilton. Screenplay, Joseph Morhaim, Andre Szots; camera (color), Bernard Daillencourt; music, Patrick Juyet; editor, J. Van Effenterre; artistic and technical director, Szots; sound, B. Ortion. Reviewed at the Marignan-Concorde theatre, Paris, Jan. 3, 1980. Running time: 90 MINS.
Saras Moore . . . . Maud Adams
Laura Moore . . . . Dawn Dunlap
Paul Wyler . . . . James Mitchell

Still photographer David Hamilton's second foray into filmmaking (his first being "Bilitis" in 1977) centers on a successful sculptor living and working in the south of France. He becomes intrigued by the lovely young daughter of an old girl friend and wants to make a sculpture of her. The girl's jealous mother won't allow her to pose and instead provides the artist with photos from which to work. An accident blinds him before he can finish the statue.

Disobeying her mother's stricture, the girl visits him and guides him in the completion of his work through the sole use of his hands. He regains his vision. Mother and daughter, reconciled, go off together.

The them of the artist's aloofness and his renewed contact with life seems only a pretext for Hamilton, who's interested in giving a temporal extension to his photographic work. The cinematography captures the essence of his work, his subjects are attractive and Patrick Juvet's pretty score oozes mood and melancoly. But "Laura" is unsatisfying as film, remaining something less than a "motion" picture. —Len.

La Familia, Bien, Gracias
(The Family, Fine, Thanks)
(SPANISH-COLOR)

Madrid, Jan. 12.
Pedro Maso P.C. - Impala S.A. production. Directed by Pedro Maso. Features entire cast. Screenplay, Pedro Maso, Rafael Azcona; camera (Eastmancolor), Alejandro Ulloa; music, Juan Carlos Calderon; sets, Ramiro Gomez; editor, Alfonso Santacana. Reviewed at Cine Rialto (Madrid), Jan. 11, '80. Running time: 106 MINS.
Cast: Alberto Closas, Jose Luis Lopez Vazquez, Maria Jose Alfonso, Jaime Blanch, Francisco Benlloch, Lola Forner, Julita Martinez, Carlos Pinar, Julieta Serrano, Paco Valledares, Margot Cottens.

This is the third part of a trilogy which Pedro Maso began 20 years ago with "La Gran Familia" and followed by "La Familia y Uno Mas." The first two installments, comedies revolving around a typical lower-middle class Madrid family, were immensely popular in Spain reflecting as they did popular attitudes and myths salted with some funny situations.

Present pic also has some good touches of humor, and some zany situations as well, but there's an undercurrent of pathos and nostalgia running through it as Maso uses clips of the former films which hark back to what for him, at least, were happier days. There was a rightwing saying "We lived better under Franco," which was countered with "A few lived better under Franco," and the indisputable "We were all younger under Franco." These three "truths" are mixed into the film, though the former and latter are underlined.

In addition to its sometime comic situations, pic in effect portrays the gradual disintegration of the family in Spain. Harking back to former times Maso evokes the happy, Catholic family of yore, and contrasts it with the speedy, emancipated living of a widower's children today.

The paterfamilias who has raised 16 children (played by Alberto Closas), after foolishly giving up his apartment upon retiring from his job, must now quest about for lodgings among his brood, in company with the children's godfather (Jose Luis Lopez Vazquez). Most are married to rather stand-offish spouses, one has become a nun, two are missionaries, and one's studying medicine in New York.

The two aging friends make the rounds, only to find that for one reason or another they are incompatible with the lives of the newer generation. The children visited range from a successful architect who's a ruthless go-getter, to a son who manages a hotel cum brothel.

Lopez Vazquez puts in an amusing performance as he contorts his face in the familiar way and blunders into awkward situations, Closas is okay as the alternately loving and disenchanted father, but the supporting cast is wooden.

Also implicit in the script are dozens of old prejudices and tacit assumptions. The elderly twosome are scandalized when a daughter blithely announces she's flying to London for an abortion, but then condemn a straitlaced son in law who upbraids them for their loose language.

Pic should appeal to non-youth audiences and those who can relate to the displacement of the elderly friends. In contrast to most Maso pix, there's almost no sex or nudity in pic, except for a few scantily-dressed girls. Item has some funny parts in it, but youth audiences may be put off by Maso's value judgments on modern Spain versus that of 20 years ago. —Besa.

El Crimen De Cuenca
(The Cuenca Crime)
(SPANISH-COLOR)

Madrid, Jan. 11.
An Incine - Jet Films production. Directed by Pilar Miro. Exec producer, Alfredo Matas. Features entire cast. Screenplay, Salvador Maldonado, Pilar Miro, based on idea by Juan Antonio Porto; camera (Eastmancolor), Hans Burmann; editor, Jose Luis Matesanz; sets, Fernando Sanez; music, Anton Garcia Abril. Reviewed at Incine screening room, Madrid, Jan. 10, '80. Running time: 90 MINS.
Varona . . . . Amparo Soler Leal
Isasa . . . . Hector Alterio
Congressman Contreras . . . Fernando Rey
Gregorio . . . . Daniel Dicenta
Leon . . . . Jose Manuel Cervino
Juana . . . . Mary Carrillo
Master . . . . Eduardo Calvo
Taboada . . . . Francisco Casares
Don Rufo . . . . Jose Vivo
Secretary . . . . Felix Rotaeta

Startling, beautifully filmed and

superbly acted pic by femme helmer Pilar Miro who tops the considerable talent she had shown in her first work, "La Peticion," in this memorable account of political conniving and the miscarriage of justice in the Spain of 1913.

Some of the torture scenes by Civil Guards have caused this film to be temporarily banned in Spain (*Variety* Jan. 16), but it is sure to surface soon, if not at local houses then on the international fest circuit.

Torture scenes are realistically acted out, about 15 minutes of them, and are not for the squeamish. They are, however, justified in the context and form an integral part of the plot, though they may cause not a few viewers to avert their eyes. The "crime" involves the disappearance of a shepherd from a small village in the rural province of Cuenca. Charges are trumped up by a local rightwing congressman and an ambitious district judge, who have two unruly recalcitrant troublemakers rounded up by the Civil Guards. The latter are told to "do their duty" to extract confessions from the accused miscreants and determine what they have done with the shepherd's body after supposedly robbing him.

The ensuing tortures never help to clarify their depositions, and the exhuming of corpses doesn't help either.

At the ensuing trial, the state-appointed counsel for the defense puts in a plea of guilty, with which they get off with a 15-year sentence. Six years later they manage to get out of jail on probation, and two years later (the story is a true, documentated one), their putative victim shows up in a neighboring village.

Thesping throughout is of a high order, with stellar performances by the two accused, Daniel Dicenta and Jose Manuel Cervino, who are new to Spanish screens, and topnotch supports by Fernando Rey, Hector Alterio, Amparo Soler Leal and others. Garcia Abril's score is spellbinding, and direction and editing imaginative.

Pic should do excellent biz in Spain once it's released, and might chalk up kudos abroad as well as proof of what modern Spanish cinema is capable of. —*Besa.*

Silent Scream
(COLOR)

Formulized but frightening fan-pleaser.

Hollywood, Jan. 18.
American Cinema Releasing release of a Jim and Ken Wheat production. Executive producers, Joan and Denny Harris. Features entire cast. Directed by Denny Harris. Screenplay, Ken and Jim Wheat; camera (MGM Color), Michael D. Murphy. David Shore; editor, Edward Salier; sound, Larry Goga; production design, Christopher Henry; special effects, Steve Karkus; music, Roger Kellaway. Reviewed at the Fox Theatre, Hollywood, Jan. 18, 1980. (MPAA Rating-R). Running time: 87 MINS.
Scotty . . . . Rebecca Balding
Lt. McGiver . . . . Cameron Mitchell
Sgt. Rusin . . . . Avery Schreiber
Victoria . . . . Barbara Steele
Jack . . . . Steve Doubet
Mason . . . . Brad Reardon
Peter . . . . John Widelock
Doris . . . . Juli Andelman
Mrs. Engels . . . . Yvonne de Carlo

A group of vulnerable youngsters imperiled by a homicidal maniac in a spooky old house is not the freshest of frameworks. Nevertheless, Denny Harris' moody, menacing direction and a solid cast combine to make "Silent Scream" a real chiller that should perform solidly on the shriek circuit.

Arriving too late to get college housing, Rebecca Balding, Steve Doubet, John Widelock and Juli Andelman are forced to take rooms in the daffy domicile of young Brad Reardon and his weird mother, Yvonne De Carlo. And strange 1950s music coming from upstairs somewhere.

The major obstacle from such a formula start, of course, is that every leap ahead will be totally predictable. But Harris never falls into the trap, building suspense with many surprises.

The major obstacle from such a formula start, of course, is that every leap ahead will be totally predictable. But Harris never falls into the trap, building suspense with many surprises.

Good performances by the likable four youngsters are an added strength, leaving the audience to actually care which survive — and which don't. Balding and Andelman are both especially good, as is Barbara Steele who turns out to be the mysterious presence upstairs.

Cameron Mitchell and Avery Schreiber are also fine as the police team investigating the murders. And Reardon is best of all as the involuntary weirdo of the house.

Tech credits are strictly low-budget, but there are several moments of really good photography. And there is one outstanding scene combining the screams of love-making with the screams of a simultaneous murder that would

be a credit to any film of a much bigger budget.

Naturally, as in all such stories, the plot ultimately depends on Balding doing something totally illogical — with a murderer on the loose, she follows a dark stairway up from the basement all alone. Though many potential companions are elsewhere in the house.

But if everyone sat around being logical in fright films, they never would go anywhere at all. —*Har.*

Fatso
(COLOR)

Gluttony themed film falters between hilarity and pathos.

Hollywood, Jan. 22.
A Twentieth Century-Fox release of a Brooksfilms Ltd. production. Produced by Stuart Cornfeld. Directed, written by Anne Bancroft. Stars Dom DeLuise. Camera (DeLuxe color), Brianne Murphy; editor, Glenn Farr; music, Joe Renzetti; production design, Peter Wooley; set decoration, Linda DeScenna; costumes, Patricia Norris; sound, Al Overton Jr.; assistant director, Mark Johnson. Reviewed at Twentieth Century-Fox Studios, L.A., Jan. 22, 1980. (MPAA Rating: PG.) Running time: 94 MINS.
Dominick DiNapoli . . . . Dom Deluise
Antoinette . . . . Anne Bancroft
Frankie . . . . Ron Carey
Lydia . . . . Candice Azzara
Charlie . . . . Michael Lombard
Vito . . . . Sal Viscuso
Ida Rendino . . . . Delia Salvi
Johnny . . . . Robert Costanzo
Mrs. Goodman . . . . Estelle Reiner
Sonny . . . . Richard Karron

"Fatso" is as bumbling and sluggish as its title would suggest, a lamentable affair which ricochets uncontrollably between attempts at hilarity and pathos. Actually a problem drama with an unpalatable comedic frosting, pic might initially attract fans of the Mel Brooks brand of humor, but world of lack of laughs should spread quickly.

After an interminable opening reel which sees the death of an obese cousin at an early age, Dom DeLuise half-heartedly decides he'd better start slimming down or face the consequences. A meek type with virtually no will-power, DeLuise caves in to temptation at every opportunity, and film is filled with conversation about food and close-ups of starchy delights of every variety.

Even a supposedly rigorous group called Chubby Checkers is no match for the hero's appetite, as he and two cohorts clean out his kitchen in a nocturnal orgy of abandon and DeLuise alone later eats his way thorugh $40 worth of Chinese food intended for a whole group of card players.

Only a sweet Polish-Catholic girl, nicely played by Candice Azzara, is able to momentarily distract the

obsessed Italian boy's attention away from his stomach, but typical of writer-director Anne Bancroft's strategies is having the shy couple kiss for the first time after Azzara has evidently stepped in dog droppings on the street.

Script's best line probably comes when DeLuise asks his girl out for a date. Queried re what he has in mind, he immediately replies to the effect that, "Maybe we can go to Chinatown and have a meal or two," which gives some indication of level of humor.

Beloved by his inamorata in his current condition (which is not nearly as fat as his colleagues in Chubby Checkers), DeLuise finally arrives at the realization that he is what he is, that it's futile to change what nature obviously intended for him. Tell that one to his late cousin.

Aside from a widely obvious indulgence in constant repetition, Bancroft's biggest problem is controlling the tone. Opening childhood montage, which features little Dom getting a squirt of urine in his face from his baby brother, clues audience to expect typical Brooksian hijinx, but subsequent funeral scene is played for overwrought emotionalism. Pic never steadies itself except for short interludes between the romantic leads.

DeLuise tries hard and is not unappealing, but needs more guidance. Aside from Azzara, remainder of cast is nondescript, with Bancroft herself unusually shrill as lead's constantly pleading sister. Tech credits are okay. —*Cart.*

Guyana: Cult Of The Damned
(MEXICAN-SPANISH-PANAMA-COLOR)

Cyanide & grape cola holocaust. Marginal shocker.

Hollywood, Jan. 18.
Universal Pictures release. Produced and directed by Rene Cardona Jr. Features entire cast. Screenplay, Carlos Valdemar and Cardona Jr; camera (color), Leopoldo Villasenor; editor, Earl Watson; music, Nelson Riddle, Bob Summers, George S. Price; sound, Simon Coke, Stephen Purvis, Dessy Markovsky; assistant director, Robert Schlosser. No other credits available. Reviewed at Universal Studios Screening Room, Universal City, Jan. 18, '80. (MPAA Rating: R). Running time: 90 MINS.
Rev. James Johnson . . . . Stuart Whitman
Congressman Lee O'Brien . . . Gene Barry
Dave Cole . . . . John Ireland
Richard Gable . . . . Joseph Cotten
Doctor Gary Shaw . . . . . Bradford Dillman
Anna Kazan . . . . Jennifer Ashley
Susan Ames . . . . Yvonne De Carlo

By the time Stuart Whitman's followers take their lethal doses of cyanide and die en masse in "Guyana Cult Of The Damned," audiences will probably be too bored to be horrified. The Universal pickup centering on the massacre at Jonestown over a year ago falls somewhere between stiff documentary and cheap drama, never succeeding on either level. As such, boxoffice success is dubious, since there's not enough shock material for the action crowd and a sparsity of intellectual stimulation for those who might want to learn something.

Pic is a coproduction of Conacine Mexico, Izaro Films in Spain and Panama-based Care Prods. Lensed in Mexico City, photography by Leopoldo Villasenor is mostly fine as scene shifts from Whitman's supposed nirvana-like village in Guyana to locales in the U.S. where government reps are deciding how to investigate the mythical "Johnsontown."

Problem comes with translation of the story. Screenplay by Carlos Valdemar and producer-director Rene Cardona Jr. depends entirely too much on narration by one of Whitman's followers, giving more the feeling of a current events lecture than a dramatic presentation.

When actors are given scenes the tendency is to shamelessly overplay, much in the style of the typical disaster pic. But because in this case the events actually occurred, the broad characterizations are not even acceptable on a humorous level.

Cardona has assembled a passel of names such as Whitman, Gene Barry, Joseph Cotten, Bradford Dillman and Yvonne De Carlo for some marquee value. Suffice it to say none are able to save the film, one reason being frequent out-of-synch dialog that makes it difficult to even remain interested in what they are saying.

The producer-director seems to have gotten around any possible factual errors with a disclaimer that although "the story is true," the names have been changed. While that might protect him from libel it won't make this film any more than it is — an attempt to capitalize on a tragic situation. —Berg.

American Gigolo
(COLOR)

Gere scores with the ladies but may have a tougher time at the b.o.

Hollywood, Jan. 28.
Paramount Pictures release of a Freddie Fields production. Executive producer, Freddie Fields. Produced by Jerry Bruckheimer. Stars Richard Gere. Written and directed by Paul Schrader. Camera (Metrocolor), John Bailey; art director, Ed Richardson; editor, Richard Halsey; music, Giorgio Moroder; set decorator, George Gaines; sound, Barry Thomas;

sound effects editors, Ray Alba, Bert Schoenfeld; asst. director, Peter Bogart; publicist, Gary Kalkin. Reviewed at Paramount Studios, Hollywood, Jan. 28, 1980. (MPAA Rating-R). Running time: 117 MINS.
Julian . . . . Richard Gere
Michelle . . . . Lauren Hutton
Sunday . . . . Hector Elizondo
Anne . . . . Nina Van Pallandt
Leon Jaimes . . . . Bill Duke
Charles Stratton . . . . Brian Davies
Lisa Williams . . . . K Callan
Mr. Rheiman . . . . Tom Stewart
Judy Rheiman . . . . Patti Carr
Lt. Curtis . . . . David Cryer
Mrs. Dobrun . . . . Carole Cook
Mrs. Sloan . . . . Carol Bruce
Mrs. Laudner . . . . Frances Bergen
Hollywood actor . . . . . . Macdonald Carey
Michelle s lawyer . . . . William Dozier
Julian's lawyer . . . . Peter Turgeon
Floyd Wicker . . . . Robert Wightman
Mr. Williams . . . . Richard Derr
Jill . . . . Jessica Potter

A hot subject, cool style and overly contrived plotting don't all mesh in "American Gigolo." Paul Schrader's third outing as a director is betrayed by a curious, uncharacteristic evasiveness at its core which renders film both less corrosive and, at times, more ridiculous than it might have been. Despite chic appointments and spicy elements which could arouse initial interest, b.o. prospects would seem mixed.

Things begin to go awry, both for Gere and the picture, when Senator's wife Lauren Hutton begins taking more than a passing interest in her man-for-hire and when a kinky sex murder is laid at his door.

It's not that either event in such a life is implausible, but rather that Gere's character has been portrayed with such moral and emotional ambivalence, which makes caring about his predicament and ultimate fate difficult. Finale attempts to lift tale into a story about the redemption of a lost soul, but a couple of unfortunate missteps and less-than-precise acting cause pic to come up short even when it might still have been saved.

As with several of Schrader's other scripts, this one charts the course of a loner, a solo driver navigating in a sea of sharks ready to eat him alive. Pic remains relatively engrossing as long Gere is making his daily rounds, but audience sympathy diminishes in inverse ratio to extent plot forces emotional investment in character's destiny.

Rarely offscreen, Gere is notably convincing in look and manner, conveying the necessary self-confidence without seeming too narcissistic or overbearing. Very low-keyed, Lauren Hutton is not quite up to the very difficult part of a woman-who-has-everything who throws it all over for her questionable lover, a role which might more

profitably have been played by a slightly older actress.

John Bailey's sleek cinematography, Giorgio Moroder's heaving electronic music, production design by Fernando Scarfiotti (billed as "visual consultant"), art direction of Ed Richardson and costuming from various sources are all crucial to film's chic visual look. Sound work was at times below par, at least in print caught, as some line readings were inaudible. —Cart.

In Search Of Historic Jesus
(COLOR)

Another of the Sunn Classic items which exploits a theme, and saturates airwaves.

A Schick Sunn Classic Productions release, produced by Charles E. Sellier Jr. and James L. Conway. Directed by Henning Schellerup, written by Marvin Wald and Jack Jacobs based on the novel by Lee Roddy and Sellier Jr. Features entire cast. Assoc producer, Bill Cornford: camera, (Technicolor) Paul Hipp; editor, Kendall S. Rase; music, Bob Summers, the New London Orchestra: production designer, Paul Staheli: special effects, John Carter; set decorator, Randy Staheli; art, Doug Vandergrift. Reviewed at the Coliseum Theatre, N.Y., Jan. 21, '80. (MPAA Rating: G). Running time: 91 MINS.
Jesus . . . . John Rubinstein
Caiaphas . . . . John Anderson
Herod Antipas . . . . Nehemiah Persoff
Narrator . . . . Brad Crandall
Apostle John . . . . Andrew Bloch
Mary . . . . Morgan Brittany
Joseph . . . . Walter Brooke
Mary Magdalene . . . . Annette Charles
Prophet . . . . Royal Dano
Peter . . . . Anthony De Longis
Pontius Pilate . . . . Lawrence Dobkin
Thomas . . . . Jeffrey Druce

Schick Sunn Classic Productions Inc. has its own brand of "showmanship," carrying a selected theme to selected situations of its own and heavily, indeed lavishly, backed by saturation blurbing on television and radio. Typically the films make money and typically they mock the art of film. Such is the new instance, "In Search Of Historic Jesus."

The central novelty deals with the "Shrowd of Turin," which scientists not long ago examined as a remnant of Christ in the tomb.

Some may consider such an exercise in pictorialized rhetoric as harmless; others may see exploitation of the mass audience in a deplorable sense. The film's "theology" will not bear scrutiny. The narrative trick is to repeatedly ask questions. Was Jesus the Son of God? Did he work miracles? One scene has John Rubinstein, son of the great piano virtuoso, walking on water in the title role.

Narrator Brad Crandall would be more convincing perhaps if his wig didn't show. The performers' per-

formances need not engage critical attention. The art in a Sunn classic is not on the screen but in the media blitz.

Night Games
(COLOR)

Fuzzy psychology. Poor outlook.

Hollywood, Jan. 9.
An Avco Embassy Pictures release of a Pan Pacific production. Produced by Andre Morgan, Roger Lewis. Exec producer, Raymond Chow. Directed by Roger Vadim. Features entire cast. Screenplay, Anton Diether, Clarke Reynolds, based on a story by Diether and Barth Jules Sussman: camera (Technicolor), Dennis Lewiston: editor, Peter Hunt; music, John Barry: production design, Robert Laing; art direction. Frank Israel; sound, Danny Daniel: special effects, Gene Grigg: assistant director, Denys Grenier de Ferre. Reviewed at Directors Guild of America, Hollywood, Jan 9, 1979. (MPAA Rating: R.) Running time: 100 MINS.
Valerie . . . . Cindy Pickett
Julie . . . . Joanna Cassidy
Jason . . . . Barry Primus
Sion . . . . Paul Jenkins
Timothy . . . . Gene Davis
Alicia . . . . Juliet Fabriga
Jun . . . . Clem Parsons

Expatriate directors haven't had an easy time of adjusting to Stateside filmmaking as of late, and on the basis of "Night Games," Roger Vadim doesn't prove an exception. The Avco Embassy release, financed by Raymond Chow's Golden Harvest Films, has the look of a foreign feature dubbed in English, with results that provoke more laughs than chills. The vaunted erotic touch from Vadim is certainly present, but boxoffice embrace from domestic audiences looks to be less than passionate.

Vadim's latest "discovery," tv actress Cindy Pickett, is fine in her feature debut as a terrorized Bev-Hills housewife, whose lingering memories of a childhood rape jeopardizes her relationship with spouse Barry Primus and anyone else wearing pants. It's just a matter of time until Pickett is left alone in the oversized manse, where the line separating fantasy from reality becomes as fuzzy as the dialog.

Since Pickett spends most of the pic screaming her lungs out at the mere approach of another human being. "Night Games" leaves surprisingly little to the imagination. Vadim has inserted some potent lovemaking scenes, in which a mysterious intruder materializes garbed in outlandish costumes, but given the inevitable trimming to obtain an R rating, effect is more of cinematic foreplay.

Supporting cast is particularly weak, with Joanna Cassidy drawing unintended chuckles as Pickett's concerned friend, and Gene Davis limning the most unlikely teenage sexpot since John Travolta in "Moment By Moment."

Best attribute of "Night Games" is John Barry's unusual and distinctive score, which uses counterpoint and dreaminess with excellent results. Peter Hunt's strange editing removes what little suspense remains in convoluted screenplay by Anton Diether and Clarke Reynolds.

While use of Manila and other Philippine locations are well meshed with scattered BevHills shots, "Night Games" really falls apart in the post-production looping, making it look like just another shoddy European import. Vadim deserves a better shot than this, but on the basis of "Night Games," it may be hard for him to get it.

—*Poll.*

Midnight Madness
(COLOR)

Juvenile hijinx could have some initial b.o. impact.

———

Hollywood, Jan. 25.
A Buena Vista release. Produced by Ron Miller. Directed by David Wechter, Michael Nankin. Features entire cast. Screenplay, Wechter and Nankin; camera (Technicolor), Frank Phillips; music, Julius Wechter; editors, Norman R. Palmer, Jack Sekely; art direction, John B. Mansbridge, Richard Lawrence; sound, Herb Taylor; set direction, R. Chris Westlund, Roger M. Shook; special effects, Danny Lee. Reviewed at the Chinese Theatre, Hollywood, Jan. 25, 1980. (MPAA Rating: PG.) Running time: **110 MINS.**
Adam .... David Naughton
Laura .... Debra Clinger
Wesley .... Eddie Deezen
Lavitas .... Brad Wilkin
Donna .... Maggie Roswell
Harold .... Stephen Furst
Mrs. Grimhaus .... Irene Tedrow
Scott .... Michael J. Fox
Flynch .... Joel P. Kenney
Leon .... Alan Solomon

———

"Midnight Madness" is an overly-long, juvenile comedy centering on the unlikely participation of a group of college students in an all-night competition with mere victory as their only reward. Although humor will no doubt occasionally appeal to the basest of adolescent instincts, script by firsttimers David Wechter and Michael Nankin, also co-directors, lacks enough continued punch or irreverence needed to carry the theme over 110 minutes. Result should spell initial boxoffice magic among youngsters that could fade once the word gets around.

A Buena Vista release, pic is the first in-house Walt Disney production to go out without the Disney name. Somewhat "off-color" nature of film was given as the reason, but if anything picture is not bold enough. Wechter and Nankin too often hold back the raunch and settle for wide-eyed exchanges that probably don't go on among junior high schoolers. While that's not bad in itself, it doesn't seem to be what's needed here, especially in a market of filmgoers.

Basic plot line has gamester Alan Solomon luring diverse group of his fellow collegiates to participate in the "ultimate game" he has concocted after a year of careful planning.

Resistent at first, all eventually agree to captain a team that will be sent through the Los Angeles area beginning at midnight to unravel variety of clues that will ultimately lead them to the finish line by morning.

Leaders fulfill all the usual stereotypes, with David Naughton as the clean-cut hero, Stephen Furst acting the nasty fatty, Eddie Deezen once again limning the

know it-all intellectual, Maggie Roswell projecting a pushy sorority sister and Brad Wilkin stuck as the obnoxious jock. All perform what's expected.

Several actors do score fine bits, most notably Joel P. Kenney as an at-first naive freshman and Michael J. Fox, believably sensitive as Naughton's younger brother.

As directors, Wechter and Nankin keep the action moving although they're no threat with the written word. Jokes aside, it is difficult to understand how a miniature golf course, a piano museum, the Griffith Park Observatory, or the Pabst brewery (complete with tour guides) could all be open in the middle of the night.

Frank Phillips does a fine job photographing a variety of locales, and editing by Norman R. Palmer and Jack Sekely gives pic a cohesive feel. Julius Wechter's music is appropriately youthful. —*Berg.*

The Last Married Couple In America
(COLOR)

———

Dirty words do not a comedy make.

———

Century City, Jan. 31.
A Universal Pictures release, produced by Edward S. Feldman and John Herman Shaner. Exec producers, Gilbert and Joseph Cates. Directed by Gilbert Cates. Screenplay, John Herman Shaner; camera (Technicolor), Ralph Woolsey; editor, Peter E. Berger; sound, Don Sharpless; production design, Gene Callahan; art direction, Peter Smith; assistant director, Thomas Lofaro. Reviewed at Plitt Theatre, Century City, Jan. 31, 1980. (MPAA Rating: R.) Running time: **103 MINS.**
Jeff Thomson .... George Segal
Mari Thomson .... Natalie Wood
Marv Cooper .... Richard Benjamin
Sally Cooper .... Arlene Golonka
Al Squib .... Allan Arbus
Alice Squib .... Allan Arbus
Alice Squib .... Marilyn Sokol
Max Dryden .... Oliver Clark
Helena Dryden .... Priscilla Barnes
Walter Holmes .... DomDeLuise
Barbara .... Valerie Harper
Howard .... Bob Dishy
Tom .... Mark Lonow
Lainy .... Sondra Currie
Rick .... Robert Wahler
Rebecca .... Catherine Hickland
Oriana .... Charlene Ryan

———

"The Last Married Couple In America" is basically a 1950s comedy with cursing. But it at least marks the full screen maturity of Natalie Wood, who started out so sweet as a child star and now uses the R-winning word on camera. Whether that will be a big audience draw remains debatable.

If ribald dialog doesn't sell, then there isn't much left in the picture at all. Certainly, John Herman Shaner's script offers not a single new idea about divorce in suburbia

and doesn't even develop the cliches well.

Gilbert Cates' direction consists largely of letting his stars reenact favorite roles of the past. So Wood plays the nice pretty lady who wants a happy, faithful marriage to George Segal, who plays the nice, handsome husband befuddled by the world around him.

Richard Benjamin is again the neurotic modern male and Dom DeLuise the likable, nutty fat guy, while Valerie Harper is essentially Rhoda running rampant, tresses turned blonde from the sheer excitement of it all.

Segal and Wood don't understand why all their friends are getting divorced while they remain happy. What's worse, they don't understand why they are happy. Unfortunately, neither do Shaner and Cates so there's not much to care about when Harper breaks them up.

Not for a moment, of course, is there any doubt they will get back together once this misunderstanding is cleared up. And they do, without learning anything except that they missed each other.

There are so many couples and characters that nobody else gets much chance to show off in the minor roles. But no one is really bad either and Bob Dishy gets a good turn as a womanizing divorce lawyer and Mark Lonow is funny as a swinger, helped by Sondra Currie as his reluctant wife.

Good production work give the picture the sleek, chi-chi look the subject matter demands, winding through the glamorous homes and watering spots of BevHills. These same backdrops have been used and reused in tales of middle-aged emptiness. Yet they remain peopled and patronized by the same characters as film like this is supposed to expose.

So who cares — except maybe those who live the life and are able to make movies about themselves.
—*Har.*

Hero At Large
(COLOR)

———

John Ritter television fans will probably support this one adequately.

———

Hollywood, Jan. 16.
A Metro-Goldwyn-Mayer release, produced by Stephen Friedman. Directed by Martin Davidson. Features entire cast. Screenplay, A.J. Carothers; camera (Metrocolor), David M. Walsh; editor, David Garfield, sound, Tommy Overton; production design, Albert Brenner; assistant director, Jack Roe; art direction, Norman Baron; music, Patrick Williams. Reviews at MGM Studios, Culver City,

Calif., Jan. 16, 1980. (MPAA Rating: PG.)
Running time: **98 MINS.**
Steve Nichols . . . . John Ritter
J. Marsh . . . . Anne Archer
Walter Reeves . . . . Bert Convy
Calvin Donnelly . . . . Kevin McCarthy
Eddie . . . . Harry Bellaver
Mrs. Havacheck . . . . Anita Dangler
Gloria . . . . Jane Hallaren
Mayor . . . . Leonard Harris
Milo . . . . Rick Podell

More often than not, sitcom stars failed to carry films because their characters were too different on the big screen. But John Ritter's followers on "Three's Company" will find him unchanged in "Hero At Large" — only difference here is two less girls and one more costume. Big MGM promotion and Ritter's popularity should pay off.

The costume is one worn by Ritter as an unemployed actor hired to make personal appearances as a cartoon character, "Captain Avenger," defender of the weak and an enemy of crime. On the way home in costume one night, Ritter stops at the corner grocery and surprises two holdup men, routing them into the night.

The whole city then goes crazy in hopes that a Captain Avenger has really come to save them, tempting Ritter into the streets again to foil a crime. It also tempts political hacks Bert Convy and Kevin McCarthy to find Ritter and employ his deception on behalf of Mayor Leonard Harris.

Up to this point, scripter A. J. Carothers and director Martin Davidson had a chance to handle some interesting points in a whimsical, yet serious way. Certainly, the basic premise is a good one: The yearning for heroes in an age of despair and hopelessness.

But Carothers and Davidson never get a handle on the story, mainly because they are constantly distracted by a stupid love affair between Ritter and Anne Archer that's even less believable — and certainly far less interesting — than the idea that an ordinary good guy in a goofy union suit can uplift the world.

As noted, Ritter is quite adequate in his nice-guy role. And Convy is solid once again in a greasy creep part, though it's time for him to reach for something tougher. But everyone else is stereotyped.

Ritter's involvement with the slimy guys ultimately brings forth his exposure and disgrace and the public turns against him, ready for the tar-and-feathers. And here the picture falls back on a plot device that's hard to forgive. With the whole town out for his head, Ritter goes home to pack and sneak away. But does he change out of his Captain Avenger costume? Of course not. If he did, he wouldn't be properly dressed later when he comes

upon a fire and makes the big rescue, restoring his image.

All told, this hero is a sandwich of interesting plausibility and pointed satire, with too much baloney and ham in between. —Har.

Journeys From Berlin 1971
(COLOR & B/W-16m)

Cerebral material on Germany's terrorists phase of 1970s. Fairly well done for selective handling.

Directed and edited by Yvonne Rainer. Camera (color/black & white), Carl Teitelbaum, Michael Steinke, Wolfgang Senn, Jon Else, Shinichi Tajiri; sound, Larry Sider, Helene Kaplan, Dan Gillham, Christian Moldt. Financed by the British Film Institute, Deutscher Akademischer Austauschdienst, New York State Council on the Arts, Center for Advanced Visual Studies M.I.T., Christophe de Menil, Beard's Fund Inc., Rockefeller Foundation. Reviewed at Bleecker St. Cinema, New York, Jan. 25, 1980. Running Time: **125 Mins.**
Cast: Annette Michelson, Ilona Halberstadt, Gabor Vernon, Chad Wollen, Amy Taubin, Vitto Acconci, Lena Hyun, Yvonne Rainer, Ruth Rainero, Leo Rainer, Cynthia Beatt, Antonio Skarmeta.

Though a bit too abstract to make complete sense, Yvonne Rainer's "Journey From Berlin-1971" represents an interesting attempt to correlate explicit public events with the more personal, everyday aspects of life. Fashioned as an at times fascinating, at times confusing melange of sequences, the picture manages to hold an audience, albeit a cerebrally inclined one, even though to many, the director's intent may not be that obvious.

The ideas and images that recur throughout concern the political terrorism that swept West Germany during the last decade along with its historical precedents in pre-Bolshevik Russia and early 20th Century America, posited against the stream of consciousness meanderings of a woman undergoing a psychoanalytic session. Annette Michelson provides an effective performance in this role, alternating between intimate introspection and comic gibberish quite well.

Michelson's material alludes to suicide, violence, and aspects of sexual and political power, and this is picked up in related and contrasted voice-overs in which a couple discusses specific political events, such as the exploits of the Baader-Meinhof terrorists, in relation to more philosophical questions regarding social justice as well as such mundane areas as food preparation and personal relationships.

Aerial views of Stonehenge, the Berlin wall, street scenes, a recurring but slowly changing tracking

shot of various cultural artifacts on a mantlepiece, and short news items concerning Germany's response to political violence also figure in the mix, as does a sequence of jump shots in which a man and a woman walking seem almost choreographed in their disjunct steps.

Considering the rather sober metier of the subject matter, Rainer is not without humor, as much of Michelson's role contains comic revelations, as well as what might be considered the world's first Stalinist obscene phone call, as a woman answering her phone is greeted by a heavily breathed harangue of Leon Trotsky.

To Rainer's credit, however disparate her elements, she manages to convey a clear linear sense, and this helps to sustain a viewer's interest. This impression is however, a misleading one as one is never quite sure where one is being led, because the correlations between public and private are never made concrete enough. —Roso.

The Ninth Configuration
(COLOR)

Mental confusion theme. Slow development but strong ending helps.

Hollywood, Jan. 22.
A Warner Bros. release. Produced by William Peter Blatty. Exec producer, William Paul. Features entire cast. Directed by Blatty, who wrote screenplay from his novel. Camera (color), Gerry Fisher; editor, T. Battle Davis, Peter Lee-Thompson, Roberto Silvi music, Barry DeVorzon; production design, Bill Malley, J. Dennis Washington; set decoration, Sydney Ann Kee; sound, Marvin Walowitz, Andrew London; assistant director, associate producer, Tom Shaw. Reviewed at Chinese Theatre, Hollywood, Jan. 22, '80. (MPAA Rating: R.) Running time: **105 MINS.**
Colonel Kane . . . . Stacy Keach
Captain Cutshaw . . . . Scott Wilson
Lieutenant Reno . . . . Jason Miller
Colonel Fell . . . . Ed Flanders
Groper . . . . Neville Brand
Captain Fairbanks . . . . . . George DiCenzo
Major Nammack . . . . Moses Gunn
Lieutenant Bennish . . . . . . Robert Loggia
Spinell . . . . Joe Spinell
Lieutenant Gomez . . . . Alejandro Rey
Sergeant Krebs . . . . Tom Atkins
1st Cyclist . . . . Steve Sandor
2d Cyclist . . . . Richard Lynch

"The Ninth Configuration" is an often confusing story concerning the effects of a new "doctor" on an institution for crazed military men which manages to effectively tie itself together in the end. Problem is the William Peter Blatty film takes entirely too long to explain itself, with the crux of the picture mired in mysterious dialog, images and plot twists that are almost consistently more infuriating than intriguing. That alone should spell serious trouble at the boxoffice which will probably be frequented by only the

most loyal Blatty admirers after opening week.

Blatty makes his directorial debut here in addition to performing producing and writing chores (he had latter duties on his 1973 blockbuster, "The Exorcist"). Unfortunately, in being given the sole responsibility of adapting a script from his novel and translating its message to the screen he has lost a sense of the filmgoer along the way.

Stach Keach limns an army colonel who has been brought Stateside to play psychiatrist to a compound of disturbed military men that include Scott Wilson, Jason Miller, Moses Gunn, Alejandro Rey and Joe Spinell, among others. From the beginning it's apparent Keach is infinitely more disturbed than any of the men he is supposed to be treating, making the actor's monotone, robot-like state unbearably grating on the nerves only minutes after his appearance.

Much time is given to the inmates in absurdist scenes that every so often create needed comic relief, particularly in the case of Miller and Spinell. Primary focus is on Wilson, who gets closest to Keach as a former astronaut hero gone bonkers. Although Wilson's long speeches are hopelessly obscure most of the time, he does so well with the difficult role that he, and supervising medico Ed Flanders, finally become the only lights at the end of a dark and cumbersome story tunnel.

Blatty should be credited for concocting a terrific series of concluding scenes where scruffy cyclists Steve Sandor and Richard Lynch terrorize Keach and Wilson. It's the one outstanding moment in the pic and suggests he has more potential as a director than the rest of the film lets on. Also top notch is use of Barry DeVorzon's haunting music.

The "Ninth Configuration" attempts to grapple with tough issues like religion, love, faith and normalcy, but Blatty fails to make his points in a coherent enough fashion for the film to be affecting or even appealing. He finally manages to overcome his closeness to the material with both a straightforward and powerful conclusion but by that time only a precious few will be interested in figuring out what it all means. —Berg.

Just Tell Me What You Want
(COLOR)

High class fluff. Will probably do satisfactory grosses.

Hollywood, Jan. 29.
A Warner Bros release, produced by Jay Presson Allen and Sidney Lumet. Exec

producer, Burtt Harris. Directed by Sidney Lumet. Stars Ali MacGraw, Alan King. Screenplay, Jay Presson Allen from her own novel; camera/(Technicolor), Oswald Morris; editor, John J. Fitzstephens; sound, James J. Sabat, production design, Tony Walton; assistant director, Alan Hopkins; art direction, John Jay Moore, music, Charles Strouse. Reviewed at the Chinese Theatre, Hollywood, Jan. 29, 1980. (MPAA rating: R). Running time: 112 MINS.

Bones Burton	Ali MacGraw
Max Herschel	Alan King
Stella Liberti	Myrna Loy
Seymour Berger	Keenan Wynn
Mike Berger	Tony Roberts
Steven Routledge	Peter Weller
Cathy	Sara Truslow
Baby	Judy Kaye
Connie Herschel	Dina Merrill
Dr. Coleson	Joseph Maher

With "Just Tell Me What You Want," Jay Presson Allen has adapted her trashy novel into a trashy picture. But it's good trash and nobody — least of all director Sidney Lumet — seems deceived into thinking it's anything else. Since the book itself was not as strong as other best-sellers-turned-movie, "Want" won't do big business, but will probably have an adequate existence.

Good-natured feel of the pic lies largely in the preposterous character of Alan King, playing a powerful mogul who collects companies, art and lots of young girls whom he molds to his own liking.

Chief of the harem is Ali MacGraw, nurtured from youth and now a successful tv producer while still tied to King's bedstead. Naturally, King has to have an arch-rival and that's Keenan Wynn, himself aided by his sinister son, Tony Roberts, a gay Hollywood studio exec.

The landscape is further populated by Myrna Loy, delightful as King's secretary; Peter Weller as MacGraw's lover and Dina Merrill as King's alcoholic wife. It isn't worth trying to tell what all these people have to do with each other, since it's all top silly and senseless.

But it's fun to watch them carry out their plots and counterplots and get so upset with each other. King is good as a man going through life enjoying himself, since that seems to be precisely what he's actually doing in getting through the story. MacGraw has a role which makes no demands on her acting ability and she gets a couple of good physical-comedy scenes. The technical credits are all smooth.

But the one worth watching is Loy, a veteran of so many really good pictures of the past, maintain her charm and dignity while those about her pepper the air with racy dialog. The septuagenarian actress looks as if she's constantly amazed at the kinds of films getting made these days. And she's absolutely right. —Har.

Deathwatch
(FRANCO-W. GERMAN-COLOR)

Paris, Jan. 30.

A Planfilm release of a Selta Films-Little Bear-Antenne 2-Sara Films-Gaumont-SFP-TV 13 (Munich) co-production. Produced by Gabriel Boustani and Janine Rubeiz. Stars Romy Schneider, Harvey Keitel. Co-produced and directed by Bertrand Tavernier. Written by Tavernier, David Rayfiel, based on novel, "The Continuous Katherine Mortenhoe" (U.S. title: "The Unsleeping Eye"), by David Compton; camera (Panavision-Fujicolor), Pierre-William Glenn; music, Antoine Duhamel; editors, Armand Psenny, Michael Ellis; art director, Tony Pratt; sound, Michel Desrois. Reviewed at Club 13, Paris, Jan. 10, 1980. Running time: 128 MINS.

Katherine Mortenhoe	Romy Schneider
Roddy	Harvey Keitel
Vincent Ferriman	Harry Dean Stanton
Tracey	Therese Liotard
Gerald Mortenhoe	Max Von Sydow
(English-language version)	

After four profoundly French films, Bertrand Tavernier has taken a gamble with "Deathwatch," an English-language film based on an American science-fiction novel and performed by an international cast.

The film works admirably, in part because the production decisions seem less a function of commercial expediency than of conception necessity, but more importantly because Tavernier, rather than trying to extend himself in ways alien to his sensibility, has shaped his source material to his own temperament and talent. Thus, despite its genre and production circumstances, "Deathwatch" remains quite European in treatment, tone and pace. It should do nicely in foreign markets, especially given Tavernier's overseas reputation, but it's not "Star Wars."

The story, shrewdly crafted by Tavernier and American screenwriter David Rayfiel from a novel by David Compton, is a throatcatcher. In a future society (represented here in the gloomy banality of contemporary Glasgow, Scotland) people die of old-age, science having almost completely banished disease.

A cunning tv producer, Vincent Ferriman, hits on the idea of a television program that would cover live the last days of an individual who has managed to contract a terminal illness. Ferriman, played with chillingly unctuous serenity by Harry Dean Stanton, is a businessman with his finger on the pulse of a society rendered morbid from lack of death.

Ferriman's proposed subject is Katherine Mortenhoe (finely played by Romy Schneider), whose fierce independence and sensitivity would seem to provide poignant fodder for the camera eye. But Katherine, after signing a contract, flees the city, intent on seeing her former husband, with whom she is still in love. The husband, who does not appear until the last part of the film, is marvelously incarnated by Max Von Sydow, an island of acting truth unto himself.

But Ferriman has foreseen this and has hired a young man named Roddy (played with inhabitual boyish candour by Harvey Keitel) to intercept her and work his way into her confidence. Roddy has had a miniature camera implanted in his brain, so that all that he sees is immediately filmed and relayed back to the tv station, where it is edited and broadcast.

Generally free of science-fiction bombast (the technological exposition is dispensed with adroit economy), "Deathwatch" is a compelling drama centered on the human implications of its fanciful premise, as well as a harsh indictment of the media's role in society. Too, Tavernier's human camera is a cruel satire on a certain kind of filmmaker, the immature, moral innocent for whom cinema is a game, or a question of technique.

Pierre-William Glenn's cinematography suits image to the theme and renders Glasgow as a forbidding, joyless urban shell. Antoine Duhamel has come up with an imaginative musical score, and art director Tony Pratt has worked some wonders, including a labyrinthine open air flea market especially constructed for one of the film's most visually exciting sequences.

— Len.

Le Voyage en douce
(Travels On The Sly)
(FRENCH-COLOR)

Paris, Jan. 14.

A Gaumont release of a Prospectacle - Gaumont - Elefilm coproduction. Produced by Maurice Bernart. Stars Dominique Sanda, Geraldine Chaplin. Written and directed by Michel Deville, with literary collaboration of: Francois-Regis Bastide, Camille Bourniquel, Muriel Cerf, Jean Chalon, Pierrette Fleutiaux, Patrick Gainville, Yves Navarre, Jacques Perry, Maurice Pons, Beatrice Privat, Suzanne Prou, Frederic Rey, Dominique Rolin, Isaure de Saint-Pierre. Camera (Fujicolor), Claude Lecomte; sound, Henry Moline, Joel Beldent; editor, Raymonde Guyot; art director, Catherine Ardouin; music by Brahms and Beethoven; additional music, Quentin Damanne. Reviewed at Gaumont screening room, Neuilly, dec. 21, 1979. Running time: 98 MINS.

Helene	Dominique Sanda
Lucie	Geraldine Chaplin

After an unusual detour into the impersonal mechanics of espionage ("Dossier 51"), Michel Deville is back in warmer realms with this casual, funny-cruel portrait of two young women and their symbiotic friendship.

Dominique Sanda and Geraldine Chaplin provide the right physical and emotional complement to each other as two girl friends, both married, who go down to the south of France together. Chaplin, impulsive and seemingly insecure, has walked out on her husband and has come to her friend to confide her hurt and anger. Sanda, apparently stronger and well-balanced, invites her to come down south with her and help find a summer house.

The right house is quickly found, but the women decide to extend their stay and enjoy their marital truancy. They wander and explore, talk and tease, exchanging memories, fantasies and regrets. When they return to Paris, Chaplin rejoins her husband, while Sanda now feels uncomfortable about her own marriage.

Out of this plotless, almost inconsequential outline, which suggests nothing more than fodder for some insipid women's magazine, Deville has made an engagingly witty and perceptive comedy about feminine relationships, eroticism and fantasy.

The director may draw some feminist ire for depicting such volatile, at times adolescently cruel, women, but it's the kind of intimate, very French, film that could go over well in foreign markets, where such product has a certain public.

One of the film's qualities is that it is of a piece, despite its undramatic progression. Consider the genesis of the script: Deville asked 15 reputable French writers (both male and female) to provide him with an anecdote, sexual or sensual in nature. He then worked these contributions into his scenario, adroitly erasing any feeling of patchwork arbitrariness.

Thus, writer Muriel Cerf is responsible for a marvelously funny and erotic scene in a hotel room where Chaplin sexually teases the young waiter who brings the breakfast. He impetuously responds while Sanda coaches him from the sidelines on the intricate procedures of that all-important "first kiss."

An anonymous contributor furnished an unnerving account of a rape in a parking lot. Rather than have Chaplin relate what happened (she may well have invented it), Deville lets us hear the rape on the soundtrack, while we watch the two women promenade through beautiful, sun-drenched landscapes. The effect is chilling.

Credit Deville, cinematographer Claude Lecomte and editor Raymonde Guyot for a sequence of pure visual pleasure in which Chaplin, sheds all her self-consciousness and inhibitions, along with her clothing, as Sanda snaps photos of her momentary transformation into a creature of alluring beauty. —*Len.*

Al Tejruba
(The Experiment)
(IRAQI-COLOR)

Berlin, Jan. 19.

An Iraqi General Organization for Cinema production. Baghdad: world rights, Iraqi General Organization for Cinema. Baghdad. Features entire cast. Written and directed by Fuad al Tohami. Camera (color), L. Salih. Reviewed at Deutsche Werbung Screening Room, Berlin, Jan. 19, '80. Running time: **90 MINS.**

Cast: Salima Khudhair. Semar Mohammed, Sami Kaftan.

A debut pic by a vet docu filmer, Fuad Al Tohami, "The Experiment" pairs two stories on the theme of change — dealing, again, with that period of the military dictatorship under General Kassem (1958-63), just before the Revolution that brought the present government to power.

The first story is about a village of farmers who submit to the will of rich landowners and leave their lands on the pretext that there's too much salt in the earth, whereby the government takes over. The villagers slowly awaken to the reality that they should return to their land to work for the removal of salt from the earth, but other farmers feel it is too restricted under governmental control and leave the land — until the dawn of a new day, the Revolution, comes.

The second story deals with a pregnant girl, who fights against her angry relatives for the right to keep her baby and even the right to live (in view of old tribal laws that demand her death). The girl's struggle for change forecasts the new society of today.

Pic is well acted, and stories are self-contained "shorts" that hold together well from beginning to end. "The Experiment" deserves an unspooling at Iraqi film weeks and the line. —*Holl.*

Al Raas
(The Head)
(IRAQI-COLOR)

Berlin, Jan. 18.

An Iraqi General Organization for Cinema production. Baghdad: world rights, Iraqi General Organization for Cinema. Baghdad. Features entire cast. Written and directed by Faisal Al Yassiry. Camera (color), Majid Kamil. Reviewed at Deutsche Werbung Screening Room, Berlin, Jan. 18, '80. Running time: **100 MINS.**

Cast: Kasim Mohammed, Kaid Al Nomani, Sami Kafan, Z. Al Rubain.

The first feature film produced by the Iraqi General Organization for Cinema, Faisal Al Yassiry's "The Head" (1977) — the same director later made "The River" (1978) and "The Sniper" (1979) — is based on a true story of an archaeological-treasure theft that also provided the theme of a commendable documentary film. Yassiry principle faults are a too-slick script and a style of direction that imitates the typical television-oriented detective thriller.

Pic begins with a sequence set in Hatra in 180 B.C. This "city of the sun" in the north of present-day Iraq was the capital of the First Arab Kingdom, and for that reason its ruins and archaeological treasures (diggings are still being undertaken) are of more than passing interest to Arab peoples. The bust, or "head," of the last reigning monarch of Hatra before the city's downfall is preserved at the original site.

As the story goes, this head was stolen by an Iraq living on the border and then smuggled out of the country. The treasure, however, proved too hot to handle and couldn't be sold to prospective buyers. Interpol was brought into the case, and the thief traced from Iraq across Syria to Beirut in Lebanon, where the head was recovered.

Good beginning for a budding Iraqi film industry. —*Holl.*

Demons du midi
(Demons of the South)
(FRANCO-SPANISH-BELGIAN-COLOR)

Paris, Jan. 7.

A Gaumont release of a C.P. Production (France)/2000 Production (Belgium)/Imago International (Spain) co-production. Features entire cast. Produced and directed by Christian Paureilhe. Screenplay, Paureilhe and Sylvie Coste; camera (Eastmancolor), Georges Barsky, Lionel Legros; editor, Delphine Desfons; music, Michel Bernolhc. Reviewed at the Paramount Elysees cinema, Paris, Dec. 11, 1979. Running time: **103 MINS.**

Francois .... Pierre Mondy
Rose .... Micheline Presle
Helene .... Sylvie Coste

Yet one more road film about world-weariness and the quest for renewal, "Demons du midi" tells of a disgruntled, middle-aged Parisian (played with pugnacious appeal by Pierre Mondy) who turns his back on the ruins of his life and takes to the southern roads in search of something else.

That something else turns out to be the errant life of an outlaw, as Mondy, accompanied by a young actress he has picked up, robs stores and banks to subsidize this new freedom. After a dispute the couple breaks up. Mondy heads for Spain where he is shot down in cold blood by the police.

The film is trite and superficial. Director-writer Christian Paureilhe, who has previously worked in an avant-garde vein, tries unsuccessfully to mix in a touch of the bizarre and the fantastic, particularly in the scene of Mondy's death, though the action remains predominantly and flatly realistic. Micheline Presle, as an old girlfriend of Mondy, and coscripter Sylvie Coste, as the actress, do the best they can with underwritten roles. —*Len.*

Haine
(Hate)
(FRENCH-COLOR)

Paris, Jan. 3.

A Gaumont release of a Radio-Cine/S Productions co-production. Stars Klaus Kinski, Maria Schneider. Written and directed by Dominique Goult. Camera (color), Roland Dantigny; music, Alain Jomy; editor, Jean-Claude Bonfanti. No other credits provided. Reviewed at the Gaumont screening room, Neuilly, Dec. 20, 1979. Running time: **90 MINS.**

Stranger .... Klaus Kinski
Madeleine .... Maria Schneider
Truckdriver .... Patrice Melennes

"Haine," a first feature by Domique Goult, is a conventional action tale heavily dressed up in metaphysics and social comment. Klaus Kinski plays a motorcyclist whose bike breaks down in a small French town where a little girl has just been run down, ostensibly by a cyclist. Suspicions focus on Kinski, who finds sympathy in the person of Maria Schneider, socially ostracized by the comunity for having an illegitimate child. Led by a burly, demonic truck driver, several of the townsmen form a lynch mob, hunt the cyclist down and kill him.

Goult's script is a multi-level muddle. A murky amalgam of Fritz Lang's "Fury," "Easy Rider," Steven Spielberg's "Duel" and the New Testament, "Haine" shapes up as a religious parable with Kinski playing Christ against Schneider's Mary Magdalena. It ends, of course, in a "crucifixion," with Kinski being hung up on an electric generator and given the juice!

As director, Goult shows more auspicious ability when he isn't indulging a penchant for hyperbolic visions. He can ably create an atmosphere of sustained menace and compose shots of intriguing ambiguity. He directs the action sequences reasonably well. Best of all, he has cast well, using his actors more for their presence than for their acting talents. (In this respect Schneider and Patrice Melennec, as Kinski's brutal antagonist, are fine). Kinski, in an unusual change from his diabolical, hell-bent personae, taps a stream of quiet warmth that is refreshing. —*Len.*

Prune Des Bois
(The Wolf-cubs of Niquoluna)
(BELGIAN-COLOR)

Brussels, Jan. 16.

C.D.E.C. release of Violette and Jacques Vercruysen production. Directed by Marcel Lobet. Features entire cast. Screenplay, Kathleen de Bethune, Marielle Paternostre, adapted by Marcel Lobet; camera (Eastmancolor), Michel Baudour; music, Pierre Perret; production design, Viviane Fleming; sound, Henri Morelle; editor, Anne Christophe. Reviewed at Passage 44, Brussels, Jan. 16, 1980. Running time: **81 MINS.**

Gaspard .... Christian Marin
Grandmother .... Arlette Biernaux
Teacher .... Bonbon Lamy
Emilien's Father .. Alexandre von Sivers
Police Superintendant ...... Michel Castel
Florette .... Julie Dubart
Charlie .... Quentin Staes
Emilien .... Alexandre Chikowsky
Julie .... Maud Noerdinger
Felicite .... Emmanuelle Taymans
Charlotte .... Isabelle Bourgeois

A rarity in Belgian film production: a children's film and what is even more exceptional, one that avoids the pitfalls of the genre in being neither maudlin nor childish. Young unprofessional players, devoid of inhibitions and with a certain amount of spontaneity, act pleasantly enough. (But perhaps the greatest asset of this fairy-tale is in the fact that there is an over-all freshness, proof that is Marcel Lobet, whose first feature it is, has an understanding of the juvenile mentality. Only the adults tend to bring an artificiality to their parts. Many are out of tune with the younger set.

It concerns four children of about 10 who discover an abandoned babe in the woods and decide to look after it without telling anyone (a la "The Little Kidnappers"-Ed.). This compels them to act not only with increased caution, but also to shed some of their good little devils status, in view of complications created but their elders. Nevertheless all ends well.

A little on the longish side but charmingly done and technically sound. Shown in world premiere on the eve of the Belgian Film Festival and received enthusiastically by an invited audience of youngsters and parents.—*Flor.*

Tous Vedettes
(All Stars)
(FRENCH-COLOR)

Paris, Jan. 9.

A Gaumont release of a Gaumont International/Productions Marcel Dassault co-production. Produced by Alain Poire. Features entire cast. Written and directed by Michel Lang. Music, Mort Shuman; songs, Shuman, Lang, Claude Lemesle; camera (Eastmancolor), Daniel Gaudry; editor, Helene Plemiannikov; sound, Alain Sempe; art director, Bernard Evein; costumes, Annie Perier. Reviewed at the Gaumont screening room, Neuilly, Jan. 8, 1980. Running time: **120 MINS.**

Cast: Leslie Caron, Remi Laurent, Kitty Kortes-Lynch, Jerome Foulon, Francoise

Pinaud, Claude Swieca, Daniel Ceccaldi, Robert Webber.

———

"Tous Vedettes' is a vapid American-style musical comedy with French-dressing. Writer-director Michel Lang, who scored with audiences here with youth comedies like "A Nous les Petites Anglaises" and "L'Hotel de la Plage," shows little aptitude at concocting one of those ethereal, joyous confections to which Hollywood held the recipe.

Just so the viewer won't be mistaken about his models, Land dusts off the old Let's-Put-On-A-Show plot and sets it in the world of the Paris music conservatory. And not only does he get Leslie Caron to play a secondary role, he also comes up with a young American dancer and actress, Kitty Kortes-Lynch, who's a dead ringer for Caron. Naturally they are cast as mother and daughter.

"Tous Vedettes" has plenty of youthful energy, but it almost completely lacks humor, invention and charm. The direction is all push-and-shove, making the boys rather obnoxious and the girls insipid — only young Francoise Pinaud, as a pretty Conservatory student from the provinces, manages to exude some personality and appeal. The music, by Frenchified Yank composer Mort Shuman, is plastic and forgettable. The choreography is pure amateurism.

Caron, still elfinly attractive and looking marvelously fit, has a perfectly thankless role as an ex-Hollywood star who enjoys a guiltless fling with her daughter's boy friend while awaiting the return of estranged hubby Robert Webber, a hot-shot producer. She sings a little and dances, briefly, only at the conclusion, along with the rest of the cast. Rather than give the film an aura, Caron's presence reminds us of what this sorry affair is not.
—*Len.*

Bangalore Fest

Kummatty
(Bogeyman)
(INDIAN-COLOR)

———

Bangalore, Jan. 29.
General Pictures release and production. Features entire cast. Directed by G. Aravindan. Screenplay, K.N. Pannicker. Aravindan: camera (color), Shaji; editor, Rameshan. Reviewed at Bangalore Film Fest, Jan. 14, '80. Running time, 90 MINS.
With: Ramunni, Ashokan, Vilasini Reema, Kothara Gopalkrishnan.

———

Ostensibly a children's film, G. Aravindan has given this a lyrical mounting, an insight into child fantasy that should make it one for adults as well.

Made in a little village, it concerns the play of its children, their running about, their detachment from local things until a sort of scary holy man turns up whom they all take to.

Childhood seems a sacred part of Indian life, especially rurally, and here, in this Malayalam film from Southern India, this is vividly portrayed. One day the holy man, whom the children see is also a mortal, changes them all into animals for a brief time to feel the freedom of this state and then changes them back before going off.

But one boy, as a mongrel dog, is chased by another dog and so remains in the canine state. He is picked up by a rich young girl for an amusing stay among large pedigreed dogs who resent him.

He finally gets home and is recognized by his mother. But no exorcism will help. Then the Holy Man, played with rambunctious good nature by musician and dancer Ramunni, returns to turn the boy back into his own shape.

G. Aravindan has a poetic flair and this film should find its way at festivals and could be a specialized entry for children and adults on its beauty and feeling for childhood fantasy. Color, lensing, playing are all assets. —*Mosk.*

Ekdin Pratidin
(And Quiet Rolls the Day)
(INDIAN-COLOR)

———

Bangalore, Jan. 29.
Mrinal Sen Productions release and production. Features entire cast. Written and directed by Mrinal Sen from a story by Amalendu Chakraborty. Camera (Color), K.K. Mahajan; editor, G. Naskar. Reviewed at Bangalore Film Fest, Jan. 16, '80. Running time, 95 MINS.
Woth: Gita Sen, Mamata Shankar, Satya Banerjcee, Srila Majundar.

———

Mrinal Sen is probably the only other Indian filmmaker, besides Satyajit Ray, to have some international standing. However Sen's is mainly through festival outings without the number of prizes and releases in Western countries that have made Ray a world film figure.

Sen's new film might just give him some chances in getting specialized outlets in more world markets as well as emerging a surefire festival film that should make its way on the world fest circuits this year.

Often his films have been full of anger and political and social overkill on such themes as unemployment, social adjustment, poverty and changing mores. Here he is more measured and effective in dealing with a family crisis that mirrors the fragile structure of a lower middle-class family on the border of economic chaos.

They live in an old house and are supported by the older daughter who works in an office. There is the put upon mother, a teenage daughter studying at school, an unemployed older son, two younger children and the unemployed father.

One evening the breadwinner is late and this sets off the simmering doubts in the family about themselves rather than real worry about the daughter. There are frantic calls to her office, and visits to the morgue, hospitals and the police all to no avail.

It enlists the help, curiosity and resentment of others in this old, once elegant house as well as riling the stuffy old landlord who feels it an affront to his house and order.

The daughter finally comes home, having tried to call a local store to relay the message that she would be late but no one had answered. The family first treats her with disdain, having had to face up to its problems of inertia and evasion, but eventually does appear to come to grips with these problems.

The film is well acted and has a fine insight into the simple human dilemmas that still go deep in a society beset by economic woes, a certain stasis and a look at emerging women workers who are suspect and often forced to give up their own lives to maintain a family.

Fine hues, shrewd ensemble playing aid the well-honed directorial control of this dramatic yarn that is universal in theme as well as remaining resolutely Indian in its treatment. —*Mosk.*

The Great Indian Film Bazaar
(INDIAN/DOCU-COLOR-B&W)

———

Bangalore, Jan. 29.
Kshirsagar release and production. Written and directed by Sridhar Kshirsagar. Camera (Color), S.D., Deodhar; editor, Javed Sayyed. Reviewed at Bangalore Film Fest, Jan. 16, '80. Running time, 150 MINS.

———

A compilation film that tries to give an indication of the usual diversity of Indian films, two are made a day, and a history of it all as well. It is hard to judge about choices but it does give a picture of the background and various kinds of films from its many filmmaking sections.

The Bombay musical extravaganzas are there as well as Satyajit Ray and his more revealing films on Indian life. There are interviews with many top names and it adds up to a film worth using in Indian Film Weeks.

But aside from its information and generally well selected scenes and interviews, film remains didactic and is mainly for its own shores.

School, archive and museum use are indicated with tv possibilities also inherent in this interesting though necessarily diffuse look at the immense Indian film industry.
—*Mosk.*

Ma Bhoomi
(Our Land)
(INDIAN-B&W)

———

Bangalore, Jan. 29.
Production Co., C. Chitra release and production. Features entire cast. Directed by Goutam Ghose. Screenplay, Kishan Chander, Partho Bannerji, Narasing Rao; camera, Kamal Naik; editor, Raj Gopal. Reviewed at Bangalore Film Fest, Jan. 10, '80. Running time, 150 MINS.
With: Siachand, Bhpal Reddy, Yadagini, Kakarala.

———

A forceful film that has enough feel for personal revolt and achieving consciousness to stave off social realism and emerge a rare Indian film of political probity.

However, its familiar tale may make this more a local item though it could find mileage at festivals.

In the early Forties, before independence in the Southern area of Andrha Pradesh where Telegu is spoken, a young boy of peasant stock shows some independence at the cruel ways of the Nizma landowners who treat the peasants as serfs.

Grown up, he leaves when his girl has to give into a landlord's sex demands. He finally meets a kindly Marxist activist who instills him with a new outlook. But his village has been devastated by butchery when the peasants take over the land after independence.

However, landlords are again installed after the state is formed and the struggle goes on. Perhaps familiar, but still effective despite its one-sided outlook and marking an interesting new director in Goutam Ghose. —*Mosk.*

Akramana
(The Conquest)
(INDIAN-B&W)

———

Bangalore, Jan. 29.
S. Sainath Productions, Prod. Co. release and production. Features entire cast. Directed by Girish Kasaravalli. Screenplay, G.S. Sadashiv; camera, S. Ramahchandra; music, B.V. Karanth. Reviewed at Bangalore Film Fest, Jan. 11, '80. Running time, 121 MINS.
With: Vijaya Kashi, Vaishali Kasaravilli.

———

One of the rare films from Kannada in Southern India leaving the villages for a contemporary subject in the big city. It concerns a young man's romantic education.

Film has some flair in detailing youthful romantic problems but is familiar, surface and finally arbitrary in its delineating the various affairs.

One man falls for an older woman who has left her husband. But he is too callow to extricate her from the need to return to her husband when he can offer nothing to her.

Another is taken in by a flighty girl. Pic marks a welcome change from the more somber Indian films, yet seems somewhat dated for chances outside its borders.

— *Mosk.*

Grihapravesh
(The Housewarming)
(INDIAN-COLOR)

———

Bangalore, Jan. 29.
Production Co. release and production. Stars Sanjeev Kumar, Sharmila Tagore. Written and directed by Basu Bhattacharya. Camera (Color). Adeep Tandon; editor, Om Prakash Takkar; music, Kanu Roy; lyrics , Gular. Reviewed at Bangalore Film Fest, Jan. 13, '80. Running time: 144 MINS.
Husband ....Sanjeev Kumar
Wife .... Sharmila Tagore
Girl .... Sarika

———

Basu Bhattacharya is a Bengali working in the nationally more accessible Hindi films in Bombay. Entertainment is the thing, and here he cloaks a romantic triangle in some shrewd plotting, agile dialog and evasive eroticism but still remains on surface in a film with mainly local chances.

A fairly successful white collar worker, with a lovely wife and child, finds himself pursued by the office lovely whom he at first ignores. Love blooms, with secret meetings and kisses, still forbidden in local pix, blocked by scarves, etc. He finally is won back by his wife. Though mainly a local item, director Bhattacharya is to be watched when he decides to take on more challenging subjects.—*Mosk.*

Cruising
(COLOR)

———

Too sexplicit, despite R rating.

———

Hollywood, Feb. 12.
United Artists release of a Lorimar presentation. Produced by Jerry Weintraub. Stars Al Pacino. Written and directed by William Friedkin, based on the novel by Gerald Walker. Camera (color), James Contner; music, Jack Nitzsche, performed by The Cripples; production designer, Bruce Weintraub; art director, Edward Pisoni; editor, Bud Smith; asst. director, Alan Hopkins. Reviewed at MGM Studios, Culver City, Calif., Feb. 11, 1980. (MPAA Rating: R) Running time: 106 MINS.
Steve Burns .... Al Pacino
Capt. Edelson .... Paul Sorvino
Nancy .... Karen Allen
Stuart Richards............Richard Cox
Ted Bailey ....Don Scardino
Patrolman DiSimone .... Joe Spinell
Skip Lee .... Jay Acovone
Det. Lefransky ....Randy Jurgensen
Dr. Rifkin .... Barton Heyman
Da Vinci ....Gene Davis
Det. Blasio ....Sonny Grosso

From a trade standpoint, "Cruising" may be remembered in the future as a picture that caused exhibitors more concern over the rating system than it agitated the gay community. If this is an R, then the only X left is actual hardcore — and that will kill business in the broad marketplace, leaving whatever dollars the big dispute can generate in urban playoff.

To put it bluntly, if an R allows the showing of one man greasing his fist followed by the rising ecstasy and pain of a second man held in chains by others, then there's only one close-up left for the X.

That is but one of many similar scenes "Cruising" has to offer as writer-director William Friedkin explores the S&M life of New York City. Like any approach to the bizarre, it is fascinating for about 15 minutes. After that, it suffers from the same boring repetition that makes porno so uninteresting generally.

In many respects, "Cruising" resembles the worst of the "hippie" films of the 1960's, lingering endlessly on the trappings of a different lifestyle without employing them for dramatic advantage.

Taking away the kissing, caressing and a few bloody killings, Friedkin has no story, though picture pretends to be a murder mystery combined with a study of Al Pacino's psychological degradation.

But there is no suspense and Pacino's Tee-shirt-and-leather-jacket scenes with others all seem designed to show who can best play Marlon Brando.

First-scene Pacino is an innocent young cop chosen by detective chief Paul Sorvino to go underground in search of a killer who's been taking sadism to the ultimate.

For the first half of the picture, Pacino literally walks through his part, wandering from one kinky enclave to another.

Finally, he picks up a false trail, causing his fellow cops to brutalize an innocent young gay in hopes of a confession. (Throughout the film New York police are pictured as either slow and stupid, or sadistic — which could make for an interesting picket line if they chose to join the gays out front.)

Pacino ultimately zeroes in on the culprit but by now is almost as far around the bend as his prey, which seems to be the thought Friedkin finds interesting. But that's not saying much more than the old maxim: "he who lies down with dogs gets up with fleas."

That saying, of course, is always unfair to the dogs, just as "Cruising" is probably unfair to some people. The film just takes longer to make its mistakes. —*Har.*

Verden er fuld af boern
(It's A World Full Of Children)
(DANISH-COLOR)

———

Copenhagen, Feb. 2.
An A/S Panorama (Just Betzer) production and release. State Film Institute production consultants, Sven Methling and Frits Raben. Written by Aase Schmidt and Henrik Herbert. Directed by Aase Schmidt. Features entire cast. Camera (Eastmancolor) Henrik Herbert; production design, Palle Arestrup; editor, Lizzi Weischenfeldt; music, Henning Christiansen; main title lyrics, Niels Lund. Reviewed at Palladium, Copenhagen, Feb. 1, 1980. Running time: 99 MINS.
Susanne .... Karen-Lise Mynster
Morten .... Jasper Christensen
Bo .... Kurt Ravn
Lisbeth .... Lane Lind
Frank .... Per Pallesen
Birthe .... Solbjoerg Hoejfeldt

———

Susanne, a journalist, and Morten, a cellist, very much want a child. Whose fault is it when Susanne remains non-pregnant? It is obviously a cause for much discussion, many tears. Later, the situation leads to more or less desperate acts, a little drunkenness, solace for her with a nice, discreet lover, etc. But the title's observation that this is "A World Full Of Children" leads Aase Schmidt's first feature towards a sunlit ending.

Schmidt, who cowrote the original story and script with her cinematographer-husband Henrik Herbert, has a very honest and relevant everyday story to tell and she tells it with a blend of solid information smacking of documentarism and keen eye as well as ear for the way middlebrow intellectuals like Susanne and Morten and their friends and relations go through life's strained situations.

Although the actors perform well (and Karen-Lis Mynster as Susanne even strongly), they are given

---

so many obviously good lines and opinions to air that audiences too often will feel themselves removed from theatre to classroom in either drama, gynecology or sociology school. Distribution handling with a view to specialized situations could however move "A World Full Of Children" safely across a few borders. —*Kell.*

Savithri
(The Wife)
(INDIAN-COLOR)

———

Bangalore, Jan. 29.
Production Co., Hamzu Films release and production. Features entire cast. Directed by T.D. Ranga. Screenplay, Ram Sha, Ranga; camera (Color), Barun Mukherjee; editor, J. Stanley; music, Gunasingh. Reviewed at Bangalore Film Fest, Jan. 9, '80. Running time: 102 MINS.
With: H.G. Somashekara, Anil Thakker, Vasant Kumar, Ashwini.

———

The village in this film evokes cruelty as well as love. Sometimes the village is treated lyrically as a place where one is in harmony with nature as a place where caste, power and rivalries are destructive.

Film is made in a measured way and in the form of a tragedy bringing to mind "Romeo and Juliet." The lovely girl of a rich landowner and a new schoolteacher are pawns in the enmity of her father and another village bigwig who have been conducting a vendetta for years.

The girl loves the teacher but he is of lower caste. The girl is abducted by the girl's father's enemy and married off to the teacher. The father manages to have the teacher jailed and then murders him when he comes back to claim her and a child she has had by him.

Pic is solidly made, but somewhat repetitive and slow. Theme is worthy but too discursive to make its tragic denouement effective as a catharis of man's inhumanity brought on by old enmities and backward ways. —*Mosk.*

Pacific High
(COLOR)

———

All about a sailboat race. Limited outlook.

———

Hollywood, Feb. 5.
Produced by Roy Edward Disney. Directed by Michael Ahnemann. Camera (Metrocolor), Stephen H. Burum; editors, Thomas Stanford, Michael Ahnemann; sound, Peter Pilafian; music, Robert F. Brunner. Reviewed at MGM Studios, Culver City, Feb. 5, 1980. (MPAA rating: R). Running time: 90 MINS.

———

With an R rating and a title like "Pacific High," this picture could easily be mistaken for another bare-skinned story of errant west coast youth. But any theatre that books it on that basis is in for a surprise.

"Pacific High" is all about a sailboat race and what few girls there are remain fully clothed in the background. The R rating, which producer Roy Edward Disney appealed in vain, lies solely in the sailors' salty language.

As a documentarian, Disney carries on the family name quite well. (He's the son of Roy O. and nephew of Walt.) Directed by Michael Ahnemann with Stephen H. Burum guiding a crew of seven cameramen, film has a solid professional quality, capturing all of the beauty of boats under sail.

But a sailboat race at its best offers limited commercial appeal and this particular contest — an annual event from Newport Beach, Calif. to Ensenada, Mex. — is extremely void of excitement, winding up at the finish in a dead-air doldrum with the winners drifting to victory.

Disney does expose the sailing fanaticism he shares with his fellow yachtsmen, but too much of the visual action consists of these same fanatics rushing about on deck, yanking ropes and hauling canvas. More often than not, it's impossible for a landlubber to know what they are doing, or why.

Consequently, "Pacific High" is strictly for those who sail themselves. And they spend their weekends on water, not at the theatre.

—*Har.*

La Gueule de l'autre
(The Other One's Mug)
(FRENCH-COLOR)

Paris, Jan. 4.
An AMLF release of a Films Gibe/Sara Films/Antenne 2 co-production. Stars Jean Poiret, Michel Serrault. Directed by Pierre Tchernia. Written by Jean Poiret. Camera (color, Rene Mathelin; music, Claude Bolling; art director, Willy Holt; editor, Francoise Javet; sound, Jean-Philippe Le Roux. Reviewed at the Marignan-Concorde theatre, Paris. Jan. 3, 1980. Running time: 90 MINS.
Martial Perrin
Gilbert Brossard . . . . Michel Serrault
Constant . . . . Jean Poiret
Marie-Helene Perrin . . . . . . Andrea Parisy
Gisele Brossard . . . . Bernadette Lafont
Wilfrid . . . . Curt Jurgens

Jean Poiret, author of the phenomenally successful "Cage aux Folles," wrote and costars in this mostly mechanical, lightweight comedy about a third-rate actor who must stand in for his look-alike cousin, a politician, who's gone into hiding to avoid being gunned down by an escaped killer, out to avenge himself on his enemies.

Most of this is routine, knee-jerk comedy. But one laughs easily because the double role is dexterously filled by the imaginative Michel Serrault, who transforms two scenes into small comic gems.

The association Poiret-Serrault-"Cages aux Folles" could give film commercial viability at U.S. box-offices.

Pierre Tchernia, a tv pro who has directed two other films, wisely allows Serrault easy maneuvering amid the generally predictable comic setpieces, but pretty much ignores the secondary roles. Poiret, as a political advisor, plays straight man-catalyst to Serrault, which isn't surprising, because the two have worked in the theatre as a highly successful comedy team.

The two scenes that will regale the viewer are that in which Serrault-actor must address a political rally in playback, with the poor man ignorant of the text and the recording machine slightly out of whack!; and a climactic tv political debate in which Serrault, utterly unversed in the issues, tackles his opponent on his bad acting technique. —*Len.*

Manaos
(ITALIAN-MEXICAN-SPANISH-COLOR)

Madrid, Jan. 25.
Federico G. Aicardi (Rome). Producciones Elmes S.A. (Mexico) and Izaro Films S.A. (Madrid) coproduction. Written and directed by Alberto Vazquez Figueroa, based on his novel of the same name. Features entire cast. Exec producer, Carlos Vasallo; camera (Eastmancolor), Alejandro Ulloa; editor, Sigfrido Garcia; music, Fabio Frizzi; sets, Kliomenes Stomatiades. Reviewed at Cine Velazque, Madrid. Jan. 25, '80. Running time: 94 MINS.
Cast: Fabio Testi, Agostina Belli, Jorge Rivero, Andres Garcia, Florinda Bolkan, Alberto de Mendoza, Alfredo Mayo, Milton Rodrigues, Jorge Luke, Carlos East.

Set in 19th century Brazil, "Manaos" suffers from the shortcoming endemic to many coproductions that try to cram as much adventure into a film as they can, without ever concerning themselves with plot or character development, nor often bothering to explain the most elemental points of the story.

The "action" in "Manaos" tumbles over itself with feverish haste, with nary a dramatic situation ever built up. There are crocodiles, an infra-human rubber plantation in the jungle, Indian attacks, a rape scene, interlarded with an occasional bit of embarrassingly flat dialog. There are plantation slave revolts, a fight to the death in a raft about to plunge over a waterfall, and even an attempt at humor in a gentlemanly boxing bout, but none of it adds up to anything. We are painfully in the 20th century throughout, as the modern disco music in the background seems to suggest.

Story, what there is of it, concerns the revolt of several foreigners (seemingly American and Venezuelan) on a rubber plantation in Brazil, and their effort to flee with seeds of the rubber plant, which heretofore was a Brazilian monopoly.

Two of the brawny men, attended by an Indian guide and, what else, a young damsel who has been sorely used by the plantation owner in his brothel, make their way overland to Ecuador, a 90-day voyage condensed into a few minutes on film. They then come all the way back to Manaos, seize a Robert E. Lee typ. paddle steamer and one of them makes good his escape while the second dies at the hands of the villain.

Despite its two-dimensional infantilism, choppy editing, and poor direction item should do well in quick play-offs and in unsophisticated areas where plot considerations are unimportant and the virtually non-stop action will satisfy those with a craving for exotic spears, he-man prowess and gratifying violence. —*Besa.*

Blue Suede Shoes
(BRITISH-DOCU-COLOR)

Cannes, Jan. 23.
A Kendon Films production. Executive producer, Don Boyd. Produced by Penny Clark. Directed by Curtis Clark. Documentary on rock 'n' roll revival in Britain, featuring Bill Haley, Ray Campi and the Rockabilly Rebels, Freddie Fingers Lee, Flying Saucers, Crazy Cavan and the Rhythm Rockers, Matchbox. Camera (color), Roger Deakins; editor, Hugh Newsam; sound, Doug Turner, Ron Fawcus; production manager, Vivien Pottersman. Reviewed at the Salle de Miramar theatre, Cannes. Jan. 22, '80. Running time: 97 MINS.

Safest way to handle this documentary on the British revival of '50s rock 'n' roll would seem to be as a makeweight item in markets where confirmed fans of the music can be counted on to sit through almost any homage to crepes and drapes, however bland.

Director Curtis Clark apparently found little to comment upon in the time-warp spectacle of thousands of latter day "teddy boys" and jive-skirted girls descending on a northern English holiday camp last year for a weekend of thick hair-oil and heavy nostalgia. He's simply filmed the concerts and culled almost nothing in the way of either amusement or self-revelation from the too-few interviews with the near-religiously dedicated followers of a Neanderthal fashion.

Without a strong angle, to most tastes the theme is a husk. Seen one number, seen 'em all. Apart from some welcome archive footage of Gene Vincent and Eddie Cochran at the start of the film, and a few moments of curiosity value in veteran rock 'n' roller Bill Haley's appearance for a London concert at the end, the material mostly just grinds on.

Cinematography and stereo soundtrack are competent enough. But there's no concealing the fact that "Blue Suede Shoes" comprises only sufficient hard content to fill a short subject. In fact, radical scissoring with tv in mind may be advisable as a means of cutting both the deadwood and possible losses. —*Simo.*

Demon Lover Diary
(COLOR-DOCU-16M)

A film by Joel DeMott. (No other credits provided). Reviewed at Leacock, Pennebaker Screening Room, New York. Jan. 8, '80. Running time: 90 MINS.

Joel DeMott and her boyfriend Jeff Kreines set out with less-than-honorable intentions to observe the making of a cheapie horror film, "Demon Lover," brainchild of two Midwestern factory workers. Kreines had been hired as cameraman for the exploitation project, and DeMott trailed along with her own camera, hoping to document the endeavor.

"Demon Lover Diary" is the result, and it is an emotional, tense and jagged look at the making of both films, with more frustrations and dangerous complications than anyone anticipated.

It is clear from the start that DeMott and Kreines are at odds with the horror project, yet they persist amid the tacky sets, impromptu dialog, amateur acting, and crass enthusiasm of would-be filmmakers Don and Jerry. Among the other facets are the insurance fraud that served as sponsor for the project, the backstage rivalries and sexual games of the crew, and the unsuspecting nature of Don's religious mother.

DeMott also reveals herself, speaking directly to the camera, recording her own awkwardness and inexperience as she subverts the Midwesterner's get-rich scheme. The characters involved have enough color to make up for lapses in her filming technique.

At this point, the elemental technical credits are an asset to the veracity of "Demon Lover Diary," and interest is sustained for the length of the film. As it turned out, the diary is an infinitely more frightening and valid experience than the movie set out to be observed.

Already screened at the Whitney Museum and the Filmmakers Exposition, "Demon Lover Diary" seems a film suited for more and similar venues.— *Pege.*

Miami Film Fest

Klondike Fever
(COLOR)

Miami, Jan. 12.

A CFI Investments presentation. Produced by Gilbert W. Taylor. Directed by Peter Carter. Features entire cast. Screenplay, Charles E. Israel, Martin Lager; camera (color), Bert Dunk; editor, Stan Cole; music, Hagood Hardy; production designer, Seamus Flannery; special effects, John Thomas. Reviewed Jan. 12, 1980 at the Miami Film Festival. Running time: 60 MINS.

Jack London . . . . Jeff East
Soapy Smith . . . . Rod Steiger
Belinda McNair . . . . Angie Dickinson
Sam Steele . . . . Lorne Greene
John Thornton . . . . Barry Morse
Will Ryan . . . . Michael Hogan
Robin Gammell . . . . Merritt Sloper
Gertie . . . . Lisa Langlois
Louise . . . . Sherry Lewis

Although he was known as a novelist, American writer Jack London was basically a yarn-spinner. Peter Carter's "Klondike Fever," based on London's own exploits during the Klondike gold rush, tries hard to be story book cinema, but never succeeds in establishing the fascination that kept London's readers turning the pages as fast as they could.

The film has the look of one bound for television — and soon. It also has a bit of the Disney touch about it, but not enough of the Disney genius to make the stuff of solid G-fare.

Young, blonde Jeff East plays London as a clinched-jawed hero of high ideals and a stout heart. London and his partner (Robin Gammell) land in Skagway, Alaska, on their way to hit the Klondike trail. The young writer grits his teeth even more as he encounters the baseness of the gold-maddened men churning around him. When he sees a cruel trainer breaking dogs for the sleds, he rescues one, Buck, a good deed that leads to a string of troubles with Soapy Smith, a renegade priest who runs the town, played in steely fashion by Rod Steiger.

Angie Dickinson looks slightly silly playing one of those heart-of-gold saloon madams; Lorne Greene, almost unrecognizeable in a black mustache, stands for Canada's idea of law and order and Barry Morse is a good-guy vet who takes kindly to London's reckless mistakes.

The film is jerkily edited with some jarring transitions. Director Carter keeps losing track of the dog, leaving him out entirely in an unexciting scene in which London and company shoot some angry whitewater rapids.

"Klondike Fever" fails to caputre the spirit of adventure and excitement that drew London to the area in the first place, or the brute strength lionized in his own writings. As played by East, the adventurer-author looks as if he can hardly wait to get back to Beverly Hills. —Von.

Quatermass Conclusion
(BRITISH-COLOR)

Miami, Jan. 20.

A Euston Films Production. Produced by Ted Childs. Directed by Piers Haggard. Features entire cast. Camera (color), Ian Wilson; screenplay, Nigel Kneale; editor, Keith Palmer; music, Marc Wilkinson and Nick Rowley. Reviewed Jan. 20, 1980 at the Miami Film Festival. Running Time: 105 MINS.

Cast: John Mills, Simon MacCorkindale, Barbara Kellerman, Margaret Tyzack, Brewster Mason.

Barring reincarnation, "Quatermass Conclusion" is the final chapter in the tale of Britain's sci-fi hero, Prof. Bernard Quatermass. Nigel Kneale's screenplay first presents the genius as something of a dotard (though still capable of saving humanity), and puts the old gent out of misery forever in the last reel.

John Mills' portrayal of the sometimes eccentric scientist is a fine portrait, a definite plus in a film whose production value is firmly rooted in the ancestral '50s. Special effects are few, but their scarcity doesn't hide the lack of production value. Scenes of a death ray from space are acceptable, but an astronaut linkup is going to disappoint stateside sci-fi fanatics weaned on "Buck Rogers."

"Conclusion" has already aired on British TV and that seems its most logical future here. Some trimming will be necessary for a solo presentation. Theatrical potential may exist in some markets with a preference for the offbeat, and drive-ins.

Nonetheless, "Conclusion" is an intriguing armageddon epic. The space beam is theorized as an intergalactic straw, sucking nourishment by ionizing world youth. Screenplay and direction are just odd enough to generate interest along cult lines. Narrative style may be inconsistent, but the pic is genuinely macabre.

Quatermass disrupts a tv broadcast with an appeal to find his granddaughter, lost amid growing anarchy around the countryside. The broadcast is further bungled when an outer space docking procedure goes awry, causing the death of several dozen astronauts.

This setup is later bridged to more immediate, earthy concerns. But like several other scenes to follow, it's merely a colorful aside to the main plot.

The world's youth, fed up with bungled civilization, are drawn to prehistoric sites like Stonehenge where the beam, seen as a conveyance to a better planet, fries them for lunch. Quatermass and his cohorts eventually feed the ray an atomic bomb to cause permanent indigestion.

Mills' tireless dedication as the prof., and related efforts by Simon MacCorkindale as a freelance scientist, manage to hold attention in the absence of suspense. The classic '50s melodrama focuses on their efforts outside the military-scientific establishment, a thematic gambit with some mileage left. —Zink.

Cuba Crossing
(COLOR)

Miami, Jan. 12.

A Key West Production. Peter J. Barton, producer. Features entire cast. Written and directed by Chuck Workman. No other credits provided. Reviewed at the Miami Film Festival, Jan. 12, 1980. Running time: 90 MINS.

Capt. Tony Terracino . . . Stuart Whitman
Hudd . . . . Robert Vaughn
Bell . . . . Raymond St. Jacques
Tracy . . . . Caren Kaye
Titi . . . . Woody Strode
Veronica . . . . Sybil Danning
Maria . . . . Mary Lou Gassen
Delgato . . . . Albert Salmi
Rosselini . . . . Michael Gazzo
Bar gay . . . . Monty Rock 3d

"Cuba Crossing" sounds as if it should have sent a stir through Miami's huge Cuban population when it preemed during the Miami Film Festival, but it fell flatter than a plantainfritter.

The film is the first feature project by Tallahassee-based Peter J. Barton Productions, a successful regional studio noted for commercials and industrials. Further, pic is internationally linked with Berlin's Jack White Productions, at both financial and location ends. Crew included a sizable German contingent.

Narrative is supposedly based on a true incident, elaborated via use of the fictional "Capt. Tony" character. But it's hard to pin down exactly how true the situation is and where, or when, it occurred. There's an attempt to give the story a touch of authenticity via film clips of a cigar-chomping Castro and some phony Bay of Pigs action, but the latter are ridiculously transparent.

Most of the action takes place in Key West, where the film was lensed, and will no doubt please tourists who recognize the backgrounds. A bloated Stuart Whitman plays Capt. Tony, a hard-hitting soldier of fortune-ish bar owner who gets mixed up in a plot to assassinate Fidel.

At times the film is amateurish beyond comprehension, most scenes shot as if in rehearsal. There are hints of the erotic pleasures offered by the locale, as well as a couple of perversions. But the story never really gets into that, simply wasting footage without saying anything.

One scene in which two huge blacks wrestle before a yelling crowd, to the death, is inexcusably tasteless. The surviving gladiator attempts to claim a woman as his prize, but she's rescued by a valiant Whitman. —Von.

J-Men Forever
(BLACK & WHITE)

Miami, Feb. 5.

Produced by William Howard. Stars Phil Proctor and Peter Bergman, who also wrote the film's "scenario." No other credits provided. Reviewed at Lincoln Theatre, Miami Beach, Jan. 21, 1980 at the Miami Film Festival. Running time: 80 MINS.

Phil Proctor and Peter Bergman, one-half of the Firesign Theatre comedy troupe, have taken Woody Allen's "What's Up, Tiger Lily?" concept one step farther. In "Lily," Allen took a Japanese spy film and turned it into a comedy by over-dubbing his own dialog. In "J-Men," Proctor and Bergman use the same technique, but on adventure serials from the '30s and '40s — and have filmed themselves in black & white insert segments to keep the plot flowing smoothly.

What there is of a story is aimed straight at the midnight crowd: the central themes are rock music and drugs. Excerpts from the likes of "Captain America," "Rocket Man" and "Shazam" are used to good effect, spotlighting these heroes (J-Men all) as they do battle with the socalled Caped Madman.

The Caped Madman's mission is to pollute and destroy the world by popularizing rock 'n' roll ("I've invented the transistor, mister," he gloats). Captain Marvel's secret transformation word is no longer Shazam, but "Sh-Boom," and costumed superheroes — borrowing the tune from "off we go into the wild blue yonder — take to the air singing "Off I go wearing my tight pajamas."

The music, provided by Billy Preston and the Tubes, is almost too much for the J-Men. As a counter-attack, they develop MUSAC: Military Underground Sugared Airwaves Command. As a counter-counter-attack, the Caped Madman develops "hash gas" and distributes it via a Nazi regiment whose salute is "Shtay High!" The good guys win, and Proctor and Bergman celebrate their victory by passing a joint.

"J-Men Forever" isn't as clever or sophisticated as Firesign Theatre's record albums; it's closest to "The Further Adventures of Nick Danger" on their second disk. But it is visual, and what is most amazing is that the predominately young matinee crowd at the screening viewed was responding to the action from these 40-year old movie serials.

The humor is Proctor and Bergman's, but the trap doors, corny situations and marvelous miniatures are literally straight from the past — and still work, for a whole new generation. With proper promotion on the late-night circuit, "J-Men" should do quite well.

—*Bian.*

Human Experiments
(COLOR)

Miami, Feb. 5.
Produced by Summer Brown and Gregory Goodell. Executive producer, Edwin Scott Brown. Stars Linda Haynes, Geoffrey Lewis. Directed by Goodell. Screenplay, Richard Rothstein; camera (color), Joao Fernandes. Reviewed at the Miami Film Festival Lincoln Theatre, Miami Beach, Jan. 24, 1980. (MPAA: R). Running time: 82 MINS.
Rachel Foster .... Linda Haynes
Dr. Kline .... Geoffrey Lewis
Also: Ellen Travolta, Aldo Ray, Jackie Coogan.

The first 15 minutes of "Human Experiments" are excellent, leaking bits of information like Hitchcock at his best. Rachel Foster (Linda Haynes) is a small-time country & western singer who lugs her own amplifier to a series of one-night stands in remote towns. The opening minutes tell what her life is like: an endless string of rude patrons, lounge owners who rob her, cockroaches in motel bathrooms, paintings of velvet bullfighters above the smelly beds.

En route from one hell-hole to another, Rachel has an accident: a woman runs in front of her station wagon, and although Rachel reacts quickly, she's unsure whether she ran the woman over. Running out of her disabled car, she searches in vain for a body, but there's no sign of anyone. As she walks to the front porch of a nearby house, the camera lingers on the bushes by the roadside — and reveals the bloody corpse that Rachel failed to find.

Inside the apparently vacant home, Rachel dials the operator and asks for the police. While the phone rings, Rachel moves around the room, and a small patch of blood is visible on the wall next to the phone. Then she learns the truth: She has stumbled onto a mass murder in progress. An entire family has been killed by shotgun blasts, and is strewn about in various rooms of the house — an entire family, that is, except for the deranged little boy whom Rachel eventually finds sitting quietly in a back room, cradling his shotgun and aiming it at her. She shoots him first, the police arrive, and she is hurriedly tried and thrown into prison.

This opening sequence is carried off beautifully, without any of the cheap "scary music" that punctuates so many low-budget horror films. Unfortunately, this sequence is only a plot device to get Rachel into the prison where the "real horror" begins — and the real horror is much less convincing than the prolog.

She falls into the, clutches of a slightly deranged prison psychologist, Dr. Kline (Geoffrey Lewis), whose novel method of rehabilitation is to drive his subjects mad, erase all memories and program them with entirely new identities, memories and childhoods. To do this, he enlists the aid of the warden, and of nearly every other prisoner in the compound — an illogical and expensive way of doing things.

It does, however, allow for some memorable horror images, but the bulk of the film is illogical, an annoying admission considering the promise of the first reel.

Linda Haynes is very good as the put-upon prisoner; she looks like Season Hubley's "Hardcore" character, and brings more credibility to her part than it deserves. She deserves better — and so does the audience. —*Bian.*

Los Gusanos
(The Worms)
(CUBAN-COLOR)

Miami, Jan. 25.
A Danilo Bardisa production. Produced by Danilo Bardisa. Directed by Camilo Vila. Features entire cast. Screenplay, Camilo Vila, Danilo Bardisa from play by Eduardo Corbe; camera, (color), Ramon Saurez; editors, Stephen Sheppard, John Paul Jones; sound, Kert Vandermeulen; assistant director, Alan Martin. Reviewed at the Miami Film Festival, Jan. 25, 1980. Running Time: 95 MINS.
Pepe .... Orestes Matachena
Captain Morena .... Mario Pena
Lt. Valdez ...... Raymundo Hidalgo-Gato
Lucia .... Clara Hernandez
Ruben Rabinovich .... Marco Santiago
Garcia .... Ruben Rebasa
Caridad .... Doris Castellanos
Ricardo .... Reynaldo Medina
Theresa .... Angela Hayden
(Spanish with English subtitles)

The term "Los Gusanos" (The Worms) was a derogatory remark used by Fidel Castro to describe his political opponents. The Cuban-American drama of the same name, taken from a 1975 play first produced at the Cuban Cultural Center of New York, describes five prisoners captured by Castro forces in the early 1960s.

Made on a $24,000 budget three years ago in Santo Domingo, "Los Gusanos" played an initial engagement in Miami in late 1977 at a Spanish-speaking theatre, after which the negative and print disappeared. When it turned up damaged six months later, proceeds from its showcase were used for its reconstruction.

The narrative is a visceral prisoner-of-war drama which has propagandistic overtones, but which concerns itself primarily with both physical and emotional survival. Though claustrophobic in setting, action and dialog set a brisk pace which makes the film something of a chiller.

Pic has considerable potential in special engagement situations in major markets, with or without a heavy Latin population. Unfortunately, some portions of the negative could not be fully restored. Approximately 10 minutes of the film is grainy and washed out. The damaged footage is all in the first half of the film, involving substantial intercutting within as well as around scenes. The effect is disconcerting, though buffs and partisan viewers at a Miami Festival screening seemed willing to endure the situation without complaint. Nevertheless, an explanation with the opening credits seems apropos to avoid surprise and disappointment.

Otherwise, tech aspects are excellent, especially considering the film's budget. Photography by Ramon Suarez is clean and provocative.

Action takes place in a field headquarters in the Cuban jungle, where three male and two female prisoners undergo major tests of emotional endurance and political conviction in between bouts with a sadistic interrogator. Raymundo Hidalgo-Gato is compelling as the ambitious lieutenant seeking to "break" the captives. It's an impressive reversal: Hidalgo-Gato last portrayed an apartment handyman in "El Super."

Mario Pena offsets the horror as a concerned, humane captain in Fidel's army. Though at odds over his underling's tactics, he's just as eager to impress Soviet brass before the prisoners are transferred.

The narrative is terse, and the always-imminent threat of torture is a gnawing presence. The tale's stage roots are apparent via the pic's sense of visual as well as dramatic confinement, but its sweep of emotions, fears and ideals is fully realized in a tense, nerve-jangling tale of horror.

More importantly, the political themes are adroitly handled. Direction and screenplay tread a thin line between Castro and counter-revolutionary rhetoric. Honor is given its due, but survival is a major issue.

Emotional impact is resultingly strong from all angles. It only remains to be seen whether the film's narrative and thespic strengths can overcome the unfortunate discrepancies in print quality. —*Zink.*

Bangalore Fest

Grhana
(Eclipse)
(INDIAN-B&W)

Bangalore, Jan. 29.
Harsha Pictures, Production Co. release and production. Features entire cast. Directed by T.S. Nagabharana. Screenplay, T.S. Ranga, Kodalli, Shivaram, Nagabharana; camera, S. Ramachandra; editor, J. Stanley; music, Vijaya Bhaskar. Reviewed at Bangalore Film Fest, Jan. 6, '80. Running time: 125 MINS.
With: Anand Paricaran, Govind Rao, S.N. Rotti, B.S. Achar.

An imposing first film from the Southern Kannada section of India which was one of the best in the Indian Panorama at the Bangalore Film Festival. Film explores a strange, ancient rite with pungent effect that reveals the Indian mixture of ancient ways and modern inroads.

Though a film about moral stands and action, it builds up its tale with fine visual observation. Exotic, and seemingly dealing with residues of old ways, film still makes a potent statement on India's existing caste systems that can lead to inhumanity.

A village has a yearly ritual in which six untouchables are chosen to be high caste figures for two weeks. But they have to mortify themselves in the process. One dies and it seems he cannot be buried by Brahmins or untouchables.

The son of the village chief revolts against this and calls the police who cart off the body. At this breach of religious propriety, his father commits suicide and the son joins the untouchables. But he cannot really get to them, and when the ritual comes again, even the son of man he had buried joins in.

The latter however, regrets it and comes to him and admits it. The man tells him to run off and takes his place. But the untouchables toss him to an unruly crowd who beat him to death for his defiance of village and religious ways.

A film that transcends its strange milieu to make a statement on man's inhumanity to man in a terse style sans florid touches. Film is another to mark an unusual new director in T.S. Nagabharana.

—*Mosk.*

22nd June, 1897
(INDIAN-COLOR)

Bangalore, Jan. 29.
Nachiket Jayoo release and production. Features entire cast. Written and directed by Nachiket and Jayoo Patwardhan. Camera (Color), Navroze Contractor; editor, Madhu Sinha; music, Anand Modak. Reviewed at Bangalore Film Fest, Jan. 9, '80. Running time: 120 MINS.

With: Prabhakar Patankar, Ravindra Mankani, Udayan Dixit, Rod Gilbert.

A well-carpentered look at a true incident when three brothers murdered an English Civil Servant due to hatred of British ways and the inroads of Christianity.

Blown up from 16m, the subtle hues aid this mainly surface rendering of the incident. Made by a husband and wife team who are architects and film buffs, Nachiket and Jayoo Patwardhan, they could be film assets with more knowhow in dramatizing an incident.

The brothers, Hindu Brahmins, led a group who felt the English were threatening their ways and religion. Highhanded methods in fighting a plague, though ironically effective, led to a determination to kill the man in charge, Walter Rand.

They succeed but are hunted down by British police. Though not always clear, film still has finely etched portrayals of mainly surface characters and is a rare historical item worth including in Indian film weeks and specialized festivals.

Film appears a blueprint rather than a more incisive look into this incident of active rather than passive resistance to the Raj in 1897.
—*Mosk.*

Jhor
(The Storm)
(INDIAN-COLOR)

Bangalore, Jan. 29.
DPICA Production Co. release and production. Features entire cast. Written and directed by Utpal Dutt. Camera (Color), Dinen Gupta; editor, H. Mukhopadhya; music, P. Bhattacharya. Reviewed at Bangalore Film Fest, Jan. 15, '80. Running time: **100 MINS.**
With: Ujjal Sengupta, Indrami Mukhopadya, Sagarika Adhikari.

Utpal Dutt is a noted theatrical name in Bengal with his leftist oriented theatre. He is an actor as well as director. In this film he deals with the sudden, heady flowering of western rationalism in the early 1820s that brought on a flowering of social and artistic progress until it came into conflict with orthodox ways.

Film is too floridly played and didactic but does have some unusual feeling for a time of change put down by age old status and the use of religious outlooks by unscrupulous men.

It deals with a school run on European lines by a Portuguese-Indian, Derozio, who trained many of the future art and political names in Bengal history. The students save a woman from being committed to the funeral pyre of her husband, the suttee ritual now outlawed.

This leads to conflict with the authorities and his final losing battle, though he has implanted a need for change in his pupils. Mainly a local item, but Dutt may be more effective when he finds a visual way to treat his basically didactic yet interesting subject matter.—*Mosk.*

Peruvaziambalan
(A Dead End)
(INDIAN-B&W)

Bangalore, Jan. 29.
Bhadra Movie Makers. Production Co. release and production. Features entire cast. Written and directed by P. Padmarajan. Camera, Kannan Narayanan; editor, Ravi; music, M.G. Radhakishman. Reviewed at Bangalore Film Fest. Jan. 10, '80. Running time: **120 MINS.**
With: Gopi, Ashok, Lalitha, Aziz, Jose Prakash, Adoor Bhavani.

Another Indian film in b&w set in a village with a dramatic tale underscoring the Indian acceptance of injustice until a sudden burst of violence counteracts the kharma of fate and compliance.

However, the characters are broad and surface. Based on theme and treatment, film looks to make more inroads at home than abroad. It still marks new director P. Padmarajan a promising newcomer when he gains more visual control and depth in his narration.

A village bully, with wife and children, preys on young women while the whole town accepts and fears him. Returning from a short jail term for rape, he beats up the man who testified against him.

He then begins to go after two sisters of a young, slightly simple young man who tries to stand up to him. The bully goes after the boy with a knife. Latter, in a frenzy, manages to kill the man.

The villagers are relieved and one man who hated the bully hides him. But the boy decides to face life and see his sisters and finds the villagers afraid to help him. The boy goes to the bully's family for understanding as the film ends.

The film castigates cowardice but does so in a literary way and obscures the theme which should have been clearer in its visual telling.
—*Mosk.*

Ashwathama
(Wandering Soul)
(INDIAN-B&W)

Bangalore, Jan. 29.
Mohan Mohammed Films. Prod. Co. release and production. Features entire cast. Directed by K.R. Mohaman. Screenplay, P. Raman Nair from the book by Madampu Kunjukuttan; camera, Madhu Ambat; music, A. Padmanabhan. Reviewed at Bangalore Film Fest. Jan. 5, '80. Running time: **120 MINS.**
With: Madampu Kunjukuttan, Vidhubala, Vatsala, Ravi Menon.

Based on a book, with a contemporary updating of a mythological figure cursed to wander the earth as a mortal for 3000 years, film is languid but displays an incisive directorial pacing to make K.R. Mohaman a man to watch.

A college teacher comes afoul of outmoted religious, human and bureaucratic ways. But, as an Indian, his revolt remains individual and more an evasion than trying to cope or stand up to corrupt things he can not bide.

This makes the lead character, played with intensity by Madampu Kunjukuttan, author of the book on which the picture is based, somewhat phlegmatic and self destructive as he turns to drink, a prostitute and alienating his friends.

However, he decides suddenly to try to conform and marries a woman of family choice. She is good but an epileptic and cannot hold him in check as he again ruins a new job by returning to drink when the headmaster tries to influence his ways and teaching.

It ends with him in stasis as the society around him. Film is shot in chiaroscuro b&w that adequately reflects the internal pattern of this tortured but aimless character. Mainly a local item, but worthy of use at festivals or film weeks.
—*Mosk.*

Palermo-Wolfsburg
(WEST GERMAN-COLOR)

Berlin, Jan. 30.
A Thomas Mauch Film Production, Berlin. Features entire cast. Written and directed by Werner Schroeter. Dialog assistance, Giuseppe Fava; camera (color), Thomas Mauch; sound, Heiko von Swieykowski; sets & costumes, Alberte Barsaq, Magdalena Montezuma, Roberto Lagana; editing Schroeter. Reviewed at Geyer Screening Room, Berlin, Jan. 30, '80. Running time: **180 MINS.**

Nicola	Nicola Zarbo
Father	Calogero Arancio
Priest	Padre Pace
Land Owner	Cavaliere Comparato
Brigitte Hahn	Brigitte Tilg
Brigitte's Mother	Gisela Hahn
Antonio	Antonio Orlando
Giovanna	Ida de Benedetto
Lawyer	Magdalena Montezuma
State Attorney	Otto Sander
Judge	Johannes Wacker
Jury Member	Ula Stoeckl
Witness	Tamara Kafka
House Owner	Harry Baer
Translater	Ines Zamurovic

Werner Schroeter left the "underground" experimental field one film ago when he made the critically praised feature, "Kingdom of Naples" (1978), lensed in Italy with an Italian-speaking cast. Now he's in the running at the Berlin Film festival with a kind of sequel, "Palermo-Wolfsburg," shot in Sicily and West Germany. It's about a young foreign-worker leaving Palermo to work in the Volkswagen factory in Wolfsburg, an isolated industrial town near Hannover and the East German border.

Pic has three parts. The first section takes place in a poverty-stricken corner of Sicily, where religious superstition and patriarchal underdevelopment play a de-humanizing role in people's lives. The second focuses on the trip by train across the Italian boot to Northern Europe, where he finds ready employment in the automobile plant. And the third takes place in a German courtroom, after the lad has killed two toughs with his knife after his honor was challenged. Altogether, Schroeter had some 6-8 hours of film, which he edited to the present three-hour version.

The Palermo portrait is a gem, once again offering ample evidence that Schroeter is at his best when landscapes and atmosphere set style and tone. The boy's father is a drunkard, who has to be carried home to bed on occasions; his younger brother crawls into his bed for warmth and comfort on the day before the inevitable departure; a frightening, blood-splurged Passion Play is enacted as a fatalistic ritual; and a young wife decides to leave Sicily for West Germany too to find her husband who hasn't returned home or written.

These Mediterranean scenes of family-devotion are then contrasted with life in the cold North. The boy arrives at the station with an address in his hand, but can't communicate with passers-by to find lodging for the night, at the home of an acquaintance. When he finally gets there, the Sicilian is married to a German and he can't stay overnight, so he sleeps outdoors. Finally, an outgoing German girl working as an auto-mechanic helps him out, only to fall in love with her later.

Two Latins on the job befriend him, and he shares quarters in a barracks for foreign-workers. A former Italian prostitute now running a cafe also offers advice and substitutes for home by her kindness. But two toughs in the area take to teasing and tormenting, until one day he is pushed too far after losing his girlfriend — and he kills the German boys in a daze of vengeance.

The rest is the trial, which takes on a satirical edge to show how justice is sometimes blind and a mockery of human respect. The film shifts to filmed theatre (Schroeter directed legit productions in Bochum and Hamburg on the experimental-theatre side), and thereby gets hopelessly bogged down in rhetoric and sentiment.

There are some fine sketches in "Palermo-Wolfsburg," and Schroeter has an excellent eye for character roles. Nicola Zarbo as the lead, a nonprofessional, gives the bitter tale complete credibility, but even he gets lost in the crowded courtroom at the end. Lenser-producer Thomas Mauch contributes a flawless hand as usual.

A good bet for summer festival circuit and art houses. —*Holl.*

Der Preis Fuers Ueberleben
(The Price for Survival)
(WEST GERMAN-COLOR)

Berlin, Feb. 4.

A DNS-Film/Popular - Film — Les Films 66 Production, in collaboration with the Bayerischer Rundfunk, Munich. Producer, Veith von Fuerstenberg. Stars Michel Piccoli. Written and directed by Hans Noever. Dialog, Noever, Christian Watton, Patrick Roth; camera (color), Walter Lassally; music, Joe Haider; sets, Toni Luedi; editing, Christa Wernicke. Reviewed at Studio am Kudam, Berlin, Feb. 3, '80. Running time: **107 MINS.**

Rene Winterhalter	Michel Piccoli
Joseph C. Randolph	Martin West
Betty Randolph	Marilyn Clark
Kathleen Randolph	Suzie Galler
Thomas Randolph	Daniel Rosen
Old Jim	Ben Dova
Jim Maiello	Kurt Weinzierl
John Myers	Michael Stumm
State Attorney	Roger Burget
Mayor	Al Christy
Investigator	William Kuhlke
Sheriff	Charles Jones
Mr. Handcott	Henry Effertz
Henderson	Leonard Belove
Mulligan	John Haseltine
Smith	Charles Devault
Nixon	Paul Murphy

(English soundtrack)

Perhaps the clearest indication that "Author's Cinema" (Autoren-Kino) in West Germany has shot its wad is Hans Noever's "The Price for Survival," the opener at this year's Berlin Film Festival. Noever has done what Wim Wenders, Werner Herzog, and Wolfgang Peterson have been promising for some time — he shot a feature film about Americans in English in America. Further, he did it with an international star, Michel Piccoli, and an Oscar-winning lenser, Berlin-born Walter Lassally, as part of his team to guarantee commercial chances.

This gutsy, low-budget pic (by international standards), costing $1,-500,000, has "writer" stamped all over it. The very title owes a great deal to the detective genre, which Noever has an affinity for since making the docu, "Bannister Has Disappeared" (1974), in the States and the feature, "A Night with Chandler" (1978) (unspooled in the fest's "German Series"). The Chandler hard-boiled novels appear to be the "mean streets" he learned his trade on, for Noever began his own film career first as a writer and novelist.

The scene is Jefferson City, Missouri, the time is summer. A top-ranking employe (Martin West) in a fictitious IME (electronics) company is fired from his job one morning for no reason at all (company cutback), but he doesn't take it lying down — he goes out, purchases a gun, and in cold blood kills five

managers in the firm. Upon turning himself over to the police, he admits only to having killed "machines," instead of human beings. West is both convincing and moving as killer and victim.

His wife then also goes into shock, and is later committed to a mental clinic. The son is driven to suicide when his college chums ostracize him at a stock-car race. The daughter, who likes boyfriends a bit too much, straightens herself out to face the town's petty narrow-mindedness, but also hankers to leave for Chicago. And from Chi-Town comes a Swiss reporter, Rene Winterhalter, to investigate, and write on, the incident.

Michel Piccoli, as the Swiss reporter, figures the police are covering up the real facts by committing the killer to a mental institution. He says politely that "a madman would not have done what Mr. Randolph did," and just as obligingly gets a hired killer of his own on his tail. A friendly old taxi-driver, a Yank immigrant from Nazi Germany (played superbly to the hilt by Ben Dova), pals with the reporter and Randolph's reformed daughter to snoop out the reason for the hush-up — the company officials, it turns out, were all guilty of a poison-dumping scandal in the area some 20 years ago. Now that Piccoli has the story-behind-the-story, the only trick left in the bag is getting this scoop to his Chicago office.

Shot in six weeks with a mixed cast of Europeans and Americans, "The Price for Survival" is somewhat ragged around the story-edges, but still sufficiently offbeat to win fest auds in the manner Corman-Hellman-Cassavetes pix did a few decades back. The lack of drive usually associated with the detective thriller is more than compensated for by a tongue-in-cheek, love-hate yen for the American Way of Life. Thesps and lensing bring polish to this tale based on a real incident that occurred in the States.

Noever has proven he is a Teutonic helmer to watch in the future, and he has offered more evidence that Europeans can film features Stateside with few difficulties on limited budgets, provided the story fits. —*Holl.*

Winterreisen Im Olympiastadion
(Winter Trip in the Olympic Stadium)
(WEST GERMAN-COLOR)

Berlin, Feb. 4.

A Klaus Michael Grueber film production, in collaboration with Spender Freies Berlin (SFB). West Berlin, based on a Schaubuehne am Halleschen Ufer legit prod in the Berlin Olympic Stadium. Features entire cast. Text fragments, Friedrich Hoederlin's "Hyperion, or The Hermit in Greece;" artistic advisor, Bernard Pautrat, Ellen Hammer; images, An-

tonio Recalcati; camera (color), Wolfgang Knigge. Reviewed at Sender Fries Berlin Screening Room, Feb. 3, '80. Running time: **70 MINS.**

Cast: Armin Baumert, Andreas Eisenschenk, Thomas Foelsch, Wolfram Goetz, Hans-Peter Jaeggi, Heiko Neumann, Hans-Joachim Schulze, Martin Szafranski, Rainer Stender, Tina Engel, Eberhard Feik, Guenter Lampe, Felix Prader, Werner Rehm, Paul Burian, Gerd David, Ruediger Hacker, Jan Kauenhowen, Michael Koenig, Wolf Redl, Sabine Andreas, Grischa Huber, Christine Oesterlein, Otto Maechtlinger, Ruth Walz, Libgart Schwarz, Willem Menne.

Coincidentally, in this time of the threatened Olympic boycott, Klaus Michael Grueber's filmed adaptation of his own legit prod at the Schaubuehne am Halleschen Ufer in West Berlin, "Winter Trip in the Olympic Stadium," focuses on the 1936 Olympic Games in Berlin when Hitler attempted to bend sport to political pomp. But don't be fooled — the play itself was utilized to ponder the depths of Nazi Socialism in German traditions and culture.

Legit director Grueber became interested in tv-adaptations of his work while staging with the perfectionist Schaubuehne ensemble a series of plays on Germany's history, culture, and tradition: "Empedocles — Reading Hoederlin" (1975), "Winter Trip in the Olympic Stadium" (1976) (based on Hoederlin's novel "Hyperion"), and "Rudi" (1979) (based on one of Bernhard von Brentano's "Berlin Stories"). He rehearsed with his actors on "Empedocles" by recording scenes on videotape, almost a prerequisite in our present phase of "total theatre" productions.

Gruber also picked up some pointers while supervising, and directing, the tv-adaptation on electronic-tape of his Euripides production at the Schaubuehne, "The Bacchae" (1974), staged in a pavilion on the Berlin Fair Grounds. On that occasion, he broke all the accepted rules of "filmed theatre" by placing the camera right in the middle of the action and using appropriate "shots" to match both the dialog and the sense of the text. If critics had the chance to examine the finesse with which this legit-tv-film helmer lensed "Bacchae," "Empedocles," and "Winter Trip," the name Klaus Michael Grueber would be better known on the international film scene.

Just as "The Bacchae" was staged in a large pavilion, so "Empedocles" utilized a gigantic reproduction of Caspar David Friedrich's painting, "The Wreck of the Hope," as the central motif for the uncompleted drama in the Schaubuehne itself. From there Grueber went to the Berlin Olympic Stadium for his second Hoederlin adaptation, "Winter Trip" (Hyperion), on misty November-to-February

nights, then to an abandoned hotel, the Esplanada, on the Berlin Wall.

On the broad field of the Olympic Stadium, and against a reproduction of the Anhalter Bahnhof ruin and a military cemetery, the play unfolds in segments that actually reflect several scenes of German history associated with this structure and the downfall of the Third Reich. A must for offshore campus German departments. —*Holl.*

Coal Miner's Daughter
(COLOR)

Sissy Spacek captures the essence of Loretta Lynn. Good outlook beyond country fans.

Hollywood, Feb. 15.

A Universal pictures release of a Bernard Schwartz production. Directed by Michael Apted. Exec producer, Bob Larson. Stars Sissy Spacek. Screenplay, Tom Rickman, based on the autobiography by Loretta Lynn with George Vescey; camera (color), Ralf D. Bode; editor, Arthur Schmidt; production design, John D. Bode; music, Owen Bradley; sound, Jim Alexander; set decoration, John M. Dwyer; assistant director, Dan Kolsrud. Reviewed at the Century Plaza Theatre, Century City, Feb. 15, 1980. (MPAA Rating: PG.) Running time: 125 MINS.
Loretta . . . . Sissy Spacek
Doolittle (Mooney)
Lynn . . . . Tommy Lee Jones
Patsy Cline . . . . Beverly D'Angelo
Ted Webb . . . . Levon Helm
Clara Webb . . . . Phyllis Boyens
Lee Dollarhide . . . . William Sanderson
Bobby Day . . . . Robert Elkins
Charlie Dick . . . . Bob Hannah
The Webb children: Bill Anderson Jr., Foister Dickerson, Malla McCown, Pamela McCown, Kevin Salvilla.
Loretta and Mooney's children: Sissy Lucas, Pat Patterson, Brian Warf, Elizabeth Watson.
Doc Turner . . . . David Gray

"Coal Miner's Daughter" is a thoughtful, endearing film charting the life of singer Loretta Lynn from the depths of poverty in rural Kentucky to her eventual rise to the title of "queen of country music." Thanks in large part to superb performances by Sissy Spacek and Tommy Lee Jones, film mostly avoids the sudsy atmosphere common to many showbiz tales and emerges as both a wonderful love story and convincing portrayal of one woman's life. As such the Universal release is in store for some healthy, long-lasting boxoffice action that should reach beyond the realm of country music fans.

Lensed on location in Kentucky and Tennessee, Ralf D. Bode's camera effectively utilizes the scenic surroundings as it picks up on 13-year old Spacek and her life in Butcher Hollow. Her parents and five brothers and sisters live in a crowded, broken-down shack, she shoulders much of the responsibility for caring for her siblings and her future appears to hold only the problems and very occasional joys of those who have lived in the mining town before her.

Difference for Spacek, illustrated almost from the beginning, is her attraction to Jones, a magnetic local boy just back from the Armed Forces who takes a liking to the adolescent. Rising above the depressing atmosphere, the pair generate irresistible romantic sparks, whether it be in frequent sarcastic dialogs or an occasional meeting of the eyes. Jones is Spacek's ticket to love and a better

life, and despite her youth she is allowed to marry and eventually leave town with her new husband.

Film then begins its second section, with more mature Spacek (of 19), the head of her own household with a brood of children. Constantly pushing his wife to improve herself, Jones recognized Spacek's musical talent and buys her a guitar. In short order he has her successfully performing at a local honky tonk and soon decides to hit out on the road and make his wife a singing star.

Rest of picture takes on more of a rags to riches tone as Spacek begins to charm almost everyone across the country with her music and finds, once at the top of the heap, that the pressures put a crimp in her personal happiness.

Director Michael Apted has a lot of ground to cover here but despite film's 125-minute length, he has competently kept the action going. There is seldom a slow moment in the picture, although towards the end short shrift is given to Spacek's bout with drugs, nervous breakdown, marriage troubles and death of her best friend, Beverly D'Angelo, who turns in a stellar if abbreviated performance as country singer Patsy Cline.

Spacek also gets fine support from Phyllis Boyens and Levon Helm as her long-suffering parents, latter tearfully accurate as the proverbial poor but decent working man.

Tom Rickman has honestly adapted Lynn's autobiography, which she penned with the help of George Vescey. Only drawback is there seems to be some pulling of punches, especially when Lynn's life takes a turn for the worse.

Still, Spacek's on-target capturing of the Lynn character is so powerful and pervasive that it picks up any sagging moments in the script. Ditto Jones as her husband, whose ornery nuances don't conceal the fact that in the final analysis he places Spacek above all else.

Both Spacek and D'Angelo deserve a special nod of credit for doing all of their own singing with style and accuracy. Although Cline's career is now a memory, Lorretta Lynn is still very much a factor in the country music world. That Spacek manages to get inside the Lynn character so completely is what makes "Coal Miner's Daughter" a film that audiences will probably find irresistible.
—Berg.

Yawmun Akher
(Another Day)
(IRAQI-COLOR)

Berlin, Jan. 18.

An Iraqi General Organization for Cinema production, Baghdad. World rights, Iraqi General Organization for Cinema, Baghdad. Features entire cast. Directed by Sahib Haddad. Screenplay, Sabah Attwan, Mohammed Shoukry Jamil; camera (color), Majid Kamil. Reviewed at Deutsche Werbung Screening Room, Berlin, Jan. 18, '80. Running time: 90 MINS.
Cast: Khalil Shawki, Nahida Al Raman, Shaidha Salim, Talib Al Forati.

The best feature pic to emerge from the Iraqi General Organization for Cinema (IGOC) since Mohammed Shoukry Jamil's prizewinning "Thirst" back in 1971, Sahib Haddad's "Another 'Day" (1979) had script help from Jamil in sketching a portrait of the 1958 overthrow of the monarchy by way of a revealing film metaphor. The story is also a true one, which adds to the enjoyment so far as uninformed auds are concerned.

The son of a rich landowner has an eye for pretty ladies and likes having his way a bit too much — he kills a young woman who resists his advances. The husband of the girl swears revenge, which he gets when he surprises the culprit in the tent of a gypsy girl, and stabs him. The killing in the gypsy camp, however, throws the blame on innocent people.

The gypsies try to flee, but they don't get far when the rich man and his hired thugs swoop down on them and kill the whole party — save for a young man and his girlfriend who were away at the time. The needless slaughter arouses the population, the rich man is overpowered, and justice is done. The landowner, however, is left to live "another day" to remember his misdeeds, instead of being dispatched in the manner he dished out to others.

Pic has a "wild west" character and style of pacing in the storytelling. Helmer Haddad, formerly an editor, shows he learned his trade well. Thesps perform well, although overacting is unfortunately still in vogue these days throughout all the Arab countries. "Another Day" deserves exposure at fests and Iraqi Film Weeks. —*Holl.*

Saturn 3
(COLOR)

Pic should hit-and-run, like its robot villain does.

Associated Film Distribution release presented by Lord Lew Grade and Elliott Kastner. Produced and directed by Stanley Donen. Exec producer Martin Starger. Features entire cast. Screenplay, Martin Amis, from story by John Barry; camera (color), Billy Williams; music, Elmer

Bernstein; editor, Richard Marden; production design, Stuart Craig; art direction, Norman Dorme; special effects, Colin Chilvers; music performed by Royal Philharmonic Orchestra with orchestrations by Christopher Palmer. Reviewed at the Ziegfeld Theatre, N.Y., Feb. 15, '80. (MPAA Rating: R) Running time: 88 MINS.
Alex . . . . Farrah Fawcett
Adam . . . . Kirk Douglas
Benson . . . . Harvey Keitel
Capt. James . . . . Douglas Lambert
Harding . . . . Ed Bishop
2nd Crewman . . . . Christopher Muncke

It's hard to say what's going on in "Saturn 3," another Elliott Kastner-Distributor inspired run for the money, this time backed by Lord Lew Grade. An Associated Film release, Grade may want a word with the costumer who put patches on the sci-fi uniforms that look like the Columbia Pictures logo.

Somewhere in deepest, darkest space, Kirk Douglas and Farrah Fawcett jog around through a space station that looks suspiciously like Bloomingdale's after closing. The pair are scientists doing important work, when bad guys Harvey Keitel shows up.

Not much to recommend on this one — the audience at the Ziegfeld in N.Y. hooted after it was over. So the indications are hit and run.

Douglas is sprightly, but he has to handle some pretty awful lines in this Martin Amis script. Keitel's dialog, if quoted, would be on a par.

Life goes on in this shopping mall of lights constructed by Stuart Craig and Norman Dorme, till Keitel reprises his standard wacko role. He builds Hector, the mad robot, whose tubes and lights and hubcaps develop goosebumps for Farrah.

Semi-conductors flashing, Hector chases everyone about, first lopping off Keitel's hand — which added to a split second flash earlier of Farrah's upper torso needlessly got this pic an R rating. Keitel's brains take over the robot, and Hector lumbers after Douglas and Fawcett til Douglas dunks Hector in what must be the sewage system and they both explode. Farrah gets a new hair-do and takes the trip to Earth she always wanted.

Best scene in the entire effort is Hector's resurrection after he has been dismantled for being randy. The parts find each other and reconnect which is more than this film does. —*Jac.*

Action
(ITALIAN-COLOR)

Rome, Feb. 4.

Released by CIDIF for Ars Cinematografica production. Stars Luc Merenda. Directed by Giovanni Tinto Brass. Screenplay, Giancarlo Fusco, Roberto Lerici, Tinto Brass; camera (Eastmancolor), Silvano Ippolti; art director, Claudio Cinini; editor, Tinto Brass; music, Riccardo Giovannini. Reviewed at Quirinale Cinema,

Rome, Feb. 3, 1980. Running time: **123 MINS.**
Bruno Martel . . . . Luc Merenda
Gas station owner . . . . Adriana Asti
"Ophelia" . . . . .Susanna Javicoli
"Garibaldi" . . . . Alberto Sorrentino

———

An offensive, grating, but occasionally vital and provocative film by Giovanni Tinto Brass, whose hallucinatory movie career stretches from the wonderful New Wave "Who Works Is Lost" to the inferno of last year's "Caligula." Brass puts a gloss of soft-core porn (lots of frontal nudity of both sexes but no grotesque couplings) over a disconnected story that tries to say everything and isn't too clear. The film succeeds when the characters' rage and disgust is so great it dominates the filth, violence and general evil on the screen.

Playing on the double sense of its title, "Action" starts by taking us behind the sordid scenes of the skin flick trade with a down-on-his-luck actor. Luc Merenda is handsome but rather cold in the difficult role of the idealist in doubt about the meaning of life. In a series of violent episodes hung together by editing alone he travels through a surrealistic England. He spends a night in jail, rescues the charming Ophelia (Susanna Javicoli in a good, multi-layered performance) from being forced to evacuate for the camera on the porno set, is raped in a garbage dump by maddened punk rockers, saves an old man who thinks he's Garibaldi (good character acting here too by Alberto Sorrentino), watches helplessly as Susanna jumps from the window of a nightmarish madhouse and ends up pumping gas for Adriana Asti in the middle of nowhere.

The film overflows with film references and Freudian fantasies (some clever) which give it a feeling of belonging to the angry, experimental pictures of '68; in 1980, it seems dated and indulgent. Doing his own editing, Brass crafts a rough but extremely personal picture that could do well at film festivals. It seems too bizarre and incoherent for the usual porn-goer.

The photography, shot in 16m and blown up, is so painfully grainy some of the characters are unrecognizable. It certainly is not kind to excellent veteran actress Adriana Asti, who romps naked through the wheatfields like a pasty, lumpish ghost of the exuberant young 60s cinema. Camerawork, on the other hand, is often elegant in its framing and long shots.

"Action" might be taken as Brass's self-critique as porn-purveyor, taking a compassionate attitude toward mistreated and exploited actors who, for all their prostituted - all - my - life exterior,

are really wistful Ophelias underneath, mad dreamers in a destructive world. —*Yung.*

———

Sarvasakshi
(The Omniscient)
(INDIAN-B&W)

———

Bangalore, Jan. 29.
Giriraj Pictures, Production Co. release and production. Features entire cast. Written and directed by Ramdas Phutane. Camera, Sharad Navle; music, Bhaskar Chandawarkar. Reviewed at Bangalore Film Fest, Jan. 14, '80. Running time: **135 MINS.**
With: Smita Patil, Jayram Hardikar, Anjali Paigankar, Vijay Joshi.

———

Progressive idealism against superstition in village life is simply but effectively dealt with in this unevenly made film.

A progressive schoolteacher helps fight a local epidemic by getting children inoculated to bring on the enmity of the local bhagat, a sort of witchdoctor.

His wife, who had lost a child, goes to the bhagat but he demands a human sacrifice. The wife is horrified and later dies in childbirth and her husband is accused of the bhagat's resorting to child sacrifice for a local village bigwig.

He is exonerated but left in doubt about his brush with superstition. Film again delves into village backwardness alongside the growing worldiness of India. A worthy theme but not transcending it for a more potent, universal statement.
—*Mosk.*

———

Unter Verschluss
(Under Lock And Key)
(WEST GERMAN-COLOR)

———

Berlin, Dec. 24.
An Artus-Film Production, Munich, Dr. Harald Mueller. Features entire cast. Written and directed by Wilma Kottusch. Camera (color), Gerard Vandenberg, Jochen Rademacher; sound, Klaus Eckelt; music, Edgar Froese; costumes, Franziska Liphart; sets, Gerd B. Fleischer. Reviewed at Deutsche Werbung Screening Room, Berlin, Dec. 23, '79. Running time: **90 MINS.**
Cast: Lisa Kreuzer (Angela Aschmann, Doctor), Juergen Prochnow (Volker Schwarz, Doctor), Rudolf Schuendler (Walter Dross, Patient), Edith Schulze-Westrum (Marguete Wimmer), Isolde Barth (Irmhild Becker), Dieter Schidor (Harald Wegner), Michaela May (Lore Brunner), Vera Tschechova (Katrin Wiedemann), Thomas Astan (Jochen Wiedemann), Kurt Raab (Guenter Vogel).

———

"Under Lock and Key" deals with the sterilized world of clinics, this one for people in extreme-care wards where the real and the unreal (or surreal) clash to rub out the sanity lines for both patients and doctors. Wilma Kottusch, latest name in a line of talented femme helmers in West Germany, did her internship in television (mostly

documentaries) before attempting this cinematic portrait of a modern Underworld. It works, and she's now one to watch in the future.

Not much happens in this "drama of the corridors" — save for the major question of who's the sick and who's the well: the patients or the doctors? But that's more than enough to engross the viewer in a labyrinth of modern medicine, as seen, more or less, through the experiences of a sensitive female doctor new to the ward and a psychic patient doomed to spend his last days in this purgatory. Another doctor who has "lost his way" and cannot feel with the patients anymore is also awakened to the reality about him through a personal crisis.

Anyone who has visited — or better, worked in — a locked-up psychiatric ward will appreciate the insights the filmmaker offers without resorting to extra, superfluous commentary on the whys and wherefores for such inhumane medical treatment in large modern clinics. Take the problem of schizophrenia, alone, or the Laing and Frankel psychiatric approaches to the soul of the individual, or the recent string of movies, from Kenneth Loach's "Family Life" to Milos Forman's "One Flew over the Cuckoo's Nest" — and the importance of this fiction-documentary is clear.

Kottusch has obviously spent a good deal of time researching her theme. The crew went into a real clinic for a short shooting span with actors prepared to improvise real scenes as they went along. Types were registered as focal points: doctors, nurses, a suicidal case, working personnel, defenseless patients, even a morbid undertaker. Some scenes work well, others don't — but the whole is a mosaic to be appreciated and studied. —*Holl.*

———

Bad Timing
(BRITISH-COLOR)

———

Looks nice but ultimately a downer.

———

London, Feb. 12.
Rank Film Distributors release of a Recorded Picture Co. production. Produced by Jeremy Thomas. Directed by Nicolas Roeg. Stars Art Garfunkel, Theresa Russell, Harvey Keitel, Denholm Elliott. Screenplay, Yale Udoff; camera (color), Anthony Richmond; editor, Tony Lawson; musical director, Richard Hartley; art director, David Brockhurst; sound, Tony Jackson; associate producer, Tim Van Rellim; production manager, Aivar Kaulins; asst. director, Niel Vine-Miller. Reviewed at Bob's Place preview theatre, London, Feb. 11, '80. (BBFC Rating: X). Running time: **123 MINS.**
Dr. Alex Linden . . . . Art Garfunkel
Milena Flaherty . . . . Theresa Russell
Inspector Fredrich Netusil . Harvey Keitel
Stefan Vognic . . . . Denholm Elliott

Foppish Man . . . . .Daniel Massey
Amy . . . . .Dana Gillespie

Director Nicolas Roeg's new film is an enervating experience. Technically flashy, and teeming with degenerate chic, the downbeat tale of two destructively selfish lovers at large in Vienna (briefly in Morocco) is unrelieved by its tacked-on thriller ending, and deals purely in despair.

With little hope that young audiences will find much identification with any of the characters, who are either over-privileged, overdosed or over the hill, likeliest commercial strategy would seem to be hefty promotion of the names and sex-angle — no disappointment on the latter score, contrary to the "family film" image of the Rank Organization — followed by fast playoff. "Bad Timing" will doubtless be cherished as an artfilm by some older buffs, but ordinary sensibilities may well feel ordinary life offers them a better time.

Top quality craftsmanship is a continuing hallmark of Roeg's work, and regular collaboration with cinematographer Anthony Richmond is still fruitful. Every scene is shot with at least one eye and one ear to the editing table: results are generally masterful but at times obtrusively pretentious. Roeg's visual sense remains a peculiar talent challenged by few, if any, contemporary directors.

No amount of aesthetic virtuosity, however, can hide the superficiality of Yale Udoff's screenplay. It plots the often brutal love-affair exhaustively in terms of what the parties do to each other, but seldom why — beyond the fact that he (a lecturer in psychoanalysis, with apparently no comment to make on his own condition) is the possessive type and she isn't.

Most milestones are missing along the presumably tortuous psychological route by which his jealousy reaches such a pitch of hatred that he ravishes the girl's drugged and senseless body instead of calling an ambulance. So with only Art Garfunkel's low-key performance to go on, alienation sets in early. He starts and finishes as a cold fish, riddled with self-regard and hypocrisy; and much of the action seems contrived or simply exploitative.

Theresa Russell's warmer-blooded character occasionally transcends those problems to evoke real sympathy. She's well cast, looking convincingly ingenue one moment and like a far-gone tart the next. Modishly dressed as a male-fantasy figure, with an expensive line in hairstyles, she makes the shallow role compelling in the tough scenes by sheer guts.

How a long-haired American (Harvey Keitel) comes to be working with the Viennese police needs more explanation. He has an Austrian name, but seemingly none of the lingo. Denholm Elliott, as Russell's deserted Czech husband, is strictly one-dimensional — a suffering face. Overall credibility of the proceedings is further impaired by the coincidence of Garfunkel being hired to analyze a political file on Elliott. Plotwise, what's more, the contrivance leads nowhere.

"Bad Timing," in fact, is a big tease. What interest is generated during the first hour — by incisive cross-cutting between time-passages, by the dazzling "look" of each new sequence, by Richard Hartley's disquieting musical score — is dissipated during the second when it becomes clear the dominance-versus-dependence theme is merely repeating itself.

Had the makers been less obsessed with the refinements of carnality, and more concerned with authentic present-day stresses on two more accessible people, their traumatic trip would have seemed more modern and less menopausal. —Simo.

Blomstrande tider
(Flourishing Times)
(SWEDISH-COLOR)

Malmoe, Feb. 8.
A Swedish Film Institute/Drakfilm Three Leaf Clover production, AB Europa distribution, foreign sales Swedish Film Institute. Written and directed by John Olsson. Features entire cast. Camera (Eastmancolor), Hanno Fuchs; executive producer, Hans Iveberg; editor, Christin Loman; music, Bjoern Isfaelt. Reviewed at Rio, Malmoe, Sweden, Feb. 7, 1980. Running time: 98 MINS.
Jussi . . . . Kristen Henriksson
Goete . . . . Carl-Gustaf Lindstedt
Dallas . . . . Halvar Bjoerk
Henry . . . . Keve Hjelm
Doris . . . . Essy Persson

"Flourishing Times" is a curious little non-film in which writer-director John Olsson uses a small rural community as a microcosm of welfare Sweden of the mid-'70s. A non-film because Olsson with such conscious care defuses all and any plot possibility for visual impact so that audiences are left with a series of dramatically and dimly-lit snapshots of people, places and moods. A chosen few may take pleasure in such a portrayal of the ordinary as dull Evil. Feature's boxoffice potential would seem nil at home and abroad.

The plot framework is hardly new. As Frank Sinatra got off the bus as a discharged soldier in "Some Came Running," here perpetually morose-miened Krister Henriksson (Jussi) does the same. And again to find things in the old home-town changed for the

worse. Jussi cannot seem to regain his footing in either love or work. A former sweetheart now prefers the owner of the gas station where self-service has taken care of the attendant's job Jussi once held. He stumbles into work for Goete, local wheeler-dealer owner of a used car and wreckage lot. He tries to have Goete exposed for some petty license plate shenanigans but gets no help from his elderly friend Henry, the local newspaper editor.

Jussi has no luck, either, with the town's bike racing team of which he was formerly leader and hero. He drifts into a love affair with a married woman (Essy Persson, as impressive now of face as she once was of body in the early "I, A Woman" films), but his heart is not in it. He gets beaten up by his own bike pals. So he packs up and leaves town on the same bus that brought him in. Since Kristen Henriksson has done nothing as an actor to make us care one way or another about Jussi.

Bjoern Isfaelt has supplied twangy music to stress the point that Sweden is fast being swallowed up by American-style pop and consumerism. Otherwise all is a blur of non-comedy, non-tragedy and - nothing. —Kell.

The Changeling
(CANADIAN-COLOR)

Toronto, Jan. 30.
A Pan-Canadian release (AFD in US), produced by Joel B. Michaels and Garth H. Drabinsky. Exec producers, Mario Kassar and Andrew Vajna. Directed by Peter Medak. Features entire cast. Screenplay, William Gray, Diana Maddox, from a story by Russell Hunter; camera (Panavision), John Coquillon; production designer, Trevor Williams; art director, Reuben Freed; music, Rick Wilkins; editor, Lilla Ledersen; sound, Patrick Drummond, Dennis Drummond, Robert Grieve; special effects, Gene Grigg; assistant director, Irby Smith. Reviewed at the Varsity Cinema, Toronto, Jan. 29, '80. Running time: 107 MINS.
John Russell . . . . George C. Scott
Claire Norman . . . . Trish Van Devere
Sen. Joe Carmichael . . . . . Melvin Douglas
De Witt . . . . John Colicos
Joanna Russell . . . . Jean Marsh
Dr. Pemberton . . . . Barry Morse
Eugene Carmichael . . . . . . James Douglas
Mrs. Norman . . . . Madeleine Thornton-Sherwood
Eva Lingstrom . . . . Roberta Maxwell
Prof. Robert Lingstrom . . Bernard Behrens
Elizabeth Grey . . . . Frances Hyland
Minnie Huxley . . . . Ruth Springford
Leah Harmon . . . . Helen Burns
Albert Harmon . . . . Eric Christmas

"The Changeling" is a superior haunted house thriller that should add boxoffice credibility to the burgeoning Canadian film industry. The film has tremendous technical polish and weaves a complex plot, that despite lapses, should have audiences guessing about the full mystery to the last frame.

The story centers on George C. Scott, a recently widowed music professor, who has moved to Seattle to forget his personal tragedy. His new residence is an old home owned by the local historic society. After moving in, the house begins to do strange things.

The range of loud morning banging, unturned flowing water taps and other oddities lead Scott to a boarded room. With the aid of Trish Van Devere of the historic society, he begins to uncover the house's dark past.

It turns out that the noisy spirit is a young sickly boy who was murdered at the turn-of-the-century. The child's father could not collect an inheritance unless the boy reached the age of 21. After the murder a changeling was put in the boy's place.

The changeling is still alive and the dead child wants to wreak his vengeance on him. Only problem is that the substitute, played by Melvin Douglas, is a powerful industrialist who assumes Scott is trying to blackmail him. He sends his goons to cover up his past but the child's spirit proves mightier than their strong-arm tactics.

The film begins as a tale of a malevolent house but promptly switches into the area of an avenging spirit story. The filmmakers take full advantage of horror set pieces like seances and nocturnal grave digging and the mystery-shrouded script manages to cover over any implausibilities.

A child's playing ball provides an eerie embodiment of the spirit's power and there's a terrifying chase involving Van Devere and the dead child's wheelchair.

Scott and Douglas register the strongest performances with Van Devere coming off rather wooden in the background. The supporting cast gets limited use with Jean Marsh disappearing before the main credits. Best cameos are John Colicos' brutish cop and Ruth Springford as an historic society busy body.

Director Peter Medak is best known for stage adaptations like "The Ruling Class," but makes an easy change to the horror venue. The picture is greatly enhanced by John Coquillon's rich camerawork and first-rate sets by Trevor Williams.

Ultimate guilt or innocence of Douglas is left to audience which some may find an unsatisfying conclusion. Nonetheless, film should have strong boxoffice appeal based on the name cast and the exemplory look of the production. —Klad.

Unversoehnliche Errinnerungen
(Irreconcilable Memories)
(WEST GERMAN-COLOR-DOCU-16m)

Mainz, Feb. 1.
A Journal-Film Klaus G. Volkenborn production, in collaboration with Zweites Deutsches Fernsehen (ZDF), Mainz; distributed by Basis-Film-Verleih, Berlin. Directed by Klaus G. Volkenborn, Johann Feindt, Karl Siebig; tv-producers, Eckhart Stein. Annegret Even; music, Andi Brauer. Reviewed at ZDF Screening Room, Mainz, Feb. 1, '80. Running time: 92 MINS.

The Golden Dove winner at the Leipzig Docu Fest in East Germany last November, "Irreconcilable Memories" by a collective team of West Berlin helmers was the first such honor paid to the West Germans by the German Democratic Republic. The kudo was not only deserved, but this document on Fascism as an historical period and portrait of West Germany today should make the rounds of fests and campuses throughout the coming season.

Zweites Deutsches Fernsehen (ZDF) has been producing a series of docus in the "Witness of Or Times" series, this one aired last September in the late-hour, "Kleines Fernsehspiel," Thursday-night slot. The reaction in the press and at the tv-station was immediate and contradictory, some critics calling the docu "a lesson in German history" and others referring to it as "a class-struggle film" The result — "Irreconcilable Memories" is now skedded for theatres and selection in the German Series at the Berlin Fest (which fortunately means English subtitling for export purposes).

Two men in their seventies fought as Germans on both sides during the Spanish Civl War, and they recall the past — thus, "irreconcilable memories — in monologues before the camera. One was a simple mason who volunteered to fight on the side of the Republican Army; as a Communist in the unions, he had to leave Germany in a hurry after Hitler came to power. The other is a retired air force general, a member of the Condor Legion on Franco's side that bombed Guernica; he reached the rank of general in the postwar years and still has close contacts with the West German military.

It may appear to be a stroke of luck that these three filmmakers, graduates of the Berlin Film & Television Academy, found two such compelling personalities and natural storytellers. But the truth is that they had to do a lot of research and talking to finally convince both parties to unlock that storehouse of information and memories on a sore spot so far as national feelings and politics go.

After getting the interviews, the team cut the interviews together to reach a kind of dialectical commentary on both the times and the gentlemen in question. The mason comes across as a forgotten individual, one who sacrificed his life for an ideal ("I'm a Marxist," he says at the end); while the general took to flying like a not-to-be-missed adventure, especially since he came from a family of military officers, and came out on top ("I had a lot of luck," he states frankly).

It would be easy to say that the filmmakers knew where their sympathies lay in the first place between the two individuals, but they refused at the same time to offer any commentary or judgments of their own. Each man tells his story as he lived it, determining the very contents of the film. That the general proved to be a bit too gullible and vain in the process is the fun-and-games of cinema-verite, or direct-cinema, interview-documentaries.

In addition to the broad amount of information this timely docu delivers, the ironies of fate and life's small tragedies surface at every turn. For one thing, it is clear that the Condor Legion brought more rewards in time than the International Brigade. The mason and his wife are living on a small pension and recount, in a shabby and embarrassing moment, how the Remscheid town officials won't recognize his 50th wedding anniversary — simply because the Nazis forced his wife to sign a divorce paper during her husband's internment.

As for the retired general, he left the military as a First Lieutenant at the end of the war, then re-entered service in 1956 when West Germany was re-armed — he was promoted to Colonel instalntly, as though he had, in fact, served in the military over the intervening eleven years of inactivity. And, as a result, his retirement pay offers an easy, comfortable existence in Frankfurt due to the high pension.

The moral that morality doesn't pay, however, is secondary to the individuals themselves. Both men take stands that they would not have had in their lives otherwise, should they live them again. It's the cards laid openly on the table that wins the viewers' respect — that, and the realization that this late chapter to "Spanish Earth" has come just in time. A must for film and history buffs. —Holl.

The Legend Of Julian Makabayan
(FILIPINO-COLOR)

Manila, Jan. 29.
An Ian Film Productions release. Produced by Romy Ching. Story and script by Marina Feleo-Gonzales based on her story "Dahong Palay" (Ricefield Snake). Directed by Celso Ad. Castillo. Features entire cast. Camera (Color). Romeo Vitug; music, Lutgardo Labad; editor, Abelardo Hulleza; art director, Peter Perlas. Reviewed at the Cultural Center of The Philippines, Manila, Dec. 21, 1979. Running time: 150 MINS.
Cast: Christopher de Leon, Celso Ad. Castillo, Charo Santos, Eddie Garcia, Tony Santos, Johnny Delgado, Perla Bautista.

Director Celso Ad. Castillo is notorious for improvising on written scripts and he has overdone it this time. So says writer Marina Feleo Gonzales who scripted "The Legend Of Julian Makabayan."

Film is a historical drama set in the 1920s when peasants were restless for relief from oppressive Spanish friars and landowners.

Julian, played by director Castillo, is imprisoned on suspicion of organizing a union to fight the landlords. Pleading for his release, his newly wedded wife is raped by the influential friar. Julian does not realize that his child is the son of the friar.

Midway in the story, Julian dies but it is implied that his son, Julian II, will continue the cause he started. A new plot develops, Julian II's romance with a rich Spaniard's daughter. The theme of the film, quest for agrarian reform, is overlooked by Castillo. In the end of the story, Julian is killed not because of any heroic deed but because he ran away with the rich man's daughter.

The glaring flaw, however, is — the entire picture does not have the characteristics of a legend. It could have been a very good film if Castillo had been more cohesive. But he also dwells lengthily on picturesque local color and neglects the development of the story.

Cinematographer Vitug excels in artistic shots of the idyllic rural scenery in Sta. Rosa, Nueva Ecija where the film was shot entirely. The period costumes, folkways, songs and rituals, are something foreigners will find interesting.
—Giro.

Das gefrorene Herz
(The Frozen Heart)
(SWISS-W. GERMAN-AUSTRIAN-COLOR)

Zurich, Feb. 2.
Columbus Film AG Zurich release of a Fernsehen DRS (Swiss TV), ZDF (2nd German TV) and ORF (Austrian TV) co-production, produced by Cine Group Zurich. Stars Sigfrit Steiner. Written and directed by Xavier Koller, from a short story by Meinrad Inglin. Camera (Eastmancolor). Hans Liechti; music, Hardy Hepp; editor, Fee Liechti; art direction, Rolf Engler; costumes, Sylvia de Stoutz. Reviewed at Alba Theatre, Zurich, Feb.2, '80. Running time: 108 MINS.
Basket Maker .... Sigfrit Steiner
Rosi ....Emilia Krakowska
Umbrella Mender ....Paul Buehlmann
Reichmuth .... Otto Maechtlinger
Betschart ....Heinz Buehlmann
Parson 1 .... Erwin Kohlund
Uerech ....Giovanni Frueh
Coffin Maker ....Volker Prechtel
Gwerder ....Guenter Lamprecht
Theres .... Vera Schweiger
Mettler .... Herbert Leiser

"Das gefrorene Herz" (The Frozen Heart) is a whimsical Swiss winter's tale, set in an icy mountain region, about a frozen corpse, a sly hobo, a village prostie and a bunch of narrow-minded, stingy village notables duped in an unexpected way. Written and directed with style and gusto by Xavier Koller, the film, made on a production budget of $830,000, should make its way on the Swiss market and may be also abroad.

Commissioned by the Swiss TV and coproduced with the 2d German TV network, ZDF, and the Austrian television, ORF, it is thus destined primarily for video consumption. In Germany and Austria, this is the way it will be handled. In Switzerland, however, the Swiss TV has agreed — for the first time, incidentally, in the case of a commissioned tv film — to a theatrical release to begin with. A "generous" gesture which seems to pay off as the picture has reaped favorable reviews and started off well at the boxoffice.

The story concerns two elderly tramps, one a basket maker and the other an umbrella mender. After too much booze at a village inn, the latter makes his way through the snowy night to the neighboring village to see his old flame, the village prostie. He falls asleep in the snow and is found by his buddy the next morning, frozen to death. It turns out the body lies on the borderline of the two villages whose notables refuse to pay for the burial. The corpse is moved to and fro until the basket maker thinks up a plan, involving a false will, which not only secures his dead pal a Christian burial, but works out to his own benefit and leaves the villagers duped.

Characterizations are uniformly excellent. Sigfrit Steiner as the surviving tramp and Paul Buehlmann as the frozen one handle their tailormade roles with aplomb, paired with subtlety, especially Steiner. Emilia Krakowska as the goodnatured prostie, Otto Maechtlinger, Heinz Buehlmann and Erwin Kohlund as villagers and particularly Giovanni Frueh as the mistreated village idiot are all firstrate.

Other important assets are the atmospheric, subdued camera work by Hans Liechti, the plausible, well-timed editing job by Fee Liechti and a delightful musical score by Hardy Hepp. —Mezo.

El Curso En Que Amamos A Kim Novak
(The Semester We Loved Kim Novak)
(SPANISH-COLOR)

Madrid, Feb. 1.
A Togapor Productions film. Directed by Juan Jose Porto. Screenplay, J.J. Porto, Carlos Puerto; camera (Eastmancolor), Miguel F. Mila. No other credits available. Reviewed at Cine Carlton, Madrid, Feb. 1, '80. Running time: 85 MINS.
Cast: Miguel Ayones, Miguel Arribas, Kity Manver, Cecilia Roth, Beatriz Elorrieta, Antonio Gamero, Roxanne Bach.

Modest little nostalgia film set in Salamanca in the late 1950s anent student lives and loves. One of the college kids has a crush on actress Kim Novak whom he sees in "Vertigo" and "Picnic" and plasters the walls of his boarding house room, which he shares with another student, with pix of her.

At a party he spots a girl somewhat in the Novak style, but is too timid to accost her till the end of the film. Some nice nostalgia lensing in Salamanca, tuna music and a few mild sex scenes provide some interest, but on the whole story and dialogs are too pedestrian to arouse any excitement. Thesping and technical credits are okay, but story is too slight and ingenuous to draw attention. —Besa.

Mani Di Velluto
(Velvet Hands)
(ITALIAN-COLOR)

Rome, Feb. 4.
A Cineriz release, produced by Mario Cecchi Gori for Capital Film. Stars Adriano Celentano, Eleanora Giorgi. Written and directed by Castellano and Pipolo. Camera (Eastmancolor). Alfio Contini; art director, Bruno Amalfitano; editor, Antonio Siciliano; music, Nando De Luca. Reviewed at Cinema Reale, Rome, Feb. 3, 1980. Running time: 102 MINS.
Guido Quiller ....Adriano Celentano
Tilli .... Eleanora Giorgi
The butler ....John Sharp
Mrs. Quiller .... Olga Karlatos

What can be said about the rousing box office success of "Velvet Hands" but the compatibility of its two popular stars, singer Adriano Celentano and ex-sex starlet Eleanora Giorgi, the latter recently gone legit in Brusati's fine "To Forget Venice." Celentano is still cashing in on the youth appeal that has seemed inexhaustible since he appeared as a wild rock 'n' roller in "La Dolce Vita." Clearly secondary in this Italian formula comedy are a weak, cliche-ridden story and direction by Castellano and Pipolo as a helming team. Commercially, "Hands" is sweeping in a lot of chips in Italy but could have limitations exporting its national stars and humor to more demanding audiences.

The reversible Cinderella plot (rags to riches, riches to rags) switches between the impossibly palatial and the picturesque poverty of a Milan ghetto (fun sets by Bruno Amalfitano.) Guido Quiller (Celentano) is a likable, goofy millionaire industrialist whose bazooka-proof plate glass has made him the enemy of thieves and Swiss insurance brokers alike, but hasn't given him the one thing he really wants — the disinterested love of a beautiful woman. One day, riding to work on the subway (?), Guido's Rolex is lifted by the loveliest of pickpockets, Tilli (Giorgi). When fate brings them together again, Tilli mistakes Guido for a humble pursesnatcher and their common vocation inspires her tenderness. Smitten with love, Guido must spend half the movie hiding his true identity from his beloved and her rollicking family of thieves.

Giorgi, well cast as the thief with heart of gold, proves herself an amiable comedienne, though it is the stronger Celentano who steals the scene every time. Playing the Cary Grant role of the man who tries to be misunderstood in the athletic slapstick style of Jerry Lewis, Celentano turns the silly story into a pretext for bizarre mini-song and dance numbers whenever a likely set presents itself. His best skits are mute body-language.

The best current Italian comedy, in fact (Nichetti's "Ratataplan" is a leader), seems to be getting its inspiration from silent movies instead of the tired formulas of the past (of which, in its entirety, "Hands" is but one more weary example).

The peppy Muzak-style soundtrack is best underheard; camerawork and editing are nondescript; and there are some good supporting performances by John Sharp as Quiller's maggiordomo-confidant and Olga Karlatos, as the eternal over-madeup heavy.
—*Yung*.

La Patata Bollente
(Hot Potato)
(ITALIAN-COLOR)

Rome, Jan. 30.
A CIDIF release, produced by Achille Manzotti for Irrigazione Cinematografica. Stars Renato Pozzetto, Edwige Fenech, Massimo Ranieri. Directed by Steno. Screenplay. Giorgio Arlorio. Enrico Vanzina, Steno; camera (Telecolor). Emilio Loffredo; art director. Mauro Passi; editor. Raimondo Crociani; music. Tato Savio. Reviewed at Esperia Cinema. Rome. Jan. 30. '80. Running time: 105 MINS.
Gandi .... Renato Pozzetto
Maria .... Edwige Fenech
Claudio .... Massimo Ranieri
Doorman .... Mario Scarpetta

"Come Saturday night, what the working class wants is to have some fun," says dissatisfied filmgoer Edwige Fenech, coming out of "Working Man," too late to make the discotheque. The last thing a waitress in the factory lunch line wants to do with her night off is watch subtitled Bulgarian films about politics. "Hot Potato" then proceeds to relieve her boredom.

Uplifting theme is hardhat and party intolerance to gays. Capra-style solution to the film gives the hypocritical union straights in the paint dept. a valuable comedy lesson in human rights.

The attempt seems to work. "Hot Potato" is doing well in Italy, where a third of election votes go to the communists and where a hero who sleeps with giant portraits of Marx and Lenin over his bed has wide comic appeal.

The choice of Milanese comedian Renato Pozzetto and Neapolitan actor-singer Massimo Ranieri (not to mention sexy Edwige Fenech) must also be credited for calculated audience draw in Italy. If recent French hit on gays, "La cage aux folles," is a parallel, "Potato" could also prove hot in the U.S. Foreign markets may be limited less by homosexual theme than by heavy political farce, though a possible go for art houses with its offbeat story and politics & entertainment strategy. Good on characters and setting, "Potato's" script is stronger than its direction or dialogue, too heavy-handed for hearty laughs.

Star of the film is flaccid-faced, bad-tempered Pozzetto, whose cranky monotone and under-played comic persona is right for the part of the deadly earnest, party-line communist Gandi.

Fenech plays the buxom, dumb waitress in an absolutely natural way: pixieish Ranieri charms as the uneffeminate "different one" Gandi saves from a beating by a group of fascist punks and unsuspectingly takes home. Nasty insinuations appear on the factory wall and Maria becomes suspicious after catching sight of her virile friend in a gay bookstore. Then his comrades thoughtfully arrange a week in Russia to cure the presumed malady. Though much seems possible nothing very unspeakable happens to anyone in the film, gay or otherwise.

Though many jokes are mistimed, some classic bits go over well — Mario Scarpetta's knowledgeable doorman and his drinking wife; the slip on the banana peel routine protracted into a minute's worth of slow motion. Sets cleverly contrast "masculine" and gay ambiances with comic license.

Camerawork is of the turn-on-all-the-lights school. Editing seems determined to make its points long and repeatedly, lest some five-year-old mistake obvious facial clues. —*Yung*.

Agenzia Riccardo Finzi... Praticamente Detective
(Detective Riccardo Finzi)
(ITALIAN-COLOR)

Rome, Jan. 29.
A Titanus release. produced by Galliana Juso for Cinemaster film production. Stars Renato Pozzetto. Directed by Bruno Corbucci. Screenplay. Bruno Corbucci, Mario Amendola; camera (Technicolor). Giovanni Ciarlo; art director. Claudio Cinnini; editor. Daniele Anabiso; music. Guido and Maurizio De Angelis. Reviewed at Gregory Cinema. Rome. Jan. 29. 1980. Running time: 94 MINS.
Riccardo Finzi .... Renato Pozzetto
Mr. Moser .... Silvano Tranquilli
Mrs. Moser .... Olga Karlatos
Ex-carabiniere .... Enzo Cannavale

Formula comedy with a premolded star, murder for laughs, and a boy's comic book fantasy of quickie adventure and instant success sell "Detective Riccardo Finzi," which should do very well nationally though limitations of star draw and local humor may make it a hard bid abroad.

Keeping its distance from deep belly laughs, the film settles for a tone of mild amusement under the tutelage of popular comedy star Renato Pozzetto. Lombard version of a grown-up Harry Langdon moving slowly through adulthood with a perpetually puffy face and delayed reactions.

His bumbling private eye passes through modern Milan like an electric knife through melted butter, solving an improbable murder case as easily as he surmounts the more difficult problems of finding an apartment, clients, and beautiful girls, who throw themselves successively if not successfully on his demi-twin bed.

The script is topical in its references to terrorism, rent laws, dead policemen. Southern immigrants and left-wing students, exploiting them for quick one- and two-liners. Setting in Milan, the star's hometown and source of much of his b.o. appeal in Italy, is emphatic, if irrelevant.

A morosely genial Pozzetto, with the face of a dazed fruit vendor and the agility of a stunned elephant, arrives in the Northern capital to hang his shingle after completing a correspondence course in private investigating.

Saving valuable plot time he heads directly for a night club where he finds a house, in invitation home from a snooty 19-year-old whose perplexing behavior can only be explained as an advanced case of nymphomania. Her death on a lonely highway, which he reads about in the morning paper, becomes his first case.

But the plot is a MacGuffin, there only for the sake of form. The star's the thing, and if you don't get off on Pozzetto you can leave right after the suitcase full of bricks lands on his head. One of those rare birds, an Italian underactor, Pozzetto is likable in his unflagging mediocrity and continuous sarcasm, seemingly a pushover and a wimp but unbending — a flattering view of a certain species of overfed Italian male who never tires of imagining stunning young girls in disco garb attacking him in public places.

Enzo Cannavale, the retired carabiniere side-kick, is surprisingly efficient as an info-gatherer, who provides the mandatory bathroom joke.

This amusing romp is held together by standard unobtrusive editing and camerawork which have no ambition to outflash their material. A repetitive and determinedly cheery musical motif by Maurizio and Guido De Angelis remains unaltered in scenes of dramatic, erotic and comic intent.
—*Yung*.

Neem Annapurna
(Bitter Morsel)
(INDIAN-B&W)

Bangalore, Jan. 30.
Calcutta release and production. Features entire cast. Directed by Buddhadeb Das Gupta. Screenplay. Kamal Kumar Majumdar. Das Gupta; camera. Kamal Nayekleditor. G. Naskar. Reviewed at Bangalore Film Fest. Jan. 8. '80. Running time. 95 MINS.
With: Manidipa Ray. Sunil Mukhopadhyaya. Jayita Sarkar. Manojit Lahiri.

Film is a bit tenuous in its look at the difficulties of a family that comes to the big city and sinks into poverty. But director Buddhadeb Das Gupta shows a flair for character delineation and makes his points without undue pathetics.

The family had existed honorably in a small town but moved to the big city when the husband lost his job. Here he cannot find work and they let out a part of their hovel to an old beggar.

The little girl of the family is caught stealing birdseed from a parrot and the older girl is near giving in to men who offer her food.

The mother feels the beggar is hoarding something and when she is caught in his room, while taking his bag of rice, the beggar has an attack and dies.

The however does nothing. After the body is gone, she gives her family a big rice meal. But she cannot eat and goes to the door to throw up as the film ends. The director may be a bit too distanced to make the more dramatic, more angered comment called for.

Item shows a filmmaker with flair who should be heard from with subjects more fitting to his seemingly intellectual temperament.

—*Mosk.*

Berlin Festival

Transit
(ISRAEL-COLOR)

Tel Aviv, Feb. 6.

A Transit Film Production. Produced by Yaakov Goldwasser. Directed by Daniel Wachsmann. Features entire cast. Screenplay, Daniel Horowitz, Daniel Wachsmann; camera (color). Ilan Rosenberg; editors: Asher Tlalim. Levy Zini; musical score, Shlomo Gronich; sound, Danny Natowitz; art director, Danny Verete. Reviewed in Tel Aviv, Feb. 6, 1980. Running time: 87 MINS.

Erich Nussbaum . . . . Gedalia Besser
Diskin . . . . Yitzhak (Picho) Ben-Zur
Yael . . . . Liora Rivlin
Michael . . . . Yair Elazar
Emmanuel . . . . Amnon Meskin
Willy . . . . Gideon Singer

The first feature to be backed by the Fund for Encouragement of Quality Films, Danny Wachsmann's first effort is enjoying a nice start as it has already been accepted for the Berlin Film Festival after having been sold to the first West German TV channel.

It deals with a German-born Jew, chased from Berlin by the Nazis before the war, who finds it difficult to make a place for himself and adjust to the life he finds in his new-old homeland, Israel. The film's main section deals with his inner struggle whether to drop everything he has achieved during his 30-40 years in Tel Aviv, and head back to Europe.

The subject is a particularly relevant one for Israel, whose population of immigrants from all corners of the world, faces these dilemmas daily. Adaptation to new surroundings have proved to be one of the main problems the new state has to face in order to achieve a truly homogeneous population, and it may take some time until this is achieved.

Wachsmann, who has won awards in the past for short subjects, is clear enough in presenting his theme, even it he doesn't place it in an exact time context. Each has its own importance when the realities of this area are delt with, as each year is different from the one before and the one after it.

The rift separating the main character (Erich Nussbaum) from his estranged wife, Yael, his teenage son. Michael and his neighbourhood, is clearly etched, as is the atmosphere of people of German origin, living in an unreal world and trying to behave as though they have never left the old country. But as the story unfolds and Nussbaum leaves home, the story becomes muddled into a detailed portrait of a shabby milieu, and the more atmospheric the treatment, the less it seems to lead the story forward.

Taking into account the incredible budget difficulties encountered by the feature, which took more than a year to shoot, with months of inactivity between sessions during which it was desperately looking for money to go on, it is a wonder that the project has been completed. There is no doubt that the pic is sincere, and a real effort has been made to measure up to the considerable task. But production problems could not be kept out of the way. Narration, added probably in order to close gaps in the story, sounds less than natural or convincing, the quality of the 16m print, blown up for the Festival, may not be comparable to commercial standards; and acting, while on the whole satisfactory, could have been improved, if more time and money would have been available.

Altogether, this is a valiant effort and its acceptance at Berlin has proven that it is starting on the right foot. Still, this is no run-of-the-mill commercial venture, and it will have to be very carefully handled, in art houses, film festivals and special events, if the right audience is to be found. —*Edna.*

Bizalom
(Confidence)
(HUNGARIAN-COLOR)

Pecs, Feb. 26.

Hungarofilm release of Mafilm-Objektiv Studio Production. Features entire cast. Written and directed by Istvan Szabo from a story by Erika Szanto. Szabo; camera (Eastmancolor), Lajos Koltai. Reviewed at Pecs Film Fest. Feb. 5, '80. Running time: 117 MINS.

Kata . . . . Ildiko Bansagi
Janos . . . . Peter Andorai

In "Bizalom," competing at current Berlin Fest, Istvan Szabo again uses war as an epic background that changes the lives of his protagonists. Latter are isolated because of war but react in personal terms to create an unusual, romantic yet never mannered tale on human conduct in the vacuum of hiding out and new adjustments. Pic sizes up as Szabo's best.

Subtle, haunting imagery, fine acting and directorial concern make this almost Kafkaesque film an absorbing drama. This could be another Magyar film, after Pal Gabor's "Angi Vera," to attract world notice.

A woman going home from a movie, where the scene has been set by a newsreel on the current World War 2, is stopped by a man who tells her the police are there but her daughter and husband are safe. The husband had probably been involved in some sort of resistance unknown to her.

A seemingly simple woman attached to her family, she is tearfully whisked to a doctor who sets up a false name and identity card for her. She is to stay with a man as his wife in the house of an old couple.

The man had been involved in leftist causes in his youth and had been in hiding often. He, too, is married but had developed a furtiveness and mistrust that at first sets them at odds. Slowly they adjust, work together to deceive the old couple and finally her need for human commitment brings love.

It is real love, unusual and unexpected. The film has a sharp erotic edge not often apparent in Szabo's films. She gets some news of her husband and goes to see him and spends a night with him to find her old ways.

But it is the other man she needs so she must return. The rise and ebb of their love is deftly detailed and counterpointed by the war outside and their few fearful forays outside that always lead to worry and dread.

The war nears its end and the Russians finally arrive. There is talk of terrible reprisals by the people against the rich. The man goes off. She is found by her husband though she is awaiting the other. The latter is seen calling her false name to a line of people waiting for newspapers. —*Mosk.*

Simon
(COLOR)

Brickman's first goody without Woody.

An Orion release through Warner Bros., produced by Martin Bregman. Written and directed by Marshall Brickman. Features entire cast. Exec producer, Louis A. Stroller. Camera (Technicolor), Adam Holender; editor, Nina Feinberg; sound, Steve Scanlon; production design, Stuart Wurtzel; assistant director, Michael Rauch; costumes, Santo Loquasto; music, Stanley Silverman. Reviewed at the Directors Guild Theatre, Hollywood, Feb. 19, 1980. (MPAA Rating: PG.) Running time: 97 MINS.

Simon . . . . Alan Arkin
Becker . . . . Austin Pendleton
Lisa . . . . Judy Graubart
Fichandler . . . . William Finley
Barundi . . . . Jayant
Van Dongen . . . . Wallace Shawn
Hundertwasser . . . . Max Wright
Korey . . . . Fred Gwynne
Cynthia . . . . Madeline Kahn
Commune leader . . . . Adolph Green

After writing three pictures with Woody Allen, Marshall Brickman ventures out on his own with "Simon," which proves to be a frisky Allenande of a comedy, with strange turns at every step. "Simon" will score strong with devoted Allen fans, but Orion and WB should spell out the Brickman-Allen linkage for the broad marketplace.

Which shouldn't be too hard, however, once the screenwriting/collaborations of "Sleeper," "Annie Hall" and "Manhattan" are mentioned, especially since the satirical targets of "Simon" are much the same and the point of attack almost identical. Only major difference is that Brickman foregoes — or can't come up with — the snappy one-liners that pepper the other pictures.

But "Simon" is funny and a fine start for Brockman, who is directing and writing solo for the first time. Once again, the absurdities of the intelligentsia, addled academia and upper-class pretensions are up for derision and Brickman is a sharp needler.

Alan Arkin has his best role in a long time in the title part, a self-important but hopelessly inept college professor who falls into the hands of a band of genius zanies in a "think tank." Led by Austin Pendleton, who's terrific, the nation's best minds are supposed to be solving world problems, but actually spend their time amusing themselves with bizarre projects.

They brainwash Arkin into thinking he's an alien from outerspace and the plot proceeds wackily from there with Arkin finally escaping to a commune led by Adolph Green ("a former programming executive with ABC"), who reads to his young flock from TV Guide while they chant commercial jingles.

Brickman's script works well because it never becomes unbelievable, though often weird to the extreme. Exaggerated almost to the point of stereotype, the think tankers — William Finley, Jayant, Wallace Shawn and Max Wright are hilarious, nonetheless, especially Finley. Top-billed, Madeline Kahn has only a brief role as another scientist in cahoots with them, but she's fine.

Unfortunately, Brickman relies too much sometimes on cliche targets, such as Muzak and the military, although Fred Gwynne is good as the commander of troops out to shoot Arkin on sight. Television, too, is an overworked subject, but Brickman still pumps laughs out of it with the help of Green and the communers. Judy Graubart is solid as Arkin's lady-love.

Cinematographer Adam Holender and production designer Stuart Wurtzel make good use of New York locations and Stanley Silverman's score is fun all the way. From a production standpoint, Brickman and crew have obviously learned one Allen lesson well: keep the costs low, the quality high and the laughs long — and the profits will take care of themselves. Without doubt, there will be more Brickman pix to come.

— Har.

The Baltimore Bullet
(COLOR)

Father-son pool hustlers. Weak script.

Hollywood, Feb. 8.
An Avco Embassy release. Produced by John F. Brascia. Directed by Robert Ellis Miller. Features entire cast. Exec producers, William D. Jekel, Norman G. Rudman. Written by Brascia and Robert Vincent O'Neill; Camera (Eastmancolor), James A. Crabe; editor, Jerry Brady; sound, Jacque Nosco; production design, Herman Blumenthal; art director, Adrian Gortoux; music, Johnny Mandel; costumes, Patricia Ann Norris. Reviewed at Goldwyn Studios, L.A., Feb. 7, 1980 (MPAA Rating: PG). Running time: **103 MINS.**

Nick Casey .... James Coburn
The Deacon .... Omar Sharif
Billie Joe Robbins ...... Bruce Boxleitner
Carolina Red .... Ronee Blakely
Max .... Jack O'Halloran
Snow White .... Clavin Lockhart
Paulie .... Michael Learner
Cosmo .... Paul Barselou
Sugar .... Cisse Cameron
Sportscaster .... Jeff Temkin
Sportscaster .... Willie Mosconi

"The Baltimore Bullet" could be categorized as "Rocky II Goes To The Pool Hall" except for the fact that it has none of the charm, wit or pathos of the Sylvester Stallone entertainment. What the picture does have is numerous cardboard characters whisking in and out of hopelessly contrived situations. It also

has pool — lots of it. Light tone maintained throughout could draw some initial response for Avco Embassy.

James Coburn and Bruce Boxleitner limn a kind of father-son pool hustling team (Coburn "adopted" a downtrodden Boxleitner while in his heyday) who make their living traveling through the country taking advantage of local would-be billiard sharks. They do occasionally enter tournaments, one of which will enable Coburn to reunite with his arch nemesis Omar Sharif, a classy hustler who seems to have the ability to emerge victorious at almost every game known to man.

Coburn has to raise $20,000 and win the big tourney in order to have a rematch with Sharif. Latter is being stalked by a not so nice killer Jack O'Halloran; one of the many people he has managed to emerge victorious over. Needless to say everyone meets at the big game.

Coburn and Boxleitner work well together although the former looks and speaks more like someone sipping champagne aboard a yacht than a journeyman dashing through an endlessly array of hick towns. Ronee Blakely is picked up by the pair along the way for moral support and fulfills the limited duties asked of her.

Problem here is script by Robert Vincent O'Neill and John Brascia, latter also producer. Situations are just too inane to take seriously (especially one elongated scene where Boxleitner gets cheated at a card game) and not funny enough to be laughed at. Director Robert Ellis Miller moves things along but what's presented never really seems to go anywhere.

Especially juvenile are a number of offensive references to women which should serve to thoroughly alienate any potential femme patrons. Picture is the first feature presentation for Filmfair, maker of numerous television commercials. — Berg.

The Black Marble
(COLOR)

Wambaugh's best, but won't roll as far as it might have.

Hollywood, Feb. 17.
An Avco Embassy Picture release, produced by Frank Capra Jr. Directed by Harold Becker. Features entire cast. Screenplay, Joseph Wambaugh, from his novel; camera (DeLuxe Color), Owen Roizman; editor, Maury Winetrobe; sound, Jeff Wexler; production design, Alfred Sweeney; asst. director, Tom Mack; music, Maurice Jarre. Reviewed at MGM Studios, Culver City, Feb. 17, 1980 (MPAA rating: PG.) Running time: **113 MINS.**
Valnikov .... Robert Foxworth
Natalie .... Paula Prentiss
Philo .... Harry Dean Stanton
Madeline .... Barbara Babcock
Clarence .... John Hancock
Capt. Hooker .... Raleigh Bond
Pattie Mae .... Judy Landers
Itchy Mitch .... Pat Corley
Bambarella .... Paul Henry Itken
Alex .... Richard Dix
Fiddler .... James Woods

With "The Black Marble," Joseph Wambaugh at last comes close to presenting police as human, even humorous, beings, capable of balancing remorse, regret and romance without becoming the total psychotics of his previous books (and films, with or without the Wambaugh credit.) At the same time, he will not gloss over the unpleasant aspects of policework, which once again creates a tough picture to market.

At the box-office, "The Black Marble" looks to be "Onion Field" plus, which won't be bad. The lighter touch and a happy ending should make the difference.

For nearly 10 minutes before the opening titles, Robert Foxworth stumbles drunkenly through a church congregation to a painful climax in a scene that establishes both the fun and pathos that will envelop his character throughout. As a troubled cop who has seen too much and expects nothing good, Foxworth is outstanding, anchoring the picture soundly.

Transferred out of homicide after too much exposure to a string of child murders, Foxworth is teamed on a burglary detail with Paula Prentiss, who doesn't relish a drunk for a partner. At first, and as usual, Prentiss tries too hard to establish her character, leaving the actress exposed. Eventually, though, her special charm takes over and she settles down into a believable relationship with Foxworth.

As with the book, "Marble" is buoyed by the fact that the crime at hand is either terribly serious or impossibly trivial, depending on your love of animals. Barbara Babcock's showdog is kidnapped and she proves superb in the role of a lonely, sex-starved woman with her whole life wrapped up in her schnauzer.

Director Harold Becker is at his best in maneuvering carefully through the minefields of animal worship and his handling of a raccoon funeral at a pet cemetery says everything without once taking a position.

Much of the credit for making the picture work goes to Harry Dean Stanton as the dognapper, driven to his dirty deed by debt. Stanton's character is not a bad man and he does a good job of conveying the hurt of his own actions, while also creating the most laughs in the picture as he bumbles along.

If Wambaugh and Becker were content to present a Foxworth-

Prentiss romance against this bent background, the result would have clearly been light comedy with a happy resolution. But the tone never lifts that high. There are many somber scenes as Foxworth wrestles with his bloody memories and a gruesome episode as Stanton tortures the dog, all the more chilling for what is unseen and left to the imagination. And a final fight between him and Foxworth is violent beyond the general context. It's all creditable realism, but ultimately costs the film much in classification.

In addition to the pet cemetery, "Marble" has many fetching settings, the best of which are realistically satirical, like the dog show itself. Becker and cinematographer Owen Roizman both have a good eye for the essential seediness of modern Hollywood, where much of the action takes place.

James Woods, who scored so solidly in "Onion Field" for Wambaugh, has no more than a bit part in this one, though he's billed as a guest star. But that's just one more oddity in an odd picture. — Har.

Cocktail Molotov
(FRENCH-COLOR)

Paris, Feb. 20.
An AMLF release of an Alexandre Films/Antenne 2 co-production. Features entire cast. Directed by Diane Kurys. Written by Kurys, Philippe Adrien and Alain Le Henry; camera (color), Philippe Rousselet; sound, Bernard Aubouy; art direction, Hilton McConnico, Tony Egry; editor, Joelle Van Effenterre; music, Yves Simon; songs performed by Murray Head. Reviewed at the Colisee Theatre, Paris, Feb. 18, '80. Running time: **100 MINS.**
Anne .... Elise Caron
Frederic .... Philippe Lebas
Bruno .... Francois Cluzet

Diane Kurys, the modestly observant chronicler of adolescent growing pains, follows up her first film, "Peppermint Soda," with another minor but agreeable, looseknit tale of young people in contemporary France.

"Cocktail Molotov," despite the violent intimations of its title, is a basically undramatic and somewhat politically naive road movie set against the backdrop of the May 1968 student-worker uprisings.

Film follows the peregrinations of three youths: Anne, 18 (perhaps the heroine of "Peppermint Soda" five years later), who leaves home after a violent quarrel with her mother, intent on living in a kibbutz; Frederic, her boy-friend and first sex partner, and his friend, Bruno.

After Anne's departure from home, the boys go after her, hoping to dissuade her from her course. In Venice, where she is to catch her boat, their car and her belongings are stolen. News of the events in

France begin to reach them and they decide to hitch back home. Their curiosity about the political situation is almost completely eclipsed by their smaller-scale problems of emotional growth and adaptation, which is basically all that the director is really concerned with here.

Kurys again shows herself to be an unaffectedly competent recorder of adolescent joys and ills although the opening up, both socially and geographically, works against her talents as an intimist director. "Peppermint Soda" was richer in convincing detail, as it was set in and around the specific, huis clos setting of a Parisian high school. "Cocktail" has failed to recreate the success here of "Peppermint Soda" and will need hard sell for overseas markets.

Kurys, herself an actress, again shows a firm guiding hand with her performers. The three principals are played by three new film faces: Elise Caron, Philippe Lebas and Francois Cluzet. Caron and Lebas are merely fine; Cluzet is a strongly present young talent who's definitely going places. —*Len.*

The Young Master
(HONG KONG-COLOR)

Hong Kong, Feb. 15.
A Leonard Ho Production for Golden Harvest. Directed by Jackie Chan. Stars Chan, Yuan Biao, Wei Pai, Whong In Sik, Lily Li, Shek Kin, Feng Ke-An, Li Hai-Sheng, Tien Feng and Feng Feng. Screenplay, Lau Tin-Chee, Tung Lu, Tang Kin-Sang; action choreographers, Jackie Chan, Feng Ke-An; music, Frankie Chan; camera (color), Chen Ching-Chueh. Reviewed at Golden Harvest preview room, Hong Kong, Feb. 14, '80. Running time: **120 MINS.**

(Cantonese dialogue, English sub-titles)

Raymond Chow's Golden Harvest has hit another gold mine in Asia's reigning current King of Kung Fu — Jackie Chan, known locally as Sing Lung. Directed and starring Chan, "The Young Master's" release has been timed with the Chinese Lunar New Year celebration which assures its boxoffice success. In fact, anything with Chan will likely stir the interest of the locals and quality has nothing to do with it. In only two days, plus special midnight shows, "Master" showed its B.O. strength with a record-breaking HK$1.9 mil.

"The Young Master" is the debut of Chan as director and he has made the picture to showcase period costumes, fancy and novel martial arts techniques, local color, colloquial jokes and a string of fight sequences. Chan, is an ex-stuntman discovered by Lo Wei ("New Fist Of Fury"), catapulted to full stardom by Ng Sze Yuen ("Snake In

The Eagle's Shadow") and then to superstardom by Raymond Chow. But Chan has full control of "Young Master," of new production abroad is underway for international release through the Golden Harvest network.

Master begins with the colourful Lion Dance tournament in a small town of Yungning. It is climaxed by a stunning lion dance contest between the town's two competing martial arts school. For years, the Ching Fung School has been winning because of a student called Tiger. But he is unable to play and the school's number two student Dragon (Jackie Chan) takes over to lead the team against the Wai Yee School. Dragon loses and later it is discovered that Tiger accepted a bribe to betray his school. Tiger is suspended and leaves, then his friend Dragon decides to follow in order to convince him to return.

The film lacks story content and intelligent characterizations but stars the acrobatic new Hong Kong hero of the 80's. So it does not really matter whether there are reasons for the antics, low and tasteless humour and practically non-existent storyline because Chan is so physically vibrant with his funny kung fu that the 8-to-80 year-old Chinese viewers will be definitely captivated.

Showing prominence despite Chan's presence are Yuan Bian and actress Lily Li, who finally blossoms into something more than a decorative starlet. She plays the daughter of the county Sheriff.

"The Young Master" is no Jackie Chan classic. He has the stamina of an Olympic athlete alright but lacks the maturity, expertise and good taste to direct a full-length movie of merit. His youthful boy innocent look is almost gone. It is obvious that he still needs a master like director Ng Sze Yuen to fully showcase his abilities as kung fu artist, acrobat and comedian as a man of 27 years. The film is now being re-edited, refined, rehashed and practically re-done for international release. The film reviewed above is the Cantonese version for Southeast Asian release and consumption.—*Mel.*

Foxes
(COLOR)

Sizable teen appeal.

Hollywood, Feb. 26.
United Artists release of a Casablanca Record & Filmworks production. Produced by David Puttnam and Gerald Ayres. Stars Jodie Foster. Directed by Adrian Lyne. Screenplay, Gerald Ayres; camera (Technicolor), Leon Bijou; original music composed and conducted by Giorgio Moroder; art director, Michael

Levesque; editor, Jim Coblentz; asst. director, Stuart Gross; unit publicist, Susan Alschuler; special effects, Robert Horvatich. Reviewed at MGM Studios, Feb. 19, 1980. (MPAA Rating - R). Running time: **106 MINS.**

Jeanie	Jodie Foster
Brad	Scott Baio
Mary	Sally Kellerman
Jay	Randy Quaid
Mrs. Axman	Lois Smith
Bryan	Adam Faith
Annie	Cheri Currie
Madge	Marilyn Kagan
Deirdre	Kandice Stroh
Loser	Jon Sloan
Sissie	Jill Barrie Bogart
Frank	Wayne Storm
Gladys	Mary Margaret Lewis
Greg	Grant Wilson
Bobby	Fredric Lehne
Scott	Robert Romanus
Counsellor	Roger Bowen

Also — Buddy Foster, E. Lamont Johnson, Mary Ellen O'Neill, Ben Frank, Kay A. Toroborg, Scott Garrett, Laura Dern, Michael Taylor, Gino Baffa, Charles Shull, Tony Termini, Jeff Silverman, Mae Williams, R Scott Thomson, Ron Lombard, Steve Jones, Jon M. Benson, Tom Pletts, Ken Novick, Angel.

"Foxes" is an ambitious attempt to do a film relating to some of the not so acceptable realities among today's teenagers that ends up delivering far less than it is capable of. Story of four teenage girls and their battles with parents, drugs, sex and life in general, seems to get so caught up in expressing problems that it often becomes a depressing, one-sided and melodramatic treatise on American youth. Still, the style of the Casablanca Filmworks project coupled with some dynamic music from its stable of talent should cinch sizable interest among teens. Given boxoffice clout of the latter, pic could cash in at the ticket window despite almost nil adult appeal.

Jodie Foster shows more talent than ever in a difficult role as leader of the group of four girls. Opening scene where camera pans across Foster's bedroom to the tune of the Donna Summer hit, "On The Radio," (pic's effective recurring theme) establishes a wonderfully accurate tone that continues as the group awakens and prepares for school.

It soon becomes clear this is not the same gaggle of girls portrayed as typical American teenagers. Cherie Currie is a stoned-out former hooker, Marilyn Kagan is an unhappy, overweight fat girl longing to shed her parents' protective shell, Kandice Stroh is a lying, confused flirt and Foster is a level-headed intellect who has her hands full in both caring for herself and dealing with the problems of everyone around her. Because each actress is so expert at making her role come alive the film manages to work extremely well in selected spots.

Difficulties arise as picture progresses to explore each character particularly Currie and her battle to

flee a crazed father and straighten her life out.

Gerald Ayres' script (he also co-produced) does quite well early on in pointing out the problems, but tends to lose focus and consequently interest when dramatizing them. Constant switching of action between the girls causes Stroh's character to be lost mid-way through and Foster's identity to never fully be explored despite the fact she's the focal point throughout.

Although it seems somewhat acceptable to portray adults as the villains for their children's plight, neither the kids or anyone else in the film appear the kind of person any intelligent, sensitive human being would want to become. It's fine to paint a not so rosy picture of life, but it's a little difficult to accept that the entire world is bad as the film would have audiences believe.

In what seems like a solution to all of this, Ayres uses a questionable tragic plot twist to tie up the loose ends and an even more dubious projection into the future as a concluding scene. Neither does the job.

Director Adrian Lyne has done excellent work in capturing the mood of a segment of today's youth and Leon Bijou's photography provides a beautiful backdrop from which to explore the issues. Ditto original music composed and conducted by Giorgio Moroder.

There are also some fine supporting performances, most notably Randy Quaid as Kagan's boyfriend, Sally Kellerman as Foster's mother.

"Foxes" ultimately disappoints artistically because it could have been much more than a film with good music that relates to teenagers. However, there's a chance that what it is could very well be enough to make it a financial success. —*Berg.*

Le Soleil en face
(Face To The Sun)
(FRENCH-COLOR)

Paris, Jan. 28.
A UGC release of an Odyssey-FR 3 coproduction. Produced by Humbert Balsan, Serge Marquand, Stephane Tchalgadjieff. Features entire cast. Directed by Pierre Kast. Screenplay, Kast, Alain Aptekman; camera (color), Gerard de Battista; music, Sergio Godinho; editor, Nicole Berckmans. Reviewed at the UGC Biarritz theatre, Paris, Jan. 26, 1980. Running time: **95 MINS.**

Marat	Jean-Pierre Cassel
Genevieve	Stephane Audran
Sandra	Alexandra Stewart
Catherine	Beatrice Bruno

Pierre Kast, an intellectual writer and filmmaker, co-wrote and directed this oddly relaxed tale about the death of an intellectual, played with seductive appeal by Jean-Pierre Cassel.

Cassel is Marat, a celebrated novelist who has produced nothing of import in years. He now lives in hedonistic semi-retirement in a villa in southern Portugal, surrounded by a bevy of adoring women, including his wife (Stephane Audran) and two pretty nieces. He makes love to one of his nieces regularly.

Marat's doctor informs his wife that the writer is dying of cancer. With the complicity of friends and family, she tries to keep Marat in ignorance of his condition and make things as agreeable as possible for him.

But he finds out. His first reaction is one of outrage and despair. Then he calms down and takes things in hand, determined to order his death as he has his life. One lovely afternoon he gathers everyone together and has them read from his favorite authors, like Epicurus and Boris Vian. In the course of this mise-en-scene he ceremonially swallows a pill, lies down and dies.

There's little that's murky or despairing here but the film's tonelessness and resolutely glib resolution leave one emotionally and intellectually hungry. There are some pictorially lovely things, like the series of poignant tracking shots through a cemetery of ships' anchors that punctuate the proceedings like a refrain from a poem, but Kast's attempt to demystify an age-old theme is finally not very probing. —*Len.*

Rude Boy
(BRITISH-COLOR)

Punk music and apathy, but it holds.

London, Feb. 21.

A Michael White presentation of a Buzzy Enterprises production. Produced and directed by Jack Hazan, David Mingay. Stars Ray Gange. Screenplay, Mingay, Gange, Hazan; camera (color), Hazan; editors, Mingay, Peter Goddard; music, Joe Strummer, Mick Jones; sound, Greg Bailey, Bob Edwards, Garth Marshall; production services, Solus Enterprises; asst. director, Goddard. Review at the Century screening room, London Feb. 20, '80. (BBFC Rating: X). Running time: 133 MINS.

Ray	Ray Gange

The Clash: Joe Strummer (singer), Mick Jones (lead guitar), Paul Simonon (bass), Nicky Headon (drums)

Road manager	John Green
Roadie	Barry Baker
Terry	Terry McQuade
Clash girlfriend	Caroline Coon
Ray's girlfriends	Elizabeth Young, Sarah Hall
CID officer	Colin Bucksey
Sex shop customer	Colin Richards
Byron	Lizard Brown
Drum	Hicky Etienne
Inch	Inch Gordon
Eel	Lee Parker
Solicitor's clerk	Kenny Joseph
Guest Singer	Jimmy Pursey

"Rude Boy" is a remarkable mix of character-study, rock-opera and social documentary. It features The Clash, one of the original, and most plausible, British punk bands. It is not, however, a vehicle to hype the act. It also features Tory prime minister Margaret Thatcher. Needless to say, it doesn't hype her act either.

What it does is plot the frustrations of a late '70s rebel without a cause. The uncouth youth of the title is a typical enough English fellow just out of his teens — not educated for anything more than a dead-end job, but not too stupid to be oppressed by its futility; with just enough pride to be irked by welfare, yet too soft to turn to serious crime or violence. To their credit, filmmakers Jack Hazan and David Mingay make more than two hours of such apparently glum material seem less.

On homeground in the U.K., "Rude Boy" will likely profit from its direct appeal to the prime filmgoing age-group. Elsewhere, prospects are bound to be spottier, with the chance of a hit here and there given strategic placing and careful local promotion. It's no rave, but it could win gut-responses from kids who identify, plus more thoughtful consideration from older types who'll see it as a politico artfilm. Audiences with an aversion to round language or loud music (there's a lot of both) won't be amused. As for the strong London dialect, the film's impact is principally visual and does not rely on what's said.

As with their earlier (1975) feature about painter David Hockney and his circle, "A Bigger Splash," Hazan and Mingay took years rather than weeks to shoot their new one, lacing the narrative and central character into actual events up and down Britain, such as political rallies, and various Clash concerts. Most dialog has the authentic ring of good improvisation, and even the scripted sequences carry a strongly naturalistic, documentary "feel."

Ray Gange is credible, watchable and sympathetic as the archetypal "blank generation" washout, first seen spitting from a highrise tenement window as the Queen's Silver Jubilee celebrations grind on below. Hired by The Clash as a roadie — his sole ambition — he fails to make out, antagonizes the band members he once idolized, still dogs them on tour even though he's been fired, gets drunk all the time and is finally kicked out for good.

The depressing tale succeeds dramatically, against considerable odds, because it conveys precisely, and often wittily, the tensions felt by the young in a formerly complacent country that's skidding into economic decline and disillusionment. The Clash's hard, unglamorous music may be no kind of entertainment, but it's one hell of an event. All filmed live, the numbers' vivid, protesting lyrics inject essential energy into the main vein of apathy.

A notable bonus, in addition to some good performances by the non-professional cast, is that "Rude Boy" is technically highly proficient. And if the definiton of a fine image is that it communicates more than it actually contains, Hazan (who also directed photography) has composed some firstrate frames. —*Simo.*

Salut I Forca Al Canut
(Catalan Cuckold)
(SPANISH-COLOR)

Madrid, Feb. 9.

Prozesa production. Directed by Francesc Bellmunt. Features entire cast. Screenplay, M. Sanz, J. Puigcorbe, F. Bellmunt; camera (Eastmancolor), Tomas Pladevall; editor, Anastasi Rinos; music, Josep Maria Duran; sets, Francesc Candini; exec producer, J.A. Perez Giner. Reviewed at Cine Luchana (Madrid), Feb. 9, '80. Running time: 94 MINS.

Joan	Juanjo Puigcorbe
Laura	Alicia Orozco
Anna	Isabel Mestres
Lluis	Pepon Coromina
Pacient	Joan Borras
Dona Pacient	Carme Molina
Lola	Anna Lizaran
Dr. Capmany	Josep Maria Loperena

(Versions in Catalan and Castilian)

Contemporary sex comedy with a few droll situations and an occasional laff, but too rambling and talky to sustain much interest. Shot mostly in Barcelona studios and interiors. Most of the humor is sophomoric and very local. The few serious subjects touched upon — marriage, sex education, feminism — are slushed off with an anecdote or a caricature.

Yarn concerns a sex counsellor whose own marriage is going on the rocks. His wife takes up with a friend while the doc pursues a loose-living nurse. There are some improbable and loquaciously dull party scenes, some discreetly simulated sex scenes, tame frontal nudity and lotsa "frank" talk

Helmer Bellmunt sprinkles in some touches of humor too, but it's all done rather clumsily. There are even two gratuitous and out-of-place caricatures of Argentinians, thrown in, it seems, just to fill out the tenuous script. Direction, thesping and technical credits are on the amateurish side. Item is fodder purely for the local market.—*Besa.*

C'est pas moi c'est lui
(It's Not Me, It's Him)
(FRENCH-COLOR)

Paris, Feb. 14.

A CCFC release of a Fideline Films production. Stars Pierre Richard, Aldo Maccione. Directed by Richard. Screenplay, Richard, Alain Godard; camera (Fujicolor), Claude Agostini; music, Vladimir Cosma; editor, Noelle Boisson; art director, Jean-Baptiste Poiret; sound, Bernard Bats. Reviewed at the Marignan Theatre, Paris, Feb. 8, 1980. Running time: 90 MINS.

Pierre	Pierre Richard
Aldo	Aldo Maccione
Valerie	Valerie Mairesse
Vallier	Henri Gardin

Pierre Richard's new comedy, which he also co-wrote and directed, has a few amusing gags & ideas and a lot of exotic color — it was shot mostly on location in Tunisia — to fill up the time.

Richard plays the ghost writer for a successful comic scenarist who assumes the latter's identity and bluffs his way into a collaboration with a hot-shot Italian movie star. They head for the solitude of Tunisia for their work sessions but fall prey to a series of misadventures, both amorous and professional.

Richard has again teamed up with Aldo Maccione, the husky, macho buffoon who appeared in his last effort, "Je Suis Timide Mais Je Me Soigne," and with whom he makes a breezy comic duo. But the film's script is biscuit-thin and wheezes predictably once the characters hit North African soil.

Richard needs better material and cannier directorial sense to make his comic vehicles sturdy enough for international markets. —*Len.*

Cordelia
(FR. CANADIAN-COLOR)

Montreal, Feb. 18.

A National Film Board of Canada production, distributed by la Corporation des Films Mutuels. Producer, Jean-Marc Garand. Directed by Jean Beaudin. Features entire cast. Screenplay, Jean Beaudin, Marcel Sabourin, from "La Lampe dans la Fenetre" by Pauline Cadieux; camera, (color), Pierre Mignot; editor, Jean Beaudin; art direction, Denis Boucher, Vianney Gauthier; sound, Jacques Blain; music, Maurice Blackburn. Reviewed at the Dauphin cinema, Montreal, Feb. 18, 1980. Running time: 118 MINS.

Cordelia Viau	Louise Portal
Samuel Parslow	Gaston Lepage
Isidore Poirier	Pierre Gobeil
M. Leduc	Gilbert Sicotte
Joseph Fortier	Raymond Cloutier
Judge Tascherau	Jean-Louis Roux
Hangman Radcliff	James Blendick
Jailer Groulx	Rolland Bedard

Beautifully shot but weak on story, this effort by Jean Beaudin (whose "J.A. Martin, Photographe" won Monique Mercure the Best Actress award at Cannes in 1978) used up most of the 1979 budget for the French production section of the National Film Board of Canada. Whether it was worth it is debatable — though the production values are stunning and the acting in general well above average.

"Cordelia" is taken from a French-Canadian book, "The Lamp In the Window," which deals with the only murder conviction in Canada based solely on circumstantial evidence. In 1899, a young woman from a Quebec village, Cordelia Viau, and her handyman, Samuel Parslow, are accused of murdering the woman's husband, Isidore Poirier. The husband, just returned from working in California, is found in his bed with his throat cut. Parslow and Cordelia both have alibis for the night in question, so the Crown's case hangs on the conflicting testimony of two witnesses on whether a lamp in the Poirier window was lit. Joseph Fortier, an old friend of the accused and the court notary, played with lascivious nastiness by Raymond Cloutier, denies the lamp was lit, and condemns Cordelia to death.

Cordelia Viau is portrayed as something of a non-conformist, inviting parties of gay blades to her house for musical soirees, whether or not her husband was present. It is apparent that the historical Cordelia was railroaded to her death by the distrust and dislike of her puritanical village and by the harangues of sensationalist journalism, which labeled the couple as murderers even before their arrest. The double hanging was enthusiastically attended by crowds from all over Canada, the United States, and even from France.

Despite this unsavoury look at 19th century justice, however, director Jean Beaudin makes the same mistake as Cordelia's historical lawyer; while insisting on the innocence of these two victims of society, he makes no attempt to explain the murdered man. Moreover, many of the key indications of plot are thrown away or only comprehensible in hindsight. Cordelia's character is given sparse indications in the script, but is given a lot of life of not much development (by Louise Portal, a plump, hairy, pugnosed girl who is sometimes sensual, sometimes repellent. Cordelia is eccentric, but after the murder she becomes first a cipher, a victim, and then, astonishingly enough, the martyred saint of a Catholic morality play.

Parslow, the sub-normal handyman, is portrayed by Gaston Lepage as a hollow-eyed, openmouthed rustic with overlapping teeth and just the right amount of dawning sensitivity. James Blendick, as the hangman Radcliff, one of the two anglophones in the film (both unspeakably depraved), puts in an exaggerated, frothing display of necrophilia when describing his double-hanging technique. This effectively repels the audience for the latter part of the film, whose claustrophobic, surrealist tone clashes with the smooth, natural style of the first part.

Despite the minimal amount of audience identification with the characters, the film after the murder is rather a harrowing experience. The camera work of Pierre Mignot, however, is worth the trip; he knows how to create visual beauty without being obtrusive. The film has the slow pace and cultured look of a European work; reviews in Montreal have been generally favorable, and "Cordelia" may find an art-film market. —Dres.

On A Vole la Cuisse de Jupiter
(Somebody's Stolen the Thigh of Jupiter)
(FRENCH-COLOR)

Paris, Feb. 17.
A CCFC release of an Ariane Films/Mondex Films/FR3 coproduction. Produced by Alexandre Mnouchkine, Georges Dancigers and Robert Amon. Stars Annie Girardot, Philippe Noiret. Directed by Philippe de Broca. Written by De Broca, Michel Audiard, based on the personage of Commissioner Tanquerelle created by Jean-Paul Rouland and Claude Olivier; camera (Eastmancolor), Jean-Paul Schwartz; sound, Jean Labussiere; music, Georges Hatzinassios; art director, Eric Moulard, Mikes Karapiperis; editor, Henri Lanoe. Reviewed at the Normandie Theatre, Paris, Feb. 14, 1980. Running time: 102 MINS.
Lise Tanquerelle . . . . Annie Girardot
Antoine Lemercier . . . . Philippe Noiret
Pochet . . . . Francis Perrin
Agnes Pochet . . . . Catherine Alric
Spiratos . . . . Marc Dudicourt

Philippe de Broca's latest is a picture postcard adventure comedy starring Philippe Noiret, Annie Girardot and some stunning Greek landscapes. It's a sequel to his 1977 "Dear Detective," and tries to muster up some of the daredevil antics of his old hit, "That Man From Rio."

Noiret and Girardot appealingly recreate their roles of Antoine Lemercier, professor of classical Greek, and Police Commissioner Lise Tanquerelle.

Films begin in France with their wedding, as Girardot rushes into the town hall straight from a police raid. Straightaway they depart for Greece for their honeymoon, where Noiret gets to show off his erudition.

They cross paths with an excitable young archaeologist (Francis Perrin) who's unearthed a statue fragment, the buttocks of Venus Heroclitus (and not, as the film title states, Jupiter's thighs). Thanks to the machinations of Perrin's dissatisfied wife (Catherine Alric) the statue is stolen by a young Greek sailor, who is murdered. Noiret and Perrin are indicted for the killing but escape to track down the true culprit, a specialist in classical wares (played, by the way, by producer Alexandre Mnouchkine) who wants to reconstitute the entire statue for his own gain.

Once again, Michel Audiard is co-scripter with De Broca which accounts for the incidental sparkle of the dialogue and the overall sloth of the script, which is freewheeling but predictable.

De Broca's direction is nimble and airy, which, along with the performances, makes for a painless, but unmemorable sitting. Film probably won't bear comparison with the old de Broca-Belmondo "Rio" pic (the thrills in "Jupiter," particularly the climax, are factitious and anti-climactic), or even "Dear Detective," but its well-sustained good-humour and eye-filling backgrounds should give it some interest in foreign markets. —Len.

Stone Cold Dead
(CANADIAN-COLOR)

Toronto, Feb. 20.
Dimension release (in the U.S.) of a Ko-Zak Productions presentation. Executive Producer, Peter Wilson. Producers, George Mendeluk, John Ryan. Directed by Mendeluk. Features entire cast. Screenplay, Mendeluk, based on novel "The Sin Sniper" by Hugh Garner; camera, (color), Dennis Miller; editor, Martin Pepler; art direction, Ted Watkins; set decoration, Jac Bradette. Reviewed at Quinn Labs screening room, Toronto, Feb. 20, 1980. Running time: 97 MINS.
Sergeant Boyd . . . . Richard Crenna
Julius Kurtz . . . . Paul Williams
Monica Page . . . . Linda Sorenson
Sandy MacAuley . . Belinda J. Montgomery
Sergeant Tony Colabre . Charles Shamata
Olivia Page . . . . .Alberta Watson
Doctor Bouvier . . . . .Monique Mercure
Bernice Carnival . . . . . Andree Cousineau
Teddy Mann . . . . Frank Moore
Rosie . . . . George Chuvalo
Inspector Webb . . . . George Touliatos
Danny De Lion . . . . Dennis Strong
Claudia Grissom . . . . .Jennifer Dale

Behind the grimy facade of an urban main street, a maniacal crime boss runs the prostie trade, a shadowy sniper guns down the girls one by one, and a lone cop fights them all.

That's the tale of this pic. It's suitable for action houses, a suspenseful enough screen debut for director George Mendeluk. A trick whodunit ending and the slammer for the crime boss rounds it all up neatly at the finish.

Richard Crenna turns in a workmanlike job as the cop. Belinda J. Montgomery breezes through her role as an undercover cop with a pleasant singing voice. Too bad she gets bumped off soon. The same goes for Jennifer Dale who does a strip act only to leave the building and get shot.

Linda Sorenson is a pert, mature, mother-figure hooker with a slight yen for Crenna. But Frank Moore and Alberta Watson as a prof and she the sniper (and Sorenson's daughter) don't deliver. Paul Williams comes across terse, over tough and even slightly humorous playing prostie boss Kurtz. Other credits are okay. —Adil.

Schilten
(SWISS-COLOR)

Berlin, Feb. 16.
A Beat Kuert and Barbara Riesen Film Production, in coproduction with the Film-Kollektiv Zurich. Features entire cast. Directed by Beat Kuert. Screenplay, Kuert, Michael Maassen, based on Hermann Burger's novel of the same name; camera (color), Hansueli Schenkel; music, Cornelius Wernle. Reviewed at Film Studio am Kudam, Berlin, Feb. 16, '80. Running time: 90 MINS.
Cast: Michael Maassen (Armin Schildknecht), Gudrun Geier (Elvira Schuepfer), Norbert Schwientek (Wiederkehr), Kaarina Schenk (Adelheid Binswanger), Rudolf Ruf (Dr. Kraehenbuehl), Peter Schweiger (Inspector), Ferdinand Mattmann (Postman Friedli), children from the Ruedertal (students).

Described in a press release as "a story in pictures," Beat Kuert's "Schilten" is based on Hermann Burger's novel with the same title that cast a bad reputation on a corner of Switzerland, the Ruedertal. Helmer Kuert went there to do a tv-pic on the area, more or less to see if Burger was justified in his writings, and stayed over a half-year to reconstruct the book's atmosphere in a stream-of-consciousness style of filmmaking.

"Schilten" refers to the area itself, and since the author's thoughts deal with a real place and definite time, the film does little more than contrast fantasy with reality as seen and felt by the novel's complex central figure, a schoolteacher isolated from everything in the provinces. Considering the pic's modest budget, both the style and the shred of a story are enough to hold the attention for the span of a feature pic.

The schoolteacher, Schildknecht, comes to the area to take over a one-room schoolhouse after the place is seemingly abandoned by others. The reason is simple: any rational being would be driven to madness, the writer and filmmaker say, by the inhuman society he comes into contact with on a daily, unrelenting basis. The spiritual bareness and drab existence are, theoretically, overwhelming.

Nevertheless, the film is just too pretty to be offensive. The area may be poor, and the inhabitants spiritually deprived, but the beauty of nature, carefully lensed, wipes out all the lines after a while — until the teacher's growing madness seems to be all his own fault on the surface. Since it's stated in the literary source that "Schilten" is about a man's fear of being buried alive, flashes of surreal fantasy and the motiv, oft repeated, of a gravedigger working in a cemetery finally destroy the story entirely.

—*Holl.*

La Legion Saute Sur Kolwezi
(Operation Leopard)
(FRENCH-COLOR)

Paris, Jan. 19.

A CCFC release of a Bela Productions/SNC/FR3 co-production. Produced by Georges de Beauregard. Features entire cast. Directed by Raoul Coutard. Screenplay, Andre G. Brunelin, based on book by Pierre Sergent; camera (color), Georges Liron; editor, Michel Lewin; sound, Michel Laurent; music, Serge Franklin. Reviewed at Club 13, Paris, Jan. 7, 1980. Running time: **100 MINS.**

Sgt.-MajorFederico .... Giuliano Gemma
Pierre Delbart . . . . Bruno Cremer
Damremont . . . . Laurent Malet
Ambassador . . . . Jacques Perrin
Annie Debruyn . . . . Mimsy Farmer

Cinematographer Raoul Coutard directed this lackluster account of the French Foreign Legion's intervention in Zaire in the spring of 1978, where they rescued 3,000 European and American civilians held hostage by Kantangese rebels in the mining town of Kolwezi. Of limited commercial interest outside of markets directly concerned with this event and evidently not recommended for viewers whose hearts don't flutter at the sight of military valour.

Scenarist Andre Brunelin has adapted Pierre Sergent's book about the incident with platitudinous indifference, conventionally alternating scenes of civilian ordeal at the hands of the rebels and sequences of military preparation and rescue.

Coutard keeps the camera close to his characters to play down the epic aspects of the action, but all this does is magnify the banality of the script and performances. The cinematography, credited to Georges Liron, is far beneath what one expects from a film boasting Coutard's participation.

Coutard won praise as director back in 1969 with the prize winning "Hoa Binh." Here his lack of irony, humour and distance have tripped him up, and we are thus subject to such ludicrous moments such as when a wounded African paratrooper gasps: "I'm not black, Major, I'm a Legionnaire." —*Len.*

Die Kinder Aus No. 67
(The Children from No. 67)
(WEST GERMAN-COLOR)

Berlin, Feb. 7.

A Road Movies Film Production, Berlin. Renee Gundelach, in collaboration with Zweites Deutsches Fernsehen (ZDF), Wolfgang Patzschke, and support from Kuratorium Junger Deutscher Film and the Stiftung Deutsche Jugendmarke. Features entire cast. Written and directed by Usch Barthelmess-Weller and Werner Meyer. Camera (color), Juergen Juerges, Hans-Guenther Buecking; sets, Maciej Putowski, Thomas Irmscher; editing, Helga Borsche, Thorsten Naeter; music, Andi Brauer. Reviewed at Studio am Kudam, Berlin, Feb. 7, '80. Running time: **103 MINS.**

Cast: Elfriede Irall, Tilo Prueckner, Bernd Riedel, Martina Krauel, Peter Franke, Rene Schaaf, Rainer-Goetz Otto.

One of those $1,000,000 budget pix with backing from several subsidy sources, and based on a set of children's stories with the same title, Usch Barthelmess-Weller and Werner Meyer's "The Children From No. 67" (subtitled "Heil Hitler, I'd Like a Couple Horse Apples") has everything going for it, save a vet helmer's hand to iron out the wrinkles and draw the laughs it's supposed to get, per title-joke. Direction is stiff and inimaginative, but lensing more than makes up for deficiencies under Juergen Juerges's steady and gifted hand.

Kid-pic is about a group of youngsters living in one of those large tenement houses in Berlin, whose courtyard serves as a kind of small-scale Grand Central Station. Every kind of political and social milieu is described during these first years under Hitler's Third Reich, when the Right and the Left were still having it out with each other. One poor family are committed Socialists, another confirmed Nazis, and a third about to swing from the former to the latter if things don't get better. The kids, of course, play their adult games to keep the plot moving, but not enough to overcome cliches and stereotypes.

—*Holl.*

Pratyusha
(Before Dan)
(INDIAN-B&W)

Bangalore, Jan. 29.

Swairi Films release and production. Features entire cast. Directed by V.N. Jatla. Screenplay, Siva Reddy; camera, R.S. Agarwal; editor, Ravishankar Patnaik. Reviewed at Bangalore Film Fest, Jan. 14, '80. Running time, **100 MINS.**

With: Kadambini, Gangaram.

The custom of turning a village woman into the town prostitute in the name of a Goddess was prevalent up to the forties in some parts of India. This film uses a crude technical and film approach to bring out all of the custom's injustice and inhumanity.

Film, using non-actors, manages to seem a part of the life being recreated and as such should find outlets for ethnic use, specialized film festivals and film weeks.

The practice, called Jogu, usually had the woman picked by a local possessed woman. One such woman wants to spare her daughter, who is singled out by the possessed woman. She does appeal to village patriarchs and wins but cannot pay a fine. Rather than let her daughter suffer, she kills her.

No attempt is made to create a storyline and the people are just shown going about their lives. But film does create a forceful feel for the woman's plight at the beginning though getting somewhat repetitive and bogged down.

Film is an unusual, unsettling look at human indignity in the guise of religion. Not included in the Indian Panorama, it should have been. —*Mosk.*

All-Hungarian Fest

Utkozben
(On The Move)
(HUNGARIAN-COLOR)

Pecs, Feb. 7.

Hungarofilm release of Mafilm, Dialog Studio production. Stars Delphine Seyrig. Directed by Marta Meszaros. Screenplay, Meszaros, Jan Nowicki, Marek Piwowski; camera (Eastmancolor), Tamas Andor; music, Zygmunt Konieczny. Reviewed at Pecs Film Fest, Feb. 6, '80. Running time, **104 MINS.**

Barbara . . . . Delphine Seyrig
Marek . . . . Jan Nowicki
Husband . . . . Djoko Rosic
Wife . . . . Beata Tyszkiewiz

Marta Meszaros is one of the more prolific filmmakers locally. She has lately gone in for using mature French actresses in her tales about women adjusting to men, family life, personal needs and work, usually in the midst of a crisis.

After Anna Karina and Marina Vlady, she now has Delphine Seyrig as a fortyish attractive woman with grown children suddenly breaking her ties due to the death of a friend in an accident.

Seyrig, who had come from Poland as a child, and whose husband heads a clinic and whom she sees only weekends, with their relationship withering, suddenly gets in her car and goes off to Poland to visit her mother's tomb.

Looking for an old friend, she meets a seductive actor, Jan Nowicki (who has been in several of Meszaros's films), and an affair develops. But the actor is too unsettled, too unreliable, and, besides, he is married. She goes back.

A brief meeting with the actor, between planes, again seems to shake her equilibrium though she had taken up her life where she left off.

Film is somewhat schematic and Meszaros tends to repeat herself with these female traumas.

Seyrig brings more manerisms than depth to her performance of a biologist who is sudden prey to a break in her life. It is a reappraisal that is more whim than a decision, or in any way enlightening on this important dramatic time in a woman's life. —*Mosk.*

Czontvary
(HUNGARIAN-COLOR)

Pecs, Feb. 26.

Hungarofilm release of Hunnia production. Features entire cast. Directed by Zoltan Huszarik. Screenplay, Istvan Csaszar; camera (Eastmancolor), Peter Jankura. Reviewed at Pecs Film Fest, Feb. 6, '80. Running time: **110 MINS.**

Czontvary . . . . Ichak Fintzi
Actor . . . . Istvan Holl
Wife . . . . Andrea Drahota
Mother . . . . Margit Dayka
Nurse . . . . Agnes Bantalvi

Chalk up another visionary director from the Eastern European countries in Zoltan Huszarik of Hungary. His first film, "Szinbad," was about a man who lived an interior life of adventure and self realization. Now Huszarik deals with the life of a Hungarian painter who was only recognized posthumously. Czontvary lived from 1854-1919.

Film is not the familiar autobiographical one of the painter as martyr or romantic hero. It instead opts for an impression of the artist's calling, the aching need to create that can lead to sacrifice and suffering as well as moments of intense truth about the world and himself that could only spring from his work.

Czontvary's immense frescoes of Hungarian life, of ruins in Italy and life around them, were only exposed after his death. When the country went Communist, his work was ignored, but he was eventually rehabilitated in the 1950s.

Besides the painter, the film deals with a sort of alter ego or perhaps an actor who tries to understand the painter's life. This man watches the painter, and, like him, tries to break with his regular life and change it. Czontvary, at age 40, left a pharmacy to roam the world and paint.

Featured are fragmented looks at his work, run-ins with majestic nature, foreign lands, a woman who tries to deflect him from his work and moments of intense joy as well as misery. He is catapulted into the present at times and this mirrors the life of an actor, Zoltan Latinovits, who was supposed to have played the painter but committed suicide.

Huszarik put the script away for a couple of years and then incorporated him into the script as a man trying to understand the artist. Both were psychologically unbalanced and their roles are intertwined and counteroint each other. A scene in an asylum deals with both of them as well as their cutting themselves off from friends and families.

This is not an easy film, but one with a high visual flair, a film with an insight into creativeness.

It needs careful handling, but seems sure to catch attention at festivals with its beauty and visual bravura. Delighting some, turning off others, it is hard to ignore.
—*Mosk.*

Ajandek Ez A Nap
(A Priceless Day)
(HUNGARIAN-COLOR)

Pecs, Feb. 26.
Hungarofilm release of Mafilm-Budapest Studio production. Features entire cast. Written and directed by Peter Gothar from an idea by Peter Zimre. Camera (Eastmancolor), Lajos Koltai; music, Gyorgy Selmeczi. Reviewed at Pecs Film Fest, Feb. 6, '80. Running time: **87 MINS.**
Iren . . . . Cecilia Esztergalyos
Attila . . . . Pal Hetenyi
Anna . . . . Judit Pogany
Andras . . . . Lajos Szabo
Gabor . . . . Janos Dersi

Full of handheld camera work, sardonic, obsessed people and a rousing though often arbitrary look at human pettiness, this first film won Hungary's national and film critic nod as the best film of the year.

Success might be due to its brashness, for it lacks a point of view and cannot quite decide whether to be a comedy, satire or a more probing look at moral ambiguity. Peter Gothar does have a breezy directorial touch and should be watched when he achieves more coherence between style and content.

Perhaps film's sheer impishness acts as tonic here these days, alongside the more taxing re-enacted political tales of small town apparatchniks, the more visionary tales on history and painters, the classical films of private adjustment and war films.

A thirtyish woman, a kindergarten teacher is having an affair with a married man. She shares her little house with an old lady. When the old woman dies she thinks she will have it but brazen relatives break in, rifle everything and take over the place.

She now must find an apartment and defiles herself to get one, including a marriage in name only which leads to the husband de-

manding his marital rights. She even offers herself to men to get her apartment paid for while also realizing that her lover will never leave his wife.

She meets his wife and the two have a heart-to-heart talk which is one of the best bits in the film. They both feel they are friends and wonder how to get rid of their husbands to have their own places.

Film is refreshingly cynical for home audiences, but perhaps somewhat heavyhanded for outings abroad, though its rakishness might just find audiences in some offshore areas. Playing is rightly overwrought in keeping with the theme and treatment. —*Mosk.*

Oktoberi Vasarnap
(A Sunday in October)
(HUNGARIAN-W. GERMAN-B&W)

Pecs, Feb. 26.
Hungarofilm release of MafilmDialog Studio, ZDF (Mainz) production. Features entire cast. Written and directed by Andras Kovacs. Camera (black and white), Istvan Lugossy. Reviewed at Pecs Film Fest, Feb. 7, '80. Running time: **99 MINS.**
Geza . . . . Ferenc Bacs
Alvincy . . . . Tibor Tancos
Lacko . . . . Laszlo Pataky
Valkay . . . . Laszlo Peredy
Edit . . . . Marianne Moor

Film, a coproduction with West German tv, is a solid but stolid restaging of a historic incident near the end of World War 2 when Hungary tried to get out of the German Axis.

The Hungarian Regent, Admiral Horthy, sensed defeat and attempted secret negotiations for a separate peace with Russia to save the country and perhaps keep it intact after the war.

The Germans got wind of it and finally aborted the affair. There are personal sidelights of an officer running the secret talks and his affair with a nobleman's wife plus a German officer, posing as a friend, who is really in intelligence.

There is also good stock footage of the destruction of Budapest. But, as happens at times, these scenes are so alive and dynamic impact that they make the posey tactics concerning the events somewhat flat.

It remains, despite its virtues, a little known event, clearly presented, and which could have an impact as video fodder, though limited for theatrical use. —*Mosk.*

Majd Holnap
(Maybe Tomorrow)
(HUNGARIAN-COLOR)

Pecs, Feb. 26.
Hungarofilm release of Mafilm, Hunnia Studio release. Features entire cast. Directed by Judit Elek. Screenplay, Gyorgy

Petho: camera (eastmancolor), Elemer Ragalyi. Reviewed at Pecs Film Fest. Feb. 8, '80. Running time, **104 MINS.**
Eszter . . . . Judit Meszleri
Istvan . . . . : . . . . Andor Lukats
Husband . . . . Istvan Szoke
Wife . . . . : . . Eszter Szakacs
Kalman . . . . Istvan Novak
Emmi . . . . Erzsi Gaal

The social, emotional and love problems of two people over 30, each married and with a family, are treated without condescension or prudery. Eastern European films, or at least Hungarian ones, have left hokum morality and social realism behind.

The lovers have an apartment and meet there regularly. They keep up their own family lives though it seems their mates know and may even have their own affairs going.

They just cannot make that decision to break out and leave all behind to live together completely. The early part is handled with dexterity by director Judith Elek, in her second feature after some notable documentaries.

The man is bequeathed a house in the country by an aunt. This may be their out, a place for a new life. They go to see it. But some highstrung relatives, most of whom had designs on the house, create an impossible situation and they go back to town.

Maybe they will still try for the house, maybe not, maybe they will tomorrow. Meanwhile they go on in the old way. The country segment is somewhat confused and evasive instead of adding a dramatic note to the impasse of the protagonists.

Perhaps it is about people who cannot decide things, or are trying to have it both ways even it is straining family ties and affecting the children. Film needed a more pungent comment on these factors, somewhat eluded by the country excursion.

The problems of adjustment exist in the country too, but it throws off the balance of a film that is otherwise well played. Its promising first half, the candor about extramarital love, tasteful love scenes might make this an item for specialized playoff abroad. —*Mosk.*

Vasarnapi Szulok
(Sunday Parents)
(HUNGARIAN-COLOR)

Pecs, Feb. 26.
Hungarofilm release of Mafilm-Objektiv Studio production. Features entire cast. Directed by Janos Rosza. Screenplay, Istvan Kardos; camera (Eastmancolor), Levente Szorenyo; music, Elemer Ragalyi; music, Levente Szorenyi. Reviewed at Pecs Film Fest, Feb. 5, '80. Running time, **100 MINS.**
Juli . . . . Julianna Nyako
Cabal . . . . Melinda Szakacs
Gypsy . . . . Julianna Balogh
Andrea . . . . : . . . . Andrea Blizik
Aranka . . . . Erszi Pasztor

Gizi . . . . Agi Kakasi
Luci . . . . Sergei Elistratov

Teenage girls in an institution is not a new theme, but a fairly rare one in Eastern European films. Director Janos Rosza has here used non-actresses extremely well.

Film is mainly about a 16-year-old girl searching for roots and family sans overdone dramatics or didactics on institutional life.

Julianna Nyako has been put there with her sister by an alcoholic father who could not support them. She has to stay there until she is of age. Having become somewhat delinquent, she repeatedly escapes and gets punished by being put in a cell when she is caught or comes back on her own.

Her continuing forays outside always meet with rebuffs from her father, now just an alcoholic, and even from her sister's husband. She finally finds some workers who offer to help her if she becomes a trainee in their factory.

But an affair with the son of one of them sends her back in the clink. One night there is a strange party during which the girls get drunk, leading to an eerie suicidal slashing of wrists, fortunately not fatal.

The girl is finally left to decide whether she will accept an arranged marriage to escape as others have done. Pic ends without her decision.

Direction has verve and the problems treated are endemic to most societies. The only drawback is the surface characterization, except for the lead. Nyako should become a regular actress after her knowing handling of this role of a girl who is tough but not completely hardened by her hard knocks.

Some playoff is indicated, in addition to the festival and film week routes, for this sober tale of youthful disarray. —*Mosk.*

Harcmodor
(Strategy)
(HUNGARIAN-COLOR)

Pecs, Feb. 26.
Hungarofilm release of Mafilm-Dialog Studio production. Features entire cast. Directed by Istvan Darday. Screenplay, Gyorgyi Szalai; camera (Eastmancolor), Lajos Koltai, Ferenc Papp. Reviewed at Pecs Film Fest, Feb. 9, '80. Running time, **164 MINS.**
Dr. Toth . . . . Ida Piri
Jazsef . . . . Tivadar Kovacs
Kalman . . . . Kalman Feher
Halapi . . . . Janos Molnar
Mihaly . . . . Janos Hegedus

Istvan Darday is the most effective filmmaker in a film movement called "the film novel" here. It consists of using non-actors to play actual incidents or placing them in concocted ones where they play people of their own kind. Film is one of the latter types.

Perhaps not new, but still effective with the right blend of characters and theme, this film looks at bureaucracy with a sharp, barbed insight.

A woman doctor gets interested in the plight of old people in her country district, where she effectively interviews some oldsters who live alone, neglected, lonely and forgotten, eventually resolving to build a home for them. A reverse of the usual Western treatment of old folks' homes.

She gets project rolling by promising various farm co-ops and districts places for their old people in line with contributions and labor. But as costs mount, and higher-ups come into it, problems develop. However she uses pull and wiles and finally gets it done, just as many who opposed her ironically take credit for it.

Whether this kind of filmmaking is more effective than a fiction film is arguable. But as long as the characters do not have to be portrayed in depth, and are mainly involved in set situations, some sharp feeling for the reality of a situation as it often is here, can be reached.

Item is somewhat long, but has a worthy theme and some savory characters to make it a worthy film festival entry. —*Mosk.*

Elve Vagy Halva
(Dead or Alive)
(HUNGARIAN-COLOR)

Pecs, Feb. 26.

Hungarofilm release of Mafilm. Budapest Studio production. Features entire cast. Directed by Tamas Renyi. Screenplay, Renyi, Peter Zimre; camera (Eastmancolor), Gabor Szabo; music, Geza Berki. Reviewed at Pecs Film Fest, Feb. 8, '80. Running time, **83 MINS.**

Moszlopy	Lajos Balazsovits
Soldier	Gyorgy Cserhalmi
Old Soldier	Deszo Garas
Engineer	Karoly Mecs
Szentgroti	Geza Tordy
Inventor	Zoltan Vadusz

A historical film done in the mode of a western with action the thing and verisimilitude unimportant. It deals with a group of men going up against the Emperor Franz Josef of the Austro-Hungarian Empire himself, in a sort of "Magnificent Seven."

An ex-leader in the aborted 1848 uprising against Austria escapes from jail three years later. He is still fanatical and rounds up some old comrades.

The idea is to capture the Emperor during a triumphant procession he is doing around Hungary and force him to give the country its independence. It leads to their demises but not until they have inflicted plenty of damage despite their small number, seven.

The leader even gets into the Emperor's carriage but it is a dummy, or perhaps a symbol. There are some sound and attention-holding preparations for the caper, but film is a local item at best due to cardboard characters and fair but rote direction. —*Mosk.*

Koportos
(HUNGARIAN-COLOR)

Pecs, Feb. 26.

Hungarofilm release of Hunnia Studio-ZDF Mainz production. Features entire cast. Directed by Livia Gyarmathy. Screenplay, Gyarmathy Joszef Balazs from the book by Balazs; camera (Eastmancolor), Ferenc Papp. Reviewed at Pecs Film Fest, Feb. 7, '80. Running time, **88 MINS.**

Balog	Mihaly Rostas
Bogdan	Ferenc Bogdan
Rozalia	Rozalia Demeter
Halier	Lajos Szabo
Priest	Jiri Menzel

A gypsy worker in the city goes back to the little town of Koportos to bury his pretty young wife. There he runs into trouble with his own people, apparently for wanting to give his wife a beautiful burial.

He must promise the priest some raffia baskets for a regular service. People scoff at the lovely casket he buys and he is robbed by the man who brings the coffin to the cemetery. The burial turns out to be a fiasco.

But the man must pay his debt to the priest, for the best part of the film which keeps it from being a rather familiar tale of racism. Most of the raffia has been cut but he finds some on a muddy hill on the other side of the river. He is almost drowned and takes all sorts of chances but finally secures the coveted raffia.

His own people, however, either annoyed at his airs or feeling it is against their acceptance of their lot, beat him up and seize the raffia as he goes back to the city.

Livia Gyarmathy, who usually makes satirical comedies or dramas about youthful adaptation, has left this sketchy and unfocused though she has created a memorable character in the determined man and his quest for some beauty, be it only his wife's funeral.

—*Mosk*

La Terrazza
(The Terrace)
(ITALIAN-COLOR)

Rome, Feb. 28.

A United Artists Europa release. Produced by Pio Angeletti and Adriano De Micheli for Dean Film and Les Artistes Associes. Stars Ugo Tognazzi, Vittorio Gassman, Jean Louis Trintignant, Marcello Mastroianni, Stefania Sandrelli, Carla Gravina, Stefano Satta Flores, Serge Reggiani. Directed by Ettore Scola. Screenplay, Age-Scarpelli-Scola; camera, (Technicolor), Pasqualino De Santis; art director, Luciano Ricceri; editor, Raimondo Crociani; music, Armando Trovajoli. Reviewed at Cinema Barberini, Rome, Feb. 28, 1980. Running time: **158 MINS.**

Amedeo	Ugo Tognazzi
Mario	Vittorio Gassman
Enrico	Jean Louis Trintignant
Luigi	Marcello Mastroianni
Giovanna	Stefania Sandrelli
Carla	Carla Gravina
Tizzo	Stefano Satta Flores
Sergio	Serge Reggiani

After a series of critical and commercial successes, Ettore Scola has fashioned a remorseful comment on intellectual life in the '70s as a companion piece to "Those Were the Days." The UA entry (on a prefinancing deal for Italy, Spain and Scandinavia), moves from his previous nostalgic, bittersweet canvas of postwar Italian life to a sombre satire on aging and decline of what was once a flourishing, radically-oriented Roman intelligentsia. Filmmaker's personal involvement and anguished indulgence temper sporadic brilliance of insights and deft irony to circumscribe film market impact in its present form at home and abroad. Whittled down to 120 mins., this outlook could be reversed.

Framework for pic is a couple of dinner receptions on an old Roman terrace — hangout of prominents in the intellectual community as a device to flesh out key characters in flashbacks or flashforwards and to underpin interdependent relationships as well.

In singling out depressed screenwriter Enrico (Jean Louis Trintignant), film producer Amadeo (Ugo Tognazzi) and his ex-actress wife (Ombretta Colli), turned art film sponsor, disoriented mag editor Luigi (Marcello Mastroianni) and his estranged journalist wife Carla (Carla Gravina), public tv exec Sergio (Serge Reggiani) and communist intellectual member of Parliament Mario (Vittorio Gassman) who has a late-in-life fling at infedelity with Giovanna (Stefania Sandrelli) — bored wife of a tv commercial producer, "The Terrace" probes the why's and wherefore's for the sad state today of the brain set and why these talented pals compromised, sold out or just ran out of steam in the devitalizing confusion of the Italian '70s.

Looking past the principals, Scola brings the mass media milieu into derisive focus as part of the more general washout — with two exceptions. His women are under the aggressive spell to achieve self-fulfillment — a disconcerting novelty for the Italian male. And he shows youth symbolically as a contrast to the terrace-full of uneasy middle-aged decliners. Pic closes (too obviously) on a clean-cut young couple who look like winners in a new dawn. Gap ominously leaves them worlds apart with all links severed.

In a script calling for ensemble as well as individual performances, cast shines bright and clear. Vittorio Gassman as the Communist unable to cope, day in day out, with his party's puritanical code, is matched by Ugo Tognazzi as a selfmade producer — who makes it on instinct and muscle rather than on higher education. Marcello Mastroianni joins them as a editor out of step when his man's world is challenged by ex-wife who wants her share of it. Trintignant, a comedy screenwriter pounded into keyboard doodling by tired repeats, is zany but vivid.

Scola skillfully lets his women — Sandrelli, Gravina, Colli and others — emerge from under the male umbrella with verve as an irresistible sign of the times and the female cast contingent sparkle.

Scola holds it all together with incisive intelligence, but script is too demanding. Complex conglomeration wears thin in time. Local references to the living and dead are merely "in" moments. Excess half-hour or so works against this forthright satire comedy of the sour '70s.

Credit for plush mounting extends to all departments — from lenser Pasqualino De Santis to composer Armando Trovajoli.

—*Werb.*

Hoito Rabu
(White Love)
(JAPANESE-COLOR)

Tokyo, Feb. 23.

A Toho release of a Toho-Hori Pro co-production. Produced by Tsugunobu Hori, Hideo Sasai. Directed by Shusei Kotani. Features entire cast. Screenplay, Toshiya Fujita, Tatsuo Kobayashi, based on work by Nichiko Nakagawa, camera (color) Kenji Hagiwara; sound, Neobumasa Fukushima; art direction, Mugen Sakaguchi; editor, Osamu Inoue; asst. director, Yoshihisa Nakagawa. Reviewed at Teatro Ikebukuro, Tokyo, Feb. 23, 1980. Running time: **110 MINS.**

Shinobu Uemura	Momoe Yamaguchi
Ken Yamanobe	Tomokazu Miura
Yoichiro Yamashita	Kazuo Kitamura
Taeko Nogawa	Bunjaku Han
Keisuke Uemura	Yoshiki Kobayashi
Ritsuko Uemura	Kaneko Iwasaki
Noriko Takeuchi	Saeko Nagashima

Twenty-year-old actress Momoe Yamaguchi and 27-year-old actor Tomokazu Miura have already been paired together in more films than were Judy Garland and Mickey Rooney.

In this, the tenth is a succession of b.o. hits that began with the release of "Izu No Odoriko" (Izu Dancer) in 1974, Yamaguchi portrays a stylist and Miura a Spanish instructor and parttime pimp. They discover each has a connection with Spain: her father deserted hearth and home for the country years ago, while it was there that Miura's career as a legitimatebusinessman came to an end along with his affair with a Japanese girl studying flamenco dancing.

The two take off for Spain, where she has a tearful reconcilation with Pop, who has been supporting himself all these years making guitars, and he a reunion with old flame Bunjaku Han, now reduced to giving Oriental messages. Pop dies and Bunjaku falls to her death, leaving a son, fathered by Miura's ex-boss, for the couple to rear.

For all its heart-tugging silliness, "White Love" is tolerably entertaining. At this stage in their partnership, Miura and Yamaguchi are a natural and relaxed romantic team. In addition, both have developed from mere teen dreamboats into attractive, photogenic adults, an important consideration given that either his or her or both their faces are on screen almost constantly. Further, Yamaguchi has developed more dramatic breadth, while Miura, who speaks very passable Spanish, has toned down his tendency to cloying winsomeness.

In his first crack at directing this twosome, Shusei Kotani shows himself a competent craftsman, equally adept at helming love, action scenes, cosmic and sad scenes. Spanish locaiton shots are effective, but too brief. Surprisingly, Yamaguchi, a top-selling vocalist, does not sing on the sound track.
—Bail.

Rejs
(The Cruise)
(POLISH-B&W)

A Tor unit production. No American distributor. Features entire cast. Directed by Marek Piwowski. Screenplay, Janusz Glowacki. Marek Piwowski, with cooperation of Andrzej Barszczynski, Jerzy Karaszkiewicz; camera (black and white), Marek Nowicki; music, Wojciech Kilar; set design, Wieszaw Aniadecki; costumes, Tadeusz Urbanowicz. Reviewed at Rizzoli Screening Room, New York, Feb. 27, 1980. as part of the Hunter College Polish Cinema Series. Running time: **65 MINS.**

Cast: Stanislaw Tym, Jolanta Lothe, Wanda Stanislawska-Lote, Andrzej Dobosz, Feridun Erol, Jan Himilsbach, Zdzislaw Maklakiewicz.

Marek Piwowski, like almost all Polish filmmakers, has a considerable background in short subjects. This 1970 effort, his first feature, is being shown during the Hunter College Polish Cinema series in what appears to be a somewhat truncated version, although the simple tale has no more plot to it than one of the stories on "Fantasy Island."

Meant to be a satire on certain aspects of Polish life, experimental in form, it consists of a short cruise on a river steamer that throws the usual assortment of passengers into a brief mini-world. The emphasis is on humor and the visual gags come across easily, being rather broad in nature. However, the dialog loses whatever humor it contains with the static subtitles provided.

Exposure outside the Polish-speaking community would appear very limited. The black and white camerawork, however, is crisp and attractive and is a major asset to the film. —*Robe.*

Survival Run
(COLOR)

Should have a short life span.

Hollywood, Feb. 29.
Film Ventures International release of a Spiegel-Bergman production. Produced by Lance Hool. Directed Larry Spiegel. Exec producer. Ruben Broido. Mel Bergman. Features entire cast. Screenplay, Spiegel, G.M. Cahill, based on a story by Cahill and Fredric Shore; camera (Deluxe Color). Alex Phillips, Jr.; music, Gary William Friedman; editor, Chris Greenbury. No other credits available. Reviewed at the World Theatre, Hollywood, Feb. 29, 1980. (MPAA Rating: R). Running time: **90 MINS.**

Stars: Peter Graves, Ray Milland, Vincent Van Patten, Pedro Armendariz Jr., Alan Conrad. Anthony Charnota. Gonzalo Vega, Cosie Costa. Randi Meryl. Marianne Sauvage; Robby Weaver. Danny Ades and Susan Pratt O'Hanlon.

Scenario for "Survival Run" is a familiar enough exploitation theme. Take a group of California teens, pile them in a van for a weekend of fun and frolic, let the auto break down in the middle of nowhere and have the kids stumble on a group of baddies who like to kill people who "know too much." What's missing from the formula is the sex and/or blood 'n' guts that aficionados of this genre pay to see. Sparse inclusion of those elements should severely curtail boxoffice action.

Vincent Van Patten leads the group of boys and girls through the Arizona desert (it's actually filmed in Mexico) after his friend manages to wreck his van. With no food or water they happen to stumble on to a campsite where Peter Graves, Ray Milland and their scurvy cronies are about to complete an illegal $2,000,000 deal. The kids think they're rescued, the crooks know they're in trouble.

Screenplay by Larry Spiegel and G.M. Cahill is not bad if it is assumed it is an exploitation film they've set out to make (in light of some of the lines the writers should be given the benefit of the doubt). That being the case, Spiegel, who also directs, should have made a few more visual accommodations to capture the audience he's aiming for.

At least one-third of the film serves to introduce a nice group of kids having fun, and even when there's real trouble later on many of the grisly scenes are avoided or left to the imagination. Alfred Hitchcock can get away with that. Spiegel can't.

That's not to say the picture is without appealing elements. Spiegel manages to keep the plot line moving, Alex Phillips Jr. provides clear and precise photography and appropriate mood music is set by Gary William Friedman. There are also several intriguing sidelights, most notably how the villanous Milland manages to keep his pearly white suit spotless after what has had to have been an extremely messy trek through the desert.

Unfortunately, those good points will not be enough to sell a picture of this nature. The basic failing of "Survival Run" is that it doesn't play by the bloodthirsty rules of the exploitation game. —*Berg.*

Tiergarten
(WEST GERMAN-COLOR-16m)

West Berlin, Feb. 17.
Produced, written, directed, photographed, and edited by Lothar Lambert, with additional poetry by Dagmar Beiersdorf and archive music; world rights, Lambert. Features entire cast. Reviewed at Studio am Kudam, West Berlin, Feb. 17, '80. Running time: **80 MINS.**

Cast: Steven Adamczewski, Dagmar Beiersdorf, Erich Foertsch, Marion Herschel, Mustafa Iskandarani, Alfredo Julian, J.W. Kurth, Dorothea Moritz, Erika Rabau, Uwe Sange, Ulrike Schirm, Roland Stoos, and Beate Hasenau.

The seventh film in a series of delightfully whacky, low-low-budget "Berlin pix" by film critic Lothar Lambert — the previous were "Ex und Hopp" (1972), "Sein Kampf" (1973), "1 Berlin-Harlem" (1975) (these three in collaboration with Wolfram Zobus), "Faux Pas de Deux" (1976), "Late Show" (1978) (using a fragment from an uncompleted film by Harry Puhlmann), and "Now or Never" (1979) — "Tiergarten" is his best to date and even has a chance for a respectable theatre run. Not bad for a home-made pic that cost less than $10,000 to make with no pretentions to be other than it is — a portrait of Berlin-Tiergarten.

For those who never visited Berlin before the last war, Tiergarten was the diplomatic section in the heart of the city that was surrounded by spacious parks and known for its luxurious villas. A broad main thoroughfare cuts its way through the area, which used to serve for parades and celebrations, but today that boulevard stops abruptly at the Brandenburg Gate where East Berlin begins. Tiergarten, after the war, was left in ruins and had to be completely replanted to restore some of its lost lustre.

Lambert describes in docu-fiction terms what goes on in the parks and along the boulevard on summer nights and weekends. This is a haven for prosties, pickups, drunkards, gays, transvestites, and such deviates as sex-killers — the murder of a well known female cabaretist a few years ago, in fact, supplies one thread of the story. The rest is a study of loneliness — each character in "Tiergarten" represents in an exaggerated way an outsider in society who requests the park,in addition, of course, to normal individuals, mostly senior citizens and children, who bask and play in the sun during the day.

There's a young married woman with a wooden stick for a husband, who sits by the canals writing mushy romantic poetry until she is gradually driven to fulfill her fantasies and join the ladies of the night on the boulevard. Another is a femme wino living in the gutter (played by the Berlin Film Fest's ace photog, Erika Rabau), who insults everyone who happens along the way but particularly homos and foreigners (Tiergarten's residential area, tucked away in the background, quarters Turks in crowded tenement houses). And there's a tipsy would-be cabaretsinger, who just goes out and grabs any passing "Turk" whenever she has the itch.

Other "fates" touched on in Lambert's compassionate human comedy are a mother with a son whose speech defect is bad enough to hinder friendships, so he turns to injections; an old man whose wife has recently died, who takes in a prostie when her pimp beats her; and several heavy-accented outsiders like a Turk, and Yank cowboy, a black, an Afghan, and whomever else you are liable to run into here on a Sunday afternoon — one, in all likelihood, following the other around.

Lambert, due to the private, hot-tip "runs" his prior pix have had in those tiny, mobbed studio cinemas in Berlin, now gets actors and non-professionals lining up for him when he begins a new experiment in improvisation. In Berlin, these are "camp" pix. Once the character types were established and the thesps engaged ("everyone works for the fun of it"), Lambert phoned them from time to time, after his own critic chores are over, to meet him in the park (if available) and shoot a scene. Each thesp brings to his personal "fate" what he or she chooses to fatten out the role, and it's in the spontaneous dialog where most of the laughs lie.

"Tiergarten" does on pennies what the pompous subsidy-film fails to do on bundles of marks — it charms the pants off an audience that likes its film fare peppered with a little sass and Freudian sex. Try and catch it somewhere. —*Holl.*

Cinco Tenedores
(Five Forks)
(SPANISH-COLOR)

Madrid, Feb. 20.

A Bridas S.A. production for Izaro Films. Directed by Fernando Fernan Gomez. Features entire cast. Screenplay. Esmeralda Adam. Manuel Ruiz Castillo; camera (Eastmancolor). Carlos Suarez; music. Anton Garcia Abril; editor. Rosa Salgado. Exec producer. Juan L. Isasi. Reviewed at Cine Velazquez. Madrid. Feb. 20. '80. Running time: **95 MINS.**
Maruja ....Concha Velasco
Aurelio ....Jose Sazatornil
Chema ....Rafael Alonso
Agustin ....Agustin Gonzalez
Herman ....William F. Sully
Miguel ....Manuel de Benito
Also: Alicia Sanchez. Manuel de Blas. Maribel Ayuso. Ana Frigola et al.

"Five Forks" is the designation given to deluxe restaurants in Spain, in one of which much of the action of this comedy-farce takes place. Pic gets off to a quick enough start, with some nice touches of humor and a bit of political ribbing as well; but pace then thins out as scripters seem to become befuddled about just where they're going. Some excellent story possibilities are never followed up and the end result is an occasionally wry but ultimately muddled film which never delivers the waited-for punch.

Story concerns the owner of a posh Madrid restaurant whose German chef, on the last night before summer closing, chops off the head of his meretricious wife on his meat block. The owner, taking pity on the chef's only child, a high school student, puts him up in his house. But the boy plays it fast and loose with his godmother, leaves her pregnant (hubby is sterile) and takes off with a female math tutor. The chef rather pointlessly turns up every now and then, and we're fed false leads that other mayhem may be in the offing. Instead, the restaurateur organizes a mammoth dinner in which he sports a hat with the cuckold's horns and everyone winds up dancing.

Some excellent thesping by Concha Velasco and Jose Sazatornil and good lensing by Carlos Suarez aren't enough to offset the weaknesses of the script. Pic might so some biz at local wickets, but is hardly apt for offshore marts. —*Besa.*

Monarch
(W. GERMAN-COLOR-DOCU)

Berlin, Feb. 7.

Produced by Regina Ziegler. Directed. written. photographed. sound-recorded. and edited by Fluetsch & Stelzer. Reviewed at Studio am Kudam, Berlin, Feb. 7. '80. Running time: **80 MINS.**

This remarkable docu by the team self-tagged as Fluetsch & Stelzer (to prevent critics from praising one individual's work over the other's) is about a professional slot-machine player — "Monarch" picked up his moniker after scoring on his first automat (as slots are referred to in Germany). It's a kind of cinema-verite account of his daily adventures seeking out, and beating consistently, a slot machine presently marketed under a "Mint" tag.

How Monarch does it is kept pretty much a secret, although it is evident there's nothing illegal about his method in beating the slots — in fact, a cop could stand right next to him as he cleans out five or six each evening to the tune of a cool $600 a machine. Monarch, in other words, proves that the eye and the thumb (punching a stop button on the slot-machine) are quicker than the mechanism itself — he and three other slot-pros make a comfortable living (taxes do have to be paid on chance-winnings, however) by travelling from one bar or inn to another in search of the kind of machine that allows the easiest winnings. Since the slots 'are in operation for a usual three-year stretch at a time. this docu had to be held back for over a year in order to make a deal with Monarch to film him in action and still not betray his racket.

This is a fascinating document. Our hero worked once as an ordinary salesman. but his love for playing the slots, since his days in an orphanage (where he always won in games of chance), led him to experimenting and discovering a method for beating the machines. Neither the film itself nor the helmers give away a thing (does Monarch really use only his eyes and the swiftness of his thumb, or is there a trick involved?), but it is obvious that his fortune depends solely on cleaning out a machine, completely, within an hour's time each evening before proceeding on to the next.

Monarch is well dressed in tailored suits (he tells his personal tailor in one scene to strengthen the pockets on the new suit), drives a classy Mercedes, and charms his film audience with rounded, refined phrases of an intellectual, even philosophical, manner. A born storyteller with dry humor and a sense for timing a phrase with a twist in it, he travels through Germany from north to south with the camera crew. The "road pic" thus offers a portrait of another side of the country, seldom seen in the typical feature or documentary.

As he tells the story, Monarch practices until his leathered thumb and Deerslayer-eye beat his first automat — "winning is more fun than playing," he observes coyly. He finds "scouts" to case an area thoroughly the day before (they get paid $50 bucks plus free food and drink) in search of the willing "Mint" machines. He has a method too for knowing how loaded the machine is, for buttering up the bar owner and the clientele (to avoid suspicion), for scoring with 2-mark and 5-mark pieces ("hitting the jackpot with 1-mark pieces makes too much noise"), and for knowing in which direction to travel next after winning sufficiently in a city or area.

Still. Monarch is anything but happy and has few friends. It's a job like any other, it turns out, requiring long hours and little time for women or other pleasures. Drinking stale beer and wearing smoke-drenched clothes, the loneliness of this nomadic life itself, and the fear that automation (eliminating the "stop" button) will eventually put him out of business — these factors, and others, apparently opened the door to making the docu in the first place.

A hit at the recent Hof Film Fest, "Monarch" has been selected for the German series to be exported abroad. —*Holl.*

L.A. Filmex Reviews

A Small Circle of Friends
(COLOR)

Now, if everyone would just relax.

Hollywood, Feb. 29.

United Artists release of a Tim Zinnemann production. Produced by Tim Zinnemann. Directed by Rob Cohen. Stars Brad Davis, Karen Allen, Jameson Parker. Screenplay. Ezra Sacks; camera (Technicolor). Michael Butler; production designer. Joel Schiller; editor. Randy Roberts; music composed by Jim Steinman; music arranged by Steven Morgoshes; asst. director. Michael Haley; set designers, Al Kemper, Nicolas Laborczy; set decorator. Rick Simpson; sound editor, Victoria Rose Sampson; special effects, Larry Cavanaugh, Joe Lombardi, Rudy Liszcak; unit publicist. Stanley Brossette. Reviewed at Disney Studios. Burbank, Calif., Friday, Feb. 29. 1980. (MPAA Rating - R). Running time: **112 MINS.**
Leo DaVinci ....Brad Davis
Jessica ....Karen Allen
Nick Baxter ....Jameson Parker
Alice ....Shelley Long
Haddox ....John Friedrich
Greenblatt ....Gary Springer
Harry ....Craig Richard Nelson
Jimmy The Cook ....Harry Caesar
Mrs. Baxter ....Nan Martin
Crazy kid ....Dan Stern
Dorm Proctor ....Jason Laskay
Karate student ....Jamie Squire
Also: Mary Margaret Amato, David Hollander. Frank Rich, Pamela Cresant, Nick Kairis. Severn Darden, Jonathan Moore, Nancy Penoyer, Deborah Offner, John Peters. Doug Llewelyn.

An ambitious attempt to pull off a "Jules. And Jim At Harvard," "A Small Circle Of Friends" engages attention through sheer energy and abundance of incident before falling apart in the final half-hour. Debut directorial effort of former producer Rob Cohen is excessively hyper and anxious to please, but displays enough talent to indicate that better could be in store down the line if he would relax enough to let his characters and situations breathe. Mixed results here, in addition to late 1960s setting, would suggest a tough sell for this UA release.

Small circle of title refers to ongoing, changeable relationships among 1967 Harvard freshmen Brad Davis, Karen Allen and Jameson Parker. Davis is a manic attention-getter with journalistic ambitions. Allen a sharp, sassy chick dabbling in painting but headed toward law, and Parker a super-straight pre-med student who manages to keep his bearings throughout the socio-political turmoil of the period.

A few other characters come and go as symptoms of the age, notably a Texas hick who mutates into a far-left terrorist, but pic's focus seldom strays from the central three. Unlike "The Paper Chase," for example, school itself is rarely mentioned or shown, save for a brief lecture by "relevant" art professor Severn Darden, as characters pursue their personal and sexual quests and presumably let the rest take care of itself.

Davis' super-charged, if hardly subtle, performance establishes momentum for film's first hour, as he romances Allen and both perpetrate numerous campus shenanigans. Along the way, LBJ bows out and hippiedom hits with a vengeance, but Davis finally gets stuck with a low draft lottery number, which triggers his descent and serious entry into Allen's life. Parker, long Davis' best friend, has been waiting for years on the sidelines for his chance with her.

Energy level (not to mention decible level of the soundtrack) is so high that a third-act burn-out is not surprising. Point of no return for Ezra Sacks' script comes when Allen suggests a menage a trois and men silently agree. Door closes on this and, despite subsequent "design for living" three-way cohabitation, new ground rules for the relationship are never explained or shown, making entire turn of events a cheat. Same applies to an absurdist bomb blast which shortly thereafter kills one of the principals — it just doesn't play, so final resolution emerges as woefully unsatisfactory.

If anything, pic is overdirected, as if Cohen was afraid to let interest sag for even a moment. Characters shout, run instead of walk, and strain to make themselves understood for fear of being left out of whatever is happening. If one feels compelled to make comparisons to "Jules And Jim" or any other classic triangular love story, one might also point out that Allen lacks the luminosity necessary for such a relationship's focal point, although she convinces as a representative woman of her time and circumstances. Parker is solid and believable as the least extreme of the threesome.

As pic is a period-piece, verisimilitude of details can be called into question. A major sequence takes place on the John Hancock skyscraper, which didn't exist at the time. Neither did the Orson Welles Cinema, where characters see "The Graduate."

Furthermore, fourth-billed Shelly Long appears to have been given short shrift in the editing, as what's set up as a sub-plot between her and Parker disappears entirely.

Like the film, Jim Steinman's score is loud and incessant, giving proceeding a curious heroic dimension which seems questionable. If nothing else, film has courage of its convictions, but ultimately suffers from an energy overload while at the same time shortcircuiting on ill-advised climactic events.

Tech credits are good.

"Small Circle" is the closing film entry in Filmex." —Cart.

The Great Rock 'N' Roll Swindle
(BRITISH-COLOR)

Hollywood, Feb. 11.
A Kendon Film production in association with Matrix Best and Virgin Records. Produced by Jeremy Thomas, Don Boyd. Features entire cast. Directed and writen by Julian Temple. Camera (Kay Laboratories Ltd. color), A. Barker-Mills; editors, R. Bedford, M.D. Maslin, G. Swire; music, The Sex Pistols; sound, John Lundsten, John Sanders, B.R. White, John Pierre Louvre; asst. directors, G. White, Patrice Vanoni. Reviewed at the Burbank Studios, Burbank, Feb. 11, 1980. (No MPAA Rating.) Running time: 103 MINS.
Cast: Malcolm McLaren, Johnny Rotten, Sid Vicious, Steve Jones, Paul Cook, Ronnie Biggs, Liz Fraser, Jess Conrad, Mary Millington, Julian Holloway, James Aubrey, Johnny Shannon, Helen of Troy, Tenpole Tudor, Faye Hart, Alan Jones, Irene Handl.

"The Greak Rock 'N' Roll Swindle" is the "Citizen Kane" of rock 'n' roll pictures. An incredibly sophisticated, stupefyingly multi-layered portrait of the 1970s phenomenon known as The Sex Pistols, unstintingly cynical pic casts a jaundiced eye at the entire pop culture scene and, if nothing else, represents the most imaginative use of a rock group in films since The Beatles debuted in "A Hard Day's Night." A sure bet for a substantial cult following, "Swindle," with its unexpected quality and broad range of commentary, could also stir interest among those who may never even have heard of The Sex Pistols while they were together (and all alive).

Group was the progenitor of the entire punk movement of the latter half of the late decade and perpetrated numerous outrages against almost everyone with whom it came in contact.

Each successive scandal — such as getting booted off both EMI and A&M Records, swearing on tv, being banned by the BBC, and playing their subversive version of "God Save The Queen" on a boat in the Thames during the Silver Jubilee celebration — merely generated that many more front page headlines. Pic, which stars and is narrated after a fashion by Pistol's manager Malcolm McLaren, begins with the basic premise that the campaign of shock tactics was premeditated from the very beginning by the admittedly devious McLaren, and continues from there to wildly illustrate the chaotic history of the short-lived sensation.

A bubbling brew of devices and styles somehow mesh under first-time helmer Julian Temple's wizardly direction to amplify McLaren's thesis on how to create a rock sensation in 10 easy lessons. Among his dicta are: Demonstrate To Record Companies The Enormous Potential Of A Band That Can't Play; Make It As Hard As Possible For The Press To See It; Insult Your Audiences As Much As Possible, and Cultivate Hatred. Cash register jingles melodiously as each step is taken, with McLaren walking away with bulging pockets as his creation dissolves.

Evidently made without the blessing of lead singer Johnny Rotten, film presents remainder of the group playing themselves. Docu footage of Rotten and the band playing numerous dates throughout their career, including the U.S. tour, offers opportunity to hear a host of tunes in their entirety, McLaren fills in a number of blanks himself, and some enormously clever animation covers some of the group's more infamous antics, such as its alleged trashing of the A&M London office.

Title tune from Russ Meyer's aborted Pistols feature, "Who Killed Bambi?," is given an hilarious rendition by one Tenpole Tudor, and some scenes of Steve Jones and Paul Cook in Rio with a Mr. Martin Bormann and Ronnie Biggs, latter one of the perpetrators of the Great Train Robbery who here collaborates on cutting a record, may have been originally planned for Meyer's opus. Filmmakers also managed to capture Sid Vicious delivering his astonishing version of "My Way" at a Paris venue before he succumbed to his self-destructive streak last year.

If all this — and there is truly much, much more — might seem like an impossible hodgepodge, triumph of the film rests in the sharp control of all its effects. Unlike some of the way-out filmmaking of the late 1960s, in which anything went, usually to diminishing returns, Temple's work is tremendously film-wise, refusing to allow anything that doesn't contribute to the overall scheme. In a conventional sense, "Swindle" goes too far on any number of occasions, but it all adds up in the end.

Technical accomplishment is of a high order. A. Barker-Mills' cinematography, like that for the Monty Python films, is strongly expressive on limited means, and editing of R. Bedford, M.D. Maslin and G. Swire makes all the disparate elements of the jigsaw puzzle fit tightly.

Produced by Jeremy Thomas and Don Boyd and presently without a U.S. distrib, pic preems at Filmex March 6. —Cart.

In For Treatment
(Opname)
(DUTCH-COLOR)

Hollywood, Feb. 9.
A Het Werkteatre production. Produced, screenplay by the Het Werkteatre. Directed by Erik van Zuylen, Marja Kok. Camera (uncredited color), Robby Muller; editor, Hans van Dongen. Reviewed at Universal Studios, Universal City, Feb. 9, 1980. (No MPAA Rating.) Running time: 99 MINS.
Features: Helmert Woundenberg, Frank Groothof, Joop Admiraal.
(English subtitles)

Myriad films from "Camille" to "Love Story" and beyond have chronicled the physical deterioration of sympathetic characters, but rarely has an illness been so excruciatingly scrutinized and the unpleasantness of hospitalization so thoroughly conveyed as in "In For Treatment." Effort of the Dutch cooperative Het Werkteatre is admirably sober and full of quiet conviction, but subject matter will limit it to similar-minded audiences.

Opening couple of reels put both the mild-mannered, 40-ish protagonist and the viewer through the wringer, as Helmert Woundenberg endures any number of painful medical examinations to determine the exact nature of his malady.

Although it turns out he has cancer, the most grisly of the tests are over early, and remainder of the picture is an even-handed, accurate evocation of how boring, irritating and undignified hospital life can be for long-term patients.

Hypocrisy of doctors and institutional personnel are brought under increasingly severe attack, as patients, systematically kept in the dark as to test results, is always the last to know the fact about his own body and ultimate fate and is never given a direct answer to his persistent question of how long he's going to be cooped up.

Done in subtle, understated style rather than as a hysterical diatribe, collective, under nominal direction of Erik van Zuylen and Marja Kok, score a number of congent points which culminate in a rather moving finale. But it is rough going at times, and anyone with a phobia about hospitals or disease is forewarned to avoid this treament.
—Cart.

The Space Movie
(BRITISH-COLOR)

Hollywood, Feb. 24.
A Virgin Films Ltd. production. Produced by Richard Branson, Simon Draper. Directed and written by Tony Palmer. Music, Mike Oldfield; editors, Graham Bunn, John Beech. Reviewed at Paramount Studios, Hollywood, Feb. 24, 1980. (No MPAA Rating.) Running time: 78 MINS.

Undoubtedly designed initially as a "head trip" picture for kids who weren't yet born when the first astronauts blasted off, "The Space Movie" could be hitting the market at just the right time to benefit from the revival of patriotism and renewed interest in the space program promulgated by Tom Wolfe's best-selling "The Right Stuff." As such, b.o. possibilities for this powerfully interesting feature could exist beyond the stoned midnight crowd.

Consisting entirely of footage from NASA and the U.S. National Archives, pic tells story of America's space effort with the expected minimum of narration and verbiage. This is one case, however, where a picture is truly worth a thousand words, as shot after hitherto unseen shot astonishes through its beauty, startling detail and literal unearthliness. One never dares take one's eyes off the screen for fear of missing the next visual wipeout.

With JFK speech excerpts and

some cursory background on the soviet space program and Mercury missions serving as an introduction, body of film concentrates on the 1969 Apollo 11 moon shot. Television certainly didn't show it like this, as liftoff alone is stretched out over several slow-motion minutes, with dozens of angles of the event finally overwhelming through sheer mass of telling details. Tubes and cables fall away, hundreds of crewcut technicians sweat it out, tons of thrust pound the ground and tourists watch with binoculars as the giant ship arcs skyward. It's a genuinely thrilling sequence, even without suspense re the outcome.

Astronauts' hijinx on the moon conjure up both amusement and awe, and, while watching, anyway, one can only feel that the entire space program was a magnificent accomplishment, regardless of cost. Without making a point of it, film strongly conveys the enormous amount of work and attention to minute detail that went into meeting a titanic challenge.

A couple of miscues pop up along the way, such as inserted longshots of the Mercury spacecraft during what is supposed to be preparation for the Apollo mission and a shot, which upon reflection must be phony, of the moon landing vehicle flying in the foreground with the mother ship behind it. Where was the camera?

Coda to the moon effort is provided by brief looks at the U.S.-USSR docking exercise in 1975, the Skylab program and the current Space Shuttle.

Backdropping it all is a "Space Symphony" by rock composer Mike Oldfield. Music is generally an enhancement, thankfully subdued at times, and is immaculately presented in Dolby Stereo.

As often happens, it took a foreigner, Briton Tony Palmer, to create this stirring homage to an American adventure. Material he had to work with is admittedly some of the most spectacular stuff ever committed to celluloid, but he's done a fine job stitching it together into striking form. —Cart.

Os Mucker
(The Mucker)
(BRAZILIAN-W. GERMAN-COLOR)

Hollywood, Feb. 5.
A Stopfilm, Ltd. production. Produced, directed by Wolf Gauer, Jorge Bodanzky. Features entire cast. Screenplay, Gauer; camera (uncredited color). Bodanzky; editor, Renato Volpato. Reviewed at the Burbank Studios, Burbank, Feb. 5, 1980. (No MPAA Rating. Running time: 106 MINS.
Jakobine Mentz ...... Marlise Saueressig
Dr. Abilio .... Jose Lewgoy

Captain Dantas ...... Paulo Cesar Pereio
Rudolf .... Ricardo Hoepper
(English subtitles)

"Os Mucker" is one of those unendurable items that inevitably seems to turn up at any film festival. Somehow, pix like this, in which shaky camerawork, junk stock color, stoned acting and vaguely revolutionary politics are equated with artistic purity and ideological correctness, always sneak in to provide ammunition to those who would put down fests in general for showing this kind of stuff. All should be spared this one.

"Relevance" of film will undoubtedly be cited, as situation bears parallels to last year's Jim Jones massacre, with remaining members of an officially despised religious cult killing each other off at the end rather than waiting for authorities to do the job. Audience has put up with so much by this time that final sacrifices could accurately be called mercy killings.

Story is purportedly based on real-life happenings in the Brazilian wilderness towards the end of the last century, when persecution of a fundamentalist, earth-working, free-sex, socialist-type group quickly degenerated into its systematic elimination by the local government and military.

Peasant sect followers took their leader, a homely, other-worldly preacher played with grim conviction by Marlise Saueressig, to be Jesus Christ reincarnated, and like others of her ilk, she did nothing to dispel the rumor. Nor did she see anything wrong with having flings with her parishioners on the side.

Tech credits are abysmal, with color processing looking to have been done in a septic tank. —Cart.

Les Turlupins
(Rascals)
(FRENCH-COLOR)

Hollywood, Feb. 5.
A Gilbert de Goldschmidt production. Produced by Gilbert de Goldschmidt. Directed by Bernard Revon. Features entire cast. Screenplay, Bernard Revon. Didier Bouquet-Nadaud, in collaboration with Michel Zemer. Claude de Givray; camera (Fujicolor). Jacques Loiseleux. Gerard de Battista; editor. Georges Klotz; music. Roland Romanelli; sound. Bernard Rochut. Reviewed at the Burbank Studios. Burbank. Feb. 5, 1980. (No MPAA Rating.) Running time: 93 MINS.
Bernard .... Bernard Drieux
Didier .... Thomas Chabrol
Marie-Helene .... Pascale Rocard
Headmaster .... Etienne Draber
Vincent .... Sebastien Drai-Dietrich
Satan .... Pierre Vial
Aline .... Brigitte Chamak
(English subtitles)

Mildly risque sexcapades seem to be what Americans are looking for in the way of French imports these days, so "Les Turlupins," a sort of "Peppermint Soda" from the

male p.o.v., might have a chance in foreign markets as well as on its home turf.

Well-made pic is generally amusing throughout and quite precocious sexually, with girls barely past puberty baring all and acting like incipient Emmanuelles, while the boys lag behind and don't know exactly what to do with their frank and forthright female counterparts.

Set at an isolated school during the air raids and German occupation of World War II, film details the academic and emotional tribulations of a pair of pranksters bent on twisting the rules to their own advantage and scoring with the desmoiselles from the girls' school across the road.

Dialog is crisp and determinedly clever, although stereotypes of the absent-minded professor, blustery old cleric, eternally flustered headmaster and the like are extravagantly indulged in, making for easy laughs at their expense.

Kids are also instantly recognizable as "types," although prolonged exposure to them, if nothing else, bring them sufficiently to life to engage some emotional connection. Despite wartime setting, answers to most of life's difficulties and mysteries come pretty easily to characters here, ultimately rendering pic an enjoyable trifle rather than any kind of hard, insightful look at the process of growing up.

Directorial debut of Bernard Revon, who has previously worked in various capacities for several major helmers and co-wrote the Truffaut films, "Stolen Kisses" and "Bed And Board," is confident and assured, as he deftly achieves the relatively modest aims he set for himself.

Young cast members seem to have fun with their parts, which rubs off comfortably on audience. Older, more studious of the two leads is played by Thomas Chabrol, son of French helmer Claude. Girls were effectively cast for their sex appeal, with Pascale Rocard bearing a passing resemblance to Sylvia Kristel. —Cart.

Berlin Festival

Solo Sunny
(EAST GERMAN-COLOR)

Berlin, Feb. 23.
A DEFA Film Production. Group Babelsberg. East Berlin: world rights. DEFA Aussenhandel, East Berlin. Features entire cast. Directed by Konrad Wolf and Wolfgang Kohlhaase. Screenplay, Kohlhaase: camera (color). Eberhard Geick: editing, Evelyn Carow: sets, Alfred Hirschmeier: music. Guenter Fischer. Reviewed at Berlin Film Fest

(Competition). Feb. 23, '80. Running time: 102 MINS.
Sunny .... Renate Kroessner
Ralph .... Alexander Lang
Harri .... Dieter Montag
Norbert .... Klaus Brasch
Christine .... Heide Kipp

One of the most critical and refreshingly entertaining pix to emerge from the German Democratic Republic. Konrad Wolf's "Solo Sunny" put East Germany squarely in the running for fest sweepstakes — it's a portrait of Socialist society in a positive and rewarding context in addition to being a warm and human story of a femme pop singer.

Sunny is from an orphanage and came up the hard way via a factory job to realize her dream of a pop singer, although her talent is clearly limited and she gets by on guts and figure alone. She also likes male companionship, but when and where she chooses, and has a heart for friends and colleagues in a business that is male-oriented and tough to crack. Her apartment in Berlin offers little consolation after long tours on the road, while love is the only thing that cuts effectively through the everyday loneliness. Now that she's no longer young, she faces the end of her career and a possible return to the factory job she had to escape from in the first place, where she was known as Ingrid Sommer.

Pic, like "Svan Klang's Combo" (Sweden), shows the seamy, boring, and funny side of travelling with a fourth-rate band from hotel to ballroom to factory party to whatever celebration will have them. Sunny's act is in the direction of Liza Minnelli, but she can't warble above a low C and loses her temper when a member of the band paws her and insults her about her age and talent.

One day a "diplome philosopher" subs for a sax-player with a fat lip, and Sunny falls in love with him. She, in turn, is loved by a Berlin taxi driver who dotes on her when she's in town. Sunny hopes that her new acquaintance, who lives alone and likes to listen to Old Indian Music, will prove to be the Prince Charming she is seeking and even write lyrics for her act that another member of the band could transpose to music.

However, while on the road, she has a run-in with the band leader about her fiery temper and itch to tell her tormenters off, and returns home to her new boyfriend unexpected — he's sleeping with another chick this evening. Without a job and a lover, and unable to accept the taxi-suitor or going back to the factory, she attempts suicide—only to be saved by a stomach-pump. In the end, she pulls herself back together and joins a new band of youths practicing in an abandoned factory in the middle of winter.

Pic's realism owes much of scripter and co-director Wolfgang Kohlhaase, who wrote several screenplays for Wolf and did a series of "Berlin Stories" for Gerhard Klein in the fifties. His dialog and the thesp performances, particularly Renate Kroessner as Sunny, plus Wolf's usual sharp direction, make this a winner in every category. A cinch to cop a Berlin fest kudo and/or nail down an aud cite in popularity, "Solo Sunny" signals a bright new trend in East German feature pix for the 1980s.

Try to catch it on the fest circuit.
— Holl.

Race D'Ep
(The Homosexual Century)
(FRENCH-COLOR/B&W-16m)

Berlin, March 4.
Little Sisters Productions release and production. Features entire cast. Directed by Lionel Soukaz. Screenplay, Soukaz, Guy Hocqenghen; camera (Color, b&w), Jerome De Missolz. Soukaz; editor, Soukaz. Reviewed at Berlin Film Fest. Feb. 22, '80. Running time: 95 MINS.
With: Elizar Von Efenterre, Copi, Remy Germain.

A sketch film of four episodes on homosexuality that are informative but a bit diffuse and overindulgent. Gays may find it a big self-pitying these days. There are still some interesting revelations that could slant this for specialized situations, and, of course, fests.

The first part concerns a well-known turn-of-the-century German photographer who liked to photograph Sicilian peasant boys in ancient Roman costumes and poses. It is supposedly commented by one of his old lovers. Seg amusingly sends up early gay reticence.

Second deals with the first homosexual movement and study center in Germany in the '30s that tried to treat it as a social reality. The office was destroyed by the Nazis and the founder, Magnus Hirschfield, shipped off to a concentration camp.

Then came the sixties when young men stepped out of closets worldwide. This is a sort of series of postcards sent by a young American to friends on his breezy gay trip around Europe and Africa.

Final one takes place in a gay cafe today and deals with a mythomaniacal gay who tells a friends of a meeting with an American that is fantasized out of proportion to what happened. Film is talky but visually acceptable.

The title "race D'Ep" is a play on an old slang word for gays,

"rasedep," made into what seems to imply a sort of race. The English title was given by the makers.
—Mosk.

Deutschland Bleiche Mutter
(Germany, Pale Mother)
(WEST GERMAN-COLOR)

Berlin, Feb. 20.
A Helma Sanders Film Production, in coproduction with Literarisches Colloquium, Berlin, and Westdeutscher Rundfunk (WDR), Cologne; producer, Ursula Ludwig. Written and directed by Helma Sanders-Brahms. Features entire cast. Camera (color), Juergen Juerges; sets, Goetz Heymann; music, Juergen Knieper; editing, Elfi Tillack, Uta Periginelli. Reviewed at Berlin Film Festival (Competition), Feb. 20, '80. Running time: 130 MINS.
Helene .... Eva Mattes
Hans .... Ernst Jacobi
Hanne .... Elisabeth Stepanek
Lydia .... Angelika Thomas
Ulrich .... Reiner Friedrichsen
Aunt Ihmchen .... Gisela Stein
Uncle Bertrand .... Fritz Lichtenhahn
Anna (at different ages) .... Anna Sanders, Sonja Lauer, Miriam Lauer

Femme helmer Helma Sanders worked her way up through the documentary — "Angelika Urban, Salesgirl, Engaged" (1970), "The Industrial Reserve Army" (1971), "The Employee" (1972), and "The Machine" (1973) and the tv-film, "Gewalt" (1971), to the feature film by the mid-1970s, always staying close to fem themes but adapting to the latest trends at the same time.

For the record, her feature pix: "The Last Days of Gomorrah" (1974), "The Sand Under the Cement" (1975), "Shirin's Wedding" (1976), and "Heinrich" (1977). Her latest, "Germany, Pale Mother," unspooled in the Berlin Film Fest — a long-winded, two-hours-plus recollection of her childhood (she was born in 1940), and beyond, during the Nazi Years and the critical postwar period. It comes across as a pale copy of Rainer Werner Fassbinder's "The Marriage of Maria Braun" in the long run, although private family stories are the privilege of every film-author.

Pic has but a thread of a narrative to keep it moving, saved for the most part by docu scenes of a wartorn Germany to place the chronological times-frames in the foreground. The personal accounts — the "this-really-happened-to-my-mother" bits — were better off discarded, for they serve neither the director nor the film, and are often downright embarrassing. From the viewpoint of women's lib, the pickings are also too slim, less the argument here that an all-women production somehow advances the cause.

Pic was shot entirely in Berlin,

principally at the Literarisches Colloquium in the city. Lensing a strong plus. —Holl.

Die Ortliebschen Frauen
(The Ortlieb Women)
(WEST GERMANY-COLOR)

Berlin, Feb. 18.
A Solaris/von Vietinghoff Film Production, in coproduction with Pia Frankenberg Music and Film Production, Hamburg, Westdeutscher Rundfunk (WDR), Cologne. Features entire cast. Directed by Luc Bondy. Screenplay, Bondy, Libgart Schwarz, based on motifs in Franz Nabl's novel, "The Grave of the Living;" camera (color), Ricardo Arnovich; music, Peer Raben. Reviewed at Berlin Film Fest (Forum), Feb. 18, '80. Running time: 106 MINS.
The Mother .... Edith Heedegen
Josefine .... Libgart Schwarz
Anna .... Elisabeth Stepanek
Walter .... Klaus Pohl

After Peter Handke's "The Left-Handed Woman" (1977), based on his own novel, it's only natural that another literary adaptation of the same sort should come along — Luc Bondy's "The Ortlieb Women." Based on Austrian writer Franz Nabl's "The Grave of the Living," and with Libgart Schwarz of the Berlin Schaubuehne (also Handke's wife) playing one of the leads, this opener of the Berlin Forum's program attracted critical attention.

Tale, as book-title indicates, is a bloodless, pessimistic portrait of contemporary life, particularly the "inner world" Teutonic cinema and theatre are so fond of. Its time and place are almost irrelevant, although the costumes appear to be from the thirties and the area just might be Austria (the accents indicate West Germany).

The father of a closely-knit family has died, leaving behind a feeble-minded mother, a sick but strong-willed daughter, Josefine, and her sister and brother. Josefine decides that she has to keep the family together at all costs, and proceeds to force the others to do things as she wants. Thus the mother retreats into the background, the other sister becomes the maid, and the gimping, slow-witted brother is finally locked into the cellar (the symbolic "grave of the living") because it's supposed to be "best" for him.

Very much of a literary adaptation and directed with the heavy hand of a theatre helmer (Bondy, the son of writer-essayist Francois Bondy, is prominent in German theatre), "The Ortlieb Women" will probably bow at a couple more fests on the summer circuit, then succomb to the laws of gravity. On the stage the thesps might have saved a couple of scenes with their undeniable talent, but as a film "The Ortlieb Women" is clumsy and un-

imaginative, even downright embarrassing due to the subsidy bucks invested in it. —Holl.

Moskwa Sljesam Nje Jerit
(Moscow Does Not Believe In Tears)
(RUSSIAN-COLOR)

Berlin, Feb. 27.
Mosfilm release and production. Features entire cast. Directed by Vladimir Menshov. Screenplay, Valentin Tschernych; camera (Sovcolor), Igor Slabnjewitsch; editor, Jelene Mischajova. Reviewed at Berlin Film Fest (Competing), Feb. 26, '80. Running time: 145 MINS.
Katerina .... Vera Alentova
Goscha .... Alexei Batalov
Ludmilla .... Irina Murawjova
Antonia .... Raissa Rjasanova
Rudolf .... Juri Wassiliev

Three girls come to Moscow from the country to find new lives and challenges. Men outweight politics and their work in factories. One ends up with an illegitimate child, another does not marry, and one has a good simple marriage.

It starts in 1958 and then goes into 1978. A bit sprawling, overlong and indulgent, film still has an easygoing attitude towards the more forthright love scenes, albeit covered up. It indicates there are class distinctions due to standing in the work hierarchy and brings in an almost overheroic, unassuming worker who wins over the unwed mother, now the director of a big factory.

Film is engagingly played and directed with ease. Perhaps a bit reminiscent of American romantic comedies of the thirties, but without their more dynamic pacing, bite and tongue-in-cheek innocence. Manliness means a need to fight when necessary when the new lover chastises five hoodlums attacking the daughter's latest suitor because one is also courting the girl.

Not really a thaw, but still a more forthright modern comedy about Soviet life where men and women relationships are the thing. A certain preciosity sometimes clouds its more outspoken look at love in a socialist state. Worth fest sorties but not the film for any Soviet breakthrough outside the Eastern Bloc orbit. —Mosk.

Seitensprung
(Escapade)
(EAST GERMAN-COLOR)

Berlin, Feb. 21.
A DEFA Film Productions, Group Babelsberg, East Berlin; world rights, DEFA Aussenhandel, East Berlin. Features entire cast. Directed by Evelyn Schmidt. Screenplay, Regina Weicker, Schmidt; camera (color), Juergen Kruse; sets, Georg Wratsch; music, Peter Rabenalt; editing, Helga Emmrich. Revised at Berlin Film Fest (Forum), Feb. 21, '80. Running time: 89 MINS.
Cast: Renate Geissler (Edith), Uwe Zerbe (Wolfgang), Annette Voss (Sandra),

Tobias Zander (Danilo), Renate Reinicke, Karin Beewers, Ursula Braun, Angela Brunner, Johanna Clas.

Evelyn Schmidt's "Escapade" at Berlin's Forum introduces a gifted femme helmer from the German Democratic Republic, a former student of East German director Konrad Wolf (whose "Solo Sunny" bowed in the Berlin competition). Not so much a femme theme as a portrait of Socialist society, pic deserves more international exposure on the upcoming fest circuit.

This is the story of a man with two wifes, one legally and one on the side, and with two children, the older of whom is the fruit of his "escapade." The odd relationship has been going on for years, without the real wife knowing anything save that her husband once had an affair, long pardoned, that produced an offspring, Sandra, now 12-years-old. For the wife, a postal employee, her marriage to a worker in a department store means a four-year-old son of her own, the regular vacation, and perfume on "woman's day."

Pic opens with wife bragging of her idyll, then the husband, Wolfgang, bringing perfume and his company, first, to the girlfriend and, then, to the wife, pleading extra work as the reason for the delay in not getting home on time for dinner. Shortly thereafter, however, the mistress dies in an accident and the girl, quite naturally, comes to her father for lack of another close relative. The family takes her in, but it's only a matter of time before the girl lets slip that her father visited her mother on the sly quite often.

Confronted by the news, he reacts by stating a man can have two loves — to which his wife forces him to choose now between his wife and son, and the illegitimate daughter. The girl is sent to an orphanage, the wife suffers from a nagging conscience, and the father sends letters to the girl and visits her on the side. Finally, the girl is readmitted to the family circle just before the vacation begins, but it's clear that she's still an outsider in the end.

Script has leaks in it, but thesps and lensing are a plus. Another of those strong GDR features of late that puts East Germany in the forefront of Socialist cinema. —Holl.

Les Bons Debarras
(Good Riddance)
(FR. CANADIAN-COLOR)

Berlin, Feb. 26.
Les Productions Prisma release and production. Features entire cast. Directed by Francis Mankiewicz. Screenplay, Rejean Ducharme; camera (Eastmancolor), Michel Brault; editor, Andre Corriveau.
Reviewed at Berlin Film Fest, Feb. 20, '80. Running time, 109 MINS.
Manon .... Charlotte Laurier
Michelle .... Marie Tifo
Guy .... Germain Houde
Madame .... Louise Marleau
Maurice .... Gilbert Sicotte

French Canadian film would need subtitles for France. It has the twangy, lower-class dialect symptomatic of its naturalistic slice-of-life look at a family trio eking out life as well as an observant study of a precocious 10-year-old girl reacting to it.

The film has an episodic air as their fairly tragic lot is played out. It records but rarely gives a more visual transmuting of thier life into a more incisive narrative flair this is mainly a home item, but still denotes a director with possibilities in Francis Mankiewicz.

The mother is drifting into an affair with the local policeman whom her pert, independent little daughter does not like. There is also the woman's backward epileptic brother who is harmless but finally destroyed by a well-meaning love for a rich woman that frightens her rather than lets her understand he has no bad intentions.

The little girl sasses everybody but is full of love and rebels when her mother becomes pregnant and thinks of settling down. She runs off but comes back. The brother is killed in an accident and these muted lives will go on.

The acting is good and it is a film with a realistic spark and worth festival slotting. It just lacks a more filmic probing of these fairly barren lives. It does indicate the beginning of the destruction of this little girl's love that will make her like the others with their mixture of despair and delight in life's more trivial and pleasurable aspects.
— Mosk.

La Viuda De Montiel
(The Widow Montiel)
(MEXICAN-CUBAN-
VENEZUELAN-
COLOMBIAN-COLOR)

Berlin, March 4.
Omnifilms release of Universidada Veracruzana-Macuto Films-ICAIC-Macondo Films production. Features entire cast. Directed by Miguel Littin. Screenplay, Jose Augustin, Littin from a story by Garcia Marquez; camera (Eastmancolor), Patricio Castilla; editor, Nelson Rodriguez; music, Leo Brower. Reviewed at Berlin Film Fest, Feb. 21, '80 (Competing). Running time: 105 MINS.
Adelaida .... Gerladine Chaplin
Montiel .... Nelson Villagra
Carmichael .... Ernesto Gomez Cruz
Alacaide .... Alejandro Parodi
Mama Grande .... Katy Jurado

Based on some short stories by the noted Latin American writer Garcia Marquez, film is somewhat literary and earthbound. It lacks the adroit mixture of myth and reality, the racy metaphorical quality of Marquez's work.

Geraldine Chaplin is the bereft widow of a man she insists made her happy though he was hated by all. Perhaps it wants to show the backwardness and blindness of Latin life alongside its harsh realities.

Film is somewhat posey, pretty but finally dirge-like in its mixture of flashbacks and the growing realisation of the widow that she had lived a life of delusion. Her husband collaborated with each revolutionary regime and became rich by selling out people.

Film is ambiguous, perhaps mirroring Latin American politics and life, but does not manage to hit the poetic and probing vein groped for which turns this into a series of tableaus instead of a more potent distillation of the Latin experience.

It is very ambitious which explains its festival appearances, though pic looks slanted more for Latin American chances than for more worldwide commercial possibilities. —Mosk.

Postav Dom, Zasad Strca
(Build A House, Plant A Tree)
(CZECHOSLOVAK-COLOR)

Berlin, Feb. 26.
Czech State Film release of Bratislava production. Features entire cast. Directed by Juraj Jakubisko. Screenplay, Nikulas Kovac, Lydia Ragatova; camera (Eastmancolor), Stanislav Dorsic, Vladimir Hollos; music, Petr Hapka. Reviewed at Berlin Film Fest, Feb. 20, '80. Running time: 90 MINS.
Pavel .... Josef Matus
Helena .... Jana Siniakova
Ziga .... Ondrej Pavelka
Gustav .... Virsitzender Simiak

Juraj Jakubisko, a Slovak, once made an unusual lyrical film about the violent side of war and revolution, "The Deserter and the Nomads," that held its own with the Czech spate of films in the 60s, that, until aborted by the Soviet invasion in '68, captured world attention and film awards.

Not heard from the last few years, Jakubisco comes up with a robust film on a loner fringe character that might be a harbinger of more outspoken films from that country. Such early notables as Jiri Menzel, Vera Chytilova and Jaromil Jires managed to make some acceptable though conventional films since '68.

Jakubisko has his freighthopping thirtyish anti-hero hopping off a train in a mountain village. He helps find a lost child and gets adopted by the people. He decides to stay and win the daughter of the village chairman.

But her father dislikes him and is against their idyll. The interloper also wins over her son, she is a divorcee. He promises to build her a house for his motto is "build a house, have a son, plant a tree."

He gets people he works with together to help him build the house. He uses shrewd tactics in liberating materials lying about unused and faking receipts. But her father gets wind of things and brings the police. He is killed trying to dump the few goods he has actually stolen when his truck falls into a deep gorge.

Though he gets his comeuppance, the film has him emerging an engaging character who shows up the waste of the system and some of its hypocrisy. Potent love scenes, fine playing, a robust narrative style mark Jakubisko in form again.

Film may be more for fests than for general release, but it is a welcome sign of returning vigor on the once fine Czechoslovak film scene.
—Mosk.

Hungerjahre
(Hunger Years)
(WEST GERMAN-B&W)

Berlin, Feb. 22.
A Jutta Brueckner Film Production, in coproduction with Zweites Deutsches Fernsehen (ZDF), Mainz. Features entire cast. Written and directed by Jutta Brueckner. Camera (black and white), Joerg Jeshel, Rainer Maerz; music, Johannes Schmoelling; editing, Anneliese Krigar; tv producer, Sybille Rahn. Reviewed at Berlin Film Fest (Forum), Feb. 22, '80. Running time: 114 MINS.
Cast: Sylvia Ulrich (Mother), Britta Pohland (Daughter), Claus Jurichs (Father), Hilda Preuss, Ismail Mahdu, Heidi Joschko, Helga Lehner, Cordula Hubrich, Viola Recklies, Tobias Meister.

Jutta Brueckner, a femme filmer with a Ph.D. on the side, prefers to make a type of pic with a sociopolitical message somewhere in the background. This one, "Hunger Years," is about the postwar Adenauer period and has something in common with Rainer Werner Fassbinder's "The Marriage of Maria Braun" and Helma Sander's "Germany, Pale Mother" (in the fest's competition program) in that it treats those 1950s when the country — West Germany, that is — got back on its feet.

Plenty of docu footage sets the story in focus, and there are years cited from 1953 on to keep the commentay going in a studious manner. Brueckner's main thesis seems to be that, after two work wars and the interim reconstruction years, those who were 40 in the '50s had lost their youth and only wanted to live out the few remaining years in peace. Thus, Konrad Adenauer was the kind of political leader required for the times.

Footage on the building of the wall between the two Germanies, beauty contests, and the rearmament policy with corresponding riots in the streets are well worth the viewer's time. The rest is about a complex relationship in a family between a withdrawn and awkward daughter and her parents, during which questions about he past are posed — such as why the father, a bit of a resistance-fighter against Nazisms in the early 1930s, went along with the conforming masses later. In the end, the girl commits suicide.

Plodding two-hour pic for the knowing insiders, but a nutcracker for foreign auds. Offshore chances are nil.—*Holl.*

Nijinsky
(BRITISH-COLOR)

Beautifully lensed but slow-paced bio of famed dancer, constructed as a homosexual romantic tragedy. Sophisticated bookings indicated. No "Turning Point" this.

Paramount Pictures release of a Hera Production. Directed by Herbert Ross. Produced by Nora Kaye & Stanley O'Toole. Screenplay. Hugh Wheeler, based on "Nijinsky" by Romola Nijinsky and "The Diary of Vaslav Nijinsky." Stars Alan Bates. George De La Pena. Leslie Browne. Exec producer. Harry Saltzman: camera (Metrocolor). Douglas Slocombe: film editor. William Reynolds: assoc.producer. Howard Jeffrey: music adapted and conducted by John Lanchbery: production design. John Blezard: costume design. Alan Barrett. Reviewed at Magno Review Theatre. N.Y.. March 7, '80. (MPAA Rating: R.) Running time: **125 MINS.**

Sergei Diaghilev	Alan Bates
Vaslav Nijinsky	George De La Pena
Romola De Pulsky	Leslie Browne
Baron De Gunzberg	Alan Badel
Tamara Karsavina	Carla Fracci
Vassili	Colin Blakely
Igor Stravinsly	Ronald Pickup
Leon Bakst	Ronald Lacey
Emilia Marcus	Janet Suzman
Lady Ripon	Sian Phillips

This exceedingly handsome treatment of legendary Russian dancer Vaslav Nijinsky's gradual disintegration from the pinnacle of his art to the dregs of madness is probably a lot more significant in terms of a Hollywood studio's big-budget commitment to a seriously crafted portrait of a homosexual relationship than as a major artistic or commercial achievement on its own merits.

With several Nijinsky projects developed and put on hold over the years, it was obviously the commercial success of director Herbert Ross's "The Turning Point" which hinted there might be more than a one-shot market for ballet backgrounded features.

But for all its exotic background and characters, "Turning Point" was basically a superbly crafted soap opera in which easily identifiable emotions were tied to conventional romantic pairings and parental conflicts.

In "Nijinsky," however, Ross and scripter Hugh Wheeler have constructed nothing less than a male-to-male romantic tragedy; one that may have temporarily reversed Hollywood's general closeting of these themes, but doesn't stand much chance of intensely involving general audience emotions or concerns. Urban art houses, especially in areas rich in balletomanes, are in order.

Leaving the details of Nijinsky's (George De La Pena) final 33 years of psychiatric confinement to a printed epilog, the film takes the form of a broad flashback covering only two critical years (1912-13) in the young dancer's early 20s. Beginning at the height of favor with both the European public and his mentor-lover Sergei Diaghilev (Alan Bates), the period charts Nijinsky through his first lambasted choreographic efforts for the Ballets Russes; his growing megalomania as his mind begins to unhinge. and his gradual romantic estrangement from Diaghilev.

Included in the latter equation is Nijinsky's gradual allegiance to a wealthy homosexual patron — brilliantly etched by Alan Badel — whose largesse makes his showcasing possible; and the successful attempt of worshipful Hungarian aristocrat Romola de Pulsky (Leslie Browne) to work her way into the company and eventually catch Nijinsky on his briefly heterosexual rebound from Diaghilev (whose thoughts turned to younger stars, like Leonid Massine) and marry him.

(Although the film's background publicity and key ad art make much of the La Pena-Brown-Bates "triangle," there's no real contest here. The love story is Bates's and La Pena's own; anything else is incidental.)

Central theme of Wheeler's script (based on Mrs. Nijinsky's bio as well as the dancer's own diaries) is that Diaghilev's obsessive love for Nijinsky clouded his otherwise shrewd taste, showmanship and business sense and put a mind-bending burden of expectations on the dancer. This is well developed in Bates's firing of chief choreographer Mikhail Fokine over latter's jealous (and obscene, hence the R-rating) putdown of his protege, as well as Stravinsky's (Ronald Pickup) distaste at having his "Sacre Du Printemps" choreographed (and booed off the stage at its premiere) by a tone-deaf novice.

The film paints the ballet world as a pragmatically manipulated business that eventually serves Art, but is largely driven by lustful allegiances and petty professional jealousies. Characters spout bitchy aphorisms as casually as they pop peppermints and the overriding homosexual mileu may be intriguing at first, but eventually pales. As the tragedy plays itself out, the film becomes bottom heavy, extremely talky and eventually tiring.

Most surprising facet of "Nijinsky" is that in only one stunningly intense segment (in which La Pena's mind begins to warp as he dances "Afternoon of a Faun" and winds up masturbating on stage) does Ross pay strict attention to a performance itself. Unlike "Turning Point," where generous segments of several ballets were beautifully caught, snippets (e.g. "Spectre of the Rose," "Scheherazade," "Petrouchka" and "Sacre Du Printemps") are the order and extent of the day.

De La Pena, who dances with American Ballet Theatre (as does Browne) has the intensity and ambiguous sexual aura to make him a credible Nijinsky, though the character's inherent weakness and unpleasantness make his tragic plunge less than disturbing. Bates is excellent as Diaghilev (especially in his guilty approach-avoidance of La Pena as the youth begins to burn himself out). Browne is the weakest element in the film and looks like she's walking through a lavishly costumed school play.

The film's production design (by John Blezard) is literally breathtaking, ranging from the salons and opera houses of Budapest and Paris to the elegance of Monte Carlo, and the set designs of the actual ballets. Music, costumes and the like are appropriately perfect. with the overall beauty of the film largely a function of Douglas Slocombe's excellent cinematography. —*Step.*

Defiance
(COLOR)

Emotionally effective but a tough sell.

Hollywood, March 6.
An American International Pictures release of a Necta film production. Produced by William S. Gilmore, Jr. and Jerry Bruckheimer. Directed by John Flynn. Exec producer. Robert J. Wunsch. Screenplay. Thomas Michael Donnelly based on a story by Donnelly and Mark Tulin. Stars Jan Michael Vincent. Camera (color). Ric Waite: editor. David Finfer: production design. Bill Malley: music. Basil Poledouris: original songs and additional score. Gerard McMahon: set decoration. Rick T. Gentz: costumes. Ellis Cohen: sound. William Nelson: assistant director. Peter Bogart. Reviewed at AIP Screening Room. March 5, '80. MPAA Rating: PG. Running time: **102 MINS.**

Tommy	Jan Michael Vincent
Marsha	Theresa Saldana
Kid	Fernando Lopez
Carmine	Danny Aiello
Abe	Art Carney
Paolo	Santos Morales
Abbie Jackson	Don Blakely
Herbie	Frank Pesce
Angel Cruz	Rudy Ramos
Bandana	Lee Fraser
Tito	Randy Herman
Slagg	Alberto Vazquez
Luis	Church Ortix
El Bravo	East Carlo
Whacko	Lenny Montana

It is easy to see why the violence that erupted in reaction to several gang-oriented films last year dissuaded American International Pictures from releasing "Defiance." Despite several characters and plot twists that take on an unrealistic, melodramatic tone, overall result is a terse, tension-filled statement on changing urban neighborhoods virtually controlled by a single group of hoodlums. Even considering natural exhib trepidation to play such an outing, pic will still be a tough sell since it is much more than a mindless action feature, but not quite the sociological exercise needed to attract the more sophisticated filmgoer.

Jan Michael Vincent is thoroughly convincing as a merchant seaman who moves into a decaying neighborhood in New York's lower east side while awaiting his assignment on board a new ship. Hating the city and the depressing atmosphere in which he lives, Vincent slowly becomes accepted as part of the small community of "civilized" inhabitants that have stayed around despite the rise to power of a local gang, The Souls.

Vincent at first tries to stay out of the way of the gang, but slowly begins to change his attitude as he views the way the Souls are terrorizing everyone around him. His emergence as the one person with the guts and ability to fight back inspires the locals to unofficially anoint him as a kind of messiah who is capable of leading them out of their unfortunate turmoil.

The conflicts within Vincent on whether to stay and fight or leave to pursue the life that he is most comfortable with are expertly fleshed out by the actor. The slow evolution of the character is the core to the film and Vincent is largely responsible for its effectiveness.

Also outstanding are the various gang members, led by Rudy Ramos in a controlled but powerful performance, Fernando Lopez as the street-smart youngster Vincent befriends and Danny Aiello as a long-winded neighbor who is eventually changed for the better by Vincent. Art Carney's storekeeper is okay but largely unexplored.

Some problems do arise with Thomas Michael Donnelly's screenplay. Plot also tends to focus more on the physical occurrences than on the actual reasons behind them. Result is a picture that evokes fear, but leaves too many questions to satisfy anyone taking the time to analyze the goings-on.

Additionally, several characters just don't work in the scheme of things, especially Theresa Saldana as the kooky Jewish girl who serves as Vincent's romantic involvement. Saldana brings what she can to the role but she's just too out-of-place in the surroundings to take seriously. Also dubious is that while the Souls are beating up and destroying everyone and everything important to Vincent, they never approach Saldana or her unusually

tasteful tenement apartment, which is just upstairs from Vincent's.

John Flynn creates the needed conflicts with some careful direction although tendency is to go back and forth in moods rather than build to the potent albeit somewhat contrived finale. Basil Poledouris' music, supplemented by contributions from Gerard McMahon appears in all the right spots and Ric Waite's camera captures the grittiness of Gotham.

"Defiance" has more than its share of faults, but it ultimately succeeds by tugging on emotions. Whether that will translate at the ticket window depends on how carefully it is sold and how willing audiences will be to accept yet another picture on the gang situation.—*Berg*.

Rising Damp
(BRITISH-COLOR)

Modest sitcom okay for the home market.

London, March 6.
ITC release of a Cinema Arts International Production for Black Lion Films, produced by Roy Skeggs. Exec producer, Brian Lawrence. Directed by Joe McGrath. Features entire cast. Screenplay, Eric Chappell; photography (color), Frank Watts; music, David Lindup; editor, Peter Weatherley; sound, Alan Kane; assistant director, Roger Simons. Reviewed at Classic Haymarket, London, March 5, '80. (BBFC rating: A). Running time: **96 MINS.**
Rigsby .... Leonard Rossiter
Miss Jones .... Frances de la Tour
Philip .... Don Warrington
John .... Christopher Strauli
Seymour .... Denholm Elliott
Sandra .... Carrie Jones
Cooper .... Glynn Edwards
Bert .... John Cater
Alec .... Derek Griffiths

"Rising Damp," another of those British television stretch jobs, is a fairly sharp little comedy. Too parochial to travel much, but it should playoff prosperously in the home market and possibly some foreign territories where the vid-series also airs.

Leonard Rossiter is very funny as a bigoted rooming house landlord. Frances de la Tour, Don Warrington, Christopher Strauli and Denholm Elliott are all fine as the motley lodgers.

The plot's little more than a series of sketches with a running joke, Rossiter's pomposity and feckless efforts to woo spinster passion flower de la Tour, who in turn only has eyes for Warrington (passed off as the son of an African tribal chief) but who ultimately is bedded by Elliott as a down-at-the-heels con artist. Sounds otherwise, but actually the film's devoid of sex, which is one of its modest charms.

At least for attuned ears, Eric

Chappell's screenplay offers a good blend of snappy dialog to go with some wacky sight gags, one of which has the ceiling collapse just as de la Tour and Elliott are about to go to it in the sack.

John McGrath's direction is witty and well-paced. Though it's mostly for laughs, pic also offers some nicely understated social comment, not least about racial attitudes.

Nothing remarkable about the tech credits, but they're all polished —*Pit*.

The Trials Of Alger Hiss
(U.S.-DOCU-COLOR/B&W-16M)

Fascinating new look at an old dispute, but only for special theatrical situations.

A History on Film presentation. Produced and directed by John Lowenthal. Camera (color/black and white), Steven L. Alexander, Adam Giffard, Vic Losick, Mark Obenhaus, Edward Gray, William G. Markle; editor, Marion Kraft; sound, Richard Brick, Robert Funk, Francis Daniel, Ronald S. Yoshida. Reviewed at Embassy 72d St. Theatre, New York, March 7, 1980. (No MPAA rating.) Running time: **166 MINS.**

Newly-edited documentary, "The Trials of Alger Hiss," was coproduced, in a sense, by the U.S. Congress, which recently passed the Freedom of Information legislation by which Hiss evidence, suppressed for almost 30 years, has become accessible to the public.

Using such new revelations of old secrets, plus new interviews with surviving participants from that Hiss era of the late 1940's, producer John Lowenthal has compiled a film that surely is a kind of milestone in American documentary, of broad length and scope, a major work despite Lowenthal's low-key pro-Hiss bias.

Lowenthal is heard and seen occasionally in the film. Film is an outgrowth of his interest in the Hiss trials as a lawyer and as a professor for 13 years at the School of Law at Rutgers U. (This is his first film.)

New Hiss film connects to other recent documentaries re-examining political trials, including "Hollywood on Trial," "The Wobblies," and "The Unquiet Death of Ethel and Julius Rosenberg."

Hiss film seems a natural for specialized situations, especially in cities with strong university presence. But it is obviously not a relaxed pop-entertainment item, as it requires attentive listening to non-stop testimony and interviews, much of it loaded with fascinating facts, insight and character revelation.

"Trials of Alger Hiss" raises

doubts about the evidence used to convict Hiss, the motives of his accusers, but refrains from making final judgments about the guilt and innocence of Hiss, prominent U.S. State Dept. officer who was convicted of perjury after two lengthy trials in 1950. Hiss served three years and eight months in Federal prison at Lewisburg, Pa.

Interviews with many strong spokesmen, pro and con, are used in the film. Hiss, House Un-American Activities Committee investigator Robert Stripling (who also figured in the Hollywood 10 trials), jurors, witnesses, FBI personnel and others appear. Richard Nixon, then a rising young Congressman from California, who became Senator the year His entered prison, declined to participate, as did Hiss' ex-wife Priscilla and the widow of Hiss' accuser, the late Whittaker Chambers. Both Nixon and Chambers appear in stock footage, however.

After his prison term and early release for good behavior, Hiss is now at liberty and is topic of numerous scholarly articles and books reconstructing the trials. Hiss was disbarred at the time, but recently has been restored as a lawyer by the Massachusetts Bar. He is now 74 and is seeking formal cancellation of his conviction.

In the film, Hiss reads aloud from Chambers's detailed hand-written statements of his homosexuality, statements made to the FBI months before the conviction of Hiss, but only recently made known per the release of new Hiss-Chambers documents under the Freedom of Information Act. Film arouses speculation that an unreciprocated "homosexual crush" by Chambers on Hiss may have motivated Chambers's accusations against Hiss, which spanned a decade, and his suicide attempts. Chambers' repeated references before newsreel cameras that he is doomed to self-destruction are particularly dramatic and unsettling. Jurors interviewed in the film confirm that they would have voted differently, for the acquittal of Hiss, had they had such suppressed facts about Chambers' emotional instability. Also, doctored FBI evidence in regard to that fatal typewriter figures in the film.

Film uses 40-minutes of stock footage, about one-quarter of its length, reconstructing background to the Hiss trials — the Depression of the 1930's, World War II, and the subsequent Cold War. Remaining 75% is new material updating the Hiss chronicle, shot by Lowenthal, who occasionally appears on camera questioning jurors, et al.

Complex sound and picture editing is especially commendable, by Marion Kraft, who was one of several editors of "Memory of Justice" by Marcel Ophuls.

"The Trials of Alger Hiss" was screened in December at the annual convention of the American Historical Assn. in New York. Except for that, Embassy opening March 9 was the world premiere. Lowenthal may do 35m blow-up of his 16m original. Budget for film is $400,000. Financing was private, but with some aid from the Samuel Rubin Foundation. —*Hitch.*

Nothing Personal
(COLOR)

Nothing much.

Hollywood, March 7.
An American International Pictures release. Produced by David M. Perlmutter. Directed by George Bloomfield. Exec producers. Alan Hamel, Jay Bernstein and Norman Hirschfield. Stars Donald Sutherland and Suzanne Somers. Screenplay, Robert Kaufman, camera (Movielab Color), Laszlo George, Arthur Ibbetson; editor, George Appleby; art direction, Mary Kerr; set decoration, Mark Freeborn, Anthony Greco; costumes, Lynda Kemp; sound, Chris Large; assistant director, R. Martin Walter. Reviewed at the Topanga Theatre, Woodland Hills, March 7, '80. (MPAA Rating: PG). Running time: 97 MINS.
Professor
Roger Keller .... Donald Sutherland
Abigail Adams .... Suzanne Somers
Robert Ralston .... Lawrence Dane
Mr. Paxton .... Roscoe Lee Browne
Tom Dickerson .... Dabney Coleman
Peter Braden .... Saul Rubinek
Janet Samson .... Catherine O'Hara
Kancok .... Maury Chakin
Audrey Seltzer .... Kate Lynch
Ralph Henry Emerson .... Hugh Webster
Jake Barnes .... Sean McCann

A handful of curiosity seekers will no doubt be attracted to "Nothing Personal" since it presents television's Suzanne Somers in her first major film role. But that's the only noteworthy aspect of this amateurish, superficial and implausible romantic comedy.

So nonsensical and tedious are the situations presented that even the most avid fans of Somers' tv series may have trouble sitting through this one. Boxoffice prospects seem poor, beyond the first week or so, but Somers' name should help Canadian investors recoup some of their money through ancillary markets.

Like Farrah Fawcett before her, Somers is attempting to make the jump from vidstar-poster queen to film actress with material impossible to bring dignity to. She cannot be faulted for her performance as a Harvard-graduate sexpot lawyer trying to help college professor Donald Sutherland stop a heartless corporation from killing innocent baby seals.

After discovering at the film's outset that the seals are being destroyed, Robert Kaufman's script immediately takes Sutherland to Washington, D.C., where he gets in to see top military and political brass in order to stop the brutality within first 10 minutes of the pic. So much for the rumor that there is a bureaucracy in the nation's capital.

A few minutes later Kaufman introduces Somers, a voluptuous magna cum laude alumna from one of the country's top law schools who can't get a client despite the fact that she seems to have interned with some of the best legal minds to be found. Only through some brainy demonstrations and a healthy bit of feminine persuasion (of course) does she land Sutherland.

The pair's quest for justice has them fighting with corporation topper Lawrence Dane and his buffoon-like assistant Dabney Coleman, looking to hotel owner Roscoe Lee Browne for help and embarking on the unavoidable ending chase scene for the only Indian in the U.S.

Kaufman's writing leaves so many plot gaps, George Bloomfield's direction is so unimaginative and George Appleby's editing is so sloppy that virtually nothing can draw commendation.

Laszlo George and Arthur Ibbetson have done a fine job of photographing Somers but most of her scenes suggest she's spent hours finding just the right position for each part of her anatomy before the cameras were allowed to roll.

"Nothing Personal" does succeed at fostering the notion the films made under a tax shelter basis are nothing more than business deals with little or no artistic merit. That's too bad since there have to be numerous projects that could put both Somers and the money to better use. —*Berg.*

The Fifth Floor
(COLOR)

Champaign, March 3:
A Film Ventures International release, a Hickmar Productions film. Produced and directed by Howard Avedis. Executive producer, Marlene Schmidt. Screenplay, Meyer Dolinsky. Story by Avedis and Schmidt; camera (color) Dan Pearl; editor, Stanford Allen; music, Casablanca Records and Filmworks. Reviewed at Rialto Theatre, Champaign, IL, March 2, '80. (MPAA rating: R) Running time: 87 MINS.
Carl .... Bo Hopkins
Kelly McIntire .... Dianne Hull
Cathy Burke .... Patti D'Arbanville
Melanie .... Sharon Farrell
Dr. Coleman .... Mel Ferrer
Nurse .... Julie Adams
Ronnie Denton .... John David Carson
Disco singer .... Patti Brooks
Benny .... Robert Englund

Disco therapy seems to be the key to "The Fifth Floor," a low-level mixture of shock elements from "Cuckoo's Nest" and musical taste from "Thank God It's Friday," but without any integration of talent, metaphor, or music.

Conditions in mental wards haven't looked this bad or unbelievable since "Shock Corridor," as Hull is mistakenly locked up for examination when she freaks out from drugs unknowingly ingested during her act as a disco dancer.

Confronted with the resident insane, Hull can't tell the patients from the doctors without a scorecard, and neither can the audience. Robert Englund walks around in white coat and stethoscope amiably, but he's crazy. Bo Hopkins attempts rape of patients, blackmails nurses for lesbian indiscretions, and tortures women, but he's the hospital guard. "It's us against them," Hopkins reminds the nurse.

Dr. Coleman (Mel Ferrer) does nothing but sit in his office and offer condescending noises. Entirety of film revolves around Hull's attempts to escape, and she does manage to evoke some sympathy amid the rest of the gargoyle thespians in the overwrought cast. Consistent action elements include an escape for a pregnant patient, a leering exploitative scene in the shower, the suicide of one despondent girl, various examples of shock treatment (described as "frying brains"), and other unsavory episodes.

The shock and gore pendulum swings fairly evenly in this otherwise unstylish picture, with many musical excuses for the patients to dance their troubles away (since, not surprisingly, the music is supplied by Casablanca). For a movie with such musical pretentions, the sound quality is poor.

Tasteless moments keep audience alert, with laughter being the primary response, although it is done at the expense of a stereotyped mentally ill. Anger is generated at expense of doctors, all of whom appear dense or cruel, and climax results from a scissors stab in Hopkins's abdomen. "The Fifth Floor" is likely to survive its spotty playoffs, but it's nothing to cheer about. —*Pege.*

The Wizard Of Waukesha
(DOCU-16m-COLOR)

Hollywood, March 8.
A Stray Cat production. Produced by Catherine Orentreich. Directed by Catherine Orentreich, Susan Brockman; camera (color), Mark Obenhaus, Don Lenzer, Ed Gray; editor, Susan Brockman; sound, Ron Yoshida, Danny Michael, Franklin Haber. Reviewed at the Beverly Hills Screening Room, L.A., Mar. 7, 1980. (No MPAA Rating:) Running time: 59 MINS.
Features: Les Paul.

Wizard is the word for Les Paul. Standout performer, electric guitar designer and inventor of eight-track recording system is given a lively appreciative profile by documentarists Catherine Orentreich and Susan Brockman; and awe in which he is held by young musicians overflows the screen. Pic is an excellent bet for fests, campus showings and tv.

Framed by a recent concert appearance, hour-long docu traces Paul's quick rise on the radio during the 1930s, his years with Fred Waring, period of hit records with wife Mary Ford, sign-up with Gibson to craft electric guitars and 1950s innovations in multi-track recording.

Spiked with interesting footage, from Paul's appearance as himself in a Monogram quickie, "Sarah Goes To College," to contempo rock guitarists singing Paul's praises and trying some of his creations on for size, film is nonetheless dominated by the man's own solid, rightfully proud personality.

Paul surveys his achievements in highly articulate fashion while demonstrating his theories of guitar design and giving some virtuoso musical demonstrations, and fully impresses as a genuinely multi-faceted talent, as at home with electronics as onstage.

Orentreich and Brockman did their homework and filmmaking well, having come up with a picture as winning as their subject. —*Cart.*

North China Commune
(CANADIAN-COLOR)

Vancouver, Feb. 1.
A National Film Board of Canada release. Produced by Tom Daly. Executive produced by Arthur Hammond and Barrie Howells. Features people of the Wuxing Commune in the People's Republic of China. Directed by Tony Ianzelo, Boyce Richardson. Narration, Donald Sutherland; researched and written by Boyce Richardson; camera (color), Tony Ianzelo, John Dyer; editor, Ginny Stikeman; sound editors, Margaret Wong, Jacqueline Newell. Reviewed at the National Film Board Theatre, Vancouver, Feb. 1, 1980. Running time: 80 MINS.

Taking advantage of a rare opportunity, Canada's National Film Board sent a top-flight production team for a month-long look at life in the People's Republic. The result, "North China Commune," is documentary filmmaking at its best, a no-nonsense close-up of contemporary China.

A text book study in journalistic objectivity, the picture is a fact-filled feature that is informative without being inflammatory and stimulates thought without sensationalizing. Sophisticated audiences, particularly in college and specialty film situations, will appreciate the straightforward approach, sans special pleading to either the left or the right.

The opportunity came as a result of meetings between the NFB and Chinese ministry of culture officials. An exchange program was devised and both nations playing host to one another's government-sponsored filmmakers.

The production reunited director/cameraman Tony Ianzelo, a 20-year NFB veteran, with freelance writer/director Boyce Richardson, 25 years a journalist. The team previously produced the prize-winning 1974 documentary, "Cree Hunters of Mistassini."

(Among Ianzelo's other credits are "High Grass Circus" and "Blackwood," both nominees for the best short subject Oscar.)

Since 80% of China's people live in rural settlements, the team asked for permission to film in a commune, one located in a part of the country where the climate and crops are similar to those in Canada. What they wanted, and eventually got, was an average, thoroughly typical collective, one that would fairly represent not the ideal but the reality.

"Reality" is the Wuxing commune, some 240 kms south of Peking and 40 kms from the provincial capital of Shijiazhuang. Five Canadians (Ianzelo, Richardson, asst. cameraman John Dyer, electrician Guy Remillard and soundman Hans Oomes) and an entourage of up to 15 Chinese officials commuted daily from the nearby city for more than a month to record a harvest cycle.

In exploring the minutiae of everyday life, the filmmakers made some amazing discoveries. Though it has no sewage system, Wuxing is almost preternaturally clean. Absolutely everything is recycled, including body wastes. All human and animal excrement — about 100,000 metric tons a year — is returned to the land, which is actually increasing in fertility while producing two crops a year.

In a series of interviews, the filmmakers heard that things have never been better. Filmgoers will notice, though, that it is the older people, the commune members with pre-Communist (or, as they phrase it, "pre-Liberation") memories who are the most enthusiastic.

The younger Chinese, the generation with no pre-1949 recall, are less outspoken. Without coming right out and saying it, the film makes it clear that there are problems even within this highly motivated society.

The narration, spoken by actor Donald Sutherland, works hard to maintain a low-key, matter-of-fact tone. Although "North China Commune" touches on a host of contemporary topics — energy, housing, unemployment, medical care,

population control — it forces no conclusions on its audience. It is a documentary in the best sense.

—*Wals.*

Ecstatic Stigmatic
(COLOR-B/W-16M.)

Produced by GSMC. Directed and edited by Gordon Stevenson. Camera (color/black and white), Joanne Heey. No other credits provided. Reviewed at Bleecker St. Cinema, New York, Feb. 22, 1980. Running time: **55 MINS.**

Cast: Mary Kathryn Cervenka, Arto Lindsay, Johnny O'Kane, Brenda Bergman, Anita Paltrinieri.

In "Ecstatic Stigmatic," director Gordon Stevenson is apparently attempting to create allusions between religious fervor, the development of cults and the seeming showbiz nature of these phenomena. With symbolism that is so obtuse as to be practically pointless, this little film would have difficulty attracting even a cult following of its own.

The specific individual referred to by the title, that is, the one who is marked with wounds due to her intense absorbtion in her own divinity, is the Little Rose, a young, crippled girl who is represented by the filmmaker to have been a cult figure of the 1930s. Purporting to follow a documentary fashion, the picture has little mention at all of the child's actual work as such a figure, and confines itself to being a conglomeration of psychological mumbo-jumbo imposed on some scenes reflecting Rose's upbrining.

While little is actually explained or documented, it seems that the girl, played by Mary Kathryn Cervenka, had a father who was a tattoo artist, and who used her as a model for a hula dancer figure, a mother who was a stripper, whose body was covered with tattoos, and was herself raped by an emcee at the joint where her parents worked. In one of the few sync sound sequences, the emcee, played by Johnny O'Kane, wears black makeup over half his face and has a rather silly interracial conversation with himself.

The meaning of blood, particularly in regard to the crucifixion, comes in for frequent, but never particularly clear discussion. Rose bleeds rather profusely from her mouth and hands, as do the sailors who are tattooed, one in particular who is stabbed with a fork, seemingly for fooling around with the stripper-mother. Some sort of relationship is inferred between the lesions suffered by Rose, Christ's wounds and the sort of desecration of the body that tattooing may represent.

Rose is also often pictured lying in bed positioned like Christ on the cross. As to what any of this may be

intended to mean, your guess is as good as anyone else's.

With the exception of these few bizarre scenes, most of the film is rather static in terms of camera work, and the narration and voice-overs tend to drone on and on. What little acting there is is pretty awful, with the exception of Cervenka's portrayal of Rose, in which she does a decent impression of a little girl.

—*Roso.*

Berlin Festival

Heartland
(U.S.-COLOR)

Berlin, Feb. 28.

Wilderness Women's Productions-Filmhaus production. Features entire cast. Directed by Richard Pearce. Screenplay, Beth Ferris based on the books and papers of Elinore Randall Stewart; camera (color), Fred Murphy; editor, Bill Yahrus; music, Charles Gross. Reviewed at Berlin Film Fest (Competing). Feb. 27, '80. Running time: **95 MINS.**

Elinore	Conchata Ferrell
Stewart	Rip Torn
Jack	Barry Primus
Oma	Lilia Skala
Jerrine	Megan Folsom

"Heartland," which shared the top prize at Berlin this year, is a film with heart about the tribulations of homesteading life in Wyoming circa 1910. The entire budget of $600,000 was backed by the National Endowment for the Humanities.

The ruggedness of ranch life is mainly shown from the viewpoint of a hearty, strong but never overbearing widow with a 10-year-old child who goes to a ranch in an isolated part of Wyoming to be the housekeeper for a taciturn Scottish rancher.

She is set on going on her own and soon puts a down payment on her own homestead near the Scotsman's. But they marry and a hard winter follows, during which she gives birth alone to a child which dies.

The birth of a calf, after the loss of most of their herd however gives couple a feeling of hope, without any undue sentimentality or overdone dramatic epiphany. Conchata Ferrell and Rip Torn are effective as the unlikely couple with Lilia Skala as a brusque but understanding old rancher, Barry Primus as a knowing hand and Megan Folsom as the daughter also are effective.

The seasons are neatly etched by lenser Fred Murphy and Beth Ferris's perceptive script, based on the books of the real widow Elinore Randall Stewart, is also an asset.

Richard Pearce, who has made many docus and some tv films, handles this simple tale with a nice

balance of regional feel and elemental drama that make him a director to watch.

Film needs careful treatment, but should find a place with receptive audiences through proper handling. It remains to be seen if its sharing of the Berlin Golden Bear will get it the attention it deserves on its home grounds for both theatrical and tv usage. —*Mosk.*

Marmeladupporet
(The Marmalade Revolution)
(SWEDISH-COLOR)

Berlin, Feb. 28.

Swedish Film Institute release of Josephson & Nykvist HB-SFI-Svensk Filmindustri production. Stars Erland Josephson, Bibi Andersson. Directed by Erland Josephson, Sven Nykvist. Screenplay, Josephson; camera (Eastmancolor), Nykvist; editor, Sylvia Ingemarrsson; music, Antoine Forqueray. Reviewed at Berlin Film Fest (Competing), Feb. 27, '80. Running time, **91 MINS.**

Eller	Erland Josephson
Anna	Bibi Andersson
Maj	Marie Goranzon
Edvard	Jan Malmsjo
Aina	Kristina Adolphson
Ellen	Susanna Hellberg

A fairly flimsy theme of a seemingly well off, middleaged man copping out of life does not have the necessary visual embroidery to counteract its mainly verbal, and often verbose, treatment.

Mainly a home item on its allusions of unrest in the welfare consumer state, it has a theatrical flair in its reliance on dialog rather than any insights into a sudden personal revolt which is rarely explored.

Interest, it has the man, played by Erland Josephson who has also co-directed with cinematographer Sven Nykvist, falling into the hands of a newspaper reporter, Bibi Andersson, who soon gets him some transient notoriety as a "new single." He even embarks on a series of lectures to insist people wake up to their basic humanity and shake off the stultifying drabness of middle-class reality.

But soon the media lose interest and his attempt at seducing the newswoman fails. His wife also fails at seducing a cousin who had always coveted her. It seems it was her inaccessibility that excited him. The revolutionary returns home and finds his daughter has gone off to find herself.

Josephson also wrote this tale which might have some tv chances on its basically talky look at social restiveness. Nykvist has given his usual clear and finely hued lensing to this disarming but essentially surface rendition, in uneven terms, of restlessness in an affluent society. —*Mosk.*

Das Versteck
(The Hiding Place)
(EAST GERMAN-COLOR)

Berlin, Feb. 29.

A DEFA, Group Johanisthal, Film Production, in collaboration with the Fernsehen der DDR; world rights, DEFA Aussenhandel, East Berlin. Stars Jutta Hoffmann, Manfred Krug. Directed by Frank Beyer. Screenplay, Jurek Becker; camera (color), Juergen Brauer; music, Guenther Fischer. Reviewed at Berlin Film Fest (Market), Feb. 29, '80. Running time: 101 MINS.

Cast: Jutta Hoffmann (Wanda Brink, bookkeeper), Manfred Krug (Max Brink, architect), Dieter Mann (Lutz Bibow, department manager), Alfred Mueller, Marita Boehme.

Helmer Frank Beyer and scripter Jurek Becker last collaborated on "Jacob the Liar" (1975), an East German prod that reached the Oscar nominations a few seasons back and won a Silver Bear at the Berlin Film Festival. They immediately went to work on "The Hiding Place" (1976), which only briefly saw the light of day in the German Democratic Republic before it was pulled from the theatres due to thesp Manfred Krug's departure for residence in West Germany.

Reports had it that "The Hiding Place" did very well in East German cinemas during its brief run, due to its comic situation and the light, satirical play in the dialogue. In any case, the teams of Beyer and Becker, Krug and Hoffmann, augured well for a commercially successful cinema that could appeal to both Germaines. The pic did quite well on its run in West Germany last autumn.

A couple without children have decided to part after a marriage that featured too many squabbles, but the husband still loves her after moving out — so he schemes to spend a week in her apartment while "hiding out" from the police. She takes him in for old times' sake, although her new boyfriend suspects something right from the beginning. The plot is set in motion by revealing at the start that the police search warrant of the woman's apartment has been staged by the former husband with the aid of a fellow architect at his office.

Then begins a play in one-upmanship between wife and husband, husband and friend, friend and wife. Flashbacks explain what went wrong in the recent past, and how the romance got underway when love was blind. The real meat, however, is the jokes about Socialist society — architectural boners, living standards, consumer society, etc. — that are the staple of every sitcom show.

Great fun for those clued in on life in the German Democratic Republic, but credits in general are tops. Deserves exposure on fest circuit. —Holl.

On Company Business
(U.S.-DOCU-16m)

Berlin, Feb. 27.

A Howard Dratch, Allan Francovich, Isla Negra/Blanca Films Production, San Francisco. Written and directed by Allan Francovich. Research, Howard Dratch, Allan Francovich, Kathleen Weaver; camera (color), Kevin Keating; editing, Veronica Selver, Alice Erber; editing assistance, Deborah Hoffman; sound, Peter Van Dyke. Reviewed at Berlin Film Fest (Forum), Feb. 27, '80. Running time: 180 MINS.

Allan Francovich's "On Company Business" ranks with Patricio Guzman's "The Battle of Chile" and Marcel Ophuls's "The Sorrow and the Pity" and "Memories of Justice" as a skillfully constructed compilation documentary, this one on the Central Intelligence Agency and U.S. foreign policy, as hinted in a press release on the three-hour film (conveniently divided into hour-long segments for tv runs). When it has its Yank preem (after being completed in the nick of time for the International Forum of Young Cinema at the Berlin Film Fest) at L.A.'s Filmex this month, several observers will surely comment on what's left out — but it's what is packed into the tight documentary that astonishes, plus the orderly manner in which the vital information is gathered and presented.

Francovich shuns the narrative, subjective opinion line, relying instead on interviews and archive material to tell the story through selection and editing for dialectic effect and an underscoring of relevant statements. Such a method requires a vast knowledge of the material at hand, which helmer Francovich, producer Howard Dratch, fellow-researcher Kathleen Weaver, and other members of the team obviously have as a collective unit.

The CIA cover was blown in 1975 at the time of the Watergate Hearings: the 18-month Congressional investigation involved a possible indictment of the agency's director, Richard Helms, followed by further revelations, some in books, by former agents. Between 1975 and 1978 the team studied governmental and news sources and ended up with some 120 hours of filmed interviews with key figures in and out of the CIA.

The problem, of course, was to cut it down to three hours. Equally difficult as a film historian is to know when someone is tooting his own horn, or hedging on the facts to cover up. Also, dealing with any government undercover agency is like reading the Old Testament in original Hebrew. Since secret agents are usually the bad guys, this account leaves no one in doubt that power is a dehumanizing and seductive bitch.

In order of appearance, the CIA agents introduced within the first few minutes are Phillip Agee, James Wilcott, William Colby (CIA-director, 1973-75), Victor Marchetti and Joseph B. Smith. Helms makes his appearance through the Congressional Hearings. Other insiders include agents Paul Sakwa, David Atlee Phillips, John Stockwell, as well as news correspondents, Congressmen, secretaries, diplomats, eye-witnesses to atrocities, and involved public officials. In all, there are 29 personalities interviewed.

The first section treats the founding of the CIA in the Cold War Years amid the McCarthy Red Scare. There are clips on the striking labor unions in Europe and the involvement of the AFL/CIO in CIA activities, the Bay of Pigs disaster and foiled plans to assassinate Castro, and, most important of all, the manner in which the Chief Executives in the postwar years stuck their thumbs in the espionage pie.

The second section views Latin America as a vassal of the Good Neighbor to the north, and here Francovich appears to be on favorite ground in recounting activities of the CIA in Brazil, Argentina, Chile, and Uruguay, where torture and terror, in particular, were in the cards. The important segment here is a description via interviews of how an agent is trained for his job.

The third section focuses on Chile and the Helms case that resulted in a reprimand during the hearings, followed by CIA activities in Angola and a closing passage on how to police a police-agency that's meddling in foreign affairs.

"On Company Business" scores as a dramatic report on the postwar era. For those who haven't read the printed accounts of the CIA caper, this is a most effective teaching aid. For those well informed, here is a further argument that bad counter-intelligence often stops the flow of intelligence and even disgraces the role of democracy in a free world. —Holl.

Exit Sunset Boulevard
(WEST GERMAN-COLOR-16m)

Berlin, Feb. 24.

A Bastian Cleve Film Production, Hamburg; distribution, CINE-PRO, Osnabrueck. Stars Elke Sommer. Written, directed, photographed (color), and edited by Bastian Cleve. Assistance and sound, Alf Olbrisch; assistance and still-photos, Inga Di Mar-Wendnagel; production assistant, Marlies Cleve. Reviewed at Berlin Film Fest (Market), Feb. 24, '80. Running time: 94 MINS.

Small-budget feature pic made by experimental filmer Bastian Cleve in Los Angeles and Southern California, "Exit Sunset Boulevard" deals with a German citizen arriving in the city to claim an inheritance of a few thousand dollars that also involves property in the desert. The American Way of Life overpowers him, however, and he simply flips out when he reaches an identity crisis. First he pays a visit to Elke Sommer in her villa-cum-swimming-pool, then he flirts with a black woman he meets on roller-skates (who rejects his pawing on an oceanside beach), and finally puts in a long-distance call from quarters from Death Valley while on a rented-car outing to say he can't come home again.

The irony is that such things happen to hard-working, middle-class Europeans when they finally reach their dream land in the California sun, as Basitian Cleve undoubtedly knows as a German presently living and working in Los Angeles. This gives the film a realistic edge.

The other aspect is the optical-printing process Cleve uses to blur the edges of the images as though the eye were catching the movements of people in space and slow-motion. The effect is a kind of restless dream world that comes after eating too much herring and ice-cream with pickles as dessert. Everything seems so real, and yet it's a nightmare.

A poetic, stylistically innovative feature film (produced with funds from a German Film Prize last year), "Exit Sunset Boulevard" could do well in Germany and Stateside in Underground cinemas, studio-theatres, and the like, where form is giving equal billing with content. —Holl.

Lagerstrasse Auschwitz
(Auschwitz Street)
(W. · GERMAN-COLOR-DOCU-16m)

Berlin, Feb. 27.

A Suedwestfunk TV Production, Baden-Baden; tv-producer, Klaus Simon. Written and directed by Ebbo Demant. Camera (color), Juergen Bolz; editing, Eva Maria Kramm; music, Christobal Halffter; sound, Harald Lill, Manfred Schmidt. Reviewed at Berlin, Film Fest (German Series), Feb. 27, '80. Running time: 60 MINS.

Arguably the most important film screened at this year's Berlin Film Fest, although, in truth, this is purely a television production, Ebbo Demant's "Auschwitz Street" deals with the reality of the past in such a manner that the very word "Auschwitz" (like "Hiroshima") stirs deep-felt and searing emotions in the viewer. Docu belongs to a series titled "People and Streets," which accounts for the title.

Demant visited four individuals on life-term prison sentences to interview them on Auschwitz, three of whom agreed to talk openly about being "killers" at Auschwitz. The irony is that these old men went on trial only in the early 1960s, and they have never before spoken in public about the crimes that took place there. In other words, the pic is a quarter-century late.

It should also be noted that, only a few weeks ago, three old Nazis involved in Jewish exportation in France during the last war were sentenced after a lengthy trial, one of whom was the mayor of a small Bavarian town (he stepped down from office when the sentence was delivered). The Majdanek trial is still going on in Dusseldorf, and it will certainly be the subject of major docus when it winds down to judgment in the not too distant future. Thus pix on the "Holocaust" and "Auschwitz" and "Majdanek" are just beginning to appear in Germany.

The honesty of these docus, however, is compelling. Further, there have been several strong docus shown on West (and East) German television on the extermination camps, but eye-witness accounts and personal interviews with both the victims and the criminals have been rare. The ice was finally broken after the "Holocaust" airing last year, which was then followed by actual testimonies of aging German prisoners in Spiegel magazine.

First of all, Demant takes the position that "Auschwitz can only be expressed through itself, through the testimonies of the victims and the reports of the culprits. I spoke with the latter in a German prison ... They had never before spoken in public, still less on film, about what they had done. I had never before sat down with anyone who had killed other human beings. And here I was, speaking with three men who had been sentenced for murdering, or complicity in the murdering of, dozens and even hundreds of innocent people."

For the record, the "witnesses for the prosecution" were Oswald Kaduk, Josef Klehr, and Josef Erber, all admitting to killing and gassing in Auschwitz. Two prisoners of Auschwitz, Stanislav Klodzinski and Mieczyslav Kieta, testify from the victims' viewpoint, the latter a witness of his father being chosen for the gas chamber by one of the above criminals.

Put this drama in an interview form, and a pin could be heard dropping in the Academy of Fine Arts during the Berlin fest screening of "Auschwitz Street," the stillness made all the more dramatic due to the presence of school classes

for the program. Undoubtedly, the tv-premiere back in April 1979 has resulted in this docu getting wide release as a film since then, and the English-subtitled print should now be made available to offshore film and tv outlets.

As for the interviews, they speak for themselves. One man tells how he gave deadly injections, another describes the horrors of the 10-minute gassing ritual, and a prisoner reports on the selective murder of his father. The realization that killing can be so clinical and coldly objective is matched by the non-judgmental attitude taken by documentarist Demant in drawing the truth from sub-humans whose intelligence and moral code leave so much to be desired.

As for the "street" part of the film, shots of present-day Auschwitz accompany the interviews and give the whole a timeless eternity. Anyone who has never visited Auschwitz should do so once in his life after seeing this docu. A must for historian and filmgoer.—Holl.

Die Nacht Mit Chandler
(The Night with Chandler)
(WEST GERMAN-COLOR-16m)

Berlin, Feb. 26.
An Olga-Film Production, Munich, in collaboration with Bayerischer Rundfunk, Munich. Features entire cast. Written and directed by Hans Noever. Camera (color), Kurt Lorenz; editing, Helga Beyer; music, Ton Steine, Sherben, Rio Reiser; sound, Vladimir Vizner; production manager, Elvira Senft. Reviewed at Berlin Film Fest (German Series), Feb. 26, '80. Running time: 87 MINS.
Cast: Agnes Dueneisen (Yvonne), Rio Reiser (Rio), Thomas Schuecke (Tommy), Vania Vlers (Raymond Chandler, watch salesman), Ray Verhaege (drugs salesman), Tommy Wieghand (Yvonne's brother), Remy Eyssen (Man in Eye-Glasses Shop).

Since Wim Wenders' "Kings of the Road" (1976) and Adolf Winkelmann's "On the Move" (1978), German road-movies have been very popular at home, precisely because they are improvised and have a free-and-easy manner about them that appeals to the younger crowd. Hans Noever's "The Night with Chandler" (lensed in 16m) also has much in common with Monte Hellman's "Two Lane Black Top" and such Hollywood Chandler pix as Howard Hawks's "The Big Sleep," in which the story somehow hangs together without necessarily making sense.

Pic preceded Noever's "The Price of Survival," which was shot in six weeks in Jefferson City, Missouri, and opened the Berlin Film Fest in the competition program. This is a filmmaker who likes to tell a story and prefers a swift-paced editing style to get the job done un-

der maximum conditions as quickly as possible.

The story is an excuse for moving across the country. Yvonne seeks information on who killed her brother in a demonstration, and puts an ad in the newspaper offering a reward of $4,000 for clues to the murder. Two chums, Rio and Tommy, are low on cash and decide to provide the clues but in a different manner than expected — they leave secret notes to entice Yvonne from Munich to Aachen to Belgium to Charleroi and the French Atlantic Coast.

All along the way, humorous and absurd things take place. A drug salesman tries to strike up an acquaintance with the girl and offers car transportation and dinner dates as lures. Rio (a jazz musician who appeared earlier in "Johnny West") beats on a piano from time to time, while Tommy hustles a few marks from Yvonne's cash resources to keep the game going. And, towards the end, the pair pick out a watch salesman with the fortunate name of "Raymond Chandler" as the man they, and Yvonne, are after. She spends the night with Chandler, and the caper is over.

Well made low-budget pic, this whacky in-joke was a hit at the Hof Film Fest last October and is doing some business with the young crowd in Germany. Thesps are a major plus, but it's the lensing and editing style that keeps the auds musing in their seats on the next twist in the narrative.

A natural for German Film Weeks and the like, but offshore chances are otherwise slim. —Holl.

Bildnis Einer Trinkerin
(Portrait of a Female Drunkard)
(WEST GERMAN-COLOR)

Berlin, Feb. 26.
An Autoren-Film Production, Berlin; production manager, Marianne Gassner. Features entire cast. Written, directed and photographed (color), by Ulrike Ottinger. Editing, Ila von Hasperb; costumes and assistant director, Tabea Blumenschein; music, Peet Raben; sound, Margit Eschenbach. Reviewed at Berlin Film Fest (German Series), Feb. 26, '80. Running time: 108 MINS.
Cast: Tabea Blumenschein (She), Lutze (Woman Drunkard at Zoo), Magdalena Montezuma (Social Question), Orpha Termin (Exact Statistics), Monika von Cube (Healthier Common Sense), Paul Glauer (Dwarf), Nina Hagen (Singer), Guenter Meisner (Director Willy), Kurt Raab (Chef), Volker Spengler (Transvestite), Eddie Constantine, Ginka Steinwachs, Mercedes Vostell, Wolf Vostell.

Take a low-low-budget femme helmer and raise her to a prestige producer overnight, and you come up with an indefinable "Portrait of a Female Drunkard" made by Ulrike Ottinger (director, scriptwriter, camerawoman) and Tabea

Blumenschein (main thesp, costumes, assistant director), who collaborated on the merry "Madame X" (1977) with a group of women friends and the support of ZDF's "Little TV-Play" series.

It's the tale of a well-dressed lady of rare beauty arriving at Berlin-Tegel airport to forget the past and live out her destiny as a drunkard. The portrait of Berlin offers some amusement, as do several personalities in the city and the film and culture scene. But nothing else clicks — not even that odd, surreal, absurd, and entertaining sense of humor that pasted their other experimental pix together. This one even does a disservice to the thriving Women's Lib movement in West Germany by squandering the subsidized coin on self-indulgence.
—Holl.

Marigolds in August
(SOUTH AFRICAN-COLOR)

Berlin, Feb. 24.
Serpent (Southern) Productions-R-M Productions production. Features entire cast. Directed by Ross Devenish. Screenplay, Athol Fugard; camera (Color), Michael Davis; editor, Lionel Selwyn. Reviewed at Berlin Film Fest (Competing), Feb. 26, '80. Running time: 87 MINS.
Daan .... Winston Ntshona
Melton .... John Kani
Paulus .... Athol Fugard

(In English)

Athol Fugard, the well-known South African playwright whose "Boesman and Lena" won the New York Critics Award in 1972, now collaborates for the third time on a film with director Ross Devenish on their home grounds.

The first, "Boesman," dealt with coloreds, that is mulattos, the second, "The Guest," with white consciousness and now this one with blacks who find that their humanity may be in jeopardy unless they can understand their fellow man's problems.

Film is a human fable about man's adjustment in times of crisis. And also to go beyond this in the untenable situations caused by government ways, especially the policy of apartheid, that separate races from each other.

The deceptively simple handling, fine playing and Devenish's spare but observant direction help this avoid sentimentality and repetition. The bigger theme of adaptation is made on a simple human level that is more effective than a more dramatic or flamboyant treatment.

A gardener, Daan (Winston Ntshona), walks miles to work every day in a white section where he does a different house every day. He is happy even though he must plant marigolds in the winter, which means they will have a short life, a metaphor for his own position which might be destroyed any day for he really does not have the right pass to work where he does.

An unemployed man, Melton (John Kani), appears on the scene and awakens Daan's fears that the man may get his job or even rob a closed supermarket he has looked into. He runs him off the place and goes with him to an itinerant white poacher and snake hunter played by Fugard himself.

There the two men are made to face up to their own lack of insight into themselves or their fellow men. Fugard plays the amiable hunter with the right mixture of knowingness and humanity. Melton, who had not thought of robbing the store, now does so and Daan has realized he must help him by sharing his job, though only once, if they are to survive and eventually face up to injustices.

Its theme and treatment slant this for definite tv play, but there could be some theatrical usage with careful handling of this rare South African film that deals in racial realities with concern.

Incidentally, film played the Berlin Fest without a flag due to early Russian objections to the festival that South Africa had no right to appear in international competitions. When informed that Fugard's plays had played many East European countries, the Russians withdrew their objections but director Devenish concurred in playing here without a national tag.

Film won a special jury nod for Fugard and was tagged a film made under difficult circumstances and one to encourage independent filmmakers. Jury also lauded the fest for showing it in competition. Film is well blown up from 16m. —Mosk.

L.A. Filmex Reviews

Stronger Than The Sun
(BRITISH-COLOR-16m)

Hollywood, Feb. 9.
A BBC production. Produced by Margaret Matheson. Directed by Michael Apted. Features entire cast. Screenplay, Stephen Poliakoff; camera (color), Elmer Cossey; editor, David Martin; music, Howard Blake; costumes, Amy Roberts, Reviewed at the Universal Studios, Universal City, Feb. 9, 1980. (No MPAA Rating.) Running time: 101 MINS.
Kate .... Francesca Annis
Alan .... Tom Bell

A timely message picture played out as an obsessive personal drama, "Stronger Than The Sun" represents a relatively tame attempt to grapple with the press-

ing issue of the dangers inherent in nuclear energy. Produced by the BBC in 1977, pic gets most of its mileage out of Francesca Annis' compelling performance, but is a bit too laborious and small-scaled to score strongly on the big screen.

Just as "The China Syndrome" anticipated the Three Mile Island mishaps, "Sun" bears an eerie resemblance to the Karen Silkwood affair. Annis portrays a suspicious worker at a Yorkshire nuclear plant who, initially prodded by cohort Tom Bell, is driven to her demise through her frustrated attempts to inform the press and public of the possibility of a radioactive leak at the facility.

Basically an intimate drama, Stephen Poliakoff's script has Bell chickening out at an early stage, leaving Annis, a somewhat unstable loner, to carry the ball herself. Story's greatest success comes in drawing a portrait of an increasingly obsessed, infuriated woman, although pic wears down significantly as Annis slips closer to the end of her tether.

Direction by Michael Apted, who has since moved on to "Agatha" and "Coal Miner's Daughter," is vigorous but at the same time rather bland, as it fails to weave a rich texture or inject any point of view beyond cautionary stance of the script.

Howard Blake's score is an active, effective plus. —Cart.

The Beneficiary
(BRITISH-B&W-16m)

Hollywood, Feb. 26.
A National Film School (U.K.) production. Features entire cast. Directed, screenplay by Carlo Gebler, based on the Anton Chekhov story, "In The Ravine;" camera (black and white), Pascoe Macfarlaine; editor, Alan Tyrer; music, sound, Trevor Jones; art direction, Celia Barnett; assistant director, Maggie Brooks. Reviewed at Filmex projection room, Los Angeles, Feb. 26, 1980. (No MPAA Rating.) Running time: 47 MINS.
Features: Marian Richardson, Desmond Fenell.

Adapted from a Chekhov short story, "The Beneficiary" nonetheless plays like a curdled O. Henry tale. Assembly of five distinct acts merely sets characters and audience up for the big fall and subsequent quick revenge. Made at the British National Film School by a young Irish director, featurette displays some discreet visual and storytelling talent, but helmer needs a bit more experience with actors. Fests and specialized academic slots are only possible venues for this one.

Realized in stark, almost Griffithian b&w, pic somberly tells tale of the unnatural rise and fall of the McCarthy family in County Gal-

way, circa 1900. Father's favorite son brings home a small fortune, enabling miserly clan to establish itself as landed gentry.

Twist is that most of the loot has been forged, immediately rendering these nouveau riches virtually penniless. Vengeance by a second son's long-suffering wife is swift and merciless, and family is reduced to joining the lower classes in constructing stone walls on land they used to own.

Writer-director Carlo Gebler successfully establishes his own methodical rhythms but fares less well with his relatively inexpressive actors, who speak in both English and (subtitled) Gaelic. In keeping with the unsavory yarn, Gebler's Ireland is totally oppressive, unrelieved by the slightest bit of gaiety or mirth, and uncommunicativeness of the characters is almost abstract in its fulsomeness.
—Cart.

Paco The Infallible
(Paco L'infaillible)
(FRENCH-SPANISH-COLOR)

Hollywood, March 1.
A Filmoblic/Lotus Films/Bloody Mary/Tanagra/Record Film production. Produced by Hubert Niogret, Luís Mendes. Directed by Didier Haudepin. Features entire cast. Screenplay, Haudepin, Nadie Feuz; dialog, Haudepin, Jose M. Forque, based on the novel by Andras Naszlo; camera (Fujicolor), Gilberto Azevedo; editor, Alberto Yaccelini; music, Serge Perathoner; set decoration, Wolfgang Burman; wardrobe, Antonio Munoz; sound, Jaime Velasco, Alix Comte; asst. directors, Philippe Leriche, Gerardo Herrero Perez. Reviewed at the Paramount Studios, Hollywood, March 1, 1980. (No MPAA Rating.) Running time: 90 MINS.
Paco .... Alfredo Landa
Pocapena .... Patrick Dewaere
Maria .... Christine Pascal
Ambroise .... Jean Bouise
(English Subtitles)

An amusingly original and quietly provocative first film by Didier Haudepin, "Paco The Infallible" is good enough to make one wish it were better than it really is. With confident helming, uniformly droll performances and nicely caught sense of time and place, pic misses the top rung through overly languid pacing and perhaps less gossing toward comedy than necessary.

Curious tale presents the waning days of middle-aged title character, a glass manufacturer in Madrid, circa 1928, with a lucrative sideline as a hired stud for aspiring wet nurses from the provinces. Per the title, Paco is an invariably reliable old chap with a highly understanding, even cooperative, wife — she even spreads a tablecloth over the bed for him before he gets down to business.

Meeting Paco in a bar, young ne'er-do-well Patrick Dewaere

sings the older man's praises and volunteers to become his partner in the after-hours enterprise, adding that he would require no fee for his contributions. Unfortunately, Paco shortly thereafter experiences his first failure in the sack, tarnishing his reputation and paving the way for the younger generation to take over his chores.

Given the self-evident control on display, there's little doubt that Haudepin, a former thesp and film critic who at age nine played Jeanne Moreau's son in Peter Brook's "Moderato Cantabile," has achieved the artistic results he sought. However, treatment seems a bit too restrained, lacking the gusto that might have brought the inherently ribald, if ultimately melancholy, yarn fully to life.

Additionally, film's ending is disturbingly abrupt and disruptive of the careful calculation of that which has gone before.

Actors all fit the bill perfectly, with Alfredo Landa evoking numerous chuckles through his almost stoical approach to his work. Dewaere bringing an Errol Flynn-like devil-may-care attitude to the young pretender and Christine Pascal exhibiting fine comic timing as the supposedly sterile wife who surprises her husband by becoming pregnant.

Tech credits are uniformly excellent, particularly Gilberto Azevedo's lensing and evocative score by Serge Perathoner. —Cart.

Little Miss Marker
(COLOR)

What price, Damon Runyon?

Hollywood, March 18.

A Universal Pictures release, produced by Jennings Lang. Directed and written by Walter Bernstein, based on a story by Damon Runyon. Stars Walter Matthau, Julie Andrews. Exec producer, Walter Matthau. Camera (Technicolor). Philip Lathrop; editor, Eve Newman; sound, John Carter; production design, Edward C. Carfagno; set decoration, Hal Gausman; assistant director, Ronald J. Martinez; costumes, Ruth Morley; music, Henry Mancini. Reviewed at the Writers Guild Theatre, Beverly Hills, Calif., March 13, 1980. (MPAA rating: PG.) Running time: 103 MINS.

Sorrowful Jones	Walter Matthau
Amanda	Julie Andrews
Blackie	Tony Curtis
Regret	Bob Newhart
Kid	Sara Stimson
Judge	Lee Grant
Herbie	Brian Dennehy
Brannigan	Kenneth McMillan
Carter	Andrew Rubin
Benny	Joshua Shelley
Mrs. Clancy	Nedra Volz
Lola	Jacquelyn Hyde

There is something irresistible about the story of a darling little girl left in the care of colorfully kind gamblers, which explains why this is the fourth attempt to bring Damon Runyon's story of "Little Miss Marker" to the screen. But writer-director Walter Bernstein blows his directorial debut completely and audiences will have to be very forgiving and very forgetful to respond.

It's a shame, because seemingly if ever there was an actor who should play "Sorrowful Jones" it's Walter Matthau and Bob Newhart should have been a wonderful "Regret," while Tony Curtis could have been a respectable antagonist.

But they are all flat in their parts and that has to be Bernstein's fault. Even worse, if any of Runyon's 1934 Broadway flavor was to be retained, Julie Andrews is woefully miscast with her British accent and Lee Grant gets no more than a bit part as a judge.

The only really decent thing about the picture is little Sara Stimson, absolutely adorable and a talent to watch. (not surprisingly, Shirley Temple was also the best character in the original.)

The basic short story, of course, allows filmmakers plenty of room for embroidery and certainly director Sidney Lanfield's 1949 version of "Sorrowful Jones" with Bob Hope and Lucille Ball stretched the framework much farther than Bernstein, not to mention "40 Pounds of Trouble" with Curtis & Suzanne Pleshette in the leads. But the hokum and characterization which made their versions successful in precisely what this version lacks so desperately.

Early moments after Wayne Fitzgerald's nice opening titles are fine as Matthau is established as the dour, stingy bookie from whom the deadly Curtis wants $50,000 to open a gambling casino in the widowed Andrews mansion. And there's a nice touch of character development when, after Curtis shoots Matthau's collie as a warning, Matthau tells a sidekick to see if he can sell the dog's fur as fox.

But the key to the picture must be the relationship of Matthau and Stimson, whose care he inherits after her father leaves her as security for a bet and never returns. Runyon himself was uncertain why this grizzled character would be softened by a tyke, so explicitly isn't important. But feeling is and Bernstein never really brings off a scene between man and girl that doesn't seem contrived.

Ditto the developing romance between him and Andrews, whose character is so completely beyond the original story that it's impossible to believe she would ever deign to talk to Sorrowful, much less marry him to keep the kid out of an orphanage.

Everything about the look of the period piece, though, is first rate, thanks mainly to Philip Lathrop's photography and Edward C. Carfagno's production design. And Henry Mancini's score fits neatly, too. But it's all dull and no fun when the actors get into the scenery and the climactic confrontation between Matthau and Curtis is incredibly lame, as is the soapy courtroom resolution of the kid's fate.

Incidentally, if Matthau gets one more script calling for him to be stranded outdoors in undies or women's clothes, he should take that as a hint and junk it. —Har.

Town Bloody Hall
(DOCU-16m-COLOR)

Hollywood, Feb. 25.

A Pennebaker Inc. production. Produced by D.A. Pennebaker. Directed by D.A. Pennebaker, Chris Hegedus. Features entire cast. Camera (uncredited color), D.A. Pennebaker, Jim Desmond; editor, Chris Hegedus; associate producer, Shirley Broughton. Reviewed at the American Film Institute, Beverly Hills, Feb. 25, 1980. (No MPAA Rating.) Running time: 88 MINS.

Features: Norman Mailer, Germaine Greer, Diana Trilling, Jacqueline Ceballos, Jill Johnston.

Streamlined, 88-minute representation of much publicized 1971 confrontation between Norman Mailer and four leading feminists proves interesting mostly as a period piece, with the macho man and his adversaries verbally slugging it out to the exhortations and protestations of the blood-thirsty intellectual crowd. As a curiosity item, film could attract some specialized audiences, although most natural outlets would be in nontheatrical field and on public tv.

Despite serious announced intentions of the New York Town Hall evening, wherein Mailer's just-published "The Prisoner Of Sex" was supposed to be discussed by Germaine Greer, Diana Trilling, Jacqueline Ceballos and Jill Johnston, event hardly stood a chance of becoming anything more than a stunt. Audience was clearly there for fireworks, with some rabble-rousers in attendance providing some of their own in the early going.

Greer lights on provocative territory in describing the masculine artist, i.e. Mailer, as "the pinnacle of the masculine elite," but writer and then-militant lesbian Johnston soon introduces a bit of Living Theatre by rolling around and making out onstage with a couple of girlfriends. Capping what was naturally the event's most publicized incident, Mailer tells her to "act like a lady," whereupon she exits the hall.

Sensing that proceedings had strayed a bit from their intended path, Mailer soon thereafter launches into the most eloquent, impassioned address of the evening, trying to cut to the essence of a question relevant to all present, that of human liberty and the threat of totaliarianism from both the right and especially, in his view, the left.

It's no one's fault, really, as the circumstances begged outrageousness rather than evenly weighed judgments, but the mud starts flying again, with comments from the audience ranging from the lovely (Susan Sontag) to the ridiculous (Lucy Comsar). All one can do at the end is shrug and head outside, where the daily struggle continues, regardless of which witty highbrow got off the best one-liners.

Technical quality, both picture and sound, is substandard, as hand-held cameras jiggle constantly and some of the repartee is garbled and inaudible. —Cart.

Hide In Plain Sight
(COLOR)

Dull tone should cause pic to elude many.

Hollywood, Feb. 27.

United Artists release of a Metro-Goldwyn-Mayer film. Produced by Robert Christiansen, Rick Rosenberg. Directed by James Caan. Stars Caan. Screenplay, Spencer Eastman, based on a book by Leslie Waller; camera (Metrocolor), Paul Lohmann; editor Fredric Steinkamp, William Steinkamp; music, Leonard Rosenman, production design, Pato Guzman; set decoration, Mary Swanson; assistant director, David McGiffert. Reviewed at MGM Studios, Culver City, Feb. 27, 1980. (MPAA Rating: PG). Running time: 92 MINS.

Thomas Hacklin, Jr.	James Caan
Alisa	Jill Eikenberry
Jack Scolese	Robert Viharo
Matty Stanke	Joe Grifasi
Ruthie Hacklin	Barbara Rae
Sam Marzetta	Kenneth McMillian
Sal Carvello	Danny Aiello
Bobby Momisa	Thomas Hill
Frankie Irish	Chuck Hicks
Andy Hacklin	Andrew Gordon Fenwick
Junie Hacklin	Heather Bicknell
Detective Reilly	David Margulies

"Hide In Plain Sight" has some of the makings of a good, honest film. It tells the true story of a working man's fight against the system, features several poignant moments between a father and his children not often seen on screen, and makes a number of political messages in an effective yet unobtrusive manager. But in his directorial debut, James Caan never musters the energy or emotion needed to break the unbearably slow, dismal tone present throughout the picture. Given the pacing and the basically non-commercial subject, film should be a tough sell for distrib United Artists.

Caan is wonderfully accurate as the factory worker who becomes an innocent victim of a new witness relocation program that gives a new identity to any person (and his family) who informs on organized crime. In this case, two-bit mobster Robert Viharo testifies against his cronies and the authorities relocate him, his wife (who happens to be Caan's former spouse), and her two children by Caan to another state. Caan is given no advance warning, finding his children missing from an empty house when he goes to visit them one day.

The frustration of the almost hopeless search Caan attempts could have been excellent fodder for a gripping, human drama. However, Caan remains almost on one level throughout in both his direction and his acting, never properly building to the proverbial climax. When his character does occasionally break under pressure, it is in abbreviated or meaningless circumstances that are dramatically unsatisfying. Picture was filmed on location in Buffalo and coupled with fine production design by Pato Guzman and expert photography by Paul Lohman overall effort nicely captures the working class look. Editing by Fredric Steinkamp and William Steinkamp is tight but unimaginative. Screenplay by Spencer Eastman, based on a book by Leslie Waller, seems true to its subject but somehow fails to create enough dramatic sparks with a rather meaty subject.

Supporting performers are capable, and, at times touching. Jill Eikenberry is heart-warming as

Caan's girlfriend and eventual wife. Robert Viharo is properly offensive but still human as the relocated mobster and Barbara Rawe manages a large dose of realism as Caan's ex, who is torn between Viharo. Caan and what is best for her children.

Although Caan's direction leaves much to be desired in the final analysis, he has managed to create an atmosphere and stay true to his subject. Hopefully, his next effort will be a little bit more interesting to watch.—*Berg.*

Dusman
(The Enemy)
(TURKISH-COLOR)

Berlin, Feb. 29.
A Guney Filmcilik Production & release; world rights. Guney Film & Focus Films, Istanbul. Features entire cast. Directed by Zeki Okten. Screenplay, Yilmaz Guney; camera (color), Cetin Tunca; music, Yavuz Top; editing, Okten. Reviewed at Berlin Film Fest (Competition), Feb. 29, '80. Running time: **157 MINS.**
Cast: Aytac Arman (Ismail), Gungor Bayrak, Guven Sengil, Kamil Sonmez, Sevket Altug, Fahamet Atilla, Atiye Oklu, Ahmet Acar, Fehmi Yasar, Huseyin Kutman, Lutfu Engin.

Yilmaz Guney has been a sort of martyr figure at international fests since 1977, when both the San Remo fest and the Berlin Forum of Young Cinema featured retros of his, till then, practically unknown pix, in which he starred as well as writing the scripts and directing. A national figure who shot a man in apparent self-defense, Guney has been serving a long prison stretch that could be shortened via parole — and each film script, directed by friend and collaborator Zeki Okten, obviously helps the cause. Last year, their "The Herd" won the Grand Prix at Locarno.

The second Guney-Okten collaboration, "The Enemy," leaves something to be desired, although several scenes are striking in a documentary point-of-view. In "The Herd" a family's destiny carried the film from start to finish; "The Enemy," as the title hints, is a revolutionary theme with the message buried in metaphors from time to time. The enemy, in other words, is unemployment.

The scene is Istanbul and its surroundings. An out-of-work laborer, with an education, living on the European side of the Bosphorus, crosses on the ferry to the Asian side in search of work on the labor exchange — a page out of "On the Waterfront," but Turkish-style. Ismail has a lovely but embittered wife, an ailing mother-in-law, and a young daughter — all of which tears at his heart when he notices that a young woman in the city has been forced into prostitution. A worker is

also killed trying to leap on a passing truck carrying day-jobbers, and his body is left under a soggy newspaper in a downpour.

For lack of anything else, he accepts a job killing stray dogs with poisoned food, but it is too humiliating and leaves him with nightmares. Then his wife's nagging drives him to return to the land he left to request his inheritance in advance from his father and brother; the confrontation leads to a fight, and Ismail's wife leaves him shortly thereafter.

Now left alone, our hero begins to fight back. Labor unions are being formed to defend the rights of workers, and he is ready to join in the struggle against the enemy: unemployment and exploitation.

At a length of two-and-a-half-hours, "The Enemy" loses dramatic force and involves too many people and problems to score a b.o. hit. But the Guney theme of human rights for the downtrodden is evident every step of the way. Thus this statement on man's inhumanity to man will likely lead to reconsideration of his parole, as film critics have requested on several occasions over the past two years.

Thesp performances and lensing are up to fest standards for the upcoming fest circuit. Pic won a special mention at Berlin fest for scripter Guney. —*Holl.*

Little Darlings
(COLOR)

Puppy love gets itself R-rated. Good performances but credulity strained.

Hollywood, March 14.
A Paramount Pictures release, produced by Stephen J. Friedman. Directed by Ronald F. Maxwell. Features entire cast. Screenplay, Kimi Peck, Dalene Young; camera (Metrocolor), Fred Batka; editor, Pembroke J. Herring; sound, John Speak; production design, William Hiney; set decoration, Charles Forian; assistant director, Michael Daves; music, Charles Fox. Reviewed at Paramount Studios, Hollywood, March 14, 1980. (MPAA Rating: R.) Running time: **92 MINS.**
Ferris .... Tatum O'Neal
Angel .... Kristy McNichol
Gary ....Armande Assante
Randy ....Matt Dillon
Cinder .... Krista Errickson
Dana ....:...... Alexa Kenin
Chubby ....Abby Bluestone
Sunshine .... Cynthia Nixon
Carrots ....Simone Schacter
Bright ....Maggie Blye
Whitney ....Nicolas Coster
Miss Nichols ....Mary Betten

"Little Darlings" makes an honest effort to deal with the sexual stirrings of two teen-age girls, but many adults are likely to dismiss the effort as puppy love with appeal to prurient interests. Big ques-

tion is how pic will strike teens themselves and there the R rating may be a major obstacle, since the 15-year-olds it is about can't readily attend.

Tatum O'Neal and Kristy McNichol are both excellent as virgins of widely different social backgrounds who meet at summer camp. O'Neal is a sheltered rich girl and McNichol the poor, streetwise urchin but their different upbringings — and the instant antagonism they have for each other — do not release their shared hesitancy about making love for the first time.

At camp, they meet a sophisticated teen-age model, enjoyably played by Krista Errickson, who not only brags of her own experience but taunts the pair into a contest over who will succumb first during vacation, with the rest of the camp placing bets.

For males of previous generations, and possibly some females, it's hard to say whether such sexual blatantness among otherwise innocent 15-year-old girls is true or not, even though this is supposed to be an age of different attitudes. Femme scripters Kimi Peck and Dalene Young obviously consider their plot plausible and believe today's young audience will relate to it.

Maybe they will. In any case, leaving the precise setting aside, the writers do a good job of constructing the young girls' doubts and fears and the two young actresses are superb in conveying them.

But it isn't all dreariness and the rest of the camp company, Alexa Kenin, Abby Bluestone, Cynthia Nixon and Simone Schachter, are variously terrific, egging the contestants on while hiding fears of their own. One antic — a raid on a filling station for contraceptives — is hilarious, though probably largely responsible itself for the "R" rating. On the other hand, a food fight is blatantly imitative of other screenplays and unworthy.

In his feature debut, director Ronald F. Maxwell isn't perfect with the difficult assignment. But he gets several fine scenes from his performers, especially when O'Neal deals with her love interest, counselor Armande Assante, when McNichol deals with her love interest, teenager Matt Dillon and, best of all, when O'Neal and McNichol finally level with each other.

Tech credits are solid and Georgia locations are appealing. Charles Fox' score is good. —*Har.*

Die Laughing
(COLOR)

No-laff monkeyshines.

Hollywood, March 20.
An Orion Pictures release through Warner Brothers of a Jon Peters production. Produced by Mark Canton, Robby Benson. Executive producer, Jon Peters. Stars Robby Benson. Directed by Jeff Werner. Screenplay, Jerry Segal, Robby Benson, Scott Parker, based on a story by Parker; camera (Technicolor), David Myers; editor, Neil Travis; original music, Robby Benson, Jerry Segal; music scoring, Craig Safan; production design, James H. Spencer; set decoration, Doug Von Koss; costumes, Nancy McArdle; sound, David McMillan; assistant director, David Whorf. Reviewed at the Burbank Studios, Burbank, March 20, 1980. (MPAA Rating: PG.) Running time: **108 MINS.**
Pinsky .... Robby Benson
Amy .... Linda Grovenor
Arnold .... Charles Durning
Sophie ......:........ Elsa Lanchester
Mueller .... Bud Cort
Thelma .... Rita Taggart
Friend .... Marty Zagon
Bock .... Larry Hankin
Zhukov .... Sammuel Krachmalnick

"Die Laughing" is deadly. Lame attempt at black comedy provokes about two-and-a-half laughs, and as Robby Benson has spread himself around as star, coproducer, cowriter and composer of three songs, blame must be placed squarely at his feet. Some bad star-vehicle comedies have done well before, and literal monkeyshines helped lift "Every Which Way But Loose" to huge grosses last year, so ad campaign focus on a simian could bring this one along as well. But it's hard to imagine anyone will be vastly amused.

To detail every ludicrous twist and turn in this concoction would amount to an exercise in pointlessness. Suffice it to say that Benson plays a charmless oaf who's left holding the bag and the gun when a top nuclear scientist is murdered, and that he's chased for all too long by young Hitler-type Bud Cort and his henchmen, Charles Durning's combat taxi fleet, the commies, the cops and the FBI, while all he really wants to do is win an amateur music contest, which he manages to accomplish despite banality of his compositions.

Entire enterprise reeks of calculation. Music in pix is in, so why not include some punk rockers and a disco act to flesh out the record album? Monkeys are big b.o., so let's make one the center of attention. Excrement jokes worked for Mel Brooks, so let's have Benson slide facefirst into animal droppings in the middle of a circus ring.

At one point, the little spider monkey jumps up and down on some typewriter keys, banging out a few lines. Benson's g.f., Linda Grovenor, says, "It's just jibberish," to which he replies, "What'd you expect, Shakespeare?" No, but something better than this. —*Cart.*

Last Rites
(COLOR)

Hollywood, March 14.

Cannon release of a New Empire Features production. Directed by Domonic Paris. Produced by Kelly Van Horn. Features entire cast. Screenplay, Ben Donnelly and Paris; camera (Deluxe), Paris; editor, Elizabeth Lombardo; music, Paul Jost, George Small. No other credits available. Reviewed at the Holly Theatre, March 14, 1980. (MPAA Rating: R.) Running time: **88 MINS.**

Cast: Patricia Lee Hammond, Gerald Fielding, Victor Jorge, Michael Lally, Mimi Weddell.

"Last Rites" is proof that they don't make horror films like they used to. At one-time vampires stalked beautiful young ladies in the night and romantically enticed them into donating a few pints of blood. In this picture they sit by a radio and wait to hear about a not quite dead accident victim who might have a few live corpuscles remaining before they decide to venture out for an evening. Diehard horror fans will be disappointed. The uninitiated will be either bored or nauseated.

Not only does director Domonic Paris (who co-wrote with Ben Donnelly and served as sole photographer) take away the romance from blood-sucking, he comes up with names for his characters that lure audiences far from the action. The head of this vampire coven is a mortician named Lucard (that's Dracula spelled backwards without the "a") and the couple he continually haunts are called the Fondas. Bad choices. Once the origin of Lucard's name is figured it's almost impossible not to imagine he's somehow after Henry, Peter and Jane.

After it becomes apparent that the doctor, sheriff and mortician in town are all after live blood, audiences are left to see whether they'll triumph over the Fondas. It's a tough battle, with Mrs. Fonda eventually succumbing to some vampire romance.

Because Lucard bears some kinship to the notorious Count (even if it's in name only), some viewers root for him if only for old times sake. Because of the Fonda family's popularity, a healthy bunch could hope they emerge victorious. Bit if anyone is really enticed at all there can be one set of winners — the filmmakers who've gotten away with this mess. —*Berg.*

L'Avare
(The Miser)
(FRENCH-COLOR)

Paris, March 11.

An AMLF release of a Films Christian Fechner production. Produced by Christian Fechner. Stars Louis de Funes. Directed by Jean Girault. Screenplay, based on the play by Moliere; camera (color), Edmond Richard; sound, Paul Laine; editor, Michel Lewin; music, Jean Bizet; art director, Sydney Bettex. Reviewed at the Marignan-Concorde theatre, Paris, March 10, 1980. Running time: **120 MINS.**

Harpagon .... Louis de Funes
Cleante .... Frank David
Elise .... Claire Dupray
Valere .... Herve Bellon
Maitre Jacques .... Michel Galabru
Frosine .... Claude Gensac

Undaunted by its rigid, self-conscious theatricality, France's most successful film comic, Louis de Funes, has made a film of Moliere's great prose comedy, "The Miser." The text is left untouched and played in its entirety.

It's canned theatre, of course. But there's good canning and bad canning. This one is poorly tinned, with all the play's rich comic juices leaked out before long.

Though faithful to the text, De Funes multiplies the settings for the action, ineffectually adding some exteriors, pantomimic extensions and naively playing on several levels of realism and stylization, such as incorporating into the decor huge blow-ups of portraits of Moliere and covers from academic paperback editions of the play. All this is aggravated by Jean Girault's poor technical direction.

But what obviously matters here is De Funes in the role of Harpagon, a part he has dreamed of playing for years. Despite the preconceived outrage of some purists, De Funes' febrile, purely buffoonish interpretation of a man so avaricious he steals his horses' oats is no betrayal of Moliere.

Still, he is disappointing. De Funes, in the hands of a good director, can be effective. Here he is, in effect, directing himself and there is less the feeling of a role being composed than of a comedian taking inventory of his grimaces and grunts for the pleasure of his inumerable and undemanding fans. —*Len.*

Serial
(COLOR)

A comedic feast for faddists.

Hollywood, March 21.

Paramount Pictures release of a Sidney Beckerman Production. Produced by Sidney Beckerman. Directed by Bill Persky. Features entire cast. Screenplay, Rich Eustis, Michael Elias, based on the novel by Cyra McFadden; camera (Movielab Color), Rexford Metz; editor, John W. Wheeler; sound, Jack Solomon; art direc-

tion, Bill Sandell; set decoration, Bob Gould, Paul Dal Porto; music, Lalo Schifrin; assistant director, Jerry Sobul. Reviewed at Paramount Studios, Hollywood, March 21, 1980. (MPAA Rating: R.) Running time: **91 MINS.**

Harvey .... Martin Mull
Kate .... Tuesday Weld
Joan .... Jennifer McAlister
Bill .... Sam Chew, Jr.
Martha .... Sally Kellerman
Stokeley .... Anthony Battaglia
Angela .... Nita Talbot
Sam .... Bill Macy
Carol .... Pamela Bellwood
Vivian .... Barbara Rhoades
Rachel .... Ann Weldon
Leonard .... Peter Bonerz
Wong .... Jon Fong
Luckman/Skull .... Christopher Lee
Stella .... Patch Mackenzie
Marlene .... Stacey Helkin
Spike .... Tom Smothers
Spenser .... Clark Brandon
Paco .... Clyde Ventura

"Serial" is a wonderfully funny film that manages to satirize every '70s fad from hot tubs to religious cults with an almost undying and irresistible fervor. The fast-paced script by Rich Eustis and Michael Elias based on Cyra McFadden's novel on the hedonistic lives of residents in the affulent northern California suburb of Marin County, is relentless in its send-up while maintaining a subtle sense of intelligence throughout.

Despite pic's comedic success, overriding question is how willing today's mass audiences will accept a subject matter that deals with an era that is clearly yesteryear. There lingers a slight possibility the Paramount release may be a little late in coming.

Scripters' image of Marin is a place where residents believe their psyche will improve by not letting others "invade their space" and their bodies will remain healthy by taking the right dose of drugs and advice from an off-the-wall therapist. In between those concerns, there is also the insane fear that lack of participation in temptations like oriental sex techniques, vegetarianism, disco dancing and "rap" sessions will cause incurable stagnation, if not disapproval from the neighbors.

In the center of all of this is Martin Mull, terrifically caustic and witty as one of the few people who resists keeping up with the Joneses. Mull is married to Tuesday Weld, who seems to have gone overboard with the Marin life. Ditto their teen daughter Jennifer McAlister.

Strength of the feature is interplay between Mull and his family with the other residents in the area. Bill Macy gives a healthy dose of realism of the straight-laced exec who is swayed to join the faddist fold and Nita Talbot provides verve as his long-suffering wife. Sally Kellerman is properly uncontrollable as a woman who must try

everything and Peter Bonerz is scathing in his portrayal of the "too-hip" therapist.

Also affecting are Barbara Rhoades, Pamela Bellwood, Anthony Battaglia and Ann Weldon is lesser roles.

A large dose of credit should go to John W. Wheeler's editing, which consistently keeps the action moving without losing a sense of story, and Lalo Schifrin's mood-setting score. Theme song of "A Changing World," penned by Schifrin and Norman Gimbel is also a winner.

In his feature directorial debut tv vet Bill Persky heroically performs the task of keeping everything in some semblance of order. There are certain stylistic suggestions of his background in situation comedy, but they seem appropriate to what's presented.

Film's only stumbling block to boxoffice success is whether it's subject is fresh enough to catch on like the fads it imitates. But given its comedic value, there should be any number of faddists out there who will latch onto it. —*Berg.*

Salto Nel Vuoto
(Leap Into the Void)
(FRENCH-ITALIAN-COLOR)

Rome, March 18.

A Cineriz release, produced by Silvio and Annamaria Clementelli for Clesi Cinematografica (Rome) and M.K. 2 productions (Paris). Stars Michel Piccoli, Anouk Aimee, Michele Placido. Directed by Marco Bellocchio. Screenplay, Marco Bellocchio, Piero Natoli, Vincenzo Cerami; camera (Eastmancolor), Beppe Lanci; art director, Andrea Crisanti, Amedeo Fago; editor, Roberto Perpignani; music, Nicola Piovani. Reviewed at Capranichetta Cinema, Rome, March 16, 1980. Running time: **120 MINS.**

Mauro .... Michel Piccoli
Marta .... Anouk Aimee
Sciabola .... Michele Placido
Anna .... Gisella Burinato

Marco Bellocchio, whose helming debut in 1966 with "Fists in His Pockets" labeled him an important new talent and the "angry young man" of '60s cinema, has calmed down into a sort of optimistic depression in a film that returns to the theme of the family as a destructive force.

Though "Salto nel vuoto" achieves a delicately balanced tone between the funereal, the gently humorous and the forward-looking and deals sensitively with issues like feminism, incest, hereditary madness — it fails as a whole to move its slow script in any very clear direction and ends up a go-nowhere atmosphere picture that loses a lot of viewers in the first quarter hour. Pic will undoubtedly make festival lists anyway (it's already invited to Cannes) on the basis of Bellocchio's reputation, the excellent performances of its two principals, and the "seriousness" of its theme. As a commercial venture it seems lukewarmish.

Mauro, a neurotic judge, and Marta, his slightly mad sister, are two unmarried siblings who have passed into middle age sharing the memory-filled house of their childhood. The side-stepped incest issue has little to do with Bellocchio's real interest here, which is to investigate the crisis of the family as an institution and the life of the couple, whose dependence on one another blocks happiness and personal fulfillment.

Anouk Aimee is excellent as the insecure sister. Years of cloister in a dark apartment with nothing to do but wash, cook and iron has driven her a bit batty. Michel Piccoli is equally fine as the unsound, obsessed brother, locked in a destructive love-hate relationship with Marta. Unable to deal any longer with his sister's behavioral oddities, Mauro tries to get Sciabola, a shabby young theatre actor who has pushed his lover to suicide, to get rid of Marta for him in the same way. But tables turn and by the end of the film Marta has begun to set out on her own, first in a relationship with Sciabola and then in a simple day out with her only friend, the housemaid.

Unfortunately, pic lacks the technical energy necessary to fashion an engrossing film out of its heavy thematic material. Despite some bravura sequences, shooting seems for the most part lifeless, heavy, and stilted. The hard-to-follow storyline that keeps viewers guessing about the relationship of characters, the chronological order of events, and the status of a particular sequence as dream, memory, fantasy or reality, combines with the photographic obscurity of the image to cloud over rather than illuminate or enrich basic qualities.

Referred to by some as "Leap in the Dark" for its determinedly murky photography, pic suffers from monotonous underlighting, though camerawork is fine and precise. Art direction works with a '30s decor and dominating triple-locked front door in a house as prison set. —*Yung.*

Un Sacco Bello
(Fun Is Beautiful)
(ITALIAN-COLOR)

Rome, March 9.
A Medusa release. Produced by Romano Cardarelli for Rafran Productions. Stars Carlo Verdone. Directed by Carlo Verdone. Screenplay, Leo Benvenuti, Piero De Bernardi, Carlo Verdone; camera (Eastmancolor), Ennio Guarnieri; art director, Carlo Simi; editor, Eugenio Alabiso; music, Ennio Morricone. Reviewed at Fiammetta Cinema, Rome, March 9, 1980. Running time: **99 MINS.**

Enzo, Ruggero, Leo . . . . Carlo Verdone
Marisol . . . . Veronica Miriel
Ruggero's father . . . . Mario Brega
Sergio . . . . Renato Scarpa

Carlo Verdone, who came into the public eye three years ago via his own sketches in tv and theatre, shows off his multiple talents as director, co-scripter and star comic for a variety of character sketches in a shoestring-budgeted film doing extremely well at the national b.o. "Un Sacco Bello" looks like the start of a successful career and could catch on abroad if its Romanness is not a barrier.

Verdone headlines the three principal roles in parallel stories that are rather arbitrarily edited into each other. Together they capture the tenor of everyday life in the center of Rome on a special day — August 15, an Italian holiday more successful in clearing the city of inhabitants than Attila ever was.

Leo, a talkative but shy mama's boy, is trying to leave the city to join his mother at the seaside when a beguiling Spanish tourist takes him over; Ruggero's father spends the day trying to convert his long-haired son away from a religious sect; Enzo's projected sex-hunt in Poland is cut short by his companion's need for emergency surgery in a roadside hospital.

Each story begins with a departure and ends where it started, which is all the film really has to say about its sad characters. In between though are some very funny moments of looking at "typical" Roman citizens as obsessed as New Yorkers with their individual-collective madnesses.

Verdone's originality lies in his ability to create characters that are not repetitively autobiographical. The characterization of Leo, the homely repairman unwillingly falling in love while keeping his mother at bay in Dispoli, reaches deepest in its human observation and even strikes a note of comic pathos. The episode with Enzo as the macho hot-rodder who stuffs his pants and prances to himself in front of the mirror is quickest to get a laugh. Verdone's tour-de-force triple performance is so good one starts looking closely to see if he isn't playing some of the secondary characters too.

Unfortunately dialog and gags coscripted by the director-star are not all on the same high level, but Verdone's performance appeal bridges most of the slow stretches. Certainly the camerawork adds little to the comedy, loaded with closeups and overlit. Nor is that Ennio Morricone signature on the soundtrack a particular aural asset — though music in this film belongs in the background anyway. Sets, cluttered with the paraphernalia of real life, are a plus. —*Yung.*

Lena Rais
(WEST GERMAN-COLOR)

Berlin, Feb. 29.
A Christian Rischert Film Production, Multimedia, Munich, and Zweites Deutsches Fernsehen (ZDF), Mainz. Features entire cast. Directed by Christian Rischert. Screenplay, Manfred Grunert; camera (color), Gerard Vandenberg; music, Eberhard Schoener; editing, Annette Dorn; sets, Hans Gailling. Reviewed at Berlin Film Fest (German Series), Feb. 29, '80. Running time: **116 MINS.**
Cast: Krista Stadler (Lena), Tilo Prueckner (Albert), Nikolaus Paryla (Rohlfs), Kai Fischer (Hella), Werner Asam (Weber), Manfred Lehmann (Policeman), Rolf Schimpf (Policeman), Tana Schanzara (Mother), Dan Van Husen (Harry).

One of the hits of the recent Hamburg Film Fest, Christian Rischert's "Lena Rais" is the story of a housewife married to a building foreman with three children who comes to the realization that life doesn't offer much in middle-age. Her husband uses her mostly as a sex object, and she wants to be emancipated before it's too late — but she simply doesn't know how to go about it.

A docu filmer at heart, Rischert has researched his theme at length and had an excellent script to lean on by Manfred Grunert, but it's the acting performances that make everything work in the end. Long ago, in 1966, Rischert was one of the hopes of New German Cinema with "Kopfstand, Madam," another pic with a personal view of a human problem. His return to prominence with a bitter, comical, sometimes sentimental and terrifying story of a woman's silent revolution in the kitchen is most welcomed in this era of pretensive social dramas aimed at saved auds. This howler should be seen to be believed.

Lena wants to leave at the very beginning when Albert starts pawing her before she even has a chance to warm to the occasion, but the man of the house refuses to let go, and there's always the kids and the home to appeal to that will soften Lena up in the long run. As a worker in the post office, she has only a few friends who will help, but one at least will take her in when a family quarrel gets rough.

And rough it is — for the more Lena rebels by withdrawing entirely into herself without words or defense, the tougher Albert gets in shaking and beating her, to return his wife to her former submissive self. A lark with her girlfriend one evening sets Albert to thinking that there's another man in her life, but she then reacts by having an affair with a passing policeman. He mauls her too in a brutal manner, and she goes into nervous shock. That leads to psychotherapy and a meeting with a muddled writer who encourages her to make the family break before it's too late. She does, and all hell breaks loose at home — but she's on the way to a self-identity.

Thesps Krista Stadler and Tilo Prueckner and lensing are big pluses. —*Holl.*

Gilda Live
(COLOR)

Tube to Broadway to screen. Youthful appeal.

Warner Bros. release of a Broadway Pictures Presentation. Directed by Mike Nichols. Produced by Lorne Michaels. Written by Anne Beatts, Lorne Michaels, Marilyn Suzanne Miller, Don Novello, Michael O'Donoghue, Gilda Radner, Paul Shaffer, Rosie Shuster, Alan Zweibel; camera (Technicolor), Ted Churchill, James Contner, Alan Metzger, Peter Norman; music produced by Howard Shore; choreography, Patricia Birch; production design, Franne Lee, Akira Yoshimura; editors, Ellen Hivde, Lynzee Klingman, Muffie Meyer. Reviewed at Sutton Theatre, N.Y.C., March 24, '80. (MPAA Rating: R.) Running time, **90 MINS.**
Cast: Gilda Radner, Father Guido Sarducci (Don Novello), Diana Grasselli, Myriam Valle, Maria Vidal, Paul Shaffer, Bob Christianson, Nils Nichols, John Caruso, Howard Shore, G.E. Smith.

Although filmed from Gilda Radner's one-woman show on Broadway last summer, the pedigree and virtually all the material in "Gilda Live" revert back to NBC's "Saturday Night Live," on which Radner has honed her act for the past five years. Strength of her large video following hints at a theoretically large youth audience. Prime question is whether previous exposure of much of this material might prompt a "why pay for something we can get free" attitude.

The show, dynamically transcribed in film by director Mike Nichols, amounts to a fast-moving reprise of all Radner's crowdpleasing characterizations from the weekly tv show. Added treat here is that language and bawdiness haven't had to toe network broadcast standards, which could be a particular lure to the younger crowd.

Still, even the best of this show's material (penned by the "Saturday Night" writing stable) is no better than the best of Radner's more popular turns on the tube. And, in the case of many of her characterizations — her punk rock parody, her Marvin Hamlisch-crazed nebbish adolescent and her Jewish American Princess routine — lack of usual interaction with other stock characters from the tv show dilutes the net effect.

Nonetheless, as a showcase for Radner's talents — which include some aggressive mock hoofing, enthusiastic singing and incredible stamina — the virtual one-woman show has been cannily constructed and works surprisingly intimately on screen.

Nichols used five cameras over four separate performances to knit together a seamless event that avoids the usual pitfalls of filmed concerts (mercifully, one never sees a single camera) and manages through close-ups and caught, off-hand moments to show the good time (and nice funny soul) Radner seems to be having.

Featured in between Radner's turns as crude news-hen Roseanne Roseannadanna, ghetto school teached Emily Litella, "nerd" Lisa Loopner, and their ilk, is actor Don Novello, plying his best material yet as Father Guido Sarducci, gossip columnist for the Vatican newspaper; Paul Shaffer, who triples as comedian-composer-musician in the show's several musical sidebars; and the backup groups Rouge and Candy Slice.

Considering it was all filmed "in vivo" at the Winter Garden Theatre under legit, not filmic, conditions, technical aspects are pretty good, though occasionally grainy. *—Step.*

Retour En Force
(Return in Bond)
(FRENCH-COLOR)

Paris, Feb. 5.

A Gaumont release of a Gaumont International/FR3 coproduction. Produced by Alain Poire. Features entire cast. Directed by Jean-Marie Poire. Written by Poire and Josiane Balasko; camera (color), Yves Lafaye; editor, Marie-Josephe Yoyotte; art direction, Gerard Viard; sound, Pierre Lenoir; music, William Sheller. Reviewed at the Concorde-Marignan theatre, Paris, Feb. 4, 1980. Running time: 100 MINS.
```
Adrien Blausac ........... Victor Lanoux
Teresa ................ Bernadette Lafont
Roger ................... Pierre Mondy
```

Yet one more comic caper highlights this pleasant but unmemorable comedy about a home coming ex-con who finds his wife living with a dull bus driver and his grown up kids picking up dirty habits.

His attempts to straighten out his home life are complicated by the murderous assaults of his ex-partners in crime, who don't want to hand over his cut of the loot from the job that landed him in the clink. Despite his intentions to stay clean, the ex-con plans the burglary of the criminal chief's well-guarded manor, using his own son as an accomplice.

The break-in is successful, but the pickings are slim. No money, just the blueprints of a major city bank. Film ends on the preparations for a new caper.

The caper sequence, which takes up the entire last quarter of the film, is basically clever and amusing (with the two men, equipped in mountain-climbing gear, clambering fly-like along the walls, above a floor wired to an alarm system), but finally not rich enough to make it genuinely satisfying in comedy or suspense. What precedes it is an insufficiently varied domestic comedy needing stronger comic treatment to make it truly marketable abroad.

Jean-Marie Poire's direction is clean but unexciting. Victor Lanoux is okay as the family-minded ex-con. As the wife, Bernadette Lafont unpacks the usual bag of tics she saves for uninspired roles. Pierre Mondy gives the right touch of bemused middle-class-mindedness to the wife's lover.—*Len.*

Target: Harry
(COLOR)

Corman oldie finally hits the screen.

Hollywood, March 19.

An ABC Pictures International release of a Corman Company production. Produced by Gene Corman. Directed by Henry Neill (Roger Corman). Stars Vic Morrow, Suzanne Pleshette, Victor Buono, Cesar Romero, Stanley Holloway. Screenplay, Bob Barbash; camera (uncredited color), Patrice Pouget; editor, Monte Hellman; music, Les Baxter. Reviewed at the Tower Theatre, L.A., March 19, 1980. (MPAA Rating: R.) Running time: 81 MINS.
```
Harry Black ............... Vic Morrow
Diane Reed .......... Suzanne Pleshette
Mosul Rashi ............. Victor Buono
Lt. Duval ............... Cesar Romero
Jason Carlyle ......... Stanley Holloway
Ruth Carlyle ........ Charlotte Rampling
Milos ............... Michael Ansara
Francesca ................ Anna Capri
```

After more than 12 years on the shelf, "Target: Harry," shot under the title "What's In It For Harry?," is finally hitting theatre screens, however humbly. Caught on the bottom half of a double bill in downtown L.A. for the record, film is more interesting historically than for its intrinsic merits, as it was one of Roger Corman's last helming jobs before abandoning the director's chair for the executive suite in 1971.

Produced by Gene Corman in the late 1960s for ABC, film was reportedly deemed too violent for the tube by the network. With a couple of nude scenes added, it was later advertised in trade ads as "How To Make It," but evidently never saw the light of day, at least domestically. One Henry Neill presently receives onscreen directing credit, but appearance by Roger Corman in a couple of shots, along with reliable accounts by his collabora-

tors, certifies his involvement with the project.

Played out against colorful Monte Carlo and Istanbul backdrops, mild suspenser increasingly unfolds as another "The Maltese Falcon" redo, with American tough guy Vic Morrow caught between sinister factions trying to lay their hands on two paper money printing plates stolen from the British mint.

Victor Buono stylishly plays a Middle Eastern Sidney Greenstreet type, and Suzanne Pleshette ultimately emerges as a carbon copy of Mary Astor, scheming unsuccessfully to worm her way into Morrow's bed to win an advantage over her competitor Buono.

Heavy travelog angle, numerous chases by foot and car, and various corpulant heavies, not to mention Les Baxter's wildly derivative score, vividly recall the spate of James Bond imitations of the period, of which this is decidedly one. Done on the cheap with natural sets and locations, film is routine but competent on every level and would have served satisfactorily as a tv pic. —*Cart.*

Korpinpolska
(The Raven's Dance)
(FINNISH-COLOR)

Berlin, Feb. 26.

SFI release of Suomi-Filmi Oy-SFI-Television Lulea production. Features entire cast. Written and directed by Markku Lehmuskallio. Camera (Fujicolor), Lehmuskallio, Bekka Martevo; editor, Juho Gartz. Reviewed at Berlin Film Fest (Competing), Feb. 19, '80. Running time: 80 MINS.

With: Pertti Kalinainen, Paavo Katajsarri, Hilkka Matikainen.

The film begins with a long, poetic, stunning evocation of nature in the Finnish North. But this is not a documentary. It is more a meditation on a rare situation where man, though a hunter, is in harmony with nature, which is destroyed by man.

But there is no didacticism here. Rather it displays good intentions as well as obtuseness in man's handling of his natural environment.

Plot involves a family that lives off the land in this far-off part of the country with neighbors far away. It consists of an old man with many memories of the hunt, but now reaching the end, and a younger, childless couple. There is a great moose that moves majestically through its habitat that the younger hunter is after but rarely can get at.

Add the birds of prey, the other animals, in what is not an Eden but a fairly controlled blend of man using nature to live by rather than to destroy. A tree falls in the forest from old age — later contrasted to

cutting them down by man as new roads are planned.

There are policemen even here and one tickets the young hunter for setting traps. Later the hunter's gun is confiscated and that leads to abandonment of the house

Though blown up from 16m, it looks fine, with excellent color. Playing is rightly solid and restrained in keeping with these simple characters. A film that has fest earmarks and also for showings at any ecology discussions as well as for tv and limited, selective situations.

Director Markku Lehmuskallio bears watching and Finland, not too often heard from at fests, makes a nice impression with this visually beautiful film. *—Mosk.*

Take It To The Limit
(DOCUMENTARY-COLOR)

Well, not that far.

Hollywood, March 11.

A Variety International Pictures release of a Peter Starr Film. Produced and directed by Peter Starr. Features entire cast. Exec producer, Leroy Lefkowitz. Written by Charles Michael Lorre, Starr; camera (Deluxe Color), Michael Chevalier, Jeremy Lepard, Mark Zavad; editor, John Bryant; animation, Jon Wokuluk; sound, Todd-AO, Bob Glass, William Knudson, Don MacDougall; original songs by Foreigner, Jean Luc Ponty, Arlo Guthrie, John McEuen, Tangerine Dream, Starwood. Reviewed at Variety International Pictures' Screening Room, Century City, March 11, 1980. (MPAA Rating: PG.) Running time: 95 MINS.

Cast: Barry Sheene, Russ Collins, Steve Baker, Scott Autrey, Mike Hailwood, Kenny Roberts.

Motorcycle enthusiasts will enjoy watching the endless array of bike races and listening to the expert commentary in "Take It To The Limit," but the picture certainly won't create many converts to the sport. Despite a sometimes engaging rock 'n' roll score, film is a straight-forward documentary that will generate little more than boredom on the part of the uninitiated halfway through its 95 minutes. Still, careful playoff in markets where racing is popular could produce some healthy b.o. action.

Some effort is made to explain the makings of a cycle champion through interviews with several racers who tell why they're drawn to the sport and how they manage to keep winning race after race. Interspersed are shots of various competitions, trick riding and narration by Alan Oppenheimer. A number of sections are backed by popular music which will at the very least create a diversion for those who have lost interest in the subject.

Photography by Michael Chevalier, Jeremy Lepard and Mark Zavad captures the action effectively although there appears to be a grainy quality to the entire feature. Peter Starr, who directed and co-wrote, latter with Charles Michael Lorre, was honest to his limited subject.

Most engaging in the entire project is a short animation scene by Jon Wokuluk htat parodies a short Arlo Guthrie cult tine on cycling (Guthrie himself sang and appeared briefly in the picture). Wokuluk's work shows great promise in its field as.well as serving as a wonderful change of pace.
—*Berg.*

80 Blocks From Tiffany's
(U.S.-DOCU-16m-COLOR)

Hollywood, Feb. 28.
An Above Average production. Produced, directed by Gary Weis. From a story by Jon Bradshaw; camera (color), Joan Churchill; editor, Michael Goldman; sound, John Hampton. Reviewed at the American Film Institute, Beverly Hills, Feb. 27, 1980. (No MPAA Rating.) Running time: 62 MINS.

Going 80 blocks north from Tiffany's lands you in the South Bronx, which is where producer-director Gary Weis went for this look at real-life gang members. While just skimming the surface of problems and their causes in the ghetto, Weis is clearly enamored of many of its denizens, their irreverent attitudes and wild speech, which makes for amusing, if a bit lightweight, viewing. Intended for network showing, pic was banned by NBC for its rough language, so will have to fight for daylight in specialized spots.

After a "West Side Story"-like aerial opening, hour-long film introduces such kids as Fly, Crazy Joe 'and 'D.S.R.,' members 'of leading Gotham gangs the Savage Nomads and Savage Skulls. Glimpsed on their home turf and in their hideouts, youths pose and attitudinize for the camera while rationalizing their lifestyles, putting down the cops and venting their spleen about social injustices which have made them what they are.

Community workers, police, reformed gang members, a priest and other locals contribute their two cents worth, although most engaging talker is undoubtedly a hefty former area club owner known as Heavy, who most articulately sketches a partial history of the neighborhood and at one point drives around in an outrageous Cadillac, complete with built-in loudspeaker, which even Super Fly would envy.

Weis tries to pull it all together by climaxing with a block party which at times threatens to degenerate into anarchy due to pent-up tensions of a few kids. As portrayed, area verges on becoming a war zone, but a wider discussion of society's ills does not come under consideration here.

Pathetic sight of young blacks and Latinos uncomprehendingly brandishing swastikas gives pause, but by inclination and "entertainment" necessity, Weis has concentrated upon the more unusual and, probably, smarter spokesmen for the gangs, and thus ends up with a more positive and likable result than is probably warrented. It's a good show rather than a disturbing probe, and as such would be relatively digestible by a mass viewership. —*Cart.*

Die Herren Machen Das Selber, Dass Ihnen Der Arme Mann Feyndt Wird
(It's the Rich Man's Fault that the Poor Man Is His Enemy)
(W. GERMAN-COLOR-DOCU-16m)

Berlin, Feb. 28.
A Wendlaendische Filmkooperative, Marleben, Production. Direction, sound, and editing by Roswitha Ziegler, Niels-Christian Bolbrinker, and Bernd Westphal, in collaboration with Thomas Wittenberg. Camera (color), Bolbrinker. Reviewed at Berlin Film Fest (German Series), Feb. 28, '80. Running time: 126 MINS.

Strong docu that describes what has been going on at the Gorleben atom-plant project from 1977 to 1979, when even the farmers in the community collectively demonstrated for their rights in the manner of a Peasants' Revolt. Documentarists Roswitha Ziegler, Niels-Christian Bolbrinker, and Bernd Westphal followed the events from start to the present, and the story is still not over — further, their documentary has temporarily been refused airing privileges on West German television stations, it's reported, which is one reason why it was put in the German Series at the Berlin fest.

High point of the documentary was a mass-demonstration march to Hannover to protest the local government's decision to use an area near the East German border for storage of nuclear waste and a reprocessing plant. The local inhabitants rose in arms upon hearing the news. Pic features several interviews with the common people on the matter, which could be dynamite on tv with the ecologists (the "Green") running for national election this year. Worth a peep if you like socially engaged docus.
—*Holl.*

Hussy
(BRITISH-COLOR)

A Kendon Films production. Executive producer, Don Boyd. Produced by Jeremy Watt. Directed by Matthew Chapman. Stars Helen Mirren, John Shea. Screenplay, Chapman; camera (color), Keith Goddard; editor, Bill Blunden; music, George Fenton; sound, John Sanders; production designer, Hazel Peiser; production manager, Buzz Besgrove; asst. director, Gino Marotta Reviewed at Paramount preview theatre, London, March 17, '80. (BBFC Rating: X). Running time: 95 MINS.

Beaty Simons	Helen Mirren
Emory	John Shea
Max	Murray Salem
Alex	Paul Angelis
Vere	Jenny Runacre
Billy	Daniel Chasin
Tama	Patti Boulaye
Nadine	Marika Rivera
Hope	Jill Melford
Olivia	Sandy Ratcliff
Laurie	Malcolm Reynolds
Fat Man	William Hootkins

Somewhere in scripter-director Matthew Chapman's first feature there's a valid love story trying to get out. It stays buried for lack of an objective eye — that of an experienced producer, perhaps — to see the pitfalls of an acceptably lightweight project that strives for serious significance. What should have been a sharp little yarn about an offbeat affair plays long and lugubrious.

While the sex angle is the obvious choice for promotion, with Helen Mirren making apt visual copy as a club escort and call girl, overselling it could backfire with some audiences since the semi-explicit stuff disappears around halfway. Thereafter, with the introduction of some new characters (Murray Salem and Paul Angelis as melodramatic nasties), a drug-smuggling plotline takes precedence. That then resolves into a sugary ending.

John Shea's performance as Mirren's lover, a transient American working as spotlight operator at the London stripjoint where she hosts and hooks, is mostly bland, but occasionally effective in hinting at a murkier past than his guileless looks suggest. Mirren, a proven stage actress with limited experience in film, would have come off better had she been directed towards a less ponderous conception of the role, and photographed more sympathetically by Keith Goddard.

Neither lead is helped by dialog which badly needed that ruthless impartial eye; and it is, there are some leaden, even laughable, moments. Atmosphere in the club scenes, both at the tables and backstage, is nicely seedy. But the drug-handover sequences, shot in the contrastingly atmospheric flat-

lands of Britain's east coast, suffer from dull light and pedestrian cuttings. —*Simo.*

The Visitor
(Il Visitatore)
(ITALIAN/AMERICAN-COLOR)

Champaign, Ill., March 7.
Ovidio Assonitis presents an International Picture Show Company release. Distributed by Marvin Films. Directed by Michael J. Paradise (Giulio Paradisi). Features entire cast. Story, Paradise, Assonitis; screenplay, Lou Comici, Robert Mundy; camera (color), Ennio Guarnieri; editing, Robert Curi; art direction, Frank Venorio; music composed and conducted by Franco Mikalizzi; animation by Bozzetto. Reviewed at Market Place Cinema No. 3, Champaign, Illinois, March 7, 1980. Running time: 90 MINS.

Cast: Mel Ferrer, Glenn Ford, Lance Henriksen, John Huston, Joanne Nail, Sam Peckinpah, Shelley Winters, Paige Conner.

Hybrid international horrors such as "The Visitor" threaten to necessitate new genre definitions. Too preposterous to be called camp, "The Visitor" features a big name cast and the kitchen sink method of derivation. Set in Atlanta, this compendium of fright effects includes a child monster with a Southern accent, slow-motion suspense and destruction on a basketball court, an apocalypse of pigeons, lots of breaking glass, more Hitchcockian borrowings than one can count, a rape setting, Shelley Winters' incessant singing, and John Huston appearing as a very literal deus ex machina.

Visually garish, pic nonetheless maintains an accelerating force with such increasingly bizarre situations. It comes hard to believe that such plot elements (including the theologically offensive conclusion, by almost anyone's standards) are being acted out by such familiar and respectable faces. Glenn Ford comes to a particularly gruesome finish as the detective investigating the misdeeds inflicted by the young girl upon her mother and others. After having his eyes pecked out by birds, his auto wraps around a tennis fence and explodes.

Mel Ferrer plays an Atlanta sports owner who is in league with some mysterious multi-national (or extra-terrestrial) demonic force, which wishes him to impregnate his wife again, since she carries powerful demonic genes unwittingly. She is unwilling, and the tortures of father and daughter commence.

Film is technically full of spark, which compensates for lapses in credulity. With a surplus of wide angles, zooms and effective pans, plus several parallel editing sequences of laughable tension, "The Visitor" backs excessive camera calisthenics with an ostentatious musical blend of "Star Wars" and "A Fifth of Beethoven." Although Sam Peckinpah's name figures largely in ad credits, this writer saw only one character (from the back) who might have been him: an abortionist who stifles the scheme of the maleficent committee. Roles of other name actors are formidable, however.

The daughter Katie is played by Paige Conner, who offers little threat to other budding child actresses. "The Visitor" holds no stock in nuance, and might be called an extreme mix of Fellini, "The Omen," and the casting call. It is hard to say which audience this was aimed at, since either the very gullible or the exhaustedly blase might find it most amusing. —*Pege.*

Filmex Fest Reviews

Return Of The Secaucus Seven
(U.S.-COLOR-16m)

Hollywood, Feb. 20.
A Salsipuedes production. Produced by Jeffrey Nelson, William Aydelott. Directed, written, edited by John Sayles. Features entire cast. Camera (Du Art Film Labs color), Austin de Besche; music, K. Mason Daring. Reviewed at the American Film Institute, Beverly Hills, Feb. 20, 1980. (No MPAA Rating.) Running time: **110 MINS.**
Jeff .... Mark Arnott
Chip .... Gordon Clapp
Frances .... Maggie Cousineau
Norman Gaddis .... Brian Johnston
J.T. .... Adam LeFevre
Mike ....:...... Bruce MacDonald
Irene .... Jean Passanante
Kate .... Maggie Renzi
Howie .... John Sayles
Ron .... David Strathairn
Maura .... Karen Trott

Avoiding numerous pitfalls and surmounting considerable limitations, notably a $60,000 budget, John Sayles has fashioned an admirable postmortem of the 1960s student left in "Return Of The Secaucus Seven." Virtually the whole cast and crew make their feature debut here, and while not all the work is on an entirely professional level, earnestness and intelligence of the enterprise carry the day and validate the thought and feeling inherent in the script. While likely to play well to contemporaries of the 30ish characters, film will still be a tricky sell, ideal for an adventurous distributor ready to try to lick a marketing challenge.

Structured like a well-built three-act play, drama is set at eight-year reunion of seven student activists who were arrested together in Secaucus, N.J. on their way to a Washington demonstration. As old cohorts and a few new companions gather at the New Hampshire farm

of one of the couples, complicated history of romantic relationships within the group begins to be unravelled. A diagram of past and present liaisons would prove as dense as that for any soap opera.

Fortunately, Sayles, scripter of several Roger Corman actioners, refuses to indulge in overt melodrama, just as he avoids the spectacle of a bunch of over-the-hill radicals crying in their beer about the good old days of Vietnam, Nixon and the draft. Despite bond provided by the past, characters are fully alive in the present, and entanglements become even more knotted as film progresses.

Keynote of the drama is that characters are irrevocably wedded to their common experience without being smothered by it. Some, like the farm couple, still live by the basic hippie ideals even if they have taken conventional jobs. Others, like two who work for Washington politicians, rationalize their co-option by arguing that they're now just trying to change the system from within rather than from without. Some have not yet fully faced the responsibilities inherent in adulthood, but all have had to confront the realities of making a living and maturing emotionally.

More like some European films than much domestic product, film is virtually wall-to-wall talk, all of it interesting and much of it rather witty. Despite production primitiveness and some rough edges, Sayles still manages to sneak in some elegance of direction which promises better to come under more favorable circumstances.

Acting is adequate, with none of the first-timers really standing out and a couple proving weaker than the rest, but an overall directness and modesty of performance push across even the more difficult scenes.

Pic is a shade overlong at 110 minutes, with an extended bar scene and some "action" exteriors, latter undoubtedly intended to break up the conversation, padding things out. Some judicious trimming might let it play even better.

Ultimately, however, Sayles has accomplished what many aspiring directors talk about doing but somehow never get around to undertaking — going off in the woods with some friends, a camera, some film and no money and producing something worthwhile. Pic represents an infrequent reminder that it can be done. —*Cart.*

A Woman Like Eve
(Een Vrouw Als Eva)
(NETHERLANDS-COLOR)

Hollywood, Feb. 12.
A Sigma Films B.V. production. Produced by Matthijs van Heyningen. Directed, written by Nouchka van Brakel. Features entire cast. Camera (color), Nurith Aviv; editor, Ine Schenkkan; music, Laurens van Rooyen; art direction, Inger Kolff; assistant director, Hans Kemna. Reviewed at the MGM Studios, Culver City, Feb. 12, 1980. (No MPAA Rating.) Running time: **101 MINS.**
Eve .... Monique van de Ven
Liliane .... Maria Schneider
Sonja .... Marijke Merckens
Ad .... Peter Faber
(In Dutch with English subtitles)

A sort of bisexual "Kramer Vs. Kramer," Dutch production "A Woman Like Eve" takes the possibilities for child custody melodrama in feature films one step further by examining a family breakdown occasioned by a middle-class wife and mother running off with another woman. Highlighted by another excellent performance by Dutch star Monique van de Ven, well-made pic is seriously undermined by a completely inexpressive appearance by Maria Schneider as van de Ven's seductress. A hit in the Netherlands, film possesses some Stateside potential thanks to off-beat premise and topicality.

Excelling in a more inward, sober role than usual, van de Ven plays an Amsterdam housewife whose horizons have never been expanded beyond her home and family until she meets commune hippie Schneider on a brief vacation in the South of France. Naively embracing latter's friendliness and live-off-the-land lifestyle, Dutch beauty vacillates for awhile before realizing, to her considerable surprise, that she's in love.

Instead of suppressing her feelings, van de Ven uncharacteristically abandons her family for a long French sojourn, only to suddenly return to wrest custody of her two kids.

A long court battle ensues, with one ruling later being overturned and youngsters flip-flopping between mother and father. It's a touchy matter, to be sure, with both parents plausibly arguing for their own rights. Although the husband understandably flips out at one point over the situation, and despite pic's self-evident approval of the lesbian love affair, husband is never made out to be the baddie, as writer-director Nouchka van Brakel bends over backwards to paint him as a nice guy and to fairly represent male p.o.v.

However, van de Ven's infatuation quickly appears preposterous

due to Schneider's vapid, somnolent performance. Although character as written, refuses to accept any **responsibility whatsoever, considering her g.f.'s children a nuisance,** Schneider herself is a complete drag. Perfect as Brando's partner in "Last Tango In Paris," she proves an insurmountable liability here.

Billed as the Netherlands' only female director, van Brakel tells her story well and displays a sure hand with all the performers save for Schneider, although the nonverbal posturing of Schneider's lesbian clique is a bit arch. —*Cart.*

Heartland Reggae
(CANADIAN-COLOR-16m)

Hollywood, Feb. 27.
A Canada Offshore Cinema Ltd. production. Produced, directed by J.P. Lewis. Features entire cast. Screenplay, J.P. Lewis, John Sutton Smith; camera (color), J.P. Lewis, John Swabey, T. Marsh; editors, J.P. Lewis, Randal Torno, John Mayes. Reviewed at the American Film Institute, Beverly Hills, Feb. 27, 1980. (No MPAA Rating.) Running time: **87 MINS.**
Features: Bob Marley and the Wailers, Peter Tosh, Jacob Miller and the Inner Circle Band, Althea and Donna, Dennis Brown, Little Jr. Tucker, Judy Mowat, The I-Threes, U-Roy.

At least in print screened for press, "Heartland Reggae" looks about as unprofessional as a film can be. Miserable sound, constantly shaking camera, Scotch tape-type editing and other irritating technical aspects effectively prevent any enjoyment of the infectious music on display. Reggae has yet to break through with American listeners in a major way, and die-hard aficionados will comprise only audience for this one.

Framed around a 1978 concert marking 12th anniversary of Jamaican visit by late Emperor Haile Selassie, figurehead of the native rasta religion, documentary features an assortment of reggae artists showing their stuff. Only one to at all surmount heavy liability of oppressive technique is Bob Marley, best-known of the lot, who would seem irrepressible under any circumstances.

Highlight of the "One Love Peace Concert" is saved for near the end, when Marley calls to the stage Jamaica's prime minister Michael Manley and opposition leader Eddie Seaga and proceeds to dance madly between the two. It's a unique moment, the only memorable one in the entire show.

Film is work of Canadian J.P. Lewis. Print on view looked as though it had been dragged through the mud, although better was promised at Filmex unspooling.
—*Cart.*

A Summer Rain
(Chuvas de Verao)
(BRAZILIAN-COLOR)

Hollywood, Feb. 19.
An Alter Filmes production. Produced by Luis Fernando Goulart. Directed, written by Carlos Diegues. Camera (color), Jose Meteiros; editor, Mair Tavares. Reviewed at the Burbank Studios, Burbank, Feb. 19, 1980. (No MPAA Rating.) Running time: **87 MINS.**
Alfonso Silva . . . . Jofre Soares
Also: Rodolfo Arena, Cristina Ache, Luiz Antonio, Paolo Cesar Pereio.
(Portuguest soundtrack; English subtitles)

A "Street Scene"-type comedy-drama with some unexpected twists, "A Summer Rain" is an upbeat, life-affirming tale forwarding the theory that life begins at 65. Genial, crisply told and spicy at times, film trades in a safe non-conformism that makes it the "commercial" sort of fest entry that could catch public's fancy.

After a perfunctory retirement party, old Alfonso looks forward to nothing in life but lolling around in his pyjamas and watching the world go by as represented on his little city block. His expectations of tame twilight years are quickly jarred when he discovers his young maid hiding her terrorist boyfriend in an upstairs room. Initially outraged, he nonetheless allows himself to protect the couple over a long, incident-filled weekend, during which he also discovers his son-in-law in drag, stumbles across a child murderer right across the street, and violates his celibacy by taking up with a spinster from down the way.

Far-fetched yarn is told in sprightly, good-natured manner which cheerfully thumbs its nose at solemnity and gloom which threatens to cloud over consideration of old age and its problems.

Carlos Diegues' direction is warm without being soft-hearted, and Jofre Soares' gruffness lends some believable rough edges to the leading role, which could have been portrayed with too much wise recognition under less controlled guidance. Entire cast performs with a boistrous energy which keeps things moving in jovial fashion. —*Cart.*

King Of The Joropo
(El Rey Del Joropo)
(VENEZUELAN-COLOR)

Hollywood, Feb. 22.
A Balumba Films C.A. production. Produced by Edmundo Aray. Directed and written by Carlos Rebolledo, Thaelman Urguelles, based on the book "Los Cuentos de Alfredo Alvarado, 'El Rey del Joropo,'" by Edmundo Aray. Stars Tito Aponte, Oscar Martinez, Alfredo Alvarado. Camera (color), Jose Antonio Ventura Jr.; editor, Justo Vega; music, Leo

Brouwer. Reviewed at the Disney Studios, Burbank, Feb. 21, 1980. No MPAA Rating. Running time: **92 MINS.**
Alfredo As A Youth . . . . .Tito Aponte
Journalist . . . . Oscar Martinez
Alfredo As A Man . . . . . . Alfredo Alvarado
TV Director . . . . Fausto Verdial
Director's Secretary . . . . Rosario Val
Alfredo As A Child . . . . . Alfredo Carrasco
(English soundtrack)

A potentially great subject is pretty thoroughly sabotaged in "King Of The Joropo." Ambitiousness and artlessness walk hand in hand in convoluted telling of commercial Venezuelan television's effort to unfold the "real story" of former Public Enemy No. One Alfredo Alvarado. Not many films from Venezuela reach these shores, so film is of some interest in light of its attempt to deal with country's own folk legends, but result comes up way short.

Opening title informs the Alvarado, who plays himself, is a celebrated performer of the joropo, the national dance, who for 40 years made headlines through his scandalous, even criminal, behavior.

Now venerated and near 60, Alvarado here agrees to participate in a tv rendition of his life story, and he carefully tries to tell the truth, which often contradicts and, more seriously, diminishes the wild tales that have surrounded his activities for years.

Difficulties between Alvarado and tv exec mount up until coming to a head when network insists on sensationalizing his life by giving viewers what it thinks they want, i.e., more sex and violence. A man is thus subjected to watching his life reduced to pulp melodrama, a terrific Pirandellian premise which is, unfortunately, just thrown up on the screen without having been mastered.

Helming by Carlos Rebolledo and Thaelman Urguelles is frantic and slapdash. Acting is generally loud, lensing looks garish and even subtitles are far from perfect.

Jabs are made in the direction of local government authorities, as tv producers point out that still-extant officials and institutions can't be publicly attacked, even if they may have figured prominently in Alvarado's true life story. Pic may or may not be daring for Venezuela, but such targets have been barbed to death in the cinemas of many other countries, so foreign viewers are likely to be unimpressed. —*Cart.*

Pentimento
(NETHERLANDS-COLOR)

Hollywood, Feb. 26.
Produced, directed and written by Frans Zwartjes. Camera (Color), Zwartjes; editor, Zwartjes. Stars Aimee, Marianne, Monique, Toebosch, Helen Hedy. No other

credits provided. Reviewed at AFI Hall, Beverly Hills, Feb. 26, 1980. (No MPAA Rating). Running time: **72 MINS.**
(English Subtitles)

It's a crime that a film as poor and offensive as "Pentimento" is getting the opportunity to play at a film festival. Accepting the fact that not every fest entry is a professional package of cinematic expertise, there is nothing interesting, unique, creative, innovative or remotely literate about this picture from the Netherland's Frans Zwartjes. It is badly photographed, badly scored, badly edited, badly written (if there ever was a script) and badly directed. There are no commercial prospects.

What Zwartjes has assembled are a series of scenes where women are transported, dragged about, beaten up and occasionally raped, mostly by Oriental men. It is notably a disgusting and vulgar use of film but horribly offensive to women, Orientals and probably anyone else with a sense of taste.

Zwartjes is known for being avant-garde, a term used to describe those in the arts who produce material that is bizarre, extremist or experimental. In this case the term does not apply. "Pentimento" is unadulterated garbage. —*Berg.*

On the Nickel
(U.S.-COLOR)

Hollywood, Feb. 6.
A Rose's Park production. Produced, directed, written by Ralph Waite. Features entire cast. Camera (TVC Labs color), Ric Waite; editor, Wendy Greene Bricmont; music, Fredric Myrow; costumes, Patrick Norris; sound, Don Matthews; associate producer, William Bushnell; assistant director, Ralph Ferrin. Reviewed at 20th Century-Fox Studios, L.A., Feb. 6, 1980. (No MPAA Rating.) Running time: **96 MINS.**
Sam . . . . Donald Moffat
C.G. . . . . Ralph Waite
Paul . . . . Hal Williams
Rose . . . . Penelope Allen
Bad Mood . . . . Jack Kehoe

Produced independently over a long period and about to enter limited self-distribution, "On The Nickel" is the sort of "worthy" little picture which will undoubtedly be embraced in some quarters simply because of its off-beat subject matter and undeniable earnestness. But despite a strong, tough performance by Donald Moffat in the lead, Skid Row melodrama is a clinker, overly sentimental, woefully indulgent and, if anything, too slick for the milieu it attempts to penetrate. Even with the careful handling planned for it, film faces an uphill struggle in the marketplace.

Pic valiantly tries to bring alive

and humanize seldom-examined denizens of every American big city, the Skid Row winos and derelicts who live mainly on the streets and are widely shunned and ignored by society. Producer-director-writer Ralph Waite thus gives himself a big head start in eliciting audience generosity, but quickly loses ground through scene after irritating scene depicting aimless drunkenness and pathetic shiftlessness of the characters.

First half is dominated by the imposing Moffat, who plays a former alcoholic who's managed to lift himself up from the "nickel," or Skid Row, but has nowhere in particular to go. He's drawn back down by news that his old friend, C.G., is around and in danger of slipping over the edge, and main dramatic thrust of second half lies in Moffat's futile effort to save his pal while trying to avoid being sucked back into his hopeless old way of life.

Unfortunately, Waite the director has exercised little control over Waite the actor, and long stretches are filled with painfully indulgent close-ups of Waite, playing C.G., delivering sodden, bleary-eyed monologs. Just as Moffat is stretched almost to his patience's end by him, so is the audience. Inevitable climax is a long time coming.

Style veers toward the glossy and even falsely upbeat when more trenchant probing would have been in order. Moffat, who bears a physical and thespian resemblance to Robert Duvall, is constantly commanding. A few good sequences stand out, notably when an entire group of locals is called before a judge and some of them don't even realize where they are, but most of the street scenes misfire.

While knocking the police for insufficient understanding, Waite fortunately doesn't sermonize about how society-at-large is responsible for the plight of these misfits, keeping things on a personal scale and ultimately saying that every individual is accountable for his or her own fate. But Waite's strenuous effort to get inside and justify his unfortunate characters makes entire enterprise a bit patronizing. It's not within shouting distance of what is still the most corrosive slum on film, Luis Bunuel's "Los Olvidados." —*Cart.*

The Shillingbury Blowers
(BRITISH-COLOR)

Hollywood, Feb. 17.
An Inner Circle Films production. Produced by Greg Smith. Directed by Val Guest. Stars Tervor Howard. Screenplay, Francis Essex; camera (color), Frank Watts; editor, Bill Lenny; music, Ed

Welch: art direction, Albert Witherick; sound, Laurie Clarkson; assistant director, Vic Priggs. Reviewed at the MGM Studios, Culver City, Feb. 17, 1980. (No MPAA Rating.) Running time: **82 MINS.**

Dan 'Saltie' Wicklow ..... Trevor Howard
Peter .... Robin Nedwell
Sally .... Diane Keen
Jake .... Jack Douglas
Reggie .... Sam Kydd
Sam .... Eric Francis
Harvey .... Joe Black
Basil .... Tony Sympson
Council Chairman ..... John Le Mesurier

It's almost impossible to believe that "The Shillingbury Blowers" was made today instead of some 30 years ago. With its quaint picture of English village life, crotchety but lovable old crones and no pressing concerns outside the maintenance of the community brass band, time seems to have passed this one by. Proudly proclaiming old-fashioned virtues, pic could appeal to generations brought up on such films, but youthful viewers would scoff. The tube seems a better bet than paying venues.

Shillingbury is an Olde English paradise, with trim little cottages, chiming bells and immaculate rose gardens. It's the perfect place for pop musician Robin Nedwell and his wife to retreat to from the city, but he's soon called in to shape up the town band, which is so bad that people flee whenever it sets to playing.

Shunted aside in the shakeup is longtime bandleader, old "Saltie," Trevor Howard. In revenge, players refuse to put anything extra into their music, agreeing only to simply play the notes. This improves the group immeasurably, to the extent that they qualify for the national championship, stupefying all of Shillingbury in the process.

A marginal work to say the least, film's unashamed sentimentality will charm those who indulge it and be dismissed by those looking for any substance. Trevor Howard has long since mastered this kind of sweet old codger role. Val Guest's direction is appropriately modest.
—*Cart.*

Vengeance Is Mine
(Fukushu Suruwa Ware Ni Ari)
(JAPANESE-COLOR)

Hollywood, Feb. 7.

A Shochiku Co. Ltd. production. Produced by Kazuo Inoue. Directed by Shohei Imamura. Features entire cast. Screenplay, Masaru Baba, based on the book by Ryuzo Saki; camera (color), Shinsaku Himeda; editor, Keiichi Uraoka; music, Shinichiro Ikebe. Reviewed at 20th Century-Fox Studios, L.A., Feb. 7, 1980. (No MPAA Rating.) Running time: **128 MINS.**

Iwao Enokizu .... Ken Ogata
Shizuo Enokizu .... Rentaro Mikuni
Kayo Enokizu .... Chocho Mikayo
Kazuko Enokizu .... Mitsuko Baisho
Haru Asano .... Mayumi Ogawa
Hisano Asano .... Nijiko Kiyokawa
(Japanese soundtrack-English subtitles)

Unfolding through multiple flashbacks something like a Japanese "In Cold Blood," Shohei Imamura's "Vengeance Is Mine" has to be counted among the major Japanese films to have reached American shores in recent years. Extremely violent, sociologically probing and packed with incident, picture won a parcel of top critics awards in its own country last year and should prove substantially more accessible to American audiences than most Japanese films.

Inspired by real-life story of a notorious criminal who murdered two small-time money collectors and then led police on a wild goose chase across Japan, pic is a red-hot examination of personal rage and insolence toward society. Killer's rationale is not unearthed as much as his contemptuous attitude is vividly portrayed, with his physical lust and brutal hostility being acted out in equal measures.

After the rough crimes of the opening reel, film starts jumping back in time to show his pathetic youth and increasingly anti-social young manhood. Stuck in prison, he begins to suspect his wife and father of having an affair and later, as a fugitive, enters into a destructive mad love relationship with a prostitute and her mother.

As erotic as it is violent, pic is ravishingly made and momentum never flags over the long running time. Artistically, work cannot be faulted, with only reservation being that Imamura might have sacrificed something in the realm of clarity and distinct point-of-view through inclusion of so much accumulated detail and decade-spanning time jumps.

But film possesses real force and power and Imamura, a director since the late 1950s but relatively unknown outside Japan, certainly becomes a name to reckon with. Ken Ogata dominates proceedings with a ferocious performance which superbly complements the supple muscularity of the tale's telling. Like "In Cold Blood," script is based on a "non-fiction novel," by Ryuzo Saki.—*Cart.*

Forbidden Zone
(U.S.-B&W)

Hollywood, March 15.

A Carl Borack production. Produced, directed by Richard Elfman. Executive producer, Gene Cunningham. Features entire cast. Screenplay, Richard Elfman, M. Bright, Martin W. Nicholson, Nick Jones; camera, (black and white), Gregory Sandor; editor, associate producer, assistant director, Martin W. Nicholson; music, Danny Elfman (Oingo-Boingo); production design, Marie-Pascale Elfman; art direction, David M. Makler; set design, Ken Corrone. Reviewed at the Century Plaza Theatre, L.A., March 15, 1980. (No MPAA Rating.) Running time: **76 MINS.**

King Fausto .... Herve Villechaize
Queen .... Susan Tyrrell
Frenchy .... Marie-Pascale Elfman
Ex-Queen .... Viva

"Forbidden Zone" could put to the test even the most fanatical followers of its creators, the Mystic Knights of the Oingo Boingo. Musically lively and imaginative, this self-styled cult pic aims for far-out humor in the dialog scenes but can't produce more than one or two real laughs. Failed zaniness comes off as just silly, and b.o. prospects beyond the midnight circuit would appear nil.

Richard Elfman's Oingo Boingo group has enjoyed a following on the nitery circuit for several years and has regularly impressed with its sophisticated, witty musicianship. Wild tunes and production numbers easily emerge as highlights of this, group's first feature, which is accurately described by producer-director Elfman as "a human cartoon."

Against humorously and self-consciously expressionistic cardboard and plaster sets overseen by Marie-Pascale Elfman, who also stars, story takes whacked-out earthlings on a tour of the Sixth Dimension, underground domain in which Herve Villechaize and Susan Tyrrell preside over an assortment of loony demons, ogres, cretins and assorted humans in chains awaiting sexual abuse by their captors.

Shot in b&w with deliberate emphasis on tackiness, pic looks like a cheap "Flash Gordon" serial juiced up by a parade of fancy opticals and herky-jerk stop-motion photography. Basic problem is that pic immediately announces its intention to outrage and boggle the mind but never delivers on the promise. —*Cart.*

Todo Modo
(ITALIAN-COLOR)

Hollywood, Feb. 17.

A Nu-Image Film release of a Cinevera S.P.A. production. Produced by Daniele Senatore. Stars Gian Maria Volonte, Marcello Mastroianni, Mariangela Melato; Directed by Elio Petri. Screenplay, Elio Petri, Berto Pelosso; camera (Eastmancolor), Luigi Kuweiller; editor, Ruggio Mastroianni; music, Ennio Morricone. Reviewed at the MGM Studios, Culver City, Feb. 17, 1980. (No MPAA Rating). Running time: **112 MINS.**

President .... Gian Maria Volonte
Don Gaetano ...... Marcello Mastroianni
Giacinta .... Mariangela Melato
Excellency .... Michel Piccoli
(Italian with English subtitles)

"Todo Modo" is the Italian "Quintet." Futuristic, purposely convoluted and pointlessly obscure, Elio Petri's 1976 production, reviewed now for the record, boasts about half of its country's top stars and trades relentlessly in the age-old state versus religion controversy. Acquired for domestic distribution by Nu-Image Film, this political fantasy would appear to offer little of meaning to American audiences.

Set in the 'near' future, pic has cleric Marcello Mastroianni presiding over a retreat for upper echelon Christian Democrats being held at a modernistic concrete bunker, redolent with plaster icons and seminary-like cubicles for meditation.

Mastroianni's announced intention is to make politicos confront their sins and get back in touch with God, but one by one the powerful men begin dropping dead. Once it appears that a wholesale slaughter is underway, Mastroianni himself commits suicide, and question of who is manipulating whom comes to fore without at all being answered.

Admittedly, Italy's political condition, now as when film was made, is confusing and chaotic, but this film hardly helps either to clarify mhos or to provide meaningful poetic amplification of existing circumstances.

After the heated polemics of such early 1970s pix as "Investigation Of A Citizen Above Suspicion" and "The Working Class Goes To Heaven," Petri tries for a cooler, more abstract style here. despite some bravura acting by the principals, "Todo Modo" adds up to nothing. —*Cart.*

The Demise Of Herman Durer
(De Verworking van Herman Durer)
(DUTCH-COLOR-16m)

Hollywood, Feb. 20.

A Virginia Films B.V. production. Produced by Hans Klap. Directed, screenplay by Rene Seegers, Jean van de Velde, Leon de Winter, based on a novel by de Winter; camera (color), Sjoerd Jansen; editor, Rene Seegers; music, Angelo Branduardi; sound, Jan Musch. Reviewed at the American Film Institute, Beverly Hills, Feb. 20, 1980. (No MPAA Rating). Running time: **108 MINS.**

Herman Durer .... Felix-Jan Kuipers
Mother .... Alma
Father .... Albert Abspoel
Jacques .... Ed van Gils
Joyce .... Miek Smit
Sister .... Vivan Lampe
(Dutch soundtrack-English subtitles)

Pix describing the banality of modern life and the disaffectedness of youth have flowed so regularly from Europe for the last 20 years that themes have become cliches. It's therefore to the credit of the three writer-directors involved that they've at least hit upon a new approach to the material in "The

Demise Of Herman Durer." Rather slow and ultimately depressing, film deserves fest-type exposure but is a long shot for commercial playoff.

Title character bears outward trappings of a typical teenage punk, complete with criminal record and no inclination to hold a job. Once he reads the 18th century novel, "The Life Of A Good-For-Nothing," however, kid develops a rich, if single-minded, fantasy life.

Emulating character in the book, young Herman decides to run away from Amsterdam for the greener pastures of Italy. Getting as far as Munich, he's told by an immigrant that the Mediterrean country's not what it used to be and he's urged to give up his dream of the idle gentleman's life in the South.

Throughout, stark reality of industrialized Europe is contrasted with the idealized past of Herman's imagination, a somewhat crude device handled with gentleness and happy lack of polemics. Film succeeds at getting inside the head of an undernourished, potentially bright wastrel left by society's wayside, even if the sociological insights are nothing new.

Three filmmakers are all in their mid-20s and picture marks the first time Dutch Ministry of Culture has entirely financed a fictional feature, which represents an accomplishment in itself. Work displays a respectable seriousness without self-importance, and craft elements are solid on meagre means. —Cart.

Tusk
(FRENCH-COLOR)

Hollywood, March 20.

A Yang Film-Films 21 production. Produced by Eric Rochat. Executive producers, Eric Rochat, Sylvio Tabet, Jean-Jacques Fourgeaud. Directed by Alexandro Jodorowsky. Features entire cast. Screenplay, Nick Niciphor, Jeffrey O'Kelly, Alexandro Jodorowsky, based on novel, "Poo Lorn Of The Elephants," by Reginald Campbell; camera (Technicolor), Jean-Jacques Flori; music original theme, Jean-Claude Petit; additional music, Guy Skornik; editor, Jean-Philippe Berger; art direction, Philip King; sound, Raymond Adam; second unit director, Peter Ferguson' assistant directors, Francois Mimet, Serge Menard, Eric Rochat Jr., Vijay Talwar, Jimmy Kacy. Reviewed at the Century Plaza Theatre, L.A., Mar. 20, 1980. (No MPAA Rating.) Running time: **119 MINS.**
Elise . . . . Cyrielle Clair
John Morrison . . . . Anton Diffring
Greyson . . . . Serge Merlin
Richard Cairn . . . . . Christopher Mitchum
Shakley . . . . Michel Peyrelon
The Maharajah . . . . Sukumar Anhana
Deepak . . . . B. Chandrasherkhra
Elise, 5 years old . . . . Oriole Henry
The Reverend . . . . Andy Jenny
The Maharand . . . . Krake
Tusk . . . . Tusk the Elephant

(English soundtrack)

This elephant is a two-ton turkey.

Grandiose, pretentiously simple, tonally inconsistent and with the narrative spine of a mollusk, "Tusk" sets out to be a family epic with mystical overtones, but falls in an artistic no-man's-land. Film will confuse children and frustrate devoted members of the Alexandro Jodorowsky cult, so turgid b.o. looms.

Rousing potential of a good, old-fashioned colonial days elephant adventure is undercut by Jodorowsky's apparent desire to fashion a different sort of film, one devoted to nonsensical digressions and misguided surrealism.

Based upon a reportedly straightforward novel describing the parallel lives of a British girl in turn-of-the-century India and an exceptional bull elephant, tale here retains some small promise as long as director concentrates on his tableaux of elephants working and making their way around the plantation. Rather remarkable opening shot, showing the beasts being rounded up and then heading out in line, lasts a full five minutes, but persistent overuse of arcing crane shots, clearly meant to convey a tour de force effect, ultimately proves wearying.

Lack of directorial control comes clear once characters open their mouths. Lines themselves are virtually unspeakable, and problem is compounded by an international cast whose thespian approaches are as varied as their origins. On past evidence, Anton Diffring and Christopher Mitchum can act, but they must have been told by Jodorowsky to forget everyting they knew. As Diffring's grown-up daughter, Cyrielle Clair is clearly in need of guidance to lift her out of her play-acting. But rock bottom is hit by Serge Merlin, Michel Peyrelon and Andy Jenny as two buffoonish traders and a cleric, all of whom appear to be dropouts from the Three Stooges school of performing. Satiric caricature is one thing, slobbering lampooning quite another, and Jodorowsky indulges them as if delivering the inside scoop on colonial degeneracy.

Pic has an impressive physical aspect, with striking locations, colorful natural sets and a hyped-up stereo soundtrack in service of a varied score and loud trumpetings of the elephants.

But woeful incoherence of the storytelling is tacitly acknowledged in the final credits, in which Jeffrey O'Kelly is noted for his adaptation, Nick Niciphor is cited for his rewrite, and Jodorowsky is credited for "final screenplay."

Jodorowsky's admitted mentor is Luis Bunuel, but the student has ignored the master's most elemental rule of basing his flights of fancy on solid ground. There's no escaping that "Tusk" is a botched job.
—Cart.

Demon Pond
(Yashaga Ike)
(JAPANESE-COLOR)

Hollywood, Feb. 15.

A Shochiku Co. Ltd. production. Produced by Kanji Nakagawa, Shigemi Sugisaki, Yukio Tomizawa. Directed by Masahiro Shinoda. Features entire cast. Screenplay, Haruhiko Minura, Takeshi Tamura, based on a story by Kyoka Izumi; camera (color), Masao Kosugi, Noritaka Sakamoto; editors, Zen Ikeda, Sachiko Yamachi; music, Isao Tomita. Reviewed at the Fox Little Theatre, L.A., Feb. 14, 1980. (No MPAA Rating.) Running time: **124 MINS.**
Yuri/Princess
Shirayuki . . . . Tamasaburo Bando
Akira Hagiwara . . . . Go Kato
Gakuen Yanasawa . . . Tsutomi Yamazaki
Priest Shikami . . . . Koji Nanbara
(English Subtitles)

Occasional great images and a self-evident ambitiousness provoke a continued extension of credit and patience throughout most of this exceedingly bizarre fantasy, but it ultimately goes unrewarded. Erratic, if always interesting, director Masahiro Shinoda here tries to mesh Kabuki style, supernatural legend, a little history and mega-special effects in a work more successful in its parts than as a coherent whole. Helmer's admirers will generally leave disappointed while any more general audiences would undoubtedly be mystified.

Set in 1913, tale has an explorer coming upon an old friend and his wife in a remote area of Japan. Pal takes the city dweller down to the demon pond, ghosts and monsters of which lie dormant as long as couple rings a magic bell.

Visit disturbs pond's inhabitants, as pic veers into wild fantasy. Once superstitions have been violated, nature unleashes its fury upon offending locals, sending a monumental tidal wave down upon the village. Clearly designed as a tour de force, sequence has its own power, but by this time all potential meaning has fallen by the wayside, and climax stands as an empty exercise in technique.

Most sustained point of interest is performance of famed kabuki actor Tamasaburo Bando who, harking back to tradition, plays both the wife and the demon princess. Even in close-up, Bando is entirely convincing as a woman, making it possible for the uninformed to watch entire film without realizing performer is a man. Go Kato is also commanding as the husband.
—Cart.

The Alien
(De Plaats van de Vreemdeling)
(DUTCH-DOCU-COLOR-16m)

Hollywood, March 7.

A Movies Filmproductions B.V. production. Directed by Rudolf van den Berg. Camera (color), Theo van de Sande; editor, Ton de Graaf; music, Louis Andriessen. Reviewed at the Century Plaza Theatre, L.A., March 6, '80. (No MPAA Rating). Running time: **89 MINS.**
(English Subtitles)

A strange, lethargic, rather out of focus documentary, "The Alien" begins by asking all the tough questions about what it means to be a Jew: is there a race, distinct identity, unique history and culture involved in being a member of the religion? How do the current politics of the Israeli state jibe with the ideals and needs of Jews around the world? Coming up with cogent answers is even tougher, which is something the film has trouble doing. Outlets for it are extremely limited, and American Jews, not to mention Zionists, are bound to be displeased.

Opening section asks the questions and presents a brief picture of the Jew as the eternal displaced person, oppressed in most societies historically and victims of the world's most horrendous holocaust only 40 years ago.

Once cameras move to the Holy Land, however, film's thesis goes astray, as a mixed bag of interviews with soldiers, inhabitants of the bleak West Bank and Golan Heights and Palestinians creates a Tower of Babel of politics which is virtually impossible to sort out, given the imprecise directorial strategy. Perhaps the confusion of the film accurately represents the dire state of Middle Eastern politics today, but film is not helpful in delineating the issues; serving more as a depressant than a stimulant to further thought.

A recurring dinner party among Jewish Dutch intellectuals articulates many sides of the issue, but concrete evidence on view in Israel just blurs it again. Film aspires to heavy meaning, but emerges as a hodgepodge of points of view, feebly assembled. —Cart.

Bells Of Autumn
(RUSSIAN-COLOR)

Hollywood, March 3.

A Sovexportfilm release of a Maxim Gorky Studios production. Directed by Vladimir Gorikker. Features entire cast. Screenplay, Alexander Volodin, based on the poem by Alexander Pushkin; camera (color), Lev Rogozin; musical mounting, A. Kogan; sound, A. Izbutsky. Reviewed at the 20th Century-Fox Studios, W. Los Angeles, March 2, 1980. No MPAA Rating. Running time: **77 MINS.**

Features: Irina, Alferova, Alexander Kirillov, Ludmilla Drebneva, Natalia Saiko.

(English Subtitles)

"Bells Of Autumn," translated as "Autumn Chimes" in on-screen titles, plays as a safe, respectful live-action version of Pushkin's "Tale Of The Dead Princess And The Seven Knights," better known as "Snow White And The Seven Dwarfs." Like a familiar ballet, material needs a new angle to bring it alive, but filmmakers add little but a slight charm. Interest for most audiences is therefore minimal.

Told virtually without dialog but with a fair amount of voiceover poetry, tale has an adolescent princess' evil stepmother banishing her from the rural tsardom on the eve of the young one's marriage to a dashing prince. Behind it all is the Tsarina's vanity, insulted by the famous mirror which informs her that the princess now outdoes her in the looks department, a claim which unfortunately is not supported by the casting. Tsarina is a real stunner.

Princess soon finds herself in the cabin of seven brotherly, hardly dwarf-like he-men who, along with the long-searching prince, ultimately save the day.

Vladimir Gorikker's direction strives for prettiness and old-world elegance, but is hampered by dark and somewhat grainy photography. Pic looks almost identical to the unfortunate U.S.-USSR co-production "The Blue Bird" of some years back and is not dissimilar in tone.

Amiable enough in parts, film still has difficulty sustaining undivided attention despite short running time. —*Cart.*

The Plumber
(AUSTRALIAN-16m-COLOR)

Hollywood, Feb. 26.

A South Australian Film Corp./Australian Film Commission/TCN production. Produced by Matt Carroll. Features entire cast. Directed, screenplay by Peter Weir. Camera (Colorfilm color), David Sanderson; editor, G. Tunney-Smith; music, Gerry Tolland; art direction, Ken James, Herbert Pinter; sound, Rod Pascoe. Reviewed at the American Film Institute, Beverly Hills, Feb. 26, 1980. (No MPAA Rating.) Running time: **76 MINS.**

Jill Cowper .... Judy Morris
Brian Cowper .... Robert Coleby
Max, the plumber .... Ivar Kants
Meg .... Candy Raymond
Department Head .... Henri Szeps

Ultimately emerging as a chilling study of the residual class structure in modern Australia, Peter Weir's "The Plumber" plays, for most of its running time, as a teasingly provocative cat-and-mouse tale which only occasionally steps beyond credulity.

Made on a tiny budget in three weeks for Australian television, short comic suspenser shows its limited means and is less visually lush than helmer's previous efforts, but represents further confirmation of his talent. Theatrical release prospects would appear limited to very specialized venues, but pic might fit into some U.S. tv formats.

A stinging indictment of the phony liberalism of young intellectuals, film features a simple premise: a swarthy, unsolicited plumber shows up at the apartment of a young university couple, claiming pipes have to be fixed. He ends up staying for days, dropping tidbits about how he's done time for rape, and generally making life increasingly impossible for the working wife.

Only cliche indulged is that of the distracted hubby who doesn't have time to help his wife through the crisis, while a more significant irritant lies in couple's not checking out the menacing plumber through his employment agency or the building manager. But, as John Ford said, if the Indians shot the horses pulling the stagecoach, the picture would end right there, and Weir's ends more than justify the somewhat contorted means.

Leading Australian helmer's first solo screenplay, like "The Last Wave," includes references to aboriginal mysticism, and also features a very funny disrupted dinner part among Third World scholars. To accommodate the tube, Weir uses close-ups more than usual, but timing and pitch of Judy Morris, Robert Coleby and Ivar Kants in the leads and of Candy Raymond as woman's best friend are precise and on target.

Despite the laughs and sense of dread, film is finally about the incompatibility of intellectuals and the working class, a 1960s ideal, ashes of which have been little discussed. It's a good, tart little picture. —*Cart.*

Where The Buffalo Roam
(COLOR)

Latest in 1960s nostalgia misses despite good show by Bill Murray.

Hollywood, April 1.

A Universal release. Produced, directed by Art Linson. Stars Peter Boyle, Bill Murray. Screenplay, John Kaye; camera (Technicolor), Tak Fujimoto; editor, Christopher Greenbury; music, Neil Young; production design, Richard Sawyer; set decoration, Barbara Krieger; costume supervision, Eddie Marks, Gilda Texter; sound, Peter Hliddal; assistant director, Gene Law. Reviewed at the Village Theatre, Los Angeles, March 29, 1980. (MPAA Rating: R). Running time: **96 MINS.**

Lazlo .... Peter Boyle
Hunter S. Thompson .... Bill Murray
Marty Lewis .... Bruno Kirby
Harris .... Rene Auberjonois
Judge Simpson .... R.G. Armstrong
Porter .... Danny Goldman
Rojas .... Rafael Campos
Desk Clerk .... Leonard Frey
SuperFan .... Leonard Gaines
Man .... De Wayne Jessie
Dooley .... Mark Metcalf
Billy Kramer .... Jon Matthews
Willins .... Joseph Ragno

"Where The Buffalo Roam" is the latest entry in what is fast becoming a mini-genre — late 1960s nostalgia. Based on the self-described antics of flip journalist Hunter S. Thompson, who cooperated as "executive consultant," pic features a number of amusing set-pieces of irreverent lunacy, but lack of serious substance to back up the strenuous facetiousness renders film too frivolous and detached from reality. Fascinating, highly-adept performance by Bill Murray is here to provide b.o. bait, although it has yet to be proved that today's audiences are anxious to look back at the domestic scene of 10 years ago.

A free-wheeling, somewhat fictionalized look at how Thompson, an outrageous personality and excellent journalist, came up with some of his more celebrated stories, film establishes its tone in the opening scene, as writer tries to finish a piece while downing full glasses of Wild Turkey and flailing about his Colorado cabin filled with oxygen tanks, a Nixon dummy and odd paraphernalia of all kinds.

Clad in Las Vegas-style shirts, cut-offs, sneakers, shades and omnipresent cigarette holder, Thompson is later seen making the rounds at a dope trial, a guerrilla gun-running effort, Super Bowl VI and finally on the 1972 campaign trail, scandalizing establishment types with his incessant boozing, pill-popping and rowdiness while running up huge bills and damages and making his "Blast" magazine editor sweat out deadlines.

Although a few snippets of Thompson's prose is heard voice-over, one misses hearing just what he made out of the chaotic events on view. Even more seriously, pic suffers by not giving writer any moral or intellectual code which could justify or explain his approach to life and work. Caustic, irreverent journalists have been a mainstay of the American tradition from Benjamin Franklin through Ben Hecht and H.L. Mencken, but there were always some principles backing up their attitudes. Only thing fortifying Thompson here are drink, drugs and the search for the insane in American culture.

Debuting director Art Linson attempts to make up for lack of narrative spine and intellectual core by emphasizing comedic aspects of his hero's adventures, but actual laughs are relatively few and far between.

Sole exceptional element is Murray's clearly studied but provocatively off-beat performance, which rings absolutely true despite complete absence of psychological underpinnings. His work is a triumph of the improvisational, Second City style of performing, all mannerisms, tics, subtle timing and low-keyed scene-stealing.

Peter Boyle is more conventionally outrageous as a radical attorney-turned-revolutionary, while remainder of the actors are in for little more than cameos. For the record, Richard M. Dixon appears in a classic men's room encounter between the presidential candidate and the intrepid reporter.

Tech credits are solid, with Neil Young's score consisting basically of an electronic variation on the old standard of the title. —*Cart.*

Spetters
(DUTCH-COLOR)

Amsterdam, March 17.

A Tuschinski Film Distribution release of a VSE production. Directed by Paul Verhoeven. Features entire cast. Produced by Joop Van den Ende. Written by Gerard Soeteman; camera (Eastmancolor), Jost Vacano; editor, Ineke Schenkkan; music, Ton Scherpenzeel & KAJAK; sound, Wim Wolf & Dieter Schwarz; art direction, Dick Schillemans; unit publicist, Gysbert Versluys. Reviewed at Tuschinski Theatre, Amsterdam, Holland, Feb. 29, 1980. Running time: **115 MINS.**

Rien .... Hans van Tongeren
Fientje .... Renee Soutendijk
Eef .... Toon Agterberg
Hans .... Maarten Spanjer
Maja .... Marianne Boyer
Angel .... Hugo Metsers
Docter .... Kitty Courbois
Witkamp .... Rutger Hauer
Henkhof .... Jeroen Krabbe

"Spetters" (meaning oil-spray, but also vaguely referring to an ejaculation) conforms to a well-tried Dutch recipe: as much sex as possible, without crossing into hardcore relieved with quick action so the audience never feels like a voyeur.

Director Paul Verhoeven and

screenwriter Gerard Soeteman used the formula in such successes as "Turkish Delight" (nominated at the time for a "best foreign feature" Oscar) and "Soldier of Orange" (released recently in the U.S.). In these earlier films they teamed with producer Rob Houwer, but with "Spetters," newcomer Joop Van den Ende took over production. The new team seems to have taken no sisk on this $1,700,000 feature. They pull all the tricks the formula allows.

Story is set in the outskirts of Rotterdam harbor and follows the fortunes of five youngsters with a common interest in sex and motorcycles.

There are some motorcycling scenes in the picture, but it is not really an issue. One of the boys meets with an accident and loses the use of his legs. Sexually incapacitated, he commits suicide by driving his wheel chair into the traffic on a highway.

A girl becomes a Jesus-adept after a very active sexlife. Another boy makes a living by beating up homosexuals, and blackmailing them. He becomes gay himself after he has been raped by a gang of four in one of the most effective scenes in this picture.

Another girl will sleep with almost anybody to advance her career in the fish-and-chips business (hence the title of the picture). She ends up happy ever after with the remaining of the five youngsters.

Director Verhoeven draws very strong performances from his youthful cast. Older actors on the other hand (like Rutger Hauer and Jeroen Krabbe) are disappointing in their small appearances.

Dramatic development in the story, characterizations and even the hard-fisted "action" are disappointments, too. Even though Verhoeven manages to insult several minority groups, he has however the blessing of the huge majority: they paid $2,000,000 at the boxoffice in the first three weeks of release in Holland — Vers.

When Time Ran Out
(COLOR)

A genre whose time has come and gone.

Hollywood, March 28.

Warner Bros. release of an Irwin Allen Production. Produced by Irwin Allen. Directed by James Goldstone. Stars Paul Newman, Jacqueline Bisset, William Holden. Screenplay, Carl Foreman, Stirling Silliphant based on the novel "The Day The World Ended" by Gordon Thomas and Max Morgan Witts, camera (Technicolor), Fred J. Koenekamp; editor, Edward Biery, Freeman A. Davies; production design, Philip M Jeffries; music, Lalo Schifrin; special photographic effects, L.B. Abbott; art direction, Russell C. Menzer; costumes, Paul Zastup-

nevich; set decoration, Stuart Reiss; assistant director, L. Andrew Stone. Reviewed at the Fox Theatre, Hollywood, March 28, 1960. (MPAA Rating: PG.) Running time, 121 MINS.

Hank Anderson	Paul Newman
Kay Kirby	Jacqueline Bisset
Shelby Gilmore	William Holden
Brian	Edward Albert
Francis Fendly	Red Buttons
Iolani	Barbara Carrera
Rose Valdez	Valentina Cortesa
Nikki	Veronica Hamel
Tiny Baker	Alex Karras
Rene Valdez	Burgess Meredith
Tom Conti	Ernest Borgnine
Bob Spangler	James Franciscus
Webster	John Considine
Mona	Sheila Allen
Sam	Pat Morita

The only description for "When Time Ran Out..." is that it is the latest in that well-known genre of pictures — the Irwin Allen disaster film. The man who brought the public "Towering Inferno," "Poseidon Adventure," "The Swarm" and even "Beyond The Poseidon Adventure" has once again gathered some heavy boxoffice names, thrown them into seemingly hopeless peril and dared them to get out alive. Given the public's ever increasing resistance to these kinds of offerings, pic's stay at theatres should be relatively brief.

This time the gift from Allen's bottomless bag of disasters is a luxury resort island's gurgling volcano, acting up after years of dormancy. As usual, opinion is split among the cast as to whether to prepare for the worst and try to leave the surroundings or ignore the goings-on and stay where they are. Most choose the latter, supporting the notin that there is a decided lack of common sense in the world.

Among those with some smarts is oil driller Paul Newman, who leads a troupe of people to a high spot of the island that offers the best hope for safety. His party includes love interest Jacqueline Bisset, William Holden, owner of the island's posh digs, island native Edward Albert, Burgess Meredith and Valentina Cortesa as a romantic elderly couple, and Red Buttons and Ernest Borgnine as a supposed swindler and the detective who is after him.

The gang's jaunt through the island once the real peril starts provides several terrifying elements, but nothing out of the ordinary for fans of the genre. As a matter of fact, all seem to be replays of disasters.

James Franciscus is somewhat effective in portraying the villain who refuses to give into impending doom (there's always one in every crowd) and appropriately both he and his mistress Barbara Carrera get their just desserts in the end.

James Goldstone has directed in the genre style and Carl Foreman and Stirling Silliphant scripted from the novel "The Day The World Ended," (the original title for the

film) with many of the catch phrases.

Edward Biery and Freeman A. Davies seem to have edited much of the character development out of the script in favor of the action, a not-so-costly decision since few of the pic's fans will expect or want to know the inner workings of any individuals presented anyway. Fred J. Koenekamp's photography is adequate but L.B. Abbott's special effects photographics are unimaginative.

"When Time Ran Out..." has several of the unintentional jokes characteristic to most disaster pix and a handful of semi-scary scenes. But it basically stands as a poor imitation of a type of picture that Allen was much more astute at producing some years ago. —Berg.

Lille Virgil og Orla Froesnapper
(Little Virgil and Frogeater Orla)
(DANISH-COLOR)

Copenhagen, March 27.

A Metronome Film production and release, based on Ole Lund Kirkegaard's childrens' books. Written by Hans Hansen, Gert Fredholm, Peter Hoimark. Directed by Gert Fredholm. Features entire cast. Camera (Eastmancolor) Jeppe Jeppesen; editor, Anker; production design and special effects; Peter Hoimark; costumes, Jette Trmann; music, Peter Bastian, Anders Koppel; lyrics, Benny Andersen. Reviewed at the Palads, Copenhagen, March 27, 1980. Running time, 90 MINS.

Virgil	Bror Bodtker-Naess
Oskar	Christian Honore
Frogeater Orla	Allan Olsen
Sille	Ktinka Bodtker-Naess
Blacksmith	Karl Stegger
Madam Madsen	Elin Reimer
Vagabond-Clown	Jesper Klein
Mr. Strong	Claus Nissen
Grocery-manager	Gotha Andersen
Mrs. Oskar	Inger Hovmand
Mr. Oskar	Peter Schroeder

There is no moralistic point at all to the late Orla Lund Kirkegaard's baroque, even mildly absurd childrens' books about "Little Virgil and Frogeater Orla," a seven-year-old village boy and his teenager bully plus other children and adults around them in a never-never fairy tale world.

Danish parents have been guffawing loudly while reading these books aloud to their younger offspring. Same guffawing is sure to be heard in theatres showing Gert Fredholm s feature version of the fun, which is sure to mark the beginning of a new family film series.

Episodes concerning the children's continuous frustration of the bully-boy's schemes and otherwise their happy negligence of all adult behaviour standards are told in rapidly moving sequences, some of which hit their target with pre-

cision, others tend to vanish in thin air.

Production designer Peter Hoimark has created such animals as a cock, a duck, a dog and a dragon, all of them very openly mechanical, all of them also very funny. Child actors as well as adult professional thesps seem to be having a glorious time.

This is the first feature from Bent Fabricius-Bjerre's newly-established Metronome Films. Company is already tuned to make a "Little Virgil" sequel. Production values are handsome. Voice-over narration would be needed for foreign sales which would probably reach tv screens in episodic series format rather than the regular theatre circuit. —Kell.

Tom Horn
(COLOR)

McQueen blows it.

Hollywood, March 26.

A Warner Bros. release of a First Artists picture, produced by Fred Weintraub. Exec producer, Steve McQueen. Directed by William Wiard. Stars McQueen. Screenplay, Thomas McGuane, Bud Shrake, based on "Life of Tom Horn, Government Scout and Interpreter" by Horn, camera (Technicolor), John Alonzo; editor, George Grenville; sound, Jerry Jost, Joe Kite; art direction, Ron Hobbs; assistant director, Cliff Coleman; costumes, Luster Bayless; set decoration, Rick Simpson; music, Ernest Gold. Reviewed at The Burbank Studios, Burbank, March 26, 1980. (MPAA rating: R.) Running time: 98 MINS.

Tom Horn	Steve McQueen
John Coble	Richard Farnsworth
Glendolene Kimmel	Linda Evans
Joe Belle	Billy Green Bush
Sam Creedmore	Slim Pickens

Steve McQueen's "Tom Horn" is a sorry ending to the once high hopes of the star-studded founding of First Artists Prods. And if it turns out there's any money in this picture at the boxoffice, then McQueen's name is the magic draw that's worth the millions he demands up front. Still, you can't fool all the people all the time and this one, combined with his previous FAP flop "Enemy Of The People," may bring the price down.

If rumor be true, McQueen did not want to do "Horn" as his third pic to fulfill his founder's commitment, but was forced into it. True or not, he certainly looks like he's walking through the part and the picture as a whole is such a technical embarrassment, the rest of the credits must have walked with him.

Imagine a film that opens up with dialog that can't be heard at all, then proceeds to build up to a fist-fight that's never seen, that cuts away to sunsets to fill in other scenes that have no dramatic point, that presents a mean where the sounds of knives and forks drowns.

out what's being said, and you have just the beginning of what's wrong with "Tom Horn."

It's the kind of picture where the exhibition of craftsmanship is so poor, it's impossible to place blame. For example, the editing is terrible, but editor George Grenville is a man of many fine credits. Is it possible he could slip so far or did he just not have the shots to work with? If so, maybe he's a hero for doing anything with the mess at all. In any case, it's his name that's finally on the film.

The director of record — one William Wiard — is largely unknown and may remain so since the press book accompanying the release doesn't even mention him in the section called "about the film-makers" and no bio is included in the package. So if the whole thing is his fault, he may have a chance to change names and start over.

Pic takes up in the final days of the life of the legendary Western hero, as he's hired by cattleman to hunt down and kill rustlers. And the only plus at all is a couple of good, bloody shoot-out sequences.

McQueen's costars are largely wasted in flat dialog and Linda Evans is probably to be pitied for what's done to her in a confusing series of romantic flashbacks. Among them all, only Slim Pickens gets a good chance to act in his role of a sheriff sympathetic to Mc-Queen after he's framed and facing the hangman's noose.

Among the most ridiculous plot developments, McQueen manages to escape the heavily guarded jail and make his way through town past several horses. But does he get on one and ride away? No, he runs on foot into the desert until he's captured again.

Into the desert, indeed. —*Har.*

Silver Dream Racer
(BRITISH-COLOR)

Action on two wheels with medium legs.

London, March 25.
Rank Film Distributors release of a David Wickes production. Produced by Rene Dupont. Directed by David Wickes. Stars David Essex, Cristina Raines, Beau Bridges. Screenplay, Wickes; camera (color), Paul Beeson; editor, Peter Hollywood; music, Essex; musical direction, John Cameron; art director, Malcolm Middleton; sound, John Mitchell; costumes, Judy Moorcroft; asst. director, Ken Baker. Reviewed at the Dominion Theatre, London, March 24, 1980. (BBFC Rating: AA). Running time: 111 MINS.
Nick Freeman ....David Essex
Bruce McBride ....Beau Bridges
Julie Prince ....Cristina Raines
Cider Jones...............Clarke Peters
Wiggins ....Harry H. Corbett
Tina ....Diane Keen
Jack Freeman............Lee Montague
Carol ....Sheila White
Ben Mendoza ....David Baxt

Al Peters ....Ed Bishop
Jack Davis ....Nick Brimble
Clarke Nichols ....Stephen Hoye
Bank Manager ...........T.P. McKenna
Journalist ....Richard Parmentier
Benson ....Patrick Ryecart

It's about motorcycle racing. Fully-financed by the Rank Organization, it's set in Britain, but made with uppermost determination to reach an international audience. Two out of the pic's three topliners are American, production trimmings are uppercase, and there are just enough thrills to commend it as okay drivein and hardtop fare in most markets.

Prospects could have been brighter yet, but for one glaring omission. Among all the biking footage in a yarn about a "revolutionary" prototype which challenges and, natch, licks all world championship comers, there's not one memorable shot of the machine in action.

That's a big pity, as the model — a genuine prototype built by Britisher Barry Hart — will certainly whet the appetites of two-wheel fans. But the film's action sequences prove generally disappointing. Editor Peter Hollywood clearly worked hard to develop pace and tension, but the material delivered him by director David Wickes and cinematographer Paul Beeson remains uninspired, however briskly cut together. Apart from some rider's point-of-view shots (nicely stomach-churning) and standard closeups (encased in wraparound helmets, the faces don't reveal much), the racetrack scenes could almost have been photographed by a news camera crew.

Plot is routine, but no worse than many, and the acting does favors for the dialog. Popstar David Essex evidences once again he can sustain a characterization: he's a natural as the ingenuous-looking Cockney fellow who can turn on a sneer when needed. Per the story, he inherits the dream-bike from his brother, another motorcycle freak who's been building it at home under wraps, but who's killed before he can put it through its paces.

Conventional as they are, the stresses surrounding Essex's decision to go for the 500 c.c. trophy — his girlfriend leaves him, he quits his job, he stands to forfeit the bike to his financier if he loses — are less contrived than the "tragic twist" ending, which involves him inexplicably in a fatal crash just after passing the chequered flag. Lack of clarity in the direction may be part of the problem there, as it is at other points in the film where the action becomes disconcertingly confused.

Beau Bridges is fine as the loud-mouthed American Goliath against whom David pits his derided British

mount. Bridges is reputed to fight dirty on the track, but the camera never quite shows how. Cristina Raines does the best she can with a role that's fraught with inconsistent motivations.

A number of local names turn in well-judged performances in small parts. Diane Keen, an established tv comedienne, shows she's excellent casting against type as Essex's grieving sister-in-law; and Lee Montague, as his father, does little but conveys plenty in one of the film's most successful scenes.

Essex penned and sang some numbers for the soundtrack, and arranger John Cameron's additional music lends much-needed lustre to the action. The tiein album should be a saleable package. —*Simo.*

Ma Cherie
(My Dearest)
(FRANCO-BELGIAN-COLOR)

Paris, March 20.
A Films Moliere release of a Films Moliere-Challenge Productions-Pierre Films (Brussels) co-production. Produced by Tony Moliere. Stars Marie-Christine Barrault. Directed by Charlotte Dubreuil. Written by Dubreuil, Judith Goldblath and Edouard Luntz; camera (Eastmancolor). Gilbert Duhalde; music, Jean-Pierre Mas; song "Ma Cherie" written and sung by Anne Sylvestre; editor, Michele Maquet; sound, Alix Comte. Reviewed at the Marignan-Concorde Theatre, Paris, March 15, 1980. Running time: 90 MINS.
Jeanne ....Marie-Christine Barrault
Sarah .... Beatrice Bruno

"Ma Cherie," an intimate study in mother-daughter harmonics and discord, is a tender, bittersweet and eminently likeable little film that could find a limited but real public in foreign markets. Director Charlotte Dubreuil, who has made a previous feature and coauthored scripts with Claude Goretta and Bertrand Tavernier, wrote the first draft of this film with her teenage daughter. The resultant dialectical scripting, underlined by clear-eyed direction, helps give the film its quiet ring of modest truths.

The plotless action opens with Jeanne, an independent, divorced woman in her mid-30's, taking her 16-year-old daughter to the doctor in order to prepare her for the use of birth-control pills (even though no prospective boyfriends are yet in sight). It ends some months later as the young girl gets ready to leave her mother's apartment to live with some girlfriends.

In-between these two moments one sees the gradual dissolution of their old order of things, based of course on profound love but also on a sometimes thorny mutual interdependence of a middle-class household devoid of male presence.

What Dubreuil represents on-

screen is an almost exclusively female world. We never see Jeanne's ex-husband, with whom she maintains contact, or her current boyfriend, with whom she has a casual sexual relationship. Only male to get screen time is the appealing younger man with whom Jeanne enjoys a tender but unpassionate affair while her daughter is away on vacation. The daughter's sexual initiation is non-reprepresented and unstressed, suggesting her healthy assumption of her sexuality.

Marie-Christine Barrault sensitively projects the difficulties of a woman and mother trying to keep her balance on shifting grounds. Beatrice Bruno is charming and vivacious as the daughter. The whole is framed in Gilbert Duhalde's mellow color photography and there is a lovely end-title song by Anne Sylvestre. —*Len.*

Sweet William
(BRITISH-COLOR)

London, March 24.
A Kendon Films production. Executive producer, Don Boyd. Produced by Jeremy Watt. Directed by Claude Whatham. Stars Sam Waterston, Jenny Agutter. Screenplay, Beryl Bainbridge, from her novel; camera (color), Les Young; editor, Peter Coulson; production designer, Eileen Diss; sound, Simon Okin; asst. director, Gino Marotta. Reviewed at the Bijou screening room, London, March 24, '80. (BBFC Rating: AA). Running time: 92 MINS.
William ....Sam Waterston
Ann ....Jenny Agutter
Edna ....Anna Massey
Pamela ....Geraldine James
Mrs. Walton ....Daphne Oxenford
Mrs. Kershaw ....Rachel Bell
Vicar ....David Wood
Gerald ....'........Tim Pigott-Smith
Daisy ....Emma Bakhle
Actress ....Sara Clee

As a low key, soft centred sex comedy with almost no visible sex, though plenty implied, "Sweet William" should appeal to a middle of the road audience of widish age range, with women the obvious promotion target. Given a carefully-pitched, sophisticatedly teasing ad campaign, plus magazine editorial hype of its best asset, Sam Waterston, the Don Boyd production could look to steady prospects in medium-capacity situations.

Nice, ordinary English girl Jenny Agutter meets wild, romantic Scots divorcee Waterston when her regular live-in man is called away to the U.S. on earnest academic business. Sadly for her — though the tone is never more than just slightly bitter-sweet — his romantic nature includes having a wildly on-off relationship with the truth. He's a wolf with two not-so-ex-wives, and a compulsion to bed down her friends, neighbors and anything else he sees move. But he gets away with it because he never doffs his sheep's clothing.

Transparent as that is to her, she's still smiling when he leaves her literally holding the baby. But she has one last laugh when she realizes it's not Waterston, but the departed stalwart, who's the father.

Adapted from her own novel by British authoress Beryl Bainbridge, whose taste for female sexual irony has won her a cult following, the screenplay is diligent without being distinguished. The same goes for Claude Whatham's direction, which tends to prefer lingering realism to dramatic pace, and thus to set up apparent significance where there is none.

Even more tantalizing, some clearly significant pointers are not followed up, as in the character of Agutter's hen-pecked father. Comedian Arthur Lowe's virtually wordless cameo begs fascinating questions about the suffocation of middleclass life, but he's gone before they're answered. Nonetheless, the Christmastide Agutter spends in a joyless seaside town with Lowe and her mother (Daphne Oxenford's portrayal is a contrasting caricature) remains one of the film's most resonant sequences.

Agutter is well cast, and good in that her seduction by the outlandish Waterston is entirely believable. He scores commendably in a role about which the script reveals little beyond what's seen through her eyes. His Scottish accent is better than many attempts by non-Scots on either side of the Atlantic, and carries the bonus of being intelligible.

Of the other supports, Anna Massey is standout as one of the waiting wives — a very English lady, her upper lip stiff with age-conscious makeup.

Cinematographer Les Young has generally lit the principals well despite the rigors of location interiors, and designer Eilenn Diss displays a fine eye for the trappings of London apartment life. The score is easy-listening chamber music, an upmarket touch which avoids sentimentality.—*Simo.*

Inferno
(ITALIAN-COLOR)

Rome, March 25.
A 20th Century-Fox release. Produced by Claudio Argento for Produzioni Intersound. Features entire cast. Written and directed by Dario Argento. Camera (Technicolor), Romano Albani; art director, Giuseppe Bassan; editor, Franco Fraticelli; music, Keith Emerson. Reviewed at Triomphe Cinema, Rome, Mar. 24, 1980. Running time: 107 MINS.
Rose Elliot .... Irene Miracle
Mark Elliot .... Leigh McCloskey
Sara .... Eleonora Giorgi

Countess Elise .... Daria Nicolodi
Also: Alida Valli.

A lavish, no holds barred witch story whose lack of both logic and technical skill are submerged in the sheer energy of the telling. Cult following of the Grand Guignol assures b.o. on these shores where helmer Dario Argento is horror king, with possible export success to violence and gore markets, plus maybe the midnight circuit.

Freely cribbing classics from "Rosemary's Baby" to "Fall of the House of Usher," "Inferno" synthesizes the most violent and spectacular elements of Gothic horror unfettered by concern with realism or coherence in plot (outrageously entangled, it is never sorted out even in the end). Sets exude a high baroque fantasy, characters are flatter than pancakes (unaided by actors' even flatter performances) and all is driven forward by Keith Emerson's pounding rock track.

Story links lovely young heroines Irene Miracle in New York and Eleonora Giorgi in Rome through the curse of the "Threz Mothers," whose discovery will lead them on Nancy Drew-like searches through haunted places and grisly deaths at the hand of a black-gloved assassin.
New York by an interrupted phone call, will be left to piece together the mystery of his sister's disappearance with the help of an ailing Countess and the hindrance of a host of sinister villains. When all the good characters are dead the script begins to kill off the bad ones, giving viewer the satisfaction of seeing the crippled bookseller eaten by rats and Alida Valli plunge in flames from a fifth-floor window. Pic ends in an apocalyptic holocaust that resolutely refuses to answer even the most fundamental questions posed in the preceding hour and a half, which is disappointing.

Argento's unmistakable technical style has a unique kind of cheap vulgarity that borrows heavily from Hollywood classics like Hitchcock, maximizing viewers' emotions through identification and point of view shots, and directing every minute of screen time to getting an "effect." It fails mainly because it lacks restraint in setting up the terrifying moment, using close-ups and fancy camera angles gratuitously with no relevance to the story. It is also full of clumsy shots that cannot be edited together. The blazing, red-tinted Technicolor photography seems quite successful, on the other hand, in rendering an atmosphere of plush Hollywood horror.

With all its technical errors (and with a plot so contrived audiences burst out laughing), "Inferno" is a fast-paced and entertaining film. Argento, a relatively young director who has made his reputation in only 10 years of filming, needs some decent scriptwriters and he will be well worth watching. —*Yung.*

Eleftherios Venizelos
1910-1927
(GREEK-COLOR)

Athens, March 9.
A Yannis Horn and Greek Film Centre production. Directed and written by Pantelis Voulgaris. Features entire cast. Camera (color), George Arvanitis; music by Loukianos Kelaedonis; sets and costumes, Dionyssis Fotopoulos; editing, Takis Yannopoulos. Reviewed at the Palace Cinema, Athens, March 6, 1980. Running time: 150 MINS.
Cast: Menas Christides, Yannis Voglis, Dimitris Myrat, Manos Katrakis, Olga Karlatos, Anna Kalouta.

This is reportedly the most ambitious and expensive Greek pic ever made, directed by Pantelis Voulgaris, one of the best helmers of the New Greek Cinema. Based on his own screenplay, Voulgaris scores again with this pic, which renders a part of the life of Eleftherios Venizelos, a great Greek stateman who lived and governed the country during one of the most important periods in Greece's history.

To those with an intimation of the man, the times and their historical aspects, the pic is not an efficient portrayal of the stateman, though the general public ignored this and the pic is a boxoffice winner.

The film depicts the political situation in Greece during the first decade of this country. The Army liaison, realizing that the royal court and the political parties were not concerned with the country's fate but were absorbed rather with their intrigues and their political interests, asked Cretan leader and politician Venizelos to come to Athens and take over. As Prime Minister Venizelos led the country into victorious Balkan wars, greatly extending its boundaries. Soon he became the idol of the Greek People, later daring to take a strong stand against the king's friendly feelings for Germany (Queen Sophia being a daughter of the Kaiser), foreseeing that Greece's interests were with the Allies. Through his leadership he won great benefits for his country after World War I, but his oppostion to the Court resulted in his losing the election. He left the country to his successors, who led it to many misfortunes, the consequences of which were borne by the Greek people until recently.
The flaw in this film lies in the screenplay, which does not include important episodes in Venizelos' life

and policy, which would complete the image of the man and enrich the pic with more dramatic tension. But Voulgaris claims that he did not make an historical film but a pic based on a part of the life of a great man. And he made it very well. Despite his insistence on rhetorical heroism and too many interior scenes, he depicts the turmoil that swept the country during that period well when his hero ruled and sturggled dreaming of a "great Greece." Excellently photographed by Greek cameraman George Arvanitis, the film is a delight for the eye.

Menas Christides, as Venizelos, effectively carries most of the pic's impact. His portrayal, however, lacks the passion and spirit of the famous stateman and leader.

Also worthy of mention are the performances of Dimitris Myrat as King George I, Yannis Voglis as the Crown Prince and later, King Constantine I, Manis Katrakis as an old Cretan fighter, of Anna Kalouta as a stage actress.

Film is effectively scored by Loukianos Kelaedonis and the sets and costumes by Dionyssis Fotopoulos excellently evoke the period adding to the pic's assets.

All other technical credits are top rate.—*Rena.*

Im Herzen Des Hurrican
(In the Heart of the Hurricane)
(WEST GERMAN-COLOR)

West Berlin, Feb. 8.
A Hamburger Kino Kompanie Hark Bohm Film Production, Hamburg; producer, Natalia Bowakow, in coproduction with Zweites Deutsches Fernsehen (ZDF), Mainz; world rights, Filmverlag der Autoren, Munich. Directed by Hark Bohm. Features entire cast. Screenplay, Bohm, in collaboration with Gerhard Kelling; camera (color), Jaroslav Kucera; sets, Heidi and Toni Luedi; music, Irmin Schmidt; editing, Susanne Paschen. Reviewed at CCC-Screening Room, West Berlin, Feb. 8, '80. Running time: 103 MINS.
Christopher Schidrosky ...... Uwe Bohm
Indian .... Dschingis Bowakow
Abigail .... Brigitte Strohbauer
Batseba .... Jelka Bouvy
Micha .... Verich von Bork
Father .... Marquard Bohm
Walter .... Dieter Thomas
Sylvia .... Hendrieke von Sydow

Hark Bohm's "family pix" have been regular boxoffice winners in Germany throughout the '70s, while several self-centered "author" helmers can't pull a week's run outside the large cities with budgets twice as large. Bohm, in the past, has made children and youth pix — "Chetan, the Indian Boy" (1972), "North Sea Is Death Sea" (1975), and "Moritz, Dear Moritz" (1977) — with his two adopted sons, Uwe and Chengis (the latter of Mongolian, or "Indian," blood), until the boys grew into young manhood for their fourth adventure-film together.

"In the Heart of the Hurricane" also stars an elk, a full-grown, majestic beast theoretically driven from his natural habitat in the far North down to West Germany by some fictional environmental malfunction. Since elks stay close to water, the Schleswig-Holstein province north of Hamburg keeps the story at the beginning within the realm of reality — but as the animal moves continually southwards, to the Kassel area and finally to the Frankfurt airport region, his presence supplies a metaphor on our times.

Two lads, Christopher and "Indian," are in pursuit of the elk, the former with a gun and the latter with a camera, both intent on "shooting" the animal. Chris is an unruly teenager, whose anger at not finding acceptance as a natural-born mechanic is taken out by shooting deer illegally, and then selling the meat to greedy customers for a few bucks. Our mysterious Indian, described as a "disco-freak," prefers living with nature rather than ordinary people, thus another kind of dropout from society with respect for living things.

Two Hamburg youths on a lark is enough to keep the story going, but Bohm this time has added more — a sardonic view of West German society that, in the end, places the pursuers in the role of the hunted, the same situation as the elk lost in strange country. It is the twists in the story that make for entertainment and several hearty laughs along the way.

First, Christopher, as an illegal poacher with a gun he constructed himself, is fired upon by officious hunters stalking the same deer from a game-tower, is badly wounded in the side, and attracts a police investigation while recovering in a hospital. Upon running away, he is commissioned by his trophy-hungry benefactor to find and kill the elk on the loose, and so he sets out on the hunt — pursued by the police who have his faked motorcycle license plates on file. Later, he and Indian have it out when the elk is located, Christopher losing, but then the pair join hands as trouble surfaces — in the form of a Jesus Cult, bent on duping youths into signing away their freedom and possessions by simply inviting them to a religious repast and then chloroforming them.

Equally dangerous for the duo is holing up with a garage co-op of left wingers after they have discovered that the elk has happened on a watering-hole poisoned by a nearby chemical plant, which is killing cattle in the area. The police have picked up the elk in a van to transport him elsewhere, which allows for the side-adventure — this time, a police raid on the garage co-op in Frankfurt, apparently in suspicion of the newcomers belonging to a terrorist organization. The result is a shoot-first-and-ask-questions-later situation, like in a typical Western or gangster pic. Bohm, however, is also hinting that recent legal protection for trigger-happy public guardians is suspect, to say the least.

A must for the summer fest circuit, although lacking professional polish and dialogue to score on its own. —Holl.

Emperor Chien Lung And The Beauty
(HONG KONG-COLOR)

Hong Kong, March 1.
A Run Run Shaw Production. Produced by Mona Fong. Written and directed by Li Han-hsiang. Camera (color), Lin Chiao; editor, Chiang Hsing-lung; musical director, Eddie Wang; martial arts instructor, Tang Chia, Huang Pei-chi. Reviewed at Pearl Theatre, Hong Kong, March 1, 1980. Running Time: 120 MINS.
Emperor Chien Lung .... Liu Ying
Li Po-erh .... Hui Ying-hung
Lady Three .... Pan Ping-chang
Liu Yung .... Li Kung
Mrs. Wan .... Liu Hui-Ling
Ng Yung-An .... Chiang Nan

(Mandarin soundtrack-English subtitles)

The continuation of Li Han-hsiang's series on the adventures and times of Emperor Chien Lung in his 21st year of reign, circa 1756. Last year's effort was "The Voyage of Emperor Chien Lung." Light-hearted in concept, the film beautifully recreates the colorful period of the Emperor's rule with amusing sidelights on his eating, loving, gambling, personal habits and informal visits to unprincely places.

The Emperor (Liu Yung) travels incognito with his two devoted ministers, the fussy Lord Ngo (Chiang Nan) and smug scholar Liu Ying (Li Kun).

Director Li is renowned for his carefully researched costumed extravaganzas ("Empress Dowager," "The Last Tempest") and scholarly historical epics. Emperor Chien Lung's latest adventure is in the same high quality even when burdened with trivia.

In this one, The Emperor gets involved with a famous courtesan in Soochow called Lady Three (Pan Ping-Chang), helps out the victims of an earthquake and rights the wrongs in a shady gambling den. Liu Ying as Emperor Chien Lung is both arresting and charming in his portrayal of a very human Emperor. The production and technical aspects are all in the high tasteful level. It is definitely one of the better ones from the Shaw studios who now alternate between stale kung fu and sordid sexpics. Foreigners with the help of subtitles can savour many of the light renderings of Chinese history with fictional paddings and amusing Chinese humour of subdued quality.

Properly promoted and re-hashed with cultural adaptation in mind the film can make it in select art houses and college circuit as it reflects on the visual splendour of a lost era, from cuisine, brothels, dens, clothes and other points of interest to amuse addicts of things Asian, Chinese or Hong Kong.

—Mel.

Baranski
(WEST GERMAN-B&W-16m)

Berlin, Feb. 24.
A Munich Film & TV Academy Production. Features entire cast. Directed by Werner Masten. Screenplay, Klaus Eichhammer, Masten, Michael Breining; camera (black and white), Eichhammer; sets, Andrea Oechsner; music, Breining. Reviewed at Berlin Film Fest (German Series), Feb. 24, '80. Running time: 68 MINS.
Cast: Jan Groth (Baranski), Nikolaus Pichler (Niki Zellner), Rick Schulz (Herr Zellner), Thussy Marini (Frau Zellner), Wolf Ackva (von Gretzbach) Edgar Wenzel (House Superintendent), Werner Masten (Taxi Driver), Mark Pouliv (Sieber), Jadwiga Czerwinska (Polish Woman), Albert Sandner (Customer).

Well-meaning diploma pic by Munich Film Academy student, Werner Masten's "Baranski" conjures up the the ghosts of the Auschwitz past in this tale of a former concentration camp victim meeting his tormentor whom he long considered dead. The gentle Baranski, meanwhile, makes friends with a boy in the apartment building he occupies, although he's still looked upon as dirt by the Germans in the city. In the end, he dies after a hit-and-run accident, and thus goes as mysteriously as he came.

Jan Groth as Baranski keeps pic moving over rough spots quite smoothly. —Holl.

L'Homme A Tout Faire
(FRENCH CANADIAN-COLOR)

Montreal, April 1.
Produced by Corporation Image Ltee, with financial participation of the Canadian Film Development Corporation and l'Institut Quebecois du cinema. Rene Malo, producer. Micheline Lanctot, director. Features entire cast. Screenplay, Lanctot; camera (color), Andre Gagnon; art direction, Normand Sarazin; editor, Annik de Bellefeuille; music, Francois Lanctot. Reviewed at the Parisien cinema, Montreal, March 25, 1980. Running time: 99 MINS.
Armand .... Jocelyn Berube
Therese .... Andree Pelletier
Cocul'oeil .... Paul Dion
Bernard .... Gilles Renaud
Georges ....:..... Marcel Sabourin

Very little happens in this gentle film, the directorial debut of Quebec actress Micheline Lanctot, but it leaves a pleasant aftertaste.

The story is about a passive, gentle handyman from the Gaspe who moves to Montreal after his 10-month-old marriage breaks up. Besides being abandoned by his wife and her two young sons, Armand (Jocelyn Berube) is rejected by a high school nymphet after a short affair, and then falls in love with a middle-class housewife who fills her empty days with renovation projects on the basement.

Therese, the wife, played to fine, nervous perfection by Andree Pelletier, turns to Armand out of boredom and confusion, but ends up staying with her brutish, irritable husband. Aside from frustrated romances, Armand's world is populated by a hustling, no-account friend named Cocul'oeil, played with wonderful crassness by Paul Dion, and a wistful homosexual chauffeur who rents a room in Armand's apartment. Georges, played by the well-known Quebec actor Marcel Sabourin, spends his evenings swilling Orange Nehis and gazing longingly at Armand.

The film is slow, especially before the affair with Therese. The lead-up to every action is too attenuated, and plot connections are not always as clear as one could wish. Over-all, however, it has a smooth, professional feel; the shooting is fine, the acting firstrate, and there are several delightful scenes.

The picture as a whole belongs to Berube. He plays the part with sweetness and vulnerability.

Original music by Francois Lanctot, the director's brother, is witty and effective, but a coy theme song by Quebecois folk-hero Gilles Vignault over Armand shuffling along a riverbank almost ruins the ending. Fortunately, the film carries on after this faux pas, and ends on a freeze-frame of a cop about to rescue Armand from a bridge girder, where he's fallen asleep after a broken-hearted night with a case of beer.

This is regional filmmaking, and certainly closer to portraying a national identity than any of the pseudo-American thrillers and horror films winning Canadian film awards. The Quebecois accents are very strong, however, and the film would probably have to be dubbed or at least partially sub-titled for distribution even in France, which limits its market. Still, French and even English audiences could do worse than spending an evening with a gentle, unpretentious film like this. —Dres.

Il Ladrone
(The Good Thief)
(FRENCH-ITALIAN-COLOR)

Rome, March 14.

An Italian International Film release, produced by Fulvio Lucisano for Daimo Cinematografica (Rome) — Italian International Film (Rome) — Carthago Film (Paris) with the collaboration of RAI television. Stars Enrico Montesano, Edwige Fenech, Bernadette Lafont. Directed by Pasquale Festa Campanile. Screenplay; Pasquale Festa Campanile, Renato Ghiotto, Ottavio Jemma, Stefano Ubezio, from a novel by Festa Campanile; camera (Telecolor), Giancarlo Ferrando; art director, Enrico Fiorentini; editor, Alberto Galletti; music, Ennio Morricone. Reviewed at Europa Cinema, Rome, March 12, 1980. Running time: **98 MINS.**

Caleb . . . . Enrico Montesano
Deborah . . . . Edwige Fenech
Apula . . . . Bernadette Lafont
Roman soldier . . . . Enzo Robutti

Prolific helmer Pasquale Festa Campanile tosses off his fourth and highest grossing pic of '79 in this religio-comic crowd pleaser. The sex and laughs makes for a product probably too home-grown for easy export beyond France and Italy, where its stars are well known b.o. movers.

With the idea of following the public life of Christ through the eyes of a roguish Palestinian hustler who ends up himself on the adjoining cross, "Good Thief" adroitly lifts the flashiest Bible bits (starting with all the miracles and including some excellent lines of dialog) and unblinkingly turns them into pointless Italian comedy. In trying to have it both ways "Thief" muffs what could have been either a wicked National Lampoon spoof or a genuinely pious tale, settling for the commercially certain middle ground.

Edwige Fenech, a national version of Raquel Welch, has such unsinkable charm as a prostitute Jesus cures of leprosy that her limited acting range matters not at all. Popular light comedian Enrico Montesano gives a predictably ingratiating performance as the doe-eyed, good-hearted thief, while the mischievously appealing Bernadette Lafont hasn't much of a role to work with.

Both actresses are all-but-completely exposed as frequently as possible, which is probably no small factor in pic's popularity; Jesus is shot at a respectful distance and infrequently. To some eyes pic offer grazes sacrilege and though local audience seemed to take this in stride, "Thief" would need a lot of editing for more sensitive offshore eyes.

Gorgeous location work in Tunisia and exotic sets don't hurt; editing is as routine as the script.
— *Yung.*

5 + 5
(ISRAEL-COLOR)

Tel Aviv, March 16.

A Shapira Films release of a Roll Films Production. Produced by Yair Pradelsky, Israel Ringel. Directed by Shmuel Imberman. Features entire cast. Screenplay, Avi Koren, Shmuel Imberman, from play by Aharon Megged; executive producer: Asher Gat; camera (color), Nissim (Nitcho) Leon; editor: Tova Neeman; costumes, Sarah Wiener; music: Benny Nagari; lyrics, Avi Koren; choreography, Yaakov Kalusky. Reviewed in Tel Aviv, March 16, 1980. Running time: **89 MINS.**

Cast: Soldiers: Dalik Wollinitz, Menahem Eyni, Eli Gorenstein, Yoni Chen, Mati Seri, Avi Dor; Girls: Liron Nirgad, Gilat Ankori, Maya Rotschild, Shula Chen, Shlomit Rieger, Lilach Glicksman; Villagers: Zaharira Harifai, Gideon Singer, Yaakov Bodo, Rachel Attas, Shmuel Wolf, Haim Polani; Officers: Moshe Timor, Yoel Libe.

Going back to origins may be a good idea, in a period of crisis when new subjects, if available, aren't always a safe commercial bet. This was probably the idea behind Roll Films' decision to revive an old stage warhorse.

Basically, a light musical play written for an Army Entertainment Group, it has been, with different music and lyrics, updated to serve the purposes of 1980 audience. The flimsy story has remained more or less the same, a group of soldiers visits a village, meets the girls and there and the ensuing romance is laced with jokes about life on the farm, and a lightweight conflict between generations.

All this is strung together more or less in a kind of vaudeville style, slight dialogs serving mainly to push story from one song to the next one, the whole thing being intended mostly as popular entertainment without any additional levels. For many years, this was the accepted official style of the variety ensembles entertained by the army which used to be enormously popular with the civilian public as well. Since the Army decided last year to put a stop to this activity, the film is probably intended first of all for that public.

While it may not meet American standards, musically or choreographically, and it falls short of a full-fledged musical, both in the combination of story and music and the direction of the dance numbers, it relies mostly on the charm of a young cast, and the basic premise that hte Israeli public, thirsts for escapist entertainment. Judging by the first days of release, the premise proves correct, if measured by public response.

Entire film has been shot on location, in a real village, not far from Tel Aviv and quality of production shows that more than usual effort has been made in order to avoid the modest looks of films produced by an industry suffering from a perenial lack of funds. — *Edna.*

La Citta' Delle Donne
(City of Women)
(ITALIAN-FRENCH-COLOR)

Rome, March 27.

A Gaumont release produced by Renzo Rossellini for Opera Film-Gaumont S.A. Stars Marcello Mastroianni, Anna Prucnal, Bernice Stegers, Donatella Damiani, Iole Silvani, Ettore Manni. Directed by Federico Fellini. Screenplay, Federico Fellini, Bernardino Zapponi, with collaboration of Brunello Rondi; camera, (Eastman) Giuseppe Rotunno; art director, Dante Ferretti; editor, Ruggero Mastroianni; music, Luis Bacalov; costumes, Gabriella Pescucci. Reviewed at Fono Roma, Roma, March 27, 1980. Running time: **140 MINS.**

Snaporaz . . . . Marcello Mastroianni
Wife . . . . Anna Prucnal
Lady On Train . . . . Bernice Stegers
Ingenue . . . . Donatella Damiani
Motorcyclist . . . . Iole Silvani
Dr. Katzone . . . . Ettore Manni

Federico Fellini's psychadelic trip into the bowels of womanhood is another visual tour-de-force in an elaborate dream framework — narrative-thin, overlength and finally, overweight. "City Of Women" will rally Fellini fans and Marcello Mastroianni fans at home and abroad though a problematic entry for general U.S. marketing beyond the foreign pic circuits — depending on size of Gaumont investment in promotion and launch.

With Mastroianni as his bait and Ettore Manni as Mastroianni's alter ego, Fellini tries to cover all terrain on the subject of woman today — from fringe feminists to generic husband-wife ruptures. Filtering through Fellini's surreal probe is the filmmaker's vision of man as a legendary hunter of the opposite sex. By instinct, human nature or whatever, man is sexually aggressive and woman his prey.

Today, however, the legendary hunt has become mobile warfare between the sexes as outraged womanhood bands together in countless sects and cults, all pyramiding into a power movement for liberation or outright assault.

In the big early episode showing Mastroianni trapped at a feminist convention, the filmmaker not only illustrates the countless attitudes within the pyramid movement — too many and too long — but accents the threatened male faced with ominous challenge to his historic sport as a conquistador and his irrepressive dream to become the perfect macho.

Equally overlong is a subsequent segment dealing with pothappy, rock-happy female adolescents — a subculture threat to Mastroianni as emblem of the male species. Katzone (Ettore Manni) offers refuge in a villa, constructed inch by inch for sexual pleasure. Fellini takes us slowly down the mausoleum corridor — filled with midnight sounds of ecstatic orgasms once seconded by Mastroianni's host. Lengthy sequence, highlighted by a revel to celebrate Katzone's 10,000th conquest, ends with an eruption by female militia to tear the big deed and big dream apart.

After a brief reunion with his estranged wife (Anna Prucnal), to recap past disenchantment, Fellini sends Mastroianni down the steepest bend on a spectacular loop-the-loop in easy stages as both go back in time to childhood and juve recollections of the road to puberty and beyond.

At the end of the ride is a trap door to Mastroianni's trial before a feminist tribunal — giving him one more futile chance at the ingenue turning up at odd moments in the film. Futile, as he is shot down by a sweet young terrorist. Final fall is the bad dream's end but abrupt return to finale normalcy, Fellini predicts, will only be a realistic repeat of the dream cycle.

Perhaps the weakness of Fellini's latest film is his failure to integrate theme and spectacle. "City of Women" is highly spectacular though some of the fantasy is stamped with motifs original in his previous pix. The theme of women's lib has been chewed and rechewed at such length in the past decade that all of Fellini's noncommittal situations and discussion related to it do not seem to engender a bond between screen and spectator.

Tempered editorially to around two hours, (from 140 mins.) "City of Women" could eliminate weighty lags and favor both spectacle and the assortment of down to earth erotica to strengthen appeal for the average as well as the discriminate filmgoer.

Editing would also heighten the impact of the technically creative contribution by lenser Giuseppe Rotunno, production designer Dante Ferretti and costume designer Gabriella Pescucci. Luis Bacalov, who replaced the late Nino Rota at the start of production, composed the score only partially in his own vein and generally followed the Rota pattern Fellini wanted — though the dream structure of "City" offered far greater opportunities for Bacalov's talent.

Mastroianni plays himself from beginning to end and the impersonation is almost flawless — perhaps too much of a good thing in sequences running past the appointed splice. The late Ettore Manni (he died midway through production) proved he was good casting as champ fornicator of all times. Fellini's choice of Bernice Stegers as a feminist with bitter memories and an unflinching pro-

gram, is a happy one. So is his nod to Anna Prucnal, the spirited Polish actress playing Mastroianni's ex-wife who wanted only communion and a fulfilling relationship.

"City of Women" is Fellini at his best, but also Fellini satisfying all his whims — some excessive or pointless. A long, static medium closeup of a big nude backside looked like a Fellini travesty of Lina Wertmuller imitating Fellini. Overall, his creative input is admirable. Refashioning it with appropriate discards and tightened sequences could make a big difference in foreign markets. —Werb.

Fernand
(FRENCH-COLOR)

Paris, March 3.
A UGC release of a Films Arquebuse-C.A.A. Maison de la Culture de la Seine Saint-Denis co-production. Produced by Rene Feret, Michelle Plaa. Directed by Feret. Features entire cast. Written by Feret, Christian Drillaud, Robert Guediguian; camera (color) Gilberto Azevedo; sound, Alix Comte; art direction, Juan Carlos Conti; costumes, Hilton McConico, music, Michel Coeuriot; editor, Christiane Lack. Reviewed at Club 13, Paris, Feb. 22, 1980. Running time: 90 MINS.
Fernand .... Bernard Bloch
Nina .... Jany Gastaldi
Mickey .... Yves Reynaud
Marguerite .... Dominique Arden
Romeo .... Roland Amstutz

Rene Feret, whose last film, "La Communion Solenelle," an evocative cinematic family album, represented France at the 1977 Cannes fest, comes a cropper with this pale black comedy about a hapless clod, fresh out of prison, who wants to go straight. He succeeds in falling into the hands of only twisted, dishonest and brutal associates. After being gulled, deceived and physically maimed he finds refuge in a police paddy wagon.

The film's tragic-comic mechanism never meshes. The actors, recruited from the theatre, are competent, but cannot build anything on the vacuity of their scenario, which deliberately deploys a string of cliches without giving a new dimension. —Len.

Deutscher Fruehling
(German Spring)
(AUSTRIAN-W. GERMAN-SWISS-COLOR-16m)

Austrian Institute screening of an ORF (Austrian Broadcasting Corp.) production. Features entire cast. Directed by Dieter Berner. Screenplay, Peter Turrini, Wilhelm Pevny, Dieter Berner; camera (color) Michael Ballhaus; editor, Erika Geiger; art director, Herta Fischinger-Hareiter, Fritz Hollergschwandtner; sound, Rolf Schmidt-Gentner, Kurt Schwarz; asst. director, Burgl Mattuschka, Markus Heltschl; music, Peer

Raben. Reviewed at Rizzoli Screening Room, N.Y., April 4, 1980. Running time: 105 MINS.
Maria Hubert .... Elisabeth Stepanek
Hubert .... Manfred Lukas-Luderer
Michael Hubert .... Karl Kroepfl
Hans Huber .... Bernd Spitzer
Herr Goldstein .... Hans Thimin
His daughter .... Paola Loew

Despite the title, "Deutscher Fruehling" (German Spring) has no connection with the pretty postcard "heimat" films which the Austrians turn out by the dozens. The film, which deals with Hitler's invasion of Austria in the spring of 1938, is the fifth segment of a television series, "Alpensaga," made by the Austrian television in collaboration with West German and Swiss tv. The entire series covers the first half of the 20th century in Austrian history.

Unremittingly outspoken this segment deals with the general capitulation and the scanty resistance of the Austrian people towards the German conquerors. Perhaps due to their Germanic background they'd be more expected to embrace the German onslaught than their Slavic neighbors. The film deals with a family of Austrian farmers, the daughter engaged to a local boy who is eager to become a Nazi. Her brother is a resister and is arrested. Most of the drama in the film deals with her trying to locate him and becoming slowly aware of the political changes. At the end she returns to the farm, the brother is shipped to Dachau and the fiance has switched to a more amenable fraulein.

Like some of the new German filmmakers, director Dieter Berner makes no apologies for his countrymen. As a result, much of the usual outside audience sympathy is lost. Perhaps the film would have more impact on American audiences had they had the opportunity to see other segments of the series. Technically, the film is excellent. Michael Ballhaus's color camerawork is like a poster in its lovely capturing of the Austrian countryside. For a change, an Austrian film does not include Vienna or Salzburg and there isn't a Vienna choirboy in earshot. But it's still a stunning country. —Robe.

Rising Sun
(HONG KONG-DOCU-B&W)

Hong Kong, March 2.
An Edwin Kong production. released by Edko Enterprises-Joey Kong. No producer or writer with credits. Written and edited by Edwin Kong; music selected by Kong. No other credits provided. Reviewed at Pathe Preview Theatre, International Bldg., Hong Kong, March 1, 1980. Running time: 100 MINS.

The surprise hit of the year is a black-and-white documentary on

the rise and fall of Japanese militarism, 1920-1945. Assembled by Edwin Kong, (son of Hong Kong film distrib Joey) in collaboration with an L.A.-based film partner. This well-done war picture begins with the end and ends with the beginning ... the bombing of Hiroshima. So far, "Rising Sun" showing in 10 theatres has garnered HK$7 million and is still strong at B.O. in four houses.

Kong's picture powerfully moves the emotions and immensely deepens one's understanding of how the Japanese got trapped in endless conflicts that brought about their campaign to conquer Asia through military aggression. The superbly paced sequences or rare and authentic footage are arranged in chronological, neat, and easy to follow fashion and is a main asset. Other technical plus points include slick editing, informative but not boring script and the appropriate "stock" soundtrack music.

The title though is misleading for it only implies the rise but not the downfall of the Japanese empire. The Chinese translation of the title is more appropriate — The Tragedy of War. The first part of "Rising Sun" details Japan's invasion of China's major cities, while the second half is the arrival and eventual participation of the Allied Forces.

Kong plans to distribute the film throughout Southeast Asia with possibly some cultural adaptation and highlight the prime interest of the various territories. There are still immense footage that could be utilized for a follow-up venture when necessary.

The sequences are unbelievably clear but the show's weakest segment is the bombing of Pearl Harbour. The English sound track version will be released later and will surely draw another wave of viewers. "Rising Sun's" selling byline is — A War Picture unfolding the horror and tragedy of the war. Though its budget is miniscule, this unpretentious local production will surely overpower the biggies now showing — "1941," "Apocalypse Now."

The Kong family plans to set a series of screenings in Cannes this May. —Mel.

Pi Hua Kad
(The Headless Ghost)
(THAI-COLOR)

Bangkok, March 28.
A Sri Syarm Productions release. Produced by Sathit Klongvesa. Directed by Vichit Usahajitr. Features entire cast. Story, Thawee Wisanukorn; screenplay, Songpet Senibodin; camera (color), Sophon Jaenphanit; music & sound, S. Klongvesa. Reviewed at Athens Theatre, Bangkok, March 28, '80. Running time: 100 MINS.

Keow .... Sorapong Chatri
Nampon .... Vasana Sittivej
Adjan Koi .... Lor Tok
Loy .... Setta Sirachaiya
Bua .... Ruangnapha Kromkom
Moh Pi .... Promain Sibunruang

Horror pix are very much in vogue here, with quite a number of imports as well as local products in this genre turning out to be sleepers and smash hits.

Thai filmmakers have been experimenting with the horror comedy genre. Add a bit more gore and a large dose of fantasy, and the result is the current big hit "Pi Hua Kad" (Headless Ghost), with Sorapong Chatri in the title role.

Sorapong has never played a ghost before, and cast as a headless one to boot, he's a powerful b.o. draw. Children double up with laughter even in violent scenes. The absence of film ratings here lets children of all ages see the film.

The special effects were done in Tokyo, and they cost money. It was worth it. Pic is what's known locally as "nang talat" (for the local market). The beheaded victim (Sorapong) returns from the dead to execute in turn all those responsible for his cruel fate. What viewers enjoy most is that fact that Sorapong's head and the rest of his body go about their separate ways scaring both Sorapong's enemies and friends, before the head attaches itself back to the body for the final confrontation between Sorapong and his killers. —*Cano.*

El Qanas
(The Sniper)
(IRAQI-COLOR)

Baghdad, March 18.
An Iraqi Film Production. Baghdad; world rights. State Establishment for Cinema & Theatre, Baghdad. Features entire cast. Written and directed by Faisal Alyassiry. Camera (color). Abdul-Lateef Salin. Shakeeb Rasheed; music, Talib El-Qaraghooli; editor, Irena El-Adhadh; production, Ramadhan Katie Mozan; production manager, Dhia El-Baiaty. Reviewed at Baghdad Film Festival, March 18. '80. Running time: 88 MINS.
Cast: Roge Assaf. Amal Aufaish, Sami Oaftan. Gazwah El-Khalidi, Sulaman El-Basha. Muhshin El-Azawi, Hassan Dahmesh, Oasim El-Mallak, Hani Hani, Nizar Qabbani.

"The Sniper" is Faisal Alyassiry's third Iraqi feature, following "The Head" (1977) and "The River" (1978), and it's the best pic to emerge from this new film producing land since Mohammed Shoukry Jamil's "Thirst" (1971) — although that statement should be qualified by pointing out that only seven Iraqi features have been produced to date and most of them deal with sociopolitical and historical events not easily known to the Westerner.

This is the story of a day in contemporary Beirut. It's about a nationalist fanatic, a Christian Lebanese, who joins a Rightist Group, goes on maneuvres on weekends with other armed citizens, and cleans his rifle every day waiting for action because it's his "duty." His sister berates him for pointing the rifle at everything in the house, including herself, when he should be out doing something useful.

The sniper, getting jittery, takes to the Beirut roofs in areas where the "enemy" lives. He first zeroes in on a couple with child at a window, misses his target, and then wanders the streets to haunt cafes and size up the situation at close hand. In short, he's a bit loco.

It's when he visits a girl friend with the gun wrapped in a tennis bag that the worst takes place. While the girl is preparing a meal, he prepares the rifle and takes to the balcony — she catches him and bawls him out, but "duty" allows him to sneak back to the balcony at the first opportunity, pick out a new victim, and shoot and kill a defenseless man who stopped at a kiosk to buy a book for a little girl.

The little girl, in a flashback, is shown to be an earlier victim of the Beirut skirmishes, who lost her parents and was taken by a sympathetic doctor, who is now shot by the fanatic. After the police and ambulance arrive to take care of the bleeding man on the sidewalk, the bystanders who have taken cover leave their holes — and the kiosk owner deftly takes the victim's car keys left on his counter, gets in, and simply drives away on a lark of his own. The sniper, meanwhile, has a spat with the girl friend, and that's the end of that, too.

Pic is impressive because of its timely portrait of a city constantly under seige from snipers on the roofs and would-be vigilantes. It has extra docu value due to its filming in Beirut.

What "The Sniper" lacks, however, is the psychological depth such theme demands, and the story loses on motivation as soon as the sniper himself (well played by Roge Assaf) is out of the picture. The ending is left in the air as well.

Pic should find its way to an international fest on the circuit, and is a must for Iraqi Film Weeks. Credits and thesps are a good cut above the average in Arab lands. —*Holl.*

Don't Answer The Phone
(COLOR)

Another psycho killer. For those who fancy strangling themes.

Hollywood, April 11.
A Crown International Pictures release of a Scorpion production. Produced, screenplay by Robert Hammer, Michael Castle. Directed by Robert Hammer. Features entire cast. Executive producer, Michael Towers; camera (Metrocolor), James Carter; editor, Joseph Fineman; music, Byron Allred; art direction, Kathy Cahill; sound, Jan Brodin; assistant director, David Osterhout. Reviewed at the Paramount Theatre, Hollywood, April 11, 1980. (MPAA Rating: R.) Running time: 94 MINS.
Chris McCabe ..... James Westmoreland
Dr. Lindsay Gale .... Flo Gerrish
Hatcher .... Ben Frank
Kirk Smith .... Nicholas Worth
Adkins .... Stan Haze
John Feldon .... Gary Allen
Sue Eilen .... Pamela Bryant

Psycho killer in this one is saddled with just about every cliched affliction in the book — he's a tormented Catholic who's into leather and chains, a Vietnam vet with scars on the brain, and a narcissist bodybuilder who compensates for his inability to relate to women by strangling them. Trouble is, audience knows all this after five minutes, so opportunities for suspense and character development are thrown out the window. "Don't Answer The Phone" has already opened briskly in several major markets, and Crown International's strong sell should continue the pattern throughout the spring.

Derivative in virtually every respect, pic seesaws between series of killings by self-styled he-man Nicholas Worth and perfunctory police work by detectives James Westmoreland and Ben Frank. Although cops comment extensively on gruesomeness of the crimes, murders as shown are relatively tame by today's standards.

By default, only point of interest and amusement is Worth's outrageous performance as the maniac. Changing personality every 10 seconds, actor obviously relishes stewing in character's completely poisonous juices and manages to enliven the otherwise monotonous proceedings whenever he's on screen.

Shot as "The Hollywood Strangler" and clearly inspired by L.A.'s recent crime wave, pic, which has nothing to do with its present title, at least has a memorable final line. After Westmoreland, who comes off as the new Jack Palance, blows Worth away, he watches the beefy body sinking slowly in a swimming pool and mutters, "Adios, creep." —*Cart.*

La Campanada
(Leaving It All)
(SPANISH-COLOR)

Madrid, April 2.
A Jose Frade production. Directed by Jaime Camino. Features entire cast. Screenplay, Roman Gubern, Jaime Camino; camera (Eastmancolor) Jose Luis Alcaine; editor, Teresa Alcocer. Reviewed at Cine Paz, April 1, 1980. Running time: 102 MINS.
Cast: Juan Luis Gallardo, Fiorella Faltoyano, Ovidi Montllor, Jose Maria Forn, Martin Galindo, Felix Moix, Luis Iriondo, Fermin Reixach, Jose Maria Loperena, Maria Asquerino.

Jaime Camino, who has helmed such firstrate pix as "A Winter in Mallorca" and "The Long Vacations of '36," now turns his attention to a subject often treated in cinema: the besieged, middle-aged ad executive who has clambered up the ladder of "success" only to find that the "top" is suffocating and stultifying and seeks to break with job, wife and children.

Unfortunately, Camino doesn't add anything to this classic dilemma and after letting his exec sock a traffic cop as his exasperation with modern life bubbles over in a monumental traffic jam, scripters don't seem to know where to go from there. Exec gets bailed out of the clink, befriends a bank robber, invites him to his house, but nothing conclusive ever happens as the exec wrangles with his wife and the family situation.

Despite a few touches of would-be humor, "La Campanada" drags along its wordy way, aimlessly wandering from bedroom scenes to an almost mock suicide intent, leaving the pic pretty much where it began.

Though direction is okay, script is weak and often maudlin. The only bright part of the pedestrian shenanigans comes when Ovidi Montllor as the bank robber makes his too-brief appearances on screen, giving the whole film a temporary lift. Rest of pic drifts along lackadaisically. Commercial outlook is poor. —*Besa.*

Death Ship
(CANADIAN-COLOR)

Awful but entertaining.

Hollywood, April 10.
Avco Embassy release of an Astral Bellevue-Pathe-Bloodstar production. Produced by Derek Gibson, Harold Greenberg. Directed by Alvin Rakoff. Features entire cast. Exec producer, Sandy Howard. Screenplay, John Robins; camera (CFI), Rene Verzier; editor, Mike Campbell; art directors, Chris Burke, Michel Proulx; special effects, Mike Albrechtsen; sound, Henri Blondeau; assistant director, Charles Braive. Reviewed at FCI Screening Room 3, Hollywood, April 10,

1980. (MPAA Rating: R.) Running time: **91 MINS.**
Ashland .... George Kennedy
Trevor Marshall .... Richard Crenna
Nick .... Nick Mancuso
Margaret Marshall ..... Sally Ann Howes
Sylvia .... Kate Reid
Lori .... Victoria Burgoyne
Robin .... Jennifer McKinney
Ben .... Danny Higham
Jackie .... Saul Rubinek

"Death Ship" is a contrived, un-inspired bit of filmmaking with one redeeming feature — it has enough unintentional chuckles to keep audiences entertained almost throughout its 91 minutes. So un-likely and absurd are the situations in John Robins' screenplay about a ship set on killing its inhabitants that at times it's difficult not to be perversely intrigued with what could possibly occur to top the pre-ceding event. That should parti-cularly amuse some thriller fans and account for some decent b.o. activity in initial weeks, particu-larly on outdoor screens.

Beginning action sets up nine crew and passengers of a luxury liner that soon explodes after collid-ing with a mysterious vessel. Mira-culously, the next shot has eight of them safely floating on a lifeboat with the ninth, particularly strange and insidious ship captain George Kennedy, surfacing near the boat after an extended stay underwater.

The gang is peacefully drifting when all of a sudden Richard Cren-na, a seaman who was supposed to replace Kennedy on the luxury ves-sel, deftly spots a gigantic black ship that happens to be floating by. Although the color should have been a sure tip-off of evil, they all get on board mistakenly thinking they've been rescued.

The killer boat wastes no time in systematically trying to murder each of the nine passengers, who probably make some of the most in-ane strategic mistakes of any set of characters in any disaster-type pic-ture. Crenna and wife Sally Ann Howes leave their children to sleep alone in a room after numerous in-stances of the ship's wrath, Kate Reid is hungry and eats some 40-year-old candy that causes her to break out in indescribably disgust-ing sores, and no one seems at all concerned about the incessant evil look in Kennedy's eye throughout the film.

Alvin Rakoff moves the feature along but he's left enough loose ends in the action to disturb even the most spaced-out filmgoer. The ac-tors do what they can with what they've been given but their char-acters' stupidity easily sways audience sympathy to the ship, which seems almost fair since it is the real star of the picture anyway.
—*Berg.*

Yesterday
(CANADIAN-COLOR)

Montreal, March 19.
A Cinepix release of a Dal Productions film. Directed by Larry Kent. Produced by John Dunning and Andre Link. Features entire cast. Screenplay, Bill Lamond, John Dunning, from an original idea of Dun-ning; a.d. Don Buchsbaum, art direction, Roy Forge Smith, camera (color) Rich-ard Ciupka, sound, Patrick Rousseau; editor Debra Karen. Reviewed at a pri-vate screening, Montreal, March 19, 1980. Running time: **97 MINS.**
Gabrielle Daneault .... Claire Pimpare
Matt Kramer .... Vince Van Patten
Bart Kramer .... Eddie Albert
Tony .... Nicholas Campbell
Claude Daneault .... Daniel Gadouas
M. Daneault .... Jacques Godin
Prof. Saunders .... Gerald Parkes

This maudlin and predictable soap opera about love between a handsome American student and a French-Canadian girl doesn't leave a dry eye in the house. Produced by the makers of "Meatballs," it has something for everyone except ser-ious filmgoers.

The story, which moves along at a quick pace once the scene is set, involves a radical arts student from a working-class home in the French East End of Montreal. She meets a rich American studying at McGill whose father was killed in World War II. The drama revolves around whether or not he should go to fight in Vietnam. He eventually does. But not before a good dose of Animal House antics, tentative and adoles-cent love scenes, a separatist bombing accident involving her brother, and a parading of all the prejudices which such a scenario offers (French-English, Protest-ant-Catholic, Canadian-Ameri-can, convervative vs. liberal, etc.)

As he leaves for war, she realizes she is pregnant, a fact which she keeps from him. Promises of marriage don't materialize, and when she finally learns of his death, she puts her life on hold and raises her baby, reconciled once again with her family.

But it doesn't end here. Years later, a chance visit to his home town and to his family reveals that he is not dead but just terribly maimed. Fade in to the hospital, the reunion ... and happiness forever after, presumably.

The film is weak on many levels that it is a miracle it works at all. But work it did with preview audi-ences, thanks mainly to the strength of the Quebecois actors — Claire Pimpare in the lead and Jac-ques Godin as her father — who pull the film through when the dramatic scenes count.

Cloris Leachman and Eddie Albert play the American family, and deliver good performances. Direction is by Larry Kent who has made other low budget films for producers Andre Link and John Dunning. Dunning originated the idea for the story. —*Tads.*

Breaker Morant
(AUSTRALIAN-COLOR)

Sydney, April 17.
A South Australian Film Corporation presentation. Producer, Matt Carroll. Di-rector, Bruce Beresford. Stars Edward Woodward, Jack Thompson. Screenplay, Beresford, Jonathon Hardy, David Stev-ens, based on a play by Kenneth Ross; camera (Eastmancolor, Panavision), Don McAlpine; sound, Gary Wilkins; editing, William Anderson; prod. manager, Pamela Vanneck; asst. director, Mark Edgerton; art direction, David Copping; costume design, Anna Senior; special ef-fects, Monty Fieguth, Chris Murray; music, Phil Cunneen; stunts, Heath Har-ris, Tony Smart. Previewed at the Road-show Theatrette Sydney, Jan. 24, '80. (Commonwealth censorship rating NRC). Running Time: **106 MINS.**
Lt. Harry Morant .... Edward Woodward
Major J. F. Thomas ..... Jack Thompson
Captain Alfred Taylor .... John Waters
Lt. Peter Handcock .... Bryan Brown
Major Charles Bolton ...... Rod Mullinar
Lt. George Witton ..... Lewis Fitz-Gerald
Lt. Col. Denny .... Charles Tingwell
Captain Simon Hunt .... Terence Donovan
Col. Ian Hamilton .... Vincent Ball
Dr. Johnston .... Frank Wilson
Lord Kitchener .... Alan Cassell
Christiaan Botha .... Russell Kiefel
Mrs. Shiels .... Judy Dick
Mrs. Bristow .... Barbara West

Undeniably a handsome film, "Breaker Morant" also contains some of the best performances yet seen in Australian film.

Director Bruce Beresford has shaped a very 'talky' subject into an action picture with a serious com-ment upon the ways of men at war — and how they are used by their superiors. It is the story of a side is-sue in a backwater war, an infini-tesimal snag on the fabric of Em-pire.

Harry "The Breaker" Morant (Edward Woodward) was an Eng-lishman who went to Australia in the last century and got his nick-name from his way with wild horses. When Britain and the Boers squared off against each other in South Africa, he and a number of other Australians volunteered and were absorbed into the non-regu-lar army contingent. As the Boers refused to fight formally, and took to guerrilla tactics, the Australians began fighting on the Boers terms. A highly flexible and mobile militia developed quickly and Morant was a prime mover.

The nature of the war made pri-soner taking a difficult business logistically, and while the film in no way tries to justify the killing of them, it does make clear that the Establishment's blind-eye can be-come very quickly healed. And when it is politically expedient, in-deed, becomes positively 20-20 in hindsight.

As an example to others, Morant and two other Australians, Hand-cock (Bryan Brown) and Witton (Lewis Fitz-Gerald) were tried by court martial. Morant and Hand-cock were convicted and sentenced to death by firing-squad; Witton to a life sentence.

The execution sequence as handled by Beresford and the two actors is profoundly affecting. The writer-director has structured the film to have by then developed his two main protagonists and their story and brought all his various elements together. How Beresford then deals with them turns his audience into an unwitting jury; as a sheer exercise in manipulation, it approaches the masterful and is extremely effective.

As stated, the events are a forgotten episode in an obscure conflict, but what emerges are the characters, and these emerge powerfully due in great part to the strength of the performances. Standout are Woodward, Jack Thompson's bewildered and frustrated defense attorney and Rod Mullinar's straight-backed, by the book prosecutor.

Tech credits are excellent with Don McAlpine's cinematography particularly fine. Commercial prospects at home are contingent on snagging the Aussie psyche; after that, timing and word of mouth should do their work. Down under it will be a most talked about film. Elsewhere, despite the fact that it is clearly a prestige piece, marketing may not be easy.

—*Miha.*

Foolin' Around
(COLOR)

Innocuous recycling of classic romantic farces is spring filler.

Hollywood, April 9.
A Columbia Pictures release. Produced by Arnold Kopelson. Directed by Richard T. Heffron. Stars Gary Busey, Annette O'Toole. Screenplay, Mike Kane, David Swift, based on a story by Swift; camera (DeLuxe color), Philip Lathrop; editor, Peter Zinner; music, Charles Bernstein' production design, Fernando Carrere; set decoration, Darrell Silvera; costume design, Joe Tompkins; sound, Michael Evje; associate producer, Deborah Castle; assistant director, Craig Huston. Reviewed at the Burban Studios, Burbank, April 9, 1980. (MPAA Rating: PG.) Running time: 101 MINS.
Wes .... Gary Busey
Susan .... Annette O'Toole
Whitley .... John Calvin
Daggett .... Eddie Albert
Samantha .... Cloris Leachman
Peddicord .... Tony Randall
Clay .... Michael Talbott
Aunt Eunice .... Shirley Kane
Bronski .... W.H. Macy
Rickie .... Beth Bosacker
Blue .... Roy Jenson
Paul .... Gene Lebell

"Foolin' Around" emerges from its rather lengthy stay on the shelf as an innocuous entry which sporadically evokes the madcap ro-

mantic farces of the 1930s. Thesps manage to convey some charm in the midst of increasingly hokey material, but it's strictly filler fare.

Pic is too irretrievably entrenched in conventions of the past to find its own footing in the present, as country bumpkin Gary Busey stumbles into the rarified world of WASP heiress Annette O'Toole and finally wins her with his goofy grin and unshakable persistance. Some modern films have successfully recycled old formulas, but this one offers up a little "It Happened One Night" here, some Harold Lloyd, Buster Keaton or Preston Sturges there, and even a touch from "The Graduate" in the finale, without ever accumulating much conviction of its own.

Busey and O'Toole invest their stock roles with as much energy as they can muster, but all the supporting parts are unbelievable throwbacks to standard Hollywood types, from John Calvin's lame-brained, impeccably attired fiance, to Eddie Albert's tycoon grandfather, who identifies more with working man Busey than with transparently ambitiious Calvin, to Cloris Leachman's status conscious, much-married society matron, and most of all to Tony Randall's seemingly straight-laced butler who's really a dirty old man under the tux.

David Swift was originally set to direct his own story and script, but idsputes led to a rewrite and entry of helmer Richard T. Heffron, who tries to keep things in high spirits but lets it all spin out of control in final, contrived reel.

Tech credits are adequate.

—*Cart.*

Kvindesind
(Inside Woman)
(DANISH-COLOR)

Copenhagen, April 1.
A Crone Film/Stig Bjoerkman in association with The Danish Film Institute (Esben Hoilund Carlsen) production. Obel Film ApS release. Features entire casts. Written and directed by Stig Bjoerkman. Camera (Eastmancolor) Dirk Bruel; production designer, Soeren Krag Soerensen; costumes, Nico; editor, Grete Moeldrup; music, Anne Linnet, Ralph Lundsten, Eric Satie; executive producer, Nina Crone. Reviewed at the Alexandra, Copenhagen, April 1, 1980. Running time, 75 MINS.
Lene .... Lotte Tarp
Steen .... Peter Schroeder
Michael .... George Bamford
Allan .... Kim Magnusson
Bente .... Ghita Noerby

Sweden's Stig Bjoerkman went to Denmark to once more prove his sensitivity as to portrayals of a woman's heart and soul. He has formerly impressed critics with such Swedish features as "The White Wall," and, to a lesser de-

gree, "Walk On Water If You Can."

Bjoerkman wrote and directed "Inside Woman" (no final English title has been decided upon yet) as a vehicle for Danish actress and former sex star Lotte Tarp. She makes the most of her role which has her up against a dilemma to be solved between dawn and night: She has long been wanting to try herself in a new life, but is running away with an American lover (George Bamford) at the cost of an emotionally dried-up life with child and cliche-patterned, mildly male chauvinist husband the right way of doing it?

New York's Bamford does not really work up to a threat to the woman's former mode of life. He may be solid, but he is also stolid. The husband (Peter Schroeder) is a likewise condescendingly described standard male, although better played. Director Bjoerkman's sympathy (and empathy) is so squarely with the woman that the film never gets a chance to tell anything new.

Production design and camerawork serves film's moods excellently. Flashbacks and a few inner visions are not used in so consistent a way as to nourish real interest.

At the end, the woman drives away alone through a winter landscape, leaving, literally, everybody and especially audiences behind. Beyond tv sales and the minor festival circuit, offshore exposure would appear unlikely. —*Kell.*

The Watcher In The Woods
(BRITISH-COLOR)

Bette Davis, at large again, and scary.

Buena Vista Distribution release of a Walt Disney Production. Produced by Ron Miller. Stars Bette Davis. Directed by John Hough. Screenplay, Brian Clemens, Harry Spalding, Rosemary Anne Sisson, based on Florence Engel Randall's novel, "A Watcher In The Woods"; camera (Technicolor), Alan Hume; co-producer, Tom Leetch; music, composed and conducted by Stanley Myers; film editor, Geoffrey Foot; production designer, Elliot Scott; art director, Alan Cassie; set decorator, Ian Whittaker; sound editor, Jim Shields; asst. director, Richard Hoult; special effects, John Richardson. Reviewed at Ziegfeld Theatre, New York, April 16, 1980. (MPAA Rating-PG). Running time: 100 MINS.
Mrs. Aylwood .... Bette Davis
Helen Curtis .... Carroll Baker
Paul Curtis .... David McCallum
Jan Curtis .... Lynn-Holly Johnson
Ellie Curtis .... Kyle Richards
John Keller .... Ian Bannen
Tom Colley .... Richard Pasco
Mary Fleming .... Frances Cuka
Mike Fleming .... Benedict Taylor
Mrs. Thayer .... Eleanor Summerfield
Young Mrs. Aylwood ..... Georgina Hale
Karen Aylwood .... Katherine Levy

There are some moments in this British-made Disney effort when

the film almost turns into "The Changeling Goes To Disneyland," but most of the time recovers enough to keep the mild layer of suspense actively building. Although Bette Davis has star billing there's not much reason for it as the film revolves around teenager Lynn-Holly Johnson who just happens to resemble the long-lost daughter of Davis.

Johnson's family (Carroll Baker, David McCallum and Kyle Richards) rent the huge country house belonging to Davis who lives in a nearby cottage and depends on the big-house rentals for income. The pretitle sequences establishes the house and woods (which actually appears to encroach on the house at times) with being something less than fun city. Whatever is out there, however, remains undiscovered even after the film has ended.

The acting and writing are barely professional but the art direction, especially Alan Hume's stunning camerawork, gives the pic a gloss that will keep parents awake, at least, while the youngsters are screaming their way through a second box of popcorn. There are brief hints of black magic but never enough to offend anyone — mostly it's left to the viewer's individual imagination what makes up the mystery.

Evidently Buena Vista has faith in the pic. Besides a very expensive benefit premiere, "Watcher" goes it alone for at least four weeks at the big Ziegfeld. And to premiere a Disney film in New York is something of an event, in itself.

—*Robe.*

Kagirinaku Tomei Ni Chikai Buruu
(Almost Transparent Blue)
(JAPANESE-COLOR)

Tokyo, March 26.
A Toho release of a Kitty Film Corporation production. Produced by Hidenori Taga, Kei Ijisato. Written and directed by Ryu Murakami, based on his book. Features entire cast. Camera (color), Shuya Sekigawa; lighting, Kanji Akiyama; sound, Koichi Beniya; art direction, Hiroshi Wada; editor, Hatoko Yamaji; music, Masaru Hoshii; asst. director, Tomoya Yoshitomi. Reviewed at Nichigeki Bunka, Tokyo, March 18, 1980. Running time: 103 MINS.
Ryu .... Kunihiko Mitamura
Lilly .... Mari Nakayama
Yoshiyama .... Haruhiko Saito
Kei .... Keiko Wakasa
Okinawa .... Togo Igawa
Reiko .... Narumi Tokura
Moko .... Yuri Takase
Kazuo .... Goro Masaki

The Kitty Film Corp. production, based on the '76 prize-winning novel of the same title, was written and directed by the author, Ryu

Murakami. In his directorial debut, Murakami demonstrates a remarkable assurance, a sure hand with actors and an unfailing eye for arrestingly composed scenes.

As was the book, the film is an episodic portrait of alienated Japanese youth of the late '60s. The film does, however, make major departures, with sex having been toned down considerably, characters added and subtracted, incidents inserted or withdrawn.

Still, much of what has been retained is impressively presented, including an early, chilling bar scene establishing the tenuous relationships between the major characters and an extended scene in which hero Ryu (Kunihiko Mitamura) and older lover Lily (Mari Nakayama) drive through the rain and then make love near an American airbase runway, under the influence of mescaline. Moments like these involve the viewer in a way they never could on the printed page. Perhaps Murakami should consider abandoning the author's pen for the director's megaphone.
—*Bail.*

ffolkes
(BRITISH-COLOR)

North Seas hijack caper.

Universal release of an Elliott Kastner production, Exec producer, Moses Rothman. Directed by Andrew V. McLaglen. Stars Roger Moore, James Mason, Anthony Perkins, Michael Parks. Screenplay, Jack Davies, based on his novel, "Esther, Ruth & Jennifer;" camera (Technicolor), Tony Imi; film editor, Alan Strachan; special effects, special sequences, John Richardson; art director, Bert Davey; asst. director, Brian Cook; stunt supervisor, Eddie Stacey; set decorator, Simon Wakefield; sound editor, Alan Sones; publicity, Jenny Craven; music composed and conducted by Michael J. Lewis. Reviewed at Eastside Theatre, N.Y., April 15, 1980. (MPAA Rating - PG) Running time: **99 MINS.**
ffolkes .... Roger Moore
Admiral Brinsden .... James Mason
Kramer .... Anthony Perkins
Shulman .... Michael Parks
King .... David Hedison
Olafsen .... Jack Watson
Fletcher .... George Baker
Tipping .... Jeremy Clyde
Herring .... David Wood
Prime Minister .... Faith Brook
Sanna .... Lea Brodie
Ackerman .... Anthony Pullen Shaw
Webb .... Philip O'Brien
Dawnay .... John Westbrook
Sarah .... Jennifer Hilary
Also John Lee, Brook Williams, Tim Bentinck, Saburo Kimura, Eiji Kusuhara, David Landbury, Alastair Llewellyn Sean Arnold, Eric Mason, Thane Bettany, George Leach, Richard Graydon.

This high seas hijack caper should find sufficient numbers in the regular booking pattern to give it a measure of success, especially if Roger ("James Bond") Moore is properly exploited. It's a handsome production with some economical touches that only the keen-eyed will spot (the ocean oil rigs are miniatures - good ones, but still miniatures).

The biggest attraction in "ffolkes" (that's Moore's name—film is called "North Seas Hijack" in Britain) is the banter between Moore and the various types with whom he comes in conflict during his preparations to save a hijacked supply ship (Esther) which the villainous Tony Perkins and accomplices have taken over, threatening to destroy a drilling rig (Ruth) and its sister production platform (Jennifer) unless a ransom is paid.

A misogynistic but dedicated frogman, whose private crew of frogmen are the only seeming rescuers of the ship, Moore is today's ideal male chauvinistic pig. And delights in it. He doesn't even mind telling the British Prime Minister (a lady, of course) what he thinks of the situation.

He's ably supported by James Mason as a by-the-books admiral. Mason is also given star billing and almost builds his role into deserving it but Perkins and especially Michael Parks certainly belong below the title. Perkins plays his usual low-keyed neurotic, a role on which he's practically earning a monopoly.

The action sequences are tense and well-handled, especially the underwater work. Among the supporting roles that stand out are Jack Watson as the Norwegian ship's captain, David Wood as the cowardly press officer who helps the kidnappers get aboard the ship, David Hedison (remember "The Fly"?) as the head man on Jennifer and Lea Brodie as the young, pretty ship's cook who provides Moore's one moment of embarrassment.

Jack Davies' screenplay, based on his own novel, "Esther, Ruth & Jennifer," might have been better off as an out and out comedy caper than this semi-serious attempt that is most attractive when it's lighthearted. Moore and Mason's names should help initial promotion if that dreadful title doesn't hold up things too much.—*Robe.*

L'Oeil du Maitre
(His Master's Eye)
(FRENCH-COLOR)

Paris, March 25.
A Gaumont release of a Sabre Films production. Produced by Quentin Raspail. Features entire cast. Directed by Stephane Kurc. Written by Kurc, Pierre Geller; camera (color), Georges Campana; sound, Philippe Lemenuel; editor, Monique Prim; music, Pierre Jansen; art director, Bruno Beauge. Reviewed at the Quintette Theatre, Paris, March 23, 1980. Running time: **95 MINS.**
Marc .... Patrick Chesnais
Francois .... Olivier Granier
Helene .... Dominique Laffin
Isabelle .... Marina Vlady
Ferazzi .... Michel Aumont
Samuel .... Daniel Gelin
Cazeau .... Jean-Claude Brialy

The focus is on French television news presentation in "His Master's Eye," a first theatrical feature by Stephane Kurc, whose own experiences in tv are the ostensible basis for the script. Of probable interest only in those countries in which television is controlled by the state, and particularly valuable as a foundation for public debate and discussion.

Two young men, Francois and Marc, work in the news department of a regional tv station. Francois, opportunistic and amenable, is promoted to cohelmer of a weekly current events program for the Paris station. He offers his friend the chance to do a reportage on an Algerian immigrant camp, though well aware of Marc's intransigent leftist sympathies. Sure enough, the program is too politically barbed. The network brass, themselves responding to exterior influences, pressure Francois to edit the reportage. Marc walks out in disgust, but not before sabotaging the transmission by replacing the censored version with the offending outtakes.

The film is moderately interesting, adequately acted and directed, but suffers from a marked lack of ambition in the writing.

Kurc wants to make things too clear and reduces the complex workings of a news bureau to a few conveniently numbered cogs and pulleys. Though important as the first theatrical film in France to confront the subject, "His Master's Eye" is at best a first draft for a good piece of filmic muckraking.
—*Len.*

The Little Convict
(AUSTRALIAN-ANIMATED-COLOR)

Sydney, April 9.
Yoram Gross presents a Roadshow release. Produced and directed by Yoram Gross. Stars Rolf Harris. Screenplay, John Palmer; animation director, Paul McAdam; character design, Athol Henry, Paul McAdam. Reviewed at Roadshow Theatrette, Sydney, April, '80. (Censorship rating G). Running time: **90 MINS.**

Using a mixture of live backgrounds and animated characters in combination with a real actor (Rolf Harris), Yoram Gross has created a charming tale, set in Sydney Town in its early days when the place was settled by convicts. Harris, born in Perth, West Australia, but living in Britain since 1954, where he has had a tv variety show, brings to the part of "Grandpa" his characteristic, ingratiating presence while adding a touch of humor.

Plotline is uncomplicated enough, with a 13-year old animated hero, Toby, who was sentenced to be transported because he was convicted of holding the horse of a highway man back in England.

In line with the nation's concept of its heritage, the characters line up with the convicts as roughish good guys, the guards as stupid and harsh, and the Governor a bumbling idiot with a heart. If somewhat predictable that the convicts will rescue the Governor's snooty wife from danger and that the guards will get their come-uppance, it is none the less still pleasant to watch. Harris singing an assortment of traditional songs and some he self-penned adds to the ethos.

A long way from a fairy tale, it's still a story that has all the right virtues, and in the right places. The plot moves right along untaxingly, and the characters develop nicely. Backgrounds were shot in and around Old Sydney Town, a modern replication of the look of the period, just outside Sydney.

Stylistically, the look of the animated characters owe more to modern tv techniques than the lush, painstaking creatures of Disney, but to a contemporary child's eye this wouldn't be noticable. The cartoon characters they see on the small screen may not have meticulous lip-synch, but the story isn't hurt by that. Nor is it here.

While parochial and at times a bit preachy for local audiences, pic should do well overseas where the novelty of the locale and story is less familiar. —*Miha.*

Pasi
(Hunger)
(INDIAN-COLOR)

Madras, April 8.
Produced by G. Lalitha for Sunitha Cine Arts, Madras 86. Features entire cast. Original story, screenplay, and direction, Durai. Camera (color), V. Ranga; editor M. Vellachami; music, Shanker-Ganesh. Reviewed in Madras, March 21, 1980. Running time: **165 MINS.**
MuniIan .... Delhi Ganesh
Rangan .... Vijayan
Street begger .... Surulirajan
Kanniah .... Narayanan
Kuppamma .... Shoba
Valliamma .... Tambaram Lalitha
Chellamma .... Sathya
Rakkamma .... S.N. Parvathy
Gowri .... Jayabharathi
Rupe .... Pravenna

G. Lalitha has produced for Sunitha Cine Arts the Tamil-language film, "Pasi" (Hunger) which can well satisfy the hunger in the intelligent cinegoer to see a picture with accent on realism.

Though many of the ideas used by director Durai are not original, his distinction lies in their proper correlation and use in a telling and effective manner.

"Pasi" has no songs, a must for any Indian film, though there is enough music in the film. The attempts of cycle shop owner Kanniah to play old records appropriate to the moods of the heroine, as she passes before his shop, to draw her towards him not only provide music but also exhibit the calf-love married men harbor for any pretty girl. The pathetic character of Kanniah, the warfish cycle shop owner, makes one compare him with the hunchback of Notre Dame.

It is character studies, more than any story line, which carry this film about the sordid life led in equally sordid environments on a highly entertaining level and help narrow down and ultimately obliterate all differences between the dirty slum area and the posh locality of a major city like Madras, even dovetailing them into each other.

While most Tamil film directors have been trekking to villages to find appeal for their films, Durai, who takes credit for the original story and screenplay, has proved that the city slum could be as entertaining as the pastoral regions, V. Ranga's camera work has pictured in colour the slum areas with quiet intimacy, without inflicting any shocked contacts!

Durai's "Pasi" lays emphasis o nthe fact that inside the sordid slum there is as much hunger for values and verities of life as elsewhere in the universe. —*Eswa.*

Toi Ashita
(Faraway Tomorrow)
(JAPANESE-COLOR)

Tokyo, March 26.

A Toho release. Produced by Osamu Tanaka. Directed by Tatsumi Kamishiro. Features entire cast. Screenplay by To Baba, based on a novel by A.J. Cronin; camera, (color), Kazumi Hara; art direction, Yukio Higuchi; sound, Noboru Kamikura; lighting, Shinji Kojima; music, Kawachi Kuni; editor, Michiko Ikeda; assistant director, Ippei Imamura. Reviewed at Ikebukuro Scalaza, March 20, 1980. Running time: 95 MINS.

Akira Tagawa	Tomokazu Miura
Junko Baba	Ayumi Ishida
Yoshie Eigawa	Junko Miyashita
Shiro Iwasa	Tomisaburo Wakayama
Manzo	Taiji Tomoyama

Tomokazu Miura is an actor who has specialized in playing what is referred to by the Japanese as a "naisu gai," or nice guys. To anyone accustomed to Western styles of acting, he appears natural, yet, at a second glance, his naturalism turns out to be wholly superficial and mannered.

In his latest film he is no more

Mr. Nice Guy and all the better for it. He portrays a young man who engages in a concerted campaign to prove the innocence of his father, a convicted "murderer."

Assisting him is newspaper proprietor Tomisaburo Wakayama. Strong and sympathetic, he is a warm father figure to Miura, who feels a sense of loss when Wakayama confesses to the murder in question and commits suicide.

Tomokazu's real father (Nobuo Kaneko), it turns out, is a disgusting boozer and womanizer who probably would have benefitted from a few more years of rehabilitative incarceration. At film's end, Miura makes a move as if to walk away from his old man, then resignedly joins him for a stroll down neon-lit streets.

Tatsumi Kamishiro directed this downbeat tale with ease and restraint. His depiction of the industrial wasteland that is the southern Japanese city of Kita Kyushu indicates more than a passing familiarity with Antonioni's "Red Desert." Serving as Kameshiro's Monica Vitti is Ayumi Ishida, a beauty in her own right, who here looks completely and appropriately haggard. As Wakayama's lover, she gives an effective, ego-free performance. —*Bail.*

Chain Reaction
(AUSTRALIAN-COLOR)

Sydney, March 2.

A Hoyts Distribution release of a Palm Beach Picture, produced by David Elfick. Written and directed by Ian Barry. Features entire cast. Associate producers George Miller and Ross Matthews. Production manager, Lynn Gailey; assistant directors, Ross Matthews, Chris Maudson, P.J. Jones; camera (color), Russell Boyd; underwater photography, George Greenough; sound, Lloyd Carrick; art direction, Graham Walker; stunt coordination, Max Aspin; editor, Tim Tim Wellburn; original music, Andrew Thomas Wilson. Previewed at Hoyts, Sydney, March 2, '80. (Censorship rating M). Running time: 87 MINS.

Larry	Steve Bisley
Carmel	Arna-Maria Winchester
Heinrich	Ross Thompson
Gray	Ralph Cotterill
Oates	Patrick Ward
Police Sgt. McSweeney	Laurie Moran
Junior Constable Piggott	Richard Moir
Eagle	Hugh Keays-Byrne
Doctor	Michael Long
Waitress	Lorna Lesley

A face-paced actioner, this is David Elfick's fourth production and director Ian Barry's feature debut. The latter's uncertainty shows at times, but the plot development moves so quickly that any lacunae are easily overlooked until later. Story establishes an accident at a central repository for nuclear waste in central Australia. Spillage **pollutes a water supply and a technician is terminally exposed to radiation.**

The plant worker (Ross Thompson) evades capture and attempts to warn public, but during his escape he wrecks a car and loses his memory. He arrives at the weekend shack of a custom car shop owner, Larry, whose lady, Carmel, takes pity on him. Whie she is dressing Heinrich's injuries, Larry drives to town to report the accident.

This brings him to the attention of security agents Gray and Oates who are anxious to keep the lid on the situation and find Heinrich before he can expose the accident. However, Heinrich has warned Eagle (Hugh Keays-Byrne) who travels to the remote village to obtain more information. Gray seals off the area, but is is clear that the couple have been exposed to radiation.

Russell Boyd's camerawork gives the film a stylish look which allows Barry to exploit the location in which it was shot — an ex-mining town, now an industrial ruin. Tech credits are all fine, with an especial nod to the sound department. Wilson's music aptly suits the mood and the context, underlining the plot by skillful, sole use of electronic sources.

Editing, as stated, is fast, and there are clear indications of heavy post-production hours at the moviola. Car chase sequences are expertly handled and are genuinely exciting.

Finance came from Australian Film Commission, Victorian Film Corp. and Hoyts.—*Miha.*

L'Empreinte des Geants
(The Imprint of Giants)
(FRENCH-W. GERMAN-COLOR)

Paris, March 4.

An SNC release of a Filmel/SNC/FR3/-Rialto Film (Berlin) co-production. Produced by Eugene Lepicier and Gerard Beytout. Features entire cast. Directed by Robert Enrico. Written by Enrico and Francois Chevallier, from the novel, "La Marie-Marraine," by Hortense Dufour; camera (color), Didier Tarot; art director, Jean-Claude Gallouin; editor, Patricia Neny; music, Karl Heinz Schafer. Reviewed at the Ponthieu screening room, Paris, Feb. 29, 1980. Running time: 140 MINS.

Meru	Mario Adorf
Eleonore	Zoe Chauveau
Dromner	Patrick Chesnais
Germaine	Andrea Ferreol
Jo Hansen	Raimund Harmstorf
Lucie	Dominique Laffin
Lucien	Philippe Leotard
Fouldroule	Serge Reggiani
La Marraine	Anne Waizemsky

The cliches roll in early in Robert Enrico's "The Imprint of Giants," an overlong, lumpy, pseudo-epic highlighting life on a highway construction site in France in 1965. The grandeur and poetry inherent in the subject matter (the

"giants" of the title refer to the great steam-shovels and bulldozers, and, by association, to the men who drive them) are absent in the writing and realization and the numerous personages are a collection of uninteresting stereotypes.

Enrico adapted a novel by a young woman who had first hand knowledge of various construction sites. But despite almost 150 minutes of screen time he fails to give a convincing picture of this harsh nomadic existence, to get under the skin of these men and their families and fathom the psychological and emotional effects of their life style.

Enrico's direction is earnest and plodding in its literalness, without the breadth needed to encompass the material. The performances are at best mediocre. For all its honest ambition "The Imprint of Giants" leaves only a smudgy impression. —*Len.*

Touched By Love
(COLOR)

Warm tale of therapeutic love could register with teens.

Hollywood, April 14.

A Columbia Pictures release. Produced by Michael Viner. Directed by Gus Trikonis. Executive producer, Peter E. Strauss. Stars Deborah Raffin, Diane Lane. Screenplay, Hesper Anderson, based on book "To Elvis With Love" by Lena Canada; camera (Metrocolor), Richard H. Kline; editor, Fred Chulack; music, John Barry; art direction, Claudio Guzman; set decoration, Ray Molyneaux; costume design, Moss Mabry; sound, David Ronne; assistant director, Bert Gold. Reviewed at the Burbank Studios, Burbank, April 14, 1980. (MPAA Rating: PG). Running time: 95 MINS.

Lena Canada	Deborah Raffin
Karen	Diane Lane
Dr. Bell	Michael Learned
Tony	John Amos
Amy	Cristina Raines
Margaret	Mary Wickes
Don Fielder	Clu Gulager
Monica	Twyla Volkins
Topper	Clive Shalom

Known during production as "To Elvis With Love," "Touched By Love" is an earnest, respectable drama of nicely restrained sentimentality which mines similar veins as "The Miracle Worker." Pointedly a real-life tale of how a young nursing trainee breaks through the recalcitrance of a young cerebral palsy victim, film will have to be carefully guided through the marketplace to reach the teenaged girls who probably comprise its most receptive audience.

Set in a beautiful, secluded mountain area (actually Banff, Alberta), pic has a deglamorized Deborah Raffin arriving to work with c.p. children. Soon fascinated by completely uncommunicative loner Diane Lane, Raffin, over the protests of boss Michael Learned, devotes all her available time to the abandoned girl, persisting until finally drawing her out of her shell.

From here on, focus shifts to Lane's dramatic progress, as she learns to write, play and eventually find an outlet for her emotions through a surprising correspondence with Elvis Presley. Her endless waits for the rock idol's replies are nicely conveyed, and depth of her happiness when they finally arrive provides meaning both to her short life and the film.

Gus Trikonis' direction of Hesper Anderson's careful, intelligent script is graceful, even-handed and placid, agreeable conveying the primary aspects of the material without plunging deeply into profoundly troubling or clinical waters. It's a clean job which, by opting for understatement, somewhat mutes the obvious moving qualities of the uplifting tragedy, but at the same time avoids many of the sticky pitfalls.

Same description could be applied to Raffin's well-judged, unemphatic performance. Lane here scores once again, strongly putting across the poor kid's emotional hurt and suspicion of others, and rejoicing winningly at the requited affection of her illustrious pen-pal.

Members of small supporting cast, including Learned, John Amos and Clu Gulager as therapists, and Cristina Raines as Raffin's man-minded roommate, all register with conviction. Standout among the kids, played by actual patients, is Clive Shalom as a precocious genius type.

Richard H. Kline's lensing is lovely, taking unforced advantage of the scenic backdrop, and John Barry's score tends toward lulling romanticism.—*Cart.*

Keow
(Miss Keow)
(THAI-COLOR)

Bangkok, April 3.
A New Five Star Productions release. Produced by Kiat Iampungporn. Directed and edited by Piac Poster. Features entire cast. Story and screenplay, Piac Poster, Boonyarak Nilawong: camera (color), Chome Bunnag: sound, Rewat Puthinan: music, Saravuth Pachaiyo; original song, "Pleng Rak Priac Ha" (When Love Calls You) by Vinai Pantarak, performed by Oriental Funk; continuity, Pichit Niyomsiri: asst. director, Boonyarak Nilawong. Reviewed at Athens theatre, Bangkok, April 3, '80. Running time: 112 MINS.
Keow . . . . Rinda Katancharoen
Natee . . . . Toon Hiranyasap
Nittaya . . . . Srisalai Suchartboot
Taweesak . . . . Kanchit Timkul
Keow's Mother . . . . . Marasri Issarangkul
Na Ayudhya
Mem . . . . Morakot Chanyadee

Alternately marketed as a disco-themed picture and a love story, "Keow," per director Piac Poster is "more of a film about broken-hearted people."

The new love team of Rinda Katancharoen and Toon Hiranyasap benefit from making their film debuts with Piac, an expert at handling new stars. He did it first with Pairoj Sangvoributr and Lalana Sulawan in the "Wai Ola-won" (Only Sixteen) series.

Comical scenes make up the first half, then story shifts to a melodramatic subject: a familiar love triangle between the young lovers (Toon and Rinda) and a rich businessman (Kanchit Timkul), the heroine's former sugar dad.

For most viewers, the acting by the screen newcomers must be good. That comes first and everything else is of secondary importance. On the basis of their debuts, there seems to be a bright future ahead for Rind and Toon, provided Piac decides to build them up. —*Cano.*

Desde El Abismo
(From The Abyss)
(ARGENTINE-COLOR)

Buenos Aires, April 12.
An Aries Cinematografica Argentina S.A. release. Produced by Hector Olivera and Luis Repetto. Directed by Fernando Ayala. Features entire cast. Screenplay Eduardo Gudino Kieffer, Fernando Ayala, based on Teresa Gondra's memoirs, "Desde la Septima Tiniebla" (From the Seventh Shadow), camera (color), Victor Hugo Caula; editor, Carlos Piaggio; sound, Norberto Castronuovo; sets, Emilio Basaldua: assistant directors, Americo Ortiz de Zarate, Alberto Lecchi: Vidal Rivas; music, Oscar Cardozo Ocampo. Reviewed at the Petit Atlas screening room, Buenos Aires, March 24, 1980. (Forbidden in Argentina for minors under 18.) Running time: 100 MINS.
Marta . . . . Thelma Biral
Miquel . . . . Alberto Argibay
Man in bar . . . . Hector Pellegrini
Neighbor . . . . Adriana Parets
Pablo . . . . Raul Rizzo
Laura . . . . Olga Zubarry
Barbara . . . . Marta Albertini
Carlos . . . . Nestor Hugo Rivas
Elena . . . . Cristina Murta
Ernesto . . . . Boy Olmi
Diego . . . . Luis Garparini
1st Whore . . . . Cristina Fernandez
2nd Whore . . . . Betty Couceiro
1st Maid . . . . Analia Agullo
2nd Maid . . . . Estela de la Rosa

A quality Argentine film on the evils of drink, described through the story of a well-off woman who slips into alcoholism, loses her job, the custody of her son, her self-respect and almost her sanity, is variously reformed by hospital treatment and by Alcoholics Anonymous, falls back again and again into the pit, and finally appears to pull herself together for keeps.

This film has been officially designated to be sent by Argentina to this year's Karlovy Vary festival in Czechoslovakia.

A fundamental reason for the film's relative success is the performance of Thelma Biral as the tormented woman who goes to any lengths to obtain a drink after her money has run out. There is a real erotic tinge to a scene in which she and a barkeeper engage in a tug-of-war over a bottle of booze.

An impact, for Argentine audiences at least, who are normally "protected" from this kind of thing by the censors, is a sequence in which a man whom the fallen heroine has picked up, but later attempts to send packing from a hotel bed, roughly flips her over onto her belly and begins to pull down clothing as the camera moves in for a closeup of her face which screams in pain. This kind of intercourse had hitherto not been acknowledged to exist in the Argentine cinema, and isn't all that frequent in non-porno films from other nations, either.

Pic's main drawback is a screenplay which at times leans towards the overtly didactic and moralistic, bringing back memories of the naive anti-booze shorts produced around 1900, complete with views of a crucifix reverently shot while bathed in a diagonal ray of sunlight. But overall the film makes audience feel along with the tortured central character, with considerable style. —*Olas.*

Rag. Arturo De Fanti, Bancario-Precario
(The Precarious Bank Teller)
(ITALIAN-COLOR)

Rome, April 3.
Produced and distributed by Produzioni Atlas Cinematografica (P.A.C.). Stars Paolo Villaggio, Catherine Spaak. Directed by Luciano Salce. Screenplay, Luciano Salce, Augusto Caminito. Ottavio Alessi: camera (Technicolor), Sergio Rubini: art director, Elio Micheli: editor, Antonio Siciliano: music, Piero Piccioni. Reviewed at Fiammetta Cinema, Rome. March 30, 1980. Running time: 94 MINS.
Arturo De Fanti . . . . Paolo Villaggio
Elena . . . . Catherine Spaak
Vanna . . . . Annamaria Rizzoli
Maid . . . . Enrica Bonaccorti

A fly-weight comedy that draws more groans than guffaws, "Bancario-Precario" is highly precarious as a commercial entry other than for Paolo Villaggio fans at home. Social-sexual satire which sometimes lifts helmer Luciano Salce's simple pix is so thin here it is nothing but a script pretext, while jokes are so unrealistically contrived they lose all punch.

Humble bank teller Villaggio finds himself unable to maintain his large country house. The maid, owed several hundred thousand lire in back pay, lounges in front of the tv all day while wife Catherine Spaak scrubs floors. This good bourgeois couple swallow their moral scruples and take in the husband's mistress, whose cabaret earnings fail, however, to balance the family budget. Next they offer a place to the wife's lover, a judo coach, whose wife returns from Africa with her lover, and so on. The repetitive plot doesn't hold up very long, as gags about bed partners tend to get old fast.

Villaggio, with the victimized everyman face and squat form that gave life to a pair of successful Salce pix based on the character Fantozzi, is a good comedian in a bad comedy. Cast as the sexual interest of elegant Spaak and sex starlet Rizzoli (who both caricature their parts) the Villaggio character loses credibility and sympathy. Only the cynical maid, well handled by Enrica Bonaccorti, shows a bit of originality and humor.

Script wavers between blasting characters' hypocritical morality and greed, and bemoaning the financial plight of bank tellers. In the end, it does neither. Predictably, it settles for easy solutions and gags — using terrorism, hold-ups, muggings and feminism as fodder for one-liners.

With undistinguished technical work, pic has little to boast about.
— *Yung.*

Mis Dias con Veronica
(My Days With Veronica)
(ARGENTINE-COLOR)

Buenos Aires, March 24.
A Disprofilm release. Produced by Tilt Producciones Cinematograficas. Directed by Nestor Lescovich. Features entire cast. Screenplay, Jorge Martinez: camera (Eastmancolor), Miguel Rodriguez: editor, Julio Di Risio: sound, Abelardo Kushnir: music, Luis Maria Serra. Reviewed at the Ideal theatre, Buenos Aires, March 13 (Argentine Film Institute rating: banned for under-18s). Running time: 85 MINS.
Cast: Dora Baret, Oscar Cruz, Susu Pecoraro, Hector Bidonde, Chela Ruiz.

The first international-class Argentine film of 1980 is this feature by Nestor Lescovich, a romantic story with big drawbacks as well as some strong assets, and which taken as a whole has the earnestness of purpose and the occasional flights of poetic fancy which make it natural film festival fodder. In fact it was sent to the recent international film fest in Cartagena, Colombia.

The story concerns a love affair between a 30-year-old man with a superficial view of life and a 42-year-old woman with plenty of aplomb, sensibility and good sense. Primarily responsible for the degree of success achieved by the picture as an artistic enterprise is the acting, especially of Dora Baret and Oscar Cruz in the leads, and of Hector Bidonde as their harried employer; and the clear color photography of Miguel Rodriguez, one of Argentina's handiest persons with a lens. Regarding the acting of the lead couple, if it features somewhat too much smiling at their first encounter to feel quite right, it is probably the fault of the script which may have called on them to do so beyond the point they would have gone if based on their own judgement as actors.

Script is good enough for its purpose in overall conception and ends with a nicely fake-complacement but ultimately cynical touch, but it errs in method by making it all depend too much on a voice-over narration which should have been unnecessary and is also corny.

In a nutshell: a wistful love story for thinking but not too demanding audiences. —*Olas.*

Le Roi et l'Oiseau
(The King and the Mockingbird)
(FRENCH-ANIMATION-COLOR)

Paris, April 1.

A Gaumont release of a Paul Grimault Films/Gibe Films/Antenne 2 co-production. Directed by Paul Grimault. Written by Grimault and Jacques Prevert; music, Wojciech Kilar; songs by Prevert and Joseph Kosma; camera (color), Gerard Soirant, editor, Grimault; set designs by Grimault, Lionel Charpy and Roger Duclent; artistic collaborator, Pierre Prevert; sound effects Henri Gruel. Reviewed at the Hautefeuille cinema, Paris, April 1, 1980. Running time: 87 MINS.

With the voices of: Jean Martin, Pascal Mazzotti, Raymond Bussieres, Agnes Viala, Renaud Marx, Hubert Deschamps, Roger Blin, Philippe Derrez, Albert Medina, Claude Pieplu.

"Le Roi et l'Oiseau" is that rarity, a French animated theatrical feature — and it's a gem. Children will respond happily to it, but it is the adult audience that will most appreciate this multi-faceted array of wit, graphic elegance, charm and melancholy.

The creators are Paul Grimault, a gifted animation artist whose work merits an audience byond connoisseur circles, and, Jacques Prevert, the poet and master screenwriter, who died in 1977. Their long-standing friendship and collaboration produced several delectable animation shorts and, belatedly, this sole feature.

Belatedly, because this film was first conceived more than 30 years ago. An earlier 62-minute version was released in 1953 under the title "La Bergere et Le Ramoneur." Grimault, whose bitter dispute with the producer led to his expulsion from the project, immediately disowned the film as his work. In 1967 he bought the negative, stripped it of all footage not his own, and set to completing it as originally envis-

ioned. It was finished only last year and promptly awarded the Louis Delluc Award.

The basis for the story is a fairy tale by Andersen, "The Shepherdess and the Chimney Sweep." With a superb blend of naivete and sophistication, delicate fantasy and raucuous humour, the authors have elaborated it into a richly textured fable about tyranny and freedom.

In the kingdom of Takicardie, a cross-eyed, pinched-face tyrant, King Charles V + III = VIII + VIII = XVI, loves a charming shepherdess. But she loves and is loved by a little chimneysweep. Aided by a wily impertinent mockingbird, who wears a top-hat and nests above the king's private apartments with his children, the lovers escape to the sunless lower city, but are soon captured. The bird instigates a revolt in the lion's den where he and the sweep have been cast, saves the shepherd, and destroys the royal palace with the aid of king's secret weapon, a huge robot.

Few cartoons have enjoyed such literate witty scripting. The Prevertian esprit is warmly aglow with its simple poetry and verbal playfulness, and the film echoes with remembrances of the old Prevert-Carne films.

Graphically, Grimault's style is classic, like Disney's, but much different in tone and untainted by treacly sentiment. In particular he has a genius for detail and his backgrounds are marvelously rich — teeming with invention like a frame from a Jacques Tati comedy.

The masterpiece of design here is his visualization of the royal palace: an outlandish 96-story amalgam of classic, medieval, Renaissance and purely fanciful architectural forms.

Special mention to Polish composer Wojciech Kilar, who had written a lovely score and to the late Joseph Kosma, who is responsible with Prevert for three fine songs. And a warm nod to Pierre Prevert, the poet's brother, himself a filmmaker, who selected the delightful voices. —*Len.*

Humanoids From The Deep
(COLOR)

Fifties monsters return for more bodies and coin.

Hollywood, April 15.

A New World Pictures release of a Roger Corman production. Produced by Martin B. Cohen, Hunt Lowry. Directed by Barbara Peeters. Features entire cast. Screenplay, Frederick James, based on a story by Frank Arnold, Martin B. Cohen; camera (Metrocolor), Daniele Lacambre; editor, Mark Goldblatt; music, James Horner; art direction, Michael Erler; humanoid designs, Rob Bottin; sound, Mark Harris; as-

sistant director/second unit director, James Sbadellari. Reviewed at the Palms Theatre, L.A., April 15, 1980. (MPAA Rating: R.) Running time: 80 MINS.

Jim Hill . . . . Doug McClure
Dr. Susan Drake . . . . Ann Turkel
Hank Slattery . . . . Vic Morrow
Carol Hill . . . . Cindy Weintraub

With "Humanoids From The Deep," Roger Corman has come full circle back to his very first production, "Monster From The Ocean Floor." Despite costing 100 times as much, new pic has similar premise and same raison d'etre, that of pocketing a profit from drive-in dates. Backed by an effectively lurid campaign, New World release (UA overseas) has already opened well in the Midwest, and presence of more nudity and gore than carried by any exploitationer in recent memory should insure continued solid results.

Tried-and-true formula of countless sci-fiers of the 1950s is revived once again, as gruesome, amphibious creatures rise from the ocean to stalk and destroy terrified humans. General pattern here has monsters systematically killing the guys and raping the girls, although at least one of the beasts betrays different predilictions as it takes its pleasure with a gent when plenty of nubile young ladies are available nearby.

Meaningless, quasi-environmentalist human plot has baddie Vic Morrow pushing for construction of a cannery along the picturesque California coast against the protestations of a young native Indian. Local fisherman Doug McClure helps out visiting scientist Ann Turkel as she investigates the reasons behind the alien invasion.

Monsters, which look like the creature from the black lagoon with moss, make their first real appearance after half-an-hour, and the last couple of reels are filled with their wholesale assault on a dockside carnival. Sequence features more screaming than will be heard in the audience, but massive scale of the slaughter, not to mention a highly effective final tag, lifted directly from "Alien," should give action crowd what it's looking for.

Given the nonsensical script and fact that considerable footage was added to director Barbara Peeters' original footage, editor Mark Goldblatt did a good job in making disparate elements at least hang together and play coherently. James Horner's highly active score also makes it seem that more is happening onscreen than actually takes place. Daniele Lacambre's photography is on the murky, bluish side, but special mention should be made of Rob Bottin's creature costume

designs, which emerge as relatively convincing under the circumstances.

Irony of the entire production, which will confound feminist-minded critics, is that a female helmer was behind one of the more woman-degrading pix to come down the pike in some seasons. Also worth noting are several glimpses of public hair, supposedly a no-no, if not with the MPAA, with several major theatre chains. —*Cart.*

McVicar
(BRITISH-COLOR)

Authentic prison-escape drama, with the score as the biggest hook.

London, April 25.

A Curbishley-Baird production for The Who Films and Polytel. Executive producers, David Gideon Thomson, Jackie Curbishley. Produced by Roy Baird, Bill Curbishley, Roger Daltrey. Directed by Tom Clegg. Stars Roger Daltrey, Adam Faith. Screenplay, John McVicar, Clegg; camera (color), Vernon Layton; music, Jeff Wayne; editor, Peter Boyle; art director, Brian Ackland-Snow; sound, David Crozier; associate producer, John Peverall; production manager, Ray Corbett; asst. director, Barry Langley. Reviewed at the Bijou screening room, London, April 24, 1980. (BBFC Rating: X). Running time: **111 MINS.**

McVicar .... Roger Daltrey
Probyn..................... Adam Faith
Sheila .... Cheryl Campbell
Harrison .... Steven Berkoff
Stokes .... Brian Hall
Johnson .... Jeremy Blake
Collins .... Leonard Gregory
Harris .... Peter Jonfield
Rabies .... Tony Haygarth
Principal Officer .... Ralph Watson
Kate .... Georgina Hale
Frank .... Malcolm Tierney
Joey Davis .... Billy Murray
Russell McVicar .... Ricky Parkinson
Hitchens .... Ian Hendry

New feature from The Who Films, produced by the Roy Baird-Bill Curbishley team with Polytel backing, is a conscientious reconstruction of several crucial months in the life of John McVicar, who escaped from the high-security wing of an English prison where he was serving eight years for robbery with violence. He was later caught and jailed again on an extended sentence, having been dubbed "Public Enemy No. 1" by the British press while on the run.

Now paroled, he's a mature student at a local university, and the author of a book, "McVicar By Himself," which was used as the basis of the film. He had a hand in the script, initially drafted by director Tom Clegg, and was on set as "technical advisor" during much of the shooting. So too was another ex-prisoner, Wally Probyn, who escaped with McVicar (though he was recaptured immediately) and is also now out on parole.

The result is an honest, unsensational picture with strongest appeal to U.K. audiences and considerable commercial prospects in key markets elsewhere. Critics may deem it middle-of-the-road — neither blockbuster material, nor artily interesting — but it provides enough food for thought to generate valuable word of mouth.

The music, produced, arranged and conducted by New Yorker Jeff Wayne, is scintillating, often suggesting emotional depths the straightforward action on its own can't convey. Ironically, airplay of some numbers written by Billy Nicholls and others shape to act as a cornerstone of promotion campaigns far more effectively than the soundtrack of The Who's first feature, "Quadrophenia," even though in the earlier case it was the album that spawned the film. As increasingly expected nowadays, the Dolby-enhanced sound quality is firstrate.

Roger Daltrey, who proved himself to be charismatic on screen in Ken Russell's "Tommy" and "Lisztomania," but left unanswered the bigger question as to whether this rock singer can act, sorts out the query by his performance in the title role. He can.

With his normally abundant curls dramatically scissored for the part, and his physique in almost muscle-bound trim, he projects a disquieting mix of danger and vulnerability.

Moreover, his characterization goes a long way towards supplying — in the absence of the analytical passages which make McVicar's book so revealing — the sense of a mind at work behind the uncompromising, bony face and the thuggish look in the eyes. This villain is no glamorous Clyde Barrow. He's synthetic because the reasons for what he does are profoundly confused; and, in the course of the film, he's bright enough to realize it. Daltrey succeeds in making that turning-point clear.

Clegg's firm direction is unflamboyant, at times almost austerely plain. Although much of the drama certainly doesn't call for obtrusive style, there are moments when more panache would not have come amiss. Studio interiors (prison scenes) in particular could have done with subtler and more atmospheric lighting by cinematographer Vernon Layton, but action sequences are notably well shot.

Only general criticism of the storytelling is that some of the screentime up to the breakout drags, and the scenes when Daltrey's on the run seem all-too-brief by comparison. That's despite an excellent, humorous performance by Adam Faith as Probyn, and a chillingly manic one by Steven Berkoff, in a role modelled on an actual inmate whose name has been changed to protect someone from someone.

Cheryl Campbell, a plaudited tv actress with a useful range of expression, spanning wilful aggression to abject pathos, turns in a touching portrayal of McVicar's common-law wife in her theatrical debut. —*Simo.*

Flygniva 450
(Flight Level 450)
(SWEDISH-COLOR)

Lund, April 16.

A Tax Productions, AB Europa Film, Swedish Film Institute production, AB Europa Film release. Original story and script, Sandro Key-Aberg, Torbjoern Axelman. Directed by Torbjoern Axelman. Features entire cast. Camera (Eastmancolor). Tony Forsberg, Lars Svanberg; editor, Darek Hodar; executive producer, Bjoern Henricson; music, Ralph Lundsten. Reviewed at Reflex, City of Lund, Sweden, April 16, 1980. Running time: **100 MINS.**

Goeran .... Thomas Hellberg
Lisa .... Ann Zacharias
Giron .... Ernst-Hugo Jaeregaard
Andre .... Hakan Serner

In the near future, Torbjoern Axelman's "Flight Level 450," says, Sweden exists in a turmoil of wanton terrorism, protest marchers in environment's cause, and government plotting to nationalize energy sources, join the OPEC and gain control over the sabotage-stricken U.S. oil company IORF, engaged in drilling off the Swedish Baltic coast.

A young woman journalist and the pilot of a plane spraying insecticide join forces to thwart an air force general's plans towards a coup d-etat.

Theme might have made "Flight Level 450" into a Swedish answer to "The China Syndrome," but Axelman tells his story in curiously flat, very talkative sequences and a cinematography that looks right out of the childhood of color prints.

Interpolated are short spurts of extremely, violent and bloody action, energetic in an ugly way, but only half-heartedly pursued.

The actions of most characters is also unfortunate, as they move only according to plot purposes and to underline this morality tale's high-minded points. An exception is Ernst-Hugo Jaeregaard's General Giron. Jaeregaard is an excellent actor and he takes full advantage of the few chances he is given to appear more than one-dimensional. But on the whole, this film would seem outdated even on the international circuit specialized in themes of political paranoia.—*Kell.*

Fame
(COLOR)

... is the name of the game.

United Artists release of a Metro-Goldwyn-Mayer presentation. Produced by David De Silva and Alan Marshall. Features entire cast. Directed by Alan Parker. Screenplay, Christopher Gore; camera (Metrocolor), Michael Seresin; original music, Michael Gore; production designer, Geoffrey Kirkland; editor, Gerry Hambling; choreography, Louis Falco; asst. director, Robert F. Colesberry; costumes, Kristi Zea; sound editor, Les Wiggins; art director, Ed Wittstein; set decorator, George DeTitta; publicist, John Kane. Songs, music by Michael Gore, Dominic Bugatti, Frank Musker, Paul McCrane; lyrics, Dean Pitchford, Robert F. Colesberry, Lesley Gore, Dominic Bugatti, Frank Musker, Dean Pitchford, Paul McCrane. Reviewed at Loews Astor Plaza, N.Y., April 24, 1980. (MPAA Rating - R). Running time: **134 MINS.**

Angelo .... Eddie Barth
Coco .... Irene Cara
Bruno .... Lee Curreri
Lisa .... Laura Dean
Hilary .... Antonia Franceschi
Michael .... Boyd Gaines
Shorofsky .... Albert Hague
Mrs. Finsecker .... Tresa Hughes
Francois Lafete .... Steve Inwood
Montgomery .... Paul McCrane
Mrs. Sherwood .... Anne Meara
Miss Berg .... Joanna Merlin
Ralph .... Barry Miller
Farrell .... Jim Moody
Leroy .... Gene Anthony Ray
Doris .... Maureen Teefy

The idea behind Metro's "Fame" is that it is supposed to tell the story, via its actors, of New York's venerable High School of Performing Arts. In truth, the educational institution would have none of the project, so producers David De Silva and Alan Marshall had to do with second best — the street outside the school. Ironically, the exterior of the actual 46th Street building is never seen in the films and those portals, purportedly of the high school, are actually the doorways of an Episcopal church on the same block.

So much for an informed film about a rarity among public schools. What director Alan Parker has come up with is exposure for some of the most talented youngsters seen on screen in years. There isn't a bad performance in the lot and the handful of older actors are hard put not to be overwhelmed by the outpouring of sheer energy of the colorful admixture of boys, girls, whites, blacks, Puerto Ricans and the cross-sections that make up New York teenagers.

The format is done in five sections — auditions, and each year of school through to graduation. The great strength of the film is in these school scenes — when it wanders away from the scholastic side as it does with increasing frequency as the overlong feature moves along, it loses dramatic intensity and slows the pace with stereotype vignettes. (It is here, and undoubtedly in the street language, that the plot structure must have provided the reasons for the Board of Education's turndown of the project.)

The "audition" opening is well worth the price of admission by itself as it does indeed capture the spirit of Performing Arts (this school shares the same block as *Variety* and its students are familiar figures — the entrance requirements are high so the admission of some borderline illiterates, as in the film, could never occur). The opening allows the film to settle into the several vignettes it continues to pursue throughout — the timid boy, the mother-dominated girl, the tough Puerto Rican, the rich kid, and others.

With all this talent, there are two individuals who are so outstanding that they dominate every scene they're in — and some of these are together. Gene Anthony Ray, plays Leroy — a superb natural dancer, but resentful of anyone trying to help, especially a white. His continuing fight with English teacher Mrs. Sherwood (Anne Meara) is the most believable plotline in the entire film. It's easily Meara's best role and should encourage every New York schoolteacher who has been faced with the same student problems. A no nonsense lady, she never loses a round in her bout with this talented, but militant street kid who defies anyone to help.

Other strong performances are turned in by Irene Cara as Coco, and "I know where I'm going and nobody better get in my way" tough Puerto Rican kid, talented in every department — singing, dancing and acting. She gets temporarily sidetracked in a semi-porno bit near the end. Lee Curreri as Bruno, an Italian-American kid who tries to introduce a synthesizer and his own compositions into the music department, is effective in his underplaying as most of his fellow students come on like gangbusters.

The dramatic pair (Paul McCrane as the gay student and Laura Dean as the mother-dominated type who doesn't know what she wants) are effective in a quieter key than the rest of the cast.

There are dozens of outstanding cameos by mostly unknown talent and the casting problem for the film must have been horrendous. Eddie Barth's Angelo gets out of hand at times but is firstrate in his key scenes.

All technical aspects of the film are excellent. Christopher Gore gets sole screen credit for the screenplay, but the production notes said that the story was originally developed by coproducer De Silva (which may account for the changes in storyline). Parker, who proved he could handle kids in "Bugsy Malone," runs a tight ship.

Michael Seresin's camerawork, considering the restricted Times Square area in which he had to work, has captured most of the color of the scene and his interiors are amazing use of borrowed spaces and cramped quarters. Geographically, numerous licenses are taken with the action, but only Gothamites are likely to catch the changes.

As of the showing caught, the film is too long, and there are numerous overlong speeches that could be shortened. Some of the incidents that border on bad taste could be exised with little damage to the overall structure. It's a rousing, lively production, bursting out of the screen with talent and exuberance and it would be most worthwhile to make the effort to clean it up so that the kids at Performing Arts could see what their life is supposed to be (on screen). —*Robe.*

Happy Birthday, Gemini
(COLOR)

Strident, vulgar, mostly unfunny version of Broadway hit. Limited appeal.

United Artists release of a King-Hitzig Production. Written and directed by Richard Benner. Based on the play "Gemini" by Albert Innaurato. Features entire cast. Produced by Rupert Hitzig. Exec Producer, Alan King; camera (color), James B. Kelly; editor, Stephen Fanfara; music, Rich Look, Cathy Chamberlain; production design, Ted Watkins. Reviewed at Preview Theatre, N.Y., April 23, '80. (M-PAA Rating: R). Running Time, 107 MINS.
Bunny Weinberger ...... Madeleine Kahn
Lucille Pompi .... Rita Moreno
Nick Geminiani .... Robert Viharo
Francis Geminiani ...... Alan Rosenberg
Judith Hastings .... Sarah Holcomb
Randy Hastings....David Marshall Grant
Herschel Weinberger ....Timothy Jenkins
Sam Weinberger ...... David McIllwraith
Mary O'Donnel .... Maura Swanson

Drawn from Albert Innaurato's "Gemini," the still-running Broadway comedy about the Harvard-schooled scion of a lower class Philadelphia-Italian family who's plagued by fears that he's gay, "Happy Birthday, Gemini" is a shrill, frequently tasteless and ultimately obnoxious feature that stand little chance of broad commercial support, even with the play's reputation behind it.

Like many properties transposed from the stage, this one has a hard time translating its contrived situations and semi-absurdist caricatures (elements that in a "theatrical" setting tend to gain from audiences' willing suspension of disbelief) to the realism of film. And when it does eventually shift gears to reveal the "humanity" underlying its otherwise gross or pathetic characters, no one will believe it for a minute.

Story revolves around its mixed up hero's (Alan Rosenberg's) distress at being surprised on the eve of his 21st birthday by his best friend at Harvard (WASP-ish David Marshall Grant) and the latter's sister (Sarah Holcomb), whom he bedded twice and then rejected.

Beyond the obvious culture-clashes between the moneyed visitors and Rosenberg's aggressively life-loving and virile father (Robert Viharo), latter's longtime girlfriend (Rita Moreno) and the blowsy, affectionate tramp (Madeline Kahn) who lives next-door with her corpulent retarded son (Timothy Jenkins), principal catalyst to the action is Rosenberg's admission that he spurned his girlfriend because he's in love with her brother.

Until the matter is resolved at fadeout (everyone is so understanding and will love him no matter what he decides to be), the film is little more than a series of farcical encounters between the principals, usually played at a pitch of screaming frenzy, heavily dependent on ethnic slurs, Kahn's colorful carnal vocabulary, and disconcerting running jokes at the expense of her kid's slowness, fatness, asthma and ability to throw fits on cue.

Pic was scripted and directed by Richard Benner (apparently hired because he did a good job at melding humor and pathos in pairing a schizoid girl and transvestite hairdresser in "Outrageous"). Though "Gemini" shares that pic's low-budget look and technical feel, occasional insights and honest emotions are nowhere in evidence here.

Cast is generally good, with Viharo coming off best because his part was written with more realism than most, and Kahn having some infectious fun as the golden-hearted trollop. Rosenberg's self-pitying sulks and outbursts of bitchiness hardly make him a character to root for, even assuming you could believe him as an Italian-American. —*Step.*

The Long Riders
(COLOR)

Latest shot at a Western just a bit off-target.

Hollywood, April 29.
A United Artists release. Produced by Tim Zinnemann. Directed by Walter Hill. Executive producers, James Keach, Stacy Keach. Screenplay, Bill Bryden, Steven Phillip Smith, Stacy Keach, James Keach; camera (Technicolor), Ric Waite; editors, David Holden, Freeman Davies; music, Ry Cooder; production design, Jack T. Collis; art direction, Peter Romero; set decoration, Richard Goddard; costume supervision, Tom Bronson; sound, James Webb, Chris McLaughlin; assistant director, Peter Gries. Reviewed at the Burbank Studios, Burbank, April 29, 1980. (MPAA Rating: R). Running time: 100 MINS.
Cole Younger ....David Carradine
Jim Younger .... Keith Carradine
Bob Younger ....Robert Carradine
Jesse James .... James Keach
Frank James .... Stacy Keach
Ed Miller .... Dennis Quaid
Clell Miller .... Randy Quaid
John Younger .... Kevin Brophy
George Arthur .... Harry Carey Jr.
Charlie Ford .... Christopher Guest
Bob Ford .... Nicholas Guest
Annie Ralston .... Shelby Leverington
Mr. Reddick .... Felice Orlandi
Belle Starr .... Pamela Reed
Sam Starr .... James Remar
Mrs. Samuel................. Fran Ryan
Zee .... Savannah Smith
Beth .... Amy Stryker
Mr. Rixley .... James Whitmore Jr.
Mortician .... John Bottoms
McCorkindale .... West Buchanan

"The Long Riders" represents Hollywood's latest shot at revitalizing the moribund genre of the Western. Attempted by young hands, pic is striking in several ways, not the least of which being the casting of actor brothers as historical outlaw kin, but narrative is episodic in the extreme and disparate artistic qualities fail to completely jell into satisfactory whole. Despite interesting try, this wouldn't appear to be the film to get Westerns off the ground again.

Yarn opens in bang-up fashion with a bank robbery, after which trigger happy Dennis Quaid is kicked out of the Younger-James-Miller gang for needlessly murdering a man during stick-up. With no time frame provided, pic proceeds by alternating scenes of further crimes, the men at play in whorehouses and courting women, and the law bungling initial attempts to capture the troublemakers but ultimately closing in on them.

As before, director Walter Hill's work acknowledges many influences, here most notably those of Howard Hawks, Akira Kurosawa and Sam Peckinpah, but still retains its own distinctive, bracingly austere tone. Hill resolutely refuses to investigate the psychology or motivations of his characters, explaining away men's life of banditry as a "habit" acquired in wake of the Civil War, and also declines much sociological exploration, indicating only that the legends of the outlaws were built through their ability to elude justice and the persistent reporting of their activities in the press.

In the absence of deep characterization and solid history, what's left is some effectively spare visual poetry and lyrical, freshly conceived renditions of classical western material. Set-pieces of particular interest are a gorgeously executed train robbery, a curious barroom fight with long knives, and the decisive, ill-prepared Northfield, Minnesota, raid, which is protracted for all it's worth not only with slow-motion visuals but slow-motion sound, the bullets approaching their victims with an agonizing but inevitable drone.

Considering the sheer number of principals, Hill and writers Bill Bryden, Steven Phillip Smith and Stacy and James Keach have split up screen time fairly, as well as providing room for some of the women, particularly Pamela Reed and Amy Stryker, to create strong impressions.

Idea of casting David, Keith and Robert Carradine as the Youngers, James and Stacy Keach as Jesse and Frank James, Dennis and Randy Quaid as the Miller boys and Christopher and Nicholas Guest as the turncoat Ford brothers was an inspired stroke which, given the vicissitudes of Hollywood schedules, billing requirements and artistic suitability, is a small miracle to have pulled off. Cast is uniformly excellent, with David Carradine and Randy Quaid throwing off the most humor and the Keaches balancing that with a grimmer, almost Puritanical streak.

What's ultimately missing is hardly style, but a definable point of view which would tie together the myriad events on display and fill in the blanks which Hill has methodically imposed on the action by sapping it of emotional or historical meaning. Only character which noticeably changes over pic's duration is Jesse James, who becomes something of an authoritarian dandy with his increased celebrity. By refusing to implicate himself or the audience in fates of the men, either pro or con, Hill leaves a void on the screen, with characters living and dying to little apparent result. This kind of fancy existentialism worked with the anonymous gang members in "The Warriors," but comes up short when applied to the legendary figures of American history and folklore.

Tech credits are outstanding all around, with top marks going to Ric Waite's rich camerawork, Ry Cooder's active score, Jack T. Col-

lis' impressive production design and Craig Baxley's crucial work with a large team of stuntmen.
—*Cart.*

We're Going To Eat You
(HONG KONG-COLOR)

Hong Kong, April 15.
A Seasonal Film Corporation release. Produced by Ng See Yuen. Directed by Tsui Hark. Features entire cast. Production manager, Richard Cheung; martial arts choreography, Yuen Kwei, Chien Yue-Sheng. Reviewed at Olympia Theatre, Hong Kong, April 15, '80. Running Time: 92 MINS.
Agent 999 .... Tsui Siu-Chang
The Concubine .... Cheung Mu-Lian
The Thief .... Han Kuo-Tsai
The Security Chief .... Kao Shiung
Rolex, Chief's Assistant .... Mel Wong
Cantonese or Mandarin soundtrack available with English sub-titles.

This is not an erotic film from Chinatown Hong Kong. It is the very disappointing second feature of Hark Tsui, who showed great promise last year with "The Butterfly Murders." While Tsui's debut had a striking originality by combining past and futuristic elements in martial arts, his latest project badly damaged his image. "We're Going To Eat You" is an ill-conceived combination of horror-comedy-gone-kung fu with satire added.

The story introduces an agent for China's Central Surveillance Agency, Agent 999 (Tsui Siu-Ching), going to an island to apprehend a bandit known as Rolex. On his way he is attacked by masked men but escapes. A young woman gives him refuge and medication, before he continues on his search mission.

Little did the agent know that the town is inhabited by cannibalistic residents. The concept is interesting, but things go haywire after the first 15 minutes and its downfall could not be salvaged by blood, decapitations, and violence. It is overlong with flashes of unnecessary, repetitious kung fu fights.

This pic will be screened at the Cannes film market by Seasonal Films.
—*Mel.*

Beyond Evil
(COLOR)

Some initial b.o. interest.

Hollywood, May 2.
An IFI/Scope III release. Producers, David Baughn, Herb Freed. Exec producer, Roven Akiba. Directed by Herb Freed. Features entire cast. Screenplay, Freed, Paul Ross based on a story by David Baughn; camera (Metrocolor), Ken Plotin' editor, Rick Westover. Reviewed at the Hollywood Screening Room, Hollywood, May 2, 1980. (MPAA Rating: R.) Running time: 94 MINS.
Larry .... John Saxon
Barbara .... Lynda Day George
Del .... Michael Dante
Albanos .... Mario Milano
Alma .... Janice Lynde
Dr. Solomon .... David Opatoshu
Leia .... Anne Marisse
Esteban .... Zitto Kazaan

"Beyond Evil" is an above average horror yarn in terms of plot, but never delivers enough tension, suspense or general grossness to satisfy genre fans. Still, acting and tech credits are better than usual for this type of offering, and saturation bookings should bring in financial payoffs for the first few weeks of release.

Film seems to adapt the old adage of "hell hath no fury like a woman scorned." Plot centers on the 100-year-old spirit of Alma, who once lived in a charming island mansion with her philandering husband. Because he was such a baddie, Alma began to dabble in the occult and eventually became so powerful (it's rumoured she made a pact with the Devil) that she was able to rise from the dead to kill her husband.

John Saxon and Lynda Day George play an innocent couple who have been given Alma's house as a present by friend Michael Dante. Alma, not liking company, does everything she can to possess George and destroy everyone within her reach.

George and Saxon seem a bit too goody-good in their characterizations but manage to perform their functions within the story. Director Herb Freed, who co-wrote with Paul Ross based on a story by David Baugh, attempts to build to several suspenseful payoffs, but there are too many sagging moments in between the scares.

Janice Lynde's characterization of Alma provides most of the interest, coming off as both menacing and sensitive. It is her presence that gives the feature its energy and will ultimately attract audiences.
—*Berg.*

Leo And Loree
(COLOR)

Three L's—Leo, Loree and Lame.

Hollywood, April 14.
A United Artists release, produced by Jim Begg. Exec producer, Ron Howard. Directed by Jerry Paris. Features entire cast. Screenplay, James Ritz; camera (CFI Color), Costa Petals; editor, Ed Cotter; sound, Robbie Robinson; art direction, Linda Pearl; assistant director, Cheryl Downey; associate producer, James Ragan; music, Lance Rubin. Reviewed at United Artists, Culver City, April 14, 1980. (MPAA rating: PG.) Running time: 97 MINS.
Leo .... Donny Most
Loree .... Linda Purl
Dennis .... David Huffman
Tony .... Jerry Paris
Christina .... Shannon Farnon
Jarvis .... Allan Rich
Cindy .... Susan Lawrence

"Leo And Loree" is not a bad film at all — except there's really no rea-

son to have made it. United Artists picked it up, probably considering the tv pull of Donny Most and Linda Purl, but the risks look minimal and the rewards about average.

The sun comes up in the east and sets in the west and actors and actresses have a terrible time getting established in Hollywood. Given this trio of truths, exec producer Ron Howard and director Jerry Paris have chosen the third to make a film about, adequately pinning down the point without adding one whit to what's been dealt with time and time again.

Most journeys west in search of an acting career, bunking initially with David Huffman, the only solid character as the suffering friend who puts up with Most's insufferable intrusions. In fact, the worst part about this picture is that Most is presented initially as so unlikeable that he has to struggle through last half to make amends. The fact that he is able to do so is a credit worth noting.

Purl portrays the daughter of Oscar-winner Shannon Farnon who has a headstart because of mother. Purl's early success naturally causes problems for her lasting love affair with Most and there are lots of wistful wanderings around the ball field where their romance first blossomed.

The ending is happy, which might be a plus in the marketplace. But there is no marketplace for this one, except as they say, in the ancillary sales shelves. —*Har.*

The Nude Bomb
(COLOR)

Recycling of Don Adams as Maxwell Smart. The tv reruns are better.

Hollywood, May 1.
Universal Pictures release of a Jennings Lang production. Produced by Lang. Directed by Clive Donner. Features entire cast. Screenplay, Arne Sultan, Bill Dana, Leonard B. Stern based on characters created by Mel Brooks and Buck Henry; camera (Technicolor), Harry L. Wolf; editor, Walter Hannemanni, Phil Tucker; music, Lalo Schifrin; production design, William Tuntke; set decoration, Marc E. Meyer, Jr. sound, Lowell Harris; costumes, Burton Miller; assistant director, Don Zepfel. Reviewed at the Samuel Goldwyn Theatre, Beverly Hills, May 1, 1980. (MPAA Rating: PG.) Running time: 94 MINS.
Maxwell Smart .... Don Adams
Agent 34 .... Sylvia Kristel
Edith Von Secondberg ...Rhonda Fleming
Chief .... Dana Elcar
Agent 36 .... Pamela Hensley
Agent 22 .... Andrea Howard
Carruthers .... Norman Lloyd
Jonathon Levinson Seigle ...... Bill Dana
Jerry Krovney .... Gary Imhoff
Pam Krovney .... Sarah Rush
Nino Salvatore Sebastiani .... Vittorio Gassman
American Ambassador ... Walter Brooke
President .... Thomas Hill
Landlady .... Ceil Cabot
Agent 13 .... Joey Forman

Resurrection of bumbling secret agent Maxwell Smart from television heaven seems at the very least to suggest a sorry lack of original ideas for feature film fodder. Although Don Adams still manages to retain the humor of the character he brought to national attention via "Get Smart," the hit sixties vidseries, "The Nude Bomb" bears little of the scathing staire and sharp dialog that lured audiences to the original. Pic has its moments but it is questionable how many Smart fans are left in the filmgoing public.

Television nostalgia buffs will no doubt be appreciative to producer Jennings Lang for giving Smart another chance but disappointed that so little of the show's original elements are left. Sadly lacking are Barbara Feldon's Agent 99 and Ed Platt (now deceased) as the Chief, as well as many of Smart's enemies from his counter org, KAOS. Unfortunately, their original portrayals are too much an integral part' of the engaging ambience of Smart for this version not to suffer.

In terms of attention to the original gimmicks, some attempt is made to resurrect original Smart paraphernalia (e.g. use of Adam's infamous shoe phone is first-rate) but it is given short shrift in favor of the new story.

That wouldn't be so bad had writers Arne Sultan, Bill Dana and Leonard B. Stern, all of whom were involved in the original, presented something at least up to par with "Get Smart." Plot line of Smart's attempt to prevent a villain from launching missiles that will cause everyone in the world to be naked, is initially amusing but weak, turning entirely into the latter as the pic progresses.

Andrea Howard provides some pleasant moments as Adams' new spy partner and Clive Donner directs the script ably. But fans of the vidshow will derive much more enjoyment by crowding around their television sets with a bowl of popcorn watching "Get Smart" reruns.—*Berg.*

La Battala de Chile - III
(The Battle Of Chile, Part III:
(The Power Of The People)
(CHILE-CUBA-DOCU-16m-B&W)

Hollywood, April 24.

A Unifilm release of an Equipo Tercer Ano production, in collaboration with the Cuban Film Institute. Directed by Patricio Guzman; camera (b&w), Jorge Muller; editor, Pedro Chaskel; sound, Bernardo Menz; assistant director, Jose Pino. Reviewed at the Nuart Theatre, W. Los Angeles, Apr. 24, 1980. (No MPAA Rating.) Running time: **83 MINS.**

(In Spanish with English subtitles and narration).

"The Battle Of Chile, Parts I & II," completed in 1976 and released domestically as one picture in 1978, stands as one of the more remarkable film and political documents of the 1970s, charting in minute and incisive detail the rise and fall of President Salvador Allende.

Final section of the trilogy, finished by refugee Patricio Guzman and his small group, based now in Cuba, shares the earnestness and commitment of the first two parts and cannot detract from their power, but it can hardly be considered their equal. Docu will attract fest and specialized audiences more because of holdover interest in earlier works than for intrinsic value of this one.

Memory lingering most strongly from first installments is the highly articulate political sophistication of the Chilean populace at large. Be they from the right, center or left, workers, intellectuals and politicos all spoke with impressive expressiveness on the events sweeping their country.

It is thus by contrast that the uniformly party line rhetoric of those interviewed in "Part III" comes as a distinct letdown. Given even the admitted left-wing bias of the entire venture, initial sections allowed a complexity of viewpoint which has been flattened out here, as workers, and especially the narrator, spout overused Marxist slogans and simplistic philosophy at odds with the intelligent shadings and nuances voiced earlier in the epic work.

In effect, this section runs parallel to "Part II," in that it focuses almost exclusively on workers' efforts to counteract a right-imposed strike at the same time Allende, who is only briefly glimpsed here, fought his losing battle with the military and outside interference. Factory workers are seen taking over their facilities even as executives stay away, and grass-roots food distribution methods are improvised in face of truckers walking off the job. It's a noble, if ultimately ponderous, picture of perseverance against overwhelming odds.

Technically, pic is at one with previous segments, as b&w images evoke sincerity and limited means of the enterprise. Many subtitles, however, are irritatingly lost against white backgrounds. —*Cart.*

Sadan Er Jeg Ogsaa
(That's Me, Too)
(DANISH-COLOR)

Copenhagen, April 12.

A Focus Film production. A/S Asa Film release. Written and directed by Lise Roos. Features entire cast. Camera (Eastmancolor) Jan Weincke); production designer, Finn Karlsson; editor, Edith Toreg; executive producer, Erik Overbye. Reviewed at Palladium, Copenhagen, April 12, 1980. Running time, **90 MINS.**

Cast: Stine Sylverstersen, Preben Kaas, Avi Sagild, Inger Stender, Annelise Gabold.

Lise Roos, one of Denmark's many woman filmmakers, used the child Stine Sylvestersen at ages 8 and 11 for a couple of shorter features and has now put Stine, age 18, in front of the camera again. She has acquired luminous qualities as a film face and displays obvious talents as an actress. Roos, however, seems mired in her very special set of convictions as to how a film should be made: mostly as filmed talks, improvised talks at that, framed into a whole by more or less professional actors cavorting in charicatures of roles.

Pic follows the girl Stine in all kinds of situations pitting herself for or against family and society norms, manners and morals. She undresses a lot, joins protest marchers, steps lively at the discotheques and has fun and sexual games with various boys. A lot of this rings true, but also has the flat tone of authenticity not inspired by any individual artistic viewpoint.

"That's Me. Too" would appear suitable for tv youth programming in more modest situations beyond Denmark's borders. —*Kell.*

Liar's Dice
(COLOR)

Nice first effort for fest genre.

San Francisco, April 29.

No distrib. Produced by Butros Makdissy and Ed Eubanks. Directed by Issam B. Makdissy. Features entire cast. Screenplay, Terry Eubanks-Makdissy; camera (color), Douglas Murray; editor, Issam B. Makdissy; music, Coleman Burke and Gary Yamani; sound, David Bacon; lighting, Robert Shoup. Reviewed at the Surf Theatre, San Francisco, April 19, '80. (No MPAA Rating.) Running time: 95 MINS.

Joe .... Robert Ede
Anne .... Terry Eubanks-Makdissy
Samir .... Issam B. Makdissy
Jack .... Frank Triest
Pete .... D.G. Buckles
Dottie .... Norma Small
Janice .... Phran Gauci
Jamil .... Rafik Assad
Sharon .... Shirley James
Tony .... Phil De Carla
Mel .... Jerry La Rue
Boy .... Judd Strelo
New waitress .... Jeannette Mignola
Boy's father .... John Lovell

This shoestring production, unspooled at Bay Area Filmmakers' Week, a Frisco film fest spinoff, is most noted for the protean talents of the director's wife, Terry Eubanks-Makdissy, nominally an artist, but involved here as screenwriter and leading lady. (Her paintings provide the backdrop for the credits, and a few more of her works are seen during the film.)

Her yarn is built around the significant theme of loneliness, a downer thesis to be sure, yet one with great contemporary pert- inence, one not yet explored fully on the screen.

Her character, an artist-cocktail waitress, is the pivotal figure of a loosely hatched triangle: a married foreign student, portrayed by director Issam B. Makdissy, and an old man, etched with competence by Robert Ede, whose sense of isolation comes through more than that of the two younger people.

Eubanks-Makdissy can't figure out how to handle the conclusion to her tale and opts for a death and an argument, neither of which work too well. But she's on the right track, particularly in her performance. A major would be wise to employ this woman's versatility.

Makdissy himself, considering his budgetary limitations, has done nice work with his first feature, although his acting leaves a bit to be desired.

This is the sort of picture which with more time, more money and a couple of b.o. names could be quite commercial, considering the relevance of its theme. As it stands, it's a solid festival film and evidence that creativity can do an awful lot with only $40,000. —*Herb.*

Stuckey's Last Stand
(COLOR)

Not even for moppets.

St. Louis, April 19.

Royal Oak Film Corp. release of a Summer Camp Company production. Produced, directed and written by Lawrence G. Goldfarb. Features entire cast. Executive producer, Erich Von Forbes. Camera (color), Arthur J. Fitzsimmons; music, Carson Whitsett; Dixieland music, the St. Louis Ragtimers; art director, Julia Norris; editors, Arthur J. Fitzsimmons, Ethan Edwards; asst. director, Peg Berry. Reviewed at Wehrenberg Screening Room, St. Louis, April 19, 1980. (MPAA Rating, PG). Running time: **92 MINS.**

Whit .... Whit Reichert
Russ .... Ray Anzalone
Will .... Will Shaw
Pete .... Tom Murray
Duke .... Richard Cosentino
Billie .... Marilyn Terschluse
Marianne .... Jeanne L. Austin
Gordon .... John Zimmerman
Angry Father .... Dan Dierdorf
Angry Mother .... Pat Ball

"Stuckey's Last Stand" does not refer to a vanishing roadside restaurant chain, though that subject probably would have made a more amusing film. Instead, the St. Louis-written, directed and acted feature, picked up for distribution by Royal Oak Film Corp., of Salt Lake City, is a dull, repetitious, poorly plotted comedy of summer camp.

A "Meatballs" it isn't, nor does it seem to be much of anything else. Boxoffice outlook seems meager, with little in the action to attract mass audiences. Primary outlook might be for Saturday morning kiddie shows in shopping centers.

Plot involves a day at a day camp

for rather well-to-do nine-year-olds, and Stuckey is the head counselor, as inept as his staff. Story is told in flashback as Whit, one of the counselors, visits a psychiatrist to discuss his well-deserved feelings of inadequacy.

From this extremely original beginning, it's easy to see what happens next. In between, perhaps to entertain those slightly older than nine, a young male counselor tries to make points with a young female counselor. Marilyn Terschluse looks good in a bathing suit, but dialog between her and John Zimmerman is about as interesting as watching grass grow, and their deliveries are right in style.

With the exception of Ellis Rice, a young black who is sympathetic, all the counselors are vacuums. Richard Cosentino stands out, however, with pitch helmet and military bearing that psychs the kids nicely and offers the only real appeal to an audience.

The others, Whit Reichert, Tom Murray and Will Shaw, along with Ray Anzalone in the title role, are losers, and they have neither the personality nor the comedic ability to become appealing.

Lawrence G. Goldfarb, producer, writer and director (his father, under a pseudonym, is executive producer), fails to show any charm in either the kids or the counselors, and the incidents are badly contrived and poorly paced.

For some reasons, it was decided that a PG rating was necessary, so a couple of the kids use the necessary language.

Technical credits are fair, just about in line with all other aspects. —*Japo*.

Hayam Ha'Acharon
(The Last Sea)
(ISRAELI-DOCU-B&W)

Tel Aviv, April 3.

A Teudah Films & Lohamei HaGetaot House Production. Produced by Benny Shilo, Yehezkel Avneri. Directed by Haim Guri, Jaquot Erlich, David Bergman. Camera (black and white), Emil Knebel; advisers: Yehuda Bauer, Gavriel Cohen; editing board, Yoske Rabinovitz, Yehuda Hellman, Itzhak Sternberg, Uzi Harpaz; music, Yossi Mar-Haim; musical advisers, Gil Aldema, Eliahu Hacohen. Reviewed Tel Aviv Museum, April 3, 1980. Running time: **100 MINS.**

To all purposes, this should be the companion piece to the same team's previous documentary, "The 81st Blow," using similar techniques taking off where the first one ended. Now Guri, Erlich and Bergman are at it again, continuing from where they left off, to tell of the struggle through which Holocaust survivers managed, between the end of the war, 1945, and the creation of the State of Israel, in 1948, to reach the shores of what they came to regard as the only place on earth for them.

To do so, the trio gathered some 30 hours of filmed documents and recorded close to 300 hours of interviews with witnesses who had lived through this period. Editing the enormous mass of material into a manageable quantity, and juxtaposing the visuals and the sound required years of painstaking labor, much of it invested in the sound, which is finally used almost to the point of manipulation, as specific phrases have been stuck to specific visuals, even if there is no connection between the speaker and the frame on the screen.

There is no doubt of the authenticity of the raw material here, and the film tries to cover as much ground as possible in describing the crises of various communities throughout Europe and North Africa and demonstrating that they had no choice but to look for a homeland of their own, a conclusion which seems to carry serious propaganda value by itself. But the real problem is that as far as filmed documents are concerned, they are of a rather indifferent nature, with some exceptions and they are hardly capable of riveting the public to the screen for 100 minutes, while the system of editing testimonies in small pieces may cause admiration for the dexterity of the editor but no identification with the witnesses. If it is very commendable not to use a narrator who would force conclusions into the public's mind, the alternate solution should not muddle the issues as it sometimes tends to do here. And what is worse, a tiresome, interminable score, slightly reminiscent of Kurt Weill, gives a kind of melodramatic patina to the whole thing it could easily do without.

The real importance of the film, finally, seems to be in its being done. The material gathered is of great importance for anyone who will wish to trace an audio-visual history of the State of Israel, and for that, Guri, Erlich and Bergman should be thanked.

As for the film itself, which some additional trimming, and substantial deletion of music, it could become a useful documentary for any self-respecting tv station, and a must for any archive. —*Edna*.

La Muchacha De Las Bragas De Oro
(The Girl With The Golden Panties)
(SPANISH-VENEZUELAN-COLOR)

Madrid, March 28.

A Morgana S.A. (Barcelona) Prozesa (Barcelona) and Proa Cinematografica C.A. (Caracas) coproduction. Directed by Vicente Aranda. Features entire cast. Exec producers Jose Antonio Perez Giner, Carlos Duran; camera (Eastmancolor), Jose Luis Alcaine; screenplay, Vicente Aranda, Santiago San Miguel and Mauricio Wallerstein, based on novel by Juan Marse; editor, Alberto Torija; music, Manuel Camp; sets, Josep Rosell. Reviewed at Real Cinema, Madrid, March 28, '80. Running time: **101 MINS.**

Luis Forest .... Lautaro Murua
Mariana .... Victoria Abril
Also Isabel Mestres, Hilda Vera, Perla Vonasek, Pep Munne, Palmiro Aranda, Consuelo de Nieva.

———

Catalan helmer Vicente Aranda scored three years ago with "Cambio de Sexo" and has followed up with a more complex film which is sure to be seen on the international fest circuit and is one of the best made in Spain over the past year.

Item, based on an award-winning novel by Juan Marse, is at once intellectualized and bawdy and has enough brooding twists to bide audiences over a slow start and a seeming tendency towards pedantry. Aided by superb thesping by Lautraro Murua and Victoria Abril, crisp lensing by Jose Louis Alcaine and a finely penned script, Aranda handles the relation between an old fascist and his iconoclastic hippie niece with expertise and taste.

Story unrolls in coastal resort of Sitges where an elderly militant of the Old Order is writing his memoirs and trying to pick through the broken strands of his former life. Unexpectedly descending on the introspective staidness of his life are two young, uninhibited girls, one his niece, the other a neurotic beatnik photographer who never speaks a word. Ostensibly they have been set by the former's mother to do a reportage on the elderly man.

Aranda skillfully develops the relationship between Luis and Mariana, as former starts to peep out of his intellectual cocoon and latter develops an interest in him. His conservative ways are contrasted with her sexually taunting, pixyish manners. Through a large part of the film she runs about barebreasted, and tries to incite or scandalize him by her actions and language. He becomes increasingly fascinated.

There are moments when the plot and insinuations of Louis's past thicken so much as to be hard to follow. Excerpts of his former life are intercut in flashbacks, chronicling his attempts to break away from the fascist fold and come to terms with an unhappy marriage.

In its first two weeks of release in Barcelona, pic has reportedly done very well. It must certainly be counted in the scant list of Spanish quality films made recently. Item is a natural for fest circuits and could do well in sophisticated markets, though it might run into censorship snags in countries like Argentina, Chile, etc. All technical credits are excellent and lensing and thesping is of a higher order. —*Besa*.

Harlequin
(AUSTRALIAN-COLOR)

Sydney, April 2.

A Greater Union Organization release of William Fayman's presentation of an Antony I. Ginnane Production. Produced by Tony Ginnane. Executive Producer, Bill Fayman. Directed by Simon Wincer. Stars Robert Powell, Carmen Duncan, David Hemmings. Associate Producer, Jane Scott; screenplay, Everett De Roche; camera (Panavision-Eastman colour) Gary Hansen; music, Brian May; editing, Adrian Carr; production design, Bernard Hides; special effects, Conrad Rothmann; asst. director, Mike McKeag; sound, Gary Wilkins. Previewed at State Theatre, Sydney, April 1, '80. (Commonwealth censorship rating: M). Running time: **96 MINS.**

Gregory Wolfe .... Robert Powell
Sandra Rast .... Carmen Duncan
Nick Rast .... David Hemmings
Doc Wheelan .... Broderick Crawford
Mr. Bergier .... Gus Mercurio
Mr. Porter ....;.... Alan Cassell
Alex Rast .... Mark Spain
Benny Lucas .... Sean Myers
Robinson .... Bevan Lee
Dr. Barthelemy .... Neville Teede
Dr. Lovelock .... John Frawley
Edith Twist .... Mary Mackay
Alice .... Alyson Best
Mabel Wheelan .... Nita Pannell
Prison Officer .... Murray Ogden
Arthur .... Claus Schultz
Godfrey .... Peter West
Jepson .... David Hough

———

"Harlequin" is a conscious attempt by producer Tony Ginnane to make an international picture; contemporary drama that could take place anywhere and in which elements of Australiana have no relevance. In that, he has succeeded admirably; perhaps too well at times because the anonymity created by this deliberate de-location contributes a strange sterility to Aussie eyes.

The plot concerns an up and coming politician, Nick Rast (David Hemmings), set to be the new head of government when the existing one disappears while scuba diving. He is being groomed for the role by political manipulator Doc Wheelan. Latter is disturbed by Rast's wife's growing attachment to Wolfe, a mysterious faith healer who has a beneficial effect on the couple's son stricken with leukemia.

Wolfe's arrival coincides with a period of remission which increases the bonding between him and the boy — and the wife. Wheelan takes steps to remove Wolfe from the scene, and the mystery man responds by unleashing supernatural powers.

If it all sounds very much like the Rasputin-Alexandra-Tsar Nicholas story, that's pretty much what it is; but it is sufficiently removed into the present to give it the contemporary elements required to make the story new, if not the plot.

Simon Wincer's direction shows a firmer hand than his previous (first) feature, and indicates that he's a talent to keep an eye on. Tony Ginnane, as usual, invests his picture with excellent production values, and Gary Hansen's Panavision cameras give the atmosphere an even richer feel.

Thesping is fine with Carmen Duncan giving a remarkable performance as the initially ambivalent wife whose filial love overtakes her better judgement. Robert Powell creates in Wolfe a twist on the Rasputin character because there are no apparently evil intentions. The bad guy is clearly Broderick Crawford as Doc Wheelan, and he exploits the role for all it's worth.

Brian May's music is excellent; likewise all other tech' credits. Pic was shot in West Australia.

"Harlequin" has already been pre-sold in a number of markets: Greater Union have it for Australia. Financing came from Australian Film Commission, Ace Theatres, Perth, W.A., and West Australian Film Council, whose first feature production investment it was. —*Miha.*

Jula Treekul
(Jula Treekul River)
(THAI-COLOR)

Bangkok, April 20.
An Apex Productions release. Produced by Nanta Tansacha. Directed by Pornpoj Kanitkasen. Features entire cast. Story, Panom Thien; screenplay, Thanachai Chinotai and Banjerd Thavee; camera (color), Sophon Jaenphanit; sound, Kasem Militachinda; music, Prachin Songpao; art direction, Urai Srisombat; costumes, Adjarn Soodsai Smitinan; asst. director, Apichat Pornpairoj. Reviewed at Indra theatre, Bangkok, April 20, '80. Running time: 105 MINS.
Ariyawat .... Sorapong Chatri
Dararai 2 .... Nawarat Yukthanan
Katiya .... Piya Trakulrat
Apasra .... Vasana Sitthivej
Kara Singha .... Pisan Akaraseni
Prachao Kasih .... Manop Assawathep
Tewati .... Marasri Issrangkul
Na Ayudhya
Dararai 2 .... Anchalee Chaisri

Budgeted at 7,000,000 baht (about $350,000), or thrice as expensive as an average Thai pic, "Jula Treekul" toplines two of the most popular Thai young love teams — Sorapong Chatri and Nawarat Yukthanan as one, Piya Trakulrat and Vasana Sitthivej the other.

. Today's audiences react differently to the familiar plot, now open to ridicule and laughter. Even as an Eastern fairy tale, with everybody dressed up as Indians, "Jula Treekul" lacks wit and charm; whatever humor is present appears unintentional.

A queen is sentenced to death by drowning in the Jula Treekul River in the opening sequence. Twenty years later, her daughter suffers a similar fate. In both cases, queen and daughter are found guilty of an illicit love. The two deaths are visually alike.

Recurring theme is the failure of true lovers to find long-lasting

happiness, seemingly responsible for making main players look morose and dejected most of the time. Forced to marry against her will, Vasana gets the lion's share of lovesick moments.

Pic's battle scenes employ shots of wounded and dying warriors as a substitute for man to man combat, but cannot hide the fact that the battles as staged are incoherent and unimpressive.

Prachin Songpao copped the best musical scoring prize of both the Suphannahong and Tukatatong film awards for his work here.

Expensive costumes indicate where a major portion of pic's budget went. —*Cano.*

We Are The
Guinea Pigs
(DOCU-COLOR-16m)

Strong protest against nuclear power.

A release by Parallel Films. Produced by Ralph Klein. Directed by John Harvey. Camera (color). Tom Hurwitz; edited by Joan Harvey and Trudy Bagdon; sound by Albee Gordon. Reviewed at Loeb Center, New York University, March 28, 1980. No MPAA rating. Running time: **90 MINS.**

One year to the day, March 28, after the near-catastrophe at Three Mile Island nuclear facility in Harrisburg, Pennsylvania, a film about that event premiered to an overflow crowd at the Loeb Center of New York. Both the film and the crowd were clearly anti-nuclear.

Title for "We Are The Guinea Pigs" is also its theme, as Harrisburg residents in on-camera interviews complain about having been deceived by nuclear authorities. Families echo identical protest, that they and the nation are victims of the greed of private power, governmental bungling, the arms race and insane technology. TMI is seen as symbolic forewarning of huge upcoming nuclear-accident catastrophe in U.S. generally.

Offering scientific testimony in "Guinea Pigs" are experts of various persuasions — doctors, physicists, environmentalists, local and state politicians, and spokespersons for the Nuclear Regulatory Agency.

Film is product of large team of independent filmmakers and private citizens. Total budget is $230,000, of which $95,000 are deferred salaries of crew and creative personnel as yet unpaid. Of $135,000 in debts and out-of-pocket costs, about $50,000 has been granted by several small foundations and by individual contributors.

Parallel Films was created for production of "Guinea Pigs" and the company will handle distribution to U.S. and foreign tv, also to the 16m market. Blow-up to 35m for theatrical exposure is in planning.

Producer of "Guinea Pigs," Ralph Klein, a New York psychologist and teacher, has no previous experience in cinema. Cameraman Tom Hurwitz is N.Y.U. professor with previous credits on "Harlan County U.S.A.," "Alambrista" and other New York independent productions. John Amato composed and performed score for "Guinea Pigs," themed to antinuclear protest.

Director of "Guinea Pigs" is Joan Harvey, whose theatre work in New York as actress, writer and director is well known. Although having many credits in cinema and television as actress and writer, "Guinea Pigs" is Harvey's first film as a director. —*Hitch.*

Viva La Clase Media
(Long Live the Middle Class)
(SPANISH-COLOR)

Madrid, April 10.
A Garci-Sinde Acuarius Films production. Directed by Jose Maria Garcias Sinde. Features entire cast. Screenplay, Jose Luis Garci, Jose Maria Garcia Sinde; camera (Eastmancolor), Hans Burman; editor, Miguel Gonzalez Sinde; exec producer, Jose Luis Garci. Reviewed at Cine Richmond, Madrid April 10, 1980. Running time: 99 MINS.
Cast: Emilio Gutierrez Caba, Enriqueta Carballeira, Maria Casanova, Irene Gutierrez Caba, Jose Luis Garci, Raul Fraile, Maria Vico, Charo Soriano, Javier Beringola.

The team that made "Asignatura Pendiente," "Solos en la Madrugada" and "Las Verdes Praderas" have now come up with a pic which looks somewhat nostalgically back upon the days when the Communist Party was still outlawed in Spain and everyone knew who the "bad" guy was. Item, set in period from 1961 to 1965, tells story of group of friends making up a Communist cell in Madrid. They all come from "middle class" backgrounds, and the Garci-Sinde tandem tells of their personal and ideological struggles, but mostly in a whimsical way.

Authors do not attempt any plot development and eschew efforts at dramatizing situations, which gives pic a plodding talkiness which slows it down as we are served up long dialogs, only occasionally interrupted by leftwing escapades as the cell distributes illegal leaflets in the streets or at a soccer game. The occasional use of Federico Chueca's zarzuela music as background casts an almost nostalgic mantle over the rather pointless doings of the cell, as though the writers were still yearning for the good old bad days of yore.

Certainly a paucity of militancy among the Communists is evinced, and the only reason put forth why the middle-class sympathizers join the Party is that "one has to do something" to fight the Franco re-

gime. Though pic is rather too talky and drawn out and motivations are not sufficiently underlined, item does come across as a sincere effort at pinpointing a period and those who 15 years ago lived through it.

Film ends on a melancholy, if not mawkish, note as the cell is finally apprehended by police and the politically lukewarm protagonist is led off to jail with his wife and child looking on in tears. Item is well directed, but thesping, especially Emilio Gutierrez Caba's, lacks emphasis. Item might have some limited commercial chances abroad, especially in East Bloc countries.
—*Besa.*

The Psychotronic Man
(COLOR)

Psychic barber runs amok in Chicago. For the product hungry only.

Chicago, April 17.
International Harmony Corp. release of a Spelson Productions and Jack M. Assoc. production. Producer, Peter Spelson. Director, Jack M. Sell. Features entire cast. Screenplay, Spelson and Sell, based on Spelson's original story; camera (Astro Color Labs). Sell; score, Tommy Irons; art director, Fred Becht; sound, Bob Bennett, Diane Haglund, Karl Navarette; special effects, Bob Vanni; editor, Bill Reese. Reviewed at Astro Color Labs, Chicago, April 17, 1980. (MPAA Rating: PG). Running time: 90 MINS.
Rocky Foscoe ....Peter Spelson
Lt. Walter O'Brien ....Christopher Carbis
Sgt. Chuck Jackson ....Curt Colbert
Kathy .... Robin Newton
Dr. Steinberg ....Paul Marvel
Officer Maloney .... Jeff Caliendo
Mrs. Foscoe .... Lindsey Novak
Professor .... Irwin Lewin
SIA Agent Gorman .... Corney Morgan
Old Man .... Bob McDonald

The only arresting aspect of this inept, rock-bottom-budget entry is its Chicago origination. Saga of a suburban barber driven by special psychic force to murder and mayhem was produced, created and lensed completely in and around the Windy City, a site not known as a source of original feature product. Pic may provide the only chance you'll ever have to witness a climactic shootout on Michigan Ave.

A word about its creators. Peter Spelson, who produced, coscripted and toplines in "The Psychotronic Man," has been tangentially involved in local film productions, and has an interest with his brother in a local insurance business. Jack Sell formed his own production outfit three years ago and has worked almost exclusively as a tv commercial helmer. Pic cost under $500,000, and was shot in 17 days in Chi and suburbs with a mixed union crew.

It would be reassuring to report that Spelson and Sell defied their extreme budget limitations. Unfortunately, "The Psychotronic Man" is threadbare both creatively and technically, emerging as a lame entry in the psychic phenomena-actioner sweepstakes. Playoff looms limited to only the most product-starved situations in non-urban areas.

Pic from Spelson and Sell's undernourished plot line has the former portraying a potbellied, monosyllabic barber beset by forces from his subconscious impelling him to bolt out of his shop and search for murder victims. Pic is a bit confused about precisely how the character's psychic drives are manifested — mostly he blinks, holds his head, stares intently at victims who in turn stumble to the ground or out a handy window.

The barber visits a psychiatrist, who advises, "now, Rocky, you gotta lay off the booze." In the film's most rationally-motivated scene, the barber employs his unspecified power to have the shrink tossed out a window.

Pic quickly cuts to a seemingly endless chase, and Chi buffs will get a kick out of seeing police cars barrel past the Water Tower and down Wacker Drive. In a misguided moment, director Sell lensed some of the chase in fast motion, lending silent-movie slapstick quality to what is supposed to be an edge-of-the-chair climax.

Other performers suffer from talent limitations and/or lack of direction. Christopher Carbis plays an Irish cop, complete with brogue; Curt Colbert grimaces a lot as latter's sidekick; and Paul Marvel twirls his glasses as the put-upon psychiatrist. General production values are adequate. Director Sell reports he intends to make a comedy next. It's not unking to suggest that with "The Psychotronic Man," he already has. —*Sege.*

Kosadate Gokko
(The Proper Way)
(JAPANESE-COLOR)

Tokyo, March 26.
A Dokuritsu Film Center release of a Satsukisha-Haiyuza Eiga Hoso co-production. Produced by Enzaburo Honda, Seiji Matsuki and Daishiro Miura. Features entire cast. Directed by Tadashi Imai. Screenplay, Naoyuki Suzuki, based on the book by Kyozo Miyoshi; camera (color), Kazumi Hara; lighting, Toshio Takashima; music, Shinjiro Ikebe; sound, Shin Watae; art direction, Yokoo Kiyoshi and Saburo Abe; editor, Tatsuji Nakajo; asst. director, Masao Nagai. Reviewed at Tokyo Scalaza, March 21, 1980. Running time: 118 MINS.
Shinkichi Yoshii .... Go Kato
Yoko Yoshi .... Komaki Kurihara
Takumi Hoshizawa .... Yoshi Kato
Rika Hoshizawa .... Chio Ushiwara
Toshie Nakagawa ...... Misako Watanabe
Tateno .... Iichiro Zaiitsu
Masakichi Sekide .... Toyoji Fukuda

Director Tadashi Imai has been branded by his detractors as an opportunist. A leftist sympathizer

before World War II, he directed blatant pro-government propaganda films during the war, then joined the Communist Party after the war and began turning out left-thinking features. In his latest effort, he is once again the opportunist, this time taking every opportunity to wring tears while lauding the greater glories of the classroom.

Shinkichi Yoshii (Go Kato) and wife Yoko (Komaki Kurihara), both primary school teachers in northern Japan, persuade author Takumi Hoshizawa (Yoshi Kato) to let them handle, for a brief period, the education of his daughter Rika (Chio Ishihara). The girl, the result of a liaison between Hoshizawa and a bar hostess, proves incorrigible. Indulged by her father, an advocate of "freedom" in learning, Rika lags far behind her classmates in reading ability, is willful, inattentive and, in general, a disruptive influence.

Gradually, however, a bond of affection develops between Rika and the childless Yoshiis. When it comes time for the girl, who has become a model pupil, to return to Tokyo and her father, neither she nor her teachers/surrogate parents wants to say goodbye. A sad parting at a train station is the first of many heart-rending scenes leading to the pic's lump in the throat conclusion.

The film unflaggingly plumps for institutionalized education over other alternative, and suspect, methods of learning. Rampant individuality, especially in the classroom, is looked upon with horror, while group-think is lauded. Kiddies who willingly submit to the system are cheerful and learn a lot while those who don't are morose and dull. Unsurprisingly, "Kosadate Gokko" has earned the seal of approval of Japan's nationwide PTA.

Coupled with this high level of enthusiasm for public schools is a gently needling anti-intellectualism. Author Hoshizawa, whose beret confirms his membership in the ranks of Japan's intelligentsia, is a figure of fun, a bad-mannered buffoon played by one of the most unattractive character actors in the Japanese cinema. His ostentatious name-dropping inspires chuckles and he coasts on his reputation, his output having dried up.

Its "dear old golden rule days" propagandizing aside, there is much to like about the film. Its performances are generally, and effectively low-keyed and its sentimentality, of which there is a great deal, never gets excessively sticky. — *Bail.*

...Y Al Tercer Ano Resucito
(...And the Third year, He Resuscitated)
(SPANISH-COLOR)

Madrid, April 12.
Cinco Films production. Directed by Rafael Gil. Features entire cast. Screenplay, F. Vizcaino Casas, based on his own novel; camera, (Eastmancolor) Jose F. Aguayo; music, Gregorio Garcia Segura; editor, Jose Luis Matasanz. Reviewed at Cine Fuencarral, Madrid, April 12, 1980. Running time: 88 MINS.
Cast: Mary Begona, Jose Badalo, Francisco Cecilio, Florinda Chico, Tip and Coll, Antonio Garisa, Isabel Luque, Fernando Sancho, Juan Luis Galiardo, Jose Sancho, Jose Nieto, Adrian Ortega, Juan Santamaria.

This political spoof, made for the most part by right-wing sympathizers and old-guard Franco supporters, is turning out to be one of the biggest b.o. hits of the year. But the rightwing ideology, though certainly implicit, is never obtrusive. Vizcaino Casas is adept enough at poking his finger at many of Spain's current ills, but he also keeps audiences amused as he ribs everyone from Santiago Carrillo of the Communists to Premier Adolfo Suarez.

The anecdotal story kicks off as we see an aged hitchhiker outside Franco's resting place, the Valley of the Fallen, who purportedly is the old Caudillo, resuscitated exactly three years after his death in 1975.

In a Madrid press agency a cub reporter mistakes a news item that the French franc (franco in Spanish) has resuscitated on international money markets as that Franco has resuscitated. Rest of pic takes us through different sectors of Spanish society where the news is received with dismay or joy; but mostly it prompts leaders to flee or dig out their old fascist togs.

Everyone comes in for lampooning, but mostly the labor unions, the separatists, the gays and other groups that have come to the fore since Spain became democratic. Bombs go off in the street, groups strike for "free vitamins," labor leaders can't find a spare day in the calendar for a new strike, prostitutes form a union as "workers in love," bank robbers stroll away from a holdup and a village, under the mistaken notion that an army on maneuvers is an advance column of Nationalists akin to those in 1936, receives them jubilantly with Spanish flags and fascist salutes.

The news mistake is finally caught, but not before thousands mass in the traditional square in front of the palace in Madrid to shout "Franco, Franco, Franco." They doubtless bring a twinge of nostalgia to Old Guard audiences. But no one appears on the balcony of the palace, and the old man hitch-

hikes back to the tomb outside Madrid.

Being laden with references to the local political and social situation, pic would be difficult for a foreigner to understand, but given its success here it might prove of some interest to minority sectors abroad. Technical credits are good. Pic is too episodic for any of the thesps to get their teeth into the parts. Most of the overtones wuld probably be lost to non-Spaniards.—*Besa.*

The Happenings
(HONG KONG-COLOR)

Hong Kong, April 3.
A Raymond Chow Production. Production supervision, Kitty Ip. Director, Yim Ho. Features entire cast. Screenplay, Shu Kei, Yim Ho; camera (color), Cheung Yiu Cho; editor, Cheung Yiu Chung; theme songs written by Stanley Pong and Ambrose Lo; sung by Patricia Chan; assistant directors, Shu Kei, Jobic Wong. Reviewed at State Theatre, Hong Kong, April 3, 1980. Running time: 100 MINS.
Cast: Cheung, Kwok Keung, Lisa Yuen, Yim Chow Wah, Pejola Chu, Yim Chun Wah, Dick Keung.
(Cantonese soundtrack with English subtitles).

"The Happenings" is the first feature of tv director and ex-Film Force (Bang Bang) member Yim Ho at Raymond Chow's Golden Harvest. And the company must be congratulated for risking on a relatively new talent and a very un-Chinese simple scenario about some of Hong Kong's restless, unruly youths on the prowl.

The storyline centers on the perambulations of four young men and two girls. They are full of life, very westernized and quite uncertain of their place in society. The group is composed of Cream (Cheung Kwok Keung), Ah Ying (Lisa Yuen), Ah Bee (Yim Chow Wah), Peter Pan (Pejola Chu), The Kid (Yim Chun Wah), King Kong (Dick Keung).

Meeting at a popular disco, director Yim Ho introduces the characters in a long exploratory sequence and segues to their robbing a gasoline station, killing the attendant, escaping in a stolen car and finally hiding in a friend's publication office. All this happens in one night.

"The Happenings" is a fascinating film in the sense that it sheds some light on the "now" Hong Kong youth subculture. But it is also irritating and maddening because the occasional insights are not properly developed and what comes off are fragments of a mosaic that does not jell.

The film's plus points include the casting of talented frisky performers who have the potent mix of innocence, sensitivity and ferocity. The cinematography has some highs in showing the city of Hong Kong at dawn and midnight to please prospective tourists. It also shows vividly the American influence on today's younger set (disco, sunglasses at night, mod dresses). Violence and savagery are also prevalent in some sequences Yim Ho is a director to watch but blase moviegoers may detect his exposure to such films like "American Graffiti," "Halloween," "Midnight Express," and some youth-oriented pics from Japan.

"Happenings" has an unclear ending which according to the director was intentional. He wanted to convey that some of Hong Kong's younger people really have no definite purpose in life, no sense of belonging and the future leaves them uncertain as the cosmopolitan, progressive British colony is still living on borrowed time despite reassurances that everything will be alright. The film is part of the current genre to lure and capture more young people to theatres with contemporary subjects they can relate to. It should have some appeal in foreign college towns and other youth predominant spots where commercial films can be intellectualized to mean more than what it prominently shows. —Mel.

Gorp
(COLOR)

'Meatballs' copy with overdone meat.

Hollywood, April 18.

An American Internation Pictures/Fimways release of a Jeffery Konvitz production. Produced by Jeffrey Konvitz, Louis S. Arkoff. Directed by Joseph Ruben. Features entire cast. Screenplay, Konvitz, based on a story by Konvitz and Martin Zweiback; camera (Movielab), Michael Hugo; editor, Bill Butler; assistant director, Chuck Russell. Reviewed at Goldwyn Studios, Hollywood, April 18, 1980. (MPAA Rating: R.) Running time: 90 MINS.
Kavell ....Michael Lembeck
Mad Grossman ....Dennis Quaid
Bergman ....Philip Casnoff
Evie ....Frank Drescher
Walrus Wallman ......David Huddleston
Rabbi Blowitz ....Robert Trebor
Federman....................Lou Wagner
Ramirez ....Richard Beauchamp
Fred The Chef ....Julius Harris
Vicki ....Lisa Shure
Barbara ....Debi Richter
Judy ....Rosana Arquette
Irvington ....Dale Robinette
Lobser Newburg ....Mark Deming

An obvious ripoff of such lucrative youth comedies as "Animal House" and "Meatballs," "Gorp" would seem an obnoxious and insipid enough picture to attract those audiences amused by food fights, fat jokes and adolescent references to sex. Its major failing though is that it is simply not funny, something all of the zaniness in the world can't cover up. Boxoffice prospects are dismal beyond first-week curiosity seekers.

"Gorp" could be written off as just a poor imitation of a successful type of film were it not so terribly insulting and morally bankrupt. It's sad to think that serving disguised pork to a camp full of religious Jews, attempting to lace children's food with speed, and drugging an overweight nurse with Quaaludes in order for her to serve as the object of desire for two oversexed waiters, is what certain filmmakers see as amusing nowadays.

Producers Louis S. Arkoff and Jeffrey Konvitz, latter of whom scripted, ably demonstrate there is no limit to bad taste.

Actors fill all of the necessary stereotypes as the various characters in the camp, trapped in a premise that never really goes anywhere. Joseph Ruben directs with a decided lack of imagination and Bill Butler's editing doesn't have a chance of appearing successful since the entire film is basically a series of juvenile vignettes.

Film is billed as a picture by American International, a Filmways company. It can be hoped that "Gorp" will not be the kind of thing that Filmways will continue to aspire to. —Berg.

Simone Barbes ou la Vertu
(Simone Barbes, or Virtue)
(FRENCH-COLOR)

Paris, April 1.

An MK 2 release of a Diagonale production. Produced and edited by Paul Vecchiali. Features entire cast. Written and directed by Marie-Claude Treilhou. Camera (Fujicolor). Jean-Yves Escoffier. sound. Yves Zlotnicka; art director. Benedict Beauge. Reviewed at Saint Andres des Arts cinema, Paris, April 1. 1980. Running time: 77 MINS.
With: Ingrid Bourgoin, Martine Simonet, Michel Delahaye.

Newcomer Marie-Claude Treilhou. 32, takes her first tentative directing steps with this funny-sad film inspired by her experience as an usherette in a porno film house. To insure the right tone she has cast in the title role a fellow usherette, Ingrid Bourgoin (who has since been promoted to projectionist at the cinema!)

Her script, cautious in form yet assured in its dialog, breaks into three distinct acts (with a minimum of revision it could be recast as a stage play): the first third shows Simone Barbes on the job in a Montparnasse porno complex, where, in the neon-gaudy lobby, she and a colleague banter continuously while trying to avoid more than perfunctory contact with the mostly diffident and embarrassed clientele.

Off-duty at midnight, she goes down the street to the third-rate lesbian nightclub where her girlfriend is employed. After killing time there she leaves and heads home on foot.

In the last act, a depressed middle-aged man, cruising in his car in search of sexual solace, picks her up but makes no physical advances. They drive around and Simone, in almost exclusively one onesided conversation, manages to impart some guarded empathy and comfort. They drive to her home where she tactfully says good night and the film ends.

Despite its clumsy direction and ragged editing, "Simone Barbes" is a wryly compassionate midnight-to-dawn tour through an urban netherworld of listless nightlife and loneliness. If author-director Treilhou can get firmer control of the medium she could grow as a complete filmmaker.

Bourgoin, unpretty and ill-postured, is appealingly right as the cool-headed, uncouth young woman who as acquired flexible safeguards against the seedy loneliness of her environment. Michel Delahaye, a Cahiers du Cinema critic who sometimes moonlights as actor, is quietly touching as the man in the car.

Film was produced, incidentally, by Paul Vecchiali, an eclectic independent director-producer who is dedicated to helping new filmmakers over the hurdle of that all-important first film. —Len.

The System
(HONG KONG-COLOR)

Hong Kong, April 8.

Trinity Asia Ltd., directed and produced by Peter Yung. Features entire cast. Screenplay, Peter Yung, Lee Sien; camera (color) Peter Yung, Tom Lau; art directors, Oliver Wong. David Chan; editor, Wong Yee Shuen; music, Lam. Reviewed at the City Hall, HOng Kong.g. April 8, 1980. Running time: 100 MINS.
Cast: Pak Ying, Shek Kin, Chiao Chiao, Erwin Panos, Peter Brent. Mike Lovatt.
(Cantonese soundtrack with English subtitles)

Another Cantonese film about Chinese cops and the underground society? Yes, but more because it is distinguished with the direction of a well-known Hong Kong photographer — cinematographer trained by the late James Wong Howe and ad-man turned filmmaker — Peter Yung. He belongs to the new breed of filmmakers who are currently changing the local film scene, style and tastes.

Slated for a Cannes unveiling, and to be distributed world-wide by Seasonal Films. "The System" centers on Inspector Chan, a narcotics bureau detective as he tries to catch the big fish of the Hong Kong drug ring. Foreigners interested in knowing how the organized Mafia-type syndicates operate and their relationship with the police force and other government agencies will find this picture enlightening. It is in essence a straightforward "cinema verite" film about chasing the drug dragon with touches of commercial ingredients.

Yung, as director, has a clear story-telling style and superb street sense, but still lacks the full development of his major characters to assure the audience's empathy and full interest. Yung is the main creative force behind this well-researched project and remarkably this is his first feature-length film. There are lapses in the pacing, but can be cured with "cultural adaptations" when shown abroad.

Talky at times, one of the film's best and most exciting moments is trailing of heroin couriers by the undercover agents. The exotic and fascinating Hong Kong backdrops would make the Hong Kong Tourist Assn. proud of the city's remaining off-beat audiovisual delights. There are some good moments of revelation, tragedy, sadness, drama, courage enacted by a well-selected cast of professionals and real street people.

Overall, "The System" has that professional documentary and glossy informative "feel" that one often misses in Hong Kong-made productions. It may have some interest in art houses outside the Chinatown circuit and would certainly be of value in the non-theatrical market and college circuit interested in seeing more than what Han Su Yin and Suzie Wong showed the other generation about the "now" Hong Kong that we often hear about but rarely see. —Mel.

Ordnung
(Order)
(WEST GERMAN-B&W)

Frankfurt, April 10.

A Marten Taege Film Production, Wiesbaden, in collaboration with Zweites Deutsches Fernsehen (ZDF), Mainz; world rights. Cine-International, Munich. Stars Heinz Lieven, Dorothea Moritz. Directed by Sohrab Shahid Saless. Screenplay, Saless, Dieter Reifarth, Bert Schmidt; camera (black & white), Ramin Molai; music, Rolf Bauer; editing, Yvonne Koelsch. Reviewed at Kommunales Kino Frankfurt. Frankfurt, April 10, '80. Running time: 96 MINS.
Herbert Sladkovsky ....Heinz Lieven
Maria Sladkovsky ......Dorothea Moritz
Heidi ....Ingrid Domann
Juergen ....Peter Schuetz
Doctor ....Dagmar Hessenland
Head of Clinic ....Dieter Schaad

Sohrab Shahid Saless, the exiled Iranian helmer living in, first, West Berlin, and, now, Munich and Wiesbaden, has made four films in Germany that won him local and international praise: "Far from Home" (1975), "Coming of Age" (1976), "Diary of a Man in Love" (1977), "Order," and plus the documentary, "The Long Vacation of Lotte H. Eisner" (1979). Each of his features can be viewed as pessimistic portraits of West Germany today, save that they are also human portraits of lonely individuals.

"Order" is about a dropout — from the prosperous middle class, something that can be viewed as "unusual" in duty-bound German circles. Herbert Sladkovsky, a former engineer, simply stopped going to work one day, and he prefers instead to sit alone in the bathroom and smoke a cigaret. He hardly says a word — save when it's early Sunday morning, a time when he walks into the quiet streets of Frankfurt and yells "Get Up!" in front of his more industrious neighbors' windows.

His wife Maria is distraught, but she faithfully goes to work to earn the bread and gently tries to win him back to seeking a job. Two friends, Heidi and Juergen (an architect), offer sympathy and understanding, but Herbert is not to be won over. Is it passive resistance, or a bad case of mental depression? Saless is hinting it is the former, while the psycho experts end up recommending a stay in a clinic where medication is the rule of thumb.

It has taken Herbert a time to agree to his wife's wishes to enter the clinic (she is close to a breakdown when he botches a last attempt to get a job), and that's when the story takes a different turn than expected. One morning he rises in the clinic, goes quietly into the corridors, and yells "Auschwitz" instead of "Get Up!" (both words are pronounced almost the same in German at the beginning of each syllable, thus producing an unnerving juxtaposition). He is carried away by attendants and given a hard dose of drug pacification.

Order has thereby defeated the passive Don Quixote, a silent revolutionary if there ever was one in the modern world of white-robed clinics and cure-all drugs that tend to damage the soul as they quiet the mind and body. Saless has taken a a mental case, however, and transferred it to a sociopolitical plane — for instance, this is probably the first time, that the world "Auschwitz" has been uttered as a metaphor for alienation and horror in the contemporary sphere.

Credits, as usual with Saless, are top-grade. Thesps are right for their parts down to the last and least important role, and lensing in b&w has a rich visual texture. Pic is slated for the Directors Fortnight section at the upcoming Cannes fest, where it should get the legs it needs to venture beyond the fest circuit into the art houses open to such esthetic and ascetic fare. —*Holl.*

The Empire Strikes Back
(COLOR)

The Force Is Still With It.

Hollywood, May 7.

A 20th Century-Fox release, produced by Gary Kurtz. Exec producer, George Lucas. Directed by Irvin Kershner. Screenplay, Leigh Brackett and Lawrence Kasdan, based on story by Lucas; camera (Rank Film Color/Deluxe Prints), Peter Suschitzy; editor, Paul Hirsch; sound (Dolby Stereo), Peter Sutton; special visual effects, Brian Johnson, Richard Edlund; associate producers, Robert Watts, James Bloom; art direction, Leslie Dilley, Harry Lange, Alan Tomkins; set decoration, Michael Ford; make-up and special creature design, Stuart Freeborn; costumes, John Mollo; design consultant, Ralph McQuarrie; music, John Williams. Reviewed at 20th Century-Fox, May 7, 1980. MPAA rating: PG. Running time: 124 MINS.

Luke Skywalker .... Mark Hamill
Han Solo .... Harris Ford
Princess Leia .... Carrie Fisher
Darth Vader .... David Prowse
C3PO .... Anthony Daniels
Chewbacca .... Peter Mayhew
R2-D2 .... Kenny Baker
Yoda .... Frank Oz
Lando Calrissian ...... Billy Dee Williams
Ben Kenobi .... Alec Guinness
Other cast: Jeremy Bulloch, John Hollis, Jack Purvis, Des Webb; Kathryn Mullen; Clive Revill, Kenneth Colley, Julian Glover, Michael Sheard, Michael Culver, John Dicks, Milton Johns, Mark Jones, Oliver Maguire, Robin Scobey, Bruce Boa, Christopher Malcom, Dennis Lawson, Richard Oldfield, John Morton, Ian Liston, John Ratzenberger, Jack McKenzie, Jerry Harte, Norman Chancer, Norwich Duff, Ray Hassett, Brigitte Kahn, Burnell Tucker.

Additional Production Credits
Production supervisor, Bruce Sharman; studio second-unit direction, Harley Cokliss, John Barry; studio second-unit camera, Chris Menges; location second-unit direction, Peter MacDonald; location second-unit camera, Geoff Glover; assistant directors, David Tomblin, Dominic Fulford, Bill Westley, Ola Solum; mechanical effects supervision, Nick Allder; sound design, Ben Burtt.

Miniature and Optical Effects Unit Credits
Effects photography, Dennis Muren; optical photography, Bruce Nicholson; art direction-visual effects, Joe Johnston; stop motion animation, Jon Berg, Phil Tippet; matte painting, Harrison Ellenshaw; model maker, Lorne Peterson; animation and rotoscope, Peter Kuran; visual effects editing, Conrad Buff.

"The Empire Strikes Back" is a worthy sequel to "Star Wars," equal in both technical mastery and characterization, suffering only from the familiarity with the effects generated in the original and imitated too much by others. Only boxoffice question is how many earthly trucks it will take to carry the cash to the bank.

From the first burst of John Williams' powerful score and the receding opening title crawl, we are back in pleasant surroundings and anxious for a good time — like walking through the front gate of Disneyland, where good and evil are never confused and the righteous will always win.

This is exec producer George Lucas' world. Though he has turned the director's chair over to the capable Irvin Kershner and his typewriter to Leigh Brackett and Lawrence Kasdan, there are no recognizable deviations from the path marked by Lucas and producer Gary Kurtz.

Having already introduced their principal players, the filmmakers now have a chance to round them out, assisted again by good performances from Mark Hamill, Harrison Ford and Carrie Fisher. And even the ominous Darth Vader (David Prowse) is fleshed with new — and surprising — motivations. Killed in the original, Alec Guinness is limited to ghostly cameo.

Responding, too, to the audience's obvious affection for the non-human sidekicks, "Empire" makes full use of Chewbacca (Peter Mayhew), C3PO (Anthony Daniels) and R2D2 (Kenny Baker). Among the new characters, Billy Dee Williams gets a good turn as a duplicitous but likeable villain-ally and Frank Oz is fascinating as sort of a guru for the Force. How this dwarfish character was created and made to seem so real is a wonder, but it's only one of many visual marvels.

There are new creatures like the Tautaun on the ice planet Hoth and dreadful new mechanical menaces such as the giant four-legged, walking juggernauts, plus the usual array of motherships and fighter craft, odd space stations and asteroids.

But it's all believable given the premise, made the more enjoyable by Lucas' heavy borrowing — with a splashing new coat of sci-fi paint — from many basic film frameworks. The juggernaut attack on infantry in the trenches with fighter planes counterattacking overhead is straight out of every war film ever made.

Even more than before, Lucas and Kershner seem to be making the comparisons obvious. Vader's admirals look now even more dressed like Japanese admirals of the fleet intercut with Hammill's scrambling fighter pilots who wouldn't look too out of place on any Marine base today.

Oz's eerie jungle home would not confuse Tarzan and the carbon-freezing chamber that threatens Ford could be substituted for any alligator pit in a Lost Temple. Naturally, too, the laser saber battles of the first are back again even more, along with the wild-west shootouts and aerial dogfights.

At 124 minutes, "Empire" is only three minutes longer than its predecessor, but seems to be longer than that, probably because of the overfamiliarity with some of the space sequences and excessive saber duels between Vader and Hamill.

Reaching its finish, "Empire" blatantly sets up the third in the "Star Wars" trilogy, presuming the marketplace will signify its interest. It's a pretty safe presumption. —*Har.*

Friday The 13th
(COLOR)

Inept horror exploitationer.

Paramount Pictures Release of a Sean S. Cunningham Film. Produced and directed by Cunningham. Screenplay, Victor Miller; camera, Barry Abrams; editor Bill Freda; music, Harry Manfredini; art direction, Virginia Field; special effects and stunts, Tom Savini; associate producer, Stephen Miner. Reviewed at Loews Astor Plaza, N.Y., May 9, '80. (MPAA Rating: R). Running time: 95 MINS.

Mrs. Vorhees .... Betsy Palmer
Alice .... Adrienne King
Bill .... Harry Crosby
Brenda .... Laurie Bartram
Ned .... Mark Nelson
Marcie .... Jeannine Taylor
Annie .... Robbi Morgan
Jack .... Kevin Bacon
Jason .... Ari Lehman

Paramount will have to do a yeoman's selling job to squeeze major cash from the sprockets of this sporadically gory but utterly suspenseless pickup. Lowbudget in the worst sense — with no apparent talent or intelligence to offset its technical inadequacies — "Friday the 13th" has nothing to exploit but its title and whatever oomph Par puts into the campaign. Quick, in-and-out playoff is in order.

Another teenager-in-jeapordy entry, contrived to lure the profitable "Halloween" audience (no hope of that), this one is set at a crumbling New Jersey summer camp, shuttered for 20 years after a history of "accidental" deaths and other spooky stuff, and about to be reopened for the summer.

Six would-be counselors arrive to get the place ready, despite overacted warnings from local villagers, then are progressively dispatched by knife, hatchet, spear and arrow during a relentless storm. Since Betsy Palmer gets top billing and still hasn't shown up more than halfway through the pic, even slow learners will correctly peg her as the murderer long before fadeout.

(Her only son was drowned at the camp, while his counselors made love, hence the vendetta).

Producer-director Sean S. Cunningham ("Last House on the

Left"), telegraphs the six murders too far ahead to keep anyone in even vague suspense, gives one grand guignol closeup of each atrocity, then moves on the the next power failure without building a modicum of tension in between.

For the record, the six dispatched counselors are Adrienne King, Harry Crosby (Bing's son), Laurie Bartram, Mark Nelson, Jeannine Taylor and Kevin Bacon. Sole survivor is Robbi Morgan. Murky production values and poor lighting help mask the pic's poor continuity.—*Step.*

Babylon
(BRITISH-COLOR)

Fiery, firstrate debut feature on an inflammable theme.

London, May 1.

A Diversity Music production in association with the National Film Finance Corp., Chrysalis Group and Lee (Electric) Lighting. Produced by Gavrik Losey. Directed by Franco Rosso. Features entire cast. Screenplay, Martin Stellman, Franco Rosso; camera (color), Chris Menges; editor, Thomas Schwalm; music, Denis Bovell. Aswad; art director, Brian Savegar; sound, Ed Pise; associate producer, Stellman; production manager, Ray Corbett; asst. director, Raymond Day. Reviewed at EMI screening room, London, April 30, '80. Running time: **95 MINS.**

Blue	Brinsley Forde
Ronnie	Karl Howman
Beefy	Trevor Laird
Spark	Brian Bovell
Lover	Victor Romero Evans
Errol	David N. Haynes
Dreadhead	Archie Pool
Wesley	T. Bone Wilson
Alan	Mel Smith
Elaine	Beverly Michaels
Woman At Lockup	Maggie Steed
Man On Balcony	Bill Moody
Fat Larry	Stephan Kaliphi
Sandra	Beverley Dublin
Sandra's Father	Granville Garner
Carlton	Mark Monero
Sir Watts	David Cunningham
Rastaman	Kosmo Laidlaw

Here's to a British film with more heart and soul than any home-produced feature of the last 20 years. Like the reggae music that pulses through it, "Babylon" is rich, rough and real. And like the streetlife of the young black Londoners it portrays, it's threatening, touching, violent and funny. Defying English traditions of cool, cerebral appeal, this one seems to explode in the gut with a powerful mix of pain and pleasure.

Perhaps the most remarkable achievement by scripter Martin Stellman and coscripter-director Franco Rosso with their first feature is that although it deals uncompromisingly with racial tension — painting neither side as unduly sympathetic — and although the ending involves brutal murder of a white by a black, the picture's overall "feel" is irrepressibly upbeat.

Returns look to be handsome from aggressively promoted playoff in cities with identifiable black communities.

Though blacks aren't the only likely audience, cautious handling would seem advisable in markets where to depict a bunch of young rebellious immigrants as ostensible "heroes" could be read as provocative.

In that regard, it's worth noting that the Stellman-Rosso screenplay was originally commissioned as a BBC-TV play, which the public broadcaster then refrained from producing, reportedly on the grounds that the treatment of the subject was potentially inflammatory. Subsequent rewrites, while triumphantly upgrading it to the level of big-screen fare, have at the same time sharpened rather than softened that controversial angle.

But whatever the risks, they were worth taking. Earlier black-predicament dramas from Britain have tended to be either downbeat "problem" pix ("Flame In The Streets") or genial, once-over-whitely interludes ("Black Joy"). "Babylon," which carries the infectious vigor of Jamaican features like "The Harder They Come" and "Rockers" into a close to home setting of sunless urban realism, could well outstrip the cult status of any of those titles and become a smash in some situations.

Plot is simple enough, although the lifestyle revealed won't be universally familiar. "Toasting," Rastafarian-themed chanting and scat-singing to a reggae backing track, is a competitive activity apparently exclusive to black discos. At the start of the film, two "sound systems" — groups of youths with truckloads of portable p.a. equipment — vie together in a London tournament semifinal. Thereafter for the winning teammates, during preparations in the days and nights before the final, a number of confrontations occur to change the life of the chief toaster in particular.

Brinsley Forde plays the slowburn but ultimately central role of a young, dreadlocked fellow whose problems at the outset are no more than everyday irritants: rows with his father, unsuccessful attempts to make his kid brother go to school, mild racial tension with the chargehand at the garage where he works. By the end, however, he's lost his job; been chased, picked up and beaten by police on unfounded suspicion; witnessed some friends mugging a white homosexual; discovered the precious sound equipment has been ripped to pieces at the group's backstreet base by nearby white residents who've been disturbed once too often by late-night music; and he's plunged a screwdriver into the stomach of the man he knows is responsible.

Forde's performance is fine, but no less compelling are those of other group members and many of the supports as well. Almost all professional actors, they prove that Britain's stock of black talent has gotten a lot healthier in recent years.

Archie Pool as the group's languorous fixer, Trevor Laird, volatile and aptly named Beefy, Stephan Kaliphi as a foxy music dealer, and Beverly Michaels as the girlfriend Forde takes too much for granted, are standouts among characterizations generally distinguished by sharp definition, natural wit and rare, vibrant screen presence.

Less likely to emerge as cult-figures, but still good, are the whites, of whom the most prominent is Karl Howman as Forde's workmate (and the sound system's temporarily adopted brother). He's unsentimentally moving when mounting racial hatred causes the group to turn irrationally against him.

One key to the film's success is its lack of an overt social or political message. It presents a hard-edged narrative centered on three-dimensional characters, most of whom are black — and the chain of events appears to develop its own momentum, rather than one imposed by script or direction. That way, there are no stereotypes, and none of the action seems contrived in order to make a point. Nor is the Rastafarian significance of the title dwelt upon, although it permeates the atmosphere like the ever-present ganga smoke.

Denis Bovell, who composed and arranged the bulk of the score (local combo Aswad did the sound system tracks), has upped the music's dramatic impact by frequently twisting and squeezing the basic reggae style into angular rhythms and menacing instrumentations. Pity that the slim budget did not stretch to a stereo mix on the film, but the Chrysalis Records soundtrack album figures to be strong package.

Tight purse-strings have not evidently limited technical standards in other respects. Producer Gavrik Losey, together with cinematographer Chris Menges and editor Thomas Schwalm merit organizational and creative achievement plaudits for turning out far more than $1,000,000-worth of meaty entertainment with only that much cash, most of which came from the state-funded National Film Finance Corp.

Release prints are due to be subtitled on a few sequences where the patois is too impenetrable for a general audience. That will certainly help to clarify some early scenes. But to judge from the print reviewed, Rosso and Stellman can still take big credit for a picture that's visual enough to be gripping even without the verbal aid.

—*Simo.*

Night Of The Juggler
(COLOR)

Needs another hand.

A Columbia Picture release, produced by Jay Weston. Exec producer, Arnold Kopelson. Directed by Robert Butler. Screenplay, Bill Norton, Sr. and Rick Natkin, from novel by William P. McGivern. Camera (Technicolor), Victor J. Kemper; editor, Argyle Nelson; sound, Dennis Maitland, Sr.; production design, Stuart Wurtzel; stunt coordinator, Chris Howell; assistant directors, Mike Haley, Ron Walsh, Mel Howard; associate producer, Stephen F. Kesten; music, Artie Kane. Reviewed at The Burbank Studios, May 6, 1980. MPAA Rating: R. Running time: **100 MINS.**

Sean Boyd	James Brolin
Gus Soltic	Cliff Gorman
Lt. Tonelli	Richard Castellano
Kathy Boyd	Abby Bluestone
Sgt. Otis Barnes	Dan Hedaya
Marie	Julie Carmen

"Night Of The Juggler" is a relentlessly preposterous picture which never gives its cast a chance to overcome director Robert Butler's passion for mindless action. Car-chase lovers look to be the limited audience.

According to the production notes, the early auto wreckage of more than 30 cars took 20 days to shoot in New York City and the result is a classic example of how filmmakers can get so ga-ga over hardware that they forget their story must still remain believable.

The chase is not only no better or more exciting than many before it, the sheer impossibility that it could ever take place for so long over sidewalk and grass in crowded Gotham destroys the pointed, plausible urban conflict of William P. McGivern's novel.

This is supposed to be the story of James Brolin's frantic pursuit of a kidnapper who grabs his daughter on the way to school and takes off with her in a car, with Brolin encountering all sorts of obstacles trying to track him down.

But who cares if the performers are never allowed to make the characters come true? The closest they get is a good opening sequence establishing the warm relationship between divorced Brolin and daughter Abby Bluestone, good enough so that the approaching menace of Cliff Gorman is initially worrisome.

Once Bluestone is mistakenly nabbed, however, the film simply falls apart. During the chase as Gorman wrecks cars and drags her endlessly up and down the city streets in daylight with Brolin hot behind, she seems to have ample opportunities to get away. But she never even calls for help.

As a frustrated, racist psychotic seeking revenge for the deterioration of his Bronx neighborhood, Gorman tries to shade his character, but is trapped by the script's needs for him to be so loony you might actually believe in him.

But Brolin gets an even worse break as the ex-cop truckdriver who simply won't be stopped until he finds his daughter hidden among the city's millions by a stranger.

In addition to getting beaten up over and over by porno bouncers and street gangs and knifed by Gorman and crashed into by dozens of cars (none of which slows him down a whit), Brolin can't even count on being a former policeman because one of his old colleagues on the force wants to kill him and complicates his search by chasing him through downtown crowds firing away with a rifle.

Richard Castellano is more rounded as a sympathetic cop, but his function is to be too stupid to catch Gorman. And in her feature debut, Julie Carmen displays a nice screen presence, but is outrageously far-fetched as a stranger who decides to tag along with Brolin as he risks death to find his daughter.

Also a film debutante, Bluestone shows promise, too, maintaining sympathy in a couple of scenes with her captor.

Naturally, there's no doubt ever of the outcome and the final shootout in the sewer system again demonstrates Butler's fascination with background and action while allowing his characters to interact ridiculously.

Technically, the film looks terrific and obviously shows each individual shot was approached with intense concentration on the craft of filmmaking. Which is exactly what's wrong with the picture.
—*Har.*

Cannes Festival

The Big Red One
(COLOR)

Smashing war yarn from Samuel Fuller.

Hollywood, April 21.
A United Artists release of a Lorimar production. Produced by Gene Corman. Directed, screenplay by Samuel Fuller. Executive producers, Merv Adelson, Lee Rich. Stars Lee Marvin, Mark Hamill. Camera (uncredited color), Adam Greenberg; supervising film editor, David Breatherton, editor, Morton Tubor; music,

Dana Kaproff; art direction, Peter Jamison; sound, Cyril Collick; assistant director, Arne Schmidt; second unit director, Lewis Teague. Reviewed at the MGM Studios, April 21, 1980. (MPAA Rating: PG.) Running time: **111 MINS.**

Sergeant	Lee Marvin
Griff	Mark Hamill
Zab	Robert Carradine
Vinci	Bobby DiCicco
Johnson	Kelly Ward
Walloon	Stephane Audran
Schroeder	Siegfried Rauch
Rensonnet	Serge Marquand
General/Captain	Charles Macaulay
Broban	Alain Doutey
Vichy Colonel	Maurice Marsac
Dog Face POW	Colin Gilbert

"The Big Red One" has emerged from two years in the making and 35 years in Samuel Fuller's head as a terrific war yarn, a picture of palpable raw power which manages both intense intimacy and great scope at the same time.

The story of the First Infantry Division's exploits in North Africa and Europe between 1942-45, fast-paced pic attempts to tell entire story of the European land war through the eyes of five foot soldiers and pulls it off to a great degree. Logistics are hardly those of "The Dirty Dozen" or "Apocalypse Now," and World War II tales seem to have somewhat lost public's favor of late, but intelligent sell should allow film to reach both those who will respond to Fuller's artistry and mass audience looking for strong action.

It's a rare treat when a dream project, as this has been for Fuller, comes to such successful fruition. Based on writer-director's own experiences as a GI, pic was announced as a John Wayne-starrer in the late 1950s and came close to realization on many other occasions, but only came together when producer Gene Corman found means to make it almost entirely in Israel. Under circumstances, variety of locations and terrain is impressive and backgrounds serve nicely for such historical battlegrounds as African desert, Sicily, Omaha Beach, Belgium, Germany and Czechoslovakia.

Although presenting the army in microcosm of group repped by sergeant Lee Marvin and four young recruits, played by Mark Hamill, Robert Carradine, Bobby DiCicco and Kelly Ward, approach eschews usual sociological analysis used in so many war pix of the past. These men are there for one reason only, to survive the war, and toughness of Fuller's attitude makes World War II come alive again on the screen.

Through accumulation of images of sweat, dust, wind, sand, and rock, as well as wild animals and insects, men are seen as just one of the basic materials with which the earth is made and populated. By reducing conflicts to their most elemental levels, Fuller unsenti-

mentally makes it clear what war is all about, flip-flopping every cliche on its back and thumbing his nose at every opportunity for mildewed liberal cant.

Shot after shot and sequence after sequence pushes the previous one off the screen through sheer force. One classic scene has small band of men hiding in a cave as German tanks rumble by hardly 10 feet away, and effect is strong enough to make one realize the horrible power of the vehicles as if for the first time. D-Day invasion has Marvin sending his boys relentlessly to the cliffs and watching them get systematically gunned down until one finally clears a path through the barbed wire.

All the confrontations, however, build to climactic episode in which Hamill, unable until then to bring himself to kill, finds a Nazi soldier hiding in the oven of an overrun concentration camp. At long last, Hamill recognizes true horror of the war to an extent Marlon Brando was never able to provide for Martin Sheen in "Apocalypse," and subsequently blasts the German to hell with a whole wartime's supply of bullets.

Fuller has been subject of an intense cult of admirers for over two decades, but as he's only been able to make two, admittedly minor, films since 1964, this has to be counted as a welcome comeback and estimable return to form. No excuses need be made on any level, as film startles with its visual beauty and economy of storytelling.

Marvin lends a strong backbone to tale in a role which seems made to order for him. Hamill, Carradine (as a cigar chomping writer in the Fuller mode), DiCicco and Ward play follow the leader without undue heroics, and nicely convey the youth and not yet totally formed personalities of draftees immediately confronted with men's jobs.

Adam Greenberg's cinematography is shimmering, vastly superior to anything he's done before. Supervising editor David Breatherton and editor Morton Tubor have admirably compressed a mountain of material to under two hours running time, and Dana Kaproff's score is appropriately subdued. —*Cart.*

Fantastica
(CANADIAN-FRENCH-COLOR SONGS-DANCE)

Cannes, May 13.
Gaumont release of E.I. Productions (Paris), Les Productions Du Verseau (Montreal). Stars Carole Laure, Lewis Furey, Serge Reggiani, Claudine Auger, John Vernon. Written and directed by Gilles Carle. Words and music, Lewis

Furey. Camera (Color), Francois Protat; editor, Hugues Darmois; choreography, Larry Gradus; art director, Jocelyn Joly. Reviewed at Cannes Film Fest (competing), May 8, '80. Running time: **104 MINS.**

Lorca	Carole Laure
Paul	Lewis Furey
Euclide	Serge Reggiani
Johanna	Claudine Auger
Jim	John Vernon
Emma	Denise Filiatrault
Hector	Claude Blanchard
Louis	Michel Labelle

"Fantastica" is a travelling revue, a musical show. The film does not live up to its title. It is a mixture of backstage showbiz loves and travail, a mixed up star trying to come of age, and a pitch for ecological balance that do not mesh. Film is a rambling affair uneven on most levels due to rote direction, playing, and music.

Lorca (Carole Laure) is the star of the show who is in love with the director, creator, lyricist, director and composer of the affair, Lewis Furey. But she feels dissatisfied and finds a cause and a lyrical love for an aging ecological hero in the town they stop at. He is bucking the big town entrepreneur who is preparing to build a factory on the site of the ecologist's paradise of a clear stream stocked with fish and saved flora.

She decides to help the ecologist who in turn pulls out after he confesses that he loves her but cannot requite it and that she is also the image of his one and only love. She carries on the fight, and almost does in the show. But she loses and rejoins the show as a more humble star.

Laure is a pretty lissom lass and she does her French and English songs acceptably but without any personal drive or effectiveness. Ditto for Furey whose music echoes Broadway shows but does not stay with one afterwards.

Director Gilles Carle does not give the bucolic war the needed lift of brashness and folk levity it calls for. The show numbers remain stagebound with the choreography simple but lacking luster and ingenuity.

Film might have legs on its home grounds due to the names and attempt to fuse an underpinning of a timely theme on a travelling show saga. Otherwise it is hampered by its lack of focus. The backwater, lilting Canadian accents, sometimes difficult for French ears, is toned down as it is a Canadian-French coproduction.

French actor Serge Reggiani gives the ecological hero some measure of dignity as he bows out of the comic war with the invading capitalists with grace. —*Mosk.*

The Missing Link
(FRANCO-BELGIAN-ANIMATED-COLOR)

Paris, April 29.

An SND release of a Pils Films - SND coproduction. Produced by Picha, Jenny Gerard, Michel Gast. Designed and directed by Picha. Written for the screen by Tony Hendra, from a story by Picha, Pierre Bartier and Jean Collette; songs, Leo Sayer; musical arrangements, Roy Budd; editor, Claude Cohen; sound track, Roy Baker; recorded in Dolby stereo; art directors, Jean Lemens, Claude Lambert, Jean-Jacques Maquaire. Reviewed at the Club 13, Paris, April 28, 1980. Running time: **95 MINS.**
With the voices of: Ron Venable, John Graham, Bob Kaliban, Christopher Guest, Clark Warren, Mark Smith.
(English-language track)

———

Picha, the irreverent 34-year-old Belgian cartoonist who took the Tarzan legend down a few branches in "Shame of the Jungle," now has it in for Darwin in "The Missing Link," a $3,000,000 Franco-Belgian animated feature made, like the former pic, in English.

This new film is richer, more elaborate, funnier. The prehistoric setting, natural follow-up to the background in "Shame of the Jungle," gives Picha a larger frame for his exuberant imagination, with its Rabelaisian verve and bracing disdain for good taste.

With its marvelously naive graphic delirium, picture should find wide response in international markets, particularly among the younger sectors. The wacky English-soundtrack, written by veteran lampoonist Tony Hendra, will help open up the English-speaking countries.

Film takes the form of an odyssey on the part of O., human evolution's missing link, as he seeks the tribe of beings that had cast him out as a baby. The loose story shape allows Picha to present a huge gallery of creations, human, animal or otherwise.

Picha marks the fateful date as Wednesday, May 25, 196,303 B.C. when O. is born into a tribe of degenerate troglodytes so deplorably stupid that their social standing is somewhere beneath that of the mollusk. Since O. is pink and doesn't sport a three-day beard, he is rejected as a freak.

O. grows up in the shadow of a paternal brontosaurus named Igua, and a sassy pterodactyl named Croak. The day he discovers that he doesn't resemble his foster parent, O. departs in search of his own kind.

There follows a series of encounters with strange creatures like the No-Lobes, jolly pear-shaped beings who work all day and spout cliches; the Felines, a cannibalistic tribe of catlike Amazons, a colony of carnivorous ants; and a hapless dragon with a bad case of gas, among others. O. also happens upon the Garden of Eden at a fateful moment.

By the time O. finds his tribe, he has picked up all the basic knowledge and abilities necessary to launch Man on the road to that great bog called Civilization.

Credit must go to the task force of animators who helped execute Picha's warped visions of prehistory, to Roy Baker for his effective aural ambiance; to Roy Budd for the orchestrations, particularly the musical pastiches underlining Picha's parodies of films like "Jaws," "Star Wars" and "2001," musicals and horror films. Leo Sayer composed a handful of okay songs to fill out certain passages. The whole is recorded in Dolby Stereo.

(Incidentally, Italian animator Bruno Bozzetto gave his own cartoon version of evolution in his unforgettable and underrated "Allegro Non Troppo" a few years back.) —*Len.*

Poseban Tretman
(Special Treatment)
(YUGOSLAV-COLOR)

Cannes, May 13.

Yugoslavia Film release of Centar Film, Dan Tana Productions production. Features entire cast. Directed by Goran Paskaljevic. Screenplay, Paskaljevic, Dusan Kovacevic, Filip David; camera (Eastmancolor), Aleksander Petkovic. Reviewed at Cannes Film Fest (competing), May 12, '80. Running time: **94 MINS.**
With: Ljuba Tadic, Milena Dravic, Dusica Zegarac, Danilo Stojkovic, Petar Kralj, Milan Srdoc, Radmilla Zivkovic.

———

Director Goran Paskaljevic lives up to early promise in his fourth and best film to date. A bright, focused tale of hypocrisy and misuse of power in the special treatment of a group of hospitalized alcoholics who may or may not want to kick their habits.

A tyrannical doctor uses psychodrama, music of Wagner, physical training and an apple diet as the core of his treatment. He decides to take his group of six patients on a test outing to perform their psychodrama at a brewery where many of the workers and executives have drinking problems.

The lushes are made up of an ex-prostitute, an emotionally disturbed man, an actor who only loses his stutter when drunk, an aging lottery ticket seller, a woman whose children were taken from her by her husband and a musician who can only play well when looped.

The doctor, played with harsh directness by Ljuba Tadic, turns out to be a hypocrite who is a closet drinker and probably an alcoholic himself. His wife had left him with his young son whom he carts around with them.

Apparently his rage at her is assuaged by his treatment of his wards whose human rights are infringed upon in his almost cruel handling of them. The salty old lottery man brings about the doctor's downfall and maybe that of the others as well, or perhaps their liberation.

The gentle but pertinent observation, the fine script and the excellent ensemble acting by many of the top Yugoslav actors from big to small roles make this comedy-drama touching, funny and revealing. Film is a crucible look at totalitarian type actions in the treatment of disturbed people that may spring from private problems as well as insensitivity or a desire for power.

The brewery has a fidgety public relations woman, played expertly by popular actress Milena Dravic. She is seduced by the doctor who exploits her private hangups and lack of self-confidence.

The testy lottery man has swiped a bottle of booze and injected their apples with it. He gets drunk and there is a fine scene of him passing out these apples. The others first munch with disdain and then joy as the liquor takes hold. One of the women even clinks apples with him.

They get looped, and lock the doctor's man, an informer, in the shower. The doctor has to take the latter's part in the show that goes awry as he reveals himself in a speech that evinces his problems, hurts and disarray.

They depart in their bus, and the doctor stops them in the country, insisting on some exercise. He leaves his son with the woman who lost her children and might cure herself. He goes off with the others as they follow him into the hills, flapping their arms like birds, a part of their exercises.

There is no didacticism in the film and characters never fall into stereotypes. A film that could have sleeper potential at home and abroad, it should also help the Yugoslav image at film festivals. It might be up in the running come prize time at the present Cannes Fest where it is in competition. Excellent technical values also help.
—*Mosk.*

Oggetti Smarriti
(Lost And Found)
(ITALIAN-COLOR)

———

Cannes, May 13.

20th Century-Fox release of Fiction Cinematografica production. Stars Mariangela Melato, Bruno Ganz; features Renato Salvatori, Laura Morante. Written and directed by Giuseppe Bertolucci. Camera (Color), Renato Tafuri; art director, Paolo Biagetti. No other credits available. Reviewed at Cannes Film Fest (Director Fortnight), May 12, '80. Running time, 94 **MINS.**
Marta . . . . Mariangela Melato
Werner . . . . Bruno Ganz
Davide . . . . Renato Salvatori
Sara . . . . Laura Morante
Gina . . . . Maria Luisa Santella

———

Giuseppe Bertolucci is Bernardo's younger brother. He worked on Bernardo's films and even did a documentary on the making of the epic "1900." Now Guiseppe does his second film and is on his own. Besides, comparisons at best are odious as someone once said.

There may be influences of his brother and his brother's mentor the late Pier Paolo Pasolini. There are some sub-proletariat figures and a rather flamboyant group of upper and middle class types and most seem more archetypes than real.

At any rate, the characters are going through a state of change, an ordeal, they are facing a time in life that has to be dealt with or end in chaos. It is really a married woman's story. She has to travel a fair distance and pick up her eight-year-old daughter staying with her grandmother.

Her husband will not fly so they decide to take the train. He gets off to buy magazines and she runs into her hippy-type lover who is coming along. Her husband misses the train and she jumps off. But the husband does not see her and goes off thinking she is still on the train.

The rest of the film takes place almost totally in the Milan railroad station. And what a place it is! She meets a man who seems to know her and her thoughts. He is a German she may have met on a beach as a child and did not have the courage to play his strange, morbid games.

She is pulled down from her set ways of some women's lib and progressiveness while still complying with middle class ways. She takes drugs, drinks, and falls for the strange German played with mysterious grace by Bruno Ganz.

Mariangela Melato has an off-beat beauty that fits her character and her slow fall into wild love that ends with the German's suicide under a train. Dressed in his clothes, her family, reunited, does not recognize her. But the precocious, flippant, impossible daughter does and takes her home where she may come back to her senses.

But all this seems like notes tossed from the underground. There is an ambivalence in this weird tale that remains clouded, without coming to grips with character or personal emancipation.

Tag it promising but somewhat too obtuse, convoluted and finally too private a film for more than festival chances. But mark brother Bertolucci an effective craftsman and perhaps making his own first name, as the saying goes, with more effective material and treatment. But he does make a railroad station seem exciting and mysterious — trains have always been photogenic. —*Mosk.*

Die Reinheit Des Herzens
(Purity Of Heart)
(WEST GERMANY-COLOR)

A Bavaria Atelier Production with Project Film Production in Filmverlag der Autoren. Features cast. Written and directed by Robert Van Ackeren. Camera (color), Dietrich Lohmann; sets, O. Jochen Schmidt; costumes, Janken Janssen; editing, Hannes Nikel, Eva Seyfried; music, Peer Raben; producer, Peter Maerthesheimer. Reviewed at Berlin Film Market Screening Room, May 6, '80. Running time: **104 MINS.**
Cast: Elisabeth Trissenaar (Lisa), Matthias Habich (Jean), Heinrich Giskes (Karl), Marie Colbin (Bini), Herb Andress, Isolde Barth.

For fans of the "decadent' side of German cinema (as cued by pix of Rainer Werner Fassbinder, Robert Van Ackeren, Rosa von Praunheim, Lothar Lambert), "Purity of Heart" skedded in the Directors Fortnight at Cannes should bring home the bacon and find some supporters abroad, particularly since Van Ackeren has recently been honored with a complete retro at the Cinematheque Francaise in Paris and his latest is soberly dedicated to Erich von Stroheim.

"Purity of Heart" does not depart from the abstracted emotional content and stilted dialog that characterized New German Cinema in its embryo stage: words are not so much spoken as pried from the mouth, as the main character, an estranged husband and impotent writer, forces his bourgeois wife into an illicit affair with a passing bum to suffer real pain and symptoms of self-destruction for the first time.

This style of cinema amply supports stories of an esoteric, erotic nature whereby the plot is unfolded in the first couple of scenes and the viewer has only nuances to take it from there. In this case, the main figure of a successful, burnt-out writer, living in Munich's concrete Olympic Village (the country retreat, however, is only 20-minutes distant) and surrounded by a mixed bag of cultured hangers-on, offers the proper dispassionate, alienated hero common to Teutonic cinema since Fassbinder began reworking Douglas Sirk's sentimental melodramas.

As the husband hits the skids, the wife finds herself captivated by her brutish lover with scars on his face, whose main occupation as a petty thief is stealing books that he would never read to sell them in turn to ready customers around town. The wife, who also works in one of the bookstores he steals from, catches him in the act, and the liaison begins — it ends when she stabs him in the back during a coupling scene in a seedy hotel, after she has left husband, daughter, and social standing to experience a "purity of heart" in her relationship to her husband, family, and self.

Credits are a plus. Pic should find its way to New German Cinema outlets specializing in the offbeat and erotic. —*Holl.*

The Blood Of Hussain
(PAKISTANI-COLOR)

Cannes, May 13.
Parindah Films release and production. Written, directed and edited by Jamil Dehlavi. Camera (Color), Walter Lassally, Dehlavi. Reviewed at Cannes Film Fest (Director Fortnight), May 11, '80. Running time: **112 MINS.**
With: Kika Markham, Salman Peerzada, Jamil Dehlavi.

Reportedly in trouble on its home grounds, where it would probably be forbidden, film is a well-made tale of an aborted uprising by a group of poor and disinherited people against a military dictator led by a man from an important family.

Based on a legend about the grandchild of the prophet Mohammad who led an uprising, film concerns one, Hussain, a hairlipped child, to whom a passing sage informs of his destiny to help disenfranchised people. Hussain's brother is an important economics advisor after they grow up but Hussain remains an outsider.

After the military coup d'etat, Hussain's brother goes along even though he knows his wife, who is English, is having an affair with the cold, haughty military commander played by director Jamil Dehlavi himself.

Hussain is finally tracked down and murdered with his newborn child and his men. Film has a professional brio and takes a stand against totalitarianism which may explain its problems on the home front.

However, it remains superficial and predictable and its hopeless romantic revolt is in keeping with its legendary derivation. Walter Lassally has added lush lensing and it is played with forthright ability by a cast conscious of its more allegorical than flesh and blood characters.

Playoff is indicated in most climes on its action, theme and execution through somewhat too flamboyant for more demanding commercial slotting.—*Mosk.*

Gaijin-Caminos Da Liberdade
(Strangers — The Road To Liberty)
(BRAZILIAN-COLOR)

Cannes, May 13.
Embrafilme release of CPC, Embrafilme, Igreja, Mundial Do Brazil, Societa Brasilera De Cultura Japonesa production. Features entire cast. Directed by Tizuka Yamasaki. Screenplay, Jorge Duran, Yamasaki; camera (Color), Edgar Maura; music, John Neschling. Reviewed at Cannes Film Fest (Director Fortnight), May 11, '80. Running time, **105 MINS.**
With: Kyoko Tsukamoto, Antonio Fagundes, Jiro Kawarasaki, Gianfrancesco Guarnieri.

A Japanese woman director, Tizuka Yamasaki, who has lived in Brazil for some years, comes up with a familiar but no less potent look at that rich topic of emigration. In this case the Japanese who went to Brazil in the early 1900s.

For a first film, there is strong visual drive that keeps this adventurous as well as making its points about exploitation and human waste. A sort of "Grapes of Wrath" without the poetry.

Film mainly concerns a lovely young woman who has married in name only a man who wanted to travel with her and her brother. After the trip, they land on a coffee plantation with brutal overseers, a company store that overcharges them and face problems of adjustment, language and saving money.

The woman and her husband fall in love and act married and they have a child. They work hard and find they are being done out of their money and insist on their rights. Some decide to leave after an epidemic which kills the woman's husband.

Helped by a sympathetic Brazilian, they manage to get away. Some stay and others go back to Japan. The woman stays behind, works, and later meets the Brazilian who helped her earlier, who's now fighting for worker rights.

The theme is relevant today. Effective period feel also helps as well as the adroit rendition of two cultures intermingling in a land still being formed. Good acting also helps makes this believable despite the predictable pattern.
—*Mosk.*

Cauchmars
(Nightmares)
(FRENCH-COLOR)

Cannes, May 13.
Diagonale Films release and production. Features entire cast. Written and directed by Noel Simsolo. Camera (Eastmancolor), Armon Suarez; editor, Khadicha Barha. Reviewed at Cannes Film Fest (French Perspective-non-competing), May 9, '80. Running time, **98 MINS.**
With: Pierre Clementi, Helene Surgere, Beatrice Bruno, Dominique Erlanger, Monique Melinand, Andre Thorent.

Noel Simsolo, a sort of filmic gadfly who has dabbled in criticism and attacks on fellow critics, acted, made some shorts and helped in other productions, now does his first film. And he shows a quirky, unusual visual style and a feel for atmosphere and fragmented storytelling that still keeps up interest throughout despite his sometimes obtuse meanderings.

A haunted looking, lovely young girl lives in a section of a ruined house. She ambles about, sometimes steals precious old comic books from a store that specializes in them. She wanders into a tacky bar one day and sits down and plays beautifully at the piano. Then she goes off.

Somebody is looking for this girl and a thin, mysterious looking man hears about a girl who played a piano so well. He finds out where it was and ends up killing the regular piano player and closing in on the girl. The man chauffeurs 2 woman about town.

They find the girl and it is her stepmother who is after her. Maybe the girl killed her brother who played the violin with her. The idea is to get her to play again. There is a strange thing being worked out by the woman and an impresario to make up a record of her work and that of the dead boy.

More for cult usage, it does show some straining under a tight budget. But the film is intriguing and has a hallucinatory quality that amply parallels the girl's stage and final self-destructiveness.

Perhaps a bit indulgent, but a needed show of inventiveness on the French film scene and a director who might be heard from with some backing and less romping in ambiguity for its own sake. —*Mosk.*

Cet Age Sans Pitie
(This Age Without Pity)
(FRENCH-COLOR)

Cannes, May 13.
Rush Production release and production. Features entire cast. Written and directed by Edouard Niermans. Camera (Eastmancolor), Bernard Lutic; editor, Yves Deschamp; music, Alain Jomy. Reviewed at Cannes Film Fest (French Perspective-non-competing), May 12, '80. Running time, **90 MINS.**
With: Bruno Cremer, Jean Bouise, Roland Bertin, Jean-Paul Dubois, Jerome Zucca.

A Jesuit school for young boys is the scene of a dramatic attempt by a priest to uphold the need of love in the face of post-war changes in morality. It is 1952, and pic concerns youthful antagonisms as well as official decisions to save face after a loss of funds and give in to changing ways.

A first film by actor Edouard Niermans, film is somewhat taut, sketchy and didactic and not always able to draw deeper facets of characterization in this tale of the final betrayal of a priest who may not be able to keep up with the times.

He finds one boy who seems to respond to his deep spiritual ways. But the boy has his own personal problems and finally turns on the priest as the boys brutally haze the priest with his help as the school director looks on without lifting a finger.

Niermans gets good acting out of the cast but the tale is somewhat glacial and emerges more a promising first effort than a pic with much chance outside the festival orbit this summer. —*Mosk.*

Moemoea
(The Dream)
(TAHITIAN-COLOR-16M)

Cannes, May 13.
Hitimarama Films release and production. Features entire cast. Written and directed by Dominique Arnaud. Camera (Color), Jean-Claude Boshel; editor, Eugene Haoa; music, Tokiri. Reviewed at Cannes Film Fest (French Perspective-non-competing), May 10, '80. Running time, **85 MINS.**
With: Richmond Terorohauepa.

Tahiti is part of French Polynesia and so this film was eligible for the French Perspective section at the Cannes Film Fest. It is a simple tale done with tact and visual inventiveness that make it more than just an exotic item from a semitropical island.

A convict looks out of his cell bars. Then he overcomes a guard bringing him food and escapes. He roams about living off his wits and even walks into a house with two lovely girls in bed and makes love to one as the other sleeps on. He is accepted.

He then goes into the jungle and builds himself a house with only a radio and animals to keep him happy. But he is at ease with nature until he suddenly hears approaching steps as the law catches up.

Back behind his bars, it might have all been a dream. Directed with inventiveness, this fable of poverty driving a man to criminality is not overdone or didactic. It is a free and easy film that is worth festival interest though perhaps not of the calibre for offshore commercial bookings. But check Dominique Arnaud as a director worth watching on her visual knowhow that keeps this anecdote of interest throughout. —*Mosk.*

Vacances Royales
(Royal Vacation)
(FRENCH-COLOR)

Cannes, May 13.
Forum Films, Les Films Du Sioux release and production. Features entire cast. Directed by Gabriel Auer. Screenplay, Auer, Carlos Andreu; camera (Eastmancolor), Robert Alazraki; editor, Joelle Hache; music, Francois Tusques, Andreu. Reviewed at Cannes Film Fest (French Perspective-non-competing), May 10, '80. Running time, **86 MINS.**
With: Agnes Chateau, Didier Sauvegrain, Francisco Curto, Emilio Sanchez Ortiz.

A sort of fictionalized documentary approach is employed in an interesting film on a subject that remains topical. In 1976 several Spanish dissidents were sent to a posh hotel on an island during the visit of King Carlos to France.

Film involves a Canadian tv director doing a film on the Spaniards and their reliving of the event plus a young man of Hispano origins, who was also among them and who might have turned into a terrorist.

Gabriel Auer blends all this fairly neatly and documents the interviews, the actual forced stay on the island and the terrorist's appearance and decision ot depart. However it is a bit bland and looks slated mainly for specialized festivals and releases. —*Mosk.*

The Hollywood Knights

Compendium of gross-outs as avoidable as drive-in food.

Hollywood, May 15.
A Columbia Pictures release of a PolyGram Pictures production. Produced by Richard Lederer. Executive producer, William Tennant. Directed by Floyd Mutrux; screenplay, Mutrux, based on a story by Mutrux, Lederer, Tennant; camera (Metrocolor), William A Fraker; supervising editor, Danford B. Greene; editors, Stan Allen, Scott Conrad; art direction, Lee Fischer; set decoration, Bruce Kay; costumes, Darryl Levine; sound, Bill Randall; assistant director, Luigi Alfano. Reviewed at the Chinese Theatre, Hollywood, May 14, 1980. MPAA Rating: R. Running time: **91 MINS.**

Sally	Fran Drescher
Jacqueline Freedman	Leigh French
Wheatly	Randy Gornel
Jimmy Shine	Gary Graham
Officer Clark	Sandy Helberg
Smitty	James Jeter
Dudley Laywicker	Stuart Pankin
Simpson	P.R. Paul
Suzie Q	Michelle Pfeiffer
Rimbeau	Gailard Sartain
Nevans	Richard Schaal
Newbomb Turk	Robert Wuhl
Duke	Tony Danza

If the redoubtable Ayatollah ever needs further evidence that films and music are degenerate Western forms that should be disposed of, "The Hollywood Knights" can readily provide it. Experiencing this 90-minute paean to jerkdom is akin to sitting in a car while someone else is continuously punching up different stations on the AM band. Like any audience that turns out for it, all those concerned with this one will want to forget about it as quickly as possible.

Given the virtually identical conceit, wall-to-wall vulgarity of this film merely makes one realize how truly fine "American Graffiti" really was. Set on Halloween night 1965, excuse for a plot has the moronic members of a car club getting back at the equally idiotic Beverly Hills matrons and city fathers for closing down berg's only remaining drive-in eatery.

Among the gang's clever revenge ploys: scribbling obscenities on a high school rally banner; persuading some hapless blacks to wreak havoc on an elegant garden with their truck; urinating into a punch bowl headed for an adult reception, and, straight out of "Graffiti," sabotaging a cop car so it will take off like a bucking bronco.

Film displays not one iota more intelligence than the characters it depicts and seems determined to set the Guinness Book record for most gross-outs ever packed into one feature. Again like "Graffiti," pic makes use of a double album's worth of period pop tunes, which are all cheapened by the context in which they are placed, and even has a stand-in for Wolfman Jack

spinning the disks from a Watts sidewalk cubicle.

Floyd Mutrux showed some sensitivity and affection for the basic elements of pop culture in "American Hot Wax," but this represents 10 steps back from that one foot forward. —*Cart.*

Kill Or Be Killed

Should please karate fans.

Hollywood, May 17.
Film Ventures International release. Produced by Ben Vlok. Directed by Ivan Hall. Screenplay, C.F. Beyers-Boshoff. Camera (TVC), Mane Eotha; editor, Brian Varaday; karate sequences staged by Norman Robinson. Reviewed at the Hollywood Pacific Theatre, Hollywood, May 16, 1980. MPAA Rating: PG. Running time: **90 MINS.**
Cast: James Ryan, Norman Combes, Charlotte Michelle, Danie DuPlessis.

Anyone whose idea of a good time is watching a series of karate champions engage in almost constant battle should enjoy "Kill Or Be Killed," latest offering from Film Ventures International. Pic has already done well in selected engagements across the country and should continue pleasing the action crowd as its release pattern broadens.

Framework for the fight sequences is an ex-Nazi general/karate coach seeking revenge on the Japanese coach who organized the martial arts team that beat the Germans during World War II. It seems the general was the coach for the Nazis and Hitler banished him from the Reich because he failed to spur his guys on to victory.

Using a rare diamond as bait, he persuades the gentleman from Japan to participate in a rematch using the top karate champs from around the world. If the German team wins the general gets a public apology and regains his "honor."

Story line is superfluous to the energetic battles, ably led by James Ryan as the top karate master. Norman Robinson's staging of numerous fight sequences will thrill genre fans, although the battles will no doubt become tedious for those not caught up with karate.

But they probably won't be in the audience anyway.—*Berg.*

Der Sprung von der Bruecke
(The Leap from the Bridge)
(SWISS-COLOR)

Zurich, May 11.
Starfilm GmbH Zurich release of a Blackbox AG Zurich (John Winistoerfer) production. Written and directed by Adrian Baenninger. Features entire cast. Camera (color), Pio Corradi; editor, Franziska Wirz; sound, Robert Jansa; music, Mar-

kus Fischer; art direction, Catherine Scholz, Rolf Engeler, Edith Peyer. Reviewed at the Piccadilly, Zurich, May 9, '80. Running time: 95 MINS.

Cast: Bruno Signer, Stefan Rainer, Sammy Ruegsegger, Benedict Freitag, Nicole Pozzi, Christa Ettlin, Lea Joannidis, Bruno Eberle, Beneo Abbuehl, Mike Zweifel, Otto Dornbierer, Rene Scheibli, Franziskus Abgottsson, G.P. Huber, Hans Suter, Ruth Bannwart, Maria Dornbierer, Guenter Gube, Monika Imhof, Rudi Nater.

"The Leap from the Bridge" is Swiss director Adrian Baenninger's first feature film. Made on a shoestring budget, with mostly unknown players and/or young amateurs, it aims at a true-to-life depiction of today's juveniles in a Swiss smalltown, their aimless drifting, their bragging, boredom and false ideals (drugs, although a growing problem here, remain unmentioned).

One of the lads announces his intention to jump from the town's high bridge as a test of courage or act of bravado. He finally shies away from the leap, while another boy jumps in his place and to his death. But even after this shock event, nothing seems changed for the other youngsters or their parents.

All this may have looked reasonably promising on paper, but on the screen, it just doesn't work out. The script is full of loopholes, character development is practically non-existent and direction is clumsy. The choppy editing and obtrusive music are other negative factors. Camera work by Pio Corradi is among the more professional contributions. The same cannot be said of the mixed cast of pros and amateurs. Although the guys' and gals' obviously eager and devoted efforts add an occasional note of authenticity, they would have deserved a better script and firmer direction. — Mezo.

Prong Nee Chan Ja Rak Koon
(I'll Love You Tomorrow)
(THAI-COLOR)

Bangkok, April 30.

A Sibunruang Films production and release. Produced by Dao Noi Sibunruang. Directed and edited by Promsin Sibunruang. Features entire cast. Story, Suwanee Sukhontha; screenplay, Sojirat Sibunruang; camera (color), Sawaeng Disayawan; sound, Maitree Janjarasskul; music, Okawee Sathakovit and Samarn Kanehanapalin; art director, Prakob Yaisiri; costumes, Outlook Tailoring and Sukanya Boutique. Reviewed at Stella theatre, Bangkok, April 30, '80. Running time: 130 MINS.

Phanat .... Sombat Metanee
Nee On .... Jarunee Suksawat
Nond .... Jatuporn Puapirom
Supak .... Ampha Pusit
Neville .... Lord Enzo
Nesalao .... Yordsoi Komarachoon
Saijai .... Choosri Misomon
Fashion Model ... Rungnapha Kromkrom

So sweet is the screen image of Jarunee Suksawat that not even Promsin Sibunruang, who discovered her for the local screen, can toy with the idea of making her a sex symbol in his remake of an earlier hit, "Prong Nee Chan Ja Rak Koon" (the original teamed up Paowanna Chanajitr and Yodchai Megsuan nine years ago).

Early scenes give the impression that one look at Jarunee and men go crazy, wanting to bed and rape her. At a bus stop one rainy night, she is accosted by a young man who offers to escort her home. She flees in a taxi driven by a sex maniac (Bu Vibulnan).

Bu happens to be a comedian, thus foreshadowing the fact that he wouldn't succeed in raping her. Jatuporn Puapirom suspects that Bu is up to no good, follows the taxi, and spends the night watching over Jarunee, who wakes in the morning thinking she's lost her virginity to Jatuporn. The script keeps postponing a second meeting between Jatuporn and Jarunee.

Local producers and directors perpetuate myths. Stories are never altered to favor mature players over the younger talent. The decision is left to the fans.

Since the majority of remakes of love stories which were previous blockbusters also proved to be moneymakers, and "Prong Nee" is no exception, more future remakes in this genre are in store for local viewers. —Cano.

The Gong Show Movie
(COLOR)

Bong.g.g.g.g.

Hollywood, May 14.

A Universal Pictures release, produced by Budd Granoff. Directed by Chuck Barris. Screenplay, Barris, Robert Downey; camera (CFI Color), Richard C. Glouner; editor, James Mitchell; sound, William Marky; art direction, Robert K. Konoshita; assistant director, William H. White; music, Milton De Lugg. Reviewed at the Chinese Theatre, Hollywood, May 13, 1980. MPAA rating: R. Running time: 89 MINS.

Himself .... Chuck Barris
Red .... Robin Altman
Mabel .... Mabel King
Mama .... Lillie Shelton
Herself .... Jaye P. Morgan
Buddy Didlo .... James B. Douglas
Maitre D' .... Rip Taylor

"The Gong Show Movie" is a bad film, but not bad for the reasons it should have been bad, which would have been good. It's bad for all the wrong reasons — and that's bad because the loonies that might have liked it may not, leaving it no audience at all.

It's hard to believe but director-coscripter Chuck Barris has actually tried to make a serious drama, starring himself as a sen-

sitive soul being driven mad by the craziness he has unleashed in a tv show that encourages the weak and lame-brained to show off in public.

That's an acting assignment Dustin Hoffman couldn't bring off under the direction of Robert Benton. It's an assignment that Marlon Brando directed by Francis Ford Coppola couldn't bring off. It's an assignment that Jack Nicholson directed by Milos Foreman couldn't bring off.

But Chuck Barris obviously thought he could do it with Chuck Barris.

The result is that nobody in the long and lustrous career of "The Gong Show" itself ever appeared more ridiculous than Barris does here, abbetted in his folly by generally poor crew work and a less than inspiring performance by Robin Altman as his girlfriend.

For all its faults, the television show does offer the sane people of the world a certain sadistic comfort in knowing they could be worse off and gives the unstable a modicum of assurance that they aren't alone. The film might have done the same, but doesn't.

Presumably, "Gong Show" fans might have been drawn to a more vulgar version, but Barris has given them only enough to qualify for an R rating. There are, of course, many acts featured but only in flashes that don't allow any to demonstrate their full nuttiness.

The goofies, in fact, are little more than punctuation marks between long stretches of self-pitying posturing by Barris, which hardcore "Gong" followers may not appreciate even if they understand it. Certainly, the crowd of show participants invited to a special screening here seemed subdued and restless half way through the picture.

And if they don't like it, it's simply a question then of who will.
—Har.

The Convict Killer
(HONG KONG-COLOR)

Bangkok, May 9.

A Shaw Bros. production and release. Produced by Run Run Shaw. Directed by Chu Yuan. Features entire cast. Executive producer, Mona Fong; story, Chu Yu; screenplay, Chin Yu; camera (color), Wang Cheh; editors, Chiang Hsing Lung and Yu Hsiao Feng; sound and music director, Eddie Wang; art director, Chiang Hsing Lung; martial art instructors, Tang Chia and Huang Pei Chi; makeup, Wu Hsu Ching. Reviewed at Warner Theatre, Bangkok, May 7, '80. Running time: 95 MINS.

Teng Piao .... Ti Lung
Kao Pai Yeh .... Pai Piao
Tu Fu Chun .... Liu Yung
Shan Lin .... Ching Li
Kuei Lan Feng .... Chen Man Na
Lan .... Ching Miao
Sung Yu .... Ku Kuan Chung
Captain Chi .... Ai Fei

Asian Fest 1979 best actor, Ti Lung, has played mostly action roles, with little or no romantic respite between fights. Apparently, that's what most patrons pay to see.

In director Chu Yuan's "The Convict Killer," Ti Lung plays an ex-con who spent 15 years in prison after being framed as a drug pusher. The action begins on the day he goes free. Armed with the same iron chain which shackled him in jail, he searches for his archenemy called "Leopard," whose identity can only be established by the leopard tattoo on his chest.

As the strong, silent type, Ti Lung barely speaks to anybody, but does get himself into one fight after another at the mere hint of animosity from anybody, including a young woman with a couple of daggers hidden in her shoe.

Perhaps to keep audiences from getting bored watching Ti Lung continuously wielding a chain as a weapon, he stops using it about half way into the pic. At first he drops it in the dark, but is shown wearing it around his neck soon afterward, as is his wont each time he takes five. Sometime later, though, the chain completely disappears without an explanation.

When the chain is gone, Ti Lung temporarily recedes into the background, thus giving Liu Yung a chance to demonstrate the latter's incredible skill at knife throwing. It appears that Liu Yung is being groomed for chop-socky stardom.

The main setting is an elegant Chinese inn with beautiful courtyards. None of the expensive stuff gets demolished during the deadly encounters, but there's lots of breaking bannisters, windows and cheap furniture to sustain action.

Plot twists swarm inevitably in a story where the identity of the villain is unknown. As it happens here, Ti Lung is not the only one seeking revenge on the "Leopard."

Chock-full of surprises, friends at one minute become enemies the next. Loyalties keep on shifting. The thinking behind it is quite simply, the more the plot twists, the more viewers can enjoy the pic.

The ultimate twist is anticlimactic, if only because there's nothing to match the concluding showdown with Ti Lung and Liu Yung allied against the true "Leopard" — the most thrilling fight sequence in an almost nonstop action pic — set in a barn and its surrounding area as snow is softly falling upon the trio of combatants, two against one, and all of whom whirl, leap, kick and box all over the place. —Cano.

Je Vais Craquer!
(The Rat Race)
(FRENCH-COLOR)

Paris, April 28.

A CCFC release of a Trinacra - FR3 co-production. Produced by Yves Rousset-Rouard. Features entire cast. Directed by Francois Leterrier. Screenplay, Leterrier and Gerard Lauzier, from the "Rat Race" comic strip by Lauzier; camera (color), Jean-Francois Robin; art director, Serge Douy; editor, Marie-Josephe Yoyotte; music, Jean-Pierre Sabar. Reviewed at the Publicis screening room, April 28, 1980. Running time: 105 MINS.
Jerome .... Christian Clavier
Brigitte .... Nathalie Baye
Natacha .... Maureen Kerwin
Liliane .... Anemone

A caustic observer of the mores and pretensions of the French middle and intelligentsia classes, satiric cartoonist Gerard Lauzier co-scripted this textually faithful, but directorially diluted screen adaptation of his "Rat Race" cartoon strip, first published in book form in 1978.

Lauzier's poison pencil sketched the dilemmas of a seemingly placid and happily married young business executive who runs into an old schoolmate, now an unemployed, down at the heels actor. But one glance at the latter's pruriently enticing bohemian life style fills Jerome with envy, reminding him of the artist he once wanted to be.

When Jerome is suddenly fired from his job shortly after, he sees his chance. Virtually ignoring wife and kids, he adopts the pose of the struggling writer, though he spends most of his time partying, pursuing a rather stand-offish svelte beauty (actually an ex-call girl), and himself fleeing the neurotic adoration of a homely girl whom he bedded once and now can't get rid of. But he is duped and used by everyone, loses his wife (who ends up part of the demi-monde he aspires to) and winds up back in the nine-to-five set, now married to the homely girl, whom he doesn't love.

As a live-action film with much too appealing actors, the cartoonist's bite — trenchant to his admirers, nasty and vulgar to his detractors — loses many of its teeth. Francois Leterrier's direction lacks ferocity and merely tickles where Lauzier aims to burn.

Still, "the Rat Race" remains a safely amusing entertainment that should do well locally and which could have good possibilites in other markets, thanks chiefly to the snarling brashness of Lauzier's dialog and a talented cast.

Christian Clavier, though he doesn't qualify as the flesh and blood embodiment of the cartoon's long-toothed protagonist, has credible energy as Jerome. Nathalie Baye, as his wife, and Anemone, as the homely girl, provide sincerity to roles that are essentially facile cliches. —Len.

Der Kandidat
(The Candidate)
(WEST GERMAN-COLOR-DOCU)

A Pro-ject Film in Filmverlag der Autoren, Bioskop-Film, and Kairos-Film Production. Directed by Stefan Aust, Alexander von Eschwege, Alexander Kluge, and Volker Schloendorff. Camera (color), Igor Luther, Werner Luering, Joerg Schmidt-Reitwein, Thomas Mauch, Bodo Kessler; editing, Inge Behrens, Beate Mainka-Jellinghaus, Jane Sperr, Mulle Goetz-Dickopp; sound, Manfred Meyer, Vladimir Vizner, Anke Apelt, Martin Mueller. Reviewed at Die Kurbel, Berlin, May 6, '80. Running time: 129 MINS.

Back at the 1978 Berlin Film Festival, Alexander Kluge, Volker Schloendorff, Bernhard Sinkel, Rainer Werner Fassbinder, and several other German filmmakers collaborated on an omnibus film, "Germany in Autumn," that was self-produced via the auspices of the Filmverlag der Autoren (owned by Rudolf Augstein, publisher of "Spiegel" magazine). It dealt with the hysteria surrounding the deaths of the Baader-Meinhof terrorists in the Stammheim prison and the burial of the murdered Hanns Martin Schleyer, a public official.

Now, in time for this year's Cannes Film Festival, Kluge, Schloendorff, Stefan Aust (a tv-reporter), and Alexander von Eschwege (research-documentarist) have collaborated on "The Candidate" — again self-produced (without film or television subsidies) and dealing with a political hot potato; the candidacy of Franz Josef Strauss for Chancellor in the upcoming German national election Oct. 5. It's arguably the best film to emerge from Germany this season, and should easily find its way abroad for wide circulation on both the academic and commercial levels.

For this is not just the story of a political figure, but a portrait too of postwar Germany — a history lesson via a compilation documentary that holds pretty much to the chronological line while offering analytical conclusions, political juxtapositions, and a non-polemical approach to the man selected by the CDU/CSU to run for the highest post in the land this fall.

With regard to the candidate himself, this docu recalls Hollywood's efforts to stop the election of Upton Sinclair as Governor of California in 1934, combining the efforts of newspaper magnate William Randolph Hearst and Metro. There's one major difference: "The Candidate" does not resort to slanted views, but simply unravels two hours of film and tv clips garnered from newsreels, archives and foreign broadcasting stations (the German tv-stations refused to allow the team to plumb their own archives, due to the political pressure of an election year), salt-and-peppered with the filmers' own comments and side remarks at appropriate intervals.

The amazing factor is how much Aust, von Eschwege, Kluge, and Schloendorff were able to collect from the sources available to them. Just as in Emile de Antoni's "Millhouse" (dealing with Richard Nixon's political career), the spotted career of Franz Josef Strauss offers plenty of political ammunition via the facts alone and those several occasions when the media was able to peep behind the curtain. Further, their research has been so accurate that little resistance is expected from opposing parties, and apparently for that reason the film was invited to participate in Cannes out-of-competition, but in the main program.

Born in 1915, Strauss is the son of a village butcher who had a distinguished university career, excelling in Latin, Greek, and history, and was also a champion bicycle-racer. He served in the Army on the Russian front, was captured by the Americans at the end of the war, served as a translator, was given appointments in the American sector before entering local politics in 1945, cofounding the Christian Socialist Union (CSU) (a revival of the Catholic Bavarian People's Party), was elected to Parliament in 1949, became a Special Minister under Adenauer in 1952, the "Atom Minister" in 1953-'54, and, a year later, the Minister of Defense — with predicted chances to become Chancellor after Adenauer stepped down.

Then followed a series of scandals, coupled by Strauss's penchant for making as many enemies as friends in high places. The "Fibag," "Uncle Alois," "Spiegel," and "Starfighter" affairs smacked of kickbacks as well as raw, authoritarian, undemocratic use of political power. Just one of these scandals was enough to put an end to Strauss's political career, but his iron-hand control of the CSU in Bavaria allowed him to bounce back into the limelight on each occasion. The biggest scandal, the "Spiegel-Affair," however, cost him his post as Defense Minister.

In October 1962, Spiegel printed a cover story by Conrad Ahlers attacking Strauss's defense policy, some information coming from military leaks. Strauss lost his head and ordered middle of the night arrests and a raid on the Spiegel office in Hamburg. The mag's publisher, Rudolf Augstein, was detained in prison for more than three months, while Conrad Ahlers was arrested by Spanish police on vacation in Spain.

The resulting uproar in the press and the prompt resignation of the Minster of Justice — Strauss had secretly telephoned to Spain on the night of the arrests, informed none of the other Cabinet members, and was then forced to admit his complicity in a Parliamentary Hearing — forced Strauss to resign his post and thus embarrassed Chancellor Adenauer, who had defended his actions until then.

That's only one of the docu's high points. Others are the opening shots of Bonn on the Rhine River (peaceful, save for helicopters surveying the area), a recent Strauss-rally in Passau, private newsreel/glimpses of the young Strauss at home and on the prowl, his recent support of the Pinochet regime in Chile, among several others. —Holl.

Shigaon Shel Moledeth
(Homeland Fever)
(ISRAELI-DOCUMENTARY-BLACK & WHITE)

A United Studios Production; producer, Itzhak Kol; writter-director, Yoram Levy; editor, Nissim Mussak; narration, Dan Almagor and Yossi Banai; narrator, Banai, music, Yoav Kutner, Nir Hakhlili. Reviewed in Tel Aviv, April 10. Running time: 90 MIN.

Twenty years of weekly newsreels have supplied the material for this documentary, which attempts to provide a composite picture of Israel from its independence to the Six Days War. The point of view is determined by the attitude of the cinema newsreel, the only visual media covering Israel until the late '60s, when the first telecasts from Jerusalem were inaugurated.

While there is no attempt to analyze the facts presented, or to organize them in anything but an associative way, some conclusions are inescapable. The most evident is the loss of innocence which has changed the nature of Israeli reporters, politicians, the public and the rapid modernization accompanied by materialism and accentuated individualism. Neither the way Yoram Levy organizes snippets from the numerous newsreels, nor the photo choices explain these developments. For anyone familiar with Israeli reality, they will probably be evident.

The goal seems to be entertainment, a hectic rhythm being imposed in order to avoid any chance of boredom, with many selections picked for their humor. The narration sometimes tries too hard, as the **original newsreel soundtrack,** whenever left intact, beats anything which could be written today.

For a non-Israeli public, subtitles may be insufficient. Even younger Israelis who did not live through the period, will miss much. Still, it should raise interest, and is certainly a most useful item for any archive. —*Edna.*

Chere Inconnue
(I Sent A Letter To My Love)
(FRENCH-COLOR)

Paris, May 5.
A Gaumont release of a Cineproduction production. Produced by Lise Fayolle & Giorgio Silvagni. Stars Simone Signoret, Jean Rochefort, Delphine Seyrig. Directed by Moshe Mizrahi. Screenplay by Mizrahi and Gerard Brach, based on the novel "I Sent A Letter To My Love" by Bernice Rubens. Camera, Ghislain Cloquet. Editor, Francoise Bonnot. Music, Philippe Sarde. Sound, Michel Vionnet and Claude Villand. Art director, Bernard Evein. Reviewed at the Marignan theatre, Paris, April 25, 1980. Running time: **96 MINS.**
Louise .... Simone Signoret
Gilles .... Jean Rochefort
Yvette .... Delphine Seyrig
Beatrice ....Genevieve Fontanel
Catherine .... Dominique Labourier

Insensitive direction and unconvincing performances ruin an interesting dramatic idea in Moshe Mizrahi's "Chere Inconnue," starring Simone Signoret, Jean Rochefort and Delphine Seyrig. The script by Mizrahi and Gerard Brach, based on a British novel "I Sent A Letter To My Love" by Bernice Rubens, isn't very subtle (or plausible for that matter), but it's of the kind from which strong acting talent can sometimes make sparks fly. No such luck here.

Rochefort and Signoret are cast as a brother and sister leading a wretchedly lonely existence in the family home on the coast of Britanny. He has been paralyzed in the legs since childhood and is restricted to a wheelchair. She has sacrificed her own happiness to look after him. They measure out their monotonous days in sibling love-hate spats and excursions along the windy cliffs. Their only contact with the outside world is through the feather-brained friend (Seyrig) who brings them bread each morning.

When lovelorn Signoret puts an anonymous ad in the regional paper seeking male companionship, she receives only one reply — from her brother! At first horrified, she nevertheless decides to continue the correspondence under an assumed name and invented biography, as her brother's desperately erotic prose helps fill up some of her own emptiness.

Rather than drop her imposture

when Rochefort becomes insistent on a rendezvous, Signoret frantically hires a local actress to fill in. The meeting is disastrous and the brother turns his attentions to Seyrig, who eventually responds to his courtship. On the day of the marriage, Rochefort finds the I.D. card Signoret had tricked up to claim his letters at the post office and realizes the whole awful situation. Film ends at the church were Rochefort turns to stare at his sister before taking his marriage vows.

Mizrahi's direction is heavy-handed and what should have been a film of restrained emotional horror and jagged poignancy is reduced to glum dime-novel bathos that will offend nobody. His handling of the actors is also poor. Seyrig and Rochefort are merely miscast and ill at ease, but it is Signoret who comes out the worst. Not only is her performance unmoving and barely credible, it is at times grotesque, as in one of the several (awful) post office sequences, when she strides pompously up to the clerk to claim a letter as if she were the Queen of England.

Film is a hit locally, but will need special delivery to foreign markets. Evoking the previous Mizrahi-Signoret picture "Madam Rosa" will obviously be a key device in publicity push. —*Len.*

Cannes Festival

Kagemusha
(The Double)
(JAPANESE-COLOR)

Cannes, May 15.
Toho, 20th Century-Fox release of Toho, Kurosawa Productions production. Features entire cast. Directed by Akira Kurosawa. Screenplay, Kurosawa, Masato Ide; camera (Eastmancolor), Kazuo Miyagawa, Asaichi Nakai; art director, Yoshiro Muraki; music, Shinichiro Ikebe. Reviewed at Cannes Film Fest (Competing), May 14, '80. Running time: **179 MINS.**
Takeda Kagemusha ..... Tatsuya Nakadai
Katsuyori .... Tsutomu Yamazaki
Son .... Kenichi Hagiwara
Takemaru .... Kota Yui
Yamagata .... Hideji Otaki
Baba .... Hideo Murata
Oda .... Daisuke Ryu

Akira Kurosawa, has made this a sweeping epic of the times of clan wars in 16th century Japan as well as etched particular lives of men involved in the decisions that brought turmoil until a victor emerged to consolidate the country.

Twentieth has the film for the world outside of Japan where it is handled by Toho, which produced the film with Kurosawa. An English version is to be supervised by

Francis Coppola and George Lucas who were go-betweens for Kurosawa and 20th. Formula allowed the film to be made, for it would otherwise have been too expensive for Japan alone.

It cost $6,000,000, not much by Hollywood standards but immense in Japan. The money is there on the screen with its meticulous costuming and reconstruction of an era and its battle scenes. Film is mainly the tale of a "Kagemusha," literally a warrior shadow or a double.

There was one clan leader, Shingen Takeda, who used doubles to take his place seated on a hill overlooking the battlefields. The seemingly constant presence of Takeda always finally unnerved his foes.

His younger brother, his usual double, has found a petty thief whom he saved from execution who looks exactly like Takeda. The incredible resemblance pleases Takeda and he is taken on as a new Kagemusha.

Then Takeda is wounded by a rifle when he goes to overlook a siege. He dies but this is kept secret and the thief is groomed to replace him for three years, per Takeda's last wishes, so as not to demoralize his people or give the enemies advantages.

There is an unusual metamorphosis as the double, tutored by the brother, gains dignity and even convinces Takeda's family that he is the real leader. But an older son, who is let in on the secret, refuses to go along and decides to storm a stronghold of one of the main enemy clans.

The double's visit to the battlefield, where he just sits on a hill as soldiers ward off enemy attacks, wins a victory. However Takeda's grandson, to whom he has become attached, talks him into riding a savage horse that only Takeda could handle and he is thrown. The concubines discover he is not Takeda when they treat him for a scar Takeda has is missing.

He is banished but follows as the older son attacks again and the whole army is wiped out in a futile series of charges against guns.

The Kagemusha grabs a battle banner and is shot down and staggers to a lake where Takeda has been buried and falls into it and floats away.

Tatsuya Nakadai is extraordinary as the leader and his double. There is a subtle scene of comic undertones as a past illness is evoked to let the concubines know he cannot be with them plus his change into a man of presence, range and strength.

The majestic pace, the court intrigues, the ritual and battles give this a tragic and human stature. It

will of course need careful handling and perhaps a little tightening for foreign shores but should make an impact on its beauty and tragic dignity in man's endless wars and intrigues as nations evolved.

Kurosawa, at 70, shows himself young indeed in the impressive handling of this historical drama laced with shrewd insights into the almost Shakespearean intrigues of power.

Kurosawa has copped two Oscars, for "Rashomon" and "Dersu Uzala," plus top awards at the Venice and Moscow Film Fests for them. He has had one film at Cannes before and no awards. Film is technically brilliant all down the line. —*Mosk.*

Une Semaine De Vacances
(A Week's Vacation)
(FRENCH-COLOR)

Cannes, May 13.
Parafrance release of Sara Films, Little Bear, A2 production. Features entire cast. Directed by Bertrand Tavernier. Screenplay, Tavernier, Colo Tavernier, Marie-Francoise Hans: Camera (Eastman-color), Pierre William Glenn; editor, Armand Psenny, Sophie Cornu; music, Pierre Papadiamandis. Reviewed at Cannes Film Fest (competing), May 13, '80. Running time: **102 MINS.**
Laurence ....Nathalie Baye
Pierre .... Gerard Lanvin
Mancheron .... Michel Galabru
Descombes ....Philippe Noiret
Sabouret .... Philippe Leotard
Anne ....Flore Fitzgerald
Father ....Jean Daste
Mother ....Marie-Louise Ebeli

Bertrand Tavernier returns to his native city of Lyons for his latest film. He made his first film "The Watchmaker of St. Paul" there, which launched him as one of the most proflific new filmmakers on the local scene and also copped the coveted annual critic prize Le Prix Louis Delluc.

"Watchmaker" was about a father trying to find a footing with his son who has killed a fascistic foreman who made advances to his girl, using his position to intimidate her.

In his new film, Tavernier is more delicate in dealing with a young teacher's near breakdown as she comes to an emotional and personal impasse. Sudden personal disarray is a topic cropping up in films from many countries.

The teacher has respect, lives with a talky but attractive man selling prefabricated houses though he does not like them. That is where the money is. He wants a child by her but she is not ready.

She begins to find a lack of purpose in her work and her life and gets sensitive to loneliness and troubles around her. A psychiatrist prescribes a week's vacation as the teacher tries to probe her problems.

Friendship ensues with a like-able father of one of her troubled students; but his fumbled pass at her is not what she needs. She visits her parents and sees her father sinking into senility and thinks back over incidents in her life.

In the background is a knowing feel for the city itself. There is also a hearty meal with the student's father and the father from the "Watchmaker" who talks of his son still in prison and his disappointment in youth but still hope for his grandchild.

Nathalie Baye, the teacher, is a sensitive actress, but borders on mannerisms held at bay by neat character touches and revealing situations. Film is a tender appraisal of a time of personal decisions.

Careful handling is called for but it has plusses in its fetching treatment and human insights without resorting to sentimentality.

Film is well lensed and smoothly edited. —*Mosk.*

Orokseg
(The Heritage)
(HUNGARIAN-FRENCH-COLOR)

Cannes, May 11.
Gaumont, Hungarofilm release of Mafilm, Hunnia Studio, Gaumont production. Stars Isabelle Huppert, Lili Monori, Jan. Nowicki. Directed by Marta Meszaros. Screenplay, Ildiko Korody, Meszaros; camera (Eastmancolor), Elemer Ragalyi; editor, Kovacs Gyorgy. Reviewed at Cannes Film Fest (Competing), May 10, '80. Running time: 100 MINS.
Irene . . . . Isabelle Huppert
Sylvia . . . . Lili Monori
Akos . . . . Jan Nowicki
Terez . . . . Zita Perzel
Father . . . . Sandor Szabo

Marta Meszaros has made a series of films on women that are not socalled women's films or femme lib diatribes for that matter. They are dramas from a woman's point of view and lately dealt with times of crisis as maternal needs, pregnancy and birth, couples in difficulty, middleaged needs, even a little girl's infatuation with a man, not equivocal, and now sterility.

For the first time she uses a period setting and again a French name for one of the leading roles, Isabelle Huppert, as she has done in three preceding pix with Marina Vlady, Anna Karina and Delphine Seyrig. This film is also a coproduction with France.

Actually she has often received more recognition abroad than at home and especially in France. It is 1936 and a rich sterile woman, married to a dashing military officer, needs an heir to inherit her father's money. She meets a young Jewish woman who paints, works in a shop and is ambitious.

The woman gets the idea of get-ting her to have a child with her husband. At first rebuffed by both, her insistence finally brings it off. A child is born. The real mother is paid off.

It is 1944 and the husband has taken up with the Jewish girl and has a child by her. Though he sympathizes with the Nazi cause and Hungary's alliance, he is against the racist aspects. He bets his wife to lend her papers to keep the woman from being deported, for Hungarian Jews are now being rounded up.

But the woman turns her in and the Jewish woman is deported, her husband arrested and the other child is turned over to her. Isabelle Huppert mixes strength and vulnerability as the finally martyred Jew and Lili Monori, usually playing proletarian free living women, is effective as the highborn woman torn by maternal needs, her love for her husband and jealousy.

Jan Nowicki is rightly haughty, slightly arrogant, but with an underlying decency, as the husband who loves both women but is finally drawn to the more fecund one as bitterness grows between him and his real wife over their half natural legal child.

Meszaros has perhaps reduced film's impact a bit putting it in such dramatic historical surroundings. The Huppert character is perverted by money, saved by love but destroyed by events and the psychological results of sterility and fecundity reacting on each other and the husband and lover.

Period recreation is good
—*Mosk*

Constans
(Constancy)
(POLISH-COLOR)

Cannes, May 13.
Polski Film release of TOR Unit production. Features entire cast. Written and directed by Krzysztof Zanussi. Camera (Eastmancolor). Slawomir Idziak; editor, Wieslawa Dembinska. Reviewed at Cannes Film Fest (competing), May 12, '80. Running time, 92 MINS.
Witold . . . . Tadeusz Bradecki
Mother . . . . Zofia Morzowska
Graznya . . . . Malgorzata Zajaczowska
Stefan . . . . Cezary Morawaski

Krzysztof Zanussi is a film author in creating his own themes and scripts plus direction. Most of his films deal in facing up to death, that of loved ones or one's self, and just coping in life that is usually beset by everyday corruption that is either accepted and dealt with or fought.

Zanussi's characters usually fight them. But they are not prissy, sanctimonious or self indulgent. They are trying to find a way of life. This has caused Zanussi, as well as noted fellow Polish director An-drjez Wajda, some problems with the censors.

But things seem to be easing as all the films are showing up at festivals or in Western theatres. Zanussi again deals with a young man facing up to death, this time that of his mother, and the petty corruption at his job that finally leads to him being framed and robbed of his one great desire to climb mountains in the himalyas as his father did and where he died when the hero, Tadeusz Bradecki, was a boy.

Bradecki does manage to get a job and help his sick mother through some influential friends of his father. But his mother's death and his final dismissal and frame-up leads to disarray, but then a final decision to go on.

There is more compassion here than usual in Zanussi's tales of adjustment and human rather than political dissidence. It does not aim for big dramatic scenes but makes its points in subtle treatment and a careful blending of sensitive acting, well drawn characters and perceptive direction.

A film that could find theatrical outlets on its forceful emotional range not to forget festival impact and another plus for the Polish film output these last few years at international film festivals. —*Mosk.*

Bye Bye Brazil
(BRAZILIAN-FRENCH-COLOR)

Cannes, May 17.
Gaumont release of Aries Cinematografica, Luiz Barreto, Lucy Barreto, Gaumont production. Features entire cast. Written and directed by Carlos Diegues. Camera (Eastmancolor), Lauro Escorel Filho; editor, Mair Tavares; music, Chico Buarque, Roberto Menescal, Dominguinhos. Reviewed at Cannes Film Fest (Competing). May 16, '80. Running time: 100 MINS.
Salome . . . . Betty Faria
Cigano . . . . Jose Wilker
Cico . . . . Fabio Junior
Dasdo . . . . Zaira Zambelli

Carlos Diegues was part of the Brazilian Cinema Novo movement in the '60s that brought film specialist and festival interest to the country. They delved into political, social and economic aspects of this sprawling, growing, changing country. That is now history and Brazil has had only intermittent impact at festivals since then.

It seems the survivors of that heroic film period are turning to more accessible, exotic themes that still pay surface attention to potent subjects. Here, in the guise of a road film concerning a seedy, intinerant travelling show, the backwardness of many areas, the growth of big cities, Indian genocide are touched on.

But the main interest is in a cunning magician, the head of the be-draggled troupe, his sexy dancer and a couple picked up on the way, a young accordion playing peasant and his pregnant wife.

The peasant falls for the older dancer and the magician has his way with the wife some time after the birth of the child. They pick up some itinerant Indians, lose their truck and go their own ways only to make it individually by talent for the musician and conniving by the magician not above prostituting the women.

Though somewhat surface, and not quite finding the mixture of social comment and ironic insight into smalltime carny life, film is colorful, flashy and exotic and could find international outlets as did that tale of small town repression, "Dona Flora and Her Two Husbands," also produced by Luis Barreto who gave this new one fine production dress. —*Mosk.*

Poseban Tretman
(Special Therapy)
(YUGOSLAV-COLOR)

Cannes, May 17.
A Centar Film/Dan Tana Film Production; world sales, Yugoslavia Film, Belgrade. Features cast. Directed by Goran Paskaljevic. Screenplay, Dusan Kovacevic, Filip David, Paskaljevic; camera (color), Aleksandar Petkovic. Reviewed at Cannes Film Festival (Competition), May 16, '80. Running time: 90 MINS.

Cast: Ljuba Tadic (Dr. Ilich), Dusica Zegarac, Milena Dravic, Danilo Stojkovic, Petar Kralj, Milan Srdoc, Radmila Zivkovic, Bora Todorvic, Predrag Bijelic.

Goran Paskaljevic has been noted as a comer for some time now — his first feature pic, "Beach Guard in Winter" (1976) and "The Dog That Liked Trains" (1978), bowed at the Berlin Film Fest, while a 16m pic for tv, "The Days Are Passing" (1979) was one of the talked-about films at last year's Pula Film Festival. Now his "Special Treatment" is in the sweepstakes at Cannes, a film that presents this young graduate of the Prague Film School (FAMU) as a filmmaker to watch closely on the international scene.

"Special Therapy" is about treating alcoholism, but it's much more: this is a sardonic, often hilarious satire on the human species and that unpredictable animal's penchant for grandiose schemes, like miraculous cure-alls for ails of heart and soul.

A specialist at a drying-out clinic, Dr. Ilich (Laubo Tadic, the Belgrade Shakespearean thesp in one of his best film roles), feels he can cure his herd of alcoholics via physical training (running in circles and flapping the arms like grounded birds), munching on apples, soaking up Wagner's music ("Tristan und Isolde" and "Ride of the Walkuere"), and performing psychodramas (dramatizing a scene at a railroad station, in which all the patients interpret their own past back-sliding). He is so convinced of his special therapy that he is ready and willing to demonstrate its effectiveness at a nearby brewery.

Off the busload of patients go with the doctor and his young son to the brewery to do their stuff. Along the way it becomes clear that one is a hopeless, but comical, relapse, another is an ex-prostitute, a third has a "capo" mentality in watching over the others, and a fourth is a mother of two children with a tragic separation from her family behind her. It also becomes clear that Dr. Ilich has more than a few skeletons in his own closet, is in truth a tyrant, and soothes his own nerves with secret snorts now and then.

The "special therapy" begins to backfire almost from the beginning. At a wayside inn one patient swipes a bottle of hard liquor and, using a syringe, injects the apples with doses of kickapoo juice. Then, at the brewery, the patients go secretly on a binge while the doctor is succumbing to weaknesses of the flesh with a lonely lady manager (whose boss is only interested in pleasures of the stomach).

As for the brewery, efficiency has been cut down by swigging on the job, so the psychodrama performance before the company workers is viewed as the solution to increase production. In addition, the brewery's badge of distinction is a giant, three-story-high glass of beer before the entrance.

To say more is to give away the side-splitting ending, during which the doctor's pretentious walls of resistance come crumbling down. Ace thesp performances and top credits make this a winner on the domestic scene. With proper handling it could get legs for offshore run in Yank art houses. —*Holl.*

Kaltgestellt
(Put On Ice)
(WEST GERMAN-COLOR)

Cannes, May 10.
An ABS-Film/Von Vietinghoff Film production. Features entire cast. Directed by Bernhard Sinkel. Screenplay, Sinkel, Alf Brustellin; camera (Color), Dietrich Lohmann; sets, Winfried Hennig; editing, Annette Dorn; music, Charly Mariano, Jasper Van T'Hoft, Mike Thatcher. Reviewed at Cannes Film Festival (competing) May 10, '80. Running time: **100 MINS.**
Brasch . . . . Helmut Griem
Franziska . . . . Angela Molina
Koerner . . . . Martin Benrath
Sokolowski . . . . Friedhelm Ptok
Roeder . . . . Hans-Guenther Martens
Anna . . . . Meret Becker

Bernhard Sinkel's "Put on Ice" has its roots in the omnibus film, "Germany in Autumn" (1978), in which several directors contributed vignette passages to an overall concept that dealt with hysteria in the land after the kidnapping of a public official (Hanns Martin Schleyer) and the sudden deaths of members of the Baader-Meinhof terrorist group in prison. Fear is still the subject in 1980, and the film was selected for the Competition sweepstakes at the Cannes film fest.

(By coincidence, another pic stemming from "Germany in Autumn" is on view at Cannes: Alexander Kluge's "The Patriot" in the Directors' Fortnight.)

Pic opens with a mass street demonstration in Berlin, protesting the stabbing of a Turkish schoolteacher (the city is heavily populated with foreign workers) on the street by an extremist group of Turks. At the rally a group of students from a secondary trade school distribute Leftist political propaganda under the guise of the Right-oriented "Bild" newspaper; the bogus newspaper had been printed in the school illegally. The National Security Bureau (an equivalent of the FBI) is on to the trick, via an informer among the boys, who commits suicide the next day.

Both the teacher (Helmut Griem) and the security agent (Martin Benrath) are pulled into the melee thereafter as opponents, the former out of liberal convictions and the latter out of sheer hate and the ruthlessness of his job. A third party, a French-speaking femme photographer (Angela Molina), gets involved because she's doing a picture-essay on "Berufsverbot" (job-blacklisting) and finds the perfect subject in the teacher who loses his job for following his conscience; she also just happens to have taken pictures of the security agent taking pictures of the youths.

When the teacher is given the dead boy's diary with the evidence that the National Security Bureau was involved, he takes it to the press and sets off a scandal, whereby in turn is relieved of his job and the guilty security agent is fired. The agent decides to instill fear in the teacher and his new girlfriend, the former an easy victim due to our liberal hero's broken marriage and the troubles he faces caring for a daughter at home.

In the end, the agent feels pressure on himself too (the National Security Bureau wants him out of town), and he delivers evidence to the teacher of the government's complicity in illegal procedures — just before he hops a train to leave West for East Berlin (supposedly to change employers). The teacher then decides to confront the city's Senator in charge of Education with the proof as to why he was fired, but the Bureau intervenes at a prearranged meeting-place, and our hero is shot by a nervous policeman while fleeing.

Comparisons with Reinhard Hauff's "Knife in the Head" can be easily made, but it's better to say that "Put on Ice" deals with questions — blacklisting, illegal bugging, shoot-to-kill police actions — that are regularly covered in the German press and hotly discussed by liberals just before election time. There are too many gaps in the story, however, to allow the uninformed to capture several salient political points, and at times helmer Sinkel has hedged on his bets by changing gears to a political thriller just when the plot requires a clearly stated point-of-view.

Further, Sinkel is not a dialog director, one who can turn stiff words into emotional feeling and conviction. Martin Benrath, as the heavy, gives the story the tense, nervous edge it needs to be convincing. Dietrich Lohmann's dark, moody lensing edge it needs to be convincing. Dietrich Lohmann's dark, moody lensing also pitches some scenes into complete darkness, although the drab landscapes and battered, divided city do contribute metaphorical strength.

Worthy of Cannes' competing slot on theme alone, this is another example of the strong political line taken lately in Germany cinema on prominent public issues. It should do well on the summer fest circuit.
—*Holl.*

Jaguar
(FILIPINO-COLOR)

Cannes, May 14.
Atienza release and production. Features entire cast. Directed by Lino Brocka. Screenplay, Jose Lacaba, Richardo Lee; camera (Color), Conrado Balthazar; editor, Rene Tala; music, Max Jocson. Reviewed at Cannes Film Fest (Competing). May 13, '80. Running time **90 MINS.**
Poldo . . . . Phillip Salvador
Cristy . . . . Amy Austria
Sonny . . . . Menggie Cobarrubias
Mother . . . . Anita Linda
Direk . . . . Johnny Delgado
Jing . . . . Tonio Gutierrez

Lino Brocka is the one Filipino director known outside his country. His "Insiang" captured attention in the non-competing Director Fortnight at the Cannes Festival last year and now he is in competition for the first time this year with "Jaguar." It is also the first Filipino film ever to compete at Cannes.

While "Insiang" stayed within the poor ghetto of Manila, and was a tale of mother and daughter rivalry, here Brocka deals with a young man who wants out of the poverty he was born to. But he is a victim of a shady rich man who uses and then discards him.

The film has an icy rage that reflects on the effects of poverty and overcomes the obvious shoe-string budget problems. There is a probable influence of the classic American gangster and so-called black films of people trapped by their environment but well assimilated to life in the Philippines today.

"Jaguar" is the slang name for a security guard. The hero, Phillip Salvador, works guarding a high class apartment house. He supports his mother and two sisters and keeps put of trouble with local gangs where he lives.

One night he helps a rich tenant attacked by an irate shady night club owner and his henchmen. Jaguar subdues them all and finds a job with the man he helped as his guard and helper. The man is rich and publishes raunchy magazines, comic books and fashion mags.

His boss and former attacker are at odds again over a girl. The girl is hidden and guarded by the Jaguar. Though she is the boss's girl, love grows into a well made love scene.

Another fight makes Jaguar a killer and he is hunted down and captured. The rich man promises to help him and his family if he does not mention his name.

Jaguar's restrained rage, his try for a decent life frustrated by corruption and moral shabbiness, has him running amok as he almost kills the man before he is subdued by the police. He is now a criminal.

The script is workmanlike and acting acceptable. The feeling for the poor quarter, the lack of outlets and the film's concern lift it above just another social thriller.

Film was refused for export but allowed to be shown at Cannes when the festival insisted on it. Its Cannes showing may help it get released from its export ban at home. More a playoff item, film shows a forceful director in Brocka, with an insight into social forces which could lead to more potent films with more important budgets. —*Mosk.*

Mon Oncle d'Amerique
(My American Uncle)
(FRENCH-COLOR)

Paris, May 8.
A Films Galatee/Gaumont release of a Philippe Dussart/Andrea Films/TF 1 co-production. Produced by Philippe Dussart. Stars Gerard Depardieu, Nicole Garcia and Roger Pierre. Directed by Alain Resnais. Written by Jean Gruault, inspired by the writings of Henri Laborit. Camera, Sacha Vierny. Music, Arie Dzierlatka. Sound,

Jean-Pierre Ruh and Jacques Maumont. Art director, Jacques Saulnier. Costumes, Catherine Leterrier. Editor. Albert Jurgenson. Reviewed at the Ariane screening room. Paris. May 7. 1980. Running time: 125 MINS.
Rene Ragueneau ......Gerard Depardieu
Janine Garnier ....Nicole Garcia
Jean Le Gall ....Roger Pierre
Therese Ragueheau .... Marie Dubois
Arlette Le Gall .... Nelly Bourgeaud
Henri Laborit ....Himself

In his new film "Mon Oncle d'Amerique," Alain Resnais again tackles a favorite theme of his — the convoluted workings of the human psyche — but perhaps because the approach is in good part so dry and baldly clinical, it proves to be one of his least satisfying pictures.

Resnais has made a film based on the scientific writings of Henri Laborit, the renowned research scientist whose work on the structure of the human brain and social behavior is the immediate inspiration for the script.

With his scenarist Jean Gruault, Resnais has fashioned three fictional case histories. Actual historical figures were first considered, but ordinary contemporary characters were finally decided on in order to underline typical patterns of behavior rather than exceptional ones.

Resnais then intercuts, in voice-over or in a direct interview, Dr. Laborit expounding his theories on comportment and his tripartite notion of growth: flight, struggle, inhibition.

The three biographies Resnais traces dramatically play out these stages. Each character breaks with family and leaves home, each undergoes a social or emotional struggle elsewhere and each ends up in a deadlock that results in desperate action.

Gerard Depardieu plays a peasant who leaves the family enterprise to find work in an urban textile firm where he lands an important post. When the company is swallowed by a larger firm, he finds himself transferred to another position in a different region. Separated from his wife and children and crushed by responsibilities he feels incapable of handling he tries unsuccessfully to commit suicide.

Nicole Garcia plays a young Parisian of working class upbringing who strives to become an actress. She meets and falls in love with a state functionary for French radio, played by Roger Pierre, he of provincial middle class background. The latter's wife plots successfully to suparate them, though Garcia later returns to make one last claim on her former lover.

Despite the competent performances and the unusual central concept, an impression of banality hangs over the film. The decision to anchor action in the commonplace with a resolutely realistic story has dramatically flat and uninvolving results. The incorporation of Laborit into the film's structure is more discordant than stimulating. And Resnais' occasional attempts at humor (flashes of scenes are reviewed with actors dressed up as white mice) are superfluous and trite.

Still, no Resnais film is cinematically uninteresting and "Mon Oncle d'Amerique" (title refers to a mythical Godot-like relation evoked by the central characters) has its share of subtle associations of image and idea, realized through Sacha Vierny's subdued but excellent cinematography, and resonant ambiguities.

Resnais demonstrates his usual impressive technical skill and once again manipulates dramatic structure with his fragmented, irrational, often subliminal editing. However there is nothing here stylistically that he has not used before.

Commercial assessment is difficult to make. Though picture seems one of Resnais' least abstract and most accessible efforts, its academic aspects may scare off the general public. —Len.

Histoire D'Adrien
(Adrien's Story)
(FRENCH-COLOR-16M)

Cannes, May 13.
Denis release and production. Features entire cast. Directed by Jean-Pierre Denis. Screenplay, Denis, Francoise Dudognon; camera (Color). Denis Gheerbrant; editor, Catherine Madilat, Patrick Genet, Danielle Lacoste. Reviewed at Cannes Film Fest (Cannes Critic Week), May 12, '80. Running time: 90 MINS.
Adrien (child) ......Bertrand Sautereau
Adrien (adult) .... Serge Dominique
Father .... Pierre Dienaide
Mother ....Marcelle Dessalles
Shepherd ....Marie Vergoat
Marguerite ....Nadine Reynaud
Roger .... J.P. Geneste

Jean-Pierre Denis may be the herald of needed new directorial blood on the French film scene. He shows he can spin a famliar epic period story on country life without falling into the traps of stereotypes, melodramatics or forced local color.

Film's feeling for landscape, plus its good acting by mainly non-pros, also attest to a promising new director. It is a rare regional film made in its provincial dialect, Occitone, which might call for French subtitles even though a good part of the dialog can be made out.

Perhaps it does evoke the prize-winning Italian film "The Tree of Wooden Clogs" of Ermanno Olmi. But Denis has his own outlooks and feel for the land and people. If he was influenced by Olmi, Denis had assimilated rather than aped it. The French film is also on a more modest scale.

It deals with the life of a bastard boy, born to a farm girl who was seduced by a shepherd. He grows up with his grandparents after his mother dies giving birth while she is alone in the fields.

World War I and a great railroad strike are used in the background of the boy's odyssey. He runs off when his grandfather treats him as a bastard, is taken in by another family and then leaves to work on the railroad as a young man.

An idyl with a girl is shattered by her bigotted father, and the title character continues his wanderings through life in the early part of this century.

Made with grants from this provincial region and the national government, the film never has the feel of patronage or static qualities. Film flows smoothly and should go on to other fests and find specialized outings on its feeling for place, time and characters quite unusual from a new director.

Though shot in 16m, it could easily be blown up for better theatrical chances abroad. It reflects timeless personal, social and political conflicts not to forget that age-old extension of politics called war. —Mosk.

Jukyu-Sai No Chizu
(The Plan of His 19 Years)
(JAPANESE-COLOR)

Cannes, May 20.
GUNRO release and production. Features entire cast. Written and directed by Mitsuo Yanagimachi from a book by Kenji Nakagami. Camera (Eastmancolor), Katsumi Sakakibara; editor, Eiko Yoshida; art director, Shunichi Hiraga; music, Fumio Itabashi. Reviewed at Cannes Film Fest (Cannes Critics Week), May 12, '80. Running time: 110 MINS.
Masaru ....Yuji Honma
Konno .... Keizo Kanie
Maria ....Hideko Okiyama
Boss .... Hatsuo Yamaya
Wife ....Chisako Hara

The Cannes Critic Week has a Japanese film about youthful disarray for the third year in a row. The first depicted a bloody patricide and fratricide, the second strange sex habits of a youth in the subway and now a game played by a young worker that might have repercussions in later life.

Adaptation of youth in this economically fecund country appears troubled. Old repressions, alongside new ways, often lead to difficulties besides the creation of a yearning poorer class alongside a richer one.

The 19-year-old boy works for a married couple delivering newspapers for them. The delivery boys get a percentage on all subscriptions and on the collections from them. He is seen running every morning, sometimes stealing milk from doorsteps and meeting different kinds in his attempts to collect money.

He keeps a secret plan, tries to prepare himself for the university and also has friends among his fellow workers. They all live with the couple. His scheme is a series of assessments on the people he has to deal with in his work.

There is usually disapproval on the part of most. They either evade paying, are too patronizing or have vicious barking dogs and can rarely please the youth. He has a lack of patience and after warning the dog owners he actually hangs it up before their door.

Phones are his weapon for he can be incognito and frighten people by threats of bombs, or revealing things he has found out about them. Sometimes treating it as a joke, he is also upset by what he sees around him.

There is a prostitute with a badly scarred leg who is the loved one of his friend, a petty criminal. When his friend robs for her and is jailed he almost drives her to suicide by his disdain. It might be a portrait of a future fascist or a violent policeman as he does have visions of himself in some kind of uniform.

Sometimes he is overwhelmed but mainly he is being formed as a harsh man who will judge others and perhaps refuse more human ways of life. Film is well lensed and played. More fest outlets in the cards but perhaps somewhat hermetic and repetititve for much foreign theatrical use. But it does show a new personal filmmaker to watch in Mitsuo Yanagimachi. —Mosk.

Aktorzy Prowincjonalni
(Provincial Actors)
(POLISH-COLOR)

Cannes, May 10.
A Film Polski Production, Group "X," Warsaw. Features entire cast. Directed by Agnieszka Holland. Screenplay, Holland, Witold Zatorski; camera (Color), Jacek Petrycki; music, Andrzej Zarycki; assistant director, Bogdan Soelle. Reviewed at Cannes Film Festival (Critics Week), May 10, '80. Running time: 108 MINS.
Cast: Halina Labonarska, Tadeusz Huk, Iwona Biernacka, Ewa Dalkowska, Slawa Kwasniewska. Kazimierz Nogajowna, Janina Ordezanka, Krystyna Wachelko, Zaleska.

One of the most talented directors to emerge from East Europe during the past decade, Agnieszka Hollan has yet to hit her full stride, but will be watched closely hereafter by international critics after her second feature, "Provincial Actors," which opened Critics Week at the

Cannes Film Festival. Her debut pic, "Sunday Parents" (1978), won recognition at San Remo, while her segment in the omnibus film, "Test Shots" (1978), featured her in one scene together with her mentor, Andrzej Wajda, for whom she also wrote the script for "Rough Treatment" (also known as "Without Anaesthesia"), unspooled at last year's Cannes fest in the competition.

"Provincial Actors," like "Sunday Parents" before it, is a comedy that has the aura of the Prague Film School (FAMU) about it, where Holland studied — and apparently learned a great deal from Milos Forman in the process. It's about the life, times, cares, and foibles of playing theatre in the deepest provinces, so true to life that the viewer laughs and cries at the same time during some scenes. And because everything is taken in dead earnestness at times, one feels a great deal of compassion for these "born losers" who, despite ignominy and defeat after defeat, refuse to give up even when the odds are, once again, stacked against them.

The setting is a small town near Warsaw, to which a young up and coming legit director comes to produce a classic in a modern vein. Everyone in the production gets his usual stereotyped role, as expected from the theatre manager, but the aging matinee idol of the ensemble senses opportunity knocking at his door — he will give the performance of his life, given half the chance, that is. The young director, however, knows that everything is already in the bag — in fact, a friendly Warsaw critic attends the first discussions on the production.

What follows is agony and travail for our leading man, however, as he tries to fatten his role by restoring cut lines and imposing his own vision on the director by discussing key scenes in detail. Meanwhile, his all-suffering wife listens to his fears, complains, and frustrations, while resigning herself to a fading career behind the scenes of a children's puppet theatre (part of the troupe). The manager is also fearful of losing his "star," while other actors go through similar stomach pains during rehearsals for the production.

Best of all, "Provincial Actors" offers a rib-tickling metaphor on the cultural scene in Poland, or any country — even the political arena, if one accepts the saying that "the whole world is a stage." There are also deeply profound and human scenes. There's one in which the wife-puppeteer meets an old friend, now well-to-do, in Warsaw. They discuss over tea and in cryptic phrases the course of their lives, the "actress" in actuality giving the performance of her life. There's also a premiere — with a naked woman in a mask ascending a modernized set.

Great fun — and a memorable film. —Holl.

Immacolata E Concetta: L'Altra Gelosia
(Immacolata and Concetta: The Other Jealousy)
(ITALIAN-COLOR)

Rome, May 5.

A Titanus release, produced by Enzo Porcelli for ANTEA productions. Stars Ida Di Benedetto and Marcella Michelangeli. Directed by Salvatore Piscicelli. Screenplay: Carla Apuzzo, S. Piscicelli. Camera (Eastmancolor), Emillo Bestetti; art director, Giovanni Dionisi; editor, Roberto Schiavone; music, Remo Ugolinelli. Reviewed at Salsomaggiore Festival, April 17, 1980. Running time: **92 MINS.**

Immacolata . . . . Ida Di Benedetto
Concetta . . . . Marcella Michelangeli

An unusual, well-made and engrossing first film by former film critic Salvatore Piscicelli, "Immacolata and Concetta" tells with talent and intelligence the old story of passion, jealousy and murder in a small southern Italian town. The "twist," that the lovers are two women, is more than a gimmick: it underlines the ironic contradictions of the old southern culture swept by modern industrial society and then by challenges to the new standards of conduct.

Already a multiple festival winner, pic is headed for Cannes and is a good bet for other class showplaces. It's feminist theme could also attract a women's market. Pic's short-lived commercial run in Italy may be explained by the fact that dialog is spoken in a Neapolitan dialect incomprehensible to most Italians. Nonetheless, material is dramatic and, with X-rated inserts spaced evenly through the film, should appeal to wider audiences once it is subtitled.

More in the somber tradition of "Kingdom of Naples" than the gay stereotypes of Neapolitan life, pic tells of two lower class women, one (Immacolata) the owner of an unsuccessful butcher shop and mother of a young daughter, the other (Concetta) a laborer and declared lesbian. They meet and become lovers in jail, where both are doing time for sex-related crimes: Immacolata for leading a young girl into prostitution, Concetta for shooting at her lover's angry husband.

Out of prison this incongruous couple find they are bound by real love. Braving the public scandal and the threats of Immacolata's husband, Concetta moves in with her friend. But it is Immacolata who really has an open view of the relationship and her own sexuality: though loving Concetta, she continues to see a male friend. Concetta, consumed by jealousy and fear when she learns Immacolata is pregnant, kills her in the butcher shop.

Both Ida Di Benedetto and Marcella Michelangeli turn in excellent performances, underplaying their roles with strong, hard faces that never sentimentalize their characters. Photographer Emilio Bestetti gives a beautiful cold light to the little country town near Naples where the action takes place, virtually all of it shot on location.

Though acting, sets and use of dialect are highly realistic, the plot is frankly melodramatic and linked to the tradition of Neapolitan film and theatre. Coscripted by Carla Apuzzo and Piscicelli, "Immacolata" gives an intimate sense of the lives and passions of its characters without falling into documentary naturalism. The frankness of the love-making scenes between the two women has an honest eroticism that is almost shocking, and far away from hardcore.

Clean editing and lensing contribute much to the power of the film. The story is told in blocks rather than having events run smoothly into each other, a technique that distances the highly-charged dramatic material somewhat. In the end it is the film's themes that absorb the viewer. —Yung.

Carny

Absorbing, offbeat tale of outsiders. A tricky sell.

Hollywood, May 16.

A United Artists release. Produced by Robbie Robertson. Executive producer, Jonathan Taplin. Directed by Robert Kaylor. Stars Gary Busey, Jodie Foster, Robbie Robertson. Screenplay, Thomas Baum, based on a story by Phoebe Kaylor, Robert Kaylor, Robbie Robertson, camera (Technicolor), Harry Stradling Jr.; music, Alex North; editor, Stuart Pappe; production design, William J. Cassidy; art direction, Josan F. Russo; set decoration, Ray Molyneaux, Charles R. Pierce; sound, Bill Kaplan; assistant director, William Scott; second unit director, Garth Craven. Reviewed at the Goldwyn Studios, Hollywood, May 15, 1980. MPAA Rating: R. Running time: **105 MINS.**

Frankie . . . . Gary Busey
Donna . . . . Jodie Foster
Patch . . . . Robbie Robertson
Gerta . . . . Meg Foster
Heavy . . . . Kenneth McMillan
On-Your-Mark . . . . Elisha Cook
Nails . . . . Theodore Wilson
Skeet . . . . John Lehne
Sugaree . . . . Tina Andrews
Delno . . . . Bert Remsen
Willie Mae . . . . Alan Braunstein
Dill . . . . Bill McKinney
W.C. Hannon . . . . Woodrow Pargrey
Mickey . . . . Craig Wasson

An excitingly eccentric, nervously energetic work, "Carny" is an intriguing look at an infrequently examined American subculture which emerges as more impressive in its various, sometimes brilliant, parts than as a satisfying whole. Although it ultimately lacks the nerve to completely follow through on the daring exhibited in its opening reels, pic has much to commend it on several levels and should at least attract some critical and cult attention, even if it may present too dark and turbulent a vision to be palatable to a large public.

Edgy tale of three born outsiders living on a tightrope vividly recalls, both in style and content, the doom-laden 'films noir' of the late 1940s. Although the performances and sexual frankness are resolutely modern, the seedy milieu and hardened characters, as well as Harry Stradling Jr.'s shadowy lensing and Alex North's moody score, strongly evoke the dangerous, fateful world caught in so many sordid, powerful postwar melodramas.

Gary Busey here plays, not a geek like Tyrone Power in "Nightmare Alley," but a slightly demented bozo in a cage who mercilessly taunts spectators trying to dump him into water by throwing baseballs. Busey hooks up with runaway Jodie Foster, engendering the initial resentment of best friend and carnival con man and manager Robbie Robertson.

As the carny makes its way through the South, Foster is gradually assimilated into the band of outcasts and a three-way relationship develops, just as the traveling show comes under unpleasant pressure from local mobsters to cut them in on proceeds for right to operate in their territory.

While the personal story unfolds satisfactorily, criminal subplot reroutes tale onto more conventional melodramatic ground, forcing third act to wrap up too many surface plot loose ends in a manner somewhat routine compared to compelling iconoclasm of the first hour. Filmmakers bracingly plunge into deep, choppy waters in the beginning, only to swim closer to shore by wrap-up.

Even so, pic remains provocative throughout, in no small measure due to standout performances down the line. Busey is tremendous as the sideshow attraction who rather miraculously retains his equilibrium despite his lunatic job. Foster, ostensibly playing her first "adult" role complete with semi-nude love scenes with both men, works wonders with a somewhat underwritten part.

In his first dramatic role, producer and story-coauthor Robertson puts across the same somewhat jaded, wasted persona he projected as "himself" in "The Last Waltz." He's completely convincing. Supporting turns, notably those by Kenneth McMillan, Bill McKinney, Elisha Cook and Meg Foster, not to mention the wide assortment of "freaks" on view, are all on target.

A documentary filmmaker for 20 years and best-known for "Derby," director Robert Kaylor displays an unnerring eye for atmosphere and detail and more than proves his talent with actors. Plot problems notwithstanding, scripter Thomas Baum has created excitingly randy, colloquial dialog which is all delivered adroitly.

Technical contributions are outstanding. Stradling and North's work is among the best of their respective careers, Stuart Pappe's editing has real snap and William J. Cassidy's production design enormously aides feeling of overall verisimilitude.—*Cart.*

Sonntagskinder
(Sunday Children)
(WEST GERMAN-B-&-W)

Cannes, May 16.
A Sentana Film Production, Munich, Michael Verhoeven; world rights, Eginhart Hillenbrand, Munich. Features entire cast. Directed by Michael Verhoeven. Screenplay, Gerlind Reinshagan, Verhoeven; camera, Gero Erhardt; editor, Dagmar Hirtz. Reviewed at Cannes Film Festival (Directors' Fortnight), May 15, '80. Running time: **103 MINS.**
Cast: Nora Barner, Erika Pluhar, Gerd Seid, Pola Kinski, Mario Fischel, Elisabeth Schwarz, Rudolf Wessely, Ruth Maria Kubitschek, Carolin Orner, Christoph Quest, Pierre Franckh, Maria Hartmann, Friedrich von Thun, Hartmut Becker, Santiago Ziesmer, Dieter Prochnow.

The primary credit for "Sunday Children," unspooled at the Directors' Fortnight, goes to dramatist Gerlind Reinshagan, whose play was adapted to the screen by Michael Verhoeven. Reinshagan is best known in the States via the "Berlin Now" program in Gotham sponsored by the Goethe Institute back in 1977, where her "Heaven and Earth" play won critical praise for its human treatment of the old and sick in a cancer ward.

"Sunday Children" deals with the war years, 1939-45, from the viewpoint of teenage children in a small provincial town. Lensed in black and white with fade outs after each segment in blazing whiteness (to mark, mostly, the passages of years), pic centers on the remembrances of Elsie, age 14 (the author?), with the focus on the

experiences of a group of school classmates.

As the war commences, the tragedy begins to strike home in ways unexpected to townspeople normally far from the center of action: the girlfriends and the servant-girl meet a prisoner, one suffers near rape by a soldier returning disfigured from the front, another commits suicide together with a teacher she loves, a pro-Nazi youth returns home a cripple in a wheelchair while an anti-Nazi youth dies during a bombing attack, and a mother convinces a teacher to promote her daughter in school by comparing the family death list to "match" who is suffering the most. That's just a few of the strong scenes this meditative film has to offer on what it was really like to live through the war in a Germany scarred by National Socialism.

The young thesps shine in "Sunday Children" amid all-around top performances. Lensing is also a plus. This is a must for history fans, one of several good pix of late — others are "David" and "Torch High" — that mark a trend to review the Nazi years with integrity and compassion for all who lived and died during that period. —*Holl.*

Hazal
(TURKISH-COLOR)

Cannes, May 13.
Umut Film release and production. Features entire cast. Directed by Ali Ozgenturk. Screenplay, Onat Kutlar, Ozgenturk; camera (Eastmancolor), Muzaffer Turan; music, Arif Sag. Reviewed at Cannes Fest (Director Fortnight), May 10, '80. Running time: **90 MINS.**
With: Turkan Soray, Talat Bulut, Meral Cetinkaya, Husedin Peyda, Keriman Ulusoy.

Old ways versus new ways and beautiful rocky landscapes are becoming standard stuff in the Turkish films that have been making inroads at major festivals lately. Here is another more melodramatic and less powerful than its predecessors but still attesting Turkey is worth festival interest for auxiliary sections at least.

Yilmaz Guney, writing films in prison and practically directing them by remote control through another, is responsible for growing interest in Turkish films. But those following up have to achieve his more dynamic treatment, dramatic power and sincere protest.

This one has a lovely girl married off whose husband dies soon afterwards. She becomes the property of her in-laws and is to be married to the 12-year-old brother of the deceased. This is colorful but leads to trouble when a young man falls for her.

There is also a road to be built by the village which will join them to the more modern world. The muslim religious leaders oppose it but the man enamored of the widow joins in the work and manages to get to her only to have both killed by the irate villagers for going against tradition.

More picturesque than dramatically effective, film still has a worthy theme and acceptable though still slogging direction and dramatic pitch. It will probably remain in the festival circuits without showing much legs outside of its own and other muslim countries. Acting is passable though the heroine, Hazal, is somewhat too well made up for the life in this village.
—*Mosk.*

The Shining
(COLOR)

But not bright.

Hollywood, May 22.
A Warner Bros. release. Produced and directed by Stanley Kubrick, in association with The Producers Circle Co. Exec producer, Jan Harlan. Features entire cast. Screenplay, Stanley Kubrick and Diane Johnson, based on the novel by Stephen King; camera (no color credited), John Alcott; editor, Ray Lovejoy; sound, Ivan Sharrock, Richard Daneil; production design, Roy Walker; art direction, Les Tomkins; assistant director, Brian Cook; make-up, Tom Smith; costumes, Milena Canonero; music, Bela Bartok. Reviewed at The Burbank Studios, Burbank, May 21, 1980. (MPAA rating: R.) Running time: **146 MINS.**

Jack Torrance	Jack Nicholson
Wendy Torrance	Shelley Duvall
Danny	Danny Lloyd
Halloran	Scatman Crothers
Ullman	Barry Nelson
Grady	Philip Stone
Lloyd	Joe Turkel
Doctor	Anne Jackson
Durkin	Tony Burton

Given the intense audience interest in "The Shining" prior to its opening, this may be Warner Bros. biggest boxoffice disappointment since "Exorcist II." With everything to work with, director Stanley Kubrick has teamed with jumpy Jack Nicholson to destroy all that was so terrifying about Stephen King's bestseller.

The truly amazing question is why a director of Kubrick's stature would spend his time and effort on a novel that he changes so much it's barely recognizable, taking away whatever originality it possessed while emphasizing its banality.

The answer, presumably, is that Kubrick was looking for a commercial "property" he could impose his own vision on and Warner Bros., not having learned its lesson with "Barry Lyndon," was silly enough to let him do it.

In his book, King took a fundamental horror formula — an innocent family marooned in an evil dwelling with a grim history — and built layers of ingenious terror upon it. The father, a nice enough fellow given too much to drink and violent outbursts, is gradually possessed by the demonic, desolate hotel he's hired to caretake for the winter.

With dad going mad, the only protection mother and child have is the boy's clairvoyance — his "shining" — which allows him an innocent understanding and some ability to outmaneuver the devils with the help of a rush-to-the-rescue by an old black cook who understands both the boy's gift and the perils he faces.

But Kubrick, as his devoted followers so often note, sees things his own way, throwing 90% of King's creation out to concentrate on Nicholson as the mentally deteriorating father. But mugging and grinning and arching his eyebrows in that wacky way he finds so charming, Nicholson is almost a certified nut from the very beginning.

What's worse, the crazier he gets, the more idiotic he looks until it's hard to believe he's taking any part of this role seriously. As so often noted, Nicholson started his career playing crazy for American International Pictures and it looks like he's gone home again, without learning anything along the way.

Without exception, in every scene Nicholson has that should be building the terror and suspense, he blows it and it's hard to reconcile what's on screen with Kubrick's vaunted reputation for demanding 50 takes until he gets what he wants.

If Nicholson's performance is what the director wants after 50 takes, it's no wonder he demands the final cut: It's impossible to imagine what the 49 takes he threw away could look like.

Kubrick fares no better with Shelley Duvall who transforms the warm, sympathetic wife of the book into a simpering, semiretarded hysteric whom nobody could be locked up with for the winter without harboring murderous thoughts.

Only young Danny Lloyd and Scatman Crothers — who share the shining — offer any hope for the plot and Kubrick minuses the former while practically ignoring the latter, up to and including killing him off pointlessly despite the fact that he's supposed to be the hero.

But Kubrick is still a visual artist and with the help of cameraman John Alcott and Roy Walker's production design, the atmosphere of the old hotel is properly menacing and glamorous. The scenes, in fact, are constantly set for something to start happening.

But it never does, even after nearly two-and-a-half hours. Compared to the exciting — if somewhat corny — conclusion to King's novel — Kubrick might as well have finished with blank film. In fact, he almost did.

There are, to be sure, some special effects that are momentarily horrifying and these are being used in the tv commercials to capitalize on the readers' interest in the film. But the effects are never used for any real purpose in the picture and at some point — as Warner Bros. learned before — the public just won't be fooled for long. —*Har.*

Achalta Ota
(You've Been Had ... You Turkey!)
(ISRAEL-COLOR)

Tel Aviv, May 8.
A Candid Production, produced by Yehuda Barkan. Directed by Yehuda Barkan and Igal Shilon. Stars Yehuda Barkan. Screenplay, Shimon Israeli, Yehuda Barkan. Camera; (color) Gadi Danzig, Beni Carmeli; music, Ilan Mochiach; editor Zion Avramian. Reviewed in Tel-Aviv, April 26, 1980. Running time: **90 MINS.**
Cast: Karolin Langford; Arie Moskuna, Dvora Bakon, Uri Gross.

Judging by the initial public response to this candid camera comedy, Israelis seem to be desperate for some laughs. Not the kind of laughter which would provoke any kind of thought process, but simply the kind of belly laugh achieved by having someone slip on a banana peel. An attitude which may be quite understandable, if the everyday reality of Israel is kept in mind.

Yehuda Barkan, the man in charge of almost all aspects of this film, is a natural choice, as besides his career as screen actor and stage comic, he has had a long and successful line of radio programs using the candid microphone to poke fun at people's credulity.

The enormous success, last year of a candid camera feature film, "It's a Funny, Funny World" was proof enough that an investment of this kind pays off on the local market, whatever its absolute value. Once again, it seems that following trends was a shrewd decision.

Barkan's approach to the hidden camera is more good-natured than the one adopted by his predecessors. He is less prone to nasty remarks, and seeks mostly to show how unaware we are of the way the world around us works: a bunch of people pushing a train because they're told this is the way to start it, or a bank-o-mat talking to its customers and telling them they won't get any money unless they ask nicely.

A flimsy story line, built around a candid camera team and girl joining up with them, is intended to keep all the jokes together in some form of unity, not necessary and not very convincing. —*Edna.*

La Verdad Sobre El Caso Savolta
(The Truth On the Savolta Affair)
(SPANISH-FRENCH-ITALO-COLOR)

Madrid, May 7.
A Domingo Pedret P.C. (Barcelona), Nef Diffusion (Paris), Filmalpha (Rome) coproduction, directed by Antonio Drove. Features cast. Exec producer, Andres Vicente Gomez; screenplay, Antonio Drove and Antonio Larreta based on novel by Eduardo Mendoza; camera (Eastmancolor), Gilberto Azevedo; music, Egisto Macchi; sets, Louis Arguello; editor, Guillermo Maldonad. Reviewed at Cine Penalver (Madrid), May 6, '80. Running. time: **120 MINS.**
Pajarito . . . . Jose Luis Lopez Vazquez
Leprince . . . . Charles Denner
Miranda . . . . Ovidi Montllor
Savolta . . . . Omero Antonutti
Teresa . . . . Stefania Sandrelli
Also: Ettore Manni, Alfred Pea, Rogelio Ibanez, Virginia Billetdoux, Pan Garsabell, others.

Fascinating, excellently-limned and often hard hitting behind the scenes expose of a famous scandal set at the end of World War I in Barcelona involving an arms manufacturer and confrontations between anarchist labor unions and big business.

Though most of the pic was directed by Antonio Drove, whose credit appears to beginning it is known that Argentinian helmer Diego Santillan also worked on the film for a while during disputes arising between Drove and the producers. But whoever the credit may be due to, outcome is an intelligent and effective film with topnotch technical credits all down the line and excellent thesping by all the principals.

Story concerns a Catalan arms manufacturer, Savolta, who on the one hand is trying to obtain new war contracts with the French and on the other is grappling with mounting labor unrest. A French rep of the firm, Leprince, however, has been secretly selling arms to the Germans and smuggling goods and falsifying bills. Some of the dirty dealings are discovered by Savolta's key accountant and info finally reaches the hands of a penurious journalist, who threatens an expose unless union demands are met. He accuses Savolta, not realizing that it is Leprince who's behind all the dirty schemes.

Through a mixture of conniving duplicity and the murder of key adversaries through paid thugs, including ultimately the journalist, his wife, various labor leaders, and Savolta himself — with blame laid to the anarchist unions — Leprince wrests controls of the company and dominates the scene. Pic ends by outlining the bloodbath caused by the murder of union leaders between the end of World War I and the advent of the Primo de Rivera dictatorship in Spain.

Though item runs a bit long, the intrigue and political action and street violence keep the pace lively. The twists in the plot never get out of hand, as they usually do in this sort of film, but on the whole are comprehensible. Pic is a fine political thriller that could find a ready market in offshore sales, except perhaps in sites where the left-wing union sympathies would be objectionable. —*Besa.*

Bon Voyage, Charlie Brown
(And Don't Come Back)
(ANIMATED-COLOR)

Great kid fare, as usual.

Hollywood, May 23.
Paramount Pictures release of a Lee Mendelson-Bill Melendez production. Produced by Lee Mendelson, Bill Melendez. Directed by Melendez; codirector, Phil Roman. Screenplay, Charles M. Schulz, based on his "Peanuts" characters; camera Movielab color, Nick Vasu Inc.); music, Ed Bogas, Judy Munsen; animation, Sam Jaimes, Hank Smith, Al Pabian, Joe Roman, Ed Newmann, Bill Littlejohn, Bob Carlson. Dale Baer, Spencer Peel, Larry Leichliter, Sergio Bertolli; sound, Producers' Sound Service. Reviewed at Paramount Studio Theatre, May 22, 1980. (MPAA Rating: G.) Running time: **75 MINS.**
Character voices: Daniel Anderson, Scott Beach, Casey Carlson, Debbie Muller, Patricia Patts, Laura Planting, Arrin Skelley, Bill Melendez, Annalisa Bortolin, Roseline Rubens, Pascale De Bardlet.

"Bon Voyage, Charlie Brown (And Don't Come Back)" brings the wonderful "Peanuts" gang back to the bigscreen in a fourth animated theatrical outing sure to pull in all of the devout Charlie Brown fans. Collaboration of writer/creator Charles M. Schulz and producers Lee Mendelson and Bill Melendez, latter of whom directed, has served the characters well through past tv and film efforts and does not disappoint here. Although no longer quite the "in" rage it once was, Schulz' cartoon is timeless and should draw fine summer kid biz.

Plot line for current pic is slightly different from others in that it transports some of the gang to France to spend two weeks as foreign exchange students. Charlie Brown and Linus are invited to stay at a mysterious chateau that becomes a vehicle for a small amount of danger not often seen in "Peanuts" pix.

Everything is merrily resolved in the finale, which should be a relief to the many who take pleasure in the dependable happy endings cartoons offers.

Particularly endearing in the pic are several scenes of kindness between Woodstock and Snoopy and exploits of the latter as he finds himself traveling first class on the airplane and, in a stopover in England, playing tennis at Wimbledom.

Sole disappointment is absence of CB's arch nemesis, Lucy, but Peppermint Patty serves well in taking over those chores.

As usual, animation is a step above most other outfits and music by Ed Bogas provides effective background. Film has been in production for three years and tech credits show it. —*Berg.*

Dear Boys
(Lieve Jongens)
(NETHERLANDS-COLOR)

Hollywood, May 23.
A Sigma Films production. Produced by Matthijs van Heijningen. Directed by Paul de Lussanet. Features entire cast. Screenplay, Chiem van Houweninge, based on a novel by Gerard Reve; camera (uncredited color), Paul van den Bos; editor, Hans van Dongen; music, Laurens van Rooyen. Reviewed at the Redd Foxx Screening Room, Hollywood, May 22, 1980. (No MPAA Rating.) Running time: **88 MINS.**
Wolf .... Hugo Metsers
Muskrat .... Hans Dagelet
Tiger .... Bill Van Dijk
Albert .... Albert Mol

"Dear Boys" which world preemed last week at the Seattle Film Festival, is another gritty Dutch look at sexuality, this one dealing with the problem of older homosexuals have holding onto their younger lovers. Based on a tome by controversial Dutch writer Gerard Reve, film is very candid in presenting cruel, selfish behavior of its principles. Despite some dramatic problems, frank treatment of topical theme makes pic a possibility for other fests and specialized markets.

Wolf is a temperamental, temporarily dried-up writer living with a lad called Tiger. Eyeing a foxy fellow named Muskrat in a bar, Wolf invites this youngster and his older companion, more conventionally named Albert, to his country home for an indefinite stay. With his dream being the ultimate conquest of Muskrat, Wolf encourages a fling between the two boys, while doing everything possible to eliminate the ineffectual Albert from the scene. Just as the sexual and emotional ramifications of all these maneuverings seem to be coming to a head, however, tale bogs down in a succession of literary digressions, halting plot's unfolding and forestalling psychological insights that might have been provided.

As convincingly played by Hugo Metsers, Wolf is both self-pitying and confidently abrasive, an interesting character to the extent that he flagrantly mistreats his boys and still gets away with it. Unfortunately, the Albert character is conveniently caricatured as a thoroughly helpless aging queen, while younger men are believable targets for older men's lechery.

Director Paul de Lussanet, recently represented at Filmex by

his first feature, "Mysteries," created a believable atmosphere and takes pic about as far as it can go without crossing over into hardcore. Laurens van Rooyen's score is a lovely asset. —*Cart.*

Harukanaru Yama No Yobigoe
(A Distant Cry From Spring)
(JAPANESE-COLOR)

Tokyo, May 7.
A Shochiku release. Produced by Kiyoshi Shimazu. Directed by Yoji Yamada. Screenplay, Yoji Yamada, Yoshitaka Asama; from a story by Yamada. Camera (color), Tetsuo Tekaba; art direction, Mitsuo Idegawa; music, Masaru Sato. Reviewed at Shochiku Central, April 27, 1980. Running time: **124 MINS.**
Kosaku Tajima .... Ken Takakura
Tamiko Kazami .... Chieko Baisho
Takeshi Kazami ......Hidetaka Yoshioka
Shunichiro Tajima .... Mizuho Suzuki
Taro Abuta .... Hajime Hana
Jiro Abuta .... Hideo Jimbo
Saburo Abuta .... Go Awazu

For all the excitement generated by Akira Kurosawa's return to filmmaking, it is Yoji Yamada who is consistently hot stuff at the domestic b.o. The two films he directed for Shochiku last year were that company's biggest moneymakers, and his '77 smash, "Shiawase No Kiiroi Hankachi" (The Yellow Handkerchief of Happiness) won the first Japan Academy Award for best picture.

A Frank Capra-like director, he lets sentiment run rampant and is concerned with big-hearted "little people." His latest work contains not only the requisite number of Capraesque touches, but large snatches of George Stevens' "Shane," as well as dollops of Yamada's own "Shiawase no Kiiroi Hankachi."

To the father- and husband-less farm of widow Chieko Baisho and son Hidetaka Yoshioka comes Ken Takakura, a mysterious drifter looking for work and asking payment next to nothing. It's obvious from the outset that Takakura is running from something in his past, the exact details of which are revealed only after he has worked on the farm long enough to gain his employer's trust and confidence. After she tells him that she no longer thinks of him as a stranger and that he need no longer take his meals alone in his room, he asks that he be allowed to move on because the police are after him for the murder of a loan shark who hounded his wife to suicide.

On the gray, misty morning following Takakura's account of his crime, the police drive up and take him away, prompting little Yoshioka, a la Brandon de Wilde in "Shane," to run after his surrogate

father, shouting, "Where are you going?"

Yamada, though no artist, is a nonpareil manipulator of emotions, and while his manipulations are easy to criticize, they're equally difficult to resist. His screenplay, which he co-authored with Yoshitaka Asama, is an accumulation of minor incidents, each designed to better acquaint and favorably impress us with his major characters. Only occasionally does he stoop to the cornball slapstick and in-jokes seemingly endemic to Japanese cinema. —*Bail.*

Cannes Festival

Loulou
(FRENCH-COLOR)

Cannes, May 27.
Gaumont release of Gaumont-Action Films production. Stars Isabelle Huppert, Gerard Depardie. Directed by Maurice Pialat. Screenplay, Arlette Langmann, Pialat; camera (Eastmancolor), Pierre William Glenn, Jacques Loiseleux; editor, Yann Dedet, Sophie Coussein. Reviewed at Cannes Film Fest (Competing), May 22, '80. Running time, 110 MINS.
Nelly .... Isabelle Huppert
Loulou .... Gerard Depardieu
Andre .... Guy Marchand
Michel .... Humbert Balsan
Remy .... Bernard Tronczyk
Pierrot .... Christian Boucher

Maurice Pialat is probably one of the most perceptive directors practicing in France today. Somewhat erratic, a sort of maverick, he is a rare populist filmmaker, in the good sense of reflecting ordinary people in a dramatic, insightful way.

That has led to extraordinary probing dramas on childhood ("Nude Childhood"), the breakup of a couple ("We Will Not Grow Old Together"), the impact of death on a family ("The Mouth Agape") and working class students ("Get Your Diploma First").

With "Loulou," Pialat deals with a couple formed of a fringe semidelinquent colossus (Gerard Depardieu), the "Loulou" of the title, and a frail but headstrong middle-class girl, Isabelle Huppert. They make an engaging couple who love and fight and may eventually make it together and even grow old together.

Huppert sometimes slips back to her former lover, who is also her boss in an ad agency. Guy Marchand is effective as a self-indulgent type who cannot see what she can possibly see in Depardieu.

Depardieu leads her in the looting of a warehouse of electronic goods, he gets stabbed in a bar fight over a

girl and she gets pregnant. He is not one for work but promises he will when the baby is born. But she is not sure and has an abortion. He feels she should have had confidence in him as the film ends on her helping him home after he gets drunk.

There is a luminous quality about this film. There is humor that springs from situations and character. Pialat may be giving a modern continuance of the French prewar poetic, naturalistic dramas with worker and sub-proletariat types.

But he has eschewed the romanticism and added sharp modern language and an acceptance of conditions with perhaps a possibility of changing them. But circumstances may have to change to.

Pialat lives up to promise and this film could have legs with the right handling. It should also go on to other festivals and marks Pialat a needed personal, probing filmmaker on the local scene. —*Mosk.*

Sauve Qui Peut La Vie
(Everyone For Himself In Life)
(SWISS-FRENCH-COLOR)

Cannes, May 27.
MK2 release of Sara Films-Sonimage-Saga-MK2 production. Stars Isabelle Huppert, Jacques Dutronc, Nathalie Baye. Directed by Jean-Luc Godard. Screenplay, Godard, Jean-Claude Carriere, Anne-Marie Mieville. Camera (Eastmancolor), Renato Berta, William Lubtchansky; music, Gabriel Yared. Reviewed at Cannes Film Fest (Competing), May 21, 1980. Running time, **88 MINS.**
Isabelle .... Isabelle Huppert
Godard .... Jacques Dutronc
Denise .... Nathalie Baye

Jean-Luc Godard, that controversial New Waver who gave jump cuts artistic merit, helped upset straight narrative with asides, commentary chapter headings and doing one's own thing, and then went into politico tracts after the May '68 events, is now back with his first feature after almost eight years devoting himself to making video films.

It is good to have him back for he still irritates, annoys and even titillates as most of the ex-Wavers have gone in for more academic films and themes that they once attacked when they were all critics.

However, Godard does not add much new to his repertoire of old. He seems to have replaced the jump cut by suddenly going into image by image analyses of some motions within an action. In fact, there is a superficial resemblance to the script of fellow filmmaker Alain Resnais's "My Uncle From America" which was also at Cannes.

Godard similarly takes three people who at times cross each others' lives. But there the resemblance ends. Godard does not explain their childhoods or them but puts them into scenes. Jacques Dutronc seems to work at a hotel taking care of important guests, even escorting them to airports. One, an opera singer, never stops singing.

Nathalie Baye is his current girlfriend upset with his vacillating ways. He runs into an innocent-looking prostitute one day with whom he spends a nice night. Godard has always been digging away at the ways of prostitution, one pic had a joy girl heroine, "To Live Her Life," and another housewives doing it at times for needed grocery money, "Two or Three Things I Know About Her."

Here Isabelle Huppert, usually a romantic or ill adjusted innocent, plays the joy girl with accepting yet curious attitudes towards her clients, gangsters preying on her and the demands of the different buyers.

Dutronc also has an estranged wife and a bitter teenage daughter. Godard was born in France but brought up in Switzerland and went back to Switzerland to shoot this one.

Film should draw more selective audiences but will turn off more general ones. If Godard has not added much new to his ways of looking at life's dissenters, he remains provocative, disturbing, a filmmaking original who takes risks. —*Mosk.*

Out of the Blue
(COLOR)

Cannes, May 27.
Robson Street Productions release and production. Stars Linda Manz, Dennis Hopper, Sharon Farrell, Raymond Burr, Don Gordon. Directed by Dennis Hopper. Screenplay, Leonard Yakir, Gary Jules Jouvenat; camera (Color), Marc Champion; editor, Doris Dyck; music, Tom Lavin; exec producer, Paul Lewis. Reviewed at Cannes Film Fest (Competing), May 20, '80. Running time, 94 MINS.
CeBe .... Linda Manz
Kathy .... Sharon Farrell
Don .... Dennis Hopper
Brean .... Raymond Burr
Charlie .... Don Gordon

Dennis Hopper, whose "Easy Rider" turned out to be the hit low budget '60s delineation of the counter culture, and who then came-a-cropper with an over indulgent try at getting to the core of film mythology with "The Last Movie," directs for the first time since 1971.

Hopper also stars in this terse drama of what the '70s drug culture and dregs of the counter culture would have wrought on those easy riders who got off their bikes and tried to conform and had children. The child of the union of an ex-leather bikey turned truck driver and a drug addict, looseliving

mother ends up destroying the whole family.

There may be some critical rejection of this drama which takes place in a midwestern city in North America. It was made in Canada with Canadian money and there has been some contention about Canada accepting its nationality for tax benefits. The thinking may be American but English-speaking Canada has always been heavily affected by U.S. culture.

Linda Manz has tart authority as a streetwise 15-year-old. She had been in a terrible accident while driving with Hopper, her father, who, in playing and joking with her while bowling along in his truck, plows into a school bus stalled in the middle of the road, killing many of the kids.

Hopper has been sentenced to five years in prison. He has become a hero to his daughter who has fanaticized the late Elvis Presley into another hero. Her mother, on drugs, is the mistress of the man who owns a restaurant she works in.

Hopper comes out but Manz's hopes for a new life go awry. Her father gets a job driving a tractor in a garbage dump. But the father of a kid who died in the accident gets him fired. Hopper, backed by a violent friend, attacks the man, robs him and comes home drunk and even tries to force his friend on the daughter.

But the girl reveals a memory of Hopper himself molesting her as a child and kills him and blows up herself and her mother in the wrecked truck of the accident which sits in their back yard.

A certain harshness, a certain forced gloom as these fallouts from the hectic '60s and '70s destroy themselves may relegate this to playoff. But it could catch youthful and perhaps older interest on its relentless look at the blighted aftermath of those in the days of revolt and change who could not afterwards adjust to the new times.

Hopper is restrained, Sharon Farrell is effective as the harried, vulnerable, pretty but neurotic mother while Manz is uncannily shrewd, sharp yet innocent, as the daughter who finally explodes into destruction of self and family when pushed beyond being able to endure or understand their ways.

Dramatically economical, pic captures urban overcrowding, personal problems and violence but sans excess. Hopper reportedly took over direction after film started but worked with the writer on changes to fit his own personal outlooks. —*Mosk.*

Non-Competing Cannes Films

The Man With Bogart's Face
(COLOR)

Gimmick with strong exploitable b.o. potentiality.

Cannes, May 14.
20th-Fox release of a Melvin Simon Productions presentation. Produced by Andrew J. Fenady. Directed by Robert Day. Stars Robert Sacchi, Franco Nero, Michelle Phillips, Olivia Hussey, Misty Rowe, Victor Buono, Sybil Danning, Herbert Lom. Screenplay, Fenady based on his novel; camera (CFI) Richard C. Glouner; editor, Eddie Saeta; music, George Duning; set designer, Richard McKenzie; sound, James J. Klimger; costumes, Oscar Rodriguez, Jack Splangler, Voulee Giokaris; assistant director, David McGiffert. Reviewed at Cannes film festival, May 14, 1980. Running time: 106 MINS.
Sam Marlow .... Robert Sacchi
Hakim .... Franco Nero
Gena ....Michelle Phillips
Elsa .... Olivia Hussey
Duchess .... Misty Rowe
Commodore Anastas .... Victor Buono
Mr. Zebra .... Herbert Lom
Lt. Bumbera .... Dick Bakalyan
Cynthia .... Sybil Danning
Sgt. Hacksaw ....Gregg Palmer
Wolf Zinderneuf ....Jay Robinson
Petey Cane ....George Raft
Teresa Anastas .... Yvonne de Carlo
Himself .... Mike Mazurki
Mr. Chevalier .... Henry Wilcoxon
Mr. Wing .... Victor Sen Yung
Jock .... Joe Theismann
Mother .... Alshia Brevard
Nicky .... Buck Kartalian

For Robert Sacchi, his face has led him to stardom; for the audience, happily, he displays ample talent and a wry sense of humor as the Bogart look-alike in the role of Sam Marlow, private eye. Producer Andrew J. Fenady, whose script is based on his own novel, has sprinkled his involved plot with a continuous flow of laugh lines which will keep audiences chuckling for most of the time.

Clearly and intentionally the picture is a gimmick, Sacchi plays Bogart as Bogart himself might have portrayed Sam Marlow, always relating incidents and personalities to stars and films of yesteryear. It adds up to a lot of fun, not always sustained, but good enough to ensure potent boxoffice possibilities.

As the film opens, the star has just undergone facial surgery, and immediately sets up shop as a private eye, hiring Misty Rowe as his luscious but scatterbrained secretary. Business is slack until his photograph appears in a newspaper following a shooting incident, and then he's overwhelmed with inquiries, all involving skulduggery over the disappearance of

a priceless pair of matching blue sapphires which are reputedly used as the eyes of the bust of Alexander the Great who died in the third century, B.C.

Involved in the caper to lay their greedy hands on the gems are Franco Nero, as a Turkish magnate, Victor Buono a Greek shipping magnate, who uses his daughter to trick the private eye into helping him, Herbert Lom as a commission man and Jay Robinson, who started it all by talking about the sapphires while serving a 17-year term in a Greek jail as a Nazi war criminal.

First victim of the ensuing thuggery is a German refugee who answers to the delightful name of Horst Borsht, whose daughter, Olivia Hussey, enlists the aid of the private eye to help her father. She survives through most of the picture, but finally gets mown down when tricked out of her home on a phony phone call.

However, it is Michelle Phillips who is mostly involved with Sacchi, both emotionally and in helping to locate the gems. They're involved in a very funny sequence in the hall of mirrors at the Hollywood Wax Museum when the thugs become trigger happy.

The action — and there is plenty of it — is played against some handsome backgrounds, including expensive yachts and the palace-like home of Nero, with his bevy of belly dancers. And the finale, on Catalina and a boat, where the two chief bidders each offer $1,000,000 for the prize gems, and are then forced to strip down to their underpants, while the commission man is sacrificed to a hungry shark, is more amusing than convincing. But that hardly matters.

All told, the principal players seem to be enjoying the romp. Sacchi himself, agile with his gun and with a powerful fist, strikes the right balance between action and comedy. Nero, Buono and Herbert Lom try to out-maneuver each other with their own brand of dirty tricks, Phillips (who always reminds Sacchi of Gene Tierney) has style and vivacity, Hussey does well in a role of more limited scope, but Rowe milks her part for all it's worth. She's the perfect dumb blonde with a passion for banana splits. Also stunning to look at is Sybil Danning as the Turk's unscrupulous secretary.

Robert Day's direction is slick and lively, and technical credits are up par. The title song and "Looking at You," both with lyrics by the producer and music by George Duning, are sung by Armando Compean over the credits, and get the pic off to a pleasing start. —*Myro.*

Dedicatoria
(Dedicated To...)
(SPANISH-COLOR)

Cannes, May 23.
An Elias Querejeta production. Directed by Jaime Chavarri. Features entire cast. Screenplay, Elias Querejeta, Jaime Chavarri; camera (Eastmancolor), Teo Escamilla; editor, Pablo G. del Amo; sets, Antonio Belison; sound, Bernardo Menz. Reviewed at Palais de Festival (Cannes), May 22, 1980. Running time: **99 MINS.**

Juan	Jose Luis Gomez
Clara	Amparo Munoz
Carmen	Patricia Adriani
Paco	Francisco Casares
Falcon	Luis Politti
Aurora	Helene Peycherand
Josefina	Marie Mansart
Donato	Claude Legros

Topnotch thesping, excellent direction by Jaime Chavarri and the usual high technical standards of all Elias Querejeta productions are not enough to offset a weak and rambling script which never quite makes its point. There is really no plot to this film. It rambles on from vague bedroom scenes to talky dialogs without ever getting under the surface of the characters. Motivations and actions are not made clear.

Pic revolves around a newshound apparently hunting down the story of a man doing a three-year jail sentence. Former seduces the man's daughter, who seems to be running a kennel, visits the prisoner and chats inconclusively with him, and has a fling with his editor's wife. The prisoner commits suicide, and the reporter winds up with the daughter, who had been involved incestuously with the deceased.

Pacing is very slow and scripters don't ever explain why the man is in jail, why he commits suicide, what sort of usable story the reporter expects to get from all his running around, or how a mere journalist can live so splendidly and carefreely on a writer's wages. Especially fine thesping by Gomez, Adriani and Politti, sensitive helming by Chavarri, but all of it unfortunately exerted in a pointless cause. — *Besa.*

The Long Good Friday
(BRITISH-COLOR)

Tautly-told tale of a gangster vs. the IRA.

Cannes, May 18.
A Calendar Production for Black Lion Films (Associated Communications Corp.) Produced by Barry Hanson. Directed by John Mackenzie. Stars Bob Hoskins, Helen Mirren. Screenplay, Barrie Keeffe; camera (color), Phil Meheux; editor, Mike Taylor; music, Francis Monkman; art director, Vic Symonds; sound, David John; asst. director, Simon Hinkly. Reviewed at the Olympia Theatre, Cannes, May 17, '80. (No BBFC Rating.) Running time: **105 MINS.**

Harold	Bob Hoskins
Victoria	Helen Mirren
Parky	Dave King
Alan	Brian Hall
Charlie	Eddie Constantine
Tony	Stephen Davies
Jeff	Derek Thompson
Harris	Bryan Marshall
Razors	P.H. Moriarty
Colin	Paul Freeman
Eric	Charles Cork
Erroll	Paul Barber
Carol	Patti Love

In many respects a conventional thriller set in London's underworld, "The Long Good Friday" is much more densely plotted and intelligently scripted by Barrie Keeffe than most such yarns. Besides being a safe bet as playable action face in most situations, it shapes to win a degree of upmarket response from audiences in search of something more than simple escapism.

Moreover, some nicely observed performances among the uncommonly large range of featured roles further help to distinguish Barry Hanson's production for ACC's Black Lion Films as a classy item. Bob Hoskins, an already much-praised British tv actor who here displays natural, and sizable, big-screen presence, works out first-rate in the anchor role of a gangland boss faced with a series of seemingly gratuitous reprisals by unknown ill-wishers against his waterfront empire.

He starts as a larger-than-life figure, confidently negotiating American finance for a massive land development project linked to the 1988 London Olympics. (Eddie Constantine makes a welcome appearance as the key backer, whose confidence that Hoskins can guarantee the area will be free of "trouble" is the lynch-pin of the deal.) But Hoskins' overweening exterior crumples by the hour during an Easter weekend, as some of his best men are murdered and explosions mess up his property.

When it becomes clear that his adversary is none other than the provisional Irish Republican Army, he pits his Mafia-style muscle against the IRA's professional terrorism — and loses.

In the U.K. particularly, the plot's mainspring could be seen as politically hot, though that won't dent its general appeal. What turns out is that a government planning department is regularly funding the IRA with protection money against incitement of construction stoppages by the predominantly Irish labor force. When part of a cash consignment is filched en route, the provos reply with a string of typically vicious warnings. Hoskins is the target. That initially baffles him, since although he has the planning authority chief in his pock-et, he is not aware of the blackmail arrangements.

While the film's overall viewpoint, that Ireland's anti-British irregulars operate a uniquely well-organized and superior network of assassins, may appear unacceptably "Boy's Own" to some, in the milieu conjured up by Keeffe's screenplay it seems fearsomely credible. So the dog-eats-dog confrontation carries substantial dramatic weight.

The absorbing, fast-paced narrative is steered competently enough by director John Mackenzie, but with a visual style that's rather too stolid to lend due gut-impact to the complex unravellings: Keeffe's somewhat overworked dialog could have been offset to advantage by more sweeping, cinematic flow. More movement might have created a sense of restlessness, and thus more menace.

Within its limits, cinematographer Phil Meheux's contribution is thoroughly pro. Print viewed was a work-copy with unfinished soundtrack, but Francis Monkman's score was still an appreciable plus.

Pic's completion has been delayed by indecision within ACC as to whether it should be played off theatrically or via the tube. Attempts to scissor the more violent sequences (and violent they are) for telecast apparently failed, but the finally-agreed version will not be handled by ACC's distribution arm, ITC. Instead, independent Osprey Films has been appointed as world-wide sales rep. —*Simo.*

Breaking Glass
(BRITISH-COLOR)

Smashing showcase for some marketable new talents.

Cannes, May 15.
GTO release (Paramount in U.S.) Allied Stars presentation of a Film & General production. Executive producer, Dodi Fayed. Produced by Davina Belling, Clive Parsons. Directed by Brian Gibson. Stars Phil Daniels, Hazel O'Connor, Jon Finch. Screenplay, Brian Gibson; camera (color), Stephen Goldblatt; editor, Michael Bradsell; original songs, Hazel O'Connor; musical director, Tony Visconti; sound, Bruce White; art director, Evan Hercules; choreography, Eric G. Robarts; production supervisor, John Comfort; asst. director, Roger Simons. Reviewed at the Palais Des Festivals, Cannes, May 15, '80. (BBFC Rating: AA). Running time: **104 MINS.**

Danny	Phil Daniels
Kate	Hazel O'Connor
Woods	Jon Fich
Ken	Jonathan Pryce
Mick	Peter-Hugo Daly
Tony	Mark Wingett
Dave	Gary Tibbs
Campbell	Charles Wegner
Fordyce	Mark Wing-Davey
Davis	Hugh Thomas
Brian	Nigel Humphreys
Publican	Ken Campbell
Policeman (Shaw)	Peter Tilbury
Guitarist	Gary Holton
Andy	Derek Thompson
Jackie	Janine Duvitski
Jane	Lowri Ann Richards
Drunk Guy	Gary Olsen

Bright commercial prospects loom for this distinctly uppercase British feature, and an even brighter future for its lead actress-cum-singer-songwriter, newcomer Hazel O'Connor, whose screen magnetism is as evident as her robust and individual musical style. Further, producers Davina Belling and Clive Parsons have herewith broken in a most gifted new British director, ex-tv helmer Brian Gibson.

Principal appeal of "Breaking Glass," which presents a cynical, off-the-peg, view of the post-punk record business, must be to the prime movie-going and disk-buying age-group, so cross-promotion potential of the picture and the A & M soundtrack figures to be massive. Dialog and action have been kept carefully sanitized despite the subject, in the sense that there's nothing in either to warrant unduly restrictive ratings on grounds of violence or sex. In all, it's a sharp, saleable package which does credit to the British production industry.

Cast opposite O'Connor, who's seen initially as a two-bit teenage performer playing a handful of her own numbers around lousy London gigs, is Phil Daniels, recent topliner of The Who Films' "Quadrophenia." Here he's a hustling would-be manager who teams with O'Connor to put together a decent backing group, then grabs interest in the act (name of which is the pic's title) from a diskery by dint of some arm-twisting of execs for whom he formerly did dirty work as a plugger.

Ensuing success undermines the pair's tentative romantic partnership and, with the arrival on the scene of Jon Finch as an overly smooth-mannered producer, their professional interdependence as well. With more than a small nod in the direction of "The Rose," Gibson's screenplay finally plots the predictable physical effects of fame on O'Connor, who's last glimpsed hospitalized and virtually catatonic.

Relentlessly fast-paced, the yarn relates to reality in much the same way as a fashion photo — that is, it works as an image-conscious reflection of a time and milieu, but does not purport to portray life as it really is. "Breaking Glass" is thick with high-gloss images which capture the essence of a tacky but strangely exhilarating era. To that end, the one-dimensional characters and one-level plot development are blatantly manipulated.

For the most part, the results of that approach are extraordinarily effective. Gibson's smart eye for essentials is well served by Stephen Goldblatt's dazzlingly stylish, hyper-real cinematography (he's new to features, too), and by O'Connor's ability to enliven many an ordinary dramatic situation with a naturally likable personality that goes much deeper than her outlandish garb and face-paint.

Only when the film seems to exploit prevalent social themes just a little too casually does it jar both artistically and as entertainment. Delineations of the police as automatically depersonalized agents of harassment, and of blacks as hardly more than token set-dressing, betrays a degree of simplistic superficiality out of key with Gibson's generally hip sense of judgment. An incidental shot, all-too obviously staged, of a drunken black bum clambering through uncollected garbage on a London street, is one that belongs on the cutting room floor.

Of the supports, top honors go to Jonathan Pryce as the combo's saxophonist. Gibson's concept of the role — a bearded, wasted-looking pro who's older than the others and partly deaf — is one of the picture's finest pluses.

Pryce has many of the best lines (including a running gag on his deafness which pays off nicely) and certainly the most telling scene; when public acclaim has started to take its toll on the band, he's shown helplessly searching a room for the heroin to which he's now addicted but which the other members have hidden. Throughout, this established stage and tv actor proves himself to be yet another likely features talent launched by the film.

Surprisingly, Daniels is somewhat disappointing, forfeiting sympathy by coming across as both mannered and monotonous. But with okay performances by all others concerned, notably Peter-Hugo Daly as the group's drummer, and top quality craftsmanship on the technical side, Allied Stars can justly regard its classy, though far from lavishly budgeted, first venture with pride.

Per deals already firmed, release in the U.S. is via Paramount, in the U.K. via GTO. —*Simo.*

Manoa
(VENEZUELAN-GERMAN-COLOR)

Cannes, May 21.
A Helkon Films-Xanadu Films and Bayerischer Rundfunk coproduction. Directed by Solveig Hoogesteijn. Features entire cast. Screenplay, Hoogesteijn;
camera, (color), Hector Rios; editors Giuliano Ferioni, Bruno Bianchini; music, Victor Cuica. Reviewed at Cannes Film Fest (Directors' Fortnight) May 21, '80. Running time: 102 MINS.
With Victor Cuica, Diego Silva, Azdrubal Melendez, Hector Duvauchelle, Emilia Rojas, Julio Mota, Kiki Mendive.

The apparent intent is to show two contrasting Venezuelans, of different race, and social class, with music as the only bond between them, who leave Caracas, the modern capital and set out on what could be both a search for personal identity and discovery of their country.

The director, Solveig Hoogesteijn, is a Venezuelan who was born in Sweden of a German mother and Dutch father. Her pic starts off very effectively with a well-filmed police roundup in Caracas, followed by a chase through the city's streets. After that, however, it's downhill all the way. Overlong and underdeveloped, only isolated scenes (like a provincial radio station) have a minimum of interest, and there is next to no connection between the filmmaker's stated intent and what is shown on the screen. Film simply meanders without any sense of an objective, either storywise or in its meaning. The two main characters are also far too flat.

Financial help from German TV can be important for Latin-American cinema, but experiences like this one are likely to slay the goose that lays the Bavarian eggs. —*Amig.*

Lightning Over Water
(Nick's Movie)
(WEST GERMAN-SWEDISH-U.S.-COLOR)

Cannes, May 14.
Pari Films release of Road Movies, Viking Film production. With Nick Ray, Wim Wenders. Directed and conceived by Nick Ray, Wim Wenders. Camera (Movielab); Ed Lachman; editor, Peter Przgodda; music, Ronnie Blakley. Reviewed at Cannes Film Fest (Non-competing official section) May 13, '80. Running time: 116 MINS.
With: Nicholas Ray, Wim Wenders, Ronee Blakley.

The late American film director Nicholas Ray and the West German filmmaker Wim Wenders decided to make a film together while Ray was dying of cancer. Film is not morbid, nor is it a documentary or an analysis of Ray's work. Rather it is an unfocused look at a man trying to finish his life at work and others trying to help him.

Wenders himself plays in it and seems ill at ease for, as he notes, it is about a close friend's death and not his attitude toward it. They talk of a possible script, Ray gives a lecture at a university where some excerpts are shown of one of his own favorite films, "The Lusty Men," which, to him, reflected the American desire of having one's own home.

Wenders' wife Ronee Blakley sings, does a scene as Ray's daughter coming to see him and both trying to face their feelings for each other on his coming demise. Ray is seen mounting a play based on a Kafka tale, dealing with students and parts of a film he made with them while a professor.

There is a Chinese junk that ploughs the East River with an unmanned camera and Moviola, seemingly symbolizing Ray's passing, creativeness and the escape hatch that might have taken him to Asia to find a cure for himself.

Ray is physically ravaged and obviously often in pain. He talks to his entourage, is hospitalized, and Wenders is even seen in his place at times as he tries to understand and feel for his friend, but cannot really do much except try to observe and record.

Ray had become a cult figure in Europe and has left a body of work worthy of respect and study. He will eventually get a firmer place on the historical film scene. This film is a document that could have festival, archive, school possibilities, with some theatrical usage indicated with proper handling.

It is well shot and uses some video additions well. It just does not quite come to grips with Ray's reaction to his condition and death, but that might have been impossible.

At any rate, film shows a harrowingly debilitated man going on till the end. Ray died midway through this look at plans for making a film and his friends, mainly part of the crew, filled in by talking about him, their reaction to the film they were making and their own ideas about it. —*Mosk.*

Causa Kralik
(The Rabbit Case)
(CZECH-COLOR)

Cannes, May 17.
Czech State Film release of Barrandov Studios production. Directed by Jaromil Jires. Screenplay, Jaroslav Dietl; camera (Eastmancolor), Jaromir Sofr; music, Vadim Petrov. Reviewed at Cannes Film Fest (Non-competing-A Certain Look), May 16, '80. Running time, 85 MINS.
With: Milos Kopecky, Alena Vranova, Zlata Adamovska, Marie Brozova, Jaroslav Satoransky, Martin Ruzek.

Czechoslovak films have caused rare stirs at film festivals since their spate of unusual directors and outspoken films for 1963-'68. Since the Russian putdown of the so-called Socialism with a human face the Czech film has sombered.

But the few good ones were usually made by those who had emerged in that fecund film era and who could still make films. The themes were of course more muted, but at least pj . were well made and did not return to the social realism that marked most of the films.

Now there could be an easing of controls. Jaromil Jires, one of the early '60s talents, here does a simple film on an aging, sick lawyer who takes a post in the country. He runs into some small cases that are more signs of personal corruption than a mirroring of national outlooks.

The film's main case is about an old woman whose nephew has bilked her of her life's savings and will not repay, saying it was a present. She counters it was a loan. The old lady can only pay the lawyer with rabbits.

The case is won but the old lady is won over by the nephew and so he will escape the repayment and perhaps even the court costs. The lawyer accepts it philosophically

Film is simple, ruefully human, and allows its characterizations to come out in action. It does not have deeper penetration into the characters and will not provoke undue theatrical interest abroad. — *Mosk.*

The Lucky Star
(CANADIAN-COLOR)

Cannes, May 20.
Tele-Metropole International presentation of a Claude Leger Production. Executive Producer, Andre Fleury. Produced by Claude Leger. Directed by Max Fischer. Stars Rod Steiger, Louise Fletcher, Lou Jacobi. Camera (color), Frank Tidy; screenplay, Fischer, Jack Rosenthal from original idea by Roland Topor; music, Art Philipps; editor, Yves Langlois. Reviewed at Les Ambassades, Cannes, May 19, 1980. Running Time: 110 MINS.
Colonel Gluck . . . . Rod Steiger
Loes Bakker . . . . Louise Fletcher
Elia Goldberg . . . . Lou Jacobi
David Goldberg . . . . Brett Marx
Rose Goldberg . . . . Helen Hughes
The Burgomaster . . . . Yvon Dufour

Here, finally, is a sweetheart of a picture made under Canada's tax shelter. It is charming, heart-tugging, handsomely photographed (partially in Holland) like a series of Dutch paintings, and smoothly acted and directed.

A family pic but not for the very young, it tells the story of a Jewish boy whose parents are captured by the Nazis and the kid, a lover of old Wild West films, gets hidden as a farm hand in Rotterdam and winds up in grand style capturing a German colonel.

In the finish, the boy is shown "High Noon" style with the German colonel (now free) regretting the outcome.

Simple and direct in approach, "The Lucky Star" boasts some fine performances; curly-haired blond Brett Marx (the young hero) making a splendid screen debut, Rod

Steiger as the crusty but sympathetic colonel, Lou Jacobi and Helen Hughes as the boy's parents, Louise Fletcher as the rich farm lady, and Yvon Dufour as the town's frightened burgomaster.

Cheers, too, for director Max Fischer and his cameraman Frank Tidy. "The Lucky Star" should be their breakthrough calling card. If anything, editing could be a bit tighter, but the careful pacing presents no real problem.

It's a pic with obvious wide audience appeal from the opening shot of a dumpy Jewish cabaret (songs of Jews aware of their fate) to the windup. Pic should clean up. It's a bundle of joy peppered with light comedy and affection. No sex, no violence. Just a direct hit down the middle. —*Adil.*

Nezha Nao Hai
(Nezha Defeats the Dragon)
(CHINESE-ANIMATION-COLOR)

Cannes, May 14.
Shanghai Animation Studios release and production. Directed by Wang Shucken, Yang Dingxian, Jingda. Screenplay, Wang Wang; camera (Color), Duang Hsiaohsian, Tchiang Youyi, Jing Tchetchen. Reviewed at Cannes Film Fest (non-competing) May 13, '80. Running time: **61 MINS.**

China's first entry in the official section of the Cannes Film Festival is an engaging full-length cartoon. It is non-competing, but augurs a step into the prizerunning section for mainland China in the future.

The animation is classic and perhaps reminiscent of Walt Disney in the humanization of animals and mythical creatures and the easy movements of the humans. Yet it never gets coy or moralistic and should be a fine item for moppet shows and also interest adults.

Delicate oriental backgrounds enfold this tale of a little boy born to a king who also has ties with celestial beings. He is born of an egg that turns into a flower and then gives up a tiny boy who can already walk and cavort.

He is a favorite of a venerated God. But he does get into trouble with the evil Dragon King who lives under the sea. But the boy's strength, celestial aid and shrewdness have him overcoming the four dragon leaders and bringing peace and joy to his father who at one time almost sacrifices him to appease the dragons.

The fights and acrobatics are beholden to the classic Peking Opera and well assimilated to animated use. It should find outlets on its sheer visual beauty and unfolding of a fable without affectation or overdoing the humanized creatures.
—*Mosk.*

Gibbi West Germany
(WEST GERMAN-COLOR)

Cannes, May 15.
A Bioskop Film Production, Munich, in collaboration with Westdeutscher Rundfunk (WDR); world rights, Filmverlag der Autoren, Munich. Features cast. Written and directed by Christel Buschmann. Camera (color), Frank Bruehne; songs, Paul Millns; editing, Jane Sperr; sets, Winfried Hennig; production, Eberhard Junkersdorf; tv-producer, Wolf-Dietrich Bruecker. Reviewed at Cannes Film Festival (Market), May 14, '80. Running time: **90 MINS.**
Cast: Joergen Pfennigwerth (Gibbi), Eva Maria Hagen (His Mother), Eric Burdon, Rosalia de Kulessa, Angelika Kulessa, Martin Kippenberger, Soma Weissenseel, Hans Noever, Guenter Meissner, Claus-Dieter Ossenkoff, Martha Sievers.

Christel Buschmann, one of several femme helmers on the German scene making their debuts of late, worked with Reinhard Hauff as coscripter of "The Main Actor" (1977). That was a story of a youth's losing struggle to be accepted into society on his own terms. Buschmann's "Gibbi West Germany" is about a similar dropout, this time about one facing a sure deadend.

Gibbi is a young man, already with a child behind him, plus a mother he somehow blames for everything that has gone wrong — although it is clear from the beginning that he has nobody to destroy but himself. He jumps ship in Hamburg and "comes home" to St. Pauli, where his mother operates a snack-bar. There he slowly lets out all the rage pent up inside him, is arrested by the police, and is finally committed to an asylum — each time he manages to escape, or is released by his mother, whom he finally kills, along with himself, in the bar. Who really caused this double-murder is the pic's open frank question. —*Holl.*

Sono Fotogenico
(I'm Photogenic)
(ITALIAN-FRENCH-COLOR)

Cannes, May 13.
A United Artists release, produced by Pio Angeletti and Adriano De Micheli for Dean Film (Rome) and Film Marceau Cocinor (Paris). Stars Renato Pozzetto and Edwige Fenech. Directed by Dino Risi. Camera (Eastmancolor), Tonino Delli Colli; art director, Ezio Altieri; editor, Alberto Galliti; music, Manuel De Sica. Reviewed at Esperian Cinema, May 11, 1980. Running time: **118 MINS.**
Antonio .... Renato Pozzetto
Cinzia .... Edwige Fenech

Helmer Dino Risi's latest effort, a well-shot comedy with a great subject like the film business, should have been funnier and more interesting than it is. "Photogenic" seems to have been cranked out pretty half-heartedly by the master of the commedia all' italiana, lacking the zest and careful observation that even minor directors put

into pix describing the world in which they live and work.

Without taking pains to give a clear picture of what goes on behind the scenes of a film set, pic manages to cover all its show biz characters with a dull sliminess that includes even cameoing vets like Mario Monicelli, Vittorio Gassman and Ugo Tognazzi. Risi's bitter cynicism has not sold well in Italy, where stars Pozzetto and Fenech should have drawn crowds, and its chances abroad may be calculated accordingly.

Antonio (Renato Pozzetto) is an aspiring actor from a Northern provincial town who packs his bags one day and heads for Cinecitta with his family's blessings and cash. But soon he discovers pix are a cynical and heartbreaking business after an unsuccessful romance with beautiful actress Cinzia (Fenech), giving most of his money to a greedy agent, being importuned by a gay acting coach and crashing through a bunch of bit parts. He ends up back north crippled after a film stunt, working in a bank to support Cinzia's twins.

Though professionally shot (by Tonino Delli Colli) and well edited, pic's production values can't efface a weak script that dives for easy targets like agents and producers and has no strong story line to keep it moving along.

The blackness with which Risi paints the film biz would be more convincing if the script had a breath of realism in it.

Instead, it relies on dull-faced comic Pozzetto for its moving force, backed by a host of cliched characters (numerous stereotype gays who talk in falsetto) and jokes about Fenech's large breasts.

The idea that a simple slob from the provinces who has neither talent nor sensibility can't make it in Italian films seems cause for rejoicing, rather than the contrary. —
— *Yung.*

A Few Days In The Life Of I.I. Oblomov
(RUSSIAN-COLOR)

Cannes, May 28.
Sovexport release of Mosfilm production. Features entire cast. Directed by Nikita Mikhalkov. Screenplay, Mikhalkov, Alexandre Adabachiane from book by Ivan Gontcharov; camera (Sovcolor), Pavel Lebechev. No other credits available. Reviewed at Canpes Film Fest (Non-Competing Market Section), May 16, '80. Running time: **150 MINS.**
With: Oleg Tabakov, Elena Soloyei, Andrei Popov, Youri Bogatyrev.

Younger Russian directors handle pre-Soviet times and especially classics with unusual tenderness and understanding. Nikita Mikhalkov has already dealt well with

Chekhov's "Platanov" as "The Mechanical Pianos," and now creates a touching, perceptive film based on Ivan Gontcharov's "Oblomov."

The main character is so human that someone exclaims that he and his way of life can be applied to a sickness or state called "oblomovism." But oblomov is not a stereotype but reflects such traits as evasiveness, the fear of commitment to life and the anxiety of rejection that cut into actions that so many may have in some degree.

Oblomov loved his mother as a child but she often travelled and when she came back she slept late as he waited to see her. He had one friend with a German background who was more solid and outgoing. Oblomov as a man spends a lot of time in bed looked after by a slavish adoring servant.

A woman comes into his life who could love him but here again he cacillates and loses her to his friend. A commentary fits this twilight world of small landowners who would be swept away. But film is never disdainful but captures the mood of the times and is visually right and effective.

Film could be pruned somewhat and then could find festival and perhaps some specialized outlets abroad. Mikhalkov made that acclaimed look at filmmaking and life at the beginning of the Russian revolution, "Slave of Love," and is one of the more accessible filmmakers on the Russian scene these days. —*Mosk.*

The Apple
(U.S.-GERMAN-COLOR)

Cannes, May 15.
A Cannon Group Inc. presentation of a N.F. Geria III Production. Produced by Menahem Golan and Yoram Globus. Written and directed by Menahem Golan. Story, Iris and Coby Recht; camera (color), David Gurfinkel; production design, Jurgen Kiebach; costumes, Ingrid Zore; editor, Alain Jacubowicz; music Coby Recht; lyrics by Iris Recht and George Clinton; choreography, Nigel Lythgoe. Reviewed in Cannes (non-competing), May 14, '80. Running time: **90 MINS.**
CAST: Catherine Mary Stewart, George Gilmour, Joss Ackland, Gladek Sheybal, Grace Kennedy, Allan Love, Ray Shell.

Menahem Golan's first large scale musical, "Kazablan" was one of the top Israeli bestsellers ever. This time, he tries to go one step further, on the international scale, shooting the whole production in Berlin, and once again using funds made available by the German Senate.

The story, set in 1994, is definitely indebted, visually and narratively, to the comic book radiation of science fiction, while the musical numbers have the kind of synthetic touch associated with the latest in disco decor.

The heroes are a couple of innocent balladeers, almost tricked by the villainous impresario Mr. Buggallow, into a life of sin and dissipation, Mr. Buggalow being a mephistophelic character who runs not only the pop business, but the whole wide world as well.

Starting with a Worldvision Song Contest, a transparent send-up of the very popular Eurovision tv song contests, in which Buggallow rigs the results to have his loud, flashy and heavy bit group, putting on a pseudo Donna Summer act, beat the appealingly unknown duo of Alphie and Bibi, who almost sweep the public away with a love song, and it goes on to show how Buggallow actually plots to swallow up the two youngsters from the backwoods of Canada.

The girl is tempted by the promise of a brilliant career she is promised by joining Buggallow's roster, the boy refuses to fall into the trap, and finally after being beaten up by goons in the impresario's pay, being seduced by the impresario's star, and being almost blown out of his mind by the variety of drugs he swallows in the impresario's mansion, he gets his love back and they escape to a colony of protesters living under a bridge, and rejecting the pop world around them.

Whatever this world might be like is not quite clear, as the futuristic aspects are restricted to some exaggerated make up, some trendy costumes and some customized cars. For the rest, there is little in Golan's version of 1994, which we don't already know from every day reality. Any questions about how people live or what they do in 1994 will have to remain unanswered, as the only visible activities around are pop-concerts. As for the mystical message in the last reel, when a magical Mr. Topps appears literally out of the blue, clad in white, and setting all wrongs to right, one wonders about the nature of these wrongs, plus the style of music they have engendered.

Characters and story are flimsy and seem intended as mere pegs on which to hang the musical numbers. Golan, who seems to believe that more is better, slips into songs and dances at the slightest excuse, without worrying whether they are integrated into story or not.

No expense seems to have been spared to make this as big a showpiece as possible, with dancers galore, huge orchestrations, costumes from glittering disco through Nazi orgiastic style, to Dr. Moreau kind of animalism, while sets

spread in all directions.

The choreography generates a lot of energy, but its frantic tempo doesn't always compensate for lack of imagination. The same may be said about the music, which includes some pretty tunes, some trendy rhythms and some old-fashioned Paul Anka-styled ballads, but rarely rises above the average pop product.

Catherine Mary Stewart and George Gilmour, in the leading parts of the innocent duo, are not asked to do much more than be nice. Vladek Sheybal overplays Mr. Buggallow into some kind of grotesque parody and so does Ray Shell as his evil assistant.

Technically, film is impressive, David Gurfinkel's camera work profusely using every trick in the business, every filter and lighting device, to hold attention up at all times. Alain Jacubowicz cuts with the same intention in mind, which makes for a rather nervous and restless film even in its quieter moments.

Intended mostly for a very young audience, the dances have some very lewd and suggestive poses, but the production has been careful enough to avoid any kind of nudity so rating may ultimately not be very harsh. —*Edna.*

Kaerleken
(Love)
(SWEDISH-COLOR)

Cannes, May 21.
An AB Cinematograph/Europa Film/-Swedish Film Institute production, Film Institute release. Features entire cast. Based on Theodor Kallifatides' novel. Script, Jeannette Donner and Kallifatides. Directed by Kallifatides. Camera (Eastmancolor), Bille August; editor, Sylvia Ingemarsson; music, Monica Dominique; executive producer, Katinka Farago. Reviewed at Cinema Le Regent, Cannes, May 21, 1980. Running time: 71 MINS.
Johannes . . . . Per Ragnar
Lena, his wife . . . . Lena Olin
Li, his mistress . . . . Anna Godenius
Markku, his son . . . . Erik Tamm
Lars . . . . , Mathias Henrikson
Erland . . . . Erland Josephson

Can husband and wife and seven-year old son, otherwise nicely compatible, expand their circle of three to include also the man's new lady love? The latter seems to think so. The wife is reluctant at first, then agrees and the quartet goes off on a trial holiday by the sea.

These people are all articulate intellectuals except maybe the kid who is being near-mobbed at school for being half-Finnish. At film's end, he seems the only one sure to suffer from the unusual set-up, although he has already proven to be of tough fibre.

The three grown-ups of Greek, but Sweden-based, novelist Theodor Kallifatides' first feature film,

"Love," soon get very tense and nervous. The man cannot get around to sleeping with either woman. Things come to a minor boil, but by then Kallifatides has run completely out of steam and audiences are left pretty much holding the bag.

Film's all-over production dress is handsome, the stamp of Ingmar Bergman's production company Cinematograph is on it. Cinematography by Denmark's Bille August would take top honors anywhere. Acting, too, is finely tuned to plot's and dialog's needs by Per Ragnar, Lena Olin, Anna Godenius (the mistress) and Erik Tamm (the boy). Erland Josephson and Mathias Henrikson as a couple of spurned lovers also know exactly what they are doing.

The Bergman production stamp (applied by Bergman veteran Katinka Farago) might help "Love's" foreign sales, but on its own merits, film is a let-down by merely scratching a very provocative surface question. —*Kell.*

Virus
(JAPANESE-COLOR)

Cannes, May 23.
Haruki Kadokawa Films presentation (Toho release in Japan). Produced by Kadokawa. Directed by Kinji Fukasaku. Features entire cast. Screenplay, Koji Takada, Gregory Knapp. Fukasaku, based on novel by Sakyo Komatsu; camera (color), Daisaku Kimura; miniature consultant, Gregory Jein; music, Teo Macero; theme song, Janis Ian. Reviewed at Cannes Festival Market, May 22, 1980. Running time: 155 MINS.
Dr. Yamauchi . . . . Sonny Chiba
Captain Maccloud . . . . Chuck Connors
Sarah Baker . . . . Stephanie Faulkner
Richardson . . . . Glenn Ford
Dr. Mayer . . . . Stuart Gillard
Marit . . . . Olivia Hussey
Admiral Conway . . . . George Kennedy
Yoshizumi . . . . Masao Kusakari
Dr. Latour . . . . Cecil Linder
Dr. Nakanishi . . . . Isao Natsuki
Professor Tsuchiya . . . . Ken Ogata
Captain Lopez . . . . Edward J. Olmos
Garland . . . . Henry Silva
Major Carter . . . . Bo Svenson
Noriko . . . . Yumi Takigawa
Barkley . . . . Robert Vaughn

(English soundtrack)

Japanese producer Haruki Kadokawa, who branched out from book publishing to filmmaking about four years ago, makes his first major essay into the international arena with this expensive disaster epic (reputedly costing in excess of $15,000,000), which is based on a book published by his own company, and which was produced jointly with the Tokyo Broadcasting System, the country's leading commercial network.

Presented in the Cannes market as a "work in progress," and due to preem in Tokyo at the end of June, "Virus" has its share of plusses and minuses, but with more attention to

editing — at 155 minutes it is overlong — and a possible reworking of the climactic sequences, which in their present form strain credulity to breaking point, film could make a commercial breakthrough internationally for a Japanese film.

The version reviewed here was in the English language, and establishes the desire (as well as the need) for international exploitation. And the story itself has world wide interest, with location lensing in many countries, highlighted by superb sequences filmed in Antarctica, which add a rare touch of beauty.

Looked at realistically, this is a double disaster pic, first the annihilation by a plague of virtually the world population (save for 858 men and eight women on Antarctica) and secondly, the total destruction of the world by a nuclear blast-off, triggered by an earthquake in the vicinity of Washington.

The events leading up to the two disasters have dramatic potentialities which are not consistently realized by the uneven direction of Kinji Fukasaku. However, there are some potent and moving sequences, notably in the White House where a dying president broadcasts a message to the survivors in Antarctica, advising them that they are safe as long as they remain put, as the virus is dormant in icy conditions, and counselling them not to admit outsiders who have been infected.

Latter advice leads to a poignant scene in which a Soviet submarine commander appeals for permission to land his sick crew, and the argument is brought to a grim conclusion when the Russian vessel is blown up by a British sub.

The second disaster is triggered off by the U.S. Chief of Staff who, against presidential orders, sets the American nuclear system to the "on" position, as he's convinced the whole thing is a Soviet plot to destroy the world. But the Russians have done the same thing, and an attempt by an American major and a Japanese scientist to get to Washington to cut out the nuclear device before it is set off by the earthquake fails by minutes.

For the few hundred survivors in Antarctica, rests the responsibility of building a new world, and it is up to the eight women to play their part in repopulating the world. It is explained that in the circumstances, there is no room for one-for-one relationships, and before long all the eight are cradling infants in their arms.

With its mixed cast of American and Japanese artists, film has recognizable names for Western as well as Asian territories, and this will help at the boxoffice.

The performances do not always equal the dramatic potentialities of the story, but are generally more than adequate. Olivia Hussey is attractive as the first of the survivors to give birth, though the father is killed in vaguely explained circumstances.

Glenn Ford is impressive as the American president, and Robert Vaughn, as the senator who exposes the U.S. involvement in the production of the deadly virus, stands out in a few brief scenes.

Chuck Connors as the commander of the British sub, Stuart Gillard as the American scientist who is put away in a mental institution when he tries to warn of the dangers of the virus, Henry Silva as the deranged chief of staff, Bo Svenson as the U.S. officer who volunteers to go to Washington, and George Kennedy as the senior officer in Antarctica, give routine performances which sustain the action.

Of the Japanese cast, Masao Kusakari has the plum role as the scientist who predicts the earthquake which leads to the second disaster, and after the failure to stop the nuclear blast in Washington, he somehow succeeds in making his way across a continent littered with skeletons and debris, straight into the arms of Olivia Hussey. This must rate among the most puerile climaxes of all time, and desperately needs to be revised.

Yumi Takigawa, as one of the last survivors in Tokyo, is a nurse who takes her infant charge by boat into Tokyo Bay, and both take an overdose of pills to anticipate the inevitable. She's a looker, and a competent performer. Lesser parts are adequately filled by Ken Ogata and Isao Natsuki.

Technically, the pic has some commendable special effects and, as mentioned, magnificently lensed sequences of the ice and snow of Antarctica. Weakest link is the editing, but as the version reviewed is still being worked on, hopefully the production will be tightened.

All the action takes place in the first two or three years of the present decade. —*Myro.*

Ballad of Tara
(IRANIAN-COLOR)

Cannes, May 27.
Lissar Film Group release and production. Features entire cast. Written and directed by Bahram Beiz'i. Camera (color), Mehrdad Fakhimi; editor, Beiz'i; Reviewed at Cannes Film Fest (Non-competing A Certain Look), May 20, '80. Running time: **103 MINS.**

Tara	Sussan Taslimi
Warrior	Manoutchehr Farid
Ghelitch	Reza Babak
Achub	Siamak Atlassi

Bahram Beiz'i weaves a fable of an ancient warrior condemned to roam until he finds his lost sword to avenge a defeat. The sword is owned by a beauteous widow. The ghost and she fall in love only to have it finally broken by the demands of life.

Film was almost finished under the regime of the deposed Shah and then wound after the revolution. Whether it reflected political repressiveness is not clear. It does show a solid pictorial flair and some outsize dramatic confrontations as the woman and the warrior finally go their ways to their respective eras.

Film sometimes exploits its tale for the picturesque. No denying Beiz'i's visual flair but this one is mainly for festival and curio playoff and not up to more effective films he has had at other events.
—*Mosk.*

Double Negative
(CANADIAN-COLOR)

Cannes, May 13.
A Quadrant Films presentation. Produced by Jerome Simon, David Main. Features entire cast. Directed by George Bloomfield; executive producer, David Perlmutter; screenplay, Thomas Hedley Jr., Charles Dennis, Janis Allen, based on "The Three Roads" by Ross Macdonald. Camera (color) Rene Verzier; editor, George Appleby; art direction, Mary Kerr; sound, Douglas Ganton; music. Paul Hoffert. Reviewed at les Ambassades, May 12, Cannes, France. **Running Time: 96 MINS.**

Michael Taylor	Michael Sarrazin
Paula West	Susan Clark
Lawrence Miles	Anthony Perkins
Lester Harlen	Howard Duff
Mrs. Swanscott	Kate Reid
D'Allasandro	Al Waxman
Frances	Elizabeth Shepherd
Dr. Webber	Kenneth Welsh
Maury Chaikin	Rawlins

"Double Negative" is a mystery-thriller of tremendous complexity which is severely hampered by an absence of logic.

Script by Thomas Hedley, loosely based on Ross MacDonald's "The Three Roads," submerges reason beneath a steady stream of bizarre characters, oblique flashbacks and improbable conveniences. Static direction further impairs the possibility of suspense or audience involvement.

Photo-journalist Michael Sarrazin has been placed in a mental institution after a nerve-wracking assignment in the Mid-East, coupled with his discovery of the brutal rape-murder of his wife on his return to Canada. He was going to ask for a divorce and his designer-lover Susan Clark now must retrieve him.

Sarrazin's investigation uncovers new facts. Meanwhile, Clark puts a private detective on his tail in the event he freaks out again.

The prime suspect is Anthony Perkins who may have been acting on Clark's instructions. Perkins was the wife's lover and is blackmailing Clark for some past sin.

The real story is that amnesiac Sarrazin caught Perkins and wife in bed and strangled his spouse. As a similiar incident happened to his father, he has blocked this painful memory. Clark has swept the truth under the rug, but Perkins wants money for his silence.

Director George Bloomfield tackles film in straightforward fashion with little left to the imagination. The effect is a plodding series of contrived incidents with long pauses to fill in the story inconsistencies.

Sarrazin's central performance is overly bland for a man with a time-bomb ticking under the surface. While he remains laid back, Perkins invests his villain with enough quirks to wipe out the entire cast but only gets detective Howard Duff who plays a very flat-footed gumshoe.

Clark comes off best of the leads but this role is not likely to enhance her screen career. Al Waxman as a sleazy disco owner provides real energy in an all too brief cameo.

Technical work is uninspired but professional. Rene Verzier's images are murky like the script, editing lulls one to sleep and the music pulls out familiar ambiance of thriller. —*Klad.*

Le Risque De Vivre
(The Risk of Living)
(FRENCH-DOCU-COLOR)

Cannes, May 27.
Roissy Films release of Les Films Du Jeudi production. Directed by Gerald Calderon. Screenplay, Dominique Ludes, Cyril De Klem, Calderon; camera (Eastmancolor), Jean-Marie Baufle; music, Georges Prost; commentary by Andre Langaney, spoken by Michel Lonsdale. Reviewed at Cannes Film Fest (Non-competing), May 22, '80. **Running time, 85 MINS.**

It starts with what looks like a great luminous dome. It is a magnified drop of water and the early life forms teeming in it are microscopically shown. The film has a stolid commentary underlining some fine scenes of all sorts of animals and birds in their habitats.

The idea is to show that all life forms seemed programmed by heredity actions and then slowly, during evolution, actual learning began as exemplified finally by an orangutan breaking a coconut to get its juice and pulp.

Akin to the apes in Stanley Kubrick's "2001, a Space Odyssey" adapting to using a bone as a club for defense and aggression, film's fine lensing and animal work could have this of use for schools and some specialized docu outlets.

It won the Technical prize at the Cannes Fest. —*Mosk.*

Mr. Patman
(CANADIAN-COLOR)

Cannes, May 18.
A Film Consortium of Canada Production. Produced by Bill Marshall and Alexander MacDonald. Stars James Coburn. Directed by John Guillermin; executive producer, Henk Van der Kolk; screenplay by Thomas Hedley. Camera (color) John Coquillon; editors, Max Benedict, Vince Hatherly; production design, Trevor Williams; sound, Brian Simmons; music, Paul Hoffert. Reviewed at les Ambassades, May 17, Cannes, France. **Running Time: 105 MINS.**

Patman	James Coburn
Peabody	Kate Nelligan
Abadaba	Fionnula Flanagan
Abernathy	Les Carlson
Mrs. Beckman	Candy Kane
Dr. Turley	Michael Kirby
Dr. Bloom	Alan McRae
Vrakatas	Jan Rubes
Wolfe	Hugh Webster
Monica	Lyn Griffin
Montgomery	Tabitha Herrington
The Director	Lois Maxwell

James Coburn has a strong role as Mr. Patman, a sly, slightly deranged, Irish orderly on a hospital psychiatric ward. Despite some strong performances and an intriguing premise, the picture is sunk by pedestrian direction from vet John Guillermin.

The film takes several wrong turns before setting a path for itself. Coburn is being trailed by a mystery man in the opening and carrying on with his landlady, Fionnula Flanagan while her husband is off at work.

Later, he is working a hospital night shift with Nelligan, another lover. The character's charm has made him a favorite with patients but his rebellious streak creates friction between him and the hospital staff.

His affinity with patients is not made clear. One commits suicide, another dies of a heart attack on release and a third, who is cured, tells him he's as bonkers as his wards.

It becomes increasingly apparent that Coburn is suffering from delusions of paranoia. His stalker is fictitious and his belief Nelligan has been killed in a car accident, a figment of his over active imagination.

His nasty pranks toward an insensitive doctor finally get him fired. He engineers a patient's escape and flees to California with Nelligan.

Things turn sour and the couple returns. Coburn is rejected by Flanagan, kills his cat, reveals to a slightly mad priest that his pursuer is a dead patient and winds up on the inside as a patient.

Guillermin directs the entire film on a persistent one-key note. Whatever emotion existed in the planning stages has been virtually erased.

Coburn musters all his charm for this thankless role. Physically and emotionally he is a perfect choice for the renegade part and injects credibility to the meandering plot. Both Nelligan and Flanagan are good as his women with roles that need some expansion. Michael Kirby is also strong as a posturing physician winding up the butt of Coburn's practical jokes.

John Coquillon's photography adds an ominous quality to the majority night shooting in Vancouver. The pic needs tighter editing and some restructuring. As it stands the film will require careful handling if it hopes to reach beyond art specialty houses. —Klad.

Middle Age Crazy
(CANADIAN-COLOR)

Cannes, May 15.
A 20th Century-Fox release of a Tormont Film Production. Produced by Robert Cooper, Ronald Cohen and John Eckert. Stars Bruce Dern, Ann-Margret. Directed by John Trent; exec producers, Sid and Marty Krofft. Screenplay by Carl Kleinschmidt; camera, (color), Reginald Morris; editor, John Kelly, art direction, Karen Bromley; sound, David Lee; music, Matthew McCauley. Reviewed at les Ambassades, May 14, Cannes, France. Running time: 89 MINS.
Bobby Lee . . . . Bruce Dern
Sue Ann . . . . Ann-Margret
J.D. . . . . Graham Jarvis
Tommy . . . . Eric Christmas
Ruth . . . . Helen Hughes
Greg . . . . Geoffrey Bowes
Nancy . . . . Deborah Wakeham
Titus . . . . Michael Kane

"Middle Age Crazy" is the newest chapter in the ever growing book of male mid-life crisis pix. The film has strong commercial prospects based on an appealing cast and a strong first hour. Regrettably, the story turns to mush at the close, though not before some very humorous insights.

This time, Houston is the site of this social comedy although the setting differs little from Boston ("Starting Over"), San Francisco ("Serial"), New York ("Something Short of Paradise") and Los Angeles ("10;" "Last Married Couple in America").

Bobby Lee (Dern) is a successful building contractor on the verge of his 40th birthday. He is getting hung up on his milestone date as a result of his wife's persistence that he's still the old stud she married.

Constant reminders from friends and family of his dependability eventually drive him to change his style. He buys a Porsche, dresses up like a drugstore cowboy, and has a brief fling with a Dallas Cowgirl.

The first hour mirrors the middle age nightmare in comic fantasies with traces of pain. Dern's surprise party and a fantasized valedictory emerge as comic high points. However, he's still stuck in his suburban cubbyhole.

The turning point occurs when his

father dies. Suddenly, the entire family dumps its collective problems in his lap. He escapes to Dallas on a job but chucks everything after he meets cowgirl Deborah Wakeham.

At first, Dern likes a life with no strings, but changes his tune when he discovers Wakeham with another man. He finally decides family and responsibility aren't so bad after all.

The revelation is pat and steeped in sentimentality. A quick resolution would have been more in keeping with the movie's acerbic wit.

Dern finally gets his best romantic lead on film. He emerges a likable family man with deep reservations about his lot in life. The actor is equally convincing dressed in three piece suits or denim and boots.

Ann-Margret as his wife is also outstanding. She pulls off the difficult task of portraying life with Ann-Margret as slightly less than a bed of roses.

Supporting roles and technical credits are all strong and there's nothing which gives away the fact that most of the film was shot in Toronto.

Carl Kleinschmidt's script inspired by the Jerry Lee Lewis song, which gives the pic its title but not played, deftly outlines Dern's midlife crisis even if it opts for a conventional solution. John Trent's direction is assured.

"Middle Age Crazy" should fare well despite the familiarity of the premise. Fox is planning an early fall break. —Klad.

Portrait Of A 60% Perfect Man
(FRENCH-COLOR-DOCU-16m)

Cannes, May 27.
Janus Film release of Action Film production. Interview by Michel Ciment. Directed by Annie Tresgot. Camera (color), Gary Graver; editor, François Ceppi. No other credits available. Reviewed at Cannes Film Fest (Non-competing-A Certain Look), May 17, '80. Running time: 58 MINS.
With: Billy Wilder, Jack Lemmon, Walter Matthau, Michel Ciment.
(In English)

Billy Wilder is not exactly a cult director but he is highly respected for his wit, eclecticism and script and directorial savvy. A recent retrospective of his work at the Berlin Film Festival gained him new converts as will this revealing, entertaining and astute interview with Wilder on his life and work by French critic Michel Ciment.

Director Annie Tresgot is also helpful in bringing is sidelight talks with actors Jack Lemmon and Walter Matthau and scripter I.A.L. Diamond. But it is Wilder who car-

ries this off with his anecdotes, his refusal to be pigeonholed into anything but a professional filmmaker who insists that there are other things in his life besides films.

A fine document that is a natural for tv usage and could find some outings in specialized spots to entice film buffs with another medium length film oriented docu.

Wilder seems ripe for more historical interest and reassessment of his work. This film will certainly be a help. Wilder is as entertaining as most of his films, not to forget a more dramatic background in his flight from Hitlerism and readjustment in a new language and country that give his more dramatic films potency. —Mosk.

Ate a ultima gota
(To The Last Drop)
(BRAZILIAN-DOCU-COLOR)

Cannes, May 21.
A Mariza Leao production directed by Sergio Rezende. Screenplay, Rezende; camera, (Eastmancolor) Jose Joffily; editor, Vera Freire; music, Paul de Castro; narration, Hugo Carvana. Reviewed at Cannes Film Fest (Market) May 20, '80. Running time: 70 MINS.

According to Sergio Rezende's hardhitting documentary, blood is a $200,000,000 a year business in Brazil and, in all of Latin America, has an annual volume of 3,000,000 litres which, explains a doctor, is an amount equivalent to the blood of 500,000 people.

Only 25% of the "merchandise" collected in Brazil is used in actual transfusions: the rest is put to industrial use by multinational drug companies in the manufacture of items such as albumine and gammaglobulin.

This documentary, through a series of interviews, also shows how selling their own blood becomes a last resort for the down and out, ranging all the way from the out of work who have to support their families, to drunks who just want money to continue drinking.

Blood banks are described as utterly unscrupulous, paying very little for blood, and, even worse, accepting donors in poor health and even in a state of inebriation. This, in many cases, leads to hepatitis after transfusions to the sick.

Donors are paid very little for their blood, but the price charged on the market is exorbitant and, says Rezende, "reproduces the pattern of international economics whereby underdeveloped countries are suppliers for raw materials which developed countries buy cheaply and transform into costly manufactured goods which, when reexported to the third world (items like gammaglobulin in this case) are prohibitively expensive."

At its best, the film accumulates little-known facts and also impressive testimonials from blood donors that clearly insinuate the social background that makes the whole racket possible. The stories of those who had to pay huge prices for transfusions in Brazilian hospitals and of a hepatitis victim are equally strong. Actual reporting was not extended, however, to blood bank owners and executives of the multinationals that deal in blood, in order to round out the picture, but it certainly opens up new vistas on a subject that, although on occasion dealt with in press exposes, is little known.

Well photographed, and thoroughly professional on a technical level, the film is weaker when it editorializes the facts and testimonials in themselves are more convincing. —Amig.

La Femme-Enfant
(The Child Woman)
(FRENCH-COLOR)

Cannes, May 14.
Gaumont release of Alma Films, GPFI, Gaumont production. Features entire cast. Written and directed by Raphaele Billetdoux. Camera (Eastmancolor), Alaine Derobe; editor, Genevieve Winding; music, Vladimir Cosma. Reviewed at Cannes Film Festival (Non-competing), May 13, '80. Running time, 100 MINS.
Elisabeth . . . . Penelope Palmer
Marcel . . . . Klaus Kinski
Father . . . . Michel Robin
Mother . . . . Helene Surgere

Raphaele Billetdoux won a prize for a novel and has been a film editor. Now for her first film she shows a flair for atmosphere in a strange tale of a 14 year old girl finding some solace from a loveless home with a mute older man.

The relationship is tender and child-like rather than sexual though some ambiguity remains. They meet secretly every morning before she goes to school. Klaus Kinski as the man somewhat overdoes his silent reactions and misses a more natural tone.

With him, the girl can be demanding, pampered and overindulged. She soon begins to tire of Kinski's demands and fears that others might find out about them.

She is sent away to work for a family and study music too for she is a fine organist. Kinski, pining for her, comes to get a shave at her parents' shop. He overhears talk of her work and musical advances and during the shave suddenly grabs her father's hand and cuts his own throat.

The girl comes back and pays a last visit to Kinski's farm where they played so romantically and innocently. Her father who has since found a notebook of Kinski's, follows her on her last visit to the house, but his berating her is useless, for she has passed this stage and will now go her own way.

Film is overindulgent in its strange relationships, but should find festival interest this summer and marks Billetdoux a possibly promising newcomer. Penelope Palmer, American but having grown up in France, is rightly nymphet-like with an engaging pug face and assurance and another promising factor in this offbeat film. —*Mosk.*

Dani Od Snova
(Days of Dreams)
(YUGOSLAV-COLOR)

Cannes, May 27.
Yugoslavia Film release of Centar, Dan/Tana Productions production. Features entire cast. Written and directed by Vlatko Gilic. Camera (Eastmancolor), Branko Ivatovic; music, Ksenija Zecevic. Reviewed at Cannes-Film Fest (Non-competing-A Certain Look), May 18, '80. Running time: 92 MINS.
With: Vladislava Milosavljevic, Boris Komnenic, Ljiljana Krstic.

Vlatko Gilic has had a fine documentary career, his shorts have won prizes at many festivals. Turning to features (this is his second) he has a tendency toward too much explanation and repetitive explicitness that may be acceptable in documentaries but bog down features and have a tendency to try to blow up a simple theme out of proportion.

Here a nubile teenage girl goes to shepherd sheep in a remote hillside part of the country. There is a secret air base nearby and one pilot buzzes her interminably while she is lying in the sun partly clad tending her sheep. He comes to show her the photos and an idyll develops that will go on or be forgotten after the summer.

There are some poetic scenes of the countryside, a feel for the peasant woman who lives with her memories and some flair for intimate, innocent scenes of youthful initiation to first love and friendship.

But it is all mainly surface and pretty, and Gilic, with a definite visual flair, has to shed his documentary distance, come to grips with more dramatic scripts and deeper characterizations before he can truly graduate from a fine documentarist to a more robust fiction film director. —*Mosk.*

Jag ar Maria
(I Am Maria)
(SWEDISH-COLOR)

Cannes, May 10.
A Drakfilm AB/Swedish Film Institute/Three Leaf Clover HB Production, Europa Film release (Sweden), Swedish Film Institute release (Foreign territories). Features entire cast. Script, edited and directed by Karsten Wedel. Based on novel by Hans-Eric Hellberg; Co-scripter Goeran Setterberg; Camera (Eastmancolor) Rune Ricsson; Micha Gavrjusjov; music, Bengt Edquist, Boerje Sandquist; Production design, Anders Barreus; Executive producer, Hans Iveberg; Production managers, Lisbeth Wikner, Bengt Wendin. Reviewed at Cinema Le Regent (non-competing) May 10, '80. Running time: 90 MINS.

Maria . . . . .Lise Lotte Hjelm
Jon . . . . Peter Lindgren
Lennart . . . . Frej Lindquist
Maj-Britt . . . . Helena Brodin
Maria's mother . . . . .Claire Wikholm

Karsten Wedel, a Sweden-based Dane, has a solid career as a film editor and maker of advertising shorts behind him before his auspicious debut as a feature director with "I Am Maria," the story of a pre-teenage girl's short-lived friendship with an old recluse, generally considered either a drunk or the village idiot after his loss years ago of his wife and two children in a train crash.

The old man Jon turns out to be a painter of the naif school and a very good one, too. Newspapers and tv invade his home to which only Maria has otherwise been admitted. The intruders make Jon explode in rage. Guided by Maria, he agrees to be transferred to an old people's home. Maria returns from the industrial-provincial town, where she has been the charge of a rather narrowminded married couple related to her mother who seems to be between men and generally in a confused state of mind back in Stockholm.

The story of the recluse-painter, feared by the burghers but a soul of pure sweetness & light as seen by Maria, is rather predictable. It is Wedel's insights in the naturally offbeat workings of Maria's mind that will capture audiences. So, also, will the subdued playing in the title role of Lise Lotte Hjelm plus the often very inventive and rhythmically right editing by the director himself.

In general, film works it way too slowly through its story to appeal to other than rather special audiences on the international cinema circuit, but it could gain some popular appeal via tv sales. —*Kell.*

Circle Of Two
(CANADIAN-COLOR)

Cannes, May 16.
A Film Consortium of Canada production in association with Jerome Simon and Milton Zysman productions. Produced by Henk Van der Kolk. Stars Richard Burton, Tatum O'Neal. Directed by Jules Dassin. Executive producer, Bill Marshall. Screenplay by Thomas Hedley, based on "A Lesson in Love" by Marie Terese Baird; camera (Color) Lazlo George; production design, Claude Bonniere; art direction, Francois de Lucy; editor, David Nochols; sound, Owen Langevin; music, Paul Hoffert; assistant director, Timothy Rowse. Reviewed at les Ambassades, May 15, Cannes, France. Running Time: 105 MINS.
Ashley St. Clair . . . . .Richard Burton
Sarah Norton . . . . Tatum O'Neal
Claudia Aldrich . . . . Nuala FitzGerald
Mr. Norton . . . . Robin Gammell
Mrs. Norton . . . . .Patricia Collins
Dr. Emily Reid . . . . Kate Reid
Smitty . . . . Donann Cavin
Paul . . . . Michael Wincott
Raspoli . . . . Norma Dell'Agnese

"Circle of Two" presents a brief romantic, but not sexual, interlude between a 60-year-old artist and a 16-year-old student. The principals are Richard Burton and Tatum O'Neal.

The coupling may have been intended to attract two different audiences. However, the pic will have better response from an older crowd making it an iffy commercial sell.

O'Neal first stumbles on Burton at a porno movie she's been dared to see by school chums. Later, he hides her at a restaurant where she's ditched a former boyfriend. In the pornohouse, two celeb extras can be noted, Ryan O'Neal (Tatum's father) and Lee Majors.

The infatuation has Burton encouraging her to pursue her writing and him taking up the paint brush after a 10-year hiatus. Their secret is uncovered with Burton facing ridicule and O'Neal virtually imprisonment by her parents.

Unfortunately, nothing happens between the two because of Burton's cold feet. O'Neal is certainly willing and even pursues him to New York where he decides they have no future. A realistic, though hardly dramatic assessment.

Jules Dassin has directed a charming, earnest movie which promises but does not deliver a grand, emotional statement. The mood is highly reflective and insular.

Burton gives one of his best performances in recent memory. He is sympathetic and vulnerable as a painter with an enormous creative block. His paintings were actually the work of noted Canadian artist Harold Town.

Tatum O'Neal, however, is never convincing as the catalyst for his new-found strength. She has a tendency to posture and smile and comes off prettier than she is inspiring. Audiences are likely to choke on her brief nude scene while she poses to be painted.

Nuala FitzGerald plays Burton's former lover and long time supporter in the art community with conviction and Robin Gammell and Patricia Collins score well as O'Neal's concerned and devoted parents.

The production has a uniform bright, clean veneer which would have been better suited to the small screen. The script by Thomas Hedley never delves beneath the surface of the two characters, creating a superficial still life.

Nonetheless, Dassin maintains audience attention and gets considerable mileage from his slight material. "Circle of Two" will still have a hard climb to lure audiences. —*Klad.*

Can't Stop The Music
(COLOR)

Take this Carr to the bank.

Sydney, June 3.

Associated Film Distribution release of an Allan Carr production. Features entire cast. Produced by Allan Carr, Jacques Morali, Henri Belolo. Directed by Nancy Walker. Screenplay, Bronte Woodard, Allan Carr; camera (Panavision-Metrocolor), Bill Butler; music composed by Jacques Morali; musical staging, choreography, Arlene Phillips; costumes, Jane Greenwood; art director, Harold Michelson; editor, John F. Burnett; asst. director, Bill Beasley; set decorators, Marvin March; Victoria Hugo; special effects, Michael Sullivan; music arrangements, Horace Ott; unit publicist, Gary Kalkin. Reviewed at the Paramount Theatre, Sydney, June 1, 1980. (MPAA Rating - PG). Running time: **118 MINS.**

Village People	Ray Simpson, David Hodo, Felipe Rose, Randy Jones, Glenn Hughes, Alex Briley
Samantha Simpson	Valerie Perrine
Ron White	Bruce Jenner
Jack Morell	Steve Guttenberg
Steve Waits	Paul Sand
Sydney Channing	Tammy Grimes
Helen Morell	June Havoc
Norma White	Barbara Rush
Alicia Edwards	Altovise Davis
Lulu Brecht	Marilyn Sokol
Richard Montgomery	Russell Nype
Benny Murray	Jack Weston
Claudia Walters	Leigh Taylor-Young
Record store manager	Dick Patterson
Bread woman	Bobo Lewis
Stick-up lady	Paula Trueman
Law Office Receptionist	Portia Nelson

Music — "Can't Stop The Music," "Liberation," "I Love You To Death," music by Jacques Morali, lyrics by Henri Belolo, Phil Hurtt, Beauris Whitehead; "YMCA," "Magic Night," "Milk Shake," music by Morali, lyrics by Belolo, Victor Willis; "Give Me A Break," music by Morali, lyrics by Belolo, Vera Brown, Dodie Draher, Jacqui Smith-Lee.

"Can't Stop The Music" calls itself "the musical event of the '80s" and if that seems somewhat premature since the decade has hardly begun, it's a fair bet that at current costs, it will be a while before another $20,000,000 is spent as lavishly as Allan Carr has done so this time out. Cost aside, the boxoffice prospects seem promising.

Writers Carr and Bronte Woodard have recreated the old "I know, we'll put on a show" gimmick to hinge their story on. Valerie Perrine plays the ex-model with a heart of gold who has quit at the top of her profession. Her roommate is an aspiring pop composer (Steve Guttenberg) whom she helps after his debut as a disco disk jockey.

She recruits various friends to sing on a demo tape she's going to present to ex-lover and president of Marrakesh Records, Steve Waits, (Paul Sand), who gives a picture-selling performance as a man at the end of a telephone and his tether.

.The people she brings into the act just happen to be an Indian, a cowboy, a singing policeman — you guessed it. So this is the way that hot disco group got together? If it isn't, what the heck? This is showbiz.

On the way she meets a staid young tax lawyer (Bruce Jenner) who she finally gets on the side of the righteous, aided and abetted by June Havoc and Barbara Rush, respectively playing the mothers of the composer and the lawyer. And on the way to the fade out, it's girl gets boy, boy briefly loses girl, boy and girl get group. What could be more updated than that?

Among the standout sequences is the "Y.M.C.A." number, replete with a chorus line of young males at the pool's edge, side-diving just like in an Esther Williams aquastravaganza at MGM in the '50s.

In fact, and clearly Carr's contribution, the picture is full of allusions to film history with recognizable references to "It Happened One Night" (the hitchhike scene), "Gone With The Wind" ("I'll think about it tomorrow") and others. Also splendid is a speech by Perrine which is entirely composed of recent hit song titles.

Musical numbers are staged with high energy and plenty of verve, and the art direction gets top marks for style and imagination. It's the scenes in between where the film fails to maintain the standard.

Director Nancy Walker's way with actors is one thing, but she clearly had trouble with the nonactors in the cast. While they're doing their schtick on stage, The Village People are fine for their kind, but along with ex-Olympic decathlon champion Jenner, they've a long way to go in the acting stakes. Some scenes one could pulp and thereby solve the world paper shortage, they're so wooden.

However, that doesn't really matter much because the overall atmosphere of the film is as eager to please as a puppy. There are bonuses for the film buffs and sly remarks that couldn't be described as double-entendres, though it might be argued that any mild salaciousness is in the ear of the audience.

Whatever, with a popular group in its first film and a lot of visual pizzazz, Carr has got a hot property that will doubtless appeal widely: maybe he's already considering a sequel to be called "Can't Stop The Money." —*Miha.*

Laemna mig inte ensam
(Leave Me Not Alone)
(SWEDISH-COLOR)

Cannes, May 18.

A Europa Film — RI Films — Swedish Film Institute production, Europea (for Sweden) and Swedish Film Institute (foreign) release. Features entire cast. Original story and script, Jan Halldoff, Rune Hjelm. Directed by Jan Halldoff. Camera (Eastmancolor) Sten Holmberg, Dan Myrman; editor, Tomas Taeng; music, Lennart Sjoeholm; executive producer, Rune Hjelm; production design, Mona Forsen. Reviewed at Cinema Le Regent, Cannes, May 18, 1980. Running time: **92 MINS.**

Sofi	Lena Loefstroem
Pia	Anki Liden
Jens	Nicola Janic
Magnus	Pelle Lindbergh
Sofi's mother	Gunvor Ponten
Sofi's father	Nils Duebeck
"Irland"	Carl-Axel Heiknert

Through the ages, intellectuals and artists have busied their minds with the psychology of the prostitute. Writer-director Jan Halldoff, an accomplished filmmaker, adds only confusion to the issue with "Leave Me Not Alone," the story of a 15-year-old girl, Sofi, who starts turning tricks to get quick money for an Ibiza holiday with her amateur boxer boyfriend.

From press releases, it would seem that Halldoff aims at pinning the blame for Sofi's venture into prostitution on her parents. His film does in no way show the parents as anything but nice, the father more than sensitive to what a daughter might need in the way of confidence.

And we see Sofi (in a morose performance by Lena Loefstroem) as a tough character who performs professionally from the very night she moves in with a pimp & hooker team. She is dull in her responses to customers such as "Irland" who is more in search of psychiatric than sexual help, but the drowning .of a kid she does not know or the death of a friend's dog move her to anger at whoever stands closest.

Anki Liden and Nicola Janic give very striking performances as prostitute and pimp. It is the pimp's abuse of Pia that finally decides Sofi on quitting street-walking, not the sorrow of her parents or her boyfriend's turning. his back to her. Audiences are left behind with a vague feeling that young Sofi has her own fate well in hand, what-, ever direction it may now take.

In spite of a fine production look, "Leave Me Not Alone" fared badly on its home ground and cannot be told any bright fortunes. —*Kell*.

The Island
(COLOR)

More violent than suspenseful. Initial b.o. looms big.

Universal Pictures release of a Zanuck-Brown Production. Directed by Michael Ritchie. Produced by Richard D. Zanuck and David Brown. Features entire cast. Screenplay, Peter Benchley, from his novel; camera (color), Henri Decae; production design, Dale Hennesy; film editor, Richard A. Harris; music, Ennio Moricone; special visual effects, Albert Whitlock; costumes, Ann Roth; set decorations, Robert de Vestel. Reviewed at Rivoli Theatre, N.Y., June 2, 1980. (MPAA Rating: R). Running time: **114 MINS.**

Maynard	Michael Caine
Nau	David Warner
Beth	Angela Punch McGregor
Windsor	Frank Middlemass
Rollo	Don Henderson
Dr. Brazil	Dudley Sutton
Hizzoner	Colin Jeavons
Wescott	Zakes Mosae
Stark	Brad Sullivan
Justin	Jeffrey Frank

Following chronologically — and qualitatively — in the wake of "Jaws" and "The Deep," this latest summertime tale from the water-obsessed pen of Peter Benchley will have audiences in the palm of its hand for its first third or so, proceeding to squeeze them in a fistful of graphically detailed violence as suspense gives way to gut-level sadism aimed at the lowest common audience denominator.

Based on the earlier pics and its own book sales, early biz promises to be very big. But word-of-mouth may well reduce longterm b.o. to the hardcore action crowd, and more genteel types, especially parents who still guide their kids viewing, could drop off fairly quickly, fueling arguments against the film's overly generous R-rating along the way.

As noted, the venture gets off to a bristling start as a charter boatload of boozy business types is ambushed by something or someone that leaves hatchets planted in their skulls and severed limbs scattered aboard. Cut to British journalist Michael Caine, who persuades his editor that his latest Bermuda Triangle-type ship disappearance — one of some 600 reported in recent years — justifies his personal research. Stuck with son Jeffrey Frank for the weekend, he drives to Miami, then charters a plane which crashlands on a small island, leaving them stranded.

At this point, audiences have had their expectations craftily manipulated by a couple of ship attacks, a plotline bristling with mystery and a trenchantly witty script that meshes nicely with director Michael Ritchie's sarcastic visual style. But once the mystery is banally resolved — the island is inhabited by a tribe of buccaneers who've been inbreeding for 300 years and prey on pleasure ships for sustenance and booty — the film degenerates to a violent chase melodrama. Pirates want Frank as leader-successor to David Warner and cruelly brainwash the kid into renouncing his real father, while Caine is tortured into submission as a sexual slave forced to bring strong outsider semen to the one remaining fertile woman (Angela Punch McGregor) in the tribe.

Film's N.Y. preview was marked by a stream of patron walkouts as Frank's eyes were stretched open with pegs, Caine stung by jellyfish and bled by leeches, and a schooner-load of young American dope smugglers brutally picked off with muskets, sabres, grappling hooks, etc. This ship storming segment — and Caine's climactic machine-gunning of the entire tribe after they've massacred a Coast Guard cutter — is quite effectively staged, and both segs combine to re-generate enough excitement to save the pic and even generate mild applause.

If the story had been tackled at a slightly more classy level, the patent silliness of these pirating "living fossils" might have been forgiven. But their bizarre dress, rituals and pidgin-English banter is more laughable than fear-inspiring. Expectedly, overacting is the order of the day, though Caine provides a strong, heroically concerned focus. Ritchie's witty direction is abandoned in the violence and periodic efforts to revive the built-in comedy fall flat. Technical work — Albert Whitlock's Grand Guignol special effects, Henri Decae's crisp lensing and Ennio Morricone's dignified score — is tops all the way. —*Step.*

Theo Gegen Den Rest Der Welt
(Theo Against the Rest of the World)
(WEST GERMAN-COLOR)

Cannes, May 21.
Altura-film, Munich, Popular-Film, Hans H. Kaden, Stuttgart, and Trio-Film, Duisburg; in coproduction with West-deutscher Rundfunk (WDR), Cologne, world rights, Cine-International, Munich. Features entire cast. Directed by Peter F. Bringmann. Screenplay, Matthias Seelig; camera (color), Helge Weindler; editing, Annette Dorn; sets, Goetz Heymann; music, Lothar Meid; production manager, Michael Wiedemann; executive producer, Alena Rimbach. Reviewed at Cannes Film Festival (Market), May 21, '80. Running time: 106 MINS.

Cast: Marius Mueller-Westerhagen (Theo), Guido Gagliardi (Enno), Claudia Demarmels (Ines), Carlheinz Heitmann, Peter Berling, Eolo Capritti, Ricardo Parisio Perotti, Marquard Bohm.

A comedy (one of the few these days in German cinema) with plenty going for it, Peter F. Bringmann's "Theo Against the Rest of the World" is about a truck driver with a chip on his shoulder who is doomed to defeat from the very beginning, for Theo is a bull-headed, bone-headed con-man whose heart and feelings are always getting in his way.

Theo has just bought a new truck and has a fistful of payments to meet, together with his Italian-born friend Enno, but just before arriving home in Herne on a trip with illegal wares, the truck is stolen while he's visiting a comfort station. So he commandeers a car to chase after the crooks, which belongs to a Swiss miss returning home from college on a vacation (she flunked her exams); she and partner Enno then join Theo in his private fight against theft and misfortune as they whackily pursue hunches that bring them to Switzerland, then to Milan, Genoa, and Naples.

In turn, they are pursued closely by a crooked bill-collector, whose strength is awesome enough to crack bones at will to get what he wants. The truck is finally located on a disembarking boat to somewhere, but even then there's a twist to keep things still going without an end in sight.

Although this tickling comedy has plenty of non sequiturs to unhinge the film afficionado, Peter K. Bringmann is a director to watch and thesp Marius Mueller-Westernhagen sparkles in the lead, as do his backup actors, Guido Garliardi and Claudia Demarmels as the Italian and the Swiss counterparts. Bringmann, by the way, scored on tv recently with another offbeat pic — "The Day That Elvis Came to Bremerhaven," using actual docu footage of the rock star arriving in West Germany to begin military duty in the 1950s.

"Theo Against the Rest of the World" deserves more exposure on the upcoming fest circuit. It's a comic oddity on German scene. —*Holl.*

Urban Cowboy
(COLOR)

Too much bull, but bully nonetheless.

Hollywood, May 28.
A Paramount Pictures release, produced by Robert Evans and Irving Azoff. Features entire cast. Directed by James Bridges. Exec producer, C.O. Erickson. Screenplay, James Bridges, Aaron Latham, based on Latham's story; camera (Movielab Color), Ray Villalobos; editor, Dave Rawlins; sound, Willie Burton; production design, Stephen Grimes; art direction, Stewart Campbell; choreography, Patsy Swayze; assistant director, Kim Kuramada; music, Ralph Burns. Reviewed at Paramount Studios, May 28, 1980. (MPAA rating: PG.) Running time: 135 MINS.
Bud .... John Travolta
Sissy .... Debra Winger
Wes .... Scott Glenn
Pam .... Madolyn Smith
Uncle Bob .... Barry Corbin
Aunt Corene .... Brooke Alderson
Marshall .... Cooper Huckabee
Steve Strange .... James Gammon
Musical appearances by Mickey Gilley, Johnny Lee, Bonnie Raitt and Charlie Daniels Band.

Though "Urban Cowboy" does its best to toss John Travolta into the dust, he hangs on through sheer tenacity and the pictures promises to be a solid commercial hit, but far short of "Saturday Night Fever" and "Grease."

Undoubtedly, there's widespread interest now in country & western in general, and Texas specifically, and director James Bridges has ably captured the atmosphere of one of the most famous chip-kicker hangouts of all: Gilley's Club on the outskirts of Houston.

Assertedly, Gilley's is the largest honky-tonk in America, where hundreds and sometimes thousands of gooxold-boys gather nightly to fight, dance, drink and pretend to themselves that modern life is still full of frontier excitement.

It's also a place for their women, Texas lovelies just now learning the first news of feminism while still accustomed to accepting a good clout from the old man for being late with dinner.

Enter Travolta, fresh from a West Texas farm and working his first job in an oil refinery, quickly learning that Gilley's is where everybody heads after work. Unfortunately, this is not an easy part for Travolta, whose commercial successes have been completely founded in translating his tv character of Vinnie Barbarino for the bigscreen, with dancing.

Try as you might, it's hard to completely accept Travolta as a redneck and his Texas accent is not quite right. Still, there's no denying he has a strong screen magnetism and as he presses forward, determined to carry it off, the disbelief is almost suspended.

Fortunately, he's surrounded by a very good cast of supporting characters, especially Debra Winger, Scott Glenn, Madolyn Smith, Barry Corbin and Brooke Alderson.

Winger is outstanding as a fetching little slut who hangs out at Gilley's and marries Travolta after a quick, hostile courtship, only to lose him almost as quickly to Smith, properly haughty and sexy as the oilman's daughter slumming for sex.

Winger leaves Travolta to move in with Glenn, excellent as a lanky, evil ex-con, who mistreats her, while Smith moves in with Travolta. That's the love story, broken into four sides and none of it is quite believable either. But, again, the power of the four personalities makes up for the holes in the script.

In one way or another, the quadrangle revolves around Gilley's mechanical bucking bull, a menacing device that tests the courage of all the would-be cowboys. (And cowgirls, too, for that matter.) Winger manages to use it for a romantic triumph that presents one of the most erotic moments seen in a PG film.)

But city-slicker teenagers in the audience may grow a bit bored with all the bull ridings, along with all the other trapings at Gilley's. Ceratinly, the dancing that goes on there is mainly a variation on the old two-step and while Travolta does it well, it's nothing to equal the flash of "Fever" or "Grease."

After two hours, the amount of padding with riding, dancing and cavorting in big hats becomes pretty tedious, raising the question again why today's "major" features feel they must go on and on, after the story's been told.

"Cowboy" would be solid entertainment at 90 minutes. The longer version just uses the time to accent the flaws. —*Har.*

Prostitute
(BRITISH-COLOR)

Cannes, May 17.
A Kestrel Films production. Produced and directed by Tony Garnett. Features entire cast. Screenplay, Garnett; camera (color), Charles Stewart; editor, Bill Shapter; art director, Martin Johnson; costumes, Monica Howe; music, The Gangsters; sound, Malcolm Hirst; asst. director, Raymond Day. Reviewed at the Star Theatre, Cannes, May 16, '80. (No BBFC Rating). Running time: 96 MINS.
Sandra .... Eleanor Forsythe
Louise .... Kate Crutchley
Jean .... Kim Lockett
Rose .... Nancy Samuels
David Selby .... Richard Mangan
Amanda .... Ann Whitaker
Mr. Hanson .... Paul Arlington
Carol .... Carol Palmer
Mrs. T .... Brigid Mackay
Griff .... Colin Hindley
Winston .... Count Prince Miller
Martin .... Howard Dickenson
London Detective .... Paul Moriarty
TV Researcher .... Mary Waterhouse

A few months in the life of an English provincial girl with aspirations to improve her lot by moving up the prostitution market is the theme of tv and film director Tony Garnett's first feature as director. Committedly downbeat, "Prostitute" (which he also researched and scripted) displays the deceptively loose-knit, "tell it like it is" approach familiar from the work of British director Ken Loach, Garnett's longtime collaborator.

Telling it like it is entails exploration of much of the central character's working life, so restricted admission is inevitable where censorship applies. Certain scenes included in the print screened at Cannes — a highly explicit massage parlor sequence in particular — will need toning down for public exhibition in most markets even wtih an adult rating.

But Garnett's aim is serious realism, not exploitation. Running parallel with the girl's doleful progress from Birmingham to London in hopes (ultimately dashed) of exchanging a scratached living on the street for classier, and safer, assignments with loaded Arabs and the like, there's a plotline concerning a female welfare worker of roughly the same age.

The two women are friends, strangely matched yet interdependent. During Sandra's sojourn in the capital, Louise sets about drumming up support in Birmingham for a review of the U.K.'s prostitution laws, which she believes to be hypocritical and commonly an incitement to corruption.

That, of course, is the film's principal message. Scripter-director's evident intention is to invite sober consideration of a controversial topic, not simply to entertain. Notwithstanding that there are plenty of incidental distractions arising out of Garnett's humorous insight into the quirks, indignities and offhand obscenities inherent in the world's oldest profession, the picture's playoff prospects must be seen as limited, though probable festival honors in due course could provide a handle for promotion as specialized fare.

In the key roles, Eleanor Forsythe as the basically ordinary, vulnerable girl who's all-too slow to realize the game is strictly for losers, and Kate Crutchley as, in a sense, the other side of the same idealistic coin, both turn in touching, naturalistic performances. Feminists should approve Garnett's intelligent treatment of the view that society offers most women two life-options: to be ripped off as men's playthings, or risk scorn as their naive competitors.

Directorial style is predictably self-effacing. Many sequences have the ring of part-improvisation, and plain pictorial composition frequently lends a documentary look to the drama. Not that technical aspects are scrappy Cinematographer Charles Stewart's lighting is notably proficient, in that while no scene appears lit, most settings convey a distinct and well-judged mood. (Release prints are firstrate blowups from Super 16m gauge negative).

Supporting actors, not all of them professionals, sustain the realistic tone admirably, making it genuinely hard to believe some scenes were staged. Especially well cast are Colin Hindley as a ludicrously earnest sociologist with whom Crutchley develops a romantic liaison scarcely more passionate than Forsythe's resigned encounters; and Ann Whitaker as a successful London whore on whose lived-in face the hatred required for survival seems to have been deeply etched. —*Simo.*

L'Affaire Coffin
(FRENCH-CANADIAN-COLOR)

Cannes, May 17.
A Corporation des Films Mutuels release of a production by Films Cine Scene and Les Productions Videofilms. Produced by Robert Menard. Features entire cast. Directed by Jean-Claude Labrecque. Editor, Andre Corriveau; camera (color), Pierre Mignot; music, Anne Laubert; sound, Alain Corneau. Reviewed at Les Ambassades, Cannes, May 16, 1980. Running time: 100 MINS.
Wilbert Coffin ...... August Schellenberg
Capitaine Forget .... Yvon Dufour
Maureen Patterson ... Micheline Lanctot
Ben Menard .... Jean-Marie Lemieux
Alain Courtemanche .....Gabriel Arcand
Chauffeur de taxi ..... Raymond Cloutier

Quebec's Gaspe peninsula is the backdrop for Jean-Claude Labrecque's feature, "The Coffin Affair." It is a sober re-telling of one of the province's most notorious trials and much too talky.

In 1953, Wilbert Coffin was tried and convicted of killing three American hunters. He was a prospector from an English-speaking community in the French-speaking province, and was proven to be near the site of the shootings. Coffin admitting stealing from the hunters, but refused any responsibility in the crime.

Coffin is tracked through the woods as he first aids the detectives and then arrested for the crime. The pic documents his trial at length, his subsequent escape from jail, and shows his lawyer convincing him to return to jail, and the ultimate failures of his appeals. It ends with the sound of his hanging against a black screen.

The very direct, unemotional approach to the subject will be a handicap with many audiences. Labrecque refers to the period — the period in Quebec when intense nationalism and political and religious oppression reigned — but fails to recreate it. An uninformed audience will miss many of the signposts, crucial to understanding the characters. References to the CIA, the tourist industry in the Gaspe and Quebec premier Maurice Duplessis are too vague.

Labrecque, a topnotch Quebec documentary maker and cinematographer. In Coffin, he fails to make a successful transition to a dramatic feature: the film remains static, faithful no doubt to its subject but hardly the stuff to attract a wide audience. August Schellenberg is adequate as Coffin but not forceful enough to carry the film alone into the realm of high drama. Only the scenes with Micheline Lanctot as his mistress ring with warmth. —*Tads.*

Den enes doed ...
(One Man's Loss ...)
(SWEDISH-COLOR)

Cannes, May 15.
A Movie Makers Sweden AB/Europa AB/Swedish Film Institute production, Swedish Film Institute release. Features entire cast. Written and directed by Stellan Olsson. Based on Poul Oerum's novel "The Unforgiving"; camera (Fuji color), Odd Geir Saether, Torbjoern Andersson; editor, Lasse Lundberg; Music, Christer Boustedt; Executive producer, Bert Sundberg; Production manager, Gustav Wiklund. Reviewed at Cinema Le Regent (non-competing), Cannes, May 15, '80. Running time: 106 MINS.
Ralf .... Jan Waldecranz
Sara .... Agneta Ekmanner
Lorenz .... Christer Boustedt
Herman .... Anders Granstroem
Johansson .... Gunnar Oehlund

Staying close to Danish novelist Poul Oerum's book, director Stellan Olsson has undertaken to deliver the crime thriller "One Man's Loss" with an almost infinite sadness of tone. This makes for a very interesting, softspoken and definitely non-commercial departure from what audiences anywhere in the world will comply with in the given genre.

Without said sadness plus a fine sketching in of small provincial town people and moods, plot would be pretty run-of-the-mill, but obviously of better striking power as entertainment.

Young Ralf returns to his home town after having served time for a bank robbery from which the loot has never been found. He is met with mixed emotions all around. He tries to renew an affair of the past with Sara who has stayed unhappily married to Lorenz, Ralf's robbery accomplice who got scot free.

Clearly, Lorenz has something to hide. There was a third accomplice, Herman, and where is Herman now? And how did Lorenz get the money to open his own new service station? Johansson, an elderly man of community power, seems to have something on his mind, too. Does it weigh heavily enough upon him for him to have been the one who one day caused Lorenz' death in an accident?

Young Ralf wants to get to the bottom of it all. He does so, literally, in a sequence of eerie gravedigging. The police, meanwhile, has Ralf picked for the guilty part all along.

Ralf and Sara, however, are finally seen as survivors, walking together into a new life of not too much promise of splendor. That's it. There is fine playing in all roles, especially by leads Jan Waldecranz, Agneta Ekmanner and Christer Boustedt. Bousted also did film's jazz-toned music score.
—*Kell.*

The Happy Hooker Goes Hollywood
(COLOR)

But no farther.

Hollywood, May 30.
A Cannon Films release, produced by Menahem Golan and Yoram Globus. Features entire cast. Directed by Alan Roberts. Screenplay, Devi Goldenberg; camera (color), Stephen Gray; sound, Douglas Vaughan. (No other credits available). Reviewed at the Pacific I Theatre, Hollywood, May 30, 1978. (MPAA rating: R.) Running time: 85 MINS.
Cast: Martine Beswicke, Adam West, Phil Silvers, Richard Deacon, Edie Adams, Chris Lemmon.

Having shown us the sights of New York and Washington, "The Happy Hooker Goes Hollywood" now, probably taking her same boxoffice followers along. But it's hard to imagine why they keep coming back to these travelogs, since so little is seen of the world outside the bedrooms.

"Hollywood" starts off well enough, as Martine Beswicke, in the title role, ventures forth in a limo with a handsome driver. Out the car's window, there are educational shots of the Hollywood sign, the Brown Derby, the Beverly Wilshire Hotel and the Chinese Theatre.

Unfortunately, Beswicke persuades the driver to pull over and drink champagne until we see the limo rocking back and forth vigorously, suggesting the shock absorbers are probably gone and the tour is over.

Sure enough, from then on director Alan Roberts is forced to rely on Beswicke to try to be funny with Adam West, Phil Silvers and Richard Deacon, an exercise that demonstrates just how entertaining the Hollywood sign was.

For an R picture, the language is very mild and the amount of skin exposed hardly provides the surface area for a good tan. But Adam West does get to dress up in women's clothes.

He's almost the best-looking thing in the picture. —*Har.*

Arabische Naechte
(Arabian Nights)
(WEST GERMAN-COLOR)

Cannes, May 15.
An Albatros-Production Michael Fengler, Munich, in coproduction with Popular-Film, Stuttgart, and Trio-Film, Duisburg; world rights, Atlas International, Munich. Features entire cast. Written and directed by Klaus Lemke. Camera (color), Ruediger Meichsner; editing, Inez Regnier; music, Juergen Kniepor; executive producer, Christian Hohoff. Reviewed at Cannes Film Festival (Market), May 14, '80. Running time: 94 MINS.
Cast: Cleo Kretschmer, Wolfgang Fierek, Dolly Dollar, Michael Lampert,

Horatius Haeberle, Jonny Badr, Zora Z., King Herbert, Guenni, El Hodjem.

Klaus Lemke has earned a reputation on tv and in cinemas with a series of odd-ball comedies starring Cleo Kretschmer, the best known being "The Sweethearts" (1976), "Some Saint" (1978) (introducing her equally dizzy partner, Wolfgang Fierek), and now "Arabian Nights" (also known as "For a Few Barrels More"). Cleo is a scatter-brained "Irma" or "Lucy" type who gets into unpredictable situations, only to come out with bells on her toes and rings on her fingers — as befits a lady of her type. As for Wolfgang, he can't get sentences to come out right either and shouldn't be let loose near a china shop — of course, in a Lemke pic that's just about where he'll end up.

Cleo and Wolfgang are operating a gas station in a hick town, when the rise in oil prices puts them out of business — this angers Cleo enough to go to London with a sexy girlfirend (her frontage profile drives the boys crazy) to find her own sheik and thus stay on top of the situation. She sends a postcard back to Wolfgang, who naturally goes looking for his lost love in bazaars and on camels in North Africa. Later, rejoined in London, they finish off the pic with an Arabian Nights party, thus allowing for another lavish change in Cleo's costumes for her growing fan club.

Worth a peep, although this is heavy Teutonic humor in spots.
—*Holl.*

Kindaichi Kosuke No Boken
(Kosuke Kindaichi's Adventure)
(JAPANESE-COLOR)

Tokyo, May 25.
A Toei release of a Kadokawa Production. Produced by Haruki Kadokawa. Features entire cast. Directed by Nobuhiko Obayashi. Screenplay, Koichi Saito, Tomoaki Nakano, based on novel by Seishi Yokomizo; dialog writer, Kohei Tsuka; animation, Makoto Wada; camera (color), Taisaku Kimura; lighting, Shinji Kojima; sound, Nobu Miyanaga; editing, Shinya Inoue; ass't director, Nobuaki Inozaki; music, Katsumi Kobayashi. Reviewed at Togeki Theatre, Tokyo, May 18, 1980. Running time: 113 MINS.
Kosuke Kindaichi . . . . .Ikko Furuya
Detective Todoroki . . . . Kunie Tanaka
Fumie Akechi . . . . .Hideko Yoshida
Goemon Ishida . . . . , ... Jiro Sakagami
Maria . . . . Miyuki Kumaya
Punch . . . . Toshio Egi

The fictional exploits of private investigator Kosuke Kindaichi, created by best-selling author Seishi Yokomizo, have been brought to the screen on numerous occasions over the past nearly five decades, most recently by Kon Ichikawa, who has directed an entire series of

b.o. smashes centered around the durable detective, beginning with "Inugami-ke No Ichizoku" (The Inugami Family) in '76. There is much about these mysteries that could, indeed deserves to be — parodied, but "Kosuke Kindaichi's Adventure" fails to do the job.

Ripe for the parodist's art are such recurring elements in the Kindaichi mysteries as plots that are almost laughably labyrinthine, requiring the assistance of a qualified geneaologist to unravel; deaths as bizarre as they are frequent; and weird collections of rustics and easily misled officers of the law. Truly successful parody is not, as the makers of this film seem to think, a matter of pulling no punches and offending no parties.

This is the third feature film directed by Nobuhiko Obayashi and it suffers from many of the same problems that affected his debut work, "House," a putative horror pic that was, in fact, nothing more than a compendium of the stylistic conventions of the tv commercial. As in "House," inconsequential narrative — here, a bit of piffle having to do with Kindaichi's efforts to recover the missing head of a statue — is fragmented by what are touted as parodies of commercials, tv series and movies, but are, in fact, mere references to the same.

There is however nothing in any of the references to commercial concerns or tv programs or films to upset the most officious pr man. Obayashi, who got his start as a director of commercials, knows how to imitate the old, but not how to initiate anything new. And it's difficult to imagine that he was urged to be creatively acerbic by producer Haruki Kadokawa, whose productions are object lessons in commercial tie-ins, which means avoiding any nastiness about manufacturers that helped you put your film together. —*Bail.*

Blue Lagoon
(COLOR)

Lovely to look at, but Shielded from excitement.

Hollywood, June 5.
A Columbia Pictures release, produced and directed by Randal Kleiser. Features entire cast. Screenplay, Douglas Day Stewart, based on the novel by Henry DeVere Stacpoole; camera (Colorfilm), Nestor Almendros; editor, Robert Gordon; sound, Paul Clark; art direction, Jon Dowding; costumes, Jean-Pierre Dorleac; assistant director, Peter Bogart; underwater photography, Ron Taylor, Valerie Taylor; music, Basil Poledouris. Reviewed at The Burbank Studios, June 5, 1980. (MPAA Rating: R). Running time: 102 MINS.
Emmeline . . . . Brooke Shields
Richard . . . . .Christopher Atkins
Paddy . . . . : . . . . .Leo McKern
Arthur . . . . William Daniels
Young Emmeline . . . . .Elva Josephson
Young Richard . . . . Glenn Kohan

"The Blue Lagoon" is a beautifully mounted production, a low-keyed love story stressing the innocent eroticism of Brooke Shields and newcomer Christopher Atkins. Given the media interest in watching Shields grow up, this may be enough for boxoffice success. But audiences may also reject the film as an outrageous cheat.

Following the 1949 version with Jean Simmons and Donald Houston, this is the second adaptation of the 1903 novel by Henry DeVere Stacpoole about two shipwrecked children who grow from childhood in an isolated South Seas paradise.

Given R-rated latitude, producer-director Randal Kleiser takes the pair through puberty and into parenthood with a charming candor that stresses natural, instinctive sexual development without leering at it.

In one touching sequence, for example, Shields is alarmed and terrified at the first sign of her womanly development, yet instinctively makes it a mystery for Atkins, who reacts with a hurt, masculine befuddlement that has separated the sexes forever.

Their romance is enhanced by Nestor Almendros' exquisite photography (and Basil Poledouris' score), as is the stunning beauty of the Fiji island where it was filmed. Working with an underage actress, however, there is only so far that Kleiser can go in his candor, which makes the film oddly unnatural for a story that strives to be so. Much is made, for instance, about the children growing up quite accustomed to seeing each other without clothes. Yet the point is consistently made with a minimum of real nudity (presumably using a double for Shields), and many suggestive camera angles. More disconcertedly, the pair swim and frolic as often with clothes as without, with no apparent point in the story.

Forgiving Kleiser that practical limitation, there is on the other hand less charity for the film's lack of excitement. If the couple faced no real danger and the story was only one of personal development, then no action could be tolerated.

But from almost the very beginning, Kleiser makes constant and threatening allusions to the presence of cannibals in the island paradise — complete with menacing drums in the distant and bloody sacrificial altars. He never passes up a chance to suggest that ultimately this will be a real peril for the young innocents.

It never happens.

Similarly, their ultimate distress at mistakenly drifting back into the open ocean is resolved with a completely anticlimactical rescue. Consequently, there's a big letdown where the uplift should have been.—*Har.*

Bronco Billy
(COLOR)

Clint clix.

Hollywood, June 4.
A Warner Bros. release. Produced by Dennis Hackin and Neal Dobrofsky. Exec producer, Robert Daley. Stars Clint Eastwood. Directed by Clint Eastwood. Screenplay, Dennis Hackin; camera (Deluxe Color), David Worth; editors, Ferris Webster, Joel Cox; sound, Bert Hallberg; art direction, Gene Lourie; associate producer, Fritz Manes; assistant director, Tom Joyner; music, Snuff Garrett. Reviewed at the Samuel Goldwyn Theatre, Beverly Hills, June 4, 1980. (MPAA rating: PG.) Running time: 119 MINS.
Bronco Billy . . . . Clint Eastwood
Antoinette Lily . . . . .Sondra Locke
John Arlington . . . . Geoffrey Lewis
Doc Lynch . . . . Scatman Crothers
Lefty LeBow . . . . Bill McKinney
Leonard James . . . . .Sam Bottoms
Chief Big Eagle . . . . .Dan Vadis
Lorraine Running Water . Sierra Pecheur
Sherrif Dix . . . . Walter Barnes
Dr. Canterbury . . . . .Woodrow Parfrey
Irene Lily . . . . Beverlee McKinsey
Edgar Lipton . . . . William Prince
Mitzi Fritz . . . . .Tessa Richarde
Doris Duke . . . . Tanya Russell

Oh how good it is to have a comedy around for the summer as genuinely funny as "Bronco Billy," which is sophisticated enough and common enough to appeal to a broad audience, perhaps introducing Clint Eastwood to new fans as a comic actor and director, even if he doesn't need them.

In the title role, Eastwood plays an ex-N.J. shoe salesman who has trained himself to live out a fantasy as a sharpshooting, knife-throwing, stunt-riding cowboy, with only a couple of major problems: For one thing, he is only about 90% perfect at his craft; for another, there's no place to practice it except as the leader of a run-down Wild West show touring tank towns and county fairs.

The others in the troupe are also definitive losers of varying talents whom Eastwood has recruited in various places, including prison. (How Eastwood got to prison is one of the loudest laughlines of the picture so won't be revealed here.)

Bronco Billy is in large part a caricature of many of the strong, taciturn western heroes whom Eastwood has played in many other pix and he's obviously having a wonderful time with the satire, never slipping once.

What's more, it's really an interesting character, this man who on the one hand realizes the fable of his existence while, on the other, living it so sincerely. He is far from a fraud in setting himself as an example "to all the little pardners and buckaroos" in the audience, putting on charity shows at orphanages and sternly lecturing one gang of youngsters on the value of going to school and the evil of truancy. Typical of his character, however, the lecture falls on a Saturday.

He is also the only anchor for his travelling, rarely paid performers (all excellently portrayed), Scatman Crothers the ringmaster; Bill McKinney of the one-hand ("I told you that shotgun act would never work," says Eastwood); Sam Bottoms the Army deserter turned rope artist; Dan Vadis the oft-bitten Indian snake dancer and his wife Sierra Pecheur.

Eastwood also has a problem keeping helpers for his gun and knife act, picking up local bimbos along the way and losing them almost as quickly to slight mishaps. In brief appearances, Tessa Richarde and Tanya Russell are both delightful as his terrified assistants.

Along the same highways, however, come Sondra Locke, an arrogant spoiled heiress, and Geoffrey Lewis, delightful as the idiotic husband she has just married only to protect her inheritance. Fed up with Locke's mistreatment, Lewis abandons her without a dime in a motel near Eastwood's tent and she winds up — quite reluctantly — as his helper.

This is the third picture together for Eastwood and Locke and the chemistry is still working as their relationship evolves from initial hostility to romance. She's quite good at both ends of the transformation from despicable to embraceable.

As director, Eastwood gets good performances even from the briefest of bit characters and Walter Barnes, Woodrow Parfrey and Beverlee McKinsey all add to the fun.

To say too much about what these characters are up to, of course, would spoil the enjoyment. But it's well worth finding out. —*Har.*

Koncert Na Konci Leta
(Concert at the End of Summer)
(CZECHOSLOVAK-COLOR)

Cannes, May 23.
A Czechoslovak Film Production, Studio Barrandov, Prague; world rights, Czechoslovensky Filmexport, Prague. Features entire cast. Directed by Frantisek Vlacil. Screenplay, Zdenek Mahler; camera (color), Jiri Marak; sets, Jindrich Goetz; music, Jaromil Burghauser, archives. Reviewed at Cannes Film Festival (Market). May 23, '80. Running time: **102 MINS.**
Cast: Josef Vinklar (Antonin Dvorak). Jana Hlavackova (Anna Dvorakova). Jana Hlavacova (Josefina Kounicova), Svatopluk Benes (Kounic), Vlasta Fabrianova (Eleonora Kounicova), Frantisek Nemec (Kent). Bohus Zahorsky (Heiliberg). Ondrej Pavelka (Suk). Ladislav Bambas (Nedbal), Ondrej Havelka (Fenix).

One of two Czech pix on music and famous personalities (the other is Jiri Krejcik's "Divine Emma," about the opera diva Emma Destinn), Frantisek Vlacil's "Concert at the End of Summer" deals with the life of Antonin Dvorak, the composer matched only by Bedrich Smetana as the leading exponent of Czech music in the 19th century. Dvorak wrote nine symphonies and was equally famous for his Slavonic Dances and Rhapsodies. It's his "Requiem," however, that serves as the film's main theme, a sort of meditation on life and death.

Pic opens with the composer in London (he went nine times to England, twice to America, and often to other European cities): Dvorak drops a concert he is supposed to conduct in the evening and returns home to Czechoslovakia immediately. While on the journey, and with musical tones constantly repeating themselves in his head as a warning (of death?), Dvorak recalls his past, in particular his relationship with two women who inspired and influenced him: the actress Josefina, who married Count Kouni; and her sister Anna, who became the composer's wife.

Helmer Frantisek Vlacil (also known as a talented painter) and scripter Zdenek Mahler (who also wrote the screenplay for "Divine Emma") focused on four weeks following Dvorak's return home from London, intertwining three dreamlike flashbacks to touch on the composer's musical inspiration. On several occasions, Dvorak's "Requiem" plus other musical pieces embellish the story, but on the whole it's a tour-de-force for thesp Josef Vinklar, who fills the role more than adequately of a spiritually troubled individual. Pic's

main drawback is that more of the composer's music could have been used, and less nods to the rigours of an interpretative, documentary-like script.

A natural for Czech film weeks. —*Holl.*

The Stunt Man
(COLOR)

Careful handling a must for unusual look at filmmaking world. Standout perf by Peter O'Toole.

Hollywood, June 4.
A Melvin Simon production. Produced, directed by Richard Rush. Executive producer, Melvin Simon. Stars Peter O'Toole, Steve Railsback, Barbara Hershey. Screenplay, Lawrence B. Marcus, adaptation by Richard Rush, based on novel by Paul Brodeur; camera (Metrocolor), Mario Tosi; editors, Jack Hofstra, Caroline Ferriol; music, Dominic Frontiere; art direction, James Schoppe; set decoration, Richard Spero; costume design, Rosanna Norton; sound, Jim Tanenbaum; associate producer, Paul Lewis; assistant director, Frank Beetson. Reviewed at MGM Studios, Culver City, June 4, 1980. (MPAA Rating: R). Running time: **129 MINS.**
Eli Cross . . . . Peter O'Toole
Cameron . . . . Steve Railsback
Nina Franklin . . . . Barbara Hershey
Sam . . . . Allen Goorwitz
Jake . . . . Alex Rocco
Denise . . . . Sharon Farrell
Raymond Bailey . . . . Adam Roarke
Ace . . . . Philip Bruns
Chuck Barton . . . . Chuck Bail

Strikingly well-made and considerably ambitious, "The Stunt Man" is one of the most unusual domestic pictures to come along in some time, delivering goods quite different than its title might suggest. Film for some reason has been languishing on the shelf for a couple of years and is still without a distributor, although exec producer Melvin Simon will try a test engagement in Seattle starting June 27. In the right hands, pic could find a wider audience than the cult following it is certain to attract.

A number of actors stack the cards against standard commercial acceptability from the outset: world-of-filmmaking setting, intentionally convoluted narrative, self-conscious "truth vs. illusion" theme, and lack of strong b.o. names.

However, from the opening virtuoso scene, helmer Richard Rush puts the audience on its toes and, through a dazzling display of kinetic direction which he manages to sustain, with only a couple of lapses, for more than two hours, fascinates with an impressive cinematic juggling act.

Off-beat tale, based on Paul Brodeur's 1970 novel, has Vietnam vet Steve Railsback on the lam and accepting refuge from both benevolent and sinister film director Pe-

ter O'Toole, who puts the fugitive through some highly dangerous paces as a stunt man while shielding him from the cops.

His hair died blond to match the actor for whom he is doubling and immediately beholden to his director, Railsback becomes totally immersed in the process of putting fiction on film, an event which Rush paints in bold, swift strokes, emphasizing the trickery, egos and power trips of insular world's habitues.

As he gets caught up in the swirl, Railsback becomes suspicious of his collaborators' motives and intentions, going so far as to imagine that O'Toole intends to actually kill him in film's climactic stunt. As story is basically told from Railsback's p.o.v., odd mood of somewhat whimsical paranoia develops into state of genuine tension by the finale.

Precise fragmentation of Lawrence B. Marcus' screenplay recalls same writer's work on "Petulia," as does the prevailing tone of disenchanted romanticism. Marcus and Rush are least successful in making full credible the relationship between Railsback and film-within-the-film star Barbara Hershey, with his disillusionment upon discovering that she once had a fling with O'Toole playing as particularly unconvincing. Most surprising, actually, is that latter would have been interested in her, as subtext and subtle clues hint that director character probably prefers guys to gals.

For his part, O'Toole is excellent in his best, cleanest performance in years. Commanding as always, he smashingly delineates an omnipotent, godlike type whose total control over those around him makes him seem almost unreal, which is very much in accord with the point of the film.

Railsback is forceful, confused and pliable by turns as a mere piece of driftwood caught up in a whirlpool. Hershey, despite a certain lack of visible motivations, is engagingly flakey and radiant at the same time. Supporting turns, notably those by Allen Goorwitz as a writer resigned to being dominated by O'Toole, Alex Rocco as a threatening sheriff and Chuck Bail as a senior stunt expert, are all on target.

Technical work is superlative, from Mario Tosi's ravishing lensing and Jack Hofstra and Caroline Ferriol's split-second editing to Dominic Frontiere's rich score and the elaborate helicopter, crane and stunt work by many worthy hands.—*Cart.*

Roadie
(COLOR)

Meat Loaf is a pleasure in wide-eyed look at rock scene.

Hollywood, June 6.
A United Artists release of an Alive Enterprises/Vivant production. Produced by Carolyn Pfeiffer. Directed by Alan Rudolph. Features entire cast. Executive producer, Zalman King. Screenplay, Big Boy Medlin, Michael Ventura, based on story by Medlin, Ventura, King, Rudolph; camera (Technicolor), David Myers; coeditor, Tom Walls; supervising editor, Carol Littleton; music, Craig Hundley; production design, Paul Peters; set decoration, Richard Friedman; costumes, Jered Edd Grenn, Gail Bixby; sound (Dolby), Richard Goodman; associate producer, John E. Pommer; assistant director, Ed Ledding. Reviewed at MGM Studios, Culver City, June 6, 1980. (MPAA Rating: PG.) Running time: 105 MINS.
Travis W. Redfish . . . . Meat Loaf
Lola Bouilliabase . . . . Kaki Hunter
Corpus C. Redfish . . . . Art Carney
B.B. Muldoon . . . . Gailard Sartain
Mohammed Johnson . . . . . . Don Cornelius
Alice Poo . . . . Rhonda Bates
Ace . . . . Joe Spano
George . . . . Richard Marion
Bird . . . . Sonny Davis
As themselves: Alice Cooper, Blondie (Deborah Harry, Chris Stein, Clem Burke, Jimmy Destri, Nigel Harrison, Frank Infante), Roy Orbison, Hank Williams Jr., Merle Kilgore, Ramblin' Jack Elliot, Ray Benson, Sheryl Cooper, Alvin Crow.

A sort of "Pilgrim's Progress" through the crazy world of rock 'n' roll, "Roadie" makes for a goofy good time. High-spirited pic also marks a turn towards the commercial mainstream for helmer Alan Rudolph, working here for the first time outside the Robert Altman stable. Although perhaps too unassuming to become a major b.o. entry, it should please enough teens and music fans to perform solidly during the summer months.

This particular life's parade is seen through the eyes of rotund pop-star Meat Loaf, who plays an innocent Texas boy unwittingly recruited as a driver-gofer-handyman, or roadie, for a touring band. What leads him astray at first is self-styled groupie Kaki Hunter, unique among her ranks by virtue of her status as a virgin who's saving herself for Alice Cooper. Meat Loaf is such a dope that he thinks Alice is one of "Charlie's Angels," but Kaki puts up with him anyway, just as he tolerates her jabbering about the glories of rockdom.

Meat, or Loaf, leads as charmed a life as Dorothy in "The Wizard Of Oz" and encounters just as many weird characters along the road to his discovery that there's no place like home. Lordly promotor Mohammed Johnson, as slickly embodied by "Soul Train" host Don Cornelius, decides Meat has the knack of solving any problem that crops up on tour, so the ample lad is quickly catapulted into orbit with the likes of Blondie and Alice Cooper, who similarly appreciate his talents.

Since p.o.v. is that of a wide-eyed innocent, view of the hairy rock world is unusually benign and prevailing tone is rolicking and whimsical. Even more unusual, however, is the gentle visual stylization. Most contempo music pix featuring live acts take a documentary tack, but Rudolph, whose "Welcome To L.A." and "Remember My Name" were nothing if not existentially abstracted, has eschewed the expected in favor of a pleasingly subjective approach, which both heightens the irreality and conveys the bemused distance from which Meat Loaf views the proceedings.

Script by journalists Big Boy Medlin and Michael Ventura is full of resonant colloquialisms and knows of what it speaks. Cooper, Deborah Harry, Roy Orbison and Hank Williams Jr. Step off the stage to blend effortlessly with the actors, all of whom perform with plenty of energy.

Meat Loaf is rarely offscreen and is fortunately a highly engaging personality. Some may be disappointed that he doesn't perform musically in this context, but he's an unusual type to topline in a feature and a constant pleasure to watch. Newcomer Hunter is believable, if at times intentionally shrill, as the mixed-up camp follower, while Art Carney fills in as Meat Loaf's off-center father, playing him, like a latter-day Lionel Barrymore, almost entirely confined to his chair.

Film is very smooth technically, with David Myers' lensing looking outstanding and the Dolby sound work playing beautifully. Soundtrack album should have potential, as many artists not actually seen are heard in background. —*Cart.*

Don't Go In The House
(COLOR)

Gruesome exploitationer.

Film Ventures Int. release of a Turbine Films production. Produced by Ellen Hammill. Directed by Joseph Ellison; screenplay, Ellison, Hammill, Joseph Masefield; camera (Deluxe), Oliver Wood; editor, Jane Kurson; music, Richard Einhorn. Remaining credits not available. Reviewed at Cinerama Theatre, N.Y., June 6, '80. (MPAA rating: R). Running time: 82 MINS.
Cast: Dan Grimaldi, Robert Osth, Ruth Dardick.

Through the grammatically skewered title of this lowbudget horror entry implies a stern warning to recently housebroken poodles, it's actually meant to keep trusting young women out of reach of the film's hero, a vengeance-prone victim of child abuse with a penchant for fire. After a quick spurt of summer business, exhibitors can expect audiences to shun their houses as well.

Plotline revolves around a mother-dominated professional incinerator employee (Dan Grimaldi) whose mommy used to punish him by holding his arms over the stove. When she dies, he gets his own back by burning her corpse to a crisp, dressing it in finery, and wandering off to lure a half dozen other females to his specially equipped firing room.

Though the pic ostensibly carries an anti-child abuse message (it ends with Grimaldi's vengeful "voices" urging another beaten boy to eventual revenge) sole motivation is to exploit the gruesomely explicit carnage and femme nudity for all they're worth. Though technically more polished than many of its ilk, the film winds up as another venture whose cash-flow depends not on quality, but on the strength of its ad campaign and competing product. —*Step.*

Up The Academy
(COLOR)

Play hookey from this one.

Hollywood, June 7.
Warner Bros. release of a Marvin Worth/Danton Rissner Production. Produced by Worth and Rissner. Directed by Robert Downey. Features entire cast. Exec producer, Bernie Brillstein. Screenplay, Tom Patchett, Jay Tarses; camera (Technicolor), Harry Stradling; editor, Bud Molin; music, Jody Taylor Worth; production design, Peter Wooley; set decoration, Mary Swanson; sound, Marty Bolger; assistant director, James J. Quinn. Reviewed at the AVCO Center Cinema, Westwood, Calif., June 7, 1980. (MPAA rating R.) Running time: 96 MINS.
Major . . . . Ron Liebman
Ike . . . . Wendell Brown
Hash . : . . . . Tom Citera
Oliver . . . . J. Hutchinson
Chooch . . . . Ralph Macchio
Ververgaert . . . . Harry Teinowitz
Sisson . . . . Tom Poston
Commandant Caseway . . . . Ian Wolfe
Candy . . . . Stacy Nelkin
Candy . . . . Barbara Bach
Keck . . . . Leonard Frey
Coach . . . . Antonio Vargas

Although Ron Liebman has surely earned a free course in good taste for starring in a film as offensive and poorly done as "Up The Academy," he deserves some praise for managing to not have his name in the credits and advertising. This Mad Magazine presentation for Warner Bros. release has retained some of the irreverence of the veteran humor publication without any of the wit and inventiveness the magazine is known for. Adolescent comedies have shown some boxoffice muscle in the past, but film is so devoid of entertainment value that it should be in and out of theatres in short order.

The joyfully hideous Alfred E. Neuman character is briefly utilized in pic's opening and closing sequences but that's about the only thing writers Tom Patchett and Jay Tarses have done right here. What they've done wrong is to take an already tired premise, a group of dumb adolescents wreaking havoc in a mythical school, and attempt to build on it with a combination of tired sexual innuendo and bathroom jokes.

The band of teens, each from various ethnic groups, is being victimized by Liebman's moronically sadistic military school major. Film shows no shame in capitalizing on almost every cultural, social and physical stereotype around which should manage to alienate, not amuse, even the most liberal. More importantly, none of the barbs are even funny.

Robert Downey has directed this childish effort with a decided lack of flair although new wave soundtrack, supervised by Jody Taylor Worth, bears a listening. Too bad it serves as a background to so little.

Wendell Brown, Tom Citera, J. Hutchinson, Ralph Macchio and Harry Teinowitz, the young actors linning various characters sentenced to the fictional military school, never have a chance against the inane script. Ditto better known Barbara Bach, Leonard Frey and Tom Poston, latter in a particularly tasteless portrayal of a limp-wristed dance instructor. Ditto the film audience. —*Berg.*

The Last Flight Of Noah's Ark
(COLOR)

Two by two, they creepeth upon the screen.

Hollywood, May 30.
A Buena Vista release. Produced by Ron Miller. Directed by Charles Jarrot. Features entire cast. Screenplay, Steven W. Carabatsos, Sandy Glass, George Arthur Bloom, based on story by Ernest K. Gann; camera (Technicolor), Charles F. Wheeler; editor, Gordon D. Brenner; sound, Henry A. Maffett; coproducer, Jan Williams; art direction, John B. Mansbridge; production design, Preston Ames; special effects, Art Cruickshank, Eustace Lycett, Danny Lee; assistant director, Richard Learman; music, Maurice Jarre. Reviewed at Samuel Goldwyn Theatre, Beverly Hills, May 30, 1980. (MPAA Rating: G.) Running time: 97 MINS.
Noah Dugan . . . . Elliott Gould
Bernadette Lafleur . . . . Genevieve Bujold
Bobby . . . . Ricky Schroder
Julie . . . . Tammy Lauren
Stoney . . . . Vincent Gardenia
Cleveland . . . . John Fujioka
Hiro . . . . Yuki Shimoda
Coslough . . . . John P. Ryan
Benchley . . . . Dana Elcar

"The Last Flight of Noah's Ark" is a family picture teaching fundamental values, mainly that every human being should be willing to risk their life for an animal, or even a chicken if the chance arises. Presumably, the normal number of Disney families will turn out to hear the message.

In case the parents don't heed the word, however, the picture stresses a subsidiary hint for the little ones: If you don't get your way, whine and cry a lot and maybe the old folks will give in.

Full responsibility for this lesson is given to little Ricky Schroder, who managed to fill the screen with tears over just one horse in "The Champ." This time he has a B-29 full of critters to cry over and doesn't waste a single opportunity.

The animals are aboard the plane because missionary Genevieve Bujold desperately wants to airlift them to a needy island in the South Pacific. On the lam from loan-sharks, grizzled Elliott Gould agrees to fly the old crate, neither knowing that Schroder and cute Tammy Lauren have stolen aboard at the last moment to make sure the animals are well cared for.

The plane flies off course and crashes on a remote island, watched over by two Japanese soldiers, John Fujioka and Yuki Shimoda, who don't know World War II is over. After some slapstick encounters, East and West make peace and team up to get off the island.

Despite a noticeable lack of lathes and drill presses, they manage to convert the airplane into a sailboat. There is, to be sure, some doubt in Gould's mind about how much weight this makeshift Queen Mary can carry. So he wants to leave the animals behind.

But Schroder and Lauren throw a tantrum and call him a bad man, forcing him to relent and take the animals aboard. (Philosophically speaking, it's interesting that the animals are never asked if they would prefer to leave this idyllic island with food and room aplenty to sail off to possible death with the humans. But since this is not a Disney cartoon, they couldn't answer anyway.)

Once afloat, Schroder causes more problems until he finally falls into the ocean because he disobeyed the elders' orders. The big shark almost eats him, but Gould pulls him out just in time and for some odd reason, Schroder does not cry over the shark.

More perils are faced and finally Schroder's pet bull gets bad sick, causing the boy to burst into tears again and there's a tense discussion of whether the bull must be shot. But just in time, the Coast Guard arrives; the bull gets well and Gould and Bujold get married.

Charles Jarrot directs this fribble as if it might all have some purpose and Gould and Bujold largely go along with it but seemingly caugious at all time that none of the animals step on their feet. Or their careers. —Har.

Ran & Ran
(Run & Run)
(JAPANESE-COLOR)

Tokyo, May 25.
A Fuji Films release. Produced by Hisao Masuda. Directed by Junzen Nemoto. Features entire cast. No writing credits. Camera (color), Kitsuru Kuroyanagi; sound, Takashi Miyamoto; editor, Koichi Atami; musical director, Eikichi Yazawa. Reviewed at Milanoza, Tokyo, May 20, 1980. Running time: **98 MINS.**

Eikichi Yazawa is perhaps Japan's one pop phenomenon. A genuine superstar, the 30-year-old native of Hiroshima has, since embarking on a solo career in '75, released eight top-selling LPs and given scores of concerts for which baseball stadiums have proved too small to accommodate his fans. He never performs on television and hardly needs too. In 1978, he was, per the National Tax Agency, Japan's top money-earning entertainer, dropping, in '79, to the number two position.

Anyone hoping for insights into the whys and wherefores of the Yazawa phenomenon won't find them in "Run & Run," a celluloid sermon to the converted. For fans only, who neither need nor ask for edification.

As superficial and imperfect as this feature is, it manages to convey a little of what Yazawa has that turns the hordes on. While the range of his vocals is limited, their raspily emotive quality is not. And if Japan is a speed culture, then Yazawa, with his staccato, machine gun bursts of energy, is its truly representative performer.

For those who already know who Yazawa is, "Run & Run" is the film to run & run to; for those who'd like to know more about him, it's a film to run & run away from. —Bail.

Le Guignolo
(The Guignolo)
(FRENCH-COLOR)

Paris, April 28.
A Gaumont-Cerito Rene Chateau release of a Gaumont — Cerito Films production. Produced by Alain Poire. Stars Jean-Paul Belmondo. Directed by Georges Lautner. Screenplay, Jean Herman and Michel Audiard; camera (color), Henri Decae; music, Philippe Sarde. No other credits available. Reviewed at the Gaumont Ambassade Theatre, Paris, April 25, 1980. Running time: **105 MINS.**
With: Jean-Paul Belmondo, Michel Galabru, Georges Geret, Michel Beaune, Charles Gerard, Carla Romanelli, Mirella D'Angelo.

In his newest comedy-action vehicle, Jean-Paul Belmondo again radiates the nonchalant charm, sexual magnetism and unsimulated derring-do that have endeared him to millions. No surprise then that "Le Guignolo" is currently breaking b.o. records on its home territory.

In their newest collaboration with the star, scripter Michel Audiard and director Georges Lautner again display the same maddening indifference to their functions that characterized Belmondo's previous hit "Cop or Hood" — which should limit this product too to compulsive consumers of Bebel (as the star is affectionately known locally).

The tired tale casts Belmondo as a swindler who joshes his way through a poorly-knotted series of intrigues involving con jobs and the pursuit of a missing microfilm that has wound up in his possession. There are the usual hordes of horizontally-disposed beauties and gun-wielding uglies (many of whom are put away with a kick to the groin, which the makers of this film seem to find a rich source of merriment). Venice, in all its touristy splendor, provides the frame for most of the mischief.

As is expected of him, Bebel stunts for himself. His numbers here include driving a speedboat out of the canal and crashing it through the facade of a luxury hotel (he's checking in); and soaring high over Venice clutching a trapeze suspended from a helicopter. Pretty dangerous. And pretty dull, since they remain just stunts and lack any real context of situation and tension.

With Belmondo becoming something of a national institution will the Eiffel Tower one day be replaced by the Tower of Bebel?
—Len.

Cloud Dancer
(COLOR)

Dizzying pic with cloudy outlook

Hollywood, May 30.
Blossom Pictures release of a Melvin Simon Production. Produced and directed by Barry Brown. Features entire cast. Exec producer, Melvin Simon. Screenplay, William Goodhart, based on a story by Brown; Daniel Tamkus and Goodhart; camera (MGM Color), Travers Hill; editor, Marshall Borden; sound, Michael Evje; technical advisor and chief pilot, Tom Poberezny; flying sequences conceived and created by Brown; music, Fred Karlin; assistant director, Don Klune. Reviewed at the Adikoff screening Room, Beverly Hills, May 30, 1980. (MPAA Rating: PG). Running time: **108 MINS.**
Bradley Randolph .... David Carradine
Helen St. Clair .... Jennifer O'Neill
Tom Loomis .... Joseph Bottoms
Cindy .... Colleen Camp
Ozzie Randolph .... Albert Salmi
Jean Randolph .... Salome Jens
Edith Randolph .....Arnette Jens Zerbe
Dr. Putnam ....Norman Alden
Caroline Sheldon ...... Nina Van Pallandt

Picked up by indie distrib Blossom Pictures almost two years after its completion for Melvin Simon Productions, Barry Brown's "Cloud Dancer" has just begun to open in selected markets across the country. One of Simon's first forays into film financing in 1977, picture is essentially the personal vision of aerobatic enthusiast Brown, who produced, directed, cowrote the story and even created the flying sequences. Tale concerning life changes of a champion stunt flier at times emerges as touching but overemphasis on the sport severely diminishes audiences for what is ultimately a well-intentioned, but slow-moving effort. B.o. prospects are dubious.

David Carradine limns his usual anti-hero in the form of an aerobatic expert who selfishly and successfully pursues his sport to the exclusion of those who care about him. Although he uses his own set of morales in order to justify some not so nice behavior, Carradine's devotion to his retarded brother and time spent straightening out drug-dealing apprentice flier Joseph Bottoms make him an appealing character.

Problems arise when pic explores his relationship with writer/photog Jennifer O'Neill, who wanders back into his life after having their child. Carradine doesn't know about the tyke and O'Neill doesn't have the nerve to tell him. Because the couple's love relationship is never fully established, most of their scenes take on a contrived feeling that lingers throughout the picture.

This leaves the view to focus on Carradine's flying adventures, which should prove quite dizzying to the uninitiated. Brown clearly is enamored of the sport, which is fine, but it is doubtful whether many others will take pleasure in seeing Carradine and his cohorts ceaselessly circling through the sky with almost no end in sight.

Travers Hill has managed to capture some beautiful scenery with the camera, particularly in the opening, and Fred Karlin's music provides a lovely mood. Many of the stunts Brown has conceived appear daring but his love of flying does not serve him well as a director. As Editor Marshall Borden seems to have responsibility of condensing the material and providing a balance between the sport and the plot line. Borden, un-

doubtedly under some guidance from Brown, wrongly opts to snip the story instead of the air show.
—*Berg.*

Clan of the White Lotus
(HONG KONG-COLOR)

Bangkok, May 22.
A Shaw Bros. production and release. Produced by Run Run Shaw. Executive producer, Mona Fong. Directed by Lo Lieh. Features entire cast. Screenplay, Wong Tien; camera (color), Ao Chin-chin; editors, Chiang Hsing-lung and Li Yin-hoi; music, Eddie Wang; art direction, Johnson Tasao; martial arts instructor, Liu Chia-liang; make-up, Wu Hsu-ching. Reviewed at Warner theatre, Bangkok, May 22, '80. Running time: **95 MINS.**
Hung Wen-ting . . . . Liu Chia-hui
Abbot of White Lotus . . . . Lo Lieh
Piao's Wife . . . . Hui Ying-hung
Kao Chin-chung . . . . Huang Lung-wei
Hu Nai-cheng . . . . Lin Hui-huang
Piao . . . . Ching Chu
Ching Miao . . . . Li Bai-hsiang

Most Asian film stars who turn to film directing combined with a starring role play the good guy. It's quite a change when a director-star plays the villain instead, as Lo Lieh does in Shaw's "Clan of the White Lotus." Perhaps that's because Lo Lieh is one of the most in-demand baddies of Chinese cinema.

Main emphasis is Liu Chia-hui's search for a fighting technique to vanquish Lo Lieh, aged for his role in what appears as a terrific make-up job. Much of the interest is not on the hero Liu's physical prowess, but rather on just how invincible the old man supposedly is.

Liu's long and arduous training period offers Lo Lieh more opportunity for directing alone rather than directing and acting at the same time. Still, Lo Lieh's role is easily the more engrossing and complex one. All the tedious nonsense about weeding out supporting baddies, so much a part of other pix in this genre, is dropped.

Initially, the hero must learn embroidery, to develop a subtle form of attack which, understandably enough, is taught to him by a woman. Then, he needs another vital technique, and the piece de resistance comes when the hero discovers how to employ acupuncture in a deadly manner. The climax shows the hero plucking scores of needles from his braided long hair and sticking them all over his opponent, thus making the latter look like a human procupine.

The main setting is a spacious and ornate Chinese temple, complete with a large swimming pool. Spectacular backgrounds are shunned. Eddie Wang's score consists of pleasantly orchestrated western music rather than traditional Chinese melodies. While that may seem strange in a Chinese period pic, it's probably the only way to call some attention to the background music. Ordinarily, the sound effects of mortal combat are all the majority of viewers hear or expect to hear. —*Cano.*

Zo Monogatari
(Elephant Story)
(JAPANESE-DOCU-COLOR)

Tokyo, May 20.
A Toho-Towa release of a Kurahara Production. General supervision by Koreyoshi Kurahara. Directed by Koretsugu Kurahara and Seido Hino. Narrative script by Jinichi Mimura; camera, Yoshio Mamiya, Masao Tochizawa and Sadanori Shibata; editor, Akira Suzuki; music, Makato Kawaguchi; theme song, Ryudo Uzaki; lyrics, Yoko Aki; narration, Eiji Okada. Reviewed at the Nichigeki, Tokyo, May 11, 1980. Running time: **112 MINS.**

Confronting those who would make a feature-length documentary about elephants are certain inherent dramatic problems, problems which those who did make "Zo Monogatari" failed to deal with entirely satisfactorily.

First of all, the elephant is a peaceful animal whose only natural enemies are man and disease. Thus, the possibility of conflict is fairly well eliminated. Indeed, to quote wildlife expert Roger Caras, this magnificent beast "confines its attention to herd behavior, migrations, foraging and seeking water," actions which, whatever else you may say about them, are not particularly cinematic.

Directors Koretsugu Kurahara and Seido Hino, under the "general supervision" of Koreyoshi Kurahara, could easily have compensated for their subject's dramatic limitations by editing the 1,000,000 feet of film they shot over a seven-year period to a more manageable length.

("The Hellstrom Chronicle," to cite an example deserving of emulation, deals informatively and entertainingly with a seemingly infinite variety of insects in but 90 minutes).

Instead the filmmakers chose to try and distract attention from these limitations with extraneous, putatively more interesting material that serves only to convince the viewer that the 112-minuted film will go on for as long as elephants are mistakenly assumed to live. Even worse, much of the non-pachydermal footage included only serves to perpetuate animal kingdom myths — i.e., the lion, in actuality a snoozer lacking the stamina and speed of its prey, is presented as an ever-vigilant, swift monarch.

Considering that it deals with an animal whose life style is orderly in the extreme, the film is a jumble, only beginning to take shape about thirty minutes after it begins. Granted that the camera crew worked under less than ideal conditions, the cinematography is often disappointingly pedestrian, characterized by jerky overhead shots and a reliance on seemingly countless shots of bee-yoo-di-ful African sunsets.

While it is praiseworthy that few attempts have been made to prettify nature, surely scenes of man-initiated carnage and elephantine sex are not suitable for the children to whom distributor Toho-Towa is making such a concerted pitch.

The musical score is an eclectic hodgepodge, alternating what sound like Tomita out-takes with authentic tribal chants, a direct lift from "Baby Elephant Walk" and the pic's theme song, sung in Japanese, the chorus in English and featuring Sinatra-like scatty do-dos. —*Bail.*

Panische Zeiten
(Panic Times)
(WEST GERMAN-COLOR)

Cannes, May 12.
A Udo Lindenberg Production in collaboration with Amazonas Film, Roba Music, and Regina Ziegler Film Production; world rights, Filmverlag der Autoren, Munich. Stars Udo Lindenberg. Directed by Udo Lindenberg, in collaboration with Peter Fratzscher. Screenplay, Lindenberg, Kalle Freynik; idea, Horst Koenigstein, Kalle Freynik, Lindenberg; camera (color), Bernd Heinl; music, Udo Lindenberg; editing, Helga Borsche; sets, Toni Luedi; production manager, Michael Wiedemann. Reviewed at Cannes Film Festival (Market), May 12, '80. Running time: **101 MINS.**
Cast: Udo Lindenberg, Leata Galloway, Walter Kohut, Vera Tschechova, Felix Scholtz, Klaus Kauroff, Otto Wanz, Hark Bohm, Beate Jensen, Eddie Constantine, Rudolf Beiswanger, Peter Ahrweiler, Fritz Rau, Heinz Domez, Werner Boehm, Willi Hermann, Renate Schubert, Egon Mueller, Juergen Baumgarten, Karl Dall, Ingeborg Thomsen, Werner Veigel.

A fun film about Hamburg's original pop singer, Udo Lindenberg (who made "Uncle Poe's Carnegie Hall" a national institution back in spring 1973 when he first appeared there), "Panic Times" is directed by Lindenberg, based on his own script plus freely improvised dialog, uses his music plus concert performances, and stars himself in a double-roll together with his friends, such as helmer Hark Bohm and cabaretist Karl Dall. All in all, it sounds like an ego trip — save that Lindenberg is a very original talent.

The story leans heavily on Yank pix of the Thirties for effects, particularly the Bogart private-eye genre. A famous concert singer, Lindenberg, is kidnapped under the eyes of fumbling bodyguards (a midget and two heavies) by a scheming secret government agent who feels his style of pop music is harmful to the country — but something could be saved for humanity if Udo recants his ways and becomes a straight-arrow singer. Once the kidnapping takes place, guess who's on the trail? Private-eye Lindenberg.

The police, naturally, stay out of the affair, citing the free advertising a kidnapping can get for a pop-singer, while the manager dutifully wrings his hands in anticipation of the worst. Detective Udo, meanwhile, confers with his friend, Lemmy Caution (Eddie Constantine), on clues to follow, which lead him through all the backstreets of waterfront Hamburg: the dives, Herbert Street (with the girls in the windows), the night clubs, even a tv-talkshow on "National Security" with leading politicians, one of whom is the culprit. His three side-kicks are always in attendance, adding to the gags.

As for pop-singer Udo, he has to be spirited out of the country, but leaps from a plane over the North Sea with a parachute to land in the water and swim to a lighthouse, where "environmentalists" are erecting an energy-powered defense plant. Due to a shortcircuit in the plant's cable wiring, Udo gives an oration on what he would do if elected Chancellor; his message goes out on nation-wide broadcasting — and he gets elected Chancellor! All his friends, in the end, are appointed to jobs in the cabinet.

A comedy from Germany, rare enough — this one, on occasion, a howler. Credits, particularly lensing and tricks, are plusses. "Panic Times" should at least be a b.o. winner in Hamburg. —*Holl.*

Un homme en fuite
(A Man on the Run)
(SWISS-FRENCH-COLOR)

Zurich, May 29.
Citel Films Distribution SA Geneva release of a Video Programs Geneva-SSR Geneva-Action Films SA Paris co-production. Directed by Simon Edelstein. Written by Edelstein, in collaboration with Anita Peyrot, Xavier Torre and Gy de Belleval. Features entire cast. Camera (color), Hans Liechti; editor, Martine Barraque; music, Pierre Jansen; executive producer, Claude Richardet. Reviewed at the Studio Nord-Sued, Zurich, May 29, '80. Running time: **91 MINS.**
Cast: Roger Jendly, Malene Sveinbjornsson, Florence Giorgetti, Jaroslav Vizner, Maurice Aufair.

Simon Edelstein comes from the same French-speaking region of Switzerland as Alain Tanner, Claude Goretta and Michel Soutter. His first feature film, "Les Vilaines Manieres" (The Awful Manners), made seven years ago, remained practically unnoticed except at some festivals.

"Un homme en fuite" (A Man on the Run), his second film, is a proof of talent, no more, no less. Sensitive treatment of a basically vapid, stagnant script, atmospheric, though often sombre camerawork by Hans Liechti and acceptable performances are among the assets. But the picture's climate and style are so vague as to border on indifference, and characterizations are clearly underdeveloped.

A drifting painter is falsely accused of murder and released for lack of proof. But he continues to be shadowed as he is still being suspected. He meets a 12-year-old girl who has seen him the night of the murder and could prove his innocence. She, too, is on the run, having left home for fear of her father. They develop a half-innocuous, half-sexual relationship until she leaves him when he sleeps with a woman. He continues his escape alone.

Roger Jendly as the painter and Malene Sveinbjornsson as the precocious child-woman would be just right with a little more help from a more incisive script and sharper direction. —*Mezo.*

Pochti Lyubovna Istorya
(Almost A Love Story)
(BULGARIA-COLOR)

Cannes, May 22.
A Bulgarofilm Production, Suvrremenik Film Group, Sofia; world rights, Bulgarofilm, Sofia. Features entire cast. Directed by Eduard Zahariev. Screenplay, Zahariev, Georgi Danailov, Georgi Mishev; camera (color), Georgi Nikolov; sets, Peter Goranov; music, Mitko Sterev. Reviewed at Cannes Film Festival (Market), May 22, '80. Running time: 90 MINS.
Cast: Marianna Dimitrova (Pavlina), Yavor Spassov (Vlado), Grigor Vachkov (the Father).

Back in 1976, at the November Tehran Film Festival, Bulgarian thesps Marianna Dimitrova and Grigor Vachkov garnered kudos for their costarring performances in Eduard Zahariev's ''Manly Times,'' a tale of the mountains penned by Nikolai Haitov that dealt with a kidnapping of a bride by a rugged, soft-hearted brigand. Now they're back again in Zahariev's ''Almost A Love Story'' as opponents in a kind of Romeo-and-Juliet story.

Billed as a psychological drama, pic deals with a working girl in a cannery who falls in love with the factory director's son, whom the father wants to go to the university and make something out of himself. The father even pays his hired help to kidnap the girl after a lovers' meeting and take her home to her own parents in a distant village, but the stubborn girl is back again to prove she can't be pushed around easily. Then the potential father-in-law tries to bribe her, which doesn't

work either, and finally he hopes she will simply listen to his reasons for preferring that his son marry a city-girl. When everything else fails, he fires her — but personal friends at the factory rise up in protest to protect her.

The twist is that the son isn't mature enough to know what's going on about him. When he attempts to bring the girl into his own circle of better educated friends, the passion begins to cool — and the scene is set for a tragic, sentimental ending.

Credits are top grade, but story starts to go downhill about the middle when things become a bit too predictable. Zahariev has made better, but the traces of a fine storyteller are there just the same. A natural for Bulgarian Film Weeks. —*Holl.*

Hog Wild
(CANADIAN-COLOR)

Chicago, June 6.
Avco Embassy Pictures release of a Filmplan International production. Features entire cast. Executive producers, Pierre David, Victor Solnicki, Stephen Miller. Produced by Claude Heroux. Directed by Les Rose. Screenplay, Andrew Peter Marin based on an original concept by Victor Solnicki, Stephen Miller; camera (color), Rene Verzier; art director, Carol Spier; editor, Dominique Boisvert; asst. director, John Fretz; sound, Don Cohen. Reviewed at Ford City Theatre, Chicago, June 6, 1980. (MPAA Rating — PG). Running time: 97 MINS.
Tim.................... Michael Biehn
Angie .... Patti D'Arbanville
Bull ....Tony Rosato
Bean .... Angelo Rizacos
Shadow .... Martin Doyle
Chrome .... Matt Craven
Lead ....Matt Birman-Feldman
Indian ....Claude Philippe
Veel ....Thomas C. Kovacs
Tina ....Jacoba Knaapan
Pete .... Michael Zelniker
Brenda...................Karen Stephen
Gil .... Jack Blum
Sarah .... Stephanie Miller
Vern .... Keith Knight
Polly .... Mitch Martin
Stiff .... Robin McCulloch

As summer exploitation fluff, this Canada-originated pic — pitting bikers against highschoolers against a comedic backdrop — ranks towards the bottom of the barrel. A largely inept stab at goofball humor, ''Hog Wild'' may have modest potential in ozoners and less selective hardtops hungry for filler, but that's about it.

Produced by Claude Heroux — with some Canadian Film Development Board funding — pic has several strikes against it. It expects its principal characters, a band of obnoxious, Hells Angels-style bikers, to be menacing, cruel and funny at the same time. As depicted, the cyclists are none of the above.

Pic, as scripted by Andrew Peter Martin, is confusingly episodic

thus precluding any chance for even minimal character development, which could have enhanced yock possibilities. As directed by Les Rose, the cast of little-knowns seems incapable of stamping individual identities on their roles.

This is the kind of pic in which the actors appear to having more funs with their antics than the audience probably will. Tony Rosato, an actor with various Second City troupes in Canada, tries hard to lend a comic edge to his part as the sinister but finally likable bike gang leader.

Rosato is a partly, extremely-limited performer who isn't helped any by the director and scripter's insistence that he mumble — literally — rather than speak his lines. Given the low quality of Marin's script, Rosata may have had the last laugh after all. The audience certainly doesn't.

Michael Biehn plays a headstrong highschooler who fights back, and Patti D'Arbanville plays his girl. They, like most of the cast portraying youths, are much too old for their parts — they barely look young enough to play collegians.

Production values are chintzy—pic was lensed entirely in the Montreal area — and even a climactic motorcycle race is a yarner. —*Sege.*

Ot Nishto-Neshto
(Something Out Of Nothing)
(BULGARIAN-COLOR)

Cannes, May 21.
A Bulgarofilm Production, Hemus Film Group, Sofia; world rights, Bulgarofilm, Sofia. Features entire cast. Directed by Nikola Roudarov. Screenplay, Nikolai Nikiforov; camera (color), Georgi Georgiev; sets, Vladimir Lekarski; music, Boris Karadimchev. Reviewed at Cannes Film Festival (Market), May 21, '80. Running time: 90 MINS.
Cast: Anetta Sotirova (Veneta), Stefan Danailov (Pancho), Assen Angelov (Tashev).

Light comedy dealing with town mores and misunderstandings, Nikolai Roudarov's ''Something Out Of Nothing'' is about a tv-personality who happens into a small village in the country to visit a friend. The reporter is recognized immediately wherever he goes, a discomfort added to by the fact that his boyhood chum is not at home — so he has to stay overnight. This makes the wife nervous, for what will the neighbors say.

Then, when our hero falls into an open pit in the yard in the middle of the night to answer the call of nature, the wife tries to get him out and falls in herself. The husband, returning home in the morning, finds them together — but country politeness requires him to kill the

family cow to celebrate the occasion of his schoolmate's visit. And so on, from one situation to another common to Yank sitcom tv-series. Comedy team keeps pic afloat. —*Holl.*

Fuori Stagione
(Off Season)
(ITALY-COLOR)

Rome, June 1.
Produced by Gianni Minervini and Antonio Avati for A.M.A. Film productions. Features entire cast. Written and directed by Luciano Manuzzi. Camera (Eastmancolor), Nino Celeste; art director, Laura Ferri; editor, Ugo De Rossi; music, Amedeo Tommasi. Reviewed at Florence Film Festival, May 22, 1980. Running time: 95 MINS.
Nicola .... Nicola Di Pinto
Saura ....Saura Fabbri
Kidnapper ....Ciro Severi
Luigi......................Gigio Morra

What the natives do in a small resort town when the tourists leave is the subject of this imaginative first film by Luciano Manuzzi. But pic is more a flight of fantasy than a sociological study. Shown at the Florence Independent Festival and a contender for this year's Rizzoli prize, "Off Season" may be too offbeat for commercial markets with its peculiar comic-horror tone, though helmer bears watching.

A foolish young couple, Saura and Luigi, are passing through a seasidetown when they are separated by an argument. The boy falls into the hands of an improvised band of local kidnappers, who bungle the job and then accidentally kill him. The girl goes off on a mini-romance with Nicola (a local practical joker) and later accidentally dies. Their bodies are buried regretfully by the parties involved and soon the tourist season starts again.

A strange little film, with Dim and unpleasant characters, with improbable and grotesque events, is animated by black-humored fantasy bordering on farce. Resolutely refusing to make a moral judgment on the incidents in the film (if anything the victims are sleazier than their aggressors), Manuzzi uses his native town as a metaphor for the desolation and emptiness all the characters share. Without past or future, their only goal is to pass the time playing dangerous criminal games, which have no sense even to them. Deaths occur casually; drama is wholly lacking from the film.

Pic was made for $20,000, with a cast of local actors and a technical crew of three, including the director. Technical look reflects tiny budget in lighting, camerawork and editing — a poverty akin to film's theme. Pic subsequently received a much larger assist from A.M.A.

Film Productions in the dubbing stage, enabling Manuzzi to complete "Off Season." —*Yung.*

Maledetti Vi Amero'
(To Love the Damned)
(ITALY-COLOR)

———

Rome, June 1.
A Filmalpha release, produced by the "Jean Vigo" Cooperative. Stars Flavio Bucci. Directed by Marco Tullio Giordana. Screenplay, Tullio Giordana and Vincenzo Caretti. Camera, (color), Giuseppe Pinori; art director and music, Tullio Giordana; editor, Sergio Nuti. Reviewed at Florence Film Festival, May 24, 1980. Running time: 110 MINS.
Svitol .... Flavio Bucci
Commissioner .... Biagio Pelligra
Heroin addict .... Pasquale Zito

———

One of the year's busy festival entrants (Cannes' "Certain Regard," Florence Independents and Rizzoli), "To Love the Damned" is that rare bird of 1980, a political film.

Young hero returns to Italy after five years abroad and looks at the chaos. Marco Tullio Giordana's first helming effort has been warmly greeted by young audiences who identify with characters, but is still untried in the general market. Its virtue of specificity to a particular place and time, Milan today, may limit exportability, though style is innovative and resh enough to jump language barriers into foreign markets.

Project failed to get producer backing but pic's script interested popular actor Flavio Bucci, whose clumsy and slightly comical presence dominates the film in the role of the disillusioned political activist Svitol. After a long period of emigration in South America, Svitol returns to Italy to find the country radically changed. His old friends in the "movement" have become businessmen, used clothes dealers, drug addicts — in the political climate of fear, retreat and confusion provoked by terrorism. Unable to find a place for himself in this new society, Svitol chooses suicide.

Fortunately this pessimistic-sounding portrait is shot with great verve and liveliness that actively contradicts the stagnation of its characters and keeps interest alive. Ironic, irreverent dialog reaches its peak in scene where Svitol's friend updates him on right and leftwing fads and figures.

Many scenes head toward comedy in their careful observation of people and events, such as Svitol's hopeless attempt to sell strange Peruvian headgear to the chic Milanese.

Pic makes excellent use of its minimal budget, which seems not to have handicapped it in any way. Technical use of very short scenes ended with fadeouts, create a fast pace and a rush of ideas that tumble into each other. Only a few extraneous images (a homage to Louise Brooks??) creep in to slow it down.

Very well lensed by Giuseppe Pinori and scored with classical music and nostalgia pieces, "To Love the Damned" attains poetic intensity at times, as in the scene of the handsome addict who shoots up by candlelight speaking street dialect and singing a medieval song.

In spite of a few forced edges, script is consistently intelligent and faithful in its exploration of contemporary Italy, its violence and desperation. —*Yung.*

———

P.S.
(EAST GERMAN-COLOR)

———

Tashkent, May 27.
A DEFA Film Production, East Berlin; world rights, DEFA Aussenhandel, East Berlin. Features entire cast. Directed by Roland Graef. Screenplay, Helga Schuetz; camera (color), Claus Neumann. Reviewed at Tashkent Film Festival (Market), May 27, -80. Running time: 90 MINS.
Cast: Andrzej Pieczynski (Peter), Jutta Wachowiak (Margot), Sigrid Roehl-Reintsch (Sabine), Franziska Troegner (Marlies), Dieter Franke (the Director).

———

Scripter Helga Schuetz (wife of writer-director Egon Guenther) penned "P.S." a decade before it was filmed by helmer Roland Graef, apparently because it was then considered too frank in its portrait of a loner in Socialist society. (Schuetz also did the script for Lothar Warneke's "Addio, Piccola Mia" last year, a portrait of the revolutionary writer Georg Buchner during his last days on the run from authorities).

Story is about a lad from an orphanage (played by Polish actor Andrzej Pieczynski, a young-looking Daniel Olbrychski), who ventures out into the world at 18 without any roots or social ties to speak of, save for a tiny flat in East Berlin, a grandmother in West Berlin (who visits on occasion), and a construction job that is viewed as a step towards truckdriving.

Since the boy has a hand for mechanical things and an eye for the fair sex due to his good looks, he uses the latter only to make gains towards the former — then learns about life the hard way through relationships with three different women.

The first is a girl Peter grew up with in the orphanage, Marlies, a kind of sister in the school's rather humane surroundings under a kindly director. She refuses, however, to serve as a family ersatz and ducks Peter whenever she shows up at home or on the job. The second, Sabine, loves Peter, makes advances, gets pregnant, and decides (against her parents' will) to have the child without even informing the lad that he is the father. The third woman in his life, Margot, serves as both lover and mother-figure; she is the social worker assigned to him who has already suffered a broken marriage and is trying to raise a daughter of her own.

Peter's main interest is motors — when he is near a car or motorbike, he loses all interest in anything else. Neither Sabine nor Margot can get near him in the long run, so the former attempts suicide with sleeping pills (her second try at self-destruction) and the latter decides to leave the lad when he's away on a motorbike trip to the seashore. Her "P.S." in a letter informs him that he has a child by Sabine, who has now taken the dose of sleeping tablets and is recovering in a hospital. Peter tries to make amends, but realizes that a university student has moved in on his former girlfriend in the meantime.

Pic ends with Peter teaching his infant son how to walk up stairs, a positive note hinting that he has decided to join society rather than warring against it. Well worth a once-over at East German Film Weeks.—*Holl.*

———

Klincz
(Clinch)
(POLISH-COLOR)

———

Cannes, May 11.
A Film Polski production, Kadr Unit, Warsaw. World rights, Film Polski, Warsaw. Features entire cast. Directed by Piotr Andrejew. Screenplay, Filip Bajon, Andrejew; camera (color), Jacek Mieroslawski, Zbigniew Wichlacz; sets, Janusz Sosnowski. Reviewed at Cannes Film Fest (Market), May 11, 1980. Running time: 96 MINS.
Cast: Tomasz Lengren, Boleslaw Smela, Janusz Sykutera, Janusz Tesarz, Wieslaw Golas, Agyei Johnson.

———

Helmer Piotr Andrejew has made a short on boxing (unspooled at Oberhausen's Sport Film Festival) and his script collaborator, Filip Bajon, a feature on wrestling. "Clinch" reflects the young helmer's intense interest in sports, but it's also a commendable debut pic by a filmer with an eye for the formal elements of his craft, such as cutting, camera angles, and fragmented dialog. But, for all of these reasons, pic lacks that needed commercial edge to put it over.

A young factory worker takes up boxing as a way to find himself and advance his chances for the future. But the difficulties of sorting himself out in the crooked boxing milieu hold him back in the beginning — until he arrives in Chicago for a tournament where he can prove himself. In the end, he wins over his Yank opponent, an amateur below his ranking, and is back in the factory demonstrating his technique to friends but still trying to prove himself.

Scenes in Chicago offer some breathing space in the pic, but it's hardly enough to straighten out the complicated story-line in the long run. Fight scenes are well handled, as are the shots in the gym where the lad learns the ropes the hard way. Well worth a peep, "Clinch" deserves exposure at Polish Film Weeks abroad. —*Holl.*

———

Die Wunderbaren Jahre
(The Wonderful Years)
(WEST GERMAN-COLOR)

———

Cannes, May 23.
A Franz Seitz Film Production, Munich, and Caro-Film, Starnberg; world rights, Franz Seitz, Munich. Features cast. Written and directed by Rainer Kunze. Features entire cast. Camera (color), Wolfgang Treu; music, Rolf Wilhelm; editing, Barbara von Weitershausen. Reviewed at Cannes Film Festival (Market), May 23, '80. Running time: 90 MINS.
Cast: Rolf Boysen, Dietrich Mattausch, Christine Wlodetzky, Gabi Marr, Martin May.

———

Author Rainer Kunze, an East German writer, now living in West Germany, wrote "The Wonderful Years" as a portrait of the German Democratic Republic after the 1968 Prague Invasion, against which he personally protested by leaving the Writers' Union and taking a job as a truckdriver. The book became famous; then when the Wolf Biermann incident occurred in Germany a few years back, he and his family (his wife is a doctor) came permanently to the West. It was only a matter of time before the offer came from producer Franz Seitz to film his book, a job he took on himself as a debut helmer.

Pic, unfortunately, is stiffly directed although visually well mounted. Story centers on the Kunze family as tanks enter Prague (the writer was there and translates Czech and Serbo-Croat literature into German), then jumps chronologically ahead to the daughter's teenage years and her problems in high school with the Pioneer authorities (without membership in which it's hard to be promoted academically).

One of the daughter's close friends is a youth who is musically talented, but his love for organ music places him too close to the Evangelical Church and a pastor who stands for moral principles and religious traditions in life. Eventually, the boy stands up for himself, is forced out of the Pioneers, and loses his chance to study music as a result. The end is suicide — which thus triggers a crisis in the daughter's life.

As a chapter in modern German history, "The Wonderful Years" should be seen by film buffs and history students alike. There are even moments when a film peeps from behind the clouds of polemics.

— *Holl.*

Mater Amatisima
(Mother, Dearly Beloved)
(SPANISH-COLOR)

Madrid, May 29.
An Imatco S.A. production. Written and directed by J.A. Salgot, based on story by Bigas Luna. Features entire cast. Exec producer, Ricardo Munoz-Suay; camera (color), Jaume Peracaula; producer, J. Cuxart Guardia; editor, Anastasi Rinos; sets, Carlos Riart; music, Vangelis. Reviewed at Cine Amaya, Madrid, May 29, 1980. Running time: **93 MINS.**
Juan .... Julito de la Cruz
Clara .... Victoria Abril
Ana .... Consuelo Tura
Ramon .... Jaime Sorribas
Clara's mother .... Carmen Contreras
Clara's father .... Carlos Lucena

Obsessive, powerful, weird and strangely oppressive film written and dircted by newcomer J.A. Salgot but heavily bearing the indelile imprint of Bigas Luna, credited only with supplying the story, but whose technique in "Caniche" and "Bilbao" is here emulated, but with a far more satisfying result.

Using almost only close-ups, interiors, night scenes and eerie music, Salgot immediately creates a mood of tension and unpleasantness which he maintains throughout pic creating an absorbing and often terrifyingly claustrophobic world for his characters, the main one being an autistic child (i.e. one given to morbid daydreaming and introspection, uninfluenced by objective reality).

Technically, Salgot's pic has a grainy quality about it, but this is more than offset by a spellbinding performance by the child and thesping by Victoria Abril which surely entitles her to the distinction of actress of the year especially after her provocative portrayal of "The Girl With the Golden Panties."

With often repulsive realism and obsession for detail, Salgot tells story of an unwed mother who gives birth to an abnormal child (we graphically see the moment of birth); rather than commit her offspring to a hospital, she opts for bringing him up on her own. Since the child is utistic, he is unpredictable and, if left on his own is as liable to spend hours mesmerized sitting in front of his tropical fish tank as setting the apartment on fire. However, as the young mother tries to bring up the boy, her own life starts to disintegrate and she increasingly withdraws from society and is sucked into her son's autistic ways. The withdrawal finally ends in incest.

Salgot's technique is anything but simple; he often focusses on the boy's obsession with the moon, television programs such as the astronauts landing on the moon or tv scenes of Frankenstein and Pinocchio. Pic has a vicious quality about it which fuses morbidity and sensitivity. It is also, at times, an apt mirroring of modern Spain: the girl is a keypunch operator, she goes on hard narcotics, eats fast food, loses her job, while trying to understand society around her, but then sinking into unremitting apathy. Pic ends in a memorable scene in which, after having made love to her son under the sheets of the bed, she feeds him a fatal dose of pills.

Being such an offbeat pic, it's difficult to evaluate commercial prospects; given right release pic could prove a hit as a cult item for those seeking the offbeat film. —*Besa.*

Vsichko e Lyubov
(All Is Love)
(BULGARIAN-COLOR)

Cannes, May 11.
A Bulgarofilm Production, Hemus Film Group, Sofia; world rights, Bulgarofilm, Sofia. Features entire cast. Directed by Borislav Sharaliev. Screenplay, Boyan Papazov; camera (color), Stefan Trifonov; sets, Georgi Ivanov; music, Vesselin Nikolov. Reviewed at Cannes Film Festival (Market), May 11, 1980. Running time: **90 MINS.**
Cast: Ivan Ivanov (Rado), Janina Kasheva (Benni), Maria Stefanova (Benni's mother), Vulcho Kamarashev (Bocher), Yordan Spirov (the director).

Despite its sentimental title, Borislav Sharaliev's "All Is Love" is a strong social statement on teenage problems and juvenile delinquency in Sofia today. Some critics feel it deserves a festival slot somewhere, having missed by a hair, per reports, making it to Berlin.

"All Is Love" features Ivan Ivanov, in the role of a good "bad boy" who always has a chip on his shoulder and finds he can boss just about anyone around among his pals. But when he turns on the girlfriend from the well-to-do, who both loves and understands him, then he can't contend with his deeper emotions. Add to this the problem of being a loner in a society with proclaimed social responsibilities, and you have a frank question being posed by Bulgarian cinema.

Critical points in the film are the boy's treatment by officials and grown-ups, who look upon him as a born loser. Although some offer to help and try to understand his problems, it is the pregnancy of the girlfriend and her subsequent miscarriage that shakes him to his senses — he runs away from the correction home to arrive, frozen and exhausted, on her doorstep.

Well acted with credits on the plus side, "All Is Love" lacks but a sharp edge to be a winner. —*Holl.*

Panel Story
(Prefab Story)
(CZECHOSLOVAK-COLOR)

Cannes, May 12.
A Czechslovak Film Production, Studio Barrandov, Prague; world rights, Czechoslovensky Film, Prague. Features entire cast. Directed by Vera Chytilova. Screenplay, Eva Kacikova. Only credits available. Reviewed at Cannes Film Fest (Market), May 12, '80. Running time: **90 MINS.**
Cast: Lukas Bech, Eva Kacirkova, J. Kode.

A light comedy by Vera Chytilova, the original Czech title, "Panel Story," offers more to chew on than its given English translation, "Prefab Story." It refers to a construction site and the erection of an apartment building via prefabricated panels. Each of the new tenants moving into the incompleted apartment building, in other words, has his or her own story to tell in the manner of a human comedy. "Panel Story" offers an mosaic of life in Prague today.

The biggest joke is when the occupants start moving into the building before the insides, even the outsides, are completed, due to the fact that Prague citizens must wait unusually long for a free apartment. Because several have promised to move out of old dwellings at a stipulated time, and because construction deadlines are not kept, this is a ready-made comedy from start to finish with cliches and predictable situations. Nothing functions like it should: a wife has a hit-and-run affair with a plaster-worker while he's "on the job;" rains turn the grounds into a mudhole; an old man keeps trying to inform everyone that one of their neighbors has died (it turns out that she's merely asleep at the window); and so forth.

Chytilova's sarcastic puns and jabs are delightful.—*Holl.*

Educatore Autorizzato
(Authorized Instructor)
(ITALIAN-COLOR)

Ischia, May 30.
Produced by RAI Television, Channel 2. Stars Gianfranco De Grassi. Directed by Luciano Odorisio. Screenplay, L. Odorisio from a book by Armando Rossini; camera (Eastmancolor), Massimo Sallusti; art director, Mario Grazzini; editor, Giancarlo Cersosimo; music, Egisto Macchi. Reviewed at the Rizzoli Prize Festival, Ischia, May 30, 1980. Running time: **120 MINS.**
Gianni Frontini .... Gianfranco De Grassi

Blue-ribboned with the Angelo Rizzoli award for new Italian filmmakers, Luciano Odorisio's pic about an ex-inmate turned reform school instructor shows the long years of tv apprenticeship that went into crafting helmer's first feature. "Authorized Instructor" has a restrained and mature style at work on a solid script, and a simple realism that communicates well with audiences. It received general public's as well as jury's vote during the Rizzoli Awards, despite serious subject and two-hour length.

Taken from an autobiographical book by Armando Rossini, "Instructor" recounts how Gianni, a young man who has been in a reformatory, becomes a teacher in another where he tries to replace the old repressive system with humane treatment of the boys. But when a boy who has been his friend and lover in the old reformatory turns up, Gianni only knows how to use violence to protect himself, and loses the trust of the other boys. He is unable to use his experience to break out of the system and becomes a part of it.

Script follows classic list of reformatory/boarding school incidents — instructor referees boys' sports, organizes a play, has a run-in with the President over his new methods, catches boys smoking dope in the bathroom. Pic reworks the chestnuts with a sociological realism of style — including heavy Neapolitan dialect — to put its message across.

Pic avoids sentimentalism, though inmates and their cheerless lives (one boy commits suicide on Christmas) have more weepy potential than De Sica's "Shoeshine."

Instead Odorisio keeps a hard head about his characters, very convincingly limned by a group of juveniles with wonderfully expressive faces. Gianfranco De Grassi as Gianni seems too conventionally handsome for tough guy role, but handles character's transition to authoritarianism well.

Photography has an austere gray-blue tinge that conveys a sense of the poverty and routine of the reformatory. Visual elegance of the polished camerawork is marred by a preponderance of detail shots, closeups and zooms, presumably part of helmer and crew's tv heritage. Generally pic's technical side is backgrounded to story; low production budget doesn't hurt film at all.

Produced by RAI television, "Instructor" has been aired as a longer 200-minute program, while theatrical version awaits distrib deal.
— *Yung.*

Lekcja Martwego Jezyka
(Lesson of a Dead Language)
(POLISH-COLOR)

Cannes, May 22.
A Film Polski Production, Zespoly Filmowe & Tor Film Units, Warsaw; world rights, Film Polski, Warsaw. Features entire cast. Written and directed by Janusz Majewski, based on Andrzej Kusniewicz's novel. Camera (color), Zygmunt Samosiuk; music, Andrzej Kurylewicz;

sets, Janusz Sosnowski; editing, Elzbieta Kurkowska; production manager, Tadeusz Drewno. Reviewed at Cannes Film Festival (Market), May 22, '80. Running time: 99 MINS.

Cast: Olgierd Lukaszewicz (Lt. Alfred Kiekiertiz), Ewa Dalkowska, Malgorzata Pritulak, Gustaw Lutkiewicz, Juliusz Machulski, Irena Karel, Marek Kondrat, Piotr Pawlowski, Mieczyslaw Voit, Wlodzimierz Borunski, Zygmunt Malanowicz.

Heavy, symbolic, and literary film, Janusz Majewski's "Lesson of a Dead Language" is nonetheless engrossing as a meditation on the meaning of life during a time of war. Since the pic's hero, an Austrian officer of Polish birth, is doomed to die of tuberculosis and knows it, his presence in a small railroad town as the only guest in the hotel (run by a Jewish proprietor) in the autumn and winter of 1918, just as World War One draws to a close, is taken by the townspeople as momentous and he himself looks upon the short stay as an opportunity to "experience" putting someone else to death — as a hunter stalks his prey. The officer "hunts" a young prisoner in the nearby woods; in the end, he dies himself.

Pic becomes talky when a second lieutenant arrives on the scene while on leave. This is where the conversations on death take on an eerie tone, as experimenting with killing prisoners took place in this area only a few decades hence in the Nazi concentration camps. Thus, "Lesson of a Dead Language" is a commentary on the Holocuast, with the death of the Austrian-Polish officer on the hallway floor of the Jewish hotel serving as a metaphor.

Well acted and strikingly mounted, pic deserves the once-over in Polish Film Weeks. —Holl.

Huset ved Havet
(The House By The Sea)
(DANISH-COLOR)

Cannes, May 19.
A Danish Film Studio — Skagen Kommune — Claus Weeke production, Danish Film Studio release. Written and directed by Claus Weeke. Features entire cast. Camera (Eastmancolor) Dirk Bruel; editor, Lars Brydesen; music, Hans Dal. Reviewed at Cinema Le Star-2, Cannes, May 19, 1980. Running time: 80 MINS.

Cast: Kurt Ravn, Lea Broegger, Lene Scharling, Dick Kaysoe, Claus Strandberg.

Something went terribly awry when Paris-based, sometime Claude Chabrol observer-assistant Claus Weeke returned last summer to Denmark to do his own first full-length feature, "The House By The Sea," which he had co-scripted with Chabrol's regular writer Paul Gegauff.

After much reediting and paring down, "House" remains in part a beautifully-filmed psychological mystery story but also a completely vulgar and senseless mess of folksy sing-along, talkathon cliches the rest of the way. Even cinematographer Dirk Bruel seems to have given up here.

There was, for a time, promise of something better, but that was soon destroyed by Weeke's complete inability to make his actors talk and move naturally. The inner psychology of the outward plot is equally loud and jerky.

A young man wakes up in a hospital after we have seen him having a beautiful rendezvous, sexual and otherwise, with a mysterious young woman named Jessica, who then disappears. The young man's friends do not believe his story and they all travel together to the remote house by the sea, where they work at opposite ends.

Some want to prove their friend a common subject of deja-vu, others string along and start believing him. The local population of the village gang up on the young man, who is beaten up, but immediately afterwards they all get together for a great seaside feast, singing, dancing, eating, dancing and yelling like Vikings.

In the early morning, the young man walks away from the party to explore an old German fortification in which he finds, wonder of wonders, the dead body of his dream-girl Jessica. A gothic tale has turned more ghastly by then.

Film has as yet no solid distribution deal sealed for its home territory. —Kell.

Pelnia
(Full Moon)
(POLISH-COLOR)

Cannes, May 15.
A Film Polski Production, Warsaw; world rights, Film Polski, Warsaw. Features entire cast. Written and directed by Andrzej Kondratiuk. Camera (color), Witold Leszczynski; editing, Kryzsztof Osieki; music, Wlodzimierz Nahomy. Reviewed at Cannes Film Fest (Directors' Fortnight), May 15, '80. Running time: 100 MINS.

Cast: Tomasz Zaliwski, Anna Seniuk, Iga Cembrzynska, Tadeusz Fijewski.

Andrzej Kondratiuk is warmly remembered by film buffs and devotees of Polish cinema as the brilliant, sardonic, acid wit behind Roman Polanski's short, "Mammals," on which script he collaborated. Polanski then put in a personal plug for Kondratiuk's own "Shave, Please" (1965), which copped a prize at the Oberhausen Short Film Festival; it dealt with a murder by strangling in a barber-shop of a man-on-the-run with money stashed in a suitcase, the guilty barber then taking off with the loot —

with another mysterious car in pursuit.

"Full Moon," Kondratiuk's fourth feature, unspooled in the Directors' Fortnight section at Cannes, is one of the finest pix to emerge from Poland in a season that sparkles with outstanding feature films. It's set in the lovely lake-country just north of Warsaw, where several artists and professional people own rustic retreats during the warm summer months for free weekends. And it's about an architect who realizes that the drive for profit, success, and fame does not compare in an industrialized society with the joys of a Waldon Pond existence.

This is an old story and an ancient truth, but it's how Kondratiuk handles the loosely connected scenes, initiates dialog that (seemingly) goes nowhere, and places the individuals leisurely against the landscape as in a Flaherty-style narrative-documentary. Lenser Witold Leszczynski's camera is outstanding in filming the lake-country (he made the feature pic, "Days of Mathew," here back in 1968), and the actors — some professionals, some people from the region — render muted, understated performances whereby nuances capture the eye and ear rather than dramatic tension.

The striking scenes are those dealing with the everyday life of a fisherman, the dropout's new commitment to life, and the dignity of leisure. His contact with people (a drunkard, an old man, several types from the village) leads in the end to a simple, philosophical statement on life, and its demand for human fulfillment. It's when the man's wife, a professional singer, arrives for a visit between theatre engagements in Warsaw that the pieces begin to fall into place, followed later by a confrontation with death when a stranger knocks on the door to spend the night.

A pic that mixes humor with sadness, "Full Moon" entertains and meditates at the same time. It should find its way to other fests.
—Holl.

Szansa
(Chance)
(POLISH-COLOR)

Cannes, May 11.
A Film Polski Production, X Film Unit, Warsaw. World rights, Film Polski, Warsaw. Features entire cast. Written and directed by Feliks Falk. Camera (color), Edward Klosinski; music, Jan Kanty Pawluslziewicz; sets, Teresa Smus-Barska. Reviewed at Cannes Film Festival (Market), May 11, 1980. Running time: 94 MINS.

Cast: Krzysztof Zaleski, Jerzy Stuhr, Elzbieta Kakoszka, Ewa Kolasinska, Slawa Kwasniewska, Iwona Biernacka, Andrzej Buszewicz, Jerzy Nowak.

Feliks Falk has been a director to watch since his "Top Dog" (1977), which won critical praise at the Paris fest and the Forum of Young Cinema in Berlin. That one was a satirical view of Polish society via a seedy master-of-ceremonies job at nightclubs on the circuit; it headlined the able Jerzy Stuhr in the role of rapacious climber. Stuhr then played the lead in Krzysztof Kieslowski's "Camera Buff" (1979), a prizewinner at last year's Moscow fest; this time he was a naive amateur cameraman whose obsession drives him to the brink of catastrophe. Then he was the greasy critic in Agnieszka Holland's "Provincial Actors" (1979).

Now he's back with Falk again in "Chance," playing a secondary schoolteacher with a sensitive outlook on life and a soft spot for students who like art and literature as passionately as he does. The main figure in the film, however, is another "heavy" — this time a possessed sports instructor at the school who knows only too well how athletic victories, particularly handball wins, can up his reputation to such a point that he controls young lads both on and off the court, terrorizes the school authorities into letting him do what he wants, and receives all the side-benefits he needs to make the team — and himself — look good (presumably because he has suffered a crippling knee-injury and needs a substitute to satisfy his ego).

The handball instructor wins the confidence of the young team by leading them to their first victories, then slowly indoctrinates them into the art of winning via extra-hour practices and cheating methods, until finally one of the heroes on the team, a sensitive boy with a love for music, rebels and is driven to a suicide attempt. The big "chance" of winning the handball crown in the Sparticade is thus cancelled out, the instructor is sent packing (he will worm his way back in somewhere else, surely), and the arts teacher (Stuhr) muses on the vicissitudes of life in the end.

Pic has some weaknesses in the plot and dialog, and the ending is left too much up in the air to be convincing, otherwise, this is a well-acted pic with several technical plusses to recommend it. — Holl.

Rough Cut
(BRITISH-COLOR)

Could use some polishing.

Hollywood, June 13.
Paramount Pictures release of a Siegel film. Produced by David Merrick. Directed by Donald Siegel. Stars Burt Reynolds. Screenplay, Francis Burns based on Derek Lambert's "Touch The Lion's Paw;" camera (Movielab), Freddie Young; editor, Doug Stewart; production design, Ted Haworth; music, Nelson Riddle, adapted from the music of Duke Ellington; art direction, Tim Hutchinson; set decoration, Peter James; sound, John Mitchell; assistant director, David Tringham. Reviewed at the Paramount Studio Theatre, June 13, 1980. (MPAA Rating: PG.) Running time: **112 MINS.**

Jack Rhodes . . . . Burt Reynolds
Gillian Bromley . . . . . . Lesley-Anne Down
Chief Inspector Cyril Willis . . David Niven
Nigel Lawton . . . . Timothy West
Ernst Mueller . . . . Patrick Magee
Ferguson . . . . Al Matthews
Sheila . . . . Susan Littler
Inspector Vanderveld . . . . . . Joss Ackland
Mrs. Willis . . . . Isobel Dean
De Gooyer . . . . Wolf Kabler
Pilbrow . . . . Andrew Ray

Having more than its share of production problems in the two and a half years since it was announced as a film project, "Rough Cut" emerges as an undistinctive, frothy romantic comedy that will charm a few and probably miss the eye of many. Love match of Burt Reynolds and Lesley-Anne Down works only in selected spots and frame of the story, intrigue over a $30,000,-000 diamond heist, is hard-pressed to sustain interest. Reynolds' mere presence casts enough boxoffice muscle to snag a few good weeks for distrib Paramount, but pic might have some difficulty competing with other summer products.

Blake Edwards was originally scheduled to direct the picture for David Merrick in 1977 with Larry Gelbart scripting and Reynolds toplining. Edwards eventually bowed out and Reynolds took on other films until Don Siegel was signed to helm last year. Siegel was fired and rehired by Merrick and pic finally wound.

Trouble began this year when Merrick decided he wanted a new ending and Siegel insisted he had the final cut. Result was Merrick hiring Robert Ellis Miller to shoot a fourth finale. Siegel receiving official screen credit, and Francis Burns, a presumed pseudonym of Gelbart's, being the screenwriter of record.

Miraculously, all of the difficulty does not result in a disjointed feeling to the picture. Problem instead seems to lie in much of the dialog, which comes across as both wooden and contrived. Reynolds and Down do what they can to keep things going but their attempts at witty banter never appear natural.

Reynolds shows promise in his segue into sophisticated comedy that began with last year's "Starting Over," also from Paramount, as does Down. But lack of strong material even manages to put a crimp in performance of David Niven, whose wry comedic style as a retiring Scotland Yard inspector can't quite save the film from tedium.

Siegel has directed the effort with a light touch that manages to move things along, but he never manages to inject enough wit or drama into the proceedings. Ted Haworth's production design is eye-catching, thanks to nice support from Tim Hutchinson and Peter James who provide art and set decoration. Nelson Riddle has also set a nice mood with his adaption of a number of Duke Ellington's tunes.

"Rough Cut" is a harmless enough venture but it would seem an unlikely candidate to have created such a stir among its top personnel. As for the ending, it hardly seems to have been worth the hassle. —*Berg.*

The Blues Brothers
(COLOR)

Lots of footage, not all fun.

Hollywood, June 12.
A Universal release. Produced by Robert K. Weiss. Executive producer, Bernie Brillstein. Directed by John Landis. Stars John Belushi, Dan Aykroyd. Screenplay, Dan Aykroyd, John Landis; camera (Technicolor), Stephen M. Katz; editor, George Folsey Jr.; production design, John J. Lloyd; art direction, Henry Larrecq; set decoration, Hal Gausman, Leslie McCarthy-Frankenheimer; costume design, Deborah Nadoolman; sound, Bill Kaplan; associate producers, George Folsey Jr., David Sosna; assistant directors, David Sosna, Jerram Swartz. Reviewed at the Samuel Goldwyn Theatre, Beverly Hills, June 12, 1980. (MPAA Rating: R). Running time: **133 MINS.**

Joliet Jake . . . . John Belushi
Elwood . . . . Dan Aykroyd
Reverend Cleophus James . James Brown
Curtis . . . . Cab Calloway
Ray . . . . Ray Charles
Mystery Woman . . . . Carrie Fisher
Soul Food Cafe Owner . . . Aretha Franklin
Sommelier . . . . Henry Gibson
Burton Mercer . . . . John Candy
Murph . . . . Murphy Dunne
Steve "The Colonel"
Cropper . . . . Steve Cropper
Donald "Duck" Dunn . . . . Donald
"Duck" Dunn
Willie "Too Big" Hall . . . . Willie Hall
"Bones" Malone . . . . Tom Malone
"Blue" Lou Marini . . . . Lou Marini
Matt "Guitar" Murphy . . . . . Matt Murphy
Corrections Officer . . . . Frank Oz
Sister Mary Stigmata . Kathleen Freeman
Trooper Daniel . . . . Armand Cerani
Trooper Mount . . . . Steve Williams
Tucker McElroy . . . . Charles Napier
Maury Sline . . . . Steve Lawrence
Chic Lady . . . . Twiggy
Cook County Clerk . . . . . . Steven Spielberg

If Universal had made it 35 years ago, "The Blues Brothers" might have been called "Abbott & Costello in Soul Town." Level of inspiration is about the same now as then, the humor as basic, the enjoyment as fleeting. But at $30,000,-000, as much as was undoubtedly spent on the complete works of Laurel & Hardy, The Marx Brothers and Abbott & Costello combined, this is a whole new ballgame. Diverting, but not hilarious, farce has enough to offer to draw sizable crowds but as always with such inflated enterprises, extent of ultimate payoff is questionable.

Opinions will certainly vary greatly as to whether all the intensely energetic shenanigans on display are exhilarating or just exhausting, but it's indisputable that few pictures have ever been crammed with so much action, music, noise and general running around, or been subject to such a wide extent of influences. It's a bubbling stew pot of ingredients, with the chefs having thrown in not only the kitchen sink but the pots and pans, Brillo pads and the catering truck.

Enacting Jake and Elwood Blues roles created for their popular concert and recording act, John Belushi and Dan Aykroyd use the slenderest of stories — attempt to raise $5,000 for their childhood parish by putting their old band back together — as an excuse to wreak havoc on the entire city of Chicago and much of the Midwest.

While comedy duo, hidden virtually at all times behind jet black shades and looking, as one character points out, like CIA men, may representing principal selling point, film's greatest pleasure comes from watching the likes of James Brown, Cab Calloway, Ray Charles and especially Aretha Franklin do their musical things. Redoubtable Blues Brothers band also cooks on several occasions and overall the music can be said to have saved the day, as humor is rarely more than mildly amusing and is often overcome by sheer logistics.

And what logistics. Surely no city has been besieged by a film to such an extent since "Is Paris Burning?" and Chicago hasn't seen so many cops, soldiers and crazies in its streets since the summer of 1968. Reverberations from this one, which has the brothers' pursuit by the fuzz, the Army, the Nazis, some good ole boys and heavily armed Carrie Fisher climaxing in the courtyard of the Civic Center, could set Mayor Richard Daley spinning in his grave.

To be sure, many of the elaborate and crunchingly damaging stunts are physically amazing, particularly an unprecedented one in which the Pinto of Hitlerite Henry Gibson seems to fall from thousands of feet to crash to a deserved hell beneath the city streets. Work of stunt coordinator Gary McLarty and his team, as well as the regiment of drivers, must be duly noted, even if its ultimate effect is to make one ponder what the bills looked like.

Given all the chaos, director and, with Aykroyd, cowriter, John Landis manages to keep things reasonably controlled and in a straight line, displaying a good eye and eager-to-please nature. As much as anything else, pic plays as a spirited tribute by white boys to black musical culture, which was inspiration for the Blues Brothers act in the first place.

Credits are as long as any in recent memory, so without singling them out, all hands can be said to have contributed solidly. Neither "Animal House" at one extreme or "1941" at the other, film offers modest pleasures considerably at odds with bloated physical baggage.
— *Cart.*

Mueda
(MOZAMBIQUE-B&W)

Tashkent, May 29.
Produced by the Mozambique Film Organization. Features entire cast. Directed by Ruy Guerra, assisted by Jose Pedro Pimenta. Screenplay, Calisto Dos Lagos. Only credits available. Reviewed at Tashkent Film Festival, May 29, '80. Running time: **90 MINS.**
Cast: Filipe Gunoguacala, Romao Canapoquele, Balthasar Nohilema.

The most talked about film unspooled at the Tashkent Film Festival in the main program, Ruy Guerra's "Mueda" deals with an incident on the Mozambique border to Tanzania 20 years ago: the villagers of Mueda demanded their rights from the Portuguese colonial magistrate in the area, which led to a massacre of some 600 people when things got out of hand.

Guerra, one of the founders of Brazil's "Cinema Novo," shot the pic in just two days on the same location where it all took place. He needed only one day to assemble the villagers for a dramatization of the events on an open space before the colonial headquarters, filming the "play" like a Soviet agitprop production on the October Revolution (the similarity to the street-play origin of Eisenstein's "October" is striking).

Once that was done, he shot the scenes inside the building on the next day, using a satirical approach in portraying the Portuguese officer's office and manner. Then he added interviews with people who witnessed, and were involved in, the massacre (one person a former soldier who fired into the crowd).

Pic may appear primitive, but its raw authenticity and intelligent juxtaposition of past and present, real and fictional, lend force to this experiment in narrative continuity. "Nueda" appears, in fact, to be a twin to Guerra's earlier "The Guns" (Brazil, 1964), also a treatise on power and violence.

Pic should find its way to international fests as first political document to emerge from revolutionary Mozambique. —Holl.

Brubaker
(COLOR)

Too good for its own good.

Hollywood, June 3.
A 20th Century-Fox release, produced by Ron Silverman. Exec producer, Ted Mann. Directed by Stuart Rosenberg. Stars Robert Redford. Screenplay, W.D. Richter; camera (Deluxe Color), Bruno Nuytten; editor, Robert Brown; sound, Charles Wilborn; art direction, J. Michael Riva; assistant director, Jon C. Andersen; associate producer, Gordon Webb; music, Lalo Schifrin. Reviewed at 20th Century-Fox, June 3, 1980. (MPAA Rating: R). Running time: 130 MINS.

Brubaker	Robert Redford
Coombes	Yaphet Kotto
Lillian	Jane Alexander
Deach	Murray Hamilton
Bullen	David Keith
Walter	Morgan Freeman
Purcell	Matt Clark
Rauch	Tim McIntire
Abraham	Richard Walsh
Zaranska	Jon Van Ness
Woodward	M, Emmet Walsh
Poke	Albert Salmi
Carol	Linda Haynes
Caldwell	Everett McGill
Wendel	Val Avery

"Brubaker" is a successfully grim and brutal drama which, unfortunately, has written its own commercial epitaph with its message: The public at large does not care about prison reform.

Even with a sharp cast topped by the star power of Robert Redford, it's hard to imagine a broad audience wanting to share the two hours of agony in this one, all the way to a downbeat ending with Redford the loser in his righteous battle.

For the squeamish, the first half hour is rough going, indeed, as Redford is inducted into a small state prison, isolated in the farmlands near a hamlet. (Though shot at an abandoned prison in Ohio, exact location of prison is never identified, but is apparently based on situations a few years back in Arkansas).

Joining the ranks, Redford discovers one horror after another. The prison administration is in corrupt cahoots with townspeople, leasing prisoners as slave labor; brutal trustees administer the discipline to fellow convicts, gaining good time for killing some off; minimally decent food and privileges must be bought for cash, with wormy gruel going to those who can't afford it.

Just when it seems any hope is beyond these men, Redford reveals himself as the prison's new warden, brought to the job by Jane Alexander, good as an assistant to a reform-minded governor never seen.

Despite his authority, however, Redford is immediately confronted and confounded by the inmates' own cynicism and acclimation to corruption. In this regard, the strongest part of the picture is Redford's relationship with Yaphet Kotto, a trustee-guard who, while wanting the prison to be better, believes Redford's naive meddling will only make it worse.

Persevering, Redford gradually imposes reforms and improved conditions that are not fully appreciated by the prisoners while outraging the citizens of the town and politicians in the state, especially prison commissioner Murray Hamilton, familiar in another weasel role.

In a no-win situation, Redford finds the more he gains the prisoners' trust, the more he loses the support of those responsible for his job until even Alexander cannot help him, especially when he insists on exposing a series of long-ago murders at the prison.

In all of this, Redford gets good acting support from David Keith, Morgan Freeman, Matt Clark, Tim McIntire and Richard Ward as various friends and enemies. Linda Haynes is also noteworthy as a town chippie.

All tech credits are strong and Stuart Rosenberg has directed W.D. Richter's thought-provoking script with a sure hand after coming aboard in mid-picture.

But mention a prison and today's public probably thinks first and is more aggravated by the country-club images of the facilities enjoyed by the Watergate villains. "Brubaker" says they should care more about the other kids, which probably they should. But odds are, they won't. —Har.

My Bodyguard
(COLOR)

Lots of muscle.

Hollywood, June 9.
A 20th Century-Fox release. Produced by Don Devlin. Exec producer, Melvin Simon. Directed by Tony Bill. Features entire cast. Screenplay, Alan Ormsby; camera (Deluxe color), Michael D. Margulies; editor, Stu Linder; sound, Nat Boxer, Ray Cymoszinski; production design, Jackson de Govia; assistafv director, Michael Daves; associate producer, Phillip Goldfarb; music, Dave Grusin. Reviewed at 20th Century-Fox, June 9, 1980. (MPAA rating: PG.) Running time: 97 MINS.

Clifford	Chris Makepeace
Linderman	Adam Baldwin
Moody	Matt Dillon
Gramma	Ruth Gordon
Peache	Martin Mull
Carson	Paul Quandt
Mike	Hank Salas
Shelley	Joan Cusack
Griffith	Craig Richard Nelson
Dobbs	John Houseman
Ms. Jump	Kathryn Grody
Hightower	Dean R. Miller
Koontz	Tim Reyna
Dubrow	Richard Bradley
Leilani	Denise Baske

"My Bodyguard" could be this summer's sleeper, appealing to the same "Breaking Away" audience that likes a well-crafted dramatic comedy about real kids whose problems are not resolved by throwing food.

In his directorial debut, Tony Bill has assembled a truly remarkable cast of youngsters with little or no previous acting experience whose natural abilities would put to shame some of the flash-in-the-pan "personalities" currently bombing in other pix.

Chris Makepeace is superb as the slightly built kid coming anew to a Chicago high school dominated by extortionist gang leader Matt Dillon, also terrific in his part. But Bill's real discovery is Adam Baldwin, a gentle giant who makes everything in the picture work so neatly.

First met, Baldwin is a standoffish, uncommunicative brute rumored throughout the school to be a psychotic weirdo who has killed cops and other kids. Dillon and gang use the rumors to demand payment for smaller fellows for "protection" from Baldwin, but in truth are terrified of him themselves.

But Makepeace will not pay up and takes his lumps until befriended by Baldwin, thereby beginning a warm friendship that leads to surprising turns in the plot, climaxed by a totally satisfying finish that audiences are likely to love.

In lesser parts, Paul Quandt is delightful as Makepeace's even smaller, more timid buddy and Joan Cusack is fine as a sympathetic friend.

On the adult side, the performers are mainly present for comic relief — but are not buffoons or villains. In a role that comes perilously close to repeating the daffy old lady of "Where's Papa?," Ruth Gordon is nonetheless a charmer as Makepeace's amorous grandmother. (And John Houseman has an unusual cameo for him as one of her potential one-night stands.)

Martin Mull is good as the distracted father who manages a luxury hotel where the family lives, too bothered by the possibility Gordon will cost him his job to pay much attention to Makepeace's school problems. And Craig Richard Nelson adds to the fun as an assistant manager after Mull's job.

Technically, picture sometimes shows the threads of low-budget shooting, especially in the dubbing. But the distractions are minor and are a price worth paying for proof again that big money is no guarantee of success. Bill and Alan Ormsby's script and a good cast, which is more than enough. —Har.

Tryptych
(SOVIET-COLOR)

Tashkent, May 30.
An Uzbekfilm Studio Production, Tashkent, Uzbekistan Republic, Soviet Union; world rights, Sovexport Film, Moscow. Features entire cast. Written and directed by Ali Khamraev. Camera (color), Yuri Klimenko. Only credits available. Reviewed at Tashkent Film Festival (market) May 30, '80. Running time: 100 MINS.
Cast: Gula Khamrayova.

The Grand Prix winner at the recent San Remo Film Festival, Ali Khamraev's "Tryptych" impressed foreign critics at Tashkent as well, although the official word on this pic is said to be negative with regard to the filmmaker's pessimistic viewpoint on life in Uzbekistan in the immediate postwar years.

Khamraev, born in Uzbekistan of a Uzbek father and Ukrainian mother, has made more than a dozen feature films, several of which have helped to put his republic on the map as a budding film production center: "White, White Storks" (1967), "Dilorom" (1969), "Without Fear" (1971), "The Man Who Follows the Birds" (1975), "Tryptych" (1978), and "The Bodyguard" (1979) (produced at the neighboring Tadzhikfilm Studio, where Khamraev made his first features).

"Tryptych" is the story of three women. The first is an illiterate girl who wants to build a house even though it's not permitted by custom without her husband (who returned home from the war to work in a neighboring factory-town without informing his wife).

The second is a schoolteacher who represents authority coming to this village in the north of Uzbekistan, where traditions and strict Moslem practices have kept the people subjugated. The third is an old woman who was kidnapped in her youth by a poor peasant from her rich family, thereby making her his property; she dies, blaming her husband for not fulfilling his promises and mourning the loss of an only son in the war. The portrait of these three women accounts for the film's title.

"Tryptych" has a dark tone. The camera moves slowly across drab landscapes and tired, worn faces in a period of Soviet history when optimism was something to be found only on the screen. Khamraev did his own research on the film, drawing on accounts given by real people at the time in such villages. There are scenes, such as the simple girl's rape by a visiting male, that are handled delicately but with a flare for experimental visual images. Thesp performances by real actors and nonprofessionals are a good cut above the average in Soviet cinema today. There's a parallel here to Andrei Tarkovsky's films, in which inner anguish has become a film genre in itself.

"Tryptych" places Khamraev in the forefront of Soviet cinema and assures his status as the best Uzbek director on the scene today, possibly the most talented in the Soviet Middle Asian republics. Pic is well worth the once-over on fest circuit or at Soviet Film Weeks. —Holl.

Abu Raihan Beruni
(SOVIET-COLOR)

Tashkent, May 30.
An Uzbekfilm Studio Production, Tashkent, Uzbekistan Republic, Soviet Union; world rights, Sovexport Film, Moscow. Features entire cast. Directed by Shukhrat Abbasov. Screenplay, Pavel Bulgakov, Abbasov; camera (color, widescreen), Khatam Faisiev. Reviewed at Tashkent Film Festival (Market), May 30, '80. Running time: 150 MINS.
Cast: Pulat Saidkasymov, Bikhtiar Shukurov, Razzak Khamraev, Bimbulat Vataev.

Shukhrat Abbasov has achieved a reputation in the budding Uzbek-film Studios as director with a flair for the historical epic, the film that made him known abroad being "Abu Raihan Beruni" (1974). Beruni (973-1048) was the "Da Vinci of the East" — philosopher, historian, geographer, traveller, astronomer, mathematician, physicist, linguist, and poet. This enlightened figure of the Moslem world, however, had his troubles with the conservative religious leaders of the day, just as Galileo was to suffer the same a few centuries later. He is today, along with the philosopher Avicenna, one of the national heroes of Uzbekistan and the eastern Moslem world.

Lensing is a strong plus, but pic lacks dramatic realism to break loose from the costume straitjacket. If only to acquaint Western auds with the fame of Beruni, pic should be included in Uzbek Film Weeks. —Holl.

Eqipaj
(The Crew)
(SOVIET-COLOR)

Cannes, May 20.
A Mosfilm Production, Moscow; world nights, Sovexport Film Moscow. Features entire cast. Directed by Alexander Mitta. Screenplay, Yuri Donsky, Valery Fried, Mitta, in collaboration with Boris Urinowsky; camera (Eastmancolor), Valery Shuvalov. Reviewed at Cannes Film Festival (Market), May 20, '80. Running time: 150 MINS.
Cast: Georgy Jenov, Anatony Vassiliel, Alexandra Yakovleva, Leonid Filatov, Irina Akulova.

Lensed in Eastmancolor, Alexander Mitta's "The Crew" has obviously been commissioned with Western standards in mind and thus seems a natural for an upcoming fest on the summer circuit, perhaps Karlovy Vary or San Sebastian. It's an adventure pic, reminiscent of Hollywood's "The High and the Mighty" (1954) in that a great part of the action takes place on a crippled airliner trying to make it back in time to a safe landing-field before the entire craft drops in flames with crew and passengers.

"The Crew" focuses chiefly on four members of the Soviet Airlines plane crew: the aging captain-pilot, charged with the safety of all abroad; the flight engineer, whose family suffers from a divorce that wasn't his fault; a steward and a stewardess, formerly lovers and now estranged although the philandering male has now seen the error of his ways. Among the passengers are the remarried, former wife of the flight engineer and their son — thus adding to the psychological dimension as the action and thrills pile one on top of the other. The first 90 minutes concentrates on the family fates of the crew; the last hour (this is a two-part pic unspooled with a pause in Soviet theatres) has all the thrills of "will the liner land in one piece at the Moscow airport?"

First part, surprisingly enough, has a gratuitous nude scene, as the steward and stewardess get better acquainted in the former's Moscow apartment. There's also a strain of comedy here, for an old girlfriend happens on the scene later and a gimmick whereby music is triggered by seating on the wrong cushion highlights a spat between the two lovers because of the old girlfriend's rather innocent presence. Mitta has a deft hand for comedy, and there should have been more of it — instead of, for example, the sentimental tears showered on a divorce scene wherein the husband (the flight engineer) is maligned but unable to defend umself.

Second part has a science-fiction touch to boot: the plane makes a trip to some unstated Third World country where, at Bibra, Soviet technicians are constructing something (oil refinery?) for the populace — the area is carved out of a mountainside, looks Latin America-ish, but is probably in the Arab Near East. While the crew is on the ground to pick up passengers, an earthquake takes place that sets off explosions and landslides killing hundreds and igniting molten mountains of flame. Our crew bides their time, gets everyone possible aboard, then takes off just in time as rocks, flames, and falling towers nearly engulf the aircraft as it angles down the runway to a last-minute escape.

The danger isn't over yet — for fissures in the crippled tail of the airliner threaten to cut the craft in two on the flight home to Moscow (why not a landing at the nearest airport isn't explained). The flight engineer and the steward save the day, however, by climbing out of the plane in mid-flight and tying the loose ends together. Just as the plane touches down in safety, the tail is torn from the body — and our stewardess is a heroine by rescuing the flight engineer's son (who was sleeping innocently in the back rows during all the excitement).

Despite the exaggerations along the way, pic does have some quality lensing and trick photography, plus set designs to make the eyes pop. "The Crew" should be seen in the West, and could draw a camp of cult following. —Holl.

The Trap
(SYRIAN-COLOR)

Tashkent, May 29.
A Syrian Film Production, Damascus. Features entire cast. Directed by Wadi Yossef. Screenplay, Ali Ogla Ursan. Only credits available. Reviewed at Tashkent Film Festival, May 29, '80. Running time: 90 MINS.
Cast: Samar Sami, Osama Khuluki, Addulhadi Sabbag.

A Syrian melodrama, Wadi Yossef's "The Trap" uses conventional stage techniques to tell the story of a lovely girl from the poor side of the tracks who gets seduced by a doctor she works for. She becomes a call girl with secret tape-recording equipment to elicit important information from clients in the construction business.

Script is stiff and unimaginative, acting is often embarrassingly overdone, and lensing in studio suffers from improper lighting. In the end, the girl decides to go straight and reveals the secret information to authorities after blackmailing her erstwhile patrons — only to get bumped off with her hardworking boyfriend (who has returned home from abroad to claim his true love) by a mysterious car that runs them down on the street. —Holl.

Sindoor
(NEPAL-COLOR)

Tashkent, May 29.
A Nepal Film Production. Features entire cast. Written and directed by Prakash Thapa. Only credits available. Reviewed at Tashkent Film Festival, May 29, '80. Running time: 90 MINS.
Cast: Beenakshi, Biswa Basnet, Prakash Thapa.

Nepal cinema borrows freely from India from time to time. For this commercial hit in home theatres, Prakash Thapa, the writer-director-actor, relied on proven musical numbers interspersed with comedy and romance to bring home the bacon.

The singing, often enough, is outdoors via playback done in the studios afterwards. Some social problems are thrown in on the side, in this case a woman emancipating herself from old traditions and prejudices. —Holl.

The Patriot Game — A Decade Long Battle for The North of Ireland
(FRENCH-B/W-16M-DOCU)

Frankly biased pro-I.R.A. film provides new facts and insight on Irish struggle.

A production of Iskra Films, Paris, released in U.S. by Icarus Films, with Cinema Perspectives, both of New York. Directed by Arthur Mac Caig. Camera (black and white), MacCaig, Theo Robichet; editor, MacCaig, Dominique Greussay; commentary voice, Winnie Marshall. Reviewed at Preview Theatre, New York, May 28, 1960. (No MPAA rating). Running time: 93 MINS.

New French feature documentary, "The Patriot Game," deals dramatically with events in Northern Ireland. It is not at all reticent about its passionate pro-IRA bias. Accordingly, film faces mixed audiences in U.S., and may have disqualified itself from being picked up for broadcast by American television.

"The Patriot Game" provides important historical background to the Irish war — and the film does call it warfare, as 2,000 Irish civilians and hundreds of British soldiers have died since the bombings and shootings began in 1968. It's a conflict with deep roots, entangling religion, culture and politics. Not surprisingly, the film interprets the struggle in terms of economics, as perceived by young Marxists.

Most of "The Patriot Game" was shot clandestinely by the Iskra crew, with additional footage bought from Eire's RTE Television, France's Antenne 2, and British TV. By coincidence, film arrives in New York as Paramount is releasing "The Outsider," new fiction feature about the violence in Northern Ireland.

U.S. distributors of "The Patriot Game" hope for lively specialized screenings in the U.S., including campuses. Six-city tour follows its New York screening several weeks ago as fund-raiser for the Irish Northern Aid Committee. Abroad, film has screened at festivals in Switzerland, Italy, and France, and in some theatrical situations in the U.K.

Director of "The Patriot Game" is an American, Arthur MacCaig, 32, from Jersey City. MacCaig is ex of anthropological studies at the U. of Hawaii, was later 1977 graduate from the IDHEC film school in Paris, on a scholarship from the French government. He now lives in Paris although he came briefly to the U.S. for the launch of his film.

—Hitch.

Wholly Moses!
(COLOR)

Wholly cow.

Hollywood, June 11.
A Columbia Pictures release. Produced by Freddie Fields. Executive producer, David Begelman. Directed by Gary Weis. Stars Dudley Moore, Laraine Newman, James Coco, Paul Sand, Jack Gilford. Screenplay, Guy Thomas; camera (Metrocolor, Panavision), Frank Stanley; editor, Sidney Levin; music, Patrick Williams; production design, Dale Hennesy; set design, Diane Wager; set decoration, Robert De Vestel; costume design, Guy Verhille; sound, John Speak; assistant director, L. Andrew Stone. Reviewed at the Burbank Studios, Burbank, June 11, '80. (MPAA Rating: PG.) Running time: 109 MINS.
Harvey/Herschel . . . . Dudley Moore
Zoey/Serelda . . . . Laraine Newman
Hyssop . . . . James Coco
Angel of the Lord . . . . Paul Sand
Tailor . . . . Jack Gilford
Shadrach . . . . Dom DeLuise
Archangel . . . . John Houseman
Sorceress . . . . Madeline Kahn
Beggar . . . . David L. Lander
Pharaoh . . . . Richard Pryor
Devil . . . . John Ritter

There's little as embarrassing as failed comedy, and blank reaction prompted by "Wholly Moses!" makes it impossible to mistake the film for anything different. Deadly dullness of both writing and execution render pointless any attempt to single out blame for misfire, which leaves many talented performers flailing about in desperate attempts to generate laughs. Premise and names could draw initially, but any b.o. legs are shackled.

Casting of Dudley Moore as false ancient religious saviour named Herschel, who overhears God's instructions to Moses and assumes the assignment to lead his people out of slavery, conjures up memories of last year's popular, and controversial, "Life Of Brian," but similarity ends there.

Whatever else can be said for

"Brian," it was mostly inventive and alive comically and visually. By contrast, "Moses" is excessively tame, tired, predictable and, at close to two hours, ultimately exhausting.

Not bad prolog has Moore meeting Laraine Newman on a tour bus in the Holy Land. During a desert stopover, pair discovers a hidden scroll, the unknown Book of Herschel, which recounts hapless life of slave James Coco's son as he stumbles from his career as an idol maker to the summit of Mount Sinai and ultimately into the court of Pharaoh Richard Pryor, only to find that Moses has long since made his getaway.

Guest turns by the likes of Pryor, Dom DeLuise, Madeline Kahn and John Ritter are as brief as they are perfunctory, playing like those occasional "surprise" appearances of stars on television specials who just happen to be in the next studio taping their own shows.

If "10" represented Dudley Moore's first real splash as a leading man, this one provides him with an unmitigated sophomore jinx. A couple of okay slapstick moments remind of how funny he can be, but in the long run there's nothing he can do with the material. Laraine Newman comes and goes without creating much of an impression, while Coco and Paul Sand's work is more elaborate than amusing.

Best that can be said for debut screenwriter Guy Thomas and first-time feature director Gary Weis is that they both have a few things to learn. Tech credits are acceptable, with California desert locations doubling reasonably for Middle Eastern settings, although slow pacing quickly becomes war-ing.

—Cart.

Underground U.S.A.
(COLOR-16M)

Strictly static.

A New Cinema Production. Produced, directed, written by Eric Mitchell. Features entire cast. Camera (color-16m), Tom DiCillo; editor, J.P. Roland-Levy; music, James White & the Blacks, Lounge Lizards, Walter Stedding; sound, Jim Jarmusch; co-producer, Erdner Rauschalle; assistant director, Becky Johnston. Reviewed at St. Marks Cinema, New York City, June 22, 1980. (No MPAA Rating). Running time: 85 MINS.
Vickie . . . . Patti Astor
Hustler . . . . Eric Mitchell
Kenneth . . . . Rene Ricard
Frank . . . . Tom Wright
Roommate . . . . Jackie Curtis
Also: Cookie Mueller, Taylor Mead, Duncan Smith, Steve Mass, Terry Toye, John Lurie.

The latest retelling of the familiar "Sunset Boulevard" story is a New York indie shot on a microscopic budget. Director Eric Mitchell, in his third outing after "Kidnapped" (1978) and "Red Italy" (1979), harks back to the Andy Warhol method of one shot per scene. However, use of scripted dialog and artificially posed acting robs the pic of the explosive confrontations found in Warhol's improvised films. Cast largely plays straight, avoiding material's camp potential.

A street hustler (ineffectively played as a zombie by Mitchell himself) is thrown out by his roommate and inveigles his way into the entourage of a fading movie star (Patti Astor). Despite the protective insulation from the truth of her decline that is provided by her loyal manager (Rene Ricard), she gradually spirals towards suicide. Satirical representatives of the New York art community and underground look on with disdain.

Styled with a platinum blonde hairdo to resemble Kim Novak, Astor comes off more like a wayward Hope Lange. Comic turns by Warhol vets Jackie Curtis and Rene Ricard offer relief to the general tedium. Music track moves fitfully from new wave to rock tunes of the '60s. Film's usage is limited to midnight movies and college circuits.

—Lor.

Tout Depend des Filles
(It All Depends On Girls)
(FRENCH-COLOR)

Paris, June 15.
An SNC release of a Bela Productions/SNC/Credo/FR3 coproduction. Produced by Georges de Beauregard. Features entire cast. Written and directed by Pierre Fabre. Camera (Eastmancolor), Alain Masseron; sound, Raymond Saint-Martin; music, Michel Bernholc; art director, Daniel O'Nillon; editor, Jean-Claude Bonfanti. Reviewed at Studio 28, Paris, May 15, 1980. Running time: 94 MINS.
Jean-Luc . . . . Jean-Luc Bideau
Mathieu . . . . Jean-Pierre Sentier

Celine . . . . Christine Murillo
Anna . . . . Tonie Marshall
Lucien . . . . Michel Galabru
Beety . . . . Michelene Presle

Screenwriter Pierre Fabre makes his directing debut with this piece of pleasant fluff which he also wrote. Its chief merits are its pert, humorous dialog and a happy-go-lucky cast headed by Jean-Luc Bideau, Jean-Pierre Sentier and Christine Murillo.

Bideau and Sentier play a pair of eccentric ne'er-do-wells living and working (sometimes) in a still villagy quarter of Montmartre. Bideau, who lives off his bric a brac carpentry, dreams of writing mystery novels and moving to the country. Sentier is an unsuccessful sculptor plagued with indecision; he can't get around to marrying his eternal fiancee, whom he has stood up at the church several times.

This is the basis for a typically French romantic comedy worked out in brisk parlays of love and amity. It's all charm and insouciance, though spun out too much and at times too indulgently. Fabre is an agile writer of dialog so taken with the pleasure of writing that he neglects to develop a rigorous editing sense of his own work. This lack of discipline extends to his directing, which muffs the more visual sequences with its uncertainty of camera maneuvering and editing.

But this is essentially an actor's film and the performers, especially Bideau, with his irresisttibly laid-back manner, and Murillo, natural and appealing as the independent young woman he doggedly woos, are engaging company for ninety-five mintues. Film's modest intentions make it seemingly for local consumption though its Gallic humour and nonchalance might carry some appeal in foreign markets. —Len.

Aria Dla Atlety
(Aria for an Athlete)
(POLISH-COLOR)

Cannes, May 16.
A Film Polski Production, Film Unit Tor, Warsaw; world rights. Film Polski, Warsaw. Features entire cast. Written and directed by Filip Bajon. Camera (color), Jerzy Zielinski; music, Zdzislaw Szostak. Reviewed at Cannes Film Fest (Market), May 10, '80. Running time: 108 MINS.
Cast: Krysztof Majchrzak, Pola Raksa, Roman Wilhelmi, Bogusz Bilewski, Wojciech Pszoniak, Ryszard Pietruski, Zdzislaw Wardejn.

Filip Bajon belongs to that talented group of young helmers emerging from Poland at the beginning of the new decade — others include Feliks Falks, Agnieszka Holland, Piotr Andrejew, Piotr Szulkin, and Janusz Kijowski. His "Aria for an Athlete" bowed at the

Rotterdam fest earlier in the year to critical accalim, after which it was slotted in the Forum sidebar at the Cannes fest.

Set at the turn of the century, this is the story of a famous Polish wrestler, Wladyslaw Goralewicz, tagged "the world's strongest man," based on true-life accounts of three such wrestlers. It begins in a small town, where a travelling circus attracts a shy boy into its phony wrestling game to please the crowds. The youth, however, takes his strength seriously and eventually defeats a name wrestler in a fair match, incurring the anger of the circus manager, who fires him. He is happy to leave in any case, due to the cruelty of two circus wrestlers, the Abs brothers, who torment him just for the fun of it.

The wrestler goes on to fame, performing in the world's top arenas, and, one day, he is serenaded by an operatic tenor in the crowd. Fame brings him women and admirers, but he is uncompromising in his profession; he gains a beautiful wife and a collection of valuable sculptures. He also has his revenge on one of the Abs brothers by defeating him in the ring.

One day, while attending a match in his tuxedo on a night's outing, he is challenged by the other Abs brother to enter the ring just as he is in a fight to the finish. In the course of the match, the brutal wrestler forces the otherwise clean-fighting Goralewicz to fight on his terms, just as our hero was about to be defeated. Goralewicz kills Abs in the ring, and thus his career is ended.

Strong film and unusual topic (particularly for East Europe), plus topnotch credits on the technical side, make this a modest winner. A tighter script might have produced a hit.—*Holl.*

Aguila
(Eagle)
(FILIPINO-COLOR)

Manila, June 18.
Bancom Audiovision Corporation release and production. Written and directed by Eddie Romero. Features entire cast. Camera (color), Mike de Leon and Rody Lacap; editor, Ben Barcelon; music, Ryan Cayabyab; art director, Mel Chionglo. Reviewed at Los Banos-Agrix Theatre, Manila, June 6, 1980. Running time: **210 MINS.**
Daniel Aguila . . . . Fernando Poe, Jr.
Sally . . . . Charo Santo
Jose Mari . . . . Christopher de Leon
Don Simoun . . . . Eddie Garcia
Isabel . . . . Amalia Fuentes
Liliam . . . . Elizabeth Oropesa
Osman . . . . Jay Ilagan

After 35 years in the business, Eddie Romero comes up with his most ambitious work, a 3½ hour dramatization in epic scale.

"Aguila" is an attempt to intelli-

gently present a parallelism between a man's inner conflicts and that of his country. The main character, Daniel, goes through an 80-year odyssesy to search for "life's meanings."

The story opens at a family reunion of the wealthy Aguila clan to celebrate the birthday of 88-year old patriarch Daniel who has been missing for 10 years. His three sons are now prominent figures and Jose Mari is the industrial magnate and former senator.

During the gathering, Mari is told that his father may still be alive somewhere in Mindanao. He packs up for a long search and in the course of his travels recalls several episodes flashed on the screen about his father's past and the life and times of the country covering a period of eight decades.

Romero's story has some historical inaccuracies and loose strands because of too many flashbacks and several sub plots but these are minor flaws that can be remedied through editing.

All in all, "Aguila" comes as a rare treat to local audiences saturated by exploitation fare produced nowadays. —*Giro.*

To Live A Long Life
(SOVIET-COLOR)

Tashkent, May 29.
An Armenfilm Studio Production, Erevan, Armenian Republic, Soviet Union; world rights, Sovexport Film, Moscow. Features entire cast. Directed by Frunze Dovlatyan. Screenplay, Shagen Tatikyan, Dovlatyan; camera (color), Albert Yavuryan; music, Martyn Vertazaryan. Reviewed at Tashkent Film Festival, May 29, '80. Running time: **95 MINS.**
Cast: Armen Dzhigarkhanyan, Violetta Gevorkyan, Ovanes Vanyan.

Armenia's best-known director, Frunze Dovlatyan, scored a commercial hit back in 1965, "Hello, It's Me!" Now, at Tashkent, his "To Live a Long Life" was the best film in the Main Program from a Soviet republic.

"To Live a Long Life" is the story of a woman dying of cancer who wants to be sure the child she is caring for, an adopted daughter of about six, is placed in the hands of her kindly grandfather. What the grandpa doesn't know is that this is his real granddaughter, which complication forms the unravelling thread of the story.

It turns out that the dying woman was seduced and betrayed by the grandpa's son, now a high minister in the government, then she aborted a pregnancy at the seducer's request. Later, after he got another girl pregnant, the heroine cared for the unlucky girl and later took the child into her home as her own. Her impending death, however, leads her to seek out a new parent, so she

chooses her former lover's father and real grandfather of the child, **who is now living alone after the death of his wife.**

The grandfather, however, doesn't know at first what to make of learning he has a grandchild, for this is bitter news to him. He didn't know that his son, the apple of his mother's eye, was in truth a scoundrel — a situation that deepens when the minister-son showers slander on the innocent woman fortaking in his own child rather than leaving it in an orphanage. When the old man learns the truth about everything, he rejects his first son and seeks out his second son, whom he himself had neglected and wronged long ago. Together they care for the dying woman until her death by sharing an apartment, another circumstance that makes the innocent parties appear suspect in the eyes of the uninformed neighbors.

Well acted and directed, "To Live a Long Life" leaves some questions open at the end — for instance, the rotten minister escapes his comeuppance. Well worth a once-over at Soviet or Armenian Film Weeks. —*Holl.*

Aziza
(TUNISIAN-ALGERIAN-COLOR)

Taskent, May 29.
A SATPEC, Tunisia, Coproduction with Radio Television Algeria and LATIF, producer, Hassen Daldoul. Features entire cast. Directed by Abdel Latif Ben Ammar. Screenplay, Ben Ammar, Tawfik Jebali; camera (color), Youssef Sharaqui; editor, Moufida Tlatli; music, Ahmed Malek; production manager, Lotfi Layouni. Reviewed at Tashkent Film Festival, May 29, '80. Running time: **90 MINS.**
Cast: Yasmine Khlat (Aziza), Raouf Ben Amor (Ali), Dalila Rames (Aicha), Mohamed Zinet (Bechir), Tawfik Jebali (Brahim), Mouna Nourredine (Jamila).

Unspooled both at Cannes in the Directors' Fortnight and at Tashkent in the Main Program, Abdel Latif Ben Ammar's "Aziza" deals with the emancipation of a working class woman in Tunis today, which may also serve as a symbol for a developing country attaining its own identity. Pic was received well in both international fests and should make it elsewhere on the summer circuit featuring femme, Arab, or Third World pix.

Aziza, who has lost her father and family as a child in the revolutionary years, accompanies her uncle and cousin Ali to the capital of Tunis, where Ali hopes to make it in business after forcing the family's move from the village to the city. While Ali burns up the family savings with pipe dreams, the uncle rises early to work on a distant job and Aziza tends to the household

chores as customary with Arab women. The uncle, however, is weakened by arduous work and bad health, falls fatally ill, and is hospitalized.

Aziza decides to go to work in a textile factory, where she slowly awakens to the necessity of determining her own life. Ali forces a showdown at home, whereupon she moves out and lives with neighbors — one of whom, Aicha, becomes the companion of an oil sheik whom Ali has been wooing for one of his schemes. When the uncle dies and Ali comes crawling back to weep on her shoulder, Aziza is now a fully emancipated and responsible individual, who can go it alone at the textile-mill. Her future is left open at the end, the last image a freeze-shot of her on the job.

Thesp Yasmine Khlat gives pic a convincing authenticity, while "Aziza" is also visually well mounted. Weak spots are in the script, its all too predictable story line, and overplaying of family scenes. Writer-director Adbel Latif Ben Ammar, who made "Sejnane" (1974) and "Simple Story" (1970), is a helmer to watch in the Arab countries. —*Holl.*

How To Beat The High Cost Of Living
(COLOR)

Well-dressed middle class types turn to robbery. Taint funny.

Hollywood, June 17.
An American International/Filmways release of a Jerome M. Zeitman/Robert Kaufman production. Produced by Jerome M. Zeitman, Robert Kaufman. Executive producer, Samuel Z. Arkoff. Directed by Robert Scheerer. Stars Susan Saint James, Jane Curtin, Jessica Lange, Richard Benjamin. Screenplay, Robert Kaufman, from a story by Leonora Thuna; camera (Movielab color), Jim Crabe; editor, Bill Butler; production design, Larry Paull; set decoration, Peg Cummings; associate producer, Robin Krause; assistant director, Irby Smith. Reviewed at the AIP/Filmways Screening Room, Beverly Hills, June 17, 1980. (MPAA Rating: PG) Running time: **110 MINS.**
Jane . . . . Susan Saint James
Elaine . . . . Jane Curtin
Louise . . . . Jessica Lange
Albert . . . . Richard Benjamin
Robert . . . . Fred Willard
Max . . . . Eddie Albert
Jack Heintzel . . . . Dabney Coleman
Gas station attendant . . . . Art Metrano
Bill Pike . . . . Ronnie Schell
Power & Light man . . . . . . Garrett Morris
Natalie . . . . Cathryn Damon
Charlotte . . . . Sybil Danning
Tim Lundy . . . . Al Checco
Mama Figueroa . . . . Carmen Zapata
Harriet . . . . Dru Wagner

Stir a little women's lib sensibility into "Fun with Dick And Jane" and you have "How To Beat The High Cost Of Living," one of the last pix produced under Samuel Z. Arkoff's auspices at American

International. It's difficult to imagine how any genuinely impoverished viewers will react to spectacle of generally well dressed and appointed middleclass trio of Susan Saint James, Jane Curtin and Jessical Lange being driven to robbery because of financial need, and topicality of the flat, overlong effort hardly compensates for its being thuddingly unfunny. More money can be seen onscreen than will probably be found in b.o. coffers.

Less outrageous than usual premise from scripter Robert Kaufman has divorcee Saint James needing more dough for her kids, Curtin left with nothing (save her house, nice car and clothes) when her husband skips out and Lange trying to take up the slack when hubby Richard Benjamin can't continue supporting her chic but unprofitable antique store.

Threesome therefore conspire to rob bills from a huge plastic ball located in a suburban shopping center. They're no pros, of course, but nonetheless pull off the caper after bungling just about every step along the way.

None of it convinces, but worse, Robert Scheerer's direction is terribly stagy and pacing is laggard, which leaves plenty of time to ponder the essential ridiculousness of the proceedings.

Of the actresses, Lange comes off best, in no small measure because her character has it more together than either Saint James, who essays a stock flustered housewife, or Curtin, who alternates between delivering sexual challenges and lewd taunts. Benjamin has a couple of decent comic moments, but Dabney Coleman has greatest success as a cop who never knows whether to score with Curton or arrest her.

Tech credits are routine, and some judicious cutting to speed things along would have helped considerably. —Cart.

Early Cranes
(SOVIET-COLOR)

Tashkent, May 27.
A Kirghizfilm Studio Production, Frunze, Kirghizian Republic, Soviet Union, in coproduction with Lenfilm, Leningrad; world rights, Sovexport Film, Moscow. Features entire cast. Directed by Bolotbek Shamshiev. Screenplay, Chinghiz Aitmatov, Shamshiev, based on a story by Aitmatov. Only credits available. Reviewed at Tashkent Film Festival, May 27, '80. Running time: 100 MINS.
Cast: Emil Boronchiev, Suimenkul Chikmorov, Gulsara Adjibekova, Hassan Abraimov, Akil Kulambaev.

Several of Chinghiz Aitmatov's stories have been adapted to the Soviet screen: Larissa Shepitko's "Heat" (1962), Andrei Mikhalkov-Konchalovsky's "The First Teacher" (1965), Tolomush Oreev's "The

Red Apple" (1976), and Bolotbek Shamshiev's "The White Ship" (1975). They were all produced at the Kirghizfilm Studio in Frunze, where the Kirghizian writer lives and (for a time) ran the film studio, thus bringing a breath of fresh air from the steppes in Middle Asia into Soviet cinema. Shamshiev, Kirghizia's best known helmer abroad (his "The White Ship" unspooled at the Berlin fest in 1976), adapted "Early Cranes" from another Aitmatov story.

This is the tale of two young boys from a small village in Kirghizia at the time of the Second World War, when the elder men were leaving for the front. One lad of 14, Sultanmurat, stays behind as the only remaining man in the family, a circumstance that requires him to drop his boyish pranks and grow up during separate tests of his manhood.

As in the best of Aitmatov's writings, it is these tests of manhood amid human weakness and moral corruption from outside that count the most. In the dead of winter the boy must search for hay for starving horses, but he is not above showing off how well, and badly, he rides in front of village girls — thus injuring one of the animal's legs. His own uncle, he discovers, is involved in stealing and reselling hay at higher prices, but this lesson comes after he has been duped by the family relative. Sultanmurat, in the end, proves himself to be a man, but at a cost of losing his innocence.

A worthy pair to Aitmatov-Shamshiev's earlier "White Ship," "Early Cranes" has the open space of the harsh Kirghizian steppes to recommend it, for lensing is a strong plus. —Holl.

De Witte Van Sichem
(Whitey)
(BELGIAN-COLOR)

Antwerp, June 6.
A New Star Distribution of a New Star-Visie production. Produced by Henk Van Soom and Roland Verhavert. Directed by Robbe de Hert. Features entire cast. Screenplay, Fernand Auwera, Robbe de Hert, Gaston Durnez, Louis-Paul Boon, based on work of Ernest Claes; camera (color), Walter Van den Ende, Theo van de Sande (Fastmancolor); editor, Ton de Graaf; sound; Andre Patrouillie; art direction, Philippe Graff; costumes, Ann Verhoeven. Set decoration, Andre Fonteyne; music, Jurgen Knieper; songs, Wannes van de Velde, Walter Heynen. Reviewed at Rex Theatre, Antwerp, April 26, 1980. Running time: 106 MINS.
Whitey .... Eric Clerckx
Farmer Coene .... Paul S. Jongers
Father of Whitey .... Blanka Heirman
Mother of Whitey .... Blanka Heirman
Heinke, Whitey's brother .....Jos Verbist
Liza, daughter of Coene . Magda De Winter
Nis, older brother of Whitey ... Ralf Troch
Priest Munte .... Luc Philips
Rozalien .... Martha Dewachter
Teacher ....Paul-Emiel Van Royen
Wannes Rasp .... Bert Struys

Young Flemish helmer Robbe de Hert (38) after making numerous shorts and a couple of documentaries makes his debut as a feature director with this good example of New Belgian Cinema.

Pic is a remake loosely based on a novel, by Ernest Claes, that has been translated into several languages. It was a smash hit as a film in 1934 and was the first Flemish talkie. Robbe de Hert and his co-scripters approach the literary stuff from a social distance. It is to their credit and that of Walther van den Ende and Theo Van de Sande, directors of photography, that an excellently composed and artistically sound picture was made, one that the Ministry of Flemish Culture (participating with $500,000) is likely to be proud of.

The story focuses on the difficult upbringing of a young boy (Eric Clerckx) in the poor Flemish countryside of Flanders at the beginning of the 1930s. He doesn't like going to school and he hates going to work on the farm, where he has to help out. From the first day everything turns out wrong.

His older brother courts the farmer's daughter thus causing a social conflict since rich and poor don't mix. The kid discovers the world of literature and works out his fantasies with his friends in big battle-scenes stimulated by a popular book "The Lion of Flanders."

He steals and borrows to buy books and gets found out and punished. Later he tries to commit suicide but doesn't succeed.

The moral of the story is that life in those good old days wasn't so good. Worse, the last shot of the film gives the impression that nothing much has changed.

Item is well paced, although some scenes just fade away among others as when Clerckx tries to trip his neighbour in church, or when he duels with the priest. But these minor faults, caused by the lack of experience, don't spoil the rest of this outstanding pic.

Besides good performances from Clerckx and the supporting roles, there's excellent production design by Philippe Graff and Andre Fonteyne. Film has a handsome period look.

The effect is ensemble film-making at its best. Jurgen Knieper's fine score is completed with some beautiful ballads by Wannes van de Velde, popular folksinger.

The low budget venture has possibilities for a foreign play-off. It has grossed more than $900,000 locally in its first six weeks of release. — Dave.

Pursuit In The Steppe
(SOVIET-COLOR)

Tashkent, May 26.
A Kazakhfilm Studio Production, Alma-Ata, Kazakhstan Republic, Soviet Union; world rights, Sovexport Film, Moscow. Features entire cast. Directed by Abdulla Karsakbaev. Screenplay, Anatoly Stephanov. Only credits available. Reviewed at Tashkent Film Festival, May 26, '80. Running time: 100 MINS.

Director Abdulla Karsakbaev made a name with his first feature film upon graduating from VGIK (Moscow Film School), "My Name Is Kozha" (1964), about a boy in a village that captured life on its simplest, most direct level in Kazakhstan. Other Karsakbaev pix are "The Anxious Morning" (1968) and "Journey into Childhood" (1970); he is known for liking images of striking beauty.

"Pursuit in the Steppe" shows the rugged landscape of the steppes in full splendor in this "Eastern" set during the Civil War period, when the Red Army in the early 1920's was fighting bandits and the like to bring the Revolution to this distant republic bordering on China. It's the story of Hamit, commander of a Red Army detachment, pursuing and fighting an armed band of outlaws led by the cunning Kudre.

Lots of action and top-grade lensing of the desert area in Kazakhstan merit a once-over. —Holl.

Opera Prima
(First Effort)
(SPANISH-FRENCH-COLOR)

Madrid, June 9.
A La Salamandra (Madrid) and Les Films Moliere (Paris) coproduction. Features entire cast. Directed by Fernando Trueba. Producer, Fernando Colomo. Screenplay, Fernando Trueba, Oscar Ladoire; camera (Eastmancolor), A. Luis Fernandez; music, Fernando Ember; editor, M.A. Santamaria. Reviewed at Cine Paz (Madrid), June 9, 1980. Running time: 92 MINS.
Matias .... Oscar Ladoire
Violeta .... Paula Molina
Leon .... Antonio Resines
Nicky .... Luis Gonzalez Regueral
Ana .... Kitty Manver
Zoila Gomez .... Marisa Paredes

This light upbeat comedy aimed at an articulate youth market has been chalking up excellent b.o. in Madrid for the past eight weeks, and shows no sign of flagging. Item was produced, scripted and acted by a group of relatively unknown young Spaniards, who have succeeded in making a sprightly comedy which is fully attuned to today's Spanish society, at least the "under 30s."

Despite a few slow parts and aimlessness in the plot, pic comes across charmingly, largely thanks to a wonderful performance by newcomer Oscar Ladoire and snappy, clever dialogs. Story is shot mostly in the old part of Madrid and in a garret apartment and has an authentic ring to it throughout. Several sex scenes are handled with expertise and good taste, the emphasis being on humor, which is sophisticated enough to probably appeal to educated audiences in all markets.

Title of pic is a play on words. "Opera prima" means "first work" in Latin, but in Spanish "prima" also means "cousin" and "Opera" can refer to a Madrid subway station adjacent to the opera building (in truth, a concert hall). Pic kicks off with a young man encountering his cousin (played by Paula Molina, who is thesp Angela Molina's sister, but could almost be her double). After various encounters between Matias, who is divorced, and the girl he moves into her top-floor apartment. She is studying atonal music with a longhair weirdo; he works for a news agency and does interviews with a photographer buddy, who counsels him on sex practices. Finally, the girl and the longhair decide they're going to charter off to Peru for a hippie-type encounter, but the girl changes her mind at the last minute, while going up the airport escalator. After a zany misencounter boy gets girl and they embrace in front of the opera as some derelicts and musicians are improvising jazz in the street.

Oscar Ladoire as Matias is a major discovery in the way of Spanish talent; supporting cast too is excellent. In all, pic has enough going for it that it might click in offshore sophisticated markets. —Besa.

Twelve Months
(JAPAN-COLOR-ANIMATION)

Tashkent, May 26.
A Japanese Film Production. An animated feature-length cartoon. Directed by Yasuhiro Yamaguchi. Screenplay, Kimio Yabuki. Only credits available. Reviewed at Tashkent Film Festival, May 26, '80. Running time: 90 MINS.

Feature-length animated cartoons have been popular in Japan for some two decades now. When Japanese fairy tales were exhausted, craftsmen like Kimio Yabuki turned to adapting "Fables from Hans Christian Andersen" (1969). It is Yabuki who wrote the script for "Twelve Months," another Western-oriented children's story about a little girl living in the household of a cruel mother and daughter who does all the work. Nearby, just beyond the forest, is an orphan queen of the same age, who likes having her own way.

She orders April flowers to be brought to her on New Year's Day, offering a reward to the lucky finder. This is just the excuse the evil stepmother needs to send the innocent little waif out into the snow to find the flowers. Just when she's about to die in a snowbank, the spirits of the Twelve Months appear around a fire — out of kindness they turn the calendar in this part of the forest to spring. Of course, the presence of the April flowers in court causes due curiosity, and everyone ventures out into the forest to meet with the spirits again — each receiving what's coming to him or her in the end.

Lovely drawings owing a nod to Disney, but quite Oriental in shading, texture, and coloring, make "Twelve Months" worth a peep for cartoon fans. Direction by Yasuhiro Yamaguchi has spirit and humor. —Holl.

Mamito
(FRENCH-COLOR)

Paris, June 6.
A Rush Distribution release of a Caraibes Production. Produced by Anne Dolanec. Features entire cast. Written and directed by Christian Lara. Camera (Fujicolor), Jean-Claude Couty; music, Emilhenco, Francisco Charles, Richard Cassin; editor, Martine Rousseau-Carrere; sound, Pierre Befve. Reviewed at the Palais des Arts, Paris, May 6, 1980. Running time: 90 MINS.
With: Lucrece Saintol, Greg Germain, Roger Tannous, Francisco Charles, Ibo Simon, Odette Laurent, Francois Maistre.

"Mamito" is the third in a series of features by Christian Lara, who is interested in fixing on film the social realities of his native Guadalupe. As in his first West Indian depiction, "Coco la Fleur," Lara again ensures a certain surface realism by casting local non-professionals with his professional actors, keeping his dialogue mostly in creole, and shooting in natural decors.

"Mamito" tells the story of an aging West Indian woman who, following the road accident that kills her doctor son and hospitalizes her (white) daughter-in-law, is obliged to end her retirement and return to the city to find work, in order to support her grandchildren.

She comes up against the serious unemployment and social ills that belie a picture postcard image of this French overseas department. She befriends a motley group of young natives intent on purchasing a plot of land and setting up a farm collective, thus affirming an economic independence out of key with the social structure of the island. The money is finally found after the daughter-in-law has a stormy reunion with her father, a rich landowner who had disowned

her for marrying a black. He has a change-of-heart and decided to finance the venture.

Lara's aim is didactic and the film suffers, beyond its cinematic ordinariness, from sketchiness in characterization and an uneasy control of narrative. But what makes "Mamito" a sympathetic and often informative film is the well-done weave of cultural notations and social types. The humor and generosity of spirit of the West Indian people give the film its true appeal, which could help give it footing in overseas markets. —Len.

Miskhak Makhbuim
(Hide 'n Seek)
(ISRAELI-COLOR)

Cannes, May 18.
A Jeff Justin-Dan Wolman Production. Written and directed by Dan Wolman. Features entire cast. Camera (color), Ilan Rosenberg; Editor, Shoshana Wolman; music, Amnon Wolman; art director, Ruth Dar. Reviewed Olympia Cinema, Cannes, May 17, 1980. Running time: 90 MINS.
Cast: Gila Almagor, Doron Tavori, Chaim Hadaya, Efrat Lavie, Binyamin Armon, Rachel Shor.

This is Dan Wolman's fourth feature film and obviously his most personal one. The story is set in Jerusalem, some 35 years ago and its main character is a 12-year-old boy. As Wolman himself lived at that time, and still lives, in Jerusalem, and was more or less in the same age bracket, it is not very difficult to see the relationship.

Uri, the boy, lives with his grandfather, as his parents are constantly away on political missions connected with the turmoil following Second World War, prior to the Independence of the State of Israel. Feeling neglected, he compensates by ignoring his duties at school and organizing a gang of children who would like to help in the struggle against the British and Arabs, without understanding too well what is really going on.

As the story unfolds a tutor is brought in by the grandfather to help Uri improve his standard at school, and the development of the relationship between the kid and the tutor, from mistrust to deep sympathy, to suspicion and finally total dismay, are the core of the film.

Uri learns to admire the young man who teaches him, refuses to believe that he may be involved in any possible way with Arabs and he can't cope until the very end with the fact that such a relationship does exist, but has nothing to do with treason, as Uri and his friends suspected.

While the story seems to be wavering, in the first part of the film, and deviates in a number of directions, it concentrates in later stages and becomes well defined.

But no less important than the main narrative line is the background, very suggestively etched, but never forced on the audience. Wolman shows a society in which tolerance is impossible, because dangers from outside rule out any kind of tolerance.

He points out the wide variety of ingredients forming this society, escapees from the Holocaust and political activists who are fighting in every possible way to achieve their goal, Israel's independence, at the cost of their private lives, he doesn't forget the nostalgia for the "old country and the old culture" left behind in Europe and the coarse bringing up of youth which already made some of the older generation complain that "this is a country where people don't let you live in peace."

Shot on a shoestring budget in 14 days, in 16m, and later blown up (the copy viewed in Cannes will have to be improved upon), the style of the film is very intimate, the acting subdued and mostly convincing and natural, and the Jerusalem scenery is used in its less known but more authentic aspects.

Technically the film is not entirely flawless, which may be only natural taking into consideration the conditions of its production. The film has to be handled carefully, it will most certainly have a career in festivals and art houses, and is definitely a credit to Wolman and to the Fund for the Encouragement of Quality Films which helped the project all along. —Edna.

Herbie Goes Bananas
(COLOR)

That car goes South.

Hollywood, July 1.
A Buena Vista release of a Walt Disney production. Produced by Ron Miller. Directed by Vincent McEveety. Features entire cast. Co-produced by Kevin Concoran, Don Tait. Screenplay, Tait, based on characters created by Gordon Buford; camera (Technicolor), Frank Phillips; editor, Gordon D. Brenner; music, Frank De Vol; songs, De Vol; art direction, John B. Mansbridge, Rodger Maus; set decoration, Norman Rockett, Roger M. Shook; special effects, Art Cruickshank, Danny Lee; matte artist, Constantine Ganakes; second unit director, Michael Dmytryk; assistant director, Win Phelps. Reviewed at the Walt Disney Studios, Burbank, June 27, 1980. (MPAA Rating: G.) Running time: 100 MINS.

Aunt Louise .... Cloris Leachman
D.J. .... Charles Martin Smith
Prindle ....John Vernon
Pete .... Stephan W. Burns
Melissa .... Elyssa Davalos
Paco .... Joaquin Garay III
Captain Elythe .... Harvey Korman
Shepard .... Richard Jaeckel
Quinn .... Alex Rocco
Chief Stewart .... Fritz Feld

Only so much coin can be wrung from the antics of a magical Volkswagen. The law of diminishing returns has applied to Disney's "Herbie" series, and the newly-released fourth entry, "Herbie Goes Bananas," should follow that trend to okay but less-than-thrilling b.o. results. Mildly amusing summer programmer relies on a thumbnail script and sight gags that have run out of steam.

First of the series, "The Love Bug," was a smash hit in 1969, bringing in domestic rentals of $23,050,000. "Herbie Rides Again" in 1974 did $17,500,000, and "Herbie Goes To Monte Carlo" netted $14,-000,000 in 1977. Vincent McEveety, who directed the last two in the series, is a competent but uninspired hand who doesn't have the wit and visual panache of Robert Stevenson, director of the first two.

Episodic, meandering plot of "Herbie Goes Bananas" follows itinerant young gringos Charles Martin Smith and Stephan W. Burns on a Central American trek with the magical VW en route to a Brazilian road race which, anticlimactically, is never seen in the film. Promise of another entry in the series may not leave audiences panting with expectation.

Most of the amusement is provided by the customarily expert comic turns of Cloris Leachman, Harvey Korman, and Fritz Feld. The visual stunts vary widely in comic invention. Highlight is an amusing scene in a bull ring, with the car challenging a bull. Too many of the sight gags, though, are not built with enough care for pacing and surprise.

Smith, the only cast principal of "American Graffiti" whose career didn't take off like a rocket, finally is getting parts that enable him to keep developing his light-comedy skills. His role here isn't much of a challenge but is amiable enough to guarantee him continued exposure. Burns is less at ease, while ingenue Elyssa Davalos is pleasant within the confines of a badly antiquated part. Moppet Joaquin Garay III is so cloyingly cute he'll make adult viewers' teeth ache.

With this unimaginative rehash of a once-popular formula, Disney seems to be marking time until it figures out how to recapture its hold on the kiddie audience. Studio is prepping some projects that promise a bolder approach to the marketplace than endless "Herbie" pix, the kind of films which ultimately send viewers back to the tube. —Mac.

Dr. Heckyl & Mr. Hype
(COLOR)

Perverse horror spoof hits funny bone.

Hollywood, June 27.
A Cannon Films release of a Golan-Globus production. Produced by Menahem Golan, Yoram Globus. Directed, screenplay by Charles B. Griffith. Stars Oliver Reed. Camera (Metrocolor), Robert Carras; editor, Skip Schoolnik; music, Richard Band; production design, Maxwell Mendes; art direction, Bob Ziembiki; set decoration, Maria Delia Javier; sound, Rob Newell; assistant director, Peter Manoojian. Reviewed at the Celluloid Services Screening Room, Hollywood, June 27, 1980. (MPAA Rating: R.) Running time: 99 MINS.

Dr. Heckyl/Mr. Hype .... Oliver Reed
Coral Careen .... Sunny Johnson
Miss Finebum .... Maia Danziger
Dr. Hinkle .... Mel Welles
Lt. Mac Druck, 'Il Topo' ...... Virgil Frye
Dr. Lew Hoo .... Kedrick Wolfe
Sgt. Fleacollar .... Jackie Coogan
Pizelle Puree .... Corinne Calvet

The title is dubious, Oliver Reed's face looks like a moldy melon with a half-eaten carrot for a nose and topped by a used Brillo pad, and director Charles B. Griffith has rarely worked outside the Roger Corman shop before. So against all odds, "Dr. Heckyl & Mr. Hype" has emerged as a real rib-tickler, a massively perverse comedy which pumps new life into an overworn basic premise.

Sharp looking pic is not horrific in the least, so sales job consists of tipping off prospective customers that this is closer to "Love At First Bite" than to another Jekyll and Hyde variation. But laughs are to be had by those who tune into this weird tale.

Reed first materializes as a gruesomely deformed podiatrist (and, needless to say, foot fetishist) working at the hip clinic of wigged-but Mel Welles. Attempting suicide by drinking a bottle of one of Welles' potions, which is seen to have changed 300-pound women into sleek model types overnight, Reed doesn't die but instead is transformed into ... dashing Oliver Reed. Looking into the mirror for the first time to witness his new face, he exclaims with mock seriousness, "My God, I'm beautiful."

Reborn man then embarks on a mad dash to lose his long-unwanted virginity but ends up killing his prey, as a result of his new evil nature, before consummating the act. Police begin trailing him at the same time as the burly Mr. Hype starts moving in on his dream girl, Sunny Johnson.

Natch, Sunny prefers the sweet personality of ugly Dr. Heckyl to the nasty Mr. Hype. The whole thing becomes more and more convoluted until the outrageous climax, which has another medic, the swishy Dr. Hoo, taking the potion, turning into the ravishing Maia Danziger and beginning to make passionate love to the by-now desperately virginal Mr. Hype. In mid-act, of course, both transform back into their former selves, and assuredly don't live happily ever after.

Everyone involved has entered into the rollicking spirit of the entire enterprise. Reed is actually somewhat touching as his monster half, and has a field day playing a parody of a macho leading man as Mr. Hype. Welles, Virgil Frye as a literally flat-footed private eye and Jackie Coogan as a desk sergeant at a dungeon-like jail also contribute significantly to the frequent hilarity.

This film undoubtedly reps "purest" expression of writer-director Charles B. Griffith's zany personality since his scripts for Corman's "A Bucket Of Blood" and "The Little Shop Of Horrors" 20 years ago (script credit comes "with apologies to Robert Louis Stevenson"). Visuals here, aided by Robert Carras' pro lensing, Maxwell Mendes' fine production design and a highly active fog machine, are also extremely pleasing.

Overall, film is one of those nice surprises that occasionally pop up in the exploitation field. —Cart.

Premier Voyage
(First Voyage)
(FRENCH-COLOR)

Paris, June 19.
A Planfilm release of a Fildebroc/Oliane Productions/Antenne 2 coproduction. Produced by Michelle de Broca, Marie-Laure Reyre. Stars Marie and Vincent Trintignant. Directed by Nadine Trintignant. Written by Trintignant, Henriette Jelinek; camera (Eastmancolor), William Lubtchansky; music, Georges Delerue; editor, Carol Marquand; sound, Pierre Gamet. Reviewed at 7 Parnassiens Theatre, Paris, April 29, 1980. Running time: 90 MINS.

Marie Lambert .... Marie Trintignant
Vincent Lambert .... Vincent Trintignant
Yan Lambert .... Patrick Chesnais
Aunt Jeanne .... Lucienne Hamon
Jean Decaze ....Richard Berry
Motorist .... Philippe Rouleau

Nadine Trintignant, wife of actor Jean-Louis Trintignant and a filmmaker with five previous features to her credit, directed this often touching tale about two children in search of a father following the death of their mother. She has cast her own children, Marie, 19, and Vincent, 5, in the main roles. Some local critics have dismissed it as a home-movie in 35m, but few home-movies have the delicate emotion that this picture emanates in its best moments.

The screenplay, by Trintignant and Henriette Jelinek (who collaborated with Jeanne Moreau on her "L'Adolescente"), is thin. Following the sudden death of their mother in a southern French town, two children escape from the tight-fisted custody of an unsympathetic aunt. Marie yearns to find the father whose departure years earlier has left her deeply wounded. Her little brother is too young to remember him.

Avoiding the police, they make their way through the countryside, headed for Antibes, where the father works as a skipper on a private yacht. Several days and several adventures later they arrive at the port and succeed in locating him.

The film's real achievement is that though one is conscious of the way it's designed to work on the lachrymal glands, there is no shame of succumbing to its wistful charms. Credit for this must go to Trintignant, who directs with discretion, restraint and, of course, love. And she has fine support from cinematographer William Lubtchansky, composer Georges Delerue and editor Carol Marquand.

Fine supporting actors help sharpen the film's poignancy. Lucienne Hamon is excellent as the iron-fisted aunt whose austerity repels the children. Richard Berry lends a sensitive presence to the figure of a young writer who puts them up for a night. Philippe Rouleau effectively composes, without worn psychotic frills, a disturbed motorist. Patrick Chesnais, as the long-lost father, is nice and relaxed, a welcome relief from the psychologically constipated roles he usually gets.

The Trintignant children move credibly, and photogenically, through the various adventures, particularly Vincent, a delicious little cupcake whom mother Trintignant directs with special acuity.

"Premier Voyage" is nothing to trumpet about, but it has a bittersweet little melody that could have siren appeal in small-scale bookings abroad. —*Len.*

Airplane
(COLOR)

Can't stop the laughs.

Hollywood, June 6.
A Paramount Pictures release of a Howard W. Koch production. Produced by Jon Davison. Features entire cast. Executive producers, directed, written by Jim Abrahams, David Zucker, Jerry Zucker. Camera (Metrocolor), Joseph Biroc; editor, Patrick Kennedy; music, Elmer Bernstein; production design, Ward Preston; set design, Joe Hubbard; set decoration, Anne D. McCulley; costume design, Rosanna Norton; sound, Tom Overton; assistant director, Aren Schmidt. Reviewed at Paramount Studios, Hollywood, June 6, 1980. (MPAA Rating: PG.) Running time: **88 MINS.**

Ted Striker . . . . .Robert Hays
Elaine . . . . .Julie Hagerty
Murdock . . . . Kareem Abdul-Jabbar
McCroskey . . . . Lloyd Bridges
Captain Oveur . . . . Peter Graves
Dr. Rumack . . . . Leslie Nielsen
Randy . . . . ,. Lorna Patterson
Kramer . . . . Robert Stack
Johnny . . . . Stephen Stucker

"Airplane" is what they used to call a laff-riot. Made by team which turned out "Kentucky Fried Movie" a couple of seasons back, this spoof of disaster features beats any other film on the horizon for sheer number of comic gags and lines and may prove to be just what audiences and exhibs are looking for in the way of a good-time sleeper hit.

Writer-directors Jim Abrahams, David Zucker and Jerry Zucker leave no cliche unturned as they lay waste to the "Airport"-style disaster cycle, among other targets. From the clever, "Jaws" take-off opening to the final, irreverent title card, laughs come thick and fast, and only audience frustration may come from not being able to hear all the dialog above the audible reaction.

Plot is derived from a 1957 Paramount release called "Zero Hour!" starring Dana Andrews, Sterling Hayden and Linda Darnell and has former pilot Robert Hays, now terrified of flying due to wartime malfeasance, boarding an L.A.-to-Chicago flight in pursuit of ex-girlfriend stewardess Julie Hagerty.

When flight personnel, including sexually-deviant pilot Peter Graves and co-pilot Kareem Abdul-Jabbar, contract food poisoning on board, Hays is called upon to land the craft safely, an effort not made easier by fact that air controller Lloyd Bridges is completely crazed

and the man talking him down, Robert Stack, hates him for his wartime conduct.

All of this is just a rack upon which the Zuckers and Abrahams hang their determinedly flipped-out conceits, many of which may be thin but which are so relentless as to keep the laughter more or less continuous.

Desired effect, which has been achieved, is that of watching a bad 1950s drama in which characters carry all the absurdly pressurized situations to their furthest comic extremes. That this works is largely due to astute casting of such recognizable types as Lloyd Bridges, Robert Stack, Peter Graves and Leslie Nielsen in sort of roles they've played frequently in the past, but never in this fashion.

Along with Abdul-Jabbar as a flyer, wacky cameos include Ethel Merman as a hospital patient who sits up in her bed and sings "Everything's Coming Up Roses," Maureen McGovern as a nun and tax-cut fanatic Howard Jarvis as a victimized taxi passenger.

Pic has been extremely well produced on low budget by Jon Davison under production banner of Howard W. Koch, and attention to detail is exemplary not only in casting but in subtle nuances, such as wonderfully overdone score by Elmer Bernstein, heavy contrast "studio"-style lensing by Joseph Biroc and having jet airliner give off noise of a prop plane, which helps evoke the 1950s ambiance.

Robert Hays and Julie Hagerty hit the proper mock-earnest tone as the quarreling lovers pushed together through mutual jeopardy, but can't help but seem the straights in a world full of zanies. Parody may be the lowest form of humor, but few comedies in ages have rocked the laugh meter this hard. —*Cart.*

Used Cars
(COLOR)

Also used jokes.

Hollywood, June 25.
A Columbia Pictures release. Produced by Bob Gale. Directed by Robert Zemeckis. Features entire cast. Executive producers, Steven Spielberg, John Milius. Screenplay, Zemeckis and Gale; camera (Metrocolor), Donald M. Morgan; editor, Michael Kahn; music, Patrick Williams; production design, Peter M. Jamison; set decoration, Linda Spheeris; sound, Ronald G. Cogswell; second unit director, stunt coordination, Terry J. Leonard; assistant director, Richard Luke Rothschild. Reviewed at the Samuel Goldwyn Theatre, Beverly Hills, June 25, 1980. (MPAA Rating: R.) Running time: **113 MINS.**

Rudy Russo . . . . .Kurt Russell
Roy L. Fuchs/
Luke Fuchs . . . . Jack Warden
Jeff . . . . Gerrit Graham
Jim the Mechanic . . . . Frank McRae

Barbara Fuchs . . . . Deborah Harmon
Sam Slaton . . . . .Joseph P. Flaherty
Freddie Paris . . . . .David L. Lander
Eddie Winslow . . . . Michael McKean
Mickey . . . . .Michael Talbott
Carmine . . . . Harry Northup
Manuel . . . . Alfonso Arau
Judge Harrison . . . . Al Lewis
Mr. Chertner . . . . .Woodrow Parfrey
Charlie . . . . Andrew Duncan
Tucker . . . . .Dub Taylor
Al . . . . Claude Earl Jones
Stanley Dewoski . . . ; . . . . . . Dan Barrows
Margaret . . . . Cheryl Rixon

What might have looked like a great idea on paper — a no-holds-barred comedy about cut-throat sellers of what are euphemistically called "pre-owned vehicles" — has been tackled by filmmakers who haven't expanded it much beyond the one joke inherent in the premise. A few targets are inevitably hit through the shotgun blast approach, resulting in some laughs along the way, but "Used Cars," overlength by about half-an-hour, is ultimately swallowed up in the crassness it relentlessly exposes. Pic could perform well for awhile in undemanding situations, but tank wasn't filled up for a long trip.

Plot has fat cat car dealer Jack Warden desperate, for some reason, to knock out negligible competition provided by an insolvent jalopy shop across the street, owned by a brother also portrayed by Warden. Latter dies early on but operator Kurt Russell and partners Gerrit Graham and Frank McRae disguise the fact to prevent their slimey neighbor from inheriting the property and then embark on a series of outrageous promotions, including, in pic's funniest scenes, a nude commercial and the jamming of a Presidential address to get one of their spots on nationwide television.

To boot, team takes advantage of their former boss' daughter, Deborah Harmon, to further their own ends and Russell eagerly schemes with local machine to become a political candidate simply by paying a modest entry fee.

Like much further downscale exploitation fare, film gets most of its mileage out of exposing the venality and essential corruption of "the system," but cynically takes the attitude, "if you can't beat it, join it." Not only is the slogan rapturously endorsed, but great glee is taken in presenting the various manners in which the public can be systematically ripped off, an attitude which quickly becomes depressing and can hardly support the length with which it is indulged.

Scripters Robert Zemeckis and Bob Gale have provided very little context or societal texture for their unmodulated tale, which disagreeably seeks to find humor in characters' humiliation, embarrassment and even death.

Nonetheless, Zemeckis has directed with undeniable vigor, if insufficient control and discipline, and Russell, Warden, Graham, McRae and Harmon, to name only the principals, have responded with energetic performances which help smooth over some of the more unpalatable moments. Al Lewis is a momentary stand-out as an imposing judge presiding over the climactic fraud trial, and Dub Taylor and Dan Barrows have nice bits.

Tech credits are okay, and special mention should be made of Terry J. Leonard's contribution as second unit director and stunt coordinator. —*Cart.*

Der Aufstand
(The Uprising)
(WEST GERMAN-COLOR)

Berlin, June 14.
An Istmo Film Production, in coproduction with Provobis, von Vietinghoff Film, and Zweites Deutsches Fernsehen (ZDF), Munich-Berlin, San Jose (Costa Rica). Features entire cast. Directed by Peter Lilienthal. Screenplay, Lilienthal, Antonio Skarmeta; camera (color), Michael Ballhaus. Only credits available. Reviewed at Atelier am Zoo, Berlin, June 14, '80. Running time: **90 MINS.**

Cast: Carlos Catania, Oscar Castillo, Guido Saenz, Agustin Pereira.

Winner of a German Film Prize, Peter Lilienthal's "The Uprising" takes up where, in a sense, his "La Victoria" (1973) and "The Country Is Calm" (1975) (winner of a GFP in 1976) left off. All three are political portraits of Latin American countries in turmoil, the first two dealing with Chile before and after the military coup. "The Uprising" focuses on the fall of the Somoza regime in Nicaragua last year, filmed on the spot just four months after the event.

First half deals with a family in Leon (Nicaragua's former capital), whose favorite son is a soldier in the dictator's army and wants to desert—but the boy's captain threatens to kill the family and neighbors should he do so. When the fighting in the streets gets heavy, however, Agustin joins his sister in the Sandinist National Liberation Front (FSLN) as the attack on the city's headquarters takes place. The father is on the son's side, no matter what happens.

The second half concentrates on the actual fighting in the streets, all reconstructed as it happened via eyewitnesses. In the end, Captain Flores attempts to break out of the blazing compound by taking hostages, one the boy's father to get his revenge. Then the captain and the soldier die in a shoot-out.

Docu footage added to storyline gives some needed immediacy, and Lilienthal's taste for visual images over dialogue keeps the whole from getting boring. Still, since everything in the story is either known or predictable, the film drags when it should be offering something new or striking instead of repetition for its own sake. Docus on the uprising in Nicaragua were more convincing.

Lilienthal is a top tv director, one who can work with nonprofessionals and draw strong, unassuming performances. He has a poetic sense that makes his political tracts clear and dramatic, although everything is drawn from life and real events as they happened. How he is able to shoot in crowded areas with masses is an enviable secret and a sure sign of a talented director. Lilienthal can match German helmers like Herzog, Fassbinder, and Wenders almost at will, given half the chance. —*Holl.*

Les Sous-Doues
(The Under-Gifted)
(FRENCH-COLOR)

Paris, June 19.
An AMLF release of a Films 7 production. Stars Michel Galabru, Maria Pacome, Daniel Auteuil. Produced and directed by Claude Zidi. Written by Zidi, Didier Kaminka, Michel Fabre, camera (Fujicolor), Paul Bonis; music, Bob Brault, sound, Jean-Louis Ughetto; editor, Nicole Saunier. Reviewed at Marignan-Concorde Theatre, Paris, June 13, 1980. Running time: **92 MINS.**
With Maria Pacome, Hubert Deschamps, Tonie Marshall, Michel Galabru, Daniel Auteuil, Raymond Bussieres, Philippe Taccini, Catherine Erhardy.

Claude Zidi's "Les Sous-Doues," which is providing a big shot in the arm to the French boxoffice of the end of the season, is a classroom hijinks comedy in tune with current public forum debate here on modern education and the value of the French Baccalaureat (or "Bac"). But Zidi has no purpose other than good mindless fun, and that's what he delivers, though this package seems designed basically for local tastes.

Zidi is one of the more competent exponents of "Saturday Night" entertainment films. As director he knows his craft fluently and this latest effort has crisp cinematic movement, helped by a mostly young and personable cast. As writer he is less secure, but "Les Sous-Doues," built on a tradition of schoolboy humour that goes back to "Zero for Conduct" (1933) by Jean Vigo, has a several amusing gags knowingly interspersed with its more tired antics.

Film is set in Versailles in a private school where less-gifted students prepare for the baccalaureat exams. But this particular establishment, run by Maria Pacome and Hubert Deschamps, is cursed with a bunch of students for whom

academic failure is the highest ideal.

When a student prank ends in the dynamiting of the entire school, the judge, before whom the students are brought up, puts forth two equally chilling alternatives: prison or success at the Bac exams. They opt for the latter, but plot cunningly to cheat every inch of the way.—*Len.*

Gross Und Klein
(Big and Little)
(W. GERMAN-COLOR-16m)

Berlin, June 16.
A Regina Ziegler Film Production, in collaboration with the Schaubuehne am Halleschen Ufer, Berlin, and in coproduction with Sender Freies Berlin (SFB). Features entire cast. Directed by Peter Stein. Screenplay, Botho Strauss, adapted from his play with the same title; camera (color), Michael Ballhaus; sets. Fred Berndt; editing, Clarissa Ambach. Reviewed at Studio am Kudam, Berlin, June 16, '80. Running time: **240 MINS.**
Cast: Edith Clever (Lotte), Gunter Berger, Gerhard Bienert, Tina Engel, Johanna Hofer, Jutta Lampe, Hans Madin, Wilhelm Menne, Elke Petri, Udo Samel, Meray Uelgen, Hildegard Wensch.

Made for tv and adapted directly from a successful Schaubuehne Ensemble legit production in Berlin a few seasons back, Peter Stein's filming of Botho Strauss's "Big and Little" could awaken some interest among theatre buffs, possibly even a film fest that places its chips on the esoteric. Stein and Stauss have the same appeal on home ground as novelist-filmer Peter Handke ("The Left-Handed Woman") and legit director-filmer Luc Bondy ("The Ortlieb Women").

Play is over four hours long, and deals with meandering around Saarbruecken of Lotte, a modern Goethe-heroine lost in the maze of stuffy well-to-do, the artist colony, and the tears- and-fears of the German psyche. Strauss's brittle text offers moments of listening pleasure (like a radio play), but a static camera and frozen stage acting by the principles doesn't make a film.

This is, however, a fine play and superbly acted, particularly by Edith Clever in the lead as Lotte. Stein also gives evidence of having come a long way since shooting "Summer Guests" (1975), based on Gorky (Strauss reworked the play for Stein and the Schaubuehne), and "The Farewell Trilogy" (1979), another Strauss play at the Schaubuehne. The opening scene, lensed in a deluxe hotel in Morocco on location, plus other exterior scenes, give the film buoyancy and breathing space over the long stretch.
Credits are tops, especially lenser Michael Ballhaus. —*Holl.*

The Morning Star
(MONGOLIA-B&W)

Tashkent, May 26.
A Mongolian Film Production. Features entire cast. Directed by Zhemyangiin Buntar. Only credits available. Reviewed at Tashkent Film Festival, May 26, '80. Running time: **90 MINS.**
Cast: Sh. Davaasamba, J. Suhuyag, Ts. Damagindorj, J. Delgerjargal.

The Mongolian cinema has yet to produce a filmmaker or a film of world standard. At the 40th anni of the Mongolkino Studios in 1976, emphasis was placed on contemporary themes, such as the emancipation of women, family problems, and Socialist society, for the rest of the decade's production.

Director Zhamyangiin Buntar, who made with G. Zhigzhidsuren the historical epic, "The Legend of the Oasis," deals with a collective farm in "The Morning Star." Pic drags along at a snail's pace without any dramatic high points or striking visual images to redeem it, although some black and white shots of the vast grazing lands and wheat fields aptly fit the widescreen format. —*Holl.*

Babek
(SOVIET-COLOR)

Tashkent, May 27.
An Azerbaidzhanfilm Studio Production. Baku, Azerbaidzhan Republic, Soviet Union; world rights, Sovexport Film, Moscow. Features entire cast. Directed by Eldar Kuliev. Screenplay, Anver Mamedkhanli. Only credits available. Reviewed at Tashkent Film Festival, May 27, '80. Running time: **120 MINS.**
Cast: Rasim Belaev, Amalia Panakhova, Tamara Yandieva.

An historical pic about a national hero, Eldar Kuliev's "Babek" tells the story of how the Azerbaidzhan people repelled foreign invaders in the Middle Ages. There's plenty of action, horses, costumes, and the like in this epic, but the whole lacks the dramatic force to make it memorable. It should perhaps be noted that the Djafar Djabarly Studio (named for national poet and writer who wrote national classics and penned the script for the republic's first feature film in the 1930's) produces four-five feature pix a year, with the main emphasis on national, historical heroes like Babek. —*Holl.*

Naomi
(Naomi)
(JAPANESE-COLOR)

Tokyo, June 15.
A Toei Central Film Production. Released by Toei. Produced by Toei Central Film. Directed by Yoichi Takabayashi. Features entire cast.

Screenplay, Takabayashi, based on "Chijin No Ai," by Junichiro Tanizaki; camera (color), Sotaro Takamura; sound, Toshiya Ban; lighting, Kazuo Yamada; art direction, Hitoshi Nojiri; editing, Osamu Tanaka. Reviewed at the Yuraku Cinema, Tokyo, June 15, 1980. Running time: **100 MINS.**
Naomi .... Yuki Mizuhara
Joji Kawai .... Makoto Saito
Hamada .... Akihiro Mitsuda
Nakamura .... Takashi Tanaka
Yoshida .... Tsutomu Kuroda
Seki .... Eiji Tsuyama
Haruno .... Ai Mori

The plot of this execrable pic has the eponymous heroine (Yuki Mizuhara), at age 16, being sweet-talked into a living-together relationship with a businessman 14 years her senior (Makoto Sato). At first the innocent party, the young woman eventually comes to terms with her own sexuality and subsequently begins using it so expertly that Sato is enthralled by her. So much so, in fact, that, despite her doing him wrong time and again, by pic's end the two are determined to stay together.

Based on a work by one of Japan's most respected novelists, the pic is characterized by an abundance of predictable dialog. Visual cliches abound as well: to suggest wide-eyed innocence, Mizuhara simply widens her eyes; when the cuckolded Sato is told of his lover's consorting with other men, he envisions Mizuhara in various ecstatic positions with various males.

Even accounting for technical restraints imposed by its apparently miniscule budget, "Naomi" is a chicken. Lighting is glaringly bright, sound recording is poor and the camera work is far too stationary. Of the acting of the two principals, the less said the better.
—*Bail.*

Two Champions of Shaolin
(HONG KONG-COLOR)

Bangkok, June 19.
A Shaw Bros. production and release. Produced by Run Run Shaw. Executive producer, Mona Fong. Directed by Chang Cheh. Features entire cast. Story and script, Chang Cheh and I Kuang; camera (color), Tsao Hui Chi; art direction, Johnson Tsao; music and sound, Eddie Wang; editors, Chiang Hsing Lung and Li Ying Hoi; martial art instructors, Lu Feng, Chiang Sheng and Kuo Che. Reviewed at Warner theatre, Bangkok, June 19, 1980. Running time: **29 MINS.**
Tung Chien Chin .... Lo Meng
Wu Hui Kan ....Chiang Sheng
Chin Tai Lai .... Sun Chien
Li Pa Shan ....Wang Li
Li Erh Huan ....Wen Hsueh Erh
Kao Chin Chung ....Lu Feng
Wei Hsing Hung ....Chien Hsiao Hao
Chin Pi Erh .... Yang Ching Ching
Li De Chung .... Yu Tai Ping
Chih Shan .... Kuan Tsung
San Te .... Liang Yao Wen

Shaw's most prolific action helmer, Chang Cheh, now busily builds up young new screen heroes, perhaps because these past four years Shaw hasn't come up with an action superstar, except Alexander Fu Sheng, who himself is Cheh's protege.

With last year's "Shaolin Heroes," Cheh introduced several new action stars, including Lo Meng and Sun Chien, both of whom now regularly work with Cheh. Another promising find, Chiang Sheng, plays one of the "Two Champions," and billed as "specially introducing" is Chien Hsiao Hao, for whom Cheh appears to have bigger roles in mind next time.

It's difficult to tell if any of these newcomers will become a superstar. Apparently, the strength of their performances lies on good teamwork more than anything else. None is them is outstanding, although of course Cheh includes scenes like the one where Lo Meng uproots a big tree with his bare hands which makes it impossible for the viewer to forget who did that.

Nonetheless, Lo Meng has yet to develop his acting style. He's laughable in doleful scenes, particularly when he mourns the murder of his bride and her brother. It might have been better if that embarrassing scene was lopped off.

The future of Shaw's new stars completely depends on Cheh. No-one else can determine who stays and who exits among this new blood. Only certainty is the fact that Cheh favors actors with Chinese martial arts expertise who can also work as fighting instructors (as actor Kuo Chue does this time).

Over the years, Cheh and co-writer I Kuang have stayed close to variations of one single format — a feud between two factions. The viewer must choose sides, but Cheh makes it easy by usually putting the majority of the winning fighters on one side.

Cheh himself casts a harsh, impartial eye on the antagonists. In "Two Champions," for example, the Shaolin and Wutang clans are at odds due to clashing loyalties, but nevertheless both short-lived winners and born losers litter the screen at the close. Pic ends in a draw.

Nor does Cheh let dramatic moments run unabated — he times them. He would never make it big with tearjerker fans. The double tragedy involving two pairs of lovers consumes less than ten minutes.

The inevitability of Chien Hsiao Hao's suicide at film's end, in atonement for betraying his girl friend, is clinched by a flashing memory of the two of them sitting side by side throwing stones in a pond. There's no such earlier scene in the pic. Instead, there's one where Hao sits by himself throwing stones in the pond, looking enormously pleased. Viewers must supply the missing parts of the romantic subplot which Cheh curtails perfectly. —Cano.

Die Flucht
(The Escape)
(W. GERMAN-YUGOSLAV-B&W)

Berlin, June 10.
A CCC Kunstfilm production with Avala Film, Belgrade. World Sales, Omnia Deutsche Film Export. Directed by Edwin Zbonek. Features entire cast. Screenplay, Sigmund Bendkover, Al Bronsowy based on an idea by Robert Azderball; camera (black and white), Nenad Jovicic. Reviewed at CCC screening room, Berlin, June 10, 1980. Running time: 80 MINS.
Cast: Gunther Ungeheuer, Goetz George, Helmut Oeser, Alexander Allerson, Katinka Hoffmann, Helmut Sobotka.

Goetz George plays a Nazi concentration camp vict'm in this surprisingly good little black-and-white film. Action sees him being mistreated among his fellow sufferers in the compound and, in flashback, how he came to the camp where his brother (Gunther Ungeheuer) is the commandant. His escape to freedom is breathtaking.

The simple story, shot militant frills and edited to an extraordinarily fast pace, is grabbing and exciting.

The actors are all excellent and well-known in Germany. That their names and faces will mean nothing in other countries is even helpful in that their anonymity will heighten the realism of the film.
—Koci.

The Sea Wolves
(BRITISH-COLOR)

Okay charge of stiff-uppered wartime heroics.

London, July 4.
Rank Film Distributors release of a Lorimar presentation, produced by Euan Lloyd. Directed by Andrew V. McLaglen. Stars Gregory Peck, Roger Moore, David Niven. Exec producer, Chris Chrisafis; screenplay by Reginald Rose (based on James Leasor's novel "The Boarding Party"); camera (color), Tony Imi; editor, John Glen; music, Roy Budd; production design, Syd Cain; art direction, Maurice Cain; associate producer, Harold Buck; ass't director, Bert Batt. Reviewed at the Leicester Sq. Theatre, London, July 3, 1980. (BBFC rating: A). Running time: 120 MINS.

Col. Lewis Pugh	Gregory Peck
Capt. Gavin Stewart	Roger Moore
Col. Bill Grice	David Niven
Jack Cartwright	Trevor Howard
Mrs. Cromwell	Barbara Kellermann
Maj. Crossley	Patrick MacNee
Colin Mackenzie	Patrick Allen
Underhill	Bernard Archard
Montero	Martin Benson
Doris Grice	Faith Brook
Melborne	Allan Cuthbertson
Wilton	Kenneth Griffith
Hilliard	Donald Houston
Peters	Glyn Houston
Dennison	Percy Herbert
Barker	Patrick Holt
Trompeta	Wolf Kahler
Malverne	Terence Longdon
Radcliffe	Michael Medwin
Finley	John Standing
Manners	Graham Stark
MacLean	Jack Watson
Breene	Moray Watson
Butterworth	Brook Williams
Ram das Gupta	Mark Zuber
Capt. Rofer	George Mikell
Lovecroft	Morgan Sheppard
Lumsdaine	Edward Dentith
Sloane	Clifford Earl
U-boat captain	Robert Hoffmann
First officer	Dan Van Husen

How a band of pip-pip British civilians rallied to King and country, tucked in their pot bellies and knocked out a German spy nest that was playing havoc with wartime Allied ships in the Indian Ocean is the subject of "Sea Wolves." The Lorimar presentation, for United Artists in U.S.-Canada, teems with romantic heroism routinely told. Some choice playing time may help pic turn up trumps with general audiences.

Producer Euan Lloyd, a quoted believer in the "star system," has Gregory Peck, Roger Moore and David Niven toplining in performances that don't stretch any of them but suffice for popular appeal under Andrew V. McLaglen's competent direction.

Touted as "the last great untold action story of the war," film was scripted by Reginald Rose from James Leasor's novel "The Boarding Party" and shot principally on locations in India. Tony Imi's cinematography often helps convert the routine into something more, including atmospheric moments harking back to British colonial rule — a game of cricket, streets congested with humanity, English contempt for the indigenous "darky" population, etc.

"Sea Wolves" otherwise is unabashed flag-waving, a salute to the Calcutta Light Horse, a parttime regiment whose membership consisted mainly of colonial business types way past draft age but recruited as volunteers for the ticky mission in question, namely the destruction of three German freighters interned in coastal waters off the then-neutral Portuguese colony of Goa.

Rose's scenario delays most of the suspense and action to the final bloody minutes when those ships are vanquished with a big bang, with credit to Kit West and Nick Allder for slick special effects. For a caper with negligible sub-plotting and minimal characterization, the pace could be quicker.

Peck's a Britisher in this one, but the affected accent won't fool anyone. He and Moore are regular army. The stiff-uppered civvy retreads, headed by Niven, include Trevor Howard and Patrick MacNee. Patrick Allen portrays a pragmatic military commander, and Barbara Kellermann, a British beauty of the "English rose" variety, and good actress to boot, appears as a German spy who has a romantic fling with Moore.

Tech credits are all accomplished, including John Glen's editing and Roy Budd's music, with end-title credits by Maurice Binder. A deja vu touch is provided by the strains of Richard Addinsell's "Warsaw Concerto," a screen theme of 40 years back.

For those who complain they don't make them like that no more, this one's a reasonably entertaining answer. —Pit.

Queridas Amigas
(Dear Friends)
(ARGENTINE-COLOR)

Buenos Aires, June 17.
Distributed by Producciones Imperial. Produced by Juan Jose Luciano. Directed by Carlos Orgambide. Features entire cast. Screenplay, Miguel Stocki, Orgambie; based on story by Elena Antoniette, Orgambide; camera (Eastmancolor), Juan Carlos Lenardi; music, Victor Proncet. Reviewed at the Astro cinema, Buenos Aires, June 5, 1980. (Argentine Film Baord rating: banned for under-18s). Running time: 90 MINS.

Esther	Luisina Brando
Mary	Graciela Dufau
Isabel	Dora Baret

Plus Rodolfo Ranni, Carlos Estrada, Marcela Lopez Rey and Hector Pellegrini.

The two main drawbacks of Argentine films, overcome only by a select number of top productions, have traditionally been weak plot development and phony-sounding dialog. Of these two hurdles, Carlos

Orgambide's first featurelength film to achieve commercial release (following a quarter century of uncompleted or unreleased features, short subjects, and jobs as cameraman on other people's films) totally vanquishes the latter and puts up a very creditable fight against the former, until a last-minute slip-up.

The story follows three women, formerly close friends who have since drifted apart, in their family and work lives. One (Isabel) is a doctor who has set up practice in an impoverished part of rural Argentina; of the other two, who have remained in Buenos Aires — where over one-third of all Argentines live — one has married a rich man and the other an average guy. The film's core interest lies in its true-sounding depictions of the problems and day-to-day lifestyles encountered in those three milieus.

One day the two city mice decide to pay a visit to the country mouse, at the invitation of the latter, who has lost her husband in an accident, but is in an advanced stage of pregnancy. After 20 years, the trio meets, and after initial effusions, sparks soon begin to fly.

Then, suddenly, the picture draws to a fake denouement and halts in its tracks. At this point the spectator may feel a bit cheated, not because the film has an open ending, which would be perfectly permissible — though it would have been interesting to follow the rubbing together of these three flinty characters until a final shape had emerged. The trouble is that the film seems to think it did somehow close the story, by ending with a strong (and, in itself, effective) scene which apparently offers catharsis; but in actual fact it doesn't.

Possibly the reason for this abrupt, sham ending is that the film essentially has a situation it wishes to described rather than a yarn it wishes to spin. Nevertheless, the overall balance is certainly positive as the description is fairly absorbing and rich in authenticity. For discriminating audiences. —Olas.

The Children
(COLOR)

———

Rotten kids; horror cheapie probably money-maker on lower levels.

———

World-Northal release of an Albright Films production. Produced by Carlton J. Albright; coproducer, Max Kalmanowicz. Directed by Kalmanowicz. Features entire cast. Screenplay, Carlton J. Albright, Edward Terry; camera (color), Barry Abrams; editor, Nikki Wessling; music, Henry Manfredini; sound, W.A. Grive-Smith; makeup, Carla White; asst. director, William Medsher. Reviewed at UA Rivoli Theatre, N.Y., July 4, '80. (MPAA Rating: R.) Running time: **90 MINS.**
John Freemont . . . . Martin Shakar
Sheriff Billy Hart . . . . Gil Rogers
Cathy Freemont . . . . Gale Garnett
With: Jessie Abrams, Tracy Griswold, Joy Glaccum, Suzanne Barnes, Rita Montone, Michelle Le Mothe, Shannon Bolin, Clara Evans, Jeptha Evans, Sarah Albright, Nathanael Albright, Julie Carrier, Edward Terry.

———

Another horror film using children as the monsters, "The Children" needed and lacked a workable script, yet despite it numerous shortcomings, this indie cheapie should prove profitable at the box office, where low budget horror pics remain at least risky form of investment.

Borderline science fiction premise is lifted from "The Incredible Shrinking Man" as an orange, radioactive cloud released from a nearby nuclear power plant engulfs a busload of school children. (Pregnant mother Gale Garnett is also caught in the cloud, setting up pic's predictable epilog.) The affected kids turn into zombie-like terrors, shambling around the little village of Ravensback to embrace unwary parents and others with lethal hugs. Lacking any special effects budget to come up with "Village of the Damned" eyes, director Max Kalmanowicz settles for unimpressive black nail polish to differentiate the deadly kids. Children on the rampage followed by a search-and-destroy mission by our heroes to stop them sums up the film's entire plot.

Failure of "The Children" to exploit potential of either childbirth fears or offspring — parents' rivalry gives the film zero value in the horror genre. Measure of this failure is that the scenes of kids killing their parents are ho-hum, while only a brief scene of an affected child stalking his unaffected buddy achieves any panache. As the sheriff who incredibly discovers how to destroy the bullet-proof tykes, Gil Rogers turns in a bug-eyed, embarrassing performance. Stalwart hero Martin Shakar has similar trouble handling his reaction shots. Gale Garnett is fine as his pregnant wife and may relieve Talia Shire from the burden of handling such thankless roles in the future.

Tech credits are standard, with Carla White's makup providing the requisite gore. With little else in view to get off on, genre fans may dig the display of severed limbs right and left, recalling better times when Hammer dominated the horror film field. —Lor.

Kronprinsen
(Crown Prince)
(NORWEGIAN-COLOR)

———

Sydney, June 24.
An EMI Production, Norway. Features entire cast. Directed by Pal Bang-Hansen. Screenplay, Bang-Hansen, from story by Bjorn Gunnar Olsen; camera (color). Bjorn Jegerstedt. Only credits available. Reviewed at the Sydney Film Festival. June 23, 1980. Running time: **91 MINS.**
Cast: Bjorn Sundquist, Reidun Nortvedt, Trini Lund, Bjorn Floberg.

At base, the "Crown Prince" of the title is a young aspiring politician who is caught up in a scandal before he has the time-in-job to get cynical ... or shifty. His destruction comes when it is learned that the Central Intelligence Agency of U.S. had been funding the Young Labor Party of Norway, a fact that had for years been well covered up. In the era of new villains, the CIA serves very nicely to shorthand the bad guys. But in so far as the picture was made (in 1979), and thus pre-Afghanistan and Teheran Embassy take-over, the main thrust is by now surely somewhat blunted.

The apochryphal Eleventh Commandment ("Thou shalt not get caught") is nowhere more brutally enforced than in politics, and since the story is set in an election year, it is obvious that there has to be a scapegoat. Roald (Bjorn Sundquist) by being all too willing to compromise literally talks himself into taking the heat. Indeed, Pal Bang-Hansen's screenplay has a hard time working in English subtitles because it is very wordy.

Film is interestingly shot by Bjorn Jegerstedt, who gets fine use out of unusual locations. Tech credits are all fine. Fine Festival fare, but distinctly dicey for all but the oddity art houses and more esoteric end of the non-theatrical circuit. —Miha.

Phooying
(A Woman)
(THAI-COLOR)

———

Bangkok, June 19.
An Apex production and release. Produced by Nanta Tansacha. Written and directed by Tipayachatr Chartchai. Features entire cast. Camera (color), Wanlop Srisamarng; asst. camera, Sanit Rujiratikul; sound and musical director, Jaratphong Janjarasskul; art direction, Patanachat Rakpipat; costumes, Pimpham Buranaphim. Reviewed at Siam Theatre, Bangkok. June 19, '80. Running time: **96 MINS.**
Salita . . . . Nawarat Yukthanan
Met . . . . Sorapong Chatri
Danai . . . . Aporn Tonnawannij
Mot . . . . Chakris Hanvichai
Uan . . . . Needa Suksawat
Salita's Mother . . . . . . Tanipha Gantatum
Met's Parents . . Tirawan Ruapiyakul and Metta Ruapiyakul

———

Fourteen songs are featured in "Phooying," mostly as background music, only a couple performed as musical numbers. Each song was paid 20,000 baht (about $1,000) or a total of 280,000 baht (about $140,000) for the lot. The mixture of both old and new hits can be boring. Most of the time, you can't hear what the actors are saying.

It seems intentional that the music drowns out the dialog. Along with the music, pretty teak houses, pretty mountain views, pretty flowers abound. (This is the fifth pic in a row by Tipayachatr Chartchai, lensed in Northern Thailand, where the climate is much cooler than the rest of the country.)

Nawarat and Sorapong play newlyweds. She is smothered with kindness by her mother-in-law, who, when not purchasing diamonds for Nawarat sees to it that the latter never has to lift a finger at home. (There are servants for all household chores.) Poor Nawarat, presumably a good cook, secretly hates her mother-in-law.

Nawarat then tries to convince Sorapong that they should move to their own house, even if they have to rent. Sorapong agrees but meets parental opposition. Nawarat quarrels with Sorapong and leaves. Enter Aporn. The moment Nawarat decides to be alone, she's again in danger of being gang-raped as in her earlier pix, but this time runs straight into Aporn's protective arms.

The love triangle and family conflict promises drama, suspense and perhaps even violence. But nothing of the sort occurs. The minute she can cook to her heart's content, everybody's happy. —Cano.

Ma'Agalim
(Circles)
(ISRAELI-COLOR)

———

Cannes, May 16.
A Yehezkel Aloani Presentation. Produced by Yehezkel Aloani and Yaakov Kotzky. Written and directed by Idith Schehori. Camera (color). Nurith Aviv; additional photography, Gad Danzig; edited by Ludmilla Goliath. Reviewed in Cannes, May 15, '80. Running time: **84 MINS.**
Cast: Galith Roitman, Hava Ortman, Noa Cohen-Raz, Rachel Schein.

———

Idith Schehori first appeared on the Israeli film scene a couple of years ago, presenting a short based on a traumatic event she had lived through: a love affair which turned sour when she discovered that her boyfriend was homosexual. The favorable reviews encouraged the young filmmaker, still in her mid-20s, to start work on her first feature project, and after many financial vagaries and some imposed artistic compromises, she finally got her wish.

The story attempts to reflect the events, the moods and the crises in the life of four girls, between 20 and 30, as they go through one weekend together. All four seem to belong to a certain fringe of the bohemian world, all of them would like to be considered entirely liberated and independent, but, as it turns out at the end, none is really liberated and independent, nor really capable of coping with the loneliness, the fits of despair and anxiety inherent in this kind of life.

The introduction presents the four girls, one by one, as they join forces together. The camera follows them through their attempts to pick out the right partners for the weekend, the right party and the right atmosphere.

After a night of drinking, dancing, fencing with each other and the company around them, after a short violent sexist incident in a night club and a nude swim, at dawn, the four find themselves in the apartment where the whole thing started, each facing her own defeat.

One of them realizes she cannot cure a broken heart and a broken marriage by gallivanting around, the second leaves her boyfriend because he is too square for her newfound indentity, which puts her clearly in line for the same kind of miseries her girlfriends are already facing, the third shows clear lesbian attitudes which bother the others who send her away, and the fourth, actually the leading character, the one who puts on the toughest show, has to come to terms with the unhappiness she tries to conceal from herself.

Altogether, the film is quite reminiscent of a certain kind of Nouvelle Vague films of 20 years ago, made on similar themes, exposing the same kind of dissipated youth and moralizing about the senseless life in an alienated society of consummerism. Schehori certainly seems to know what she is talking about, even if she still lacks the dexterity to bring off this kind of film.

The characters are not strong enough in the script, and the quartet of young actresses is still very conscious of the camera, with the director doing too little to take their mind off it. A shortage of funds is also evident.

Very well shot however in 16m by Paris-based Israeli camera woman Nurith Aviv, and later blown up to 35m, the film's texture has a real feeling to it, the background being more convincing in this instance than the foreground. Appeal seems mostly to young audiences. —*Edna.*

Honeysuckle Rose
(COLOR)

Should be big, unless there really is a backlash.

Hollywood, July 3.
A Warner Bros. release, produced by Gene Taft. Exec producer, Sydney Pollack. Directed by Jerry Schatzberg. Screenplay, Carol Sobieski, William D. Wittliff, John Binder; camera (Technicolor), Robby Muller; editors, Aram Avakian, Norman Gay, Marc Laub, Evan Lottman; sound (Dolby Stereo), Arthur Rochester; production design, Joel Schiller; assistant director, David McGiffert; costumes, Jo Ynocencio; music, Willie Nelson, Richard Baskin. Reviewed at The Burbank Studios, July 3, 1980. (MPAA Rating: PG). Running time: 119 MIN.
Buck .... Willie Nelson
Viv .... Dyan Cannon
Lily .... Amy Irving
Garland .... Slim Pickens
Jamie .... Joey Floyd
Sid .... Charles Levin
Rosella .... Priscilla Pointer
Cotton .... Mickey Rooney, Jr.
Rooster .... Pepe Serna
Brag .... Lane Smith
Jeanne .... Diana Scarwid
Emmylou .... Emmylou Harris
Tex .... Rex Ludwick
Kelly .... Mickey Raphael

A down-home, country treasure, "Honeysuckle Rose" is about as good as this kind of film is ever going to get, which means it should easily equal the $59,000,000 grossed to date by "Coal Miner's Daughter." If it doesn't then there must indeed be some kind of mysterious backlash this summer against redneck films.

One caveat: This is not a picture for anybody who doesn't like Willie Nelson, so completely does he dominate the two hours. But his legions of recording and concert fans should be delighted with a picture that so adroitly blends his musical performances with a gently dramatic acting job in an old-fashioned love story. (Pic is in fact a credited remake of "Intermezzo," the Swedish and later Selznick vehicle for Ingrid Bergman. —Ed.)

As he demonstrated briefly in "The Electric Horseman," Nelson is a natural before the cameras — at least so long as he's essentially playing himself, or somebody close to it. In "Honeysuckle," he plays a fictional character, but there's so much of Nelson's own biography built in, it's almost always surprising when any of the other characters call him "Buck."

Picture catches Nelson at that point in his career about 10 years ago when his touring band was wildly popular in Texas and nearby regions, but he had yet to break out with the big hit that would make him nationally famous. Consequently, this is not the story of a superstar like Bette Midler in "The Rose," though comparisons could be made between the two pix, but a more commonplace story of a nice-enough family man who loves his wife and son. But he's also a musician who loves liquor, the open road — and maybe another woman now and then — just as much.

Dyan Cannon and Joey Floyd nicely set up Nelson's approaching conflict as the wife and son who wait affectionately at home for him to finish his periodic tours. When the three are together, there's no question this is a happy family, though always haunted by the next approaching departure date.

Nelson's second family, of course, is his band and his connubial equivalent there is Slim Pickens, right on target as the guitar-picking sidekick who's rousted around with Nelson for all the lean years.

Whatever the problems, Nelson has maintained a balance between these opposing forces — until Pickens decides to retire and his young daughter, Amy Irving, takes his place on the road. Irving is near perfect as the instinctively seductive woman who has adored Nelson since girlhood and now has a chance to fulfill her fantasies — no matter what the consequences.

Director Jerry Schatzberg deftly wedges this eternal triangle into a mosaic of musical numbers and vivid portraits of the people and places still along the backroads of America. Most importantly, he and a large crew of editors neatly avoid the talk-awhile, sing-awhile bounciness that can hurt a picture like this, consistently overlapping the music with the dramatic sequences.

Entire cast is right for their assignments and technical credits are first-rate down the line, with special note for Robby Muller's camera and Arthur Rochester's sound work. —*Har.*

Manganinnie
(AUSTRALIA-COLOR)

Sydney, July 1.
A GUO Film Distributors' Release of a Tasmanian Film Corp. production. Produced by Gilda Baracchi. Executive producers, Gil Brealey and Malcolm Smith. Directed by John Honey. Screenplay Ken Kelso; camera (Eastmancolor), Gary Hansen; editor, Mike Woolveridge. Reviewed at the GUO Theaterette, Sydney, June 27, '80. (Commonwealth Censorship Rating: G). Running time: 91 MINS.
Manganinnie ......Mawuyul Yathalawuy
Joanna Waterman .... Anna Ralph
Edward Waterman .... Phillip Hinton
Margaret Waterman ..... Elaine Mangan
Meenopeekameena .... Buruminy
                            Dhamarrandji
Quinn .... Reg Evans
Simon Waterman .... Jonathan Elliott
William Waterman .... Timothy Latham

The white man's encroachment upon and ill-treatment of the aboriginal is a constant theme in Australian literature, and while few local films so far have done little more than treat it in passing, those that have — such as "The Chant of Jimmie Blacksmith" and "The Last Tasmanian" (a documentary) — have been powerful and highly dramatic.

The Tasmanian Film Corp.'s initial foray into the feature film field must have looked as good on paper as it does on the screen, although the drama seems forced and the suspense comes over false. Story is of a very young girl who, in the 1830s, gets lost and is taken in hand by an aboriginal woman. Neither speaks the other's language, but communication is soon established and together they roam over Tasmania, following the ancient trails as Manganinnie, the woman, searches for her lost tribe.

Director John Honey's first feature, the film concentrates on the growing relationship which is dramatically valid, but the problem is that there is no drama in it. Basically, the film spends a lot of its time watching Manganinnie intoning aboriginal chants while the wide-eyed little Joanna looks on. Much of the rest of the film is taken up with footage of the stunning scenery on the island: so much so that the abounding views could be accused of overacting.

The script simply doesn't offer enough substance to sustain what is, in effect, a non-dialog two-hander. And however undeniably pretty the countryside is, it doesn't bridge the gap. The film's final scenes are its finest moments and are moving.

Actress Mawuyul Yathalawuy's debut is difficult to evaluate because the role calls more for behavioral than thespic skills. Moppet Anna Ralph does well and genuinely appears to know what is going on. Tech credits are all above reproach.

Film's appeal is aimed at the family audience, but the whole thing is drawn out to the point where television-reared kids of today would be aching to switch channels. —*Miha.*

The Final Countdown
(COLOR)

Documents USS Nimitz. Remarkable Naval close-up. Okay summer fare, if reminiscent of tv.

Hollywood, July 11.
United Artists release of a Bryna Co. production. Stars Kirk Douglas, Martin Sheen, Katharine Ross, James Farentino, Ron O'Neal, Charles Durning. Produced by Peter Vincent Douglas. Exec producer, Richard R. St. Johns. Directed by Don Taylor. Screenplay, David Ambrose & Gerry Davis and Thomas Hunter & Peter Powell,

from a story by Hunter & Powell and Ambrose; camera (Technicolor) Victor J. Kemper; second-unit camera. David L. Butler, Stan Lazan; music, John Scott; editor, Robert K. Lambert, production designer, Fernando Carrere; set decorator, Dennis Peeples; sound, Bruce Bisenz, Robert J. Litt, David J. Kimball, Howard S. Wollman; special visual effects and storm sequence, Maurice Binder; second-unit directors, David Jones, Robert K. Lambert; assistant director, Pat Kehoe. Reviewed at MGM Studios, July 10, 1980. (MPAA Rating: PG). Running time: 103 MINS.

Capt. Matthew Yelland ..... Kirk Douglas
Warren Lasky .... Martin Sheen
Laurel Scott .... Katharine Ross
Cmdr. Richard Owens .. James Farentino
Cmdr. Dan Thurman .... Ron O'Neal
Sen. Samuel Chapman ..Charles Durning
Black Cloud .... Victor Mohica
Lt. Perry .... James C. Lawrence
Simura .... Soon-Teck Oh
Cmdr. Damon .... Joe Lowry
Kajima .... Alvin Ing
Cpl. Kullman .... Mark Thomas

———

As a documentary on the USS Nimitz, "The Final Countdown" is wonderful. As entertainment, however, the United Artists release has the feeling of a telepic that strayed onto the big screen. The magnificent production values provided by setting the film on the world's largest nuclear-powered aircraft carrier can't transcend the predictable cleverness of a plot that will seem overly familiar to viewers raised on "Twilight Zone" reruns. Yet the Bryna Co. production, starring Kirk Douglas and produced by his son Peter with Richard R. St. Johns exec producing, is okay summer program fare.

In his debut as a producer, young Douglas (fourth in the family to produce, after Kirk, his wife Anne, and son Michael) pulled off a genuine coup in getting permission to film on the mammoth carrier, and the film seems not to have missed an inch of the vessel in its exhaustive visual coverage. Presumably the Soviet Union is already thoroughly familiar with the inside and outside of the Nimitz; if they aren't, they're sure to find this film fascinating in the Kremlin screening room. Actually, from the Pentagon's point of view, the film is probably seen as a valuable commercial for American military power in this day of uneasiness over the country's degree of preparedness.

The liberal sympathies typical of the work of Kirk Douglas are evident, however, in his characterization of the ship's commander as a man whose sense of military honor will not allow him to take the opportunity provided him by a mysterious storm — and his ship and crew find themselves transported back in time from the contemporary world to Dec. 6, 1941, between Pearl Harbor and the Japanese fleet heading to destroy the American naval base and send the U.S. into World War II. Douglas' character decides that to take preemptive act-

ion would be wrong because doing so would mean the U.S. attacked Japan first, rather than the other way around.

The philosophical issues raised by the film hardly bear much examination, however, because the patchwork screenplay by two teams of writers paints each character in too schematic a function. There's the impulsive black officer, Ron O'Neal, who wants to blow the Japanese to kingdom come; the ambitious senator, Charles Durning, who vacillates due to expediency; his bubbleheaded assistant, Katharine Ross, whom everyone describes as a brilliant woman far ahead of her time; the crazed Japanese pilot, Soon Teck-Oh, who shoots up the ship in banzai style; the resident World War II expert, James Farentino, who conveniently has all the facts at his command; and the resident intellectual, Martin Sheen, who argues for an attack because it tickles his imagination.

Sheen has the kind of part Kirk Douglas used to play in his younger days — the fanatical idealist — and as such he has much more to work with than Douglas, who seems uncharacteristically and unprofitably subdued.

As always happens on "The Twilight Zone," the opportunity to rewrite history winds up causing history to happen the same way we knew it did before we went into the theatre. The ending seems anticlimactic here, because the film has been building up to a huge battle, and all we get is a quick montage of documentary stock footage of the Pearl Harbor attack mixed with flashes of "Tora, Tora, Tora." The straight, serious tone followed by director Don Taylor often makes the film seem unintentionally comic.

While the documentary details of the ship's functions are fascinating and provide most of the genuine interest of the film, so much screen time is devoted to technical details that the thin, hokey nature of the plot becomes stretched way too thin for suspension of disbelief. The film was ably served by second-unit directors David Jones and Robert K. Lambert, but the special visual effects by Maurice Binder often look cheap and cartoon-like in contrast to the veracity of the setting, and Victor Kemper's lensing has so many color inconsistencies that the trickery becomes too hard to swallow. —Mac.

———

Telephone Public
(FRENCH-DOCU-COLOR)

———

Paris, July 2.
A Gaumont release of a Prospectacle production. Produced by Maurice Bernart

& Claudie Ossaro. Stars the rock group, Telephone. Directed by Jean-Marie Perier. Camera (Eastmancolor-Cinemascope), Lionel Legros and Alain Masseron; editor, Thierry Derocles; sound, Harald Maury, Laurent Pele, recorded in Dolby stereo. Reviewed at the Marignan-Concorde theatre, Paris, July 1, 1980. Running time: 100 MINS.
With: the Telephone rock group (Jean-Louis Aubert, Corine Marienneau, Richard Kolinka and Louis Bertignac).

———

"Telephone" is a currently hot French rock group that first appeared on the scene here in 1976 and has enjoyed some live concert exposure in Britain and the U.S. Director Jean-Marie Perier (son of actor Francois Perier) conceived this performance film around two of their major concerts in Paris last year and padded it out with interviews with its four components (of whom one, the oldest, is a girl).

Film is clearly geared to fans of the group; others will find only Dolby doldrums. (To this reviewer's ears their music is without distinction.) Chances in U.S. markets look slight.

As film, as reportage, as musical document, it's poor. Perier insists on using bi- and tri-partite split screen projection, even for the interviews. Good, conventional editing would have easily preserved the theatrical energies of the performers, but Perier's device merely tires the eye.

The interviews are dreary. All four appear colorless personalities off-stage and mouth the usual contemporary platitudes one often finds in interviews with pop figures.
—Len.

———

Oh Heavenly Dog
(COLOR)

Benji's third pic adds Chevy Chase for young crowd. Special selling needed.

———

Hollywood, July 9.
Twentieth Century-Fox release of a Mulberry Square Production. Stars Chevy Chase and Benji. Produced and directed by Joe Camp. Screenplay, Rod Browning, Camp; camera (DeLuxe Color), Don Reddy; music, Evel Box; songs, Elton John, Gary Osborne, Paul McCartney; editor, Leon Seith; production design, Garrett Lewis; art director, George Richardson; sound, Colin Charles, Don Bassman, Pat Egan, Chris Carpenter; assistant director, Derek Cracknell; dog trainers, Frank Inn, Juanita Inn. Reviewed at 20th-Fox Studios, July 9, 1980. (MPAA Rating: PG.) Running time: 103 MINS.

Benjamin Browning .... Chevy Chase, Benji
Jackie Howard .... Jane Seymour
Malcolm Bart .... Omar Sharif
Bernie .... Robert Morley
Freddie .... Alan Sues
Montanero .... Donnelly Rhodes
Higgins .... Stuart Germain
Alistair Becket .... John Stride
Margaret .... Barbara Leigh-Hunt
Lady Chalmers ..... Margaret Courtenay
Mr. Easton .... Frank Williams
Pelican Man .... Albin Pahernik
German Clerk .... Susan Kellerman

Carlton .... Lorenzo Music
Patricia Elliot ..... Marguerite Corriveau

The original "Benji" in 1974 attracted wide following from subteens and older (over-30) adults, but few viewers in the prime filmgoing age range, 13-30, showed interest in the emotive G-rated pooch pic. Sequel, "For The Love Of Benji" in 1977, was a disappointment, doing $5,000,000 to the $12,000,000 domestic rentals of the first. Hence, for the latest Benji pic, producer-director Joe Camp has added a youth market star, Chevy Chase, and enough profanity and sexual innuendo to get a mild PG rating. Problem is that the original Benji audience may be offended, while the 13-30 group may be turned off by the predominant juve aspects of the pic. Looks like a tricky sell for the 20th-Fox release.

The script by Camp and Rod Browning, which seems heavily influenced by Warren Beatty's "Heaven Can Wait," has gumshoe Chase reincarnated as a dog after being murdered while investigating a complicated London politics-and-sex intrigue. The mystery unravels tediously whenever Benji — marvelously handled, as usual, by trainers Frank and Juanita Inn — surrenders the screen to Chase's lackadaisical clowning. Actor basically bookends the part, and in the middle does a running v.o. for the dog. (Universal's Dick Powell-starrer "You Never Can Tell" of 1951 used same man reincarnated as dog premise. —Ed.)

Most the humor comes from placing the dog in a romantic situation with human emotions, as Chase pursues pretty magazine reporter Jane Seymour without her realizing he inhabits the body of her faithful pooch. Benji/Chase is thus able to jump in the bubble bath with Seymour, snuggle up in her lap while she is being wooed by a human suitor, etc., which makes for some amiable moments in the midst of a generally slow and laborious film. The language and visual innuendos are not unusually vulgar for a PG film, but parents taking their kids in the expectation of seeing a typical Benji film may find cause to complain.

Camp, here releasing through a major distrib for the first time after previously handling his pix himself, gets good production value out of Montreal, London, and Paris locations, with Montreal unobtrusively doubling for London during much of the film due to restrictive animal quarantine regulations which made it hard to film in England. Supporting cast of English players is adept, but Omar Sharif and Donnelly Rhodes seem oddly miscast in the setting.

Tech aspects are okay, particularly the bouncy score by Leon Seith, but Don Reddy's lensing, while attractive, sometimes seems too dark and somber for a comedy. Problem may be with the entire conception, however, which awkwardly attempts to blend elements that just don't mesh. —*Mac.*

No Nukes
(COLOR-DOCU)

Concert film with propaganda angle. Presumed youth appeal.

A Warner Bros. release of a MUSE (Musicians for a Safe Environment) presentation. Produced by Julian Schlossberg and Danny Goldberg. Directed by Julian Schlossberg, Danny Goldberg and Anthony Potenza. Features Jackson Browne, Crosby, Stills & Nash, Doobie Bros., John Hall, Graham Nash, Bonnie Raitt, Gil Scott-Heron, Carly Simon, Bruce Springsteen, James Taylor, Jesse Colin Young. Technical director, Mark Pines; documentary footage director, Anthony Potenza; cinematographer, Haskell Wexler; sound mixers, Mark Berger, Richard Beggs; creative coordinator, David Silver. Reviewed at Warner Bros. Screening Room, N.Y., July 10, '80. (MPAA Rating: PG). Running time: **103 MINS.**

"No Nukes" is a concert film with a message. The message, an attack on the use of nuclear power, comes across, but the audience the film should attract is essentially youths interested in the impressive rock and folk lineup of performers.

The concert footage, mainly from the five "No Nukes" concerts at Madison Square Garden, N.Y., last September, is similar to that of other concert films, except that there are more acts involved and, therefore, less footage on each. However, there are many interesting instances of top artists performing together as well as backstage shots of them going over unfamiliar charts.

A notable exception is the material on Bruce Springsteen, the biggest draw of the series, whose fun seg brings the only genuine laughs of the film. Anti-nuclear material also is prominent, from sincere comments by artists, such as John Hall and Graham Nash, offhandedly and in press conference, to speeches and comments by such anti-nuclear spokesmen as Ralph Nader and Jane Fonda, to parts of a dated U.S. Army film extolling the safety of atomic weapons. Telling footage on Three-Mile Island and those opposed to nuclear energy from different parts of the country is also effective.

Actually, this footage elevates the film above the concert-film level, but interest will be drawn by such name concert acts as Springsteen, James Taylor, Carly Simon, Doobie Bros., Stills & Nash, Bonnie Raitt, etc. The closing is the most-impressive concert section, from an outdoor rally at Battery Park, N.Y., that reportedly drew more than 250,000. A stirring Hall song on preserving the environment against nuclear energy is followed by a group sing, including many in the audience, of the Jesse Colin Young-led "Get Together." There also are many other performers, not credited up front, such as the Joy Ryder & Davis Davis Band, whose "No More Nukes" excerpt at the Battery Park rally gives the film its New Wave element, plus Paul Simon, Chaka Khan, Rosemary Butler, and Steven Tyler of Aerosmith.

"No Nukes," because of the handling of the message is one of the better pop concert films. It may draw enough youths to get the message across. —*Kirb.*

Stir
(AUSTRALIA-COLOR)

Sydney, July 4.
A Hoyts Distribution release of a Smiley Films production. Produced by Richard Brennan. Directed by Stephen Wallace. Screenplay, Bob Jewson; camera (Eastmancolor) Geoffrey Burton; editor, Henry Dangar; music, Cameron Allan; special effects, Chris Murray. Reviewed at Hoyts' Theaterette, Sydney, July 3, '80. Commonwealth Censorship Rating: R). Running time: **100 MINS.**

China	Bryan Brown
Norton	Max Phipps
Redford	Dennis Miller
Andrew	Michael Gow
Alby	Phil Motherwell
Dave	Gary Waddell
Chalmers	Ray Marshall
Partridge	Ted Robshaw
Webster	James Marsh
McIntosh	Paul Sonkkila
Tony	Keith Gallasch
Riley	Robert Noble
Old Bob	Syd Heylen
Lewis	Peter Kowitz
Governor	Robert "Tex" Morton
Visiting Judge	Tony Wager
Hogan	Les Newcombe
Chickenman/Barber	Morris Saidi
Prisoner's	
Spokesman No. 1	Dave Taylor
TV Interviewer	Margaret Throsby

Others: Christ Smith, Ian Gray, Peter Barton, James Cameron, Greg Smith, Dennis Hunt.

"Stir" is a film of extraordinary power that never lets up from its first sequence. It sets the theme with a television interview of China (Bryan Brown) about his role in some recent prison riots. Then a simple super, "Three Years Later," over a similar head-shot tells you that he's back inside. Interplay between prisoners in a van sets up very economically how the pecking order will evolve.

For a first feature, Stephen Wallace has made a stunning directional debut. He exhibits a control over his actors that approaches mastery because the whole thing is played at such an intense pitch. The cold, apparently random brutality of the warders establishes not only the violence of the action, but also of the language. It is this uncompromising harshness of every aspect of the prison ecology that infuses the film with its shocking immediacy.

Geoffrey Burton's photography of Lee Whitmore's cool, blue-toned production design effectively underlines the jail atmosphere, enhancing the dourness of actuality, in fact, since the picture was shot wholly on location in a real prison (in South Australia) which has been vacant for five years.

But the initial accuracy lies in Bob Jewson's screenplay, based on his own experience in jail where he was serving a sentence in 1974 at Bathurst when the riots there occurred. There are clear echoes of Attica and more recently New Mexico in the film which, while delineating the augmenting petty frustrations of the entire population of the prison — warder and jailed — makes heroes of neither. And inarticulation of the problem, caused by a lack of common communication forms (the "us vs. them" syndrome in action), leads to a total breakdown and the inevitable culminating riot and destruction. The futility of it all is stated: Wallace and Jewson leave any judgments to the audience.

The acting is superlative — the best ensemble performance by a cast of an Australian film emerges. Standout is lead Bryan Brown who fulfills all predictions as topline talent; likewise, newcomers Ted Robshaw and Paul Sonkkila turn in devastatingly memorable thesping. Latter can look forward to a career as a heavy given the strength of menace he exudes in this one.

Interestingly a number of the extras were recruited from the ranks of ex-cons. For example: Les Newcombe, a notorious real-life escapee, plays against experience in the Hogan character who connives with the authorities. This sort of careful orchestration of verisimilitude is a major factor in conveying the realism of the picture.

Producer Brennan reaffirms his ability to make a dime look like a dollar, investing the picture with really terrific production values that Wallace exploits in an understated way to great effect.

Technical credits, as noted, are superior. For the local circuits the film may have a hard time initially because of the sensitivity of Australian audiences — they don't like "difficult" pictures. For elsewhere it will have to be "re-voiced," because as yet the rest of the world is unattuned to the Aussie accent. However the power of the piece is sufficient to overcome any diminution fiddling the soundtrack might create.

It is another of those occasions when a nation of immigrants like Australia is cursed by having English as its Mother tongue — much as the American accent was before Hollywood talkies made it universally comprehensible.

It was politically a brave move on the part of the New South Wales Film Corporation to develop and fund the project since there is in the film an implicit criticism of the prison system. However it is also true that what is wrong in N.S.W. is as wrong or more so elsewhere — from which is not to be implied that the film moralizes on any level; it emphatically does not. Nor does it purport to suggest an alternative. What it does do is create in the mind a nagging question. —*Miha.*

Sir Henry At Rawlinson End
(BRITISH — B&W)

Comedy of 1950. British flavor. Special audiences.

London, July 7.
A Charisma Films production. Executive producer, Martin Wesson. Produced by Tony Stratton Smith. Directed by Steve Roberts. Stars Trevor Howard. Screenplay, Vivian Stanshall, Steve Roberts; camera (b&w), Martin Bell; editor, Chris Rose; music, Vivian Stanshall; art director, Jim Acheson; sound, Keith Desmond; associate producer, Peter R. Smith; asst. director, Raymond Day. Reviewed at the Oxford Film Festival, New Theatre, Oxford, July 6, '80. Running time: **72 MINS.**

Sir Henry Rawlinson	Trevor Howard
Reverend Slodden	Patrick Magee
Mrs. E	Denise Coffey
Old Scrotum	J.G. Devlin
Buller Bullethead	Harry Fowler
Florrie	Sheila Reid
Hubert	Vivian Stanshall
Candice	Suzanne Danielle
Rafe	Daniel Gerroll
Lord Tarquin of Staines	Ben Aris
Lady Philippa of Staines	Liz Smith
Peregrine	Jeremy Child
Porcelain	Susan Porrett

Designed to recall the flavor of British film comedies churned out in the '50s by Ealing studios, "Sir Henry At Rawlinson End" is a surreal slice of eccentric English life that could score as a returning cult favorite on home ground and in certain very select markets elsewhere.

Essentially an artfilm, the Charisma Films production (company is an offshoot of London-based independent diskery Charisma Records) is idiosyncratic enough to be acclaimed as a work of genius by some English-speakers, and dismissed by others as pretentious or merely incomprehensible. Hard to see that rendering into another language, via dubbing or subtitles, would leave more than a dim impression of the original, since zany verbiage is the mainspring of the humor.

Nevertheless director-coscripter Steve Roberts has done a remarkable job of transferring Vivian Stanshall's story, initially written and recorded for radio and disk, to the screen. Helpful factors are Trevor Howard's spirited central performance as a resolutely drunken English aristocrat whose lifestyle is a gross and fantastical reflection of his addled brain; Jim Acheson's aptly preposterous art direction; and Martin Bell's black-and-white cinematography, which is stylish beyond the call of simple comic duty.

Plot, such as it is, concerns the antics of Howard's bizarre household in a bid to exorcise a family ghost, namely that of Howard's brother (played by Stanshall). Latter was unwittingly shotgunned down by Howard while wearing no pants — having been surprised in flagrante delicto — and must be re-trousered if his spirit is to rest. Patrick Magee offers services as a charlatan demon-operative, but the undead is reclad with unexpected success, Magee's ulterior criminal motives are thwarted more by accident than anything, and Rawlinson End life returns to the relative calm of its normal insanity.

For dedicated Monty Python followers, lavatory-joke afficionados, and lovers of puns and relentless literary gagging, there are laughs a-plenty. Pace of some of the prattle (and audibility problems at the screening under review) caused a good many possible gems to go unappreciated, but that could make for repeat admissions from determined fans.

Denise Coffey, Sheila Reid, Harry Fowler and Jeremy Child contribute bravura supporting caricatures. Technically handsome in most departments, and edited by Chris Rose with gratifying lack of indulgence, the film's low budget is well masked by general professional competence. The feeble score, which Stanshall also penned, is the one disappointing area. Shortish running time could limit playoff in some situations. —*Simo.*

Touch And Go
(AUSTRALIA-COLOR)

Sydney, July 1.

A GUO Film Distributors' release of the Mutiny Pictures production. Produced by John Pellatt. Executive producers Peter Maxwell and Peter Yeldham. Directed by Peter Maxwell. Screenplay by Peter Yeldham (from an original story by Maxwell and Yeldham); production manager, Michael McKeag; camera (Eastmancolor) John McLean; editors, Sara Bennett and Paul Maxwell. Reviewed at the GUO Theaterette, Sydney, June 17, '80. (Commonwealth Censorship Rating: NRC). Running time: **92 MINS.**

Eva Gilmour .... Wendy Hughes
Fiona Latham .... Chantal Contouri
Millicent Hoffman ...... Carmen Duncan
Gina Tesoriero .... Jeanie Drynan
Helen Preston .... Liddy Clark
Sue Fullerton .... Christine Amor
Frank Butterfield .... Jon English
Anatole Sushinsky .... John Bluthal
George Latham .... Brian Blain
Steve Godfrey .... Vince Martin
Julia Henderson ...... Barbara Stephens
Miss Pringle .... Pamela Norman
Daphne Sushinsky .... Cynthia Cooper
Housewife .... Beryl Cheers

"Touch and Go" is a comedy heist film with the twist that the "villains" are a sextet of shapely women who do their robberies to provide funds for charities. Moralities aside, the plot idea was perhaps a good one, but the screenplay result would be shallow even for a teevee quickie. Previously highly competent actresses on this outing aren't given enough characterization to make them play convincingly.

Film is neither sexy nor funny enough, reaching for guffaws without even delivering titters. In the light of today's competition on either level, the picture needed strengthening to make it thoroughly viable in the marketplace.

The story is of three dishy ladies — an actress, a socialite and (would you believe?) a locksmith — who connive to rob in order to keep a kindergarten solvent. When more coin is needed, they recruit more distaff specialists and plan to knock over one of Queensland's off-shore island resorts.

While the plot is remarkably similar to the Margarethe von Trotta flick, "Das Zweite Erwachen der Christa Klages" (*Variety* June 21, 1978) which treated virtually the same story as social realism, in treatment, however, "Touch and Go" perhaps owes more to the 1960 Lewis Milestone-Sinatra Rat Pack pic, "Ocean's Eleven," the denouement of which has echoes here. The fade-out sequence offers the only really humorous line in the film.

(Just starting in U.S. is "How To Beat the High Cost of Living," of like plot concept. —Ed.)

Aussie actor John Bluthal clearly had a good time with his sauvely Rumanianlike resort director. He almost single hits the right pitch in what really was intended as a light drama played at a farce pace. Peter Maxwell's direction tends to bog down when the girls are sitting around luncheon tables in superbly scenic suburbs of Sydney. On those occasions the three principals (Hughes, Contouri and Duncan), seem to be almost angular in their dialog scenes together, bespeaking uncertainty and unease.

The action moves briskly enough, but the interplay between Contouri and husband Blain is stilted, and somehow local pop-rock superstar Jon English's gardener seems

tacked on to widen the comedy and improve the appeal. Yeldham's script in the result delivers only a fine character in Sushinsky, and an interesting concept of a comic plot.

Production values are excellent, and physically the film has a certain glamour. Technical aspects are all up to scratch, but the whole is short of the sum of the parts.

Finance was through the Queensland Film Corporation, the Australian Film Corporation and private sources including the Greater Union Organization. —*Miha.*

Dressed To Kill
(COLOR)

Stylish, graphic exercise in Hitchcockiana. Slick, very commercial package.

A Filmways Pictures release of a Samuel Z. Arkoff presentation of a Cinema 77 film. Produced by George Litto. Stars Michael Caine, Angie Dickinson and Nancy Allen. Written and directed by Brian De Palma. Camera (Technicolor), Ralf Bode; editor, Jerry Greenberg; music, composed by Pino Donaggio, conducted by Natalie Massara; production design, Gary Weist; costumes, Ann Roth; costume design, Gary Jones. Reviewed at Magno Preview Theatre, N.Y., July 14, '80. (MPAA Rating: R). Running time: **105 MINS.**

Dr. Robert Elliott .... Michael Caine
Kate Miller .... Angie Dickinson
Liz Blake .... Nancy Allen
Peter Miller .... Keith Gordon
Detective Marino .... Dennis Franz
Dr. Levy .... David Margulies
Warren Lockman .... Ken Baker
Cleveland Sam .... Brandon Maggart
Bobbi .... Susanna Clemm

Brian De Palma goes right for the audience jugular in "Dressed to Kill," the director's latest stylish exercise in ersatz-Hitchcock suspense-terror. Despite some major structural weaknesses, the cannily manipulated combination of mystery, gore and kinky sex adds up to a slick commercial package that stands to draw some rich blood money.

Borrowing in almost equal measure from Hitchcock (notably "Psycho") and his own features (notably "Carrie"), De Palma has spun a convoluted horror tale of a sexually unsatisfied suburban housewife (Angie Dickinson) whose days and nights are tortured by heavy erotic fantasies that turn to grisly reality on the one occasion she actually follows through with a casual pickup.

Possibly more than any other "A" film in recent memory, "Dressed" fully milks the erotic boundaries of its R-rating and was, in fact, trimmed down to avoid a probable 'X.'

Carefully laying the seeds of the plot, the film begins with a steamy auto-erotic shower scene (fantasized while Dickinson's husband is going through a slapdash boudoir performance), and segues to a session between Dickinson and psychiatrist Michael Caine in which she outlines her frustrations, makes an incomplete pass at Caine and is advised to indulge herself in an extramarital fling.

In a masterful scene of sexually tense approach-avoidance, Dickinson, alternately attracts and repels a fellow museum visitor, finally allowing herself to be scooped into a waiting cab, orally ravished by the stranger in the back seat, and swept into an afternoon of sexual dalliance that seems idyllic until she discovers that her paramour (a) is a virulent carrier of venereal disease, and (b) has apparently copped her diamond ring.

(Typically, these last facts are merely two red herrings out of the shoals that float through the film to help compound the already intensely complex plot.)

Matters begin in earnest when she enters the elevator to retrieve the ring and is razor-sliced to death by what seems to be a large, blond-wigged woman. Enter high-priced hooker Nancy Allen who finds Dickinson's body and is caught razor-in hand with no alibi, smack into the arch Hitchcockian position of a circumstantially involved "innocent" forced to clear herself by discovering the real murderer.

Paralleling her search is Caine's attempt to track down one of his patients — a male-turned female transsexual — whom he suspects as the murderer. Through inordinately complicated plot twists (some of them patently ridiculous), Allen, Dickinson's genius son (Keith Gordon) and the cops eventually turn to a luridly unlikely candidate as the sexually split personality who's periodically "Dressed to Kill."

Even audiences who figure out where Caine figures into the puzzle (though De Palma doesn't play fair with the kinds of clues and red herrings he sets up), will presumably have fun watching the manhunt unfurl.

Fortunately, the wholesale lapses in logic are usually bathed in a lush directorial style that manages to pull viewers through the film on a sheerly emotional gut level. Instances of patent manipulation or cheating (and the film's stolen ending from "Carrie") are generally more annoying in retrospect than while they're happening.

Dickinson, whose up-to-a-point nudity alone should draw every "Policewoman" fan in the country (she has an abdominal stand-in for the steamier segments) is used exceptionally well as the sexually torn, quickly disposed-of heroine. Caine, until the film's internal logic breaks down, is excellent as the suave shrink. Allen and Gordon are okay.

Technically the film is beautifully honed and satisfyingly seamless, alternating De Palma's sensous, lulling dolly and tracking shots with staccato bursts of sudden shock and violence. Work of cinematographer Ralf Bode, editor Jerry Greenberg and composer Pino Donaggio adds considerably to the net effect. —*Step.*

Lulu
(FRANCO-GERMAN-ITALIAN-COLOR)

Paris, June 26.

A Parafrance release of a TV 13 (Munich)-Capitol Films, Medusa (Rome)-Elephant Production and Whodunit (Paris) coproduction. Produced by Ralph Baum. Written, designed and directed by Walerian Borowczyk, based on "Earth Spirit" and "Pandora's Box" by Frank Wedekind. Camera (Fujicolor), Michael Steinke; sound, Wolfgang Kapst. Reviewed at the Paramount Elysees theatre, Paris, June 25, 1980. Running time: **95 MINS.**
Lulu .... Ann Bennent
Schwarz .... Michele Placido
Goll .... Jean-Jacques Delbo
Schon .... Heinz Bennent
Alwa .... Hans Jurgen Schatz
Geschwitz .... Beate Kopp
Jack the Ripper .... Udo Kier

Walerian Borowczyk's new screen treatment of Frank Wedekind's "Lulu" sex tragedies, basis for G. W. Pabst's classic "Pandora's Box" with Louise Brooks, is torpid and vacuous, of small interest as art film or erotic item. The director's deteriorating sense of aestheticism becomes increasingly anaesthesizing.

Borowczyk's script, in German, at first appears more faithful to the play than did Pabst's version: he restores the play's first act, involving Lulu's liaison with a painter. But later he executes an ellipse by lopping off the action that takes place between the death of Schon, the influential editor who cannot rid himself of Lulu's grasp, and the climactic London act where Lulu, symbol of sexual freedom, falls prey to the representative of repression, Jack the Ripper.

Borowczyk's direction is stagey, listless and sometimes plain silly (why show Lulu's entrails hanging out ludicrously following her murder?). Ann Bennent, daughter of actor Heinz Bennent (who plays Schon), and sister of David Bennent, (the diabolical little boy in "The Tin Drum"), is inadequate in the demanding central role. The rest of the cast flap about like beached fish. —*Len.*

Cheech And Chong's Next Movie
(COLOR)

Misfired reunion of "Up In Smoke" comedy duo.

Hollywood, July 16.

Universal Pictures release of a C&C Brown Productions film. Stars Richard Marin and Thomas Chong. Produced by Howard Brown. Directed by Thomas Chong. Screenplay by Chong and Cheech Marin; camera (Technicolor), King Baggot; editor, Scott Conrad; music, Mark Davis; production designer, Fred Harpman; set decorator, Bob Benton; sound, Darin Knight, Bill McCaughey, Bob Harman; assistant director, Newton Arnold;

special visual effects, Albert Whitlock; animation designer, Paul Power; associate producer, Peter MacGregor-Scott. Reviewed at Universal Studios, July 16, 1980. (MPAA Rating: R.) Running time: **99 MINS.**
Cheech/Red .... Richard Marin
Chong .... Thomas Chong
Donna .... Evelyn Guerrero
Candy .... Betty Kennedy
Mr. Neatnick .... Sy Kramer
Gloria .... Rikki Marin
Chicken Charlie .... Bob McClurg
Gloria's Mother .... Edie McClurg
Pee Wee Herman/
Desk Clerk .... Paul Reubens

Cheech & Chong's debut pic, "Up In Smoke," was a happy sleeper hit that gained in amusement from its fresh, amateurish, slapdash filming style. Unfortunately, the wacked-out duo's second effort, "Cheech & Chong's Next Movie," is a laborious disappointment in which the freshness has vanished and the laughs come few and far between. You didn't have to be a dope freak or a Cheech & Chong fan to enjoy "Up In Smoke;" it's hard to imagine even people in those categories finding much enjoyment in this one. The Universal release should open well before quick fall-off once word-of-mouth spreads.

It's hard to pinpoint exactly where the film went wrong, since so little of it is on target. Perhaps the fundamental problem is the lack of the simple, one-track-minded story thread that "Up In Smoke" used to hang its riotous jokes. In the earlier film Cheech & Chong were monomaniacally in search of the perfect high; in the new one, they wander through L.A. in search of whatever happens next. Result is an increasing sense of tedium and shapelessness that makes the 99-minute film seem interminable.

Another difference between "Smoke" and "Next Movie" is that Cheech & Chong had a director in their first film. Lou Adler's direction was a mess, but an amiable mess, and there was at least some creative tension operating. Here, Chong takes director reins and holds them so loosely that there's no sense of pacing, timing, or design, all factors necessary for any kind of comedy, even a nutty comedy about potheads. "Next Movie" lacks the performing dynamism and manic energy that gave the first film its lift.

Supporting cast is allowed to mug to their hearts' delight, but not the audience's. Nobody stands out except in competition for most obnoxious cast member, a distinction probably taken by Paul Reubens as an unfunny Pinky Lee-type comic, with Edie McClurg's imbecilic rich matron a close second. Under the circumstances, though, cast deserves pity more than censure. Cheech & Chong soon become tiresome doing their by now overfamiliar routines.

Tech credits are routine, except for a few standout effects shots by Albert Whitlock in sequences showing Cheech & Chong in outer space. —*Mac.*

Caddyshack
(COLOR)

No "Animal House," though biz should be good in same market. Names will help.

Orion Pictures release (thru Warner Bros.) of a Jon Peters Production. Produced by Douglas Kenney. Exec producer, Jon Peters. Directed by Harold Ramis. Written by Brian Doyle-Murray, Ramis, Kenney. Features entire cast. Camera (Technicolor), Steven Larner; editor, William Carruth; supervising editor, David Bretherton; production design, Stan Jolley; music, Johnny Mandel; original songs, Kenny Loggins. Reviewed at National Theatre, N.Y., July 11, '80. (MPAA rating: R). Running time: **90 MINS.**
Ty Webb .... Chevy Chase
Al Czervik .... Rodney Dangerfield
Judge Smalls .... Ted Knight
Danny Noonan .... Michael O'Keefe
Carl Spackler .... Bill Murray
Maggie O'Holligan .... Sarah Holcomb
Tony D'Annunzio .... Scott Colomby
Lacey Underall .... Cindy Morgan
Dr. Beeper .... Dan Resin
The Bishop .... Henry Wilcoxon
Mrs. Noonan .... Elaine Aiken
Mr. Noonan .... Albert Salmi

In its unabashed bid for the mammoth audience which responded to the anti-establishment outrageousness of "National Lampoon's Animal House," this vaguely likable, too-tame comedy stands to fall short of the mark, though its own business should be brisk within the relative doldrums of the current summer. Marquee value of Chevy Chase and Bill Murray bodes well for initial turnstyle action.

This time, the thinly plotted shenanigans unfold against the manicured lawns and posh backdrop of a restricted country club, generally pitting the free-living youthful caddies against the uptight gentry who employ them. After the frat-house familiarity of "Animal House" and the widely shared summer camp experience of "Meatballs," commercial question arises as to how large an audience is going to get off on this more limited setting.

Stock characters include Chase as resident golf-pro, whose golfing acumen has no relation to his off-links physical stumbling and verbal malapropisms; club prexy and jurist Ted Knight in a well-played extension of his pompously inadequate persona from the Mary Tyler Moore tv series; and Rodney Dangerfield as the perfectly cast and very funny personification of anti-social, nouveau riche grossness.

Beyond Chase, prime lure for the kid market will be Bill Murray (who became bankable with

"Meatballs") as a foul-habited, semi-moronic groundskeeper, constantly aroused by the cellulite-draped thighs of older femme golfers, and waging an increasingly violent battle against a cute, furry gopher who's ruining the lawns. Nominal plotline has ambitious caddy Michael O'Keefe trying to wangle a golf scholarship by brown-nosing Knight, with predictably disastrous results.

Pic's verbal hijinks and sight gags runs the gamut of sex, drugs and other counter-culture icons, though the net effect is far tamer, less vicious and considerably less uniformly funny than "Animal House." Penned by producer Doug Kenney ("Animal House"), director Harold Ramis ("Groove Tube," "Second City TV") and Brian Doyle-Murray ("Saturday Night Live"), film should have milked its combo of gross-outs, property destruction, juvenalia and raunchiness to greater effect.

Already in debt to so many sources (particularly the home tube where most of its cast was weaned), "Caddyshack's" best moment is a wonderful parody of the shark attacks in "Jaws" (complete with pounding musical score) as the camera sinks to swimming pool water-level to limn the murderous panic when a scatological look-alike (actually a chocolate candy bar) is thrown into the water. Technical credits are fine. —*Step.*

From The Life Of The Marionettes

(W. GERMAN-B&W/COLOR)

Could be Ingmar Bergman's most commercial entry to date.

London, July 14.
ITC Film Distributors release of an ITC Entertainment production. Executive producers, Lord Grade, Martin Starger. Directed by Ingmar Bergman. Features entire cast. Screenplay, Ingmar Bergman; camera (b&w-color), Sven Nykvist; editor, Petra Voelffen; music, Rols Wilhelm; production designer, Rolf Zechetbauer; art director, Herbert Strabel; costumes, Charlotte Fleming; assts. to the director, Trudy V. Trotha, Johannes Kaetzler. Reviewed at the Oxford Film Festival, New Theatre, Oxford, July 13, '80. (BBFC Rating: X). Running time: 104 MINS.
Peter Egerman . . .•. . . . . Robert Atzorn
Katarina . . . . Christine Buchegger
Mogens Jensen . . . . Martin Benrath
Ka . . . . Rita Russek
Cordelia Egerman . . . . Lola Muethel
Tim . . . . Walter Schmidinger
Arthur Brenner . . . . Heinz Bennent
Nurse . . . . Ruth Olafs
Interrogator . . . . Karl Heinz Pelser
Secretary . . . . Gaby Dohm
Doorman . . . . Toni Berger

With this formal analysis of a man's psyche under excruciating sexual pressure, Ingmar Berg-man, 35 years a director and possibly the world's best-known minority-appeal filmmaker, gives the impression of a master holding his cinematic artistry in check. Devotees of the auteur may be disappointed by its comparative lack of virtuosity, but given the right promotional hooks, "From The Life Of The Marionettes" looks to pull audiences from a wider spectrum than just diehard disciples.

Episodically, relentlessly, Berg-man's screenplay probes the hinterland of an ostensibly irrational crime — the killing and anal ravishment of a young prostitute by a well-heeled, well-married business executive.

The film opens with depiction of the actual event, in color. Everything else — scenes from the preceding weeks, and extracts from the inquiry that follows — is shot black-and-white, until color returns at the very end for a sequence plotting the minutes immediately before the murder. It's as if the body of the film is in parentheses.

On a realistic level, Bergman pieces together a fearsomely credible explanation of the man's mental cataclysm. The superficial success of his marriage is shown to overlay a subtext of ritualized antagonism now so far gone that there's no way back for either partner from the profound lovelessness they've created.

Part of the problem seems to be the man's repressed homosexuality, but to what extent that is a cause or an effect of his wife's frigidity is a question to which the uncompromising script offers no facile answer.

Either way, it's the man who is the logical victim. More sensitive than the woman to the depth of their alienation, and less able to take refuge in his work (she's sharply portrayed heading a fashion house, while his financial dealings are left undefined), he dreams of murdering her as a means of ultimately possessing her. But even with his fuse running dangerously short, some warmth is needed to spark the explosion. The prostitute, routine as her favors are, awakens just enough of the fire long absent from the marriage bed, and unwittingly diverts the nightmare onto herself.

Probably only Bergman could get away with the contrivance of having the girl share a first name with the wife; and the symbolism whereby in a frantic attempt to escape his own impending deed, the man finds all exit doors from the place of assignation — a luridly-appointed peepshow parlor — locked against him.

For those with a taste for a wider than realistic interpretation, the film also works as a devastating image of emotional aridity (and its potential effect) insidiously induced by "normal" life in a comfortable, materialistic society. Bergman seems to indicate that the man in question is merely one hapless puppet drawn from a world of similarly-manipulated marionettes.

It goes almost without saying that casting is spot-on, and performances precisely measured to the director's characteristic cool style.

Robert Atzorn is a fine choice for the central role, achieving the required equation between conventional good looks and total facelessness. Rita Russek's natural sweetness as the prostitute perfectly counterpoints the cumulative chill exuded by the picture's other two principal women, Christine Buchegger as the wife (is that concern in her eyes, or simply pity?) and Lola Muethel as Atzorn's rancorous mother.

Sven Nykvist's cinematography, hallmark of many of Bergman's films, is in stunning form here for the dream sequences — minimal dark shapes in limbo on a bled-white background. Even the frequent scenes which amount to no more than "talking heads" are vested with dramatic urgency by dint of meticulous composition and art-concealing-art lighting.

Pic is wordy, but subtitling of the German dialog on the print viewed was competent and not unduly obtrusive. —*Simo.*

Prom Night
(COLOR)

Scary plot for summertime youth appeal.

Hollywood, July 15.
Avco Embassy release of a Simcom Production. Produced by Peter Simpson. Directed by Paul Lynch. Features entire cast. Screenplay, William Gray from a story by Robert Gunza Jr.; camera (Medallion), Robert New; editor, Brian Ravok; music, Carl Zittrer, Paul Zaza; art direction, Reuben Freed; sound, Brian Day; assistant director, Steve Wright. Reviewed at CFI Screening Room 10, Hollywood, July 15, 1980. (MPAA Rating: R.) Running time: 91 MINS.
Mr. Hammond . . . . Leslie Nielsen
Kim . . . . .•. . . . . Jamie Lee Curtis
Nick . . . . Casey Stevens
Wendy . . . . Eddie Benton
Mrs. Hammond . . . . Antoinette Bower
Alex . . . . Michael Tough
Sykes . . . . Robert Silverman
Vicki . . . . Pita Oliver
Lou . . . . David Mucci
Drew . . . . Jeff Wincott
Kelly . . . . Marybeth Rubins
Jude . . . . Joy Thompson
Children . . . . Brock Simpson,
Debbie Greenfield, Tammy Bourne.
Dean Bosacki, Leslie Scott,
Karen Forbes, Joyce Kite.

"Prom Night" is a scary enough suspenser aimed squarely at the lucrative summer teen market.

Borrowing shamelessly from "Carrie" and any number of gruesome exploitationers in past history, pic manages to score a few horrific points amid a number of sagging moments. It also produces some deliciously ridiculous situations that will entice fans of this genre and consequently ensure some nice initial boxoffice action for distrib Avco Embassy.

Pic opens with the falling death of a 10-year-old girl brought on by unmerciful teasing on the part of four of her peers. There is something glaringly tasteless about a band of children surrounding the tyke yelling "Kill, kill, kill," but once that scene is out of the way rest of pic nobly concentrates on a mysterious killer seeking to avenge the girl's death.

It's six years later and prom night for the surviving kiddies and each is slated to meet an unsavory fate due to past exploits — unbeknownst to anyone. Once the masked killer gets going it becomes a guessing game of who is the ax-wielding avenger and which, if any, of the four scheduled victims will escape.

Director Paul Lynch seems to have captured the spirit of the genre here, but spends a little too much time setting up each murder, thus eliminating some suspense. Script by William Gray manages to tie lots of subplots together in a fairly tight package, helped partly by some tight editing by Brian Ravok.

Leslie Nielsen and Jamie Lee Curtis, latter making a kind of reputation for herself as a stock suspense character, are top-billed names but all cast members contribute to the sometimes menacing mood. That atmosphere is at times broken by the emphasis on the prom's discotheque look in latter part of pic, a factor that seems to have dated the film before its release. Thankfully, the killer was not forced to do the hustle. —*Berg.*

Hopscotch
(COLOR)

Star strength should hold this one up.

Hollywood, July 14.
An Avco Embassy release, produced by Edie and Ely Landau. Exec producer, Otto Plaschkes. Features entire cast. Directed by Ronald Neame. Screenplay, Brian Garfield, Bryan Forbes, based on Garfield novel; camera (Movielab Color), Arthur Ibbetson; editor, Carl Kress; sound, Derek Ball, Oliver Moss; production design, William Creber; assistant directors, Patrick Clayton, William Hassell; music, Ian Fraser. Reviewed at the Samuel Goldwyn Theatre, Beverly Hills, July 14, 1980. (MPAA rating: R.) Running time: 104 MINS.
Miles Kendig . . . . Walter Matthau
Isobel von Schmidt . . . . . . Glenda Jackson
G.P. Myerson . . . . Ned Beatty
Cutter . . . . Sam Waterston

Mikhail Yaskov	Herbert Lom
Ross	David Matthau
Westlake	George Baker
Ludlum	Ivor Roberts
Carla	Lucy Saroyan

"Hopscotch" is a high-spirited caper comedy which, unfortunately, reaches its peak too soon. But while it may sag, it never sinks and should be a respectable program filler for summer's end, especially with solid star attractions.

Grizzled as usual, Walter Matthau plays CIA agent whose independent ways are too much for this finicky, double-dealing boss, Ned Beatty. So Matthau is relieved of his job in the field and put in charge of the files.

But he never shows up for the new assignment, deciding instead to hide out and write a book that will embarrass not only the CIA but spies in every country, making himself a target for extinction from several directions.

In Brian Garfield's novel, and in some earlier script versions reportedly, this was serious stuff. But no more. Now it's all for laughs as Matthau evades the hunters while dreaming up additional ways to make fools of them.

It works well enough in the beginning, thanks in large part to Beatty, thoroughly a dislikable foil who takes all the trappings of espionage seriously while prattling on about the problems of renting his house in the country.

Hiding out, Matthau takes up with Glenda Jackson, an ex-agent herself who has since left the trade and widowed wealthily. They are old flames and their initial moments together serve up the same good bantering chemistry of "House Calls."

Also essential to the chase are Sam Waterston, good as Matthau's former friend and protege now in charge of the pursuit and Herbert Lom, another old friend who happens to be the chief Russian agent and also anxious to run Matthau down before he tells too much. Lucy Saroyan also has a brief but nice part as a pilot who helps Matthau play hide-and-seek.

Having nicely introduced and set up the action for all these characters, director Ronald Neame hits full stride when he hides Matthau as a tenant in Beatty's house, ultimately bringing on the FBI and CIA to shoot up the gingerbread while Matthau slips away.

But that's as funny as the picture ever gets and it comes much too soon. Though the chase continues, it remains only mildly amusing and climaxes in a finish that isn't worthy of what came before. What's worse, Jackson largely disappears long before the finale, in spirit if not in fact. —*Har.*

Borderline
(U.S.-COLOR)

Bronson vehicle with prospects.

London, July 13.

ITC Film Distributors release of an ITC Entertainment presentation. Executive producer, Martin Starger. Produced by James Nelson. Directed by Gerrold Freedman. Stars Charles Bronson. Screenplay, Steve Kline, Gerrold Freedman; camera (color), Tak Fujimoto; editor, John Link; art director, Michael Levesque; music, Gil Melle; sound, Gene Cantamessa; production manager, Christopher Seiter; asst. director, Chuck Myers. Reviewed at the Oxford Film Festival, New Theatre, Oxford, July 12, '80. Running time: **97 MINS.**

Jeb Maynard	Charles Bronson
Jimmy Fante	Bruno Kirby
Elena Morales	Karmin Murcelo
Carl Richards	Bert Remsen
Arturo	Enrique Castillo
Scooter Jackson	A. Wilford Bramley
Henry Lydell	Michael Lerner
Hotchkiss	Ed Harris
Willy	Norman Alden
Munroe	John Ashton
Andy Davies	Larry Casey
Benito	Panchito Gomez

In welcome contrast to the several star-heavy feats of implausibility produced by ITC of late, this new Charles Bronson vehicle works fine. It tackles a serious subject — the profiteering in illicit Mexican immigration — with workmanlike dramatic skill and a notable preference for realism over hokum.

Assured of strong returns in Bronson's customary markets, pic's theme and treatment could also qualify it for favorable attention in the U.S. and elsewhere. Notwithstanding Bronson's convincing performance, the nicely spare script by Steve Kline and Gerrold Freedman endorses the view that an indispensable above-the-line element of a worthwhile package is a good story, plausibly told. This one is also well directed by Freedman.

The film's big name, in fact, is self-effacing almost to the point of elusiveness. As a long-serving, compassionate border patrolman, Bronson is hunched and hated virtually throughout. Given the preponderance of night shooting and, in day sequences, cinematographer Tak Fujimoto's reliance on available light (mainly vertical sun), Bronson's deep-lined face is mostly masked by heavy shadow.

That hardly damages his enduring charisma, however, and the actor's apparent commitment to conveying the reality of the role is a definite plus.

The professionally-honed, conventional plot pits him against a younger, ruthless racketeer who runs wetbacks across the border at an exploitative price on behalf of a U.S. business corporation. Per the ironic ending, while the battle predictably results in a victory for justice (and Bronson gets his man), eventual acquittal of the behind-the-scenes boss shows the war is far from won.

Newcomer Ed Harris is memorable as the frontline villain, displaying screen presence to match the star's and thus injecting a powerful sense of danger.

Karmin Murcelo is good, unobvious casting for the only featured female role of an illegal immigrant given a promise of tacit help by Bronson after leading him to his quarry. Along with Bruno Kirby, A. Wilford Bramley and Michael Lerner, also stand out in support, she contributes handsomely to the action's general believability.

So, too, does Fujimoto's naturalistic camerawork, which resorts to none of the overlit effects all-too familiar in night scenes, but rather ups the tension by frequently using only those light sources present. The relatively few sequences shot day-for-night are carefully handled and less than commonly distracting.

Gil Melle's musical score is traditional but effective. —*Simo.*

Today Is For
The Championship
(DOCUMENTARY-COLOR)

Going nowhere at top speed.

Hollywood, June 26.

A Breakthrough Racing release, produced and directed by Dan Weisburd. Exec producer, Daniel Miller. Camera (Foto-Kem color), Peter Smiokler; editor, James Oliver; sound, Robert Eber; music, Buddy Collette. Reviewed at Adikoff Screening Room, Hollywood, June 26, 1980 (MPAA rating: PG.) Running time: **110 MINS**).

If racing cars could run on hot air, "Today Is For The Championship" would at least be credited for solving the fuel shortage. But like the cars, this four-wall documentary about the application of nonsense to tough tasks just goes in circles. Outlook: Grim would be good.

In two hours that seem like four, film focuses on the latest brainstorm of Werner Erhard, the founder of est, as he attempts to apply his philosophies to the mastery of race-car driving, a sport he has never attempted before.

One of the foundations of Erhard's success to date, of course, is his sheer charismatic genius, unequalled in his ability to elevate pristine dribble into a message that thousands will willingly follow. If there's any value to the film at all, it's the fun of watching him say so sincerely and convincingly.

"The stuff that could make a major difference in your life isn't thinkable."

Or, "The appropriate context of life is that life shall work for everyone."

The amazing thing about Erhard and est, to be sure, is that it sometimes seems to work for people, even if they themselves can't explain why. And, sure enough, once he gets into the racing business, talking to the cars and everyone around him, he actually begins to win.

When things do go wrong, nobody ever blames a bad carburetor or a stubborn fuel pump. They all sit around reexamining their own personal relationships and "acknowledging" whatever it is the other person is trying to say. They also cry a lot and apologize.

Along the way, they also wonder if the secret they obviously possess couldn't somehow be packaged and sold to major corporations.

But the only person with any plain understanding in the whole picture speaks up and says, "The heads of the Fortune 500 companies wouldn't understand anything Erhard says."

He's right. —*Har.*

The Mountain Men
(COLOR)

Bloody wilderness pic may have trouble finding an audience.

Hollywood, July 17.

Columbia Pictures release of a Martin Ransohoff Production. Stars Charlton Heston, Brian Keith. Produced by Martin Shafer, Andrew Scheinman; exec producer, Richard R. St. Johns. Directed by Richard Lang. Screenplay, Fraser Clarke Heston; camera (Metrocolor), Michel Hugo; second-unit camera, Herb Pearl; music, Michel Legrand; editor, Eva Ruggiero; production designer, Bill Kenney; set decorator, Rick T. Gentz; sound, Glenn Anderson, Les Fresholtz; second-unit director, Joe Canutt; associate producer, Cathleen Summers. Reviewed at The Burbank Studios, July 17, 1980. (MPAA Rating: R.) Running time: **102 MINS.**

Bill Tyler	Charlton Heston
Henry Frapp	Brian Keith
Running Moon	Victoria Racimo
Heavy Eagle	Stephen Macht
Nathan Wyeth	John Glover
La Bont	Seymour Cassel
Medicine Wolf	David Ackroyd
Cross Otter	Cal Bellini
Jim Walker	Bill Lucking
Fontenelle	Ken Ruta
Iron Belly	Victor Jory

Does anyone want to see Charlton Heston as Grizzly Adams? That's the question arising from Columbia's lethargic new wilderness pic, "The Mountain Men," which plays like a Schick Sunn Classics four-waller uncomfortably spiced up with violence and profanity. If the film had a G or PG rating it might be salable to the family market, but with its well-deserved R rating, film may have trouble finding an audience. The Martin Ransohoff production, exec produced by Richard R. St. Johns and produced by Martin Shafer and Andrew Scheinman, is a limp feature debut for director Richard Lang.

Screenplay by star's son Fraser Clarke Heston is loaded with vulgarities that seem excessive for the genre, and scene after scene dwells on bloody hand-to-hand battles between Indians and the grizzled trappers played by Heston and sidekick Brian Keith. The emphasis on crudity and sadism may be in keeping with the setting, but this kind of wilderness adventure pic uauslly has to click with family viewers to make money. "Jeremiah Johnson" broke out to wider audiences, and Col may hope to repeat its success, but that one had Robert Redford and striking direction by Sydney Pollack in contrast to tired marquee names here and Lang's rambling treatment.

Heston, festooned with long hair and beard and bedecked in furs, looks awkward and uncomfortable as he struggles through the strenuous role with his customary earnestness. Keith, in the Denver Pyle part, hams it up for comic effect but comes off as an irritant, particularly since he is saddled with most of the tiresome profanity.

Film takes ages to drag from one plot development to another, though the Indian battles are thrown in with sufficient regularity to keep the audience from snoozing. Basic storyline is Heston's courtly protection of runaway Indian squaw Victoria Racimo and the violent attempts by her former Indian mate Stephen Macht to win her back. Racimo livens up the screen whenever she appears, but unfortunately she's absent for long stretches and the film becomes a yawn.

Lensing by Michel Hugo is attractive, though not first-rate. The spectacular settings in the Bridger-Teton National Forest and Shoshone National Forest provide most of the visual interest. Michel Legrand's score is bombastic and not always appropriate, but it works hard to keep the film afloat.

Best tech work was done by production designer Bill Kenney, set decorator Rick T. Gentz, and costumers Thomas S. Dawson and Kathleen McGregor, who combine their efforts to give the film authentic-looking physical trappings. —Mac.

Living Legend
(COLOR)

Not about whom you think, or anything else.

Hollywood, July 17.
A Maverick Pictures International release, produced by Earl Owensby. Di-rected by Worth Keeter. Features entire cast. Screenplay. Tom McIntyre; camera (CFI Color). Darrell Cathcart; editor. Richard Aldridge. (No other credits supplied). Reviewed at Holly Vine Screening Room. Hollywood, July 17, 1980. (MPAA Rating: PG). Running time: 92 MINS.

Eli Canfield	Earl Owensby
Jim Cannon	William T. Hicks
Jeannie Loring	Ginger Alden
Chad	Jerry Rushing
Teddy	Greg Carswell
Dean	Toby Wallace
Susan	Kristina Reynolds

"Living Legend" starts off with a title card disclaiming that any resemblance to a person living or dead is purely coincidental. Any resemblance to a professional feature film is even more so.

This is not necessarily a detraction, however. Earl Owensby produces and stars in dedicatedly amateur films that presumably must make money out in the hinterlands or else he wouldn't have been able to make a dozen of them in his own studio in North Carolina.

In "Living Legend," Owensby acts like Elvis Presley, dresses like Elvis Presley and even has a girl friend played by Ginger Alden, who was Elvis Presley's girlfriend at the time of his death.

So much for disclaimers.

There is, however, no real danger of mistaking Owensby for Presley since Owensby would have to be an actor to bring that off. And Owensby is no actor. Fortunately, though, he picked his costar well and Alden is no actress either. Together, as they are through much of the picture, they make their own screen history..

Rest of the regional cast is a bit better and William T. Hicks is almost fairly good as the conniving, selfish, dominant manager, surely not meant to be Col. Tom Parker. And Jerry Rushing and Greg Carswell are convincing as Owensby's friends.

The plot, several hundred years old, involves Owensby's mental and physical deterioration under the pressure of stardom. Crazed by drugs, he is driving away all of his real friends while falling further and further under the evil spell of Hicks, who is willing to risk the singer's life to keep him on the concert tour.

Finally, Owensby collapses enroute and is taken away from the Atlanta airport by ambulance. That's what the sign on the tower says as the plane lands — Atlanta. But he's driven away by a "Scotland County Ambulance." Atlanta is in Fulton County, which gives some idea of the technical level of the picture.

On the plus side, Owensby does lip-synch some pretty good songs, actually sung by Roy Orbison. But this also is a technical problem that director Worth Keeter couldn't han-dle. When Owensby "sings" you see the crowd going wild. But you can't hear them at all.

It's that kind of picture. —Har.

The Little Dragons
(COLOR)

Kiddie karate item lacks snap.

Hollywood, July 15.
An Aurora Film Corp. release of an Eastwind production. Produced by Hannah Hempstead. Curtis Hanson. Executive producers. Tony Bill. Robert Bremson. Directed by Curtis Hanson. Features entire cast. Screenplay. Harvey Applebaum, Louis G. Atlee, Rudolph Borchert, Alan Ormsby; camera (uncredited color), Stephen Katz; music. Ken Lauber; art direction. Spencer Quinn; sound. Trevor Black; assistant director. Rick Whiting. Reviewed at Nosseck's Screening Room. L.A.. July 15. 1980. (MPAA Rating: PG.) Running time: 90 MINS.

J.J.	Charles Lane
Angel	Ann Sothern
Zack	Chris Petersen
Woody	Pat Petersen
Carol	Sally Boyden
Dick Forbinger	Rick Lenz
Ruth Forbinger	Sharon Weber
Yancey	Joe Spinell
Carl	John Chandler
Sheriff	Clifford A. Pellow
Lunsford	Stephen Young
Karate Instructor	Pat Johnson
The Master	Master Bong Soon Han
Motorcycle Gang Leader	Donnie Williams
Niles	Tony Bill
Deputy	Brad Gorman

A rather lackadaisical, if amiable, suspenser clearly intended a palatable antidote to more violent action fare, "The Little Dragons" might be more at home on the tube than on theatre screens but still could prove a serviceable entry in situations hungry for unobjectionable family fare. Having bowed Friday (18) in several markets, pic possesses salable elements, even if they materialize rather blandly in film itself.

Basic idea of having kiddie sleuths proving more effective than the fuzz in solving rural kidnapping plot isn't at all bad, but quartet of writers relies mostly on stock characterizations and hasn't embellished the tale with sufficient imagination or wit to lift it above the routine.

Simple situation has real cutie Sally Boyden, vacationing in the boonies with her city-folk parents, abducted by buffoonish Joe Spinell and John Chandler, two hicks living in a junk heap with mama Ann Sothern. Local cops aren't able to come up with many leads, so blond chop-socky devotes Chris and Pat Petersen, with some incidental help from roving Hell's Angels, take it upon themselves to rescue the girl from her peril.

Given the initial attention to karate training and the PG, rather than G, rating, one hopes for at least a little climatic action, but eventual triumph over the baddies plays as mildly as the rest of the picture. too bad since coincidental congregation of many martial arts moppets at a lakeside retreat provides opportunity for some good-spirited mayhem in routing the dim-witted evil-doers.

Direction by Curtis Hanson, former film mag editor who previously helmed "Sweet Kill" for Roger Corman, is serviceable and sympathetic, but never gets close enough to any of the characters to generate a great deal of personal involvement. Only vet character actor Charles Lane comes up with much elaboration of his role, that of the kids' kooky, almost hippie-like grandfather who plays along with their independent tracking of the villains.

Stories featuring tykes successfully undertaking adult functions should never be underestimated for their potential appeal to youngsters, so pic could make it with under-14 crowd. But a stronger script and deeper characterizations could have broadened its audience.

Tech credits are okay. —Cart.

Fatty Finn
(AUSTRALIA-COLOR)

Sydney, July 8.
A Hoyts Distribution release of a Children's Film Corp. production. Produced by Brian Rosen. Executive producer. John Sexton. Directed by Maurice Murphy. Screenplay. Bob Ellis and Chris McGill. from an original idea by Ellis; camera (Eastmancolor). John Seale; editor. Bob Gibson; music. Graham Bond and Rory O'Donohue. Reviewed at Hoyts' Theater-ette. Sydney. July 8. 1980. (Commonwealth Censorship. Rating: not yet rated). Running time: 91 MINS.

Fatty Finn	Ben Oxenbould
Mr. Finn	Bert Newton
Mrs. Finn	Noni Hazelhurst
Tiger Murphy	Gerard Kennedy
Bruiser Murphy	Greg Kelly
Maggie McGrath	Lorraine Bayly
Mr. Zilch	Henri Szeps
Lord Mayor	Frank Wilson
Teacher	Peter Carroll
Radio Announcer	Ross Higgins

The eponymous hero is as classic to the Australian comic strip as the Katzenjammer Kids were to America in that same distant, innocent age; and just as dated. "Fatty Finn" is the ultimate in Australian parochial filmmaking; even for ears attuned to the local dialect, words are lost. Beyond that, there is the bewildering urgency of the plot which involves gang rivalry among small children in an inner Sydney suburb in the late stages of the Depression.

Derived as it is from a comic strip, one can accept a certain overemphasis, and over-statement. However the director has allowed every character to "go over the top" to such a stage in delivery that the line between inability to act, overacting and inept direction becomes blurred. The whole film is over-blown and frequently in danger of going completely off the edge in search of cuteness. Fact is a comic-strip frame can't blow up to a 16-foot screen without a great deal more content.

Scriptwriters Bob Ellis (whose original idea it was to do the film) and Chris McGill (director of the still-unreleased "Maybe This Time") simply haven't invested enough substance in the film to make it pay off as anything other than an expensive exercise in nostalgia. While social realism certainly isn't called for, something less than high-camp opera might have created a more acceptable result.

That the film was made at all must be regarded as a manifestation of the country's current phase of cultural self-examination and resurgent nationalism in the arts. Overseas, it could be considered only as a curiosity, and in fact the Henry Szeps characterization of the local pawnbroker might well be considered offensive.

Clearly it was the intention to exaggerate, and while the allure of the memories the subject has for the adults who made and financed it — such things as crystal sets, goat cart races, a coprological fascination with outdoor toilets and other quaint aspects of urban Aussie life in the Thirties — it must be considered doubtful in the extreme that a generation assaulted by the marvels of the electronic age will share the wistfulness of the grown-ups.

As a sort of live cartoon, it might be considered a noble academic failure; but the hard facts are that the film will be released here at Christmas against opposition that, given today's kids' tastes, is bound to annihilate it at the boxoffice. Other than those dragged by keenly nostalgic parents and grandparents, the bulk of "Fatty Finn's" audience will be made up of those who couldn't get into "Empire Strikes Back" and "Superman II." Overseas the film stands even less chance. —Miha.

L'Entourloupe
(The Swindle)
(FRENCH-COLOR)

Paris, July 8.
A CCFC release of a Cathala production. Produced by Norbert Saada. Stars Jean-Pierre Marielle and Jacques Dutronc. Directed by Gerard Pires. Screenplay by Jean Herman and Michel Audiard, based on the novel "Nos Intentions Sont Pacifiques" by Francis Ryck. Music, Django Reinhardt; camera (Fujicolor), Pierre William Glenn; editor, Jacques Witta; Sound, Guy Rophe. Reviewed at U.G.C. Biarritz Theatre, Paris, June 14, 1980. Running time: 90 MINS.

Casterlard .... Jean-Pierre Marielle
Olivier .... Jacques Dutronc
Roland .... Gerard Lanvin
Valerie .... Anne Jousset

Gerard Pires' "L'Entourloupe" falters as satiric comedy but it does contain some cruelly hilarious scenes and one sterling performance. Picture has been a hit locally, perhaps in part due to its star names, but probably doesn't have enough impact to give it impetus in overseas markets.

Based on a novel by Francis Ryck (best known here for his thrillers), films tells of two young urban layabouts (well portrayed by Jacques Dutronc and Gerard Lanvin) who sign up to peddle useless family medical encyclopedias to peasant families that neither need them nor can afford them.

The script by Jean Herman and Michel Audiard begins well but wobbles dramatically once the early setpieces of the young men's induction into their new milieu have been effectively put across.

These induction sequences are the best in the film and they all share a common denominator: Jean-Pierre Marielle, as the head of the dubious sales enterprise. To watch Marielle use his theatrical cunning to breach the peasant wall of hardened innocence is a spectacle in itself; and, thanks in good part to Audiard's brittle dialog, his composition of an unctuous, bigoted, unstoppable seducer-shyster is the best thing this fine actor has done in some time. —Len.

Karlovy Fest

Iluzia
(Illusion)
(BULGARIAN-COLOR)

Karlovy Vary, July 5.
A Bulgarofilm Production, Sofia; world rights, Bulgarofilm, Sofia. Features entire cast. Directed by Lyudmil Staikov. Screenplay, Konstantin Pavlov; camera (Eastmancolor), Boris Yanakiev, art direction, Zahari Ivanov; music, Goergi Genkov. Reviewed at Karlovy Vary Film Festival (Competition), July 5, '80. Running time: 90 MINS.
Cast: Roussi Chanev (Poet), Lyuben Chatalov (Artist), Suzanna Kocurikova (Actress), Peter Slabakov (Danil).

Prizewinner at Karlovy Vary, Lyudmil Staikov's "Illusion" is less a fiction feature than a tract on the nature of art in its social and moral context. Staikov earlier made "Amendment of the Defence-of-State Act" (1977), set in the troublesome year of 1923 when the September Uprising was put down by a government bent on dictatorship. This is the poetic reflection on those same events, a sequel that makes

more sense if the former is kept in mind.

Scripter Konstantin Pavlov is also a comer to watch in the Bulgarian film industry. He wrote the screenplays for Lyubomir Sharlandjiev's "Memory of the Twin Sister" (1976) and Stefan Dimitrov's "Hark to the Cock!" (1977), both having memory, flashbacks, and reflections on abstract ideas in the foreground. He addresses himself to the perceptive viewer who likes his cinema with an intellectual challenge.

"Illusion," as the title indicates, is succession of poetic images, some related in time and history, others applying to questions of truth, moral conviction, and social responsibility. The three principle figures in the story — the artist, the poet, and the actress — have their own illusions, not the least of which is a love both men have for the same woman. The poet and artist, in turn, look differently at the political scene after 1923, when the uprising against fascism was put down with brutal force.

The poet is killed on the street by a hired assassin's bullet, at the same time as the artist is painting flowers of every kind in his studio while working in splendid isolation. The death of his friend, however, triggers an act of resistance at the public exhibition of his paintings when he discovers that the government's cultural minister has proclaimed his flowers as models to be imitated — the painter bites the ear of the minister! Then he goes back to an empty canvas to start over, presumably on a revolutionary theme.

Several other poetic juxtapositions are found in "Illusion" — the question of artistic and sexual impotency, for instance, when the artist tries to paint a portrait of the actress. There's also a prophet, Danil, who talks with the artist about events that took place in his village, the figure and the story probably referring to the historical past when Bulgaria was an agrarian, patriarchal society. The prophet's story (pouring from Danil's memory in bursts of inspiration, it seems) is sketched in absurd, Hieronymus Bosch images and features a Dance of Death across the horizon when an impish harlequin appears to court the naive and innocent away from the Prophet's own, heavenly-inspired "Book of Revelation" (in fact, a lexicon of encyclopedia).

"Illusion" cannot be fully grasped without some knowledge of Bulgarian history, but there is enough on the surface in any case to fascinate for the first hour or so,

then the pic tends to bog down in repetition and metaphoric symbol for its own sake. Worth a looksee at Bulgarian Film Weeks. —Holl.

Die Verlobte
(The Fiancee)
(EAST GERMAN-COLOR)

Karlovy Vary, July 4.
A Coproduction between DEFA-Studio for Feature Films and GDR-Television; world rights. DEFA Aussenhandel, Berlin, GDR. Features entire cast. Directed by Guenter Reisch and Guenther Ruecker. Screenplay, Guenther Ruecker, based on the novel trilogy, "The House with the Heavy Doors," by Eva Lippold; camera (color), Juergen Brauer; art direction, Dieter Adam; music, Karl-Ernst Sasse; editing, Erika Lemphul; artistic manager, Hans Muencheberg. Reviewed at Karlovy Vary Film Festival (Competition), July 4, '80. Running time: 105 MINS.
Cast: Jutta Wachowiak (Hella), Regimantas Adomaitis (Reimers), Slavka Budinova (Lola), Christine Gloger (Frenzel), Inge Keller (Irene), Kaethe Reichel (Olser), Hans-Joachem Hegewald (Hensch), Barbara Zinn (Elsie), Katrin Sass (Barbara), Ewa Zieteck (Hilde), Ursula Braun (Naudorf), Katrin Martin (Konrad), Reinhard Straube (Rimer's comrade), Friedrich Richter (Official), Johannes Wieke (Reimer's father), Rolf Ludwig (Prison doctor).

Grand Prix winner at the Karlovy Vary fest, "The Fiancee" was begun by director Guenter Reisch and finished by scripter Guenther Ruecker when Reisch fell seriously ill. Among the fest entries it deserved the top kudo, but pic also compares well with the director's earlier "Wolz" (1974) and "Anton the Magician" (1977) — a trilogy in that all three pix deal with "outsiders" who maintain their personal integrity at all costs and thus contribute significantly to society and the common good.

"The Fiancee" is based on a true-life incident as recorded in the three-part novel, Eva Lippold's "The House with the Heavy Doors," that served as the inspirational source of the fiction-document; in fact, the author, who spent 10 years in a Nazi prison from 1935 to the end of the war, was present during the shooting to add to the authenticity.

It's the story of a young, dedicated woman working in the underground Communist movement in Germany together with the man she loves. When she is arrested and he isn't, the lover requests the right to marry her while she serves the 10-year sentence. It is refused, but letters and messages keep her hopes alive throughout the rigors and inhumanity of prison treatment. Her spirit and courage win the respect of other inmates, most of whom have been sentenced for murder and crimes of a more serious nature than hers.

Towards the end of the war, her accomplice on the outside is also arrested and condemned to death by the Gestapo; she is allowed to visit him for the first and final time since the incarceration. That scene, indeed, makes the picture — movingly played by Jutta Wachowiak as the fiancee who, unable to speak, must transmit her emotions by gesture and expression. Then, upon her release, the nearly shattered woman leaves the prison in a daze to return to the places of her memories, only to find that there is nothing left to fulfill her hopes and dreams.

More a film about loneliness, isolation, and prison life than the hinted (in the title) love story, or the destiny of a committed revolutionary, "The Fiancee" contains a profounder message that surfaces more than once in the depiction of everyday work routines and punishments designed to strip the victim of decency and humanity. Credits in every category are a strong plus, and pic deserves further exposure at fests and East German Film Weeks. —*Holl.*

Fabian Balint Talalkozasa Istennel
(Balint Fabian Meets God)
(HUNGARIAN-COLOR)

Karlovy Vary, July 15.
Hungarofilm release of Dialog Studio production. Features entire cast. Written and directed by Zoltan Fabri from book by Jozsef Balazs. Camera (Eastmancolor), Gyorgy Illes; music, Gyorgy Vukan. Reviewed at Karlovy Vary Film Fest (non-competing). July 6, '80. Running time, 113 MINS.
Balint .... Gabor Koncz
Anna .... Vera Venczel
Andras .... Istvan Szabo
Istvan .... Gyorgy Szatmari
Joszi .... Jozsef Ivanyi
Karoly .... Matyas Lisztics

A ruggedly honed tale of the life of a peasant in Hungary going through World I and its aftermath with the short lived commune and the hunting down of the men involved in this first attempt at communism in Hungary. These events affect and finally destroy the life of the main character, Balint Fabian, who is not up to understanding and being able to cope with the effects on his own ways and family life.

Director Zoltan Fabri is one of the deans of Magyar filmmaking. He does this in a solid academic style which fits this tale of interior anguish and one man's inability to deal with changing ways. It is a tale of woe but sidesteps melodrama to lay out its tale in carefully detailed scenes.

Fabian kills an Italian in hand-to-hand fighting in the war and it haunts him afterwards. His sons have killed a priest who became his wife's lover during the war. This has driven the wife mad and she finally dies and his sons go off as he hangs himself to the church bell

when he finds out his sons have killed the priest and also a man who tried to reveal the tale to him.

Balint does not go along with the revolutionary days of the commune but later helps get some of his fellow villagers saved from hanging by the local nobleman for whom he works. He finally feels that only God can help him but even here he finds no solace and finally kills himself.

Film is a "prequel," that is about the earlier days of characters Fabri treated in his previous film, "The Hungarians," about the sons who emigrated. This one is too stolid and lacking the dramatic visiual epiphany that Fabri achieved in earlier films. But it is a good picture of the epoch and has fest if not commercial possibilities abroad. —*Mosk.*

Boszka Ema
(Divine Ema)
(CZECHOSLOVAK-COLOR)

Karlovy Vary, July 15.
Czech State film release of Barrandov Studio production. Features entire cast. Directed by Jiri Krejcik. Screenplay, Zdenek Mahler, Krejcik; camera (Eastmancolor), Miroslav Ondricek; art director, Jindrich Goets; music, Zdenek Liska. Reviewed at Karlovy Vary Film Fest (non-competing), June 28, '80. Running time, 110 MINS.
Ema .... Bozidara Turzonovova
Viktor .... Juraj Kukura
Samuel .... Milos Kopecky
Colonel .... Jiri Adamira
Lieutenant .... Joszef Somr

Reportedly one of the leading local hits this season, it is quite understandable. Film is a well-done tale about a famed Bohemian opera diva who was accused of espionage during the First World War. Her country, later to become Czechoslovakia, was part of the Austro-Hungarian Empire fighting alongside Germany.

Film has a neat timeless patriotic flair, fine period atmosphere and the right flamboyant thesping. Bozidara Tursonovova is touching, haughty, lovely, vulnerable and yet loving and strong (and well dubbed in her singing), as the diva who is finally forced into a tragic solitude after the war.

Director Jiri Krejcik has not stinted on the gloss and sheen that makes it reminiscent of the Hollywood period bios of the Thirties. It is played straight which gives it charm. The singer is first seen on a triumphant tour of America. Europe is at war and the U.S. is still keeping aloof.

She decides to go home and a man gives her a coat and says someone will claim it on arrival. She accepts it absentmindedly but on arrival in Bohemia Austro-Hungarian officers arrest her for there has been a leak. A code is found in the coat and she is saved

from execution by the Kaiser himself.

She remains virtually a prisoner in her own home and is not allowed to sing. But one day she embarks on a tour of the country singing patriotic songs. The caretaker of her home, who was her lover, has probably been killed and she resists an offer to go to America to spy, for it seems the U.S. will soon be in the war. She resists and faces her future solitude at home.

Film might be worth some playoff and even fest outings on its disarming treatment of a real life singer accused of spying, though the actual affair has always been unclear. It takes romantic liberties to make it an entertaining opus.
—*Mosk.*

Gnezdo Na Vetru
(Nest in the Wind)
(SOVIET-COLOR)

Karlovy Vary, June 30.
A Tallinfilm Studio production, Tallin, Estonia, USSR; world rights, Goskino, Moscow, USSR. Features entire cast. Directed by Olev Neuland. Screenplay, Isaak Fridbergas, Gegori Kanovichius; camera (color), Arvo Ikho; music, Lepo Sumera. Reviewed at Karlovy Vary Film Festival (Opera Prima), June 30 '80. Running time: 95 MINS.
Cast: Rudolf Allabert (Yuri Pijr), Nelli Taar (Roozi Pijr), Evald Aavik (the Stranger), Tynu Kark (Tijt Palysamaa), Anne Maayik (Liza Pijr).

The best of the debut pix unspooled in the "Opera Prima" section of this Czech fest, Olev Neuland's "Nest in the Wind" deserved the first (sectional), prize award by the international jury. It's a complex but moving tale of the social and political conflicts that took place in the Balkan republic of Estonia in the Soviet Union in the autumn and winter of 1946, when the country (free between 1920 and 1940) was torn apart by warring parties as though the war had never really finished.

In a lonely peasant farmer's cottage on the edge of the woods, the tragic central figure, Yuri Pijr, is warned under pain of death by the hostile, nationalistic, and fiercely independent Forest Fraternity (fellow Estonians refusing to join either the Germans or the Soviets in the Second World War) not to deliver grain to the Soviet Secretary who has recently arrived in town. To add to his troubles, a deaf-and-dumb stranger arrives at the farm, who turns out later to be an Austrian deserter from the German Wehrmacht.

These four opposing positions lead to several unexpected turns of events. The stranger is sent by the farmer to deliver the grain to the Soviet Secretary, and is nearly killed (the horse is killed instead).

The farmer's daughter-in-law is a widow (the farmer's son was killed in the war); she marries the Austrian deserter and becomes pregnant. In an attack on the farmer, the Austrian kills two members of the Forest Fraternity ("brothers" of the Estonian farmer). Then the Soviet Secretary arrives with an armed patrol and a shoot-out takes place, killing the farmer and several others on both sides. In the end, the Austrian is taken away with members of the Forest Fraternity — undoubtedly to certain death or Siberian exile.

The last scene shows the farmer's daughter caring now for two children that are fatherless, and the Estonian peasant woman is also without her man. A bleak moment, but with a ray of hope for the future in the idyllic spring atmosphere.

"Nest in the Wind" should receive more fest exposure. Not only are all the credits top-grade, but the subject matter and general compassion for all the losers in the film are of particular interest to Soviet film buffs and European history fans. As for helmer Neuland, his 10-year experience in television and string of docus under his belt prepared him well for this remarkable debut effort. —*Holl.*

Laski Mezi Kapkami Deste
(Love Between the Raindrops)
(CZECHOSLOVAK-COLOR)

Karlovy Vary, July 15.
Czech State Film release of Barrandov Studio production. Features entire cast. Directed by Karel Kachyna. Screenplay, Jan Otcenasek, Vladimir Kalina; camera (Eastmancolor), Jan Curik; music, Lubos Fiser. Reviewed at Karlovy Vary Film Fest (non-competing), June 29, '80. Running time, 106 MINS.
Burski .... Vladimir Mensik
Kajda .... Lukas Vaculik
Pepan .... Jan Hrusinski
Paja .... Tereza Pokorna
Vera .... Zlata Adamovska
Fanka .... Eva Jakoubova

Director Karel Kachyna has usually summed up the Czechoslovak film strengths in adding an edge of fantasy to any period, fine treatment of young love without sentimentality and the coming of age. Here these are all neatly dovetailed for a most beguiling film that looks at a poor worker family from 1925-1939 in the worker suburbs of Prague.

Kachyna had a hiatus from 1970 to '75 but is now working regularly. He adds a good balance to the usually rote work, except for a few exceptions by those who made up the heyday of unusual Czech films from '63-68, that has been coming out in the country since '68.

A brash, self dramatizing, colorful shoemaker moves his family into a sprawling apartment house in Prague from the country. He is soon done in by a big shoe company, his wife dies, his daughter leaves home and his two sons grow up in the streets. But no melodrama here but a rousing human comedy that should find its way on world screens.

The younger boy still goes to school and meets a most delightful teenager who dreams of being a dancer. They find a garden outside the house of a rich old pharmacist. It becomes their Eden and they are allowed to come as long as they do not touch certain grapes. But the older brother also woos the girl and when shown the garden takes the grapes which are bitter. They are thrown out.

The brothers fight over her and the older one wins. The other goes off saying goodbye to his childhood.

The fine overall playing, the mixture of comedy and human revelation, the envelope of a gaudy cabaret symbolizing the depression, fascist encroachment and war all weld this into a most entertaining comedy-drama. —Mosk.

Buna Seara, Irina
(Good Evening, Irina)
(RUMANIAN-COLOR)

Karlovy Vary, July 6.
A Romaniafilm Production, Bucharest; world rights, Romaniafilm, Bucharest. Features entire cast. Directed by Tudor Marascu. Screenplay, Timotei Ursu; camera (color), Mirian Iordache, Dumitru Truica. Only credits available. Reviewed at Karlovy Vary Film Festival (Opera Prima), July 6, '80. Running time: 90 MINS.
Cast: Valeria Seciu, Stefan Iordache, Emil Hossu, Radu Panamerenco, Bogdan Carp.

Slated in the competitive debut section at Karlovy Vary, Tudor Marascu's "Good Evening, Irina" deals with an officer on an ocean vessel, whose family life is laid on ice for four months of the year as a consequence of his job. His wife, Irina, works in an engineering institute, is pursued by another man in private life, and is now considering a divorce. She leaves the apartment just as the husband is returning home.

Since both parties still love each other, it's a question of resolving the differences of opinion on what constitutes a marriage. The first step in the right direction is made by the husband in trying to win her back. Then, when she visits the ship in port, he is involved in a rescue operation to free the vessel from an underwater snag, which involves a dangerous diving-suit operation. The officer comes out a hero and receives his own ship to captain, the youngest in the fleet. All seems for the better in the end.

Helmer Marascu is a vet tv-director with experience in musicals and comedy programs, and has also done stage directions. "Good Evening, Irina" fulfills its aim to entertain with touches of comedy and tenderness on the side. —Holl.

Minden Szerdan
(Every Wednesday)
(HUNGARIAN-COLOR)

Karlovy Vary, July 15.
Hungarofilm release and production. Features entire cast. Directed by Livia Gyarmathy. Screenplay, Guyka Marosi, Gyarmathy; camera (Eastmancolor), Ferenc Papp. Reviewed at Karlovy Vary Film Fest (competing), July 1, '80. Running time: 90 MINS.
Boy .... Janos Ban
Old Man .... Miklos Markovics
Ibolya .... Judit Mezlery
Husband .... Tiber Szilagi

Add another film on youthful disarray that seems a steady theme in much world production these days. Here a young man, heading for delinquency, gets straightened out by a friendship with a crusty old man.

Director Livia Gyarmathy does not overstress the boy's problems with a sluttish mother, hypocrisy around him and a callow side to his childish revolt which consists of breaking into a supermarket.

The old man had seen the boy and sees him again when the boy comes to wash windows at his house. They begin to talk and the boy makes other visits and also becomes involved in the old man's family disorders.

After the old man's death he walks out on it all with a seemingly newfound maturity and perhaps new ways to tackle life.

Mainly a local film. —Mosk.

The Squeeze
(ITALIAN-COLOR)

Van Cleef looms large in otherwise routine programmer.

Hollywood, July 17.
A Maverick Pictures International release of a Dritte Centama GmbH production. Produced by Turi Vasile. Executive producer, Raymond R. Homer. Stars Lee Van Cleef, Karen Black. Directed by Anthony M. Dawson (Antonio Margheriti). Screenplay, Simon O'Neil, Marc Princi, Paul Costello; camera (Technicolor), Sergio D'Offizi; editor, Robert Sterbini; music, Paolo Vasile; art direction, Francesco Bronzi, Hans Zillman; costume design, Adrianna Berselli; sound, Miro Branoti; assistant director, Ignazio Dolce. Reviewed at the Holly Vine Screening Room, Hollywood, July 17, 1980. (MPAA Rating: R.) Running time: 100 MINS.
Chris .... Lee Van Cleef
Clarisse .... Karen Black
Jeff .... Edward Albert
Sam Epstein .... Lionel Stander
Donati .... Robert Alda
Inspector .... Angelo Infanti
Jessica .... Antonella Murgia
Von Stratten .... Peter Carsten
(English soundtrack)

In many ways a rather cheesey rehash of countless caper pix of the 1960s, "The Squeeze" is nonetheless a passably enjoyable programmer due entirely to Lee Van Cleef's almost continual presence onscreen. Just as the great studio stars often carried pictures which were otherwise woefully deficient, this vet character actor, long a standby in European actioners, commands attention here despite familiarity of all that surrounds him. Film is b.o. filler by definition.

Italo production, on which Carlo Ponti gets presentor credit, has shifty, unsavory Edward Albert recruiting retired ace safecracker Van Cleef for the irresistible one last heist. Tipped off by Albert that the German ringleaders intend to bump him off as soon as the job is pulled, clever Van Cleef manages to turn situation to his own advantage, killing the "Krauts" and making off with the entire load of diamonds himself.

All of this occupies film's first half, which is tight, to the point and aided by some incidental comic relief from on-the-ball pawnbroker Lionel Stander. Unfortunately, Van Cleef is injured during his getaway, after which he holes up to recuperate in an apartment building, only other occupant of which is seemingly innocent Karen Black, who helps robber through his recovery.

Despite fun Black has with part by affecting an exaggerated Brooklyn accent, it becomes a different pic mid-way, with Van Cleef lying flat on his back and Black bringing him soup and cigars. It all sort of ties together in the end, but not before interest and momentum have long since sagged irretrievably.

Though an actor of admittedly limited range, Van Cleef simply has one of those faces that the camera loves. Hawklike and ravaged by experience, he can effortlessly convey the impression of being one up on anyone else in any situation, and it's a pleasure to watch him outwit his nasty cohorts in crime. As long as he's on top of the game, pic sails effortlessly along, but seeing him laid up in second half is akin to witnessing a bird of prey cooped up in a cage.

Film's griminess is accentuated by location lensing in a particularly nasty New York winter. Sound work is occasionally marred by dubbing, and score consists of one disco strain repeated endlessly. —Cart.

The Hunter
(COLOR)

Another summer big-star misfire.

Hollywood, July 24.
A Paramount Pictures release of a Rastar-Mort Engelberg production. Produced by Mort Engelberg. Directed by Buzz Kulik. Stars Steve McQueen. Screenplay, Ted Leighton, Peter Hyams, based on the book by Christopher Keane and the life of Ralph Thorson; camera (Metrocolor), Fred J. Koenekamp; editor, Robert Wolfe; music, Michel Legrand; production design, Ron Hobbs; set design, Jim Tocci; set decoration, George Gaines, Rick Simpson; sound, Al Overton Jr.; assistant director, Richard Learman. Reviewed at the Paramount Studios, Hollywood, July 24, 1980. (MPAA Rating: PB.) Running time: 117 MINS.
Papa Thorson .... Steve McQueen
Ritchie Blumenthal .... Eli Wallach
Dotty .... Kathryn Harrold
Tommy Price .... LeVar Burton
Sheriff Strong .... Ben Johnson
Spota .... Richard Venture
Rocco Mason .... Tracey Walter
Bernardo .... Tom Rosales
Winston Blue .... Theodore Wilson
Luke Branch .... Ray Bickel
Matthew Branch .... Bobby Bass
Billie Joe .... Karl Schueneman

If ever a star vehicle delivered the exact opposite of what waiting fans want and expect to see, "The Hunter" does. Given all the hands a property must pass through these days in order to get made, it's amazing that no one along the way noticed that this one has no story, introduces at least a dozen characters who are then dropped or used in completely inexplicable ways, and succeeds in destroying a screen image Steve McQueen has spent 20 years cultivating. Audiences hoping for a reborn "Bullitt" might flock at first, until they realize it's yet another of this summer's big-star misfires.

Fact that the overlong pic is based on adventures of a modern-day bounty hunter may have hampered filmmakers' imagination, as attempt to render contradictions of real-life Ralph "Papa"

Thorson. who's into classical music and astrology as well as hauling in fugitives from justice. has made for an annoyingly unrealized and childish onscreen character.

McQueen may have felt that the time had come to revise his persona a bit. but what's involved here is desecration. Given star's rep since "Bullitt" as a terrific driver. someone thought it might be cute to make him a lousy one here, but seeing him crash stupidly into car after car throughout the film runs the gag into the ground, just as his status as a man born 100 years after his time seems awfully old hat by now and only underlines notion that "The Hunter" is a western in disguise.

Typical of film's inane use of characters is progression of LeVar Burton from a young dude apprehended by McQueen in the opening scene to an unexplained fixture in latter's household who's always seen sitting around trying to fix something mechanical. while a totally mysterious bunch of loudmouths is invariably lolling around playing cards.

Once in awhile. when pregnant g.f. Kathryn Harrold isn't busy prodding McQueen into attending La Maze natural childbirth classes or trying to get him to pay attention to her rather than to his toy collection. star heads off for an assignment. One trip takes him to Nebraska. where a couple of hayseeds in a Trans Am (Ray Bickel. Bobby Bass) engage McQueen. aboard a harvesting machine. in a chase through cornfields. Shot mainly from an aerial p.o.v.. which makes it look as though crops are being vacuumed. this has to be one of the most ludicrous action set-pieces ever concocted.

Only sequence which remotely delivers the goods the action crowd is looking for, has McQueen chasing a gun-toting maniac on the Chicago "el." Despite the fancy stunts, passage is played out in relatively perfunctory fashion, and pic's finale. which has star fainting when Harrold gives birth, merely puts capper on overall misconception.

Contributions of all hands in front of and behind camera are way below what they've offered in the past. —*Cart.*

Jane Austen In Manhattan
(U.S.-COLOR)

London, July 22.

Contemporary Films release of a Merchant-Ivory production. Produced by Ismail Merchant. Directed by James Ivory. Features entire cast. Screenplay. Ruth Prawer Jhabvala; camera (color). Ernest Vincze; music, Richard Robbins; settings. Michael Yeargan; costumes. Jenny Beavan. Reviewed at the Century screening room. London. Jly 21. '80. (B-BFC Rating: A). Running time: 108 MINS.
Lilianna . . . . Anne Baxter
Pierre . . . . Robert Powell
Ariadne . . . . Sean Young
Victor . . . . Kurt Johnson
Katya . . . . Katrina Hodiak
Jamie . . . . Tim Choate
Jenny . . . . Nancy New
Billie . . . . Chuck McCaughan
Gregory . . . . John Guerrasio
George Midash . . . . Michael Wager

The prolific team of director James Ivory, producer Ismail Merchant and writer Ruth Prawer Jhabvala, who pick original themes and milieus for their staunchly independent features, have made uncharacteristic heavy weather of their latest venture.

Premise is initially intriguing, as the auction of a little-known Jane Austen playscript triggers off a bout of infighting in an incestuous pocket of New York's avant-garde theatre society. A promising starting-point for a sendup of the whole pretentious scene. But pace flags early on. Relationships and flamboyant personalities lose focus and the meandering plot runs out of punch and credibility.

Cautious art house playoff is indicated, in markets where Merchant-Ivory productions have scored before. Cofinanced by Polytel and London Weekend TV, pic was first shown on tv in the U.K., then bowed theatrically in London in Contemporary Films shortly after.

Robert Powell's mocking eyes make him apt casting as an "experimental" stager whose hold over the minds and wallets of his troupe topically aligns him with those self-styled gurus of modish, quasi-religious sects. But the dramatic edge of his eventual exposure as a charlatan is dulled by the fact that his rival for the rights to the play — Anne Baxter, as a contrastingly altruistic teacher-producer — is hardly less preposterous. or more sympathetic. What's more, there seems little to choose between her presentation of the piece as a stiff operetta and Powell's concept of it as slapstick on a stage covered in foam rubber.

So. with no way of telling if the forgotten manuscript (written when Austen was 12 years old, based on an 18th century Samuel Richardson novel) was worth putting on at all. the film offers scant involvement. although committed performances among the supports create a number of touching moments. Sean Young and Kurt Johnson are standout as a married couple of acting hopefuls rifted by Powell's seduction of Young into his commune.

Technically fine. with an elegant chamber music score by Richard Robbins. the film is distinguished by Irvory's customary cool style of direction. A nice flight of fancy is a kidnapping sequence. shot like a clip from a period romance. which is inserted whenever the recurrent theme of abduction crops up.
—*Simo.*

Battle Beyond the Stars
(COLOR)

Sci-fi with a sense of humor.

Chicago, July 25.

New World Pictures release of its own production. Produced by Ed Carlin; exec producer. Roger Corman. Stars Richard Thomas, George Peppard. Robert Vaughn. John Saxon. Darlanne Fleugel. Directed by Jimmy T. Murakami. Screenplay, John Sayles based on a story by Sayles and Anne Dyer: camera (color). Daniel Lacambre; score. James Horner: set decorator. John Zabrucky; costumes. Durinda Rice Wood: lighting supervisor. Paul Turner: miniature photographic effects. C. Comisky: miniatures designed by Mary Schallock. Reviewed at McVickers Theatre. Chicago. July 25. '80. (MPAA Rating: PG.) Running time: 104 MINS.
Shad . . . . Richard Thomas
Gelt . . . . Robert Vaughn
Sador . . . . Darlanne Fleugel
Cowboy . . . . George Peppard
St. Exmin . . . . Sybil Danning
Dr. Hephaestus . . . . Sam Jaffe
Cayman . . . . Morgan Woodward
Quopeg . . . . Steve Davis
Nestor #1 and #2 . . . . Earl Boen.
                                   John McGowans
Kelvin . . . . Larry Meyers. Laura Cody
Nell . . . . Lynne Carlin
Zed . . . . Jeff Corey
Mol . . . . Julia Duffy
Feh . . . . Eric Morris
Lux . . . . Marta Kristen
Pok . . . . Doug Carleson
Dab . . . . Ron Ross
Gar . . . . Terrence McNally
Cush . . . . Don Thompson
Pez . . . . Daniel Carlin
Wok . . . . Ansley Carlin

The fascination of watching how the defenseless cope with marauding barbarians is put to the test with New World's production of "Battle Beyond the Stars." Akira Kurosawa realized the explosive potential of the subject in his 1954 classic. "The Seven Samurai." With this pic. producer Roger Corman has shifted the setting from 16th-century Japan to outer space.

"Battle." with a nod to Kurosawa. emerges from the transformation as a late-summer. sci-fi exploitationer with moderate b.o. potential. especially since "Empire Strikes Back" is beginning to show signs of firstrun fatigue.

"Battle." other than in its genre, doesn't resemble "Empire" much and occasionally the difference is refreshing. An obviously lavish outing by New World standards, pic boasts of credible special effects — mostly involving miniatures of space vehicles shot in closeup — and a pleasant sort of brashness resulting from its blending of several pic styles.

In unfolding its saga of how the peace-loving bunch on a small planet rebuffs a genetically deficient but vicious band of bad guys. "Battle" incorporates touches of an old fashioned Western (not surprising since "Samurai" was recycled as a 1960 oater by director John Sturges. "The Magnificent Seven"), horror pics and even a touch of contemporary softcore, which doesn't threaten the pic's PG rating.

Despite the expense involved. the pic appears not to take itself too seriously. Principal characterizations are skin deep. John Sayles' dialog (script is based on Sayles' and Anne Dyer's story) takes the form of relaxed banter with a minimum of homilies. And, to its credit. a sense of humor pervades "Battle," especially in its casting of supporting players.

George Peppard has fun as a Scotch-tippling cowboy frm earth who turns up as one of the mercenaries hired by the planet's earnest young soldier (Richard Thomas). Robert Vaughn turns up as a jaw-jutting hired gunman with heart of plutonium. John Saxon. sporting makeup out of "The Rocky Horror Picture Show." is hilarious as the chief of the bad guys. Sybil Danning is sexy as a female mercenary who becomes sexually titillated during combat.

Director Jimmy Murakami moves the characters around expeditiously, cuing their actions to special effects from a platoon of technicians. John Zabrucky's sets are inventive in a comic book vein; and Daniel Lacambre's photography milks Paul Turner's facile lighting techniques.

Special nods should go to Durinda Rice Wood's inventive costumes of the planetary principles; to actor Sam Jaffe's bit as a weapons supplier (we only see his head); and to James Horner's effective but unobtrusive musical score.

"Battle" knows its severe limits and works well within them; it should please unfussy sci-fi and action buffs. In any case, it marks a somewhat ambitious turns for New World. a company that has provided more than a few low-level cinematic surprises in its 10 years of existence. —*Sege.*

Zombie
(ITALIAN-COLOR)

Enough gore to generate solid grosses on the horror circuit.

Jerry Gross Organization release of a Variety Film production. Features entire cast. Produced by Ugo Tucci and Fabrizio de Angelis. Directed by Lucio Fulci. Screenplay and story. Elisa Briganti; camera (Technicolor). Sergio Salvati; editor. Vincenzo Tomassi; music. Fabio Frizzi. Giorgio Tucci: special effects and makeup supervision. Gianneto de Rossi. Reviewed at UA East theatre, N.Y., July 26. '80. (Self-imposed X Rating). Running time: 91 MINS.

Ann Boles .... Tisa Farrow
Peter West .... Ian McCulloch
Dr. David Menard ...... Richard Johnson
Brian .... Al Cliver
Susan Barrett .... Annetta Gay
Mrs. Menard .... Olga Karlatos
Nurse .... Stefania D'Amario

A summer of 1979 hit in Italy, "Zombie" has been imported by Jerry Gross to capitalize on the public's fancy for gory horror films. State-of-the-art makeup effects by Gianneto de Rossi are sure to please fans of this form, and far-out-distance the wildest dreams of '60s gore pioneer Herschell Gordon Lewis ("Blood Feast").

Pic was shot as an unauthorized followup to George A. Romero's hit "Dawn of the Dead," which was released in Europe under the title "Zombie." New pic is called "Zombie 2" in Italy, but qualifies for original "Zombie" tag in the U.S.

Story has Tisa Farrow traveling from New York to the tiny island of Matul, near St. Thomas, in search of her father, whose sailboat mysteriously returned to New York harbor with only zombies aboard. Accompanying her is an intrepid reporter Ian McCulloch (hinted comically to be working for the Post) and the handsome couple (Al Cliver and Annetta Gay) who charter their boat.

Island doctor Richard Johnson is coping with the zombie epidemic, blamed on local voodoo rites. Stealing implausibly from Romero's mythos in his "Dead" films, these zombies can be destroyed by a gunshot in the head. Film's open-ending sets up a sequel, as the zombies overrun New York City (staged cheaply via a radio news report and a single shot of the zombies shambling along the George Washington bridge).

Director Fulci adopts a leisurely pace and goes after daylight horror, playing off the grisly, cannibalistic zombie attacks against picture postcard beauty of the island and the New York harbor. Emphasis on blood reaches the ludicrous extreme of 400-year old zombie conquistadores bleeding profusely when shot down, fresh from their graves.

Though the makeup's the star, Farrow is appealing as the vulnerable heroine, styled here as the spitting image of sister Mia. Having made a dozen Italian films, British character actor Richard Johnson has all the worried, bedraggled expressions down pat, while Ian McCulloch fails to make an impression. Pleasant nude turns by Gay and Karlatos fit with the self-imposed X rating, as Jerry Gross has copied Romero's successful marketing strategy for "Dawn of the Dead." —*Lor.*

The Earthling
(COLOR)

Sydney, July 24.

A Roadshow release of a Filmways presentation of the Earthling Productions film. Stars William Holden, Ricky Schroder. Producer Elliot Schick. Directed by Peter Collinson. Executive producer Stephen Sharmat. Screenplay, Lanny Cotler; production supervisor, John Weiley; camera (Panavision-color), Don McAlpine; production designer, Bob Hilditch; editor, Nick Beauman; assistant directors, Mark Egerton, Steve Andrews, Chris Williams; sound, Don Connolly; 2nd unit director, David Le Maistre. Previewed at Roadshow Theatrette, Sydney, July 23, 1980. (Commonwealth censorship rating: NRC). Running time: 97 MINS.
Patrick Foley .... William Holden
Shawn Daley .... Ricky Schroder
Ross Daley .... Jack Thompson
Bettina Daley .... Olivia Hamnett
Christian Neilson .... Alwyn Kurts
Bobby Burns .... Redmond Phillips
R.C. .... Willie Fennell
Parnell .... Ray Barrett
Meg Neilson .... Pat Evison

William Holden as an irascible old curmudgeon with a terminal illness and Ricky Schroder as a lost child is fairly safe billing for a movie aimed at the kidult market. In this instance the teaming works because both are really quite fine actors as displayed in this made-in-Australia Elliot Schick production.

The novelty of the Australian bush to Yank eyes is shamelessly exploited; local flora and fauna in a profusion and in circumstances that would only raise the eyebrows of a naturalist. Fact is, much of Australia is picturesque; and for all the local cultural cringing at yet another koala filmed for overseas consumption, it'll be a while yet before that side of the country becomes a cliche offshore.

Plot has Schroder orphaned in an accident while holidaying with his parents in remote country. Holden, returning to his birthplace to die, meets up with him and knowing time is short puts the kid through a basic training course in bushmanship. The rest has the pair of them playing contrasts which they do so well that it is evident that there were times when director Collinson thought it prudent not to intrude.

Another big contribution to the style of the picture, that Collinson was wise to take advantage of, is veteran local cinematographer Don McAlpine's powerful feel for the terrain which provides the film with its visual power. The technical crew were all Australians, and the standards are high.

Producer Schick got a lot of back-of-camera talent, choosing as he could from the best available Down Under. Slick editing by Nick Beauman, however, can't mask the considerable amount of post-production that is evident. Problem there might have been with the British director's conception of

Yank writer Lanny Cotler's original screenplay which started out set in America.

The boy's gradual awakening to the environment and his grudging but growing relationship with Holden are well-handled, and towards the end most affecting. The schmaltz is there, to be sure, but it's not all that burdensome. It's the transformation of the kid that is the core of the story, and that comes over.

With Schroder top-lined, pic should have great appeal for the market it is aimed at, and relying on the ability of moppets to identify, it should get good word of mouth. In less self-conscious and needlessly sensitive markets than is Australia, it should perform well, but the embarrassment of all those cute furry Aussie animals might affect local acceptance. Pity, that, because there is some good family-style entertainment that will be missed if the pre-conceptions aren't overcome. —*Miha.*

Contes Pervers
(Perverse Tales)
(FRANCO-ITALIAN-COLOR)

Paris, July 16.

A UGC release of a Belstar/Cathala/New Movie (Rome) coproduction. Features entire cast. Written and directed by Regine Deforges. Camera (Fujicolor), Alain Derobe; editor, Michel Valio; sound, Alain Curvelier; music, Martial Carceles. Reviewed at the U.G.C. Ermitage theatre, Paris, July 15, 1980. Running time: 90 MINS.
Cast: Françoise Gayat, Beatrice, Carina Barone, Genevieve Omini, Salima Bahloul, Gerard Lauzier.

"Contes Pervers" only shows that an erotic picture concocted and directed by a woman can be as untitilating and puerile as that made by a male director. Writer Regine Deforges, a specialist in erotic literature, makes her film debut here as screenwriter and helmer and tries to put on film her own fantasies, which turn out to be extremely banal and boring.

The three tales — title evidently designed to play off Walerian Borowczyk's "Immoral Tales" — concern a businessman's wife in Japan getting involved in a sexually-staked dice game in a seedy gambling den; a Spanish businessman with a thing about nuns who hires a high class whore to help him play out his ecumenical fantasies; and an Italian truck-driver who treats himself to an expensive callgirl but then finds he is impotent in an upper class environment.

Deforges shows no aptitude for screenwriting or directing. In fact the picture leaves the impression that its author was rather embarrassed by what she had written and

hurried to be done with it, particularly in the editing stages. Technically the film is mediocre and most of the performers look unhappy about being caught with their pants down. —*Len.*

Almost Human
(Milano Odia: La Polizia non puo' Sparare)
(ITALIAN-COLOR)

A Joseph Brenner release of a Dania production. Features entire cast. Produced by Luciano Martino. Directed by Umberto Lenzi. Camera (Eastmancolor), uncredited; editor, Eugenio Alabiso; music, Ennio Morricone. No other credits available. Reviewed at UA East, N.Y., July 20, '80. (MPAA Rating: R). Running time: 92 MINS.
Julio Sacchi .... Tomas Milian
Inspector Walter
Grandi .... Henry Silva
Iona Tucci .... Anita Strindberg
Carmine .... Raymond Lovelock
Mary Lou .... Laura Belli
Mary Lou's father .... Guido Alberti

To exploit the inexhaustible public appetite for horror pics, Joseph Brenner has taken a 1974 Italo crime potboiler and sold it as a monster film in the "Alien" vein. Only hit-and-run bookings can sustain this marketing ploy.

One of the innumerable "police are powerless" Italian crime films of the mid-70s, "Almost Human" was originally titled "The Kidnap of Mary Lou" for English-language markets. Storyline has incredibly vicious street thug Tomas Milian duping his girlfriend Anita Strindberg to help him kidnap her rich boss's daughter Mary Lou (Laura Belli) for 500,000,000 lira ransom. Milian and two male accomplices go on an orgy of indiscriminate carnage until frustrated police inspector Grandi (Henry Silva) finally overrules the law and executes Milian himself. Cynical final credit notes that Grandi got 20 years in jail for this public service.

Main wonderment of the film is how scruffy, unappealing, and hammy Milian ever became a local superstar on the basis of roles like this one. His sadistic behavior and ruthless shooting down of any man, woman or child in his way makes the charismatic antiheroes of past decades look like saints. Of the rest of the cast, Silva gives a tired, poorly-dubbed (with his own voice, however) walkthrough mouthing "Dirty Harry" platitudes. Technical credits are standard for the chase and shoot genre, with Ennio Morricone recycling music from his earlier, uppercase Sergio Sollima pics "Violent City" and "Revolver." —*Lor.*

5% de Risque
(5% Risk)
(FRENCH-BELGIAN-COLOR)

Paris, July 10.
A Gaumont release of a Unite 3/Framo Diffusion/Orion/Paradise Films (Brussels) coproduction. Produced by Alain Dahan. Stars Bruno Ganz, Jean-Pierre Cassel, Aurore Clement. Directed by Jean Pourtale. Screenplay, Pourtale, Jean Bany, Jean-Pierre Beaurenaud, Gilles Thibaut, based on the novel by David Pearl; camera (color), Jean Penzer; editors, Caludine Merlin and Helene Muller; music, Eric de Marsan; art directors, Yves Bernard, Danka Semenowiecz; sound, Henri Morelle; stunts, Remy Julienne. Reviewed at the Marignan-Concorde theatre, Paris, July 8, 1980. Running time: **100 MINS.**
Cast: Bruno Ganz, Jean-Pierre Cassel, Aurore Clement, Pierre Michael, Fernand Guiot, Chantal Akerman.

———

There's about 5% credibility in this lame suspense tale about a physics professor who scientifically plots and executes a "perfect crime" in order to rid a politician friend of a blackmailer.

The central premise is this: the professor, who has a tight daily schedule which includes driving from the suburban university where he teaches to the research center where he works, plans to make a wide detour, pot the blackmailer as he exits from his office building, then speed on to the center where his arrival time is noted daily.

The crux of the scheme is to do all this in so brief a time that the police would never suspect he could commit the murder and yet arrive at the center just minutes later.

Much screen time is spent documenting the professor's months of mad rehearsal as he attempts to do record time speeding across the super-highways outside Paris. It's all preposterous and too repetitive to be truly engrossing, even if the prof and his blackmailed friend are portrayed by Bruno Ganz and Jean-Piere Cassel, two fine actors who are rarely dull, even in such skimpy roles as these. Aurore Clement gets star billing as well, though she's asked to do nothing more than look concerned and smile sadly once in a while, a mild variation on the zombie-like women she usually plays. —*Len.*

———

Hangar 18
(COLOR)

Barely plausible premise on unidentified flying objects.

———

Hollywood, July 25.
Sunn Classic Pictures release. Producer, Charles E. Sellier, Jr. Director, James L. Conway. Features entire cast. Screenplay, Steven Thornley, based on a story by Tom Chapman and Conway. Camera (Technicolor), Paul Hipp; editor, Michael Spence; special effects, Harry Woolman; optical effects supervisor, John Forrest. Reviewed at the Vine Theatre, Hollywood, July 25, 1980. (MPAA Rating: PG.) Running time: **93 MINS.**
Cast: Darren McGavin, Robert Vaughn, Gary Collins, James Hampton, Philip Abbott, Joseph Campanella, Pamela Bellwood, Tom Hallick, Steven Keats, William Schallert, Cliff Osmond, Andrew Bloch.

"Hangar 18" is where Sunn Classic Pictures would have audiences believe the U.S. government is successfully hiding an Unidentified Flying Object that happened to collide with a NASA satellite during a routine mission. Following Sunn's formula of taking a barely plausible premise and stretching it even further, pic emerges as both a dramatic bore and an intellectual waste of time. Although Sunn is known for accuracy of its audience research, "Hangar 18" should have trouble remaining in flight more than one or two weeks.

Feature takes on a bit of a documentary stance as astronauts Gary Collins and James Hampton try to unravel the real mystery behind the satellite crash they are unfairly being blamed for. At the same time, White House staffer Robert Vaughn is doing his best to hide the alien craft in "Hangar 18" and to cover-up the UFO incident in order to secure the election for the current U.S. president. (It seems that the chief exec had at one time insulted his competitor for believing in UFO's and would look foolish if now proved wrong).

Needless to say, themes of political corruption and outer space adventures have been more cleverly presented in countless other pix. Screenplay by Steven Thornley is full of loose ends and long stretches of mediocrity. However, Thornley and director James L. Conway seem to realize the ridiculousness of their endeavors by occasional use of tongue-in-cheek approach to some of the occurrances.

When one space expert examines the UFO and notes that "they (aliens) didn't get this equipment in Radio Shack," there is some momentary amusement in how absurd the entire approach of this film is.

But it is only momentary.
— *Berg.*

———

Esperando A Papa
(Waiting For Daddy)
(SPANISH-COLOR)

———

Madrid, July 9.
An Aspa P.C. and Penta Films production. Directed by Vicente Escriva. Screenplay, Alvaro Lyon de Petre, Vicente Escriva; camera (Eastmancolor), Johnny Cabrera; music, Julio Iglesias and Rafael Ferro; editor, Soledad Lopez; exec producer, Vicente Escriva Jr.; sets, Adolfo Lofino. Reviewed at Cine Luna, Madrid, July 9, '80. Running time: **100 MINS.**
Cast: Arturo Fernandez, Teresa Rabal, Maria Silva, Josele Roman, Mary Carmen Prendes, Angel Picazo, Javier.

———

Riding on the "Kramer Vs. Kramer" crest, this Spanish item about divorce and children, despite its occasional cliches, comes across as an absorbing and entertaining film apt for unsophisticated audiences with a penchant for the plangent from Madrid to Buenos Aires. Characterizations are on the simplistic side and the five-year-old boy is rather too articulate to be entirely convincing, but pic should have a broad appeal and is handled with enough adroitness to perhaps reap some of the benefits of its American model.

Scene is set in the highest stratum of Madrid society: a bored, fur-clad and scrupulously faithful wife; a charming, irresponsible playboy husband who'll bed down with any woman at the slightest encouragement; a father (on wife's side) who heads a big banking trust; and two cutesy kids, aged four and five, who are the victims of matrimonial strife.

Playboy hubby evinces a particularly strong attachment to the little boy, which is reciprocated in spades by the moppet. Even after a separation, daddy breezes in and out of the household, until one day the girl's father learns just what a cad he is and kicks him out of the company's comfy swivel chair and sends him packing to Latin America with a blank check.

The melodramatic and sometimes maudlin interludes are well handled by thesps and director, and "daddy" manages to wheedle the sympathies and pity of the audience as he alternates from the role of party buffoon to pathetic, empty-shelled outcast. The man is a wastrel, but simpatico nonetheless. A short courtroom scene with an ecclesiastic judge takes a swipe at divorce proceedings in Spain. Thesping, especially by Arturo Fernandez and the little boy, are satisfactory. All technical credits up to crack. —*Besa.*

———

Final Cut
(AUSTRALIA-COLOR)

———

Sydney, July 4.
A GUO Film Distributors' release of a Wilgar production. Produced by Mike Williams. Executive producer Frank Gardiner. Directed by Ross Dimsey. Screenplay, Jonathan Dawson and Ross Dimsey, from an original idea by Dawson; camera (Eastmancolor) Ron Johanson; editor, Tony Patterson; music written and performed by Howard Davidson. Reviewed at the GUO Theaterette, Sydney, July 3, '80. (Commonwealth Censorship Rating: M). Running time: **82 MINS.**
Chris ....Louis Brown
Dominic ....David Clendenning
Sarah ....Jennifer Cluff
Yvette ....Narelle Johnson
Julie/Lyn ....Carmen J. McCall
Mick ....Thaddeus Smith

The problem with "Final Cut" is that it starts with a good premise — investigative video-journalist's intrepid examination of enigmatic Aussie entrepreneur — but fails ultimately to deliver. One suspects that a cheat is in the wind when the opening sequence intercuts the showman, arrival of Dominic, and hovering press, against close-up shots of the assembly of what is patently a camera, but is clearly meant to suggest a weapon of more sinister mien.

In an effort to keep the tension going, the co-writer-director seems himself to have become confused about what is happening. After a showbiz triumph overseas, Dominic returns to Queensland, his Onassis-size yacht and vast penthouse apartment. Into these opulent surroundings he permits a reporter, Chris, on a freelance assignment for some unnamed network. The reporter is accompanied by his girl-friend, also a Fourth Estater, and both are really out to get the goods on Dominic, who in his past has dabbled in porno movies.

Just to add spice, Dominic lets drop that there are other darker secrets (these turn out to be his predeliction for "snuff" movies), and hints he may have not only made them in the past, but still may be. The yacht is populated with naked nubility in all shapes and form, all of it behaving in such a way as to give the impression that they are acting in a movie. The picture probably has as broad an acreage of female flesh in it as the average skin-flick, but at least those don't have the pretense of serious thriller content.

"Final Cut" clothes its poverty of invention with the semblance of a story which, upon closer examination, reveals behaviour of such preposterousness as to negate the intention. Even given a reasonable suspension of disbelief, the plot won't hold.

The quality of acting is dubious at best, with David Clendenning going in for extensive eye-rolling and Narelle Johnson simulating sensuality by moving around inside her silk jumpsuit as though infested with fleas.

Director Ross Dimsey uses a lot of now-you-see-it-now-you-don't intercuts from the point of view of the main protagonists who seem perpetually to be drugged by Dominic or in bed together wondering aloud about what they've gotten themselves into. The obligatory lesbian sequences are tastefully-handled as befits a film set in the only state in Australia with a board of censorship rating review, and which still bans Playboy.

In the technical area, the film is fine, and Howard Davison's electronic soundtrack is excellent. Pic is the first all-Queensland feature film funded by the Queensland Film Corporation. who financed in conjunction with the Australian Film Commission and private investors.
—*Miha.*

Charlie Bravo
(FRENCH-COLOR)

Paris, July 25.

A Gaumont release of a Shagrila Productions 'Gaumont co-production. Features entire cast. Directed by Claude Bernard-Aubert. Screenplay. Bernard-Aubert, Pascal Jardin; camera. (Eastmancolor), Pierre Fattori; editor. Gabriel Rongier, Robert Rongier; sound. Lucien Yvonnet; music. Alain Goraguer. Reviewed at Gaumont screening room. Neuilly, July 15. 1980. Running time: 104 MINS.

Lt. Brissac	Bruno Pradal
Girard	Jean-Francois Poron
Catherine	Karine Verlier
Magnan	Gerard Boucaran
Chaumont	Georges Chelon

"Charlie Bravo" is a conventionally violent war picture that is initially interesting because it comes out of France and deals with this nation's own tragic involvement in Southeast Asia during the early 1950's. As an actioner it usually succeeds in holding the attention in its lurid concern for the gruesome details of jungle warfare, (shot on location in Ceylon) but the film quickly winds down into the nth variation of John Ford's "The Lost Patrol," heavily dosed with post-Peckinpah gore.

Screenplay and direction are by Claude Bernard-Aubert (novelist Pascal Jardin wrote the dialogue). The director based the film on his own experience as a photo-journalist in the Indochina War, where he says he witnessed the massacre of an entire village by French troops.

(Bernard-Aubert's first film "Patrouille de Choc," in 1956, was also a war pic about Vietnam: the first French film, in fact, to treat the conflict, which earned it a run-in with the censors. It preceded, by eight years, Pierre Schoendoerffer's "The 317th Platoon" in '64.)

In "Charlie Bravo," a 13-man commando unit parachutes into North Vietnam on a rescue mission during the very last days of the war. The supposedly important French prisoner turns out to be a Red Cross nurse. They free her, and as they have orders to leave no witnesses, massacre villagers and Vietcong prisoners alike. They even shoot their own men when they are seriously wounded and cannot be transported without slowing down their retreat to the coast. In the course of the film the entire unit is wiped out by the Vietcong.

The film is muddled, thematically and morally. Beginning as a harsh recreation of an ignoble action and its executants, it then chickens out for more facile blood 'n' guts effects, leaving its personages unprobed and its politics glib (the commando mission is suicidal and strategically pointless, a propaganda ploy by French top brass to package some heroes and martyrs as buffer to the ignominy of armistice).

Bernard-Aubert's direction oscillates between good and awful, and goes incredibly corny in the final sequence, when the four remaining characters find themselves on the beach surrounded by hundreds of vengeful Vietcong. The French exchange ambiguous smiles and lunge towards the camera, guns blazing. Freeze frame. Yup, it's "Butch Cassidy and the Sundance Kid" in khaki!
— *Len.*

Warui Yatsura
(Bad Sorts)
(JAPANESE-COLOR)

Tokyo, June 10.

A Shochiku release. Produced by Kotaro Nomuramm. Koki Nomura. Features entire cast. Screenplay. Masato Ide. based on a book by Seicho Matsumoto. Directed by Kotaru Nomura. Camera (color). Noboru Kawamata; art direction, Kohei Morita; music. Satoshi Akutagawa; recording. Tadahiko Yamamoto; editing. Kazuo Ota; assistant director. Toshinori Oryo. Reviewed at Shochiku Screening Room. Tokyo. May 29. 1980. Running time: 129 MINS.

Shinichi Toya	Takao Kataoka
Takako Makimura	Keiko Matsuzaka
Chise Fujishima	Meiko Kaji
Tatsumko Yokotake	Mariko Fuji
Toyo Terishima	Junko Miyashita
Keiko Tanaka	Ai Kanzaki
Sakuo Shimomizawa	Makoto Fujita
Detective Inoue	Ken Ogata

Of the 12 pictures released by Shochiku last year, seven were over two hours in length, as were six of the 20 films released by Toho and 12 of the 32 films released by Toei. By contrast, of the 109 American pics released here in '79, only nine topped the 120-minute mark.

Whatever the reason for this tendency to celluloid windiness, it only serves to unnecessarily prolong the death throes of bad films and to blunt the effectiveness of good ones. In the latter category is "Warui Yatsura" — at 129 minutes.

Takao Kataoka is a doctor with an unusual bedside manner, romancing certain patients and speeding others into the hereafter. He gives lover Mariko Fuji a special potion with which to dispatch her elderly husband, and then, with the assistance of nurse (and lover) Junko Miyashita, rids himself of Mariko when the latter becomes too demanding.

Kataoka performs the same Instant Widowhood service for mistress Meiko Kaji, who has promised, in return, to loan the good doctor 30,000,000 yen to pay off his estranged wife. Soon thereafter, nurse Miyashita comes to a violent end after complaining to Kataoka about his dalliance with designer Keiko Matsuzaka.

Up to this point, "Warui Yatsura" is a study of a libertine's progress that is as likely to inspire admiration of his power over women as horror at his misdeeds. Then, in a cleverly constructed reversal, it is Kataoka who is made a dupe and seemingly innocent women are revealed to be "bad sorts."

Though it's difficult to accept Katoaka as a rake, he remains a fine actor with an appropriately seductive manner of speaking. The ever-reliable Ken Ogata is entertaining as a police detective and Junko Miyashita gives a Bette Davis-like, tempestuous performance. —*Bail.*

The Bodyguard
(SOVIET-COLOR)

Tashkent, May 29.

A Tadzhikfilm Studio Production. Dushanbe. Tadzhik Republic. Soviet Union; world rights. Sovexport Film, Moscow. Features entire cast. Directed by Ali Khamraev. Only credits available. Reviewed at Tashkent Film Festival. (market). May 29. '80. Running time: 90 MINS.

Cast: Alexander Kaidanovsky, Anatoly Solonitsyn, Gula Khamrayova.

An excellent "Eastern" (the "Western" in partisan or revolutionary clothing) Ali Khamraev's "Bodyguard" strikes home like a cross between a Samurai film and "Shane" in that only one man faces all the bad guys. In this case the hero is a former bodyguard to a sultan, he fights to bring his master safely to the Red Army, instead of letting him fall into the hands of bandits representing the old independent traditions.

The scene is the rugged, mountainous terrain of Tadzhik, formerly a part of Uzbekistan directly on the border with Afghanistan. The time is the early 1920's during the Civil War, but also the period of Revolution in Middle Asian republics. The bodyguard, played by Alexander Kaidanovsky, and the sultan played by Anatoly Solonitsyn, were both last seen in Andrei Tarkovsky's remarkable "Stalker" (1979). Director Khamraev is considered one of the best "Eastern" helmers in the Soviet Union who usually works out of Uzbekistan. He and the Tarkovsky-thesps were "on loan" to the Tadzhik Studios to make the film.

"The Bodyguard" opens with a detachment of the Red Army in the mountains faced with the task of getting a ruling sultan to the main forces, but the unknown terrain full of canyons, rocky cliffs, and desert area requires a special individual to achieve the task. The sultan's bodyguard is given the job — Kaidanovsky must take Solonitsyn, his daughter, and two other companions through the enemy territory. The bad guys have guns and horses, but they are also led by a bewitching, evil devil-goddess who dominates her chieftain husband.

Although the weak on both sides die along the way. the superhuman bodyguard manages to scale the faces of cliffs, cross canyons by ropes, and fight it out hand-to-hand with snakes and the leader of the gang to bring his master to the Red Army. At times, he seems all but lost, yet singlehandedly, like a Tarzan or a Toshiro Mifune, or Odysseus, he accomplishes each Herculean task set before him.

In the end. after being injured in a fight with the gang leader, it's the sultan who carries him the last distance to safety — in return, he receives the sultan's talisman identifying the bearer as the rightful leader of the people. With this authority-symbol tied about his neck, the bodyguard returns to his people in the mountains.

An action pic with few faults, "The Bodyguard" with any luck will find its way to a prominent fest or Soviet Film Week, where both the film and the filmmaker could win the critical backing to achieve some market in the West. Khamraev is an Uzbek helmer to watch closely in the future. —*Holl.*

Karlovy Fest

Temne Slunce
(Dark Sun)
(CZECHOSLOVAK-COLOR)

Karlovy Vary, July 15.

Czech State Film release of Barrandov Studio production. Features entire cast. Directed by Otakar Vavra. Screenplay. Jiri Sotala, Vavra from the book by Karel Capek; camera (Eastmancolor), Miroslav Ondricek; music, Martin Kratochvili; art director, Karel Lior. Reviewed at Karlovy Vary Film Fest (non-competing), June 27, '80. Running time, 135 MINS.

Prokop	Radoslav Hrzobohaty
Ludek	Jiri Tomas
Carson	Rudolf Hrusinsky
MKris	Magda Vasaryova
Holz	Gunther Naumann
Tomes	Vladimir Sneral

Otakar Vavra, oldtime filmmaker and now a revered teacher, takes a tumble in this would-be cautionary tale about the misuse of atomic power. Based on a book by writer Karel Capek, Vavra made it once before in 1947 as "Krakitat." Capek's visionary tale was updated to reflect on World War II and is now again moved in time to the present for a Bondish caper kind of film.

Vavra's previous version had a dreamlike almost surreal quality that made it visually impressive and an acceptable humanist metaphor on man's potential for self annihilation. But now it is rather straight, and, though glossily told, a rather shambling affair about a well meaning inventor who has found a form of matter that can be compressed into a ball the size of a Ping Pong ball with the effects of an H Bomb.

A multinational org, seemingly based on the U.S. (one office scene has the Manhattan skyline in the distance) is after it. But a friend has also taken his papers and on his own transformed it into a bomb that will only kill people and not destroy buildings.

The scientist is recruited into the company, has an affair with the director's niece but then tries to back out. He finds his friends who sets off the bomb that destroys a city. The professor has escaped and comes to a small town where people still exist as man gets another chance to start over.

Neither effective actioner or parable, film remains primarily a local item. —*Mosk.*

Ah! Nomugi Toge
(Nomugi Pass)
(JAPANESE-COLOR)

Karlovy Vary, July 15.
Yamamoto release and production. Features entire cast. Directed by Satsuo Yamamoto. Screenplay, Yoshi Hatori, Shigemi Yamamoto; camera (Fujicolor), Setsuo Kobayashi; music, Masaru Sato. Reviewed at Karlovy Vary Film Film Fest (competing), June 29, '80. Running time: 145 MINS.
With: Shinobu Otake, Mieko Harada, Chikako Yuri, Yuko Kotegawa, Takeo Jii, Akira Ninishimura.

Satsuo Yamamoto was an early practitioner of neo-realism in Japanese films and made two that have made dents with buffs and film specialists, "Sunless District" in a twenties strike and "War and People" on militarism. Now he does a detailed, exhaustive look at sweatshop silk-spinning mills in the early part of the century.

Young girls were sent over a hazardous mountain pass to work in the mills. They came from small towns where poverty forced families to indenture girls to the mills for needed money and to remove a mouth to feed.

Film follows a few on a trek one winter, scenes adroitly intercut shots of monied government and industrial people waltzing at a party. A group of girls are picked out to deal with and in the background is

the Japanese-Russian War, dependence on the U.S. as the top silk market, and growing militarism.

The girls are harshly treated. They have only about 20 minutes to eat, work long hours and are badly paid. They are also preyed on by a sadistic foreman who often beats them as well as tries to seduce them, as does the boss's son. One is driven to suicide, another promised marriage by the director's son but sent off when pregnant and the main character becomes a successful worker who earns more than the others.

Film builds up a feeling for the people and though predictable is still effective and holds attention. The skilled worker's illness and death is especially moving as her friends for once brave the harsh directors to pay homage to her. It is a statement about general inhumanity and worker and social problems of the past but transcends its period to make a statement on the past that can have resonances today.

Perhaps too long and familiar, film has the stamina, sincerity and fine playing and technical tone for lingo and specialized chances.
—*Mosk.*

Olimpiada 40
(Olympics 40)
(POLISH-COLOR)

Karlovy Vary, July 22.
Polski Film release of X Production Unit production. Features entire cast. Directed by An drej Kotkowski. Screenplay, Michal Kamar, Kotkowski; camera (Eastmancolor), Witold Adamek; music, Andrej Korynski. Reviewed at Karlovy Vary Film Fest (competing), July 8, '80. Running time, 103 MINS.
Piotr . . . . Mariusz Benoit
Jacques . . . . Jerzy Bonisak
Leon . . . . Tadeusz Galia
Andrej . . . . Krystof Jancsar
Sharlppke . . . . Rysiard Kotys
Schultz . . . . Wojiech Psioniak

A timely idea indeed in these times of the Olympics becoming a political gambit. Hard to know if the idea was spawned by the U.S.-sponsored boycott of the coming Moscow Olympics over the Soviet invasion of Afghanistan or whether it had been planned beforeband. It is supposedly based on a real incident.

No matter, the film is ambiguous in re the politico or human aspects of the Olympics. What it does is deal with a clandestine olympiade held in a German prisoner of war camp during World War 2, housing mainly Poles but also French and Britishers. And it is a rousing, sharply-made, taking film of men showing their ingenuity and cohesion under trying circumstances.

A spit and polish German lieu-

tenant is added to the staff of a prison camp. He sees a Pole, the acknowledged head of the Polish prisoners, against whom he had competed in the Berlin Olympics of 1936. He asks the Pole to train with him but is refused. The Pole points out he is a prisoner and nothing more.

But a germ takes hold and the Pole proposes an Olympics 40 to be held among the prisoners. They ingeniously make a flag and medals. Shot puts are made from sledges, purloined bikes are made to roll on rollers and speeds clocked and a crouching hop race is unwittingly organized by a German prison guard who uses it as torture.

The German lieutenant knows something is going on but cannot find it. They finally do and the Polish chief is sent off to a concentration camp but the others disobey orders and salute his leaving as the sound of machineguns is heard.

Film does show how morale is lifted by the games and how it overcomes differences among the prisoners themselves. But it is also a political act of defiance of their captors. At any rate, director Andrzej Kotkowski shows a sure hand in creating the atmosphere of the camp and neatly etching character without falling into stereotype.

A film that further illuminates a growing number of talented new filmmakers in Poland with good themes and knowing craftsmanship. Kotkowski is to be watched and his first film, on its theme, timelessness and fine treatment, could find this specialized outings besides the usual festival routes.
—*Mosk.*

Paciorki Jednego Rozanca
(The Beads of One Rosary)
(POLISH-COLOR)

Karlovy Vary, July 22.
Polski Film release of Kadr Unit production. Features entire cast. Written and directed by Kazimierz Kutz from the book by A. Siekierski. Camera (Eastmancolor), Wieslaw Zdort; music, Wojiech Kilar. Reviewed at Karlovy Vary Film Fest (competing), July 7, '80. Running time, 116 MINS.
Habryka . . . . Augustyn Halotta
Habrykowa . . . . Marta Straszna
Zosia . . . . Ewa Wisniewska
Jery . . . . Fransiczek Pieczka
Antek . . . . Jan Bogdol
Leszek . . . . Jerzy Rzepka

The showing of new Polish directors at recent film festivals has been amply noted in *Variety*. But the older ones are no slouches either. Andrezj Wajda was nominated for an Oscar with his poetic "The Young Girls of Wilko" and now Kazimierz Kutz comes up with a touching tale of an old miner standing up to what he feels is unjust progress.

The film has great charm in its

fine acting and shrewd dissection of a theme that has been seen around. It is given new freshness, human comedy dash and unsentimental drama by Kutz's obviously committed feeling to his natal area of Silesia and its people.

The crusty hero, Augustyn Halotta, is an old miner who has won many worker medals and is now retired with his youngest son and the latter's family living with him. To build new apartment dwellings, the old houses are being bought out, the residents given apartments in the new houses, and being cleared away.

But Halotta refuses to sell. He thinks his house has too much history, many generations of his family have lived there, and he will not leave even if the apartments have more modern facilities. Everybody tries to convince him. His son's wife leaves, he is threatened but to no avail. Finally he gives in when the irate head of the mine decides he is a noted worker and gives him and his wife a new model house.

But it is in a remote location and the many gadgets confuse the wife. They are lonely. He finally dies peacefully in his sleep. Kutz executes a slow pan across the bed with the big eiderdown and holy pictures behind it. No tearjerking here. It is not necessary, for here is a man who had a good life and gone his own way.

He gets a giant funeral as an homage to one of the oldest miners in the district. His dog comes to the grave after the others leave. Film should find interest in many climes on its sheer charm and depiction of a rugged individualist's passing, shown without mawkishness.

The old man does point out that they are building needed housing, rushing in people but seem to be forgetting adequate schools, stores and other things needed for better living conditions. Film, surprisingly. is said not to be doing well on its home grounds where more forceful, polemic themes are draws rather than this deceptively simple look at the passing of a good man.
—*Mosk.*

Vpervye Zamuzhem
(Married for the First Time)
(SOVIET-COLOR)

Karlovy Vary, July 15.
Sovexport release of Lenfilm production. Features entire cast. Directed by Iosif Heifits. Screenplay. Pavel Nilin. Heifits; music. O. Karavaychuk. No other credits available. Reviewed at Karlovy Vary Film Fest (competing), June 30, '80. Running time, 92 MINS.
Tonya . . . . Yevgenie Glushenkova
Yefim . . . . Nikolai Volkov
Galya . . . . Valentina Telichkin
Tamara . . . . Svetlana Smirnov
Valery . . . . Igor Starygin

Iosif Heifits has arguably made some of the best films adapted from the works of Anton Chekhov as "The Lady With the Dog" and "The Town of S." Here, at 75, he turns to a contemporary tale of an unwed mother who finally turns against the sacrifices and self denial she had taken on as her daughter grew up.

Perhaps there is a certain naivete in this woman who gives up school, advancement and men because her child insists the stork brought her and usually does not like the men who approach her. But they live adequately as the mother does menial work and only gets to a restaurant when her daughter gets married. She foots the bill, too.

The mother is well limned and played and does gain stature to avoid sentimentality. She finally is driven out of the flat by her daughter's shiftless husband and roams the streets one night. A friend gives her the address of a man who wants to get married and it works out. She will live in the country, be fulfilled, perhaps, and be married for the first time.

Fetching performances, good direction aid this otherwise old fashioned tale of virtue rewarded. On the Heifits name it could have some fest outings though it leaves the insight that made his Chekhov films on the human condition so revealing.—*Mosk.*

Suria Dighal Bari
(The Ominous House)
(BANGLADESH-B&W)

Karlovy Vary, July 22.
Bangladesh Film release and production. Features entire cast. Written and directed by Massiouddin Shaker. Shiekh Niamat Ali from a book by Abu Ishak; camera, (black and white), Answar Hosen, Alaouddin Ali. Reviewed at Karlovy Vary Film Fest (competing), July 10, '80. Running time: 130 MINS.
With: Dolly Anwar, Flora, Keramat Mulla, Sajib, Roushan Jami.

A rare film from Bangladesh and worth reviewing for the record as well as for a feel for place, time and character that perhaps promises some future films of interest. This one is somewhat too drawn out, a bit primitive technically and directorially, for more than specialized festival outings.

It takes place during a time of famine when people went to the city. A family, a woman and teenaged daughter and son, decide to go back to their land, considered haunted by past tragedies.

They try to cope but lack of work and the woman coveted by but fending off a village head lead to their going back to the city. The film

deals with everyday life and relations that give an acceptable insight into the land and people.
—*Mosk.*

Maluala
(CUBAN-COLOR)

Karlovy Vary, July 15.
ICAIC release and production. Features entire cast. Directed by Sergio Giral. Screenplay, Jorge Sotolongo, Giral; camera (Color), Raul Rodriguez; editor, Roberto Bravo; music, Sergio Vitier. Reviewed at Karlovy Vary Film Fest (competing), July 2, '80. Running time, 105 MINS.
With: Samuel Claxton, Miguel Navarro, Roberto Blanco, Miguel Guitierrez.

Black slavery seems a staple theme in Cuban films. Director Sergio Giral alone here does his third film on the subject. 19th-century tale concerns slaves who escaped and built up communities in an isolated part of the country called Maluala.

The Spanish Governor sends word through the Church and businessmen who deal with the ex-slave communes that he will pardon the leaders if they return but it would be some time before others are released from slavery.

Some decide to give in but others hold out and film concerns an army attack on the two holdouts which ends in the defeat of one but the routing of the army by the others. Stop action and slow motion is used in battle scenes to try to give this a more momentous underlining of the meaning of revolt and the need to resist tyranny.

But film remains sketchy in characters and is more a series of epic tableaus and surface treatment of slave breakaway communal life that robs this of a needed dramatic sweep and more probing revelation of the times. It could find further international fest outlets but that is about it. Latino markets are naturals, however, not to forget the third world orbit. Technically good with other credits acceptable. —*Mosk.*

Proba De Microfon
(Mike Test)
(RUMANIAN-COLOR)

Karlovy Vary, July 15.
Romaniafilm release of Three production. Features entire cast. Written and directed by Mircea Daneliuc. Camera (Color), Ion Marinescu; editor, Maria Neagu; music, Maja Stepanenco. Reviewed at Karlovy Vary Film Fest (noncompeting), July 3, '80. Running time, 108 MINS.
With: Mircea Daneliuc, Tora Vasilescu, Gina Patrichi, Geta Grapa, Gheorghe Negoescu, Maria Junghieta.

Rumanians seem to be counting on this film to establish some Western interest in their films

which has lagged of late. It does have an easygoing, free-wheeling treament but stays a bit too surface and unfocused to make that desired breakthrough. It does, however, unveil a new film author in Mircea Daneliuc who has written, directed and played the main character.

Daneliuc is a tv cameraman for a show that does outside interviews. In a railroad station they focus on a girl who did not have a train ticket and just wants to pay her fine. She later calls him and he meets her and there is an attraction. He even destroys her interview.

But the director of the show, an older woman, with whom Daneliuc also has a liaison, though accepting the film was lost, decides to find the girl who may make for a good human interest story. They track her down but Daneliuc gives away their plans and she disrupts any way of going on with the tv show.

After an affair with her, and finding out her need for money is to help a sick brother and that she is a non-conformist which also makes it hard for her to get a job, he drifts awy from her. He cannot find a way of morally coping with his love both for her and the other woman.

Film does lay out moral dilemmas, has a fresh style for introducing and revealing the characters but finally just comments on these problems rather than finding a more intense, revealing insight into the problems and actions of its characters. It should find some festival interest. —*Mosk.*

Kjaerleikens Ferjreiser
(A Commuter Kind of Love)
(NORWEGIAN-COLOR)

Karlovy Vary, July 15.
Nordisk Film release and production. Features entire cast. Written and directed by Hans Otto Nicolaysen from the book by Edvard Hoem; camera (color), Halvor Naess. No other credits available. Reviewed at Karlovy Vary Film Fest (competing), July 4, '80. Running time: 92 MINS.
With: Froydis Armand, Eilif Armand, Per Jansen, Karen Randers Person, Sigrid Huun, Sylvia Salvesen.

A small settlement nestled in the valley of a hilly island, a mile or so from the mainland, is threatened by the takeover of North Sea oil company. Film uses this vague ecological background to sketch out some human crises among the island people before a move is made to fight the takeover by a petition.

Film is somewhat bland and directed without a more dynamic blend of the various incidents. A waitress has come back pregnant by a son of a rich family and tries for an abortion. A housewife is suffering a nervous breakdown, a couple is at the breaking point and an

old retired postman observes all this and tries to help.

The lack of a more forceful drive makes this primarily a local item but does show more potent timely themes surfacing on the Norwegian scene. They will just need more talent and dramatic savvy than is evidenced in this well meaning but finally surface film that does not quite have the insights into the small human dramas or the bigger ones of a possible uprooting by a big financial corporation bent on buying out all the residents. Technically acceptable. —*Mosk.*

Signum Laudis
(The Medal)
(CZECHOSLOVAK-COLOR)

Karlovy Vary, July 15.
Czech State Film release of Barrandov Studio, Slovak Film Studio production. Features entire cast. Directed by Martin Holly. Screenplay, Valdimir Kalina, Jiri Krizan; camera (Eastmancolor), Frantisek Uldrich; music, Zdenek Liska. Reviewed at Karlovy Vary Film Fest (competing), July 1, '80. Running time: 85 MINS.
Hoferik .... Vlado Muller
General .... Ilja Prachar
Reischl-Dad .... Jan Skopecek
Lorisch .... Jiri Zahajsky
Kostolany .... Jiri Kodet
Konig .... Josef Blaha

Perhaps somewhat too demonstrative in wanting to make a point about military injustice and the basic dehumanization of war, film is still kept afloat by fine acting and Martin Holly's direction that recreates the fighting in World War I between the Austro-Hungarian and Russian forces.

A sergeant takes over a company and carries out futile charges against Russian guns following orders. Despite the loss of men and hardly any capture of land, he is picked out to get a special decoration only given to officers designed by the Emperor to buck up sagging morale.

Vlado Muller is effective as the burly sergeant, an ex-horse dealer, who is rough with the men and who is hated by them but grudgingly followed due to his knowhow. After his decoration and coddling by a new General to the annoyance of other officers, he is put in charge of retreat as the Russians encircle their forces.

Muller insists that the officers follow him thru the woods to get to safety in their lines. But he has to kill the horses and the trek deteriorates. Some officers convince the General Muller is getting too powerful and leading them to their deaths.

A court martial is trumped up and Muller summarily executed, the men sent to their deaths as the officers go forth to surrender. The film ends on a freeze shot of their walk to prison camps rather than death.

Somewhat schematic, but with effective feeling for the times and a destruction of a man by blind compliance rather than more human appraisals of man's actions even in wartime. Worth film fest attention.
—*Mosk.*

Bis Dass Der Tod Euch Scheidet
(Until Death Do Us Part)
(EAST GERMAN-COLOR)

Karlovy Vary, July 10.
A DEFA-Film Production, Babelsberg Group, Berlin, GDR; world rights, DEFA Aussenhandel, Berlin, GDR. Features entire cast. Directed by Heiner Carow. Screenplay, Guenther Ruecker; camera (color), Juergen Brauer; sets, Harry Leupold; music, Peter Gotthardt; production manager, Erwin Albrecht. Reviewed at Karlovy Vary Film Festival (Market), July 10, '80. Running time: **100 MINS.**
Cast: Karin Sass (Sonja), Martin Seifert (Jens), Renate Kroessner (Tilli), Angelika Domroese (Jens's Sister), Peter Zimmermann (Conny), Horst Schulze (Sales Manager), Werner Godemann (Construction Foreman).

"Until Death Do Us Part" is the third in a series of socially-engaged films on contemporary East Germany made by Heiner Carow, the others being "The Legend of Paul and Paula" (1972), scripted by Ulrich Plenzdorf, and "Icarus" (1975), scripted by Klaus Schlesinger. This latest effort was done in collaboration with screenplay writer Guenther Ruecker, who also worked with Guenter Reisch on "The Fiancee" (Grand Prix at Karlovy Vary).

"Until Death Do Us Part" is the story of a bumpy marriage set amid the working class. It begins with the wedding of a construction worker to a salesgirl, who is asked to quit her job when the child comes because the husband, remembers his own loveless childhood under a working mother. The girl, however, is intelligent and bored, so she finds work on the sly and even completes a management course to better her position.

When the hubby finds out what has been done behind his back, he takes to drinking and beating the better half, but always returning in the end to beg for forgiveness and support to overcome the drinking problem and his own insecurity. To add to the family problems, the sister of the husband, married to a well-to-do executive, is having an affair with another who doesn't return the affection — in other words, the same sort of misguided love, but on a different plane of relations.

The upshot comes when the husband flunks a promotion course and realizes his wife is still working

parttime. After beating and raping her in a drunken attack, she becomes pregnant again — and has an abortion. The marriage is then completely on the rocks, but rescued again via a family tragedy. The husband, by mistake, drinks cleaning fluid in a beer bottle that the wife, intentionally, left laying around — his vocal chords are burnt and he can never speak again, nor yell and scream at the woman he loves. He defends her during a confession on the truth at a closing wedding party.

Pic could have been a winner if properly cast as apparently intended in the screenplay. The husband was conceived as a swaggering brute and the wife as a timid lamb — the roles changing when the latter becomes stronger in will and the former weaker in purpose. As Carow pegged his film, however, the working husband is a handsome pip-squeak to begin with, and the wife a healthy specimen of femininity that contradicts her vacillation. Clamor instead of realism, but still well worth a onceover.
—*Holl.*

Me Vang Nha
(When Mother Is Out)
(VIETNAMESE-B&W)

Karlovy Vary, July 22.
Vietnam Feature Film Enterprise release and production. Features entire cast. Written and directed by Khanh Du from a book by Neguyen Thi. Camera, Ngoc Lan. Reviewed at Karlovy Vary Film Fest (competing), July 10, '80. Running time: **80 MINS.**
With Van Dung, Hong Phuong, Ngoc Thu.

Vietnam still has its past long wars, especially with the U.S., as a staple film theme. But here it remains in the background. Film looks at children behaving naturally and most entertainingly as they wait for their mother, who often has to go off to fight, to get back home.

Director Khanh Du displays an unusual flair for handling five children ranging from 12 to a baby without descending into gratuitous cuteness or exploiting them in the context of theme or propaganda.

The older girl does her chores, others try to learn from her, and when mother comes back it is a joyous reunion. But soon, when a helicopter is heard or guns, she is off again.

There are some over-heroic shots of the mother in action as the children imagine it and even a harrowing one of a napalmed cow, burning, running madly through fields.

Film looms mainly for fests and perhaps some specialized ethnic and children events. But it does mark a director with a fine visual knowhow who might be heard from

in turning from the eternal war themes to more contemporary subjects. —*Mosk.*

Bushkhugin Ulger
(The Story of a Good Guy)
(MONGOLIAN-COLOR)

Karlovy Vary, July 8.
A Mongolian Film Production, Ulan Bator; world rights, Mongolia Film, Ulan Bator, Mongolia. Features entire cast. Written and directed by Purev Tsogzol. Camera (color), L. Sharadorzh; music, T. Namsraizhav; art direction, Tsogzol. Reviewed at Karlovy Vary Film Festival (Competition), July 8, '80. Running time: **90 MINS.**
Cast: O. Ganbat (Bushkhu), S. Gedzhen (the Khan), T. Sainsana (the Princess), N. Daiyrane, N. Suvda, D. Dolgorsuren.

A children's film based on an old Mongolian legend, Purev Tsogzol's "The Story of a Good Guy" uses trick photography and special effects to charm audiences. It was a winner at home and is the best Mongolian pic to bow at international fests to date.

Filmed in color, helmer Tsogzol worked together with technicians on every phase of the story and the execution of trick photography from beginning to end, often having to solve problems neither he nor his team had anticipated at the outset. There's enough here to amuse special-effects buffs as well as auds interested in folk traditions, fairy tales, and fantasy for its own sake.

The Good Guy is Bushkhu, an orphan who hired himself out as a shepherd, and is later given a single sheep for his services. On his return home, he frees an enchanted chamois and a princess appears: since he is pure of heart, she has asked the Ruler of the Waters to grant him a wish, advising the lad to take a magic bone as his reward for freeing her enchanted sister. He does so, guided again by his heart to pick the right bone from the three offered to him.

The next morning, Bushkhu finds himself surrounded by splendor and the princess herself for his wife; but before the lad woke up, the last button had not yet been sewed onto his cloak — which means misfortune for the time being. That occurs when a despotic Khan decides he wants the princess for his own son and requires that the rivals must first pass tests to win her hand. The tests require shooting arrows over great distances and bringing back the sun in a box. Bushkhu wins out in the end, after many adventures.

A lovely pic that deserves invites to children's fests. —*Holl.*

Duios Anastasia Trecea
(Anastasia Passed By)
(RUMANIAN-COLOR)

Karlovy Vary, July 6.
A Rumaniafilm Production, Film Group One, Bucharest; world rights, Romaniafilm, Bucharest. Features entire cast. Directed by Alexandru Tatos. Screenplay, D.R. Popescu, based on his short story with the same title; camera (color), Florin Mihailescu; sets, Andrei Both; music, Lucian Metianu; editing, Iolanda Mintulescu. Reviewed at Karlovy Vary Film Festival (Competition), July 6, '80. Running time: **100 MINS.**
Cast: Anda Onesa (Anastasia), Amza Pellea, Laszlo Tarr, Levente Biro, Christian Ghita, Razvan Onesa, Catalin Ciornei, Gheorghe Teasca, Daniel Petrescu, Stefan Kofalvy, Imola Gaspar, Dumitru Bordeianu, Ernest Kantor.

Alexandru Tatos's "Anastasia Passed By" (original title translates a poetic "Gently Was Anastasia Passing") draws upon a short story adapted to the screen by the same writer, D.R. Popescu, with clear references to the classical Sophocles' tragedy, "Antigone." It's this frame of reference that gives the story something extra and makes it one of the best pix to emerge from Rumania in recent years.

The setting is a border town on the Danube across from Yugoslavia. It is 1944 and the German Wehrmacht comes grinding along the roads and into the village. The youths of the town are enlisted into a Folks Army to fight on the side of the Germans, but several choose instead to escape across the river and join the Yugoslav partisans.

The occupied village is told to elect the new collaborating mayor, who in turn is surrounded by a cohort of ready collaborators, and hires the village strongman, an idiot, to be his henchman. Meanwhile, the partisans raid the area one night and disappear back over the Danube — but a hiding Serbian is killed, and then dragged into the village as a warning to the populace. The body is dumped on a platform at the crossroads; anyone who buries the corpse is threatened with death.

The schoolteacher Anastasia refuses to obey the command — thus the Antigone drama proceeds to unfold. The mayor attempts to reason with her, followed by his son, her lover, who is in hiding like a coward rather than fight on either side of the ongoing conflict. The old cronies in the inn also lend their comments but refuse to act — the villagers hide in fear. She buries the corpse, then is strangled by the mayor's brutal bodyguard. Her body is dumped into a limepit, the murder witnessed by a young boy who reveals the crime that was passively approved by the chorus of old cronies.

Considering how often of late

Greek tragedies and Shakespearean plays have been used to comment on the present, "Anastasia Passed By" is even more remarkable because it argues for human dignity by totally revamping the usual action-packed partisan theme (the so-called "Eastern") into a compact drama that leaves the Nazis almost completely out of the picture. Further, it's the Rumanian collaborators who are the heavies, while Anastasia is a victim because she follows her human instincts.

Lensing is a plus, but thesps and direction are additional factors that pay dividends. Pic should be included in Rumanian Film Weeks abroad and deserves further exposure on the fest circuit. —*Holl.*

Cardena Perpetua
(Vicious Circle)
(MEXICAN-COLOR)

Karlovy Vary, July 22.
Conacine release and production. Directed by Arturo Ripstein. Features entire cast. Screenplay, Vicento Lenaro, Ripstein, camera (color), Jorge Stahl; music, Miguel Pons. Reviewed at Karlovy Vary Film Fest (competing), July 9, '80. Running time: **90 MINS.**
With Pedro Armendariz Jr., Narciso Busquets, Ernesto Gomez Cruz, Ana Martin, Angelica Chain, Ana Ofelia Marguia, Roberto Cobo.

A grim tale of an ex-con, one-time pimp and thief, who has gone straight. Though with a good job, wife and children, he is hounded back to criminality by a venal, blackmailing detective who recognizes him in the street one day.

Arturo Ripstein's direction is fluid. But the playing, surface detailing of lowlife ways and the sketchy characterizations lose the edge of social protest it strives at getting over.

Pedro Armendariz Jr. is handsome but lacks his late father's forcefulness to make a more complex character of this macho lout who learns a lesson in prison. He is too easily undone and film evades the real issue of social responsibility by having the boss absent when Armendariz needs him.

He runs around for a long time, but cannot find his boss who might have helped him. He resorts to thieving again to get the money for the blackmailing detective.

Film could have Latin legs on its brisk handling but misses the probing and revealing insight into a valid theme for more offshore chances. Pity, for it is well made and well meaning. —*Mosk.*

Zendabad
(Long Live...)
(IRANIAN-B&W)

Karlovy Vary, July 22.
Iran Film release and production. Written and directed by Khosrow Sinai. Features entire cast. Camera (black and white), Fereidun Kavanlu. No other credits available. Reviewed at Karlovy Vary Film Fest (competing), July 7, '80. Running time: **100 MINS.**
With Soroyya Kasemi, Mehdi Hashemi, Gholanreza Tabataba, Ema il Mohammadi, Ahmad Kashani.

One of the first Iranian films made after the overthrow of the Shah and the revolution to come to a festival, it does not shed much light on the events. Film is a familiar thriller about a simple household beset by an intruder who changes their ways. In this case it is a student revolutionary.

The film does have a good flair for action and building some suspense as well as underlining its simply treated but universal theme of the need to take sides during historic change.

Here a man has made good and is comfortably installed in a nice house with wife, two young daughters and his father. Revolts have started in the streets, with brutal police reprisals. But the man wants no part of it. Events however, force him into a commitment.

Sent to shop, he gets caught up in street battles and manages to get home, only to find a student has slipped in, too. First against him, he soon remembers that at one time he too was in revolt but gave it up when he saw that, when things changed, the revolutionaries sold out, becoming like their forerunners.

Soon he gets fond of the man, and when a plainclothes man comes into the house on a search, the enraged father, helped by the student, kills him. In the end they are both killed themselves.

Mainly a home item but showing a filmic feel for action and perhaps a future for director Khosrow Sinai when he can work the knowhow into more potent themes and material. —*Mosk.*

Ein April Hat 30 Tage
(April Has 30 Days)
(EAST GERMAN-COLOR)

Karlovy Vary, June 27.
A DEFA Film Production, Babelsberg, GDR; world rights, DEFA Aussenhandel, Berlin, GDR. Features entire cast. Directed by Gunther Scholz. Screenplay, Carlos Cerda, Scholz; camera (color), Guenter Haubold; music, Udo Zimmermann. Reviewed at Karlovy Vary Film Festival (Opera Prima), June 27, '80. Running time: **90 MINS.**
Cast: Angelika Waller (Marie), Jurie Darie (Alvaro), Ronald Kubenz (Micha), Bert Brunn, Peter Slakakov.

Debut director Gunther Scholz came up through television and legit productions to make "April Has 30 Days," at DEFA. It's a solidarity-style pic for and about Latin American refugees living in East Germany, framed within a love story that only lasts through the month of April. The relationship is between Uruguayan exile leader and a divorced German woman with a young son.

The pair meet in the elevator of an apartment building both are moving into; since they live on the same floor, a borrowed light bulb leads to a candlelight supper and the first casual acquaintance. Maria is a factory worker, still young and lovely, but also lonely; Alvaro, a Party official, knows that he can be changed to another post and even back to South America if he's needed. Within 30 days the couple become intimate lovers, then the relationship has to be broken off for the predictable fateful reason. Alvaro says goodbye at the airport, presumably headed for the Latin American underground.

Pic has some nice touches as two cultures blend awkwardly with each other in the beginning, but over the long stretch the principles remain stereotypes instead of flesh-and-blood individuals with a heartbreaking problem on their hands. Lensing and thesps (the Bulgarian ace bit player, Peter Slabakov, passes neatly as a Latin in this one) hint that director Scholz has learned his trade in the tv-studios. —*Holl.*

Dvoynikat
(The Double)
(BULGARIAN-COLOR)

Karlovy Vary, July 5.
A Bulgarian Film production, "Suvremenik" Film Group, Sofia; world rights, Bulgarofilm, Sofia. Features entire cast. Directed by Nikolai Volev. Screenplay, Mormarev Brothers; camera (color), Venko Kableshkov; art directions, Nikolai Surchadjiev; music, Johann Sebastian Bach. Reviewed at Karlovy Vary Film Festival (Opera Prima), July 5, '80. Running time: **90 MINS.**
Cast: Todor Kolev (Ivan Denev and The Double), Yordanka Kouzmanova (Cortinska), Lyuben Kalinov (Roussev), Radosveta Vassileva (Shivacheva), Pavel Poppandov (Peyev).

Unspooled in Karlovy Vary's "Opera Prima" section, this Bulgarian debut pic, "The Double," aims to be a comedy and toplines one of the country's best dramatic comedians, Todor Kolev (of the Sofia Theatre), in the double role of a famous scientist and his fun-loving look-alike. Anyone who has seen Danny Kaye or Stan Laurel pix of the same nature can anticipate the gags in the film — still they work their magic all the same.

Script by the Mormarev Brothers, Bulgaria's top comic writers, features a scientist aching for more time to himself for research work. Since he happens to have a cousin who looks exactly like him, he invites the latter to Sofia to attend the official meetings in his place. The double, however, likes to smoke and drink — the opposite of the scientist — and has a way of using his intelligent half's reputation to win a new popularity on the public media and further the cause of Bulgarian science by organizing an international congress on his own.

The snowball keeps growing in size, but as it does so, the stuffy scientist begins to learn that life has other pleasures besides research and a romantic interest is one of them. Helmer Nikolai Volev has a light hand with the comic situations and could develop into a talent in this genre. —*Holl.*

La Triple Mort Du Troisieme Personnage
(The Triple Death of the Third Character)
(FRENCH-COLOR)

Karlovy Vary, July 15.
Babylone Films release of Babylone Films, Producciones Zeta production. Features entire cast. Directed by Helvio Soto. No other credits available. Reviewed at Karlovy Vary Film Fest, Jun 30, '80. Running time, **95 MINS.**
With: Jose Sacristan, Andre Dussolier, Patricio Guzman, Brigitte Fossey.

Helvio Soto is a Chilean political refugee filmmaker living in France. He made the routine reenactment film on the fall of Chilean Marxist President Allende, "It Rains on Santiago." Now he does an unusual, convoluted, intellectual film delving into the mind of a writer who had been tortured in some Latin American country.

The writer is in the forbidding railroad station of Antwerp. He is afraid. Various incidents take place that emanate from a book he had written on his experiences. The film weaves in the meeting with an old flame who is with a group in Spain, some sort of governmental secret service org (French, Belgian, U.S.?), working to find out who the men in a torture cell mentioned in the book were and their fates.

Film is perhaps not crystal clear, but is done with an icy directorial control that makes this descent into political refugee fears rather engrossing. —*Mosk.*

Steel
(COLOR)

With careful sell gutsy story should play well in action markets.

Hollywood, July 30.
World-Northal Films release of a Peter S. Davis/William N. Panzer production. Produced by David, Panzer. Directed by Steven Carver. Features entire cast. Exec producer, Lee Majors. Screenplay, Leigh Chapman; camera (Movielab), Roger Shearman; editor, David Blewitt; production design, Ward & Preston; music, Michael Colombier; set decoration, Lloyd Linean; special effects, Roger George; stunt coordinator, James Arnett; costumes, Doris Lynch, Sydney Gilbert; sound, William Griffith; assistant directors, Tom Connors, Richard Hashimoto. Reviewed at the ABC Entertainment Complex VIP Room, Century City, July 30, 1980. (MPAA Rating: PG). Running time: **99 MINS.**

Mike Catton	Lee Majors
Cass Cassidy	Jennifer O'Neill
Pignose Moran	Art Carney
Lew Cassidy	George Kennedy
Eddie Cassidy	Harris Yulin
Harry	Redmond Cleason
Valentino	Terry Kiser
Dancer	Richard Lynch
The Kid	Ben Marley
Lionel	Roger Mosley
Tank	Albert Salmi
Cherokee	Robert Tessier
Surfer	Hunter Von Leer
Kellin	R.G. Armstrong
Tom	Joseph DeNicola

Despite more than its share of production and distribution problems, "Steel" emerges as a grabbing drama with an abundance of energy and emotional gutsiness. The World-Northal domestic pickup concerning an all-star group of construction workers laboring to finish nine floors of a skyscraper before the bank closes in, has enough heart to entice sophisticates and enough action to play the exploitation market. Although pic might be a tough sell outside the latter, careful release could generate word of mouth needed to cut into a broader audience. Clearly, the material is there.

"Steel" began lensing in Lexington, Ky. in 1978 and during production famed stuntman A.J. Bakunis died doing a tricky maneuver (pic has since been dedicated to him). New Line Cinema sold foreign rights to Columbia and pic has played abroad for over a year. Col was originally supposed to domestic distribute in April, but producers Peter S. Davis and William N. Panzer wanted a summer release. Col bowed out and World-Northal picked up the feature more than a month ago.

Lee Majors stars and exec produces (he was also involved in financing) and his well-crafted, restrained portrayal as the leader of the constructioners provides a solid base for a series of involving relationships. In what is easily one of the more outstanding supporting appearances in recent history, George Kennedy dominates the first 15 minutes as a gruff but good-hearted company owner supervising the going-on. Kennedy has not forsaken his blue collar roots and joins workmen atop a building to pound some steel. There is an explosion and, in trying to aid a fear-stricken novice clinging to a girder, Kennedy plunges to a tragic death.

Daughter Jennifer O'Neill is then left to take on the task of completing the project, which will be cut off by the bank in three weeks unless nine floors are completed. Lack of time, dedicated workers and the wrath of Kennedy's villainous brother all make the effort near impossible. Kennedy's friend Art Carney suggests O'Neill search out Majors to coordinate the job, and he in turns travels around the country and rounds up the most famed workers in the business.

What unravels is a rightly-directed story and true-to-life character study of endearing personalities interacting against outside forces in order to achieve a shared goal. Steven Carver turns in an impressive helming performance, foremost keeping the action moving but also providing enough nuances to flesh out their varied individuals. Leigh Chapman has provided him with a well-constructed script, although occasional attempts at allusions to a romance between Majors and O'Neill come off as a bit forced.

A variety of non-stars turn in stellar perfs as the workers, particularly Roger Mosley and Hunter Von Leer as best friends who come to an unfortunate separation. Stunt work supervised by James Arnett is exceptional as is David Blewitt's careful editing.

Outstanding point concerning "Steel" is that its history and subject matter seem to suggest the makings of a financial and artistic disaster. That it comes off as such an outstanding work is a rare and welcome surprise.—*Berg.*

Why Would I Lie?
(COLOR)

Another instance of strong cast, weak script.

Hollywood, July 30.
An MGM release through United Artists, produced by Pancho Kohner. Exec producers, Rich Irvine, James L. Stewart. Directed by Larry Peerce. Features entire cast. Screenplay, Peter Stone, based on the novel, "The Fabricator," by Hollis Hodges; camera (Metrocolor), Gerald Hirschfeld; editor, John C. Howard; sound, Bud Alper; art direction, James Schoppe; assistant director, Steve Barnett; music, Charles Fox. Reviewed at MGM Studios, Culver City, July 30, 1980. (MPAA rating: PG.) Running time: **105 MINS.**

Cletus	Treat Williams
Kay	Lisa Eichhorn
Jeorge	Gabriel Swann
Mrs. Bok	Valerie Curtin
Faith	Anne Byrne
Amy	Susan Heldfond
Mrs. Crumpe	Jocelyn Brando
Walter	Nicolas Coster
Dr. Barbour	Severn Darden
Paul	Sonny Davis

"Why Would I Lie?" is another one of those pictures, and there have been too many of late, that assembles a good cast to struggle with a bad script. Commercially, the big question lies not in the title but with the filmgoer who must ask, "Why Would I Bother?"

Right from the start, Treat Williams is a troublesome, ill-defined character, preventing his siblings from sharing a $1,000,000 inheritance for no good reason other than his own irresponsible kookiness. He is also a compulsive liar who makes up stories because he believes they make everyone's life more exciting.

In other words, Williams is not the sort of person anybody would want to be around very long. But director Larry Peerce and writer Peter Stone plan to fix this fairly soon by giving the hero something sympathetic to do. And that's where they really go awry.

Though he absolutely lacks any qualifications for the job, Valerie Curtin hires Williams as a social worker. He thus becomes embroiled in the case of young Gabriel Swann, taken away from his mother while she was wrongfully jailed and now about to be transferred from a foster home to permanent adoption.

Instead of delivering the lad to his new parents, however, Treat takes the boy home. Does Curtin investigate? Does the court? Do the expectant adoptive parents ever question what happened to their new son? Of course not. The story must simply roll on so Williams can meet Lisa Eichhorn.

Eichhorn works at a feminist retreat that was once the post-prison stopping place for Swann's mother, for whom Williams is so desperately searching so he can give back the kid he stole. Once Williams and Eichhorn meet, it's only a matter of time until all the mysteries unravel — and not a single word of it is believable, up to and including the corny ending.

Unfortunate this is, because Williams and Eichhorn make an attractive couple and young Swann is a delight in his film debut. And the rest of the cast is also strong: Anne Byrne as Williams' sister, Susan Heldfond as a more-than-casual housemate for Eichhorn, and Nicolas Coster and Sonny Davis as the impatiently greedy brothers.

There was, in sum, a lot of talent to work with. But nowhere to start and nowhere to go. —*Har.*

Raise The Titanic
(COLOR)

Poor script and direction handicap big name players.

Hollywood, July 30.
Associated Film Distribution release, produced by William Frye. Exec producer, Martin Starger. Features entire cast. Directed by Jerry Jameson. Screenplay, Adam Kennedy, adapted by Eric Hughes, from the novel by Clive Cussler; camera (DeLuxe Color), Matthew F. Leonetti, Rex Metz (second unit), Jack Cooperman (underwater inserts), Bob Steadman (model unit), Arthur Wooster (Malta sequences); music, John Barry; edited by J. Terry Williams, Robert F. Shugrue; production designer, John F. DeCuir; art direction, John F. DeCuir Jr.; set decoration, Mickey S. Michaels, Raphael Breton (Washington, D.C.) Ian Whittaker (Europe); sound, Dean Gilmore, John Mitchell (Europe), John K. Wilkinson, Robert W. Glass Jr., Robert Thirlwell; second-unit director, Mickey Moore; model and mechanical effects supervisor (Europe), John Richardson; model unit director (Europe), Ricou Browning; special effects supervisor, Alex Weldon; assistant director, Jim Westman. Reviewed at Academy of Motion Picture Arts & Sciences, BevHills, July 21, 1980 and Directors Guild Theatre, Hollywood, July 30, 1980. (MPAA Rating: PG.) Running time: **112 MINS.**

Admiral James Sandecker	Jason Robards
Dirk Pitt	Richard Jordan
Dr. Gene Seagram	David Selby
Dana Archibald	Anne Archer
John Bigalow	Alec Guinness
Capt. Joe Burke	J.D. Cannon
Capt. Andre Prevlov	Bo Brundin
MCPO Vinnie Giordino	M. Emmet Walsh

"Raise The Titanic" wastes a potentially intriguing premise with dull scripting, a lackluster cast, laughably phony trick work, and clunky direction. As usual, the Lew Grade-Martin Starger release will undertake to recoup its inflated cost overseas, but U.S. prospects for the AFD release look dubious.

Half of the 112-minute running time (at least) is devoted to underwater miniature shots of submarines and other apparatus trying to dislodge the long-lost luxury liner Titanic from its deepsea resting place. The trickery, while undoubtedly time-consuming and expensive to film, is glaringly obvious and may provoke derision among viewers when enormous air bubbles drift past ships that look like plastic models floating in a bathtub. Plus, it's an eternity before the one truly spectacular scene occurs — the Titanic finally exploding to the surface.

The ridiculously expository screenplay by Adam Kennedy, adapted by Eric Hughes from the novel by Clive Cussler, spends most of its time having characters repeatedly explain what will happen, why it's happening (some folderol about minerals on the Titanic coveted for weaponry by both the U.S. and the Russians), and how it's going to happen. It evidently never occurred to Kennedy, producer William Frye and director Jerry Jameson that all the gabbing was a bore and could have been more profitably converted into the creation of interesting characters.

The actors adopt various strategies for coping with their unspeakable dialog and cardboard characterization. Jason Robards, as an unscrupulous admiral behind the salvage project, walks around with a smirk on his face; Richard Jordan, as a master technician uncomfortably saddled with the B-movie hero name of "Dirk Pitt," tries for nonchalance without totally guying the part (it doesn't work); David Selby, as a coldly sinister think-tank type', quickly becomes unbearable because he takes it all so seriously and tries so hard; and Anne Archer, as a reporter improbably involved with both Jordan and Selby, seems to be repressing hysteria over having nothing sensible to do in the film.

Others handle their parts in standard fashion, aside from Alec Guinness, who provides a dramatic highlight with a lovely scene as a retired old salt who served on the Titanic's crew and vividly recalls her brief glory.

After being previewed, pic was cut by 10 minutes and rescreened for reviewers. —Mac.

___

Il Cappotto Di Astrakan
(The Persian Lamb Coat)
(ITALIAN-COLOR)

___

Rome, July 10.
A Cineriz release, produced by Franco Cristaldi and Nicola Carrara for Vides Productions (Rome) and Les Film Ariane (Paris). Stars Johnny Dorelli, Andrea Ferreol, Carole Bouquet. Directed by Marco Vicario. Screenplay, Vicario and Sandro Parenzo from the novel by Piero Chiari; camera (Eastmancolor), Ennio Guarnieri; editor, Nino Baragli; music, Bruno Nicolai. Reviewed at America Cinema, Rome, July 9, 1980. Running time: 100 MINS.
Piero ....Johnny Dorelli
Mme Lenormand ....Andrea Ferreol
Valentine ....Carole Bouquet

___

A gentle charm and whimsical story distinguish what might otherwise be another lightweight comedy in "The Persian Lamb Coat," adapted from a Piero Chiari novel about an Italian wastrel who takes a vacation in Paris. Good performances by principals Johnny Dorelli and Andrea Ferreol and solid scripting account for a positive showing in Franco-Italian production lands. More a commercial property than a festival entry, "Coat" has the well-penned humor and touristic locales that could pull it through in other territories.

Small-town loafer Piero waves goodbye to buddies and boards the train for a wicked week in Gay Paree. Mistaken for a thief he spends the first night in jail, the second in the home of lonely Mme. Lenormand who is struck by his resemblance to her husband Maurice, himself in jail for a real robbery. Piero moves into the husband's room and becomes a pale copy of the ghostly Maurice, reading his books, working on his inventions, possessing wife and mistress and wearing his enormous Persian lamb coat. When Maurice returns unexpectedly one night Piero scurries back to his little town on the lake, where he can recount exotic tales of his Parisian adventures to his friends.

Conformism theme doesn't stop "Coat" from some tired moments of rehashed Italian comedy (Dorelli being one of its princes), like the ill-boding opener of Piero's suitcase springing open as he boards the train.

Pic gets more mileage out of its mystery angle. Who Maurice is and how far Piero goes in assuming the absent man's identity is something he and the audience discover only gradually by other people's reactions to him. Maurice's mistress Valentine (played appropriately by Carole Bouquet, one of the Cochitas of "Obscure Object of Desire") embodies the film's doubling idea in her work of copying famous paintings. Andrea Ferreol gives the most subtle performance in pic as Maurice's wife, living in a house filled with antiques and herself a relic from the '40s.

Feature stays engrossing throughout, though it loses unity of space and time when Valentine goes to Italy to find Piero after his return. This unnecessary epilog robs some of the force of the second train sequence, where Piero's cowardice leads him to accept the sexual propositions of a strange man. Ending defuses the sexual surrender with a milder life-goes-on finish, the standard closing of Italian comedy.

Excellent photography by Ennio Guarnieri and sets by Andrea Crisanti give "Coat" a strong technical boost, adding a note of class to Paris and a touristic charm to the lake town. A nice touch are the Pasolini low-life actors who cameo as jewel thieves. —Yung.

___

Melech Leyom Echad
(King for a Day)
(ISRAELI-COLOR)

___

Tel Aviv, June 28.
A Nachshon Films presentation. Produced by Isaac Shani and Naotali Alter. Stars Gabi Amrani, Carolyn Langford, Hanan Goldblatt. Directed by Assaf Dayan. Screenplay, Dayan and Alter; camera (color), Ilan Rosenberg; editor. Reuven Kornfeld; costumes, Sara Wiener; music, Alter; lyrics; Dayan; sound, Yaakov Goldstein. Released in Tel Aviv, June 28, 1980. Running time: 85 MINS.
Cast: Gabi Amrani, Carolyn Langford, Hanan Goldblatt, Eyal Geffen, Irith Mohar, Uri Alter, Yohanan Raviv, Danny Segev, Rivka Michaeli, Yosef Shiloach, Miriam Fuchs.

___

The most obvious credit is missing here, as no one bothered to recall on screen the name of Damon Runyon, whose "Madame La Gimp" has been the obvious inspiration for the scripters. Even the title is a clear take-off on Frank Capra's first screen adaptation of this story, the 1933 classic "Lady for a Day." Capra liked it enough to do it again, less successfully, as "A Pocketful of Miracles" in 1961, and now the Assaf Dayan-Naftali Alter tandem are trying to move the action from the streets of New York to the beach-resort town of Nethanyia, not far from Tel Aviv. They have also switched the sex of the leading character (now it is a man instead of a woman) but the story remains basically the same. The doorman of a Nethanyia hotel has left a daughter in America, during his short passage there. She is now in her early twenties and hasn't seen her father for 15 years. As he is ashamed of just being a porter, he has invented, in his letters to her, a new personality for himself, that of a successful and terribly busy tycoon.

Then the daughter arrives without warning to visit, and with a little help from his friends, he succeeds in keeping on the appearance of a big time operator, in order to impress her accordingly. The love interest is supplied by a local never-do-well who is always trying to romance lady tourists out of their money and removes his dilapidated wolf skin, when his help is required for the game of deceit.

Altogether the film seems to be put together rather lackadaisically, the introduction is far too long and not funny enough, dialogs sound like ad libs invented on the spur of the moment, when camera started to roll, laughs are elicited mostly by these ad libs, as the director's main concern is watching his characters talk. Needless to say, the richness and variety of the Runyon types is sadly missed here.

Most of the action is shot at the Nethanyia Blue Bay Hotel, which was put at the disposition of the filmmakers, as a promotional stunt, before official opening. The inn was paid back handsomely, as its name is repeatedly featured on screen, sometimes through the most transparent techniques of commercials. The city of Nethanyia and its soccer team, this year's champions in Israel, are also

promoted, even if their presence is not relevant or consistent with the story. ◆

Gabi Amrani, as the doorman-parent, has some nice moments, when he doesn't have to strain to be funny, and Carolyn Langford is nicely natural as his daughter, but should be spared the singing, which doesn't suit her too well. The rest of the cast is just hamming it up.

Intended as light summer fare, shot in 16m and blown up to 35m, it was hoped the film will follow in the steps of previous Dayan-Alter successful ventures of the same kind, but initial public response, for the first couple of weeks seems less than enthusiastic. —Edna.

___

Hasereth Festival Hayeladim
(The Children Song Festival - The Movie)
(ISRAEL-COLOR-DOCU)

___

Tel Aviv, June 14.
A Classipop Production. Produced by Avshalom Rubin and Alex Barnea. Executive producer, Tommy Lang. Directed by Ilan Eldad. Camera (color), Yehiel Neeman, Amnon Salomon, Danny Schneur, Yaakov Eisenman, Avi Daphna; edited by Rachel Yagil; musical direction: Uri Kariv; conducted by Itzhak Graziani. Reviewed in Tel Aviv, June 14, 1980. Running time: 84 MINS.
Adult Singers: Mike Burstein, Igal Bashan, Rikki Gal, Dori Ben-Zeev, Ariel Zilber, Sexta, Ruchama, Dudu Zakkai,Jerry Heyman, Suzy Miller. Children singers: Rachel Levin, Aharon Israeli, Jenny Blum, Ravith Berger, Limor Nachum. M.C.'s: Israel Gurion, Ezra Dagan, Dorinne Caspi.

___

Practically a tv show dedicated to the tenth annual Children Song Festival, the film has been released theatrically due to the enormous success of the show itself, and the record-breaking sales of the disks, both supplying ample proof of the popularity of this festival.

In a long-oriented kid market, which swallows up greedily anything that might pleasure the tots, the production of such a film was to be expected and timing its release to coincide with the summer holidays is only natural.

Using some of the best cameramen in the ocuntry, director Ilan Eldad focuses his attention on the stage activity, most of the footage being centered on the performance per se, during the Festival, from different angles, some behind the scenes, but most of them from the traditional point of view of the public.

To relieve uniformity, Eldad escapes from time to time from the closed quarters of the Tel Aviv Mann Auditorium, to show parents pushing their children towards stardom, as some 5,000 competitors are doing their best to get a shot at one of the 10 songs featured finally in the concert. Auditions, repetitions and public reactions have all their small share, but after all, what the film offers first and foremost, are the songs, some performed once by the grownups, some twice, when the children offer their own version, and some even three times, if the song is a winner and gets an award at the end.

As there is no attempt to go deeper in any of the possible issues raised by such a festival, from selection of entries to commercialization of children, there is nothing to be said about Eldad as director, except that he does a very clean and efficient job. Footage shot in 16m has been excellently blown up to 35m and sound is usually OK, except for some mixing which lets orchestra overpower the inexperienced vocals of the younger participants.

At home, the film stands a good chance of turning into a hit, as it is unpretentious enough, and supplies efficiently the equivalent of a live concert at a much lower price. Abroad, outlook is more chancy, as musical standard is professional but not original and the document doesn't really try to get under the surface of anything. —*Edna.*

Septemberweizen
(September Wheat)
(WEST GERMAN-COLOR-
DOCU-16m)

Mainz, July 18.
A Teldok Film, Freiburg, production, in collaboration with ZDF (Second Channel), Mainz: world rights, Peter Krieg, Teldok, Freiburg. Written, directed and edited by Peter Krieg. Assistant director and sound, Heidi Knott; music, Rolf Riehm. No other credits. Reviewed at ZDF Screening Room, Mainz, July 18, '80. Running time: **90 MINS.**

Peter Krieg and Heidi Knott have collaborated on several docus dealing with hunger and health problems in the underdeveloped countries of the world, several sponsored by the World Council of Churches in conjunction with John Taylor in the Film and Visual Arts section. For "September Wheat" Eckart Stein and Annegret Even of West Germany ZDF (Second Channel) web took an interest and cosponsored the project for the "Kleine Fernsehspiel" series. Pic made such an impact at the initial airing in June that it will now find its way to docu fests and the like as a fave in the ecology movement.

Krieg's "September Wheat" hits hard as a montage docu, rather than being polemic or preachy. Since the subject is hunger, matched with the riches of the American grain belt, the didactic element is in the presentation of facts, sometimes juxtaposing dif-

ferent information on the soundtrack than what is presented via images. The blame for the world's hungry is placed on no one in particular; still, the John Heartfield-style of picture montage leaves little doubt that the "system" is at the bottom of trouble and misery.

"September Wheat" (the term refers to wheat contracts on the trade exchange) begins with the harvest season in Kansas in 1979; in the first episode, the farmers are shown to be on the edge of bankruptcy despite the abundance of wheat due to rising costs and stagnating prices. For the second chapter, Krieg then shifts to the use of satellites to determine world wheat harvest on computers, contrasted with the world of scientists to find a hybrid form of wheat that would resist agricultural pests and plagues — all the findings of which come to naught due to concerns buying out the seed companies to prevent the use of a hybrid seed that would, in effect, eliminate seed companies altogether.

Next, Krieg visits the Cargill silos in Middle America, the largest in the world, and the wheat exchange in Chicago, where 90% of the world's business is in the hands of speculators. Then comes the manufacturing of the cheapest form of bread on the market, damaging to health in the long run, and the selling of wheat to the countries who can buy, the rest "dumped" instead of being used to feed the world's starving. Finally, hunger in America is shown, a paradox that has been commented on as far back as Edward R. Morrow's famous tv-report on Thanksgiving Day in the 1950s.

"September Wheat," if nothing else, forces the viewer to pause and reflect on a mass of information intelligently compiled and presented. And some of the images — one of a preacher with a Bible standing in a sea of wheat reading the passage about Joseph in the land of Egypt preparing for the seven lean years in the midst of the seven fat ones — stick to the mind to prick the conscience. As for a solution, however, both the system and the starving are still with us — without much hope in sight that things will change for the betterment of mankind. —*Holl.*

The Kidnapping of
the President
(CANADIAN-COLOR)

Good action pic with fair prospects.

Crown International release of a Sefel Pictures International production. Produced by George Mendeluk, John Ryan. Exec producer, Joseph Sefel. Directed by Mendeluk. Stars William Shatner, Hal Holbrook, Van Johnson, Ava Gardner. Screenplay, Richard Murphy, from novel by Charles Templeton; camera (DeLuxe color), Mike Molloy; music, Paul J. Zaza; editor, Michael McLaverty; art direction, Douglas Higgins; special effects, Peter Hutchinson, Richard Albain; assistant director, Gerry Arbeid. Reviewed at Preview 4 screening room, N.Y., Aug. 6, '80 (MPAA Rating: R). Running time: **113 MINS.**

Jerry O'Connor	William Shatner
President Adam Scott	Hal Holbrook
V.P. Ethan Richards	Van Johnson
Beth Richards	Ava Gardner
Roberto Assanti	Miguel Fernandes
Linda Steiner	Cindy Girling
MacKenzie	Michael J. Reynolds
Joan Scott	Elizabeth Shepherd
Deitrich	Gary Reineke
Harvey Cannon	Maury Chaykin

A fine action-suspense film shot last winter in Canada, "The Kidnapping of the President" has good topical prospects in this presidential campaign year. Lack of b.o.-exploitable names in the familiar cast could be a stumbling block, however.

Functional script by Richard Murphy from Charles Templeton's novel has Third World terrorists devising a plot to bring America to its knees by kidnapping the president. Hot issue of whether one should ever accede to terrorists' demands is pic's central theme.

After an unpromising, needlessly bloody opening set in South America, film settles down to gripping tale of terrorists, led by chilling psychotic Miguel Fernandes, snatching president Hal Holbrook, who is wading through a crowd in downtown Toronto. Handcuffing himself to Holbrook, Fernandes believably makes off with his hostage by threatening to detonate explosives strapped to his vest. Plausibility of this well-directed staging drives home the fact that any politician routinely risks death in public appearances from some deranged person willing to forfeit his own life in the bargain.

Storing the prexy in a booby-trapped security truck, Fernandes holds up the U.S. Government for $100,000,000 ransom. Secret Service head William Shatner, vying with the CIA for jurisdictional authority, is faced with the tough decision. Excellent last-reel pacing leads to suspenseful resolution.

Key subplot involves veep Van Johnson also under pressure, first faced with a "Billygate"-type bribery scandal and secondly ambi-

valent about saving Holbrook, as wife Ava Gardner eggs him on to take a stand.

After the fiasco of his first feature, "Stone Cold Dead," director George Mendeluk has come back with a solid action film, which wisely doesn't hide its Canadian origins. Murphy's script marks a welcome return to features by the screenwriter of "Boomerang," "Panic in the Streets" and "Compulsion," Mike Molloy's budget-stretching photography in the oval office set and on Toronto locations is outstanding.

Shatner and Holbrook are effective in their central roles, but the film's real star is Fernandes, creating a spellbinding anti-hero as the lead terrorist. Elizabeth Shepherd is quite affecting in her small role as the First Lady. Guestars Van Johnson and Ava Gardner form an attractive couple as veep and wife in their first featured teaming in 35 years, since "Three Men In White." (Duo were skedded to make Italo pic "The Concorde Affair" together in 1978 but project went through cast changes.) It makes one wonder why MGM never paired them during their salad days at the studio. —*Lor.*

Those Lips Those Eyes
(COLOR)

Summer stock comedy could be a sleeper.

Hollywood, Aug. 8.
United Artists release of a Herb Jaffe production. Stars Frank Langella. Directed by Michael Pressman. Produced by Steven-Charles Jaffe and Michael Pressman; executive producer, Herb Jaffe. Screenplay, David Shaber; camera (Technicolor), Bobby Byrne; original music composed and conducted by Michael Small; musical staging and choreography, Dan Siretta; film editor, Millie Moore; production designer Walter Scott Herndon; set decorator, Cloudia; publicist, Earl Wingard. Reviewed at Samuel Goldwyn Theatre, Beverly Hills, Aug. 8, 1980. (MPAA Rating: R). Running time: **107 MINS.**

Harry Crystal	Frank Langella
Ramona	Glynnis O'Connor
Artie Shoemaker	Thomas Hulce
Sherman Sprat	George Morfogen
Mr. Shoemaker	Jerry Stiller
Mrs. Shoemaker	Rose Arrick
Dr. Julius Fuldauer	Herbert Berghof
Mickey Bellinger	Kevin McCarthy
Mr. Henry	William Robertson
Fibby Geyer	Joseph Maher
Cooky	Marshall Colt

"Those Lips, Those Eyes" is a solid picture that accomplishes its limited goals very well. On the other hand, its sights are not set very high and it would seem to face a number of obstacles in today's marketplace.

Not only is the title unfortunately vague, the story about backstage life in summer stock is hard to summarize and perhaps limited in interest, even if it had anything new to say about the heartbreaks of acting, which it doesn't. Finally, the trio of stars, Frank Langella, Glynnis O'Connor and Thomas Hulce, are hardly boxoffice heavyweights.

Those probably fatal illnesses aside, "Lips" is charmingly simple and straightforward, thanks to a good script by David Shaber, sensitive direction by Michael Pressman and the uncomplicated performances of the stars.

Though Langella gets top billing, most of the scenes fall on young Hulce, who ably brings off the role of a stagestruck young pre-med student, working part time — 'for the first time — as prop boy in an outdoor summer theatre in Ohio.

Hopelessly incompetent at his initial tasks and severely bullied and berated by stage director George Morfogen, Hulce is defended and befriended by Langella, likable as the star of the stock company who has enough talent for tank towns but tortures himself with futile dreams of making it to Broadway.

But in Hulce's eyes, Langella is a marquee idol to be envied, especially for the different girls he goes home with every night. And thanks to Langella's largesse, Hulce lucks into his own over-his-head romance with O'Connor, who nicely plays a dancer from the chorus with very practical ideas about romance on the road.

Jerry Stiller and Rose Arrick are also good as Hulce's parents, the proverbial worriers about his taking up with showbiz instead of medicine. And Kevin McCarthy is okay, but limited to a brief appearance, as the big-time agent who's the focal point of Langella's dreams.

Tech credits are all good in setting up the somewhat seedy atmosphere of the summer theatre. In sum, "Lips" is a film about the backwaters of the world of legitimate theatre and ironically itself falls into the backwaters of commercial filmmaking. —*Har.*

The Fiendish Plot
Of Dr. Fu Manchu
(COMEDY)

Sad epitaph to Sellers' career.

Hollywood, Aug. 5.
An Orion Pictures release through Warner Brothers of a Zev Braun production. Produced by Zev Braun, Leland Nolan. Executive producer, Hugh M. Hefner. Stars Peter Sellers. Directed by Piers Haggard. Screenplay, Jim Moloney, Rudy Dochtermann, based on characters from the Sax Rohmer novels; camera (Technicolor), Jean Tournier; editors, Russell Lloyd, Claudine Bouche; music, Marc Wilkinson; production design, Alex Trauner; costume design, John Bloomfield; sound, Daniel Brisseau; associate producer, Yannoulla Wakefield; assistant directors, Paul Feyder, Jerry Toomey. Reviewed at the Directors Guild of America Theatre, L.A., Aug. 5, 1980. (MPAA Rating: PG.) Running time: 98 MINS.
Fu Manchu/Nayland Smith . Peter Sellers
Alice Rage . . . . Helen Mirren
Sir Roger Avery . . . . David Tomlinson
Joe Capone . . . . Sid Caesar
Robert Townsend . . . . .Simon Williams
Peter Williams . . . . .Steve Franken
Ismail . . . . .Stratford Johns
Perkins . . . . .John Le Mesurier

Sadly, Peter Sellers' last film is a misfire from beginning to end. Feature has no reason to exist except for the star to try on some new accents and makeup. Sellers' many fans will certainly choose to regard "Being There" as his final testament and this should accordingly slip from sight before long.

Reportedly plagued by production problems, partially written and directed by Sellers himself, and cut just before opening by about 10 minutes, pic begins with a nifty kung fu credit sequence but it's all downhill from there. Set in early 1930s, shaky story has 168-year-old Oriental super-villain pulling off robberies of the Crown Jewels and other priceless items, necessary ingredients for a youth-restoring elixir.

Pitted against him is a group of sleuths led by a mild-mannered retired English detective, also portrayed by Sellers. Unfortunately, lumpy screenplay, which never finds proper form or tone, is largely filled with digressive material, including some pointless musical numbers, so what should have had contours of a streamlined suspenser, albeit with comedic slant, just clunks along to no discernable end.

Macabre note is also struck throughout in that many scenes feature the evil but feeble doctor, desperately awaiting delivery of rare materials for his serum, being tentatively snatched from death's doors by electrification, which sends Sellers into wild, twitching spasms. Totally inane ending, mercifully abbreviated, has star celebrating his regained youth by impersonating Elvis Presley, belting out something called "Rock A Fu."

Sellers unexpectedly selected an upper-class British accent, for Fu Manchu, while vocal and physical aspects of the shrewd inspector seem virtually those of the actor himself. Both were intriguing choices, but performances remain concepts rather than fully fleshed out characterizations.

Helen Mirren gives it a good shot as an undercover agent who becomes the Asian's concubine, but no one shines under flat direction credited to Piers Haggard.

Tech contributions, particularly Alex Trauner's handsome production design, are elaborate but only provide fancy dressing for the dispiriting endeavor. —*Cart.*

Willie & Phil
(COLOR)

Pleasant but low-key Paul Mazursky film about romantic threesome. Faces mild b.o. prospects.

Hollywood, Aug. 7.
Twentieth Century-Fox release. Produced by Paul Mazursky and Tony Ray. Written and directed by Mazursky. Features entire cast. Camera (DeLuxe Color), Sven Nykvist; music, Claude Bolling, with additional music from "Jules Et Jim" by Georges Delerue; editor, Donn Cambern; production designer, Pato Guzman; set decorators, Ed Stewart, Ernie Bishop; sound, Dennis Maitland, Arthur Piantadosi, Les Fresholtz, Michael Minkler; associate producer/assistant director, Terry Donnelly. Reviewed at Solari Theatre, BevHills, Aug. 6, 1980. (MPAA Rating: R.) Running time: 116 MINS.
Willie Kaufman . . . . Michael Ontkean
Jeannette Sutherland . . . . Margot Kidder
Phil D'Amico . . . . Ray Sharkey
Mrs. Kaufman . . . . .Jan Miner
Mr. Kaufman . . . . Tom Brennan
Mrs. D'Amico . . . . .Julie Bovasso
Mr. D'Amico . . . . Louis Guss
Mrs. Sutherland . . . . . Kathleen Maguire
Patti Sutherland . . . . Kaki Hunter
Rena . . . . .Kristine DeBell
Zelda Kaufman #4 . . . . Alison Cass Shurpin
Zelda Kaufman #3 . . . . . . .Christine Varnai
Wilson . . . . Laurence Fishburne III
Park Bum . . . . .Walter N. Lowery
Karen . . . . .Jerry Hall
Used Car
 Salesperson . . . . Helen Hanft
Black Kid . . . . Hubert J. Edwards
Natalie Wood . . . . .Natalie Wood

Though it doesn't satisfy all the ambitions it sets for itself, Paul Nazursky's "Willie & Phil" is an amiable and humane film about a menage-a-trois spanning the decade just passed. Mazursky's compassionate eye for character and his wry wit balance out a tendency to overromanticize and sentimentalize his characters' situation, but the film is not provocative enough to augur more than modest b.o. returns. The 20th-Fox release is a prestige item that ought to go over with the kind of audience that enjoys foreign sexual souffles like "Cousin, Cousine" or "Get Out Your Handkerchiefs."

Michael Ontkean and Ray Sharkey play the title characters — roles once intended for Woody Allen and Al Pacino — and Margot Kidder completes the romantic triangle, which forms in Greenwich Village at the beginning of the 1970s and winds up in Malibu nine years later. Along the way, Mazursky deftly traces changing sexual mores and other social values while portraying the trio, despite their adventurous entertainment, as typical representatives of their generation's hopes and confusions.

Beginning rather coyly with the two men meeting at a Bleecker Street Cinema screening of Truffaut's classic 1962 film about a menage-a-trois, "Jules Et Jim," Mazursky then has the two become friends so inseparable that they have trouble deciding who should board with Kidder. She gravitates more to Ontkean, whom she eventually marries and has a child with, but they share at least one night as a sexual threesome, and when the marriage falters, she mores in with Sharkey.

It's all handled in very civilized and low-key fashion by Mazursky and his characters, with none of the emotional peaks and valleys that made Truffaut's film such a memorable experience. The suspicion persists that all the unpleasant moments in the lives of Willie & Phil & Jeannette must have occurred off-screen. Mazursky honestly depicts the ultimate impossibility of making such a complex relationship last, but since he is dealing with a decade in which most twosomes found it hard to deal with each other, let alone threesomes, the approach seems evasive.

Some of the evasiveness comes in the treatment of sex. American films dealing with this kind of theme usually seem strangely reluctant to level with the audience about what actually happens in bed, and after a big buildup, this pic discreetly cuts away before anything really happens. Audience is left unclear as to the exact dynamics of the triangular character relationship, with several loose ends left unexamined, such as the hints that at least on Willie's side, the feelings between the two men may not be entirely platonic.

Since parting creative company with his former writing partner Larry Tucker, with whom he crafted his first and still best film as a director, "Bob & Carol & Ted & Alice," Mazursky has softened his satirical approach and his pix have become fuzzier around the edges. The treatment of Sharkey's affluent Malibu lifestyle is surprisingly mild and approving from a director who in the past has fashioned many hilarious barbs at Southern California.

The earlier Mazursky might have found satiric leverage in the realization that relationships such as the one portrayed here, while shockingly avant-garde at the beginning of the decade, were progressively aped and co-opted by the middle class until by the late 1970s there was nothing more than mildly titillating about them. None of that comes across here, since Mazursky so warmly cuddles his three loveable characters he rubs all the rough edges off them.

Sharkey scores triumphantly with his touching and bouyantly funny portrayal of the kind of Hollywood character who proudly labels himself "street-smart" while wholeheartedly embracing all the L.A. trendiness. Mazursky's satiric instincts falter more with Ontkean, who sincerely but rather limply plays a meandering misfit constantly in search of an answer; unfortunately, his quest is rendered in strictly external terms and the film never gets far inside his head. Kidder, though warm and sexy, doesn't have the magnetism necessary to keep two men under her spell for so long, and her Kentucky accent is as uncertain as her emotions. But she convincingly captures the painfully growing self-awareness of women in the 1970s.

Tech aspects are first-rate, particularly the rich and inventive lensing by Sven Nykvist and the unobtrusive sense of changing time conveyed by production designer Pato Guzman. Tony Ray coproduced with Mazursky. —Mac.

Xanadu
(COLOR)

Mystical fantasy. Poor prospects despite Newton-John.

A Universal Pictures release, produced by Lawrence Gordon. Exec producer, Lee Kramer. Features entire cast. Directed by Robert Greenwald. Screenplay, Richard Christian Danus, Marc Reid Rubel. Camera (Technicolor), Victor J. Kemper; editor, Dennis Virkler; sound (Dolby Stereo), Robert Gravenor; coproducer, Joel Silver; production design, John W. Corso; costumes, Bobbie Mannix; choreography, Kenny Ortega, Jerry Trent; assistant director, Dan Kolsrud; animation, Don Bluth; visual effects, Richard Greenberg; music, Barry DeVorzon; songs, Jeff Lynne, John Farrar, performed by Olivia Newton-John and Electric Light Orchestra. Reviewed at Chinese Theatre, Aug. 8, 1980. (MPAA rating: PG.) Running time: **93 MINS.**
Kira .... Olivia Newton-John
Danny McGuire .... Gene Kelly
Sonny Malone ....Michael Beck
Simpson .... James Sloyan
Helen .... Dimitra Arliss
Sandra .... Katie Hanley
Richie .... Fred McCarren
Jo .... Ren Woods

After cancelling its scheduled critics' screening Wednesday (6), Universal Pictures opened "Xanadu" cold Friday (8), suggesting rumor be true that the studio has little hope for the picture. Tsk, tsk for such faint-of-heart. After all, who else this summer has Olivia Newton-John starring as a roller-skating lightbulb?

When it gets on the small screen, as it surely will soon, don't miss "Xanadu," however. It is truly a stupendously bad film whose only salvage is the music (which has already provided four hit singles.) In a sense, the music is well-integrated into the film, if well-integrated means it comes somewhere

between the start of the picture and the finish.

Olivia Newton-John plays a muse, first seen with her eight sisters painted on a wall. Suddenly, they all come alive, with glowing stuff all around them, singing and zipping hither and yon, apparently looking for a script that will never be found.

Newton-John's task is to inspire Michael Beck in his work as an artist. For this she stops glowing and he thinks she's a real girl, despite the sun dress she wears with roller skates and rags around both ankles.

Beck in turns meets millionaire Gene Kelly, who once played the clarinet before he got rich in the construction business. Way back in 1945, he too had been wooed by the same muse, as shown in a flashback, but she had her hair up then and wore an army suit. She disappeared back then and he's still carrying a torch for her, as they said in those days, but doesn't recognize her when she comes around with Beck. But it's not the roller-skates; Kelly has a pair of those himself. It may be the rags on her feet.

Anyway, Kelly dreams of someday opening another little soft-music joint of his own while Beck would like to open a rock palace and Newton-John is neutral so long as she gets to go opening night. So they compromise on a roller-derby disco.

But love is threatening and Newton-John decides it's best for all if she skips opening night and goes back into the painting on the wall, so she starts glowing again and bids Beck farewell. But he gets up a head of steam and skates into the wall after her and winds up somewhere near Mt. Olympus where he gets to glow, too, and talk to Zeus — and Mrs. Zeus.

Everything turns out okay, though, and he gets to take Newton-John to the roller disco, where there are people with pink hair and so many other bizarre costumes that nobody would notice if she's glowing or not. So she just sings a jillion songs, with different costumes on for each and then disappears again.

Beck is sad for just a moment until he meets a waitress who looks just like Newton-John. Yes, he really does. And the picture is over.

The small audience at one of the first opening-day screenings went out humming. Or maybe groaning. Sometimes it's hard to tell. —Har.

Third World, Prisoner in the Street
(FRENCH-DOCU-COLOR)

Paris, July 28.
A Mediane Films release of an Island International and Mediane Films production. Stars the Reggae group Third World. Written and directed by Jerome Laperrousaz. Camera (color), Etienne Fauduet; editor, Roselyne Petit, Noun Serra; music, Third World. Reviewed at the Saint-Severin Studio, Paris, July 26, 1980. Running time: **80 MINS.**
With: The Third-World musicians (Michael Cooper, Stephen Coore, Bunny Rugs, Richard Daley, Irwin Jarret, William Stewart).
(English Soundtrack)

This portrait of a leading Jamaican Reggae group, Third World, falls easy on the ears, and, thanks to the warm colors of Etienne Fauduet's cinematography, is equally pleasing to the eye. Director Jerome Laperrousaz' aim is modest: he conventionally records concert numbers, discreetly and without editorial fuss, and alternates them with casual sequences of the musicians at ease, riffing, smoking, joking, jogging, explaining to the camera what Reggae means to them, and to the environment that nurtured it.

The group's music is pulsating and engaging, the musicians affable and charming in that mellifluous West Indian manner of speaking. One is quickly won over by the vivacity and high spirits of the group and the rhythmic way they live in their music even when they aren't performing. As social record, picture is thin and doesn't probe any further than what the musicians tell us about harsh life of the lower social classes.

Entire picture is, of course, in English and should do well in specialized booking abroad, particularly in non-commercial and university situations. —Len.

The Octagon
(COLOR)

Colorful chopsocky actioner with Chuck Morris should please fans of genre.

Hollywood, Aug. 8.
American Cinema release, produced by Joel Freeman; exec producers, Michael Leone and Alan Belkin. Features entire cast. Directed by Eric Karson. Screenplay, Leigh Chapman, from a story by Paul Aaron, Chapman; camera (CFI Color), Michel Hugo; music, Dick Halligan; editor, Dann Cahn; production designer, James Schoppe; set decoration, Jim Hassinger; sound, Glenn Anderson; karate fight choreography, Chuck Norris, Aaron Norris; stunt coordinator, Aaron Norris; assistant director, Skip Surguine. Reviewed at CFI Lab, Hollywood, Aug. 8, 1980. (MPAA Rating: R). Running time: **103 MINS.**
Scott James .... Chuck Norris
Justine .... Karen Carlson
McCarn .... Lee Van Cleef

A.J. .... Art Hindle
Aura .... Carol Bagdasarian
Nancy .... Kim Lankford
Seikura .... Tadashi Yamashita
Doggo .... Kurt Grayson
Katsumoto .... Yuki Shimoda
Tibor .... Larry D. Mann
Isawa .... John Fujioka
Sharkey .... Jack Carter

American Cinema has done good business with its two previous chopsocky films starring Chuck Norris, "Good Guys Wear Black" and "A Force Of One," and its new one, "The Octagon," ought to keep the fans happy. A bizarre plot involving the Ninja cult of Oriental assassins with international terrorism provides plenty of chances for Norris and other martial arts experts to do their stuff, and pic has a nicely stylized look with excellent lensing and music.

Subtleties of writing and performing are not this film's selling points, so it would be misleading to belabor those inadequacies. What producer Joel Freeman and exec producers Michael Leone and Alan Belkin set out to deliver are frequent and elaborately staged action sequences (however far-out and improbable), dollops of Oriental mysticism to give the mayhem a facade of higher meaning, and stolid integrity from Norris, an actor of limited resources but a likable person as the Clint Eastwood of kung-fu.

Screenwriter Leigh Chapman, working from a story she wrote with Paul Aaron, weaves a wildly incredible but entertaining tale of retired martial arts champ Norris being recruited by wealthy Karen Carlson to rub out the terrorists who have earmarked her for death. Norris is reluctant to get involved in somebody else's problems, but he comes around when he realizes his nemesis is Tadashi Yamashita, his sworn enemy from their youthful days as chopsocky pupils. The vendetta culminates in a pitched battle at the octagonal training compound of the Ninja cult, which serves as a school for terrorists of all types.

Director Eric Karson keeps the film moving briskly and colorfully with the aid of Michel Hugo's strikingly attractive photography, crisp editing by Dann Cahn, and inventive music by Dick Halligan. Chuck and Aaron Norris were responsible for the effective action choreography.

Supporting cast is well chosen, including a trio of attractive leading ladies who succeed each other as they die one by one, an unusual narrative gambit. Wholesome Kim Lankford is a dancer unexpectedly mixed up in terrorism, classy Karen Carlson is the rich target, and sultry Carol Bagdasarian is a terrorist trainee who helps Norris destroy the compound. Bagdasarian, a stunning beauty, makes the most impact of the three. Lee Van Cleef has fun with an eccentric role of a mysterious mercenary, Art Hindle is suitably boorish as Norris' undisciplined brother, and Yuki Shimoda has authority as the Ninja master. —*Mac.*

The Saviour
(HONG KONG-COLOR)

Hong Kong, July 29.
A Pearl City Films production by Teddy Robin. Produced by Teddy Robin. Directed by Ronny Yu. Stars Pak Wing-Ying, Danny Ng, Gigi Wong, Nick Cox; story, Ronny Yu; screenplay, Alfred Chow; camera (color, Tony Hope; music, Teddy Robin. (No other credits provided).
Reviewed at State Theatre, Hong Kong, July 28, 1980. Running time: **87 MINS.**
(Cantonese dialog with English sub-titles).

There are three saviors in "The Saviour" and they all survive with high marks in this modern Cantonese film laden with carefully jumbled jigsaw, cinema puzzles that seem all too familiar yet different.

The first is a hard-working Hong Kong police inspector who wakes up early every morning and prepares himself with routine precision in the same manner that a performer would for a stage appearance. He tries to rid society of its crimes and assorted sins through job dedication.

The second savior is a rich young man, emotionally handicapped by a gruesome childhood vision of seeing his mother driven to suicide by the adulterous affairs of his father. As a form of revenge he dispatches prostitutes with a knife to satisfy his distorted perception about women's sexual relationship with men.

The third savior is Ronny Yu, a talented and Americanized Chinese director, one of the few saviors of the Hong Kong film industry, a comatose industry numbed with dried up kung-fu jabs, colorless chop suey comedies and tall promises of local companies trying to be international but yet to produce a film of merit.

What makes "The Saviour" unique is the frisky presentation and fancy direction of Yu, a local version of Brian De Palma.

Yu, as a director, is definitely a man to watch and though he tends to imitate at present, his true style will eventually emerge with the passing of years.

Vigor, red herrings, vibrant, creative flair, comedic touches mixed with sensitivity and flamboyance are other qualities viewers will discover in this cops and robbers versus madman on the prowl genre.

All told, "The Saviour" is a calculated thriller that makes the flesh creep with pleasurable screen perils. It saves the dry local movie spell of summer 1980. —*Mel.*

Exterieur Nuit
(Exterior Night)
(FRENCH-COLOR)

Paris, July 28.
A Films Noirs production. Features entire cast. Directed and edited by Jacques Bral. Written by Bral, Jean-Paul Leca, Julien Levi, from an original idea by Noel Burch; camera (color), Pierre-William Glenn; music, Karl-Heinz Schafer. Reviewed at Club 13, Paris, June 15, 1980. Running time: **110 MINS.**
With: Christine Boisson, Andre Dussolier, Gerard Lanvin, Jean-Pierre Sentier.

Jacques Bral's "Exterieur nuit" drew considerable attention in the "Perspectives on French Cinema" parallel event at this year's Cannes Festival, where it won a newly-created sidebar prize, "The Chance of Cannes," which guarantees picture major fall release on all of the three major French circuits.

Award was merited and should help put a spotlight on a talented 32-year-old director (who has already made three previous features) and the fine young cast of this brooding drama about urban loneliness and emotional misalliance. Film could have chances in foreign situations and festivals.

Script, by Bral, Jean-Paul Leca and Julien Levi, follows a slightly blase young musician who breaks completely with his usual lifestyle and takes up temporary refuge with a writer-friend. One night he allows himself to be picked up an aggressive young woman cabbie. They meet night after night, playing out a volatile, troubled relationship against a backdrop of nocturnal Paris bars, clubs and streets. The writer, who allows them to use his apartment, wants the girl as well, but is put off by her barely concealed violent nature. She finally disappears completely one day, apparently headed for other climes.

Bral describes with force and emotion a night world he seems to know only too well. The true excellence of much of the film (which is somewhat overlong, though never dull) is that he gets beyond a facile, brute realism to find a genuine resonance in his personages and their environment. Bral's acute filmic sense, for example, is evident in the manner in which he uses the taxi cab as an extension of the girl's troubled nature, giving it a dramatic and symbolic value without straining for effect.

Christine Boisson, a diminutive 23-year-old actress whose first major role this is, is stunning as the aggressive young woman scarred by barely-contained rage and desperation, violent enough to beat up difficult passengers or mug them for their wallets.

Another relative newcomer, Gerard Lanvin, 29, remarked at Cannes for his performance in Bertrand Tavernier's "Une Semaine de Vacances," has presence and power as the musician. Andre Dussolier, 34, a well-known face to French tv and theatre audiences (in film, he was the radiant Sir Gawain in Eric Rohmer's "Perceval"), is appealingly forlorn as the writer.

The excellent color photography is the work of Pierre-William Glenn. —*Len.*

Qua La Mano
(Give Me Five)
(ITALIAN-COLOR)

Rome, July 28.
A Titanus release, produced by Luigi and Aurelio De Laurentiis for Filmauro productions. Stars Adriano Celentano, Enrico Montesano. Directed by Pasquale Festa Campanile. Screenplay, Enrico Oldoini, Ottavio Jemma; camera (Eastmancolor), Giancarlo Ferrando; art director, Enrico Fiorentini and Enrico Tovaieri; editor, Alberto Galletti; music, Detto Mariano. Reviewed at Adriano Cinema, Rome, July 28, 1980. Running time: **120 MINS.**
Dancing priest . . . . Adriano Celentano
Mayor . . . . Renzo Montagnani
Orazio . . . . Enrico Montesano
The Pope . . . . Philippe Leroy

The season's Italian boxoffice leader this fluffy two-episode comedy can thank a pair of top comic stars and some nice story ideas for its phenomenal popularity. Enrico Montesano, headlining the saga of a Roman cabdriver who gets to know the Pope, and Adriano Celentano, hero of "The Dancing Priest" SEG, never appear on screen together but star in separate stories glued back-to-back.

They are united by scriptwriters' and helmer's simple humor and sizable narrative gifts that keep audiences tuned in to the overly long stories. Export success for such a pure-bred package of Italian comedy is hard to predict where stars are not a major drawing card.

In first episode, a poor horse-and-buggy driver fakes an accident to meet the Pope, and on subsequent acquaintanceship develops. His dream of standing in the window behind the Pope at the Sunday blessing — and waving to his friends — sums up the pathetic aspirations of the character.

Great moments are rare but this modern-day fairy tale is well-conceived and remains amusing. Philippe Leroy is a dignified and worthy foreign Pope, complete with accent and retinue of French nuns. Montesano, ideal choice for Papal groupie, Orazio, is a likable young comedian able to get laughs out of a suitable script.

Second episode is so completely dominated by powerhouse Cele-

ntano, celebrated singer and entertainer, it could be a spin-off from one of his tv specials. A nonconformist parish priest transforms himself into disco king on Saturday night, happily rock 'n rolling incognito until the matter is brought to the bishop's attention. At the last minute he will be saved by that comprehensive deus-ex-machina, The Pope, who has seen him on a tv dance contest.

On of "Five's" more uproarious scenes is Celentano's secret kitchen boogeying while he prepares supper, the first time we see him "in action." By the end of the hour not even his considerable balletic and comic talents can keep the predictable, repetitive situations from waltzing some viewers off toward dreamland.

Though the subplot about the town's need for trees is weak, supporting actor Renzo Montagnari as the dieting town mayor aids whenever he is on the screen. His role could have been beefier as ideological antagonist to Celentano per the Don Camillo novels he is taken from. Typically "Five" chooses the adolescent humor of practical jokes to more sophisticated comedy, which may be one of its limiting factors on foreign markets.

This innocent "religious comedy" is most interesting for its obsession-awe toward the great foreign Pope (only common element of the two stories) who dominates Rome the way Elizabeth Taylor and Charlton Heston once did the Via Veneto. The order of episodes is right in showing how the people's response to the openness and humanity of the Pontiff leads naturally to a loosening up in the lower orders of the clergy — one of the secrets of "Five's" very conemporary and national appeal.

A subject for meditation is the relation of production quality to the pic's success: from haphazard lighting and imprecise camerawork to heavy sloughed off dialog, technical credits in "Five" barely rate a "2" — and you would think no one noticed. —*Yung.*

Yugoslav Festival

Tajna Nikole Tesle
(The Secret of Nikola Tesla)
(YUGOSLAV-COLOR)

Pula, Aug. 12.
Yugoslavia Film release of Zagreb Film-Kinematografi production. Features entire cast. Directed by Krsto Papic. Screenplay, Ivo Bresan, Ivan Kusan, Papic; camera (Eastmancolor), Ivica Rajkovic; art director, Veljko Despotovic; music, Andelko Klobucar. Reviewed at Pula Film Fest, July 30, '80. Running time: **120 MINS.**
With: Petar Bozovic, Orson Welles, Strother Martin, Dennis Patrick, Oja

Kodar, Boris Buzancic, Charles Millot, Ana Karic.

(In English)

A too reverent bio film on the great Yugoslav electrical genius Nikola Tesla who did all his work in America at the turn-of-the-century. Film intimates his interest in perhaps getting in touch with extra-terrestrial forces and his attempt to find a source of new energy from space.

But it remains didactic rather than breaking away from exposition to a more enticing insight into this man who has become the guiding force of some modern-day sects and who some feel is alive on another planet today.

Tesla was a sort of Howard Hughes figure who could not stand being touched, though, unlike Hughes, there did not seem to be any women in his life. Film has some solid Yank character actors involved, playing people in Tesla's life, that could help it for some play-off and then tv usage abroad on Tesla's unusual character, life and theories.

Orson Welles is a shrewd, helpful but then finally selfish financier as J.P. Morgan who withdraws his help for Tesla's final project when he, Welles, thinks it will not serve his purpose. The late Strother Martin is George Westinghouse who helped Tesla and was aided in return, and Dennis Patrick is a mean, vindictive Thomas Edison who held up Tesla's recognition when Tesla's superior ac current showed more strength than his, Edison's, dc.

The film is directed simply, but sometimes the American idiom and pace escapes filmmaker Krsto Papic. Specialized and school usage are there for this well made but sometimes solid tale of an eccentric but great man's life. —*Mosk.*

Petrijin Venac
(Petrija's Wreath)
(YUGOSLAV-COLOR)

Pula, Aug. 12.
Yugoslavia Film release of Centar Film production. Features entire cast. Directed by Srdan Karanovic. Screenplay, Karanovic from the book by Dragoslav Mihakilovic; art director, Miodrag Miric; music, Zoran Simjanovic. Reviewed at Pula Film Fest, Aug. 28, '80. Running time: **97 MINS.**
With: Mirjana Karanovic, Dragan Maksimovic, Marko Nicolic, Pavle Vujisic.

A sober, dense film about the life of an illiterate peasant woman before, during and after the last war. Fraught with trauma and tragedy, the film avoids falling into melodrama or bathos by adroit direction by Srdan Karanovic and expert acting down the line.

Based on a book using the life of a real woman, film starts with her first marriage to a hardhearted peasant. She does not get along with the mother-in-law who leads to the first tragic event when she, the mother, does not come in time to cut the umbilical cord after the birth of the first child.

The woman has the child alone and knew nothing of what to do. She has a daughter who dies of disease during the war and she is thrown out by her husband. She is helped by a tavern owner who becomes her lover and she then marries a miner.

She remains superstitious, and, working by mistake on a religious holiday after the war, she hears of her husband's accident. She blames it on herself. But she faces up and tries to help him as he grows bitter and finally dies of his wounds. The mine is closed but she stays in this almost deserted village waiting to join her child and last husband whom she appears to see at times.

A lifetime odyssey of intense perception that gives this a deep ring of authenticity. Not an easy film, but one that could find outlets with proper handling on its depiction of a life that was caught up in its time.

The film will also surely make the fest circuits this year, and, in fact, has already been invited to the Venice Film Fest later this month. It should make an impact though it is specialized and demanding.

—*Mosk.*

Nasvidenje V. Naslednji Vojni
(See You In The Next War)
(YUGOSLAV-COLOR)

Pula, Aug. 12.
Yugoslavia Film release of Viba Film, Vesna Film production. Features entire cast. Written and directed by Zivojin Pavlovic from book by Vitomil Zupan. Camera (Eastmancolor), Tomoslav Pinter; music, Bojan Adamic. Reviewed at Pula Film Fest, July 29, '80. Running time: **113 MINS.**
With: Metod Pevec, Hans Christian Blech, Milan Puzic, Boris Juh, Tanja Poberznik, Ruth Gassman.

A demystification of the usual zealously romantic, revolutionary partisan films comes at a time when this genre has about been exhausted. Film is a good epitaph for it is a meditation on war and revolution and the Yugoslav experience in World War II touched on both.

A onetime Yugoslav partisan and an ex-German soldier meet during a vacation in Spain. They talk and the Yugoslav relives his partisan experiences. He sees it as something he had to do and did not understand its political side while the German, who once voted for Hitler but turned against him, has become a pacifist.

The German is writing a book and notes he once saw a dead partisan and a dead German soldier. The former seemed emaciated and Christ-like but the German remained a soldier.

The Yugoslav admits to an obsession with those days and even remembrances of a fleeting glory and adventurousness as well as the killing of some instincts, namely love, rather than fortifying them. His slogging lovemaking with a dedicated communist girl is only endured by her and his actions are rote.

The war scenes are done with dash and insight and there are the dedicated revolutionaries, the dogmatic ones and others in for it was war. There are echoes of the Spanish Civil War and its disillusion also.

Zivojin Pavlovic is a virile director and excellent in narrative flair. The film emerges as pacifistic but looking at the mechanics of a just war. This gives the film a dramatic clout and an ambivalence that makes it intriguing and unusual. Another impressive Yugoslav film that should find fest footing and perhaps offshore legs as war films, romantic, questioning and abstract, seem to be gaining audience interest again. —*Mosk.*

Splav Meduze
(The Medusa Raft)
(YUGOSLAV-COLOR)

Pula, Aug. 12.
Yugoslavia Film release of Viba Film-Televizija Beograd production. Features entire cast. Directed, photographed (Eastmancolor) and edited by Karpo Godina. Reviewed at Pula Film Fest, July 29, '80. Running time: **93 MINS.**
With: Olga Kacjan, Vladilava Jevic, Boris Komnenic, Erol Kadic, Franco Lasic, Radmila Zilkovic, Petar Kralj.

The film reveals a rapturous feel for the early 1920s when the world seemed to be marking time before the Depression and ruinous wars. It has the romantic elan of dreamers caught up in changing realities that they approach as a sort of game or theatrically, making it reminiscent of the Russian film, "Slave of Love."

But director Karpo Godina goes his own way as two bored school teachers in a small town are visited by a colorful set of would-be revolutionaries. They are imbued with the early Russian revolutionary freedom of creation which makes them decide to do a show to stage in the streets to inculcate people to new changes in politics and society.

They recruit a strong man who can hold back two cars going in different directions by holding chains in the crook of each arm. Slowly this joyful odyssey turns tragic as two women fight over the strong man, one couple is destroyed when the man is accidentally killed and they split up.

One girl ends up teaching blind children and she becomes practically a saint. The film came in for some attacks as being anti-communist by some local critics. But it is more a look at a zeal for change cloaked in dreams rather than reality and not against it, per se.

On its grace, inventiveness and charm film could find outlets abroad outside the fest circuits where it would be preaching to the converted. —*Mosk.*

Snovi, Zivot, Smrt Filipa Filipovic
(Dreams, Life, the Death of Filip Filipovic)
(YUGOSLAV-COLOR)

Pula, Aug. 12.
Yugoslavia Film release of CFS Kosutnjak - Oour Avala Film - Televizija Beograd production. Features entire cast. Directed by Milos Radivojevic. Screenplay, Slobodan Stojanvic, Milovan Vitezovic, Alesander Popovic, Novica Savic, Misa Stanislavjevic, Radivojevic; camera (Eastmancolor), Bozidar Nikolic; music, Kornelije Kovac. Reviewed at Pula Film Festival, July 26, '80. Running time, **100 MINS.**
With: Aleksander Bercek, Milena Dravic, Bata Zivojinovic, Drago Cuma, Predrag Ejdus.

Milos Radivojevic has been doing mainly experimental films. After a harsh tale of youthful run-ins with simmering violence, a wordless film about a man reliving his life and an uneven romantic item about a man trying to find his own morality in a hamstrung life he now goes in for a sort of chamber look at the life and death of the first secretary of the Yugoslav Communist Party who was killed in Stalin's purges in Russia in 1938.

There is the constant traveling, the constant prison forays as this man, Filip Filipovic, tries to create a leftist movement in Yugoslavia before and after World War 1. The film is told through Filipovic's work on his own memoirs.

Interspersed with meetings, his brief stays with his sister and his aid from his father, are stock footage of wars and the starvation in Russia after the revolution. It might mean more on its home grounds due to all its allusions to historical personages and events.

A wide angled lens is used in most of the scenes he reminisces about which distort things as perhaps does memory. The film is talky but finally gets a measure of visual finesse as two soldiers take him out in the snow to kill him. Mainly a local item, but film does possess an unusual sense of period in its scenes of meetings and demonstrations.

— *Mosk.*

Prkosna Delta
(Defiant Delta)
(YUGOSLAV-COLOR)

Pula, Aug. 12.

Yugoslavia Film release of Sutjeska Film production. Features entire cast. Written and directed by Vesna Ljubic. Camera (Eastmancolor), Dragan Resner; music, Vangelius Papatanisu. Reviewed at Pula Film Fest, Aug. 1, '80. Running time: **90 MINS.**

With: Glorica Popovic, Ante Vican, Ivica Klenenc, Jadranka Matkovic, Spaso Papac.

Vesna Ljubic was the only femme director to make a film in Yugoslavia this year. It deals with survival in the last, and early part of this, century as different armies came through a small town on a delta.

The film is reserved and has a fine feel for the land and traditions slowly being destroyed by enemy incursions that take young men, rape the women and also requisition food and livestock. Besides the everlasting wars, there is occasional flood.

One woman feels that only explosives can make a tunnel to relieve the floods though they can not damn up mankind's follies. She approaches soldiers asking for explosives. She gives into some for them but never gets any, is raped by one who is killed by the townspeople as many are shot for it, and is finally shot herself when caught trying to steal explosives and nobody will listen to her reasons.

Perhaps a bit reserved for a more forceful poetic drive and dramatic epiphany, the film has a fine feeling for the times and traditional life and could show up at specialized festivals though not incisive enough for much general chances abroad.

—*Mosk.*

Osam Kila Srece
(Eight Kilos of Happiness)
(YUGOSLAV-COLOR)

Pula, Aug. 12.

Yugoslavia Film release of Radna Organizacija Film Cetedesetprva - Avala Film - Televizija Beograd production. Features entire cast. Written and directed by Purisa Dordevic. Camera (Eastmancolor), Zika Milic; music, Vojkan Simic. Reviewed at Pula Film Fest, Aug. 1, '80. Running time, **70 MINS.**

With: Milena Dravic, Dragan Maksimovic, Maja Lalevic, Predrag Kristovic.

An unassuming fable about an incident during the last war when a gypsy girl sacrifices herself for her young lover, a partisan who has taken French leave for a while. Somewhat too convoluted to bring it off, the film might be more effective on tv in its close-quarter, freewheeling style where a lack of background may be accepted.

There are gypsy songs under-

lying this love affair. The Germans have decided to kill 50 hostages when one of their men is killed by partisans. They need one more and when they come on the girl and the deserter partisan she insists she will go for his hand has said he must live when she read its lines.

Film is charming but finally lightweight and a bit too cluttered to fuse it into the poetic statement on war and love it aims at. Oldtimer Purisa Dordevic has made some original films in the partisan genre earlier and this new approach is lacking the fusion of feeling, wartime demands and an inventive edge the others possessed. —*Mosk.*

Olovna Brigada
(The Lead Brigade)
(YUGOSLAV-COLOR)

Pula, Aug. 12.

Yugoslavia Film release of Vardar Film-Makedonia Film production. Features entire cast. Directed by Kiril Cenevski. Screenplay, Cenevski; camera (Eastmancolor), Miso Samoilovski; music, Ilija Pejovski. Reviewed at Pula Film Fest, July 30, '80. Running time: **100 MINS.**

With: Miralem Zupcevic, Darko Dameski, Milja Vujanovic, Aco Janovski, Pavle Vujisic.

Director Kiril Cenevski moves his camera with precision and creates a strange, murky look at miners at work as well as singling out an engineer with personal as well as work trouble.

He neglects stopping long enough to make much sense out of this tale. It seems that an old part of a mine may have some new important ore worth mining. But it is dangerous and the men feel underpaid. Some are trapped studying the possibilities for a time of proving themselves as they try to get out.

The engineer has left his two-timing wife but misses his kid. He tries to go back to her but fails and loses a lovely mistress, too. But all this is opaque, utterly contrived and heavygoing and it remains a truly local film for it is hard to find anything but technique for its own sake in this would-be look at the hard life of miners and their personal problems. —*Mosk.*

Svetozar Markovic
(YUGOSLAV-COLOR)

Pula, Aug. 12.

Yugoslavia Film release of CFS Kosutnjak-Oour Avala Film — Televizija Beograd — Televizija Novi Sad production. Features entire cast. Directed by Eduard Galic. Screenplay, Momcilo Milankov, Milan Secerovic; camera (Eastmancolor), Aleksander Petkovic; music, Zoran Hristic. Reviewed at Pula Film Fest, July 27, '80. Running time: **109 MINS.**

With: Lazar Hristovski, Petar Kralj, Ljuba Tadic, Gojko Santic, Milan Strljic, Branislav Lecic.

Another bio-film based on a turn-of-the-century famous Yugoslav political figure. It is Svetozar Markovic who led to the founding of the socialist party. Film is somewhat too local in allusions, characters and treatment though it does evoke an unusual selfless figure destroyed by illness and the obtuseness, self-indulgence and machiavellianism around him.

It does not manage to evoke much feeling for the times and emerges more a mouthpiece than a truly assimilated political drama. It is talk rather than actions and visual indications that make the points about the need for new systems.

Many figures of the era including the Russian anarchist Bukinin parade by with often ill-fitting beards and moustaches. Film is a spinoff from a tv series which may explain its gaps and lack of contact with the times and the things surrounding the hero's ways, outlooks and final death in a foreign country from tb. Acting is acceptable though the film is technically uneven with color often unbalanced in different shots in the same scene.

—*Mosk.*

Smokey And The Bandit II
(COLOR)

Disappointing sequel to Burt Reynolds' hit should do excellent biz on echoes of the original.

Hollywood, Aug. 14.

Universal Pictures release of a Rastar/Mort Engelberg Production, produced by Hank Moonjean. Stars Burt Reynolds. Directed by Hal Needham. Screenplay, Jerry Belson and Brock Yates, from story by Michael Kane, based on characters created by Needham, Robert L. Levy; camera (Technicolor), Michael Butler; music supervison, Snuff Garrett; editors, Dann Cambern, William Gordean; production designer, Henry Bumstead; art direction, Bernie Cutler, set decoration, Richard De Cinces; sound, Jack Solomon, Donald O. Mitchell, Bill Nicholson, Rick Kline; stunt coordinator, Richard Ziker; assistant director, David Hamburger. Reviewed at Universal Studios, Universal City, Aug. 13, 1980. (MPAA Rating: PG.) Running time: **101 MINS.**

Bandit .... Burt Reynolds
Buford T. Justice/Reginald Van Justice/
Gaylord Justice .... Jackie Gleason
Cledus .... Jerry Reed
Doc .... Dom DeLuise
Carrie .... Sally Field
Little Enos .... Paul Williams
Big Enos .... Pat McCormick
John Conn .... David Huddleston
Junior .... Mike Henry
Governor .... John Anderson
Nice Lady .... Brenda Lee
Themselves ....The Statler Brothers,
        Don Williams, Terry Bradshaw,
        "Mean Joe" Greene, Joe Klecko
Fairground Owner .... Mel Tillis

Sally Field tells Burt Reynolds in "Smokey And The Bandit II" that he is no longer having fun doing what used to come naturally. If that's true, it's too bad, and this stale sequel seems to be evidence of going through the motions for money instead of fun. "Smokey II" has only intermittent flashes of the high spirits and rollicking action comedy that made the original such a popular hit (more than $60,000,000 domestic rentals). Enough good will was generated by the first one to ensure a hefty profit on the sequel, but the Universal release is bound to disappoint audiences' expectations.

A very weird film in all respects, "Smokey II" not only lacks the nonstop car chase action of the first one, concentrating instead on sluggish and mostly overdone attempts at roadside comedy skits, but it doesn't even bother to have Reynolds and Fields play the same characters they played so engagingly in the original.

Culprits include writers Jerry Belson and Brock Yates, who scripted from a story by Michael Kane, but director Hal Needham also deserves blame for imitating himself so badly.

Fans of the original will recall that CB trucker Reynolds was hired to run an illegal load of beer through the South, with sheriff Jackie Gleason on his trail and runaway bride

Field along for the thrill of it all. Here, Reynolds is hired to haul a pregnant elephant to the Republican convention (why he is under great time pressure to do so is not explained), and Gleason continues his vendetta, this time while split unfunnily into three characters.

The heavy reliance on elephant gags quite literally slows down the film, and though it's always enjoyable to watch an animal on screen, up-staging Reynolds to this extent is unhelpful as well as cloyingly cute. Kids will enjoy the film (which has an excess of verbal vulgarity that becomes tedious), but adults may wish for more action and romance and less elephant clowning.

A similar mistake is made in the car chase action, largely saved up here for the 10-minute finale, billed as the most elaborate ever staged. Dozens of cars and trucks slam into each other in badly timed shots that resemble outtakes from "The Blues Brothers."

The original "Smokey" was a cheap-looking film that looked like it was a riot to make for all concerned. But the enjoyment communicated itself to the viewers, which doesn't happen here.

Reynolds and Field carp at each other throughout the film, which picks their characters up after a separation of several months. He's become a drunk and she will only come back to help him for money. None of this has anything remotely to do with the characters they established in the original.

Ironically, the best part of the film is the unusual end credit sequence, a gag reel which shows the actors having fun when they blow lines in outtakes. That spirit got lost en route to the film itself. —*Mac.*

La Petite Sirene
(The Little Siren)
(FRENCH-COLOR)

Paris, Aug. 5.
A UGC release of an Apple Films/FR 3/-J. Roitfeld Productions/Les Lyons/Stephan Films coproduction. Produced, written and directed by Roger Andrieux. Features entire cast. Based on the novel "Les Petites Sirenes," by Yves Dangerfield; camera (color), Robert Alazraki; music, Alain Jomy; sound, Pierre Lorain; art director, Jean-Baptiste Poirot; costumes, Christian Gasc; editor, Kenout Peltier. Reviewed at Club 13, Paris, July 29, 1980. Running time: **104 MINS.**
Isabelle .... Laura Alexis
Georges . . . . .Philippe Leotard
Nelly .... .Evelyne Dress
Benedicte .... .Marie Dubois

Films about adolescent love tend often towards false fairytale sweetness. Roger Andrieux's "The Little Siren" marks a harsh rectification by recalling that fairy tales, despite their appeal, are frequently fundamentally horrible. Pic is an entry in the Montreal Film Festival.

Andrieux's film is about the incompatibility of a young girl's attempt to impose a fairy tale on her perceptions of the world with the realities of adult life. Film's originality and force come from Andrieux inscribing the tale in a banal contemporary setting yet telling the story with beguiling fairy tale simplicity in which a veneer of charm barely conceals a strong undercurrent of anxiety.

Entire film operates cunningly on this skillfully-honed double-edge as we watch the attempts of a 14-year-old girl of cozy middle class background to make her life conform to the Hans Andersen fairy tale ("The Little Siren") in which she has projected all her emotional needs.

When she comes across a 40-year-old garage mechanic, who has playfully whistled at her, she decides that he is her Prince and devotes all her wiles and energies into luring him into her private world. The mechanic is drawn uncomprehendingly towards the little enchantress, whose freshness and vivacity seems to fill a void in him, but, when he finally lets himself go to abide completely by her vision, he is destroyed by the impossibility of the liaison.

For all the admirable economy and rigour of Andrieux's script (adapted from a novel by Yves Dangerfield) and direction, the viewer wouldn't buy the premise if it were not for the alluring bulldozer charm of Laura Alexis (a 16-year-old American girl who has been living in France for several years; who gives her role an extraordinary blend of mystery and banality. Philippe Leotard is fine as the mediocre working-class mechanic who doesn't know what's hit him.

Picture has excellent contributions from cinematographer Robert Alazraki, editor Kenout Peltier and composer Alain Jomy. "The Little Siren" works on enough levels to earn it good commercial playoff and should be snapped up quickly for overseas distribution. —*Len.*

Berlin - Dein Filmgesicht
(Berlin - Your Film Profile)
(GERMAN-B&W/COLOR-DOCU)

Berlin, Aug. 11.
A Film Collage on the History of the German Sound Film from 1929 to 1979, produced by Kaeguruh-Film, Hans-Henning Borgelt, Detlef Gumm, and Hans-Georg Ullrich. Written and directed by Hans Borgelt, in collaboration with Edmund Luft. Reviewed at Berlin Film Fair Screening Room, August 11, '80. Running time: **95 MINS.**

After such well-known and appreciated compilation docus on Hollywood like Robert Youngson's "The Golden Age of Comedy" and the musical-collage "That's Entertainment" that opened the Cannes fest a few years back, it was only a matter of time before a portrait of another of the world's great film cities would be made.

Hans Borgelt's "Berlin - Your Film Profile" was made to celebrate the 50-year birthday of the German sound film last year, and it comes across not only as an historical document (the first sound-film experiments took place here in Berlin) but also as a nostalgic look over the shoulder to some of the highlights of German talkies.

For the record, a system known as Tri-Ergon was perfected by three Berlin inventors — Guenther Vogt, Erich Engl, and Josef Massole — as early as 1918. This system led to sound being recorded on film photographically, rather then recorded on synchronized disks (the first system used by Warner Brothers in the making of "The Jazz Singer"), and the Tri-Ergon rights were purchased by the Fox Company to be matched with De Forrest Phonofilm system (for which Fox also brought the rights). Fox used the system for the first time in 1926 in the making of "What Price Glory?"

Last November, Borgelt presented his collage-film of 46 excerpts from feature films on the city of Berlin at a public showing sponsored by the Berlin Senate. The feature presentation was accompanied by a short, "How Sound Came to Film and Film to Sound," in which an oldtime Berliner, actor Ewald Wenck (88-years-old), recalled the highlights of the Tri-Ergon invention. One of those highlights was when the three engineer-inventors presented the first docu with scenes using realistic sound at the Alhambra theatre in Berlin in September 1923, a film titled "Life in a Village." A further attempt to do the same with a feature film, the Ufa fairy-tale, Ulrich Kayser's "Das Maedchen mit den Schwefelhoelzen" (The Girl with the Box of Matches) in 1925, flopped as an experiment, and the invention was temporarily shelved.

Then Fox came along and bought the rights, whereby the American film industry moved to the forefront of the sound film. The first authentic German production, using the applied invention of the Berlin inventors, was "Dich hab' ich geliebt" in a November 1929 preem, the event the Berlin Senate celebrated in fashion with Borgelt's docu.

Helmer Hans Borgelt took a no-commentary approach to his theme, choosing instead to offer a profile of the city in various feature films treating the subject in an historical-chronological fashion — that is, Berlin shown from the time of the Great Kurfurst and Prussia's first king, Friedrich I. at the beginning of the 18th century.

Both the titles and the directors are too numerous to mention. Borgelt also refused to be critical about the meaning some of these pix had in German history, for several of them **were produced during the Nazi Years to serve as effective** propaganda for one purpose or another. These feature pix, forbidden by the Allies after the war, have only recently surfaced in restored or returned copies sent back to West Germany from the Library of Congress, where contraband films were stored and intelligently cared for).

Another aspect of Borgelt's docu is the presentation of destroyed monuments (Schlueter's Schloss Berlin), entire streets and squares (Potsdamer Platz), and sections of the city (the Wedding ruins, where the former workers' section was that offered such an important backdrop for novels and paintings). Make no mistake, this is a nostalgic pic that will wet the eyes of anyone who had visited Berlin in the Roarin' '20s and Tragic '30s.

There's also another reason to take a peep at "Berlin — Your Film Profile" — the German film buff can catch glimpses of top stars of the early sound period: Grethe Weise, Heinrich George, Rotraut Richter, Heinz Ruhmann, Viktor de Kowa, Willi Forst, Lilian Harvey, Willy Fritsch, Gustav Froehlich, and others. Among the directors are Josef von Baky, Slatan Dudow, Veit Harlan, Helmut Kautner, Carl Froelich, Theo Lingen, Richard Oswald, Robert Wiene, and several other oldtimers. A forgotten chapter in German film history. —*Holl.*

Scandal
(Shuban)
(JAPANESE-B&W)

Entertainment Marketing Corp. release of a Shochiku production. Produced by Takashi Koide. Directed by Akira Kurosawa. Features entire cast. Screenplay, Akira Kurosawa, Ryuzo Kikushima; camera (black and white), Toshio Ubakata; music, Fumio Hayasaka. No other credits provided. Reviewed at New York screening room, Aug. 18, 1980. (No MPAA rating). Running time: 105 MINS.
Cast: Toshiro Mifune, Yoshiko Yamaguchi, Takashi Shimura.
(Japanese with English subtitles)

This 1950 film by Japanese master Akira Kurosawa, just now being released in the U.S. by Entertainment Marketing Corp. is one of the director's first post-war attempts to emulate the American film but which comes off today as a Japanese version of a soap opera. The trite story is saved only by first-rate black-and-white camerawork by Toshio Ubakata and the acting of a very young Toshiro Mifune. The classic "Rasho-mon" was to follow the same year and establish Kurosawa internationally.

The attempts to ape western idioms are most apparent in the musical score of Fumio Hayasaka and the use of western tunes — Yoshiko Yamaguchi portrays a concert singer who uses "Connais tu le pays" in a practice session; later she sings "Stille nacht" at a Christmas Eve gathering and a group of celebrants in a bar sing "Auld lang syne." All in Japanese, of course.

Mifune, an artist, and Yamiguchi are slandered by a scandal-type magazine and they engage Takashi Shimura (who still had "Ikiru" ahead of him) as their lawyer. A weak, vacillating man with a tubercular daughter, he sells out to the enemy and, of course, comes through at the last minute with a witness-stand confession. This film belongs in the same company as "Sarah and Son" and "Stella Dallas" but is worth seeing just to watch the talented cast wring every tear out of the terrible story. —*Robe*.

Dead Man's Float
(AUSTRALIAN-COLOR)

Sydney, Aug. 7.

A Greg Lynch Film Distributors release of an Andromedia Production. Features entire cast. Produced by Tom Broadbridge. Director, Peter Sharp. Screenplay, Roger Carr, based on a novel by Carr; camera (color), David Eggby, assistant director, Michael McKeag; sound Gary Wilkins; editor, Clifford Hayes. Reviewed at Palm Beach Screening Rooms Sydney, Aug. 4, 1980. (Commonwealth Censorship Rating: G). Running time: **75 MINS**.

Anne	Sally Boyden
Johnny	Greg Rowe
Sue	Jacqui Gordon
Pete	Rick Ireland
Eddie Bell	Bill Hunter
Shirley Bell	Sue Jones
Captain Collins	John Heywood
Mr. Dobraski	Gus Mercurio
Rex Coates	Brian Hannan
Mr. Luth	Marcel Cugola
Snarks	Ernie Sigley
Parish	Bunney Brooke
Heavy	Chris Hayward

As a piece of good, entertaining kidult fare, "Dead Man's Float" is fine: nothing much is demanded of its target market whose ability to suspend disbelief is depended upon. The main characters are an attractive quartet of neo-adolescents with high identifiability factors for the younger audiences. The plot is neatly divided between the good guys and the baddies (with a couple of good-bad guys to help make everything come out right), and the environment in which it is set is a novel one — at least for non-Aussies.

The four youngsters are keen surfies and in the opening scenes

the sexual lines are drawn with Boyden and Gordon both seeking the attention of the American visitor, Pete (Rick Ireland). They live on a fairly remote stretch of coast, but are rudely invaded by adults who are seeking to bring to the surface a cache of drugs. The shades of Arthur Penn's "Night Moves" are faint, however, because this one moves quickly to a confrontation with the eager investigator (Greg Rowe) and the evil ones; parents rally to the rescue and by the fade out all's right with the world.

Performances are in tune with the intention as is the direction and script; production values are good. Both the girls convey the right level of coy concupiscence and there are moments when Jacqui Gordon defines fetching; however, Sally Boyden, playing the spoiled sibling, gives as little as possible away.

Of the boys the more experienced Greg Rowe convinces better, perhaps largely because the Pete character is meant to be awkward (with both girls vying for his favors) and for a neophyte cast as he is as a Yank, the accent seems at times out of Ireland's reach. Gus Mercurio as his father will appeal to local kids because of his associations here, but his warmth should also come over elsewhere. Bill Hunter as Rowe's dad balanced nicely as the loving-gruff style parent, however neither of the maternal characters registers much.

As noted, tech credits are good and the pic should be solid school holiday fare Down Under. Elsewhere it could happen given some care, and it's a natch for the small screen where "re-voicing" probably would be a less necessary factor. —*Miha*.

Locarno Fest

Retour a Marseille
(Return to Marseilles)
(FRENCH-COLOR)

Locarno, Aug. 19.

Gaumont release of Action Films-FR3-Filmproduktion Janus production. Features entire cast. Written and directed by Rene Allio. Camera (Eastmancolor), Renato Berta; music, Lucien Bertolina, Georges Boeuf. Reviewed at Locarno Film Fest, Aug. 9, '80. Running time: **117 MINS**.

Michel	Raf Vallone
Cece	Andrea Ferreol
Charles	Jean Maurel
Le Mino	Paul Allio
Charlot	Rene Fontanarava
Claudia	Danielle Durand

Director Rene Allio is originally from Marseilles and he obviously felt a personal identification with this film about a man returning to this busy port after a long absence due to a favorite aunt's funeral.

But he has cast this in the form of a chase film — criss-crossed with the theme of a man on the run and the meeting of old memories. A rather contrived script and ordinary direction do not bring the themes together.

Raf Vallone, the Italo actor who speaks very good French with a slight accent, has been living in Italy for many years. Actually, his family was originally Italian which explains his accent. He comes in with his good Italo car which is taken by the 17-year-old nephew he has never seen.

But things get serious when the car is not returned and his nephew's shady friends find a briefcase in which there are unstamped bills from his associates. Obviously his partners went in for cheating.

Vallone will not call the police, one of the men tries to blackmail him but he finally gets back his papers helped by the mother of his nephew's girl. But the boy himself is killed by police when he kills a watchman in an attempted holdup.

The boy may be what Vallone was once but he, Vallone, had changed by hard work, raising a family and success. But all this is drawn out and lacks the visual drive to make it gel. It might be an okay home item with foreign chances limited. —*Mosk*.

Melodrama?
(GREEK-COLOR/B&W)

Locarno, Aug. 19.

Christos Mangos release and production. Features entire cast. Written and directed by Nikos Panayotopoulos. Camera (Color, B&W), Stavros Hassapis; editor, Andreas Andreadakis. Reviewed at Locarno Film Fest, Aug. 5, '80. Running time, **93 MINS**.

With: Lefteris Voyatzis, Maria Xenoudaki, Kostas Kokakis, Aliki Georgouli, Eleonora Stathopoulou, Aleka Paizi.

This personal look at a young man's return home, his coping with internal problems and love, has all the earmarks of a first film in its insistence on private symbolism, a slow tempo and a refusal to make clear whether this is a melodrama, interior musing or a dream.

On this score it looms mainly for film weeks or fests on its arresting but unclear assertions and even adolescent quirks of a grown young man.

The more interesting aspect of it all is that it is director Nikos Panayotopoulos's second film. His first, "Idlers of the Fertile Valley," was an intriguing, harsh look at human sloth made with firm directorial insights that won the grand prize at Locarno in 1978.

His latest copped nothing but was felt an unusual probing of youthful decision as a young man who has lived in America for several years comes back to see his sick mother.

He falls for a girl who leaves him for an older man and kills his mother who is terminally ill. It may be all allegory in a man's need to face and break with his past.

Film is mainly in black and white with only the first and last shots in color. —*Mosk*.

Parceiros De Aventura
(Partners of Adventure)
(BRAZILIAN-COLOR)

Locarno, Aug. 19.

Embrafilme release of A.F. Sampaio Prod. Art production. Features entire cast. Written and directed by Jose Arujo De Madeiros, from the book by Joao Falicio. Camera (Eastmancolor), Madeiros; editor, Raphael Valverde; music, Paulo Moura. Reviewed at Locarno Film Fest, Aug. 5, '80. Running time: **90 MINS**.

With: Vinicios, Paula Moura, Ana Madelena, Paulo, Catalina Bonak, Reginaldo Faria, Luiz Armando Quieroz.

A Brazilian film going in for the familiar theme from many climes of small-time criminals and unemployed people caught up with this element. Film remains somewhat surface and predictable but does have some engaging local color though not adding much to this overworked theme. A Latino item at best.

An unemployed, decent bus driver refuses to pass a picket line. He is friendly with some petty drug pushers and they get him involved. But when he steals a needed car there is a little girl in the back and he is killed by police as a kidnapper.

There is a musician in the group who gets out but must compromise on his music. Film does have some engaging albeit typed characters and is ably helmed by first timer Jose Arujo De Madeiros. —*Mosk*.

Exit ... Nur Keine Panik
(Exit — But No Panic)
(AUSTRIAN-COLOR)

Locarno, Aug. 19.

Film Production. Terra Film-Kunst release and production. Features entire cast. Directed by Franz Novotny. Screenplay, Gustav Ernst, Novotny; camera (Eastmancolor), Alfio Contini; editor, Eliska Stibrova; music, Otto M. Zykan. Reviewed at Locarno Film Fest, Aug. 4, '80. Running time, **100 MINS**.

With: Eddie Constantine, Hanno Poschl, Ulrich Neumann, Konrad Becker, Sabrina Thurm, Beatrice Frey, Peter Weibel.

A raunchy Teutonic vulgarity highlights this Austrian film on subproletariat, semi-delinquent types. A growing theme these days as societies seem to spawn these kinds. But the film lays it on a bit thick and indulges in everything from random violence and destructiveness to free sex and homosexuality.

The anti-hero reveals more in macho male companionship and

his sex seems more aimed at impressing friends than for its own sake. Is he a latent gay? But he does kick a gay, who makes a pass at him, in the face.

A wild joy ride in a stolen car with a boat attached to it ends this tale of the life and times of a sort of social, semi-criminal rebel who would really like to just own an espresso shop and settle down.

Not much use outside exploitation playoff abroad but still denoting some brisk directorial flair in Franz Novotny when he can temper it with taste. Players are okay and Eddie Constantine, the Yank who made a top European career for himself playing undercover men in French films, still displays his exceptional filmic presence as a shady Frenchman who still has vestiges of honor. —*Mosk.*

Le Chemin Perdu
(The Lost Way)
(SWISS-COLOR)

Locarno, Aug. 19.
Cactus Film release of Saga Production production. Features entire cast. Written and directed by Patricia Moraz. Camera (Eastmancolor), Sacha Vierny; editor, Thierry Derocles; music, Moraz. Reviewed at Locarno Film Fest, Aug. 9, '80. Running time, 107 MINS.
With: Charles Vanel, Magali Noel, Delphin Seyrig, Christine Pascal, Vania Vilers, Clarisse Barrere, Charles Dudoignon.

This Swiss film uses mainly French thesps and technicians even though shot entirely in Switzerland. Patricia Moraz believes in longheld shots and slow progression to allow her characters to express themselves and to play on their surroundings.

It makes for slowness but this film does have a revealing tone that makes its tale of a 12-year-old girl's self realization affecting. Some woodenness in acting may be due to trying to show the adults through the girl's eyes. It is not clear.

She loves her Communist grandfather who often speaks homilies to her and her little brother. She respects her parents who are taxidermists. After her grandfather's death, and disillusion when the man he picked to deliver his funeral oration does not come, the girl finds him with the girlfriend of her dead grandfather and runs off.

She provokes a fight between her parents who she now sees as evading life's issues by their work which holds back time by giving lifelike feeling to dead animals. Somewhat too measured, film remains more for the fest route but marks director Moraz worth watching due to her insight into change and childhood though more visual bite and sharper pacing would help. —*Mosk.*

Polenta
(SWISS-COLOR)

Locarno, Aug. 19.
Release and production of Eos Film-SSR production. Stars Bruno Ganz. Directed by Maya Simon. Screenplay, Jean-Marc Lovay. Camera (Eastmancolor), Maurice Giraud; editor, Marc Blavet. Reviewed at Locarno Film Fest, Aug. 1, '80. Running time, 133 MINS.
Jules .... Bruno Ganz
Hector .... Jean-Marc Stehle
Girl .... Aude Eggimann
Sister .... Marina Golovine
Guard .... Guy Touraille
Driver .... Jean-Marc-Lovay

A hermetic, repetitive film dealing with the very bare bones of life, but still manages to exert a hypnotic influence despite running over two hours. It evokes Samuel Beckett in the almost larvae-like state of its three personnages as well as a sort of concentrationary, always wintery, world.

So it's not an easy film but has a dedicated spark that should slant it for more festival outings, though its commercial chances are restricted. Director Maya Simon, who studied at the Moscow Film Institute, does create a visual drive by staking out the bleak lives of the personnages, though Soviet officialdom would look askance at the film's treatment and intimations of imprisoned lives.

Bruno Ganz, the German actor who has scored in films on his own grounds and many other countries, is fine as the sort of spokesman of the film. He has dreams of sometimes killing or cutting the tongue out of his hirsute, loud roommate in a cabin in a compound surrounded by barbed wire and with lights flashing by at night.

An adolescent girl comes for help for her young sister who dies and is carted off by two men dressed in plastic. She then comes into the lives of these two haunted men. Ganz's friend always insists he is being attacked by owls and does show stigmatic wounds at times.

The film has the dead girl reappear as its sidelight look at death in sterile lives.

This Swiss oddity, made in French, does show a new director with temperament in Simon who may be heard from when she essays more accessible forms but hopefully does not attenuate her strong personal outlooks and visual flair. Film is technically good and thesps fit this parable on basic human behavior or allegory on life and death. —*Mosk.*

Clarence and Angel
(U.S.-COLOR-16m)

Locarno, Aug. 19.
Robert Gardner Representative release of Robert Gardner Representative-Clarence and Angel Productions production. Features entire cast. Written and directed by Robert Gardner. Camera (color), Doug Harris; editor, Jonathan Weld; music, Philip Wilson. Reviewed at Locarno Film Fest, Aug. 7, '80. Running time, 72 MINS.
Clarence .... Darren Brown
Angel .... Mark Cardova

An unassuming film that uses sentiment without mawkishness and delves into the world of pre-teenagers and school life without condescension or false moves. It could well find a definite niche for school use and snag youthful audiences and older ones in specialized outlets with savvy treatment.

No doubt school and institutional and non-commercial use would also be appropriate, not to forget educational tv. Film takes place in a partly segregated public school with mainly black and Puerto Rican students and staff.

The two title characters spend most of their time in the hall outside their respective classrooms. Angel, a Puerto Rican, for being too brash and noisy and Clarence, a black, for not being able to read as well as the others. But Clarence cannot read and needs extra help which the understaffed school cannot give him.

It is Angel, a kung fu buff, who teaches Clarence to read in between his endless prattling. The kids are exceedingly well handled and Robert Gardner directs this with a nice feeling for their dream-like world without exploiting it. Pic is simple but devoid of violence and even the daydreams are disarming and rightly child-like as Clarence's final breakthrough in his reading to the dumbfounded teacher. It copped one of the top prizes at the Locarno Fest. —*Mosk.*

So Weit Das Auge Reicht
(As Far As The Eye Sees)
(WEST GERMAN-COLOR)

Locarno, Aug. 19.
Cactus Film release of Prokino, Films Du Losange-Cactus Film-Swiss TV-DRS production. Features entire cast. Written and directed by Erwin Keusch. Camera (color), Dietrich Lohmann; editor, Bettina Lewertoff. Reviewed at Locarno Film Fest, Aug. 8, '80. Running time, 137 MINS.
Robert .... Bernd Tauber
Anna .... Aurore Clement
Alex .... Jurgen Prochnow
Iris .... Antonia Reininghaus
Kuhl .... Hans-Michael Rehberg

Film is a carefully worked-out attempt to bring off a sort of melodrama about love over money, full of rife coincidene, cupidity, and murder as the protagonists go in and out of outlandish, highly coincidental situations and meetings. But all this is too contrived and hollow to get the needed inventiveness, light hearted romantics and final winning out of inno-

cence it strives desperately to achieve.

The hero, a simple masseur and parttime singer, is afflicted with bad hearing. It might be a dramatic, tragic flaw but is also used for some misunderstandings. He inherits a fortune in stocks from his father who left his now-dead mother.

But some conniving stock market types are after him to get the money. The young man charged with finding the inheritor even sets up an elaborate idea to get his own girl to seduce and marry the man to get the money and then divorce him. But the latter ends up with another girl, is charged with murder the other commits but is finally rid of all of them as he leaves the girl he perhaps loved who insists she really loved him despite being in on the elaborate affair.

Home grounds might take to this. Its excessive plotting and careful but stolid direction might give it some playoff, though it's otherwise limited and does not enhance the cries of the West German renaissance that still spill plenty of critical ink in many countries. Acceptable thesps cannot overcome the elephantine handline of what should have been a sprightly adventure tale of innocence overcoming cupidity. —*Mosk.*

Kilas
(Killer)
(PORTUGUESE-COLOR-16m)

Locarno, Aug. 19.
IPDC release of Film Forum production. Features entire cast. Directed by Jose Fonseca e Costa. Screenplay, Costa, Sergio Godinho, Tabajara Ruas; camera (Color), Mario Barroso; editor, Manuel Tomas. Reviewed at Locarno Film Fest, Aug. 6, '80. Running time, 125 MINS.
With: Mario Viegas, Lia Gama, Luis Lello, Milu, Paula Guedes, Duarte, Natalia Do Vale, Francisco Pestana.

Portugal makes film appearances mainly at smaller festivals. Primarily a tale of small-time delinquents and criminals, film rings in some sidelight looks at a still uneven political keel since Portugal's emergence from long years of dictatorship.

The title character, Kilas, names himself after the killers in U.S. gangster films. He takes up with a fading singer and indulges in small robberies and begins to get a name as he forges a gang. He is used by a mysterious man who wants him to watch a house where secret meetings go on.

When the place is blown up, Kilas finds it was a meeting place for Communists and a rightist had executed the explosion. He finally gets into trouble with one of his cohorts and ends up being badly beaten and his girl leaving him.

Rather derivative of the many lowlife films these days but worth reviewing for the record plus also denoting that director Jose Fonseca e Costa does have a busy directorial style and might be seen at other fests when he gets more original material to work with. Technically acceptable. —*Mosk.*

Sey Seyeti
(A Man, Some Women)
(SENEGALESE-COLOR)

Locarno, Aug. 19.
Ben Diogaye release and production. Features entire cast. Written and directed by Ben Diogaye Beye. Camera (color), Beye; editor, Andree Daventure. Reviewed at Locarno Film Fest, Aug. 4, '80. Running time: **77 MINS.**
With: El Abaye Seck, Dienaba Niang, Fatim Diagne.

Polygamy in Muslim Senegal in black Africa has been treated before in the dean of black African filmmaker Ousmane Sembene's films. Here it is a bit splintered, meandering but finally coming to grips with the theme that seems to be as much of a problem to the men as to the women.

There are many early scenes of gossiping women, children from various wives of one man and their relationships and finally singling out the case of one man whose bickering wives almost drive him to a breakdown and thoughts of divorce.

There is also a teenage girl, in love with a young man, forced to marry an older man as his second wife. She finally breaks away but will not be the second wife of her former lover, who has since married, for she wants to go her own way.

Despite its sometimes lumbering look, film does make its points on this outmoded practice with comic and human insight. However, its lack of a firm narrative slants this more for fests and ethnic events than for more commercial usage outside of Africa or other places where polygamy may still be in force. Playing is fresh and director Ben Diogaye Beye is not to be written off. —*Mosk.*

The Big Brawl
(COLOR)

Amusing chopsocky actioner with Jackie Chan has potential beyond usual audience for genre.

Hollywood, Aug. 20.
Warner Bros. release of a Golden Harvest presentation. Exec produced by Raymond Chow. Stars Jackie Chan. Produced by Fred Weintraub, Terry Morse Jr. Directed by Robert Clouse. Screenplay, Clouse, from story by Clouse, Weintraub; camera (Technicolor), Robert Jessup; music, Lalo Schifrin; editor, George Grenville; art direction, Joe Altadonna; set decoration, Jack Marty; sound, Bob Wald, Bob Litt; stunt coordinator, Pat Johnson; assistant director, Craig Huston. Reviewed at Academy of Motion Picture Arts & Sciences, BevHills, Aug. 19, 1980. (MPAA Rating: R.) Running time: **95 MINS.**
Jerry ....Jackie Chan
Dominici ....Jose Ferrer
Nancy ....Kristine De Bell
Herbert ....Mako
Leggetti ....Ron Max
Morgan ....David Sheiner
Mae ....Rosalind Chao
John ....Lenny Montana
Carl ....Pat Johnson
Dominici's Mother ....Mary Ellen O'Neill
Kiss ...................H.B. Haggerty
Kwan ....Chao-Li Chi
Miss Wong ....Joycelyne Lew

Hong Kong martial arts star Jackie Chan makes an amiable American film debut in Warner Bros.' "The Big Brawl," an amusing chopsocky actioner whose appeal is not limited to the usual audience for this genre. Key ingredient here is humor, as the cartoonish plot takes full advantage of Chan's light-hearted approach to his chopsocky mastery. Coproducer Fred Weintraub and writer-director Robert Clouse, who collaborated on WB's enormously successful "Enter The Dragon," may have found another winner in this pic made under the aegis of Raymond Chow's Golden Harvest.

The diminutive Chan, whose Hong Kong pix have made him a potent b.o. draw there, has dazzling physical skills but, unlike the late Bruce Lee, never comes off as menacing, specializing instead in a winking complicity that invites the audience to share his own amusement. Chopsocky pix typically are outlandishly plotted, but since this one makes no bones about playing for outright laughs, those who find the genre alien to their tastes may have a pleasant surprise.

Story by Weintraub and Clouse is set in Chicago, 1938, filmed with engagingly artificial style that resembles vintage gangster pix of the period, right down to show-offish optical wipes. Epicene gangster lord Jose Ferrer runs his terrain with the aid of his foul-mouthed, cigar-chomping mother Mary Ellen O'Neill. Attempts to strong-arm Chinese restaurateur Chao-Li Chi run afoul when his son, Chan,

gets into the act with chopsocky skills he has been practicing with an uncle, Mako. Chan eventually is recruited by Ferrer to be his entrant into a Texas free for all (the "big brawl" of the title) which pits him against an incredibly sadistic brute played by H.B. Haggerty.

Chan's physical prowess grows from scene to scene, as the actor intelligently holds back on his expertise in the earlier scenes, which are played mostly for laughs, saving the flashiest stuff for the finale. Director Clouse never forgets he has to satisfy the action audience, but keeps a sure hand on the blend of comedy and violence.

Supporting cast is chosen with a sense of whimsy befitting the story. In addition to vets Ferrer and Mako, who play their campy parts with zest, Kristine De Bell is nonchalantly sexy as Chan's highly improbable Caucasian girlfriend. De Bell, attempting to segue these days from her sexpo "Alice In Wonderland" image into a career in regular Hollywood pix, hasn't yet found a role that capitalizes fully on her hoydenish charm, but this one is a better showcase for her than "The Main Event" or "Willie & Phil."

Tech credits are good, Lalo Schifrin's bouncy score is particularly effective in sustaining the predominantly comic mood. —*Mac.*

Le Chemin Perdu
(The Lost Way)
(FRENCH-SWISS-BELGIAN-COLOR)

Paris, July 25.
An MK2 release of an Abilene Production-MK2 (Paris)/Saga Productions (Lausanne)/Cactus Film (Zurich)/F3 (Brussels) co-production. Features entire cast. Written and directed by Patricia Moraz. Script collaborator, Serge Schoukine; camera, (color), Sacha Vierny; editor, Thierry Derocles; music, Patrick Moraz; art directors, Alain Nicolet, Pierre Gattoni. Reviewed at Studio 43, Paris, July 25, 1980. Running time: **107 MINS.**
With: Charles Vanel, Delphine Seyrig, Magali Noel, Clarisse Barrere, Charles Dudoignon, Vania Vilers, Remo Girone, Christine Pascal.

Patricia Moraz, a Swiss director in her late 30s, made a promising debut in 1977 with "Les Indiens Sont Encore Loin" which irritated with some of its experimentations but was generally disturbing in dealing with the alienation and suicide of a Swiss high-school girl (played by Isabelle Huppert).

"The Lost Way," her second feature, still has its share of annoyances, but is often rich and perceptive in its evocation of a 10-year-old girl's initiation into the ways of familial disobedience. Moraz gets beyond the conventionally coy portraits of childhood and with a particularly subtle sense of camera

expression, renders the girl's vision of the world with considerable lyricism. Tone is deliberately restrained and humourless, marking picture essentially for festival and art house playoffs.

Film describes the situation of a Swiss girl growing up between parents who are too involved in each other to pay sufficient attention to their children, and a watchmaker-grandfather who seeks to insure that his grandchildren continue in his militant left-wing footsteps.

Moraz deploys a good deal of symbolism, some of it deft and nicely woven underneath the action, some of it trite and labored (the parents, who are taxidermists, are as dull and lifeless as the animals they stuff).

Among the film's loveliest sequences are those with 87-year-old Charles Vanel, memorable as the beloved grandfather, whose most cherished memory is of having shook hands with Lenin. Opposite him, Clarisse Barrere offers the right dreamy-faced quality as the granddaughter who finally betrays his legacy.

Moraz gets less satisfying results from the other players like Delphine Seyrig and Vania Vilers, as the parents, who never get beyond vaguely caricatural outlines. Most of the secondary actors are wooden. Christine Pascal appears briefly in two sequences, but her role (a crippled cinema usherette) weighs the film down crudely.

Sacha Vierny provides excellent cinematography and the other technical contributions are first-grade. —*Len.*

Galaxina
(COLOR)

Space spoof a good premise, but never gets into orbit on characterizations or story line. Limp b.o. in prospect.

Kansas City, Aug. 20.
Crown International Pictures Inc., release of a Marimar Production. Produced by Marilyn J. Tenser, George E. Mather, associate producer. Written and directed, William Sachs. Features entire cast. Camera (color), Dean Cundy; production designer, Tom Turlley; editor, Larry Bock; supervisor Special Photographic Effects, Chuck Colwell. Reviewed at Midland 3 Theatre, K.C., Aug. 19, 1980. (MPAA Rating: R). **95 MINS.**
Thor ....Stephen Macht
Galaxina ....Dorothy R. Stratten
Buzz ....James David Hinton
Captain Butt ....Avery Schreiber
Ordric ....Ronald Knight
Maurice ....Lionel Smith
Sam Wo ....Tad Horino
Rock Eater, Kitty, Ugly
Alien Woman ....Herp Kaplowitz
Elexia ....Nancy McCauley
Commander ....Fred D. Scott
Horn Man ....George E. Mather

On paper the idea of spoofing the wealth of galactic films which currently abound is a potent premise, but writer-director William Sachs little more than scratches the surface of the idea. The film had further potential in casting former Playboy Playmate, and now the late, Dorothy Stratten, as the title character, but even as a robot her contribution is a wooden portrayal.

The film may derive some patron interest on the Stratten score, her body having been discovered Friday (15), the day the film opened, an apparent victim of her estranged husband, who is supposed also to have killed himself. Some lingering curiosity on the part of those wanting to see this last film of the 20-year-old beauty may prove of some benefit to the film.

A few laughs spurt through the lethargic pace, mostly to the credit of Avery Schreiber as the nutty craft commander, but even devoted space buffs will find it difficult to glean much from the thinly profiled characters and scanty action.

The picture was not given a press preview or trade screening, but opened here Aug. 15 in a showcase combining indoor and outdoor theatres to moderate biz, about all that can be expected of it.

Well ahead into the year 3008 the firmament is glutted with spacecrafts and abandoned hardware to the point space must be patrolled. That's the job of the huge spacecraft. The Infinity, a police cruiser in space chasing unidentified craft, checking on galactic beer halls and brothels and tying up behind a lighted signboard on a convenient asteroid at times. Stratten is the beauteous robot who guides the craft with just a touch of her fingertips on the push buttons.

After seven years in space and now assigned to a run to Altar I which will take 28 more years, Stephen Macht becomes enamored of the beautiful robot, who obliges with some programming herself with some additional parts so she can speak and have emotions. When Macht discovers their love cannot be consummated because the robot was not provided with the necessary female equipment, she eases his fears by telling him the missing parts may be obtained through her parts catalog. She appears throughout encased in a space-type jump suit, even at one point wears ballet dancer leggings, all of which doesn't seem appropriate use of a gorgeous beauty on film.

The jaunt to Altar I is in search of the "Blue Star" with which evil hands might want to control the universe. The star is retrieved by Stratten after close encounters with a rough motorcycle gang, a "High Noon" shoot out with a Darth Vader-like character in the decrepit Western town. Custard's Last Stand. "Star Wars," "Star Trek," "Close Encounters," "Buck Rogers" and other films come in for humorous spoofs, but the net result is inconsistent and superficial treatment of what could have been a howling success. The lumps have to go to the writing and direction for not getting the idea off the launch pad and not making better use of Stratten.

To the film's credit it has some good technical effects in the design of the mother ship, the ghoulish mutations which appear in the orbital house of ill-repute and the infra red setting of Custard's Last Stand. The "R" rating stems from a few cusswords needlessly thrown in, possibly to give a space film a down-to-earth effect. —*Quin.*

El Infierno Tan Temido
(So Feared a Hell)
(ARGENTINE-COLOR)

Buenos Aires, Aug. 8.

A Dispro Film release. Produced by Pino Farina Producciones. Stars Graciela Borges, Alberto de Mendoza. Directed by Raul de la Torre. Screenplay, Raul de la Torre, Oscar Viale, based on story by Juan Carlos Onetti; executive producer, Kiko Tenebaum; camera (Eastmancolor) Juan Carlos Desanzo; editing, Juan Carlos Macias; production design, Graciela Galan; assistant director, Carlos Obes; costumes, Graciela Galan; music, Astor Piazzolla. Reviewed at the Gran Savoy cinema, Buenos Aires, August 7, 1980. (Forbidden in Argentina for children under 18). Running time: 113 MINS.
Juan Rizzo .... Alberto de Mendoza
Gracia Cesar .... Graciela Borges
Tana .... Beba Bidart
Nona .... Nora Cullen
With Cacho Spindola, Enrique Almada, Arturo Garcia Buhr.

Raul de la Torre is one of Argentina's top directors and the number one screen delver into female psyches, and Graciela Borges is his favorite leading actress. In Juan Carlos Onetti's story the director found a theme which is closely attuned to his sensibility: a woman's flipped-out reaction to her lover's lack of understanding. He is an older man, an old-school Buenos Aires male, in other words rather formal, very conscious of his dignity, and irreductibly a male chauvinist.

Juan is utterly incapable of condoning or even comprehending Gracia's method of exorcizing a previous lover — going to bed with him to prove to herself that she no longer feels a thing for him. Rejected by Juan, Gracia bombards him with dirty photographs of herself in a kind of blackmail whose only purpose is moral punishment.

Beautifully photographed, particularly the nude scenes — which show a daring amount of skin for Argentina, even if they have been lightened from the director's original conception. The film has a rich Buenos Aires atmosphere, not least thanks to the tango music of Astor Piazzolla as well as more traditional practitioners. There is a certain amount of padding in the second half, and a totally superfluous chorus-like commentary by one auxiliary character (played by Enrique Almada) towards the end. Nevertheless the overall balance is strongly positive. A fully exportable adult product, with a modern, non-linear editing idiom. —*Olas.*

He Knows You're Alone
(COLOR)

Low-budget thriller could pay off.

Hollywood, Aug. 26.

An MGM release through United Artists of a Lansbury/Beruh production. Produced by George Manasse, Robert Di Milia, Nan Pearlman. Executive producers, Edgar Lansbury, Joseph Beruh. Directed by Armand Mastroianni. Features entire cast. Screenplay. Scott Parker; camera (Metrocolor), Gerald Feil; editor, George T. Norris; music, Alexander Peskanov, Mark Peskanov; art direction, Susan Kaufman; sound, Rolf Pardula; assistant director, Costa Mantis. Reviewed at the M-G-M Studios, Culver City, Aug. 20, 1980. (MPAA Rating: R.) Running time: 92 MINS.
Marvin .... Don Scardino
Amy .... Caitlin O'Heaney
Nancy .... Elizabeth Kemp
Killer .... Tom Rolfing
Gamble .... Lewis Arlt
Joyce .... Patsy Pease
Professor .... James Rebhorn
Elliot .... Tom Hanks
Diana .... Dana Barron
Ralph The Tailor .... Joseph Leon
Daley .... Paul Gleason
Phil .... James Carroll

At this point in the killer-with-a-knife sweepstakes, after the mammoth success of Par's pick-up "Friday The 13th," every company in Hollywood is trying to get into the act before the market becomes saturated. More ingenuity is going into titles and campaigns than into the films themselves, and MGM's acquisition "He Knows You're Alone" is neither markedly better nor worse than similar horror items that have come before. If audiences are still hungry for more of the same, pic will clean up; if the fancy is cooling off, relatively low expenditure should still insure a profit to all concerned.

Given the rate at which these revenge-themed, nocturnal slasher suspensers are being churned out, "Carrie" and "Halloween" may emerge as the most influential pix of the late '70s. Main challenge now lies in inventing new and imaginative ways of scaring or killing off characters, and this one, among its many methodical applications of minor jolts, displays at least two good ideas among its seven murder scenes.

Film offers a compendium of genre conventions for aficionados and/or scholars, perhaps not a good thing in that their predictability makes it play at times like a parody, which is probably the next and inevitable step in the process given the essential foolishness of horror situations.

There's the group of nubile teenaged girls which is reduced in number like clockwork by the sex-starved psychopath who has killed before and will kill again; the ineffectual efforts of the police to keep up with the murderer; the tongue-in-cheek awareness of "Psycho" as the granddaddy of all these films, and the nerdy kid, this time an employe at the local morgue, who proves he's really a man by saving the day at the last second.

Like the most recent hit in the genre, "Prom Night," pic is relatively low on real gore even if the body count is fairly high. Director Armand Mastroianni (for the record. Marcello's American-born cousin) crosses the line between scariness and ridiculousness a few times too often, but Caitlin O'Heaney. Elizabeth Kemp and Patsy Pease nicely fill the bill as the three principal femme targets of the maniac, whose motivation is that he was spurned by his bride-to-be some years back.

Pic was mainly, if not exclusively shot on Staten Island. Tech credits are adequate to the demands of the form. —*Cart.*

Golge
(WEST GERMAN-COLOR)

Berlin, Aug. 11.

A coproduction between the Berlin Film & Television Academy (DFFB) and Sender Freies Berlin (SFB). Features entire cast. Written and directed by Sema Poyraz and Sofoklis Adamidis. Camera (color), Adamidis; sound, Nana Gravesen, Hanjo Bred.rmann; editing, Thomas Balkenhol, Eduard Genart; music, Jo Liebau. Reviewed at Berlin Film Fair Screening Room, August 11, '80. Running time: 92 MINS.
Cast: Semru Uysal (Golge), Yuksel Topcugurler (father), Birgul Topcugurler (mother), Fatos Alkan (the sister), Asil Basyildiz (the Turkish friend).

"Golge"—a girl's name (in Turkish it means "Shadow") — is the diploma film of two students at the Berlin Film & Television Academy, Sema Poyraz from Turkey and Sofoklis Adamidis from Greece. Perhaps some observers would be astonished at the collaboration between a Turk and a Greek, but this is a film about foreign workers in West Berlin and has a universal implication for all nationalities "far from home."

It is, in fact, one of the finest diploma works to emerge from the

Berlin Film School, and was rightly chosen by SFB-TV moderator Michael Strauven for his "Projections" series on Berlin filmmakers on this summer's Third Channel nationwide hook-up. Pic now goes into the Off-Kudam studio art houses for a run, which in turn will hopefully open the door for fest invites and the like.

Golge is a teenager who now belongs more to the German milieu she was raised in from school-age than to her parents' Turkish background. Both the parents are working people, whose two daughters are bilingual and suffer the fate of all Second Generation children, particularly the older and more intelligent and sensitive Golge. At school, she does better in German history than the German born-and-bred students, and decides one day to become an actress.

The father is totally against his daughter's ambitions, simply because this is not the thing a nice young girl would do back home in Turkey. The mother tries to compromise the situation by allowing Golge to stay out more with her friends and have "outside-the-family" experiences at parties and gatherings. The father, in a moment of fury, forbids the girl to leave the house, although she does more of the housekeeping chores than any other in the family and is quite sensible in her choice of friends and contacts.

Since the story reflects the personal experiences of scripter-director Sema Poyraz, it has an authenticity that is striking and convincing. Only one other German pic on the foreign-workers (Gastarbeiter) matches it — "Far From Home," by the Iranian exiled director Sohrab Shahid Saless. It, too, was set in Berlin.

"Golge" takes the viewer into the crowded two room flats where four individuals must live out their destinies with few chances for privacy or intimacies of any kind. There are meetings of Turks, during which the men tell their jokes in one room and the women collect for chatting and sewing in another, as in the Old Country. The father, upon returning home in the evening from work, turns first to his Turkish newspaper and music on a record, together with a consoling bottle of spirits, before eating his evening meal.

The girl eventually breaks away from these surroundings — first in dreams of a surrealistic nature that deal with love and passion, and then in a normal relationship with a new Turkish acquaintance, a young man with Leftist leanings and an **understanding of the ways of the Western world. The future now has a ray of hope.**

Well scripted and finely lensed and acted, "Golge" deserves as much critical and fest attention as it can get on the circuit. And the directors, Poyraz and Adamidis, are names to watch should either of them ever get a second chance to make another feature film. —*Holl.*

La Discoteca Del Amor
(The Disco of Love)
(ARGENTINE-COLOR)

Buenos Aires, Aug. 5.

An Aries Cinematografica Argentina release. Production: Aries-Baires-Microfon. Produced by Fernando Ayala and Hector Olivera. Stars Cacho Castana, Monica Gonzaga, Ricardo Darin. Directed by Adolfo Aristarain. Original screenplay, Aristarain; executive producer, Eva Harguindey de Cuesta; camera (Eastmancolor), Horacio Maira; editing, Carlos Piaggio; sound, Daniel Castronuovo; sets, Oscar Piruzanto; assistant directors, Alejandro Pimentel, Armando Pronzato; costumes, Katy Saavedra; music, Emilio Kauderer. Reviewed at the Aries screening room, Buenos Aires, Aug. 4, 1980. (No viewing restrictions for any age group in Argentina). Running time: **93 MINS.**
Lucas .... Cacho Castana
Gloria .... Monica Gonzaga
Eddie .... Ricardo Darin
Lugosi .... Tito Mendoza
"Orejas" (Ears) .... Marcos Woinsky
  With Tincho Zabala, Stella Maris Lanzani, Silvia Perez, Carlos del Burgo.

This is the fourth in a locally popular series of films with the words "del Amor" in the title and plenty of songs in the sound track, and contrary to expectations — and tradition — the series is actually improving in quality. Clearly responsible for this is the inclusion as writer and director of Adolfo Aristarain, who surprised everybody with his first feature, two films back in his career, called "La Parte del Leon" (The Lion's Share) — a rock-solid thriller in the "film noir" mode.

A greater part of this picture's public will be the fans of the singers who appear in it — Camilo Sesto, Angela Carrasco, Franco Simone, Tormenta, Jose Jose, Sonia Rivas and lead star Cacho Castana. But the story woven around them, involving music pirates, has enough funny moments in it to stand up on its own. Hardly likely to win writing awards in international competition, but well above the norm for the genre, and not bereft of genuinely deft touches.

A standout is the character of the chief hoodlum, called Lugosi, who is a head shorter than everybody else, reads "The Films of James Cagney," and practices the grapefruit-in-the-face routine on a store-window dummy. —*Olas.*

Ko To Tamo Peva
(Who's That Singing
Over There?)
(YUGOSLAV-COLOR)

Pula, Aug. 12.

Yugoslavia Film release of Centar Film production. Features entire cast. Directed by Slobodan Sijan. Screenplay, Dusan Kovacevic; camera (Eastmancolor), Bozidar Nikolic; music, Vojislav Kostic. Reviewed at Pula Film Fest, July 28, '80. Running time, **84 MINS.**
  With: Pavle Vujisic, Dragan Nikolic, Aleksander Bercek, Neda Aneric, Slavko Stimac, Bora Stepanovic, Tasko Nacic.

A robust, raunchy road film about the trip of a brokendown country bus across practically non-existent roads a day before the war came to Yugoslavia in 1941. Full of familiar types played by popular and good actors, film is witty and reflective of things to come as the various people react under the stress of constant breakdowns, interruptions and the final arrival the day the city is bombed and only two gypsy musicians survive the bus when it is hit by a bomb.

There is the newlywed peasant couple whose love trysts at the numerous stops are spied on, battles between right and left factions, an orderly type, a ladies' man, a maladroit hunter and others in this funny trip which has shrewdly assimilated such U.S. westerns as "Stagecoach" and others.

It does get repetitive and bogs down a bit before the sudden tragic denouement. But it is inventive most of the way and sparks a director to watch in Slobodan Sijan whose first film this is. He has a sense of action and character, even if they are sometimes stereotyped, which keeps this afloat most of the way. Film should do well at home and might even have the wheels for some playoff spotlighting abroad on its broad human comedics. —*Mosk.*

Daj Sto Das
(Whatever You Can Spare)
(YUGOSLAV-COLOR)

Pula, Aug. 12.

Yugoslavia Film release of Jadran Film-Croatia Film release. Features entire cast. Directed by Bogdan Zizic. Screenplay, Kruno Quien, Zizic; camera (Eastmancolor), Zeljko Guberobid; music, Ozren Depolo. Reviewed at Pula Film Fest, July 27, '80. Running time: **96 MINS.**
  With: Sreten Mokrovic, Slobodan Milovanovic, Zonvko Lepetic, Vjera Zagar, Nardelli, Fabian Sovagovic.

A tale of young love that is somewhat contrived in scripting and somewhat lacking in directorial perception. There are class differences involved, parental silliness and freely given love as opposed to ambition.

But all this is somewhat too rote to give an insight into its worthwhile theme of what can destroy love no matter how ill assorted the couple.

It takes a young man on his new motorcycle running into the heroine during her father's funeral for them to meet. A forced meeting cute gambit. She is a sort of free-loving and giving girl and he has hangups from his social climbing family. He is also a social psychology major.

But love blooms and he is unthawed after he even makes a suicide pact with her and they take sleeping pills. Cured, they get married but it does not work and he ends up using his liaison for his thesis.

She, on the other hand, will go on and have the baby and go her own way. Film might find pupularity at home but just lacks the balance of direction and more probing scripting to give it the social revelations it strives after. —*Mosk.*

Luda Kuca
(A Mess In The House)
(YUGOSLAV-COLOR)

Pula, Aug. 12.

Yugoslavia Film release of Jadran Film production. Features entire cast. Directed by Ljubisa Ristic. Screenplay, Nermina Ferizegovic, Nada Kokotovic, Lazar Stojanovic, Ristic; camera (Eastmancolor), Enes Midzic. Reviewed at Pula Film Fest, July 27, '80. Running time: **105 MINS.**
  With: Miodrag Krivokapic, Zvonimir Zoricic, Zdenka Hersak, Ratko Buljan, Janez Bormez, Stane Potisk, Petar Dobric, Jelica Lovric.

A rare comedy set during the last war when a puppet state was set up in Croatia by the German army. It is a crucible affair of larger-than-life types in an apartment house. Perhaps a bit overcharged, film is still an inventive affair.

A Communist hiding in the apartment of two resistance leaders is killed by the local police. His wife escapes but the baby is left and the police decide to use it as a hostage. But the children of the house kidnap it and take care of it until the mother and the resistance rescue the child.

Film skirts that difficult field of black comedy but never falls into bad taste or questionable ethnics. Charges by local critics that it was fascist are ill-founded.

It just shows an unusual gallery of types who would be hard to handle anywhere and is more a human comedy than one of theory or heroics. There are madcap chases, a bewildered German who moves into the house, a lovesick married man and others.

Somewhat theatrical film still has some visual bite and a good rhythm that make theatre director Ljubisa Ristic worth watching when he gets an even more filmic feel for his material which remains still charged with theatrical acting.

A home item but a welcome new attitude towards the eternal war themes. —*Mosk.*

Montreal Fest

Health
(U.S.-COLOR)

Altman goes to a Florida health foods convention. Amusing but overdrawn.

Montreal, Aug. 23.
Twentieth Century-Fox release of a Lion's Gate Films production. Stars Carol Burnett, Glenda Jackson, James Garner, Lauren Bacall. Directed by Robert Altman. Screenplay, Frank Barhydt, Paul Dooley and Altman. Camera (color), Edmond Koons; sound, Bob Gravenor; editor, Dennis M. Hill. No other credits provided. Reviewed at Cinema Parisien, Montreal, Aug. 23, 1980. Running time: **102 MINS.**
Cast: Glenda Jackson, Carol Burnett, James Garner, Lauren Bacall, Dick Cavett, Paul Dooley, Henry Gibson.

Since producer-director Robert Altman completed production early last year of this arch look at a Florida health foods bash, the pic has gradually been stigmatized in the trade as the best known unreleased, major company film in some time. It's a bad rap: "Health" is overdrawn and thin in too many spots, but the pic is a genuinely humorous effort that affords its good cast often-seized opportunities for incisively funny performances.

Twentieth should take the pic off the shelf and, election year or not, test the exhibition waters. Careful playoff plus a canny campaign could yield modest, if not substantial wicket results. What's left of Altman's faithful following should be cheered since this is his most satisfactory outing since "A Wedding."

Like that pic, and "Nashville," the rambling format of "Health" puts a contingent of dotty characters against a frenzied social backdrop. Altman's clever handling of that backdrop — he is best at lending credibility to even the oddest of circumstances; what's seen here really looks like a convention, any large convention — permits the cast to develop broad characterizations that most often work.

In his apparent desperation to get the pic into release, Altman has made much of the all-too-facile connection of "Health's" plot to the recent major-party political conventions. The value of the pic isn't its political moralizing, even as subtly presented here, but the cast's (and Altman's) funny way of poking fun at the character types presented.

The convention is set in a gar-

ishly statuesque southern Florida hotel, and Altman (considering his satirical intent) somehow got some 100 health food companies to provide their wares in the pic's highly detailed and immensely clever sets. Lauren Bacall plays a well-preserved 83-year-old health authority who claims she's stayed so remarkably fit (Bacall resembles herself off-screen; there's no attempt to age her) by maintaining her virginity.

Bacall regularly lapses into catatonia, a condition signalled by the raising of her right arm which remains stiffly upraised. She's running for the presidency of the health foods org. that runs the convention, against a vaguely masculine, cigar puffer (Glenda Jackson) with a fondness for Adlai Stevenson and taping her own conversations.

Carol Burnett is the film's real surprise. She's firstrate as a sexually frustrated White House health emissary sent to the convention to gladhand the Presidential candidates. Burnett splendidly combines the sexiness (she's rarely looked better onscreen), temerity and political idealism of her character without forgetting that she's supposed to be funny.

Dick Cavett plays himself in a supporting part, covering the convention for his tv gab show. Altman cleverly puts him in a hotel room on two occasions, lying in underwear and wistfully watching Johnnie Carson. James Garner is appropriately droll as Burnett's ex-husband, a political p.r. type hustling Bacall's candidacy. Paul Dooley overdoes it a bit as a disgruntled, third-party candidate, but Henry Gibson puts in a very funny bit as a political dirty trickster who resorts to eavesdropping in elevators in drag.

Altman shifts back and forth between this brood. Nothing much is resolved and no big political statements are made. Altman has always been known as a director who gives much leeway to actors. That's a dangerous practice (John Cassavetes' films are a case in point), but with "Health," it works.

Altman's keen satirical eye gives the film shape and the quality of the cast takes it from there. "Health" is in competition at Montreal's World Film Festival. Perhaps it will emerge with the attention it deserves and the release date Altman has had to wait for. Given the soggy series of this summer releases, 20th could do a lot worse.
—*Sege.*

Dikaia Okhota Korolia Stakha
(Wild Hunting of King Stakh)
(USSR-COLOR)

Montreal, Aug. 24.
Sovexportfilm Release of a Studios Bielarousfilm production. Directed by Valeri Roubinchik. Features entire cast. Screenplay, Vladimir Korotkevitch; camera (color), Tatiana Loguinova. No other credits provided. Reviewed at Cinema Parisien, Montreal, Aug. 24, '80. Running time: **135 MINS.**
Cast: Boris Plotnikov, Elena Dimitrova, Boris Khmelnitski, Valentina Chendrikova.

An early contender for top prize in the feature competition at Montreal's World Film Fest has to be this Soviet offering from director and coscripter Valeri Roubinchik. "Wild Hunting of King Stakh" is a handsomely mounted, superbly executed work that turns an somewhat obscure subject into a firstrate suspenser that just doesn't let up.

This is a considerable accomplishment given the pic's time and setting — the turn of the century in Polesse in Byelorussia. A young folklorist arrives at the beginning of the film at a forbidding castle. He's in search of local color; the castle's inhabitants, what remains of a long line of Russian aristocrats, are concerned with something else.

Seems that 300 years previous, one of the family's less considerate progenitors murdered the King Stakh of the title, a beneficent local monarch interested in improving the lot of the poor via land reform. The folklorist learns, to his instant disbelief, that the ghost of the slain king has been riding roughshod over the land intent on picking off generation after generation of the aristocratic family.

Director Roubinchik turns this spooky premise into a gripping battle between folklorist and the spirits and folklorist and local police officials intent on ignoring this "blood feud." In the process, the director gives the ghostly combatants — who ride thunderously on white horses — a ominous credibility that underscores the pic's horror and suspense elements.

Roubinchik succeeds largely because of his sensuous treatment of the drama. Tatiana Loguinova has beautifully photographed the rustic surroundings, helping Roubinchik make his plot points visually. Crisp editing shifts scenes long before they tire, a device that makes the two-hours-plus running time fly by.

Thanks to the fest's sketchy cast listings, it's difficult to parcel out credit to the pic's excellent cast. Boris Plotnikov is fine as the ethnologist, skillfully rendering the

character's shift from wide-eyed credibility to steely determination. Elena Dimitrova handles her difficult part — as the understandibly crazed young noblewoman who's last on the ghostly king's hit list. She too nicely conveys her character's shift from resentment and terror to love (for the folklorist) and a different sort of determination.

The remainder of the cast — right down to the most minor character parts — is excellent, always a sure sign of a first-rate effort. Settings are also superb, and cannily exploited by Roubinchik and Loguinova. Much credit should go to the composer of the score; it's dramatic, compelling and good enough to stand apart from the film.

This beauty of a pic could with the proper sendoff be viable in a commercial setting. U.S. distribution should at least be explored. It's an excellent find, and Montreal fest officials deserve credit for its selection.— *Sege.*

Gui Xin Shi Jian
(Anxious to Return)
(CHINA-COLOR)

Montreal, Aug. 23.
China Film Export & Import Corp. release of a August First Film Studio production. Directed by Li Jun. Features entire cast. Screenplay, Li Keyi; camera (color), Yang Guangyuang. No other credits provided. Reviewed at Cinema Parisien, Montreal, Aug. 23, 1980. Running time: **110 MINS.**
Cast: Zhao Erkang, Siquin Gaowa, Ma Zhigang.

This pic, about a stalwart anti-Japanese guerrilla's dedication to duty, is inevitably more interesting for political rather than esthetic reasons. Essentially a plodding, one-note meller, "Anxious to Return" is nonetheless a significant sign that the People's Republic of China is highly anxious to join the major leagues of world cinema.

Pic is relatively new — it was lensed last year — and has been entered in competition at the Montreal Film fest. To oversee the entry, China sent along a delegation from China Film Export & Import Corp., equipped with glossy promo brochures (unheard of from the Chinese previously) pushing the pic as entertainment rather than propaganda.

Politics haven't been completely shunted aside. "Wei Desheng (the pic's central character portrayed by Zhao Erkang) is not the kind of hero lauded by the Gang of Four," reads one line from the promo material. But the pic's political values are muted — this is a story of human beings rather than tractors.

Set in 1939 during the bitter Japanese-Chinese war, "Anxious To Return" follows the guerrilla soldier's gruelling combat experiences with a small command unit, and his equally difficult period as a war prisoner and refugee. The combat footage opening the pic is reasonably well accomplished although still rudimentary by contemporary Western pic standards — editing is uneven, zoom shots are overused and there appears to be a lack of extras leaving the viewer a bit confused as to just who is fighting whom.

Offsetting these limitations somewhat is Erkang's strong performance as the hero, who resists the lures of money (proferred by a gang of gold prospectors operating outside political apparati) and of the heart and flesh. Thanks to a series of implausible coincidences (set forth in Li Keyi's simplistic script), the warrior manages to connect at film's end with the beautiful daughter (portrayed by either Siquin Gaowa or Ma Zhigang; the credits are not clear) ofo the elderly leader of the gold prospectors encountered earlier in the pic.

The daughter happens to be very beautiful and, as portrayed, is a warm, enticing and emotionally forthright woman. She also happens to be a widow with a cute, young son — an ideal domestic situation since the warrior falls for the woman and becomes deeply attached to the boy.

His perceived sense of duty to rid China of the Japanese — presented as unmitigated bad guys — moves the warrior to leave again for the front, promising to return. Although "Anxious to Return" provides theoretical justification for such dedication (both the warrior and his family had been strung up and tortured for such heinous crimes as not paying the rent), the concluding decision begs credibility. That's especially so since the romantic liaison with the widow provides the pic's most genuinely moving moments.

Whatever its flaws, "Anxious to Return" should be seen by as wide as audience as possible. Its focus on human relationships and its attempt to create action onscreen sans political moralizing is a big step — one of which the Chinese behind this film should take justified pride. —Sege.

Saellskapsresan
(The Charter Trip)
(SWEDISH-COLOR)

Malmoe, Aug. 19.

A Viking Film/Europa Film/RiFilm production. A/B Europa Film release. Story and script. Lasse Aberg. Bo Jonsson. Directed by Lasse Aberg. Features entire cast. Technical director, Peter Hald; production manager, Christer Abrahamsen. Gisela Bergquist; camera (Eastmancolor). Joergen Persson; production design. Bo Lindgren; costumes, denise Gruenstein; music. Bengt Palmers; editor. Sylvia Ingemarsson. Reviewed at International Film Days. Malmoe. Sweden, Aug. 19, 1980. Running time. 104 MINS.
Stig Olsson ....Lasse Aberg
Majsan Lindberg ....Lottie Ejebrandt
Doctor Levander ....Magnus Haerenstam
Goesta Angerud ....Roland Jansson
Siv Aberg ....Kim Anderzon
"Berra" Olsson ....Sven Melander
"Partille" Soederberg ..Weiron Holmberg
Jose Rodriguez ....German Perez
Ole Bramsrud ....Jon Skolmen
Lasse Lundberg ....Ted Astroem

Writer-director-actor Lasse Aberg must by now be considered an established master of the elusive genre, the human comedy-cum-farce, that defied language barriers through the early works of Milos Forman and Jacques Tati to both of whom Aberg is unabashedly indebted. Aberg's new work, "The Charter Trip," should travel equally well. The dialog is beautiful, but much of the feature's fun will be evident even for its frames and visual indications alone. A minimum of subtitles will be needed in whatever market.

Aberg, whose earlier film comedy, "The Call-Up," about middle-aged men called up in arms for two weeks of annual maneuvers, clearly loves the people he again so hilariously depicts in warm and witty situations during The Sun Trip Charter Travels' Christmas flight and stay at one of the Canary Islands, where much inexpensive liquor, too much sun and a great deal of haphazard love affairs are enjoyed and more or less skillfully dealt with by a group of mostly jolly naives.

The farcical possibilities around such a trip could easily lead a lesser light than Aberg astray, but his fun in never labored, never flat-footed. It is never overly intellectual in satirical approach, either. Aberg is loyal to his characters, he never betrays them nor exposes them. They are seen and heard as richly comical, but equally rich in their human frailty and quiet strength.

Aberg himself leads a perfect cast as the lanky, shy electrician who (in a subtly worked plot device) is exploited by a real estate entrepreneur in a money smuggling deal that backfires badly for the bad guy while the electrician, his new girl friend, the parking meter watchwoman and another couple made up of the girl friend's lusty sister and gimmick-happy, kind-hearted Norwegian, with a clear conscience can proceed on a non-charter voyage to Rio.

The Rio ending is, however, just a throw-away footnote, while the real meat and heart of Aberg's film is the sweet way in which all his characters react to the various situations and fates they stumble into.

Not a single episode from attitude to air travel to fiesta-bound dancing and drunkenness is treated with anything less than wry humor and often with outright tenderness.

While no Keaton stone face, Aberg is a comedy actor of the almost mutely appealing kind. Although wildly exuberant, Norway's Jon Skilmen is no less appealing. Without being chorus girls or pin-ups, Lottie Ejebrandt and Kim Anderzon manage to radiate healthy sexiness in the leading girl roles.

Film buffs will particularly enjoy semi-quotes from Tati's "Mr. Hulot's Holiday" and one (sun tanning by stop watch) from John Schlesinger's "Darling," but such fun does not really add anything to Aberg's own original way of viewing and recording the commonplace.

Technical credits are up several notches this time from "The Call-Up," possibly due to the work of cowriter/producer Bo Jonsson and directorial aide de camp Peter Hald. "The Call-Up" proved a major money maker in most of Scandinavia. —Kell.

Bereketli Topraklar Uzerinde
(On the Fertile Land)
(TURKISH-COLOR)

Locarno, Aug. 9.

Focus Films release of a Doga Film. Polar Film production. Features entire cast. Directed by Erden Kiral. Screenplay, Kiral from a story by Orhan Kemal; camera (Color). Jan Perhson. Reviewed at Locarno Film Fest, Aug. 8, '80. Running time: 130 MINS.
With: Tuncel Kurtiz, Erkan Yucel. Yaman Okay. Nur Surer. Meanderes Samanci. Ozcan Ozgur, Selcuk Ulyerguven.

Turkey won the grand prize at the Locarno Fest last year with a film of rage and dramatic edge against the poverty, backwardness and political excesses of the times with "The Flock." Its writer, Yilmaz Guney, still in prison for manslaughter, practically directed it by remote control from prison. He obviously has influenced other filmmakers.

This film deals with worker exploitation in cotton mills, cotton farms and other occupations. It follows three men who leave their towns to go to work but encounter low wages, overwork and harsh conditions.

There is some fine feeling for the work, the land and many of the people. But the film just stands back and records rather than giving more character insight and a more acceptable dramatic pitch that Guney's films have achieved before. Mainly of fest interest, but still showing a growing body of committed films, Turkey may show more successful ones at other festivals.

This item is obviously sincere but without a more coherent pace, dramatic flair and taut epiphany to give it more than a well meaning albeit finally familiar look. —Mosk.

Fontamara
(ITALIAN-COLOR)

Montreal, Aug. 26.

SACIS release of a Rai-Radiotelevisione Italiana Erre Cinematographica production. Executive producer, Edmondo Ricci. Directed by Carlo Lizzani. Features entire cast. Screenplay. Lizzani, Luciano De Caro; camera (Technospes). Mario Vulpiani; score. Roberto DeSimone. No other credits provided. Reviewed Aug. 26, '80, at Cinema Parisien, Montreal. Running time: 134 MINS.
Cast: Michele Placido, Antonella Murgia. Ida di Benedetto; Imma Piro. Antonio Orlando. Diddi Savagnone. Marcello Monti. Enzo Monteduro, Lino Coletta. Liliana Gerace. Franco Javarone, Dino Sarti. Franco Ferri.

This Carlo Lizzani item, in competition in Montreal, is a worthy, engrossing look at how a small village (of the title) fared under the Fascist regime. While an assuredly handsome slice of Italian-peasant-life, Lizzani has approached his material with an emotional reserve that lends the pic a slightly preachy aspect.

The director-coscripter has given his actors plenty of room to emote, but "Fontamara" fails to deliver the accumulated emotional wallop it should. By contrast, for example, Franco Rosi's handling of similar material in "Christ Stopped at Eboli" maintains a constricted key throughout but unleashes strong emotion at the conclusion. That's missing here.

Fontamara is a hillside village in the Abruzzi, which can easily withstand electricity failures (the town hadn't paid its bills in some time) but can't live with officialdom's diverting of its water supply. Among the townspeople is a man in his late twenties (Michele Placido) of unusual physical strength, a large sense of humor and given occasionally to buffoonery.

He tries repeatedly to rally the locals against the regional officials, but, tiring takes off for Rome. There he's unable to get work, and is picked up on trumped-up agitation charges by the Fascists. He rebels in captivity, is tortured and finally killed. A companion confesses, is set free by the Fascists, hikes back to Fontamara, begins effective organizing of the populace by printing up literature telling the actual story of the young man's demise.

Lizzani spends much time giving the audience entertaining but diverting looks at peasant life. He paints the townsfolk in bold colors, emphasizing their simplicity, independence and sense of humor. Things get serious, we know, when the characters begin squabbling amongst themselves when water gets short.

Unfortunately, some of these diversions prolong the pic's excessive two hours plus running time without advancing action. Placido is strong as the heroic young man, carefully managing a broad portrayal without overacting.

Production values are firstrate, and Mario Vulpiani's photography is beautiful without being slick. Pic is best when it shows Placido among the townsfolk. It's when the Nazis step in that tendention threatens. Perhaps given Lizzani's point of view, that's exactly what we're supposed to come away with.

—Sege.

Right Out Of History — The Making Of Judy Chicago's Dinner Party
(COLOR-DOCU-16m)

Hollywood, Aug. 25.
A Phoenix Films release. Produced by Thom Tyson. Directed by Johanna Demetrakas. Camera (color). Baird Bryant; editors. Demetrakas. Nina Toumanoff; music. Catherine MacDonald; sound. Tyson. Demetrakas. Reviewed at the American Film Institute. Beverly Hills. Aug. 25. 1980. (No MPAA Rating.) Running time: 75 MINS.

Filmmakers have always complained that theirs is the most expensive art form, but radical feminist artist Judy Chicago gave them a run for their money with "The Dinner Party," an elaborate, five-year undertaking involving 400 volunteers and over $250,000. An effort to reassert the role of women in history, project consisted of a triangular table. 48 feet on a side, with 39 individually designed needlework place settings and painted porcelain plates for selected · female historical heavyweights, and was first presented at the San Francisco Museum of Modern Art in March, 1979.

Johanna Demetrakas recorded much of the process on film, with an unusual emphasis on feminist acrimoniousness over sisterly harmony or the artistic evoltuion of the bulky piece. Despite placid, visually unexciting aspect of working with fabric and china, 75-minute docu

holds the interest due to tension created by Chicago's "benevolent hierarchy" in which her ego and ideological priorities invariably take precedence over the needs of the hundreds of anonymous workers taken under wing to execute her grand design. Due to dual angles of art world and feminism, pic should have some commercial life in the right specialized situations before hitting non-theatrical circuit.

While a great deal of planning and skill was obviously required to produce the immaculate and precise objet d'art finally achieved, circumstances of its creation here are made to seem distinctly unprofessional, as volunteers are simultaneously required to do as they are told to become a cog in the machine but also to voice their grievances and innermost feelings at weekly rap sessions, where latent frustrations of both Chicago and her entourage spill to the surface.

Other curious aspect of the enterprise is that Chicago forthrightly declares that she is creating art for what is often considered the least assured and most egotistical of reasons — posterity. As far as she's concerned, women's achievements have always been systematically erased from history by male bias, and she is determined to go to enormous lengths.to assure that her work doesn't meet the same fate. Ironically, even after the record-breaking three-month run in S.F., "The Dinner Party" has had trouble finding other museums to book it, often because of its unwieldiness.

Determination of Chicago's artistic accomplishment is another matter entirely, although it must be said that virtually all of the plate designs in commoration of famous women are glorified interpretations of the female sexual organ. Demetrakas has succeeded with her work to the extent that she has focused attention strongly upon the subject at hand and has managed to preserve what can only be certain aspects of a monumental project for all time. Of that, at least, Chicago can be assured to approve.

—Cart.

La Banquiere
(The Woman Banker)
(FRENCH-COLOR)

Paris, Aug. 28.
A Gaumont release of a Partners/FR 3 co-production. with the participation of the Societe Francaise de Production. Produced by Ariel Zeitoun. Stars Romy Schneider. Directed by Francis Girod. Screenplay. Girod and Georges Conchon; camera (color). Bernard Zitzermann; music. Ennio Morricone; art director. Jean-Jacques Caziot; costumes. Jacques Fonteray; editor. Genevieve Winding; sound. Jean-Pierre Ruh. Reviewed at the

Gaumont Ambassade theatre, Paris, August 27. 1980. Running time: 125 MINS.
Emma Eckert .... Romy Schneider
Vannister .... Jean-Louis Trintignant
Cisterne .... Jean-Claude Brialy
Largue .... Claude Brasseur
Lecoudray .... Daniel Mesguich
Colette Lecoudray .. Marie-France Pisier

Romy Schneider is the poised center of attraction in Francis Girod's "La Banquiere," a glossy, dramatically lacklustre retelling of the rise and fall of Marthe Hanau, a woman journalist and banker who dominated French financial circles in the late 1920's before being crushed by a series of scandals that ended with her suicide in 1935.

Girod has surrounded his star with name talent — Jean-Louis Trintignant as the dandyish competitive banker who engineers Hanau-Schneider's destruction, Jean Carmet as the diffident but ruthless scandal sheet reporter, Claude Brasseur as the unscrupulous district attorney who snares her, Jean-Claude Brialy as her faithful lawyer friend, Daniel Mesguich as her idealistic lover, and Marie-France Pisier as Mesguich's wife who shunts aside jealousy to side with her rival.

There are also top-grade technicians like cinematographer Bernard Zitzermann, composer Ennio Morricone, art director Jean-Jacques Caziot and costume designer Jacques Fonteray. All this star shine and production luxuriance is a sound guarantee for local success and will probably facilitate overseas pickup of the film.

But "La Banquiere" is just one more heavily embellished cardboard period piece in which art direction is mistaken for content and a shallow, conventional sense of characterization and narrative betrays any presumptions of psychological and social analysis.

Girod and his coscreenwriter Georges Conchon draw a naively romanticized portrait of Hanau (here called Emma Eckert) and affix their sympathies without nuance. Rather than focus on intimate drama they opt for gaudy brush strokes and effects, as in the final sequence when Schneider dies, not by her own hand, but under the bullets of a hired assassin during a public meeting, as she stirringly tells her investors that they will be fully reimbursed. Girod adds directorial schmaltz by catching her dying all in slow motion and consecrating her martyrdom with that cheapest of film cliches, the freeze frame.

Schneider poses handsomely in her many outfits but her performance is mannered and empty. The other actors are passable, ex-

cepting Jean Carmet, who provides the film's rare moments of imaginative acting in a sparely written role. —Len.

La Mano Negra
(The Black Hand)
(SPANISH-COLOR)

Madrid, Aug. 20.
La Salamandra. Ogro Films and Incine coprodiction. Directed by Fernando Colomo. Features entire cast. Screenplay, Fernando Trueba. Fernando Colomo; camera, (Eastmancolor), Angel Luis Fernandez; editor, Miguel Angel Santamaria; music, Jose Nieto; sound, Pierre Gamet; exec producer, Ramiro G. Bermudez de Castro. Reviewed at Cine Luchana. Madrid. Aug. 20. 1980. Running time: 94 MINS.
Cast: Inigo Gurrea, Joaquin Hinojosa, Virginia Mataix, Carmen Maura, Mary Carrillo, Manuel Alexandre, Fabio Testi, Emilio Urdiales.

Delightul, tongue-in-cheek spoof of the spy thriller genre scripted by the two leading young Spanish talents of the day, Fernando Colomo and Fernando Trueba, the latter the director of this year's local comedy hit, "Opera Prima." Throughout, dialog sparkle, as droll take-offs on the spy genre succeed each other, but in a homespun sort of Spanish way which never takes itself quite seriously. Thesping is down to earth and natural and lines are delivered via direct sound and without the usual stilted style typifying the bulk of Spanish films.

Story concerns a 33 year old ex-student who spends his life loafing about his parents' house and trying to make various girlfriends. Latter endeavor provides some of the funniest scenes in the film. One morning he meets an old school friend in a record store. The friend, a seeming man of the world, tells him he has led a mysterious life, mentions a broken marriage in London, shows a scar from an anarchist clash in Germany, and claims to be the author of a famous spy bestseller, a la Graham Greene or John Le Carre, written in English, published by Penguin and then translated into Spanish.

The student swallows the story and renews contacts with his old buddy, as bombs go off, cars follow him in the street and assassins try to kill the mysterious pal. Till the very end audience is in doubt whether the pal is really a secret agent or is simply guilty of a monumental bluff. The action scenes are discreet but the clowning comes across well thanks to spontaneity and freshness of these relatively unknown thesps, and a live-wire script.

Item may do exceedingly well in Spain, following in the steps of "Opera Prima." Pic is a natural for the fest circuit (it's unspooling at Montreal) and could chalk up some sales in specialized circuits; though no explicit sex scenes are included, some of the language and situations might have to be toned down for countries with tough censorship. —Besa.

Kung-Fu
(POLISH-COLOR)

Locarno, Aug. 8.

Film Polski release of Film Unit X production. Features entire cast. Written and directed by Janusz Kijowski. Camera (Eastmancolor), Krysztof Wyszynski; editor, Irena Choryinska; music, Jacek Bednarek. Reviewed at Locarno Film Fest, Aug. 7, '80. Running time: 112 MINS.
With: Teresa Sawicka, Piotr Fronczewski, Daniel Olbrychski, Andrzej Sewerynm. Krzysztof Janczar.

The new Polish directors have focused attention of the Polish cinema at various festivals with their outspoken, well-made looks at corruption in many facets of life there today. This one fits in with the movement though somewhat convoluted in delving into the past as well as present of its assorted characters.

Film does not have the bite of some of its predecessors but cogently looks at a well-regarded engineer in a big enterprise suddenly hounded by trumped up attacks on his integrity when he delves too deeply into how bonuses are handled by higher-ups.

He gets into an argument with a guard and is arrested and then fired. An old friend, a journalist, tries to sort it out but the victim's hard headedness and past problems with his wife that crop up again lead to losses for both, though his railroading is uncovered.

Janusz Kijowski directs with a bit too much distance from his setting up of the characters and their problems. The result is an obscuring of clarity and motivations. But the film does pack a wallop in its statement though not always in its direction and characterizations.

Not as clear cut for offshore chances as the other Polski pix that have made dents at fests this year but a natural for film weeks and not hurting the growing impact of Polski pix abroad at all. —Mosk.

Wahnsinn, Das Ganze Leven Ist Wahnsinn
(Madness, The Whole Life Is Madness)
(WEST GERMAN-COLOR)

Berlin, Aug. 23.

A C & H Film production, Berlin in collaboration with Zweites Deutsches Fernsehen (ZDF), Wiesbaden-Mainz. Features entire cast. Directed by Petra Haffter. Screenplay, Haffter, Richard Claus; camera (color), Richard Claus.

Only credits available. Reviewed at Arsenal-Kino, Aug. 23, '80. Running time: 90 MINS.
Cast: Germaine Riedinger (Karen Q), Ronni Ranner (Robert), Andrea Schurig (Evelyn), Ludwig Kaschke (Richard), Ellen Esser (Karin's mother).

Petra Haffter's "Madness, the Whole Life Is Madness" followed a typical formula of the Berlin School: take a social theme like a diary of a slow-witted 16-year-old girl with boys on her mind, then cast a normal and good looking lass in the role of the mixed-up teenager and forget about fiction dialog to rely solely on the social document for effect (and discussion, apparently, wit teenagers afterwards). It doesn't work, but pic is an example of how the Berlin women filmmakers have continued the social line of the previous Berlin "worker" films of the last decade.

More of a docu than a feature. Haffter's "Madness" is headed for L.A. in a Women's Filmmakers package shortly. —Holl.

Babylone-XX
(RUSSIAN-COLOR/B&W)

Locarno, Aug. 9.

Sovexport release of Alexander Dov-Zhenko Studio production. Features entire cast. Directed by Ivan Mikolaitchouk. Screenplay, Vassili Zemliak, Mikolaitchouk from the book by Zemliak; camera (Sovcolor-B&W), Youri Gartman. Reviewed at Locarno Film Fest, Aug. 6, '80. Running time, 98 MINS.
With: Lubov Politchchouk, Ivan Mikolaitchouk, Les Surdak, Yaraslov Gavriluk, Ivan Taissia Litvinenko, Raissa Nedachkovskaia.

A mixture of folklore, poetics and political change that do not quite mesh due to excess in each and a visual flamboyance that is pretentious and undigested rather than effective.

Made by an actor who had a role in blacklisted and once-jailed director Serge Paradjanov's noted film of the same kind, "In The Shadow of Our Ancestors," director Ivan Mikolaitchouk did not quite absorb his predecessor's talents.

A little town called Babylone gets its first reps of the recent Russian Revolution. Attempts to communize it meet with resistance from the still rich elements ending in murder but a final quelling of the rebellion by the Red Army.

There are colorful characters, lovely women and some fine atmospheric scenes of virtue. But the characters range from the stereotyped to the exaggerated and film is more an exercise in style than bringing off a highly flavored folk fable with a revolutionary background.

Film uses black-and-white for night scenes which might have

avoided problems and is acceptable. Playing is posey. But this richly atmospheric affair might still carry some more fest and film week potential though not one to raise hopes for the Ukrainian films after the fine work of Paradjanov and the great early Ukrainian genius Alexander Dovzhenko.
—Mosk.

Soulsister
(Soul Sister)
(WEST GERMAN-B&W)

Mainz, Aug. 22.

A Dietmar Buchmann Production, Berlin, in collaboration with Zweites Deutsches Fernsehen (ZDF), Wiesbaden-Mainz. Features cast. Written and directed by Dietmar Buchmann. Only credits available. Reviewed at ZDF Screening Room, Mainz, August 22, '80. Running time: 90 MINS.
Cast: Tatjana Blacher (Monika), Holmes McHenry (Paul), Eberhard Feik (Father), Edith Elsholtz (Mother), Dieter Stolz (Fiancee).

Dietmar Buchmann, a graduate of the Berlin Film & Television Academy, made "Soul Sister" for Second Channel Television (ZDF) in 1978, but pic also had an echo as in studio cinemas here due to its scenes set in Gotham's Harlem and the Yank military barracks scattered across West Germany. It has stateside potential in view of a Yank thesp, Holmes McHenry, playing the lead of a black GI in a situation that is rather common among soldiers stationed abroad.

Monika, a dentist-assistant in a "garrison town," falls in love with Paul, a black GI with more sensitivity than her fiance and parents. After meeting casually, they become lovers and decide to brave the hostile reactions of friends and acquaintances and live together as much as it is possible under the circumstances. Paul is transferred to a large city, and Monika follows him — then his tour of duty runs out, and she follows him back to the States when his letters stop coming. Upon reaching Harlem and visiting Paul's mother without being able to locate the ex-GI, she gives up the search and returns home.

Buchmann telis his story simply and directly, eliminating polemics as a whole and concentrating on the relationship. Thesps Tatjana Blacher and Holmes McHenry carry the story and film by staying close to the realities of the doomed relationship. Worth a onceover at German Film Weeks. —Holl.

Atlantic City, U.S.A.
(CANADIAN-FRENCH-U.S.-COLOR)

Venice, Sept. 3.

Planfilm release of Selta Films-Elie Kfouri-Cine Neighbor Inc.-FR3-SDICC production. Stars Burt Lancaster, Susan Sarandon, Michel Piccoli. Directed by Louis Malle. Screenplay, John Guare; camera (Color), Richard Ciupka; editor, Suzanne Baron; music, Michel Legrand, song "Atlantic City, My Old Friend" by Paul Anka; produced by Dennis Heroux, Gabriel Boustani. Reviewed at Venice Film Fest, Sept. 2, '80. Running time: 104 MINS.

Lou	Burt Lancaster
Sally	Susan Sarandon
Grace	Kate Reid
Joseph	Michel Piccoli
Chrissie	Hollis MacLaren
Dave	Robert Joy
Alfie	Al Waxman
Singer	Robert Goulet

Louis Malle, one of the best French film craftsmen, long talked of leaving France which he felt he could no longer respond to or make films about. He did go off to make a tv series and a film on Indian poverty and then "Pretty Baby" in the U.S.

Now he again makes a film in the U.S., a dramatically taking tale with the rebirth of Atlantic City as a gambling resort in the background.

Malle easily adapts to the rhythms of the English lingo and brings a French flair for observation and even an existential look at his characters that is effective in a tale that brushes nostalgia and sentimentality but avoids them.

Film is blessed with a spare, intriguing script by Yank John Guare, who worked on Milos Forman's first U.S. film, "Taking Off," which always skirts impending cliches and predictability by finding unusual facets in his characters and their actions.

Besides the work of Malle and Guare, the film is well limned by Burt Lancaster as a smalltime, mythomaniacal, aging mafia hood, Susan Sarandon as an ambitious young woman, Kate Reid as a fading moll and Robert Joy and Hollis MacLaren as Sarandon's husband and young sister who are catalysts in this drama.

Atlantic City is also a character as Malle adroitly uses decrepit old facades and the new ones thanks to gambling when New Jersey voted to allow it at this once proud resort which had boasted gangsters, prohibition capers and big show attractions.

Lancaster takes care of bedridden Kate Reid, who may be shamming it, widow of a fellow hood. He even services her sexually at times. He also takes numbers, and likes to watch Sarandon who always washes herself down with lemon juice to remove the smell of fish from an oyster bar where she works.

Into this comes Joy, Sarandon's husband whom she had left, dragging along her kid sister now pregnant by him. Joy has heisted some heroin from a drop. They move in on Sarandon.

Joy meets Lancaster and asks him to help him sell the stuff. The dope is hidden in Lancaster's room, but after the first delivery Joy is killed by the two hoods who owned the dope and have tracked him down.

Lancaster is now flush and helps Sarandon, is drawn to her and maybe she to him. The hoods come after them and Lancaster kills them with his old gun. This is really the first time he ever had killed anyone though he had boasted he had in his heyday.

He goes off with Sarandon but she steals a lot of the money and leaves to perhaps become a croupier in France for which she had been studying at a special school.

Lancaster lets her go and comes back to take up with Reid and sell off the last bit of dope. Michel Piccoli, noted French actor, adds a lively bit as the croupier teacher.

Well shot, this drama of smalltimers achieves a solid dramatic rightness.

Primarily made as a Canadian feature, it does have Sarandon and MacLaren and Joy from the backwaters of Canada which makes acceptable the latter two's fairly old fashioned hippy garb and talk of Indian religion.

Film is not a hybrid for all is well meshed. It might well have sleeper potential on its Atlantic City background and its observant, sympathetic but never condescending treatment of its characters.

Film makes a bow to "The Killers," Lancaster's first film, for he might have become this kind of character if he had lived, and even an homage to the great German filmmaker F.W. Murnau via a scene in which Lancaster helps an old gangster chum now working in a men's toilet. —*Mosk.*

Deux Lions Au Soleil
(Two Lions in the Sun)
(FRENCH-COLOR)

Venice, Sept. 3.
Gaumont release of Basta Films, FR3 production. Features entire cast. Written and directed by Claude Faraldo. Camera (Eastmancolor). Bernard Lutic; editor. Dominique Gallieni; music, Albert Marcoeur. Francois Ovide. Reviewed at Venice Film Fest. Sept. 2, '80. Running time: 110 MINS.

Rene .... Jean-Pierre Sentier
Paul .... Jean-Francois Stevenin
Babette ....Catherine Lachens
Woman .... Martine Sarcey
Husband .... Michel Robin
Wife .... Valerie Kling
Agent .... Alain Doutey
Procureur .... Jean-Pierre Tailhade

Claude Faraldo is one of the rare original French filmmakers who came from worker ranks, albeit he had studied acting and had done some theatrical work.

His first film, to make an impact "So What!", was an anarchic look at workers who decide to opt out, a father and son who also share the same woman.

Another one on worker alienation and a need for liberty, "Themroc," emerged a more expressionistic film about worker revolt against the system. Now again, after two films that did not click, Faraldo goes back to workers who need more than bread alone to live by.

The result is a sometimes strained, sometimes touching tale of two homosexuals, both semiskilled workers, who had previously been married and had children. They are a fine match but decide to stop work and live by expediency when they feel their lives are lacking a needed edge of freedom.

In these days of growing worker controversies, writer-director Faraldo skirts and politics and just deals in two people drifting into petty, sloppy attempts at crime. They do find a blissful moment when both share a woman barmaid whose husband is in prison.

Jean-Pierre Sentier, as the more tender member of the two, is effective and balanced by Jean-Francois Stevenin's more headstrong character who brings on the actions.

Faraldo is a personal filmmaker with an itchy, iconoclastic attitude towards cliche social attitudes and the sanctity of work.

His workers are not fighting for more money but dignity. However, Faraldo does not achieve the anarchic bite, the grace and rightness of its sentiments, with a comic envelope, of his other films. He could use a scripter to help tighten his sprawling stories of people searching for their place in the sun.

The film's intensity of mood, its offbeat treatment and subject could insure fest outings though commercial chances outside its home grounds are chancey.

The film is technically fine down the line. —*Mosk.*

C'Est La Vie!
(That's Life)
(FRENCH-COLOR)

Venice, Aug. 30.
MK2 release of Diagonale Productions production. Features entire cast. Written and directed by Paul Vecchiali. Camera (Eastmancolor). Georges Strouve; music, Roland Vincent. Reviewed at Venice Film Fest. Aug. 30, '80. Running time, 90 MINS.
Ginette .... Chantal Delsaux
Richard ....Jean-Christophe Bouvet
Rachah .... Cecile Clairval
Simone................. Ingrid Bourgoin
Delordre .... Helene Surgere
Beatrice .... Beatrice Bruno
L'Agent ....Michel Delahaye

Paul Vecchiali is one of those French film mavericks. He makes and produces his own films, and those of others. He has built up a specialized following at home. But he has yet to get attention abroad, despite festivals, and this talky look at female confession and suburban life will also get mainly token festival appearances outside France.

Vecchiali here obviously opted for spontaneity and perhaps a good deal of improvisation.

Verbose affair does have insights into personal problems but lacks the visual edge that Vecchiali was able to achieve in his best film, "Femmes, Femmes," about two middleaged women living together.

A highly specialized item but one perhaps having the barrage of ideas and insights into female adaptation that may net it specialized archive, school and sponsored chances though regular commercial outings look chancey. —*Mosk.*

Times Square
(COLOR)

Teenage walk on the wild side doesn't convince. Music promo major sales angle.

Hollywood, Sept. 6.
An EMI Films release (AFD in U.S.-Canada) of a Butterfly Valley N.V./RSO Films Ltd. production. Produced by Robert Stigwood. Jacob Brackman. Executive producers. Kevin McCormick, John Nicolella. Features entire cast. Directed by Alan Moyle. Screenplay. Jacob Brackman, based on a story by Alan Moyle, Leanne Unger; camera (DeLuxe color). James. A. Contner; editor. Tom Priestley; production design, Stuart Wurtzel; set decoration. Leslie Bloom; costumes, Robert de Mora; sound. Les Lazarowitz; asst. director. Alan Hopkins; second unit directors. Edward Bianchi, John Nicolella. Reviewed at the Paramount Theatre, Hollywood. Sept. 6. 1980. (MPAA Rating: R) Running time: 111 MINS.
Johnny Laguardia .... Tim Curry
Pamela Pearl .... Trini Alvarado
Nicky Marotta ....Robin Johnson
David Pearl .... Peter Coffield
Dr. Huber ....Herbert Berghof
Dr. Zymansky ....David Margulies
Rosie Washington .. Anna Maria Horsford

"Times Square" is a film about and for those urban creatures who walk the streets lugging around huge tape players. It's also a pseudo-punk picture which doesn't dare speak that lifestyle's name, thereby making it seem curiously synthetic despite the furious effort made for documentary veracity. Studded by a double album's worth of current sounds, grungy tale of New York runaways comes off as neither entertaining nor convincing and reps a considerable sales challenge for RSO Records and domestic distrib AFD to put it across even with ever-hungry adolescent audience.

Betraying shades of "Hardcore" but with no real sense of danger or menace, pic limns unlikely tale of a surly delinquent girl who induces a rather withdrawn, upper-class daughter of a N.Y. City Commissioner to take to the streets. Conveniently. Papa is also in charge of Mayor's Redevelopment Program for 42d Street area, setting up a dialectical angle which is never coherently articulated beyond the juvenile level of portraying liberal adults as uncomprehending morons and implicitly suggesting that Times Square ought to be preserved as a playground for good-time kids.

Literally hovering over it all from his high rise perch is cynical radio d.j. Tim Curry, who somehow manages to chronicle adventures of the teenie-bopper duo and even gives them air time on occasion.

After assorted shenanigans, including making off in a city ambulance and dropping tv sets off of buildings, street girl finally starts channeling her anarchic personality into music, which allows tale to climax with an outrageously implausible punk mini-conc rt by the "Sleez Sisters" on top o a Times Square theatre marquee'

Canadian director Alan Moyle is clearly a devotee of the current British "high energy" school of filmmaking, but that can't compensate for his frequently haphazard cutting and storytelling style. Jacob Brackman's script is loaded with contempo street jargon but makes many illogical jumps and, more seriously, doesn't develop a firm p.o.v. despite obvious pro-youth slant.

Much rides on the appeal of the kids, and here again pic comes up short. As the tough-break urchin, Robin Johnson displays a real spirit and, along with her Jagger-Travolta lips, somewhat resembles a rough-hewn Simone Signoret. But as Moyle has not seen fit to curb her incessant moving and fidgeting, she becomes a bit much well before overlong pic finally fades out. Trini Alvarado is demurely appealing as her well-bred companion, and Curry, making a break with his "Rocky Horror Picture Show" image, is good as the late-night voice on the airwaves.

All-important soundtrack is comprised of 20, mostly new wave, tunes from English and Yank groups. Despite fact that film never declares itself as punk, it remains to be seen whether or not this sort of music will help or hurt pic's attempt to cross over to mainline teen crowd. —Cart.

Pile ou Face
(Heads or Tails)
(FRENCH-COLOR)

Paris, Sept. 2.
GEF/CCFC release of an FDR/Antenne 2 coproduction. Produced by Georges Cravenne. Stars Philippe Noiret, Michel Serrault. Directed by Robert Enrico. Screenplay, Enrico, Marcel Jullian, Michel Audiard, based on the novel. "Baroni," by Alfred Harris; camera, (Eastmancolor), Didier Tarot; editor, Patricia Neny; sound, Alain Lachassagne, Jean Neny; art director, Jean-Claude Gallouin; music, Lino Leonardi. Reviewed at UGC Ermitage Theatre, Paris, Sept. 2, 1980. Running time: 105 MINS.
Baroni .... Philippe Noiret
Morlaix .... Michel Serrault
Laurence .... Dorothee
Larrieu .... Andre Falcon

Canny packaging of two top leading men, Michel Serrault and Philippe Noiret, and a made to order police thriller script with polished dialog by Michel Audiard, has produced a boxoffice hit locally with "Heads or Tails," which marks publicist Georges Cravenne's initial foray into production and director Robert Enrico's first commercial success since "The Old Gun" (1975).

International standing of its stars should make film (based on an Am-

erican detective novel) a viable commodity in overseas markets, though it proves to be a rather contrived and finally disappointing affair that is shallow despite its air of psychological astuteness. It will probably satisfy a public not too concerned to look beyond surfaces and taken with the over-emphatic performances of its stars.

Noiret plays a Bordeaux police inspector, a widower and nearing retirement, and Serrault a henpecked accountant whose vertigo wife falls to her death from their apartment window. The police class the affair as an accident, but Noiret is convinced that the man pushed her.

Noiret begins to hound Serrault, trailing him and prying into his past, though latter makes no attempt to complain against the persecution, a game of cat and mouse ensues with the two widowers finally forming an odd couple. When Noiret's retirement is prematurely imposed on him by his corrupt superiors — his professional integrity has become an obstacle to influential drug dealers — he accepts a fat bribe and sails for the South Seas with Serrault, who has always dreamt of escape to a sun-drenched island there.

One is deliberately left in the dark as to what motivates the peculiar behavior of the two men until the last minute of film, when "The Surprise Ending" arrives to illuminate it all. It's pretty gimmicky, not especially surprising, and doesn't make what has preceded more credible or interesting.

Both Noiret and Serrault lack subtlety and play for effects, which is in keeping with Enrico's insistent direction. At times their scenes seem an unconscious parody of the Noiret-Jean Rochefort relationship in Bertrand Tavernier's "The Clockmaker." —Len.

Heinrich Heine Revue
(WEST GERMAN-COLOR-16m)

Berlin, Aug. 23.
A PTP Peter Thomas Production, Duesseldorf. Features entire cast. Directed by Guenther Fiedler. Based on Guenther Buech's Revue at the Kammerspiele Duesseldorf. Text, Heinrich Heine; camera (color), Juergen Schuermann; sets, Lioba Winterhalder; music, Peter Jassens, Peter Frass-Wolfsburg; choreography, Marlis Gruenberg; sound, Werner Vitalis; lighting and assistance, Hans Hoffmann. Reviewed at Arsenal-Kino, Berlin, August 23, '80. Running time: 90 MINS.
Cast: Katrin Schoenermark, Dagmar Soerensen, Ilona Wiedem, Georg Cadalbert, Klaus Jaegel, Manfred Repp, Michael Thiele.

At a time when several tv adaptations of legit prods are finding their ways to the screens of German film fests and small art

houses, among them Peter Stein's "Big and Little" and Klaus Michael Grueber's "Winter Journey," don't fail to catch the "Heinrich Heine Revue" at your local Goethe Institute, or German Film Week, or any anniversary celebrating the birth or death of the greatest German poet since Goethe. The filmed theatre production of the Duesseldorf musical and theatrical revue (it has been performed at the Kammerspiele Duesseldorf over 300 times since the preem in 1972) has relevance in light of the fact that the city fathers in Heine's birthplace, Duesseldorf, have refused to name the university there after the famous poet.

Heinrich Heine (born 1797, died 1856) spent most of his adult life in exile in Paris. As the poor cousin of a wealthy Jewish family who was rejected in love, he felt himself an outsider wherever he went, but Paris at least offered the opportunity to pour out his thoughts in an endless stream of verses, travelogues, autobiographical memoirs, satirical letters, and sketches of every kind. Several romantic songwriters used his texts, and these composers made his poetry so popular that, during the time of Hitler, the songs were marked "Poet Unknown" to save the Third Reich embarrassment. Heine's satirical pen still embarrasses Germans enough today to avoid naming the university in Duesseldorf after him.

Favorite audience passages in the revue with 59 scenes are those from the "Memoirs" (his family is believed to have destroyed part of the manuscript after his death), "Buch der Lieder" (the reservoir for song-texts), "Pictures of Travel" (descriptions of landscapes with people from an irreverent viewpoint), "Germany: A Winter's Tale" (satire), and "Atta Troll" (satire), in addition to the letters and autobiographical sketches (often penned as a journalist for the newspaper feuilleton section). The original title for the revue, in fact, was from a Heine comment "When I Think of Germany ..." that ends with a night tossing in bed.

Any Heine fan or friend of German literature can pick his own passages. The staging is visually oriented to underscore the verbal puns and satirical barbs in the revue. Pic opens with candles being lit, as at a cocktail party or masquerade ball; it ends with the candles burned down, the thesps departing in ordinary street clothes that represent various walks of modern life, from conservative-minded to radical-oriented to whatever fits Heine's own conception of himself as a homeless "Doppelgaenger" warring with himself as much as society.

Cast and credits are of the same

quality as the legit prod under Buech and Thomas nearly a decade ago, which is still going strong.
—Holl

Os Anos JK — Uma Trajetoria Politica
(The JK Years — A Political Trajectory)
(BRAZILIAN-COLOR)

Rio de Janeiro, Aug. 28.
Embrafilme release of a Terra Filmes production. Features newsreels, documents and interviews. Directed by Silvio Tendler. Camera (color), Lucio Kodato; editor, Francisco Sergeio Moreira; research, Francisco Quental, Antonio Paulo Ferraz; text, Claudio Bojunga; narrator, Othon Bastos; music, Caique Botkay; sound, Christiano Maciel; asst. director and editor, Francisco Sergio Moreira; asst. research, Olga d'Arc Pimentel, Silvia Bregman. Reviewed at Caruso Cinema, Rio de Janeiro, Aug. 28, 1980. Running time: 110 MINS.

When elected President of Brazil back in 1955, the physician Juscelino Kubitschek de Oliveira did not yet have the popularity that he was to gain during his term. The political crisis, which dramatically materialized with the suicide of President Getulio Vargas a year before, had led the country into deep perplexity. Kubitschek was elected on a platform based on energy and transportation, as well as democratization and economic development, both particularly appealing under the circumstances. In just a few years he built Brasilia, the new capital, shifting the center for political decisions from crowded Rio de Janeiro to an arid and forgotten land 1,000 miles to the interior. He left the government under democratic elections in 1960 almost as a hero, already preparing his return for 1965.

Four years later, a military coup deposed Joao Goulart, vice-president who had taken over after the resignation of Janio Quadros, elected successor of Kubitschek. In just a few weeks, latter had his political rights suspended by the military government and was sent into exile to Europe after a web of incriminations and policial inquiries. The dossier was prepared by Col. Joao Baptista Figueiredo, then an officer at the National Intelligence Service.

Kubitschek died in 1976 in an automobile accident. In 1979 the now General Figueiredo was made fifth President of the revolution. All Kubitschek's "faults" were forgiven; post-mortem, military awards and orders were returned to his family.

Silvio Tendler, 30, a Rio professor and occasional filmmaker, has been searching for an answer to these contrasts since he went to

Paris, some seven years ago. Back in Brazil, he managed to accumulate almost 30 hours of filmed documents, speeches, struggles and interviews. Such material was reduced to slightly less than two hours.

Tendler's resulting documentary is one of the most faithful and honest works of such kind made recently in Brazil. The collected material can be considered the best possible in the absence of organized Brazilian film archives. Facts are narrated in a didactic yet never academic way, and the text allows the spectator an easy comprehension of the Brazilian political life in the last 35 years.

Newsreel and official films are often used, as well as recent interviews with former members of Vargas, Quadros, Kubitschek and military governments. Certainly, Tendler exercises his right to ideologize his material, although always interpreting rather than distorting it. —*Hoin.*

Moon In Taurus
(SWISS-COLOR).

Zurich, Aug. 29.
Starfilm GmbH Zurich release of an Alive Film Productions GmbH Zurich production. Produced, written and directed by Steff Gruber. Features entire cast. Camera (color), Andy Humphreys; sound, Jim Hawkins; editors, Gruber, Beni Mueller, Daniel Koch; music, "Cordoba" from "Iberia" by Isaas Albeniz, played by Ruedi Burkhalter; musical advice, Paul Fischli; assistant cameraman, Billy Sherrill. Previewed at the Le Paris, Zurich, Aug. 29, '80. Running time: 100 MINS.
Wanda .... Wanda Linn Wester
Jack .... Jack Wright
Bonnie .... Bonnie T
Steff .... Steff Gruber
(English soundtrack)

"Moon In Taurus," first feature film by a young Swiss filmmaker, Steff Gruber, is an oddity: a Swiss film made entirely in English and filmed in the U.S. (Athens, Ga.), without a story in the usual sense and with a non-pro cast of four playing themselves. In fact, Gruber aimed at coming to grips with his emotional problems, resulting from an unhappy affair with a Georgia girl, by analyzing the reasons for the failure through talks with her and her ex-husband. She had, since the affair with Gruber five years before, been married and divorced.

Obviously, this is a special film for specialized audiences, talky to be sure, but constantly interesting, intelligent and mature. Edited down from 24 hours of filmed material to an acceptable 100 minutes, "Moon" meets professional standards also in Andy Humphreys' effective lensing job. The danger of monotony, always inherent in an excessive amount of dialog, is avoided by visual interceptions of an often symbolic nature.

Gruber wisely resisted the pitfalls of an ego trip by focusing on the girl and her ex-hubby rather than on himself, although it is clear that the discussions he either takes part in or witnesses, are mind-openers to him, too. Not an easy film, but a noteworthy one. —*Mezo.*

Attentat
(Assassination)
(DANISH-COLOR)

Copenhagen, Aug. 18.
An A/S Panorama (Just Betzer) production. A/S ASA release. Story and script, Poul-Henrik Trampe, based on his novel. Directed by Bent Christensen. Features entire cast. Production manager, John Hilbard; camera (Eastmancolor) Erik Wittrup Willumsen; editor, Maj Soya; production design, Palle Arestrup, Viggo Bentzon; music, Ole Hoeyer; stunt action, Jen Sheppard, Stunt Inc., England. Reviewed at the EBC screening room, Copenhagen, Aug. 18, 1980. Running time: 88 MINS.
Police Lt. Joergensen .. Jesper Langberg
Police Intelligence
Commissioner Hein ...... Bent Mejding
Police Sgt. Holm .... Claus Strandberg
Martin Lindberg ...... Joern Fauerschou
Michael Wilnsdorf ..... Peter Eszterhas
Tove Madsen .... Anne-Lise Gabold
Gladys Soerensen ...... Susanne Heinrich

The real culprit in this expensively produced crime meller with political overtones is scriptwriter Poul-Henrik Trampe who has almost totally neglected to correct a major weakness of his novel, "Assassination," before turning it into a film of the same name. Director Bent Christensen has tried to right the wrong, but too feebly so. In the novel as in the film, the person who does it remains the total shadow of a supporting player even when finally found out and arrested.

Whatever ire the spectator may have generated through a multi-layered plot thus ends up as a punch into thin air. It is all right for Trampe to indicate that the political arm of Denmark's law enforcement turn to brutality and that it is suffering from its own political paranoia. This may or may not be so. But it is not all right to have audiences guessing without purpose amongst all suspects presented with any touch of characterization.

Plot has a guard in the State Parliament take a bullet that to all intents and purposes appears to have been aimed at the Energy Minister.

Lt. Joergensen, played with subdued strength and the tired conviction of a Maigret (we get to see a good deal of his family life, too) by Jesper Langberg, does his best to contain the rough methods and the paranoic thinking of his Police Intelligence counterparts (they appear to be a kind of independent FBI), while general panic is said (not shown) to be spreading via the media.

The Intelligence guys, one smoothly mean (Bent Mejding), the rest the usual ape types, are seen pursuing all their wrong leads and driving at least one innocent suspect to his death. Joergensen plods less spectacularly along, following his own hunch in quite another direction. He pauses now and then to speak up for common sense and is despairing of the Danish people having any such left.

"Assassination" has several chase sequences involving autos and either sneaking or dashing around hospital corridors. None of them work very well although Ken Sheppard and some of his men from Stunt Inc. came over from England to do the running and jumping. Standing still is what this film does most of the time.

Obviously, producer Just Betzer has had hopes for across-the-border sales of "Assassination." Re-couping his costs (the State Film Institute chipped in with a substantial guarantee) at home may prove hard enough. —*Kell.*

Venice Film Fest

Melvin And Howard
(U.S.-COLOR)

Unusual comedy-drama about unlikely hero Melvin Dummar scores artistically but presents tough sell.

Hollywood, Aug. 29.
A Universal release of a Linson Phillips Demme production. Produced by Art Linson, Don Phillips. Directed by Jonathan Demme. Stars Paul Le Mat, Jason Robards. Screenplay, Bo Goldman; camera (Technicolor), Tak Fujimoto; editor, Craig McKay; music, Bruce Langhorne; production design, Toby Rafelson; art direction, Richard Sawyer; set decoration, Bob Gould; sound, David Ronne; associate producer, Terry Nelson; assistant director, Don Heitzer; second unit director, Evelyn Purcell. Reviewed at the Universal Studios, Universal City, Aug. 29, 1980. (MPAA Rating: R.) Running time: 93 MINS.
Melvin Dummar .... Paul Le Mat
Howard Hughes .... Jason Robards
Lynda Dummar .... Mary Steenburgen
Jim Delgado .... Jack Kehoe
Little Red .... Michael J. Pollard
Bonnie Dummar .... Pamela Reed
Judge Keith Hayes ..... Dabney Coleman
2nd Attorney (Freese) .... John Glover
Ventura .... Charles Napier
Darcy Dummar ......Elizabeth Cheshire
Bus Depot Counterman Melvin E. Dummar
Mrs. Sisk .... Gloria Grahame
Chapel Owner .... Susan Peretz
Easy Street Announcer ...... Danny Dark
Realty Agent .... Martine Beswicke
Mrs. Worth .... Charlene Holt
Sherry Dummar ...... Melissa Williams
Melvin's Lawyer .... Rick Lenz
1st Attorney (Maxwell) ... Joseph Ragno

A pungent fable about the elusiveness of the American Dream, "Melvin And Howard" is a richly textured, highly individualistic look at Melvin Dummar, a man in over his head both before and after becoming the beneficiary of $156,000,000 via Howard Hughes' socalled Mormon will. Jonathan Demme's tour-de-force direction, Bo Goldman's imaginative screenplay and top-drawer performances from a huge cast fuse in an unusual, original creation which nonetheless presents a tough sell in the marketplace. Latest, and best, Universal release to derive from folk history of the immediate past needs top reviews to give it a commercial toe-hold, after which slow playoff to generate word of mouth would seem the wisest course. World preemed at the Venice Film Festival, film will launch N.Y. Fest Sept. 26.

Dummar's chance encounter with a man representing himself as the reclusive tycoon occupies first reel or so and, despite Jason Robards' amusing portrait of Hughes as a grizzled old coot, pic takes awhile generating a full head of steam. As his two-time bride and divorcee, Mary Steenburgen says, when leaving him, Melvin is a loser, and early footage focusing upon his inability to cope with family or jobs makes for somewhat uncertain p.o.v. and difficult viewer entry into the mixed-tone proceedings.

Once the couple remarries in a hilarious Las Vegas ceremony and Steenburgen goes on to win $10,000 in an even funnier game show sequence, Preston Sturges-like tale comes into its own, as modern society is seen to hold success and prosperity out on a carrot stick in front of people who gamely keep chasing it but can never rise above their own limitations nor the constrictions of the class-economic structure.

Hughes angle, which consists of impoverished Dummar giving billionaire a lift to Las Vegas and throwing in a quarter in the bargain, merely serves as a wild bookend which lifts otherwise mundane lives to an extraordinary level.

Among its other virtues, film is exemplary for its rare concentration on the quality, and lack of it, in Middle American life, and incisive, if indirect, examination of the no win syndrome for contemporary proletariat. Pic is highly mindful of working conditions, false bonhomie between haves and have nots, people living beyond their means, and vague, pervasive dissatisfaction among the hoipolloi which stops short of being articulated in any meaningful personal or political way save for simply leaving one's mate or job.

Oblique critique of contempo society is matched by Demme's off beat visual style, distancing of which prevents a real warming up to the characters but, as in his earlier "Handle With Care," allows for a rewarding intermingling of personalities as well as for unexpected comedy. In league with responsive cinematographer Tak Fujimoto, director has developed a penchant for spectacular, Bertolucci-esque crane and tracking shots, although style remains at service of the material and never seems unnaturally imposed upon it.

Like several of Preston Sturges' unlikely heroes of the 1940s, Paul Le Mat's Dummar "has greatness thrust upon him," but perhaps it's a sign of the times that reality has punctured the American Dream to the extent that no guardian angel or happy twist of fate comes along to save Melvin from himself. Many things happen to him but, despite numerous opportunities, he never manages to turn his chances to his own advantage.

Le Mat's essential affability makes Melvin's perpetual loser status palatable in context of the askance approach, while Mary Steenburgen gives pic a very welcome center of warmth and humanity. Crowding the screen with personality is a terrific array of supporting players, which most notably includes Pamela Reed as Melvin's new wife, Michael J. Pollard, amusingly in as lead's good friend, Jack Kehoe as a short fused boss, Elizabeth Cheshire as one of the Dummar's daughters, Danny Dark as the outrageous game show host and Susan Peretz as a Vegas chapel owner.

Behind the scenes contributions are equally outstanding, including Craig McKay's sharp editing, Toby Rafelson's highly attentive production design and particularly Bruce Langhorne's flavorsome score, which is abetted by numerous w.k. tunes.

Due to somewhat sidelong approach to Dummar's odyssey and unemphatic point-making, "Melvin And Howard" remains more engaging than compelling, more satisfying for its many small pleasures than dazzling for any knock out punches. That it dares to be modest and quietly observant makes it relatively unique among American pix these days. —Cart.

Gloria
(U.S.-COLOR)

Venice, Sept. 9.
Columbia Pictures release and production. Stars Gena Rowlands. Written and directed by John Cassavetes. Camera (Color). Fred Schuler; editor, George C. Villasenor; music, Bill Conti; producer, Sam Shaw. Reviewed at Venice Film Fest, Sept. 4, '80. Running time: 123 MINS.
Gloria . . . . Gena Rowlands
Phil . . . . John Adames

Jack . . . . Buck Henry
Jeri . . . . Julie Carmen

"Gloria" is a glorious broad perhaps pushing 40. She has been in prison but now has her nestegg and just wants to be let alone with her cat, friends and a fairly economically carefree life. But the way things happen she has to put her neck out again, and for a precocious kid, half Puerto Rican, whom she has inadvertently pledged to help.

Director-actor John Cassavetes eases up on his unusually probing, darting camera and closeups studying human problems and disarray. Here instead he stands back and churns out a chase film that pits Gloria and the kid against the powerful Mafia no less.

Do they win? Maybe. The ending seems a happy one but it may just be a daydream. Gloria goes to borrow a cup of coffee from her pretty Puerto Rican friend in a big sprawling apartment house. She finds the family trying to get out for they have been staked out for death by the Mafia.

Buck Henry, the husband, has been a bookkeeper for the gangs and taken notes in a book that could give away many covert financial matters. The Mafia has sent its men. Gloria is begged to take the kids, there is a seven-or eight-year-old boy and an older girl.

The girl will not go but the boy finally follows her, reluctantly, when his father insists he must for he will be the man of the family. Gloria gets him away but hoods kill the family and she is on the run with the kid, also has his father's book.

Gena Rowlands is excellent as the tired woman who decides to take her chances for the boy, even if he is annoying at first, as a sort of romantic gesture against the cold murder of a while family.

The kid is a right blend of understanding and childish tantrums. The look at New York during the chases is also a pictorial asset for this breezy actioner which substitutes a good-looking, mature woman for the usual man-on-the-run plus another fillip to the genre in the well-observed relationship of the boy and woman that grows without any forced sentimentality.

A vigorous campaign might help turn the film into a solid performer at the wickets at home as well as elsewhere. It is an enjoyable return to film basics of two uplikely people — outwitting organized crime. There is canny revelation of the characters of the woman and the boy who can get no help and depend only on their own resources.

Technically fine, with all the secondary characters assets despite their fleeting apparitions. —Mosk.

Uomini E No
(Men or Not Men)
(ITALIAN-COLOR)

Venice, Sept. 9.
Italnoleggio Cinematografico release of Ager Cinematografica — RAI Rete 2 production. Features entire cast. Directed by Valentino Orsini. Screenplay, Faliero Rosati, Giuliana De Negri, Orsini from the book by Elio Vittorini; camera (color). Franco De Giacomo; editor, Roberto Perpigini; music, Ennio Morricone. Reviewed at Venice Film Fest, Sept. 4. Running time, 102 MINS.
N2 . . . . Flavio Bucci
Lorena . . . . Ivana Monti
El Paso . . . . Massimo Foschi
Cane Negor . . . . Renato Scarpa

A war resistance film and love story, film is economically told but does not add anything new or get a more dramatic edge into its worthy theme. Made as a film for Italo tv, it seems more a telefilm than a theatrical one in its pared down story, tight and simple characterizations and bypassing more background bolstering of the Resistance moves and times.

It is Milan in 1944 and the Italian replica of the Nazi SS is brutally engaging in reprisals against Italian Resistance fighters. Bodies are laid out in town squares. The leader of one Resistance group meets a woman he loved but lost contact with during the war.

She is married but love now blooms again. The man, however, is tracked down and holed up in a top story of a house as the woman, after leaving her husband, tries to join him. It may be a bow to Marcel Carne's classic pre-war French pic, "Daybreak," as the man barricades himself in.

But here he wraps dynamite around himself and manages to get the sadistic leader of the Italo Black Guards by flinging himself out the window and exploding together with him.

Film is solidly made but too schematic and rote for more than local chances and perhaps video outings abroad. —Mosk.

Guns
(FRENCH-COLOR)

Venice, Sept. 9.
SND release of Quasar production. Features entire cast. Written and directed by Robert Kramer. Camera (Eastmancolor). Richard Kopans, Eric Pittard, Claude Michaud, Louis Bihi; editor, Valeria Sarmiento, Claudio Martinez; executive producer, Helene Vager. Reviewed at Venice Film Festival, Sept. 3, '80. Running time, 95 MINS.
Tony . . . . Patrick Bauchau
Margot . . . . Juliet Berto
Lil . . . . Peggy Frankston
Katrin . . . . Hermine Karagheuz
Marie . . . . Beatrice Lord
Destrez . . . . Stephane Fey
Robin . . . . Robert Kramer

Robert Kramer has made, in all probability, one of the most intensive, revelatory films about youthful revolt in the late '60s and early '70s in the U.S.A. in response to new political consciousness and changes wrought by the unpopular Vietnam war.

The U.S. director's last fiction film, "Milestones," in 1976, was an unusual look at what had happened to the revolutionary-prone characters of his earlier films, "The Edge" and "Ice." Now, after a sojourn and a documentary in Portugal, he makes his first film in France as a French film.

It is a sort of mosaic ringing in a group of people who have ties with each other on the background of the political intrigue of gun-running to some oil-rich Arab spot apparently secretly underwritten by the government to secure continued oil shipments.

It all remains a bit mysterious and is reflected by the work of a freelance journalist who senses a big story. He lives with an American woman who has an American friend, played by director Kramer himself, who lives off some so-called black labor, helps political refugees and is a sculptor.

There is also an actress, an old friend of the reporter, staying with her mother in Marseilles to help her die. The mother wants to go her own way from her cancer without medical help.

The film is somewhat mysterious, even hermetic at times, with shafts of insight into the mixed nationality characters and an oblique reaction to some obscure political machinations in a country the filmmaker is now living in and reflected through his outlooks rather than those of the natives of the country he is observing.

It is also sometimes cold, with a rather slow but revealing tempo as the characters criss-cross each other's lives. The actress is a friend of the journalist and he can console her in Marseilles where he is making his studies for his story.

The film looks headed for other festivals and might catch more selectives audiences abroad with good placement and handling on its observation of people caught up in new lives abroad or in obscure political events. —Mosk.

Spasatel
(The Life Guard)
(RUSSIAN-COLOR)

Venice, Sept. 9.
Sovexport release of Mosfilm production. Features entire cast. Written and directed by Sergei Soloviov. Camera (Sovcolor). Pavel Lebsev; editor, A. Abramova; music, Isaak Svarc. Reviewed at Venice Film Fest, Sept. 3, '80. Running time, 101 MINS.
Anja . . . . Tatiana Drubic
Vilja . . . . Vasili Miscenko

Larikov .... Sergei Sakurov
Olija .... Olga Beljavskaya
Ganin .... Vjaselav Konenko
Varaskin .... Alejsandr Kajdonovski

A slow, disarming but finally listless rather than dramatically-taking film comes out of this tale of a few young people coming of emotional age. There are intimated love scenes between a young man and his best friend's girl and a young married woman's crush on her ex-professor which is never consummated.

Perhaps it is outspoken for a Russian film, but just lacking the dramatic punch to make it more pointed and give the characters more depth. As is, they remain stereotyped. The husband of the woman who has the crush on her idealistic professor thinks of killing the man but only in thought. However that thought is graphically shown.

The professor has affected all his students and one of them, now a tv director, thinks of doing 2 documentary on him but none of his ex-students will collaborate. The woman tries to commit suicide and is saved by the man who had an affair with his friend's girl and is a lifeguard.

It leads to the two talking out their problems and an understanding of themselves. Film spotlights upbeat social realism rather than a more robust insight into human motivations, but a neat and smooth directorial style does emerge which makes director Sergei Soloviov worth watching when he shakes off his establishment approach to personal human outlooks and change. —*Mosk.*

Il Mistero Di Oberwald
(The Mystery of Oberwald)
(ITALIAN-COLOR)

Venice, Sept. 9.
RAI release of Rai Rete 2 production. Stars Monica Vitti. Directed by Michelangelo Antonioni. Screenplay, Antonioni, Tonino Guerra from "The Eagle Has Two Heads" by Jean Cocteau; camera (color), Luciano Tovoli; editor, Francesco Grandoni. Antonioni. Reviewed at Venice Film Fest. Sept. 3. '80. Running time: 123 MINS.
La Regina .... Monica Vitti
Sebastian .... Franco Branciaroli
Fohn .... Paolo Bonacelli
Di Berg .... Elisabetta Pozzi
Willenstein .... Luigi Diberti
Tony .... Amad Saha Alan

Backed entirely by Italian television, this is basically a telefilm. Made by noted director Michelangelo Antonioni and so shown as a film at the recent Venice Film Festival, item is essentially a fairly inconclusive experiment on the use of video in filmmaking today.

Film is more a technological than esthetic problem. Antonioni has not made a film since his 1975 "The Passenger," and perhaps was tempted by the offer from Italo tv when several feature projects fell through. The idea was to make it entirely by electronic means and then put it on film.

All this seems to be begging the question. For actually, what emerges from the film is an attempt to make video seem like film. So why not shoot it on film and avoid all the intricate problems? Theoretically, video is supposed to do things with color that might add to film technique.

But not much of this is in evidence in this hoary Ruritanian romantic melodrama about a queen whose husband was assassinated on the day of their marriage and lived hidden from her country ever since.

One night a man breaks in who has been selected to kill her due to unrest among many factions in the country. But they fall in love. (He is also a dead ringer for the dead King.) However, his attempt to help her take over the country and do good is foiled by the police chief's blackmail and he ends up taking poison and then killing the Queen when she goads him into it.

Monica Vitti does not quite have the regal stature and bearing to make much of the role of the bereaved and then lovesick queen and others are adequate in stereotyped roles. And how about the color?

A reddish hue in the early sequences of the would-be killer being chased by police is effective, but could just as easily been done with film. There are times when one character is bathed in blue or in b&w lensing while another part of the screen is in regular color. Perhaps it does give some color indication of a character or of a scene or mood but does not seem worth all the trouble.

Video appears most effective when it is just put right on film with its wavy definition making vegetation look like expressionistic paintings.

Video has been used before by Jean-Luc Godard in his "Number Two," albeit with much use of split and multi-screen frame.

Antonioni does have his deft directorial feelings intact and there are some scenes that are effective as those depicting the kitchen life in the castle.

The late Jean Cocteau also filmed his play, "The Eagle Has Two Heads," and memory serves, it was more aptly kitchy and melodramatically outrageous than this one. Film has some interest as an attempt to wed electronic and film techniques but is too inconclusive and finally too mannered to give this old-hat tale more than curio interest at festivals and for tv use on the Antonioni name. —*Mosk.*

Richard's Things
(BRITISH-COLOR)

Venice, Aug. 31.
Southern Pictures Ltd. release and production. Stars Liv Ullmann. Directed by Anthony Harvey. Screenplay, Frederic Raphael from his own book; camera (Color), Freddie Young; editor, Lesley Walker; music, Georges Delerue. Reviewed at Venice Film Fest. Aug. 30. '80. Running time, 104 MINS.
Kate .... Liv Ullmann
Josie .... Amanda Redman
Peter .... Tom Piggott-Smith
Mrs. Sells .... Elizabeth Spriggs
Bill .... Michael Maloney
Richard .... Mark Eden

Liv Ullmann seems to still be in Ingmar Bergman territory in this tale of a dedicated, reserved, decent woman suddenly shaken to her roots and bringing out her true facets when she finds her beloved husband has had a heart attack in a hotel room with a mistress. He dies.

Adapted from his own book by Frederic Raphael, film remains literary as the characters talk out their problems in cars, at tables, generally somewhat more forced than springing from a viable, visual fusion of ideas and action.

Ullmann finds a book of poetry in her husband's bag and finally tracks down the fact he was with a pretty young girl from his office. The woman goes to see the girl and a relationship springs up between them for they were both, it seems, the husband's objects rather than really blending respect, love and more mutual relationships.

Director Anthony Harvey uses Ullmann's wide open face to reflect her growing change as she finds an almost lesbianic relationship with the girl, beds down her husband's partner who has always loved her and finally goes her own way when the girl leaves. But too much is implied rather than growing into more effective dramatic revelation.

There is a rather forced scene with a burglar chased out by an enraged Ullmann who finally breaks out of her Nordic passiveness. There is also an underlying antagonism with her mother-in-law.

But film lacks Bergman's taut, nervous, pared down reflections of married relations that he brought to his "Scenes From a Marriage" out to a film from a tv series.

Comparison may be unfair and maybe it is mainly Ullmann's presence that brings it on. But here it is death and not divorce that forces her to face her own self that was somewhat drowned in her fairly happy marriage, or she felt it was good even if he did cheat at times which she was unaware of until his untimely death.

Amanda Redman is somewhat too brittle to give the supposedly hip young girl the needed charm to seduce both husband and wife. Others are more shadowy figures in this fairly surface look at marital upset. Made with tv coin, film might fare better on tv than on theatrical screens. —*Mosk.*

Phobia
(CANADIAN-U.S.-COLOR)

Venice, Sept. 1.
Spiegel-Bergman Films release and production. Features entire cast. Directed by John Huston. Screenplay, Ronald Shusett, Gary Sherman, Lew Lehman, James Sangster, Peter Bellwood; camera (Color), Reginald Morris; editor, Stan Cole; music, Andre Gagnon. Reviewed at Venice Film Fest. Aug. 29. '80. Running time, 94 MINS.
Dr. Ross .... Paul Michael Glaser
Barnes .... John Colicos
Jenny .... Susan Hogan
Barbara .... Alexandra Stewart
Bubba .... Robert O'Ree
Henry .... David Bolt
Johnny .... David Eisner
Laura .... Lisa Langlois

Another film churned out by the Canadian investment handouts which allow for a few notable American creative names to be incorporated in the Canadian move for development of a potent film industry. John Huston has turned out a fairly familiar potboiler in the "Psycho" and "Spellbound" syndrome where the theme might be something like "doctor cure yourself."

Huston has not cheated and has given this a good gloss. But it is hard to overcome a fairly routine script and mixture of whodunit and psychological problems. The medical reasoning is surface at best as it follows an experiment of a young psychologist on homicidal people driven to their deeds by phobias, be it vertigo, agoraphobia, effects of a rape, fear of snakes and overriding guilt complexes.

Paul Michael Glaser, who became a tv name stateside with the "Starsky and Hutch" series, (he played Starsky), is somewhat too smooth for the role of the experimental scientist. But he does have a phobia, too, so his evasive playing is acceptable.

One of his patients who he has sent to face crowds, though she fears them, is blown up in his office when she opens her file drawer while waiting for him. Is one of his patients after him? A bitter ex-mistress, or, as a brutish police inspector begins to feel, is it the doctor himself? No fair giving it away though it is not hard to guess.

Film has some degree of suspense as the murders mount, the usual love interest and some interesting aspects of the doctor's methods mainly concerned with making his patients face their phobias by appearing before a giant film screen which mirrors their problems. Would that Glaser had tried out this method himself.

This type of film on homicidal deranged characters has caught public fancy of late and "Phobia" might shape up to a good fast playoff item with a well designed pub campaign. Otherwise it is a rote Huston film that may still find some cult reverberations in Europe.

The French have a theory that Huston's main theme is failure though fighting it is considered the important thing. The film could fit this perhaps true, but perhaps arbitrary look at Huston's work. Technically good. —*Mosk.*

La Ragazza Di Via Millelire
(The Girl From Millelire Street)
(ITALIAN-COLOR)

Venice, Sept. 1.

RAI release of RAI 2 TV production. Features entire cast. Directed by Gianni Serra. Screenplay, Tomaso Sherman, Serra; camera (Color), Dario Di Palma; editor, Maria Di Mauro; music, Luis Bacalov. Reviewed at Venice Film Fest. Aug. 30, '80. Running time. **119 MINS.**

Betty .... Oria Conforti
Verdiana .... Maria Monti
Luisa .... Lisa Policaro
Carmela .... Lucia Sturiale
Tonino .... Ugo Campanile

Entirely backed by Italy's RAI-TV film is a first feature helmed by documentarist and news tv director Gianni Serra. Film is somewhat disparate and rambling but does manage to give a disturbing yet humanly observed look at fringe subproletarian life in a big industrial city, in this cast Turin.

Hastily thrown up outskirt housing developments for people coming from farms or the south have developed into instant slums and bred a sort of semi-delinquent youth without roots in the metropolis.

Film is both universal and quintessentially Italian in its acceptance of adversity with dramatic inchoate revolt or lively, good humored sometimes dramatically tinged acceptance. The protagonist, a jauntly, bubble gum-chewing 13-year-old girl, keeps escaping from and coming back to a social settlement house which tries to cope with the disoriented youth and old people.

She gets involved with a macho tyrannical youth who is not above forcing her to give in to friends and some drug-pushing, thieving types. But she gets away from them all and finds some haven with the head of a settlement, a sorely beset but understanding woman.

Item is somewhat rambling, and shows director Serra's tv background in docus and news features. Sometimes scenes just run on too long or do not always clarify the theme of the dispossessed who may go the way of delinquency or beat it by sheer grit. He does avoid didactics and film is disturbing in its look at moral breakdown.

Pic marks director Serra a man to watch in the feature field when he gets a more narrative fluidity to balance his sharp documental flair for observation and revelation of people in a social and personal bind.

Film could certainly have some institutional, school and tv use and might be worth some consideration for selected commercial outlets with some effective pruning. Non-pro thesps in cast, as is usual in Italy, are all good especially Oria Conforti as the rebellious, hard bitten but human adolescent trying to survive amidst moral chaos, family alienation and changing ways. —*Mosk.*

Aulad El Rih
(Children of the Wind)
(ALGERIAN-COLOR)

Venice, Aug. 28.

DPFN-ONC release and production. Features entire cast. Written and directed by Brahim Tsaki. Camera (Eastmancolor), Mustapha Beimihoub; editor, Rachid Soufi; music, Djilali Detto Carlos. Reviewed at Venice Film Fest. Aug. 27, '80. Running time: **79 MINS.**

With: Djamel Youbi, Bennani Broualem, Si-Ahmed, Si-El Hadj De Hassi.

An exemplary film to come from a so-called Third World nation. Real decors, real people, especially children, are used with flair by new director Brahim Tsaki who makes a memorable bow for his first film.

Three sketches look at a child or children in a city, a small town and a desert work area to make a statement on borderline poverty as seen through the children. No accusations or false bravado or melodrama here, but a forceful feel for children who react with inchoate rebellion or unusual inventiveness to make their lives bearable.

The first episode, "Hardboiled Eggs," is about a little boy who sells eggs in town cafes and his drunken father who makes toy mice which flit about on a string. The boy finally goes into a temper tantrum as his father plays childishly with the toy mice as the boy is boiling eggs.

The second, "Djamel in the Country of Images," deals with a little boy who sells sand flowers and spends his nights looking at tv while his father works as a night watchman. He has problems in school and finally runs off with money he made selling a flower while his father chases him.

Last, "The Box in The Desert," shows children creating unusual wire toys from shreds gleaned from a barbed wire fence. Their absorption, their inventiveness give a note of unusual observation to children making the best of their situation and showing natural joy in their own creations.

Some children do stare out at the audience but it is not in accusation but curiosity. The implied social criticism is muted and springs from fine visuals rather than forced didactics or melodrmatics. There is no word spoken except for a father calling his son's name, or calling him a name while chasing him.

There is also a little song sung at the end over the image of a child laughing in his joy of his handmade toy asking what the child will be tomorrow and what others have done to help. The lack of dialog is not forced but a part of these taciturn lives.

A natural for UNICEF operations, festivals and specialized fund operations. Its fine filmic approach, its graceful insight into children, be they poor or not, might also find this some commercial specialized outlets where it might well be helped by critics and word-of-mouth. A bit slight and frail but still engaging.

Actually, Algeria has scored with more ambitious films at fests and copped the grand prize in Cannes in '76 for the epic look at the Algerian War "The Day of the Burning Embers" of Mohamad Lakhdar Hamina. This more modest entry is also a plus for Algeria. —*Mosk.*

Oxala
(Leave It To God)
(PORTUGUESE-COLOR-16m)

Venice, Sept. 9.

V.O. Films release and production. Features entire cast. Written and directed by Antonio Pedro Vasconcelos. Camera (color), Joao Rocha; editor, Antoine Bonfanti. Reviewed at Venice Film Fest. Sept. 2, '80. Running time: **145 MINS.**

With: Manuel Baeta Neves, Marta Reynolds, Laura Soveral, Judith Magre, Rue Furtado, Karen Blangueron, Lia Gama, Teresa Madruga, Adelaide Joao.

A personal film about political exile, a timely subject today. Film may be a bit rambling but balances a tendency toward the French penchant for overabundant dialog with a more terse visual treatment.

The director, Antonio Pedro Vasconcelos, puts the film in a sort of literary format, dividing it into chapters, which makes its meandering style and constant shifts between Paris and Portugal acceptable.

The protagonist is a young Portuguese deserter from the colonial army who had lived in Paris for eight years. He had gotten a job as secretary to the widow of a well-known Latin American writer and become her lover.

The coup d'etat in his home country sends him back to see a woman he had a child by and his family. He does not take sides and watches a rich family crumble on the fringe of the changes. He has an affair with his young sister in law but finally decides to become a writer and stay in France.

The director has a feel for succinct dialog that enhances rather than slows down the action and gets a good feel of the life of an exile in Paris and his inability to get involved with the changes in his old country. Obviously influenced by the ex-French New Wavers, he goes his own way in a film that could stand some pruning but should find its way at other fests. —*Mosk.*

Montreal Fest

Second-Hand Hearts
(U.S.-COLOR)

Second-rate Ashby. Lovely to look at and that's it.

Montreal, Aug. 31.

Lorimar presentation of a Caribou production of a Northstar International picture. Produced by James William Guercio. Stars Robert Blake, Barbara Harris. Directed by Hal Ashby. Screenplay, Charles Eastman; camera (Technicolor), Haskell Wexler; editor, Amy Holden Jones; music, Willis Alan Ramsey; art director, Richard Carter; production designer, Peter Wooley; assistant director, David Hamburger; assoc. producer unit prod. mgr., Charles Mulvehill. Reviewed at Cinema Parisien, Montreal, Aug. 31, 1980. (MPAA Rating; PG.) Running time: **98 MINS.**

Cast: Robert Blake, Barbara Harris, Sondra Blake, Bert Remsen, Shirley Stoler, Collin Boone, Amber Rose Gold.

The slimmest of plot lines combined with the broadest of lead performances sink this Hal Ashby outing, formerly titled "The Hamster of Happiness." Lorimar Productions seems in no rush to release this pic, since selling points, other than Ashby's participation, are hard to come by.

"Second Hand Hearrts" was a last-minute addition at the Montreal World Film Fest., and played to an unenthusiastic house (walkouts were rife) the night before closing. It rounded out a Yank slate of pics, most notable for problems in getting distribution deals and/or release dates.

Robert Blake and Barbara Harris appear here as two down-and-nearly-out Texans engaged in making a paper marriage a real one, both emotionally and physically. Pic's premise — losers redeemed by mutual love — has promise, but the performances by Blake and Harris negate the best script intentions.

Their performances are memorably bad. Both affect Texas accents so impenetrable that much of the dialog is unintelligible. Blake gestures maniacally throughout, attempting to inject some physical humor into the proceedings. Harris is quirky, not especially interesting to look at, although she seems a bit more controlled than Blake. Many of their scenes together have the needlessly prolonged feel of actors' improvisation, a dubious sign in any film.

Worst of all, the lead performances patronize rather than elucidate their characters, a blowsy, fifth-rate night club singer with three young children and the none too bright car washer who married her apparently in a drunken stupor.

Plot is sketchy at best, and has the couple trekking to California in a beat-up jalopy that occasionally manages to hit 80 miles-per-hour. What little action there is involves various encounters with local types, both good and malevolent, that offer good parts for the supporting cast. Bert Remsen, for one, is fine as a friendly general store proprietor.

By pic's end, the love after marriage premise is nicely worked out, although the pic's few rewarding moments — tender scenes between the two principals and the children — are much too late in coming.

Production values are excellent, however. Haskell Wexler's photography is truly stunning, giving a visual opulence to the most mundane highway scenes. Wexler's work is so good, the viewer hates to see it largely wasted on this outing.

Especially effective is Willis Alan Ramsey's country-and-western score that energetically bridges many scenes that lack any trace of energy whatever. —Sege.

Masoch
(ITALIAN-COLOR)

Montreal, Sept. 1.
Difilm S.r.l. release of a Difilm S.r.l.-Tierre S.A.S. (Rome) production. Stars Paolo Malco, Francesca De Sapio. Director, Franco Brogi Taviani. Screenplay, Taviana; camera (Eastmancolor), Angelo Bevilacqua; score, Gianfranco Plenizio; producers, Taviani, Giancarlo di Fonzo, Tonino Paoletti. No other credits provided. Reviewed at Cinema Parisien, Montreal, Sept. 1, 1980. Running time: 109 MINS.
Cast: Paolo Malco, Francesca DeSapio, Fabrizio Bentivoglio, Inga Alexandrova, Dario Mazzoli, Remo Remotti, Valeria D'Obici, Stefano Calanchi, Franca Lumachi, Claudio Sorrentino, Stefano Stefanelli, Farris Fabio.

Just how much of this handsome and riveting pic, from the 39 year old Italo producer-director-scripter Franco Brogi Taviani, is based on actual fact is open to conjecture. Enough said that its title refers to Leopold von Sacher-Masoch, a 19th century German novelist whose themes often dealt with pain and humiliation and whose name lives on to describe the sexual deviation opposite to the one inspired by the Marquis de Sade.

"Masoch," shown out of competition at the Montreal World Film fest., is a daring work about a queasy subject that will have audiences squirming a bit. But the film is also a firstrate accomplishment, a stylistic triumph for Taviani (third and youngest member of the Taviani brothers), who manages to bring its two central characters sharply into focus via superb performances by Paolo Malco as Masoch and Francesca De Sapio as his over-accommodating wife, Wanda.

Pic has interesting playoff possibilities thanks to its sensational subject matter and classy production values. Warning: there's beaucoup nudity, explicit language, whippings, beatings. Out-and-out torture is shown with little reservation. Getting "Masoch" into U.S. exhibition without an X rating would be impossible without the kinds of cuts that would virtually gut the pic's content.

That's a shame since the pic is essentially a searing look at the man-woman dynamics of a fascinating if bizarre marriage. Taviani isn't out for sexual titillation (the pic is not pornographic in any sense). Rather, the director-scripter explores the limits of a strange union that finally falters when its precarious emotional balance is tipped too far in the wrong direction.

The plot line is fairly simple. Masoch is presented here as a prominent writer living in Austria at the turn of the century. (For the record, the real Sacher-Masoch died in 1895 at 59.) A Svengali of the first order, he turns an encounter with a beautiful, lower-class woman (De Sapio) into a long-term union (two children are produced), sealed by a strange pact.

In order to keep his somewhat overwrought imagination fueled, Masoch (Malco) insists that the woman suborn her conventionally romantic nature to become the dominant half of a mistress-slave relationship. Until the marriage collapses at pic's end — after she takes on lovers openly at his urging — she administers beatings and other indignities in keeping with Masoch's fantasies.

Through inventive use of his excellent cast, Taviani brings out the subtleties of this unusual union, and actually makes the principal characters plausible if not sympathetic. He also keeps viewer interest high by carefully alternating scenes, developed as dramatic set pieces punctuated by abrupt but effective screen dissolves.

The technical aspects of this pic — costume and set designs, Angelo Bevilacqua's lush color photography, Gianfranco Plenizio's score — beautifully support Taviani's episodic approach. Performances are strong in all categories although Malco and DeSapio dominate (no pun intended) "Masoch," and justifiably so.

In all, a knockout of a film that surprisingly turns rough subject matter into an exquisite esthetic experience. —Sege.

Los Miedos
(Fears)
(ARGENTINE-COLOR)

Montreal, Aug. 25.
Isla Cinematographica production. Directed by Alejandro Doria. Features entire cast. Screenplay, Doria, Cernadas Lamadrid; camera (color), Miguel Rodriguez; score, Luis Maria Serra; editor, Silvia Ripoll. No other credits provided. Reviewed at Cinema Parisien, Montreal, Aug. 25, 1980. Running time: 100 MINS.
Cast: Tita Merello, Soledad Silveyra, Miguel Angel Sola, Maria Leal, Sandra Mihanovich, Anibal Morixe, Littl Gonzalez.

With this brittle and unpleasant pic, director Alejandro Doria attempts to ensnare the viewer into a cinematic nightmare about a plague that hits a modern South American city and the stereotypically theatrical bunch which take off for the south to murderous result. "Los Miedos" may or may not be laden with political allegory, but it's essentially a cheapo disaster pic not up to the worst of Irwin Allen or Jennings Lang.

A pregnant blonde finds herself in a brassy disco when she happens to notice boils and other blemishes on one of the femme dancers. She immediately takes off to a local supermarket, stocks up on victuals, and then contrary to local police fiat, decides to take off. The plague has hit, and she wants out.

Along her escape route, she links up with — how's this for "Airport" casting? — a nun, a sleazy leather-jacketed type who totes a gun, a prostitute, a garrulous elderly woman, a mental retard and a more or less (by the overly theatrical standards of this pic) an average Joe. Each of course, brings along built-in personality problems, and the audience is not spared hearing about their angst.

The plot is similarly unenlightening, and even less interesting. Once the band of would-be survivors escapes the trigger-happy gendarmes, they take off to various refuges and begin making each other unhappy. The pregnant woman winds up slaying the leather-jacketed wearer and the prostie (the first because he has murderous intentions of his own; the second, because she gives dumb answers, and shoves the average Joe off a cliff after he delivers his opinion that the woman had murdered her own husband.

Pic's finale has the woman giving birth on a beach with the retard slated — until he too comes down with the plague at the last minute — to act as midwife. Concluding close-ups of the infant are at least momentarily arresting.

The cast generally is that kind that maintains its coiffures and bright smiles in what's supposed to be an escape trek of grueling proportions. Only the actress (she's not singled out in credits) who plays the prostie shows spark, but even she overdoes things before she's bumped off.

Cameraman Luis Maria Serra's work is solid, but director Doria attempts to patch up the script's vacuousness by cheap effects — tricky camera shots, loud noises (screams, police sirens and even what passes as routine conversation) and much theatrical attitudinizing on the part of the cast.

Trick ending has the woman actually waking up in a spic-and-span hospital, so the audience is left to ponder whether what went on in the pic's previous 99 minutes was really a nightmare or something else. Viewers very likely won't care.
—Sege.

Dyrygent
(The Orchestra Conductor)
(POLISH-COLOR)

Montreal, Sept. 1.
Film Polski-United X production. Stars John Gielgud, Krystyna Janda, Andrzej Serveryn. Director, Andrzej Wajda. Screenplay, Andrzej Kijowski; camera (color), Slawomir Idziak; sound, Piotr Zawadzki; editor, Halina Prugar. No other credits provided. Reviewed Cinema Parisien, Montreal, Sept. 1, 1980. Running time: 101 MINS.
Cast: John Gielgud, Krystyna Janda, Andrzej Seweryn.

The presence of John Gielgud, some footage shot in New York City and Beethoven's Fifth Symphony on the soundtrack lend some interest to this lightweight look at the classical music world by Polish director Andrzej Wajda. Overall, there's not much going for it, least of all commercial playoff possibilities in the U.S.

How Gielgud wound up in the case is anyone's guess. Much of his part, as a world-renowned symphony conductor, involves soliloquies in English. His dialogs with Polish actors are clumsily dubbed, giving his portrayal an unintentinally humorous slant.

Protagonist here is a winsome violinist in a provincial Polish orch (Krystyna Janda), whose husband (Andrzej Seweryn) is the conductor of the ensemble. On a visit to the U.S., she ties up with the Gielgud character — resembling an effete Georg Solti — who, it turns out, was once in love with the violinist's mother.

The big-time conductor is also being dogged by an American tv crew for reasons not quite made clear, but the pursuit permits Gielgud to snap off a few choice lines about over-eager journalists.

Contrived plot has the big time conductor, a slightly unstable hypochondriac, returning to Poland to lead the provincial orchestra. He also tries to revive his old love affair, using the violinist as a surrogate for her own mother.

The husband, an aggressively bumbling type who has trouble keeping his orchestra in rein, is resentful of the Gielgud character — for both personal and professional reasons. At pic's end, the violinist sees her husband in his true, crassly ambitious light and gives him the heave-ho.

Janda is pretty as the violinist, Seweryn overacts as the conductor of the local orchestra, and Gielgud, who should look like a big-time conductor, instead looks somewhat bewildered by his inclusion in this pic. It would also help if he conducted the local orchestra to the rhythm of the music heard on the soundtrack.

Technical points are generally shoddy. Color quality is flat, sound work is clumsy and Slawomir Idziak's photography is as dull and listless. —*Sege.*

Cafe Express
(ITALIAN-COLOR)

Montreal, Aug. 31.
Vides Cinematrogafica S.p.A. production, produced by Franco Cristaldi and Nicola Carraro. Stars Nino Manfredi. Director, Nanni Loy. Screenplay, Manfredi, Loy and Elvio Porta; camera (Technospes color). Claudio Cirillo; score, Giovanna Marini. No other credits provided. Reviewed at Cinema Parisien, Montreal, Aug. 31, 1980. Running time: **105 MINS.**
Cast: Nino Manfredi, Adolfo Celi, Vittorio Mezzogiorno, Marzio C. Honorato, Gigi Reder, Luigi Basagaluppi, Marisa Laurito, Vittorio Marsiglia, Vittorio Caprioli.

This pic. about a gypsy expresso vendor illegally working Italy's express trains, permits Nino Manfredi to do another of his turns as a stalwart, lovable laborer inveighing against seemingly insurmountable odds. Manfredi has the part down to

perfection, giving "Cafe Express" a classily humorous sheen that makes the pic suitable for Yank distribution.

Unlike Franco Brusati's "Bread and Chocolate" (Pane e Cioccolata), which had Manfredi as a displaced Italo waiter working in Switzerland, this Nanni Loy pic couches no large social statement in comedy.

This time, Manfredi's comic adversaries are Italian bureaucrats, various low life pickpockets and rich folk who take turns in trying to frustrate, expose or otherwise thwart his resourceful expressoselling operation.

To tug at the heart strings a bit, script (coauthored by Manfredi) includes some harmless bathos relating to the expresso man's son — he has asthma and needs an operation — and the man's own physical handicap. His paralysed left hand, concealed in a black glove, is passed off as a war wound.

Essentially a chase caper, "Cafe Express" has Manfredi working the trains and outwitting the officious conductors and bureaucrats at nearly every turn. The antics are broad, very funny and often involve bathroom humor.

It's Manfredi's show all the way, although there are some fine character portrayals here. Production values are general slick, especially Claudio Cirillo's color photography. It's to his and Loy's credit that the pic is visually cluid and has none of the claustrophobic feel of a second-class train compartment.

In all, a nifty, unpretentious comedy that Manfredi milks to a fare-thewell. Has good possibilities for successful Yank distribution.
—*Sege*

Mo Hoozue Wa Tsukanai
(No More Easy Going)
(JAPAN-COLOR)

Montreal, Aug. 29.
Angle-ATG production. Producers, Takashi Arima, Hidehiro Kudo. Director, Yoichi Higashi. Screenplay, Higashi, Tatsuo Kobayashi; camera (color), Koichi Kawakami; sound. Yukio Kubota; score, Michi Tanaka. No other credits provided. Reviewed at Cinema Parisien, Montreal, Aug. 29, 1980. Running time: **113 MINS.**
Cast: Kaori Momoi, Eiji Okuda, Leo Morimoto, Sakura Kamo, Akemi Negishi, Juzo Itami.

Director Yoichi Higashi has a knack for visually capturing the sense and time of a place through attention to detail. Unfortunately, with his "No More Easy Going," a Japanese competitive entry at the Montreal Film Fest, he's overlooked such niceties as a worthwhile script and compelling character development.

This is a minute look at the tangled romantic affairs of a pretty

but slightly slutty young Japanese student. Her involvements with another (and, alas, a somewhat unattractive) student and a freelance reporter with dubious ties to the Japanese underworld are presented in relentless detail.

A problem: she's not an especially interesting woman and neither are her two consorts. Helmer Higashi gets around this slightly by using Koichi Kawakami's handsome color photography to set moods and get across small details revealing at least minimal character change.

Essentially the pic is a meller, saved from soaper proportions by Higashi's intelligent technical approach. The young girl is truly enamored of the strange journalist, but puts up with the obnoxious student. Points are made about men being casually selfish, but no large feminist statement is offered. A fairly explicit love scene, and a measure of nudity, enliven things.

Most interesting are two minor characters. A philandering man married to a beauty shop owner is gracious after his wife, who discovers his extra-marital liaisons, stabs him in the leg with a pair of scissors. Husband forgives her, drops charges. Otherwise, "No More Easy Going" is an exercise without much of a point, and stays with an audience long after it's worn out its welcome mat. —*Sege.*

Toronto Festival

Union City
(COLOR)

Rock star Deborah Harry's dramatic debut disappoints. Tough sell for beautifully-shot but limp pic.

A Kinesis Ltd. production and release. Produced by Graham Belin. Features entire cast. Directed by Mark Riechert. Screenplay, Reichert, from story by Cornell Woolrich; camera (color), Ed Lachman; supervising editor, Eric Albertson; editors, Lana Tokel, J. Michaels; music, Chris Stein; art direction, George Stavrinos; sound, Luke Yersin. Reviewed at Preview 9 screening room, N.Y.C., Aug. 27, '80. (MPAA Rating: PG). Running time: **87 MINS.**
Harlan .... Dennis Lipscomb
Lillian .... Deborah Harry
Contessa .... Irina Maleeva
Larry Longacre .... Everett McGill
Young vagrant .... Sam McMurray
Evelyn, secretary .... Terina Lewis
Jeanette .... Pat Benatar
Alphonse .... Tony Azito
With: Paul Andor, Taylor Mead, Cynthia Crisp, Charles Rydell.

Writer-director Mark Reichert's indie film, "Union City," is a handsomely shot *film noir*, featuring rock star Deborah Harry of

the group Blondie in her dramatic screen debut. Straddling the line between melodrama and camp, the pic emerges as too studied and lifeless to break out of its underground peg into commercial environs.

Woolrich's dark and fetishistic material is both a source of strength and the undoing of "Union City." His story is similar to Poe's "The Telltale Heart" in structure and while helmer Reichert exploits its strangeness very well, he fails to flesh out the short, one actor sketch into a full length feature.

Set in Union City, N.J., arbitrarily in March, 1953, pic concerns a paranoid businessman (Dennis Lipscomb), obsessed with catching the mysterious culprit who steals a drink out of his milk bottle that is delivered every morning. His setting a trap for the miscreant is very amusing, while his plain, vapid wife Lillian (Deborah Harry) puts up with his increasingly bizarre behavior.

Ultimately, he captures a young, war vet vagrant (Sam McMurray) in the act and releases his pent-up anger and frustration by beating the man's head bloodily on the floor as the vagrant taunts him for impotency re: wife Lillian. The Hitchcockian body removal footage provides fine black humor as Lipscomb hides the corpse in a Murphy bed in the vacant apartment next door.

Meanwhile, Lillian is two-timing him with building super Larry (Everett McGill) and in the last reel bleaches her dark brown hair blonde, to finally assume some of her rock star image. When new neighbors move in next door, Lipscomb is driven to suicide by his fear of discovery, leading to an ironic conclusion.

Film is carried by stage actor Lipscomb, always credible in his physical interpretation of the "driven little man" lead role.

Harry, after appealingly playing herself in "Roadie," is virtually unrecognizable here in brown wig and plain, unflattering makeup. Painfully underdirected and robbed of her icon image as "Blondie," Harry plays most of the film awkwardly. Her best moments come in two silent, autoerotic scenes, well-backed by an "after hours" jazz score by Blondie teammate Chris Stein and an unidentified sax soloist.

Irina Maleeva, a Fellini actress, steals Harry's thunder in her support role as a wacked-out neighbor.

While Reichert's script is lacking, his direction is mainly on-target, making the most of a low budget by limiting the action to the apartment house, the street outside, a nearby bar and Lipscomb's tiny office.

The real talent to emerge from

"Union City" is cinematographer Ed Lachman. After an apprenticeship, usually as assistant cameraman, with Werner Herzog, Wim Wenders and Sven Nykvist, plus *films noirs* "Scalpel" and "The Last Embrace," Lachman has a major achievement. His handsome compositions, pastel lighting and precise camera movements display a talent ready for the big solo assignments. —*Lor.*

Loving Couples
(U.S.-COLOR)

Fast-paced comedy on today's marriage mores. Looks like a winner.

Toronto, Sept. 4.
A 20th Century-Fox release, produced by Renee Valente. Exec producer, David Susskind. Features entire cast. Directed by Jack Smight. Screenplay, Martin Donovan; camera (Metrocolor), Philip Lathrop; editors, Grey Fox, Frank Urioste; sound, Lee Alexander; art direction, Jan Scott; assistant director, Carl Olsen; associate producer, Andrew Susskind; music, Fred Karlin. Reviewed at the Toronto Film Festival, Sept. 4, 1980. MPAA rating: PG. Running time: **97 MINS.**
Evelyn .... Shirley MacLaine
Walter .... James Coburn
Stephanie .... Susan Sarandon
Gregg .... Stephen Collins
Mrs. Liggett .... Sally Kellerman
Nurse .... Nan Martin
Duley .... Shelly Batt

"Loving Couples" ought to pack them in. Film opens with a snappy cute meet. Shirley MacLaine is riding a horse and Stephen Collins, driving along in a sports car, stares at her, misses a turn in the road, and crashes. She rides over to the prone Collins and rips open his pants. Well, she's a doctor.

After hospitalization, young stud Collins tries to put the make on her but she reminds him of T. S. Eliot's line about life ending with a whimper and not a bang. Not too long after he gets it.

She's not getting much attention from her work-obsessed doctor husband, James Coburn, who learns of her affair from Collins' live-in friend, Susan Sarandon, a daffy tv weathergirl.

And they, in turn, fall into a motel bed.

The two roaming couples meet underwater in a resort swimming pool in one of the film's more hilarious scenes. MacLaine throws Coburn out and Collins moves in. Coburn and Sarandon bunk in together. But neither new couple lasts long.

The script by Martin Donovan moves swiftly and finally the two original couples come back together, with Coburn on horseback chasing teary-eyed MacLaine driving along a freeway in her sports car.

It's all fun and sexual games played off against today's mores. Direction by Jack Smight is assured and never lags.

However, except for a disco tune or so, original tunes (ballads) are soppy in context and deter from the pic's general move-it-along beat.

MacLaine is in top form, sassy and sweet in turn and softly lit by cameraman Philip Lathrop.

Coburn, white teeth flashing almost throughout, delivers a casually effective light comedy performance. Sarandon is topnotch, especially when doing weather reports which in themselves are a sendup of attractive but not so bright small-screen newscasters.

Sally Kellerman weighs in with a purposely hammy role as a sex-hungry doctor's wife who takes Collins to bed, the factor that leads to his breakup from MacLaine, who decides she's more for old-fashioned monogamy.

And Collins suitably maintains his part, that of a shallow handsome stud getting exactly what he wants and when.

Pic might annoy moralists and monogamists. It's a modern day fairy tale with this moral: You can stray if long married and that is okay because you get back together in the end.

Also, it's quite funny and winningly played off and made.

The pic had its world preem at the Toronto Festival of Festivals and is being released by 20th Century-Fox on Oct. 24. —*Adil.*

Resurrection
(COLOR)

Uneven pic with Ellen Burstyn as faith healer faces doubtful commercial future.

Hollywood, Aug. 27.
Universal Pictures releases, produced by Renee Missel, Howard Rosenman. Stars Ellen Burstyn, Sam Shepard. Directed by Daniel Petrie. Screenplay, Lewis John Carlino; camera (Technicolor), Mario Tosi; special visual sequences, Tony Silver, Richard Greenberg, Robert Greenberg; music, Maurice Jarre; editor, Rita Roland; production designer, Paul Sylbert; art direction, Edwin O'Donovan; set decoration, Bruce Weintraub; sound, John Kean, Richard Portman; assistant director, Craig Huston. Reviewed at Universal Studios, Aug. 27, 1980. (MPAA Rating: PG.) Running time: **103 MINS.**
Edna McCauley .... Ellen Burstyn
Cal Carpenter .... Sam Shepard
Esco .... Richard Farnsworth
John Harper .... Roberts Blossom
George .... Clifford David
Margaret ...... Pamela Payton-Wright
Joe McCauley .... Jeffrey DeMunn
Grandma Pearl .... Eva Le Galliene
Kathy .... Lois Smith
Ruth ..... Madeleine Thornton-Sherwood
Earl Carpenter .... Richard Hamilton
Suzy Kroll .... Carlin Glynn
Don .... Lane Smith
Ellie .... Penelope Allen
Hank Peterson .... Ebbe Roe Smith

Films about evil running rampant have been cleaning up at the b.o. for the last few years, as witness the current slate of highly profitable horror films. But films about the transcendent power of goodness are not only rare, they usually are shaky commercial propositions. Universal's "Resurrection," an unusual supernatural drama about a faith healer, gives Ellen Burstyn a shot at a tour-de-force performance, but never comes into strong enough focus dramatically or philosophically to work as more than an oddity item. Film bowed last Saturday at the Montreal Film Festival and opens in the Southwest later this month.

It's difficult to tell what the audience for this film might be. The resurgence of religious feeling in the last few years may help, although orthodox believers could be offended by the film's negative treatment of fundamentalism. Skeptics may find the film's matter-of-fact insistence on the credibility of psychic healing hard to swallow. The Renee Missel-Howard Rosenman production may fall in between the cracks without attracting much of a following.

Burstyn, who clearly exerted a major creative influence on the film, is one of America's finest film actresses, and any chance to see her in such a sizable role is a treat. However the overly prosaic style of director Daniel Petrie and the underdeveloped screenplay by Lewis John Carlino inhibit her from exerting her full range of emotions until the latter sections, which become genuinely moving through sheer cumulative power.

She begins as a somewhat improbably affluent L.A. housewife who gives her husband a sports car for his birthday, only to have it cause his death in a crash which leaves her legs paralyzed. During her laborious recovery period in her native Kansas, she discovers that her close brush with death has given her the power of healing by the laying on of hands.

Burstyn's character increasingly alienates the more doctrinaire elements among the locals, including her father Roberts Blossom and her b.f. Sam Shepard, by her refusal to ascribe her healing powers to divine influence and by her unwillingness to drop her earthier pleasures. Carlino's script makes the telling point that mankind cannot bear too much sanctity without trying to destroy it.

But the drama is slowly paced and muted by its repetitiveness. There is commendably little sensationalism, but not enough thoughtful exploration of the meaning of her powers. Petrie's filming makes the pic resemble a soap opera (Burstyn is a very weepy, particularly in the earlier sections), which gets in the way of the philosophical premise, though the approach could help female audiences, in particular, to identify with the character.

Supporting cast is well chosen, particularly Shepard, who scores impressively with his brooding portrait of a not-too-intelligent but sincere smalltown man way out of his depth in a relationship with the unorthodox Burstyn. Eva Le Galliene, in a rare film appearance, is affecting as Burstyn's grandmother, and Richard Farnsworth has a good scene as a kind of John The Baptist to Burstyn's female Christ figure. Bit parts and extras, cast from townsfolk around the Texas locations, add plentifully to the film's Grant Wood look.

However, it is off-putting that the film is supposed to be taking place in Kansas when the setting and the people are so obviously Texan.

Tech credits are good, with Mario Tosi's lensing capturing the windswept, overcast location flavor and Paul Sylbert's production design giving the film a feeling of downhome starkness. Maurice Jarre's score is both mystical and sensuous in keeping with the film's provocative, if somewhat muddled, theme. —*Mac.*

The Awakening
(COLOR)

Mummy rises from the crypt, but not soon enough to provide many thrills. Quick playoff.

Hollywood, Sept. 12.
An Orion Pictures release through Warner Bros. of a Robert Solo production. Produced by Robert Solo. Andrew Scheinman. Martin Shafer. Stars Charlton Heston. Directed by Mike Newell. Screenplay, Allan Scott, Chris Bryant, Clive Exton, based on the novel "The Jewel Of Seven Stars" by Bram Stoker; camera (Technicolor), Jack Cardiff; editor, Terry Rawlings; music, Claude Bolling; production design, Michael Stringer; art direction, Lionel Couch; costume design, Phyllis Dalton; sound (Dolby), Brian Simmons; associate producer, Harry Benn; assistant director, Neill Vine-Miller. Reviewed at The Burbank Studios, Burbank, Sept. 12. 1980. (MPAA Rating: R.) Running time: 102 MINS.
Matthew Corbeck .... Charlton Heston
Jane Turner .... Susannah York
Anne Corbeck .... Jill Townsend
Margaret Corbeck ... Stephanie Zimbalist
Paul Whittier ....Patrick Drury
Dr. Khalid .... Bruce Myers
Dr. El Sadek .... Nadim Sawalha
Dr. Richter .... Ian McDiarmid

Dracula, Frankenstein, zombies, Hitler clones, child devils and berserk automobiles have all had a field day on the screen in recent years, and werewolves are due back soon, so why not give equal time to one of the oldest ghouls of all, the redoubtable mummy? "The Awakening" may be able to ride the crest of the horror wave to decent opening figures, but fast playoff is essential for Orion's latest.

It seems that there was once a certain Egyptian Queen Kara whose father, following the custom of the day, induced her into an incestuous relationship. In revenge, Kara killed him and proceeded to have slaughtered everyone in the land who had even spoken with the late pharoah. Dead at 18, the evil queen was buried, amidst the usual riches, in an isolated tomb bearing a "do not disturb" sign.

Story possesses a strange fascination for archeologist Charlton Heston, who finally penetrates the chamber centuries later. Kara's nasty spirit transforms neatly to Heston's baby daughter, born at the same instant Heston pries open the ancient coffin. So it's only a matter of time until Kara begins wreaking havoc once again via the innocent conduit of Stephanie Zimbalist.

It's hokum through and through. As ultimate payoff is telegraphed in the opening quarter-hour, with middle section devoted to rather dry scientific and domestic exposition, long wait for expected results will tax genre fans by now primed for regular applications of jolts.

Heston takes his obsessed Egyptologist role all too seriously. He's supposed to be a bright fellow, so the fact the audience is ahead of him all the way doesn't help credibility. Furthermore, a simple line of dialog establishing him as an American working abroad would have gotten him off the hook of having to affect a British accent. Zimbalist is okay as his daughter, while Susannah York and Jill Townsend have thankless parts.

Veteran lenser Jack Cardiff contributes a highly professional sheen, particularly to the 40 minutes set in Egypt, but first-time feature director Mike Newell exhibits a jumpy, visually disjointed style which is becoming increasingly apparent as the common denominator among the new crop of British commercials and tv helmers. Violence, not graphic, is disagreeable.

Pic opened this summer in Europe through EMI in a slightly different version. For domestic release, Orion trimmed about five minutes and reportedly added some new visual and sound effects.
— Cart.

Ordinary People
(COLOR)

Excellent directorial debut by Robert Redford. Good b.o. seen despite heavy seriousness.

Hollywood, Sept. 8.
A Paramount release of a Wildwood Enterprises production. Produced by Ronald L. Schwary. Directed by Robert Redford. Stars Donald Sutherland, Mary Tyler Moore, Judd Hirsch, Timothy Hutton. Screenplay, Alvin Sargent, based on the novel by Judith Guest; camera (Technicolor), John Bailey; editor, Jeff Kanew; music adaptation, Marvin Hamlisch; art direction, Phillip Bennett, J. Michael Riva; set decoration, Jerry Wunderlich, William Fosser; costume design, Bernie Pollack; sound, Charles Wilborn; assistant director, Steven H. Perry. Reviewed at Paramount Studios, L.A., Sept. 8, 1980. (MPAA Rating: R.) Running time: 123 MINS.
Calvin .... Donald Sutherland
Beth .... Mary Tyler Moore
Berger .... Judd Hirsch
Conrad .... Timothy Hutton
Swim Coach .... M. Emmet Walsh
Jeannine .... Elizabeth McGovern
Karen .... Dinah Manoff
Lazenby .... Fredric Lehne
Ray .... James B. Sikking
Sloan .... Basil Hoffman
Ward .... Quinn Redeker
Audrey .... Mariclare Costello
Grandmother .... Meg Mundy
Ruth .... Elizabeth Hubbard
Stillman .... Adam Baldwin
Grandfather .... Richard Whiting

A powerfully intimate domestic drama, "Ordinary People" represents the height of craftsmanship across the board. Robert Redford, well-suited for Donald Sutherland's role, stayed behind the camera to make a remarkably intelligent and assured directorial debut that is fully responsive to the mood and nuances of Alvin Sargent's astute adaptation of Judith Guest's best seller. Careful nurturing by Paramount should make this a solid b.o. performer through the fall season.

While not ultimately downbeat or despairing, tale of a disturbed boy's precarious tightrope walk through his teens is played out with tremendous seriousness, thereby setting it apart from many other recent films trading in snideness and cynicism. Pic possesses a somber, hour of the wolf mood, with characters forced to definitively confront their own souls before fadeout.

Dilemma of the youth, who at first glimpse has recently attempted suicide in remorse for not having saved his older brother from drowning and thereafter proves a heavy burden for both himself and his normally complacent parents, may be too grim for some viewers, but total conviction in the storytelling and performances will grab many who have lived through their own variations on the domestic turmoil here portrayed.

Timothy Hutton, son of the late actor Jim Hutton, is up to the considerable demands of the central role. Unable to slide back into his old routine, he embarks upon a believably tentative romance with very cute schoolmate Elizabeth McGovern and begins seeing shrink Judd Hirsch. Psychiatric chit chat often reps a writer's easy way out, explaining things when they should be dramatized, and while a couple of the sessions in pic's middle go on a bit long, device for once seems valid in terms of story dynamics.

At the same time, things go from bad to worse at home. Hutton isn't convinced his parents, who always favored the dead brother, truly care about him, and the tragedy of this suburban saga is that he might be right.

Sutherland tries to communicate and ultimately sees the falseness in his life in the process of coming to grips with his troubled son. On the other hand, Mary Tyler Moore, as the mother, has centered her life for too many years on surface values and automatic avoidance of emotion to perhaps ever change, systematically rejecting any attempt to get to the heart of the matter.

Moore's part is undoubtedly the most brilliantly written and observed, as her distress over her family's deterioration is seen more as social concern over form and neighborhood acceptability than as result of deep feeling. Backing down from any intense probing, one senses that this woman could live her entire life without ever questioning its basic components.

It's an actors' picture, but in addition to his sensitive touch with the players Redford keenly evokes the darkly serene atmosphere of Chicago's affluent North Shore and effectively portrays this WASP society's prediliction for pretending everything is okay even when it's not.

Aside from the curious note struck by design of Hirsch's office, which seems a bit on the seedy side for chic Highland Park, tech contributions, from John Bailey's subtle camerawork to Jeff Kanew's precise editing to Marvin Hamlisch's classical music adaptation, are all of a piece with Redford's highly controlled, well-ordered approach.
—Cart.

Anti-Clock
(BRITISH-B&W/COLOR)

IFEX release of a Kendon Film (Boyd's Co.) presentation of a Jack Bond production. Produced by Bond. Features entire cast. Directed by Jane Arden, Bond. Screenplay, Arden; camera (color, b&w, video), Mike Davis, Nic Knowland, others; editor, uncredited; music, Mihai Dragutescu; songs, Arden; video concepts, Robert Parker; executive producer, Don Boyd; associate producer, Louise Temple. Reviewed at Art Theatre, N.Y.C., Sept. 10, '80. (No MPAA Rating). Running time: 97 MINS.
Joseph Sapha,
Prof Zanof .... Sebastian Saville
Sapha's sister .... Liz Saville
Sapha's mother .... Suzan Cameron
Madame Aranovitch ..... Louise Temple
Poker dealer .... Tom Gerrard

The British underground filmmaking team of Jane Arden and Jack Bond, previously responsible for "Separation" (1967) and other pix, have devised an anti-rational, mystical exercise in science fiction called "Anti-Clock." Using both video and film techniques, pic surprisingly lacks much visual invention. Even devotees of experimental films will be dismayed at the over-reliance upon soundtrack dialog and narration.

Science fiction premise is an offshoot of George Lucas's "THX1138" for Warners, as murmuring technicians' voices establish that Joseph Sapha's mind has been programmed to follow set behavior patterns. As Sapha attempts to rebel against this deterministic universe and claim some freedom of choice, the viewer is treated to a barrage of distorted video images, old newsreels, and some token bland film footage of events Sapha either experiences or imagines. The fragmentary presentation reflects the film's off and on shooting and editing schedule, which stretched over a three-year period.

As with many faddists and hoaxers, the filmmakers take scientific principles and draw absurd conclusions from them out of context. In "Anti-Clock," the theories of physics formulated by Heisenberg and Einstein to explain the properties of subatomic particles are fatuously applied to issues of human behavior. This gives Arden and Bond license to rail out against sexism and materialism, but their "we are all one" philosophy is strained. Despite contributions by some talented cameramen, film is a technical shambles. —Lor.

Divine Madness
(COLOR-DOCU)

Bette Midler's concert film, though uneven, should please her fans.

Hollywood, Sept. 9.

A Ladd Company release through Warner Bros., exec produced by Howard Jeffrey. Produced and directed by Michael Ritchie. Stars Bette Midler. Written by Jerry Blatt, Midler, Bruce Vilanch; camera (Technicolor). William A. Fraker; additional photography, Bobby Byrne; concert lighting. E.H.B. ("Chip") Monck; editor. Glenn Farr; music arrangement and supervision. Tony Berg, Randy Kerber. choreography, Toni Basil; additional choreography, Marla Blakey; production design, Albert Brenner; sound, Don Rush, Billy Youdelman, Bill Darlington, Bob Litt, Steve Maslow, Elliot Tyson; assistant director, Jack Roe. Reviewed at Academy of Motion Picture Arts & Sciences theatre, Bev.Hills, Sept. 9, 1980. (MPAA Rating: R). Running time 91 MINS.
The Divine Miss M . . . . .Bette Midler
The Harlettes . . . . .Jocelyn Brown, Ula
Hedwig, Diva Gray
Head Usher . . . . .Irving Sudrow
Band Vocalists . . Tony Berg, Jon Bonine,
Joey Carbone, Randy Kerber

Though it might more logically have preceded "The Rose" to the screen, Bette Midler's concert film, "Divine Madness," (which was also the closer for the Toronto Film Fest) is a worthy follow-up to her starring debut and a surefire pleaser for her fans. Quibbles about uneven pacing and performance tend to pale under the glow of her truly amazing personality. First production of the Ladd Co., released through Warner Bros., the raunchy R-rated pic should turn a nice profit.

After years of honing her act in gay baths and on concert stages, Midler last February committed it to film in four days at the Pasadena, Calif., Civic Auditorium, with Howard Jeffrey exec producing and Michael Ritchie producing and directing. "Because this is the time capsule version of my show," she tells the aud. "I might as well do everything I know." Well, she doesn't quite do everything (a couple of her w.k. numbers are excluded), but she does not stint on energy and showmanship.

The film has a more carefully designed and visually opulent look than most concert pix, which tend to be hastily lensed under less than optimum conditions. Here, Ritchie and his supervising cameraman, William A. Fraker, employed a 30-man camera team to shoot more than 1,000,000 feet of film, winnowed down to a brisk 94 minutes of screen time.

Midler amply demonstrated her dramatic talents in "The Rose," and perhaps more than anything else this film is a stunning display of her comic abilities. Her monologs between songs, largely blue material familiar to devotees of her show, are uproariously funny and she delivers them with infectious physical panache that will serve her well in future screwball comedy stints on screen. Material was scripted by Midler with Jerry Blatt and Bruce Vilanch.

As for her voice, Midler is no Streisand, but she has a solid personality to back up her songs, and her versatility is one of her strongest assets. She ranges from camp presentations of cornball standards (in the guise of "Delores DeLago, The Toast of Chicago," her tacky lounge singer character) to straightforward ballads delivered with considerable force ("The Rose," "Stay With Me," "I Shall Be Released"), and even a punk number ("Leader Of The Pack").

But it is her personality and her comedy that create the strongest impression, particularly in a routine full of zingers about the British Royal Family and in a tribute to Sophie Tucker's dirty jokes. The language is not quite as risque as Midler's stage show has become on occasions, but it is strong enough to divide her fans from the unconverted, if any of the latter may happen to wander into the theatre.

Ritchie, Fraker, concert lighting director "Chip" Monck, production designer Albert Brenner, editor Glenn Farr, choreographer Toni Basil and rest of the crew have combined forces to provide a graphically arresting look to the film. Some of the numbers, however, fall below par, such as Midler's tedious old-lady skit or the punk routine, tending to create occasional dead spots that disrupt but don't destroy the generally snappy rhythm.

In addition to Midler, cast includes her adept backup trio, The Harlettes, comprising Jocelyn Brown, Ula Hedwig, and Diva Gray; on-stage musicians and vocalists; and a hilarious credit sequence appearance by Irving Sudrow as an ultra-square head usher briefing his crew for the evening's entertainment.

For the record, this is Midler's fourth film appearance, though studio publicity omits any mention of her low-budget pic of the early '70s, "The Divine Mister J." She also had a bit part in "Hawaii" before achieving film stardom with "The Rose." —Mac.

Le Dernier Metro
(The Last Subway)
(FRENCH-COLOR)

Paris, Sept. 5.

Gaumont release of Films du Carrosse/SEDIF/TF1/SFP co-production. Stars Catherine Deneuve, Gerard Depardieu, Jean Poiret. Directed by Francois Truffaut. Screenplay, Truffaut, Suzanne Schiffman, Jean-Claude Grumberg; camera (Fujicolor), Nestor Almendros; art director, Jean-Pierre Kohut-Svelko; sound, Michel Laurent; music, Georges Delerue; costumes, Lisele Roos; editors, Martine Barraque, Marie-Aimee Debril, Jean-Francois Gire. Reviewed at the Ponthieu screening room, Paris, Sept. 3, 1980. Running time: 130 MINS.
Marion Steiner . . . . . . Catherine Deneuve
Bernard Granger . . . . . Gerard Depardieu
Jean-Loup Cottins . . . . .Jean Poiret
Lucas Steiner . . . . .Heinz Bennent
Arlette Guillaume . . . . .Andrea Ferreol
Germaine Fabre . . . . Paulette Dubost
Nadine Marsac . . . . .Sabine Haudepin
Daxiat . . . . .Jean-Louis Richard
Raymond . . . . .Maurice Risch

Francois Truffaut's 19th feature is his richest, most satisfying film in years and could earn him the joint critical-commercial success that has been eluding him of late. On its most undemanding level it is adroit dramatic entertainment, gracefully romantic and uplifting. But it is also a fascinating chronicle of Paris life under the German Occupation — its daily terror, material deprivation, opportunism, cowardice, denunciation, as well as its quiet heroism and unexpected moments of laughter — as such will be one of the most-discussed films of the year.

"Le Denier Metro" follows the difficulties of a small Paris theatre struggling to stay open under the constraints of the Nazi occupants. In a way, it's "Day for Night" recast for the theatre, once again examining the sycophantic interplay of art and reality, this time in a specific historical context. And it's no less a subtle valentine to Truffaut's mentor, Jean Renoir, who celebrated the theatre in all its literal and metaphoric expression throughout his work.

Truffaut has been inspired foremost by the autobiography of Jean Marais, which provides an important compendium of theatrical life in Paris during the War. Many of Marais' recollections are deftly woven into the script.

Cinematically, Truffaut's model is not Renoir, but Lubitsch. The latter's "To Be Or Not To Be" (1942) is a film that Truffaut adores, and the core of his script, a romantic triangle, reflects the mainspring of Lubitsch's classic.

An exiled German Jewish director (Heinz Bennent) has gone into hiding in the cellar of the Paris theatre he had been running prior to the Nazi invasion. His non-Jewish wife (Catherine Deneuve) has taken over management of the troupe, which is rehearsing a Norwegian play, the reception of which will decide the company's future.

Deneuve must maneuver among the internal problems of the company, the emotional difficulties with her husband, whom she visits secretly every evening, and the impending menace in form of a virulently anti-semitic drama critic who prowls around the theatre when he is not busy spewing hate in his column or on the radio. Further emotional complications arise with the arrival of a new actor (Gerard Depardieu), a compulsive womanizer who moonlights as a Resistance fighter.

Truffaut, aided by his usual collaborator Suzanne Schiffman, and dramatist Jean-Claude Grumberg, have successfully wrestled with a mountain of factual material and compressed it into a memorable gallery of composite personages and incidents. The first part of the film threatens to sacrifice character to anecdote, but once it finds its equilibrium, the narrative flows smoothly, with its full weight of emotion.

Truffaut's direction is uncharacteristically restrained, his mise-en-scene almost classical in its invisible camerawork and sober editing. Inevitably, he indulges his penchant for filmic references (which include an opening scene paraphrasing, aptly enough, the first scene in "Children of Paradise," and a silhouette lifted right out of "Rules of the Game"), but rarely have they seemed more appropriate.

The acting is fine down the line, with Deneuve giving one of her most accomplished performances, particularly in her scenes with Bennent, forlorn and appealing, and Depardieu, who displays vigorous range. Jean Poiret (author of "La Cage Aux Folles"), Andrea Ferreol, Sabine Haudepin, Paulette Dubost and Maurice Risch, as the other members of the theatre, all register strongly.

But film's top performance comes from a new face: Jean-Louis Richard, whose portrayal of the fascist critic is so finely drawn and nuanced that one is almost moved by this essentially odious personality.

Nestor Almendros is behind the camera, so it seems superflous to add that the film looks lovely. The other technical credits are excellent. —Len.

Le Cheval d'Orgeuil
(Horse of Pride)
(FRENCH-COLOR)

Paris, Sept. 9.

A Planfilm release of a Bela production. Produced by Georges de Beauregard.

Stars Jacques Dufilho. Bernadette Le Sache. Francois Cluzet. Directed by Claude Chabrol. Screenplay, Chabrol. Daniel Boulanger, from book by Pierre-Jakez Helias; camera (Eastmancolor), Jean Rabier; music. Pierre Jansen; costumes. Magali Dray; art director. Hilton McConnico; editor. Monique Fardoulis. Reviewed at Publicis screening room. Paris. Sept. 4, 1980. Running time: **120 MINS.**

Cast: Jacques Dufilho, Bernadette Le Sache. Francois Cluzet. Paul Le Person, Pierre Le Rumeur, Michel Robin, Dominique Lavanant, and the voice of Georges Wilson.

———

The films of Marcel Pagnol excepted, local pictures about regional and rural life have never been great boxoffice in France and such films as Jean Renoir's "Toni" (1935), Georges Rouquier's classic "Farrebique" (1947), Louis Daquin's "Le Point du Jour" (1949) and Rene Allio's "Moi, Pierre Riviere..." (1975) remain isolated, commercially unsuccesssful masterpieces in a predominantly middle class, Paris-centered film industry. To date, rural life in commercial films here has usually been represented contemptuously as a hotbed of ignorance, intolerance and irrational violence.

"Le Cheval d'Orgueil" may make a difference at the boxoffice here, not because it has found a potent new approach — aesthetically it's derivative of, and inferior to, the above mentioned films — but because it's based on a phenomenal best-seller, Pierre-Jakez Helias' "Horse of Pride," a semi-autobiographical chronicle of peasant life in Britanny during the first four decades of this century. To date it has sold over 1,500,000 copies in France (it was published in 1975) and the film may have a ready public.

Picture will make it abroad for no other reason than that it's directed by Claude Chabrol, who has abandoned his role as the antagonist of the indiscreet bourgeoisie for that of the bucolic ethnographer.

Chabrol's film is clean, honest, unpretentious and made with an evident love for its subject. The direction is characterized by sobriety and self-effacing patience, unusual qualities for one of the master wizards of virtuosic directing. Some of the film's descriptive passages of peasant mores and customs are handled with a genuine lyricism.

But for all these qualities material remains rather remote and frequently monotonous as Boulanger and Chabrol steer clear of dramatization. It's a film of beautiful surfaces that will evoke more admiration than emotion.

There are script problems, particularly with focus. Although books' 40-year span is reduced to a mere decade (1908-1918), it's still too diffuse, relying rather conventionally on voice-over narration. The poor peasant family that serves as film's point of reference has little relief. Its members are convincingly portrayed by professional actors (Jacques Dufilho, Francois Cluzet and Bernadette Le Sache, who don't look incongruous among the many indigent non-professional players and extras).

Some scenes are misconceived, like those centered on the peasant oral tradition. Chabrol and Boulanger upstage the Breton storytellers by representing their tales cinematically, rather than sitting the camera down with the other peasant auditors and recording the speaker, who is as much the subject as his tales of amine, death and the supernatural.

The production looks splendid. Jean Rabier's color photography is beautiful without being glossy and the often stark beauty of the Breton countryside is one of the picture's most eloquent elements. —*Len.*

Brothers And Sisters
(BRITISH-COLOR)

———

London, Sept. 10.

A British Film Institute production. Executive producer, Peter Sainsbury. Produced by Keith Griffiths. Directed by Richard Woolley. Features entire cast. Screenplay, Richard Woolley, Tammy Walker; camera (color), Pascoe Macfarlane; editor. Mick Audsley; music. Trebor Jones; art director. Miranda Melville; sound, Alf Bower; production supervisor. Jim Pearse. Reviewed at the British Academy of Film and Television Arts. Sept. 9, '80. Running time: **96 MINS.**

Theresa Bennett, Jennifer Collins	Carolyn Pickles
David Barratt	Sam Dale
James Barratt	Robert East
Sarah Barratt	Elizabeth Bennett
Tricia Snow	Jenifer Armitage
Pete Gibson	Barry McCarthy
Helen Dawson	Barrie Shore
Father	Norman Claridge
Mother	Mavis Pugh
Detective	Fred Gaunt
Constable	Nick Jensen
Client	Jack Platts
2d Prostitute	Mary Wray
2d Policeman	David Theakston
Winston	Nelson Fletcher

———

Richard Woolley's commendable debut feature as writer-director, the biggest financial undertaking to date by the British Film Institute's grant allocating production board, is still a very slim budget effort that calls for sympathetic handling.

Ripe for some lowkey art house exposure in English-speaking markets, its best hopes probably lie in Europe. Prospects in foreign language territories won't be inhibited by accent and dialect, nor by the strongly northern English urban setting since the mystery theme is not unduly parochial.

Plot's whodunit element, pivoted on the murder of a parttime prostitute, acts as catalyst in Woolley's ambitious Chinese puzzle of a screenplay. Particularly ambitious is that it defiantly risks leaving audiences unsatisfied — the killer's identity ultimately remains uncertain.

But, as the title implies, the film is principally an investigation of contemporary relationships — filial, communal, sexual — among a bunch of characters marginally connected with the victim. It uses the murder investigation merely as a returning narrative link designed to be more interesting for its consequences than in itself.

Although finally the device does not quite come off (largely due to some unconvincing, or shakily directed, performances), the brave attempt to cut across conventional storyline expectations offers, en route, much intelligent challenging of conventional prejudices about character-types.

Robert East, for example, starting out as an uppercrust cad you love to hate, and emerging as prime suspect for the crime, is gradually revealed as a cad you hate to love, fundamentally more honest than his superficially more likable, if saccharine-liberal, younger brother.

For too long early on, it's unclear just how seriously Woolley expects the characters to be taken, especially members of a semi-communal household on which much of the action — and contrived dialog — centers. The intended tone of gentle satire at the expense of almost every familiar, angst-ridden situation only settles down after a splendid scene in which the "nice" brother confesses infidelity to his regular girlfriend (Jenifer Armitage). As the supposedly "talked through," quasi brother-sister relationship is threatened, it's fun to watch both parties abandon rational responses when faced with the possessiveness problem.

Besides East, the strong performances come from Sam Dale as his brother, and Carolyn Pickles as both the prostitute and her sister, who's covertly involved with Dale. Cinematography by Pascoe Macfarlane, notably of night exteriors, is mostly excellent, with occasional lapses into an inappropriate artiness.

Pic is included in the "British Film Now" section of the upcoming New York fest. Cineastes should enjoy its references to Nicolas Roeg's "Bad Timing," Ingmar Bergman's yet to be released "From The Life Of The Marionettes," and no doubt other similar-themed titles. —*Simo.*

The Exterminator
(COLOR)

———

Violent vigilante meller is for undiscriminating grind houses only.

———

Avco Embassy release of an Interstar production. Produced by Mark Buntzman. Features entire cast. Directed by James Glickenhaus. Screenplay, Glickenhaus; camera (color), Bob Baldwin; editor. Corky O'Hara; music. Joe Renzetti; sound (Dolby stereo). Bill Daly; special effects. Tom Brumberger; assistant director. Jane Hershcopf. Reviewed at National theatre. N.Y.C. Sept. 10, '80. (MPAA Rating: R). Running time: **101 MINS.**

Det. James Dalton	Christopher George
Dr. Megan Stewart	Samantha Eggar
John Eastland	Robert Ginty
Michael Jefferson	Steve James

With: Tony Di Benedetto, Dick Boccelli, Patrick Farrelly, Michele Harrell, David Lipman, Cindy Wilks, Dennis Boutsikaris.

———

The violent, vigilante revenge cycle of films has a new entry in "The Exterminator." For his second pic, writer-director James Glickenhaus commits the major sin of shooting an action film with little action. Contrived script instead opts for grotesque violence meted out by the titular antihero in a series of glum, distasteful scenes.

After a pre-credits Vietnam teaser sequence that relies heavily on Dolby stereo, "The Exterminator" returns to New York City for a listlessly paced tale of Robert Ginty suddenly deciding to avenge his war buddy, paralyzed from an encounter with a youth gang. Absence of proper transition scenes and script's frequent reliance upon coincidence loses credibility for Ginty's actions early on.

Unlike previous antiheroes, Ginty is styled as a sadist, not content to just exterminate criminals, but devising ludicrously gruesome deaths for them. This condescending catering to the action crowd's baser instincts won't wash.

Cynical, nullifying ending of the CIA shooting both Ginty and the policeman (Christopher George) who has hunted him down is preposterous, and audiences may hoot down the phony, sequel-baiting tag which follows.

Ginty cannot overcome the unplayable role of "sympathetic sadist," whose supposedly most noble moment is when he pulls the plug on the hospital's life support system for his paralyzed buddy. George's walkthrough as a policeman is regrettable. while Samantha Eggar as both the buddy's doctor and George's girlfriend must have calculated that this travesty would never be released. Tech credits are standard. —*Lor.*

Mais Qu'est-Ce Que J'Ai Fait Au Bon Dieu Pour Avoir Une Femme Qui Boit dans Les Cafes Avec Les Hommes!?
(What Did I Ever Do To The Good Lord To Deserve A Wife Who Drinks in Cafes with Men!?)
(FRENCH-COLOR)

Paris, Sept. 2.

A UA release of a Sofracima - UA coproduction. Produced by Giselle Rebillon and Catherine Winter. Features entire cast. Directed by Jan Saint-Hamont. Screenplay, Jan and Daniel Saint-Hamont. Alain Le Henry; technical advisor. Christian Bricout; camera (color), Maurice Fellous; sound, Paul Laine; editor. Michel Lewin; music. Georges and Pierce-Marie Baux. Reviewed at the Gaumont Colisee Theatre. Paris. Sept. 1. 1980. Running time: **90 MINS.**
With: Robert Castel. Antoinette Moya. Michel Boujenah.

Prolix title only conceals a commercial comedy that is short on ideas and humor. The director is Jan Saint-Hamont, who co-wrote last year's French sleeper, "Le Coup de Sirocco," first picture to deal, in a serio-comic vein, with the "Pieds-Noir," those Algerians of European extraction who were repatriated to France following Algerian independence in 1962. Film struck a nerve in France's large Pied-Noir community and cleaned up.

This one sort of picks up on "Coup de Sirocco" and again presents a Pied-Noir family, but one that has succeeded in business. Script ribs the ineffectual macho tyranny of family head, Robert Castel, as his wife decides to pack up and leave. Hamont's direction is a feeble as the story. Presence of Michel Boujenah, young Tunisian Jewish comic who had a hit one-man show in Paris last season, does nothing for film or Boujenah's career.

Pic has gotten off to fairly decent commercial start locally, proof that Pied-Noir theme still has b.o. clout, though it may be waning quickly.
—*Len.*

Mas Alla Del Terror
(The Hereafter of Terror)
(SPANISH-COLOR)

Madrid, Sept. 1.

Cinevision Production (Madrid). Directed by Tomas Aznar. Features entire cast. Screenplay. Tomas Aznar. Miguel Lizondo, Alfredo Casado; camera (Eastmancolor) Julio Bragado; editor. Maruja Soriano; sets, Gumersindo Andres; exec producer. Alfredo Casado. Reviewed at Cine Luchana. Madrid. Sept. 1. '80. Running time: **80 MINS.**
Chema . . . . Francisco Sanchez Grajera
Lola . . . . Raquel Ramirez
Nico . . . . Emilio Siegrist
Jorge . . . . Antonio Jabalera

Linda . . . . Alexia Loreto
Andras . . . . David Forrest

Youth-slanted actioner combining elements of juvenile delinquent violence with supernatural trappings and gore; item has been racking up brisk sales in its home market. Though production values and thesping are of the most elemental sort, pic may appeal to unsophisticated audiences seeking thrills of young hoods going rampant and then receiving bloody retribution from the ghosts of those they've brutally slain.

Pic starts (before titles) with a young knife-toting girl stabbing a businessman to death in a deserted country plot and robbing him; this is followed by her and three other youths racing off on choppers to an isolated road diner which they hold up and in a shoot out kill two cops who happen to pass by as well as all those in the diner, minus a couple who are taken along as "hostages." The nasty goings-on continue with the mob (minus one, who get himself shot) storming into a peaceful country house. After robbing it, they set the place ablaze, with an old woman and a child inside perishing in the flames.

Second and slower-paced half of pic then takes a turn to the supernatural as the fleeing hoods seek refuge in an abandoned monastery and are stalked one by one by the ghosts of those they've murdered and by some half-decomposed skeletons they find in the catacombs of the church.

A few relatively mild sex scenes, a touch of sacrilege, but especially the violence, got film an "S" rating (more or less equivalent to our "X") for Spain. Item could make apt fodder for exploitation circuits.
—*Besa.*

Der Tag, An Dem Elvis Nach Bremerhaven Kam
(The Day Elvis Came To Bremerhaven)
(WEST GERMAN-COLOR)

Berlin. Aug. 21.

A Tura-Film production. Munich, in collaboration with Westdeutscher Rundfunk (WDR). Cologne. Directed by Peter F. Bringmann. Features entire cast. Screenplay. Horst Koenigstein; camera (color). Axel Block; editing. Stefan Arnsten; sets. Goetz Heymann. Reviewed at Sender Freies Berlin Screening Room. Berlin. August 21. '80. Running time: **103 MINS.**
Cast: Wolfgang Drygalla (Karl-Heinz Teschner). Petra Bigaj (Monika). Michael Shelley (Joe). Margret Homeyer (Ilse Teschner). Michael Rehberg (Herbert Teschner). Hannelore Hoger (Elisabeth Keller). Susanne Schnur (Jutta Teschner). Marcus Mueller (Werner Keller).

Director Peter F. Bringmann made a name for himself immedi-

ately upon making "The Day Elvis Came to Bremerhaven" (1979), and he has scored again recently with "Theo Against the Rest of the World" (1980), unspooled in the film market at the Cannes fest. He is now a talent to watch, particularly with regard to the narrative style of cinema fostered by Germany's new generation of filmmakers.

"The Day Elvis Came to Bremerhaven" has an autobiographical thread running through it — scripter Horst Koenigstein grew up in Bremerhaven in the '50s, his family renting quarters in their home to American GIs stationed in the port city. He was on hand as a teenager when Elvis Presley arrived in Bremerhaven on Oct. 1, 1958, to serve his tour of duty as a soldier in West Germany. Like several other German teenagers at the time. he looked upon rock-'n'-roll and c-&-w music as well as jazz and blues as a way of life; further, from the port city. he watched several German families emigrate to Canada and the United States in search of a better existence.

Bringmann is careful to maintaint he atmosphere of the '50s in dress. costumes. sets, and even choice of actors (none of whom are known to tv and film audiences). The story itself is a chronicle of the times in several important details. Basically a love story, it's about a lad of 17 in love with a more mature woman of 19, who in turn has an affair with a black GI as a kind of protest against the anti-Yankee feeling in the area because of the town's "garrison" character. When the black GI is beaten one night by white soldiers. the German lad (who has befriended him together with the girl) is there to help. The three form a trio of outsiders. When Elvis arrives on the in-coming boat, the tv cameras are there with actual footage, while the lad and the girl discover their love for each other in a brief night of companionship.

Nostalgia for the '50s in the best sense and a winner as a fiction docu.
—*Holl.*

Sverige at Svenskarna
(Sweden For The Swedes)
(SWEDISH-COLOR)

Malmoe, Aug. 20.

A Mats Helge Olsson Filmproduktion/-Per Oscarsson production. AB Europea Film release. Original story and script and directed by Per Oscarsson. Features entire cast. Camera (Eastmancolor) Jiri Tirl; executive producers. Robert Ekman. Ake Brandhild. Dan Krantz; production design. Per Oscarsson. Dick Ljunggren, Jiri Kotlar; editors, Per Oscarsson. Henrik Ahlen; music. Carl-Axel Dominique. Reviewed at the Rio. Malmoe. Aug. 20. 1980. Running time: **113 MINS.**
Gustav Klosterhjerta . . . . . . Per Oscarsson
King Jean Louis . . . . Per Oscarsson

King Karl Brecht . . . . Per Oscarsson
King Wilfred
  Himmelthrill . . . . Per Oscarsson
Gustav's squire . . . . Ernst Gunther
Inga-Lill . . . . Sonya Hedenbratt
Traveling surgeon . . . . Allan Edwall
Finance minister . . . . . Monica Zetterlund
German messenger . . . . Lena Nyman
Swedish monk . . . . Bjoern Skifs
Another monk . . . . Martin Ljung

"Sweden For The Swedes" took three years of almost everybody involved's spare time and untold million of Kroner for semi-amateur producer Mats-Helge Olsson to carry through. Name actors put in cameo performances. Now fewer than 13 women designed film's costumes. Add to all this the vastly diversified talents and/or energies of Per Oscarsson, a 1956 Cannes Golden Palm winner for best actor (in Henning Carlsen's Danish feature "Hunger"), and you come up with a bulky historical-satirical farce of 14th Century farce.

Oscarsson, privately, is a soft touch for every liberal or left wing cause. This has in some ways hurt his career on stage and screen (he is a former "Hamlet" who once did an unscheduled frontal nudity strip in a tv family-aimed program), but he is also sincere and mild-mannered and audiences here still seem willing to go a long way with him. On this. he has made his huge bet with "Sweden For The Swedes." The same Swedes. however, have sat through his film in stony silence or stayed massively away from it since its opening some weeks ago.

In the credits, Oscarsson is listed as coproducer. author, director, production codesigner, coeditor plus he plays the film's four leading roles. Only as a production designer does he succeed.

"Sweden For The Swedes" has the fine looks of a major historical romance. Jiri Tirl's cinematography is also first-rate. The rest is a mess and a shambles of corny. school play dialog and gags, clumsy plot construction and wildly unfunny mugging replacing acting by Oscarsson in all his roles. Among the cameos. only Allan Edwall defies all odds and puts in a superior and subdued comedy performance as a traveling hack surgeon.

Plot has the Kings of France, England and Germany, all blithering. dithering idiots and all played by Oscarsson, waiting in the wings while hoping for Gustav, the equally idiotic Swedish throne pretender, to stumble before the Crown can be put upon his head. When Gustav (Oscarsson again, of course) stumbles plenty but does not fall, the three Kings have their armies invade Sweden where they fight a decisive battle with Gustav's forces. The latter are made up of thieves and imbeciles, such talent being alone in volunteering. This to indicate the satirical level of Oscarsson's anti-military stance in a film that cannot be salvaged.

—Kell.

Le Bar du Telephone
(The Telephone Bar)
(FRENCH-COLOR)

Paris, Sept. 1.

AMLF release of an A.T.C. 3000 production. Produced by Benjamin Simon. Features entire cast. Directed by Claude Barrois. Screenplay, Claude Neron; camera (color), Bernard Lutic; music, Vladimir Cosma; art director, Didier Haudepin; editor, Nicole Saunier; sound, Bernard Bats. Reviewed at the Paramount Elysees Theatre, Paris, Aug. 29, 1980. Running time: **93 MINS.**

With: Daniel Duval, Francois Perier, Georges Wilson, Julien Guiomar, Raymond Pellegrin, Valentine Monier, Christophe Lambert, Richard Anconina.

Claude Barrois, Claude Lelouch's habitual editor, directed this routine crime thriller freely inspired by the October, 1978 underworld massacre of the inhabitants of a Marseille bar. Screenwriter Claude Neron, best known for his collaboration with Claude Sautet, has retained the bloody incident as the film's centerpiece but has transferred the action to Paris and imagined an intrigue that has nothing to do with the real-life case.

Echoes of French film noir master Jean-Pierre Melville abound in this tale of vicious gang warfare that brings face-to-face three generations of gangsters. Violence is triggered by the brazen provocation of a self-styled loner hood (credibly played by filmmaker/actor Daniel Duval) who steps on the well-manicured toes of a firmly rooted criminal family (headed by Raymond Pellegrin). Pellegrin hires a pack of young amateur hoods to eliminate Duval at a suburban bar-restaurant, but they muff the job, killing everyone but Duval. Latter tracks down the amateurs' chief (Christophe Lambert), talks him over to his side and together they confront their underworld elders. No one survives the final shootout.

Francois Perier is also on hand as a canny police inspector who bides his time as the warring hoods wipe each other out. Perier and Pellegrin are both Melville veterans and here do re-runs of roles they performed in Melvilel thrillers.

Despite its conventional show of criminal ruthlessness picture trips over its simplistic formula and a nonsensical sentimentality — Duval is clearly the most cold-blooded of the lot, but he has Barrois and Neron's approbation, because he's a romantic loner and not middle-class-minded like Pellegrin and his

kind. Barrois' direction aggravates the attitude, particularly in the closing sequence when a musical motif used earlier for some drippy love scenes between Duval and his girl gets impasted on images of Duval and Lambert, who has acquired a misty-eyed admiration for the outlaw. —*Len.*

Von Wegen "Schicksal"
(Is This "Fate"?)
(W. GERMAN-B&W-DOCU-16m)

Berlin, Aug. 18.

A Literarisches Colloquium, Deutsche Film-und Fernsehakademie, and Second German Television (ZDF) coproduction, Berlin. Directed by Helga Reidemeister. Screenplay, Irene Rakowitz. Reidemeister; camera, (black and white), Axel Brandt. Reviewed at Arsenal-Kino, West Berlin, August 18, '80. Running time: **110 MINS.**

This docu, slated for the sister city program, Berlin-Los Angeles, in L.A. this November, goes beyond the typical "women's film" emerging from Berlin these days. It tells the story of a mother of four children, now divorced, trying to become independent despite the series of setbacks that plague her from year to year.

Since a strip of documentary footage existed from a typical working-class family scene back in 1972, which shows Irene Rakowitz with her husband and kids in a daily-life routine, director Helga Reidemeister could research a broken marriage under the "Is This 'fate'?" title. Docu won a German Film Prize this year for the debut helmer's work.

There's also another twist. The woman in question, Irene, also happens to be a former film-cutter, or editor, so we see her sitting at a cutting table viewing sequences and scenes Reidemeister has shot with her and members of her family. Since the three older girls are now teenagers, and two have moved out of the house in a kind of protest, and the divorced father lives in the apartment below the now-reduced "family" of three (mother, daughter, son), the portrait of a social condition rises quickly to the surface to intrigue and captivate the viewer.

Irene is not a happy woman, and she has her emotional problems. She can't explain exactly what her dreams were when she married 22 years ago, but her life with a coalminer was not easy — and when the mines closed down and there wasn't work anymore in the industrial Ruhr Valley area, the family decided to move to Berlin. Then the father has a serious accident on his new construction job and is lamed for life, receiving a pension.

The elements of "fate" are intertwined with how the mother, the

father, and the older daughters view the entire situation. It's rather painful, indeed, to watch the lady in question view what her children say, quite impolitely and negatively, about her and her way of life — Irene herself can't take it and nearly breaks down in tears. Save for this moment, however, the docu is open to every opinion expressed and doesn't try to reconstruct a "truth" out of the proceedings. Well worth a onceover at docu and women fests. —*Holl.*

Was Soll'n Wir Denn Machen Ohne Den Tod?
(What Should We Do Without Death?)
(W. GERMAN-COLOR-DOCU-16m)

Berlin, Aug. 23.

An Oh Muvie production, Berlin, in collaboration with Zweites Deutsches Fernsehen, Wiesbaden-Mainz. Directed by Elfi Mikesch. Reviewed at Arsenal-Kino, Berlin, Aug. 23, '80. Running time: 105 MINS.

Cast: Anke-Rixa Hansen, Barbara Gold, Brigitte, Christa Weisenseel, Christian Sievers, Edith London, Elfi Mikesch, Gabi Gysel, Joscha, Kaethe, Katharina Rosa, Liebchen, Los Seitz, Maria, Maya Farber-Jansen, Petra, Renate Merck, Soma, Traute, Ursula Weck, Uschi Gerhard Jensen, Steve Adamschevski.

Elfi Mikesch ranks with Helke Sander at the top of the list of Berlin Women Filmmakers. She won a German Film Prize for "I Often Think of Hawaii" (1978), a docu about the dreams of a young girl in Berlin whose mother is a scrub woman and father an American soldier, who deserted the family long ago, leaving behind mementoes from Hawaii. Then she made the very impressive docu on an old peoples home in Hamburg, "What Should We Do Without Death?"

Mikesch excels in the camera department. She is a trained photographer with an eye for composition and for catching nuances that reveal character. In "What Should We Do without Death?" she concentrates on portraits of individuals in the old peoples home, letting the patients tell their own stories about their past and present. One does not except such a docu to be anything but pessimistic; however, even when the subject of "death" comes up, the feeling is that it's a natural consequence of a full life. One patient, in fact, is over 100 years old; another dies in the course of the filmmaking; and others seem to view the film project as a kind of "testament."

The elderly women selected for the film all possess fresh memories or nostalgic recollections of the past. A sepia tone is used for reflective scenes of the women, while the colors of a lovely summer day on

the banks of the Alster in Hamburg show the objective reality. Music that pertains to the daydreams of certain individuals, such as a Turkish working-woman, is used to accent other impressions of the mansion's atmosphere. Best of all, the people caring for the aged gently prompt responses on questions about life, death, growing old, love, companionship, and other aspects that pertain to human dignity.

Docu is going to the Berlin-Los Angeles sister city exchange in L.A. this November. It should be seen by any who like docus at their observant and unobtrusive best. —*Holl.*

Die Macht Der Maenner Ist Die Geduld Der Frauen
(The Power of Men Is the Patience of Women)
(W. GERMAN-COLOR-16m)

Berlin, Aug. 18.

A Sphinx-Film production, Berlin; world rights, Basis Film, Berlin. Features entire cast. Written and directed by Cristina Perincioli. Camera (color), Katia Forbert Petersen; editing, Helga Schnurre; music, Flying Lesbians. Reviewed at Arsenal-Kino, West Berlin, Aug. 18, '80. Running time: 75 MINS.

Cast: Elisabeth Walinski (Addi), Eberhard Feik (her husband), Dora Kuerten, Christa Gehmann, Hilde Hessmann, Barbara Stanek.

Swiss-born Cristina Perincioli, a grad of the Berlin Film & Television Academy, made "The Power of Men Is the Patience of Women" (1979) with a group of women filmmakers and based the story entirely on the experiences of women who have been beaten by their husbands. Pic is now slated for the Berlin-Los Angeles "sister-city" exchange in L.A. this November on the occasion of the city's 200th anniversary.

A fiction-documentary, pic seldom stays far from home base in telling this story of a mother with a child who has an intolerable egoist with a bad temper for a husband. Their child is now at kindergarten age, but still wets his pants and cannot adjust to being away from home, which adds an extra burden to the affair. Further Addi, our heroine, wants to win a bit of independence as a salesgirl, her former profession, but the odds are against her under the present circumstances.

Addi finally goes looking for help when the beatings get to be too frequent and shamelessly brutal. She takes the child and moves out of the apartment to a "Frauen-Haus," a place where other women, in the same position, can advise and help her. But when she applies for a divorce, neither the lawyer nor the social workers accept the facts and take her side — instead, the sonny-boy of a husband makes the favorable impression. He even kidnaps his son to force Addi to come back — to more beatings.

It's only when Addi is hospitalized that the film's point has been completely made. The rest is how the group of defenseless women organize to such a degree that the picture now looks rosy and more realistic for all concerned, although this is only one story among many.

Although there's is hardly a plot, the documented side of a woman's case-history under an oppressing husband allows for a loose and convincing interpretation by the principal thesps, who know only too well what they're talking about. A natural for Women Film Fests. —Holl.

Venice Festival

Berlin Alexanderplatz
(W. GERMAN-ITALO-COLOR)

Venice, Sept. 2.
Bavaria Atelier, RAI-TV2 release and production. Features entire cast. Written and directed by Rainer Werner Fassbinder from the book by Alfred Doblin in 13 episodes for tv. Camera (color), Xaver Schwarzenberger; editor, Juliane Lorenz; music, Peer Raben; art director, Barbara Baum. Reviewed at Venice Film Fest, Aug. 30-Sept. 5. Running time, 75 MINS. per tv episode or 975 MINS. in all.
Franz .... Gunter Lamprecht
Eva .... Hanna Schygulla
Meck .... Franz Buchrieser
Reinhold .... Gottfried John
Mieze .... Barbara Sukowa
Wirt .... Claus Holm
Lina .... Elisabeth Trissenaar
Mrs. Bast .... Brigitte Mira
Bruno .... Roger Frotz
Pums .... Volker Spengler
Rudi .... Ivan Desny

Rainer Werner Fassbinder emerged from a cult figure and festival idol to a hot commercial filmmaker with his highly accessible "The Marriage of Maria Braun." So all eyes are on his latest project, an ambitious tv series based on a well-known German book of the Twenties. Showing segs in pairs of twos and threes, it was one of the events of the recent Venice Film Festival.

Fassbinder seems to have been faithful to the novel in transposing it to visual terms. There is the use of interior monolog, commenting on the actions and an expressionistic approach that was in fashion in that period of the late '20s.

He exteriorizes the protagonist's feelings, needs and problems and makes him a sort of archetype Teutonic man who is molded by events and broken down to a survivor that may have made him easy bait for the rising Nazi Party in this period.

Gunter Lamprecht is extraordinary as the lumpen worker and

highly reminiscent of such heavyweight German actors of the period as Emil Jannings. In fact, he looks like him and may have studied his films, such as "Variety" and "The Blue Angel." But it is all assimilated into a powerful performance in its own right.

Lamprecht, a porter, had killed his mistress in a fit of jealousy. He is seen leaving prison and experiencing terror as he sees his city so new and strange now. He is taken in hand by an Hassidic Jew who tries to assuage his fears.

He finally gets to his old rooms and then tries to take up his life again. He visits his dead mistress' sister whom he seduces with all his clothes still on. A heavy, erotic, bear-like aspect is evident in Lamprecht, a sometimes well meaning type but too often taken over by instincts, fears and problems.

He meets a Polish woman who lives with him and decides he will try to be straight and lead a good life. But circumstances will not have it so. He is betrayed by friends, joins a gang and loses an arm in a getaway. But he still wants no vengeance and ends up being kept by his new woman, a prostitute.

She is killed by the man who betrayed him in the holdup and led to his accident. But he feels at least she has not crossed and left him. He ends up in prison and has a breakdown and seems to see death. He survives, but as a sort of shell that seems to anticipate the promises of Nazism that will be accepted by his kind and bring on the horrors that ensued.

Fassbinder was right in not trying to pull a film out of this taut, personal look at a man mauled, destroyed, put together again by the times and its ethics. As a tv series, it is at first opaque and harsh, but slowly builds into an unusual look at the Germany that was able to go on to its Nazi stages.

Extremely demanding but absorbing tv fare with public service webs sure to find a selective audience for it. It holds its own on a big screen and does emerge a sort of merging of tv and film techniques with its barrage of characters coming into the life of the protagonist, all sketched in short scenes with the city of Berlin finely and stylistically recreated in its last decadence and surface flash before the advent of Nazism.

Perhaps a specialized house might try this on for cult chances in showing a few episodes at a time. Producers announce it as a series of 13 episodes but at Venice they varied from 75 minutes to one hour and had 14 in the series. They can be honed perhaps to wanted lengths for there is a flow between the epi-

sodes that does not make each a complete entity.

Fassbinder, like many other of the brighter German filmmakers, seems to be going back to the techniques of the great German period of the '20s, but gives them a fresher look despite using the same period at times or World War II or contemporary subjects.

Fassbinder continues to be the most prolific of the German filmmakers and has already started a new film. His many regular actors all dress up this series well and it has an expensive look. There is sometimes a dark hue to the colors which might need to be lightened for the tube but are acceptable on the big screen.

Chalk this up as an unusual tv event, perhaps too demanding in some areas, but certainly an advance as a video series trying to blend entertainment and even gloss with important themes. —Mosk.

O Megalexandros
(Alexander The Great)
(GREEK-ITALIAN-COLOR)

Venice, Sept. 16.
RAI Rete 2-ZDF-Anghelopulos Productions release and production. Features entire cast. Written and directed by Theodoros Anghelopulos. Camera (Color), Ghiorgos Arvanitis; music, Christodulos Halaris. Reviewed at Venice Film Fest, Sept. 8, '80. Running time, 230 MINS.
Alessandro .... Omero Antonutti
Figliastra .... Eva Kotmanid
Maestro .... Grigoris Evanghelatos
Anarchist .... Norma Mozzato

Theodoros Anghelopulos, who has made a mark at film festivals among buffs and film critics, and some respectable specialized outings in Japan and France, now wins his first major prize at a leading competitive international film festival.

His Greek entry won a Golden Lion for its innovative qualities. Actually, Anghelopulos goes in for long-held shots, posey acting patterned on Greek tragedy and allegories and symbolical themes also beholden to ancient Greek dramas but commenting on Greece politics, ethos and society over this century so far.

Alexander the Great, that great historical figure who overran a good part of Eastern Europe and the Near East, has usually been identified as a liberal bringing hope to the oppressed. But here he is a bandit figure in 1900 who escapes from prison with his men.

He is against the government of the time and kidnaps some British aristocrats in for celebrating British interests in the country as well as the new century. He holds them for amnesty. He goes back to a town he ruled and finds an idealistic teacher had brought in

communal living against his harsh, authoritarian rule balanced by adherence to his rules of behavior and life.

One of his soldiers trying to rape a British hostage is hung at once. Alexander comes into conflict with the teacher but then they have to fight against governmental soldiers and the people 'are defeated, the village razed and all destroyed except a young boy who escapes on Alexander's white horse and 'indicates the spirit of Alexander may go on.

Editors may get itchy fingers watching this film, but nothing can be touched without destroying the hypnotic, ritualistic rhythm that Anghelopulos succeeds in evoking and makes his films effective despite their length, overlong shots and postured playing.

Some feeling for Greek history could help but is not necessary for the film creates a human comedy of man's adaptation that transcends its borders. For selective audiences, universities and festivals film depicts a literary, individual talent that uses the visuals of film on its own terms and succeeds despite its often portentous, relentlessly held shots. —Mosk.

Pilgrim, Farewell
(U.S.-COLOR)

Venice, Sept. 9.
Post Mills Productions Inc. release and production. Features entire cast. Written and directed by Michael Roemer. Features entire cast. Camera (color), Franz Rath; editor, Terry Lewis; producer, Stanley Plotnick. Reviewed at Venice Film Fest, Sept. 1.-80. Running time: 102 MINS.
Kate .... Elizabeth Huddle
Paul .... Christopher Lloyd
Ann .... Laurie Prange
Rebecca .... Lesley Paxton
Maggie .... Shelley Wyant
Doctor .... Elizabeth Franz
Luke .... Robert Brown

Using that untractable theme of death, and by cancer, that seems to be showing up in films and tv of late, Michael Roemer has utilized it more as a catalyst than treating the factor of imminent death itself.

It makes the film somewhat ambiguous and perhaps overcharged despite the fact that the situation must bring on facing up to it, to one's self and to those around one. But everything is brought to a boil at once and the film does not quite achieve the poignance, dramatic epiphany and fresher insight into the painful situation it strives for.

Film is helped by some fine ensemble acting and especially Elizabeth Huddle as the headstrong victim who has never accepted depending on anyone or dependence on her. This has led to a neurotic daughter of 19 she left with her in-laws when her unstable husband committed suicide.

There is also a younger sister who had looked up to her but never gotten the love she wanted and a taciturn cabinet maker she lives with who she saved from a monk-like life and little reward for his fine work. She makes pottery.

Film starts with Huddle getting the news she has little time left. The daughter has come to see her but cannot face up to it and her sister has arrived pregnant. Huddle gets jealous of her sister who she suspects wants to stay with her man after her death and cannot find a way to her daughter though she wants to.

There are bouts of extreme pain, levity and finally breakthroughs with the few important people in her life. Director Roemer made the heralded tv docu, "Dying," and does not overdo the physical side though it is harrowing at times.

This independent film is well produced and could find its way at specialized wickets on its restraint though it would call for careful launching. A touchy theme treated with obvious sincerity but just missing the grace to add a new dimension to this oft-treated and eternal theme. It is technically sound.

—*Mosk.*

Con Fusione
(Con-fusion)
(ITALIAN-COLOR)

Venice, Aug. 31.
A Gaumont Italia film, produced by Azione Cinematografica. Written and directed by Piero Natoli. Features entire cast. Camera (color). Giuseppe Lanci; editor, Anna Napoli; music, Arturo Annecchion. No other credits. Running time: 100 MINS..
Carlotta .... Carlotta Natoli
The father .... Piero Natoli
The girl .... Luisa Maneri

An unabashedly autobiographical second feature by young helmer Piero Natoli narrates his relations with his eight-year-old daughter and an independent young woman (Luisa Maneri) they meet on a summer vacation. Both Natoli and daughter Carlotta are natural, unselfconscious actors making their screen debut here; with pro actress Luisa Maneri they create a film out of their personal story that is surprisingly successful for this dangerous sort of undertaking. Very well shot but with some dead spots where scenes are stretched too long.

When Carlotta's mother leaves her in the care of the estranged father for a summer, the young man finds himself uncomfortable with the necessity of living in close contact with the girl, an active and clever child with a very individual personality. Unable to pawn her off on girlfriend or grandmother, he buys a camper and the two take off

for a vacation at the seaside. They pick up a pretty 20-year-old hitchhiker, whose exclusive relationship with the father is gradually transformed into a friendship with the child. His self-esteem wounded, the father sinks into moody isolation; but by the end of the film the three overcome their individual problems in a harmonious relationship.

Pic's saving grace is probably the ironic view helmer-father is able to take of his own role. Strongest are scenes tracing father-daughter relations, carefully scripted (the child is credited for dialog consultation) and acted with spontaneith and good comic timing.

Despite some empty minutes in overly long scenes and the basic slightness of the story, "Confusion" shows an unpretentious and very filmic talent behind it that should bear watching. —*Yung.*

A Idade Da Terra
(The Age of the Earth)
(BRAZILIAN-COLOR)

Venice, Sept. 9.
Embrafilme. Glauber Rocha Communicacoes Artisticas release and production. Features entire cast. Written and directed by Glauber Rocha. Camera (Color). Roberto Pires; editor, Carlos Cox, Raul Soares, Ricardo Miranda; music, Rogerio Duarte. Reviewed at Venice Film Fest, Sept. 1, '80. Running time. 158 MINS.
With: Mauricio Do Valle, Jece Valadao, Norma Benguel; Tarcisio Meira, Antonio D'El Rey, Danuza Leao, Carlos Petrovich.

Glauber Rocha was the kingpin in the unusual Cinema Novo movement in Brazil in the late '60s and early '70s that made an impact at festivals with its romantic, allegorical, poetic fusion of political and social themes.

The movement died out some years ago and Rocha went back after several years of exile and making films abroad. Now he surfaces with a loud, didactic, surface mixture of his old themes which now seem repetitious and overdone rather than making the impact of yore.

Rocha still sometimes hits an unusual image and a frenetic interpretation of revolutionary zeal lost in social and political changes. It starts with exotically dressed Indians writhing in sexual freedom and song and then cuts to the Mardi Gras which may reflect the early tribal days of the country.

Then a political demagogue, his rival, exotic women representing eternal truths alternate in this grabbag of visual ideas with one long explanation of the past Brazilian political changes by an historian in the exotic, modernistic capital of Brasilia which is a leitmotif in the film.

The excitement of his films on romantic bandits, "Antonio Das

Mortes," "Black God and White Devil," or his dynamic political poem "Land in Trance," are just echoes in this overlong film which may have been worth fest outing on Rocha's past brilliance but not having the coherence for much theatrical interest outside Latino climes.

Rocha's visual inventiveness is there at times, though lost in this massive ferment of images, music and folk characters mingling in this overripe mosaic look at the past, present and future of this bustling country which lately has eased its repressive governmental tactics.

Film raised pros and cons but was worth festival outing on its sheer visual bravado and perhaps heralding the last gasp of that old cinema novo movement. Now it remains to be seen if Rocha can curb and refine his robust directorial flair to more modern and accessible themes or at least clarify his historical fragmented style. —*Mosk.*

Rasskaz O Neisvestnom Celoveke
(Story of an Unknown Man)
(RUSSIAN-COLOR)

Venice, Sept. 9.
Sovexport release of Mosfilm production. Features entire cast. Written and directed by Vitautas Zalakjavicjus from a story by Anton Chekhov. Camera (Sovcolor), A. Kuznetcov; music, A. Firtic. Reviewed at Venice Film Fest, Sept. 1, '80. Running time: 99 MINS.
Zinaida .... E. Simonova
Vladimir .... A. Kajdanovski
Orlov .... G. Taratorkin

Anton Chekhov, and most other classic Russian writers and playwrights, have systematically been filmed by Soviet filmmakers. Checkhov, with his humanistic but lost characters, never pitied or sentimentalized, has been a special favorite of many filmmakers.

This one, based on a short story, is a bit skimpy in narrative format but is lovingly though academically made by Lithuanian director Vitautas Zalakjavicjus. A nice period feel and good acting help this tale of a vengeance that is thwarted by illness, change of heart and love.

A naval officer, whose friends had been broken by a general after an aborted uprising, gets a job as a valet in the general's son's house. He becomes a confidant of the son who takes a woman to live with him. The valet admires the woman who is finally jilted by the son while she is pregnant.

The doddering old general visits the house but the valet, now ill with t.b., cannot do anything and takes out his hurt on a complacent, patronizing visitor to the house. He goes off with the woman to France for his health. He confesses his love but it cannot be consummated. She

dies in childbirth and he brings back the little girl which the real father will not accept.

Somewhat literary, the film looms more for possible tv usage and some university outings, not having the more robust filmic insights and treatment for theatrical outings. —*Mosk.*

Venezia, Ultima Serata Di Carnevale
(Venice: Last Night of Carnival)
(ITALIAN-COLOR-DOCU)

Venice, Aug. 28.
Produced and distributed by the Third Channel of RAI-TV. Directed by Carlo Tuzii. Camera (color). Nino Celeste; editor. Carlo Valerio. No other credits. Running time: 50 MINS.

Opening the Venice Film Biennale this year was director Carlo Tuzii's short, uneasy documentary on what he saw earlier at the Biennale Theatre's Carnival revival. The official attempt to reanimate an ancient popular tradition, the Carnival that celebrates the end of Lent with raucous merrymaking in the streets, was invaded by thousands of young people from all over the country.

Helmer's restless camera captures some striking images from the giant masked celebration. However·gratifying the unexpected response to the initiative must have been to organizers of Biennale Theatre, the unleashing of mass energy sounds also a desperate note for the filmmaker.

The wild, rather sinister side of Carnival comes out in the dancing crowds overflowing St. Mark's Square and particularly in the performances of small theatre groups informally performing before the public. An exceptionally performed and filmed Medieval allegory, "Merrymaking in Times of Plague," and a New York punkstyle "If Venice Were a Metropolis" miming a kidnapping, have the paranoiac tone of the latest news reports. —*Yung.*

Toronto Fest

Love In A Taxi
(US-COLOR)

Toronto, Sept. 12.
A Davey Company production. No distributor. Produced and directed by Robert Sickinger. Screenplay by Michael Kortchmar. Stars Diane Sommerfield and James Jacobs. Camera (color). Joseph Mangine; art direction, Steven Vickers; editor, Bill Freda; sound. Dale Whitman; music, Susan Minsky. Reviewed at Toronto Festival of Festivals at Famous Players screening room. Toronto. Sept. 8. '80. Running Time: 90 MINS.

Corinne .... Diane Sommerfield
Sam .... James H. Jacobs
Gary .... Earl Monroe
Davey .... Malik Murray
Marian .... Lisa Jane Persky
Jimmy ....Lyle Kessler
Norma .... Karen Grannum
Mel .... Phil Rubinstein
Monk .... Al Fann
Hoods ....Bill Moor
Hannibal Penney, Jr., Tony Capra
Dowager .... Dorothy Leon

"Love in a Taxi" is a low-budget debut picture filled with warmth, skill and humor, one of those happy surprises which proves big-budgets are not the only way to get quality product.

The $350,000 film observes the blossoming relationship between Jewish New York City cabbie James Jacobs and struggling black bank clerk Diane Sommerfield. They are brought together by Sommerfield's precocious son, Malik Murray, who appears in Jacob's cab one afternoon. Director Robert Sickinger carefully details the growing attraction between these two people with compassion. The obvious color and cultural tensions are handled without pain or breast-beating. The overall effect is a real upper for audiences.

Layered into the main story are some wonderful stories involving cabbie cronies and a dope-dealing scam which Jacobs and Sommerfield inadvertently becoming party to. The latter sub-plot is somewhat awkward but essential to the plot flow. Charming, witty and with production values considerably beyond its modest resources, the film has polish and heart.

Sickinger has an assured visual style and has integrated natural locations to strong dramatic purpose. A chase through the Museum of Natural History is one of the most exciting and freshest seen in recent films. "Love in a Taxi" is actually several years old but has gone through a post-production reworking and could emerge as a commercial prospect with carefully placed distribution.

Jacobs, best known as a writer of the original "Grease," is an affable screen personality and Sommerfield is sheer magic on screen. The supporting cast is outstanding with special nods to Lisa Jane Persky as a tough female cabbie and Lyle Kessler as Jacobs' wise-cracking buddy. —*Klad.*

Temps Morts
(Dead Times)
(FRENCH-DOCU-COLOR-16m)

Toronto, Sept. 16.
Les Films Du Sabre-Centre Georges Pompidou release and production. Conceived, directed and photographed (color) by Claude Godard. Editor, C. Tronquet. Reviewed at Toronto Film Fest, Sept. 12, '80. Running time. **76 MINS.**

Claude Godard, apparently no relation to ex-New Waver Jean-Luc, has made a documentary on very aged people in a home. There is no music, no dialog, no commentary, only background sounds and voices. Film is haunting, never gratuitous or shocking but emerges more an album of photos than giving insight into the twilight time of approaching death from old age.

Most just lie about and are washed or cared for by nurses and doctors. Others doze at tables but others do some work such as making labels for companies and some even make their way to a local cafe.

The institution looks dreary, decrepit, dying likes its inhabitants. But Godard, despite a fine visual flair and an acceptable editing of his scenes, does not give an inkling of an attitude, a feeling of reaction to what he is filming.

It may be useful for geriatric conferences, institutions, festivals, of course, and, perhaps, some public service tv outlets. But despite its arresting imagery, film's attempt to find beauty as well as distress in knarled limbs and bodies emerges as overlong, ambiguous and even voyeuristic in its refusal to make a statement on this eerie haven for people slipping into senility and death.

Things can be read into it in re care of these people, but film needed a more implicit treatment. Godard, only 22, shows a flair for individual images and may be a filmmaker to watch. —*Mosk.*

Suzanne
(CANADIAN-COLOR)

Toronto, Sept. 12.
An Ambassador (Canada) film release of an RSL production. Produced by Robert Lantos; executive producer Stephen J. Roth. Directed by Robin Spry. Stars Jennifer Dale. Winston Rekert, Gabriel Arcand. Screenplay. Robin Spry. Ronald Sutherland, based on novel, "Snow Lark," by Sutherland; camera (color). Miklos Lente; art director, Vianney Gauthier; costume design. Louise Jobin; editor. Fima Noveck; music. Francois Cousineau, theme by Luc Plamondon and Francois Cousineau. Reviewed at Toronto Festival of Festivals at Elgin Theatre, Toronto, Sept. 9, '80. Running time: **114 MINS.**
Suzanne McDonald ....Jennifer Dale
Nicky Callaghan .... Winston Rekert
Georges Laflamme ...... Gabriel Arcand
Andrew McDonald .... Ken Pogue
Yvette McDonald ..... Michelle Rossignol
Kathy .... Marianne McIsaac
Jimmy .... Michael Ironside
Marilyn .... Gina Dick
Pierre .... Pierre Curzi
Greg .... Gordon Thompson
Brenda Callaghan .... Helen Hughes
Andre .... Adam Chase

"Suzanne" is a weepy, true romance tale set in the 1950s amid the backdrop of French-English strife in Montreal. The subject may sound ambitious and original, but the resulting film is a disaster from beginning to end.

It's impossible to tell where the project misfired. Almost every aspect of production is wrongheaded. The accent is on the obvious and the overplayed.

The film opens at a Roman Catholic religious parade in 1944. This prolog attempts to explain that cultural tension is an ongoing aspect of daily life. Abruptly, the action flashes ahead 10 years into the world of football, rock 'n' roll and "good girls don't."

Suzanne McDonald, as played by Jennifer Dale, is a young woman with a Quebecois mother and a stern Scot father. She is betwixt and between, pursued by Winston Rekert, sensitive and misunderstood under his macho front.

The stormy affair ends in Suzanne's pregnancy and Rekert's imprisonment for petty thievery. Then, a past Quebecois friend returns to offer Suzanne love and education. All seems well and resolved. Once again the action flashes forward to 1965 when Rekert returns from jail. Rekert and Gabriel Arcand, Suzanne's husband, clash but Rekert's love for his **son brings him back to his senses and the picture ends on a tearful note.**

Director Robin Spry has a solid reputation in documentaries and docu-dramas and it's difficult to understand his presence in this highly romantic piece. At times he strains to give the production a realistic mood destroying the precious quality of the material.

Spry co-wrote the screenplay with Ronald Sutherland who wrote the novel which formed the film's basis. The two have produced almost two hours of painful dialog and clumsy dramatic situations.

Dale emerges as radiant and valiant. It's easy to see a potential as a film actress given better material. Rekert is faced with a role which is all image and no substance. His dialog is insalvageable and his handling of the character is without balance.

The best performances are Arcand's and Michelle Rossignol as Suzanne's mother. Both manage to ease back from the intense material and root their work in a more natural style.

"Suzanne" is set for Canadian release this month and will be trimmed to tone down some of the laughter-generating dialog. The curiously out-of-step production will have a tough market to crack locally and will probably be viewed with curiosity on the international scene. —*Klad.*

Somewhere In Time
(COLOR)

Christopher Reeve terrific in change of pace from "Superman." Beautifully crafted romantic drama involving time travel.

Hollywood, Sept. 16.
Universal release of a Rastar Stephen Deutsch production. Produced by Deutsch. Stars Christopher Reeve. Directed by Jeannot Szwarc. Screenplay. Richard Matheson, from his novel "Bid Time Return;" camera (Technicolor). Isidore Mankofsky; music. John Barry, with "Rhapsody On A Theme Of Paganini" by Rachmaninoff; editor, Jeff Gourson; production designer. Seymour Klate; set decorator. Mary Ann Biddle; sound, Charles L. King III, Roger Heman, Earl M. Madery, Rex A. Slinkard; associate producer, Steven Bickel; assistant director, Burt Bluestein. Reviewed at Universal Studios. North Hollywood. Sept. 15, 1980. (M-PAA Rating: PG.) Running time: 103 MINS.
Richard Collier .... Christopher Reeve
Elise McKenna .... Jane Seymour
W.F. Robinson ..... Christopher Plummer
Laura Roberts .... Teresa Wright
Arthur .... Bill Erwin
Dr. Gerald Finney ..... George Voskovec
Older Elise .... Susan French
Arthur's Father .... John Alvin
Genevieve .... Eddra Gale
Yount Arthur .... Sean Hayden
Astonished Man ...... Richard Matheson

A charming, witty, passionate romantic drama about a love transcending space and time. Universal's "Somewhere In Time" is an old-fashioned film in the best sense of that term. Which means it's carefully crafted, civilized in its sensibilities, and interested more in characterization than in shock effects. Christopher Reeve is smashing in his first film outing since "Superman," and his commercial appeal, plus careful handling, could help this Rastar/Stephen Deutsch production find the audience it deserves.

The film harks back to such 1940s Hollywood romantic classics as "Portrait Of Jennie" and "The Ghost And Mrs. Muir," in which people from different eras managed to overcome all physical obstacles to their love. This kind of film has always been a matter of taste, with some finding the genre enchanting and others finding it insufferably corny. Some lines may be drawn here, too, but the pic is made with impeccable taste and intelligence.

In the finely wrought screenplay by veteran fantasy writer Richard Matheson, based on his own novel "Bid Time Return," Reeve sheds his "Superman" cloak for contemporary garb as a promising young Chicago playwright who becomes mysteriously fascinated by a 1912 photo of a stage actress, Jane Seymour. She has visited him as an old lady with the cryptic words

"Come back to me." and after her death, Reeve is drawn to a hotel on Mackinac Island in Michigan, where it transpires they actually did meet and have an affair at the time the photo was taken. Reeve's journey back in time and the bitter-sweet resolution of the romance form the main part of the film.

If this type of time-travel story also seems reminiscent of "The Twilight Zone." that's because Matheson was a frequent contributor to that series and helped set its tone. "Somewhere In Time" is elevated above tv series fare by its extraordinarily attractive cast, its subtly detailed writing, and the sumptuous production values of the period hotel setting.

The elements are beautifully controlled and orchestrated by director Jeannot Szware, who, in his third feature, finally seems to be on ground he finds congenial ("Bug" and "Jaws 2" in retrospect seem like impersonal commercial assignments). Szware guides Reeve and Seymour through the deliriously romantic story with a sure hand that allows touches of irony and playfulness but never sacrifices the essentially sincere and emotionally moving tone.

If anyone had any doubt after "Superman" that Reeve is a fine actor with both star power and versatility, this film should firmly establish his credentials. As a first-rate and exciting romantic lead, able to handle both comedy and drama with equal skill, Reeve has a terrific screen career in the making. Seymour is lovely and mesmerizing enough to justify Reeve's grand romantic obsession with her, and Christopher Plummer ably sketches in the purposely shadowy figure of her Svengali. Among the supporting cast, which includes solid appearances by Teresa Wright and Bill Erwin, most engaging perhaps is a small boy, Sean Hayden, who plays Erwin's character as Reeve knew him in 1912.

The romantic mood is well served and sustained by all tech elements, including Isidore Mankofsky's nostalgic lensing; John Barry's lush score with a theme from Rachmaninoff; alluring production design by Seymour Klate, set decoration by Mary Ann Biddle; and costumes by Jean-Pierre Dorleac. And the main location, the Grand Hotel on Mackinac Island, is a visual feast virtually worth the price of admission. —Mac.

Mother's Day
(COLOR)

Mommie dearest and her two evil kids.

United Film Distribution Company release of a Michael Kravitz and Charles Kaufman production. Features entire cast. Directed by Charles Kaulman. Screenplay. Charles Kaufman. Warren D. Leight; camera (color). Joe Mangine; associate producers. Lloyd Kaufman, Michael Heriz; music. Phil Gallo. Clem Vicari. No other credits provided. Reviewed at Gemini Theatre. New York. Sept. 19. 1980. (No MPAA rating.) Running time. 98 MINS.

Abbey	Nancy Hendrickson
Jackie	Deborah Luce
Trina	Tiana Pierce
Ike	Holden McGuire
Addley	Billy Ray McQuade
Mother	Rose Ross
Ted	Kevin Loew
Brad	Karl Sandys
Doorman	Ed Battle
Charlie	Stanley Knapp
Terry	Marsella Davidson
Tex	Robert Carnegie
Storekeeper	Scott Lucas
Ernie	Bobby Collins

This bit of gore, aimed at the Tobe Hooper market and released on the same day it was trade-screened, is par for the course. Lots of bloodletting, lots of suggestions of rape and violence (neither ever consummated on screen), and the usual inane dialog and plot situations. For the intended market, it should do well and those few more sophisticated members of the audience who find themselves trapped in the theatre can have fun talking back to the screen.

These films follow formula. Several innocents put themselves into jeopardy, lots of nasty things happen to them and, on occasion, they escape. The survival score here is two out of three or so we're led to believe until we remember that the murderous mama has a sister.

Three former college gals go camping somewhere in New Jersey and are captured by two retarded brothers who drag them home to present to mama. After a period of fun and games, the two surviving femmes turn the tables and bring about the gruesome resolution.

Technically, it's not bad. Dramatically, it's dreadful. These performances are more than likely going to be omitted in the cast's resume when they next go job-hunting. —Robe.

Without Warning
(COLOR)

AIP lives on.

Hollywood, Sept. 23.
A Filmways Pictures release, produced and directed by Greydon Clark. Features entire cast. Exec producers. Skip Steloff, Paul Kimatian. Screenplay. Lyn Freeman. Daniel Grodnik. Ben Nett. Steve Mathis; camera (Movielab color). Dean Cundy: editor. Curtis Burch: sound. Bob Dietz; assistant director. Caren Singer; associate producers. Curtis Burch. Milton Spencer; music. Dan Wyman. Reviewed at Filmways Pictures. Beverly Hills. Sept. 16. 1980. (MPAA rating: R.) Running time: 89 MINS.

Taylor	Jack Palance
Fred	Martin Landau
Sandy	Tarah Nutter
Greg	Christopher S. Nelson
Hunter	Cameron Mitchell
Leo	Neville Brand
Aggie	Sue Ane Langdon
Scoutmaster	Larry Storch
Dave	Ralph Meeker
Beth	Lynn Theel
Tom	David Caruso
Randy	Darby Hinton

"Without Warning" is without distinction in the current horror-film derby, but the story is dumb enough, the acting bad enough, the killings slurpy enough and often enough to hold its own. In any case, it proves Filmways Pictures can make films just as bad as its predecessor American International Pictures. Which is probably good.

As Hansel & Gretel in goofball land, young Tarah Nutter and Christoper S. Nelson go up to the lake for an outing with their friends, Lynn Theel and David Caruso, stopping for gas at a station run by crazy old coot Jack Palance.

Palance warns them to stay away from the lake because something evil is afoot. And he's right because Cameron Mitchell is already up there hunting with fey son Darby Hinton, not far from where Larry Storch is hiking with his cub-scout troop.

Suddenly, Mitchell is attacked by these flying pancake things that stick to his body and big red peppers come out and penetrate the skin as the soundtracks goes slurp and gloopety gloop until Mitchell falls dead. It's just awful.

An instant later, the pancakes have gotten Hinton and Storch, too, quickly taking care of two of the seven major stars Filmways is advertising.

Once they get up to the lake, Theel and Caruso disappear and Nutter and Nelson finally find them hanging on hooks in a shed with the other three bodies (but luckily no cubscouts, who seem to have gotten home on their own somehow.) The corpses have all been eaten on and glooped on and look just terrible.

The young couple retreat under pancake attack to a saloon where crazy Martin Landau. Neville Brand, Ralph Meeker and Sue Ane Langdon hear their unhappy story. This one scene, albeit somewhat extended, takes care of three more of the seven major stars and Brand. Meeker and Langdon never appear again.

Consequently, it's up to the kids. Landau and Palance to go after the alien being that's been tossing the pancakes. But the chase is very confusing since Landau thinks the young couple are aliens in disguise and keeps shooting at them while Palance enjoys prying the pancakes off himself with a big knife. Everytime he cuts into one, yellow egg yolks run out in abundance and there's more slurping and gloopety glopping and it's just more awful then ever.

Somewhere along the way, Landau reminds the others, "Aliens ain't human, you know," which marks the intellectual highspot in the script by Lyn Freeman, Daniel Grodnik, Ben Nett and Steve Mathis, which Greydon Clark produced and directed. There's a post-script at the end, reminding us that there are more of these inhuman aliens out there in the stars.

Where they will hopefully stay, but don't bet on it. —Har.

Fist of Fear
Touch of Death
(COLOR)

Bruce Lee, where are you?

Chicago, Sept. 15.
An Aquarius Releasing Inc. release of an Aquarius Promotions Production. Produced by Terry Levene. Stars Fred Williamson. Ron Van Clief and old film clips of Bruce Lee. Directed by Matthew Mallinson: Screenplay. Ron Harvey, based on an original story by Harvey and Mallinson; camera (color). John Hazard; score. Keith Mansfield; editor. Mallinson and Jeffrey Brown: sound, Jimmy Kwei: stunt coordinators. Ron Van Clief. Bill Louis. Reviewed at Woods Theatre. Chicago. Sept. 15. '80. (MPAA Rating: R) Running time: 90 MINS.
Cast: Fred Williamson. Ron Van Clief. Adolph Caesar. Aaron Banks. Bill Louis. Teruyuki Higa. Gail Turner. Richard Barathy. Hollywood Browde. Louis Neglia. Cydra Karlyn. Annett Bronson. Ron Harvey. John Flood.

The martial arts grind circuit is one of the few remaining exhibition avenues that tolerates promotional flim-flammery, and "Fist of Fear Touch of Death" takes full advantage of audience credulity. Billed as a chop-sock extravaganza with Bruce Lee, the Aquarius production and release boils down to a so-so actioner covering a martial arts exhibition a couple of years ago at New York's Madison Square Garden.

B.o. action for the outing has been solid, mostly because of the Bruce Lee connection. The late kung-fu titan's appearance here is limited to brief clips from Lee pics showing him delivering bits of dialog often with a snarl. These clips have been dubbed and refitted into an interview format showing Lee supposedly conversing with inquisitors (Adolph Caesar and Aaron Banks) about his martial arts methodology.

Aquarius has also dug up some old Oriental film footage and passes it off as biographical information about Lee as a youth and about his supposed samurai (samurai? - Lee was Chinese -Ed.) grandfather — nonsensical stuff that attempts to bolster the all-to-tenuous Lee connection.

The chicanery doesn't stop there. Fred Williamson is billed as a topliner even though is part is more cameo — as a black lothario of remote martial arts connection who sits in the audience at the Madison Square Garden during the kung-fu doings.

Ron Van Clief (don't confuse him with Lee Van Cleef) is the only genuine martial arts principal, and his participation is limited to some scenes showing workouts and valiant defenses of women joggers in Central Park.

Then what is this picture about? It's concerned with that stock footage of the kung-fu tournament providing the bulk of the action for martial arts buffs. Aquarius has simply spiked up routine footage with the ersatz Bruce Lee connection and dragged in Williamson — who's capable of much better things — and Van Clief as afterthoughts. And so it goes on the martial arts grind. Production values are generally okay. —*Sege.*

The Gamekeeper
(BRITISH-COLOR-16m)

An ATV Network Ltd. production. Directed by Kenneth Loach. Features entire cast. Screenplay, Loach; adapted by Barry Hines from novel by Hines; camera (color), Chris Menges, Charles Stewart; editor, Roger James; music, none; sound, Andrew Boulton, Peter Rann; art director, Martin Johnson, Graham Tew; costumes, Maxine Henry. Reviewed at Magno screening room, N.Y.C., Sept. 8, 1980, as part of the British Film Now scene. (No MPAA rating.) Running time: **84 MINS.**
George Purse .... Phil Askham
Mary .... Rita May
John .... Andrew Grubb
Ian .... Peter Steels
Bob .... Michael Hinchcliffe
With: Philip Firth, Lee Hickin, Jackie Shinn, Paul Brian, Ted Beyer, Chick Barratt, Willoughby Gray, Mark Elwes.

Ken Loach's latest film, bankrolled by the ATV television network in Britain, is a perceptive study of a young gamekeeper and family man toiling on a private estate, trapped within a class system as rigid as in feudal times. Eschewing the cute and dramatized approach of the local "Country Matters" tv series, Loach treats his material with the tough, direct social realism which marked him as a director of stature a decade ago in "Kes."

Phil Askham, a personable, seeming nonactor, portrays the title character, going his rounds at raising pheasants, trapping and hunting rabbits, escorting the lords on grouse hunts and watching for poachers. Though his wife (a solid, no-nonsense turn by Rita May) and village pals understandably grumble about the paternalistic system run by the wealthy landowners,

Askham is an outspoken supporter of the established order. He treats both poachers and trespassing children to stern lectures on respecting private property.

Only one scene, with Askham chatting up a neighbor on his tractor, reveals the repressed hostility of the gamekeeper, as he declares: "we'll have to get rid of 'em; they won't give the land away," in reference to the wealthy lords of the manors.

Loach's simple directorial style and way with his players, especially the always believable children, make for a subtle, though austere film. Ace lighting cameramen Chris Menges and Charles Stewart bring to life a green and brown rural paradise, bolstering the pic's theme of complacency preventing a revolution. Lack of dramatics and Loach's uncompromising use of sometimes unintelligible local accents limit this fine film to tv and college circuit usage. —*Lor.*

Agee
(DOCU-COLOR/B&W-16m)

Hollywood, Sept. 15.
A James Agee Film Project production. Produced, directed, written by Ross Spears. Features entire cast. Camera (color b&w), Anthony Forma; music, Kenton Coe; associate producer, Jude Cassidy. Reviewed at the Nuart Theatre, W. Los Angeles, Sept. 15, 1980. (No MPAA Rating.) Running time: **98 MINS.**
Features Jimmy Carter, Father James Flye, Robert Saudek, Olivia Wood, Dwight Macdonald, Robert Fitzgerald, Elizabeth Tingle, Mae Burroughs, Alma Neuman, Mia Agee, John Huston, Earl McCarroll (as voice of James Agee), voice of Walker Evans.

Balanced and intelligent full length docu study of James Agee effectively charts the trajectory of late writer's life, from his deeply religious Tennessee upbringing, his formative years at Harvard, extended stint as a journalist and film critic in New York, work as a screenwriter, to his premature death at age 45. Film is appropriate for fests and some specialized commercial slots, but more viewers lie down the line in non-theatrical and public tv markets.

Unlikely lead-off interviewee is President Jimmy Carter, who has never seemed more sincere nor perceptive than here praising the social and poetic merits of Agee's long-neglected 1940 look (with photographer Walker Evans) at impoverished southern sharecroppers, "Let Us Now Praise Famous Men." Producer-director, writer Ross Spears journeyed to Alabama to interview some of Agee's subjects, who still remember him after nearly 40 years and confess to having greatly missed him once he departed from their midst.

Bearing expert witness to restless scribe's professional activities are critic Dwight Macdonald, who helped arrange for his friend's first job, at Fortune magazine; poet-historian Robert Fitzgerald, who vividly conjures up Agee's turbulent mind and manners, and John Huston, in excellent form recalling pair's teaming on "The African Queen" and allowing that physical punishment of non-stop writing and tennis playing, not to mention incessant smoking and drinking, led to Agee's first heart attack during their collaboration.

Father James Frye, a mentor from writer's childhood on, lends continuity to what he sees as an unfulfilled life, while Agee's three wives testify to his intensely romantic nature as well as his working habits, which were irregular enough to understandably place an enormous burden on home life.

For such an expanded treatment of the man's career, certain omissions are inexplicable, such as any reference to circumstances of the writing of "A Death In The Family" or his fascinating work on Charles Laughton's "The Night Of The Hunter." But the shrewdly edited interviews, as well as the aptly chosen excerpts from Agee's prose, manage to bring a personality to life and provide a solid basis for further inquiries into his career. —*Cart.*

Cheaper To Keep Her
(COLOR)

Mediocre sex investigative plot.

Hollywood, Sept. 19.
American Cinema release. Produced by Lenny Isenberg. Directed by Ken Annakin. Exec producer, Jerry Frankel. Features entire cast. Screenplay, Timoth Harris, Herschel Weingrod; camera (Metrocolor), Roland (Ozzie) Smith; editor, Edward Warschilka; sound, (Fast) Eddie Mahler; music, Dick Halligan; set decoration, Charles Rutherford; assistant director, Rafael Elortegui. Reviewed at Celluloid TV Center, Hollywood, Sept. 19, 1980 (MPAA Rating: R.) Running time: **92 MINS.**
Bill Dekker .... Mac Davis
K.D. Locke .... Tovah Feldshuh
Tony Turino .... Art Metrano
Dr. Alfred Sunshine .... Ian McShane
Theresa .... Priscilla Lopez
Ida Bracken .... Rose Marie
Stanley Bracken .... Jack Gilford
The Landlord .... J. Pat O'Malley

"Cheaper To Keep Her" is poorly-conceived, poorly written and poorly executed. It's leering view of sexuality and demeaning characterizations of men, women, Mexican-Americans and gays, among other groups, combine for an offensive and interminable 92 minutes. There should be some initial marquee value for star Mac Davis in light of his impressive debut in last year's "North Dallas Forty."

Davis limns a just divorced detective who is hired by hard-nosed lady lawyer Tovah Feldshuh to investigate a list of men who have not been paying alimony. His spot checks are quickly handled with some amateurish scene editing, with Davis naturally checking out anything resembling a femme figure. Not surprisingly, the dialog he uses to lure the ladies back to his abode creates something less than sexual satisfaction.

Story drifts until he begins investigating hedonistic BevHills sex doctor Ian McShane. Feldshuh's estranged husband unbeknownst to Davis, and seemingly down-on-his luck storekeeper Jack Gilford. From there on plot alternates between the two scenarios with an equal amount of imprecision.

Scripters Timothy Harris and Herschel Weingrod deserve blame for invoking some of the worst stereotypes around for the people in this picture. Priscilla Lopez' loud, ill-mannered Mexican secretary, Davis' impersonation of a limp-wristed homosexual and Feldshuh's supposedly smart lawyer who is blinded to the faults of an obviously scurvy spouse seem to have been conceived before minority groups ever heard of civil rights and dignity.

Director Ken Annakin does a substandard job of tying the film together (although it would have been a near impossible feat) while producer Lenny Isenberg and exec producer Jerry Frankel demonstrate a colossal waste of time and money.

American Cinema ultimately carries the overall responsibility and is no doubt anticipating Davis' name will foster at least a few weeks of boxoffice action. Whether that works is for audiences to decide. —*Berg.*

The Hearse
(COLOR)

More moody than scary.

Hollywood, Sept. 13.
A Crown International release of a Marimark production. Produced by Mark Tenser, Charles Russell. Executive producer, Newton P. Jacobs. Directed by George Bowers. Screenplay, Bill Bleich, from an idea by Tenser; camera (Metrocolor), Mori Kawa; editor, George Berndt; music, Webster Lewis; art direction, Keith Michl; sound, Jan Brodin; assistant director, John Curran. Reviewed at the UA Cinema Center, W. Los Angeles, Sept. 13, 1980 MPAA Rating: PG. Running Time: **95 MINS.**
Jane Hardy .... Trish Van Devere
Walter Pritchard .... Joseph Cotten
Tom Sullivan .... David Gautreaux
Reverend Winston .... Donald Hotton
Features Med Flory, Perry Lang.

"The Hearse" is a perfectly decent scare picture — for the late 1950s. Director George Gowers has crafted a nice mood piece, but after "The Exorcist," "The Amityville Horror," and any number of other modern haunted house shockers, mere bumps in the night aren't quite enough. Pic has played off throughout most of the country, and is reviewed for the record.

Recovering from a breakdown, San Franciscan Trish Van Devere makes off for a small town to recuperate in a home willed her by her late aunt. Suspicious locals look at her strangely and try to have as little to do with her as possible, and Van Devere eventually learns the reason why — auntie was believed to be a witch possessed by Satan and it seems that Trish looks almost exactly like her.

In the absence of much other company, Van Devere warms to the romantic overtures of elegant gentleman caller David Gautreaux, just as she's disturbed by a vintage hearse that keeps knocking her off the road and appearing outside the house at night. Not helping matters either is grouchy old Joseph Cotten, realtor who can't wait for her to leave town.

Despite somewhat leisurely pace and fact that denouncement comes as no great surprise, film's craftsmanship and consistant tone manage to hold the interest. But overall impact is rather negligible, given deja vu aspect of basic material.

Van Devere comes off as a bit of a goody-two-shoes but fills the bill nonetheless, while both Gautreaux and Donald Hotton, as the local pastor, possess a slightly bent quality which adds texture to their otherwise standard roles.

Behind-the-scenes contributions are all admirable, notably those of lenser Mori Kawa and composer Webster Lewis, who penned a lovely romantic theme for piano, a nice change of pace from the synthesized scores which generally accompany such genre pieces these days. —*Cart.*

Mar De Rosas
(Sea of Roses)
(BRAZILIAN-COLOR)

Embrafilme/Unifilm release of an Embrafilme production. Produced by Mario Volcoff. Features entire cast. Directed by Ana Carolina. Screenplay, Carolina; camera (color), Lauro Escorel; editor, Vera Freire; music, Paulo Herculano; assistant director, Paulo Adario. Reviewed at Bleecker St. Cinema, N.Y.C., Sept. 11, '80. (No MPAA Rating). Running time: **90 MINS.**

Felicidade . . . . Norma Benguel
Sergio . . . . Hugo Carvana
Daughter . . . . Cristina Pereira
Orlande, the pursuer . . . . Otavio Augusto
Dentist . . . . Ary Fontoura
Dentist's wife . . . . Miriam Muniz

Shown as part of a two-day Public Cinema series of recent Brazilian films, Ana Carolina's 1977 pic, "Sea of Roses," is a devastating black comedy attacking any and all institutions, including the family. Focusing on the bizarre and explosive behavior of her talented microcosmic cast, Carolina delivers a "comedy to offend everyone;" what MGM's all-star "The Loved One" only promised.

Film begins in a road movie format, with Felicidade (Norma Benguel) and her horrid adolescent daughter (Cristina Pereira) fleeing after mom slashes her husband brutally with a razor blade during an argument in their motel room. They soon team up with a friendly pursuer (Otavio Augusto) sent by the husband, who has seemingly survived the bloodletting.

Fast pace of the opening reels bogs down when the trio stop off in a small town and rest at the home of a dentist while Felicidade recuperates from nearly being hit by a bus. Ensemble gabfest which ensues contains many highs and lows, but is kept lively by broad playing and explosive humor.

Symbolic climax has trio fleeing on a train and the murderous daughter pushing her mother and Augusto off to ride on alone.

Norma Benguel as the mother gives an intense, riveting performance, all the more effective than just playing for laughs. Otavio Augusto, a sort of latin John Belushi, is an excellent, mainly deadpan foil for her.

Standing out in the well-chosen ensemble is young actress Cristina Pereira as the "bad seed" daughter. Whether playing violent practical jokes or merely flaring her dangerous looking teeth, Pereira is an unforgettable young monster and an expert scene-stealer. Her transition to an adult career is problematical.

Count Ana Carolina as a helmer to watch, with a great facility for handling actors while giving them plenty of room for invention. Tech credits are good —*Lor.*

Gdansk Festival

Wizja Lokalna 1901
(Inspection of the Scene of a Crime 1901)
(POLISH-COLOR)

Gdansk, Sept. 14.

A Film Polski production for Film Unit, Warsaw; world rights, Film Polski, Warsaw. Features entire cast. Written and directed by Filip Bajon. Camera (color), Jerzy Zielinski; music, Zdzislaw Szostak; sets, Andrzej Kawalczyk. Reviewed at Gdansk Film Fest, Sept. 14, '80. Running time: **98 MINS.**

Cast: Tadeusz Lomnicki (Mossembach), Daniel Olbryschski (Father Paczkowski), Jerzy Stuhr (Concellor Wagner), Henryk Bista (Rector Fedtke), Wieslaw Drzewicz (Inspector Winter), Zdzislaw Wardejn (Teacher Koralewski), Zygmunt Bielawski (Teacher Pohl), Jerzy Trela, Stanislaw Igar, Mieczyslaw Voit, Stanislaw Michalski, Janusz Michalski.

Considered by many to be the best talent on the scene among the young generation of Polish filmmakers, Filip Bajon gained some attention abroad with his last feature film, "Aria for an Athlete" (1978). He is also a writer with collected stories and a novel to his credit.

"Inspection of the Scene of a Crime 1901" deals with a children's strike in Wrzesnia near the Prussian-Russian border, a famous incident that occurred in a schoolroom in 1901. Strikes of this nature apparently happened across partitioned Poland between 1901 and 1905, and of course the reference to the present strike is coincidental. Nevertheless, this was one of the Main Prize winners at Gdansk and one of the high moments of the festival.

The issue is the teaching of religion in German in the schools, a decision by the German authorities that draws a protest from Polish deputies in the parliament. There's also the local priest who invoked the strike and continues to back the children when they refuse to participate in the lessons, even under beatings, threats, and the like. Finally, the parents march on the school when their kids are beaten and kept after hours for a form of psychological torture. Support comes from items printed in newspapers about the striking children, reaching as far as Berlin, and what started out to be a protest becomes a national event.

One by one, the children give in to the tyrannical authorities. The leaders of the strike are broken, but the last images show a slaughtering of a flock of geese on a meadow that heralds the coming First World War. This is highly stylized and poetic cinema, as was "Aria for an Athlete," but there are several strong passages that carry the film over the long run. One drawback is the stereotyped Prussian teacher who becomes the heavy throughout, but another is that this is less a film than a semi-documentary.

Ace lensing and handling of young, nonprofessional tesps are on the plus side of the ledger. A must of the fest circuit and Polish Film Weeks. —*Holl.*

Na Wlasna Prosbe
(At Your Own Request)
(POLISH-COLOR)

Gdansk, Sept. 10.

A Poltel (Polish Television) production, Warsaw; world rights, Poltel, Warsaw. Written and directed by Ewa and Czeslaw Petelski, based on a novel titled "No Problem" by Janina Wieczerska. Only credits available. Reviewed at Gdansk Film Fest, Sept. 10, '80. Running time: **60 MINS.**

Ewa and Czeslaw Petelski's tv-film, "At Your Own Request," was made in 1979 and then immediately put on the shelf until the present screening at the Gdansk Fest, where it was shown in a late-night slot after a last-minute decision to present the film. Of more than passing interest to public and critics it's based on a novel, "No Problem," by a journalist and writer living in Gdansk, Janina Wieczerska.

This is one of the those social-problem pix with a moral bent: it deals with the subtle process of getting rid of a troublesome, although esteemed, worker who won't go along with the usual corruption and conformity. "At Your Own Request" tells the story of an engineer in a conflict with his superior; it is raised to the heights of drama when the hero is left entirely on his own amid indifference and ineptitude by his fellow-workers and the management. Even the party secretary and the trade union are against him. A hot pic in view of the strikes at Gdansk and the present corruption leaks of higher-ups, the dialog scenes nevertheless drag. This is an inside story for Polish auds.

The Petelski husband-wife team have been making films for nearly three decades in Poland, and have practically founded a personal cinema of moral concern. This is arguably their best pic. —*Holl.*

Grzeszny Zywot Franciszka Buly
(The Sinful Life of Franciszek Bula)
(POLISH-COLOR)

Gdansk, Sept. 10.

A Film Polski production, Silesia Film Unit, Warsaw; world rights, Film Polski, Warsaw. Features entire cast. Written and directed by Janusz Kidawa. Camera (color), Zdzislaw Kaczmarek; sets, Jerzy Muller; music, Zygmunt Zgraja; production manager, Wanda Wojnar-Iliew. Reviewed at Gdansk Film Fest, Sept. 10, '80. Running time: **106 MINS.**

Cast: Andrzej Grabarczyk (Franciszek Bula), Jarek Antonik (Franciszek as child), Jerzy Cnota (Wilik Lizon), Miroslaw Krawczyk (Stanik), Adam Baumann (Zaglebiak), Henryk Stanek (Gajda), Henryk Skolik (Gajdy), Tadeusz Cjrostek (Jugler), Ginter Benkariek (Fakir), Irena Moczygemba (Hejdla).

One of the Main Prize winners at Gdansk, Janusz Kidawa's "The Sinful Life of Franciszek Bula" is set as usual in the director's native Silesia, the coalmining area of the country he depicted in several docus before turning to the feature film. "Horizontal Landscape" (1978) was his only other venture into the narrative feature after nearly two decades of docu filmmaking. Pic justly deserved its prize, as it was one of the best of the fest.

As the title hints, this is an epic on life in Polish Silesia, where folk traditions and a peculiar native dialect play a central role in life and living. The period is in the 1920s and 1930s, between the two world wars, and the hero is a street performer from the so-called "lumpenproletariat" of Polish Silesia. Franciszek Bula is one of those quick-witted con-men belonging to a troupe of wandering actors and swindlers who roam the countryside after the First World War, just as the land was returned back to the Poles but conflicts with German-speaking natives were still frequent.

To a degree, this is a black comedy. When Franciszek is about to be born, his mother insists he be born Polish — which means that the war raging outside the window has to drift during the birth itself in Poland's favor, and so the midwife belts a room-invading German soldier over the head with a frying-pan to guarantee the lad's citizenship at the last minute.

As the boy grows up, he doesn't do well in school but has a way with his pals and the girls that endears him at once to nearly everyone. His "first love" occurs in short pants: he helps out a rich girl in the neighborhood and becomes her playing companion on the sly. When she moves away, he never forgets her — although girls, in turn, are after him, and he is treated to the glories of the sinful life by a prostitute making the rounds of the country fairs. Franciszek's muscular feats of daring also win him acceptance with the travelling troupe of street actors, and it is more or less through his experiences that we come to know the land, its customs, and its traditions. Then the next war comes.

Well worth a onceover on the fest circuit. —Holl.

Spotkanie Na Atlantyku
(Chance Meeting on the Ocean)
(POLISH-COLOR)

Gdansk, Sept. 11.
A Film Polski production. Kadr Film Unit, Warsaw; world rights, Film Polski, Warsaw. Features entire cast. Directed by Jerzy Kawalerowicz. Screenplay, Boleslaw Michalek, Kawalerowicz; camera (color), Jerzy Lukaszewicz; music, Piotr Figiel; production manager, Urszula Orczykowska, Zygmunt Wojcik. Reviewed at Gdansk Film Fest, Sept. 11, '80. Running time: 110 MINS.
Cast: Teresa Budzisz-Krzyzanowska (Magda), Malgorzata Niemirska (Irena), Ignacy Gogolewski (Nowak), Marek Walczewski (Walter), Feliks Parnell (Stary), Waclaw Ulewicz (Priest), Marek Lewandowski (Zbyszek), Gustaw Lutkiewicz, Jerzy Braszka.

Director Jerzy Kawalerowicz and scripter Boleslaw Michalek last collaborated on the historical epic, "Death of the President," (1977), and now they're back together again on "Chance Meeting on the Ocean." Tale bears a strong similarity to Kawalerowicz's "Night Train" (1959), this time the entire action taking place on an ocean liner from Canada to Poland instead of a train from Warsaw to the Baltic Sea.

This is not vintage Kawalerowicz, but there's more than enough to satisfy his fans and others who like easy entertainment. It's the story of several people with pasts and problems placed in the uncomfortable position of confronting others with pasts and problems. The chief confrontation is between a Polish doctor with a heart condition meeting a man he knew long ago; both recognize each other, but neither is willing to spell out their differences back in their college days. In any case, the meeting torments the doctor enough to take to drinking heavily, releasing his pent-up emotions in public, and having a heart attack that is fatal after a ship's party.

Other guests with related crises are the doctor's girlfriend, who is not his wife as listed; a fading chanteuse; the lonely traveler who triggers the confrontation in the first place; and an aging passenger who wonders at the feat of a 70-year-old sailing around the world in a one-man display of courage. Something for everyone, but nothing to really sink your teeth into, save the viewer gets a feeling of what it's like to cross the ocean on the liner Stephan Bathory. —Holl.

Zamach Stanu
(Coup d'Etat)
(POLISH-COLOR)

Gdansk, Sept. 12.
A Film Polski production. Profil Film Unit, Warsaw; world rights, Film Polski, Warsaw. Features entire cast. Directed by Ryszard Filipski. Screenplay, Ryszard Gontarz; camera (color), Jacek Stachiewski; music, Piotr Marczewski; sets, Czeslaw Siekiera. Reviewed at Gdansk Film Fest, Sept. 12, '80. Running time: 176 MINS.
Cast: Ryszard Filipski (Jozef Pilsudski), Jerzy Sagan (Wincenty Witos), Gabriel Nehrebecki, Lech Bijald, Wlodzimierz Wiszniowski, Jerzy Ziotnicki, Zygmunt Malanowicz, Jozef Pieracki, Arkadiusz Bazak, Jozef Fryzlewicz, Henryk Boukolowski, Wlodzimierz Borunski, Henryk Machalica, Andrzej Krasicki, Czeslaw Wollejko, Kazimierz Wichniarz, Tomasz Zaliwski, Tadeusz Janczar, Jozef Nowak.

Ryszard Filipski's "Coup d'Etat" is the story of General Jozef Pilsudski's takeover of an ineffectual Polish government on May 11, 1926 and what happened in the years afterwards under his military dictatorship (with his friend Ignacy

Moscicki serving as a figurehead President of Poland). Pilsudski died in 1935, and even then his influence was felt in the continued dictatorship under Moscicki until 1939 at the outbreak of the Second World War.

Since Pilsudski is a controversial political figure in Poland, it was not easy to present a chronicle of his years of power. The first time he appeared stage-center in a Polish historical epic was in Jerzy Kawalerowicz's "Death of a President" (1977), dealing with events in 1923 when Poland formed a republic with a constitutional government and parliament via a plebiscite. That may have been the test run for an historical epic on Pilsudski himself.

To put the historical record straight: upon his release from German imprisonment during the First World War, Pilsudski appeared in Warsaw and took charge of the army and, in 1918, declared himself chief of state. The Treaty of Versailles in 1919 tried to fix Poland's boundaries according to economic, ethnographic, and strategic lines, and Poland found herself a republic once again after the humiliation of the partitions among Germany, Austria, and Russia. This did not prevent Pilsudski, however, from fighting and winning a war against the Red Army over disputes about the eastern border with Russia. The Treaty of Riga in 1921 confirmed Poland's claims to an historic border approximately the previous one of 1772, before the partition was made. Pilsudski then retired from the scene upon the adoption of a republican constitutions in 1922.

Quarrels among the radicals and conservatives in parliament, however, led Pilsudski out of retirement in 1926 to engineer the coup d'etat. Thereafter, a second constitution reduced the parliament to a rubber-stamp government until his death in 1935 and after. These events are covered in the nearly three-hour-long recreation of history. It's a weary stretch to soak in everything, but there are some rewards if the viewer is a student of history and can read between the lines. In general, however, this "official" version of the Pilsudski era will be hotly discussed (as it was in Gdansk) by Polish and history experts. —Holl.

Venice Films

Linea D'Ombra
(Shadow Line)
(ITALIAN)

Venice, Sept. 1.
Produced by Antoniana Film productions. Stars Giorgio Giacomin. Written and

directed by Maurizio Targhetta and Gerardo Fontana. Camera (color), Sergio Fontana; editing, Emanuele Foglietti; music, Manuel De Sica, Friedrich Handel. Reviewed at Venice Film Festival, Sept. 1, 1980. Running time: about 90 MINS.
Pierfrancesco . . . . Giorgio Giacomini

Terrorism is the background rather than the theme of this sober psychological study of a weak intellectual who takes part in a political shooting and finds himself unable to face the consequences. Young directors Maurizio Targhetta and Gerardo Fontana handle first feature well, although pic seems too introverted and staid to be much of a b.o. hit. A dignified entry in the Venice Biennial's all-Italian "Controcampo" section.

Pierfrancesco (Giorgio Giacomin) is a bearded and bespectacled art history professor whose adherence to the terrorist movement is more emotional than political. Wounded during a gun fight, his mask slips off but he gets away, shunned by old friends who have seen him on the evening news. He goes clandestine. The Hamletian professor cannot decide to slip across the border. A final gunshot is heard. Did it kill Pierfrancesco or a girl terrorist? A frustrating finale.

The simple story is complicated by continual flashbacks that flow like the depressed and unhappy terrorist's stream of consciousness. Recurring images of a girl walking away into the distance, his wife and child, the cultured world of art intersect the main action without illuminating it much.

The character inevitably brings to mind political science professor Toni Negri (like the directors, from Padua) currently accused of participation in terrorist actions, but using his tie to recent events, pic moves in the personal direction of psychological portraiture, sidestepping both action and politics. Professor as a terrorist, is incidental to the story. Regrettable, since pic is listless and could have gained strength in grappling with bigger issues.

Lensing is neat — tapping beauty of natural landscapes. —Yung.

Alcool
(Alcohol)
(ITALIAN-COLOR)

Venice, Aug. 31.
Produced by Augusto Tretti for the Province of Milan. Features entire cast. Written and directed by Augusto Tretti, with the consultation of Dario De Martis. Camera (color), Maielli. Reviewed at Venice Film Festival, Aug. 31, 1980. Running time: 110 MINS.
Chronic drunk . . . . Mario Grazioni

A bizarre and irritating offering on the problem of alcoholism by ex-Fellini assistant Augusto Tretti. Pic's unusual production circumstances (it was financed at clearly minimal cost by the Province of Milan after being turned down by film and tv) have raised a certain amount of unjustified interest in it. Wavering between moralizing didacticism and obvious attempts at humor, helmer's third feature fails to find a voice for itself.

Pic bills itself as "essentially informative, educational and preventive" while it aims at avoiding documentary dullness with the fictional structure of an "auteurist" film; result of this admirable intention is a hodge-podge of sketches (drunken housewives, gas company men, movie stars, etc.) whose potential humor is wrecked every time by amateur execution. Lighting, actors, dialog and editing all contribute their bit to the chaos. Every 20 minutes a group of four deadpan young "professionals," presumably psychologists and sociologists, break into the narrative to mouth statistical data.

With a non-professional cast of alcoholics from country towns around Milan and collaboration on the script by a registered psychiatrist, "Alcohol" might have made a great Woody Allen pic in the old days.

Presented out of competition in the Panorama of Italian Cinema.

—*Yung.*

Feste, Farina E ...
(Festa, Flour and ...)
(ITALIAN-COLOR)

Venice, Sept. 2.
A RAI-Television Channel 2 film, produced by Cooperativa Celimontana. Stars Vittorio De Bisogno. Written and directed by Nino Russo. Camera (color), Massimo Lupi; art direction, Mimma Russo; editing, Mario Gargiulo and Marcello Malvestiti. Reviewed at Venice Film Festival, Sept. 2, 1980. Running time: 120 MINS. (2 episodes).
Pippo Ciotola .... Vittorio De Bisogno

Subtitled "a Neapolitan metaphor in two acts," This RAI-TV production of two hour-long sketches written and directed by Nino Russo was the best comic entry seen in the Controcampo section at Venice. Both skits have penniless young actor Pippo Ciotola (Vittorio De Bisogni) as central figure and Neapolitan "festas" as the background in which ancient traditions clash with modern technology, popular culture with the new "mass" culture of TV and radio. An exceptional documentary on the city and its people while fictional structure keeps pic lively and amusing.

"How many people in the street," the first episode, shows Ciotola and his friend Pasquale Pellecchia setting off to do an improvised radio spot on a religious pilgrimage. Pippo attempts to interview the swarm of people thronging the streets, but the tape recorder is a pilgrim barrier. He meets a girl dressed in the white and blue costume of the faithful, falls for her, but loses her in the crowd. In the end Pippo and his sound man head home as the sun set over Vesuvius, outlining an industrial landscape of oil refineries.

In the second part, "Noted artists of the RAI-TV will be appearing." Pippo and Pasquale unsuccessfully try to crash a little cabaret show set up in a dingy square in the city. Around them the real show is provided by housewives leaning out the window haranguing the neighborhood and elderly gentlement protesting street noise hindering tv reception. Only some humble trattoria musicians and P.A. of a famous Neapolitan singer succeed in momentarily uniting the populace.

The disturbing effect massmedia technology has had on local traditions is humorously suggested by the Chaplinesque ballet of Pippo and Pasquale trying to handle the batteries and cord of their simple tape recorder. Over and over they must explain to their primping interviewees "There's no video" — ultimate ambition of the tv culture which coexists uneasily with mass processions to the Virgin where the icons are decorated with pearl necklaces and where pilgrims by the hundreds fall into fleeting "trances."

Russo's camera captures Naples with the immediacy of great documentaries, mixing actors and story with real pilgrims and locals. Dialect mingles with the cries of water vendors and the songs of strolling musicians to give pic a singular authenticity. De Bisogno impersonates Pippo like a young version of Toto, never defeated for long and ever flowing with ideas for finding his identity as actor-singer-composers.

"Festa" may be taken to task only for a few overly long scenes that wear down and some flat moments in Pippo's endless monologues. Sound track is a mixture of traditional Neapolitan songs and radio pop music — an incongruous cultural babble. —*Yung.*

La Brace Dei Biassoli
(The Biassoli Embers)
(ITALIAN-COLOR)

Venice, Sept. 1.
A RAI-Television Channel 2 production. Stars Anna Maria Gherardi, Luigi Di Berti. Directed by Giovanni Fago. Screenplay, Giovanni Fago, Mario Tobino, from novel by Mario Tobino; camera, (color), Sandro Messina; art direction, Emilio Voglino. Reviewed at Venice Film Festival, Sept. 1, 1980. Running time: 147 MINS.
Mother .... Anna Maria Gherardi
Andrea Tobino .... Luigi Di Berti
Alfeo .... Remo Girone
Federico .... Gianni Garko
Ippolito .... Giuseppe Anatrelli
Aunt Virginia .... Angelina Quinterno
Oscare .... Bruno Zanin
Clementina .... Gisella Burinato

One of the most carefully crafted pix presented at the Venice Biennial in the Controcampo section, "The Biassoli Embers" is an unabashedly nostalgic journey into a family's past in a small Northern Italian town. Adapted from the autobiographical history of his family by Mario Tobino, the RAI-TV produced film traces the life of Tobino's mother through her memories recounted to him on her deathbed. Result is an intimate fresco of the times when the extended family of relatives, servants, friends and peasants made up a warm and protective world unto itself; a sort of middle-class "Tree of Wooden Clogs" but lacking the religious thrust of Ermanno Olmi's peasant epic.

Signora Maria, last of the line of the Biassolis, returns to the town she was born in and falls ill. In the weeks preceding her death she relives memories of her childhood in a rich landowning family: her sisters, the strange characters who populated the village, the joys of excursions in the country with her children. Running through the whole story are the son's memories of his own childhood and his awakening consciousness of the world.

Shot in classic style with loving attention to detail and atmosphere, pic has the feeling of looking through an old family photo album. Viewing is a total immersion in the harmonious existence of times gone by, an idealized and sentimentalized world where a strong family structure acted as a shield against the cruelties of life and death.

Performances are sensitive and uniformly excellent, beginning with Anna Maria Gherardi as the mother, whose sweet old-fashioned face ideally reflects the sentiment of the film. The period is reverently reconstructed in costumes, sets, breathtaking pastoral images and musical comment — exemplary use of a low tv budget.

Though the overall sweetness of pic and its literary tone becomes selfconsciously dated at times, film as a whole rises to an exalting purity of sentiment in delineating the simplicity and moral strength of its heroine. —*Yung.*

Oh, God! Book II
(COLOR)

Very mild followup to the George Burns hit. Modest b.o. likely.

A Warner Brothers production and release. Produced by Gilbert Cates. Stars George Burns. Directed by Cates. Screenplay, Josh Greenfeld, Hal Goldman, Fred S. Fox, Seaman Jacobs, Melissa Miller from a story by Greenfeld; camera (Technicolor), Ralph Woolsey; editor, Peter E. Berger; music, Charles Fox; production design, Preston Ames; set decorator, Chris Westlund; sound, Don Sharpless; assistant director, Tom Lofaro. Reviewed at Warner Brothers screening room, N.Y.C., Sept. 18, '80. (MPAA Rating: PG). Running time: 94 MINS.
God .... George Burns
Paula .... Suzanne Pleshette
Don .... David Birney
Tracy .... Louanne
Shingo .... John Louie
Dr. Whitley .... Howard Duff
Dr. Barnes .... Hans Conried
Mr. Benson .... Conrad Janis
Dr. Jerome Newell ...... Anthony Holland
Judge Miller .... Wilfrid Hyde-White
With: Hugh Downs, Joyce Brothers, Marian Mercer, Bebe Drake Massey, Mari Gorman, Vernon Weddle, Alma Beltran.

"Oh, God! Book II" is not a sequel to the hit 1977 Warner Brothers release (which amassed $31,000,-000 in domestic rentals) but rather an alternate approach to the same basic premise: what would happen if God were to appear to an ordinary person with instructions to "spread my message." Absence this time of John Denver, his chemistry with lead George Burns, and the original's solid comedy material lead to a bland, unstimulating film.

Script, collectively credited to five writers, has a pleasant moppet (Louanne) meeting God (George Burns) in the lounge of a Chinese restaurant. It seems that Burns (heard pre-credits voicing over his problems with mankind on Earth) has decided to enlist a child "with belief in things you can't see" to remind people that God is still around. Since Louanne's dad (David Birney) is an adman, she sets out to concoct a slogan which will "make God a household name." Burns' quaint program is to first win over the children and then get on with various environmental projects (e.g., fight pollution and cool off volcanoes).

Louanne recruits her cute Japanese playmate Shingo (John Louie) and other classmates to spread her "Think God" slogan via posters and graffiti. This leads to her suspension from school, and when she is seen talking to the invisible (to everyone but her) Burns, the child is brought before psychiatrists to be committed to an institution. Climax has Burns materializing as a literal deus ex machina to protect Louanne at the roundtable of shrinks.

Burns is fine once again, a master of the throwaway line and well-suited to tone down the religious philosophy in the script. More screen time, however, is allotted to debuting Louanne, a pleasant and talented youngster who holds one's sympathy.

Suzanne Pleshette and David Birney as her estranged parents who reconcile before the final freeze-shot are effective in limited roles, with Pleshette's beauty and strong screen presence under-utilized. Supporting parts are all well-limned.

Director Cates is hamstrung by the talky, largely unfunny script, which contains little dramatic content and only one scene involving physical action (Burns giving Louanne a motorcycle and sidecar ride). Except for recurring gags about "boobs" the mild script is too squeaky-clean for the film's good. By not expanding upon the first film, "Oh, God! Book II" is extraneous. Tech credits are routine.

—Lor.

Stardust Memories
(BLACK & WHITE)

The worm finally turns ... too late.

Hollywood, Sept. 23.
A United Artists release, produced by Robert Greenhut. Written and directed by Woody Allen. Exec producers, Jack Rollins, Charles H. Joffe. Camera (b&w), Gordon Willis; editor, Susan E. Morse; sound, James Sabat; production design, Santo Loquasto; assistant director, Frederic B. Blankfein; art direction, Michael Molly; various songs and music credited. Reviewed at United Artists, Culver City, Calif., Sept. 23, 1980. (MPAA rating: PG.) Running time: **89 MINS.**
Sandy Bates ....Woody Allen
Dorrie ....Charlotte Rampling
Isobel ....Marie-Christine Barrault
Daisy ....Jessica Harper
Jack Abel ....John Rothman
Shelley ....Amy Wright
Vivian Orkin ....Helen Hanft
Actor ....Daniel Stern
Tony ....,.Tony Roberts
Sister ....Anne Desalvo

Like a cute little puppy that's been petted too much, Woody Allen turns with a snarl in "Stardust Memories," snapping at everybody who has befriended him in the past. It is indeed a curious choice at the peak of his career — and highly risky from any commercial viewpoint.

While Allen has teased with auto-biography in "Manhattan" and "Annie Hall," he drops all pretense here. No effort is made to pretend that his character of Sandy Bates is anybody but Allen himself — a filmmaker first adored for wacky comedies, then gradually appreciated as a cinematic genuis.

But Bates-Allen does not appreciate the appreciation. He thinks those who like his early comedies more than his later "deeper" pictures are buffoons; he thinks those who try to sift through the meaning of his later works are intellectual lamebrains and — with a final move at checkmate — he makes clear that any attempt to analyze "Stardust Memories" itself would be the heighth of pompous pretension.

Though there are laughs along the way, even a few guffaws, this is a truly mean-spirited picture. Once a sympathetic nebbish, Allen now sees himself as a put-upon, embittered genuis, disdainful of everything around him.

Or is that a joke, too? If so, is it ridiculous to look for the point or punchline? These and scores of similar mocking questions hang over the whole last half of "Stardust" and when the actors in the film itself appear as themselves to scoff the whole enterprise, the audience may well feel it was invited to the party and puked upon.

The tone is not evident at the start. For a while, it looks like Allen is going to have some old-fashioned, yet thoughtful, fun with his success as a filmmaker. Surely, success does bring its problems, some of which interfere with the same creative process that brought on the success.

For the trade and no one else, there's a good inside joke when UA topper Andy Albeck cameos as a studio exec decrying the fact that the director's new film isn't funny. And, like all Allen films, interesting faces abound, many belonging to all kinds of caricatures besieging the director at a film buffs' retrospective of his work.

At first, the powerful lady film critic and her pretentious friends are funny; the babbling film buffs are funny; the charitable solicitations are funny; the film executives are funny. But soon it is apparent that Allen is not having fun with his characters; he truly hates them without reservation or any sympathy for their foibles.

The women in his life, Charlotte Rampling, Marie-Christine Barrault and Jessica Harper, are no longer the wondrous objects that have confused and inspired him in the past. He no longer likes them much either, except as adoring companions for his continuing neuroses.

In the end, Allen says, it has been for nothing, this least of all. It's a shame he feels that way, or so clearly seems to. *—Har.*

In God We Trust
(COLOR)

A comedy with no laughs.

Hollywood, Sept. 24.
A Universal release of a Howard West - George Shapiro production. Produced by West, Shapiro. Executive producer, Norman T. Herman. Stars, directed by Marty Feldman. Screenplay, Feldman, Chris Allen; camera (Technicolor), Charles Correll; editor, David Blewitt; music, John Morris; song, "Good For God," by Harry Nilsson; production design, Lawrence G. Paull; set decoration, Peg Cummings; costume deisgn, Ruth Myers; sound, "Fast Eddie" Mahler; associate producer, Lauretta Feldman; assistant director, Stephen Barnett. Reviewed at Universal Studios, Universal City, Sept. 24, 1980. (MPAA Rating: PG.) Running time: **97 MINS.**
Brother Ambrose .... Marty Feldman
Dr. Melmoth .... Peter Boyle
Mary .... Louise Lasser
God ....Richard Pryor
Armageddon T.
   Thunderbird .... Andy Kaufman
Abbot Thelonious .... Wilfrid Hyde-White
Priest .... Severn Darden

"In God We Trust" is a rare achievement — a comedy with no laughs. This distinction prompts speculation on how a film can be called a comedy when there's no merriment to be found, but leave that to the semanticists. Ticket sale action should prove even less swift than that for the last religioso-themed "comedy" backfire, "Wholly Moses."

This one has totally innocent monk Marty Feldman cast out into the mean and nasty world on the same mission as the Blues Brothers — to raise some quick cash to keep his monastery in business, he ends up on Hollywood Blvd., where in his robe and sandals he fits in pretty well but where his religious beliefs prove no match for the sinful temptations at hand.

Object of his search is outrageous tv evangelist Armageddon T. Thunderbird, he of the Conway Twitty hairdo and head of the Church of Divine Profit, who puts off the meek man of God for the longest time before taking him in as a partner, only to later turn against him when Feldman wins the ear of G.O.D., as Thunderbird calls his master, Richard Pryor.

At the same time, Feldman takes a tumble or two with gold-hearted prostie Louise Lasser, which provides opportunity to repeat two or three lame sex jokes several times each. Finally, of course, he makes it back to the monastery, where the only palatable character in the picture, Abbot Wilfrid Hyde-White, greets him with open arms.

Beneath all the strained attempts at humor, there's a germ of sweetness in Feldman's innocent led astray, but as a director he's unable to give it any play. Nor does he do any favors for the remainder of the cast, as Kaufman's potentially great appearance remains just a good idea and Pryor, as a hipster Almighty, is seen almost exclusively on a tiny tv screen.

Technically, film is a near-shambles and bears a cheap back-lot look. Especially appalling is the staging of crowd scenes. In one sequence, Feldman and Lasser are surrounded by extras after Feldman knocks down an assailant. Cut to the next shot of the pair making off into the night and there's not a soul around. Which is likely to be the case in theatres where pic plays.

— Cart

One Trick Pony
(COLOR)

Paul Simon scores neat hat trick as writer, composer and star. Music biz setting possible onus.

Hollywood, Sept. 29.
A Warner Brothers release. Produced by Michael Tannen, Michael Hausman. Directed by Robert M. Young. Features entire cast. Screenplay, music by Paul Simon; camera (Technicolor), Dick Bush; editors, Edward Beyer, Barry Malkin, David Ray; production design, David Mitchell; art direction, Woods Macintosh; set decoration, Justin Scoppa; costumes, Hilary Rosenfeld; sound (Dolby), Chris Newman, Larry Jost; asst. director, Michael Hausman. Reviewed at the Burbank Studios, Burbank, Sept. 29, 1980. (MPAA Rating: R.) Running time **98 MINS.**
Jonah ....Paul Simon
Marion ....Blair Brown
Walter Fox ....Rip Torn
Lonnie Fox ....Joan Hackett
Cal Van Damp .... Allen Goorwitz
Modena Dandridge ...Mare Winningham
Matty Levin ....Michael Pearlman
Steve Kunelian .... Lou Reed
Danny Duggin ....Steve Gadd
Lee-Andrew Parker..........: Eric Gale
John Dibatista ....Tony Levin
Clarence Franklin ....Richard Tee
Bernie Wepner ....Harry Shearer
With: the B-52's, the Lovin Spoonful, Sam and Dave, Tiny Tim.

Transparently yet another look at the contempo music scene, "One-Trick Pony" is also an engaging and emotionally sympathetic study of a popular artist's premature mid-life crisis. While pic would ordinarily seem to have solid trappings of a success, recent flops of such inside the biz tuners as "Honeysuckle Rose" and "Roadie" necessarily cast some doubt on genre's general appeal, no matter what the quality of individual film.

Like Paul Simon's music, "One-Trick Pony" possesses a softer, less rambunctious tone than other pop music pix, and therefore could prove accessible to non-fans as well as inveterate record buyers. Subplot concerning singer's reluctant divorce and continuing, poignant relationship with wife and young son immediately brings to mind "Kramer Vs. Kramer," albeit without the suspense and single-minded concentration.

Playing a role about as dissimilar from his real self as the characters Woody Allen has played of late, Simon is seen as a heavyweight pop figure from 10 years ago now reduced to opening act status for punk bands in clubs who's under respectful but firm pressure from his label to come up with a top-40 hit. No one questions his talent, but he hasn't changed with the times and is in danger of being permanently relegated to the golden oldies shelf unless he comes up with a new hook.

Seconding the accusations of the record company is estranged wife Blair Brown, who's tired of waiting for Simon to grow out of adolescence. Domestic scenes nicely avoid the inherent potential for standard bitchiness and I'm just doing what I gotta do cliches and lend film a spine of emotional veracity.

Openly contemptuous of chart hit maker Allen Goorwitz's philistinism and precariously becoming involved with label topper Rip Torn's wife, Joan Hackett, Simon against his better judgment allows vogueish producer Lou Reed to corrupt his new recording with a string section, background singers and the like before coming to grips with what he truly cares about. Hyped-up confrontations and temper tantrums are studiously avoided in favor of a natural ebb and flow of momentary feelings, which sacrifices dramatic urgency but agreeably heightens believeability.

Respecting intimate quality of Simon's script, former documentary filmmaker Robert M. Young doesn't push scenes for histrionic overkill and has elicited nicely underplayed performances across the board. Not at all like the slick type he seemed in his small part in "Annie Hall," Simon wins sympathy from his earliest scenes and is never overshadowed even by such pros as Torn and Goorwitz, both of whom are on target as industry biggies whose real life counterparts will provide some chuckles for those in the know.

Blair Brown, somewhat resembling a new Maureen O'Hara, strongly conveys the two minds her character has about her wandering minstrel husband, and Hackett and Mare Winningham score as two of his incidental bedmates.

While not, as the film fully admits, the sound of the moment, Simon's collection of 11 new tunes reps a strong accomplishment, with two or three standing out from the rest as possessing possible durability.

Tech credits are all excellent.
— Cart.

The Elephant Man
(BRITISH-BLACK & WHITE)

Freakish man sensitively depicted by filmmakers. Period drama needs careful selling.

Hollywood, Sept. 23.

Paramount Pictures release of a Brooksfilms Production. Exec producer, Stuart Cornfeld. Produced by Jonathan Sanger. Stars Anthony Hopkins, John Hurt. Directed by David Lynch. Screenplay, Christopher DeVore, Eric Bergren, Lynch, based on "The Elephant Man And Other Reminiscences" by Sir Frederick Treves and in part on "The Elepant Man: A Study In Human Dignity" by Ashley Montagu; camera (b&w, processed by Rank Laboratories), Freddie Francis; editor, Anne V. Coates; music, John Morris, with "Adagio For Strings" by Samuel Barber; production designer, Stuart Craig; art director, Bob Cartwright; set decorator, Hugh Scaife; sound, Alan Splet, Lynch, Robin Gregory; assistant director, Anthony Waye. Reviewed at Paramount Studios, Hollywood, Sept. 22, '80. (MPAA Rating: PG.) Running time: 125 MINS.

Frederick Treves	Anthony Hopkins
John Merrick	John Hurt
Mrs. Kendal	Anne Bancroft
Carr Gomm	John Gielgud
Mothershead	Wendy Hiller
Bytes	Freddie Jones
Night Porter	Michael Elphick
Mrs. Treves	Hannah Gordon
Princess Alexandra	Helen Ryan
Fox	John Standing
Bytes' Boy	Dexter Fletcher
Nora	Lesley Dunlop
Merrick's Mother	Phoebe Nicholls, Lydia Lisle

Treating its bizarre subject with compassion, "The Elephant Man" is a moving glimpse into the dark alleys of human existence. Those seeking shock and sensationalism will be disappointed and, hopefully, chastened by the experience. Director David Lynch has created an eerily compelling atmosphere in recounting a hideously deformed man's perilous life in Victorian England. The Paramount release of a Brooksfilms Production needs special handling to maximize its commercial potential.

Though the film, produced by Jonathan Sanger, went into production after the Bernard Pomerance play of the same title paved the way by becoming a hit in London and N.Y., it is not based on the play, per an end-title and ad copy disclaimer added in settlement of a legal dispute. Screenplay by Christopher DeVore, Eric Bergren, and Lynch was based on two books about the real-life Elephant Man, one written by his protector, Sir Frederick Treves, played in the film by Anthony Hopkins.

Hopkins is splendid as always in a subtly nuanced portrayal of a man torn between humanitarianism and qualms that his motives in introducing the Elephant Man to society are no better than those of the brutish carny who exhibited him in a freak show. The center-piece of the film, however, is the virtuoso performance by the almost unrecognizable John Hurt as the title character.

Like Quasimodo in "The Hunchback Of Notre Dame," the Elephant Man gradually reveals suppressed depths of humanity as he responds to the kindness of his protector, despite the desires of others to torment and exploit him. But the scenes dealing with the cruelties of human nature are less interesting for that comparatively conventional theme than for Lynch's poetic exploration of how it feels to go through life as a monster, isolated from normal experiences.

With evocative b&w lensing by the veteran Freddie Francis and expert production design on a limited budget by Stuart Craig, Lynch recreates Victorian England as a shadowy world of starkly contrasted brutalization and culture, in which the Elephant Man stands as a potently symbolic conjunction of the two extremes.

Seen only in furtive glimpses by the camera in the early part of the film, Hurt is gradually revealed in makeup by Christopher Tucker (applied by Wally Schneiderman) that becomes less shocking as his inner sensitivity becomes apparent. Acting largely with his eyes, voice, and posture, Hurt memorably conveys the character's progression from torment to ultimate happiness.

Lynch commendably avoids summoning up feelings of disgust, as he did in his loathsome first feature, "Eraserhead," which dealt with a man's destruction of his deformed child. In fact, he treats the Elephant Man so compassionately that if the film falters at all, it is in its slight fastidiousness in avoiding tricky areas such as the Elephant Man's sexual urges.

The play depicted the stage actress who befriends him as being perversely aroused by him, while in the film, the character as played by Anne Bancroft seems merely a do-gooder, which robs her role of dimensions. Scenes of her lavishing affection on Hurt have a somewhat uncomfortably patronizing tone, much less interesting than the bracing impact of Hopkins' agonizing assumption of responsibility.

But by and large, "The Elephant Man" stands out in today's market as an unusually serious and gripping treatment of a subject that could have easily been cheapened. Rather than pandering to the worst in humanity, it attempts to enlarge the audience's sense of human worth. —Mac.

The Life And Times Of Rosie The Riveter
(U.S.-DOCUMENTARY-B&W)

Produced and directed by Connie Field. Photographed by Cathy Zheutin, Bonnie Friedman, Robert Handley, Emiko Omori. Edited by Lucy Massie Phenix and Field. Review at Alice Tully Hall, N.Y., Sept. 27, 1980. Running time: 60 MINS.

With Lola Weixel, Wanita Allen, Gladys Belcher, Lyn Childs, Margaret Wright.

Connie Field looks back in this well-produced and edited documentary to the women who worked in the heavy war industries as riveters, welders, machine tool operators and whatnot and then, with victory and demobilization, were indiscriminately dropped in favor of returning soldiers. If it sounds like propaganda, it is. But beguilingly managed, rather lovable and good humored.

There are a number of clips from the old "March of Time," both urging women to enroll in the factories and foundries and shipyards for patriotic reasons and then urging them, also for patriotic reasons, to get back into the kitchen, or into the hay to make babies. The implication, in part, is that women were "conned" by the Luce newsreel, the Office of War Information, the Writers War Board and whoever else was then involved. This was substantially true, though justified then and now as a war that had to be won because if it wasn't won nothing else would be very important.

Field and her editor, Lucy Massie Phenix, cross-cut to various women, several of them very persuasive black gals. They recall their wartime experiences with telltale detailing of hypocrisy and doubletalk and due confession of going on shopping sprees with the war wages rather than saving for later.

Attempts to exclude blacks even when the economy was desperate for workers are stressed. The role of the unions in forcing bosses to rise above color blindness was but one aspect. Often it was not the bosses but white employes who practiced racial shutout, as per a near-riot when one black woman assumed that she, too, could use the factory showers to take a bath.

This documentary is very "entertaining," which is more than can be said for some other recent footage making the case for the second-classing of women as workers and citizens. There are many sly digs at male macho attitudes. Comments one she-worker in overalls and protective head-mask, "During the war the women were macho, too, but afterwards they were returned to inferior status."

The finale has the women, no longer the young wives of the early 40s (as shown in family photographs) now expanded in girth, many of them working again in the menial kitchen and food service jobs from which the war had allowed temporary escape to higher wages and greater satisfactions.

The audience at Alice Tully Hall was clearly delighted with this example of "jolly" history with sardonic commentary. The film is also pretty harsh on the government "line" of that day, and the falsifying of motivations. A quarter of a century later it is both amusing in a wry sort of way but, for younger people, surely instructive.

While documentaries are sometimes a hard sell in regular commercial playoff, this one has a lot going for it. The women are consistently attractive, even in their gripe citations. Indeed, the Brooklyn Jewish woman, Lola Weixel, emerges as a sort of star. She seems a fine human being and so do the rest of these who testify. —Land.

Terror Train
(CANADIAN-COLOR)

Well-made formula shocker with Jamie Lee Curtis.

Hollywood, Sept. 25.
Twentieth Century-Fox release of an Astral Bellevue Pathe Production in association with Sandy Howard Prods. Corp./Daniel Grodnik. Exec producer. Lamar Card. Produced by Harold Greenberg. Stars Ben Johnson, Jamie Lee Curtis, Hart Bochner, David Copperfield. Directed by Roger Spottiswoode. Screenplay. T.Y. Drake; camera (DeLuxe Color), John Alcott; additional photography, Rene Verzier, Al Smith, Peter Benison; editor, Anne Henderson; music, John Mills-Cockell; production designer, Glenn Bydwell; art director, Guy Comtois; sound, Bo Harwood, Dave Appleby, Dino Pigat; assistant director, Ray Sager. Reviewed at Academy of Motion Picture Arts & Sciences theatre, BevHills. Sept. 24, 1980. (MPAA Rating: R.) Running time: 97 MINS.
Carne .... Ben Johnson
Alana .... Jamie Lee Curtis
Doc .... Hart Bochner
The Magician .... David Copperfield
Kenny Hampson ...... Derek MacKinnon
Mitchy .... Sandee Currie
Mo .... Timothy Webber
Jackson .... Anthony Sherwood
Ed .... Howard Busgang
Brakeman .... Steve Michaels
Class President .... Greg Swanson
Merry .... D.D. Winters
Pet .... Joy Boushel
Engineer .... Victor Knight

Jamie Lee Curtis runs around and screams a lot in "Terror Train," so the film should make a lot of money. Canadian-made shocker follows the formula established in "Halloween" and continued in Curtis' two subsequent, highly profitable pix, "The Fog" and "Prom Night." In this one, a 20th-Fox pickup, the youngsters menaced by a psychotic are having a wild party on a train. The kill-

ings are well engineered and run right on schedule.

To give an idea of how much profit potential the majors have been discovering (belatedly) in these horror quickies, "Terror Train" has a print order of 1,000 and an ad outlay of $5,000,000 for its Oct. 3 openings. Studios have found such modest pix often pay the bills while big-budget pix go down the tubes.

"Terror Train" bears a complicated pedigree, with both American and Canadian cooks getting their hands into the lucrative broth. Harold Greenberg and Astral Bellevue Pathe, which distribs the film in Canada, made it in association with Sandy Howard Prods. and Daniel Grodnik, both of Hollywood. Roger Spottiswoode, vet editor who co-authored a respected book on the subject with Karel Reisz, makes a competent directing debut here. He's a Britisher who recently became a landed immigrant in Canada.

As in Curtis' other pix, she limns the feisty survivor character in a group of young people menaced by a psychotic. Her acting fits a narrow groove that teen viewers evidently find easy to identify with, though adults might wish for more emotional range and clearer diction. But it must be said in young thesp's favor that she has not been given the most challenging material.

Acting is perhaps the least important element in this genre anyway, and kids cast here are mostly blah. Ben Johnson does his usual sturdy turn in an offbeat role for him as the kindly conductor. It's amusing to watch him try to keep order as everyone on the train goes more and more bananas while the killer does his lurid work. David Copperfield has an effective supporting role as a magician who may have dirty tricks up his sleeve.

Efficient screenplay by T.Y. Drake quickly sets up the premise by showing a repulsive sick joke being perpetrated by college med students on a sensitive youth who goes insane as a result. Three years later the kids all take a train excursion to celebrate their graduation, and the chickens come home to roost. Plot takes several interesting twists before the actual killer is revealed.

Tech credits are good. Stanley Kubrick's lenser John Alcott contributes a smoky, eerily distorted color scheme that works well in establishing the hellish mood. Anne Henderson's editing keeps things zipping along at an increasingly frenetic pace. —Mac.

Moon Over The Alley
(BRITISH-16m-B&W)

British Film Institute production and release. Features entire cast. Directed by Joseph Despins. Screenplay, William Dumaresq; camera (b&w), Peter Hannan; editor, Despins; music, Galt MacDermot; lyrics, Dumaresq; sound, Conrad Weyns; production manager, Geoffrey Evans; assistant director, Ian Sellar. Reviewed at Paramount theatre, N.Y.C., Sept. 22, '80. (No MPAA Rating). Running time: 107 MINS.
With: Doris Fishwick, Peter Farrell, Erna May, John Gay, Sean Caffrey, Sharon Forester, Patrick Murray, Lesley Roach, Basil Clarke, Bill Williams, Vari Sylvester, Joan Geary, Norman Mitchell, Leroy Hyde, Miguel Sergides, Debbie Evans.

Amateurish 1975 filmusical from Joseph Despins, a young Canadian working in Britain, "Moon Over the Alley" is an embarrassing attempt to inject "realist" approaches to this fantasy genre. Crudely shot on a tiny BFI-generated budget, pic once again demonstrates that realistic representations on screen come after hard work and construction, not taking a camera on location and using nonactors or semi-pros.

With the pretense of showing a slice of life on London's Portobello Road, William Dumaresq's script introduced a motley group of personages in Bertha Gusset's boardinghouse. When not bursting into maudlin, middle of the road songs (which sound like '60s rejects) by Galt MacDermot, the cast bickers in best "kitchen sink" tradition. Stereotypes abound: young teenage lovers whose parents object; sturgling family from Jamaica; drunken Irish barman and his bar dancer girl; local joint-smoking "hippies."

To pave the way for a heavy-handed building demolition ending, the film suddenly drops its cute pose and segues into contrived violence, a definite novelty for a musical (other than Ken Russell's "Tommy").

Underrehearsed, one-take cast is awkward, though Erna May as Gusset is amusing in her German lady in Britain routine. Pro cameraman Peter Hannan ("Slade in Flame," "Full Circle") delivers studied expressionistic lighting inside the boardinghouse and eye-straining low light out in the alley. The BFI Production Board aims to encourage young talent, but there's little talent on display here. —Lor.

Augh! Augh!
(ITALIAN-COLOR)

Venice, Sept. 3.
Produced by Kronos Film productions. Stars Andrea Occhipinti. Directed by Marco Toniato. Screenplay. Lucio Manlio Battistrada, Toniato; camera. (color),

Cristiano Pogany; art direction, Paolo Montesi; editing, Raimondo Crociani; music, Pino Donaggio. Reviewed at Venice Film Festival, Sept. 3, 1980. Running time: 90 MINS.
Danilo Severini .... Andrea Occhipinti

Title says it all in this first film by 40-year-old Marco Toniato, an amateurish attempt at making a nonconformist pic about a rebellious boy by following the canons of normal commercial film-making badly.

Handsome young Danilo

(Andrea Occhipinti) returns to his hometown one day and instantly falls in love with a rich girl named Simona. The love is impossible because Danilo, though from a good family himself, has the habit of openly insulting everyone he meets and, in addition, has not bathed in two years. Also the girl is about to be married to a dull old count, a fate Danilo saves her from by seducing her on the wedding night under the count's eyes. The next morning the unconventional vagabond hits the road again.

Plot is highly illogical, dialog stilted and acting poor. Toniato unfortunately shows none of his character's rage for scandal in an extremely mannered shooting style lacking in originality. Technical credits don't help much either. A Panorama of Italian Cinema entry. —Yung.

Head On
(CANADA-COLOR)

Toronto, Sept. 9.
A Michael Grant film production. No distributor. Produced by Michael Grant and Alan Simmonds. Directed by Grant. Stars Sally Kellerman, Stephen Lack. Screenplay, James Sanderson, Paul Illidge; camera (color), Anthony Richmond; production designer, Antonin Dimitrov; music, Peter Mann; editor, Gary Oppenheimer; assistant directors, Mac Bradden, John Board. Reviewed at Toronto Festival of Festivals, Elgin Theatre, Toronto, Sept. 7, '80. Running time: 98 MINS.
Michelle Keys .... Sally Kellerman
Peter Hill .... Stephen Lack
Clarke Hill .... John Huston
Frank Keys .... Lawrence Dane
Gad Bernstein .... John Peter Linton
Karim .... Mina E. Mina
Stanley .... Hadley Kay
Michelle's Analyst ..... Robert Silverman
Henry .... Maxwell Moffett

"Head On" is an uneven mix of comedy and terror involving two people with a penchant for games of a sexual and psychological nature. As such, the film will require a careful campaign to reach its specialized audience.

The story gets off to a crashing start when child therapist Kellerman and psychology professor Lack collide head on in a traffic accident. After a suitable convalescence in casts, they face off in a legal battle. They resolve their differences by buying each other twin

Mercedes — one black (Lack's), the other white (Kellerman's).

Emnity evolves into attraction as the two engage in a series of encounters revolving around unique interpretations of familiar nursery rhymes. Each participant alternates at fulfilling the other's secret sexual fantasies.

Kellerman comes out the winner in audience sympathy. She is a frustrated wife whose husband (Larry Dane) is too involved in his work to notice her growing dissatisfaction. Her professional career is equally bleak. She's losing a young patient with suicidal tendencies.

Lack's background is sketchily painted. In a delightful vignette we meet his eccentric sculptor-father John Huston. Unfortunately, Huston's scenes are with Kellerman and Lack can only speak rather than demonstrate his love for Huston.

The film's high-point is a lover's encounter in an Italian restaurant. Lack struts in dressed like a Mafia hit man and holds the patrons at gunpoint as he kidnaps Kellerman. The scene is the perfect mix of bizarre comedy and unnerving tension.

However, the mood promptly turns black. The relationship hits rock bottom when Kellerman is picked up by police for prostitution in the course of a new game. She is humiliated and her husband in a rage walks out.

All seems lost but the lovers are reunited at Huston's funeral and decide to marry. Rather than a a happy resolution, the marriage ceremony which Lacks watches but does not attend, is the beginning of more cruel games. The film concludes with the same collision which began the film.

First time director Michael Grant and first time writers James Sanderson and Paul Illidge simply lack the experience to pull off their ambitious mood piece. The balance scales lean toward the bizarre and frightening with the performer's struggling to maintain their humanity in the generally dark piece.

Lack, in his first major dramatic role, almost succeeds in being funny and manic simultaneously. His natural appeal is partially muted by the material.

Kellerman emerges in a full-blown performance as crazy, sympathetic and tragic. She roots the role in very real terms and allows the film its greatest success. Dane as her husband turns in a brief, effective insight into her mania.

Production values are good certainly impressive, with Anthony Richmond's photography taking top honors.

"Head On" joins recent outlings

"Night Games" and "Bad Timing" in theme. Its future may hinge on the acceptance of the latter title in North America but it cannot escape a tag of interesting and flawed first effort. —*Klad*.

Beyond Reasonable Doubt
(NEW ZEALAND-COLOR)

Auckland, Sept. 19.

An Endeavour Productions film produced by John Barnett. Stars David Hemmings, John Hargreaves. Directed by John Laing. Screenplay, David Yallop, based on his book, "Beyond Reasonable Doubt?"; editor Michael Horton; camera (Eastman-color) Alun Bollinger; music, Dave Fraser; art director, Kai Hawkins. Reviewed at Civic Theatre, Auckland, Sept. 19, 1980. Running time: **127 MINS.**

Inspector Hutton	David Hemmings
Arthur Allen Thomas	John Hargreaves
Detective John Nughes	Martyn Sanderson
David Morris	Grant Tilly
Vivien Thomas	Diana Rowan
Kevin Ryan	Ian Watkin
Paul Temm	Terence Cooper
Constable Wyllie	Marshall Napier
Detective Murray Jeffries	John Bach
Detective Stan Keith	Bruce Allpress
Pat Vesey	Bruno Lawrence
Graham Hewson	Peter Hayden

For 10 years the New Zealand public has been living with the murder mystery surrounding the deaths of Jeannette and Harvey Crewe. After an unprecedented two trials, Arthur Thomas was found guilty. He was pardoned late in 1979 and currently a Royal Commission is sitting to determine how justice could have miscarried so badly. This public interest and topicality will all make for lively boxoffice action in its homeland, but pic will have to stand on its own merits for the rest of the world's moviegoers, who will be hearing about the Crewe murders for the first time.

As it is, the story had enough false trails and contradictions to interest Britain's investigative writer David Yallop, and his book, "Beyond Reasonable Doubt?", is credited with much of the final boost that led to Thomas' pardon. Yallop has done a workmanlike job on the book's translation to the screen, and if the aim was to persuade us that a tough cop, hellbent on a conviction, manipulated the murder evidence even to the extent of planting a cartridge case at the scene of the crime to implicate Thomas, then it strikes the bullseye.

Roles have been sharply cast to have look-alikes doubling for the real life protagonists, which will carry an extra smack of authenticity Down Under, where all the faces are very well known indeed. Imported name David Hemmings brings a chillingly vindictive venom to the role of the cop, no doubt an accurate portrayal in terms of the Yallop thesis. John Hargreaves is

suitably bewildered as Thomas, the rather simple young farmer who can't believe it's happening to him.

The soundtrack is noisy, drowning the dialog at times. John Laing's direction is mostly straight down the middle, which dispels the idea that he's deliberately following a popular trend. Captions are used to denote the passage of time and the details of how it all worked out in the end are left to a voiceover — reminders that this is fictionalized documentary and it is wrong to expect imaginative flights of creative filmmaking. —*Dub*.

Der Verlorene Engel
(The Lost Angel)
(EAST GERMAN-B&W)

East Berlin, Sept. 8.

A DEFA Film production, East Berlin; world rights, DEFA Aussenhandel, East Berlin. Features entire cast. Directed by Ralf Kirsten. Screenplay, Kirsten, Manfred Freitag, Joachim Nestler, based on novel, "Das Schlimme Jahr" (The Terrible Year), by Franz Fuehmann; camera (black and white), Claus Neumann; music, Andre Asriel; sets, Hans Poppe; dramatic advisor, Klaus Wischnewski. Reviewed at DEFA Screening Room, East Berlin, Sept. 8, '80. Running time: **59 MINS.**

Cast: Fred Dueren (Barlach), Erika Polikowsky (Frau Barlach), Erik S. Klein, Walter Lendrich, Agnes Kraus, Heidemarie Wenzel, Frank Schenk.

Unspooled at the recent Karlovy Vary fest in a salute to former FAMU grads from the Prague Film School, Ralf Kirsten's "The Lost Angel" (produced 1966, released 1970) was one of those shelved films in the mid-1960s when Socialist countries reexamined their production policies and decided against films that dealth with controversial themes. Even this cut version (about 30 minutes are gone) and possibly rewritten dialog texts of "The Lost Angel" are enough to indicate that a fine film was in the making on a theme that captivates the imagination to the present day.

"The Lost Angel" refers to an Ernst Barlach sculpture that once hung in the village church of Guestrow, a sculpture that the Nazis removed in the night in 1939 and apparently destroyed (it was never found again), because the countenance of this sculptured angel was that of Kaethe Kollwitz and the artist was suspect. Both Barlach and Kollwitz were expressionistic artists whose works were condemned as "decadent" by the Nazis. Barlach (1870-1938) died in the village of Guestrow, his home since 1910, at the dawn of the Second World War catastrophe that was to engulf half of Europe in flames.

An understanding of the film requires some historical background. Barlach was, in 1938 (the year of his death), a prominent dra-

matist, sculptor, and graphic artist, whose finest sculptures and plays, half expressionistic and half vitalistic, reflect a strong mystical belief in God's hand upon the cosmos and the human destiny. His brooding sorrow on the state of affairs under the Nazi dictatorship is expressed in the film through stream-of-consciousness dialogues with himself and an outside world that has now become alient to him..

The story is a day in the life of the aged Barlach. He leaves his studio to go to the church and peer at this sculptured angel. Nazis follow his movements from a threatening distance. A wedding takes place in the church. He goes to the countryside to watch young boys in brownshirts fighting a mock war. In the end, it is clear that the artistic has resigned and is prepared to depart from this alien world of anti-intellectuals and witch-hunters. The angel is removed from the church in the night, never to be found again. An epilog states that a second Barlach-Kollwitz angel was kilned according to sketches and documents left behind; it now hangs in its former place in the Guestrow church.

For today's audience, the fascination for this 15-year-old pic lies in its references to a universal artist who speaks to all generations of German people and elsewhere. (Chancellor Helmut Schmidt, for example, recently intended to visit Guestrow, north of Berlin, while conferring with his East German counterpart, Erich Honnecker, on relations between the two Germanys; the conference, set for late August early September, fell through at the last minute due to the other political reasons). But Kirsten's "Lost Angel" is also a compelling story, on "passion," of an isolated artist, played with dignity and insight by Fred Dueren. Thus, it is the more impressive in its shortened form. —*Holl*.

Sabine Wulff
(EAST GERMAN-COLOR)

East Berlin, Sept. 8.

A DEFA Film production, Berlin Group, East Berlin; world rights, DEFA Aussenhandel, East Berlin. Features entire cast. Written and directed by Erwin Stranka, based on a novel by Heinz Kruschel. Camera (color), Peter Brand; music, Karl-Heinz Sasse; dramatic advisor, Anne Pfeuffer. Reviewed at DEFA Screening Room, East Berlin, Sept. 8, '80. Running time: **91 MINS.**

Cast: Karen Duewel (Sabine), Manfred Ernst (Jimmi), Juergen Heinrich (Atsche), Hans-Joachim Frank (Hansel), Lars Jung (Hotte), Jutta Wachowiak (Heide Hoboha).

One of the biggest boxoffice draws in East Germany, Erwin Stranka's "Sabine Wulff" aims at the younger generation to tell their story and get a response. When it appeared in 1978, this film and another youth-oriented pic, "Seven Summer Freckles," were b.o. hits that left their competitors far behind, although better films had been made in that season.

"Sabine Wulff" is a straightforward and sometimes tough story of a young girl who leaves an orphanage that raised her to young adulthood and must now go into the cruel world to find her own way. Since she is attractive and likes the boys a bit more than average, her dreams and hopes get trampled on by one heavy-handed Prince Charming after another. The one who loves her, and plasters his walls with blow-ups of her photos, is too much of a dropout from society to suit her, but her quick temper and restless search for independence prevent her from settling down in any case.

Sabine lives in a small town, where the older and younger generation tend to clash on fundamentals — like respect for the older and wiser, behaving and minding your manners, and the like. When the bosomy lass gets angry at tormenters in a cafe, she simply raises her pullover to bare her breasts in defiance — a strong scene for film production in the German Democratic Republic. On another occasion, her understanding landlady, in the apartment where she rents a room, allows her to decorate as she pleases — foot-prints on the wallpaper and furniture — and even gives in when she secretly has boyfriends over for the night.

One of Sabine's boyfriends manhandles her; another comes from an apparently different social class; and the auto-mechanic who loves her is just not her style in the end. And on the factory job she speaks her mind once too often and is fired from her job. In the end, she decides to pull up stakes and go elsewhere, now a bit more the wiser and open to the future.

Despite narrative weaknesses, this GDR pic is well worth the once-over. —*Holl.*

Reggae Sunsplash
(W. GERMAN-JAMAICAN-COLOR)

Toronto, Sept. 8.
Aresenal Filmtheatre. Filmvertreibs Stephen Paul KG production. Directed by Stefan Paul. Camera (color). Hans Schalk, Rainer Heinzelmann, Peter Rees; editor, Hildegard Schroder; sound, Roland Engele, Amel Thomae. Reviewed at Toronto Festival of Festivals, Varsity Theatre, Toronto, Sept. 6, '80, 107 MINS.
Cast: Bob Marley, Peter Tosh, The Third World Band, Burning Spear.

Filmed at last summer's Sunsplash II Festival in Montego Bay.

Jamaica, by German tv director Stefan Paul, this music documentary places powerfully rhythmic music in its own contest; in front of a Jamaican crowd of 40,-000 which treats the occasion as one great romp.

Paul has explained that the festival used only "local sound equipment," and because the "concerts always took place at night and differing voltage systems were responsible for the fact that Bob Marley's performance was hardly lit at all." But the grainy, muted colors gives the film the raw edge of authenticity. It's as much apart of the reggae experience as the music.

Performances by Bob Marley and Peter Tosh are less structured than those North American audiences have seen in live concerts. The real musical break-through is scored by Burning Spear and The Third World Band.

In fact, "Reggae Sunsplash" is likely to benefit Third World Band the most. Its sophisticated use of vocal harmonies and the strong rhythm 'n' blues and funk influence in its music are far more in evidence here than in any of their albums so far. —*Goda.*

AC/DC: Let There Be Rock
(FRENCH-COLOR)

Toronto, Sept. 8.
High Speeds Production film. Directed by Eric Dionysius and Eric Mistler; camera, (color), Jean Francis Gorde. No other production credits available. With Angus Young, Malcolm Young, Bon Scott, Phill Rudd, Cliff Williams. Reviewed at the Toronto Festival of Festivals, Varsity Theatre, Sept. 7, '80. Running time: 95 MINS.

"Let There Be Rock," the French-made concert-documentary featuring the Australian hard-rock band, AC/DC, is not remarkable for what it shows as how it shows it.

The footage of Paris and Belgium concerts was shot, for the most part, from above or on the stage — as opposed to upwards, in the pit in front of the stage, as is the case with so many rock concert films.

This gives the hard rock audience which goes repeatedly to Led Zeppelin or Pink Floyd concert films a chance to see rock from a new angle — and see the final footage of Bon Scott, the band's lead singer who died earlier this year from alcohol poisoning.

Musically, the band tends to get stuck in a groove and this can leave any but the hardcore fan wanting something else. Visually, lead guitarist Angus Young, in his short pants and schoolboy's uniform, proves to be one of the most orig-

inal and theatrical rock performers to come by in years. His crazy, careening dances across the stage are, along with the photography, the only elements that separate this production from so many other rock films.

Some attempt has been made to broaden out the context, with one sequence showing Scott being flown in a vintage plane and then being driven a round by a "mysterious stranger" in a Porsche. But all this does is make pretentious something which, if klutzy at times, was at least open and honest about it.
—*Goda.*

Can-Cannes
(ITALIAN-COLOR)

Venice, Sept. 5.
Produced by Franco Scepi, Mario Battistoni, Andrea De Micheli, Pierluigi Ronchetti for Monolite Cinematografica Milano productions. Features entire cast. Written and directed by Franco Scepi. Camera (color), Mario Battistoni; editing, Lucio Tomaz; music, Detto Mariano; animation, Guido Manuli. Reviewed at Venice Film Festival, Sept. 5, 1980. Running time: 90 MINS.
Andrea .... Andrea De Micheli
Wizard .... Franco Scepi
The Dog .... Massimo De Rossi

Dedicated to Georges Melies, pioneer of a non-realistic fantasy cinema based on camera tricks made to look like "magic," "Can-Cannes" has the odd tone of a '60s "acid trip" sequence without the drugs. Throwing away a ready-made chance for a satire on Cannes and its denizens, pic uses film fest city as background circus for its loony but undisciplined lens and editing antics. Could click commercially with an unchoosy youth market to whom its rock music and pop images seem geared.

A young Italian trio's weekend trip to Cannes in a camper is about the only solid fact in the surrealistic pic — produced, filmed and thesped by a group of Milanese ad men. Unable to get his ideas past conservative Roman producers, former set designer Franco Scepi formed Monolite Cinematografica with other media pros, penned and helmed his debut picture. Though result is refreshingly different from mainstream Italo comedy, pic flounders in all that creative freedom and loses more than it gains with its frenetic pace and unfollowable editing.

Andrea (Andrea Di Micheli), his wife and her girlfriend, three well-to-do Milanese, take off for Cannes in a camper. While the girls sunbathe topless and form an alliance against Andrea, he wanders aimlessly around the Film Festival building having strange encounters. A stray dog takes human form and becomes his best friend. A

"magic box" turns up in which Scepi himself appears, making Andrea dream of bizarre stories from the past about a soldier, his mistress and her jealous husband. In a finale all characters appear jumbled together.

Acting is generally fine — all thespers except Massimo De Rossi as the humanized dog are well-directed non-pros. Andrea, rich, infantile and perpetually dazed, descends from that comic tradition of passive males "to whom things happen." Funniest encounter is with a little round candy salesman who likes little girls but doesn't have much success with them. —*Yung.*

Gdansk Fest

Cma
(The Moth)
(POLISH-B&W)

Gdansk, Sept. 14.
A Film Polski production, Film Unit, Warsaw; world rights, Film Polski, Warsaw. Features entire cast. Written and directed by Tomasz Zygadlo. Camera, (black & white), Jacek Zygadlo; sets, Janusz Sosnowski; music, Jan Kanty Pawluskiewicz; production manager, Andrzej Smulski. Reviewed at Gdansk Film Festival, Sept. 14, '80. Running time: 103 MINS.
Cast: Roman Wilhelmi (Jan), Anna Seniuk (Magda), Iwona Bielska (Justyna), Nela Obarska (Agata), Jerzy Trela (Soltys), Grzegorz Herominski (Tomek), Marek Probosz (Marcin), Piotr Fronczewski (psychiatrist), Jerzy Stuhr (Elegant Gentleman), Inez Fichna (Jola).

"The Moth" was made by a young brother-team: scripter-helmer Tomasz Zygadlo and lenser Jacek Zygadlo. Tomasz also doubles on occasion as an actor, for Andrzej Wajda ("Without Anaesthetic") and Agnieszka Holland("Provincial Actors"). "The Moth" is a pic that reminds one of Nathaniel West's novel, "Miss Lonely Hearts," in that both are about a concerned individual in the mass media/dealing with lonely people in the public sphere via a vicarious life-line.

Jan has his own nightly radio program, "Radio-Telephone," whereby people phone in simply to talk with him about their troubles. The people at the station, however, couldn't care less about Jan's nightly compassion for the lonely souls who are attracted to his voice like moths to a light-bulb. Instead, his fellow-employees and his boss think the program is a waste of time, and so our hero becomes increasingly disturbed that others don't understand the situation as well as he does.

In addition, Jan has a wife with a drinking problem and a girlfriend on the side during the day who doesn't understand him either. He becomes more and more irritated, loses sleep, and one night also loses complete control of himself. After a stretch in the mental clinic, he returns home to his apartment, smiling, to meet his acquaintances on and off the job sitting around a table. The Fellini-like ending hints too where the inspiration for the story might have originated.

Black and white lensing helps the film considerably in tracing a mental breakdown from a kind of neutral point-of-observation, and Roman Wilhelmi's acting carries the pic a good part of the way. Although only fringe outlets are expected for this offbeat experiment, helmer Zygadlo is a talent to watch after two feature pix under his belt.
—*Holl.*

Bez Milosci
(Without Love)
(POLISH-COLOR)

Gdansk, Sept. 10.
A Film Polski production. Iluzion Film Unit, Warsaw; world rights. Film Polski, Warsaw. Features entire cast. Written and directed by Barbara Sass. Camera (color). Wieslaw Zdort; sets. Roman Rozycki; music. Seweryn Krajewski; production manager. Ryszard Straszewski. Reviewed at Gdansk Film Fest, Sept. 10, '80. Running time: 103 MINS.
Cast: Dorota Stalinska (Ewa Bracka), Wladyslaw Kowalski (Piotr), Malgorzata Zajaczkowska (Marianna), Zdzislaw Wardjn (journalist), Malgorzata Pritulak (Piotr's wife), Jadwiga Polanowska (Malgosia), Emilian Kaminski (Marianna's boyfriend).

A debut pic by a femme helmer, Barbara Sass's "Without Love" takes its cue from Andrzej Wajda's tough-minded girl-reporter in "Man of Marble" (1976), and Feliks Falk's "Top Dog" (1977), about an M.C. entertainer clawing his way to the top of the ballrooms in the provinces to make the big time on television. Now we have Sass's version of a cub reporter, Ewa, using her feminine charms and other wily means to become a journalist on a Warsaw weekly popular magazine. She hopes to develop into a Oriana Fallaci-style political interviewer of personalities and state leaders. On the way up the ladder, however, she trips over her own shoestrings and falls just short of the goal she has been pursuing with almost fanatical energy.

Our heroine is believable as a hustler with a camera in her hand uncovering corruption at every turn, but she apparently has instant recall in writing her stories without using a tape-recorder and with seldom recourse to a typewriter between assignments. Ewa, however, does have time for judo training, walks with her infant daughter, bouts in bed with bosses, and whatever else can distract her

from learning the ropes of the trade.

All the same, she uncovers some scandals of note: doctors take money from patients on the side for better treatment; a workers' hotel for the temporarily unemployed has turned into a rundown bordello; and a kind of alter ego, a pregnant unmarried girl, has become a drunkard with tendencies to suicide due to frustration and cruelty. These revelations make for sensational news and meaty stories for the climbing Brenda Starr, but the star reporter also has a mother who happens to be an honest doctor, while she herself is heavy on drugs to keep her own adrenalin going under pressure. Further, her former true-love affair with an Italian in Rome, who later left her, offers a clue as to why she is set on becoming an international newshound.

Minus the weaknesses in the script, Sass proves that she is a femme helmer of rank in Poland. Pic is a good cub above the average in its technical credits, and it should find its way offshore on the Polish film weeks and on the fest circuit for femme directors. —*Holl.*

Ojciec Krolowej
(The Queen's Father)
(POLISH-COLOR)

Gdansk, Sept. 11.
A Film Polski production. Kadr Film Unit, Warsaw; world rights. Film Polski, Warsaw. Features entire cast. Directed by Wojciech Solarz. Screenplay. Jerzy Stefan Stawinski; camera (color). Stefan Matyjaszkiewicz; sets. Boleslaw Kamykowski; music. Maciej Malecki; production manager. Urszula Orczykowska. Zygmunt Wojcik. Reviewed at Gdansk Film Fest, Sept. 11, '80. Running time: 110 MINS.
Cast: Jan Englert (de Charentes), Dorota Pomykala (Helena Pogorzelska), Ignacy Machowski (Marquis d'Arquiem), Anna Seniuk (Queen Maria Kazimiera), Mariusz Dmochowski (King Jan III Sobieski), Ludwik Benoit (Jablonowski), Emund Fetting (Count Zierowski), Wienczyslaw Glinski (Ambassador de Vitry).

Historical tale set in the late 17th century. "The Queen's Father" was directed by veteran tv-helmer Wojciech Solarz. It deals with the alliance between Poland and Austria that resulted in the rescue of Vienna from the invading Turks by Sobieski.

As this story goes in a tongue-in-cheek fashion, it's only a question of keeping the Queen Marysienka Sobieska's father from falling into the wrong hands of three conniving foreign governments, made all the more difficult because father likes sneaking out of the palace to wine-and-cards wherever he gets the chance. The gallant knight, Chevalier de Charentes, is on hand, however, to match swords and wits with anyone set on kidnapping this important pawn on the chessboard

to prevent the eventual alliance.
Nothing of special interest, not even the swordplay. —*Holl.*

Dzien Wisly
(The Day of the Vistula)
(POLISH-COLOR)

Gdansk, Sept. 12.
A Film Polski production. Profil Film Unit, Warsaw; world rights. Film Polski, Warsaw. Features entire cast. Directed by Tadeusz Kijanski. Screenplay. Ryszard Frelek; camera (color). Mathieu Przedpelski; music. Waldemar Kazanecki; sets. Zenon Rozewica; production manager. Tadeusz Karwanski. Reviewed at Gdansk Film Festival. September 12, '80. Running time. 75 MINS.
Cast: Henryk Talar (Tadeusz), Ewa Borowik (Katarzyna), Edmund Fetting (Professor), Jerzy Kamas (Maj. Kazimierz), Emil Karewicz (Lt. Florian), Anna Milewska (Tadeusz's mother), Erwin Nowiaszek (Schultz, SS-Officer), Andrzej Preeigs (Witek, Tadeusz's brother), Mieczyslaw Voit (Samuel Blum).

Psychological war pic without much to recommend it other than its historical background, Tadeusz Kijanski's "The Day of the Vistula" is set on the right bank of the Vistual River in a suburb of Warsaw in September 1944, as the Germans were withdrawing after laying the city in ruins and the Russians were preparing to cross the river in the march on Berlin. A disabled war veteran, confined to a wheelchair since September 1939, tries to figure how to help his comrades in the Resistance during the Warsaw Uprising. First, members of the Resistance, and then Polish officers siding with the Red Army, happen on the scene, followed by a roving band of Nazi Germans who plunder and rape as they retreat.

Each individual represents a differing, contrasting point of view. What's lacking is a story to tie them all together. —*Holl.*

Urodziny Mlodego Warszawiaka
(The Birthday)
(COLOR-COLOR)

Gdansk, Sept. 8.
A Film Polski production. Iluzion Film Unit, Warsaw; world rights. Film Polski, Warsaw. Features entire cast. Directed by Ewa and Czeslaw Petelski. Screenplay. Jerzy Stefan Stawinski, based on his own novel; camera (color). Jacek Stachlewski; music. Jerzy Maksymiuk; sets. Andrzej Borecki; production manager. Zbigniew Brejtkopf. Wieslaw Grzelczak. Reviewed at Gdansk Film Fest, Sept. 8, '80. Running time: 105 MINS.
Cast: Piotr Lysak (Jerzy), Andrzej Lapicki (his father), Jolanta Grusznic (Teresa), Gabriela Kownacka (Jadzka), Hanna Skarzanka (Grandmother), Kazimierz Kaczor (Karczewski), Roman Frankl (Ziemowit), Tomasz Zaliwski (Walczak), Arkadiusz Bazak (Gustaw), Krzysztof Chamiec (Colonel), Henryk Kluba, Witold Prykosz.

Scripter and writer Jerzy Stefan Stawinski is best known to Polish

film buffs through a series of a dozen or more dynamic scripts penned for Andrzej Munk ("Man on the Track," "Eroica," "Bad Luck"), Andrzej Wajda ("Kanal"), and Aleksandar Ford ("Knights of the Teutonic Order"), among others, in the late 1950s and early 1960s. He has even directed films on occasion.

The husband-wife team of Ewa and Czeslaw Petelski have been making films together also since the 1950s, and they are contemporaries of Stawinski. "The Birthday" is based on Stawinski's autobiography, and it thus has references to Poland's recent tragic history that were shared by all. The four sequences in the film cover four days in the life of a young Warsaw lad (Stawinski) on his birthdays (September 24) in 1938, 1939, 1943, and 1944, the first of the chosen birthdays taking place when Jurek is 17-years-old.

In the first sequence, Jurek decides not to study at the Sorbonne as his parents wish, but to enlist in a Polish military school out of a sense of patriotism. The second sequence brings us to the opening shots of the Second World War as Poland is invaded and Warsaw occupied in the fatal month of September 1939. The third part, 1943, finds him working in the Underground Resistance movement. Then comes September 1944 (his 23rd birthday) and the Warsaw Uprising, during which the city is reduced to ruins.

There are family scenes and the lad's first love, lost and found in the uncertainty of the times and the resistance fighting. He marries in the last sequence in the midst of the Warsaw Uprising. All of which remind the viewer at several turns of Andrzej Wajda's "Kanal" (1957), the earlier Stawinski script based on personal experiences. The comparison only goes thus far, however, as the direction is wooden and the acting stiff. Still, it's a page of Polish history that should be continually studied, particularly when films are made by those who experienced those bitter years of the "lost generation" first-hand.
—*Holl.*

Golem
(POLISH-COLOR)

Gdansk, Sept. 10.
A Film Polski production. Perspektywa Film Unit, Warsaw; world rights. Film Polski, Warsaw. Features entire cast. Directed by Piotr Szulkin. Screenplay. Szulkin, Tadeusz Sobolewski, based on and inspired by motifs in the legend and novel by Gustav Meyrink. Camera (color). Zygmunt Samosiuk; sets. Zbigniew Warpechowski. Janusz Wlasow; production manager. J. Leszek Sobczyk. Reviewed at Gdansk Film Festival. Sept. 10, '80. Running time: 92 MINS.

Cast: Marek Walczewski (Pernat). Krystyna Janda (Rozyna). Joanna Zolkowska (Miriam). Krzysztof Majchrzak (Student). Mariusz Dmochowski (Holtrum). Wieslaw Drzewicz (Miriam's father). Henryk Bak. Wojciech Pszoniak. Jan Nowicki. Ryszard Pietruski. Andrzej Seweryn. Marian Opania. Boguslaw Sobczak.

Piotr Szulkin has made a solid reputation for himself at the short-film fests in Oberhausen, Mannheim, and Cracow; his best known shorts are "A Girl with a Devil" (1976) (Grand Prix at Mannheim and FIPRESCI Critics' Award at Cracow), "Copyright" (1977), and "Working Women" (1978) (Grand Prix at Oberhausen). Now he has turned his experimental talents to the feature film, choosing the legend of the Golem as a starting point for another philosophical reflection on the state of man in the age of technology.

"Golem" doesn't work as a feature film, but might have as a short feature in view of the well-known Golem legend and its application to the future — it's a kind of "Golem in 1984." We are placed in a terrorizing world of the future in which technology commands the movements of individuals, supervised by doctors who are carrying out a program for the improvement of the human race. Thus, instead of doctors creating a monster, the monsters are already there as the normal species of the future — but one of them is suspected by the doctors of being a human being, that is a Golem in reverse.

"Golem" has echoes of Jan Lenica's animated horror cartoon, "Labyrinth" (1962) and Kantor's pessimistic play, "The Dead Class," both of which draw on the ruins of Poland and the horrors of Auschwitz for effect. The twist in Szulkin's pic is that mass media is presently the evil everyone should fear and distrust; in our age of computers he feels that "information" can mold "reality" to its own image.

In any case, our Golem wanders through a future urban jungle in sepia tones and, occasionally, color in search of a way out of "programmed madness." Nothing much happens, however, in the way of a narrative line, but it's intriguing to puzzle over the meanings of signs and symbols. A treat for avant-garde fans, but without offshore chances. —Holl.

Jesli Msz Serce Bijace
(If Your Heart Can Feel)
(POLISH-COLOR)

Gdansk, Sept. 13.
A Film Polski production. Profil Film Unit. Warsaw: world rights. Film Polski. Warsaw. Features entire cast. Directed by Wojciech Fiwek. Screenplay. Fiwek. Konrad Frejdlich, based on Edmund de Amicis' "The Heart:" camera (color). Stefan Pindelski: sets. Tadeusz Myszorek: music. Piotr Marczewski: production manager. Wojciech Karmolinski. Reviewed at Gdansk Film Fest. Sept. 13, '80. Running time: 91 MINS.
Cast: Wladyslaw Kowalski (Henryk). Zofia Rysiowna (Madame von Golz). Alfred Struve (Prof. Hampel). Boreslaw Smela (Fisherman). Adam Probosz (Henryk).

Set at the end of the 19th century, Wojciech Fiwek's "If Your Heart Can Feel" is the story of a young boy attending school in Cracow under the Austrian administration. Since the lad comes from the provinces to begin his schooling, he boards with a merciless and stern landlady who also mistreats a servant girl his own age but without parents. In the school there's an authoritarian Austrian teacher who demands discipline above all else.

The upshot of the story is that the students slowly rebel against the teacher, particularly after one of the lads is injured in a sleigh accident and is forced to stand on legs that haven't healed as punishment in the classroom. Eventually, another goodhearted teacher takes pity on the boys when things go from bad to worse, and the offensive teacher is dismissed. Then, when there's no money to pay his board anymore, our young hero wanders the streets and is thought dead via suicide in the river. Then the father arrives in time for the happy ending.

Not much here to chew on, and the primary objection is that the film fits neither for the family nor for the children audience. —Holl.

Kobieta I Kobieta
(A Woman and a Woman)
(POLISH-COLOR)

Gdansk, Sept. 14.
A Film Polski production. Film Unit. Warsaw: world rights. Film Polski. Warsaw. Features entire cast. Written and directed by Ryszard Bugajski and Janusz Dymek. Camera (color). Janusz Kalicinski: music. Wojciech Trzcinski: sets. Teresa Snuis-Barska: production manager. Michal Szczerbic. Reviewed at Gdansk Film Fest. Sept. 14, '80. Running time: 102 MINS.
Cast: Halina Labonarska (Barbara). Anna Romantowska (Irena). Witold Debicki (Michal). Stefan Szmidt (Jerzy Domagalski). Stanislaw Jaroszynski (Jablonski). Jerzy Zelnik (Architect). Jerzy Kryszak (Kozlowski). Andrzej Gloskowski (Secretary).

A debut pic by a pair of young helmers who also collaborated on the script. Ryszard Bugajski and Janusz Dymek's "A Woman and a Woman" aims to say something about corruption in higher places but gets bogged down in sentimental tete-a-tete scenes between two women who are the best of pals, save when honesty and integrity separate them. Pic has some relevance in view of current situation in Poland.

It's the story of a femme production manager in a garment factory discovering an award is being given to the wrong person on purpose, so she stands up to the injustice — and her friend backs her position rather than the culprit, who happens to be the man she's living with. Later, the former production manager has risen to be the mayor of a resort city, where she in turn practices malfeasance and is caught in the act by her friend, who had learned honesty and decency from the good example ten years before. Good intentions don't help a bad script.
—Holl.

The Club
(AUSTRALIAN-COLOR)

Sydney, Sept. 19.
A Roadshow Distributors release of a South Australian Film Corporation and New South Wales Film Corporation production of David Williamson's "The Club." Produced by Matt Carroll. Features entire cast. Directed by Bruce Beresford; screenplay. David Williamson. Assoc. producer. Moya Iceton. Camera (Color-Panavision). Don McAlpine: art direction, David Copping: sound. Gary Wilkins: editor. William Anderson: music. Mike Brady. Reviewed at Roadshow theatrette. Sydney, Sept. 19, '80. (Commonwealth censorship rating: M). Running time. 99 MINS.

Laurie	Jack Thompson
Ted	Graham Kennedy
Jock	Frank Wilson
Danny	Harold Hopkins
Geoff	John Howard
Gerry	Alan Cassell
Susy	Maggie Doyle

Based on his play of the same name, (retitled "Players" for its brief American run), David Williamson's screen adaptation opens out the action, but in so doing somehow manages to close down the characters. The plot has to do with a football club and the behind the scenes machinations: ruthless powerplays that make what takes place on the field seem relatively tame.

The game in this case is a local aberration, confined to the State of Victoria mostly, called Australian Rules. To get most enjoyment out of the film, perhaps, no knowledge of the game is preferable. Actually the game itself plays a background role, and director Bruce Beresford has shrewdly kept the thrust of his film in the hands of his main characters.

The film's stage origins could have been a liability, but as he did with an earlier Williamson work, "Don's Party," Beresford has made what might have been confined ensemble playing into a conflict of cameos. Again, the technique works, though one has the feeling that it is better suited to television at times. In terms of the ultimate destination of the work, this will obviously be of benefit. The Seven Network are investors in the production.

As the former star, now a fading coach, Jack Thompson is fine, investing the role with no subtlety, only directed aggression. Frank Wilson's devious old player and club past president has shadings that are recognizable in similar people in other areas of activity. It is his maneuvering that precipitates the removal of the existing president, by joining forces with the ambitious administrator. Graham Kennedy as the former and Alan Cassell as the latter are both superb. Kennedy in particular shows himself as an actor of considerable range. Cassell shows flashes of Iago-like detachment, pseudo-disinterested behaviour that manipulates.

Tech credits are uniformly excellent, and McAlpine's photography is by now so routinely excellent that superlatives are superfluous. William Anderson's editing is smooth, creating un-jarring transitions between actual footage of games and that structured for the film plays.

Williamson's plays have been described as "life at the top of your lungs," and "The Club" is no exception; there are few quiet passages. One such, however, gives Kennedy a chance to invest Ted, the meat-pie manufacturer who bought his way to the presidency, with not only dignity, but integrity. Though ever a spectator, Ted loves the game. It's a classic case of what the Freudians call sublimation, and in his playing of the scene Kennedy hints at some of the deprivations that must have shaped the character.

Difficulty with many sports pictures is that they usually suffer from such even-handedness that they wind up with both the fans and anti-fans wanting more of what they think the film is about. Beresford's film won't give the fans much satisfaction, except maybe those of Collingwood Football Club, which lent facilities and has a piece of the picture.

Domestic returns seem assured. The film is being released in Melbourne, (bastion of Aussie Rules), at Grand Final time and should pick up on the general interest, and promotional chances are therefore good.

Film could also benefit from the current success of Beresford's earlier film, "Breaker Morant" which swept the Australian Film Institute Awards and garnered for Jack Thompson best actor in addition to the supporting Palme D'Or he won at Cannes in the same role. —*Miha.*

Children Of Babylon
(JAMAICAN-COLOR)

Joden Distributing release of a Rainbow Productions Ltd. production. Produced by Lennie Little-White. Features entire cast. Directed by Little-White. Screenplay, Little-White; camera (color), Franklyn St. Juste; editor, Little-White; music, Harold Butler; lyrics, Little-White; production manager, Peter Packer; sound, Oscar Lawson. Reviewed at Fifth Ave. screening room, N.Y.C. Oct. 1, '80. (No MPAA Rating). Running time: **122 MINS.**

Penny	Tobi
Rick	Don Parchment
Luke	Bob Andy
Dorcas	Leonie Forbes
Laura	Elizabeth de Lisser

Just as Italian directors revitalized the moribund American Western genre in the 1960s with a new approach, Jamaican filmmakers have brought back the U.S.-invented blaxploitation film, but with political overtones. In his feature debut, helmer Lennie Little-White has an intriguing "Children of Babylon," but lets the medium get in the way of his message.

Shot in 1979 and released this year on the island of Jamaica (and in a current test run in Brooklyn), "Babylon" portrays various archetypal characters to represent Jamaica today. Little-White likens the island to a "plantation" of ante bellum South days, and points out the emptiness of the decadent, "Babylonian" life styles and world views of his protagonists.

Penny (played by model Tobi) is a beautiful Marxist graduate student whose thesis concerns the mating habits of working class women. She falls in love with Rick (Don Parchment), a handsome artist who picks her up hitchhiking, and Luke (Bob Andy), a young plantation farmer who's into the Rastafarian faith. Dorcas (Leonie Forbes), the mute domestic at the home where they're all staying, is also sexually involved with Luke. The absentee owner of the plantation and Rick's patroness Laura (Elizabeth de Lisser), an older white Jamaican woman, is also Rick's bedmate.

Little-White mixes and matches this bunch in numerous softcore sex scenes, but eschews the violence which was a staple of domestic blaxploitation product. The overlong film errs chiefly in its highly romantic approach, stressing the beauties of the Jamaican countryside and shamelessly spotlighting Tobi in lyrical shots better suited to a Penthouse or Players magazine layout than a serious feature film. Result is that audiences (especially in the U.S.) may identify with the attractive, hedonistic life style shown in the picture and find the verbal criticisms of it either laughable or irrelevant.

Largely inexperienced cast is okay in terms of presence and physical appearance but unconvincing in dramatic scenes. Reggae-oriented musical score is quite pleasant, and the blowup from 16m to 35m is good. —*Lor.*

Here's Looking At You, Kid
(U.S.-DOCU.-COLOR)

Biomed Arts Associates Inc. release. Produced by Andrew McGuire, for the Burn Council of San Francisco General Hospital. Directed by William E. Cohen. Camera (color). Cohen. Paul Shain, Mag-

gie Cole; editor, Cohen; lighting, Barbara Dunn; sound. Jay Litvin, Andy Wiskes. Reviewed at Alice Tully Hall in New York Film Fest. Oct. 2, '80. (No MPAA Rating). Running time: **53 MINS.**
With: Maggie Cole, Rob Cole, Andrew McGuire.

"Here's Looking At You, Kid" is a well-meaning, generally engrossing documentary concerning the adjustment of a severely burned child (and his mother) to living normally in society despite his disfigurement. Film consists mainly of interviews with the mother (Maggie Cole) and Rob Cole, the burn victim, conducted by producer Andrew McGuire, head of the Burn Center and a friend of the family. Helmer William E. Cohen intercuts these with revealing footage of Maggie watching and reacting to her home movies of Rob shot mainly before the house fire incident.

Film works best through Maggie's deeply felt reactions plus footage showing Rob operating quite normally in his classroom or out in public. Pic is intentionally unpleasant in closeup footage showing Rob's physical appearance (no cosmetic surgery has yet begun in what is termed a 10 year program of operations for him) and in McGuire's frequently stupid questions, e.g., "Do you love your mother?" which are suitably ridiculed by Rob and Maggie.

The filmmakers' hearts are certainly well-located, but this overly-intrusive film combines its public education aspects with a morbid obsessiveness likely to turn off many viewers. It is difficult to strike a proper balance in films dealing with sensitive subject matter like this one, so credit McGuire and Cohen with a good try. —*Lor.*

Asphaltnacht
(Asphalt Night)
(WEST GERMAN-COLOR)

Berlin, Sept. 28.
A Tura-Film production, Munich, in collaboration with ZDF, Wiesbaden-Mainz. Features entire cast. Written and directed by Peter Fratzcher. Camera (color), Bernd Heinl; music, Lothar Meid, editor, Fratzcher; tv-editor, Sibylle Hubatschek-Rahn; producer, Alena Rimbach. Reviewed at Kant Kino, Berlin, Sept. 28, '80. Running time: **90 MINS.**
Cast: Gerd U. Heinemann (Angel), Thomas Davis (Johnny), Ralf Herrmann (Frank), Charly Wierczejewsky (L.A. Peters), Michael Zens (Kamikaze), Herbert "Rim" Rimbach (the Critic), Debbie Neon (Debbie), Gabriele Helene Ruttmann (Nelly), Christiane Plate (the Little Girl). Clemens Schkorski (84).

Another of those delightful low-budget pix (this one cost in the range of $250,000) being made these days in West Germany, Peter Fratzcher's "Asphalt Night" is about rock 'n' roll, punk attitudes, and what's like to roam the streets

of Berlin from dusk to dawn in a single night sof adventure at various hot-spots, peep-shows, recording studios, and even churches (to hear an organ played by a friend) in a common effort to nurse a song into existence. Fratzcher's other directorial credit of note was the ghost job he did on Udo Lindenberg's "Panic Times," which lensed and recorded the pop scene in Hamburg.

"Asphalt Night" is a film of mood and rhythm rather than a narrative entertainment movie, although it is also all of the latter. It begins with an aging devotee of rock, a 30-year-old guitarist who has lost his touch as a song-writer, on the verge of becoming a loser in the only profession he knows and likes. A bit down on his luck, Angel still has his drag-racer to cruise the streets, and he does just that to while the night away — only to constantly bump into Johnny, a punk-guitarist of 17 who keeps a wary eye out for cops who will collect him and send him back to his parents. Johnny is against everything and thus also a set-up for Hell's Angels types who refuse to take his lip sitting down. The two become reluctant, and then steadfast, friends.

Angel saves Johnny from pursuing cops, a motorcycle gang, and the punk-rocker's penchant for just getting into trouble with anyone he meets on the street. In return, Johnny bangs out a partial tune on his guitar, which inspires Angel to record the song he's been trying to shake out of himself all evening. In the meanwhile, there's plenty of humorous dialog and improvised scenes on original locations in Berlin. This is arguably the best pic on today's "Berlin Scene" made by young filmers.

Well acted by nonprofessional thesps, "Asphalt Night" overcomes its imperfections by aiming for the tastes of a young public and simply trying to entertain with the meagre means at its disposal. It's an entry in the San Francisco Film Fest. —*Holl.*

El Nido
(The Nest)
(SPANISH-COLOR)

Madrid, Sept. 27.
An A-Punto E.L.S.A. production, written and directed by Jaime de Arminan. Features entire cast. Camera (Eastmancolor), Teo Escamilla; editor, Jose Luis Matesanz; sets, Jean Claude Hoerner; direct sound, Bernardo Menz. Reviewed at Cine Coliseum, Madrid, Sept. 27, 1980. Running time: **97 MINS.**

Alejandro	Hector Alterio
Goyita	Ana Torrent
Eladio	Luis Politti
Sergeant	Agustin Gonzalez
Marisa	Patricia Adrani
Amparo	Maria Luisa Ponte
Manuel	Ovidi Montllor

Also Mercedes Alonso, Luisa Rodrigo, Amparo Baro, Mauricio Calvo.

Masterfully scripted and directed film by Jaime de Arminan comparable or better than the best of his past work, such as "My Dearest Senorita" and "The Love of Captain Brando." "El Nido" is that rare specimen, an intelligent, sensitive, and articulate film which features some of the best thesping seen this year in Spain.

In another acting tour de force, Hector Alterio portrays an aging hidalgo living in a swank but rustic country house near Salamanca whose barren and meaningless life is filled by computer chess, horseback-riding and an elaborate hi-fi system which he "conducts" to the sound of Haydn's "Creation." A 13-year-old village girl insinuates herself into his life and a strange relationship develops between them, patently platonic, but covertly with sexual overtones. She is bewitchingly played by Ana Torrent, the child actress in "Cria Cuervos" and "The Spirit of the Bee-Hive."

The girl, in addition, happens to be the daughter of a local Civil Guard. Her demands upon Alejandro become increasingly more elaborate as their friendship grows. He first balks, but then complies by giving her a medallion, burning his late wife's clothes, and, finally, even trying to avenge her hate for a Civil Guard sergeant.

Alterio and Torrent are magnificent, and their brilliant thesping are counterpointed by a touching performance by the late Luis Politti as an understanding, down-to-earth priest who, uncondescendingly, befriends the freethinking Alejandro.

Pic was recently entered in the Montreal fest and copped a best-thesping award for Ana Torrent. Certainly, this is one of the pick of Spain's best films so far this year.

Bright sales prospects for more discriminating markets and subtitled-fare circuits in Europe, U.S. and Latin America. Item shouldn't have any censorship problems in any area since priest and police are handled with tact. —Besa.

Shock Waves
(COLOR)

Inept 1975 horror programmer, with interesting casting. For marginal bookings only.

Joseph Brenner release of a Zopix production. Produced by Reuben Trane. Features entire cast. Directed by Ken Wiederhorn. Screenplay, John Harrison, Wiederhorn; camera (TVC color), Trane; editor, Norman Gay; music, Richard Einhorn; production manager, Jessica Sack; make-up, Alan Ormsby. Reviewed at Times Square theatre, N.Y.C., Sept. 27, '80. (M-

PAA Rating: PG). Running time: 84 MINS.
SS Commander . . . . Peter Cushing
Rose . . . . Brooke Adams
Captain . . . . John Carradine
    With: Fred Buch, Jack Davidson, Luke Halprin, D.J. Sidney, Don Stout.

Filmed in Florida as a low budget indie in 1975 under the title "Death Corps," this one is an amateurish horror film never tradescreened, and reviewed here as "Shock Waves" for the record. Aspiring filmmakers (with producer Reuben Trane doubling as cameraman) managed to sign a solid cast of leading players, but fumbled in scripting and executing a basically interesting premise.

Brooke Adams narrates this tall tale in flashback, as presumably the sole survivor when a yachting party, under captain John Carradine, is shipwrecked on an island after colliding with a mysterious freighter. On the island they encounter old, scarred SS Commander Peter Cushing at a decrepit hotel and he fills in the plot exposition.

It seems the Nazis were experimenting to create invincible soldiers, and Cushing was put in command of a corps of zombie submariners. Unfortunately these SS men were recruited from the ranks of murderers and proved unreliable, so were not activated. Cushing and his undead were still awaiting orders at war's end, and he sank them in his boat in 1945.

The zombies are an arresting creation; blonde figures in SS uniforms and dark goggles who arise from the water to threaten the cast. The goggles protect them from (for these zombies) lethal rays of the sun.

Tactical error which kills the film's horror potential is that the SS men don't really do anything. They either choke or drown unlucky cast members, but are not really scary in strictly unarmed combat scenes.

Horror pros Cushing and Carradine are okay in context, but the film is really a showcase for Brooke Adams, before her rise to prominence in "Days of Heaven" and subsequent major pix. Clad mainly in a yellow bikini, Adams is an appealing presence even in these tawdry circumstances of shoestring filmmaking. Rest of the cast is acceptable, but film technically is a joke. —Lor.

Hard Knocks
(AUSTRALIAN-COLOR)

Sydney, Sept. 20.
Greg Lynch Film Distributors Pty Ltd presents an Andromeda Production. Pro-

duced by Don McLennan and Hilton Bonner. Features entire cast. Directed by Don McLennan. Screenplay, McLennan, Hilton Bonner; camera (color) Zbigniew Friedrich; editor, Friedrich; assistant director, Rod McNicol; sound, Lloyd Carrick; costume design, Julie Cutler and Penelope Hester. Reviewed at Hoyts' Theaterette, Sydney, Sept. 19, 1980. (Commonwealth Censorship Rating: M.) Running time: 85 MINS.

Sam . . . . Tracey Mann
Wally . . . . John Arnold
Brady . . . . Bill Hunter
Newman . . . . Max Cullen
Barry . . . . Tony Barry
Frank . . . . Hilton Bonner
Debbie . . . . Kirsty Grant

"Hard Knocks" is a tough city drama about tough city people. Director Don McLennan as done a superlative job in maintaining the pressure and despite a low budget achieving some remarkable production values. The Melbourne-made film was originally shot on 16m and has been blown up to 35m; the ensuing graininess is at times distracting, but on the other hand it also imparts a cinema-verite immediacy that increases verisimilitude.

Tracey Mann won this year's Australian Film Institute Best Actress award for her portrayal of Sam, the delinquent whose determination to improve herself after a jail term, is eroded by both the police and her former associates. The film evolves from and revolves around Sam, and Mann's performance dominates every scene, ranging from the crewcut punk moll to the lissome mannequin she eventually — if briefly — becomes.

McLennan and producer Hilton Bonner's screenplay has a tendency to episodic exposition but this is neatly muted by McLennan's use of flashback. It is especially effective in the opening sequences which establish the contrast between Sam the punk moll and Samantha as is. Because no reference terms have been established, there is created a sort of time-disassociation that is resolved gradually through subsequent plot and character development; and, thus, retains interest for the entire 85 minutes, if not concern.

Supporting cast is well-chosen; mainly new faces among the young, but established actors in the heavier roles — none more heavy than Bill Hunter's unrelentingly morally-corrupt cop, Brady. Indeed, it is only the film's stance as viewing events from Sam's side of things that prevents Hunter's performance from seeming parody. Zbigniew Friedrich's lensing aids immeasurably here, imparting a subjectivity that underlines point of view.

For all its apparent despair, "Hard Knocks" isn't a depressing

film — largely because Mann invests Sam with a resilience that recognizes that for her and her kind, life is never going to be easy. Upward achievers at that level of society need either to compromise or be possessed of such determination as to be undaunted by setbacks. That particular state Sam seems close to approaching, but one feels she'll be so case hardened by the time she is 30, she'll be a fascinating character to unravel. But that's another film.

Melbourne seems to be emerging as almost an Australian equivalent of Germany in terms of its cinema: small-budget dramas of social relevance like "Mouth To Mouth," "In Search of Anna" and "Hard Knocks" indicate a definite potential for sociological neo-realism exists among the talent there.

With Sydney's filmmakers appearing to go more for bigger-budgeted productions, the dichotomy will doubtless provide academics and future film historians something to chew on in the next decade. Whatever the reason, it will be films with the power of "Hard Knocks" that will define any trend. —Miha.

Private Benjamin
(COLOR)

Sporadically funny about female soldiers, Hollywood style.

Warner Bros. release of a Meyers-Shyler-Miller production. Executive producer and star Goldie Hawn. Written and produced by Nancy Meyers, Charles Shyer, Harvey Miller. Directed by Howard Zeiff. Camera (Technicolor), David M. Walsh; production designer, Robert Boyle; film editor, Sheldon Kahn; music, Bill Conti; asst. director, Jerry Sobul, sound, Martin Bolger; art director, Jeff Howard; set decorator, Arthur J. Parker; special effects, Robert Peterson; unit publicist, Joan Eisenberg. Reviewed at Beekman Theatre, New York, Oct. 1, 1980. (MPAA Rating-R). Running time: 109 MINS.
Judy Benjamin . . . . Goldie Hawn
Capt. Doreen Lewis . . . . . Eileen Brennan
Henri Tremont . . . . Armand Assante
Col. Clay Thornbush . . . . . Robert Webber
Teddy Benjamin . . . . Sam Wanamaker
Harriet Benjamin . . . . Barbara Barrie
Pvt. Mary Lou Glass . . . . Mary Kay Place
Sgt. Jim Ballard . . . . . Harry Dean Stanton
Yale Goodman . . . . Alberta Brooks

Goldie Hawn's venture in producing her own film is actually a double feature — one is a frequently funny tale of an innocent who is conned into joining the U.S. Army and her adventures therein; the other deals with the same innocent's personality problems as a Jewish princess with only an intermittent chuckle to help out.

The trouble may be with the use of too many screenwriters who have been told to always keep their star's image uppermost in their scribblings. There's little doubt that

Hawn is a very funny lady when given the proper material — "Foul Play" more than established that. But she's not so gifted that she can carry a heavy load of indifferent material on her own two little shoulders. without considerable sagging.

Another script problem is that the supporting characters are. even when they start out sympathetically. turned into unlikable types — and that includes Eileen Brennan as a feisty Army captain. Robert Webber as a gung-ho colonel, Sam Wanamaker and Barbara Barrie as Benjamin's upper-middle-class Jewish parents and Albert Brooks as her second husband who dies during coitus on their wedding night. Harry Dean Stanton is thrown away on a brief bit as an Army recruiting sergeant who cons Hawn into the military bit.

The Army sequences which provide most of the fun are pure Hollywood and should. in themselves. provide lots of laughs for military personnel. One wonders what the two U.S. Army technical advisors did in return for their screen credit. There's a bit of bad taste displayed in a scrappable bit about fellatio in a car that adds nothing to the film. Armand Assante starts off great as a handsome French doctor who seems to be Hawn's great romance but is shot down with a shoddy bit about his being a security risk because of a brief flirtation with the Communist party.

Technically. the film is top-flight. David M. Walsh's color photography gives the picture a professional gloss that makes the vapid storyline seem even thinner than it is.

Initial outlook should be good based on the great Hawn vibes left over from "Foul Play" but whether the film has legs will depend on what the competition is this fall.
—*Robe.*

Coast To Coast
(COLOR)

———

A long haul.

———

Hollywood, Sept. 30.
Paramount Pictures release. exec produced by Terry Carr. Produced by Steve Tisch, Jon Avnet. Directed by Joseph Sargent. Screenplay. Stanley Weiser; camera (Movielab Color). Mario Tosi; second-unit camera. Joel King; editor. George Jay Nicholson; music. Charles Bernstein; art director. Hilyard Brown; set decorator. Ira Bates; sound. Gene S. Cantamessa. John T. Reitz. David Campbell. David Hudson; associate producer. Vince Cannon; assistant director. Michael Daves. Reviewed at Mann's Chinese Theatre. Hollywood. Sept. 29. 1980. (MPAA Rating. PG.) Running time: 95 MINS.
Madie Levrington ....Dyan Cannon
Charlie Callahan ....Robert Blake
Benjamin Levrington ....Quinn Redeker
Dr. Froll ....Michael Lerner
Sam Klinger ....Maxine Stuart
Jules .... Bill Lucking
Nurse #1 ....Ellen Gerstein
Nurse #2 ....Patricia Conklin
Chester ....David Moody
Orderly ....Rozelle Gayle
Albert....................Martin Beck
Callahan's Wife ....Karen Rushmore

"Coast To Coast" is a forced, strident attempt at romantic comedy. Dyan Cannon and Robert Blake share one of those "zany" romances that only happens on screen, and with good reason. They are so dissimilar and have so little chemistry together they seem to be acting in different films. The Steve Tisch-Jon Avnet production, is strictly program fodder.

The synthetic package is loaded with the kind of superficially commercial elements that could have been spewed out of a computer: a road setting. a couple thrown together by adversity. baddies chasing them, the comedy of mismatch (he's a redneck trucker. she's a rich lady on the lam from her husband), and the poignancy of their ultimate attraction. The Stanley Weiser screenplay is phony as a three-dollar bill and is never remotely credible even by the artificial standards of the screwball comedy genre.

Cannon is simply unbearable in her hysterical performance, and it's no wonder that Blake constantly tries to ditch her on the road from N.Y. to L.A. Her husband Quinn Redeker is supposed to have tried to drive her crazy in order to avoid expensive divorce proceedings, and Cannon is so shrill and mindless in the part, she almost makes one sympathize with Redeker.

Blake. by contrast. gives a very good. low key performance whose only drawback is that the film is supposed to be a comedy. not a drama. He's laconic and likable as a trucker driven to desperate measures and dubious moral choices (he almost turns Cannon in for reward money) but economic hardship and the violent harassment of a bill collector.

An actor who seems incapable of any phony behavior on screen. Blake brings an inherent sadness to any role he plays. which gives this part a depth not present in the script but has the side-effect of undercutting the comedy. However, his disgust at Cannon's idiotic behavior provides an enjoyable running putdown of the shallow mentality responsible for the film.

Director Joseph Sargent also seems miscast in the genre. He handles comedy with all the delicacy of an 18-wheeler running over a beer can. Most surprisingly. given the opportunities the subject provides for movement and varied backgrounds, most of the film consists of boringly unimaginative two-shots of Cannon and Blake sitting glumly in the cab of the truck.

Probably unintentionally. the film does succeed in one respect. It accurately captures the monotony and fatigue of driving from coast to coast. —*Mac.*

Venice Films

Vacanze In Val Trebbia
(Vacations in Val Trebbia)
(ITALIAN-COLOR)

———

Venice, Aug. 29.
Produced by Enzo Porcelli for Antea-Odissya productions. Features entire cast. Written and directed by Marco Bellocchio. Camera (color). Luigi Verga; art direction, Gianluigi Olmi; editing, Anna Napoli; music, Nicola Piovani. Reviewed at Venice Film Festival, Aug. 29, 1980. Running time: 50 MINS.
With Piergiorgio Bellocchio, Gisella Burinato, Marco Bellocchio, Gianni Schicchi, Beppe Ciavatta.

———

Marco Bellocchio, one of the leading lights of Italian cinema in the '60s and '70s, filmed a 50-minute documentary-fantasy two years ago during his summer vacation. Result is a personal look into the director's imagination (the fantasy parts) alternated with home movies of a pretty boring vacation (docu side). Of interest to Bellocchio fans only.

Helmer himself appears as protagonist of a fake family spat with wife Gisella, while son Giorgio (now a child actor in great demand) takes part in country plays. Friends arrive for nightly get-togethers of city folk and local peasants.

Fantasy shots: girls sleeping on iron beds that float dangerously down the river rapids; Indians on horseback and Roman soldiers throwing dice at the foot of a cross, to which a young boy is tied. In the end the real life Bellocchio makes a difficult raft trip throuh the symbolic tunnel.

A minor work, "Vacations" has the virtue of its oddity and a few eerie moments. Idea of mixing reality, memory and imagination with helmer's emotional crisis is an interesting one — approached as a personal diary. —*Yung.*

Stupende Le Mie Amiche
(My Fabulous Girlfriends)
(ITALIAN-COLOR)

———

Venice, Sept. 7.
Produced by Clara Gallini, Sergio Martinat. Domenico Vizzari, Alessandro Scalco and Luisa Corsini. Features entire cast. Written and directed by Alessandro Scalco. Camera (color). Maurizio Calvesi; editing. Enzo Meniconi; music. Gioele and Elvio Boeri. Reviewed at Venice Film Festival. Sept. 7, 1980. Running time: 95 MINS.
With: Luigi Fioravante, Maurizio

Lembo. Orazio Marino, Claudio Moscatelli. Ferdinando Moscatelli, Sergio Moscatelli. Toni Zaza.

Sociological slice of life in a heretofore unexplored area — the lives of young gays in Turin who have emigrated from the South and are now practically integrated in Northern culture, here the gay lifestyle of the city. Fascinating overall, Alessandro Scalco's helming debut has heady moments of high cinematic realism following characters around on a typical Saturday; other stagnant parts killed by an incomprehensible soundtrack. An interesting entry for fest circuits.

Film is fiction but shows a strong documentary impulse, noticeable in the predisposition for very long takes and still camerawork. Six heroes. presumably non-pros picked off the street as in neorealism's heyday, are allowed free reign to improvise in front of the camera. Direct sound recording, rare in an Italian production, gives dialoge authenticity and immediacy. though much is lost owing to a bad recording job.

The two characters who stand out are the squat Afro-haired truck driver with a scrappy personality and enormous shaggy dog, and a sensitive young man, the group's natural leader, who spends Saturday night at home in a fit of melancholy while his friends go to the opening of a giant new disco.

At the hairdresser's and in a boutique, fixing spaghetti in a decrepit ghetto apartment and on a lark through the streets, camera follows its subjects with an unobtrusive style that lets situations and characters speak for themselves.

Pic's strong point is its arresting images: the truckdriver dresses up as Marilyn Monroe in his squalid apartment; he drives his car in frenetic circles in an empty field; the solitude of the boy who abstains from the disco as he prepares for bed, shot from outside the window; the final free frame on the disco dancers all strangely turned to look into the camera as an apocalyptic wind rises on the soundtrack.
—*Yung.*

Nella Citta' Perduta Di Sarzana
(In the Lost City of Sarzana)
(ITALY-COLOR)

———

Venice, Sept. 2.
A RAI-Television Channel 2 production. Features entire cast. Directed by Luigi Faccini. Screenplay. Luigi Faccini, Piero Anchisi; camera (color), Nevio Sivini; music, Vittorio, Gianni Nocenzi. Reviewed at Venice Film Festival, Sept. 2, 1980. Running time: 100 MINS.
With: Franco Graziosi, Riccardo Cucciolla, Bruno Corazzari, Bruno Cattaneo,

Ernesto Colli, Roberto Posse, Ezio Marano, Marisa Mantovani, Claudio Gora.

Helmer Luigi Faccini, whose sensitive period film, "Red Carnation," made the fest circuits a few years back, gives another proof of his feel for good politically-toned drama in "Lost City of Sarzana." Produced by RAI-TV, pic gets a lot of mileage from a moderate budget in recreating a massive fascist attack on a Tuscan town in 1921, when Mussolini had not yet taken control of the government. But real note of pic is intellectual suspense: Faccini alternates action scenes with the political jockeying for power surrounding the incident. A specialized item indicated for more fest appearances.

On a July night in 1921 a group of 600 armed fascists march along the railroad tracks to "clean up" Sarzana, a socialist town. The farmers resist, seconded by the small police force. Fifteen fascists are killed in the clash and the attack repulsed.

Meanwhile the Italian Parliament is debating the conservative Bonomi program of government. Bonomi promises the socialists the repression of fascism if they will adhere to his program and sends a police inspector, Trani, to gather proof of fascist aggression in Sarzana. Bonomi's government passes without the socialist vote and Trani is replaced with a Fascist sympathizer. Mussolini creates the legend of the "fascist martyrs of Sarzana." Sarzana's population is repressed and their spontaneous self-defense is turned into a defeat.

Film fascinates with its many-sided analysis of a historical event and its demonstration of the political machinations going on behind the scenes, though this inevitably slows down its adventurous side. It has no main character but a collection of "Leaders" who come to the forefront one after another. Technically competent in all departments. —*Yung.*

Desideria, La Vita Interiore
(Desire, the Interior Life)
(ITALIAN-GERMAN-COLOR)

Rome, Sept. 18.

A Cinemaster release, produced by Galliano Juso for Cinemaster (Rome). Medusa Cinematografica (Rome). and Lisa Film (Munich). Stars Stefania Sandrelli. Lara Wendel. Klaus Lowitsch. Directed by Gianni Barcelloni. Screenplay. Enzo Ungari and Barcelloni. from novel by Alberto Moravia; camera (Eastmancolor). Claudio Cirillo; art direction, Ferdinando Giovanoni; editing. Daniele Alabiso; music. Pino Donaggio. Reviewed at Barberini Cinema. Rome. Sept. 16. 1980. Running time: 105 MINS.
First Desideria . . . . Rosana Marra
Desideria . . . . Lara Wendel
Viola . . . . Stefani Sandrelli
Administrator . . . . Klaus Lowitsch
Eros Occhipinti . . . . . Vittorio Mezzogiorno

Often riveting in spite of its overblown melodramatic plot, this adaptation of Alberto Moravia's "The Inner Life" is held together by performances of young actress Lara Wendel and Stefania Sandrelli, daughter and mother with a tense relationship. At its best, pic poignantly describes the inner hell of a poor little rich girl who learns to use her developing sexuality as a weapon against her mother. Rest of story slips into a bad B-film plot with modern gangsters — pimps, kidnappers, terrorists — who do not merge with pic's psychological angle.

Attempt to rev up a delicate emotional drama and appeal to action pic audiences makes "Desideria" a strange animal indeed that risks disappointing high-brow circuits looking for Moravia's Freudian eroticism and the sex and violence market, who are in for slim pickings.

Pic opens with a great supporting performance by a fat, stringy-haired little girl (Rosana Marra plays the ugly duckling Desideria with a sense of humor) who eats compulsively as a substitute for mother love. Glamorous millionairess mom, Viola (Stefania Sandrelli) is a neurotic single parent physically repulsed by the homely child. One climactic night daughter catches mom, her administrator and the French maid in bed together; furious, Viola tells Desideria she bought her from a prostitute because she was unable to have children of her own.

This unlikely story turns out to be true, though it reads like the child's fantasy for most of the film. Desideria attempts suicide but recovers as the gracious Lara Wendel, slimmed down, desirable, and bent on revenge. With Eros (Vittorio Mezzogiorno), a lowlife police informer, she schemes to kidnap Viola, but plan backfires and Eros is killed. Desideria and Viola drive off together into the sunset.

Explicit sex scenes will be an important element in pic's sell and a censorship menace. Though legitimately called for by the theme, bedroom sequences are rushed through and their psychological import often lost, as in the key mother-daughter "incest" scene that is just thrown away in the middle of the romance-connivance between Desideria and Eros. Other scenes are unintentionally comic. Pic curiously mixes explicitness (Wendel's abundant nudity and insistence on Mama's particular erotic preferences) with a desire to photograph everything in attractive shadow and to tastefully suggest. In fact, biggest shock is last reel discovery that Desideria is still a virgin.

Fine performances by Sandrelli as the playgirl — tightroping between motherly over-protection and self-indulgence. Vittorio Mezzogiorno as the weak boyfriend, and Wendel in the main role. This serious-faced young actress, not conventionally pretty, sustains intensity and single-mindedness to finale in her plans for revenge.

Helmer Gianni Barcelloni shows a preference for elegant shots and subtleties that generally work fine in this pic. Technical credits are all a plus, for millionaire sets by Ferdinando Giovanoni to Claudio Cirillo's subdued lighting. —*Yung.*

Panagulis Zei
(Panagoulis Lives)
(ITALIAN-COLOR)

Venice, Aug. 30.

A RAI-Television Channel 2 film. produced by Cine 2000 productions. Stars Stathis Giallelis. Pupella Maggio. Directed by Giuseppe Ferrara. Screenplay. Ferrara. Piergiovanni Anchisi. Riccardo Iacona. Gianfrancesco Ramacci. with collaboration of Tanassis Valtinos; camera (color). Silvio Fraschetti; music. Dimitri Nicolau. Reviewed at Venice Film Festival. Aug. 30. 1980. Running time: 100 MINS.
Allessandro Panagulis . . . Stathis Giallelis
Mother . . . . Pupella Maggio
Statis Panagulis . . . . Victor Cavallo
Hadzizidis . . . . Adalberto Maria Merli
Teofilo Jannakos . . . . Cristiano Censi
Babalis . . . . Luigi Montini
Orjana Fallaci . . . . Marcella Michelangeli

A classic of its kind, the Greek freedom fighter's bio is a 100-minute theatrical version of miniseries "Panagoulis Lives," an uncritical elegy to Alekos Panagoulis, imprisoned and tortured by the Colonels for a failed attempt on the life of P.M. Papadopoulos. Concentrating on his years in prison, story lacks tension to keep hero's fate of prime interest until his murder. Inspiring theme will be main b.o. draw.

Stormy production history included fierce contestation by Panagoulis' companion, Oriana Fallaci, who insisted she had exclusive rights to film the story of her friend, and worked with the current Greek government opposed to a Balkan shoot. Crew filmed Parthenon and Athenian street scenes surreptitiously, while interiors were reconstructed in Rome. Pic will be aired on RAI-TV in a longer four-hour version.

After an abortive attempt on P.M. Papadopoulos in 1968, Panagoulis (well played by lookalike Stathis Giallelis) is arrested and tortured for several months before being condemned to death. World protest prevents the Colonels from carrying out the sentence; instead Panagoulis begins five terrible years of imprisonment. hunger strikes. failed escape attempts, and inhuman living conditions. His mother and brothers carry on the struggle for human rights and Alekos' release. Finally Panagoulis is granted amnesty. He is interviewed by Italian journalist Oriana Fallaci and they become friends. When the Colonels are ousted Panagoulis is elected to Parliament, but dies in a mysterious car accident just as he is about to release secret documents compromising members of Parliament. His funeral is attended by an immense crowd shouting "Panagoulis lives."

Helmer Giuseppe Ferrara has a lot of good dramatic material going for him, but routine handling defuses much of it; pic has difficulty getting inside characters' motivations. Panagoulis and his brothers are unflinchingly dedicated to the cause to the point of masochism (Alekos doesn't want to accept amnesty and stop being a symbol for the people.) Neapolitan theatre actress Pupella Maggio plays the courageous mother, whose fears for her son are transformed into active militancy. In the end one suspects what pic lacks is precisely Fallaci's insight into the private world of the Greek hero.
—*Yung.*

O Passado E O Presente
(The Past and the Present)
(PORTUGUESE-COLOR)

Figueira da Foz. Sept. 21.

A Manoel de Oliveira Film production. Oporto. Features entire cast. Written. and directed by Manoel de Oliveira. adapted from a play by Vincente Sanches. Camera (color). Acacio de Almeida; music. Mendelssohn; editing. Oliveira. Reviewed at Figueira da Foz Film Festival. Sept. 21. '80. Running time: 120 MINS.
Cast: Maria de Saisset. Mauela de Freitas. Barbara Maria. Alberto Inacio. Pedro Pinheiro.

Manoel de Oliveira's "The Past and the Present" (1971) is one of his three productions — the other two are "Benilde, or the Virgin Mary" (1975) and "Love of Perdition" (1978) — based on theatrical works. either original plays or legit prods based on literary classics. The three films should be viewed as a kind of trilogy, since their styles are similar and all three examine Portugese bourgeois society at close range.

"The Past and the Present" has been compared by Oliveira admirers to Jean Renoir's "La Regle du Jeu" and Luis Bunuel's "The Exterminating Angel" and rightly so — it takes place in a manor-house for the most part, where acquaintances gather, it appears, to console a lady who has lost her husband, who fell out a window into the garden below (a suicide?). Later, the husband appears upstairs to confront the wife about what happened in the past, and we have what appears to be a flashback to explain why the death took place at all. But as the conversation lengthens, it becomes apparent that not very much of it makes sense, nor is it supposed to.

The· events and the conversations in the house are disembodied manifestations of petty meanness, one-upmanship, insults, putting-others-down, bragging, trading lovers, ego trips, and whatever else occupies the rich and idle with time on their hands. At the beginning of the film, a burial service seems to be the order of the day; at the end, everyone is searching for the right wedding in a church, while (in a closing shot) an organ-player with an outrageous hair-do is solemnly pressing the keyboards. Throughout, Mendelssohn's music adds further ironic touches to the goings-on.

All in all, this is an intellectual tickler that should be seen by anyone who likes Bunuelian excursions into the surreal, the subconscious, and cultural pretense for the sake of the decadent bourgeoisie.
— *Holl.*

Parallels
(CANADIAN-COLOR)

Toronto, Sept. 9.

A Group 3 films production of a Creswin Films release. Produced by Jack Wynters. Directed by Mark Schoenberg. Features entire cast. Screenplay by Schoenberg and Jaron Summers; camera (color), Douglas Cole; art direction, Drew Borland; music, Don Archbold; editor, Marke Slipp; sound, Don Paches. Reviewed at Toronto Festival of Festivals, Festival Theatre, Toronto, Sept. 8, '80. Running Time: 92 MINS.
Father Robert Dane .... David Fox
Judith Del 'Assandro ...... Judith Mabey
Steven Del'Assandro ..... Gerard Lepage
Claire .... Kyra Harper
Philip Calder .... David Ferry
Bishop Teller .... Walter Kaasa
Father Clifford .... Howard Dallin
Marianne .... Jennifer Riach
Paul .... Stephen Walsh

"Parallels" is a first film from stage director Mark Schoenberg. It's a brooding drama about people confronting personal responsibility after years of avoidance. A diffi-

cult film dramatically and stylistically which may find its audience in alternate cinemas and on television.

David Fox plays a Catholic priest who is rector of a boys' college. He is confronting a growing dissatisfaction with the church aggravated by his liberal views on issues like abortion and discipline.

A new student played by Lepage is creating tension among the seniors. His rival is Ferry who holds a personal grudge created because Lepage steals Ferry's girlfriend.

The situation is complicated because Fox was involved with Lepage's mother before he joined the priesthood.

The convoluted plot is the ideal vehicle for lots of personal angst. It evolves into a predictable conclusion with the boys squaring off and Fox turning his collar around.

That Schoenberg has created a watchable, often moving film is a major accomplishment. Made on a budget of ($300,000) with mostly staged-based performers speaking often embarrassing dialog, "Parallels" is guided through its awkwardness by an assured hand.

The performances by and large are well observed with only a small degree of stiffness in characterization. The production values are well-beyond the film's humble means.

"Parallels" will probably have a difficult time finding conventional distribution. The theme and presentation have no ready market. However, Schoenberg's film talent is obvious and should find an outlet in the marketplace. —*Klad.*

Zielone Lata
(Salad-Days)
(POLISH-COLOR)

Gdansk, Sept. 10.

A Film Polski production. Silesia Film Unit, Warsaw; world rights, Film Polski, Warsaw. Features entire cast. Directed by Stanislaw Jedryka. Screenplay, Jerzy Przezdziecki, based on his own book; camera (color), Jacek Korcelli; sets, Boleslaw Kamykowski; music, Andrzej Korzynski; production manager, Jerzy Owoc. Reviewed at Gdansk Film Fest, September 10, '80. Running time: 102 MINS.
Cast: Tomasz Jarosinski (Wojtek), Jacek Bryniarski (Abramek), Agnieszka Konopczynska (Erna), Malgorzata Pritulak (Wojtek's Mother), Krzysztof Kiersznowski (Wojtek's Father), Anna Chodakowska (Abramek's Mother), Zygmunt Hobot (Abramek's Father), Irena Laskowska (Erna's Mother).

Children's pic with heavy overtones. Stanislaw Jedryka's "Salad-Days" will appeal more to adult auds and, in particular, those interested in war history. Set in Silesia, the focus is on a friendship among three 10-year-old children living in the town of Sasnowiec: a Polish boy, a Jewish lad, and a German girl. The period is 1939 and shortly thereafter, when the Nazi

troops separate the companions but not their friendship and loyalty to each other.

The Jewish boy's parents are killed and he is wounded and left for dead, but saved by the other two: the Polish boy sees his baby brother taken from the mother's arms to be raised by an Aryan family, after Polish Resistance members are found in his home and shot down in the street; and the German girl leaves with her parents to live in Germany far from Silesia, after braving family pressure to henceforth associate only with brown-shirted, German-bred companions.

"Salad-Days" is well played by the young thesps in the juvenile roles, but the caricatures of the grown-ups are too pat and events are too black-and-white for the pic to score as anything other than a children's film, albeit with cruelty and inhumanity as primary instructional realities. Still, the story is fascinating and memorable as an indictment on the horrors inflicted on every nationality and creed during the German Occupation of Poland. —*Holl.*

Fade To Black
(COLOR)

Films weren't this lad's best form of entertainment.

American Cinema release of an Irwin Yablans. Sylvio Tabet production. Stars Dennis Christopher. Written and directed by Vernon Zimmerman. Executive producers, Irwin Yablans, Sylvio Tabet. Producers, George Braunstein, Ron Hamady. Camera (color), Alex Phillips Jr.; asst. director, Ron Fury; film editor, Howard Kunin; set decorator, Loma Lee Brookbank; special effects, James Wayne; publicity, Solters & Roskin. Reviewed at Magno Park Avenue Screening Room, New York, Sept. 29, 1980. (MPAA Rating - R) Running time: 100 MINS.
Eric .... Dennis Christopher
Marilyn .... Linda Kerridge
Dr. Moriarity .... Tim Thomerson
Gary Bialy .... Morgan Paull
Bart .... Hennen Chambers
Doreen .... ·.... Marya Small
Aunt Stella .... Eve Brent Ashe
Rev. Shick .... Bob Drew
Anne .... Gwynne Gilford
Sam .... John Steadman
Richie .... Mickey Rourke
Talk show hostess .... Melinda Fee
Go-fer .... Jane K. Wiley
Joey Madona .... Peter Horton
Morty Berger .... Norman Burton
Gallagher ....·........... James Luisi
Dee Dee .... Anita Converse
Stacy .... Marcie Barkin
Counterman ..... Gilbert Lawrence Kahn

Vernon Zimmerman may have been inspired by Walker Percy's "The Moviegoer" when he wrote and directed "Fade To Black," but somewhere along the way, his treatise on a young man obsessed by film became a routine horror film, replete with violence, bloodletting and the usual shocker ingredients — plus a generous helping

of clippings from some old, classic films.

Eric (Dennis Christopher) is a shiftless, layabout young man who lives for one thing — the movies. He's a thorn in the side of his aunt (mother?), his employer and his fellow employes.

Romance comes into his life when he spots a young Australian actress (Linda Kerridge) who bears a striking resemblance to Marilyn Monroe. Why she is attracted to him is highly illogical as he's most unlikeable. Transported into his fantasy world of old pix at the least hint, Eric most strongly identifies with Cody Jarrett, the criminal played by James Cagney in "White Heat," but it doesn't take much to shift himself into Richard Widmark in "Kiss of Death," Bela Lugosi in "Dracula," William Boyd in any of the Hopalong Cassidy films or Boris Karloff in "The Mummy."

In these various guises he revenges himself on real and imagined insults, ranging from his murder of his aunt to various other enemies. It takes a lot of acceptance by the viewer to stay interested in another person's fixations and non-violent film buffs are likely to feel that their area of interest has been highly insulted by turning it into a violence gambit.

Beyond the erratic, over-imaginative script, the ineffectual acting of most of the cast, particularly Christopher, is the film's biggest obstacle. Most effective is Kerridge whose resemblance to Monroe is amazing. She has not only the facial resemblance but has evidently done a great job of studying the mannerisms.

There's plenty of violence once the central character gets into it so most of the interest must come from that type audience, fortunately for the distributor a big one at the moment. The ultimate reaction is, however, indifference and a great waste of really interesting film clips. All technical aspects of the film are firstrate. —*Robe.*

Manha Submersa
(Morning Mist)
(PORTUGUESE-COLOR)

Figueira da Foz, Sept. 17.

A Lauro Antonio production. Portuguese Institute of Cinema, Lisbon. Features cast. Written and directed by Lauro Antonio, based on a novel by Vergilio Ferreira. Camera (color), Elso Roque; editing, Antonio; music, Verdi, Gregorian Chant. Reviewed at Figueira da Foz Fest, Sept. 17, '80. Running time: 127 MINS.
Cast: Eunice Munoz (Dona Estefania), Vergilio Ferreira (the Rector), Caato e Castro (Antonio), Jacinto Ramos, Carlos Wallenstein, Joaquim Manuel Dias.

Unspooled initially at the Directors' Fortnight in Cannes on the last day of that sidebar last May, Lauro

Antonio's "Morning Mist" was marked by several critics as the best pic to emerge from Portugal since the April 1974 Revolution — for the simple reason that it offers an allegorical portrait of Salazar Regime, the dictator who ruled the country without a democratically elected opposition from 1945 to 1968.

But the film is more than that — as a lyrical, stylistic debut pic, it introduces a new talent on the European directorial scene who should be closely watched in the years to come.

"Morning Mist" is the story of an underprivileged youth in a small village chosen by the town's patroness to study at a seminary for the priesthood. That the boy doesn't have a vocation, or that he doesn't wish to leave his own mother (a widow with younger children to care and feed) to study at the seminary, means little to his patroness and the church authorities. This is simply the way things were done in Portugal for generations in a state-church society, particularly under Salazar — who lived, by the way, such a meagre puritan-existence in his office of benevolent dictator and maintained a close relationship to the Archbishop of Lisbon, a former school-companion.

Shortly after Ferreira wrote the book, based on his own childhood experiences in such a school (he left the seminary in his twenties), "Morning Mist" was censored and banned by the government.

Pic follows Antonio from his home to the seminary with a group of other 12-year-old youths, where the priests introduce them to the rituals of a monastic way of life from dawn to dusk. The boy makes friends during recreation periods with another disillusioned seminarian, and they both plan to leave the institution within a year. When the boy confides to his mother his loneliness and desire to return home, the letter is opened by an instructor with the result that he is sent to the rector to talk over the problem (the rector is played by writer Vergilio Ferreira himself). In the end, that means he will stay at the seminary and leave everything else up to God. Also, when he returns home to his village, the patroness takes him in under her roof and further indoctrinates him into the personal glories, as it were, of having a priest ordained from the village.

With the advent of puberty, Antonio takes notice of the housemaid's affairs with the masters of the house and, once, stumbles on a coupling scene in the doorway to the maid's room. Back in the seminary, his friend takes ill and dies; the burial on the seminary grounds is attended by priests and fellow-students. Antonio recalls his friend's prediction to "leave the seminary"

within the year, and this in turn motivates an intentional hand injury while home on the next occasion. His seminary days are over.

Quietly directed, acted with conviction by thesps and nonprofessionals, and lensed in a manner that relates to still-life compositions, "Morning Mist" etches several unforgettable images on the memory and leaves the viewer with the feeling of knowing what it was like to live in a closed-society atmosphere under Salazar in pre-revolutionary Portugal. Catch it on the fest circuit and at Portuguese Film Weeks. —Holl.

Eroina
(Heroin)
(ITALIAN-COLOR)

Venice, Aug. 30.

Produced by Benedetto Conversi and Patrizia Tonon for Samar Film productions. Stars Helmut Berger, Corinne Clery. Written and directed by Massimo Pirri. Camera (color). Sergio Martinelli; music, The Pretenders. Reviewed at the Venice Film Festival, Aug. 30, 1980. Running time: 90 MINS.
Marco .... Helmut Berger
Pina .... Corinne Clery
Tobia .... Marzio C. Honorato
Pusher .... Franco Citti

One of the most successful pix presented in the Panorama of Italian Cinema, Massimo Pirri's "Heroin" works its two stars, Helmut Berger and Corinne Clery, into a rigorously realistic story with a strong social thrust. Pirri, a young director on his fourth feature, knows how to use the camera and achieves a technical professionalism that leaves pic a clear field for commercial marketing. With the speedy pace of an Italian police film and the horrible fascination akin to watching a bloody car accident close up, pic has good b.o. prospects that could go beyond these shores.

Story follows three characters in search of their daily fix: Marco (Berger), a middle-class ex-teacher clearly in a state of decline, his girlfriend Pina (Clery) in hippie clothes and Tobia, a lighthearted street thief (Marzio Honorato). Marco takes Pina to a pusher's house and shoots up. She prostitutes herself in the next room; he gets a fix for a friend in the hospital. Pina informs the police of a pusher in exchange for a small quantity of dope. Script underlines the degradation of the ceaseless hunt for money to support their habit that doesn't stop at prostitution, stealing from each other, recruiting child addicts. Their lives consecrated to the ritual of flame, spoon and syringe, they seem lost creatures waiting only for the end which comes on schedule when they attempt to rob a big-time supplier.

Berger and Clery function surprisingly well, both playing down

their glamour and playing up the toughness of their personalities, but with fleeting moments of tenderness that make them touching. Living in an abandoned bus in a junk yard where they are prey to the violence of relatives and underworld toughs alike, the addicts emerge as more pitiable than despicable, victims of a killing habit impossible to break.

Pirri's choice of a realistic style without authorial "comments" unveils the hell of an addict's life much more effectively than an educational documentary or the usual simplifications of tv shows that show a trip to the clinic as the solution. Here the hospitals are only drug stores where those forced there for a "cure" can find a cheap fix sold in the waiting room.

The Italian Minister of Health has endorsed pic as a "valuable document" on the evils of heroin. Good technical work and a particularly strong rock music track by The Pretenders give story a boost.
—Yung.

A Culpa
(The Fault)
(PORTUGUESE-COLOR)

Figueira da Foz, Sept. 19.

An Antonio Victorino d'Almeida. Vindobona Film production. Lisbon. Features cast. Written and directed by Antonio Victorino d'Almeida. Camera (color). Hanus Polak; music, Antonio Victorino d'Almeida; editing, Daniela Klein. Victor Silva. Reviewed at Figueira da Foz Film Festival. Sept. 19. '80. Running time: 140 MINS.
Cast: Sinde Filipe, Mario Viegas, Estrela Novais, Lia Gama, Paula Guedes.

Antonio Victorino d'Almeida, whose position in the Ministry of Culture as a cultural attache at the Portuguese Embassy in Vienna and as a music composer with his own television program in Portugal makes him a national figure, ventured into filmmaking with "The Fault," a debut pic with plenty of narrative weaknesses but a flair nevertheless for comedy and pungent satire.

"The Fault" is a portrait of Salazar's Portugal. Helmer d'Almeida presents a family of means in the bourgeoisie in stereotyped caricatures: the father is a member of parliament, where voting is just a formality and functions are non-existent; the oldest son is a playboy, whose main interests are chasing the housemaid; the second son is a cripple, who was injured in one of the conflicts plaguing the colonies; the third son is a Marxist, who is constantly priming the pump with revolutionary slogans that have little or no meaning.

In addition, there's also jokes about religous and state realities under Salazar, who is reported to have been a puritan to the core con-

sumed by cares for the "destiny" of his country. Every Portuguese member of the audience understood the references to Fatima, where an apparition of the Virgin is said to have taken place, and to PIDE, the secret police always on the lookout for revolutionaries intent on overthrowing the dictatorship before April, 1974 (when the Revolution actually did take place). One of d'Almeida's standing jokes is a PIDE-inspector always checking his shoes to see if he stepped into dog-dung on the street.

Too long for general release, a cut version could make the rounds of fests and Portuguese Film Weeks as an example of first satirical polit-pic made in Portugal after the Revolution. —Holl.

Palac
(The Palace)
(POLISH-COLOR)

Gdansk, Sept. 14.

A Film Polski production. Perspektywa Film Unit, Warsaw; world rights. Film Polski, Warsaw. Features entire cast. Directed by Tadeusz Junak. Screenplay. Wieslawa Mysiliwskiego, based on a novel by W. Mysliwski; camera (color). Ryszard Lenczewski; music, Leszek Orlewicz; sets. Elzbieta Karwanska, Jerzy Michalak, Tadeusz Cielewica. Stefan Burzynski: production manager, Halina Kawecka. Reviewed at Gdansk Film Fest. Sept. 14. '80. Running time: 95 MINS.
Cast: Janusz Michalowski (Jakub), Danuta Kisiel, Wiktor Sadecki, Halina Gryglaszewska, Elzbieta Karkoszka, Teresa Budzisz-Kezyzanowska, Zdzislaw Kozien, Roman Stankiewicz, Stanisalw Frackowiak, Stefan Szmidt.

Prolific tv-helmer, Tadeusz Junak turns to the cinema for the first time with "The Palace." The debut pic, however, gets lost among symbols and time-projectsthat have meaning for Polish auds but otherwise seem to be slight-of-hand tricks to mystify, rather than, explain anything.

The settting is 1944 (according to the program), and a shepherd boy enters an abandoned palace he has seen from a distance since he was a boy. Once he enters the palace, strange things happen as though he were dreaming the events rather than living them; most of the people he encounters force him to make decisions and take action on life-and-death situations. A philosophical tract more than a narrative story, "The Palace" is only remarkable for its rich decorative settings. —Holl.

Przed Odlotem
(Break Away)
(POLISH-COLOR)

Gdansk, Sept. 11.

A Film Polski production, Silesia Film Unit. Warsaw; world rights. Film Polski, Warsaw. Features cast. Directed by Krzysztof Rogulski. Screenplay. Ryszard Sadaj; camera (color). Jacek Prosinski;

sets. Tadeusz Kosarewicz; music. Elzbieta Sikora; production manager. Michal Zablocki. Reviewed at Gdansk Film Fest. Sept. 11. '80. Running time: **96 MINS.**

Cast: Mariusz Benoit (Wiktor Siennicki), Grazyna Szapolowska (Ewa), Jerzy Kryszak (Marek). Igor Przegrodzki. Henryk Boukolowski. Jozef Fryzlewic. Ewa Dec. Mieczyslaw Milecki. Marek Siudym. Marcin Tronski. Stanislaw Michalski. Teresa Sawicka. Eugeniusz Kujawski. Alfred Freudenheim. Ewa Zietek.

Feature film debut by a promising director, Krzysztof Rogulski's "Break Away" is the story of a biologist working on an anti-cancer serum against all kind of odds from officials about him in the institute. The young doctor believes he is on the right track in his research, but the tests have not yet been tried on humans — until he himself comes down with cancer and takes the medicine himself, only to die in spite of the promising results in his own unusual case of the fatal disease.

Meanwhile. he fights it out with his colleagues and marries just before being struck down at the peak of success. There's too much in this melodrama to be taken seriously, although pace and narrative style of helmer hints that all he needs next time is a good script to have a winner. —*Holl.*

Smak Wody
(The Taste of Water)
(POLISH-COLOR)

Gdansk, Sept. 9.

A Film Polski production. Profil Film Unit. Warsaw: world rights. Film Polski. Warsaw. Features entire cast. Written and directed by Leszek Wosiewicz. Camera (color). Wladyslaw Nagy; sets. Andrzej Kowalczyk; music. Leszek Orlewicz; production manager. Jerzy Szebesta. Reviewed at Gdansk Film Fest. Sept. 9. '80. Running time: **74 MINS.**

Cast: Magda Teresa Wojcik (Maria Szara). Zdzislaw Kozien (Jozef Szary). Jadwiga Hanska (His Mother). Eugeniusz Kojawski (the Physician). Edwin Petrykant (Dance Leader). Emilia Krakowska (Maria's Sister). Halina Buyno-Loza (Housewife). Daria Trafankowska (Cleaning woman). Andrzej Kozak (Godek). Wiktor Grotowicz (Gynaecologist).

Debut pic unspooled in the Info Show of the Gdansk Fest of Polish FEature Films, Leszek Wosiewicz's "The Taste of Water" plods along on a single psychological note: a middle-aged wife. is expecting a baby that the husband neither expected to have nor wishes to complicate his settled family routine in the future.

The wife, in order to have the child, leaves home one night for the Baltic Coast to be alone on its barren, wintery shores to think over the problem and resolve the marital relationship. When she returns home, the husband is waiting and, presumably, the mid-life crisis is over. Although packed with sound psychology and well acted by

Magda Teresa Wojcik in the lead, the story is too thin to hold up beyond the stretch of a short feature. —*Holl.*

Wyrok Smierci
(Sentence of Death)
(POLISH-COLOR)

Gdansk. Sept. 8.

A Film Polski production. Silesia Film Unit. Warsaw: world rights. Film Polski. Warsaw. Features entire cast. Directed by Witold Orzechowski. Screenplay. Jerzego Gieraltowskiego. based on a story by Jerzy Gieraltowski: camera (color). Kazimierz Konrad: sets. Adam Kopczynski: production manager. Ryszard Jasionowski. Reviewed at Gdansk Film Fest. Sept. 8. '80. Running time: **105 MINS.**

Cast: Wojciech Wysocki (Smukly) Jerzy Bonczak (Nurek). Doris Kunstmann (Christine Mueller). Stanislaw Igar (von Dehl). Slawomira Lozinska (Zyta): Piotr Dejmek (Lt. Zyndram). Leon Niemczyk (Maj. Rawicz). Holger Mahlich (hans Frank). Erich Thiede (Heinrich Himmler). Klaus-Peter Thiele (Foerster).

A run of the mill spy thriller set in 1943 when the Polish Resistance was bumping off SS-officers and collaborators in Lublin and Zamosc. "Sentence of Death" is a curiosity in that a West German actress (Doris Kunstmann) plays an "officer's lady" who falls in love with a Polish gunman in the Underground while he's setting up her boyfriend for his sentence of death. In the end. our hero loses out to a collaborator living in the apartment next door. Pic was unspooled in the Info Show of Gdansk Fest. — *Holl.*

Cerromaior
(PORTUGUESE-COLOR)

Figueira da Foz, Sept. 19.

A Prole Films production. Lisbon. Features cast. Written and directed by Luis Filipe Rocha, based on a novel by Manuel da Fonseca. Camera (color). Joao Abel Aboim: music. Constanca Capdeville: editing. Jose Nascimento. Reviewed at Figueira da Foz Film Fest. Sept. 19. '80. Running time: **90 MINS.**

Cast: Carlos Paulo. Santos Manuel. Clara Joana. Rui Fortado. Titus Faria. Elsa Wallenkamp.

The Grand Prix winner at the Figueira da Foz fest. Luis Filipe Rocha's "Cerromaior" deserved its prize in view of Lauro Antonio's competing "Morning Mist" having already won recognition at the Directors' Fortnight in Cannes last May. "Cerromaior" cost a meagre $160,000 to shoot on 16m, which was then blown up to 35m for export to fests and home consumption.

Set in the period of the Spanish Civil War and adapted from a novel by Manuel da Fonseca, the title refers to a village in the south of Portugal where a rich landowner subjugates peasants to his will. The entire film deals with the theme of rebellion, but not just in open and violent conflict (which, in fact, oc-

curs only once on the screen). The question here is how a people "rebel" via drunkeness. fear and madness. and self-resignation to the point of suicide. On the surface, this is a kind of Brazilian "Cine Novo" Western: beneath the surface, the psychological tensions point to the dawn of a new day in the not too distant future.

The novel belongs to the Portuguese "neorealist movement" after World War Two. Although generally considered to be poor literature. Manuel da Fonseca's "Cerromaior" had a political bent that mirrored the times under the Salazar dictatorship. The key moment in both the film and the book is the news of the bombing of Guernica reaching the Alentejo villagers over the radio — matched with another scene that shows the gentry more interested in the news about a soccer match in Lisbon, also being broadcast.

The film is largely without a narrative thread. Real-life farmers in the area play scenes that describe the on-going conflicts between the exploiters (the bourgeoisie) and the exploited (the landless peasants). It begins with the adolescent son of a landowner being brought back by force to the home he has tried to run away from: this, in turn. is matched with peasants herded down a road by policeguards because they are without work and are thus considered dangerous vagrants. The youth, Adrian, the symbol of both the landowners and the exploited, doesn't fit in anywhere on either side, and rage mounts inside him even when he can't prove his sexual prowess to the housemaid or the village "lady" who courts his attention openly. Meanwhile, a small uprising takes place when a man is beaten by the oppressor, until a peasant comes to the victim's aid with a club in his hand. Times will change, the film says, but land reform may never arrive. Sharply lensed with an eye for compositions and dynamic images that say everything without the assistance of dialogue, the landscape in "Cerromaior". sets the style and mood of the pic — the barren, sun-scorched plains remind the viewer of the plight of the Oakies in "Grapes of Wrath." Rocha, whose earlier debut pic, "The Escape" (1976), was set in a prison and dealt with political prisoners, is now the leading sociopolitical voice in Portuguese cinema. —*Holl.*

Oejeblikket
(The Moment)
(DANISH-COLOR)

Copenhagen, Oct. 2.

A Panorama (Just Betzer) production and release. Features entire cast. Written and directed by Astrid Henning-Jensen. Camera (Eastmancolor) Lasse Bjoerne:

production design. Palle Arestrup: editors. Grete Moeldrup. Astrid Henning-Jensen: music. "Greensleeves" and Lars Henning Jensen. Reviewed at Palads. Copenhagen. Oct. 2. 1980. Running time: **90 MINS.**

Line . . . . Ann-Mari Max Hansen
Leif . . . . Soeren Spanning
Child Hoene . . . . Kathrine Helmuth
Child Torben . . . . Torbjorn Rafn
Grandmother . . . . Lisbeth Movin
Anne . . . . Helle Merete Soerensen

Veteran director Astrid Henning-Jensen scored beautifully at home and in several foreign territories with "Winterborn." The hospital milieu inspired her mightily and so did Dea Trier's novel on which film was based.

That inspiration has, however. turned deadly now that Henning-Jensen has tackled the subject of how to live with a terminal cancer. The young nuclear family in "The Moment" makes it all look suspiciously loke a tv commercial.

Henning-Jensen has been so nobly serious-minded about the whole project that solid research and tact succeed in killing off any vestige of natural drama within the subject matter.

The young family is at first seen near a commonplace breakup, but the moment the first small sign of a malignancy in the woman's breast is recorded, the Bravery of Ordinary People (everything is spelled out with capital letters in this film) takes over, leading straight to the moment where the woman dies and is reincarnated as a flower.

Of course, the young couple are handsome people. Their two small children are something out of a Shirley Temple nightmare. Everybody speaks his lines as if being tested for the Royal stage. True drama is manifested only in the occasional breaking of a mirror or a vase.

Ann-Mari Max Hansen in the lead remains a Danish answer to Romy Schneider, but still without her promises anywhere near fulfilled. Lasse Bjoerne's cinematography is bathed in beautiful sunshine and simmering light. The classical-sounding musical score is used with such discretion that it unwittingly calls too much attention to itself.

The Moment's" pretty production values and its reverential treatment of a serious subject might rate this feature exposure at some minor festivals. Commercially, it would seem a dud even on home territory. —*Kell.*

Ukryty W Sloncu
(Hidden in the Sunlight)
(POLISH-COLOR)

Gdansk, Sept. 9.

A Film Polski production. Iluzion Film Unit. Warsaw: world rights. Film Polski. Warsaw. Features entire cast. Directed by Jerzy Trojan. Screenplay. Ireneusz Iredynski. based on his own book: camera (color). Wieslaw Zdort; music, Zbigniew Namyslawski; sets, Tadeusz Kusarewicz, Barbara Komosinska; production manager, Zbigniew Tolioczko. Reviewed at Gdansk Film Fest, Sept. 8, '80. Running time: 91 MINS.

Cast: Jan Englert (Janek), Gabriela Kownacka (Joanna), Ewa Dalkowska (Maria), Eugen-iusz Priwiezencew (Robert), Teresa Sawicka (Reviewer), Dorota Pomykala (Beata), Kazimierz Kaczor (Examing Officer), Mieczyslaw Voit (Professor).

Debut pic by a thesp turned helmer, Jerzy Trojan's "Hidden in the Sunlight" takes place on a busy street corner in the course of a day's waiting for a date to show up. When the girl doesn't come, the young artist on the corner gets restless and begins to imagine all kind of things that could have happened to the girl he loves. The audience discovers in the flashbacks that he is responsible for several messy incidents in the past — among them palming his girl off on others for favors — but it's in his imagination as to what could happen to the girl if and when she shows up (in one sequence she gets hit by a car while crossing the street in a hurry to reach him) that revelations of character are revealed and ponderously meditated on by the director. The experimental aspects falter midway in this tiring feature. —*Holl.*

Velhos Sao Os Trapos
(Only Their Clothes Are Old)
(PORTUGUESE-COLOR)

Lisbon, Sept. 22.
A Monique Rutler, Filmforum production, Lisbon. Features entire cast. Written and directed by Monique Rutler. Camera (color) Mario de Carvalho. Only credits available. Reviewed at Portugese Film Institute, Lisbon, Sept. 22, '80. Running time: 83 MINS.

Cast: Joao Guedes, Luis Santos, Luisa Neto.

Debut pic by femme helmer Monique Rutler, "Only Their Clothes Are Old" is a fiction documentary about old people living from hand-to-mouth in the old section of Lisbon. Chief figure is an old rag-picker who sells enough paper to buy the necessities of life and a bottle of booze on the side. One day, he is struck down by a car while crossing the street, and taken to a hospital. In a surrealistic scene, we seem him hanging himself in the inhuman environs of the clinic, apparently because he has been "condemned" to old age.

Another thread of the story is about an aged pair who meet each other in the park, and thereafter follows a romance that shows the pair to be young at heart. In the end, they are lovers in the courtly sense of the word.

Rutler intersperses interviews with old people in a documentary manner to offer contrast with the two fiction stories. This works well

in the beginning, but pic doesn't hold up over the long run when her statement on life and the aged becomes repetitious. Pic could find a slot at women's fests. —*Holl.*

Arrebato
(Rapture)
(SPANISH-COLOR)

San Sebastian, Sept. 18.
Nicolas Astiarraga P.C. production. Written and directed by Ivan Zulueta. Features entire cast. Camera (Eastmancolor). Angel Luis Fernandez; editor, Jose Luis Pelaez, sets, Ivan Zulueta, Carlos Astiarraga, Eduardo Eznarriaga; music, Ivan Zulueta. Reviewed at Cine Miramar, San Sebastian, Sept. 18, 1980. Running time: 115 MINS.
Jose Sirgado . . . . Eusebio Poncela
Ana . . . . Cecilia Roth
Pedro . . . . Will More
Marta . . . . Marta Fernandez-Muro

The less said about this self-indulgent, amateurish and masturbatory film the better. Those with the patience and endurance to sit through its excruciating nigh-two-hour run are served up an unintelligible story about a demented young Super-8 filmmaker living in the country, another equally unsuccessful "auteur" who becomes intrigued by the former, and a miscellany of girls.

Thesps spend most of pic sucking cocaine up their noses, making passes at each other and watching footage by the moronic Super-8 home-cinema director who slouches about in a greatcoat, dances by himself in the fields and is obsessed by his Canon camera. Item ran for two weeks in a small location in Madrid before it was yanked. —*Besa.*

L'Ebreo Fascista
(The Fascist Jew)
(ITALIAN-COLOR)

Venice, Sept. 2.
A Gaumont release produced by Enzo Boetani and Giuseppe Collura for Dionysio Cinematografica productions. Stars Ray Lovelock, Martine Brochard, Silvia Dionisio. Directed by Franco Mole. Screenplay by Piero Regnoli and Luigi Preti, based on Preti's book "A Jew During Fascism." Camera (color), Fausto Zuccoli; art direction, Vera Cozzolino; editing, Luigi Russo; music, Aldo Salvi. Reviewed at Venice Film Festival, Sept. 2, 1980. Running time: 96 MINS.
Oberdan Rossi . . . . Ray Lovelock
Elena Miotti . . . . Marine Brochard
Rosa Calzolari . . . . Silvia Dionisio
Morselli-Cyclone . . . . . . Adalberto Rosseti
Marino . . . . Jose Quaglio

A dignified, well-made and slightly stuffy entry in Venice's Italo film section, "The Fascist Jew" marks celluloid helming debut of Franco Mole — theatre writer, director and actor. This quality drama about race discrimination in the upper classes in late 30's Italy covers much the same ground as "Garden of the Finzi-Continis." Adapted from a novel by

co-scripter Luigi Preti, pic remains bound by literary elements and theatrical staging that make it seem a bit cold and formal. Lacks a key to get inside characters and story and bring them alive. Production values should get pic off to a good start on local markets but might not stir offshore bid.

Handsome blank-faced son of a Jewish father and non-Jewish mother, Oberdan Rossi (Ray Lovelock) marries Rosa (Silvia Dionisio), scion of another wealthy family, in 1935. He enthusiastically enrolls in Mussolini's Ethiopian campaign but returns depressed by the atrocities committed by his co-nationals. Oberdan's troubled memories of this period appear in dazzling stark images of the desert, shock-effect flashbacks in the midst of his silver spoon life "back home."

When Rosa refuses to follow him to Bologna where he finds work as a journalist, Oberdan goes alone, making friends with Morselli, another journalist, and falling in love with Elena, a secretary. As race laws tighten, Oberdan is forced to leave the paper. Morselli and Elena are determined to resist encroaching Fascism but Oberdan, unable to find a publisher for his novel, kills himself.

Pic boasts good period atmosphere — particularly in late Bologna sequences, and distinct full-bodied characters who compensate for lackluster acting in the main roles. With hero looking and feeling more like a poker-faced Fascist than a literate Jewish writer, problems arise with audience identification that throw film off-balance. Oberdan theoretically gets more sympathetic in Bologna but there Adalberto Rosseti as the high-spirited prankster, Morselli, steals the show with his manic personality. Suicide finale fails to register emotionally.

Pic's saving grace is its historical and geographical sweep that anchors story firmly in its period and maintains interest. —*Yung.*

Amor Der Perdicao
(Love Of Perdition)
(PORTUGUESE-COLOR)

Figueira da Foz, Sept. 19.
A Portuguese Film Institute production, Lisbon. Features entire cast. Written and directed by Manoel de Oliveira, adapted from the novel with the same title by Camilo Castelo Branco. Camera (color), Manuel Costa e Silva; music, Joao Paes, Handel. Reviewed at Figueira da Foz Film Festival, Sept. 19, '80 Running time: 260 MINS.
Cast: Cristina Hauser (Teresa Albuquerque), Antonio Sequeira Lopes (Simao Botelho), Elsa Wallenkamp (Mariana), Antonio J. Costa, Henrique Viana, Maria Dulce.

Manoel de Oliveira, Portugal's best known director, was recently honored with a retro at the Cinema-

theque Francaise. His "Love of Perdition" (1978) was unspooled at the Forum of the Berlin Film Fest last February, and that was followed by an Oliveira colloquium at the Figueira da Foz fest in Portugal this September. He is truly an undiscovered talent, whose films have only just surfaced on the international scene.

"Love of Perdition," financed by the Portuguese Film Institute, is Oliveira's fifth feature. Nearly all his films are based in his native city of Oporto (or Porto), and this one is no different: the author of the famous novel on which the film is based, Camilo Castelo Branco (1825-1895), was a native of this seaport city. Oliveira has lensed Castelo Branco's famous classic in a lovingly faithful four-hour version.

"Love of Perdition" (written in 1862) is the story of an unhappy love affair between the adolescent children of two aristocratic families antagonistically disposed toward one another. When the hand of the girl, Teresa, is offered to her cousin instead of her lover, Simao, the latter kills his rival and is sentenced to a ten-year exile. Both youths die shortly thereafter — Teresa in a convent and Simao on a deportation ship as it leaves Oporto. The story has other intricate subplots, but it's the Romeo-and-Juliet frame that lifts it to the heights of romantic tragedy.

As a novel, "Love of Perdition" tells much about Portuguese society in the middle of the last century. The autobiographical traits are also of interest: author Castelo Branco, already famous as a bohemian journalist and serial writer, was deeply hurt when his favorite mistress left him to marry a rich merchant; he entered a seminary for a time to study for the priesthood, then persuaded his true love to\leave her husband and join him in Lisbon, where they later married. His novel about the affair was a scandal and commercial success.

Slow moving but beautifully lensed, "Love of Perdition" deserves retro programming and more exposure at fests and Portuguese Film Weeks. —*Holl.*

Rycerz
(The Knight)
(POLISH-COLOR)

Gdansk, Sept. 12.
A Film Polski production, Profil Film Unit, Warsaw; world rights, Film Polski, Warsaw. Features entire cast. Written and directed by Lech J. Majewski. Camera (color), Czeslaw Swirta; sets, Jerzy Szeski; music, Zdzislaw Szostak; production manager, Jerzy Nitecki. Reviewed at Gdansk Film Fest, Sept. 12, '80. Running time: 85 MINS.
Cast: Piotr Skarga (the Knight), Daniel Olbrychski (Hierofant), Katarzyna Ko-

zak. (the Princess), Czeclaw Meissner (the Monk), Andrzej Hudziak (the Youngest Monk), Stanislaw Holly (the old Monk), Irena Jun (the Widow).

Debut helmer, Lech J. Majewski favors a static camera style in this tale of medieval quest for a golden harp titled (perhaps metaphorically) "The Knight."

The attractive side of the project is the relation to medieval paintings and other works of art stemming from the Middle Ages and picture-book romances, inclusive of knightly trappings and scenic backdrops across dunes, through forests, and the like. The tiring aspect, however, is a poetic, rather than prose, story that leave breathing room only for images over the long stretch. Recommended for art lovers and Age of Romanticism buffs. —Holl.

Danmark er lukket
(Denmark Closed Down)
(DANISH-COLOR)

Copenhagen, Oct. 3.
A Focus Film production. A/S Nordisk Film release. Based on Benny Andersen's stage play "Orfeus In The Underground." Script by Andersen and Dan Tschernia. Directed by Tschernia. Features entire cast. Camera (Eastmancolor), Claus Loff; production managers, Erik Overbye, Erik Nissen; editor, Anker; music and lyrics, Benny Andersen. Reviewed at Palads, Copenhagen, Oct. 3, 1980. Running time: 85 MINS.
Orfeus Jensen . . . . Christoffer Bro
Eurydice Jensen . . . . Anne Linnet
Apple . . . . Claus Ryskjaer
Tomato . . . . Paul Hagen
Swee'Pea . . . . Jess Ingerslev
Radio announcer . . . . Ove Sprogoe
The Brain . . . . Olaf Ussing
Alberto . . . . Peter Steen

Having finished a novel in deep seclusion in Sweden, Orfeus Jensen finds it impossible to return to his native Denmark. The EEC has decided, he is told (we don't see it), to close down the Kingdom, exile all its citizens and turn the entire area over to an atomic warfare proving ground. The Danish language is now illegal.

In Dan Tschernia's first feature, "Denmark Closed Down," Orfeus now proceeds through the remaining EEC countries in search of his wife Eurydice. He joins the underground Danish Liberation Forces. When he does find Eurydice, a Women's Lib consciousness has turned her away from him.

Film is set up as a political satire, but also as a comedy with tragic undertones. Shot entirely on Hamburg, Paris and Rome locations, it emerges as a jerkily put together series of feeble sketches. There is no cinematic fluency anywhere and most actors are made to ham it up mightily.

Only Christoffer Bro in the Orfeus role manages to appear slightly human, but this may be against

the director's intentions judging from the amateurish performances of the rest of an otherwise highly professional cast.

The gist of the satire is the old saw that the Common Market kills off all individuality of its member nations. The very location shooting of "Denmark Closed Down" dispute any such claim. Paris and Rome are seen in full possession of everything that remains Parisian and Roman from architecture to the varieties of foods.

Anti-EEC diehards will want to laugh at Benny Andersen's and Dan Tschernia's satire, but even they will find it hard to find the jokes within the stiff workings of a stagy scenario with too many words and too little action. —Kell.

Kilas, O Mau Da Fita
(The Killers)
(PORTUGUESE-COLOR)

Lisbon, Sept. 22.
A Filmforum production, Lisbon. Features entire cast. Directed by José Fonseca e Costa. Screenplay, Jose Fonseca e Costa, Sergio Godinho, Tabajara Ruas; camera (color), Antonio H. Escudeiro, Mario Barrosa; music, Sergio Godinho. Reviewed at Portuguese Film Institute, Lisbon, Sept. 22, '80. Running time: 125 MINS.
Cast: Mario Viegas, Lia Gama, Luis Lello, Milu, Paula Guedes, Francisco Pestana, Adelaide Ferreira.

"Kilas," the title for Jose Fonseca e Costa's detective pic, is slang for "Killers" — the reference is to the cine noir style of Yank thrillers and the hardboiled detective stories admired by readers in Portugal and on the European Continent in general. The small-time con-man and pimp in the film is called "Kilas," and his moll known as "Pepsi Rita," keeps him in style by working the nite-spots as torch-singer and lady-for-a-night pickups.

Gradually, however, the film turns from parodying the American thriller genre to a try at the real thing, as our hero gets deeper into an espionage ring than he expected. He is beaten to a pulp by a bigger gang in the end. Meanwhile, sex and impotence has supplied leers and laughs for the gentry in the balcony. —Holl.

Razza Selvaggia
(Savage Breed)
(ITALIAN-COLOR)

Venice, Sept. 2.
A Titanus film, produced by Luigi Borghese for Cinematografica Alex productions. Stars Saverio Marconi, Stefano Madia. Directed by Pasquale Squitieri. Screenplay, Squitieri, De Concini; camera (color), Giulio Albonico; art direction, Marco Canevari; editing, Mauro Bonanni; music, Tullio De Piscopo. Reviewed at Venice Film Festival, Sept. 2, 1980. Running time: 95 MINS.

Mario . . . . Saverio Marconi
Umberto . . . . Stefano Madia

A fast-moving, rather conventional actioner with a social theme: the emigration of Southerners to the North's industrial cities and their loss of cultural identity. Helmer Pasquale Squitieri's medium budget pic looked expensive amid other entries at Venice's fest, and in fact shows astute use of a commercial genre, the police film, that could get its message across to a broad national audience and open up distrib channels offshore.

Mario (Saverio Marconi), a young southerner working in a factory on the outskirts of Turin, feels like a fish out of water in the north, where he lives with his sister and niece. His bond of friendship for Umberto (Stefano Madia), who has become a rich nightclub owner, is the only traditional value that has not crumbled in the poverty and ugliness of ghetto life. But after a weekend in the city he is disillusioned to learn that Umberto is involved in the underworld and a drug addict, his old girlfriend Anna is Umberto's kept woman and his sister and niece prostitutes themselves. Umberto dies under the eyes of indifferent policemen after a knife fight while Anna and Mario return to the south.

With flashing police headlights, a constantly moving camera and drum roll of the violent urban ghetto on the soundtrack, "Savage Breed" has the virtues and faults of the popular Mafia films. Squitieri, a native Neapolitan who has made numerous actioners on the Mafia and other southern themes, knows how to get and hold interest in his story, but finally pic seems too slick to probe the problem deeply. Finally with sun coming up over Naples as train pulls in rings awfully pat.

Marconi, familiar to Yank audiences from "Padre Padrone," again makes good use of his serious child's face in playing another southerner struggling (here unsuccessfully) to rise socially by exchanging his native dialect for Italian. For Squitieri it is the wrong path, however. Here individual's choice to return to his roots is a rejection of northern "progress" and debasement of values.

Pic occasionally rises to visual eloquence. One classic shot shows Mario's arrival in the cold gray city as he stands under its monuments to heroic generals and soldiers, shot from below to contrast their power with Mario's frail human dimensions. —Yung.

Semmelweis
(ITALIAN-SWISS-COLOR)

Venice, Sept. 2.
A RAI-Television Channel 1 (Italy) and RTSI-Television (Switzerland) film, produced by Gaspare Palumbo and Giuseppe Tortorella for Milano Cinema productions. Stars Giulio Brogi, Alain Cuny. Directed by Gianfranco Bettetini. Screenplay, Bettentini and Aldo Grasso; camera (color), Lamberto Caimi; art direction, Paolo Bregni; editing, Gaspare Palumbo and Jolanda Adamo; music, Gino Negri. Reviewed at Venice Film Festival, Sept. 2, 1980. Running time: 100 MINS.
Semmelweis . . . . Giulio Brogi
Skoda . . . . Alain Cuny
Hebra . . . . Pier Paolo Capponi
Scanzoni . . . . Tino Carraro
Markusovsky . . . . Umberto Ceriani

Inspired by a book by Celine and helmed by film theorist Gianfranco Bettetini, this Italo-Swiss TV coproduction is a pleasant if routine bio of the life of Ignazio Filippo Semmelweis, a Hungarian doctor who worked on the theory that microscopic germs are the source of illness before Pasteur. "Semmelweis" deviates from classic Hollywood elegies to great scientists mainly in being artificially complicated with flashbacks and fond of repeating shots, ideas, and bits of plot. Result is a pic that seems padded to twice its natural length.

Film opens with a group of elderly doctors discussing death of colleague Semmelweis (Giulio Brogi) from an infection contracted when he cut himself dissecting a cadaver, thus dramatically proving his own theory of the transmission of germs. The villains of the story are up in the gallery, rejecting scientifically proven Truth. Through post-mortem comments by Alain Cuny as Dr. Skoda and a long series of flashbacks, we learn that the brilliant young Hungarian discovered the cause of puerperal fever in pregnant women through his analytic powers and use of new statistical methods. Solution to the scientific mystery (which we are given at the beginning of pic) is that the hospital's medical students don't wash their hands between dissection class and gynecological exams.

Coupling this simple story with a flashback structure, pic only succeeds in disorienting viewer in deciding where Semmelweis is and what stage his research has reached. Suspense is half-heartedly built into the query: When will Semmelweis find the cure?

Film's inherent interest is based on an unusual main character. Brogi succeeds in conveying the obsessions and moral fibre of the ill-mannered doctor. Cuny is perfectly cast as his teacher-turned-defender. But without narrative development and climaxes, pic constantly returns to the category of educational TV programs and classroom aids.

Some good photography

brightens conventional period sets and costumes . An unforgettable crane shot over a courtyard with a line of medical students intersecting a file of nurses is squeezed dry in flashback repeats. —*Yung.*

Intoarcerea Lui Voda Lupusneanu
(The Return of the Banished)
(RUMANIAN-COLOR)

San Sebastian, Sept. 16.
Maison de Films Trois production. Written and directed by Malvina Ursianu. Features entire cast. Camera (color) Alexandru Intorsureanu, Gheorghe Fischer, editor, Margareta Anescu; music, Anatol Vieru. Reviewed at Cine Victoria Eugenia, San Sebastian. Sept. 16. 1980. Running time: **148 MINS.**
Cast: Georges Motoi, Silvia Popovici, Valeriu Paraschiv, Cornel Coman.

Rumanian epic drama set in the 16th century anent exile, return to power and bloody rule in Moldavia of Alexandru Lapusneau, last of the Musatini princes. Extremely slow pacing, confusing flashbacks, static lensing and interminably long dialogs make this overlong setpiece hard to digest, despite some good thesping.

Story traces life and ruthless rule of a Moldavian king, but never really gets into any of the characters. Nor does femme helmer Malvina Ursianu succeed in building even a minimum of dramatic tension. Gabby, stilted dialogs are sometimes broken when the king decides to decapitate one of his faithless followers, or has the boyars slaughtered at a feast. But it's all handled like a schoolboy unemphatically reading a history book out loud. Outlook zilch. —*Besa.*

Last Hurrah For Chivalry
(HONG KONG-COLOR)

Bangkok, Sept. 15.
A Raymond Chow presentation of a Golden Harvest production and release. Executive producer, Louis Sit. Features entire cast. Written and directed by John Y.S. Woo. Camera (color), Chang Yao Chua; fight sequences arranged by Feng Ke An; production manager, Catherine Cheung. Reviewed at Siam theatre, Bangkok. Sept. 15. '80. Running time: **100 MINS.**
Cast Wei Pai, Liu Sung Chen, Wei Chiu Hua, Liu Chiang.

Kung fu filmmakers in Hong Kong and Taiwan now have to watch out for John Y.S. Woo, who seems to be doing the most exciting work. in the Chinese martial arts and swordplay genre. "Last Hurrah For Chivalry" makes no pretensions about being anything else but a succession of brilliantly arranged fight sequences.

The pleasure of watching Woo's work largely comes from the way he uses familiar material to evolve a personal style. He is a much better director than writer, and wastes no time on complicated plotting. It seems that he works best with characters who are dim-witted and caricaturish. The minute they start to fight, however, these same insipid people are then transformed into valiant screen idols.

Imperfect heroes, comical and often lonely, are popularly accepted in kung fu comedies. Champion fighters are usually shown as heavy drinkers. No different is Liu Sung Chen in this pic; always exacting vengeance in a drunken state. There's also a drowsy swordsman, to cite another example, who's liable to fall asleep during a fight. Combining lethal skill with comic antics is much more acceptable to viewers rather than pure action or pure comedy.

Comedy relief and romance are fine, but sometimes a casually flippant line can throw everything out of whack. For instance, when Liu Sung Chen says in the penultimate fight scene, "I'm not going to die now, the movie isn't finished yet," the audience laughs, but at the same time such a remark decreases one's enjoyment of the realistic and dazzling fights.

In Bangkok, "Last Hurrah" further capitalizes on the enormous popularity of Chinese tv serials. Woo's work is far superior, of course, but his mastery of the genre must encompass original storytelling before mass audiences can notice the difference between his work and other mass-produced kung fu pix. —*Cano.*

Wsciekly
(Mad Dog)
(POLISH-COLOR)

Gdansk, Sept. 9.
A Film Polski producton. Iluzion Film Unit, Warsaw; world rights. Film Polski, Warsaw. Features entire cast. Written and directed by Roman Zaluski, based on motifs in a story by Jerzy Romuald Milicz. Camera (color), Janusz Pawlowski; sets, Jerzy Sniezawski; music, Jerzy Matula; production manager, Tadeusz Urbanowicz. Reviewed at Gdansk Film Fest. Sept. 9, '80. Running time: **102 MINS.**
Cast: Bronislaw Cieslak (Capt. Zawada), Barbara Brylska (Golewiczowa), Liliana Glabczynska (Ewa), Halina Gryglaszewska (Prynikowa), Ewa Kania (Anna Piotrowska), Tadeusz Borowski (Institute Director), Zbigniew Buczkowski (Piotrowski), Andrzej Chrzanowski (Golewicz).

Detective thriller about a killer loose in the crowds, "Mad Dog" follows a sniper on his rounds looking for victims, while a police inspector, with few clues at hand, has to figure out the motif for the killings as well as who the psychopath is and where he might strike next. It's established midway through the film that the mentally deranged sniper can't stand seeing people happy together in public places.

His weapon is a rifle that can be dismantled and stuffed in a handbag, and the "mad dog" has an itch to return for burial services after commiting the crime. The case is solved in the end according to the usual tv-formula for this genre. Helmer Roman Zaluski is the Polish specialist for television serials and entertainment pix.
— *Holl.*

It's My Turn
(COLOR)

Could turn a nifty profit.

Hollywood, Oct. 16.
Columbia Pictures release of a Rastar-Martin Elfand production. Produced by Martin Elfand. Directed by Claudia Weill. Stars Jill Clayburgh. Michael Douglas. Exec producer, Jay Presson Allen. Screenplay. Eleanor Bergstein; camera (Metrocolor), Bill Butler: editors, Byron (Buzz) Brandt, Marjorie Fowler. James Coblenz; production design. Jack Delovia; music. Patrick Williams; sound. Pat Somerset, Jeff Bushelman; costumes. Ruth Myers; assistant director. David McGiffert. Reviewed at the Samuel Goldwyn Theatre. Beverly Hills. Oct. 16. 1980. (MPAA Rating: R.) Running time: **91 MINS.**

Kate Gunzinger	Jill Clayburgh
Ben Lewin	Michael Douglas
Homer	Charles Grodin
Emma	Beverly Garland
Jacob	Steven Hill
Maryanne	Teresa Baxter
Rita	Joan Copeland
Hunter	John Gabriel
Jerome	Charles Kimbrough
Flicker	Roger Robinson
Maisie	Jennifer Salt
Cooperman	Daniel Stern

A wonderfully witty yet realistic look at love relationships, "It's My Turn" is a cut above most of the romantic comedies coming down the studio pike as of late. Buoyed by an original, well-crafted script from Eleanor Bergstein and inspired performances by topliners Jill Clayburgh, Michael Douglas and Charles Grodin, the Columbia release of a Rastar-Martin Elfand production should have no trouble achieving a nice return on its money. In fact, word-of-mouth might very well keep it in theatres until the onslaught of Christmas product.

In her second feature, director Claudia Weill has managed to zero in on both the funny and tragic sides of falling in love while keeping the action moving and the story intact. If there is a tendency for the editing to be a bit choppy and the camera shots a tinge forced or unimaginative, Weill is a pro with actors. Clayburgh, Douglas and Grodin are each allowed freedom to project essentially interesting, humane, likable people placed at various sides of the romantic triangle. That, in itself, is a rarity nowadays.

Clayburgh limns an offbeat but intellectually over-achieving mathematics professor residing with perpetually humorous building developer Grodin in Chicago. Although she claims she is happy that the pairing provides her with lots of "space," she quickly finds herself in the arms of Douglas during a trip to New York.

Douglas is an ex-baseball player whose mother is marrying Clayburgh's father. He is immediately entranced and pursues the tentative Clayburgh, but begins to retreat as she slowly begins to take more positive steps to further their relationship.

Probably the most endearing aspect here is the way action so easily moves from screwball to intellectual humour and then on to numerous emotionally touching moments. Clayburgh has added some irresistible nuances to Eleanor Bergstein's well-rounded character and the performance ranks with much of the superior work she has done in the last few years. Douglas underplays it just enough as an emotionally confused but eternally ''good guy'' and Grodin is amusing but not ridiculous as the live-in mate. Beverly Garland and Steven Hill provide a healthy dose of old-fashioned romance as the middle-aged newlyweds.

Bill Butler's camera features some nice shots of New York and Ruth Myers has fashioned some particularly eye-catching costumes, especially for Clayburgh. Music by Patrick Williams is appropriate but much-ballyhooed theme song sung by Diana Ross leaves something to be desired.

There might be some complaints about the hopeful but abrupt ending to a film whose characters are as well-developed as this one. But Weill seems to have cut the story off at a point that is both artistically and commercially palatable. —Berg.

Motel Hell
(COLOR)

Was This Trip Necessary?

Hollywood, Oct. 21.
United Artists release of a Camp Hill production. Executive producer. Herb Jaffe. Features entire cast. Produced and written by Steven-Charles Jaffe and Robert Jaffe. Directed by Kevin Connor. Camera (color). Thomas Del Ruth; editor. Bernard Gribble; music. Lance Rubin; art director. Joseph M. Altadonna; first assistant director. Jack Barry; special effects. Adams R. Calvert. Reviewed at Samuel Goldwyn Theatre. Beverly Hills. Calif.. Oct. 17. '80 (MPAA Rating-R). Running time: 106 MINS.
Vincent Smith . . . . Rory Calhoun
Bruce Smith . . . . Paul Linke
Ida Smith . . . . Nancy Parsons
Terry . . . . Nina Axelrod
Reverend Billy . . . . Wolfman Jack
Edith Olson . . . . Elaine Joyce
Guy Robaire . . . . Dick Curtis
Debbie . . . . Monique St. Pierre
Suzi . . . . Rosanne Katon
Bob Anderson . . . . E. Hampton Beagle
Ivan . . . . Michael Melvin

If ''Motel Hell'' were as funny throughout as it is in the final ten minutes. this send-up of horror films might have the potential of an ''Airplane.'' But the rewards are too long arriving and United Artists faces a tough sell, maybe having to settle for gradual returns from cultists.

Rory Calhoun is delightful as the kindly proprietor of an out of the way motel where he also smokes up a line of ''Farmer Vincent'' meats that are the most delicious in the territory. Portly Nancy Parsons is also a lot of fun as Calhoun's gluttonous little sister, who helps run the motel and the packing plant.

Calhoun and Parsons round up their meat at night out on the highway, where they invent clever ways to run cars off the road. The passengers are then buried alive up to their necks to await their turn in the smokehouse.

Nina Axelrod is the exception and after her motorcycle mishap they keep her around the house on the hoof to help out. Naturally, Calhoun's younger brother, Paul Linke, falls in love with her but she's already smitten by Calhoun, because he's fatherly and sweet and brings along great food for picnics.

Calhoun also recruits potential porkchops through ads in kinky magazines and Elaine Joyce and Dick Curtis have a good turn as a couple who show up for a wild night of abandon and get more masochism than they planned on.

All of this has potential, but director Kevin Connor fails to solve the basic problem he confronts: all horror movies are so absurd, it's hard to know for at least an hour whether ''Motel Hell'' is kidding or not.

Connor drops hints of a send-up but they don't fully register as Calhoun and cast try so hard to establish a deadly earnest foundation for what's to come. It's only when the picture fully commits itself to wackiness that it starts to work.

Finale features a chainsaw duel between Calhoun and Linke as the bound-up Axelrod is propelled toward a meat-slicer, while the other unburied victims assault the house. Curtis the kinky one in his dirty plastic ladies underwear.

That and Calhoun's long monolog as he lays dying — with the chainsaw sticking out of his side — are. as they say. worth seeing. But not necessarily worth the wait. —Har.

First Deadly Sin
(COLOR)

Sinatra's first pic in 10 years a downbeat affair. Questionable b.o.

Hollywood, Oct. 21.
Filmways Pictures release of an Elliott Kastner presentation of an Artanis-Cinema 7 production. Stars Frank Sinatra, Faye Dunaway. Executive producers. Frank Sinatra. Elliott Kastner. Producers. George Pappas. Mark Shanker. Directed by Brian Hutton. Screenplay. Mann Rubin; based on novel by Lawrence Sanders; camera (color). Jack Priestley; art director. Woody Mackintosh; costume designer. Gary Jones; film editor. Eric Albertson; first asst. director. Joe Napolitano; set decorator. Robert Drumheller; music, Gordon Jenkins. Reviewed at Filmways screening room. Bevhills. Calif., Oct. 20, 1980. (MPAA Rating-R). Running time: 112 MINS.
Edward Delaney . . . . Frank Sinatra
Barbara Delaney . . . . Faye Dunaway
Daniel Blank . . . . David Dukes
Dr. Bernardi . . . . George Coe
Monica Gilbert . . . . Brenda Vaccaro
Christopher Langley . . . . Martin Gabel
Doorman . . . . Joe Spinell
Sgt. Fernandez . . . . Jeffrey De Munn
Capt. Broughton . . . . Anthony Zerbe
Dr. Sanford Ferguson . . James Whitmore
Delivery man . . . . Fred Fuster

Otherwise a fairly routine and turgid crime meller, ''The First Deadly Sin'' commands some interest as Frank Sinatra's first film in 10 years and the first one in some time more that he appears to have taken with complete seriousness. With little else to recommend it, main question is whether or not star's name still has the drawing power it held throughout most of the 1950s and 1960s.

Pic presents audience with considerable barriers to involvement from the outset, as first few reels consist predominantly of a bloody operation, a violent murder, dialog conducted over mutilated bodies in an autopsy room and unappetizing hospital scenes. Established tone is therefore distinctly unpleasant, and drama encompassing it isn't sufficiently unusual or compelling to justify such detailed attention to the grim and grisly.

Plot has Sinatra, a cop within weeks of retirement, latching onto an apparent series of arbitrary murders. Advised to leave it alone, he nonetheless pursues the case, determining, with the aid of museum armaments curator Martin Gabel, that the murder weapon is an unusual mountain climber's ice ax, discovery of which eventually leads to reasonably compelling confrontation with demented, insecurity-ridden killer David Dukes.

Paralleling the straightforward crime-and-detection yarn, and slowing down the entire proceedings, are Sinatra's visits to wife Faye Dunaway, who's not recovering well from a kidney operation. Rarely in recent memory has a major star saddled herself with such a thankless and unbecoming role, as Dunaway literally spends the entire picture on her back in a hospital bed, adorned by tubes and sickly makeup.

Obviously designed to humanize Sinatra's character. husband-wife interludes tie in not at all with main drama, and time devoted to them might more profitably have been spent further building up jockeying between cop and killer.

Sacrificed in the balance is any insight into the killer who. despite Dukes' strengths as a performer, comes off as a high tech weirdo who might have wandered in from the set of ''Cruising.'' Standouts among the supporting players are Joe Spinell, as a street-wise security apartment doorman bribed by Sinatra. and Gabel, whose deadpan enthusiasm for esoteric weapons provides only comic relief from the omnipresent grimness.

As for Sinatra. he's serious. direct and not at all the wise guy amounting to a decent performance, even if the role might seem to have called for a more obsessive and desperate attitude in the face of his career and wife slipping away from him simultaneously. The way he plays it, one can read the underlying feelings into his behavior, which might have worked to greater advantage had the telling of the tale possessed a more compelling edge.

Brian G. Hutton has done a workmanlike job as director. Save for a few synthesized effects, Gordon Jenkins' music recalls the heavy sauce scores of the 1950s. and some of lenser Jack Priestley's night scenes are so dark one wonders how they'll show up on drive-in screens. —Cart.

Lady Grey
(COLOR)

Success ain't everything. So what else is new?

Hollywood, Oct. 9.
A Maverick Pictures International release. Produced by Earl Owensby. Directed by Worth Keeter. Features entire cast. Screenplay, Tom McIntyre; camera (DeLuxe Color). Darryl Cathcart; editor. Jim Laudenslager; music. Arthur Smith. Clay Smith; art direction, Sam Robbins; sound, John Dellinger, Emil Neroda; assistant director. William Olsen. Reviewed at the Academy of Motion Picture Arts & Sciences Screening Room. Beverly Hills. Oct. 9, 1980. (No MPAA Rating.) Running time: 100 MINS.
Lady Grey . . . . Ginger Alden
Balck Jack Donovan . . . . David Allen Coe
Don Sands . . . . Paul Ott
Johnny Nyland . . . . Herman Bloodsworth
Hubbard Jackson . . . . Ed Grady
Pru . . . . Paula Baldwin

''Lady Grey'' is a ''Coal Miner's Daughter'' without good music, performances, atmosphere or drama. Regionally indigenous in that it was made at producer Earl Owensby's studio in North Carolina with local talent, latest cautionary tale about the cold bitch goddess success is a bland, overpadded affair about an aspiring country singer who gets what she wants but can't find happiness in the bargain. Potential outlets for this one would seem restricted to Bible belt ozoners.

Only conceivable rationale for the rags to riches saga is as a star vehicle. Lady in question is Ginger Alden, who made her name as Elvis Presley's last female companion and has appeared before for

Owensby. While attractive, her chirping is monotonous and script seems to bend over backwards to avoid getting her involved with a man. She's just not interested, period, and lack of any romantic or emotional thread to the story renders lead character strangely inhuman and unsympathetic.

Sure, she suffers her share of hard knocks. Slimy manager Herman Bloodsworth wrests Alden away from her family and rapes her after seemingly knocking her out and later turns her sister Paula Baldwin into a traumatized prostie for some of his good ole boys. At the same time, country star David Allen Coe lectures her on how it took him 30 years to make it and why she shouldn't complain if she doesn't become a headliner overnight.

But it's all pretty pallid stuff, not helped by the fact that half the film is stuffed with colorless tunes, which are sometimes audaciously repeated to further reduce impact.

Cast gives it the college try, while tech credits, except for some all too obvious post-synch work, are passable. Even with allowances made for pic's origins, however, just getting something up there on the screen is not enough. —Cart.

Kontrakt
(Contract)
(POLISH-COLOR)

Gdansk, Sept. 8.

A Film Polski release of a Prf Unit production. Features entire cast. Written and directed by Krzysztof Zanussi. Camera (color), Tadeusz Wybult; music. Wojciech Kilar. No other credits provided. Reviewed at Gdansk Film Fest, Sept. 8, 1980. Running time: 100 MINS.

Cast: Leslie Caron, Maja Komorowska, Tadeusz Lomnicki, Magda Jaroszowna, Krzysztof Kolberger, Beata Tyszkiewicz.

A surprise pic at the Gdansk Film Fest, Krzysztof Zanussi's "Contract" was shown on the fest's opening night at the same time as it was unspooled (Sept. 8) at the Venice Film Festival. This tv film is next on San Francisco's fest schedule.

The globetrotting director made "Contract" at the same time as he was lensing "Constans," his entry at the Cannes fest last May; in fact, the films were shot simultaneously. It is a praiseworthy feat by any standards, but the director is obviously now at the height of his powers and almost anything of quality and/or relevance can be expected of him at the moment.

"Contract" has a deceptively simple story to work from, but like Luis Bunuel's moral fables, it bursts its seams to become a sardonic comedy on the Polish Party bourgeoisie, one of the finest and bitterest films Zanussi has made to date. It reminds this viewer of his

early "Camouflage" (1976). Most of the film takes place in a Warsaw villa owned by a well-to-do doctor on the occasion of a family wedding — or what appears to be a wedding, for while the happy couple agreed on their vows before the civil authorities, the girl backs out of marrying the doctor's son at the church altar because the young egoist is not interested in having children and only has his career on his mind.

The other thread of the story is equally perverse. Leslie Caron, playing an aging relative of the family, a former star ballerina, comes to Warsaw for the wedding and to shore up her sagging popularity. Her daughter accompanies her, but it's obvious from the beginning that the two don't get along — rather, the girl is a trollop type, and our famous ballerina is a kleptomaniac who snatches jewelry and purses at parties. The wedding party is thus ready made for her wiles, where she gets caught at the height of the celebrations — the scene is a ripe one for Caron's talents, and she plays it to the hilt.

The party begins to degenerate in the church, when the girl walks off in a huff with the angry bridegroom in hot pursuit. The rest retire to the villa to celebrate anyway, some foreign guests stripping to the buff to try out the sauna in the basement and to romp in the snow outdoors. Deals are made on the side between corrupt officials, the atmosphere of the villa with all its Western touches fairly exuding blackmarketing at higher levels in government and industry. The doctor, in fact, prefers getting paid off inside the leaves of books, since he has quite a collection of rare publications in his library. One of the doctor's acquaintances also oils his way around the villa like he is comparing Greek vases in an art-collector's mansion.

In the end, the son has to be crated away to a hospital because he has attempted suicide, or has simply thrown an hysterical fit, in keeping with the degeneration of the wedding celebration as it slips into a drunken orgy. A great show, one of the best pix to emerge from Poland this season. —Holl.

Schizoid
(COLOR)

Creepy atmospherics but not enough shock for the horror crowd.

Hollywood, Oct. 10.

Cannon Group release of a Golan-Globus Production. Produced by Menahem Golan, Yoram Globus. Stars Klaus Kinski, Mariana Hill, Craig Wasson. Written and directed by David Paulsen. Camera (TVC Color), Norman Leigh; music, Craig

Hundley; editors, Robert Fitzgerald, Dick Brummer; art direction, Kathy Curtis Cahill; sound, Kenard King; associate producer, Christopher Pearce; assistant director, Caren Singer. Reviewed at Pacific's Vine Theatre, Hollywood, Oct. 10, 1980. (MPAA Rating: R.) Running time: **91 MINS.**

Dr. Peter Fales	Klaus Kinski
Julie	Mariana Hill
Doug	Craig Wasson
Alison Fales	Donna Wilkes
Donahue	Richard Herd
Jake	Joe Regalbuto
Gilbert	Christopher Lloyd
Pat	Flo Gerrish
Rosemary	Kiva Lawrence
Francoise	Claude Duvernoy
Sally	Cindy Dolan

The presence of Klaus Kinski in a low-budget Hollywood shocker suggests that the filmmaker may have more on his mind than doing a typical entry in the current horror cycle, and such is the case with "Schizoid." Kinski's moody presence as a sinister psychiatrist carries far more interest than the formula murder scenes of women being sliced up by a psychopath. The Cannon Group release is exploitable, though too slow and not scary enough for maximum b.o. impact in its market.

Writer-director David Paulsen may have wanted to do a classier film than this one turned out to be, since the scenes with Kinski and Donna Wilkes as his disturbed teenage daughter have a dramatic and even visual resonance the rest of the film lacks. The main plot about advice-to-the-lovelorn columnist Mariana Hill and the rest of Kinski's group therapy patients being menaced one by one seems like a concession to commercial expediencies.

The killing are unpleasantly blunt and distastefully misogynistic, which isn't saying anything new for this genre, but the relentless and predictable killing of women with a pair of scissors (the camera taking the murderer's p.o.v.) shows a poverty of imagination.

On a pure scream level, pic doesn't sustain its scares sufficiently, simply throwing in murder scenes every once in a while to provide kicks for the yahoo crowd. Absence of a teenaged audience identification figure (the victims are all middle-aged women) probably is also a hindrance in the market.

Paulsen shows a real flair for offbeat casting, not only in using Kinski, but in finding the talented young Wilkes and in giving the gorgeous Mariana Hill one of her rare large parts. After catching the eye as a Howard Hawks protegee back in the '60s, Hill has had far too little to do on screen, and she proves herself a solid dramatic performer in the central part here despite the banality with which too many scenes were conceived.

Hill receives a series of threatening letters that make her wonder whether Kinski is bumping off his own patients (maybe she has seen "Dressed To Kill" and "Phobia," two recent shockers in that vein), but evidence also points to Wilkes and to Hill's estranged husband, Craig Wasson, whose performance is a bit overblown even for an erratic character.

There's a genuine sense of eeriness in the quiet scenes of Kinski prowling restlessly through his house, spying on his daughter as she showers, and having "Last Tango"-like sexual encounters with his patients. Possessor of perhaps the creepiest face in films today, Kinski can be disturbing without doing or saying much, as this film proves. Unfortunately, his character and that of his daughter are never sufficiently developed to pay off on their promise.

Production values of this Menahem Golan-Yoram Globus pic, shot under the title of "Murder By Mail," are on the threadbare side, but Paulsen and lenser Norman Leigh work hard to provide atmosphere. —Mac.

Cabaret Mineiro
(Mineiro Cabaret)
(BRAZILIAN-COLOR)

Rio de Janeiro, Sept. 24.

An Embrafilme release of a Cinematografica Montesclarense production, with Zoom Cinematografica, Corisco Filmes and Embrafilme. Features entire cast. Written and directed by Carlos Alberto Prates Correia. Cmera (Eastmancolor), Murilo Salles; art direction and costume design, Carlos Wilson; music, Tavinho Moura; sound, Walter Goulart; editing, Ide Lacreta; executive production, Lacreta, Paulo Henrique Souto. Reviewed at screening room, Hotel Meridien, Rio de Janeiro, Sept. 23, 1980. Running time: **90 MINS.**

Cast: Nelson Dantas, Tamara Taxman, Tania Alves, Helber Rangel, Louise Cardoso, Eliete Narduchi, Dora Pellegrino, Luiza Clotilde, Carlos Wilson, Maria Silvia, Saira Zambelli, Thelma Reston, Nildo Parente, Paschoal Villaboim, Sonia Santos, Nena Ainhoren, Celia Maracaja.

Minas Geraes is for Brazil what Sicily is for Italy. Its people get together no matter where in the world they are. Minas inhabitants (the "Mineiros") help each other mutually because they seem not to trust anybody else. Not even their secrets, their hopes, their expectations. No wonder they reached a clear hegemonic position in Brazilian finances and politics. Indeed, Humberto Mauro became the biggest name of Brazilian cinema back in the Twenties working in the small town of Cataguases, Minas Geraes.

A recent hommage to Mauro and Minas, "A Noiva da Cidade" (The Bride of the City) was shot by critic and filmmaker Alex Viany and became a commercial failure in part because "the Mineiro spirit could not spread but to Mineiros themselves" as a critic in Rio noted. Such possibility does not seem to bother Prates Correia, who had made a remarkable film on prostitution a few years ago, "Perdida" (Lost Woman). His new film is the orchestration of a number of Mineiro situations and behaviors, as well as a hallucinated view of a man comprised between his dreams and the reality, the romant.c values of the past, the coldness of the present and an anguishing world in-between.

Dialog is often poetic and the whole story develops in its own space. Reality is recodified on all its levels and one is never positive about when it appears to be similar to our patterns, although it often does. Perhaps the film is turned into such a regional work that even Brazilian audiences of different origins will have difficulty understanding its meaning; perhaps, on the contrary, it becomes as universal as, say, the Sicilian code of honor is: one does not have to live it in order to understand it.

Technically, at least, "Cabaret Mineiro," is certainly universal. Cinematographer Murilo Salles photographed "Dona Flor and Her Two Husbands"; music by Tavinho Moura is as competent as the composer's group (which includes Milton Nascimento) used to be; Nelson Dantas, though more active on stage than on screen, is a first-rank actor; and both editing and sound are quite professional.

There are not many films, among a production of nearly 100 a year, that are able to show something of the Brazilian soul or even a fraction of it. "Cabaret Mineiro" is certainly an exception, even though not as easy to digest as fashionable stereotypes are. —Hoin.

The Hounds...Of Notre Dame
(CANADIAN-COLOR)

Regina, Sask., Oct. 10.
A Fraser film production. Released by Pan-Canadian film distributors. Produced by Fil Fraser. Directed by Zale Dalen. Features entire cast. Screenplay, Ken Mitchell; camera (color), Ron Orieux; art direction, Richard Hudolin; editor, Tony Lower; music, Maurice Marshall; asst. director, Joan Board. Reviewed at the Saskatchewan Centre of the Arts, Regina, Canada. Oct. 10. 1980. Running Time: 95 MINS.
Father Athol Murray .. Thomas Peacocke
Mother Therese .... Frances Hyland
Archbishop Williams .... Barry Morse
Ron Fryer .... David Ferry
Tom Howard .... Lawrence Reese
Lila Petri .... Lenore Zann
Bob Cormack .... Phil Ridley
Terry Gladwell .... Dale Heibein
Frank Lasuisse .... Paul Bougie
Ben McCauley .... Rob MacLean

Stephen Kessler .... Bill Sorenson
Bashinsky .... Bill Morton

"The Hounds of Notre Dame" is an affectionate tribute to Pere Murray, founder of the College of Notre Dame in Saskatchewan, Canada. The feature drama was largely financed by Notre Dame grads but can hardly be considered an in-house document.

Rather than attempt an exhaustive history of the college or a biography of Murray, the script by playwright Ken Mitchell looks at two days at the college in the winter of 1940. The opening frames establish the Murray of legend — a hard drinking, salty tongued, anti traditional priest. To raise money for his school Murray does radio broadcasts denouncing the CCF (Socialist) party popular in the region.

The early days of Notre Dame (established in 1927) are far from an educational mecca. Student dorms are glorified shacks heated by coal, the classrooms require a coat be worn at all times and the cafeteria rarely features meat.

Nonetheless, the setting vaguely resembles Boys Town. A major subplot involves the taming of a tough kid. The rapid transition from rebel to team leader by Fryer (David Perry) strains all credibility.

However, the main body of the film is a series of anecdotes revolving around Murray. Murray believed in a strong mixture of education and athletics and fostered a championship hockey team called the Hounds.

The vignettish quality of the film provides an awkward pacing to the action. The film opens strongly but a lack of focus and a series of diverting subplots weaken what should have been a dramatic conclusion.

This is director Zale Dalen's second feature. His debut, "Skip Tracer," won him the Canadian film award for promising newcomer and although "The Hounds of Notre Dame" attests to his competent handling of the material, it's hardly a breakthrough picture.

Dalen is particularly good with the non-professional actors who play the Hounds. Apart from Thomas Peacocke, who plays Murray, the remaining roles are all supporting parts. Peacocke gives a full-bodied performance as the chain-smoking, no-nonsense founder of Notre Dame. Whatever focus exists in the film derives from the actor's performance, a remarkable feat for a film debut.

The low-budget feature (about $1,200,000) has strong production values particularly from Ron Orieux's stunning camerawork. There are some curious continuity

lapses in the film even considering its budget and clumsy narrative transitions.

The film has similar market possibilities to producer Fraser's earlier "Why Shoot the Teacher." However, it's unlikely "The Hounds of Notre Dame" will equal the earlier picture's market penetration.
—Klad.

San Francisco Fest

The Ninth Heart
(CZECH-COLOR)

San Francisco, Oct. 14.
Czeskoslovensky Filmexport (Prague) release and production. Stars Ondrej Pavelka, Anna Malova, Juraj Kukura. Directed by Juraj Herz. Screenplay, Herz; story, Josef Hanzlik; camera (color), Jiri Machane; design, Vladimir Labsky; music, Petr Hapka. Reviewed at Palace of Fine Arts Theater, San Francisco Film Festival, Oct. 14, 1980. Running time: 90 MINS.
Martin .... Ondrej Pavelka
Princess .... Julie Juristova
Toncka .... Anna Malova
Clown .... Frantisek Filipovsky
Principal .... Josef Kemr
Astrologist .... Juraj Kukura
Grand Duke .... Premyal Koci
Grand Duchess .... Ruzena Rudnicka
Captain .... Josef Somr

This is a fetching, lavishly designed fairy tale from the director of last year's "Beauty and the Beast." Problem is, in terms of U.S. distribbing, where's the audience? Dubbing might sell it to moppets, for it has all the elements to attract the kids: a handsome, underdog hero; his sweet gypsy girlfriend; a beautiful blonde princess; a sympathetic clown-sidekick, and as nasty a villain as you'll want to find — an astrologer who steals hearts literally.

The tale is slow to develop, but once the hero (a student named Martin) begins his year-long effort to free the princess from the spell of the nasty astrologer, the tale moves along effortlessly.

Vladimir Labsky, the set designer, emerges as the real hero of the picture. He's concocted a cavernous castle for the villain which s also true, so stunning, that you expect to find it on a Draculean real estate market.

Technical credits all are swell. If only a market could be found for this professional piece of lavish craftsmanship. —Herb.

Il Casotto
(The Beach House)
(ITALIAN-COLOR)

San Francisco, Oct. 14.
Medusa Film (Rome) release and production. Features entire cast. Produced by Mauro Berardi. Directed by

Sergio Citti. Screenplay, Citti and Vincenzo Cerami; camera (color), Tonino Delli Colli; music, Gianni Mazza. Reviewed at Palace of Fine Arts Theatre, San Francisco Film Festival, Oct. 14, 1980. (No MPAA Rating.) Running time: 114 MINS.
Tersina .... Jodie Foster
Grandfather .... Paolo Stoppa
Grandmother .... Flora Mastroianni
Cerquette .... Ugo Tognazzi
Client .... Mariangela Melato
Bachelors .... Michele Placido,
Luigi Proietti

Sergio Citti, an assistant director on nearly all of the films of Pier Paolo Pasolini, has missed badly on this near-sexpo, beach house farce which more closely resembles languid burlesque-legit than a pic.

All the action, except the opening, is confined to a large changing room at Ostia Beach and adds up to a nude sitcom. Principals keep entering and exiting, dressing and undressing, and neither they nor their situations are either interesting or compelling.

Catherine Deneuve is wasted in an absurd dream sequence, while Jodie Foster, as a pregnant teen whose grandparents scheme to find her a husband, has little to do but thrust out her chest. Ugo Tognazzi, an insurance man who prefers at least two women at once but wears a chastity belt to inhibit his lust, is ultimately forced into a downright silly, raving confessional.

Screenplay, which goes from worse to worse as it stagnates along, offers such delights as a priest with two sex organs, dirty feet, dog feces and sunburned lovers.

Little of the farce works, although Michele Placido and Luigi Proietti, as a pair of grease monkey bachelors, somehow manage to rise above the ineptitude of the yarn.

"Casotto" seemed out of place at a festival. Neither hard nor soft, it's simply badcore. —Herb.

Grimaces
(HUNGARIAN-COLOR)

San Francisco, Oct. 13.
Hungarofilm (Budapest) release and production. No distributor. Stars Istvan Geczy, Tundi Kassai, Rita Baranyai, Gabor Lontay. Co-directed and cowritten by Ferenc Kardos and Janos Rozsa. Camera, (color), Sandor Sara; music, Andras Szollosy. Reviewed at the Palace of Fine Arts Theatre, San Francisco Film Festival, Oct. 13, 1980. Running time: 77 MINS.

This oft-surreal, 14 year old comedy from Hungary was booked into the "rediscovery" section of this year's Frisco fest. Originally unveiled at Cannes' critics' week seg, and heretofore unreviewed, "Grimaces" has been in limbo for more than a decade. Co-makers Ferenc Kardos and Janos Rozsa split after this pic and now direct individually.

Tale of moppets was patterned

after French new wave style and thus has a dated, albeit technically sound, look to it. Yarn centers on a six-year-old boy starting school and his fantasies about emergence into the world, all told from his point of view. Most fascinating segs center on moppet's view of big people, a prediction of the loss of innocence to come.

The once-innovative style of blending reality with fantasy works only some of the time when reviewed in 1980. But the moppets are downright delightful and many of their pranks amusing.

There's an "Alice in Wonderland" feeling dissipated only by excessive slapstick. Although pic was initially aimed for an adult audience, it might (and should) have more impact on a kid audience, except for the fact that dubbing would be mandatory for U.S. distrib. It appears that "Grimaces" will serve only as occasional "rediscovery" fest fodder. —*Herb.*

Esthappan
(INDIAN-COLOR)

San Francisco, Oct. 12.

General Pictures (Kerala, India) release and production. No distributor. Cast all non-pro. Directed by Aravindam. Screenplay, Aravindam, Isaac Thomas Kottukapally and Kavalam; camera (color), Shaji; music, Aravindam, Janardhan and Kottukapally. Reviewed at Castro Theater, San Francisco Film Festival, Oct. 12, 1980. Running time: 93 MINS.

Pic arrived at the Frisco Fest without sub-titles, and a narrator from the U. of California, Berkeley, was on hand with a mike for the unspooling at the Castro Theater. Interestingly, although the narration was spare, and not always audible, walkouts were minimal. "Esthappan" told its own story quite well; trouble was, the story was a bit thin.

Premise is the existence of an immortal man, a combination mystic and Christ-like fisherman, in a coastal village south of Bombay. This ageless holy man, named Esthappan, has the ability to change his appearance, walk on water, heal by the laying on of hands, survive a hanging, turn stones into cookies, chug-a-lug a fifth of whiskey without getting a hangover and print his own money.

Screenplay interviews several villagers with the inquiry: What's Esthappan really like? For real? A fakir? A nut?

The yarn has a certain, albeit thin, charm, and there's a sense of reality to the pic because all the performers are non-pro and quite unaffected. Technical credits are firstrate; color quite compelling.

Director Aravindam made the film as a moonlight project. He works full-time for a government rubber combine and has now made five pix in six years. Off his latest, he clearly rates a niche internationally. With better screenplay development, "Esthappan" might have had commercial promise.
—*Herb.*

Hinotori
(JAPANESE-COLOR)

San Francisco, Oct. 16.

Toho International Co., Ltd., release of a Toho-Hinotori production. Exec producers Kiichi Ichikawa, Kunihiko Murai. Features entire cast. Directed by Kon Ichikawa. Screenplay, Shuntaro Tanikawa; original story, Osamu Tezuka; camera, Kiyoshi Hasegawa; special effects, Teruyoshi Nakano; animation, Tezuka Production; music, Michel Legrand, Jun Fukamachi. Reviewed at Palace of Fine Arts Theatre, San Francisco Film Festival, Oct. 16, '80. (No MPAA Rating). Running time: 137 MINS.

With: Tomisaburo Wakayama, Masao Kusakari, Kaoru Yumi, Reiko Ohara, Mieko Takamine, Tatsuya Nakadai.

Here's a send-up, with the underlying message that life is to be lived and must go on, of every samurai film ever lensed. Some of it — with dropins of animation, split screen, slomo and stop-action — is good fun. Trouble is, the yarn is endless. Everybody alive at the pic's start dies by the end — usually very violently. There's such an excess of people-animal carnage that the senses are dulled early on. Even with this comic book approach, the tale is too unwieldy to succeed at this length.

Focus is on the mythic phoenix and attempts by a variety of warriors to capture it so that the bird's blood may be quaffed en route to eternal life. In animation, the phoenix emerges as a combo Woody Woodpecker-Big Bird.

Yarn takes places circa 180 A.D. Tribes knock off each other in bloody raids. There's a heroic little boy and his mentor, a great warrior whose nose reaches mega-Pinocchio length after 72 hours in a wasp pit.

As fillips, director Kon Ichikawa offers a volcano and earthquake, not to mention the decapitation of a platoon of cavalry horses.

Any severe cutting would make the story incomprehensible, because everything builds to the regeneration of Japan. As a Saturday matinee serial, "Hinotori" could run for months. —*Herb.*

Joni
(COLOR)

Real-life inspirational saga excellent for type. Could work with unconverted auds with right sell.

Hollywood, Oct. 24.

A World Wide Pictures release. Produced by Frank R. Hacobson. Executive producer, William F. Brown. Features entire cast. Directed and written by James F. Collier, based on the book by Joni Eareckson. Camera (Metrocolor), Frank Raymond; editor, Duane Hartzell; music, Ralph Carmichael; art direction, Bill Ross; sound, Dean Gilmore; assistant director, Stephen Lim. Reviewed at the UA Cinema Center, W. L.A., Oct. 24, 1980. (MPAA Rating: G.) Running time: 108 MINS.

Joni	Joni Eareckson
Mr. Eareckson	Bert Remsen
Jay	Katherine De Hetre
Dick	Cooper Huckabee
Doctor	John Milford
Don	Michael Mancini
Steve	Richard Lineback

Also: Jay W. MacIntosh, Louise Hoven, Cloyce Morrow, Sarah Rush, Jeff Austin, Cheryl Harvey, Ernie Hudson, Barbara Mallory, Jane Ralston, Betsy Jones-Moreland, Stephen Parr.

Overcoming any upfront skepticism about the potential quality of a forthrightly evangelical picture, "Joni," based on the real-life struggle of Joni Eareckson and starring same, emerges as an involving and highly believable account of a young woman surmounting a terrible handicap and making something of her life. By going the four-wall, quick saturation route to reach the already converted, pic runs the risk of missing out on the wider general audience which patronized "The Other Side Of The Mountain." It has already opened in some markets to fair results.

At age 17, Joni (pronounced "Johnny") breaks her spine in a diving accident. Undergoing relatively unproductive operations and a long period of rehabilitation, she must come to grips with fact that she'll never regain use of her arms or legs. After reaching depths where suicide looks like the best solution, she finally returns to her family's lovely Maryland farm and begins sketching and painting, holding the implements in her mouth.

Hints of her eventual religious conversion are sprinkled along the way, but healthily, for drama's sake, doubts and cynicism are hard to overcome. Two boyfriends, one from before the accident and another who at first appears as an impossible shining knight, are shown to be unable, in their different ways, to deal with the physical limitations imposed on their relationships with her.

James F. Collier's solid, colloquial script is also mindful of the social context, showing racism in the hospital and drawing real economic lines between the various characters found there and elsewhere.

When it comes, religious embrace seems as logical a climax as any other, with Joni seen speaking to increasingly larger crowds (one of which includes film's backer Billy Graham). Only unfortunate note is struck by pic's coda, featuring a lushly orchestrated theme song sung by Joni herself as she rides her electrical wheelchair around a country road.

Despite sound story construction and Collier's straightforward direction, film would be nothing without Eareckson's own compelling presence. Extremely attractive, she registers both her doubt and later belief with equal conviction. Few people have ever played themselves to such effect.

Although lensing could be better, tech qualities are otherwise good, and lack of a certain Hollywood slickness perhaps works to film's advantage. —*Cart.*

Land Og Synir
(Land And Sons)
(ICELANDIC-COLOR)

Isfilm (Reykjavik) release of a Jon Hermannsson production. Features entire cast. Directed by Agust Gudmundsson. Screenplay, Gudmundsson, based on a novel by Indridi G. Thorsteinsson; camera (color), Sigurdur Sverrir Palsson; music, Gunnar Raynir Sveinsson. No other credits provided. Reviewed at the Museum of Modern Art, Oct. 24, 1980. Running time: 94 MINS.

Cast: Sigurdur Sigurjonsson, Jon Sigurdbjornsson, Gudny Ragnarsdottir, Jonas Tryggvason.

The filmmaking company, Isfilm, is from one of the world's oldest countries, Iceland, and one of the world's newest filmmaking nations. It may be a late starter but this early Icelandic effort is a worthy attempt at trying a new approach to an old theme and, for the most part, it works. The relationship is between a farmer and his son and the unavoidable separation of the generations. The boy, at least, hangs on to the family farm until after his father's death but can't wait much longer to shed his ties with the land and the people who work it. What he will seek in the city isn't defined but it's the change that is important.

Young director-screenwriter Agust Gudmundsson did his apprenticeship at the National Film School in London and at home on television. This first feature shows the result of sticking to the first law of filmmaking — surround yourself with skilled technicians. Sigurdur Sverrir Palsson's color camerawork makes what is generally considered a cold land look warm and inviting. Indeed, one wonders if any other farms (possibly in New Zealand) have such a combination of rich land and spectacular scenery.

Most of the film's acting falls on the sturdy shoulders of young Sigurdur Sigurjonsson but he's given plenty of support by a stunningly beautiful young actress, Gudny Ragnarsdottir (a teenage Candice Bergen). Most of the character people are also topnotch. A very worthy beginning. —*Robe.*

Formynderne
(The Guardians)
(NORWEGIAN-COLOR)

Norsk Film, Jar, Norway release of an Harald Ohrvik production. Directed by Nicole Mace. Features entire cast. Screenplay, Kirsten Bryhni, based on two novels by Amalie Skram; camera (color), Paul Rene Roestad; music, Synne Skouen; editor, Edith Toreg; art director, Sven Wickman. Reviewed at Museum of Modern Art, New York, Oct. 20, 1980. Running time: 104 MINS.
Cast: Vibeke Lokkeberg, Helge Reiss, Odd Furoy.

Although the setting for this 1978 Norwegian film is a mental institution, the theme is less about mental health than the emergence of the feminist movement in Norway. Femme director Nicole Mace has taken for the storyline two novels written in 1895 by Amalie Skram, based on her own experiences in trying to follow an artistic career and maintain a household at the same time.

In the film version, obviously truncated as the first novel dealt with the horrendous Professor Hieronimus and the second with the patient's stay at St. Jorgen Hospital, there is lots of exposition to set one up for the strain on the heroine's nerves — what is really the problem is that she has an artistic block in trying to complete a painting which leads to what would be called today "a nervous breakdown" — and agrees to a stay in a mental hospital.

The rest of the film is the struggle between the unfeeling hospital head (who rules her insane because she chooses unpleasant subjects as the themes of her paintings) and the strong-willed woman. Along the way she finds the solution for her painting — the hospital head becomes the evil spirit which would lead one to believe that incarceration did do some good after all. She loses her husband but keeps her sanity.

One would sympathize with Vibeke Lokkeberg's problems more if she looked or acted a bit feminine but she's more masculine than the husband — and that's a problem the film doesn't deal with.

Technically, the film is firstrate

with Paul Rene Roestad's color camerawork outstanding. There's supposed to be a lengthy time period but one sees foliage throughout of a single season. Incidentally, the leading lady is also a director, having her own film, "The Revelation," also in the Museum's "New Scandinavian Films" series.
—*Robe.*

Taiyo o Nusunda Otoko
(The Man Who Stole The Sun)
(JAPANESE-COLOR)

Kitty Films production. Directed by Kazuhiko Hasegawa. Features entire cast. Screenplay, Leonard Schrader, Kazuhiko Hasegawa; camera (color), Tatsuo Suzuki; music, Takayuki Inoue. No other credits provided. Reviewed at Japan House, New York, Oct. 10, 1980. Running time: 130 MINS.
Cast: Kenji Sawada, Bunta Sugawara, Kimiko Ikegami, Yonusuke Ito.

Casting Japanese pop singer Kenji Sawada opposite yakuza veteran Bunta Sugawara is about the equivalent of putting Mick Jagger opposite Robert Mitchum — interesting and offbeat casting that doesn't always work.

The fault with the black comedy is that a thin, but good idea, is expanded into more than two hours of action cliches. Indeed, the story holds up very well through a series of capers until it goes ridiculous with the villain-hero recapturing the homemade atom bomb from the police and starting over with his silly demands. This is more than likely the fault of scripter American Leonard Schrader (brother of Paul Schrader) and writer-director Kazuhiro Hasegawa.

Sawada is a science teacher in a Tokyo school who manufactures an atom bomb in his apartment (while using his classroom lectures as trials for the project) and, completed, starts making demands on the government. Through an unintentional heroic act at the film's beginning (he helps capture a nut who has held his bus full of students captive), he makes the acquaintance of chief detective Bunta Sugawara. This begins a low-scale "Crime and Punishment" relationship between the two which leads up to the erratic and bloody (and completely unbelievable) finale.

Some of the concepts are both funny and original. His first demand is that the television network not stop the telecast of baseball games at a certain hour by government edict whether the game is completed or not. His big coup is to specify a concert in Japan by the Rolling Stones (banned from that country because of Keith Richards' drug record), which also leads to his downfall.

A farfetched romance with a

pretty but addlebrained female disk jockey pads out the overlong footage. Technically the film is superior with Tatsuo Suzuki's color camerawork giving the city of Tokyo a vibrancy that makes it an additional character in the film.

Extensive editing would help a great deal. The film is the first in Japan House's "High Tide, Low Tide" (effects of the New Wave in Japanese cinema) series. —*Robe.*

Bloodeaters
(COLOR)

Gore film for horror addicts only.

Parker National release of a CM production. Produced and directed by Chuck McCrann. Features entire cast. Screenplay, McCrann; camera (Movielab color), David Sperling; editors, McCrann, Sperling; music, Ted Shapiro; production manager, C.A. Harris; sound, James McGonigal, Jr.; assistant director, Jenny Lee; makeup, Craig Harris, Gerald Cullen. Reviewed at Rivoli Theatre, N.Y.C., Oct. 23, '80. (MPAA Rating: R). Running time: 84 MINS.
Cole .... Charles Austin
Polly .... Beverly Shapiro
Hermit .... Dennis Helfend
Briggs .... Paul Haskin
Phillips .... John Amplas

Using the paraquat controversy as a plot peg, "Bloodeaters" is a very low budget horror pic joining the hundreds of gore films inspired by George Romero's "Night of the Living Dead" hit. Pic was filmed in Pennsylvania in 1979 under the working title "Forest of Fear."

A set of young criminals are harvesting a $2,000,000 crop of marijuana when a Federal agency orders the forest sprayed with Dromax, an experimental herbicide. Chemical turns the sprayed humans into bloodthirsty, zombie-like monsters who prey on unwary victims in the remote forest.

Film's main subplot deals with corrupt government agents, but by film's end the morality of heroes, villains and zombies is foolishly subordinated to audience-baiting "survival is everything" tactics.

Grainy 35m blowup of a film shot in 16m is a tipoff to the amateur efforts here on all artistic and technical levels. McCrann's corny script consists largely of vamping between gore scenes, with plenty of blood and ugliness for what used to be called the "slob" trade in the heyday of William Mishkin pix. Zombies emit dumb grunting sounds comically reminiscent of Soupy Sales' old White Fang and Black Tooth tv sketches.

Acting in "Bloodeaters" varies from the monotone of nonpros to very hammy comic relief, the latter including Hariet Miller's turn as a shrewish wife of the cropduster. It is distressing to see John Amplas, who received critical kudos in the ti-

tle role of Romero's "Martin" (shot in 1976), reduced to playing a stock heavy in another regional production. —*Lor.*

Fat Angels
(U.S.-SPANISH — COLOR)

Madrid, Oct. 6.
An Impala (Madrid) and Mambru Movies (New York) coproduction. Directed by Manuel Summers. Features entire cast. Screenplay, M. Summers, Chumy Chumez, Leon Tchaso, Joe Gonzalez based on story by M. Summers; camera (Eastmancolor), Manuel Rojas; music, Bob Dorough; show "A Night of Love," conceived and written by Jose Raul Bernardo; direct sound, Neelon Crawford; sets, Ramiro Gomez; editor, Gloria Pineyro; exec producer, Jose Vicuna. Reviewed at Impala screening room, Madrid, Oct. 6, 1980. Running time: 92 MINS.
Mike .... Farnham Scott
Mary .... January Stevens
Frank .... Jack Aaron
Alison .... Amy Steel
Jackie .... Robert Reynolds
Also: B. Constance Barry, Peter Bogyo, Nina David, Sanford Seeger, Robert Caus.
(English Soundtrack)

Mike, a cherub-faced, overweight young man of 28, grinds out his living as a piano player in an off-Broadway show, and makes some extra income tickling the ivories in a ballet school. He's cheerful, good-natured and lonely because those extra pounds make him self-consciously diffident when it comes to girls. A candy store owner suggests a pen-pal club, and sure enough Mike strikes up a missive passion for another "fat angel" living in Miami. She's a nursemaid to a dowager's lap dog. Except that each doesn't know the other is fat.

Pic, with variations on the Cyrano theme and the oldtime comedy of errors, lurches along somewhat anticlimactically as both Mike and Mary send off pictures of friends; the confusion is compounded when Mary and her retinue unexpectedly hit Gotham, and the stand-ins on both sides engage in a sexual romp. After a good deal of further confusion, the two "fat angels" finally meet up at the very end of the film and are left walking towards asphalt felicity, promising that some day they'll go on a diet.

Pleasant low key thesping by Farnham Scott and January Stevens, okay direction by Summers and a non-commital script skimming blandly over both pathos and thin humor, give item a somewhat wistful air. Little emotion is generated by the characters.

Item might do some biz in select playoffs in the U.S. and abroad. All technical credits up to crack. On-scene Gotham-lensing could help sales along as well. — *Besa*

Namida o Shishi no Tategami
(Tears On The Lion's Mane)
(JAPANESE-COLOR)

Shochiku release of a Masahiro Shinoda film. Features entire cast. Directed by Masahiro Shinoda. Screenplay, Shuji Terayama, Ichiro Mizunuma, Masahiro Shinoda; camera (color), Masao Kosugi; music, Toru Takemitsu. Reviewed at Japan House, New York, Oct. 24, 1980. Running time: 91 MINS.

Cast: Takashi Fujiki, Komi Nambara, Kyoko Kishida, Mariko Kaga, So Yamamura.

This 1962 effort by Masahiro Shinoda, though followed by much better films such as "Buraikan," could have been subtitled "Rebel without a cause on the waterfront."

Singer Takashi Fujiki, cast as a young gullible Yokohama dock worker (he's not really a worker as much as a gofer for a company boss), has a limited acting range which abandons him when it calls for a display of emotion, such as anger, disappointment or even naivete. The film is for the most part, an imitation of American "rebel" films but not even a good copy. It can often turn ridiculous especially when Fujiki's one release is to pick up a guitar and sing — when it's ersatz rock, it's terrible; when it's imitation Aznavour, it's rather good.

All technical aspects are fine with the Yokohama docks and waterfront providing a much more colorful setting than the silly plot does serves. —Robe.

The Rebel Intruders
(HONG KONG-COLOR)

Bangkok, Oct. 2.
A Shaw Bros. production and release. Produced by Runme Shaw. Directed by Chang Cheh. Features entire cast. Executive producer, Mona Fong; screenplay, Yi Huang and Chang Cheh; camera (color) Hui Chi Tsao; art direction, Johnson Tsao; music, Eddie Wang; martial art instructors, Kuo Chue, Chiang Sheng and Lu Feng. Reviewed at Warner Theatre, Bangkok, Oct. 2, '80. Running time: 95 MINS.
Wang Hsui . . . . Kuo Chue
Yu Han Sheng . . . . .Chiang Sheng
Chin Cheng Ping . . . . Lo Meng
Chen Tsu Kuang . . . . .Lu Peng
Ten Yun Tung . . . . Sun Chien
Pan Feng . . . . .Wang Li
Hung Ling . . . . Chu Hsiang Yun
Chang Hsia Hu . . . . Yang Hsiung
Fang Cheng Hua . . . . Yu Tai Ping
Chen Tsung Yao . . . . Tan Chen Tu

A brotherhood pact is the recurring theme of the new series of films helmed by Chang Cheh, Shaw's top action filmmaker, who has been working consistently now with a group of young new actors, Kuo Chue, Chiang Sheng, Lo Meng, Lu Feng, Sun Chien and others. The heroic triumvirate of Kuo, Chiang and Lo pay homage at a shrine,

then drink from the same cup of wine mixed with each other's blood — an obligatory ceremony foreshadowing subsequent encounters that put their blood compact to the test.

Story is set in China's warlord period, with the three heroes cast as refugees from South China trying to find a new home in Northern China. They discover the existence of different pugnacious factions, and each must choose which one to join. For easy identification, you can tell the groups apart by their uniforms — white, black, red and brown. Betrayal and treachery are again the main excuse for chases and fights.

The fights are only briefly interrupted by whatever else is going on. There's a hint of romance between Kuo and a courtesan (Chu Hsiang Yun), but whatever little there is of it is poignant.

Kuo Chue, the most impressive martial artist among Chang's new proteges, uses only a bench to protect himself against enemy swordsmen at first, but subsequently arms himself with a stick and chain weapon reminiscent of Bruce Lee, except that Chang does not let this particular weapon seem as lethal as in Bruce Lee pix, and in fact there's a demonstration of how it could be subdued by means of spears in the climactic battle scene.

These new actors in Chang's films have apparently been picked on the basis of their actual fighting skills in real life. Kuo, Lu and Chiang are listed in the credits as martial art instructors, and sometimes work only as fight arrangers when not appearing in a movie.

They are all of average height and average looks, and their very ordinariness works in their favor. Empathy and identification with them seem a lot easier, since what's special about them is their fighting ability and with proper training, such skills can be acquired. —Cano.

Tango Durch Deutschland
(Tango Through Germany)
(WEST GERMAN-COLOR)

Duesseldorf, Sept. 23.
A Lutz Mommartz Film production, in collaboration with ZDF (Second Channel). "Das kleine Fernsehspiel." Only credits available. Reviewed at Filmfest '80, Duesseldorf. Sept. 23, '80. Running time: 90 MINS.
With Eddie Constantine, Maya Farber-Jansen.

Yank actor Eddie Constantine has made a career in Europe, as anyone who follows the "Film Noir" tradition knows at the drop of a hat. His figure of Lemmy Caution, in fact, dominated the French "Film Noir" scene in 1954-55 at the height of the American influence in Paris, and Lemmy Caution's adventures in Jean-Luc Godard's

"Alphaville" (1965), perhaps Constantine's best film, paralleled the paperback detective stories carrying his tired, battered face on the cover.

After France, Constantine worked in Switzerland and Belgium while receiving offers to work in West Germany as a film actor and cabaret singer. His best role in Germany is considered to be the anarchist in Peter Lilienthal's "Malatesta" (1969). He also did Rainer Werner Fassbinder's "Third Generation." Now he's back in the public eye again with Lutz Mommartz's "Tango through Germany," Mommartz's first attempt at a feature film afer making a series of impressive shorts and experimental pix.

"Tango Through Germany" deals wqith the fate of a film idol, Constantine himself as Lemmy Caution, who leaves a kind of museum as a resurrected mummy. Everywhere he goes he confronts his film image and past glory as a tough gangster type, which he in real life isn't. He gets pushed around on the street, is afraid of being recognized in bars by fans of the genre, and finds some solace in the company of a television production manager (Maya Farber-Jansen, his present wife) who doesn't know anything about his past image.

Pic, however, doesn't hold up beyond the first half, when it's clear what's happening and the thesp is left, repeating himself in different settings. —Holl.

Mosch
(WEST GERMAN-B&W)

Duesseldorf, Sept. 24.
A Westdeutscher Rundfunk film production. Cologne. Features entire cast. Directed by Tankred Dorst. Screenplay, Dorst, Ursula Ehler; camera (B&W), Juergen Juerges; music. Peer Raben; sets. Guenther Naumann; editing, Liesgret Schmitt-Klink; tv-production manager, Hartwig Schmidt. Reviewed at Filmfest '80, Duesseldorf. Sept. 24, '80. Running time: 105 MINS.
Cast: Marius Mueller-Westernhagen (Arno). Valter Taub (Mosch). Katharina Thalbach (Billy). Ulrich Wildgruber (Paul). Rosel Zech (Adele). Sonja Karzau (the Aunt). Rudolf Voss (Herr Kolb). Ernst Konarek (Konarek). Franz-Adolph Rampelmann (Gerhard). Marie-Luise Marjan (Singer). Horst Laube.

Tankred Dorst, house author at the Bochum Schauspielhaus over the past decade, borrowed freely from that theatre's departing ensemble to make a tv film based on an original screenplay, "Mosch," which has its sequel in his play, "The Villa," presently on the boards of the Duesseldorf Schauspielhaus. Pic was shown on the opening night of Filmfest '80 in Oberhausen. "Mosch" was an oddity at the fest in that it was a pure tv

production and could be seen on the tube at the same time as in the fest theatres.

This is another of those triste views of the immediate postwar years that are being cranked out like sausages these days after the success of Rainer Werner Fassbinder's "The Marriage of Maria Braun."

"Mosch" is the story of a young man who goes to the city of Wuppertal to take over a rundown soap-factory left to him by his grandfather. What he doesn't know, but soon finds out, is Herr Mosch, a long-term employe in the factory, runs the business the way he sees fit and won't brook any interference from the new manager. The tug-of-war between the two incapable individuals leads in the end to Mosch's death in his bed by freezing to death after the pipes in his room burst in sub-zero weather, all because the old man is too stingy to repair the leaking radiators. Mosch is left frozen like a human icicle, an appropriate image or symbol (take it as you wish) of both the times and the alienation that was supposedly rampant then.

Ace lensing by Juergen Juerges, one of the best cameramen in West Germany, is pic's saving grace.
—Holl.

Encore
(HONG KONG-COLOR)

Hong Kong, Oct. 15.
Produced by Philip Chan and Elaine Sung through Promotion Center. Directed by Clifford Choi. Screenplay, Choi, Philip Chan. Original songs and music by Danny Chan. No other credits provided by the producers. Reviewed at Queen's Theatre, Hong Kong. Oct. 10, 1980. Running Time: 90 MINS.
Cast: Danny Chan. Leslie Cheung, Mary Yung. Winnie Yu. Paul Chung. Elizabeth Tam. Yang Kwan. Philip Chan with cameo appearance of local television and radio personalities.
(English subtitles)

Lightweight and youth oriented, "Encore" brings about the acting debut of popular baby-faced singer Danny Chan and the producing team of actor Philip Chan and Elaine Sung. For first timers, the film proved to be a success to all concerned. The boxoffice receipts reached HK $3 million in about 15 days.

"Encore" is a pleasant example of a Cantonese comedy-tearjerker about that old fashioned first love with tuneful ditties then capped with a memorable theme song penned by Chung. The film creates that "Breaking Away" youth appeal, corny at times but always sensible and tasteful. For a wholesome presentation that is like a peck on the cheek the warm Hong Kong reception surprised even the producers.

Giving a new twist to his acting career is producer Philip Chan who appears as the sympathetic beer-addicted uncle. He shows that he is finally evolving into a mature character actor. Clifford Choi directs with ease which minimizes the effect of the copious tears raining down the young hero's cheeks while his lush romantic song is played on the soundtrack. It is all predictable and calculated but captivating to watch.

The film may find some markets in Asia with a promo campaign directed to the soda pop brigade. The setting may be Hong Kong but the family situations, the value of friendship, growing up pains, competitive school spirit, westernized Asian youths, filial frictions and adolescent romance are universal themes. The memorable finale song performed by Chan at the talent quest contest sequence is good. "Encore's" cinematography evoke freshness. As for clean-cut Chan as actor, he makes a charming movie personality and deserves an encore from the producers. —*Mel.*

Per Jom Phen
(Per, Jom and Phen)
(THAI-COLOR)

Bangkok, Oct. 14.
A Saha Mongkol Films production and release. Produced by Somsak Techaratanaprasert. Directed by Sompong Tribupa. Features entire cast. Story and screenplay. Laem Bandit; camera (color), Saravuth Vudhichai; asst. camera. Suwan Julavutr; sound, Maitree Janjarasskul; music, Buan Savatcho; art director, Chuwit Permpohem; continuity, Khun Pao. Reviewed at Stella Theatre, Bangkok, Oct. 14, '80. Running time: 125 MINS.
Per .... Thep Thienchai
Jom .... Long Kaomonkadee
Phen .... Buan Savatcho
Jookjarng .... Supansa Nuangpirom
Poojah .... Suda Puavilai
Pan .... Choosri Misonion
Tiang .... Sitao
Dr. Saengthong .... Poonsawat Timakorn
Lung Mee .... Sompong Pongmitr
Pah Mah .... Jantree Sarikavutr
Toh .... Thep Po Ngarm
Jin .... Jin Po Ngarm

Since last year, local comedians have been getting more work, following the success of a spate of comedies. Most producers prefer to finance comedies these days, and local comedians now get starring roles. The tables have turned: popular romantic stars now only co-star or lend support to toplined comedians.

Thep Thienchai, Long Kaomonkadee and Buan Savatcho play three inseparable friends named Per, Jom and Phen, respectively, in Sompong Tribupa's new movie comedy. The comic situations are mostly cribbed from other recent comedies, but it makes no difference to local viewers.

The opening sequence shows the comic trio working as partners in a temple fair, playing jokes on unsuspecting customers. Viewers are supposed to laugh harder with repetition of this type of joke, which is what the movie does. It caters to the provincial market.

Invisibility has become a cheap trick in Thai comedies. Worse, it's combined here with mafiosi-type goings-on. Movie closes with a long chase between a red convertible with no visible occupants and several limousines driven by the heavies. A climax where the leading characters are invisible completely loses sight of their importance. At the same time, the comic villains don't get a good build-up prior to the protracted chase, and thus can only make viewers laugh mechanically.
—*Cano*

Paraguelia
(GREEK — COLOR)

Thessaloniki, Sept. 28.
A Pavlos Tassios-Greca Film, M. Lefakis and Greek Film Centre production. Written and directed by Pavlos Tassios. Camera, (color) Sakis Maniatis. Costas Papayannakis; music by Kyriavos Sfetsas; editing. Yannis Tsitsopoulos; reviewed at an Athens cinema, Sept. 28, 1980. Running time 95 MINS.
Cast: Antonis Antoniou, Katerina Gogou, Sophia Roubou, Nikitas Tsakirooglou, Olia Lazaridou, Antonis Kaftzoglou, Vicki Vanita.

This picture swept most of the prizes at the Thessaloniki Film Festival including best picture, best actor, music, editing and sound. Based on a true story and directed by Pavlos Tassios, it is his fourth picture. With this one he emerges as one of the top Greek helmers. His film is a well-made drama loaded with passion and violence plus bouzouki music and should have good boxoffice possibilities here and abroad.

The title word "Paraguelia" has a meaning at the popular bouzouki places, of an order a customer gives to the orchestra to play for him to dance alone. Not anyone else is allowed to dance with him and if he does a trouble follows. That's what really happened a few years ago at such a place. Two brothers went in a bouzouki place with their girl friends. One of them paid the orchestra to play for him to dance alone. But someone from another group got up too, and insisted on dancing. A trouble followed and a fight with both brothers killing two persons and wounding six others. The killers got away but were caught later and sentenced to death.

Tassios marks with this film a turning point in his career presenting a picture far better from his previous ones. Though his script does not explore his characters deeply, giving only vague hints about them, he directs crisply never allowing the spectator's interest to lag, especially in the first half. The sequence of the "slaughter" is exceptionally well made and is repeated at the scene of the trial in slow motion. But in the second half of the picture the action and tension drops as well as the quality. Some poems written and recited by Katerina Gogou, meant to serve as a link between the several segments of the story and provide a relief when passion reached great height, are sometimes out of place having no relation to the sequence over which her voice is heard.

Antonis Antiniou as the elder brother and killer, winner of the best actor prize at the festival, is really excellent. Olia Lazaridou, Katerina Gogou, Vicki Vanita, Antonis Kafetzopoulos and Nikitas Tsakiroglou are turning also good performances. The music by Kyruacos Sfetsas, winning a prize at the festival is effectively underlining the scenes of the picture enriching it with many bouzouki songs.

Other technical credits are good.
—*Rena.*

Santa Esperanza
(USSR-COLOR)

San Sebastian, Sept. 15.
A mosfilm production. Directed by Sebastian Alarcon. Features entire cast. Screenplay, Alarcon, Vladimir Amlinski; camera (color), Vadim Allissov; art direction, Irina Chreter; music, Gabriel Casto; Ramiro Soriano and Adrian Chamorro. Reviewed at San Sebastian Film Festival, Sept. 15, 1980. Running time: 94 MINS.
Borislav Brondoukov, Pavel Kadotchinikov, Evgueni Leonov-Gladychev;

"Santa Esperanza" is a Soviet film set in a fictional South American country. A heavily allegoric tale, it centres on life in a remote desert labor camp. It is a surprisingly bleak picture with little hope offered for escape or change for the prisoners.

The story unfolds with almost no detail offered for the camp's existence or the prisoner's crimes. It can be assumed most of the occupants are political dissidents. There are several attempts to break out by individuals but all fail miserably.

The film moves at a relentlessly slow pace. The final riot where the prisoners manage to take-over the radio room and transmit a message to the outside world is an explosion of action which occurs far too late in the film. In any event, it proves to be a fruitless exercise as the camp is closed and everyone is moved to another location.

Director Sebastian Alarcon, a Chilean living in Moscow, displays a strong visual sense in the second feautre. However, his story remains overly oblique and unfolds without drama or tension.

The blend of Russian and South American elements may spur some curiousity interest. However, the film is unlikely to find any acceptance in Latin America. —*Klad.*

El Hombre De Moda
(Man of Fashion)
(SPANISH-COLOR)

San Sebastian, Sept. 21.
A Niebla films production released by In-Cine. Directed by Fernando Mendez Leite. Screenplay, Leite and Manuel Marji. Features entire cast. Camera (color), Porfirio Enriquez; editor, Nieves Martin; sound, Julian Del Santo; music, Luis Eduardo Aute. Reviewed at San Sebastian film festival. Sept. 21, 1980. Running time: 113 MINS.
With: Xabier Elorriaga (Pedro), Marilina Ross (Aurora), Maite Blasco, Isabel Mestre, Alicia Sanchez, Carmen Maura, Francisco Merino.

"El Hombre de Moda" is a bittersweet tale of a man ruled almost entirely by intellect. It is a fascinating study which suffers from an inability to delineate how the central character was stripped of his emotions and a far too leisurely pacing.

Pedro is a teacher of literature at a girl's school. He has a genuine interest in providing his students with an outlet to examine writing and authors. Aurora, an Argentinian exile, becomes his most vocal student.

The two meet by coincidence at a party and their relationship grows but is abruptly stopped by Pedro. Pedro subsequently becomes involved with the wife of another teacher and is briefly reunited with his ex-wife.

The women appear to be attracted by Pedro's level-headedness. However, he retreats at the slightest hint things are becoming serious. He appears to be biding time but it is unclear what he ultimately intends to do with his life.

Director Fernando Mendez Leite makes no attempts to provide deep insights into Pedro's character and although he retains the central focus, he is the least satisfying character in the film.

The women, chiefly Argentinian actress Marilina Ross and Isabel Mestre, provide their roles with a deep felt passion. Ross particularly is touching in her attempts to bring Pedro out of his shell.

There is an amusing cameo from Spanish director Francisco Merino ("The Savolta Affair") as a frustrated movie critic.

"El Hombre de Moda" lacks the drama and insight to reach foreign audiences. Even with some judicious trimming, it's unlikely to spark the imagination of overseas viewers. It is nonetheless a work of talent and one should expect Leite's next film to make a major international breakthrough. —*Klad*.

Ke Xana Pros Ti Doxa Trava
(He Is Heading To The Glory Again)
(GREEK-COLOR)

Thessaloniki, Sept. 28.
A Studio "S" and Greek Film Centre production. Written by George Stampoulopoulos, Yannis Kakoulides. Directed by George Stampoulopoulos. Camera (color) Sakis Maniatis; music, Mimis Plessas; editing, George Triantafyllou; sound, Thanassis Arvanitis, Nicos Achladis. Reviewed at the Thessaloniki Film Festival, Sept. 28, 1980. Running time: 105 MINS.
Cast: Vera Krouska, Costas Arzoglou, Mimi Denissis, Yannis Floriniotes.

George Stampoulopoulos, a filmmaker with one picture to his credit, "Open Letter," which won a prize at the Thessaloniki Film Festival some years ago, disappointed with this picture. The film, his second, is a halfway effort with good intentions which are not realized in the end. The result is an insignificant picture with limited local draw possibilities and no prospects abroad.

With this picture Stampoulopoulos tries to present an unusual reflection of many aspects of modern life through a central character, a popular singer who has become the idol of the people, A female tv reporter tries to find out the motives of his sudden success which is not justified by an equal talent.

Through her search the director tries to satirize many odd things and conditions of modern life: the way popular singers are launched by the record companies; the hunt for an easy way to success and wealth; the political corruption; cheap tv propaganda; the miserable life of people in rural territories and their search for work; the old cheap melodramatic pictures; and many other conditions of life in this country. In the end of the picture the singer reaches the height of his success. A political party appoints him candidate to the next government elections to the astonishment of the tv reporter.

Stampoulopoulos narrates this well-meaning but uneven story with a directorial know-how but with a tighter script he might have made a better picture. The screenplay, though it won a prize at this festival, is sketchy and loosely knit with many flashbacks, some of them in black and white. The di-rector trying to satirize as many odd situations as possible, jumps from one topic to the other treating them only on the surface. His satire does not come off effectively.

The singer-idol is portrayed by Yannis Floriniotis, a singer-idol himself, who inspired the filmmaker to make this picture. Floriniotis portrays himself effectively and signs some of his hit songs. Vera Krouska as the tv reporter carries skillfully most of the acting burden while the rest of the actors and actresses are adequate.

Worthy of mention is the photography by Sakis Maniatis and the music by Mimis Plessas. —*Rena*.

Kapos Etsi
(Somewhat Like This)
(GREEK-COLOR)

Thessaloniki, Sept. 28.
An Agamemnon Ditsas picture. Written and directed by himself. Features entire cast. Camera (color), Vaguelis Nassopoulos; editing, Popi Alkouli; music, L. Kelaedonis; sound, I. Stavrou, K. Kittou. Reviewed at the Thessaloniki Film Festival, Sept. 28, 1980. Running time: 110 MINS.
Cast: An. Antoniou, K. Liacopoulos, A. Dounias, I. Avgoustidou and A. Constantopoulou.

This is the first picture of Agamemnon Ditsas, an architect, written and directed by himself. For a first effort Ditsas shows a promising start though his picture, based on a thin screenplay, suffers from an uneven treatment and structure. The result is a talky downbeat picture meant for local limited consumption with slim sales possibilities abroad.

The loosely-knit plot depicts two parties living in a modern city. The first includes people well established and the other workers and poor people. The main characters in both parties are a worker, a group of cultural people, a foreman, a lonely man, a company's manager and a group of children. We see them in their every day life until tragedy strikes.

But the storyline is so poorly developed jumping from endless political discussions to social criticism that fails to show the deadlock in which one modern society had reached as the filmmaker wanted to show.

Most of the festival audience had not understood when the film ended and left the theatre wondering what this picture would like to say.
· Performances are adequate as are all technical credits. —*Rena*.

Con El Culo Al Aire
(Caution To The Wind)
(SPANISH-COLOR)

San Sebastian, Sept. 14.
An Ascle-Globe-Andro production of a Globe Film release. Produced by Juan Andreu. Direction and screenplay by Carlos Mira. Features entire cast. Camera (color), Hans Burmann; editor, Pablo del Amo; art direction, Alejandro Soler; music, Juan C. Senante. Reviewed at San Sebastian film festival. Sept. 14, 1980. Running Time: 97 MINS.
Cast: Ovidi Montllor (Juan), Eva Leon (Esperanza), Maria Jose Arenos (Sister Angustias), Juan Monleon, Juan Carlos Serante, Antonio Morant, Rosita Amores, Jorge Seguij.

"Con El Culo Al Aire" (being translated as "Caution to the Wind") is a local entry with serio-comic intentions which largely fail to elicit laughter or pathos. The film has an intriguing premise but confines much of its humor to strictly provincial jokes which are likely to carry beyond the border.
Juan is a young, inexperienced man living in a Spanish village. During a local festival he meets Esperanza, a voluptuous singer who fronts a group of blind musicians. They spend the evening together and then she departs for her next engagement.

Juan is found by his family the next day silent and inert. He winds up in an asylum run by a tyrannical nun. Juan finds life in the asylum to his liking despite the odd inconvenience. However, when Esperanza appears in a vision to him he rebels causing a riot among the inmates and leading to a down-beat ending.

The film appears to join a recent crop of films inspired by "One Flew Over the Cuckoo's Nest." The basic notion is that it's becoming more difficult to distinguish the patients from the keepers in the institutions. "Con El Culo al Aire" offers no new insights into the problem.

Aside from strong technical credits and a fine central performance from local actor Ovidi Montllor the film passes without note. The film has opened in Spain to less than enthusiastic reviews and box-office. —*Klad*.

Oficio De Tinieblas
(MEXICAN-COLOR)

San Sebastian, Sept. 20.
A Conacito Dos presentation. Direction and screenplay by Archibaldo Burns, based on a novel by Rosario Castellanos. Features entire cast. Camera (color), Miguel Garzon; music, Manuel Enriquez. Reviewed at San Sebastian film festival, Sept. 20, 1980. Running Time: 96 MINS.
With: Enrique Lizalde, Julissa, Manuel Ojeda, Monica Miguel, Lilia Prado.

"Oficio de Tinieblas" is a poorly-made, muddle-headed tale from Mexico about the ill treatment accorded natives by powerful land barons. The film jerks along awkwardly in an attempt to mix social comment, melodrama and sex into a meaningful document.

It's difficult even to attempt a simple plot synopsis. The film opens with a dramatically unmotivated rape. It is presented more for titillation than as a symbol of how the Indian women are being economically pillaged.

Set in 1934, although few attempts are made to disguise modern automobiles or clothing, the film chronicles a government official's attempts to redistribute the land. There is obvious resistance from the landowners and tremendous opposition from the superstitious natives.

The final section of the film is a poorly executed revolt by the Indians who crucify a young boy to create a local Christ figure. The rebellion is quashed when their new order is revealed to have no power over the senors' guns.

"Officio de Tinieblas" has apparently been banned in Mexico for political reasons. There is little reason to be offended by any message the film may have to offer. Director Archibaldo Burns executes his ideas poorly and crudely and is unlikely to find any converts to his cause. —*Klad*.

Cork Fest

Hordubal
(CZECH-COLOR)

Cork, Oct. 28.
Czech State Film review of Barrandov Production production. Features entire cast. Directed by Jaroslav Balik. Screenplay, Vaclav Nyvit from the book by Karel Capek; camera (Color), Viktor Svoboda; music, Karel Mares. Reviewed at Cork Film Fest. Oct. 15, '80. Running time, 92 MINS.
Hordubal . . . . Anatoli Kuznezov
Polana . . . . , ... Luibuse Geptrova
Hafia . . . . Klara Pollertova
Stepan . . . . Sandor Oszter

A stolid rural drama that indicates Czech films are still looking backwards. Direction is plodding and misses the intensity needed to stave off repetitiveness.

The jury at the Cork Festival seemed pleased by the film and handed it best art direction and photography awards. Film does recreate bucolic life in the thirties well.

A man comes back from America to his farm. A local notary had robbed money he sent home and a handyman had been living with his wife.

To stave off local talk, he promises his 13-year-old daughter to the handyman. He gets ill and is found stabbed to death and the wife and handyman are arrested. It is intimated the mistreated daughter might have done it.

The Karel Capek tale misses the irony, insights into motivations and actions that the story might have had in book form. Mainly a local item, but, with the usual Czech technical excellence that has gotten it fest airings though not having the dramatic force for other outlets. —*Mosk.*

Fabian
(WEST GERMAN-COLOR)

Cork, Oct. 28.
United Artists release of Regina Ziegler Filmproduktion production. Features entire cast. Directed by Wolf Gremm. Screenplay. Gremm, Hans Borgalt from the book by Erich Kastner; camera (color). Jurgen Wagner; editor. Sigrun Jager; music. Charles Kalman. Reviewed at Cork Film Fest, Oct. 17, '80. Running time: 116 MINS.
With: Hans-Peter Hallwachs, Hermann Lause, Silvia Janisch, Mijanou Van Baarzel, Brigitte Mira, Ivan Desny.

United Artists might have a sleeper with this bittersweet look at the Germany of the late 20s as unemployment, moral slippage and permissiveness were leading to Nazism rather than better economic and democratic ways.

It builds up an arresting look at these days through a young man who keeps seeing the injustices building up but enjoys the freewheeling life that a rich friend and easy women bring his way.

The crowds seem to be sleepwalking in both their pleasures and few attempts at facing up to the hard times. The hero's friend commits suicide when a thesis he worked on is turned down. It was supposedly a trick by a petty professor for the thesis had gotten fine marks.

The protagonist finds love but she leaves him for a film producer. He goes home and may take a job with a Nazi newspaper. He had been a publicity man before he lost his job. Trying to save a boy who has fallen into a river he drowns. The ending is taken from the book from which it is adroitly adopted.

Two lines on the screen note that he tried to save the boy but could not swim. He drowned. He might not really have been able to swim through the approaching Nazi days. Director Wolf Gremm shows a neat balance of humor, fine blending of scenes and an unforced reflection of the times that led to the war and Nazi ways.

Film was held up from the Berlin Fest but was turned down by Cannes and finally ended up at Cork where it got mixed reactions. But it does denote a director with a flair for dovetailing narrative, characterization and finding a serio-comic edge that makes it an unusual look at this period.

Gremm has made four films and on the basis of this deserves attention. Though made before noted fellow filmmaker Werner Rainer Fassbinder's massive 17-hour tv series on the same period, Gremm's film goes its own way in showing the effects of the times on the central character as Fassbinder also did.

It needs careful handling for its points are subtle and made obliquely rather than giving them a more obvious dramatic edge. Film makes an impact and gathers timeliness on the disturbing resurfacing of Neo-Nazi groups in Europe today. —*Mosk.*

Criminal Conversation
(IRISH-COLOR-16m)

Cork, Oct. 28.
BAC Films, RTE release and production. Features entire cast. Directed by Kieran Hickey. Screenplay, Philip Davison. Hickey; camera (Color), Sean Corcoran; editor. J. Patrick Duffner. Reviewed at Cork Film Fest, Oct. 12. '80. Running time: 61 MINS.
Frank . . . . Emmet Bergin
Margaret . . . . Deirdre Donnelly
Charlie . . . . .Peter Caffrey
Bernadette . . . . Leslie Lalor
Susan . . . . .Kate Thompson
Student . . . . .Garrett Keogh

Irish films are rare and this buoyant 61-minute, 16m film coproduced with tv holds its own on a theatrical screen. It has acceptable ensemble acting, surface but recognizable characters and passably perceptive direction in its treatment of marital and human problems.

The film title, "Criminal Conversation," is a legal term for adultery for divorce is against the law in Ireland. It also means a wronged husband can sue a man who dallied with his wife for depriving him of her services. This gives it more bite on its home grounds.

Otherwise, it is a familiar tale of suburban dalliance, male machos with a built-in irony that a couple who have reached a lack of comprehension cannot easily . break with each other.

One Christmas eve two couples, old friends, drink and let things out of the bag. One man has been having an affair with the other's wife. The latter is upset by her husband's harmless flirting despite her own ways. The adulterer's wife knows but feels it is alright if it is kept among them.

It winds in an impasse. Film mainly depends on the long comic and then dramatic scene of confrontation and lacks more depth in characterization. Besides home chances, it could find more festival outings as a first harbinger of growing fiction films from Ireland.
—*Mosk.*

American Odyssey
(DOCU-16m-COLOR)

Pleasant travelog study of runners and outdoors enthusiasts.

A McKinley Productions Inc./Media America release. Exec producer, Suzanne Beffa. Written and directed by Ambrose Salmini. Camera (uncredited color), Ambrose Salmini, Steve Marts, Peter Salmini. Norv Knight; editor, Ambrose Salmini; sound. Kathy Emerick; narrator. Gerard Bocker; associate producer. Peter Salmini. Reviewed at Preview 9 theatre, N.Y.C., Oct. 24. '80. (No MPAA Rating). Running time: 87 MINS.
With: Melody Mayer, Todd Gay. Leon Henderson, Linda Macias.

Sports documentarist Ambrose Salmini organized and shot this entertaining cross country holiday, using the 1979 New York City Marathon as his starting point. Centering on three runners and exercise enthusiasts, he extols the value of outdoor sports while treating the viewer to the beauties of many unspoiled U.S. locations. Though the commercial market of late has given support to mainly controversial docus (e.g., "Harlan County, U.S.A."), this pleasant pic could find an audience as did Bruce Brown's carefree films of a decade or so ago. "The Endless Summer" and "On Any Sunday."

Melody Mayer, a teacher from Sandusky, Ohio, Todd Gay. and Leon Henderson, a farmer from Eugene, Oregon, are three young believers in the virtue of vigorous physical exercise. After running in the 1979 N.Y.C. Marathon, they embark with Salmini's camera crew on a journey by van across America, stopping off at scenic sites for running. cycling and local sports activities. Salmini also intercuts footage of earlier races and his protagonists at home before the trek.

Highlights of the trip include kayaking on the Little Tennessee River, visiting hospitable and self-reliant family of beekeepers in Blairsville, Georgia, a 50-mile bike tour near Tulsa, Oklahoma, hot air ballooning in Colorado, rock-climbing out west, racing on foot in San Francisco's "Bay to Breakers" competition, a visit to the Navajo cliffs, and running through the Grand Canyon.

A fourth participant, Linda Macias, joins the trio in Wyoming. Though Mayer stresses the importance of running and cycling as solitary pursuits by which she gains independence, she and Todd fall in love during the tour. Trip winds up at the U. of California at Davis, where trio, especially Mayer, prove exceptional in testing at the Human Performance Lab. Salmini proselytizes on the healthful effects of vigorous sport and exercise, e.g., cutting down on cardiovascular disease, but his film's message is clearly summed up in a bit of narration: "We were healthy, we shared friendship, we were free."

Using pleasant library and pop music for a soundtrack, film boasts sharp 16m photography (with emphasis on wideangle lens shots), which may sustain a blowup to 35m without much loss of definition.

—*Lor.*

The Idolmaker
(COLOR)

Powerhouse performance by Ray Sharkey as creator of 1950-'60s teen rock idols. Good outlook for UA's period drama.

Hollywood, Oct. 31.
United Artists release, produced by Gene Kirkwood, Howard W. Koch Jr. Directed by Taylor Hackford. Screenplay, Edward Di Lorenzo; camera (Technicolor), Adam Holender; music and lyrics, Jeff Barry; editor, Neil Travis; art direction, David L. Snyder; set decorator, Barbara Kreiger; sound, Buzz Knudson, Don MacDougall, Bob Glass, Peter Hliddal; choreography, Deney Terrio; associate producers, R.J. Louis, David Nichols; assistant director, Clifford C. Coleman. Reviewed at MGM Studios, Culver City, Oct. 28, '80. (MPAA Rating: PG.) Running time: 107 MINS.
Vincent Vacarri .... Ray Sharkey
Brenda Roberts .... Tovah Feldshuh
Caesare .... Peter Gallagher
Tommy Dee .... Paul Land
Gino Pilato .... Joe Pantoliano
Ellen Fields .... Maureen McCormick
Paul Vacarri .... John Aprea
Uncle Tony .... Richard Bright
Mrs. Vacarri .... Olympia Dukakis
Mr. Vacarri .... Steven Apostlee Peck
Luchetti .... Leonard Gaines
Jerry Martin .... Deney Terrio
Jesse .... Charles Guardino
Ed Sharp .... Michael Mislove

"The Idolmaker" is an unusually compelling film about the music business in the late 1950s and early '60s. The flip side of "Grease," it shows how teen idols were created, promoted, and discarded by entrepreneurs cynically manipulating the adolescent audience. Ray Sharkey is superb in the title role. Though it's marred by an overly melodramatic and dubious finale, the United Artists release should be an impressive entry in the fall market.

Edward DiLorenzo's script is a roman-a-clef of the career of Bob Marcucci, who, along with Dick Clark, guided Frankie Avalon to stardom and then created Fabian as Avalon's successor. Marcucci, listed in the credits only as "technical advisor," talked Gene Kirkwood into producing the film (with Howard W. Koch Jr.) and managed to get the jump on Clark, whose feature project on the period hasn't yet reached the cameras.

Viewers will have no trouble recognizing Paul Land as the Avalon figure or Peter Gallagher as Fabian, though the names and a few of the circumstances have been altered. Michael Mislove does a very brief appearance as the Clark figure, but the bulk of the story revolves around the Marcucci character, the frustrated singer turned personal manager played by Sharkey.

The manufacturing of pop idols during the early days of rock 'n' roll is a marvelous subject, since it allows the filmmakers to view the period from a double perspective: showing the genuine innocence of the fans who made the rock revolution possible, but admitting the almost Pavlovian role of the men who pulled the strings behind the scenes. Talent was often secondary to good looks, and if the white teen idol couldn't sing, a black back-up combo could always be hired to drown out his meager voice with a strong beat. And to make everything absolutely certain, there was payola.

All of these elements are shown in believable detail by DiLorenzo and director Taylor Hackford, though the payola and organized crime elements of the record industry are shown affecting the lower levels of the business but are not indicated on the higher levels, an unfortunate omission. Just how does Sharkey persuade "National Bandstand" host "Ed Sharp" to put the marginally talented "Caesare" on national tv? The viewer will have to draw his own inferences.

Sharkey, who made a strong impression earlier this year in "Willie & Phil," shows the full range of his talents here in a part that could elevate him to stardom. As a kind of "Rocky" figure who fights his way to the top through surrogates, Sharkey captures all the frustrations, rage, and drive that it takes to succeed in such a business. When he gradually comes to the awareness that he must find his fulfillment by marketing his own talents, rather than those of other people, Sharkey keeps the character believable even if the ending seems dictated by a phony need for an "upbeat" finale.

Land and Gallagher are both very good in their film debuts as the pop singers, though in the latter sections Gallagher and Sharkey are compelled to tear their passions to tatters in a shrill display of Italian arm-waving and shouting. The film suffers somewhat from pretension, and the feeling that everyone is going all-out to win Oscars rather than relaxing and treating the subject with the perspective it deserves. More humor would have helped.

The romantic subplot involving Tovah Feldshuh as a fan mag editor who pushes Gallagher while bedding Sharkey seems inadequately

developed and leads to an unbelievable resolution. The whole film really revolves around Sharkey and his ferocious energy, which reduces the supporting cast to shadows of his act.

Tech elements are good, especially the art direction by David L. Snyder and costuming by Rita Riggs that effectively capture the period on a modest budget. Original songs by Jeff Barry are polished, but they often have too contemporary a sound, a decision that may have been calculated to appeal to today's teen audience rather than to express the period with accuracy. Too bad, since the film is otherwise faithful to details. —*Mac.*

Sus Anos Dorados
(Their Golden Years)
(SPANISH-COLOR)
Seville, Oct. 22.
Produced, directed and written by Emilio Martinez Lazaro; exec producer, Jesus Martinez Leon; camera (Eastmancolor), Porfirio Enriquez; music, Suburbano; editor, Nieves Martin; direct sound, Julian del Santo and Miguel Angel Rospir; sets, Matoya del Real. Reviewed at Multiplex Cine 3 (Seville), Oct. 21, '80. Running time: 98 MINS.
Luis .... Jose Pedro Carrion
Maria .... Patricia Adriani
Carmen .... Marisa Paredes
Fermin .... Luis Politti
Miguel .... Pep Munne
Lola .... Mireia Ros

Confused, rambling pic never really comes to grips with the shifting characters it portrays due to weak script and virtual non-plot.

Item touches upon the lives of today's Spanish "lost generation" who seem to spend all their time smoking pot and sleeping with any girl they happen to be near. When main character, who's a dropout and a loser is asked what he wants out of life, he merely shrugs his shoulders. Not even the titillations of leftwing politics for these bored and boring yawners.

Only time pic comes alive a little is when the late Luis Politti steps in front of the cameras. But his part is too short and ill-scripted. Sales prospects nil for this self-indulgent work of "auteurship." —*Besa.*

Farodokument 1979
(Faro Document 1979)
(SWEDISH-COLOR)

Cinematograph production and release. Written and directed by Ingmar Bergman. Camera (color), Arne Carlsson; editor, Sylvia Ingemarsson; music, Svante Pettersson, Sigvard Hultdt, Dag & Lena, Ingmar Nordstroms, Strix Q, others. No other credits provided. Reviewed at Museum of Modern Art, N.Y., Oct. 30, 1980. Running time: 103 MINS.
Cast: Inhabitants of Faro island.

This 1979 updating of Ingmar Bergman's 1969 documentary of the

same title, made for Swedish television, is vastly more optimistic than the earlier look at life on the island of Faro, located in the Baltic Sea, and home for Bergman since he went there to shoot "Through A Glass Darkly." Although he's now situated in Munich, West Germany, for his film enterprises, he still considers Faro home and the film more than shows his affection for the island and his concern for its future.

The earlier Faro document ended on a somewhat downbeat note with most of the young people interviewed indicating that their departure for bigger and grander locales couldn't come soon enough. Ironically, those youngsters interviewed 10 years later seem to have decided to stay home after all and today's kids, while curious about the world, sound and look more content with life on Faro, despite its limited resources and (as the film was shot during the winter and the non-tourist season) its rather bleak look.

What is beautiful about Faro Document 1979 is the people in it. They're all serious, hardworking, a bit resigned to getting the short end of the budget and in every way, strong. One example is a handsome elderly farmer-lumberjack-fisherman-chef (you name it, he does it) named Valter Broman. He's so capable in every thing he does (and invariably without any help) that it comes as a shock to be told he's also a diabetic.

Bergman says he'll update it in 1989. You'd better believe it.

—*Robe.*

Honningmane
(In My Life)
(DANISH-COLOR)

Konsortiet Honningmane (Copenhagen) production. Written and directed by Bille August. Features entire cast. Camera (color), Dirk Bruel; editor, Janus Billeskov Jensen; art director, Erling Jorgensen; music, Fuzzy. Reviewed at Museum of Modern Art, N.Y., Oct. 30, 1980. Running time: 108 MINS.
Cast: Claus Strandberg (Jens), Kirsten Olesen (Kirsten), Jens Okking, Grethe Holmer, Poul Bundgaard.

Bille August's 1978 opera prima, "In My Life," is intended, if one believes the production notes, to show the "echoing emptiness of the welfare society — a society fuelled by the eternal vicious circle of production and consumption."

As portrayed, however, one gets the impression that this dull young couple wouldn't make a successful match in the happiest of situations. Claus Strandberg's factory worker is supposed to be under a strain of monotony — his work is certainly routine but his labors don't look all that strenuous and apparently he takes home enough money from the job to afford marriage and a nice apartment.

On the other hand, Kirsten Olesen is the daughter of two "ordinary people" types who have pampered her but don't resist her falling in love and marrying a factory worker. The real doldrums begin when the marriage starts. The best part of August's film is the satirical treatment of the wedding and reception — he has a real comedy sense — but then it goes back to the turgid pace of the beginning. For a first film, it's an interesting effort but there's plenty of room for growth.

One wonders if the Swedish morality hasn't been too strong an influence on this Danish filmmaker (he did the camerawork on Jorn Donner's "Men Can't Be Raped"). Still quite young, there's promise and a chance for improvement. He'd be wise to tackle a comedy. —*Robe.*

Le Coeur a l'Envers
(My Heart is Upside-Down)
(FRENCH-SPANISH-COLOR)

Paris, Oct. 12.

SN Prodis release of a 5 Continents - JL. Tafur (Madrid) coproduction. Produced by Bernard Lenteric. Stars Annie Girardot, Laurent Malet. Directed by Franck Apprederis. Screenplay, Odile Barsky, Apprederis, Gerard Brach; camera (color), Charlet Recors; sound, Bernard Ortion; music, Jean Musy; art director, Gerard Daoudal; editor, Laurence Leinenger. Reviewed at UGC Biarritz theatre, Paris, Sept. 30, 1980. Running time: **93 MINS.**

Laure .... Annie Girardot
Julien .... Laurent Malet
Guillaume .... Charles Denner
Jeanne .... Stephane Audran

Annie Girardot and Laurent Malet star in this dull drama about a mother-son relationship that veers dangerously close to incestuous consequences.

Girardot is a complacent, successful child psychiatrist whose life is upset by the return of her itenerant 24-year-old son, whom she has not seen since her divorce 12 years earlier. After a troubled reconciliation, the two take off for Spain where Girardot must attend a convention, but she soon abandons her professional obligations to enjoy a deceptively idyllic vacation with Malet. When she suddenly awakens to the ambiguities of their rapport, she panics and flees back to Paris, while her son returns disconsolately to the road.

The script by Odile Barski, Franck Apprederis and Gerard Brach is too meek in its treatment of a much worn and delicate subject to give film any intensity or conviction, and Apprederis' direction is equally bland.

This is the second attempt to package Malet as star material opposite Girardot. It's a marriage made neither in heaven nor at the pay windows, and both players again hand in mannered, superficial performances. Only supporting players Stephane Audran and Charles Denner manage to connect in silhouette roles. —*Len.*

Tiro Al Aire
(Unpredictable Guy)
(ARGENTINE-COLOR)

Buenos Aires, Oct. 22.

Distributed by Maxifilm. Produced by Rey Films. Producer, Toto Rey. Features Hector Alterio. Director, Mario Sabato. Original screenplay, Sabato. Camera (Eastmancolor), Leonardo Rodriguez Solis. Sets, Marchegiani - Olivo; Costumes, Marta de Serpi; Music, Victor Proncet. Reviewed at the Petit Atlas screening room, Buenos Aires, Oct. 1, 1980. Running time: **104 MINS.**

Nestor .... Hector Alterio
Sebastian .... Adrian Ferrario
Maria Jose .... Graciela Duffau
Marisa .... Graciela Alfano

Also: Aldo Barbero, Hector Bidonde, Julio de Grazia, Diana Ingro, Enrique Pinti, Rodolfo Ranni, Elena Sedova, Fernando Siro, Luis Tasca, Marcos Zucker, Paula Dominguez, Antonio Gasalla.

Aimed at the family market, this comedy with moments of anguish marks the return to Argentine film production of noted local actor Hector Alterio, star of "La Tregna," which was nominated for an Oscar in 1975, after some years spent working in Spain, notably in Carlos Saura films.

The comedy comes from the observation of everyday detail and of the character of Nestor Cegaglia (Alterio), a good for nothing dreamer, plus the contrast between the latter and his model son, Sebastian, aged 11. The moments of anguish come when the son becomes seriously ill (the father being too incompetent even to call the doctor in time). These episodes are an all too obviously synthetic plot insert to allow the soft hearted in the audience to exercise their tear ducts — so obviously, in fact, that the ducts are likely to retain their fluid.

The rest, however, is entertaining enough. The title character, while bungling everything else, does manage to pick up his son's beauteous schoolteacher, played by the Argentine cinema's reigning pretty face, Graciela Alfano — another attraction for home audiences. Abroad, the plot provides sufficient pleasant moments to deserve general-audience screenings. —*Olas.*

Le Coup du Parapluie
(The Umbrella Coup)
(FRENCH-COLOR)

Paris, Oct. 15.

Gaumont release of a Gaumont International production. Produced by Alain Poire. Stars Pierre Richard. Directed by Gerard Oury. Written by Oury, Daniele Thompson; camera (color), Henri Decae; music, Vladimir Cosma; editor Albert Jurgenson; art director, Jean Andre; sound, Alain Sempe. Reviewed at the Gaumont Ambassade theatre, Paris, Oct. 13, 1980. Running time: **90 MINS.**

Gregorie .... Pierre Richard
Otto Krampe .... Gerd Frobe
Bunny .... Valerie Mairesse
Josyane .... Christine Murillo

No surprises concerning the local success of "Le Coup du Parapluie," new film comedy starring Pierre Richard and directed by Gerard Oury, who has engineered some of the biggest grossing film farces in French cinema, including the 1973 "Adventures of Rabbi Jacob" (with Louis de Funes) and especially the 1966 "La Grande Vadrouille," which boasted the double-barreled headliners: De Funes and Bourvil, and has been seen by more than 17,000,000 spectators to date.

"Le Coup du Parapluie," concocted by Oury and his usual script collaborator Daniele Thompson (his daughter), is pleasant enough nonsense that maintains its pace with an unfaltering cheeriness and, even if you don't exactly respond to this kind of humor, it's hard not to admire the sheer technical skill with which it is made. Like another leading comedy director, Claude Zidi, Oury is a pro who understands how to give a gag, even a second-rate one, shape, rhythm and punch.

The script is amusing if not terribly original — yet one more spy spoof, it tells of a third-rate actor (Richard) who wanders by mistake into the office of a mafioso chief, who he believes to be a talent agent, and gets himself a "contract." The gangster thinks Richard will knock off an important arms dealer (Gerd Frobe); Richard thinks he's got a leading role in a big budget thriller pic.

After that the quid-pro-quos unfurl at a furious pace and climax in a manic imbroglio around the swimming pool of Saint-Tropez's Byblos Hotel (admirably reconstructed in a studio by veteran art director Jean Andre, who died of a heart attack at age 62 during the early weeks of film's shooting).

Richard bounces frenetically through the film with rubbery appeal and the supporting players, particularly the gifted Christine Murillo, as Richard's equally frenzied, jealous girlfriend, provide effective foils to the star's capers.

Film is, again, technically first-rate, with Henri Decae behind the camera and Albert Jurgenson at the editing table. —*Len.*

Kara Kafa
(Blinders)
(TURKISH-COLOR)

Berlin, Oct. 27.

A Korhan-Film production, Istanbul. Features entire cast. Directed by Korhan Yurtsever. Screenplay, Yurtsever, Bulent Oran; camera (color), George Becker, Salin Dikisci; editing, Yurtsever; sets, Kemal Yurt. Reviewed at Sender Freies Berlin Screening Room, Oct. 27, '80. Running time: **90 MINS.**

Cast: Betul Ascioglu (Hacer), Savas Yurttas (Cafer), Cuneyt Kaymat (Kerem), Oslem Guler (Zeynep), Macit Floroun (Rifat), Markus Ueberhoff (Uli).

Korhan Yurtsever's "Blinders" (the original Turkish title translates "Schwarzkopf" in German and something like "Black Sheep" into English) describes the plight of Turkish workers now living for more than a decade in West German cities. They are the "Gastarbeiter" in factories who do unskilled labor. One of the best pix on the subject due to its inside angle on abuses and family tragedies, this is also a human document that deserves some attention on the fest circuit.

Yurtsever made an impact at the San Remo fest a couple years back with "The Evil Spirit of the Euphrates," a small-budget Turkish pic dealing with exploitation of peasants by landowners in the arid, mountain regions of southeastern Turkey. He also did a photoessay on the migration of Turks to West Germany, which provided the basis for a successful tv film by a German femme helmer. Now, with meagre funds again, he has made "Blinders" to tell the migration story in such a way as to inform his country year of the psychological and social pressures placed on Turks living abroad for a more or less permanent stay. (When "Blinders" was shown recently in a cinema in Istanbul, a furor broke out as Rightists protested its political viewpoint. Now West German television is considering the merits of an airing with possible feedback discussion afterwards).

The story concerns a hardworking Turk in a steel foundry in Duisburg, an industrial city in the Ruhr Valley. The worker decides to bring his wife and two children to live with him in West Germany, a possibility that is quite realistic in view of his salary and living conditions (he has an apartment of his own). However, when the family arrives, he finds that he was "blind" to the quirks of fate: first he gets laid off from work and then has to go on unemployment compensation, which barely serves the family needs. His wife has to go to work, but she in turn liberates herself from her Oriental past and those restricting customs of obedience to the man in the house. Since she is now working and he isn't, that triggers the first family conflict.

The upshot is that the wife emancipates herself and shows her husband the way at the end by threatening to leave him. The worker also realizes he has to begin to fight for his rights in a foreign country that is now practically his own due to long-term residence. Several dialog scenes zero in on the working conditions and the conflicts between East and West cultures.

Quality lensing and a fluid narrative style make "Blinders" a winner as a human, social document on foreign workers in Western German cities. —Holl.

Ke Ha See Dang
(The Red Mansion)
(THAI-COLOR)

Bangkok, Oct. 21.
An Apex Productions release. Produced by Nanta Tansacha. Written and directed by Prince Tipayachatr Chartchai. Features entire cast. Executive producer, Orasee Chartchai; story, Princess Sawat Watanadom Pravit; camera (color), Prayong Mongkolmuang; music, Prajin Songpao; sound director, Pong Asvinikul. Reviewed at Siam Theatre, Bangkok, Oct. 21, '80. Running time: **120 MINS.**
Arya . . . . Nawarat Yukthanan
Moh Ruj . . . . Aporn Tonnawannij
Chalie . . . . Toon Hiranyasap
Sawaroje . . . . Ampha Pusit
Pakinai . . . . Projetr Ganpetr
Pakinee . . . . Nantaporn Amphaparint
Maids . . . . . Malee Wetprasert, Sulaliwan
                Suwanatat, Choosri Misomon
Ampha . . . . Marasri Nabangchang

No Thai filmmaker has done love stories more consistently in the past few years than Prince Tipayachatr Chartchai. "Ke Ha See Dang" is his third film released through Apex Productions this year. Most of his films have starred Nawarat Yukthanan in love triangles usually set in Chiang Mai, where it is possible to pick urban locations similar to Bangkok and pretty mountainside scenery at the same time.

"Ke Ha See Dang" is picturesque. Nawarat this time has three, instead of two suitors. They are Aporn Tonnawannij, Toon Hiranyasap and Pojetr Ganpetr.

Making her film debut in "Ke Ha See Dang" is Nantaporn Amphaparint. She plays an invalid, a sympathetic character who could have been the heroine, except that the script limits her role. On the other hand, Ampha Pusit is cast as a haughty and vindictive young lady, who displays her erudition by speaking in English.

Providing a number of comic scenes are Malee Wetprasert, Sulaliwan Suwanatat and Choosri Misomon. —Cano.

Vienna Fest

Io sono Anna Magnani
(I Am Anna Magnani)
(BELGIAN-DOCU-COLOR & B&W)

Vienna, Oct. 24.
A Chris Vermorcken/Pierre Film production. Pierre Film (Bruxelles) release. Directed by Chris Vermorcken. Executive producer, Jacqueline Pierreux. Spoken commentaries, Leonor Fini and Liliane Becker. Research and production assistants, Louise Rocco. Agnes Rombaut. Music, Willyl de Maesschalk. Edited by Eva Houdova. Available in Cinemascope format. Reviewed Oct. 24 at Kuensteerhaus Kino, Vienna, as official Vienna fest entry. Running time. 105 MINS.

With commentaries spoken in French, English subtitles and most interviews conducted in Italian, Chris(tina) Vermorcken's tight and warm hearted feature length Anna Magnani montage is already in theatrical release in Belgium and soon will be in France, too. "Io sono Anna Magnani" is such an accomplished work of documentary filmmaking that, carefully placed, it could turn out as a minor hit in specialized situations. Later tv sales are not only inevitable, rights will be fought for.

Using clips mostly from Anna Magnani's more important films and mixing them into a dramatic whole with clips from interviews with directors, actors and with the great "Nannarella" herself, Chris Vermorcken brings forth a portrait of a thorough professional whose bursts of violent emotion were reserved for the screen. At least, she was very disciplined on the set although she did very often suggest new interpretations of her roles which, as Luchino Visconti says, it was not always smart to listen to.

Much is made of what Visconti scenarist Suso Cecchi d'Amico calls the Italian film industry's boycott of Anna Magnani when her America-made features failed to do well at the boxoffice. No actual proof of any such boycott is entered, but the actress's son Luca Magnani (now an architect and handling her estate) says that she, during her later years, received mostly trashy scripts. The falling out of Magnani and Carlo Ponti when she refused to play mother to Sophia Loren in "La Ciociara" is interpreted in an openly prejudiced way.

The general warmth and strong use of documentary dramatics should not only further sales of Chris Vermorcken's film, but may

also stir interest in the complete Magnani oeuvre at revival houses. Film is also an entry at the Chicago Film Fest. —Kell.

Menschenfrauen
(Woman Rhymes With Human)
(AUSTRIAN-COLOR)

Vienna, Oct. 23.
A Valie Export and Top Film production. Top Film (Vienna) release. Features entire cast. Features entire cast. Script and structural assistance, Peter Weibel. Co-scripter and directed by Valie Export. Camera, (Eastmancolor), Wolfgang Dickmann, Karl Kases; editors, Tina Frese, Friedl Mayer. No music credits. Reviewed at Oefram Film screening room, Vienna, on Oct. 23, 1980 before entry in official Viennale program. Running time, 116 MINS.
Barmaid Elizabeth . . . . Renee Felden
Teacher Gertrud . . . . Maria Martina
Wife Anna . . . . Susanne Widl
Nurse Petra . . . . Christiane von Aster
Journalist Franz . . . . Klaus Wildbolz

Valie Export (a pseudonym for Waldtraud Hoellinger) does the skinny Austrian feature film output proud with this deftly-fashioned story about "Menschenfrauen" (no English title has been chosen, but the play on words is an ironic stressing of women being human, too). Export has been a keen student of Alain Resnais, Jean-Luc Godard, et al., and while she adds nothing new technically, she does very well with her interpolations of events in time and place and also occasionally with her use of graphics.

The Menschenfrauen of the title are Elizabeth, Gertrud, Anna and Petra, who are either married to, pregnant by or in other ways, attached to one man, Franz, who seems nice and easy going while he is also a false face and somewhat of a whiner. For a long time, he gets understanding all around, but in the end the women revolt. While Franz is not completely an outright male chauvinist caricature, the women, being allowed to indulge in over acting, sometimes do resemble vicious takeoffs. This was hardly the intention.

Picture is overlong and thematically bogged down by self pity, but it also has strength and obvious visual impact.

If the flood tide of women's films are not at an ebb by now, situations catering to such features may show "Menschenfrauen" to a profit. The risk is, however, that even militant women today will find the ending with the two pregnant women bathing their faces in the clean ocean water and entering a future of sisterly love together just plain tacky. —Kell.

The Pioneers
(NATIONAL CHINA/ TAIWAN-COLOR)

Vienna, Oct. 21.
A Central Motion Picture Corporation (Taipei. Taiwan) production and release. Written by Chang Yung-Hsiang, Chang Yi. Directed by Richard Y. Chen. Features entire cast. Camera (Eastmancolor, Cinemascope) Lin Wen-Chin; music, Oun Ching-Shi. Reviewed on official Viennale program at the Kuensterhaus Kino, Vienna, Oct. 21, 1980. Running time. 102 MINS.
Wu Lin-fang . . . . Wang Tao
Chaing Wan . . . . Hsu Feng
A.P. Karns . . . . John Philip Law
Teacher Tu . . . . Shih Chun
Wu's father . . . . Tien Yeh
Yueh-chun . . . . Lin Yueh-yun

Judging from the massive turnout of Vienna's Chinese community for the Viennale showing of University of California Film Class graduate Richard Y. Chen's "The Pioneers," this action-meller about the search for oil in the last half of the 19th century in Taiwan would seemed assured of happy audiences wherever these are Chinese in sufficient numbers. In other situations, film's fate may be more dubious.

Chen fills his every Cinemascope frame with either violent, blood-curling action or teary melodrama, but he never follows through on any of his many dramatic promises. As abruptly as some developments is put into high gear, it is again abandoned, sometimes only with "Fillers" of folkloristic or historical curio interest.

Story has first a father, then a son pursue the quest for oil on Taiwan. They are otherwise engaged in the dyeing business. There is much family interfighting and also some conflict between the mainland Chinese settlers and Taiwan's long-haired aboriginals. America's Standard Oil has a nice, well-meaning engineer (John Philip Law wearing formal Dickensian clothes) enter the picture, but he is soon out of it again. It would seem that the story is based on actual events. Production dress is of the highest order. —Kell.

Johnny Unser
(Our Johnny)
(AUSTRIAN — COLOR)

Vienna, Oct. 22.
An Arge Fi/Li/Po with Cinecoop-Film (Vienna) production and release. Features entire cast. Original story, script and directed by Tone Fink and Robert Polak. Camera (Eastmancolor, 16m, available in 35m). Herbert Link; edited, Robert Polak; music, Dieter Kaufmann, Bela Koreni. Clockwork. Reviewed on the official Viennale program at the Kuenstlerhaus Kino, Vienna, Oct. 21, 1980. Running time, 85 MINS.
Andrea . . . . Antonio Limacher
Paul . . . . Hagnot Elischka

Austrian features are rare birds, and this one is about a cat. The cat is supposed to relieve the humdrum life of a married couple. Soon everything in the household of Andrea and Paul turns around "Our Johnny" as the cat is called. It finally gets to be too much of a cat-race for Paul. At that time, however, Andrea has turned her mind to a more independant career while Paul goes in the opposite direction. He, rather than the cat, has been thoroughly domesticated.

The little everyday comedy would have served better as a half-hour tv sitcom, but Robert Polak and Tone Fink want to be on their way as regular ·feature film-'makers. They have financed "Our Johnny" themselves (and have only now gotten official money for 35m blow-up versions), and their work has yet too many earmarks of the home movie.

What Polak and Fink miss is any kind of personal style or even artistic or other viewpoint on their material. They have a vivid sense of the absurd which, with better production control, should help them on their future way. As it stands, "Our Johnny" will be lucky to get even limited tv exposure after an even more limited theatrical run. —*Kell.*

Raging Bull
(B&W AND COLOR)
―――

Great boxing scenes but De-Niro's character a turnoff. May have wobbly legs.

Hollywood, Nov. 7.
United Artists release of a Chartoff-Winkler Production, produced by Irwin Winkler and Robert Chartoff in association with Peter Savage. Directed by Martin Scorsese. Screenplay, Paul Schrader, Mardik Martin, from the book "Raging Bull" by Jake La Motta with Joseph Carter and Savage; camera (b&w and color, prints by Technicolor), Michael Chapman; editor, Thelma Schoonmaker; music, from prerecorded classical and pop sources; production designer and visual consultant, Gene Rudolf; art directors, Alan Manser, Kirk Axtell (L.A.), Sheldon Haber; (N.Y.); set decorators, Fred Weiler, Phil Abramson; sound, Les Lazarowitz, Michael Evje, Donald Q. Mitchell, Bill Nicholson, David J. Kimball; associate producer, Hal W. Polaire; stunt coordinator, Jim Nickerson; boxing technical advisor, Al Silvani; technical advisor, Frank Topham; assistant directors, Allan Wertheim, Jerry Grandey. Reviewed at Warner-Hollywood Studio, Nov. 6, 1980. (MPAA Rating: R.) Running time: 119 MINS.
Jake La Motta ....Robert DeNiro
Vickie La Motta ....Cathy Moriarty
Joey La Motta ....Joe Pesci
Salvy ....Frank Vincent
Tommy Como ....Nicholas Colosanto
Lenore ....Theresa Saldana
Patsy ....Frank Adonis
Mario .... Mario Gallo
Toppy .... Frank Topham
Sugar Ray Robinson ..... Johnny Barnes
Other Fighters: ....Floyd Anderson,
Kevin Mahon, Ed Gregory,
Louis Raftis, Johnny Turner

Martin Scorsese makes pictures about the kinds of people you wouldn't want to know. In his mostly b&w biopic of middleweight boxing champ Jake La Motta, "Raging Bull," the La Motta character played by Robert DeNiro is one of the most repugnant and unlikeable screen protagonists in some time. But the boxing sequences are possibly the best ever filmed, and the film captures the feverish intensity of a boxer's life with considerable force. The United Artists release, a Robert Chartoff-Irwin Winkler production, should do well in class situations but may flounder in the mass market due to the offputting character.

As in other Scorsese pix, the director excels at whipping up an emotional storm but seems unaware that there is any need for quieter, more introspective moments in drama. Every scene is all-out hysteria. This bravura tendency makes the boxing scenes so viscerally intense that the viewer will be almost reeling, but Scorsese unfortunately shoots every other kind of scene as if it's a boxing match too.

Scorsese here blends the work of the screenwriters of "Mean Streets" and "Taxi Driver," Mardik Martin and Paul Schrader, into

a film which takes the emotionally tangled N.Y. Italian milieu of the former and shows it creating the psychotic DeNiro of the latter. Here DeNiro's antisocial violence is channeled into the socially accepted role of a prizefighter, but in the end he has ruined his body and alienated everyone who ever cared about him, including the audience.

The relentless depiction of the downward slide of La Motta from a trim contender in 1941 to a shockingly bloated slob introducing strippers in a sleazy nightclub in 1964 has the morbid quality of a German expressionist film. By the time DeNiro — who actually gained 50 pounds for the latter scenes — sits at a dressing-room mirror looking at his puffy face and trying to close the tuxedo collar around his swollen neck, he's become as grotesque as Emil Jannings in "The Blue Angel."

The film is not a conventional biopic in that it skips over important stages in its character's life (such as his rise to fame, his divorce and remarriage, all covered in a quick montage of home movies) in order to concentrate on building up selected emotional high (or low) lights. That would be fine, since the contemporary audience doesn't know or care much about La Motta going in, except that the scenes it does choose to show are almost perversely chosen to alienate the audience.

Scorsese and DeNiro made a similar miscalculation in "New York, New York," in which the lead character also did nothing but rant and abuse his wife for the entire film. There it seemed especially unpleasant because the audience had other expectations raised by the musical genre, but here it works more often because boxing pix are expected to be rough and violent.

Aside from the customary genre plot of a boxer selling out to the mob, what seems to be on the minds of Scorsese and his screenwriters is an exploration of an extreme form of Catholic sadomasochism. La Motta's violence toward himself and other people seems to stem from the deep repression of his sexual tendencies, as his brother-manager Joe Pesci hints in one scene, suggesting if La Motta would sleep with his wife more often, he'd hit her and other people less often. All of the unsatisfactory sexual encounters between DeNiro and wife Cathy Moriarty take place underneath prominently displayed crucifixes and religious paintings, providing a pervasive feeling ·of guilt and frustration.

Schrader's fascination with self-destructive characters, and his ability to make them compellingly real, give Scorsese and DeNiro some scenes of high emotional vol-

tage to work with, such as when La Motta acts out his insane jealousy of his wife, but Scorsese never makes credible why a woman would put up with such incredible abuse for so long. The inarticulate performance of newcomer Moriarty, who has an interesting sullen quality when she remains silent, never adequately fills in the blanks of the character.

The boxing scenes regularly punctuate the drama, with printed titles keeping track of the time and place. DeNiro, with his dedication to believability, trained himself into a completely convincing fighter, with La Motta's crouched, in-close style. The other fighters in the pic, notably Johnny Barnes as recurring opponent Sugar Ray Robinson, are also top-notch under the supervision of boxing technical advisor Al Silvani.

Not since "The Harder They Fall" in 1956 have boxing scenes been filmed with such terrific intensity, and "Raging Bull" outdoes that and other classics of the genre such as "The Set-Up" and "Body & Soul" in conveying the punishing physicality of boxing from the fighter's p.o.v. — quite literally so in the amazing finale to the third Robinson fight, in which LaMotta takes a horrible beating that the viewer feels with him. Lenser Michael Chapman makes spectacular contributions to the brilliance of the fight scenes, as do the sound crew with their surreal heightening of the sounds of punches and crowd noise. Scorsese and editor Thelma Schoonmaker also make highly effective use of slow motion in the fights and elsewhere to take the film out of objective reality into the subjectivity of La Motta's mind.

Though the film is almost completely in b&w, which fits the subject and time period perfectly, color is used briefly in the home movies sequence, and the main title card is also in color. Technicolor did the superb print job.

When screened for the trade press, the film was not completely mixed or timed, and the titles were incomplete, but UA indicated no other changes would be made before the openings. —*Mac.*

Trois Hommes a Abattre
(Three Men to Destroy)
(FRENCH-COLOR)
―――

Paris, Nov. 5.
A UGC release of an Adel Productions - Antenne 2 coproduction. Produced by and starring Alain Delon. Directed by Jacques Deray. Screenplay, Deray and Christopher Frank, based on a novel by Jean-Patrick Manchette. Camera (color), Jean Tournier. Sound, Kean Labussiere. Music, Claude Bolling. Art director, Jacques Brizio. Editor, I. García de Herreros. Production manager, Henri Jaquillard. Re-

viewed at the UGC Normandie Theatre, Paris; Oct. 31, 1980. Running time: **90 MINS.**

Michel Gerfaut .... Alain Delon
Bea .... Dalila DiLazzaro
Emmerich .... Pierre Dux
Leprince .... Michel Auclair
Madam Gerfaut .... Simone Renant

Alain Delon's latest is a routine thriller about a professional gambler who finds himself the prey of killers after having come to the aid of one of their quarries, whom he ignorantly believed to be the victim of a road accident. After one of Delon's friends is accidentally murdered, the hunted becomes the hunter. Delon, whipped into fury, fills his role of avenger with such brutal efficiency that his chief tormentor, a ruthless, influential arms dealer (Pierre Dux) thinks he is a pro at mayhem and tries to buy his allegiance. Delon refuses and is later murdered.

Jacques Deray directed and co-scripted with novelist Christopher Frank. Deray keeps the film moving and forestalls boredom, but the script, laden with action cliches and trite characterizations, is an unstimulating rehash of a classic thriller situation.

Delon's role is a bare outline, dependent on the star's presence for its cohesion and force. Unfortunately, Delon is so icily bland that he never gets the necessary purchase on audience sympathies and the supposedly tragic denouement falls flat.

Delon fans may buy it, but others will be left hungry for better crafted thrills. —*Len.*

Det Andre Skiftet
(The Second Shift)
(NORWEGIAN-COLOR)

Marcusfilm A/S production. Produced by Oddvar Bull Tuhus. Directed by Lasse Glomm. Screenplay, Glomm, from stories by Espen Hraavardsholm; camera (color), Erling Thurmann-Andersen; editors, Fred Sassebo, Christian Hartkopp; music, Arne Garvang; art director, Frode Krogh; assistant director, Aamund Johannesen. Reviewed at Museum of Modern Art, New York, Nov. 4, '80. Running time: **78 MINS.**

Margot Amundsen .... Mona Malm
Trond Amundsen ..... Gunnar Enerkjaer
Olof Vikan .... Nils Gaup
With Frode Rasmussen, Rolf Nielsen.

Lasse Glomm's 1978 first film, "The Second Shift," is an intense romantic triangle story, masquerading as a social document. Sketchy script degenerates into repetitive situations, making film seem much longer than its barely feature-length running time.

Flashback tale has Olof Vikan, a 23 year-old, arriving in an industrial town for a job at the state-run steel works. He befriends an older worker, Trond Amundsen and his wife Margot. Trond, 30 years Olof's senior, is a loyal union member, re-

sistant to the current petition-circulating protestors, while both Olof and Margot identify with the dissenters. For his pains, Trond gets little respect at work, being treated like a shirker by a foreman one day when he takes a break due to stomach problems.

Working on separate shifts, Trond and Olof are ultimate both serviced sexually by Margot, while male duo remain the best of buddies as long as the deception lasts. When Trond finally gets wise, violence erupts.

Glomm fails to make his point about working conditions by not showing the effects of the union unrest; all one gets is a series of verbal arguments. Threesome's dramatic action is well-directed, with excellent cinematography by Erling Thurmann-Andersen, contrasting dramatic character close-ups with awesome visuals of the steelmaking process and the vast reindeer roundups Olof used to work with.

It is left to intrusive narration to establish the disillusionment that has set in since the works opened in 1946 with plans for workers' control. Narrator sums up with "It's not a question of what the state owns, but who owns the state;" a telling point, but not integrated properly into the film's melodramatic narrative. —*Lor.*

Final Assignment
(CANADIAN-COLOR)

Chicago, Nov. 4.
An Inter Ocean Film Sales Ltd. release, financed by Canadian Film Development Corp., Famous Players Ltd., and CTV Television Network Ltd. A Persephone Productions Ltd. production, produced by Lawrence Hertzog and Gail Thomson. Features Genevieve Bujold, Michael York, Burgess Meredith and Coleen Dewhurst. Directed by Paul Amond. Screenplay, Marc Rosen; camera (color), John Coquillon; score, Peter Germyn; editor, Debbie Karin; sound, Henri Blondeau; exec producers, James Shavick and Arnold Kopelson. Reviewed at Chicago Film Festival screening room, Chicago, Nov. 4, '80. (No MPAA Rating reported). Running time: **101 MINS.**

Nicole Thomson .... Genevieve Bujold
Lyosha Petrov .... Michael York
Zak .... Burgess Meredith
Dr. Valentine Ulanova . Colleen Dewhurst
Sam O'Donnell .... Alexandra Stewart
Bowen .... Richard Gabourie

"Final Assignment" seen at the Chi Film Fest is a Canadian pic with a troubled plot. The film is supposed to be set in Moscow and Leningrad, but was transparently shot in what looks like a four-square block area of Montreal, home base of Persephone Productions, which is responsible for "Final Assignment."

Pic has an idealistic tv journalist (Genevieve Bujold) on assignment in the Soviet Union covering a visit by the Canadian prime minister to

discuss disarmament treaties, among other issues. Along the way Bujold has a romantic encounter with a Soviet press bureaucrat (Michael York) and unearths a rather nasty Russian scientific experiment involving the use of steroids on young children.

"Final Assignment" was apparently designed as a romantic foreign intriguer pitting Bujold against the entire KGB and a reluctant York in spiriting out of Russia an incriminating videotape recording of the results of those nasty experiments.

To further complicate matters, scripter Marc Rosen also has Bujold in league with a scientist involved in the experiments (Colleen Dewhurst) to smuggle out of Russia the scientist's young daughter, who needs a brain operation in Los Angeles. To help in the escape attempt, Bujold turns to an old family friend, a Jewish fur merchant (Burgess Meredith), who happens to be in Leningrad at the time on a buying trip.

All this comes across on film as silly as it probably reads. Enough said that "Final Assignment" is loaded from start to finish with unintentionally funny lines, settings and entire scenes. The name cast tries hard enough, but there's just no way of endrunning Paul Almond's lackluster direction and Rosen's banal script.

Bujold, usually an interesting actress, here resorts to or is directed to use frantic hand gestures and facial expressions to make something of her ill-conceived part. York lapses into pigeon Russian in an unsuccessful try to make his part at least minimally credible. Meredith is simply miscast and Dewhurst is simply wasted.

General production values are inadequate. A boom mike is spotted in one scene; color quality is washed out in others. It's hard too to recall one bar of Peter Germyn's score. Why this pic wound up in the 16th anni Chi Film Fest is impossible to explain. "Final Assignment" made its world preem at the Fest, and will be released via Pan-Canadian in November in Canada. —*Sege.*

Falling In Love Again
(COLOR)

Nostalgic, warm romantic comedy. Needs careful handling.

The International Picture Show of Atlanta release of an O.T.A. production. Produced and directed by Steven Paul. Exec producer, Hank Paul. Features Elliott Gould, Susannah York, Stuart Paul, Michelle Pfeiffer, Kaye Ballard. Screenplay, Steven Paul, Ted Allan, Susannah York; camera (color), Michael Mileham, Dick Bush, Wolfgang Suschitzky; editors, Bud Smith, Doug Jackson, Jacqueline Cambas; music, Michel Legrand; songs, music by Legrand, lyrics by Sammy Cahn, Carol Connors, Dennis Lambert; co-producer, Patrick Wright; assoc. producers, Dan Murphy, Dorothy Koster-Paul. Reviewed at Rizzoli screening room, N.Y.C., Aug. 7, 1980. (MPAA Rating: PG). Running time: **103 MINS.**

Harry Lewis .... Elliott Gould
Sue Lewis .... Susannah York
Pompadour (Young Harry) ...Stuart Paul
Sue Wellington ....Michelle Pfeiffer
Mrs. Lewis .... Kaye Ballard
Mr. Lewis .... Robert Hackman
Stan the Con .... Steven Paul
Alan Childs .... Todd Helper
Mr. Wellington .... Herb Rudley
Mrs. Wellington .... Marion McCargo
Hilary Lewis .... Bonnie Paul

Though spiralling production and promotion budgets currently conspire against the "small picture," Steven Paul's "Falling in Love Again" demonstrates that unpretentious, personal filmmaking is far from dead. Largely a family project for the Paul clan, this modestly budgeted romance could find an audience as a people-intensive film, with warm, easy-to-identify-with characters rather than currently fashionable shock values.

Elliott Gould, in his perhaps best, most comfortable performance in several years, is perfectly cast as Harry Lewis, a New Yorker entering middle age, suffering the usual crisis and recalling the good old days of his youth. On a cross-country trip by car with his family, en route to a high school reunion in the Bronx, Gould narrates flashbacks of his romance with Susannah York (played by Michelle Pfeiffer as teenager) in the '40s.

Lewis (played by Stuart Paul as a youth) went after and married the beautiful, "unattainable" rich girl. His hopes of career success did not materialize, with duo currently owning a clothing business which York runs while Gould dreams of becoming an architect.

Crosscut with present-day footage, the '40s scenes feature fine ensemble comedy of Stuart Paul and friends' antics, as well as their serious effort to mount a local scrap drive to support the war. Nostalgic approach includes a well-directed seduction sequence as Paul succumbs to the wiles of a beautiful young (but older than he) housewife (played by the stunning Cathy

Tolbert). Jewish milieu is well-delineated, with a brassy Kaye Ballard very funny as Paul's mom.

After inevitable conflicts erupt during the trip, Gould is disillusioned upon arrival in New York, with the deterioration of his old neighborhood. Film climaxes with an incisive, beautifully-played scene in a restaurant where Gould is shooting his mouth off with his old buddies. York slips in unnoticed to silently observe, and in a very well-judged switch, Gould suddenly turns serious and pours out his true feelings regarding York and his goals in life. With York an almost ghost-like presence here, both thesps shine.

Young actor-turned director Steven Paul shot "Falling in Love Again" last year at age twenty, but his feel for a past era and emphasis upon old-fashioned (but still effective) picture values bely his youthful status. Pic artfully captures the '40s look and feel, with color stock-footage an effective budget-stretcher for shots of old New York beyond the neighborhood. Michel Legrand's score works well in whipping up sentiment, though he lapses into a corny pastiche of Bill Conti's "Rocky" theme during an action sequence.

Gould and York, reteamed after their "The Silent Partner" stint, have been allowed by the young helmer to actively collaborate in the filming, with York receiving a co-scripting credit. Film benefits from their personal involvement, with Gould a very sympathetic central figure and York selflessly alternating supportive scenes with confrontational outbursts, all designed to help the film rather than steal the spotlight. Interesting structure has some flashback material late in the pic presented from her point-of-view, departing from the "Gould's story" premise.

Michelle Pfeiffer makes a strong impression as York's younger self, with a dreamy look in her eyes which is quite distinctive. Stuart Paul is convincing as Gould's young ego and the director acquits himself well as a negative influence in the old neighborhood. —*Lor.*

Alligator
(COLOR)

More teeth than legs, but maybe some b.o. bite.

Hollywood, Nov. 11.
A Group 1 Films release, produced by Brandon Chase. Exec producer, Robert S. Bremson. Directed by Lewis Teague. Screenplay, John Sayles; camera (Deluxe Color). Joseph Mangine. (No other credits provided by distributor). Reviewed at the Joe Shore Screening Room, Los Angeles, Nov. 11. 1980. (MPAA rating: R.) Running time: **94 MINS.**

David Madison	Robert Forster
Marisa	Robin Riker
Police chief	Michael Gazzo
Kelly	Perry Lang
Mayor	Jack Carter
Col. Brock	Henry Silva
Reporter	Bart Braverman
Tycoon	Dean Jagger

"Alligator" is bloody and boisterous but may bite off a bit of business. It at least has the distinction of featuring the only man-eating monster in memory named "Ramone."

First seen, Ramone is a little baby alligator on a reptile farm in Florida, soon to be bought as a pet and taken to Missouri by sweet little Marisa who loves snakes. But dad gets mad and dumps Ramone down the toilet.

Fast forward 12 years and Marisa (Robin Riker) has grown up to be a world-famous herpatologist, while down below in the sewer Ramone has grown up unnoticed to be a 36-foot, one-ton, mean-tempered alligator.

Ramone developed his size and personality eating dead dogs thrown into the sewer by a chemical company experimenting on them in search of growth-inducing hormones. Ultimately tired of dog meat, the alligator starts to eat sewer workers and pet-store owners and policemen and finally a newspaper reporter dedicated enough to keep snapping pictures while chewed alive.

Until the camera was found, nobody believed detective Robert Forster's story that it was a big alligator that ate his partner, Perry Lang. Even Riker didn't believe him, though she did remember papa flushing the baby down the drain.

Pursued by everyone, poor Ramone is forced to flee the sewer and hide in a suburban swimming pool, where he apparently looks to the homeowners like nothing more than a big log because they let the kids play by the pool until the log eats one.

But, when not in bed, Forster and Riker are a match for the menace, finally driving him back down to his nest in the sewer and blowing him up in a mist of methane gas. But not before he wrecked the wedding party and ate mayor Jack Carter, assorted waiters and waitresses and crushed the limo containing the drug-company tycoon, Dean Jagger.

Dumb as it is, director Lewis Teague brings some plusses to the pic. Forster and Riker are amiable leads, never taking the film too seriously. Tech credits are cheap but serviceable and the finale of the pic is actually a bit exciting. Exploitation fans will also be glad to see the return of Sue Lyon and Angel Tompkins, cameoed as news reporters.

Finally, the title creature in one of these films outperforms the rest of the cast. —*Har.*

The Day Time Ended
(COLOR)

Nice special effects and creatures in a throwaway film. No b.o. potential.

Compass Int'l/Manson Int'l release of a Vortex production. Produced by Wayne Schmidt. Steve Neill. Exec producer, Charles Band. Directed by John (Bud) Cardos. Features entire cast. Screenplay, Schmidt, J. Larry Carroll, David Schmoeller; camera (Metrocolor), John A. Morrill; editor, Ted Nicolaou; music, Richard Band; ass't director. Bob Shug; art director, Rusty Rosene; special visual effects, Paul W. Gentry, David Allen, Randy Cook; animation effects supervisor, Pete Kuran; "City of Light" visual effects, Jim Danforth; stop-motion animation, Lyle Conway; models design, Lain Liska; models execution, Greg Jein. Reviewed at RKO 86th St. Theatre, N.Y.C., Nov. 15. 1980. (MPAA Rating: PG). Running time: **79 MINS.**
With: Jim Davis, Christopher Mitchum, Dorothy Malone. Marcy Lafferty, Scott Kolden. Natasha Ryan. Roberto Contreras.

Filmed in 1978 under the working title "Vortex," "The Day Time Ended" is a very low-budget science fiction film which gives every indication of being unfinished, but released anyway for some fast playoff bucks. The effects crew has conjured up some very diverting visuals, but complete absence of a workable script will have the fans complaining.

Sketchy storyline concerns a family led by patriarch Jim Davis moving into their modernistic, solar-powered home out in the desert. Meanwhile, a trinary supernova (three stars exploding some hundreds of years ago) has just visibly reached Earth observers and its radiation is presumably causing some strange occurrences.

The family's young daughter, Natasha Ryan, finds a glowing green pyramid out by their corral. Object later shrinks and is brought into the house by Ryan as a toy. From then on, script gets loose, and though helmer John (Bud) Cardos tries to maintain suspense and dramatic tension, film disintegrates into a series of inexplicable events.

A cute, tiny humanoid creature appears to Ryan (and later to mom Dorothy Malone), performing stop-motion animated ballet moves and seeming to ask for help. It is followed by a sinister, miniature spaceship, which destroys bullets or objects aimed at it, but does nothing positive or harmful to our heroes.

Using the all-purpose gimmick that the house has passed into a "time-space warp," filmmakers have two upright, dinosaur-type monsters appear and fight to the death out in the backyard. Finally, amidst numerous colorful UFO sightings (reminiscent of Doug Trumbull's beautiful work in "Close Encounters of the Third Kind"), cast strolls hopefully over the next ridge to a "City of Light" for what may be an idyllic future for them. Davis is stuck at the finish with that corny line: "Maybe this was all meant to be," but by this time the fans will be ready to riot over the pointless nonsense preceding.

Live-action cast is to be pitied, having to essay innumerable reaction shots to effects or monster scenes added later in a seemingly arbitrary fashion. Cardos never gets his players to display the proper degree of awe or terror to match what they're supposed to be looking at. Chris Mitchum, though a lead player, is oddly written out of most of the script, only to come back pointlessly at the end, all evidence of the film's "unfinished" nature. Malone is looking good, but both she and a pre-"Dallas" Jim Davis have no characters with which to work.

The special effects team deserves credit for their fine achievements here, with the stop-motion animated monsters particularly well-done and without the jerky movements one normally identifies with the process. Too bad they couldn't have toiled on a project with even minimal scripting logic.
—*Lor.*

Fico D'India
(Prickly Pears)
(ITALIAN-COLOR)

Rome, Oct. 24.
A Titanus release, produced by Achille Manzotti for Intercontinental Film Co. Stars Renato Pozzetto, Aldo Maccione and Gloria Guida. Directed by Steno. Screenplay by Enrico Vanzina, Steno. Renato Pozzetto, Sandro Continenza. Raimondo Vianello. Camera, Carlo Carlini; art director, Paola Comencini; editor, Raimondo Crociani; music, Giancarlo Chiaromello. Reviewed at Cola Di Rienzo Cinema. Rome. Oct. 21. 1980. Running time: **98 MINS.**

Lorenzo Millozzi	Renato Pozzetto
His wife	Gloria Guida
Arrigo Buccilli	Aldo Maccione

The popularity of the Italian comedy, by now a genre with its own fixed rules, characters and situations, has sent "Prickly Pears" soaring on national top grosser charts. Prototypical pic is almost a textbook on vices and virtues of the trend. Jealous husband suspects wife of playing around. Devoid of originality but likable in moments of greatest absurdity, "Pears" would make an excellent test case to see how provincial Italo comedy fares in more sophisticated markets abroad.

Basic situation of veteran helmer Steno turns up on schedule: two male comics clown around the "straight" female, who has a minimal role. Renato Pozzetto, pudgy and puritanical, plays the mayor of a small town happily married to sexy Gloria Guida, the kind of housewife who does the dusting in high heels, make-up and St. Laurent. Playing off against Pozzetto, as the self-righteous oaf, is Aldo Maccione in a fine and credible performance as a rather greasy local Lothario who leaves a fish with a rose in its mouth after his amorous visits. Gloria is the only faithful wife in town, but is believed only after mayor and Lothario are photographed together in bed.

The importance of gratuitous female nudity in this kind of comedy (Guida has the face and body of an emaciated Barbie doll) is equalled only by the mandatory transvestite scene. Homosexual pairing is suggested and then emphatically denied when the mayor's fear of being cuckolded yields to the warmth of comradeship after several bottles of champaign. Pozzetto's unpleasant rotundity is revealed in bra, panties and garter belt in one of pic's funnier sequences.

Laughs are principally built around visual jokes — potential plus for export. Pozzetto being chased by a gang of juvenile delinquents, setting up "anti-cuckold" mechanisms around the house, making magic costume changes into waiters, butlers etc., are a few. Verbal jokes are tied to bathroom dialogue.

Pic's situations are not bad but the jealous husband idea is simply tiring, as is the happy ending of Guida chastizing the men for the way they treat women. Five-man writing team (too many cooks at work on the same broth?) must have congratulated themselves there.

The children's music that accompanies pic is a total irritation but pretty aptly mirrors film's backwoods atmosphere. Ditto sets featuring "Italian style" interior decorating at its most pedestrian. —*Yung.*

Un Escargot Dans la Tete
(Snails in the Head)
(FRENCH-COLOR)

Paris, Nov. 6.

A Gaumont release of a Link production. Produced by Maurice Molina and Andre de Blanzy. Features entire cast. Written and directed by Jean-Etienne Siry. Camera (Eastmancolor), Francois About. Editor, Antoinette Perraud. Sound, Jean-Luc Rault Cheynet. Art directors, Kim Doan and Patrice Mercier. Reviewed at the Quintette, Paris, Oct. 1, 1980. Running time: **90 MINS.**
Cast: Florence Giorgetti, Renaud Verley, Jeanne Allard, Jean-Claude Buoillon, Charles Dubois, Marcel Gassouk.

Newcomer Jean-Etienne Siry says he had a nightmare about snails and felt impelled to write this film, which begins as a psychological drama and climaxes as a gasteropodous horror pic in which one of the main characters is apparently killed by the creeping crawlers.

Script relates how two young artists (Florence Giorgetti and Renaud Verley) meet in a psychiatric hospital where both are recovering from severe emotional crises — she has been through a painful divorce, he is responsible for a car accident that killed his wife and child. Once released they continue to see each other. But Verley is still morbidly obsessed by the past and is inexplicably fixated on snails, which begin to invade the woman's dreams as well.

A rupture comes brutally when Giorgetti's ex-husband commits suicide, throwing her into solitary depression. Verley, rejected, himself retires into delirious seclusion. When Giorgetti later comes to his country home seeking a reconciliation, she finds Verley's body being feasted upon by the colony of snails he has been raising. She is recommitted to a mental hospital.

The initial premise is interesting and the snails work well as a symbol of the characters' sexual and emotion repulsion, but Siry has clearly not bothered to think his film out. He merely sets us up for a series of eerie effects that culminate in the shot of Verley's body infested with a horde of rebellious molluscs. The transition from the symbolic to the literal is confused and more ludicrous than chilling and the picture ends with nothing being explained. A good nightmare doesn't automatically make a good screenplay. —*Len.*

Shogun Assassin
(JAPANESE-COLOR)

Slick Americanization of two Japanese actioners with much bloodshed. Possible attraction for both cults and masses.

Hollywood, Nov. 11.

A New World Pictures release of a Toho Company-Katsu production. Executive producer, Peter Shanaberg. Original version produced by Shintaro Katsu, Hisaharu Matsubara. American version produced by David Weisman. Original version directed by Kenji Misumi. American version directed by Robert Houston. Screenplay, Robert Houston, David Weisman, Kazuo Koike, based on an original story by Koike, Goseki Kojima; camera (Metrocolor), Chriski Makiura; original editor, Toskio Taniguchi; American editor, Lee Percy; music, W. Michael Lewis, Mark Lindsay; sound (Dolby), Tsuchitaro Hayaski; associate producers, Larry Franciose, Michael Maiello, Albert Ellis Jr., Joseph Ellis. Reviewed at the Warner-Hollywood Studios, Hollywood, Nov. 11, 1980. (MPAA Rating: R.) Running time: **86 MINS.**
Lone Wolf . . . . Tomisaburo Wakayama
Daigaro, The Son . . . Masahiro Tomikawa
The Supreme Ninja . . . . Kayo Matsuo
The Masters of Death . . . . Minoru
Ohi, Shoji Kobayashi, Shin Kishida
Voices by Lamont Johnson, Marshal Efron, Sandra Bernhard, Vic Davis, Lennie Weinrib, Lainie Cook, Sam Weisman, Mark Lindsay, Robert Houston, David Weisman. Voice of Daigaro by Gibran Evans.

"Shogun Assassin" is a real curiosity item. A fast-paced, almost absurdly bloody actioner, pic is fashioned of footage from a 1974 Japanese item "Baby-Cart At The River Styx," second in the highly popular "Baby-Cart" series, as well as 12 minutes from the first entry in the series, "Sword Of Vengeance." With new editing, deliberate lip-sync dialog and fancy music and sound effects, result is very slick and very playable on the exploitation circuit. As the first of a kind, it's likely to catch on as a cult item, but whether or not it makes it with more mainstream audiences is impossible to say. Film has already opened in Detroit, with best results in black-oriented houses.

Filled with incident but little real plot, tale has a demented Shogun's "Official Decapitator" seeking revenge on the Shogun and his hordes of Ninja warriors for murdering his wife. The fearless Lone Wolf travels the land with his young son in tow in a baby-cart, slaughtering his predators by the hundreds via dazzling displays of swordmanship.

Reediting job has made the film a satisfying series of violent confrontations, wherein Lone Wolf dispatches dozens of samurai at a time. A first for Yank audiences never before exposed to these Japanese actioners will be the sight of blood literally gushing and spraying from victims of the hero's lightning sword, sometimes covering the lens with red liquid.

However, because of the almost cartoon-like quality of the violence, bloodletting isn't upsetting in the least, and stylized quality gives the action virtually no visceral impact, which may disappoint domestic audiences primed on realistic mayhem and gore.

American producer David Weisman, director Robert Houston and editor Lee Percy have taken enormous pains to carefully lip synch the minimal dialog, and have also added elaborate sound effects and a lush, largely electronic, score. Unfortunately, tone of the new script falls somewhere in between the spare toughness of Sergio Leone's Italian westerns and the outright hilarity of Woody Allen's Japanese dub job, "What's Up, Tiger Lily?," so that viewers may not know exactly how they're supposed to react to the proceedings.

Perhaps because of the combination of all the post-production work, the disembodied voices and the inherent unreality of the material, a certain distancing sets in between picture and audience, taking the edge off the enjoyment of action for its own sake and making it less exciting than it might have been.

Nonetheless, fact that violence almost never stops may be enough for undiscriminating viewers, and entire project is sufficiently unusual to perhaps carve a niche with the hipsters.

Among the vocalists, director Lamont Johnson's rich baritone lends Lone Wolf great strength, and Gibran Evans does a charming job as the infant son, who is also narrator of the piece. —*Cart.*

Der Erfinder
(The Inventor)
(SWISS-COLOR)

Zurich, Nov. 10.

Rex Film AG Zollikon/Zurich release of a Kurt Gloor production, in collaboration with ZDF (2nd German TV), Swiss TV, Jean Frey AG and Dr. A. Eric Scotoni. Written and directed by Gloor, from a play by Hansjoerg Schneider. Stars Bruno Ganz, Walo Luond, Verena Peter. Camera (Fujicolor), Franz Rath; editor, Stefanie Wilke; music, Jonas C. Haefeli; sound, Hans Kuenzi; art direction, Bernhard Sauter; costumes, Regina Baetz. Reviewed at Frosch Cinema, Zurich, Nov. 8, '80. Running time: **97 MINS.**
Jakob Nuessli . . . . Bruno Ganz
Otti . . . . Walo Luond
Martha Nuessli . . . . Verena Peter
Seppli Nuessli . . . . Oliver Diggelmann
Kobi . . . . Thomas S. Ott
Phillipp Nuessli . . . . Klaus Knuth
Lisbeth Nuessli . . . . Babett Areans
Viktor . . . . Inigo Gallo
Manufacturer . . . . Erwin Kohlund
Doctor . . . . Klaus Steiger
Reverend . . . . Walter Ruch
Speculator . . . . Mathias Gnaedinger
Boss . . . . Ettore Cella
Herta . . . . Margrit Rainer
Colonel . . . . Guido Bachmann
Engineer . . . . Rene Scheibli
Teacher . . . . Michael Gempart
Controller . . . . Ernst Stiefel

"The Inventor" is described by scripter-director Kurt Gloor as "a memorial to all those who had a good idea at the wrong time." In this case, it's a World War I factory worker in a Swiss village who invents a caterpillar-type carriage, not knowing that his "invention" has just been put into use by the war powers as the tank. Always regarded by the villagers as a weirdo, this blow breaks his resistance against being put away in a asylum by the authorities.

Based on a play by Hansjoerg Schneider, produced at the Schauspielhaus in Zurich seven years ago, the film version clearly rises above the stage edition, which was a near-miss. While the latter unsuccessfully tried to combine two themes into a single drama, Gloor's script is a clear cut, straightforward job, not particularly imaginative or inspired, but plausible. The same goes for his direction. Gloor has an eye and ear for atmosphere and characterization, both hitting the right note most of the time. "The Inventor" was made on a modest (by international standards) budget of $970,000.

Bruno Ganz as the quietly stubborn inventor delivers a restrained, most convincing performance free from any false histrionic fireworks, in line with his recent remarkable appearances in films by such directors as Peter Stein, Eric Rohmer, Wim Wenders, Reinhard Hauff and Werner Herzog. Walo Luond as his pal, who shares his obsession, is also excellent.

Verena Peter as the inventor's wife is a fresh new face. Secondary roles are all satisfactory. Technically, the film is professional all the way, especially Franz Rath's color lensing and Stefanie Wilke's editing. —*Mezo.*

The Boogey Man
(COLOR)

Another Kill-Kill-Kill film.

Hollywood, Nov. 14.

A Jerry Gross Organization release, produced, directed and written by Ulli Lommel. Exec producer, Wolf Schmidt. Camera (Metrocolor), David Sperling, Jochen Breitenstein. (No other credits available). Reviewed at the Pacific Theatre, Hollywood, Nov. 14, 1980. (MPAA rating: R). Running time: **79 MINS.**
Lacy . . . . Suzanna Love
Jake . . . . Ron James
Doctor . . . . John Carradine

If the market for "creative killing" hasn't been saturated by now, "Boogey" may boogie on down to the bank.

There's these two little kids, you see, whose mother has a boyfriend who likes to tie little brother up while he makes out with mom. Little sister takes a big knife and cuts him loose and then watches in the mirror while boy cuts up the boyfriend.

Some 20 years later, the sister, Suzanna Love, is still suffering from the memorable night while brother won't talk, even to his collection of snakes and spiders. Love's husband, Ron James, thinks she's a bit addled and takes her to doctor John Carradine, who suggests a visit back to the murderous old home place will cheer her up.

Unfortunately, it doesn't. Allowed entrance by the two teenage girls and their snotty little brother who live there, Love goes to look in mom's old bedroom and immediately spies the ghost of the dead boyfriend in the mirror. So she picks up a chair and smashes it.

This makes James suspect his wife is loonier than ever and he, being the sane one, decides to pick up all the pieces of the mirror and take it home and paste them back together so Love will know the world isn't so odd after all.

Unfortunately, he leaves one piece behind on the floor and it starts glowing red and breathing heavy and before you know it, one sister has stabbed herself in the throat with her scissors, the brother is choked to death by a window and the other sister — well, it's a surprise.

Back at the farm, the brother has almost strangled the girl who came to get eggs, then painted all their mirrors black, but none of this is very important compared to James mirror-patching project. Once he's finished, Love looks at the fractured reflections and concedes she can't see any spooks. So she decides to take her kid fishing.

But the mirror wants to go fishing, too, so a piece fastens onto the boy's shoe sole and away they go. Unhappily for them, four teenagers are frolicking nearby at the lake and just as one girl starts to do something nasty, a beam of light bounces upon her from the kid's tennies and soon she and her boyfriend are spiked together in an eternal kiss.

Back at the farm, hayforks are flying through the air and the mirror is madder than ever. Uncle Earnest says, "This is unbelievable," but nobody's listening, least of all producer-director-writer Ulli Lommel.

Finally, Love gets a piece of glass in her eye and aunt-and-uncle are hayforked to death out at the barn. Love turns green and bloodies James and the priest, which is enough to shock brother into his first words in 20 years.

"Throw the mirror down the well," he shouts.

Oh, if he had only spoken sooner.
—*Har.*

Rendez-Moi Ma Peau
(Give Me Back My Skin)
(FRENCH-COLOR)

Paris, Nov. 13.

A CCFC release of a Chloe Production-Parano Films coproduction. Produced by Jean-Pierre Fougeau. Feature entire cast. Written and directed by Patrick Schulmann. Camera (color) Jacques Assuerus and Andre Zarra. Sound, Alix Comte. Editor, Aline Asseo. Art director, Marc Heyden. Special effects, Bertrand Bellouin. Reviewed at the UGC Biarritz, Paris, Nov. 12, 1980. Running time: **110 MIN.**
Cast: Bee Michelin, Erik Colin, Chantal Neuwirth, Jean-Luc Bideau, Alain Flick.

Patrick Schulmann, who came upon the French film scene last year with a hugely successful sex comedy, "Et la tendresse?... Bordel!", is back with more. And this time more is less.

The crotch humorist in Schulmann is unrepentant. In this one two young people, strangers to each other, run into an irate witch on a highway and promptly find themselves transplanted into the body of the other. Think of all the predictable guffaws you can mine out of this situation and you have half the script.

The other half concerns the quest of a detective and his assistant, hired by the two victims of witchcraft, to track down the sorceress and have the spell reversed. This allows Schulmann to run the gamut of humor to be found in a limp-brained satire on paranormality and religious sects.

Of course it's vulgar and tasteless, but that wouldn't matter if the material was at least inspired in its uncouthness. But this is bottom-of-the-barrel puerility.

Schulmann wrote, directed and composed the music, all with small incompetence. At least his first film had a certain brio and one refreshing performance (by Bernard Giraudeau) but here the desert has no oasis. And Schulmann will go down in film history as the first director to spoof a scene from a Louis de Funes comedy. —*Len.*

Nedtur
(If Music Be the Food of Love)
(NORWEGIAN-COLOR)

Norsk Film production. Produced by Harald Ohrvik. Written and directed by Hans Lindgren. Features entire cast. Camera (color), Halvor Naess; editor, Ola Solum; music, Christian Reim; art director, Ingeborg Kvamme. Reviewed at Museum of Modern Art, N.Y.C., Nov. 16, 1980. Running time: **91 MINS.**
Nils . . . . Nils Sletta
Elin . . . . Sigrid Huun
Christian Henning . . . . . Froydis Armand
Kari Henning . . . . Helge Jordal

"If Music Be the Food of Love" is a 1980 Norwegian "sax film" (a story of a young man and his saxophone) which tries very hard to examine empty human relationships in a critical manner. Heavy soul-searching dialog rapidly sinks this well-meaning but gauche pic.

Story concerns Nils, a young tenor player who is too self-centered to give of himself in his relationship with Elin, a former junkie. His best pal, Christian, is a still photographer who works in advertising and for porno magazines. Christian can't get along with his wife Kari, as "free love" is something they can't cope with.

Downer of a script contrives to have both couples break up, with Elin going back on the hard drugs and overdosing at film's climax, Nils having trouble on the bandstand and landing in jail, and Christian railing out against his job and meaningless existence. Hokey open-ending presents Nils with a new opportunity to start up a permanent relationship with a woman, but leaves hanging whether he has matured sufficiently to handle it.

Nils Sletta creates a sullen, intriguing (though unsympathetic) protagonist, sort of a Nordic Robbie Robertson. Unfortunately, his tenor playing is mediocre, giving the film very little interest to jazz fans. In fact, when he's on the bandstand soloing in front of a huge blowup photo of the great Dexter Gordon, one can't help think that an authentic story of the jazz experience would be preferable to this gimmicky "express my emotions with my horn" approach.

Supporting cast is good, though hampered by the heart-on-sleeve self-examining dialog. Tech credits are excellent, but debuting helmer Hans Lindgren would do well to devise an interesting, more subtle script next time out. —*Lor.*

Mormor og de atte ungene i byen
(Grandma and the Eight Children in Town)
(NORWEGIAN-COLOR)

Vampyrfilm and Norsk Film production. Produced by Hans Lindgren, Gunnar Svensrud. Stars Anne-Cath Vestly. Written and directed by Espen Thorstenson, from novels by Anne-Cath Vestly. Camera (color), Halvor Naess; editors, Leif Leif Erisboe, Thorstenson; art director, Sven Wickman. No other credits provided. Reviewed at Museum of Modern Art, N.Y.C., Nov. 15, 1980. Running time: **96 MINS.**
Grandma . . . . Anne-Cath Vestly
Mother . . . . Eli Ryg
Father . . . . Jon Eikemo
Henrik . . . . Nils Sletta
Neighbor Hulda . . . . Kari Simonsen
Morten . . . . Grim Snorre Langen

Intermittently cute but generally tedious, "Grandma and the Eight Children in Town" is a Norwegian family film tailored strictly for the home market. Shot in 1976, it is derived from popular children's books by Anne-Cath Vestly (who also stars in the pic version), and local familiarity with the material made the film a hit, even commanding a sequel. Film's charm does not extend readily to the uninitiated.

Writer-director Espen Thorstenson has chosen enough story material and character interaction to justify perhaps a 30 minute short, but with his snail's pace and unfocused direction stretch it to feature length. Three segment structure consists of the kids' adventures searching for their dad's stolen truck, grandma's visit to town with the kids teaching her how to cope with traffic, and grandma's hitchhiking trek back to the old folk's home.

Shot in a largely realistic, "heavy" style at odds with both comedy or children's films, pic gains its warmth and value from the playing of star Vestly and the ebullient, nonactor children. The antics of the youngest, Morten (played by a cherub named Grim Snorre Langen) yield the film's brightest fantasy moments, as he communes with an imaginary cloud or indulges in funny practical jokes.

Concept of finding adventure in the commonplace is okay, but Vestly and Thorstenson have not devised enough interesting situations to flesh out this comical "slice of life." The implicit thematic question of why lovable grandma has to live at an old folks' home instead of with the parents and kids is unconvincingly sidestepped by having the mother say "If only we had more room you could stay with us for good," to granny at the finish.

Tech credits are okay, but dubbing would probably remove what charm the kids have in the original Norwegian soundtrack version.
— *Lor.*

Seitseman Veljesta
(Seven Brothers)
(FINNISH-ANIMATED-COLOR)

Nelimarkka/Seeck production. Produced and directed by Riitta Nelimarkka and Jaakko Seeck. Screenplay adapted by Nelimarkka from novel by Aleksis Kivi; camera (Eastmancolor), Seeck; editors, Kaija Ahopelto, Pipsa Valavaara; music, Pekka Jalkanen; watercolor backgrounds, Nelimarkka; cut-out animation, Seeck; sound mix, Pauli Vellnonen; voice director, Kari Franck; narrator, Esko Salminen. Reviewed at Museum of Modern Art, N.Y.C., Nov. 10, 1980. Running time: **80 MINS.**

Touted as Finland's first animated feature film, "Seven Brothers" (1979) is too much, too soon. Painfully tedious and disjointed, the film at first arouses interest via its combination of watercolor backgrounds and manipulated cut-out paper character figures, but the primitive technique cannot sustain an hour or more of running time.

Story is an episodic set of folktales, set in Finland during the mid-1800s. Lack of continuity makes the film difficult to follow, but it is basically concerned with the picaresque adventures and fantasies of seven orphaned brothers. They farm, play hookey from school and generally avoid adult responsibilities.

Riitta Nelimarkka's backgrounds are in generally drab colors, while Jaakko Seeck's foreground figures move in jerky motions not likely to win favor with animation buffs. The brothers are not well differentiated, offering little competition to popular cartoons. Animals are treated realistically, except for a bear which gets drunk and a fantasy of oxen dressed as the faithful congregation, carrying on a service with prayer books and grammar books "in hand."

Best moments in the film, which is separated into three related sections, are fantasies, including the legend of a cyclops-like ogre who preys upon the "Wan Maiden" in the forest, and a very quaint trip to the moon escorted by the devil (to see the Earth below explode like a popped balloon) in one of the brother's nightmares. Subtitling presented focussing problems (trying to get both background and titles simultaneously in focus) on the print screened; dubbing would be more appropriate. —*Lor.*

Akitsu Onsen
(Affair at Akitsu)
(JAPANESE-COLOR)

A Shochiku production. Exec produced by Masao Shirai; planned by Mariko Okada. Directed by Yoshishige Yoshida. Features entire cast. Screenplay, Yoshida, from a story by Shinji Fujiwara; camera (color), Toichiro Narushima; music, Hikaru Hayashi; art director, Tatsuo Hamada; costumes, Mariko Okada. Reviewed at Japan House, N.Y.C., Nov. 9, '80. Running time: **113 MINS.**
Shinko .... Mariko Okada
Shusaku Kawamoto ..... Hiroyuki Nagato
With: Sumiko Hidaka, Taiji Tonoyama, Masako Nakamura, Jinkichi Uno, Eijiro Tono, Fukuko Sayo, Teruo Yoshida.

An impressively shot star vehicle made in 1962, "Affair at Akitsu" is a lavish soap opera, with the issue of changing moods and mores in postwar Japan as its subtext. Stark beauty and thesping ability of Mariko Okada, later to marry the director, is pic's raison d'etre.

Tale spans 1945-62 period, commencing with a frail student, Kawamoto, stopping at a health spa located at Akitsu near the end of the war. He is befriended and nursed back to health by a lovely teenager, Shinko. News of Japan's surrender brings them to tears, and after an incongruously hopeful segment of their looking forward to a new life together, leads enter into a suicide pact. Their unsuccessful attempt at carrying out the deed is directed with delightful black humor, but unfortunately renders **the ensuing hour of footage as anticlimactic.**

Director Yoshishige Yoshida proceeds to run the soap opera changes, with Kawamoto leaving town, marrying and becoming successful, but iteratively returning to Akitsu to commune with this first love. Shinko's suicide 17 years later is a decidedly Japanese variant of the Hollywood "woman's film" genre, and really played to the hilt.

Yoshida is a master of widescreen composition, often dwarfing his actors and story with stunning shots.

"Akitsu" is unfortunately sabotaged by the sentimental musical score by Hikaru Hayashi, in which a couple of corny themes are repeated dozens of times. Tech credits are all excellent. —*Lor.*

Aquella Casa En Las Afueras
(That House In the Outskirts)
(SPANISH-COLOR)

Madrid, Oct. 31.
A Kalender Films International S.A.k production. Directed by Eugenio Martin. Features entire cast. Screenplay, Manuel Summers, Antonio Cuevas, Jose G. Castrillo, Eduardo Alvarez, Eugenio Martin and Manuel Matji; camera (Eastmancolor), Manuel Rojas; exec producer, Antonio Cuevas; music, Carmelo Bernaola; editor, Pablo G. del Amo; sets, Jose Maria Alarcon. Reviewed at Cine Conde Duque Madrid, Oct. 31, 1980. Running time: **101 MINS.**
Joaquin .... Javier Escriva
Nieves .... Silvia Aguilar
Isabel .... Alida Valli
   Also features Mara Goyanes, Carmen Maura.

This is a well-scripted, taut and on the whole absorbing suspense thriller which avoids the excessive gore and sadism of many pix in the genre, while still piling on enough suspense to keep audiences riveted in their seats, especially during the last half hour. Item never goes off the deep end; satisfactory explanations are offered for all mystifications.

Plot concerns a 22-year-old girl from the provinces who's brought to Madrid by a devoted husband. Latter has rented an old-fashioned house in the outskirts for himself and his six-months pregnant wife. When driven to the house, rather then being pleasantly surprised, Nieves is horrified. It turns out house was formerly run by a clandestine abortionist and his girlfriend nurse. Nieves herself had undergone a traumatic abortion here five years early, but had never mentioned it to hubby.

Story moves along nicely, with ominous hints along the way as the upstairs lady tenant (Isabel), who pretends to befriend Nieves, turns out to be the former abortionist's aide, and now a homocidal schizoid to boot, who has kept all of the abortionist's trappings and paraphernalia in the attic of the house, including the jars containing the foeti. At the end, nurse goes berserk, reaping mayhem on those around her, but Nieves comes through unscatched.

Excellent production values, good thesping by all, and sufficient terror should enable the pic to chalk up sales in all territories, even those down on violence. Pic has been doing brisk biz in its Spanish release, and commercial prospects offshore are good. Alida Valli's name may help. —*Besa.*

Un Mauvais Fils
(A Bad Son)
(FRENCH-COLOR)

Paris, Nov. 5.
Parafrance release of a Sara Films Antenne 2 SFP coproduction. Produced by Alain Sarde. Stars Patrick Dewaere. Directed by Claude Sautet. Written by Sautet, Daniel Biasini and Jean-Paul Torok. Camera (color) Jean Boffety. Music, Philippe Sarde. Editor, Jacqueline Thiedot. Art director, Dominique Andre. Sound, Pierre Lenoir. Reviewed at the Paramount Elysees, Paris, Nov. 1, 1980. Running time: **110 MINS.**
Bruno Calgagni .... Patrick Dewaere
Rene Calgagni .... Yves Robert
Catherine .... Brigitte Fossey
Adrien Dussart .... Jacques Dufilho
Madeleine .... Claire Maurier

Claude Sautet's latest probing of conventional people in conventional settings is "A Bad Son." The film is itself rather conventional, but made with sincerity, feeling and talent, and even those detractors who have found Sautet's recent pictures stodgy and soporific may respond to this one's uncluttered lines of emotion. As far as "quiet dramas" go, this one has possibilities in the English-language market.

Patrick Dewaere stars and he is unostentatiously good in one of his less eccentric roles. (The pic's publicity poster merely displays a pencil drawing of Dewaere, seated and pensive, a Metro ticket in his hand — it not only gives the tone of his performance but also loads the film's ad campaign on Dewaere's image).

Dewaere plays a young man returning to France from the U.S., where he has just served a five-year prison term for drug trafficking. Film begins with his arrival in Paris. The drama ensues from his difficulties of readjustment: social (his attempt to find satisfactory employment), familial (a difficult reconciliation with his working-class father, who blames the recent death of Dewaere's mother on his shameful incarceration), emotional (his affair with a young woman, an ex-addict like himself, who still shoots up from time to time in moments of stress).

Sautet, steering clear of the sensational and the over-dramatic, succeeds in giving a touching relief ot his personages and their difficulties in getting from one day to the next without losing balance. His direction is subtle and intelligent and his penchant for staging scenes around dinner and cafe tables doesn't become exasperating for the viewer. Apparently, dropping his sights down a few notches on the social scale (from middle to working class) has sharpened his narrative abilities.

Yves Robert, drawn away from performance in recent years by his producing and directing activities, makes an affecting comeback as the embittered, lonely father. Brigitte Fossey has timorous delicacy as Dewaere's girlfriend, precariously rehabilitated from her drug habit. In precisely written supporting roles, Claire Maurier, as Robert's mistress, and Jacques Dufilho, as a music-loving bookseller who employs Dewaere and Fossey, are excellent.

Film is well-photographed, edited and scored by Jean Boffety, Jacqueline Thiedot and Philippe Sarde. —Len.

Chicago Fest

Eugenio
(ITALIAN-FRENCH-COLOR)

Chicago, Nov. 13.

A coproduction of Intercontinental Film Company (Rome) and Les Films Du Losange — Gaumont — Moonfleet (Paris). Produced by Achille Manzotti. Features cast. Directed and written by Luigi Comencini. Camera (color) by Carlo Carlini. Art director and costumes, Paoli Comencini. Editor, Nino Baragli. Music, Romano Checcacci. Associate producers, Margaret Menegoz, Simon Mizrahi. Reviewed at the Chi Film Fest screening room, Nov. 13, 1980. Running time: 105 MINS.
Giancarlo . . . . Saverio Marconi
Fernanda . . . . Dalila Di Lazzaro
Grandfather Eugenio . . . . . Bernard Blier
Eugenio . . . . Francesco Bonelli
Milena . . . . Carole Andre
Baffo (Mustachio) . . . . Meme Perlini
Grandmother Anna . . . . Dina Sassoli
Grandmother Edvige . . . . . . .Gisella Sofio
Tristano . . . . Jose Luis De Villalonga
Guerrino . . . . Alessandro Bruzzese

Luigi Comencini has been a prodigious filmmaker for 30 years, but for reasons unknown he has never caught the international brass ring and his reputation lies primarily in his native Italy. If he is known at all in the U.S. it is for "Til Marriage Us Do Part," which was heavily cut (by others) to show off the considerable form of Laura Antonelli. Among the Comencini films that remain offshore, but are considered to have U.S. potential, are the 1972 "Lo

Scopone Scientifico" with Bette Davis, Joseph Cotten, Alberto Sordi and Silvana Mangano; "The Adventures of Pinocchio" (1971) and "Casanova, an Adolescent in Venice" (1969).

What is puzzling about the geographical distribution restraints that have hampered Comencini's work is that, if "Eugenio" is an example, they are complex but easily accessible films dealing with universal concerns. There is no point in positioning him in the pantheon of international directors at this time, but there is absolutely no doubt that he is a prodigious director and appears to have been for some time.

"Eugenio" is the story of boy of 10 and his relationship with his young, separated parents. Comencini treats the trio with compassion, treats them as they are and as they see each other, and generally intertwines their lives and behavior into a filmic tapestry about modern marriage. Eugenio (Francesco Bonelli) and his parents, Giancarlo (Saverio Marconi) and Fernanda (Dalila Di Lazzaro) are caught in a dilemma called marriage and parenthood, the former an anachronism per Comencini and the latter a place with no exit. They all try to make the best out of a bad deal and none of it works.

This is a tapestry peopled with richly-drawn figures: Eugenio (through whom we see much of the story) is a perceptive child, but not so wise that he couldn't be the kid down the street. Giancarlo loves the boy, just as he does his wife, but they both impinge upon the life he would like to lead. Fernanda seeks feminist liberation and makes some progress in that direction, but she can't separate her own hangups from societal restraints.

There are other acutely-limmed characters: Meme Perlini as the eccentric radical Mustachio who sets off the chain of events by abandoning Eugenio on a country road when the boy irritates him. Bernard Blier as the caring and pragmatic Grandfather Eugenio and Dina Sassoli as the caring but careful Grandmother Anna. These are complicated people who do the same things for different reasons and different things for the same reason.

The story is told in a series of multiple flash-backs, sometimes out of sequence, depending upon what Comencini has to say. He is much more interested in matching up comparable or contrasting situations than he is in following the easily-discernible narrative. The result is a powerful film with a long aftertaste and the pervasive and

disturbing feeling that it will be hard to look at any marriage the same after seeing this film. —Mor.

Perro de Alambre
(Wire Dog)
(SPANISH-VENEZUELAN-COLOR)

Chicago, Nov. 10.

Fernandez-Cid/Poleo-Urdaneta production. Directed by Manuel Cano. Features entire cast. Screenplay, Cano and C.A. Montaner; color (camera), Hans Burman; no other credits provided. Reviewed at Chicago International Film Festival screening room, Chicago, Nov. 10, '80. Running time: 120 MINS.

This is the sort of film that gives film festivals and revolution a bad name — a tediously-long 120-minute exercise in empty-headed political rhetoric and melodramatic Hispanic longueurs. There may be some playoff for it in Spanish markets used to this ham-handed treatment of characters, plot and ideas that mark this Spanish-Venezuelan coproduction, but other viewers are likely to find it heavy going.

It is possible that the (bad) subtitles tended to further simplify through compression a film that at best is not very complex or subtle. Bad grammar and poor spelling can make a difference when one is looking for meaning.

The "unnamed Caribbean dictatorship" of the film's promotional material is clearly Castro's Cuba, a country that undoubtedly was as repressive as this portrayal, but in recent years appears to be making a pitch for international respectability. It is no defense of whatever repression that goes on there today to guess that this representatin plays fast and loose with the facts.

The truth is something else, and that seems to be the point that the picture tries to make. But the distance between the apparent facts and the truth is too great. The fictional country a/k/a Cuba has been loaded with almost every element of tyranny known to history. The closing crawl has quotes from Amnesty International obviously relating to political prisoners everywhere which, in this context, makes them all appear to be in Cuban jails.

This is a dreadfully earnest film and maybe all is fair when the counter-revolution comes. The problem is that dogma is both boring and unconvincing.—Mor.

At Dere Tor!
(Stop It!)
(NORWEGIAN-COLOR)

Chicago, Nov. 10.

Marcusfilm A/S production. Directed by Lasse Glomm. Features entire cast. Screenplay by Glomm, based on a novel by

Espen Haavardsholm; camera (color), Erling Thurmann-Andersen; no other credits provided. Reviewed at Chicago International Film Festival screening room, Chicago, Nov. 10, '80. Running time: 100 MINS.
Cast: Eirik Kvale, Ole Moystad, Eindride Eidsvold, Wenche Bjornstad, Kristin Hauge, Karen Randers-Pherson.

Lasse Glomm is a 36-year-old producer-scriptwriter (he worked as an assistant to Joseph Losey on "A Doll's House") with two directoral efforts under his belt: "The Second Shift" and this outing, lensed earlier this year. Based on his efforts with "At Dere Tor," Glomm's career as a director doesn't show a great promise.

A dreary tale of callow Norwegian youth versus society, this pic has little to recommend it. Glomm extracts barely functional performances from a young, undistinguished cast, and can't make the plot's all-too obvious points with any clarity or precision.

Briefly, film focusses on a somewhat obnoxious teenager whose cohort was shot by police after stealing a car. Most of the pic is devoted to the teenager's conflicting views about his friend's death (was it a brutal manifestation of a heavyhanded authoritarianism?) and the youth's troubled relationships on the job, with his hard-working mother and with his girlfriends.

What the pic adds up to is an overlong, unengaging treatment of overly familiar material without redeeming directoral skill. Glomm's banal script, from a novel by Espen Haavardsholm doesn't help either.

Production values are generally passable. Commercial possibilities for this Scandinavian entry at the Chi International Film Festival are hard to imagine. Perhaps unkindest cut of all was the fact that at screening caught, festival's jury walked out shortly before pic was half unspooled. —Sege.

Heaven's Gate
(COLOR)

Cattle barons plot to exterminate immigrants of 1890. Big production, meagre entertainment. A problem picture.

A United Artists release, directed and written by Michael Cimino. Producer. Joann Carelli. Executive in charge of production. Denis O'Dell, Charles Okum. Features entire cast. Camera (Technicolor). Vilmos Zsigmond; editors, Tom Rolf, William Reynolds, Lisa Fruchtman. Gerald Greenberg; art director. Tambi Larsen; music. David Mansfield; costumes, Allen Highfill; choreographer, Eleanor Fazan; production managers, Charles Okum. Bob Grand. Peter Price; assistant directors. Michael Grillo, Brian Cook; sound editors. Richard W. Adams, Winston Ryder. Reviewed at Cinema 1. New York City. Nov. 18, 1980 (MPAA Rating R). Running time: 219 MINS.
Averill . . . . Kris Kristofferson
Champion . . . . Christopher Walken
Irvine . . . . John Hurt
Canton . . . . Sam Waterston
Mr. Eggleston . . . . Brad Dourif
Ella . . . . Isabelle Huppert
The Reverend Doctor . . . . . Joseph Cotten
John H. Bridges . . . . Jeff Bridges
Beautiful Girl . . . . Roseanne Vela
Wolcott . . . . Ronnie Hawkins
Trapper . . . . Geoffrey Lewis

The first scenes of "Heaven's Gate" are so energetic and beautiful that anyone who has followed the saga of the $35,000,000 epic might begin to think it was going to be worth every penny. Unfortunately the balance of director Michael Cimino's newest film, is so confusing, so overlong at three and a half hours and so ponderous that it fails to work at almost every level, all credit to the stunning photography notwithstanding. The trade must marvel that directors now have such power that no one, in the endless months since work on the picture began, was able to impose some structure and sense. Too much of the film is incoherent.

What structure the film does have is based on the Johnson County wars which took place in the 1890's in Wyoming.

The story deals with a group of established cattlemen headed by Canton (Sam Waterston) who are convinced their herds of cattle are being looted by immigrant settlers. With the approval of the state, the operators of the large cattle ranches draw up a death list of 125 poor immigrants in Johnson County who are supposedly doing the "rustling." They then hire a band of men to go out and summarily murder the alleged thieves.

Jim Averill (Kris Kristofferson) is the county's Federal marshal, and though he comes from the same class as the cattle barons, a fact which is established by his graduation from Harvard at the opening of the film, he is opposed to their violent, self-serving tactics.

But it's never really explained why Kristofferson has turned against his class or what he's doing as a Federal marshal. Other relationships in the picture are similarly unclarified.

Kristofferson's love affair with Eva (Isabelle Huppert), a local brothel madam. sheds little light on his character. As for this delicate French actress it's hard to accept her as running a house of prostitution in the turn of the century U.S. west.

Kristofferson's former friendship with Champion (Christopher Walken) is also fuzzy since, until the very end of the film, the latter appears to befriend the very cattle barons whom his friend detests, and beyond that, Walken is also in love with Huppert.

From the beginning the plot line and the characters are so unclear that it's literally difficult to decipher what-if anything-is happening. The plot seems to wander from the marshal's romance to scenes depicting life in the early west and the evils suffered by the poor, until the film finally culminates in a bloody confrontation between the immigrants and the cattle barons, three hours and one intermission later.

In the scenes of frontier life, Cimino's attempts to draw a portrait of the plight of the Ukrainian and Eastern European immigrants in the west in that period are done with such broad strokes and are so impersonal, that none of the victims ever get beyond pat stereotypes.

In counterpoint, the scenes between Kristofferson and Huppert at first seem more interesting. Both performers work very hard to make themselves credible, but there's no way to overcome the incongruity of an 1890's affair with dialog straight out of the 1970's.

One advantage of those love scenes at least is that the dialog is audible, but unfortunately other scenes with dialog which should supply plot and background information are either almost incomprehensible, or else so abrupt that they do little to "explain" what's going on.

In one scene at a railway station when the marshal arrives in the west, apparently having lived a number of years in St. Louis, the sound effects of the trains so overwhelm the dialog that it's almost impossible to hear his explanation of what he had done in the interim since Harvard and why he has come west.

Cimino, who wrote the script himself, has simply not provided enough details for his story, leaving his audience guessing. As a result, the characters and events aren't

sufficiently defined to be either credible or interesting. Kristofferson and Huppert do the best they can, given very difficult roles.

John Hurt's role as Irvine, the drunken cattle baron, whose heart is in the right place, but who does not have the character to oppose his peers, is also handicapped as an actor, since he seems to appear and disappear in the tale with no real purpose.

Jeff Bridges does a good job as the sympathetic bartender of "Heaven's Gate," who staunchly supports Kristofferson.

Much of the cinematography is wonderful. Vilmos Zsigmond has done an excellent job, but the music by David Mansfield, which is at first interesting, is so overused that it grows corny after a while.

Most of the writer-director's scenes are overlong and the viewer grows impatient with the self-indulgent editing. Film trade hears the director was hard pressed by United Artists to reduce the length of the film and fought against it.

The big battle sequences at the end of the film are beautifully shot and edited, but by the time they happen, one is already wondering how much longer the film can last.
—*Geri.*

The Alternative Miss World
(BRITISH-DOCU-COLOR)

Chicago, Nov. 17.
A James Street Ltd. production. Stars Divine. Produced and directed by Richard Gayer. Camera (color). Mike Davis, Mike Dodds, Nick Knowland, Mike Lensvelt, Bob Smith, Clive Tickner; sound, Malcolm Stuart; editor. Rob Small; lighting. Stephen Goldblatt; associate producers. Michael Davis, Simon Mallin, Toni Tye Walker; executive producer, Judy McDonald. Reviewed at the Carnegie Theatre. Chicago. Nov. 17. '80. Running time: 114 MINS.
Cast: Divine, Andrew Logan, Sophia Parkin, Nigel Adey, Riccardo de Velasco, John Thomas, Rosemary Gibb, Rebecca du Pont de Bie, Jenny Runacre, Stevie Hughes, James Birch, Sarah Parkin, Golinda Von Regensburg, Joanie de Vere Hunt, Jill Bruce, John Maybury, Emma Harrison, William Waldron, Janet Slee, John Hopwood, Stephen Holt, Bob Anthony. Maruice. Bobby Claridge, Lynn O'Liam.

At first glance a homophobe's nightmare, this British-made docu about the elaborate staging of a drag beauty contest emerges as fairly amusing if slightly overdone entry that flaunts its bad taste almost as much as the innocence of its intentions. That said, however, it must be added that the pic appears a highly chancy commercial prospect at best, although canny playoff before homosexual audiences might produce results.

Lensed last year in England, pic takes the viewer inside a tent where

under the supervision of one Andrew Logan an "Alternative Miss World" contest unfolds amidst a large, rapt and fun-loving audience. Before the contest concludes, the obvious conviviality of the occasion seeps through to those not usually keen on viewing men ornately made up as women or women burlesquing their own sexuality.

Although the docu blessedly doesn't take itself seriously, it perceptively brings home the care and consideration shown by contest organizers (it's a yearly event) and contest participants, both men and women. This is an earnest exercise of a totally frivolous sort.

As in "straight" beauty pageants, contestants here parade around in full costume (often cleverly conceived ensembles designed strictly for humorous effect), in something skimpy (bathing suits or less) and are asked a number of banal questions ("What do you like to do best?" or "Who's your favorite film star?"). Divine, the porcine "star" of drag, supervises the latter to generally harmless result.

Although Divine is heavily billed here, (his, her?) appearance is largely limited to a brief but funny vamp turn complete with wildly gesticulating tongue. Logan is the emcee in charge. In perhaps the pic's sole metaphorical reference, Logan's costume is one half a military parade outfit, the other half a sequined evening dress.

The contestants are introduced by name (Miss Snowwhite, Miss Proposition 13, Miss Slightly Misanthropic, and so on), then are forced to descend a sharply-banked stairway that claims several unsurefooted casualties before the event is concluded. Voices of the judges are heard on the soundtrack commenting on each contestant via bitchy but occasionally funny references.

Pic's only malevolent touch developed from what appears to have been an accident. A bewildered-looking donkey is led onto the semicircular stage to bear the contest winner off in glory. Unfortunately, the donkey stumbled into the orchestra pit, taking the winner along. Both survived uninjured.

Technical credits are touch-and-go although extensive use of hand-held cameras went smoothly. Use of record music is generally effective. At some 114 minutes, the pic runs too long. Pre and post-contest segments featuring Logan rattling around what he calls "the alternative Tower of London" could be excised. Pic preemed at Cannes and made its U.S. bow at the 16th annual Chicago International Film Festival. —*Sege.*

Nikudan
(Human Bullet)
(JAPANESE-B&W)

———

ATG release. Directed by Kihachi Okamoto. Features entire cast. Screenplay, Kihachi Okamoto; camera (black and white), Hiroshi Murai. No other credits provided. Reviewed at Japan House, New York, Nov. 22, 1980. Running time: **109 MINS.**

Cast: Minoru Terada, Naoko Otani, Chishu Ryu, Tanie Kitabayashi, Yunosuke Ito.

———

Kihachi Okamoto's "Human Bullet," made five years after his 1963 "Warring Clans," manifests considerable growth in maturity, being a powerful statement against war, especially Japan's involvement in it. He leavens the message with a wonderfully touching, often comic, performance by the young hero who finds himself elected to be a "human bullet" — he's to guide a torpedo into the nearest enemy ship when the expected invasion of Japan starts. He quickly becomes a forgotten man, finally being told many days later by a passing fisherman that the war is over. His sacrifice is for nothing and Okamoto's satirical windup has today's Japanese swimming and water-skiing in Tokyo Bay as if nothing had happened.

Minoru Terada, a skinny, bespectacled and fanatically dedicated young soldier, is slow to react to circumstances — even his discovery that a pigtailed schoolgirl he encounters and falls in love with is really the operator of a brothel takes a long time to sink in — but he reacts bravely and wisely to the deprivations caused by the drawn-out war effort. A fascinating film. —*Robe.*

Pendin Heng Kuam Rak
(The Land Of Love)
(THAI-COLOR)

———

Bangkok, Nov. 12.

A Nantanakorn Films production and release. Produced and directed by Charin Nantanakorn. Features entire cast. Story, Saengpetr Senabodin; screenplay, Khun Prasai; camera (color), Pipak Payaka; asst. camera, Virat Dakasa; music, Chalie Intravijit, Smarn Kanjanaparint and Bang Lach; sound, Kasem Militachinda; production design, Charoen Rakdakrom; asst. director, Nantawat. Reviewed at Chalerm Thai theatre, Bangkok, Nov. 12, '80. Running time: **130 MINS.**

Malinee	Jarunee Sooksawat
Tiew	Rawin Buralak
Thong	Sor Asanachinda
Toey	Kanchai Gemangkang
Ton	Lak Apichat
Bancha	Promsin Siburnruang
Kamnan	Prachuab Lerkyamdi
Kamnan's Son	Jirasak Issarangkul, Na Ayudhya
Poodyakarn	Tuam Toranong

———

"Pendin Heng Kuam Rak" seems to satisfy rural needs thoroughly, while also capitalizing on Jarunee Sooksawat's popularity nationwide.

All comic sequences are repeated or extended as much as possible. Waves of laughter from the audience rise higher with every collision and actors' expression of pain.

"Pendin Heng Kuam Rak" looks like one of the big comedy winners of the year. The fact that Jarunee again plays a tomboy with a destructive streak in her — a stereotyped role as widely accepted as repetitious jokes — is perhaps a key factor. In other words, when the public enjoys something, they ask not for something different, but for more of the same. —*Cano.*

Seems Like Old Times
(COLOR)

———

An extremely commercial film.

———

Hollywood, Nov. 19.

Columbia Pictures release of a Ray Stark Production. Produced by Ray Stark. Directed by Jay Sandrich. Features entire cast. Exec producer, Roger M. Rothstein. Screenplay, Neil Simon; camera (Metrocolor) David M. Walsh; editor, Michael A. Stevenson; production design, Gene Callahan; music, Marvin Hamlisch; art direction, Pete Smith; set decoration, Lee Poll; costumes, Betsy Cox; assistant director, Jack Aldworth. Reviewed at Burbank Studios, Room 5, L.A., Nov. 19, 1980 (MPAA Rating: PG). Running time: **102 MINS.**

Glenda	Goldie Hawn
Nick	Chevy Chase
Ira	Charles Grodin
Fred	Robert Guillaume
Judge	Harold Gould
Governor	George Grizzard
Aurora	Yvonne Wilder
Chester	T.K. Carter
Dex	Judd Omen
Bee Gee	Marc Alaimo

———

The onscreen reunion of Goldie Hawn and Chevy Chase and the ample flow of comedic barbs from scripter Neil Simon, makes "Seems Like Old Times" a sweet, witty, escapist and above all extremely commercial film. If there must be a suspension of reality in order to accept the very flimsy premise, chemistry between the two stars, dialog and array of physical mishaps sets a fast-paced yet romantic comedic tone. Although it sometimes plays like an elongated tv sitcom, topliners' proven b.o. appeal and upbeat atmosphere should make Columbia release of the Ray Stark production a major holiday boxoffice hit.

The name of the game here is pure entertainment with Hawn limning a wide-eyed liberal lawyer with a weakness for giving refuge to anyone she has ever been involved with. Writer ex-husband Chase intrudes into her affluent life with staid district attorney, Charles Grodin, after two robbers force him to hold up a bank. He wants help and she, still with an obvious weakness for him, is torn.

Those looking for anything more in the way of plot won't find much beyond the aforementioned. Majority of the picture consists of vignettes where Chase mugs, pratfalls and snidely addresses anyone who'll listen, Hawn wringing her hair in comical despair as her life begins to unravel around her and Grodin trying to maintain his place in Hawn's life amid the romantic sparks.

Robert Guillaume provides nice support as Grodin's associate as does Harold Gould as a harried judge and Yvonne Wilder as a kind of stereotypical but amusing Mexican maid.

In his first feature, Jay Sandrich has relied basically upon Neil Simon's script, often funny but thin on development, to carry things. The result is a picture that is amusing on the surface but very typical in terms of its setups. Michael A. Stevenson's editing often appears to intrude on the action as does Marvin Hamlisch's uninspiring mood music. Betsy Cox's costumes are eye-catching, especially for Hawn.

Of course, none of the pic's drawbacks much matter thanks to the extremely engaging rapport between Chase and Hawn. They seem to be capable of injecting warmth and laughs into just about anything. Business being what it is, they will no doubt be back in front of the cameras before too long. —*Berg.*

Milionario e Ze Rico na Estrada da Vida
(Milionario and Ze Rico in The Highway of Life)
(BRAZILIAN-COLOR)

———

Brasilia, Oct. 30.

An Embrafilme release of a Villafilmes Producoes Cinematograficas production. Features entire cast. Produced by Dora Suerner Vilals Boas, Luiz Carlos Villas Boas. Directed by Nelson Pereira dos Santos. Screenplay, Chico de Assis; music director, Dooby Ghizzy; camera (Eastmancolor), Francisco Botelho; sound, Juarez Dagoberto; editor, Carlos Alberto Camuyrano. Reviewed at Cine Brasilia, First International Fair of Brazilian Film, Oct. 30, 1980. Running time: **100 MINS.**

Cast: Milionario, Jose Rico, Nadia Lippi, Silvia Leblon, Raimundo Silva, Turibio Ruiz, Jose Raimundo.

———

Nelson Pereira dos Santos is generally acknowledged as the father of the new Brazilian Cinema. His first two films, "Rio 40 Graus" (Rio 40 Degrees) and "Rio Zona Norte" (Rio North Side), made in the mid-1950s, were predecessors of the urban drama which would become a movement almost 10 years later. "Vidas Secas" (Barren Lives), a 1963 production marked the "Cinema Novo" and the intellectual turning point · in the Brazilian film conscience. Pic's success freed dos Santos from the strong influence and stigma of neo-realism, and ever since he has been encouraging new filmmakers to do the same, as well as trying his own style in such different films as "Quem e Beta" (Who is Beta) (1972) and "Tenda dos Milagres" (Tent of Miracles) (1976). A common denominator, if any, has been his ever-increasing approach to the popular, towards a language that can be easily understood regardless of social or cultural class.

"In the Highway of Life" is certainly a climax of this ambition. Milionario and Jose Rico are an actual country music duo, most popular inland and among construction workers in Sao Paulo, yet almost unknown by the middle class. Country duos are an impressive cultural and commercial phenomenon in Brazil; they sell hundreds of thousands of albums, but no city radio station would dare to play one of their songs; their pics regularly draw filmgoers like no one else in Brazil, yet such films are barely seen in the capital, nor is country music a subject discussed in academic groups.

Yet dos Santos chose to do so, and has dramatized the real story of this duo, one of dozens. His credentials as a respected intellectual allowed the filmmaker to go further in his search for the popular (he had dealt with bandits and religious mysticism in his two previous films) and perhaps will bring his subject even more respectability and make it "fashionable."

Both Milionario and Jose Rico are wall painters with artistic ambitions in "Highway" and they meet in Sao Paulo by chance. Both are looking for work. Busy on the same construction job, they are able to rehearse their act at lunchtime until fired for diverting attention of their colleagues. They even record an album but dishonest entrepreneurs help it fail and the duo is forced to keep on painting walls. Ultimately, however, religiosity is the key to their success: they make a promise to a saint, and a miracle brings them fame and fortune.

One could not think of a less sophisticated way to tell such a story. Pereira fills it with almost 20 of the duo's tunes, far more than the average big city spectator would have heard in all his life. Narrative is deliberately primitive, as are photography and special effects, often "quoting" old Mexican pics, which were indeed a common presence at the inland theatres of the state of Sao Paulo some 20 years ago.

Though item seems questionable for general (and international) audiences, dos Santos' cinema remains as personal as ever in his realistic reflection of the culture of his country. —*Hoin.*

The Private Eyes
(COLOR)

Knotts and Conway - more of same.

Champaign, Ill., Nov. 21.

A New World Pictures release of a Tri-Star Pictures Production. Produced by Lang Elliott and Wanda Dell. Directed by Lang Elliott. Stars Tim Conway, Don Knotts. Screenplay, Tim Conway, John Myhers; camera (Color), Jacques Haitkin; editor, Fabien Tordjmann; art director, Vincent Peranio; music, Peter Matz. Reviewed at Virginia Theatre, Champaign, Ill., Nov. 21, '80. (MPAA rating: PG.) Running time: **91 MINS.**

Dr. Tart	Tim Conway
Inspector Winship	Don Knotts
Mistress Phyllis Morley	Trisha Noble
Justin	Bernard Fox
Nanny	Grace Zabriskie
Jock	Irwin Keyes
Hilda	Susie Mandel
Tebit	Stan Ross
Mr. Uwatsum	John Fujioka
Lord Morley	Fred Stuthman
Lady Morley	Mary Nell Santacroce

Don Knotts and Tim Conway continue to stuff their silly antics into the shells of old genres. "The Private Eyes" mingles and mangles the inept inspector angle with an old dark house setting, coming up with enough low comedy hooks to keep turnstiles rotating steadily.

Like the previous New World release for the pair, "The Prize Fighter," the technical aspects have the same degree of adequacy, with largely the same team at work. Pic keeps to essentially a single set, a 250-room Victorian mansion outside London in the 1920's (actually filmed at Biltmore House in Asheville, North Carolina). The single exception is a filling station scene at the outset, when a deadpan attendant (Patrick Cranshaw) observes the dumb duo grease up faces and set the place on fire.

Inspector Winship (Knotts) and his assistant Dr. Tart (Conway) investigate the murders of Lord and Lady Morley, on orders from Scotland Yard. The house staff consists of a ghoulish lot of suspects: a samurai cook, a Quasimodo character, a mass-murderer butler, a filthy groundskeeper, a busty maid, and so forth. This supporting cast is given only enough time to walk on for a minimal appearance, then is killed off ungracefully, one by one.

Apart from the predictably recycled gags, the slammed fingers and knocked heads, some running jokes include bumbler Tart's pigeon messages to the Yard which never get off the ground, clues left in rhyming notes and off-color rhymes, Winship's "time gun" invention which is supposed to go off

every hour, and a remarkable series of nauseating descriptions.

The shocks which should develop in the labyrinthine passages and trap doors of the semi-haunted house never appear, and the murder mystery itself causes no gasps. It's the dark ramble from prop to prop that "The Private Eyes" depends upon, with caped figures in tunnels, portraits with moving eyes, getting trapped in a garbage presser, an inventive torture chamber, a clumsy suit of iron, a bolt-upright body in a coffin, and an incongruous monster called a Wookalar, inserted for the finale (resembling a distant outer-space relative with a similar name).

Conway and Knotts find the killer, through no expert sleuthing of their own, mostly playing off each other's wrinkled brow to the loyal fans, who ask for no more.

— *Pege.*

Crew Cut
(DUTCH-COLOR)

Chicago, Nov. 18.

Roissy Films (Paris) release. Producer, Gerrit Visscher. Features entire cast. Directed by Guido Pieters. Screenplay, Pieters, Karin Loomans; camera (color), Eduard Van Der Enden. No other credits provided. Reviewed at Carnegie Theatre, Chicago, Nov. 18, '80. Running time: **105 MINS.**

Cast: Derek De Lint, Tingue Dongelmans, Cristel Braak, Guus Oster.

This technically polished but essentially foolish film can't quite make up its mind whether it's a soap opera, softcore sex farce or a grim look at a young artist who becomes mentally unhinged in wartime Holland. By attempting to mesh these disparate elements, director-coscripter Guido Pieters sinks his project although he does so with a good measure of style.

"Crew Cut" (presumably the pic's original title; skimpy credits aren't clear on the point) marks its U.S. preem at the Chicago Film Festival, and the first fest exposure of the pic anywhere. Beyond its technical merit (Eduard Van Der Enden's photography is good and an uncredited musical score is firstrate), it's hard to see why Fest director Michael Kutza picked the film for showing here.

The setting is 1944 when the Allied troops have Germans on the run in Holland. The wartime doings don't figure all that prominently, though, in the actions of a sexually-charged young painter (Derek De Lint), who's emotionally at odds with his family, his girlfriends and his employer (the young man paints seascapes on lampshades).

Turns out the protagonist is most bothered by an ugly scalp scar, which he hides underneath a long and unkempt hair style, the result of

a childhood accident (for which the painter blames his parents, with seeming good reasons). The painter's rather brutish father, viewer is informed, thwarted the boy's attempts to hide the scar by insisting on repeated and cruelly-administered haircuts (thus the title). Pic, in fact, opens with a tough-to-watch title scene showing a boy tearfully getting shorn.

Whatever, the painter is depicted initially as an eager lothario who seduces a comely but shy librarian and a Jewish coworker, much to the consternation of the employer, who has lascivious intentions of his own. Sex scenes are boldly handled with beaucoup nudity, although not especially erotic.

At its best, "Crew Cut" boasts of some farcical scenes showing dour but libidinous bourgeoise slyly on the make. Dialog is often surprisingly raunchy, fully the match of pic's almost explicit sex scenes.

But the pic veers sharply back to the protagonist's angst, exemplified by his not-so-gradual mental and emotional deterioration. Finally, his esthetic and sexual leanings fuse to the point where — in the pic's most sensational and incredible scene — he simulates copulation with a statue of a Venus de Milo type he had particularly admired. At pic's end, our protagonist is mowed down by local police as some sort of violent loon (no wonder since he had, minutes before, strangled the Jewish coworker to death).

Beyond its generally good production values, and that score, there's not much to recommend "Crew Cut." Commercial prospects in the U.S. augur little.

—*Sege.*

Naeste Stop Paradis
(Next Stop Paradise)
(DANISH-COLOR)

Copenhagen, Nov. 14.

An Obel Film production (with the Danish Film Institute/Erik Crone) and release. Features entire cast. Original story, written and directed by Jon Bang Carlsen. Camera (color), Alexander Gruszynski; editor, Kasper Schyberg. Anders Refn; production manager, Michael Christensen; music, Gunnar Moller Pedersen. Reviewed at Alexandra, Copenhagen, Nov. 14, 1980. Running time: **95 MINS.**

Dagmar	Karen Lykkehus
The Major	Preben Lerdorff Rye
Dagmar as young	Suzett Kempf
Frederiksen	Ole Larsen
Ellen	Jessie Rindom
Kurt Larsen	Peter Boesen

Jon Bang Carlsen, a documentarist noted for his fine artistic feeling and technical originality, enters the feature field with "Next Stop Paradise" which emerges as a minor work, but one of nicely controlled humor and compassion in the description of the alumni at an old people's home.

Actually, Bang Carlsen has a two-in-one film, alternating rather haphazardly between presentday Dagmar and her dream incarnations of herself as a young girl. The young Dagmar was a farm girl turned, reluctantly at first, later quite lustily, to stripper in a travelling tent show.

At the Old People's Home, Dagmar suffers the usual indignities of regimentation and creeping senility, but she has some spark of revolt left in her and one night sneaks away with a male inmate for an amourous stay at a seedy hotel.

Bang Carlsen has used professional actors along with regular old people's home inmates to very good effect. The baroque viewpoint is taken more often than the sentimental. He has also used Alexander Gruszynski's cinematography in an unusual way, preferring to place audiences smack into completed picture frames rather than having them move along with the action.

Television sales and presentations at minor fests are predicted for this quaint and handsome little item rather than extensive sales to theatrical situations. —*Kell.*

Hamiskhak Ha'Amiti
(The Real Game)
(ISRAELI-COLOR)

Tel Aviv, Nov. 15.

A Kayitz Films Production. Produced by David Tour. Associate Producer: Amos Mokadi. Stars Yossi Polack, Michal Bat-Adam, Gabi Amrani. Directed by Avi Cohen. Written by Avi Cohen and Jonathan Aroch; camera (color), Danny Schneur; music, Alona Tur-El; editor, Anath Luberski; sound, Amnon Ben-Yaakov. Reviewed in Tel Aviv, Nov. 15, 1980. Running time: **90 MINS.**

Shaul Raz	Yossi Polack
Alma	Michal Bat-Adam
Shimon Tzuri	Gabi Amrani
Aharon Brener	David Ram
Haim Caspi	Izhak Haviss

Avi Cohen's maiden effort has the distinction of being the first Israeli feature dealing frontally with the political life here, and hinting at some of the juicier scandals that have hit front pages during the last years, even if it does not identify directly the culprits or the other persons involved.

Shaul Raz, the leading character, is a successful businessman in his late 30s, who decides to volunteer, out of purely idealistic motives, and join the political apparatus of a party fighting governmental corruption and purporting to bring back to public life the good old honest mores. It takes only 90 minutes, the length of the film, for Raz to learn the rules of the "real game" and to turn out to be a through-and-through bastard, selling his conscience and his friends for a better position and a safer chance at the next elections.

First of all, Cohen's script fails to give the main part enough substance, so his political involvement would be clear, and it certainly springs the changes in his behavior without too much psychological preparation. As for the background on which he evolves, the least that could be said is that compared to real life, Cohen's characters are tame and innocent in their conniving shenanigans. Finally, the love interest which was supposed to develop side by side with the political plot, is rather forced, with Michal Bat-Adam playing straight person to the rest of the case, and diffusing obvious truths once in a while.

This leads to Cohen's second, and not less serious problem, that of acting. Yossi Polack, a stage actor of some renown here, is cast against character and has a lot of trouble conveying the slick, self-assured executive he is supposed to play, as he is by nature inclined to play much heavier and more introverted parts. David Ram, no professional actor, looks just that, trying to make believe he is a charismatic politician, and the only one to come out with flying honors is Gabi Amrani, an old hand in local comedies who has no trouble reacting to the camera as the folksy labor leader who has taken the law once too often in his own hands.

Cohen has all the possible mitigating circumstances for not coming up to par on his first try, production having gone through all kinds of trouble, from money shortage to lead Polack breaking his leg. The subject he has picked is certainly worthwhile and he tries to measure up to it seriously, but for the time being he seems to lack the necessary experience and know-how to pull the project through. Box office prospects are chancy at best.
—*Edna.*

The Thin Line
(ISRAELI-COLOR)

Chicago, Nov. 25.

Isram Film Corp. release of a G.U.Y. Film Productions Ltd. production. Produced by Avi Kleinberger and Gideon Amir. Stars Gila Almagor, Alex Peleg and Liat Panski. Directed by Michal Bat-Adam; screenplay, Bat-Adam; camera (color), Nurith Aviv; set design, Gaby Klasmer; sound, Dany Natovich; no other credits provided. Reviewed at Chicago Film Festival screening room, Chicago, Nov. 25, '80. Running time: 93 MINS.
Cast: Gila Almagor, Alex Peleg, Liat Panski.

Director-scripter Michal Bat-Adam's second film (first was "Each Other" as it was known domestically; it was titled "Moments" abroad) is a finely etched, carefully detailed look at an Israeli family's losing battle against psychosis — specifically, the manic depression suffered by Pola (Gila Amagor), wife of a hardworking and supremely patient camera shop operator (Alex Peleg) and the mother of two young daughters.

Much of the film is seen from the point of view of the younger daughter, 10-year-old Nilli (Liat Panski), a splendid actress whose somber mien conceals a range of strong emotion.

Her performance — Panski brings to mind the not-easily-forgotten visage of Ana Torrent, the riveting child actress of several recent Spanish films — and those of the other principal players are first-rate, an indication that helmer Bat-Adam is a director capable of creating and sustaining powerful and intricate characterizations.

She is, however, less assured at pacing her film. "The Thin Line" marks the downward spiral of a woman into the mentally and emotionally unreachable — at pic's end she cannot recognize her own daughter. Bat-Adam's journey is a grueling one that, although occasionally relieved by winning character touches in specific scenes, doesn't provide a catharsis or even a minimal emotional escape hatch. The viewer is at once fascinated and trapped.

Several scenes are standouts, especially those showing the young girl fondling her mother's naked body in a playful exercise in sexual education; the father and mother staging an improbably graceful waltz amidst a cluttered kitchen; the father's controlled but desperate attempts to get his insomniac wife to sleep.

The performers blend so completely into their roles that it's not possible to resist the reality of their situation. Specifics of life in Tel Aviv and at the Kibbutz, where the young girl is sent to school, ring as completely realistic. Amagor is particularly good at capturing the

mother's inability to control her demons; Peleg plays the father as a warm, somewhat reserved character in way over his head.

Bat-Adam tosses aside the characterization of the older daughter who's seen almost continuously in flight from the family's painful situation. In general, production values are excellent.

Nurith Aviv's photography is as sharply etched as Bat-Adam's characters. Gaby Klasmer's sets nicely reflect the cluttered family condition. An uncredited score, however, is pleasant in itself but a bit too lyrical given the subject

"The Thin Line" is an impressive effort and was easily one of the better pics screened at the Chicago International Film Festival, where it was world preemed. It's not an easy film to watch but the director's careful and specific presentation of a difficult family condition earns respect and admiration. Michal Bat-Adam is a helmer to watch.
—*Sege.*

Superman II
(COLOR)

Solid sequel with worldwide b.o. prospects of steel.

A Warner Brothers release of an Alexander Salkind presentation of an International Film Production/Alexander and Ilya Salkind Production. Executive producer, Ilya Salkind. Produced by Pierre Spengler. Features entire cast. Directed by Richard Lester. Screenplay, Mario Puzo, David Newman, Leslie Newman; story, Puzo, based on characters created by Jerry Siegel and Joe Shuster; creative consultant, Tom Mankiewicz; camera (Technicolor), Geoffrey Unsworth, Robert Paynter; editor, John Victor-Smith; music, Ken Thorne, from original material composed by John Williams; production design, John Barry, Peter Murton; supervising art director, Maurice Fowler; special effects director, Colin Chilvers; second-unit directors, David Tomblin, Robert Lynn; sound mixer, Roy Charman; costumes, Yvonne Blake, Susan Yelland; production manager, Vincent Winter; assistant director, Dusty Symonds; makeup, Stuart Freeborn. Reviewed at Warner Brothers screening room, N.Y.C., Dec. 1, 1980. (Not yet MPAA rated). Running time: 127 MINS.

Additional Special Effects Unit Credits

Supervisor of optical and visual effects, Roy Field; additional flying sequences and director of miniature effects, Derek Meddings; flying unit special effects director, Zoran Perisic; flying unit director of photography, Denys Coop; director of miniature photography, Paul Wilson; optical and special effects editor, Peter Watson; zoptic operator, David Speed; flying effects, Bob Harman; optical printers, Dick Dimbleby, David Docwra; matte artists, Ivor Beddoes, Doug Ferris; aerial camera sequences, Wesscam; Wesscam photography, Ronald Goodman; matte camera operators, Peter Harman, Peter Hammond; New York process stills, Cervin Robinson; special lighting effects, The

Lightflex system; astronautical consultant, Harry Lange.

Lex Luthor	Gene Hackman
Superman/Clark Kent	Christopher Reeve
Otis	Ned Beatty
Perry White	Jackie Cooper
Ursa	Sarah Douglas
Lois Lane	Margot Kidder
Non	Jack O'Halloran
Eve Teschmacher	Valerie Perrine
Lara	Susannah York
Sheriff	Clifton James
The President	E.G. Marshall
Jimmy Olsen	Marc McClure
General Zod	Terence Stamp

For all the production halts, setbacks, personnel changeovers and legal wrangling that paved its way to the screen, "Superman II" has finally emerged as a solid, classy, cannily constructed piece of entertainment that already bodes a long hot boxoffice summer domestically, preceded by burly overseas prospects through the winter and spring.

Although the caped hero's high-flying magic may have lost some of its technological surprise and lustre in two years since the original appeared, "Superman II" makes some distinct gains in the plot department, spinning off a barrage of imaginative and lavish action segments that will form the core of a broad audience base.

One of the major things the sequel has going for it is the ability to take completely for granted an audience's familiarity with the characters and relationships of the original. Without the first film's mammoth scene-setting requirements, "Superman II" has the luxury of getting down to action almost immediately, having a crisply economical recap of the original's highlights dispensed with under the opening credits.

Although original plans called for lensing the first two "Superman" features simultaneously, the sequel is reportedly 80% newly shot footage, with Richard Lester finally emerging owner of full and sole director's credit, after original helmer Richard Donner ankled the project during one of the longer limbo periods.

Surprisingly, there's ultimately little in the way of any director's personal stamp on the sequel, though Lester has done a bravura job of melding grandiose action with a core of heart-tickling romance and an ample overlay of tongue-in-cheek humor. Whether he or the script bears primary blame for some of the campier low-comedy excesses that the original managed to avoid is an open question.

The new film does an especially good job of picking up the strings of unexplored characters and plot seeds left dangling from the first pic, taking its core plot from the three Kryptonian villains — Terence Stamp, Jack O'Halloran and Sarah Douglas — briefly glimpsed in the first pic before Krypton explodes.

Here, they're liberated from perpetual imprisonment in a bizarre time-warp by an H-bomb, explosion in outer space — a terrorist bomb, intended to destroy Paris, is hurled into space by Superman from its perch in the Eiffel Tower — and head for Earth, where their superpowers are at least equal to the titled hero's. Visions of world domination quickly begin dancing in their heads.

Meanwhile, as the sadistic trio wreak increasing havoc and quickly bring the earth's leaders to their knees, fate intrudes in the guise of heavy romance. Once Lois Lane (Margot Kidder) finally catches on that Christopher Reeve's mild-mannered Clark Kent and Superman are one and the same, they fly off to his arctic fortress where Reeve decides to eternally give up his powers for the sake of worldly coupling with Kidder.

Predictably, mortality doesn't sit too well with him (among other things, a brutal bully kicks the kryptonite out of him in a roadside diner brawl) and when Reeve realizes it's a tossup between his sex life and the future of the world, he gets a second chance at being the celibate man of steel he once was.

The film builds quickly to a climactic battle between Reeve and the three supervillains in midtown Manhattan (the Empire State Building notches up its best film credit since the original "King Kong" in the process), finally resolved in true comic book fashion back at Superman's Fortress of Solitude. Fate of the villains is left somewhat dangling, but then "Superman III" is already in the works.

Lively script is again credited to Mario Puzo, David Newman and Leslie Newman, with Robert Benton the only one of the original lineup not reprising.

Reeve again scores better as the benignly cocky caped hero, than as the falsely awkward mild-mannered reporter. Shifting of the film's exclusive focus on him to the three arch-foes wisely puts less premium on what amounts to a slimly dimensional role. Stamp is power-crazed evil incarnate, the giant O'-Halloran is pure dumb brute strength, and Douglas flexes well as a leather-clad dominatrix-type.
Kidder is as sexy and petulant as ever as the eternally unrequited

star reporter, while Gene Hackman has some relatively brief but highly enjoyable turns as the affably villainous. Lex Luthor. Virtually cut into nonexistence are his sidekicks Valerie Perrine and (mercifully) the bumbling Ned Beatty. Susannah York reprises nobly as Superman's holographic mommy, gaining from the complete (and not missed) write-out of papa Marlon Brando.

Granted that both "Superman" pics carry more charm and good-heartedness than any of their special-effects ilk, the overall magic is still largely in the hands of the vast technical crew. The film completely retains the light-suffused images of the late cinematographer Geoffrey Unsworth, who retains prime lensing credit, with Bob Paynter credited as director of photography. Ken Thorne has done an excellent job of scoring the film from John Williams' original themes The film is a first-class achievement right down the line. —Step.

Squeeze
(NEW ZEALAND-COLOR)

Chicago, Nov. 25.
Trilogic Film Productions (Auckland, N. Zealand). Produced and directed by Richard Turner. Features entire cast. Screenplay, Turner; camera (color), Ian Paul; editor, Jamie Selkirk; score, Toy Love and the music of The Features, Streetplayer & Hagan & Young; no other credits provided. Reviewed at Chicago Film Festival screening room, Chicago, Nov. 26, '80. Running time: 82 MINS.
Cast: Robert Shannon, Paul Eadv. Donna Akersten, Peter Heperi, David Herkt, Fay Flegg, Lynn Robson, Dinah Russell, Eileen Swann, Bruce Weston, Don Farr, Sandy Gauntlett, Martyn Sanderson, Ian Westbury, Arthur Wright.

Despite the virtual establishment of the gay rights movement with its insistence on sexual self-declaration, the plight of the "closet" homosexual managing in a "straight" world remains a provocative topic, one that's not often treated intelligently on the screen. Although it claims to address that subject, "Squeeze" boils down to homosexual soap opera that teeters dangerously on the edge of softcore sensationalism.

It's for undiscriminating, homosexual audiences only.
Rather than clearly focus on the self-imposed dilemma faced by a successful young businessman (Robert Shannon) — he is about to be married to a somewhat frumpish, not so young woman (Donna Akersten) but instead falls for a wispy, blond gay (Paul Eady) — Richard Turner's film gives the viewer a tiresome look of homo-

sexual nightlife in downtown Auckland, New Zealand, the pic's country of origination.

Cardboard characters abound: the earnest protagonist who shuns promiscuity; the bitchy "queens" who hustle customers at homosexual bars; brutish, nonunderstanding parents; the put-upon but woefully unobservant fiance; the vulnerable young gay and his fey friends. Turner presents all these without elaboration, as though the very fact of their sexual persuasion makes them intrinsically interesting. They're not and neither is Turner's film.

The producer, director and scripter tries to enliven things by adding gratuitous, all-male bed scenes, but he would be well-advised to leave such doings to more gamy and accomplished filmmakers such as Wakefield Poole.
—Sege.

Tribute
(CANADIAN-COLOR)

Deserves one.

Hollywood, Nov. 25.
A 20th Century-Fox release, produced by Joel B. Michaels and Garth B. Drabinsky. Directed by Bob Clark. Features entire cast. Exec producers, Lawrence Turman, David Foster, Richard S. Bright. Screenplay, Bernard Slade, based on his stage play; camera (Medallion Film Laboratories color), Reginald H. Morris; editor, Richard Halsey, sound, David Lee; productions design, Trevor Williams; art direction, Reuben Freed; assistant director, Ken Goch; associate producer, Hannah Hempstead; music. Ken Wannberg, Barry Manilow, Jack Feldman, Bruce Sussman, Jack Lemmon, Alan Jay Lerner. Reviewed at 20th Century Fox, L.A., Nov. 25, 1980. (MPAA rating: PG). Running time: 123 MINS.
Scottie Templeton . . . . Jack Lemmon
Jud Templeton . . . . Robby Benson
Maggie Stratton . . . . Lee Remick
Sally Haines . . . . Kim Cattrall
Gladys Petrelli . . . . Colleen Dewhurst
Lou Daniels . . . . John Marley
Hilary . . . . Gale Garnett

When Jack Lemmon opened "Tribute" on Broadway, people said it would be impossible to imagine any other actor in the role and sure enough the show shuttered when he departed. It's equally impossible to imagine anyone but Lemmon in the film version, which can obviously be around forever — and probably will.
The complex role of Scottie Templeton has been tailored for Lemmon's oft-proclaimed talents for both comedy and heavy drama. On the one hand, he must be a flippant, shallow ne'er-do-well; on the other, terrified by his own fatal illness and aware of the waste of his life; and, most importantly, be both willing and unwilling to change.
Working from his own stage script, and with an able assist from

director Bob Clark, writer Bernard Slade uses film to deepen and enrich Templeton's story, which begins with his learning of his illness just as the young son he hasn't seen for several years arrives for a visit.

Robby Benson is excellent in the equally complex part of the intellectual, introspective boy, both repelled by his father's superficial, even pimpish, existence as a Broadway press agent and attracted, as everyone is, to his charm. Most of all, he's resentful of the years lost since Lemmon divorced mother Lee Remick.
In the smallest of the three major parts, Remick nonetheless turns in a solid performance as the ex-wife who still loves him but learned long ago he wasn't worth putting up with. But she shares the terror of his impending death and desperately wants to witness a reconciliation between father and son, with time running short.
As a taut father-mother-son drama, "Tribute" has more than a little in common with "Ordinary People," but the gag-it-up nature of Lemmon's character adds a buoyancy to this one without diluting the heartpull. And the fact that Lemmon ultimately accepts medical help to prolong his life and resolves his conflicts with Benson provides a much more up-beat ending.
Though Lemmon may be unique to the project, he nonetheless gets first-rate help throughout the cast. Kim Cattrall adds a lot as the young girl involved closely with father and son; Colleen Dewhurst is strong as Lemmon's doctor-friend and John Marley catches fire in the second half of the film as Lemmon's partner and defender.

Gale Garnett also is quite accomplished in one of the film's best parts, a hooker who admires and appreciates Lemmon, especially after he stages a retirement dinner for her, complete with gold watch.
There is a minority around that initially saw Slade's play as thinly obvious melodrama and Lemmon on the edge of overacting. It's not likely they will like the film any better. But they'll also still be in the minority. —Har.

Zucchero, Miele E Peperoncino
(Sugar, Honey and Pepper)
(ITALIAN-COLOR)

Rome, Nov. 14.
A Medusa release, produced by Luciano Martino for Dania Film productions. Stars Renato Pozzetto, Edwige Fenech, Pippo Franco. Directed by Sergio Martino. Screenplay, Castellano and Pipolo; camera (Eastmancolor), Giancarlo Ferrando; art director, Adriana Bellone;

editor, Eugenio Alabiso; music, Detto Mariani. Reviewed at Europa Cinema, Rome, Nov. 11, 1980. Running time: 113 MINS.

Milanese	Lino Banfi
Maila	Edwige Fenech
Giuseppe	Pippo Franco
Wife	Dagmar Lassander
Plinio	Renato Pozzetto
Girl	Patrizia Garganese

In three sketches of "light viewing" Italian comedy put together by veteran scribes Castellano and Pipolo, helmer Sergio Martino scores a high average in a package film that is (luckily) sweeter (funnier) than it is spicy. Whatever the deficiencies of logic and short-cuts on the technical side, "Sugar" has fattened its producer with its seemingly unsinkable formula of sexy women and bumbling males that is so to the taste of Italo audiences. Better thesping, than is commonly found in the genre, gives pic some distinction, but offshore palates will still have to adjust to the native humor.

Pic's recipe is to exaggerate ills besetting three innocent victims of fate who wind up in court before the judge, with relatives throwing tomatoes or smiling encouragement from the gallery. Highlight of first tale of woe is character actor Lino Banfi, who subtly limns a man mistaken for a wanted killer and "kidnapped" by Edwige Fenech, reporter in search of a scoop. Fenech's gifts are principally physical — her fans will never find her lovelier than in "Sugar" — and she is used strictly for the easy gag. Fine character actor Enzo Robutti as the hysterical police chief if a frenetic Keystone Kop pushed a bit too far beyond the limits of credibility — another easy laugh.

Best results are wrestled from the central story of a starving Pippo Franco, balding, clown-faced and ready to consume his parrot, who finds a job at last disguised as a maid. He valiantly fights against his lust for the operaticly appealing lady of the house, but is at last unmasked by her jealous and brutal husband. Here the mandatory transvestite scene works better than in most current comedies, perhaps because it is so pathetically motivated. Camera technique, or lack of it, mercifully recedes into the background and lets Franco carry the show

Even Renato Pozzetto, a top b.o. star whose stock Milanese character is as unwavering as Dolomites, comes to life a little more than usual in the role of an independent cab driver who sleeps with his tax until it is highjacked by a Sicilian trio on their way to enforce a shotgun wedding. Pozzetto in his wedding suit offering bonbons to the judge is just the right touch to keep the ending from seeming arbitrary.

The "pepper" is again supplied by a small pinch of "nice" softcore from tv soubrette Patrizia Garganese, who is very pretty. Helmer Martino has a particularly loving way of photographing his three very different actresses, though it's a pity he makes no attempt to get performances out of them. —*Yung*.

Flash Gordon
(BRITISH-COLOR)

Pretty but dumb sci-fi pic for Christmas family trade.

Hollywood, Nov. 21.

Universal Pictures release of a Dino De Laurentiis production, exec produced by Bernard Williams. Produced by De Laurentiis. Directed by Mike Hodges. Features entire cast. Screenplay, Lorenzo Semple Jr., adapted by Michael Allin from characters created by Alex Raymond; camera (Technicolor), Gil Taylor; editor, Malcolm Cooke; production, costumes, and set design, Danilo Donati; music, Howard Blake, Queen; supervising art director, Frank Van Der Veer; special effects supervisor, George Gibbs; second-unit director, William Kronick; sound, Ivan Sharrock, Gerry Humphreys, Robin O'Donoghue; assistant direcior, Brian Cook. Reviewed at Universal Studios, North Hollywood, Nov. 19, '80. (MPAA Rating: PG.) Running time: 110 MINS.

Additional Special Effects Unit Credits
Photographic effects assistant, Barry Nolan; special effects consultant, Glen Robinson; art director (models), Norman Dorme; special effects (models and skies), Richard Conway; coordinator of action and movement, Bill Hobbs; Zarkov brain-drain sequence director, Denis Postel; special effects editor, Chris Kelly; illustrators, Mentor Huebner, Emanuela Alteri, Giovanna Lombardo; sculptors, Giulio Tomassy, Peter Voysey, Arthur Healey, Galliano Donati; assistant art directors, Giorgio Postiglione, Tony Reading, Steve Spence, Kent Court, Ted Clements, John Fenner; scenic artist, Ted Michell; additional photography, Harry Waxman; lighting cameraman (skies and clouds), Harry Oakes; skies and clouds artists, Count Ul De Rico, Tom Adams; special effects assistants, Dave WAtson, Pierre Tilley, Michael White; special effects (flying), Derek Botell; model makers, Martin Bower, Christine Overs, Bill Pearson, Don Sargent; optical effects, Van Der Veer Photo Effects, R/Greenberg Associates Inc.; blue screen composites, Greg Van Der Veer; optical cameramen, Hugh Wade, Ray Monahan; matte paintings, Lou Lichtenfield, Bob Scifo.

Flash Gordon	Sam J. Jones
Dale Arden	Melody Anderson
Dr. Hans Zarkov	Topol
The Emperor Ming	Max Von Sydow
Princess Aura	Ornella Muti
Prince Barin	Timothy Dalton
Prince Vultan	Brian Blessed
Klytus	Peter Wyngarde
Kala	Mariangela Melato
Arborian Pirest	John Osborne
Fico	Richard O'Brien
Luro	John Hallam
Zogi, The High Priest	Philip Stone

The expensive new version of "Flash Gordon" is a lot more gaudy, and just as dumb, as the original serials starring Buster Crabbe. Sam J. Jones in the title role has even less thespic range than Crabbe showed in the old Saturday matinee sci-fi cliffhangers, but audiences may find the badness of his performance part of the fun of the film. The sets, costumes, and photography are eye-filling, and there's enough sex in the PG film to keep parents entertained as well as kids. The Dino De Laurentiis production, a Universal release, should be a good holiday moneymaker.

It's certainly a commentary on the evolution of Hollywood that the B serials of the 1930s have become the big-budgeted pix of today. This film is hyped as having cost $35,-000,000, but more reliable sources peg the actual cost at around $20,-000,000, still a hefty outlay of money for such frivolity.

"Flash Gordon" lacks the wit and verve of "Superman," whose virtues loom larger in retrospect, and rather than trying to update its characters and situations, as "Superman" did so well, "Flash" is content to recycle its comic book hero and his adventures with minimal dramatic alterations. The big differences between this film and the old serial are the lavish sets and costumes, beautifully executed by Danilo Donati, best known for his work with Federico Fellini, and the colorful lensing by Gil Taylor, who also did "Star Wars."

Director Mike Hodges isn't able to do much to animate Jones, a big hunk of beefcake whose blond-dyed hair gives him a comically epicene look which may or may not have been intentional. Jones, a former "Playgirl" nude centerfold whose only previous film role was the husband of Bo Derek in "10," lumbers vacantly through the part of Flash Gordon with the naivete, fearlessness, and dopey line readings familiar from the 1930s serials. (Another actor, uncredited, reportedly redubbed Jones' entire part, to little avail.)

Scripter Lorenzo Semple Jr., who wrote De Laurentiis' "King Kong" remake in similarly campy vein, never takes the situations seriously in this derivation from the Alex Raymond cartoon strip. He throws in occasional smirking allusions to women's lib, jock slang, and contemporary sexual deviations, as he did in "Kong," and though it's not the highest level of humor, it should amuse the intended audience.

Typical of the script's humor are the parallels drawn implicitly between Flash Gordon, who is supposed to be quarterback of the N.Y. Jets football team before heading for outer space, and Joe Namath, another good-natured dumb jock type whom the ladies can't resist. The ladies panting after Jones are the very sexy Melody Anderson, in the Dale Arden role, and Ornella Muti, as Princess Aura, both of whom are much more than incidental decorations.

Film also benefits greatly from the adroit performance of Max Van Sydow as Emperor Ming. Von Sydow, who probably made more money for this one part than for all of his Ingmar Bergman pix combined, plays the part almost exactly the way Charles Middleton did in the serials, but brings his own finely honed sense of timing and menace to Ming's baroque villainy.

The plot draws as heavily on "Star Wars" as it does on Alex Raymond, with Flash rallying enemies of Ming to overthrow him, much the way Luke Skywalker combats Darth Vader in the Lucas film. And, naturally, the door is left open for a sequel at the end, with the suggestion that Ming may have survived after all.

Ming's opponents are effectively limned by dashing Timothy Dalton and burly Brian Blessed, while his loyalists are played with suitable creepiness by Peter Wyngarde and Mariangela Melato. Chaim Topol makes an amusing Dr. Zarkov, and the sequence (directed by Denis Postle) in which Ming tries to empty Zarkov's brain of its memory images is the best thing in the film.

Tech credits, including a large effex staff, are very good, and the music by Howard Blake and the rock group Queen keeps the film zipping along, even over the vacuum created by its star. —*Mac*.

Sengoku Yaro
(Warring Clans)
(JAPANESE-B&W)

Toho release. Directed by Kihachi Okamoto. Features entire cast. Screenplay, Takeshi Sano, Kihachi Okamtoro, Shinichi Sekizawa; camera (black and white), Uzuru Aizawa; music, Masaru Sato. No other credits provided. Reviewed at Japan House, New York City, Nov. 21, 1980. Running time: 97 MINS.
Cast: Yuzo Kayama, Ichiro Nakatani, Makoto Sato, Yuriko Hoshi.

If Akira Kurosawa's samurai films are the Japanese equivalent of John Ford's westerns, then this comic actioner by Kihachi Okamoto could be compared to a Gene Autry or Roy Rogers western, complete with Gabby Hayes and Smiley Burnette types. This 1963 actioner, like all of Okamoto's fast-paced efforts, was popular with Japanese youth. For more discriminating filmgoers, it might be considered a lesser effort.

A solitary Shane-like figure, disillusioned by the actions of some of his employers, takes off for parts unknown and finds himself involved in the double action of a group of porters and a band of pirates, the latter led by a beautiful princess. There are many scenes of action, none lasting very long, which appears to be an Okamoto trait — his pseudo-Godardian editing even leaves the sweep of a sword arm suspended in the air while he cuts to the beginning of another scene.

Between skirmishes two separate romances find time to flourish but it's the often comic action scenes that make this effort memorable. Uzuru Aizawa's black and white camerawork is a triumph of chiaroscuro. —*Robe.*

Stir Crazy
(COLOR)

Poitier directs a pryor-ized comedy. Saleable.

Hollywood, Nov. 28.

Columbia release of a Hannah Weinstein production. Produced by Hannah Weinstein. Directed by Sidney Poitier. Features entire cast. Exec producer, Melville Tucker. Screenplay, Bruce Jay Friedman; camera (Metrocolor), Fred Schuler; editor, Harry Keller; production design, Alfred Sweeney; music, Tom Scott; sound, Glen Anderson; set decoration, Arthur Jeph Parker; assistant director, Daniel J. McCauley. Reviewed at Burbank Studios, L.A., Nov. 28, 1980. (MPAA Rating: R.) Running time: **111 MINS.**
Skip Donahue .... Gene Wilder
Harry Monroe .... Richard Pryor
Rory Schultebrand .... Georg Stanford Brown
Meredith .... Jobeth Williams
Jesus Ramirez .... Miguelangel Suarez
Deputy Ward Wilson ..... Craig T. Nelson
Warden Walter Beatty ..... Barry Corbin
Blade .... Charles Weldon
Warden Henry Sampson ... Nicolas Coster
Len Garber .... Joel Brooks
Jack Graham .... Jonathan Banks
Grossberger .. Erland Van Lidth De Jeude
Guard No. 1 .... Lewis Van Bergen
Susan .... Lee Purcell

The extensive comedic talents of Richard Pryor take a below average film like "Stir Crazy" and make it into an often funny and definitely saleable picture. Pryor's idle mugging, coupled with his clever reactions to the very ridiculous on-screen situation, provide an immeasurable dose of polish to Bruce Jay Freidman's distinctly vacant script.

With the undeniable interest in Pryor since his well-publicized personal difficulties and the already sizable audience for the reteaming of him and Gene Wilder, the Columbia release should capture a healthy share of the holiday boxoffice.

Story setup has down on their luck New Yorkers Pryor and Wilder deciding to blow the city for what they think are the promising shores of California. Driving cross country they land in a small town where they take a job dressing up as woodpeckers in a local bank in order to make some cash. Two baddies they met in a bar use the woodpecker suits to rob the bank, leaving Pryor and Wilder 120-year prison sentences and no alibi.

Majority of the action focuses on the antics of prison life, with Pryor and Wilder at the center of a group of fairly stereotypical jail characters. Much of the comedy rests not in the story or dialog but with the visual mishaps of the pair as they get accustomed to life behind bars. and plan their eventual escape.

Director Sidney Poitier's chief role seems to be providing enough space for Pryor and Wilder to do their schtick without going too far afield from the scant storyline. He performs this responsibility reasonably well, although Wilder is allowed a little too much freedom, delivering a fairly one-note performance as the naive neurotic he's often limned in the past.

Because the script offers so little, supporting players are nothing but perennial straight men for the two comics. Erland Van Lidth De Jeude is sometimes amusing as a fat, scary murderer Wilder somehow tames but Georg Stanford Brown is particularly offensive in a major role as a lisping, limp-wristed gay inmate. Latter is a surprising characterization for a film made in 1980.

Harry Keller's editing keeps some sense of the proceedings but even those allowing creative license will be wondering how an oaf like Wilder can be an expert bronco buster, can get away with his stupidity without being lynched and why he and not Pryor ever gets to see their lawyer.

Although there is some nice musical assist from Tom Scott, it can easily be said that "Stir Crazy" succeeds because of Pryor. His pained look into the camera when he's sentenced to jail, his hopeless reactions to Wilder's eccentricities and his overall stance as the famed fool make a flimsy feature like "Stir Crazy" worth seeing. To quote an often used line, "that takes talent."
—*Berg.*

Tomas - et barn, du ikke kan naa
(Tomas - A Child You Cannot Reach)
(DANISH-DOCU-COLOR)

Copenhagen, Nov. 1.

An HTM production with the Danish Film Institute (Erik Crone), HTM Film release. Stars Lone Hertz and Tomas Stroebye. Written and directed by Mads Egmont Christensen and Lone Hertz. Camera (Eastmancolor/Widescreen) Bille August and Alexander Gruszynski; editor, Janus Billeskov Jansen; executive producer, production manager, Tivi Magnusson. Reviewed at Dagmar Bio, Copenhagen, Nov. 1, 1980. Running time: **100 MINS.**

"Tomas - A Child You Cannot Reach" is a kind of documentary parallel to any dramatized Helen Keller story, but without the latter's periods of conclusions of relief. The title says it all. There is practically no hope for Tomas, a physically almost adult child who is seriously retarded, possibly insane and suffering from epileptic attacks.

Tomas is now and again taken from the institution where he lives to a remote seaside village for a week of holidays-cum-instruction with his mother, actress Lone Hertz, who is of the conviction that Tomas (she has three normal children) would have stood a better chance if he had not had his "education" neglected when he was a small child. Specialists then had deemed his case hopeless.

What is then shown is the mother's obdurate although also loving struggle to have the boy work at least minimally with his mind. They have endless sessions together with pictures to select and similar exercises. Tomas would rather giggle (he cannot speak) and exchange kisses with his mother, but she never gives up until at least some kind of minuscule (even just token?) result has been gained.

It should be noted that Tomas, when his face is at ease and when he is smiling, is a bewilderingly good-looking, even charming and definitely normal-looking boy.

Film contains no spoken commentary, no experts are brought in and no moral is preached. "Tomas" is an item to be used on lecture circuits and shown in numerous specialized situations. In Denmark it is even enjoying a fairly good theatrical run. Film has been chosen to represent Denmark in the documentary category of the next Academy awards. It is a strange and unusual work of high documentary as well as artistic merit. —*Kell.*

The Competition
(COLOR)

Tasteless film on classical music. Hard going.

Hollywood, Nov. 26.

Columbia Pictures release of a Rastar-William Sackheim production, exec produced by Howard Pine. Produced by Sackheim. Stars Richard Dreyfuss, Amy Irving, Lee Remick. Directed by Joel Oliansky. Screenplay, Oliansky, from story by Oliansky, Sackheim; camera (Metrocolor), Richard H. Kline; original music, Lalo Schifrin; song, "People Alone," by Schifrin, Wilbur Jennings; music by Ginastera, Brahms, Chopin, Prokofiev, and Beethoven, performed by Eduardo Delgado, Ralph Grierson, Lincoln Mayorga, Daniel Pollack, Chester B. Swiatowski and the L.A. Philharmonic Orchestra; editor, David Blewitt; production design, Dale Hennesy; set decorator, James Payne; set designer, Dianne Wager; sound, John Speak, Les Fresholtz, Tex Rudloff, Asron Rochin; piano instructor-music consultant, Jean Evensen Shaw; assistant director, Jon C. Anderson. Reviewed at The Burbank Studios, Burbank, Nov. 25, '80. (MPAA Rating: PG.) Running time: **129 MINS.**
Paul Dietrich .... Richard Dreyfuss
Heidi Schoonover .... Amy Irving
Greta Vandemann .... Lee Remick
Erskine .... Sam Wanamaker
Jerry DiSalvo .... Joseph Cali
Michael Humphries .... Ty Henderson
Tatiana Baronov .... Vickie Kriegler
Mark Landau .... Adam Stern
Mme. Gorshev .... Bea Silvern
Mr. Dietrich .... Philip Sterling
Mrs. Dietrich .... Gloria Strcock
Mrs. DiSalvo .... Delia Salvi
Mrs. Donellan .... Priscilla Pointer

"The Competition" is a disappointment which may be taken seriously in some quarters because it deals with the world of classical music. Writer-director Joel Oliansky's glibly cynical view of the performing world and his dreary character portraits are matched in clumsiness by his ugly visual style and lack of genuine feeling for music. Richard Dreyfuss and Amy Irving waste their talents in this Rastar-William Sackheim production, a Columbia release with limited commercial appeal.

The film, which includes piano music by several classical composers, needed a conductor and composer of background music with a sensitivity to the classical field, but instead it has Lalo Schifrin. His noisy, bombastic style is a measure of the ham-handed tastelessness of this film.

The classical pieces are subjected to condensation, an unconscionable violation by a film which purports to be a serious treatment of classical music. The footage devoted to actual performing reportedly was shortened after screenings for exhibs, on the dubious theory that the pic might do better commercially by downplaying its actual subject. "The Turning Point" proved that such material can be commercial.

The story, by debuting director Oliansky and producer Sackheim, could have been the genesis of a good film if the other elements had lived up to its promise. There is, in fact, one terrific scene near the end of the film which shows what "The Competition" tries to be and could have been.

Dreyfuss, as an aging paino wunderkind making one last shot at recognition before giving up performing for teaching, is reunited at a San Francisco music competition with Irving, a less driven but more gifted young woman he had impressed briefly at an earlier festival. She tries to rekindle their attraction, but Dreyfuss is too absorbed in his music at first to respond; finally he does, which leads to a crisis when she beats him in the competition.

The standout scene comes after

Irving's victory, when Dreyfuss' deep disappointment and sense of failure overcome his capacity to love her, and he cannot help but reject her. There's a sense of painful truth here, conveyed with devastating emotional impact by the actors, who finally have material worthy of their potential.

But the rest of the film is tedious and predictable, curiously portraying music as a grim and joyless profession for these youngsters. Oliansky makes much of how they're pushed into competing by their elders — in Dreyfuss' case, by his dying pop Philip Sterling, and in Irving's, by her grotesquely rapacious teacher Lee Remick — and the film never suggests that they could actually love music for its own sake. The film thus becomes a symptom of a malaise it purports to criticize.

Endless boring and irritating scenes are devoted to the Dreyfuss family's melodramatic hand-wringing, Remick's crass materialistic monologs, and assorted other cardboard filler material such as an unnecessary subplot about a defecting Russian, cheap gags with a stereotyped gay black pianist, and the hammy theatrics of yet another family of Italian over-actors. The dialog is mystifyingly crude, particularly as in the offensive scene of Remick urging Irving to reject Dreyfuss in favor of the young Italian stud Remick describes as "a human vibrator."

While some may take the film's potshots at the classical music world as hard-hitting realism; the film actually indulges in shallow attacks at easy targets, such as the dilettantism of the lecherous conductor played by Sam Wanamaker or Remick's ludicrous attempts to corrupt her protegee.

Irving is such a lively and attractive actress that she manages to keep whatever scenes she is in watchable and occasionally even amusing. Dreyfuss, on the other hand, seems unduly leaden even considering the strain his character is supposed to be undergoing. In his recent pix, the once-vigorous Dreyfuss has appeared haggard and lethargic, and he's lost the cocky brio that made him a star in the first place.

After the film comes briefly to life with its one riveting scene, the filmmakers cop out by allowing Dreyfuss to make an unmotivated return to Irving as the entire cast boogies under the end credits to an awful disco number by Schifrin. It's one of the most appalling lapses of artistic integrity, and seems the result of a compromise solution in which two endings were considered, neither won out, and both

were included. It makes nonsense of the story.

Production credits are subpar, especially the murky lighting by Richard F. Kline and the drab production design by Dale Hennesy. Dreyfuss and Irving competently mime their own piano playing, which is dubbed by Chester B. Swiatowski and Daniel Pollack, respectively. —*Mac.*

Tendres Cousines
(Tender Cousins)
(FRENCH-COLOR)

Paris, Nov. 25.

An AMLF release of a Stephan Films/Filmedis coproduction. Features entire cast. Directed by David Hamilton. Screenplay, Pascal Laine, Josiane Leveque, Claude D'Anna; camera (color), Bernard Daillencourt; sound, Pierre Befve; art director, Aric Simon; editor, Jean-Bernard Bonis. Reviewed at the UGC Biarritz theatre, Paris, Nov. 22, 1980. Running time: 90 MINS.
Cast: Anja Shute, Thierry Teveni, Macha Meril, Catherine Rouvel, Pierre Vernier, Jean Rougerie.

Photographer David Hamilton's third theatrical film venture, is, again, pretty and pretty dull. This one has a scenario by novelist Pascal Laine ("The Lacemaker"), another trite tale of the sexual initiation of a 15-year-old boy on his parents' summer property where adults and children, masters and servants mingle in a predictable roundelay of sexual flirtations and petty heartaches. The flimsy through-line of the story — which is set during the summer of 1939 — is the boy's attempts to win the affections of his cousin. After tipping into the hay with most of the maidservants in the house, he finally conquers her.

Technically, "Tendres Cousines" is Hamilton's most accomplished pic, and his best acted. But his problem as a filmmaker still remains an unwillingness to look deeper than the photogenic possibilities of his characters, who remain vaguely appealing silhouettes.

That war breaks out two-thirds of the way through the film couldn't interest Hamilton less — its just a narrative point that allows him to clear the slate and prepare new visual combinations. Theme and content have little place in Hamilton's scheme of things, which is dedicated to pursuit of the purely photographic. —*Len.*

Laong Dao
(Miss Laong Dao)
(THAI-COLOR)

Bangkok, Nov. 18.

A Visit Mingwattanaboon production and release. Produced by Wanchai Termjitaree. Written and directed by Pisan

Akaraseni; based on original story by Suphan Pramphan. Features entire cast. Camera (color), Vichien Ruangwittayakul; sound, Union Lab (Hong Kong); songs sung by Tanongsap Pakdithiwa; production design, VC Promotion; asst. director, Kitti Akaraseni. Reviewed at Ambassador theatre, Bangkok, Nov. 18, '80. Running time: 125 MINS.
Korakot .... Pisan Akaraseni
Laong Dao .... Nawarat Yukthanand
Radachamai .... Rinda Katancharoen
Chartchai .... Montri Jaenaksorn
Yord Rak .... Jamrak Chamnanpadit
Mae Ban ... Ratanaporn Indrakamhaeng
Sadej Praong Ying .. Marasri Issarangkul
Na Ayudhaya
Mom Chao Sadayoo ..... Uthen Boonyong
Chao Kam-in .... Siriwat Kongkaketr
Family Administrator ... Singh Milintasai

The love team of Pisan Akaraseni and Nawarat Yukthanand has appeared in several pics during the past few years, one of the few local screen couples that have survived fluctuations in public acceptance and the considerable loss of popularity of love stories here since more than a year ago when the demand for comedies rose higher.

"Laong Dao" is a remake of a previous hit starring Sombat Metanee and Pisamai Wilaisak. The plot has many similarities to other pix that Pisan and Nawarat have done before.

Depiction of life among the rich and royalty in pic lacks attention to detail. The portrait of Pisan's father, often used, shows Pisan himself with gray hair, which is unintentionally funny.

Pisan also disappears during the final portion, and it turns out that he went to a Buddhist temple. But he doesn't go there to enter monkhood. He just loiters in the vicinity until Nawarat comes to fetch him. Monkhood requires shaving one's head, and Pisan, who's busy making other films, couldn't afford that. —*Cano.*

Mamma Dracula
(FRENCH-BELGIAN-COLOR)

Paris, Nov. 25.

A UGC release of a Valisa Films Productions-SND production. Produced and directed by Boris Szulzinger. Stars Louise Fletcher, Maria Schneider. Screenplay, Szulzinger, Pierre Sterckx and M. H. Wajnberg; English dialog, Tony Hendra; camera (color), Willy Kurant; editor, Claude Cohen; make-up, Pascale Kellen; costumes, Mouchy Houblinne; music, Roy Budd. Reviewed at the Elysees Cinema, Paris, Nov. 21, 1980. Running time: 90 MINS.
Mamma Dracula .... Louise Fletcher
Nancy Hawaii .... Maria Schneider
Vladimir .... Marc-Henri Wajnberg
Ladislas .... Alexander Wajnberg
Van Bloed .... Jimmy Shuman
Rosa .... Michel Israel
Superintendent .... Jess Hahn
(English Soundtrack)

More fooling around with Dracula. This latest, and hopefully last, vampire spoof was produced, co-written and directed by Boris Szul-

zinger, the Belgian filmmaker who directed Picha's "Shame of the Jungle" (1975), and was made in English with a cast of American, Belgian and French actors including Louise Fletcher and Maria Schneider, who share star billing. Professional lampoonist Tony Hendra wrote the English dialog.

Despite all the above factors, "Mamma Dracula" is an utterly anemic farce, plodding and unfunny, directed without invention and acted without style. It's hard to see what Szulzinger and his collaborators thought they had in the way of a new idea that would warrant this film.

Fletcher plays the title role, a modern day fashion-conscious vampire immune to sunlight, crucifixes, garlic, stakes, whose only true need, in order to remain young, is a periodic bath in the blood of virgins.

Since virgins are in short supply in today's decadent society, Fletcher buys the services of a scientist who is working on a formula for artificial blood and sequesters him in the castle lab, while her two sons continue to kidnap young girls in the fashion boutique she runs in town. Investigating the disappearance of the women are two police inspectors.

Fletcher has virtually nothing to do except look elegant and speak her lines in one of those tedious pastiche accents. Her two wacky sons are played by creepy-looking twin brothers, Marc-Henri and Alexander Wajnberg, one of whom shares writing credits. They flap around and grimace a lot and seem to have quite a good time, but they're no funnier than the wheezing gags they're involved in. Maria Schneider, as one of the police inspectors who eventually becomes Fletcher's daughter-in-law, looks profoundly bored. The other actors fare no better.

Pic offers some small visual pleasure in the actual art nouveau decors that serve as interiors of the vampire's castle, adequately photographed by Willy Kurant. But "Mamma Dracula" looks destined to the graveyard of commercial trends that have overstayed their welcome. —*Len.*

You Better Watch Out
(COLOR)

Sharp handling of controversial theme could give grim drama b.o. strength. Possible best route would be down horror road.

Pittsburgh, Nov. 13.

Edward R. Pressman presentation. Produced by Burt Kleiner and Pete Kameron. Associate producer, Michael Levine.

Directed and written by Lewis Jackson. Features entire cast. Editors, Corky O'Hara, Linda Leeds; camera (color), Ricardo Aronovich; costumes, Dierdre Williams; production designer, Lorenzo Jodie Harris. Reviewed at Squirrel Hill Theatre, Pittsburgh, Nov. 13, 1980. (No MPAA rating.) Running time: 100 MINS. No distributor yet.

Harry Stadling	Brandon Maggart
Jackie Stadling	Dianne Hull
Fletcher	Scott McKay
Frank Stoller	Joe Jamrog
Grosch	Peter Friedman
Gleason	Ray Barry
Gottleib	Bobby Lesser
Grilla	Sam Gray
Harry's mother	Ellen McElduff
Moss' mother	Patty Richardson

"You Better Watch Out" creeps along for the first 11 minutes with no action except for one scene that will give it a R rating and does nothing to indicate the grim unrelenting drama that unfolds during the film's 100 minutes. How audiences accept the Santa Claus figure as a murdering psychotic will determine the ultimate success of the picture.

The part is a tour de force for Brandon Maggart and could mean a future career. He is dynamic, believable and well-directed on the collision course that was designed for him by an innocent eavesdropping in early childhood.

Writer-director Lewis Jackson has given his best effort to Maggart and bogs down in handling cast members in secondary roles. Production design, art direction and many tiny touches stand out. Jackson is a real comer even though he wastes his ending by indulging in a little whimsy. However, it could be he wanted to break the stern grip that Maggart had put on the audience during most of the film. Film is a fantasy that makes sense with the unlikely character of a murdering Santa Claus dominating the picture. There are many horrific moments when Santa Claus kills and this horror aspect will probably be the guide to financial success. The cult audiences will be easy. This picture could make it in the commercial market. Outstanding part of the production is the work of cinematographer Ricardo Aronovich in his first American film. —*Lit.*

La Locandiera
(ITALIAN-COLOR)

Rome, Nov. 24.

A CIDIF release, produced by Giulio Scanni for DADA Film productions and RAI Film. Stars Claudia Mori, Adriano Celentano, Paolo Villaggio. Directed by Paolo Cavara. Screenplay Leo Benvenuti, Pietro De Bernardi, Lucia Demby, based on Carlo Goldoni play; camera (Eastmancolor), Mario Vulpiani; sets and costumes, Giancarlo Bartolini Salimbeni; editing, Angelo Curi; music, Detto Mariano. Reviewed at Esperia Cinema, Rome, Nov. 17, 1980. Running time: 111 MINS.

Mirandolina	Claudia Mori
The Cavaliere	Adriano Celentano
The Marchese	Paolo Villaggio
Fabrizio	Gianni Cavina

Helmer Paolo Cavara shoots a competent light version of the famous Goldoni play, but loses points on the jazzed up song and dance numbers all'italiana and in liberties taken to popularize the leading man roles, played by entertainer Adriano Celentano and comedian Paolo Villaggio. This particular classics for the masses formula has done extremely well at local boxoffice but will almost certainly be a limiting factor abroad, where the two comedians are less beloved and where the glory of the American musical is a standard of comparison.

Lenser Mario Vulpiani's rich brown-beiges and excellent period costumes by Giancarlo Bartolini Salimbeni give production a compensating quality look. Light-hearted tale has an aristocratic woman-hater, the Cavaliere, fall for beautiful Florentine innkeeper Mirandolina. She artfully wins his love and almost loses her faithful Fabrizio. Both Claudia Mori as the proud hotel keeper and Gianni Cavina as her mooning servant give their characters subtleties that make them believably real.

Celentano's Cavaliere and, still more, Villaggio's fat and penniless Marchese rely on close-ups of their well-known facial expressions and mannerisms to modernize their parts, turning them into simple caricatures.

A more serious distraction are the poorly lensed and choreographed musical numbers that overdose time worn local color. Celentano, strangely, neither sings nor dances in the film, though many lesser talents do. Otherwise, film is well shot and story flows sans sags.

The 18th century playwright Carlo Goldoni, appears as a character in a striking opening sequence showing his midnight arrival at the inn and signing the registry book with a flourishing "Carlo Goldoni, Venetian." Subsequent appearance of a wandering theatrical troupe of the period is not up to snuff in creating either mood or an art-as-life atmosphere, as in Jean Renoir's "Golden Coach" which it strongly recalls.

Geared to the taste of Italian musical comedy audiences, "Locandiera" remains pretty much a middle of the road product with a few classy moments. —*Yung.*

Le Rebelle
(The Rebel)
(FRENCH-COLOR)

Paris, Nov. 15.

A Films Moliere release of a Roc/Pelical Films/Films Moliere/Auditrust/Telcipro coproduction, with the participation of Antenne 2. Produced by Louis Duchesne. Directed by Gerard Blain. Features entire cast. Written by Blain and Andre Debaecque; camera (Eastmancolor), Emmanuel Machuel; editor, Jean-Philippe Berger; sound, Alex Pront; music, Catherine Lara. Reviewed at the Marignan-Concorde theatre, Paris, Nov. 13, 1980. Running time: 105 MINS.

Cast: Patrick Norbert, Michel Subor, Isabelle Rosais, Jean-Jacques Aublanc, Francoise Michaud.

Gerard Blain's "The Rebel" is one of those Loners-Against-Society dramas in which the dice are loaded from the start and heavily cast. The difference here, and an essential one for Blain's supporters, is that it is treated with a quasi-Bressonian austerity which, if one plays ball with the idea, is supposed to transcend the stark schematism of the screenplay and deepen the moral significance of its events.

But all the stylistic attitudinizing in the world can't hide the platitudes of situation and dialog and the arrant sentimentality that lurks at every turn of this scornfully predictable tale. Blain may be sincere in his anger but his film is nonetheless claptrap social melodrama in which what you see on the screen is all that you get.

An orphaned young man (Patrick Norbert) of working class background commits robberies to support his young sister. Resolutely unwilling to work for a society in which he can discern no good, Norbert is nevertheless put in a tight spot when his sister is threatened with placement in a State home unless he can show adequate employment.

Propositioned by Communist and left wing terrorist supporters who want to channel his rage to their own uses, the young man rejects his supposed sympathizers and their rhetoric and follows his rebelliousness to its logical conclusion: he shoots down a powerful homosexual businessman, (Michel Subor) who has offered him work papers in exchange for sexual favors. He is arrested and definitively separated from his sister.

Although the solemnity of tone and the subdued performances are meant to belie the fact, "The Rebel" is a blatant sympathy monger that, ironically, never connects emotionally. Norbert's love for his sister is pure and unselfish and sanctions his hate. Everyone else is either rotten, hypocritical or fickle. So what else is new?

Blain's direction is okay, but his purported stylistic rigor is surprisingly gratuitous at times, particularly in his use of close-ups. Norbert and especially Subor give taut, credible performances under Blain's steely control. —*Len.*

Mababangong Bangungot
(The Perfumed Nightmare)
(FILIPINO-COLOR-16m)

A Zoetrope Studios release of a Kidlat Tahimik production. Produced, directed and written by Kidlat Tahimik. Features entire cast. Camera (color, 8m), Tahimik, Harmut Lerch; editor, Tahimik; music, traditional (Filipino). Reviewed at Bleecker St. Cinema Agee room, Nov. 30, 1980. Running time: 95 MINS.

With: Kidlat Tahimik, Dolores Santamaria, Mang Fely, Georgette Baudry, Katrin Muller.

Kidlat Tahimik's first film, "The Perfumed Nightmare," is an amateur effort, offering very slim commercial returns in its domestic release via Francis Coppola's Zoetrope Studios. The filmmaker's fashionable anti-American and anti-technological progress sentiments could whip up some fringe following.

Shot silent in 8m, pic relies heavily on added soundtrack (including star-director's English language first-person narration and comical radio broadcasts in English) for both narrative and gags. Tahimik plays himself, a jitney-driver in the small Filipino town of Balian who idolizes America and especially immigrant Werner von Braun and the NASA program. His father was killed for "trespassing" by an American sentry and he keeps as a totem a horse carved by his mother from his dad's rifle butt. He has a friend, with a prominent butterfly tattoo on his chest, who offers him homespun traditional philosophy, but spurred on by American radio broadcasts, Tahimik is anxious to reach the paradise of America.

A young American businessman takes him to Paris where Tahimik services the man's chain of street gumball machines. A side-trip to Bavaria has him befriending a pregnant woman who names her baby after him. Returning to Paris, he comes to reject the advanced technology which has growing supermarkets crowding out of business a kindly woman street peddler he had known. In an unconvincingly militant finale, he resigns his presidency of the von Braun fan club and rejects an opportunity to travel via Concorde to the U.S., instead fantasizing his own space trip in one of the new plastic Parisian chimneys being erected nearby.

Tahimik's rejection of American technology and influence is a banal theme familiar from many Third World filmmakers. Extremely poor technical quality of his blown-up-to-16m home movie footage makes watching "The Perfumed Nightmare" a chore. It is possible to identify with his theme of turning inward and becoming self-reliant, but making the NASA program whipping boy for U.S. domination of the economies and consciousness of other peoples in the world is both facile and misleading. Typical of Tahimik's sophomoric approach is that two benign institutions of international goodwill, the Boy Scouts and topical stamp collecting, are recurring targets of his satire.

What's wrong with "The Perfumed Nightmare" conceptually is evident in the awfully "cute" end-credits sequence: credits cards are adorned with space stamps from Sharjah, Panama, Paraguay and sundry other topical-specializing nations of yore, culminating in a hand-drawn mythical Filipino stamp picturing Tahimik on his space chimney. As with other issues raised (and dealt with on a quick gag level) in the pic, corrupt and exploitative stamp-issuing policies are a controversial and complex problem for philatelists, but mere fodder for laughs in this painfully naive film. —Lor.

Popeye
(COLOR)

Cartoon character, fleshed out, unpredictable outlook.

Hollywood, Dec. 9.

Paramount Pictures Corp. release of a Paramount Pictures and Walt Disney Productions presentation of a Robert Evans production. Executive producer, C.O. Erickson. Stars Robin Williams, Shelley Duvall. Directed by Robert Altman. Screenplay, Jules Feiffer; camera (color), Giuseppe Rotunno; music and lyrics, Harry Nilsson; production designer, Wolf Kroeger; supervising editor, Tony Lombardo; costumes, Scott Bushnell; based on E.C. Segar's "Popeye" characters; choreography, Sharon Kinney, Hovey Burgess. Lou Wills; sound, Robert Gravenor; film editors, John W. Holmes, David Simmons; set decorator, Jack Stephens; publicist, Bridget Terry. Reviewed at Chinese Theatre, Hollywood, Dec. 6, 1980. (MPAA Rating - PG). Running time: 114 MINS.

Popeye	Robin Williams
Olive Oyl	Shelley Duvall
Poopdeck Pappy	Ray Walston
Wimpy	Paul Dooley
Bluto	Paul L. Smith
Geezil	Richard Libertini
The Taxman	Donald Moffat
Cole Oyl	MacIntrye Dixon
Nana Oyl	Roberta Maxwell
Castor Oyl	Donovan Scott
Rough House	Allan Nicholls
Swee'pea	Wesley Ivan Hurt

It is more than faint praise to say that "Popeye" is far, far better than it might have been, considering the treacherous challenge it presented. But avoiding disaster is not necessarily the same as success. In any case, its outlook clearly rests with teens and under, who are an unpredictable lot.

Compared to characters like Superman and Flash Gordon, Popeye is obviously a much more difficult hero to adapt to human dimen-

sions, both physically and dramatically. For story purposes, Popeye and those around him are simple drawings whose whole existence is manifested in broad action.

Though producer Robert Evans and director Robert Altman have struggled admirably — with essential help from Robin Williams and Shelley Duvall — they fail to bring the characters to life at the sacrifice of a large initial chunk of the film. It's only when they allow the characters to fall back on their cartoon craziness that the picture works at all.

If the whole film had enjoyed the zest of the last half, there's no question Paramount and Disney (which will distribute overseas) would have a solid commerical hit, regardless of the faults. It's that first hour — which should have been a half hour at best — that remains troubling.

To the eye, Williams is terrifically transposed into the squinting sailor with the bulging arms. But to the ear, his mutterings are not always comprehensible and, more importantly, what he has to say is not terribly compelling. (Paramount now contends its premiere screening was marred by technical sound difficulties that are being cured.)

In Jules Feiffer's script, Popeye comes to the quaint village of Sweethaven in search of a father who abandoned him and this is supposed to be his underlying motivation for whatever happens as he first meets Olive Oyl and acquires his own abandoned baby, Swee'pea.

That's just too much for a cartoon to carry, even with some generally good songs by Harry Nilsson and a wacky, colorfully created town for a backdrop.

Though Duvall makes a delightful Olive Oyl and Paul L. Smith a perfectly jealous Bluto, the triangular formula that was standard for the cartoon is initially so studiously avoided that when Popeye and Bluto have their first fight, Popeye not only doesn't take to the spinach to save himself — the creators go out of their way to establish he hates spinach.

Finally, however, Olive Oyl and Swee'pea are kidnapped by Bluto and the picture starts to work because of its very familiarity. It's fun to see Popeye in pursuit with Olive screaming for help in her screeching voice. And the wacky, exaggerated fisticuffs and action are sure to follow, which they admirably do. They should have been there sooner.

From a craft standpoint, the film is firstrate, allowing much credit for Wolf Kroeger's production design, Scott Bushnell's costumes and Giuseppe Rotunno's pho-

tography, though the question remains about the quality of the sound.

Popeye says, "I yam what I yam" and the film is what it is, which is a lot but not enough. —Har.

Tell Me A Riddle
(COLOR)

Strong treatment of commercially questionable subject.

Hollywood, Dec. 1.

A Filmways Pictures release of a Godmother production, produced by Mindy Affrime, Rachel Lyon and Susan O'Connell. Exec producer, Michael Rosenberg. Directed by Lee Grant. Screenplay, Joyce Eliason, Alev Lytle; based on Tillie Olsen novella; camera (CFI Color), Fred Murphy; editor, Suzanne Pettit; sound, David McMillan; production manager, Tony Wade; production design, Patrizia Von Brandenstein; assistant director, Peter Schindler; music Sheldon Shkolnik. Reviewed at Filmways Pictures, Beverly Hills, Dec. 1, 1980. (MPAA rating: PG.) Running time: 90 MINS.

David	Melvyn Douglas
Eva	Lila Kedrova
Jeannie	Brooke Adams
Mrs. Mays	Lili Valenty
Vivi	Dolores Dorn
Sammy	Bob Elross
Mathew	Jon Harris
Paul	Zalman King
Hannah	Winifred Mann
Phil	Peter Owens
Nancy	Deborah Sussel

Since taking over American International Pictures, Filmways Pictures has strived to associate itself with quality pictures and people and there's no question "Tell Me A Riddle" fits that description. But "Riddle" also raises the question of whether Filmways has retained AIP's eye on the marketplace.

Excellently directed by Lee Grant in her feature debut and ably performed, "Riddle" is nonetheless a very morose story about very old people and thus a challenge to today's commercial judgment. Indeed, if it should take off, all involved can lay claim to genius.

Written almost 20 years ago, Tillie Olsen's novella was a forerunner of some of today's feminist concerns, dealing with the reawakenings of an old woman, Lila Kedrova, locked in an unfulfilling marriage for 40 years and now nearing death.

For years Kedrova has lived within herself with childhood memories of Russia and her love of books and music, shutting out husband Melvyn Douglas. Increasingly feeble, he secretly sells the home where they raised their children, knowing that it's all she has left but no longer able to care for it himself.

Kedrova doesn't know she's dying but the family does and they persuade her to take a long trip to visit the children, winding up with granddaughter Brooke Adams in San Francisco. Exposed to this

modern young woman, Kedrova sees even more clearly the voids in her own life.

Grant and the players construct one fine scene after another, especially a belated reconciliation between Douglas and Kedrova, until her end finally comes. Though the picture obviously struggled along for production money, technical work turns out just fine.

—Har.

The Formula
(COLOR)

Brando and Scott in a lost plot. Trouble.

Hollywood, Dec. 2.

A Metro-Goldwyn-Mayer release. Produced and written by Steve Shagan from his novel. Stars George C. Scott, Marthe Keller, Marlon Brando. Directed by John G. Avildsen. Camera (Metrocolor), James Crabe; editors, David Bretherton, John G. Avildsen, John Carter; sound, Al Overton; art direction, Hans-Jurgen Keibach; production design, Herman A. Blumenthal; assistant director, Dwight Williams; music, Bill Conti. Reviewed at MGM, Culver City, Dec. 2, 1980 (MPAA rating: R.) Running time: 117 MINS.

Barney Caine	George C. Scott
Lisa	Marthe Keller
Adam Steiffel	Marlon Brando
Hans Lehman	John Van Dreelen
Sgt. Yosuta	Calvin Jung
Dr. Esau	John Gielgud
Kay Neeley	Beatrice Straight
Kladen/Tedesco	Richard Lynch
Major Nelley	Robin Clarke
Tony	Ike Eisenmann
Nolan	Alan North
Siebold	Ferdy Mayne
Chauffeur	Gerry Murphy
Obermann	David Byrd
Franz Tauber	Wolfgang Preiss
Clements	G.D. Spradlin

Fed up with corporate corruption, "The Formula" makes a daring attack on the world's giant oil cartels that might hit them where they're most vulnerable: if films keep getting as bad as this one, people will never leave their homes to drive to theatres.

Director John Avildsen has already complained publicly that MGM refused to let him take his name off this picture, which just proves how cruel and merciless big companies can be.

According to Avildsen, this is not his original cut, nor producer-writer Steve Shagan's cut, but sort of a combination of the two, plus a few snips and patches by MGM president David Begelman. That allows at least three pair of feet to look under for the film that contains the plot that isn't on the screen.

Given the combined efforts of 14 Oscar nominees and a solid bestseller to start from, it's truly amazing that "The Formula" is such a clump of sludge, impossible to understand for at least an hour before it grinds to a halt.

Oddly enough, "The Formula" starts off so well it promises to be one of those cases where the advance bad-mouthing could be wrong, but unfortunately isn't. Initial sequences solidly establish the closing hours of World War II when a German general, Richard Lynch, is entrusted with top secret documents — including a formula for synthetic fuel — to take to Switzerland in hopes the Nazis can use them to bargain for amnesty.

But Lynch is captured by a U.S. major, Robin Clarke, who recognizes what the secrets will be worth in the postwar world of commerce and the two soldiers are last seen going off together to sift through the papers for future riches.

Cut forward 35 years and Clarke is a fresh corpse, murdered in his bed. Apparently, his access to the secrets of so long ago did not make him rich because he's a retired police official who has to supply his wealthy friends with cocaine to get invitations to their parties.

Anyway, George C. Scott is called in to investigate the murder of his old friend and before long his old friend's ex-wife, Beatrice Straight. Scott soon establishes Clarke had some mysterious dealings with oil supertycoon Marlon Brando and goes to talk to him. (This is Scene No. 1 for Brando; for those who care about such things, he has three scenes in all in the picture, for which he was paid $1,000,000 each.)

The picture continues to hold together as Scott picks up the trail of the missing formula and heads for Germany to investigate further. It would be nice to report he was never seen again, but unfortunately that's not the case.

Though Scott snarls and growls a lot, he never seems to be able to ask anybody a question that would help the audience understand what's going on. When somebody volunteers helpful information, in fact, Scott usually cuts short the conversation and then that person gets killed.

Marthe Keller turns up as the spy for somebody, but it's not clear who; John Gielgud rants through one scene as the formula's inventor; and finally Lynch shows up again as an old man, mumbling key clues unintelligibly.

By the time Scott returns to the U.S. for a grand confrontation with Brando, only those two — and maybe not even them — have any idea what they're talking about. But even in Chinese, this long scene between two once-fine actors is worth watching, just for the business that goes on between them.

Appearing grotesquely fat and ridiculous, Brando apparently thinks he's making some visual comment on the nature of his char-

acter. But it's so overdone, those seeing it are more likely to be so taken by how big Brando has gotten, they'll never think about the corporate fat cats at all.

As everyone knows, of course, both Brando and Scott have taken well-publicized stands against accepting Academy Awards for their work. So at least one plus for "The Formula" is that it's not likely to allow either gentleman another chance to turn Oscar down, sparing them the aggravation. —*Har.*

Rockshow
(COLOR)

An on-screen concert album. Good fan-fodder.

A Miramax release. Produced by MPL Communications. No director credit. Camera, Jack Priestley; editor, Robin Clark; sound mix, Chris Thomas, Paul McCartney. Reviewed at Ziegfeld Theatre, N.Y., Dec. 5, 1980. (MPAA Rating: PG). Running time: 105 MINS.
Features: Paul McCartney, Linda McCartney, Jimmy McCulloch, Joe English, Denny Laine.

With no pretense of any higher purpose than to capture the high-voltage singing and musical talents of former-Beatle Paul McCartney and his Wings group, "Rockshow" is a straightforward film replay of the band's U.S. tour act that bodes a concentrated fan turnout provided it sticks to quick, in-and-out bookings.

State-of-the-art Dolby recording technique has made the sound infinitely superior to the pic's visuals, which should be no hardship to the band's legions of fans. Most will still see more than they ever will from a concert seat (more likely standing) and will probably get a better earful as well.

The show, which features polished, high-spirited renditions of such Wings hits as "Band on the Run," "Jet," and "Silly Love Songs," also lets McCartney get into some nicely recalled Beatles-era hits, including "Lady Madonna," "The Long and Winding Road" and "Maybe I'm Amazed." Something even for the revisionists.

Pic lacks anything that could pass for style (appropriately, it doesn't bear a director's credit) randomly moving from performer to performer with a 95% focus on McCartney, intercut with screaming and swooning audience shots.

In sum, it may be fun, but amounts less to a film than to an expensively produced record album with liner photos that move around and go "Yeah" a lot.
—*Step.*

Altered States
(COLOR)

A massive "upper" from Ken Russell. Big b.o. likely.

Warner Brothers release and production. Produced by Howard Gottfried. Exec producer, Daniel Melnick. Directed by Ken Russell. Stars William Hurt, Blair Brown, Bob Balaban, Charles Haid. Screenplay, Sidney Aaron, from novel by Paddy Chayefsky; camera (Technicolor), Jordan Cronenweth; editor, Eric Jenkins; music, John Corigliano; production designer, Richard McDonald; assoc. producer, Stuart Baird; assistant director, Gary Daigler; sound (Dolby) consultant, Stephen Katz; special effects, Chuck Gaspar; special visual effects, Bran Ferren; special optical effects, Robbie Blalack, Jamie Shourt; time-lapse photography, Lou Schwartzberg; costumes, Ruth Myers; makeup, Dick Smith. Reviewed at Ziegfeld theatre, N.Y.C., Nov. 7, 1980. (MPAA Rating: R). Running time: 102 MINS.
Edward Jessup .... William Hurt
Emily Jessup .... Blair Brown
Arthur Rosenberg .... Bob Balaban
Mason Parrish .... Charles Haid
Eccheverria .... Thaao Penghlis
Primal Man .... Miguel Godreau
Sylvia Rosenberg .... Dori Brenner
Hobart .... Peter Brandon
The Brujo .... Charles White Eagle
With: Drew Barrymore, Megan Jeffers, Jack Murdock, Frank McCarthy, Deborah Baltzell, Evan Richards, Hap Lawrence, John Walter Davis, Cynthia Burr, Susan Bredhoff, John Larroquette.

"Altered States" is an exciting combo science fiction-horror film, well-timed to exploit the under-30 market's current enthusiasm for this genre. Direction by Ken Russell has energy to spare, with appropriate match-up of his baroque visual style to special effects-intensive material. With repeat attendance a definite possibility, Warner Bros. could have a major hit via this $15,000,000 budgeter.

Producers Howard Gottfried and Daniel Melnick weathered stormy pre-production problems, including the ankling of director Arthur Penn late in 1978, departure soon after of special effects wiz John Dykstra, and transfer of project from Columbia to Warners as proposed budget grew.

Screenplay credited to Sidney Aaron (after Paddy Chayefsky insisted that his name be removed) follows the Chayefsky novel very closely, retaining much of the dialog and crucial incidents. Tall tale concerns a young psychophysiologist, Edward Jessup (William Hurt), working in New York and later at Harvard on dangerous experiments involving human consciousness. Despite his having visions of Christ during his childhood, he takes a strictly rationalist, "God is dead" stance in his search for a meaning behind man's existence.

Using himself as the subject, Jessup makes use of a sensory deprivation tank (sealing off light, sound, gravity, etc.) to hallucinate back to

the event of his birth and beyond, regressing into primitive stages of human evolution.

As Hurt, a physically-commanding young actor, becomes increasingly obsessed, his wife Emily provides the film's human balance. She is an anthropologist with a career of her own, portrayed empathetically by the redhead beauty Blair Brown, previously on view in "One-Trick Pony," shot after "Altered States."

Jessup ventures to Mexico, engaging in a mystical Indian rite. Bringing home the Indians' hallucinogenic compounds, he escalates his tank sessions until physically changing into an apelike monster, killing a security guard and escaping into the primitive environment of a nearby zoo.

Returning to normal in "Jekyll and Hyde" fashion, Jessup continues in his folly until wife Emily is also involved, with duo's love romantically conquering the physical (and perhaps psychological) effects, making for a surprisingly hopeful conclusion.

Russell has downplayed much of Chayefsky's heady philosophy by having the actors, especially Hurt, rattle off their jargon-laden speeches at breakneck speed. In fact, the thesps' tendency to declaim or shout is the film's weakest element. Countering this defect are the film's impressive visual hallucinations, akin to the "ultimate trip" light-shows in Stanley Kubrick's "2001: A Space Odyssey." Shattering use of Dolby stereo effects conspires with the images to give the viewer a vicarious LSD-type experience sans drugs. While not for all tastes, this aspect of the pic should win over the youth audience.

Film's action scenes are also potent, with Eric Jenkins' top-notch editing bringing it all in at under 100 minutes. Dick Smith's makeup is outstanding, and combines with the physical agility of Miguel Godreau as the apeman to suspend disbelief during the most outrageous horror scenes.

William Hurt's feature film debut is arresting, especially during the grueling climactic sequence. Hopefully, he will be given a chance to relax in future roles. Blair Brown is warm and appealing, while also up to the physical demands of nudity and mayhem typical of Russell's approach. Charles Haid's gruff, southern-fried medico creates solid comic relief between action crescendos.

A newcomer to films, classical composer John Corigliano has penned an atonal score which more than holds its own amidst a barrage of sound effects. Effects men and the whole technical crew

deserve kudos, including cameraman Jordan Cronenweth for his lighting and tracking. Their combined efforts should "zap" audiences with a theatrical film experience they can't get at home.
—*Lor.*

Inside Moves
(COLOR)

Look at the handicapped suffers from too conventional approach. Lukewarm b.o.

Hollywood, Nov. 18.
An Associated Film Distribution release of a Goodmark Production. Produced by Mark M. Tanz, R.W. Goodwin. Directed by Richard Donner. Features entire cast. Screenplay, Valerie Curtin, Barry Levinson, based on the novel by Todd Walton; camera (Technicolor), Laszlo Kovacs; editor, Frank Morriss; music, John Barry; Production design, Charles Rosen; set design, Boyd Willat; set decoration, Dick Goddard; costume design, Ron Talsky; sound, Willie D. Burton; assistant director-second unit director, Michael F. Grillo. Reviewed at the Samuel Goldwyn Theatre, Beverly Hills, Nov. 18, 1980. (MPAA Rating PG.) Running time: 113 MINS.

Roary	John Savage
Jerry	David Morse
Louise	Diana Scarwid
Ann	Amy Wright
Lucius Porter	Tony Burton
Blue Lewis	Bill Henderson
Burt	Steve Kahan
Max	Jack O'Leary
Stinky	Bert Remsen
Wings	Harold Russell
Herrada	Pepe Serna
Alvin Martin	Harold Sylvester
Benny	Arnold Williams

Inoffensive and essentially compassionate, "Inside Moves" is also a highly conventional and predictable look at handicapped citizens trying to make it in everyday life. Pic telegraphs its message about the indominability of the human spirit practically from the beginning, and any rough edges are inevitably softened by fadeout. Unless it somehow grabs some top reviews, small scale drama will face a troublesome b.o. future.

Flip flopping from "Superman" to a set of physically impaired characters, director Richard Donner focuses on the intermittently tense relationship between insecure, failed suicide John Savage and volatile David Morse, who's only a knee operation away from a dreamed-about basketball career.

Basic plot movement has Savage, permanently hobbled in the legs after jumping off a building, gradually regaining confidence by running a bar patronized mainly by other cripples, only to suffer emotional setbacks in frustrated romance with waitress Diana Scarwid. At the same time, Morse alienates his old friends when his career skyrockets after surgery but all is harmoniously resolved by fadeout.

Well intentioned pretext for the entire enterprise is that there's no reason the handicapped can't live relatively normal lives, secondarily arguing that the emotionally crippled may suffer more in the long run than those with physical impediments. Unfortunately, the situation is considerably more complex than that, and Valerie Curtin and Barry Levinson's screenplay eschews any intimations or tragedy better to posit a naively optimistic, feel good attitude. Pic even avoids any socio-economic comment on the financial and employment problems of the handicapped, which surely should have been a basic consideration if subject was to be dealt with at all honestly.

Pic does offer up some scenes of dramatic potency, notably these detailing Savage and Scarwid's reluctance to become sexually involved despite mutual desire, and somewhat standard confrontations with a black pimp who steals Morse's girlfriend, effectiveness of which are largely due to Tony Burton's super-cool incarnation of unadulterated evil. But as befits this rose-colored look at worldly problems, even he gets his comeuppance at the hands of life's ostensible losers.

Performances can't be faulted, with Savage seeming truly disturbed at the start, only to slowly come to terms with himself and those around him. In his feature debut, Morse puts across the called-for ambition and later shallowness, Scarwid hits the right notes as a "normal" young woman forced to confront her own limitations via her relationships with the outwardly afflicted, and Amy Wright impresses once again as Morse's junkie-prostie roommate.

In basically for comic relief are Bill Henderson, Bert Remsen and Harold Russell (last seen in his double Oscar-winning role as the paraplegic war vet in "The Best Years Of Our Lives") as three card playing regulars at Max's Bar, which has been nicely created by production designer Charles Rosen. All other contributions, from Laszlo Kovacs' lensing to John Barry's music, are modest, while Frank Morriss' editing, like Donner's direction, veers a bit toward the overactive. —*Cart.*

The Jazz Singer
(COLOR)

Third rendition of old chestnut has professional sheen but doesn't convince. Questionable b.o.

Hollywood, Dec. 1.
An Associated Film Distributors release of a Jerry Leider production. Produced by Jerry Leider. Directed by Richard Fleischer. Stars Neil Diamond, Laurence Olivier. Screenplay, Herbert Baker; adaptation, Stephen H. Foreman, based on the play by Samson Raphaelson; camera (Deluxe color), Isidore Mankofsky; supervising film editor, Frank J. Urioste; editor, Maury Winetrobe; original song score, Neil Diamond; incidental music, Leonard Rosenman; production design, Harry Horner; art direction, Spencer Deverill; set design, Christopher Horner, Mark Poll; set decoration, Ruby Levitt, Robert de Vestel; costume design, Albert Wolsky; sound (Dolby), T.G. Overton; assistant directors, James Turley, Robert M. Webb; associate producer, Joel Morwood. Reviewed at the Samuel Goldwyn Theatre, Beverly Hills, Dec. 1, 1980. (MPAA Rating: PG). Running time: 115 MINS.

Jess Robin	Neil Diamond
Cantor Rabinovitch	Laurence Olivier
Molly Bell	Lucie Arnaz
Rivka Rabinovitch	Catlin Adams
Bubba	Franklyn Ajaye
Keith Lennox	Paul Nicholas
Eddie Gibbs	Sully Boyar
Leo	Mike Kellin
Paul Rossini	James Booth
Teddy	Luther Waters
Mel	Oren Waters
Timmy	Rod Gist

A vanity production from the word go, this third screen version of "The Jazz Singer" asks the same question as the 1927 Al Jolson history maker and the 1952 Danny Thomas update — can a nice cantor's son break with family and tradition to make it as a popular entertainer? No one's going to get sweaty palms waiting for the answer, as contempo dramatization of Samson Raphaelson's venerable chestnut lacks urgency and plausible incidental detail.

Curiously, femme-slanted music biz tales, such as "A Star Is Born," "The Rose" and "Coal Miner's Daughter," have performed well commercially, while male starrers have generally belly-flopped of late. Neil Diamond enjoys a wide and seemingly loyal following, and there's no doubt that the soundtrack album will be around a long time. It remains to be seen, however, if his fans crave seeing the disk's visual rendering.

Screenplay, credited to Herbert Baker, with adaptation by Stephen H. Foreman, but reportedly having passed through many other hands, follows general line of earlier incarnations. However, elimination of the mother character in favor of a traditional wife k.o.'s any attempt at a reprise of "Mammy," even if Diamond does amusingly appear in blackface early on.

Story jerks along from one crisis to another with little dramatic build-up, as any warm or humanizing conversation is eschewed in favor of constant repetition of Diamond's advancing dilemmas, first of which comes when, against his orthodox father's wishes, he hies to California, where some black buddies have arranged for his music to be recorded. .

Not pleased with his tune's punk-

ish rendition, Diamond leaves it to promoter Lucie Arnaz to make him a star, which she more or less accomplishes in an astounding two weeks. From then on he can't help himself, allowing his marriage and relationship with his father to disintegrate while reaping the rewards of fame and fortune and having a baby with Arnaz.

Eventually, however, his shiksa g.f. pushes him into going home again to sustain tradition by singing "Kol Nidre" at a Yom Kippur service. Soon thereafter, even his father becomes a fan, clapping along with the crowd at a big Pantages concert.

Central issue of the original story — that of Jews becoming successfully assimilated into fabric of American society — seems significantly less problematic today, lending drama an anachronistic quality, and matters aren't helped much by fact that Diamond comes off as rather selfish and uncaring, which certainly couldn't have been said for Jolson. Given the ease with which he casts off from his family, it's hard to feel that his roots run very deep despite having lived with his father for 30-plus years.

Pic also glosses over the intricacies of the music biz, making ascendency to stardom look as easy as pie. At the same time, most amusing performance in the film comes from Sully Boyar, as a middle-aged recording honcho who can't stand loud music but still knows a good thing when he sees one.

In other roles, Catlin Adams effectively defends the conservative view of what her marriage to Diamond is supposed to be, while Arnaz is sprightly as his West Coast playmate and collaborator. Using his Old World Jewish accent for the fourth time in recent years, Lord Laurence Olivier, as the elderly cantor, seems to take the job of acting a lot more seriously than anyone else around him, which places his scenes on a completely different level of intensity.

Richard Fleischer took over the reins from Sidney J. Furie mid-way through shooting, and the best that can be said for the direction is that there's no disruption of the prosaic, by-the-numbers style. Technically, however, effort has an impressive pro sheen, from Isidore Mankofsky's filtered photography to Harry Horner's production design and, notably, to the impeccable sound recording of the musical numbers. On the debit side is a lot of overcutting within simple dialog scenes, making for occasional mis-matching and choppiness.

Of Diamond's numbers, "Love On The Rocks" penned with Gilbert Becaud, is already in the chart top ten, and "America," which bookends the pic, also gets a rousing rendition.

The unanswered $64,000 question is, what is jazz to Neil Diamond and Neil Diamond to jazz? Old title has nothing to do with music on display here and would seem meaningless to modern audiences. —Cart.

The Dogs Of War
(BRITISH-COLOR)

Intelligent actioner about mercenaries looks a strong bet — overseas.

Hollywood, Dec. 9.

United Artists release of a Norman Jewison/Patrick Palmer production. Directed by John Irvin. Features entire cast. Screenplay, Gary DeVore, George Malko, based on a novel by Frederick Forsyth; camera (Panavision-Technicolor), Jack Cardiff; production design, Peter Mullins; film editor, Antony Gibbs; first asst. directors, Candace Suerstedt-Rehmet, Michelle Marx; music, Geoffrey Burgon; costumes, Emma Porteous; unit publicist, Mike Russell; art director, John Siddall, Bert Davey; special effects, Larry Cavanaugh, Rudi Liszczak, Steve Lombardi, Mike Collins. Reviewed at the Cinedome Theatre, Orange, Calif., Dec. 6, 1980. (MPAA Rating-R) Running time: 122 MINS.

Shannon	Christopher Walken
Drew	Tom Berenger
North	Colin Blakely
Endean	Hugh Millais
Derek	Paul Freeman
Michel	Jean-Francois Stevenin
Jessie	JoBeth Williams
Capt. Lockhart	Robert Urquhart
Dr. Okoye	Winston Ntshona
The Major	Pedro Armendariz
Richard	Harlan Cary Poe
Terry	Ed O'Neill
Evelyn	Isabel Grandin
Warner	Ernest Graves
The Black boy	Kelvin Thomas
Dr. Oaks	Shane Rimmer
Priest	Father Joseph Konrad
Shop manager	Bruce McLane
Col. Bobi	George W. Harris
Endean's man	David Schofield
Hackett	Terence Rigby
Bank vice president	Tony Mathews

"The Dogs Of War" is an intelligent and occasionally forceful treatment of a provocative but little-examined theme, that of mercenary warrior involvement in the overthrow of a corrupt black African dictatorship. Since these apolitical guns for hire are almost by definition expendable characters, audiences are likely to feel somewhat removed from the unsavory proceedings, but subject is sufficiently unusual to attract some interest. Moderate b.o. is probably in store domestically, although this is the kind of pic that could clean up in many overseas territories.

Set to open in London Dec. 19, film was caught at an advertised preview, at which it was indicated that some changes could be made in advance of U.S. openings in February. Some radical cuttings seem

already to have been done, however, as second-billed Tom Berenger hasn't much important screen time and Helen Shaver, as his wife, was evidently instrumental in a sub-plot which has now disappeared.

Deviating in several substantial ways from Frederick Forsyth's novel, script by Gary Devore and George Malko focuses almost exclusively on Christopher Walken, an "irresponsible" American who seems to have led a normal life at times but is drawn to the mercenary's loner, adventurous life.

After a smash action opening wherein a bunch of fighters make it out of a war-torn country on the proverbial last plane out, pic settles down to detail intricacies of planning insurrection against a tiny west African country. Paid by big businessman Hugh Millais, who sees big profits to be made there given the right puppet regime, Walken visits the pathetic nation posing as a nature photographer, gradually arousing official suspicion and finally being imprisoned, tortured and deported.

Temporarily fed up with his way of life, Walken unsuccessfully attempts a reconciliation with his wife back in the States. but is then lured back by Millais to lead a nocturnal invasion of the meagerly-defended nation.

Story's substantial center section is therefore relatively low-keyed, reminding of nothing so much as any number of "secret agent" telepisodes wherein Patrick McGoohan felt his way through the treacherous minefields of unstable banana republics, without, in this case, a strongly developed rooting interest. Amoral motives among all the characters, as well as the refusal to delve into Walken's psychology, makes for general sense of detachment, even if most of the maneuvers on view are still interesting in themselves.

Because Walken's intelligence and style make the character seem something of an aberration in his field, and because other roles are given such little prominence, film fails to really get at the heart of the whys and hows of mercenary life, and also rejects the idea of generating any sense of camaraderie among the men. Pic displays their extreme form of machismo without indulging it, while emphasizing their political, moral and emotional isolation.

Touchy subject of contempo African dictatorships has rarely been confronted by commercial features, and details of life in such a country, from the bribery and censorship to the military strongarming and oppressive economic conditions, have been effectively sketched here. Leader, briefly seen

but frequently discussed, comes off as a cross between two recently-ousted tyrants, Idi Amin of Uganda and Bokassa of the Central African Empire, and pic displays the political realities without editorializing.

Expected pay-off comes in climactic invasion of the presidential military compound, and spectacular fireworks should be satisfying to the action crowd. Beyond that lies a neat switcheroo ending which, if possible, given the various unpalatable alternatives, manages to resolve matters on a somewhat upbeat note.

While commanding and at times nicely unpredictable, Walken is nonetheless rather limited by the indecisive tack given his character in the writing. Millais makes for an imposing heavy, while none of the other characters is given more than a moment or two to emerge from the background, save for Colin Blakely as an alcoholic British journalist who hounds Walken.

John Irvin, just off his splendid job on the "Tinker, Tailor, Soldier, Spy" miniseries, handles his feature debut with strong assurance and, when called upon, a secure sense of logistics.

Behind-the-scenes contributions, notably Jack Cardiff's expectedly outstanding lensing, Geoffrey Burgon's excellent score and various special effects and stunt work, are all top-notch. —Cart.

Der Gelbe Stern
(The Yellow Star)
(WEST GERMAN-DOCU-B&W)

Berlin, Nov. 30.

A Chronos-Film production. Berlin; world distribution, Chronos-Film, Berlin. Bengt von zur Muehlen. Written and directed by Dieter Hildebrandt. Research consultant, Gerhard Schoenberner; assistant director, Manfred Helling; compilation editor, Helga Kruska; camera sequences, Nicolas Joray; narrators, Friedhelm Ptok, Heidemarie Theobald, Heinz Rabe. Reviewed at Gloria Palast, Berlin, Nov. 30, '80. Running time: 90 MINS.

Docu on Nazi crimes during the 1930s and 1940s, Dieter Hildebrandt's "The Yellow Star" is exceptional in that it follows the theme of the Jewish Question from beginning to end, sparing no criticism of the nation's collective guilt.

It also includes footage never seen to date on the treatment of Jews under the Third Reich that was recently discovered in film archives. And the unusual factor about the docu's appearance at this time is worth noting: without West Germany's awakening to the plight of German Jews via the Yank-made tv series, "Holocaust," there probably would not have been "The

Yellow Star" aimed at the home market.

As it was, the film was hard to get made in the first place. Dieter Hildebrandt, a former Dramaturg at the Schiller Theater and a talented director-writer, worked for months to mount footage found in the Chronos-Film archive in Berlin and at more than a dozen other national archives in East and West Europe. Taking an historian's approach, he used the best source on the subject: Gerhard Schoenberner's standard book, "The Yellow Star," an oft-translated volume of compiled documentation on Hitler's planned extermination of the Jews. The name of Schoenberner, who recently served as director of the Goethe Institute in Israel and is presently with the International Forum of Young Cinema at the Berlin Fest, thus guarantees that all the facts in this documentary are accurate, down to important analyses and assumptions on social responsibilities (even when a complacent nation is threatened by the listing of these facts).

Anyone who has seen "Night and Fog" or "Mein Kampf" or "Holocaust" has images burnt into memory about one of the greatest sins in history committed against the human race. It is to Hildebrandt's credit that he tells the story with unassuming objectivity: sometimes a word spoken by the commentator says everything important; at other times it's simply a shocking, moving, questioning, accusing photo, or a strip of film footage, which lays the irritating truth at the viewer's own doorstep.

One is grateful to see a German documentary cover the field so expertly and at the proper distance, with commitment to the historical events as they happened. (By an odd coincidence, a tv documentary titled "History in Opposition" on WDR's Third Channel was aired on the same day as "The Yellow Star:" the former dealt with the Nazi treatment of Soviet prisoners of war (2,000,000 dead), while the latter detailed the fate of the 500,000 German Jews and several million more who died in the gas chambers at Auschwitz.) "The Yellow Star" is divided into 19 sequences: The Shock, The Escaping Point, The Ambush, The Law, The Trespassing, The Threat, The Flight, The Hate, The War, The Ghetto, The Panic, The Villa, The Stars, The Wagons, The Present, The Murderer, The Transport, The Camp, and The Victims.

The most moving sequence of all is still the infamous story of the Warsaw Ghetto. That the camera could not turn away in shame before the spectacle of 500,000 Jews slowly and systematically being starved to death says much about the callous nature of recording wars and destruction for posterity. Hopefully, this film will have an impact on audiences in, and outside, Germany.

The amazing, disturbing aspects of the film don't occur on the screen, however. Producer Bengt von zur Muehlen states openly in the film's program notes that the subsidy grants came from Bavaria and the Federal Film Board — not, according to an interview, from the Berlin Film Fund or the Ministry of the Interior — "because of lack of commercial potential!"

Documentaries like "The Yellow Star," and others, such as Ebbo Demant's "Auschwitz Street," and Klaus G. Volkerborn, Karl Siebig, and Johann Feindt's "Irreconcilable Memories," all made in West Germany in the two years since "Holocaust" appeared on tv screens here, should be booked, singly or collectively, into festivals, archives, and campus programs. They are musts for the student of contemporary history. —*Holl.*

Windwalker
(COLOR)

Superior wilderness pic about Indians.

Hollywood, Dec. 5.

Pacific International Enterprises release of a Windwalker Prods. film. Produced by Arthur R. Dubs, Thomas E. Ballard. Stars Trevor Howard. Directed by Kieth Merrill. Screenplay, Ray Goldrup, from the novel by Blaine M. Yorgason; camera (CFI Color), Reed Smoot; music, Merrill Jensen; production designer, Thomas Pratt; editors, Stephen J. Johnson, Janice Hampton, Peter L. McCrea. Reviewed at CFI screening room, Hollywood, Dec. 3, '80. (MPAA Rating: PG.) Running time: **108 MINS.**
Windwalker . . . . Trevor Howard
Smiling Wolf/Twin Brother/
Narrator . . . . Nick Ramus
Windwalker (Young Man) . James Remar
Tashina . . . . Serene Hedin
Dancing Moon . . Dusty Iron Wing McCrea
Little Feather . . . . Silvana Gallardo
Crow Scout . . . . Billy Drago
Crow Eyes . . . . Rudy Diaz
Crow Hair . . . . Harold Goss-Coyote
Wounded Crow . . . . Roy J. Cohoe
Horse That Follows . . . . Jason Stevens
Happy Wind . . . . Roberta Deherrera
Windwalker (Child) Wamni-OmniSka-
                              Romideau
(Cheyenne and Crow Indian languages — English subtitles and narration).

"Windwalker" is a dramatic feature for the wilderness market which transcends that genre with its genuine visual beauty and its unusually authentic treatment of American Indian culture. Flawed in that regard only by casting Trevor Howard in the title role of a dying Indian patriarch, the subtitled film was made in the Cheyenne and Crow languages by director Kieth Merrill, a sensitive filmmaker who won an Oscar for his feature docu, "The Great American Cowboy." This Pacific International Enterprises release is a sleeper which could play art houses as well as the wilderness market.

The use of Indian languages on the soundtrack throughout (with only an occasional use of English by a narrator for voice-overs in flashbacks) makes "Windwalker" rare if not unique for a western. Coupled with the absence of non-Indian characters in the film, which takes place in the 18th century, this gives the Indians on screen a dignity they have been denied previously, even in the most sympathetic of westerns.

While the casting of Howard, a fine actor, may be partially justifiable for commercial reasons, this single lapse in authenticity is a painful one, since the filmmakers went so far in the right direction. Try as he might, Howard is never totally convincing as a Cheyenne, and one wishes the film had a genuine Indian actor such as Chief Dan George or Will Sampson in the role.

In a day when producers would not think of casting white people in black roles, it's still possible, evidently, to get away with a white man wearing dark makeup playing an Indian. The uneasy suspicion lingers that producers Arthur R. Dubs and Thomas E. Ballard might have felt white audiences needed at least one member of their race on screen for them to identify with the story.

Too bad, for the story taken from a novel by Blaine M. Yorgason is an absorbing one, and Ray Goldrup's screenplay is effective in its spareness and simplicity. Title character on his deathbed tells his grandchildren about the death of his young wife (Serene Hedin) and the abduction of one of his twin sons (both played by Nick Ramus) by the Cheyennes' traditional antagonists, the Crows. After the old man dies, he mysteriously comes back to life to prevent the destruction of what remains of the family by the missing son, whom he recognizes before returning to the land of the dead and being reunited with his wife.

Filmed in Utah, mostly in snowy mountain country, film has first-rate lensing by Reed Smoot which captures the glories of landscape and weather without indulging in the sentimental visual cliches typical of this genre. Merrill's visual style at its best evokes the westerns of John Ford and Anthony Mann, with a stark clarity which makes the most of a limited budget.

Howard brings a rugged grandeur and, at times, a sly humor to his part, and the rest of the cast is well chosen and effective right down to the smallest parts. Ramus is fine in his double role but if some English narration by the Howard character was necessary, it's too bad Ramus' voice was used and not Howard's familiar voice. James Remar and Serene Hedin are attractive and emotionally compelling as the ill-fated young couple.

Excellent musical score by Merrill Jensen was performed by the London Philharmonic evidently due to the Hollywood musicians' strike. Rest of tech credits are good, too, in this lovely film. —*Mac.*

La Provinciale
(The Provincial)
(FRENCH-SWISS-COLOR)

Zurich, Nov. 29.

Citel Films SA Geneva release of a Phenix Productions-Gaumont-Fr 3-S.S.R. production. Directed by Claude Goretta. Stars Nathalie Baye, Angela Winkler. Produced by Yves Peyrot, Raymond Pousaz. Screenplay, Goretta, Jacques Kirsner, Rosine Rochette; adaptation and dialog, Goretta, Kirsner. Camera (color), Philippe Rousselot, Dominique Bringuier; music, Arie Dzierlatka; editors, Joele Van Effenterre, Xavier Castano; art direction, Jacques Bufnoir; sound, Pierre Gamet, Bernard Chaumeil. Reviewed at the Studio Nord-Sued, Zurich, Nov. 29, '80. Running time: **107 MINS.**
Cast: Bruno Ganz, Patrick Chesnais, Dominique Paturel, Pierre Vernier.

"La Provinciale" (The Provincial), Swiss director Claude Goretta's first feature film since his internationally successful "The Lacemaker," is a fine example of modern filmmaking of a type that has become comparatively rare: artful, but not "arty," simple, but not simplistic, moving, but not maudlin. Moreover, it may mean for its star, Nathalie Baye, what Goretta's countryman Alain Tanner's "The Salamander" meant for Bulle Ogier and, especially, "The Lacemaker" for Isabelle Huppert: a career.

The title character is a 31-year-old building designer leaving her native Lorraine for Paris to change her sheltered, but dreary life. She has trouble finding a job as she refuses to give in to leering propositions by prospective employers. A casual meeting with a Swiss pharmaceutical marketing expert leads to a passionate, but short, affair as he leaves for Japan to further his career.

She strikes up a friendship with a jobless actress tired of struggling to make ends meet and live in debt, who ends up as a high-class callgirl. Refusing to make compromises against her outlook on life and disgusted with the isolation and hypocrisy of big city life, she returns to her provincial town.

Goretta wraps up his criticism of modern society in a melancholy tale about a bunch of people torn between hope and disillusionment. Paris and Parisians have rarely been so bleak and disenchanted in a film, except perhaps in some of Marcel Carne's classic prewar films of poetic realism There's hardly any poetry left in Goretta's 1980 Paris.

In sharp and certainly purposeful contrast, initial scenes when the girl leaves her hometown, radiate human warmth. Her relationship with the Swiss looks like love at first, but is later revealed as primarily sexual Her actress-friend is a superficial egotist The girl herself is not beyond reproach either during an evening spent with a neurotic exec, she fails to see that he's desperately in need of human help and he commits suicide after she has left him

These considerations notwithstanding, "La Provinciale" is an important film of quiet beauty, sensitively directed and with an excellent cast. Baye's expressive face and radiant smile linger in memory long after the film has ended. Bruno Ganz as her lover and German actress Angela Winkler, who first came to prominence with "The Lost Honor of Katharina Blum," as the actress-friend both deliver finely etched characterizations. The subdued color photography by Philippe Rousselot is firstrate, as is Joele Van Effenterre's and Xavier Castano's editing. —*Mezo.*

Any Which Way You Can
(COLOR)

Sequel to Eastwood's biggest hit delivers same goods, but with gentler tone. Big initial b.o. assured.

Hollywood, Dec. 8.

A Warner Brothers release. Produced by Fritz Manes. Executive producer, Robert Daley. Directed by Buddy Van Horn. Stars Clint Eastwood. Screenplay, Stanford Sherman, based on characters created by Jeremy Joe Kronsberg; camera (DeLuxe color), David Worth; editors, Ferris Webster, Ron Spang; music supervision, Snuff Garrett; production design, William J. Creber; set decoration, Ernie Bishop; costume supervision, Glenn Wright; sound, Bert Hallberg; assistant director, Tom Joyner. Reviewed at the Chinese Theatre, Hollywood, Dec. 8, 1980. (MPAA Rating: PG.). Running time: 116 MINS.

Philo Beddoe . . . . Clint Eastwood
Lynne Halsey-Taylor . . . . . Sondra Locke
Orville . . . . Geoffrey Lewis
Jack Wilson . . . . William Smith
James Beekman . . . . Harry Guardino
Ma . . . . Ruth Gordon
Patrick Scarfe . . . . Michael Cavanaugh
Fat Zack . . . . Barry Corbin
Moody . . . . Roy Jenson
Dallas . . . . Bill McKinney
Elmo . . . . William O'Connell
Cholla . . . . John Quade
Tony Paoli Sr. . . . . Al Ruscio
Frank . . . . Dan Vadis
Hattie . . . . Camila Ashlend

"Any Which Way You Can" is a benign continuation of "Every Which Way But Loose." At over $50,000,000 in film rentals, latter pic stands as star Clint Eastwood's biggest hit, and since Warners is opening follow-up in a record 1,560 theatres Dec. 17, some big numbers are assured, at least at the start. Each subsequent film in Eastwood's two previous series, the "Dollars" westerns and the Dirty Harry actioners, grossed more than the one before, and only time will tell if the pattern repeats itself with these monkeyshines.

Eastwood, Sondra Locke, Geoffrey Lewis, Ruth Gordon and numerous supporting players all repeat their characterizations from the first outing to similar effect. Main difference is that, where everyone in the original was an undiluted redneck macho or machoette, individuals this time seem almost forgiving, loving and considerate, which substantially moderates the reckless violent tone of "Loose," bringing it closer to the genial nice-guy mood of star's last pic, "Bronco Billy." Even the villainous Nazi bikers finish by telling their nemesis, "You take care now."

After an initial bare-knuckled boxing bout, Eastwood's Philo Beddoe swears off his lucrative sideline career, better to settle down with Ma Ruth Gordon, a significantly tamed Sondra Locke and orangutan chum Clyde. However, the mob makes him an offer he can't refuse to battle he-man William Smith, and the two, despite having become good pals, end up in an epic brawl straight out of "The Quiet Man" which sprawls through all the bars, streets and parks of Jackson Hole, Wyo.

Filled with plenty of monkey business, first half is pretty funny as these things go, but film runs out of steam after mid-way highlight, which has Clyde's motel room seduction of an abducted female ape intercut with Eastwood bedding Locke, an elderly mid-western couple getting it on for the first time in years and the motel manager chasing Gordon, who in one trick shot he literally sees as a combination of Gordon's face and Bo Derek's body. Although overlength didn't stop "Loose," same flaw here is even more irritating due to protracted finale and lack of any continuing tension in Eastwood-Locke relationship. In this one, she's just along for the ride.

Original ape from "Loose" was not available to Eastwood here, but substitute performs heroically, swigging beer like a pro, giving the raspberry and the finger and knocking out cops and hoods on cue. Clearly, this sort of thing exists on a plane either beyond or beneath criticism, and as it seems to be the main reason for the enduring popularity of "Loose," there's no reason to believe that it won't prove equally satisfying to audiences who come back for more.

Technically, and stunt-wise, sequel's on a par with the original, and has Fats Domino and Glen Campbell in for Palomino Club numbers. One of the more unusual end-title details seen recently warns to the effect that viewers should not imitate any of the stunts seen in pic. In the case of some of the ape's activities, both in and out of the bedroom, there shouldn't be much danger of that. —Cart.

Delitto A Porta Romana
(Crime At Porta Romana)
(ITALIAN-COLOR)

Rome, Nov. 28.

A Titanus release. Produced by Giovanni Di Clemente for Cleminternazionale Productions. Stars Tomas Milian. Directed by Bruno Corbucci. Screenplay, Mario Amendola, Bruno Corbucci; camera (Technicolor), Giovanni Ciarlo; art director, Claudio Cinini; editor, Daniele Alabiso; music, Franco Miccolizzi. Reviewed at Cola Di Rienzo Cinema, Rome, Nov. 25, 1980. Running time: 94 MINS.

Inspector Giraldi . . . . Tomas Milian
His wife . . . . Olimpia Di Nardo
Grandma . . . . Nerina Montagnani
Thief . . . . Bombolo

Latest effort by action helmer Bruno Corbucci has again succeeded in cashing in on the immense popularity of Tomas Milian as an anti-cop done for laughs, following the long collaboration of actor and director in the "Anti-Squad" series of recent years. Here the method is to alternate lightning-edited chase scenes and sports matches with a lot of colorful language jokes in a loose detective story frame. Chases work fine; street jargon seems destined to titillate local ears only. A strong national showing heralds sequels

Milian runs away with pic in spite of cast's general bravura. Out of a few stringy ringlets, an aged jogging suit and a pair of sneakers he creates a nonchalant and uncouth policeman who must have Serpico writhing in his Swiss hideout.

The hippy cop is a police inspector here, called to Milan to investigate a murder case for no reason other than that he "grew up" in the same ghetto as the suspect — who was hiding under the bed when the victim was strangled. The trail leads through a soccer game, an ice hockey match, a roller skating rink and a strip joint, for local color which Corbucci knows how to exploit visually. The chase between two fully-outfitted hockey players is the more excellent for being brief, while the sequence of Milian chasing a car through the city on roller skates deserves to be anthologized.

Weakness is suspense promised in the title. Writers are loose with logic and coherency. Instead, they concentrate on street (or gutter) dialog including puns on all the raw language in modern Italian. This strategy cheapens pic and detours scenes for laughs.

Supporting thesps who play Milian's pregnant wife and deaf mother-in-law are a help. So is the petty thief (limned by character actor Bombolo), weepily fighting off the amorous advances of his cellmate.

Pic remains lively, fast and unpretentious till the end (no surprise: childbirth in the camper during the climactic chase). Best tech credits go to editor Daniele Alabiso for pacing, which keeps the plodding solution to the murder from turning sour. —Yung.

The Mirror Crack'd
(BRITISH-COLOR)

Amiable Agatha Christie comedy-mystery with a cast of 1950s stars.

Hollywood, Dec. 11.

AFD release of an EMI Films presentation. Produced by John Brabourne, Richard Goodwin. Stars Angela Lansbury, Geraldine Chaplin, Tony Curtis, Edward Fox, Rock Hudson, Kim Novak, Elizabeth Taylor. Directed by Guy Hamilton. Screenplay, Jonathan Hales, Barry Sandler, from the novel, "The Mirror Crack'd From Side To Side," by Agatha Christie; camera (Technicolor), Christopher Challis; music, John Cameron; editor, Richard Marden; production designer, Michael Stringer; art direction, John Roberts; sound, Bill Rowe, John Richards, John Mitchell; assistant director, Derek Cracknell. Reviewed at Directors Guild of America Theatre, Hollywood, Dec. 10, 1980. (MPAA Rating: PG). Running time: 105 MINS.

Miss Marple . . . . Angela Lansbury
Ella Zielinsky . . . . Geraldine Chaplin
Marty N. Fenn . . . . Tony Curtis
Inspector Craddock . . . . Edward Fox
Jason Rudd . . . . Rock Hudson
Lola Brewster . . . . Kim Novak
Marina Rudd . . . . Elizabeth Taylor
Margot Bence . . . . Marella Oppenheim
Cherry . . . . Wendy Morgan
Mrs. Bantry . . . . Margaret Courtenay
Bates, The Butler . . . . Charles Gray
Heather Babcock . . . . . . Maureen Bennett
Miss Giles . . . . Carolyn Pickles
The Major . . . . Eric Dodson
Vicar . . . . Charles Lloyd-Pack
Cast of Film Within
Film . . . . Anthony Steel, Dinah Sheridan, Oriana Grieve, Kenneth Fortescue, Hildegarde Neil, Allan Cuthbertson, George Silver, John Bennett, Nigel Stock

A worthy if more leisurely successor to "Murder On The Orient Express" and "Death On The Nile," EMI's third Agatha Christie mystery, "The Mirror Crack'd," is a nostalgic throwback to the genteel British murder mystery pix of the 1950s. Film is, in fact, set in the '50s, with a cast of stars from that period playing roles which frequently veer from melodrama into camp. But somehow the curious concoction works, though the film's appeal may be primarily to older audiences. AFD releases the John Brabourne-Richard Goodwin production in the U.S. and Canada.

Though Angela Lansbury is top-billed in the role of Christie's famed sleuth Jane Marple (a role the late Margaret Rutherford played in four earlier pix), the central part really is Elizabeth Taylor's. Taylor comes away with her most genuinely affecting dramatic performance in years as a film star attempting a comeback following an extended nervous breakdown.

The script by Jonathan Hales and Barry Sandler follows Christie's 1962 source novel, "The Mirror Crack'd From Side To Side," with fidelity, but whether by coincidence or design the tragedy which caused the actress' breakdown is exactly identical to a real-life one which struck Gene Tierney. Tierney revealed in her recent autobiog the particulars of the tragedy (to discuss it here would be to give away the mystery plot), and the use of a World War II flashback in "The Mirror Crack'd" makes the events depicted even more directly identical to Tierney's story than the novel was.

Suffice it to say that the Taylor character and those close to her have been haunted by the memory of an apparently accidental catastrophe which, during the course of the film, proves to have been caused by one of the minor characters they meet in the small English village where they are locationing with a film company.

As two murders result and the mystery unfolds under the prodding of Lansbury and her Scotland Yard inspector nephew Edward Fox, the film gradually takes on a darker mood. Taylor has some compelling emotional scenes which never become overdone. The earlier parts of the film are much lighter in tone, broadly spoofing the pomposities and professional rivalries among the film company and their uneasy interaction with the sheltered local residents.

Taylor has an uproarious good time (and so will the audience) as she trades bitchy insults with Kim Novak, wife of producer Tony Curtis, who insists on grossly miscasting Novak as Queen Elizabeth I in the film they're making of "Mary, Queen Of Scots." Proving themselves very good sports, Taylor and Novak pelt each other with hilarious zingers about their physical appearances and screen images.

Adroit supporting performances are given by Curtis, Rock Hudson as Taylor's husband and director, and Geraldine Chaplin as Hudson's secretary and probable lover. While the satirizing of the film company is broad, it also hits most of its targets. And the recalling of a bygone time in the British film industry is pleasantly nostalgic.

Director Guy Hamilton, not usually given a chance to direct much besides actioners recently, handles the proceedings with an indulgent but able hand. Christopher Challis' glossy lighting is a suitable recapturing of the mood of the period, as is the lush score by John Cameron. A particularly poignant and amusing touch is having Taylor make her grand entrance to the tune of a local brass band playing "There's No Business Like Show Business."

The American visitors have the gaudiest parts, but Lansbury and Fox are highly effective in their quieter ways, and among many solid British performers playing villagers, Wendy Morgan is a standout as Lansbury's maid and Maureen Bennett is just right as an overzealous fan of Taylor's who becomes embroiled in the tragic events.

Lansbury plays Miss Marple without the buffoonery so delightfully added to the character by Rutherford, instead going about her business with crisp, witty efficiency. Fox is a delight as a film buff who uses his knowledge of the company's past careers to help crack the case.

Buffs in the audience will also enjoy some nostalgic casting reunions in the film. Taylor and Hudson have their first teaming since playing husband and wife in "Giant," and Taylor and Lansbury were sisters in "National Velvet." Such reverberations are perfectly suited to the deja vu themes of the film. —Mac.

Nine To Five
(COLOR)

Will get paid handsomely for overtime at the b.o.

Hollywood, Dec. 4.
Twentieth Century-Fox release of an IPC Films production. Produced by Bruce Gilbert. Directed by Colin Higgins. Stars Jane Fonda, Lily Tomlin, Dolly Parton. Screenplay, Higgins and Patricia Resnick, based on Resnick's story; camera (Deluxe). Reynaldo Villalobos; editor, Pembroke J. Herring; production design, Dean Mitzner; music, Charles Fox; sound, Nicholas Eliopoulos; costumes, Ann Roth; art direction. Jack Gammon Taylor, Jr.; set decoration, Anne McCulley; special effects, Chuck Gaspar, Matt Sweeney; animation. Mishkin, Hellmuch, Virgien & Friends; assistant director, Gary Daigler. Reviewed at the Darryl F. Zanuck Theatre, L.A. Dec. 4, 1980. (MPAA Rating: PG.) Running time: **110 MINS.**

Judy Bernly	Jane Fonda
Violet Newstead	Lily Tomlin
Doralee Rhodes	Dolly Parton
Franklin Hart, Jr.	Dabney Coleman
Tinsworthy	Sterling Hayden
Roz	Elizabeth Wilson
Hinkle	Henry Jones
Dick	Lawrence Pressman
Missy Hart	Marian Mercer
Barbara	Ren Woods
Betty	Norma Donaldson
Maria	Roxanna Bonilla-Giannini
Margaret	Peggy Pope

Anyone who has ever worked in an office will be able to identify with the antics in "Nine To Five," Twentieth Century-Fox's offbeat, amusing holiday comedy starring Jane Fonda, Lily Tomlin and Dolly Parton.

Although it can probably be argued that Patricia Resnick and director Colin Higgins' script at times borders on the inane, the bottom line is that this picture is a lot of fun. Fonda, Tomlin and Parton provide charm and distinction to their sketchy characters and Dabney Coleman gives new meaning to the word chauvinist as their villainous boss. Critics may dismiss it, but universal theme and heavy marquee value of topliners should gain the picture recognition of a wide audience.

Original story was concocted by Resnick for Fonda's IPC Films and Higgins later came in and reworked the script as director. Result concerns a group of office workers (Tomlin the all-knowing manager who trained the boss but can't get promoted, Fonda the befuddled newcomer and Parton the alluring personal secretary everyone presumes is having an affair with Coleman) who band together to seek revenge on the man who is making their professional lives miserable. It's the fantasy of almost any employee and as such immediately gives the picture a strong commercial hook.

In terms of execution, once the penchant for nitpicking is dismissed and the idea is dropped that any of this could actually occur in real life, "Nine To Five" is an effective escapist feast with lotsa funny physical schtick.

After the typically constricting conditions within the corporation are established, the three women have a pot party and fantasize what each would like to do Coleman in (Tomlin's sequence as an evil Snow White poisoning Coleman with the approval of some animated friends is a scream). Higgins then cleverly finds a way to make each fantasy almost come true and when Coleman wises up to the situation the women kidnap and tie him up in order to figure out a plan. In his absence the office improves immeasurably.

Although it looks like Coleman will ultimately outfox the women those suppressed by unfathomably awful superiors will delight in the conclusion. It could only happen in the movies, but then again, that's one of the reasons people go to films.

In the three pivotal roles, Tomlin comes off best in the most appealing role as the smart yet underappreciated glue in the office cement. She has an uncanny ability to give a knowing glance in the camera that does far more to explain a situation than a mountain of dialog and transmits a bit of intelligence into the wacky goings-on.

Parton makes a delightful screen debut in a role tailored to her already well-defined country girl personality. That innocence casts a natural screen presence that should cause filmgoers to take her to heart in much the same way as her music fans. Her rendition of title song she wrote is an added plus.

Surprisingly, Fonda, the most honored actress of the bunch and initiator of the project, emerges as the weakest. Although she fits in with the action, there is still a residual hardness to her voice and manner that don't jibe with her character.

Supporting cast, including Elizabeth Wilson as a nasty office snitch, aforementioned Coleman and Marian Mercer as his semi-dizzy wife (latter pair reunited from their tube days on "Mary Hartman, Mary Hartman"), are all fine.

Higgins has done a respectable job of keeping linear sense of what could have been an unwieldy subject while also managing to sustain a quick pace throughout. He's helped by Pembroke J. Herring's fine editing and Dean Mitzner's accurate production design. Ann Roth's costumes, however, seem a little too snappy for the surroundings.

A complaint worth noting about the entire project is the fact that there is not a man in the picture who comes off as anything close to admirable. In fact, most are really rather nasty, one level, obnoxious buffoons. But after all the time women have spent, to rid the screen of cardboard female characterizations, it's a perversely entertaining to see the tables turned just this once. —Berg.

Sunday Lovers
(FRENCH-ITALIAN-COLOR)

Paris, Nov. 27.
A S.N. Prodis release of a Viaduc Productions (Paris) — Medusa Distribuzione (Rome) coproduction. Produced by Leo Fuchs. Stars Lino Ventura, Roger Moore, Ugo Tognazzi, Gene Wilder, Lynn Redgrave. Directed by Edouard Molinaro, Bryan Forbes, Dino Risi and Gene Wilder. Screenplays, Francis Veber, Leslie Bricusse, Age & Scarpelli and Wilder. French Segment: Camera (Color), Claude Agostini, sound, J.-P. Mugel; editor, R. Isnardon. English Segment: Camera (color), C. Lecomte; sound, D. Brisseau; editor, P. Shaw. Italian Segment: Camera (color), T. Delli Colli; sound, V. Massi; editor, A. Gallitti. American Segment: Camera (color) J. Hirschfeld; sound, P. Mitchell; editor, C. Greenbury. Music for entire film, Manuel de Sica. Reviewed at the Empire Theatre, Paris, Nov. 27, 1980. Running time: **125 MINS.**

FRANCE

Francois Querole	Lino Ventura
Henry Morrison	Robert Webber
Christine	Catherine Salviat

ENGLAND

Harry	Roger Moore
Parker	Denholm Elliott
Lady Davina	Lynn Redgrave
Donna	Priscilla Barnes

ITALY

Armando	Ugo Tognazzi
Clara	Rossana Podesta
Zira	Sylva Koscina
Marisa	Beba Loncar

AMERICA

Skippy	Gene Wilder
Lauri	Kathleen Quinlan
Maggie	Dianne Crittenden

"Sunday Lovers" produced by Paris-based Yank producer Leo Fuchs is an international sketch film written, directed and performed by name talent. A common denominator for the four sketches is that they describe the weekend amorous adventures of four men, all middle-aged. Another common denominator is that they are all mediocre, although one sketch works up some real charm.

The English and Italian segments are straight-forwardly farcical. The English sketch, written by Leslie Bricusse and directed by Bryan Forbes, is a leering little comedy about the skirt-chasing chauffeur of an English lord who profits from his employer's business weekends abroad to bed whichever of his air stewardess girlfriends is in town, passing himself off as a lord to dazzle them.

On this particular weekend he has a new prospect, a bird-brained California beauty, but complications arise when, in the midst of his pleasures, a high-blooded lady friend of Moore's employer (Lynn Redgrave) drives up hot on seeking stud service from the virile chauffeur.

Had Bricusse pushed the vulgarity of the situation further, and had Forbes given the sketch the snappy direction it needs, and had the chauffeur been played by someone other than Moore, hard to accept either as chauffeur or comic actor, the segment would have been entertaining. Redgrave and Denholm Elliott, as a helpful butler, are wasted.

The Italian segment shows director Dino Risi and scripters Age and Scarpelli at their most dully insignificant. Ugo Tognazzi, in bland form, plays a married man whose spouse takes off one weekend in response to a sick mother's call. Bored, Tognazzi comes across an old address book and decides look up his luscious girlfriends of yesteryear. Needless to say, one disappointment follows upon another and the chastened hubby returns to wife and hearth.

The script and direction of the French section, by Francis Veber and Edouard Molinaro, are only slightly better. Lino Ventura plays a French industrialist who, to insure the security of an important business contract with a boorish American businessman (Robert Webber) reluctantly agrees to bring to dinner his pretty temporary secretary, whom the American is eager to bed. But Ventura, gradually drawn to the girl's wily sweetness and charm, finally tells Webber what he can do with the contract and leaves with the secretary.

The sketch is the best of the four, simply because it stars the never indifferent Ventura and casts him opposite a charming young actress from the Comedie-Francaise, Catherine Salviat. Together the two manage to create some fragile bittersweet moments.

The American segment presents us Gene Wilder possessed, a la Woody Allen, by the demon of Seriousness. He is writer, director, star. Alas, alas, alas.

Wilder plays a patient in a psychiatric hospital, interned there following a suicide attempt that has climaxed a long history of sexual inadequacy. When he meets a girl (Kathleen Quinlan) at a hospital dance to whom he is drawn, his case officer decides to give him a weekend pass to consummate a promis-

ing romance. The two lonely people move cautiously but successfully to fully satisfying sex. But the idyll is broken when the girl confesses that she is still deeply in love with her estranged husband. Wilder returns to the clinic, crushed but not beaten, ready to try again.

Wilder couldn't have picked a subject more diametrically opposed to his abilities. His script is just a heap of shallow sexually candid dialog appointed to case-book silhouettes. His performance is as inadequate as his personage's emotional past.

Only Quinlan's skillful performance keeps the sketch from being an insufferable bore. —Len.

Below The Belt
(COLOR)

Sleazy but affecting pic about female wrestlers.

Hollywood, Dec. 5.
Atlantic Releasing Corp. release of an Aberdeen/RLF/Tom-Mi Prods. film. Exec produced by Joseph Miller. Produced and directed by Robert Fowler. Features entire cast. Screenplay, Fowler, Sherry Sonnett, from the novel "To Smithereens" by Rosalyn Drexler; camera (TVC Color), Alan Metzger, with additional photography by Misha Suslov; editor, Stephen Zaillion; music, Jerry Fielding; song lyrics by Fielding and David MacKechnie. Reviewed at UA cinema Center, West L.A., Dec. 5, '80. (MPAA Rating: R.) Running time: 91 MINS.
Rosa Rubinsky .... Regina Baff
Herself .... Mildred Burke
Promoter .... John C. Becher
The Beautiful
    Boomerang .... Annie McGreevey
Terrible Tommy .... Jane O'Brien
Verne Vavoom .... Sierra Pecheur
    Also: Frazer Smith, Shirley Stoler, Dolph Sweet, Ric Mancini, K.C. Townsend, and the voices of the Firesign Theatre.

As sleazy-looking as its subject, "Below The Belt" is a curiously endearing little film about female wrestlers. The most but real virtues the film possesses are not in subtleties of story or performance, but in the documentary-like texture producer-director Robert Fowler brings to the milieu, and his sympathy for the miserable people he portrays. The film's threadbare look and the general market resistance to pix about wrestling will make it a hard sell, but it could do okay in some markets.

The film was lensed mostly in 1974, with an additional ten days of shooting after completion money was finally obtained this year by Fowler and exec producer Joseph Miller. Atlantic Releasing Corp. is giving it a one-week Oscar-qualifying run in L.A. on the hopes that the late Jerry Fielding's last musical score might be recognized by the Academy.

While the spate of recent films about wrestling have not over-

come the industry tradition that wrestling is an uncommercial subject (a tradition based on very few examples, in comparison to the wealth of boxing pix), "Below The Belt" has a certain novelty value in dealing with distaff bruisers. MGM will certainly be paying attention to the film's reception, since it is currently lensing a pic on the subject, "All The Marbles."

Basing his story on a novel by Rosalyn Drexler, "To Smithereens," Fowler, who coscripted with Sherry Sonnett, limns the comic-pathetic tale of N.Y. City waitress Regina Baff's attempts to reach stardom on the Dixie grunt-and-groan circuit as "Rosa Carlo, The Mexican Spitfire." After training with former world champ Mildred Burke, Baff tarvels with a rag-tag group of hardboiled femmes and finally has her big chance in a match against the meanest woman in the business. Jane O'Brien.

The dramatic values are thin, the acting is highly uneven, and the dialog is second-rate Paddy Chayefsky. But Fowler, a former documentary filmmaker, has a keen eye for human faces and for evocative surroundings, and this keeps the film continually interesting.

Baff has a forlorn, winsome charm and a believably ordinary appearance, though she seems rather slight of frame to make it as a wrestler, and her ring action is not particularly convincing. But when she goes up against the brutish O'Brien, the audience will be rooting for her in an irresistible female David-and-Goliath situation.

The film's look has been aptly compared with the photographs of Diane Arbus, and its main fascination is its parade of geeks and grotesques, totally devoid of any traditional film glamorization. Shirley Stoler, Sierra Pecheur, and Annie McGreevey make strong impact as other femme wrestlers.

The film is suffused with an awareness of the humiliation and frustration of these people's lives on the fringes of society, but it is a tribute to Fowler's sense of perspective that he never lets the film slide into bathos, keeping a comic edge throughout and investing his characters with their own piculiar brand of dignity.

Aside from Fielding's lively score, and the punchy songs he wrote with David MacKechnie, sung by Billy Preston and others, film has bottom-level tech credits, with lensing that looks like it was done on Super 8 film and blown up for the big screen. But in some ways the film's lack of slickness is its major asset. —Mac.

Fantozzi Contro Tutti
(Fantozzi Against the World)
(ITALIAN-COLOR)

Rome, Dec. 1.
A Titanus release, produced by Bruno Altissimi and Claudio Saraceni for Maura Film productions. Stars Paolo Villaggio. Directed by Paolo Villaggio, Neri Parenti. Screenplay, Leo Benvenuti, Piero De Bernardi, Villaggio, Parenti; camera (Technicolor), Claudio Cirillo; sets, Umberto Turco; editing, Sergio Montanari; music, Fred Bongusto. Reviewed at Reale Cinema, Rome, Nov. 30, 1980. Running time: 97 MINS.
Fantozzi .... Paolo Villaggio
Mrs. Fantozzi .... Milena Vukotic

The legendary little guy, Accountant Fantozzi, returns to the screen in a third version that miraculously loses none of its vitality in recounting more of his slapstick misadventures and dismal humiliations. Closer in spirit to Keaton and Tati than to current Italian comedy, Fantozzi's is a type of humor that could jump national lines and prove its amiability in mass markets abroad.

Fantozzi is a universal symbol of the losing battle fought by the guy at the bottom against everyone higher up from the director of his office to the group leader of his vacation trip. And Fantozzi always loses.

The formula remains the same: a loose collection of episodes that pit the sweet beaten-down face of Fantozzi against 1) a ski expedition with his coworkers to a snowless mountain; 2) a sadistic Swiss doctor whose hospital is a prison and who orders 20 days of fasting for his patient; 3) his wife's flirtation with a 6--foot Neapolitan baker; 4) the death of the office director and his replacement by a fascistic cycling enthusiast; 5) a 35-mile forced cycling race; 6) an invitation to spend a vacation on the president's yacht — swabbing the deck, as it turns out; and a final humiliation by his no-good company prexy.

Conducting thread is a bitter satire on office bureaucracy and social snobbery. Splendid opening sequence shows the dedicated office workers playing ping pong on their desks until the clock strikes 5, when they lower ropes from the windows to exit more quickly. Pic has the surrealistic tone of an animated cartoon or a silent comedy where the characters always survive intact. A dead-pan voice-over narration comments on the action like silent titles of old.

Basically Fantozzi clicks as a prototypical loser, joined by a pathetically homely, but good-hearted wife, (excellently played by Milena Vukotic) and a brutally ugly daughter (actually a bewigged boy) in a precarious united front against forces that continually demolish their fragile dignity. The oppressed little clan musters almost as much sympathy as Chaplin and the Kid against the policeman with the big stick.

Lone disappointment this time around is pic's tone-down of black humor; somehow the world doesn't seem as cruel as in the 1975 original helmed by Luciano Salce.

Codirection by Villaggio and Neri Parenti shows fine comic timing that never loses the audience for a minute; a well-handled camera adds a lot unobtrusively to Villaggio's excellent slapstick. Accidentally knocking people down with a pair of skis is older than the cinema, but the vision of Fantozzi arriving late at the train station in his new plastic ski outfit and 10 ton moon boots carries the gag.

The creators feel no shame in repeating themselves, relying on new situations to hit the same successful notes as previous trials. Villaggio's routine of swiping food and surreptitiously chewing it while the doctor's head is turned is even funnier in the context of the 20-day diet than the actor's identical bit as an impoverished Marquis in "La Locandiera," a pic still on firstrun release in Italy. —*Yung*.

Grabbes Letzter Sommer
(Grabbe's Last Summer)
(WEST GERMAN-COLOR-16m)

Bremen, Dec. 4.

A Radio Bremen Production, Bremen; executive producer, Juergen Breest. Features entire cast. Directed by Sohrab Shahid Saless. Screenplay, Thomas Valentin; camera (color), Rolf Romberg; sets, Guenther Naumann; costumes, Ute Burgmann; editing, Anna Koudelka; production manager, Hans-Calixt Krug. Reviewed at Radio Bremen Screening Room, Bremen, Dec. 4, '80. Running time: **203 MINS.**

Cast: Wilfried Grimpe (Christian Dietrich Grabbe), Renate Schroeter (Luise Grabbe), Sonja Karzau (Dorothea Grabbe), Marta Holler (Wilhelmine), Ulrich von Bock (Moritz Petri), Uwe Meister (Ziegler), Gabriele Fischer (Sophie Moeller), Boris Guradze (Gottlieb), Eberhard Fechner (Piderit), Gunther Malzacher (Althaus), Alexander Radzum (Bergius), Heinz Rabe (Stedtfeld), Axel Ganz (Dr. Rosen), Ruediger Schulzki (Runnenberg), Kurt Ackermann (Gladbach), Jens Scholkmann (Scholz), Norbert Kollakowsky (Pustkuchen), Frank Helmholz (Kroeger), Heinz Lieven (Preuss).

This is the first television film made by the Iranian exiled filmmaker, Sohrab Shahid Saless, who has now probably won more international film festival prizes and awards for his seven feature pix (two in Iran, five in Germany) than all but a small handful of New German Cinema filmmakers. "Grabbe's Last Summer," a 210-minute epic biography on the last days of poet-dramatist Christian Dietrich Grabbe (born 1801, died 1836), is not exactly Saless's best film, and is lacking that special vision common to his original screenplays, but

it is suitable fare for fest devoted to the art film.

First, a preamble on literary adaptations in West Germany. This is a peculiar form of tv entertainment: film adaptations of plays or novels, as well as stories about the authors themselves (often slated by tv executives to celebrate anniversaries). In general, literary adaptations have a bad name in Germany as far as film art is concerned — the assigned directors of these project-films rarely go beyond supporting the text with appropriate photographed images (although there are notable exceptions to this rule).

Radio Bremen's "house author," Thomas Valentin, wrote the screenplay for "Grabbe's Last Summer" a few years ago; then he published a novel on the cantankerous writer from nearby Detmold, which, in turn, set the stage for the present tv-film. Both Valentin and tv-editor Juerger Breest (a screenplay writer in his own right) had seen prizewinning films of Saless at the Berlin Film Festival, and they decided that, thematically, this was the director they were looking for. Shortly after finishing "Order" earlier this year, Saless went to work trying to whittle "Grabbe's Last Summer" down to his own size.

Valentin's script is so spread out, and enriched with so many historical references, that the author, rather than the director, is the victor in this artistic, visionary tug-of-war. Yet it should be said too that this is one of the best "literary films" made here. Not only is it an engaging, tragic tale about a controversial writer of the past century — Saless has also fully captured the spirit of the times, all the more remarkable because he is hardly a student of German letters.

Grabbe's best known work is "Comedy, Satire, Irony, and Deeper Meaning," a literary and social comedy that is often performed as a play; it puts down the sacred cows of German culture, particularly the Goethe syndrome that provincialized German letters in the early 19th century. The viewer should perhaps be aware that some of the country's greatest literary talent of the time — Lenz, Kleist, Heine, and Grabbe — had an uphill struggle to prominence in the pessimistic days before the 1848 rebellion.

Saless, as an outsider in German filmmaking today (he is not named in "official" lists of German filmmakers and filmmaking prepared by critics Pflaum & Prinzler and critic Peter W. Jansen), more or less identifies with his subject; thus he underlines those scenes satirizing culture, officialdom, and bur-

eaucracy with stylistic flourishes. He found a look-alike, Wilfried Grimpe (engaged as actor-director in Wiesbaden), to portray Grabbe, who plays the role to the hilt and carries the viewer easily over the three hours-plus stretch.

And there are unmistakeable Saless touches for fest fans: the best is at the bedside of the alcohol-driven poet, when he rises from delirium to see in his mother a figure of death. The moment is worth a whole film. —*Holl*.

London Film Fest

To Woody Allen, From Europe With Love
(BELGIAN-COLOR-DOCU)

London, Dec. 9.

Iblis Film, BRT release and production. Conceived and directed by Andre Delvaux. Camera (color), Michael Badour, Walther Van Den Ende; editor, John Reznikov. Annette Wauthoz; music, Egisto Macchi. Reviewed at London Film Fest, Nov. 27, '80. Running time: **40 MINS.**

(In English)

Belgian director Andre Delvaux has composed a valentine documentary to Woody Allen. There is no attempt to make a comment on his work of prod Allen with questions or attempt to criticize his work. Delvaux apparently likes all of Allen's films.

Allen talks about his films, those he likes, especially "Love and Death," and is seen at work on his latest film, "Stardust Memories," which has come into heavy criticism on its home grounds.

Delvaux, a director with a buff and festival following, spends a lot of footage on his own efforts to edit the footage and get a grasp of Allen through the juxtaposition. It is more time-filling than revealing.

The film shows Allen at work and repose and could find tv usage, though it lacks sufficient analysis of Allen for more interest for schools or theatrical outings. Item is well shot and, as the title indicates, mainly aimed at confirmed Allen fans. —*Mosk*

Hirok Rajar Deshe
(The Kingdom of Diamonds)
(INDIAN-COLOR)

London, Dec. 9.

GOVWB release and production. Features entire cast. Written, directed and music by Satyajit Ray. Camera (color), Soumendu Roy; editor, Dulal Dutta; art director, Ashoke Bose; lyrics, Ray. Reviewed at London Film Fest, Nov. 30, '80. Running time: **118 MINS.**

With: Soumitra Chatterji, Utpal Dutt, Rabi Ghose, Tapen Chatterji, Samtosh Dutta.

Satyajit Ray, whose human probing films on life in India in the past and present, in villages and cities, among upper and lower classes have gotten him worldwide renown, has also peppered his output with so-called children's films. Lately he has been at play with these films and, ironically, they are more popular in India (though not abroad) than his so-called serious films.

Ray does not consider them as intended only for children; they can also be savored by adults due to their fine craftsmanship, inventive settings and deceptively simple themes. Here there is a political undertone in the tale of the fall of an authoritarian monarch in a colorful India of the past.

Actually, this is a sequel to Ray's "Adventures of Goopy and Bagha" where two simple men achieved weddings to a maharajah's daughters by the use of magic shoes. Now they are bored, feel they are getting old and have a chance to leave their pampered lives on a state visit to a rich monarch whose country contains diamond mines.

There they use their magic to help dissident people fight the monarch who uses brainwashing to keep his exploited subjects in hand. There is a lot of singing, which has a bouncy catchy air in its mixture of Indian and Western music.

The monarch himself is finally made to see the evil of his ways and helps pull down his own statue. Political aspects notwithstanding, this is a witty, disarming film bolstered by a fine director enjoying himself. Ray has recreated his grandfather's noted children's magazine recently and perhaps this has led to his return to these kind of films. His last one, "The Elephant God," was also in this genre.

But it is time for Ray to get back to more adult-oriented films. This one may be too wistful, charming and deceptively simple for much theatrical impact outside its home grounds but is ample fest fodder and could emerge in specialized so-called children's shows which might give attendant adults a boost also.

Ray has also done the sprightly music and lyrics for this disarming adventure politico fable on the Indian past most outsiders are accustomed to from Hollywood days. —*Mosk*.

Le Dernier Melodrame
(The Last Melodrama)
(FRENCH-COLOR-16m)

London, Dec. 9.

FR3 Marseille release and production. Features entire cast. Directed by Georges Franju. Features screenplay, Bernard Dimey from an idea by Pierre Brasseur; camera (Eastmancolor), Marcel

Fradetal; editor, Fernand Mannella. Reviewed at London Film Fest, Nov. 26, '80. Running time, **80 MINS.**

With: Michel Vitold, Edith Scob, Raymond Bussieres, Juliette Mills, Luis Masson.

———

Georges Franju believes in good old theatrical melodrama that deals juicily with basic human drama without kitsch or satire. He proves it in this engaging tv film about one of the last travelling legit companies of this type in the fifties.

A bit hampered by 16m, Franju still paints a disarming picture of this company playing the small hamlets around France. The scenes from the hoary old plays are never laughable though the audiences react both for and against them.

In one small town the drama comes to a head. A woman who wants to leave her innkeeper husband and go off with the troupe is refused by them. She goads her husband into trying to burn down the travelling theatre. But she does it herself and the founder perishs and the last theatre is over.

Acting is appropriately as melodramatic as the repertoire of this musty but dedicated legit company. Franju has made a film that may lack vigor for more demanding theatrical use but should find tv outings abroad, more fests and perhaps some specialized outings on its shrewd insights into the ironic emotinal concepts of melodrama. It is time for Franju to return to mre theatrical films. —*Mosk.*

Brussels-Transit
(BELGIAN-B&W-16m)

———

London, Dec. 9.

Paradise Films release and production. Features entire cast. Written and directed by Samy Szlingerbaum. Camera, Michael Houssiau; editor, Eva Houdova. Reviewed at London Film Fest, Nov. 23, '80. Running time: **80 MINS.**

With: Helene Laplower, Brois Lehman, Jeremy and Micha Wald.

———

Film mixes acted segments and a surrounding documentary filling of railroads, cars and stations and streets today though the time is over 30 years ago. It creates a languid yet unusual look at immigrants and adaptation.

Director Samy Szlingerman is an editor and his first film is a tale of his parents' leaving Poland in 1947. The commentary is delivered by his mother in Yiddish and the film, despite the final settling into life in Brussels, gives a feeling of people still living between two worlds.

There is the arrival in Brussels and staying there. Scenses of a visit by a postman they cannot handle because of language, the mother's troubles with people sharing a kitchen, a determined attempt to try to get a bakery to put a Polish delicacy into their oven articulate the problems of adaptation in human terms.

Film is somewhat slight and more geared for tv and some specialized houses due to its intime treatment. But it shows director Szlingerman has a flair for building human dramatic scenes without affectation. He needs more cohesive scripts but is worth watching on the strength of this simple, touching look at people in transit. — *Mosk.*

Joe Albany ... A Jazz Life
(U.S.-COLOR-DOCU-16m)

———

London, Dec. 9.

Carole Langer Productions release and production. Conceived and directed by Carole Langer. Camera (color), Jonathon Smith, editor, Michael Schenkein. Reviewed at London Film Fest, Nov. 25, '80. Running time: **60 MINS.**

With: Joe Albany.

———

Joe Albany was involved in the great days of the bop jazz movement in the Forties. He is a rare survivor as the others disappeared in dope and early death. This canny interview pic erases the talking-head syndrome by bringing out the charm and insight of Albany into his own life and problems and those of the more noted people of the era as Charlie Parker, Lester Young, Billie Holliday and others.

Albany was a rare white pianist who worked with these past greats. He wryly gives out with his own fall into drugs and prison under the pressures but also the feeling of the times that brought a new high in jazz before its fall to other types of music.

Well constructed, with Albany talking with a deejay, at home and on a bus and seen at work. He is not bitter about his small gigs and is now finally getting some renown and making records. Carole Langer has neatly edited this into a jazz portrait that mirrors the lives and times of this movement.

It is a natural for tv, of course, but also has a fine mood and insight into the times and Albany himself that could get it commercial attention with another medium-length jazz film. School and specialized use are also indicated. —*Mosk.*

Dialogue With a Woman Departed
(U.S.-DOCU-COLOR/B&W-16m)

———

London, Dec. 9.

Leo Hurwitz Productions release and production. Written and directed by Leo Hurwitz. Camera (color/b&w), Hurwitz; editor, Hurwitz. Reviewed at London Film Fest, Nov. 23, '80. Running time: **270 MINS.**

———

Leo Hurwitz, who made the noted study of American labor persecu-tion in the 30s, "Native Land," came through blacklisting in the 50s and helped found the film department at NYU in New York, now has made an almost four-hour intimate summing up of his work and outlooks.

Film took eight years to make and is a ruminative attempt to express his feelings for his late wife, Peggy Lawson, by recalling the times they went through together.

There are scenes of the city, nature and poetic attempts at conjuring up his feelings for his wife. The film traces the times from the Depression to the divisive Vietnam War through Hurwitz's own films which encompass the events going on during her lifetime.

She was also committed to social and political engagement and worked with Hurwitz on his later films. Film has a tendency to ramble despite the old footage which gives familiar but sharp glimpses of the Depression, World War II, racism and civil rights in the U.S. and the Vietnam War as well as showing stills of his wife and commenting on her development within her family and her life on her own.

Film becomes repetitive and too private despite an unusual visual attempt to mix an act of love and remembrance with documentary aspects of the times. They do not really mesh. A film that is special, demanding and more for fests, school and public tv use than more general theatrical outlets. —*Mosk.*

A Change Of Seasons
(COLOR)

———

Marital boredom theme getting tiresome. Dubious outlook despite Bo Derek in cast.

———

Hollywood, Dec. 17.

Twentieth Century-Fox release of a Film Finance Group Ltd. Martin Ransohoff production, exec produced by Richard R. St. Johns. Produced by Martin Ransohoff. Stars Shirley MacLaine, Anthony Hopkins, Bo Derek. Directed by Richard Lang. Screenplay, Erich Segal, Ronni Kern, Fred Segal, from a story by Erich Segal, Ransohoff; camera (DeLuxe Color), Philip Lathrop; second-unit camera, Dick Kratina, Rexford Metz, Joe Jackman; ski photographer, Scott Miller; music, Henry Mancini; song, "Where Do You Catch The Bus For Tomorrow?," by Alan & Marilyn Bergman, Mancini; editor, Don Zimmerman; production designer, Bill Kenney; set decorator, Rick T. Gentz; sound, Richard Gragg, Robert Knudson, Don MacDougall, Robert Glass; associate producer, Cathleen Summers; second-unit director, Michael Moore; assistant director, Donald Heitzer, James Weatherill. Reviewed at 20th-Fox Studios, L.A., Dec. 16, '80. (MPAA Rating: R.) Running time: **102 MINS.**

Karen Evans	Shirley MacLaine
Adam Evans	Anthony Hopkins
Lindsey Rutledge	Bo Derek
Pete Lachapelle	Michael Brandon
Kasey Evans	Mary Beth Hurt
Steven Rutledge	Ed Winter
Paul Di Lisi	Paul Regina
Alice Bingham	K Callan
Sam Bingham	Rod Colbin
Lance	Steve Eastin
Fritz	Christopher Coffey

———

During production, "A Change Of Seasons" was frequently confused with "Loving Couples," another Fox pic about marital musical chairs starring Shirley MacLaine, and it's likely the public will have a similar reaction. "Loving Couples" didn't make it, and "Seasons" can avoid that fate only if the presence of Bo Derek, in her first role since "10," can stir some audience interest. The Martin Ransohoff production, exec produced by Richard St. Johns, is a tired rehash of themes that might have been provocative a decade ago.

So far, the only hit in the marital boredom sex cycle has been "10," with such entries as "Loving Couples," "Middle Age Crazy," and "The Last Married Couple In America" falling by the wayside. While such themes may appeal to middle-aged filmmakers in Hollywood, they generally leave the predominantly youthful filmgoing audience cold. The success of "10" could be due to the fact that it was basically comic, but it was also an unusually fine film, and as such transcended the formula.

It would take the genius of a Lubitsch to do justice to the incredibly tangled relationships in "A Change Of Seasons," and director Richard Lang, who replaced Noel Black after two weeks of shooting, is no Lubitsch. The switching of couples seems arbitrary and mechanical, and more sour than amusing. The script by Erich Segal and others strives too hard for cuteness.

MacLaine emerges as the most sympathetic person in the film, the wife of new England college professor Anthony Hopkins, whose philandering with coed Derek shatters the complacency of their marriage. MacLaine retaliates by taking a young lover, Michael Brandon, and they all head off on a Vermont skiing vacation (filmed in Colorado) together in a dubious demonstration of open-mindedness which another character aptly labels "a kind of commune for the Geritol generation."

There's not a moment in this film which wasn't anticipated, and bettered, 10 years ago by Paul Mazursky and Larry Tucker in "Bob & Carol & Ted & Alice," the progenitor of this increasingly tedious cycle. While Mazursky neatly satirized his characters' frenetic attempts to find happiness by swinging, the makers of "Seasons" seem to take the characters at face value without realizing how joyless their sexual experimentation really is. The issues between men and women have progressed considerably beyond what is shown here.

Bo Derek fanciers who have been panting to see her in the buff since "10" will be pleased by the opening nude sequence which has her and Hopkins romping in slow-motion in a hot tub. That's about all the sexual charge the film carries, however, for with the exception of some peek-a-boo glimpses of Derek showering, all the eroticism is dissipated in talk.

Hopkins, who seems at times to be doing a comic impersonation of Richard Burton in "Virginia Woolf," comes off as a totally self-centered boor who never engages audience sympathy. He spends most of his time adjusting his oversized glasses and muttering pompous howlers such as "Men are different; our needs, for example, are more baroque."

MacLaine has a keen wit and innate sense of dignity which prevent her from being totally sucked into the lame comic and dramatic mechanisms of the script, but Brandon is an irritant throughout with his leftover hippie mannerisms. The film ultimately shows that neither Hopkins nor MacLaine can make it work with their young lovers, but that point seemed obvious without having to sit through 102 minutes of phony suspense on the subject.

Derek doesn't do anything here which proves she can act. It's possible that Blake Edwards, by keeping her almost entirely in the realm of fantasy in "10," made the perfect use of her limited talents. When she is asked to pretend to be a real person, she loses all of her lustre. Mousy-looking Mary Beth Hurt virtually steals the film in the latter sections as the emotionally confused but clear-minded daughter of MacLaine and Hopkins.

Production values are surprisingly old-fashioned, with Philip Lathrop's lensing relying too much on process shots and studio-bright interior lighting. Henry Mancini's gooey score is not helped by the addition of one of Alan & Marilyn Bergman's lesser songwriting efforts. —Mac.

There Goes The Bride
(BRITISH-COLOR)

A Vanguard Releasing Inc. release of a Cooney-Schute production. Produced by Ray Cooney and Martin Schute. Features entire cast. Directed by Terence Marcel. Screenplay, Cooney, Marcel, from play by Cooney, John Chapman; camera (Rank Film Laboratories color), James Devis; editor, Alan Jones; music, Harry Robinson; production design, Peter Mullin; art direction, John Siddall; choreography, Gillian Gregory. Reviewed at Quad Cinema, N.Y.C., Dec. 6, 1980. (MPAA Rating: PG). Running time: **88 MINS.**

Timothy Westerby	Tom Smothers
Polly	Twiggy
Mr. Babcock	Martin Balsam
Ursula Westerby	Sylvia Syms
Bill Shorter	Michael Whitney
Gerald Drimond	Geoffrey Sumner
Rossi	Graham Stark
Daphne Drimond	Hermione Baddeley
Judy Westerby	Toria Fuller
Mrs. Babcock	Margot Moser
Nicholas Babcock	John Terry
Mr. Perkins	Jim Backus
Psychiatrist	Phil Silvers
Gas station attendant	Broderick Crawford
Mr. Ramirez	Gonzales Gonzales
Mrs. Ramirez	Carmen Zapata
Church organist	Steve Franken

"There Goes the Bride" is a lame Midatlantic filmization of the 1974 West End farce, which originally starred Bernard Cribbins and featured Trudi Van Doorn on the stage. Shot in 1979 at Pinewood Studios and on Vero Beach, Florida exteriors, pic lacks the sex comedy and nudity of previous Ray Cooney efforts (e.g., "Not Now, Darling") and is woefully out-of-step with the commercial realities for feature films today. "Bride" faces very grim prospects in domestic release.

The old chestnut of wedding day problems constitutes the picture's sitcom basis. Florida parents Tom Smothers (incredibly miscast with his boyish looks in Cribbins' role) and Sylvia Syms are trying to wed daughter Toria Fuller to Texan John Terry, son of Martin Balsam and Margot Moser. Psychiatrist Phil Silvers (an embarrassing cameo) and Italian waiter Graham Stark recall the wedding day slapstick mishaps in a rickety flashback structure.

With the bride and groom roles barely pencilled in, film revolves solely around a comedy premise lifted from "Topper." Ad man Smothers, working on a brassiere campaign for magnate Jim Backus, uses a '20s-era photo of then-model Twiggy for inspiration (!). Upon bumping into doors, addle-brained Smothers imagines Twiggy has come to life again, causing sitcom humor since she is invisible to the rest of the cast. A final reel crash on the head removes Smothers' fantasy girl and the wedding comes off after all.

Unfunny script, credited to Cooney and helmer Terence Marcel, leaves the laughs (some unintentional) for the spectacle of Smothers imagining himself as the answer to Fred Astaire (with Twiggy looking smashing in a white satin gown as his Ginger Rogersesque dancing partner). In two routine song-and-dance numbers, Smothers' sincere terping and warbling seem to be essayed in earnest rather than bumbling, and rate as pure camp.

Despite her billing, Twiggy is saddled with a merely decorative non-role and comes off as cute and harmless. Unfortunately, all her footage is shot with fog filters for an irritating soft-focus effect, designed insipidly to cue the fans that "she's not real." Pic's few amusing moments (intended) are provided by the mugging of Syms' British parents played by Geoffrey Sumner (holdover from the original play's cast) and Hermione Baddeley. Various guest cameos fizzle.

The production and technical team, encoring from a previous Cooney film, "Why Not Stay for Breakfast?," contributes a subpar job. Errors (Smothers' prop eyeglasses keep disappearing from his face in reverse shots) and antiquated painted backdrops for studio-shot exteriors attest to the project's microscopic budget. —Lor.

Hawk The Slayer
(BRITISH-COLOR)

Soft sword and sorcery.

London, Dec. 16.
ITC Film Distributors release of a Chips Production presentation, produced by Harry Robertson. Exec producer, Bernard J. Kingham. Directed by Terry Marcel. Features entire cast. Screenplay, Terry Marcel, Harry Robertson; camera (color), Paul Beeson; music, Harry Robertson; editor, Eric Boyd Perkins; art direction, Michael Pickwoad; stunts, Eddie Stacey; special effects, Effects Associates. Reviewed at Odeon Marble Arch Theatre, London, Dec. 15, 1980. (BBFC rating - A). Running time: **93 MINS.**

Voltan	Jack Palance
Hawk	John Terry
Gort	Bernard Bresslaw
Crow	Ray Charleson
Baldin	Peter O'Farrell
Ranulf	Morgan Sheppard
Sister Monica	Cheryl Campbell
Abbess	Annette Crosbie
Eliane	Catriona MacColl
Drogo	Shane Briant
High Abbot	Harry Andrews
Fitzwalter	Christopher Benjamin
Innkeeper	Roy Kinnear
Old Man	Ferdy Mayne
Sparrow	Graham Stark
Scar	Warren Clarke
Sped	Declan Mulholland
Ralf	Derrick O'Connor
Black Wizard	Peter Benson

Sword & sorcery as a blossoming fantasy-action genre has yet to cut it in the marketplace, and "Hawk the Slayer" is no prospect to upset the odds. Otherwise efficient and well-paced, what it lacks are striking elements of style and story. Tradition has prevailed over innovation. Figure it useful for circuit programming with promotion angled to fans of s&s pulp literature.

The forces of light and darkness are herein personified by, respectively, John Terry and Jack Palance, as brothers in name only contending for "the power," a family heirloom in the form of a magical flying sword. Also in the plot is a nunnery and the kidnap of its abbess by Palance in exchange for ransom gold and his brother's scalp.

Comic relief and moral parallels for our time do not seriously impede the action and kicks. Arrows fly as fast as bullets. Swordplay is deployed intermittently, often in slow motion. Gore is minimal (and some viewers may thus feel cheated), but the ultimate moral is that violence is violence even in bloodless slowmo.

The script by director Terry Marcel and producer Harry Robertson is long on soft-lens atmosphere and stop-action, short on imaginative narrative. Direction is adequate, but the pic is certainly well-assembled.

Palance as the facially-disfigured Voltan in headmask offers a polished study in snarl and venom. Terry, on the other hand, is not much more than a pretty face whose bland American accent sticks out in the company of some fine, but wasted, British secondary performers — Harry Andrews, Roy Kinnear, Patrick Magee, Annette Crosbie, Bernard Bresslaw and Patricia Quinn, among others.

Paul Beeson's lensing is pretty, and there are some good special effects, ditto physical stunting as arranged by Eddie Stacey. The original hopped-up score, a good one, is also credited to Harry Robertson. There are, to repeat, some effective things in the film, but they don't add up in any compelling way. And that means no bang at the box-office either. —Pit.

O Anthropos Me To Garyfallo
(The Man With The Red Carnation)
(GREEK-COLOR)

Athens, Dec. 19.

An Arma Film's production. Written and directed by Nicos Tzemas. Featuring entire cast. Camera (color), Nicos Kavoukides; music Mikis Theodorakis; sets and costumes, Ersi Dryni, Tassos Zografos; editing, Petros Lycas; sound, George Nicalaedes. Reviewed at the Galazias Cinema of Athens, Dec. 12, 1980. Running Time: 120 MINS.

Cast: Manos Katrakis, Alecos Alexandrakis, Costas Kazacos, Anguelos Antonopoulos, Peter Fyssoun, Vaguelis Kazan, Emilia Ipsilanti, Mirca Papaconstantinou, Phoebus Guicopoulos.

This film is breaking all-time records in Greece with an unprecedented b.o. response. As an entry at the recent Thessaloniki Film Festival it shared a best picture prize with "Melodrama" but writer-director Nicos Tzemas refused to accept it.

It is a political drama set in one of the most critical periods of the recent Greek history. The real story of a young underground hero, Nicos Beloyannis, who was arrested as a Communist spy, sentenced and executed by a court martial in Athens in 1952.

The picture, too politically specialized, calls for careful handling abroad because it will not have the same tremendous b.o. response by foreign audiences not familiar with the times and its historical aspects. The story is set in Athens after the Civil War in 1950-52. Beloyannis arrives from abroad and starts underground activity against foreign intervention which was trying to overthrow the democratic government General Nikolaos Plasteras. He is arrested with some comrades, tortured and brought to trial. Sentenced to death with three others, in spite of appeals by many foreign personalities to save his life, he was executed with three others. During his trial and at his execution he wore a red carnation in his buttonhole. His young pregnant wife, who was on trial with him, was spared.

Nicos Tzemas' work, which in the past dealt with social topics, now marks a turning point. He directed with an undeniable simplicity evoking the period and environment well. His screenplay has a stolidity in construction depicting simply the historical events. Though he adds a melodramatic aspect in the last sequences he does not take any political stance.

He is very much helped by a cast of top Greek thespians even in secondary roles who delivering convincing performances as historical persons, still living or dead. Manos Katrakis is excellent as General Plasteras, as well as Alecos Alexandrakis, Mirca Papaconstantinou, Anguelos Antonopoulos, Vaguelis Kazan, Costas Kazacos, Emilia Ipsilanti.

The title role is performed by an amateur, Phoebus Guicopoulos, who gives a convincing performance though it lacks the brightness needed. He is a professor of Italian Literature in real life and was picked up by Tzemas for his resemblance to Beloyannis, after Italian actor Gian Maria Volonte turned down the part.

All technical credits are good. The color photography by Nikos Kavoukides captures nicely the neighbourhoods of Athens as they were then. The music by Mikis Theodorakis underscores effectively the events. The sets and costumes as well as the editing are up to standard. —Rena.

Nous Etions Un Seul Homme
(We Were One Man)
(FRENCH-COLOR)

Chicago, Dec. 1.

Philippe Vallois production. Written and directed by Vallois. Features entire cast. Camera (Eastmancolor), Francois About; editor, Vallois; sound, Alain Villeval; score, Jean Jaques Ruhlmann; no other credits provided. Reviewed at Chicago Film Festival screening room, Chicago, Dec. 1, '80. Running time: 90 MINS.
Guy .... Serge Avedikian
Rolf .... Piotr Stanislas
Janine .... Catherine Albin

This French outing from producer-director-scripter and editor. Philippe Vallois is a keenly crafted pic clouded by its essentially homosexual orientation. Set in rural France at the close of World War II, pic tells of the developing emotional and physical bond between a wounded German soldier (Piotr Stanislas) and a hermetic and mentally-uncertain young French provincial (Serge Avedikian), who saves the soldier's life.

Vallois's static narrative sandwiches in some obvious themes — especially a love-across-the-barricades statement, with a homoerotic twist — but fails to lay sufficient groundwork to make its finale (a lyrically staged but nonetheless graphic boy-boy love scene) as movingly credible as it's supposed to be. The explicitness of the scene is jarring, and throws the pic somewhat out of kilter.

Vallois takes great and rewarding pains to individually establish his two principals, both sealed off in different ways from their respective cultures. The provincial is an escaped mental patient holed up in an abandoned farmhouse scratching out childlike drawings in between strenuous odd jobs.

The soldier emerges as a more enigmatic figure. A product of the Nazi military regimen since youth, he confesses to friendlessness and an emotional (and literal) isolation. As presented, he may or may not be a deserter; Vallois isn't clear on the point. It's the soldier who finally pushes the relationship into sexuality, thus confirming a cinematic stereotype of many Nazis as closet homosexuals.

Vallois is at his best at presenting the duo as oddly compatible friends, gamboling about the handsome French countryside, cutting down trees, fishing and adopting a stray dog. But the director's work here is marred by his penchant for self-consciously "arty" visual effects — sunsets glowing across serene lakes, slow motion and stop-action sequences and unnervingly odd camera angles.

But through it all, Vallois manages to lend the relationship a life of its own, keeping the viewer engaged with most of its erratic emotional turns. In pic's earlier parts, Vallois displays a bold streak of barnyard physicality, exemplified in questionable taste by a defecation scene turned into a political statement (don't ask, it must be seen firsthand).

The director-scripter adds a welcome but slightly confusing note by introducing a shapely, extremely agreeable young village woman, superbly portrayed by Catherine Albin. What's confusing is that she is presented as the mentally unstable provincial's enthusiastic sexual partner.

Rather than debate fine points of bisexuality, Vallois has the pliant young woman accepting the homosexual liaison and, by pic's end, offering by implication to make things a menage a trois. Pic winds on a downbeat note; enough said the soldier is mowed down accidentally after being hauled off by French resistance types, who are presented as obnoxious and brutal.

Vallois elicits excellent performances from his three principals, but after carefully establishing his characters through canny use of detail, he throws his pic into the cocked hat of sensationalism. Production credits, especially Jean Jaques Ruhlmann's score, are first-rate. Pic was preemed in the U.S. at the recent Chi Film Fest, where it received a silver "Hugo" prize.
—Sege.

Barna fran Blasjofjaellet
(The Children From Blue Lake Mountain)
(SWEDISH-COLOR)

Malmoe, Nov. 21.

A Moviemakers/Sandrews/Swedish Film Institute production. Sandrews Film release (Sweden), Swedish Film Institute (outside Sweden). Script, Bjoern Norstroem and Jonas Sima, based on their book. Directed by Jonas Sima. Camera (Fujicolor), Rune Ericson; production manager, Gustav Wiklund; editor, Lasse Lundberg; music, Bernt Rosengren; title song, Torgny Bjoerk. Reviewed at Sandrews 1, Malmoe (Sweden), Nov. 20, 1980. Running time: 92 MINS.
Ante .... Anders Edvinsson
Lena .... Carina Linder
Anna-Lisa .... Yvonne Danielsson
Manke .... Kent Ivar Frederiksson
Paer-Erik .... Martin Isaksson
Maerta-Stina .... Lova Sima

"The Children From Blue Lake Mountain" are sisters and brothers (to say nothing of the goat) who make their way on skis from Northern Sweden to Stockholm. Their mother died unexpectedly. Their father is a worker on the expansion of Stockholm's subway system. Welfare workers, aided by helicopter pilots, the military, etc., are in hot pursuit of the children, deeming it best to have them forced into the security of an institution. Along their route, the children and their pet goat encounter various nice-enough ordinary grownups. They survive a minor avalanche. Strange but nice characters loom in the various landscapes. The latter are given all due credit in Fujicolored frames of very little mobility.

Jonas Sima, a former film critic and Ingmar Bergman scholar, tried his hand successfully on several documentaries (mostly for tv) before this utterly failed venture into feature filmmaking. Like so many other documentarists, he may be good at following and recording actual events, but he is at a complete loss in staging live action. He cannot even compose frames that serve as natural springboards for movement,

An attempt to juxtapose action with meaningful dialog disguised as comedy repartee has the same lethargy as the sole result. And the bony finger of educational intent comes through as embarrassing left-wing parody. But since there is no dramatic structure to anything, neither dialog nor action, in this film, a sensation of general helplessness prevails to the exclusion of any other impression, positive or negative.

The children chosen for the leads are just pretty faces with nothing to distinguish them as individual characters. Such showbiz notables as Lasse Poeysti, Gunnar Wiklund, Monica Zetterlund, Bebbe Wolgers, Pierre Lindstedt, Halvar Bjoerk and Lars-Olof Loethwall are badly served with cameos of inane buffoonery. Only Norway's Rolv Wesenlund forces his way through with a spoken punch-line you must suspect to be of his own desperate, last-minute making.—*Kell.*

Total Vereist
(Totally Frozen)
(WEST GERMAN-COLOR)

Munich, Dec. 3.

A DNS-Film-Production. Munich, in collaboration with Bayerischer Rundfunk, Munich. executive producer. OLGA-Film. Munich, distributed in Germany by Skylight. Berlin. Features entire cast. Directed by Hans Noever. Screenplay, Noever. Ursula Jeshel; camera (color), Jacques Steyn; sound. Olof Griepenkerl, Peter Kellerhals; sets. Georg von Kieseritzky; editing. Christine Leyrer; production manager. Elvira Senft. Reviewed at Studio-Meister. Munich. Dec. 3. '80. Running time: **80 MINS.**

Cast: Rio Reiser (Hans N.), Adam Alexander Kaz (Adam N.), Juergen von Alten (Grandfather), Renate Reiche (Elisabeth), Silvia Janisch (Sophie), Ginka Steinwachs (Hetti), Ursula Wachnowski (Aunt Johanna), Kurt Raab (Herr Muench), Hanns Zischler (Pilot), Margie Subee (Frau Froese), Albert Heins (Herr Hermkes), Dominic Raacke (Frau Froese's son).

Hans Noever burst on the German film scene a few years back with a series of fest oddities that put him in the front lines of Teutonic filmers: "The Woman Across The Way" (1977), the opener at the Week of the Critics in Cannes; "The Night with Chandler" (1978), a hit at last year's Hof fest; and "The Price of Survival" (1979), the opener at last year's Berlin fest. Both "The Woman across the Way" and "The Price of Survival" were lensed by Britain's Walter Lassally, a former Oscar-winner, which made the pix something a bit out of the ordinary — further, "Survival" was lensed in Jefferson City, Missouri.

Now the energetic Noever is back with "Totally Frozen," a low-budget seems to have a lot in common with "The Night with Chandler" — it's a fun pic leaning heavily on improvisations for effect and even features the Noever regular, Rio Reiser, from the "Chandler" jaunt across Europe. "Totally Frozen" — the direct translation from the original German title — is a little too heavy and thereby misleading; a loose translation would be something "Like a Block of Ice" or "Completely Crazy," to get the point across.

Noever wants to present us with a Bunuelian stringer about the German middle-class bourgeoisie, albeit in a Marx Brothers mode or the old Olsen & Johnson comic routines. Picture a Berlin villa that is big enough to hold an entire film crew for a couple weeks, add a thread of a story about the Master of the House kicking the bucket on the toilet-seat while listening to, and conducting, Puccini on the radio, and then apply the salt-and-pepper shakers as the impulse takes you — the result is a film without a narrative and one that only makes sense if you are living in Germany.

The best joke is the center-piece motif: the cast with the body on view in the living room surrounded by distracted family members — a surrealist touch. —*Holl.*

Legend Of The Fox
(HONG KONG-COLOR)

Hong Kong, Nov. 30.

A Shaw Brothers production and release. Produced by Mona Fong. Directed by Chang Cheh. Features entire cast. Screenplay, Chang Cheh, Erh Kuang; camera (color), Tsao Hui Chi; music director, Eddie Wang; fighting instructors, Lu Feng, Chiang Sheng, Kuo Chui. Reviewed at Jade Cinema, Hong Kong. Nov. 30, 1980. Running time: **100 MINS.**

Cast: Chien Hsiao Hao, Chiang Sheng, Linda Chu, Kuo Chui, Lu Feng.

(Mandarin with English subtitles)

Once upon a time there was a feud between three big families in China, the Hu, Miao and Tien filial groups. The fathers of Chiang Sheng and Kuo Chui kill each other while fighting over one of the precious swords. Chiang frames Lu Feng for a murder and a series of duels occur until everyone gets killed in the process. But that is not the end of this dripping legend because a baby boy survives and years later he rights the wrongs, avenges the death of his parents and re-establishes the tarnished reputation of his family.

This undistinguished costumed swordplay item marks the return of Shaw's contract director, Chang Cheh, to the energetic world of period kung fu epics, but with no success. It is yet another assembly-line Shaw product with the usual prolonged duels with chats, gimmick fights, fantastic trampoline leaps and elaborate weaponry.

As often seen in Cheh's past efforts, like "Heroes Two" and his Shaolin series, the piece revolves round the diverse poles of two male protagonists with touches of self-sacrifice for honor's sake. "Legend of The Fox" sadly disintegrates into a talky and boring legend with bits and pieces of martial arts here and there to awaken sleepy viewers. To say more would be saying much that Chang Cheh, as a director and discoverer of action stars, seems to have run out of steam. —*Mel.*

The Beast
(HONG KONG-COLOR)

Hong Kong, Dec. 1.

A Pearl City Films Ltd. production and release. Executive producer. Teddy Robin Kwan. Produced by Wallace Cheung. Directed by Dennis Yu. Features entire cast. Camera (color), Bob Thomson. No other credits provided. Reviewed at Queen's Theatre, Hong Kong. Dec. 1, 1980. Running time: **90 MINS.**

Cast: Patricia Chong, Paul Chung, Wong Ching, Eddy Chang, Juk Sze, Chan Sing.

(Cantonese with English subtitles)

Just when local film goers think that the Chinese cinema of cruelty, voyeurism and violence is out of steam, another hybrid comes along to fill the theatres. This time it is "The Beast," not a horror film but a thriller plagiarizing "Deliverance," "Straw Dogs," "Friday the 13th," then finishing it with "Death Wish." As can be expected, it is garnished with Hong Kong-version gore and sick sex, then assembled to look like an original.

Picture this: five teenagers leave the city for a weekend of camp picnic in the countryside in search of peace, sunshine and fresh air. Pauline and Ken, carefree lovers, make it in the tall grass, leaving the virginal Ah Ling alone washing dishes by the stream to be gang raped by five men. Ah Wah, her protective brother, is killed while in pursuit of the gang. That is the first half.

The second segment is devoted to Ah Ling's father, the strong, violent but silent type in his quest for vengeance after being told by the police that the law cannot gather sufficient evidence to charge the culprits. Violence erupts often as he kills the human beasts one by one.

Those who enjoy brutal murders, complete with either decapitated or dangling corpses, group sex, ingenious instruments guaranteed to kill, and other novel means of murdering, will drool over the unnecessary sequences.

Director Dennis Yu may believe that he was making a compelling and gripping revenge story but in fact he merely created an exploitation pic in order to satisfy the current craving for screen bloodbath as kung fu acrobatics die out.

The design and casting are good, the cinematography glossy but erratic. But the scenario could have used originality, subtlety and less desire to shock. Others have obviously managed to play better on the theme of the beastly aspects of man. It can be a curio piece abroad as an example of Chinese sadism, masochism on celluloid. —*Mel.*

Ato de Violencia
(Act of Violence)
(BRAZILIAN-COLOR)

Brasilia, Nov. 2.

An Embrafilme release of a Linxfilm/Embrafilme production. Produced by Cesar Memolo Jr. Directed by Eduardo Escorel. Features entire cast. Screenplay, Escorel and Roberto Machado; camera (Eastmancolor), Lauro Escorel Filho; music, Egberto Gismonti; editor, Gilberto Santeiro; sound, Victor Raposeiro; art direction, Paulo Chada; vocal, Pepe Castro Neves. Reviewed at First International Fair of Brazilian Film, Convention Center, Brasilia, Nov. 2, 1980. Running time: **112 MINS.**

Cast: Nuno Leal Maia, Selma Egrei, Renato Consorte, Eduardo Abbas, Liana Duval, Antonio Petrin, Oscar Felipe, Luis Serra, Ruthnea de Morais, Chico Martins, Abrahao Farc.

A man kills a woman with no apparent reason and does not try to escape. He is sentenced to 20 years but good behavior contributes to reduce his penalty in half and he gets conditional freedom after eight years in jail. He marries and is given a job but by no means is happy with his new life. After two years under such situation, he murders a prostitute in similar conditions to those of the first crime. The man is still in his early thirties and knows the next conviction will be for life.

Eduardo Escorel was an editor for many important films during the Cinema Novo period ("Terra em Transe," "Macunaima") and later ("Der Leone Have Sept Cabecas," "Sao Bernardo"). His first feature as director, "Licao de Amor" (Lecture on Love), produced five years ago, was intended to support the idea that the new Brazilian cinema should be understood by most audiences and made according to generally acknowledged technical standards. The picture accomplished that, but did not manage to escape a frozen, literary narrative, with little audience involvement.

Written with Roberto Machado, a professor of philosophy in Rio, Escorel's story talks about the failure of a man to feel any emotion, i.e. the definitive absence of love and hate. The man, Antonio (performed by Nuno Leal Maia), does not have the slightest idea of why and how he kills. He had no reason to do so in the light of any criminal code: he did not know the victims before, did not rob them, did not have any discussion with them, he is not sexually disturbed and so forth. All psychological tests reveal an ordinary mind. No Freudian problems, no compulsions and a good capacity to learn an office, which he does in jail.

Interestingly enough, Escorel chooses a thriller-oriented narrative — we follow the criminal and the law pursuing. Nevertheless, focus is not on the plot but on the character. Antonio defies all moral standards for crime and punishment, for there is no guilt.

Antonio's saga is inspired by the real-life case of Francisco da Costa Rocha, alias "chopped Chico," who strangled two women between 1966 and 1976. Justice could never find a plausible reason for that and Francisco is still waiting judgment in a Sao Paulo penitentiary.

Universal in its theme, "Act of Violence" was shot in Sao Paulo and Rio suburbs and manages to quite accurately interpret some familiar and professional relationship situations. Egberto Gismonti, who signs the musical score, is a well known jazz musician and composer. Editing is precise and acting convincing. Photography by Escorel's brother, Lauro, helps turn "Act of Violence" into a particularly competent work in the recent effort for re-industrialization of the Brazilian cinema. —*Hoin.*

La Cage Aux Folles II
(ITALIAN-FRENCH-COLOR)

Paris, Dec. 22.

UA release of a DaMa Produzione (Rome) — United Artists (Paris) coproduction. Produced by Marcello Danon. Stars Michel Serrault and Ugo Tognazzi. Directed by Edouard Molinaro. Written by Danon, Jean Poiret, Francis Veber; camera (Technicolor), Armando Nannuzzi; costume, Ambra Danon; music, Ennio Morricone; editor, Robert Isnardon; makeup, Piero Antonio Mecacci; sound, Mario Dallimonti; art director, Francesco Saverio Chianese. Reviewed at UGC Opera Theatre, Paris, Dec. 22, 1980. Running time: 100 MINS.

Renato	Ugo Tognazzi
Albin	Michel Serrault
Broca	Marcel Bozzuffi
Charrier	Michel Galabru
Mrs. Baldi	Paola Borboni
Jacob	Benny Luke
Milan	Giovanni Vettorazzo
Luigi	Glauco Onorato
Ralph	Roberto Bisacco

The Abbott and Costello of gaydom are back with new limp-wristed adventures. But the law of sequels applied to "La Cage Aux Folles II" — it's markedly inferior to number one.

The very title gives you an idea of the singular lack of effort that's gone into its packaging. Ironically, though the first picture was filmed theatre, it was a better film, more competently made, a neater, more satisfying commercial product. Jean Poiret's original stage play, described by the author as the flip side of Charles Dyer's "The Staircase," was really much closer in form to the sure-fire formula of Kaufman and Hart's "You Can't Take It With You."

Nevertheless producer Marcello Danon and his collaborators (the same as in number one), if slothful about making a good film, have programmed it shrewdly so as to give "Cage Aux Folles" enthusiasts what they want. What they want is obviously Michel ("Zaza Napoli") Serrault in all his shrill effeminate splendor. That's what they'll get in variety and abundance. Pic has opened stronger in Paris than "Superman II" and it looks certain to cash in big in the U.S.

Danon takes coscripting credits with Poiret and Francis Veber. They have mechanically embroiled Serrault and costar Ugo Tognazzi in a dull espionage plot that lacks surprise and comic ingenuity. It looks as if further sequels may amount to little more than genre grafts, exactly like in the old Abbott and Costello features. Don't be surprised if Serrault and Tognazzi next meet Dracula, go to Mars, or become buck privates.

Story begins when a deeply offended Serrault sets out to prove to his companion that he's still got sex appeal. Decked out in his finest (women's) wear he is promptly picked up on a cafe terrace, not by an excited admirer, but by a spy fleeing enemy agents. He whisks Serrault off as a cover. Pretty soon there are a couple of dead spies and a roll of microfilm winds up in Serrault's pill case, unknown to him.

With French agents trying to use them as decoys and foreign agents out to torture or kill them for the recovery of the film, Tognazzi and Serrault head for the (Italian) hills where they find temporary refuge on the farm of Tognazzi's mother, dismayed at the shabby specimen of womanhood her son has married. Finally all the spies converge on the couple, the French get the microfilm, the foreign espionage network is destroyed and Serrault and Tognazzi make up (without kissing, of course. This is a family picture. And don't believe what's written about how "La Cage Aux Folles" promotes tolerance and understanding of homosexuals).

Almost all the comedy rests on the splendid comic talents of Serrault. The role is a cinch for him and he's perfected it flamboyantly. Film is basically a Michel Serrault drag variety show with such amusing numbers as Zaza doing the "Blue Angel" act (in blackface), Zaza and the killer, Zaza trying to be macho, Zaza and Italian peasant tradition, and so on.

There's little else here of interest or competence.

Tognazzi has less to do than before and just fades into the background. Ditto for rest of the cast, including Marcel Bozzuffi, as the French espionage chief, and Michel Galabru, repeating his role as luckless in-law and politician. Benny Luke is again on hand as Jacob, the dainty servant.

Edouard Molinaro's direction is pedestrian. He did a snappier job on number one, working hard to keep the material from looking stagey. Robert Isnardon's editing is often sloppy and Armando Nannuzzi's lensing is ugly, washed out Technicolor (at least in print reviewed).

Ennio Morricone wrote the dull score. Other credits are blah.
—*Len.*

Nestbruch
(Nest Break)
(SWISS-COLOR)

Zurich, Dec. 10.

Rialto-Film AG Zurich release of a Kuert-Riesen/Filmkollektiv Zurich AG production. Directed by Beat Kuert. Produced by Barbara Eva Riesen. Features entire cast. Screenplay, Michael Maassen, Kuert; music, Cornelius Wernle, Collettivo Teatrale Operaio, Wolfgang Amadeus Mozart; camera (color). Hansueli Schenkel, Bernhard Lehner; editor, Kuert; sound, Florian Eidenbenz, Hanspeter Fischer; art direction, Hans Gloor, Charles Moser; lighting, Hans Meier, Markus Fischer; costumes, Marion Steiner; exec producer, Rolf Schmid. Reviewed at the Movie 1, Zurich, Dec. 10, '80. Running time: 93 MINS.

Frau Walti	Anne-Marie Blanc
Kaethi	Therese Affolter
Peter	Michael Maassen
Herr Meier	Hans Madin
Urs	Jost Osswald
Music Group	Collettivo Teatrale Operaio

Youthful unrest, street riots, vandalism and violence, increasingly frequent in Switzerland, and especially Zurich, since mid-1980, are cracks in the wall of Swiss prosperity, saturation and self-indulgence. "Nestbruch" (Nest Break), by Swiss helmer Beat Kuert, although not a film about youth revolt, means to show up a climate of such icy, heartless perfection that it almost inevitably produces rebellion. It fails to convince, though.

A retired German from Frankfurt, tired of big city life, comes to Switzerland with his driver to visit an old friend, who is mysteriously absent. An efficient, but impersonal housekeeper takes care of the guests and of her two grownup children. By and by, menacing or seemingly inexplicable happenings scratch the facade of the house's glacial hospitality. At the end, the housekeeper's son pushes his mother down the stairs to her death, while the daughter leaves for good and the German returns home.

A basically worthwhile theme is overlaid by vague allusions and bloodless symbolism. The script, written by Kuert and Michael Maassen, who plays the driver, is too literary. Direction is static and often stagy, with too many meaningless "pregnant" pauses.

Lowkey photography by Hansueli Schenkel is no big help either, Kuert himself did the editing.

Performances are uneven, but must, at least to some extent, be blamed on script deficiencies. The more convincing ones come from oldtimers Hans Madin as the visiting German and Anne-Marie Blanc as the almost frighteningly perfect housekeeper. —*Mezo.*

First Family
(COLOR)

Misfired lampoon of White House domestic doings.

Hollywood, Dec. 26.

Warner Bros. release of an Indie-Prod Production, produced by Daniel Melnick. Stars Gilda Radner, Bob Newhart, Madeline Kahn. Written and directed by Buck Henry. Camera (Technicolor), Fred J. Koenekamp; music, John Philip Sousa, adapted and conducted by Ralph Burns; editors, Stu Linder; Susan Martin; art director, William Hiney; set decorator, Rick Simpson; sound, Les Fresholtz, Tex Rudloff, Dick Alexander, Kevin F. Cleary,

Gerry Jost; sacrificial dance choreo-graphed by Toni Basil; associate pro-ducers, Phil Rawlins, Leslie Hill; assistant director, Skip Beaudine. Reviewed at The Burbank Studios, Dec. 26, '80. (MPAA Rating: R.) Running time: **104 MINS.**
Gloria Link . . . . Gilda Radner
President Manfred Link . . . . Bob Newhart
Constance Link . . . . Madeline Kahn
Press Secretary Bunthorne . . . .
. . . . Richard Benjamin
Vice-President Shockley . . . . . . Bob Dishy
U.N. Ambassador Spender . . . .
. . . . Harvey Korman
Alexander Grade . . . . . . Austin Pendleton
JCS Chairman G.E. Dumpston . . Rip Torn
Presidential Asst. Feebleman . . . . Fred Willard
Ambassador Longo . . . . Julius Harris
President Mazai Kalundra . John Hancock
Arab Delegate . . . . Maurice Sherbanee
Father Sandstone/TV Anchorman . . Buck Henry
African Dancers . . . . Shatsmi Sarumi Dance Troupe

Despite its amusing premise of Bob Newhart as a dim-witted President of the United States and Gilda Radner as his sex-starved daughter trying desperately to lose her virginity, "First Family" falls flat on its face. Much more was ex-pected of writer-director Buck Henry's solo directing debut than this glum attempt at comedy, which overstretches its thin plot and blunders into racist offensiveness when the characters go on an African trip. The R-rated Warner Bros. release, produced by Daniel Melnick, opened on Christmas Day, and if films could be returned like disappointing presents, the cus-tomers would be standing in line to exchange it.

Henry's reputation as a drolly satiric writer holds up in many one-liners sprinkled through the film, and in some enjoyably outlandish situations, but his screenplay does not adequately sustain or develop the characters, who quickly become one-note gags. His visual timing and sense of camera place-ment are weak, and the film has tacky production values which call attention to the lack of filmmaking expertise on display here.

Not modelled directly on any re-cent First Family, but somewhat resembling the Gerald Ford clan, the Newhart family also includes tippling wife Madeline Kahn, whose inebriated header into a limousine is one of the biggest laughs in the film. She and Newhart adroitly capture the vacantly pompous rhetoric presidential couples often displayed on tv, and, in Henry's comic conceit, at home as well.

Gilda Radner's comic flair, how-ever, does not translate well from tv onto the big screen, particularly since her character is made up and dressed to look as unattractively juvenile as possible. The first couple of times she grabs at the nearest available man are amusing; after that the gag becomes increasingly tiresome and depressing.

Furthermore, too many of what are intended to be funny ideas ir-ritate rather than amuse because they just don't make sense even on their own terms. Newhart is sup-posed to have been elected only be-cause the opposing candidate died in an automobile crash — but in such a case, the party would nom-inate a substitute. Radner is ab-ducted in Africa without any Secret Service men in sight, and not a **single tv camera or reporter** accompanies the family on the trip.

After enjoyably setting up some extreme contrasts between the manners of African envoy Julius Harris and the ultra-WASPish Newhart, the film goes haywire when Henry clumsily tries to emu-late Evelyn Waugh's classic satire "Black Mischief" in lampooning the primitive African country of Upper Gorm. The characteriza-tion of the Africans is on the most animalistic level, and the screen-play lacks the genuine wit to keep the cultural differences from seem-ing to be a smug comic putdown of blacks.

In a dismal spoof of "King Kong," the natives abduct Radner after learning she is a virgin and sacri-fice her maidenhood to a giant phallic statue. As if that isn't crude or silly enough, Henry then has Newhart make a deal with the Africans to trade middle-class white Americans as slaves in ex-change for a tank of dung with mag-ical plant-growing properties.

Anyone still hanging in there with the film by this point will be hard pressed to find laughs in the cli-mactic sequences revolving around an assassination attempt on New-hart. After negative preview re-action, WB reshot the ending to have Newhart survive. The film doesn't. —*Mac.*

Inspecteur la Bavure
(Inspector Blunder)
(FRENCH-COLOR)

Paris, Dec. 20.
An AMLF release of a Renn Produc-tions-FR3 production. Produced by Claude Berri. Stars Coluche, Gerard Depardieu. Directed by Claude Zidi. Written by Zidi and Jean Bouchaud; camera (color), Henri Decae; editor, Nicole Saunier; sound, Bernard Aubouy; art director, Jean-Baptiste Poirot; music, Vladimir Cosma. Reviewed at the Marignan-Con-corde Theatre, Paris, Dec. 15, 1980. Run-ning time: **100 MINS.**
Michel Clement . . . . Coluche
Roger Morzini . . . . Gerard Depardieu
Marie-Anne
Prossant . . . . Dominique Lavanant
Vermillot . . . . Julien Guiomar

Comedy director Claude Zidi has another commercial smash with this occasionally amusing vehicle for popular music-hall comedian, Coluche, who's being packaged as a new comic genius in the line of Raimu and Bourvil.

Coluche and his collaborators will have to do much better than this to support such big claims, but the plump comic shows an appealing screen presence and creates some funny moments. Claude Berri, who produced pic, already has an ex-clusive four-picture contract with the clown and will himself direct his next comedy.

Rather than transpose Coluche's caustic stage image, Zidi has cast him in an utterly conventional com-ic mold: the timid, slow-witted bumbler who fails at everything but triumphs ingeniously when the chips are down.

Here he is a rookie police inspec-tor, the son of a police hero, who constantly mucks up the pursuit of a dangerous public enemy (Gerard Depardieu). When the criminal kid-naps a young woman journalist who has been accompanying Coluche on patrol and seeking a scoop inter-view with the hood, the young de-tective is galvanized into perform-ing a spectacular single-handed rescue.

Script is patchy as if Zidi and co-scripter Jean Bouchaud were not quite certain as to the presentation of their star. Zidi's direction suffers as well, taking certain sections at a brisk farcical pace, then slowing down to accommodate Coluche as an actor. Depardieu and Domini-que Lavanant, as the over-eager journalist, provide good foils to Co-luche's blundering   nenticesh;

Der Rote Strumpf
(The Red Stocking)
(WEST GERMAN-COLOR)

Berlin, Dec. 20.
An Aspekt Telefilm Produktion, Markus Trebitsch, producer, Berlin, in collabora-tion with Zweites Deutsches Fernsehen (ZDF), Martin Buettner, Redakteur, Mainz. Features entire cast. Directed by Wolfgang Tumler. Screenplay, Elfie Don-nelly; camera (color), Petrus Schloemp; sound, Gunther Kortwich; music, Eber-hard Weber, Rainer Brueninghaus; edit-ing, Peter Przygodda. Reviewed at Studio am Kudam, Berlin, Dec. 20, '80. Running time: **92 MINS.**
Cast: Inge Meysel (Frau Maria Pala-cek), Julie Tumler (Marie), Ulrike Blei-fert (Mother), Peter Bauer (Father), Inge Wolffberg (Grandmother), Dorothea Moritz (Seamstress).

Lively children's film that was an immediate winner with young and old at its preem in Berlin at the Stu-dio am Kudam, Wolfgang Tum-ler's "The Red Stocking" should find its way without much diffi-culty to international kid-fests starting with the Berlin Film Festi-val in February. Pic has much in common with the lighthearted an-tics found in those specials from the Children's Film Foundation in Great Britain, which may have set an example in the past.

"The Red Stocking" stays com-pletely within the world of chil-dren, avoiding social messages or stereotypes and cliches. It's the story of a young girl about nine-years-old who makes friends with an elderly citizen from a nearby psychiatric clinic; since both hap-pen to be named "Maria" and "Marie," there's already some-thing in common. But the young Marie is also in the curiosity, asking-questions stage, so she swiftly discovers things about the elderly lady that belie the "crazy" tag put upon her by grown-ups and kids in the neighborhood. Further, the girl meets her elderly friend regularly in the park after school, thereby setting the stage for adven-ture in the wooded residential area of Berlin, where Old Peoples Homes are plentiful.

After the two become friends, Marie stands up for the elderly woman's idiosyncrasies and de-fends her before her playmates and "normal" people looking upon Frau Panacek as a kook who gets let out of the clinic every now and then to sit on a park bench. One of the lady's idiosyncrasies is a non-matching pair of stockings, the "red stocking" referring to one leg that feels colder than the other and is thus warmed by the red color. Also, both Maria and Marie discover they don't like fish — the younger be-cause her grandmother always serves it on Friday when the duti-ful family visit is paid, and the older because her own fish-store was taken over by her son-in-law when she was forcefully admitted to the clinic. The old woman is even sure someone's trying to poison her, per-haps even in the fish served at meals, so she runs away from the Home.

The young Marie, of course, takes her new friend into her own home and bedroom for the night, where she is discovered by the par-ents the next morning. But the father and mother are quickly won over by the charm of the two com-rades so that, in the end, the family has a "Sunday relative" to share their lives with. Meanwhile, the father's job at the local television station in the props-and-costumes section allows for plenty of merry monkey-business for the young audience, and there's also a scene in which the authoritarian grand-mother gets her comeuppance at the dinner table as spaghetti is served and then eaten by everyone else with the fingers.

Inge Meysel, a vet thesp on tv in motherly roles, proves once again that she's a fine mime, while Julie Tumler (the helmer's own daughter) cake-walks through the pic as a natural charmer. "The Red Stocking" — together with Wolfgang Becker's adaptation of Max von the Gruen's "Vorstadt Krokodile" (The Suburban Crocodiles) (1977) and Haro Senft's "A Day with the Wind" (1978) — is an encouraging sign that the West Germans are now seriously contending for the domain of the kid-pic, a genre left in the past to the Socialist countries and Britain's unique Children's Film Foundation. —*Holl.*